THE WESTERN HERITAGE

Property of
BOARD OF EDUCATION
BAY VILLAGE, OHIO

THE WESTERN HERITAGE
Seventh Edition

COMBINED VOLUME

DONALD KAGAN
YALE UNIVERSITY

STEVEN OZMENT
HARVARD UNIVERSITY

FRANK M. TURNER
YALE UNIVERSITY

Prentice Hall

UPPER SADDLE RIVER, NEW JERSEY 07458

Library of Congress Cataloging–in–Publication Data

Kagan, Donald
    The Western heritage / Donald Kagan, Steven Ozment, Frank M. Turner.—
    Combined Volume, 7th ed.
         p.   cm.
    Includes bibliographical references and index.
    ISBN 0-13-027718-5
    1. Civilization, Western. I. Ozment, Steven E. II. Turner, Frank M. (Frank Miller), 1944-III. Title.
    CB245.K28 2001
    909'.09812—dc21   00-026148

Editorial Director: Charlyce Jones Owen
Editor-in-Chief, Development: Susanna Lesan
Development Editor: Roberta Meyer
Director of Production
   and Manufacturing: Barbara Kittle
Production Editor: Joseph Scordato
Prepress and Manufacturing Manager:
   Nick Sklitsis
Prepress and Manufacturing Buyer: Lynn Pearlman

Creative Design Director: Leslie Osher
Interior and Cover Designer: Nancy Wells
Electronic Page Layout: Scott Garrison, Joh Lisa,
   Thomas Benfatti
Photo Director: Beth Boyd
Photo Research: Barbara Salz
Cartographer: Carto-Graphics
Copy Editor: Write With, Inc.
Art Manager: Guy Ruggiero

Cover Art: "Scuola Olandese" (Dutch School), *Fiume gelato con pattinatori* (Frozen river with ice
    skaters). Galleria Sabauda, Torino/Art Resource, NY

This book was set in 10/12 Trump Mediaeval by the HSS in-house formatting
and production services group and was printed and bound by RR Donnelley & Sons.
The cover was printed by Phoenix Color Corp.

© 2001, 1998, 1991, 1987, 1983, 1979 by Prentice-Hall, Inc.
Pearson Education
Upper Saddle River, New Jersey 07458

All rights reserved. No part of this book may
be reproduced, in any form or by any means,
without permission in writing from the publisher.

Printed in the United States of America
10 9 8 7 6 5 4 3

ISBN 0-13-027718-5

Prentice-Hall International (UK) Limited, *London*
Prentice-Hall of Australia Pty. Limited, *Sydney*
Prentice-Hall Canada Inc., *Toronto*
Prentice-Hall Hispanoamericana, S.A., *Mexico*
Prentice-Hall of India Private Limited, *New Delhi*
Prentice-Hall of Japan, Inc. *Tokyo*
Pearson Education Asia Pte. Ltd., *Singapore*
Editora Prentice-Hall do Brasil, Ltda., *Rio de Janeiro*

TIME LINE PHOTO CREDITS:

Time Line 1: page 0, (left) Gary Cralle/The Image Bank;
(right) Winfield I. Parks Jr./National Geographic Image Collection; page 1, The Granger Collection; page 2, *Battle of Alexander the Great at Issus.* Roman mosaic. Museo Archeologico Nazionale, Naples, Italy. Scala/Art Resource; p. 3, Robert Frerck/Woodfin Camp & Associates.

Time Line 2: page 192, Marvin Trachtenberg; page 193, Bayeus, Musée de l'Eveche. "With special authorization of the City of Bayeaux." Giraudon/Art Resource.

Time Line 3: page 288, *Elizabeth I, Armada Portrait*, c. 1588 (oil on panel) by George Gower (1540–96) (attr. to). Woburn Abbey, Bedfordshire, UK/Bridgeman Art Library, London/New York; p. 289, The Granger Collection.

Time Line 4: page 586, Philosopher, dramatist, poet, historian, and populizer of scientific ideas, Voltaire (1694–1778). Bildarchiv Preussischer Kulterbesitz; page 587, By Permission of Musée de la Legion d'Honneur.

Time Line 5: page 778, Corbis; page 779, The Bridgeman Art Library International.

Time Line 6: page 992, (left) Hulton Getty/Archive Photos; (right) Franklin D. Roosevelt Library; page 993, (left) Corbis Sygma Photo News; (right, top) John Launois/Black Star; (right, bottom) Reuters/Natalie Behring/Archive Photos.

Brief Contents

Detailed Contents

Documents

Maps

Art & the West

The West & the World

Preface

As we enter the twenty-first century, the heritage of Western civilization is a major point of departure for understanding our own epoch. The unprecedented globalization of daily life has occurred in large measure through the spread of Western technological, economic, and political influences. From the sixteenth through the end of the twentieth century the West exerted vast influences throughout the globe for both good and ill, and the global citizens of this new century live in the wake of that impact. It is the goal of this book to introduce its readers to the Western heritage so that they may be better informed and more culturally sensitive citizens of the emerging global age.

Since *The Western Heritage* first appeared, we have sought to provide our readers with a work that does justice to the richness and variety of Western civilization. We hope that such an understanding of the West will foster lively debate on its character, values, institutions, and global influence. Indeed, we believe such a critical outlook on their own culture has characterized the peoples of the West since its earliest history. Through such debates we define ourselves and the values of our culture. Consequently, we welcome the debate and hope that *The Western Heritage*, seventh edition, can help to foster a genuinely informed discussion through its overview of Western civilization, its strengths, weaknesses, and the controversies surrounding it.

Human beings make, experience, and record their history. In this edition as in past editions, our goal has been to present Western civilization fairly, accurately, and in a way that does justice to that great variety of human enterprise. History has many facets, no one of which alone can account for the others. Any attempt to tell the story of the West from a single overarching perspective, no matter how timely, is bound to neglect or suppress some important part of that story. Like all authors, we have had to make selections for an introductory text, but we have attempted to provide the broadest possible coverage suitable to that task of introduction. To that end we hope that the vast array of documents included in this book will allow the widest possible spectrum of people over the course of the centuries to give personal voice to their experience and to allow our readers to enter into that experience.

We also believe that any book addressing the experience of the West must also look beyond its historical European borders. The students reading this book are drawn from a wide variety of cultures and experiences. They live in a world characterized by highly interconnected economies and instant communication between cultures. In this emerging multicultural society it seems both appropriate and necessary to recognize the ways in which Western civilization has throughout its history interacted with other cultures, influencing other societies and being influenced by them. Examples of this two-way interaction, such as that with Islam, appear throughout the text. To further highlight the theme of interaction, *The Western Heritage* includes a series of comparative essays, *The West & the World*. (For a fuller description, see below.)

Goals of the Text

Our primary goal has been to present a strong, clear narrative account of the central developments in Western history. We have also sought to call attention to certain critical themes:

- The capacity of Western civilization from the time of the Greeks to the present to generate transforming self-criticism.
- The development of political freedom, constitutional government, and concern for the rule of law and individual rights.
- The shifting relations among religion, society, and the state.
- The development of science and technology and their expanding impact on thought, social institutions, and everyday life.
- The major religious and intellectual currents that have shaped Western culture.

We believe that these themes have been fundamental in Western civilization, shaping the past and exerting a continuing influence on the present.

FLEXIBLE PRESENTATION   *The Western Heritage*, seventh edition, is designed to accommodate a variety of approaches to a course in Western civilization, allowing teachers to stress what is most important to them. Some teachers will ask students to read all the chapters. Others will select among them to reinforce assigned readings and lectures. We have reorganized and rewritten the last two chapters (30 and 31) to permit instructors to end their course by emphasizing either social or political factors in the twentieth-century experience.

INTEGRATED SOCIAL, CULTURAL, AND POLITICAL HISTORY *The Western Heritage* provides one of the richest accounts of the social history of the West available today, with strong coverage of family life, the changing roles of women, and the place of the family in relation to broader economic, political, and social developments. This coverage reflects the explosive growth in social historical research in the past quarter century, which has enriched virtually all areas of historical study. In this edition we have again expanded both the breadth and depth of our coverage of social history through revisions of existing chapters, the addition of major new material, and the inclusion of new documents.

While strongly believing in the study of the social experience of the West, we also share the conviction that internal and external political events have shaped the Western experience in fundamental and powerful ways. The experiences of Europeans in the twentieth century under fascism, national socialism, and communism demonstrate that influence, as has, more recently, the collapse of communism in the former Soviet Union and eastern Europe. We have also been told repeatedly by teachers that no matter what their own historical specialization, they believe that a political narrative gives students an effective tool to begin to organize their understanding of the past. Consequently, we have made every effort to integrate the political with the social, cultural, and intellectual.

No other survey text presents so full an account of the religious and intellectual development of the West. People may be political and social beings, but they are also reasoning and spiritual beings. What they think and believe are among the most important things we can know about them. Their ideas about God, society, law, gender, human nature, and the physical world have changed over the centuries and continue to change. We cannot fully grasp our own approach to the world without understanding the intellectual currents of the past and their influence on our thoughts and conceptual categories.

CLARITY AND ACCESSIBILITY Good narrative history requires clear, vigorous prose. As in earlier editions, we have paid careful attention to the quality of our writing, subjecting every paragraph to critical scrutiny. Our goal was to make our presentation fully accessible to students without compromising vocabulary or conceptual level. We hope this effort will benefit both teachers and students.

Changes in the Seventh Edition

INTRODUCING *ART & THE WEST* A beautiful and important new feature enhances students' understanding of the artistic heritage of the West. In every chapter we highlight a work of art or architecture and discuss how the work illuminates and reflects the period in which it was created. In Chapter 5, for example, a portrait of a young woman on the wall of a house in Pompeii and the accompanying essay provide a glimpse into the life of well-to-do young women in the Roman Empire (p. 161). In Chapter 7, two views of Salisbury Cathedral illustrate an essay on Gothic architecture (p. 248). In Chapter 16, two paintings tell contrasting stories about domestic life in eighteenth-century France (p. 526), and in Part 4, works by Turner, Manet, and Seurat illustrate both the power of the new industrialism and its effects on European social life. Part 5 includes discussions of paintings by Grosz, Magritte, and Picasso. In Chapter 30, *Bread*, painted by the Soviet realist Tatjiana Yablonskaya, and Jackson Pollock's *One (Number 31, 1950)*, offer starkly contrasting views of twentieth-century culture (p. 1040). (See p. xxiv for a complete list of *Art & The West* essays.)

THE WEST & THE WORLD In this feature, we focus on six subjects, comparing Western institutions with those of other parts of the world, or discussing the ways in which developments in the West have influenced cultures in other areas of the globe. In the seventh edition, the essays are:

Part 1: Ancient Warfare (new) (p. 186)

Part 2: The Invention of Printing in China and Europe (new) (p. 284)

Part 3: The Columbian Exchange (new) (p. 582)

Part 4: The Abolition of Slavery in the Transatlantic Economy (p. 736)

Part 5: Imperialism: Ancient and Modern (p. 928)

Part 6: Energy and the Modern World (new) (p. 1116)

RECENT SCHOLARSHIP As in previous editions, changes in this edition reflect our determination to incorporate the most recent developments in historical scholarship and the concerns of professional historians. Of particular interest are expanded discussions of:

• **Women in the history of the West.** Adding to our longstanding commitment to the inclusion of the experience of women in Western civilization, this edition presents new scholarship on women in the ancient world and the Middle Ages, women and the scientific revolution, and women under the authoritarian governments of the twentieth century. (See, especially, chapters 3, 4, 5, 7, 14, 30.)

- **The Scientific Revolution.**   Chapter 14, which addresses the rise of the new science, has been wholly revised and rewritten to clarify the new scientific theory arising from the Copernican revolution, the new understanding of the Galileo case, the role of women in the new science, and the social institutions of the new science.

- **The Dutch Golden Age.**   A new section in Chapter 15 discusses the United Netherlands during the seventeenth and eighteenth centuries.

- **Africa and the transatlantic economy.**   An extensive section in Chapter 17 explores the relationship of Africa to the transatlantic economy of the sixteenth through eighteenth centuries. We examine the role of African society and politics in the slave trade, the experience of Africans forcibly transported to the Americas, and the incorporation of elements of African culture into the New World.

- **Jewish thinkers in the Enlightenment.**   A new section in Chapter 18 discusses the thought of Spinoza and Moses Mendelsohn as they relate to the role of Jewish religion and society in the wider European culture.

- **The Holocaust.**   The discussion of the Holocaust has been significantly expanded in two ways. Chapter 29 provides more analysis of the causes of the Holocaust, and Chapter 30 includes an extensive new narrative of the particular case of the destruction of the Jews of Poland.

- **Twentieth-century social history.**   The seventh edition of *The Western Heritage* presents the most extensive treatment of twentieth-century social history available in a survey text. We examine, in Chapter 30, the experiences of women under authoritarian governments, the collectivization of Soviet agriculture, the destruction of the Polish Jewish community, and European migration. The chapter concludes with a new section on the coming of the computer and the impact of new technology on European life.

- **The history of the Cold War and Europe at the start of the twenty-first century.**   Chapter 31, on the Soviet–American rivalry and the collapse of communism, has been wholly rewritten and includes the conflict in the former Yugoslavia. Instructors may close their course with either of the twentieth-century chapters, depending on the issues they wish to emphasize.

Chapter-by-Chapter Revisions

Chapter 1   The treatment of the origins of humankind has been completely rewritten to reflect the newest scholarship.

Chapters 3, 4, 5 contain new sections on Women in Homeric Society; Aspasia, Pericles' Common-law Wife; Greek Slavery; Women in Early Rome; Women of the Upper Classes in later Roman history.

Chapter 9 contains a discussion of medieval Russia.

Chapter 12 includes a shorter, rewritten discussion of The Thirty Years' War.

Chapter 14 has a wholly rewritten discussion of the Scientific Revolution and of the impact of the Scientific Revolution on philosophy, new or extensively rewritten sections on women and early modern science, the new institutions associated with the emerging scientific knowledge, religious faith and the new science, with an expanded discussion of the Galileo case.

Chapter 15 contains an extensive new section on the Dutch Golden Age, including the impact of its overseas empire on its prosperity.

Chapter 16 has a new section on The Impact of the Agricultural and Industrial Revolutions on Working Women.

Chapter 17 includes a much expanded and revised section on African Slavery, the experiences of Africans in the Americas, and the cultural institutions they brought with them.

Chapter 18 has a new section on Jewish Thinkers in the Age of Enlightenment with emphasis on Spinoza and Moses Mendelsohn.

Chapter 22 has a refocused discussion of Karl Marx's thought.

Chapter 25 expands the treatment of racial thinking and the non-Western world.

Chapter 28 includes a rewritten discussion of the Soviet Experience in the 1930s.

Chapter 29 expands the discussion of the Holocaust.

Chapter 30 is a largely new chapter on twentieth-century social history, with major new sections on state violence, women under authoritarian governments, the collectivization of Soviet agriculture, the destruction of the Polish Jews, and the impact of the computer.

Chapter 31 has been extensively rewritten and reorganized to reflect the latest scholarship on the Cold War through the collapse of communism. It ends with a discussion of Europe at the Opening of the Global Century.

The last two chapters are written so that instructors, though teaching both chapters, may choose to close their course with either, depending upon their personal emphasis. Those instructors wishing to emphasize social history might end the course with Chapter 30 and those wishing to emphasize political development and great power relations may choose to conclude with Chapter 31.

MAPS AND ILLUSTRATIONS   To help students understand the relationship between geography and history, we have added relief features to approximately one-half of the maps. All 90 maps have been carefully edited for accuracy. The text also contains close to 500 color and black and white illustrations, many of them new to the seventh edition.

PEDAGOGICAL FEATURES   This edition retains the pedagogical features of the last edition, including part-opening comparative timelines, a list of key topics at the beginning of each chapter, chapter review questions, and questions accompanying the more than 200 source documents in the text. Each of these features is designed to make the text more accessible to students and to reinforce key concepts.

- **Illustrated timelines** open each of the six parts of the book summarizing, side-by-side, the major events in politics and government, society and economy, and religion and culture.

- **Primary source documents**, more than one third new to this edition, acquaint students with the raw material of history and provide intimate contact with the people of the past and their concerns. Questions accompanying the source documents direct students toward important, thought-provoking issues and help them relate the documents to the material in the text. They can be used to stimulate class discussion or as topics for essays and study groups.

- Each chapter includes an **outline**, a **list of key topics**, and an **introduction**. Together these features provide a succinct overview of each chapter.

- **Chronologies** follow each major section in a chapter, listing significant events and their dates.

- *In Perspective* sections summarize the major themes of each chapter and provide a bridge to the next chapter.

- **Chapter review questions** help students review the material in a chapter and relate it to broader themes. They too can be used for class discussion and essay topics.

- **Suggested readings lists** following each chapter have been updated with new titles reflecting recent scholarship.

A NOTE ON DATES AND TRANSLITERATIONS   This edition of *The Western Heritage* continues the practice of using B.C.E. (before the common era) and C.E. (common era) instead of B.C. (before Christ) and A.D. (*anno domini*, the year of the Lord) to designate dates. We also follow the most accurate currently accepted English transliterations of Arabic words. For example, today Koran is being replaced by the more accurate Qur'an; similarly Muhammad is preferable to Mohammed and Muslim to Moslem.

Ancillary Instructional Materials

The ancillary instructional materials that accompany *The Western Heritage* include print and multimedia supplements that are designed to reinforce and enliven the richness of the past and inspire students with the excitement of studying the history of Western civilization.

Print Supplements for the Instructor

INSTRUCTOR'S MANUAL WITH TEST ITEMS   The Instructor's Manual contains chapter summaries, key points and vital concepts, and information on audio-visual resources that can be used in developing and preparing lecture presentations. Also included is a test item file that offers multiple-choice, identification, and essay test questions.

PRENTICE HALL CUSTOM TEST   This commercial-quality computerized test management program, for Windows and Macintosh environments, allows users to create their own tests using items from the printed Test Item File. The program allows users to edit the items in the Test Item File and to add their own questions. Online testing is also available.

TRANSPARENCY PACKAGE   This collection of full-color transparency acetates provides the maps, charts, and graphs from the text for use in classroom presentations.

ADMINISTRATIVE HANDBOOK by Jay Boggis provides instructors with resources for using *The Western Heritage* with Annenberg/CPB telecourse, *The Western Tradition*.

Print Supplements for the Student

STUDY GUIDE, VOLUMES I AND II   The study guide includes commentaries, definitions, and a variety of exercises designed to reinforce the concepts in the chapter. These exercises include: identification, map exercises, and short-answer and essay questions.

DOCUMENTS SET, VOLUMES I AND II   This carefully selected and edited set of documents provides over 100 additional primary source readings. Each document includes a brief introduction as well as questions to encourage critical analysis of the reading and to relate it to the content of the text.

MAP WORKBOOK   This brief workbook gives students the opportunity to increase their knowledge of geography through identification and other map exercises. It is available free to students when shrink-wrapped with the text.

HISTORICAL ATLAS OF THE WORLD   This four-color historical atlas provides additional map resources to reinforce concepts in the text. It is available for a nominal fee when shrink-wrapped with the text.

UNDERSTANDING AND ANSWERING ESSAY QUESTIONS Prepared by Mary L. Kelley, San Antonio College. This brief guide suggests helpful study techniques as well as specific analytical tools for understanding different types of essay questions and provides precise guidelines for preparing well-crafted essay answers. This guide is available free to students when shrink-wrapped with the text.

READING CRITICALLY ABOUT HISTORY: A GUIDE TO ACTIVE READING   Prepared by Rose Wassman and Lee Ann Rinsky. This guide focuses on the skills needed to learn the essential information presented in college history textbooks. Material covered includes vocabulary skills, recognizing organizational patterns, critical thinking skills, understanding visual aids, and practice sections. This guide is available free to students when shrink-wrapped with the text.

THEMES OF THE TIMES   *The New York Times* and Prentice Hall are sponsoring *Themes of the Times*, a program designed to enhance student access to current information of relevance in the classroom. Through this program, the core subject matter provided in the text is supplemented by a collection of current articles from one of the world's most distinguished newspapers, *The New York Times*.

These articles demonstrate the vital, ongoing connection between what is learned in the classroom and what is happening in the world around us. To enjoy the wealth of information of *The New York Times* daily, a reduced subscription rate is available. For information call toll-free: 1-800-631-1222.

Prentice Hall and *The New York Times* are proud to co-sponsor *Themes of the Times*. We hope it will make the reading of both textbooks and newspapers a more dynamic, involving process.

TELECOURSE STUDY GUIDE, VOLUMES I AND II, by Jay Boggis correlates *The Western Heritage* with the Annenberg/CPB telecourse, *The Western Tradition*.

Multimedia Supplements

HISTORY ON THE INTERNET   This guide focuses on developing the critical thinking skills necessary to evaluate and use online sources. The guide also provides a brief introduction to navigating the Internet, along with complete references related specifically to the History discipline and how to use the *Companion Website*™ available for *The Western Heritage*. This supplementary book is free to students when shrink-wrapped with the text.

COMPANION WEBSITE™
ADDRESS: WWW.PRENHALL.COM/KAGAN
Students can now take full advantage of the World Wide Web to enrich their study of Western Civilization through *The Western Heritage Companion Website*™. Features of the website include, for each chapter in the text, objectives, study questions, map labeling exercises, related links, and document exercises. A faculty module provides material from the Instructor's Manual and the maps and charts from the text in Powerpoint™ format.

POWERPOINT™ IMAGES CD ROM   Available for Windows and Macintosh environments, this resource includes the maps, charts, and graphs from the text for use in Powerpoint™ . Organized by chapters in the text, this collection of images is useful for classroom presentations and lectures.

IRC WESTERN CIVILIZATION CD ROM   Available for Windows 95 and 3.1, this lecture and presentation resource includes a library of over 3000 images, each with a descriptive caption, plus film clips, maps, and sound recordings. A correlation guide lists the images as they correspond to the chapters of *The Western Heritage*. Contact your local Prentice Hall representative for information about the adoption requirements for this resource.

COURSE MANAGEMENT SYSTEMS   For instructors interested in distance learning, Prentice Hall offers fully customizable, online courses with enhanced content, www links, online testing, and many other course management features using the best available course management systems available, including WebCT, Blackboard, and ecollege online course architecture. Contact your local Prentice Hall representative or visit our special Demonstration Central Website at http://www.prenhall.com/demo for more information.

Acknowledgments

We are grateful to the scholars and teachers whose thoughtful and often detailed comments helped shape this revision:

Lenard R. Berlanstein, University of
  Virginia, Charlottesville
Margaret Bostwick, John Jay College
Stephanie Christelow, Idaho State University
Samuel Willard Crompton, Holyoke
  Community College
Mary Beth Emmerichs, University of Wisconsin-
  Sheboygan
Robert L. Ervin, San Jacinto Community College
Benjamin Foster, Yale University
Joseph Gonzales, Moorpark College
Victor Davis Hanson, California State
  University, Fresno
John Hinde, Malaspina University -College
William I. Hitchcock, Wellesley College
Pardaic Kenny, University of Colorado, Boulder
Raymond F. Kierstead, Reed College

Steven Leibo, Russell Sage College
David Lindberg, University of
  Wisconsin, Madison
Eleanor McCluskey, Palm Beach Atlantic College
  and Broward Community College
Robert J. Mueller, Hastings College
John Nicols, University of Oregon, Eugene
W. Gary Nichols, The Citadel
Sandra J. Peacock, State University of New York,
  Binghamton
John Powell, Pennsylvania State University
Richard R. Rivers, Macomb Community College
Robert A. Schneider, Catholic University
Hugo Schwyzer, Pasadena City College
Sidney R. Sherter, Long Island University
Roger P. Snow, College of Great Falls
Ilicia J. Sprey, Blue Ridge Community College
Racel Stocking, Southern Illinois University at
  Carbondale

Finally, we would like to thank the dedicated people who helped produce this revision. Our acquisitions editor, Charlyce Jones Owen; our development editor, Roberta Meyer; our production editor, Joe Scordato; Nancy Wells, who created the handsome new design of this edition; Scott Garrison, who formatted the pages; Lynn Pearlman, our manufacturing buyer; and Barbara Salz, photo researcher.

D.K.
S.O.
F.M.T.

About the Authors

DONALD KAGAN is Hillhouse Professor of History and Classics at Yale University, where he has taught since 1969. He received the A.B. degree in history from Brooklyn College, the M.A. in classics from Brown University, and the Ph.D. in history from Ohio State University. During 1958–1959 he studied at the American School of Classical Studies as a Fulbright Scholar. He has received three awards for undergraduate teaching at Cornell and Yale. He is the author of a history of Greek political thought, *The Great Dialogue* (1965); a four-volume history of the Peloponnesian war, *The Origins of the Peloponnesian War* (1969); *The Archidamian War* (1974); *The Peace of Nicias and the Sicilian Expedition* (1981); *The Fall of the Athenian Empire* (1987); and a biography of Pericles, *Pericles of Athens and the Birth of Democracy* (1991); and *On the Origins of War* (1995). He is coauthor, with Frederick W. Kagan of *While America Sleeps* (2000). With Brian Tierney and L. Pearce Williams, he is the editor of *Great Issues in Western Civilization*, a collection of readings.

STEVEN OZMENT is McLean Professor of Ancient and Modern History at Harvard University. He has taught Western Civilization at Yale, Stanford, and Harvard. He is the author of ten books. *The Age of Reform, 1250–1550* (1980) won the Schaff Prize and was nominated for the 1981 American Book Award. *Magdalena and Balthasar: An Intimate Portrait of Life in Sixteenth Century Europe* (1986), *Three Behaim Boys: Growing Up in Early Modern Germany* (1990), *Protestants: The Birth of a Revolution* (1992), and *The Burgermeister's Daughter: Scandal in a Sixteenth Century German Town* (1996) were selections of the History Book Club, as is his most recent book, *Flesh and Spirit: Private Life in Early Modern Germany* (1999).

FRANK M. TURNER is John Hay Whitney Professor of History at Yale University, where he served as University Provost from 1988 to 1992. He received his B.A. degree at the College of William and Mary and his Ph.D. from Yale. He has received the Yale College Award for Distinguished Undergraduate Teaching. He has directed a National Endowment for the Humanities Summer Institute. His scholarly research has received the support of fellowships from the National Endowment for the Humanities and the Guggenheim Foundation and the Woodrow Wilson Center. He is the author of *Between Science and Religion: The Reaction to Scientific Naturalism in Late Victorian England* (1974), *The Greek Heritage in Victorian Britain* (1981), which received the British Council Prize of the Conference on British Studies and the Yale Press Governors Award, and *Contesting Cultural Authority: Essays in Victorian Intellectual Life* (1993). He has also contributed numerous articles to journals and has served on the editorial advisory boards of *The Journal of Modern History, Isis,* and *Victorian Studies.* He edited *The Idea of a University,* by John Henry Newman (1996). Since 1996 he has served as a Trustee of Connecticut College.

Part 1

1,000,000 B.C.E.–400 C.E.

	POLITICS AND GOVERNMENT	SOCIETY AND ECONOMY	RELIGION AND CULTURE
1,000,000– 3500 B.C.E.		ca. 1,000,000– 10,000 B.C.E. **Paleolithic Age**	ca. 30,0000– 6000 B.C.E. **Paleolithic art**
		ca. 8,000 B.C.E. **Earliest Neolithic settlements**	
3500– 2200 B.C.E.	ca. 3100– 2700 B.C.E. **Egyptian Early Dynastic Period; unification of Upper and Lower Egypt**	ca. 3500 B.C.E. **Earliest Sumerian settlements**	ca. 3000 B.C.E. **Invention of writing**
	ca. 2800– 2340 B.C.E. **Sumerian city– states' Early Dynastic period**	ca. 3000 B.C.E. **First urban settlements in Egypt and Mesopotamia; Bronze Age begins in Mesopotamia and Egypt**	ca. 3000 B.C.E. **Temples to gods in Mesopotamia; development of ziggurat temple architecture**
	2700–2200 B.C.E. **Egyptian Old Kingdom**		2700–2200 B.C.E. **Building of pyramids for Egyptian god-kings, development of hieroglyphic writing in Egypt**
	ca. 2370 B.C.E. **Sargon established Akkadian Empire**	ca. 2900– 1150 B.C.E. **Bronze Age Minoan society on Crete; Helladic society on Greek mainland**	
2200– 1600 B.C.E.	2200–2052 B.C.E. **Egyptian First Intermediate Period**	ca. 2000 B.C.E. **Hittites arrive in Asia Minor**	2200–1786 B.C.E. **Rise of Amon-Re as chief Egyptian god**
	2052–1786 B.C.E. **Egyptian Middle Kingdom**	ca 1900 B.C.E. **Amorites in Babylonia**	ca. 1900 B.C.E. **Traditional date for Hebrew patriarch Abraham**
	1792–1760 B.C.E. **Reign of Hammurabi; height of Old Babylonian Kingdom; publication of Code of Hammurabi**		
	1786–1575 B.C.E. **Egyptian Second Intermediate Period**		
	ca. 1700 B.C.E. **Hyksos' invasion of Egypt**		
1600– 1100 B.C.E.	ca. 1600 B.C.E. **Fall of Old Babylonian Kingdom**		Sumerian clay tablet
	1575–1087 B.C.E. **Egyptian New Kingdom (or Empire)**		
	ca. 1400– 1200 B.C.E. **Height of Hittite Empire**		
	ca. 1400– 1200 B.C.E. **Height of Mycenaean power**		
	1367–1350 B.C.E. **Amenhotep IV (Akhenaten) in Egypt**		1367–1360 B.C.E. **Religious revolution led by Akhenaten makes Aton chief Egyptian god**
			1347–1339 B.C.E. **Tutankhamen restores worship of Amon-Re**
		Queen Nefertiti	
	ca. 1250 B.C.E. **Sack of Troy (?)**	ca. 1200 B.C.E. **Hebrews arrive in Palestine**	
	1087–30 B.C.E. **Egyptian Post-Empire Period**		

THE FOUNDATIONS OF WESTERN CIVILIZATION IN THE ANCIENT WORLD

1,000,000 B.C.E.–400 C.E.

	POLITICS AND GOVERNMENT	SOCIETY AND ECONOMY	RELIGION AND CULTURE
1100–500 B.C.E.	ca. 1000–961 B.C.E. **Reign of King David in Israel**	ca. 1100–750 B.C.E. **Greek "Dark Ages"**	
	ca. 961–922 **Reign of King Solomon in Israel**	ca. 1000 B.C.E. **Italic peoples enter Italy**	
	ca. 1100–615 B.C.E. **Assyrian Empire**	ca. 800 B.C.E. **Etruscans enter Italy**	
	ca. 800–400 B.C.E. **Height of Etruscan culture in Italy**	ca. 750–700 B.C.E. **Rise of *Polis* in Greece**	ca. 750 B.C.E. **Hebrew prophets teach monotheism**
	ca. 650 B.C.E. **Spartan constitution formed**	ca. 750–600 B.C.E. **Great age of Greek colonization**	ca. 750 B.C.E. **Traditional date for Homer**
	722 B.C.E. **Israel (northern kingdom) falls to Assyrians**	ca. 700 B.C.E. **Invention of hoplite phalanx**	ca. 750 B.C.E. **Greeks adapt Semitic script and invent the Greek alphabet**
	ca. 700–500 B.C.E. **Rise and decline of tyranny in Greece**		ca. 750–600 B.C.E. **Panhellenic shrines established at Olympia, Delphi, Corinth, and Nemea; athletic festivals attached to them**
	621 B.C.E. **First written law code in Athens**		
	612–539 B.C.E. **Neo-Babylonian (Chaldean) Empire**		ca. 700 B.C.E. **Traditional date for Hesiod**
	594 B.C.E. **Solon's constitutional reforms, Athens**	ca. 600–550 B.C.E. **Spartans adopt new communitarian social system**	ca. 675–500 B.C.E. **Development of Greek lyric and elegiac poetry**
	586 B.C.E. **Destruction of Jerusalem; fall of Judah (southern kingdom); Babylonian Captivity**	ca. 600–500 B.C.E. **Athens develops commerce and a mixed economy**	ca. 570 B.C.E. **Birth of Greek philosophy in Ionia**
	ca. 560–550 B.C.E. **Peloponnesian League begins**		ca. 550 B.C.E. **Oracle of Apollo at Delphi grows to great influence**
	559–530 B.C.E. **Reign of Cyrus the Great in Persia**		ca. 550 B.C.E. **Cult of Dionysus introduced to Athens**
	546 B.C.E. **Persia conquers Lydian Empire of Croesus, including Greek cities of Asia Minor**		539 B.C.E. **Restoration of temple in Jerusalem; return of exiles**
	539 B.C.E. **Persia conquers Babylonia; temple at Jerusalem restored; exiles return from Babylonia**		
	521–485 B.C.E. **Reign of Darius in Persia**		
	509 B.C.E. **Kings expelled from Rome; Republic founded**		
	508 B.C.E. **Clisthenes founds Athenian democracy**		
500–336 B.C.E.	490 B.C.E. **Battle of Marathon**	ca. 500–350 B.C.E. **Spartan population shrinks**	ca. 500–400 B.C.E. **Great age of Athenian tragedy**
	485–465 B.C.E. **Reign of Xerxes in Persia**	ca. 500–350 B.C.E. **Rapid growth in overseas trade**	469–399 B.C.E. **Life of Socrates**

Hercules taming Cerberus, Greek, 530 B.C.E.

1,000,000 B.C.E.–400 C.E.

POLITICS AND GOVERNMENT	SOCIETY AND ECONOMY	RELIGION AND CULTURE

500–336 B.C.E. (cont.)

POLITICS AND GOVERNMENT	SOCIETY AND ECONOMY	RELIGION AND CULTURE
480–479 B.C.E. **Xerxes invades Greece**	477–431 B.C.E. **Vast growth in Athenian wealth**	ca. 450–400 B.C.E. **Great influence of Sophists in Athens**
478–477 B.C.E. **Delian League founded**		ca. 450–385 B.C.E. **Great age of Athenian comedy**
ca. 460–445 B.C.E. **First Peloponnesian War**		448–432 B.C.E. **Periclean building program on Athenian acropolis**
450–449 B.C.E. **Laws of the Twelve Tables, Rome**		
431–404 B.C.E. **Great Peloponnesian War**	431–400 B.C.E. **Peloponnesian War casualties cause decline in size of lower class in Athens, with relative increase in importance of upper and middle classes**	429–347 B.C.E. **Life of Plato**
404–403 B.C.E. **Thirty Tyrants rule at Athens**		ca. 425 B.C.E. **Herodotus' history of the Persian Wars**
400–387 B.C.E. **Spartan war against Persia**		ca. 400 B.C.E. **Thucydides' history of the Peloponnesian War**
398–360 B.C.E. **Reign of Agesilaus at Sparta**		ca. 400–325 B.C.E. **Life of Diogenes the Cynic**
395–387 B.C.E. **Corinthian War**		386 B.C.E. **Foundation of Plato's Academy**
392 B.C.E. **Romans defeat Etruscans**		384–322 B.C.E. **Life of Aristotle**
378 B.C.E. **Second Athenian Confederation**		
371 B.C.E. **Thebans end Spartan hegemony**		
362 B.C.E. **Battle of Mantinea; end of Theban hegemony**		
338 B.C.E. **Philip of Macedon conquers Greece**		

336–31 B.C.E.

POLITICS AND GOVERNMENT	SOCIETY AND ECONOMY	RELIGION AND CULTURE
336–323 B.C.E. **Reign of Alexander III (the Great)**		336 B.C.E. **Foundation of Aristotle's Lyceum**
334 B.C.E. **Alexander invades Asia**		342–271 B.C.E. **Life of Epicurus**
330 B.C.E. **Fall of Persepolis; end Achaemenid rule in Persia**	Alexander the Great & Darius III	335–263 B.C.E. **Life of Zeno the Stoic**
323–301 B.C.E. **Ptolemaic Kingdom (Egypt), Seleucid Kingdom (Syria), and Antigonid Dynasty (Macedon) founded**	ca. 300 B.C.E.– 150 C.E. **Growth of international trade and development of large cities in Hellenistic/Roman world**	ca. 287–212 B.C.E. **Life of Archimedes of Syracuse**
287 B.C.E. **Laws passed by Plebeian Assembly made binding on all Romans; end of Struggle of the Orders**		ca. 275 B.C.E. **Foundation of museum and library make Alexandria the center of Greek intellectual life**
264–241 B.C.E. **First Punic War**		
218–202 B.C.E. **Second Punic War**	ca. 218–135 B.C.E. **Decline of family farm in Italy; growth of tenant farming and cattle ranching**	ca. 250 B.C.E. **Livius Andronicus translates the *Odyssey* into Latin**
215–168 B.C.E. **Rome establishes rule over Hellenistic world**		106–43 B.C.E. **Life of Cicero**

1,000,000 B.C.E.–400 C.E.

	POLITICS AND GOVERNMENT	SOCIETY AND ECONOMY	RELIGION AND CULTURE

336–31 B.C.E. (cont.)

POLITICS AND GOVERNMENT

154–133 B.C.E. **Roman wars in Spain**

133 B.C.E. **Tribunate of Tiberius Gracchus**

123–122 B.C.E. **Tribunate of Gaius Gracchus**

82 B.C.E. **Sulla assumes dictatorship**

60 B.C.E. **First Triumvirate**

46–44 B.C.E. **Caesar's dictatorship**

43 B.C.E. **Second Triumvirate**

31 B.C.E.– 400 C.E.

31 B.C.E. **Octavian and Agrippa defeat Anthony at Actium**

27 B.C.E.–14 C.E. **Reign of Augustus**

14–68 C.E. **Reigns of Julio-Claudian Emperors**

69–96 C.E. **Reigns of Flavian Emperors**

96–180 C.E. **Reigns of "Good Emperors"**

180–192 C.E. **Reign of Commodus**

284–305 C.E. **Reign of Diocletian; reform and division of Roman Empire**

306–337 C.E. **Reign of Constantine**

330 C.E. **Constantinople new capital of Roman Empire**

361–363 C.E. **Reign of Julian the Apostate**

379–395 C.E. **Reign of Theodosius**

376 C.E. **Visigoths enter Roman Empire**

SOCIETY AND ECONOMY

ca. 150 B.C.E. **Growth of slavery as basis of economy in Roman Republic**

The Roman Forum

ca. 150–400 C.E. **Decline of slavery and growth of tenant farming and serfdom in Roman Empire**

ca. 250–400 C.E. **Coloni (Roman tenant farmers) increasingly tied to the land**

301 C.E. **Edict of Maximum Prices at Rome**

RELIGION AND CULTURE

ca. 99–55 B.C.E. **Life of Lucretius**

86–35 B.C.E. **Life Sallust**

ca. 84–54 B.C.E. **Life Catullus**

70–19 B.C.E. **Life of Vergil**

65–8 B.C.E. **Life of Horace**

59 B.C.E.–17 C.E. **Life of Livy**

43 B.C.E.–18 C.E. **Life of Ovid**

9 B.C.E. **Ara Pacis dedicated at Rome**

ca. 4 B.C.E. **Birth of Jesus of Nazareth**

ca. 30 C.E. **Crucifixion of Jesus**

64 C.E. **Christians persecuted by Nero**

66–135 C.E. **Romans suppress rebellions of Jews**

ca. 70–100 C.E. **Gospels written**

ca. 150 C.E. **Ptolemy of Alexandria establishes canonical geocentric model of the universe**

ca. 250–260 C.E. **Severe persecutions by Decius and Valerian**

303 C.E. **Persecution of Christians by Diocletian**

311 C.E. **Galerius issues Edict of Toleration**

312 C.E. **Constantine converts to Christianity**

325 C.E. **Council of Nicaea**

348–420 C.E. **Life of St. Jerome**

354–430 C.E. **Life of St. Augustine**

395 C.E. **Christianity becomes official religion of Roman Empire**

This limestone statue depicts the head of Queen Nefertiti (about 1348–1345 B.C.E.), wife of the rebel pharaoh Akhenaten of the Eighteenth Egyptian Dynasty in the period of the New Kingdom. It was discovered at the modern site called Tell el-Amarna, the ancient city of Akhetaten founded by the pharaoh as his new capital and the center of the new worship of Aten, the disc of the sun. The queen appears to have had unusual importance, serving, along with the pharaoh, as one of the only mediators between the god and the people.

Gary Cralle/The Image Bank

The Birth of Civilization

K E Y   T O P I C S

- The earliest history of humanity, including the beginnings of human culture in the Paleolithic Age, the agricultural revolution and the shift from food gathering to food production, and the emergence of civilization in the great river valleys of the Near East and Asia

- The ancient civilizations of Mesopotamia and Egypt

- The great Near Eastern empires, 1500–539 B.C.E.

- The emergence of Judaism

- The difference in outlook between ancient Near Eastern civilization and ancient Greek civilization

History, in its two senses—as the events of the past that make up the human experience on earth and as the written record of those events—is a subject of both interest and importance. We naturally want to know how we came to be who we are, and how the world we live in came to be what it is. But beyond its intrinsic interest, history provides crucial insight into present human behavior. To understand who we are now, we need to know the record of the past and to try to understand the people and forces that shaped it.

For hundreds of thousands of years after the human species emerged, people lived by hunting, fishing, and collecting wild plants. Only some 10,000 years ago did they learn to cultivate plants, herd animals, and make airtight pottery for storage. These discoveries transformed them from gatherers to producers and allowed them to grow in number and to lead a settled life.

About 5,000 years ago humans learned how to control the waters of great river valleys, making possible much richer harvests and supporting a further increase in population. The peoples of these river valley societies created the earliest civilizations. They invented writing, which, among other things, enabled them to keep inventories of food and other resources. They discovered the secret of smelting metal to make tools and weapons of bronze far superior to the stone implements of earlier times. They came together in towns and cities, where industry and commerce flourished. Complex religions took form, and social divisions increased. Kings— considered to be representatives of the gods or to be themselves divine—emerged as rulers, assisted by priests and defended by well-organized armies.

The first of these civilizations appeared among the Sumerians before 3500 B.C.E. in the Tigris–Euphrates Valley we call Mesopotamia. From the Sumerians to the Assyrians and Babylonians, a series of peoples ruled Mesopotamia, each shaping and passing along its distinctive culture, before the region fell under the control of great foreign empires. A second early civilization emerged in the Nile Valley around 3100 B.C.E. Egyptian civilization developed a remarkably continuous pattern, in part because Egypt was largely protected from invasion by the formidable deserts surrounding the valley. The essential character of Egyptian civilization changed little for nearly 3000 years. Influences from other areas, however, especially Nubia to the south, Syria–Palestine to the northeast, and the Aegean to the north, may be seen during many periods of Egyptian history.

By the fourteenth century B.C.E., several powerful empires had arisen and were vying for dominance in regions that included Egypt, Mesopotamia, and Asia Minor. Northern warrior peoples, among them the Hittites, the Kassites, and the Mitannians, conquered and ruled peoples in various areas. The Hittites dominated in Asia Minor, the Kassites in southern Mesopotamia, and the Mitannians in northern Mesopotamia and Syria. For two centuries, the Hittite and Egyptian Empires struggled with each other for control of Syria–Palestine. By about 1200 B.C.E., however, both these empires had collapsed. Beginning about 850 B.C.E., the Assyrians arose in northern Mesopotamia and ultimately established a mighty new empire, even invading Egypt in the early seventh century B.C.E. The Assyrians were dominant until the late seventh century B.C.E., when they fell to a combination of enemies. Their vast empire was overtaken by the Babylonians, but these people, too, would soon become only a small, though important, part of the enormous empire of Persia.

Among all these great empires nestled a people called the Israelites, who maintained a small independent kingdom in the region between Egypt and Syria for several centuries. This kingdom ultimately fell to the Assyrians and later remained subject to other conquerors. The Israelites possessed little worldly power or wealth, but they created a powerful religion, Judaism, the first certain and lasting worship of a single god in a world of polytheism. Judaism was the seedbed of two other religions that have played a mighty role in the history of the world: Christianity and Islam. The great empires have collapsed, their power forgotten for millennia until the tools of archaeologists uncovered their remains, but the religion of the Israelites, in itself and through its offshoots, has endured as a powerful force.

Early Humans and Their Culture

Scientists estimate that the earth may be as many as 6 billion years old and that creatures very much like humans appeared perhaps 3 to 5 million years ago, probably in Africa. Some 1 to 2 million years ago, erect and tool-using early humans spread over much of Africa, Europe, and Asia. Our own species, *Homo sapiens*, probably emerged some 200,000 years ago, and the earliest remains of fully modern humans date to about 90,000 years ago.

Humans, unlike other animals, are cultural beings. *Culture* may be defined as the ways of living built up by a group and passed on from one generation to another. It includes behavior such as courtship or child-rearing practices; material things such as tools, clothing, and shelter; and ideas, institutions, and beliefs. Language, apparently a uniquely human trait, lies behind our ability to create ideas and institutions and to transmit culture from one generation to another. Our flexible and dexterous hands enable us to hold and make tools and so to create the material artifacts of culture. Because culture is learned and not inherited, it permits rapid adaptation to changing conditions, making possible the spread of humanity to almost all the lands of the globe.

The Paleolithic Age

Anthropologists designate early human cultures by their tools. The earliest period—the Paleolithic (from Greek, "old stone")—dates from the earliest use of stone tools some one million years ago to about 10,000 B.C.E. During this immensely long period, people were hunters, fishers, and gatherers, but not producers, of food. They learned to make and use increasingly sophisticated tools of stone and

In Chauvet cave, near Avignon, France, Paleolithic artists decorated the walls with exquisite drawings of animals. Jean Clottes/Corbis Sygma Photo News

perishable materials like wood; they learned to make and control fire; and they acquired language and the ability to use it to pass on what they had learned.

These early humans, dependent on nature for food and vulnerable to wild beasts and natural disasters, may have developed responses to the world rooted in fear of the unknown—of the uncertainties of human life or the overpowering forces of nature. Religious and magical beliefs and practices may have emerged in an effort to propitiate or coerce the superhuman forces thought to animate or direct the natural world. Evidence of religious faith and practice, as well as of magic, goes as far back as archaeology can take us. Fear or awe, exultation, gratitude, and empathy with the natural world must all have figured in the cave art and in the ritual practices, such as burial, that we find evidenced at Paleolithic sites around the globe. The sense that there is more to the world than meets the eye—in other words, the religious response to the world—seems to be as old as humankind.

The style of life and the level of technology of the Paleolithic period could support only a sparsely settled society. If hunters were too numerous, game would not suffice. In Paleolothic times, people were subject to the same natural and ecological con-straints that today maintain a balance between wolves and deer in Alaska.

Evidence from Paleolithic art and from modern hunter–gatherer societies suggests that human life in the Paleolitic Age was probably characterized by a division of labor by sex. Men engaged in hunting, fishing, making tools and weapons, and fighting against other families, clans, and tribes. Women, less mobile because of childbearing, gathered nuts, berries, and wild grains, wove baskets, and made clothing. Women gathering food probably discovered how to plant and care for seeds. This knowledge eventually made possible the development of agriculture and animal husbandry.

The Neolithic Age

Only a few Paleolithic societies made the initial shift from hunting and gathering to agriculture. Anthropologists and archaeologists disagree as to why, but however it happened, some 10,000 years ago parts of what we now call the Near East began to change from a nomadic hunter–gatherer culture to a more settled agricultural one. Because the shift to agriculture coincided with advances in stone tool technology—

At Ain Ghazal, a Neolithic site in Jordan, several pits contained male and female statues made of clay modeled over a reed framework. Similar figures have been found at Jericho and other sites, all from the same period, about 8500–7000 B.C.E. They were probably used in religious rituals, perhaps connected with ancestor worship, as were plastered skulls, masks, carved heads, and other artifacts. Archeological Museum, Amman, Jordan,kingdom/Art Resource. ©Photograph by Erich Lessing

the development of greater precision, for example, in chipping and grinding—this period is called the Neolithic Age (from Greek, "new stone"). Productive animals, such as sheep and goats, and food crops, such as wheat and barley, were first domesticated in the mountain foothills where they already lived or grew in the wild. Once domestication had taken place, people could move to areas where these plants and animals did not occur naturally, such as the river valleys of the Near East. The invention of pottery during the Neolithic enabled people to store surplus foods and liquids and to transport them, as well as to cook agricultural products that were difficult to eat or digest raw. Cloth was made from flax and wool. Crops required constant care from planting to harvest, so Neolithic farmers built permanent dwellings. The earliest of these tended to be circular huts, large enough to house only one or two people and clustered in groups around a central storage place. Later people built square and rectangular family-sized houses with individual

storage places and enclosures to house livestock. Houses in a Neolithic village were normally all the same size and were built on the same plan, suggesting that most Neolithic villagers had about the same level of wealth and social status. A few items, such as stones and shells, were traded long distance, but Neolithic villages tended to be self-sufficient.

Two larger Neolithic settlements do not fit this village pattern. One was found at Çatal Höyük, in a fertile agricultural region about 150 miles south of Ankara, the capital of present-day Turkey. This was a large town covering over fifteen acres, with a population probably well over 6,000 people. The houses were clustered so closely that they had no doors, but were entered by ladders from the roofs. Many were decorated inside with sculptures of animal heads and horns, as well as paintings that were apparently redone regularly. Some appear to depict ritual or festive occasions involving men and women. One is the world's oldest landscape picture, showing a nearby volcano exploding. The agriculture, arts, and crafts of this town were astonishingly diversified and at a much higher level of attainment than other, smaller settlements of the period. The site of Jericho, an oasis around a spring near the Dead Sea, was occupied as early as 12,000 B.C.E. Around 8000 B.C.E. a town of eight to ten acres grew up, surrounded by a massive stone wall with at least one tower against the inner face. Although this wall may have been for defense, its use is disputed because no other Neolithic settlement has been found with fortifications. The inhabitants of Neolithic Jericho had a mixed agricultural, herding, and hunting economy and may have traded salt. They had no pottery, but plastered the skulls of their dead to make realistic memorial portraits of them. These two sites show that the economy and the settlement patterns of the Neolithic period may be more complicated than many scholars have thought.

Throughout the Paleolithic Age, the human population had been small and relatively stable. The shift from food gathering to food production may not have been associated with an immediate change in population, but over time in the regions where agriculture and animal husbandry appeared, the number of human beings grew at an unprecedented rate. One reason for this is that farmers usually had larger families than hunters. Their children began to work and matured at a younger age than the children of hunters. When animals and plants were domesticated and brought to the river valleys, the relationship between human beings and nature was changed forever. People had learned to control nature, a vital prerequisite for the emergence of civilization. But farmers had to work harder and longer than hunters did, and they had to stay in one place. Herders, on the other hand, often moved from place to place in search of pasture and water, returning to their villages in the spring. Some scholars refer to the dramatic changes in subsistence, settlement, technology, and population of this time as the "Neolithic Revolution." The earliest Neolithic societies appeared in the Mideast about 8000 B.C.E., in China about 4000 B.C.E., and in India about 3600 B.C.E. Neolithic agriculture was based on wheat and barley in the Mideast, on millet and rice in China, and on corn in Mesoamerica, several millennia later.

The Bronze Age and the Birth of Civilization

Neolithic agricultural villages and herding cultures gradually replaced Paleolithic culture in much of the world. Then another major shift occurred, first in the plains along the Tigris and Euphrates Rivers in the region the Greeks and Romans called Mesopotamia (modern Iraq), later in the valley of the Nile River in Egypt, and somewhat later in India and the Yellow River basin in China. This shift was associated initially with the growth of towns alongside villages, creating a hierarchy of larger and smaller settlements in the same region. Some towns then grew into much larger urban centers and often drew population into them, so that nearby villages and towns declined. The urban centers, or cities, usually had monumental buildings, such as temples and fortifications. These were vastly larger than individual houses and could be built only by the sustained effort of hundreds and even thousands of people over many years. Elaborate representational artwork appeared, sometimes made of rare and imported materials. New technologies, such as smelting and the manufacture of metal tools and weapons, were characteristic of urban life. Commodities like pottery and textiles that had been made in individual houses in villages were mass produced in cities, which also were characterized by social stratification—that is, different classes of people based on factors such as control of resources, family, religious or political authority, and personal wealth. The earliest writing is also associated with the growth of cities. Writing, like representational art, was a powerful means of communicating over space and time and was probably invented to deal with urban problems of management and record keeping. These attributes—urbanism; technological, industrial, and social change; long-distance trade; and new methods of symbolic communication—are defining characteristics of the form of human culture called *civilization*. At about the time the earliest civilizations were emerging, someone discovered how to combine tin and copper to make a stronger and more useful material—bronze. Archaeologists coined the term Bronze Age to refer to the period 3100–1200 B.C.E. in the near East and eastern Mediterranean.

Early Civilizations to about 1000 B.C.E.

By 4000 years B.C.E., people had settled in large numbers in the river-watered lowlands of Mesopotamia and Egypt. By about 3000 B.C.E., when the invention of writing gave birth to history, urban life and the organization of society into centralized states were well established in the valleys of the Tigris and Euphrates Rivers in Mesopotamia and of the Nile River in Egypt.

Much of the population of cities consists of people who do not grow their own food, so urban life is possible only where farmers and stockbreeders can be made to produce a substantial surplus beyond their own needs. Also, some process has to be in place so that this surplus can be collected and redeployed to sustain city dwellers. Efficient farming of plains alongside rivers, moreover, requires intelligent management of water resources for irrigation. In Mesopotamia, irrigation was essential, because in the south (Babylonia), there was not enough rainfall to sustain crops. Furthermore, the rivers, fed by melting snows in Armenia, rose to flood the fields in the spring, about the time for harvest, when water was not needed. When water was needed for the autumn planting, less was available. This meant that people had to build dikes to keep the rivers from flooding the fields in the spring and had to devise means to store water for use in the autumn. The Mesopotamians became skilled at that activity early on. In Egypt, on the other hand, the Nile River flooded at the right moment for cultivation, so irrigation was simply a matter of directing the water to the fields. In Mesopotamia, villages, towns, and cities tended to be strung along natural watercourses and, eventually, man-made canal systems. Thus, control of water could be important in warfare, because an enemy could cut off water upstream of a city to force it to submit. Since the Mesopotamian plain was flat, branches of the rivers often changed their courses, and people would have to abandon their cities and move to new locations. Archeologists once believed that urban life and centralized government arose in response to the need to regulate irrigation. This theory supposed that only a strong central authority could construct and maintain the necessary waterworks. However, archeologists have now shown that large-scale irrigation appeared only long after urban civilization had already developed, so major waterworks were a *consequence* of urbanism, not a cause of it.

Mesopotamian Civilization

The first civilization appears to have arisen in Mesopotamia. The region is divided into two ecological zones, roughly north and south of modern

Baghdad. In the south (Babylonia), as noted, irrigation is vital; in the north (Assyria), agriculture is possible with rainfall and wells. The south has high yields from irrigated lands, while the north has lower yields, but much more land under cultivation, so it can produce more than the south. The oldest Mesopotamian cities seem to have been founded by a people called the Sumerians during the fourth millennium B.C.E. in the land of Sumer, which is the southern half of Babylonia. By 3000 B.C.E., the Sumerian city of Uruk was the largest city in the world (see Map 1–1). Colonies of people from Uruk built cities and outposts in northern Syria and southern Anatolia. One of these, at Habubah Kabirah on the Euphrates River in Syria, was built on a regular plain on virgin ground, with strong defensive walls, but was abandoned after a few generations and never inhabited again. No one knows how the Sumerians were able to establish colonies so far from their homeland or even what their purpose was. They may have been trading centers.

From about 2800 to 2370 B.C.E., in what is called the Early Dynastic period, several Sumerian city–states existed in southern Mesopotamia, arranged in north–south lines along the major watercourses. Among these cities were Uruk, Ur, Nippur, Shuruppak, and Lagash. Some of the city–states formed leagues among themselves that apparently had both political and religious significance. Quarrels over water and agricultural land led to incessant warfare, and in time, stronger towns and leagues conquered weaker ones and expanded to form kingdoms ruling several city–states.

Peoples who, unlike the Sumerians, mostly spoke Semitic languages (that is, languages in the same family as Arabic and Hebrew) occupied northern Mesopotamia and Syria. The Sumerian language is not related to any language known today. Many of these Semitic peoples absorbed aspects of Sumerian culture, especially writing. At the western end of this broad territory, at Ebla in northern Syria, scribes kept records using Sumerian writing and studied Sumerian word

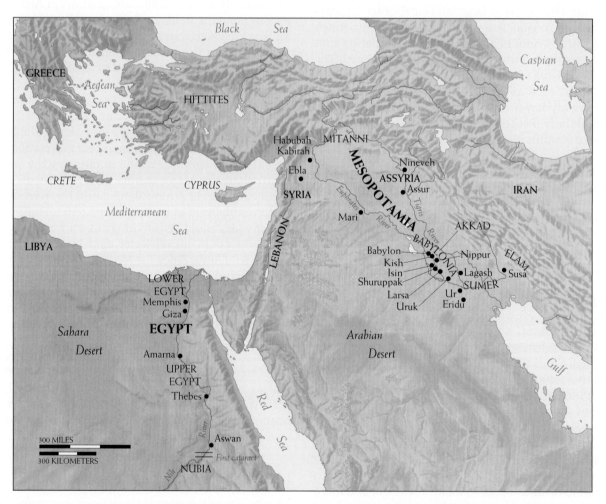

MAP 1–1 THE ANCIENT NEAR EAST *There were two ancient river valley civilizations. While Egypt was united into a single state, Mesopotamia was long divided into a number of city–states.*

lists. In northern Babylonia, the Mesopotamians believed that the large city of Kish had the first kings in history. In the far east of this territory, not far from modern Baghdad, a people known as the Akkadians established their own kingdom at a capital city called Akkade, under their first king, Sargon, who had been a servant of the king of Kish.

The Akkadians conquered all the Sumerian city–states and invaded southwestern Iran and northern Syria. This was the first empire in history, having a heartland, provinces, and an absolute ruler. It included numerous peoples, cities, languages, and cultures, as well as different ecological zones, under one rule. Sargon's name became legendary as the first great conqueror of history. His grandson, Naram-Sin, ruled from the Persian Gulf to the Mediterranean Sea, with a standardized administration, unheard-of wealth and power, and a grand style that to later Mesopotamians was a high point of their history. Naram-Sin even declared himself a god and had temples built to himself, something no Sumerian ruler had ever done. (See "Art and the West.") External attack and internal weakness destroyed the Akkadian empire, but several smaller states flourished independently, notably Lagash in Sumer, under it's ruler Gudea.

About 2125 B.C.E. the Sumerian city of Ur rose to dominance, and the rulers of the Third Dynasty of Ur established an empire built on the foundation of the Akkadian empire, but far smaller. In this period, Sumerian culture and literature flourished. Epic poems were composed, glorifying the deeds of the ancestors of the kings of Ur. A highly centralized administration kept detailed records of agriculture, animal husbandry, commerce, and other matters. Over a hundred thousand of these documents have been found in the ruins of Sumerian cities. After little more than a century of prominence, the kingdom of Ur disintegrated in the face of famine and invasion. From the east, the Elamites attacked the city of Ur and captured the king. From the north and west, a Semitic-speaking people, the Amorites, invaded Mesopotamia in large numbers, settling around the Sumerian cities and eventually founding their own dynasties in some of them, such as at Uruk, Babylon, Isin, and Larsa.

The fall of the Third Dynasty of Ur put an end to Sumerian rule, and the Sumerians gradually disappeared as an identifiable group. The Sumerian language survived only in writing as the learned language of Babylonia taught in schools and used by priests and scholars. So great was the respect for Sumerian, that seventeen centuries after the fall of Ur, when Alexander the Great arrived in Babylon, Sumerian was still used as a scholarly and religious language there.

This statue of Gudea, city ruler of Lagash after the fall of the Akkadian empire, shows him as a pious Sumerian ruler. It was carved of very hard imported black stone. A brief historical inscription is visible on his cloak. Gudea built a major temple to a local deity at Lagash, Ningirsu, and describes the work, step by step, in one of the longest Sumerian poems known today. Scala/Art Resource, NY

For some time after the fall of Ur, there was relative peace in Babylonia under the Amorite kings of Isin, who used Sumerian at their court and considered themselves the successors of the kings of Ur. Eventually, another Amorite dynasty at the city of Larsa contested control of Babylonia, and a period of warfare began, mostly centering around attacks on strategic points on waterways. A powerful new dynasty at Babylon defeated Isin, Larsa, and other rivals and dominated Mesopotamia for nearly 300 years. Its high point was the reign of its most famous king, Hammurabi (r. ca. 1792–1750 B.C.E.), best known today for the collection of laws that bears his name. Hammurabi destroyed the great city of Mari on the Euphrates and created a kingdom embracing most of Mesopotamia.

A Monument to a King's Triumph:
The Victory Stele of Naram-Sin

The Victory Stele of the Akkadian ruler Naram-Sin commemorates the king's campaign against the Lullubi, a people living in the northern Zagros Mountains, along the eastern frontier of Mesopotamia. Kings set up monuments like this one in the courtyards of temples to record their deeds. They were also left in remote corners of the empire to warn distant peoples of the death and enslavement awaiting the king's enemies. On a slab of limestone over six feet high, the sculptor posed Naram-Sin so that the ruler's size and placement dominate the scene. The king, wearing the horned helmet denoting divine power, strides forward at the head of his army. Beneath his feet are the trampled bodies of defeated Lullubi. He seems oblivious to the hide-clad survivors to the right, who beg for mercy. Originally, a cuneiform inscription describing the king's triumph occupied much of the sky area, but it is now so abraded that it is barely visible.

The mountain summit bears a second cuneiform inscription, this one added in the twelfth century B.C. when the Elamites captured the stele and took it back to their capital of Susa, in southwestern Iran. The seizure of artifacts as war booty was common practice in the ancient world, with monuments often being destroyed or mutilated in the process. This piece was spared that fate, as was the Stele of the Laws of Hammurabi, which the Elamites also brought to Susa. Modern archaeologists discovered both stelae, along with other Mesopotamian works of art, in the ruins of Susa.

The Stele of Naram-Sin is one of the finest sculptures to survive from the Akkadian period. The Akkadians built the first empire known to history, and new features in their art, many of which we can see in this piece, reflect that imperialism. Sumerian art confined figures to horizontal rows, or registers. Here Naram-Sin and his army move diagonally across the space, energetically ascending and conquering. For the first time, Mesopotamian art shows a sense of landscape, with the rocky terrain and gnarled trees signaling how far distant from Mesopotamia Naram-Sin has pushed the borders of his empire. The human figures, even those of the enemy, are naturalistically modeled, in sharp contrast to the Sumerian emphasis on gesture at the expense of anatomy.

The portrayal of the gods on this stele is especially striking. They appear at the top, three stars symbolizing Naram-Sin's patron deities. In a comparable Sumerian victory stele, made just a few generations earlier, the god of the successful city, shown in anthropomorphic form, occupies nearly one entire side, holding enemy prisoners in a net. In contrast, the Akkadian focus here is on Naram-Sin, warrior–king and deified ruler.

The Victory Stele of Naram–Sin, King of Akkad, over the mountain-dwelling Lullubi, Mesopotamian, Akkadian Period, c. 2230 B.C.E. (pink sandstone). Louvre, Paris, France. The Bridgeman Art Library International Ltd.

Collections of laws existed as early as the Third Dynasty of Ur, and Hammurabi's owed much to earlier models and different legal traditions. His collection of laws, now referred to as the Code of Hammurabi, reveals a society divided by class. There were nobles, commoners, and slaves, and the law did not treat all of them equally. In general, punishments were harsh, based literally on the principle of "an eye for an eye, a tooth for a tooth," whereas Sumerian law often levied fines instead of bodily mutilation or death. Disputes over property and other complaints were heard in the first instance by local city assemblies of leading citizens and heads of families. Professional judges heard cases for a fee and held court near the city gate. In Mesopotamian trials, witnesses and written evidence had to be produced and a written verdict issued. False testimony was punishable by death. Sometimes the contesting parties would submit to an oath before the gods, on the theory that no one would risk swearing a false oath. In cases where evidence or oath could not establish the truth, the contesting parties might take an ordeal, such as being thrown into the river for the god to decide who was telling the truth. Cases of capital punishment could be appealed to the king. Hammurabi was closely concerned with the details of his kingdom, and his surviving letters often deal with minor local disputes.

About 1600 B.C.E., the Babylonian kingdom fell apart under the impact of invasions from the north by the Hittites, Hurrians, and Kassites, all non-Mesopotamian peoples.

GOVERNMENT   From the earliest historical records, it is clear that the Sumerians were ruled by monarchs in some form. The earliest Sumerian rulers are shown in their art leading an army, killing prisoners, and making offerings to the gods. The type of rule varied at different times and places. In later Assyria, for example, the king served as chief priest, while in Babylonia the priesthood was separate from royalty. Royal princesses were sometimes appointed as priestesses of important gods. One of the most famous of these was Enheduanna, daughter of Sargon of Akkad. She is the first author in history whose writings can be identified with a real person. Although she was an Akkadian, she wrote complicated, passionate, and intensely personal poetry in the Sumerian language, in which she tells of important historical events that she experienced. In one passage, she compares the agony of writing a poem to giving birth.

The government and the temples cultivated large areas of land to support their staffs and retinue. Laborers of low social status who were given rations of raw foods and other commodities to sustain them and their families did some of the work on this land. Citizens leased some land for a share of the crop and a cash payment. These lands were carefully surveyed, and sometimes the crop could be estimated in advance. The government and temples owned large herds of sheep, goats, cattle, and donkeys. The Sumerian city–states exported wool and textiles to buy metals, such as copper, that were not available in Mesopotamia. Families and private individuals often owned their own farmland or houses in the cities, which they bought and sold as they liked.

A Letter Home

In this letter from a son to his mother, the young man argues for a new suit of clothes.

❖ *What seems to be the most important reason he needs new clothes? Are his old ones worn out? In Mesopotamia, when you wrote a petition, you saved the strongest argument for last. What does he hope will really move his mother? If you were his mother, how would you respond to his letter?*

Tell the Lady Zinû: Iddin-Sin sends the following message:

May the gods Shamash, Marduk, and Ilabrat keep you forever in good health for my sake.

From year to year, the clothes of the [young] gentlemen here become better, but you let my clothes get worse from year to year. Indeed, you persisted(?) in making my clothes poorer and more scanty. At a time when in our house wool is used up like bread, you have made me poor clothes. The son of Adad-iddinam, whose father is only an assistant of my father, (has) two new sets of clothes...while you fuss even about a single set of clothes for me. In spite of the fact that you bore me and his mother only adopted him, his mother loves him, while you, you do not love me!

From translation by A. Leo Oppenheim in *Letters from Mesopotamia* (Chicago: The University of Chicago Press), p. 85.

The Babylonian Story of the Flood

The passage that follows is part of the Babylonian Epic of Gilgamesh. *It did not form a part of the original Epic, but was added at some point from an earlier independent Babylonian* Story of the Flood, *which suggested that the gods sent a flood as a drastic effort at population control because there were too many people on the earth. The gods realized their mistake when there were no more people to provide for them, so they made sure that everyone would die sooner or later, and they restricted childbirth through various social and medical means. A version of this story was later combined with the* Epic of Gilgamesh. *Gilgamesh was a legendary king who became terrified of death when his best friend and companion died. He resolved to locate Utanapishtim, who, with his wife, was the only survivor of the great flood, in order to ask him how he, too, could escape death. After many adventures, Gilgamesh crossed the distant ocean and the "waters of death" to ask Utanapishtim the secret of eternal life. In response, Utanapishtim narrated the story of the great flood, to show that his own immortality derived from a one-time event in the past, so that Gilgamesh could not share his destiny. Note the similarities between this and the biblical story of Noah, as well as the important differences between them.*

❖ *How is this tale similar to the story of Noah in the* Book of Genesis *in the Hebrew Bible? How is it different?*

Six days and seven nights
The wind continued, the deluge and windstorm
   levelled the land.
When the seventh day arrived,
The windstorm and deluge left off their battle,
Which had struggled, like a woman in labor.
The sea grew calm, the tempest stilled, the deluge ceased.
I looked at the weather, stillness reigned,
And the whole human race had turned into clay.
The landscape was flat as a rooftop.
I opened the hatch, sunlight fell upon my face.
Falling to my knees, I sat down weeping,
Tears running down my face.
I looked at the edges of the world, the borders
   of the sea,
At twelve times sixty double leagues the periphery emerged.

The boat had come to rest on Mount Nimush,
Mount Nimush held the boat fast, not letting
   it move.
One day, a second day Mount Nimush held the
   boat fast, not letting it move.
A third day, a fourth day Mount Nimush held
   the boat fast, not letting it move.
A fifth day, a sixth day Mount Nimush held the
   boat fast, not letting it move.
When the seventh day arrived,
I brought out a dove and set it free.
The dove went off and returned,
No landing place came to its view, so it
   turned back.
I brought out a swallow and set it free,
The swallow went off and returned,
No landing space came to its view, so it
   turned back.

WRITING AND MATHEMATICS   Government, business, and scholarship required a good system of writing. The Sumerians invented the writing system now known as *cuneiform* (from the Latin *cuneus*, "wedge") because of the wedge-shaped marks they made by writing on clay tablets with a cut reed stylus. At first the writing system was sketchy, giving only a few elements of a sentence to help a reader remember something that he probably already know. Later, people thought to write whole sentences in the order in which they were to be spoken, so writing could communicate new information to a reader. The Sumer-

ian writing system used several thousand characters, some of which stood for words and some for sounds. Some characters stood for many different sounds or words, and some sounds could be written using a choice of many different characters. The result was a writing system that was difficult to learn. Sumerian students were fond of complaining about their unfair teachers, how hard their schoolwork was, and their too-short vacations. Sumerian and Babylonian schools emphasized language and literature, accounting, legal practice, and mathematics, especially geometry, along with memorization of much abstract knowledge that

I brought out a raven and set it free.
The raven went off and saw the ebbing of the
    waters.
It ate, preened, left droppings, did not turn back.
I released all to the four directions,
I brought out an offering and offered it to the
    four directions.
I set up an incense burner on the summit of
    the mountain,
I arranged seven and seven cult vessels,
I heaped reeds, cedar, and myrtle in their bowls.
The gods smelled the savor,
The gods smelled the sweet savor,
The gods crowded round the sacrificer like flies.
As soon as the Belet-ili arrived,
She held up the great fly-ornaments that Anu
    had made in his ardor:
    'O ye gods, as surely as I shall not forget
    these lapis pendants on my neck,
    'I shall be mindful of these days and not for-
    get, not ever!
    'The gods should come to the incense burner,
    'But Enlil should not come to the incense
    burner,
    'For he, irrationally, brought on the flood,
    'And marked my people for destruction!'
As soon as Enlil arrived,
He saw the boat, Enlil flew into a rage,
He was filled with fury at the gods:
    'Who came through alive? No man was to
    survive destruction!'
Ninurta made ready to speak,
Said to the valiant Enlil:
    'Who but Ea could contrive such a thing?
    'For Ea alone knows every artifice.'
Ea made ready to speak,

Said to the valiant Enlil:
    'You, O valiant one, are the wisest of the gods,
    'How could you, irrationally, have brought
    on the flood?
    'Punish the wrong-doer for his wrong-doing,
    'Punish the transgressor for his transgression,
    'But be lenient, lest he be cut off,
    'Bear with him, lest he [...].
    'Instead of your bringing on a flood,
    'Let the lion rise up to diminish the
    human race!
    'Instead of your bringing on a flood,
    'Let the wolf rise up to diminish the
    human race!
    'Instead of your bringing on a flood,
    'Let famine rise up to wreak havoc in the land!
    'Instead of your bringing on a flood,
    'Let pestilence rise up to wreak havoc in
    the land!
    'It was not I who disclosed the secret of the
    great gods,
    'I made Atrahasis have a dream and so he
    heard the secret of the gods.
    'Now then, make some plan for him.'
Then Enlil came up into the boat,
Leading me by the hand, he brought me up too.
He brought my wife up and had her kneel be-
    side me.
He touched our brows, stood between us to
    bless us:
    'Hitherto Utanapishtim has been a human
    being,
    'Now Utanapishtim and his wife shall be-
    come like us gods.
    'Utanapishtim shall dwell far distant at the
    source of the rivers.'

"The Babylonian Story of the Flood" from "The Babylonian Epic of Gilgamesh", in *The Epic of Gilgamesh*, translated by Benjamin R. Foster. Copyright © 2001 by W.W. Norton &Company. Used by permission of W.W. Norton & Company, Inc.

had no relevance to everyday life. The ability to read and write was restricted to an elite who could afford to go to school. Success in school, however, and factors such as good family connections, meant that a literate Sumerian could find employment as a clerk, surveyor, teacher, diplomat, or administrator.

The Sumerians also began the development of mathematics. The earliest Sumerian records suggest that before 3000 B.C.E. people had not yet thought of the concept of number independently of counting specific things. Therefore, the earliest writing used different numerals for counting different things, and the nu-

merals had no independent value. (The same sign could be 10 or 18, for example, depending on what was counted.) Once an independent concept of number was established, mathematics developed rapidly. The Sumerian system was based on the number 60 ("sexagesimal"), rather than the number 10 ("decimal"), the system in general use today. Sumerian counting survives in the modern 60-minute hour and the circle of 360 degrees. By the time of Hammurabi, the Mesopotamians were expert in many types of mathematics, including mathematical astronomy. The calendar the Mesopotamians used had twelve lunar months of thirty days each. To keep it in accordance with the solar year and the seasons, the Mesopotamians occasionally introduced a thirteenth month.

RELIGION   The Sumerians and their successors worshiped many gods and goddesses. They were visualized in human form, with human needs and weaknesses. Most of the gods were identified with some natural phenomenon such as the sky, fresh water, or storms. They differed from humans in their greater power, sublime position in the universe, and immortality. The Mesopotamians believed that the human race was created to serve the gods and to relieve the gods of the necessity of providing for themselves. The gods were considered universal, but also residing in specific places, usually one important god or goddess in each city. Mesopotamian temples were run like great households where the gods were fed lavish meals, entertained with music, and honored with devotion and ritual. There were gardens for their pleasure and bedrooms to retire to at night. The images of the gods were dressed and adorned with the finest

materials. Theologians organized the gods into families and generations. Human social institutions, such as kingship, or crafts, such as carpentry, were associated with specific gods, so the boundaries between human and divine society were not always clearly drawn. Since the great gods were visualized like human rulers, remote from the common people and their concerns, the Mesopotamians imagined another more personal intercessor god who was supposed to look after a person, rather like a guardian spirit. The public festivals of the gods were important holidays, with parades, ceremonies, and special foods. People wore their best clothes and celebrated their city and its gods. The Mesopotamians were religiously tolerant and readily accepted the possibility that different people might have different gods.

The Mesopotamians had a vague and gloomy picture of the afterworld. The winged spirits of the dead were recognizable as individuals. They were confined to a dusty, dark netherworld, doomed to perpetual hunger and thirst unless someone offered them food and drink. Some spirits escaped to haunt human beings. There was no preferential treatment in the afterlife for those who had led religious or virtuous lives—everyone was in equal misery. Mesopotamian families often had a ceremony to remember and honor their dead. People were usually buried together with goods such as pottery and ornaments. In the Early Dynastic period, certain kings were buried with a large retinue of attendants, including soldiers and musicians, who apparently took poison during the funeral ceremony and were buried where they fell. But this practice soon disappeared. Children were sometimes buried under the floors of houses. Some families used burial vaults, others large cemeteries. No tombstones or inscriptions identified the deceased. Mesopotamian religion focused on problems of this world and how to lead a good life before dying.

The Mesopotamian peoples who came after the Sumerians believed that the gods revealed a person's destiny to those who could understand the omens, or indications of what was going to happen. The Babylonians therefore developed an elaborate science of divination based on chance observations, such as a cat walking in the street, and on ritual procedures, such as asking a question of the gods then slaughtering a sheep to examine its liver and entrails for certain marks and features. Some omens, such as monstrous births or eclipses, were thought to apply to the government, while others, such as birds flying over a person's house, were thought to apply to the individual. Thousands of omens, including both the observation and the outcome thereof, were compiled into huge encyclopedias that scholars could consult.

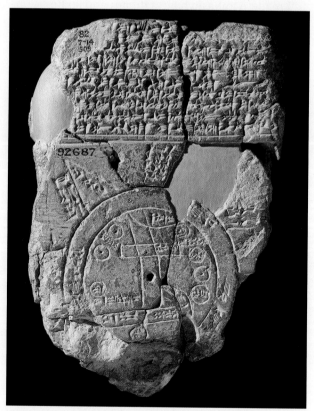

This clay tablet from the Neo-Babylonian period (612–539 B.C.E.) shows a map of the world as seen by the Babylonians. The "Salt Sea" is shown as a circle. An arc inside it is labeled "Mountains." Below it is a rectangular box marked "Babylon," and to the right of the box is a small circle marked "Assyria." Courtesy of the Trustees of the British Museum. © The British Museum

Divination was often done before making major decisions and to discover the causes of illness, unhappiness, and failure. The hope was to avert unfavorable future events by discovering them in time and carrying out rituals or avoiding certain actions. Diviners were paid professionals, not priests. Witchcraft was also widely feared and blamed for illnesses and harm to people. There were many rituals against witchcraft, such as making a figurine of a witch and burning it, thereby burning up the witchcraft.

Religion played a large part in the literature and art of Mesopotamia. Epic poems told of the deeds of the gods, such as how the world was created and organized, of a great flood the gods sent to wipe out the human race, and of the hero–king Gilgamesh, who tried to escape death by going on a fantastic journey to find the sole survivor of the great flood. (See "The Babylonian Story of the Flood.") There were also many literary and artistic works that were not religious in character, so we should not imagine that religion dominated all aspects of the Mesopotamians' lives. Religious architecture took the form of great temple complexes in the major cities. The most imposing religious structure was the *ziggurat*, a tower in stages, sometimes with a small chamber on top. The terraces may have been planted with trees to resemble a mountain. Poetry about ziggurats often compares them to mountains, with their peaks in the sky and their roots in the netherworld, linking heaven to earth, but their precise purpose is not known. Eroded remains of many of these monumental structures still dot the Iraqi landscape. Through the Bible, they have entered western tradition as "the tower of Babel."

Society Hundreds of thousands of cuneiform texts from the early third millenium B.C.E. until the third century B.C.E. give us a full and detailed picture of how peoples in ancient Mesopotamia conducted their lives and of the social conditions in which they lived. From the time of Hammurabi, for example, there are many royal letters to and from the various rulers of the age, letters from the king to his subordinates, administrative records from many different cities, and numerous letters and documents belonging to private families.

Categorizing the laws of Hammurabi according to the aspects of life with which they deal reveals much about Babylonian life in his time. The third largest category of laws deals with commerce, relating to such issues as contracts, debts, rates of interest, security, and default. Business documents of Hammurabi's time show how people invested their money in land, moneylending, government contracts, and international trade. Some of these laws regulate professionals, such as builders, judges, and surgeons. The second largest category of laws deals with land tenure, especially land given by the king to soldiers and

This stele preserves the laws of Hammurabi. In the relief carving at the top, Hammurabi, standing prayerfully to the left, receives a rod and ring, perhaps symbols of justice, from the sun god, who is seated and wears the special crown of the gods. The text of the laws is inscribed below "to administer the law of the land, to prescribe the ordinances of the land, to give justice to the oppressed." Reunion des Musèes Nationaux

marines in return for their service. The letters of Hammurabi that deal with land tenure show that he was concerned to uphold individual rights of landholders against powerful officials who tried to take their land from them. The largest category of laws relates to the family and its maintenance and protection, including marriage, inheritance, and adoption.

Parents usually arranged marriages, and betrothal was followed by the signing of a marriage contract. The bride usually left her own family to join her husband's. The husband-to-be could make a bridal payment, and the father of the bride-to-be provided a dowry for his daughter in money, land, or objects. A

Key Events and People in Mesopotamian History	
ca. 3500 B.C.E.	Development of Sumerian cities, especially Uruk
ca. 2800–2370 B.C.E.	Early Dynastic period of Sumerian city–states
ca. 2370 B.C.E.	Sargon establishes Akkadian dynasty and empire
ca. 2125–2027 B.C.E.	Third Dynasty of Ur
ca. 2000–1800 B.C.E.	Establishment of Amorites in Mesopotamia
ca. 1792–1750 B.C.E.	Reign of Hammurabi
ca. 1550 B.C.E.	Establishment of Kassite Dynasty at Babylon

An Assyrian Woman Writes to Her Husband, ca. 1800 B.C.E.

The wives of early Assyrian businessmen were often active in their husbands' business affairs. They made extra money for themselves by having slave girls weave textiles that the husbands then sold on business trips. Their letters are one of the largest groups of women's records from the ancient world. The woman writing this letter, Taram-Kubi, complains of her husband's selfishness and points out all the matters she has worked on during his absence on business.

❖ *What functions did this woman perform on behalf of the family? How do you judge her real power in regard to her husband? On what evidence do you base that judgment? What does this document reveal about the place of women in Assyrian society?*

You wrote to me saying, "You'll need to safeguard the bracelets and rings which are there so they'll be available [to buy] food." In fact, you sent [the man] Ilum-bani a half pound of gold! Which are the bracelets you left me? When you left, you didn't leave me an ounce of silver, you picked the house clean and took away everything! After you left, there was a severe famine in the city. Not so much as a quart of grain did you leave me, I always had to buy grain for our food. Besides that, I paid the assessment for the divine icon(?); in fact, I paid for my part in full. Besides that, I paid over to the Town Hall the grain owed [the man] Atata. What is the extravagance you keep writing to me about? There is nothing for us to eat—we're the ones being extravagant? I picked up whatever I had to hand and sent it to you—today I'm living in an empty house. It's high time you sent me the money realized on my weavings, in silver, from what you have to hand, so I can buy ten quarts of grain!

Translation, Benjamin R. Foster, 1999.

marriage started out monogamous, but a husband whose wife was childless or sickly could take a second wife. Sometimes husbands also sired children from domestic slave women. Women could own their own property and do business on their own. Women divorced by their husbands without good cause could get their dowry back. A woman seeking divorce could also recover her dowry if her husband could not convict her of wrongdoing. A married woman's place was thought to be in the home, but hundreds of letters between wives and husbands show them as equal partners in the ventures of life. (See "An Assyrian Woman Writes to Her Husband, ca. 1800 B.C.E.") Single women who were not part of families could set up in business on their own, often as tavern owners or moneylenders, or could be associated with temples, sometimes working as midwives and wetnurses, or taking care of orphaned children.

SLAVERY: CHATTEL SLAVES AND DEBT SLAVES   There were two main types of slavery in Mesopotamia: chattel and debt slavery. Chattel slaves were bought like any other piece of property and had no legal rights. They had to wear their hair in a certain way and were sometimes branded or tatooed on their hands. They were often non-Mesopotamians bought from slave merchants. Prisoners of war could also be enslaved. Chattel slaves were expensive luxuries during most of Mesopotamian history. They were used in domestic service rather than in production, such as fieldwork. A wealthy household might have five or six slaves, male and female.

Debt slavery was more common than chattel slavery. Rates of interest were high, as much as $33\frac{1}{3}$, so people often defaulted on loans. One reason the interest rates were so high was that the government periodically canceled certain types of debts, debt slavery, and obligations, so lenders ran the risk of losing their money. If debtors had pledged themselves or members of their families as surety for a loan, they became the slave of the creditor; their labor went to pay the interest on the loan. Debt slaves could not be sold, but could redeem their freedom by paying off the loan. True chattel slavery did not become common until the Neo-Babylonian period (612–539 B.C.E.).

Although laws against fugitive slaves or slaves who denied their masters were harsh—the Code of Hammurabi permits the death penalty for anyone who sheltered or helped a runaway slave to escape—Mesopotamian slavery appears enlightened compared with other slave systems in history. Slaves were generally of the same people as their masters. They had been enslaved because of misfortune from which their masters were not immune, and they generally labored alongside them. Slaves could engage in business and, with certain restrictions, hold property. They could marry free men or women, and the resulting children would normally be free. A slave who acquired the means could buy his or her freedom. Children of a slave by a master might be allowed to share his property after his death. Nevertheless, slaves were property, subject to an owner's will and had little legal protection.

Egyptian Civilization

As Mesopotamian civilization arose in the valley of the Tigris and Euphrates, another great civilization emerged in Egypt, centered on the Nile River. From its sources in Lake Victoria and the Ethiopian highlands, the Nile flows north some 4,000 miles to the Mediterranean. Ancient Egypt included the 750-mile stretch of smooth, navigable river from Aswan to the sea. South of Aswan the river's course is interrupted by several cataracts—rocky areas of rapids and whirlpools.

The Egyptians recognized two sets of geographical divisions in their country. Upper (southern) Egypt consisted of the narrow valley of the Nile. Lower (northern) Egypt referred to the broad triangular area, named by the Greeks after their letter "delta," formed by the Nile as it branches out to empty into the Mediterranean. (See Map 1–2.) They also made a distinction between what they termed the "black land," the dark fertile fields along the Nile, and the "red land," the desert cliffs and plateaus bordering the valley.

The Nile alone made agriculture possible in Egypt's desert environment. Each year the rains of central Africa caused the river to rise over its floodplain, cresting in September and October. In places the plain extends several miles on either side, while elsewhere the cliffs slope down to the water's edge. When the floodwaters receded, they left a rich layer of organically fertile silt. The construction and maintenance of canals, dams, and irrigation ditches to control the river's water, together with careful planning and organization of planting and harvesting, produced agricultural prosperity unmatched in the ancient world.

The Nile served as the major highway connecting Upper and Lower Egypt. There was also a network of desert roads running north and south, as well as routes across the eastern desert to the Sinai and the Red Sea. Other tracks led to oases in the western desert. Thanks to geography and climate, Egypt was more isolated and enjoyed far more security than Mesopotamia. This security, along with the predictable flood calendar, gave Egyptian civilization a more optimistic outlook than

One of the hallmarks of the early river civilizations was the development of techniques to increase harvests. This statue from the Old Kingdom in Egypt (ca. 2700–2200 B.C.E.) shows a woman grinding wheat for bread. Kenneth Garrettings/National Geographic Society

the civilizations of the Tigris and Euphrates, which were more prone to storms, flash floods, and invasions.

The 3,000-year span of ancient Egyptian history is traditionally divided into thirty-one royal dynasties, from the first, said to have been founded by Menes, the king who originally united Upper and Lower Egypt, to the last, conquered by Alexander the Great in 332 B.C.E. (as we shall see in Chapter 3). Ptolemy, one of Alexander's generals, founded the Ptolemaic Dynasty, whose last ruler was Cleopatra. In 30 B.C.E. the Romans defeated Egypt, effectively ending the independent existence of a civilization that had lasted three millennia.

The unification of Upper and Lower Egypt was vital, for it meant that the entire river valley could benefit from an unimpeded distribution of resources. Three times in its history, Egypt experienced a century or more of political and social disintegration, known as Intermediate Periods. During these eras, rival dynasties often set up separate power bases in Upper and Lower Egypt until a strong leader reunified the land.

The three largest pyramids of Egypt, located at Giza, near Cairo, are the colossal tombs of pharaohs of the Fourth Dynasty (ca. 2640–2510 B.C.E.): Khufu (right), Chafre (center), and Menkaure (left). The small pyramids and tombs at their bases were those of the pharaohs' queens and officials. Pictor

THE OLD KINGDOM (2700–2200 B.C.E.)   The Old Kingdom represents the culmination of the cultural and historical developments of the Early Dynastic period. For over 400 years, Egypt enjoyed internal stability and great prosperity. During this period, the pharaoh (the term comes from the Egyptian for "great house," much as we use "White House" to refer to the President) was a king who was also a god. From his capital at Memphis, the god–king administered Egypt according to set principles, prime among them being *maat*, an ideal of order, justice, and truth. In return for the king's building and maintaining temples, the gods preserved the equilibrium of the state and ensured the king's continuing power, which was absolute. Since the king was obligated to act infallibly in a benign and beneficent manner, the welfare of the people of Egypt was automatically guaranteed and safeguarded.

Nothing better illustrates the nature of Old Kingdom royal power than the pyramids built as pharaonic tombs. Beginning in the Early Dynastic period, kings constructed increasingly elaborate burial complexes in Upper Egypt. Djoser, a Third Dynasty king, was the first to erect a monumental six-step pyramid of hard stone. Subsequent pharaohs built other stepped pyramids until Snefru, the founder of the Fourth Dynasty, converted a stepped to a true pyramid over the course of putting up three monuments.

His son Khufu (Cheops in the Greek version of his name) chose the desert plateau of Giza, south of Memphis, as the site for the largest pyramid ever constructed. Its dimensions are prodigious: 481 feet high, 756 feet long on each side, and its base covering 13.1 acres. The pyramid is made of 2,300,000 stone blocks averaging 2.5 tons each. It is also a geometrical wonder, deviating from absolutely level and square only by the most minute measurements using the latest modern devices. Khufu's successors, Khafre (Chephren) and Menkaure (Mycerinus), built equally perfect pyramids at Giza, and together, the three constitute one of the most extraordinary achievements in human history. Khafre also built the huge composite creature, part lion and part human, which the Greeks named the Sphinx. Recent research has shown that the Sphinx played a crucial role in the solar cult aspects of the pyramid complex.

The pyramids are remarkable not only for the great technical skill they demonstrate, but also for the concentration of resources they represent. They are evidence that the pharaohs controlled vast wealth and had the power to focus and organize enormous human effort over the years it took to build each pyramid. They also provide a visible indication of the nature of the Egyptian state: The pyramids, like the pharaohs, tower above the land, while the low tombs at their base, like the officials buried there, seem to huddle in relative unimportance.

Originally, the pyramids and their associated cult buildings contained statuary, offerings, and all that the pharaoh needed for the afterlife. Despite great precautions and ingenious concealment methods, tomb robbers took nearly everything, leaving little for modern archeologists to recover. Several full-size wooden boats have been found, however, still in their own graves at the base of the pyramids, ready for the pharaoh's journeys in the next world. Recent excavations have uncovered remains of the large town built to house the thousands of pyramid builders, including the farmers who worked at Giza during the annual flooding of their fields.

Numerous officials, both members of the royal family and nonroyal men of ability, aided the god–kings. The highest office was the *vizier* (a modern term from Arabic). Central offices dealing with granaries, surveys, assessments, taxes, and salaries administered the land. Water management was local rather than on a national level. Upper and Lower Egypt were divided into *nomes*, or districts, each governed by a *nomarch*, or governor, and his local officials. The kings could also appoint royal officials to oversee groups of nomes or to supervise pharaonic land holdings throughout Egypt.

THE FIRST INTERMEDIATE PERIOD AND MIDDLE KINGDOM (2200–1630 B.C.E.)

Towards the end of the Old Kingdom, for a combination of political and economic reasons, absolute pharaonic power waned as the nomarchs and other officials became more independent and influential. About 2200 B.C.E. the Old Kingdom collapsed and gave way to the decentralization and disorder of the First Intermediate Period, which lasted until about 2025 B.C.E. Eventually, the kings of Dynasty 11, based in Thebes in Upper Egypt, defeated the rival Dynasty 10, based in a city south of Giza.

Amunemhet I, the founder of Dynasty 12 and the Middle Kingdom, probably began his career as a successful vizier under an Eleventh Dynasty king. After reuniting Upper and Lower Egypt, he turned his attention to making three important and long-lasting administrative changes. First, he moved his royal residence from Thebes to a brand new town, just south of the old capital at Memphis, signaling a fresh start rooted in past glories. Second, he reorganized the nome structure by more clearly defining the nomarchs' duties to the state, granting them some local autonomy within the royal structure. Third, he established a coregency system to smooth transitions from one reign to another.

Amunemhet I and the other Middle Kingdom pharaohs sought to evoke the past by building pyramid complexes like those of the later Old Kingdom rulers. Yet the events of the First Intermediate Period had irrevocably changed the nature of Egyptian kingship. Gone was the absolute, distant god–king; the king was now more directly concerned with his people. In art, instead of the supremely confident faces of the Old Kingdom pharaohs, the Middle Kingdom rulers seem thoughtful, careworn, and brooding.

Egypt's relations with its neighbors became more aggressive during the Middle Kingdom. To the south, royal fortresses were built to control Nubia and the growing trade in African resources. To the north and east, Syria and Palestine increasingly came under Egyptian influence, even as fortifications sought to prevent settlers from the Levant from moving into the Delta.

THE SECOND INTERMEDIATE PERIOD AND THE NEW KINGDOM (1630–1075 B.C.E.)

For some unknown reason, during Dynasty 13, the kingship changed hands rapidly and the western Delta established itself as an independent Dynasty 14, ushering in the Second Intermediate Period. The eastern Delta, with its expanding Asiatic populations, came under the control of the Hyksos (Dynasty 15) and minor Asiatic kings (Dynasty 16). Meanwhile, the Dynasty 13 kings left their northern capital and regrouped in Thebes (Dynasty 17).

Though much later sources describe the Hyksos ("chief of foreign lands" in Egyptian) as ruthless invaders from parts unknown, they were almost certainly Amorites from the Levant, part of the gradual infiltration of the Delta during the Middle Kingdom. Ongoing excavations at the Hyksos capital of Avaris in the eastern Delta have revealed architecture, pottery, and other goods consistent with that cultural

Seated Egyptian scribe, height 21" (53 cm.) painted limestone, fifth dynasty, c. 2510–2460 B.C.E. One of the hallmarks of the early river valley civilizations was the development of writing. Ancient Egyptian scribes had to undergo rigorous training, but were rewarded with a position of respect and privilege.
Musée de Louvre, Paris. © Giraudon/Art Resource, N.Y.

Love Poems From the New Kingdom

Numerous love poems from ancient Egypt reveal the Egyptians' love of life through their frank sensuality.

❖ *How does the girl in the first poem propose to escape the supervision of her parents? What ails the young man in the second poem?*

SHE: Love, how I'd love to slip down to the pond, bathe with you close by on the bank.
Just for you I'd wear my new Memphis swimsuit, made of sheer linen, fit for a queen—
Come see how it looks in the water!
Couldn't I coax you to wade in with me? Let the cool creep slowly around us?
Then I'd dive deep down and come up for you dripping,
Let you fill your eyes with the little red fish that I'd catch.
And I'd say, standing there tall in the shallows:
Look at my fish, love, how it lies in my hand,

How my fingers caress it, slip down its sides...
But then I'd say softer, eyes bright with your seeing:
A gift, love. No words.
Come closer and look, it's all me.

HE: I think I'll go home and lie very still, feigning terminal illness.
Then the neighbors will all troop over to stare, my love, perhaps, among them.
How she'll smile while the specialists snarl in their teeth!—
she perfectly well knows what ails me.

From *Love Songs of the New Kingdom*, translated from the Ancient Egyptian by John L. Foster, copyright © 1969, 1970, 1971, 1972, 1973, and 1974 by John L. Foster, p. 20 and p. 72. Reprinted by permission of the University of Texas Press.

background. After nearly a century of rule, the Hyksos were expelled, a process begun by Kamose, the last king of Dynasty 17, and completed by his brother Ahmose, the first king of the Eighteenth Dynasty and the founder of the New Kingdom.

During the Eighteenth Dynasty, Egypt pursued foreign expansion with renewed vigor. Military expeditions reached as far north as the Euphrates in Syria, with frequent campaigns in the Levant. To the south, major Egyptian temples were built in the Sudan, almost 1,300 miles from Memphis. Egypt's economic and political power was at its height.

Egypt's position was reflected in the unprecedented luxury and cosmopolitanism of the royal court and in the ambitious palace and temple projects undertaken throughout the country. Perhaps to foil tomb robbers, the Eighteenth Dynasty pharaohs were the first to cut their tombs deep into the rock cliffs of a desolate valley in Thebes, known today as the Valley of the Kings. To date, only one intact royal tomb has been discovered there, that of the young Eighteenth Dynasty king Tutankhamun, and even it had been disturbed shortly after his death. The thousands of goods buried with him, many of them marvels of craftsmanship, give an idea of Egypt's material wealth during this period.

Following the premature death of Tutankhamun in 1323 B.C.E., a military commander named Horemheb assumed the kingship, which passed in turn to his own army commander, Ramses I. The Ramessides of Dynasty 19 undertook numerous monumental projects, among them Ramses II's rock-cut temples at Abu Simbel, south of the First Cataract, which had to be moved to a higher location when the Aswan High Dam was built in the 1960s. There and elsewhere, Ramses II left textual and pictorial accounts of his battle in 1285 B.C.E. against the Hittites at Kadesh on the Orontes in Syria. Sixteen years later, the Egyptians and Hittites signed a formal peace treaty, forging an alliance against an increasingly volatile political situation in the Mideast and Eastern Mediterranean during the thirteenth century B.C.E.

Merneptah, one of the hundred offspring of Ramses II, held off a hostile Libyan attack, as well as incursions by the Sea Peoples, a loose coalition of Mediterranean raiders who seem to have provoked and taken advantage of unsettled conditions. One of Merneptah's inscriptions commemorating his military triumphs contains the first known mention of Israel.

Despite his efforts, by the end of the Twentieth Dynasty, Egypt's period of imperial glory had passed. The next thousand years witnessed a Third Intermediate Period, a Saite Renaissance, Persian domination, conquest by Alexander the Great, the Ptolemaic period, and finally, defeat at the hands of Octavian in 30 B.C.E.

LANGUAGE AND LITERATURE. Writing first appears in Egypt about 3000 B.C.E. While the impetus for the first Egyptian writing probably came from Mesopotamia, the Egyptians may have invented it on their own. The writing system, dubbed *hieroglyphs* ("sacred carvings") by the Greeks, was highly sophisticated, involving hundreds of picture signs that remained relatively constant in the way they were rendered for over 3,000 years. Many of them formed a syllabary of one, two, or three consonantal sounds, while some conveyed a word's meaning or category, either independently or added to the end of the word. Texts were usually written horizontally from right to left, but could be written from left to right, as well as vertically from top to bottom in both horizontal directions. A cursive version of hieroglyphs was used for business documents and literary texts, which were penned rapidly in black and red ink. The Egyptian language, part of the Afro–Asiatic (or Hamito–Semitic) family, evolved through several stages—Old, Middle, and Late Egyptian, Demotic, and Coptic— thus giving it a history of continuous recorded use well into the medieval period.

Egyptian literature includes narratives, myths, books of instruction in wisdom, letters, religious texts, and poetry, written on papyri, limestone flakes, and postherds. (See "Love Poems from the New Kingdom.") Unfortunately only a small fraction of this enormous literature has survived, and many texts are incomplete. Though they surely existed, we have no epics or dramas from ancient Egypt. Such nonliterary documents as lists of kings, autobiographies in tombs, wine jar labels, judicial records, astronomical observations, and medical and other scientific texts are invaluable for our understanding of Egyptian history and civilization.

RELIGION: GODS AND TEMPLES Egyptian religion encompasses a multitude of concepts that often seem mutually contradictory to us. Three separate explanations for the origin of the universe were formulated, each based in the philosophical traditions of a venerable Egyptian city. The cosmogony of Heliopolis, north of Memphis, held that the creator sun god Atum (also identified as Re) emerged from the darkness of a vast sea to stand upon a primeval mound, containing within himself the life force of the gods he was to create. At Memphis, it was the god Ptah who created the other gods by uttering their names. Further south, at Hermopolis, eight male and female entities

The Egyptians believed in the possibility of life after death through the god Osiris. Aspects of each person's life had to be tested by 42 assessor-gods before the person could be presented to Osiris. In this scene from a papyrus manuscript of the Book of the Dead *the deceased and his wife (on the left) watch the scales of justice weighing his heart (on the left side of the scales) against the feather of truth. The jackal-headed god Anubis also watches the scales, while the ibis-headed god Thoth keeps the record.* British Museum, London/The Bridgeman Art Library International Ltd.

within a primordial slime suddenly exploded, and the energy that resulted created the sun and Atum, from which the rest came.

The Egyptian gods, or pantheon, similarly defy neat categorization, in part because of the common tendency to combine the character and function of one or more gods. Amun, one of the eight entities in the Hermopolitan cosmogony, provides a good example. Thebes, Amun's cult center, rose to prominence in the Middle Kingdom. In the New Kingdom, Amun was elevated above his seven cohorts and took on aspects of the sun god Re to become Amun-Re.

Not surprisingly in a nearly rainless land, solar cults and mythologies were highly developed. Much thought was devoted to conceptualizing what happened as the sun god made his perilous way through the underworld in the night hours between sunset and sunrise. Three long texts trace Re's journey as he vanquishes immense snakes and other foes.

The Eighteenth Dynasty was one of several periods during which solar cults were in ascendancy. Early in his reign, Amunhotep IV promoted a single, previously minor aspect of the sun, the Aten ("disk") above Re himself and the rest of the gods. He declared that the Aten was the creator god who brought life to mankind and all living beings, with himself and his queen Nefertiti the sole mediators between the Aten and the people. For religious and political reasons still imperfectly understood, he went further, changing his name to Akhenaten ("the effective spirit of the Aten"), building a new capital called Akhetaten ("the horizon of the Aten") near Amarma north of Thebes, and chiseling out the name of Amun from inscriptions everywhere. Shortly after his death, Amarna was abandoned and partially razed. A large diplomatic archive of tablets written in Akkadian was left at the site, which give us a vivid, if one-sided, picture of the political correspondence of the day. During the reigns of Akhenaten's successors, Tutankhamun (born Tutankhaten) and Horemheb, Amun was restored to his former position, and Akhenaten's monuments were defaced and even demolished.

In representations, Egyptian gods have human bodies, possess human or animal heads, and wear crowns, celestial disks, or thorns. The lone exception is the Aten, made nearly abstract by Akhenaten, who altered its image to a plain disk with solar rays ending in small hands holding the hieroglyphic sign for life to the nostrils of Akhenaten and Nefertiti. The gods were thought to reside in their cult centers, where, from the New Kingdom on, increasingly ostentatious temples were built, staffed by full-time priests. At Thebes, for instance, successive kings enlarged the great Karnak temple complex dedicated to Amun for over 2,000 years. Though the ordinary person could not enter a temple precinct, great festivals took place for all to see. During Amun's major festival of Opet, the statue of the god traveled in a divine boat along the Nile, whose banks were thronged with spectators.

WORSHIP AND THE AFTERLIFE   For most Egyptians, worship took place at small local shrines. They left offerings to the chosen gods, as well as votive inscriptions with simple prayers. Private houses often had niches containing busts for ancestor worship and statues of household deities. The Egyptians strongly believed in the power of magic, dreams, and oracles, and they possessed a wide variety of amulets to ward off evil.

The Egyptians thought that the afterlife was full of dangers, which could be overcome by magical means, among them the spells in the *Book of the Dead*. The goals were to join and be identified with the gods, especially Osiris, or to sail in the "boat of millions." Originally only the king could hope to enjoy immortality with the gods, but gradually this became available to all. Since the Egyptians believed that the preservation of the body was essential for continued existence in the afterlife, early on they developed mummification, a process that took seventy days by the New Kingdom. How lavishly tombs were prepared and decorated varied over the course of Egyptian history and in accordance with the wealth of a family. A high-ranking Dynasty 18 official, for example, typically had a Theban rock-cut tomb of several rooms embellished with scenes from daily life and funerary texts, as well as provisions and equipment for the afterlife, statuettes of workers, and a place for descendants to leave offerings.

WOMEN IN EGYPTIAN SOCIETY   It is difficult to assess the position of women in Egyptian society, because our pictorial and textual evidence comes almost entirely from male sources. Women's prime roles were connected with the management of the household. They could not hold office, go to scribal schools, or become artisans. Nevertheless, women could own and control property, sue for divorce, and, at least in theory, enjoy equal legal protection.

Major Periods in Ancient Egyptian History (Dynasties in Roman Numerals)	
3100–2700 B.C.E.	Early Dynastic Period (I–II)
2700–2200 B.C.E.	Old Kingdom (III–VI)
2200–2025 B.C.E.	First Intermediate Period (VII–XI)
2025–1630 B.C.E.	Middle Kingdom (XII–XIII)
1630–1550 B.C.E.	Second Intermediate Period (XIV–XVII)
1550–1075 B.C.E.	New Kingdom (XVIII–XX)

This painting from the Theban tomb of a high-ranking Eighteenth Dynasty official shows him, accompanied by his wife and daughter, on a hunting trip through the papyrus marshes, an activity the family enjoyed during their lives on earth and would continue in the afterlife. Courtesy of the Trustees of the British Museum. Copyright The British Museum

Royal women often wielded considerable influence, particularly in the Eighteenth Dynasty. The most remarkable was Hatshepsut, daughter of Thutmosis I and widow of Thutmosis II, who ruled as pharaoh for nearly 20 years. Many Egyptian queens held the title "god's wife of Amun," a power base of great importance.

In art, royal and nonroyal women are conventionally shown smaller than their husbands or sons (see illustration above). Yet it is probably of greater significance that they are so frequently depicted in such a wide variety of contexts. Much care was lavished on details of their gestures, clothing, and hairstyles. With their husbands, they attend banquets, boat in the papyrus marshes, make and receive offerings, and supervise the myriad affairs of daily life.

SLAVES Slaves did not become numerous in Egypt until the growth of Egyptian imperial power in the Middle Kingdom (2052–1786 B.C.E.). During that period, black Africans from Nubia to the south and Asians from the east were captured in war and brought back to Egypt as slaves. The great period of Egyptian imperial expansion, the New Kingdom (1550–1075 B.C.E.), vastly increased the number of slaves and captives in Egypt. Sometimes an entire people was enslaved, as the Bible says the Hebrews were.

Slaves in Egypt performed many tasks. They labored in the fields with the peasants, in the shops of artisans, and as domestic servants. Others worked as policemen and soldiers. Many slaves labored to erect the great temples, obelisks, and other huge monuments of Egypt's imperial age. As in Mesopotamia, slaves were branded for identification and to help prevent their escape. Slaves could be freed in Egypt, but manumission seems to have been rare. Nonetheless, former slaves were not set apart and could expect to be assimilated into the mass of the population.

This Egyptian wallpainting, in the tomb of Menna, shows men carrying grain while, in the background, two slaves fight over the leftovers. Menna was scribe of the fields and estate inspector under Pharaoh Thutmosis IV 15th century B.C.E. (18th Dynasty). Archaeological Site, Luxor–Thebes, Egypt. © Photograph by Erich Lessing. Art Resource

MAP 1–2   THE NEAR EAST AND GREECE ABOUT 1400 B.C.E.   *About 1400* B.C.E., *the Near East was divided among four empires. Egypt went south to Nubia and north through Palestine and Phoenicia. Kassites ruled in Mesopotamia, Hittites in Asia Minor, and the Mitannians in Assyrian lands. In the Aegean, the Mycenaean kingdoms were at their height.*

Ancient Near Eastern Empires

In the time of the Eighteenth Dynasty in Egypt, new groups of peoples had established themselves in the Near East: the Kassites in Babylonia, the Hittites in Asia Minor, and the Mitannians in northern Syria and Mesopotamia. (See Map 1–2.) The Kassites and Mitannians were warrior peoples who ruled as a minority over more civilized folk and absorbed their culture. The Hittites established a kingdom of their own and forged an empire that lasted some 200 years.

The Hittites

The Hittites were an Indo-European people, speaking a language related to Greek and Sanskrit. By about 1500 B.C.E., they established a strong, centralized government with a capital at Hattusas (near Ankara, the capital of modern Turkey). Between 1400 and 1200 B.C.E., they emerged as a leading military power in the Mideast and contested and contested Egypt's ambitions to control Palestine and Syria. This struggle culminated in a great battle between the Egyptian and Hittite armies at Kadesh in northern Syria (1285 B.C.E.) and ended as a standoff. The Hittites also broke the power of the Mitannian state in northern Syria. The Hittites adopted Mesopotamian writing and many aspects of Mesopotamian culture, especially through the Hurrian peoples of northern Syria and southern Anatolia. Their extensive historical records are the first to mention the Greeks, whom the Hittites called Ahhiyawa (the Achaeans of Homer). The Hittite kingdom disappeared by 1200 B.C.E., swept away in the general invasions and collapse of the Mideastern nation–states at that time. Successors to the empire, called the Neo-Hittite states, flourished in southern Asia Minor and northern Syria until the Assyrians destroyed them in the first millennium B.C.E.

The government of the Hittites was different from that of Mesopotamia in that Hittite kings did not claim to be divine or even to be the chosen representatives of the gods. In the early period, a council of nobles limited the king's power, and the assembled army had to ratify his succession to the throne.

THE DISCOVERY OF IRON   An important technological change took place in northern Anatolia, somewhat earlier than the creation of the Hittite Kingdom, but perhaps within its region. This was the discovery of how to smelt iron and the decision to use it to manufacture weapons and tools in preference to copper or bronze. Archaeologists refer to the period after 1100 B.C.E. as the Iron Age.

The Kassites

The Kassites were a people of unknown origin, speaking their own Kassite language, who established a dynasty at Babylon that ruled for nearly 500 years. The Kassites were organized into large tribal families and carved out great domains for themselves in Babylonia. They promoted Babylonian culture, and many of the most important works of Babylonian literature were written during their rule. Under the Kassites, Babylonia became one of the great nation–states of the late Bronze Age, along with Mitanni on the Upper Euphrates, Assyria, Egypt, and the empire of the Hittites in Anatolia. The kings of these states wrote frequently to each other and exchanged lavish gifts. They supported a military aristocracy based on horses and chariots, the prestige weaponry of the age. Though equally matched in power, the kings of this time conspired against each other, with Egypt and the Hittites hoping to control Syria and Palestine, and Babylonia and Assyria testing each other's borders, but wars were often inconclusive.

The Mitannians

The Mitannians belonged to a large group of people called the Hurrians, some of whom had been living in Mesopotamia and Syria in the time of the kings of Akkad and Ur. Their language is imperfectly understood, and the location of their capital city, Washukanni, is uncertain. The Hurrians were important mediators of Mesopotamian culture to Syria and Anatolia. They developed the art of chariot warfare and horse training to a high degree and created a large state that reached from the Euphrates to the foothills of Iran. The Hittites destroyed their kingdom, and the Assyrian empire eventually incorporated what was left of it.

The Assyrians

The Assyrians were originally a people living in Assur, a city in northern Mesopotamia on the Tigris River. They spoke a Semitic language closely related to Babylonian. They had a proud, independent culture heavily influenced by Babylonia. Assur had been an early center for trade, but emerged as a political power during the fourteenth century B.C.E., after the decline of Mitanni. The first Assyrian empire spread north and west against the Neo-Hittite states, but was brought to an end in the general collapse of Near Eastern states at the end of the second millennium. A people called the Arameans, a Semitic nomadic and agricultural people originally from northern Syria who spoke a language called Aramaic, invaded As-

This eighth-century B.C.E. relief of a hero gripping a lion formed part of the decoration of an Assyrian palace. The immense size of the figure and his powerful limbs and muscles may well have suggested the might of the Assyrian king. Giraudon/Art Resource, N.Y.

syria. Aramaic is still used in parts of the Near East and is one of the languages of medieval Jewish and Mideastern Christian culture.

The Second Assyrian Empire

After 1000 B.C.E., the Assyrians began a second period of expansion, and by 665 B.C.E. they controlled all of Mesopotamia, much of southern Asia Minor, Syria, Palestine, and Egypt to its southern frontier. They succeeded thanks to a large, well-disciplined army and a society that valued military skills. Some Assyrian kings boasted of their atrocities, so that

their names inspired terror throughout the Near East. They constructed magnificent palaces at Nineveh and Nimrud (near modern Mosul, Iraq), surrounded by parks and gardens. The walls of the reception rooms and hallways were decorated with stone reliefs and inscriptions proclaiming the power and conquests of the king.

The Assyrians organized their empire into provinces with governors, military garrisons, and administration for taxation, communications, and intelligence. Important officers were assigned large areas of land throughout the empire, and agricultural colonies were set up in key regions to store up supplies for military actions beyond the frontiers. Vassal kings had to send tribute and delegations to the Assyrian capital every year. Tens of thousands of people were forcibly displaced from their homes and resettled in other areas of the empire, partly to populate sparsely inhabited regions, partly to diminish resistance to Assyrian rule. People of the kingdom of Israel, which the Assyrians invaded and destroyed, were among them.

The empire became too large to govern efficiently. The last years of Assyria are obscure, but civil war apparently divided the country. The Medes, a powerful people from western and central Iran, had been expanding across the Iranian plateau. They were feared for their cavalry and archers, against which traditional Mideastern armies were ineffective. The Medes attacked Assyria and were joined by the Babylonians, who had always been restive under Assyrian rule, under the leadership of a general named Nebuchadnezzar. They eventually destroyed the Assyrian cities, including Nineveh in 612 B.C.E., so thoroughly that Assyria never recovered. The ruins of the great Assyrian palaces lay untouched until archaeologists began to explore them in the nineteenth century.

The Neo-Babylonians

The Medes did not follow up on their conquests, so Nebuchadnezzar took over much of the Assyrian empire. Under him and his successors, Babylon grew into one of the greatest cities of the world. The Greek traveler Herodotus described its wonders, including its great temples, fortification walls, boulevards, parks, and palaces, to a Greek readership that had never seen the like. Babylon prospered as a center of world trade, linking Egypt, India, Iran, and Syria–Palestine by land and sea routes. For centuries, an astronomical center at Babylon kept detailed records of observations that were the longest-running chronicle of the ancient world. Nebuchadnezzar's dynasty did not last long, and the government passed to various men in rapid succession. The last independent king of Babylon set up a second capital in the Arabian desert and tried to force the Babylonians to honor the Moon-god above all

Key Events in the History of Ancient Near Eastern Empires

ca. 1400–1200 B.C.E.	Hittite Empire
ca. 1100 B.C.E.	Rise of Assyrian power
732–722 B.C.E.	Assyrian conquest of Syria–Palestine
671 B.C.E.	Assyrian conquest of Egypt
612 B.C.E.	Destruction of Assyrian capital at Nineveh
612–539 B.C.E.	Neo-Babylonian (Chaldean) Empire

other gods. He allowed dishonest or incompetent speculators to lease huge areas of temple land for their personal profit. These policies proved unpopular—some said that the king was insane—and many Babylonians may have welcomed the Persian conquest that came in 539 B.C.E. After that, Babylonia began another, even more prosperous phase of its history as one of the most important provinces of another great Eastern empire, that of the Persians. We shall return to the Persians in Chapter 2.

Palestine

None of the powerful kingdoms of the ancient Near East had as much influence on the future of Western civilization as the small stretch of land between Syria and Egypt, the land called Palestine for much of its history. The three great religions of the modern world outside the Far East—Judaism, Christianity, and Islam—trace their origins, at least in part, to the people who arrived there a little before 1200 B.C.E. The book that recounts their experiences is the Hebrew Bible.

The Canaanites and the Phoenicians

Before the Israelites arrived in their promised land, it was inhabited by groups of people speaking a Semitic language called Canaanite. The Canaanites lived in walled cities and were farmers and seafarers. They had their own writing system, an alphabet that may have originated among people who were impressed by Egyptian writing, but wanted something much simpler to use. Instead of the hundreds of characters required to read Egyptian or cuneiform, their alphabet used between twenty and thirty. The Canaanites, like the other peoples of Syria–Palestine, worshiped many gods, especially gods of weather and fertility, whom they thought resided in the clouds atop the high mountains of northern Syria. The invading Israelites destroyed various Canaanite cities and holy places and may have forced some of the population to move north and west, though Canaanite and Israelite culture also intermingled.

The Phoenicians were the descendants of the Canaanites and other peoples of Syria–Palestine, especially those who lived along the coast. They played an important role in Mediterranean trade, sailing to ports in Cyprus, Asia Minor, Greece, Italy, France, Spain, Egypt, and North Africa, as far as Gibraltar and possibly beyond. They founded colonies throughout the Mediterranean as far west as Spain. The most famous of these colonies was Carthage, near modern Tunis in North Africa. Sitting astride the trade routes, the Phoenician cities were important sites for the transmission of culture from east to west. The Greeks, who had long forgotten their older writing system of the Bronze Age, adopted a Phoenician version of the Canaanite alphabet that is the origin of our present alphabet.

The Israelites

The history of the Israelites must be pieced together from various sources. They are mentioned only rarely in the records of their neighbors, so we must rely chiefly on their own account, the Hebrew Bible. This is not a history in our sense, but a complicated collection of historical narrative, pieces of wisdom, poetry, law, and religious witness. Scholars of an earlier time tended to discard it as a historical source, but the most recent trend is to take it seriously while using it with caution.

According to tradition, the patriarch Abraham came from Ur and wandered west to tend his flocks in the land of the Canaanites. Some of his people settled there, and others wandered into Egypt. By the thirteenth century B.C.E., led by Moses, they had left Egypt and wandered in the desert until they reached and conquered Canaan. They established a united kingdom that reached its peak under David and

The Israelites

ca. 1000–961 B.C.E.	Reign of King David
ca. 961–922 B.C.E.	Reign of King Solomon
722 B.C.E.	Assyrian conquest of Israel (northern kingdom)
586 B.C.E.	Destruction of Jerusalem; fall of Judah (southern kingdom); Babylonian Captivity
539 B.C.E.	Restoration of temple; return of exiles

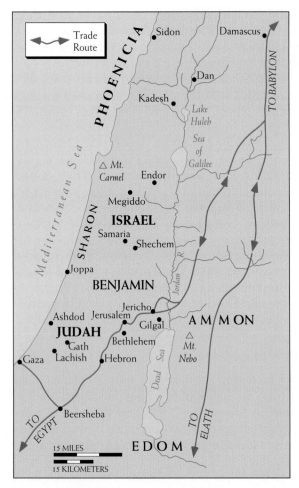

MAP 1–3   ANCIENT PALESTINE   *The Hebrews established a unified kingdom in Palestine under Kings David and Solomon in the tenth century B.C.E.. After the death of Solomon, however, the kingdom was divided into two parts—Israel in the north and Judah, with its capital, Jerusalem, in the south. Along the coast, especially to the north, were the great commercial cities of the Phoenicians, such as Sidon and Tyre.*

Solomon in the tenth century B.C.E. The sons of Solomon could not maintain the unity of the kingdom, and it split into two parts: Israel in the north and Judah, with its capital at Jerusalem, in the south. (See Map 1–3.) The rise of the great empires brought disaster to the Israelites. The northern kingdom fell to the Assyrians in 722 B.C.E., and its people—the "ten lost tribes"—were scattered and lost forever. Only the kingdom of Judah remained. It is from this time that we may call the Israelites Jews.

In 586 B.C.E., Judah was defeated by the Neo-Babylonian king Nebuchadnezzar II. He destroyed the great temple built by Solomon and took thousands of hostages off to Babylon. When the Persians defeated Babylonia, they ended this Babylonian captivity of the Jews and allowed them to return to their homeland. After that, the area of the old kingdom of

the Jews in Palestine was dominated by foreign peoples for some 2,500 years, until the establishment of the State of Israel in 1948 C.E.

The Jewish Religion

The fate of the small nation of Israel would be of little interest were it not for its unique religious achievement. The great contribution of the Jews is the development of monotheism—the belief in one universal God, the creator and ruler of the universe. This idea may be as old as Moses, as the Jewish tradition asserts, and it certainly dates as far back as the prophets of the eighth century B.C.E. The Jewish God is neither a natural force nor like human beings or any other creatures; He is so elevated, that those who believe in Him may not picture Him in any form. The faith of the Jews is given special strength by their belief that God made a covenant with Abraham that his progeny would be a chosen people who would be rewarded for following God's commandments and the law He revealed to Moses. (See "The Second Isaiah Defines Hebrew Monotheism.")

A novelty of Jewish religious thought is the powerful ethical element it introduced. God is a severe, but just, judge. Ritual and sacrifice are not enough to achieve His approval. People must be righteous, and God Himself appears to be bound to act righteously. The Jewish prophetic tradition was a powerful ethical force. The prophets constantly criticized any falling away from the law and the path of righteousness. They placed God in history, blaming the misfortunes of the Jews on God's righteous and necessary intervention to punish the people for their misdeeds. The prophets also promised the redemption of the Jews if they repented, however. The prophetic tradition expected the redemption to come in the form of a Messiah who would restore the house of David. Christianity, emerging from this tradition, holds that Jesus of Nazareth was that Messiah.

Jewish religious ideas influenced the future development of the West, both directly and indirectly. The Jews' belief in an all-powerful creator (who is righteous Himself and demands righteousness and obedience from humankind) and a universal God (who is the father and ruler of all peoples) is a critical part of the Western heritage.

General Outlook of Mideastern Cultures

Our brief account of the history of the ancient Mideast so far reveals that its various peoples and cultures were different in many ways. Yet the distance between all of them and the emerging culture of the Greeks

The Second Isaiah Defines Hebrew Monotheism

The strongest statement of Hebrew monotheism is found in these words of the anonymous prophet whom we call the Second Isaiah. He wrote during the Hebrew exile in Babylonia, 597–539 B.C.E.

❖ *How is the deity in this passage different from the deities of the Mesopotamian and Egyptian societies? Are there any similarities? Many peoples have claimed that a single god was the greatest and the ruler over all others. What is there in this selection that claims a different status for the Hebrew deity?*

42

⁵Thus says God, the Lord
who created the heavens and stretched them out,
who spread forth the earth and what comes
    from it,
who gives breath to the people upon it and spirit
to those who walk in it:
⁶"I am the Lord, I have called you in right-
    eousness,
I have taken you by the hand and kept you;
I have given you as a covenant to the people, a
    light to the nations,
⁷to open the eyes that are blind,
to bring out the prisoners from the dungeon,
from the prison those who sit in darkness.
⁸I am the Lord, that is my name;
my glory I give to no other,
nor my praise to graven images.
⁹Behold, the former things have come to pass,
    and new things I now declare;
before they spring forth I tell you of them."

44

⁶Thus says the Lord, the King of Israel and his
    Redeemer, the Lord of hosts:
"I am the first and I am the last; besides me
    there is no god.
⁷Who is like me? Let him proclaim it,
let him declare and set it forth before me.
Who has announced of old the things to come?
Let them tell us what is yet to be.
⁸Fear not, nor be afraid;
have I not told you from of old and declared it?

And you are my witnesses!
Is there a God besides me?
There is no Rock; I know not any."

49

²²Thus says the Lord God:
"Behold, I will lift up my hand to the nations,
and raise my signal to the peoples;
and they shall bring your sons in their bosom,
and your daughters shall be carried on their
    shoulders
²³Kings shall be your foster fathers,
and their queens your nursing mothers.
With their faces to the ground they shall bow
    down to you,
and lick the dust of your feet.
Then you will know that I am the Lord;
those who wait for me shall not be put to
    shame."
²⁴Can the prey be taken from the mighty, or the
    captives of a tyrant be rescued?
²⁵Surely, thus says the Lord:
"Even the captives of the mighty shall be taken,
and the prey of the tyrant be rescued,
for I will contend with those who contend
    with you
and I will save your children.
²⁶I will make your oppressors eat their own flesh,
and they shall be drunk with their own blood as
    with wine.
Then all flesh shall know
that I am the Lord your Savior,
and your Redeemer, the Mighty One of Jacob."

Bible, Revised Standard Version (New York: Division of Christian Education, National Council of Churches, 1952).

(Chapter 2) is striking. We can see this distance best by comparing the approach of the other cultures with that of the Greeks on several fundamental human problems: What is the relationship of humans to nature? To the gods? To other humans? These questions involve attitudes toward religion, philosophy, science, law, justice, politics, and government in general.

Humans and Nature

For the peoples of the Mideast, there was no simple separation between humans and nature or even between animate creatures and inanimate objects. Humanity was part of a natural continuum, and all things partook of life and spirit. These peoples imagined the universe to be dominated by gods more or less in the shape of humans, and the world they ruled was irregular and unpredictable, subject to divine whims. The gods were capricious because nature seemed capricious.

A Babylonian story of creation makes it clear that humanity's function is merely to serve the gods. The creator Marduk says:

I shall compact blood, I shall cause bones to be,
I shall make stand a human being, let "Man" be
    its name.
I shall create humankind,
They shall bear the gods' burden that those
    may rest.[1]

In a world ruled by powerful deities of this kind, human existence was precarious. Disasters that we would think human in origin the Mesopotamians saw as the product of divine will. Thus, a Babylonian text depicts the destruction of the city of Ur by invading Elamites as the work of the gods, carried out by the storm god Enlil:

Enlil called the storm.
The people mourn.
Exhilarating winds he took from the land.
The people mourn.
Good winds he took away from Sumer.
The people mourn.
He summoned evil winds.
The people mourn.
Entrusted them to Kingaluda, tender of storms.
He called the storm that will annihilate the land.
The people mourn.
He called disastrous winds.
The people mourn.
Enlil—choosing Gibil as his helper—
Called the (great) hurricane of heaven.
The people mourn.[2]

The vulnerable position of humankind in the face of divine powers is clearly shown in both the Egyptian and the Babylonian versions of the destruction of mankind. In one Egyptian tale, Re, the god who had created humans, decided to destroy them because they were plotting evil against him. He sent the goddess Sekhmet to accomplish the deed, and she was resting in the midst of her task, having enjoyed the work and waded in a sea of blood, when Re changed his mind. He ordered 7,000 barrels of blood-colored beer poured in Sekhmet's path. She quickly became too drunk to continue the slaughter and thus preserved humanity. In the Babylonian story of the flood, the motive for the destruction of humanity is given as follows:

The land had grown numerous, the peoples
    had increased,
The land was bellowing like a bull.
The god was disturbed by their uproar,
The god Enlil heard their clamor.
He said to the great gods,
"The clamor of mankind has become burdensome
    to me,
"I am losing sleep to their uproar!"[3]

Utanapishtim and his wife survived because he was friendly with Enki, the god of wisdom, who helped him to pull through by a trick.

In such a universe, humans could not hope to understand nature, much less control it. At best, they could try by magic to use uncanny forces against others. An example of this device is provided by a Mesopotamian incantation to cure sickness. The sufferer tries to use magical powers by acting out the destruction of the powers he thinks caused his illness:

As this garlic is peeled off and thrown into
    the fire,
[And the Fire God] burns it up with fire,
Which will not be cultivated in a garden patch,
Whose roots will not take hold in the ground,
Whose sprout will not come forth nor see the sun,
Which will not be used for the repast of god or king,
[So] may the curse, something evil, revenge,
    interrogation,
The sickness of my suffering, wrong-doing,
    crime, misdeed, sin
The sickness which is in my body, flesh, and sinews
Be peeled off like this garlic,
May [the Fire God] burn it with fire this day,
May the wicked thing go forth, that I may see light.[4]

Humans and the Gods, Law, and Justice

Human relationships to the gods were equally humble. There was no doubt that the gods could destroy human beings and might do so at any time for no good reason. Humans could—and, indeed, had to—try to win the gods over by prayers and sacrifices, but there was no guarantee of success. The gods were bound by no laws and no morality. The best behavior and the greatest devotion to the cult of the gods were no defense against the divine and cosmic caprice.

[1]Benjamin R. Foster, *From Distant Days, Myths, Tales, and Poetry of Ancient Mesopotamia* (Bethesda, MD: CDL Press, p. 38).

[2]Thorkild Jacobsen in Henri Frankfort et al., *Before Philosophy* (Baltimore: Penguin, 1949), pp. 154.

[3]Foster, pp. 170–171.

[4]Foster, p. 412.

In the earliest civilizations, human relations were guided by laws, often set down in written codes. The basic question about law concerned its legitimacy: Why, apart from the lawgiver's power to coerce obedience, should anyone obey the law? For Old Kingdom Egyptians, the answer was simple: The king was bound to act in accordance with *maat*, and so his laws were righteous. For the Mesopotamians, the answer was almost the same: The king was a representative of the gods, so that the laws he set forth were authoritative. The prologue to the most famous legal document in antiquity, the Code of Hammurabi, makes this plan:

I am the king who is preeminent among kings;
my words are choice; my ability has no equal.
By the order of Sharnash, the great judge of heaven
    and earth,
may my justice prevail in the land;
by the word of Marduk, my lord,
may my statutes have no one to rescind them.[5]

The Hebrews introduced some important new ideas. Their unique God was capable of great anger and destruction, but He was open to persuasion and subject to morality. He was therefore more predictable and comforting, for all the terror of His wrath. The biblical version of the flood story, for instance, reveals the great difference between the Hebrew God and the Babylonian deities. The Hebrew God was powerful and wrathful, but He was not arbitrary. He chose to destroy His creatures for their moral failures, for the reason that

the wickedness of man was great in the earth, and that every imagination of the thought of His heart was evil continually...the earth was corrupt in God's sight and the earth was filled with violence.[6]

When He repented and wanted to save someone, He chose Noah because "Noah was a righteous man, blameless in his generation."[7]

That God was bound by His own definition of righteousness is neatly shown in the biblical story of Sodom and Gomorrah. He had chosen to destroy these wicked cities, but felt obliged by His covenant to inform Abraham first.[8] In this passage, Abraham calls on God to abide by His own moral principles, and God sees Abraham's point.

In such a world, there is the possibility of order in the universe and on this earth. There is also the possibility of justice among human beings, for the Hebrew God had provided His people with law. Through

his prophet Moses, He had provided humans with regulations that would enable them to live in peace and justice. If they would abide by the law and live upright lives, they and their descendants could expect happy and prosperous lives. This idea was quite different from the uncertainty of the Babylonian view, but like it and its Egyptian partner, it left no doubt of the certainty of the divine. Cosmic order, human survival, and justice were all dependent on God.

Toward the Greeks and Western Thought

Greek thought offered different approaches and answers to many of the concerns we have been discussing. Calling attention to some of those differences will help convey the distinctive outlook of the Greeks and the later cultures within Western civilization that have drawn heavily on Greek influence.

It is important to recognize that Greek ideas had much in common with the ideas of earlier peoples. The Greek gods had most of the characteristics of the Mesopotamian deities, magic and incantations played a part in the lives of most Greeks, and Greek law, like that of earlier peoples, was usually connected with divinity. Many, if not most, Greeks in the ancient world must have lived their lives with notions similar to those held by other peoples. The surprising thing is that some Greeks developed ideas that were strikingly different and, in so doing, set a part of humankind on an entirely new path.

As early as the sixth century B.C.E., some Greeks living in the Ionian cities of Asia Minor raised questions and suggested answers about the nature of the world that produced an intellectual revolution. In their speculations, they made guesses that were completely naturalistic and made no reference to supernatural powers. One historian of Greek thought, discussing the views of Thales, the first Greek philosopher, put the case particularly well:

In one of the Babylonian legends it says: "All the lands were sea...Marduk bound a rush mat upon the face of the waters, he made dirt and piled it beside the rush mat." What Thales did was to leave Marduk out. He, too, said that everything was once water. But he thought that earth and everything else had been formed out of water by a natural process, like the silting up of the Delta of the Nile....It is an admirable beginning, the whole point of which is that it gathers into a coherent picture a number of observed facts without letting Marduk in.[9]

By putting the question of the world's origin in a naturalistic form, Thales, in the sixth century B.C.E.,

---

[5]James B. Pritchard, *Ancient Near Eastern Texts Related to the Old Testament*, 3d ed. (Princeton: Princeton University Press, 1969), pp. 164.

[6]Genesis 6:5–11.

[7]Genesis 6:9.

[8]Genesis 18:20–33.

[9]Benjamin Farrington, *Greek Science* (London: Penguin Books, 1953), p. 37.

may have begun the unreservedly rational investigation of the universe and, in so doing, initiated both philosophy and science.

The same relentlessly rational approach was used even in regard to the gods themselves. In the same century as Thales, Xenophanes of Colophon expressed the opinion that humans think of the gods as resembling themselves, that, like themselves, they were born, that they wear clothes like theirs, and that they have voices and bodies like theirs. If oxen, horses, and lions had hands and could paint like humans, Xenophanes argued, they would paint gods in their own image; the oxen would draw gods like oxen and the horses like horses. Thus, Africans believed in flat-nosed, black-faced gods, and the Thracians in gods with blue eyes and red hair.[10] In the fifth century B.C.E., Protagoras of Abdera went so far in the direction of agnosticism as to say, "About the gods I can have no knowledge either that they are or that they are not or what is their nature."[11]

This rationalistic, skeptical way of thinking carried over into practical matters as well. The school of medicine led by Hippocrates of Cos (about 400 B.C.E.) attempted to understand, diagnose, and cure disease without any attention to supernatural forces or beings. One of the Hippocratics wrote, of the mysterious disease epilepsy,

It seems to me that the disease is no more divine than any other. It has a natural cause, just as other diseases have. Men think it divine merely because they do not understand it. But if they called everything divine which they do not understand, why, there would be no end of divine things.[12]

By the fifth century B.C.E., it was also possible for the historian Thucydides to analyze and explain the behavior of humans in society completely in terms of human nature and chance, leaving no place for the gods or supernatural forces.

The same absence of divine or supernatural forces characterized Greek views of law and justice. Most Greeks, of course, liked to think that, in a vague way, law came ultimately from the gods. In practice, however, and especially in the democratic states, they knew very well that laws were made by humans and should be obeyed because they represented the expressed consent of the citizens. Law, according to the fourth-century-B.C.E. statesman Demosthenes, is "a general covenant of the whole State, in accordance with which all men in that State ought to regulate their lives."[13]

In Perspective

The statement of the following ideas, so different from any that came before the Greeks, opens the discussion of most of the issues that appear in the long history of Western civilization and that remain major concerns in the modern world. What is the nature of the universe, and how can it be controlled? Are there divine powers, and if so, what is humanity's relationship to them? Are law and justice human, divine, or both? What is the place in human society of freedom, obedience, and reverence? These and many other matters were either first considered or first elaborated on by the Greeks.

The Greeks' sharp departure from the thinking of earlier cultures marked the beginning of the unusual experience that we call Western civilization. Nonetheless, they built on a foundation of lore that people in the Near East had painstakingly accumulated over millennia. From ancient Mesopotamia and Egypt, they borrowed important knowledge and skills in mathematics, astronomy, art, and literature. From Phoenicia, they learned the art of writing. The discontinuities, however, are more striking than the continuities.

The great civilizations of the river valleys were ruled by hereditary monarchies often elevated by the aura of divinity. Powerful priesthoods presented yet another bastion of privilege that stood between the ordinary person and the knowledge and opportunity needed for freedom and autonomy. Religion was an integral part of the world of the ancient Near East, in the kingdoms and city–states of Palestine, Phoenicia, and Syria just as in the great empires of Egypt and Mesopotamia. The secular, reasoned questioning that sought understanding of the world in which people lived—that tried to find explanations in the natural order of things rather than in the supernatural acts of the gods—was not characteristic of the older cultures. Nor would it appear in similar societies at other times in other parts of the world. The new way of looking at things was uniquely the product of the Greeks. We now need to see whether there was something special in their experience that made them raise fundamental questions in the way that they did.

REVIEW QUESTIONS

1. How would you define "history"? What different academic disciplines do historians rely on, and why is the study of history important?
2. How was life during the Paleolithic Age different from that in the Neolithic Age? What advancements in agriculture and human development had

[10]Henri Frankfort et al. *Before Philosophy* (Baltimore: Penguin, 1949), pp. 14–16.

[11]Hermann Diels, *Fragmente der Vorsokratiker*, 5th ed., ed. by Walter Krantz (Berlin: Weidmann, 1934–38), Frg. 4.

[12]Diels, Frgs. 14–16.

[13]Demosthenes, *Against Aristogeiton*, 16.

taken place by the end of the Neolithic era? Is it valid to speak of a "Neolithic Revolution"?

3. Describe, generally, the differences in the political and intellectual outlooks of the civilizations of Egypt and Mesopotamia. Compare especially their religious views. In what ways did geography influence the religious outlooks of these two civilizations?

4. To what extent did the Hebrew faith bind the Jews politically? Why was the concept of monotheism so radical for Near Eastern civilizations?

5. Why were the Assyrians so successful in establishing their Near Eastern empire? How did their empire differ from that of the Hittites or Egyptians? In what ways did this empire benefit the civilized Middle East? Why did the Assyrian Empire ultimately fail to survive?

6. In what ways did Greek thought develop along different lines from that of Near Eastern civilizations? What new questions about human society were asked as a result of Greek influence?

SUGGESTED READINGS

J. BAINES AND J. MÁLEK, *Atlas of Ancient Egypt* (1980). An authoritative, well-illustrated guide to archaeological sites and cultural matters, with special treatment of thematic issues.

W. V. DAVIES, *Egyptian Hieroglyphs* (1987). A good introduction to the ancient Eygptian language, scripts, and grammar of ancient Egyptian.

R. DE VAUX, *Ancient Israel: Its Life and Institutions* (1961). A fine account of social institutions.

M. EHRENBERG, *Women in Prehistory* (1989). An account of the role of women in early times.

H. FRANKFORT ET AL., *Before Philosophy* (1949). A brilliant examination of the mind of the ancients from the Stone Age to the Greeks.

O. R. GURNEY, *The Hittites* (1954). A good survey.

W. W. HALLO AND W. K. SIMPSON, *The Ancient Near East: A History* (1998). A fine survey of Egyptian and Mesopotamian history.

W. W. HALLO AND L. YOUNGER, ED., *The Context of Scripture, Canonical Compositions from the Biblical World* (1997). A good collection of literary works translated from Egyptian, Hittite, Sumerian, Babylonian, and other ancient Near Eastern languages, with introductions and explanatory notes.

G. HART, *Egyptian Myths* (1990). A clear presentation of major myths and religious literature.

D. C. JOHNSON AND M. R. EDEY, *Lucy: The Beginnings of Mankind* (1981). A study of the first human creatures based on remains found in Africa.

B. J. KEMP, *Ancient Egypt: Anatomy of a Civilization* (1989). A thought-provoking assessment of Egypt's social and intellectual history.

S. N. KRAMER, *The Sumerians: Their History, Culture and Character* (1963). A readable general account of Sumerian history.

A. KUHRT, *The Ancient Near East, c. 3000–330 B.C.* (1995). The best compact and reliable history of the ancient Near East, including Egypt and Israel, with extensive bibliographies.

S. LLOYD, *The Archaeology of Mesopotamia*, rev. ed. (1984). An account of the material remains of Mesopotamia and their meaning from the Old Stone Age to the Persian Conquest.

K. R. NEMET-NEJAT, *Daily Life in Ancient Mesopotamia* (1998). Excellent introduction for the general reader.

D. OATES AND J. OATES, *The Rise of Civilization* (1976). A study of the emergence of urban life in southern Mesopotamia, placed in a broad context and well illustrated with photographs.

J. OATES, *Babylon*, rev. ed. (1986). An introduction to the history and archaeology of Babylonia, revised to make use of newly discovered evidence.

J. N. POSTGATE, *The First Empires* (1977). A fine account of Mesopotamian history from the dawn of history to the Persian conquest.

J. N. POSTGATE, *Early Mesopotamia* (1992). An excellent study of Mesopotamian economy and society from the earliest times to about 1500 B.C.E., helpfully illustrated with drawings, pictures, and translated documents.

D. B. REDFORD, *Akhenaten* (1987). A new study of the controversial pharaoh.

C. L. REDMAN, *The Rise of Civilization* (1978). An attempt to use the evidence provided by anthropology, archaeology, and the physical sciences to illuminate the development of early urban society.

G. ROBINS, *Women in Ancient Egypt* (1993). A comprehensive study of the role of women in Egyptian society.

N. K. SANDARS, *The Sea Peoples* (1985). A lively account of the collection of peoples who disrupted established Mediterranean civilization in the thirteenth century B.C.E.

D. C. SNELL, *Life in the Ancient Near East, 3100–332 B.C.E.* (1997). Imaginative study focusing on social and economic history.

A. J. SPENCER, *Early Egypt: The Rise of Civilisation in the Nile Valley* (1993). An up-to-date account of the latest research on the Predynastic and Early Dynastic periods.

B. G. TRIGGER ET AL., *Ancient Egypt: A Social History* (1982).

M. Van De Mieroop, *The Ancient Mesopotamian City* (1997). Written for the general historian, a concise survey of Mesopotamian urban life, including political and social structures, economy, government, and the arts.

Chapter 2

The ruins of the sanctuary of Apollo at Delphi, dating from the sixth century B.C.E. Greeks and foreigners traveled great distances to worship Apollo and to consult the famous Delphic oracle for clues to the future. Josè Fuste Raga/The Stock Market

The Rise of Greek Civilization

KEY TOPICS

- The Bronze Age civilizations that ruled the Aegean area before the development of Hellenic civilization
- The rise, development, and expansion of the *polis*, the characteristic political unit of Hellenic Greece
- The early history of Sparta and Athens
- The wars between the Greeks and the Persians

About 2000 B.C.E., Greek-speaking peoples settled the lands surrounding the Aegean Sea and established a style of life and formed a set of ideas, values, and institutions that spread far beyond the Aegean corner of the Mediterranean Sea. Preserved and adapted by the Romans, Greek culture powerfully influenced the society of western Europe in the Middle Ages and dominated the Byzantine Empire in the same period. It would ultimately spread across Europe and cross the Atlantic to the Western Hemisphere.

At some time in their history, the Greeks of the ancient world founded cities on every shore of the Mediterranean Sea. Pushing on through the Dardanelles, they placed many settlements on the coasts of the Black Sea in southern Russia and as far east as the approaches to the Caucasus Mountains. The center of Greek life, however, has always been the Aegean Sea and the islands in and around it. This location at the eastern end of the Mediterranean very early put the Greeks in touch with the more advanced and earlier civilizations of Mesopotamia, Egypt, Asia Minor, and Syria–Palestine.

The Greeks acknowledged the influence of these predecessors. A character in one of Plato's dialogues says, "Whatever the Greeks have acquired from foreigners they have, in the end, turned into something finer."[1] This is a proud statement, but it also shows that the Greeks were aware of how much they had learned from other civilizations.

The Bronze Age Minoan culture of Crete contributed to Greek civilization, and the mainland Mycenaean culture, which conquered Minoan Crete, contributed even more. Both these cultures, however, had more in common with the cultures of the Near East than with the new Hellenic culture established by the Greeks in the centuries after the end of the Bronze Age in the twelfth century B.C.E.

The rugged geography of the Greek peninsula and its nearby islands isolated the Greeks of the early Iron Age from their richer and more culturally advanced neighbors, shaping, in part, their way of life and permitting them to develop that way of life on their own. The aristocratic world of the "Greek Dark Ages" (1150–750 B.C.E.) produced impressive artistic achievements, especially in the development of painted pottery and most magnificently, in the epic poems of Homer. In the eighth century B.C.E., social, economic, and military changes profoundly influenced the organization of Greek political life; the Greek city–state, the polis, *came into being and thereafter dominated the cultural development of the Greek people.*

This change came in the midst of turmoil, for the pressure of a growing population led many Greeks to leave home and establish colonies far away. Those who remained often fell into political conflict, from which tyrannies sometimes emerged. These tyrannies, however, were in all cases transitory, and the Greek cities emerged from them as self-governing polities, usually ruled by an oligarchy, broad or narrow. The two most important states, Athens and Sparta, developed in different directions. Sparta formed a mixed constitution in which a very small part of the population dominated the vast majority, and Athens developed the world's first democracy.

The Bronze Age on Crete and on the Mainland to about 1150 B.C.E.

The Bronze Age civilizations in the region that the Greeks would rule arose on the island of Crete, on the islands of the Aegean, and on the mainland of Greece. Crete was the site of the earliest Bronze Age settlements, and modern scholars have called the

civilization that arose there Minoan, after the legendary king of Crete. A later Bronze Age civilization was centered at the mainland site of Mycenae and is called Mycenaean.

The Minoans

With Greece to the north, Egypt to the south, and Asia to the east, Crete was a cultural bridge between the older civilizations and the new one of the Greeks. The Bronze Age came to Crete not long after 3000 B.C.E., and the Minoan civilization, which powerfully influenced the islands of the Aegean and the mainland of Greece, arose in the third and second millennia B.C.E.

Scholars have established links between stratigraphic layers at archaeological sites on Crete and specific styles of pottery and other artifacts found in the layers. On this basis they have divided the Bronze Age on Crete into three major periods—Early, Middle, and Late Minoan—with some subdivisions. Dates for Bronze Age settlements on the Greek mainland, for which the term *Helladic* is used, are derived from the same chronological scheme.

(a)

(b)

(a) The Minoan-period Palace at Cnossus on the island of Crete. (b) A fresco painting from the east wing of the palace. The fresco shows acrobats leaping over a charging bull. It is not known whether such acrobatic displays were only for entertainment or part of some religious ritual.

(a) D. A. Harissiadis Photography, Benaki Museum, Photographic Department; (b) Leaping bull. Minoan fresco. Archeological Museum, Heraklion, Crete, Greece. Scala/Art Resource, N.Y.

[1]Plato, *Epinomis*, 987 d.

During the Middle and Late Minoan periods in the cities of eastern and central Crete, a civilization developed that was new and unique in its character and beauty. Its most striking creations are the palaces uncovered at such sites as Phaestus, Haghia Triada, and, most important, Cnossus. Each of these palaces was built around a central court surrounded by a labyrinth of rooms. Some sections of the palace at Cnossus were as tall as four stories high. The basement contained many storage rooms for oil and grain, apparently paid as taxes to the king. The main and upper floors contained living quarters, as well as workshops for making pottery and jewelry. There were sitting rooms and even bathrooms, to which water was piped through excellent plumbing. Lovely columns, which tapered downward, supported the ceilings, and many of the walls carried murals showing landscapes and seascapes, festivals, and sports. The palace design and the paintings show the influence of Syria, Asia Minor, and Egypt, but the style and quality are unique to Crete.

In contrast to the Mycenaean cities on the mainland of Greece, Minoan palaces and settlements lacked strong defensive walls. This evidence that the Minoans built without defense in mind has raised questions and encouraged speculation. Some scholars, pointing also to evidence that Minoan religion was more matriarchal than the patriarchal religion of the Mycenaeans and their Greek descendants, have argued that the civilizations of Crete, perhaps reflecting the importance of women, were inherently more tranquil and pacific than others. An earlier and very different explanation for the absence of fortifications was that the protection provided by the sea made them unnecessary. The evidence is not strong enough to support either explanation, and the mystery remains.

Along with palaces, paintings, pottery, jewelry, and other valuable objects, excavations have revealed clay writing tablets like those found in Mesopotamia. The tablets, preserved accidentally when a great fire that destroyed the royal palace at Cnossus hardened them, have three distinct kinds of writing on them: a kind of picture writing called *hieroglyphic*, and two different linear scripts called Linear A and Linear B. The languages of the two other scripts remain unknown, but Linear B proved to be an early form of Greek. The contents of the tablets, primarily inventories, reveal an organization centered on the palace and ruled by a king who was supported by an extensive bureaucracy that kept remarkably detailed records.

This sort of organization is typical of early civilizations in the Near East, but as we shall see, is nothing like that of the Greeks after the Bronze Age.

A Linear B tablet from Cnossus, dated about 1200 B.C.E. *First discovered late in the nineteenth century, Linear B was not deciphered until 1952, when a brilliant young Briton, Michael Ventris, demonstrated that it was an early Greek dialect. This tablet is part of a palace inventory. It survived because it was hardened in a fire when the palace at Cnossus was destroyed by invaders.*
Hirmer Fotoarchiv

Yet the inventories were written in a form of Greek. If they controlled Crete throughout the Bronze Age, why should Minoans, who were not Greek, have written in a language not their own? This question raises the larger one of what the relationship was between Crete and the Greek mainland in the Bronze Age and leads us to an examination of mainland, or Helladic, culture.

The Mycenaeans

In the third millennium B.C.E.—the Early Helladic Period—most of the Greek mainland, including many of the sites of later Greek cities, was settled by people who used metal, built some impressive houses, and traded with Crete and the islands of the Aegean. The names they gave to places, names that were sometimes preserved by later invaders, make it clear that they were not Greeks and that they spoke a language that was not Indo-European (the language family to which Greek belongs).

Not long after the year 2000 B.C.E., many of the Early Helladic sites were destroyed by fire, some were abandoned, and still others appear to have yielded peacefully to an invading people. These signs of invasion probably signal the arrival of the Greeks.

All over Greece, there was a smooth transition between the Middle and Late Helladic periods. The invaders succeeded in establishing control of the entire mainland. The shaft graves cut into the rock at the royal palace–fortress of Mycenae show that they prospered and sometimes became very rich. At Mycenae, the richest finds come from the period after 1600 B.C.E. The city's wealth and power reached their peak during this time, and the culture of the whole mainland during the Late Helladic Period goes by the name *Mycenaean*.

The presence of the Greek Linear B tablets at Cnossus suggests that Greek invaders also established themselves in Crete, and there is good reason to believe that at the height of Mycenaean power (1400–1200 B.C.E.), Crete was part of the Mycenaean world. Although their dating is still controversial, the Linear B tablets at Cnossus seem to belong to Late Minoan III, so what is called the great "palace period" at Cnossus would have followed an invasion by Mycenaeans in 1400 B.C.E. These Greek invaders ruled Crete until the end of the Bronze Age.

MYCENAEAN CULTURE   The excavation of Mycenae, Pylos, and other Mycenaean sites reveals a culture influenced by, but very different from, the Minoan culture. Mycenae and Pylos, like Cnossus, were built some distance from the sea. It is plain, however, that defense against attack was foremost in the minds of the founders of the Mycenaean cities. Both Mycenae and Pylos were built on hills in a position commanding the neighboring territory. The Mycenaean people were warriors, as their art, architecture, and weapons reveal. The success of their campaigns and the defense of their territory required strong central authority, and all available evidence shows that the kings provided it. Their palaces, in which the royal family and its retainers lived, were located within the walls; most of the population lived outside the walls. Usually paintings covered the palace walls, as on Crete, but instead of peaceful scenery and games, the Mycenaean murals depicted scenes of war and boar hunting.

About 1500 B.C.E., the already impressive shaft graves were abandoned in favor of *tholos* tombs. These large, beehivelike chambers were built of enormous well-cut and fitted stones and were approached by an unroofed passage (*dromos*) cut horizontally into the side of the hill. The lintel block alone of one of these tombs weighs over one hundred tons. Only a strong king whose wealth was great, whose power was unquestioned, and who commanded the labor of many people could undertake such a project. His wealth probably came from plundering raids, piracy, and trade. Some of this trade went westward to Italy and Sicily, but most of it was with the islands of the Aegean, the coastal towns of Asia Minor, and the cities of Syria, Egypt, and Crete. The Mycenaeans sent pottery, olive oil, and animal hides in exchange for jewels and other luxuries.

Tablets containing the Mycenaean Linear B writing have been found all over the mainland; the largest and most useful collection was found at Pylos. These tablets reveal a world very similar to the one shown by the records at Cnossus. The king, whose title was *wanax*, held a royal domain, appointed officials, commanded servants, and kept a close record of what he owned and what was owed to him. This evidence confirms all the rest; the Mycenaean world was made up of several independent, powerful, and well-organized monarchies.

THE RISE AND FALL OF MYCENAEAN POWER   At the height of their power (1400–1200 B.C.E.), the Mycenaeans were prosperous and active. They enlarged their cities, expanded their trade, and even established commercial colonies in the East. They are mentioned in the archives of the Hittite kings of Asia Minor. They are named as marauders of the Nile Delta in Egyptian records. Sometime about 1250 B.C.E. they probably sacked Troy, on the coast of northwestern Asia Minor, giving rise to the epic poems of Homer—the *Iliad* and the *Odyssey*. (See Map 2–1.) Around 1200 B.C.E., however, the Mycenaean world showed signs of great trouble, and by 1100 B.C.E. it was gone. Its palaces were destroyed, many of its cities were abandoned, and its art, pattern of life, and system of writing were buried and forgotten.

What happened? Some recent scholars, noting evidence that the Aegean island of Thera (modern Santorini) suffered a massive volcanic explosion in the middle to late second millennium B.C.E., have suggested that this natural disaster was responsible. According to one version of this theory, the explosion occurred around 1400 B.C.E., blackening and poisoning the air for many miles around and sending a monstrous tidal wave that destroyed the great palace at Cnossus and, with it, Minoan culture. According to another version, the explosion took place about 1200 B.C.E., destroying Bronze Age culture throughout the Aegean. This second version conveniently accounts for the end of both Minoan and Mycenaean civilizations in a single blow, but the evidence does not support it. The Mycenaean towns were not destroyed all at once; many fell around 1200 B.C.E., but

MAP 2–1 THE AEGEAN AREA IN THE BRONZE AGE *The Bronze Age in the Aegean area lasted from about 1900 to about 1100 B.C.E. Its culture on Crete is called Minoan and was at its height about 1900–1400 B.C.E. Bronze Age Helladic culture on the mainland flourished from about 1600–1200 B.C.E.*

some flourished for another century, and the Athens of the period was never destroyed or abandoned. No theory of natural disaster can account for this pattern, leaving us to seek less dramatic explanations for the end of Mycenaean civilization.

THE DORIAN INVASION Some scholars have suggested that piratical sea raiders destroyed Pylos and, perhaps, other sites on the mainland. The Greeks themselves believed in a legend that told of the Dorians, a rude people from the north who spoke a Greek dialect different from that of the Mycenaean peoples. According to the legend, the Dorians joined with one of the Greek tribes, the Heraclidae, in an attack on the southern Greek peninsula of Peloponnesus, which was repulsed. One hundred years later they returned and gained full control. Recent historians have identified this legend of "the return of the Heraclidae" with a Dorian invasion.

Archaeology has not provided material evidence of whether there was a single Dorian invasion or a series of them, and it is impossible as yet to say with any certainty what happened at the end of the Bronze Age in the Aegean. The chances are good, however, that Mycenaean civilization ended gradually over the century between 1200 B.C.E. and 1100 B.C.E. Its end may have been the result of internal conflicts among the Mycenaean kings combined with continuous pressure from outsiders, who raided, infiltrated, and eventually dominated Greece and its neighboring islands. There is reason to believe that Mycenaean society suffered internal weaknesses due to its organization around the centralized control of military force and agricultural production. This rigid organization may have deprived it of flexibility and vitality, leaving it vulnerable to outside challengers. In any case, Cnossus, Mycenae, and Pylos were abandoned, their secrets to be kept for over 3,000 years.

The Greek "Middle Ages" to about 750 B.C.E.

The immediate effects of the Dorian invasion were disastrous for the inhabitants of the Mycenaean world. The palaces and the kings and bureaucrats who managed them were destroyed. The wealth and organization that had supported the artists and merchants were likewise swept away by a barbarous people who did not have the knowledge or social organization to maintain them. Many villages were abandoned and never resettled. Some of their inhabitants probably turned to a nomadic life, and many perished. The chaos resulting from the collapse of the rigidly controlled palace culture produced severe depopulation and widespread poverty that lasted for a long time.

Greek Migrations

Another result of the invasion was the spread of the Greek people eastward from the mainland to the Aegean islands and the coast of Asia Minor. The Dorians themselves, after occupying most of the Peloponnesus, swept across the Aegean to occupy the southern islands and the southern part of the Anatolian coast.

These migrations made the Aegean a Greek lake. Trade with the old civilizations of the Near East, however, was virtually ended by the fall of the advanced Minoan and Mycenaean civilizations; nor was there much internal trade among the different parts of Greece. The Greeks were forced to turn inward, and each community was left largely to its own devices. The Near East was also in disarray at this time, and no great power arose to impose its ways and its will on the helpless people who lived about the Aegean. The Greeks were allowed time to recover from their disaster and to create their unique style of life.

Our knowledge of this period in Greek history rests on very limited sources. Writing disappeared after the fall of Mycenae, and no new script appeared until after 750 B.C.E., so we have no contemporary author to shed light on the period. Excavation reveals no architecture, sculpture, or painting until after 750 B.C.E.

The Age of Homer

For a picture of society in these "Dark Ages," the best source is Homer. His epic poems, the *Iliad* and the *Odyssey*, emerged from a tradition of oral poetry whose roots extend into the Mycenaean Age. Through the centuries bards had sung tales of the heroes who had fought at Troy, using verse arranged in rhythmic formulas to aid the memory. In this way some very old material was preserved into the eighth century B.C.E., when the poems attributed to Homer were finally written down. Although the poems tell of the deeds of Mycenaean Age heroes, the world they describe clearly differs from the Mycenaean world. Homer's heroes are not buried in *tholos* tombs, but are cremated; they worship gods in temples, whereas the Mycenaeans had no temples; they have chariots, but do not know their proper use in warfare. Certain aspects of the society described in the poems appear rather to resemble the world of the tenth and ninth centuries B.C.E., and other aspects appear to belong to the poet's own time, when population was growing at a swift pace and prosperity was returning, thanks to important changes in Greek agriculture, society, and government.

GOVERNMENT   In the Homeric poems, the power of the kings is much less than that of the Mycenaean rulers. Homeric kings were limited in their ability to make important decisions by the need to consult a council of nobles. The nobles felt free to discuss matters in vigorous language and in opposition to the king's wishes. In the *Iliad*, Achilles does not hesitate to address Agamemnon, the "most kingly" commander of the Trojan expedition, in these words: "you with a dog's face and a deer's heart." Such language may have been impolite, but it was not treasonous. The king, on the other hand, was free to ignore the council's advice, but it was risky for him to do so.

The right to speak in council was limited to noblemen, but the common people could not be ignored. If a king planned a war or a major change of policy during a campaign, he would not fail to call the common soldiers to an assembly; they could listen and express their feelings by acclamation, though they could not take part in the debate. Homer shows that even in these early times the Greeks, unlike their predecessors and contemporaries, practiced some forms of limited constitutional government.

The "Trojan Horse," depicted on a seventh-century B.C.E. Greek vase. According to legend, the Greeks finally defeated Troy by pretending to abandon their siege of the city, leaving a giant wooden horse behind. Soldiers hidden in the horse opened the gates of the city to their compatriots after the Trojans had brought it within their walls. Note the wheels on the horse and the Greek soldiers holding weapons and armor who are hiding inside it. Greek 10th–6th B.C.E. Trojan Horse and Greek Soldiers. Relief from neck of an earthenware amphora (640 B.C.E.) from Mykanos, overall ht. 120 cm. Archeological Museum, Mykonos, Greece. Photography by Erich Lessing

Society Homeric society, nevertheless, was sharply divided into classes, the most important division being the one between nobles and everyone else. We do not know the origin of this distinction, but we cannot doubt that at this time Greek society was aristocratic. Birth determined noble status, and wealth usually accompanied it. Below the nobles were three other classes: *thetes*, landless laborers, and slaves. We do not know whether the *thetes* owned the land they worked outright (and so were free to sell it) or worked a hereditary plot that belonged to their clan (and was therefore not theirs to dispose of as they chose).

The worst condition was that of the free, but landless, hired agricultural laborer. The slave, at least, was attached to a family household and so was protected and fed. In a world where membership in a settled group gave the only security, the free laborers were desperately vulnerable. Slaves were few in number and were mostly women, who served as maids and concubines. Some male slaves worked as shepherds. Few, if any, worked in agriculture, which depended on free labor throughout Greek history.

Homeric Values The Homeric poems reflect an aristocratic code of values that powerfully influenced all future Greek thought. In classical times, Homer was the schoolbook of the Greeks. They memorized his texts, settled diplomatic disputes by citing passages in them, and emulated the behavior and cherished the values they found in them. Those values were physical prowess; courage; and fierce protection of one's family, friends, property, and, above all, personal honor and reputation. Speed of foot, strength, and, most of all, excellence at fighting make a man great, and all these attributes serve to promote personal honor. The great hero of the *Iliad*, Achilles, refuses to fight in battle, allowing his fellow Greeks to be slain and almost defeated, because Agamemnon has wounded his honor by taking away his battle prize. He returns not out of a sense of duty to the army, but to avenge the death of his dear friend Patroclus. Odysseus, the hero of the *Odyssey*, returning home after his wanderings, ruthlessly kills the many suitors who had, in his long absence, sought to marry his wife Penelope; they had dishonored him by consuming his wealth, wooing Penelope, and scorning his son.

The highest virtue in Homeric society was *arete*—manliness, courage in the most general sense, and the excellence proper to a hero. This quality was best revealed in a contest, or *agon*. Homeric battles are not primarily group combats, but a series of individual contests between great champions. One of the prime forms of entertainment is the athletic contest, and the funeral of Patroclus is celebrated by such a contest.

The central ethical idea in Homer can be found in the instructions that Achilles' father gives him when he sends him off to fight at Troy: "Always be the best and distinguished above others." The father of another Homeric hero has given his son exactly the same orders and has added to them the injunction: "Do not bring shame on the family of your fathers who were by far the best in Ephyre and in wide Lycia." Here in a nutshell we have the chief values of the aristocrats of Homer's world: to vie for individual supremacy in *arete* and to defend and increase the honor of the family. These would remain prominent aristocratic values long after Homeric society was only a memory.

Women in Homeric Society In the world described by Homer the role of women was chiefly to bear and raise children, but the wives of the heroes also had a respected position, presiding over the household, overseeing the servants, and safeguarding the family property. (See "Husband and Wife in Homer's Troy.") They were prized for their beauty, constancy, and skill at

Husband and Wife in Homer's Troy

Homer's poems provide a picture of early Greek ideas and institutions. In the Iliad, *the poet tells of the return from the battle of the Trojan hero Hector. He is greeted by his loving, "warm, generous wife," Andromache, who is carrying their baby son. Hector reaches for the boy, who is frightened to tears by the plume on his father's helmet. The father removes the helmet and prays that his son will grow up to be called "a better man than his father … a joy to his mother's heart." The rest of the scene reveals the character of their marriage and the division of responsibility between men and women in their world.*

❖ *How does Homer depict the feelings of husband and wife toward one another? What are the tasks of the aristocratic woman revealed in this passage? What can be learned about the attitude towards death and duty?*

So Hector prayed and placed his son in the arms of his loving wife. Andromache pressed the child to her scented breast, smiling through her tears. Her husband noticed, and filled with pity now, Hector stroked her gently, trying to reassure her, repeating her name: "Andromache, dear one; why so desperate? Why so much grief for me? No man will hurl me down to Death, against my fate. And fate? No one alive has ever escaped it, neither brave man nor coward, I tell you—it's born with us the day that we are born. So please go home and tend to your own tasks, the distaff and the loom, and keep the women working hard as well. As for the fight-ing, men will see to that, all who were born in Troy but I most of all."

Hector aflash in arms took up his horsehair-crested helmet once again. And his loving wife went home, turning, glancing back again and again and weeping live warm tears. She quickly reached the sturdy house of Hector, man-killing Hector, and found her women gathered there inside and stirred them all to a high pitch of mourning. So in his house they raised the dirges for the dead, for Hector still alive, his people were so convinced that never again would he come home from battle, never escape the Argives' rage and bloody hands.

From *The Iliad* by Homer, translated by Robert Fagles, copyright © 1990 by Robert Fagles. Used by permission of Viking Penguin, a division of Penguin Putnam Inc.

weaving. All these fine qualities are combined in Penelope, the wife of Odysseus, probably the ideal Homeric woman. For the twenty years of her husband's absence, she put off the many suitors who sought to marry her and take his place, remained faithful to him, preserved his property, and protected the future of their son. Far different was the reputation of Agamemnon's wife, Clytemnestra who betrayed her husband while he was off fighting at Troy and murdered him on his return. Homer contrasts her with the virtuous Penelope in a passage that reveals a streak of hostility to women that can be found throughout the ancient history of the Greeks. (See "Hesiod Tells of the Creation of Woman.")

Not so did the daughter of Tyndareus fashion
  her evil
deeds, when she killed her wedded lord, and a
  song of loathing
will be hers among men, to make evil the reputation
of womankind, even for those whose acts are
  virtuous.[2]

Unlike Greek women in later centuries, the women of the higher class depicted in Homer are seen moving freely about their communities in town and country. They have a place alongside their husbands at the banquets in the great halls and take part in the conversation. In the *Odyssey*'s land of Phaeacia, admittedly a kind of fairyland, the wise queen Arete can decide the fate of suppliants and sometimes is asked to settle disputes even between men. A good marriage is seen as essential, admirable, and desirable. The shipwrecked Odysseus tries to win the sympathy of Arete's young daughter by wishing for her "all that you desire in your heart":

A husband and a home and the accompanying
  unity of mind and feeling
Which is so desirable, for there is nothing nobler
  or better than this,
When two people, who think alike, keep house
As man and wife; causing pain to their enemies,
And joy to their well-wishers, as they themselves
  know best.[3]

[2]*Odyssey* 24.199–202, trans. by Richmond Lattimore (Chicago: University of Chicago Press, 1965).

[3]Homer, *Odyssey*, 6.181–185, translated by M. Dillon and L. Garland, *Ancient Greece*, Routtledge, London and New York.

The *Polis*

The characteristic Greek institution was the *polis*. The common translation of that word as "city–state" is misleading, for it says both too much and too little. All Greek *poleis* began as little more than agricultural villages or towns, and many stayed that way, so the word "city" is inappropriate. All of them were states, in the sense of being independent political units, but they were much more than that. The *polis* was thought of as a community of relatives; all its citizens, who were theoretically descended from a common ancestor, belonged to subgroups, such as fighting brotherhoods or phratries, clans, and tribes, and worshiped the gods in common ceremonies.

Aristotle argued that the *polis* was a natural growth and that the human being was by nature "an animal who lives in a *polis*." Humans alone have the power of speech and from it derive the ability to distinguish good from bad and right from wrong, "and the sharing of these things is what makes a household and a *polis*." Therefore, humans who are incapable of sharing these things or who are so self-sufficient that they have no need of them are not humans at all, but either wild beasts or gods. Without law and justice, human beings are the worst and most dangerous of the animals. With them, humans can be the best, and justice exists only in the *polis*. These high claims were made in the fourth century B.C.E., hundreds of years after the *polis* came into existence, but they accurately reflect an attitude that was present from the first.

Development of the *Polis*

Originally the word *polis* referred only to a citadel—an elevated, defensible rock to which the farmers of the neighboring area could retreat in case of attack.

Hesiod Tells of the Creation of Woman

Hesiod was a farmer and a poet who lived in a village in central Greece about 700 B.C.E.. His poem Theogony *tells stories of how the gods came to be as they were. In one of these tales Zeus, as part of his conflict with the titan Prometheus, the divine benefactor who brought fire and other gifts to man, creates woman as a punishment. The story is an example of a hostile attitude towards women that is found in many early societies. Zeus orders the craftsman–god Hephaestus to create a woman out of clay and to have it made beautiful by the goddess Athena.*

❖ *What are the specific complaints Hesiod makes of women? What does he see as the advantages and disadvantages of marriage? What does this dark picture of women tell us about the society in which it emerged?*

Then the gods and mortal men were struck with amazement when they beheld this sheer inescapable snare for men. From her descend the race of women, the feminine sex; from her come the baneful race and types of women. Women, a great plague, make their abodes with mortal men, being ill-suited to Poverty's curse but suited to Plenty. Compare how the honey bees in the protected cells of the hives garner food for the drones, conspirers in evil works—all day long they are active until the sun goes down busily working and storing white honey during the daylight —while the drones keep within the protected cells of the hives and garner into their stomachs the food that others have worked for. Even so Zeus the Thunderer on High created women as an evil for men and conspirers in troublesome works. And in exchange for a good he gave a balancing evil. Whoever flees from marriage and women's mischievous works, being unwilling to wed, comes to baneful old age with no one to care for his needs, and though he has plenty to live on while he is living, collateral heirs divide his possessions when he is dead. As for the man who is fated to marry, if he obtains a virtuous wife, one endowed with good sense, throughout his life evil and good alternate endlessly. But that man who obtains a wife who is thoroughly bad lives having deep in his breast a pain which never subsides fixed in his innermost heart, and this is an evil incurable. Thus to deceive Zeus's mind is impossible or to get around it, for not even the son of Iapetos, crafty Prometheus, avoided his deep wrath, but in spite of his shrewdness suffers under compulsion great inescapable bondage.

Excerpt from *The Histories* by Herodotus, translated by Aubrey de Selincourt, revised by John Marincola (Penguin Classics, 1954, Second revised edition 1996), copyright © Aubrey de Selincourt, 1954. Revised edition copyright © John Marincola, 1996. Reprinted by permission of Penguin Books Ltd.

The Acropolis in Athens and the hill called Acro-corinth in Corinth are examples. For some time, such high places and the adjacent farms made up the *polis*. The towns grew gradually and without planning, as their narrow, winding, and disorderly streets show. For centuries they had no walls. Unlike the city–states of the Near East, they were not placed for commercial convenience on rivers or the sea. Nor did they grow up around a temple to serve the needs of priests and to benefit from the needs of worshipers. The availability of farmland and of a natural fortress determined their location. They were placed either well inland or far enough away from the sea to avoid piratical raids. Only later and gradually did the *agora*—a marketplace and civic center—appear within the *polis*. The *agora* was to become the heart of the Greeks' remarkable social life, distinguished by conversation and argument carried on in the open air.

Some *poleis* probably came into existence early in the eighth century B.C.E. The institution was certainly common by the middle of the century, for all the colonies that were established by the Greeks in the years after 750 B.C.E. took the form of the *polis*. Once the new institution had been fully established, true monarchy disappeared. Vestigial kings survived in some places, but they were almost always only ceremonial figures without power. The original form of the *polis* was an aristocratic republic dominated by the nobility through its council of nobles and its monopoly of the magistracies.

Just as the *polis* emerged from sources within Greek society after the Bronze Age, striking changes also appeared in the creation and decoration of Greek pottery. A stunning example of the shift to the new Geometric style is the *Dipylon Vase*, discussed in "Art & the West" on p. 47.

About 750 B.C.E., coincident with the development of the *polis*, the Greeks borrowed a writing system from one of the Semitic scripts and added vowels to create the first true alphabet. This new Greek alphabet was easier to learn than any earlier writing system, leading to much wider literacy.

The Hoplite Phalanx

A new military technique was crucial to the development of the *polis*. In earlier times, the brunt of fighting had been carried on by small troops of cavalry and individual "champions" who first threw their spears and then came to close quarters with swords. Toward the end of the eighth century B.C.E.,

however, the hoplite phalanx came into being and remained the basis of Greek warfare thereafter.

The hoplite was a heavily armed infantryman who fought with a spear and a large shield. These soldiers were formed into a phalanx in close order, usually at least eight ranks deep. So long as the hoplites fought bravely and held their ground, there would be few casualties and no defeat; but if they gave way, the result was usually a rout. All depended on the discipline, strength, and courage of the individual soldier. At its best, the phalanx could withstand cavalry charges and defeat infantries not as well protected or disciplined. Until defeated by the Roman legion, it was the dominant military force in the eastern Mediterranean.

The usual hoplite battle in Greece was between the armies of two *poleis* quarreling over a piece of land. One army invaded the territory of the other when the crops were almost ready for harvest. The defending army had no choice but to protect its fields. If the army was beaten, its fields were captured or destroyed and its people might starve. In every way, the phalanx was a communal effort that relied not on the extraordinary actions of the individual, but on the courage of a considerable portion of the citizenry. This style of fighting produced a single decisive battle that reduced the time lost in fighting other kinds of warfare; it spared the houses, livestock, and other capital of the farmer–soldiers who made up the phalanx, and it reduced the number of casualties as well. It perfectly suited the farmer–soldier–citizen, who was the backbone of the *polis*, and, by keeping wars short and limiting their destructiveness and expense, it helped the *polis* prosper.

The phalanx and the *polis* arose together, and both heralded the decline of the kings. The phalanx, however, was not made up only of aristocrats. Most of the hoplites were farmers working small holdings. The immediate beneficiaries of the royal decline were the aristocrats, but because the existence of the *polis* depended on small farmers, their wishes could not long be wholly ignored. The rise of the hoplite phalanx created a bond between the aristocrats and the yeomen family farmers who fought in it. This bond helps explain why class conflicts were muted for some time. It also guaranteed, however, that the aristocrats, who dominated at first, would not always be unchallenged.

The Importance of the *Polis*

The Greeks looked to the *polis* for peace, order, prosperity, and honor in their lifetime. They counted on it to preserve their memory and to honor their de-

A Funeral Scene in Eighth-Century B.C.E. Greece: The Dipylon Vase

*H*ellenic civilization proper, as opposed to the more generally Mediterranean culture of the Minoan and Mycenaean periods of the Bronze Age, took shape in the four centuries from about 1100 to about 700 B.C.E. These are sometimes referred to as the Greek Dark Ages, chiefly because of how little is known about them, for there are no written sources for this period. There is better evidence for the history of art, for archaeology has turned up small sculptures in clay and bronze and a great deal of painted pottery that illuminate the development of the new culture.

Although the potters and vase painters of the early part of this period clearly learned much from their Mycenaean forerunners, their sharp break with the past is evident not only in the abandonment of older shapes and the development of new ones, but, most strikingly, in the style of their painting. The new style is called Geometric, from the dominant use of geometric forms—circles, rectangles and triangles—placed in parallel bands around the vases, instead of the freer forms favored by the Mycenaeans. The earliest and simplest examples are called Proto-Geometric. The next development was toward more complicated and fuller use of the geometric shapes and, finally, the appearance of human and animal figures alongside the geometric patterns.

The *Dipylon Vase* is a splendid example of the fully developed style. Its date is about 750 B.C.E., when the *polis*—the fully developed political community that would characterize Hellenic civilization—was just coming into being in a few places, when the Greeks were beginning to adapt the Phoenician alphabet to write their own language, and when Homer's great epic poems were taking shape. The vase, about 3½ feet tall, was found in the ancient cemetery outside the Dipylon gate to the ancient city of Athens. It is one of several large vases that served as burial monuments.

The painting depicts the funeral of an important person. At the center of the top band, or register, the body of the dead person is placed on a high platform. On either side, male and female mourners place their hands on the tops of their heads, as though tearing their hair in grief. In the lower register appears a funeral procession with horse-drawn chariots and soldiers carrying shields.

Although the bottom of the vase has holes that allow liquid offerings to pour through to the dead, the Greeks did not share the Egyptians' belief in an afterlife where the dead continue to engage in activities they enjoyed while alive. The Greek idea of death, on the contrary, was grim, and dark, and final.

Sources: Janson, *History of Art*, (New York: Prentice Hall and Harry N. Abrams, 1997), 110–112; Marilyn Stokstad, *Art History*, rev. ed. (Upper Saddle River, NJ: Prentice Hall, 1999), pp. 152–161.

The Dipylon Vase, c. 750 B.C.E. The Metropolitan Museum of Art, Rogers Fund, 1914. (14.130.14) Photograph © 1996 The Metropolitan Museum of Art.

scendants after death. Some of them came to see it not only as a ruler, but as the molder of its citizens. Knowing this, we can understand the pride and scorn that underlie the comparison made by the poet Phocylides between the Greek state and the capital of the great and powerful Assyrian Empire: "A little *polis* living orderly in a high place is stronger than a block-headed Nineveh."

Expansion of the Greek World

From the middle of the eighth century B.C.E. until well into the sixth century B.C.E., the Greeks vastly expanded the territory they controlled, their wealth, and their contacts with other peoples. A burst of colonizing activity placed *poleis* from Spain to the Black Sea. A century earlier, a few Greeks had established trading posts in Syria. There they had learned new techniques in the arts and crafts and much more from the older civilizations of the Near East.

Magna Graecia

Syria and its neighboring territory were too strong to penetrate, so the Greeks settled the southern coast of Macedonia and the Chalcidic peninsula. These regions were sparsely settled, and the natives were not well enough organized to resist the Greek colonists. Southern Italy and eastern Sicily were even more inviting areas. Before long, there were so many Greek colonies in Italy and Sicily that the Romans called the whole region *Magna Graecia*, "Great Greece." The Greeks also put colonies in Spain and southern France. In the seventh century B.C.E., Greek colonists settled the coasts of the northeastern Mediterranean, the Black Sea, and the straits connecting them. About the same time, they established settlements on the eastern part of the North African coast. The Greeks now had outposts throughout the Mediterranean world. (See Map 2–2.)

The Greek Colony

The Greeks did not lightly leave home to join a colony. The voyage by sea was dangerous and uncomfortable, and at the end of it were uncertainty and danger. Only powerful pressures like overpopulation and hunger for land drove thousands from their homes to establish new *poleis*.

The colony, although sponsored by the mother city, was established for the good of the colonists rather than for the benefit of those whom they left behind. The colonists tended to divide the land they settled into equal shares, reflecting an egalitarian tendency

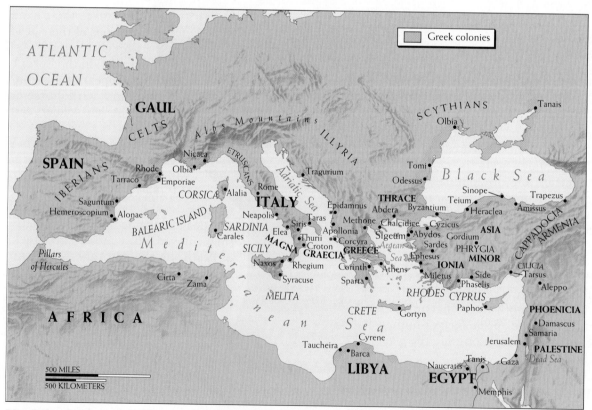

MAP 2–2   GREEK COLONIZATION   *The height of Greek colonization was between about 750 and 550 B.C.E. Greek colonies stretched from the Mediterranean coasts of Spain and Gaul (modern France) in the west to the Black Sea and Asia Minor in the east.*

inherent in the ethical system of the yeoman farmers in the mother cities. They often copied their home constitution, worshiped the same gods as the people of the mother city at the same festivals in the same way, and carried on a busy trade with the mother city. Most colonies, though independent, were friendly with their mother cities. Each might ask the other for aid in time of trouble and expect to receive a friendly hearing, although neither was obligated to help the other.

The Athenians had colonies of this typical kind, but introduced innovations during their imperial period (478–404 B.C.E.). At one point they began to treat all the colonies of their empire as though they were Athenian settlements, requiring them to bring an offering of a cow and a suit of armor to the Great Panathenaic festival, just like true Athenian colonies. The goal may have been to cloak imperial rule in the more friendly garb of colonial family attachment.

The best known exception to the general rule of friendly relations between colony and mother city was the case of Corinth and its colony Corcyra, which quarreled and fought over more than two centuries. Thucydides tells of a fateful conflict between them that played a major role in causing the Peloponnesian War.

Colonization had a powerful influence on Greek life. By relieving the pressure of a growing population, it provided a safety valve that allowed the *poleis* to escape civil wars. By confronting the Greeks with the differences between themselves and the new peoples they met, colonization gave them a sense of cultural identity and fostered a Panhellenic ("all-Greek") spirit that led to the establishment of a number of common religious festivals. The most important ones were at Olympia, Delphi, Corinth, and Nemea.

Colonization also encouraged trade and industry. The influx of new wealth from abroad and the increased demand for goods from the homeland stimulated a more intensive use of the land and an emphasis on crops for export, chiefly the olive and the wine grape. The manufacture of pottery, tools, weapons, and fine artistic metalwork, as well as perfumed oil, the soap of the ancient Mediterranean world, was likewise encouraged. New opportunities allowed some men, sometimes outside the nobility, to become wealthy and important. The newly enriched became a troublesome element in the aristocratic *poleis*, for, although increasingly important in the life of their states, they were barred from political power, religious privileges, and social acceptance by the ruling aristocrats. These conditions soon created a crisis in many states.

The Tyrants (about 700–500 B.C.E.)

In some cities—perhaps only a small percentage of the more than 1,000 Greek *poleis*—the crisis produced by new economic and social conditions led to or intensified factional divisions within the ruling aristocracy. In the years between 700 and 500 B.C.E., the result was often the establishment of a tyranny.

THE RISE OF TYRANNY A tyrant was a monarch who had gained power in an unorthodox or unconstitutional, but not necessarily wicked, way and who exercised a strong one-man rule that might well be beneficent and popular.

The founding tyrant was usually a member of the ruling aristocracy who either had a personal grievance or led an unsuccessful faction. He often rose to power because of his military ability and support from the hoplites. He generally had the support of the politically powerless group of the newly wealthy and of the poor farmers. When he took power, he often expelled many of his aristocratic opponents and divided at least some of their land among his supporters. He pleased his commercial and industrial supporters by destroying the privileges of the old aristocracy and by fostering trade and colonization.

The tyrants presided over a period of population growth that saw an increase especially in the number of city dwellers. They responded with a program of public works that included the improvement of drainage systems, care for the water supply, the construction and organization of marketplaces, the building and strengthening of city walls, and the erection of temples. They introduced new local festivals and elaborated the old ones. They were active in the patronage of the arts, supporting poets and artisans with gratifying results. All this activity contributed to the tyrant's popularity, to the prosperity of his city, and to his self-esteem.

In most cases, the tyrant's rule was secured by a personal bodyguard and by mercenary soldiers. An armed citizenry, necessary for an aggressive foreign policy, would have been dangerous, so the tyrants usually pursued a program of peaceful alliances with other tyrants abroad and avoided war.

THE END OF THE TYRANTS By the end of the sixth century B.C.E., tyranny had disappeared from the Greek states and did not return in the same form or for the same reasons. The last tyrants were universally hated for the cruelty and repression they employed. They left bitter memories in their own states and became objects of fear and hatred everywhere.

Besides the outrages committed by individual tyrants, there was something about the very concept of tyranny that was inimical to the idea of the *polis*. The notion of the *polis* as a community to which every member must be responsible, the connection of justice with that community, and the natural aristocratic hatred of monarchy all made tyranny seem alien and offensive. The rule of a tyrant, however beneficent, was arbitrary and unpredictable. Tyranny came into being in defiance of tradition and law, and the tyrant governed without either. He was not answerable in any way to his fellow citizens.

From a longer perspective, however, the tyrants made important contributions to the development of Greek civilization. They encouraged economic changes that helped secure the future prosperity of Greece. They increased communication with the rest of the Mediterranean world and cultivated the crafts and technology, as well as the arts and literature. Most important of all, they broke the grip of the aristocracy and put the productive powers of the most active and talented of its citizens fully at the service of the *polis*.

The Major States

Generalization about the *polis* becomes difficult not long after its appearance, for although the states had much in common, some of them developed in unique ways. Sparta and Athens, which became the two most powerful Greek states, had especially unusual histories.

Sparta

At first Sparta seems not to have been strikingly different from other *poleis*. About 725 B.C.E., however, the pressure of population and land hunger led the Spartans to launch a war of conquest against their western neighbor, Messenia. (See Map 2–3.) The First Messenian War gave the Spartans as much land as they would ever need. The reduction of the Messenians to the status of serfs, or Helots, meant that the Spartans did not even need to work the land that supported them.

The turning point in Spartan history came about 650 B.C.E., when, in the Second Messenian War, the Helots rebelled with the help of Argos and other Peloponnesian cities. The war was long and bitter and at one point threatened the existence of Sparta. After the revolt had been put down, the Spartans were forced to reconsider their way of life. They could not expect to keep down the Helots, who outnumbered them perhaps ten to one, and still maintain the old free and easy habits typical of most Greeks. Faced with the choice of making drastic changes and sacrifices or abandoning their control of Messenia, the Spartans chose to introduce fundamental reforms that turned their city forever after into a military academy and camp.

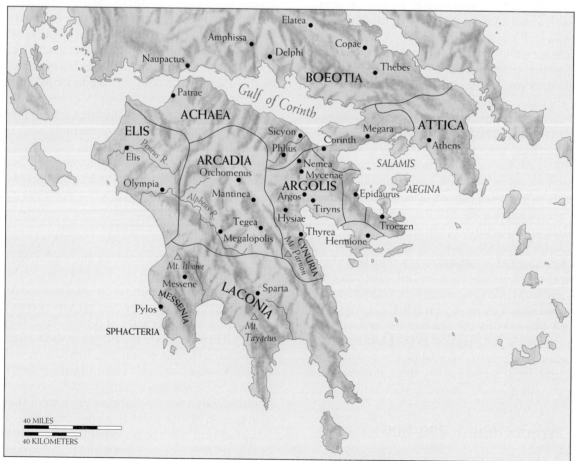

MAP 2–3   THE PELOPONNESUS   *Sparta's region, Laconia, was in the Peloponnesus. Nearby states were members of the Peloponnesian League under Sparta's leadership.*

Chronology of the Rise of Greece

ca. 2900–1150 B.C.E.	Minoan period
ca. 1900 B.C.E.	Probable date of the arrival of the Greeks on the mainland
ca. 1600–1150 B.C.E.	Mycenaean period
ca. 1250 B.C.E.	Sack of Troy (?)
ca. 1200–1150 B.C.E.	Destruction of Mycenaean centers in Greece
ca. 1100–750 B.C.E.	"Greek Dark Ages"
ca. 750–500 B.C.E.	Major period of Greek colonization
ca. 725 B.C.E.	Probable date when Homer flourished
ca. 700 B.C.E.	Probable date when Hesiod flourished
ca. 700–500 B.C.E.	Major period of Greek tyranny

SPARTAN SOCIETY The new system that emerged late in the sixth century B.C.E. exerted control over each Spartan from birth, when officials of the state decided which infants were physically fit to survive. At the age of seven, the Spartan boy was taken from his mother and turned over to young instructors. He was trained in athletics and the military arts and taught to endure privation, to bear physical pain, and to live off the country, by theft if necessary. At twenty the Spartan youth was enrolled in the army, where he lived in barracks with his companions until the age of thirty. Marriage was permitted, but a strange sort of marriage it was, for the Spartan male could visit his wife only infrequently and by stealth. At thirty, he became a full citizen, an "equal." He took his meals at a public mess in the company of fifteen comrades. His food, a simple diet without much meat or wine, was provided by his own plot of land, worked by Helots. Military service was required until the age of sixty; only then could the Spartan retire to his home and family.

This educational program extended to women, too, although they were not given military training. Female infants were examined for fitness to survive in the same way as males. Girls were given gymnastic training, were permitted greater freedom of movement than among other Greeks, and were equally indoctrinated with the idea of service to Sparta.

The entire system was designed to change the natural feelings of devotion to family and children into a more powerful commitment to the *polis*. Privacy, luxury, and even comfort were sacrificed to the purpose of producing soldiers whose physical powers, training, and discipline made them the best in the world. Nothing that might turn the mind away from duty was permitted. The very use of coins was forbidden lest it corrupt the desires of Spartans. Neither family nor money were allowed to interfere with the only ambition permitted to a Spartan male: to win glory and the respect of his peers by bravery in war.

A large Spartan plate from the second quarter of the sixth century B.C.E. It shows traders weighing silphium, a medicinal plant from North Africa, before King Arcesilas of Cyrene, seated on the deck of a ship. Below them, workers pile cargo into the ship's hold. The monkey at the top of the scene and the lizard at the left suggest the location. Hirmer Fotoarchiv

The Greek and Persian Ways of War—Autocracy versus Freedom under the Law

The Greek historian Herodotus, who wrote his account of the wars between the Greeks and Persians more than half a century after they ended, was very interested in the differences between the ways of the Greeks and other peoples of the world. In the following passage he describes a conversation between Demaratus, an exiled king of Sparta, and Xerxes, the Great King of Persia. Demaratus had come to Xerxes' court after his exile. Xerxes received him kindly and made him a royal adviser.

❖ *On what does Xerxes rely for Persian military success? What is the source of Demaratus' confidence in the Spartans? Does the claim he makes hold for other Greeks as well as the Spartans? How is it possible to reconcile freedom with obedience to the laws?*

"How is it possible that a thousand men, or ten thousand, or fifty thousand, should stand up to an army as big as mine, especially if they were not under a single master, but all perfectly free to do as they pleased? Suppose them to have five thousand men: In that case we should be more than a thousand to one! If, like ours, their troops were subject to the control of a single man, then possibly for fear of him, in spite of the disparity in numbers, they might show some sort of factitious courage, or let themselves be whipped into battle; but, as every man is free to follow his fancy, it is not conceivable that they should do either. Indeed, my own opinion is that even on equal terms the Greeks could hardly face the Persians alone. We, too, have this thing that you were speaking of—I do not say it is common, but it does exist; for instance, amongst the Persians in my bodyguard there are men who would willingly fight with three Greeks together. But you know nothing of such things, or you could not talk such nonsense."

"My lord," Demaratus answered, "I knew before I began that if I spoke the truth you would not like it. But, as you demanded the plain truth and nothing less, I told you how things are with the Spartans. Yet you are well aware that I now feel but little affection for my countrymen, who robbed me of my hereditary power and privileges and made me a fugitive without a home—whereas your father welcomed me at his court and gave me the means of livelihood and somewhere to live. Surely it is unreasonable to reject kindness; any sensible man will cherish it. Personally I do not claim to be able to fight ten men—or two; indeed I should prefer not even to fight with one. But should it be necessary—should there be some great cause to urge me on—then nothing would give me more pleasure than to stand up to one of those men of yours who claim to be a match for three Greeks. So it is with the Spartans; fighting singly, they are as good as any, but fighting together they are the best soldiers in the world. They are free—yes—but not entirely free; for they have a master, and that master is Law, which they fear much more than your subjects fear you. Whatever this master commands they do; and his command never varies: it is never to retreat in battle, however great the odds, but always to stand firm, and to conquer or die. If, my lord, you think that what I have said is nonsense—very well; I am willing henceforward to hold my tongue. This time I spoke because you forced me to speak. In any case, I pray that all may turn out as you desire."

Xerxes burst out laughing at Demaratus' answer, and goodhumouredly let him go.

Excerpt from *The Histories* by Herodotus, translated by Aubrey de Selincourt, revised by John Marincola (Penguin Classics, 1954, Second revised edition 1996), copyright © Aubrey de Selincourt, 1954. Revised edition copyright © John Marincola, 1996. Reprinted by permission of Penguin Books Ltd.

SPARTAN GOVERNMENT   The Spartan constitution was mixed, containing elements of monarchy, oligarchy, and democracy. There were two kings, whose power was limited by law and also by the rivalry that usually existed between the two royal houses. The origins and explanation of this unusual dual kingship are unknown, but both kings ruled together in Sparta and exercised equal powers. Their functions were chiefly religious and military. A Spartan army rarely left home without a king in command.

The oligarchic element was represented by a council of elders consisting of twenty-eight men over the age of sixty, elected for life, and the kings. These elders had important judicial functions, sitting as a court in cases involving the kings. They also were consulted before any proposal was put before the assembly of Spartan citizens. In a traditional society like Sparta's, they must have had considerable influence.

The Spartan assembly consisted of all males over thirty. Theoretically, they were the final authority, but in practice, debate was carried on by magistrates, elders, and kings alone, and voting was usually by acclamation. Therefore, the assembly's real function was to ratify decisions already taken or to decide between positions favored by the leading figures. In addition, Sparta had a unique institution, the board of *ephors*. This consisted of five men elected annually by the assembly. Originally, boards of ephors appear to have been intended to check the power of the kings, but gradually they gained other important functions. They controlled foreign policy, oversaw the generalship of the kings on campaign, presided at the assembly, and guarded against rebellions by the Helots.

The whole system was remarkable both for the way in which it combined participation by the citizenry with significant checks on its power and for its unmatched stability. Most Greeks admired the Spartan state for these qualities and also for its ability to mold citizens so thoroughly to an ideal. Many political philosophers, from Plato to modern times, have based utopian schemes on a version of Sparta's constitution and educational system.

THE PELOPONNESIAN LEAGUE   By about 550 B.C.E. the Spartan system was well established, and its limitations were made plain. Suppression of the Helots required all the effort and energy that Sparta had. The Spartans could expand no further, but they could not allow unruly independent neighbors to cause unrest that might inflame the Helots.

When the Spartans defeated Tegea, their northern neighbor, they imposed an unusual peace. Instead of taking away land and subjugating the defeated state, Sparta left the Tegeans their land and their freedom. In exchange, they required the Tegeans to follow the Spartan lead in foreign affairs and to supply a fixed number of soldiers to Sparta on demand. This became the model for Spartan relations with the other states in the Peloponnesus. Soon Sparta was the leader of an alliance that included every Peloponnesian state but Argos; modern scholars have named this alliance the Peloponnesian League. It provided the Spartans with the security they needed, and it also made Sparta the most powerful *polis* in Hellenic history. By 500 B.C.E., Sparta and the league had given the Greeks a force capable of facing mighty threats from abroad. (See "The Greek and Persian Ways of War—Autocracy versus Freedom under the Law.")

Athens

Athens was slow to come into prominence and to join in the new activities that were changing the more advanced states. The reasons were several: Athens was not situated on the most favored trade routes of the eighth and seventh centuries B.C.E., its large area (about 1,000 square miles) allowed population growth without great pressure, and the unification of the many villages and districts within this territory into a single *polis* was not completed until the seventh century B.C.E. (See Map 2–4.)

ARISTOCRATIC RULE   In the seventh century B.C.E., Athens was a typical aristocratic *polis*. Its people were divided into four tribes and into several clans and brotherhoods (*phratries*). The aristocrats held the most land and the best land and dominated religious and political life. There was no written law, and decisions were rendered by powerful nobles on the basis of tradition and, most likely, self-interest. The state was governed by the Areopagus, a council of nobles deriving its name from the hill where it held its sessions. Annually the council elected nine magistrates, called *archons*, who joined the Areopagus after their year in office. Because the *archons* served for only a year, were checked by their colleagues, and looked forward to a lifetime as members of the Areopagus, it is plain that the aristocratic Areopagus, not the *archons*, was the true master of the state.

PRESSURE FOR CHANGE   In the seventh century B.C.E., the peaceful life of Athens experienced some disturbances, caused in part by quarrels within the nobility and in part by the beginnings of an agrarian crisis. In 632 B.C.E., a nobleman named Cylon attempted a coup to establish himself as tyrant. He was thwarted, but the unrest continued.

In 621 B.C.E., a man named Draco was given special authority to codify and publish laws for the first time. In later years Draco's penalties were thought to be harsh—hence the saying that his laws were written in blood. (We still speak of unusually harsh penalties as Draconian.) Draco's work was probably limited to laws concerning homicide and was aimed at ending blood feuds between clans, but it set an important precedent: The publication of laws strengthened the hand of the state against the local power of the nobles.

The root of Athens' troubles was agricultural. Many Athenians worked family farms, from which they obtained most of their living. It appears that they planted wheat, the staple crop, year after year without rotating fields or using enough fertilizer. Shifting to more intensive agricultural techniques and to the planting of trees and vines required capital, leading the less successful farmers to acquire excessive debt.

MAP 2–4   ATTICA AND VICINITY   *Citizens of all towns in Attica were also citizens of Athens.*

To survive, some farmers had to borrow from wealthy neighbors to get through the year. In return, they promised one-sixth of the next year's crop. The deposit of an inscribed stone on the entailed farms marked the arrangement. As their troubles persisted, debtors had to pledge their wives, their children, and themselves as surety for new loans. Inevitably, many Athenians defaulted and were enslaved. Some were even sold abroad. Revolutionary pressures grew among the poor, who began to demand the abolition of debt and a redistribution of the land.

REFORMS OF SOLON   In the year 594 B.C.E., as tradition has it, the Athenians elected Solon as the only *archon*, with extraordinary powers to legislate and revise the constitution. Immediately, he attacked the agrarian problem by canceling current debts and forbidding future loans secured by the person of the borrower. He helped bring back many Athenians enslaved abroad and freed those in Athens enslaved for debt. This program was called the "shaking off of burdens." It did not, however, solve the fundamental economic problem, and Solon did not redistribute the land.

In the short run, therefore, Solon did not put an end to the economic crisis, but his other econom-

ic actions had profound success in the long run. He forbade the export of wheat and encouraged that of olive oil. This policy had the initial effect of making wheat more available in Attica and encouraging the cultivation of olive oil and wine as cash crops. By the fifth century B.C.E., the cultivation of cash crops had become so profitable that much Athenian land was diverted from grain production, and Athens became dependent on imported wheat. Solon also changed the Athenian standards of weights and measures to conform with those of Corinth and Euboea and the cities of the east. This change also encouraged commerce and turned Athens in the direction that would lead it to great prosperity in the fifth century B.C.E. Solon also encouraged industry by offering citizenship to foreign artisans, and his success is reflected in the development of the outstanding Attic pottery of the sixth century B.C.E.

Solon also significantly changed the constitution. Citizenship had previously been the privilege of all male adults whose fathers were citizens; to their number he added those immigrants who were tradesmen and merchants. All these Athenian citizens were divided into four classes on the basis of

The Rule of the Tyrant Pisistratus

Although tyranny came to have a bad reputation, the first tyrants were often popular because they broke the unchallenged domination of the aristocrats. Their careers were sometimes remembered fondly because their achievements contrasted favorably with those of their successors. So it was with the Athenian view of the reign of their first tyrant, Pisistratus, as suggested by this passage from Aristotle's Athenian Constitution, *written two centuries after the events described.*

❖ *What were the bases of Pisistratus' power? If he was a tyrant, why is his rule portrayed as a golden age? If it was a golden age, why did the Athenians after his death pass a law against the establishment of tyranny? What was the relation between the tyranny at Athens and the rule of law?*

Such was the origin and such the vicissitudes of the tyranny of Pisistratus. His administration was temperate, as has been said before, and more like constitutional government than a tyranny. Not only was he in every respect humane and mild and ready to forgive those who offended, but, in addition, he advanced money to the poorer people to help them in their labours, so that they might make their living by agriculture. In this he had two objects, first that they might not spend their time in the city but might be scattered over all the face of the country, and secondly that, being moderately well off and occupied with their own business, they might have neither the wish nor the time to attend to public affairs. At the same time his revenues were increased by the thorough cultivation of the country, since he imposed a tax of one-tenth on all the produce. For the same reasons he instituted the local justices, and often made expeditions in person into the country to inspect it and to settle disputes between individuals, that they might not come into the city and neglect their farms. It was in one of these progresses that, as the story goes, Pisistratus had his adventure with the man of Hymettus, who was cultivating the spot afterwards known as "Tax-free Farm." He saw a man digging and working at a very stony piece of ground, and being surprised he sent his attendant to ask what he got out of this plot of land. "Aches and pains," said the man; "and that's what Pisistratus ought to have his tenth of." The man spoke without knowing who his questioner was; but Pi-sistratus was so pleased with his frank speech and his industry that he granted him exemption from all taxes. And so in matters in general he burdened the people as little as possible with his government, but always cultivated peace and kept them in all quietness. Hence the tyranny of Pisistratus was often spoken of proverbially as "the age of gold;" for when his sons succeeded him the government became much harsher. But most important of all in this respect was his popular and kindly disposition. In all things he was accustomed to observe the laws, without giving himself any exceptional privileges. Once he was summoned on a charge of homicide before the Areopagus, and he appeared in person to make his defense; but the prosecutor was afraid to present himself and abandoned the case. For these reasons he held power long, and whenever he was expelled he regained his position easily. The majority alike of the upper class and of the people were in his favour; the former he won by his social intercourse with them, the latter by the assistance which he gave to their private purses, and his nature fitted him to win the hearts of both. Moreover, the laws in reference to tyrants at that time in force at Athens were very mild, especially the one which applies more particularly to the establishment of a tyranny. The law ran as follows, "These are the ancestral statutes of the Athenians; if any persons shall make an attempt to establish a tyranny, or if any person shall join in setting up a tyranny, he shall lose his civic rights, both himself and his whole house."

Aristotle, Athenian Constitution, 16, from *The Greek Historians* by Francis R.B. Godolphin, editor. Copyright 1942 and renewed 1970 by Random House, Inc. Reprinted by permission of Random House, Inc.

wealth, measured by annual agricultural production. The two highest classes alone could hold the *archonship*, the chief magistracy in Athens, and sit on the Areopagus.

Men of the third class were allowed to serve as *hoplites*. They could be elected to a council of 400 chosen by all the citizens, 100 from each tribe. Solon seems to have meant this council to serve as a check on the Areopagus and to prepare any business that needed to be put before the traditional assembly of all adult male citizens. The *thetes* made up the last class. They voted in the assembly for the *archons* and the council members and on any other business brought before them by the *archons* and the council. They also sat on a new popular court established by Solon. This new court was recognized as a court of appeal, and by the fifth century B.C.E. almost all cases came before it. In Solon's Athens, as everywhere in the world before the twentieth century, women took no part in the political or judicial process.

PISISTRATUS THE TYRANT Solon's efforts to avoid factional strife failed. Within a few years contention reached such a degree that no *archons* could be chosen. Out of this turmoil emerged the first Athenian tyranny. Pisistratus, a nobleman, leader of a faction, and military hero, briefly seized power in 560 B.C.E. and again in 556 B.C.E., but each time his support was inadequate and he was driven out. At last, in 546 B.C.E. he came back at the head of a mercenary army from abroad and established a successful tyranny. It lasted beyond his death, in 527 B.C.E., until the expulsion of his son Hippias in 510 B.C.E.

In many respects, Pisistratus resembled the other Greek tyrants. His rule rested on the force provided by mercenary soldiers. He engaged in great programs of public works, urban improvement, and religious piety. Temples were built and religious centers expanded and improved. Poets and artists were supported to add cultural luster to the court of the tyrant.

Pisistratus sought to increase the power of the central government at the expense of the nobles. The newly introduced festival of Dionysus and the improved and expanded Great Panathenaic festival helped fix attention on the capital city, as did the new temples and the reconstruction of the agora as the center of public life. Circuit judges were sent out into the country to hear cases, weakening the power of the local barons. All this time Pisistratus made no formal change in the Solonian constitution. Assembly, councils, and courts met; magistrates and councils were elected. Pisistratus merely saw to it that his supporters dominated these bodies. The intended effect was to blunt the sharp edge of tyranny with the appearance of constitutional government, and it worked. The rule of Pisistratus was remembered as popular and mild. The unintended effect was to give the Athenians more experience in the procedures of self-government and a growing taste for it. (See "The Rule of the Tyrant Pisistratus.")

Aristogeiton and Harmodius were Athenian aristocrats slain in 514 B.C.E. after assassinating Hipparchus, brother of the tyrant Hippias. After the overthrow of the Pisistratus in 510 B.C.E., the Athenians erected a statue to honor their memory. This is a Roman copy. Scala/Art Resource, N.Y.

SPARTAN INTERVENTION Pisistratus was succeeded by his oldest son, Hippias, who followed his father's ways at first. In 514 B.C.E., however, his brother Hipparchus was murdered as a result of a private quarrel. Hippias became nervous, suspicious, and harsh. The Alcmaeonids, one of the noble clans that Hippias and Hipparchus had exiled, won favor with the influential oracle at Delphi and used its support to persuade Sparta to attack the Athenian tyranny. Led by their ambitious king, Cleomenes I, the Spartans marched into Athenian territory in 510 B.C.E. and deposed Hippias, who went into exile to the Persian court. The tyranny was over.

The Spartans must have hoped to leave Athens in friendly hands, and indeed Cleomenes' friend Isagoras, a rival of the Alcmaeonids, held the leading position in Athens after the withdrawal of the Spartan army. Isagoras, however, faced competitors, chief among them Clisthenes of the restored Alcmaeonid clan. Clisthenes lost out in the initial political struggle among the noble factions. Isagoras seems then to have tried to restore a version of the pre-Solonian aristocratic state. As part of his plan, he carried through a purification of the citizen lists, removing those whom Solon or Pisistratus had enfranchised and any others thought to have a doubtful claim.

Clisthenes then took an unprecedented action—he turned to the people for political support and won it with a program of great popular appeal. In response, Isagoras called in the Spartans again; Cleomenes arrived and allowed Isagoras to expel Clisthenes and many of his supporters. But the fire of Athenian political consciousness, ignited by Solon and kept alive under Pisistratus, had been fanned into flames by the popular appeal of Clisthenes. The people refused to tolerate an aristocratic restoration and drove out the Spartans and Isagoras with them. Clisthenes and his allies returned, ready to put their program into effect.

CLISTHENES, THE FOUNDER OF DEMOCRACY   A central aim of Clisthenes' reforms was to diminish the influence of traditional localities and regions in Athenian life, for these were an important source of power for the nobility and of factions in the state. He immediately restored to citizenship those Athenians who had supported him whom Isagoras had disenfranchised, and he added new citizens to the rolls. In 508 B.C.E. he made the *deme*, the equivalent of a small town in the country or a ward in the city, the basic unit of civic life. The *deme* was a purely political unit that elected its own officers. The distribution of *demes* in each tribe guaranteed that no region would dominate any of them. Because the tribes had common religious activities and fought as regimental units, the new organization also increased devotion to the *polis* and diminished regional divisions and personal loyalty to local barons.

A new council of 500 was invented to replace the Solonian council of 400. The council's main responsibility was to prepare legislation for discussion by the assembly, but it also had important financial duties and received foreign emissaries. Final authority in all things rested with the assembly of all adult male Athenian citizens. Debate in the assembly was free and open; any Athenian could submit legislation, offer amendments, or argue the merits of any question. In practice, political leaders did most of the talking. We may imagine that in the early days the

Key Events in the Early History of Sparta and Athens	
ca. 725–710 B.C.E.	First Messenian War
ca. 650–625 B.C.E.	Second Messenian War
632 B.C.E.	Cylon tries to establish a tyranny at Athens
621 B.C.E.	Draco publishes legal code at Athens
594 B.C.E.	Solon institutes reforms at Athens
ca. 560–550 B.C.E.	Sparta defeats Tegea: Beginning of Peloponnesian League
546–527 B.C.E.	Pisistratus reigns as tyrant at Athens (main period)
510 B.C.E.	Hippias, son of Pisistratus, deposed as tyrant of Athens
ca. 508–501 B.C.E.	Clisthenes institutes reforms at Athens

council had more authority than it did after the Athenians became more confident in their new self-government.

It is fair to call Clisthenes the father of Athenian democracy. He did not alter the property qualifications of Solon, but his enlargement of the citizen rolls, his diminution of the power of the aristocrats, and his elevation of the role of the assembly, with its effective and manageable council, all give him a firm claim to that title.

As a result of the work of Solon, Pisistratus, and Clisthenes, Athens entered the fifth century B.C.E. well on the way to prosperity and democracy. It was much more centralized and united than it had been, and it was ready to take its place among the major states that would lead the defense of Greece against the dangers that lay ahead.

Life in Archaic Greece

Society

As the "Dark Ages" ended, the features that would distinguish Greek society thereafter took shape. The roles of the artisan and the merchant grew more important as contact with the non-Hellenic world became easier. The great majority of people, however, continued to make their living from the land. Wealthy aristocrats with large estates, powerful households, families, and clans led very different lives from those of the poorer countryfolk and the independent farmers who had smaller and less fertile fields.

This terra-cotta figurine from Boeotia is a rare ancient Greek representation of the lives of ordinary people. It shows Boeotian women laundering clothes. Musée du Louvre, Paris

FARMERS   Ordinary country people rarely leave a written record of their thoughts or activities, and we have no such record from ancient Greece. The poet Hesiod (ca. 700 B.C.E.), however, was certainly no aristocrat. He presented himself as a small farmer, and his *Works and Days* gives some idea of the life of such a farmer. The crops included grain—chiefly barley, but also wheat; grapes for the making of wine; olives for food, but mainly for oil used for cooking, lighting, and washing; green vegetables, especially the bean; and some fruit. Sheep and goats provided milk and cheese. The Homeric heroes had great herds of cattle and ate lots of meat, but by Hesiod's time land fertile enough to provide fodder for cattle was needed to grow grain. He and small farmers like him tasted meat chiefly from sacrificial animals at festivals.

These farmers worked hard to make a living. Although Hesiod had the help of oxen and mules and one or two hired helpers for occasional labor, his life was one of continuous toil. The hardest work came in October, at the start of the rainy season, the time for the first plowing. The plow was light and easily broken, and the work of forcing the iron tip into the earth was backbreaking, even with the help of a team of oxen. For the less fortunate farmer, the cry of the crane that announced the time of year to plow "bites the heart of the man without oxen." Autumn and winter were the time for cutting wood, building wagons, and making tools. Late winter was the time to tend to the vines, May the time to harvest the grain, July to winnow and store it. Only at the height of summer's heat did Hesiod allow for rest, but when September came, it was time to harvest the grapes. No sooner was that task done than the cycle started again. The work went on under the burning sun and in the freezing cold.

Hesiod wrote nothing of pleasure or entertainment, but his poetry displays an excitement and pride that reveals the new hopes of a rural population more dynamic and confident than we know of anywhere else in the ancient world. Less austere farmers than Hesiod gathered at the blacksmith's shop for warmth and companionship in winter, and even he must have taken part in religious rites and festivals that were accompanied by some kind of entertainment. Nonetheless, the lives of yeoman farmers were certainly hard and their pleasures few. (See "Hesiod's *Farmer's Almanac*.")

ARISTOCRATS   Most aristocrats were rich enough to employ many hired laborers, sometimes sharecroppers, and sometimes even slaves, to work their extensive lands. They were therefore able to enjoy leisure for other activities. The center of aristocratic social life was the drinking party, or *symposium*. This activity was not a mere drinking bout, meant to remove inhibitions and produce oblivion. The Greeks, in fact, almost always mixed their wine with water, and one of the goals of the participants was to drink as much as the others without becoming drunk.

This scene on an Attic jar from late in the sixth century B.C.E. shows how olives, one of Athens' most important crops, were harvested. Courtesy of the Trustees of the British Museum. © The British Museum

Hesiod's *Farmer's Almanac*

Hesiod was a farmer and poet who lived in a village in Greece about 700 B.C.E. His poem Works *and* Days *contains wisdom on several subjects, but its final section amounts to a farmer's almanac, taking readers through the year and advising them on just when each activity is demanded. Hesiod painted a picture of a very hard life for Greek farmers, allowing rest only in the passage that follows.*

❖ *What might be Hesiod's purposes in writing this poem? What can be learned from this passage about the character of Greek farming? How did it differ from other modes of agriculture? What are the major virtues Hesiod associates with farming? How do they compare with the virtues celebrated by Homer?*

But when House-on-Back, the snail, crawls
    from the ground up
the plants, escaping the Pleiades, it's no longer
    time for vine-digging;
time rather to put an edge to your sickles, and
    rout out your helpers.
Keep away from sitting in the shade or lying in
    bed till the sun's up
in the time of the harvest, when the sunshine
    scorches your skin dry.
This is the season to push your work and bring
    home your harvest;
get up with the first light so you'll have enough
    to live on.
Dawn takes away from work a third part of the
    work's measure.
Dawn sets a man well along on his journey, in
    his work also,
dawn, who when she shows, has numerous
    people going their ways; dawn who puts the
    yoke upon many oxen.
But when the artichoke is in flower, and the
    clamorous cricket
sitting in his tree lets go his vociferous singing,
    that issues

from the beating of his wings, in the exhausting
    season of summer,
then is when goats are at their fattest, when the
    wine tastes best,
women are most lascivious, but the men's
    strength fails them
most, for the star Seirios shrivels them, knees
    and heads alike,
and the skin is all dried out in the heat; then, at
    that season,
one might have the shadow under the rock, and
    the wine of Biblis,
a curd cake, and all the milk that the goats can
    give you,
the meat of a heifer, bred in the woods, who has
    never borne a calf,
and of baby kids also. Then, too, one can sit in
    the shadow
and drink the bright-shining wine, his heart
    satiated with eating
and face turned in the direction where Zephyros
    blows briskly,
make three libations of water from a spring that
    keeps running forever
and has no mud in it; and pour wine for the
    fourth libation.

Hesiod, *Works and Days*, trans. by Richmond Lattimore © 1959 University of Michigan Press, pp. 87, 89. Reprinted by permission of University of Michigan Press.

The *symposium* was a carefully organized occasion, with a "king" chosen to set the order of events and to determine that night's mixture of wine and water. Only men took part; they ate and drank as they reclined on couches along the walls of the room. The sessions began with prayers and libations to the gods. Usually there were games, such as dice or *kottabos*, in which wine was flicked from the cups at different targets. Sometimes dancing girls or flute girls offered entertainment. Frequently the aristocratic participants provided their own amusements with songs, poetry, or even philosophical disputes. Characteristically, these took the form of contests, with some kind of prize for the winner, for aristocratic values continued to emphasize competition and the need to excel, whatever the arena.

This aspect of aristocratic life appears in the athletic contests that became widespread early in the sixth century. The games included running events; the long jump; the discus and javelin throws; the *pentathlon*, which included all of these; boxing; wrestling; and the chariot race. Only the rich could afford to raise, train, and race horses, so the chariot race was a special preserve of aristocracy. Wrestling, however, was also especially favored by the nobility, and the *palaestra*, or fields, where they practiced became an important social center for the aristocracy. The contrast between the hard, drab life of the farmers and the leisured and lively one of the aristocrats could hardly have been greater.

Religion

Like most ancient peoples, the Greeks were polytheists, and religion played an important part in their lives. A great part of Greek art and literature was closely connected with religion, as was the life of the *polis* in general.

OLYMPIAN GODS   The Greek pantheon consisted of the twelve gods who lived on Mount Olympus. These were

- Zeus, the father of the gods
- Hera, his wife

Zeus' siblings:

- Poseidon, his brother, god of the seas and earthquakes
- Hestia, his sister, goddess of the hearth
- Demeter, his sister, goddess of agriculture and marriage

and Zeus' children:

- Aphrodite, goddess of love and beauty
- Apollo, god of the sun, music, poetry, and prophecy
- Ares, god of war
- Artemis, goddess of the moon and the hunt
- Athena, goddess of wisdom and the arts
- Hephaestus, god of fire and metallurgy
- Hermes, messenger of the gods, connected with commerce and cunning

These gods were seen as behaving very much as mortals behaved, with all the foibles of humans, except that they were superhuman in these as well as in their strength and immortality. On the other hand, Zeus, at least, was seen as a source of human justice, and even the Olympians were understood to be subordinate to the Fates. Each *polis* had one of the Olympians as its guardian deity and worshiped that god in its own special way, but all the gods were Panhellenic. In the eighth and sev-

enth centuries B.C.E., common shrines were established at Olympia for the worship of Zeus, at Delphi for Apollo, at the Isthmus of Corinth for Poseidon, and at Nemea once again for Zeus. Each held athletic contests in honor of its deity, to which all Greeks were invited and for which a sacred truce was declared.

IMMORTALITY AND MORALITY   Besides the Olympians, the Greeks also worshiped countless lesser deities connected with local shrines. They even worshiped human heroes, real or legendary, who had accomplished great deeds and had earned immortality and divine status. The worship of these deities was not a very emotional experience. It was a matter of offering prayer, libations, and gifts in return for protection and favors from the god during the lifetime of the worshiper. There was no hope of immortality for the average human, and these devotions involved little moral teaching.

Most Greeks seem to have held to the common-sense notion that justice lay in paying one's debts. They thought that civic virtue consisted of worship-

This Attic cup from the fifth century B.C.E. shows the two great poets from the island of Lesbos, Sappho (right) and Alcaeus.   Hirmer Fotoarchiv

Sappho the Poet

Sappho was born at Mytilene on the island of Lesbos about 612 B.C.E. After a period of exile in Sicily, she returned and became a central figure in a thiastos, *a company of revelers who sang and danced in honor of a god. Sappho's group was made up of young girls who gave honor to Aphrodite and the Muses, the goddesses of the fine arts. They lived together intimately and affectionately. Sappho wrote poems to and about them and to celebrate their marriages. Her poems were highly admired in antiquity, winning her a position among the greatest lyric poets, but they are preserved only in fragments. The following selection illustrates one type of her poetry.*

❖ *How does the mood and style of the poem compare with the excerpts from Homer and Hesiod in this chapter? Since we have little reliable information about Sappho outside the fragments of her poems, what does the selection tell us about her life and activities?*

Fragment 94

"and honestly I want to die"
—so sobbing, many times, she left me
and she said this [to me]
"My god! what awful things are happening to us:
Sappho, I swear I am leaving you against my
　　will."
And I replied to her in these words:
"Go with a light heart, and with memories
of me, for you know how we cherished you.
And if not, then I want to
remind you [　　]
[　　] and we had good times
For ma[ny garland]s of violets
and roses [　　] together

and [　　] you put on beside me
And many garlands
woven from flowers about your soft neck
[　　] fashioned
And with m[uch] myrrh
from rich flowers [　　]
and royal you rubbed your skin
And on soft beds
tender [　　]
you would satisfy desire [　　]
And there was no [　　] nothing
holy nor [　　]
from which [we] kept away
No grove [　　]
[　　] sound
[　　]"

From Sappho, *Fragment 94*, trans. by Ewen Bowie, in J. Boardman, J. Griffin, and O. Murray, *The Oxford History of the Classical World* (Oxford and New York: Oxford University Press, n.d.), p. 104.

ing the state deities in the traditional way, performing required public services, and fighting in defense of the state. To them, private morality meant to do good to one's friends and harm to one's enemies.

THE CULT OF DELPHIAN APOLLO In the sixth century B.C.E., the influence of the cult of Apollo at Delphi and of his oracle there became very great. The oracle was the most important of several that helped satisfy the human craving for a clue to the future. The priests of Apollo preached moderation; their advice was exemplified in the two famous sayings identified with Apollo: "Know thyself" and "Nothing in excess." Humans needed self-control (*sophrosynē*). Its opposite was arrogance (*hubris*), brought on by excessive wealth or good fortune. *Hubris* led to moral blindness and, finally, to divine vengeance. This theme of moderation and the dire consequences

of its absence was central to Greek popular morality and appears frequently in Greek literature.

THE CULT OF DIONYSUS AND THE ORPHIC CULT The somewhat cold religion of the Olympian gods and of the cult of Apollo did little to assuage human fears or satisfy human hopes and passions. For these needs, the Greeks turned to other deities and rites. Of these deities, the most popular was Dionysus, a god of nature and fertility, of the grapevine, drunkenness, and sexual abandon. In some of his rites, this god was followed by *maenads*, female devotees who cavorted by night, ate raw flesh, and were reputed to tear to pieces any creature they came across.

The Orphic cult, named after its supposed founder, the mythical poet Orpheus, provided its followers with more hope than did the worship of the twelve Olympians. Cult followers are thought to

Theognis of Megara Gives Advice to a Young Aristocrat

Theognis was born about 580 B.C.E. and lived to see his native city Megara torn by social upheaval and civil war. His poems present the political and ethical ideas of the Greek aristocracy.

❖ *What does Theognis claim is the source of virtue among human beings? What role does he give to education in improving the character of people? What does he mean by "judgment"? What are the political and constitutional implications of his way of thinking?*

Do not consort with bad men, but always hold to the good. Eat and drink with them. You will learn good from good men, but if you mingle with the bad you will lose such wisdom as you already have. Therefore consort with the good and one day you will say that I give good advice to my friends.

We seek thoroughbred rams asses and horses, Cyrnus, and a man wants offspring of good breeding. But in marriage a good man does not decline to marry the bad daughter of a bad father, if he gives him much wealth. Nor does the wife of a bad man refuse to be his bedfellow if he be rich, preferring wealth to goodness. For they value possessions and a good man marries a woman of bad stock and the bad a woman of good. Wealth mixes the breed. So do not wonder, son of Polypaus, that the race of your citizens is obscured since bad things are mixed with good.

It is easier to beget and rear a man than to put good sense into him. No one has ever discovered a way to make a fool wise or a bad man good. If God had given the sons of Asclepius the knowledge to heal the evil nature and mischievous mind of man, great and frequent would be their pay. If thought could be made and put into a man, the son of a good man would never become bad, since he would obey good counsel. But you will never make the bad man good by teaching.

The best thing the gods give to men, Cyrnus, is judgment; judgment contains the ends of everything. O happy is the man who has it in his mind; it is much greater than destructive insolence and grievous satiety. There are no evils among mortals worse than these—for every evil, Cyrnus, comes out of them.

From *Sources in Greek Political Thought From Homer To Polybuis*, Donald Kagan, Editor. Copyright © 1965 by The Free Press, A Division of Simon & Schuster. Adapted with permission of the publisher.

have refused to kill animals or eat their flesh and to have believed in the transmigration of souls, which offered the prospect of some form of life after death.

Poetry

The great changes sweeping through the Greek world were also reflected in the poetry of the sixth century B.C.E. The lyric style—poetry meant to be sung, either by a chorus or by one person—predominated. Sappho of Lesbos, Anacreon of Teos, and Simonides of Cos composed personal poetry, often relating the pleasure and agony of love. (See "Sappho the Poet.") Alcaeus of Mytilene, an aristocrat driven from his city by a tyrant, wrote bitter invective.

Perhaps the most interesting poet of the century from a political point of view was Theognis of Megara. He was an aristocrat who lived through a tyranny, an unusually chaotic and violent democracy, and an oligarchy that restored order, but ended the rule of the old aristocracy. Theognis was the

spokesperson for the old, defeated aristocracy of birth. He divided everyone into two classes, the noble and the base; the former were the good, the latter bad. Those nobly born must associate only with others like themselves if they were to preserve their virtue; if they mingled with the base, they became base. Those born base, on the other hand, could never become noble. Only nobles could aspire to virtue, and only nobles possessed the critical moral and intellectual qualities—respect or honor and judgment. These qualities could not be taught; they were innate. Even so they had to be carefully guarded against corruption by wealth or by mingling with the base. Intermarriage between the noble and the base was especially condemned. These were the ideas of the unreconstructed nobility, whose power had been destroyed or reduced in most Greek states by this time. Such ideas remained alive in aristocratic hearts throughout the next century and greatly influenced later thinkers, Plato among them. (See "Theognis of Megara Gives Advice to a Young Aristocrat.")

The Rise of Persia

559–530 B.C.E.	Reign of Cyrus the Great
546 B.C.E.	Persians conquer Lydia
530–522 B.C.E.	Reign of Cambyses
522–521 B.C.E.	Civil war in Persia
521–485 B.C.E.	Reign of Darius
485–465 B.C.E.	Reign of Xerxes

The Persian Wars

The Greeks' period of fortunate isolation and freedom ended in the sixth century B.C.E. They had established colonies along most of the coast of Asia Minor from as early as the eleventh century B.C.E. The colonies maintained friendly relations with the mainland but developed a flourishing economic and cultural life independent of their mother cities and of their eastern neighbors. In the middle of the sixth century B.C.E., however, these Greek cities of Asia Minor came under the control of Lydia and its king, Croesus (ca. 560–546 B.C.E.). Lydian rule seems not to have been very harsh, but the Persian conquest of Lydia in 546 B.C.E. brought a less pleasant subjugation.

The Persian Empire

The Persian Empire had been created in a single generation by Cyrus the Great, the founder of the Achaemenid dynasty. In 559 B.C.E. he came to the throne of Persia, then a small kingdom well to the east of the lower Mesopotamian Valley. He unified Persia under his rule, made an alliance with Babylonia, and led a successful rebellion toward the north against the Medes, the overlords of Persia. (See Map 2–5.) In succeeding years he expanded his empire in all directions, in the process defeating Croesus and occupying Lydia. Most of the Greek cities of Asia Minor sided with Croesus and resisted the Persians. By about 540 B.C.E., however, they had all been subdued. The western part of Asia Minor was divided into three provinces, each under its own *satrap*, or governor.

MAP 2–5   THE PERSIAN EMPIRE   *The empire created by Cyrus had reached its fullest extent under Darius when Persia attacked Greece in 490 B.C.E. It extended from India to the Aegean and even into Europe. It included the lands formerly ruled by Egyptians, Hittites, Babylonians, and Assyrians.*

Persian nobles pay homage to King Darius in this relief from the treasury at the Persian capital of Persepolis. Darius is seated on the throne; his son and successor Xerxes stands behind him. Darius and Xerxes are carved in larger scale to indicate their royal status.
Courtesy of the Oriental Institute of the University of Chicago

The Ionian Rebellion

The Ionian Greeks (those living on the central part of the west coast of Asia Minor and nearby islands) had been moving toward democracy and were not pleased to find themselves under the monarchical rule of Persia. That rule, however, was not overly burdensome at first. The Persians required their subjects to pay tribute and to serve in the Persian army. They ruled the Greek cities through local individuals, who governed their cities as "tyrants." Most of the "tyrants," however, were not harsh, the Persian tribute was not excessive, and the Greeks enjoyed general prosperity. Neither the death of Cyrus fighting on a distant frontier in 530 B.C.E. nor the suicide of his successor Cambyses, nor the civil war that followed it in 522–521 B.C.E. produced any disturbance in the Greek cities. When Darius emerged as Great King (as the Persian rulers styled themselves) in 521 B.C.E., he found Ionia perfectly obedient.

The private troubles of the ambitious tyrant of Miletus, Aristagoras, ended this calm. He had urged a Persian expedition against the island of Naxos; when it failed, he feared the consequences and organized the Ionian rebellion of 499 B.C.E. To gain support, he overthrew the tyrannies and proclaimed democratic constitutions. Then he turned to the mainland states for help, petitioning first Sparta, the most powerful Greek state. The Spartans, however, would have none of Aristagoras' promises of easy victory and great wealth. They had no close ties with the Ionians and no national interest in the re-

gion. Furthermore, they were terrified at the thought of leaving their homeland undefended against the Helots for a long time while their army was far off.

Aristagoras next sought help from the Athenians, who were related to the Ionians and had close ties of religion and tradition with them. Besides, Hippias, the deposed tyrant of Athens, was an honored guest at the court of Darius, and the Great King had already made it plain that he favored the tyrant's restoration. The Persians, moreover, controlled both sides of the Hellespont, the route to the grain fields beyond the Black Sea that were increasingly vital to Athens. Perhaps some Athenians already feared that a Persian attempt to conquer the Greek mainland was only a matter of time. The Athenian assembly agreed to send a fleet of twenty ships to help the rebels. The Athenian expedition was strengthened by five ships from Eretria in Euboea, which participated out of gratitude for past favors.

In 498 B.C.E. the Athenians and their allies made a surprise attack on Sardis, the old capital of Lydia and now the seat of the *satrap*, and burned it. This action caused the revolt to spread throughout the Greek cities of Asia Minor outside Ionia, but the Ionians could not follow it up. The Athenians withdrew and took no further part. Gradually the Persians reimposed their will. In 495 B.C.E. they defeated the Ionian fleet at Lade, and in the next year they wiped out Miletus. They killed many of the Miletan men, transported others to the Persian Gulf, and enslaved the women and children. The Ionian rebellion was over.

MAP 2–6   THE PERSIAN INVASION OF GREECE   *This map traces the route taken by the Persian king Xerxes in his invasion of Greece in 480 B.C.E. The gray arrows show movements of Xerxes' army, the purple arrows show movements of his navy, and the green arrows show movements of the Greek army and navy.*

The War in Greece

In 490 B.C.E. the Persians launched an expedition directly across the Aegean to punish Eretria and Athens, to restore Hippias, and to gain control of the Aegean Sea. (See Map 2–6.) They landed their infantry and cavalry forces first at Naxos, destroy-

ing it for its successful resistance in 499 B.C.E. Then they destroyed Eretria and deported its people deep into the interior of Persia.

MARATHON   Rather than submit and accept the restoration of the hated tyranny of Hippias, the Athenians chose to resist the Persian forces bearing

This bronze helmet was dedicated to Zeus by Miltiades to commemorate the Athenian victory over the Persians in 490 B.C.E. Deutsche Archäologisches Institut, Athens

The Greek Wars against Persia

ca. 560–546 B.C.E.	Greek cities of Asia Minor conquered by Croesus of Lydia
546 B.C.E.	Cyrus of Persia conquers Lydia and gains control of Greek cities
499–494 B.C.E.	Greek cities rebel (Ionian rebellion)
490 B.C.E.	Battle of Marathon
480–479 B.C.E.	Xerxes' invasion of Greece
480 B.C.E.	Battles of Thermopylae, Artemisium, and Salamis
479 B.C.E.	Battles of Plataea and Mycale

cian. During his *archonship* in 493 B.C.E., Athens had already taken the first step in that direction by building a fortified port at Piraeus. A decade later the Athenians came upon a rich vein of silver in the state mines, and Themistocles persuaded them to use the profits to increase their fleet. By 480 B.C.E. Athens had over 200 ships, the backbone of a navy that was to defeat the Persians.

Of the hundreds of Greek states, only thirty-one—led by Sparta, Athens, Corinth, and Aegina—were willing to fight as the Persian army gathered south of the Hellespont. In the spring of 480 B.C.E., Xerxes launched his invasion. The Persian strategy was to march into Greece, destroy Athens, defeat the Greek army, and add the Greeks to the number of Persian subjects. The huge Persian army needed to keep in touch with the fleet for supplies. If the Greeks could defeat the Persian navy, the army could not remain in Greece long. Themistocles knew that the Aegean was subject to sudden devastating storms. His strategy was to delay the Persian army and then to bring on the kind of naval battle he might hope to win.

The Greek League, founded specifically to resist this Persian invasion, met at Corinth as the Persians were ready to cross the Hellespont. They chose Sparta as leader on land and sea and first confronted the Persians at Thermopylae, the "hot gates," on land and off Artemisium at sea. The opening between the mountains and the sea at Thermopylae was so narrow that it might be held by a smaller army against a much larger one. The Spartans sent their king, Leonidas, with 300 of their own citizens and enough allies to make a total of about 9,000.

Severe storms wrecked many Persian ships while the Greek fleet waited safely in a protected harbor. Then Xerxes attacked Thermopylae, and for two days the Greeks butchered his best troops without serious loss to themselves. On the third day, how-

down on them and risk the same fate that had just befallen Eretria. Miltiades, an Athenian who had fled from Persian service, led the city's army to a confrontation with the Persians at Marathon.

A Persian victory at Marathon would have destroyed Athenian freedom and led to the conquest of all the mainland Greeks. The greatest achievements of Greek culture, most of which lay in the future, would never have occurred. But the Athenians won a decisive victory, instilling them with a sense of confidence and pride in their *polis*, their unique form of government, and themselves.

THE GREAT INVASION   Internal troubles prevented the Persians from taking swift revenge for their loss at Marathon. Almost ten years elapsed before Darius' successor, Xerxes, in 481 B.C.E., gathered an army of at least 150,000 men and a navy of more than 600 ships for the conquest of Greece. In Athens, Themistocles, who favored making Athens into a naval power, had become the leading politi-

A Greek hoplite attacks a Persian soldier. The contrast between the Greek's metal body armor, large shield, and long spear and the Persian's cloth and leather garments indicates one reason the Greeks won. This Attic vase was found on Rhodes and dates from ca. 475 B.C.E.
The Metropolitan Museum of Art, Rogers Fund, 1906

ever, a traitor showed the Persians a mountain trail that permitted them to come on the Greeks from behind. Many allies escaped, but Leonidas and his 300 Spartans all died fighting. At about the same time the Greek and Persian fleets fought an indecisive battle at Artemisium. The fall of Thermopylae, however, forced the Greek navy to withdraw.

After Thermopylae, the Persian army moved into Attica and burned Athens. If an inscription discovered in 1959 is authentic, Themistocles had foreseen this possibility before Thermopylae, and the Athenians had begun to evacuate their homeland before they sent their fleet north to fight at Artemisium.

DEFEATING THE PERSIANS The fate of Greece was decided in a sea battle in the narrow waters to the east of the island of Salamis, to which the Greek fleet withdrew after the battle at Artemisium. The Peloponnesians were reluctant to confront the Persian fleet at this spot, but Themistocles persuaded them to stay by threatening to remove all the Athenians from Greece and settle them anew in Italy. The Spartans knew that they and the other Greeks could not hope to win without the aid of the Athe-

nians. Because the Greek ships were fewer, slower, and less maneuverable than those of the Persians, the Greeks put soldiers on their ships and relied chiefly on hand-to-hand combat. In the ensuing battle the Persians lost more than half their ships and retreated to Asia with a good part of their army, but the danger was not over yet.

The Persian general Mardonius spent the winter in central Greece, and in the spring he unsuccessfully tried to win the Athenians away from the Greek League. The Spartan regent, Pausanias, then led the largest Greek army up to that time to confront Mardonius in Boeotia. At Plataea, in the summer of 479 B.C.E., the Persians suffered a decisive defeat. Mardonius died in battle and his army fled toward home.

Meanwhile the Ionian Greeks urged King Leotychidas, the Spartan commander of the fleet, to fight the Persian fleet at Samos. At Mycale, on the coast nearby, Leotychidas destroyed the Persian camp and its fleet offshore. The Persians fled the Aegean and Ionia. For the moment, at least, the Persian threat was gone.

In Perspective

Hellenic civilization, that unique cultural experience at the root of Western civilization, has powerfully influenced the peoples of the modern world. It was itself influenced by the great Bronze Age civilization of Crete called Minoan, and emerged from the collapse of the Bronze Age civilization on the Greek mainland called Mycenaean. These earlier Aegean civilizations more closely resembled other early civilizations in Egypt, Mesopotamia, Syria–Palestine, and elsewhere than the Hellenic civilization that sprang from them. They had highly developed cities; a system of writing; strong, centralized monarchical systems of government with tightly organized, large bureaucracies; hierarchical social systems; professional standing armies; and a regular system of taxation supporting all this. To a greater or lesser degree, these early civilizations tended toward cultural stability—changing little over time—and uniformity—all sharing many structural features. The striking thing about the emergence of Hellenic civilization is its sharp departure from this pattern.

The collapse of the Mycenaean world produced a harsh material and cultural decline for the Greeks. Cities were swept away and replaced by small farm villages. Trade all but ended, and communication among the Greeks themselves and between them and other peoples was sharply curtailed. The art of writing was lost for more than three centuries. During this "Dark Age," the Greeks—poor, small in number, isolated, and illiterate—were ignored by the rest of the world and left alone to develop their own society and the matrix of Hellenic civilization.

During the three-and-a-half centuries from about 1100 to 750 B.C.E., the Greeks set the foundations for their great achievements. The crucial unit in the new Greek way of life was the polis, *the Hellenic city-state. There were hundreds of them, and each evoked a kind of loyalty and attachment by its citizens that made the idea of dissolving one's own* polis *into a larger unit unthinkable. The result was a dynamic, many-faceted, competitive, sometimes chaotic world in which rivalry for excellence and victory had the highest value. This agonistic, or competitive, quality marks Greek life throughout its history. Its negative aspect was constant warfare among the states. Its positive side was an extraordinary achievement in literature and art; competition, sometimes formal and organized, spurred on poets and artists.*

Kings had been swept away with the Mycenaean world and the poleis *were republics. Since the Greeks were so poor, the difference in wealth among them was relatively small. Therefore, class distinctions were less marked and important than in other civilizations. The introduction of a new mode of fighting, the hoplite phalanx, had further leveling effects, for it placed the safety of the state in the hands of the average farmer. Armies were made up of citizen–soldiers, who were not paid and who returned to their farms after a campaign. As a result, political control was shared with a relatively large portion of the people, and participation in political life was highly valued. There was no bureaucracy, for there were no kings and not much economic surplus to support bureaucrats. Most states imposed no regular taxation. There was no separate caste of priests and little concern with any life after death. In this varied, dynamic, secular, and remarkably free context there arose speculative natural philosophy based on observation and reason, the root of modern natural science and philosophy.*

Contact with the rest of the world increased trade and wealth and brought in valuable new information and ideas. Greek art was powerfully shaped by Egyptian and Near Eastern models that were always adapted and changed rather than copied. Changes often produced social and economic strain, leading to the overthrow of traditional aristocratic regimes by tyrants. But monarchic rule was anathema to the Greeks, and these regimes were temporary. In Athens, the destruction of the tyranny brought the world's first democracy. Sparta, on the other hand, developed a uniquely stable government that avoided tyranny and impressed the other Greeks.

The Greeks' time of independent development, untroubled by external forces, ended in the sixth century, when Persia's powerful Achaemenid dynasty conquered the Greek cities of Asia Minor. When the Persian kings tried to conquer the Greek mainland, however, the leading states managed to put their quarrels aside and unite against the common enemy. Their determination to preserve their freedom carried them to victory over tremendous odds.

REVIEW QUESTIONS

1. Describe the Minoan civilization of Crete. How did the later Bronze Age Mycenaean civilization differ from the Minoan civilization in political organization, art motifs, and military posture?
2. What are the most important historical sources for the Minoan and Mycenaean civilizations? Most particularly, what is Linear B, and what problems does it raise for the reconstruction of Bronze Age history? How valuable are the Homeric epics as sources of early Greek history?
3. Define the concept of a *polis*. What role did geography play in its development and why did the Greeks consider it a unique and valuable institution?
4. Compare the fundamental political, social, and economic institutions of Athens and Sparta about 500 B.C.E. Why did Sparta develop its unique form of government?
5. What were the main stages in the transformation of Athens from an aristocratic state to a democracy between 600 and 500 B.C.E.? In what ways did Draco, Solon, Pisistratus, and Clisthenes each contribute to the process?
6. Why did the Greeks and Persians go to war in 490 and 480 B.C.E.? What benefit could the Persians have derived from conquering Greece? Why were the Greeks able to defeat the Persians and how did they benefit from the victory?

SUGGESTED READINGS

A. ANDREWES, *Greek Tyrants* (1963). A clear and concise account of tyranny in early Greece.

A. R. BURN, *The Lyric Age of Greece* (1960). A discussion of early Greece that uses the evidence of poetry and archaeology to fill out the sparse historical record.

J. CHADWICK, *The Mycenaean World* (1976). A readable account by an author who helped decipher Mycenaean writing.

J.M. COOK, *The Persian Empire* (1983). A valuable study of Persian history based on archeological and literary evidence.

O. DICKINSON, *The Aegean Bronze Age* (1994). A fine survey of Bronze Age culture in the Aegean region.

R. DREWS, *The End of the Bronze Age: Changes in Warfare and Catastrophes ca. 1200 B.C.* (1993). A scholarly and fascinating examination of the theories explaining the fall of the late Bronze Age civilizations.

V. EHRENBERG, *From Solon to Socrates* (1968). An interpretive history that makes good use of Greek literature to illuminate politics.

J. V. A. FINE, *The Ancient Greeks* (1983). An excellent survey that discusses historical problems and the evidence that gives rise to them.

M. I. FINLEY, *World of Odysseus*, 2d. ed. (1978). A fascinating attempt to reconstruct Homeric society.

W. G. FORREST, *The Emergence of Greek Democracy* (1966). A lively interpretation of Greek social and political developments in the archaic period.

P. GREEN, *The Greco-Persian Wars* (1998). A lively and stimulating history of the Persian wars.

V. D. HANSON, *The Western Way of War* (1989). A brilliant and lively discussion of the rise and character of the hoplite phalanx and its influence on Greek society.

V. D. HANSON, *The Other Greeks* (1995). A revolutionary account of the invention of the family farm by the Greeks and the central role of agrarianism in shaping the Greek city-state.

C. HIGNETT, *A History of the Athenian Constitution* (1952). A scholarly account, somewhat too skeptical of the ancient sources.

J. M. HURWIT, *The Art and Culture of Early Greece* (1985). A fascinating study of the art of early Greece in its literary and cultural context.

S. ISAGER AND J. E. SKYDSGAARD, *Ancient Greek Agriculture: An Introduction* (1993). A new study of a fundamental subject.

D. KAGAN, *The Great Dialogue: A History of Greek Political Thought from Homer to Polybius* (1965). A discussion of the relationship between the Greek historical experience and political theory.

H. D. F. KITTO, *The Greeks* (1951). A personal and illuminating interpretation of Greek culture.

W. K. LACEY, *The Family in Ancient Greece* (1984).

P. B. MANVILLE, *The Origins of Citizenship in Ancient Athens* (1990). An examination of the origins of the concept of citizenship in the time of Solon of Athens.

L. G. MITCHELL AND P. J. RHODES, eds., *The Development of the* Polis *in Archaic Greece* (1997). A collection of articles on the emergence and development of the Greek city-state.

I. MORRIS AND B. POWELL, eds., *A New Companion to Homer* (1997). A collection of articles treating Homeric questions in an accessible style.

O. MURRAY, *Early Greece* (1980). A lively and imaginative account of the early history of Greece to the end of the Persian War.

A. T. OLMSTEAD, *History of the Persian Empire* (1960). A thorough survey.

C. ROEBUCK, *Ionian Trade and Colonization* (1959). An introduction to the history of the Greeks in the East.

R. SALLARES, *The Ecology of the Ancient Greek World* (1991). A valuable study of the Greeks and their environment.

D. M. SCHAPS, *Economic Rights of Women in Ancient Greece* (1981).

A. M. SNODGRASS, *The Dark Age of Greece* (1972). A good examination of the archaeological evidence.

C. G. STARR, *The Economic and Social Growth of Early Greece, 800–500 B.C.E.* (1977).

A. G. WOODHEAD, *Greeks in the West* (1962). An account of the Greek settlements in Italy and Sicily.

W. J. WOODHOUSE, *Solon the Liberator* (1965). A discussion of the great Athenian reformer.

D. C. YOUNG, *The Olympic Myth of Greek Athletics* (1984). A lively challenge to the orthodox view that Greek athletes were amateurs.

Chapter 3

The Winged Victory of Samothrace. This is one of the great masterpieces of Hellenistic sculpture. It appears to be the work of the Rhodian sculptor Pythokritos, about 200 B.C.E. The statue stood in the sanctuary of the Great Gods on the Aegean island of Samothrace on a base made in the shape of a ship's prow. The goddess is seen as landing on the ship to crown its victorious commander and crew. Marble figure (190 B.C.E.) from Rhodos, Greece. Height 328 cm, MA 2369, Lourve, Dpt. des Antiquities Grecques/Romaines, Paris, France. © Photograph by Erich Lessing. Art Resource.

Classical and Hellenistic Greece

KEY TOPICS

- The Peloponnesian War and the struggle between Athens and Sparta
- Democracy and empire in fifth-century B.C.E. Athens
- Culture and society in Classical Greece
- The struggle for dominance in Greece after the Peloponnesian War
- The Hellenistic world

The Greeks' remarkable victory over the Persians in 480–479 B.C.E. won them another period of freedom and autonomy. They used this time to carry their political and cultural achievement to its height. In Athens, especially, it produced a great sense of confidence and ambition.

Spartan withdrawal from active leadership against the Persians left a vacuum that was filled by the Delian League, which soon turned into the Athenian Empire. At the same time as it tightened its hold over the Greek cities in and around the Aegean Sea, Athens developed an extraordinarily democratic constitution at home. Fears and jealousies of this new kind of state and empire created a split in the Greek world which led to a series of major wars that impoverished Greece and left it vulnerable to conquest. In 338 B.C.E. Philip of Macedon conquered the Greek states, putting an end to the age of the polis.

Aftermath of Victory

The unity of the Greeks had shown strain even in the life-and-death struggle against the Persians. Within two years of the Persian retreat it gave way almost completely and yielded to a division of the Greek world into two spheres of influence, dominated by Sparta and Athens. The need of the Ionian Greeks to obtain and defend their freedom from Persia and the desire of many Greeks to gain revenge and financial reparation for the Persian attack brought on the split.

The Delian League

Sparta had led the Greeks to victory, and it was natural to look to the Spartans to continue the campaign against Persia. But Sparta was ill-suited to the task, which required both a long-term commitment far from the Peloponnesus and continuous naval action.

Athens had become the leading naval power in Greece, and the same motives that led the Athenians to support the Ionian revolt prompted them to try to drive the Persians from the Aegean and the Hellespont. The Ionians were at least as eager for the Athenians to take the helm as the Athenians were to accept the responsibility and opportunity.

In the winter of 478–477 B.C.E., the islanders, the Greeks from the coast of Asia Minor and from some other Greek cities on the Aegean, met with the Athenians on the sacred island of Delos and swore oaths of alliance. As a symbol that the alliance was meant to be permanent, they dropped lumps of iron into the sea; the alliance was to hold until these lumps of iron rose to the surface. The aims of this new Delian League were to free those Greeks who were under Persian rule, to protect all against a Persian return, and to obtain compensation from the Persians by attacking their lands and taking booty. League policy was determined by a

MAP 3–1   CLASSICAL GREECE   *Greece in the Classical period (ca. 480–338 B.C.E.) centered on the Aegean Sea. Although there were important Greek settlements in Italy, Sicily, and all around the Black Sea, the area shown in this general reference map embraced the vast majority of Greek states.*

vote of an assembly in which each state, including Athens, had one vote. Athens, however, was clearly designated the leader.

From the first, the league was remarkably successful. The Persians were driven from Europe and the Hellespont, and the Aegean was cleared of pirates. Some states were forced into the league or were prevented from leaving. The members approved coercion because it was necessary for the common safety. In 467 B.C.E., a great victory over the Persians at the Eurymedon River in Asia Minor routed the Persians and added several cities to the league.

The Rise of Cimon

Cimon, son of Miltiades, the hero of Marathon, became the leading Athenian soldier and statesman soon after the war with Persia. Themistocles appears to have been driven from power by a coalition of his enemies. Ironically, the author of the Greek victory over Persia of 480 B.C.E. was exiled and ended his days at the court of the Persian king. Cimon, who was to dominate Athenian politics for almost two decades, pursued a policy of aggressive attacks on Persia and friendly relations with Sparta. In domestic affairs Cimon was conservative. He accepted the democratic constitution of Clisthenes, which appears to have become somewhat more limited after the Persian war. Defending this constitution and his interventionist foreign policy, Cimon led the Athenians and the Delian League to victory after victory, and his own popularity grew with his successes.

The First Peloponnesian War: Athens against Sparta

The Thasian Rebellion

In 465 B.C.E., the island of Thasos rebelled from the Delian League, and Cimon put it down after a siege of more than two years. The revolt of Thasos is the first recorded instance in which Athenian interests alone seemed to determine league policy, a significant step in the league's evolution into the Athenian Empire.

When Cimon returned to Athens from Thasos, he was charged with taking bribes for having refrained from conquering Macedonia, although conquering Macedonia had not been part of his assignment. He was acquitted; the trial was only a device by which his political opponents tried to reduce his influence. Their program at home was to undo the gains made by the Areopagus and to bring about further changes in the direction of democracy. In foreign policy, these enemies

of Cimon wanted to break with Sparta and to contest its claim to leadership over the Greeks. They intended at least to establish the independence of Athens and its alliance. The head of this faction was Ephialtes. His supporter, and the person chosen to be the public prosecutor of Cimon, was Pericles, a member of a distinguished Athenian family. He was still young, and his defeat in court did not do lasting damage to his career.

The Breach with Sparta

When the Thasians began their rebellion, they asked Sparta to invade Athens the next spring, and the *ephors*, the annual magistrates responsible for Sparta's foreign policy, agreed. An earthquake, however, accompanied by a rebellion of the Helots that threatened the survival of Sparta, prevented the invasion. The Spartans asked their allies, the Athenians among them, for help, and Cimon persuaded the Athenians to send it.

The results of this policy were disastrous for Cimon and his faction. While Cimon was in the Peloponnesus helping the Spartans, Ephialtes stripped the Areopagus of almost all its power. The Spartans, meanwhile, fearing "the boldness and revolutionary spirit of the Athenians," ultimately sent them home. In 462 B.C.E., Ephialtes was assassinated and Pericles replaced him as leader of the democratic faction. In the spring of 461 B.C.E. Cimon was ostracized, and Athens made an alliance with Argos, Sparta's traditional enemy. Almost overnight, Cimon's domestic and foreign policies had been overturned.

The Division of Greece

The new regime at Athens, led by Pericles and the democratic faction, was confident and ambitious. When Megara, getting the worst of a border dispute with Corinth, withdrew from the Peloponnesian League, the Athenians accepted the Megarians as allies. This alliance gave Athens a great strategic advantage, for Megara barred the way from the Peloponnesus to Athens. Sparta, however, resented the defection of Megara to Athens, leading to the outbreak of the First Peloponnesian War, the first phase in a protracted struggle between Athens and Sparta. The Athenians conquered Aegina and gained control of Boeotia. At this moment Athens was supreme and apparently invulnerable, controlling the states on its borders and dominating the sea. (See Map 3–2.)

About 455 B.C.E., however, the tide turned. A disastrous defeat met an Athenian fleet that had gone to aid an Egyptian rebellion against Persia. The great loss of men, ships, and prestige caused rebel-

MAP 3–2   THE ATHENIAN EMPIRE ABOUT 450 B.C.E.   *The Athenian Empire at its fullest extent shortly before 450 B.C.E. We see Athens and the independent states that provided manned ships for the imperial fleet, but paid no tribute; dependent states that paid tribute; and states allied to, but not actually in, the empire.*

lions in the empire, forcing Athens to make a truce in Greece to subdue its allies in the Aegean. In 449 B.C.E., the Athenians ended the war against Persia.

In 446 B.C.E., the war on the Greek mainland broke out again. Rebellions in Boeotia and Megara removed Athens' land defenses and brought a Spartan invasion. Rather than fight, Pericles, the commander of the Athenian army, agreed to a peace of thirty years by the terms of which he abandoned all Athenian possessions on the Greek mainland outside of Attica. In return, the Spartans gave formal recognition to the Athenian Empire. From then on, Greece was divided into two power blocs: Sparta with its alliance on the mainland, and Athens ruling its empire in the Aegean.

Classical Greece

The Athenian Empire

After the Egyptian disaster, the Athenians moved the Delian League's treasury to Athens and began to keep one-sixtieth of the annual revenues for themselves. Because of the peace with Persia, there seemed no further reason for the allies to pay tribute, so the Athenians were compelled to find a new justification for their empire. (See "The Delian League Becomes the Athenian Empire.") They called for a Panhellenic congress to meet at Athens to discuss rebuilding the temples destroyed by the Persians and to consider how to maintain freedom of the seas. When Sparta's reluctance to participate prevented the congress, Athens felt free to continue to collect funds from the allies, both to maintain its navy and to rebuild the Athenian temples. Athenian propaganda suggested that henceforth the allies would be treated as colonies and Athens as their mother city, the whole to be held together by good feeling and common religious observances.

There is little reason, however, to believe that the allies were taken in or were truly content with their lot. Nothing could cloak the fact that Athens was becoming the master and its allies mere subjects. By 445 B.C.E., when the Thirty Years' Peace gave formal recognition to an Athenian Empire, only Chios, Les-

Key Events in Athenian History between the Persian War and the Great Peloponnesian War

478–477 B.C.E.	Delian League founded
ca. 474–462 B.C.E.	Cimon leading politician
467 B.C.E.	Victory over Persians at Eurymedon River
465–463 B.C.E.	Rebellion of Thasos
462 B.C.E.	Ephialtes murdered; Pericles rises to leadership
461 B.C.E.	Cimon ostracized
461 B.C.E.	Reform of Areopagus
ca. 460 B.C.E.	First Peloponnesian War begins
454 B.C.E.	Athens defeated in Egypt; crisis in the Delian League
449 B.C.E.	Peace with Persia
445 B.C.E.	Thirty Years' Peace ends First Peloponnesian War

(a)

(b)

An Athenian silver four-drachma coin (tetradrachm) from the fifth century B.C.E. (440–430 B.C.E.). On the front (a) is the profile of Athena and on the back (b) is her symbol of wisdom, the owl. The silver from which the coins were struck came chiefly from the state mines at Sunium in southern Attica. Hirmer Foto archive

bos, and Samos were autonomous and provided ships. All the other states paid tribute. The change from alliance to empire came about because of the pressure of war and rebellion and largely because the allies were unwilling to see to their own defense. Although the empire had many friends among the lower classes and the democratic politicians in the subject cities, it came to be seen more and more as a tyranny. Athenian prosperity and security, however, had come to depend on the empire, and the Athenians were determined to defend it at any cost.

Athenian Democracy

Even as the Athenians were tightening their control over their empire, they were expanding democracy at home. Under the leadership of Pericles, they evolved the freest government the world had yet seen.

DEMOCRATIC LEGISLATION Legislation was passed making the *hoplite* class eligible for the *archonship*, and in practice no one was thereafter prevented from serving in this office on the basis of property class. Pericles himself proposed a law introducing pay for jury members, opening that important duty to the poor. Circuit judges were reintroduced, a policy making swift impartial justice available even to the poorest residents in the countryside.

Finally, Pericles himself introduced a bill limiting citizenship to those who had two citizen parents. From a modern perspective this measure might be seen as a step away from democracy, and, in fact, it would have barred Cimon and one of Pericles' ancestors. In Greek terms, however, it was quite natural. Democracy was defined as the privilege of those who held citizenship, making citizenship a valuable commodity. The decision to limit it would have increased its value. Thus, the bill must have won a large majority. Women, resident aliens, and slaves were also denied participation in government in all the Greek states.

HOW DID THE DEMOCRACY WORK? Within the citizen body, the extent of Athenian democracy was remarkable. Every decision of the state had to be approved by the popular assembly—a collection of the people, not their representatives. Every judicial decision was subject to appeal to a popular court of not fewer than 51, and as many as 1,501, citizens, chosen from an annual panel of jurors widely representative of the Athenian population. Most officials were selected by lot without regard to class. The main elected officials, such as the ten generals (the generalship was an office that had both political and military significance) and the imperial treasurers, were usually nobles and almost always rich men, but the people were free to choose otherwise. All public officials were subject to scrutiny before taking office and could be called to account and removed from office during their tenure. They were held to compulsory examination and accounting at the end of their term. There was no standing army, no police force, open or secret, and no way to coerce the people.

Pericles was elected to the generalship fifteen years in a row and thirty times in all, not because he was a dictator but because he was a persuasive speaker, a skillful politician, a respected military leader, an acknowledged patriot, and patently incorruptible. When he lost the people's confidence, they did not hesitate to depose him from office. In 443 B.C.E., however, he stood at the height of his power. The defeat of the Athenian fleet in the Egyptian campaign and the failure of Athens' continental campaigns had persuaded him to favor a conservative policy, seeking to retain the empire in the Aegean and live at peace with the Spartans. It was in this direction that he led Athens' imperial democracy in the years after the First Peloponnesian War. (See "Athenian Democracy: An Unfriendly View.")

The Women of Athens: Legal Status and Everyday Life

Greek society, like most societies all over the world throughout history, was dominated by men. This was true of the democratic city of Athens in the great days of Pericles, in the fifth century B.C.E., no less than of other Greek cities. The actual position of women in classical Athens, however, has been the subject of much controversy.

The bulk of the evidence, coming from the law, from philosophical and moral writings, and from information about the conditions of daily life and the organization of society, shows that women were excluded from most aspects of public life. They could not vote, could not take part in the political assemblies, could not hold public office, and could not take any direct part in politics. Since Athens was one of the few places in the ancient world where male citizens of all classes had these public responsibilities and opportunities, the exclusion of women was all the more significant.

The Acropolis was both the religious and civic center of Athens. In its final form it is the work of Pericles and his successors in the late fifth century B.C.E. This photograph shows the Parthenon and to its left the Erechtheum. Meredith Pillon, Greek National Tourism Organization

The Delian League Becomes the Athenian Empire

In the years after its foundation in the winter of 478–477 B.C.E., the Delian League gradually underwent changes that finally justified calling it the Athenian Empire. In the following selection, the historian Thucydides explains why the organization changed its character.

❖ *Why did some allies choose to pay money rather than supply ships and men? Since membership in the league was originally voluntary, why did the allies refuse to meet their obligations? Who was responsible for converting a voluntary league of allies into the Athenian Empire?*

The causes which led to the defections of the allies were of different kinds, the principal being their neglect to pay the tribute or to furnish ships, and, in some cases, failure of military service. For the Athenians were exacting and oppressive, using coercive measures towards men who were neither willing nor accustomed to work hard. And for various reasons they soon began to prove less agreeable leaders than at first. They no longer fought upon an equality with the rest of the confederates, and they had no difficulty in reducing them when they revolted. Now the allies brought all this upon themselves; for the majority of them disliked military service and absence from home, and so they agreed to contribute a regular sum of money instead of ships. Whereby the Athenian navy was proportionally increased, while they themselves were always untrained and unprepared for war when they revolted.

Thucydides, *The Peloponnesian War*, Vol. 2, trans. by Benjamin Jowett, in *The Greek Historians*, ed. by F. R. B. Godolphin (New York: Random House, 1942), p. 609.

The same sources show that in the private aspects of life women were always under the control of a male guardian—a father, a husband, or some other male relative. Women married young, usually between the ages of twelve and eighteen, whereas their husbands were typically over thirty. In many ways, women's relationships with men were similar to father–daughter relationships. Marriages were arranged; women normally had no choice of husband, and their dowries were controlled by male relatives. Divorce was difficult for women to obtain, for they needed the approval of a male relative who was willing to serve as guardian after the dissolution of the marriage. In case of divorce, the dowry returned with the woman but was controlled by her father or the appropriate male relative.

The main function and responsibility of a respectable Athenian woman of a citizen family was to produce male heirs for the *oikos*, or household, of her husband. If, however, her father's *oikos* lacked a male heir, the daughter became an *epikleros*, the "heiress" to the family property. In that case, she was required by law to marry a relative on her father's side in order to produce the desired male offspring. In the Athenian way of thinking, women were "lent" by one household to another for bearing and raising a male heir to continue the existence of the *oikos*.

Because the pure and legitimate lineage of the offspring was important, women were carefully segregated from men outside the family and were confined to the women's quarters in the house. Men might seek sexual gratification outside the house with prostitutes of high or low style, frequently recruited from abroad. Respectable women stayed home to raise the children, cook, weave cloth, and oversee the management of the household. The only public function of women—an important one—was in the various rituals and festivals of the state religion. Apart from these activities, Athenian women were expected to remain at home out of sight, quiet and unnoticed. Pericles told the widows and mothers of the Athenian men who died in the first year of the Peloponnesian War only this: "Your great glory is not to fall short of your natural character, and the greatest glory of women is to be least talked about by men, whether for good or bad."

The picture of the legal status of women derived from these sources is largely accurate. It does not fit well, however, with other evidence from mythology, from pictorial art, and from the tragedies and comedies by the great Athenian dramatists. These often show women as central characters and powerful figures in both the public and the private spheres, suggesting that the role played by Athenian women may have been more complex than their legal status suggests. In

Athenian Democracy: An Unfriendly View

The following selection comes from an anonymous pamphlet thought to have been written in the midst of the Peloponnesian War. Because it has come down to us among the works of Xenophon, but cannot be his work, it is sometimes called "The Constitution of the Athenians" by Pseudo-Xenophon. It is also common to refer to the unknown author as "The Old Oligarch"—although neither his age nor his purpose is known—because of the obviously antidemocratic tone of the work. Such opinions were common among members of the upper classes in Athens late in the fifth century B.C.E. *and thereafter.*

❖ *What are the author's objections to democracy? Does he describe the workings of the Athenian democracy accurately? How would a defender of the Athenian constitution and way of life meet his complaints? Is there any merit in his criticisms?*

Now, in discussing the Athenian constitution, I cannot commend their present method of running the state, because in choosing it they preferred that the masses should do better than the respectable citizens; this, then, is my reason for not commending it. Since, however, they have made this choice, I will demonstrate how well they preserve their constitution and handle the other affairs for which the rest of the Greeks criticise them.

Again, some people are surprised at the fact that in all fields they give more power to the masses, the poor and the common people than they do to the respectable elements of society, but it will become clear that they preserve the democracy by doing precisely this. When the poor, the ordinary people and the lower classes flourish and increase in numbers, then the power of the democracy will be increased; if, however, the rich and the respectable flourish, the democrats increase the strength of their opponents. Throughout the world the aristocracy are opposed to democracy, for they are naturally least liable to loss of self control and injustice and most meticulous in their regard for what is respectable, whereas the masses display extreme ignorance, indiscipline and wickedness, for poverty gives them a tendency towards the ignoble, and in some cases lack of money leads to their being uneducated and ignorant.

It may be objected that they ought not to grant each and every man the right of speaking in the Ekklesia and serving on the Boule, but only the ablest and best of them; however, in this also they are acting in their own best interests by allowing the mob also a voice. If none but the respectable spoke in the Ekklesia and the Boule, the result would benefit that class and harm the masses; as it is, anyone who wishes rises and speaks, and as a member of the mob he discovers what is to his own advantage and that of those like him.

But someone may say: "How could such a man find out what was advantageous to himself and the common people?" The Athenians realise that this man, despite his ignorance and badness, brings them more advantage because he is well disposed to them than the ill-disposed respectable man would, despite his virtue and wisdom. Such practices do not produce the best city, but they are the best way of preserving democracy. For the common people do not wish to be deprived of their rights in an admirably governed city, but to be free and to rule the city; they are not disturbed by inferior laws, for the common people get their strength and freedom from what you define as inferior laws.

Aristotle and Xenophon on Democracy and Oligarchy, trans. with introductions and commentary by J. M. Moore (Berkeley and Los Angeles: University of California Press, 1975), pp. 37–38. Reprinted by permission of the University of California Press.

Aeschylus's tragedy *Agamemnon*, for example, Clytemnestra arranges the murder of her royal husband and establishes the tyranny of her lover, whom she dominates.

As a famous speech in Euripides' tragedy *Medea* makes clear, we are left with an apparent contradiction. In this speech, Medea paints a bleak picture of

the subjugation of women as dictated by their legal status. (See "Medea Bemoans the Condition of Women.") Yet Medea, as depicted by Euripides, is herself a powerful and terrifying figure who negotiates with kings. She is the central figure in a tragedy bearing her name, produced at state expense before most of the Athenian population and written by one of Athens'

Greek Women at Leisure. Most Greek women of the upper classes appear to have led a secluded and confined existence, but there is some evidence that suggests a somewhat richer social and cultural life. The picture of these women comes from a water-jar of the mid-fifth century B.C.E. Women used them to bring water into the house from wells or fountains, where ancient comedies portray them as gathering and conversing. This scene, however, is indoors, in the women's quarters of the house. The seated woman reads from a scroll; another holds a chest containing other works of literature on scrolls while the remaining two listen attentively. The British Museum

greatest poets and dramatists. She is a cause of terror to the audience and, at the same time, an object of their pity and sympathy as a victim of injustice. She is certainly not, what Pericles recommended in his *Funeral Oration*, "least talked about by men, whether for good or for bad. At the same time, it is important to remember that she is a foreigner with magical powers, by no means a typical Athenian woman."

AN EXCEPTIONAL WOMAN: ASPASIA Pericles' life did not conform to his own prescription. After divorcing his first wife, he entered a liaison that was unique in his time, to a woman who was, in her own way, as remarkable as the great Athenian leader. His companion was Aspasia, a young woman who had left her native Miletus and come to live in Athens. The ancient writers refer to her as a *hetaira*, a kind of high-class courtesan who provided men with both erotic and other kinds of entertainment. She clearly had a keen and lively intellect and may well have been trained in the latest ideas and techniques of discussion in her native city, the home of the Greek enlighten-

ment. Socrates thought it worth his time to talk with her in the company of his followers and friends. In the dialogue *Menexenus*, Plato jokingly gives her credit for writing Pericles' speeches, including the *Funeral Oration*. There should be no doubt that she was taken seriously by both Pericles and the men in his circle.

In every way, Aspasia represented something very different from Athenian women. She was not a child, not a sheltered and repressed creature confined to the narrow world of slave women, children, and female relatives, but a beautiful, independent, brilliantly witty young woman capable of holding her own in conversation with the best minds in Greece and of discussing and illuminating any kind of question with her husband. There can be no doubt that he loved her dearly and passionately. He took her into his house, and whether or not they were formally and legally married, he treated her as his one and only beloved wife. Each morning when he left home and every evening when he returned, he embraced her and kissed her tenderly, by no means the ordinary greeting between an Athenian man and woman.

For an Athenian to consort with courtesans was normal—to take one into his house and treat her as a concubine, perhaps only a little less so. What was by no means normal, but was shocking and, to many, offensive, was to treat such a woman, a foreigner, as a wife, to lavish such affection on her as few Athenian wives enjoyed, to involve her regularly in conversation with other men, and to discuss important matters with her and treat her opinions with respect. The scandal was immense, and the comic poets made the most of it. Enemies claimed that Pericles was enslaved to a foreign woman who was using her hold over him for political purposes of her own. The Samian War, which arose over a quarrel between Aspasia's native Miletus and Samos, intensified these allegations, for the story spread that Pericles had launched the war at her bidding. After Pericles' death, Aristophanes would pick up these old charges and work them around comically to blame Aspasia for the Peloponnesian War as well.

To some degree, the reality of women's lives in Ancient Greece must have depended on their social and economic status. Poorer women necessarily worked hard at household as well as agricultural tasks and in shops. They also went out to the wells and fountains to fetch water, and both vase paintings and literature show women gathering and chatting at these places. Aristotle asks "How would it be possible to prevent the wives of the poor from going out of doors?"[1] Women of the better classes, however, had no such duties or opportunities. They were more easily and closely supervised. Our

[1]Aristotle, *Politics*, 1300a.

Medea Bemoans the Condition of Women

In 431 B.C.E., Euripides (ca. 485–406 B.C.E.) presented his play Medea *at the Festival of Dionysus in Athens. The heroine is a foreign woman who has unusual powers. Her description of the condition of women in the speech that follows, however, appears to be an accurate representation of the condition of women in fifth-century B.C.E. Athens.*

❖ *Apart from participation in politics, how did the lives of men and women differ in ancient Athens? How well or badly did that aspect of Athenian society suit the needs of the Athenian people and the state in the Classical Age? Since men had a dominant position in the state, and the presentation of tragedies was managed and financed by the state, how do you explain the sympathetic account of the condition of women Euripides puts into the mouth of Medea?*

Of all things which are living and can form a
    judgment
We women are the most unfortunate creatures.
Firstly, with an excess of wealth it is required
For us to buy a husband and take for our bodies
A master; for not to take one is even worse.
And now the question is serious whether we
    take
A good or bad one; for there is no easy escape
For a woman, nor can she say no to her mar-
    riage.
She arrives among new modes of behavior and
    manners,
And needs prophetic power, unless she has
    learned at home,
How best to manage him who shares the bed
    with her.
And if we work out all this well and carefully,

And the husband lives with us and lightly bears
    his yoke,
Then life is enviable. If not, I'd rather die.
A man, when he's tired of the company in his
    home,
Goes out of the house and puts an end to his
    boredom
And turns to a friend or companion of his
    own age.
But we are forced to keep our eyes on one alone.
What they say of us is that we have a peace-
    ful time
Living at home, while they do the fighting in
    war.
How wrong they are! I would very much
    rather stand
Three times in the front of battle than bear
    one child.

From Euripides, *Medea in Four Tragedies*, trans. by Rex Warner, copyright ©1955, The Bodley Head. Reprinted by permission of Random House Group, Ltd.

knowledge of the experience of women, however, comes from limited sources that do not always agree. Different scholars arrive at conflicting pictures by emphasizing one kind of a source rather than another. While the legal subordination of women cannot be doubted, the reality of their place in Greek society remains a lively topic of debate.

Slavery

The Greeks had some form of slavery from the earliest times, but true chattel slavery was initially rare. The most common forms of bondage were different kinds of serfdom in relatively backward areas such as Crete, Thessaly, and Sparta. As noted in Chapter 2, the Spartans conquered the natives of their region and reduced them to the status of Helots, subjects who belonged to the Spartan state and worked the

land for the benefit of their Spartan masters. Another early form of bondage involving a severe, but rarely permanent, loss of freedom resulted from default in debt. In Athens, however, at about 600 B.C.E., such bondsmen, called *hektemoroi*, were sold outside their native land as true slaves until the reforms of Solon put an end to debt bondage entirely.

True chattel slavery began to increase about 500 B.C.E. and remained important to Greek society thereafter. The main sources of slaves were war captives and the captives of pirates. Like the Chinese, Egyptians, and many other peoples, the Greeks regarded foreigners as inferior, and most slaves working for the Greeks were foreigners. Greeks sometimes enslaved Greeks, but not to serve in their home territories.

The chief occupation of the Greeks, as of most of the world before our century, was agriculture. The great majority of Greek farmers worked small holdings too poor to support even one slave, but some had as many as one or two slaves to work alongside them. The upper classes had larger farms that were let out to free tenant farmers or worked by slaves, generally under an overseer who was himself a slave. Large landowners generally did not have a single great estate, but possessed several smaller farms scattered about the *polis*. This arrangement did not encourage the amassing of great numbers of agricultural slaves such as those who would later work the cotton and sugar plantations of the New World. Industry, however was different.

Larger numbers of slaves labored in industry, especially in mining. Nicias, a wealthy Athenian of the fifth century B.C.E., owned one thousand slaves whom he rented to a mining contractor for profit, but this is by far the largest number known. Most manufacturing was on a very small scale, with shops using one, two, or a handful of slaves. Slaves worked as craftsmen in almost every trade, and, like agricultural slaves on small farms, they worked alongside their masters. A significant proportion of slaves were domestic servants, and many were shepherds. Publicly held slaves served as policemen, prison attendants, clerks, and secretaries.

The number of slaves in ancient Greece and their importance to Greek society are the subjects of controversy. We have no useful figures of the absolute number of slaves or their percentage of the free population in the classical period (fifth and fourth centuries B.C.E.) that range from twenty thousand to one hundred thousand. Accepting the mean between the extremes, sixty thousand, and estimating the free population at its height at about forty thousand households, would yield a figure of fewer than two slaves per family. Estimates suggest that only a quarter to a third of free Athenians owned any slaves at all.

Some historians have noted that in the American South during the period before the Civil War—where slaves made up less than one-third of the total population and three-quarters of free Southerners had no slaves—the proportion of slaves to free citizens was similar to that of ancient Athens. Because slavery was so important to the economy of the South, these historians suggest, it may have been equally important and similarly oppressive in ancient Athens. This argument has several problems.[2] First, it is important to make a distinction between the cotton states of the American South before the Civil War, where a single cash crop, well suited for exploitation by large groups of slaves, dominated the economy and society, and Athens, where the economy was mixed, the

crops varied, and the land and its distribution were poorly suited to massive slavery.

Quite different, too, was the likelihood that a slave would become free. Americans rarely freed their slaves, but in Greece liberation was common. The most famous example is that of the Athenian slave Pasion, who began as a bank clerk, earned his freedom, became Athens' richest banker, and was awarded Athenian citizenship. Such cases were certainly rare, but gaining one's freedom was not.

It is important also to distinguish the American South, where skin color separated slaves from their masters, from the very different society of classical Athens. Southern masters were increasingly hostile to freeing slaves and afraid of slave rebellions, but in Athens slaves walked the streets with such ease that class-conscious Athenians were offended.

Even more remarkable, the Athenians sometimes considered freeing all their slaves. In 406 B.C.E., their city facing defeat in the Peloponnesian War, they freed all slaves of military age and granted citizenship to those who rowed the ships that won the battle of Arginusae. Twice more at crucial moments, similar proposals were made, although without success.

The Great Peloponnesian War

During the first decade after the Thirty Years' Peace of 445 B.C.E., the willingness of each side to respect the new arrangements was tested and not found wanting. About 435 B.C.E., however, a dispute in a remote and unimportant part of the Greek world ignited a long and disastrous war that shook the foundations of Greek civilization.

Causes

The spark that ignited the conflict was a civil war at Epidamnus, a Corcyraean colony on the Adriatic. This civil war caused a quarrel between Corcyra and her mother city and traditional enemy, Corinth, an ally of Sparta. The Corcyraean fleet was second in size only to that of Athens, and the Athenians feared that its capture by Corinth would change the balance of power at sea and seriously threaten Athenian security. As a result, they made an alliance with the previously neutral Corcyra, angering Corinth and leading to a series of crises in the years 433–432 B.C.E. that threatened to bring the Athenian Empire into conflict with the Peloponnesian League.

In the summer of 432 B.C.E., the Spartans met to consider the grievances of their allies. Persuaded, chiefly by the Corinthians, that Athens was an insatiably aggressive power seeking to enslave all the Greeks, they voted for war. The treaty of 445 B.C.E.

---

[2] M.I. Finley, "Was Greek Civilization Based on Slave Labor?," *Historia* 8 (1959): 151.

specifically provided that all differences be submitted to arbitration, and Athens repeatedly offered to arbitrate any question. Pericles insisted that the Athenians refuse to yield to threats or commands and that they uphold the treaty and the arbitration clause. Sparta refused to arbitrate, and in the spring of 431 B.C.E. its army marched into Attica, the Athenian homeland.

Strategic Stalemate

The Spartan strategy was traditional: to invade the enemy's country and threaten the crops, forcing the enemy to defend them in a *hoplite* battle. Such a battle the Spartans were sure to win because they had the better army and they outnumbered the Athenians at least two to one. Any ordinary *polis* would have yielded or fought and lost. Athens, however, had an enormous navy, an annual income from the empire, a vast reserve fund, and long walls that connected the fortified city with the fortified port of Piraeus.

The Athenians' strategy was to allow devastation of their own land to prove that Spartan invasions could not hurt Athens. At the same time, the Athenians launched seaborne raids on the Peloponnesian coast to show that Sparta's allies could be hurt. Pericles expected that within a year or two—three at most—the Peloponnesians would become discouraged and make peace, having learned their lesson. If the Peloponnesians held out, Athenian resources were inadequate to continue for more than four or five years without raising the tribute in the empire and running an unacceptable risk of rebellion.

The plan required restraint and the leadership only a Pericles could provide. In 429 B.C.E., however, in the wake of a devastating plague and a political crisis that had challenged his authority, Pericles died. After his death, no dominant leader emerged to hold the Athenians to a consistent policy. Two factions vied for influence: one, led by Nicias, wanted to continue the defensive policy, and the other, led by Cleon, preferred a more aggressive strategy. In 425 B.C.E., the aggressive faction was able to win a victory that changed the course of the war. Four hundred Spartans surrendered. Sparta offered peace at once to get them back. The great victory and the prestige it brought Athens made it safe to raise the imperial tribute, without which Athens could not continue to fight. The Athenians indeed wanted to continue, for the Spartan peace offer gave no adequate guarantee of Athenian security.

In 424 B.C.E., the Athenians undertook a more aggressive policy. They sought to make Athens safe by conquering Megara and Boeotia. Both attempts failed, and defeat helped discredit the aggressive policy, leading to a truce in 423 B.C.E. Meanwhile, Sparta's ablest

The Great Peloponnesian War	
435 B.C.E.	Civil war at Epidamnus
432 B.C.E.	Sparta declares war on Athens
431 B.C.E.	Peloponnesian invasion of Athens
421 B.C.E.	Peace of Nicias
415–413 B.C.E.	Athenian invasion of Sicily
405 B.C.E.	Battle of Aegospotami
404 B.C.E.	Athens surrenders

general, Brasidas, took a small army to Thrace and Macedonia. He captured Amphipolis, the most important Athenian colony in the region. Thucydides was in charge of the Athenian fleet in those waters and was held responsible for the city's loss. He was exiled and was thereby given the time and opportunity to write his famous history of the Great Peloponnesian War. In 422 B.C.E., Cleon led an expedition to undo the work of Brasidas. At Amphipolis, both he and Brasidas died in battle. The removal of these two leaders of the aggressive factions in their respective cities paved the way for the Peace of Nicias, named for its chief negotiator, which was ratified in the spring of 421 B.C.E.

The Fall of Athens

The peace, officially supposed to last fifty years and, with a few exceptions, guarantee the status quo, was in fact tenuous. Neither side carried out all its commitments, and several of Sparta's allies refused ratification. In 415 B.C.E., Alcibiades persuaded the Athenians to attack Sicily to bring it under Athenian control. This ambitious and unnecessary undertaking ended in disaster in 413 B.C.E. when the entire expedition was destroyed. The Athenians lost some two hundred ships, about 4,500 of their own men, and almost ten times as many allies. It shook Athenian prestige, reduced the power of Athens, provoked rebellions, and brought the wealth and power of Persia into the war on Sparta's side.

It is remarkable that the Athenians could continue fighting in spite of the disaster. They survived a brief oligarchic coup in 411 B.C.E. and won several important victories at sea as the war shifted to the Aegean. Their allies rebelled, however, and were sustained by fleets paid for by Persia. The Athenians saw their financial resources shrink and finally disappear. When their fleet was caught napping and was destroyed at Aegospotami in 405 B.C.E., they could not build another. The Spartans, under Lysander, a clever and ambitious general who was responsible for obtaining Persian support, cut off the food supply through the Hellespont, and the Athenians were starved into submission. In 404 B.C.E. they surrendered unconditionally; the city walls were dismantled, Athens was permitted no fleet, and the empire was gone. The Great Peloponnesian War was over.

Competition for Leadership in the Fourth Century B.C.E.

The defeat of Athens did not bring domination to the Spartans. Instead, the period from 404 B.C.E. until the Macedonian conquest of Greece in 338 B.C.E. was a time of intense rivalry among the Greek cities, each seeking to achieve leadership and control over some or all of the others. Sparta, a recovered Athens, and a newly powerful Thebes were the main competitors in a struggle that ultimately weakened all the Greeks and left them vulnerable to outside influence and control.

The Hegemony of Sparta

The collapse of the Athenian Empire created a vacuum of power in the Aegean and opened the way for Spartan leadership or hegemony. Fulfilling the contract that had brought them the funds to win the war, the Spartans handed the Greek cities of Asia Minor back to Persia. Under the leadership of Lysander, the Spartans went on to make a complete mockery of their promise to free the Greeks by stepping into the imperial role of Athens in the cities along the European coast and the islands of the Aegean. In most of the cities, Lysander installed a board of ten local oligarchs loyal to him and supported them with a Spartan garrison. Tribute brought in an annual revenue almost as great as that the Athenians had collected.

Limited population, the Helot problem, and traditional conservatism all made Sparta a less than ideal state to rule a maritime empire. The increasing arrogance of Sparta's policies alienated some of its allies, especially Thebes and Corinth. In 404 B.C.E. Lysander installed an oligarchic government in Athens, and the outrageous behavior of its leaders earned them the title "Thirty Tyrants." Democratic exiles took refuge in Thebes and Corinth and created an army to challenge the oligarchy. Sparta's conservative king, Pausanias, replaced Lysander, arranging a peaceful settlement and, ultimately, the restoration of democracy. Thereafter, Athenian foreign policy remained under Spartan control, but otherwise Athens was free.

In 405 B.C.E., Darius II of Persia died and was succeeded by Artaxerxes II. His younger brother, Cyrus, contested his rule and received Spartan help in recruiting a Greek mercenary army to help him win

the throne. The Greeks marched inland as far as Mesopotamia, where they defeated the Persians at Cunaxa in 401 B.C.E., but Cyrus was killed in the battle. The Greeks were able to march back to the Black Sea and safety; their success revealed the potential weakness of the Persian Empire.

The Greeks of Asia Minor had supported Cyrus and were now afraid of Artaxerxes' revenge. The Spartans accepted their request for aid and sent an army into Asia, attracted by the prospect of prestige, power, and money. In 396 B.C.E., the command of Sparta's army was given to a new king, Agesilaus. This leader dominated Sparta throughout its period of hegemony and until his death in 360 B.C.E. Some have argued that his consistent advocacy of aggressive policies that provided him with opportunities to display his bravery in battle may have been motivated by a psychological need to compensate for his physical lameness and his disputed claim to the throne.

Agesilaus collected much booty and frightened the Persians. They sent a messenger with money and promises of further support to friendly factions in all of the Greek states likely to help them against Sparta. By 395 B.C.E., Thebes was able to organize an alliance that included Argos, Corinth, and a resurgent Athens. The result was the Corinthian War (395–387 B.C.E.), which put an end to Sparta's Asian adventure. In 394 B.C.E., the Persian fleet destroyed Sparta's maritime empire. Meanwhile, the Athenians took advantage of events to rebuild their walls, to enlarge their navy, and even to recover some of their lost empire in the Aegean. The war ended when the exhausted Greek states accepted a peace dictated by the Great King of Persia.

The Persians, frightened now by the recovery of Athens, turned the management of Greece

The Spartan and Theban Hegemonies	
404–403 B.C.E.	"Thirty Tyrants" rule at Athens
401 B.C.E.	Expedition of Cyrus, rebellious prince of Persia; Battle of Cunaxa
400–387 B.C.E.	Spartan War against Persia
398–360 B.C.E.	Reign of Agesilaus at Sparta
395–387 B.C.E.	Corinthian War
382 B.C.E.	Sparta seizes Thebes
378 B.C.E.	Second Athenian Confederation founded
371 B.C.E.	Thebans defeat Sparta at Leuctra; end of Spartan hegemony
362 B.C.E.	Battle of Mantinea; end of Theban hegemony

Xenophon Recounts How Greece Brought Itself to Chaos

Confusion in Greece in the fourth century B.C.E. reached a climax with the inconclusive Battle of Mantinea in 362 B.C.E. The Theban leader Epaminondas was killed, and no other city or person emerged to provide the needed general leadership for Greece. Xenophon, a contemporary, pointed out the resulting near-chaos in Greek affairs—tempting ground for the soon-to-appear conquering Macedonians under their king Philip II.

❖ *What does this passage reveal about the nature of ancient Greek warfare and the customs surrounding it? How decisive were most battles in ancient Greece? Before the Macedonian conquest of Greece in 338 B.C.E., why was no state able to impose its rule over the others? Why was that possible elsewhere?*

The effective result of these achievements was the very opposite of that which the world at large anticipated. Here, where well-nigh the whole of Hellas was met together in one field, and the combatants stood rank against rank confronted, there was no one who doubted that, in the event of battle, the conquerors this day would rule; and that those who lost would be their subjects. But god so ordered it that both belligerents alike set up trophies as claiming victory, and neither interfered with the other in the act. Both parties alike gave back their enemy's dead under a truce, and in right of victory; both alike, in symbol of defeat, under a truce took back their dead. And though both claimed to have won the day, neither could show that he had thereby gained any accession of territory, or state, or empire, or was better situated than before the battle. Uncertainty and confusion, indeed, had gained ground, being tenfold greater throughout the length and breadth of Hellas after the battle than before.

Xenophon, *Hellenica*, trans. by H. G. Dakyns, in *The Greek Historians*, ed. by F. R. B. Godolphin (New York: Random House, 1942), p. 221.

over to Sparta. Agesilaus broke up all alliances except the Peloponnesian League. He used or threatened to use the Spartan army to interfere in other *poleis* and put friends of Sparta in power within them. Sparta reached a new level of lawless arrogance in 382 B.C.E., when it seized Thebes during peacetime without warning or pretext. In 379 B.C.E., a Spartan army made a similar attempt on Athens. That action persuaded the Athenians to join with Thebes, which had rebelled from Sparta a few months earlier, to wage war on the Spartans.

In 371 B.C.E., the Thebans, led by their great generals Pelopidas and Epaminondas, defeated the Spartans at Leuctra. The Thebans encouraged the Arcadian cities of the central Peloponnesus to form a league, freed the Helots, and helped them found a city of their own. They deprived Sparta of much of its farmland and of the people who worked it and hemmed it in with hostile neighbors. Sparta's population had shrunk so that it could put fewer than 2,000 men into the field at Leuctra. Sparta's aggressive policies had led to ruin. The Theban victory brought the end of Sparta as a power of the first rank.

The Hegemony of Thebes: The Second Athenian Empire

Thebes' power after the its victory at Leuctra lay in its democratic constitution, its control over Boeotia, and its two outstanding and popular generals. One of these generals, Pelopidas, died in a successful attempt to gain control of Thessaly. The other, Epaminondas, consolidated his work, making Thebes dominant over all Greece north of Athens and the Corinthian Gulf and challenging the reborn Athenian Empire in the Aegean. All this activity provoked resistance, and by 362 B.C.E. Thebes faced a Peloponnesian coalition as well as Athens. Epaminondas, once again leading a Boeotian army into the Peloponnesus, confronted this coalition at the Battle of Mantinea. His army was victorious, but Epaminondas himself was killed. With both its great leaders now dead, Theban dominance ended.

The Second Athenian Confederation, which Athens had organized in 378 B.C.E., was aimed at resisting Spartan aggression in the Aegean. Its constitution was careful to avoid the abuses of the Delian League, but the Athenians soon began to repeat them anyway. This time, however, they did not have the power to put down resistance. When the collapse of Sparta and Thebes and the restraint of Persia removed any reason for voluntary membership, Athens' allies revolted. By 355 B.C.E., Athens had to abandon most of the empire. After two centuries of almost continuous warfare, the Greeks returned to the chaotic disorganization that characterized the time before the founding of the Peloponnesian League. (See "Xenophon Recounts How Greece Brought Itself to Chaos.")

The Culture of Classical Greece

The repulse of the Persian invasion released a flood of creative activity in Greece that was rarely, if ever, matched anywhere at any time. The century and a half between the Persian retreat and the conquest of Greece by Philip of Macedon (479–338 B.C.E.) produced achievements of such quality as to justify the designation of that era as the Classical Period. (See "Art & the West.") Ironically, we often use the term "classical" to suggest calm and serenity, but the word that best describes the common element present in Greek life, thought, art, and literature in this period is "tension."

The Fifth Century B.C.E.

Two sources of tension contributed to the artistic outpouring of fifth-century B.C.E. Greece. One arose from the conflict between the Greeks' pride in their accomplishments and their concern that overreaching would bring retribution. Friction among the *poleis* intensified during this period as Athens and Sparta gath-

ered most of them into two competing and menacing blocs. The victory over the Persians brought a sense of exultation in the capacity of humans to accomplish great things and a sense of confidence in the divine justice that had brought low the arrogant pride of Xerxes. But the Greeks recognized that the fate which had met Xerxes awaited all those who reached too far, creating a sense of unease. The second source of tension was the conflict between the soaring hopes and achievements of individuals and the claims and limits put on them by their fellow citizens in the *polis*. These tensions were felt throughout Greece. They had the most spectacular consequences, however, in Athens in its Golden Age, the time between the Persian and the Peloponnesian wars.

ATTIC TRAGEDY Nothing reflects Athens' concerns better than Attic tragedy, which emerged as a major form of Greek poetry in the fifth century B.C.E. The tragedies were presented in a contest as part of the public religious observations in honor of the god Dionysus. The festivals in which they were shown were civic occasions.

Each poet who wished to compete submitted his work to the *archon*. Each offered three tragedies (which might or might not have a common subject) and a satyr play, or comic choral dialogue with Dionysus, to close. The three best competitors were each awarded three actors and a chorus. The actors were paid by the state. The chorus was provided by a wealthy citizen selected by the state to perform this service as *choregos*, for the Athenians had no direct taxation to support such activities. Most of the tragedies were performed in the theater of Dionysus on the south side of the Acropolis, and as many as 30,000 Athenians could attend. Prizes and honors were awarded to the

The Theatre of Dionysus in Athens, seen from the Acropolis. It was here, in contests held in honor of Dionysus, that the great Attic tragedies and comedies were performed for the citizens of Athens.
Meredith Pillon, Greek National Tourism Organization

Diagram of a Doric Column and Entablature:

a Corner Akroterion
b Sima with a lion's head as waterspout
c Geison (cornice)
d Tympanum
e Mutule with Guttae (drops)
f Triglyphs
g Metopes
h Regulae with guttae
i Architrave or Epistyle
k Abacus
l Echinus
m Shaft with 20 sharp-edged flutings
n Stylobate
o Krepis or Krepidoma
p Taenia

Diagram of an Ionic Column and Entablature

a Sima
b Geison (cornice)
c Tympanum
d Frieze
e Architrave or Epistyle (in three parts)
f Capital with Volutes
g Shaft with 24 flutings separated by fillets
h Attic Base with double Torus and a Trochilos
i Stylobate
k Krepis or Krepidoma

Corinthian Capital

The three orders of Greek architecture, Doric, Ionic, and Corinthian, have had an enduring impact on Western architecture.

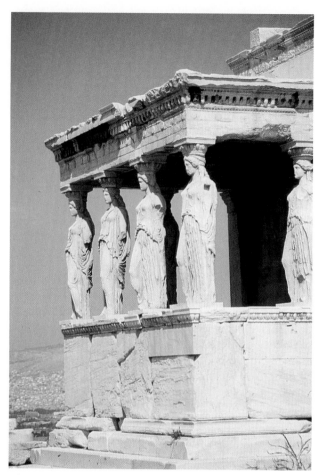

The porch of the maidens is part of the Erechtheum on the Athenian Acropolis near the Parthenon. Built between 421 and 409 B.C.E., *the Erechtheum housed the shrines of three different gods. In place of the usual fluted columns, the porch uses the statues of young girls taking part in a religious festival.* Meredith Pillon, Greek National Tourism Organization

author, the actor, and the *choragus* voted best by a jury of Athenians chosen by lot.

Attic tragedy served as a forum in which the poets raised vital issues of the day, enabling the Athenian audience to think about them in a serious, yet exciting, context. On rare occasions, the subject of a play might be a contemporary or historic event, but almost always it was chosen from mythology. Until late in the century, the tragedies always dealt solemnly with difficult questions of religion, politics, ethics, morality, or some combination of these. The plays of the dramatists Aeschylus and Sophocles, for example, follow this pattern. The plays of Euripides written toward the end of the century are less solemn and more concerned with individual psychology.

OLD COMEDY   Comedy was introduced into the Dionysian festival early in the fifth century B.C.E. Cratinus, Eupolis, and the great master of the genre called Old Comedy, Aristophanes (ca. 450–385 B.C.E.), the only one from whom we have complete plays, wrote political comedies. They were filled with scathing invective and satire against such contemporary figures as Pericles, Cleon, Socrates, and Euripides. (See "Lysistrata Ends the War.")

ARCHITECTURE AND SCULPTURE   The great architectural achievements of Periclean Athens, as much as Athenian tragedy, illustrate the magnificent results of the union and tension between religious and civic responsibilities on the one hand and the transcendent genius of the individual artist on the other. Beginning in 448 B.C.E. and continuing to the outbreak of the Great Peloponnesian War, Pericles undertook a great

Victory and Nobility in Bronze:
The Charioteer of Delphi

The Charioteer of Delphi. c. 470
B.C.E. Nimatallah/Art Resource, NY

This freestanding statue of the *Charioteer of Delphi* is one of the few full-scale bronze sculptures that survive from the fifth century B.C.E. Polyzalus, the tyrant of the Greek city of Gela in Sicily, dedicated it after winning a victory in the chariot race in the Pythian games, either in 478 or 474. The games were held at the sacred shrine of the god Apollo at Delphi, and the statue was placed within the god's sanctuary, not far from Apollo's temple. (See p. 36.) Along with the Olympic games, the Isthmian games at Corinth and the Nemean games were great athletic contests, part of religious celebrations in honor of a god. The winners in these contests were frequently memorialized in poems inspired by their victories, often by the great poet Pindar.

The statue does not represent Polyzalas, who provided the horses, chariots, and equipment, but the professional charioteer whom he hired. It is all that remains of a group that included the chariot, horses, and a groom. It is possible that it also included a statue of Polyzalas himself, standing on the chariot next to the driver.

The sculpture probably represented the scene after the race, when the winning chariot moved slowly in a victory procession.

The statue is made in what scholars call the "severe style" that emerged in Greece soon after the Persian invasion of 480–479. Compared with earlier statues from the Archaic period of Greek art, it is simple, without frills, serious, and austere. Unlike the earlier figures, which often wore a smile, the statues of the severe style wear a serious, even "moody," expression. Their sculptors seem to try to present what the Greeks called the *ethos*—the character—of the subject in their work.

One distinguished scholar makes the following observations: "It is easy to see how the charioteer could be taken as an embodiment, in the visual arts, of one of the odes of Pindar. Not only does it celebrate, like the Pythian Ode, a victory won at the festival games at Delphi, but the *ethos* which it conveys is a manifestation of Pindaric *arete...*, the 'innate excellence' of noble natures which gives them proficiency and pride in their human endeavors, but humility before the gods."[3]

[3] J. J. Politt, *Art and Experience in Classical Greece*, Cambridge University Press, Cambridge, 1972, p. 48.

Sources: J. J. Pollitt, *Art and Experience in Classical Greece* (Cambridge: Cambridge University Press, 1972), pp. 15–63. H. W. Janson and Anthony F. Janson, *History of Art*, 5th ed., rev. (Upper Saddle River, NJ: Prentice Hall, 1997), pp. 139–151.

building program on the Acropolis. (See Map 3–3.) The funds were provided by the income from the empire. The new buildings included temples to honor the city's gods and a fitting gateway to the temples. Pericles' main purpose seems to have been to represent visually the greatness and power of Athens, but in such a way as to emphasize intellectual and artistic achievement—civilization rather than military and naval power. It was as though these buildings were tangible proof of Pericles' claim that Athens was "the school of Hellas"—that is, the intellectual center of all Greece.

PHILOSOPHY   The tragic dramas, architecture, and sculpture of the fifth century B.C.E. are all indications of an extraordinary concern with human beings—their capacities, their limits, their nature, and their place in the universe. The same concern is clear in the development of philosophy.

To be sure, some philosophers continued the speculation about the nature of the cosmos (as opposed to human nature) that began with Thales in the sixth century B.C.E. Parmenides of Elea and his pupil Zeno, in opposition to the earlier philosopher Heraclitus, argued that change was only an illusion of the senses. Reason and reflection showed that reality was fixed and unchanging, because it seemed evident that nothing could be created out of nothingness. Empedocles of Acragas further advanced such fundamental speculations by identifying four basic elements: fire, water, earth, and air. Like Parmenides, he thought that reality was permanent, but he thought it not immobile; the four elements, he contended, were moved by two primary forces: love and strife—or, as we might say, attraction and repulsion.

Empedocles' theory is clearly a step on the road to the atomic theory of Leucippus of Miletus and Democritus of Abdera. According to this theory, the world consists of innumerable tiny, solid, indivisible, and unchangeable particles—or "atoms"—that move about in the void. The size of the atoms and the arrangements they form when joined produce the secondary qualities that our senses perceive, such as color and shape. These secondary qualities are merely conventional—the result of human interpretation and agreement—unlike the atoms themselves, which are natural.

Previous to the atomists, Anaxagoras of Clazomenae, an older contemporary and a friend of Pericles, had spoken of tiny fundamental particles called seeds, which were put together on a rational basis by a force called *nous*, or "mind." Anaxagoras was thus suggesting a distinction between matter and mind. The atomists, however, regarded "soul," or mind, as material and believed that everything was guided by purely physical laws. In these conflicting positions,

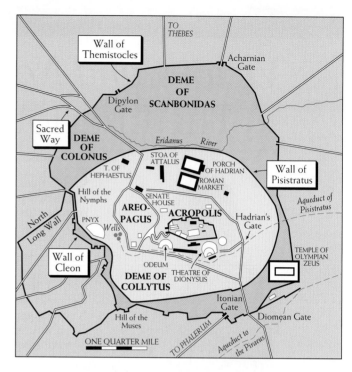

MAP 3–3   ANCIENT ATHENS   *This sketch locates some of the major features of the ancient city of Athens that have been excavated and are visible today. It includes monuments ranging in age from the earliest times to the period of the Roman Empire. The geographical relation of the Acropolis to the rest of the city is apparent, as is that of the Agora, the Areopagus (where the early council of aristocrats met), and the Pnyx (site of assembly for the larger, more democratic meetings of the entire people).*

we have the beginning of the enduring philosophical debate between materialism and idealism.

These speculations were of interest to very few people, and in fact, most Greeks were suspicious of them. A far more influential debate was begun by a group of professional teachers who emerged in the mid-fifth century B.C.E. Called *Sophists*, they traveled about and received pay for teaching such practical techniques of persuasion as rhetoric, dialectic, and argumentation. (Persuasive skills were much valued in democracies like Athens, where so many issues were resolved through open debate.) Some Sophists claimed to teach wisdom and even virtue. Reflecting the human focus characteristic of fifth-century thought, they refrained from speculations about the physical universe, instead applying reasoned analysis to human beliefs and institutions. In doing so, they identified a central problem of human social life and the life of the *polis*: the conflict between nature and custom, or law. The more traditional among them argued that law itself was in accord with nature and was of divine origin, a view that fortified the traditional beliefs of the *polis*.

Others argued, however, that laws were merely the result of convention—an agreement among people—and not in accord with nature. The laws could not pretend to be a positive moral force, but merely had the negative function of preventing people from harming each other. The most extreme Sophists argued that law was contrary to nature, a trick whereby the weak control the strong. Critias, an Athenian oligarch and one of the more extreme Sophists, went so far as to say that the gods themselves had been invented by some clever person to deter people from doing what they wished. Such ideas attacked the theoretical foundations of the *polis* and helped provoke the philosophical responses of Plato and Aristotle in the next century.

HISTORY   The first prose literature in the form of history was an account of the Persian War written by Herodotus. "The father of history," as he has been deservedly called, was born shortly before the outbreak of the war. His account goes far beyond all previous chronicles, genealogies, and geographical studies and attempts to explain human actions and to draw instruction from them.

Although his work was completed about 425 B.C.E. and shows a few traces of Sophist influence, its spirit is that of an earlier time. Herodotus accepted the evidence of legends and oracles, although not uncritically, and often explained human events in terms of divine intervention. Human arrogance and divine vengeance are key forces that help explain the defeat of Croesus by Cyrus, as well as Xerxes' defeat by the Greeks. Yet the *History* is typical of its time in celebrating the crucial role of human intelligence as exemplified by Miltiades at Marathon and Themistocles at Salamis. Nor was Herodotus unaware of the importance of institutions. There is no mistaking his pride in the superiority of the Greek *polis* and the discipline it inspired in its citizen soldiers and his pride in the superiority of the Greeks' voluntary obedience to law over the Persians' fear of punishment.

Thucydides, the historian of the Peloponnesian War, was born about 460 B.C.E. and died a few years after the end of the Great Peloponnesian War. He was very much a product of the late fifth century B.C.E. His work, which was influenced by the secular, human-centered, skeptical rationalism of the Sophists, also reflects the scientific attitude of the school of medicine named for his contemporary, Hippocrates of Cos.

The Hippocratic school, known for its pioneering work in medicine and scientific theory, placed great emphasis on an approach to the understanding, diagnosis, and treatment of disease that combined careful observation with reason. In the same way, Thucydides took great pains to achieve factual accuracy and tried to use his evidence to discover meaningful patterns of human behavior. He believed that human nature was essentially unchanging, so that a wise person equipped with the understanding provided by history might accurately foresee events and thus help to guide them. He believed, however, that only a few had the ability to understand history and to put its lessons to good use. He thought that even the wisest could be foiled by the intervention of chance, which played a great role in human affairs. Thucydides focused his interest on politics, and in that area his assumptions about human nature do not seem unwarranted. His work has proved to be, as he hoped, "a possession forever." Its description of the terrible civil war between the two basic kinds of *poleis* is a final and fitting example of the tension that was the source of both the greatness and the decline of Classical Greece.

The Fourth Century B.C.E.

Historians often speak of the Peloponnesian War as the crisis of the *polis* and of the fourth century B.C.E. as the period of its decline. The war did bring powerfully important changes: the impoverishment of some Greek cities and, with it, an intensification of class conflict; the development of professionalism in the army; and demographic shifts that sometimes reduced the citizen population and increased the numbers of resident aliens. The Greeks of the fourth century B.C.E. did not know, however, that their traditional way of life was on the verge of destruction. Still, thinkers could not avoid recognizing that they lived in a time of troubles, and they responded in various ways. Some looked to the past and tried to shore up the weakened structure of the *polis*; others tended toward despair and looked for new solutions; and still others averted their gaze from the public arena altogether. All of these responses are apparent in the literature, philosophy, and art of the period.

DRAMA   The tendency of some to turn away from the life of the *polis* and inward to everyday life, the family, and their own individuality is apparent in the poetry of the fourth century B.C.E. A new genre, called Middle Comedy, replaced the political subjects and personal invective of the Old Comedy with a comic–realistic depiction of daily life, plots of intrigue, and mild satire of domestic situations. Significantly, the role of the chorus, which in some way represented the *polis*, was very much diminished. These trends all continued and were carried even further in the New Comedy. Its leading playwright,

Lysistrata Ends the War

Aristophanes, the greatest of the Athenian comic poets, presented the play Lysistrata *in 411 B.C.E., two decades into the Great Peloponnesian War. The central idea of the plot is that the women of Athens, led by Lysistrata, tired of the privations imposed by the war, decide to take matters into their own hands and bring the war to an end. The device they employ is to get the women on both sides to deny their marital favors to their husbands, a kind of sexual strike that quickly achieves its purpose. Before the following passage, Lysistrata has set the terms the Spartans must accept. Next she turns to the Athenians. The play is a masterful example of Athenian Old Comedy, which was almost always full of contemporary and historical political satirical references and sexual and erotic puns and jokes. The references to "Peace" in the stage directions are to an actor playing the goddess Peace.*

❖ *To what historic event does the passage concerning "the Tyrant's days" refer? To what does the "Promontory of Pylos" refer? What was the real role of women in Athenian political life, and what does the play tell us about it? What is the relationship between humor and reality in this play?*

LYSISTRATA
(*Turning to the Athenians*)
—Men of Athens, do you think I'll let you
   off?
Have you forgotten the Tyrant's days, when you
   wore
the smock of slavery, when the Spartans turned
   to the spear,
cut down the pride of Thessaly, despatched the
   friends
of tyranny, and dispossessed your oppressors?
                                        Recall:
On that great day, your only allies were
   Spartans;
your liberty came at their hands, which
   stripped away
your servile garb and clothed you again in
   Freedom!

SPARTAN
(*Indicating Lysistrata*)
Hain't never seed no higher type of woman.
KINESIAS
(*Indicating Peace*)
Never saw one I wanted so much to top.
LYSISTRATA
(*Oblivious to the byplay, addressing both groups*)
With such a history of mutual benefits conferred
and received, why are you fighting? Stop this
   wickedness!
Come to terms with each other! What prevents
   you?
SPARTAN
We'd a heap sight druther make Peace, if we was
   indemnified with a plumb strategic location.
(*Pointing at Peace's rear*)
                              We'll take thet butte.

Menander (342–291 B.C.E.), completely abandoned mythological subjects in favor of domestic tragicomedy. His gentle satire of the foibles of ordinary people and his tales of lovers temporarily thwarted before a happy and proper ending would not be unfamiliar to viewers of modern situation comedies.

Tragedy faded as a robust and original form. It became common to revive the great plays of the previous century. No tragedies written in the fourth century B.C.E. have been preserved. The plays of Euripides, which rarely won first prize when first produced for Dionysian festival competitions, became increasingly popular in the fourth century and after. Euripides was less interested in cosmic confrontations of conflicting principles than in the psychology and behavior of individual human beings. Some of his late plays, in fact, are less like the tragedies of Aeschylus and Sophocles than forerunners of later forms such as the New Comedy. Plays like *Helena*, *Andromeda*, and *Iphigenia in Tauris* are more like fairy tales, tales of adventure, or love stories than tragedies.

SCULPTURE   The same movement away from the grand, the ideal, and the general and toward the ordinary, the real, and the individual is apparent in the development of Greek sculpture. To see these developments, one has only to compare the statue of the

LYSISTRATA
Butte?

SPARTAN
The Promontory of Pylos—Sparta's Back Door.
We've missed it fer a turrible spell.
(*Reaching*)

                             Hev to keep our
hand in.

KINESIAS
(*Pushing him away*)
The price is too high—you'll never take that!

LYSISTRATA
Oh, let them have it.

KINESIAS
                     What room will we have left
for maneuvers?

LYSISTRATA
                Demand another spot in exchange.

KINESIAS
(*Surveying Peace like a map as he addresses
the Spartan*)
Then you hand over to us—uh, let me see—
let's try Thessaly—
(*Indicating the relevant portions of Peace*)
                  First of all, Easy Mountain ...
then the Maniac Gulf behind it ...
            and down to Megara for the legs ...

SPARTAN
You cain't take all of thet! Yore plumb
out of yore mind!

LYSISTRATA
(*To Kinesias*)
               Don't argue. Let the legs go.
(*Kinesias nods. A pause, general smiles of
agreement*)

KINESIAS
(*Doffing his cloak*)
I feel an urgent desire to plow a few furrows.

SPARTAN
(*Doffing his cloak*)
Hit's time to work a few loads of fertilizer in.

LYSISTRATA
Conclude the treaty and the simple life is yours.
If such is your decision, convene your councils,
and then deliberate the matter with your allies.

KINESIAS
Deliberate? Allies?
                  We're over-extended already!
Wouldn't every ally approve of our position—
Union Now?

SPARTAN
               I know I kin speak for ourn.

KINESIAS
And I for ours.
               They're just a bunch of gigolos.

LYSISTRATA
I heartily approve.
Now first attend to your purification,
then we, the women, will welcome you to the
    Citadel
and treat you to all the delights of a home-
    cooked banquet.
Then you'll exchange your oaths and pledge
    your faith,
and every man of you will take his wife
and depart for home.

Aristophanes, *Lysistrata*, trans. by Douglass Parker, in *Four Comedies by Aristophanes*, ed. by W. Arrowsmith (Ann Arbor: University of Michigan Press, 1969), pp. 79–81. Reprinted by permission of the University of Michigan Press.

Striding God of Artemisium (ca. 460 B.C.E.), thought to be either Zeus on the point of releasing a thunderbolt or Poseidon about to throw his trident, or the Doryphoros of Polycleitus (ca. 450–440 B.C.E.) with the Hermes of Praxiteles (ca. 340–330 B.C.E.) or the Apoxyomenos attributed to Lysippus (ca. 330 B.C.E.).

Philosophy and the Crisis of the *Polis*

SOCRATES   Probably the most complicated response to the crisis of the *polis* may be found in the life and teachings of Socrates (469–399 B.C.E.). Because he wrote nothing, our knowledge of him comes chiefly from his disciples Plato and Xenophon and from later tradition. Although as a young man he was interested in speculations about the physical world, he later turned to the investigation of ethics and morality; as Cicero put it, he brought philosophy down from the heavens. Socrates was committed to the search for truth and for the knowledge about human affairs that he believed could be discovered by reason. His method was to go among men, particularly those reputed to know something, such as craftsmen, poets, and politicians, in order to question and cross-examine them.

The result was always the same. Those Socrates questioned might have technical information and

The striding god from Artemisium is a bronze statue dating from about 460 B.C.E. It was found in the sea near Artemisium, the northern tip of the large Greek island of Euboea, and is now on display in the Athens archaeological museum. Exactly whom he represents is not known. Some have thought him to be Poseidon holding a trident; others believe that he is Zeus hurling a thunderbolt. In either case, he is a splendid representative of the early Classical period of Greek sculpture.
National Archaeological Museum, Athens

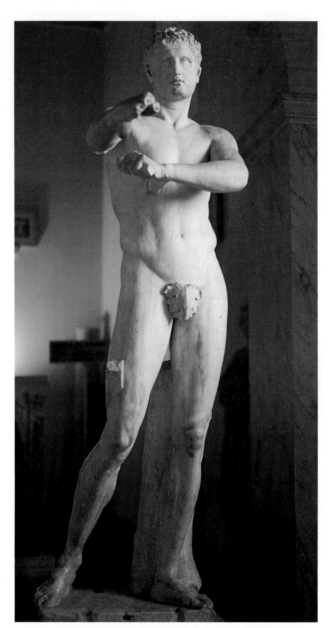

This is a Roman copy of the Apoxyomenos (the scraper) by Lysippus of Sicyon. It shows a young athlete scraping from his body the oil used for cleansing after exertion. The original was made about 330 B.C.E. Robert Miller

skills, but seldom had any knowledge of the fundamental principles of human behavior. It is understandable that Athenians so exposed should be angry with their examiner, and it is not surprising that they thought Socrates was undermining the beliefs and values of the *polis.* Socrates' unconcealed contempt for democracy, which seemingly relied on ignorant amateurs to make important political decisions without any certain knowledge, created further hostility. Moreover, his insistence on the primacy of his own individualism and his determination to pursue philosophy even against the wishes of his fellow citizens reinforced this hostility and the prejudice that went with it.

But Socrates, unlike the Sophists, did not accept pay for his teaching; he professed ignorance and denied that he taught at all. His individualism, moreover, was unlike the worldly hedonism of some of the Sophists. It was not wealth or pleasure or power that he urged people to seek, but "the greatest improvement of the soul." He differed also from the more radical Sophists in that he denied that the *polis* and its laws were mere-

ly conventional. He thought, on the contrary, that they had a legitimate claim on the citizen, and he proved it in the most convincing fashion.

In 399 B.C.E., he was condemned to death by an Athenian jury on the charges of bringing new gods into the city and of corrupting the youth. His dialectical inquiries had angered many important people. His criticism of democracy must have been viewed with suspicion, especially as Critias and Charmides, who were members of the Thirty Tyrants, and the traitor Alcibiades had been among his disciples. He was given a chance to escape but, as we are told in Plato's *Crito,* he refused to do so because of his veneration of the laws. Socrates' career set the stage for later responses to the travail of the *polis*. He recognized its difficulties and criticized its shortcomings, and he turned away from an active political life, but he did not abandon the idea of the *polis*. He fought as a soldier in its defense, obeyed its laws, and sought to put its values on a sound foundation by reason.

THE CYNICS One branch of Socratic thought—the concern with personal morality and one's own soul, the disdain of worldly pleasure and wealth, and the withdrawal from political life—was developed and then distorted almost beyond recognition by the Cynic school. Antisthenes (ca. 455–360 B.C.E.), a follower of Socrates, is said to have been its founder, but its most famous exemplar was Diogenes of Sinope (ca. 400–325 B.C.E.). Because Socrates disparaged wealth and worldly comfort, Diogenes wore rags and lived in a tub. He performed shameful acts in public and made his living by begging to show his rejection of convention. He believed that happiness lay in satisfying natural needs in the simplest and most direct way; because actions to this end, being natural, could not be indecent, they could and should be done publicly.

Socrates questioned the theoretical basis for popular religious beliefs; the Cynics, in contrast, ridiculed all religious observances. As Plato said, Diogenes was Socrates gone mad. Beyond that, the way of the Cynics contradicted important Socratic beliefs. Socrates, unlike traditional aristocrats such as Theognis, believed that virtue was a matter not of birth, but of knowledge and that people do wrong only through ignorance of what is virtuous. The Cynics, on the other hand, believed that "virtue is an affair of deeds and does not need a store of words and learning."[4] Wisdom and happiness come from pursuing the proper style of life, not from philosophy.

The Cynics moved even further away from Socrates by abandoning the concept of the *polis* entirely. When Diogenes was asked about his citizenship, he answered that he was *kosmopolites*, a citizen of the world. The Cynics plainly had turned away from the past, and their views anticipated those of the Hellenistic Age.

PLATO Plato (429–347 B.C.E.) was by far the most important of Socrates' associates and is a perfect example of the pupil who becomes greater than his master. He was the first systematic philosopher and therefore the first to place political ideas in their full philosophical context. He was also a writer of genius, leaving us twenty-six philosophical discussions. Almost all are in the form of dialogues, which

somehow make the examination of difficult and complicated philosophical problems seem dramatic and entertaining. Plato came from a noble Athenian family, and he looked forward to an active political career until the excesses of the Thirty Tyrants and the execution of Socrates discouraged him from that pursuit. Twice he made trips to Sicily in the hope of producing a model state at Syracuse under the tyrants Dionysius I and II, but without success.

In 386 B.C.E., he founded the Academy, a center of philosophical investigation and a school for training statesmen and citizens. It had a powerful impact on Greek thought and lasted until it was closed by the emperor Justinian in the sixth century C.E.

Like Socrates, Plato firmly believed in the *polis* and its values. Its virtues were order, harmony, and justice, and one of its main objects was to produce good people. Like his master, and unlike the radical Sophists, Plato thought that the *polis* was in accord with nature. He accepted Socrates' doctrine of the identity of virtue and knowledge. He made it plain what that knowledge was: *episteme*—science—a body of true and unchanging wisdom open to only a few philosophers, whose training, character, and intellect allowed them to see reality. Only such people were qualified to rule; they would prefer the life of pure contemplation, but would accept their responsibility and take their turn as philosopher kings. The training of such an individual required a specialization of function and a subordination of that individual to the community even greater than that at Sparta. This specialization would lead to Plato's definition of justice: that each person should do only that one thing to which his or her nature is best suited. (See "Plato on the Role of Women in His Utopian Republic.")

Plato saw quite well that the *polis* of his day suffered from terrible internal stress, class struggle, and factional divisions. His solution, however, was not that of some Greeks—that is, conquest and resulting economic prosperity. For Plato, the answer was in moral and political reform. The way to harmony was to destroy the causes of strife: private property, the family—anything, in short, that stood between the individual citizen and devotion to the *polis*.

Concern for the redemption of the polis was at the heart of Plato's system of philosophy. He began by asking the traditional questions: What is a good man, and how is he made? The goodness of a human being belonged to moral philosophy, and when goodness became a function of the state, it became political philosophy. Because goodness depended on knowledge of the good, it required a theory of knowledge and an investigation of what kind of knowledge was required for goodness. The answer must be metaphysical and so required a full examination of metaphysics. Even when the philosopher knew the good,

[4]Diogenes Laertius, *Life of Antisthenes*, 6.11.

however, the question remained how the state could bring its citizens to the necessary comprehension of that knowledge. The answer required a theory of education. Even purely logical and metaphysical questions, therefore, were subordinate to the overriding political questions. In this way, Plato's need to find a satisfactory foundation for the beleaguered polis contributed to the birth of systematic philosophy.

ARISTOTLE   Aristotle (384–322 B.C.E.) was a pupil of Plato's and owed much to the thought of his master, but his very different experience and cast of mind led him in some new directions. He was born at Stagirus in the Chalcidice, the son of the court doctor of neighboring Macedon. As a young man, he went to Athens to study at the Academy, where he stayed until Plato's death. Then he joined a Platonic colony at Assos in Asia Minor, and from there he moved to Mytilene. In both places he did research in marine biology, and biological interests played a large part in all his thoughts. In 342 B.C.E., Philip, the king of Macedon, appointed him tutor to his son, the young Alexander. (See the next section.)

In 336 B.C.E. Aristotle returned to Athens, where he founded his own school, the Lyceum, or the Peripatos, as it was also called because of the covered walk within it. In later years its members were called *Peripatetics*. On the death of Alexander in 323 B.C.E., the Athenians rebelled from Macedonian rule, and Aristotle found it wise to leave. He died at Chalcis in Euboea in the following year.

The Lyceum was a very different place from the Academy. Its members took little interest in mathematics and were concerned with gathering, ordering, and analyzing all human knowledge. Aristotle wrote dialogues on the Platonic model, but none survive. He and his students also prepared many collections of information to serve as the basis for scientific works. Of these, only the *Constitution of the Athenians*, one of 158 constitutional treatises, remains. Almost all of what we possess is in the form of philosophical and scientific studies, whose loose organization and style suggest that they were lecture notes. The range of subjects treated is astonishing, including logic, physics, astronomy, biology, ethics, rhetoric, literary criticism, and politics.

In each field, the method is the same. Aristotle began with observation of the empirical evidence, which in some cases was physical and in others was common opinion. To this body of information he applied reason and discovered inconsistencies or difficulties. To deal with these, he introduced metaphysical principles to explain the problems or to reconcile the inconsistencies.

Marble head of Aristotle.   Louvre, Dept. des Antiquities Grecques/Romaines, Paris, France. © Photograph by Erich Lessing/ Art Resource, NY

His view on all subjects, like Plato's, was teleological; that is, both Plato and Aristotle recognized purposes apart from and greater than the will of the individual human being. Plato's purposes, however, were contained in ideas, or forms that were transcendental concepts outside the experience of most people. For Aristotle, the purposes of most things were easily inferred by observation of their behavior in the world. Aristotle's most striking characteristics are his moderation and his common sense. His epistemology finds room for both reason and experience; his metaphysics gives meaning and reality to both mind and body; his ethics aims at the good life, which is the contemplative life, but recognizes the necessity for moderate wealth, comfort, and pleasure.

All these qualities are evident in Aristotle's political thought. Like Plato, he opposed the Sophists' assertion that the *polis* was contrary to nature and the result of mere convention. His response was to apply the teleology he saw in all nature to politics as well. In his view, matter existed to achieve an end, and it developed until it achieved its form, which was its end. There was constant development from matter to form, from potential to actual. Therefore, human primitive instincts could be seen as the matter out of which the human's potential as a political being could be realized. The

Plato on the Role of Women in His Utopian Republic

The Greek invention of reasoned intellectual analysis of all things led the philosopher Plato to consider the problem of justice, which is the subject of his most famous dialogue, the Republic. *This leads him to sketch out a utopian state in which justice may be found and where the most radical arrangements may be necessary. These include the equality of the sexes and the destruction of the family in favor of the practice of men having wives and children in common. In the following excerpts, he argues for the fundamental equality of men and women and that women are no less appropriate as Guardians—leaders of the state— than men.*

❖ *What are Plato's reasons for treating men and women the same? What objections could be raised to that practice? Would that policy, even if appropriate in Plato's utopia, also be suitable to conditions in the real world of classical Athens? In the world of today?*

"If, then, we use the women for the same things as the men, they must also be taught the same things."

"Yes."

"Now music and gymnastics were given to the men."

"Yes."

"Then these two arts, and what has to do with war, must be assigned to the women also, and they must be used in the same ways."

"On the basis of what you say," he said, "it's likely."

"Perhaps," I said, "compared to what is habitual, many of the things now being said would look ridiculous if they were to be done as is said."

"Indeed they would," he said.

"Well," I said, "since we've started to speak, we mustn't be afraid of all the jokes—of whatever kind—the wits might make if such a change took place in gymnastic, in music and, not the least, in the bearing of arms and the riding of horses."

"Then," I said, "if either the class of men or that of women show its superiority in some art or other practice, then we'll say that that art must be assigned to it. But if they look as though they differ in this along, that the female bears and the male mounts, we'll assert that it has not thereby yet been proved that a woman differs from a man with respect to what we're talking about; rather, we'll still suppose that our guardians and their women must practice the same things."

"And rightly," he said.

"Therefore, my friend, there is no practice of a city's governors which belongs to woman because she's woman, or to man because he's man; but the natures are scattered alike among both animals; and woman participates according to nature in all practices, and man in all, but in all of them woman is weaker than man."

"Certainly."

"So, shall we assign all of them to men and none to women?"

"How could we?"

"For I suppose there is, as we shall assert, one woman apt at medicine and another not, one woman apt at music and another unmusical by nature."

"Of course."

"And isn't there then also one apt at gymnastic and at war, and another unwarlike and no lover of gymnastic?"

"I suppose so."

"And what about this? Is there a lover of wisdom and a hater of wisdom? And one who is spirited and another without spirit?"

"Yes, there are these too."

"There is, therefore one woman fit for guarding and another not, or wasn't it a nature of this sort we also selected for the men fit for guarding?"

"Certainly, that was it."

From *The Republic of Plato*, (2nd ed.) translated by Allan Bloom. Copyright © 1968 by Allan Bloom. Preface to paperback edition, © 1991 by Allan Bloom, pp. 130–134. Reprinted by permission of Basic Books, a member of Perseus Books, L.L.C.

polis made individuals self-sufficient and allowed the full realization of their potentiality. It was therefore natural.

It was also the highest point in the evolution of the social institutions that serve the human need to continue the species—marriage, household, village, and, finally, *polis*. For Aristotle, the purpose of the *polis* was neither economic nor military, but moral. According to Aristotle, "The end of the state is the good life" (*Politics* 1280b), the life lived "for the sake of noble actions" (1281a), a life of virtue and morality.

Characteristically, Aristotle was less interested in the best state—the utopia that required philosophers to rule it—than in the best state that was practically possible, one that would combine justice with stability. The constitution for that state he called *politeia*, not the best constitution, but the next best, the one most suited to, and most possible for most states. Its quality was moderation, and it naturally gave power to neither the rich nor the poor, but to the middle class, which must also be the most numerous. The middle class possessed many virtues; because of its moderate wealth, it was free of the arrogance of the rich and the malice of the poor. For this reason, it was the most stable class.

The stability of the constitution also came from its being a mixed constitution, blending in some way the laws of democracy and of oligarchy. Aristotle's scheme was unique because of its realism and the breadth of its vision. All the political thinkers of the fourth century B.C.E. recognized that the *polis* was in danger, and all hoped to save it. All recognized the economic and social troubles that threatened it. Isocrates, a contemporary of Plato and Aristotle, urged a program of imperial conquest as a cure for poverty and revolution. Plato saw the folly of solving a political and moral problem by purely economic means and resorted to the creation of utopias. Aristotle combined the practical analysis of political and economic realities with the moral and political purposes of the traditional defenders of the *polis*. The result was a passionate confidence in the virtues of moderation and of the middle class and the proposal of a constitution that would give it power. It is ironic that the ablest defense of the *polis* came soon before its demise.

The Hellenistic World

The term "Hellenistic" was coined in the nineteenth century to describe the period of three centuries during which Greek culture spread far from its homeland to Egypt and far into Asia. The new civilization formed in this expansion was a mixture of Greek and Near Eastern elements, although the degree of mixture varied from time to time and place to place. The Hellenistic world was larger than the world of Classical Greece, and its major political units were much larger than the city–states, though these persisted in different forms. The new political and cultural order had its roots in the rise to power of a Macedonian dynasty that conquered Greece and the Persian Empire in the space of two generations.

The Macedonian Conquest

The quarrels among the Greeks brought on defeat and conquest by a new power that suddenly rose to eminence in the fourth century B.C.E.: the kingdom of Macedon. The Macedonians inhabited the land to the north of Thessaly (see Map 3–1), and through the centuries they had unknowingly served the vital purpose of protecting the Greek states from barbarian tribes further to the north.

By Greek standards, Macedon was a backward, semibarbaric land. It had no *poleis* and was ruled loosely by a king in a rather Homeric fashion. He was chosen partly on the basis of descent, but the acclamation of the army gathered in assembly was required to make him legitimate. Quarrels between pretenders to the throne and even murder to secure it were not uncommon. A council of nobles checked the royal power and could reject a weak or incompetent king. Hampered by constant wars with the barbarians, internal strife, loose organization, and lack of money, Macedon played no great part in Greek affairs up to the fourth century B.C.E.

The Macedonians were of the same stock as the Greeks and spoke a Greek dialect, and the nobles, at least, thought of themselves as Greeks. The kings claimed descent from Heracles and the royal house of Argos. They tried to bring Greek culture into their court and won acceptance at the Olympic games. If a king could be found to unify this nation, it was bound to play a greater part in Greek affairs.

PHILIP OF MACEDON   That king was Philip II (r. 359–336 B.C.E.), who, while still under thirty, took advantage of his appointment as regent to overthrow his infant nephew and make himself king. Like many of his predecessors, he admired Greek culture. Between 367 and 364 B.C.E. he had been a hostage in Thebes, where he learned much about Greek politics and warfare under the tutelage of Epaminondas. His talents for war and diplomacy and his boundless ambition made him the ablest king in Macedonian history. Using both diplomatic and military means, he was able to pacify the tribes on his frontiers and make his own hold on the throne firmer. Then he began to undermine Athenian control of the northern Aegean. He took Amphipolis, which gave him control of the Strymon Valley and of the gold and silver mines of Mount Pangaeus. The income allowed him to found new cities, to bribe politicians in foreign towns, and to reorganize his army into the finest fighting force in the world.

THE MACEDONIAN ARMY Philip put to good use what he had learned in Thebes and combined it with the advantages afforded by Macedonian society and tradition. His genius created a versatile and powerful army that was at once national and professional, unlike the amateur armies of citizen–soldiers who fought for the individual *poleis*.

The infantry was drawn from among Macedonian farmers and the frequently rebellious Macedonian hill people. In time, these two elements were integrated to form a loyal and effective national force. Infantrymen were armed with thirteen-foot pikes instead of the more common nine-foot pikes and stood in a more open phalanx formation than the

hoplite phalanx of the *poleis*. The effectiveness of this formation depended more on skillful use of the pike than the weight of the charge. In Macedonian tactics, the role of the phalanx was not to be the decisive force, but to hold the enemy until a massed cavalry charge could strike a winning blow on the flank or into a gap. The cavalry was made up of Macedonian nobles and clan leaders, called Companions, who lived closely with the king and developed a special loyalty to him.

Philip also employed mercenaries who knew the latest tactics used by mobile light-armed Greek troops and were familiar with the most sophisticated siege machinery known to the Greeks. With these mercenaries, and with draft forces from among his allies, he could expand on his native Macedonian army of as many as 40,000 men.

THE INVASION OF GREECE So armed, Philip turned south toward central Greece. Since 355 B.C.E., the Phocians had been fighting against Thebes and Thessaly. Philip gladly accepted the request of the Thessalians to be their general, defeated Phocis, and treacherously took control of Thessaly. Swiftly he

Demosthenes Denounces Philip of Macedon

Demosthenes (384–322 B.C.E.) was an Athenian statesman who urged his fellow citizens and other Greeks to resist the advance of Philip of Macedon (r. 359–336 B.C.E.). This passage is from the speech we call the **First Philippic,** *probably delivered in 351 B.C.E.*

❖ *Whom does Demosthenes blame for the danger facing Athens? What hope does he see of stopping Philip's advance? How important is Philip himself, according to Demosthenes, as a source of the menace to Athens and the rest of Greece?*

Do not imagine, that his empire is everlastingly secured to him as a god. There are those who hate and fear and envy him, Athenians, even among those that seem most friendly; and all feelings that are in other men belong, we may assume, to his confederates. But now they are cowed, having no refuge through your tardiness and indolence, which I say you must abandon forthwith. For you see, Athenians, the case, to what pitch of arrogance the man has advanced, who leaves you not even the choice of action or inaction, but threatens and uses (they say) outrageous language, and, unable to rest in possession of his conquests, continually widens their circle, and whilst we dally and delay, throws his net all around us.

When then, Athenians, when will ye act as becomes you? In what event? In that of necessity, I suppose. And how should we regard the events happening now? Methinks, to freemen the strongest necessity is the disgrace of their condition. Or tell me, do ye like walking about and asking one another:—is there any news? Why, could there be greater news than a man of Macedonia subduing Athenians, and directing the affairs of Greece? Is Philip dead? No, but he is sick. And what matters it to you? Should anything befall this man, you will soon create another Philip, if you attend to business thus. For even he has been exalted not so much by his own strength, as by our negligence.

Demosthenes, *The Olynthiac and Other Public Orations of Demosthenes* (London: George Bell and Sons, 1903), pp. 62–63.

turned northward again to Thrace and gained domination over the northern Aegean coast and the European side of the straits to the Black Sea. This conquest threatened the vital interests of Athens, which still had a formidable fleet of 300 ships.

The Athens of 350 B.C.E. was not the Athens of Pericles. It had neither imperial revenue nor allies to share the burden of war on land or sea, and its own population was smaller than in the fifth century B.C.E. The Athenians, therefore, were reluctant to go on expeditions themselves or even to send out mercenary armies under Athenian generals, for they had to be paid out of taxes or contributions from Athenian citizens.

The leading spokesman against these tendencies and the cautious foreign policy that went with them was Demosthenes (384–322 B.C.E.), one of the greatest orators in Greek history. He was convinced that Philip was a dangerous enemy to Athens and the other Greeks. He spent most of his career urging the Athenians to resist Philip's encroachments. (See "Demosthenes Denounces Philip of Macedon.") He was right, for beginning in 349 B.C.E., Philip attacked several cities in northern and central Greece and firmly planted Macedonian power in those regions. The king of "barbarian" Macedon was elected president of the Pythian Games at Delphi, and the Athenians were forced to concur in the election.

In these difficult times it was Athens' misfortune not to have the kind of consistent political leadership that Cimon or Pericles had offered a century earlier. Many, perhaps most, Athenians accepted Demosthenes' view of Philip, but few were willing to run the risks and make the sacrifices necessary to stop his advance. Others, like Eubulus, an outstanding financial official and conservative political leader, favored a cautious policy of cooperation with Philip in the hope that his aims were limited and were no real threat to Athens.

Not all Athenians feared Philip. Isocrates (436–338 B.C.E.), the head of an important rhetorical and philosophical school in Athens, looked to him to provide the unity and leadership needed for a Panhellenic campaign against Persia. He and other orators had been urging such a campaign for some years. They saw the conquest of Asia Minor as the solution to the economic, social, and political problems that had brought poverty and civil war to the Greek cities ever since the Peloponnesian War. Finally, there seem to have been some Athenians who were in the pay of Philip, for he used money lavishly to win support in all the cities.

The years between 346 B.C.E. and 340 B.C.E. were spent in diplomatic maneuvering, each side trying to win strategically useful allies. At last, Philip attacked Perinthus and Byzantium, the lifeline of Athenian commerce; in 340 B.C.E. he besieged both cities and declared war. The Athenian fleet saved both, and so in the following year Philip marched into Greece. Demosthenes performed wonders in rallying the Athenians and winning Thebes over to the Athenian side. In 338 B.C.E., however, Philip defeated the allied forces at Chaeronea in Boeotia. The decisive blow in this great battle was a cavalry charge led by the eighteen-year-old son of Philip, Alexander.

THE MACEDONIAN GOVERNMENT OF GREECE The Macedonian settlement of Greek affairs was not as harsh as many had feared, although in some cities the friends of Macedon came to power and killed or exiled their enemies. Demosthenes remained free to engage in politics. Athens was spared from attack on the condition that it give up what was left of its empire and follow the lead of Macedon. The rest of Greece was arranged in such a way as to remove all dangers to Philip's rule. To guarantee his security, Philip placed garrisons at Thebes, Chalcis, and Corinth.

In 338 B.C.E., Philip called a meeting of the Greek states to form the federal League of Corinth. The constitution of the league provided for autonomy, freedom from tribute and garrisons, and suppression of piracy and civil war. The league delegates would make foreign policy in theory without consulting their home governments or Philip. All this was a facade; not only was Philip of Macedon president of the league, but he was its ruler. The defeat at Chaeronea ended Greek freedom and autonomy. Although it maintained its form and way of life for some time, the *polis* had lost control of its own affairs and the special conditions that had made it unique.

Philip did not choose Corinth as the seat of his new confederacy simply from convenience or by accident. It was at Corinth that the Greeks had gathered to resist a Persian invasion almost 150 years earlier. And it was there in 337 B.C.E. that Philip announced his intention to invade Persia in a war of liberation and revenge as leader of the new league. In the spring of 336 B.C.E., however, as he prepared to begin the campaign, Philip was assassinated.

In 1977, a mound was excavated at the Macedonian village of Vergina. The structures that were revealed and the extraordinarily rich finds associated with them have led many scholars to conclude that this is the royal tomb of Philip II, and the evidence seems persuasive that they are right. Philip certainly deserved so distinguished a resting place. He found Macedon a disunited kingdom of semibarbarians, despised and exploited by the Greeks. He left it a united kingdom, master and leader of the Greeks, rich, powerful, and ready to undertake the invasion of Asia.

Alexander the Great

Philip's first son, Alexander III (356–323 B.C.E.), later called Alexander the Great, succeeded his father at the age of twenty. Along with the throne, the young king inherited his father's daring plans for the conquest of Persia.

THE CONQUEST OF THE PERSIAN EMPIRE The Persian Empire was vast and its resources enormous. The usurper Cyrus and his Greek mercenaries, however, had shown it to be vulnerable when they penetrated deep into its interior in the fourth century B.C.E. Its size and disparate nature made it hard to control and exploit. Its rulers faced constant troubles on its far-flung frontiers and constant intrigues within the royal palace. Throughout the fourth century B.C.E. they had called on Greek mercenaries to suppress uprisings. At the time of Philip II's death in 336 B.C.E., Persia was ruled by a new and inexperienced king, Darius III. Yet with a navy that dominated the sea, a huge army, and vast wealth, it remained a formidable opponent.

In 334 B.C.E., Alexander crossed the Hellespont into Asia. His army consisted of about 30,000 infantry and 5,000 cavalry; he had no navy and little money. These facts determined his early strategy—he must seek quick and decisive battles to gain money and supplies from the conquered territory, and he must move along the coast to neutralize the Persian navy by depriving it of ports. Memnon, the commander of the Persian navy, recommended the perfect strategy against this plan: to retreat, to scorch the earth and deprive Alexander of supplies, to avoid battles, to use guerrilla tactics, and to stir up rebellion in Greece. He was ignored. The Persians preferred to stand and fight; their pride and courage were greater than their wisdom.

Alexander met the Persian forces of Asia Minor at the Granicus River, where he won a smashing victory in characteristic style. (See Map 3–4.) He led a cavalry charge across the river into the teeth of the enemy on the opposite bank. He almost lost his life in the process, but he won the devotion of his soldiers. That victory left the coast of Asia Minor open. Alexander captured the coastal cities, thus denying them to the Persian fleet.

In 333 B.C.E., Alexander marched inland to Syria, where he met the main Persian army under King Darius at Issus. Alexander himself led the cavalry charge that broke the Persian line and sent Darius fleeing into central Asia Minor. He continued along the coast and captured previously impregnable Tyre after a long and ingenious siege, putting an end to the threat of the Persian navy. He took Egypt with little trouble and was greeted as liberator, pharaoh, and son of Re (an Egyptian god whose Greek equivalent was Zeus).

At Tyre, Darius sent Alexander a peace offer, yielding his entire empire west of the Euphrates River and his daughter in exchange for an alliance and an end to the invasion. But Alexander aimed at conquering the whole empire and probably whatever lay beyond.

In the spring of 331 B.C.E., Alexander marched into Mesopotamia. At Gaugamela, near the ancient Assyrian city of Nineveh, he met Darius, ready for a last stand. Once again, Alexander's tactical genius and personal leadership carried the day. The Persians were broken, and Darius fled

This sculpture of Alexander the Great, king of Macedon and conqueror of the Persian Empire, was made in the second century B.C.E. and found at the ancient city of Magnesia in Asia Minor. Alexander's conquests spread Greek culture far from its homeland, laying the foundation of the Hellenistic world. Statue from Magnesia ad Sipylum. Archeological Museum, Istanbul, Turkey. Erich Lessing/Art Resource, N.Y.

once more. Alexander entered Babylon, again hailed as liberator and king.

In January of 330 B.C.E. he came to Persepolis, the Persian capital, which held splendid palaces and the royal treasury. This bonanza ended his financial troubles and put a vast sum of money into circulation, with economic consequences that lasted for centuries. After a stay of several months, Alexander burned Persepolis to dramatize the destruction of the native Persian dynasty and the completion of Hellenic revenge for the earlier Persian invasion of Greece.

The new regime could not be secure while Darius lived, so Alexander pursued him eastward. Just south of the Caspian Sea, he came upon the corpse of Darius, killed by his relative Bessus. The Persian nobles around Darius had lost faith in him and had joined in the plot. The murder removed Darius from Alexander's path, but now he had to catch Bessus, who proclaimed himself successor to Darius. The pursuit of Bessus (who was soon caught), combined with his own great curiosity and longing to go to the most distant places, took Alexander to the frontier of India.

Near Samarkand, in the land of the Scythians, he founded Alexandria Eschate ("Furthest Alexandria"), one of the many cities bearing his name that he founded as he traveled. As part of his grand scheme of amalgamation and conquest, he married the Bactrian princess Roxane and enrolled 30,000 young Bactrians into his army. These were to be trained and sent back to the center of the empire for later use.

In 327 B.C.E., Alexander took his army through the Khyber Pass in an attempt to conquer the lands around the Indus River (modern Pakistan). He reduced the king of these lands, Porus, to vassalage, but pushed on in the hope of reaching the river called Ocean that the Greeks believed encircled the world. Finally, his weary men refused to go on. By the spring of 324 B.C.E., the army was back at the Persian Gulf and celebrated in the Macedonian style, with a wild spree of drinking.

THE DEATH OF ALEXANDER   Alexander was filled with plans for the future: for the consolidation and organization of his empire; for geographical exploration; for building new cities, roads, and harbors; and perhaps even for further conquests in the west. There is even some evidence that he asked to be deified and worshiped as a god, although we cannot be sure if he really did so or why. In June of 323 B.C.E., however, he was overcome by a fever and died in Babylon at the age of thirty-three. His memory has never faded, and he soon became the subject of myth, legend, and romance. From the beginning, estimates of him have varied. Some have seen in him a man of grand and noble vision who transcended the narrow limits of Greek and Macedonian ethnocentrism and sought to realize the solidarity of hu-

mankind in a great world state. Others have seen him as a calculating despot, given to drunken brawls, brutality, and murder.

The truth is probably somewhere in between. Alexander was one of the greatest generals the world has seen; he never lost a battle or failed in a siege, and with a modest army he conquered a vast empire. He had rare organizational talents, and his plan for creating a multinational empire was the only intelligent way to consolidate his conquests. He established many new cities—seventy, according to tradition—mostly along trade routes. These cities had the effect of encouraging commerce and prosperity, as well as of introducing Hellenic civilization into new areas. It is hard to know if even Alexander could have held together the vast new empire he had created, but his death proved that only he would have had a chance to succeed.

The Successors

Nobody was prepared for Alexander's sudden death in 323 B.C.E., and affairs were further complicated by a weak succession: Roxane's unborn child and Alexander's weak-minded half-brother. His able and loyal Macedonian generals at first hoped to preserve the empire for the Macedonian royal house, and to this end they appointed themselves governors of the various provinces of the empire. The conflicting ambitions of these strong-willed men, however, led to prolonged warfare among various combinations of them. In these conflicts three of the original number were killed, and all of the direct members of the Macedonian royal house were either executed or murdered. With the murder of Roxane and her son in 310 B.C.E., there was no longer any focus for the enormous empire, and in 306 and 305 B.C.E. the surviving governors proclaimed themselves kings of their various holdings.

Three of these Macedonian generals founded dynasties of significance in the spread of Hellenistic culture:

- Ptolemy I, 367–283 B.C.E.; founder of the Thirty-First Dynasty in Egypt, the Ptolemies, of whom Cleopatra, who died in 30 B.C.E., was the last
- Seleucus I, 358–280 B.C.E.; founder of the Seleucid Dynasty in Mesopotamia
- Antigonus I, 382–301 B.C.E.; founder of the Antigonid Dynasty in Asia Minor and Macedon

For the first seventy-five years or so after the death of Alexander, the world ruled by his successors enjoyed considerable prosperity. The vast sums of money that he and they put into circulation greatly increased the level of economic activity. The opportunities for service and profit in the East attracted

MAP 3–4 ALEXANDER'S CAMPAIGNS *The route taken by Alexander the Great in his conquest of the Persian Empire, 334–323 B.C.E. Starting from the Macedonian capital at Pella, he reached the Indus Valley before being turned back by his own restive troops. He died of fever in Mesopotamia.*

The Rise of Macedon	
359–336 B.C.E.	Reign of Philip II
338 B.C.E.	Battle of Chaeronea; Philip conquers Greece
338 B.C.E.	Founding of League of Corinth
336–323 B.C.E.	Reign of Alexander III, the Great
334 B.C.E.	Alexander invades Asia
333 B.C.E.	Battle of Issus
331 B.C.E.	Battle of Gaugamela
330 B.C.E.	Fall of Persepolis
327 B.C.E.	Alexander reaches Indus Valley
323 B.C.E.	Death of Alexander

many Greeks and relieved their native cities of some of the pressure of the poor. The opening of vast new territories to Greek trade, the increased demand for Greek products, and the new availability of desired goods, as well as the conscious policies of the Hellenistic kings, all helped the growth of commerce.

The new prosperity, however, was not evenly distributed. The urban Greeks, the Macedonians, and the Hellenized natives who made up the upper and middle classes lived in comfort and even luxury, but the rural native peasants did not. Unlike the independent men who owned and worked the relatively small and equal lots of the *polis* in earlier times, Hellenistic farmers were reduced to subordinate, dependent, peasant status, working on large plantations of decreasing efficiency. During prosperous times these distinctions were bearable, although even then there was tension between the two groups. After a while, however, the costs of continuing wars, inflation, and a gradual lessening of the positive effects of the introduction of Persian wealth all led to economic crisis. The kings bore down heavily on the middle classes, who were skilled at avoiding their responsibilities, however. The pressure on the peasants and the city laborers became great, too, and they responded by slowing down their work and even by striking. In Greece, economic pressures brought clashes between rich and poor, demands for the abolition of debt and the redistribution of land, and even, on occasion, civil war.

These internal divisions, along with international wars, weakened the capacity of the Hellenistic kingdoms to resist outside attack. By the middle of the second century B.C.E. they had all, except for Egypt, succumbed to an expanding Italian power, Rome. The two centuries between Alexander and the Roman conquest, however, were of great and lasting

importance. They saw the entire eastern Mediterranean coast, Greece, Egypt, Mesopotamia, and the old Persian Empire formed into a single political, economic, and cultural unit.

Hellenistic Culture

The career of Alexander the Great marked a significant turning point in Greek thought as it was represented in literature, philosophy, religion, and art. His conquests and the establishment of the successor kingdoms put an end to the central role of the *polis* in Greek life and thought. Some scholars disagree about the end of the *polis*, denying that Philip's victory at Chaeronea marked its demise. They point to the persistence of *poleis* throughout the Hellenistic period and even see a continuation of them in the Roman *municipia*. These were, however, only a shadow of the vital reality that had been the true *polis*.

Deprived of control of their foreign affairs, and with their important internal arrangements determined by a foreign monarch, the post-Classical cities lost the kind of political freedom that was basic to the old outlook. They were cities, perhaps—in a sense, even city–states—but not *poleis*. As time passed, they changed from sovereign states to municipal towns merged in military empires. Never again in antiquity would there be either a serious attack on or defense of the *polis*, for its importance was gone. For the most part, the Greeks after Alexander turned away from political solutions for their problems. Instead, they sought personal responses to their hopes and fears, particularly in religion, philosophy, and magic. The confident, sometimes arrogant, humanism of the fifth century B.C.E. gave way to a kind of resignation to fate, a recognition of helplessness before forces too great for humans to manage.

Philosophy

These developments are noticeable in the changes that overtook the established schools of philosophy as well as in the emergence of two new and influential groups of philosophers: the Epicureans and the Stoics. Athens' position as the center of philosophical studies was reinforced, for the Academy and the Lyceum continued in operation, and the new schools were also located in Athens. The Lyceum turned gradually away from the universal investigations of its founder, Aristotle, even from his scientific interests, to become a center chiefly of literary and especially historical studies.

The Academy turned even further away from its tradition. It adopted the systematic Skepticism of

Pyrrho of Elis. Under the leadership of Arcesilaus and Carneades, the Skeptics of the Academy became skilled at pointing out fallacies and weaknesses in the philosophies of the rival schools. They thought that nothing could be known and so consoled themselves and their followers by suggesting that nothing mattered. It was easy for them, therefore, to accept conventional morality and the world as it was. The Cynics, of course, continued to denounce convention and to advocate the crude life in accordance with nature, which some of them practiced publicly to the shock and outrage of respectable citizens. Neither Skepticism nor Cynicism had much appeal to the middle-class city dweller of the third century B.C.E., who sought some basis for choosing a way of life now that the *polis* no longer provided one ready made.

THE EPICUREANS   Epicurus of Athens (342–271 B.C.E.) formulated a new teaching, embodied in the school he founded in his native city in 306 B.C.E. His philosophy conformed to the mood of the times in that its goal was not knowledge, but human happiness, which he believed could be achieved if one followed a style of life based on reason. He took sense perception to be the basis of all human knowledge. The reality and reliability of sense perception rested on the acceptance of the physical universe described by the atomists, Democritus and Leucippus. The Epicureans proclaimed that atoms were continually falling through the void and giving off images that were in direct contact with the senses. These falling atoms could swerve in an arbitrary, unpredictable way to produce the combinations seen in the world.

Epicurus thereby removed an element of determinism that existed in the Democritean system. When a person died, the atoms that composed the body dispersed so that the person had no further existence or perception and therefore nothing to fear after death. Epicurus believed that the gods existed, but that they took no interest in human affairs. This belief amounted to a practical atheism, and Epicureans were often thought to be atheists.

The purpose of Epicurean physics was to liberate people from their fear of death, of the gods, and of all nonmaterial or supernatural powers. Epicurean ethics were hedonistic, that is, based on the acceptance of pleasure as true happiness. But pleasure for Epicurus was chiefly negative: the absence of pain and trouble. The goal of the Epicureans was *ataraxia*, the condition of being undisturbed, without trouble, pain, or responsibility. Ideally, a man should have enough means to allow him to withdraw from the world and avoid business and public life. Epicurus even advised against marriage and children. He preached a life of genteel, restrained selfishness that might appeal to intellectual men of means, but was not calculated to be widely attractive.

THE STOICS   Soon after Epicurus began teaching in his garden in Athens, Zeno of Citium in Cyprus (335–263 B.C.E.) established the Stoic school. It derived its name from the *stoa poikile*, or painted portico, in the Athenian *agora*, where Zeno and his disciples walked and talked beginning about 300 B.C.E. From then until about the middle of the second century B.C.E., Zeno and his successors preached a philosophy that owed a good deal to Socrates, by way of the Cynics. It was fed also by a stream of Eastern thought. Zeno, of course, came from Phoenician Cyprus; Chrysippus, one of his successors, came from Cilicia; and other early Stoics came from such places as Carthage, Tarsus, and Babylon.

Like the Epicureans, the Stoics sought the happiness of the individual. Quite unlike them, the Stoics proposed a philosophy almost indistinguishable from religion. They believed that humans must live in harmony within themselves and in harmony with nature; for the Stoics, god and nature were the same. The guiding principle in nature was divine reason (*Logos*), or fire. Every human had a spark of this divinity, and after death it returned to the eternal divine spirit. From time to time the world was destroyed by fire, from which a new world arose.

The aim of humans, and the definition of human happiness, was the virtuous life: a life lived in accordance with natural law, "when all actions promote the harmony of the spirit dwelling in the individual man with the will of him who orders the universe."[5] To live such a life required the knowledge possessed only by the wise, who knew what was good, what was evil, and what was neither, but "indifferent." According to the Stoics, good and evil were dispositions of the mind or soul: prudence, justice, courage, temperance, and so on were good, whereas folly, injustice, cowardice, and the like were evil. Life, health, pleasure, beauty, strength, wealth, and so on, were neutral—morally indifferent—for they did not contribute either to happiness or to misery. Human misery came from an irrational mental contraction—from passion, which was a disease of the soul. The wise sought *apatheia*, or freedom from passion, because passion arose from things that were morally indifferent.

Politically, the Stoics fit well into the new world. They thought of it as a single *polis* in which

[5]Diogenes Laertius, Life of Antisthenes, 6 11.

Plutarch Cites Archimedes and Hellenistic Science

Archimedes (ca. 287–211 B.C.E.) was one of the great mathematicians and physicists of antiquity. He was a native of Syracuse in Sicily and a friend of its king. Plutarch discusses him in the following selection and reveals much about the ancient attitude toward applied science.

❖ *Was the attitude toward science and technology attributed to Archimedes by Plutarch common in the ancient world? How can that attitude be explained? If it was common, what were the consequences? Are distinctions between the importance of pure science and applied science made in the modern world? If so, are they the same as the ancient ones? How do you explain any similarities or differences?*

Archimedes, however, in writing to King Hiero, whose friend and near relation he was, had stated that given the force, any given weight might be moved, and even boasted, we are told, relying on the strength of demonstration, that if there were another earth, by going into it he could remove this. Hiero being struck with amazement at this, and entreating him to make good this problem by actual experiment, and show some great weight moved by a small engine, he fixed accordingly upon a ship of burden out of the king's arsenal, which could not be drawn out of the dock without great labour and many men; and, loading her with many passengers and a full freight, sitting himself the while far off, with no great endeavor, but only holding the head of the pulley in his hand and drawing the cords by degrees. ... Yet Archimedes possessed so high a spirit, so profound a soul, and such treasures of scientific knowledge, that though these inventions had now obtained him the renown of more than human sagacity, he yet would not deign to leave behind him any commentary or writing on such subjects; but, repudiating as sordid and ignoble the whole trade of engineering, and every sort of art that lends itself to mere use and profit, he placed his whole affection and ambition in those purer speculations where there can be no reference to the vulgar needs of life.

From Plutarch, "Marcellus," in *Lives of the Noble Grecians and Romans*, trans. by John Dryden, rev. by A. H. Clough (New York: Random House, n.d.), pp. 376–378.

all people were children of the same god. Although they did not forbid political activity, and many Stoics took part in political life, withdrawal was obviously preferable because the usual subjects of political argument were indifferent. Because the Stoics strove for inner harmony of the individual, their aim was a life lived in accordance with the divine will, their attitude fatalistic, and their goal a form of apathy. They fit in well with the reality of post-Alexandrian life. In fact, the spread of Stoicism facilitated the task of creating a new political system that relied not on the active participation of the governed, but merely on their docile submission.

Literature

The literature of the Hellenistic period reflects the new intellectual currents, the new conditions of literary life, and the new institutions created in that period. The center of literary production in the third and second centuries B.C.E. was the new city of Alexandria in Egypt. There the Ptolemies, the monarchs of Egypt during that time, founded the museum—a great research institute where royal funds supported scientists and scholars—and the library, which contained almost half a million volumes of papyrus scrolls.

The library contained much of the great body of past Greek literature, most of which has since been lost. The Alexandrian scholars saw to it that what they judged to be the best works were copied. They edited and criticized these works from the point of view of language, form, and content and wrote biographies of the authors. Their work is responsible for the preservation of most of what remains to us of ancient literature. Much of their work proved valuable, but some of it is dry, petty, quarrelsome, and simply foolish. At its best, however, it is full of learning and perception.

The scholarly atmosphere of Alexandria naturally gave rise to work in the field of history and its ancillary discipline, chronology. Eratosthenes (ca. 275–195 B.C.E.) established a chronology of important events dating from the Trojan War, and others undertook similar tasks. Contemporaries of Alexander, such as Ptolemy I, Aristobulus, and Nearchus, wrote what were apparently sober and essentially factual accounts of his career. Most of the work done by Hellenistic historians is known to us only in fragments cited by later writers. It seems in general to have emphasized sensational and biographical detail over the kind of rigorous impersonal analysis that marked the work of Thucydides.

Architecture and Sculpture

The advent of the Hellenistic monarchies greatly increased the opportunities open to architects and sculptors. Money was plentiful, rulers sought outlets for conspicuous display, new cities needed to be built and beautified, and the well-to-do created an increasing demand for objects of art. The new cities were usually laid out on the grid plan introduced in the fifth century B.C.E. by Hippodamus of Miletus. Temples were built on the classical model, and the covered portico, or stoa, became a very popular addition to the agoras of the Hellenistic towns.

Reflecting the cosmopolitan nature of the Hellenistic world, leading sculptors accepted commissions wherever they were attractive. The result was a certain uniformity of style, although Alexandria, Rhodes, and the kingdom of Pergamum in Asia Minor developed their own distinctive stylistic characteristics. For the most part, Hellenistic sculpture moved away from the balanced tension and idealism of the fifth century B.C.E. toward the sentimental, emotional, and realistic mode of the fourth century B.C.E. These qualities are readily apparent in the marble statue called the Laocoon, carved at Rhodes in the second century B.C.E. and afterward taken to Rome.

Mathematics and Science

Among the most spectacular and remarkable intellectual developments of the Hellenistic age were those that came in mathematics and science. The burst of activity in these subjects drew their in-

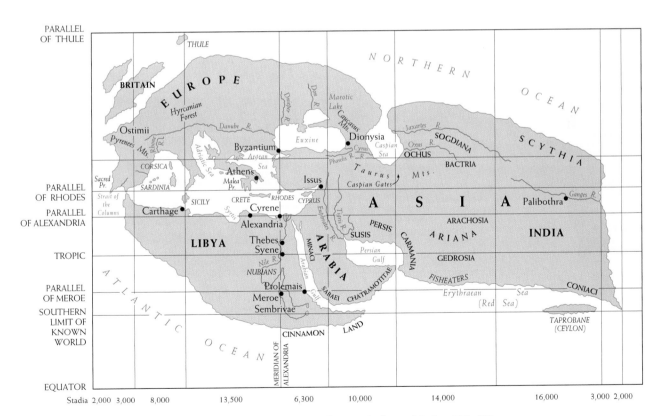

MAP 3–5   THE WORLD ACCORDING TO ERATOSTHENES   *Eratosthenes of Alexandria (ca. 275–195 B.C.E.) was a Hellenistic geographer. His map, reconstructed here, was remarkably accurate for its time. The world was divided by lines of "latitude" and "longitude," thus anticipating our global divisions.*

This is a Roman copy of one of the masterpieces of Hellenistic sculpture, the Laocoon. According to legend, Laocoon was a priest who warned the Trojans not to take the Greek's wooden horse within their city. This sculpture depicts his punishment. Great serpents sent by the goddess Athena, who was on the side of the Greeks, devoured Laocoon and his sons before the horrified people of Troy. Musei Vaticani spiration from several sources. The stimulation and organization provided by the work of Plato and Aristotle should not be ignored. To these was added the impetus provided by Alexander's interest in science, evidenced by the scientists he took with him on his expedition and the aid he gave them in collecting data.

The expansion of Greek horizons geographically and the consequent contact with Egyptian and Babylonian knowledge were also helpful. Finally, the patronage of the Ptolemies and the opportunity for many scientists to work with one another at the museum at Alexandria provided a unique opportunity for scientific work. It is not too much to say that the work done by the Alexandrians formed the greater part of the scientific knowledge available to the Western world until the scientific revolution of the sixteenth and seventeenth centuries C.E.

Euclid's *Elements* (written early in the third century B.C.E.) remained the textbook of plane and solid geometry until recent times. Archimedes of Syracuse (ca. 287–212 B.C.E.) made further progress in geometry, established the theory of the lever in mechanics, and invented hydrostatics. (See "Plutarch Cites Archimedes and Hellenistic Science.")

These advances in mathematics, once applied to the Babylonian astronomical tables available to the Hellenistic world, spurred great progress in the field of astronomy. As early as the fourth century, Heraclides of Pontus (ca. 390–310 B.C.E.) had argued that Mercury and Venus circulate around the sun and not the Earth. He appears to have made other suggestions leading in the direction of a heliocentric theory of the universe. Most scholars, however, give credit for that theory to Aristarchus of Samos (ca. 310–230 B.C.E.), who asserted that the sun, along with the other fixed stars, did not move and that the Earth revolved around the sun in a circular orbit and rotated on its axis while doing so. The heliocentric theory ran contrary not only to the traditional view codified by Aristotle, but to what seemed to be common sense.

Hellenistic technology was not up to proving the theory, and, of course, the planetary orbits are not circular. The heliocentric theory did not, therefore, take hold. Hipparchus of Nicea (b. ca. 190 B.C.E.) constructed a model of the universe on the geocentric theory; his ingenious and complicated model did a very good job of accounting for the movements of the sun, the moon, and the planets. Ptolemy of Alexandria (second century C.E.) adopted Hipparchus' system with a few improvements. It remained dominant until the work of Copernicus, in the sixteenth century C.E.

A page from On Floating Bodies. *Archimedes' work was covered over by a tenth-century manuscript, but ultraviolet radiation reveals the original text and drawings underneath.* Christie's Images, Inc.

Hellenistic scientists made progress in mapping the Earth as well as the sky. Eratosthenes of Cyrene (ca. 275–195 B.C.E.) was able to calculate the circumference of the Earth to within about 200 miles. He wrote a treatise on geography based on mathematical and physical reasoning and the reports of travelers. In spite of the new data that were available to later geographers, Eratosthenes' map (see Map 3–5) was in many ways more accurate than the one constructed by Ptolemy of Alexandria, which became standard in the Middle Ages.

The Hellenistic Age contributed little to the life sciences, such as biology, zoology, and medicine. Even the sciences that had such impressive achievements to show in the third century B.C.E. made little progress thereafter. In fact, to some extent, there was a retreat from science. Astrology and magic became subjects of great interest as scientific advance lagged.

In Perspective

The Classical Age of Greece was a period of unparalleled achievement. While the rest of the world continued to be characterized by monarchical, hierarchical, command societies, in Athens democracy was carried as far as it would go before modern times. Although Athenian citizenship was limited to adult males of native parentage, citizens were granted full and active participation in every decision of the state without regard to wealth or class. Democracy disappeared late in the fourth century B.C.E. with the end of Greek autonomy. When it returned in the modern world more than two millennia later, it was broader, but shallower. Democratic citizenship did not again imply the active direct participation of every citizen in the government of the state.

It was in this democratic, imperial Athens that the greatest artistic, literary, and philosophical achievements of Classical Greece took place. Analytical, secular history, tragedy and comedy, the philosophical dialogue, an organized system of logic, and the logical philosophical treatise were among the achievements of the Classical Age. The tradition of rational, secular speculation in natural philosophy and science was carried forward, but more attention was devoted to human questions in medicine and ethical and political philosophy. A naturalistic style of art evolved that showed human beings first as they ideally might look and then as they really looked, an approach that dominated Greek and Roman art until the late stages of the Roman Empire. This naturalistic style had a powerful effect on the Italian Renaissance and, through it, the modern world.

These Hellenic developments, it should be clear, diverge sharply from the experience of previous cultures and of contemporary ones in the rest of the world. To a great degree, they sprang from the unique political experience of the Greeks, based on the independent city–states. That unique experience and the Classical period ended with the Macedonian conquest, which introduced the Hellenistic Age and ultimately made the Greeks subject to, or part of, some great national state or empire.

The Hellenistic Age speaks to us less fully and vividly than that of Classical Greece, chiefly because it had no historian to compare with Herodotus and Thucydides. We lack the clear picture that a continuous, rich, lively, and meaningful narrative provides. This deficiency should not obscure the great importance of the achievements of the age. The literature, art, scholarship, and science of the period deserve attention in their own right.

The Hellenistic Age did perform a vital civilizing function. It spread Greek culture over a remarkably wide area and made a significant and lasting impression on much of it. Greek culture also adjusted to its new surroundings to a degree, unifying and simplifying its cultural cargo to make it more accessible to outsiders. The various Greek dialects gave way to a version of the Attic tongue, the koine, *or common language.*

In the same way, the scholarship of Alexandria established canons of literary excellence and the scholarly tools with which to make the great treasures of Greek culture understandable to later generations. The syncretism of thought and belief introduced in this period also made understanding and accord more likely among peoples who were very different. When the Romans came into contact with Hellenism, they were powerfully impressed by it. When they conquered the Hellenistic world, they became, as Horace said, captives of its culture.

REVIEW QUESTIONS

1. How was the Delian League transformed into the Athenian Empire during the fifth century B.C.E.? Did the empire offer any advantages to its subjects? Why was there such resistance to Athenian efforts to unify the Greek world in the fifth and fourth centuries B.C.E.?

2. Why did Athens and Sparta come to blows in the Great Peloponnesian War? What was each side's strategy for victory? Why did Sparta win the war?

3. Give examples from art, literature, and philosophy of the tension that characterized Greek life and thought in the Classical Age. How does Hellenistic art differ from that of the Classical Age?

4. Between 431 and 362 B.C.E., Athens, Sparta, and Thebes each tried to impose hegemony over the city–states of Greece, but none succeeded except for short periods of time. Why did each state fail? What does your analysis tell you about the components of successful rule?

5. How and why did Philip II conquer Greece between 359 and 338 B.C.E.? How was he able to turn Macedon into a formidable military and political power? Why was Athens unable to defend itself against Macedon? Where does more of the credit for Philip's success lie; in Macedon's strength or in the weakness of the Greek city–states?

6. What were the major consequences of Alexander's death? Assess the achievement of Alexander. Was he a conscious promoter of Greek civilization or just an egomaniac drunk with the lust of conquest?

SUGGESTED READINGS

M. AUSTIN AND P. VIDAL-NAQUET, *The Economic and Social History of Classical Greece* (1977). A collection of documents with commentary.

A. B. BOSWORTH, *Conquest and Empire: The Reign of Alexander the Great* (1988). An excellent, tough-minded account.

J. BUCKLER, *The Theban Hegemony, 371–362 B.C.E.* (1980). A study of Thebes at the height of its power.

W. BURKERT, *Greek Religion* (1985). A fine general study.

P. CARTLEDGE, *Agesilaus and the Crisis of Sparta* (1987). More than a biography of the Spartan king, this is a thorough study of Spartan society.

G. CAWKWELL, *Philip of Macedon* (1978). A brief, but learned, account of Philip's career.

W. R. CONNOR, *The New Politicians of Fifth-Century Athens* (1971). A study on changes in political style and their significance for Athenian society.

V. EHRENBERG, *The People of Aristophanes* (1962). A study of Athenian society as revealed by the comedies of Aristophanes.

J. R. ELLIS, *Philip II and Macedonian Imperialism* (1976). A study of the career of the founder of Macedonian power.

E. FANTHAM, H. FOLEY, N. KAMPEN, S. POMEROY, AND H. A. SHAPIRO, *Women in the Classical World* (1994). A valuable survey based on written and visual evidence.

J. R. L. FOX, *Alexander the Great* (1973). An imaginative account that does more justice to the Persian side of the problem than is usual.

Y. GARLAN, *Slavery in Ancient Greece* (1988). An up-to-date survey.

P. GREEN, *Alexander the Great* (1972). A lively biography.

P. GREEN, *From Alexander to Actium* (1990). A brilliant new synthesis of the Hellenistic period.

C. D. HAMILTON, *Agesilaus and the Failure of Spartan Hegemony* (1991). An excellent biography of the king who was the central figure in Sparta during its domination in the fourth century B.C.E.

N. G. L. HAMMOND AND G. T. GRIFFITH, *A History of Macedonia, Vol. 2, 550–336 B.C.E.* (1979). A thorough account of Macedonian history that focuses on the careers of Philip and Alexander.

M.H. HANSEN, *The Athenian Democracy in the Age of Demosthenes* (1991). An analysis of the Athenian consitution and society in the fourth century B.C.E.

R. JUST, *Women in Athenian Law and Life* (1988). A good study of the place of women in Athenian life.

D. KAGAN, *Pericles of Athens and the Birth of Athenian Democracy* (1991). An account of the life and times of the great Athenian statesman.

D. KAGAN, *The Outbreak of the Peloponnesian War* (1969). A study of the period from the foundation of the Delian League to the coming of the Peloponnesian War that argues that war could have been avoided.

G. B. KERFERD, *The Sophistic Movement* (1981). A fine study of these worldly thinkers of the Classical period.

B. M. W. KNOX, *The Heroic Temper: Studies in Sophoclean Tragedy* (1964). A brilliant analysis of tragic heroism.

D. M. LEWIS, *Sparta and Persia* (1977). A valuable discussion of relations between Sparta and Persia in the fifth and fourth centuries B.C.E.

G. E. R. LLOYD, *Greek Science after Aristotle* (1974).

A. A. LONG, *Hellenistic Philosophy: Stoics, Epicureans, Skeptics* (1974). A solid study.

R. MEIGGS, *The Athenian Empire* (1972). A fine study of the rise and fall of the empire, making excellent use of inscriptions.

J. J. POLLITT, *Art and Experience in Classical Greece* (1972). A scholarly and entertaining study of the relationship between art and history in Classical Greece, with excellent illustrations.

J. J. POLLITT, *Art in the Hellenistic Age* (1986). An extraordinary analysis that places the art in its historical and intellectual context.

S. POMEROY, *Families in Classical and Hellenistic Greece* (1998). A valuable and thorough study of the Greek family.

M. I. ROSTOVTZEFF, *Social and Economic History of the Hellenistic World*, 3 vols. (1941). A masterpiece of synthesis by a great historian.

R. SEALEY, *Demosthenes and His Time* (1993). A learned and controversial study.

B. S. STRAUSS, *Athens after the Peloponnesian War* (1987). An excellent discussion of Athens' recovery and of the nature of Athenian society and politics in the fourth century B.C.E.

B. S. STRAUSS, *Fathers and Sons in Athens* (1993). A study of tension between the generations in Classical Athens.

V. TCHERIKOVER, *Hellenistic Civilization and the Jews* (1970). A fine study of the impact of Hellenism on the Jews.

G. VLASTOS, *Socrates: Ironist and Moral Philosopher* (1991). A study of the father of Western ethical philosophy.

G. VLASTOS, *Platonic Studies*, 2d ed. (1981). A valuable collection of essays on the philosophy of Plato.

F. W. WALBANK, *The Hellenistic World* (1981). A solid history.

A. E. ZIMMERN, *The Greek Commonwealth* (1961). A study of political, social, and economic conditions in fifth-century Athens.

Chapter 4

This is a wall painting from a house in the provincial Roman town of Pompeii, near the Bay of Naples. The house was buried, and thus preserved, in a rain of ash and lava by the great eruption of Mt. Vesuvius in 79 C.E. The painting shows a well-to-do couple, the wife wearing gold jewelry and holding a stylus and wax tablet, the usual writing implements of the time. The picture seems to emphasize her status as a wife, her personal attractiveness, and her literacy.

Museo Nazionale, Napoli/Scala/Art Resource N.Y.

Rome: From Republic to Empire

KEY TOPICS

- The emergence of the Roman Republic
- The development of the republican constitution
- Roman expansion and imperialism
- The character of Roman society in the republican era
- The fall of the republic

The achievement of the Romans was one of the most remarkable in human history. The descendants of the inhabitants of a small village in central Italy, they came eventually to rule the entire Italian peninsula, then the entire Mediterranean coastline. They conquered most of the Near East and, finally, much of continental Europe. They ruled this vast empire under a single government that provided considerable peace and prosperity for centuries. Never before the Romans nor since has that area been united, and rarely, if ever, has it enjoyed a stable peace. But Rome's legacy was not merely military excellence and political organization. The Romans adopted and transformed the intellectual and cultural achievements of the Greeks and combined them with their own outlook and historical experience. The resulting Graeco-Roman tradition in literature, philosophy, and art provided the core of learning for the Middle Ages and pointed the way to the new paths taken in the Renaissance. It remains at the heart of Western civilization to this day.

Prehistoric Italy

The culture of Italy developed late. Paleolithic settlements gave way to the Neolithic mode of life only around 2500 B.C.E. The Bronze Age came around 1500 B.C.E. About 1000 B.C.E., bands of new arrivals—warlike peoples speaking a set of closely related languages we call Italic—began to infiltrate Italy from across the Adriatic Sea and around its northern end. These invaders cremated their dead and put the ashes in tombs stocked with weapons and armor. Their bronzework was of a higher quality than that of the people they displaced, and they were soon making weapons, armor, and tools of iron. By 800 B.C.E. they had occupied the highland pastures of the Apennines, and within a short time they began to challenge the earlier settlers for control of the tempting western plains. It would be the descendants of these tough mountain people—Umbrians, Sabines, Samnites, and Latins—together with others soon to arrive—Etruscans, Greeks, and Celts—who would shape the future of Italy.

The Etruscans

The Etruscans exerted the most powerful external influence on the Romans. Their civilization arose in Etruria (now Tuscany), west of the Apennines between the Arno and Tiber rivers, about 800 B.C.E. (See Map 4–1.) Their origin is far from clear, but their tomb architecture, resembling that of Asia Minor, and their practice of divining the future by inspecting the livers of sacrificial animals point to an eastern origin.

Government

The Etruscans brought civilization with them. Their settlements were self-governing, fortified city–states, of which twelve formed a loose religious confederation. At first, kings ruled these cities, but they were replaced by an aristocracy of the agrarian nobles. The latter ruled by means of a council and elected annual magistrates. The Etruscans were a military ruling class that dominated and exploited the native Italians (the predecessors of the later Italic speakers), who worked the Etruscans' land and mines and served as infantry in the Etruscan armies. This aristocracy accumulated considerable wealth through agriculture, industry, piracy, and a growing commerce with the Carthaginians and the Greeks.

Religion

The Etruscans' influence on the Romans was greatest in religion. They imagined a world filled with

MAP 4–1   ANCIENT ITALY   *This map of ancient Italy and its neighbors before the expansion of Rome shows major cities and towns as well as several geographical regions and the locations of some of the Italic and non-Italic peoples.*

gods and spirits, many of them evil. To deal with such demons, the Etruscans evolved complicated rituals and powerful priesthoods. Divination by sacrifice and omens in nature helped discover the divine will, and careful attention to precise rituals directed by priests helped please the gods. After a while the Etruscans, influenced by the Greeks, worshiped gods in the shape of humans and built temples for them.

Women

Etruscan women had a more significant role in family and society than did Greek women in the world of the *polis*. Etruscan wives appeared in public, in religious festivals, and at public banquets together with their husbands. Many of them were literate, and women both took part in athletic contests and watched them as spectators alongside of men. Inscriptions on tombs and paintings on coffins mention both father and mother of the deceased and

Much of what we know of the Etruscans comes from their funerary art. This sculpture of an Etruscan couple is part of a sarcophagus. Erich Lessing/Art Resource, N.Y.

often show husbands and wives together in respectful and loving attitudes.

Dominion

The Etruscan aristocracy remained aggressive and skillful in the use of horses and war chariots. In the seventh and sixth centuries B.C.E., they expanded their power in Italy and across the sea to Corsica and Elba. They conquered Latium (a region that included the small town of Rome) and Campania, where they became neighbors of the Greeks of Naples. In the north, they got as far as the Po Valley. These conquests were carried out by small bands led by Etruscan chieftains who did not work in concert and would not necessarily aid one another in distress. As a result, the conquests outside Etruria were not firmly based and did not last long.

Etruscan power reached its height some time before 500 B.C.E. and then rapidly declined. About 400 B.C.E., Celtic peoples from the area the Romans called Gaul (modern France) broke into the Po Valley and drove out the Etruscans. They settled this land so firmly that the Romans thereafter called it Cisalpine Gaul (Gaul on this side of the Alps). Eventually, even the Etruscan heartland in Etruria lost its independence and was incorporated into Roman Italy. The Etruscan language was forgotten, and Etruscan culture gradually became only a memory, but its influence on the Romans remained.

Royal Rome

Rome was an unimportant town in Latium until its conquest by the Etruscans, but its location—fifteen miles from the mouth of the Tiber River at the point at which the hills made further navigation impossible—gave it several advantages over its Latin neighbors. The island in the Tiber southwest of the Capitoline Hill made the river fordable, so Rome was naturally a center for communication and trade, both east–west and north–south.

Government

In the sixth century B.C.E., Rome came under Etruscan control. Led by Etruscan kings, the Roman army, equipped and organized like the Greek phalanx, gained control of most of Latium. An effective political and social order that gave extraordinary power to the ruling figures in both public and private life made this success possible. To their kings the Romans gave the awesome power of *imperium*—the right to issue commands and to enforce them by fines, arrests, and corporal, or even capital, punishment. Although it tended apparently to remain in the same family, kingship was elective. The Roman Senate had to approve the candidate for the office, and a vote of the people gathered in an assembly formally granted the *imperium*. A basic characteristic of later Roman government—the granting of great power to executive officers contingent on the approval of the Senate and, ultimately, the people—was already apparent in this structure.

In theory and law, the king was the commander of the army, the chief priest, and the supreme judge. He could make decisions in foreign affairs, call out the army, lead it in battle, and impose discipline on his troops, all by virtue of his *imperium*. In practice, the royal power was much more limited.

The Senate was the second branch of the early Roman government. According to tradition, it originated when Romulus, Rome's legendary first king, chose 100 of Rome's leading men to advise him. The number of senators ultimately rose to 300, where it stayed through most of the history of the republic. Ostensibly, the Senate had neither executive nor legislative power; it met only when summoned by the king and then only to advise him. In reality its authority was great, for the senators, like the king, served for life. The Senate, therefore, had continuity and experience, and it was composed of the most powerful men in the state. It could not lightly be ignored.

The third branch of government, the curiate assembly, was made up of all citizens, as divided into thirty groups. (In early Rome, citizenship required descent from Roman parents on both sides.) The assembly met only when summoned by the king; he determined the agenda, made proposals, and recognized other speakers, if any. Usually, the assembly was called to listen and approve. Voting was not by head, but by group; a majority within each group determined its vote, and the decisions were made by majority vote of the groups. Group voting would be typical of all future forms of Roman assembly.

The Family

The center of Roman life was the family. At its head stood the father, whose power and authority within the family resembled those of the king within the state. Over his children, the father held broad powers analogous to *imperium* in the state; he had the right to sell his children into slavery, and he even had the power of life and death over them. Over his wife, he had less power; he could not sell or kill her. In practice, his power to dispose of his children was limited by consultation with the family, by public opinion, and, most of all, by tradition. A wife could not be divorced except for stated serious offenses, and even then she had to be convicted by a court made up of her male blood relatives. The Roman woman had a respected position and the main responsibility for managing the household. The father was the chief priest of the family. He led it in daily prayers to the dead, which reflected the ancestor worship central to the Roman family and state.

Women in Early Rome

Early Roman society was hierarchical and dominated by males. Throughout her life a woman was under the control of some adult male. Before her marriage it was her father, afterwards her husband or, when neither was available, a guardian chosen from one of their male relatives. Always her right to buy or sell property or make contracts required the approval of one of them. The Roman law gave control of a woman from father to husband by the right of *manus* (hand). This was conferred by one of two formal marriage ceremonies that were typical in early Rome. Over time, however, a third form of marriage became popular that left the power of *manus* in the hands of the woman's father, even after her marriage. This kind of union was similar to what we would call common-law marriage, in which a woman could stay out of her husband's control of her and her dowry by absenting herself from her husband's home for at least three consecutive nights each year. This gave her greater rights of inheritance in her father's family and greater independence in her marriage.

Busts of a Roman couple from the period of the Republic. Although some have identified the individuals as Cato the Younger and his daughter Porcia, no solid evidence confirms this claim. Roman sculpture. Vatican Museums, Vatican State. Scala/Art Resource N.Y.

In early Rome, marriage with *manus* was most common, but women of the upper classes had a position of influence and respect greater than the classical Greeks had and more like what appears to have been true of the Etruscans. Just as the husband was *paterfamilias*, the wife was *materfamilias*. She was mistress within the home, controlling access to the storerooms, keeping the accounts, and supervising the slaves and the raising of the children. She also was part of the family council and a respected adviser on all questions concerning the family. Divorce was difficult and rare, limited to a few specific transgressions by the wife, one of which was drunkenness. Even when divorced for cause, the wife retained her dowry.

Clientage

Clientage was one of Rome's most important institutions. The *client* was "an inferior entrusted, by custom or by himself, to the protection of a stranger more powerful than he, and rendering certain services and observances in return for this protection."[1] The Romans spoke of a client as being in the *fides*, or trust, of his patron, and so the relationship always had moral implications. The patron provided his client with protection, both physical and legal. He gave him economic assistance in the form of a land grant, the opportunity to work as a tenant farmer or a laborer on the patron's land, or simply handouts. In return, the client would fight for his patron, work his land, and support him politically. These mutual obligations were enforced by public opinion and tradition. When early custom was codified in the mid-fifth century B.C.E., one of the twelve tablets of laws announced, "Let the patron who has defrauded his client be accursed."

In the early history of Rome, patrons were rich and powerful whereas clients were poor and weak, but as time passed, it was not uncommon for rich and powerful members of the upper classes to become clients of even more powerful men, chiefly for political purposes. Because the client–patron relationship was hereditary and was sanctioned by religion and custom, it was to play a very important part in the life of the Roman Republic.

Patricians and Plebeians

In the royal period, Roman society was divided in two by a class distinction based on birth. The wealthy patrician upper class held a monopoly of power and influence. Its members alone could conduct state religious ceremonies, sit in the Senate, or hold office. They formed a closed caste by forbidding marriage outside their own group. (See "Art & the West.")

The plebeian lower class must have consisted originally of poor, dependent small farmers, laborers, and artisans, the clients of the nobility. As Rome and its population grew in various ways, families that were rich, but outside the charmed circle of patricians, grew wealthy. From very early times, therefore, there were rich plebeians, and incompetence and bad luck must have produced some poor patricians. The line between the classes and the monopoly of privileges remained firm, nevertheless, and the struggle of the plebeians to gain equality occupied more than two centuries of republican history.

The Republic

Roman tradition tells us that the outrageous behavior of the last kings led the noble families to revolt in 509 B.C.E., bringing the monarchy to a sudden close and leading to the creation of the Roman Republic.

Constitution

THE CONSULS   The Roman constitution was an unwritten accumulation of laws and customs. The Romans were a conservative people and were never willing to deprive their chief magistrates of the great powers exercised by the monarchs. They elected two patricians to the office of consul and endowed them with *imperium*. They were assisted by two financial officials called *quaestors*, whose number ultimately reached eight. Like the kings, the consuls led the army, had religious duties, and served as judges. They retained the visible symbols of royalty—the purple robe, the ivory chair, and the *lictors* (minor officials), who accompanied them bearing rods and axe. The power of the consuls, however, was limited legally and institutionally as well as by custom.

The power of the consulship was granted not for life, but only for a year. Each consul could prevent any action by his colleague simply by saying no to his proposal, and the religious powers of the consuls were shared with others. Even the *imperium* was limited. Although the consuls had full powers of life and death while leading an army, within the sacred boundary of the city of Rome the citizens had the right to appeal all cases involving capital punishment to the popular assembly. Besides, after their one year in office, the consuls would spend the rest of their lives as members of the Senate. It was a most reckless consul who failed to ask the advice of the Senate or who failed to follow it when there was general agreement.

[1] E. Badian, *Foreign Clientelae* (264–70 B.C.E.) (Oxford, 1958), p. 1.

Family and Honor:
A Roman Patrician with the Busts of His Ancestors

*R*oman sculpture was heavily influenced by other cultures, first by the Etruscans and later by the Greeks of the Hellenistic period. No large sculptures remain from much before the first century B.C.E., but Roman writers reveal that from very early times it was the custom to honor leading generals and political leaders by setting up statues to them in public places. This practice continued and expanded throughout the history of Rome.

This statue of an unknown member of the Roman nobility, from late in the first century, illustrates an even more fundamental custom. He carries the images of two of his ancestors, probably his father and grandfather. The Greek historian Polybius, who lived among the leading aristocrats of Rome, tells of the funeral practice when an illustrious Roman of the upper class died. The body was placed on a platform in the Forum. If the deceased had a son, he would deliver a eulogy praising his father's virtues and achievements. After the funeral, writes Polybius, a wax image of the dead man would be placed "in the most conspicuous spot in his house, surmounted by a wooden canopy or shrine. This likeness consists of a mask made to represent the deceased with extraordinary fidelity both in shape and color. These likenesses they display at public sacrifices with much care. And when any illustrious member of the family dies, they carry these masks to the funeral, putting them on men whom they thought as like the originals as possible."[2]

At these funerals, after the speaker had praised the deceased, he went on to praise the others whose images were displayed. "The chief benefit of the ceremony is that it inspires young men to shrink from no exertion for the general welfare, in the hope of obtaining the glory which awaits the brave."[3]

The wax images, of course, did not last, so by the first century it was customary to make marble copies of them. Although the Romans admired, collected, and copied sculptures in the naturalistic style of the Hellenistic Greeks, these commemorative statues and masks had a severe and repetitive style that did not

A Roman Patrician with the busts of his ancestors. First century C.E. Musei Capitolini, Rome/Scala/Art Resource N.Y.

care about individual character and psychology. Instead, they represented a *type*—the stern and serious Roman aristocrat, the responsible father of his family, the dutiful and brave citizen and leader of his people.

[2]Polybius, *The Histories*, 6.53, translated by E. S. Shuckburgh (Bloomington, IN: Indiana University Press, 1962), pp. 503–504.
[3]Ibid.

Sources: Polybius 6.53; Janson, *Art History*, pp. 188–190. D. Kleiner, *Roman Sculpture*, (New Haven: Yale University Press, 1992).

The many checks on consular action tended to prevent initiative, swift action, and change, but this was just what a conservative, traditional, aristocratic republic wanted. Only in the military sphere did divided counsel and a short term of office create important problems. The Romans tried to get around the difficulties by sending only one consul into the field or, when this was impossible, allowing each consul sole command on alternate days. In really serious crises, the consuls, with the advice of the Senate, could appoint a single man, the *dictator*, to the command and could retire in his favor. The *dictator*'s term of office was limited to six months, but his own *imperium* was valid both inside and outside the city without appeal.

These devices worked well enough in the early years of the republic, when Rome's battles were near home. Longer wars and more sophisticated opponents, however, revealed the system's weaknesses and required significant changes. Long campaigns prompted the invention of the *proconsulship* in 325 B.C.E., whereby the term of a consul serving in the field was extended. This innovation contained the seeds of many troubles for the constitution.

The creation of the office of *praetor* also helped provide commanders for Rome's many campaigns. The basic function of the *praetors* was judicial, but they also had *imperium* and served as generals. *Praetors'* terms were also for one year. By the end of the republic, there were eight *praetors*, whose annual terms, like the consuls', could be extended for military commands when necessary.

The job of identifying citizens and classifying them according to age and property was at first the responsibility of the consuls. After the middle of the fifth century B.C.E., this job was delegated to a new office, that of *censor*. The Senate elected two *censors* every five years. They conducted a census and drew up the citizen rolls. Their task was not just clerical; the classification of the citizens fixed taxation and status, so the censors had to be men of fine reputation, former consuls. They soon acquired additional powers. By the fourth century B.C.E., they compiled the roll of senators and could strike senators from that roll not only for financial, but also for moral, reasons. As the prestige of the office grew, it came to be considered the ultimate prize of a Roman political career.

THE SENATE AND THE ASSEMBLY   With the end of the monarchy, the Senate became the single continuous deliberative body in the Roman state, greatly increasing its influence and power. Its members were prominent patricians, often leaders of clans and patrons of many clients. The Senate soon gained

Lictors, pictured here, attended the chief Roman magistrates when they appeared in public. The axe carried by one of the lictors and the bound bundle of staffs carried by the others symbolize both the power of Roman magistrates to inflict corporal punishment on Roman citizens and the limits on that power. The bound staffs symbolize the right of citizens within the city of Rome not to be punished without a trial. The axe symbolizes the power of the magistrates, as commanders of the army, to put anyone to death without a trial outside the city walls.
Alinari/Art Resource, N.Y.

control of the state's finances and of foreign policy. Its formal advice was not lightly ignored either by magistrates or by popular assemblies.

The most important assembly in the early republic was the *centuriate assembly*, which was, in a sense, the Roman army acting in a political capacity. Its basic unit was the *century*, theoretically 100 fighting men classified according to their weapons, armor, and equipment. Because each man equipped himself, this meant that the organization was by classes according to wealth.

Voting was by century and proceeded in order of classification from the cavalry down. The assembly elected the consuls and several other magistrates, voted on bills put before it, made decisions of war and peace, and also served as the court of appeal against decisions of the magistrates affecting the life or property of a citizen. In theory, the assembly had final authority, but the Senate exercised great, if informal, influence.

THE STRUGGLE OF THE ORDERS   The laws and constitution of the early republic gave to the patricians almost a monopoly of power and privilege. Plebeians were barred from public office, from priesthoods, and from other public religious offices. They could not serve as judges and could not even know the law, for there was no published legal code. The only law was traditional practice, and that existed only in the minds and actions of patrician magistrates. Plebeians were subject to the *imperium*, but could not exercise its power. They were not allowed to marry patricians. When Rome gained new land by conquest, patrician magistrates distributed it in a way that favored patricians. The patricians dominated the assemblies and the Senate. The plebeians undertook a campaign to achieve political, legal, and social equality, and this attempt, which succeeded after two centuries of intermittent effort, is called the Struggle of the Orders.

The most important source of plebeian success was the need for their military service. According to tradition, the plebeians, angered by patrician resistance to their demands, withdrew from the city and camped on the Sacred Mount. There they formed a plebeian tribal assembly and elected plebeian tribunes to protect them from the arbitrary power of the magistrates. They declared the tribune inviolate and sacrosanct; anyone laying violent hands on him was accursed and liable to death without trial. By extension of his right to protect the plebeians, the tribune gained the power to veto any action of a magistrate or any bill in a Roman assembly or the Senate. The plebeian assembly voted by tribe, and a vote of the assembly was binding on plebeians. They tried to make their decisions binding on all Romans, but could not do so until 287 B.C.E.

The next step was for the plebeians to obtain access to the laws, which they accomplished by 450 B.C.E., when early Roman custom in all its harshness and simplicity was codified in the Twelve Tables. In 445 B.C.E., plebeians gained the right to marry patricians. The main prize, the consulship, the patricians did not yield easily. Not until 367 B.C.E. did legislation—the Licinian–Sextian Laws—provide that at least one consul could be a plebeian.

Before long, plebeians held other offices—even the dictatorship and the censorship. In 300 B.C.E. they were admitted to the most important priesthoods, the last religious barrier to equality. In 287 B.C.E., the plebeians completed their triumph. They once again withdrew from the city and secured the passage of a law whereby decisions of the plebeian assembly bound all Romans and did not require the approval of the Senate.

It might seem that the Roman aristocracy had given way under the pressure of the lower class. Yet the victory of the plebeians did not bring democracy. An aristocracy based strictly on birth had given way to an aristocracy more subtle, but no less restricted, based on a combination of wealth and birth. A relatively small group of rich and powerful families, both patrician and plebeian, known as *nobiles*, attained the highest offices in the state. The significant distinction was no longer between patrician and plebeian but between the *nobiles* and everyone else.

The absence of the secret ballot in the assemblies enabled the *nobiles* to control most decisions and elections by a combination of intimidation and bribery. The leading families were in constant competition with one another for office, power, and prestige, but they often combined in marriage and less formal alliances to keep the political plums within their own group. In the century from 233 to 133 B.C.E., for instance, twenty-six families provided 80 percent of the consuls, and only ten families accounted for almost 50 percent. These same families dominated the Senate, whose power became ever greater. Rome's success brought the Senate prestige, increased control of policy, and confidence in its capacity to rule. The end of the Struggle of the Orders brought domestic peace under a republican constitution dominated by a capable, if narrow, senatorial aristocracy. This outcome satisfied most Romans outside the ruling group, because Rome conquered Italy and brought many benefits to its citizens.

The Conquest of Italy

Not long after the fall of the monarchy in 509 B.C.E., a coalition of Romans, Latins, and Italian Greeks defeated the Etruscans and drove them out of Latium for good. Throughout the fifth century B.C.E., the powerful Etruscan city of Veii, only twelve miles north of the Tiber River, raided Roman territory. After a hard struggle and a long siege, the Romans took Veii in 392 B.C.E., more than doubling the size of Rome.

Roman policy toward defeated enemies used both the carrot and the stick. When the Romans made friendly alliances with some, they gained

The Rise of the Plebeians to Equality in Rome	
509 B.C.E.	Kings expelled; republic founded
450–449 B.C.E.	Laws of the Twelve Tables published
445 B.C.E.	Plebeians gain right of marriage with patricians
367 B.C.E.	Licinian–Sextian Laws open consulship to plebeians
300 B.C.E.	Plebeians attain chief priesthoods
287 B.C.E.	Laws passed by Plebeian Assembly made binding on all Romans

new soldiers for their army. When they treated others more harshly by annexing their land, they achieved a similar end. Service in the Roman army was based on property, and the distribution to poor Romans of conquered land made soldiers of previously useless men. It also gave the poor a stake in Rome and reduced the pressure against its aristocratic regime. The long siege of Veii kept soldiers from their farms during the campaign. From that time on, the Romans paid their soldiers, thus giving their army greater flexibility and a more professional quality.

GALLIC INVASION OF ITALY AND ROMAN REACTION At the beginning of the fourth century B.C.E., a disaster struck. In 387 B.C.E. the Gauls, barbaric Celtic tribes from across the Alps, defeated the Roman army and captured, looted, and burned Rome. The Gauls sought plunder, not conquest, so they extorted a ransom from the Romans and returned to their homes in the north. Rome's power appeared to be wiped out.

By about 350 B.C.E., however, the Romans were more dominant than ever. Their success in turning back new Gallic raids added still more to their power and prestige. As the Romans tightened their grip on Latium, the Latins became resentful. In 340 B.C.E., they demanded independence from Rome or full equality and launched a war of independence that lasted until 338 B.C.E. The victorious Romans dissolved the Latin League, and their treatment of the defeated opponents provided a model for the settlement of Italy.

ROMAN POLICY TOWARD THE CONQUERED The Romans did not destroy any of the Latin cities or their people, nor did they treat them all alike. Some near Rome received full Roman citizenship. Others farther away gained municipal status, which gave them the private rights of intermarriage and commerce with Romans, but not the public rights of voting and holding office in Rome. They retained the rights of local self-government and could obtain full Roman citizenship if they moved to Rome. They followed Rome in foreign policy and provided soldiers to serve in the Roman legions.

Still other states became allies of Rome on the basis of treaties, which differed from city to city. Some were given the private rights of intermarriage and commerce with Romans, and some were not; the allied states were always forbidden to exercise these rights with one another. Some, but not all, were allowed local autonomy. Land was taken from some, but not from others, nor was the percentage taken always the same. All the allies supplied troops to the army, in which they fought in auxiliary battalions under Roman officers, but they did not pay taxes to Rome.

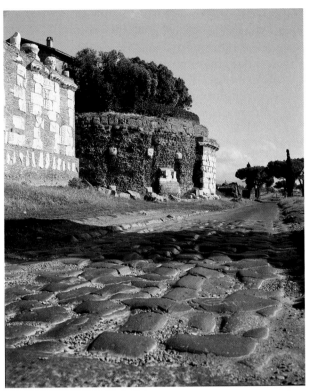

Original Roman pavement of the Via Appia, part of the network of military roads that tied all Italy to Rome. These roads enabled Roman legions to move swiftly to enforce their control of Italy. The Via Appia dates from the fourth century B.C.E. Scala/Art Resource, N.Y.

On some of the conquered land the Romans placed colonies, permanent settlements of veteran soldiers in the territory of recently defeated enemies. The colonists retained their Roman citizenship and enjoyed home rule; in return for the land they had been given, they served as a kind of permanent garrison to deter or suppress rebellion. These colonies were usually connected to Rome by a network of military roads built as straight as possible and so durable that some are used even today. The roads guaranteed that a Roman army could swiftly reinforce an embattled colony or put down an uprising in any weather.

The Roman settlement of Latium reveals even more clearly than before the principles by which Rome was able to conquer and dominate Italy for many centuries. The excellent army and the diplomatic skill that allowed Rome to separate its enemies help to explain its conquests. The reputation for harsh punishment of rebels, and the sure promise that such punishment would be delivered was made unmistakably clear: Both the colonies and military roads help to explain the reluctance to revolt. But the positive side, represented by Rome's organization of the defeated states, is at least as important. The Romans did not regard the status given each newly conquered city as permanent. They held out to loyal allies the prospect of improving their status—even of achieving the ultimate prize, full Roman citizenship. In so doing, the Romans gave their allies a stake in Rome's future success and a sense of being colleagues, though subordinate ones, rather than subjects. The result, in general, was that most of Rome's allies remained loyal even when put to the severest test.

DEFEAT OF THE SAMNITES   The next great challenge to Roman arms came in a series of wars with a tough mountain people of the southern Apennines, the Samnites. Some of Rome's allies rebelled, and soon the Etruscans and Gauls joined in the war against Rome. But most of the allies remained loyal. In 295 B.C.E., at Sentinum, the Romans defeated an Italian coalition, and by 280 B.C.E. they were masters of central Italy. Their power extended from the Po Valley south to Apulia and Lucania.

Now the Romans were in direct contact with the Greek cities of southern Italy. Roman intervention in a quarrel between Greek cities brought them face to face with Pyrrhus, king of Epirus. Pyrrhus, probably the best general of his time, commanded a well-disciplined and experienced mercenary army, which he hired out for profit, and a new weapon: twenty war elephants. He defeated the Romans twice, but suffered many casualties. When one of his officers rejoiced at the victory, Pyrrhus told him, "If we win one more battle against the Romans we shall be completely ruined." This "Pyrrhic victory" led him to withdraw to Sicily in 275 B.C.E. The Greek cities that had hired him were forced to join the Roman confederation. By 265 B.C.E. Rome ruled all Italy as far north as the Po River, an area of 47,200 square miles. The year after the defeat of Pyrrhus, Ptolemy Philadelphus, king of Egypt, sent a message of congratulations to establish friendly relations with Rome. This act recognized Rome's new status as a power in the Hellenistic world.

Roman Expansion in Italy	
392 B.C.E.	Fall of Veii; Etruscans defeated
387 B.C.E.	Gauls burn Rome
338 B.C.E.	Latin League defeated
295 B.C.E.	Battle of Sentinum; Samnites and allies defeated
275 B.C.E.	Pyrrhus driven from Italy
265 B.C.E.	Rome rules Italy south of the Po River

Rome and Carthage

The conquest of southern Italy brought the Romans face to face with the great naval power of the western Mediterranean, Carthage. (See Map 4–2.) Late in the ninth century B.C.E., the Phoenician city of Tyre had planted a colony on the coast of northern Africa near modern Tunis, calling it the New City, or Carthage. In the sixth century B.C.E., the conquest of Phoenicia by the Assyrians and the Persians left Carthage independent and free to exploit its very advantageous situation. The city was located on a defensible site and commanded an excellent harbor that encouraged commerce. The coastal plain grew abundant grain, fruits, and vegetables. An inland plain allowed sheep herding. The Phoenician settlers conquered the native inhabitants and used them to work the land.

Beginning in the sixth century B.C.E., the Carthaginians expanded their domain to include the coast of northern Africa west beyond the Straits of Gibraltar and eastward into Libya. Overseas, they came to control the southern part of Spain, Sardinia, Corsica, Malta, the Balearic Islands, and western Sicily. The people of these territories, though originally allies, were all reduced to subjection like the natives of the Carthaginian home territory. They all served in the Carthaginian army or navy and paid tribute. Carthage also profited greatly from the mines of Spain and from an absolute monopoly of trade imposed on the western Mediterranean.

An attack by Hiero, tyrant of Syracuse, on the Sicilian city of Messana just across from Italy first caused trouble between Rome and Carthage. Messana had been seized by a group of Italian mercenary soldiers who called themselves *Mamertines*, the sons of the war god Mars. When Hiero defeated the Mamertines, some of them called on the Carthaginians to help save their city. Carthage agreed and sent a garrison, for the Carthaginians wanted to prevent Syracuse from dominating the straits. One Mamertine faction, however, fearing that Carthage might take undue advantage of the opportunity, asked Rome for help.

In 264 B.C.E., the request came to the Senate. Because a Punic garrison (the Romans called the Carthaginians *Phoenicians*; in Latin the word is *Poeni* or *Puni*—hence the adjective *Punic*) was in place at Messana, any intervention would be not against Syracuse, but against the mighty empire of Carthage. Unless Rome intervened, however, Carthage would gain control of all Sicily and the straits. The assembly voted to send an army to Messana and expelled the Punic garrison. The First Punic War was on.

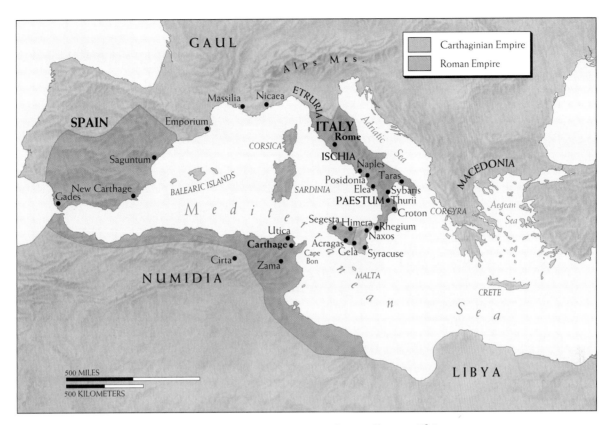

MAP 4–2 THE WESTERN MEDITERRANEAN AREA DURING THE RISE OF ROME *This map covers the theater of conflict between the growing Roman dominions and those of Carthage in the third century B.C.E. The Carthaginian Empire stretched westward from the city (in modern Tunisia) along the North African coast and into southern Spain.*

THE FIRST PUNIC WAR (264–241 B.C.E.) The war in Sicily soon settled into a stalemate until the Romans built a fleet to cut off supplies to the besieged Carthaginian cities at the western end of Sicily. When Carthage sent its own fleet to raise the siege, the Romans destroyed it. In 241 B.C.E. Carthage signed a treaty giving up Sicily and the islands between Italy and Sicily; it also agreed to pay a war indemnity in ten annual installments. Neither side was to attack the allies of the other. The peace was realistic and not unduly harsh; Rome had earned Sicily, and Carthage could well afford the indemnity. If it had been carried out in good faith, it might have brought lasting peace.

A rebellion, however, broke out in Carthage among the mercenaries, newly recruited from Sicily, who now demanded their pay. In 238 B.C.E., while Carthage was still preoccupied with the rebellion, Rome seized Sardinia and Corsica and demanded that Carthage pay an additional indemnity. This was a harsh and cynical action by the Romans; even the historian Polybius, a great champion of Rome, could find no justification for it. It undid the calming effects of the peace of 241 B.C.E. without preventing the Carthaginians from recovering their strength to seek vengeance in the future.

The conquest of overseas territory presented the Romans with new administrative problems. Instead of following the policy they had pursued in Italy, they made Sicily a province and Sardinia and Corsica another. It became common to extend the term of the governors of these provinces beyond a year. The governors were unchecked by colleagues and exercised full imperium. New magistracies, in effect, were thus created free of the limits put on the power of officials in Rome.

The new populations were neither Roman citizens nor allies; they were subjects who did not serve in the army, but paid tribute instead. The old practice of extending citizenship and, with it, loyalty to Rome thus stopped at the borders of Italy. Rome collected taxes on these subjects by "farming" them out at auction to the highest bidder. At first, the tax collectors were natives from the same province. Later they were Roman allies and, finally, Roman citizens below senatorial rank who could become powerful and wealthy by squeezing the provincials hard. These innovations were the basis for Rome's imperial organization in the future. In time, they strained the constitution and traditions to such a degree as to threaten the existence of the republic.

A Roman warship. Rome became a naval power late in its history, in the course of the First Punic War. Roman sailors initially lacked the skill and experience in sea warfare of their Carthaginian opponents, who could maneuver their oared ships to ram the enemy. To compensate for this disadvantage, the Romans sought to make a sea battle more like an encounter on land by devising ways to grapple enemy ships and board them with armed troops. In time, they also mastered the skillful use of the ram. This picture shows a Roman ship, propelled by oars, with both ram and soldiers, ready for either kind of fight. Direzione Generale Musei Vaticani.

After the First Punic War, campaigns against the Gauls and across the Adriatic distracted Rome. Meanwhile Hamilcar Barca, the Carthaginian governor of Spain from 237 B.C.E. until his death in 229 B.C.E., was leading Carthage on the road to recovery. Hamilcar sought to compensate for Carthaginian losses elsewhere by building a Punic Empire in Spain. He improved the ports and the commerce conducted in them, exploited the mines, gained control of the hinterland, won over many of the conquered tribes, and built a strong and disciplined army.

Hamilcar's successor, his son-in-law Hasdrubal, pursued the same policies. His success alarmed the Romans. They imposed a treaty in which he promised not to take an army north across the Ebro River in Spain, although Punic expansion in Spain was well south of that river at the time. Though the agreement appeared to put Rome in the position of giving orders to an inferior, it benefited both sides equally. If the Carthaginians accepted the limit of the Ebro on their expansion in Spain, the Romans would not interfere with that expansion.

THE SECOND PUNIC WAR (218–202 B.C.E.)   On Hasdrubal's assassination in 221 B.C.E., the army chose as his successor Hannibal, son of Hamilcar Barca. Hannibal was at that time twenty-five years old. He quickly consolidated and extended the Punic Empire in Spain. A few years before his accession, Rome had received an offer of alliance from the people of the Spanish town Saguntum (about one hundred miles south of the Ebro). The Romans accepted the friendship and the responsibilities it entailed, in the process violating at least the spirit of the Ebro treaty. At first, Hannibal was careful to avoid any action against Saguntum, but the Saguntines, con-

fident of Rome's protection, began to interfere with some of the Spanish tribes allied with Hannibal. When the Romans sent an embassy to Hannibal warning him to let Saguntum alone and repeating the injunction not to cross the Ebro, he ignored the warning and proceeded to besiege and capture the town. The Romans sent an ultimatum to Carthage demanding the surrender of Hannibal. Carthage refused, and Rome declared war in 218 B.C.E.

Between the close of the First Punic War and the outbreak of the Second, Rome had repeatedly provoked Carthage, taking Sardinia in 238 B.C.E. and interfering in Spain, but had taken no measures to prevent Carthage from building a powerful and dangerous empire or even to prepare defenses against a Punic attack in Spain. Hannibal saw to it that the Romans paid the price for these blunders. By September of 218 B.C.E. he was across the Alps, in Italy and among the friendly Gauls.

Hannibal defeated the Romans at the Ticinus River and crushed the joint consular armies at the Trebia River. In 217 B.C.E., he outmaneuvered and trapped another army at Lake Trasimene. The key to success, however, would be defection by Rome's allies. Hannibal released Italian prisoners without harm or ransom and moved his army south of Rome to encourage rebellion. But the allies remained firm.

Sobered by their defeats, the Romans elected Quintus Fabius Maximus dictator. His strategy was to avoid battle while following and harassing Hannibal's army. He would fight only when his army had recovered and then only on favorable ground.

In 216 B.C.E. Hannibal marched to Cannae in Apulia to tempt the Romans, under different generals, into another open fight. They sent off an army of some 80,000 men to meet him. Almost the entire

Roman army was killed or captured. It was the worst defeat in Roman history. Rome's prestige was shattered, and most of its allies in southern Italy, as well as Syracuse in Sicily, now went over to Hannibal. For more than a decade, no Roman army would dare face Hannibal in the open field.

Hannibal, however, had neither the numbers nor the supplies to besiege walled cities, nor did he have the equipment to take them by assault. To win the war in Spain, the Romans appointed Publius Cornelius Scipio (237–183 B.C.E.), later called Africanus, to the command in Spain with proconsular *imperium*. Scipio was not yet twenty-five and had held no high office. But he was a general almost as talented as Hannibal. Within a few years, young Scipio had conquered all Spain and had deprived Hannibal of hope of help from that region.

In 204 B.C.E. Scipio landed in Africa, defeated the Carthaginians, and forced them to accept a peace, the main clause of which was the withdrawal of Hannibal and his army from Italy. Hannibal had won every battle, but lost the war, for he had not counted on the determination of Rome and the loyalty of its allies. Hannibal's return inspired Carthage to break the peace and to risk all in battle. In 202 B.C.E., Scipio and Hannibal faced each other at the Battle of Zama. The generalship of Scipio and the desertion of Hannibal's mercenaries gave the victory to Rome. The new peace terms reduced Carthage to the status of a dependent ally of Rome. The Second Punic War ended the Carthaginian command of the western Mediterranean and Carthage's term as a great power. Rome ruled the seas and the entire Mediterranean coast from Italy westward.

The Republic's Conquest of the Hellenistic World

THE EAST   By the middle of the third century B.C.E., the eastern Mediterranean had reached a condition of stability based on a balance of power among the three great Hellenistic kingdoms that allowed an established place even for lesser states. This equilibrium, however, was threatened by the activities of two aggressive monarchs: Philip V of Macedon (221–179 B.C.E.) and Antiochus III of the Seleucid kingdom (223–187 B.C.E.). Philip and Antiochus moved swiftly, the latter against Syria and Palestine, the former against cities in the Aegean, in the Hellespontine region, and on the coast of Asia Minor.

The threat that a more powerful Macedon might pose to Rome's friends and, perhaps, even to Italy was enough to persuade the Romans to intervene. Philip had already attempted to meddle in Roman affairs when he formed an alliance with

Carthage during the Second Punic War, provoking a conflict known as the First Macedonian War (215–205 B.C.E.). In 200 B.C.E., in an action that began the Second Macedonian War, the Romans sent an ultimatum to Philip ordering him not to attack any Greek city and to pay reparations to Pergamum. These orders were meant to provoke, not avoid, war, and Philip refused to obey. Two years later the Romans sent out a talented young general, Flamininus, who demanded that Philip withdraw from Greece entirely. In 197 B.C.E., with Greek support, Flamininus defeated Philip in the hills of Cynoscephalae in Thessaly, ending the war. The Greek cities freed from Philip were made autonomous, and in 196 B.C.E. Flamininus proclaimed the freedom of the Greeks.

Soon after the Romans withdrew from Greece, they came into conflict with Antiochus, who was expanding his power in Asia and on the European side of the Hellespont. On the pretext of freeing the Greeks from Roman domination, he landed an army on the Greek mainland. The Romans routed Antiochus at Thermopylae and quickly drove him from Greece. In 189 B.C.E., they crushed his army at Magnesia in Asia Minor. The peace of Apamia in the next year deprived Antiochus of his elephants and his navy and imposed a huge indemnity on him. Once again, the Romans took no territory for themselves and left several Greek cities in Asia free. They continued to regard Greece, and now Asia Minor, as a kind of protectorate in which they could intervene or not as they chose.

This relatively mild policy was destined to end as the stern and businesslike policies favored by the conservative censor Cato gained favor in Rome. A new harshness was to be applied to allies and bystanders, as well as to defeated opponents.

In 179 B.C.E., Perseus succeeded Philip V as king of Macedon. He tried to gain popularity in Greece

The Punic Wars	
264–241 B.C.E.	First Punic War
238 B.C.E.	Rome seizes Sardinia and Corsica
221 B.C.E.	Hannibal takes command of Punic army in Spain
218–202 B.C.E.	Second Punic War
216 B.C.E.	Battle of Cannae
209 B.C.E.	Scipio takes New Carthage
202 B.C.E.	Battle of Zama
149–146 B.C.E.	Third Punic War
146 B.C.E.	Destruction of Carthage

Plutarch Describes a Roman Triumph

In 168 B.C.E., L. Æmilius Paullus defeated King Perseus in the Battle of Pydna, bringing an end to the Third Macedonian War. For his great achievement, the Senate granted Paullus the right to celebrate a triumph, the great honorific procession granted only for extraordinary victories and eagerly sought by all Roman generals. Plutarch described the details of Paullus' triumph.

❖ *How do you explain the particular elements displayed on each day of the triumph? What purposes do you think a triumph served? What can be learned from this selection about the values celebrated by the Romans? How are they different from the values cherished by Americans in our day? Are there any similarities?*

The people erected scaffolds in the forum, in the circuses, as they call their buildings for horse races, and in all other parts of the city where they could best behold the show. The spectators were clad in white garments; all the temples were open, and full of garlands and perfumes; the ways were cleared and kept open by numerous officers, who drove back all who crowded into or ran across the main avenue. This triumph lasted three days. On the first, which was scarcely long enough for the sight, were to be seen the statues, pictures, and colossal images which were taken from the enemy, drawn upon two hundred and fifty chariots. On the second was carried in a great many wagons the finest and richest armour of the Macedonians, both of brass and steel, all newly polished and glittering; the pieces of which were piled up and arranged purposely with the greatest art, so as to seem to be tumbled in heaps carelessly and by chance.

On the third day, early in the morning, first came the trumpeters, who did not sound as they were wont in a procession or solemn entry, but such a charge as the Romans use when they encourage the soldiers to fight. Next followed young men wearing frocks with ornamented borders, who led to the sacrifice a hundred and twenty stalled oxen, with their horns gilded, and their heads adorned with ribbons and garlands; and with these were boys that carried basins for libation, of silver and gold.

After his children and their attendants came Perseus himself, clad all in black, and wearing the boots of his country, and looking like one altogether stunned and deprived of reason, through the greatness of his misfortunes. Next followed a great company of his friends and familiars, whose countenances were disfigured with grief, and who let the spectators see, by their tears and their continual looking upon Perseus, that it was his fortune they so much lamented, and that they were regardless of their own.

After these were carried four hundred crowns, all made of gold, sent from the cities by their respective deputations to Æmilius, in honour of his victory. Then he himself came, seated on a chariot magnificently adorned (a man well worthy to be looked at, even without these ensigns of power), dressed in a robe of purple, interwoven with gold, and holding a laurel branch in his right hand. All the army, in like manner, with boughs of laurel in their hands, divided into their bands and companies, followed the chariot of their commander; some singing verses, according to the usual custom, mingled with raillery; others, songs of triumph and the praise of Æmilius' deeds; who, indeed, was admired and accounted happy by all men, and unenvied by every one that was good; except so far as it seems the province of some god to lessen that happiness which is too great and inordinate, and so to mingle the affairs of human life that no one should be entirely free and exempt from calamities; but, as we read in Homer, that those should think themselves truly blessed whom fortune has given an equal share of good and evil.

From Plutarch, "Æmilius Paullus," in *Lives of the Noble Grecians and Romans*, trans. by John Dryden, rev. by A. H. Clough (New York: Random House, n.d.), pp. 340–341.

by favoring the democratic and revolutionary forces in the cities. The Romans, troubled by his threat to stability, launched the Third Macedonian War (172–168 B.C.E.), and in 168 B.C.E. Æmilius Paullus defeated Perseus at Pydna. (See "Plutarch Describes a Roman Triumph.") The peace that followed this war, reflecting the changed attitude at Rome, was harsh. It divided Macedon into four separate republics, whose citizens were forbidden to intermarry or even to do business across the new national boundaries. Leaders of anti-Roman factions in the Greek cities were punished severely.

When Æmilius Paullus returned from his victory, he celebrated for three days by parading the spoils of war, royal prisoners, and great wealth through the streets of Rome. The public treasury benefited to such a degree that the direct property tax on Roman citizens was abolished. Part of the booty went to the general and part to his soldiers. New motives were thereby introduced into Roman foreign policy, or, perhaps, old motives were given new prominence. Foreign campaigns could bring profit to the state, rewards to the army, and wealth, fame, honor, and political power to the general.

THE WEST   Harsh as the Romans had become toward the Greeks, they were even worse in their treatment of the people of the Iberian Peninsula, whom they considered barbarians. They committed dreadful atrocities, lied, cheated, and broke treaties to exploit and pacify the natives, who fought back fiercely in guerilla style. From 154 to 133 B.C.E. the fighting waxed, and it became hard to recruit Roman soldiers to participate in the increasingly ugly war. At last, in 134 B.C.E., Scipio Æmilianus took the key city of Numantia by siege and burned it to the ground. This put an end to the war in Spain.

Roman treatment of Carthage was no better. Although Carthage lived up to its treaty with Rome faithfully and posed no threat, some Romans refused to abandon their hatred and fear of the traditional enemy. Cato is said to have ended all his speeches in the Senate with the same sentence: "Ceterum censeo delendam esse Carthaginem" ("Besides, I think that Carthage must be destroyed"). At last the Romans took advantage of a technical breach of the peace to destroy Carthage. In 146 B.C.E. Scipio Æmilianus took

the city, plowed up its land, and put salt in the furrows as a symbol of the permanent abandonment of the site. The Romans incorporated it as the province of Africa, one of six Roman provinces, including Sicily, Sardinia–Corsica, Macedonia, Hither Spain, and Further Spain.

Civilization in the Early Roman Republic

Close and continued association with the Greeks of the Hellenistic world wrought important changes in the Roman style of life and thought. The Roman attitude toward the Greeks ranged from admiration for their culture and history to contempt for their constant squabbling, their commercial practices, and their weakness. Conservatives such as Cato might speak contemptuously of the Greeks as "Greeklings" (*Graeculi*), but even he learned Greek and absorbed Greek culture.

Before long, the education of the Roman upper classes was bilingual. In addition to the Twelve Tables, young Roman nobles studied Greek rhetoric, literature, and sometimes philosophy. These studies even had an effect on education and the Latin language. As early as the third century B.C.E. Livius Andronicus, a liberated Greek slave, translated the *Odyssey* into Latin. It became a primer for young Romans and put Latin on the road to becoming a literary language.

Religion

Roman religion was influenced by the Greeks almost from the beginning. The Romans identified their own gods with Greek equivalents and incorporated Greek mythology into their own. Mostly, however, Roman religious practice remained simple and Italian, until the third century B.C.E. brought important new influences from the East.

In 205 B.C.E. the Senate approved the public worship of Cybele, the Great Mother goddess from Phrygia. Hers was a fertility cult accompanied by ecstatic, frenzied, and sensual rites that shocked and outraged conservative Romans to such a degree that they soon banned the cult. Similarly, the Senate banned the worship of Dionysus, or Bacchus, in 186 B.C.E. In the second century B.C.E. interest in Babylonian astrology also grew, and the Senate's attempt in 139 B.C.E. to expel the "Chaldaeans," as the astrologers were called, did not prevent the continued influence of their superstition.

Roman Engagement Overseas	
215–205 B.C.E.	First Macedonian War
200–197 B.C.E.	Second Macedonian War
196 B.C.E.	Proclamation of Greek freedom by Flamininus at Corinth
189 B.C.E.	Battle of Magnesia; Antiochus defeated in Asia Minor
172–168 B.C.E.	Third Macedonian War
168 B.C.E.	Battle of Pydna
154–133 B.C.E.	Roman wars in Spain
134 B.C.E.	Numantia taken

Education

The education provided in the early centuries of the Roman Republic reflected the limited, conservative, and practical nature of that community of plain farmers and soldiers. Education was entirely the responsibility of the family, the father teaching his own son at home. It is not clear whether in these early times girls received any education, though they certainly did later on. The boys learned to read, write, and calculate, and they learned the skills of farming. They memorized the laws of the Twelve Tables, learned how to perform religious rites, heard stories of the great deeds of early Roman history and particularly those of their ancestors, and engaged in the physical training appropriate for potential soldiers. This course of study was practical, vocational, and moral; it aimed at making the boys moral, pious, patriotic, law abiding, and respectful of tradition.

HELLENIZED EDUCATION   In the third century B.C.E. the Romans came into contact with the Greeks of southern Italy, and this contact produced momentous changes in Roman education. Greek teachers introduced the study of language, literature, and philosophy, as well as the idea of a liberal education, or what the Romans called *humanitas*, the root of our concept of the humanities. The aim of education changed from the mastery of practical, vocational skills to an emphasis on broad intellectual training, critical thinking, an interest in ideas, and the development of a well-rounded person.

The new emphasis required students to learn Greek, for Rome did not yet have a literature of its own. Hereafter, educated Romans were expected to be bilingual. For this purpose, schools were established in which a teacher, called a *grammaticus*, taught students the Greek language and its literature, especially the poets and particularly Homer. After the completion of this elementary education, Roman boys of the upper classes studied rhetoric—the art of speaking and writing well. For the Greeks, rhetoric was a subject of less importance than philosophy. The more practical Romans took to it avidly, however, for it was of great use in legal disputes and was becoming ever more valuable in political life.

Some Romans were powerfully attracted to Greek literature and philosophy. The important and powerful Roman aristocrat, Scipio Æmilianus, the man who finally defeated and destroyed Carthage, surrounded himself and his friends with such Greek thinkers as the historian Polybius and the philosopher Panaetius.

Equally outstanding Romans, such as Cato the Elder, were more conservative and opposed the new learning on the grounds that it would weaken Roman moral fiber. (See "Cato Educates His Son.") They were able on more than one occasion to pass laws expelling philosophers and teachers of rhetoric. But these attempts to go back to older ways failed. The new education suited the needs of the Romans of the second century B.C.E. They found themselves changing from a rural to an urban society and were being thrust into the sophisticated world of Hellenistic Greeks.

By the last century of the Roman Republic, the new Hellenized education had become dominant. Latin literature had come into being, along with Latin translations of Greek poets, and these formed part of the course of study. But Roman gentlemen still were expected to be bilingual, and Greek language and literature were still central to the curriculum. Many schools were established. The number of educated people grew, extending beyond the senatorial class to the equestrians and outside Rome to the cities of Italy.

This carved relief from the second century C.E. shows a schoolmaster and his pupils. The pupil at the right is arriving late. Alinari/Art Resource, N.Y.

Cato Educates His Son

Marcus Porcius Cato (234–149 B.C.E.) was a remarkable Roman who rose from humble origins to the highest offices in the state. He stood as the firmest defender of the old Roman traditions at a time when Hellenic ideas were strongly influential. In the following passage, Plutarch tells how Cato attended to his son's education.

❖ *What was the curriculum prepared for Cato's son? Was it suitable for the kind of life he would lead? Was his education more or less helpful and appropriate in this way than that of the average American student today? Why did Cato teach his son himself? Why did he pay so much attention to Roman history? Was he wise in doing so?*

After the birth of his son, no business could be so urgent, unless it had a public character, as to prevent him from being present when his wife bathed and swaddled the babe. For the mother nursed it herself, and often gave suck also to the infants of her slaves, that so they might come to cherish a brotherly affection for her son. As soon as the boy showed signs of understanding, his father took him under his own charge and taught him to read, although he had an accomplished slave, Chilo by name, who was a school teacher, and taught many boys. Still, Cato thought it not right, as he tells us himself, that his son should be scolded by a slave, or have his ears tweaked when he was slow to learn, still less that he should be indebted to his slave for such a priceless thing as education. He was therefore himself not only the boy's reading teacher, but his tutor in law, and his athletic trainer, and he taught his son not merely to hurl the javelin and fight in armour and ride the horse, but also to box, to endure heat and cold, and to swim lustily through the eddies and billows of the Tiber. His *History of Rome*, as he tells us himself, he wrote out with his own hand and in large characters, that his son might have in his own home an aid to acquaintance with his country's ancient traditions.

Plutarch, *Cato Major*, 20, trans. by Bernadotte Perrin (London and New York: Loeb Classical Library, William Heinemann, 1914).

In the late republic, Roman education, though still entirely private, became more formal and organized. From the ages of seven to twelve, boys went to elementary school accompanied by a Greek slave called a *paedagogus* (whence our term *pedagogue*), who looked after their physical well-being and their manners, and who improved their ability in Greek conversation. At school the boys learned to read and write, using a wax tablet and a stylus, and to do simple arithmetic with an abacus and pebbles (*calculi*). Discipline was harsh and corporal punishment frequent. From twelve to sixteen, boys went to a higher school, where the *grammaticus* undertook to provide a liberal education, using Greek and Latin literature as his subject matter. In addition, he taught dialectic, arithmetic, geometry, astronomy, and music. Sometimes he included the elements of rhetoric, especially for those boys who would not go on to a higher education.

At sixteen, some boys went on to advanced study in rhetoric. The instructors were usually Greek. They trained their charges by studying models of fine speech of the past and by having them write, memorize, and declaim speeches suitable for different occasions. Sometimes the serious student attached himself to some famous public speaker and followed him about to learn what he could. Sometimes a rich and ambitious Roman would support a Greek philosopher in his own home. His son could converse with the philosopher and acquire the learning and polished thought necessary for the fully cultured gentleman. Some, like the great orator Cicero, undertook what we might call postgraduate study by traveling abroad to study with great teachers of rhetoric and philosophy in the Greek world.

One result of this whole style of education was to broaden the Romans' understanding through the careful study of a foreign language and culture. It made them a part of the older and wider culture of the Hellenistic world, a world that they had come to dominate and needed to understand.

EDUCATION FOR WOMEN Though the evidence is limited, we can be sure that girls of the upper classes received an education equivalent at least to the early stages of a boy's education. They were probably taught by tutors at home rather than going to school, as was increasingly the fashion among boys in the late republic. Young women did not study with philosophers and rhetoricians, for they were usually married by the age at which the men were pursuing their higher edu-

This wall painting from the first century B.C.E. comes from the villa of Publius Fannius Synistor at Pompeii and shows a woman playing a cithera. Fresco on lime plaster. H. 6 ft. 1 1/2 in. W. 6 ft. 1 1/2 in. (187 x 187 cm.) The Metropolitan Museum of Art, Rogers Fund, 1903. (03.14.5) Photograph © 1986 The Metropolitan Museum of Art

cation. Still, some women found ways to continue their education. Some became prose writers and others poets. By the first century C.E., there were apparently enough learned women to provoke the complaints of a crotchety and conservative satirist:

Still more exasperating is the woman who begs as soon as she sits down to dinner, to discourse on poets and poetry, comparing Virgil with Homer; professors, critics, lawyers, auctioneers—even another woman—can't get a word in. She rattles on at such a rate that you'd think that all the pots and pans in the kitchen were crashing to the floor or that every bell in town was clanging. All by herself she makes as much noise as some primitive tribe chasing away an eclipse. She should learn the philosopher's lesson: "moderation is necessary even for intellectuals." And, if she still wants to appear educated and eloquent, let her dress as a man, sacrifice to men's gods and bathe in the men's baths. Wives shouldn't try to be public speakers; they shouldn't use rhetorical devices; they shouldn't read all the classics—there should be some things women don't understand. I myself cannot understand a woman who can quote the rules of grammar and never make a mistake and cites obscure, long-forgotten poets—as if men cared about such things. If she has to correct somebody let her correct her girl friends and leave her husband alone.[4]

(Also see "Women's Uprising in Republican Rome.")

[4]Juvenal, *Satires* 6.434–456, trans. by Roger Killian, Richard Lynch, Robert J. Rowland, and John Sims, cited by Sarah B. Pomeroy in *Goddesses, Whores, Wives, and Slaves* (New York: Schocken Books, 1975), p. 172.

Slavery

Like most ancient peoples, the Romans had slaves from very early in their history, but among the shepherds and family farmers of early Rome they were relatively few. Slavery became a basic element in the Roman economy and society only during the second century B.C.E., after the Romans had conquered most of the lands bordering the Mediterranean. In the time between the beginning of Rome's first war against Carthage (264 B.C.E.) and the conquest of Spain (133 B.C.E.), the Romans enslaved some 250,000 prisoners of war, greatly increasing the availability of slave labor and reducing its price. Many slaves worked as domestic servants, feeding the Roman upper class' growing appetite for luxury; at the other end of the spectrum, many worked in the mines of Spain and Sardinia. Some worked as artisans in small factories and shops or as public clerks. Slaves were permitted to marry, and they appear to have produced sizable families. As in Greece, domestic slaves and those used in crafts and commerce were permitted to earn money, to keep it, and, in some cases, to use it to purchase their own freedom. Manumission (the freeing of slaves) was very common among the Romans. After a time, a considerable proportion of the Roman people included freedmen who had been slaves themselves or whose ancestors had been bondsmen. It was not uncommon to see the son or grandson of a slave become wealthy as a freedman and the slave himself or his son become a Roman citizen.

The unique development in the Roman world was the emergence of an agricultural system that employed and depended on a vast number of slaves. By the time of Jesus there were between two and three million slaves in Italy, and about 35 to 40 percent of the total population, most of them part of great slave gangs that worked the vast plantations the Romans called *latifundia*. Turning from the grain that was the chief crop of the free Roman farmer, these large estates concentrated on such cash-producing products as wool, wine, and olive oil. The life of Rome's agricultural slaves appears to have been much harder than that of other Roman slaves and of slaves in other ancient societies, with the possible exception of slaves working in mines. *Latifundia* owners sought maximum profits and treated their slaves simply as means to that end. The slaves often worked in chains, were oppressed by brutal foremen, and lived in underground prisons.

Such harsh treatment led to a number of serious slave rebellions of a kind we do not hear of in other ancient societies. A rebellion in Sicily in 134 B.C.E.

Women's Uprising in Republican Rome

In 195 B.C.E., Roman women staged a rare public political protest when they demanded the repeal of a law passed two decades earlier during the Second Punic War, which they judged to limit their rights unfairly. Livy (59 B.C.E.–17 C.E.) describes the affair and the response of the traditionalist Marcus Porcius Cato (234–149 B.C.E.).

❖ *Of what did the women complain? How did they try to achieve their goals? Which of Cato's objections to their behavior do you think were most important? Since women did not vote or sit in assemblies, how can the outcome of the affair be explained?*

Amid the anxieties of great wars, either scarce finished or soon to come, an incident occurred, trivial to relate, but which, by reason of the passions it aroused, developed into a violent contention. [Two] tribunes of the people, proposed to the assembly the abrogation of the Oppian law. The tribune Gaius Oppius had carried this law in the heat of the Punic War,. . . that no woman should possess more than half an ounce of gold or wear a parti-coloured garment or ride in a carriage in the City or in a town within a mile thereof, except on the occasion of a religious festival. . . . [T]he Capitoline was filled with crowds of supporters and opponents of the bill. The matrons could not be kept at home by. . .their husbands' orders, but blocked all the streets and approaches to the Forum, begging the men as they came down to the Forum that, in the prosperous condition of the state, when the private fortunes of all men were daily increasing, they should allow the woman too to have their former distinctions restored. The crowd of women grew larger day by day; for they were now coming in from the towns and rural districts. Soon they dared even to approach and appeal to the consuls, the praetors, and the other officials, but one consul, at least, they found adamant, Marcus Porcius Cato, who spoke thus in favour of the law whose repeal was being urged:

"If each of us, citizens, had determined to assert his rights and dignity as a husband with 'respect to his own spouse, we should have less trouble with the sex as a whole; as it is, our liberty, destroyed at home by female violence, even here in the Forum is crushed and trodden underfoot, and because we have not kept them individually under control, we dread them collectively. . . . But from no class is there not the greatest danger if you permit them meetings. . . . and secret consultations.

"I should have said, 'What sort of practice is this, of running out into the streets and blocking the roads and speaking to other women's husbands? Could you not have made the same requests, each of your own husband, at home? And yet, not even at home, if modesty would keep matrons within the limits of their proper rights, did it become you to concern yourselves with the question of what laws should be adopted in this place or repealed.' Our ancestors permitted no woman to conduct even personal business without a guardian to intervene in her behalf; they wished them to be under the control of fathers, brothers, husbands; we (Heaven help us!) allow them now even to interfere in public affairs, yes, and to visit the Forum and our informal and formal sessions. Give loose rein to their uncontrollable nature and to this untamed creature and expect that they will themselves set bounds to their licence; unless you act, this is the least of the things enjoined upon women by custom or law and to which they submit with a feeling of injustice. It is complete liberty or, rather, if we wish to speak the truth, complete licence that they desire.

"If they win in this, what will they not attempt? Review all the laws with which your forefathers restrained their licence and made them subject to their husbands; even with all these bonds you can scarcely control them. What of this? If you suffer them to seize these bonds one by one and wrench themselves free and finally to be placed on a parity with their husbands, do you think that you will be able to endure them? The moment they begin to be your equals, they will be your superiors."

The next day an even greater crowd of women appeared in public, and all of them in a body beset the doors of those tribunes, who were vetoing their colleagues' proposal, and they did not desist until the threat of veto was withdrawn by the tribunes. After that there was no question that all the tribes would vote to repeal the law. The law was repealed twenty years after it was passed.

From *Livy*, trans. by Evan T. Stage (Cambridge, Mass.: Harvard University Press, 1935), XXXIV, i–iii; viii, pp. 413–419, 439.

kept the island in turmoil for more than two years, and the rebellion of the gladiators led by Spartacus in 73 B.C.E. produced an army of seventy thousand slaves that repeatedly defeated the Roman legions and overran all of southern Italy before it was brutally crushed.

Slavery retained its economic and social importance in the first century of the imperial period, but its centrality began to decline in the second. The institution was never abolished, nor did it disappear while the Roman Empire lasted, but over time it became less important. The reasons for this decline are rather obscure. A rise in the cost of slaves and a consequent reduction in their economic value seem to have been factors. More important, it appears, was a general economic decline that permitted increasing pressure on the free lower classes. More and more they were employed as *coloni*—tenant farmers—tied by imperial law to the land they worked, ostensibly free, but bonded and obligated. Over centuries, most agricultural slave labor was replaced by these increasingly serflike *coloni*. Pockets of slave labor remained as late as the time of Charlemagne, but the system of ancient slavery had essentially been replaced by the time the Roman Empire fell in the West.

Roman Imperialism: The Late Republic

Rome's expansion in Italy and overseas was accomplished without a grand general plan. (See Map 4–3.) The new territories were gained as a result of wars that the Romans believed were either defensive or preventive. Their foreign policy was aimed at providing security for Rome on Rome's terms, but these terms were often unacceptable to other nations and led to continued conflict. Whether intended or not, Rome's expansion brought the Romans an empire and, with it, power, wealth, and responsibilities. The need to govern an empire beyond the seas would severely test the republican constitution that had served Rome well during its years as a city–state and that had been well adapted to the mastery of Italy. Roman society and the Roman character had maintained their integrity through the period of expansion in Italy. But these would be tested by the temptations and strains presented by the wealth and the complicated problems of an overseas empire.

The Aftermath of Conquest

War and expansion changed the economic, social, and political life of Italy. Before the Punic wars most Italians owned their own farms, which provided the greater part of the family's needs. Some families owned larger holdings, but their lands chiefly grew grain, and they used the labor of clients, tenants, and hired workers rather than slaves. Fourteen years of fighting in the Second Punic War did terrible damage to much Italian farmland. Many veterans returning from the wars found it impossible or unprofitable to go back to their farms. Some moved to Rome, where they could find work as occasional laborers, but most stayed in the country to work as tenant farmers or hired hands. Often, the land they abandoned was gathered into large parcels by the wealthy. They converted these units, later called *latifundia*, into large plantations for growing cash crops—grain, olives, and grapes for wine—or into cattle ranches.

The upper classes had plenty of capital to stock and operate these estates because of profits from the war and from exploiting the provinces. Land was cheap, and slaves conquered in war provided cheap labor. By fair means and foul, large landholders obtained great quantities of public land and forced small farmers from it. These changes separated the people of Rome and Italy more sharply into rich and poor, landed and landless, privileged and deprived. The result was political, social, and, ultimately, constitutional conflict that threatened the existence of the republic.

The Gracchi

By the middle of the second century B.C.E., the problems caused by Rome's rapid expansion troubled perceptive Roman nobles. The fall in status of peasant farmers made it harder to recruit soldiers and came to present a political threat as well. The patron's traditional control over his clients was weakened by their flight from their land. Even those former landowners who worked on the land of their patrons as tenants or hired hands were less reliable. The introduction of the secret ballot in the 130s B.C.E. made them even more independent.

TIBERIUS GRACCHUS   In 133 B.C.E., Tiberius Gracchus tried to solve these problems. He became tribune for 133 B.C.E. on a program of land reform; some of the most powerful members of the Roman aristocracy helped him draft the bill. They meant it to be a moderate attempt at solving Rome's problems. The bill's target was public land that had been acquired and held illegally, some of it for many years. The bill allowed holders of this land to retain as many as 300 acres in clear title as private property, but the state would reclaim any-

MAP 4–3   ROMAN DOMINIONS OF THE LATE ROMAN REPUBLIC   *The Roman Republic's conquest of Mediterranean lands—and beyond—until the death of Julius Caesar is shown here. Areas conquered before Tiberius Gracchus (ca. 133 B.C.E.) are distinguished from later ones and from client areas owing allegiance to Rome.*

thing over that. The recovered land would be redistributed in small lots to the poor, who would pay a small rent to the state and could not sell what they had received.

The bill aroused great hostility. Many senators held vast estates and would be hurt by its passage. Others thought it would be a bad precedent to allow any interference with property rights, even ones so dubious as those pertaining to illegally held public land. Still others feared the political gains that Tiberius and his associates would make if the beneficiaries of their law were properly grateful to its drafters. (See "The Ruin of the Roman Family Farm and the Gracchan Reforms.")

When Tiberius put the bill before the tribal assembly, one of the tribunes, M. Octavius, interposed his veto. Tiberius went to the Senate to discuss his proposal, but the senators continued their opposition. Tiberius now had to choose between dropping the matter and undertaking a revolutionary course. Unwilling to give up, he put his bill before the trib-

al assembly again. Again Octavius vetoed. So Tiberius, strongly supported by the people, had Octavius removed from office, violating the constitution. The assembly's removal of a magistrate implied a fundamental shift of power from the Senate to the people. If the assembly could pass laws opposed by the Senate and vetoed by a tribune, if they could remove magistrates, then Rome would become a democracy like Athens instead of a traditional oligarchy. At this point many of Tiberius' powerful senatorial allies deserted him.

Tiberius proposed a second bill, harsher than the first and more appealing to the people, for he had given up hope of conciliating the Senate. This bill, which passed the assembly, provided for a commission to carry it out. When King Attalus of Pergamum died and left his kingdom to Rome, Tiberius proposed to use the Pergamene revenue to finance the commission. This proposal challenged the Senate's control both of finances and of foreign affairs. Hereafter there could be no compro-

The Ruin of the Roman Family Farm and the Gracchan Reforms

The independent family farm was the backbone both of the Greek polis *and of the early Roman Republic. Rome's conquests, the long wars that kept the citizen–soldier away from his farm, and the availability of great numbers of slaves at a low price, however, badly undercut the traditional way of farming and with it the foundations of republican society. In the following passage, Plutarch describes the process of agricultural change and the response to it of the reformer Tiberius Gracchus, tribune in 133* B.C.E.

❖ *What were the causes of the troubles faced by Roman farmers? What were the social and political consequences of the changes in agricultural life? What solution did Tiberius Gracchus propose? Can you think of any reasons, besides selfishness and greed, that people might oppose his plan?*

Of the territory which the Romans won in war from their neighbours, a part they sold, and a part they made common land, and assigned it for occupation to the poor and indigent among the citizens, on payment of a small rent into the public treasury. And when the rich began to offer larger rents and drove out the poor, a law was enacted forbidding the holding by one person of more than five hundred acres of land. For a short time this enactment gave a check to the rapacity of the rich, and was of assistance to the poor, who remained in their places on the land which they had rented and occupied the allotment which each had held from the outset. But later on the neighbouring rich men, by means of fictitious personages, transferred these rentals to themselves, and finally held most of the land openly in their own names. Then the poor, who had been ejected from their land, no longer showed themselves eager for military service, and neglected the bringing up of children, so that soon all Italy was conscious of a dearth of freemen, and was filled with gangs of foreign slaves, by whose aid the rich cultivated their estates, from which they had driven away the free citizens.

And it is thought that a law dealing with injustice and rapacity so great was never drawn up in milder and gentler terms. For men who ought to have been punished for their disobedience and to have surrendered with payment of a fine the land which they were illegally enjoying, these men it merely ordered to abandon their injust acquisitions upon being paid their value, and to admit into ownership of them such citizens as needed assistance. But although the rectification of the wrong was so considerate, the people were satisfied to let bygones be bygones if they could be secure from such wrong in the future; the men of wealth and substance, however, were led by their greed to hate the law, and by their wrath and contentiousness to hate the lawgiver, and tried to dissuade the people by alleging that Tiberius was introducing a re-distribution of land for the confusion of the body politic, and was stirring up a general revolution.

From Plutarch, "Tiberius Gracchus," in *Lives* 8–9, Vol. 10, trans. by Bernadotte Perrin and William Heinemann (London and New York: G. P. Putnam's Sons, 1921), pp. 159–167.

mise: Either Tiberius or the Roman constitution must go under.

Tiberius understood the danger that he would face if he stepped down from the tribunate, so he announced his candidacy for a second successive term, striking another blow at tradition. His opponents feared that he might go on to hold office indefinitely, to dominate Rome in what appeared to them a demagogic tyranny. They concentrated their fire on the constitutional issue, the deposition of the tribune. They appear to have had some success, for many of Tiberius' supporters did not come out to vote. At the elections a riot broke out, and a mob of senators and their clients killed Tiberius and some 300 of his followers and threw their bodies into the Tiber River. The Senate had put down the threat to its rule, but at the price of the first internal bloodshed in Roman political history.

The tribunate of Tiberius Gracchus brought a permanent change to Roman politics. Heretofore

Roman political struggles had generally been struggles for honor and reputation between great families or coalitions of such families. Fundamental issues were rarely at stake. The revolutionary proposals of Tiberius, however, and the senatorial resort to bloodshed created a new situation. Tiberius' use of the tribunate to challenge senatorial rule encouraged imitation in spite of his failure. From then on, Romans could pursue a political career that was not based solely on influence within the aristocracy; pressure from the people might be an effective substitute. In the last century of the republic, politicians who sought such backing were called *populares*, whereas those who supported the traditional role of the Senate were called *optimates* or "the best men."

These groups were not political parties with formal programs and party discipline, but they were more than merely vehicles for the political ambitions of unorthodox politicians. Fundamental questions—such as those about land reform, the treatment of the Italian allies, the power of the assemblies versus the power of the Senate, and other problems—divided the Roman people, from the time of Tiberius Gracchus to the fall of the republic. Some popular leaders, of course, were cynical self-seekers who used the issues only for their own ambitions. Some few may have been sincere advocates of a principled position. Most, no doubt, were a mixture of the two, like most politicians in most times. (See "Sallust on Factions and the Decline of the Republic.")

GAIUS GRACCHUS The tribunate of Gaius Gracchus (brother of Tiberius) was much more dangerous than that of Tiberius. All the tribunes of 123 B.C.E. were his supporters, so there could be no veto, and a recent law permitted the reelection of tribunes. Gaius developed a program of such breadth as to appeal to a variety of groups. First, he revived the agrarian commission, which had been allowed to lapse. Because there was not enough good public land left to meet the demand, he proposed to establish new colonies: two in Italy and one on the old site of Carthage. Among other popular acts, he put through a law stabilizing the price of grain in Rome, which involved building granaries to guarantee an adequate supply.

Gaius broke new ground in appealing to the equestrian order in his struggle against the Senate. The equestrians (so called because they served in the Roman cavalry) were neither peasants nor senators. A highly visible minority of them were businesspeople who supplied goods and services to the Roman state and collected its taxes. Almost continuous warfare and the need for tax collection in the provinces had made many of them rich. Most of the time, these wealthy men had the same outlook as the Senate; generally, they used their profits to purchase land and to try to reach senatorial rank themselves. Still, they had a special interest in Roman expansion and in the exploitation of the provinces. Toward the latter part of the second century B.C.E., they came to have a clear sense of group interest and to exert political influence.

In 129 B.C.E., Pergamum became the new province of Asia. Gaius put through a law turning over to the equestrian order the privilege of collecting its revenue. He also barred senators from serving as jurors on the courts that tried provincial governors charged with extortion. The combination was a wonderful gift for wealthy equestrian businessmen, who were now free to squeeze profits out of the rich province of Asia without much fear of interference from the governors. The results for Roman provincial administration were bad, but the immediate political consequences for Gaius were excellent. The equestrians were now given reality as a class; as a political unit they might be set against the Senate or be formed into a coalition to serve Gaius's purposes.

Gaius easily won reelection as tribune for 122 B.C.E. He aimed at giving citizenship to the Italians, both to solve the problem that their dissatisfaction presented and to add them to his political coalition. But the common people did not want to share the advantages of Roman citizenship. The Senate seized on this proposal as a way of driving a wedge between Gaius and his supporters.

The Romans did not reelect Gaius for 121 B.C.E., leaving him vulnerable to his enemies. A hostile consul provoked an incident that led to violence. The Senate invented an extreme decree ordering the consuls to see to it that no harm came to the republic; in effect, this decree established martial law. Gaius was hunted down and killed, and a senatorial court condemned and put to death some 3,000 of his followers without any trial.

Marius and Sulla

For the moment, the senatorial oligarchy had fought off the challenge to its traditional position. Before long, it faced more serious dangers arising from troubles abroad. The first grew out of a dispute over the succession to the throne of Numidia, a client kingdom of Rome's near Carthage.

MARIUS AND THE JUGURTHINE WAR The victory of Jugurtha, who became king of Numidia, and his massacre of Roman and Italian businessmen in the province, gained Roman attention. Although the Senate was reluctant to become involved, pressure from the equestrians and the people forced the dec-

Sallust on Factions and the Decline of the Republic

Sallust (86–35 B.C.E.) was a supporter of Julius Caesar and of the political faction called populares, *translated here as "the democratic party," opponents of the* optimates, *translated here as "the nobility." In this selection from his monograph on the Jugurthine War, Sallust tries to explain Rome's troubles in the period after the destruction of Carthage in 146 B.C.E.*

❖ *Why did Sallust think that the destruction of Carthage marked the beginning of the decline of the Roman Republic? Does his account of events seem fair and dispassionate? How would a member of "the nobility" have evaluated the same events? Is the existence of factions or "parties" inevitably harmful to a republic?*

The division of the Roman state into warring factions, with all its attendant vices, had originated some years before, as a result of peace and of that material prosperity which men regard as the greatest blessing. Down to the destruction of Carthage, the people and Senate shared the government peaceably and with due restraint, and the citizens did not compete for glory or power; fear of its enemies preserved the good morals of the state. But when the people were relieved of this fear, the favourite vices of prosperity—licence and pride—appeared as a natural consequence. Thus the peace and quiet which they had longed for in time of adversity proved, when they obtained it, to be even more grievous and bitter than the adversity. For the nobles started to use their position, and the people their liberty, to gratify their selfish passions, every man snatching and seizing what he could for himself. So the whole community was split into parties, and the Republic, which hitherto had been the common interest of all, was torn asunder. The

nobility had the advantage of being a close-knit body, whereas the democratic party was weakened by its loose organization, its supporters being dispersed among a huge multitude. One small group of oligarchs had everything in its control alike in peace and war—the treasury, the provinces, public offices, all distinctions and triumphs. The people were burdened with military services and poverty, while the spoils of war were snatched by the generals and shared with a handful of friends. Meantime, the soldiers' parents or young children, if they happened to have a powerful neighbour, might well be driven from their homes. Thus the possession of power gave unlimited scope to ruthless greed, which violated and plundered everything, respecting nothing and holding nothing sacred, till finally it brought about its own downfall. For the day came when noblemen rose to power who preferred true glory to unjust dominion: then the state was shaken to its foundations by civil strife, as by an earthquake.

Excerpt from *The Jugurthine War: The Conspiracy of Catiline* by Sallust, translated by S. A. Hanford (Penguin Classics, 1963) © S. A. Hanford, 1963.

laration of what became known as the Jugurthine War in 111 B.C.E.

As the war dragged on, the people, sometimes with good reason, suspected the Senate of taking bribes from Jugurtha. They elected C. Marius (157–86 B.C.E.) to the consulship for 107 B.C.E. The assembly, usurping the role of the Senate, assigned him to Numidia. This action was significant in several ways. Marius was a *novus homo*, a "new man"—that is, the first in the history of his family to reach the consulship. Although a wealthy equestrian, he had been born in the town of Arpinum and was outside the closed circle of the old Roman aristocracy. His earlier career had won

him a reputation as an outstanding soldier and something of a political maverick.

Marius quickly defeated Jugurtha, but Jugurtha escaped and guerilla warfare continued. Finally, Marius's subordinate, L. Cornelius Sulla (138–78 B.C.E.), trapped Jugurtha and brought the war to an end. Marius celebrated the victory, but Sulla, an ambitious though impoverished descendant of an old Roman family, resented being cheated of the credit he thought he deserved. Soon rumors circulated crediting Sulla with the victory and diminishing Marius's role. Thus were the seeds planted for a personal rivalry and a mutual hostility that would last until Marius's death.

While the Romans were fighting Jugurtha, a far greater danger threatened Rome from the north. In 105 B.C.E. two barbaric tribes, the Cimbri and the Teutones, had come down the Rhone Valley and crushed a Roman army at Arausio (Orange). When these tribes threatened again, the Romans elected Marius to his second consulship to meet the danger. He served five consecutive terms until 100 B.C.E., when the crisis was over.

While the barbarians were occupied elsewhere, Marius used the time to make important changes in the army. He began using volunteers for the army, mostly the dispossessed farmers and rural proletarians whose problems had not been solved by the Gracchi. They enlisted for a long term of service and looked on the army not as an unwelcome duty, but as an opportunity and a career. They became semiprofessional clients of their general and sought guaranteed food, clothing, shelter, and booty from victories. They came to expect a piece of land as a form of mustering-out pay, or veteran's bonus, when they retired.

Volunteers were most likely to enlist with a man who was a capable soldier and influential enough to obtain what he needed for them. They looked to him rather than to the state for their rewards. He, on the other hand, had to obtain these favors from the Senate if he was to maintain his power and reputation. Marius' innovation created both the opportunity and the necessity for military leaders to gain enough power to challenge civilian authority. The promise of rewards won these leaders the personal loyalty of their troops, and that loyalty allowed them to frighten the Senate into granting their demands.

THE WAR AGAINST THE ITALIAN ALLIES (90–88 B.C.E.) For a decade Rome avoided serious troubles, but in that time the Senate took no action to deal with Italian discontent. The Italians were excluded from the land bill for Marius' veterans. Their discontent was serious enough to cause the Senate to expel all Italians from Rome in 95 B.C.E. Four years later, the tribune M. Livius Drusus put forward a bill to enfranchise the Italians. Drusus seems to have been a sincere aristocratic reformer, but he was assassinated in 90 B.C.E. Frustrated, the Italians revolted and established a separate confederation with its own capital and its own coinage.

Employing the traditional device of divide and conquer, the Romans immediately offered citizenship to those cities that remained loyal and soon made the same offer to the rebels if they laid down their arms. Even then, hard fighting was needed to put down the uprising, but by 88 B.C.E. the war against the allies was over. All the Italians became Roman citizens with the protections that citizenship offered. However, they retained local self-government and a dedication to their own municipalities that made Italy flourish. The passage of time blurred the distinction between Romans and Italians and forged them into a single nation.

SULLA AND HIS DICTATORSHIP During the war against the allies, Sulla had performed well. He was elected consul for 88 B.C.E. and was given command of the war against Mithridates, who was leading a major rebellion in Asia. At this point, the seventy-year-old Marius emerged from obscurity and sought the command for himself. With popular and equestrian support, he got the assembly to transfer the command to him. Sulla, defending the rights of the Senate and his own interests, marched his army against Rome. This was the first time a Roman general had used his army against fellow citizens. Marius and his friends fled, and Sulla regained the command. No sooner had he left again for Asia, than Marius joined with the consul Cinna and reconquered Rome by force. He outlawed Sulla and launched a bloody massacre of the senatorial opposition. Marius died soon after his election to a seventh consulship, for 86 B.C.E.

Cinna now was the chief man at Rome. Supported by Marius's men, he held the consulship from 87

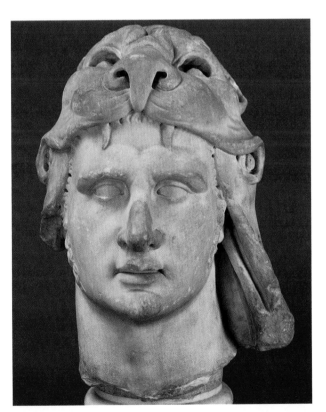

Mithridates the Great, king of Pontus. For two decades he opposed Rome's expansion. In this sculpture from the Louvre, he wears a lion's head in imitation of Hercules.
Giraudon/Art Resource, N.Y.

to 84 B.C.E. His future depended on Sulla's fortunes in the East.

By 85 B.C.E., Sulla had driven Mithridates from Greece and had crossed over to Asia Minor. Eager to regain control of Rome, he negotiated a compromise peace. In 83 B.C.E., he returned to Italy and fought a civil war that lasted for more than a year. Sulla won and drove the followers of Marius from Italy. He now held all power and had himself appointed dictator, not in the traditional sense, but for the express purpose of reconstituting the state.

Sulla's first step was to wipe out the opposition. The names of those proscribed were posted in public. As outlaws, they could be killed by anyone, and the killer received a reward. Sulla proscribed not only political opponents, but his personal enemies and men whose only crime was having wealth and property. With the proceeds from the confiscations, Sulla rewarded his veterans, perhaps as many as 100,000 men, and thereby built a solid base of support.

Sulla had enough power and influence to make himself the permanent ruler of Rome. He was traditional enough to want a restoration of senatorial government, but reformed so as to prevent the misfortunes of the past. To deal with the decimation of the Senate caused by the proscriptions and the civil war, he enrolled 300 new members, many of them from the equestrian order and the upper classes of the Italian cities. The office of tribune, used by the Gracchi to attack senatorial rule, was made into a political dead end.

Sulla's most valuable reforms improved the quality of the courts and the entire legal system. He created new courts to deal with specified crimes, bringing the number of courts to eight. Because both judge and jurors were senators, the courts, too, enhanced senatorial power. These actions were the most permanent of Sulla's reforms, laying the foundation for Roman criminal law.

Sulla retired to a life of ease and luxury in 79 B.C.E. He could not, however, undo the effect of his own example—that of a general using the loyalty of his own troops to take power and to massacre his opponents, as well as innocent men. These actions proved to be more significant than his constitutional arrangements.

The Fall of the Republic

Pompey, Crassus, Caesar, and Cicero

Within a year of Sulla's death, his constitution came under assault. To deal with an armed threat to its powers, the Senate violated the very procedures meant to defend them. The Senate gave the command of the army to Pompey (106–48 B.C.E.), who was only twenty-eight and had never been elected to a magistracy. Then, when Sertorius, a Marian general, resisted senatorial control, the Senate appointed Pompey proconsul in Spain in 77 B.C.E. These actions ignored Sulla's rigid rules for office holding, which had been meant to guarantee experienced, loyal, and safe commanders. In 71 B.C.E. Pompey returned to Rome with new glory, having put down the rebellion of Sertorius. In 73 B.C.E., the Senate made another extraordinary appointment to put down a great slave rebellion led by the gladiator Spartacus. Marcus Licinius Crassus, a rich and ambitious senator (See "Plutarch Describes How Crassus Became a Millionnaire.") received powers that gave him command of almost all Italy. Together with the newly returned Pompey, he crushed the rebellion in 71 B.C.E. Extraordinary commands of this sort proved to be the ruin of the republic.

Crassus and Pompey were ambitious men whom the Senate feared. Both demanded special honors and election to the consulship for the year 70 B.C.E. Pompey was legally ineligible because he had never gone through the strict course of offices prescribed in Sulla's constitution, and Crassus needed Pompey's help. They joined forces, though they disliked and were jealous of each other. They gained popular support by promising to restore the full powers of

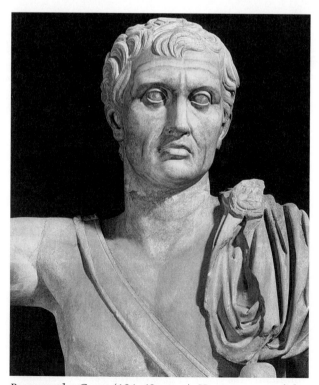

Pompey the Great (106–48 B.C.E.). He was successful in crushing rebellions against the Roman Republic.
Alinari/Art Resource, N.Y.

Plutarch Describes How Crassus Became a Millionaire

Marcus Licinius Crassus (ca. 112–53 B.C.E.) was a fine general, a powerful politician, and the richest person in Rome. There is no doubt that his wealth contributed greatly to his power. In the following selection, Plutarch describes how Crassus acquired his riches.

❖ *By what devices did Crassus become rich? Why is Plutarch critical of his techniques? How would they be described and evaluated in our own time? What does this passage tell us about the ways in which Roman society had changed since the days of the early republic?*

Most of [his wealth], if one must tell the scandalous truth, he gathered by fire and war, making the public calamities his greatest source of revenue. For when Sulla seized Rome and sold the property of those put to death by him, regarding and calling it booty, and wishing to make as many influential men as he could partners in the crime, Crassus refused neither to accept nor buy such property. Moreover, observing how natural and familiar at Rome were the burning and collapse of buildings, because of their massiveness and their closeness to one another, he bought slaves who were builders and architects. Then, when he had more than 500 of these, he would buy houses that were on fire and those adjoining the ones on fire. The owners would let them go for small sums, because of their fear and uncertainty, so that the greatest part of Rome came into his hands. But though he had so many artisans, he never built any house but the one he lived in, and used to say that those that were addicted to building would undo themselves without the help of other enemies. And though he had many silver mines, and very valuable land with laborers on it, yet one might consider all this as nothing compared with the value of his slaves, such a great number and variety did he possess—readers, amanuenses, silversmiths, stewards and table-servants. He himself directed their training, and took part in teaching them himself, accounting it, in a word, the chief duty of a master to care for his slaves as the living tools of household management.

Excerpt from Plutarch, *Life of Crassus*, trans. by N. Lewis and M. Reinhold, in *Roman Civilization*, Vol. 1, pp. 458–459. Copyright © 1955 Columbia University Press. Reprinted by permission of the publisher.

the tribunes, which Sulla had curtailed. And they gained equestrian backing by promising to restore equestrians to the extortion court juries. They both won election and repealed most of Sulla's constitution. This opened the way for further attacks on senatorial control and for collaboration between ambitious generals and demagogic tribunes.

In 67 B.C.E., a special law gave Pompey *imperium* for three years over the entire Mediterranean and fifty miles in from the coast. It also gave him the power to raise great quantities of troops and money to rid the area of pirates. The assembly passed the law over senatorial opposition, and in three months Pompey cleared the seas of piracy. Meanwhile, a new war had broken out with Mithridates. In 66 B.C.E. the assembly transferred the command to Pompey, giving him unprecedented powers. He held *imperium* over all Asia, with the right to make war and peace at will. His *imperium* was superior to that of any proconsul in the field.

Once again, Pompey justified his appointment. He defeated Mithridates and drove him to suicide. By 62 B.C.E., he had extended Rome's frontier to the Euphrates River and had organized the territories of Asia so well that his arrangements remained the basis of Roman rule well into the imperial period. When Pompey returned to Rome in 62 B.C.E., he had more power, prestige, and popular support than any Roman in history. The Senate and his personal enemies had reason to fear that he might emulate Sulla and establish his own rule.

Rome had not been quiet in Pompey's absence. Crassus was the foremost among those who had reason to fear Pompey's return. Although rich and influential, Crassus did not have the confidence of the Senate, a firm political base of his own, or the kind of military glory needed to rival Pompey. During the 60s B.C.E., therefore, he allied himself with various popular leaders.

The ablest of these men was Gaius Julius Caesar (100–44 B.C.E.). He was a descendant of an old, but politically obscure, patrician family that claimed descent from the kings and even from the goddess Venus. In spite of this noble lineage, Caesar was connected to the popular party through his aunt, the wife of Marius, and through his own wife, Cornelia, the daughter of Cinna. Caesar was an ambitious and determined young politician whose daring and rhetorical skill made him a valuable ally in winning the discontented of every class to the cause of the *populares*. Though Crassus was very much the senior partner, each needed the other to achieve what both wanted: significant military commands whereby they might build a reputation, a political following, and a military force to compete with Pompey's.

The chief opposition to Crassus' candidates for the consulship for 63 B.C.E. came from Cicero (106–43 B.C.E.), a *novus homo*, from Marius' home town of Arpinum. He had made a spectacular name as the leading lawyer in Rome. Cicero, though he came from outside the senatorial aristocracy, was no *popularis*. His program was to preserve the republic against demagogues and ambitious generals by making the government more liberal. He wanted to unite the stable elements of the state—the Senate and the equestrians—in a harmony of the orders. This program did not appeal to the senatorial oligarchy, but the Senate preferred Cicero to Catiline, a dangerous and popular politician thought to be linked with Crassus. Cicero and Antonius were elected consuls for 63 B.C.E., with Catiline running third.

Cicero soon learned of a plot hatched by Catiline. Catiline had run in the previous election on a platform of cancellation of debts; this appealed to discontented elements in general, but especially to the heavily indebted nobles and their many clients. Made desperate by defeat, Catiline planned to stir up rebellions around Italy, to cause confusion in the city, and to take it by force. Quick action by Cicero defeated Catiline.

Formation of the First Triumvirate

Toward the end of 62 B.C.E., Pompey landed at Brundisium. To general surprise, he disbanded his army, celebrated a great triumph, and returned to private life. He had delayed his return in the hope of finding Italy in such a state as to justify his keeping the army and dominating the scene. Cicero's quick suppression of Catiline prevented his plan. Pompey, therefore, had either to act illegally or to lay down his arms. Because he had not thought of monarchy or revolution, but merely wanted to be recognized and treated as the greatest Roman, he chose the latter course.

Pompey had achieved amazing things for Rome and simply wanted the Senate to approve his excellent arrangements in the East and to make land allotments to his veterans. His demands were far from unreasonable, and a prudent Senate would have granted them and would have tried to employ his power in defense of the constitution. But the Senate was jealous and fearful of overmighty individuals and refused his requests. Pompey was driven to an alliance with his natural enemies, Crassus and Caesar, because all three found the Senate standing in the way of what they wanted.

In 60 B.C.E. Caesar returned to Rome from his governorship of Spain. He wanted the privilege of celebrating a triumph, the great victory procession that the Senate granted certain generals to honor especially great achievements, and of running for consul. The law did not allow him to do both, however, requiring him to stay outside the city with his army but demanding that he canvass for votes personally within the city. He asked for a special dispensation, but the Senate refused. Caesar then performed a political miracle. He reconciled Crassus with Pompey and gained the support of both for his own ambitions. So was born the First Triumvirate, an informal agreement among three Roman politicians, each seeking his private goals, which further undermined the future of the republic.

Julius Caesar and His Government of Rome

Though he was forced to forgo his triumph, Caesar's efforts were rewarded when he was elected to the consulship for 59 B.C.E. His fellow consul was M. Calpernius Bibulus, the son-in-law of Cato and a conservative hostile to Caesar and the other *populares*. Caesar did not hesitate to override his colleague. The triumvirs' program was quickly enacted. Caesar got the extraordinary command that would give him a chance to earn the glory and power with which to rival Pompey: the governorship of Illyricum and Gaul for five years. A land bill settled Pompey's veterans comfortably, and his eastern settlement was ratified. Crassus, much of whose influence came from his position as champion of the equestrians, won for them a great windfall by having the government renegotiate a tax contract in their favor. To guarantee themselves against any reversal of these actions, the triumvirs continued their informal but effective, collaboration, arranging for the election of friendly consuls and the departure of potential opponents.

Caesar was now free to seek the military success he craved. His province included Cisalpine Gaul in the Po Valley (by now occupied by many Italian settlers as well as Gauls) and Narbonese Gaul beyond the Alps (modern Provence).

Relying first on the excellent quality of his army and the experience of his officers and then on his own growing military ability, Caesar made great progress. By 56 B.C.E. he had conquered most of Gaul, but he had not yet consolidated his victories firmly. He therefore sought an extension of his command, but quarrels between Crassus and Pompey so weakened the Triumvirate that the Senate was prepared to order Caesar's recall.

To prevent the dissolution of his base of power, Caesar persuaded Crassus and Pompey to meet with him at Luca in northern Italy to renew the coalition. They agreed that Caesar would get another five-year command in Gaul, and Crassus and Pompey would be consuls again in 55 B.C.E. After that, they would each receive an army and a five-year command. Caesar was free to return to Gaul and finish the job. The capture of Alesia in 51 B.C.E. marked the end of the serious Gallic resistance and of Gallic liberty. For Caesar, it brought the wealth, fame, and military power he wanted. He commanded thirteen loyal legions, a match for his enemies as well as for his allies.

By the time Caesar was ready to return to Rome, the Triumvirate had dissolved and a crisis was at hand. At Carrhae, in 53 B.C.E., Crassus died trying to conquer the Parthians, successors to the Persian Empire. His death broke one link between Pompey and Caesar. The death of Caesar's daughter Julia, who had been Pompey's wife, dissolved another.

As Caesar's star rose, Pompey became jealous and fearful. He did not leave Rome but governed his province through a subordinate. In the late 50s B.C.E., political rioting at Rome caused the Senate to appoint Pompey sole consul. This grant of unprecedented power and responsibility brought Pompey closer to the senatorial aristocracy in mutual fear of, and hostility to, Caesar. The Senate wanted to bring Caesar back to Rome as a private citizen after his proconsular command expired. He would then be open to attack for past illegalities. Caesar tried to avoid the trap by asking permission to stand for the consulship in absentia.

Early in January of 49 B.C.E., the more extreme faction in the Senate had its way. It ordered Pompey to defend the state and Caesar to lay down his command by a specified day. For Caesar, this meant exile or death, so he ordered his legions to cross the Rubicon River, the boundary of his province. (See Map 4–4 and "Caesar Tells What Persuaded Him to Cross the Rubicon.") This action started a civil war. In 45 B.C.E. Caesar defeated the last forces of his enemies under Pompey's sons at Munda in Spain. The war was over, and Caesar, in Shakespeare's words, bestrode "the narrow world like a Colossus."

From the beginning of the civil war until his death in 44 B.C.E., Caesar spent less than a year and a half in Rome, and many of his actions were attempts to deal with immediate problems between campaigns. His innovations generally sought to make rational and orderly what was traditional and chaotic. An excellent example is Caesar's reform of the calendar. By 46 B.C.E. it was eighty days ahead of the proper season, because the official year was lunar, containing only 355 days. Using the best scientific advice, Caesar instituted a new calendar. With minor changes by Pope Gregory XIII in the sixteenth century, it is the calendar in use today.

Another general tendency of his reforms in the political area was the elevation of the role of Italians

A bust of Julius Caesar. Alinari/Art Resource, N.Y.

Caesar Tells What Persuaded Him to Cross the Rubicon

Julius Caesar competed with Pompey for the leading position in the Roman state. Complicated maneuvers failed to produce a compromise. In the following selection, Caesar gives his side of the story of the beginning of the Roman civil war. Note that Caesar writes about himself in the third person.

❖ *This selection, of course makes the case for Caesar's actions. From your reading in this book and from any other information you have, how do you think Pompey might have replied? On constitutional and legal grounds, who had the stronger case? On grounds of practical considerations and of the welfare of the Roman state, which party, if either, deserved support? If neither did, why not?*

These things being made known to Caesar, he harangued his soldiers; he reminded them of the wrongs done to him at all times by his enemies, and complained that Pompey had been alienated from him and led astray by them through envy and a malicious opposition to his glory, though he had always favored and promoted Pompey's honor and dignity. He complained that an innovation had been introduced into the republic, that the intercession of the tribunes, which had been restored a few years before by Sulla, was branded as a crime, and suppressed by force of arms; that Sulla, who had stripped the tribunes of every other power, had, nevertheless, left the privilege of intercession unrestrained; that Pompey, who pretended to restore what they had lost, had taken away the privileges which they formerly had; that whenever the senate decreed, "that the magistrates should take care that the republic sustained no injury" (by which words and decree the Roman people were obliged to repair to arms), it was only when pernicious laws were proposed; when the tribunes attempted violent measures; when the people seceded, and possessed themselves of the temples and eminences of the city; (and these instances of former times, he showed them were expiated by the fate of Saturninus and the Gracchi): that nothing of this kind was attempted now, nor even thought of: that no law was promulgated, no intrigue with the people going forward, no secession made; he exhorted them to defend from the malice of his enemies the reputation and honor of that general under whose command they had for nine years most successfully supported the state; fought many successful battles, and subdued all Gaul and Germany. The soldiers of the thirteenth legion, which was present (for in the beginning of the disturbances he had called it out, his other legions not having yet arrived), all cry out that they are ready to defend their general, and the tribunes of the commons, from all injuries.

Having made himself acquainted with the disposition of his soldiers, Caesar set off with that legion to Ariminum, and there met the tribunes, who had fled to him for protection.

Julius Caesar, *Commentaries*, trans. by W. A. McDevitte and W. S. Bosh (New York: Harper and Brothers, 1887), pp. 249–250.

and even provincials at the expense of the old Roman families, most of whom were his political enemies. He raised the number of senators to 900 and filled the Senate's depleted ranks with Italians and even Gauls. He was free with grants of Roman citizenship, giving the franchise to Cisalpine Gaul as a whole and to many individuals of various regions.

Caesar made few changes in the government of Rome. The Senate continued to play its role, in theory. But its increased size, its packing with supporters of Caesar, and his own monopoly of military power made the whole thing a sham. He treated the Senate as his creature, sometimes with disdain. His legal position rested on several powers. In 46 B.C.E. he was appointed dictator for ten years, and in the next year he was appointed for life. He also held the consulship, the immunity of a tribune (although, being a patrician, he had never been a tribune), the chief priesthood of the state, and a new position, prefect of morals, which gave him the censorial power. Usurping the elective power of the assemblies, he even named the magistrates for the next few years, because he expected to be away in the East.

The enemies of Caesar were quick to seize on every pretext to accuse him of aiming at monarchy. A senatorial conspiracy gathered strength under the leadership of Gaius Cassius Longinus and Marcus Junius Brutus and included some sixty senators in all. On March 15, 44 B.C.E., Caesar entered the Senate, characteristically without a bodyguard, and was stabbed to death. The assassins regarded themselves as heroic tyrannicides, but did not have a clear plan of action to follow the tyrant's death. No doubt they simply expected the republic to be restored in the old way, but things had gone too far for that. There followed instead thirteen more years of civil war, at the end of which the republic received its final burial. (See "Suetonius Describes Caesar's Dictatorship.")

The Second Triumvirate and the Emergence of Octavian

Caesar had had legions of followers, and he had a capable successor in Mark Antony. But the dictator had named his eighteen-year-old grandnephew, Gaius Octavius (63 B.C.E.–14 C.E.), as his heir and had left him three-quarters of his vast wealth. To everyone's surprise, the sickly and inexperienced young man came to Rome to claim his legacy. He gathered an army, won the support of many of Caesar's veterans, and became a figure of importance—the future Augustus.

At first, the Senate tried to use Octavius against Antony, but when the conservatives rejected his request for the consulship, Octavius broke with them. Following Sulla's grim precedent, he took his army and marched on Rome. There he finally assumed his adopted name, C. Julius Caesar Octavianus. Modern historians refer to him at this stage in his career as Octavian, although he insisted on being called Caesar. In August of 43 B.C.E., he became consul and declared the assassins of Caesar outlaws. Brutus and Cassius had an army of their own, so Octavian sought help on the Caesarean side. He made a pact with Mark Antony and M. Aemilius Lepidus, a Caesarean governor of the western provinces. They took control of Rome and had themselves appointed "triumvirs to put the republic in order," with great powers. This was the Second Triumvirate, and unlike the first, it was legally empowered to rule almost dictatorially.

The need to pay their troops, their own greed, and the passion that always emerges in civil wars led the triumvirs to start a wave of proscriptions that outdid even those of Sulla. In 42 B.C.E. the triumviral army defeated Brutus and Cassius at Philippi in Macedonia, and the last hope of republican restoration died with the tyrannicides. Each of the triumvirs received a command. The junior partner, Lepidus, was given Africa, Antony took the rich and

inviting East, and Octavian got the West and the many troubles that went with it.

Octavian had to fight a war against Sextus, the son of Pompey, who held Sicily. He also had to settle 100,000 veterans in Italy, confiscating much property and making many enemies. Helped by his friend Agrippa, he defeated Sextus Pompey in 36 B.C.E. Among his close associates was Maecenas, who served him as adviser and diplomatic agent. Maecenas helped manage the delicate relations with Antony and Lepidus, but perhaps equally important was his role as a patron of the arts. Among his clients were Vergil and Horace, both of whom did important work for Octavian. They painted him as a restorer of traditional Roman values, as a man of ancient Roman lineage and of traditional Roman

A profile of Brutus, one of Caesar's assassins, appeared on this silver coin. The reverse shows a cap of liberty between two daggers and reads "Ides of March."
H. Roger-Viollet/Liason Agency, Inc.

Suetonius Describes Caesar's Dictatorship

Suetonius (ca. C.E. 69–ca. 140) wrote a series of biographies of the emperors from Julius Caesar to Domitian. In the following selection, he described some of Caesar's actions during his dictatorship in the years 46–44 B.C.E.

❖ *Why does Suetonius think Caesar deserved to be killed? To what group of Romans did his behavior give the greatest offense? How would other Romans view the pros and cons of Caesar's career?*

[Caesar's] other words and actions, however, so far outweigh all his good qualities, that it is thought he abused his power, and was justly cut off. For he not only obtained excessive honours, such as the consulship every year, the dictatorship for life, and the censorship, but also the title of emperor, and the surname of Father of His Country, besides having his statue amongst the kings, and a lofty couch in the theatre. He even suffered some honours to be decreed to him, which were unbefitting the most exalted of mankind; such as gilded chair of state in the senate-house and on his tribunal, a consecrated chariot, and banners in the Circensian procession, temples, altars, statues among the gods, a bed of state in the temples, a priest, and a college of priests dedicated to himself, like those of Pan; and that one of the months should be called by his name. There were, indeed, no honours which he did not either assume himself, or grant to others, at his will and pleasure. In his third and fourth consulship, he used only the title of the office, being content with the power of dictator, which was conferred upon him with the consulship; and in both years he substituted other consuls in his room, during the three last months; so that in the intervals he held no assemblies of the people, for the election of magistrates, excepting only tribunes and ediles of the people; and appointed officers, under the name of *praefects*, instead of the *praetors*, to administer the affairs of the city during his absence. The office of consul having become vacant, by the sudden death of one of the consuls the day before the calends of January [January 1], he conferred it on a person who requested it of him, for a few hours. Assuming the same licence, and regardless of the customs of his country, he appointed magistrates to hold their offices for terms of years. He granted the insignia of the consular dignity to ten persons of *praetorian* rank. He admitted into the senate some men who had been made free of the city, and even natives of Gaul, who were semi-barbarians. He likewise appointed to the management of the mint, and the public revenue of the state, some servants of his own household; and entrusted the command of three legions, which he left at Alexandria, to an old catamite of his, the son of his freed-man Rufinus.

He was guilty of the same extravagance in the language he publicly used, as Titus Ampius informs us; according to whom he said, "The republic is nothing but a name, without substance or reality. Sylla was an ignorant fellow to abdicate the dictatorship. Men ought to consider what is becoming when they talk with me, and look upon what I say as a law."

From Suetonius, *The Lives of the Twelve Caesars*, trans. by Alexander Thompson, revised by T. Forster, George Bell and Sons, 1903, pp. 45–47.

virtues, and as the culmination of Roman destiny. More and more he was identified with Italy and the West, as well as with order, justice, and virtue.

Meanwhile Antony was in the East, chiefly at Alexandria with Cleopatra, the queen of Egypt. In 36 B.C.E. he attacked Parthia, with disastrous results. Octavian had promised to send troops to support Antony's Parthian campaign, but never sent them. Antony was forced to depend on the East for support, and to some considerable degree, this meant reliance on Cleopatra. Octavian clearly understood the advantage of representing himself as the champion of the West, Italy, and Rome. Meanwhile he represented Antony as the man of the East and the dupe of Cleopatra, her tool in establishing Alexandria as the center of an empire and herself as its ruler. Such propaganda made it easier for Caesareans to abandon their veteran leader in favor of the young heir of Caesar. It did not help Antony's cause that he agreed to a public festival at Alexan-

MAP 4–4   THE CIVIL WARS OF THE LATE ROMAN REPUBLIC   *This map shows the extent of the territory controlled by Rome at the time of Caesar's death and the sites of the major battles of the civil wars of the late republic.*

dria in 34 B.C.E., where he and Cleopatra sat on golden thrones. She was proclaimed "Queen of Kings," her son by Julius Caesar was named "King of Kings," and parts of the Roman Empire were doled out to her various children.

By 32 B.C.E., all pretense of cooperation ended. Octavian and Antony each tried to put the best face on what was essentially a struggle for power. Lepidus had been put aside some years earlier. Antony sought senatorial support and promised to restore the republican constitution. Octavian seized and published what was alleged to be the will of Antony, revealing his gifts of provinces to the children of Cleopatra. This caused the conflict to take the form of East against West, Rome against Alexandria.

In 31 B.C.E., the matter was settled at Actium in western Greece. Agrippa, Octavian's best general, cut off the enemy by land and sea, forcing and winning a naval battle. Antony and Cleopatra escaped to Egypt, but Octavian pursued them to Alexandria, where both committed suicide. The civil wars were over, and at the age of thirty-two Octavian was absolute master of the Mediterranean world. His power was enormous, but so was the task before him. He had to restore peace, prosperity, and confidence. All of these required establishing a constitution that would reflect the new realities without offending unduly the traditional republican prejudices that still had so firm a grip on Rome and Italy.

In Perspective

The history of the Roman Republic was almost as sharp a departure from the common experiences of ancient civilizations as that of the Greek city–states. A monarchy in its earliest known form, Rome not long thereafter expelled its king, abandoned the institution of monarchy, and established an aristocratic republic somewhat like the poleis of the Greek "Dark Ages." But unlike the Greeks, the Romans continued to be in touch with foreign neighbors, including the far more civilized urban monarchies of the Etruscans. Nonetheless, the Romans clung faithfully to their republican institutions. For a long time the Romans remained a nation of farmers and herdsmen, to whom trade was relatively unimportant, especially outside Italy.

Over time, the caste distinctions between patricians and plebeians became unimportant. They were replaced by distinctions based on wealth and, even more important, aristocracy, wherein the significant distinction was between noble families, who held the highest elected offices in the state, and those outside the nobility. The Roman Republic from the first found itself engaged in almost continuous warfare with its neighbors—either in defense of its own territory, in fights over disputed territory, or in defense of other cities or states who were friends and allies of Rome.

Both internally and in their foreign relations, the Romans were a very legalistic people, placing great importance on traditional behavior encoded into laws. Although backed by the powerful authority of the magistrates at home and the potent Roman army abroad, the laws were based on experience, common sense, and equity. Roman law aimed at stability and fairness, and it succeeded well enough that few people who lived under it wanted to do away with it. It lived on and grew during the imperial period and beyond. During the European Middle Ages it played an important part in the revival of the West and continued to exert an influence into modern times.

The force of Roman arms, the high quality of Roman roads and bridges, and the pragmatic character of Roman law helped create something unique: an empire ruled by a republic, first a large one on land that included all of Italy and later one that commanded the shores of the entire Mediterranean and quite a distance inland in many places. Rome controlled an area that bears comparison with some of the empires of the East. It acquired that territory, wealth, and power in a state managed by annual magistrates elected by the male Roman citizens and by an aristocratic Senate, which had to take notice of popular assemblies and a published, impersonal code of law. It achieved its greatness with an army of citizens and allies, without a monarchy or a regular bureaucracy.

The temptations and responsibilities of governing a vast and rich empire, however, finally proved too much for the republican constitution. Trade grew, and with it a class of merchants and financiers—equestrians—that was neither aristocratic nor agricultural, but increasingly powerful. The influx of masses of slaves captured in war undermined the small farmers who had been the backbone of the Roman state and its army. As many of them were forced to leave their farms, they moved to the cities, chiefly to Rome, where they had no productive role. Conscripted armies of farmers serving relatively short terms gave way to volunteer armies of landless men serving as professionals and expecting to be rewarded for their services with gifts of land or money. The generals of these armies were not annual magistrates controlled by the Senate and the constitution, but ambitious military leaders seeking glory and political advantage.

The Fall of the Roman Republic	
133 B.C.E.	Tribunate of Tiberius Gracchus
123–122 B.C.E.	Tribunate of Gaius Gracchus
111–105 B.C.E.	Jugurthine War
104–100 B.C.E.	Consecutive consulships of Marius
90–88 B.C.E.	War against the Italian allies
88 B.C.E.	Sulla's march on Rome
82 B.C.E.	Sulla assumes dictatorship
71 B.C.E.	Crassus crushes rebellion of Spartacus
71 B.C.E.	Pompey defeats Sertorius in Spain
70 B.C.E.	Consulship of Crassus and Pompey
60 B.C.E.	Formation of First Triumvirate
58–50 B.C.E.	Caesar in Gaul
53 B.C.E.	Crassus killed in Battle of Carrhae
49 B.C.E.	Caesar crosses Rubicon; civil war begins
48 B.C.E.	Pompey defeated at Pharsalus; killed in Egypt
46–44 B.C.E.	Caesar's dictatorship
45 B.C.E.	End of civil war
43 B.C.E.	Formation of Second Triumvirate
42 B.C.E.	Triumvirs defeat Brutus and Cassius at Philippi
31 B.C.E.	Octavian and Agrippa defeat Anthony at Actium

The result was civil war and the destruction of the republic. The conquest of a vast empire moved the Romans away from their unusual historical traditions toward the more familiar path of empire trodden by older rulers in Egypt and Mesopotamia.

REVIEW QUESTIONS

1. In what ways did the institutions of family and clientage and the establishment of patrician and plebeian classes contribute to the stability of the early Roman Republic? How important were education and slavery to the success of the republic? the institution of slavery?
2. What was the Struggle of the Orders? What methods did plebeians use to get what they wanted? How was Roman society different after the struggle ended?
3. Discuss Rome's expansion to 265 B.C.E. How was Rome able to conquer and control Italy? In their relations with Greece and Asia Minor in the second century B.C.E., were the Romans looking for security? wealth? power? fame?
4. Explain the clash between the Romans and the Carthaginians in the First and Second Punic wars. Could the wars have been avoided? How did Rome benefit from its victory over Carthage? What problems were created by this victory?
5. What social, economic, and political problems did Italy have in the second century B.C.E.? What were the main proposals of Tiberius Gaius Gracchus? What questions about Roman society did they raise? Why did the proposals fail?
6. What were the problems that plagued the Roman Republic in the last century? What caused these problems and how did the Romans try to solve them? To what extent was the republic destroyed by ambitious generals who loved power more than Rome itself?

SUGGESTED READINGS

F. E. ADCOCK, *The Roman Art of War Under the Republic* (1940). A basic study of the subject.

E. BADIAN, *Foreign* Clientelae (1958). A brilliant study of the Roman idea of a client–patron relationship, extended to foreign affairs.

R. A. BAUMAN, *Women and Politics in Ancient Rome* (1992). A useful study of women's role in roman public life.

J. BOARDMAN, J. GRIFFIN, AND O. MURRAY, *The Oxford History of the Roman World* (1990). An encyclopedic approach to the varieties of the Roman experience.

P. A. BRUNT, *Social Conflicts in the Roman Republic* (1971). A fine study by a master of the subject.

T. J. CORNELL, *The Beginnings of Rome: Italy and Rome from the Bronze Age to the Punic Wars* (1995). A fine new study of early Rome.

T. CORNELL AND J. MATTHEWS, *Atlas of the Roman World* (1982). Much more than the title indicates, this book presents a comprehensive view of the Roman world in its physical and cultural setting.

M. GELZER, *Caesar: Politician and Statesman*, trans. by P. Needham (1968). The best biography of Caesar.

E. S. GRUEN, *The Last Generation of the Roman Republic* (1973). An interesting but controversial interpretation of the fall of the republic.

E. S. GRUEN, *The Hellenistic World and the Coming of Rome* (1984). A new interpretation of Rome's conquest of the eastern Mediterranean.

W. V. HARRIS, *War and Imperialism in Republican Rome, 327–70 B.C.E.* (1975). An analysis of Roman attitudes and intentions concerning imperial expansion and war.

KEAVENEY, *Lucullus: A Life* (1992). A biography of the famous Roman epicure.

S. LANCEL, *Carthage, a History.* (1995). A good account of Rome's great competitor.

J. F. LAZENBY, *Hannibal's War* (1978). An excellent military history of the Second Punic War.

F. B. MARSH, *A History of the Roman World from 146 to 30 B.C.E.*, 3d ed., rev. by H. H. Scullard (1963). An excellent narrative account.

T. N. MITCHELL, *Cicero, The Senior Statesman* (1991). An intelligent study of Cicero's later career.

C. NICOLET, *The World of the Citizen in Republican Rome* (1980). A valuable study of the meaning of Roman citizenship.

M. PALLOTTINO, *The Etruscans*, 6th ed. (1974). Makes especially good use of archaeological evidence.

J. RICH AND G. SHIPLEY, *War and Society in the Roman World* (1993). A useful collection of essays on military topics.

E. T. SALMON, *Roman Colonization under the Republic* (1970). An account of the character and importance of the Roman colony.

E. T. SALMON, *The Making of Roman Italy* (1980). The story of Roman expansion on the Italian peninsula.

H. H. SCULLARD, *A History of the Roman World 753–146 B.C.E.*, 4th ed. (1980). An unusually fine narrative history with useful critical notes.

D. STOCKTON, *Cicero: A Political Biography* (1971). A readable and interesting study.

G. WILLIAMS, *The Nature of Roman Poetry* (1970). An unusually graceful and perceptive literary study.

Chapter 5

Hadrian's entry into Rome. This carved relief from the first half of the second century C.E. shows the Emperor Hadrian at the city gates of Rome where he is greeted by the guiding spirits of the Senate and the Roman people. Late Hadrianic–early Autonine relief. Palazzo dei Conservatori, Rome, Italy. Nimatallah/Art Resource, N.Y.

The Roman Empire

KEY TOPICS

- The Augustan constitution
- The organization and government of the Roman Empire
- Culture and civilization from the late republic through the imperial period
- The early history of Christianity
- The decline and fall of Rome

The victory of Augustus put an end to the deadly period of civil strife that had begun with the murder of Tiberius Gracchus. The establishment of a monarchy, at first concealed in republican forms but gradually more obvious, brought a long period of peace. Rome's unquestioned control of the entire Mediterranean permitted the growth of trade and a prosperity in the first two centuries of the Roman Empire not to be equaled for more than a millennium.

Management of the empire outside Italy became more benign and efficient. With shared citizenship, the provinces usually accepted Roman rule readily and even enthusiastically. Latin became the official language of the western part of the empire and Greek the official language in the east. This permitted the growth and spread of a common culture, today called Classical Civilization, throughout the empire. The same conditions fostered a great outburst of ac-

tivity and excellence in the arts. The loss of political freedom, however, brought a decline in the vitality of the great Roman genre of rhetoric.

Christianity emerged in the first century C.E. as one of many competing Eastern cults. It continued to spread and attract converts, winning toleration and finally dominance in the fourth century. Christianity was powerfully shaped by the world of imperial Rome, absorbing and using classical culture even while fighting against it.

The third century C.E. brought serious attacks on several of Rome's frontiers, causing political and economic chaos. For a time, such emperors as Diocletian (r. 284–305) and Constantine (r. 306–337) instituted heroic measures to restore order. Their solutions involved increased centralization, militarization, and attempts to control closely every aspect of life. The emperors became more exalted and remote, the people increasingly burdened with heavy taxes even as the loss of economic freedom reduced their ability to pay. At last a new wave of barbarian attacks proved irresistible, and the Roman Empire in the west ended in the second half of the fifth century.

The Augustan Principate

If the problems facing Octavian after the Battle of Actium in 31 B.C.E. were great, so were his resources for addressing them. He was the master of a vast military force, the only one in the Roman world, and he had loyal and capable assistants. Of enormous importance was the rich treasury of Egypt, which Octavian treated as his personal property. He was helped by the great eagerness of the people of Italy for an end to civil war and a return to peace, order, and prosperity. In exchange for these, most people were prepared to accept a considerable abandonment of republican practices and to give significant power to an able ruler. The memory of Julius Caesar's fate, however, was still fresh in Octavian's mind. Its lesson was that it was dangerous to flaunt unprecedented powers and to disregard all republican traditions.

Octavian did not create his constitutional solution at a single stroke. It developed gradually as he tried new devices to fit his perception of changing conditions. Behind all the republican trappings and the apparent sharing of authority with the Senate, the government of Octavian, like that of his successors, was a monarchy. All real power, both civil and military, lay with the ruler—whether he was called by the unofficial title of *princeps*, or "first citizen," like Octavian, the founder of the regime, or *imperator*, "emperor," like those who followed. During the civil war Octavian's powers came from his triumviral status, whose dubious legality and unrepublican char-

acter were an embarrassment. From 31 B.C.E. on, he held the consulship each year, but this circumstance was neither strictly legal nor very satisfactory.

On January 13, 27 B.C.E., Octavian put forward a new plan in dramatic style, coming before the Senate to give up all his powers and provinces. In what was surely a rehearsed response, the Senate begged him to reconsider. At last he agreed to accept the provinces of Spain, Gaul, and Syria with proconsular power for military command and to retain the consulship in Rome. The other provinces would be governed by the Senate as before. Because the provinces he retained were border provinces that contained twenty of Rome's twenty-six legions, his true power was undiminished. The Senate, however, responded with almost hysterical gratitude, voting him many honors. Among them was the semireligious title "Augustus," which carried implications of veneration, majesty, and holiness. From this time on, historians speak of Rome's first emperor as Augustus and of his regime as the Principate. This would have pleased him, for it helps conceal the novel, unrepublican nature of the regime and the naked power on which it rested.

In 23 B.C.E., Augustus resigned his consulship and held that office only rarely thereafter. Instead, he was voted two powers that were to be the base of his rule thenceforth: the proconsular *imperium maius* and the tribunician power. The former made his proconsular power greater than that of any other proconsul and permitted him to exercise it even within the city of Rome. The latter gave him the right to conduct public business in the assemblies and the Senate, gave him the power of the veto, the tribunician sacrosanctity (immunity from arrest and punishment), and a connection with the Roman popular tradition. Thereafter, with only minor changes, Augustus' powers remained those conferred by the settlement of 23 B.C.E.

Administration

Augustus made important changes in the government of Rome, Italy, and the provinces. Most of his reforms reduced inefficiency and corruption, ended the danger to peace and order from ambitious individuals, and lessened the distinction between Romans and Italians, senators and equestrians. The assemblies lost their significance as a working part of the constitution, and the Senate took on most of the functions of the assemblies. Augustus purged the old Senate of undesirable members and fixed its number at 600. He recruited its members from wealthy men of good character, who entered after serving as lesser magistrates. Augustus controlled the elections and ensured that promising young men, whatever their origin, served the state as administrators and provincial governors. In this way, equestrians and Italians

This statue of Emperor Augustus (r. 27 B.C.E.–14 C.E.), now in the Vatican, stood in the villa of Augustus's wife Livia. The figures on the elaborate breastplate are all of symbolic significance. At the top, for example, Dawn in her chariot brings in a new day under the protective mantle of the sky god; in the center, Tiberius, Augustus' future successor, accepts the return of captured Roman army standards from a barbarian prince; and at the bottom, Mother Earth offers a horn of plenty.
Charitable Foundation/Gemeinnutzige Stiftung Leonard von Matt

who had no connection with the Roman aristocracy entered the Senate in great numbers. For all his power, Augustus was careful always to treat the Senate with respect and honor.

Augustus divided Rome into regions and wards with elected local officials. He gave the city, with its rickety wooden tenements, its first public fire department and rudimentary police force. Grain distribution to the poor was carefully controlled and limited, and organizations were created for providing an adequate water supply. The Augustan period was one of great prosperity, based on the wealth brought in by the conquest of Egypt, on the great increase in commerce and industry made possible by general peace and a vast program of public works, and on a strong return to successful small farming by Augustus's resettled veterans.

The union of political and military power in the hands of the *princeps* made it possible for him to install rational, efficient, and stable government in the provinces for the first time. The emperor, in effect, chose the governors, removed the incompetent or rapacious, and allowed the effective ones to keep their provinces for longer periods. Also, he provided for much greater local autonomy, giving considerable responsibility to the upper classes in the provincial cities and towns and to the tribal leaders in less civilized areas.

The Army and Defense

The main external problem facing Augustus—and one that haunted all his successors—was the northern frontier. (See Map 5–1.) Rome needed to pacify the regions to the north and the northeast of Italy and to find defensible frontiers against the recurring waves of barbarians. Augustus' plan was to push forward into central Europe to create the shortest possible defensive line. The eastern part of the plan succeeded, and the campaign in the west started well. In 9 C.E., however, there was a revolt led by the German tribal leader Herrmann, or Arminius, as the Romans called him. He ambushed and destroyed three Roman legions, and the aged Augustus abandoned the campaign, leaving a problem of border defense that caused great trouble for his successors.

Under Augustus, the armed forces achieved true professional status. Enlistment, chiefly by Italians, was for twenty years, but the pay was relatively good, with occasional bonuses and the promise of a pension on retirement in the form of money or a plot of land. Together with the auxiliaries from the provinces, these forces formed a frontier army of about 300,000 men. In normal times, this number was barely enough to hold the line.

The army permanently based in the provinces played a vital role in bringing Roman culture to the natives. The soldiers spread their language and customs, often marrying local women and settling down in the area of their service. They attracted merchants, who often became the nuclei of new towns and cities that grew into centers of Roman civilization. As time passed, the provincials on the frontiers became Roman citizens who helped strengthen Rome's defenses against the barbarians outside.

Religion and Morality

A century of political strife and civil war had undermined many of the foundations of traditional Roman society. Augustus thought it desirable to try to repair the damage. So he undertook a program aimed at preserving and restoring the traditional values of the family and religion in Rome and Italy. He introduced laws curbing adultery and divorce and encouraging early marriage and the procreation of legitimate children.

MAP 5–1   THE ROMAN EMPIRE, 14 C.E.   *This map shows the growth of the empire under Augustus and its extent at his death.*

He set an example of austere behavior in his own household and even banished his daughter, Julia, whose immoral behavior had become public knowledge.

Augustus worked at restoring the dignity of formal Roman religion, building many temples, reviving old cults, and reorganizing and invigorating the priestly colleges. He banned the worship of newly introduced foreign gods. Writers whom he patronized, such as Vergil, pointed out his family's legendary connection with Venus. During his lifetime he did not accept divine honors, though he was deified after his death. As with Julius Caesar, a state cult was dedicated to his worship.

Civilization of the Ciceronian and Augustan Ages

The high point of Roman culture came in the last century of the republic and during the principate of Augustus. Both periods reflected the dominant influence of Greek culture, especially its Hellenistic mode. Upper-class Romans were educated in Greek rhetoric, philosophy, and literature, which also served as the models for Roman writers and artists. Yet in spirit and sometimes in form, the art and writing of both periods show uniquely Roman qualities, though each in different ways.

The Late Republic

CICERO   The towering literary figure of the late republic was Cicero (106–43 B.C.E.). He is most famous for the orations he delivered in the law courts and in the Senate. Together with a considerable body of his private letters, these orations provide us with a clearer and fuller insight into his mind than into that of any other figure in antiquity. We see the political life of his period largely through his eyes. He also wrote treatises on rhetoric, ethics, and politics that put Greek philosophical ideas into Latin terminology and at the same time changed them to suit Roman conditions and values.

Cicero's own views provide support for his moderate and conservative practicality. He believed in a world governed by divine and natural law that human reason could perceive and human institutions reflect. He looked to law, custom, and tradition to produce both stability and liberty. His literary style, as well as his values and ideas, was an important legacy for the Middle Ages and, reinterpreted, for the Renaissance. He was killed at the order of Mark Antony, whose political opponent he had been during the civil wars after the death of Julius Caesar.

HISTORY   The last century of the republic produced some historical writing, much of which is lost to us. Sallust (86–35 B.C.E.) wrote a history of the years 78–67 B.C.E., but only a few fragments remain to remind us of his reputation as the greatest of republican historians. His surviving work consists of two pamphlets on the Jugurthine War and on the Catilinarian conspiracy of 63 B.C.E. They reveal his Caesarean and antisenatorial prejudices and the stylistic influence of Thucydides.

Julius Caesar wrote important treatises on the Gallic and civil wars. They are not fully rounded historical accounts, but chiefly military narratives written from Caesar's point of view and with propagandist intent. Their objective manner (Caesar always referred to himself in the third person) and their direct, simple, and vigorous style make them persuasive even today. They must have been most effective with their immediate audience.

LAW   The period from the Gracchi to the fall of the republic was important in the development of Roman law. Before that time, Roman law was essentially national and had developed chiefly by juridical decisions, case by case. Contact with foreign peoples and the influence of Greek ideas, however, forced a change. From the last century of the republic on, the edicts of the *praetors* had increasing importance in developing the Roman legal code. They interpreted and even changed and added to existing law. Quite early, the edicts of the magistrates who dealt with foreigners developed the idea of the *jus gentium*, or "law of peoples," as opposed to that arising strictly from the experience of the Romans. In the first century B.C.E., the influence of Greek thought made the idea of *jus gentium* identical with that of the *jus naturale*, or "natural law," taught by the Stoics. (See "Roman Law.") It was this view of a world ruled by divine reason that Cicero enshrined in his treatise on the law, *De Legibus*.

POETRY   The time of Cicero was also the period of two of Rome's greatest poets, Lucretius and Catullus, each representing a different aspect of Rome's poetic tradition. The Hellenistic poets and literary theorists saw two functions for the poet: entertainer and teacher. They thought the best poet combined both roles, and the Romans adopted the same view. When Naevius and Ennius wrote epics on Roman history, they combined historical and moral instruction with pleasure. Lucretius (ca. 99–55 B.C.E.) pursued a similar

path in his epic poem *De Rerum Natura* (*On the Nature of the World*). In it, he set forth the scientific and philosophical ideas of Epicurus and Democritus with the zeal of a missionary trying to save society from fear and superstition. He knew that his doctrine might be bitter medicine to the reader: "That is why I have tried to administer it to you in the dulcet strain of poesy, coated with the sweet honey of the Muses."[1]

Catullus (ca. 84–54 B.C.E.) was a thoroughly different kind of poet. He wrote poems that were personal—even autobiographical. Imitating the Alexandrians, he wrote short poems filled with learned allusions to mythology, but he far surpassed his models in intensity of feeling. He wrote of the joys and pains of love, he hurled invective at important contemporaries like Julius Caesar, and he amused himself in witty poetic exchanges with others. He offered no moral lessons and was not interested in Rome's glorious history and in contemporary politics. In a sense, he is an example of the proud, independent, pleasure-seeking nobleman who characterized part of the aristocracy at the end of the republic.

The Age of Augustus

The spirit of the Augustan Age, the Golden Age of Roman literature, was quite different, reflecting the new conditions of society. The old aristocratic order, with its system of independent nobles following their own particular interests, was gone. So was the world of poets of the lower orders, receiving patronage from any of a number of individual aristocrats. Augustus replaced the complexity of republican patronage with a simple scheme in which all patronage flowed from the *princeps*, usually through his chief cultural adviser, Maecenas.

The major poets of this time, Vergil and Horace, had lost their property during the civil wars. The patronage of the *princeps* allowed them the leisure and the security to write poetry; at the same time, it made them dependent on him and limited their freedom of expression. They wrote on subjects that were useful for his policies and that glorified him and his family. These poets were not mere propagandists, however. It seems clear that mostly they were persuaded of the virtues of Augustus and his reign and sang its praises with some degree of sincerity. Because they were poets of genius, they were also able to maintain a measure of independence in their work.

VERGIL   Vergil (70–19 B.C.E.) was the most important of the Augustan poets. His first important works, the *Eclogues*, or *Bucolics*, are pastoral idylls

---

[1] Lucretius, *De Rerum Natura*, lines 931 ff.

Roman Law

One of the most important achievements of Roman civilization was the establishment over a wide area of a code of law derived from experience and custom but based on principles thought to apply universally and organized according to reason. It had a powerful influence in shaping the character of Western civilization long after the fall of the empire. The following selection, from the Digest, *compiled at the order of the emperor Justinian in the sixth century* C.E., *quotes the* Institutes, *a work by Ulpian, a leading jurist of the third century* C.E. *It discusses the fundamental issues underlying the Roman conception of law in the imperial period.*

❖ *According to this document, for what reason should a Roman citizen obey the law? How does this rationale compare with the rationale for obeying the law in Hammurabi's Mesopotamia or in democratic Athens? What is the importance of the concept of natural law? What are the consequences of rejecting such an idea?*

Justice and Law

(*Ulpian Institutes I*) When a man means to give his attention to law, he ought first to know whence the term law (*ius*) is derived. Now it is so called from justice (*iustitia*). In fact, as Celsus neatly defines it, *ius* is the art of the good and fair. Of this art we may deservedly be called the priests; we cherish justice and profess the knowledge of the good and the fair, separating the fair from the unfair, discriminating between the permitted and the forbidden, desiring to make men good, not only by the fear of penalties, but also by the incentives of rewards, affecting, if I mistake not, a true and not a simulated philosophy.

This subject comprises two categories, public law and private law. Public law is that which regards the constitution of the Roman state, private law that which looks to the interest of individuals; for some things are beneficial from the point of view of the state, and some with reference to private persons. Public law is concerned with sacred rites, with priests, with public officers. Private law is tripartite, being derived from the rules of natural law, or of the law of nations, or of civil law. Natural law is that which all animals have been taught by nature; this law is not peculiar to the human race, but is common to all animals which are produced on land or sea, and to the birds as well. From it comes the union of male and female, which we call matrimony, and the procreation and rearing of children; we find in fact that animals in general, even the wild beasts, are marked by acquaintance with this law. The law of nations is that which the various peoples of mankind observe. It is easy to see that it falls short of natural law, because the latter is common to all living creatures, whereas the former is common only to human beings in their mutual relations.

"Justice and Law" from Justinian, *Digest* I, i. iii–iv, trans. by Naphtali Lewis and Meyer Reinhold, in *Roman Civilization*, Vol. 2 , p. 534. Copyright © 1955 Columbia University Press. Reprinted by permission of the publisher.

---

in a somewhat artificial mode. The subject of the *Georgics*, however, was suggested to Vergil by Maecenas. The model here was the early Greek poet Hesiod's *Works and Days*, but the mood and purpose of Vergil's poem are far different. It pays homage to the heroic human effort to forge order and social complexity out of an ever hostile and sometimes brutal natural environment. It was also a hymn to the cults, traditions, and greatness of Italy.

All this served the purpose of glorifying Augustus's resettlement of the veterans of the civil wars on Italian farms and his elevation of Italy to special status in the empire. Vergil's greatest work is the *Aeneid*, a long national epic that succeeded in placing the history of Rome in the great tradition of the Greeks and the Trojan War. Its hero, the Trojan war-

rior Aeneas, personifies the ideal Roman qualities of duty, responsibility, serious purpose, and patriotism. As the Romans' equivalent of Homer, Vergil glorified not the personal honor and excellence of the Greek epic heroes, but the civic greatness represented by Augustus and the peace and prosperity that he and the Julian family had given to imperial Rome.

HORACE Horace (65–8 B.C.E.) was the son of a freeman and fought on the republican side until its defeat at Philippi. He was won over to the Augustan cause by the patronage of Maecenas and by the attractions of the Augustan reforms. His *Satires* are genial and humorous. His great skills as a lyric poet are best revealed in his *Odes*, which are ingenious in their adaptation of Greek meters to the requirements of Latin verse. Two of the *Odes* are directly in praise of Augustus, and many of them glorify the new Augustan order, the imperial family, and the empire.

PROPERTIUS   Sextus Propertius lived in Rome in the second half of the first century B.C.E., a contemporary of Vergil and Horace. Like them, he was part of the poetic circle favored by Augustus' friend Maecenas. He wrote poetry in the form of elegies, appreciated for their grace and wit. (See "An Ideal Roman Woman.")

OVID   The career of Ovid (43 B.C.E.–18 C.E.) reveals the darker side of Augustan influence on the arts. He wrote light and entertaining love elegies that reveal the sophistication and the loose sexual code of a notorious sector of the Roman aristocracy whose values and way of life were contrary to the seriousness and family-centered life Augustus was trying to foster. Ovid's *Ars Amatoria*, a poetic textbook on the art of seduction, angered Augustus and was partly responsible for the poet's exile in 8 C.E. Ovid tried to recover favor, especially with his *Fasti*, a poetic treatment of Roman religious festivals, but to no avail. His most popular work is the *Metamorphoses*, a kind of mythological epic that turns Greek myths into charming stories in a graceful and lively style. Ovid's fame did not fade with his exile and death, but his fate was an effective warning to later poets.

HISTORY   The achievements of Augustus, his emphasis on tradition, and the continuity of his regime with the glorious history of Rome encouraged both

An Ideal Roman Woman

Just after the fall of the Roman republic, late in the first century B.C.E., the poet Propertius wrote an elegy in honor of a woman of the Roman nobility, Cornelia, the stepdaughter of Augustus, the ruler of the newly established Principate. She was married to the aristocrat Paullus and was the mother of three children. Propertius presents her as defending herself before the last judgment of Hades, kind of the underworld. Her words were written by a man, but they seem to be an accurate representation of the values of the upper classes of Rome of both sexes.

❖ *In what achievements, associations and qualities did she take pride? What might a person of our time find absent? What limits are implied by what is missing?*

I was born to this, and when the wreath of marriage
Caught up my hair, and I was a woman grown,
it was your bed, my Paullus, that I came to
and now have left. The carving on the stone
says SHE WED BUT ONCE. O fathers long respected
victors in Africa, be my defense...
I asked no favours when Paullus was
    made censor:
no evil found its way within our walls.
I do not think I have disgraced my fathers:
I set a decent pattern in these halls.
Days had a quiet rhythm: no scandal touched us
from the wedding torch to the torch beside
    my bier.
A certain integrity is proof of breeding:
the love of virtue should not be born of fear.
Whatever the judge, whatever the lot fate
    gives me,

no woman needs to blush who sits at my side—...
For my children I wore the mother's robe
    of honor;
It was no empty house I left behind.
Lepidus, Paullus, still you bring me comfort
you closed my eyes when death had made
    me blind.
Twice in the curule chair I have seen my brother;
they cheered him as a consul the day before
    I died.
And you, my daughter, think of your censor-
    father,
choose one husband and live content at his side.
Our clan will rest on the children that you
    give it,
Secure in their promise I board the boat
    and rejoice.
Mine is the final triumph of any woman,
that her spirit earns the praise of a living voice.

From Propertius, *Elegies*, 4.11, translated by Constance Carrier, *The Poems of Propertius*, Indiana University Press, copyright © 1963, pp. 191–192. Reprinted by permission of Indiana University Press.

Ruins of the Roman Forum. From the earliest days of the city, the Forum was the center of Roman life. Augustus had it rebuilt, and it was frequently rebuilt and refurbished by his successors, so most of the surviving buildings date to the imperial period. Corbis

historical and antiquarian prose works. Some Augustan writers wrote scholarly treatises on history and geography in Greek. By far the most important and influential prose writer of the time, however, was Livy (59 B.C.E.–17 C.E.), an Italian from Padua. His *History of Rome* was written in Latin and treated the period from the legendary origins of Rome until 9 B.C.E. Only a fourth of his work is extant; of the rest we have only pitifully brief summaries. He based his history on earlier accounts and made no effort at original research. His great achievement was in telling the story of Rome in a continuous and impressive narrative. Its purpose was moral, and he set up historical models as examples of good and bad behavior and, above all, patriotism. He glorified Rome's greatness and connected it with Rome's past, as Augustus tried to do.

ARCHITECTURE AND SCULPTURE Augustus was as great a patron of the visual arts as he was of literature. He embarked on a building program that beautified Rome, glorified his reign, and contributed to the general prosperity and his own popularity. He filled the Campus Martius with beautiful new buildings, theaters, baths, and basilicas; the Roman Forum was rebuilt; and Augustus built a forum of his own. At its heart was the temple of Mars the Avenger, which commemorated Augustus' victory and the greatness of his ancestors. On Rome's Palatine Hill he built a splendid temple to his patron god, Apollo, in pursuit of his religious policy.

Most of the building was influenced by the Greek classical style, which aimed at serenity and the ideal type. The same features were visible in the portrait sculpture of Augustus and his family. The greatest

A panel from the Ara Pacis (Altar of Peace). The altar was dedicated in 9 B.C.E. It was part of a propaganda campaign—involving poetry, architecture, myth, and history—that Augustus undertook to promote himself as the savior of Rome and the restorer of peace. This panel shows the goddess Earth and her children with cattle, sheep, and other symbols of agricultural wealth. Nimatallah/Art Resource, N.Y.

monument of the age is the *Ara Pacis*, or "Altar of Peace," dedicated in 9 B.C.E. Set originally in an open space in the Campus Martius, its walls still carry a relief. Part of it shows a procession in which Augustus and his family appear to move forward, followed in order by the magistrates, the Senate, and the people of Rome. There is no better symbol of the new order.

Imperial Rome, 14–180 C.E.

The central problem for Augustus's successors was the position of the ruler and his relationship to the ruled. Augustus tried to cloak the monarchical nature of his government, but his successors soon abandoned all pretense. The ruler came to be called *imperator*— from which comes our word "emperor"—as well as *Caesar*. The latter title signified connection with the imperial house, and the former indicated the military power on which everything was based.

The Emperors

Because Augustus was ostensibly only the "first citizen" of a restored republic and his powers were theoretically voted him by the Senate and the people, he could not legally name his successor. In actuality, however, he plainly designated his heirs by lavishing favors on them and by giving them a share in the imperial power and responsibility. Tiberius (r. 14–37 C.E.),[2] his immediate successor, was at first embarrassed by the ambiguity of his new role, but soon the monarchical and hereditary nature of the regime became patent. Gaius (Caligula, r. 37–41 C.E.), Claudius (r. 41–54 C.E.), and Nero (r. 54–68 C.E.) were all descended from either Augustus or his wife, Livia, and all were elevated because of that fact.

In 41 C.E., the naked military basis of imperial rule was revealed when the Praetorian Guard dragged the lame, stammering, and frightened Claudius from behind a curtain and made him emperor. In 68 C.E., the frontier legions learned what the historian Tacitus called "the secret of Empire…that an emperor could be made elsewhere than at Rome." Nero's incompetence and unpopularity, and especially his inability to control his armies, led to a serious rebellion in Gaul in 68 C.E. The year 69 saw four different emperors assume power in quick succession as different Roman armies took turns placing their commanders on the throne.

Vespasian (r. 69–79 C.E.) emerged victorious from the chaos, and his sons, Titus (r. 79–81 C.E.) and Domitian (r. 81–96 C.E.), carried forward his line, the Flavian dynasty. Vespasian was the first emperor who did not come from the old Roman nobility. He was a

tough soldier who came from the Italian middle class. A good administrator and a hardheaded realist of rough wit, he resisted all attempts by flatterers to find noble ancestors for him. On his deathbed he is said to have ridiculed the practice of deifying emperors by saying, "Alas, I think I am becoming a god."

The assassination of Domitian put an end to the Flavian dynasty. Because Domitian had no close relative who had been designated as successor, the Senate put Nerva (r. 96–98 C.E.) on the throne to avoid chaos. He was the first of the five "good emperors," who included Trajan (r. 98–117 C.E.), Hadrian (r. 117–138 C.E.), Antoninus Pius (r. 138–161 C.E.), and Marcus Aurelius (r. 161–180 C.E.). Until Marcus Aurelius, none of these emperors had sons, so they each followed the example set by Nerva of adopting an able senator and establishing him as successor. This rare solution to the problem of monarchical succession was, therefore, only a historical accident. The result, nonetheless, was almost a century of peaceful succession and competent rule, which ended when Marcus Aurelius allowed his incompetent son, Commodus (r. 180–192 C.E.), to succeed him, with unfortunate results.

The genius of the Augustan settlement lay in its capacity to enlist the active cooperation of the upper classes and their effective organ, the Senate. The election of magistrates was taken from the assemblies and given to the Senate, which became the major center for legislation and exercised important judicial functions. This semblance of power persuaded some contemporaries and even some modern scholars that Augustus had established a "dyarchy,"—a system of joint rule by *princeps* and Senate. That was never true.

Rulers of the Early Empire	
27 B.C.E.–14 C.E.	Augustus
The Julio–Claudian Dynasty	
14–37 C.E.	Tiberius
37–41 C.E.	Gaius (Caligula)
41–54 C.E.	Claudius
54–68 C.E.	Nero
69 C.E.	Year of the Four Emperors
The Flavian Dynasty	
69–79 C.E.	Vespasian
79–81 C.E.	Titus
81–96 C.E.	Domitian
The "Good Emperors"	
96–98 C.E.	Nerva
98–117 C.E.	Trajan
117–138 C.E.	Hadrian
138–161 C.E.	Antoninus Pius
161–180 C.E.	Marcus Aurelius

[2] Dates for emperors give the years of their reigns, indicated by "r."

Spoils from the temple in Jerusalem were carried in triumphal procession by Roman troops. This relief from Titus's arch of victory in the Roman Forum celebrates his capture of Jerusalem after a two-year siege. The Jews found it difficult to reconcile their religion with Roman rule and frequently rebelled. Scala/Art Resource, N.Y.

The hollowness of the senatorial role became more apparent as time passed. Some emperors, like Vespasian, took pains to maintain, increase, and display the prestige and dignity of the Senate. Others, like Caligula, Nero, and Domitian, degraded the Senate and paraded their own despotic power. But from the first, the Senate's powers were illusory. Magisterial elections were, in fact, controlled by the emperors, and the Senate's legislative function quickly degenerated into mere assent to what the emperor or his representatives put before it. The true function of the Senate was to be a legislative and administrative extension of the emperor's rule.

There was, of course, some real opposition to the imperial rule. It sometimes took the form of plots against the life of the emperor. Plots and the suspicion of plots led to repression, the use of spies and paid informers, book burning, and executions. The opposition consisted chiefly of senators who looked back to republican liberty for their class and who found justification in the Greek and Roman traditions of tyrannicide as well as in the precepts of Stoicism. Plots and repression were most common under Nero and Domitian. From Nerva to Marcus Aurelius, however, the emperors, without yielding any power, again learned to enlist the cooperation of the upper class by courteous and modest deportment.

The Administration of the Empire

The provinces flourished economically and generally accepted Roman rule easily. (See Map 5–2.) In the eastern provinces, the emperor was worshiped as a god; even in Italy, most emperors were deified after their death as long as the imperial cult established by Augustus continued. Imperial policy usually combined an attempt to unify the empire and its various peoples with a respect for local customs and differences. Roman citizenship was spread ever more widely, and by 212 C.E. almost every inhabitant of the empire was a citizen. Latin became the language of the western provinces. Although the East remained essentially Greek in language and culture, even it adopted many aspects of Roman life. The spread of *Romanitis*, or "Roman-ness," was more than nominal, for senators and even emperors began to be drawn from provincial families.

LOCAL MUNICIPALITIES   From an administrative and cultural standpoint, the empire was a collection of cities and towns and had little to do with the countryside. Roman policy during the Principate was to raise urban centers to the status of Roman municipalities, with the rights and privileges attached to them. A typical municipal charter left

MAP 5–2 PROVINCES OF THE ROMAN EMPIRE TO 117 C.E. *The growth of the empire to its greatest extent is here shown in three stages—at the death of Augustus in 14 C.E., at the death of Nerva in 98, and at the death of Trajan in 117. The insert shows the main roads that tied the far-flung empire together. The division into provinces is also shown.*

much responsibility in the hands of local councils and magistrates elected from the local aristocracy. Moreover, the holding of a magistracy, and later a seat on the council, carried Roman citizenship with it. Therefore, the Romans enlisted the upper classes of the provinces in their own government, spread Roman law and culture, and won the loyalty of the influential people. (For a glimpse into the lives of ordinary people see "Daily Life in a Roman Provincial Town: Graffiti from Pompeii.")

There were exceptions to this picture of success. The Jews found their religion incompatible with Roman demands and were savagely repressed when they rebelled in 66–70, 115–117, and 132–135 C.E. (See "The Bar-Kochba Rebellion: The Final Jewish Uprising against Rome.") In Egypt, the Romans exploited the peasants with exceptional ruthlessness and did not pursue a policy of urbanization.

Trajan's Column was erected at Rome about 110 C.E. to celebrate the emperor Trajan's (r. 98–117) victory over the Dacians beyond the Danube. Trajan pushed the boundaries of the Roman Empire to their farthest limits, defeating the Parthians in the east as well as the Dacians in the north. Carved in a spiraling relief, the column shows more than a thousand figures, accurately depicting people, buildings, flowers, animals, implements, and weapons. Scala/Art Resource, N.Y.

As the efficiency of the bureaucracy grew, so did the number and scope of its functions and therefore its size. The emperors came to take a broader view of their responsibilities for the welfare of their subjects than before. Nerva conceived and Trajan introduced the *alimenta*, a program of public assistance for the children of indigent parents. More and more the emperors intervened when municipalities got into difficulties, usually financial, sending imperial troubleshooters to deal with problems. The importance and autonomy of the municipalities shrank as the central administration took a greater part in local affairs. The provincial aristocracy came to regard public service in its own cities as a burden rather than an opportunity. The price paid for the increased efficiency offered by centralized control was the loss of the vitality of the cities throughout the empire.

The success of Roman civilization also came at great cost to the farmers who lived outside Italy. Taxes, rents, mandatory gifts, and military service drew capital away from the countryside to the cities on a scale not previously seen in the Graeco-Roman world. More and more the rich life of the urban elite came at the expense of millions of previously stable farmers.

FOREIGN POLICY   Augustus' successors, for the most part, accepted his conservative and defensive foreign policy. Trajan was the first emperor to take the offensive in a sustained way. Between 101 and 106 C.E. he crossed the Danube and, after hard fighting, established the new province of Dacia between the Danube and the Carpathian Mountains. He was tempted, no doubt, by its important gold mines, but he probably was also pursuing a new general strategy: to defend the empire more aggressively by driving wedges into the territory of threatening barbarians. The same strategy dictated the invasion of the Parthian Empire in the east (113–117 C.E.). Trajan's early success was astonishing, and he established three new provinces in Armenia, Assyria, and Mesopotamia. But his lines were overextended. Rebellions sprang up, and the campaign crumbled. Trajan was forced to retreat, and he died before getting back to Rome.

Hadrian's reign marked an important shift in Rome's frontier policy. Heretofore, even under the successors of Augustus, Rome had been on the offensive against the barbarians. Although the Romans rarely gained new territory, they launched frequent attacks to chastise and pacify troublesome tribes. Hadrian hardened the Roman defenses, building a stone wall in the south of Scotland and a wooden one across the Rhine–Danube triangle.

The Roman defense became rigid, and initiative passed to the barbarians. Marcus Aurelius was compelled to spend most of his reign resisting dangerous attacks in the east and on the Danube frontier.

Daily Life in a Roman Provincial Town: Graffiti from Pompeii

On the walls of the houses of Pompeii, buried and preserved by the eruption of Mount Vesuvius in 79 C.E., are many scribblings that give us an idea of what the life of ordinary people was like.

❖ *How do these graffiti differ from those one sees in a modern American city? What do they reveal about the similarities and differences between the ordinary people of ancient Rome and the people of today? How would you account for the differences?*

I

Twenty pairs of gladiators of Decimus Lucretius Satrius Valens, lifetime flamen of Nero son of Caesar Augustus, and ten pairs of gladiators of Decimus Lucretius Valens, his son, will fight at Pompeii on April 8, 9, 10, 11, 12. There will be a full card of wild beast combats, and awnings [for the spectators]. Aemilius Celer [painted this sign], all alone in the moonlight.

II

Market days: Saturday in Pompeii, Sunday in Nuceria, Monday in Atella, Tuesday in Nola, Wednesday in Cumae, Thursday in Puteoli, Friday in Rome.

III

Pleasure says: "You can get a drink here for an as [a few cents], a better drink for two, Falernian for four."

IV

A copper pot is missing from this shop. 65 sesterces reward if anybody brings it back, 20 sesterces if he reveals the thief so we can get our property back.

V

The weaver Successus loves the innkeeper's slave girl, Iris by name. She doesn't care for him, but he begs her to take pity on him. Written by his rival. So long.

[Answer by the rival:] Just because you're bursting with envy, don't pick on a handsomer man, a lady-killer and a gallant.

[Answer by the first writer:] There's nothing more to say or write. You love Iris, who doesn't care for you.

VI

Take your lewd looks and flirting eyes off another man's wife, and show some decency on your face!

VII

Anybody in love, come here. I want to break Venus' ribs with a club and cripple the goddess' loins. If she can pierce my tender breast, why can't I break her head with a club?

VIII

I write at Love's dictation and Cupid's instruction;

But damn it! I don't want to be a god without you.

IX

[A prostitute's sign:] I am yours for 2 asses cash.

Excerpt from *Roman Civilization*, by N. Lewis and M. Reinhold, Vol. 2, Columbia University Press, 1955. Reprinted by permission of Columbia University Press.

AGRICULTURE: THE DECLINE OF SLAVE LABOR AND THE RISE OF *COLONI* The defense of its frontiers put enormous pressure on the human and financial resources of the empire, but the effect of these pressures was not immediately felt. The empire generally experienced considerable economic growth well into the reigns of "good emperors." Internal peace and efficient administration benefited agriculture as well as trade and industry. Farming and trade developed together as political conditions made it easier to sell farm products at a distance.

Small farms continued to exist, but the large estate, managed by an absentee owner and growing cash crops, became the dominant form of agriculture. At first, as in the republican period, these estates were worked chiefly by slaves, but in the first century this began to change. Economic pressures on the free lower classes forced many of them to become tenant farmers, or *coloni*, and eventually the *coloni* replaced slaves as the mainstay of agricultural labor. Typically, these sharecroppers paid rent in labor or in kind, though sometimes they made

The Bar-Kochba Rebellion:
The Final Jewish Uprising against Rome

Unlike most conquered peoples, the Jews found accommodation to Roman rule difficult. Their first rebellion was crushed by Vespasian's son, the future emperor Titus, in 70 C.E. At that time the Temple in Jerusalem was destroyed. A second revolt was put down in 117 C.E. Finally, when Hadrian ordered a Roman colony placed on the site of Jerusalem, Simon, who was called Bar-Kochba, or "Son of the Star," led a last uprising from 132 to 135. Dio Cassius describes the brutality of its suppression.

❖ *Did the Romans treat the Jews differently from other people under their control? What special problems did the Roman conquest pose to the Jews? What problems did the Jews present to the Romans?*

At Jerusalem Hadrian founded a city in place of the one which had been razed to the ground, naming it Aelia Capitolina, and on the site of the temple of the god he raised a new temple to Jupiter. This brought on a war of no slight importance nor of brief duration, for the Jews deemed it intolerable that foreign peoples should be settled in their city and foreign rites planted there....

At first the Romans took no account of them. Soon, however, all Judaea had been stirred up, and the Jews everywhere were showing signs of disturbance, were gathering together, and giving evidence of great hostility to the Romans, partly by secret and partly by overt acts; many outside peoples, too, were joining them through eagerness for gain, and the whole world, one might almost say, was being stirred up over the matter. Then, indeed, Hadrian sent his best generals against them. Foremost among these was Julius Severus, who was dispatched against the Jews from Britain, where he was governor....[In Judaea] he was able, rather slowly...but with comparatively little danger, to crush, exhaust, and exterminate them. Very few of them in fact survived. Fifty of their most important strongholds and 985 of their most famous villages were razed to the ground; 580,000 men were slain in the various raids and battles, and the number of those that perished by famine, disease, and fire was past finding out.

From Dio Cassius, *Roman History* 59.12–14, trans. by Ernest Cary (London: Loeb Classical Library and William Heinemann, 1916).

---

cash payments. Eventually, their movement was restricted, and they were tied to the land they worked, much as were the manorial serfs of the Middle Ages. Whatever its social costs, the system was economically efficient, however, and contributed to the general prosperity.

Although the economic importance of slavery began to decline in the second century with the rise of *coloni* labor, the institution was never abolished, nor did it disappear so long as the Roman Empire lasted. Pockets of slave labor remained as late as the time of Charlemagne. (See Chapter 6.)

Women of the Upper Classes

By the late years of the Roman republic, women of the upper classes had achieved a considerable degree of independence and influence. Some of them had become very wealthy through inheritance and very well educated. (See "Art & the West.") Women conducted literary salons and took part in literary groups. Marriage without the husband's right of *manus* became common, and some women conducted their sexual lives as freely as men. (See "Rome's Independent Women: Two Views.") The notorious Clodia, from one of Rome's noblest and most powerful families, is described as conducting many affairs, the most famous with the poet Catullus, who reviles her even as he describes the pangs of his love. Such women were reluctant to have children and increasingly employed contraception and abortion to avoid childbirth.

During the Principate, Augustus' daughter and granddaughter, both named Julia, were both the subject of scandal and punished for adultery. Augustus tried to restore Rome to an earlier ideal of decency and family integrity that reduced the power and sexual freedom of women. He also introduced legislation to encourage the procreation of children, but the new laws seem to have had little effect. In the

Portrait of a Young Woman from Pompeii

The Roman provincial city of Pompeii, near the Bay of Naples, was buried by an eruption of Mt. Vesuvius in 79 C.E. As a result, the town, together with its private houses and their contents, was remarkably well preserved until recovery in the eighteenth century. Among the discoveries were a number of works of art, including pictorial mosaics and paintings. This depiction of a young woman, on a round panel from a house in Pompeii, is part of a larger painting that includes her husband holding a volume of Plato's writings. The woman is holding a stylus and a booklet of wax tablets and is evidently in the process of writing. Her gold earrings and hair net show that she is a fashionable person of some means.

This painting comes from a modest two-story house from a residential district of the town. The main streets had shops where women went, accompanied by a slave. Pompeian remains show that women decorated themselves; among the remains are jewelry and cosmetic jars, as well as the earrings and golden net worn by the woman in this painting. She and her husband represent three significant concepts: the representation of the couple, a woman's attractiveness, and female literacy. "Such an image locates a woman in a world that combines the very old traditions—marriage and female beauty—as natural and necessary—with the notion of female competence; this last is hardly surprising as a motif in. . . Pompeii. . . , a place where women own property, do business, pay for construction, hold honorific and cultic office, and go about in public."[3] There must have been many such towns and many such women in the Roman Empire.

Sources: Marilyn Stokstad, *Art History*, revised edition, Harry N. Abrams and Prentice Hall, New York, 1999, pp. 258–259; E. Fantham, H. P. Foley, N. B. Kampen, S. B. Pomeroy and H. A. Shapiro, *Women in the Classical World*, Oxford University Press, Oxford and New York, 1994, pages 340–341

Young Woman Writing, detail of a wall painting from Pompeii. Late 1st century C.E. Diameter 14 ⅝" Museo Archeologico Nazionale, Naples, Italy/Art Resource. © Photograph by Erich Lessing.

[3] Fantham et. al., *Women in the Classical World*, p. 341.

Rome's Independent Women: Two Views

In the last years of the republic and into the transition to the empire, Roman writers begin to describe what might be called the "new woman." These women are pictured as wearing makeup, dressing and behaving shamelessly, and engaging in adulterous affairs. Perhaps the most shocking of their practices was to engage in sexual activity, but to refuse to have children. The following passages reveal two different approaches to the newly popular means of birth control. The first comes from the work of Soranus, a doctor who practiced in Rome late in the first century C.E. The second comes from the poet Ovid's poems about love.

❖ *What are the opinions of the doctors as to if and when abortion and contraception are appropriate? What reasons do they have for their opinions? What arguments does Ovid make against the use of abortion? How do these ancient arguments compare with modern ones?*

Soranus

For one party banishes abortives, citing the testimony of Hippocrates who says: "I will give to no one an abortive;" moreover, because it is the specific task of medicine to guard and preserve what has been engendered by nature. The other party prescribes abortives, but with discrimination, that is, they do not prescribe them when a person wishes to destroy the embryo because of adultery or out of consideration for youthful beauty; but only to prevent subsequent danger in parturition if the uterus is small and not capable of accommodating the complete development, or if the uterus at its orifice has knobbly swellings and fissures, of if some similar difficulty is involved. And they say the same about contraceptives as well, and we too agree with them.

Ovid

She who first began the practice of tearing out her tender progeny deserved to die in her own warfare. Can it be that, to be free of the flaw of stretchmarks, you have to scatter the tragic sands of carnage? Why will you subject your womb to the weapons of abortion and give dread piosons to the unborn? The tigress lurking in Armenia does no such thing, nor does the lioness dare destroy her young. Yet tender girls do so—though not with impunity; often she who kills what is in her womb dies herself.

Soranus, *Gynecology* 1.19.60 in O. Temkin, *Soranus: Gynecology* (Baltimore: 1956).
Ovid, *Amores* 2.14.5–9, 27–28, 35–38, translated by Natalie Kampen in E. Fantham, E. P. Foley, N. B. Kampen, S. B. Pomeroy and H. A. Shapiro, *Women in the Classical World* (New York: Oxford University Press 1994), pp. 301–302.

first imperial century several powerful women played an important, if unofficial, political role. Augustus' wife Livia had great influence during his reign, and he honored her with the title Augusta in his will. Even in the reign of her son (and Augustus' stepson) Tiberius, she exercised great influence. It was said that he fled Rome to live in Capri in order to escape her domination. The Emperor Claudius' wife Messalina took part in the plot to overthrow him. The Elder Agrippina, wife of the general Germanicus, was active in opposition to Tiberius, and her daughter, also called Agrippina, helped bring her son Nero to the throne. In later centuries, women's rights were expanded by permitting them to make wills and inherit from children. At the turn of the fourth century, the Emperor Domitian freed women from the need for guardianship.

Life in Imperial Rome: The Apartment House

The civilization of the Roman Empire depended on the vitality of its cities. The typical city had about 20,000 inhabitants, and perhaps only three or four had a population of more than 75,000. The population of Rome, however, was certainly greater than 500,000, perhaps more than a million. People coming to Rome for the first time found it overwhelming and were either thrilled or horrified by its size, bustle, and noise. The rich lived in elegant homes called *domūs*. These were single-storied houses with plenty of space, an open central courtyard, and several rooms designed for specific and different purposes, such as dining, sitting, or sleeping, in privacy and relative quiet. Though only a small portion of Rome's population lived in them, *domūs* took up as much as a third of the city's space. Public space for temples, markets, baths, gymnasiums, theaters, forums, and governmental buildings took up another quarter of Rome's territory.

This left less than half of Rome's area to house the mass of its inhabitants, who were squeezed into multiple dwellings that grew increasingly tall. Most Romans during the imperial period lived in apartment buildings called *insulae*, or "islands," that rose to a height of five or six stories and sometimes even more. The most famous of them, the Insula of Febiala, seems to have "towered above the Rome of the Antonines like a skyscraper."[4]

These buildings were divided into separate apartments (*cenicula*) of undifferentiated rooms, the same plan on each floor. The apartments were cramped and uncomfortable. They had neither central heating nor open fireplaces; heat and fire for cooking came from small, portable stoves. The apartments were hot in summer, cold in winter, and stuffy and smoky when the stoves were lit. There was no plumbing, so tenants needed to go into the streets to wells or fountains for water and to public baths and latrines, or to less regulated places. The higher up one lived, the more difficult were these trips, so chamber pots and commodes were kept in the rooms. These receptacles were emptied into vats on the staircase landings or in the alleys outside; on occasion, the contents, and even

[4] J. Carcopino, *Daily Life in Ancient Rome* (New Haven, CT: Yale University Press, 1940), p. 26.

the containers, were tossed out the window. Roman satirists complained of the discomforts and dangers of walking the streets beneath such windows. Roman law tried to find ways to assign responsibilities for the injuries done to dignity and person.

In spite of these difficulties, the attractions of the city and the shortage of space caused rents to rise, making life in the *insulae* buildings expensive as well as uncomfortable. It was also dangerous. The houses were lightly built of concrete and brick and were far too high for the limited area of their foundations, and so they often collapsed. Laws limiting the height of buildings were not always obeyed and did not, in any case, always prevent disaster. The satirist Juvenal did not exaggerate much when he wrote, "We inhabit a city held up chiefly by slats, for that is how the landlord patches up the cracks in the old wall, telling the tenants to sleep peacefully under the ruin that hangs over their heads." (See "Juvenal on Life in Rome.")

Even more serious was the threat of fire. Wooden beams supported the floors, and the rooms were lit by torches, candles, and oil lamps and heated by braziers. Fires broke out easily and, without running water, were not easily put out; once started, they usually led to disaster.

When we consider the character of these apartments and compare them with the attractive public places in the city, we can easily understand why the people of Rome spent most of their time out of doors.

This is a reconstruction of a typical Roman apartment house found at Ostia, Rome's port. The ground floor contained shops, and the stories above it held many apartments.
Museo della Civitá Romana, Rome, Italy. Scala/Art Resource, N.Y.

Juvenal on Life in Rome

The satirical poet Juvenal lived and worked in Rome in the late first and early second centuries C.E. His poems present a vivid picture of the material and cultural world of the Romans of his time. In the following passages, he tells of the discomforts and dangers of life in the city, both indoors and out.

❖ *According to Juvenal, what dangers awaited pedestrians in the Rome of his day? Who had responsibility for the condition of Rome? If the situation was as bad as he says, why was nothing done about it? Why did people choose to live in Rome at all and especially in the conditions he describes?*

Who, in Praeneste's cool, or the wooded Volsinian uplands,
Who, on Tivoli's heights, or a small town like Gabii, say,
Fears the collapse of his house? But Rome is supported on pipestems,
Matchsticks; it's cheaper, so, for the landlord to shore up his ruins,
Patch up the old cracked walls, and notify all the tenants
They can sleep secure, though the beams are in ruins above them.
No, the place to live is out there, where no cry of Fire!
Sounds the alarm of the night, with a neighbor yelling for water,
Moving his chattels and goods, and the whole third story is smoking.

Look at other things, the various dangers of nighttime.
How high it is to the cornice that breaks, and a chunk beats my brains out,
Or some slob heaves a jar, broken or cracked, from a window.
Bang! It comes down with a crash and proves its weight on the sidewalk.
You are a thoughtless fool, unmindful of sudden disaster,
If you don't make your will before you go out to have dinner.
There are as many deaths in the night as there are open windows
Where you pass by; if you're wise, you will pray, in your wretched devotions,
People may be content with no more than emptying slop jars.

....

From Juvenal, *The Satires of Juvenal*, trans. by Rolfe Humphries (Bloomington, IN: Indiana University Press, 1958), pp. 40, 43.

The Culture of the Early Empire

The years from 14 to 180 C.E. were a time of general prosperity and a flourishing material and artistic culture, but one not so brilliant and original as in the Age of Augustus.

LITERATURE   In Latin literature, the period between the death of Augustus and the time of Marcus Aurelius is known as the Silver Age. As the name implies, this age produced work of high quality although probably not of so high a quality as in the Augustan era. In contrast to the hopeful, positive optimists of the Augustans, the writers of the Silver Age were gloomy, negative, and pessimistic. In the works of the former period, praise of the emperor, his achievements, and the world abounds; in the latter, criticism and satire lurk everywhere. Some of the most important writers of the Silver

Age came from the Stoic opposition and reflected its hostility to the growing power and personal excesses of the emperors.

The writers of the second century C.E. appear to have turned away from contemporary affairs and even recent history. Historical writing was about remote periods so that there would be less danger of irritating imperial sensibilities. Scholarship was encouraged, but we hear little of poetry, especially that dealing with dangerous subjects. In the third century C.E., romances written in Greek became popular and offer further evidence of the tendency of writers of the time to seek and offer escape from contemporary realities.

ARCHITECTURE   The main contribution of the Romans lay in two new kinds of buildings—the great public bath and a new, freestanding kind of amphitheater—and in the advances in engineering that made these large structures possible. While keeping the basic post-and-lintel construction used by the Greeks, the Romans added to it the principle of the semicircular arch, borrowed from the Etruscans. They also made good use of concrete, a building material first used by the Hellenistic Greeks and fully developed by the Romans. The arch, combined with the post and lintel, produced the great Colosseum built by the Flavian emperors. When used internally in the form of vaults and domes, the arch permitted great buildings like the baths, of which the most famous and best preserved are those of the later emperors Caracalla and Diocletian. (See Map 5–3.)

One of Rome's most famous buildings, the Pantheon, begun by Augustus' friend Agrippa and rebuilt by Hadrian, combined all these elements. Its portico of Corinthian columns is of Greek origin, but its rotunda of brick-faced concrete with its domed ceiling and relieving arches is thoroughly Roman. The new engineering also made possible the construction of more mundane, but useful, structures like bridges and aqueducts.

SOCIETY   Seen from the harsh perspective of human history, the first two centuries of the Roman Empire deserve their reputation of a "golden age." One of the dark sides of Roman society, at least since the third century B.C.E., had been its increasing addiction to the brutal contests involving gladiators. By the end of the first century C.E., emperors regularly appealed to this barbaric entertainment as a way of winning the acclaim of their people (see "Seneca Describes Gladiatorial Shows.") On broader fronts in Roman society, by the second century C.E., troubles were brewing that foreshadowed the difficult times ahead. The literary efforts of the time reveal a flight from the present, from reality, and from the public realm to the past, to romance, and to private pursuits. Some of the same aspects may be seen in the more prosaic world of everyday life, especially in the decline of vitality in local government.

In the first century C.E., members of the upper classes vied with one another for election to municipal office and for the honor of doing service to their communities. By the second century C.E., it became necessary for the emperors to intervene to correct abuses in local affairs and even to force unwilling

MAP 5–3   ANCIENT ROME   *This map of Rome during the late empire shows the seven hills on and around which the city was built, as well as the major walls, bridges, and other public sites and buildings.*

Seneca Describes Gladiatorial Shows

Roman society was never gentle, but by imperial times the public had become addicted to brutal public displays of violence in the form of combats involving gladiators. At first, gladiators were enslaved prisoners of war or condemned criminals, but later free men entered the combats, driven by poverty. They were all trained in schools by professional trainers. The following selection by Seneca gives an unfriendly account of the shows and of the spectators who watched them.

❖ *What does Seneca think of the gladiatorial contests? What does he think of the spectators? Who were the gladiators? What was the attitude of the spectators toward them? What do such entertainments say about the society in which they take place? Do they have any effect on the character of that society?*

I chanced to stop in at a midday show, expecting fun, wit, and some relaxation, when men's eyes take respite from the slaughter of their fellow men. It was just the reverse. The preceeding combats were merciful by comparison; now all trifling is put aside and it is pure murder. The men have no protective covering. Their entire bodies are exposed to the blows, and no blow is ever struck in vain....In the morning men are thrown to the lions and the bears, at noon they are thrown to their spectators. The spectators call for the slayer to be thrown to those who in turn will slay him, and they detain the victor for another butchering. The outcome for the combatants is death; the fight is waged with sword and fire. This goes on while the arena is free. "But one of them was a highway robber, he killed a man!" Because he killed he deserved to suffer this punishment, granted...."Kill him! Lash him! Burn him! Why does he meet the sword so timidly? Why doesn't he kill boldly? Why doesn't he die game? Whip him to meet his wounds! Let them trade blow for blow, chests bare and within reach!" And when the show stops for intermission, "Let's have men killed meanwhile! Let's not have nothing going on!"

"Seneca Describes Gladiatorial Shows" from Seneca, *Moral Epistles*, in N. Lewis and M. Reinhold, *Roman Civilization*, Vol. 2, p. 230. Copyright © 1955 Columbia University Press. Reprinted by permission of the publisher.

members of the ruling classes to accept public office. Magistrates and council members were held personally and collectively responsible for the revenues due. There were even some instances of magistrates fleeing to avoid their office, a practice that became widespread in later centuries. (For a satirical view of life in first-century C.E. Rome, see "Dinner at Trimalchio's: A Satire of the Newly Rich at Rome.")

These difficulties reflected more basic problems. The prosperity brought by the end of civil war and the influx of wealth from the east could not sustain itself beyond the first half of the second century C.E. There also appears to have been a decline in population for reasons that remain mysterious. The cost of government kept rising. The emperors were required to maintain a standing army, minimal in size, but costly, to keep the people in Rome happy with "bread and circuses," to pay for an increasingly numerous bureaucracy, and to wage expensive wars to defend the frontiers against dangerous and determined barbarian enemies. The ever-increasing need for money compelled the emperors to raise taxes, to press hard on their subjects, and to bring on inflation by debasing the coinage. These elements brought about the desperate crises that ultimately destroyed the empire.

The Rise of Christianity

Christianity emerged, spread, survived, and ultimately conquered the Roman Empire in spite of its origin among poor people from an unimportant and remote province of the empire. Christianity faced the hostility of the established religious institutions of its native Judaea. It also had to compete against the official cults of Rome and the highly sophisticated philosophies of the educated classes and against such other "mystery" religions as the cults of Mithra, Isis, and Osiris. In addition to all this, the Christians faced the opposition of the imperial government and formal persecution. Yet Christianity achieved toleration and finally exclusive command as the official religion of the empire.

Jesus of Nazareth

An attempt to understand this amazing outcome must begin with the story of Jesus of Nazareth. The most important evidence about his life is in the Gospel accounts, all of them written well after his death. The earliest, by Mark, is dated about 70 C.E. and the latest, by John, about 100 C.E. They are not, moreover, attempts at simply describing the life of Jesus with historical accuracy. Rather, they are statements of faith by true believers. The authors of the Gospels believed that Jesus was the son of God and that he had come into the world to redeem humanity and to bring immortality to those who believed in him and followed his way. To the Gospel writers, Jesus' resurrection was striking proof of his teachings. At the same time, the Gospels regard Jesus as a figure in history, and they recount events in his life as well as his sayings.

There is no reason to doubt that Jesus was born in the province of Judaea in the time of Augustus and that he was a most effective teacher in the tra-dition of the prophets. This tradition promised the coming of a Messiah (in Greek, *christos*—so Jesus Christ means "Jesus the Messiah"), the redeemer who would make Israel triumph over its enemies and establish the kingdom of God on earth. In fact, Jesus seems to have insisted that the Messiah would not establish an earthly kingdom, but would bring an end to the world as human beings knew it at the Day of Judgment. On that day, God would reward the righteous with immortality and happiness in heaven and condemn the wicked to eternal suffering in hell. Until then (a day that his followers believed would come very soon), Jesus taught the faithful to abandon sin and worldly concerns; to follow him and his way; to follow the moral code described in the Sermon on the Mount, which preached love, charity, and humility; and to believe in him and his divine mission.

Jesus won a considerable following, especially among the poor, which caused great suspicion among the upper classes. His novel message and his criticism of the religious practices connected

Dinner at Trimalchio's: A Satire on the Newly Rich at Rome

The following selection is from Trimalchio's Feast, *part of a fragmentary satire called* The Satyricon, *by Petronius, a writer of the first century C.E. The speaker is a guest at a lavish dinner given by Trimalchio, a former slave risen to great wealth at Rome. Included among the jibes and sneers is some useful information about life in this period.*

❖ *What is the source of Trimalchio's wealth? What sources of wealth were available at the time? What does this selection reveal about social mobility in the first century? What does it reveal about the range of commerce? How do you explain the tone of the narrator?*

"As for old Trimalchio, that man's got more farms than a kite could flap over. And there's more silver plate stuffed in his porter's lodge than another man's got in his safe. As for slaves, whoosh! So help me, I'll bet not one in ten has ever seen his master. Your ordinary rich man is just peanuts compared to him; he could knock them all under a cabbage and you'd never know they were gone.

"And buy things? Not him. No sir, he raises everything right on his own estate. Wool, citron, pepper, you name it. By god, you'd find hen's milk if you looked around. Now take his wool. The home-grown strain wasn't good enough. So you know what he did? Imported rams from Tarentum, bred them into the herd. Attic honey he raises at home. Ordered the bees special from Athens.

And the local bees are better for being crossbred too. And, you know, just the other day he sent off to India for some mushroom spawn. Every mule he owns had a wild ass for a daddy. And you see those pillows there? Every last one is stuffed with purple or scarlet wool. That boy's loaded!

"And don't sneer at his friends. They're all ex-slaves, but every one of them's rich. You see that guy down there on the next to last couch? He's worth a cool half-million. Came up from nowhere. Used to tote wood on his back. People say, but I don't know, he stole a cap off a hob-goblin's head and found a treasure. He's the god's fair-haired boy. That's luck for you, but I don't begrudge him. Not so long ago he was just a slave. Yes sir, he's doing all right."

From Petronius, *The Satyricon*, trans. by William Arrowsmith (Ann Arbor, MI: University of Michigan Press, 1959), pp. 35–36. Reprinted by permission of the University of Michigan Press.

Mark Describes the Resurrection of Jesus

Belief that Jesus rose from the dead after his Crucifixion (about 30 C.E.) was and is central to traditional Christian doctrine. The record of the Resurrection in the Gospel of Mark, written a generation later (toward 70 C.E.), is the earliest we have. The significance to most Christian groups revolves about the assurance given them that death and the grave are not final and that, instead, salvation for a future life is possible. The appeal of these views was to be nearly universal in the West during the Middle Ages. The church was commonly thought to be the means of implementing the promise of salvation—hence the enormous importance of the church's sacramental system, its rules, and its clergy.

❖ *Why are the stories of miracles such as the one described here important for the growth of Christianity? What is special and important about this miracle? Why is it important in the story that days passed between the death of Jesus and the opening of the tomb? Why might the early Christians believe this story? Why was belief in the resurrection important for Christianity in the centuries immediately after the life of Jesus? Is it still important today?*

And when evening had come, since it was the day of Preparation, that is, the day before the sabbath, Joseph of Arimathea, a respected member of the council, who was also himself looking for the kingdom of God, took courage and went to Pilate, and asked for the body of Jesus. And Pilate wondered if he were already dead; and summoning the centurion, he asked him whether he was already dead. And when he learned from the centurion that he was dead, he granted the body to Joseph. And he brought a linen shroud, and taking him down, wrapped him in the linen shroud, and laid him in a tomb which had been hewn out of the rock; and he rolled a stone against the door of the tomb. Mary Magdalene and Mary the mother of Jesus saw where he was laid.

And when the sabbath was past, Mary Magdalene, and Mary the mother of James, and Salome, bought spices, so that they might go and anoint him. And very early on the first day of the week they went to the tomb when the sun had risen. And they were saying to one another, "Who will roll away the stone for us from the door of the tomb?" And looking up, they saw that the stone was rolled back; for it was very large. And entering the tomb, they saw a young man sitting on the right side, dressed in a white robe; and they were amazed. And he said to them, "Do not be amazed; you seek Jesus of Nazareth, who was crucified. He has risen, he is not here, see the place where they laid him. But go, tell his disciples and Peter that he is going before you to Galilee; there you will see him, as he told you." And they went out and fled from the tomb; for trembling and astonishment had come upon them; and they said nothing to any one, for they were afraid.

Gospel of Mark 15:42–47; 16:1–8, *Revised Standard Version of the Bible* (New York: Thomas Nelson and Sons, 1946, 1952).

with the temple at Jerusalem and its priests provoked the hostility of the religious establishment. A misunderstanding of the movement made it easy to convince the Roman governor that Jesus and his followers might be dangerous revolutionaries. He was put to death in Jerusalem by the cruel and degrading device of crucifixion, probably in 30 C.E. His followers believed that he was resurrected on the third day after his death, and that belief became a critical element in the religion they propagated throughout the Roman Empire and beyond. (See "Mark Describes the Resurrection of Jesus.")

The new belief spread quickly to the Jewish communities of Syria and Asia Minor. There is reason to believe, however, that it might have had only a short life as a despised Jewish heresy were it not for the conversion and career of Saint Paul.

Paul of Tarsus

Paul was born Saul, a citizen of the Cilician city of Tarsus in Asia Minor. He had been trained in Hellenistic culture and was a Roman citizen. But he was also a zealous member of the Jewish sect known as the *Pharisees*, the group that was most strict in its insistence on adherence to the Jewish law. He took a vigorous part in the persecution of the early Christians until his own conversion outside Damascus about 35 C.E.

The great problem facing the early Christians was to resolve their relationship to Judaism. If the new faith was a version of Judaism, then it must adhere to the Jewish law and seek converts only among Jews. James, called the brother of Jesus, was a conservative who held to that view, whereas the Hellenist Jews tended to see Christianity as a new and universal religion. To force all converts to follow Jewish law would have been fatal to the growth of the new sect. Jewish law's many technicalities and dietary prohibitions were strange to gentiles, and the necessity of circumcision—a frightening, painful, and dangerous operation for adults—would have been a tremendous deterrent to conversion. Paul, converted and with his new name, supported the position of the Hellenists and soon won many converts among the gentiles. After some conflict within the sect, Paul won out. Consequently, the "apostle to the gentiles" deserves recognition as a crucial contributor to the success of Christianity.

Paul believed it important that the followers of Jesus be evangelists (messengers), to spread the gospel, or "good news," of God's gracious gift. He taught that Jesus would soon return for the Day of Judgment, and it was important that all who would should believe in him and accept his way. Faith in Jesus as the Christ was necessary, but not sufficient, for salvation, nor could good deeds alone achieve it. That final blessing of salvation was a gift of God's grace that would be granted to some, but not all.

Organization

Paul and the other apostles did their work well. The new religion spread throughout the Roman Empire and even beyond its borders. It had its greatest success in the cities and mostly among the poor and uneducated. The rites of the early communities appear to have been simple and few. Baptism by water removed original sin and permitted participation in the community and its activities. The central ritual was a common meal called the *agape*, or "love feast," followed by the ceremony of the *Eucharist*, or "thanksgiving," a celebration of the Lord's Supper in which unleavened bread was eaten and unfermented wine was drunk. There were also prayers, hymns, or readings from the Gospels.

Not all the early Christians were poor, and it became customary for the rich to provide for the poor at the common meals. The sense of common love fostered in these ways focused the community's attention on the needs of the weak, the sick, the unfortunate, and the unprotected. This concern gave the early Christian communities a warmth and a human appeal that stood in marked contrast to the coldness and impersonality of the pagan cults. No less attractive were the promise of salvation, the importance to God of each human soul, and the spiritual equality of all in the new faith. As Paul put it, "There is neither Jew nor Greek, there is neither slave nor free, there is neither male nor female; for you are all one in Christ Jesus."[5]

The future of Christianity depended on its communities' finding an organization that would preserve unity within the group and help protect it against enemies outside. At first, the churches had little formal organization. Soon, it appears, affairs were placed in the hands of boards of *presbyters*, or "elders," and *deacons*, or "those who serve." By the second century C.E., as their numbers grew, the Christians of each city tended to accept the authority and leadership of bishops (*episkopoi*, or "overseers"). Bishops were elected by the congregation to lead them in worship and to supervise funds. As time passed, the bishops extended their authority over the Christian communities in outlying towns and the countryside. The power and almost monarchical authority of the bishops were soon enhanced by the doctrine of Apostolic Succession, which asserted that the powers that Jesus had given his original disciples were passed on from bishop to bishop by ordination.

The bishops kept in touch with one another, maintained communications between different Christian communities, and prevented doctrinal and sectarian splintering, which would have destroyed Christian unity. They maintained internal discipline and dealt with the civil authorities. After a time they began the practice of coming together in councils to settle difficult questions, to establish orthodox opinion, and even to expel as heretics those who would not accept it. It is unlikely that Christianity could have survived the travails of its early years without such strong internal organization and government.

The Persecution of Christians

The new faith soon incurred the distrust of the pagan world and of the imperial government. At first, Christians were thought of as a Jewish sect and were therefore protected by Roman law. It soon became clear, however, that they were quite different, seeming both mysterious and dangerous. They denied the existence of the pagan gods and so were accused of atheism. Their refusal to worship the emperor was judged to be treason. Because they kept mostly to

---

[5] Galatians 3:28. *Revised Standard Version of the Bible.*

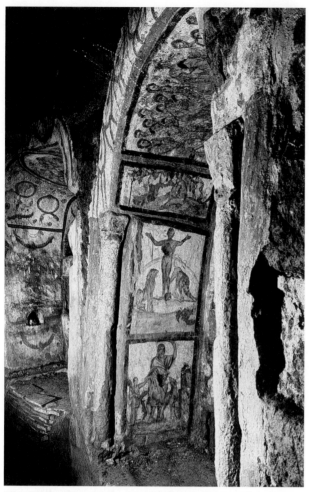

This is the Catacomb of the Jordani in Rome. The early Christians built miles of catacombs, or tunnels, in Rome. They were used as underground cemeteries and as refuges from persecution. Charitable Foundation/Gemeinnutzige Stiftung Leonard von Matt

themselves, took no part in civic affairs, engaged in secret rites, and had an organized network of local associations, they were misunderstood and suspected. The love feasts were erroneously reported to be scenes of sexual scandal. The alarming doctrine of the actual presence of Jesus' body in the Eucharist was distorted into an accusation of cannibalism.

The privacy and secrecy of Christian life and worship ran counter to a traditional Roman dislike of any private association, especially any of a religious nature. Christians thus earned the reputation of being "haters of humanity." Claudius expelled them from Rome, and Nero tried to make them scapegoats for the great fire that struck the city in 64 C.E. By the end of the first century, "the name alone"— that is, simple membership in the Christian community—was a crime.

But, for the most part, the Roman government did not take the initiative in attacking Christians in the first two centuries. When one governor sought instructions for dealing with the Christians, the emperor Trajan urged moderation. Christians were not to be sought out, anonymous accusations were to be disregarded, and anyone denounced could be acquitted merely by renouncing Christ and sacrificing to the emperor. Unfortunately, no true Christian could meet the conditions, and so there were some martyrdoms.

Most persecutions in this period, however, were started not by the government, but by mob action. Though they lived quiet, inoffensive lives, some Christians must have seemed unbearably smug and self-righteous. Unlike the tolerant, easygoing pagans, who were generally willing to accept the new gods of foreign people and add them to the pantheon, the Christians denied the reality of the pagan gods. They proclaimed the unique rightness of their own way and looked forward to their own salvation and the damnation of nonbelievers. It is not surprising, therefore, that pagans disliked these strange and unsocial people, tended to blame misfortunes on them, and, in extreme cases, turned to violence. But even this adversity had its uses. It weeded out the weaklings among the Christians, and brought greater unity to those who remained faithful. It also provided the Church with martyrs around whom legends could grow that would inspire still greater devotion and dedication.

The Emergence of Catholicism

Division within the Christian Church may have been an even greater threat to its existence than persecution from outside. The great majority of Christians never accepted complex, intellectualized opinions, but held to what even then were traditional, simple, conservative beliefs. This body of majority opinion, considered to be universal, or "catholic," was enshrined by the church that came to be called *Catholic.* The Catholic Church's doctrines were deemed *orthodox*, that is, "holding the right opinions," whereas those holding contrary opinions were heretics.

The need to combat heretics, however, compelled the orthodox to formulate their own views more clearly and firmly. By the end of the second century C.E., an orthodox canon had been shaped that included the Old Testament, the Gospels, and the Epistles of Paul, among other writings. The process of creating a standard set of holy books was not completed for at least two more centuries, but a vitally important start had been made. The orthodox declared the Catholic Church itself to be the depository of Christian teaching and the bishops to be its receivers. They also drew up creeds, or brief statements of faith to which true Christians should adhere.

In the first century, all that was required of one to be a Christian was to be baptized, to partake of the Eucharist, and to call Jesus the Lord. By the end of the second century an orthodox Christian—that is, a member of the Catholic Church—was required to accept its creed, its canon of holy writings, and the authority of the bishops. The loose structure of the apostolic church had given way to an organized body with recognized leaders able to define its faith and to exclude those who did not accept it. Whatever the shortcomings of this development, there can be little doubt that it provided the clarity, unity, and discipline needed for survival.

Rome as a Center of the Early Church

During this same period, the church in Rome came to have special prominence. As the center of communications and the capital of the empire, Rome had natural advantages. After the Roman destruction of Jerusalem in 135 C.E., no other city had any convincing claim to primacy in the church. Besides having the largest single congregation of Christians, Rome also benefited from the tradition that Jesus' apostles Peter and Paul were martyred there.

Peter, moreover, was thought to be the first bishop of Rome. The Gospel of Matthew (16:18) reported Jesus' statement to Peter: "Thou art Peter [in Greek, *Petros*] and upon this rock [in Greek, *petra*] I will build my church." Eastern Christians might later point out that Peter had been leader of the Christian community at Antioch before he went to Rome. But in the second century the church at Antioch, along with the other Christian churches of Asia Minor, was fading in influence, and by 200 C.E. Rome was the most important center of Christianity. Because of the city's early influence and because of the Petrine doctrine derived from the Gospel of Matthew, later bishops of Rome claimed supremacy in the Catholic Church. But as the era of the "good emperors" came to a close, this controversy was far in the future.

The Crisis of the Third Century

Dio Cassius, a historian of the third century C.E., described the Roman Empire after the death of Marcus Aurelius as declining from "a kingdom of gold into one of iron and rust." Although we have seen that the gold contained more than a little impurity, there is no reason to quarrel with Dio's assessment of his own time. Commodus (r. 180–192 C.E.), the son of Marcus Aurelius, proved the wisdom of the "good emperors" in selecting their successors for their talents rather than for family ties. Commodus was incompetent and autocratic. He reduced the respect in which the imperial office was held, and his assassination brought the return of civil war.

Barbarian Invasions

The pressure on Rome's frontiers, already serious in the time of Marcus Aurelius, reached massive proportions in the third century. In the east, a new power arising in the old Persian Empire threatened the frontiers. In the third century B.C.E., the Parthians had made the Iranians independent of the Hellenistic kings and had established an empire of their own on the old foundations of the Persian Empire. Several Roman attempts to conquer them had failed, but as late as 198 C.E. the Romans could reach and destroy the Parthian capital and bring at least northern Mesopotamia under their rule.

In 224 C.E., however, a new Iranian dynasty, the Sassanians, seized control from the Parthians and brought new vitality to Persia. They soon recovered Mesopotamia and made raids deep into Roman provinces. In 260 C.E., they humiliated the Romans by actually taking the emperor Valerian prisoner; he died in captivity.

On the western and northern frontiers the pressure came not from a well-organized rival empire, but from an ever-increasing number of German tribes. Though they had been in contact with the Romans at least since the second century B.C.E., they had not been much affected by civilization. The men did no agricultural work, but confined their activities to hunting, drinking, and fighting. They were organized on a family basis by clans, hundreds, and tribes. They were led by chiefs, usually from a royal family, elected by the assembly of fighting men. The king was surrounded by a collection of warriors, whom the Romans called his *comitatus*. Always eager for plunder, these tough barbarians were attracted by the civilized delights they knew existed beyond the frontier of the Rhine and Danube rivers.

The most aggressive of the Germans in the third century C.E. were the Goths. Centuries earlier they had wandered from their ancestral home near the Baltic Sea into the area of southern Russia. In the 220s and 230s C.E., they began to put pressure on the Danube frontier. By about 250 C.E., they were able to penetrate the empire and overrun the Balkan provinces. The need to meet this threat and the one posed by the Persian Sassanids in the east made the Romans weaken their western frontiers, and other Germanic peoples—the Franks and the Alemanni—

broke through in those regions. There was considerable danger that Rome would be unable to meet this challenge.

Rome's perils were caused, no doubt, by the unprecedentedly numerous and simultaneous attacks, but its internal weakness encouraged these attacks. The Roman army was not what it had been in its best days. By the second century C.E., it was made up mostly of romanized provincials. The pressure on the frontiers and epidemics of plague in the time of Marcus Aurelius forced the emperor to resort to the conscription of slaves, gladiators, barbarians, and brigands. The training and discipline with which the Romans had conquered the Mediterranean world had declined. The Romans also failed to respond to the new conditions of constant pressure on all the frontiers. A strong, mobile reserve that could meet a threat in one place without causing a weakness elsewhere might have helped, but no such unit was created.

Septimius Severus (r. 193–211 C.E.) and his successors played a crucial role in the transformation of the character of the Roman army. Septimius was a military usurper who owed everything to the support of his soldiers. He meant to establish a family dynasty, in contrast to the policy of the "good emperors" of the second century. He was prepared to make Rome into an undisguised military monarchy. Septimius drew recruits for the army increasingly from peasants of the less civilized provinces.

Economic Difficulties

These changes were a response to the great financial needs caused by the barbarian attacks. Inflation had forced Commodus to raise the soldiers' pay. Yet the Severan emperors had to double it to keep up with prices, which increased the imperial budget by as much as 25 percent. To raise money, the emperors resorted to inventing new taxes, debasing the coinage, and even selling the palace furniture. But it was still hard to recruit troops. The new style of military life introduced by Septimius—with its laxer discipline, more pleasant duties, and greater opportunity for advancement, not only in the army but in Roman society—was needed to attract men into the army. The policy proved effective for a short time, but could not prevent the chaos of the late third century.

The same forces that caused problems for the army did great damage to society at large. The shortage of workers for the large farms, which had all but wiped out the independent family farm, reduced agricultural production. As external threats distracted the emperors, they were less able to preserve domestic peace. Piracy, brigandage, and the neglect of roads and harbors all hampered trade. So, too, did the debasement of the coinage and the inflation in general. Imperial taxation and confiscations of the property of the rich removed badly needed capital from productive use.

More and more, the government was required to demand services that had been given gladly in the past. Because the empire lived hand to mouth, with no significant reserve fund and no system of credit financing, the emperors were led to compel the people to provide food, supplies, money, and labor. The upper classes in the cities were made to serve as administrators without pay and to meet deficits in revenue out of their own pockets. Sometimes these demands caused provincial rebellions, as in Egypt and Gaul. More typically, they caused peasants and even town administrators to flee to escape their burdens. The result of all these difficulties was a weakening of Rome's economic strength when it was most needed.

The Social Order

The new conditions caused important changes in the social order. Direct attacks from hostile emperors and economic losses decimated the Senate and the traditional ruling class. Their ranks were filled by men coming up through the army. The whole state began to take on an increasingly military appearance. Distinctions among the classes by dress had been traditional since the republic; in the third and fourth centuries C.E., the people's everyday clothing had become a kind of uniform that precisely revealed status. Titles were assigned to ranks in society as to ranks in the army. The most important distinction was the one formally established by Septimius Severus, which drew a sharp line between the *honestiores* (senators, equestrians, the municipal aristocracy, and the soldiers) and the lower classes, or *humiliores*. Septimius gave the *honestiores* a privileged position before the law. They were given lighter punishments, could not be tortured, and alone had the right of appeal to the emperor.

As time passed, it became more difficult to move from the lower order to the higher, another example of the growing rigidity of the late Roman Empire. Peasants were tied to their lands, artisans to their crafts, soldiers to the army, merchants and shipowners to the needs of the state, and citizens of the municipal upper class to the collection and payment of increasingly burdensome taxes. Freedom and private initiative gave way before the needs of the state and its ever-expanding control of its citizens.

Civil Disorder

Commodus was killed on the last day of 192 C.E. The succeeding year was similar to the year 69. Three emperors ruled in swift succession, Septimius Severus emerging, as we have seen, to establish firm rule and a dynasty. The death of Alexander Severus, the last of the dynasty, in 235 C.E., brought on a half century of internal anarchy and foreign invasion.

The empire seemed on the point of collapse. But the two conspirators who overthrew and succeeded the emperor Gallienus proved to be able soldiers. Claudius II Gothicus (268–270 C.E.) and Aurelian (270–275 C.E.) drove back the barbarians and stamped out internal disorder. The soldiers who followed Aurelian on the throne were good fighters who made significant changes in Rome's system of defense. Around Rome, Athens, and other cities, they built heavy walls that could resist barbarian attack. They drew back their best troops from the frontiers, relying chiefly on a newly organized heavy cavalry and a mobile army near the emperor's own residence.

Hereafter, the army was composed largely of mercenaries who came from among the least civilized provincials and even from among the Germans. The officers gave personal loyalty to the emperor rather than to the empire. These officers became a foreign, hereditary caste of aristocrats that increasingly supplied high administrators and even emperors. In effect, the Roman people hired an army of mercenaries, who were only technically Roman, to protect them.

The Late Empire

During the fourth and fifth centuries the Romans strove to meet the many challenges, internal and external, that threatened the survival of their empire. Growing pressure from barbarian tribes pushing against its frontier intensified the empire's tendency to smother individuality, freedom, and initiative, in favor of an increasingly intrusive and autocratic centralized monarchy. Economic and military weakness increased, and it became even harder to keep the vast empire together. Hard and dangerous times may well have helped the rise of Christianity, encouraging people to turn away from the troubles and dangers of this world to concern about the next.

The Fourth Century and Imperial Reorganization

The period from Diocletian (r. 284–305 C.E.) to Constantine (r. 306–337 C.E.) was one of reconstruction

A mosaic from Carthage illustrating aspects of life on the manorial estate of a certain Julian in the province of Africa. His housing, provisions, and entertainment appear to have been opulent. Social boundaries hardened in the late empire, and large fortified estates like this increasingly dominated social and economic life. Musée Nationale du Bardo

and reorganization after a time of civil war and turmoil. Diocletian was from Illyria (the former Yugoslavia). He was a man of undistinguished birth who rose to the throne through the ranks of the army. He knew that he was not a great general and that the job of defending and governing the entire empire was too great for one individual.

Diocletian therefore decreed the introduction of the *tetrarchy*, the rule of the empire by four men with power divided territorially. (See Map 5–4.) He allotted the provinces of Thrace, Asia, and Egypt to himself. His co-emperor, Maximian, shared with him the title of Augustus and governed Italy, Africa, and Spain. In addition, two men were given the subordinate title of Caesar: Galerius, who was in charge of the Danube frontier and the Balkans, and Constantius, who governed Britain and Gaul. This arrangement not only afforded a good solution to the military problem, but also provided for a peaceful succession.

Diocletian was recognized as the senior Augustus, but each tetrarch was supreme in his own sphere. The Caesars were recognized as successors to each half of the empire, and their loyalty was enhanced by marriages to daughters of the Augusti. It was a return, in a way, to the precedent of the "good emperors" of 96–180 C.E., who chose their successors from the ranks of the ablest men. It seemed to promise orderly and peaceful transitions instead of assassinations, chaos, and civil war.

Each man established his residence and capital at a place convenient for frontier defense, and none chose Rome. The effective capital of Italy became the northern city of Milan. Diocletian beautified Rome by constructing his monumental baths, but he visited the city only once and made his own capital at Nicomedia in Bithynia. This was another step in the long leveling process that had reduced the eminence of Rome and Italy. It was also evidence of the growing importance of the east.

In 305 C.E., Diocletian retired and compelled his co-emperor to do the same. But his plan for a smooth succession failed completely. In 310 there were five Augusti and no Caesars. Out of this chaos, Constantine, son of Constantius, produced order. In 324 he defeated his last opponent and made himself sole emperor, uniting the empire once again; he reigned until 337. Mostly, Constantine carried forward the policies of Diocletian. He supported Christianity, however, which Diocletian had tried to suppress.

DEVELOPMENT OF AUTOCRACY   The development of the imperial office toward autocracy was carried to the extreme by Diocletian and Constantine. The emperor ruled by decree, consulting only a few high officials whom he himself appointed. The Senate had no role whatever, and its dignity was further diminished by the elimination of all distinctions between senator and equestrian.

The emperor was a remote figure surrounded by carefully chosen high officials. He lived in a great palace and was almost unapproachable. Those admitted to his presence had to prostrate themselves before him and kiss the hem of his robe, which was purple and had golden threads going through it. The emperor was addressed as *dominus*, or "lord," and his right to rule was not derived from the Roman people, but from heaven. All this remoteness and ceremony had a double purpose: to enhance the dignity of the emperor and to safeguard him against assassination.

Constantine erected the new city of Constantinople on the site of ancient Byzantium on the Bosporus, which leads to both the Aegean and Black Seas. He made it the new capital of the empire. Its strategic location was excellent for protecting the eastern and Danubian frontiers, and, surrounded on three sides by water, it was easily defended. This location also made it easier to carry forward the policies that fostered autocracy and Christianity. Rome was full of tradition, the center of senatorial and even republican memories and of pagan worship. Constantinople was free from both, and its dedication in 330 C.E. marked the beginning of a new era. Until its fall to the Turks in 1453, it served as a bas-

tion of civilization, the preserver of classical culture, a bulwark against barbarian attack, and the greatest city in Christendom.

The autocratic rule of the emperors was carried out by a civilian bureaucracy, carefully separated from the military to reduce the chances of rebellion by anyone combining the two kinds of power. Below the emperor's court the most important officials were the *praetorian* prefects, each of whom administered one of the four major areas into which the empire was divided: Gaul, Italy, Illyricum, and the Orient. The four prefectures were subdivided into twelve territorial units called *dioceses*, each under a vicar who was subordinate to the prefect. The dioceses were further divided into almost a hundred provinces, each under a provincial governor.

The operation of the entire system was supervised by a vast system of spies and secret police, without whom the increasingly rigid organization could not be trusted to perform. In spite of these efforts, the system was corrupt and inefficient.

The cost of maintaining a 400,000-man army as well as the vast civilian bureaucracy, the expensive imperial court, and the imperial taste for splendid buildings put a great strain on an already weak economy. Diocletian's attempts to establish a uniform and reliable currency failed, leading instead to increased inflation. To deal with it, he resorted to price control with his Edict of Maximum Prices in 301 C.E. For each product and each kind of labor, a maximum price was set, and violations were punishable by death. The edict failed despite the harshness of its provisions.

Peasants unable to pay their taxes and officials unable to collect them tried to escape. Diocletian resorted to stern regimentation to keep all in their places and at the service of the government. The terror of the third century forced many peasants to seek protection in the *villa*, or "country estate," of a large and powerful landowner and to become tenant farming *coloni*. As social boundaries hardened, these *coloni* and their descendants became increasingly tied to their estates.

DIVISION OF THE EMPIRE   The peace and unity established by Constantine did not last long. His death was followed by a struggle for succession that was won by Constantius II (r. 337–361 C.E.), whose death, in turn, left the empire to his young cousin Julian (r. 361–363 C.E.). Julian was called the Apostate by the Christians because of his attempt to stamp out Christianity and restore paganism. Julian undertook a campaign against Persia with the aim of putting a Roman on the throne of the Sassanids and ending the Persian menace once and for all. He penetrated deep into Persia, but was killed

MAP 5–4   DIVISIONS OF THE ROMAN EMPIRE UNDER DIOCLETIAN   *Diocletian divided the sprawling empire into four prefectures for more effective government and defense. The inset map shows their boundaries, and the larger map gives some details of regions and provinces. The major division between east and west was along the line running south between Pannonia and Moesia.*

in battle. His death put an end to the expedition and to the pagan revival.

The Germans in the West took advantage of the eastern campaign to attack along the Rhine and upper Danube rivers. And even greater trouble was brewing along the middle and upper Danube. (See Map 5–5.) That territory was occupied by the eastern Goths, known as the Ostrogoths. They were being pushed hard by their western cousins, the Visigoths, who in turn had been driven from their home in the Ukraine by the fierce Huns, a nomadic people from central Asia. (See "Ammianus Marcellinus Describes the People Called Huns.")

The emperor Valentinian (r. 364–375 C.E.) saw that he could not defend the empire alone and appointed his brother Valens (r. 364–378 C.E.) as coruler. Valentinian made his own headquarters at Milan and spent the rest of his life fighting successfully against the

Franks and the Alemanni in the west. Valens was given control of the east. The empire was once again divided in two. The two emperors maintained their own courts, and the halves of the empire became increasingly separate and different. Latin was the language of the west and Greek of the east.

In 376 the Visigoths, pursued by the Huns, asked and received permission to enter the empire. Soon to be Christianized, they won rights of settlement and material assistance within the empire from the eastern emperor Valens (r. 364–378) in exchange for defending the eastern frontier as *foederati*, or special allies of the empire.

The Visigoths, however, did not keep their bargain with the Romans, retaining their weapons and plundering the Balkan provinces. Nor did the Romans comply: They treated the Visigoths cruelly, even forcing them to trade their children for dogs to eat. Valens attacked the Goths and died, along with most of his army, at Adrianople in Thrace in 378. Theodosius (r. 379–395 C.E.), an able and experienced general, was named coruler in the east. By a combination of military and diplomatic skills, Theodosius pacified the Goths, giving them land and a high degree of autonomy and enrolling many of them in his army. He made important military reforms, putting greater emphasis on the cavalry. Theodosius tried to unify the empire again, but his death in 395 left it divided and weak.

THE RURAL WEST   The two parts of the empire went their separate and different ways. The west became increasingly rural as barbarian invasions continued and grew in intensity. The *villa*, a fortified country estate, became the basic unit of life. There, *coloni* gave their services to the local magnate in return for economic assistance and protection from both barbarians and imperial officials. Many cities shrank to no more than tiny walled fortresses ruled by military commanders and bishops. The upper classes moved to the country and asserted ever greater independence from imperial authority. The failure of the

central authority to maintain the roads and the constant danger from bands of robbers sharply curtailed trade and communications, forcing greater self-reliance and a more primitive style of life.

The new world emerging in the west by the fifth century and after was increasingly made up of isolated units of rural aristocrats and their dependent laborers. The only institution providing a high degree of unity was the Christian Church. The pattern for the early Middle Ages in the west was already formed.

THE BYZANTINE EAST   In the east the situation was quite different. Constantinople became the center of a vital and flourishing culture we call Byzantine that lasted until the fifteenth century. Because of its defensible location, the skill of its emperors, and the firmness and strength of its base in Asia Minor, it could deflect and repulse barbarian attacks. A strong navy allowed commerce to flourish in the eastern Mediterranean and, in good times, far beyond. Cities continued to prosper, and the emperors made their will good over the nobles in the countryside. The civilization of the Byzantine Empire was a unique

MAP 5–5   THE EMPIRE'S NEIGHBORS   *In the fourth century the Roman Empire was nearly surrounded by ever more threatening neighbors. The map shows who these so-called barbarians were and where they lived before their armed contact with the Romans.*

Ammianus Marcellinus Describes the People Called Huns

Ammianus Marcellinus was born about 330 C.E. in Syria, where Greek was the language of his well-to-do family. After a military career and considerable travel, he lived in Rome and wrote an encyclopedic Latin history of the empire, covering the years 96 to 378 C.E. and giving special emphasis to the difficulties of the fourth century. Here he describes the Huns, one of the barbarous peoples pressing on the frontiers. Like most Romans, he was alarmed and appalled by the way of life of these nomadic peoples. His account is a combination of observation, hearsay, and prejudice, and it is not always easy to separate facts from fantasy.

❖ *In what ways did the culture of the Huns differ from that of the Romans? How did their way of life give them an advantage against Rome? How was it disadvantageous? Which of the writer's statements do you think are factual? Explain the reasons for your judgments.*

The people called Huns, barely mentioned in ancient records, live beyond the sea of Azof, on the border of the Frozen Ocean, and are a race savage beyond all parallel. At the very moment of birth the cheeks of their infant children are deeply marked by an iron, in order that the hair, instead of growing at the proper season on their faces, may be hindered by the scars; accordingly the Huns grow up without beards, and without any beauty. They all have closely knit and strong limbs and plump necks; they are of great size, and low legged, so that you might fancy them two-legged beasts or the stout figures which are hewn out in a rude manner with an ax on the posts at the end of bridges.

They are certainly in the shape of men, however uncouth, and are so hardy that they neither require fire nor well-flavored food, but live on the roots of such herbs as they get in the fields, or on the half-raw flesh of any animal, which they merely warm rapidly by placing it between their own thighs and the backs of their horses.

They never shelter themselves under roofed houses, but avoid them, as people ordinarily avoid sepulchers as things not fit for common use. Nor is there even to be found among them a cabin thatched with reeds; but they wander about, roaming over the mountains and the woods, and accustom themselves to bear frost and hunger and thirst from their very cradles....

There is not a person in the whole nation who cannot remain on his horse day and night. On horseback they buy and sell, they take their meat and drink, and there they recline on the narrow neck of their steed, and yield to sleep so deep as to indulge in every variety of dream.

And when any deliberation is to take place on any weighty matter, they all hold their common council on horseback. They are not under kingly authority, but are contented with the irregular government of their chiefs, and under their lead they force their way through all obstacles.

From Ammianus Marcellinus, *Res Gestae*, trans. by C. D. Yonge (London: George Bell and Son, 1862), pp. 312–314.

---

combination of classical culture, the Christian religion, Roman law, and eastern artistic influences.

While the west was being overrun by barbarians, the Roman Empire, in altered form, persisted in the east. While Rome shrank to an insignificant ecclesiastical town, Constantinople flourished as the seat of empire, the "New Rome." Indeed, the Byzantines even called themselves "Romans." When we contemplate the decline and fall of the Roman Empire in the fourth and fifth centuries, we are speaking only of the west. A form of classical culture persisted in the Byzantine East for a thousand years more.

The Triumph of Christianity

The rise of Christianity to dominance in the empire was closely connected with the political and cultural experience of the third and fourth centuries. Political chaos and decentralization had religious and cultural consequences.

RELIGIOUS CURRENTS IN THE EMPIRE   In some of the provinces, native languages replaced Latin and Greek, sometimes even for official purposes. The classical tradition that had been the basis of impe-

Reigns of Selected Late Empire Rulers (All dates are C.E.)

180–192	Commodus
193–211	Septimius Severus
222–235	Alexander Severus
249–251	Decius
253–260	Valerian
253–268	Gallienus
268–270	Claudius II Gothicus
270–275	Aurelian
284–305	Diocletian
306–337	Constantine
324–337	Constantine sole emperor
337–361	Constantius II
361–363	Julian the Apostate
364–375	Valentinian
364–378	Valens
379–395	Theodosius

rial life became the exclusive possession of a small, educated aristocracy. In religion, the public cults had grown up in an urban environment and were largely political in character. As the importance of the cities diminished, so did the significance of their gods. People might still take comfort in the worship of the friendly, intimate deities of family, field, hearth, storehouse, and craft, but these gods were too petty to serve their needs in a confused and frightening world. The only universal worship was of the emperor, but he was far off, and obeisance to his cult was more a political than a religious act.

In the troubled times of the fourth and fifth centuries, people sought powerful, personal deities who would bring them safety and prosperity in this world and immortality in the next. Paganism was open and tolerant. It was by no means unusual for people to worship new deities alongside the old and even to intertwine elements of several to form a new amalgam by the device called *syncretism*.

Manichaeism was an especially potent rival of Christianity. Named for its founder, Mani, a Persian who lived in the third century C.E., this movement contained aspects of various religious traditions, including Zoroastrianism from Persia and both Judaism and Christianity. The Manichaeans pictured a world in which light and darkness, good and evil, were constantly at war. Good was spiritual and evil was material. Because human beings were made of matter, their bodies were a prison of evil and darkness, but they also contained an element of light and good. The "Father of Goodness" had sent Mani, among other prophets, to free humanity and gain its

salvation. To achieve salvation, humans must want to reach the realm of light and to abandon all physical desires. Manichaeans led an ascetic life and practiced a simple worship guided by a well-organized Church. The movement reached its greatest strength in the fourth and fifth centuries, and some of its central ideas persisted into the Middle Ages.

Christianity had something in common with these cults and answered many of the same needs felt by their devotees. None of them, however, attained Christianity's universality, and none appears to have given the early Christians and their leaders as much competition as the ancient philosophies or the state religion.

IMPERIAL PERSECUTION   By the third century, Christianity had taken firm hold in the eastern provinces and in Italy. It had not made much headway in the west, however. (See Map 5–6.) Christian apologists pointed out that Christians were good citizens who differed from others only in not worshiping the public gods. Until the middle of the third century, the emperors tacitly accepted this view, without granting official toleration. As times became bad and the Christians became more numerous and visible, that policy changed. Popular opinion blamed disasters, natural and military, on the Christians.

About 250, the emperor Decius (r. 249–251 C.E.) invoked the aid of the gods in his war against the Goths and required that all citizens worship the state gods publicly. True Christians could not obey, and Decius started a major persecution. Many Christians—even some bishops—yielded to threats and torture, but others held out and were killed. Valerian (r. 253–260 C.E.) resumed the persecutions, partly to confiscate the wealth of rich Christians. His successors, however, found other matters more pressing, and the persecution lapsed until the end of the century.

By the time of Diocletian, the number of Christians had grown still greater and included some high state officials. At the same time, hostility to the Christians grew on every level. Diocletian was not generous toward unorthodox intellectual or religious movements. His own effort to bolster imperial power with the aura of divinity boded ill for the church, and in 303 he launched the most serious persecution inflicted on the Christians in the Roman Empire. He issued a series of edicts confiscating church property and destroying churches and their sacred books. He deprived upper-class Christians of public office and judicial rights, imprisoned clergy, and enslaved Christians of the lower classes. He placed heavy fines on anyone refusing to sacrifice to the public gods. A final decree required public sacrifices and libations. The persecution horrified many pagans, and the plight and the demeanor of the martyrs often aroused pity and sympathy.

Ancient states could not carry out a program of terror with the thoroughness of modern totalitarian governments, so the Christians and their church survived to enjoy what they must have considered a miraculous change of fortune. In 311 Galerius, who had been one of the most vigorous persecutors, was influenced, perhaps by his Christian wife, to issue the Edict of Toleration, permitting Christian worship.

The victory of Constantine and his emergence as sole ruler of the empire changed the condition of Christianity from a precariously tolerated sect to the religion favored by the emperor. This put it on the path to becoming the official and only legal religion in the empire.

EMERGENCE OF CHRISTIANITY AS THE STATE RELIGION

The sons of Constantine continued to favor the new religion, but the succession of Julian the Apostate posed a new threat. He was a devotee of traditional classical pagan culture and, as a believer in Neoplatonism, an opponent of Christianity. Neoplatonism was a religious philosophy, or a philosophical religion, whose connection with Platonic teachings was distant. Its chief formulator was Plotinus (205–270 C.E.), who tried to combine classical and rational philosophical speculation with the mystical spirit of his time. Plotinus's successors were bitter critics of Christianity, and their views influenced Julian. Though he refrained from persecution, he tried to undo the work of Constantine by withdrawing the privileges of the church, removing Christians from high offices, and introducing a new form of pagan worship. His reign, however, was short, and his work did not last.

In 394, Theodosius forbade the celebration of pagan cults and abolished the pagan religious calendar. At his death, Christianity was the official religion of the Roman Empire.

The establishment of Christianity as the state religion did not put an end to the troubles of the Christians and their church; instead, it created new ones and complicated some old ones. The favored position of the church attracted converts for the wrong reasons and diluted the moral excellence and spiritual fervor of its adherents. The problem of the relationship between church and state arose, presenting the possibility that religion would become subordinate to the state, as it had been in the classical world and in earlier civilizations. In the East, that is what happened to a considerable degree.

In the West, the weakness of the emperors prevented such a development and permitted church leaders to exercise remarkable independence. In 390 Ambrose, bishop of Milan, excommunicated Theodosius for a massacre he had carried out, and the emperor did humble penance. This act provided an important precedent for future assertions of the church's autonomy and authority, but it did not put an end to secular interference and influence in the church.

ARIANISM AND THE COUNCIL OF NICAEA

Internal divisions proved to be even more troubling as new heresies emerged. Because they threatened the unity of an empire that was now Christian, they took on a political character and inevitably involved the emperor and the powers of the state. Before long, the world would view Christians persecuting other Christians with a zeal at least as great as had been displayed against them by the most fanatical pagans.

Among the many controversial views that arose, the most important and the most threatening was Arianism. It was founded by a priest named Arius of Alexandria (ca. 280–336 C.E.) in the fourth century. The issue creating difficulty was the relation of God the Father to God the Son. Arius argued that Jesus was a created being, unlike God the Father. He was, therefore, not made of the substance of God and was not eternal. "The Son has a beginning," he said, "but God is without beginning." For Arius, Jesus was neither fully man nor fully God, but something in between. Arius' view did away with the mysterious concept of the Trinity, the difficult doctrine that holds that God is three persons (the Father, the Son, and the Holy Spirit) and also one in substance and essence.

The Arian concept had the advantage of appearing to be simple, rational, and philosophically acceptable. To its ablest opponent, Athanasius, however, it had serious shortcomings. Athanasius (ca. 293–373 C.E.), later bishop of Alexandria, saw the Arian view as an impediment to any acceptable theory of salvation, to him the most important religious question. He adhered to the old Greek idea of salvation as involving the change of sinful mortality into divine immortality through the gift of "life." Only if Jesus were both fully human and fully God could the transformation of humanity to divinity have taken place in him and be transmitted by him to his disciples. "Christ was made man," he said, "that we might be made divine."

To deal with the growing controversy, Constantine called a council of Christian bishops at Nicaea, not far from Constantinople, in 325. For the emperor the question was essentially political, but for the disputants salvation was at stake. At Nicaea, the view expounded by Athanasius won out, became orthodox, and was embodied in the Nicene Creed. But Arianism persisted and spread. Some later emperors were either Arians or sympathetic to that view. Some of the most successful missionaries to the barbarians were Arians;

MAP 5–6   THE SPREAD OF CHRISTIANITY   *Christianity grew swiftly in the third, fourth, fifth, and sixth centuries—especially after the conversion of the emperors in the fourth century. By 600, on the eve of the birth of the new religion of Islam, Christianity was dominant throughout the Mediterranean world and most of western Europe.*

as a result, many of the German tribes that overran the empire were Arians. The Christian emperors hoped to bring unity to their increasingly decentralized realms by imposing the single religion. Over time it did prove to be a unifying force, but it also introduced divisions where none had existed before.

Arts and Letters in the Late Empire

The art and literature of the late empire reflect the confluence of pagan and Christian ideas and traditions as well as the conflict between them. Much of the literature is of a polemical nature and much of the art is propaganda.

The salvation of the empire from the chaos of the third century was accomplished by a military revolution based on and led by provincials whose origins were in the lower classes. They brought with them the fresh winds of cultural change, which blew out not only the dust of classical culture, but much of its substance as well. Yet the new ruling class was not interested in leveling; it wanted instead to establish itself as a new aristocracy. It thought of itself as effecting a great restoration rather than a revolution and sought to restore classical culture and absorb it. The confusion and uncertainty of the times were tempered in part, of course, by the comfort of Christianity. But the new ruling class sought order and stability—ethical, literary, and artistic—in the classical tradition as well.

The Preservation of Classical Culture

One of the main needs and accomplishments of this period was the preservation of classical culture. Ways were discovered to make it available and useful to the newly arrived ruling class. Works of the great classical authors were reproduced in many copies and were transferred from perishable and inconvenient papyrus rolls to sturdier codices, bound volumes that were as easy to use as modern books. Scholars also digested long works like Livy's *History of Rome* into shorter versions, wrote learned commentaries, and compiled grammars. Original works by pagan writers of the late empire were neither numerous nor especially distinguished.

Christian Writers

On the other hand, the late empire saw a great outpouring of Christian writings. There were many examples of Christian apologetics in poetry as well as in prose, and there were sermons, hymns, and biblical commentaries. Christianity could also boast important scholars. Jerome (348–420 C.E.), thoroughly trained

The Triumph of Christianity	
ca. 4 B.C.E.	Jesus of Nazareth born
ca. 30 C.E.	Crucifixion of Jesus
64 C.E.	Fire at Rome: persecution by Nero
ca. 70–100 C.E.	Gospels written
ca. 250–260 C.E.	Major persecutions by Decius and Valerian
303 C.E.	Persecution by Diocletian
311 C.E.	Galerius issues Edict of Toleration
312 C.E.	Battle of Milvian Bridge; conversion of Constantine to Christianity
325 C.E.	Council of Nicaea
395 C.E.	Christianity becomes official religion of Roman Empire

in both the east and the west in classical Latin literature and rhetoric, produced a revised version of the Bible in Latin. Commonly called the Vulgate, it became the Bible used by the Catholic Church. Probably the most important eastern scholar was Eusebius of Caesarea (ca. 260–340 C.E.). He wrote apologetics, an idealized biography of Constantine, and a valuable attempt to reconstruct the chronology of important events in the past. His most important contribution, however, was his *Ecclesiastical History*, an attempt to set forth the Christian view of history. He saw all of history as the working out of God's will. All of history, therefore, had a purpose and a direction, and Constantine's victory and the subsequent unity of empire and church were its culmination.

The closeness and also the complexity of the relationship between classical pagan culture and that of the Christianity of the late empire are nowhere better displayed than in the career and writings of Augustine (354–430 C.E.), bishop of Hippo in North Africa. He was born at Carthage and was trained as a teacher of rhetoric. His father was a pagan, but his mother was a Christian and hers was ultimately the stronger influence. He passed through several intellectual way stations—skepticism and Neoplatonism among others—before his conversion to Christianity. His training and skill in pagan rhetoric and philosophy made him peerless among his contemporaries as a defender of Christianity and as a theologian.

His greatest works are his *Confessions*, an autobiography describing the road to his conversion, and *The City of God*. The latter was a response to the pagan charge that Rome's sack by the Visigoths in 410 was caused by the abandonment of the

This late-Roman ivory plaque shows a scene from Christ's Passion. The art of the late empire was transitional between the classical past and the medieval future.
Crucifixion, carving, c. 420 A.D. (ivory). British Museum, London, UK/Bridgeman Art Library, London/New York

old gods and the advent of Christianity. The optimistic view held by some Christians that God's will worked its way in history and was easily comprehensible needed further support in the face of the Visigoths' sack of Rome. Augustine sought to separate the fate of Christianity from that of the Roman Empire. He contrasted the secular world, the City of Man, with the spiritual, the City of God. The former was selfish, the latter unselfish; the former evil, the latter good.

Augustine argued that history was moving forward, in the spiritual sense, to the Day of Judgment, but there was no reason to expect improvement before then in the secular sphere. The fall of Rome was neither surprising nor important. All states, even a Christian Rome, were part of the City of Man and were therefore corrupt and mortal. Only the City of God was immortal, and it, consisting of all the saints on earth and in heaven, was untouched by earthly calamities.

Though the *Confessions* and *The City of God* are Augustine's most famous works, they emphasize only a part of his thought. His treatises *On the Trin-* *ity* and *On Christian Education* reveal the great skill with which he supported Christian belief with the learning, logic, and philosophy of the pagan classics. Augustine believed that faith is essential and primary (a thoroughly Christian view), but it is not a substitute for reason (the foundation of classical thought). Instead, faith is the starting point for, and liberator of, human reason, which continues to be the means by which people can understand what faith reveals. His writings constantly reveal the presence of both Christian faith and pagan reason, as well as the tension between them, a legacy he left to the Middle Ages.

The Problem of the Decline and Fall of the Empire in the West

Whether important to Augustine or not, the massive barbarian invasions of the fifth century put an end to effective imperial government in the west. For centuries people have speculated about the causes of the collapse of the ancient world. Every kind of reason has been put forward, and some suggestions seem to have nothing to do with reason at all. Exhaustion of the soil, plague, climatic change, and even poisoning caused by lead water pipes have been suggested as reasons for Rome's decline in population, vigor, and the capacity to defend itself. Some blame the institution of slavery and a resulting failure to make advances in science and technology. Others blame excessive government interference in the economic life of the empire and still others the destruction of the urban middle class, the carrier of classical culture.

Perhaps a simpler and more obvious explanation can be found. It might begin with the observation that the growth of so mighty an empire as Rome's was by no means inevitable. Rome's greatness had come from conquests that provided the Romans with the means to expand still further, until there were not enough Romans to conquer and govern any more peoples and territory. When pressure from outsiders grew, the Romans lacked the resources to advance and defeat the enemy as in the past. The tenacity and success of their resistance for so long were remarkable. Without new conquests to provide the immense wealth needed for the defense and maintenance of internal prosperity, the Romans finally yielded to unprecedented onslaughts by fierce and numerous attackers.

To blame the ancients and the institution of slavery for the failure to produce an industrial and economic revolution like that of the later Western world (one capable of producing wealth without taking it from another) is to stand the problem on its head. No one yet has a satisfactory explanation for those revolutions. So it is improper to blame any institution or society for not achieving what has been achieved only once in human history. Perhaps we would do well to think of the problem as Gibbon did:

The decline of Rome was the natural and inevitable effect of immoderate greatness. Prosperity ripened the principle of decay; the cause of the destruction multiplied with the extent of conquest; and, as soon as time or accident had removed the artificial supports, the stupendous fabric yielded to the pressure of its own weight. The story of the ruin is simple and obvious; and instead of inquiring why the Roman Empire was destroyed, we should rather be surprised that it had subsisted so long.[6]

[6] Edward Gibbon, *The History of the Decline and Fall of the Roman Empire*, 2d ed., Vol. 4, ed. by J. B. Bury (London: 1909), pp. 173–174.

In Perspective

Out of the civil wars and chaos that brought down the republic, Augustus brought unity, peace, order, and prosperity. As a result, he was regarded with almost religious awe and attained more military and political power than any Roman before him. He ruled firmly, but with moderation. He tried to limit military adventures and the costs they incurred. Augustus supported public works that encouraged trade and communication in the empire. He tried to restore and invigorate the old civic pride, and in this he had considerable success. He was less successful in promoting private morality based on family values. He patronized the arts so as to beautify Rome and glorify his reign. On his death, Augustus was able to pass on the regime to his family, the Julio-Claudians.

For almost two hundred years, with a few brief interruptions, the empire was generally prosperous, peaceful, and well run. But problems were growing. Management of the many responsibilities assumed by the government required the growth of a large bureaucracy that placed a heavy and increasing burden on the treasury, required higher taxes, and stifled both civic spirit and private enterprise. Pressure from barbarian tribes on the frontiers required a large standing army, which was also very costly and led to further rises in taxation.

In the late empire, Rome's rulers resorted to many devices for dealing with their problems. Policies came to include putting down internal military rebellions led by generals from different parts of the empire. More and more, the emperors' rule and their safety depended on the loyalty of the army, so they courted the soldiers' favor with gifts of various kinds. This only increased the burden of taxes; the rich and powerful found ways to avoid their obligations, making the load on everyone else all the heavier. The government's control over the lives of its people became ever greater and the society more rigid as people tried to flee to escape the crushing load of taxes. Expedients were tried, including inflating the currency, fixing farmers to the soil as serfs or coloni, building walls to keep the barbarians out, and bribing barbarian tribes to fight for Rome against other barbarians. Ultimately, all these measures failed. The Roman Empire in the west fell, leaving disunity, insecurity, disorder, and poverty. Like similar empires in the ancient world, it had been unable to sustain its "immoderate greatness."

REVIEW QUESTIONS

1. Discuss the Augustan constitution and government. What solutions did Augustus provide for the problems that had plagued the Roman Republic? Why was the Roman population willing to accept Augustus as head of the state?
2. How was the Roman Empire organized and why did it function smoothly? What role did the emperor play in the maintenance of political stability?
3. How did the literature in the Golden Age of Augustus differ from that of the Silver Age during the first and second centuries C.E.? How did the poetry of Vergil and Horace contribute to the stability of Augustus' rule?
4. In spite of unpromising beginnings, Christianity was enormously popular by the fourth century C.E. Why were Christians persecuted by Roman authorities? What were the more important reasons for Christianity's success?
5. What were the political, social, and economic problems that beset Rome in the third and fourth centuries C.E.? How did Diocletian and Constantine deal with them? Were they effective in stemming the tide of decline and disintegration in the Roman Empire? What problems were they unable to solve?
6. Discuss three theories that scholars have advanced to explain the decline and fall of the Roman Empire. What are the difficulties involved in explaining the fall? What explanation would you give?

SUGGESTED READINGS

T. BARNES, *The New Empire of Diocletian and Constantine* (1982). A study of the character of the late empire.

A. R. BIRLEY, *Hadrian the Restless Emperor* (1997). A biography of an important emperor.

P. BROWN, *Augustine of Hippo* (1967). A splendid biography.

P. BROWN, *The World of Late Antiquity, C.E. 150–750* (1971). A brilliant and readable essay.

P. BROWN, *Power and Persuasion in Late Antiquity: Towards a Christian Empire* (1992). A fine discussion of early Christianity and its complicated relationship with the Roman Empire.

A. FERRILL, *The Fall of the Roman Empire, The Military Explanation* (1986). An interpretation that emphasizes the decline in the quality of the Roman army.

A. FERRILL, *Caligula: Emperor of Rome* (1991). A biography of the monstrous young emperor.

E. GIBBON, *The History of the Decline and Fall of the Roman Empire*, 7 vols., ed. by J. B. Bury, 2d ed. (1909–1914). One of the masterworks of the English language.

M. GRANT, *The Fall of the Roman Empire* (1990). A lively, well-written account.

A. H. M. JONES, *The Later Roman Empire*, 3 vols. (1964). A comprehensive study of the period.

D. KAGAN, ED., *The End of the Roman Empire: Decline or Transformation?* 3d. ed. (1992). A collection of essays discussing the problem of the decline and fall of the Roman Empire.

M. L. W. LAISTNER, *The Greater Roman Historians* (1963). Essays on the major Roman historical writers.

J. LEBRETON AND J. ZEILLER, *History of the Primitive Church*, 3 vols. (1962). The Catholic viewpoint.

H. LIETZMANN, *History of the Early Church*, 2 vols. (1961). From the Protestant viewpoint.

E. N. LUTTWAK, *The Grand Strategy of the Roman Empire* (1976). An original and fascinating analysis by a keen student of modern strategy.

R. MACMULLEN, *Enemies of the Roman Order* (1966). An original and revealing examination of opposition to the emperors.

R. MACMULLEN, *Roman Social Relations, 50 B.C. to A.D. 284* (1981). An interesting study of social developments.

R. MACMULLEN, *Corruption and the Decline of Rome* (1988). A study that examines the importance of changes in ethical ideas and behavior.

R. W. MATHISON, *Roman Aristocrats in Barbarian Gaul: Strategies for Survival* (1993). An unusual slant on the late empire.

F. G. B. MILLAR, *The Roman Empire and Its Neighbors* (1968). An analysis of Roman foreign relations in the imperial period.

F. G. B. MILLAR, *The Emperor in the Roman World, 31 B.C.–A.D. 337* (1977). A study of Roman imperial government.

F.G.B. MILLAR, *The Roman Near East, 31 B.C.–A.D. 337* (1993). A valuable study of Rome's relations with an important part of its empire.

A. MOMIGLIANO, ED., *The Conflict between Paganism and Christianity* (1963). A valuable collection of essays.

H. M. D. PARKER, *A History of the Roman World from A.D. 138 to 337* (1969). A good survey.

M. I. ROSTOVTZEFF, *Social and Economic History of the Roman Empire*, 2d. ed. (1957). A masterpiece whose main thesis has been much disputed.

V. RUDICH, *Political Dissidence under Nero, the Price of Dissimulation* (1993). A brilliant exposition of the lives and thoughts of political dissidents in the early empire.

E. T. SALMON, *A History of the Roman World, 30 B.C. to 138 A.D.* (1968). A good survey.

G. E. M. DE STE. CROIX, *The Class Struggle in the Ancient World* (1981). An ambitious interpretation of all of classical civilization from an idiosyncratic Marxist perspective.

R. SYME, *The Roman Revolution* (1960). A brilliant study of Augustus, his supporters, and their rise to power

Ancient Warfare

The Causes of War

War has been a persistent part of human experience since before the birth of civilization.[1] Organized warfare goes back to the Stone Age. There may be evidence of it as early as the late Paleolithic Age, but there can be no doubt that it was a significant human activity by the Neolithic Age. The earliest civilizations of Egypt and Mesopotamia added powerful new elements to the character of warfare and were from the first occupied with war, as were later Bronze and Iron Age cultures all over the world.

The earliest literary work in the Western tradition, Homer's *Iliad*, describes a long, bitter war and the men who fought it. The Rigvedic hymns of the ancient culture of India tell of the warrior god Indra, who smashes the fortifications of his enemies. The earliest civilizations of China were established by armies armed with spears, composite bows, and war chariots. The evidence is plentiful that war is one of the oldest and most continuous activities of the human species.

Ancient philosophers like Plato and Aristotle took all this for granted. They believed that men (they never thought of women in this context) were naturally acquisitive and aggressive and that governments and laws existed to curb those tendencies. The ancient Greeks, wracked as they were by perpetual war, were eager to investigate its causes. Thucydides, writing at the end of the fifth century B.C.E. set forth with great care the quarrels between the Athenians and the Peloponnesians and why they broke their treaty: "so that no one may ever have to seek the cause that led to the outbreak of so great a war among the Greeks." He provided a profound and helpful understanding of the causes of wars and of the motives of human beings in going to war. He understood war as the armed competition for power, but he thought that unusually wise and capable leaders could limit their own fears and desires and those of their people—could choose to gain and defend only so much power as was needed for their purposes.

In this struggle for power, whether for a rational sufficiency or in the insatiable drive for all the power there is, Thucydides found that people go to war out of "fear, honor, and interest."[2] That trio of motives is illuminating in understanding the origins of wars throughout history. That fear and interest move states to war will not surprise the modern reader, but that concern for honor should do so may seem strange. If we take honor to mean "fame," "glory," "renown," or "splendor," it may appear applicable to the premodern world alone. If, however, we understand its significance as "deference," "esteem," "just due," "regard," "respect," or "prestige," we will find it an important motive of nations in the modern world as well.

Wars are made by human beings who may choose different courses of action. Sometimes the decisions are made by a single individual or a small group, sometimes by a very large number. Their choices are always limited and affected by circumstances, and the closer they come to the outbreak of a war, the more limited the choices seem. Those who decide to make war always think they have good reason to fight. Although impersonal forces play a role and the reasons publicly given are not necessarily the true ones, the reasons must be taken seriously, for "the conflicts between states which have usually led to war have normally arisen, not from any irrational and emotional drives, but from almost a superabundance of analytic rationality....[I]n general men have fought during the past two hundred years neither because they are aggressive nor because they are acquisitive animals, but because they are reasoning ones: because they discern, or believe that they can discern, dangers before they become immediate, the possibility of threats before they are made."[3]

At any time in history, there has been widespread agreement that some things are desirable and worth fighting for. Liberty, autonomy, the freedom to ex-

---

[1]Arther Ferrill, *The Origins of War* (London, 1985), p. 13, says that "organized warfare appeared at least by the end of the Palaeolithic Age," but Richard A. Gabriel argues that true warfare did not come until the Bronze Age and the invention of the state and the social structure that came with it. No one, however, doubts that war is at least as old as civilization.

[2]1.75.3.

[3]*The Lessons of History* (New York, 1968), p. 81.

This mound marks the ancient city of Jericho. Thought by some to be the earliest Neolithic site in the Near East, it sprang up around an oasis about 7000 B.C.E. The thick stone walls and moat that surround it show that it was meant to be a fortress that could resist sieges, showing that warfare was common at least as early as the construction of this city. © Zev Radovan, Jerusalem, Israel

ercise one's religion, and the search for wealth have been among the most common through the ages. Fear of their opposites—slavery, subordination, religious suppression, and poverty—have probably been even greater causes of wars. All of them, however, depend on power, for the distribution of power determines who can and cannot impose his or her will on others. In one sense, there is no single cause of war, but a myriad. But in another sense, there is only one cause: Wars have rarely happened by accident or because of honest misunderstandings; most of them have resulted from calculations about power, which is valued because it can provide security, reputation, and material advantage.

In the sixth century B.C.E., the Greek philosopher Heracleitus observed that "war is the father of all things." In 1968 Will and Ariel Durant calculated that, in the previous 3,421 years, only 268 were free of war. There have been none since, suggesting that, in that respect, little has changed in more than three millennia. The reasons that have led to war in the past seem not to have disappeared. Human beings, organized into nations and states, continue to compete for a limited supply of desirable things, to seek honor and advantage, and to fear others. All too often, the result has been war.

War and Technology

The conduct of war is shaped at the deepest level by the character of the societies involved, their values, their needs, and their organization, but from the first, technology has played a vital role. Weapons and other necessities of war are the product of technological development, and war and technology have had a mutually stimulating effect from the earliest times as new technologies have helped shape the character of war and the needs of armies have provoked technological advance.

Fortress Walls

Jericho, built about 7000 B.C.E. in the Neolithic Age, already reveals the importance of warfare and the development of technology to deal with it. Jericho

This carving in low relief from the seventh century B.C.E. shows an Assyrian war-chariot and its charioteer. It comes from the palace of King Ashurbanipal at Nineveh, the capital of the mighty Assyrian Empire that dominated the Near East in his time. Erich Lessing/Art Resource, N.Y.

is surrounded by a stone wall 700 yards around, ten feet thick, and thirteen feet high, protected by a moat ten feet deep and thirty feet wide. This barrier made the town a powerful fortress that could be defeated only by an enemy who could besiege it long enough to starve it out. Nobody would have undertaken the expense and effort to build such a structure unless war was a relatively common danger. Not too many years after the rise of civilization in Mesoptamia (ca. 3000 B.C.E.) fortified Sumerian cities appeared in the south. A thousand years later, the pharaohs of the Twelfth Dynasty in Egypt devised a strategic defense system of fortresses on their southern frontier with Nubia. In early China the towns had no walls, because the surrounding plains lacked both trees and stone. During the Shang dynasty (ca.1766–1050 B.C.E.), however, towns with walls made of beaten earth appeared. Once the techniques needed to build fortresses strong enough to withstand attack were mastered, kingdoms could expand into empires that could defend their conquered lands.

The history of warfare and military technology is a story of continued change caused by a permanent competition between defense and offense. In time, construction of fortified stronghold provoked new devices and techniques for besieging them. Excavations in Egypt and Mesopotamia have uncovered scaling ladders, battering rams, siege towers (some of them mobile), and mines burrowing under fortress walls. Catapults capable of hurling stones against an enemy's walls appear in Greece in the fourth century B.C.E.; the weapon was brought to greater perfec-

tion and power by the Romans centuries later. Alexander the Great and some of his Hellenistic successors became skillful at storming fortified cities with the aid of such technology, but throughout ancient history, success against a fortified place usually came as a result of starvation and surrender after a long siege. Not until the invention of gunpowder and powerful canons did offensive technology overcome the defensive strength of fortification.

Army Against Army

A different kind of warfare, of army against army in the open field, appeared as early as the Stone Age. Scholars disagree as to whether it came in the Paleolithic Age or emerged in Neolithic times, but we know that warriors used such weapons as wooden or stone clubs, spears and axes with sharpened stone heads, and simple bows with stone-tipped arrows. The discovery of metallurgy brought the Bronze Age to Mesopotamia, perhaps as early as 3500 B.C.E., providing armies with weapons that were sharper and sturdier than stone and with body armor and helmets that brought greater safety to warriors. The Mesopotamian rulers already had wealth, a sizable population, a civilized organization, and substantial fortress walls. Now, with bronze weapons, Mesopotamian rulers could expand their empires far beyond their early frontiers. When, not much later, the Bronze Age came to Egypt, its rulers, too, used the new technology to expand and defend their wealthy kingdom.

The Chariot and the Bow

The next great revolution in warfare occurred with the inventions of the chariot and the composite bow. When these came together by about 1800 B.C.E. their users swept all before them, conquering both Egypt and Mesopotamia. The chariot was a light vehicle, a platform on two wheels pulled by a team of two or four horses that could move swiftly on a battlefield. It was strong enough to hold two men—a driver and a warrior—as it sped along on an open field. The wheels were of wood—not solid, but with spokes and a hub—and were attached to an axle; building them required great skill and experience. The warrior on the chariot wielded a new weapon: the composite bow, more powerful by far than anything that had come before it. Made of thin strips of wood glued together and fastened with animal tendons and horn, the bow was short and easy to use from a moving chariot. It could shoot a light arrow accurately for 300 yards and penetrate the armor of the day at about 100. A man on a chariot on a flat enough field, using a composite bows with a quiver full of light arrows, could devastate an army of foot soldiers. "Circling at a distance of 100 or 200 yards from the herds of unarmoured foot soldiers, a chariot crew—one to drive, one to shoot—might have transfixed six men a minute. Ten minutes' work by ten chariots would cause 500 casualties or more."[4]

For several centuries, beginning about 1800 B.C.E., peoples from the north using such weapons smashed into Mesopotamia and conquered the kingdoms they attacked. In India, the Aryans, who also spoke an Indo-European language, smashed the indigenous Indus civilization. In Egypt, the Hyksos, speakers of a Semitic language, conquered the northern kingdom. In China, the chariot-riding Shang dynasty established an aristocratic rule based on the new weapons. In Europe, the Mycenaean Greeks used chariots, although it is not clear that they had the composite bow and used the tactics that had brought such great success elsewhere.

The most sophisticated users of ancient military technology before Alexander the Great were the Assyrians. They had a wide range of devices for siege warfare, and took them along on all their campaigns. As always, new weapons made of new materials with new techniques do not in themselves constitute a revolution in military affairs. To use them effectively, armies require organizations that can devise appropriate operational plans and train their soldiers in the needed skills and discipline. The Assyrian annals suggest that by the eighth century B.C.E. their kings had turned their chariot forces into "a weapon of shock and terror, manipulated by the driver to charge at breakneck speed behind a team of perfectly schooled horses and used by the archer as a platform from which to launch a hail of arrows; squadrons of chariots, their drivers trained to act in mutual support, might have clashed much as armoured vehicles have done in our time, success going to the side that could disable the larger opposing number, while the footmen unlucky or foolhardy enough to stand in their way would have been scattered like chaff."[5]

Mounted Cavalry

In 612 B.C.E., the great Assyrian empire fell before a coalition of opponents, but it had already been weakened by enemies who commanded a new military technique: mounted cavalry. Ironically, the Assyrians themselves may have been the first to develop the critical skills of riding astride a horse while keeping both hands free to shoot with a bow. The first peoples to use the new cavalry technology to great effect were nomads from the steppes of northern Eurasia. About 690 B.C.E., a people whom the Greeks called Cimmerians flooded into Asia Minor on their warhorses, shaking the established order. Later in that century they were followed by another group of steppe-nomads called the Scythians, who came from the Altai mountains in central Asia. The Scythians overthrew the Cimmerians and then joined with more settled peoples in the battles that destroyed the Assyrian empire. This was the beginning of a series of attacks by horse-riding nomads from the steppes against the settled lands to their south that lasted for two millennia. In China there is no clear evidence for such attacks before the fourth century B.C.E. but it is possible that attacks from Mongolia and nearby areas may have brought down the western Chou dynasty in 771 B.C.E.

In the Middle East the Babylonian Empire had succeeded the Assyrian, but was soon replaced by the Persian Empire. The Persians had no other way of preventing the nomads' devastating raids than to pay other nomads to defend their frontiers, and the Chinese emperors did the same. The Chinese also developed a cavalry that carried the crossbow, more powerful than the composite bow. Another device for defending against the invaders was the Great Wall of China, built during the Ch'in dynasty (256–206 B.C.E.) and designed to keep the ravaging horsemen out. But this, too, proved ineffective.

Despite endless perturbations of the political and military relationships between grassland and plowland, peoples of the steppe enjoyed a consistent advantage because of their superior mobility and the cheapness of their military equipment. This produced a pattern of recurrent nomad conquests of civilized lands.[6]

[4]John Keegan, *A History of Warfare* (New York: Vintage Books, 1993), p. 166.

[5]*Ibid*, pp. 176–177.

[6]William H. McNeill, *The Pursuit of Power* (Chicago: University of Chicago Press, 1982), p. 16.

The Great Wall of China was originally built during the Ch'in dynasty (256–206 B.C.E.), but what we see today is the wall as it was completely rebuilt during the Ming dynasty (1368–1644 C.E.). Paolo Koch/Photo Researchers, Inc.

Iron-wielding Warriors

Even as the chariot and the warhorse were having so great an impact on the nature of ancient warfare, a far more fundamental revolution in military affairs was underway. Bronze is an alloy of copper and tin, but the latter is a rather rare metal, so it was expensive. Horses also were costly to keep. So warfare that depended on bronze weapons and horses was necessarily limited to a relatively small number of men. About 1400 B.C.E., however, in Asia Minor, someone discovered the technique of working iron to give it an edge so hard and durable that tools and weapons made of it were clearly superior to those of bronze. Iron, moreover, is far more abundant than the components of bronze, is easier to work, and is much cheaper. For the first time, it became possible for common people to own and use metal. Now a much larger part of the population could own arms and armor, and "[o]rdinary farmers and herdsmen thereby achieved a new formidability in battle, and the narrowly aristocratic structure of society characteristic of the chariot age altered abruptly. A more democratic era dawned as iron-wielding invaders overthrew ruling elites that had based their power on a monopoly of chariotry."[7]

Within two centuries, the new technology spread over the Middle East and into Europe. A new round of invasions by iron-wielding warriors swept away kingdoms and empires and brought new peoples to power. The Assyrians, combining the bureacratic organizational skills of Mesopotamian civilization with a warrior spirit and an ability to assimilate new techniques, achieved control of their own region with the aid of iron weapons, but many indigenous rulers of civilized lands were subdued or swept away. In Europe, a Greek-speaking people we call the Myceneans had ruled the Greek peninsula and the Aegean Sea with a Bronze Age civilization similar to those of the Middle East.

[7]*Ibid*, p. 12.

190

Between 1200 B.C.E. and 1100 B.C.E., however, the Mycenaeans were overthrown by a new wave of Greeks with iron weapons who obliterated the old civilization and brought a new culture based on new ways of fighting.

The Shield and the Phalanx

The heart of this new Greek civilization, which is called Hellenic, was the city state, or *polis*, hundreds of which came into being towards the end of the eighth century B.C.E. (See Chapter 2.) Their armies consisted of independent yeoman farmers who produced enough wealth to supply their own iron weapons and body armor, made cheap enough by the revolution in metallurgy. But again, these would have been of little value without organizational change. Now, a new way of warfare that made infantry the dominant fighting force on land for centuries, permitted an alliance of poor Greek states to defeat the mighty and wealthy Persian Empire. The soldiers, wearing helmets, body armor, and a heavy, large, round shield for protection, carried short iron swords, but used iron-tipped wooden pikes as their chief weapon. Arrayed in compact blocks called *phalanxes*, usually eight men deep, these freemen, well disciplined and highly motivated, defeated lesser infantries, archers, and cavalry. Adapted by the Macedonians under King Philip II and his son Alexander the Great, the hoplite phalanx remained the dominant infantry force until it was defeated by the Roman legion in the second century B.C.E.

Trireme Warfare

The Greeks also achieved supremacy at sea by improving an existing technological innovation and providing it with an effective operational plan. Oared galleys were known at Cyprus as early as about 1000 B.C.E. and the Phoenicians improved their speed and maneuverability by superimposing a second and then a third bank of rowers over the first to produce a ship that the Greeks called a *trireme*. The Greeks added outriggers for the top rowers, and it is possible that this permitted their rowers to use the full power of their strongest leg muscles by sliding back and forth as they rowed. At first, the main mode of trireme warfare was for one ship to come alongside another, grapple it, and send marines to board the enemy ship. In time, however, the Greeks placed a strong ram at the prow of each ship and learned how to row with great bursts of speed and to make sharp turns that allowed them to ram and disable their opponents by striking them in the side or rear. With such ships and tactics, the Greek triremes repeatedly sank fleets of the Egyptians and Phoenicians who rowed for the Persian Empire, thus gaining complete naval mastery.

The Macedonians came to dominate the Greek world, to conquer the Persian Empire, and to rule its successor states in the Hellenistic Period (323–31 B.C.E.), but technological innovation in military affairs played only a small part in their success. Military victories came chiefly from the quality of their leaders, the number, spirit, and discipline of their troops, and the ability to combine infantry, cavalry, and light-armed troops to win battles. Alexander's engineers also brought unprecedented skill to the use of siege weapons.

Roman Legions

The armies of the Roman Republic defeated Macedon in a series of wars in the third and second centuries B.C.E. and brought the entire Mediterranean world under Roman sway by the end of the second century. This conquest was achieved almost entirely by the power of the infantry. In time, the Roman army moved from the phalanx formation to a looser, more open order of battle based on the legion, which was divided into smaller, self-sufficient units. The Romans abandoned the pike as the chief infantry weapon, using instead the *pilum*, a heavy iron javelin that was thrown to cause disarray in the enemy line and permit the Romans to use their short, double-edged swords at close quarters. In the Imperial period, beginning especially in the third century of our era, nomadic barbarian tribes began applying the severe pressure on Rome's frontiers that would ultimately bring down the empire. Like the Chinese, the Romans built walls in some places to ease the burden of defending their extensive borders. In the empire's last years, the Romans began to use heavily armored horses ridden by knights in heavy armor, carrying lances and capable of charging an enemy with great force and effect. These armored cavalrymen, called *cataphracts* in Greek, would develop into a major new system of fighting in the Western Middle Ages, but they were too few to take a significant role in the final, futile defense of the empire.

❖ *How early is the evidence for warfare among human beings? What did Thucydides think that war was about? For what purposes did he think people went to war? Is war a rational or irrational action? Can you think of any good reason for fighting a war? How did war and technology affect one another in the ancient world?*

Part 2

476 C.E.–1300 C.E.

	POLITICS AND GOVERNMENT	SOCIETY AND ECONOMY	RELIGION AND CULTURE
300–500	315 Constantinople becomes new capital of Roman Empire 410 Visigoths sack Rome 451–453 Attila the Hun invades Italy 455 Vandals overrun Rome 476 Odovacer deposes the last Western emperor 489–493 Theodoric's Ostrogoth kingdom established in Italy	400 Cities and trade begin to decline in the West; Germanic (barbarian) tribes settle in the West	312 Constantine embraces Christianity 325 Council of Nicaea 380 Christianity becomes the official religion of the Roman Empire 413–426 Saint Augustine writes *City of God* 451 Council of Chalcedon 496 The Franks embrace Christianity
500–700	527–565 Reign of Justinian 568 Lombard invasion of Italy	533–534 *Corpus juris civilis* compiled by Justinian Interior of Hagia Sophia	529 Saint Benedict founds monastery at Monte Cassino 537 Byzantine Church of Hagia Sophia completed 590–604 Pope Gregory the Great 622 Muhammad's flight from Mecca (Hegira)
700–900	632–733 Muslim expansion and conquests 734 Charles Martel defeats Muslims at Poitiers 768–814 Reign of Charlemagne 843 Treaty of Verdun partitions Carolingian empire	632–733 Muslims disrupt western Mediterranean trade 700 Agrarian society centered around the manor predominates in the west 700–800 Moldboard plow and three field system in use 700 Islam enters its Golden Age 800 Byzantium enters its Golden Age 800 Introduction of collar harness 850 Muslims occupy parts of Spain 880s Vikings penetrate central Europe	725–787 Iconoclastic Controversy in East ca. 775 *Donation of Constantine* 782 Alcuin of York runs Charlemagne's palace school 800 Pope Leo crowns Charlemagne emperor

THE MIDDLE AGES

476 C.E.–1300 C.E.

	POLITICS AND GOVERNMENT	SOCIETY AND ECONOMY	RELIGION AND CULTURE
900–1100	918 Saxon Henry I becomes first non-Frankish king, as Saxons succeed Carolingians in Germany	900 Introduction of the horseshoe	910 Benedictine monastery of Cluny founded
	987 Capetians succeed Carolingians in France	900–1100 Rise of towns, guilds, and urban culture in West	980s Orthodox Christianity penetrates Russia
	1066 Battle of Hastings (Norman Conquest of England)		1054 Schism between Eastern and Western churches
			1075 Pope Gregory VII condemns lay investiture
		1086 *Domesday Book*	
			1095 Pope Urban II preaches the First Crusade
	1071 Seljuk Turks defeat Byzantine armies at Manzikert		
	1099 Jerusalem falls to Crusaders		
1100–1300	1152 Frederick I Barbarossa first Hohenstaufen emperor	1130 Gothic architecture begins to displace Romanesque	1122 Concordat of Worms ends Investiture Controversy
			1158 First European university founded in Bologna
	1187 Saladin reconquers Jerusalem from West		
	1204 Fourth Crusade captures Constantinople	1200 Shift from dues to rent tenancy on manors	
	1214 Philip II Augustus defeats English and German armies at Bouvines		1210 Franciscan order founded
	1215 Magna Carta		1216 Dominican order founded
	1240 Mongols dominate Russia		1265 Thomas Aquinas's *Summa Theologica* begun
	1250 Death of Frederick II (end of Hohenstaufen dynasty)		
	1257 German princes establish electoral college to elect emperor		ca. 1275 *Romance of the Rose*

Harold's crowning. The Bayeux Tapestry

The story of Adam and Eve from Genesis 1–3. Here God creates Adam and then Eve from one of Adam's ribs, then blesses and gives them both dominion over the earth—but He forbids them to eat from the tree of the knowledge of good and evil in the garden of Eden. Eve and Adam disobey God and are cast out of the garden in shame, forever thereafter to do penance in toilsome lives—Eve by bearing children, Adam by hard labor. From the Moutier-Grandval Bible. By permission of the British Library

The Early Middle Ages:
Creating a New European Society and Culture (476–1000)

KEY TOPICS

- How the fusion of Germanic and Roman culture laid the foundation for a distinctively European society after the collapse of the western Roman Empire
- The Byzantine and Islamic empires and their impact on the West
- The role of the church in Western society during the early Middle Ages
- The political and economic features of Europe under the Franks
- The characteristics of feudal society

The early Middle Ages mark the birth of Europe. This period of recovery from the collapse of Roman civilization gave rise to forced experimentation with new ideas and institutions. Greco–Roman culture combined with the new Germanic culture and an evolving Christianity to create distinctive political and cultural forms within what had been the northern and western provinces of the Roman Empire. In government, religion, and language, as well as geography, these regions grew separate from the Eastern Byzantine world and the Islamic Arab world, which extended across North Africa from Spain to the eastern Mediterranean.

The early Middle Ages have been called, not with complete fairness, a "dark age," because during these centuries western Europe lost touch with classical, especially Greek, learning and science. People the Romans somewhat arrogantly called "barbarians"—because their origins were rural and they knew no Latin—intruded on the region from the north and east. German tribes that had been settling peacefully around the empire since the first century B.C.E.

began to migrate directly into it by the fourth century. During the fifth century, these tribes turned fiercely against their Roman hosts, largely because the Romans treated them so cruelly. To the south, Arab dominance transformed the Mediterranean into an often inhospitable "Islamic lake," greatly reducing (although by no means completely severing) Western trade with the East and isolating Western people more than they had been before. Thus surrounded and assailed from north, east, and south, Europe understandably became somewhat insular and even stagnant.

On the other hand, being forced to manage by themselves, western Europeans also learned to develop their native resources. The reign of Charlemagne saw a modest renaissance of antiquity. And the peculiar social and political forms that emerged during this period—manorialism and feudalism—not only were successful at coping with unprecedented chaos on local levels, but also proved to be fertile seedbeds for the growth of distinctive Western institutions.

On the Eve of the Frankish Ascendancy

As we have already seen, by the late third century the Roman Empire had become too large for a single sovereign to govern and was failing in many respects. The emperor Diocletian (r. 284–305) tried to strengthen the empire by dividing it between himself and a co-emperor, Maximian. The result was a dual empire with an eastern and a western half, each with its own emperor and, eventually, imperial bureaucracy. A critical shift of the empire's resources and orientation to the eastern half accompanied these changes. In 284 Diocletian moved to Nicomedia (in modern Turkey), where he remained until the last two years of his reign. As imperial rule weakened in the West and strengthened in the East, it also became increasingly autocratic.

In an attempt to end the factional strife that followed Diocletian's reign and to position himself better to meet the empire's new eastern enemies, Constantine the Great (r. 306–337) briefly reunited the empire by conquest (it would be redivided by his three sons and subsequent successors) and ruled as sole emperor of the eastern and western halves after 324. In that year, he moved the capital of the empire from Rome to Byzantium, an ancient city that stood at the crossroads of the major sea and land routes between Europe and Asia Minor. On the site of this ancient city, Constantine built the new city of Constantinople, dedicated in 330. Serving as the imperial residence and the new administrative center of

the empire, Constantinople gradually became a "new Rome." The "old" Rome, suffering from internal political quarrels and geographically distant from new military fronts in Syria and along the Danube River, declined in importance. The city and the western empire were actually on the wane in the late third and fourth centuries, well before the barbarian invasions in the West began. Milan had replaced Rome as the imperial residence in 286; in 402 the seat of Western government would be moved yet again, to Ravenna. When the barbarian invasions began in the late fourth century, the West was in political disarray, and imperial power and prestige had shifted decisively to Constantinople and the East.

Germanic Migrations

The German tribes did not burst in on the West all of a sudden. They were at first a token and benign presence on the fringes of the empire and even within it. Before the massive migrations from the north and the east, Roman and Germanic cultures had commingled peacefully for centuries. The Romans had "imported" barbarians as domestics, slaves, and soldiers. Barbarian soldiers rose to positions of high leadership and fame in Roman legions.

Beginning in 376 with a great influx of Visigoths, or "west Goths," into the empire, this peaceful coexistence ended. The Visigoths, accomplished horsemen and fierce warriors, were themselves pushed into the empire by the emergence of a notoriously violent people, the Huns, from the region of what is now Mongolia. The Visigoths ultimately reached southern Gaul and Spain. Soon to be Christianized, they won rights of settlement and material assistance within the empire from the eastern emperor Valens (r. 364–378) in exchange for defending the eastern frontier as *foederati*, or the emperor's "special allies."

Instead of the promised assistance, however, the Visigoths received harsh treatment from their new allies. They had arrived in the empire an impoverished people fleeing the Huns. So bad off were they that they traded their own children to the Romans for dogs to eat. The Romans, showing no mercy, charged them one child per dog. After repeated conflicts, the Visigoths rebelled and handily defeated Roman armies led by Valens at the Battle of Adrianople in 378.

After Adrianople, the Romans passively permitted the settlement of barbarians within the very heart of the western empire. The Vandals crossed the Rhine in 406 and within three decades gained control of northwest Africa and a sizable portion of the Mediterranean. The Burgundians, who came on the heels of the Vandals, settled in Gaul. Most important for subsequent Western history were the Franks, who settled northern and central Gaul,

A Contemporary Description of Attila the Hun

In 448 a Roman envoy, Priscus, visited the home of Attila in a Scythian village at the base of the Danube River, three years before Attila's famous invasion of Italy. Knowing Attila's reputation for savagery, he was surprised to find him a simple and cultured man.

❖ *How would you account for the discrepancy between this portrait of Attila and his reputation? Has history falsely portrayed this fiercest of warriors? What does it say about the Huns' system of justice that Attila dispensed judgments on the street as he walked?*

Attila's residence...was made of polished boards, and surrounded with wooden enclosures, designed not so much for protection as for appearance's sake....I entered the enclosure of Attila's palace, bearing gifts to his wife, whose name was Kreka....Having been admitted by the barbarians at the door, I found her reclining on a soft couch. The floor of the room was covered with woolen mats for walking on....Having approached, saluted her, and presented the gifts, I went out and walked to the other houses....Attila came forth from [one of] the house[s] with a dignified strut, looking round on this side and on that....Many persons who had lawsuits with one another came up and received his judgment. Then he returned into the house and received ambassadors of barbarous peoples....

[We were invited to a banquet with Attila at three o'clock.] The cupbearers gave us a cup, according to the national custom, that we might pray before we sat down. Having tasted the cup, we proceeded to take our seats, all the chairs being ranged along the walls of the room on either side. Attila sat in the middle on a couch; a second couch was set behind him, and from it steps led up to his bed, which was covered with linen sheets and wrought coverlets for ornament, such as Greeks and Romans used to deck bridal beds. The places on the right of Attila were held chief in honor; those on the left, where we sat, were only second....

The attendant of Attila first entered with a dish full of meat, and behind him came the other attendants with bread and viands [plates of food], which they laid on the tables. A luxurious meal, served on silver plate, had been made ready for us and the barbarian guests, but Attila ate nothing but meat on a wooden trencher [a wooden plate]. In everything else, too, he showed himself temperate; his cup was of wood, while to the guests were given goblets of gold and silver. His dress, too, was quite simple, affecting only to be clean. The sword he carried at his side, the latchets of his...shoes, the bridle of his horse were not adorned with gold or gems or anything costly...like those of the other Scythians.

[After two courses were eaten and] evening fell, torches were lit and two barbarians, coming forward in front of Attila, sang songs they had composed, celebrating his victories and deeds of valor in war.

From James Harvey Robinson, ed., *Readings in European History*, Vol. 1 (Boston: Athenaeum, 1904), pp. 47–48.

some along the seacoast (the Salian Franks) and others along the Rhine, Seine, and Loire Rivers (the Ripuarian Franks).

Why was there so little Roman resistance to these Germanic tribes, whose numbers—at most 100,000 people in the largest of them—were comparatively very small? The invaders were successful because they had come upon a badly overextended western empire divided politically by ambitious military commanders and weakened by decades of famine, pestilence, and overtaxation. By the second half of the fourth century, Roman frontiers had become too vast to manage. Efforts to do so by "barbarizing" the Roman army, that is, by recruiting many peasants into it and by making the Germanic tribes key

Roman allies, only weakened it further. The eastern empire retained enough wealth and vitality to field new armies or to buy off the invaders. The western empire, in contrast, succumbed not only because of moral decay and materialism, but also because of a combination of military rivalry, political mismanagement, disease, and sheer poverty.

Fall of the Roman Empire

In the early fifth century, Italy and the "eternal city" of Rome suffered a series of devastating blows. In 410, the Visigoths, under Alaric (ca. 370–410), revolted and sacked Rome. In 452, the Huns, led by Attila—known to contemporaries as the "scourge

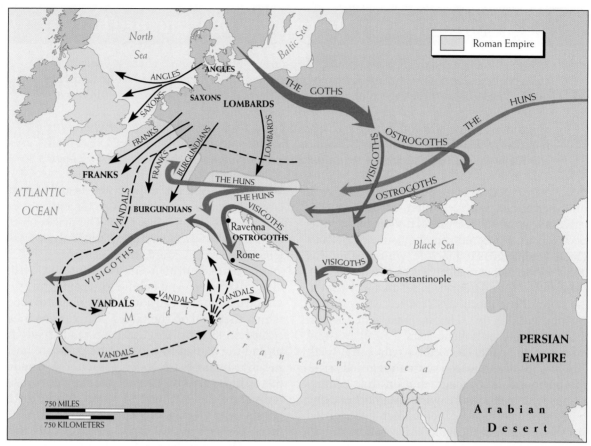

MAP 6–1   BARBARIAN MIGRATIONS INTO THE WEST IN THE FOURTH AND FIFTH CENTURIES   *The forceful intrusion of Germanic and non-Germanic barbarians into the Roman Empire from the last quarter of the fourth century through the fifth century made for a constantly changing pattern of movement and relations. The map shows the major routes taken by the usually unwelcome newcomers and the areas most deeply affected by main groups.*

of God"—invaded Italy. (See "A Contemporary Description of Attila the Hun.") And in 455 Rome was overrun yet again, this time by the Vandals.

By the mid-fifth century, power in western Europe had passed decisively from the hands of the Roman emperors to those of barbarian chieftains. In 476, the traditional date given for the fall of the Roman Empire, the barbarian Odovacer (ca. 434–493) deposed and replaced the western emperor Romulus Augustulus. The eastern emperor, Zeno (r. 474–491), recognized Odovacer's authority in the west, and Odovacer acknowledged Zeno as sole emperor, contenting himself to serve as Zeno's western viceroy. In a later coup in 493 manipulated by Zeno, Theodoric (ca. 454–526), king of the Ostrogoths, or "east Goths," replaced Odovacer. At least until the last part of his reign, Theodoric governed with the full acceptance of the Roman people and the Christian Church.

By the end of the fifth century, barbarians had thoroughly overrun the western empire. The Ostrogoths settled in Italy, the Franks in northern Gaul, the Burgundians in Provence, the Visigoths in southern Gaul and Spain, the Vandals in Africa and the western Mediterranean, and the Angles and Saxons in England. (See Map 6–1.)

Western Europe, however, was not transformed into a savage land. Its new masters were willing to learn from the people they had conquered; barbarian military victories did not result in a great defeat of Roman culture. Except in Britain and northern Gaul, Roman language, law, and government coexisted with the new Germanic institutions. In Italy under Theodoric, Roman law gradually replaced tribal custom. Only the Vandals and the Anglo-Saxons—and, after 466, the Visigoths—refused to profess at least titular obedience to the emperor in Constantinople.

That the Visigoths, the Ostrogoths, and the Vandals entered the West as Christianized people contributed to this accommodation of cultures. They were followers, however, of the Arian creed, considered heretical in the West. Arian Christians believed that Jesus Christ was not one identical being with God the Father—a point of view the Council of Nicaea had condemned in 325. (See Chapter 5.)

In spite of the hostility their Arian Christianity provoked, the Germans themselves admired Roman culture and had no desire to destroy it, although their rural lifestyle further weakened its urban foundations. Later, around 500, the Franks, under their strong king, Clovis, converted to the orthodox, or "Catholic," form of Christianity supported by the bishops of Rome. Then, as Roman Christians, the Franks helped conquer and convert the Goths and other barbarians in western Europe.

All things considered, rapprochement and a gradual interpenetration of two strong cultures—a creative tension—marked the period of the Germanic migrations. The stronger culture was the Roman, and it became dominant in a later fusion. Despite western military defeat, the Goths and the Franks became far more romanized than the Romans were germanized. The Latin language, Nicene Christianity, and eventually Roman law and government were to triumph in the West during the Middle Ages.

The Byzantine Empire

As western Europe succumbed to the Germanic invasions, imperial power shifted to the Byzantine Empire, that is, the eastern part of the Roman Empire. Emperor Constantine the Great began the rebuilding of Byzantium in 324, renaming the city Constantinople and dedicating it in 330. Constantinople became the sole capital of the empire and remained so until the successful revival of the western empire in the eighth century by Charlemagne.

Between 324 and 1453, the empire passed from an early period of expansion and splendor to a time of contraction and splintering and finally to

MAP 6–2   THE BYZANTINE EMPIRE AT THE TIME OF JUSTINIAN'S DEATH   *The inset shows the empire in 1025, before its losses to the Seljuk Turks.*

A sixth-century ivory panel depicting the Byzantine emperor Justinian as the champion of the Christian faith. From 500 to 1100, the Byzantine Empire was the center of Christian civilization. Giraudon/Art Resource, N.Y.

catastrophic defeat by the Ottoman Turks. Historians commonly divide the history of the empire into three distinct periods:

1. from the rebuilding of Byzantium as Constantinople in 324 to the beginning of the Arab expansion and the spread of Islam in 632
2. from 632 to the conquest of Asia Minor by the Seljuk Turks after the fall of Manzikert in 1071, or, as some prefer, to the fall of Constantinople to western Crusaders in 1204
3. from 1071 or 1204 to the fall of Constantinople to the Turks in 1453.

The Reign of Justinian

In terms of territory, political power, and culture, the first period of Byzantine history (324–632) was by far its greatest. The height of this period was the reign of the emperor Justinian (r. 527–565) and his brilliant wife, the empress Theodora (d. 548). (See Map 6–2.) The daughter of a bear trainer in the circus, the empress in her youth had fallen prey to the seedy side of sixth-century circus life. Her activities may have included prostitution, if the contro-

versial *Secret History* by Justinian's court historian, Procopius, is to be believed. Her background may have given her a toughness that fully matched and even exceeded her husband's. (See "The Character and 'Innovations' of Justinian and Theodora.")

An influential counselor, Theodora became a major figure in imperial government. In 532, Justinian contemplated abdication following riots against his rule that left much of Constantinople in ruins and thousands dead. Theodora stiffened his resolve, reportedly insisting that he crack down ruthlessly on the rioters and firmly reestablish his authority, which he most decisively did. In doctrinal matters, the empress clearly had a mind and will of her own. Whereas Justinian remained strictly orthodox in his Christian beliefs, Theodora lent her support to a Christian heresy known as Monophysitism, which taught that Jesus had only one nature, a composite divine–human one, not a fully human and fully divine dual nature, as orthodox doctrine taught. In the sixth century, the Monophysites formed a separate church that had a very strong influence in the eastern provinces of the empire. The imperial government persecuted them as heretics after Theodora's death, a policy that cost the empire dearly when, in the seventh century, Persian and Arab armies besieged its eastern frontiers. Bitter over their treatment, the Monophysites offered little resistance to the invaders.

LAW The imperial goal in the East—as reflected in the policy "one God, one empire, one religion"—was to centralize government and impose legal and doctrinal conformity. To this end, Justinian collated and revised Roman law. This codification had become a pressing matter because of the enormous number of often contradictory legal decrees that had piled up since the mid-second century as the empire grew increasingly Christian and imperial rule increasingly autocratic.

Justinian's *Corpus juris civilis* or "body of civil law," was a fourfold compilation undertaken by a learned committee of lawyers. The first compilation, known as the *Code*, appeared in 533. It revised imperial edicts issued since the reign of Hadrian (r. 117–138). A second compilation, the *Novellae*, or "new things," contained the decrees issued by Justinian and his immediate successors after 534. The third compilation, the *Digest*, was a summary of the major opinions of the old legal experts. The fourth compilation, the *Institutes*, was a textbook for young scholars, which drew its lessons from the *Code* and the *Digest*. These works had little immediate effect on medieval common law, but, beginning with the Renaissance, they provided the foundation for most subsequent

The Character and 'Innovations' of Justinian and Theodora

According to Procopius, their court historian and biographer, Justinian and Theodora were tyrants, pure and simple. His Secret History *(sixth century), which some historians distrust as a source, had only criticism and condemnation for the two rulers. Procopius especially resented Theodora, and he did not believe that the rule of law was respected at the royal court.*

❖ *Is Procopius being fair to Justinian and Theodora? Is the* Secret History *an ancient tabloid? How does one know when a source is biased and self-serving and when it is telling the truth? What does Procopius most dislike about the queen? Was Theodora the last woman ruler to receive such criticism?*

Formerly, when the senate approached the Emperor, it paid homage in the following manner. Every patrician kissed him on the right breast; the Emperor [then] kissed the patrician on the head, and he was dismissed. Then the rest bent their right knee to the Emperor and withdrew. It was not customary to pay homage to the Queen.

But those who were admitted [in]to the presence of Justinian and Theodora, whether they were patricians or otherwise, fell on their faces on the floor, stretching their hands and feet out wide, kissed first one foot and then the other of the Augustus [i.e., the emperor], and then retired. Nor did Theodora refuse this honor; and she even received the ambassadors of the Persians and other barbarians and gave them presents, as if she were in command of the Roman Empire: a thing that had never happened in all previous time.

And formerly intimates of the Emperor called him Emperor and the Empress, Empress....But if anybody addressed either of these two as Emperor or Empress without adding "Your Majesty" or "Your Highness," or forgot to call himself their slave, he was considered either ignorant or insolent, and was dismissed in disgrace as if he had done some awful crime or committed some unpardonable sin.

And [whereas] before, only a few were sometimes admitted to the palace...when these two came to power, the magistrates and everybody else had no trouble in fairly living in the palace. This was because the magistrates of old had administered justice and the laws according to their conscience...but these two, taking control of everything to the misfortune of their subjects, forced everyone to come to them and beg like slaves. And almost any day one could see the law courts nearly deserted, while in the hall of the Emperor there was a jostling and pushing crowd that resembled nothing so much as a mob of slaves.

From *Secret History of Procopius* translated by Richard Atwater. Copyright © 1927 by Crown Publishers, Inc. Reprinted by permission of Crown Publishers, Inc.

European law down to the nineteenth century. They especially benefitted those rulers who aspired to centralize their states.

RELIGION   Religion as well as law served imperial centralization. Since the fifth century, the patriarch of Constantinople had crowned emperors in that city. This practice reflected the close ties between rulers and the church. In 380 Christianity had been proclaimed the official religion of the eastern empire. All other religions and sects were denounced as "demented and insane."[1] Between the fourth and sixth centuries the patriarchs of Constantinople, Alexandria, Antioch, and Jerusalem acquired enormous wealth in the form of land and gold. The church, in turn, acted as the state's welfare agency, drawing on its generous endowments from pious rich donors to aid the poor and needy. The prestige and comfort of the clergy swelled the clerical ranks of the Eastern Church.

Orthodox Christianity was not, however, the only religion within the empire with a significant following. Nor did the rulers view religion as merely a political tool. At one time or another the Christian heresies of Arianism, Monophysitism, and Iconoclasm also received imperial support. Persecution and absorption into popular Christianity served to curtail many pagan religious practices.

The empire was also home, although at times a less than hospitable one, to large numbers of Jews. Non-Christian Romans saw Jews as narrow, dogmatic, and intolerant people in comparison with Christians, and

[1] Cyril Mango, *Byzantium: The Empire of New Rome* (New York: Charles Scribner's Sons, 1980) p. 88.

Hagia Sophia: A Temple Surpassing that of Solomon

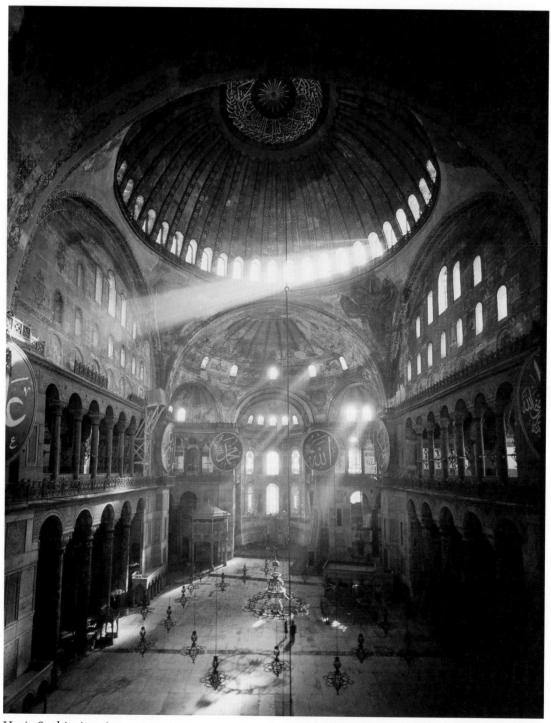

Hagia Sophia, interior. Erich Lessing/Art Resource, N.Y.

One of the greatest achievements of Emperor Justinian's reign proved also to be one of the greatest in Byzantine art and architecture: Hagia Sophia (the Church of Holy Wisdom). It was built on the spot of another Christian church begun centuries earlier by Emperor Constantine (r. 306–337) and was completed in 360, later to be enhanced by Emperor Theodosius II (408–450), builder of Constantinople's fortified wall. In 532, the Nika riots (named after the rebels' cry of "victory" [*nika*]) completely destroyed this ancient church and almost toppled Justinian and Theodora.

One of Justinian's responses was Hagia Sophia, begun in the aftermath of the riots and completed in 537. Two of the age's great architects, Anthemius of Tralles and Isidore of Miletus, designed the building and oversaw its construction by a team of equally outstanding engineers, who employed one hundred master masons with crews of one hundred workers each, 10,000 in all. The sprawling new church rose 184 feet, its key feature a massive dome, 112 feet in diameter, made from five separate pieces from bottom (pendentive) to top (cupola). Circled with numerous windows, the dome flooded the nave with light and, together with the church's many other windows, glistening mosaics, and open spaces, gave the interior a remarkable airiness and luminosity.

A contemporary record of its construction, written two decades later by the royal biographer Procopius (probably under the constraint of the emperor and as propaganda) portrays Justinian as a knowledgeable engineer who conceived the building in a divine vision. (No mention is made of Theodora, whom Procopius appears to have intensely disliked.) In all probability, Justinian did little more than provide the funds, a reported 320,000 pounds of gold. Another retrospective account, written in the ninth century and largely fictional, has Justinian destroying the older church himself so that he might build a temple surpassing that of Solomon (possibly a criticism of the hubris of rulers past and present). Such accounts, while historically inaccurate, have been seen to reflect the popular view of contemporaries and not a few modern visitors to the church today: Hagia Sophia was too magnificent to have been the work of human minds and hands alone.

With the Turkish conquest of Constantinople in 1453, Hagia Sophia was transformed into a Muslim mosque with four prominent minarets, and as with the churches of many Protestants in Western Europe, its colorful mosaics were painted over in accordance with Muslim law, which deemed the depictions of God in Byzantine art idolatrous.

Sources: H. W. Janson & A. F. Janson, *History of Art*, 5th ed. (Upper Saddle River, NJ: Prentice Hall, 1997), pp. 252–254; Cyril Mango, "Byzantine Writers on the Fabric of Hagia Sophia," in *Hagia Sophia from the Age of Justinian to the Present*, ed. R. Mark and A. S. Cakmak (Cambridge, U.K.: Cambridge University Press, 1992), pp. 41–50.

Property of
BOARD OF EDUCATION
BAY VILLAGE, OHIO

Empress Theodora and her attendants. The union of political and spiritual authority in the person of the empress is shown by the depiction on Theodora's mantle of three magi carrying gifts to the Virgin and Jesus.
Scala/Art Resource, N.Y.

they had little love for them. Under Roman law, Jews had legal protection so long as they did not proselytize among Christians, build new synagogues, or try to enter sensitive public offices or professions. Justinian (the emperor most intent on religious conformity within the empire) adopted a policy of encouraging Jews to convert voluntarily. Later emperors ordered all Jews to be baptized and granted tax breaks to those who voluntarily complied. But neither persuasion nor coercion succeeded in converting the empire's Jews.

CITIES During Justinian's reign the empire's strength was its more than 1,500 cities. The largest, with perhaps 350,000 inhabitants, was Constantinople, the cultural crossroads of the Asian and European civilizations. The large provincial cities had populations of 50,000. Between the fourth and fifth centuries, councils of about 200 members, all of whom were local wealthy landowners known as *decurions*, governed the cities. Decurions were the intellectual and economic elite of the empire. They were also heavily taxed, and for this reason they were not always the emperor's most docile or loyal servants. By the sixth century, special governors and bishops, appointed from the landholding classes, replaced the decurion councils and proved to be more reliable instruments of the emperor's will.

A fifth-century statistical record gives us some sense of the size and splendor of Constantinople at its peak. It lists five imperial and nine princely palaces; eight public and 153 private baths; four public forums; five granaries; two theaters; one hippodrome; 322 streets; 4,388 substantial houses; fifty-two porticoes; twenty public and 120 private bakeries; and

fourteen churches.[2] The most popular entertainments were the theater, frequently denounced by the clergy for nudity and immorality, and the races at the hippodrome. Many public taverns existed as well.

Eastern Influences

During the reign of Heraclius (r. 610–641) the empire took a decidedly Eastern, as opposed to Roman, direction. Heraclius spoke Greek, not Latin. He spent his entire reign resisting Persian and Islamic invasions, the former successfully, the latter in vain. Islamic armies progressively overran the empire after 632, directly attacking Constantinople for the first time in 677. Not until the reign of Leo III of the Isaurian dynasty (r. 717–740) were the Islamic armies repulsed and most of Asia Minor regained by the Byzantines.

Leo, however, offended Western Christians when he forbade the use of images in Eastern churches and tried to enforce the ban also in the West. This was an affront to Western Christianity, which had carefully nurtured the adoration of Jesus, Mary, and the saints in images and icons. Historians have speculated that Leo and his immediate successors pursued this policy under the influence of Islam, which condemned the veneration of images, perhaps hoping to placate the Muslims by joining them on this point of doctrine. Be that as it may, the banning of images was a major expression of eastern Caesaro-papism—the direct involvement of the emperor in religious dogma and practice as if he were both secular ruler and the head of the church—which, as we will see, the West-

[2]Mango, p. 76.

ern church always resisted. In addition to creating a new division within Christendom, the ban on images led to the destruction of much religious art until it was reversed in the late eighth century.

In 1071, the Byzantine Empire suffered a major defeat at the hands of the Muslim Seljuk Turks. Successful over Byzantine armies at Manzikert, the Turks rapidly overran the eastern provinces of the empire. This defeat was the beginning of the end of the empire, although the actual end—at the hands of the Seljuks' cousins, the Ottoman Turks—still lay centuries ahead. After two decades of steady Turkish advance, the eastern emperor Alexius I Comnenus (r. 1081–1118) invoked Western aid in 1092. Three years later, the West launched the first of the Crusades. A century later (1204), the Crusaders would inflict far more damage on Constantinople and Eastern Christendom than all previous non-Christian invaders had done.

Throughout the early Middle Ages, the Byzantine Empire remained a protective barrier between western Europe and hostile Persian, Arab, and Turkish armies. The Byzantines were also a major conduit of classical learning and science into the West down to the Renaissance. While western Europeans were fumbling to create a culture of their own, the cities of the Byzantine Empire provided them a model of a civilized society.

Islam and the Islamic World

A new drama began to unfold in the sixth century with the awakening of a rival far more dangerous to the West than the German tribes: the new faith of Islam. By the time of Muhammad's death (632), Islamic armies absorbed the attention and the resources of the emperors in Constantinople and rulers in the West.

At first, the Muslims were both open and cautious. They borrowed and integrated elements of Persian and Greek culture into their own. The new religion of Islam adopted elements of Christian, Jewish, and native pagan religious beliefs and practices. Muslims tolerated religious minorities within the territories they conquered, so long as these minorities recognized Islamic political rule, refrained from proselytizing among Muslims, and paid their taxes. Nonetheless, the Muslims were keen to protect the purity and integrity of Islamic religion, language, and law from any corrupting foreign influence. With the passage of time, and increased conflict with Eastern and Western Christians, this protective tendency grew stronger. Despite significant contacts and exchanges, Islamic culture would not penetrate the West as creatively as Germanic culture did, but would remain largely strange and threatening to Westerners.

Muhammad's Religion

Muhammad (570–632), an orphan, was raised by a family of modest means. As a youth, he worked as a merchant's assistant, traveling the major trade routes. When he was twenty-five, he married a wealthy Meccan widow. Thereafter, himself a wealthy man, he became a kind of social activist, criticizing Meccan materialism, paganism, and unjust treatment of the poor and needy. At about age forty, a deep religious experience heightened his commitment to reform and transformed his life. He began to receive revelations from the angel Gabriel, who recited God's word to him at irregular intervals. These revelations grew into the *Qur'an* (literally, a "reciting"), which his followers compiled between 650 and 651. The basic message Muhammad received was a summons to all Arabs to submit to God's will. Followers of Muhammad's religion came to be called *Muslim* ("submissive" or "surrendering"); the name applied to the religion itself, *Islam*, has the same derivation and means "submission."

The message was not a new one. It had been reiterated by a long line of Jewish prophets going back to Noah. According to Muslims, however, this line ended with Muhammad, who, as the last of God's chosen prophets, became "the Prophet." The *Qur'an* also recognized Jesus Christ as a prophet, but did not view him as God's coeternal and coequal son. Like Judaism, Islam was a monotheistic and theocentric religion, not a trinitarian one like Christianity.

Mecca was a major pagan pilgrimage site (the *Ka'ba*—a black meteorite that became Islam's holiest shrine—was originally a pagan object of worship). Muhammad's attacks on idolatry and immorality threatened the trade that flowed from the pilgrims, enraging the merchants of the city. Persecuted for their attacks on traditional religion, Muhammad and his followers fled in 622 to Medina, 240 miles to the north. This event came to be known as the *Hegira* and marks the beginning of the Islamic calendar.

In Medina, Muhammad organized his forces and drew throngs of devoted followers. He raided caravans going back and forth to Mecca. Also at this time he had his first conflicts with Medinan Jews, who were involved in Meccan trade. By 624 his army was powerful enough to conquer Mecca and make it the center of the new religion.

During these years the basic rules of Islamic practice evolved. True Muslims were expected (1) to be honest and modest in all their dealings and behavior; (2) to be unquestionably loyal to the Islamic community; (3) to abstain from pork and alcohol at all times; (4) to wash and pray facing Mecca five times a day; (5) to contribute to the support of the poor and needy; (6) to fast during daylight hours for one month each year; and (7) to make a pilgrimage to Mecca and visit the *Ka'ba* at least once in a lifetime. The last requirement reflects the degree to which Islam was an assimilationist religion; here it "Islamicized" a major pagan religious practice.

In another distinctive feature, Islam permitted Muslim men to have up to four wives—provided that they treated them all justly and gave each equal attention—and as many concubines as they wished. A husband could divorce a wife with a simple declaration, whereas a wife, to divorce her husband, had to have a very good reason and go before an official. A wife was expected to be totally loyal and devoted to her husband. She was allowed to show her face to no man but him.

In contrast to Christianity, Islam drew no rigid distinction between the clergy and the laity. A lay scholarly elite developed, however, that held moral authority within Islamic society and formed a kind of magisterium in moral and religious matters. This elite, known as the *ulema*, or "persons with correct knowledge," served a social function similar to that of a professional priesthood or rabbinate. Its members were men of great piety and obvious learning whose opinions came to have the force of law in Muslim society. They also kept a critical eye on Muslim rulers, seeing that they adhered to the letter of the *Qur'an*.

Islamic Diversity

The success of Islam lay in its ability to unify and inspire tribal Arabs and other non-Jewish and non-Christian people. In a world where Christianity and Judaism had reigned supreme among religions, Islam must also have appealed to Arab pride, for it made Muhammad history's major religious figure and his followers God's chosen people.

As early as the seventh century, however, disputes arose among Muslims over the shape of Islamic society that left permanent divisions within it. Disagreement over the true line of succession to Muhammad—the caliphate—was one source of discord. Another, tied to the first, was disagreement on doctrinal issues involving the extent to which Islam was meant to be an inclusive religion, open to the weak as well as to the strong. Several groups emerged from these disputes. The most radical was the Kharijites, whose leaders seceded from the camp of the caliph Ali (656–661) because Ali compromised with his enemies on a matter of principle. Righteous and judgmental, the Kharijites wanted to exclude all but rigorously virtuous Muslims from the community of the faithful. In 661 one of their members assassinated Ali.

Muslims are enjoined to live by the divine law, or Shari'a, *and have a right to have disputes settled by an arbiter of the* Shari'a. *Here we see a husband complaining about his wife before the state-appointed judge, or* qadi. *The wife, backed up by two other women, points an accusing finger at the husband. In such cases, the first duty of the* qadi, *who should be a learned person of faith, is to try to effect a reconciliation before the husband divorces his wife, or the wife herself seeks a divorce.* Cliché Bibliothèque Nationale de France, Paris

Another, more influential group was the Shi'a, or "partisans of Ali" (*Shi'at Ali*). The Shi'a looked on Ali and his descendants as the rightful successors of Muhammad not only by virtue of kinship, but also by the expressed will of the Prophet himself. To the Shi'a, Ali's assassination revealed the most basic truth of a devout Muslim life: a true *imam*, or "ruler," must expect to suffer unjustly even unto death in the world, and so, too, must his followers. A distinctive theology of martyrdom has ever since been a mark of Shi'a teaching. And the Shi'a, until modern times, have been an embattled minority within mainstream Islamic society.

A third group, which has been dominant for most of Islamic history, was the majority centrist Sunnis (followers of *sunna*, or "tradition"). Sunnis have always put loyalty to the community of Islam above all else and have spurned the exclusivism and purism of the Kharijites and the Shi'a.

Islamic Empires

Under Muhammad's first three successors—the caliphs Abu Bakr (r. 632–634), Umar (r. 634–644), and Uthman (r. 644–655)—Islam expanded by conquest throughout the southern and eastern Mediterranean, into territories mostly still held today by Islamic states. In the eighth century, Muslim armies occupied parts of Spain in the West and India in the East, producing a truly vast empire. (See Map 6–3.) The capital of this empire moved from Mecca to Damascus, and then, in 750, to Baghdad after a civil war in which the Abbasid dynasty replaced the Umayyad dynasty in the caliphate. Thereafter, the huge Muslim Empire broke up into separate states, each with its own line of caliphs, each claiming to be the true successor of Muhammad.

These conquests would not have been so rapid and thorough had the contemporary Byzantine and Persian empires not been exhausted after a long period of war. The Muslims struck at both empires shortly after the Byzantine emperor Heraclius (r. 610–641) had recovered Egypt, Palestine, Syria, and Asia Minor from the Persians. Before Heraclius died in 641, however, Arab armies had conquered Egypt, Palestine, and Syria; by 643 they had overrun most of the Persian Empire. Byzantine territory in North Africa fell by the end of the seventh century. Most of the inhabitants in the territory Heraclius had reconquered from the Persians, although Christian, were, like the Arabs, Semitic. Any religious unity they felt with the Byzantine Greeks may have been offset by hatred of the Byzantine Greek army of occupation. The Christian community was in any case badly divided. Heraclius's efforts to impose Greek "orthodox" beliefs on the Monophysitic churches of Egypt and Syria only increased the enmity between Greek and Semitic Christians. As a result, many Egyptian and Syrian Christians, hoping for deliverance from Byzantine oppression, may have welcomed the Islamic conquerors.

Although Islam gained converts from among the Christians in North Africa and Spain, its efforts to invade the heart of Christendom were in the end successfully rebuffed. In the West the ruler of the Franks, Charles Martel, defeated a raiding party of Arabs on the western frontier of Europe at Poitiers (today in central France) in 732. This victory ended any possible Arab effort to expand into western Europe by way of Spain. Beginning with Emperor Leo III (r. 717–740), the Isaurian dynasty of Byzantine rulers successfully defended Asia Minor from Islamic aggression. So effective were they that the subsequent Macedonian dynasty of

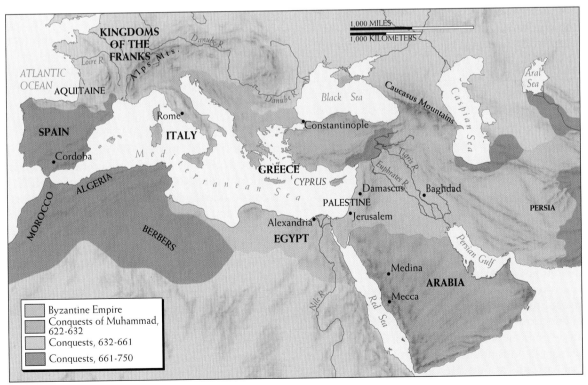

MAP 6–3   MUSLIM CONQUESTS AND DOMINATION OF THE MEDITERRANEAN TO ABOUT 750 C.E.
The rapid spread of Islam (both as a religion and as a politcal–military power) is shown here. Within 125 years of Muhammad's rise, Muslims came to dominate Spain and all areas south and east of the Mediterranean.

Byzantine rulers (867–1057) expanded militarily and commercially into Arab lands. Muslim disunity after the tenth century greatly aided Byzantine success. The Byzantine Empire would ultimately fall to the Ottoman Turks, who would continue to strike terror into Christian hearts well into the sixteenth century, but after the Seljuk Turks took the Islamic capital of Baghdad in 1055 and the Christian Crusaders captured Jerusalem in 1099, the Muslims never again posed a serious threat to Western Christendom.

The Western Debt to Islamic Culture

Despite the hostility of the Christian West to the Islamic world, there was nonetheless much creative interchange between these two very different cultures, and the West profited greatly from it. The more advanced Arab civilization, which was enjoying its golden age during the West's early Middle Ages, taught Western farmers how to irrigate fields and Western artisans how to tan leather and refine silk. The West also gained from its contacts with Islamic scholars. Thanks to Arabic translators, major Greek works in astronomy, mathematics, and medicine became available in Latin to scholars in much of the West for the first time. And down to the sixteenth century, after the works of the famous ancient physicians Hippocrates and Galen, the basic gynecological and child-care manuals followed by Western midwives and physicians were compilations by the famed Baghdad physician Al-Razi (Rhazes), the philosopher and physician ibn-Sina (Avicenna) (980–1037), and ibn-Rushd (Averröes) (1126–1198), Islam's greatest authority on Aristotle. Jewish scholars also thrived amid the intellectual culture Islamic scholars created. The famed Spanish Jewish scholar Moses Maimonides (1135–1204) wrote in Arabic as well as in Hebrew.

Western Society and the Developing Christian Church

Facing barbarian invasions from the north and east and a strong Islamic presence in the Mediterranean, the West found itself in decline during the fifth and sixth centuries. As trade waned, cities rapidly fell on hard times, depriving the West of centers for the exchange of goods and ideas that would enable it to look and live beyond itself.

In the seventh century, the Byzantine emperors, their hands full with the Islamic threat in the East, were unable to assert themselves in the West, leaving most of the region in the control of the Franks and the Lombards (a Germanic tribe that invaded Italy in the sixth century and settled in the Po Valley). Islamic dominance of the Mediterranean likewise closed the West to much trade or cultural influence from the East. As a result, western Europeans were forced to rely on their own resources and develop their Germanic and Greco-Roman heritage into their own distinctive culture.

As Western shipping declined in the Mediterranean, populations that would otherwise have been engaged in trade-related work in the cities moved in great numbers into interior regions. There they found the employment and protection they sought on the farms of the great landholders. The landholders, for their part, needed laborers and welcomed the new emigrants.

Peasants made up 90 percent of the population. Those who owned their own land were "free peasants." Some peasants became "serfs" by surrendering their land to a more powerful landholder in exchange for assistance in time of dire need, such as prolonged crop failure or foreign invasion. Basically, serfdom was a status of servitude to an economically and politically stronger person. Powerful landholders, after seizing all the agricultural land they could control, essentially reallocated it to the people who supplied labor and goods, offering them protection in return.

As the demand for agricultural products diminished in the great urban centers and as traffic between town and country declined, the farming belts became regionally insular and self-contained. Production and travel adjusted to local needs. There was little incentive for bold experimentation and exploration. The domains of the great landholders became the basic social and political units of society, and local barter economies sprang up within them. In these developments were sown the seeds of what would later come to be known as manorial and feudal society (which we will discuss in more detail). Manorial society involved a division of land and labor among lords, serfs, and other peasants for the profit of the lords and the protection of all. Feudal society involved the emergence of a special class of aristocratic warrior knights as guarantors of order.

While all of this was going on, one institution remained firmly entrenched within the cities: the Christian Church. The church had long modeled its own structure on that of the imperial Roman administration. Like the imperial government, church government was centralized and hierarchical. Strategically placed "generals" (bishops) in European cities looked for spiritual direction to their leader, the bishop of Rome. As the western empire crumbled, Roman governors withdrew, and populations emigrated to the countryside, the resulting vacuum of authority was filled by local bishops and cathedral chapters. The local cathedral became the center of urban life and the local bishop the highest authority for those who remained in the cities. In Rome, on a larger and more fateful scale, the pope took control of the city as the Western emperors gradually departed and died out. Left to its own devices, western Europe soon discovered that the Christian Church was its best repository of Roman administrative skills and classical culture.

The Christian Church had been graced with special privileges, great lands, and wealth by Emperor Constantine and his successors. In the first half of the fourth century, Christians gained legal standing and a favored status within the empire. In 391 Emperor Theodosius I (r. ca. 379–395) raised Christianity to the official religion of the empire. Both Theodosius and his predecessors acted as much for political effect as out of religious conviction. In 313 Christians made up about one-fifth of the population of the empire, and Christianity was unquestionably the strongest of the competing religions. Its main rivals were Mithraism, the religion popular among army officers and restricted to males, and the Egyptian cults of Isis and Serapis.

Challenged by Rome's decline to become a major political force, the Christian Church survived the period of Germanic and Islamic invasions a somewhat spiritually weakened and compromised institution. Yet it remained a potent civilizing and unifying force. It had a religious message of providential purpose and individual worth that could give solace and meaning to life at its worst. It had a ritual of baptism and a creedal confession that united people beyond the traditional barriers of social class, education, and gender. And alone in the West, the church retained an effective hierarchical administration, scattered throughout the old empire, staffed by the best-educated minds in Europe, and centered in emperorless Rome.

Writing after the fall of Rome, but before the emergence of Islam, Augustine (354–430) eloquently elaborated the Christian message and the force of its appeal in his chaotic times. In his *City of God*, he defended Christianity against those who held it responsible for the collapse of Roman civilization because it allegedly rejected the Roman gods and its message of love and forgiveness fostered weakness. He pointed out the empire's internal weaknesses and the constructive nature of Christian teaching, which he deemed superior to the ancient philosophies. He stressed in particular the discipline of the church and the power of its sacraments to heal and unite humankind in a new spiritual empire. The

Saint Gregory the Great, shown in a monastic scriptorium, *or study, receiving the divine word from a dove perched on his shoulder. Below him three monks are writing. The middle monk holds an inkwell in his left hand.* Kunsthistorisches Museum, Vienna

book became a favorite of the Frankish king Charlemagne nearly 400 years later.

Monastic Culture

The church enjoyed the services of growing numbers of monks, who were not only loyal to its mission, but also objects of great popular respect. Monastic culture proved again and again to be the peculiar strength of the church during the Middle Ages.

The first monks were hermits who had withdrawn from society to pursue a more perfect way of life. They were inspired by the Christian ideal of a life of complete self-denial in imitation of Christ. The popularity of monasticism began to grow as Roman persecution of Christians waned and Christianity became the favored religion of the empire during the fourth century. Monasticism replaced martyrdom as the most perfect way to imitate Christ and to confess one's faith.

Christians came to view monastic life—embracing, as it did, the biblical "counsels of perfection" (chastity, poverty, and obedience)—as the purest form of religious practice, going beyond the baptism and creedal confession that identified ordinary believers. This view evolved during the Middle Ages into a belief in the general superiority of the clergy and in the church's mission over the laity and the state. That belief served the papacy in later confrontations with secular rulers.

Anthony of Egypt (ca. 251–356), the father of hermit monasticism, was inspired by Jesus' command to the rich young ruler: "If you will be perfect, sell all that you have, give it to the poor, and follow me" (Matthew 19:21). Anthony went into the desert to pray and work, setting an example followed by hundreds in Egypt, Syria, and Palestine in the fourth and fifth centuries.

Hermit monasticism was soon joined by the development of communal monasticism. In the first quarter of the fourth century, Pachomius (ca. 286–346) organized monks in southern Egypt into a highly regimented community in which hundreds shared a life of labor, order, and discipline enforced by a strict penal code. Such monastic communities grew to contain a thousand or more inhabitants. They were little "cities of God," trying to separate themselves from the collapsing Roman and the nominal Christian world. Basil the Great (329–379) popularized communal monasticism throughout the East, providing a rule that lessened the asceticism of Pachomius and directed monks beyond their segregated enclaves of perfection into such social worldly services as caring for orphans, widows, and the infirm in surrounding communities.

Athanasius (ca. 293–373) and Martin of Tours (ca. 315–399) introduced monasticism to the West. The teachings of John Cassian (ca. 360–435) and Jerome (ca. 340–420) then helped shape the basic values and practices of Western monasticism. The great organizer of Western monasticism, however, was Benedict of Nursia (ca. 480–547). In 529 he established a monastery at Monte Cassino, in Italy, founding the form of monasticism—Benedictine—that bears his name and that quickly came to dominate in the West. It eventually replaced an Irish, non-Benedictine monasticism that was common until the 600s in the British Isles and Gaul.

Benedict wrote *Rule for Monasteries*, a sophisticated and comprehensive plan for every activity of the monks, even detailing the manner in which they were to sleep. His *Rule* opposed the severities of earlier monasticism that tortured the body and anguished the mind. Benedict insisted on good food and even some wine, adequate clothing, and proper amounts of sleep and relaxation. Periods of devotion (about four hours each day) were set aside for the "work of God." That is, regular prayers, liturgical activities, and study alternated with manual labor (farming). This program permitted not a moment's idleness and carefully nurtured the religious, intellectual, and physical well-being of the cloistered monks. The monastery was directed by an abbot, whose command had to be obeyed unquestioningly.

Individual Benedictine monasteries remained autonomous until the later Middle Ages, when the Benedictines became a unified order of the church. During the early Middle Ages, Benedictine missionaries Christianized both England and Germany. Their disciplined organization and devotion to hard work made the Benedictines an economic and political power as well as a spiritual force wherever they settled.

The Doctrine of Papal Primacy

Constantine and his successors, especially the Eastern emperors, ruled religious life with an iron hand and consistently looked on the church as little more than a department of the state. Such political assumption of spiritual power involved the emperor directly in the church's affairs, even to the point of playing the theologian and imposing conciliar solutions on its doctrinal quarrels. State control of religion was the original church–state relation in the West. The bishops of Rome, however, never accepted such intervention and opposed it in every way they could. In the fifth and sixth centuries, taking advantage of imperial weakness and distraction, they developed for their own defense the weaponry of the doctrine of papal primacy. This doctrine raised the Roman pontiff to an unassailable supremacy within the church when it came to defining all other church doctrine. It also put him in a position to make important secular claims, leading to repeated conflicts between church and state and between pope and emperor throughout the Middle Ages.

Papal primacy was first asserted as a response to the decline of imperial Rome that accompanied the shift of the imperial residence in the West to Milan and, later, Ravenna. It was also a response to the concurrent claims of the patriarchs of the Eastern Church, who, after imperial power was transferred to Constantinople, looked on the bishop of Rome as a peer, not as a superior. In 381 the ecumenical Council of Constantinople declared the bishop of Constantinople to be of first rank after the bishop of Rome "because Constantinople is the new Rome."

A ninth-century Byzantine manuscript shows an icono-clast whiting out an image of Christ. The Iconoclastic Controversy was an important factor in the division of Christendom into separate Latin and Greek branches. State Historical Museum, Moscow

be endowed with a "plentitude of power," thereby establishing the supremacy of the bishop of Rome over all other bishops in the church. During Leo's reign, an imperial decree recognized his exclusive jurisdiction over the Western church. At the end of the fifth century, Pope Gelasius I (r. 492–496) proclaimed the authority of the clergy to be "more weighty" than the power of kings because priests had charge of divine affairs and the means of salvation.

Events, as well as ideology, favored the papacy. The Germanic and Islamic invasions, just as they had isolated the West by diverting the attention of the eastern empire, also prevented both emperors and eastern patriarchs from interfering in the affairs of the Western church. Islam may even be said to have "saved" the Western church from Eastern domination. At the same time, the emergent Lombards and Franks provided the church with new political allies. Eastern episcopal competition with Rome ended as bishopric after bishopric fell to Islamic armies in the East. The power of the exarch of Ravenna—the Byzantine emperor's viceroy in the West—was eclipsed by invading Lombards, who, thanks to Frankish prodding, became Nicene Christians loyal to Rome and, increasingly, a counterweight to Eastern power and influence in the West. In an unprecedented act, Pope Gregory I, "the Great" (r. 590–604), negotiated an independent peace treaty with the Lombards, completely ignoring the Eastern emperor and the imperial authorities in Ravenna, who were too weak to resist.

The Division of Christendom

As the events just discussed suggest, the division of Christendom into Eastern (Byzantine) and Western (Roman Catholic) churches has its roots in the early Middle Ages. The division was due in part to linguistic and cultural differences between the Greek East and the Roman, Latin-speaking West. A novel combination of Greek, Roman, and Asian elements shaped Byzantine culture, giving Eastern Christianity more of a mystical orientation than Western Christianity. Compared with their Western counterparts, Eastern Christians seemed to attribute less importance to life in this world and to be more concerned about questions affecting their eternal destiny. This strong mystical orientation toward the next world may also have permitted the Eastern patriarchs to submit more passively than Western popes could ever do to royal intervention in church affairs.

As in the West, Eastern Church organization closely followed that of the secular state. A patriarch ruled over metropolitans and archbishops in the cities and provinces; and they, in turn, ruled over

In 451 the ecumenical Council of Chalcedon recognized Constantinople as having the same religious primacy in the East as Rome had traditionally possessed in the West. By the mid-sixth century, the bishop of Constantinople regularly described himself in correspondence as a "universal" patriarch.

Roman pontiffs, understandably jealous of such claims and resentful of the ecclesiastical interference of Eastern emperors, launched a counteroffensive. Pope Damasus I (r. 366–384)[3] took the first of several major steps in the rise of the Roman church when he declared a Roman "apostolic" primacy. Pointing to Jesus' words to Peter in the Gospel of Matthew (16:18) ("Thou art Peter, and upon this rock I will build my church"), he claimed himself and all other popes to be Peter's direct successors as the unique "rock" on which the Christian Church was built. Pope Leo I (r. 440–461) took still another fateful step by assuming the title *pontifex maximus*, or "supreme priest." He further proclaimed himself to

---

[3]Dates after popes' names are the years of each reign.

bishops, who stood as authorities over the local clergy. Except for the patriarch Michael Cerularius, who tried unsuccessfully in the eleventh century to free the church from its traditional tight state control, the patriarchs were normally carefully regulated by the emperor.

Contrary to the evolving Western tradition of universal clerical celibacy (which Western monastic culture encouraged), the Eastern Church permitted the marriage of parish priests (but not monks), while strictly forbidding bishops to marry. The Eastern Church also used leavened bread in the Eucharist, contrary to the Western custom of using unleavened bread, and rejected the Western doctrine of purgatory. Unlike the Roman Church, the Eastern Church accommodated the laity by recognizing divorce and by using vernacular liturgies. The Roman Church also objected to the tendency of the Eastern Church to compromise doctrinally with the politically powerful Arian and Monophysite Christians. Finally, in the background, the Eastern and Western churches both laid claim to jurisdiction over the newly converted areas in the North Balkans.

Beyond these issues, three major factors lay behind the religious break between East and West. The first revolved around questions of doctrinal authority. The Eastern Church put more stress on the authority of the Bible and the ecumenical councils of the church in the definition of Christian doctrine than on the counsel and decrees of the bishop of Rome. The claims of Roman popes to a special primacy of authority on the basis of the apostle Peter's commission from Jesus in the Gospel of Matthew were unacceptable to the East. In the East the independence and autonomy of national churches held sway. As Steven Runciman summarized, "The Byzantine ideal was a series of autocephalous state churches, linked by intercommunion and the faith of seven councils."[4] This basic issue of authority in matters of faith lay behind the mutual excommunication of Pope Nicholas I and Patriarch Photius in the ninth century and that of Pope Leo IX (through his ambassador to Constantinople, Cardinal Humbert) and Patriarch Michael Cerularius in 1054.

A second major factor in the separation of the two churches was the Western addition of the *filioque* clause to the Nicene–Constantinopolitan Creed. According to this anti-Arian clause, the Holy Spirit proceeds "also from the Son" (*filioque*) as well as from the Father. This addition made clear the Western belief that Christ was "fully substantial with God the Father" and not a lesser being.

The third factor dividing the Eastern and Western churches was the iconoclastic controversy of the first half of the eighth century. As noted in the discussion of the Byzantine Empire, after 725 the Eastern emperor, Leo III, banned the use of images in Eastern churches and attempted to enforce the ban in the West also. Images were greatly cherished in the West, and his actions met fierce official and popular resistance there. To punish the West for this disobedience, Leo confiscated papal lands in Sicily and Calabria (in southern Italy) and placed them under the jurisdiction of the subservient patriarch of Constantinople. Because these territories provided essential papal revenues, the Western church could not but view the emperor's action as a declaration of war. (Later Empress Irene made peace with the Roman Catholic Church on this issue and restored the use of images at the ecumenical Council of Nicaea in 787.)

Emperor Leo's direct challenge to the pope coincided with a renewed threat to Rome and the Western church from the Lombards of northern Italy. Assailed on two fronts, the Roman papacy seemed surely doomed. There has not, however, been a more resilient and enterprising institution in Western history than the papacy. Since Gregory the Great, who 150 years earlier had negotiated a treaty with the Lombards, popes had recognized the Franks of northern Gaul as Europe's ascendant power and had seen in them their surest protectors. In 754, Pope Stephen II (r. 752–757), initiating the most fruitful political alliance of the Middle Ages, enlisted the Franks and their ruler, Pepin III, to defend the church against the Lombards and as a Western counterweight to the Eastern emperor. This marriage of religion and politics created a new Western church and empire; it also determined much of the course of Western history into our time.

The Kingdom of the Franks

Merovingians and Carolingians: From Clovis to Charlemagne

A warrior chieftain, Clovis (ca. 466–511), who converted to orthodox Christianity around 496, founded the first Frankish dynasty, the Merovingians, named for Merovich, an early leader of one branch of the Franks. Clovis and his successors united the Salian and Ripuarian Franks, subdued the Arian Burgundians and Visigoths, and established the kingdom of the Franks within ancient Gaul, making the Franks and the Merovingian kings a significant force in western Europe. The Franks themselves occupied a broad belt of territory that extended throughout

[4]Steven Runciman, *Byzantine Civilization* (London: A. and C. Black, 1993), p. 128.

Major Political and Religious Developments of the Early Middle Ages	
313	Emperor Constantine issues the *Edict of Milan*
325	Council of Nicaea defines Christian doctrine
410	Rome invaded by Visigoths under Alaric
413–426	Saint Augustine writes *City of God*
451	Council of Chalcedon further defines Christian doctrine
451–453	Europe invaded by the Huns under Attila
476	Barbarian Odovacer deposes Western emperor and rules as king of the Romans
489–493	Theodoric establishes kingdom of Ostrogoths in Italy
529	Saint Benedict founds monastery at Monte Cassino
533	Justinian codifies Roman law
622	Muhammad's flight from Mecca (*Hegira*)
732	Charles Martel defeats Muslims at Poitiers
754	Pope Stephen II and Pepin III ally

modern France, Belgium, the Netherlands, and western Germany, and their loyalties remained strictly tribal and local.

GOVERNING THE FRANKS   In attempting to govern this sprawling kingdom, the Merovingians encountered what proved to be the most persistent problem of medieval political history—the competing claims of the "one" and the "many." On the one hand, the king struggled for a centralized government and transregional loyalty, and on the other, powerful local magnates strove to preserve their regional autonomy and traditions.

The Merovingian kings addressed this problem by making pacts with the landed nobility and by creating the royal office of *count*. The counts were men without possessions to whom the king gave great lands in the expectation that they would be, as the landed aristocrats often were not, loyal officers of the kingdom. But like local aristocrats, the Merovingian counts also let their immediate self-interest gain the upper hand. Once established in office for a period of time, they, too, became territorial rulers in their own right, so that the Frankish kingdom progressively fragmented into independent regions and tiny principalities. This centrifugal tendency was further aided by the Frankish custom of dividing the kingdom equally among the king's legitimate male heirs.

Rather than purchasing allegiance and unity within the kingdom, the Merovingian largess simply occasioned the rise of competing magnates and petty tyrants, who became laws unto themselves within their regions. By the seventh century, the Frankish king was king in title only and had no effective executive power. Real power came to be concentrated in the office of the *mayor of the palace*, spokesperson at the king's court for the great landowners of the three regions into which the Frankish kingdom was divided: Neustria, Austrasia, and Burgundy. Through this office, the Carolingian dynasty rose to power.

The Carolingians controlled the office of the mayor of the palace from the ascent to that post of Pepin I of Austrasia (d. 639) until 751, when, with the enterprising connivance of the pope, they simply expropriated the Frankish crown. Pepin II (d. 714) ruled in fact, if not in title, over the Frankish kingdom. His illegitimate son, Charles Martel ("the Hammer," d. 741), created a great cavalry by bestowing lands known as *benefices*, or *fiefs*, on powerful noblemen. In return, they agreed to be ready to serve as the king's army. It was such an army that checked the Islamic probings on the western front at Poitiers in 732—an important battle that helped to secure the borders of western Europe.

The fiefs so generously bestowed by Charles Martel to create his army came in large part from landed property that he usurped from the church. His alliance with the landed aristocracy in this grand manner permitted the Carolingians to have some measure of political success where the Merovingians had failed. The Carolingians created counts almost entirely out of the landed nobility from which the Carolingians themselves had risen. The Merovingians, in contrast, had tried to compete directly with these great aristocrats by raising landless men to power. By playing to strength rather than challenging it, the Carolingians strengthened themselves, at least for the short term. The church, by this time dependent on the protection of the Franks against the Eastern emperor and the Lombards, could only suffer in silence the usurpation of lands to which it held claim. Later, although they never returned them, the Franks partially compensated the church for these lands.

THE FRANKISH CHURCH   The church came to play a large and enterprising role in the Frankish government. By Carolingian times, monasteries were a dominant force. Their intellectual achievements made them respected centers of culture. Their religious teaching and example imposed order on surrounding populations. Their relics and rituals made them magical shrines to which pilgrims came in great numbers. And, thanks to their many gifts and internal discipline and industry, many had become very profitable farms and landed estates, their abbots rich and powerful magnates. Already in Merovingian times, the higher clergy were employed in tandem with counts as royal agents.

It was the policy of the Carolingians, perfected by Charles Martel and his successor, Pepin III ("the Short," d. 768), to use the church to pacify conquered neighboring tribes—Frisians, Thüringians, Bavarians, and especially the Franks' archenemies, the Saxons. Conversion to Nicene Christianity became an integral part of the successful annexation of conquered lands and people. The cavalry broke their bodies, while the clergy won their hearts and minds. The Anglo–Saxon missionary Saint Boniface (born Wynfrith; 680?–754) was the most important cleric to serve Carolingian kings in this way. Christian bishops in missionary districts and elsewhere became lords, appointed by and subject to the king. In this ominous integration of secular and religious policy lay the seeds of the later Investiture Controversy of the eleventh and twelfth centuries. (See Chapter 7.)

The church served more than Carolingian territorial expansion. Pope Zacharias (r. 741–752) also sanctioned Pepin the Short's termination of the vestigial Merovingian dynasty and supported the Carolingian accession to outright kingship of the Franks. With the pope's public blessing, Pepin was proclaimed king by the nobility in council in 751, while the last of the Merovingians, the puppet king Childeric III, was hustled off to a monastery and dynastic oblivion. According to legend, Saint Boniface first anointed Pepin, thereby investing Frankish rule from the very start with a certain sacral character.

Zacharias's successor, Pope Stephen II (r. 752–757), did not let Pepin forget the favor of his predecessor. In 753, when the Lombards besieged Rome, Pope Stephen crossed the Alps and appealed directly to Pepin to cast out the invaders and to guarantee papal claims to central Italy, largely dominated at this time by the Eastern emperor. As already noted, in 754 the Franks and the church formed an alliance against the Lombards and the Eastern emperor. Carolingian kings became the protectors of the Catholic Church and thereby "kings by the grace of God." Pepin gained the title *patricius Romanorum*, "patrician of the Romans," a title first borne by the ruling families of Rome and heretofore applied to the representative of the Eastern emperor. In 755 the Franks defeated the Lombards and gave the pope the lands surrounding Rome, creating what came to be known as the *Papal States*.

In this period a fraudulent document appeared—the *Donation of Constantine* (written between 750 and 800)—that was enterprisingly designed to remind the Franks of the church's importance as the heir of Rome. Many believed it to be genuine until it was definitely exposed as a forgery in the fifteenth century by the humanist Lorenzo Valla.

The papacy had looked to the Franks for an ally strong enough to protect it from the Eastern emperors. It is an irony of history that the church found in the Carolingian dynasty a Western imperial government that drew almost as slight a boundary between state and church and between secular and religious policy as did eastern emperors. Although Carolingian patronage was eminently preferable to Eastern domination for the popes, it proved in its own way to be no less constraining.

The Reign of Charlemagne (768–814)

Charlemagne, the son of Pepin the Short, continued the role of his father as papal protector in Italy and his policy of territorial conquest in the north. After decisively defeating King Desiderius and the Lombards of northern Italy in 774, Charlemagne took upon himself the title "King of the Lombards" in Pavia. He widened the frontiers of his kingdom further by subjugating surrounding pagan tribes, foremost among them the Saxons, whom the Franks brutally Christianized and dispersed in small groups throughout Frankish lands. The Muslims were chased beyond the Pyrenees, and the Avars (a tribe related to the Huns) were practically annihilated, bringing the Danubian plains into the Frankish orbit. The defeat of the Avars was so complete that the expression "vanished like the Avars" came to be applied to anything that was irretrievably lost.

By the time of his death on January 28, 814, Charlemagne's kingdom embraced modern France, Belgium, Holland, Switzerland, almost the whole of western Germany, much of Italy, a portion of Spain, and the island of Corsica—an area about equal to that of the modern European Common Market. (See Map 6–4.)

THE NEW EMPIRE Encouraged by his ambitious advisers, Charlemagne came to harbor imperial designs. He desired to be not only king of all the Franks but a universal emperor as well. He had his sacred palace city, Aachen (in French, Aix-la-Chapelle), constructed in conscious imitation of the courts of the ancient Roman and contemporary Eastern emperors. Although he permitted the church its independence, he looked after it with a paternalism almost as great as that of any Eastern emperor. He used the church, above all, to promote social stability and hierarchical order throughout the kingdom—as an aid in the creation of a great

MAP 6–4   THE EMPIRE OF CHARLEMAGNE TO 814   *Building on the successes of his predecessors, Charlemagne greatly increased the Frankish domains. Such traditional enemies as the Saxons and the Lombards fell under his sway.*

Frankish Christian Empire. Frankish Christians were ceremoniously baptized, professed the Nicene Creed (with the *filioque* clause), and learned in church to revere Charlemagne.

The formation of a distinctive Carolingian Christendom was made clear in the 790s, when Charlemagne issued the so-called *Libri Carolini*. These documents attacked the ecumenical Council of Nicaea, which, in what was actually a friendly gesture to the West, had met in 787 to formulate a new, more accommodating position for the Eastern Church on the use of images.

Charlemagne fulfilled his imperial pretensions on Christmas Day, 800, when Pope Leo III (r.

795–816) crowned him emperor. This event began what would come to be known as the Holy Roman Empire, a revival of the old Roman Empire in the West, based in Germany after 870.

In 799, Pope Leo III had been imprisoned by the Roman aristocracy but escaped to the protection of Charlemagne, who restored him as pope. The fateful coronation of Charlemagne was thus in part an effort by the pope to enhance the church's stature and to gain some leverage over this powerful king. It was, however, no papal coup d'etat; Charlemagne's control over the church remained as strong after as before the event. If the coronation benefitted the church, as it certainly did, it also served Charlemagne's purposes.

Before his coronation, Charlemagne had been a minor Western potentate in the eyes of Eastern emperors. After the coronation, Eastern emperors reluctantly recognized his new imperial dignity, and Charlemagne even found it necessary to disclaim ambitions to rule as emperor over the East.

THE NEW EMPEROR   Charlemagne stood a majestic six feet three and one half inches tall—a fact confirmed when his tomb was opened and exact measurements of his remains were taken in 1861. He was restless, ever ready for a hunt. Informal and gregarious, he insisted on the presence of friends even when he bathed. He was widely known for his practical jokes, lusty good humor, and warm hospitality. Aachen was a festive palace city to which people and gifts came from all over the world. In 802 Charlemagne even received from the caliph of Baghdad, Harun-al-Rashid, a white elephant, the transport of which across the Alps was as great a wonder as the creature itself.

Charlemagne had five official wives in succession, as well as many mistresses and concubines, and he sired numerous children. This connubial variety created special problems. His oldest son by his first marriage, Pepin, jealous of the attention shown by his father to the sons of his second wife and fearing the loss of paternal favor, joined with noble enemies in a conspiracy against his father. He spent the rest of his life in confinement in a monastery after the plot was exposed.

PROBLEMS OF GOVERNMENT   Charlemagne governed his kingdom through counts, of whom there were perhaps as many as 250. They were strategically located within the administrative districts into which the kingdom was divided. In Carolingian practice the count tended to be a local magnate, one who already possessed the armed might and the self-interest to enforce the will of a generous king. He had three main duties: to maintain a local army loyal to the king, to collect tribute and dues, and to administer justice throughout his district.

This last responsibility he undertook through a district law court known as the *mallus*. The *mallus* received testimony from witnesses familiar with the parties involved in a dispute or criminal case, much as a modern court does. Through such testimony, it sought to discover the character and believability of each side. On occasion, in very difficult cases where the testimony was insufficient to determine guilt or innocence, recourse would be taken to judicial duels or to a variety of "divine" tests or ordeals. Among these was the length of time it took a defendant's hand to heal after immersion in boiling water. In an-

other, the ordeal by water, a defendant was thrown with his hands and feet bound into a river or pond that a priest had blessed. If he floated, he was pronounced guilty, because the pure water had obviously rejected him; if, however, the water received him and he sank, he was deemed innocent.

In such ordeals God was believed to render a verdict. Once guilt had been made clear to the *mallus*, either by testimony or by ordeal, it assessed a monetary compensation to be paid to the injured party. This most popular way of settling grievances usually ended hostilities between individuals and families.

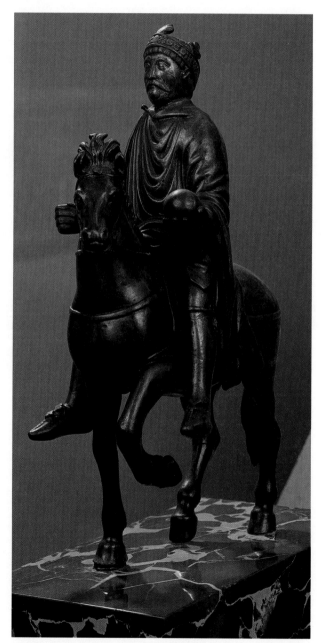

An equestrian figure of Charlemagne (or possibly one of his sons) from the early ninth century. Giraudon/Art Resource, N.Y.

As in Merovingian times, many counts used their official position and new judicial powers to their own advantage and became little despots within their districts. As the strong became stronger, they also became more independent. They began to look on the land grants with which they were paid as hereditary possessions rather than generous royal donations—a development that began to fragment Charlemagne's kingdom. Charlemagne tried to oversee his overseers and improve local justice by creating special royal envoys known as *missi dominici*. These were lay and clerical agents (counts and archbishops and bishops) who made annual visits to districts other than their own. But their impact was marginal. Permanent provincial governors, bearing the title of prefect, duke, or margrave, were created in what was still another attempt to supervise the counts and organize the outlying regions of the kingdom. But as these governors became established in their areas, they proved no less corruptible than the others.

Charlemagne never solved the problem of creating a loyal bureaucracy. Ecclesiastical agents proved no better than secular ones in this regard. Landowning bishops had not only the same responsibilities, but also the same secular lifestyles and aspirations as the royal counts. Save for their attendance to the liturgy and to church prayers, they were largely indistinguishable from the lay nobility. Capitularies, or royal decrees, discouraged the more outrageous behavior of the clergy. But Charlemagne also sensed, rightly, as the Gregorian reform of the eleventh century would prove, that the emergence of a distinctive, reform-minded class of ecclesiastical landowners would be a danger to royal government. He purposefully treated his bishops as he treated his counts, that is, as vassals who served at the king's pleasure.

To be a Christian in this period was more a matter of ritual and doctrine (being baptized and reciting the creed) than of following a prescription for ethical behavior and social service. Both clergy and laity were more concerned with contests over the most basic kinds of social protections than with more elevated ethical issues. An important legislative achievement of Charlemagne's reign, for example, was to give a free vassal the right to break his oath of loyalty to his lord if the lord tried to kill him, to reduce him to an unfree serf, to withhold promised protection in time of need, or to seduce his wife.

ALCUIN AND THE CAROLINGIAN RENAISSANCE Charlemagne accumulated a great deal of wealth in the form of loot and land from conquered tribes. He used a substantial part of this booty to attract Europe's best scholars to Aachen, where they developed court culture and education. By making scholarship materially as well as intellectually rewarding, Charlemagne attracted such scholars as Theodulf of Orleans, Angilbert, his own biographer Einhard, and the renowned Anglo–Saxon master Alcuin of York (735–804). In 782, at almost fifty years of age, Alcuin became director of the king's palace school. He brought classical and Christian learning to Aachen in schools run by the monasteries. Alcuin was handsomely rewarded for his efforts with several monastic estates, including that of Saint Martin of Tours, the wealthiest in the kingdom.

Although Charlemagne also appreciated learning for its own sake, his grand palace school was not created simply for the love of antiquity. Charlemagne intended it to upgrade the administrative skills of the clerics and officials who staffed the royal bureaucracy. By preparing the sons of the nobility to run the religious and secular offices of the realm, court scholarship served kingdom building. The school provided basic instruction in the seven liberal arts, with special concentration on grammar, logic, rhetoric, and the basic mathematical arts. It therefore provided training in reading, writing, speaking, sound reasoning, and counting—the basic tools of bureaucracy.

Among the results of this intellectual activity was the appearance of a more accurate Latin in official documents and the development of a clear style of handwriting known as Carolingian minuscule, which was far more legible than Merovingian script. By making reading both easier and more pleasurable, Carolingian minuscule helped lay the foundations of subsequent Latin scholarship. It also increased lay literacy.

A modest renaissance of antiquity occurred in the palace school as scholars collected and preserved ancient manuscripts for a more curious posterity. Alcuin worked on a correct text of the Bible and made editions of the works of Gregory the Great and the monastic *Rule* of Saint Benedict. These scholarly activities aimed at concrete reforms and served official efforts to bring uniformity to church law and liturgy, to educate the clergy, and to improve moral life within the monasteries. Through personal correspondence and visitations, Alcuin created a genuine, if limited, community of scholars and clerics at court. He did much to infuse the highest administrative levels with a sense of comradeship and common purpose.

THE CAROLINGIAN MANOR The agrarian economy of the early Middle Ages was organized and controlled through village farms known as manors. (See "the Carolingian Manor.") On these, peasants labored as tenants for a lord, that is, a more powerful landowner who allotted them land and tenements in exchange for their services and a portion of their crops. The part of the land tended for the lord was the *demesne*, on average about one-quarter to one-

The Carolingian Manor

A capitulary from the reign of Charlemagne known as "De Villis" itemizes what the king received from his royal manors or village estates. It is a testimony both to Carolingian administrative ability and domination over the countryside.

❖ *What gave the lord the right to absolutely everything? (Has anything been overlooked?) How did the stewards and workers share in the manorial life? Was the arrangment a good deal for them as well as for the lord?*

That each steward shall make an annual statement of all our income: an account of our lands cultivated by the oxen which our ploughmen drive and of our lands which the tenants of farms ought to plough; an account of the pigs, of the rents, of the obligations and fines; of the game taken in our forests without our permission; of the various compositions; of the mills, of the forest, of the fields, of the bridges, and ships: of the free-men and the hundreds who are under obligations to our treasury; of markets, vineyards, and those who owe wine to us; of the hay, fire-wood, torches, planks, and other kinds of lumber; of the waste-lands; of the vegetables, millet, panic; of the wool, flax, and hemp; of the fruits of the trees, of the nut trees, larger and smaller; of the grafted trees of all kinds; of the gardens; of the turnips; of the fish-ponds; of the hides, skins, and horns; of the honey, wax; of the fat, tallow and soap; of the mulberry wine, cooked wine, mead, vinegar, beer, wine new and old; of the new grain and the old; of the hens and eggs; of the geese; the number of fishermen, smiths [workers in metal], swordmakers, and shoemakers; of the bins and boxes; of the turners and saddlers; of the forges and mines, that is iron and other mines; of the lead mines; of the tributaries; of the colts and fillies; they shall make all these known to us, set forth separately and in order, at Christmas, in order that we may know what and how much of each thing we have.

In each of our estates our stewards are to have as many cow-houses, piggeries, sheep-folds, stables for goats, as possible, and they ought never to be without these.

They must provide with the greatest care that whatever is prepared or made with the hands, that is, lard, smoked meat, salt meat, partially salted meat, wine, vinegar, mulberry wine, cooked wine, garns, mustard, cheese, butter, malt beer, mead, honey, wax, flour, all should be prepared and made with the greatest cleanliness.

That each steward on each of our domains shall always have, for the sake of ornament, swans, peacocks, pheasants, ducks, pigeons, partridges, turtle-doves.

That in each of our estates, the chambers shall be provided with counterpanes, cushions, pillows, bed-clothes, coverings for the tables and benches; vessels of brass, lead, iron and wood; andirons, chains, pothooks, adzes, axes, augers, cutlasses and all other kinds of tools, so that it shall never be necessary to go elsewhere for them, or to borrow them. And the weapons, which are carried against the enemy, shall be well cared for, so as to keep them in good condition.

For our women's work they are to give at the proper time, as has been ordered, the materials, that is the linen, wool, woad, vermilion, madder, wool-combs, teasels, soap grease, vessels and the other objects which are necessary.

Of the food-products other than meat, two-thirds shall be sent each year for our own use, that is of the vegetables, fish, cheese, butter, honey, mustard, vinegar, millet, panic, dried and green herbs, radishes, and in addition of the wax, soap and other small products.

That each steward shall have in his district good workmen, namely, blacksmiths, goldsmiths, silver-smiths, shoemakers, turners, carpenters, swordmakers, fishermen, foilers, soapmakers, men who know how to make beer cider, berry, and all the other kinds of beverages, bakers to make pastry for our table, net-makers who know how to make nets for hunting, fishing and fowling, and the other who are too numerous to be designated.

Translations and Reprints from the Original Sources of European History, Vol. 3 (Philadelphia: Department of History, University of Pennsylvania, 1909), pp. 2–4.

The invention of the moldboard plow greatly improved farming. The heavy plow cut deeply into the ground and furrowed it. This illustration from the Luttrell Psalter (ca. 1340) also shows that the traction harness, which lessened the strangulating effect of the yoke on the animals, had not yet been adopted. Indeed, one of the oxen seems to be on the verge of choking.
The British Library/E.T. Archive

third of the arable land. All crops grown there were harvested for the lord. The manor also included common meadows for grazing animals and forests reserved exclusively for the lord to hunt in.

Peasants were treated according to their personal status and the size of their tenements. A *freeman*, that is, a peasant with his own modest allodial, or hereditary, property (property free from the claims of an overlord), became a serf by surrendering his property to a greater landowner—a lord—in exchange for protection and assistance. The freeman received his land back from the lord with a clear definition of his economic and legal rights. Although the land was no longer his property, he had full possession and use of it and the number of services and amount of goods he was to supply to the lord were carefully spelled out.

Peasants who entered the service of a lord with little real property (perhaps only a few farm implements and animals) ended up as *unfree serfs*. Such serfs were much more vulnerable to the lord's demands, often spending up to three days a week working the lord's fields. Truly impoverished peasants, those who had nothing to offer a lord except their hands, had the lowest status and were the least protected from excessive demands on their labor.

All classes of serfs were subject to various dues in kind: firewood for cutting the lord's wood, sheep for being allowed to graze their sheep on the lord's land, and the like. Thus the lord, who, for his part, furnished shacks and small plots of land from his vast domain, had at his disposal an army of servants of varying status who provided him with everything from eggs to boots. Weak serfs often fled to monasteries rather than continue their servitude. That many serfs were discontented is reflected in the high number of recorded escapes. An astrological calendar from the period even marks the days most favorable for escaping. Escaped serfs roamed the land as beggars and vagabonds, searching for new and better masters.

By the time of Charlemagne, the moldboard plow and the three-field system of land cultivation were coming into use. These developments greatly improved agricultural productivity. The older "scratch" plow had crisscrossed the field with only slight penetration and required light, well-drained soils. The moldboard plow, by contrast, cut deep into the soil and turned it to form a ridge, providing a natural drainage system and permitting the deep planting of seeds. This new type of plow made cultivation possible in the regions north of the Mediterranean, where soils were dense and waterlogged from heavy precipitation.

Unlike the earlier two-field system of crop rotation, which simply alternated fallow with planted fields each year, the three-field system increased the amount of cultivated land by leaving only one third fallow in a given year. Indeed, the third field might be reclaimed from previously passed-over heavier soils now made workable by the moldboard plow, thus increasing the amount of land under cultivation in a dramatic fashion. It also better adjusted crops to seasons. In fall, one field was planted with winter crops of wheat or rye, to be harvested in early summer. In late spring, a second field was planted with summer crops of oats, barley, lentils, and legumes, which were harvested in August or September. The third field was left fallow, to be planted in its turn with winter and summer crops. The new summer crops, especially legumes, restored nitrogen to the soil and helped increase yields.

RELIGION AND THE CLERGY   The lower clergy lived among, and were drawn from, peasant ranks. They fared hardly better than peasants in Carolingian times. As owners of the churches on their lands, the lords had the right to raise chosen serfs to the post of parish priest, placing them in charge of the churches on the lords' estates. Church law directed a lord to set a serf free before he entered the clergy.

Lords, however, were reluctant to do this and risk thereby a possible later challenge to their jurisdiction over the ecclesiastical property with which the serf, as priest, was invested. Lords preferred a "serf priest," one who not only said the mass on Sundays and holidays, but who also continued to serve his lord during the week, waiting on the lord's table and tending his steeds. Like Charlemagne with his bishops, Frankish lords cultivated a docile parish clergy.

The ordinary people looked to religion for comfort and consolation. They especially associated religion with the major Christian holidays and festivals, such as Christmas and Easter. They baptized their children, attended mass, tried to learn the Lord's Prayer and the Apostles' Creed, and received the last rites from the priest as death approached. This was all probably done with more awe and simple faith than understanding. Because local priests on the manors were no better educated than their congregations, religious instruction in the meaning of Christian doctrine and practice remained at a bare minimum. The church sponsored street dramas in accordance with the church calendar. These were designed to impart the highlights of the Bible and church history and to instill basic Christian moral values.

People understandably became particularly attached in this period to the more tangible veneration of saints and relics. The Virgin Mary was also widely revered, although a true cult of Mary would not develop until the eleventh and twelfth centuries. Religious devotion to saints has been compared to subjection to powerful lords in the secular world. Both the saint and the lord were protectors whose honor the serfs were bound to defend and whose favor and help in time of need they hoped to receive. Veneration of saints also had strong points of contact with old tribal customs, from which the commonfolk were hardly detached. (Indeed, Charlemagne enforced laws against witchcraft, sorcery, and the ritual sacrifice of animals by monks.)

But religion also had an intrinsic appeal and special meaning to those masses of medieval men and women who found themselves burdened, fearful, and with little hope of material betterment on this side of eternity. Charlemagne shared many of the religious beliefs of his ordinary subjects. He collected and venerated relics, made pilgrimages to Rome, and frequented the Church of Saint Mary in Aachen several times a day. In his last will and testament, he directed that all but a fraction of his great treasure be spent to endow masses and prayers for his departed soul.

Breakup of the Carolingian Kingdom

In the last years of his life, an ailing Charlemagne knew that his empire was ungovernable. The seeds of dissolution lay in regionalism, that is, the de-

The tenth-century crown of the Holy Roman Emperor (the title applied to rulers who succeeded to the remains of Charlemagne's empire) reveals the close alliance between church and throne. The crown is surmounted by a cross, and it includes panels depicting the great kings of the Bible, David and Solomon. Kunsthistorisches Museum, Vienna

termination of each region, no matter how small, to look first—and often only—to its own self-interest. Despite his considerable skill and resolve, Charlemagne's realm became too fragmented among powerful regional magnates. Although they were his vassals, these same men were also landholders and lords in their own right. They knew that their sovereignty lessened as Charlemagne's increased and accordingly became reluctant royal servants. In feudal society, a direct relationship existed between physical proximity to authority and loyalty to authority. Local people obeyed local lords more readily than they obeyed a glorious, but distant king.

Charlemagne had been forced to recognize and even to enhance the power of regional magnates to win needed financial and military support. But as in the Merovingian kingdom, the tail came increasingly to wag the dog. Charlemagne's major attempt to enforce transregional discipline and the subordination of local interests to royal dictates was to create the institution of the *missi dominici*—royal overseers of the king's law and justice. But these new officials themselves fell prey to narrow, regional self-interest, and this effort also proved ultimately unsuccessful.

LOUIS THE PIOUS The Carolingian kings did not give up easily, however. Charlemagne's only surviving son and successor was Louis the Pious (r. 814–840), so-called because of his close alliance with the church and his promotion of puritanical reforms. Before his death, Charlemagne secured the imperial succession for Louis by raising him to "co-emperor" in a grand public ceremony. After Charlemagne's death, Louis no longer referred to himself as king of the Franks. He bore instead the single title of emperor. The assumption of this title reflected not only Carolingian pretense to an imperial dynasty, but also Louis' determination to unify his kingdom and raise its people above mere regional and tribal loyalties.

Unfortunately, Louis' own fertility joined with Salic, or Frankish, law and Frankish custom to prevent the attainment of this high goal. Louis had three sons by his first wife. According to Salic law, a ruler partitioned his kingdom equally among his surviving sons. (Salic law forbade women to inherit the throne.) Louis, who saw himself as an emperor and no mere king, recognized that a tripartite kingdom would hardly be an empire and acted early in his reign, in the year 817, to break this legal tradition. This he did by making his eldest son, Lothar (d. 855), co-regent and sole imperial heir. To Lothar's brothers he gave important, but much lesser, appanages, or assigned hereditary lands; Pepin (d. 838) became king of Aquitaine, and Louis "the German" (d. 876) became king of Bavaria, over the eastern Franks.

In 823 Louis's second wife, Judith of Bavaria, bore him a fourth son, Charles, later called "the Bald" (d. 877). Mindful of Frankish law and custom, and determined that her son should receive more than just a nominal inheritance, the queen incited the brothers Pepin and Louis against Lothar, who fled for refuge to the pope. More important, Judith was instrumental in persuading Louis to adhere to tradition and divide the kingdom equally among his four living sons. As their stepmother and the young Charles rose in their father's favor, the three brothers, fearing still further reversals, decided to act against their father. Supported by the pope, they joined forces and defeated their father in a battle near Colmar in 833.

As the bestower of crowns on emperors, the pope had an important stake in the preservation of the revived western empire and the imperial title. Louis' belated agreement to an equal partition of his kingdom threatened to weaken the pope as well as the royal family. Therefore, the pope condemned Louis and restored Lothar to his original inheritance. But Lothar's

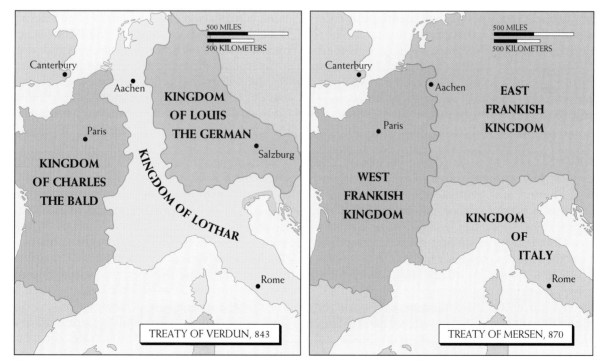

MAP 6–5 THE TREATY OF VERDUN, 843, AND THE TREATY OF MERSEN, 870 *The Treaty of Verdun divided the kingdom of Louis the Pious among his three feuding children: Charles the Bald, Lothar, and Louis the German. After Lothar's death in 855, his lands and titles were divided among his three sons: Louis, Charles, and Lothar II. When Lothar II, who had received his father's northern kingdom, died in 870, Charles the Bald and Louis the German claimed the middle kingdom and divided it between themselves in the Treaty of Mersen.*

regained imperial dignity only stirred anew the resentments of his brothers, including his stepbrother, Charles, who joined in renewed warfare against him.

THE TREATY OF VERDUN AND ITS AFTERMATH In 843, with the Treaty of Verdun, peace finally came to the surviving heirs of Louis the Pious. (Pepin had died in 838.) But this agreement also brought about the disaster that Louis had originally feared. The great Carolingian Empire was partitioned into three equal parts. Lothar received a middle section, known as Lotharingia, which embraced roughly modern Holland, Belgium, Switzerland, Alsace–Lorraine, and Italy. Charles the Bald acquired the western part of the kingdom, or roughly modern France. And Louis the German took the eastern part, or roughly modern Germany. (See Map 6–5.)

Although Lothar retained the imperial title, the universal empire of Charlemagne and Louis the Pious ceased to exist after Verdun. Not until the sixteenth century, with the election in 1519 of Charles I of Spain as Holy Roman Emperor Charles V (see Chapter 11), would the Western world again see a kingdom so vast as Charlemagne's.

The Treaty of Verdun proved to be only the beginning of Carolingian fragmentation. When Lothar died in 855, his middle kingdom was divided equally among his three surviving sons, the eldest of whom, Louis II, retained Italy and the imperial title. This partition of the partition sealed the dissolution of the great empire of Charlemagne. Henceforth, western Europe saw an eastern and a western Frankish kingdom—roughly Germany and France—at war over the fractionalized middle kingdom, a contest that has continued into modern times.

In Italy the demise of the Carolingian emperors enhanced for the moment the power of the popes, who had become adept at filling vacuums. The popes were now strong enough to excommunicate weak emperors and override their wishes. In a major church crackdown on the polygyny of the Germans, Pope Nicholas I (r. 858–867) excommunicated Lothar II for divorcing his wife. After the death of the childless emperor Louis II in 875, Pope John VIII (r. 872–882) installed Charles the Bald as emperor against the express last wishes of Louis II.

When Charles the Bald died in 877, both the papal and the imperial thrones suffered defeat. They became pawns in the hands of powerful Italian and German magnates, respectively. Neither pope nor emperor knew dignity and power again until a new western imperial dynasty—the Saxons—attained dominance during the reign of Otto I (r. 962–973).

It is especially at this juncture in European history—the last quarter of the ninth and the first half of the tenth century—that one may speak with

The Carolingian Dynasty (751–987)	
750–800	Donation of Constantine protests Frankish domination of church
751	Pepin III "the Short" becomes king of the Franks
755	Franks protect church against Lombards and create the Papal States
768–814	Charlemagne rules as king of the Franks
774	Charlemagne defeats Lombards in northern Italy
800	Pope Leo III crowns Charlemagne emperor
814–840	Louis the Pious succeeds Charlemagne as emperor
843	Treaty of Verdun partitions the Carolingian Empire
870	Treaty of Mersen allows eastern and western Frankish kingdoms to absorb the fragmented middle lands
962	Saxons under Otto I firmly established as successors to Carolingians in Germany
987	Capetian dynasty succeeds Carolingian in France

some justification of a "dark age." The internal political breakdown of the empire and the papacy coincided with new barbarian attacks, set off probably by overpopulation and famine in northern Europe. The late ninth and tenth centuries saw successive waves of Normans (North-men), better known as Vikings, from Scandinavia; Magyars, or Hungarians, the great horsemen from the eastern plains; and Muslims from the south. (See Map 6–6.)

For the people of western Europe, the Vikings were the most serious of these threats. They came in greater numbers and, thanks to their unsurpassed skills as seamen, swept over European lands from Novgorod to Gibraltar. Wherever Viking tribes settled, they brought conflict, warring among themselves when not with native peoples. In the 880s, the Vikings penetrated to the imperial residence of Aachen and to Paris. Moving rapidly in ships and raiding coastal towns, they were almost impossible to defend against and kept western Europe on edge. The Franks built fortified towns and castles in strategic locations, which served as refuges. When they could, they bought off the invaders with outright grants of land (for example, Normandy) and payments of silver. In the resulting political and social turmoil, local populations became more dependent than ever before on local strongmen for life, limb, and livelihood. This brutal reality provided the essential conditions for the maturation of feudal society in western Europe.

Feudal Society

The Middle Ages were characterized by a chronic absence of effective central government and the constant threat of famine, disease, and foreign invasion. In this state of affairs the weaker sought the protection of the stronger, and the true lords and masters became those who could guarantee immediate security from rapine and starvation. The term "feudal society" refers to the social, political, military, and economic system that emerged from these conditions.

The feudal society of the Middle Ages was a society dominated by warlords. What people needed most was the firm assurance that others could be depended on in time of dire need. Lesser men pledged themselves to powerful individuals— warlords or princes—recognizing them as personal superiors and promising them faithful service. Large warrior groups of vassals sprang up and ultimately developed into a prominent professional military class with its own code of knightly conduct. The result was a network of relationships based on mutual loyalty that enabled warlords to acquire armies and to rule over territory, whether or not they owned land or had a legitimating royal title. The emergence of these extensive military organizations—warlords and their groups of professional military vassals—was an adaptation to the absence of strong central government and the predominance of a noncommercial, rural economy.

Origins

Following the modern authority on the subject, the late French historian Marc Bloch, historians distinguish the cruder forms of feudal government that evolved during the early Middle Ages from the sophisticated institutional arrangements by which princes and kings consolidated their territories and established royal rule during the High Middle Ages (the so-called second feudal age).

MAP 6–6   VIKING, ISLAMIC, AND MAGYAR INVASIONS TO THE ELEVENTH CENTURY   *Western Europe was sorely beset by new waves of outsiders from the ninth to the eleventh century. From north, east, and south, a stream of invading Vikings, Magyars, and Muslims brought the West at times to near collapse and, of course, gravely affected institutions within Europe.*

The origins of feudal government can be found in the divisions and conflicts of Merovingian society. In the sixth and seventh centuries it became customary for individual freemen who did not already belong to families or groups that could protect them to place themselves under the protection of more powerful freemen. In this way the latter built up armies and became local magnates, and the former solved the problem of simple survival. Freemen who so entrusted themselves to others were known as *ingenui in obsequio*, or "freemen in a contractual relation of dependence." Those who gave themselves to the king in this way were called *antrustiones*. All men of this type came to be described collectively as *vassi* or "those who serve," from which evolved the term *vassalage*, meaning the placement of oneself in the personal service of another who promises protection in return.

Landed nobles, like kings, tried to acquire as many such vassals as they could, because military strength in the early Middle Ages lay in numbers. Because it proved impossible to maintain these growing armies within the lord's own household (as was the original custom) or to support them by special monetary payments, the practice evolved of simply granting them land as a "tenement." Vassals were expected to dwell on these *benefices*, or fiefs, and maintain horses and other accouterments of war in good order. Originally, vassals therefore were little more than gangs-in-waiting.

Vassalage and the Fief

Vassalage involved "fealty" to the lord. To swear fealty was to promise to refrain from any action that might in any way threaten the lord's well-being and to perform personal services for him on his request. (See "Bishop Fulbert Describes the Obligations of Vassal and Lord.") Chief among the expected services was military duty as a mounted knight. This could involve a variety of activities: a short or long military expedition, escort duty, standing castle guard, or the placement of one's own fortress at the lord's disposal, if the vassal was of such stature as to have one. Continuous bargaining and bickering occurred over the terms of service. Limitations were placed on the number of days a lord could require services from a vassal. In France in the eleventh century, about forty days of service a year were considered sufficient. It also became possible for vassals to buy their way out of military service by a monetary payment, known as *scutage*. The lord, in turn, applied this payment to the hiring of mercenaries, who often proved more efficient than contract-conscious vassals.

Beyond his military duty, the vassal was also expected to give the lord advice when he requested it and to sit as a member of his court when the latter was in session. The vassal also owed his lord financial assistance when his lord was in obvious need or distress, for example, when he had been captured by his enemies and needed to be ransomed, or when he was outfitting himself for a crusade or a major military campaign. And gifts of money might also be expected when the lord's daughters married and his sons became knights.

Beginning with the reign of Louis the Pious (r. 814–840), bishops and abbots swore fealty to the king and received their offices from him as a benefice. The king formally "invested" these clerics in their offices during a special ceremony in which he presented them with a ring and a staff, the symbols of high spiritual office. Earlier, Louis' predecessors had confiscated church lands with only modest and belated compensation to the church in the form of a tithe required of all Frankish inhabitants. Long a sore point with the church, the

A seventh-century portrayal of a vassal, who kneels before his lord and inserts his hands between those of his lord in a gesture of mutual loyalty: the vassal promising to obey and serve his lord, the lord promising to support and protect his vassal. Spanish School (7th century). Lord and vassal, decorated page (vellum). Archivo de la Corona de Aragon, Barcelona, Spain. Index/Bridgeman Art Library

Bishop Fulbert Describes the Obligations of Vassal and Lord

Trust held the lord and vassal together. Their duties in this regard were carefully defined. Here are six general rules for vassal and lord, laid down by Bishop Fulbert of Chartres in a letter to William, Duke of Aquitaine, in 1020.

❖ *What are the respective obligations of vassal and lord? Do they seem fair for each side? Why might a vassal have more responsibilities and a lord fewer?*

He who swears fealty to his lord ought always to have these six things in memory: what is harmless, safe, honorable, useful, easy, practicable. Harmless, that is to say, that he should not injure his lord in his body; safe, that he should not injure him by betraying his secrets or the defenses upon which he relies for his safety; honorable, that he should not injure him in his possessions; easy and practicable, that that good which his lord is able to do easily he make not difficult, nor that which is practicable he make not impossible to him.

That the faithful vassal should avoid these injuries is certainly proper, but not for this alone does he deserve his holding; for it is not sufficient to abstain from evil, unless what is good is done also. It remains, therefore, that in the same six things mentioned above he should faithfully counsel and aid his lord, if he wishes to be looked upon as worthy of his benefice and to be safe concerning the fealty which he has sworn.

The lord also ought to act toward his faithful vassal reciprocally in all these things. And if he does not do this, he will be justly considered guilty of bad faith, just as the former, if he should be detected in avoiding or consenting to the avoidance of his duties, would be perfidious and perjured.

From James Harvey Robinson, ed., *Readings in European History*, Vol. 1 (Boston: Athenaeum, 1904), p. 184.

presumptuous practice of the lay investiture of the clergy provoked a serious confrontation of church and state in the late tenth and eleventh centuries. At that time, reform-minded clergy rebelled against what they then believed to be a kind of involuntary clerical vassalage. Even reform-minded clerics, however, welcomed the king's grants of land and power to the clergy.

The lord's obligations to his vassals were very specific. First, he was obligated to protect the vassal from physical harm and to stand as his advocate in public court. After fealty was sworn and homage paid, the lord provided for the vassal's physical maintenance by the bestowal of a *benefice,* or fief. The fief was simply the physical or material wherewithal to meet the vassal's military and other obligations. It could take the form of liquid wealth, as well as the more common grant of real property. There were so-called money fiefs, which empowered a vassal to receive regular payments from the lord's treasury. Such fiefs created potential conflicts because they made it possible for a nobleman in one land to acquire vassals among the nobility in another. Normally, the fief consisted of a landed estate of anywhere from a few to several thousand acres. But it could also take the form of a castle.

In Carolingian times a *benefice,* or fief, varied in size from one or more small villas to several *mansi,* agricultural holdings of twenty-five to forty-eight acres. The king's vassals are known to have received *benefices* of at least 30 and as many as 200 such *mansi,* truly a vast estate. Royal vassalage with a *benefice* understandably came to be widely sought by the highest classes of Carolingian society. As a royal policy, however, it ultimately proved deadly to the king. Although Carolingian kings jealously guarded their rights over property granted in *benefice* to vassals, resident vassals were still free to dispose of their *benefices* as they pleased. Vassals of the king, strengthened by his donations, in turn created their own vassals. These, in turn, created still further vassals of their own—vassals of vassals of vassals—in a pyramiding effect that had fragmented land and authority from the highest to the lowest levels by the late ninth century.

Fragmentation and Divided Loyalty

In addition to the fragmentation brought about by the multiplication of vassalage, effective occupation of land led gradually to claims of hereditary possession. Hereditary possession became a legally recognized principle in the ninth century and laid the basis for claims to real ownership. Fiefs given as royal donations became hereditary possessions and, with the passage of time, sometimes even the real property of the possessor.

Further, vassal engagements came to be multiplied in still another way as enterprising freemen sought to accumulate as much land as possible. One man could become a vassal to several different lords. This development led in the ninth century to the "liege lord"—that one master whom the vassal must obey even to the detriment of his other masters, should a direct conflict arise among them.

The problem of loyalty was reflected not only in the literature of the period, with its praise of the virtues of honor and fidelity, but also in the ceremonial development of the very act of "commendation" by which a freeman became a vassal. In the mid-eighth century, an "oath of fealty" highlighted the ceremony. A vassal reinforced his promise of fidelity to the lord by swearing a special oath with his hand on a sacred relic or the Bible. In the tenth and eleventh centuries, paying homage to the lord involved not only the swearing of such an oath, but also the placement of the vassal's hands between the lord's and the sealing of the ceremony with a kiss.

As the centuries passed, personal loyalty and service became quite secondary to the acquisition of property. In developments that signaled the waning of feudal society in the tenth century, the fief came to overshadow fealty, the *benefice* became more important than vassalage, and freemen proved themselves prepared to swear allegiance to the highest bidder.

Feudal arrangements nonetheless provided stability throughout the early Middle Ages and aided the difficult process of political centralization during the High Middle Ages. The genius of feudal government lay in its adaptability. Contracts of different kinds could be made with almost anybody, as circumstances required. The process embraced a wide spectrum of people, from the king at the top to the lowliest vassal in the remotest part of the kingdom. The foundations of the modern nation-state would emerge in France and England from the fine tuning of essentially feudal arrangements as kings sought to adapt their goal of centralized government to the reality of local power and control.

In Perspective

The centuries between 476 and 1000 saw both the decline of classical civilization and the birth of a new European civilization in the regions of what had been the western Roman Empire. Beginning in the fifth century, barbarian invasions separated western Europe culturally from much of its classical past. Although some important works and concepts survived from antiquity and the Christian Church preserved major features of Roman government, the West would be recovering its classical heritage for centuries to come in "renaissances" that stretched into the sixteenth century. Out of the mixture of barbarian and surviving or recovered classical culture, a distinct Western culture was born. Aided and abetted by the Christian Church, the Franks created a new imperial tradition and shaped basic Western political and social institutions for centuries to come.

The early Middle Ages also saw the emergence of a rift in Christendom between the Eastern and Western branches of the church. Evolving from the initial division of the Roman Empire into eastern and western parts, this rift widened, resulting in bitter conflict between popes and patriarchs.

During this period, the capital of the Byzantine Empire, Constantinople, far exceeded in population and culture any city of the West. Serving both as a buffer against Persian, Arab, and Turkish invasions of the West and as a major repository of classical learning and science for western scholars, the Byzantine Empire did much to make possible the development of western Europe as a distinctive political and cultural entity. Another cultural and religious rival of the West, Islam, also saw its golden age during these same centuries. Like the Byzantine world, the Muslim world preserved ancient scholarship and, especially through Muslim Spain, provided a conduit for retransmitting it to the West. But despite examples of coexistence and even friendship, the cultures of the Western and Muslim worlds were too different and their people too estranged and suspicious of one another for them to become good neighbors.

The early Middle Ages were not centuries of great ambition in the West. It was a time when modest foundations were being laid. Despite a certain common religious culture, Western society remained primitive and fragmented, probably more so than anywhere else in the contemporary world. Two distinctive social institutions developed in response to these conditions: manorialism and feudalism. Manorialism ensured that all would be fed and cared for; feudalism provided protection from outside predators. Western people were concerned primarily to satisfy basic needs; great cultural ambition would come later.

REVIEW QUESTIONS

1. Trace the history of Christianity to the coronation of the emperor Charlemagne in 800. What distinctive features characterized the early church? What role did the church play in the world after the fall of the western Roman Empire?

2. Discuss the growth of the Frankish kingdom, including its relationship with the church, through the reign of Charlemagne. What were the characteristics of Charlemagne's rule? Why did Charlemagne encourage learning at his court? How could the Carolingian renaissance have been dangerous to Charlemagne's rule? Why did his empire break apart?

3. How and why was the history of the eastern half of the Roman empire so different from that of the western half? How would you assess the rule of Justinian over the Byzantine empire? How would you compare Justinian to Charlemagne?

4. What were the tenets of Islam, and how were the Muslims suddenly able to build an empire? Assess the importance of the Muslim invasions for the development of western Europe.

5. How and why did feudal society begin? What were the essential ingredients of feudalism? How easy do you think it would be for modern society to "slip back" into a feudal pattern?

SUGGESTED READINGS

G. BARRACLOUGH, *The Crucible of Europe: The Ninth and Tenth Centuries* (1976). Sweeping survey of political history.

R. BARTLETT, *Trial by Fire and Water: The Medieval Judicial Ordeal* (1986). Makes sense of these seemingly bizarre ways of letting God decide guilt or innocence.

M. BLOCH, *Feudal Society*, vols. 1 and 2, trans. by L. A. Manyon (1971). A classic on the topic and an example of historical study.

P. BROWN, *Augustine of Hippo: A Biography* (1967). Late antiquity seen through the biography of its greatest Christian thinker.

H. CHADWICK, *The Early Church* (1967). Among the best treatments of early Christianity.

R. H. C. DAVIS, *A History of Medieval Europe: From Constantine to St. Louis* (1972). Unsurpassed in clarity.

K. F. DREW (ED.), *The Barbarian Invasions: Catalyst of a New Order* (1970). Collection of essays that focuses the issues.

G. DUBY, *The Early Growth of the European Economy: Warriors and Peasants from the Seventh to the Twelfth Century* (1974). Readable, authoritative account of rural society.

H. FICHTENAU, *The Carolingian Empire: The Age of Charlemagne*, trans. by Peter Munz (1964). Strongest on political history of the era.

J. V. A. FINE, *The Early Medieval Balkans: Sixth–Twelfth Centuries* (1983). Insight into the ethnic divisions that form the background to modern conflict in the region.

F. L. GANSHOF, *Feudalism*, trans. by Philip Grierson (1964). The most profound brief analysis of the subject.

R. HODGES AND D. WHITEHOUSE, *Mohammed, Charlemagne and the Origins of Europe* (1982). Account of the social and economic history of early medieval Europe.

A. HOURANI, *A History of the Arab Peoples* (1991). A comprehensive text that includes an excellent overview of the origins and early history of Islam.

D. KNOWLES, *Christian Monasticism* (1969). Sweeping survey with helpful photographs.

M. L. W. LAISTNER, *Thought and Letters in Western Europe, 500 to 900* (1957). Among the best surveys of early medieval intellectual history.

J. LECLERCQ, *The Love of Learning and the Desire for God: A Study of Monastic Culture*, trans. by Catherine Misrahi (1962). Lucid, delightful, absorbing account of the ideals of monks.

B. LEWIS, *The Muslim Discovery of Europe* (1982). Authoritative account from the Muslim perspective.

C. MANGO, *Byzantium: The Empire of New Rome* (1980). Perhaps the most readable account of the subject.

R. MCKITTERICK, *The Frankish Kingdoms under the Carolingians, 751–987* (1983). The fate of Carolingian government.

P. MUNZ, *The Age of Charlemagne* (1971). Penetrating social history of the period.

S. RUNCIMAN, *Byzantine Civilization* (1970). Succinct, comprehensive account by a master.

P. SAWYER, *The Age of the Vikings* (1962). Among the best accounts.

R. W. SOUTHERN, *The Making of the Middle Ages* (1973). Originally published in 1953, but still a fresh account by an imaginative historian.

C. STEPHENSON, *Medieval Feudalism* (1969). Excellent short summary and introduction.

A. A. VASILIEV, *History of the Byzantine Empire 324–1453* (1952). The most comprehensive treatment in English.

W. WALTHER, *Woman in Islam* (1981). One hour spent with this book teaches more about the social import of Islam than days spent with others.

S. WEMPLE, *Women in Frankish Society: Marriage and the Cloister 500–900* (1981). What marriage and the cloister meant to women in these early centuries.

L. WHITE, JR., *Medieval Technology and Social Change* (1962). Often fascinating account of the way primitive technology changed life.

Chapter 7

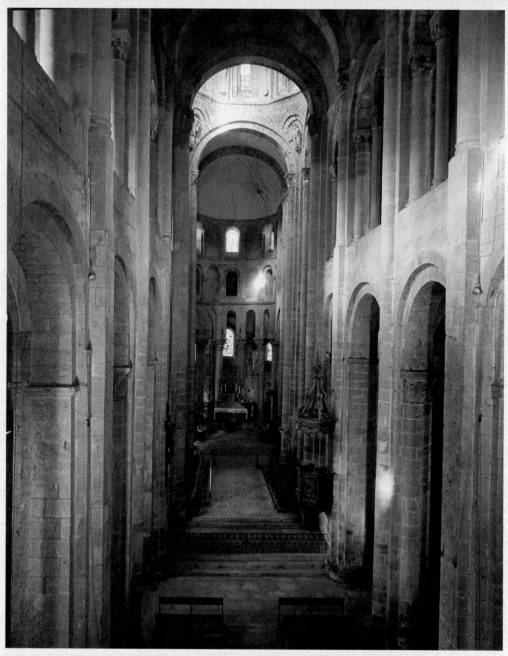

The central nave of the Romanesque abbey of St. Faith (Foy) in Conques, France, where the female saint's relics lie. Roasted alive and beheaded in the third century Gaul, she became widely revered in France, England, Italy, and Spain, and was later a popular South American saint. The interior of the abbey reveals bulky and tightly built pillars, uniform rounded arches, and the restricted lighting that are characteristic of classic Romanesque architecture. Compare and contrast the abbey of St. Faith with the Gothic cathedral of Salisbury, England on pages 248–249. Scala/Art Resource, N.Y.

The High Middle Ages:
The Rise of European Empires and States (1000–1300)

KEY TOPICS

- The revival of the Holy Roman Empire by a new German dynasty, the Saxons
- The emergence of a great reform movement in the church and the church's successful challenge to political domination by kings and emperors
- The development of strong national monarchies in England and France
- The fragmentation of Germany in the wake of a centuries-long struggle between the emperors of the Hohenstaufen dynasty and the papacy

The High Middle Ages mark a period of political expansion and consolidation and of intellectual flowering and synthesis. The noted medievalist Joseph Strayer called it the age that saw "the full development of all the potentialities of medieval civilization."[1] Some even argue that as far as the development of Western institutions is concerned, this was a more creative period than the later Italian Renaissance and the German Reformation.

The High Middle Ages saw the borders of western Europe largely secured against foreign invaders. Although intermittent Muslim aggression continued well into the sixteenth century, fear of assault from without diminished. On the contrary, a striking change occurred during the late eleventh century and the twelfth century: western Europe, which had for so long been the prey of foreign powers, became, through the Crusades and foreign trade, the feared hunter within both the eastern Byzantine world and the Muslim world.

---

[1] *Western History in the Middle Ages—A Short History* (New York: Appleton-Century-Crofts, 1955), pp. 9, 127.

During the High Middle Ages, "national" monarchies emerged. Rulers in England and France successfully adapted feudal principles of government to create newly centralized political realms. At the same time, parliaments and popular assemblies emerged to secure the rights and customs of the privileged many—the nobility, the clergy, and propertied townspeople—against the desires of kings. In the process, the foundations of modern European states were laid. The Holy Roman Empire, however, proved the great exception to this centralizing trend: Despite a revival of the empire under the Ottonians (Otto I, the most powerful member of the Saxon imperial dynasty, and his immediate successors, Otto II and Otto III), the events of these centuries left it weak and fragmented until modern times.

The High Middle Ages also saw the Latin, or Western, church establish itself in concept and law as a spiritual authority independent of monarchical secular government, thus sowing the seeds of the distinctive Western separation of church and state. During the Investiture Controversy, the confrontation between popes and emperors that began in the late eleventh century and lasted through the twelfth, a reformed papacy overcame its long subservience to the Carolingian and Ottonian kings. In this struggle over the authority of rulers to designate bishops and other high clergy and to invest them with their symbols of authority, the papacy, under Gregory II and his immediate successors, won out. It did so, however, by becoming itself a monarchy among the world's emerging monarchies, preparing the way for still more dangerous confrontations between popes and emperors in the later Middle Ages. Some religious reformers later saw in the Gregorian papacy of the High Middle Ages the fall of the church from its spiritual mission as well as a declaration of its independence from secular power.

Otto I and the Revival of the Empire

The fortunes of both the old empire and the papacy began to revive after the dark period of the late ninth century and the early tenth century. In 918 the Saxon Henry I ("the Fowler," d. 936), the strongest of the German dukes, became the first non-Frankish king of Germany.

Unifying Germany

Henry rebuilt royal power by forcibly combining the duchies of Swabia, Bavaria, Saxony, Franconia, and Lotharingia. He secured imperial borders by checking the invasions of the Hungarians and the Danes. Although much smaller than Charlemagne's empire, the German kingdom Henry created placed his son and successor Otto I (r. 936–973) in a strong territorial position.

The very able Otto maneuvered his own kin into positions of power in Bavaria, Swabia, and Franconia. He refused to recognize each duchy as an independent hereditary entity, as the nobility increasingly expected, dealing with each instead as a subordinate member of a unified kingdom. In a truly imperial gesture in 951, he invaded Italy and proclaimed himself its king. In 955 he won his most magnificent victory when he defeated the Hungarians at Lechfeld. This victory secured German borders against new barbarian attack, further unified the German duchies, and earned Otto the well-deserved title "the Great." In defining the boundaries of western Europe, Otto's conquest was comparable with Charles Martel's earlier triumph over the Saracens at Poitiers in 732.

Embracing the Church

As part of a careful rebuilding program, Otto, following the example of his predecessors, enlisted the church. Bishops and abbots—men who possessed a sense of universal empire, yet because they did not marry, could not found competitive dynasties—were made royal princes and agents of the king. Because these clergy, as royal bureaucrats, received great land holdings and immunity from local counts and dukes, they also found such vassalage to the king very attractive. The medieval church did not become a great territorial power reluctantly. It appreciated the blessings of receiving, while teaching the blessedness of giving.

In 961 Otto, who had long aspired to the imperial crown, responded to a call for help from Pope John XII (955–964), who was then being bullied by an Italian enemy of the German king, Berengar of Friuli. In recompense for this rescue, Pope John crowned Otto emperor on February 2, 962. Otto, for his part, recognized the existence of the Papal States and proclaimed himself their special protector. The church was now more than ever under royal control. Its bishops and abbots were Otto's appointees and bureaucrats, and the pope reigned in Rome only by the power of the emperor's sword.

Pope John, belatedly recognizing the royal web in which the church had become entangled, joined in Italian opposition to the new emperor. This turnabout brought Otto's swift revenge. An ecclesiastical synod over which Otto presided deposed Pope John and proclaimed that henceforth no pope could take office without first swearing an oath of allegiance to the emperor. Under Otto I, popes ruled at the emperor's pleasure.

As these events reflect, Otto had shifted the royal focus from Germany to Italy. His successors—Otto II (r. 973–983) and Otto III (r. 983–1002)—became so preoccupied with running the affairs of Italy that their German base began to disintegrate, sacrificed to imperial dreams. They might have learned a lesson from the contemporary Capetian kings, the successor dynasty to the Carolingians in France. These kings, perhaps more by circumstance than by design, pursued a very different course than the Ottonians. They mended local fences and concentrated their limited resources to secure a tight grip on their immediate royal domain, never neglecting it for the sake of foreign adventure.

The Ottonians, in contrast, reached far beyond their grasp when they tried to subdue Italy. As the briefly revived empire began to crumble in the first quarter of the eleventh century, the church, long unhappy with Carolingian and Ottonian domination, prepared to declare its independence and exact its own vengeance.

The Reviving Catholic Church

During the late ninth and early tenth centuries the clergy had become tools of kings and magnates and the papacy a toy of Italian nobles. The Ottonians made bishops their servile princes and likewise dominated the papacy. The church was about to gain renewed respect and authority, however, thanks not only to the failing fortunes of the overextended empire, but also to a new, determined force for reform within the church itself.

The Cluny Reform Movement

The great monastery in Cluny in east-central France gave birth to a monastic reform movement that progressively won the support of secular lords and German kings. In doing so, this movement enabled the church to challenge its domination by royal authority at both the episcopal and papal levels.

The reformers of Cluny were aided by widespread popular respect for the church that found expression in lay religious fervor and generous baronial patronage of religious houses. One reason so many people admired clerics and monks was that the church was medieval society's most democratic institution as far as lay participation was concerned. In the Middle Ages any man could theoretically rise to the position of pope, who was supposed to be elected by "the people and the clergy." All people were candidates for the church's grace and salvation. The church promised a better life to come to the great mass of ordinary people, who found the present one brutish and without hope.

Benedictine monks at choir. The reform movement that began at the Benedictine monastery at Cluny in northern France in the tenth century spread throughout the church and was ultimately responsible for the reassertion of papal authority. Courtesy of the Trustees of the British Library

Since the fall of the Roman Empire, popular support for the church had been especially inspired by the example set by monks. Monasteries provided an important alternative way of life for the religiously earnest in an age when most people had very few options. Monks remained the least secularized and most spiritual of the church's clergy. Their cultural achievements were widely admired, their relics and rituals were considered magical, and their high religious ideals and sacrifices were imitated by the laity.

The tenth and eleventh centuries saw an unprecedented boom in the construction of monasteries. William the Pious, duke of Aquitaine, founded Cluny in 910. It was a Benedictine monastery devoted to the strictest observance of Saint Benedict's *Rule for Monasteries*, with a special emphasis on liturgical purity. Although the reformers who emerged at Cluny were loosely organized and their demands not always consistent, they shared a determination to maintain a spiritual church. They absolutely rejected the subservience of the clergy, especially that of the German bishops, to royal authority. They taught that the pope in Rome was sole ruler over all the clergy.

No local secular rulers, the Cluniacs asserted, could have any control over their monasteries. They further denounced the transgression of ascetic piety by "secular" parish clergy, who maintained concubines in a relationship akin to marriage. (Later a distinction would be formalized between the *secular* clergy, who lived and ministered in the world [*saeculum*] and the *regular* clergy, monks and nuns withdrawn from the world and living according to a special rule [*regula*].)

The Cluny reformers resolved to free the clergy from both kings and "wives"—to create an independent and chaste clergy. The church alone was to be the clergy's lord and spouse. Thus, the distinctive Western separation of church and state and the celibacy of the Catholic clergy, both of which continue today, had their definitive origins in the Cluny reform movement.

Cluny rapidly became a center from which reformers were dispatched to other monasteries throughout France and Italy. Under its aggressive abbots, especially Saint Odo (r. 926–946), it grew to embrace almost 1,500 dependent cloisters, each devoted to monastic and church reform. In the latter half of the eleventh century, the Cluny reformers reached the summit of their influence when the papacy itself embraced their reform program.

The proclamation of a series of church decrees called the Peace of God in the late ninth and early tenth centuries reflected the influence of the Cluny movement. Emerging from a cooperative venture between the clergy and the higher nobility, these decrees tried to lessen the endemic warfare of medieval society by threatening excommunication for all who, at any time, harmed members of such vulnerable groups as women, peasants, merchants, and the clergy. The Peace of God was subsequently reinforced by the Truce of God, a church order proclaiming that all men must abstain from every form of violence and warfare during a certain part of each week (eventually from Wednesday night to Monday morning) and in all holy seasons.

Popes devoted to reforms like those urged by Cluny came to power during the reign of Emperor Henry III (r. 1039–1056). Pope Leo IX (r. 1049–1054) promoted regional synods to oppose simony (the selling of spiritual things, especially as church offices) and clerical marriage (celibacy was not strictly enforced among the secular clergy until after the eleventh century). He also placed Cluniacs in key administrative posts in Rome. Imperial influence over the papacy, however,

was still strong during Henry III's reign and provided a counterweight to the great aristocratic families that manipulated the elections of popes for their own gain. Before Leo IX's papacy, Henry had deposed three such popes, each a pawn of a Roman noble faction, and had installed a German bishop of his own choosing who ruled as Pope Clement II (r. 1046–1047).

Such high-handed practices ended soon after Henry III's death. During the turbulent minority of his successor, Henry IV (r. 1056–1106), reform popes began to assert themselves more openly. Pope Stephen IX (1057–1058) reigned without imperial ratification, contrary to the earlier declaration of Otto I. To prevent local factional control of papal elections, Pope Nicholas II (1059–1061) decreed in 1059 that a body of high church officials and advisers known as the College of Cardinals would henceforth choose the pope, establishing the procedures for papal succession that the Catholic Church still follows. With this action, the papacy declared its full independence from both local Italian and distant royal interference. Rulers continued nevertheless to have considerable indirect influence on the election of popes.

Pope Nicholas II also embraced Cluny's strictures against simony and clerical concubinage and even struck his own political alliances with the Normans in Sicily and with France and Tuscany. His successor, Pope Alexander II (r. 1061–1073), was elected solely by the College of Cardinals, although not without a struggle.

The Investiture Struggle: Gregory VII and Henry IV

Alexander's successor was Pope Gregory VII (r. 1073–1085), a fierce advocate of Cluny's reforms who had entered the papal bureaucracy a quarter century earlier during the pontificate of Leo IX. (See "Pope Gregory VII Asserts the Power of the Pope.") It was he who put the church's declaration of independence to the test. Cluniacs had repeatedly inveighed against simony. Cardinal Humbert, a prominent reformer, argued that lay investiture of the clergy—that is, the appointment of bishops and other church officials by secular officials and rulers—was the worst form of this evil practice. In 1075 Pope Gregory embraced these arguments and condemned, under penalty of excommunication, lay investiture of clergy at any level. He had primarily in mind the emperor's well-established custom of installing bishops by presenting them with the ring and staff that symbolized episcopal office.

After Gregory's ruling, emperors were no more able to install bishops than they were to install popes. As popes were elected by the College of Cardinals and were not raised up by kings or nobles,

Pope Gregory VII Asserts the Power of the Pope

Church reformers of the high Middle Ages vigorously asserted the power of the pope within the church and his rights against emperors and all others who might encroach on the papal sphere of jurisdiction. Here is a statement of the basic principles of the Gregorian reformers, known as the Dictatus Papae *("The Sayings of the Pope"), which is attributed to Pope Gregory VII (1073–1085).*

❖ *In defining his powers as pope, on what authority does Pope Gregory base his authority? How many of his assertions are historically verifiable by actual events in church history? Can any of them be illustrated from Chapters 6 and 7? Compare Gregory's statements on papal power with those of Marsilius of Padua on pp. 307.*

That the Roman Church was founded by God alone.

That the Roman Pontiff alone is rightly to be called universal.

That the Pope may depose the absent.

That for him alone it is lawful to enact new laws according to the needs of the time, to assemble together new congregations, to make an abbey of a canonry; and...to divide a rich bishopric and unite the poor ones.

That he alone may use the imperial insignia.

That the Pope is the only one whose feet are to be kissed by all princes.

That his name alone is to be recited in churches.

That his title is unique in the world.

That he may depose emperors.

That he may transfer bishops, if necessary, from one See to another.

That no synod may be called a general one without his order.

That no chapter or book may be regarded as canonical without his authority.

That no sentence of his may be retracted by any one; and that he, alone of all, can retract it.

That he himself may be judged by no one.

That the Roman Church has never erred, nor ever, by the witness of Scripture, shall err to all eternity.

That the Pope may absolve subjects of unjust men from their fealty.

From *Church and State through the Centuries: A Collection of Historic Documents*, trans. and ed. by S. Z. Ehler and John B. Morrall (New York: Biblo and Tannen, 1967), pp. 43–44. Reprinted by permission of Biblio–Moser Book Publishers.

so bishops would henceforth be installed in their offices by high ecclesiastical authority empowered by the pope. The spiritual origins and allegiance of episcopal office would thereby be made clear.

Gregory's prohibition came as a jolt to royal authority. Since the days of Charlemagne, emperors had routinely passed out bishoprics to favored clergy. Bishops, who received royal estates, were the emperors' appointees and servants of the state. Henry IV's Carolingian and Ottonian predecessors had carefully nurtured the theocratic character of the empire in both concept and administrative bureaucracy. The church and religion had become integral parts of government.

Now the emperor, Henry IV, suddenly found himself ordered to secularize the empire by drawing a distinct line between the spheres of temporal and spiritual—royal and ecclesiastical—authority and jurisdiction. But if his key administrators were no longer to be his own carefully chosen and sworn servants, then was not his kingdom in jeopardy? Henry considered Gregory's action a direct challenge to his authority. The territorial princes, on the other hand,

ever tending away from the center and eager to see the emperor weakened, were quick to see the advantages of Gregory's ruling. If a weak emperor could not gain a bishop's ear, then a strong prince might, thus bringing the offices of the church into his orbit of power. In the hope of gaining an advantage over both the emperor and the clergy in their territory, the princes fully supported Gregory's edict.

The lines of battle were quickly drawn. Henry assembled his loyal German bishops at Worms in January 1076 and had them proclaim their independence from Gregory. Gregory promptly responded with the church's heavy artillery: He excommunicated Henry and absolved all Henry's subjects from loyalty to him. This turn of events delighted the German princes, and Henry found himself facing a general revolt led by the duchy of Saxony. He had no recourse but to come to terms with Gregory. In a famous scene, Henry prostrated himself outside Gregory's castle retreat at Canossa on January 25, 1077. There he reportedly stood barefoot in the snow off and on for three days before the pope agreed to absolve him.

A twelfth-century German manuscript portrays the struggle between Emperor Henry IV and Pope Gregory VII. In the top panel, Henry installs the puppet pope Clement III and drives Gregory from Rome. Below, Gregory dies in exile. The artist was a monk; his sympathies were with Gregory, not Henry.
Thuringer Universitäts- und Landesbibliothek Jena: Ms. Bos. q. 6, Blatt 79r.

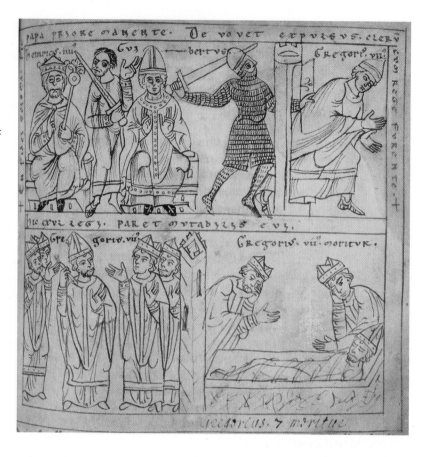

Papal power had at this moment reached a pinnacle (it would attain even greater heights during the papacy of Innocent III [r. 1198–1216], who also had rulers at his mercy). But such peaks must also be descended. Gregory's power, as he must have known when he restored Henry to power, was soon to be challenged.

Henry regrouped his forces, regained much of his power within the empire, and soon acted as if the humiliation at Canossa had never occurred. In March 1080 Gregory excommunicated Henry once again, but this time the action was ineffectual. (Historically, repeated excommunications of the same individual have proved to have diminishing returns.) In 1084 Henry, absolutely dominant, installed his own antipope, Clement III, and forced Gregory into exile, where he died the following year. It appeared as if the old practice of kings controlling popes had been restored—with a vengeance. Clement, however, was never recognized within the church, and Gregory's followers, who retained wide popular support, regained power during the pontificates of Victor III (r. 1086–1087) and Urban II (r. 1088–1099).

The settlement of the investiture controversy came in 1122 with the Concordat of Worms. Emperor Henry V (r. 1106–1125), having early abandoned his predecessors' practice of nominating popes and raising up antipopes, formally renounced his power to invest bishops with ring and staff. In exchange, Pope Calixtus II (r. 1119–1124) recognized the emperor's right to be present and to invest bishops with fiefs before and after their investment with ring and staff by the church. The old church–state "back-scratching" in this way continued, but now on very different terms. The clergy received their offices and attendant religious powers solely from ecclesiastical authority and no longer from kings and emperors. Rulers continued to bestow lands and worldly goods on high clergy in the hope of influencing them. The Concordat of Worms thus made the clergy more independent, but not necessarily less worldly.

The Gregorian party may have won the independence of the clergy, but the price it paid was to encourage division among the feudal forces within the empire. The pope made himself strong by making imperial authority weak. In the end, those who profited most from the investiture controversy were the German princes.

The new Gregorian fence between temporal and spiritual power did not prevent kings and popes from being good neighbors if each was willing. Succeeding centuries, however, proved that the aspirations of kings were too often in conflict with those of popes for peaceful coexistence to endure. The most bitter clash between church and state was still to come. It would occur during the late thirteenth century and early fourteenth century in the confrontation between Pope Boniface VIII and King Philip IV of France. (See Chapter 9.)

The First Crusades

If an index of popular piety and support for the pope in the High Middle Ages is needed, the Crusades amply provide it. What the Cluny reform was to the clergy, the first Crusades to the Holy Land were to the laity: an outlet for the heightened religious zeal of the late eleventh and twelfth centuries, Europe's most religious period before the Protestant Reformation.

Late in the eleventh century, the Byzantine Empire was under severe pressure from the Seljuk Turks, and the eastern emperor, Alexius I Comnenus, appealed for Western aid. At the Council of Clermont in 1095, Pope Urban II responded positively to this appeal, setting the First Crusade in motion. (See "Pope Urban II [r. 1088–1099] Preaches the First Crusade.") This event has puzzled some historians, because the First Crusade was a risky venture. But the pope, the nobility, and western society at large had much to gain by removing large numbers of nobility temporarily from Europe. Too many idle, restless noble youths were spending a great part of their lives feuding with each other and raiding other people's land. The pope recognized that peace and tranquility might be gained at home by sending factious aristocrats abroad with their accouterments of war (100,000 went with the First Crusade). And the nobility recognized that there were fortunes to be made in foreign wars. This was especially true of the younger sons of noblemen, who, in an age of growing population and shrinking landed wealth, saw the Crusades as an opportunity to become landowners. Pope Urban may also have envisioned the Crusade leading to a reconciliation and possible reunion with the Eastern Church.

Religion was not the only motive inspiring the Crusaders; hot blood and greed were equally influential. But unlike the later Crusades, undertaken for patently mercenary reasons, the early Crusades were to a very high degree inspired by genuine religious piety and were carefully orchestrated by the revived papacy. Popes promised participants in the First Crusade a plenary indulgence should they die in battle, that is, a complete remission of any outstanding temporal punishment for their unrepented mortal sins and hence release from suffering for them in purgatory. In addition to this direct spiritual reward, the Crusaders were also impelled by their enthusiasm for a Holy War against the hated infidel and the romance of a pilgrimage to the Holy Land. All these elements combined to make the First Crusade a rousing success, at least from the Christian point of view.

With the journeys to Jerusalem came a cleansing of European Christendom en route that would inten-

sify in the thirteenth century under Pope Innocent III and the new mendicant orders of Dominicans and Franciscans. Jewish communities along the Crusaders' routes, particularly in the lands along the Rhine, became the objects of pogroms, as Christian knights attempted to rid Europe of Jews as well as Muslims.

THE FIRST VICTORY The eastern emperor welcomed any aid against advancing Islamic armies. The Crusaders did not, however, assemble to defend Europe's borders against aggression. They freely took the offensive to rescue the holy city of Jerusalem, which had been in non-Christian hands since the seventh century, from the Seljuk Turks. To this end, three great armies—tens of thousands of Crusaders—gathered in France, Germany, and Italy. Following different routes, they reassembled in Constantinople in 1097. (See Map 7–1.)

The convergence of these spirited soldiers on the eastern capital was a cultural shock that only deepened antipathy toward the West. The eastern emperor suspected their true motives, and the common people, whom they pillaged and suppressed, hardly considered them Christian brothers in a common cause. Nonetheless these fanatical Crusaders accomplished what no eastern army had been able to do. They soundly defeated one Seljuk army after another in a steady advance toward Jerusalem, which fell to them on July 15, 1099. The Crusaders' success resulted from their superior military discipline and weaponry. It also helped that they had descended upon a politically divided and factious Islamic world that initially lacked the unity to organize an effective resistance.

The victorious Crusaders divided the conquered territory into the feudal states of Jerusalem, Edessa, and Antioch, which they held as alleged fiefs from the pope. Godfrey of Bouillon, leader of the French–German army (and after him, his brother Baldwin), ruled over the kingdom of Jerusalem. The Crusaders, however, remained only small islands within a great sea of Muslims, who looked on the Western invaders as hardly more than savages. And once settled in the Holy Land, the Crusaders found themselves increasingly on the defensive. Now an occupying rather than a conquering army, they became obsessed with fortifying their position. They built castles throughout the Holy Land, the ruins of many of which are still visible today.

Once secure within their castle enclaves, the Crusaders ceased to live off the land, as they had done since leaving Europe, and relied more and more on imports from home. The once fierce warriors became international businesspeople as they developed the economic resources of their new possessions. The Knights Templars, originally a military–religious order, became castle stewards and escorts of Western

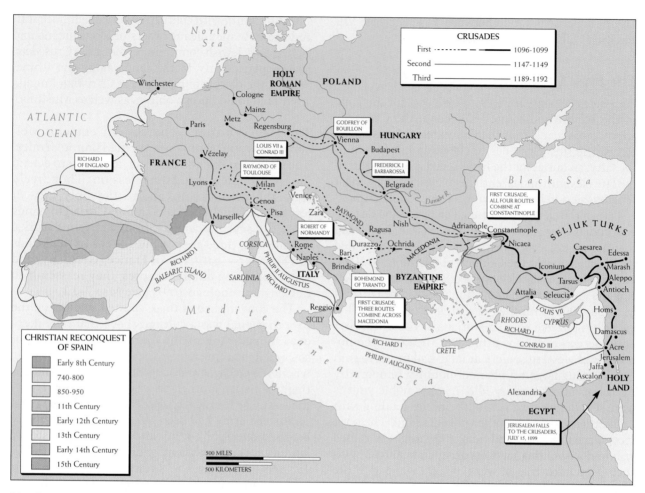

MAP 7–1   THE EARLY CRUSADES   *Routes and several leaders of the Crusades during the first century of the movement are shown. The names on this map do not exhaust the list of great nobles who went on the First Crusade. The even showier array of monarchs of the Second and Third Crusades still left the Crusades, on balance, ineffective in achieving their goals.*

pilgrims to and from the Holy Land, in the process accumulating great wealth and becoming important bankers and moneylenders.

THE SECOND CRUSADE   Native resistance finally broke the Crusaders around midcentury, and the forty-odd-year Latin presence in the East began to crumble. Edessa fell to Islamic armies in 1144. A Second Crusade, preached by the eminent Bernard of Clairvaux (1091–1153), Christendom's most powerful monastic leader, attempted a rescue, but it met with dismal failure. In October 1187, Saladin (r. 1138–1193), king of Egypt and Syria, reconquered Jerusalem itself. Save for a brief interlude in the thirteenth century, it remained thereafter in Islamic hands until modern times.

THE THIRD CRUSADE   A Third Crusade in the twelfth century (1189–1192) attempted yet another rescue, enlisting as its leaders the most powerful western rulers: Emperor Frederick Barbarossa; Richard the

Lion-Hearted, king of England; and Philip Augustus, king of France. But the Third Crusade proved a tragicomic commentary on the passing of the original crusading spirit. Frederick Barbarossa accidentally drowned while fording the Saleph River, a small stream, near the end of his journey across Asia Minor. Richard the Lion-Hearted and Philip Augustus reached the outskirts of Jerusalem, but their intense personal rivalry shattered the Crusaders' unity and chances of victory. Philip Augustus returned to France and made war on Richard's continental territories. Richard fell captive to the Emperor Henry VI as he was returning to England. (Henry VI suspected Richard of plotting against him with Henry's mortal enemy, Henry the Lion, the duke of Saxony, who happened also to be Richard's brother-in-law.)

The English paid a handsome ransom for their adventurous king's release. Popular resentment of taxes levied for this ransom became part of the background of the revolt against the English monarchy

Pope Urban II (r. 1088–1099) Preaches the First Crusade

When Pope Urban II summoned the First Crusade in a sermon at the Council of Clermont on November 26, 1095, he painted a most savage picture of the Muslims who controlled Jerusalem. Urban also promised the Crusaders, who responded by the tens of thousands, remission of their unrepented sins and assurance of heaven. Robert the Monk is one of four witnesses who has left us a summary of the sermon.

❖ *Is the pope engaging in a propaganda and smear campaign? What are the images he creates of the enemy and how accurate and fair are they? Did the Christian Church have a greater claim to Jerusalem than the people then living there? Does a religious connection with the past entitle one group to confiscate the land of another?*

From the confines of Jerusalem and the city of Constantinople a horrible tale has gone forth and very frequently has been brought to our ears, namely, that a race from the kingdom of the Persians [that is, the Seljuk Turks], an accursed race, a race utterly alienated from God, a generation forsooth which has not directed its heart and has not entrusted its spirit to God, has invaded the lands of those Christians and has depopulated them by the sword, pillage and fire; it has led away a part of the captives into its own country, and a part it has destroyed by cruel tortures; it has either entirely destroyed the churches of God or appropriated them for the rites of its own religion. They destroy the altars, after having defiled them with their uncleanness. They circumcise the Christians, and the blood of the circumcision they either spread upon the altars or pour into the vases of the baptismal font. When they wish to torture people by a base death, they perforate their navels, and dragging forth the extremity of the intestines, bind it to a stake; then with flogging they lead the victim around until the viscera having gushed forth the victim falls prostrate upon the ground. Others they bind to a post and pierce with arrows. Others they compel to extend their necks and then, attack-ing them with naked swords, attempt to cut through the neck with a single blow. What shall I say of the abominable rape of the women? The kingdom of the Greeks is now dismembered by them and deprived of territory so vast in extent that it can not be traversed in a march of two months. On whom therefore is the labor of avenging these wrongs and of recovering this territory incumbent, if not upon you? ...

Jerusalem is the navel of the world; the land is fruitful above others, like another paradise of delights. This the Redeemer of the human race has made illustrious by His advent, has beautified by residence, has consecrated by suffering, has redeemed by death, has glorified by burial. This royal city, therefore, situated at the centre of the world, is now held captive by His enemies, and is in subjection to those who do not know God, to the worship of the heathens. She seeks therefore and desires to be liberated, and does not cease to implore you to come to her aid. From you especially she asks succor, because, as we have already said, God has conferred upon you above all nations great glory in arms. Accordingly undertake this journey for the remission of your sins, with the assurance of the imperishable glory of the kingdom of heaven.

Translations and reprints from *Original Sources of European History*, Vol. 1 (Philadelphia: Department of History, University of Pennsylvania, 1910), pp. 5–7.

that led to the royal recognition of Magna Carta in 1215 (discussed later in the chapter).

The long-term results of the first three Crusades had little to do with their original purpose. Politically and religiously they were a failure, and the Holy Land reverted as firmly as ever to Muslim hands. The Crusades did, however, act for centuries as a safety valve for violence-prone Europe. More importantly, they stimulated Western trade with the East. The merchants of Venice, Pisa, and Genoa followed the Cru-saders across to lucrative new markets. The need to resupply the new Christian settlements in the Near East reopened old trade routes that had long been closed by Islamic domination of the Mediterranean and established important new ones as well.

It is a commentary on both the degeneration of the original crusading ideal and the Crusaders' true historical importance that the Fourth Crusade turned into a large commercial venture manipu-lated by the Venetians. And wherever new trading centers sprang up along the Crusader routes, cultural as well as economic commerce occurred. Western Christians learned firsthand about Islamic culture and Muslims about the Christian West.

The Pontificate of Innocent III (r. 1198–1216)

Pope Innocent III was a papal monarch in the Gregorian tradition of papal independence from secular domination. He proclaimed and practiced as none before him the doctrine of the plenitude of papal power. In a famous statement, he likened the relationship of the pope to the emperor—or the church to the state—to that of the sun to the moon. As the moon received its light from the sun, so the emperor received his brilliance (that is, his crown) from the hand of the pope—an allusion to the famous precedent set on Christmas Day, 800, when Pope Leo III crowned Charlemagne.

Although this pretentious theory greatly exceeded Innocent's ability to practice it, he and his successors did not hesitate to act on the ambitions it reflected. When Philip II, the king of France, tried unlawfully to annul his marriage, Innocent placed France under interdict, suspending all church services save baptism and the last rites. The same punishment befell England with even greater force when King John refused to accept Innocent's nominee for archbishop of Canterbury. And as we will see later in the chapter, Innocent intervened frequently and forcefully in the affairs of the Holy Roman Empire.

THE NEW PAPAL MONARCHY Innocent made the papacy a great secular power, with financial resources and a bureaucracy equal to those of contemporary monarchs. During his reign the papacy transformed itself, in effect, into an efficient ecclesio-commercial complex, which would be attacked by reformers throughout the later Middle Ages. Innocent consolidated and expanded ecclesiastical taxes on the laity, the chief of which was "Peter's pence." In England, that tax, long a levy on all but the poorest houses, became a lump-sum payment by the English crown during Innocent's reign. Innocent also imposed an income tax of 2.5 percent on the clergy. Annates (the payment of a portion or all of the first year's income received by the holder of a new *benefice*) and fees for the *pallium* (an archbishop's symbol of office) became especially favored revenue-gathering devices.

Innocent also reserved to the pope the absolution of many sins and religious crimes, forcing those desirous of pardons or exemptions to bargain directly with Rome. It was a measure of the degree to which the papacy had embraced the new money

The crusaders capture the city of Antioch in 1098 during the First Crusade. From Le Miroir Historial *(fifteenth century) by Vincent de Beauvais.* Musée Conde Chantilly. E. T. Archive, London

economy that it employed Lombard merchants and bankers to collect the growing papal revenues.

CRUSADES IN FRANCE AND THE EAST Innocent's predilection for power politics also expressed itself in his use of the Crusade, the traditional weapon of the church against Islam, to suppress internal dissent and heresy. Heresy had grown under the influence of native religious reform movements that tried, often naïvely, to disassociate the church from the growing materialism of the age and to keep it pure of political scheming. A good deal of heresy also stemmed from anticlericalism fed by real abuses of the clergy witnessed directly by the laity, such as immorality, greed, and poor pastoral service.

The idealism of these movements was too extreme for the papacy. In 1209 Innocent launched a Crusade against the Albigensians, also known as Cathars, or "pure ones." These advocates of an ascetic, dualist religion were concentrated in the area of Albi in Languedoc in southern France, but Catharism also had adherents among the laity in Italy and Spain. The Albigensians generally sought a pure and simple religious life, following the model of the apostles of Jesus in the New Testament. They opposed Christian teaching on several points. They denied the Old Testament and its God of wrath, as well as the Christian belief in God's incarnation in Jesus Christ. They conceived of the church as an invisible, spiritual force, and resisted it as a legal, financial, and dogmatic institution.

The more radical Cathars opposed human procreation, because to reproduce corporeal bodies was to prolong the imprisonment of immortal souls in dying matter. They avoided it either through extreme sexual asceticism or the use of contraceptives (sponges and acidic ointments) and even abortion. On the other hand, the Cathars' strong dualism justified latitude in sexual behavior on the part of ordinary believers, in the belief that the flesh and the spirit were so fundamentally different that it mattered little what the former did. It was in opposition to such beliefs that the church developed its social teachings condemning contraception and abortion.

The Crusades against the Albigensians were carried out by powerful noblemen from northern France. These great magnates, led by Simon de Montfort, were as much attracted by the great wealth of the area of Languedoc as they were moved by Christian conscience to stamp out heresy. The Crusades also allowed the northerners to extend their political power into the south. They resulted in a succession of massacres and ended with a special Crusade led by King Louis VIII of France from 1225 to 1226, which destroyed the Albigensians as a political entity. Pope Gregory IX (r. 1227–1241) introduced the Inquisition into the region to complete the work of the Crusaders. This institution, a formal tribunal for the detection and punishment of heresy, had been in use by the church since the mid-twelfth century as a way for bishops to maintain diocesan discipline. During Innocent's pontificate it became centralized in the papacy. Papal legates were dispatched to chosen regions to conduct interrogations and the subsequent trials and executions.

THE FOURTH CRUSADE   It was also during Innocent's pontificate that the Fourth Crusade to the Holy Land was launched. In 1202, some 30,000 Crusaders arrived in Venice to set sail for Egypt. When they were unable to pay the price of transport, the Venetians negotiated an alternative to payment: conquest of Zara, a rival Christian port city on the Adriatic. To the shock of Pope Innocent III, the Crusaders obliged. This digression of the Crusaders from their original goal proved to be only their first. They soon besieged Constantinople itself, which was completely in Western hands by 1204.

This stunning event brought Venice new lands and maritime rights that assured its domination of the eastern Mediterranean. Constantinople now became the center for Western trade throughout the Near East. Although its capture had been an embarrassment to the pope, the papacy soon adjusted to this unforeseen turn of events and shared in the spoils. The Western church had a unique opportunity to extend its presence into the East. A confidant of Innocent's became patriarch of Constantinople and launched a mission to win the Greeks and the Slavs to the Roman Church. Western control of Constantinople continued until 1261, when the Eastern emperor Michael Paleologus, helped by the Genoese, who envied Venetian prosperity in the East, finally recaptured the city. The more than fifty-year occupation of Constantinople did nothing to heal the political and religious divisions between East and West. When Constantinople returned to eastern hands, East–West relations were at a new low.

THE FOURTH LATERAN COUNCIL   Under Innocent's direction, the Fourth Lateran Council met in 1215 to formalize church discipline throughout the hierarchy, from pope to parish priest. Many important landmarks in ecclesiastical legislation issued from this council. It gave full dogmatic sanction to the controversial doctrine of transubstantiation, according to which the bread and wine of the Lord's Supper become the true body and blood of Christ when consecrated by a priest in the sacrament of the Eucharist. This doctrine has been part of Catholic teaching ever since. It reflects the influence of the Cluniac monks and those of a new order, the Cistercians. During the twelfth century, these orders made the adoration of the Virgin Mary (the patron saint of the Cistercians) and the worship of Christ in the Eucharist the centerpieces of a reformed, christocentric piety. The doctrine of transubstantiation is an expression of the popularity of this piety. It also enhanced the power and authority of the clergy, because it specified that only they could perform the miracle of the Eucharist.

In addition, the council made annual confession and Easter communion mandatory for every adult Christian. This legislation formalized the sacrament of penance as the church's key instrument of religious education and discipline in the later Middle Ages.

FRANCISCANS AND DOMINICANS   During his reign, Pope Innocent gave official sanction to two new monastic orders: the Franciscans and the Dominicans. No other action of the pope had more of an effect on spiritual life. Unlike other regular clergy, the members of these mendicant orders, known as friars, did not confine themselves to the cloister. They went out into the world to preach the church's mission and to combat heresy, begging or working to support themselves (hence the term "mendicant").

Lay interest in spiritual devotion, especially among urban women, was particularly intense at the turn of the twelfth century. In addition to the heretical Albigensians, there were movements of Waldensians, Beguines, and Beghards, each of which stressed biblical simplicity in religion and a life of poverty in imitation of Christ. Such movements were especially active in Italy and France. Their heterodox teachings—teachings that, although not necessarily heretical, nonetheless challenged church orthodoxy—and the critical frame of mind they promoted caused the pope deep concern. Innocent feared they would inspire lay piety to turn militantly against the church. The Franciscan and Dominican orders, however, emerged from the same background of intense religiosity. By sanctioning them and thus keeping their followers within the confines of church organization, the pope provided a response to heterodox piety as well as an answer to lay criticism of the worldliness of the papal monarchy.

The Franciscan order was founded by Saint Francis of Assisi (1182–1226), the son of a rich Italian cloth merchant, who became disaffected with wealth and urged his followers to live a life of extreme poverty. Pope Innocent recognized the order in 1210, and its official rule was approved in 1223. The Dominican order, the Order of Preachers, was founded by Saint Dominic (1170–1221), a well-educated Spanish cleric, and was sanctioned in 1216. Both orders received special privileges from the pope and were solely under his jurisdiction. This special relationship with Rome gave the friars an independence from local clerical authority that bred resentment among some secular clergy.

Pope Gregory IX (r. 1227–1241) canonized Saint Francis only two years after Francis's death—a fitting honor for Francis and a stroke of genius on the part of the pope. By bringing the age's most popular religious figure, one who had even miraculously received the stigmata (bleeding wounds like those of the crucified Jesus), so emphatically within the confines of the church, he enhanced papal authority over lay piety.

Two years after the canonization, however, Gregory canceled Saint Francis's own *Testament* as an authoritative rule for the Franciscan order. He did so because he found it to be an impractical guide for the order and because the unconventional nomadic life of strict poverty it advocated conflicted with papal plans to enlist the order as an arm of church policy. (See "Saint Francis of Assisi Sets Out His Religious Ideals.") Most Franciscans themselves, under the leadership of moderates like Saint Bonaventure, general of the order between 1257 and 1274, also came to doubt the wisdom of extreme asceticism. During the thirteenth century the main branch of the order progressively complied with papal wishes. In the fourteenth century the pope condemned a radical branch, the Spiritual Franciscans, extreme followers of Saint Francis who considered him almost a new Messiah. In his condemnation, the pope declared absolute poverty a fictitious ideal that not even Christ endorsed.

The Dominicans, a less factious order, combated doctrinal error through visitations and preaching. They conformed convents of Beguines to the church's teaching, led the church's campaign against heretics in southern France, and staffed the offices of the Inquisition after its centralization by Pope Gregory IX in 1223. The great Dominican theologian Thomas Aquinas (d. 1274) was canonized in 1322. His efforts to synthesize faith and reason resulted in a definitive and enduring statement of Catholic belief. (See Chapter 8.)

The Dominicans and the Franciscans strengthened the church among the laity. Through the institution of so-called Third orders, they provided ordinary men and women the opportunity to affiliate with the monastic life and pursue the high religious ideals of poverty, obedience, and chastity, while remaining laypeople. Laity who joined such orders were known as tertiaries. Such organizations helped keep lay piety orthodox and within the church during a period of heightened religiosity.

England and France: Hastings (1066) to Bouvines (1214)

In 1066 the death of the childless Anglo–Saxon ruler Edward the Confessor (so named because of his reputation for piety) occasioned the most important change in English political life. Edward's mother was a Norman, giving the duke of Normandy a hereditary claim to the English throne. Before his death, Edward, who was not a strong ruler, acknowledged the duke's claim and even directed that his throne be given to William, the reigning duke of Normandy (d. 1087). But the Anglo–Saxon assembly, which customarily bestowed the royal power, had a mind of its own and vetoed Edward's last wishes, choosing instead Harold Godwinsson. This defiant action triggered the swift conquest of England by the powerful Normans. William's forces defeated Harold's army at Hastings on October 14, 1066. (See "How William the Conqueror Won the Battle of Hastings.") Within weeks of the invasion William was crowned king of England in Westminster Abbey, both by right of heredity and by right of conquest.

Dominicans (left), and Franciscans (right). Unlike the other religious orders, the Dominicans and Franciscans did not live in cloisters, but wandered about preaching and combating heresy. They depended for support on their own labor and the kindness of the laity. Cliche Bibliothèque Nationale de France–Paris

William the Conqueror

Thereafter, William embarked on a twenty-year conquest that eventually made all of England his domain. Every landholder, whether large or small, was henceforth his vassal, holding land legally as a fief from the king. William organized his new English nation shrewdly. He established a strong monarchy whose power was not fragmented by independent territorial princes. He kept the Anglo–Saxon tax system and the practice of court writs (legal warnings) as a flexible form of central control over localities. And he took care not to destroy the Anglo–Saxon quasi-democratic tradition of frequent "parleying"—that is, the holding of conferences between the king and lesser powers who had vested interests in royal decisions.

The practice of parleying had been initially nurtured by Alfred the Great (r. 871–899). A strong and willful king who had forcibly unified England, Alfred cherished the advice of his councilors in the making of laws. His example was respected and emulated by Canute (r. 1016–1035), the Dane who restored order and brought unity to England after the civil wars that engulfed the land during the reign of the incompetent Ethelred II (r. 978–1016). The new Norman king, William, although he thoroughly subjugated his noble vassals to the crown, maintained the tradition of parleying by consulting with them regularly about decisions of state. The result was a unique blending of the "one" and the "many," a balance between monarchical and parliamentary elements that has ever since been a feature of English government—although the English Parliament as we know it today did not formally develop as an institution until the late thirteenth century.

For administration and taxation purposes William commissioned a county-by-county survey of his new realm, a detailed accounting known as the *Domesday Book* (1080–1086). The title of the book may reflect the thoroughness and finality of the survey. As none would escape the doomsday judgment of God, so none was overlooked by William's assessors.

Henry II

William's son, Henry I (r. 1100–1135), died without a male heir, throwing England into virtual anarchy until the accession of Henry II (r. 1154–1189). Son of the duke of Anjou and Matilda, daughter of Henry I, Henry mounted the throne as head of the new Plantagenet dynasty, the family name of the Angevin (or Anjouan) line of kings who ruled England until the death of Richard III in 1485. Henry tried to recapture the efficiency and stability of his grandfather's regime, but in the process he steered the English monarchy rapidly toward an oppressive rule. Partly by inheritance from his father (Anjou) and partly by his marriage to Eleanor of Aquitaine (ca. 1122–1204), Henry brought to the throne greatly expanded French holdings, virtually the entire west coast of France.

The union with Eleanor created the so-called Angevin, or English–French, Empire. Eleanor married Henry while he was still the count of Anjou and not yet king of England. The marriage occurred only eight weeks after the annulment of Eleanor's fifteen-year marriage to the ascetic French king Louis VII in March

Saint Francis of Assisi Sets Out His Religious Ideals

Saint Francis of Assisi (1182–1226) was the founder of the Franciscan order of friars. The religious principles by which he required his followers to live were stated in the Rule of the Order, *which Pope Honorius III approved in 1223. The chief principle was to lead a life of poverty. The ideal of poverty caused conflict between the order and the pope, who feared that some Franciscans carried it too far.*

❖ *Can ideals be so high that they threaten the well-being of an institution? What would have happened to the church if all clergy, including the pope, had lived a life of poverty, begging, and working with their hands, as the* Rule *of Saint Francis instructs? What provisions are there in the* Rule *to assure the pope of the order's loyalty?*

This is the rule and way of living of the Minorite brothers, namely, to observe the holy Gospel of our Lord Jesus Christ, living in obedience, without personal possessions, and in chastity. Brother Francis promises obedience and reverence to our lord Pope Honorius, and to his successors who canonically enter upon their office, and to the Roman Church. And the other brothers shall be bound to obey Brother Francis and his successors.

I firmly command all the brothers by no means to receive coin or money, of themselves or through an intervening person. But for the needs of the sick and for clothing the other brothers, the ministers alone and the guardians shall provide through spiritual friends, as it may seem to them that necessity demands, according to time, place, and the coldness of the temperature. This one thing being always borne in mind, that, as has been said, they receive neither coin nor money.

Those brothers to whom God has given the ability to labor shall do so faithfully and devoutly, but in such manner that idleness, the enemy of the soul, being averted, they may not extinguish the spirit of holy prayer and devotion, to which other temporal things should be subservient. As a reward, moreover, for their labor, they may receive for themselves and their brothers the necessities of life, but not coin or money; and this humbly, as becomes the servants of God and the followers of most holy poverty.

The brothers shall appropriate nothing to themselves, neither a house, nor a place, nor anything; but as pilgrims and strangers in this world, in poverty and humility serving God, they shall confidently go seeking for alms. Nor need they be ashamed, for the Lord made Himself poor for us in this world.

From Frederic Austin Ogg, ed., *A Source Book of Mediaeval History: Documents Illustrative of European Life and Institutions from the German Invasions to the Renaissance* (New York: Telegraph Books, 1908), pp. 375–376.

1152. Although the annulment was granted on grounds of consanguinity (blood relationship), the true reason for the dissolution of the marriage was Louis's suspicion of infidelity. (According to rumor, Eleanor had been intimate with a cousin.) The annulment was very costly to Louis, who lost Aquitaine along with his wife. Eleanor and Henry had eight children, five of them sons, among them the future kings Richard the Lion-Hearted and John.

In addition to gaining control of most of the coast of France, Henry also conquered a part of Ireland and made the king of Scotland his vassal. Louis VII saw a mortal threat to France in this English expansion. He responded by adopting what came to be a permanent French policy of containment and expulsion of the English from their continental holdings in France. This policy was not finally successful until the mid-fifteenth century, when English power on the continent collapsed after the Hundred Years' War.

Eleanor of Aquitaine and Court Culture

Eleanor of Aquitaine was a powerful influence on both politics and culture in twelfth-century France and England. She had accompanied her first husband, King Louis VII, on the Second Crusade, becoming an example for women of lesser stature, who were also then venturing in increasing numbers into war and business and other areas previously considered the province of men. After marrying Henry, she settled in Angers, the chief town of Anjou, where she sponsored troubadours and poets at her lively court. There the troubadour Bernart de Ventadorn composed in Eleanor's honor many of the most popular love songs of high medieval aristo-

	The Growing Power and Influence of the Church
910	Cluny founded by William the Pious
1059	Pope Nicholas II establishes College of Cardinals
1075	Pope Gregory VII condemns lay investiture of clergy under penalty of excommunication
1076	Emperor Henry IV excommunicated by Pope Gregory VII for defying ban on lay investiture
1077	Henry IV begs for and receives papal absolution in Canossa
1084	Henry IV installs an antipope and forces Gregory VII into exile
1095	Pope Urban II preaches the First Crusade at the Council of Clermont
1099	Jerusalem falls to the Crusaders; forty-five years of Western rule in the Holy Land begins
1122	Concordat of Worms between Emperor Henry V and Pope Calixtus II ends Investiture Controversy
1144	Islamic armies reconquer Edessa
1187	Jerusalem reconquered by Saladin, King of Egypt and Syria
1189–1192	Third Crusade fails to recover the Holy Land from Islamic armies
1202	Fourth Crusade launched; captures Constantinople instead of going to Holy Land
1209	Pope Innocent III launches Albigensian Crusade in southern France; excommunicates King John of England
1210	Pope Innocent III recognizes the Franciscan order
1215	Fourth Lateran Council sanctions doctrine of transubstantiation and mandates annual confession by all adult Christians

cratic society. Eleanor spent the years 1154 to 1170 as Henry's queen in England. She separated from Henry in 1170, partly because of his public philandering and cruel treatment of her, and took revenge on him by joining Louis VII in provoking Henry's three surviving sons, who were unhappy with the terms of their inheritance, into unsuccessful rebellion against their father in 1173. From 1179 until his death in 1189, Henry kept Eleanor under mild house arrest to prevent any further such mischief from her.

After her separation from Henry in 1170 and until Henry confined her in England, Eleanor lived in Poitiers with her daughter Marie, the countess of Champagne; the two made the court of Poitiers a famous center for the literature of courtly love. This genre, with its thinly veiled eroticism, has been viewed as an attack on medieval ascetic values. Be that as it may, it was certainly a commentary on contemporary domestic life within the aristocracy. The troubadours hardly promoted promiscuity at court—the code of chivalry that guided relations between lords and their vassals condemned the seduction of the wife of one's lord as the most heinous of offenses, punishable, in some places, by castration or execution (or both). Rather, the troubadours presented in a frank and entertaining way stories that satirized carnal love or depicted it with tragic irony while glorifying the ennobling power of friendly, or "courteous," love. The most famous courtly literature was that of Chrétien de Troyes, whose stories of King Arthur and the Knights of the Round Table contained the tragic story of Sir Lancelot's secret and illicit love for Arthur's wife, Guinevere.

Popular Rebellion and Magna Carta

As Henry II acquired new lands abroad, he became more autocratic at home. He forced his will on the clergy in the Constitutions of Clarendon (1164). These measures placed limitations on judicial appeals to Rome, subjected the clergy to the civil courts, and gave the king control over the election of bishops. The result was strong political resistance from both the nobility and the clergy. The archbishop of Canterbury, Thomas à Becket (1118?–1170), once Henry's compliant chancellor, broke openly with the king and fled to Louis VII. Becket's subsequent assassination in 1170 and his canonization by Pope Alexander III in 1172 helped focus popular resentment against the king's heavy-handed tactics. (Two hundred years later, Geoffrey Chaucer, writing in an age made cynical by the Black Death and the Hundred Years' War, had the pilgrims of his *Canterbury Tales* journey to the shrine of Thomas à Becket.)

Under Henry's successors, the brothers Richard the Lion-Hearted (r. 1189–1199) and John (r. 1199–1216), burdensome taxation in support of unnecessary foreign Crusades and a failing war with France turned resistance into outright rebellion. Richard had to be ransomed at a high price from the Holy Roman emperor Henry VI, who had taken him prisoner during his return from the ill-fated Third Crusade. In 1209 Pope Innocent III, in a dispute with King John over the pope's choice for archbishop of Canterbury, ex-

William the Conqueror on horseback urging his troops into combat with the English at the Battle of Hastings (October 14, 1066). Detail from the Bayeux Tapestry, scene 51, about 1073–1083. Musée de la Tapisserie, Bayeux, France. Giraudon/Art Resource, N.Y.

communicated the king and placed England under interdict. To extricate himself and keep his throne, John had to make humiliating concessions, even declaring his country a fief of the pope. The last straw for the English, however, was the defeat of the king's forces by the French at Bouvines in 1214. With the full support of the clergy and the townspeople, English barons revolted against John. The popular rebellion ended with the king's grudging recognition of Magna Carta, or "Great Charter" in 1215.

The Magna Carta put limits on autocratic behavior of the kind exhibited by Norman kings and their successors, the Angevin or Plantagenet kings. It also secured the rights of the many—at least, the privileged many—against the monarchy. In Magna Carta the privileged preserved their right to be represented at the highest levels of government in important matters like taxation. But the monarchy was also preserved and left strong. Some argue that just such a balancing of the one and the many, the stronger and the comparatively weaker—preserving both sides and giving real power to each—was precisely the goal of feudal government. (See "The English Nobility Imposes Restraints on King John.")

Political accident clearly had more to do with Magna Carta than political genius. Nevertheless, the English did manage to avoid both a dissolution of the monarchy by the nobility and the abridgment of the rights of the nobility by the monarchy. Although King John continued to resist the Magna Carta in every way, and succeeding kings ignored it, Magna Carta nonetheless became a cornerstone of modern English law.

Philip II Augustus

The English struggle in the High Middle Ages was to secure the rights of the many, not the authority of the king. The French, on the other hand, faced the

opposite problem. In 987, noblemen chose Hugh Capet to succeed the last Carolingian ruler, replacing the Carolingian dynasty with the Capetian dynasty. For two centuries thereafter, until the reign of Philip II Augustus (r. 1180–1223), powerful feudal princes dominated France.

During this period, after a rash initial attempt to challenge the more powerful French nobility before they had enough strength to do so, the Capetian kings concentrated their limited resources on securing the royal domain, their uncontested territory around Paris and the Île-de-France to the northeast. Aggressively exercising their feudal rights, French kings, especially after 1100, gained near absolute obedience from the noblemen in this area, and in the process established a solid base of power. By the reign of Philip II, Paris had become the center of French government and culture and the Capetian dynasty a secure hereditary monarchy. Thereafter, the kings of France could impose their will on the French nobles, who were always in law, if not in political fact, the king's sworn vassals.

In an indirect way the Norman conquest of England helped stir France to unity and made it possible for the Capetian kings to establish a truly national monarchy. The duke of Normandy, who after 1066 was master of the whole of England, was also among the vassals of the French king in Paris. Capetian kings understandably watched with alarm as the power of their Norman vassal grew. Other powerful vassals of the king also watched with alarm. King Louis VI, the Fat (r. 1108–1137), entered an alliance with Flanders, traditionally a Norman enemy. King Louis VII (r. 1137–1180), assisted by a brilliant minister, Suger, the abbot of St. Denis and famous for his patronage of Gothic architecture (see "Art & the West"), found allies in the great northern French cities and used their wealth to build a royal army.

How William the Conqueror Won the Battle of Hastings

This account of the Battle of Hastings appears in the Chronicle *of the kings of England, written by a Benedictine monk, William of Malmesbury, the son of a Norman father and an English mother. Although William wrote over a half century after the Battle of Hastings, his chronicle is our fullest account of these events.*

❖ *Where does Brother William think the winning difference lay between the two sides (Norman and English)? Might the fact that he was half Norman and a monk as well prejudice his account in favor of William the Conqueror? Are there statements in the document that suggest or deny this?*

The courageous leaders mutually prepared for battle, each according to his national custom. The English passed the night without sleep, in drinking and singing, and in the morning proceeded without delay against the enemy. All on foot, armed with battle-axes, and covering themselves in front by joining their shields, they formed an impenetrable body.... King Harold himself, on foot, stood with his brothers near the standard in order that, so long as all shared equal danger, none could think of retreating....

The Normans passed the whole night in confessing their sins, and received the communion of the Lord's body in the morning. Their infantry, with bows and arrows, formed the vanguard, while their cavalry, divided into wings, was placed in the rear. The duke [of Normandy], with serene countenance, declaring aloud that God would favor his...side, called for his arms... Then starting the song of Roland, in order that...the example of

that [early French war] hero might stimulate the soldiers, and calling on God for assistance, the battle commenced on both sides...neither side yielding ground during the greater part of the day.

Observing this, William gave a signal to his troops, that, pretending flight, they should withdraw from the field. By means of this device the solid phalanx of the English opened for the purpose of cutting down the fleeing enemy and thus brought upon itself swift destruction; for the Normans, facing about, attacked them, thus disordered, and compelled them to fly....

[The English were not] without their own revenge, for, by frequently making a stand, they slaughtered their pursuers in heaps... [Such] alternating victory, first by one side and then by the other, continued as long as Harold lived to check the retreat; but when he fell, his brain pierced by an arrow, the flight of the English ceased not until night.

From Frederic Austin Ogg (ed.), *A Source Book of Mediaeval History: Documents Illustrative of European Life and Institutions from the German Invasions to the Renaissance* (New York: Telegraph Books, 1908), pp. 235–237.

When he succeeded Louis VII as king, Philip II Augustus inherited financial resources and a skilled bureaucracy that put him in a strong position. He was able to resist the competition of the French nobility and the clergy and to focus on the contest with the English king. Confronted at the same time with an internal and an international struggle, he proved successful in both. His armies occupied all the English king's territories on the French coast except for Aquitaine. As a showdown with the English neared on the continent, however, Holy Roman Emperor Otto IV (r. 1198–1215) entered the fray on the side of the English, and the French found themselves assailed from both east and west. But when the international armies finally clashed at Bouvines in Flanders on July 27, 1214, in what history records as the first great European battle, the French won handily over the opposing Anglo–Flemish–German army. This victory

unified France politically around the monarchy and thereby laid the foundation for French ascendancy in the later Middle Ages. The defeat so weakened Otto IV that he fell from power in Germany. (It also, as we have seen, sparked the rebellion in England that forced King John to accept Magna Carta.)

France in the Thirteenth Century: The Reign of Louis IX

If Innocent III realized the fondest ambitions of medieval popes, Louis IX (r. 1226–1270), the grandson of Philip Augustus, embodied the medieval view of the perfect ruler. Coming to power in the wake of the French victory at Bouvines (1214), Louis inherited a unified and secure kingdom. Although he was endowed with a moral character that far exceeded that of his royal and papal contemporaries, he was also at times prey to naïveté. Not beset by the problems of sheer survival, and a reformer at heart, Louis found himself free to concentrate on what medieval people believed to be the business of civilization.

Generosity Abroad

Magnanimity in politics is not always a sign of strength, and Louis could be very magnanimous. Although in a strong position during negotiations for the Treaty of Paris (1259), which momentarily settled the dispute between France and England, he refused to take advantage of it to drive the English from their French possessions. Had he done so and ruthlessly confiscated English territories on the French coast, he might have lessened, if not averted altogether, the conflict underlying the Hundred Years' War, which began in the fourteenth century. Instead he surrendered disputed territory on the borders of Gascony to the English king, Henry

A depiction of the murder of Saint Thomas à Becket in Canterbury cathedral. From the Playfair Book of Hours. Victoria and Albert Museum/Art Resource, N.Y., Ms. L 475–1918

III, and confirmed Henry's possession of the duchy of Aquitaine.

Although he occasionally chastised popes for their crude political ambitions, Louis remained neutral during the long struggle between the German Hohenstaufen emperor Frederick II and the papacy (discussed later in the chapter); and his neutrality redounded very much to the pope's advantage. Louis also remained neutral when his brother, Charles of Anjou, intervened in Italy and Sicily against the Hohenstaufens, again to the pope's advantage. Urged on by the pope and his noble supporters, Charles was crowned king of Sicily in Rome, and his subsequent defeat of the son and grandson of Frederick II ended the Hohenstaufen dynasty. For such service to the church, both by action and by inaction, the Capetian kings of the thirteenth century became the objects of many papal favors.

Order and Excellence at Home

Louis's greatest achievements lay at home. The efficient French bureaucracy, which his predecessors had used to exploit their subjects, became under Louis an instrument of order and fair play in local government. He sent forth royal commissioners (*enquêteurs*), reminiscent of Charlemagne's far less successful *missi dominici*. Their mission was to monitor the royal officials responsible for local governmental administration (especially the *baillis* and *prévôts*, whose offices had been created by his predecessor, Philip Augustus) and to ensure that justice would truly be meted out to all. These royal ambassadors were received as genuine tribunes of the people. Louis further abolished private wars and serfdom within his royal domain. He gave his subjects the judicial right of appeal from local to higher courts and made the tax system, by medieval standards, more equitable. The French people came to associate their king with justice; consequently, national feeling, the glue of nationhood, grew very strong during his reign.

Respected by the kings of Europe and possessed of far greater moral authority than the pope, Louis became an arbiter among the world's powers. During his reign French society and culture became an example to all of Europe, a pattern that would continue into the modern period. Northern France became the showcase of monastic reform, chivalry, and Gothic art and architecture. Louis's reign also coincided with the golden age of Scholasticism, which saw the convergence of Europe's greatest thinkers on Paris, among them Saint Thomas Aquinas and Saint Bonaventure. (See Chapter 8.)

Louis' perfection remained, however, that of a medieval king. Like his father, Louis VIII (r. 1223–

The English Nobility Imposes Restraints on King John

The gradual building of a sound English constitutional monarchy in the Middle Ages required the king's willingness to share power. He had to be strong, but could not act as a despot or rule by fiat. The danger of despotism became acute in England under the rule of King John. In 1215 the English nobility forced him to recognize Magna Carta, which reaffirmed traditional rights and personal liberties that are still enshrined in English law.

❖ *Does the Magna Carta protect basic rights or special privileges? Does this protection suggest that there was a sense of fairness in the past? Does the granting of such protection in any way weaken the king?*

A free man shall not be fined for a small offense, except in proportion to the gravity of the offense; and for a great offense he shall be fined in proportion to the magnitude of the offense, saving his freehold [property]; and a merchant in the same way, saving his merchandise; and the villein [a free serf, bound only to his lord] shall be fined in the same way, saving his wainage [wagon], if he shall be at [the king's] mercy. And none of the above fines shall be imposed except by the oaths of honest men of the neighborhood....

No constable or other bailiff of [the king] shall take anyone's grain or other chattels without immediately paying for them in money, unless he is able to obtain a postponement at the good will of the seller.

No constable shall require any knight to give money in place of his ward of a castle [i.e., standing guard], if he is willing to furnish that ward in his own person, or through another honest man, if he himself is not able to do it for a reasonable cause; and if we shall lead or send him into the army, he shall be free from ward in proportion to the amount of time which he has been in the army through us.

No sheriff or bailiff of [the king], or any one else, shall take horses or wagons of any free man, for carrying purposes, except on the permission of that free man.

Neither we nor our bailiffs will take the wood of another man for castles, or for anything else which we are doing, except by the permission of him to whom the wood belongs....

No free man shall be taken, or imprisoned, or dispossessed, or outlawed, or banished, or in any way injured, nor will we go upon him, nor send upon him, except by the legal judgment of his peers, or by the law of the land.

To no one will we sell, to no one will we deny or delay, right or justice.

From James Harvey Robinson, ed., *Readings in European History*, Vol. 1 (Boston: Athenaeum, 1904), pp. 236–237.

1226), who had taken part in the Albigensian Crusade, Louis was something of a religious fanatic. He sponsored the French Inquisition. He led two French Crusades against the Muslims, which, although inspired by the purest religious motives, proved to be personal disasters. During the first (1248–1254), Louis was captured and had to be ransomed out of Egypt. He died of a fever during the second in 1270. It was especially for this selfless, but also useless, service on behalf of the church that Louis later received the rare honor of sainthood. Probably not coincidentally, the church bestowed this honor when it was under pressure from a more powerful and less than "most Christian" French king, the ruthless Philip IV, "the Fair" (r. 1285–1314). (See Chapter 9.)

The Hohenstaufen Empire (1152–1272)

During the twelfth and thirteenth centuries, stable governments developed in both England and France. In England Magna Carta balanced the rights of the nobility against the authority of the kings, and in France the reign of Philip II Augustus secured the authority of the king over the competitive claims of the nobility. During the reign of Louis IX, the French exercised international influence over politics and culture. The story within the Holy Roman Empire, which embraced Germany, Burgundy, and northern Italy by the mid-thirteenth century, was very different. (See Map 7–2.) There, primarily be-

Salisbury Cathedral:
A Church Filled with Light

Salisbury Cathedral, England. © Christopher Cormack/Corbis

Between 1050 and 1150 Christian churches and abbeys had been built predominately in the Romanesque style. Fortress-like, with thick stone walls and heavy rounded arches, Romanesque architecture expressed the Church's role as a refuge for the faithful and its status as a newly emerging worldy power. But beginning in France around 1140, Gothic architecture replaced Romanesque as the dominant style across most of Europe. During the next 100 years—the Age of the Great Cathedrals—numerous magnificent churches were built in England, Germany Spain, Poland and Italy.

The architects of the great Gothic cathedrals had two main goals: to give mathematical harmony to the church (an expression of divine law and a source of true beauty), and to bring more light into it than had ever been possible. By contrast with Romanesque churches, Gothic churches soared to towering heights and were filled with light. This was achieved through a new technical design. Architects and builders used ribbed, criss-crossed vaulting on the ceiling to create Gothic architecture's soaring pointed arches without having to support the arches by widening their base. Supports known today as "flying buttresses" were built into the exterior walls to shift much of the building's weight off of the walls themselves, which thus could become thinner. Because the exterior walls no longer had to carry so much weight, they could be pierced with wide expanses of stained glass windows that flooded the churches with colored light. These windows displayed both biblical and historical figures, including the church's saintly and lay patrons.

Salisbury Cathedral, shown here, is a prime example of early English Gothic architecture. Built between 1220 and 1226, the cathedral required 60,000 tons of stone, which arrived in 10 cartloads daily from March to October for 46 years, hauled by workers from a quarry 12 miles away. Note the soaring arches and the ribbed vaulting on the ceiling of the cathedral's interior. The exterior view shows the flying buttresses placed symmetrically between the arched windows on the sides of the cathedral and the intricately decorated west facade with ornamental carvings and statuary spaced evenly across the wall.

Salisbury Cathedral, England. The Image Works.

cause of the efforts of the Hohenstaufen dynasty to extend imperial power into southern Italy, disunity and blood feuding remained the order of the day for two centuries. It left as a legacy the fragmentation of Germany until the nineteenth century.

Frederick I Barbarossa

The investiture struggle had earlier weakened imperial authority. After the Concordat of Worms, the German princes were the supreme lay powers within the rich ecclesiastical territories and held a dominant influence over the appointment of the Church's bishops.

The power of the emperor promised to recuperate, however, with the accession to the throne of Frederick I Barbarossa (r. 1152–1190) of the Hohenstaufen dynasty, the most powerful line of emperors yet to succeed the Ottonians. This new dynasty not only reestablished imperial authority, but also started a new, deadlier phase in the contest between popes and emperors. Never have kings and popes despised and persecuted one another more than during the Hohenstaufen dynasty. (See "Hildegard of Binge Advises Frederick I Barbarossa.)

Frederick I confronted powerful feudal princes in Germany and Lombardy and a pope in Rome who still looked on the emperor as his creature. However, the incessant strife among the princes and the turmoil caused by the papacy's pretensions to great political power alienated many people. Such popular sentiment presented Frederick with an opportunity to recover imperial authority, and he was shrewd enough to take advantage of it. Frederick especially took advantage of the contemporary revival of Roman law, which served him on two fronts. On one hand, it praised centralized authority, that of king or emperor, against the nobility; on the other, it stressed the secular origins of imperial power against the tradition of Roman election of the emperor and papal coronation of him, thus reducing papal involvement to a minimum.

From his base of operation in Switzerland Frederick attempted to hold his empire together by invoking feudal bonds. He was relatively successful in Germany, thanks largely to the fall from power and exile in 1180 of his strongest German rival, Henry the Lion (d. 1195), the duke of Saxony. While he could not defeat the many German duchies, Frederick never missed an opportunity to remind each German ruler of his prescribed duties as one who held his land legally as a fief of the emperor. The same tactic had also been successfully employed by the Capetian kings of France when they faced superior forces of the nobility.

Italian popes proved to be the greatest obstacle to Frederick's plans to revive his empire. In 1155 he restored Pope Adrian IV (r. 1154–1159) to power in Rome

after a religious revolutionary had taken control of the city. For his efforts, Frederick won a coveted papal coronation—and strictly on his terms, not on those of the pope. Despite fierce resistance to him in Italy, led by Milan, the door to Italy had opened, and an imperial assembly sanctioned his claims to Italian lands.

As this challenge to royal authority was occurring, Cardinal Roland, a skilled lawyer, became Pope Alexander III (r. 1159–1181). In a clever effort to strengthen the papacy against growing imperial influence, the new pope had, while still a cardinal, negotiated an alliance between the papacy and the Norman kingdom of Sicily. Knowing him to be a very capable foe, Frederick opposed his election as pope and backed a rival candidate after the election in a futile effort to undo it. Frederick now found himself at war with the pope, Milan, and Sicily.

By 1167 the combined forces of the north Italian communes had driven Frederick back into Germany, and a decade later, in 1176, Italian forces soundly defeated his armies at Legnano. In the Peace of Constance in 1183, which ended the hostilities, Frederick recognized the claims of the Lombard cities to full rights of self-rule, a great blow to his imperial plans.

Henry VI and the Sicilian Connection

Frederick's reign thus ended with stalemate in Germany and defeat in Italy. At his death in 1190 he was not a ruler equal in stature to the kings of England and France. After the Peace of Constance, he seems to have accepted the reality of the empire's division among the feudal princes of Germany.

King Louis IX (1226–1270) giving justice. Louis, who was canonized in 1297, was the medieval ideal of a perfect ruler. From "Justiniani in Fortiatum," fol. 34. France, 14th C. Bibliotica Real, El Escorial, Madrid, Spain. Giraudon/Art Resource, NY

However, in the last years of his reign he seized an opportunity to gain control of Sicily, then still a papal ally, and form a new territorial base of power for future emperors. The opportunity arose when the Norman ruler of the kingdom of Sicily, William II (r. 1166–1189), sought an alliance with Frederick that would free him to pursue a scheme to conquer Constantinople. In 1186 a most fateful marriage occurred between Frederick's son, the future Henry VI (r. 1190–1197), and Constance, the heiress to the kingdom of Sicily, which promised to change the balance of imperial–papal power.

It proved, however, to be but another well-laid plan that went astray. The Sicilian kingdom became a fatal distraction for succeeding Hohenstaufen kings, tempting them to sacrifice their traditional territorial base in northern Europe to dreams of imperialism. Equally disastrous for the Hohenstaufens, the union of the empire with Sicily left Rome encircled, ensuring even greater emmity from a papacy already thoroughly distrustful of the emperor.

When Henry VI became emperor in 1190, he faced a hostile papacy, German princes more defiant than ever of the emperor, and an England whose adventurous king, Richard the Lion-Hearted, plotted against Henry VI with the old Hohenstaufen enemy, the exiled duke of Saxony, Henry the Lion.

It was into these circumstances that the future Emperor Frederick II was born in 1194. Heretofore the German princes had not recognized birth alone as qualifying one for the imperial throne, although the offspring of the emperor did have the inside track. To ensure baby Frederick's succession and stabilize his monarchy, Henry campaigned vigorously for recognition of the principle of hereditary succession. He won many German princes to his side by granting them what he asked for himself and his son: full hereditary rights to their own fiefs. Not surprisingly, the encircled papacy strongly opposed hereditary succession and joined dissident German princes against Henry.

Otto IV and the Welf Interregnum

Henry died in September 1197, leaving his son Frederick a ward of the pope. Henry's brother succeeded him as German king, but the Welf family, who were German rivals of the Hohenstaufens, put forth their own candidate, whom the English supported, while the French, beginning a series of interventions in German affairs, stuck with the Hohenstaufens. The papacy supported first one side and then the other, depending on which seemed most to threaten it. The new struggle for power soon threw Germany into anarchy and civil war.

The Welf candidate, Otto of Brunswick, outlasted his rival and was crowned Otto IV by his followers in Aachen in 1198, thereafter winning general recognition in Germany. In October 1209, Pope Innocent III (r. 1198–1216) boldly meddled in German politics by crowning Otto emperor in Rome. Playing one German dynasty against the other in an evident attempt to curb imperial power in Italy, while fully restoring papal power there, the pope had badly underestimated the ambition of the new German emperor. After his papal coronation, Otto proceeded to attack Sicily, an old imperial policy threatening to Rome. Four months after crowning Otto emperor, Pope Innocent excommunicated him.

Frederick II

Casting about for a counterweight to the treacherous Otto, the pope joined with the French, who had remained loyal to the Hohenstaufens. His new ally, French king Philip Augustus, impressed on Innocent that a solution to their mutual problem with Otto IV lay near at hand in the person of Innocent's ward, Frederick of Sicily, son of the late Hohenstaufen Emperor Henry VI, who had now come of age. Unlike Otto, the young Frederick had an immediate hereditary claim to the imperial throne. In December 1212, with papal, French, and German support, Frederick was crowned king of the Romans, in the German city of Mainz. Within a year and a half, Philip Augustus ended the reign of Otto IV on the battlefield of Bouvines, and three years later (1215), Frederick II was crowned emperor again, this time in the sacred imperial city of Aachen.

During his reign, Frederick effectively turned dreams of a unified Germany into a nightmare of disunity, assuring German fragmentation until modern times. Raised Sicilian and dreading travel beyond the Alps, Frederick spent only nine of his thirty-eight years as emperor in Germany, and six of those were before 1218. Although he pursued his royal interests in Germany, he did so mostly through representatives, seeming to desire only the imperial title for himself and his sons and willing to give the German princes whatever they wanted to secure it. It was this eager compliance with their demands that laid the foundation for six centuries of German division. In 1220 he recognized the jurisdictional claims of the ecclesiastical princes of Germany, and twelve years later (1232) he extended the same recognition to the secular princes.

Frederick's concessions were tantamount to an abdication of imperial power in Germany. Some view them as a kind of German Magna Carta in that they secured the rights of the German nobility for the forseeable future. But unlike the king of England with-

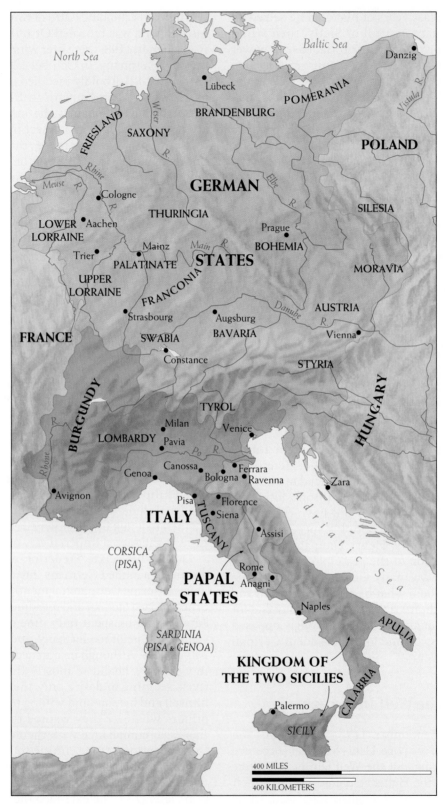

MAP 7–2   GERMANY AND ITALY IN THE MIDDLE AGES   *Medieval Germany and Italy were divided lands. The Holy Roman Empire (Germany) embraced hundreds of independent territories that the emperor ruled only in name. The papacy controlled the Rome area and tried to enforce its will on Romagna. Under the Hohenstaufens (mid-twelfth to mid-thirteenth century), internal German divisions and papal conflict reached new heights; German rulers sought to extend their power to southern Italy and Sicily.*

Hildegard of Bingen Advises Frederick I Barbarrossa

Hildegard of Bingen (1098–1179) would have been a remarkable and highly accomplished woman in any century. Sought out by contemporaries for her mystical visions, which she recorded and illustrated, she was also a recognized authority on the natural sciences and herbal medicine, composed her own original musical scores, and had a wide circle of correspondents that included many of her centuries' leading rulers and churchmen.

Born in Mainz, Germany, the tenth child of a wealthy knight, she had her first vision at six. When she was eight, her parents sent her to a local Benedictine cloister in Disibodenber, named after St. Disibod, a local seventh-century Celtic missionary to Germany. There she gained proficiency in Latin and as good an education as any woman of her time. She became a nun at fifteen, and at thirty-eight assumed the position of abbess in the cloister in which she had grown up. Declaring her visions to be divinely inspired, the archbishop of Mainz recorded them for posterity. Together with her scientific and medical writings they attracted to the cloister many who sought career advice and cures.

So many came that Hildegard left Disobodenberg to found a new convent near Bingen in 1147, where she lived out the rest of her life writing and conducting a far-flung correspondence with the admiring powerful and influential people of her age.

The following letter is one of four she wrote to Frederick I Barbarrossa, the first Hohenstaufen emperor, apparently shortly after his coronation as emperor in 1152. Frederick, on the other hand, wrote only one to her.

❖ *Why might Hildegard have written more often to Frederick than he to her? Is there anything in the letter that suggests a woman or a gifted visionary has written it? Why would a famous and powerful emperor want the advice of such a person? Did he follow her advice (see text)?*

Now, O king, pay careful attention! All lands are clouded by the plots of the many people who through the blackness of their souls put out the light of justice. Robbers and vagrants destroy the way of the Lord. O king, control with the sceptre of compassion the slothful, changeable, and wild habits of men. For you have a name of renown, since you are the king in Israel [that is, a divine king in the line of kings stemming from Old Testament times]. For your name is of high repute. Make sure, then, when the highest Judge looks at you, you will not be charged with not having rightly grasped your office, for then you must indeed blush with shame. May this be far from you! It is a well-known truth that it is right that the ruler imitate his predecessors in all that is good. For the idle morals of the princes are black indeed, since they run about in negligence and filth. Flee from this, O king! Be rather an armed fighter who bravely withstands the Devil, so that God doesn't strike you down and thereby scandal come over your earthly kingdom. God protect you from eternal destruction. May your times not be dry [that is, may they be times of growth and progress]. God guard you and may you live in eternity! So cast off all greed and choose moderation. For that is what the highest King loves.

Sources: *Hildegard of Bingen's Book of Divine Works with Letters and Songs*, ed. by Matthew Fox (Bear & Company, Santa Fe, 1987), pp. 289–290; Hildegard of Bingen, *The Book of the Rewards of Life*, trans. by Bruce W. Hozeski (Garland Publishing, Inc., New York, 1994), pp. xi–xiii.

in his realm, Frederick did little to secure the rights of the emperor in Germany. Whereas Magna Carta had the long-term consequence of promoting a balance of power between king and parliament, Frederick simply made the German princes little emperors within their respective realms. Centuries of petty absolutism, not parliamentary government, were the result.

Frederick's relations with the pope were equally disastrous, leading to his excommunication on four different occasions—the first in 1227 for refusing to

Major Political Events of High Middle Ages	
955	Otto I defeats Hungarians at Lechfeld, securing Europe's eastern border
1066	Normans win the Battle of Hastings and assume English rule
1152	Frederick I Barbarossa becomes first Hohenstaufen emperor; reestablishes imperial authority
1154	Henry II assumes the English throne as the first Plantagenet or Angevin king
1164	Henry II forces the Constitutions of Clarendon on the English clergy
1170	Henry II's defiant archbishop, Thomas à Becket, assassinated
1176	Papal and other Italian armies defeat Frederick I at Legnano
1194	Birth of future Hohenstaufen ruler Frederick II, who becomes a ward of the pope
1198	Welf interregnum in the empire begins under Otto IV
1212	Frederick II crowned emperor in Mainz with papal, French, and German support
1214	French armies under Philip II Augustus defeat combined English and German forces at Bouvines in the first major European battle
1215	English barons revolt against King John and force the king's recognition of Magna Carta
1227	Frederick II excommunicated for the first of four times by the pope; conflict between Hohenstaufen dynasty and papacy begins
1250	Frederick II dies, having been defeated by the German princes with papal support
1257	German princes establish their own electoral college to elect future emperors

finish a crusade he had begun at the pope's request. He was also determined to control Lombardy and Sicily, a policy that was anathema to the pope. The papacy came to view Frederick as the Antichrist, the biblical beast of the Apocalypse, whose persecution of the faithful signaled the end of the world.

The papacy won the long struggle that ensued, although its victory was arguably a Pyrrhic one. During this bitter contest, Pope Innocent IV (r. 1243–1254) launched the church into European politics on a massive scale, a policy that left the church highly vulnerable to criticism from both religious reformers and royal apologists. Pope Innocent organized the German princes against Frederick, who—thanks to Frederick's grand con-

cessions—were a superior force and able to gain full control of Germany by the 1240s.

When Frederick died in 1250, the German monarchy died with him. The princes established their own informal electoral college in 1257, which thereafter controlled the succession. Through this institution, which the emperor recognized in 1356, the "king of the Romans" became a puppet of the princes, and one with firmly attached strings. The princes elected him directly, and his offspring had no hereditary right to succeed him.

Between 1250 and 1272 the Hohenstaufen dynasty slowly faded into oblivion. Independent princes henceforth controlled Germany, while the imperial kingdon in Italy fell to local Italian magnates. The connection between Germany and Sicily ended forever, and the papal monarchy emerged as one of Europe's most formidable powers, soon to enter its most costly conflict of the Middle Ages with the new French and English monarchies. Internal division and the absence of a representative system of government persisted in Germany for six centuries. Even after Chancellor Bismarck created a new German empire in 1871, the legacy of the Hohenstaufen dynasty's defeat was still visible until the end of World War I.

In Perspective

With its borders finally secured, western Europe was free to develop its political institutions and cultural forms during the High Middle Ages. The map of Europe as we know it today began to take shape. England and France can be seen forming into modern nation–states, but within Germany and the Holy Roman Empire the story was different. There, imperial rule first revived (under the Ottonians) and then collapsed totally (under the Hohenstaufen dynasty). The consequences for Germany were ominous: thereafter, it became Europe's most fractured land. On a local level, however, an effective organization of society from noble to serf emerged throughout western Europe.

The major disruption of the period was an unprecedented conflict between former allies, church and state. During the Investiture Struggle and the period of the Crusades, the church became a powerful monarchy in its own right. For the first time it competed with secular states on the latter's own terms, dethroning emperors, kings, and princes by excommunication and interdict. In doing so, it inadvertently laid the foundation for the Western doctrine of the separation of church and state.

Having succeeded so brilliantly in defending its spiritual authority against rulers, popes ventured boldly into the realm of secular politics as well, especially during the pontificates of Innocent III and Innocent IV. As the sad story of the Hohenstaufen dynasty attests, the popes had remarkable, if short-lived, success there also. But the Church was to pay dearly for its successes, both spiritually and politically. Secularization of the papacy during the High Middle Ages left it vulnerable to the attacks of a new breed of unforgiving religious reformers, and the powerful monarchs of the later Middle Ages were to subject it to bold and vengeful bullying.

REVIEW QUESTIONS

1. Discuss the rise of the German Empire and the accomplishments of the Saxon king, Otto I. How was he able to consolidate political rule over the various German duchies and use the church to his advantage? Does he deserve the title "the Great"?

2. What were the main reasons for the Cluny reform movement? How do you account for its success? How important was the impact of this reform movement on the subsequent history of the medieval church?

3. Discuss the conflict between Pope Gregory VII and King Henry IV over the issue of lay investiture. What were the causes of the controversy, the actions of the contending parties, and the outcome of the struggle? What was at stake for each of the disputants, and what were the ramifications of the struggle?

4. The eighteenth-century French intellectual Voltaire said that the Holy Roman Empire was neither holy nor Roman. What did he mean? Do you agree with him?

5. What major development in western and eastern Europe encouraged the emergence of the Crusades? Why were the Crusaders unsuccessful in establishing lasting political and religious control over the Holy Land? What were the political, religious, and economic results of the Crusades? Which do you consider most important and why?

6. Hohenstaufen rule proved disastrous for Germany's development as a nation. What were some of the factors preventing German consolidation during that era? Why did Germany remain in feudal chaos while France and England eventually coalesced into reasonably strong states?

SUGGESTED READINGS

J. W. Baldwin, *The Government of Philip Augustus* (1986). An important scholarly work.

G. Barraclough, *The Origins of Modern Germany* (1946). Dated, but penetrating, political narrative setting modern Germany in the perspective of the Middle Ages.

A. Capellanus, *The Art of Courtly Love*, trans. by J. J. Parry (1941). Documents from the court of Marie de Champagne.

H. E. J. Cowdrey, *Popes, Monks, and Crusaders* (1984). Re-creation of the atmosphere that gave birth to the Crusades.

R. H. C. Davis, *A History of Medieval Europe: From Constantine to St. Louis* (1972), Part 2. Succinct, lucid survey.

E. M. Hallam, *Capetian France 987–1328* (1980). Very good on politics and heretics.

J. C. Holt, *Magna Carta*, 2d ed. (1992). The famous document and its interpretation by succeeding generations.

E. H. Kantorowicz, *The King's Two Bodies* (1957). Controversial analysis of political concepts in the High Middle Ages.

K. Leyser, *Rule and Conflict in Early Medieval Society: Ottonian Saxony* (1979). Basic and authoritative.

K. Leyser, *Medieval Germany and Its Neighbors, 900–1250* (1982). Basic and authoritative.

P. Mandonnet, *St. Dominic and His Work* (1944). On the origins of the Dominican order.

H. E. Mayer, *The Crusades*, trans. by John Gilligham (1972). Extremely detailed; the best one-volume account.

J. B. Morrall, *Political Thought in Medieval Times* (1962). Readable and illuminating account.

C. Petit-Dutaillis, *The Feudal Monarchy in France and England from the Tenth to the Thirteenth Century*, trans. by E. D. Hunt (1964). Political narrative in great detail.

S. Reynolds, *Kingdoms and Communities in Western Europe 900–1300* (1984). For the medieval origins of Western political and cultural traditions.

J. Riley-Smith, *The Crusades: A Short History* (1987). Up-to-date, lucid, and readable.

W. Roesener, *Peasants in the Middle Ages* (1992) Up to date overview.

Joseph Schatazmiller, *Jews, Medicine, and Medieval Society* (1994). Information on Jewish women physicians.

B. Tierney, *The Crisis of Church and State* (1964). Extremely useful collection of key documents.

Chapter 8

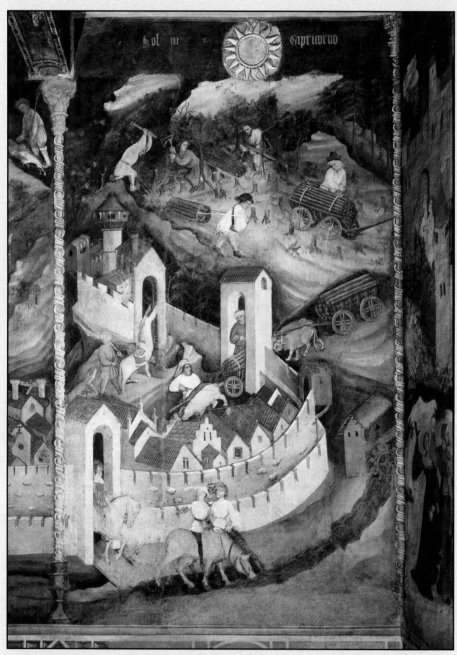

A depiction of court and countryside in thirteenth-century Italy. The oldest of three parts of Castle Buonconsiglio in Trent, Italy was built in the mid-thirteenth century (1239–1255) between the city's north and east gates, through which workers can be seen hauling wood into the city by ox cart, while royals of both sexes ride out on horseback. Scala/Art Resource, N.Y.

Medieval Society:
Hierarchies, Towns, Universities, and Families (1000–1300)

The Traditional Order of Life
Nobles
Clergy
Peasants

Towns and Townspeople
The Chartering of Towns
The Rise of Merchants
Challenging the Old Lords
New Models of Government
Towns and Kings
Jews in Christian Society

Schools and Universities
University of Bologna
Cathedral Schools
University of Paris
The Curriculum
Philosophy and Theology

Women in Medieval Society

The Lives of Children

KEY TOPICS

- The major groups composing medieval society
- The rise of towns and a new merchant class
- The founding of universities and educational curricula
- How women and children fared in the Middle Ages

Between the tenth and twelfth centuries, European agricultural production steadily improved, due to a warming climate and improved technology. With increased food supplies came something of a population explosion by the eleventh century. The recovery of the countryside in turn stimulated new migration into and trade with the long-dormant towns. A revival of old towns and the creation of new ones resulted. A rich and complex fabric of life developed, closely integrating town and countryside and allowing civilization to flourish in the twelfth and thirteenth centuries as it had not done in the West since the Roman Empire. Beginning with the Crusades, trade with distant towns and foreign lands also revived. With the rise of towns, a new merchant class, the ancestors of modern capitalists, came into being. Enormous numbers of skilled artisans and day workers, especially in the clothmaking industries, were the foundation of the new urban wealth.

Urban culture and education also flourished. The revival of trade with the East and contacts with Muslim intellectuals, particularly in Spain, made possible the recovery of ancient scholarship and science. Unlike the comparative dabbling in antiquity during Carolingian times, the twelfth century enjoyed a true renaissance of classical learning. Schools and curricula also broadened beyond the clergy during the twelfth century to educate laity, thereby greatly increasing lay literacy and the role of the laity in government and culture.

In the mid-twelfth century in France, Gothic architecture began to replace the plain and ponderous Romanesque preferred by fortress Europe during the early Middle Ages. Its new grace and beauty—soaring arches, bold flying buttresses, dazzling light, and stained glass—were a testament to the vitality of humankind as well as to the glory of God in this unique period of human achievement.

The Traditional Order of Life

In the art and literature of the Middle Ages, three basic social groups were represented: those who fought as mounted knights (the landed nobility), those who prayed (the clergy), and those who labored in fields and shops (the peasantry and village artisans). After the revival of towns in the eleventh century, there emerged a fourth social group: the long-distance traders and merchants. Like the peasantry, they also labored, but in ways strange to the traditional groups. They were freemen who often possessed great wealth, yet unlike the nobility and the clergy, they owned no land, and unlike the peasantry, they did not toil in fields and shops. Their rise to power caused an important crack in the old social order, for they drew behind them the leadership of the urban artisan groups created by the new urban industries that grew up in the wake of the revival of trade. During the late Middle Ages these new "middling classes" firmly established themselves, and their numbers have been enlarging ever since.

Nobles

As a distinctive social group, not all nobles were originally great men with large hereditary lands. Many rose from the ranks of feudal vassals or warrior knights. The successful vassal attained a special social and legal status based on his landed wealth (accumulated fiefs), his exercise of authority over others, and his distinctive social customs—all of which set him apart from others in medieval society. By the late Middle Ages, there had evolved a distinguishable higher and lower nobility living in both town and country. The higher were the great landowners and territorial magnates, long the dominant powers in their regions; the lower comprised petty landlords, the descendants of minor knights, newly rich merchants who could buy country estates, and wealthy farmers patiently risen from ancestral serfdom.

It was a special mark of the nobility that they lived off the labor of others. Basically lords of manors, the nobility of the early and High Middle Ages neither tilled the soil like the peasantry nor engaged in the commerce of merchants—activities considered beneath their dignity. The nobleman resided in a country mansion or, if he were particularly wealthy, a castle. Personal preference drew him to the countryside as much as the fact that his fiefs were usually rural manors. (See "Art & the West.")

WARRIORS Arms were the nobleman's profession; to wage war was his sole occupation and reason for living. In the eighth century the adoption of stirrups made mounted warriors, or cavalry, the key ingredient of a successful army. (Stirrups had the advantage of permitting the rider to strike a blow without falling to the ground.) Good horses (and a warrior needed several) and the accompanying armor and weaponry of horse warfare were expensive. Only those with means could pursue the life of a cavalryman. The nobleman's fief provided the means to acquire the expensive military equipment that his rank required. He maintained his enviable position as he had gained it, by fighting for his chief.

The nobility accordingly celebrated the physical strength, courage, and constant activity of warfare. Warring gave them both new riches and an opportunity to gain honor and glory. Knights were paid a share in the plunder of victory, and in time of war everything became fair game. Special war wagons, designed for the collection and transport of booty, followed them into battle. Sadness greeted periods of peace, as they meant economic stagnation and boredom. Whereas the peasants and the townspeople counted peace the condition of their occupational success, the nobility despised it as unnatural to their profession.

They looked down on the peasantry as cowards who ran and hid in time of war. Urban merchants, who amassed wealth by business methods strange to feudal society, were held in equal contempt, which increased as the affluence and political power of the townspeople grew. The nobility possessed as strong a sense of superiority over these "unwarlike" people as the clergy did over the general run of laity.

KNIGHTHOOD The nobleman nurtured his sense of distinctiveness within medieval society by the chivalric ritual of dubbing to knighthood. This ceremonial entrance into the noble class became almost a religious sacrament. The ceremony was preceded by a bath of purification, confession, communion, and a prayer vigil. Thereafter, the priest blessed the knight's standard, lance, and sword. As prayers were chanted, the priest girded the knight with his sword and presented him his shield, enlisting him as much in the defense of the church as in the service of his lord. Dubbing raised the nobleman to a state as sacred in his sphere as clerical ordination made the priest in his. The comparison is legitimate: The clergy and the nobility were medieval society's privileged estates. The appointment of noblemen to high ecclesiastical office and their eager participation in the church's Crusades had strong ideological and social underpinnings as well as economic and political motives.

In the twelfth century, knighthood was legally restricted to men of high birth. This circumscription of noble ranks came in reaction to the growing wealth, political power, and successful social climbing of newly rich townspeople (mostly merchants), who formed a new urban patriciate that was increasingly competitive with the lower nobility. Kings remained free, however, to raise up knights at will and did not shrink from increasing royal revenues by selling noble titles to wealthy merchants. But the law was building fences—fortunately, not without gates—between town and countryside in the High Middle Ages.

SPORTSMEN In peacetime, the nobility had two favorite amusements: hunting and tournaments. Where they could, noblemen progressively monopolized the rights to game, forbidding the commoners from hunting in "lords'" forests. This practice built resentment among common people to the level of revolt. Free game, fishing, and access to wood were basic demands in the petitions of grievance and the revolts of the peasantry throughout the High and later Middle Ages.

The pastime of tournaments also sowed seeds of social disruption, but more within the ranks of the nobility itself. Tournaments were designed not only to keep men fit for war, but also to provide the excitement of war without the useless maiming and killing of prized vassals. But as regions competed fiercely with one another for victory and glory, even mock battles with blunted weapons proved to be deadly. Often, tournaments got out of hand, ending with bloodshed and animosity among the combatants. (The intense emotions and occasional violence that accompany interregional soccer in Europe today may be seen as a survival of this kind of rivalry.) The church came to oppose tournaments as occasions of pagan revelry and senseless violence. Kings and princes also turned against them as sources of division within their realms. Henry II of England proscribed them in the twelfth century. They did not end in France until the mid-sixteenth century, after Henry II of France was mortally wounded by a shaft through his visor during a tournament celebrating his daughter's marriage.

COURTLY LOVE From the repeated assemblies in the courts of barons and kings, set codes of social conduct, or "courtesy," developed in noble circles. With the French leading the way, mannered behavior and court etiquette became almost as important as expertise in the battlefield. Knights became literate gentlemen, and lyric poets sang and moralized at court. The cultivation of a code of behavior and a special literature to eulogize it was not unrelated to problems within the social life of the nobility. Noblemen were notorious philanderers; their illegitimate children mingled openly with their legitimate offspring in their houses. The advent of courtesy was in part an effort to reform this situation.

Although the poetry of courtly love was sprinkled with frank eroticism and the beloved in these epics

Noblewomen watch a tournament. These mock battles were designed to provide the excitement of war without its mayhem. However, they tended to get out of hand, resulting in bloodshed and even death. University of Heidelberg

were married women pursued by those to whom they were not married, the love recommended by the poet was usually love at a distance, unconsummated by sexual intercourse. It was love without touching, a kind of sex without physical contact, and only as such was it considered ennobling. Court poets depicted those who succumbed to illicit carnal love as reaping at least as much suffering as joy from it.

SOCIAL DIVISIONS No medieval social group was absolutely uniform—not the nobility, the clergy, the townspeople, or even the peasantry. Not only was the nobility a class apart; it also had strong social divisions within its own ranks. Noblemen formed a broad spectrum—from minor vassals without subordinate vassals to mighty barons, the principal vassals of a king or prince, who had many vassals of their own. Dignity and status within the nobility were directly related to the exercise of authority over others; a chief with many vassals obviously far excelled the small country nobleman who served another and was lord over none but himself.

Illuminated Manuscripts:
The Luttrell Psalter

Sir Geoffrey Luttrell on Horseback. From *The Luttrell Psalter*, by permission of The British Library.

In the Middle Ages, religious devotion could be a very personal affair. Often, that devotion was linked to more secular interests and concerns. The illustrations on the right show a knight and his family at dinner while servants carry in the feast. The same man appears above with his wife and daughter-in-law, and, although aging, he carries the full armor of the newest fashion, the joust.

The manuscript depicts an English knight, Sir Geoffrey Luttrell, who was born in the last part of the thirteenth century. Although Sir Geoffrey bears the trappings of a knight from a medieval romance,

this image was actually painted as an illustration for a religious book known as a "Psalter," a collection of the Psalms and other religious texts for personal devotion.

The Psalter was one of the more common types of medieval illuminated manuscripts. A manuscript was made from parchment—animal skin, which when properly prepared, allowed for writing and decoration. The process required soaking the skin of a cow, goat, or sheep in different solutions and repeatedly scraping it to remove the hair. The best manuscripts came from the thinnest, whitest parchment, which took the most labor to produce. Once the parchment was prepared, it was taken to a workshop to be written upon and decorated. Manuscript workshops varied over the centuries of the Middle Ages. Manuscripts from sixth- or seventh-century monasteries might even be written outdoors, where the light was best, while later manuscripts might be copied in a well-lit room within the monastery.

In the thirteenth century, the type of person commissioning a manuscript began to change, and with that change came others, even in the kind of manuscripts produced. Lay people—not just monks and priests—wanted to own manuscripts. In cities like Paris and Oxford, workshops grew outside monasteries, and from the thirteenth to the fifteenth centuries, the number of people manufacturing and owning manuscripts steadily increased. Topics changed as well: although many were religious, there were also romances and other stories, texts for law and medicine, and genealogocal and ceremonial scrolls. Illuminated manuscripts might have real gold leaf applied to letters or pictures, the glittering reflection from which rendered them full of light, or "illuminated." Gold leaf, expensive pigments, elaborate patterns, and creative designs in the margins combined to make these illuminated manuscripts among the most expensive and desirable.

Throughout the Middle Ages almost all manuscripts were made for a specific client or patron: monastery, church, king, or member of the land-owning gentry, such as Sir Geoffrey Luttrell. In Paris, students might enter a workshop, choose the texts they desired, and have a special "economy" copy made to order. A king might commission a devotional book for his bride with illuminations on every page, perhaps even with certain pages depicting the young girl herself praying to the Virgin Mary. It is unclear exactly why Sir Geoffrey ordered his Pslater, but we can be sure that one of the most personal and most telling objects a medieval person might own was an illuminated manuscript.

When the printing press came into use for making illustrated books in the 1480s, the illuminated manuscript lost its prominence. More people could afford printed books, whose variety and number were now greater than ever before.

Sources: Alexander, J. J. G. *Medieval Illuminators and Their Methods of Work*. New Haven: Yale University Press, 1992. Backhouse, Janet. *The Luttrell Psalter*. London: British Library, 1989. Camille, M. *Mirror in Parchment: The Luttrell Psalter and the Making of Medieval England*. Chicago: University of Chicago Press, 1998. De Hamel, C. *A History of Illuminated Manuscripts*. (7th–16th centuries) London: Phaidon, 1986. Sandler, L. F. *Gothic Manuscripts, 1285–1385* (A Survey of Manuscripts Illuminated in the British Isles, General editor J. J. G. Alexander, Vol. 6), 2 vols. (London: University of Toronto Press, 1996).

[Top] *The Lord of the Manor Dining.* From *The Luttrell Psalter*, by permission of The British Library. [Bottom] *Kitchen Scene; Chopping Meat.* From *The Luttrell Psalter*, by permission of The British Library.

261

A lady and her knight going hunting. Bildarchiv Preussischer Kulturbesitz

Even among the domestic servants of the nobility, a social hierarchy developed according to assigned manorial duties. Although they were peasants in the eyes of the law, the chief stewards—charged with overseeing the operation of the lord's manor and entrusted with the care and education of the noble children—became powerful "lords" within their "domains." Some freemen found the status of the steward enviable enough to surrender their own freedom and become domestic servants in the hope of attaining it. In time, the social superiority of the higher ranks of domestic servants won legal recognition as medieval law adjusted to acknowledge the privileges of wealth and power at whatever level they appeared.

By the late Middle Ages, several factors forced the landed nobility into a steep economic and political decline from which it never recovered. Climatic changes and agricultural failures created large famines, while the great plague (see Chapter 9) brought about unprecedented population losses. Changing military tactics occasioned by the use of infantry and heavy artillery during the Hundred Years' War made the noble cavalry nearly obsolete. And the alliance of wealthy towns with the king weakened the nobility within

their very own domains. One can speak of a waning of the landed nobility after the fourteenth century. Thereafter, the effective possession of land and wealth counted far more than parentage and lineage as a qualification for entrance into the highest social class.

Clergy

Unlike the nobility and the peasantry, the clergy was an open estate. Although the clerical hierarchy reflected the social classes from which the clergy came, one was still a cleric by religious training and ordination, not by the circumstances of birth or military prowess.

REGULAR AND SECULAR CLERICS   There were two basic types of clerical vocation: the regular clergy and the secular clergy. The regular clergy was made up of the orders of monks who lived according to a special ascetic rule (*regula*) in cloisters separated from the world. They were the spiritual elite among the clergy, and theirs was not a way of life lightly entered. Canon law required that one be at least twenty-one years of age before making a final profession of the monastic vows of poverty, chastity, and obedience. The monks' personal sacrifices and high religious ideals made them much respected in high medieval society. This popularity was a major factor in the success of the Cluny reform movement and of the Crusades of the eleventh and twelfth centuries. The Crusades provided laypeople with a way to participate in the admired life of asceticism and prayer; in these holy pilgrimages they had the opportunity to imitate the suffering and perhaps even the death of Jesus, as the monks imitated his suffering and death by retreat from the world and severe self-denial.

Many monks (and also nuns, who increasingly embraced the vows of poverty, obedience, and chastity without a clerical rank) secluded themselves altogether. The regular clergy, however, were never completely cut off from the secular world. They maintained frequent contact with the laity through such charitable activities as feeding the destitute and tending the sick, through liberal arts instruction in monastic schools, through special pastoral commissions from the pope, and as supplemental preachers and confessors in parish churches during Lent and other peak religious seasons. It became the mark of the Dominican and Franciscan friars to live a common life according to a special rule and still to be active in a worldly ministry. Some monks, because of their learning and rhetorical skills, even rose to prominence as secretaries and private confessors to kings and queens.

The secular clergy, those who lived and worked directly among the laity in the world (*saeculum*), formed a vast hierarchy. At the top were the high prelates—the wealthy cardinals, archbishops, and bishops, who were drawn almost exclusively from the nobility—and below them the urban priests, the cathedral canons, and the court clerks. Finally, there was the great mass of poor parish priests, who were neither financially nor intellectually very far above the common people they served. (The basic educational requirement was an ability to say the mass.) Until the Gregorian reform in the eleventh century, parish priests lived with women in a relationship akin to marriage, and their concubines and children were accepted within the communities they served. Because of their relative poverty, it was not unusual for priests to "moonlight" as teachers, artisans, or farmers. Their parishioners also accepted and even admired this practice.

NEW ORDERS One of the results of the Gregorian reform was the creation of new religious orders aspiring to a life of poverty and self-sacrifice in imitation of Christ and the first apostles. The more important were the Canons Regular (founded 1050–1100), the Carthusians (founded 1084), the Cistercians (founded 1098), and the Praemonstratensians (founded 1121). Carthusians, Cistercians, and Praemonstratensians practiced extreme austerity in their quest to recapture the pure religious life of the early Church.

Strictest of them all were the Carthusians. Members lived in isolation and fasted three days a week. They also devoted themselves to long periods of silence and even self-flagellation in their quest for perfect self-denial and conformity to Christ.

The Cistercians (from Cîteaux in Burgundy) were a reform wing of the Benedictine order and were known as the "white monks," a reference to their all-white attire, symbolic of apostolic purity. (The Praemonstratensians also wore white.) They hoped to avoid the materialistic influences of urban society and maintain uncorrupted the original *Rule* of Saint Benedict, which their leaders believed Cluny was compromising. The Cistercians accordingly stressed anew the inner life and spiritual goals of monasticism. They located their houses in remote areas and denied themselves worldly comforts and distractions. Remarkably successful, the order could count 300 chapter houses within a century of its founding, and many others imitated its more austere spirituality.

The Canons Regular were independent groups of secular clergy (and also earnest laity) who, in addition to serving laity in the world, adopted the *Rule* of Saint Augustine (a monastic guide dating from around the year 500) and practiced the ascetic virtues of regular clerics. There were monks who renounced exclusive withdrawal from the world. There were also priests who renounced exclusive involvement in it. By merging the life of the cloister with traditional clerical duties, the Canons Regular foreshadowed the mendicant friars of the thirteenth century—the Dominicans and the Franciscans, who combined the ascetic ideals of the cloister with a very active ministry in the world.

The monasteries and nunneries of the established orders recruited candidates from among the wealthiest social groups. Crowding in the convents and the absence of patronage gave rise in the thirteenth century to lay satellite convents known as Beguine houses. These convents housed religiously earnest unmarried women from the upper and middle social strata. Cologne established 100 such houses between 1250 and 1350, each containing eight to twelve women. Several of these convents, in Cologne and elsewhere, became heterodox in religious doctrine and practice, falling prey to heresy. Among the responsibilities of the new religious orders of Dominicans and Franciscans was the "regularization" of such convents.

PROMINENCE OF THE CLERGY The clergy constituted a far greater proportion of medieval society than modern society. Estimates suggest that 1.5 percent of fourteenth-century Europe was in clerical garb. The clergy were concentrated in urban areas, especially in towns with universities and cathedrals, where, in addition to studying, they found work in a wide variety of religious services. In late fourteenth-century England there was one cleric for every seventy laypeople, and in counties with a cathedral or a university the proportion rose to one cleric for every fifty laypeople.[1] In large university towns, the clergy might exceed 10 percent of the population.

Despite the moonlighting of poorer parish priests, the clergy as a whole, like the nobility, lived on the labor of others. Their income came from the regular collection of tithes and church taxes according to an elaborate system that evolved in the High and later Middle Ages. The church was, of course, a major landowner and regularly collected rents and fees. Monastic communities and high prelates amassed great fortunes; there was a popular saying that the granaries were always full in the monasteries. The immense secular power attached to high clerical posts can be seen in the intensity of the investiture struggle. The loss of the right to present chosen clergy with the ring and staff of episcopal office was a direct threat to the emperor's control of his realm. The bishops had become royal agents and were ingratiated to that purpose with royal lands that the emperor could ill afford to have slip from his control.

[1] Denys Hay, *Europe in the Fourteenth and Fifteenth Centuries*, 2d ed. (New York: Holt, Rinehart, 1966), pp. 58–59.

During the greater part of the Middle Ages, the clergy were the "first estate," and theology was the queen of the sciences. How did the clergy come into such prominence? A lot of it was self-proclaimed. However, there was also popular respect and reverence for the clergy's role as mediator between God and humanity. The priest brought the very Son of God down to earth when he celebrated the sacrament of the Eucharist; his absolution released penitents from punishment for mortal sin. It was declared improper for mere laypeople to sit in judgment on such a priest.

Theologians elaborated the distinction between the clergy and the laity very much to the clergy's benefit. The belief in the superior status of the clergy underlay the evolution of clerical privileges and immunities in both person and property. As holy persons, the clergy were not supposed to be taxed by secular rulers without special permission from the proper ecclesiastical authorities. Clerical crimes were under the jurisdiction of special ecclesiastical courts, not the secular courts. Because churches and monasteries were deemed holy places, they, too, were free from secular taxation and legal jurisdiction. Hunted criminals, lay and clerical, regularly sought asylum within them, disrupting the normal processes of law and order. When city officials violated this privilege of asylum, ecclesiastical authorities threatened excommunication and interdict. People feared this suspension of the church's sacraments, including Christian burial, almost as much as they feared the criminals to whom the church gave asylum.

By the late Middle Ages, townspeople came increasingly to resent the special immunities of the clergy. They complained that it was not proper for the clergy to have greater privileges, yet far fewer responsibilities, than all others who lived within the town walls. An early sixteenth-century lampoon reflected what had by then become a widespread sentiment:

Priests, monks, and nuns
Are but a burden to the earth.
They have decided
That they will not become citizens.
That's why they're so greedy—
They stand firm against our city
And will swear no allegiance to it.
And we hear their fine excuses:
"It would cause us much toil and trouble
Should we pledge our troth as burghers."[2]

The separation of church and state and the distinction between the clergy and the laity have persisted into modern times. After the fifteenth century, however, the clergy ceased to be the superior class they had been for so much of the Middle Ages. In both Protestant and Catholic lands, governments progressively subjected them to the basic responsibilities of citizenship.

Peasants

The largest and lowest social group in medieval society was the one on whose labor the welfare of all the others depended: the agrarian peasantry. Many peasants lived on and worked the manors of the nobility, the primitive cells of rural social life. All were to one degree or another dependent on their lords and were considered their property. The manor in Frankish times was a plot of land within a village, ranging from twelve to seventy-five acres in size, assigned to a certain member by a settled tribe or clan. This member and his family became lords of the land, and those who came to dwell there formed a smaller, self-sufficient community within a larger village community. In the early Middle Ages such manors consisted of the dwellings of the lord and his family, the cottages of the peasant workers, agricultural sheds, and fields.

THE DUTIES OF TENANCY   The landowner or lord of the manor required a certain amount of produce (grain, eggs, and the like) and a certain number of services from the peasant families that came to dwell on and farm his land. The tenants were free to divide the labor as they wished, and what goods remained after the lord's levies were met were their own. A powerful lord might own many such manors. Kings later based their military and tax assessments on the number of manors owned by a vassal landlord. No set rules governed the size of manors. There were manors of a hundred acres or less and some of several thousand or more.

There were both servile and free manors. The tenants of the latter had originally been freemen known as *coloni*. Original inhabitants of the territory and petty landowners, they swapped their small possessions for a guarantee of security from a more powerful lord, who came in this way to possess their land. Unlike the pure serfdom of the servile manors, whose tenants had no original claim to a part of the land, the tenancy obligations on free manors tended to be limited and the tenants' rights more carefully defined. It was a milder serfdom. Tenants of servile manors were by comparison far more vulnerable to the whims of their landlords. These two types of manors tended, however, to merge. The most common situation was the manor on which tenants of greater and lesser degrees of servitude dwelt together, their services to the lord defined by their personal status and local custom. In many regions free, self-governing peasant communities existed without any overlords and tenancy obligations.

---

[2] Cited by S. Ozment, *The Reformation in the Cities* (New Haven, CT: Yale University Press, 1975), p. 36.

The livelihood of towns and castles depended on the labor of peasants. Here a peasant family collects the September grape harvest outside a fortified castle in France, most likely for the making of wine. From Les Tres Riches heures du duc de Berry, Chateau de Saumur, Musée Condé, Chantilly, France. Giraudon/Art Resource, N.Y.

The lord held both judicial and police powers. He owned and operated the machines that processed crops into food and drink. Marc Bloch, the modern authority on manorial society, has vividly depicted the duties of tenancy:

On certain days the tenant brings the lord's steward perhaps a few small silver coins or, more often, sheaves of grain harvested on his fields, chickens from his farmyard, cakes of wax from his beehives or from the swarms of the neighboring forest. At other times he works on the arable or the meadows of the demesne [the lord's plot of land in the manorial fields, between one-third and one-half of that available]. Or else we find him carting casks of wine or sacks of grain on behalf of the master to distant residences. His is the labour which repairs the walls or moats of the castle. If the master has guests the peasant strips his own bed to provide the necessary extra bed-clothes. When the hunting season comes round he feeds the pack. If war breaks out he does duty as a footsoldier or orderly, under the leadership of the reeve of the village.[3]

[3] Marc Bloch, *Feudal Society*, trans. by L. A. Manyon (Chicago: University of Chicago Press, 1968), p. 250.

The lord also had the right to subject his tenants to exactions known as banalities. He could, for example, force them to breed their cows with his bull and to pay for the privilege, to grind their bread grains in his mill, to bake their bread in his oven, to make their wine in his wine press, to buy their beer from his brewery, and even to surrender to him the tongues or other choice parts of all animals slaughtered on his lands. The lord also collected a serf's best animal as an inheritance tax. Without the lord's permission, serfs could neither travel nor marry outside the manor in which they served.

THE LIFE OF A SERF Exploited as the serfs may appear to have been from a modern point of view, their status was far from chattel slavery. It was to the lord's advantage to keep his serfs healthy and happy; his welfare, like theirs, depended on a successful harvest. Serfs had their own dwellings and modest strips of land and lived by the produce of their own labor and organization. They were permitted to market for their own profit what surpluses might remain after the harvest. They were free to choose their spouses within the local village, although the lord's permission was required if a wife or husband was sought from another village. And serfs could pass their property (their dwellings and field strips) and worldly goods on to their children.

Peasants lived in timber-framed huts. Except for the higher domestic servants, they seldom ventured far beyond their own villages. The local priest often was their window on the world, and church festivals were their major communal entertainment. Their religiosity was based in large part on the church being the only show in town, although their religious beliefs were by no means unambiguously Christian.

Despite the social distinctions between free and servile serfs—and, within these groups, between those who owned ploughs and oxen and those who possessed only hoes—the common dependence on the soil forced close cooperation. The ratio of seed to grain yield was consistently poor; about two bushels of seed were required to produce six to ten bushels of grain in good times. There was rarely an abundance of bread and ale, the staple peasant foods. Two important American crops, potatoes and corn (maize), were unknown in Europe until the sixteenth century. Pork was the major source of protein, and every peasant household had its pigs. At slaughter time a family might also receive a little tough beef. But basically, everyone depended on the grain crops. When they failed or fell short, the peasantry simply went hungry unless the lord had surplus stores that he was willing to share.

CHANGES IN THE MANOR Two basic changes occurred in the evolution of the manor from the early to the later Middle Ages. The first was the fragmentation of the manor and the rise to dominance of the single-family holding. This development was aided by such technological advances as the collar harness (ca. 800), the horseshoe (ca. 900), and the three-field system of crop rotation, which made it easier for smaller familial units to support themselves. As the lords parceled out their land to new tenants, their own plots became progressively smaller. The increase in tenants and the decrease in the lord's fields brought about a corresponding reduction in the labor services exacted from the tenants. Also, the bringing of new fields into production increased individual holdings and modified labor services. In France, by the reign of Louis IX (r. 1226–1270), only a few days of labor a year were required, whereas in the time of Charlemagne peasants had worked the lords' fields several days a week.

As the single-family unit replaced the clan as the basic nuclear group, assessments of goods and services fell on individual fields and households, no longer on manors as a whole. Family farms replaced manorial units. The peasants' carefully nurtured communal life made possible a family's retention of its land and dwelling after the death of the head of the household. In this way, land and property remained in the possession of a single family from generation to generation.

The second change in the evolution of the manor was the conversion of the serf's dues into money payments, a change made possible by the revival of trade and the rise of the towns. This development, completed by the thirteenth century, permitted serfs to hold their land as rent-paying tenants and to overcome their servile status. Although tenants thereby gained greater freedom, they were not necessarily better off materially. Whereas servile workers could have counted on the benevolent assistance of their landlords in hard times, rent-paying workers were left, by and large, to their own devices. Their independence caused some landlords to treat them with indifference and even resentment.

Lands and properties that had been occupied by generations of peasants and were recognized as their own were always under the threat of the lord's claim to a prior right of inheritance and even outright usurpation. As their demesnes declined, the lords were increasingly tempted to encroach on such traditionally common lands. The peasantry fiercely resisted such efforts, instinctively clinging to the little they had. In many regions they successfully organized to gain a voice in the choice of petty rural officials.

By the mid-fourteenth century a declining nobility in England and France, faced with the ravages of the great plague and the Hundred Years' War, tried to turn back the historical clock by increasing taxes on the peasantry and passing laws to restrict their migration into the cities. The peasantry responded with armed revolts in the countryside. These revolts became the rural equivalents of the organization of medieval cities in sworn communes to protect their self-interests against powerful territorial rulers. The revolts of the agrarian peasantry, like those of the urban proletariat, were brutally crushed. They stand out at the end of the Middle Ages as violent testimony to the breakup of medieval society. As growing national sentiment would break its political unity and heretical movements end its nominal religious unity, the peasantry's revolts revealed the absence of medieval social unity.

Towns and Townspeople

In the eleventh and twelfth centuries, towns held only about 5 percent of western Europe's population. By comparison to modern towns, they were not very large. Of Germany's 3,000 towns, for example, 2,800 had populations under 1,000. Only fifteen German towns exceeded 10,000. The largest, Cologne, had 30,000. In England, only London had more than 10,000. Paris was larger than London, but not by much. The largest European towns were in Italy; Florence approached 100,000 and Milan was not far behind. Despite their comparatively small size, towns then, as now, were where the action was. In the town, one could find the whole of medieval society and its most creative segments.

The Chartering of Towns

Towns were originally dominated by feudal lords, both lay and clerical. The lords created the towns by granting charters to those who would agree to live and work within them. The charters guaranteed their safety and gave inhabitants a degree of independence unknown on the land. The purpose was originally to concentrate skilled laborers who could manufacture the finished goods desired by lords and bishops. In this way, manorial society may be seen actually creating its urban challenger and weakening itself. Because they longed for finished goods and for the luxuries that came from faraway places, noblemen had urged their serfs to become skilled at making such things. The new skills required to do this in turn gave serfs a new importance and power. By the eleventh century, skilled serfs began to pay their manorial dues in manufactured goods, rather than in field labor, eggs, chickens, and beans, as they had earlier. In return for a fixed rent and proper subservience, serfs were also encouraged to settle and work in towns. There they gained special rights and privileges by way of the charters.

As towns grew and beckoned, many serfs fled the countryside with their skills and went directly to the new urban centers. There they found the freedom and profits that could lift an industrious craftsperson into higher social ranks. As this migration of serfs to the towns accelerated, the lords in the countryside offered them more favorable terms of tenure to keep them on the land. In that way, the growth of towns improved the lot of serfs generally. But serfs could not easily be kept down on the farms after they had discovered the opportunities of town life.

The Rise of Merchants

Not only did rural society give the towns their craftspeople and day laborers, but the first merchants themselves may also have been enterprising serfs. Certainly, some of the long-distance traders were men who had nothing to lose and everything to gain by the enormous risks of foreign trade. They traveled together in armed caravans and convoys, buying goods and products as cheaply as possible at the source, and selling them for all they could get in Western ports. (See Map 8–1.) More than anything else, it was the greed and daring of these rough-hewn men that created Western urban life as we know it today.

At first the merchants were not liked by the traditional social groups—nobility, clergy, and peasantry—who considered them an oddity. As late as the fifteenth century, we find the landed nobility still snubbing the urban patriciate. Such snobbery probably never died out among the older landed nobility, who looked down on the traders as men with poor breeding, little character, and money they did not properly earn or deserve. Over time, however, the powerful grew to respect the merchants, and the weak always tried to imitate them, because wherever the merchants went, they left a trail of wealth behind.

Challenging the Old Lords

As the traders established themselves in towns, they grew in wealth and numbers, formed their own protective associations, and soon found themselves able to challenge traditional seigneurial authority. Merchants especially wanted to end the arbitrary tolls and tariffs imposed by regional magnates over the surrounding countryside. Such regulations hampered the flow of commerce on which both merchant and craftsperson in the growing urban export industries depended. Wherever merchants settled in large numbers, they opposed the tolls, tariffs, and

The Rue du Matelas, a French street in Rouen, Normandy, was preserved intact from the Middle Ages to World War II. Note the narrowness of the street and the open sewer running down its center. The houses were built of rough cast stone, mud, and timber. H. Roger Viollet/Liaison Agency, Inc.

other petty restrictions that discouraged the flow of trade. Merchant guilds or protective associations sprang up in the eleventh century, followed in the twelfth by guilds of craftspeople (drapers, haberdashers, furriers, hosiers, goldsmiths, and so on), who worked to advance the business interests of both merchants and craftspeople, as well as to enhance the personal well-being of their members. This quickly brought them into conflict with the norms of comparatively static agricultural society.

Townspeople needed simple and uniform laws and a government sympathetic to their new forms of business activity, not the fortress mentality of the lords of the countryside. Such a need could not but create a struggle with the old nobility within and outside the towns. This conflict led towns in the High and later Middle Ages to form their own independent communes and to ally themselves with kings against the nobility in the countryside, a development that would eventually rearrange the centers of power in medieval Europe and dissolve classic feudal government.

MAP 8–1   SOME MEDIEVAL TRADE ROUTES AND REGIONAL PRODUCTS   *The map shows some of the channels that came to be used in interregional commerce and what was traded in a particular region.*

Because the merchants were so clearly the engine of the urban economy, small shopkeepers and artisans identified far more with them than with the aloof lords and bishops who were a town's original masters. Most townspeople found their own interests best served by the development of urban life in the direction the merchants wanted it to go. That is, they wanted greater commercial freedom, fewer barriers to trade and business, and a freer secular life—in sum, a less closed urban life. The lesser nobility (the small knights) outside the towns also recognized the new mercantile economy to be the wave of the future. During the eleventh and twelfth centuries, the burgher upper class increased its economic strength and successfully challenged the old urban lords for control of the towns.

New Models of Government

With urban autonomy came new models of self-government. Around 1100 the old urban nobility and the new burgher upper class merged. It was a marriage between those wealthy by birth (inherited property) and those who made their fortunes in long-distance trade. From this new ruling class was born the aristocratic town council, which henceforth came to govern towns.

Enriching and complicating the situation even more, small artisans and craftspeople also slowly developed their own protective associations or guilds and began to gain a voice in government. The towns' ability to provide opportunities for the "little person" had created the slogan, "Town air brings freedom." In the countryside the air one breathed still belonged to the lord of the land; but in the towns residents were treated as freemen. Within town walls, people thought of themselves as citizens with basic rights, not subjects liable to their masters' whim. Economic hardship certainly continued to exist among the lower urban groups despite their basic legal and political freedoms. But social mobility was at least a possibility in the towns.

KEEPING PEOPLE IN THEIR PLACES   Traditional measures of success had great appeal within the towns. Despite their economic independence, the wealthiest urban groups admired and imitated the lifestyle of the old landed nobility. Although the latter treated the urban patriciate with disdain, successful merchants longed to live the noble, knightly life. They wanted coats of arms, castles, country estates, and the life of a gentleman or a lady on a great manor. This became particularly true in the later Middle Ages, when reliable bills of exchange and international regulation of trade, together with the maturation of merchant firms, allowed merchants to conduct their business by mail. Then only the young apprentices did a lot of traveling, to learn the business from the ground up. When merchants became rich enough to do so, they took their fortunes to the countryside.

Such social climbing disturbed city councils, and when merchants departed for the countryside, towns often lost out economically. A need to be socially distinguished and distinct pervaded urban society. The merchants were just the tip of the iceberg. Towns tried to control this need by defining grades of luxury in dress and residence for the various social groups and vocations. Overly conspicuous consumption was a kind of indecent exposure punishable by law. Such sumptuary laws restricted the types and amount of clothing one might wear (the length and width of fur pieces, for example) and how one might decorate one's dwelling architecturally. In this way, people were forced to dress and live according to their station in life. The intention of such laws was positive: to maintain social order and dampen social conflict by keeping everyone clearly and peacefully in their place. (See "The Laws and Customs of Chester.")

The Laws and Customs of Chester

The following laws and customs appear in the Domesday Book *(1080–1086). They were included there because the English town of Chester was among the forty or so towns in which the king had a financial interest. The town paid a portion of the fines it collected for criminal behavior to the king's representative.*

❖ *In terms of fines and financial loss, what were the most serious crimes? Was simple negligence punished? Did religion play a role in the setting of any of these fines? Do the fines suggest vigilance or pettiness?*

If any free man of the king broke the peace which had been granted and killed a man in his house, all his land and money came to the king, and he himself became an outlaw.

He who shed blood between Monday morning and the ninth hour of Saturday compounded for it with [i.e., paid a fine of] ten shillings. From the ninth hour of Saturday to Monday morning bloodshed was compounded for with twenty shillings. Similarly any one paid twenty shillings who shed blood in the twelve days after Christmas, on the day of the Purification of the Blessed Mary, on the first day after Easter, the first day of Pentecost, Ascension day, on the Assumption or Nativity of the Blessed Mary, and on the day of All Saints....

He who committed theft or robbery, or exercised violence upon a woman in a house, compounded for each of these with forty shillings....

If fire burned the city, he from whose house it started compounded for it with three oras [about two shillings worth] of pennies, and gave to his next neighbor two shillings. Of all these forfeitures, two parts belonged to the king and the third to the earl.

A man or a woman making false measure in the city, and being arrested, compounded for it with four shillings. Similarly a person making bad ale was either placed in the ducking stool or gave four shillings to the reeve [the bailiff]. This forfeiture the officer of the king and of the earl received in the city, in whosesoever land it has been done, either of the bishop or of another man. Similarly also, if any one held the toll back beyond three nights, he compounded for it with forty shillings.

From James Harvey Robinson, ed., *Readings in European History*, Vol. 1 (Boston: Athenaeum, 1904), pp. 406–407.

Skilled workers were an integral component of the commerce of medieval towns. This scene shows the manufacture of cannons in a foundry in Florence. Scala/Art Resource, N.Y.

SOCIAL CONFLICT AND PROTECTIVE ASSOCIATIONS (GUILDS)   Despite unified resistance to external domination, medieval towns were not internally harmonious social units. They were a collection of many selfish and competitive communities, each seeking to advance its own business and family interests. Conflict between "haves" and "have-nots" was inevitable, especially because medieval towns had little concept of social and economic equality. Theoretically, poor artisans could work their way up from lower social and vocational levels, and some lucky ones did. But so long as they had not done so, they were excluded from the city council. Only families of long standing in the town who owned property had full rights of citizenship and a direct say in the town's government at the highest levels. Government, in other words, was inbred and aristocratic.

Conflict also existed between the poorest workers in the export trades (usually the weavers and woolcombers) and the economically better off and socially ascending independent workers and small shopkeepers. The better-off workers also had their differences with the merchants, whose export trade often brought competitive foreign goods into the city. So independent workers and small shopkeepers organized to restrict foreign trade to a minimum and corner the local market in certain items.

Over time, the formation of artisan guilds gave workers in the trades a direct voice in government. Ironically, a long-term effect of this gain was to limit the social mobility of the poorest artisans. The guilds gained representation on city councils, where,

to discourage imports, they used their power to enforce quality standards and fair prices on local businesses. These actions created tight restrictions on guild membership, squeezing out poorer artisans and tradesmen. As a result, lesser merchants and artisans found their opportunities progressively limited. So rigid and exclusive did the dominant guilds become that they often stifled their own creativity and inflamed the journeymen whom they excluded from their ranks. Unrepresented artisans and craftspeople constituted a true urban proletariat prevented by law from forming their own guilds or entering existing ones. The efforts by guild-dominated governments to protect local craftspeople and industries tended to narrow trade and depress the economy for all.

Towns and Kings

By providing kings with the resources they needed to curb factious noblemen, towns became a major force in the transition from feudal societies to national governments. In many places kings and towns formally allied against the traditional lords of the land. A notable exception to this general development is England, where the towns joined with the barons against the oppressive monarchy of King John (r. 1199–1216), becoming part of the parliamentary opposition to the crown. But by the fifteenth century, kings and towns had also joined forces in England, so much so that by century's end Henry Tudor (r. 1485–1509) was known as the "burgher king."

Towns attracted kings and emperors for obvious reasons. Towns were a ready source of educated bureaucrats and lawyers who knew Roman law, the tool for running kingdoms and empires. Money was also to be found in the towns in great quantity, enabling kings to hire their own armies and free themselves from dependence on the nobility. Towns had the human, financial, and technological resources to empower kings. By such alliances, towns won royal political recognition and had their constitutions guaranteed. This proved somewhat easier to do in the stronger coastal areas than in interior areas, where urban life remained less vigorous and territorial government was on the rise. In France, towns became integrated early into royal government. In Germany, they fell under ever tighter control by the princes. In Italy, uniquely, towns expanded to dominate the surrounding countryside, becoming genuine city–states during the Renaissance.

It was also in the towns' interest to have a strong monarch as their protector against despotic local lords and princes, who were always eager to integrate or engulf the towns within their expanding territories. Unlike a local magnate, a king tended to remain at a distance, allowing towns to exercise their precious autonomy. A king was thus the more desirable overlord. It was also an advantage to a town to have its long-distance trade conducted in the name of a known powerful monarch. This gave predators pause and improved official cooperation along the way. Both sides—kings and towns—gained from such alliances.

Between the eleventh and fourteenth centuries, towns had considerable freedom and autonomy. As in Roman times, they again became the flourishing centers of Western civilization. But after the fourteenth century, and even earlier in France and England, the towns, like the church before them, were steadily bent to the political will of kings and princes in most places. By the seventeenth century few would be truly autonomous, the vast majority integrated thoroughly into the larger purposes of the "state."

Jews in Christian Society

Towns also attracted large numbers of Jews. It was within the major urban centers, particularly in France and Germany, that Jews gathered between the late twelfth and thirteenth centuries. They did so both by choice and for safety in the increasingly hostile Christian world. Mutually wary of one another, Christians and Jews sought to limit their contacts with each other to exchanges between merchants and scholars. The church expressly forbade Jews from hiring Christians in their businesses and from holding any public authority over them. In the cities, Jews plied trades in their own small businesses, and many became wealthy bankers to kings and popes, as well as having private business clients among both Christians and Jews. Jewish intellectual and religious culture had always been very elaborate and sophisticated, both dazzling and threatening to Christians who viewed it from outside. These various factors—the separateness of Jews, their economic power, and their cultural strength—contributed to suspicion and distrust among Christians, whose religious teaching held Jews responsible for the death of Christ.

Between the late twelfth and early fourteenth centuries, Jews were exiled from France and persecuted elsewhere as well. Two factors were behind this unprecedented surge in anti-Jewish sentiment. The first was a desire on the part of kings to confiscate Jewish wealth and property and eliminate the Jews as economic competitors with the monarchy. (French kings acted similarly in the fourteenth century against a wealthy Christian military order known as the Knights Templars; see Chapters 7 and 9.) The other factor behind the surge in anti-Jewish sentiment was the church's increasing political vulnerability to the new dynastic monarchies. Faced with the loss of its political power, the church became more determined than ever to maintain its spiritual hegemony. With the beginning of the Crusades and the creation of new mendicant orders, the church powerfully reasserted claims to spiritual sovereignty over Europe and beyond, instigating major campaigns against dissenters, heretics, witches, and Jews at home as well as against the infidel abroad. (See "The Massacre of Jews during the First Crusade (1096).")

Schools and Universities

In the twelfth century, Byzantine and Spanish Islamic scholars made it possible for the works of Aristotle on logic, the writings of Euclid and Ptolemy, the basic works of Greek physicians and Arab mathematicians, and the larger texts of Roman law to circulate among Western scholars. Islamic scholars especially preserved these works. They also wrote extensive, thought-provoking commentaries on Greek texts, which were translated into Latin and made available to Western scholars and students. The result of this renaissance of ancient knowledge was an intellectual ferment that gave rise to Western universities.

University of Bologna

The first important Western university, established by Emperor Frederick I Barbarossa in 1158, was in Bologna. There we find the first formal organizations of students and masters and the first degree programs—the institutional foundations of the modern university. Originally, the term "university" meant simply a corporation of individuals (students and masters) who joined for their mutual protection from overarching episcopal authority (the local bishop oversaw the university) and from the local townspeople. Because townspeople then looked on students as foreigners without civil rights, such protective unions were necessary. They followed the model of an urban trade guild.

Bolognese students also "unionized" to guarantee fair rents and prices from their often reluctant hosts. And students demanded regular, high-quality teaching from their masters. In Italy, students actually hired their own teachers, set pay scales, and drew up desired lecture topics. Masters who did not keep their promises or live up to student expectations were boycotted. Price gouging by townspeople was met with the threat to move the university to another town. This could rather easily be done because the university was not yet tied to a fixed physical plant. Students and masters moved freely from town to town as they chose. Such mobility gave them a unique independence from their surroundings.

Masters also formed their own protective associations and established procedures and standards for certification to teach within their ranks. The first academic degree was a certificate that licensed one to teach, a *licentia docendi*. It granted graduates in the liberal arts program, the program basic to all higher learning, as well as those in the higher professional sciences of medicine, theology, and law, "the right to teach anywhere" (*ius ibique docendi*).

Bologna was famous for the revival of Roman law. During the Frankish era and later, from the seventh to the eleventh centuries, only the most rudimentary manuals of Roman law had survived. With the growth of trade and towns in the late eleventh century, Western scholars had come into contact with the larger and more important parts of the *Corpus juris civilis* of Justinian, which had been lost during the intervening centuries. The study and dissemination of this recovered material was now undertaken in Bologna under the direction of a learned man

The Massacre of Jews during the First Crusade (1096)

Crusades embraced the full social spectrum. Already before the First Crusade, itinerant preachers like Peter the Hermit (1050–1115) inspired popular crusades by urging peasants and artisans to seek a better life and perhaps also heaven by marching to the Holy Land along familiar pilgrim routes. So-called people's crusades both preceded and followed the First Crusade, also pillaging Jewish towns en route. The following description recounts the pillaging of the Jewish community of Speyer during the First Crusade.

❖ *How did the Crusaders justify killing Jews in Speyer? Was it Christian law or doctrine to kill Jews who refused to be baptized? Why didn't the Jews defend themselves in more aggressive ways? Is this an example of a Crusade turned mob?*

It came to pass that, when [the crusaders] traversed towns where there were Jews, they said…"Behold we journey a long way to seek the idolatrous shrine and to take vengeance upon the Muslims. But here are the Jews dwelling among us, whose ancestors killed [Jesus Christ]….Let us take vengeance first upon them. Let us wipe them out as a nation; Israel's name will be mentioned no more. Or else let them be like us and acknowledge the son born of menstruation."

Now when the [Jewish] communities heard their words, they reverted to…repentance, prayer and charity. The hands of the holy people [Jews] fell weak and their hearts melted and their strength flagged. They hid themselves in innermost chambers before the ever turning sword….They fasted three consecutive days, both day and night, in addition to daily fasts….They cried out and gave forth a loud and bitter shriek. But their Father did not answer them…

That year Passover fell on Thursday and the new moon of Iyyar on Friday. On the eight of Iyyar, on the Sabbath, the enemy [the Crusaders] arose against the Jewish community of Speyer and killed eleven [holy] souls who sanctified their Creator on the holy Sabbath day and refused to be baptised [at the hands of the Crusaders].

Copyright © 1992. From *Women's Lives in Medieval Europe*, ed. Emilie Amt. Reproduced by permission of Taylor Francis, Inc./ Routledge, Inc., http://www.routledge-ny.com

The University of Bologna in central Italy was distinguished as the center for the revival of Roman law. This carving on the tomb of a Bologna professor of law shows students attending one of his lectures. Scala/Art Resource, N.Y.

named Irnerius, who flourished in the early twelfth century. He and his students made authoritative commentaries, or glosses, on existing laws based on their newly broadened knowledge of the *Corpus juris civilis.* They thereby expanded legal knowledge. Around 1140, a monk named Gratian, also resident in Bologna, created the standard legal text in church, or canon, law, the *Concordance of Discordant Canons,* known simply as Gratian's *Decretum.*

As Bologna was the model for southern European universities (that is, those of Spain, Italy, and southern France) and the study of law, so Paris became the model for northern European universities and the study of theology. Oxford, Cambridge, and (much later) Heidelberg were among its imitators. All these universities required a foundation in the liberal arts for advanced study in the higher sciences of medicine, theology, and law. The arts program consisted of the *trivium* (grammar, rhetoric, and logic) and the *quadrivium* (arithmetic, geometry, astronomy, and music), or, more simply, the language arts and the mathematical arts.

Cathedral Schools

Before the emergence of universities, the liberal arts had been taught in cathedral and monastery schools. The purpose of these schools was to train the clergy, and their curricula tended understandably to be narrowly restricted to this goal. But by the late eleventh and twelfth centuries, cathedral schools also began to provide lectures for nonclerical students and they broadened their curricula to include some training for purely secular vocations. In 1179, a papal decree obliged cathedrals to provide teachers gratis for laity who wanted to learn.

After 1200, increasing numbers of future notaries and merchants who had no particular interest in becoming priests, but who needed Latin and related intellectual disciplines to fill their secular positions, studied side by side with aspiring priests in cathedral and monastery schools. By the thirteenth century, the demand for secretaries and notaries in the growing urban and territorial governments and for literate personnel in the expanding merchant firms gave rise to special schools for strictly secular vocational preparation. With the appearance of these schools, the church began for the first time to lose some of its monopoly on higher education.

The most famous of the cathedral schools were those of Rheims and Chartres. Chartres won fame under the direction of such distinguished teachers as Fulbert, Saint Ivo, and Saint Bernard of Chartres (not to be confused with the more famous Saint Bernard of Clairvaux). Gerbert, who later became Pope Sylvester II (r. 999–1003), guided Rheims to greatness in the last quarter of the tenth century. Gerbert was filled with enthusiasm for knowledge and promoted both logical and rhetorical studies. He did much to raise the study of logic to preeminence within the liberal arts, despite his personal belief in the greater relevance of rhetoric to the promotion of Christianity.

University of Paris

The University of Paris grew institutionally out of the cathedral school of Notre Dame, among others. King Philip Augustus and Pope Innocent III gave the new university its charter in 1200. At Paris the college, or house system, originated. At first, a college was just a hospice providing room and board for poor students who could not afford to rent rooms in town. But the educational life of the university quickly expanded into fixed structures and began to thrive on their sure endowments. University-run colleges made the overseeing and protection of students easier and gave the university a new prominence as a permanent urban institution.

In Paris, the most famous college was the Sorbonne, founded around 1257 by Robert de Sorbon, chaplain to the king, for the housing of theology students. In Oxford and Cambridge, the colleges became the basic unit of student life and were indistinguishable from the university proper. By the end of the Middle Ages such colleges had tied universities to physical plants and fixed foundations.

In this engraving, a teacher at the University of Paris leads fellow scholars in a discussion. As shown here, all of the students wore the scholar's cap and gown. Corbis

Their mobility was forevermore restricted, as was, compared with earlier times, their autonomy and freedom.

As a group, students at Paris had power and prestige. They enjoyed royal protections and privileges denied ordinary citizens. Many Parisian students were well to do, and not a few were spoiled and petulant. (See "Student Life at the University of Paris.") They did not endear themselves to the townspeople, whom they considered to be inferior. That townspeople sometimes let their resentments of such students lead to violence against them is made clear from the city's ordinances, which were highly protective of students. For example, city law forbade the beating of students. Only those students who had clearly committed serious crimes could be imprisoned. Only in self-defense might a citizen strike a student. All citizens were obligated to testify against anyone seen abusing a student. University laws also required all teachers to be carefully examined before being licensed to teach Parisian students. The law thus recognized students as both a valuable and a vulnerable resource.

The Curriculum

Before the so-called renaissance of the twelfth century, when many Greek and Arabic texts became available to Western scholars and students in Latin translations, the education available within the cathedral and monastery schools had been quite limited. Students learned grammar, rhetoric, and some elementary geometry and astronomy. They had the classical Latin grammars of Donatus and Priscian, Saint Augustine's treatise, *On Christian Doctrine*, and Cassiodorus's treatise, *On Divine and Secular Learning*. The writings of Boethius provided instruction in arithmetic and music and preserved the small body of Aristotle's works on logic then known in the West. After the textual finds of the early twelfth century, Western scholars recovered the whole of Aristotle's logic, the astronomy of Ptolemy, the writings of Euclid, and many Latin classics. By the mid-thirteenth century, almost all of Aristotle's works circulated in the West.

In the High Middle Ages, the learning process remained very basic. The assumption was that truth already existed; it was not something that one had to go out and find. It was there, requiring only to be properly organized, elucidated, and defended. Such conviction made logic and dialectic the focus of education. Students wrote commentaries on authoritative texts, especially those of Aristotle and the Church Fathers. Teachers did not encourage students to strive independently for undiscovered truth. Students rather learned to organize and harmonize the accepted truths of tradition, which were drilled into them.

Student Life at the University of Paris

As the following account by Jacques de Vitry makes clear, not all students at the University of Paris in the thirteenth century were there to gain knowledge. Students fought constantly and subjected each other to ethnic insults and slurs.

❖ *Why were students from different lands so prejudiced against one another? Does the rivalry of faculty members appear to have been as intense as that among students? What are the student criticisms of the faculty? Do they sound credible?*

Almost all the students at Paris, foreigners and natives, did absolutely nothing except learn or hear something new. Some studied merely to acquire knowledge, which is curiosity; others to acquire fame, which is vanity; others still for the sake of gain, which is cupidity and the vice of simony. Very few studied for their own edification, or that of others. They wrangled and disputed not merely about the various sects or about some discussions; but the differences between the countries also caused dissensions, hatreds and virulent animosities among them, and they impudently uttered all kinds of affronts and insults against one another.

They affirmed that the English were drunkards and had tails; the sons of France proud, effeminate and carefully adorned like women. They said that the Germans were furious and obscene at their feasts; the Normans, vain and boastful; the Poitevins, traitors and always adventurers. The Burgundians they considered vulgar and stupid. The Bretons were reputed to be fickle and changeable, and were often reproached for the death of Arthur. The Lombards were called avaricious, vicious and cowardly; the Romans, seditious, turbulent and slanderous; the Sicilians, tyrannical and cruel; the inhabitants of Brabant, men of blood, incendiaries, brigands and ravishers; the Flemish, fickle, prodigal, gluttonous, yielding as butter, and slothful. After such insults from words they often came to blows.

I will not speak of those logicians [professors of logic and dialectic] before whose eyes flitted constantly "the lice of Egypt," that is to say, all the sophistical subtleties, so that no one could comprehend their eloquent discourses in which, as says Isaiah, "there is no wisdom." As to the doctors of theology, "seated in Moses' seat," they were swollen with learning, but their charity was not edifying. Teaching and not practicing, they have "become as sounding brass or a tinkling cymbal," or like a canal of stone, always dry, which ought to carry water to "the bed of spices." They not only hated one another, but by their flatteries they enticed away the students of others; each one seeking his own glory, but caring not a whit about the welfare of souls.

Translations and Reprints from the Original Sources of European History, Vol. 2 (Philadelphia: Department of History, University of Pennsylvania, 1902), pp. 19–20.

This method of study, based on logic and dialectic, was known as *Scholasticism*. It reigned supreme in all the faculties—in law and medicine as well as in philosophy and theology. Students read the traditional authorities in their field, formed short summaries of their teaching, disputed them with their peers by elaborating traditional arguments pro and con, and then drew conclusions. Logic and dialectic dominated training in the arts because they were the tools that could discipline knowledge and thought. *Dialectic* is a negative logical inquiry, the art of discovering a truth by finding the contradictions in arguments against it. Astonishingly, medical students did no practical work; they studied and debated the authoritative texts just as law and theology students did.

Few books existed for students, and because printing with movable type did not yet exist, those available were expensive hand-copied works. So students could not leisurely master a subject in the quiet of their studies. They had rather to learn it in discussion, lecture, and debate. There was a lot of memorizing, and the ability to think on one's feet was stressed. Rhetoric, or persuasive argument, was the ultimate goal, that is, the ability to make an eloquent defense of the knowledge one had clarified by logic and dialectic. Successful students became virtual walking encyclopedias; their education both filled their heads with knowledge and gave them the ability to recite it impressively.

THE SUMMA The twelfth century saw the rise of the *summa*, an authoritative summary of allegedly all that was known about a particular subject. The summa's main purpose was to conciliate traditional authorities and heap up clarified truth. In canon law, there was Gratian's *Concordance of Discordant Canons* (around 1142), whose very title embodies the scholastic method. In theology, there was Peter Lombard's *Four Books of Sentences* (1155–1157). Embracing traditional teaching on God, the creation, Christ, and the sacraments, it was destined to become the standard theological textbook until the Protestant reformers declared it unbiblical. It had evolved from Peter Abelard's *Sic et Non* (around 1122), a much smaller work that juxtaposed seemingly contradictory statements on the same subject by revered authorities. Out of this same tradition came Saint Thomas Aquinas's magnificent *Summa Theologiae* (begun in 1265), to many the last word on theology, which the medieval summa was always intended to be. (See "Thomas Aquinas Proves the Existence of God.")

University study normally began between the ages of twelve and fifteen. Students coming to university were expected to bring with them a good knowledge of Latin gained in local schools or from a private tutor. Once there, students spent four years perfecting their Latin (particularly in the study of the *trivium*) before attaining the bachelor-of-arts degree. A master's degree thereafter might take three or four years, during which time students studied mathematics, natural science, and philosophy by way of classical texts. A degree in theology at Paris might take more than twenty years of study from beginning to end.

CRITICS OF SCHOLASTICISM Even in the heyday of Scholasticism, this kind of education had its strong critics. Prominent among them were John of Salis-

Thomas Aquinas Proves the Existence of God

People in the Middle Ages saw continuity between Earth and heaven, the world of the living and the world of the dead. For intellectuals, reason and revelation, while different, were also believed to be connected, so that reasoned argument could prove some of what the Bible revealed to faith. Thomas Aquinas, perhaps the greatest medieval theologian, here states his famous five arguments for the existence of God, which he believed any rational person would agree with.

❖ *Are these arguments persuasive? Which is the most persuasive, which the least? Are they basically the same argument?*

Is there a God?

REPLY: There are five ways in which one can prove that there is a God.

The FIRST...is based on change. Some things...are certainly in process of change: this we plainly see. Now anything in the process of change is being changed by something else....Hence one is bound to arrive at some first cause of change not itself being changed by anything, and this is what everybody understands by God.

The SECOND way is based on the nature of causation. In the observable world causes are found to be ordered in series....Such a series must however stop somewhere....One is therefore forced to suppose some first cause, to which everyone gives the name "God."

The THIRD way is based on what need not be and on what must be....Some...things...can be, but need not be for we find them springing up and dying away....Now everything cannot be like this [for then we must conclude that] once upon a time there was nothing. But if that were true there would be noth-

ing even now, because some thing that does not exist can only be brought into being by something already existing....One is forced therefore to suppose something which must be...[and] is itself the cause that other things must be.

The FOURTH way is based on the gradation observed in things. Some things are found to be more good, more true, more noble...and other things less [so]. But such comparative terms describe varying degrees of approximation to a superlative...[something that is] the truest and best and most noble of things....There is something, therefore, which causes in all other things their being, their goodness, and whatever other perfection they have. And this we call "God."

The FIFTH way is based on the guidedness of nature. An orderedness of actions to an end is observed in all bodies obeying natural laws...; they truly tend to a goal and do not merely hit it by accident....Everything in nature, therefore, is directed to its goal by someone with intelligence, and this we call "God."

Thomas Aquinas, *Summa Theologiae, I*, ed. by Thomas Gilby (Image Books, New York: 1969), pp. 67–70.

bury (ca. 1120–1180) and Saint Bernard of Clairvaux (1090–1153), who thought the scholastic method was a heartless and presumptuous way to train minds and a threat to the church.

There were critics also within the ordinary faculty ranks, the so-called *dictatores*. These professional grammarians and rhetoricians, the forerunners of later humanists, gave students practical instruction in the composition of letters and documents. They taught good writing and speaking, and in contrast to the highly abstract logic and dialectic of scholastic education, they stressed practice over theory. (The difference might be compared with that between a modern expository writing program, in which execution is the focus, and a modern English department, wherein theory is the focus.) Later humanists, establishing an approach still favored in modern liberal arts education, would urge scholars to go directly to sources in their original languages and draw their own conclusions.

Philosophy and Theology

Scholastics quarreled over the proper relationship between philosophy (which, for them, meant almost exclusively the writings of Aristotle) and theology (which they believed to be a special "science" based on divine revelation). The problem between philosophy and theology arose because, in Christian eyes, there was a lot of heresy in Aristotle's writings, especially as his teaching was interpreted by certain Islamic commentators. These commentators did not treat his work as a handmaiden to Christianity. For example, Aristotle believed in the eternality of the world (that the world had always been). This plainly called into question the Judeo–Christian teaching that the world had been created in time, as stressed in the book of Genesis. Aristotle also taught that intellect, or mind, was ultimately one, a seeming denial of individuality and hence of Christian teaching about individual responsibility and personal immortality.

When theologians took the logic and metaphysics of Aristotle over into their theologies, some critics believed that it posed a threat to biblical teaching and traditional church authority. Berengar of Tours (d. 1088), for example, was a Scholastic who applied logic to the sacrament of the Eucharist; and before long he found himself questioning the church's teaching on transubstantiation (which was not yet official dogma). Peter Abelard (1079–1142) tried to subject the Trinity to logical examination. He found that, by Aristotle's logic, three could not be one nor one three, in contrast to the church's teachings about the unity of God the Father, Son, and Holy Ghost.

The boldness of these new logicians shocked conservatives. Monastic leaders especially wondered whether the liberal arts course of study, dominated by Aristotle's writings, was more foe than ally of theological study. The love of learning had clearly gotten in the way of the love of God as far as the critics of Scholasticism were concerned.

A century of such suspicion and criticism of Aristotle's alleged undermining of Christian theology culminated in 1277 when the bishop of Paris condemned 219 philosophical propositions. The condemnation was directed against scholars who seemed to the authorities to be more interested in secular philosophy than in Christian truth. It chilled the relationship between learning and religion. Reason and revelation thereafter became two very different spheres of knowledge, much as church and state were then also being forced apart in the world of secular politics. William of Ockham (d. 1349) represented conservative opinion on the issue and signaled its future direction when he denied that essential matters of theology could be addressed as if they were empirical. To know God's mind, Christians must content themselves with biblical revelation; reason could not know God directly.

Women in Medieval Society

The image and the reality of medieval women are two very different things. The image, both for contemporaries and for us today, was strongly influenced by the views of male Christian clergy, whose ideal was the celibate life of chastity, poverty, and obedience. Drawing on classical medical, philosophical, and legal traditions that predated Christianity, as well as on ancient biblical theology, Christian theologians depicted women as physically, mentally, and morally weaker than men.

On the basis of such assumptions, medieval church and society sanctioned the coercive treatment of women, including corrective wife beating in extreme cases. Christian clergy generally considered marriage a debased state by comparison with the religious life, and in their writings they praised virgins and celibate widows over wives. Women, as the Bible clearly taught, were the "weaker vessel." In marriage, their role was to be subject and obedient to their husbands, who, as the stronger, had a duty to protect and discipline them.

This image of the medieval woman suggests that she had two basic options in life: to become either a subjugated housewife or a confined nun. In reality, the vast majority of medieval women were neither.

IMAGE AND STATUS Both within and outside Christianity, this image of women—not yet to speak of the reality of their lives—was contradicted. In chivalric romances and courtly love literature of

A fifteenth-century rendering of an eleventh- or twelfth-century marketplace. Medieval women were active in all trades, but especially in the food and clothing industries.
Scala/Art Resource, N.Y.

the twelfth and thirteenth centuries, as in the contemporaneous cult of the Virgin Mary, women were presented as objects of service and devotion to be praised and admired—even put on pedestals and treated as superior to men. If the church shared traditional misogynist sentiments, it also condemned them, as in the case of the *Romance of the Rose* (late thirteenth century) and other popular "bawdy" literature.

The learned churchman Peter Lombard (1100–1169) sanctioned an image of women that didactic Christian literature often invoked. Why, he asked, was Eve created from Adam's rib and not instead taken from his head or his feet? The answer was clear: God took Eve from Adam's side because he wanted woman neither to rule over nor to be enslaved by man, but to stand squarely at his side, as his companion and partner in mutual aid and trust. By so insisting on the spiritual equality of men and women and their shared responsibility to one another within marriage, the church also helped to raise the dignity of women.

Germanic law treated women better than Roman law had done. Women had basic rights under law that prevented their being treated as

chattels. And there was far greater equality between the sexes: Unlike Roman women, who as teens married men much older than themselves, German women married as adults and their husbands were of similar age. Another practice unknown to the Romans was the groom's conveyance of a marriage portion, or dowry, to his bride to have and to hold as her own in the event of widowhood. All the major Germanic law codes recognized the economic freedom of women, that is, their right to inherit, administer, dispose of, and confer on their children family property and wealth. They could also press charges in court against men for bodily injury and rape. Depending on the country in question, punishments for rape ranged from fines, flogging, and banishment to blinding, castration, and death.

LIFE CHOICES   The nunnery was an option for only a very few unmarried women from the higher social classes. Entrance required a dowry (*dos*) and could be almost as expensive as a wedding, although usually it was less. Within the nunnery, a woman could rise to a position of leadership as abbess or mother superior and could exercise an organizational and administrative authority denied her in much of secular life. The nunneries of the established religious orders were under male supervision, however, so that even abbesses had finally to answer to higher male authority.

Nunneries also provided women an escape from the debilitating effects of multiple pregnancies. In the ninth century, under the influence of Christianity, the Carolingians made monogamous marriage their official policy. Heretofore they had practiced polygyny and concubinage and had permitted divorce. The result was both a boon and a burden to women. On one hand, the selection of a wife now became a very special event, and wives gained greater dignity and legal security. On the other hand, a woman's labor as household manager and bearer of children greatly increased.

The aristocratic wife not only ran a large household, but was also the agent of her husband during his absence. In addition to these responsibilities, one wife now had sole responsibility for the propagation of heirs. The Carolingian wife also became the sole object of her husband's wrath and displeasure. Such demands clearly took

their toll. The mortality rates of Frankish women increased and their longevity decreased after the ninth century.

Under such conditions, the cloister could serve as a welcome refuge to women. The number of women in cloisters was never very great, however. In late medieval England, for example, it is estimated that there were no more than 3,500 cloistered women. (See "The Regulation of Prostitutes in London (1393)."]

The vast majority of medieval women were neither aristocratic housewives nor nuns, but working women. Much evidence suggests that they were respected and loved by their husbands, perhaps because they worked shoulder by shoulder and hour by hour with them. Between the ages of ten and fifteen, girls were apprenticed in a trade much as were boys, and they learned to be skilled workers. If they married, they might continue their particular trade, operating their bakeshops or dress shops next to their husbands' business, or become assistants and partners in the shops of their husbands. Women appeared in virtually every "blue-collar" trade, from butcher to goldsmith, although they were especially

The Regulation of Prostitutes in London (1393)

As with the nunnery, the brothel was also a recognized special place for women, and, again like the nunnery, the women's activities were carefully regulated by male authority, only now for social rather than theological reasons. Prostitution was deemed to be both morally repugnant and socially necessary—an outlet for single men (married men were not supposed to frequent brothels) and thereby protection for young maidens, whose virginity was important on the marriage market. A magnet for brawling and, after the fifteenth century, a known source of venereal disease (syphilis), prostitution was subjected to strict controls in medieval towns. An ordinance of 1393 describes the concerns of London authorities and their determination to restrict prostitutes to well-monitored brothels.

❖ *Why can prostitutes not have free run of the city? Is this sensible legislation or is it gender bias? What exactly does a prostitute lose if she breaks the law?*

Whereas many...broils and dissensions have arisen in times past, and many men have been slain and murdered by reason of the frequent...consorting with common harlots, at taverns, brewhouses of [peddlars], and other places of ill-fame, within the said city and the suburbs thereof...Hence we do by our command forbid, on behalf of our Lord the King, and the Mayor and Alderman of the City of London, that any such women shall go about or

lodge in the said city, or in the suburbs thereof, by night or by day; but they are to keep themselves to the places thereunto assigned, that is to say, the [bathhouses] on the other side of [the River] Thames, and Cokkeslane; on pain of losing and forfeiting the upper garment that she shall be wearing, together with her hood [the striped clothing required of all legal prostitutes, indicating their profession]..."

Copyright © 1992. From *Women's Lives in Medieval Europe,* ed. Emilie Amt. Reproduced by permission of Taylor & Francis, Inc./Routledge, Inc., http://www.routledge-ny.com

prominent in the food and clothing industries. Women belonged to guilds, just like men, and they became craftmasters. In the later Middle Ages, townswomen increasingly had the opportunity to go to school and to gain vernacular literacy.

It is also true that women did not have as wide a range of vocations as men, although the vocational destinies of the vast majority of men were as fixed as those of women. Women were excluded from the learned professions of scholarship, medicine, and law. They often found their freedom of movement within a profession more carefully regulated than a man's. Usually, women performed the same work as men for a wage 25 percent lower. And, as is still true today, women filled the ranks of domestic servants in urban households in disproportionate numbers. Still, women remained as prominent and as creative a part of workaday medieval society as men.

The Lives of Children

The image of medieval children and the reality of their lives seem also to have been two very different things. Until recently, historians were inclined to believe that parents were emotionally distant from their children during the Middle Ages. Evidence of low esteem for children comes from a variety of sources.

Depicted are two children's pastimes: catching butterflies with a net (center child) and spinning tops (lower left). The third child is using a walker, despite his appearance of being too old to need it. All three indicate contemporary recognition of children and the stages of life they go through.   The Bridgeman Art Library International

CHILDREN AS "LITTLE ADULTS"   Some historians maintain that children are rarely portrayed as different from adults in medieval art and sculpture. If, pictorially, children and adults look alike, were people in the Middle Ages aware of childhood as a separate period of life requiring special care and treatment? There was also high infant and child mortality, which, it seems, could only have discouraged parents from making a high emotional investment in their children. How could a parent dare to have a deep emotional attachment to a child who had a 30–50 percent chance of dying before age five?

During the Middle Ages, children assumed adult responsibilities early in life. The children of peasants labored in the fields alongside their parents as soon as they could physically manage the work. Urban artisans and burghers sent their children out of their homes into apprenticeships in various crafts and trades between the ages of eight and twelve. Can such early removal of children from their homes be taken for anything but low affection for children? That children were expected to grow up fast is attested to by the canonical ages for marriage, twelve for girls and fourteen for boys (although few actually married at these ages).

The practice of infanticide is an even more striking suggestion of low esteem for children in ancient and early medieval times. According to Tacitus, the Romans exposed unwanted children, especially girls, at birth. In this way, they regulated family size. The surviving children appear to have been given plenty of attention and affection. The Germanic tribes of medieval Europe, by contrast, had large families, but tended to neglect their children in comparison with the Romans. Infanticide, particularly of girls, continued to be practiced in the early Middle Ages, as shown by its condemnation in penance books and by church synods. Parents were forbidden to sleep with infants and small children to prevent them from being suffocated, either by accident or by design.

Among the German tribes, one paid a much lower *wergild*, or compensatory fine, for injury to a child than for injury to an adult. The *wergild* for injuring a child was only one-fifth that for injuring an adult. That paid for injury to a female child under fifteen was one-half that for injury to a male child—a strong indication that female children were the least esteemed members of German tribal society. Mothers appear also to have nursed boys longer than they did girls, which favored boys' health and survival. A woman's *wergild*, however, increased a full eightfold between infancy and her childbearing years, at which time she had obviously become highly prized.[4]

---

[4] David Herlihy, "Medieval Children," in *Essays on Medieval Civilization*, ed. by B. K. Lackner and K. R. Phelp (Austin, TX: University of Texas Press, 1978), pp. 109–131.

CHILDHOOD AS A SPECIAL STAGE Despite such varied evidence of parental distance and neglect, there is another side to the story. Since the early Middle Ages, physicians and theologians, at least, had understood childhood to be a distinct and special stage of life. Isidore (560–636), the metropolitan of Seville and a leading intellectual authority throughout the Middle Ages, carefully distinguished six ages of life, the first four of which were infancy (between one and seven years of age), childhood (seven to fourteen), adolescence, and youth.

According to the medical authorities, infancy proper extended from birth to anywhere between six months and two years (depending on the authority) and covered the period of speechlessness and suckling. The period thereafter, until age seven, was considered a higher level of infancy, marked by the beginning of a child's ability to speak and his or her weaning. At age seven, when a child could think and act decisively and speak clearly, childhood proper began. After this point, a child could be reasoned with, could profit from regular discipline, and could begin to train for a lifelong vocation. At seven a child was ready for schooling, private tutoring, or apprenticeship in a chosen craft or trade. Until physical growth was completed, however—and that could extend to twenty-one years of age—the child or youth was legally under the guardianship of parents or a surrogate authority.

There is evidence that high infant and child mortality, rather than distancing parents from children, actually made parents look on children as all the more precious. The medical authorities respected during the Middle Ages—Hippocrates, Galen, and Soranus of Ephesus—dealt at length with postnatal care and childhood diseases. Both in learned and in popular medicine, sensible as well as fanciful cures can be found for the leading killers of children (diarrhea, worms, pneumonia, and fever). When infants and children died, medieval parents grieved as pitiably as modern parents do. In the art and literature of the Middle Ages, we find mothers baptizing dead infants and children or carrying them to pilgrim shrines in the hope of reviving them. There are also examples of mental illness and suicide brought on by the death of a child.[5]

Clear evidence of special attention being paid to children is also found in the great variety of children's toys and even devices like walkers and potty chairs, which existed in the Middle Ages. The medieval authorities on child rearing widely condemned child abuse and urged moderation in the disciplining of children. In church art and drama, parents were urged to love their children as Mary loved Jesus. And early apprenticeships may also be interpreted as an expression of parental love and concern rather than indifference and low esteem. For in the Middle Ages, no parental responsibility was thought greater than that of equipping a child for useful and gainful work. Certainly, by the High Middle Ages if not earlier, children were widely viewed as special creatures with their own needs and rights.

In Perspective

During the High Middle Ages, the growth of Mediterranean trade revived old cities and caused the creation of new ones. The Crusades aided and abetted this development. Italian cities especially flourished during the late eleventh and twelfth centuries. Venice dominated Mediterranean trade and extended its political and economic influence throughout the Near East. It had its own safe ports as far away as Syria. As cities grew in population and became rich with successful trade, a new social group, the long-distance traders, rose to prominence. By marriage and political organization, these merchant families organized themselves into an unstoppable force. They successfully challenged the old nobility in and around the cities. A new elite of merchants gained control of city governments almost everywhere. They brought with them a policy of open trade and the blessings and problems of nascent capitalism. Artisans and small shopkeepers at the lower end of the economic spectrum aspired to follow their example, as new opportunities opened for all. The seeds of social conflict and of urban class struggle had been sown.

One very positive result of the new wealth of towns was the patronage of education and culture. These matters were given an emphasis not experienced since Roman times. Western Europe's first universities appeared in the eleventh century and universities steadily expanded over the next four centuries. There were twenty by 1300. Not only did Scholasticism flourish, but a new literature, art, and architecture developed as well, reflecting both a new human vitality and the reshaping of society and politics. For all of this, western Europeans had no one to thank so much as the new class of merchants, whose greed, daring, and ambition made it all possible.

---

[5] Klaus Arnold, *Kind und Gesellschaft im Mittelalter und Renaissance* (Paderborn, Germany: 1980), pp. 31, 37.

REVIEW QUESTIONS

1. How did the responsibilities of the nobility differ from those of the clergy and the peasantry during the High Middle Ages? In what ways did each social class contribute to the stability of society?
2. What led to the revival of trade and the growth of towns in the twelfth century? What political and social conditions were essential for a revival of trade? How did towns change medieval society?
3. From your understanding of the functions of the medieval university, assess the strengths and weaknesses of higher education in that period. Comment especially on the curriculum.
4. How would you define Scholasticism? What was the Scholastic program and method of study? Who were the main critics of Scholasticism and what were their complaints?
5. How would you assess the position of women in Germanic law and Roman law? What were the options and responsibilities for women in each social class? What are the differing theories regarding the image of children in the Middle Ages?

SUGGESTED READINGS

E. AMT (ED.), *Women's Lives in Medieval Europe: A Sourcebook* (1993). Outstanding collection of sources.

P. ARIÈS, *Centuries of Childhood: A Social History of Family Life* (1962). Pioneer effort on the subject.

J. W. BALDWIN, *The Scholastic Culture of the Middle Ages: 1000–1300* (1971). Best brief synthesis available.

M. BLOCH, *French Rural History*, trans. by J. Sondheimer (1966). A classic by a great modern historian.

J. BRUNDAGE, *Law, Sex and Christian Society in Medieval Europe* (1987). The Church's conception and regulation of sexuality.

G. DUBY, *The Three Orders: Feudal Society Imagined*, trans. by A. Goldhammer (1981). Large, comprehensive, authoritative.

E. GILSON, *Heloise and Abelard* (1968). Analysis and defense of medieval scholarly and gender values.

J. GOODY, *The Development of the Family and Marriage in Europe* (1983). Interesting effort to explain the Church's stake in the regulation of family and marriage.

B. A. HANAWALT, *The Ties That Bound: Peasant Families in Medieval England* (1986). Illuminating demographic and economic study of rural life.

B. A. HANAWALT, *Growing Up in Medieval London* (1993). Excellent, positive portrayal of parental and societal treatment of children.

C. H. HASKINS, *The Renaissance of the Twelfth Century* (1927). Still the standard account.

C. H. HASKINS, *The Rise of Universities* (1972). A short, minor classic.

D. HERLIHY, *Medieval Households* (1985). Bread-and-butter account of household structure in antiquity and the Middle Ages.

G. KÜNSTLER, *Romanesque Art in Europe* (1973). Standard survey.

G. LEFF, *Paris and Oxford Universities in the Thirteenth and Fourteenth Centuries: An Institutional and Intellectual History (1968).* Very good on Scholastic debates.

R. S. LOOMIS (ED.), *The Development of Arthurian Romance* (1963). Essays debating its meaning and significance.

R. LOPEZ, *The Commercial Revolution of the Middle Ages 900–1350* (1971). A master's brief survey.

E. MÂLE, *The Gothic Image: Religious Art in France in the Thirteenth Century* (1913). An enduring classic.

L. DE MAUSE (ED.), *The History of Childhood* (1974). Very substantive and provocative essays with an interest in the inner as well as the material lives of children.

R. I. MOORE, *The Formation of a Persecuting Society: Power and Deviance in Western Europe, 950–1250* (1987). A sympathetic look at heresy and dissent.

A. MURRAY, *Reason and Society in the Middle Ages* (1978). A view of the Middle Ages as an age of reason as well as of faith.

J. T. NOONAN, *Contraception: A History of Its Treatment by the Catholic Theologians and Canonists* (1967). Fascinating account of medieval theological attitudes toward sexuality and sex-related problems.

E. PANOFSKY, *Gothic Architecture and Scholasticism* (1951). A controversial classic.

H. PIRENNE, *Medieval Cities: Their Origins and the Revival of Trade*, trans. by F. D. Halsey (1970). A minor classic.

H. RASHDALL, *The Universities of Europe in the Middle Ages*, vols. 1–3 (1936). Dated, but still extremely useful for documents of the period.

I. S. ROBINSON, *The Papacy, 1073–1198: Continuity and Innovation* (1990). A fresh look at the papacy in this period of its reform and independence.

S. SHAHAR, *The Fourth Estate: A History of Women in the Middle Ages* (1983). A comprehensive survey, making clear the great variety of women's work.

B. STOCK, *The Implications of Literacy* (1983). How the ability to read changed medieval society.

L. THORNDIKE, *University Records and Life in the Middle Ages* (1975). Rich primary sources for both curricular and extracurricular life.

The Invention of Printing in China and Europe

The ability to put information and ideas on paper and to circulate them widely in multiple identical copies has been credited in the West with the rise of Humanism, the Protestant Reformation, the modern state, and the Scientific Revolution. In truth, the message preceded the machinery: It was a preexisting desire to rule more effectively, to shape and control the course of events that brought the printing press into existence in both China and Europe. Before there was printing, there were rulers, religious leaders, and merchants eager to disperse their laws, scriptures, and wares more widely and efficiently among their subjects, followers, and customers.

To create the needed skilled agents and bureaucrats, leaders of state, church, and business cooperated in the sponsorship of schools and education, which spurred the growth of reading and writing among the middle and upper urban classes. Literacy, in turn, fueled the desire for easily accessible and reliable information. Literacy came more slowly to the lower social classes, as authorities feared too much knowledge in the hands of the uneducated or poorly educated would only fan the fires of discontent. To the many who remained illiterate after the invention of printing, information was conveyed carefully in oral and pictorial form. Printed official statements were designed to be read to as well as read by people, and religious leaders put images and pictures in the hands of simple folk, hoping to content them with saints and charms.

Resources and Technology: Paper and Ink

Among the indispensable materials of the print revolution were sizable supplies of durable, inexpensive paper and a reliable ink. As early as the Shang period (1766–1122 B.C.E.) a water-based soot and gum ink was used across Asia. (Europe would not have such an ink until the early Middle Ages.) Also in the Shang period, official seals and stamps used to authenticate documents were made by carving bronze, jade, ivory, gold, and stone in a reverse direction (that is, in a mirror form, to prevent the print from appearing backwards).

Similar seals appeared in ancient Mesopotamia and Egypt but only for religious use, not for the affairs of daily secular life. Later, more easily carved clay or wax seals reproduced characters on silk or bamboo surfaces.

Silk in the East and parchment in the West had been early, but very expensive, print media. Bamboo and wood were cheaper, but neither was suited to large-scale printing.

A step forward occurred in the second century B.C.E, when the Chinese invented a crude paper from hemp fibers, which was used only for wrappings. Three centuries later (105 C.E.), an imperial eunuch named Ts'ia Lun combined tree bark, hemp, rags, and old fish nets into a superior paper on which one could reliably write. A better blend of mulberry bark, fish nets, and natural fibers became the standard paper mixture. By the Tang period (618–907), high-quality paper manufacturing had become a major industry.

In the eighth century, the improved Chinese recipe began to make its way west, after Chinese prisoners taught their Arab captors how to make paper. By the ninth century, Samarkand in Russian Turkestan had become the leading supplier of paper in the East. A century later, Baghdad and Damascus shipped fine paper to Egypt and Europe. Italy became a major Western manufacturer in the thirteenth century followed by Nuremberg, Germany, in the late fourteenth.

Early Printing Techniques

By the seventh century C.E., multiple copies of the Confucian Scriptures were made by taking paper rubbings from stone and metal engravings, a direct prelude to block printing. At this time in the West, the arts of engraving, and particularly of coin-casting (by hammering hot alloy on an anvil that bore a carved design), took the first steps toward printing with movable type.

The invention of printing occurred much earlier in the East than in the West. The Chinese invented "block printing" (that is, printing with carved wooden blocks) in the eighth century, almost six hundred years before the technique appeared in Europe (1395). The Chinese also far outpaced the West in printing with "movable type" (that is, with individual char-

The Diamond Sutra. This Chinese translation of a Sanskrit Buddhist work was printed in 868 and found at Tunhuang. It is the earliest dated piece of block printing yet discovered.
The Granger Collection

acters or letters that could be arranged by hand to make a page)—a technique invented by Pi Scheng in the 1040s, four hundred years before Johann Gutenberg set up the first Western press in Mainz, Germany (around 1450).

Block printing used hard wood (preferably from pear or jujube trees), whose surface was glazed with a filler (glue, wax, or clay). A paper copy of what one wanted to duplicate (be it a drawn image, a written sentence, or both) was placed face down on a wet glaze covering the block and the characters cut into it. The process accommodated any artistic style while allowing text and illustration to coexist harmoniously on a page. Once carved, the block was inked and mild pressure applied, allowing a great many copies to be made before it wore out.

The first movable type was ceramic. The printer set each character or piece in an iron form and arranged them on an iron baking plate filled with heated resin and wax which, when cooled, created a tight page. After the print run was finished, the plate was heated again to melt the wax and free the type for new settings. Ceramic and later metal type were fragile and left uneven impressions, and metal type was expensive as well and did not hold water-based Chinese inks.

Carved wooden type did not have these problems and therefore became the preferred tool. Set in a wooden frame and tightened with wooden wedges, the readied page was inked up and an impression made, just as in printing with carved wooden blocks. Cutting a complete set of type or font required much time and effort because of the complexity and enormity of Chinese script. To do the latter justice, a busy press required 10,000 individual characters, and that number could increase several-fold, depending on the project.

Printing Comes of Age

In 952, after a quarter century of preparation, a standardized Chinese text, unblemished by any scribal errors, was printed for the first time on a large scale.

That text, the Confucian Classics, was an epochal event in the history of printing. The main reading of the elite, these famous scrolls became the basis of the entry exam for a government office. In awakening people to the power of printing, the Confucian Classics may be compared to the publication of Gutenberg's Latin Bible.

The Sung period (960–1278) saw the first sustained flowering of block printing. Still today among the Chinese the phrase "Sung style" connotes high quality. Three monumental publications stand out: the Standard Histories of previous Chinese dynasties, serially appearing between 994 and 1063; the Buddhist Scriptures in scrolls up to sixty feet and longer, requiring 130,000 carved wooden blocks (971–983); and the Taoist Scriptures (early eleventh century). For the literate, but not necessarily highly educated, numerous how-to books on medical, botanical, and agricultural topics became available. Printed paper money also appeared for the first time in copper-poor Szechwan during the Sung.

There is no certain evidence that printing was a complete gift of the Far East to the West. Although some scholars believe that Chinese block printing accompanied playing cards through the Islamic world and into Europe, the actual connecting links have not yet been demonstrated. So while there was a definite "paper trail" from East to West, Europe appears to have developed its own inks and invented its own block and movable type printing presses independently.[1]

Indeed in East and West, different writing systems would favor distinct forms of printing: In China, carved wood blocks suited an ideographic script that required a seemingly boundless number of characters. Each ideograph, or character, expressed a complete concept. In contrast, European writing was based on a very small phonetic alphabet. Each letter could express meaning only when connected to other letters, forming words. For such a system, movable metal type worked far better than carved wood blocks. So while China mastered movable type printing earlier than the West, the enormous number of characters required by the Chinese language made movable type impractical.

A European Printshop. This 1568 woodcut by Hans Sachs shows typesetting (rear) and printing (front) underway in an early printshop. Printing made it possible to reproduce exactly and in quantity both text and illustrations, leading to the distribution of scientific and technical information on a scale unimaginable in the pre-print world. Houghton Library, Harvard University

Ironically, the simpler machinery of block printing did greater justice to China's more intricate and complex script, while Europe's far simpler script required the more complex machinery of movable type. Today the Chinese still face the problem of storing and retrieving their rich language in digitized form, "the space-age equivalent of movable type." In telecommunications, they prefer faxes, "the modern-day equivalent of the block print."[2]

Society and Printing

In neither East nor West do the availability of essential material resources (wood, ink, and paper) and the development of new technologies sufficiently

[1]Carter, *The Invention of Printing in China and Its Spread Westward*, pp. 143, 150, 182.

[2]Twitchett, *Printing and Publishing in Medieval China*, p. 86.

286

explain the advent of printing. Cultural and emotional factors played an equally large role. In China, the religious and moral demands of Buddhists, Taoists, and Confucians lay behind the invention of block printing. For Buddhists, copying and disseminating their sacred writings had always been a traditional path of salvation. Taoists wanted to hang protective charms or seals around their necks, printed sacred messages blessed by their priests that were up to four inches wide. These were apparently the first block prints. Confucianists, too, lobbied for standardized printed copies of their texts, which they had for centuries duplicated by crude rubbings from stone-carved originals.

In Europe, the major religious orders (Augustinians, Dominicans, and Franciscans) and popular lay religious movements (Waldensians, Lollards, and Hussites) joined with Humanists to promote the printing of standardized, orthodox editions of the Bible and other religious writings. As the numbers of literate laity steadily grew, the demand for cheap, practical reading material (calendars, newssheets, and how-to pamphlets) also rapidly increased. By 1500, fifty years after Gutenberg's invention, two hundred printing presses operated throughout Europe, sixty of them in German cities. And just as in China, the large print runs of the new presses tended to be religious or moral subjects in the early years: Latin Bibles and religious books, indulgences and Protestant pamphlets, along with decorated playing cards often bearing moral messages.

With the printing press came the first copyright laws. Knowledge had previously been considered to be "free." The great majority of medieval scholars and writers were clergy, who lived by church or other patronage and whose knowledge was deemed a gift of God to be shared freely with all. After the printing press, however, a new sense of intellectual property emerged. In Europe, primitive protective laws took the form of a ruler's "privilege," by which a ruler pledged to punish the pirating of a particular work within his or her realm over a limited period of time. Such measures had clear limits: More than half of the books published during the first century of print in the West were pirated editions, a situation that would not change significantly until the eighteenth century.

Government censorship laws also ran apace with the growth of printing. The clergy of Cologne, Germany, issued the first prohibition of heretical books in 1479. In 1485 the church banned the works of the heretics John Wycliffe and John Huss Europe-wide, and two years later the pope promulgated the first bull against any and all books "harmful to the faith." In 1521 Emperor Charles V banned Martin Luther's works throughout the Holy Roman Empire, along with their author. In 1527 the first publisher was hanged for printing a banned book of Luther's. And in 1559 the pope established the Index of Forbidden Books, which still exists.

Printing stimulated numerous new ancillary trades. In addition to the proliferation of bookstores and the rise of traveling booksellers, who carried flyers from town to town promoting particular works, there were new speciality stationery shops, ink and inkstone stores, bookshelf and reading-table makers, and businesses manufacturing brushes and other printing tools. The new print industry also brought social and economic upheaval to city and countryside when, like modern corporations relocating factories to underdeveloped countries, it went in search of cheaper labor by moving presses out of guild-dominated cities and into the freer marketplace of the countryside.

For society's authorities, the new numbers of literate citizens and subjects made changes and reforms both easier and more difficult. As a tool of propaganda, the printing press remained a two-edged sword. On the one hand, it gave authorities the means to propagandize more effectively than ever. On the other hand, the new literate public found itself in an unprecedented position to recognize deceit, challenge tradition, and expose injustice.

❖ Why did the invention of printing occur earlier in the East than in the West? Did the West inherit all of its knowledge of printing from the East? What are the differences between Chinese and European writing systems? What problems do these systems create for printing? Why might one Chinese scholar prefer to send another Chinese scholar a fax rather than an e-mail? What was the impact of printing on Chinese and European societies?

Sources: Thomas F. Carter, *The Invention of Printing in China and Its Spread Westward* (1925). Elisabeth L. Eisensrein, *The Printing Press as an Agent of Change*, I–II (1979). Rudolf Hirsch, *Printing, Selling and Reading 1450–1550* (1967). Constance R. Miller, *Technical and Cultural Prerequisites for the Invention of Printing in China and the West* (1983). Denis Twitchett, *Printing and Publishing in Medieval China* (1983).

Part 3
1300–1750

	POLITICS AND GOVERNMENT	SOCIETY AND ECONOMY	RELIGION AND CULTURE
1300–1400	1309–1377 Pope resides in Avignon 1337–1453 Hundred Years' War 1356 *Golden Bull* creates German electoral college	1315–1317 Greatest famine of the Middle Ages 1347–1350 Black Death peaks 1358 *Jacquerie* shakes France 1378 Ciompi Revolt in Florence 1381 English peasants' revolt	1300–1325 Dante Alighieri writes *Divine Comedy* 1302 Boniface VIII issues bull *Unam Sanctam* 1350 Boccaccio, *Decameron* 1375–1527 The Renaissance in Italy 1378–1417 The Great Schism 1380–1395 Chaucer writes *Canterbury Tales* 1390–1430 Christine de Pisan writes in defense of women
1400–1500	1415–1433 Hussite revolt in Bohemia 1428–1519 Aztecs expand in central Mexico 1429 Joan of Arc leads French to victory in Orleans 1434 Medici rule begins in Florence 1453–1471 Wars of the Roses in England 1469 Marriage of Ferdinand and Isabella 1487 Henry Tudor creates Court of Star Chamber	1450 Johann Gutenberg invents printing with movable type 1492 Christopher Columbus encounters the Americas 1498 Vasco da Gama reaches India	1414–1417 The Council of Constance 1425–1450 Lorenzo Valla exposes the *Donation of Constantine* 1450 Thomas à Kempis, *Imitation of Christ* 1492 Expulsion of Jews from Spain
1500–1600	1519 Charles V crowned Holy Roman emperor 1530 *Augsburg Confession* defines Lutheranism 1547 Ivan the Terrible becomes tsar of Russia 1555 *Peace of Augsburg* recognizes the legal principle, *cuius regio, eius religio* 1568–1603 Reign of Elizabeth I of England 1572 Saint Bartholomew's Day Massacre 1588 English defeat of Spanish Armada 1598 Edict of Nantes gives Huguenots religious and civil rights	1519 Hernan Cortes lands in Mexico 1519–1522 Ferdinand Magellan circumnavigates the Earth 1525 German Peasants' Revolt 1531–1533 Francisco Pizarro conquers the Incas 1540 Spanish open silver mines in Peru, Bolivia, and Mexico 1550–1600 The great witch panics Elizabeth I, The Armada Portrait	1513 Niccolo Machiavelli, *The Prince* 1516 Erasmus compiles a Greek New Testament 1516 Thomas More, *Utopia* 1517 Martin Luther's Ninety-five theses 1534 Henry VIII declared head of English Church 1540 Jesuit order founded 1541 John Calvin becomes Geneva's reformer 1543 Copernicus, *On the Revolutions of the Heavenly Spheres* 1545–1563 Council of Trent 1549 English *Book of Common Prayer*

EUROPE IN TRANSITION
1300–1750

POLITICS AND GOVERNMENT	SOCIETY AND ECONOMY	RELIGION AND CULTURE

1600–1700

POLITICS AND GOVERNMENT	SOCIETY AND ECONOMY	RELIGION AND CULTURE
1624–1642 Era of Richelieu in France	1600–1700 Period of greatest Dutch economic prosperity	1605 Bacon, *The Advancement of Learning*; Shakespeare, *King Lear*; Cervantes, *Don Quixote*
1629–1640 Charles I's years of personal rule	1600–early 1700s Spain maintains commercial monopoly in Latin America	1609 Kepler, *The New Astronomy*
1640 Long Parliament convenes	1607 English settle Jamestown, Virginia	1611 King James Version of the English Bible
1642 Outbreak of civil war in England	1608 French settle Quebec	1632 Galileo, *Dialogues on the Two Chief Systems of the World*
1643–1661 Cardinal Mazarin regent for Louis XIV	1618–1648 Thirty Years' War devastates German economy	1637 Descartes, *Discourse on Method*
1648 Peace of Westphalia	1619 African slaves first bought at Jamestown, Virginia	1651 Hobbes, *Leviathan*
1649–1652 The *Fronde* in France	1650s–1670s Commercial rivalry between Dutch and English	
1649 Charles I executed		
1660 Charles II restored to the English throne	1661–1683 Colbert seeks to stimulate French economic growth	1687 Newton, *Principia Mathematica*
1661–1715 Louis XIV's years of personal rule		1689 English Toleration Act
1682–1725 Reign of Peter the Great		
1685 James II becomes king of England	1690 Paris Foundling Hospital established	1690 Locke, *Essay Concerning Human Understanding*
Louis XIV revokes Edict of Nantes		
1688 "Glorious Revolution" in Britain		

1700–1789

POLITICS AND GOVERNMENT	SOCIETY AND ECONOMY	RELIGION AND CULTURE
1700–1721 Great Northern War between Sweden and Russia	1715–1763 Era of major colonial rivalry in the Caribbean	1739 Wesley begins field preaching
1702–1714 War of Spanish Succession	1719 Mississippi Bubble in France	1748 Montesquieu, *Spirit of the Laws*
1713 Peace of Utrecht	1733 James Kay's flying shuttle	1750 Rousseau, *Discourse on the Moral Effects of the Arts and Sciences*
1720–1740 Age of Walpole in England and Fleury in France	1750s Agricultural Revolution in Britain	
1740 Maria Theresa succeeds to the Habsburg throne	1750–1840 Growth of new cities	1751 First volume Diderot's *Encyclopedia*
1740–1748 War of the Austrian Succession	1763 Britain becomes dominant in India	1762 Rousseau, *Social Contract* and *Émile*
1756–1763 Seven Years' War	1763–1789 Enlightened absolutist rulers seek to spur economic growth	1763 Voltaire, Treatise on Tolerance
1767 Legislative Commission in Russia	1765 James Hargreaves's spinning jenny	
1772 First Partition of Poland	1769 Richard Arkwright's waterframe	1774 Goethe, *Sorrow of Young Werther*
1776 American Declaration of Independence	1771–1775 Pugachev's Rebellion	1776 Smith, *Wealth of Nations*
		1781 Kant, *Critique of Pure Reason*
		Joseph II adopts policy of toleration in Austria

Declaration of Independence

1778 France aids the American colonies

Chapter 9

The apparition of the Knight of Death, an allegory of the plague approaching a city, whose defenses against it are all too unsure. From the *Tres Riches Heures du Duc de Berry* (1284), Limbourg Brothers. Ms. 65/1284, fol. 90v. Musée Conde, Chantilly, France. Giraudon/Art Resource, N.Y.

The Late Middle Ages:
Social and Political Breakdown
(1300–1527)

KEY TOPICS

- The Hundred Years' War between England and France
- The effects of the bubonic plague on population and society
- The growing power of secular rulers over the papacy
- Schism, heresy, and reform of the church

The late Middle Ages saw almost unprecedented political, social, and ecclesiastical calamity. France and England grappled with each other in a bitter conflict known as the Hundred Years' War (1337–1453), an exercise in seemingly willful self-destruction that was made even more terrible in its later stages by the introduction of gunpowder and the invention of heavy artillery. Bubonic plague, known to contemporaries as the "Black Death," swept over almost all of Europe, killing as much as one-third of the population in many regions between 1348 and 1350 and transforming many pious Christians into believers in the omnipotence of death. A schism emerged within the church, which lasted thirty-nine years (1378–1417) and led, by 1409, to the election of no fewer than three competing popes and colleges of cardinals. In 1453, the Turks marched seemingly invincibly through Constantinople and toward the West. As their political and religious institutions buckled, as disease, bandits, and wolves ravaged their cities in the wake of war, and as Islamic armies gathered at their borders, Europeans beheld what seemed to be the imminent total collapse of Western civilization.

It was in this period that such scholars as Marsilius of Padua, William of Ockham, and Lorenzo Valla produced lasting criticisms of medieval assumptions about the nature of God, humankind, and society. Kings worked through parliaments and clergy through councils to place lasting limits on the pope's temporal power. The notion, derived from Roman law, that a secular ruler is accountable to the body of which he or she is head had already found expression in documents like the Magna Carta. It came increasingly to carry the force of accepted principle, and conciliarists (advocates of the judicial superiority of a church council over a pope) sought to extend it to establish papal accountability to the church.

But viewed in terms of their three great calamities—war, plague, and schism—the fourteenth and fifteenth centuries were years in which politics resisted wisdom, nature strained mercy, and the church was less than faithful to its mandate.

The Hundred Years' War and the Rise of National Sentiment

Medieval governments were by no means all-powerful and secure. The rivalry of petty lords kept localities in turmoil, and dynastic rivalries could plunge entire lands into war, especially when power was being transferred to a new ruler, and woe to the ruling dynasty that failed to produce a male heir.

To field the armies and collect the revenues that made their existence possible, late medieval rulers depended on carefully negotiated alliances among a wide range of lesser powers. Like kings and queens in earlier centuries, they, too, practiced the art of feudal government, but on a grander scale and with greater sophistication. To maintain the order they required, the Norman kings of England and the Capetian kings of France finetuned traditional feudal relationships, stressing the duties of lesser to higher power and the unquestioning loyalty noble vassals owed the king. The result was a degree of centralized royal power unseen before in these lands and a nascent "national" consciousness that equipped both France and England for international warfare.

The Causes of the War

The conflict that came to be known as the Hundred Years' War began in May 1337 and lasted until October 1453. The English king Edward III (r. 1327–1377), the grandson of Philip the Fair of France (r. 1285–1314), may be said to have started the war by asserting a claim to the French throne when the French king Charles IV (r. 1322–1328), the last of Philip the Fair's surviving sons, died without a male heir. The French barons had no intention of placing the then fifteen-year-old Edward on the French throne, choosing instead the first cousin of Charles IV, Philip VI of Valois (r. 1328–1350), the first of a new French dynasty that ruled into the sixteenth century.

But there was more to the war than just an English king's assertion of a claim to the French throne. England and France were then emergent territorial powers in too close proximity to one another. Edward was actually a vassal of Philip's, holding several sizable French territories as fiefs from the king of France, a relationship that went back to the days of the Norman conquest. English possession of any French land was repugnant to the French because it threatened the royal policy of centralization. England and France also quarreled over control of Flanders, which, although a French fief, was subject to political influence from England because its principal industry, the manufacture of cloth, depended on supplies of imported English wool. Compounding these frictions was a long history of prejudice and animosity between the French and English people, who constantly confronted one another on the high seas and in port towns. Taken together, these various factors made the Hundred Years' War a struggle for national identity as well as for control of territory.

FRENCH WEAKNESS   France had three times the population of England, was far the wealthier of the two countries, and fought on its own soil. Yet, for the greater part of the conflict, until after 1415, the major battles ended in often stunning English victories. (See Map 9–1.) The primary reason for these French failures was internal disunity caused by endemic social conflicts. Unlike England,

Edward III pays homage to his feudal lord Philip VI of France. Legally, Edward was a vassal of the king of France. Archives Snark International/Art Resource, N.Y.

MAP 9–1 THE HUNDRED YEARS' WAR *The Hundred Years' War went on intermittently from the late 1330s until 1453. These maps show the remarkable English territorial gains up to the sudden and decisive turning of the tide of battle in favor of the French by the forces of Joan of Arc in 1429.*

Scene from an encamped army, surrounded by a barricade of wagons, some of which contain artillery pointed outward. 15th-century Germany. Kunstammlungen der Frusten zu Waldburg-Wolfegg, fol. 54r

France was still struggling in the fourteenth century to make the transition from a fragmented feudal society to a centralized "modern" state.

Desperate to raise money for the war, French kings resorted to such financial policies as depreciating the currency and borrowing heavily from Italian bankers, which aggravated internal conflicts. In 1355, in a bid to secure funds, the king convened a representative council of townspeople and nobles that came to be known as the Estates General. Although it levied taxes at the king's request, its members also used the king's plight to enhance their own regional rights and privileges, thereby deepening territorial divisions.

France's defeats also reflected English military superiority. The English infantry was more disciplined than the French, and English archers carried a formidable weapon, the longbow, capable of firing six arrows a minute with enough force to pierce an inch of wood or the armor of a knight at two hundred yards.

Finally, French weakness during the Hundred Years' War was due in no small degree to the comparative mediocrity of its royal leadership. English kings were far the shrewder.

Progress of the War

The war had three major stages of development, each ending with a seemingly decisive victory by one or the other side.

THE CONFLICT DURING THE REIGN OF EDWARD III In the first stage of the war, Edward embargoed English wool to Flanders, sparking urban rebellions by merchants and the trade guilds. Inspired by a rich merchant, Jacob van Artevelde, the Flemish cities, led by Ghent, revolted against the French and in 1340 signed an alliance with England acknowledging Edward as king of France. On June 23 of that same year, in the first great battle of the war, Edward defeated the French fleet in the Bay of Sluys, but his subsequent effort to invade France by way of Flanders failed.

In 1346 Edward attacked Normandy and, after a series of easy victories that culminated at the Battle of Crécy, seized Calais. Exhaustion of both sides and the onset of the Black Death forced a truce in late 1347, and the war entered a brief lull. In 1356, near Poitiers, the English won their greatest victory, rout-

This miniature illustrates two scenes from the English peasant revolt of 1381. On the left, Wat Tyler, one of the leaders of the revolt, is executed in the presence of King Richard II. On the right, King Richard urges armed peasants to end their rebellion. Arthur Hacker, *The Cloister of the World.* The Bridgeman Art Library.

ing France's noble cavalry and taking the French king, John II the Good (r. 1350–1364), captive back to England. The defeat brought a complete breakdown of political order to France.

Power in France now lay with the Estates General. Led by the powerful merchants of Paris under Étienne Marcel, that body took advantage of royal weakness, demanding and receiving rights similar to those granted the English privileged classes in the Magna Carta. But unlike the English Parliament, which represented the interests of a comparatively unified English nobility, the French Estates General was too divided to be an instrument for effective government.

To secure their rights, the French privileged classes forced the peasantry to pay ever-increasing taxes and to repair their war-damaged properties without compensation. This bullying became more than the peasants could bear, and they rose up in several regions in a series of bloody rebellions known as the *Jacquerie* in 1358 (after the peasant revolutionary popularly known as *Jacques Bonhomme*, or "simple Jack"). The nobility quickly put down the revolt, matching the rebels atrocity for atrocity.

On May 9, 1360, another milestone of the war was reached when England forced the Peace of Brétigny on the French. This agreement declared an end to Edward's vassalage to the king of France and affirmed his sovereignty over English territories in France (including Gascony, Guyenne, Poitou, and Calais). France also agreed to pay a ransom of three million gold crowns to win King John the Good's release. In return, Edward simply renounced his claim to the French throne.

Such a partition of French territorial control was completely unrealistic, and sober observers on both sides knew that it could not last long. France struck back in the late 1360s and by the time of Edward's death in 1377 had beaten the English back to coastal enclaves and the territory of Bordeaux.

FRENCH DEFEAT AND THE TREATY OF TROYES After Edward's death the English war effort lessened, partly because of domestic problems within England. During the reign of Richard II (r. 1377–1399), England had its own version of the *Jacquerie*. In June 1381, long-oppressed peasants and artisans joined in a great revolt of the unprivileged classes under the leadership of John Ball, a secular priest, and Wat Tyler, a journeyman. As in France, the revolt was brutally crushed within the year, but it left the country divided for decades.

The war intensified under Henry V (r. 1413–1422), who took advantage of internal French turmoil created by the rise to power of the duchy of Burgundy. With France deeply divided, Henry V struck hard in Normandy. Happy to see the rest of France besieged, the Burgundians foolishly watched from the sidelines while Henry's army routed the opposition led by the count of Armagnac, who had picked up the royal banner at Agincourt on October 25, 1415. In the years thereafter, belatedly recognizing that the defeat of

France would leave them easy prey for the English, the Burgundians closed ranks with French royal forces. The renewed French unity, loose as it was, promised to bring eventual victory over the English, but it was shattered in September 1419 when the duke of Burgundy was assassinated. In the aftermath of this shocking event, the duke's son and heir, determined to avenge his father's death, joined forces with the English.

France now became Henry V's for the taking—at least in the short run. The Treaty of Troyes in 1420 disinherited the legitimate heir to the French throne and proclaimed Henry V the successor to the French king, Charles VI. When Henry and Charles died within months of one another in 1422, the infant Henry VI of England was proclaimed in Paris to be king of both France and England. The dream of Edward III that had set the war in motion—to make the ruler of England the ruler also of France—had been realized, at least for the moment.

The son of Charles VI went into retreat in Bourges, where, on the death of his father, he became Charles VII to most of the French people, who ignored the Treaty of Troyes. Displaying unprecedented national feeling inspired by the remarkable Joan of Arc, they soon rallied to his cause and came together in an ultimately victorious coalition.

A contemporary portrait of Joan of Arc (1412–1431) in the National Archives in Paris. 15th c. Franco-Flemish miniature. Archives Nationales, Paris, France. Giraudon/Art Resource, N.Y.

The Hundred Years' War (1337–1443)

1340	English victory at Bay of Sluys
1346	English victory at Crécy and seizure of Calais
1347	Black Death strikes
1356	English victory at Poitiers
1358	*Jacquerie* disrupts France
1360	Peace of Brétigny recognizes English holdings in France
1381	English peasants revolt
1415	English victory at Agincourt
1422	Treaty of Troyes proclaims Henry VI ruler of both England and France
1429	Joan of Arc leads French to victory at Orléans
1431	Joan of Arc executed as a heretic
1453	War ends; English retain only coastal town of Calais

JOAN OF ARC AND THE WAR'S CONCLUSION   Joan of Arc (1412–1431), a peasant from Domrémy, presented herself to Charles VII in March 1429, declaring that the King of Heaven had called her to deliver besieged Orléans from the English. The king was understandably skeptical, but being in retreat from what seemed to be a hopeless war, he was willing to try anything to reverse French fortunes. And the deliverance of Orléans, a city strategic to the control of the territory south of the Loire, would be a godsend. Charles's desperation overcame his skepticism, and he gave Joan his leave.

Circumstances worked perfectly to her advantage. The English force, already exhausted by a six-month siege of Orléans, was at the point of withdrawal when Joan arrived with fresh French troops. After repulsing the English from Orléans, the French enjoyed a succession of victories they popularly attributed to Joan. She deserved much of this credit, but not because she was a military genius. She provided the French with something military experts could not: inspiration and a sense of national identity and self-confidence. Within a few months of the liberation of Orléans, Charles VII received his crown in Rheims and ended the nine-year "disinheritance" prescribed by the Treaty of Troyes.

Charles forgot his liberator as quickly as he had embraced her. When the Burgundians captured Joan in May 1430, he was in a position to secure her release, but did little for her. The Burgundians and the English wanted her publicly discredited, believing this would also discredit Charles VII and demoralize French resistance. She was turned

Joan of Arc Refuses to Recant Her Beliefs

Joan of Arc, threatened with torture, refused to recant her beliefs and instead defended the instructions she had received from the voices that spoke to her.

❖ *In the following excerpt from her self-defense, do you get the impression that the judges have made up their minds about Joan in advance? How does this judicial process, which was based on intensive interrogation of the accused, differ from a trial today? Why was Joan deemed heretical and not insane when she acknowledged hearing voices?*

On Wednesday, May 9th of the same year [1431], Joan was brought into the great tower of the castle of Rouen before us the said judges. And [she] was required and admonished to speak the truth on many different points contained in her trial which she had denied or to which she had given false replies, whereas we possessed certain information, proofs, and vehement presumptions upon them. Many of the points were read and explained to her, and she was told that if she did not confess them truthfully she would be put to the torture, the instruments of which were shown to her all ready in the tower. There were also present by our instruction men ready to put her to the torture in order to restore her to the way and knowledge of truth, and by this means to procure the salvation of her body and soul which by her lying inventions she exposed to such grave perils.

To which the said Joan answered in this manner: "Truly if you were to tear me limb from limb and separate my soul from my body, I would not tell you anything more: and if I did say anything, I should afterwards declare that you had compelled me to say it by force." Then she said that on Holy Cross Day last she received comfort from St. Gabriel; she firmly believes it was St. Gabriel. She knew by her voices whether she should submit to the Church, since the clergy were pressing her hard to submit. Her voices told her that if she desired Our Lord to aid her she must wait upon Him in all her doings. She said that Our Lord has always been the master of her doings, and the Enemy never had power over them. She asked her voices if she would be burned and they answered that she must wait upon God, and He would aid her.

From *The Trial of Jeanne D'Arc*, trans. by W. P. Barrett (New York: Gotham House, 1932), pp. 303–304.

over to the Inquisition in English-held Rouen. The inquisitors broke the courageous "Maid of Orléans" after ten weeks of interrogation, and she was executed as a relapsed heretic on May 30, 1431. (See "Joan of Arc Refuses to Recant Her Beliefs.") Twenty-five years later (1456) Charles reopened her trial, and she was declared innocent of all the charges. In 1920 the church declared her a saint.

In 1435, the duke of Burgundy made peace with Charles. France, now unified and at peace with Burgundy, continued progressively to force the English back. By 1453, the date of the war's end, the English held only their coastal enclave of Calais.

The Hundred Years' War, with sixty-eight years of at least nominal peace and forty-four of hot war, had lasting political and social consequences. It devastated France, but it also awakened French nationalism and hastened the transition there from a feudal monarchy to a centralized state. It saw Burgundy become a major European political power. And it

encouraged the English, in response to the seesawing allegiance of the Netherlands throughout the conflict, to develop their own clothing industry and foreign markets. In both France and England the burden of the on-again, off-again war fell most heavily on the peasantry, who were forced to support it with taxes and services.

The Black Death

Preconditions and Causes

In the late Middle Ages, nine-tenths of the population worked the land. The three-field system, in use in most areas since well before the fourteenth century, had increased the amount of arable land and thereby the food supply. The growth of cities and trade had also stimulated agricultural science and productivity. But as the food supply grew, so did the population. It is estimated that Europe's population

A Renaissance portrayal of the sixth-century (590) procession of St. Gregory to St. Peter's, an effort to end a plague. From the Soane Book of Hours *(c. 1500).*
Sir John Soane's Museum. E.T. Archive, London

rapidly through Spain and southern France and into northern Europe. Areas that lay outside the major trade routes, like Bohemia, appear to have remained virtually unaffected.

Bubonic plague made numerous reappearances in succeeding decades. By the early fifteenth century, it is estimated that western Europe as a whole had lost as much as two-fifths of its population. A full recovery did not occur until the sixteenth century. (See Map 9–2.)

Popular Remedies

The plague, transmitted by rat- or human-borne fleas, often reached a victim's lungs during the course of the disease. From the lungs, it could be spread from person to person by the victim's sneezing and wheezing. Contemporary physicians had no understanding of these processes, so even the most rudimentary prophylaxis against the disease was lacking. To the people of the time, the Black Death was a catastrophe with no apparent explanation and against which there was no known defense. Throughout much of western

doubled between the years 1000 and 1300 and by 1300 had begun to outstrip food production. There were now more people than there was food available to feed them or jobs to employ them, and the average European faced the probability of extreme hunger at least once during his or her expected thirty-five-year life span.

Between 1315 and 1317, crop failures produced the greatest famine of the Middle Ages. Densely populated urban areas such as the industrial towns of the Netherlands experienced great suffering. Decades of overpopulation, economic depression, famine, and bad health progressively weakened Europe's population and made it highly vulnerable to a virulent bubonic plague that struck with full force in 1348.

This "Black Death," so called by contemporaries because of the way it discolored the body, was probably introduced by seaborne rats from Black Sea areas and followed the trade routes from Asia into Europe. Appearing in Sicily in late 1347, it entered Europe through the port cities of Venice, Genoa, and Pisa in 1348, and from there it swept

In this scene from an illustrated manuscript of Boccaccio's Decameron, *physicians apply leeches to an emperor. The text says he suffered from a disease that caused a terrible stench, which is why the physicians are holding their noses. Bleeding was the agreed-upon best way to prevent and cure illness and was practiced as late as the nineteenth century. Its popularity was rooted in the belief that a build-up of foul matter in the body caused illness by disrupting the body's four humors (blood, phlegm, yellow bile, and black bile). Bleeding released the foul matter and restored equilibrium among the humors, thus preserving good health by strengthening resistance to disease.*
Jean-Loup Charmet/Science Photo Library

MAP 9–2   SPREAD OF THE BLACK DEATH   *Apparently introduced by seaborne rats from Black Sea areas where plague-infested rodents have long been known, the Black Death brought huge human, social, and economic consequences. One of the lower estimates of Europeans dying is 25,000,000. The map charts the plague's spread in the mid-fourteenth century. Generally following trade routes, the plague reached Scandinavia by 1350, and some believe it then went on to Iceland and even Greenland. Areas off the main trade routes were largely spared.*

Europe it inspired an obsession with death and dying and a deep pessimism that endured for decades after the plague years. (See "Art & the West.")

Popular wisdom held that a corruption in the atmosphere caused the disease. Some blamed poisonous fumes released by earthquakes. Many adopted aromatic amulets as a remedy. According to the contemporary observations of Boccaccio, who recorded the varied reactions to the plague in the *Decameron* (1353), some sought a remedy in moderation and a temperate life; others gave themselves over entirely to their passions (sexual promiscuity within the stricken areas apparently ran high); and still others, "the most sound, perhaps, in judgment," chose flight and seclusion as the best medicine. (See "Boccaccio Describes the Black Death in Florence.")

Among the most extreme social reactions were processions of flagellants. These religious fanatics beat themselves in ritual penance until they bled, believing that such action would bring divine intervention. The terror created by the flagellants (whose

Images of Death
in the Late Middle Ages

The Prince of the World in the Church of St. Sebald, Nürnberg, 1320–1330. Germnisches Nationalmuseum, Nürnberg.

Throughout the Middle Ages, people perceived, and artists portrayed death both realistically and religiously: on the one hand, as a terrible, inescapable fate, and on the other, as the beginning of a new, eternal life, either in heaven or in hell. That life is death (transitory) and death is life (the afterlife) were two urgent and ironic teachings of the Christian Church. Many laity, finding the present world undesirable and death no sure release into a better one, understandably resisted. Graphic and sermonic instruction in the "Art of Dying" became the Church's response. Shown here, a sandstone sculpture, *The Prince of the World*, carries a vivid warning. When viewers looked behind this young, attractive prince, they discovered that beauty is only skin deep: His body, like everyone else's, is filled with worms and flesh-eating frogs. A serpent spirals up his left leg and enters his back—an allusion to the biblical teaching that the wages of sin are death. To drive home human mortality, the Church instructed laity to think often about the inevitability of death by visiting dying relatives and friends, watching them die and being buried, and thereafter visiting their graves often. This, in turn, would move them to resist the devil's temptations, obey the Church, avoid sin, and become eligible for heaven in the afterlife.

During the late Middle Ages, in both literature and art, the "Dance of Death" became a new reminder of human mortality and the need for Christian living and Church instruction. (It was first painted in 1424, on the wall of the Church of the Holy Innocents in Paris.) Death appeared as a living skeleton in lively conversation with mortal representatives—from pope to friar in the religious world, from emperor to laborer in the secular—none of whom, no matter how mighty, can elude Death's grasp. Even the Son of God, as an incarnate man, died a dreadful death. Although emerging in the late Middle Ages, the "Dance of Death" conveyed an old message, apparently urgently needed at the time because of the indiscipline and self-indulgence occasioned by the new horrors of the Black Death and the Hundred Years' War.

The Church's last word on death, however, was resplendently positive: Mortal men and women of true faith, like the crucified Son of God, might look forward to eternal life as shown in *The Resurrection*, from the *Isenheim Altarpiece*, 1509/10–1515.

Sources: Alberto Tenenti, "Death in History," in *Life and Death in Fifteenth Century Florence*, ed. M. Tetel et al. (Durham, NC: Duke University Press, 1989); Donald Weinstein, "The Art of Dying Well and Popular Piety in the Preaching and Thought of Girolamo Savonarola," in *ibid.*, 88–104; and James M. Clark, *The Dance of Death in the Middle Ages and the Renaissance* (Glasgow: Jackson, Son, and Col, 1950), pp. 1–4, 22–24, 106–110. Joseph L. Koerner, *The Moment of Self-Portraiture in German Renaissance Art* (Chicago, University of Chicago Press, 1993), pp. 199–200. H. W. Janson et al., *History of Art* (Upper Saddle River, NJ: Prentice Hall, 1997), p. 528.

Gruenwald, Mathias (1460–1528), *The Resurrection*. A panel from the Isenheim Altar. Limewood (around 1515), 250 × 650 cm. Musée d'Unterlinden, Colmar, France.

Boccaccio Describes the Ravages of the Black Death in Florence

The Black Death provided an excuse to the poet, humanist, and storyteller Giovanni Boccaccio (1313–1375) to assemble his great collection of tales, the Decameron. *Ten congenial men and women flee Florence to escape the plague and while away the time telling stories. In one of the stories, Boccaccio embeds a fine clinical description of plague symptoms as seen in Florence in 1348 and of the powerlessness of physicians and the lack of remedies.*

❖ *What did people do to escape the plague? Was any of it sound medical practice? What does the study of calamities like the Black Death tell us about the people of the past?*

In Florence, despite all that human wisdom and forethought could devise to avert it, even as the cleansing of the city from many impurities by officials appointed for the purpose, the refusal of entrance to all sick folk, and the adoption of many precautions for the preservation of health; despite also humble supplications addressed to God, and often repeated both in public procession and otherwise, by the devout; towards the beginning of the spring of the said year [1348] the doleful effects of the pestilence began to be horribly apparent by symptoms that [appeared] as if miraculous.

Not such were these symptoms as in the East, where an issue of blood from the nose was a manifest sign of inevitable death; but in men and women alike it first betrayed itself by the emergence of certain tumours in the groin or the armpits, some of which grew as large as a common apple, others as an egg, some more, some less, which the common folk called *gavoccioli*. From the two said parts of the body this deadly *gavoccioli* soon began to propagate and spread itself in all directions indifferently; after which the form of the malady began to change, spots black or livid making their appearance in many cases on the arm or the thigh or elsewhere, now few and large, now minute and numerous. And as the *gavoccioli* had been and still were an infallible token of approaching death, such also were these spots on whomsoever they shewed themselves. Which maladies seemed to set entirely at naught both the art of the physician and the virtues of physic; indeed, whether it was that the disorder was of a nature to defy such treatment, or that the physicians were at fault... and, being in ignorance of its source, failed to apply the proper remedies; in either case, not merely were those that recovered few, but almost all died within three days of the appearance of the said symptoms...and in most cases without any fever or other attendant malady.

From *The Decameron of Giovanni Boccaccio*, trans. by J. M. Rigg (London: J. M. Dent & Sons, 1930), p. 5.

dirty bodies may actually have served to transport the disease) became so socially disruptive and threatening even to established authority, that the church finally outlawed their processions.

Jews were cast as scapegoats for the plague. Centuries of Christian propaganda had bred hatred toward them, as had their role as society's money-lenders. Pogroms occurred in several cities, sometimes incited by the arrival of flagellants.

Social and Economic Consequences

Whole villages vanished in the wake of the plague. Among the social and economic consequences of this depopulation were a shrunken labor supply and a decline in the value of the estates of the nobility.

FARMS DECLINE As the number of farm laborers decreased, their wages increased and those of skilled artisans soared. Many serfs now chose to commute their labor services by money payments or to abandon the farm altogether and pursue more interesting and rewarding jobs in skilled craft industries in the cities. Agricultural prices fell because of lowered demand, and the price of luxury and manufactured goods—the work of skilled artisans—rose. The noble landholders suffered the greatest decline in power

A caricature of physicians (early sixteenth century). In the Middle Ages and later, people recognized the short-comings of physicians and surgeons and visited them only as a last resort. Here a physician carries a uroscope (for collecting and examining urine); cloudy or discolored urine signaled an immediate need for bleeding. The physician/surgeon wears surgical shoes and his assistant carries a flail—a comment on the risks of medical services. Hacker Art Books Inc.

from this new state of affairs. They were forced to pay more for finished products and for farm labor, but received a smaller return on their agricultural produce. Everywhere their rents were in steady decline after the plague.

PEASANTS REVOLT To recoup their losses, some landowners converted arable land to sheep pasture, substituting more profitable wool production for labor-intensive grain crops. Others abandoned the effort to farm their land and simply leased it to the highest bidder. Landowners also sought simply to reverse their misfortune—to close off the new economic opportunities opened for the peasantry by the demographic crisis—through repressive legislation that forced peasants to stay on their farms and froze their wages at low levels. In France the direct tax on the peasantry, the *taille*, was increased, and opposition to it was prominent among the grievances behind the *Jacquerie.* In 1351, the English Parliament passed a Statute of Laborers,

which limited wages to preplague levels and restricted the ability of peasants to leave the land of their traditional masters. Opposition to such legislation was also a prominent factor in the English peasants' revolt in 1381.

CITIES REBOUND Although the plague hit urban populations especially hard, the cities and their skilled industries came, in time, to prosper from its effects. Cities had always been careful to protect their interests; as they grew, they passed legislation to regulate competition from rural areas and to control immigration. After the plague, the reach of such laws was progressively extended beyond the cities to include surrounding lands belonging to impoverished nobles and feudal landlords, many of whom were peacefully integrated into urban life.

The omnipresence of death whetted the appetite for goods that only skilled urban industries could produce. Expensive cloths and jewelry, furs from the north, and silks from the south were in great demand in the second half of the fourteenth century. Faced with life at its worst, people insisted on having the very best. Initially, this new demand could not be met. The basic unit of urban industry was the master and apprentices (usually one or two), whose numbers were purposely kept low and whose privileges were jealously guarded. The craft of the skilled artisan was passed from master to apprentice only very slowly. The first wave of plague transformed this already restricted supply of skilled artisans into a shortage almost overnight. As a result, the prices of manufactured and luxury items rose to new heights, and this in turn encouraged workers to migrate from the countryside to the city and learn the skills of artisans. Townspeople in effect profited coming and going from the forces that impoverished the landed nobility. As wealth poured into the cities and per capita income rose, the cost to urban dwellers of agricultural products from the countryside, now less in demand, declined.

There was also gain, as well as loss, for the church. Although it suffered losses as a great landholder and was politically weakened, it had received new revenues from the vastly increased demand for religious services for the dead and the dying and from the multiplication of gifts and bequests.

New Conflicts and Opportunities

By increasing the importance of skilled artisans, the plague contributed to new conflicts within the cities. The economic and political power of local artisans and trade guilds grew steadily in the late Middle Ages, along with the demand for their goods and services. The merchant and patrician classes found it increasingly difficult to maintain their traditional dominance and grudgingly gave guild masters a voice in city government. As the guilds won political power, they encouraged restrictive legislation to protect local industries. These restrictions, in turn, brought confrontations between master artisans, who wanted to keep their numbers low and expand their industries at a snail's pace, and the many journeymen, who were eager to rise to the rank of master. To the long-existing conflict between the guilds and the urban patriciate was now added a conflict within the guilds themselves.

After 1350 the two traditional "containers" of monarchy—the landed nobility and the church—were politically on the defensive, to no small degree as a consequence of the plague. Kings took full advantage of the new situation, drawing on growing national sentiment to centralize their governments and economies. As already noted, the plague reduced the economic power of the landed nobility. In the same period, the battles of the Hundred Years' War demonstrated the military superiority of paid professional armies over the traditional noble cavalry, thus bringing into question the role of the nobility. The plague also killed many members of the clergy—perhaps one-third of the German clergy fell victim to it as they dutifully ministered to the sick and dying. The reduction in clerical ranks occurred in the same century in which the residence of the pope in Avignon (1309–1377) and the Great Schism (1378–1415) were undermining much of the church's popular support.

Ecclesiastical Breakdown and Revival: The Late Medieval Church

At first glance, the popes may appear to have been in a very favorable position in the latter half of the thirteenth century. Frederick II had been vanquished and imperial pressure on Rome had been removed. The French king, Louis IX, was an enthusiastic supporter of the church, as evidenced by his two disastrous Crusades, which won him sainthood. Although it lasted only seven years, a reunion of the Eastern church with Rome was proclaimed by the Council of Lyons in 1274, when the Western church took advantage of Emperor Michael Palaeologus's request for aid against the Turks. But despite these positive events, the church was not really in as favorable a position as it appeared.

The Thirteenth-Century Papacy

As early as the reign of Pope Innocent III (r. 1198–1216), when papal power reached its height, there were ominous developments. Innocent had elaborated the doctrine of papal plenitude of power and on that authority had declared saints, disposed of *benefices*, and created a centralized papal monarchy with a clearly political mission. Innocent's transformation of the papacy into a great secular power weakened the church spiritually even as it strengthened it politically. Thereafter, the church as a papal monarchy and the church as the "body of the faithful" came increasingly to be differentiated. It was against the "papal church" and in the name of the "true Christian Church" that both reformers and heretics raised their voices in protest until the Protestant Reformation.

What Innocent began his successors perfected. Under Urban IV (r. 1261–1264), the papacy established its own law court, the *Rota Romana*, which tightened and centralized the church's legal proceedings. The latter half of the thirteenth century saw an elaboration of the system of clerical taxation; what had begun in the twelfth century as an emergency measure to raise funds for the Crusades became a fixed institution. In the same period, papal power to determine appointments to many major and minor church offices—the "reservation of *benefices*"—was greatly broadened. The thirteenth-century papacy became a powerful political institution governed by its own law and courts, serviced by an efficient international bureaucracy, and preoccupied with secular goals.

Papal centralization of the church undermined both diocesan authority and popular support. Rome's interests, not local needs, came to control church appointments, policies, and discipline. Discontented lower clergy appealed to the higher authority of Rome against the disciplinary measures of local bishops. In the second half of the thirteenth century, bishops and abbots protested such undercutting of their power. To its critics, the church in Rome was hardly more than a legalized, "fiscalized," bureaucratic institution. As early as the late twelfth century, heretical movements of Cathars and Waldensians had appealed to the biblical ideal of simplicity and separation from the world. Other reformers who were unquestionably loyal to the church, such as Saint Francis of Assisi, would also protest a perceived materialism in official religion.

POLITICAL FRAGMENTATION The church of the thirteenth century was being undermined by more than internal religious disunity. The demise of imperial power meant that the papacy in Rome was no longer the leader of anti-imperial (Guelf, or propapal) sentiment in Italy. Instead of being the center of Italian resistance to the emperor, popes now found themselves on the defensive against their old allies. That was the ironic price paid by the papacy to vanquish the Hohenstaufens.

Rulers with a stake in Italian politics now directed the intrigue formerly aimed at the emperor toward the College of Cardinals. For example, Charles of Anjou, king of Sicily, managed to create a French–Sicilian faction within the college. Such efforts to control the decisions of the college led Pope Gregory X (r. 1271– 1276) to establish the practice of sequestering the cardinals immediately on the death of the pope. The purpose of this so-called conclave of cardinals was to minimize extraneous political influence on the election of new popes, but the college had become so politicized that it proved to be of little avail.

In 1294 such a conclave, in frustration after a deadlock of more than two years, chose a saintly, but inept, Calabrian hermit as Pope Celestine V. Celestine abdicated under suspicious circumstances after only a few weeks in office. He also died under suspicious circumstances; his successor's critics later argued that he had been murdered for political reasons by the powers behind the papal throne to ensure the survival of the papal office. His tragicomic reign shocked a majority of the College of Cardinals into unified action. He was quickly replaced by his very opposite, Pope Boniface VIII (r. 1294–1303), a nobleman and a skilled politician. His pontificate, however, would augur the beginning of the end of papal pretensions to great-power status.

Boniface VIII and Philip the Fair

Boniface came to rule when England and France were maturing as nation–states. In England, a long tradition of consultation between the king and powerful members of English society evolved into formal "parliaments" during the reigns of Henry III (r. 1216–1272) and Edward I (r. 1272–1307), and these meetings helped to create a unified kingdom. The reign of the French king Philip IV the Fair (1285–1314) saw France become an efficient, centralized monarchy. Philip was no Saint Louis, but a ruthless politician. He was determined to end England's continental holdings, control wealthy Flanders, and establish French hegemony within the Holy Roman Empire.

Boniface had the further misfortune of bringing to the papal throne memories of the way earlier popes had brought kings and emperors to their knees. Very painfully he was to discover that the papal monarchy

Pope Boniface VIII (r. 1294–1303), depicted here, opposed the taxation of the clergy by the kings of France and England and issued one of the strongest declarations of papal authority over rulers, the bull Unam Sanctam. This statue is in the Museo Civico, Bologna, Italy. Scala/Art Resource, N.Y.

of the early thirteenth century was no match for the new political powers of the late thirteenth century.

THE ROYAL CHALLENGE TO PAPAL AUTHORITY France and England were on the brink of all-out war when Boniface became pope in 1294. Only Edward I's preoccupation with rebellion in Scotland, which the

Boniface VIII Reasserts the Church's Claim to Temporal Power

Defied by the French and the English, Pope Boniface VIII (r. 1294–1303) boldly reasserted the temporal power of the church in the bull Unam Sanctam *(November 1302). This document claimed that both spiritual and temporal power on earth were under the pope's jurisdiction, because in the hierarchy of the universe spiritual power both preceded and sat in judgment on temporal power.*

❖ *On what does the pope base his claims to supremacy? Is his argument logical, or does he beg the question? On what basis did secular rulers attack his arguments?*

We are taught by the words of the Gospel that in this church and in her power there are two swords, a spiritual one and a temporal one....Certainly anyone who denies that the temporal sword is in the power of Peter has not paid heed to the words of the Lord when he said, "Put up thy sword into its sheath" (Matthew 26:52). Both then are in the power of the church, the material sword and the spiritual. But the one is exercised for the church, the other by the church, the one by the hand of the priest, the other by the hand of kings and soldiers, though at the will and suffrance of the authority subject to the spiritual power....For, according to the blessed Dionysius, it is the law of divinity for the lowest to be led to the highest through intermediaries. In the order of the universe all things are not kept in order in the same fashion and immediately but the lowest are ordered by the intermediate and inferiors by superiors. But that the spiritual power excels any earthly one in dignity and nobility we ought the more openly to confess in proportion as spiritual things excel temporal ones. Moreover we clearly perceive this from the giving of tithes, from benediction and sanctification, from the acceptance of this power and from the very government of things. For, the truth bearing witness, the spiritual power has to institute the earthly power and to judge it if it has not been good. So it is verified the prophecy of Jeremiah (1:10) concerning the church and the power of the church, "Lo, I have set thee this day over the nations and over kingdoms."

Reprinted with the permission of Simon & Schuster from *The Crisis of Church and State, 1050–1300* by Brian Tierney. Copyright © 1964 by Prentice-Hall, Inc., renewed 1992 by Brian Tierney.

French encouraged, prevented him from invading France and starting the Hundred Years' War a half century earlier than it did start. As both countries mobilized for war, they used the pretext of preparing for a Crusade to tax the clergy heavily. In 1215 Pope Innocent III had decreed that the clergy were to pay no taxes to rulers without prior papal consent. Viewing English and French taxation of the clergy as an assault on traditional clerical rights, Boniface took a strong stand against it. On February 5, 1296, he issued a bull, *Clericis laicos*, which forbade lay taxation of the clergy without prior papal approval and took back all previous papal dispensations in this regard.

In England, Edward I retaliated by denying the clergy the right to be heard in royal court, in effect removing from them the protection of the king. But it was Philip the Fair who struck back with a vengeance: In August 1296 he forbade the exportation of money from France to Rome, thereby denying the papacy revenues it needed to operate. Boniface had no choice but to come quickly to terms with Philip. He conceded Philip the right to tax the French clergy "during an emergency," and, not coincidentally, he canonized Louis IX in the same year.

Boniface was then also under siege by powerful Italian enemies, whom Philip did not fail to patronize. A noble family (the Colonnas), rivals of Boniface's family (the Gaetani) and radical followers of Saint Francis of Assisi (the Spiritual Franciscans), were at this time seeking to invalidate Boniface's election as pope on the grounds that Celestine V had resigned the office under coercion. Charges of heresy, simony, and even the murder of Celestine were hurled against Boniface.

Boniface's fortunes appeared to revive in 1300, a "Jubilee year." During such a year, all Catholics who visited Rome and fulfilled certain conditions had the penalties for their unrepented sins remitted. Tens of thousands of pilgrims flocked to Rome in that year, and Boniface, heady with this display of popular religiosity, reinserted himself into international politics. He championed Scottish resistance to England, for which he received a firm rebuke from an outraged Edward I and from Parliament.

But once again a confrontation with the king of France proved the more costly. Philip seemed to be eager for another fight with the pope. He arrested Boniface's Parisian legate, Bernard Saisset, the bishop of Pamiers and also a powerful secular lord, whose independence Philip had opposed. Accused of heresy and treason, Saisset was tried and convicted in the king's court. Thereafter, Philip demanded that Boniface recognize the process against Saisset, something that Boniface could do only if he was prepared to surrender his jurisdiction over the French episcopate. This challenge could not be sidestepped, and Boniface acted swiftly to champion Saisset as a defender of clerical political independence within France. He demanded Saisset's unconditional release, revoked all previous agreements with Philip in the matter of clerical taxation, and ordered the French bishops to convene in Rome within a year. A bull, *Ausculta fili*, or "Listen, My Son," was sent to Philip in December 1301, pointedly informing him that "God has set popes over kings and kingdoms."

UNAM SANCTAM (1302) Philip unleashed a ruthless antipapal campaign. Two royal apologists, Pierre Dubois and John of Paris, refuted papal claims to the right to intervene in temporal matters. Increasingly placed on the defensive, Boniface made a last-ditch stand against state control of national churches. On November 18, 1302, he issued the bull *Unam Sanctam*. This famous statement of papal power declared that temporal authority was "subject" to the spiritual power of the church. On its face a bold assertion, *Unam Sanctam* was in truth the desperate act of a besieged papacy. (See "Boniface VIII Reasserts the Church's Claim to Temporal Power.")

After *Unam Sanctam*, the French and the Colonnas moved against Boniface with force. Guillaume de Nogaret, Philip's chief minister, denounced Boniface to the French clergy as a common heretic and criminal. An army, led by Nogaret and Sciarra Colonna, surprised the pope in mid-August 1303 at his retreat in Anagni. Boniface was badly beaten and almost executed before an aroused populace liberated and returned him safely

Marsilius of Padua Denies Coercive Power to the Clergy

According to Marsilius, the Bible gave the pope no right to pronounce and execute sentences on any person. The clergy held a strictly moral and spiritual rule, their judgments to be executed only in the afterlife, not in the present one. Here, on earth, they should be obedient to secular authority. Marsilius argued this point by appealing to the example of Jesus.

❖ *How do Marsilius's arguments compare with those of Pope Boniface in the preceding document? Does Marsilius's argument, if accepted, destroy the worldly authority of the church? Why was his teaching condemned as heretical?*

We now wish...to adduce the truths of the holy Scripture...which explicitly command or counsel that neither the Roman bishop called pope, nor any other bishop or priest, or deacon, has or ought to have any rulership or coercive judgment or jurisdiction over any priest or nonpriest, ruler, community, group, or individual of whatever condition....Christ himself came into the world not to dominate men, nor to judge them [coercively]...not to wield temporal rule, but rather to be subject as regards the...present life; and moreover, he wanted to and did exclude himself, his apostles and disciples, and their successors, the bishops or priests, from all coercive authority or worldly rule, both by his example and by his word of counsel or command....When he was brought before Pontius Pilate...and accused of having called himself king of the Jews, and [Pilate] asked him whether he had said this...[his] reply included these words...."My kingdom is not of this world," that is, I have not come to reign by temporal rule or dominion, in the way...worldly kings reign.... This, then, is the kingdom concerning which he came to teach and order, a kingdom which consists in the acts whereby the eternal kingdom is attained, that is, the acts of faith and the other theological virtues; not however, by coercing anyone thereto.

Excerpt from *Marsilius of Padua: The Defender of Peace:* The Defensor Pacis, trans. by Alan Gewirth. Copyright © 1967 by Columbia University Press, pp. 113–116. Reprinted by permission of the publisher.

A book illustration of the Palace of the Popes in Avignon in 1409, the year in which Christendom found itself confronted by three duly elected popes. The "keys" to the kingdom of God, which the pope held on earth as the vicar of Christ, decorate the three turret flags of the palace. In the foreground, the French poet Pierre Salmon, then journeying via Avignon to Rome, commiserates with a monk over the sad state of the Church and France, then at war with England. Book illustration, French, 1409. Paris, Bibliotheque Nationale. AKG Photo.

to Rome. But the ordeal proved too much for him and he died a few months later, in October 1303.

Boniface's immediate successor, Benedict XI (r. 1303–1304), excommunicated Nogaret for his deed, but there was to be no lasting papal retaliation. Benedict's successor, Clement V (r. 1305–1314), was forced into French subservience. A former archbishop of Bordeaux, Clement declared that *Unam Sanctam* should not be understood as in any way diminishing French royal authority. He released Nogaret from excommunication and pliantly condemned the Knights Templars, whose treasure Philip thereafter forcibly expropriated.

In 1309 Clement moved the papal court to Avignon, an imperial city on the southeastern border of France. Situated on land that belonged to the pope, the city maintained its independence from the king. In 1311 Clement made it his permanent residence, to escape both a Rome ridden with strife after the confrontation between Boniface and Philip and

further pressure from Philip. There the papacy was to remain until 1377.

After Boniface's humiliation, popes never again seriously threatened kings and emperors, despite continuing papal excommunications and political intrigue. In the future, the relation between church and state would tilt in favor of the state and the control of religion by powerful monarchies. Ecclesiastical authority would become subordinate to larger secular political purposes.

The Avignon Papacy (1309–1377)

The Avignon papacy was in appearance, although not always in fact, under strong French influence. During Clement V's pontificate the French came to dominate the College of Cardinals, testing the papacy's agility both politically and economically. Finding itself cut off from its Roman estates, the papacy had to innovate to get needed funds. Clement expanded papal taxes, especially the practice of collecting annates, the first year's revenue of a church office, or *benefices* bestowed by the pope. Clement VI (r. 1342–1352) began the practice of selling indulgences, or pardons for unrepented sins. To make the purchase of indulgences more compelling, church doctrine on purgatory—a place of punishment where souls would atone for venial sins—also developed during this period. By the fifteenth century the church had extended indulgences to cover the souls of people already dead, allowing the living to buy a reduced sentence in purgatory for their deceased loved ones. Such practices contributed to the Avignon papacy's reputation for materialism and political scheming and gave reformers new ammunition.

POPE JOHN XXII   Pope John XXII (r. 1316–1334), the most powerful Avignon pope, tried to restore papal independence and to return to Italy. This goal led him into war with the Visconti, the most powerful ruling family of Milan, and a costly contest with Emperor Louis IV. John had challenged Louis's election as emperor in 1314 in favor of the rival Habsburg candidate. The result was a minor replay of the confrontation between Philip the Fair and Boniface VIII. When John obstinately and without legal justification refused to recognize Louis's election, the emperor retaliated by declaring John deposed and putting in his place an antipope. As Philip the Fair had also done, Louis enlisted the support of the Spiritual Franciscans, whose views on absolute poverty had been condemned by John as heretical. Two outstanding pamphleteers wrote lasting tracts for the royal cause: William of Ockham, whom John excommunicated in 1328, and Marsilius of Padua (ca. 1290–1342), whose teaching John declared heretical in 1327.

In his *Defender of Peace* (1324), Marsilius of Padua stressed the independent origins and autonomy of secular government. Clergy were subjected to the strictest apostolic ideals and confined to purely spiritual functions, and all power of coercive judgment was denied the pope. Marsilius argued that spiritual crimes must await an eternal punishment. Transgressions of divine law, over which the pope had jurisdiction, were to be punished in the next life, not in the present one, unless the secular ruler declared a divine law also a secular law. This assertion was a direct challenge to the power of the pope to excommunicate rulers and place countries under interdict. The *Defender of Peace* depicted the pope as a subordinate member of a society over which the emperor ruled supreme and in which temporal peace was the highest good. (See "Marsilius of Padua Denies Coercive Power to the Clergy.")

John XXII made the papacy a sophisticated international agency and adroitly adjusted it to the growing European money economy. The more the *Curia*, or papal court, mastered the latter, however, the more vulnerable it became to criticism. Under John's successor, Benedict XII (r. 1334–1342), the papacy became entrenched in Avignon. Seemingly forgetting Rome altogether, Benedict began construction of the great Palace of the Popes and attempted to reform both papal government and the religious life. His high-living French successor, Clement VI, placed papal policy in lockstep with the French. In this period the cardinals became barely more than lobbyists for policies favorable to their secular patrons.

NATIONAL OPPOSITION TO THE AVIGNON PAPACY As Avignon's fiscal tentacles probed new areas, monarchies took strong action to protect their interests. The latter half of the fourteenth century saw legislation restricting papal jurisdiction and taxation in France, England, and Germany. In England, where the Avignon papacy was identified with the French enemy after the outbreak of the Hundred Years' War, statutes that restricted payments and appeals to Rome and the pope's power to make high ecclesiastical appointments were passed by Parliament several times between 1351 and 1393.

In France, ecclesiastical appointments and taxation were regulated by the so-called Gallican liberties. These national rights over religion had long been exercised in fact and were legally acknowledged by the church in the *Pragmatic Sanction of Bourges*, published by Charles VII (r. 1422–1461) in 1438. This agreement recognized the right of the French church to elect its own clergy without papal

A portrayal of John Huss as he was led to the stake at Constance. After his execution, his bones and ashes were scattered in the Rhine River to prevent his followers from claiming them as relics. This pen-and-ink drawing is from Ulrich von Richenthal's Chronicle of the Council of Constance (ca. 1450). The Bettman Archive

interference, prohibited the payment of annates to Rome, and limited the right of appeals from French courts to the *Curia* in Rome. In German and Swiss cities in the fourteenth and fifteenth centuries, local governments also took the initiative to limit and even to overturn traditional clerical privileges and immunities.

JOHN WYCLIFFE AND JOHN HUSS The popular lay religious movements that most successfully assailed the late medieval church were the Lollards in England and the Hussites in Bohemia. The Lollards looked to the writings of John Wycliffe (d. 1384) to justify their demands, and both moderate and extreme Hussites to the writings of John Huss (d. 1415), although both Wycliffe and Huss would have disclaimed the extremists who revolted in their names.

Wycliffe was an Oxford theologian and a philosopher of high standing. His work initially served the anticlerical policies of the English government. He became within England what William of Ockham and Marsilius of Padua had been at the Bavarian court of Emperor Louis IV: a major intellectual spokesman for the rights of royalty against the secular pretensions of popes. After 1350 English kings greatly reduced the power of the Avignon papacy to make ecclesiastical appointments and collect taxes within England, a position that Wycliffe strongly

The Ruin of the Church during the Schism

Nicholas of Clamanges, a theologian writing around 1400, viewed the decades-long division of the papacy and the continuing growth of two separate papal courts, one in Avignon, another in Rome, as proof that the high clergy had become thoroughly corrupt. Popes and bishops had so lost face, that their threats of excommunication now fell on deaf ears. Only by ending the Schism could the church begin to restore its authority.

❖ *What incentive did either pope have to end the Schism? Did the loss of efficacy of papal disciplinary actions such as excommunication provide such an incentive? Which, if either, of the papal courts seemed to have greater validity?*

After the great increase of worldly goods...boundless avarice and blind ambition invaded the hearts of churchmen...Carried away by the glory of their position and the extent of their power [they] soon gave way to the[ir] degrading effects....Three most exacting and troublesome masters had now to be satisfied. *Luxury* demanded sundry gratifications—wine, sleep, banquets, music, debasing sports, and courtesans....*Display* required fine houses, castles, towers, palaces, rich and varied furniture, expensive clothes, horses, servants and the pomp of luxury....*Avarice*...carefully brought together vast treasures to supply the demands of the above vices....

For carrying on exactions and gathering their gains...the popes appointed their collectors in every province, those namely whom they knew to be most skillful in extracting money, owing to [their] energy, diligence, or harshness of temper....To these the popes granted the power of anathematizing anyone, even prelates, and of expelling from the communion of the faithful everyone who did not...satisfy their demands for money....Hence came suspensions from divine service, interdicts from entering a church, and anathemas a thousandfold intensified in severity.

Such things were resorted to in the rarest instances by the [Church] Fathers, and then only for the most horrible of crimes; for by these penalties a man is separated from the companionship of the faithful and turned over to Satan. But nowadays these inflictions have so fallen in esteem that they are used for the lightest offense, often for no offense at all, so that they no longer bring terror but are objects of contempt.

From James Harvey Robinson, ed., *Readings in European History*, Vol. I (Boston: Athenaeum, 1904), pp. 508–509.

supported. His views on clerical poverty followed original Franciscan ideals and, more by accident than by design, gave justification to government restriction and even confiscation of church properties within England. Wycliffe argued that the clergy "ought to be content with food and clothing."

Wycliffe also maintained that personal merit, not rank and office, was the only basis of religious authority. This was a dangerous teaching, because it raised allegedly pious laypeople above allegedly corrupt ecclesiastics, regardless of the latter's official stature. There was a threat in such teaching to secular as well as ecclesiastical dominion and jurisdiction. At his posthumous condemnation by the pope, Wycliffe was accused of the ancient heresy of Donatism—the teaching that the efficacy of the church's sacraments did not lie in their true performance, but also depended on the moral character of the clergy who administered them. Wycliffe also anticipated certain Protestant criticisms of the medieval church by challenging papal infallibility, the sale of indulgences, the authority of scripture, and the dogma of transubstantiation.

The Lollards, English advocates of Wycliffe's teaching, like the Waldensians, preached in the vernacular, disseminated translations of Holy Scripture, and championed clerical poverty. At first, they came from every social class. Lollards were especially prominent among the groups that had something tangible to gain from the confiscation of clerical properties (the nobility and the gentry) or that had suffered most under the current church system (the lower clergy and the poor people). After the English peasants' revolt in 1381, an uprising filled with egalitarian notions that could find support in Wycliffe's teaching, Lollardy was officially viewed as subversive. Opposed by an alliance of church and crown, it became a capital offense in England by 1401.

Heresy was not so easily brought to heel in Bohemia, where it coalesced with a strong national movement. The University of Prague, founded in 1348, became the center for both Czech nationalism and a native religious reform movement. The latter began within the bounds of orthodoxy. It was led by local intellectuals and preachers, the most famous of whom was John Huss, the rector of the university after 1403.

The Czech reformers supported vernacular translations of the Bible and were critical of traditional ceremonies and allegedly superstitious practices, particularly those relating to the sacrament of the Eucharist. They advocated lay communion with cup as well as bread, which was traditionally reserved only for the clergy as a sign of the clergy's spiritual superiority over the laity. Hussites taught that bread and wine remained bread and wine after priestly consecration, and they questioned the validity of sacraments performed by priests in mortal sin.

Wycliffe's teaching appears to have influenced the movement very early. Regular traffic between England and Bohemia had existed for decades, ever since the marriage in 1381 of Anne of Bohemia to King Richard II. Czech students studied at Oxford, and many returned with copies of Wycliffe's writings.

Huss became the leader of the pro-Wycliffe faction at the University of Prague. In 1410 his activities brought about his excommunication and the placement of Prague under papal interdict. In 1414 Huss won an audience with the newly assembled Council of Constance. He journeyed to the council eagerly, armed with a safe-conduct pass from Emperor Sigismund, naïvely believing that he would convince his strongest critics of the truth of his teaching. Within weeks of his arrival in early November 1414, he was formally accused of heresy and imprisoned. He died at the stake on July 6, 1415, and was followed there less than a year later by his colleague Jerome of Prague.

The reaction in Bohemia to the execution of these national heroes was fierce revolt. Militant Hussites, the Taborites, set out to transform Bohemia by force into a religious and social paradise under the military leadership of John Ziska. After a decade of belligerent protest, the Hussites won significant religious reforms and control over the Bohemian church from the Council of Basel.

The Great Schism (1378–1417) and the Conciliar Movement to 1449

Pope Gregory XI (r. 1370–1378) reestablished the papacy in Rome in January 1377, ending what had come to be known as the "Babylonian Captivity" of the church in Avignon, a reference to the biblical bondage of the Israelites. The return to Rome proved to be short lived, however.

URBAN VI AND CLEMENT VII   On Gregory's death, the cardinals, in Rome, elected an Italian archbishop as Pope Urban VI (r. 1378–1389), who immediately announced his intention to reform the *Curia*. This was an unexpected challenge to the cardinals, most of whom were French, and they responded by calling for the return of the papacy to Avignon. The French king, Charles V, wanting to keep the papacy within the sphere of French influence, lent his support to a schism, which came to be known as the "Great Schism."

On September 20, 1378, five months after Urban's election, thirteen cardinals, all but one of whom was French, formed their own conclave and elected Pope Clement VII (r. 1378–1397), a cousin of the French king. They insisted that they had voted for Urban in fear of their lives, surrounded by a Roman mob demanding the election of an Italian pope. Be that as it may, the papacy now became a "two-headed thing" and a scandal to Christendom. (See "The Ruin of the Church during the Schism.") Allegiance to the two papal courts divided along political lines. England and its allies (the Holy Roman Empire, Hungary, Bohemia, and Poland) acknowledged Urban VI, whereas France and those in its orbit (Naples, Scotland, Castile, and Aragon) supported Clement VII. The Roman line of popes has, however, been recognized de facto in subsequent church history.

Two approaches were initially taken to end the schism. One tried to win the mutual cession of both popes, thereby clearing the way for the election of a new pope. The other sought to secure the resignation of the one in favor of the other. Both approaches proved completely fruitless. Each pope considered himself fully legitimate, and too much was at stake for a magnanimous concession on the part of either. One way remained: the forced deposition of both popes by a special council of the church.

CONCILIAR THEORY OF CHURCH GOVERNMENT   Legally, a church council could be convened only by a pope, but the competing popes were not inclined to summon a council they knew would depose them. Also, the deposition of a legitimate pope against his will by a council of the church was as serious a matter then as the forced deposition of a monarch by a representative assembly.

The correctness of a conciliar deposition of a pope was thus debated a full thirty years before any direct action was taken. Advocates sought to fashion a church in which a representative council could effectively regulate the actions of the pope. The con-

Genghis Khan holding an audience. This Persian miniature shows the great conqueror and founder of the Mongol empire with members of his army and entourage as well as an apparent supplicant (lower right). E.T. Archive

ciliarists defined the church as the whole body of the faithful, of which the elected head, the pope, was only one part. And the pope's sole purpose was to maintain the unity and well-being of the church—something that the schismatic popes were far from doing. The conciliarists further argued that a council of the church acted with greater authority than the pope alone. In the eyes of the pope(s), such a concept of the church threatened both its political and its religious unity.

THE COUNCIL OF PISA (1409–1410) On the basis of the arguments of the conciliarists, cardinals representing both popes convened a council on their own authority in Pisa in 1409, deposed both the Roman and the Avignon popes, and elected a new pope, Alexander V. To the council's consternation, neither pope accepted its action, and Christendom suddenly faced the spectacle of three contending popes. Although the vast majority of Latin Christendom accepted Alexander and his Pisan successor John XXIII (r. 1410–1415), the popes of Rome and Avignon refused to step down.

THE COUNCIL OF CONSTANCE (1414–1417) The intolerable situation ended when Emperor Sigismund

prevailed on John XXIII to summon a new council in Constance in 1414, which the Roman pope Gregory XII also recognized. In a famous declaration entitled *Sacrosancta*, the council asserted its supremacy and proceeded to elect a new pope, Martin V (r. 1417–1431), after the three contending popes had either resigned or been deposed. The council then made provisions for regular meetings of church councils, within five, then seven, and thereafter every ten years.

Despite the role of the council of Constance in ending the Great Schism, in the official eyes of the church it was not a legitimate council. Nor have the schismatic popes of Avignon and Pisa been recognized as legitimate. (For this reason, another pope could take the name John XXIII in 1958.)

THE COUNCIL OF BASEL (R. 1431–1449) Conciliar government of the church peaked at the Council of Basel, when the council negotiated church doctrine with heretics. In 1432 the Hussites of Bohemia presented the *Four Articles of Prague* to the council as a basis for the negotiations. This document contained requests for (1) giving the laity the Eucharist with cup as well as bread; (2) free, itinerant preaching; (3) the exclusion of the clergy from holding secular offices and owning property; and (4) just punishment of clergy who commit mortal sins.

In November 1433 an agreement was reached between the emperor, the council, and the Hussites, giving the Bohemians jurisdiction over their church similar to that held by the French and the English. Three of the four Prague articles were conceded: communion with cup, free preaching by ordained clergy, and like punishment of clergy and laity for mortal sins.

The end of the Hussite wars and the reform legislation curtailing the papal power of appointment and taxation were the high points of the Council of Basel. The exercise of such power by a council did not please the pope, and in 1438 he gained the opportunity to upstage the Council of Basel by negotiating a reunion with the Eastern Church. The agreement, signed in Florence in 1439, was short lived, but it restored papal prestige and signaled the demise of the Conciliar Movement. The Council of Basel collapsed in 1449. A decade later Pope Pius II (r. 1458–1464) issued the papal bull *Execrabilis* (1460) condemning appeals to councils as "erroneous and abominable" and "completely null and void."

Although many who had worked for reform now despaired of ever attaining it, the Conciliar Movement was not a total failure. It planted deep within the conscience of all Western peoples the conviction that the role of a leader of an institution is to provide for the well-being of its members, not just for that of the leader.

A second consequence of the Conciliar Movement was the devolving of religious responsibility onto the laity and secular government. Without papal leadership, secular control of national or territorial churches increased. Kings asserted power over the church in England and France. In German, Swiss, and Italian cities magistrates and city councils reformed and regulated religious life. This development could not be reversed by the powerful popes of the High Renaissance. On the contrary, as the papacy became a limited territorial regime, national control of the church ran apace. Perceived as just one among several Italian states, the Papal States could now be opposed as much on the grounds of "national" policy as for religious reasons.

Medieval Russia

In the late tenth century, Prince Vladimir of Kiev (972–1015), at that time Russia's dominant city, received delegations of Muslims, Roman Catholics, Jews, and Greek Orthodox Christians, each of which hoped to see Russians embrace their religion. Vladimir chose Greek Orthodoxy, which became the religion of Russia, adding strong cultural bonds to the close commercial ties that had long linked Russia to the Byzantine Empire.

Politics and Society

Vladimir's successor, Yaroslav the Wise (1016–1054), developed Kiev into a magnificent political and cultural center, with architecture rivaling that of Constantinople. He also sought contacts with the West in an unsuccessful effort to counter the political influence of the Byzantine emperors. After his death, rivalry among their princes slowly divided Russians into three cultural groups: the Great Russians, the White Russians, and the Little Russians (Ukrainians). Autonomous principalities also challenged Kiev's dominance, and it became just one of several national centers. Government in the principalities combined monarchy (the prince), aristocracy (the prince's council of noblemen), and democracy (a popular assembly of all adult males). The broadest social division was between freemen and slaves. Freemen included the clergy, army officers, *boyars* (wealthy landowners), townspeople, and peasants. Slaves were mostly prisoners of war. Debtors working off their debts made up a large, semifree, intermediate group.

Mongol Rule (1243–1480)

In the thirteenth century, Mongol, or Tatar, armies swept over China, much of the Islamic world, and Russia. Ghengis Khan (1155–1227) invaded Russia in 1223, and Kiev fell to Batu Khan in 1240. Russian cities became dependent, tribute-paying principalities of the segment of the Mongol Empire called the Golden Horde (a phrase derived from the Tatar words for the color of Batu Khan's tent), which included the steppe region of what is now southern Russia and had its capital at Sarai, on the lower Volga. The Golden Horde stationed officials in all the principal Russian towns to oversee taxation and the conscription of soldiers into Tatar armies. Mongol rule created further cultural divisions between Russia and the West. The Mongols intermarried with the Russians and also created harems filled with Russian women. Russians who resisted were sold into slavery in foreign lands. Russian women—under the influence of Islam, which had become the religion of the Golden Horde—began to wear veils and to lead more secluded lives. The Mongols, however, left Russian political and religious institutions largely intact and, thanks to their far-flung trade, brought most Russians greater peace and prosperity than they had enjoyed before.

Liberation

The princes of Moscow cooperated with their overlords in the collection of tribute and grew wealthy under the Mongols. As Mongol rule weakened, the princes took control of the territory surrounding the city. In a process that has come to be known as "the gathering of the Russian Land," they then gradually expanded the principality of Moscow through land purchases, colonization, and conquest. In 1380, Grand Duke Dimitri of Moscow (1350–1389) defeated Tatar forces at Kulikov Meadow in a victory that marks the beginning of the decline of Mongol hegemony. Another century would pass before Ivan III, called Ivan the Great (d. 1505), would bring all of northern Russia under Moscow's control and end Mongol rule (1480). By the last quarter of the fourteenth century, however, Moscow had become the political and religious center of Russia, replacing Kiev. In Russian eyes, it was destined to become the "third Rome" after the fall of Constantinople to the Turks in 1453.

In Perspective

War, plague, and schism convulsed much of late medieval Europe throughout the fourteenth and into the fifteenth century. Two-fifths of the population, particularly along the major trade routes, died from plague in the fourteenth century. War and famine continued to take untold numbers after the plague had passed. The introduction of gunpowder and heavy artillery during the long years of warfare between England and France resulted in new forms of human destruction. Periodic revolts erupted in town and countryside as ordinary people attempted to defend their traditional communal rights and privileges against the new autocratic territorial regimes. Even God's house seemed to be in shambles in 1409, when no fewer than three popes came to rule simultaneously.

There is, however, another side to the late Middle Ages. By the end of the fifteenth century the population losses were rapidly being made up. Between 1300 and 1500, education had become far more accessible, especially to laypeople. The number of universities increased 250 percent, from twenty to seventy, and the rise in the number of residential colleges was even more impressive, especially in France, where sixty-three were built. The fourteenth century saw the birth of humanism, and the fifteenth *century gave us the printing press. Most impressive were the artistic and cultural achievements of the Italian Renaissance during the fifteenth century. The later Middle Ages were thus a period of growth and creativity, as well as one of waning and decline.*

REVIEW QUESTIONS

1. What were the underlying and precipitating causes of the Hundred Years' War? What advantages did each side have? Why were the French finally able to drive the English almost entirely out of France?
2. What were the causes of the Black Death, and why did it spread so quickly throughout western Europe? Where was it most virulent? What were its effects on European society? How important do you think disease is in changing the course of history?
3. Discuss the struggle between Pope Boniface VIII and King Philip the Fair. Why was Boniface so impotent in the conflict? How had political conditions changed since the reign of Pope Innocent III in the late twelfth century, and what did that mean for the papacy?
4. Briefly trace the history of the church from 1200 to 1450. How did it respond to political threats from the growing power of monarchs? How great an influence did the church have on secular events?
5. What was the Avignon papacy, and why did it occur? What effect did it have on the state of the papacy? What relation does it have to the Great Schism? How did the church become divided and how was it reunited? Why was the Conciliar Movement a setback for the papacy?
6. Why were kings in the late thirteenth and early fourteenth centuries able to control the church more than the church could control the kings? How did kings attack the church during this period? Contrast these events with earlier ones in which the pope dominated rulers.

SUGGESTED READINGS

C. ALLMAND, *The Hundred Years' War: England and France at War, c. 1300–c. 1450* (1988). Good overview of the war's development and consequences.

P. ARIÈS, *The Hour of Our Death* (1983). People's familiarity with, and philosophy of, death in the Middle Ages.

R. BARBER (ED.), *The Pastons: Letters of a Family in the War of the Roses* (1984). Revelations of English family life in an age of crisis.

J. LE GOFF, *The Birth of Purgatory*, trans. by A. Goldhammer (1984). Cultural impact of the idea.

J. HUIZINGA, *The Waning of the Middle Ages: A Study of the Forms of Life, Thought, and Art in France and the Netherlands in the Dawn of the Renaissance* (1924). A classic study of "mentality" at the end of the Middle Ages; exaggerated, but engrossing.

W. H. MCNEILL, *Plagues and Peoples* (1976). The Black Death in a broader context.

D. N. NICOL, *The Byzantine Lady: Ten Portraits, 1250–1500* (1994)

F. OAKLEY, *The Western Church in the Later Middle Ages* (1979). Eloquent, sympathetic survey.

S. OZMENT, *The Age of Reform, 1250–1550* (1980). Highlights of late medieval intellectual and religious history.

E. PERROY, *The Hundred Years' War*, trans. by W. B. Wells (1965). Still the most comprehensive one-volume account.

Y. RENOVARD, *The Avignon Papacy, 1305–1403*, trans. by D. Bethell (1970). The standard narrative account.

M. SPINKA, *John Huss's Concept of the Church* (1966). Lucid and authoritative account of Hussite theology.

B. TIERNEY, *The Crisis of Church and State, 1050–1300* (1964). Part IV provides the major documents in the clash between Boniface VIII and Philip the Fair.

C. T. WOOD, *Philip the Fair and Boniface VIII* (1967). Excerpts from the scholarly debate over the significance of this confrontation.

P. ZIEGLER, *The Black Death* (1969). Highly readable account.

Chapter 10

A map of America in 1596 with representations of the great Western explorers Columbus, Vespucci, Magellan, and Pizarro. Etching by Theodor de Bry, National Museum, Berlin. Bildarchiv Preussischer Kulturbesitz.

Renaissance and Discovery

KEY TOPICS

- The politics, culture, and art of the Italian Renaissance
- Political struggle and foreign intervention in Italy
- The powerful new monarchies of northern Europe
- The thought and culture of the northern Renaissance

I*f the late Middle Ages saw unprecedented chaos, it also witnessed a rebirth that would continue into the seventeenth century. Two modern Dutch scholars have employed the same word (Herfsttij, or "harvesttide") with different connotations to describe the period. Johan Huizinga has used the word to mean a "waning" or "decline," and Heiko Oberman has used it to mean "harvest." If something was dying away, some ripe fruit was being gathered and seed grain was sown. The late Middle Ages was a time of creative fragmentation.*

By the late fifteenth century, Europe was recovering well from two of the three crises of the late Middle Ages: the demographic and the political. The great losses in population were being recaptured, and increasingly able monarchs and rulers were imposing a new political order. A solution to the religious crisis, however, would have to await the Reformation and Counter-Reformation of the sixteenth century.

Although the opposite would be true in the sixteenth and seventeenth centuries, the city–states of Italy survived the century and a half between 1300 and 1450 better than the territorial states of northern Europe. This was due to Italy's strategic location between East and West and its lucrative Eurasian trade. Great wealth gave rulers and merchants the ability to work their will on both society and culture. They became patrons of government, education, and the arts, always as much for self-aggrandizement as out of benevolence, for whether a patron was a family, a firm, a government, or the church, their endowments enhanced their reputation and power. The result of such patronage was a cultural Renaissance in Italian cities unmatched elsewhere.

With the fall of Constantinople to the Turks in 1453, the shrinkage of Italy's once unlimited trading empire began. City–state soon turned against city–state, and by the 1490s the armies of France invaded Italy. Within a quarter century, Italy's great Renaissance had peaked.

The fifteenth century also saw an unprecedented scholarly renaissance. Italian and northern humanists made a full recovery of classical knowledge and languages and set in motion educational reforms and cultural changes that would spread throughout Europe in the fifteenth and sixteenth centuries. In the process the Italian humanists invented, for all practical purposes, critical historical scholarship and exploited a new fifteenth-century invention, the "divine art" of printing with movable type.

In this period the vernacular—the local language— began to take its place alongside Latin, the international language, as a widely used literary and political means of communication. And European lands progressively superseded the universal Church as the community of highest allegiance, as patriotism and incipient nationalism seized hearts and minds as strongly as religion. Nations henceforth "transcended" themselves not by journeys to Rome, but by competitive voyages to the Far East and the Americas, as the age of global exploration opened.

For Europe, the late fifteenth and sixteenth centuries were a period of unprecedented territorial expansion and ideological experimentation. Permanent colonies were established within the Americas, and the exploitation of the New World's human and mineral resources was begun. Imported American gold and silver spurred scientific invention and a new weapons industry and touched off an inflationary spiral that produced an escalation in prices by the century's end. The new bullion also helped create an international traffic in African slaves as rival African tribes sold their captives to the Portuguese. These slaves were brought in ever-increasing numbers to work the mines and the plantations of the New World as replacements for faltering American natives. The period also saw social engineering and political planning on a large scale. Newly centralized governments began to put long-range economic policies into practice, a development that came to be known as mercantilism.

The Renaissance in Italy (1375–1527)

A historian has described the Renaissance as the "prototype of the modern world." In his *Civilization of the Renaissance in Italy* (1860), Jacob Burckhardt argues that in fourteenth- and fifteenth-century Italy, through the revival of ancient learning, new secular and scientific values began to supplant traditional religious beliefs. This was the period in which people began to adopt a rational, objective, and statistical approach to reality and to rediscover the importance of the individual and his or her artistic creativity. The result, in Burckhardt's words, was a release of the "full, whole nature of man."

Other scholars have found Burckhardt's description far too modernizing an interpretation of the Renaissance and have accused him of overlooking the continuity between the Middle Ages and the Renaissance. His critics especially stress the still strongly Christian character of Renaissance humanism. They point out that earlier "renaissances," especially that of the twelfth century, also saw the revival of the ancient classics, interest in the Latin language and Greek science, and an appreciation of the worth and creativity of individuals.

Despite the exaggeration and bias of Burckhardt's portrayal, most scholars agree that the Renaissance was a time of transition from the medieval to the modern world. Medieval Europe, especially before the twelfth century, had been a fragmented feudal society with an agricultural economy, and its thought and culture were largely dominated by the church. Renaissance Europe, especially after the fourteenth century, was characterized by growing national consciousness and political centralization, an urban economy based on organized commerce and capitalism, and ever-greater lay and secular control of thought and culture, including religion.

The distinctive features and achievements of the Renaissance are most strikingly revealed in Italy from roughly 1375 to 1527, the year of the infamous sack of Rome by imperial soldiers. What was achieved in Italy during the late fourteenth to the early sixteenth centuries also deeply influenced northern Europe. (See "Art & the West.")

The Italian City–State

Renaissance society was no simple cultural transformation. It first took distinctive shape within the cities of late medieval Italy. Italy had always had a cultural advantage over the rest of Europe because its geography made it the natural gateway between East and West. Venice, Genoa, and Pisa traded uninterruptedly with the Near East throughout the Middle Ages

An Unprecedented Self-Portrait

Albrecht Dürer (1471–1528), the greatest German painter of the Renaissance, was the son of a Nuremberg goldsmith and the apprentice of the city's then most famous painter, Michael Wolgemut. Naturally gifted and trained from childhood, Dürer at thirteen could draw so lifelike a reflection of himself in a mirror, that senior artists already then recognized his genius. A dowry from his marriage at twenty-two (his wife, Agnes Frey, was nineteen) permitted him to travel to Venice, where he acquired the skills of the great Italian artists. His ability to paint realistically led contemporaries to compare him to the legendary ancient Greek painter Apelles and won him many humanistic and princely patrons. According to one story, his dog, passing by a just finished painting his master had put outside to dry, mistook the work for the master himself and gave it a loving lick, leaving a permanent mark on the painting that Dürer proudly pointed out.

The *Self-Portrait* of 1500 was one of perhaps thirty self-portraits over Dürer's lifetime. (No previous artist painted himself as often or as provocatively.) For some scholars this painting signals a change from the medieval toward a more modern worldview. The individual becomes the primary focus, supplanting God and king. Exalting the power of art and the artist, Dürer presents himself as Christ-like and full faced, a pose traditionally reserved for members of the Holy Trinity. His own autograph, placed at eye level, backs up the portrait's bold proclamation: "I, Albrecht Dürer, divinely inspired artist."

The portrait's powerful effect is achieved by strict adherence to the rules of geometric proportionality (a subject on which Dürer wrote a major book) and by painstaking attention to detail. It is a work of perfect symmetry, and each hair of his head—even the fur on his coat— seems to have been drawn individually with great care. What the viewer beholds is neither Christ nor Everyman, but the gifted individual as many Renaissance thinkers dreamed him to be: a divinely endowed person capable of great achievement.

Dürer, Albrecht (1471–1528). *Self-portrait at Age 28 with Fur Coat*. 1500. Oil on wood, 67 × 49 cm. Alte Pinakothek, Munich, Germany. Scala/Art Resource, N.Y.

Sources: Jane Campbell Hutchison, *Albrecht Dürer: A Biography* (Princeton: Princeton University Press, 1990); Joseph Leo Koerner, *The Moment of Self-Portraiture in German Renaissance Art* (Chicago, 1993), esp. pp. xviii, 8–9, 40–42.

and maintained vibrant urban societies. When commerce revived on a large scale in the eleventh century, Italian merchants quickly mastered the business skills of organization, bookkeeping, scouting new markets, and securing monopolies. During the thirteenth and fourteenth centuries, trade-rich cities expanded to become powerful city–states, dominating the political and economic life of the surrounding countryside. By the fifteenth century, the great Italian cities had become the bankers of much of Europe.

GROWTH OF CITY–STATES The growth of Italian cities and urban culture was assisted by the endemic warfare between the emperor and the pope and the Guelf (propapal) and Ghibelline (proimperial) factions that this warfare had created. Either of these might have successfully challenged the cities had they permitted each other to concentrate on that. Instead, they chose to weaken one another and thus strengthened

MAP 10–1 RENAISSANCE ITALY *The city–states of Renaissance Italy were self-contained principalities whose internal strife was monitored by their despots and whose external aggression was long successfully controlled by treaty.*

the merchant oligarchies of the cities. Unlike those of northern Europe, which tended to be dominated by kings and territorial princes, the great Italian cities were left free to expand. They became independent states, absorbing the surrounding countryside and assimilating the area's nobility in a unique urban meld of old and new rich. There were five such major, competitive states in Italy: the duchy of Milan; the republics of Florence and Venice; the Papal States; and the kingdom of Naples. (See Map 10–1.)

Social strife and competition for political power were so intense within the cities that most had evolved into despotisms by the fifteenth century just to survive. Venice was a notable exception. It was ruled by a successful merchant oligarchy with power located in a patrician senate of 300 members and a ruthless judicial body, the Council of Ten, which anticipated and suppressed rival groups. Elsewhere, the new social classes and divisions within society produced by rapid urban growth fueled chronic, near-anarchic conflict.

SOCIAL CLASS AND CONFLICT Florence was the most striking example. There were four distinguishable social groups within the city. The first was the old rich, or *grandi*, the nobles and merchants who traditionally ruled the city. The second group was the emergent newly rich merchant class—capitalists and bankers known as the *popolo grosso*, or "fat people." They began to challenge the old rich for political power in the late thirteenth and early fourteenth centuries. Then there were the middle-burgher ranks of guild masters, shop owners, and professionals—those smaller businesspeople who, in Florence as elsewhere, tended to take the side of the new rich against the conservative policies of the old rich. Finally, there was the *popolo minuto*, or the "little people," the lower economic classes. In 1457 one-third of the population of Florence, about 30,000 people, were officially listed as paupers, that is, having no wealth at all.

These social divisions produced conflict at every level of society, to which was added the ever-present fear of foreign intrigue. In 1378 there was a great revolt of the poor known as the Ciompi Revolt. It resulted from a combination of three factors that made life unbearable for those at the bottom of society: the feuding between the old and the new rich; the social anarchy that had resulted from the Black Death, which cut the city's population almost in half; and the collapse of the banking houses of Bardi and Peruzzi, which left the poor more economically vulnerable than ever. The successful revolt established a chaotic four-year reign of power by the lower Florentine classes. True stability did not return to Florence until the ascent to power of Cosimo de' Medici (1389–1464) in 1434.

Florentine women doing needlework, spinning, and weaving. These activities took up much of a woman's time and contributed to the elegance of dress for which Florentine men and women were famed.
Alinari/Art Resource

DESPOTISM AND DIPLOMACY   The wealthiest Florentine, Cosimo de' Medici, was an astute statesman. He controlled the city internally from behind the scenes, skillfully manipulating the constitution and influencing elections. Florence was governed by a council, first of six and later of eight members, known as the *Signoria*. These men were chosen from the most powerful guilds—those representing the major clothing industries (cloth, wool, fur, and silk) and such other groups as bankers, judges, and doctors. Through his informal, cordial relations with the electoral committee, Cosimo was able to keep councillors loyal to him in the *Signoria*. As head of the Office of Public Debt, he was able to favor congenial factions. His grandson Lorenzo the Magnificent (1449–1492, r. 1478–1492) ruled Florence in almost totalitarian fashion during the last quarter of the fifteenth century. The assassination of his brother in 1478 by a rival family, the Pazzi, who plotted with the pope against Medici rule, made Lorenzo a cautious and determined ruler.

Despotism was less subtle elsewhere. To prevent internal social conflict and foreign intrigue from paralyzing their cities, the dominant groups cooperated to install a hired strongman. Known as a *podestà*, his purpose was to maintain law and order. He was given executive, military, and judicial authority. His mandate was direct and simple: to permit, by whatever means required, the normal flow of business activity without which neither the old

rich, the new rich, nor the poor of a city could long survive. Because these despots could not depend on the divided populace, they operated through mercenary armies, which they obtained through military brokers known as *condottieri*.

It was a hazardous job. Not only were despots subject to dismissal by the oligarchies that hired them, but they were also popular objects of assassination attempts. The spoils of success, however, were very great. In Milan, it was as despots that the Visconti family came to power in 1278 and the Sforza family in 1450. Both ruled without constitutional restraints or serious political competition. The latter produced one of Machiavelli's heroes, Ludovico il Moro.

Political turbulence and warfare gave birth to diplomacy. Consequently, the various city–states could stay abreast of foreign military developments and, if shrewd enough, gain power and advantage short of actually going to war. Most city–states established resident embassies in the fifteenth century. Their ambassadors not only represented them in ceremonies and as negotiators, but also became their watchful eyes and ears at rival courts.

Whether within the comparatively tranquil republic of Venice, the strong-arm democracy of Florence, or the undisguised despotism of Milan, the disciplined Italian city proved a most congenial climate for an unprecedented flowering of thought and culture. Italian Renaissance culture was promoted as vigorously by despots as by republicans and as enthusiastically by secularized popes as by the more spiritually minded.

Cosimo de' Medici (1389–1464), Florentine banker and statesman, in his lifetime the city's wealthiest man and most successful politician. This portrait is by Pontormo.
Erich Lessing, Art Resource, N.Y.

Such widespread support occurred because the main requirement for patronage of the arts and letters was the one thing that Italian cities of the High Renaissance had in abundance: great wealth.

Humanism

Several schools of thought exist on the meaning of "humanism." There are those who see the Italian Renaissance as the birth of modernity, characterized by an un-Christian philosophy that stressed the dignity of humankind and championed individualism and secular values. (These are the followers of the nineteenth-century historian Jacob Burckhardt.) Others argue that humanists were the very champions of authentic Catholic Christianity, who opposed the pagan teaching of Aristotle and the ineloquent Scholasticism that his writings nurtured. Still others see humanism as a form of scholarship consciously designed to promote a sense of civic responsibility and political liberty.

An authoritative modern commentator on humanism, Paul O. Kristeller, has accused all these views of dealing more with the secondary effects than with the essence of humanism. Humanism, he believes, was no particular philosophy or value system, but simply an educational program that concentrated on rhetoric and sound scholarship for their own sake.

There is truth in each of these definitions. Humanism was the scholarly study of the Latin and Greek classics and of the ancient Church Fathers both for its own sake and in the hope of a rebirth of ancient norms and values. Humanists advocated the *studia humanitatis*, a liberal arts program of study that embraced grammar, rhetoric, poetry, history, politics, and moral philosophy. Not only were these subjects considered a joy in themselves, but they were also seen as celebrating the dignity of humankind and preparing people for a life of virtuous action. The Florentine Leonardo Bruni (ca. 1370–1444) first gave the name *humanitas*, or "humanity," to the learning that resulted from such scholarly pursuits. Bruni was a student of Manuel Chrysoloras, a Byzantine scholar who opened the world of Greek scholarship to a generation of young Italian humanists when he taught at Florence between 1397 and 1403.

The first humanists were orators and poets. They wrote original literature in both the classical and the vernacular languages, inspired by and modeled on the newly discovered works of the ancients. They also taught rhetoric within the universities. When humanists were not employed as teachers of rhetoric, their talents were sought as secretaries, speechwriters, and diplomats in princely and papal courts.

The study of classical and Christian antiquity existed before the Italian Renaissance. There were recoveries of ancient civilization during the Carolingian renaissance of the ninth century, within the cathedral school of Chartres in the twelfth century, during the great Aristotelian revival in Paris in the thirteenth century, and among the Augustinians in the early fourteenth century. These precedents, however, only partially compare with the grand achievements of the Italian Renaissance of the late Middle Ages. The latter was far more secular and lay dominated, had much broader interests, was blessed with far more recovered manuscripts, and possessed far superior technical skills than had been the case in the earlier "rebirths" of antiquity.

Unlike their Scholastic rivals, humanists were less bound to recent tradition; they did not focus all their attention on summarizing and comparing the views of recognized authorities on a text or question, but went directly to the original sources themselves. And their most respected sources were classical and biblical, not the medieval philosophers and theologians. Avidly searching out manuscript collections, Italian humanists made the full sources of Greek and Latin antiquity available to scholars during the fourteenth and fifteenth centuries. Mastery of Latin and Greek was the surgeon's tool of the humanist. There is a kernel of truth—but only a kernel—in the humanists' arrogant assertion that the period between themselves and classical civilization was a "dark middle age."

PETRARCH, DANTE, AND BOCCACCIO   Francesco Petrarch (1304–1374) was the "father of humanism." (See "Petrarch's Letter to Posterity.") He left the legal profession to pursue letters and poetry. Most of his life was spent in and around Avignon. He was involved in Cola di Rienzo's popular revolt and two-year reign (1347–1349) in Rome as "tribune" of the Roman people. Petrarch also served the Visconti family in Milan in his later years.

Petrarch celebrated ancient Rome in his *Letters to the Ancient Dead*, fancied personal letters to Cicero, Livy, Vergil, and Horace. He also wrote a Latin epic poem (*Africa*, a poetic historical tribute to the Roman general Scipio Africanus) and a set of biographies of famous Roman men (*Lives of Illustrious Men*). Petrarch's most famous contemporary work was a collection of highly introspective love sonnets to a certain Laura, a married woman whom he romantically admired from a safe distance.

His critical textual studies, elitism, and contempt for the allegedly useless learning of the Scholastics were features that many later humanists also shared. Classical and Christian values coexist, not always harmoniously, in his work, an uneasy coexistence that is seen in many later humanists. Medieval Christian values can be seen in Petrarch's imagined dialogues with Saint Augustine and in tracts written to defend the personal immortality of the soul against the Aristotelians.

Petrarch was, however, far more secular in orientation than his famous near-contemporary Dante Alighieri (1265–1321), whose *Vita Nuova* and *Divine Comedy* form, with Petrarch's sonnets, the cornerstones of Italian vernacular literature. Petrarch's student and friend Giovanni Boccaccio (1313–1375) was also a pioneer of humanist studies. His *Decameron*–one hundred often bawdy tales told by three men and seven women in a country retreat from the plague that ravaged Florence in 1348—is both a stinging social commentary (especially in its exposé of sexual and economic misconduct) and a sympathetic look at human behavior. An avid collector of manuscripts, Boccaccio also assembled an encyclopedia of Greek and Roman mythology.

Petrarch's Letter to Posterity

In old age Petrarch wrote a highly personal letter to posterity in which he summarized the lessons he had learned during his lifetime. The letter also summarizes the original values of Renaissance humanists: their suspicion of purely materialistic pleasure, the importance they attached to friendship, and their utter devotion to and love of antiquity.

❖ *Does Petrarch's letter give equal weight to classical and Christian values? Why would he have preferred to live in another age?*

I have always possessed extreme contempt for wealth; not that riches are not desirable in themselves, but because I hate the anxiety and care which are invariably associated with them....I have, on the contrary, led a happier existence with plain living and ordinary fare....

The pleasure of dining with one's friends is so great that nothing has ever given me more delight than their unexpected arrival, nor have I ever willingly sat down to table without a companion....

The greatest kings of this age have loved and courted me....I have fled, however, from many...to whom I was greatly attached; and such was my innate longing for liberty that I studiously avoided those whose very name seemed incompatible with the freedom I loved.

I possess a well-balanced rather than a keen intellect—one prone to all kinds of good and wholesome study, but especially to moral philosophy and the art of poetry. The latter I neglected as time went on, and took delight in sacred literature....Among the many subjects that interested me, I dwelt especially upon antiquity, for our own age has always repelled me, so that, had it not been for the love of those dear to me, I should have preferred to have been born in any other period than our own. In order to forget my own time, I have constantly striven to place myself in spirit in other ages, and consequently I delighted in history....

If only I have lived well, it matter little to me how I have talked. Mere elegance of language can produce at best but an empty fame.

Frederick Austen Ogg, ed., *A Source Book of Mediaeval History: Documents Illustrative of European Life and Institutions from the German Invasions to the Renaissance* (New York: American Book Company, 1908), pp. 470–473.

Dante Alighieri (1265–1321) portrayed with scenes of hell, purgatory, and paradise from the Divine Comedy, *his classic epic poem.* Scala/Art Resource, N.Y.

EDUCATIONAL REFORMS AND GOALS Humanists were not bashful scholars. They delighted in going directly to primary sources and refused to be slaves to tradition. Such an attitude not only made them innovative educators, but also kept them constantly in search of new sources of information. Magnificent manuscript collections were assembled with great care, as if they were potent medicines for the ills of contemporary society.

The goal of humanist studies was to be wise and to speak eloquently, to know what is good, and to practice virtue. Learning was not to remain abstract and unpracticed. "It is better to will the good than to know the truth," Petrarch had taught, and this became a motto of many later humanists, who, like Petrarch, believed that learning ennobled people. Pietro Paolo Vergerio (1349–1420), the author of the most influential Renaissance tract on education, *On the Morals That Befit a Free Man*, left a classic summary of the humanist concept of a liberal education:

We call those studies liberal which are worthy of a free man; those studies by which we attain and practice virtue and wisdom; that education which calls forth, trains, and develops those highest gifts of body and mind which ennoble men and which are rightly judged to rank next in dignity to virtue only, for to a vulgar temper, gain and pleasure are the one aim of existence, to a lofty nature, moral worth and fame.[1]

The ideal of a useful education and well-rounded people inspired far-reaching reforms in traditional education. Quintilian's *Education of the Orator*, the

complete text of which was discovered in 1416, became the basic classical guide for the humanist revision of the traditional curriculum. Vittorino da Feltre (d. 1446) exemplified the ideals of humanist teaching. He not only had his students read the difficult works of Pliny, Ptolemy, Terence, Plautus, Livy, and Plutarch, but also subjected them to vigorous physical exercise and games. Another famous educator, Guarino da Verona (d. 1460), rector of the new University of Ferrara and a student of the age's most renowned Greek scholar, Manuel Chrysoloras, streamlined the study of classical languages and gave it systematic form.

Humanist learning was not confined to the classroom, as Baldassare Castiglione's (1478–1529) famous *Book of the Courtier* illustrates. Written as a practical guide for the nobility at the court of Urbino, it embodies the highest ideals of Italian humanism. It depicts the successful courtier as one who knew how to integrate knowledge of ancient languages and history with athletic, military, and musical skills, while practicing good manners and exhibiting a high moral character.

Noblewomen also played a role at court in education and culture, among them none more so than Christine de Pisan (1363?–1434). The Italian-born daughter of the physician and astrologer of the French king Charles V, she received as fine an education at the French court as anyone could have. She became expert in classical, French, and Italian languages and literature. Married at fifteen and the widowed mother of three at twenty-seven, she turned to writing lyric poetry to support herself. She soon became a well-known woman of letters who was much read throughout the courts of Europe. Her most famous

---

[1] Cited by De Lamar Jensen, *Renaissance Europe: Age of Recovery and Reconciliation* (Lexington, MA: D. C. Health, 1981), p. 111.

work, *The City of Ladies*, is a chronicle of the accomplishments of the great women of history. (See "Christine de Pisan Instructs Women on How to Handle Their Husbands.")

THE FLORENTINE "ACADEMY" AND THE REVIVAL OF PLATONISM Of all the important recoveries of the past made during the Italian Renaissance, none stands out more than the revival of Greek studies, especially the works of Plato, in fifteenth-century Florence. Many factors combined to bring this revival about. An important foundation was laid in 1397 when the city invited Manuel Chrysoloras to come from Constantinople to promote Greek learning. A half century later (1439), the ecumenical Council of Ferrara–Florence, having convened to negotiate the reunion of the Eastern and Western churches, opened the door for many Greek scholars and manuscripts to enter the West.

After the fall of Constantinople to the Turks in 1453, Greek scholars fled to Florence for refuge. This was the background against which the Florentine Platonic Academy evolved under the patronage of Cosimo de' Medici and the supervision of Marsilio Ficino (1433–1499) and Pico della Mirandola (1463–1494).

The thinkers of the Renaissance were interested in every variety of ancient wisdom. They were especially attracted, however, to the Platonic tradition and to those Church Fathers who tried to synthesize Platonic philosophy with Christian teaching. The "Florentine Academy" was actually not a formal school, but an informal gathering of influential Florentine humanists devoted to the revival of the works of Plato and the Neoplatonists: Plotinus, Proclus, Porphyry, and Dionysius the Areopagite. To this end, Ficino edited and published the complete works of Plato.

Christine de Pisan Instructs Women on How to Handle Their Husbands

Renowned Renaissance noblewoman Christine de Pisan has the modern reputation of being perhaps the first feminist, and her book, The Treasure of the City of Ladies *(also known as* The Book of Three Virtues*), has been described as the Renaissance woman's survival manual. Here she gives advice to the wives of artisans.*

❖ *How does Christine de Pisan's image of husband and wife compare with other medieval views? Would the church take issue with her advice in any way? As a noblewoman commenting on the married life of artisans, does her high social standing influence her advice? Would she give similar advice to women of her own social class?*

All wives of artisans should be very painstaking and diligent if they wish to have the necessities of life. They should encourage their husbands or their workmen to get to work early in the morning and work until late....[And] the wife herself should [also] be involved in the work to the extent that she knows all about it, so that she may know how to oversee his workers if her husband is absent, and to reprove them if they do not do well....And when customers come to her husband and try to drive a hard bargain, she ought to warn him solicitously to take care that he does not make a bad deal. She should advise him to be chary of giving too much credit if he does not know precisely where and to whom it is going, for in this way many come to poverty....

In addition, she ought to keep her husband's love as much as she can, to this end: that he will stay at home more willingly and that he may not have any reason to join the foolish crowds of other young men in taverns and indulge in unnecessary and extravagant expense, as many tradesmen do, especially in Paris. By treating him kindly she should protect him as well as she can from this. It is said that three things drive a man from his home: a quarrelsome wife, a smoking fireplace, and a leaking roof. She too ought to stay at home gladly and not go off every day traipsing hither and yon gossiping with the neighbours and visiting her chums to find out what everyone is doing. That is done by slovenly housewives roaming about the town in groups. Nor should she go off on these pilgrimages got up for no good reason and involving a lot of needless expense.

Excerpt from *The Treasure of the City of Ladies* or *The Book of the Three Virtues*, by Christine de Pisan, trans. by Sarah Lawson (Penguin Classics, 1985), this translation copyright © Sarah Lawson, 1985. Reprinted by permission of Penguin Books Ltd.

The appeal of Platonism lay in its flattering view of human nature. It distinguished between an eternal sphere of being and the perishable world in which humans actually lived. Human reason was believed to belong to the former—indeed, to have preexisted in this pristine world and to continue to commune with it, to which the present knowledge of mathematical and moral truth bore witness.

Strong Platonic influence can be seen in Pico's *Oration on the Dignity of Man*, perhaps the most famous Renaissance statement on the nature of humankind. Pico wrote the *Oration* as an introduction to a pretentious collection of 900 theses. Published in Rome in December 1486, the theses were intended to serve as the basis for a public debate on all of life's important topics. The *Oration* drew on Platonic teaching to depict humans as the only creatures in the world who possessed the freedom to be whatever they chose, able at will to rise to the height of angels or to descend to the level of pigs.

CRITICAL WORK OF THE HUMANISTS: LORENZO VALLA Because they were guided by a scholarly ideal of philological accuracy and historical truthfulness, the humanists could become critics of tradition even when that was not their intention. Dispassionate critical scholarship shook long-standing foundations, not the least of which were those of the medieval church.

The work of Lorenzo Valla (1406–1457), author of the standard Renaissance text on Latin philology, the *Elegances of the Latin Language* (1444), reveals the explosive character of the new learning. Although a good Catholic, Valla became a hero to later Protestants. His popularity among Protestants stemmed from his defense of predestination against the advocates of free will, and especially from his exposé of the *Donation of Constantine*. (See Chapter 6.)

The fraudulent *Donation*, written in the eighth century, purported to be a grant of vast territories made by the fourth-century Roman emperor Constantine to the pope. Valla did not intend the exposé of the *Donation* to have the devastating force that Protestants later attributed to it. He only proved in a careful, scholarly way what others had long suspected. Using the most rudimentary textual analysis and historical logic, Valla demonstrated that the document was filled with such anachronistic terms as *fief* and that it contained material that could not be in a genuine fourth-century document. In the same dispassionate way, Valla also pointed out errors in the Latin Vulgate, still the authorized version of the Bible for the Western church.

Such discoveries did not make Valla any less loyal to the church, nor did they prevent his faithful fulfillment of the office of apostolic secretary in Rome under Pope Nicholas V. Nonetheless, historical criticism of this type served those less loyal to the medieval church. It was no accident that young humanists formed the first identifiable group of Martin Luther's supporters.

CIVIC HUMANISM Italian humanists were exponents of applied knowledge; their basic criticism of traditional education was that much of it was useless. Education, they believed, should promote individual virtue and public service. This ideal inspired what has been called civic humanism, by which is meant examples of humanist leadership of the political and cultural life. The most striking instance is to be found in Florence. There three humanists served as chancellors: Colluccio Salutati (1331–1406), Leonardo Bruni (ca. 1370–1444), and Poggio Bracciolini (1380–1459). Each used his rhetorical skills to rally the Florentines against the aggression of Naples and Milan. Bruni and Poggio also wrote adulatory histories of the city. Another accomplished humanist scholar, Leon Battista Alberti (1402–1472), was a noted architect and builder in the city. Whether it was humanism that accounted for such civic activity or just a desire to exercise great power remains a debated issue.

On the other hand, many humanists became cliquish and snobbish, an intellectual elite concerned only with pursuing narrow, antiquarian interests and writing pure, classical Latin in the quiet of their studies. It was in reaction to this elitist trend that the humanist historians Niccolò Machiavelli (1469–1527) and Francesco Guicciardini (1483–1540) adopted the vernacular and made contemporary history their primary source and subject matter.

Renaissance Art

In Renaissance Italy, as in Reformation Europe, the values and interests of the laity were no longer subordinated to those of the clergy. In education, culture, and religion, the laity assumed a leading role and established models for the clergy to imitate. This was a development due in part to the church's loss of international power during the great crises of the late Middle Ages. It was also encouraged by the rise of national sentiment, the creation of competent national bureaucracies staffed by the laity rather than by clerics, and the rapid growth of lay education during the fourteenth and fifteenth centuries. Medieval Christian values were adjusting to a more this-worldly spirit. Men and women began again to appreciate

Giotto's portrayal of the funeral of Saint Francis of Assisi. The saint is surrounded by his admiring brothers and a knight of Assisi (first on the right). Giotto's (1266–1336) work signals the evolution toward Renaissance art. The damaged areas on this fresco resulted from the removal of nineteenth-century restorations. Scala/Art Resource, N.Y.

and even glorify the secular world, secular learning, and purely human pursuits as ends in themselves.

This new perspective on life is prominent in the painting and sculpture of the High Renaissance—the late fifteenth and early sixteenth centuries, when Renaissance art reached its full maturity. Whereas medieval art tended to be abstract and formulaic, Renaissance art was emphatically concerned with the observation of the natural world and the communication of human emotions. Renaissance artists also tried to give their works a greater rational (chiefly mathematical) order—a symmetry and proportionality that reflected pictorially their deeply held belief in the harmony of the universe. The interest of Renaissance artists in ancient Roman art was closely allied to an independent interest in humanity and nature.

Renaissance artists had the advantage of new technical skills developed during the fifteenth century. In addition to the availability of oil paints, two special techniques were perfected: that of using shading to enhance naturalness (*chiaroscuro*) and that of adjusting the size of figures to give the viewer a feeling of continuity with the painting (linear perspective). These techniques permitted the artist to "rationalize" space and paint a more natural world. The result was that, compared to their flat Byzantine and Gothic counterparts, Renaissance paintings were filled with energy and life and stood out from the canvas in three dimensions.

The new direction was signaled by Giotto (1266–1336), the father of Renaissance painting. An admirer of Saint Francis of Assisi, whose love of nature he shared, Giotto painted a more natural world than his Byzantine and Gothic predecessors. Though still filled with religious seriousness, his work was no longer so abstract and unnatural a depiction of

the world. The painter Masaccio (1401–1428) and the sculptor Donatello (1386–1466) continued to portray the world around them more literally and naturally. The heights were reached by the great masters of the High Renaissance: Leonardo da Vinci (1452–1519), Raphael (1483–1520), and Michelangelo Buonarroti (1475–1564).

LEONARDO DA VINCI   More than any other person in the period, Leonardo exhibited the Renaissance ideal of the universal person. He was a true mas-

Aviation drawings by Leonardo da Vinci (1452–1519), who imagined a possible flying machine with a retractable ladder for boarding. David Forbert/SuperStock, Inc.

ter of many skills. One of the greatest painters of all time, he was also a military engineer for Ludovico il Moro in Milan, Cesare Borgia in Romagna, and the French king Francis I. Leonardo advocated scientific experimentation, dissected corpses to learn anatomy, and was an accomplished, self-taught botanist. His inventive mind foresaw such modern machines as airplanes and submarines. Indeed, the variety of his interests was so great that it could shorten his attention span, so that he was constantly moving from one activity to another. His great skill in conveying inner moods through complex facial features can be seen in the most famous of his paintings, the *Mona Lisa*, as well as in his self-portrait.

RAPHAEL A man of great sensitivity and kindness, Raphael was apparently loved by contemporaries as much for his person as for his work. His premature death at thirty-seven cut short his artistic career. He is famous for his tender madonnas, the best known of which graced the monastery of San Sisto in Piacenza and is now in Dresden. Art historians praise his fresco *The School of Athens*,

a grandly conceived portrayal of the great masters of Western philosophy, as a virtually perfect example of Renaissance technique. It depicts Plato and Aristotle surrounded by the great philosophers and scientists of antiquity, who are portrayed with features of Raphael's famous contemporaries, including Leonardo and Michelangelo.

MICHELANGELO The melancholy genius Michelangelo also excelled in a variety of arts and crafts. His eighteen-foot godlike sculpture David, which long stood majestically in the great square of Florence, is a perfect example of the Renaissance artist's devotion to harmony, symmetry, and proportion, as well as the extreme glorification of the human form. Four different popes commissioned works by Michelangelo. The most famous of these works are the frescoes for the Sistine Chapel, painted during the pontificate of Pope Julius II (r. 1503–1513), who

Portrait by Raphael of Baldassare Castiglione (1748–1529), author of the Cortegiano. Portrait (c. 1515) now in the Louvre. Cliche des Musées Nationaux

Commissioned in 1501, when the artist was 26, Michelangelo's David *became the symbol of the Florentine republic and was displayed in front of the Palazzo Vecchio. The detail shown here highlights the restrained emotion and dignity for which the statue is famous.* Michelangelo (1475–1564) David-p. (testa di profilo.) Accademia Firenze. Scala/Art Resource

These two works by Donatello, sculpted fifteen years apart, reveal the psychological complexity of Renaissance artists and their work. On the left is a youthful, sexy David, standing awkwardly and seemingly puzzled on the head of the slain Goliath. Created in 1440, it is the earliest free-standing nude made in the West since Roman times. Art Resource, N.Y *On the right, sculpted in 1454–1455 from poplar wood, is Mary Magdalen returned from her desert retreat; she is a frightful, toothless old woman, shorn of all dignity.* Scala/Art Resource, N.Y.

The frescoes of Michelangelo on the west wall ceiling of the Sistine Chapel in the Vatican Palace. Above the altar is his Last Judgment. Brett Froomer/The Image Bank

also set Michelangelo to work on the pope's own magnificent tomb. (See "Michaelangelo and Pope Julius II.") The Sistine frescoes originally covered 10,000 square feet and involved 343 figures, over half of which exceeded 10 feet in height. But it is their originality and perfection as works of art that impress most. This labor of love and piety took four years to complete. A person of incredible energy and endurance who lived to be almost ninety, Michelangelo insisted on doing almost everything himself and permitted his assistants only a few of the many chores involved in his work.

His later works are more complex and suggest deep personal changes. They mark, artistically and philosophically, the passing of High Renaissance painting and the advent of a new style known as mannerism, which reached its peak in the late sixteenth and early seventeenth centuries. A reaction against the simplicity and symmetry of High Renaissance art (which also found expression in music and literature), mannerism made room for the strange and even the abnormal and gave freer reign to the subjectivity of the artist. Mannerism acquired its name because the

artist was permitted to express his or her own individual perceptions and feelings, to paint, compose, or write in a "mannered," or "affected," way. Tintoretto (d. 1594) and especially El Greco (d. 1614) became mannerism's supreme representatives.

Slavery in the Renaissance

Throughout Renaissance Italy, slavery flourished as extravagantly as art and culture. A thriving western slave market existed as early as the twelfth century, when the Spanish sold Muslim slaves captured in raids and war to wealthy Italians and other interested buyers. Contemporaries looked on such slavery as a merciful act, since these captives would otherwise have been killed. In addition to widespread household or domestic slavery, collective plantation slavery, following East Asian models, also developed during the High Middle Ages in the eastern Mediterranean. In the savannas of Sudan and on Venetian estates on the islands of Cyprus and Crete, gangs of slaves worked sugar cane plantations, the model for later western Mediterranean and New World slavery.

After the Black Death (1348–1350) had reduced the supply of laborers everywhere in western Europe, the demand for slaves soared. Slaves now began to be imported from Africa, the Balkans, Constantinople, Cyprus, Crete, and the lands surrounding the Black Sea. Because slaves were taken randomly from conquered people, they consisted of many races: Tatars, Circassians, Greeks, Russians, Georgians, and Iranians as well as Asians and Africans. According to one source, "By the end of the fourteenth century, there was hardly a well-to-do household in Tuscany without at least one slave: brides brought them [to their marriages] as part of their dowry, doctors accepted them from their patients in lieu of fees—and it was not unusual to find them even in the service of a priest."[2]

Owners had complete dominion over their slaves; in Italian law, this meant the "[power] to have, hold, sell, alienate, exchange, enjoy, rent or unrent, dispose of in [their] will[s], judge soul and body, and do with in perpetuity whatsoever may please [them] and [their] heirs and no man may gainsay [them]."[3] A strong, young, healthy slave cost the equivalent of the wages paid a free servant over several years. Considering the lifetime of free service thereafter, slaves could be well worth the cost.

The Tatars and Africans appear to have been the worst treated. But as in ancient Greece and Rome, slaves at this time were generally accepted as family members and were integrated into households. Not a few women slaves became mothers of their masters' children. Quite a few children of such

[2] Iris Origo, *The Merchant of Prato: Francesco di Marco Datini, 1335–1410* (New York: David Godine, 1986), pp. 90–91.

[3] *Ibid.*, p. 209.

Michelangelo and Pope Julius II

Vasari here describes how Pope Julius, the most fearsome and worldly of the Renaissance popes, forced Michelangelo to complete the Sistine Chapel before Michelangelo was ready to do so.

❖ *Did Michelangelo hold his own with the pope? What does this interchange suggest about the relationship of patrons and artists in the Renaissance? Were great artists like Michelangelo so revered that they could do virtually as they pleased?*

[The pope was very anxious to see the decoration of the Sistine Chapel completed and constantly inquired when it would be finished.] On one occasion, therefore, Michelangelo replied, "It will be finished when I shall have done all that I believe is required to satisfy Art." "And we command," rejoined the pontiff, "that you satisfy our wish to have it done quickly," adding that if it were not at once completed, he would have Michelangelo thrown headlong from the scaffolding. Hearing this, our artist, who feared the fury of the pope, and with good cause, without taking time to add what was wanting, took down the remainder of the scaffolding to the great satisfaction of the whole city on All Saints' day, when Pope Julius went into that chapel to sing mass. But Michelangelo had much desired to retouch some portions of the work *a secco* [that is, after the damp plaster upon which the paint had been originally laid *al fresco* had dried], as had been done by the older masters who had painted the stories on the walls. He would also have gladly added a little ultramarine to the draperies and gilded other parts, to the end that the whole might have a richer and more striking effect.

The pope, too, hearing that these things were still wanting, and finding that all who beheld the chapel praised it highly, would now fain have had the additions made. But as Michelangelo thought reconstructing the scaffold too long an affair, the pictures remained as they were, although the pope, who often saw Michelangelo, would sometimes say, "Let the chapel be enriched with bright colors and gold; it looks poor." When Michelangelo would reply familiarly, "Holy Father, the men of those days did not adorn themselves with gold; those who are painted here less than any, for they were none too rich; besides which they were holy men, and must have despised riches and ornaments."

From James Harvey Robinson, ed., *Readings in European History*, Vol. 1 (Boston: Athenaeum, 1904), pp. 538–539.

This portrait of Katharina, by Albrecht Dürer, provides evidence of African slavery in Europe during the sixteenth century. Katharina was in the service of one João Bradao, a Portuguese economic minister living in Antwerp, then the financial center of Europe. Dürer became friends with Bradao during his stay in the Low Countries in the winter of 1520–1521. Albrecht Dürer, Portrait of the Moorish Woman Katharina. Uffizi Florence, Italy. Foto Marburg/Art Resource, NY

unions were adopted and raised as legitimate heirs of their fathers. It was clearly in the interest of their owners to keep slaves healthy and happy; otherwise they were of little use and could even become a threat. Still, slaves remained a foreign and suspected presence in Italian society; they were, as all knew, uprooted and resentful people.

Italy's Political Decline: The French Invasions (1494–1527)

The Treaty of Lodi

As a land of autonomous city–states, Italy had always relied on internal cooperation for its peace and safety from foreign invasion—especially by the Turks. Such cooperation had been maintained during the latter half of the fifteenth century thanks to a carefully constructed political alliance known as the Treaty of Lodi (1454–1455). The terms of the treaty brought Milan and Naples, long traditional enemies, into alliance with Florence. These three stood together for decades against Venice, which was frequently joined by the Papal States, to create an internal balance of power. When a foreign enemy threatened Italy, however, the five formed a united front.

Around 1490, following the rise to power of the Milanese despot Ludovico il Moro, hostilities between Milan and Naples resumed. The peace made possible by the Treaty of Lodi ended in 1494 when Naples, supported by Florence and the Borgia Pope Alexander VI (r. 1492–1503), prepared to attack Milan. Ludovico made what proved to be a fatal response in these new political alignments: He appealed for aid to the French. French kings had ruled Naples from 1266 to 1435, before they were driven out by Duke Alfonso of Sicily. Breaking a wise Italian rule, Ludovico invited the French to reenter Italy and revive their dynastic claim to Naples. In his haste to check his rival Naples, Ludovico did not recognize sufficiently that France also had dynastic claims to Milan. Nor did he foresee how insatiable the French appetite for Italian territory would become once French armies had crossed the Alps.

Charles VIII's March through Italy

The French king Louis XI had resisted the temptation to invade Italy, while nonetheless keeping French dynastic claims in Italy alive. His successor, Charles VIII (r. 1483–1498), an eager youth in his twenties, responded to Ludovico's call with lightning speed. Within five months, he had crossed the Alps (August 1495) and raced as conqueror through Florence and the Papal States into Naples. As Charles approached Florence, the Florentine ruler, Piero dé Medici, who had allied with Naples against Milan, tried to placate the French king by handing over Pisa and other Florentine possessions. Such appeasement only brought about Piero's forced exile by a population that was revolutionized then by the radical Dominican preacher Girolamo Savonarola (1452–1498). Savonarola convinced most of the fearful Florentines that the French king's arrival was a long-delayed and fully justified divine vengeance on their immorality.

Charles entered Florence without resistance. Thanks to Savonarola's flattery and the payment of a large ransom, the city was spared a threatened destruction. Savonarola continued to exercise virtual rule over Florence for four years after Charles's departure. The Florentines proved, however, not to be the stuff theocracies are made of. Savonarola's moral rigor and antipapal policies made it impossible for him to survive indefinitely. This became especially true after the Italian cities reunited and the ouster of the French invader, whom Savonarola had praised as a godsend, became national policy. Savonarola was imprisoned and executed in May 1498.

Charles's lightning march through Italy also struck terror in non-Italian hearts. Ferdinand of Aragon, who hoped to expand his own possessions in Italy from his kingdom of Sicily, now found himself vulnerable to a French–Italian axis. He took the initiative to create a counteralliance—the League of Venice, formed in March 1495—in which he joined with Venice, the Papal States, and Emperor Maximilian I against the French. The alliance set the stage for a conflict between France and Spain that would not end until 1559.

Ludovico il Moro meanwhile recognized that he had sown the wind; having desired a French invasion only so long as it weakened his enemies, he now saw Milan threatened by the whirlwind of events that he had himself created. In reaction, he joined the League of Venice, and this alliance was able to send Charles into retreat by May. Charles remained thereafter on the defensive until his death in April 1498.

Pope Alexander VI and the Borgia Family

The French returned to Italy under Charles's successor, Louis XII (r. 1498–1515). This time they were assisted by a new Italian ally, the Borgia pope, Alexander VI. Alexander was probably the most corrupt pope who ever sat on the papal throne. He openly promoted the political careers of Cesare and Lucrezia Borgia, the children he had had before he became pope, and he placed papal policy in tandem with the efforts of his powerful family to secure a political base in Romagna.

In Romagna, several principalities had fallen away from the church during the Avignon papacy. And Venice, the pope's ally within the League of Venice, continued to contest the Papal States for their loyalty. Seeing that a French alliance could give him the opportunity to reestablish control over the region, Alexander took steps to secure French favor. He annulled Louis XII's marriage to Charles VIII's sister so that Louis could marry Charles's widow, Anne of Brittany—a popular political move designed to keep Brittany French. The pope also bestowed a cardinal's hat on the archbishop of Rouen, Louis's favorite cleric. Most important, Alexander agreed to abandon the League of Venice; this withdrawal of support made the league too weak to resist a French reconquest of Milan. In exchange, Cesare Borgia received the sister of the king of

Navarre, Charlotte d'Albret, in marriage, a union that greatly enhanced Borgia military strength. Cesare also received land grants from Louis XII and the promise of French military aid in Romagna.

All in all it was a scandalous trade-off, but one that made it possible for both the French king and the pope to realize their ambitions within Italy. Louis successfully invaded Milan in August 1499. Ludovico il Moro, who had originally opened the Pandora's box of French invasion, spent his last years languishing in a French prison. In 1500 Louis and Ferdinand of Aragon divided Naples between them, while the pope and Cesare Borgia conquered the cities of Romagna without opposition. Alexander awarded his victorious son the title "duke of Romagna."

Pope Julius II

Cardinal Giuliano della Rovere, a strong opponent of the Borgia family, succeeded Alexander VI as Pope Julius II (r. 1503–1513). He suppressed the Borgias and placed their newly conquered lands in Romagna under papal jurisdiction. Julius came to be known as the "warrior pope," because he brought the Renaissance papacy to a peak of military prowess and diplomatic intrigue. Shocked, as were other contemporaries, by this thoroughly secular papacy, the

Major Political Events of the Italian Renaissance (1375–1527)	
1378–1382	The Ciompi Revolt in Florence
1434	Medici rule in Florence established by Cosimo de' Medici
1454–1455	Treaty of Lodi allies Milan, Naples, and Florence (in effect until 1494)
1494	Charles VIII of France invades Italy
1494–1498	Savonarola controls Florence
1495	League of Venice unites Venice, Milan, the Papal States, the Holy Roman Empire, and Spain against France
1499	Louis XII invades Milan (the second French invasion of Italy)
1500	The Borgias conquer Romagna
1512–1513	The Holy League (Pope Julius II, Ferdinand of Aragon, Emperor Maximilian, and Venice) defeats the French
1513	Machiavelli writes *The Prince*
1515	Francis I leads the third French invasion of Italy
1516	Concordat of Bologna between France and the papacy
1527	Sack of Rome by imperial soldiers

humanist Erasmus (1466?–1536), who had witnessed in disbelief a bullfight in the papal palace during a visit to Rome, wrote a popular anonymous satire entitled *Julius Excluded from Heaven*. This humorous account purported to describe the pope's unsuccessful efforts to convince Saint Peter that he was worthy of admission to heaven.

Assisted by his powerful allies, Pope Julius succeeded in driving the Venetians out of Romagna in 1509. Thus, he ended Venetian claims in the region and fully secured the Papal States. Having realized this long-sought papal goal, Julius turned to the second major undertaking of his pontificate: ridding Italy of his former ally, the French invader. Julius, Ferdinand of Aragon, and Venice formed a second Holy League in October 1511, and within a short period Emperor Maximilian I and the Swiss joined them. By 1512 the league had the French in full retreat, and they were soundly defeated by the Swiss in 1513 at Novara.

The French were nothing if not persistent. They invaded Italy a third time under Louis's successor, Francis I (r. 1515–1547). French armies massacred Swiss soldiers of the Holy League at Marignano in September 1515, avenging the earlier defeat at Novara. The victory won the Concordat of Bologna from the people in August 1516. The agreement gave the French king control over the French clergy in exchange for French recognition of the pope's superiority over church councils and his right to collect annates in France. This was an important compromise that helped keep France Catholic after the outbreak of the Protestant Reformation. But the new French entry into Italy also led to the first of four major wars with Spain in the first half of the sixteenth century: the Habsburg–Valois wars, none of which France won.

Niccolò Machiavelli

The period of foreign invasions made a shambles of Italy. The same period that saw Italy's cultural peak in the work of Leonardo, Raphael, and Michelangelo also witnessed Italy's political tragedy. One who watched as French, Spanish, and German armies wreaked havoc on Italy was Niccolò Machiavelli (1469–1527). The more he saw, the more convinced he became that Italian political unity and independence were ends that justified any means.

A humanist and a careful student of ancient Rome, Machiavelli was impressed by the way Roman rulers and citizens had then defended their homeland. They possessed *virtù*, the ability to act decisively and heroically for the good of their country. Stories of ancient Roman patriotism and self-sacrifice were Machiavelli's favorites, and he

lamented the absence of such traits among his compatriots. Such romanticizing of the Roman past caused some exaggeration of both ancient virtue and contemporary failings. His Florentine contemporary, Francesco Guicciardini, a more sober historian less given to idealizing antiquity, wrote truer chronicles of Florentine and Italian history.

Machiavelli also held deep republican ideals, which he did not want to see vanish from Italy. He believed that a strong and determined people could struggle successfully with fortune. He scolded the Italian people for the self-destruction their own internal feuding was causing. He wanted an end to that behavior above all, so that a reunited Italy could drive all foreign armies out.

But were his fellow citizens up to such a challenge? The juxtaposition of what Machiavelli believed the ancient Romans had been with the failure of his contemporaries to attain such high ideals made him the famous cynic whose name—in the epithet "Machiavellian"—has become synonymous with ruthless political expediency. Only a strongman, he concluded in the end, could impose order on so divided and selfish a people; the salvation of Italy required, for the present, a cunning dictator. (See "Machiavelli Discusses the Most Important Trait for a Ruler.")

It has been argued that Machiavelli wrote *The Prince* in 1513 as a cynical satire on the way rulers actually did behave and not as a serious recommendation of unprincipled despotic rule. To take his advocacy of tyranny literally, it is argued, contradicts both his earlier works and his own strong family tradition of republican service. But Machiavelli seems to have been in earnest when he advised rulers to discover the advantages of fraud and brutality, at least as a temporary means to the higher end of a unified Italy. He apparently hoped to see a strong ruler emerge from the Medici family, which had captured the papacy in 1513 with the pontificate of Leo X (r. 1513–1521). At the same time, the Medici family retained control over the powerful territorial state of Florence. The situation was similar to that of Machiavelli's hero Cesare Borgia and his father Pope Alexander VI, who had earlier brought factious Romagna to heel by placing secular family goals and religious policy in tandem. The Prince was pointedly dedicated to Lorenzo de' Medici, duke of Urbino and grandson of Lorenzo the Magnificent.

Whatever Machiavelli's hopes may have been, the Medicis were not destined to be Italy's deliverers. The second Medici pope, Clement VII (r. 1523–1534), watched helplessly as Rome was sacked by the army of Emperor Charles V in 1527, also the year of Machiavelli's death.

Machiavelli Discusses the Most Important Trait for a Ruler

Machiavelli believed that the most important personality trait of a successful ruler was the ability to instill fear in his subjects.

❖ *Why did Machiavelli maintain that rulers must be feared? Do American politicians of today appear to embrace Machiavelli's theory?*

Here the question arises; whether it is better to be loved than feared or feared than loved. The answer is that it would be desirable to be both but, since that is difficult, it is much safer to be feared than to be loved, if one must choose. For on men in general this observation may be made: they are ungrateful, fickle, and deceitful, eager to avoid dangers, and avid for gain, and while you are useful to them they are all with you, offering you their blood, their property, their lives, and their sons so long as danger is remote, as we noted above, but when it approaches they turn on you. Any prince, trusting only in their words and having no other preparations made, will fall to his ruin, for friendships that are bought at a price and not by greatness and nobility of soul are paid for indeed, but they are not owned and cannot be called upon in time of need. Men have less hesitation in offending a man who is loved than one who is feared, for love is held by a bond of obligation which, as men are wicked, is broken whenever personal advantage suggests it, but fear is accompanied by the dread of punishment which never relaxes.

From Niccolò Machiavelli, *The Prince* (1513), trans. and ed. by Thomas G. Bergin (New York: Appleton-Century-Crofts, 1947), p. 48.

Revival of Monarchy in Northern Europe

After 1450, there was a progressive shift from divided feudal to unified national monarchies as "sovereign" rulers emerged. This is not to say that the dynastic and chivalric ideals of feudal monarchy vanished. Territorial princes did not pass from the scene; representative bodies persisted and in some areas even grew in influence. But in the late fifteenth and early sixteenth centuries, the old problem of the one and the many was decided in favor of the interests of monarchy.

The feudal monarchy of the High Middle Ages was characterized by the division of the basic powers of government between the king and his semiautonomous vassals. The nobility and the towns had acted with varying degrees of unity and success through evolving representative assemblies such as the English Parliament, the French Estates General, and the Spanish *Cortés* to thwart the centralization of royal power. Because of the Hundred Years' War and the Great Schism in the church, the nobility and the clergy were in decline by the late Middle Ages and less able to contain expanding monarchies.

The increasingly important towns began to ally with the king. Loyal, business-wise townspeople, not the nobility and the clergy, increasingly staffed the royal offices and became the king's lawyers, bookkeepers, military tacticians, and foreign diplomats. This new alliance between king and town broke the bonds of feudal society and made possible the rise of sovereign states.

In a sovereign state, the powers of taxation, war making, and law enforcement no longer belong to semiautonomous vassals, but are concentrated in the monarch and are exercised by his or her chosen agents. Taxes, wars, and laws become national, rather than merely regional, matters. Only as monarchs became able to act independently of the nobility and representative assemblies could they overcome the decentralization that had been the basic obstacle to nation building. Ferdinand and Isabella of Spain rarely called the *Cortés* into session. The French Estates General did not meet at all from 1484 to 1560. Henry VII (r. 1485–1509) of England managed to raise revenues without going begging to Parliament after Parliament voted him customs revenues for life in 1485. Monarchs were also assisted by brilliant theorists, from Marsilius of Padua in the fourteenth century to Machiavelli to Jean Bodin in the sixteenth, who eloquently argued the sovereign rights of monarchy.

The many were, of course, never totally subjugated to the one. But in the last half of the fifteenth century, rulers demonstrated that the law was their creature. They appointed civil servants whose vision was no longer merely local or regional. In Castile they were the *corregidores*, in England the justices of the peace, and in France bailiffs operating through well-drilled lieutenants. These royal ministers and agents could become closely attached to the localities they administered in the ruler's name. And regions were able to secure congenial royal appointments. Throughout England, for example, local magnates served as representatives of the Tudors. Nonetheless, these new executives remained royal executives, bureaucrats whose outlook was "national" and whose loyalty was to the "state."

Monarchies also began to create standing national armies in the fifteenth century. The noble cavalry receded as the infantry and the artillery became the backbone of royal armies. Mercenary soldiers were recruited from Switzerland and Germany to form the major part of the "king's army." Professional soldiers who fought for pay and booty proved far more efficient than feudal vassals who fought simply for honor's sake. Monarchs who failed to meet their payrolls, however, faced a new danger of mutiny and banditry on the part of foreign troops.

The growing cost of warfare in the fifteenth and sixteenth centuries increased the need of monarchs for new national sources of income, but their efforts to expand royal revenues were hampered by the stubborn belief among the highest classes that they were immune from government taxation. The nobility guarded their properties and traditional rights and despised taxation as an insult and a humiliation. Royal revenues accordingly grew at the expense of those least able to resist and least able to pay.

The monarchs had several options when it came to raising money. As feudal lords, they could collect rents from their royal domains. They could also levy national taxes on basic food and clothing, such as the *gabelle*, or "salt tax," in France and the *alcabala*, or 10-percent sales tax on commercial transactions, in Spain. The rulers could also levy direct taxes on the peasantry, which they did through agreeable representative assemblies of the privileged classes in which the peasantry did not sit. The *taille*, which the French kings independently determined from year to year after the Estates General was suspended in 1484, was such a tax. Innovative fund-raising devices in the fifteenth century included the sale of public offices and the issuance of high-interest government bonds. But rulers did not levy taxes on the powerful nobility. Rather, they borrowed from rich nobles and the great bankers of Italy and Germany. In money matters, the privileged classes remained as much the kings' creditors and competitors as their subjects.

France

Charles VII (r. 1422–1461) was a king made great by those who served him. His ministers created a permanent professional army, which—thanks initially to the inspiration of Joan of Arc—drove the English out of France. And largely because of the enterprise of an independent merchant banker named Jacques Coeur, the French also developed a strong economy, diplomatic corps, and national administration during Charles's reign. These were the sturdy tools with which Charles's son and successor, the ruthless Louis XI (r. 1461–1483), made France a great power.

There were two cornerstones of French nation building in the fifteenth century. The first was the collapse of the English Empire in France following the Hundred Years' War. The second was the defeat of Charles the Bold and his duchy of Burgundy. Perhaps Europe's strongest political power in the mid-fifteenth century, Burgundy aspired to dwarf both France and the Holy Roman Empire as the leader of a dominant middle kingdom. It might have done so had not the continental powers joined in opposition.

When Charles the Bold died in defeat in a battle at Nancy in 1477, the dream of Burgundian Empire died with him. Louis XI and Habsburg emperor Maximilian I divided the conquered Burgundian lands between them, with the treaty-wise Habsburgs getting the better part. The dissolution of Burgundy ended its constant intrigue against the French king and left Louis XI free to secure the monarchy. The newly acquired Burgundian lands and his own Angevin inheritance permitted the king to end his reign with a kingdom almost twice the size of that with which he had started. Louis successfully harnessed the nobility, expanded the trade and industry so carefully nurtured by Jacques Coeur, created a national postal system, and even established a lucrative silk industry at Lyons (later transferred to Tours).

A strong nation is a two-edged sword. Because Louis's successors inherited a secure and efficient government, they felt free to pursue what proved ultimately to be a debilitating foreign policy. Conquests in Italy in the 1490s and a long series of losing wars with the Habsburgs in the first half of the sixteenth century left France by the mid-sixteenth century again a defeated nation almost as divided internally as during the Hundred Years' War.

Spain

Spain, too, became a strong country in the late fifteenth century. Both Castile and Aragon had been poorly ruled and divided kingdoms in the mid-fifteenth century. The union of Isabella of Castile (r. 1474–1504) and Ferdinand of Aragon (r. 1479–1516) changed that situation. The two future sovereigns married in 1469, despite strong protests from neighboring Portugal and France, both of whom foresaw the formidable European power the marriage would create. Castile was by far the richer and more populous of the two, having an estimated five million inhabitants to Aragon's population of under one million. Castile was also distinguished by its lucrative sheep-farming industry, run by a government-backed organization called the *Mesta*, another example of a developing centralized economic planning. Although the marriage of Ferdinand and Isabella dynastically united the two kingdoms, they remained constitutionally separated. Each retained its respective government agencies—separate laws, armies, coinage, and taxation—and cultural traditions.

Ferdinand and Isabella could do together what neither was able to accomplish alone: subdue their realms, secure their borders, venture abroad militarily, and Christianize the whole of Spain. Between 1482 and 1492 they conquered the Moors in Granada. Naples became a Spanish possession in 1504. By 1512 Ferdinand had secured his northern borders by conquering the kingdom of Navarre. Internally, Ferdinand and Isabella won the allegiance of the *Hermandad*, a powerful league of cities and towns that served them against stubborn landowners. Townspeople allied themselves with the crown and progressively replaced the nobility within the royal administration. The crown also extended its authority over the wealthy chivalric orders, a further circumscription of the power of the nobility.

Spain had long been remarkable among European lands as a place where three religions—Islam, Judaism, and Christianity—coexisted with a certain degree of toleration. This toleration was to end dramatically under Ferdinand and Isabella, who made Spain the prime exemplar of state-controlled religion.

Ferdinand and Isabella exercised almost total control over the Spanish church as they placed religion in the service of national unity. They appointed the higher clergy and the officers of the Inquisition. The latter, run by Tomás de Torquemada (d. 1498), Isabella's confessor, was a key national agency established in 1479 to monitor the activity of converted Jews (*conversos*) and Muslims (*Moriscos*) in Spain. In 1492 the Jews were exiled and their properties were confiscated. In 1502 nonconverting Moors in Granada were driven into exile by Cardinal Francisco Jiménez de Cisneros (1437–1517), under whom Spanish spiritual life remained largely uniform and successfully controlled. This was a major reason Spain remained a loyal Catholic country throughout the sixteenth century and provided a base of operation for the European Counter-Reformation.

Despite a certain internal narrowness, Ferdinand and Isabella were rulers with wide horizons. They contracted anti-French marriage alliances that came to determine a large part of European history in the sixteenth century. In 1496 their eldest daughter, Joanna, later known as "the Mad," married Archduke Philip, the son of Emperor Maximilian I. The fruit of this union, Charles I, was the first ruler over a united Spain; by his inheritance and election as emperor in 1519, he came to rule over a European kingdom almost equal in size to that of Charlemagne. A second daughter, Catherine of Aragon, wed Arthur, the son of the English king Henry VII. After Arthur's premature death, she was betrothed to his brother, the future King Henry VIII (r. 1509–1547), whom she married eight years later, in 1509. The failure of this marriage became the key factor in the emergence of the Anglican church and the English Reformation.

The new power of Spain was also revealed in Ferdinand and Isabella's promotion of overseas exploration. They sponsored the Genoese adventurer Christopher Columbus (1451–1506), who arrived at the islands of the Caribbean while sailing west in search of a shorter route to the spice markets of the Far East. This patronage led to the creation of the Spanish Empire in Mexico and Peru, whose gold and silver mines helped to make Spain Europe's dominant power in the sixteenth century.

England

The latter half of the fifteenth century was a period of especially difficult political trial for the English. Following the Hundred Years' War, a defeated England was subjected to internal warfare between two rival branches of the royal family: the House of York and the House of Lancaster. This conflict, known to us today as the Wars of the Roses (because York's symbol, according to legend, was a white rose and Lancaster's a red rose), kept England in turmoil from 1455 to 1485.

The Lancastrian monarchy of Henry VI (r. 1422–1461) was consistently challenged by the duke of York and his supporters in the prosperous southern towns. In 1461 Edward IV (r. 1461–1483), son of the duke of York, successfully seized power and instituted a strong-arm rule that lasted more than twenty years; it was only briefly interrupted, in 1470–1471, by Henry VI's short-lived restoration. Assisted by loyal and able ministers, Edward effectively increased the power and finances of the monarchy.

His brother, Richard III (r. 1483–1485), usurped the throne from Edward's son, and after Richard's death, the new Tudor dynasty portrayed him as an unprincipled villain who had also murdered Edward's sons in the Tower of London to secure his hold on the throne. The best-known version of this characterization—unjust according to some—is found in Shakespeare's *Richard III*. Be that as it may, Richard's reign saw the growth of support for the exiled Lancastrian Henry Tudor, who returned to England to defeat Richard on Bosworth Field in August 1485.

Henry Tudor ruled as Henry VII (r. 1485–1509), the first of the new Tudor dynasty that would dominate England throughout the sixteenth century. To bring the rival royal families together and to make the hereditary claim of his offspring to the throne uncontestable, Henry married Edward IV's daughter, Elizabeth of York. He succeeded in disciplining the English nobility through a special instrument of the royal will known as the Court of Star Chamber. Created with the sanction of Parliament in 1487, the court was intended to end the perversion of English justice by "over-mighty subjects," that is, powerful nobles who used intimidation and bribery to win favorable verdicts in court cases. In the Court of Star Chamber, the king's councillors sat as judges and were not swayed by such tactics. The result was a more equitable court system.

It was also a court more amenable to the royal will. Henry shrewdly construed legal precedents to the advantage of the crown, using English law to further the ends of monarchy. He managed to confiscate lands and fortunes of nobles with such success that he was able to govern without dependence on Parliament for royal funds, always a cornerstone of strong monarchy. In these ways, Henry began to shape a monarchy that would develop into one of early modern Europe's most exemplary governments during the reign of his granddaughter, Elizabeth I.

The Holy Roman Empire

Germany and Italy were the striking exceptions to the steady development of politically centralized lands in the last half of the fifteenth century. Unlike England, France, and Spain, the Holy Roman Empire saw the many thoroughly repulse the one. In Germany, territorial rulers and cities resisted every effort at national consolidation and unity. As in Carolingian times, rulers continued to partition their kingdoms, however small, among their sons. By the late fifteenth century, Germany was hopelessly divided into some 300 autonomous political entities.

The princes and the cities did work together to create the machinery of law and order, if not of union, within the divided empire. The emperor and the major German territorial rulers reached an agreement in 1356, the *Golden Bull*. It established a seven-member electoral college consisting of the archbishops of Mainz, Trier, and Cologne; the duke of Saxony; the margrave of Brandenburg; the count Palatine; and the king of Bohemia. This group also functioned as an administrative body. They elected the emperor and, in cooperation with him, provided what transregional unity and administration existed.

The figure of the emperor gave the empire a single ruler in law if not in fact. The conditions of his rule and the extent of his powers over his subjects, especially the seven electors, were renegotiated with every imperial election. Therefore, the rights of the many (the princes) were always balanced against the power of the one (the emperor).

In the fifteenth century, an effort was made to control incessant feuding by the creation of an imperial diet known as the *Reichstag*. This was a national assembly of the seven electors, the nonelectoral princes, and representatives from the sixty-five imperial free cities. The cities were the weakest of the three bodies represented in the diet. During such an assembly in Worms in 1495, the members won from Emperor Maximilian I (r. 1493–1519) an imperial ban on private warfare, the creation of a Supreme Court of Justice to enforce internal peace, and an imperial Council of Regency to coordinate imperial and internal German policy. The latter was only grudgingly conceded by the emperor because it gave the princes a share in executive power.

Although important, these reforms were still a poor substitute for true national unity. In the sixteenth and seventeenth centuries, the territorial princes became virtually sovereign rulers in their various domains. Such disunity aided religious dissent and conflict. It was in the cities and territories of still-feudal, fractionalized, backward Germany that the Protestant Reformation broke out in the sixteenth century.

The Northern Renaissance

The scholarly works of northern humanists created a climate favorable to religious and educational reforms on the eve of the Reformation. Northern humanism was initially stimulated by the importation of Italian learning through such varied intermediaries as students who had studied in Italy, merchants who traded there, and the Brothers of the Common Life. This last was an influential lay religious movement that began in the Netherlands and permitted men and women to live a shared religious life without making formal vows of poverty, chastity, and obedience.

The northern humanists, however, developed their own distinctive culture. They tended to come from more diverse social backgrounds and to be more devoted to religious reforms than their Italian counterparts. They were also more willing to write for lay audiences as well as for a narrow intelligentsia. Thanks to the invention of printing with movable type, it became possible for humanists to convey their educational ideals to laypeople and clerics alike. Printing gave new power and influence to elites in both church and state, who now could popularize their viewpoints freely and widely.

The Printing Press

A variety of forces converged in the fourteenth and fifteenth centuries to give rise to the invention of the printing press. Since the days of Charlemagne, kings and princes had encouraged schools and literacy, to help provide educated bureaucrats to staff the offices of their kingdoms. Without people who could read, think critically, and write reliable reports, no kingdom, large or small, could be properly governed. By the fifteenth century, a new literate lay public had been created, thanks to the enormous expansion of schools and universities during the late Middle Ages. (The number of universities more than tripled between 1300 and 1500, growing from twenty to seventy.)

The invention of a cheap way to manufacture paper also helped to make books economical and to broaden their content. Manuscript books had been inscribed on vellum, a cumbersome and expensive medium. (It required 170 calfskins or 300 sheepskins to make a single vellum Bible.) Single-sheet woodcuts had long been printed. This involved carving a block of wood, inking it, and then stamping out as many copies as one could make before the wood deteriorated. The end product was much like a modern poster.

In response to the demand for books created by the expansion of lay literacy, Johann Gutenberg (d. 1468) invented printing with movable type in the mid-fifteenth century in the German city of Mainz, the center of printing for the whole of western Europe. Thereafter, books were rapidly and handsomely produced on topics both profound and practical and were intended for ordinary lay readers, scholars, and clerics alike. Especially popular in the early decades of print were books of piety and religion, calendars and almanacs, and "how-to" books (for example, on child rearing, making brandies and liquors, curing animals, and farming successfully).

The new technology proved enormously profitable to printers, whose numbers exploded. By 1500, within a scant fifty years of Gutenberg's press, printing presses operated in at least sixty German cities and in more than 200 cities throughout Europe. The printing press was a boon to the careers of humanists, who now gained international audiences.

Literacy deeply affected people everywhere, nurturing self-esteem and a critical frame of mind. By standardizing texts, the print revolution made anyone who could read an instant authority. Rulers in church and state now had to deal with a less credulous and less docile laity. Print was a powerful tool for political and religious propaganda as well. Kings could now indoctrinate people as never be-

The printing press made possible the diffusion of Renaissance learning. But no book stimulated thought more at this time than did the Bible. With Gutenberg's publication of a printed Bible in 1454, scholars gained access to a dependable, standardized text, so that Scripture could be discussed and debated as never before. Reproduced by permission of The Huntington Library, San Marino, California fore, and clergymen found themselves able to mass-produce both indulgences and pamphlets. (See "The West & the World," p. 284.)

Erasmus

The far-reaching influence of Desiderius Erasmus (1466?–1536), the most famous of the northern humanists and the "prince of the humanists," illustrates the impact of the printing press. Erasmus gained fame both as an educational and as a religious reformer. His life and work make clear that many loyal Catholics wanted major reforms long before the Reformation made them a reality.

Erasmus earned his living by tutoring when patrons were scarce. He prepared short Latin dialogues for his students that were intended to teach them how to speak and live well, inculcating good manners and language by encouraging them to imitate what they read.

These dialogues were published under the title *Colloquies*; they grew in number and length in consecutive editions, coming also to embrace anticlerical dialogues and satires on popular religious superstition. Erasmus collected ancient and contemporary proverbs as well, which he published under the title *Adages*. Beginning with about 800 examples, he increased his collection to more than 5,000 in the final edition of the work. Among the locutions that the *Adages* popularized are the common modern expression "to leave no stone unturned" and the saying "Where there is smoke, there is fire."

Erasmus aspired to unite the classical ideals of humanity and civic virtue with the Christian ideals of love and piety. He believed that disciplined study of the classics and the Bible, if begun early enough, was the best way to reform both individuals and society. He summarized his own beliefs with the phrase *philosophia Christi*, a simple, ethical piety in imitation of Christ. He set this ideal in starkest contrast to what he believed to be the dogmatic, ceremonial, and factious religious practice of the later Middle Ages. What most offended him about the Scholastics, both those of the late Middle Ages and, increasingly, the new Lutheran ones, was their letting doctrine and disputation overshadow humble piety and Christian practice.

To promote his own religious beliefs, Erasmus labored to make the ancient Christian sources available in their original versions. He believed that only as people drank from the pure, unadulterated sources could moral and religious health result. He edited the works of the Church fathers and produced a Greek edition of the New Testament (1516), which became the basis for his new, more accurate Latin translation (1519).

These various enterprises did not please church authorities. They were unhappy with both Erasmus's "improvements" on the Vulgate, Christendom's Bible for over a thousand years, and his popular anticlerical satires. At one point in the mid-sixteenth century, all of Erasmus's works were placed on the *Index of Forbidden Books*. Erasmus also received Luther's unqualified condemnation for his views on the freedom of human will. Still, Erasmus's works became basic tools of reform in the hands of both Protestant and Catholic reformers.

Humanism and Reform

In Germany, England, France, and Spain, humanism stirred both educational and religious reform.

GERMANY   Rudolf Agricola (1443–1485), the "father of German humanism," spent ten years in Italy and introduced Italian learning to Germany when he returned. Conrad Celtis (d. 1508), the first German poet laureate, and Ulrich von Hutten (1488–1523), a fiery knight, gave German humanism a nationalist coloring hostile to non-German cultures, particularly Roman culture. Von Hutten especially illustrates the union of humanism, German nationalism, and Luther's religious reform. A poet who admired Erasmus, he attacked indulgences and published an edition of Valla's exposé of the Donation of Constantine. He died in 1523, the victim of a hopeless knights' revolt against the princes.

The *cause célèbre* that brought von Hutten onto the historical stage and unified reform-minded German humanists was the Reuchlin affair. Johann Reuchlin (1455–1522) was Europe's foremost Christian authority on Hebrew and Jewish learning. He wrote the first reliable Hebrew grammar by a Christian scholar and was personally attracted to Jewish mysticism. Around 1506, supported by the Dominican order in Cologne, a Christian who had converted from Judaism began a movement to suppress Jewish writings. When this man, whose name was Pfefferkorn, attacked Reuchlin, many German humanists, in the name of academic freedom and good scholarship—not for any pro-Jewish sentiment—rushed to Reuchlin's defense. The controversy lasted several years and produced one of the great satires of the period, the *Letters of Obscure Men* (1515), a merciless satire of monks and Scholastics to which von Hutten contributed. When Martin Luther came under attack in 1517 for his famous ninety-five theses against indulgences, many German humanists saw a repetition of the Scholastic attack on Reuchlin and rushed to his side.

ENGLAND   Italian learning came to England by way of English scholars and merchants and visiting Italian prelates. Lectures by William Grocyn (d. 1519) and Thomas Linacre (d. 1524) at Oxford

Thomas More (1478–1535), painted by Hans Holbein the Younger in 1527. The English statesman and author was beheaded by Henry VIII for his refusal to recognize the king's sovereignty over the English church.
The Frick Collection, New York

and those of Erasmus at Cambridge marked the scholarly maturation of English humanism. John Colet (1467–1519), dean of Saint Paul's Cathedral, patronized humanist studies for the young and promoted religious reform as well.

Thomas More (1478–1535), a close friend of Erasmus, is the best known English humanist. His *Utopia* (1516), a conservative criticism of contemporary society, rivals the plays of Shakespeare as the most-read sixteenth-century English work. *Utopia* depicted an imaginary society based on reason and tolerance that overcame social and political injustice by holding all property and goods in common and requiring everyone to earn their bread by their own work.

More became one of Henry VIII's most trusted diplomats. But his repudiation of the Act of Supremacy (1534), which made the king of England head of the English church in place of the pope (see Chapter 11), and his refusal to recognize the king's marriage to Anne Boleyn led to his execution in July 1535. Although More remained Catholic, humanism in England, as also in Germany, played an important role in preparing the way for the English Reformation.

FRANCE The French invasions of Italy made it possible for Italian learning to penetrate France, stirring both educational and religious reform. Guillaume Budé (1468–1540), an accomplished Greek scholar, and Jacques Lefèvre d'Étaples (1454–1536), a biblical authority, were the leaders of French humanism. Lefèvre's scholarly works exemplified the new critical scholarship and influenced Martin Luther. Guillaume Briçonnet (1470–1533), the bishop of Meaux, and Marguerite d'Angoulême (1492–1549), sister of King Francis I, the future queen of Navarre, and a successful spiritual writer in her own right, cultivated a generation of young reform-minded humanists. The future Protestant reformer John Calvin was a product of this native reform circle.

SPAIN Whereas in England, France, and Germany, humanism prepared the way for Protestant reforms, in Spain it entered the service of the Catholic Church. Here the key figure was Francisco Jiménez de Cisneros (1437–1517), a confessor to Queen Isabella and, after 1508, the "Grand Inquisitor"—a position that allowed him to enforce the strictest religious orthodoxy. Jiménez founded the University of Alcalá near Madrid in 1509, printed a Greek edition of the New Testament, and translated many religious tracts designed to reform clerical life and better direct lay piety. His great achievement, taking fifteen years to complete, was the *Complutensian Polyglot Bible*, a six-volume work that placed the Hebrew, Greek, and Latin versions of the Bible in parallel columns. Such scholarly projects and internal church reforms joined with the repressive measures of Ferdinand and Isabella to keep Spain strictly Catholic throughout the Age of Reformation.

Voyages of Discovery and the New Empire in the West

On the eve of the Reformation, the geographical as well as the intellectual horizons of Western people were changing. The fifteenth century saw the beginning of western Europe's global expansion and the transference of commercial supremacy from the Mediterranean and the Baltic to the Atlantic seaboard.

Gold and Spices

Mercenary motives, reinforced by traditional missionary ideals, inspired the Portuguese prince Henry the Navigator (1394–1460) to sponsor the Portuguese exploration of the African coast. His

What Columbus knew of the world in 1492 was contained in this map by the Nuremberg geographer Martin Behaim, creator of the first spherical globe of the Earth. The ocean section of Behaim's globe is reproduced here. Departing the Canary Islands (in the second section from the right), Columbus expected his first major landfall to be Japan (Cipangu, in the second section from the left). When he landed at San Salvador, he thought he was on the outer island of Japan. And when he arrived in Cuba, he thought he was in Japan. Reprinted from *Admiral of the Ocean Sea* by Samuel Eliot Morison. Copyright 1942 by Samuel Eliot Morison; renewed 1970 by Samuel Eliot Morison. By permission of Little, Brown and Company, Boston, Massachusetts

main object was the gold trade, which Muslims had monopolized for centuries. By the last decades of the fifteenth century, gold from Guinea was entering Europe by way of Portuguese ships calling at the port cities of Lisbon and Antwerp, rather than by the traditional Arab land routes. Antwerp became the financial center of Europe, a commercial crossroads where the enterprise and derring-do of the Portuguese, the Spanish, and especially the Flemish met the capital funds of the German banking houses of Fugger and Welser.

The rush for gold quickly expanded into a rush for the spice markets of India. In the fifteenth century the diet of most Europeans was a dull combination of bread and gruel, cabbage, turnips, peas, lentils, and onions, together with what meat became available during seasonal periods of slaughter. Spices, especially pepper and cloves, were in great demand, both to preserve and to enhance the taste of food.

Bartholomeu Dias (d. 1500) opened the Portuguese Empire in the East when he rounded the Cape of Good Hope at the tip of Africa in 1487. A decade later, in 1498, Vasco da Gama (d. 1524) reached the coast of India. When he returned to Portugal, he brought with him a cargo worth sixty times the cost of the voyage. Later, the Portuguese established themselves firmly on the Malabar Coast with colonies in Goa and Calcutta and successfully challenged the Arabs and the Venetians for control of the European spice trade.

While the Portuguese concentrated on the Indian Ocean, the Spanish set sail across the Atlantic. They did so in the hope of establishing a shorter route to the rich spice markets of the East Indies. But rather than beating the Portuguese at their own game, Christopher Columbus (1451–1506) came upon the Americas instead.

Amerigo Vespucci (1451–1512) and Ferdinand Magellan (1480–1521) showed that these new lands were not the outermost territory of the Far East, as Columbus died believing. Their travels proved the lands to be an entirely new continent that opened on the still greater Pacific Ocean. Magellan, in search of a westward route to the East Indies, died in the Philippines. (See Map 10–2.)

The Spanish Empire in the New World

Columbus's voyage of 1492 marked, unknowingly to those who undertook and financed it, the beginning of more than three centuries of Spanish conquest, exploitation, and administration of a vast American empire. That imperial venture produced important results for the cultures of both the European and the American continents. The gold and silver extracted from its American possessions financed Spain's major role in the religious and political conflicts of the age and contributed to European inflation in the sixteenth century.

In large expanses of both South and North America, Spanish government set an imprint of Roman Catholicism, economic dependence, and hierarchical social structure that has endured to the present day. Such influence was already clear with Columbus. On October 12, 1492, after a thirty-three day voyage from the Canary Islands, Columbus landed in San Salvador (Watlings Island) in the eastern Bahamas. He thought that he was on an outer island of Japan (or what he called Cipangu); he had undertaken his journey in the mistaken notion that the island of Japan would be the first land mass he would reach as he sailed west. This belief was based on Marco Polo's accounts of his years in China in the thirteenth century and the first globe map of the world, by Martin Behaim. That map, published in 1492, showed only ocean between the west coast of Europe and the east coast of Asia. Not until his third voyage to the Caribbean did Columbus realize that the island of Cuba was not Japan and that the South American continent beyond it was not China.

MAP 10–2 EUROPEAN VOYAGES OF DISCOVERY AND THE COLONIAL CLAIMS OF SPAIN AND PORTUGAL IN THE FIFTEENTH AND SIXTEENTH CENTURIES *The map dramatizes Europe's global expansion in the fifteenth and sixteenth centuries.*

When Columbus landed in San Salvador, his three ships were met on the beach by naked and extremely friendly natives. Like all the natives Columbus met on his first voyage, they were Taino Indians, who spoke a variant of a language known as Arawak. From the start, the natives' generosity amazed Columbus. They freely gave his men all the corn and yams they desired and many sexual favors as well. "They never say no," Columbus marveled. At the same time Columbus observed how very easily they could be enslaved.

A Conquered World

Mistaking the islands where he landed for the East Indies, Columbus called the native peoples whom he encountered "Indians." That name persisted even after it had become clear that this was a new continent and not the East Indies. These native peoples had migrated across the Bering Straits from Asia onto the American landmass many thousands of years before the European voyages of discovery, creating communities all the way from Alaska to South America. The islands that Columbus mistakenly believed to be the East Indies came to be known as the West Indies.

Native Americans had established advanced civilizations going back to as early as the first millennium B.C.E. in two parts of what is today known as Latin America: Mesoamerica, which stretches from central Mexico into the Yucatan and Guatemala, and the Andean region of South America, primarily modern-day Peru and Bolivia. The earliest civilization in Mesoamerica, that of the Olmec, dates

to about 1200 B.C.E. By the early centuries of the first millennium C.E. much of the region was dominated by the powerful city of Teotihuacán, which at the time was one of the largest urban centers in the world. The first millennium C.E. saw the flowering of the remarkable civilization of the Mayas in the Yucatan region. The Mayans built large cities with immense pyramids and achieved considerable skills in mathematics and astronomy.

The first great interregional civilization in Andean South America, that of Chavín, emerged during the first millennium B.C.E. Regional cultures of the succeeding Early Intermediate Period (100–600 C.E.) included the Nazca on the south coast of Peru and the Moche on the north coast. The Huari–Tiahuanco culture again imposed interregional conformity during the Middle Horizon (600–1000). In the Late Intermediate Period, the Chimu Empire (800–1400) dominated the valleys of the Peruvian north coast. These early Andean societies built major ceremonial centers throughout the Andes, constructed elaborate irrigation systems, canals, and highways, and created exquisite pottery, textiles, and metalwork.

At the time of the arrival of the first Spanish explorers, the Aztec Empire dominated Mesoamerica and the Inca Empire dominated Andean South America. (See Map 10–3.) Both were very rich, and their conquest promised the Spanish the possibility of acquiring large quantities of gold.

THE AZTECS IN MEXICO   The forebears of the Aztecs had arrived in the Valley of Mexico early in the twelfth century, where they lived as a sub-

Armored Spanish soldiers, under the command of Pedro de Alvarado (d. 1541) and bearing crossbows, engage unprotected and crudely armed Aztecs, who are nonetheless portrayed as larger than life by Spanish artist Diego Duran (16th century).   Codex Duran: Pedro de Alvarado (c. 1485–1541), companion-at-arms of Hernando Cortes (1485–1547) besieged by Aztec warriors. Biblioteca Nacional, Madrid, Spain. The Bridgeman Art Library International Ltd.

MAP 10–3   THE AZTEC AND INCA EMPIRES ON THE EVE OF THE SPANISH CONQUEST.

servient people. In 1428, under the leadership of Chief Itzcoatl, they rebelled against their rulers. That rebellion opened a period of Aztec conquest that reached its climax just after 1500. Their capital, Tenochtitlán (modern-day Mexico City), was located on an island in the center of a lake. By the time the Spanish conquerors arrived, the Aztecs governed many smaller tribes harshly, forcing labor and tribute from them. Believing that the gods must literally be fed with human bodies to guarantee continuing sunshine and fertility of the soil, the Aztecs also demanded and received thousands of captives each year to be sacrificed to their gods. Such policies left the Aztecs surrounded by terrorized tribes that felt no loyalty to them and longed for a liberator.

In 1519, Hernán Cortés landed on the coast of Mexico with a force of about 600 men. He opened communication with tribes nearby and then with Montezuma, the Aztec ruler. Montezuma initially believed Cortés to be a god. Aztec religion contained the legend of a priest named Quetzalcoatl who had been driven away four centuries earlier and had promised to return in the very year in which Cortés arrived. Montezuma initially attempted to appease Cortés with gifts of gold. The Indians had recently been ravaged by epidemic diseases of European origin, principally smallpox, and were in no position to oppose him. After several weeks of negotiations and the forging of alliances with subject tribes, Cortés's forces marched on Tenochtitlán, conquered it, and imprisoned Montezuma, who later died under unexplained circumstances. The Aztecs tried to drive the Spanish out, but by late 1521 they were defeated after great loss of life. Cortés proclaimed the former Aztec Empire to be New Spain.

THE INCAS IN PERU   The second great Native American civilization conquered by the Spanish was that of the Incas, located in the highlands of Peru. Like the Aztecs, they had vanquished many neighboring states and tribes and by the early sixteenth century ruled harshly over several million subject people, whom they compelled to build their roads and cities, farm their lands, and fight their wars.

In 1531, largely inspired by Cortés's example in Mexico, Francisco Pizarro sailed from Panama and landed on the western coast of South America to undertake a campaign against the Inca Empire. His force included perhaps 200 men armed with guns and swords and equipped with horses, the military power of which the Incas did not fathom.

In late 1531, Pizarro lured the Inca chief Atahualpa into a conference, where he captured him and killed many of his followers. Atahualpa attempted to ransom himself by having a vast horde of gold transported from all over Peru to Pizarro. Discovering that he could not turn Atahualpa into a puppet ruler, Pizarro executed him in 1533. Division within the ranks of the Spanish conquerors prevented effective royal control of the sprawling Inca civilization until the late 1560s.

The conquests of Mexico and Peru stand among the most brutal episodes in modern Western history. One civilization armed with advanced weaponry subdued, in a remarkably brief time, two powerful peoples. Beyond the drama and bloodshed, the conquests made it very difficult for these Native American cultures to have a major impact on Western civilization. Some scholars believe, however, that the Iroquois tribes of North America set examples of freedom of speech, assembly, and religion that may have influenced the framers of the American Constitution.

The Spanish and the Native Americans made some accommodations to each other, but in the end European values, religion, economic goals, and language dominated. No group that retained indigenous religion, language, or values could become part of the new dominant culture or of the political power elite. In that sense, the Spanish conquests of the early sixteenth century marked the beginning of the process whereby South America was transformed into Latin America.

The Economy of Exploitation

From the beginning, both the native peoples of America and their lands were drawn into the Atlantic economy and the world of competitive European commercialism. For the Indians of Latin America and somewhat later, the blacks of Africa, that drive for gain meant various arrangements of forced labor.

There were three major components in the colonial economy of Latin America: mining, agriculture, and shipping. Each of them involved labor, servitude, or a relationship of dependence of the New World economy on that of Spain.

MINING   The early *conquistadores*, or "conquerors," were primarily interested in gold, but by the middle of the sixteenth century, silver mining provided the chief source of metallic wealth. The great mining centers were Potosí in Peru and somewhat smaller sites in northern Mexico. (See "Forced Indian Labor at Potosí".) The Spanish crown was particularly interested in mining because it received one-fifth (the *quinto*) of all mining revenues. For this reason, the

Forced Indian Labor at Potosí

The Potosí range in Peru was the site of the great silver-mining industry in the Spanish Empire. The vast amount of wealth contained in the region became legendary almost as soon as mining began there in the 1540s. Indians, most of whom were forced laborers working under the mita *system of conscription, did virtually all of the work underground. The description that follows, written by a Spanish friar in the early seventeenth century, portrays both the large size of the enterprise and the harsh conditions that the Indians endured. At any one time, only one-third of the 13,300 conscripted Indians were employed. The labor force was changed every four months.*

❖ *How efficient does the description suggest the mines were? What would have been the likely effect of working so long underground surrounded by burning candles?*

According to His Majesty's warrant, the mine owners on this massive range have a right to the *mita* [conscripted labor] of 13,300 Indians in the working and exploitation of the mines, both those which have been discovered, those now discovered, and those which shall be discovered. It is the duty of the *Corregidor* [municipal governor] of Potosí to have them rounded up and to see that they come in from all the provinces between Cuzco over the whole of El Collao and as far as the frontiers of Tarija and Tomina....

The *mita* Indians go up every Monday morning to the locality of Guayna Potosí which is at the foot of the range; the *Corregidor* arrives with all the provincial captains or chiefs who have charge of the Indians assigned him for his miner or smelter; that keeps him busy till 1 P.M., by which time the Indians are already turned over to these mine and smelter owners.

After each has eaten his ration, they climb up the hill, each to his mine, and go in, staying there from that hour until Saturday evening without coming out of the mine; their wives bring them food, but they stay constantly underground, excavating and carrying out the ore from which they get the silver. They all have tallow candles, lighted day and night; that is the light they work with, for as they are underground, they have need of it all the time....

These Indians have different functions in the handling of the silver ore; some break it up with bar or pick, and dig down in, following the vein in the mine; others bring it up; others up above keep separating the good and the poor in piles; others are occupied in taking it down from the range to the mills on herds of llamas; every day they bring up more than 8,000 of these native beasts of burden for this task. These teamsters who carry the metal do not belong to the *mita*, but are *mingados*—hired.

From Antonia Vázquez de Espinosa, *Compendium and Description of the Indies [ca. 1620]*, trans. by Charles Upson Clark (Washington, DC: Smithsonian Institution Press, 1968), p. 62. Reprinted by permission of the Smithsonian Institution Press.

crown maintained a monopoly over the production and sale of mercury, required in the silver-mining process. Exploring for silver never lost predominance during the colonial era. Its production by forced labor for the benefit of Spaniards and the Spanish crown epitomized the wholly extractive economy that stood at the foundation of colonial life.

AGRICULTURE   The major rural and agricultural institution of the Spanish colonies was the *hacienda*, a large landed estate owned by persons originally born in Spain (*peninsulares*) or persons of Spanish descent born in America (*creoles*). Laborers on the *hacienda* usually stood in some re-

lation of formal servitude to the owner and were rarely free to move from the services of one landowner to another.

The *hacienda* economy produced two major products: foodstuffs for mining areas and urban centers and leather goods used in mining machinery. Both farming and ranching were subordinate to the mining economy.

In the West Indies, the basic agricultural unit was the plantation. In Cuba, Hispaniola, Puerto Rico, and other islands, the labor of black slaves from Africa produced sugar to supply an almost insatiable demand for the product in Europe.

A final major area of economic activity in the Spanish colonies was urban service occupations, including government offices, the legal profession, and shipping. Practitioners of these occupations were either *peninsulares* or *creoles*, with the former dominating more often than not.

LABOR SERVITUDE   All of this extractive and exploitive economic activity required labor, and the Spanish in the New World decided very early that the native population would supply that labor. A series of social devices was used to draw them into the new economic life imposed by the Spanish.

The first of these was the *encomienda*, a formal grant of the right to the labor of a specific number of Indians, usually a few hundred, but sometimes thousands, for a particular period of time. The institution stood in decline by the middle of the sixteenth century because the Spanish monarchs feared that the holders of *encomienda* might become a powerful independent nobility in the New World. They were also persuaded on humanitarian grounds against this particular kind of exploitation of the Indians.

The passing of the *encomienda* led to a new arrangement of labor servitude: the *repartimiento*. This device required adult male Indians to devote a certain number of days of labor annually to Spanish economic enterprises. In the mines of Peru, the *repartimiento* was known as the *mita*, the Inca term for their labor tax. *Repartimiento* service was often extremely harsh, and in some cases Indians did not survive their stint. The limitation on labor time led some Spanish managers to abuse their workers on the assumption that fresh workers would soon be appearing on the scene.

The eventual shortage of workers and the crown's pressure against extreme versions of forced labor led to the use of free labor. The freedom, however, was more in appearance than reality. Free Indian laborers were required to purchase goods from the landowner or mine owner, to whom they became forever indebted. This form of exploitation, known as *debt peonage*, continued in Latin America long after the nineteenth-century wars of liberation.

Black slavery was the final mode of forced or subservient labor in the New World. Both the Spanish and the Portuguese had earlier used African slaves in Europe. The sugar plantations of the West Indies now became the major center of black slavery.

The conquest, the forced labor of the economy of exploitation, and the introduction of European diseases had devastating demographic consequences for the Native American population. For centuries, Europeans had lived in a far more complex human and animal environment than Native Americans did. They had frequent contact with different ethnic and racial groups and with a variety of domestic animals. Such interaction helped them develop strong immune systems that enabled them to survive the ravages of measles, smallpox, and typhoid. Native Americans, by contrast, grew up in a simpler and more sterile environment and were completely defenseless against these diseases. Within a generation, the native population of New Spain (Mexico) was reduced to an estimated 8 percent of its numbers, from 25,000,000 to 2,000,000.

The Impact on Europe

Among contemporary European intellectuals, Columbus's discovery increased skepticism about the wisdom of the ancients. If traditional knowledge about the world had been so wrong geographically, how could one trust it on other matters? For many, Columbus's discovery demonstrated the folly of relying on any fixed body of presumed authoritative knowledge. Both in Europe and in the New World, there were those who condemned the explorers' treatment of American natives, as more was learned about their cruelty. (See "Montaigne on 'Cannibals' in Foreign Lands.") Three centuries later, however, on the third anniversary of Columbus's discovery (1792), the great thinkers of the age lionized Columbus for having opened up new possibilities for civilization and morality. By establishing new commercial contacts among different peoples of the world, Columbus was said to have made cooperation, civility, and peace among them indispensable. Enlightenment thinkers drew parallels between the discovery of America and the invention of the printing press—both portrayed as world-historical events opening new eras in communication and globalization, an early multicultural experiment.[4]

On the material side, the influx of spices and precious metals into Europe from the new Spanish Empire was a mixed blessing. It contributed to a steady rise in prices during the sixteenth century that created an inflation rate estimated at 2 percent a year. The new supply of bullion from the Americas joined with enlarged European production to increase greatly the amount of coinage in circulation, and this increase in turn fed inflation. Fortunately, the increase in prices was by and large spread over a long period and was not sudden. Prices doubled in Spain by midcentury, quadrupled by 1600. In Luther's Wittenberg, the cost of

---

[4] Cf. Anthony Pagden, "The Impact of the New World on the Old: The History of an Idea," *Renaissance and Modern Studies* 30 (1986): 1–11.

Montaigne on "Cannibals" in Foreign Lands

The French philosopher Michel de Montaigne (1533–1592) had seen a Brazilian native in Rouen in 1562, an alleged cannibal brought to France by the explorer Ville-gagnon. The experience gave rise to an essay on the subject of what constitutes a "savage." Montaigne concluded that no people on earth were more barbarous than Europeans, who take natives of other lands captive.

❖ *Is Montaigne romanticizing New World natives? Is he being too hard on Europeans? Had the Aztecs or Incas had the ability to discover and occupy Europe, would they have enslaved and exploited Europeans?*

Now, to return to my subject, I think there is nothing barbarous and savage in that nation [Brazil], from what I have been told....Each man calls barbarism whatever is not his own practice; for indeed it seems we have no other test of truth and reason than the example and pattern of the opinions and customs of the country we live in. There [we] always [find] the perfect religion, the perfect government, the perfect and accomplished manners in all things. Those [foreign] people are wild, just as we call wild the fruits that Nature has produced by herself and in her normal course; where really it is those that we have changed artificially and led astray from the common order that we should rather call wild. The former retain alive and vigorous their genuine virtues and properties, which we have debased in the latter by adapting them to gratify our corrupted taste. And yet for all that, the savor and delicacy of some uncultivated fruits of those countries is quite as excellent, even to our taste, as that of our own. It is not reasonable that [our human] art should win the place of honor over our great and powerful mother Nature. We have so overloaded the beauty and richness of her works by our inven-

tions that we have quite smothered her. Yet wherever her purity shines forth, she wonderfully puts to shame our vain and frivolous attempts: "Ivy comes readier without our care;/In lonely caves the arbutus grows more fair;/No art with artless bird song can compare."[1] All our efforts cannot even succeed in reproducing the nest of the tiniest little bird, its contexture, its beauty and convenience; or even the web of the puny spider. All things, says Plato,[2] are produced by nature, by fortune, or by art; the greatest and most beautiful by one or the other of the first two, the least and most imperfect by the last.

These nations, then, seem to me "barbarous" in this sense, that they have been fashioned very little by the human mind, and are still very close to their original naturalness. The laws of nature still rule them, very little corrupted by ours; and they are in such a state of purity that I am sometimes vexed that they were unknown earlier, in the days when there were men able to judge them better than we.

[1] Propertius, 1.11.10.

[2] Laws, 10.

From *The Complete Essays of Montaigne*, trans. by Donald M. Frame (Stanford: Stanford University Press, 1958), pp. 153–154.

basic food and clothing increased almost 100 percent between 1519 and 1540. Generally, wages and rents remained well behind the rise in prices.

The new wealth enabled governments and private entrepreneurs to sponsor basic research and expansion in the printing, shipping, mining, textile, and weapons industries. There is also evidence of large-scale government planning in such ventures as the French silk industry and the Habsburg–Fugger development of mines in Austria and Hungary.

In the thirteenth and fourteenth centuries capitalist institutions and practices had already begun to develop in the rich Italian cities. (One may point to the activities of the Florentine banking houses of Bardi and Peruzzi.) Those who owned the means of production, either privately or corporately, were clearly distinguished from the workers who operated them. Wherever possible, entrepreneurs created monopolies in basic goods. High interest was charged on loans—actual, if not legal, usury. And the "capitalist" virtues of thrift, industry, and orderly planning were everywhere in evidence—all intended to permit the free and efficient accumulation of wealth.

The late fifteenth and the sixteenth centuries saw the maturation of this type of capitalism together with its attendant social problems. The Medicis of Florence grew very rich as bankers of the pope, as did the Fuggers of Augsburg, who bankrolled Habsburg rulers. The Fuggers lent Charles I of Spain more than 500,000 florins to buy his election as Holy Roman Emperor in 1519 and boasted that they had created the emperor. The new wealth and industrial expansion also raised the expectations of the poor and the ambitious and heightened the reactionary tendencies of the wealthy. This effect, in turn, aggravated the traditional social divisions between the clergy and the laity, the urban patriciate and the guilds, and the landed nobility and the agrarian peasantry.

These divisions indirectly prepared the way for the Reformation as well, by making many people critical of traditional institutions and open to new ideas—especially those that seemed to promise greater freedom and a chance at a better life.

In Perspective

As it recovered from national wars during the late Middle Ages, Europe saw the establishment of permanent centralized states and regional governments. The foundations of modern France, Spain, England, Germany, and Italy were laid at this time. As rulers imposed their will on regions outside their immediate domains, the "one" progressively took control of the "many," and previously divided lands came together as nations.

Thanks to the work of Byzantine and Islamic scholars, ancient Greek science and scholarship found their way into the West in these centuries. Europeans had been separated from their classical cultural heritage for almost eight centuries. No other world civilization had experienced such a disjunction from its cultural past. The discovery of classical civilization occasioned a rebirth of intellectual and artistic activity in both southern and northern Europe. One result was the splendor of the Italian Renaissance, whose scholarship, painting, and sculpture remain among western Europe's most impressive achievements.

Ancient learning was not the only discovery of the era. New political unity spurred both royal greed and national ambition. By the late fifteenth centu-

ry, Europeans were in a position to venture far away to the shores of Africa, the southern and eastern coasts of Asia, and the New World of the Americas. European discovery was not the only outcome of these voyages: The exploitation of the peoples and lands of the New World revealed a dark side of Western civilization. Some penalties were paid even then. The influx of New World gold and silver created new human and economic problems on the European mainland. In some circles, Europeans even began to question their civilization's traditional values.

REVIEW QUESTIONS

1. Discuss Jacob Burkhardt's interpretation of the Renaissance. What criticisms have been leveled against it? How would you define the term "Renaissance" in the context of fifteenth- and sixteenth-century Italy?

2. How would you define Renaissance humanism? In what ways was the Renaissance a break with the Middle Ages, and in what ways did it owe its existence to medieval civilization?

3. Who were some of the famous literary and artistic figures of the Italian Renaissance? What did they have in common that might be described as "the spirit of the Renaissance"?

4. Why did the French invade Italy in 1494? How did this event trigger Italy's political decline? How do the actions of Pope Julius II and the ideas of Niccolò Machiavelli signify a new era in Italian civilization?

5. A common assumption is that creative work proceeds best in periods of calm and peace. Given the combination of political instability and cultural productivity in Renaissance Italy, do you think this assumption is valid?

6. How did the Renaissance in the north differ from the Italian Renaissance? In what ways was Erasmus the embodiment of the northern Renaissance?

7. What factors led to the voyages of discovery? How did the Spanish establish their empire in the Americas? Why was the conquest so violent? What was the experience of native peoples during and after the conquest?

SUGGESTED READINGS

L. B. ALBERTI, *The Family in Renaissance Florence*, trans. by R. N. Watkins (1962). A contemporary humanist, who never married, explains how a family should behave.

R. H. BAINTON, *Erasmus of Christendom* (1960). Charming presentation.

H. BARON, *The Crisis of the Early Italian Renaissance*, vols. 1 and 2 (1966). A major work, setting forth the civic dimension of Italian humanism.

C. BOXER, *Four Centuries of Portuguese Expansion, 1415–1825* (1961). Comprehensive survey by the leading authority.

G. A. BRUCKER, *Renaissance Florence* (1969). Comprehensive survey of all facets of Florentine life.

G. A. BRUCKER, *Giovanni and Lusanna: Love and Marriage in Renaissance Florence* (1986). Love in the Renaissance shown to be more Bergman than Fellini.

J. BURCKHARDT, *The Civilization of the Renaissance in Italy* (1867). The old classic that still has as many defenders as detractors.

R. E. CONRAD, *Children of God's Fire: A Documentary History of Black Slavery in Brazil* (1983). Not for the squeamish.

A. W. CROSBY, *The Columbian Exchange: Biological and Cultural Consequences of 1492* (1973). A study of the epidemiological disaster that Columbus visited upon Native Americans.

E. L. EISENSTEIN, *The Printing Press as an Agent of Change: Communications and Cultural Transformations in Early Modern Europe*, 2 vols. (1979). Bold, stimulating account of the centrality of printing to all progress in the period.

W. K. FERGUSON, *Europe in Transition, 1300–1520* (1962). A major survey that deals with the transition from medieval society to Renaissance society.

F. GILBERT, *Machiavelli and Guicciardini* (1984). The two great Renaissance historians lucidly compared.

L. HANKE, *Bartholomé de Las Casas: An Interpretation of His Life and Writings* (1951). Biography of the great Dominican critic of Spanish exploitation of Native Americans.

J. HANKINS, *Plato in the Renaissance* (1992). A magisterial study of how Plato was read and interpreted by Renaissance scholars.

D. HERLIHY, *The Family in Renaissance Italy* (1974). Excellent on family structure and general features.

D. HERLIHY, *Women, Family, and Society in Medieval Europe: Historical Essays, 1978–1991*, ed. A. Molho (1998). A major medievalist's collected essays on medieval and Renaissance society.

D. HERLIHY AND C. KLAPISCH-ZUBER, *Tuscans and Their Families* (1985). Important work based on unique demographic data that give the reader a new appreciation of quantitative history.

D. L. JENSEN, *Renaissance Europe: Age of Recovery and Reconciliation* (1981). Up-to-date and comprehensive survey.

F. KATZ, *The Ancient American Civilizations* (1972). An excellent introduction.

R. KELSO, *Doctrine of the Lady of the Renaissance* (1978). Noblewomen in the Renaissance.

C. KLAPISCH-ZUBER, *Women, Family, and Ritual in Renaissance Italy* (1985). Provocative, wide-ranging essays documenting Renaissance Italy as very much a man's world.

P. O. KRISTELLER, *Renaissance Thought: The Classic, Scholastic, and Humanist Strains* (1961). A master shows the many sides of Renaissance thought.

I. MACLEAN, *The Renaissance Notion of Women* (1980). An account of the views of Renaissance intellectuals and their sources in antiquity.

L. MARTINES, *Power and Imagination: City States in Renaissance Italy* (1980). Stimulating account of cultural and political history.

S. E. MORRISON, *Admiral of the Ocean Sea: A Life of Christopher Columbus* (1946). Still the authoritative biography.

E. PANOFSKY, *Meaning in the Visual Arts* (1955). Eloquent treatment of Renaissance art.

J. H. PARRY, *The Age of Reconnaissance* (1964). A comprehensive account of exploration in the years 1450–1650.

P. PARTNER, *Renaissance Rome, 1500–1559: A Portrait of a Society* (1976). A description of the city from an insider's perspective.

J. B. A. POCOCK, *The Machiavellian Moment in Florentine Political Thought and the Atlantic Republican Tradition* (1975). Traces the influence of Florentine political thought in early modern Europe.

I. A. RICHTER (ED.), *The Notebooks of Leonardo da Vinci* (1985). The master in his own words.

Q. SKINNER, *The Foundations of Modern Political Thought; I: The Renaissance* (1978). Broad survey, including absolutely every known political theorist, major and minor.

Chapter 11

A Catholic Portrayal of Martin Luther Tempting Christ (1547). *Reformation propaganda often portrayed the pope as the Antichrist or the devil. Here Catholic propaganda turns the tables on the Protestant reformers by portraying a figure of Martin Luther as the Devil (note the monstrous feet and tail under his academic robes). Recreating the biblical scene of Christ being tempted by the Devil in the wilderness, the figure of Luther asks Christ to transform stone into bread, to which temptation Christ responds by saying that humans do not live by bread alone.* Versucung Christi, 1547, Gemälde, Bonn, Rheinisches Landesmuseum, Inv. Nr. 58.3.

The Age of Reformation

KEY TOPICS

- The social and religious background to the Reformation
- Martin Luther's challenge to the church and the course of the Reformation in Germany
- The Reformation in Switzerland, France, and England
- Transitions in family life between medieval and modern times

In the second decade of the sixteenth century, a powerful religious movement began in Saxony in Germany and spread rapidly throughout northern Europe, deeply affecting society and politics, as well as the spiritual lives of men and women. Attacking what they believed to be burdensome superstitions that robbed people of both their money and their peace of mind, Protestant reformers led a broad revolt against the medieval church. In a short span of time, hundreds of thousands of people from all social classes set aside the beliefs of centuries and adopted a more simplified religious practice.

The Protestant Reformation challenged aspects of the Renaissance, especially its tendency to follow classical sources in glorifying human nature and its loyalty to traditional religion. Protestants were more impressed by the human potential for evil than by the inclination to do good; they encouraged parents, teachers, and magistrates to be firm disciplinarians. On the other hand, Protestants also embraced many Renaissance values, especially in the sphere of educational reform and particularly with regard to training in ancient languages. Like the Italian humanists, the Protestant reformers prized the tools that allowed them to go directly to the original sources. For them, this meant the study of the Hebrew and Greek scriptures, enabling them to root their consequent challenges to traditional institutions in biblical authority.

Society and Religion

The Protestant Reformation occurred at a time of sharp conflict between the emerging nation–states of Europe, bent on conformity and centralization within their realms, and the self-governing small towns and regions, long accustomed to running their own affairs. Since the fourteenth century, the king's law and custom had progressively overridden local law and custom almost everywhere. Many towns and territories were keenly sensitive to the loss of traditional rights and freedoms. Many townspeople and village folk perceived in the religious revolt an ally in their struggle to remain politically free and independent. The Reformation came to be closely identified in the minds of its supporters with what we today might call states' rights or local control.

Social and Political Conflict

The Reformation broke out first in the free imperial cities of Germany and Switzerland. There were about sixty-five such cities, and each was in a certain sense a little kingdom unto itself. The great majority had Protestant movements, but with mixed success and duration. Some quickly turned Protestant and remained so. Some were Protestant only for a short time. Others developed mixed confessions, frowning on sectarianism and aggressive proselytizing, and letting Catholics and Protestants live side by side with appropriate barriers.

What seemed a life-and-death struggle with higher princely or royal authority was not the only conflict cities were experiencing. They also suffered deep internal social and political divisions. Certain groups favored the Reformation more than others. In many places, guilds whose members were economically prospering and socially rising were in the forefront of the Reformation. The printers' guild is a prominent example. Its members were literate, sophisticated about the world, in a rapidly growing industry, and economically very ambitious. They also

The Reformation broke out against a background of deep social and political divisions that bred resentment against authority. This early sixteenth-century woodcut by Georg Pencz presents a warning against tyranny. It shows a world turned upside down, with the hunted becoming the hunters. The rabbits capture the hunters and their dogs and subject them to the same brutal treatment—skinning, butchering, and cooking—that the hunters and dogs routinely inflict on rabbits. The message: tyranny eventually begets rebellion. From Max Geisberg, *The German Single-Leaf Woodcut*, 1500–1550, edited by Walter L. Strauss. Hacker Art Books, 1974. Used by permission of Hacker Art Books, Inc.

had an economic stake in fanning religious conflict with Protestant propaganda, which many, of course, also sincerely believed. Guilds with a history of opposition to reigning governmental authority also stand out among early Protestant supporters, regardless of whether their members were literate.

There is, in brief, evidence to suggest that people who felt pushed around and bullied by either local or distant authority—a guild by an autocratic local government, an entire city or region by a powerful prince or king—often perceived an ally in the Protestant movement, at least initially.

Social and political experience thus coalesced with the larger religious issues in both town and countryside. A Protestant sermon or pamphlet seemed directly relevant, for example, to the townspeople of German and Swiss cities who faced incorporation into the territory of a powerful local prince, who looked on them as obedient subjects rather than as free citizens. When Martin Luther and his comrades wrote, preached, and sang about a priesthood of all believers, scorned the authority of ecclesiastical landlords, and ridiculed papal laws as arbitrary human inventions, they touched political as well as religious nerves. And this was as true in the villages as in the towns. Like city dwellers, the peasants on the land also heard in the Protestant sermon and pamphlet a promise of political liberation and even a degree of social betterment. More than the townspeople, the peasants found their traditional liberties—from fishing and hunting rights to representation at local diets—progressively being chipped away by the great secular and ecclesiastical landlords who ruled over them.

Popular Religious Movements and Criticism of the Church

The Protestant Reformation could also not have occurred without the monumental crises of the medieval church during the "exile" in Avignon, the Great Schism, the Conciliar period, and the Renaissance papacy. For increasing numbers of people, the medieval church had ceased to provide a viable foundation for religious piety. Many intellectuals and laypeople felt a sense of crisis about the traditional teaching and spiritual practice of the church. Between the secular pretensions of the papacy and the dry teaching of Scholastic theologians, laity and clerics alike began to seek a more heartfelt, idealistic, and—often, in the eyes of the Pope—increasingly heretical religious piety. The late Middle Ages were marked by independent lay and clerical efforts to reform local religious practice and by widespread experimentation with new religious forms.

A variety of factors contributed to the growth of lay criticism of the church. The laity in the cities were becoming increasingly knowledgeable about the world and those who controlled their lives. They traveled widely—as soldiers, pilgrims, explorers, and traders. New postal systems and the printing press increased the information at their disposal. The new age of books and libraries raised literacy and heightened curiosity. Laypeople were increasingly able to take the initiative in shaping the cultural life of their communities.

From the Albigensians, Waldensians, Beguines, and Beghards in the thirteenth century to the Lollards and Hussites in the fifteenth, lay religious movements shared a common goal of religious simplicity in imitation of Jesus. Almost without exception, they were inspired by an ideal of apostolic poverty in religion; that is, all wanted a religion of true self-sacrifice like that of Jesus and the first disciples. The laity sought a more egalitarian church, one that gave the members as well as the head of the church a voice, and a more spiritual church, one that lived manifestly according to its New Testament model.

THE MODERN DEVOTION   One of the most constructive lay religious movements in northern Europe on the eve of the Reformation was that of the Brothers of the Common Life, or what came to be known as the Modern Devotion. The brothers fostered religious life outside formal ecclesiastical offices and apart from formal religious vows. Established by Gerard Groote (1340–1384), the Modern Devotion was centered at Zwolle and Deventer in the Netherlands. The brother and (less numerous) sister houses of the Modern Devotion, however, spread rapidly throughout northern Europe and influenced parts of southern Europe as well. In these houses clerics and laity came together to share a common life, stressing individual piety and practical religion. Lay members were not expected to take special religious vows or to wear special religious dress, nor did they abandon their ordinary secular vocations.

The brothers were also active in education. They worked as copyists, sponsored many religious and a few classical publications, ran hospices for poor students, and conducted schools for the young, especially boys preparing for the priesthood or a monastic vocation. As youths, Nicholas of Cusa, Johann Reuchlin, and Desiderius Erasmus were looked after by the brothers. Thomas à Kempis (d. 1471) summarized the philosophy of the brothers in what became the most popular religious book of the period, the *Imitation of Christ*. This semimystical guide to the inner life was intended primarily for monks and nuns, but was widely appropriated by laity who also wanted to pursue the ascetic life.

The Modern Devotion has been seen as the source of humanist, Protestant, and Catholic reform movements in the sixteenth century. Some scholars, how-

Injustice. This woodcut by an unknown artist compares the law, represented by the court scene in the center, to a spider's web, shown in the window on the right. Just as the web traps small, weak insects, the law ensnares the poor, seen hanging on the gallows and the wheel through the window on the left. And just as the large bee flies easily through the web, the rich and powerful escape punishment for their crimes. Hacker Art Books, Inc.

ever, believe that it represented an individualistic approach to religion, indifferent and even harmful to the sacramental piety of the church. It was actually a very conservative movement. The brothers retained the old clerical doctrines and values, while placing them within the new framework of an active common life. Their practices clearly met a need for a more personal piety and a more-informed religious life. Their movement appeared at a time when the laity was demanding good preaching in the vernacular and was even taking the initiative to endow special preacherships to ensure it. The Modern Devotion permitted laypeople to practice a full religious life without surrendering their life in the world.

LAY CONTROL OVER RELIGIOUS LIFE   On the eve of the Reformation, Rome's international network of church offices, which had unified Europe religiously during the Middle Ages, began to fall apart in many areas. This collapse was hurried along by a growing sense of regional identity—incipient nationalism—and local secular administrative competence. The long-entrenched *benefice* system of the medieval church had permitted important ecclesiastical posts to be sold to the highest bidders and had left residency requirements in parishes unenforced. Such a system did not result in a vibrant local religious life. The substitutes hired by nonresident holders of *benefices* lived elsewhere, mostly in Rome. They milked the revenues of their offices, often performed their chores mechanically, and had neither firsthand knowledge of, nor much sympathy with, local needs and problems. Rare was the late medieval German town that did not have complaints about the maladministration, concubinage, or fiscalism of its clergy, especially the higher clergy (bishops, abbots, and prelates).

Communities had loudly protested the financial abuses of the medieval church long before Luther published his famous summary of economic griev-ances in 1520 in the *Address to the Christian Nobility of the German Nation*. The sale of indulgences in particular had been repeatedly attacked before Luther came on the scene. On the eve of the Reformation, this practice had expanded to permit people to buy release from time in purgatory for both themselves and their deceased loved ones. Rulers and magistrates had little objection to their sale and might even encourage it, so long as a generous portion of the income they generated remained in the local coffers. But when an indulgence was offered primarily for the benefit of distant interests, as with the Saint Peter's indulgence protested by Luther, resistance arose for strictly financial reasons, because their sale drained away local revenues.

The sale of indulgences would not end until rulers found new ways to profit from religion and the laity found a more effective popular remedy for religious anxiety. The Reformation provided the former by sanctioning the secular dissolution of monasteries and the confiscation of ecclesiastical properties. It held out the latter in its new theology of justification by faith.

City governments also undertook to improve local religious life on the eve of the Reformation by endowing preacherships. These positions, supported by *benefices*, provided for well-trained and dedicated pastors who could offer regular preaching and pastoral care that went beyond the routine performance of the mass and traditional religious functions. In many instances, these preacherships became platforms for Protestant preachers.

Magistrates also carefully restricted the growth of ecclesiastical properties and clerical privileges. During the Middle Ages, canon and civil law had come to recognize special clerical rights in both property and person. Because they were holy places, churches and monasteries had been exempted from the taxes and laws that affected others. They were treated as special places of "sacral peace" and asylum. It was considered inappropriate for holy persons (clergy) to be burdened with such "dirty jobs" as military service, compulsory labor, standing watch at city gates, and other obligations of citizenship. Nor was it thought right that the laity, of whatever rank, should sit in judgment on those who were their shepherds and intermediaries with God. The clergy, accordingly, came to enjoy an immunity of place (which exempted ecclesiastical properties from taxes and recognized their right of asylum) and an immunity of person (which exempted the clergy from the jurisdiction of civil courts).

On the eve of the Reformation, measures were passed to restrict these privileges and to end their abuses. Among them, we find efforts to regulate ecclesiastical acquisition of new property, to circumvent the right of asylum in churches and monasteries (a practice that posed a threat to the normal administration of justice), and to bring the clergy under the local tax code. Governments had understandably tired of ecclesiastical interference in what to them were strictly political spheres of competence and authority.

Martin Luther and German Reformation to 1525

Unlike France and England, late medieval Germany lacked the political unity to enforce "national" religious reforms during the late Middle Ages. There were no lasting Statutes of Provisors and Praemunire, as in England, nor a Pragmatic Sanction of Bourges, as in France, limiting papal jurisdiction and taxation on a national scale. What happened on a unified national level in England and France occurred only locally and piecemeal within German territories and towns. As popular resentment of clerical immunities and ecclesiastical abuses, especially over the selling of indulgences, spread among German cities and towns, an unorganized "national" opposition to Rome formed. German humanists had long given voice to such criticism, and by 1517 it was pervasive enough to provide a solid foundation for Martin Luther's reform.

Luther (1483–1546) was the son of a successful Thüringian miner. He was educated in Mansfeld, Magdeburg (where the Brothers of the Common Life were his teachers), and Eisenach. Between 1501 and 1505 he attended the University of Erfurt, where the nominalist teachings of William of Ockham and Gabriel Biel (d. 1495) prevailed. After receiving his master-of-arts degree in 1505, Luther registered with the law faculty, following his parents' wishes. But he never began the study of law. To the disappointment of his family, he instead entered the Order of the Hermits of Saint Augustine in Erfurt on July 17,

1505. This decision had apparently been building for some time and was resolved during a lightning storm in which Luther, terrified and crying out to Saint Anne for assistance (Saint Anne was the patron saint of travelers in distress), promised to enter a monastery if he escaped death.

Ordained in 1507, Luther pursued a traditional course of study. In 1510 he journeyed to Rome on the business of his order, finding there justification for the many criticisms of the church he had heard in Germany. In 1511 he moved to the Augustinian monastery in Wittenberg, where he earned his doctorate in theology in 1512. Thereafter, he became a leader within the monastery, the new university, and the spiritual life of the city.

Justification by Faith Alone

Reformation theology grew out of a problem then common to many of the clergy and the laity: the failure of traditional medieval religion to provide either full personal or intellectual satisfaction. Luther was especially plagued by the disproportion between his own sense of sinfulness and the perfect righteousness that medieval theology taught that God required for salvation. Traditional church teaching and the sacrament of penance proved to be of no consolation. Luther wrote that he came to despise the phrase "righteousness of God," for it seemed to demand of him a perfection he knew neither he nor any other human being could ever achieve. His insight into the meaning of "justification by faith alone" was a gradual process that extended between 1513 and 1518. The righteousness that God demands, he concluded, did not result from many religious works and ceremonies, but was given in full measure to those who believe and trust in Jesus Christ, who alone is the perfect righteousness satisfying to God. To believe in Christ meant to stand before God clothed in Christ's sure righteousness.

The Attack on Indulgences

An indulgence was a remission of the temporal penalty imposed by priests on penitents as a "work of satisfaction" for their mortal sins. According to medieval theology, after the priest absolved a penitent of guilt for the sins, the penitent remained under an eternal penalty, a punishment God justly imposed for sin. After absolution, however, this eternal penalty was said to be transformed into a temporal penalty, a manageable "work of satisfaction" that the penitent might perform here and now (for example, through prayers, fasting, almsgiving, retreats, and pilgrimages). Penitents who defaulted on such prescribed works of satisfaction could expect to suffer for them in purgatory.

A contemporary caricature depicts John Tetzel, the famous indulgence preacher. The last lines of the jingle read: "As soon as gold in the basin rings, right then the soul to Heaven springs." It was Tetzel's preaching that spurred Luther to publish his ninety-five theses. Courtesy Staatliche Lutherhalle

At this point, indulgences, which had earlier been given to Crusaders who did not complete their penances because they had fallen in battle, became an aid to laity, made genuinely anxious by their belief in a future suffering in purgatory for neglected penances or unrepented sins. In 1343 Pope Clement VI (r. 1342–1352) had proclaimed the existence of a "treasury of merit," an infinite reservoir of good works in the church's possession that could be dispensed at the pope's discretion. On the basis of this declared treasury, the church sold "letters of indulgence," which covered the works of satisfaction owed by penitents. In 1476, Pope Sixtus IV (r. 1471–1484) extended indulgences also to cover purgatory.

Originally, indulgences had been given only for the true self-sacrifice of going on a Crusade to the Holy Land. By Luther's time, they were regularly dispensed for small cash payments (very modest sums that were regarded as a good work of almsgiving). They were presented to the laity as remitting not only their own future punishments, but also those of their dead relatives presumed to be suffering in purgatory.

In 1517 Pope Leo X (r. 1513–1521) revived a plenary Jubilee Indulgence that had first been issued by Pope Julius II (r. 1503–1513), the proceeds from which were to be used to rebuild St. Peter's Basilica in Rome. Such an indulgence promised forgiveness of all outstanding unrepented sins upon the completion of certain acts. That kind of indulgence was subsequently preached on the borders of Saxony in the territories of Archbishop Albrecht of Mainz, who was much in need of revenues because of the large debts he had incurred in order to hold, contrary to church law, three ecclesiastical appointments. The selling of the indulgence was a joint venture by Albrecht, the Augsburg banking house of Fugger, and Pope Leo X, with half the proceeds going to the Pope and half to Albrecht and his creditors. The famous indulgence preacher John Tetzel (d. 1519) was enlisted to preach the indulgence in Albrecht's territories because he was a seasoned professional who knew how to stir ordinary people to action. As he exhorted on one occasion:

Don't you hear the voices of your dead parents and other relatives crying out, "Have mercy on us, for we suffer great punishment and pain. From this you could release us with a few alms.... We have created you, fed you, cared for you, and left you our temporal goods. Why do you treat us so cruelly and leave us to suffer in the flames, when it takes only a little to save us?"[1]

When, on October 31, 1517, Luther, according to tradition, posted his ninety-five theses against

[1]*Die Reformation in Augenzeugen berichten,* ed. by Helmar Junghaus (Düsseldorf: Karl Rauch Verlag, 1967), p. 44.

indulgences on the door of Castle Church in Wittenberg, he protested especially against the impression created by Tetzel that indulgences actually remitted sins and released the dead from punishment in purgatory. Luther believed that these claims went far beyond the traditional practice and seemed to make salvation something that could be bought and sold.

Election of Charles V

The ninety-five theses were embraced by humanists and other proponents of reform. The theses made Luther famous overnight and prompted official proceedings against him. In October, he was called before the general of the Dominican order in Augsburg. But as sanctions were being prepared against Luther, Emperor Maximilian I died (January 12, 1519), and this event, fortunate for the Reformation, turned attention away from heresy in Saxony to the contest for a new emperor.

The pope backed the French king, Francis I. However, Charles I of Spain, a youth of nineteen, succeeded his grandfather and became Emperor Charles V.

(See Map 11–1.) Charles was assisted by both a long tradition of Habsburg imperial rule and a massive Fugger campaign chest, which secured the votes of the seven electors. The electors, who traditionally enhanced their power at every opportunity, wrung new concessions from Charles for their votes. The emperor agreed to a revival of the Imperial Supreme Court and the Council of Regency and promised to consult with a diet of the empire on all major domestic and foreign affairs that affected the empire. These measures also helped the development of the Reformation by preventing unilateral imperial action against the Germans, something Luther could be thankful for in the early years of the Reformation.

Luther's Excommunication and the Diet of Worms

In the same month in which Charles was elected emperor, Luther entered a debate in Leipzig (June 27, 1519) with the Ingolstadt professor John Eck. During this contest, Luther challenged the infallibility of the Pope and the inerrancy of church coun-

MAP 11–1   THE EMPIRE OF CHARLES V   *Dynastic marriages and simple chance concentrated into Charles's hands rule over the lands shown here, plus Spain's overseas possessions. Crowns and titles rained down on him; his election in 1519 as emperor gave him new distractions and responsibilities.*

cils, appealing, for the first time, to the sovereign authority of Scripture alone. He burned all his bridges to the old church when he further defended certain teachings of John Huss that had been condemned by the Council of Constance.

In 1520, Luther signaled his new direction with three famous pamphlets. The *Address to the Christian Nobility of the German Nation* urged the German princes to force reforms on the Roman church, especially to curtail its political and economic power in Germany. The *Babylonian Captivity of the Church* attacked the traditional seven sacraments, arguing that only two, Baptism and the Eucharist, were biblical, and exalted the authority of Scripture, church councils, and secular princes over that of the pope. The eloquent *Freedom of a Christian* summarized the new teaching of salvation by faith alone.

On June 15, 1520, Leo's papal bull *Exsurge Domine* condemned Luther for heresy and gave him sixty days to retract. The final bull of excommunication, *Decet Pontificem Romanum*, was issued on January 3, 1521.

In April 1521 Luther presented his views before the empire's Diet of Worms, over which the newly elected Emperor Charles V presided. Ordered to recant, Luther declared that to do so would be to act against Scripture, reason, and his own conscience. On May 26, 1521, he was placed under the imperial ban and thereafter became an "outlaw" to secular as well as religious authority. For his own protection, friends hid him in a secluded castle, where he spent almost a year, from April 1521 to March 1522. During his stay, he translated the New Testament into German, using Erasmus's new Greek text and Latin translation, and he attempted, by correspondence, to oversee the first stages of the Reformation in Wittenberg.

Imperial Distractions: France and the Turks

The Reformation was greatly helped in these early years by the emperor's war with France and the advance of the Ottoman Turks into eastern Europe. Against both adversaries Charles V, who also remained a Spanish king with dynastic responsibilities outside the empire, needed German troops, and to that end he promoted friendly relations with the German princes. Between 1521 and 1559, Spain (the Habsburg dynasty) and France (the Valois dynasty) fought four major wars over disputed territories in Italy and along their borders. In 1526 the Turks overran Hungary at the Battle of Mohacs, while in western Europe the French-led League of Cognac formed against Charles for the second Habsburg–Valois war.

Thus preoccupied, the emperor agreed through his representatives at the German Diet of Speyer in 1526 that each German territory was free to enforce the Edict of Worms (1521) against Luther "so as to be able to answer in good conscience to God and the emperor." That concession, in effect, gave the German princes territorial sovereignty in religious matters and the Reformation time to put down deep roots. Later (in 1555), the Peace of Augsburg would enshrine such local princely control over religion in imperial law.

How the Reformation Spread

In the late 1520s and on through the 1530s, the Reformation passed from the hands of the theologians and pamphleteers into those of the magistrates and princes. In many cities, the magistrates quickly followed the lead of the Protestant preachers and their sizable congregations in mandating the religious reforms they preached. In numerous instances, magistrates had themselves worked for decades to bring about basic church reforms and thus welcomed the preachers as new allies. Reform now ceased to be merely slogans and became laws that all townspeople had to obey.

The religious reform became a territorial political movement as well, led by the elector of Saxony and the prince of Hesse, the two most powerful German Protestant rulers. (See "Art & the West.") Like the urban magistrates, the German princes quickly recognized the political and economic opportunities offered them by the demise of the Roman Catholic Church in their regions. Soon they, too, were pushing Protestant faith and politics onto their neighbors. By the 1530s, Protestant cities and lands formed powerful defensive alliances and prepared for war with the Catholic emperor.

The Peasants' Revolt

In its first decade, the Protestant movement suffered more from internal division than from imperial interference. By 1525, Luther had become as much an object of protest within Germany as was the Pope. Original allies, sympathizers, and fellow travelers declared their independence from him.

Like the German humanists, the German peasantry also had at first believed Luther to be an ally. Since the late fifteenth century, the peasantry had been organized against efforts by territorial princes to override their traditional laws and customs and to subject them to new regulations and taxes. (See "German Peasants Protest Rising Feudal Exactions.") Peasant leaders, several of whom were convinced Lutherans, saw in Luther's teaching about Christian freedom and his criticism of monastic landowners a point of view close to their own. They openly solicited Luther's support of their political and economic rights, including their revolutionary request for release from serfdom.

A Royal Stag Hunt

Lucas Cranach, German, 1472–1553. *Hunting Near Hartenfels Castle*, 1540. Oil on wood, 116.8 × 170.2 cm. The Cleveland Art Museum, John L. Severance Fund, 1958.425.

*I*n 1504, Lucas Cranach the Elder (1472-1553), the most famous sixteenth-century German painter after Albrecht Dürer, became court painter to the Elector of Saxony, who was one of seven German princes empowered to elect the Holy Roman Emperor. Cranach was also a close friend of Martin Luther, a best man at the reformer's wedding in 1525 and later godfather to his first son.

A court painter had many responsibilities: He painted the interiors and exteriors of his lord's residences, outfitted their rooms with portraits, tapestries, furniture, and utensils, and furnished the decorations for large celebrations—from coats of arms, flags, and tents to sketches for the court tailors of the clothing to be worn. Cranach's lord owned over a dozen residences, and Cranach worked in five of his castles.

Among the most popular of Cranach's works at the royal court were paintings of hunts, which were also social and political occasions for area royalty and nobility. In 1540, Cranach painted this major hunt, in the rich game reserve around Castle Torgau, which stands in the background. Both hunt and painting were staged events and not the candid snapshot they appear. Before the hunt began, horsemen and dogs gathered the animals to be hunted into hedge pens bounded by a bend in the Elbe River. On the day of the hunt, the hunting party arranged itself in favorable positions to kill the stags, as they were released and crossed the river.

In the lower right, Princess Sybille stands armed and ready with her group, while Elector John Frederick, dressed in dark green hunting attire, cocks his crossbow as he waits for a stag to cross the river. To the left of the elector, a young hunter can be seen with three dogs and the Saxon motto initialed on his sleeves: "May the Word of God Remain into Eternity." The hunter in the blue-gray coat in the lower left foreground is the duke and future Elector of Saxony, Maurice. The scene also shows a bear hunt occurring in the upper left corner and a boar hunt in the upper right.

Source: *Lucas Cranach: Ein Maler-Unternehmer aus Franken*, ed. by Claus Grimm, et al. (Verlag Friedrich Pustet, Regensburg, 1994), pp. 311–313.

German Peasants Protest Rising Feudal Exactions

*In the late fifteenth and early sixteenth centuries, German feudal lords, both secu-
lar and ecclesiastical, tried to increase the earnings from their lands by raising demands on their peasant tenants. As the personal freedoms of peasants were restricted,
their properties confiscated, and their traditional laws and customs overridden, massive revolts occurred in southern Germany in 1525. Some historians see this uprising
and the social and economic conditions that gave rise to it as the major historical force
in early modern history. The list that follows is the most representative and well-
known statement of peasant grievances.*

❖ *Are the peasants' demands reasonable, given the circumstances of the sixteenth
century? Are the peasants more interested in material than in spiritual freedom?
Which of the demands are the most revolutionary?*

1. It is our humble petition and desire...that in the future...each community should choose and appoint a pastor, and that we should have the right to depose him should he conduct himself improperly....

2. We are ready and willing to pay the fair tithe of grain....The small tithes [of cattle], whether [to] ecclesiastical or lay lords, we will not pay at all, for the Lord God created cattle for the free use of man....

3. We...take it for granted that you will release us from serfdom as true Christians, unless it should be shown us from the Gospel that we are serfs.

4. It has been the custom heretofore that no poor man should be allowed to catch venison or wildfowl or fish in flowing water, which seems to us quite unseemly and unbrotherly as well as selfish and not agreeable to the Word of God....

5. We are aggrieved in the matter of woodcutting, for the noblemen have appropriated all the woods to themselves....

6. In regard to the excessive services demanded of us which are increased from day to day, we ask that this matter be properly looked into so that we shall not continue to be oppressed in this way....

7. We will not hereafter allow ourselves to be further oppressed by our lords, but will let them demand only what is just and proper according to the word of the agreement between the lord and the peasant. The lord should no longer try to force more services or other dues from the peasant without payment....

8. We are greatly burdened because our holdings cannot support the rent exacted from them.... We ask that the lords may appoint persons of honor to inspect these holdings and fix a rent in accordance with justice....

9. We are burdened with a great evil in the constant making of new laws....In our opinion we should be judged according to the old written law....

10. We are aggrieved by the appropriation...of meadows and fields which at one time belonged to a community as a whole. These we will take again into our own hands....

11. We will entirely abolish the due called *Todfall* [that is, heriot or death tax, by which the lord received the best horse, cow, or garment of a family upon the death of a serf] and will no longer endure it, nor allow widows and orphans to be thus shamefully robbed against God's will, and in violation of justice and right....

12. It is our conclusion and final resolution, that if any one or more of the articles here set forth should not be in agreement with the Word of God, as we think they are, such article we will willingly retract.

From *Translations and Reprints from the Original Sources of European History*, Vol. 2 (Philadelphia: Department of History, University of Pennsylvania, 1897).

Luther and his followers sympathized with the peasants. Indeed, for several years Lutheran pamphleteers made Karsthans, the burly, honest peasant who earned his bread by the sweat of his brow and sacrificed his own comfort and well-being for others, a symbol of the simple life that God desired all people to live. The Lutherans, however, were not social revolutionaries. When the peasants revolted against their masters in 1524–1525, Luther, not surprisingly, condemned them in the strongest possible

The punishment of a peasant leader in a village near Heilbronn. After the defeat of rebellious peasants in and around the city of Heilbronn, Jacob Rorbach, a well-to-do peasant leader from a nearby village, was tied to a stake and slowly roasted to death. © Badische Landesbibliothek

terms as "un-Christian" and urged the princes to crush their revolt without mercy. Tens of thousands of peasants (estimates run between 70,000 and 100,000) died by the time the revolt was put down.

For Luther, the freedom of the Christian was to be found in an inner release from guilt and anxiety, not in a right to restructure society by violent revolution. Had Luther supported the peasants' revolt, he would not only have contradicted his own teaching, but probably would also have ended any chance of the survival of his reform beyond the 1520s. Still, many believe that his decision ended the promise of the Reformation as a social revolution.

The Reformation Elsewhere

Although Luther's was the first, Switzerland and France had their own independent church reform movements almost simultaneously with Germany's. From these movements developed new churches as prominent and lasting as the Lutheran.

Zwingli and the Swiss Reformation

Switzerland was a loose confederacy of thirteen autonomous cantons, or states, and allied areas. (See Map 11–2.) Some cantons became Protestant, some remained Catholic, and a few other cantons and regions managed to effect a compromise. There were two main preconditions of the Swiss Reformation. First was the growth of national sentiment occasioned by popular opposition to foreign mercenary service. (Providing mercenaries for Europe's warring nations was a major source of Switzerland's livelihood.) Second was a desire for church reform that had persisted in Switzerland since the councils of Constance (1414–1417) and Basel (1431–1449).

THE REFORMATION IN ZURICH Ulrich Zwingli (1484–1531), the leader of the Swiss Reformation, had been humanistically educated in Bern, Vienna, and Basel. He was strongly influenced by Erasmus, whom he credited with having set him on the path to reform. He served as a chaplain with Swiss mercenaries during the disastrous Battle of Marignano in Italy in 1515 and thereafter became an eloquent critic of mercenary service. Zwingli believed that this service threatened both the political sovereignty and the moral well-being of the Swiss confederacy. By 1518, Zwingli was also widely known for opposition to the sale of indulgences and to religious superstition.

In 1519, he entered the competition for the post of people's priest in the main church of Zurich. His candidacy was contested because of his acknowledged fornication with a barber's daughter, an affair he successfully minimized in a forcefully written self-defense. Actually, his conduct was less scandalous to his contemporaries, who sympathized with the plight of the celibate clergy, than it may be to the modern reader. One of Zwingli's first acts as a reformer was to petition for an end to clerical celibacy and for the right of all clergy to marry, a practice that quickly became accepted in all Protestant lands.

From his new position as people's priest in Zurich, Zwingli engineered the Swiss Reformation. In March 1522, he was party to the breaking of the Lenten fast—an act of protest analogous to burning one's national flag today. Zwingli's reform guideline was very simple and very effective: Whatever lacked literal support in Scripture was to be neither believed nor practiced. As had also happened with Luther, that test soon raised questions about such honored traditional teachings and practices as fasting, transubstantiation, the worship of saints, pilgrimages, purgatory, clerical celibacy, and certain sacraments. A disputation held on January 29, 1523, concluded with the city government granting its sanction to Zwingli's Scripture test. Thereafter Zurich became, to all intents and purposes, the center of the Swiss Reformation. The new regime imposed a harsh discipline that made the city one of the first examples of puritanical Protestantism.

THE MARBURG COLLOQUY Landgrave Philip of Hesse (1504–1567) sought to unite Swiss and German Protestants in a mutual defense pact, a poten-

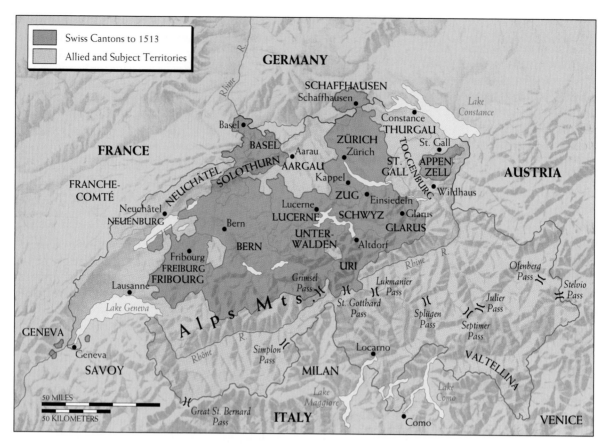

MAP 11–2   THE SWISS CONFEDERATION   *While nominally still a part of the Holy Roman Empire, Switzerland grew from a loose defensive union of the central "forest cantons" in the thirteenth century into a fiercely independent association of regions with different languages, histories, and, finally, religions.*

tially significant political alliance. His efforts were spoiled, however, by theological disagreements between Luther and Zwingli over the nature of Christ's presence in the Eucharist. Zwingli maintained a symbolic interpretation of Christ's words, "This is my body"; Christ, he argued, was only spiritually, not bodily, present in the bread and wine of the Eucharist. Luther, to the contrary, insisted that Christ's human nature could share the properties of his divine nature; hence, where Christ was spiritually present, he could also be bodily present, for his was a special nature. Luther wanted no part of an abstract, spiritualized Christ. Zwingli, on the other hand, feared that Luther had not broken sufficiently with medieval sacramental theology.

Philip of Hesse brought the two Protestant leaders together in his castle in Marburg in early October 1529, but they were unable to work out their differences on this issue. Luther left thinking Zwingli a dangerous fanatic. Although cooperation between the two sides did not cease, the disagreement splintered the Protestant movement theologically and politically. Separate defense leagues formed, and semi-Zwinglian theological

views came to be embodied in the *Tetrapolitan Confession*. This confession of faith was prepared by the Strasbourg reformers Martin Bucer and Caspar Hedio for presentation to the Diet of Augsburg (1530) as an alternative to the Lutheran Augsburg Confession.

SWISS CIVIL WARS   As the Swiss cantons divided between Protestantism and Catholicism, civil wars began. There were two major battles, both at Kappel, one in June 1529 and a second in October 1531. The first ended in a Protestant victory, which forced the Catholic cantons to break their foreign alliances and to recognize the rights of Swiss Protestants. During the second battle Zwingli was found wounded on the battlefield and was unceremoniously executed, his remains scattered to the four winds so his followers would have no relics to console and inspire them. The subsequent treaty confirmed the right of each canton to determine its own religion. Heinrich Bullinger (1504–1575), who was Zwingli's protégé and later married his daughter, became the new leader of the Swiss Reformation and guided its development into an established religion.

Anabaptists and Radical Protestants

The moderate pace and seemingly low ethical results of the Lutheran and Zwinglian reformations discontented many people, among them some of the original followers of Luther and Zwingli. They desired a more rapid and thorough implementation of apostolic Christianity—that is, a more visible moral transformation—and accused the major reformers of going only halfway. The most important of these radical groups were the Anabaptists, the sixteenth-century ancestors of the modern Mennonites and Amish. The Anabaptists were especially distinguished by their rejection of infant baptism and their insistence on only adult baptism. (The term "Anabaptism" derives from the Greek word meaning "to rebaptize.") They believed that baptism performed on a consenting adult conformed to Scripture and was more respectful of human freedom.

CONRAD GREBEL AND THE SWISS BRETHREN   Conrad Grebel (1498–1526), with whom Anabaptism originated, performed the first adult rebaptism in Zurich in January 1525. Initially a co-worker of Zwingli's and an even greater biblical literalist, Grebel broke openly with that reformer. In a religious disputation in October 1523, Zwingli supported the city government's plea for a very gradual removal of traditional religious practices.

The alternative of the Swiss Brethren, as Grebel's group came to be called, was embodied in the *Schleitheim Confession* of 1527. This document distinguished Anabaptists not only by their practice of adult baptism, but also by their refusal to go to war, to swear oaths, and to participate in the offices of secular government. Anabaptists physically separated from society to form a more perfect community in imitation of what they believed to be the example of the first Christians. Because of the close connection between religious and civic life in this period, the political authorities viewed such separatism as a threat to basic social bonds.

THE ANABAPTIST REIGN IN MÜNSTER   At first, Anabaptism drew its adherents from all social classes. But as Lutherans and Zwinglians joined with Catholics in opposition to the Anabaptists and persecuted them within the cities, a more rural, agrarian class came to make up the great majority. In 1529, rebaptism became a capital offense throughout the Holy Roman Empire. Estimates are that between 1525 and 1618 at least 1,000, and perhaps as many as 5,000, men and women were executed for rebaptizing themselves as adults. Brutal measures were universally applied against non-

conformists after Anabaptist extremists came to power in the German city of Münster in 1534–1535.

Led by two Dutch emigrants, a baker, Jan Matthys of Haarlem, and a tailor, Jan Beukelsz of Leiden, the Anabaptist majority in Münster forced Lutherans and Catholics either to convert or to emigrate. The Lutherans and Catholics left, and the city was blockaded by besieging armies. Münster transformed itself into an Old Testament theocracy, replete with charismatic leaders and the practice of polygamy. The latter was undertaken as a measure of social control, because there were so many more women, recently widowed or deserted, than men in the city. Many women revolted against the practice and were allowed to leave the resented polygynous marriages.

The outside world was deeply shocked by such developments in Münster. Protestant and Catholic armies united to crush the radicals. The skeletons of their leaders long hung in public view as a warning to all who would so offend traditional Christian sensitivities. After this episode, moderate, pacifistic Anabaptism became the norm among most nonconformists. The moderate Anabaptist leader Menno Simons (1496–1561), the founder of the Mennonites, set the example for the future.

SPIRITUALISTS   Another radical movement, that of the Spiritualists, was made up mostly of isolated individuals distinguished by their disdain of all traditions and institutions. They believed that the only religious authority was God's spirit, which spoke here and now to every individual. Among them were several former Lutherans. Thomas Müntzer (d. 1525), who had close contacts with Anabaptist leaders in Germany and Switzerland, died as a leader of a peasants' revolt. Sebastian Franck (d. 1541), a freelance critic of all dogmatic religion, proclaimed the religious autonomy of every individual soul. Caspar Schwenckfeld (d. 1561) was a prolific writer and wanderer after whom the Schwenckfeldian Church is named.

ANTITRINITARIANS   A final group of radical Protestants was the Antitrinitarians, exponents of a commonsense, rational, and ethical religion. Chief among this group were the Spaniard Michael Servetus (1511–1553), executed in 1553 in Geneva for "blasphemies against the Holy Trinity," and the Italians Lelio (d. 1562) and Faustus Sozzini (d. 1604), the founders of Socinianism. These thinkers were the strongest opponents of Calvinism, especially its belief in original sin and predestination, and have a deserved reputation as defenders of religious toleration.

John Calvin and the Genevan Reformation

In the second half of the sixteenth century, Calvinism replaced Lutheranism as the dominant Protestant force in Europe. Calvinism was the religious ideology that inspired or accompanied massive political resistance in France, the Netherlands, and Scotland. It established itself within the geographical region of the Palatinate during the reign of Elector Frederick III (r. 1559–1576). Calvinists believed strongly in both divine predestination and the individual's responsibility to reorder society according to God's plan. They became zealous reformers determined to transform and order society so that men and women would act externally as they believed, or should believe, internally and were presumably destined to live eternally.

In his famous study, *The Protestant Ethic and the Spirit of Capitalism* (1904), the German sociologist Max Weber argues that this peculiar combination of religious confidence and self-disciplined activism produced an ethic that stimulated and reinforced the spirit of emergent capitalism. According to Weber's argument, there was thus a close association between Calvinism and other later forms of Puritanism and the development of modern capitalist societies.

The founder of Calvinism, John Calvin (1509–1564), was born into a well-to-do family, the son of the secretary to the bishop of Noyon in Picardy. He received church *benefices* at age twelve, which financed the best possible education at Parisian colleges and a law degree at Orléans. In the 1520s, he associated with the indigenous French reform party. Although he would finally reject this group as ineffectual, its members contributed to his preparation as a religious reformer.

It was probably in the spring of 1534 that Calvin experienced that conversion to Protestantism by which he said his "long stubborn heart" was "made teachable" by God. His own experience became a personal model of reform that he would later apply to the recalcitrant citizenry of Geneva. His mature theology stressed the sovereignty of God over all creation and the necessity of humankind's conformity to His will. In May 1534, Calvin dramatically surrendered the *benefices* he had held for so long and at such profit and joined the Reformation.

POLITICAL REVOLT AND RELIGIOUS REFORM IN GENEVA
Whereas in Saxony religious reform paved the way for a political revolution against the emperor, in Geneva a political revolution against the local prince–bishop laid the foundation for the religious change. Genevans successfully revolted against their resident prince–bishop in the late 1520s, and the city council assumed his legal and political powers in 1527.

In late 1533, the Protestant city of Bern dispatched two reformers to Geneva: Guillaume Farel (1489–1565) and Antoine Froment (1508–1581). In the summer of 1535, after much internal turmoil, the Protestants triumphed, and the traditional mass and other religious practices were removed. On May 21, 1536, the city voted officially to adopt the Reformation: "to live according to the Gospel and the Word of God...without...any more masses, statues, idols, or other papal abuses."

Calvin arrived in Geneva after these events, in July 1536. He was actually en route to a scholarly refuge in Strasbourg, in flight from the persecution of Protestants in France, when warring between France and Spain forced him to turn sharply south to Geneva. Farel successfully pleaded with him to stay in the city and assist the Reformation, threatening Calvin with divine vengeance if he turned away from this task.

Before a year had passed, Calvin had drawn up articles for the governance of the new church, as well as a catechism to guide and discipline the people. (See "Rules Governing Genevan Moral Behavior.") Both were presented for approval to the city councils in early 1537. Because of the strong measures they proposed to govern Geneva's moral life, many suspected that the reformers were intent upon creating a "new papacy." Opponents attacked Calvin and Farel, fearing that they were going too far too fast. Geneva's powerful Protestant ally, Bern, which had adopted a more moderate Protestant reform, pressured Geneva's magistrates to restore traditional

A portrait of the young John Calvin. Bibliotheque Publique et Universitaire, Geneva

religious ceremonies and holidays that Calvin and Farel had abolished. When the reformers opposed these actions, they were exiled from the city.

Calvin went to Strasbourg, a model Protestant city, where he became pastor to French exiles and wrote biblical commentaries. He also produced a second edition of his masterful *Institutes of the Christian Religion*, which many consider the definitive theological statement of the Protestant faith.

Most important, he learned from the Strasbourg reformer Martin Bucer how to achieve his goals.

CALVIN'S GENEVA In 1540, Geneva elected syndics who were both favorable to Calvin and determined to establish full Genevan political and religious independence from Bern. They knew Calvin would be a valuable ally in this project and invited him to return. This he did in September 1540, never to leave

---

Rules Governing Genevan Moral Behavior

During Calvin's lifetime, Geneva gained the reputation of being a model evangelical city. Persecuted Protestants in the outside world considered it Europe's freest and most godly city. Strict moral enforcement made practice conform with faith. It also gave the city and the new church the order they needed to survive against their enemies. The following selections are from ordinances governing the village churches around Geneva.

❖ *Are Calvin's rules designed primarily to protect the Reformation? What do these rules suggest that he fears most? Are the penalties heavy or slaps on the wrist? Is it a sign of the failure of his reform that the Genevan people never stopped doing these things?*

Concerning the Time of Assembling at Church

That the temples be closed for the rest of the time [when religious services are not being held] in order that no one shall enter therein out of hours, impelled thereto by superstition; and if any one be found engaged in any special act of devotion therein or near by he shall be admonished for it: if it be found to be of a superstitious nature for which simple correction is inadequate, then he shall be chastised.

Blasphemy

Whoever shall have blasphemed, swearing by the body or by the blood of our Lord, or in similar manner, he shall be made to kiss the earth for the first offence; for the second to pay 5 sous, and for the third 6 sous, and for the last offence be put in the pillory for one hour.

Drunkenness

1. That no one shall invite another to drink under penalty of 3 sous.
2. That taverns shall be closed during the sermon, under penalty that the tavern-keeper shall pay 3 sous, and whoever may be found therein shall pay the same amount.

3. If any one be found intoxicated he shall pay for the first offence 3 sous and shall be remanded to the consistory; for the second offence he shall be held to pay the sum of 6 sous, and for the third 10 sous and be put in prison.
4. That no one shall make *roiaumes* [great feasts] under penalty of 10 sous.

Songs and Dances

If any one sing immoral, dissolute or outrageous songs, or dance the *virollet* or other dance, he shall be put in prison for three days and then sent to the consistory.

Usury

That no one shall take upon interest or profit more than five per cent upon penalty of confiscation of the principal and of being condemned to make restitution as the case may demand.

Games

That no one shall play at any dissolute game or at any game whatsoever it may be, neither for gold nor silver nor for any excessive stake, upon penalty of 5 sous and forfeiture of stake played for.

From *Translations and Reprints from the Original Sources of European History*, Vol. 3 (Philadelphia: Department of History, University of Pennsylvania, 1909), pp. 10-11.

the city again. Within months of his return, the city implemented new ecclesiastical ordinances that provided for cooperation between the magistrates and the clergy in matters of internal discipline.

Following the Strasbourg model, the Genevan Church was organized into four offices: (1) pastors, of whom there were five; (2) teachers or doctors to instruct the populace in, and to defend, true doctrine; (3) elders, a group of twelve laypeople chosen by and from the Genevan councils and empowered to "oversee the life of everybody"; and (4) deacons to dispense church goods and services to the poor and the sick.

Calvin and his followers were motivated above all by a desire to transform society morally. Faith, Calvin taught, did not sit idly in the mind, but conformed one's every action to God's law. The "elect" should live in a manifestly God-pleasing way if they were truly God's "elect." In the attempted realization of this goal, Calvin spared no effort. The consistory, or regulatory court, became his instrument of power. This body was composed of the elders and the pastors and was presided over by one of the four syndics. It enforced the strictest moral discipline.

Among the many personal conflicts in Geneva that gave Calvin his reputation as a stern moralist, none proved more damaging than his active role in the capture and execution of the Spanish physician and amateur theologian Michael Servetus in 1553. Earlier, Servetus had been condemned by the Inquisition. He died at the stake in Protestant Geneva for denying the doctrine of the Trinity, a subject on which he had written a scandalous book.

After 1555, the city's syndics were all devout Calvinists, greatly strengthening Calvin's position, and Geneva became home to thousands of exiled Protestants who had been driven out of France, England, and Scotland. Refugees (more than 5,000), most of them utterly loyal to Calvin, eventually made up more than one-third of the population of Geneva.

To the thousands of persecuted Protestants who flocked to Geneva in midcentury, the city was a beacon and a refuge, Europe's only free city. During Calvin's lifetime, Geneva also gained the reputation of being a "woman's paradise" because the laws there severely punished men who beat their wives.

Political Consolidation of the Lutheran Reformation

By 1530, the Reformation was in Europe to stay. It would, however, take several decades and major attempts to eradicate it, before all would recognize this fact. With the political triumph of Lutheranism in the empire by the 1550s, Protestant movements elsewhere gained a new lease on life.

The Diet of Augsburg

Emperor Charles V, who spent most of his time on politics and military maneuvers outside the empire, especially in Spain and Italy, returned to the empire in 1530 to direct the Diet of Augsburg. This meeting of Protestant and Catholic representatives assembled to impose a settlement of the religious divisions. With its terms dictated by the Catholic emperor, the diet adjourned with a blunt order to all Lutherans to revert to Catholicism.

The Reformation was by this time too firmly established for that to occur. In February 1531 the Lutherans responded with the formation of their own defensive alliance, the Schmalkaldic League. The league took as its banner the *Augsburg Confession*, a moderate statement of Protestant beliefs that had been spurned by the emperor at the Diet of Augsburg. In 1538, Luther drew up a more strongly worded Protestant confession known as the *Schmalkaldic Articles*. Under the leadership of Landgrave Philip of Hesse and Elector John Frederick of Saxony, the league achieved a stalemate with the emperor, who was again distracted by renewed war with France and the ever-resilient Turks.

The Expansion of the Reformation

In the 1530s German Lutherans formed regional consistories, judicial bodies composed of theologians and lawyers, which oversaw and administered the new Protestant churches. These consistories replaced the old Catholic episcopates. Philip Melanchthon, the "praeceptor of Germany," oversaw the enactment of educational reforms that provided for compulsory primary education, schools for girls, a humanist revision of the traditional curriculum, and catechetical instruction of the laity in the new religion.

The Reformation also entrenched itself elsewhere. Introduced into Denmark by Christian II (r. 1513–1523), Lutheranism thrived there under Frederick I (r. 1523–1533), who joined the Schmalkaldic League. Under Christian III (r. 1536–1559), Lutheranism became the official state religion.

In Sweden, King Gustavus Vasa (r. 1523–1560), supported by a Swedish nobility greedy for church lands, embraced Lutheranism, confiscated church property, and subjected the clergy to royal authority at the Diet of Vesteras (1527).

In politically splintered Poland, Lutherans, Anabaptists, Calvinists, and even Antitrinitarians found room to practice their beliefs. Primarily because of the absence of a central political authority, Poland became a model of religious pluralism and toleration in the second half of the sixteenth century.

Reaction against Protestants: The Interim

Charles V made abortive efforts in 1540–1541 to enforce a compromise between Protestants and Catholics. As these and other conciliar efforts failed, he turned to a military solution. In 1547 imperial armies crushed the Protestant Schmalkaldic League, defeating John Frederick of Saxony in April and taking Philip of Hesse captive shortly thereafter.

The emperor established puppet rulers in Saxony and Hesse and issued as imperial law the Augsburg Interim, a new order which mandated that Protestants everywhere readopt old Catholic beliefs and practices. Protestants were granted a few cosmetic concessions, for example, clerical marriage (with papal approval of individual cases) and communion in both kinds (that is, bread and wine). Although the Interim met only surface acceptance within Germany, it forced many Protestant leaders into exile. The Strasbourg reformer Martin Bucer, for example, departed to England, where he would play an important role in drafting the religious documents of the English Reformation during the reign of Edward VI. In Germany, the city of Magdeburg became a refuge for persecuted Protestants and the center of Lutheran resistance.

The Peace of Augsburg

The Reformation was too entrenched by 1547 to be ended even by brute force. Maurice of Saxony, handpicked by Charles V to rule Saxony, recognized the inevitable and shifted his allegiance to the Protestants. Confronted by fierce resistance and weary from three decades of war, the emperor was forced to relent. After suffering a defeat by Protestant armies in 1552, Charles reinstated the Protestant leaders and guaranteed Lutherans religious freedoms in the Peace of Passau (August 1552). With this declaration, he effectively surrendered his lifelong quest for European religious unity.

The Peace of Augsburg in September 1555 made the division of Christendom permanent. This agreement recognized in law what had already been well established in practice: *Cuius regio, eius religio*, meaning that the ruler of a land would determine the religion of the land. Lutherans were permitted to retain all church lands forcibly seized before 1552. An "ecclesiastical reservation" was added, however, that was intended to prevent high Catholic prelates who converted to Protestantism from taking their lands, titles, and privileges with them. Those discontented with the religion of their region were permitted to migrate to another.

The Peace of Augsburg did not extend official recognition to Calvinism and Anabaptism as legal forms of Christian belief and practice. Anabaptists had long adjusted to such exclusion by forming their own separatist communities. Calvinists, however, were not separatists and could not choose that route. They remained determined not only to secure the right to worship publicly as they pleased, but also to shape society according to their own religious convictions. While Anabaptists retreated and Lutherans enjoyed the security of an established religion, Calvinists organized to lead national revolutions throughout northern Europe in the second half of the sixteenth century.

The English Reformation to 1553

Late medieval England had a well-earned reputation for maintaining the rights of the crown against the pope. Edward I (r. 1272–1307) had rejected efforts by Pope Boniface VIII to prevent secular taxation of the clergy. Parliament passed the first Statutes of Provisors and *Praemunire* in the mid-fourteenth century, curtailing payments and judicial appeals to Rome as well as papal appointments in England. Lollardy, humanism, and widespread anticlerical sentiment prepared the way religiously and intellectually for Protestant ideas, which entered England in the early sixteenth century.

The Preconditions of Reform

In the early 1520s, future English reformers met at the White Horse Inn in Cambridge to discuss Lutheran writings smuggled into England by merchants and scholars. One of these future reformers was William Tyndale (ca. 1492–1536), who translated the New Testament into English in 1524–1525 while in Germany. Printed in Cologne and Worms, Tyndale's New Testament began to circulate in England in 1526.

Cardinal Thomas Wolsey (ca. 1475–1530), the chief minister of King Henry VIII (r. 1509–1547), and Sir Thomas More (1478–1535), Wolsey's successor, guided royal opposition to incipient English Protestantism. The king himself defended the seven sacraments against Luther, receiving as a reward the title "Defender of the Faith" from Pope Leo X. Following Luther's intemperate reply to Henry's amateur theological attack, More wrote a lengthy *Response to Luther* in 1523.

The King's Affair

While Lollardy and humanism may be said to have provided the native seeds for religious reform, it was Henry's unhappy marriage that broke the soil and allowed the seeds to take root. In 1509 Henry had married Catherine of Aragon (d. 1536), daughter of Ferdinand and Isabella of Spain, and the aunt of Emperor Charles V. By 1527 the union had produced no male heir to the throne and only one surviving child, a daughter, Mary. Henry was justifiably concerned about the political consequences of leaving only a female heir. In this period, people believed it unnatural for women to rule over men. At best a woman ruler meant a contested reign, at worst turmoil and revolution.

Henry even came to believe that his union with Catherine, who had many miscarriages and stillbirths, had been cursed by God, because Catherine had first been the wife of his brother, Arthur. Henry's father, King Henry VII, had betrothed Catherine to Henry after Arthur's untimely death in order to keep the English alliance with Spain intact. They were officially married in 1509, a few days before Henry VIII received his crown. Because marriage to the wife of one's brother was prohibited by both canon and biblical law (see Leviticus 18:16, 20:21), the marriage had required a special dispensation from Pope Julius II.

By 1527 Henry was thoroughly enamored of Anne Boleyn, one of Catherine's ladies in waiting. He determined to put Catherine aside and take Anne as his wife. This he could not do in Catholic England, however, without papal annulment of the marriage to Catherine. And therein lay a special problem. The year 1527 was also the year when soldiers of the Holy Roman Empire mutinied and sacked Rome. The reigning Pope Clement VII was at the time a prisoner of Charles V, who happened also to be Catherine's nephew. Even if this had not been the case, it would have been virtually impossible for the Pope to grant an annulment of a marriage that not only had survived for eighteen years, but had been made possible in the first place by a special papal dispensation.

Cardinal Wolsey, who aspired to become Pope, was placed in charge of securing the royal annulment. Lord Chancellor since 1515 and papal legate-at-large since 1518, Wolsey had long been Henry's "heavy" and the object of much popular resentment. When he failed to secure the annulment through no fault of his own, he was dismissed in disgrace in 1529. Thomas Cranmer (1489–1556) and Thomas Cromwell (1485–1540), both of whom harbored Lutheran sympathies, thereafter became the king's closest advisers. Finding the way to a papal annulment closed, Henry's new advisers struck a different course: Why not simply declare the king supreme in English spiritual affairs as he was in English temporal affairs? Then the king could settle the king's affair himself.

The "Reformation Parliament"

In 1529, Parliament convened for what would be a seven-year session that earned it the title the "Reformation Parliament." During this period, it passed a flood of legislation that harassed, and finally placed royal reins on, the clergy. In so doing, it established a precedent that would remain a feature of English government: Whenever fundamental changes are made in religion, the monarch must consult with and work through Parliament. In January 1531, the Convocation (a legislative assembly representing the English clergy) publicly recognized Henry as head of the church in England "as far as the law of Christ allows." In 1532 Parliament published official grievances against the church, ranging from alleged indifference to the needs of the laity to an excessive number of religious holidays. In the same year, Parliament passed the Submission of the Clergy, which effectively placed canon law under royal control and thereby the clergy under royal jurisdiction.

In January 1533 Henry wed the pregnant Anne Boleyn, with Thomas Cranmer officiating. In February 1533, Parliament made the king the highest court of appeal for all English subjects. In March 1533, Cranmer became archbishop of Canterbury and led the Convocation in invalidating the king's marriage to Catherine. In 1534, Parliament ended all payments by the English clergy and laity to Rome and gave Henry sole jurisdiction over high ecclesiastical appointments. The Act of Succession in the same year made Anne Boleyn's children legitimate heirs to the throne, and the Act of Supremacy declared Henry "the only supreme head in earth of the Church of England."

When Thomas More and John Fisher, bishop of Rochester, refused to recognize the Act of Succession and the Act of Supremacy, Henry had them executed, making clear his determination to have his way regardless of the cost. In 1536 and 1538, Parliament dissolved England's monasteries and nunneries.

Wives of Henry VIII

Henry's domestic life lacked the consistency of his political life. In 1536 Anne Boleyn was executed for alleged treason and adultery, and her daughter, Elizabeth, was declared illegitimate. Henry had four further marriages. His third wife, Jane Seymour, died in 1537 shortly after giving birth to the future Edward VI. Henry wed Anne of Cleves sight unseen on the advice of Cromwell, the purpose being to create by

An allegorical depiction of the Tudor succession by the painter Lucas de Heere (1534–1584). On Henry VIII's right stands his Catholic daughter Mary (1533–1558) and her husband Philip II of Spain. They are accompanied by Mars, the god of war. Henry's son, Edward VI (r. 1547–1553), kneels at the king's left. Elizabeth I (1558–1603) is shown standing in the foreground attended by Peace and Plenty, allegorical figures of what her reign brought to England. Sudeley Castle National Museums & Galleries of Wales

the marriage an alliance with the Protestant princes. Neither the alliance nor the marriage proved worth the trouble; the marriage was annulled by Parliament, and Cromwell was dismissed and eventually executed. Catherine Howard, Henry's fifth wife, was beheaded for adultery in 1542. His last wife, Catherine Parr, a patron of humanists and reformers, for whom Henry was the third husband, survived him to marry still a fourth time—obviously she was a match for the English king.

The King's Religious Conservatism

Henry's boldness in politics and his domestic affairs did not extend to religion. True, because of Henry's actions, the Pope had ceased to be head of the English Church and English Bibles were placed in English churches, but despite the break with Rome, Henry remained decidedly conservative in his religious beliefs. With the Ten Articles of 1536, he made only mild concessions to Protestant tenets, otherwise maintaining Catholic doctrine in a country filled with Protestant sentiment. Despite his many wives and amorous adventures, Henry absolutely forbade the English clergy to marry and threatened any clergy who were caught twice in concubinage with execution.

Angered by the growing popularity of Protestant views, even among his chief advisers, Henry struck directly at them in the Six Articles of 1539. These reaffirmed transubstantiation, denied the Eucharistic cup to the laity, declared celibate vows inviolable, provided for private masses, and ordered the continuation of auricular confession. (Protestants referred to the articles as the "whip with six stings.") Although William Tyndale's English New

Testament grew into the Coverdale Bible (1535) and the Great Bible (1539), and the latter was mandated for every English parish, England had to await Henry's death before it could become a genuinely Protestant country.

Main Events of the English Reformation	
1529	Reformation Parliament convenes
1532	Parliament passes the Submission of the Clergy
1533	Henry VIII weds Anne Boleyn; Convocation proclaims marriage to Catherine of Aragon invalid
1534	Act of Succession makes Anne Boleyn's children legitimate heirs to the English throne
1534	Act of Supremacy declares Henry VIII "the only supreme head of the Church of England"
1535	Thomas More executed for opposition to Acts of Succession and Supremacy
1535	Publication of Coverdale Bible
1539	Henry VIII imposes the Six Articles
1547	Edward VI succeeds to the throne under protectorships of Somerset and Northumberland
1549	First Act of Uniformity imposes *Book of Common Prayer* on English churches
1553–1558	Mary Tudor restores Catholic doctrine
1558–1603	Elizabeth I fashions an Anglican religious settlement

The Protestant Reformation under Edward VI

When Henry died, his son and successor, Edward VI (r. 1547–1553), was only ten years old. Edward reigned under the successive regencies of Edward Seymour, who became the duke of Somerset (1547–1550), and the earl of Warwick, who became known as the duke of Northumberland (1550–1553). During this time, England fully enacted the Protestant Reformation. The new king and Somerset corresponded directly with John Calvin. During Somerset's regency, Henry's Six Articles and laws against heresy were repealed, and clerical marriage and communion with cup were sanctioned.

In 1547 the chantries, places where endowed masses had traditionally been said for the dead, were dissolved. In 1549, the Act of Uniformity imposed Thomas Cranmer's *Book of Common Prayer* on all English churches. Images and altars were removed from the churches in 1550. After Charles V's victory over the German princes in 1547, German Protestant leaders had fled to England for refuge. Several of these refugees, with Martin Bucer prominent among them, now directly assisted the completion of the English Reformation.

The Second Act of Uniformity, passed in 1552, imposed a revised edition of the *Book of Common Prayer* on all English churches. A forty-two-article confession of faith, also written by Thomas Cranmer, was adopted, setting forth a moderate Protestant doctrine. It taught justification by faith and the supremacy of Holy Scripture, denied transubstantiation (although not real presence), and recognized only two sacraments.

All these changes were short lived, however. In 1553, Catherine of Aragon's daughter succeeded Edward (who had died in his teens) to the English throne as Mary I (r. 1553–1558) and proceeded to restore Catholic doctrine and practice with a singlemindedness that rivaled that of her father. It was not until the reign of Anne Boleyn's daughter, Elizabeth I (r. 1558–1603), that a lasting religious settlement was worked out in England.

Catholic Reform and Counter-Reformation

The Protestant Reformation did not take the medieval church completely by surprise. There were many internal criticisms and efforts at reform before there was a Counter-Reformation in reaction to Protestant successes.

Sources of Catholic Reform

Before the Reformation began, ambitious proposals had been made for church reform. But sixteenth-century Popes, ever mindful of how the councils of Constance and Basel had stripped the Pope of his traditional powers, quickly squelched such efforts to bring about basic changes in the laws and institutions of the church. They preferred the charge given to the Fifth Lateran Council (1513–1517) in the keynote address by the superior general of the Hermits of Saint Augustine: "Men are to be changed by, not to change, religion."

Despite such papal foot-dragging, the church was not without its reformers. Many new religious orders also sprang up in the sixteenth century to lead a broad revival of piety within the church. The first of these orders was the Theatines, founded in 1524 to groom devout and reform-minded leaders at the higher levels of the church hierarchy. One of the cofounders was Bishop Gian Pietro Carafa, who would be Pope Paul IV. Another new order, whose

The Ecstasy of Saint Teresa of Avila, *by Gianlorenzo Bernini (1598–1680). Mystics like Saint Teresa and Saint John of the Cross helped revive the traditional piety of medieval monasticism.* Scala/Art Resource, N.Y.

mission pointed in the opposite direction, was the Capuchins. Recognized by the Pope in 1528, they sought to return to the original ascetic and charitable ideals of Saint Francis and became very popular among the ordinary people to whom they directed their ministry. The Somaschi, who became active in the mid-1520s, and the Barnabites, founded in 1530, directed their efforts at repairing the moral, spiritual, and physical damage done to people in war-torn areas of Italy.

For women, there was the new order of Ursulines, founded in 1535. It established convents in Italy and France for the religious education of girls from all social classes and became very influential. Another new religious order, the Oratorians, officially recognized in 1575, was an elite group of secular clerics who devoted themselves to the promotion of religious literature and church music. Among their members was the great Catholic hymnist and musician Giovanni Perluigi da Palestrina (1526–1594).

In addition to these lay and clerical movements, the mystical piety of medieval monasticism was revived and popularized by the Spanish mystics Saint Teresa of Avila (1515–1582) and Saint John of the Cross (1542–1591).

Ignatius of Loyola and the Jesuits

Of the various reform groups, none was more instrumental in the success of the Counter-Reformation than the Society of Jesus, the new order of Jesuits. Organized by Ignatius of Loyola in the 1530s, it was officially recognized by the church in 1540. The society grew within the space of a century from its original 10 members to more than 15,000 members scattered throughout the world, with thriving missions in India, Japan, and the Americas.

The founder of the Jesuits, Ignatius of Loyola (1491–1556), was a heroic figure. A dashing courtier and *caballero* in his youth, he began his spiritual pilgrimage in 1521 after he had been seriously wounded in the legs during a battle with the French. During a lengthy and painful convalescence, he passed the time by reading Christian classics. So impressed was he with the heroic self-sacrifice of the church's saints and their methods of overcoming mental anguish and pain that he underwent a profound religious conversion. Henceforth, he, too, would serve the church as a soldier of Christ.

After recuperating, Ignatius applied the lessons he had learned during his convalescence to a program of religious and moral self-discipline that came to be embodied in the *Spiritual Exercises*. (See "Ignatius of Loyola's 'Rules for Thinking With the Church.'") This psychologically perceptive devotional guide contained mental and emotional

Protestant Reformation and Catholic Reform on the Continent

1513–1517	Fifth Lateran Council fails to bring about reform in the church
1517	Luther posts ninety-five theses against indulgences
1519	Charles I of Spain elected Holy Roman Emperor (as Charles V)
1519	Luther challenges authority of Pope and inerrancy of church councils at Leipzig Debate
1521	Papal bull excommunicates Luther for heresy
1521	Diet of Worms condemns Luther
1521–1522	Luther translates the New Testament into German
1524–1525	Peasants' revolt in Germany
1527	The *Schleitheim Confession* of the Anabaptists
1529	Marburg Colloquy between Luther and Zwingli
1530	Diet of Augsburg fails to settle religious differences
1531	Formation of Protestant Schmalkaldic League
1534–1535	Anabaptists assume political power in city of Münster
1536	Calvin arrives in Geneva
1540	Jesuits, founded by Ignatius of Loyola, recognized as order by Pope
1546	Luther dies
1547	Armies of Charles V crush Schmalkaldic League
1548	Augsburg Interim outlaws Protestant practices
1555	Peace of Augsburg recognizes rights of Lutherans to worship as they please
1545–1563	Council of Trent institutes reforms and responds to the Reformation

exercises designed to teach one absolute spiritual self-mastery over one's feelings. It taught that a person could shape his or her own behavior—even create a new religious self—through disciplined study and regular practice.

Whereas in Jesuit eyes Protestants had distinguished themselves by disobedience to church authority and by religious innovation, the exercises of Ignatius were intended to teach good Catholics to deny themselves and submit without question to higher church authority and spiritual direction. Perfect discipline and self-control were the essential con-

Ignatius of Loyola's "Rules for Thinking With the Church"

As leaders of the Counter-Reformation, the Jesuits attempted to live by and instill in others the strictest obedience to Church authority. The following are some of the eighteen rules included by Ignatius in his Spiritual Exercises *to give Catholics positive direction. These rules also indicate the Catholic reformers' refusal to compromise with Protestants.*

❖ *Would Protestants find any of Ignatius's "rules" acceptable? Might any of them be controversial among Catholic laity as well as among Protestant laity?*

In order to have the proper attitude of mind in the Church Militant we should observe the following rules:

1. Putting aside all private judgment, we should keep our minds prepared and ready to obey promptly and in all things the true spouse of Christ our Lord, our Holy Mother, the hierarchical Church.
2. To praise sacramental confession and the reception of the Most Holy Sacrament once a year, and much better once a month, and better still every week....
3. To praise the frequent hearing of Mass....
4. To praise highly the religious life, virginity, and continence; and also matrimony, but not as highly....
5. To praise the vows of religion, obedience, poverty, chastity, and other works of perfection and supererogation....
6. To praise the relics of the saints...[and] the stations, pilgrimages, indulgences, jubilees, Crusade indulgences, and the lighting of candles in the churches.
7. To praise the precepts concerning fasts and abstinences...and acts of penance....
8. To praise the adornments and buildings of churches as well as sacred images....
9. To praise all the precepts of the church....
10. To approve and praise the directions and recommendations of our superiors as well as their personal behaviour....
11. To praise both the positive and scholastic theology....
12. We must be on our guard against making comparisons between the living and those who have already gone to their reward, for it is no small error to say, for example: "This man knows more than St. Augustine"; "He is another Saint Francis, or even greater."...
13. If we wish to be sure that we are right in all things, we should always be ready to accept this principle: I will believe that the white that I see is black, if the hierarchical Church so defines it. For I believe that between...Christ our Lord and...His Church, there is but one spirit, which governs and directs us for the salvation of our souls.

From *The Spiritual Exercises of St. Ignatius*, trans. by Anthony Mottola. Copyright © 1964 by Doubleday, a division of Bantam, Doubleday, Dell Publishing Group, Inc., pp. 139–141. Used by permission of Doubleday, a division of Random House, Inc.

ditions of such obedience. To these were added the enthusiasm of traditional spirituality and mysticism and uncompromising loyalty to the church's cause above all else. This was a potent combination that helped counter the Reformation and win many Protestants back to the Catholic fold, especially in Austria and Bavaria and along the Rhine. (See Map 11–3).

The Council of Trent (1545–1563)

The broad success of the Reformation and the insistence of the Emperor Charles V forced Pope Paul to call a general council of the church to reassert church doctrine. In anticipation, the Pope appointed a reform commission, chaired by Caspar Contarini (1483–1542), a leading liberal theologian. His report, presented to the Pope in February 1537, bluntly criticized the fiscal practices and simony of the papal *Curia* as the primary source of the church's loss of esteem. The report was so critical, that Pope Paul attempted unsuccessfully to suppress its publication and Protestants reprinted and circulated it as justification of their criticism.

The long-delayed council of the church met in 1545 in the imperial city of Trent in northern Italy. There were three sessions, spread over eighteen years, with long interruptions due to war, plague, and imperial and papal politics. The council met from 1545 to 1547, from 1551 to 1552, and from 1562 to 1563, a period that spanned the careers of four different Popes.

Unlike the general councils of the fifteenth century, Trent was strictly under the Pope's control, with high Italian prelates prominent in the proceedings. Initially four of the five attending archbishops and twenty-one of the twenty-three attending bishops were Italian. Even at its final session in 1562, more than three-quarters of the council fathers were Italians. Voting was limited to the high levels of the clergy; university theologians, the lower clergy, and the laity were not permitted to share in the council's decisions.

The council's most important reforms concerned internal church discipline. Steps were taken to curtail the selling of church offices and other religious goods. Many bishops who resided in Rome rather than within their dioceses were forced to move to their appointed seats of authority. Trent strengthened the authority of local bishops so they could effectively discipline popular religious practice. The bishops were also subjected to new rules that required them not only to reside in their dioceses, but also to be highly visible by preaching regularly and conducting annual visitations. Trent also sought to give the parish priest a brighter image by requiring him to be neatly dressed, better educated, strictly celibate, and active among his parishioners. To this end, Trent also called for the construction of a seminary in every diocese.

MAP 11–3   THE RELIGIOUS SITUATION ABOUT 1560   *By 1560 Luther, Zwingli, and Loyola were dead, Calvin was near the end of his life, the English break from Rome was complete, and the last session of the Council of Trent was about to assemble. This map shows "religious geography" of western Europe at the time.*

Not a single doctrinal concession was made to the Protestants, however. In the face of Protestant criticism, the Council of Trent gave a ringing reaffirmation to the traditional Scholastic education of the clergy; the role of good works in salvation; the authority of tradition; the seven sacraments; transubstantiation; the withholding of the Eucharistic cup from the laity; clerical celibacy; the reality of purgatory; the veneration of saints, relics, and sacred images; and the granting of letters of indulgence. The council resolved medieval Scholastic quarrels in favor of the theology of Saint Thomas Aquinas, further enhancing his authority within the church. Thereafter, the church offered its strongest resistance to groups like the Jansenists, who strongly endorsed the medieval Augustinian tradition, a source of alternative Catholic, as well as many Protestant, doctrines.

Rulers initially resisted Trent's reform decrees, fearing a revival of papal political power within their lands. But with the passage of time and the Pope's assurances that religious reforms were his sole intent, the new legislation took hold, and parish life revived under the guidance of a devout and better-trained clergy.

The Church in Spanish America

Roman Catholic priests had accompanied the earliest explorers and the conquerors of the Native Americans. Because of internal reforms within the Spanish church at the turn of the sixteenth century, these first clergy tended to be imbued with many of the social and religious ideals of Christian humanism. They believed that they could foster Erasmus's concept of the "philosophy of Christ" in the New World. Consequently, these missionary priests were filled with zeal not only to convert the inhabitants to Christianity, but also to bring to them learning and civilization of a European kind.

A very real tension existed between the early Spanish conquerors and the mendicant friars who sought to minister to the Indians. Without conquest, the church could not convert the Indians, but the priests often deplored the harsh labor conditions imposed on Native Americans. During the first three-quarters of a century of Spanish domination, priests were among the most eloquent and persuasive defenders of the rights of native peoples in the New World.

Bartolomé de Las Casas, a Dominican, contended that conquest was not necessary for conversion. One result of his campaign was new royal regulation of conquest after 1550. Another result was the "Black Legend," which portrayed all Spanish treatment of Indians as unprincipled and inhumane. Those who held this point of view drew heavily on Las Casas's writings. (See "A Defense of American Indians.") Although largely true, the "Black Legend" nonetheless exaggerated the case against Spain and has been exploited by Spanish critics. Many of the Indian rulers had also been exceedingly cruel, as witnessed by the Aztec demands for human sacrifice, and both the Aztecs and the Incas enslaved other peoples. Had the Aztecs discovered Spain and held the upper hand there, the persecution of native Europeans would likely have been as great as that of Native Americans at the hands of the Spanish.

By the end of the sixteenth century, the church in Spanish America had become largely an institution upholding the colonial status quo. On many occasions, individual priests did defend the communal rights of Indian tribes, but the colonial church also prospered as the Spanish elite prospered. The church became a great landowner through crown grants and through bequests from Catholics who died in the New World. The monasteries took on an economic as well as a spiritual life of their own. Whatever its concern for the spiritual welfare of the Indians, the church remained one of the indications that Spanish America was a conquered world. And those who spoke for the church did not challenge Spanish domination or any but the most extreme modes of Spanish economic exploitation. By the end of the colonial era in the late eighteenth century, the Roman Catholic Church had become one of the most conservative forces in Latin America.

The Social Significance of the Reformation in Western Europe

It was a common trait of the Lutheran, Zwinglian, and Calvinist reformers to work within the framework of reigning political power. Luther, Zwingli, and Calvin saw themselves and their followers as subject to definite civic responsibilities and obligations. Their conservatism in this regard has led scholars to characterize them as "magisterial reformers," meaning not only that they were the leaders of the major Protestant movements, but also that they succeeded by the force of the magistrate's sword. Some have argued that this willingness to resort to coercion led the reformers to compromise their principles. They themselves, however, never contemplated reform outside or against the societies of which they were members. They wanted it to take shape within the laws and institutions of the sixteenth century. To that end, they remained highly sensitive to what was politically and socially possible in their age. Some scholars believe that the reformers were too conscious of the historically possible, that their reforms went forward with

A Defense of American Natives

Bartolomé de Las Casas (1474–1566), a Dominican missionary to the New World, describes the native people of the islands of the Caribbean and their systematic slaughter by the Spanish.

❖ *Is Las Casas romanticizing the American natives? Does he truly respect their native culture and beliefs?*

This infinite multitude of people was so created by God that they were without fraud...or malice.... Toward the Spaniards whom they serve, patient, meek, and peaceful, [they] lay aside all contentious and tumultuous thoughts, and live without any hatred or desire of revenge. The people are most delicate and tender, enjoying such a feeble constitution of body as does not permit them to endure labour.... The[ir] nation [the West Indies] is very poor and indigent, possessing little, and by reason that they gape not after temporal goods, [being] neither proud nor ambitious. Their diet is such that the most holy hermit cannot feed more sparingly in the wildernesse. They go naked... and a poor shag mantle...is their greatest and their warmest covering. They lie upon mats; only those who have larger fortunes lie upon a kind of net which is tied at the four corners and so fasten'd to the roof, which the Indians in their natural language call *Hamecks* [hammocks]. They are of a very apprehensive and docile wit, and capable of all good learning, and very apt to receive our Religion, which when they have but once tasted [it], they are carried [off] with a very ardent and zealous desire to make further

progress in it; so that I have heard divers Spaniards confess that they had nothing else to hinder them from enjoying heaven, but the ignorance of the true God.

To these quiet Lambs, endued with such blessed qualities, came the Spaniards like most cruel Tygres, Wolves, and Lions...for these forty years, minding nothing else but the slaughter of these unfortunate wretches...[whom] they have so cruelly and inhumanely butchered, [so] that of three millions of people which Hispaniola [modern Haiti and the Dominican Republic] itself did contain, there are left remaining alive scarce three hundred persons. And the island of Cuba...lies wholly desert, untilled and ruined. The islands of St. John and Jamaica lie waste and desolate. The Lycayan islands neighboring to the north upon Cuba and Hispaniola...are now totally unpeopled and destroyed; the inhabitants thereof amounting to above 500,000 souls, partly killed, and partly forced away to work in other places....Other islands there were near the island of St. John more than thirty in number, which were totally made desert. All which islands...lie now altogether solitary without any people or inhabitant.

Bartolomé de Las Casas, *The Tears of the Indians*, trans. by John Phillips (1656), from reprint of original edition (Stanford, CA: Academic Reprints, n.d.), pp. 2–4.

such caution that they changed late medieval society very little and actually encouraged acceptance of the sociopolitical status quo.

The Revolution in Religious Practices and Institutions

The Reformation may have been politically conservative, but by the end of the sixteenth century it had brought about radical changes in traditional religious practices and institutions in those lands where it succeeded.

RELIGION IN FIFTEENTH-CENTURY LIFE In the fifteenth century, on the streets of the great cities of central Europe that later turned Protestant (for example,

Zurich, Strasbourg, Nuremberg, and Geneva), the clergy and the religious were everywhere. They made up six to eight percent of the total urban population, and they exercised considerable political as well as spiritual power. They legislated and taxed, they tried cases in special church courts, and they enforced their laws with threats of excommunication.

The church calendar regulated daily life. About one-third of the year was given over to some kind of religious observance or celebration. There were frequent periods of fasting. On almost a hundred days out of the year a pious Christian could not, without special dispensation, eat eggs, butter, fat, or meat.

Monasteries, and especially nunneries, were prominent and influential institutions. The children of society's most powerful citizens resided there.

Local aristocrats were closely identified with particular churches and chapels, whose walls recorded their lineage and proclaimed their generosity. On the streets, friars from near and far begged alms from passersby. In the churches the mass and liturgy were read entirely in Latin. Images of saints were regularly displayed, and on certain holidays their relics were paraded about and venerated.

There was a booming business at local religious shrines. Pilgrims gathered there by the hundreds—even thousands—many sick and dying, all in search of a cure or a miracle, but also for diversion and entertainment. Several times during the year, special preachers arrived in the city to sell letters of indulgence.

Many clergy walked the streets with concubines and children, although they were sworn to celibacy and forbidden to marry. The church tolerated such relationships upon payment of penitential fines.

People everywhere could be heard complaining about the clergy's exemption from taxation and, in many instances, also from the civil criminal code. People also grumbled about having to support church offices whose occupants actually lived and worked elsewhere. Townspeople also expressed concern that the church had too much influence over education and culture.

RELIGION IN SIXTEENTH-CENTURY LIFE In these same cities, after the Reformation had firmly established itself, few changes in politics and society were evident. The same aristocratic families governed as before, and the rich generally got richer and the poor poorer. But overall numbers of clergy fell by two-thirds and religious holidays shrank by one-third. Cloisters were nearly gone, and many that remained were transformed into hospices for the sick and poor or into educational institutions, their endowments also turned over to these new purposes. A few cloisters remained for very devout old monks and nuns who could not be pensioned off or who lacked families and friends to care for them. But these remaining cloisters died out with their inhabitants.

In the churches, which had also been reduced in number by at least one-third, worship was conducted almost completely in the vernacular. In some, particularly those in Zwinglian cities, the walls were stripped bare and whitewashed to make sure that the congregation meditated only on God's word. The laity observed no obligatory fasts. Indulgence preachers no longer appeared. Local shrines were closed down, and anyone found openly venerating saints, relics, and images was subject to fine and punishment.

Copies of Luther's translation of the New Testament or, more often, excerpts from it could be found in private homes, and meditation on them was en-couraged by the new clergy. The clergy could marry, and most did. They paid taxes and were punished for their crimes in civil courts. Domestic moral life was regulated by committees composed of roughly equal numbers of laity and clergy, over whose decisions secular magistrates had the last word.

Not all Protestant clergy remained enthusiastic about this new lay authority in religion. And the laity themselves were also ambivalent about certain aspects of the Reformation. Over half of the original converts returned to the Catholic fold before the end of the sixteenth century. Whereas one-half of Europe could be counted in the Protestant camp in the mid-sixteenth century, only one-fifth would be there by the mid-seventeenth century.[2]

The Reformation and Education

Another important cultural achievement of the Reformation was its implementation of many of the educational reforms of humanism in the new Protestant schools and universities. Many Protestant reformers in Germany, France, and England were humanists. And even when their views on Church doctrine and humankind separated them from the humanist movement, the Protestant reformers continued to share with the humanists a common opposition to Scholasticism and a belief in the unity of wisdom, eloquence, and action. The humanist program of studies, which provided the language skills to deal authoritatively with original sources, proved to be a more appropriate tool for the elaboration of Protestant doctrine than did scholastic dialectic, which remained ascendant in the Counter-Reformation.

The Catholic counterreformers recognized the close connections between humanism and the Reformation. Ignatius of Loyola observed the way in which the new learning had been embraced by and served the Protestant cause. In his *Spiritual Exercises*, he insisted that when the Bible and the Church Fathers were read directly, they be read under the guidance of the authoritative scholastic theologians: Peter Lombard, Bonaventure, and Thomas Aquinas. The last of these worthies, Ignatius argued, being "of more recent date," had the clearest understanding of what Scripture and the Fathers meant and therefore should guide the study of the past.

When, in August 1518, Philip Melanchthon (1497–1560), a young humanist and professor of Greek, arrived at the University of Wittenberg, his first act was to implement curricular reforms on the

[2]Geoffrey Parker, *Europe in Crisis, 1598–1648* (Ithaca, NY: Cornell University Press, 1979), p. 50.

Brothers and sisters. While away from home at law school in Padua, Italy, nineteen-year-old Paul Behaim, Jr., the brother of Friedrich (see document on p. 381), wrote in July, 1577 to his older sisters Magdalena (22) and Sabina (21) to complain about the infrequency of their writing to him. Typical of sibling relations in every age, the letter is affectionate and joking. The sisters were then at home with their widowed mother and busy with the many chores of the self-sufficient sixteenth-century domestic household—especially, at this time of the year, gardening. Because of their alleged neglect Paul teasingly tells them that they must now do "penance" by making him two new shirts, as his were embarrassingly tattered. He indicated in the left margin the exact collar length (A) and style (B) he wishes the shirts to be. Sewing for the household was another regular domestic chore for burgher and patrician women not working in trades outside the home. But Magdalena and Sabina went even further to "cover" their brother: they also allowed him to receive income (to be repaid in the future) from their own paternal inheritances so that he might finish his legal education, on the successful completion of which the whole family depended for its future success. Geramnisches National Museum, Nuremberg, Germany, Behaim-Archiv Fasz. 106; Steven Ozment, Flesh and Spirit: Private Life in Early Modern Germany (Viking/Penguin, New York, 1999), pp. 174–176

humanist model. In his inaugural address, entitled *On Improving the Studies of the Young,* Melanchthon presented himself as a defender of good letters and classical studies against "barbarians who practice barbarous arts." By the latter, he meant the scholastic theologians of the later Middle Ages, whose methods of juxtaposing the views of conflicting authorities and seeking to reconcile them by disputation had, he believed, undermined both good letters and sound biblical doctrine. Scholastic dominance in the universities was seen by Melanchthon as having bred contempt for the Greek language and learning and as having encouraged neglect of the study of mathematics, sacred studies, and the art of oratory. Melanchthon urged the careful study of history, poetry, and other humanist disciplines.

Together, Luther and Melanchthon restructured the University of Wittenberg's curriculum. Commentaries on Lombard's *Sentences* were dropped, as was canon law. Straightforward historical study replaced old Scholastic lectures on Aristotle. Students read primary sources directly, not by way of accepted Scholastic commentators. Candidates for theological degrees defended the new doctrine on the basis of their own exegesis of the Bible. New chairs of Greek and Hebrew were created. Luther and Melanchthon also pressed for universal compulsory education so that both boys and girls could reach vernacular literacy in the Bible.

In Geneva, John Calvin and his successor, Theodore Beza, founded the Genevan Academy, which later evolved into the University of Geneva. That institution, created primarily for training Calvinist ministers, pursued ideals similar to those set forth by Luther and Melanchthon. Calvinist refugees trained in the academy carried Protestant educational reforms to France, Scotland, England, and the New World. Through such efforts, a working knowledge of Greek and Hebrew became commonplace in educated circles in the sixteenth and seventeenth centuries.

Some contemporaries decried what they saw as a narrowing of the original humanist program as Protestants took it over. Erasmus, for example, came to fear the Reformation as a threat to the liberal arts and good learning. Sebastian Franck pointed to parallels between Luther's and Zwingli's debates over Christ's presence in the Eucharist and such old scholastic disputations as that over the Immaculate Conception of the Virgin.

Humanist culture and learning nonetheless remained indebted to the Reformation. The Protestant endorsement of the humanist program of studies remained as significant for the humanist movement as the latter had been for the Reformation. Protestant schools and universities consolidated and preserved for the modern world many of the basic pedagogical achievements of humanism. There, the *studia humanitatis*, although often as little more than a handmaiden to theological doctrine, found a permanent home, one that remained hospitable even in the heyday of conservative Protestantism.

The Reformation and the Changing Role of Women

The Protestant reformers took a positive stand on clerical marriage and strongly opposed monasticism and the celibate life. From this position, they challenged the medieval tendency alternately to degrade women as temptresses (following the model of Eve) and to exalt them as virgins (following the model of Mary). Protestants opposed the popular antiwoman and antimarriage literature of the Middle Ages. They praised woman in her own right, but especially in her biblical vocation as mother and housewife. Although from a modern perspective, women remained subject to men, new marriage laws gave them greater security and protection.

Relief of sexual frustration and a remedy for fornication were prominent in Protestant arguments for marriage. But the reformers also viewed their wives as indispensable companions in their work, and this not solely because they took domestic cares off their husbands' minds. Luther, who married in 1525 at the age of forty-two, wrote the following of women:

Imagine what it would be like without women. The home, cities, economic life, and government would virtually disappear. Men cannot do without women. Even if it were possible for men to beget and bear children, they still could not do without women.[3]

John Calvin wrote this at the death of his wife:

I have been bereaved of the best companion of my life, of one who, had it been so ordered, would not only have been the willing sharer of my indigence, but even of my death. During her life she was the faithful helper of my ministry.[4]

Such tributes were intended in part to overcome Catholic criticism that marriage distracted the cleric from his ministry. They were primarily the expression of a new value placed on the estate of marriage and family life. In opposition to the celibate ideal of the Middle Ages, Protestants stressed as no religious movement before them the sacredness of home and family. This attitude contributed to a more respectful and sharing relationship between husbands and wives and between parents and children. (See "A German Mother Advises Her Fifteen-Year-Old Son (1578).")

The ideal of the companionate marriage—that is, of husband and wife as co-workers in a special God-ordained community of the family, sharing authority equally within the household—led to an important expansion of the grounds for divorce in Protestant cities as early as the 1520s. Women now had an equal right with men to divorce and remarry in good conscience—unlike the situation in Catholicism, where only a separation from bed and table, not divorce and remarriage, was permitted a couple in a failed marriage. The reformers were actually more willing to permit divorce and remarriage on grounds of adultery and abandonment than were secular magistrates, who feared that liberal divorce laws would lead to social upheaval.

Protestant doctrines were as attractive to women as they were to men. Renegade nuns wrote exposés of the nunnery in the name of Christian freedom and justification by faith, declaring that the nunnery was no special woman's place at all and that supervisory male clergy (who alone could hear the nuns' confessions and administer sacraments to them) made their lives as unpleasant and burdensome as any abusive husband. Women in the higher classes, who enjoyed new social and political freedoms during the Renaissance, found in Protestant theology a religious complement to their greater independence in other walks of life. Some cloistered noblewomen, however, protested the closing of nunneries. They believed that the cloister provided them a more interesting and independent way of life than they would have known in the secular world.

Because they wanted women to become pious housewives, Protestants encouraged the education of girls to literacy in the vernacular, with the expectation that they would thereafter model their lives on the Bible. During their studies, however, women found biblical passages which suggested that they were equal to men in the presence of God. Education also gave some women a role as independent authors in the Reformation. From a modern perspective, these may seem like small advances, but they were significant, if indirect, steps in the direction of the emancipation of women.

---

[3]*Luther's Works, Vol. 54: Table Talk*, ed. and trans. by Theodore G. Tappert (Philadelphia: Fortress Press, 1967), p. 161.

[4]*Letters of John Calvin*, Vol. 2, trans. by J. Bonnet (Edinburgh: T. Constable, 1858), p. 216.

A German Mother Advises Her Fifteen-Year-Old Son (1578)

Although only fourteen miles away from his Nuremberg home, Friederich Behaim was fifteen and on his own for the first time at the Altdorf Academy, where he would spend the next three years of his life. As there was daily traffic back and forth, mother and son could correspond regularly, and Frau Behaim could give her son needed advice and articles of clothing.

❖ *What is the mother most concerned about? What do her concerns suggest about life in the sixteenth century? Does she appear to be more strict and demanding of her son than a modern mother would be? Is the son clueless, or skillfully manipulating the mother?*

Dear son Friederich...You write that you have been unable to get by on the money [I gave you]. I will let it pass this quarter, but see that you manage on it in the future. Enclosed is another gulden.

As for your clothes, I do not have Martin [a servant] here with me now (we are quarreling), but he has begun to work on your clothes. He has made stockings for your leather holiday trousers, which I am sending you with this letter. Since your everyday trousers are so bad, wear these for now until a new pair of woolen ones can be made and sent to you, which I will do as soon as I can. Send me your old trousers in the sack I sent you the pitcher in. As for the smock that you think should be lined [for the winter], I worry that the skirt may be too short and will not keep you warm. You can certainly wear it for another summer if it is not too small for you then and the weather not too warm. Just keep it clean and brushed. I will have a new coat made for you at the earliest.

You also write about [unhappiness with] your food. You must be patient for a while. You may not at the outset lodge a complaint against [your master], and especially while you are sitting at his table. [Only] he may speak out who eats his food and is also an authority in the house. So it

would be better if the Inspector, who is there for a reason, reports it to him.

Will you once tell me who your table companions are! Also, let me know by All Saints what you have spent on beer and what you owe the tailor, so I may know how much to send you for the quarter.

As for your [sore] throat, there is nothing you can take for it but warm mead. Gargle often with it and keep your head warm. Put a muffler or scarf around your neck and wear your night coat when you are in your room. Avoid cold drinks and sit perhaps for a while by the fire. And do not forget to be bled on time [people then bled themselves once or twice a year as a health measure]...When you need paper, let me know....

I am sending some cleaning flakes for your leather pants. After you have worn them three times, put some on the knees...I will have your old coat patched and send it to you with the next carter [so that you can wear it] until the new one is made. Send me the two sacks with the next carter. You will find the [aforementioned] gulden in the trouser foot tied with a string.

Nothing more for now. God bless. 14 October, 1578.

Mrs. Paul Behaim

From *Three Behaim Boys: Growing Up in Early Modern Germany: A Chronicle of Their Lives*, ed. and trans. by Steven Ozment, pp. 107–108. Copyright © 1990 Yale University Press. Reprinted by permission of Yale University Press.

Family Life in Early Modern Europe

Changes in the timing and duration of marriage, in family size, and in infant and child care suggest that family life was under a variety of social and economic pressures in the sixteenth and seventeenth centuries. The Reformation was a factor in these changes, but not the only or even the major one.

A family has a certain force and logic of its own, regardless of the time and place in which it exists. The routine of family life conspires with basic instincts to establish characteristic patterns of behavior, reinforcing natural feelings and building expectations among family members. Time, place, and culture, however, are important. A person raised in a twelfth-century family would be different from one raised in a twentieth-century family, and growing up in Europe is not the same as growing up in China. But the differences do not lie in the ability of husbands and wives to love one another or of parents to make sacrifices for their children. They lie, rather, in the ways different cultures and religions infuse family life with values and influence the behavior of family members.

Later Marriages

Between 1500 and 1800, men and women in western Europe and England married at later ages than they had in previous centuries. Men tended to be in their mid- to late twenties rather than in their late teens and early twenties, and women in their early to mid-twenties rather than in their teens. The canonical, or church-sanctioned, age for marriage remained fourteen for men and twelve for women, and engagements might occur at these young ages, especially among royalty and nobility. As it had done throughout the high and late Middle Ages, the church also recognized as valid free, private exchanges of vows between a man and a woman at these minimal ages. However, after the Reformation, which condemned such clandestine unions, the church increasingly required both parental agreement and public vows in church before a marriage could be recognized as fully licit—procedures it had always actually preferred.

Late marriage in the West reflected the difficulty couples had supporting themselves independently. The difficulty arose because of the population growth that occurred during the late fifteenth and early sixteenth centuries, when western Europe recovered much of the population loss incurred during the Great Plague. Larger families meant more heirs and hence a greater division of resources. In Germanic and Scandinavian countries, the custom of fair sharing of inheritance among all male children worked to delay marriages, for divided inheritances often meant small incomes for the recipients. It simply took the average couple a longer time than previously to prepare themselves materially for marriage. In the sixteenth century one in five women never married, and these, combined with the estimated 15 percent who were unmarried widows, constituted a sizable unmarried female population.

A later marriage meant a marriage of shorter duration, since couples who married in their thirties would not spend as much time together as couples who married in their twenties. Such marriages also contributed to more frequent remarriage for men because women who bore children for the first time at advanced ages had higher mortality rates than younger mothers. Moreover, as growing church condemnation and the rapid growth of orphanages and foundling homes between 1600 and 1800 confirm, delayed marriage increased premarital sex and raised the number of illegitimate children.

Arranged Marriages

Marriage tended to be "arranged" in the sense that the parents customarily met and discussed the terms of the marriage before the prospective bride and bridgegroom became party to the discussions. But the wealth and social standing of the bride and the bridegroom were not the only things condsidered when parents arrange a marriage. By the fifteenth century it was not unusual for the two involved people to have known each other in advance and even to have had some prior relationship. Also, emotional feeling for one another was increasingly respected by parents. Parents did not force total strangers to live together, and children had a legal right to protest and resist an unwanted marriage. A forced marriage was by definition invalid, and parents understood that unwanted marriages could fail. The best marriage was one desired by both parties and supported by their families.

Family Size

The western European family was conjugal, or nuclear; that is, it consisted of a father and a mother and two to four children who survived into adulthood. This nuclear family lived with a larger household, consisting of in-laws, servants, laborers, and boarders. The average husband and wife had seven or eight children—a birth about every two years. Of these, however, an estimated one third died by age five, and one half by their teens. Rare is the family, at any social level, that did not experience infant mortality and child death.

Birth Control

Artificial birth control has existed since antiquity. The ancient Egyptians used alligator dung and other acidic sperm killers, and sponges were also popular. In the West, the church's condemnation of *coitus interruptus* (male withdrawal before ejaculation) during the thirteenth and fourteenth centuries suggests that a contraceptive mentality—that is, a conscious and regular effort at birth control—may have been developing at this time. But early birth control measures, when applied, were not very effective, and for both historical and moral reasons the church firmly opposed them. During the eleventh century it suppressed an extreme ascetic sect, the Cathars, whom it accused of practicing birth control. The church also opposed (and still opposes) contraception on moral grounds. According to Saint Thomas Aquinas, a moral act must always aid and abet, never frustrate, the natural end of the being or thing in question, and he believed that the natural end of sex could be only the birth of children and their godly rearing within the bounds of holy matrimony and the community of the church.

Wet Nursing

The church allied with the physicians of early modern Europe on another intimate family matter: the condemnation of women who hired nurses to suckle their newborn children, sometimes for as long as a year and a half. The practice was popular among upper-class women, who looked on it as a symbol of their high rank. Wet nurses were women who had recently had a baby or were suckling a child of their own, and who, for a fee, agreed also to suckle another child. The practice appears to have increased the risk of infant mortality, exposing infants to a strange and shared milk supply from women who were usually not as healthy as the infants' own mothers and who often lived under less sanitary conditions. But nursing an infant was a chore some upper-class women found distasteful, and their husbands also preferred that they not do it. Among women, vanity and convenience appear to have been motives for turning to wet nurses. For husbands, more was at stake in the practice. Because the church forbade sexual intercourse while a women was lactating, and sexual intercourse was also believed to spoil a lactating woman's milk (pregnancy, of course, eventually ended her milk supply), a nursing wife often became a reluctant lover. In addition, nursing had a contraceptive effect (about 75 percent effective). Some women prolonged nursing their children precisely to delay a new pregnancy, and some husbands understood and cooperated in this form of family planning. For other husbands, however, especially noblemen and royalty who desired an abundance of male heirs, nursing seemed to rob them of offspring and to jeopardize the patrimony; hence, their support of wet nursing.

Loving Families?

The traditional western European family had features that may seem cold and unloving. When children were between the ages of eight and thirteen, parents routinely sent them out of their homes into apprenticeships, off to school, or into employment in the homes and businesses of relatives, friends, and even strangers. In addition, the emotional ties between spouses seem to have been a tenuous as those between parents and children. Widowers and widows often married again within a few months of their spouses' deaths, and marriages with extreme disparity in age between partners also suggest limited affection.

Portrait of two children from the Thenn family. Frankfurt, Stadelsch. Kunstinst

In response to modern-day criticism, an early modern parent would surely have asked, "What greater love can parents have for their children than to equip them to make their way vocationally in the world?" An apprenticed child was a self-supporting child, and hence a child with a future. Considering primitive living conditions, contemporaries could also appreciate the purely utilitarian and humane side of marriage and understand when widowers and widows quickly married again. On the other hand, marriages with extreme disparity in age were no more the norm in early modern Europe than the practice of wet nursing, and they received just as much criticism and ridicule.

Literary Imagination in Transition

Alongside the political and cultural changes brought about by the new religious systems of the Reformation (Lutheranism, Calvinism, and Puritanism) and Catholic reform, medieval outlooks and religious values continued into the seventeenth century. Major literary figures of the post-Reformation period had elements of both the old and the new in their own new transitional works. Two who stand out are Miguel de Cervantes Saavedra (1547–1616), writing in still deeply Catholic Spain, and William Shakespeare (1564–1616), who wrote in newly Anglican England.

Miguel de Cervantes Saavedra: Rejection of Idealism

Spanish literature of the sixteenth and seventeenth centuries reflects the peculiar religious and political history of Spain in this period. Traditional Catholic teaching was a major influence on all aspects of Spanish life. Since the joint reign of Ferdinand and Isabella (1479–1504), the church had received the unqualified support of the reigning political power. Although there was religious reform in Spain, and genuine Protestant groups were persecuted for "Lutheranism," a Protestant Reformation never occurred there, thanks largely to the entrenched power of the church and the Inquisition.

A second influence on Spanish literature was the aggressive piety of Spanish rulers. Their intertwining of Catholic piety and political power underlay a third influence: preoccupation with medieval chivalric virtues, in particular, questions of honor and loyalty. The novels and plays of the period almost invariably focus on a special test of character, bordering on the heroic, that

threatens honor and reputation. In this regard, Spanish literature remained more Catholic and medieval than that of England and France, where major Protestant movements had occurred. Two of the most important Spanish writers of this period became priests (Lope de Vega and Pedro Calderón de la Barca). The one generally acknowledged to be the greatest Spanish writer of all time, Cervantes, was preoccupied in his work with the strengths and weaknesses of traditional religious idealism.

Cervantes (1547–1616) had only a smattering of formal education. He educated himself by wide reading in popular literature and immersion in the "school of life." As a young man, he worked in Rome for a Spanish cardinal. As a soldier, he was decorated for gallantry in the Battle of Lepanto (1571). He also spent five years as a slave in Algiers after his ship was pirated in 1575. Later, while working as a tax collector, he was imprisoned several times for padding his accounts, and it was in prison that he began, in 1603, to write his most famous work, *Don Quixote*.

Miguel de Cervantes Saavedra (1547–1616), the author of Don Quixote, *considered by many to be Spain's greatest writer.* Art Resource, N.Y.

The first part of *Don Quixote* appeared in 1605. The intent of this work seems to have been to satirize the chivalric romances then popular in Spain. But Cervantes could not conceal his deep affection for the character he created as an object of ridicule. The work is satire only on the surface and has remained as much an object of study by philosophers and theologians as by students of Spanish literature. Cervantes presented Don Quixote as a none-too-stable middle-aged man. Driven mad by reading too many chivalric romances, he had come to believe he was an aspiring knight who had to prove his worthiness by brave deeds. To this end, he donned a rusty suit of armor and chose for his inspiration a quite unworthy peasant girl (Dulcinea), whom he fancied to be a noble lady to whom he could, with honor, dedicate his life.

Don Quixote's foil—Sancho Panza, a clever, worldly-wise peasant who serves as Quixote's squire—watches with bemused skepticism as his lord does battle with a windmill (which he has mistaken for a dragon) and repeatedly makes a fool of himself as he gallops across the countryside. The story ends tragically with Don Quixote's humiliating defeat by a well-meaning friend who, disguised as a knight, bests Quixote in combat and forces him to renounce his quest for knighthood. The humiliated Don Quixote does not, however, come to his senses as a result. He returns sadly to his village to die a shamed and brokenhearted old man.

Throughout the novel, Cervantes juxtaposes the down-to-earth realism of Sancho Panza with the old-fashioned religious idealism of Don Quixote. The reader perceives that Cervantes admired the one as much as the other and meant to portray both as representing attitudes necessary for a happy life.

William Shakespeare: Dramatist of the Age

There is much less factual knowledge about Shakespeare (1564–1616) than one would expect of the greatest playwright in the English language. He married at the early age of eighteen, in 1582, and he and his wife, Anne Hathaway, were the parents of three children (including twins) by 1585. He apparently worked as a schoolteacher for a time and in this capacity gained his broad knowledge of Renaissance learning and literature. His own reading and enthusiasm for the learning of his day are manifest in the many literary allusions that appear in his plays.

Shakespeare lived the life of a country gentleman. There is none of the Puritan distress over worldliness in his work. He took the new commercialism and the bawdy pleasures of the Elizabethan Age in stride and with amusement. He was a radical neither in politics nor religion. The few allusions in his works to the Puritans seem more critical than complimentary.

That Shakespeare was interested in politics is apparent from his historical plays and the references to contemporary political events that fill all his plays. He viewed government through the character of the individual ruler, whether Richard III or Elizabeth Tudor, not in terms of ideal systems or social goals. By modern standards, he was a political conservative, accepting the social rankings and the power structure of his day and demonstrating unquestioned patriotism.

Shakespeare knew the theater as one who participated in every phase of its life—as a playwright, an actor, and part owner of a theater. He was a member and principal writer of a famous company of actors known as the King's Men. Between 1590 and 1610, many of his plays were performed at court, where he moved with comfort and received both Queen Elizabeth's and King James's enthusiastic patronage.

Elizabethan drama was already a distinctive form when Shakespeare began writing. Unlike French drama of the seventeenth century, which was dominated by classical models, English drama developed in the sixteenth and seventeenth centuries as a blending of many forms: classical comedies and tragedies, medieval morality plays, and contemporary Italian short stories.

Two contemporaries, Thomas Kyd and Christopher Marlowe, influenced Shakespeare's tragedies. Kyd (1558–1594) wrote the first dramatic version of Hamlet. The tragedies of Marlowe (1564–1593) set a model for character, poetry, and style that only Shakespeare among the English playwrights of the period surpassed. Shakespeare synthesized the best past and current achievements. A keen student of human motivation and passion, he had a unique talent for getting into people's minds.

Shakespeare wrote histories, comedies, and tragedies. *Richard III* (1593), a very early play, stands out among the histories, although the picture it presents of Richard as an unprincipled villain is viewed by some scholars as "Tudor propaganda." Shakespeare's comedies, although not attaining the heights of his tragedies, surpass his history plays in originality.

Shakespeare's tragedies are considered his unique achievement. Four of these were written within a three-year period: *Hamlet* (1603), *Othello* (1604), *King Lear* (1605), and *Macbeth* (1606). The most original of the tragedies, *Romeo and Juliet* (1597), transformed an old popular story into a moving drama of "star-cross'd lovers." Both Romeo and Juliet, denied a marriage by their warring families, die tragic deaths. Romeo, believing Juliet to be dead when she has merely taken a sleeping potion, poisons himself. When Juliet awakes to find Romeo dead, she kills herself with his dagger.

Shakespeare's works struck universal human themes, many of which were deeply rooted in contemporary religious traditions. His plays were immensely popular with both the playgoers and the play readers of Elizabethan England. Still today, the works of no other dramatist from his age are performed in theaters or on film more regularly than his.

In Perspective

During the early Middle Ages, Christendom had been divided into Western and Eastern churches with irreconcilable theological differences. When, in 1517, Martin Luther posted ninety-five theses questioning the selling of indulgences and the traditional sacrament of penance that lay behind them, he created a division within Western Christendom itself—an internal division between Protestants and Catholics.

The Lutheran protest came at a time of political and social discontent with the church. Not only princes and magistrates, but many ordinary people as well, resented traditional clerical rights and privileges. In many instances the clergy were exempted from secular laws and taxes, while remaining powerful landowners whose personal lifestyles were not all that different from those of the laity. Spiritual and secular protest combined to make the Protestant Reformation a successful assault on the old church. In town after town and region after region within Protestant lands, the major institutions and practices of traditional piety were significantly transformed.

It soon became clear, however, that the division would not stop with the Lutherans. Making Scripture the only arbiter in religion had opened a Pandora's box. People proved to have very different ideas about what Scripture taught. Indeed, there seemed to be as many points of view as there were readers. Rapidly, the Reformation created Lutheran, Zwinglian, Anabaptist, Spiritualist, Calvinist, and Anglican versions of biblical religion—a splintering of Protestantism that has endured until today.

Catholics had been pursuing reform before the Reformation broke out in Germany, although without papal enthusiasm and certainly not along clear Protestant lines. When major reforms finally came in the Catholic Church around the mid-sixteenth century, they were doctrinally reactionary, but administratively and spiritually flexible. The church enforced strict obedience and conformity to its teaching, but it also provided the laity with a better educated and disciplined clergy. For laity who wanted a deeper and more individual piety, experimentation with proven spiritual practices was now

permitted. By century's end, such measures had successfully countered, and in some areas even spectacularly reversed, Protestant gains.

After the Reformation, pluralism steadily became a fact of Western religious life. It did so at first only by sheer force, since no one religious body was then prepared to concede the validity of alternative Christian beliefs and practices. During the sixteenth and seventeenth centuries, only those groups that fought doggedly for their faith gained the right to practice it freely. Despite these struggles, religious pluralism endured. Never again would there be only a Catholic Christian Church in Europe.

REVIEW QUESTIONS

1. What were the main problems of the church that contributed to the Protestant Reformation? Why was the church unable to suppress dissent as it had earlier?

2. What were the basic similarities and differences between the ideas of Luther and Zwingli? Between Luther and Calvin? Did the differences tend to split the Protestant ranks and thereby lessen the effectiveness of the movement?

3. Why did the Reformation begin in Germany? What political factors contributed to the success of the Reformation there as opposed to France or Italy?

4. What was the Catholic reformation, and what principal decisions and changes were instituted by the Council of Trent? Was the Protestant Reformation a healthy movement for the Catholic Church?

5. Why did Henry VIII finally break with the Catholic Church? Was the "new" religion he established really Protestant? What problems did his successors face as a result of Henry's move?

6. What impact did the Reformation have on women in the sixteenth and seventeenth centuries? What new factors and pressures affected relations between men and women, family size, and child care during this period?

SUGGESTED READINGS

HAROLD BLOOM, *Shakespeare: The Invention of the Human* (1998). A modern master's complete analysis of the greatest writer in the English language.

W. BOUWSMA, *John Calvin: A Sixteenth Century Portrait* (1988). Interpretation of Calvin against background of Renaissance intellectual history.

J. DELUMEAU, *Catholicism Between Luther and Voltaire: A New View of the Counter Reformation* (1977). Programmatic essay for a social history of the Counter-Reformation.

A. G. DICKENS, *The English Reformation* (1974). The best one-volume account.

G. DONALDSON, *The Scottish Reformation* (1960). Dependable, comprehensive narrative.

E. DUFFY, *The Stripping of the Altars: Traditional Religion in England, 1400–1580 (1992)*. Strongest of recent arguments that popular piety survived the Reformation in England.

M. DURAN, *Cervantes* (1974). Detailed biography.

G. ELTON, *Reform and Reformation: England, 1509–1558* (1977). Standard political narrative.

H. O. EVENNETT, *The Spirit of the Counter Reformation* (1968). Essay on the continuity of Catholic reform and its independence from the Protestant Reformation.

B. GOTTLIEB, *The Family in the Western World* (1992). Accessible overview with up-to-date annotated bibliographies.

SCOTT HENDRIX, "Masculinity and Patriarchy in Reformation Germany," *Journal of the History of Ideas 56* (1995): 177–193. Caring males in the sixteenth century.

R. HOULBROOKE, *English Family Life, 1450–1716. An Anthology from Diaries* (1988). A rich collection of documents illustrating family relationships.

R. HOULBROOKE, *Death, Religion, and Family in England, 1480-1758)* (1998). How death was met in the early modern English family.

J. L. IRWIN (ed.), *Womanhood in Radical Protestantism, 1525–1675* (1979). Sources illustrating images of women in sectarian Protestant thought.

H. JEDIN, *A History of the Council of Trent*, vols. 1 and 2 (1957–1961). Comprehensive, detailed, and authoritative.

W. K. JORDAN, *Edward VI: The Young King* (1968). The basic biography.

A. MACFARLANE, *The Family Life of Ralph Josselin: A Seventeenth Century Clergyman* (1970). A model study of Puritan family life!

SHERRIN MARSHALL, ed., *Women in Reformation and Counter Reformation Europe: Private and Public Worlds* (1989). Lucid and authoritative presentations.

J. F. MCNEILL, *The History and Character of Calvinism* (1954). The most comprehensive account and very readable.

H. A. OBERMAN, *Luther: Man Between God and the Devil* (1989). Perhaps the best account of Luther's life, by a Dutch master.

J. O'MALLEY, *The First Jesuits* (1993). Extremely detailed account of the creation of the Society of Jesus and its original purposes.

S. OZMENT, *The Age of Reform, 1250–1550: An Intellectual and Religious History of Late Medieval and Reformation Europe* (1980). A broad survey of major religious ideas and beliefs.

S. OZMENT, *When Fathers Ruled: Family Life in Reformation Europe* (1983). A survey of sixteenth-century attitudes toward marriage and parenthood.

S. OZMENT, *Three Behaim Boys: Growing Up in Early Modern Germany* (1990). The lives of three boys in their late teens and early adulthood told in their own words.

S. OZMENT, *Flesh and Spirit: Private Life in Early Modern Germany* (1999)

R. R POST, *The Modern Devotion* (1968). Currently the authoritative interpretation.

J. G. RIDLEY, *Thomas Cranmer* (1962). The basic biography.

B. SCRIBNER, *Germany: A New Social and Economic History, 1450–1630* (1996). Collection of comprehensive essays presenting up-to-date research.

Q. SKINNER, *The Foundations of Modern Political Thought II: The Age of Reformation* (1978). A comprehensive survey that treats every political thinker and tract.

D. STARKEY, *The Reign of Henry VIII* (1985). Portrayal of the king as in control of neither his life nor his court.

L. STONE, *The Family, Sex and Marriage in England 1500–1800* (1977). Controversial but in many respects still the reigning view of English family history.

G. STRAUSS (ED. AND TRANS.), *Manifestations of Discontent in Germany on the Eve of the Reformation* (1971). Rich collection of sources of both rural and urban scenes.

G. STRAUSS, *Luther's House of Learning: The Indoctrination of the Young in the German Reformation* (1978). Account of Protestant efforts to rear children in the new faith, stressing the negative side.

MARTIN TREU, *Katherine von Bora* (1995). Short biography of Martin Luther's wife.

E. TROELTSCH, *The Social Teaching of the Christian Churches*, vols. 1 and 2, trans. by O. Wyon (1960). Old, liberal account of the Reformation and its critics, with fondness for the latter.

J. WITTE, JR., *From Sacrament to Contract: Marriage, Religion and Law in the Western Tradition* (1997). Five major legal–religious systems elucidated and compared

F. WENDEL, *Calvin: The Origins and Development of His Religious Thought*, trans. by P. Mairet (1963). The best treatment of Calvin's theology.

G. H. WILLIAMS, *The Radical Reformation* (1962). Broad survey of the varieties of dissent within Protestantism.

H. WUNDER, *He Is the Sun, She Is the Moon: A History of Women in Early Modern Germany* (1998). A model of gender history.

Chapter 12

The massacre of worshiping Protestants at Vassy, France (March 1, 1562), which began the French wars of religion. An engraving by an unidentified seventeenth-century artist. The Granger Collection

K E Y   T O P I C S

- The war between Calvinists and Catholics in France
- The Spanish occupation of the Netherlands
- The struggle for supremacy between England and Spain
- The devastation of central Europe during the Thirty Years' War

The late sixteenth century and the first half of the seventeenth century are described as the "age of religious wars" because of the bloody opposition of Protestants and Catholics across Europe. Both genuine religious conflict and bitter dynastic rivalries fueled the wars. In France, the Netherlands, England, and Scotland in the second half of the sixteenth century, Calvinists fought Catholic rulers for the right to govern their own territories and to practice their chosen religion openly. In the first half of the seventeenth century, Lutherans, Calvinists, and Catholics marched against one another in central and northern Europe during the Thirty Years' War. By the middle of the seventeenth century, English Puritans had successfully revolted against the Stuart monarchy and the Anglican Church.

Renewed Religious Struggle

During the first half of the sixteenth century, religious conflict had been confined to central Europe and was primarily a struggle by Lutherans to secure rights and freedoms for themselves. In the second half of the sixteenth century, the focus shifted to western Europe—to France, the Netherlands,

Holy Roman Empire. The Peace of Augsburg did not, however, extend recognition to non-Lutheran Protestants. Both Catholics and Lutherans scorned Anabaptists and other sectarians as anarchists, and Calvinists were not yet strong enough to demand legal standing.

Outside the empire, the struggle for Protestant religious rights had intensified in most countries by the mid-sixteenth century. After the Council of Trent adjourned in 1563, Catholics began a Jesuit-led international counteroffensive against Protestants. At the time of John Calvin's death in 1564, Geneva had become both a refuge for Europe's persecuted Protestants and an international school for Protestant resistance, producing leaders fully equal to the new Catholic challenge.

Genevan Calvinism and Catholicism as revived by the Council of Trent were two equally dogmatic, aggressive, and irreconcilable church systems. Calvinists may have looked like "new papists" to critics when they dominated cities like Geneva. Yet when, as minorities, they found their civil and religious rights denied, they became true firebrands and revolutionaries. Calvinism adopted a presbyterian organization that magnified regional and local religious authority. Boards of presbyters, or elders, representing the many individual congregations of Calvinists, directly shaped the policy of the church at large.

By contrast, the Counter-Reformation sponsored a centralized episcopal church system, hierarchically arranged from pope to parish priest, that stressed absolute obedience to the person at the top. The high clergy—the pope and his bishops—not the synods of local churches, ruled supreme. Calvinism proved attractive to proponents of political decentralization who opposed totalitarian rulers, whereas Catholicism remained congenial to proponents of absolute monarchy determined to maintain, in the words of Louis XIV, "one king, one church, one law."

The opposition between the two religions can be seen even in the art and architecture that each came to embrace. The Catholic Counter-Reformation found the baroque style congenial. A successor to mannerism, baroque art is a grandiose, three-dimensional display of life and energy. Great baroque artists like Peter Paul Rubens (1571–1640) and Gianlorenzo Bernini (1598–1680) were Catholics. Protestants by contrast opted for a simpler and more restrained art and architecture, as can be seen in the English churches of Christopher Wren (1632–1723) and the gentle, searching portraits of the Dutch Mennonite, Rembrandt van Rijn (1606–1669). (See "Art & the West.")

centuries. (See Chapter 14.) Sebastian Castellio's (1515–1563) pithy censure of John Calvin for his role in the execution of the anti-Trinitarian Michael Servetus summarized a growing sentiment: "To kill a man is not to defend a doctrine, but to kill a man."[1] The French essayist Michel de Montaigne (1533–1592) asked in scorn of the dogmatic mind, "What do I know?" And the Lutheran Valentin Weigel (1533–1588), surveying a half century of religious strife in Germany, advised people to look within themselves for religious truth and no longer to churches and creeds.

Such skeptical views gained currency in larger political circles only at the cost of painful experience. Religious strife and civil war were best held in check where rulers tended to subordinate theological doctrine to political unity, urging tolerance, moderation, and compromise—even indifference—in religious matters. Rulers of this kind came to be known as *politiques*, and the most successful among them was Elizabeth I of England. By contrast, such rulers as Mary I of England, Philip II of Spain, and Oliver Cromwell, who took their religion with the utmost seriousness and refused every compromise, did not in the long run achieve their political goals.

As we shall see, the wars of religion were both internal national conflicts and truly international wars. Catholic and Protestant subjects struggled against one another for control of the crown of France, the Netherlands, and England. The Catholic governments of France and Spain conspired and finally sent armies against Protestant regimes in England and the Netherlands. The outbreak of the Thirty Years' War in 1618 made the international dimension of the religious conflict especially clear; before it ended in 1648, the war drew every major European nation directly or indirectly into its deadly net.

The French Wars of Religion (1562–1598)

Anti-Protestant Measures and the Struggle for Political Power

French Protestants are known as Huguenots, a term derived from Besançon Hugues, the leader of Geneva's political revolt against the House of Savoy in the 1520s, a prelude to that city's Calvinist

[1]*Contra libellum Calvini* (N.P., 1562), p. E2a.

Reformation. Huguenots were under surveillance in France already in the early 1520s when Lutheran writings and doctrines began to circulate in Paris. The capture of the French king Francis I by the forces of Emperor Charles V at the Battle of Pavia in 1525 provided a motive for the first wave of Protestant persecution in France. The French government hoped thereby to pacify their Habsburg conqueror, a fierce opponent of German Protestants, and to win their king's swift release.

A second major crackdown came a decade later. When Protestants plastered Paris and other cities with anti-Catholic placards on October 18, 1534, mass arrests of suspected Protestants followed. The government retaliation drove John Calvin and other members of the French reform party into exile. In 1540 the Edict of Fontainebleau subjected French Protestants to the Inquisition. Henry II (r. 1547–1559) established new measures against Protestants in the Edict of Chateaubriand in 1551. Save for a few brief interludes, the French monarchy remained a staunch foe of the Protestants until the ascension to the throne of Henry of Navarre in 1589.

The Habsburg–Valois wars (see Chapter 11) had ended with the Treaty of Cateau-Cambrésis in 1559, after which Europe experienced a moment of peace. But the same year marked the beginning of internal French conflict and a shift of the European balance of power away from France to Spain. The shift began with an accident. During a tournament held to celebrate the marriage of his thirteen-year-old daughter to Philip II, the son of Charles V and heir to the Spanish Habsburg lands, the French king, Henry II, was mortally wounded when a lance pierced his visor. This unforeseen event brought to the throne his sickly fifteen-year-old son, Francis II, under the regency of the queen mother, Catherine de Médicis. With the monarchy so weakened by Henry's death, three powerful families saw their chance to control France and began to compete for the young king's ear: the Bourbons, whose power lay in the south and west; the Montmorency-Chatillons, who controlled the center of France; and the Guises, who were dominant in eastern France.

The Guises were by far the strongest and had little trouble establishing firm control over the young king. Francis, duke of Guise, had been Henry II's general, and his brothers, Charles and Louis, were cardinals of the church. Mary Stuart, Queen of Scots and wife of Francis II, was their niece. Throughout the latter half of the sixteenth century, the name "Guise" remained interchangeable with militant, reactionary Catholicism.

The Bourbon and Montmorency-Chatillon families, in contrast, developed strong Huguenot sympathies, largely for political reasons. The Bourbon Louis I, prince of Condé (d. 1569), and the Montmorency-Chatillon Admiral Gaspard de Coligny (1519–1572) became the political leaders of the French Protestant resistance. They collaborated early in an abortive plot to kidnap Francis II from his Guise advisers in the Conspiracy of Amboise in 1560. This conspiracy was strongly condemned by John Calvin, who considered such tactics a disgrace to the Reformation.

Appeal of Calvinism

Often for quite different reasons, ambitious aristocrats and discontented townspeople joined Calvinist churches in opposition to the Guise-dominated French monarchy. In 1561 more than 2,000 Huguenot congregations existed throughout France. Yet Huguenots were a majority of the population in only two regions: Dauphiné and Languedoc. Although they made up only about one-fifteenth of the population, Huguenots were in important geographic areas and were heavily represented among the more powerful segments of French society. More than two-fifths of the French aristocracy became Huguenots. Many apparently hoped to establish within France a principle of territorial sovereignty akin to that secured within the Holy Roman Empire by the Peace of Augsburg. In this way, Calvinism indirectly served the forces of political decentralization.

John Calvin and Theodore Beza consciously sought to advance their cause by currying favor with powerful aristocrats. Beza converted Jeanne d'Albert, the mother of the future Henry IV. The prince of Condé was apparently converted in 1558 under the influence of his Calvinist wife. For many aristocrats—Condé probably among them—Calvinist religious convictions were attractive primarily as aids to long-sought political goals.

The military organization of Condé and Coligny progressively merged with the religious organization of the French Huguenot churches, creating a potent combination that benefited both political and religious dissidents. Calvinism gave political resistance justification and inspiration, and the forces of political resistance made Calvinism a viable religious alternative in Catholic France. Each side had much to gain from the other. The confluence of secular and religious motives, although beneficial to aristocratic resistance and the Calvinist religion alike, tended to cast suspicion on the religious appeal of Calvinism. Clearly, religious conviction was neither the only nor always the main reason for becoming a Calvinist in France in the second half of the sixteenth century.

Warring Architectural Styles: Baroque vs. Plain Churches

Art and architecture portrayed the beliefs of different religious systems as effectively as did the latter's creeds and laws. The Swiss, French, and English churches that grew out of the Reformed Protestant traditions of Ulrich Zwingli and John Calvin together with the non-conformist sectarian Protestants (Anabaptists, Puritans, Quakers) opposed both Catholic

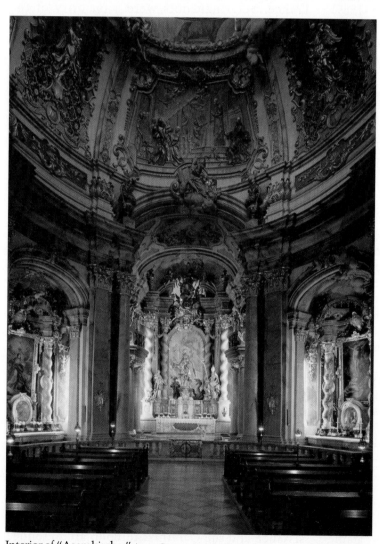

Interior of "Asamkirche," Asam Cosmas Damian (1686–1739). Saint Nepomit Church in Munich designed by the brothers Cosmas Damian and Egid Quirin Asam in 1733. The church stands next to the house the brothers built for themselves. Asamkirche (St. Johann-Nepomuk). Erich Lessing/Art Resource, N.Y.

and Lutheran retention of traditional church art and architecture and of music in churches as a serious distraction from the Word of God. Although a gifted and much-praised musician, Zwingli could find no biblical basis for any ornamentation in a Christian service of worship. In this, he had the support not only of the sectarians who condemned the more flexible Luther, but also of the Humanist Erasmus. In Zwinglian, Calvinist, and sectarian churches across Europe, the walls were stripped bare, and the only music heard was a congregational recitation of the Psalms.

In Austria, southern Germany, and elsewhere, the Catholic Counter Reformation, led by the Jesuits, embraced the exuberant baroque style of art and architecture then popular in Italy. This style permitted the Catholic faith to be displayed grandly in three-dimensions, its impact magnified by choruses and musical instruments, an artistic and musical feast. The intent was to overwhelm the worshippers' senses and move them emotionally, leaving them filled with awe and wonder at the power and glory of their Church. The new style proved effective in reassuring the doubting faithful and bringing the many who had turned Protestant back into Catholic churches.

Baroque style was also a boon to the building trades and the careers of painters, sculpters, and musicians. Great baroque artists like Peter Paul Rubens (1571–1640) and Gianlorenzo Bernini (1598–1680) were Catholics. But Protestants also had their great plain church architects, such as the Englishman Christopher Wren (1632–1723), and popular artists, such as the Dutch Mennonite Rembrandt van Rijn (1606–1669), whose works were distinguished by their simplicity and restraint.

Temple de Lyon. Bibliotheque Publique et Universitaire, Geneve

This eighteenth-century church, in Munich, is in the baroque style congenial to the Catholic Counter-Reformation. The interior explodes with energy and is filled with sculpture, paintings, and woodwork that dazzle the eyes. The intent was to give worshippers a keen sense of membership in the Church militant and move them to self-transcendence.

In stark contrast to the baroque style, this seventeenth-century Calvinist church in Lyon has no interior decoration to distract the worshipper from the Word of God. Here, the intent was to create an atmosphere of quiet introspection and reflection on one's own spiritual life in the presence of God's Word. For the Calvinists at worship in Lyon, the preacher is absolutely at center stage. There are no decorations, paintings, statuary, or elaborate stained glass. In Zwinglian churches the walls were even white-washed and no music or singing was permitted. Such simplicity contrasts dramatically with the Baroque style of contemporary Catholic churches.

Catherine de Médicis and the Guises

Following Francis II's death in 1560, Catherine de Médicis continued as regent for her minor son, Charles IX (r. 1560–1574). At a colloquy in Poissy, she tried unsuccessfully to reconcile the Protestant and Catholic factions. Fearing the power and guile of the Guises, Catherine, whose first concern was always to preserve the monarchy, sought allies among the Protestants. In 1562, after conversations with Beza and Coligny, she issued the January Edict, a measure that granted Protestants freedom to worship publicly outside towns—although only privately within them—and to hold synods. In March, this royal toleration came to an abrupt end when the duke of Guise surprised a Protestant congregation at Vassy in Champagne and proceeded to massacre several scores of worshipers. That event marked the beginning of the French wars of religion (March 1562).

Had Condé and the Huguenot armies rushed immediately to the queen's side after this attack, Protestants might well have secured an alliance with the crown. The queen mother's fear of Guise power was great at this time. But the hesitation of the Protestant leaders, due primarily to indecision on the part of Condé, placed the young king and the queen mother, against their deepest wishes, in firm Guise control. Cooperation with the Guises became the only alternative to capitulation to the Protestants.

Catherine de Médicis (1519–1589) exercised power in France during the reigns of her three sons Francis II (r. 1559–1560), Charles IX (r. 1560–1574), and Henry III (r. 1574–1589). Liaison Agency, Inc.

THE PEACE OF SAINT-GERMAIN-EN-LAYE During the first French war of religion, fought between April 1562 and March 1563, the duke of Guise was assassinated. It is a measure of the international character of the struggle in France that troops from Hesse and the Palatinate fought alongside the Huguenots. A brief resumption of hostilities in 1567–1568 was followed by the bloodiest of all the conflicts, between September 1568 and August 1570. In this period, Condé was killed and Huguenot leadership passed to Coligny. This was actually a blessing in disguise for the Protestants, because Coligny was far the better military strategist. In the Peace of Saint-Germain-en-Laye (1570), which ended the third war, the crown, acknowledging the power of the Protestant nobility, granted the Huguenots religious freedoms within their territories and the right to fortify their cities.

Perpetually caught between fanatical Huguenot and Guise extremes, Queen Catherine had always sought to balance one side against the other. Like the Guises, she wanted a Catholic France; she did not, however, desire a Guise-dominated monarchy. After the Peace of Saint-Germain-en-Laye the crown tilted manifestly toward the Bourbon faction and the Huguenots, and Coligny became Charles IX's most trusted adviser. Unknown to the king, Catherine began to plot with the

Guises against the ascendant Protestants. As she had earlier sought Protestant support when Guise power threatened to subdue the monarchy, she now sought Guise support as Protestant influence grew.

There was reason for Catherine to fear Coligny's hold on the king. Louis of Nassau, the leader of Protestant resistance to Philip II in the Netherlands, had gained Coligny's ear. Coligny used his position of influence to win the king of France over to a planned French invasion of the Netherlands in support of the Dutch Protestants. Such a course of action would have placed France squarely on a collision course with mighty Spain. Catherine recognized far better than her son that France stood little chance in such a contest. She and her advisers had been much sobered in this regard by news of the stunning Spanish victory over the Turks at Lepanto in October 1571 (to be discussed later).

THE SAINT BARTHOLOMEW'S DAY MASSACRE When Catherine lent her support to the infamous Saint Bartholomew's Day Massacre of Protestants, she did so out of a far less reasoned judgment. Her decision appears to have been made in a state of near panic. On August 22, 1572, four days after the Huguenot

Henry of Navarre had married the king's sister, Marguerite of Valois—still another sign of growing Protestant power—Coligny was struck down, although not killed, by an assassin's bullet. Catherine had apparently been party to this Guise plot to eliminate Coligny. After its failure, she feared both the king's reaction to her complicity with the Guises and the Huguenot response under a recovered Coligny. Catherine convinced Charles that a Huguenot coup was afoot, inspired by Coligny, and that only the swift execution of Protestant leaders could save the crown from a Protestant attack on Paris.

On Saint Bartholomew's Day, August 24, 1572, Coligny and 3,000 fellow Huguenots were butchered in Paris. Within three days an estimated 20,000 Huguenots were executed in coordinated attacks throughout France. It is a date that has ever since lived in infamy for Protestants.

Pope Gregory XIII and Philip II of Spain reportedly greeted the news of the Protestant massacre with special religious celebrations. Philip especially had good reason to rejoice. By throwing France into civil war, the massacre ended for the moment any planned French opposition to his efforts to subdue his rebellious subjects in the Netherlands. But the massacre of thousands of Protestants also gave the discerning Catholic world cause for new alarm. The event changed the nature of the struggle between Protestants and Catholics both within and beyond the borders of France. It was thereafter no longer an internal contest between Guise and Bourbon factions for French political influence, nor was it simply a Huguenot campaign to win basic religious freedoms. Henceforth, in Protestant eyes, it became an international struggle to the death for sheer survival against an adversary whose cruelty now justified any means of resistance.

PROTESTANT RESISTANCE THEORY   Only as Protestants faced suppression and sure defeat did they begin to sanction active political resistance. At first, they tried to practice the biblical precept of obedient subjection to worldly authority (Romans 13:1). Luther had only grudgingly approved resistance to the emperor after the Diet of Augsburg in 1530. In 1550 Lutherans in Magdeburg had published a highly influential defense of the right of lower authorities to oppose the emperor's order that all Lutherans return to the Catholic fold.

Calvin, who never faced the specter of total political defeat after his return to Geneva in September 1540, had always condemned willful disobedience and rebellion against lawfully constituted governments as un-Christian. But he also taught that lower magistrates, as part of the lawfully constituted government, had the right and duty to oppose tyrannical higher authority.

The exiled Scottish reformer John Knox, who had seen his cause crushed by Mary of Guise, the Regent of Scotland, and Mary I of England, laid the groundwork for later Calvinist resistance. In his famous *First Blast of the Trumpet Against the Terrible Regiment of Women* (1558), he declared that the removal of a heathen tyrant was not only permissible, but a Christian duty. He had the Catholic queen of England in mind.

After the great massacre of French Protestants on Saint Bartholomew's Day, 1572, Calvinists everywhere came to appreciate the need for an active defense of their religious rights. Classical Huguenot theories of resistance appeared in three major works of the 1570s. The first was the *Franco–Gallia* of François Hotman (1573), a humanist argument that the representative Estates General of France historically held higher authority than the French king. The second was Theodore Beza's *On the Right of Magistrates over Their Subjects* (1574), which, going beyond Calvin's views, justified the correction and even the overthrow of tyrannical rulers by lower authorities. (See "Theodore Beza Defends the Right to Resist Tyranny.") Finally, Philippe du Plessis Mornay's *Defense of Liberty Against Tyrants* (1579) admonished princes, nobles, and magistrates beneath the king, as guardians of the rights of the body politic, to take up arms against tyranny in other lands.

The Rise to Power of Henry of Navarre

Henry III (r. 1574–1589) was the last of Henry II's sons to wear the French crown. He found the monarchy wedged between a radical Catholic League, formed in 1576 by Henry of Guise, and vengeful Huguenots. Neither group would have been reluctant to assassinate a ruler whom they considered heretical and a tyrant. Like the queen mother, Henry sought to steer a middle course. In this effort, he received support from a growing body of neutral Catholics and Huguenots, who put the political survival of France above its religious unity. Such *politiques* were prepared to compromise religious creeds as might be required to save the nation.

The Peace of Beaulieu in May 1576 granted the Huguenots almost complete religious and civil freedom. France, however, was not ready then for such sweeping toleration. Within seven months of the Peace, the Catholic League forced Henry to return to the illusory quest for absolute religious unity in France. In October 1577, the king truncated the Peace of Beaulieu and once again circumscribed areas of permitted Huguenot worship. Thereafter, Huguenot and Catholic factions quickly returned to their accustomed anarchical military solutions. The Protestants were led by Henry of Navarre, now heir to the French throne by virtue of his marriage to Margaret of Valois, Henry III's sister.

Theodore Beza Defends the Right to Resist Tyranny

One of the oldest problems in political and social theory has been that of knowing when resistance to repression in matters of conscience is justified. Since Luther's day, Protestant reformers had urged their followers to obey established political authority. After the 1572 Saint Bartholomew's Day Massacre, however, pamphleteers urged Protestants to resist tyrants and persecutors with armed force. In 1574, Theodore Beza pointed out the obligation of rulers to act in the best interests of their subjects and the latter's right to resist them when they did not.

❖ *When does a ruler go too far, according to Beza? To whom may subjects appeal against a tyrant? Does Beza believe that individuals may take the law into their own hands?*

It is apparent that there is a mutual obligation between the king and the officers of a kingdom; that the government of the kingdom is not in the hands of the king in its entirety, but only the sovereign degree; that each of the officers has a share in accord with his degree; and that there are definite conditions on either side. If these conditions are not observed by the inferior officers, it is the part of the sovereign to dismiss and punish them....If the king, hereditary or elective, clearly goes back on the conditions without which he would not have been recognized and acknowledged, can there be any doubt that the lesser magistrates of the kingdom, of the cities, and of the provinces, the administration of which they have received from the sovereignty itself, are free of their oath, at least to the extent that they are en-titled to resist flagrant oppression of the realm which they swore to defend and protect according to their office and their particular jurisdiction?...

We must now speak of the third class of subjects, which though admittedly subject to the sovereign in a certain respect, is, in another respect, and in cases of necessity the protector of the rights of the sovereignty itself, and is established to hold the sovereign to his duty, and even, if need be, constrain and punish him....The people is prior to all the magistrates, and does not exist for them, but they for it....Whenever law and equity prevailed, nations neither created nor accepted kings except upon definite conditions. From this it follows that when kings flagrantly violate these terms, those who have the power to give them their authority have no less power to deprive them of it.

From *Constitutionalism and Resistance in the Sixteenth Century: Three Treatises by Hotman, Beza, and Mornay*, trans. and ed. by Julian H. Franklin (New York: Pegasus, 1969), pp. 111–114.

In the mid-1580s the Catholic League, supported by the Spanish, became completely dominant in Paris. In what came to be known as the Day of the Barricades, Henry III attempted to rout the league with a surprise attack in 1588. The effort failed badly, and the king had to flee Paris. Forced by his weakened position into unkingly guerilla tactics, and also emboldened by news of the English victory over the Spanish Armada in 1588, Henry successfully plotted the assassinations of both the duke and the cardinal of Guise. These assassinations sent France reeling once again. Led by still another Guise brother, the Catholic League reacted with a fury that matched the earlier Huguenot response to the Massacre of Saint Bartholomew's Day. The king now had only one course of action: He struck an alliance with the Protestant Henry of Navarre in April 1589.

As the two Henrys prepared to attack the Guise stronghold of Paris, however, a fanatical Jacobin friar stabbed and killed Henry III. Thereupon, the Bourbon Huguenot Henry of Navarre succeeded the childless Valois king to the French throne as Henry IV (r. 1589–1610). Pope Sixtus V and Philip II stood aghast at the sudden prospect of a Protestant France. They had always wanted France to be religiously Catholic and politically weak, and they now acted to achieve that end. Spain rushed troops to support the besieged Catholic League. Philip II apparently even harbored hopes of placing his eldest daughter, Isabella, the granddaughter of Henry II and Catherine de Médicis, on the French throne.

Direct Spanish intervention in the affairs of France seemed only to strengthen Henry IV's grasp on the crown. The French people viewed his right to hereditary succession more seriously than his espoused

Protestant confession. Henry was also widely liked. Notoriously informal in dress and manner—a factor that made him especially popular with the soldiers—Henry also had the wit and charm to neutralize the strongest enemy in a face-to-face confrontation. He came to the throne as a *politique*, long weary with religious strife and fully prepared to place political peace above absolute religious unity. He believed that a royal policy of tolerant Catholicism would be the best way to achieve such peace. On July 25, 1593, he publicly abjured the Protestant faith and embraced the traditional and majority religion of his country. "Paris is worth a mass," he is reported to have said.

It was, in fact, a decision he had made only after a long period of personal agonizing. The Huguenots were understandably horrified by this turnabout, and Pope Clement VIII remained skeptical of Henry's sincerity. But most of the French church and people, having known internal strife too long, rallied to the king's side. By 1596, the Catholic League was dispersed, its ties with Spain were broken, and the wars of religion in France, to all intents, had ground to a close.

The Edict of Nantes

On April 13, 1598, Henry IV's famous Edict of Nantes proclaimed a formal religious settlement. The following month, on May 2, 1598, the Treaty of Vervins ended hostilities between France and Spain.

Henry IV Recognizes Huguenot Religious Freedom

By the Edict of Nantes (April 13, 1598), Henry IV recognized Huguenot religious freedoms and the rights of Protestants to participate in French public institutions. Here are some of its provisions.

❖ *Are Huguenots given equal religious standing with Catholics? Are there limitations on their freedoms?*

We have by this perpetual and irrevocable Edict pronounced, declared, and ordained and we pronounce, declare and ordain:

Art. I. Firstly, that the memory of everything done on both sides from the beginning of the month of March, 1585, until our accession to the Crown and during the other previous troubles, and at the outbreak of them, shall remain extinct and suppressed, as if it were something which had never occurred....

Art. II. We forbid all our subjects, of whatever rank and quality they may be, to renew the memory of these matters, to attack, be hostile to, injure or provoke each other in revenge for the past, whatever may be the reason and pretext...but let them restrain themselves and live peaceably together as brothers, friends, and fellow-citizens....

Art. III. We ordain that the Catholic, Apostolic, and Roman religion shall be restored and reestablished in all places and districts of this our kingdom and the countries under our rule, where its practice has been interrupted....

Art. VI. And we permit those of the so-called Reformed religion to live and dwell in all the towns and districts of this our kingdom and the countries under our rule, without being annoyed, disturbed, molested or constrained to do anything against their conscience, or for this cause to be sought out in their houses and districts where they wish to live, provided that they conduct themselves in other respects to the provisions of our present Edict....

Art. XXI. Books dealing with the matters of the aforesaid so-called Reformed religion shall not be printed and sold publicly, except in the towns and districts where the public exercise of the said religion is allowed....

Art. XXII. We ordain that there shall be no difference or distinction, because of the aforesaid religion, in the reception of students to be instructed in Universities, Colleges, and schools, or of the sick and poor into hospitals, infirmaries, and public charitable institutions....

Art. XXVII. In order to reunite more effectively the wills of our subjects, as is our intention, and to remove all future complaints, we declare that all those who profess or shall profess the aforesaid so-called Reformed religion are capable of holding and exercising all public positions, honours, offices, and duties whatsoever...in the towns of our kingdom...notwithstanding all contrary oaths.

From *Church and State Through the Centuries: A Collection of Historic Documents*, trans. and ed. by S. Z. Ehler and John B. Morrall (New York: Biblo and Tannen, 1967), pp. 185–187. Reprinted by permission of Biblo-Moser Book Publishers.

Main Events of French Wars of Religion	
1559	Treaty of Cateau-Cambrésis ends Habsburg–Valois wars
1559	Francis II succeeds to French throne under regency of his mother, Catherine de Médicis
1560	Conspiracy of Amboise fails
1562	Protestant worshipers massacred at Vassy in Champagne by the duke of Guise
1572	The Saint Bartholomew's Day Massacre leaves thousands of Protestants dead
1589	Assassination of Henry III brings the Huguenot Henry of Navarre to throne as Henry IV
1593	Henry IV embraces Catholicism
1598	Henry IV grants Huguenots religious and civil freedoms in the Edict of Nantes
1610	Henry IV assassinated

In 1591, Henry IV had already assured the Huguenots of at least qualified religious freedoms. The Edict of Nantes made good that promise. It recognized and sanctioned minority religious rights within what was to remain an officially Catholic country. This religious truce—and it was never more than that—granted the Huguenots, who by this time numbered well over one million, freedom of public worship, the right of assembly, admission to public offices and universities, and permission to maintain fortified towns. Most of the new freedoms, however, were to be exercised within their own towns and territories. Concession of the right to fortify their towns reveals the continuing distrust between French Protestants and Catholics. As significant as it was, the edict only transformed a long hot war between irreconcilable enemies into a long cold war. To its critics, it had only created a state within a state. (See "Henry IV Recognizes Huguenot Religious Freedom.")

A Catholic fanatic assassinated Henry IV in May 1610. Although he is best remembered for the Edict of Nantes, Henry IV put in place political and economic policies that were equally important. They laid the foundations for the transformation of France into the absolute state it would become under Cardinal Richelieu and Louis XIV. Ironically, in pursuit of the political and religious unity that had escaped Henry IV, Louis XIV, calling for "one king, one church, one law," would revoke the Edict of Nantes in 1685. (See Chapter 13.) This action would force France and Europe to learn again by bitter experience the hard lessons of the wars of religion. Rare is the politician who learns from the lessons of history rather than repeating its mistakes.

Imperial Spain and the Reign of Philip II (r. 1556–1598)

Pillars of Spanish Power

Until the English defeated the mighty Spanish Armada in 1588, no one person stood larger in the second half of the sixteenth century than Philip II of Spain. Philip was heir to the intensely Catholic and militarily supreme western Habsburg kingdom. The eastern Habsburg lands of Austria, Bohemia, and Hungary had been given over by his father, Charles V, to Philip's uncle, the emperor Ferdinand I. These lands, together with the imperial title, remained in the possession of the Austrian branch of the family.

NEW WORLD RICHES Populous and wealthy Castile gave Philip a solid home base. The regular arrival in Seville of bullion from the Spanish colonies in the New World provided additional wealth. In the 1540s great silver mines had been opened in Potosí in present-day Bolivia and in Zacatecas in Mexico. These gave Philip the great sums needed to pay his bankers and mercenaries. He nonetheless never managed to erase the debts left by his father or to finance his own foreign adventures fully. He later contributed to the bankruptcy of the Fuggers when, at the end of his life, he defaulted on his enormous debts.

INCREASED POPULATION The new American wealth brought dramatic social change to the peoples of Europe during the second half of the sixteenth century. As Europe became richer, it was also becoming more populous. In the economically and politically active towns of France, England, and the Netherlands, populations had tripled and quadrupled by the early seventeenth century. Europe's population exceeded 70 million by 1600.

The combination of increased wealth and population triggered inflation. A steady two-percent-a-year rise in prices in much of Europe had serious cumulative effects by midcentury. There were more people than before and greater coinage in circulation, but less food and fewer jobs; wages stagnated while prices doubled and tripled in much of Europe.

This was especially the case in Spain. Because the new wealth was concentrated in the hands of a few, the traditional gap between the "haves"—the propertied, privileged, and educated classes—and the "have-nots" greatly widened. Nowhere did the unprivileged suffer more than in Spain, where the Castilian peasantry, the backbone of Philip II's great empire, became the most heavily taxed people of Europe. Those whose labor contributed most to making possible Spanish hegemony in Europe in the second half of the sixteenth century prospered least from it.

EFFICIENT BUREAUCRACY AND MILITARY A subjugated peasantry and wealth from the New World were not the only pillars of Spanish strength. Philip II shrewdly organized the lesser nobility into a loyal and efficient national bureaucracy. A reclusive man, he managed his kingdom by pen and paper rather than by personal presence. He was also a learned and pious Catholic, although some popes suspected that he used religion as much for political as for devotional purposes. That he was a generous patron of the arts and culture is evident in his unique retreat outside Madrid, the Escorial, a combination palace, church, tomb, and monastery. Philip also knew personal sorrows: His mad and treacherous son, Don Carlos, died under suspicious circumstances in 1568—some contemporaries suspected that Philip had him quietly executed—only three months before the death of the queen.

SUPREMACY IN THE MEDITERRANEAN During the first half of Philip's reign, attention focused almost exclusively on the Mediterranean and the Turkish threat. By history, geography, and choice, Spain had traditionally been Catholic Europe's champion against Islam. During the 1560s the Turks advanced deep into Austria, while their fleets dominated the Mediterranean. Between 1568 and 1570, armies under Philip's half-brother, Don John of Austria, the illegitimate son of Charles V, suppressed and dispersed the Moors in Granada.

In May 1571 a Holy League of Spain, Venice, and the pope, again under Don John's command, formed to check Turkish belligerence in the Mediterranean. In what was the largest naval battle of the sixteenth century, Don John's fleet engaged the Ottoman navy under Ali Pasha off Lepanto in the Gulf of Corinth on October 7, 1571. Before the engagement ended, over one-third of the Turkish fleet had been sunk or captured and 30,000 Turks had died. The Mediterranean for the moment belonged to Spain, and the Europeans were left to fight each other. Philip's armies also succeeded in putting down resistance in neighboring Portugal, which Spain annexed in 1580. The conquest of Portugal not only added to Spanish sea power, but also brought the magnificent Portuguese overseas empire in Africa, India, and the Americas into the Spanish orbit.

The Revolt in the Netherlands

The spectacular Spanish military success in southern Europe was not repeated in northern Europe. When Philip attempted to impose his will within the Netherlands and on England and France, he learned the lessons of defeat. The resistance of the Netherlands especially proved the undoing of Spanish dreams of world empire. (See Map 12–1.)

CARDINAL GRANVELLE The Netherlands was the richest area not only of Philip's Habsburg kingdom, but of Europe as well. In 1559 Philip had departed the Netherlands for Spain, never again to return. His half-sister, Margaret of Parma, assisted by a special council of state, became regent in his absence. The council was headed by Philip's hand-picked lieutenant, the extremely able Antoine Perrenot (1517–1586), known after 1561 as Cardinal Granvelle. Granvelle hoped to check Protestant gains by internal church reforms. He planned to

Titian's portrait of Philip II of Spain (r. 1556–1598), the most powerful ruler of his time. Alinari/Art Resource, N.Y.

MAP 12–1   THE NETHERLANDS
DURING THE REFORMATION   *The
northern and southern provinces
of the Netherlands. The former,
the United Provinces, were mostly
Protestant in the second half of the
sixteenth century, while the southern Spanish Netherlands made
peace with Spain and remained
largely Catholic.*

break down the traditional local autonomy of the seventeen Netherlands provinces by stages and establish in its place a centralized royal government directed from Madrid. A politically docile and religiously uniform country was the goal.

The merchant towns of the Netherlands were, however, Europe's most independent; many, like magnificent Antwerp, were also Calvinist strongholds. By tradition and habit, the people of the Netherlands inclined far more toward variety and toleration than toward obeisant conformity and hierarchical order. Two members of the council of state formed a stubborn opposition to the Spanish overlords, who now sought to reimpose their traditional rule with a vengeance. They were the Count of Egmont (1522–1568) and William of Nassau, the Prince of Orange (1533–1584), known as "the Silent" because of his extremely small circle of confidants.

Like other successful rulers in this period, William of Orange placed the Netherlands' political autonomy and well-being above religious creeds. He personally passed through successive Catholic, Lutheran, and Calvinist stages. In 1561, he married Anne of Saxony, the daughter of the Lutheran elector Maurice and the granddaughter of the late Landgrave Philip of Hesse. He maintained his Catholic practices until 1567, when he turned Lutheran. After

the Saint Bartholomew's Day Massacre (1572), Orange (as he was called) became an avowed Calvinist.

In 1561, Cardinal Granvelle proceeded with a planned ecclesiastical reorganization of the Netherlands. It was intended to tighten the control of the Catholic hierarchy over the country and to accelerate its consolidation as a Spanish ward. Orange and Egmont, organizing the Dutch nobility in opposition, succeeded in gaining Granvelle's removal from office in 1564. Aristocratic control of the country after Granvelle's departure, however, proved woefully inefficient. Popular unrest continued to grow, especially among urban artisans, who joined the congregations of radical Calvinist preachers in increasing numbers.

THE COMPROMISE   The year 1564 also saw the first fusion of political and religious opposition to Regent Margaret's government. This opposition resulted from Philip II's unwise insistence that the decrees of the Council of Trent be enforced throughout the Netherlands. William of Orange's younger brother, Louis of Nassau, who had been raised a Lutheran, led the opposition, and it received support from the Calvinist-inclined lesser nobility and townspeople. A national covenant called the *Compromise* was drawn up, a solemn pledge to resist the decrees of Trent and the Inquisition. Grievances were loudly and persistently voiced. When Regent Margaret's government spurned the protesters as "beggars" in 1566, Calvinists rioted through the country. Louis called on French Huguenots and German Lutherans to send aid to the Netherlands, and a full-scale rebellion against the Spanish regency appeared imminent.

THE DUKE OF ALBA The rebellion failed to materialize, however, because the Netherlands' higher nobility would not support it. Their shock at Calvinist iconoclasm and anarchy was as great as their resentment of Granvelle's more subtle repression. Philip, determined to make an example of the Protestant rebels, dispatched the duke of Alba to suppress the revolt. His army of 10,000 journeyed northward from Milan in 1567 in a show of combined Spanish and papal might. A special tribunal, known to the Spanish as the Council of Troubles and among the Netherlanders as the Council of Blood, reigned over the land. The counts of Egmont and Horn and several thousand suspected heretics were publicly executed before Alba's reign of terror ended.

The Spanish levied new taxes, forcing the Netherlands to pay for the suppression of its own revolt. One of these taxes, the "tenth penny," a ten-percent sales tax, met such resistance from merchants and artisans that it remained uncollectible in some areas even after a reduction to three percent. Combined persecution and taxation sent tens of thousands fleeing from the Netherlands during Alba's cruel six-year rule. Alba came to be more hated than Granvelle or the radical Calvinists had ever been.

RESISTANCE AND UNIFICATION William of Orange was an exile in Germany during these turbulent years. He now emerged as the leader of a broad movement for the Netherlands' independence from Spain. The northern, Calvinist-inclined provinces of Holland, Zeeland, and Utrecht, of which Orange was the *stadholder*, or governor, became his base. As in France, political resistance in the Netherlands gained both organization and inspiration by merging with Calvinism.

The early victories of the resistance attest to the popular character of the revolt. A case in point is the capture of the port city of Brill by the "Sea Beggars," an international group of anti-Spanish exiles and criminals, among them many Englishmen. William of Orange did not hesitate to enlist their services. Their brazen piracy, however, had forced Queen Elizabeth to disassociate herself from them and to bar their ships from English ports. In 1572, the Beggars captured Brill and other seaports in Zeeland and Holland. Mixing with the native population, they quickly sparked rebellions against Alba in town after town and spread the resistance southward. In 1574, the people of Leiden heroically resisted a long Spanish siege. The Dutch opened the dikes and flooded their country to repulse the hated Spanish. The faltering Alba had by that time ceded power to Don Luis de Requesens, who replaced him as commander of Spanish forces in the Netherlands in November 1573.

THE PACIFICATION OF GHENT The greatest atrocity of the war came after Requesens's death in 1576. Spanish mercenaries, leaderless and unpaid, ran

The Milch Cow, a sixteenth-century satirical painting depicting the Netherlands as a cow in whom all the great powers of Europe have an interest. Elizabeth of England is feeding her (England had longstanding commercial ties with Flanders); Philip II of Spain is attempting to ride her (Spain was trying to reassert its control over the entire area); William of Orange is trying to milk her (he was the leader of the anti-Spanish rebellion); and the king of France holds her tail (France hoped to profit from the rebellion at Spain's expense). Rijksmuseum, Amsterdam amok in Antwerp on November 4, 1576, leaving 7,000 people dead in the streets. The event came to be known as the Spanish Fury.

These atrocities accomplished in four short days what neither religion nor patriotism had previously been able to do. The ten largely Catholic southern provinces (what is roughly modern Belgium) now came together with the seven largely Protestant northern provinces (what is roughly the modern Netherlands) in unified opposition to Spain. This union, known as the Pacification of Ghent, was accomplished on November 8, 1576. It declared internal regional sovereignty in matters of religion, a key clause that permitted political cooperation among the signatories, who were not agreed over religion. It was a Netherlands version of the territorial settlement of religious differences brought about in

the Holy Roman Empire in 1555 by the Peace of Augsburg. Four provinces initially held out, but they soon made the resistance unanimous by joining the all-embracing Union of Brussels in January 1577. For the next two years, the Spanish faced a unified and determined Netherlands.

Don John, the victor over the Turks at Lepanto in 1571, had taken command of Spanish land forces in November 1576. He now experienced his first defeat. Confronted by unified Netherlandic resistance, he signed the humiliating Perpetual Edict in February 1577. This edict provided for the removal of all Spanish troops from the Netherlands within twenty days. The withdrawal of troops gave the country to William of Orange and effectively ended for the time being whatever plans Philip may have had for using the Netherlands as a staging area for an invasion of England.

William of Orange Defends Himself to the Dutch Estates

Branded an outlaw by Philip II of Spain, the Protestant Dutch Prince William of Orange defended himself to his countrymen in an eloquent address known as the Apology *(1581).*

❖ *Is this a rhetorical speech of the kind we still hear today—making an enemy's condemnation a badge of honor? Did being branded as an outlaw by the Spanish king put William in greater danger? If so, from whom? How did William's life end in 1584? Did the condemnation by the Spanish King have anything to do with it?*

What could be more gratifying in this world, especially to one engaged in the great and excellent task of securing liberty for a good people oppressed by evil men, than to be mortally hated by one's enemies, who are at the same time enemies of the fatherland, and from their mouths to receive a sweet testimony to one's fidelity to his people and to his obstinate opposition to tyrants and disturbers of the peace? Such is the pleasure that the Spaniards and their adherents have prepared for me in their anxiety to disturb me. They have but gratified me by that infamous proscription by which they sought to ruin me. Not only do I owe to them this favor, but also the occasion to make generally known the equity and justice of my enterprises....

My enemies object that I have "established liberty of conscience." I confess that the glow of fires in which so many poor Christians have been tormented is not an agreeable sight to me, although it may rejoice the eyes of the duke of Alba and the Spaniards; and that it has

been my opinion that persecutions should cease in the Netherlands....

They denounce me as a hypocrite, which is absurd enough....As their friend, I told them quite frankly that they were twisting a rope to hang themselves when they began the barbarous policy of persecution....

As for me personally...it is my head that they are looking for, and they have vowed my death by offering such a great sum of money [25,000 crowns]. They say that the war can never come to an end so long as I am among you....

If, gentlemen, you believe that my exile, or even my death, may serve you, I am ready to obey your behests. Here is my head, over which no prince or monarch has authority save you. Dispose of it as you will for the safety and preservation of our commonwealth. But if you judge that such little experience and energy as I have acquired through long and assiduous labors, if you judge that the remainder of my possessions and of my life can be of service to you, I dedicate them to you and to the fatherland.

From James Harvey Robinson, *Readings in European History*, Vol. 2 (Boston: Ginn and Co., 1906), pp. 177–179.

THE UNION OF ARRAS AND THE UNION OF UTRECHT
The Spanish, however, were nothing if not persistent. Don John and Alessandro Farnese of Parma, the regent Margaret's son, revived Spanish power in the southern provinces, where constant fear of Calvinist extremism had moved the leaders to break the Union of Brussels. In January 1579 the southern provinces formed the Union of Arras, and within five months they made peace with Spain. These provinces later served the cause of the Counter-Reformation. The northern provinces responded with the formation of the Union of Utrecht.

NETHERLANDS INDEPENDENCE   Seizing what now appeared to be a last opportunity to break the back of Netherlandic resistance, Philip II declared William of Orange an outlaw and placed a bounty of 25,000 crowns on his head. The act predictably stiffened the resistance of the northern provinces. In a famous defiant speech to the Estates General of Holland in December 1580, known as the Apology, Orange publicly denounced Philip as a heathen tyrant whom the Netherlands need no longer obey. (See "William of Orange Defends Himself to the Dutch Estates.")

On July 22, 1581, the member provinces of the Union of Utrecht met in The Hague and formally declared Philip no longer their ruler. They turned instead to the French duke of Alençon, Catherine de Médici's youngest son. The southern provinces had also earlier looked to him as a possible middle way between Spanish and Calvinist overlordship. All the northern provinces save Holland and Zeeland accepted Alençon as their "sovereign" (Holland and Zeeland distrusted him almost as much as they did Philip II), but with the understanding that he would be only a titular ruler. But Alençon, an ambitious failure, saw this as his one chance at greatness. When he rashly attempted to take actual control of the provinces in 1583, he was deposed and returned to France.

Spanish efforts to reconquer the Netherlands continued into the 1580s. William of Orange, assassinated in July 1584, was succeeded by his seventeen-year-old son, Maurice (1567–1625), who, with the assistance of England and France, continued Dutch resistance. Fortunately for the Netherlands, Philip II began now to meddle directly in French and English affairs. He signed a secret treaty with the Guises (the Treaty of Joinville in December 1584) and sent armies under Farnese into France in 1590. Hostilities with the English, who had openly aided the Dutch rebels, also increased. Gradually, they built toward a climax in 1588, when Philip's great Armada was defeated in the English Channel.

These new fronts overextended Spain's resources, strengthening the Netherlands. Spanish preoccupation with France and England permitted the northern provinces to drive out all Spanish soldiers by 1593. In 1596, France and England formally recognized the independence of these provinces. Peace was not, however, concluded with Spain until 1609, when the Twelve Years' Truce gave the northern provinces virtual independence. Full recognition came finally in the Peace of Westphalia in 1648.

England and Spain (1553–1603)

Mary I

Before Edward VI died in 1553, he agreed to a device to make Lady Jane Grey, the teenage daughter of a powerful Protestant nobleman and, more important, the granddaughter on her mother's side of Henry VIII's younger sister Mary, his successor in place of the Catholic Mary Tudor (r. 1553–1558). But popular support for the principle of hereditary monarchy was too strong to deprive Mary of her rightful rule. Popular uprisings in London and elsewhere led to Jane Grey's removal from the throne within days of her crowning, and she was eventually beheaded.

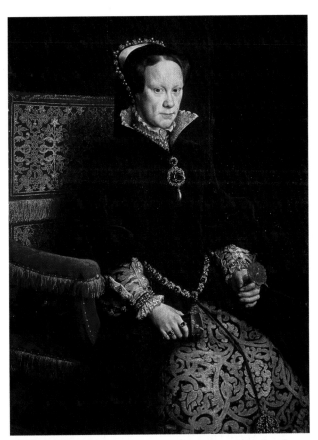

Portrait of Mary I (r. 1553–1558), Queen of England. By Sir Anthony Mor (Antonio Moro) (1517/20–76/7), Prado, Madrid. 1554 (panel). Prado, Madrid/Bridgeman Art Library, London/Index

Once enthroned, Mary proceeded to act even beyond the worst fears of the Protestants. In 1554 she entered a highly unpopular political marriage with Prince Philip (later Philip II) of Spain, a symbol of militant Catholicism to English Protestants. At his direction, she pursued a foreign policy that in 1558 cost England its last enclave on the Continent, Calais.

Mary's domestic measures were equally shocking to the English people and even more divisive. During her reign, Parliament repealed the Protestant statutes of Edward and reverted to the Catholic religious practice of her father, Henry VIII. The great Protestant leaders of the Edwardian Age—John Hooper, Hugh Latimer, and Thomas Cranmer—were executed for heresy. Hundreds of Protestants either joined them in martyrdom (282 were burned at the stake during Mary's reign) or took flight to the Continent. These "Marian exiles" settled in Germany and Switzerland, forming especially large communities in Frankfurt, Strasbourg, and Geneva. (John Knox, the future leader of the Reformation in Scotland, was prominent among them.) There they worshiped in their own congregations, wrote tracts justifying armed resistance, and waited for the time when a Protestant counteroffensive could be launched in their homelands. They were also exposed to religious beliefs more radical than any set forth during Edward VI's reign. Many of these exiles later held positions in the Church of England during Elizabeth I's reign.

Elizabeth I

Mary's successor was her half-sister, Elizabeth I (r. 1558–1603), the daughter of Henry VIII and Anne Boleyn. Elizabeth had remarkable and enduring successes in both domestic and foreign policy. Assisted by a shrewd adviser, Sir William Cecil (1520–1598), she built a true kingdom on the ruins of Mary's reign. Between 1559 and 1563, she and Cecil guided a religious settlement through Parliament that prevented England from being torn asunder by religious differences in the sixteenth century, as the Continent was. Another ruler who subordinated religious to political unity, Elizabeth merged a centralized episcopal system, which she firmly controlled, with broadly defined Protestant doctrine and traditional Catholic ritual. In the resulting Anglican Church, inflexible religious extremes were not permitted.

In 1559 an Act of Supremacy passed Parliament, repealing all the anti-Protestant legislation of Mary Tudor and asserting Elizabeth's right as "supreme governor" over both spiritual and temporal affairs. In the same year, the Act of Uniformity mandated a revised version of the second *Book of Common Prayer* (1552) for every English parish. In 1563, the issuance of the *Thirty-Nine Articles on Religion*, a revision of Thomas Cranmer's

Elizabeth I (r. 1558–1603) standing on a map of England in 1592. An astute politician in both foreign and domestic policy, Elizabeth was perhaps the most succesful ruler of the sixteenth century. National Portrait Gallery, London

original forty-two, made a moderate Protestantism the official religion within the Church of England.

CATHOLIC AND PROTESTANT EXTREMISTS Elizabeth hoped to avoid both Catholic and Protestant extremism at the official level by pursuing a middle way. Her first archbishop of Canterbury, Matthew Parker (d. 1575), represented this ideal. But Elizabeth could not prevent the emergence of subversive Catholic and Protestant zealots. When she ascended the throne, Catholics were in the majority in England. The extremists among them, encouraged by the Jesuits, plotted against her. Catholic radicals were also encouraged and later directly assisted by the Spanish, who were piqued both by Elizabeth's Protestant sympathies and by her refusal to follow the example of her half-sister Mary and take Philip II's hand in marriage. Elizabeth remained unmarried throughout her reign, using the possibility of a marriage as a political alliance very much to her diplomatic advantage.

Catholic extremists hoped eventually to replace Elizabeth with Mary Stuart, Queen of Scots. Unlike

Elizabeth, who had been declared illegitimate during the reign of her father, Mary Stuart had an unblemished claim to the throne by way of her grandmother Margaret, the sister of Henry VIII. Elizabeth acted swiftly against Catholic assassination plots and rarely let emotion override her political instincts. Despite proven cases of Catholic treason and even attempted regicide, she executed fewer Catholics during her forty-five years on the throne than Mary Tudor had executed Protestants during her brief five-year reign. She showed little mercy, however, to separatists and others who threatened the unity of her rule.

Elizabeth dealt cautiously with the Puritans, who were Protestants working within the national church to "purify" it of every vestige of "popery" and to make its Protestant doctrine more precise. The Puritans had two special grievances:

1. the retention of Catholic ceremony and vestments within the Church of England, which made it appear to the casual observer that no Reformation had occurred, and

2. the continuation of the episcopal system of Church governance, which conceived of the English church theologically as the true successor to Rome, while placing it politically under the firm hand of the queen and her compliant archbishop.

Sixteenth-century Puritans were not separatists. They enjoyed wide popular support and were led by widely respected men like Thomas Cartwright (d. 1603). They worked through Parliament to create an alternative national church of semiautonomous congregations governed by representative presbyteries (hence, "Presbyterians"), following the model of Calvin and Geneva. Elizabeth dealt firmly, but subtly, with this group, conceding absolutely nothing that lessened the hierarchical unity of the Church of England and her control over it.

The more extreme Puritans wanted every congregation to be autonomous, a law unto itself, with neither higher episcopal nor presbyterian control. They came to be known as Congregationalists. Elizabeth and her second archbishop of Canterbury, John Whitgift (d. 1604), refused to tolerate this group, whose views on independence they found patently subversive. The Conventicle Act of 1593 gave such separatists the option of either conforming to the practices of the Church of England or facing exile or death.

DETERIORATION OF RELATIONS WITH SPAIN A series of events led inexorably to war between England and Spain, despite the sincerest desires on the part of both Philip II and Elizabeth to avoid a confrontation. In 1567 the Spanish duke of Alba marched his mighty army into the Netherlands, which was, from the English point of view, simply a convenient staging area for a Spanish invasion of England. Pope Pius V (r. 1566–1572), who favored a military conquest of Protestant England, "excommunicated" Elizabeth for heresy in 1570. This mischievous act only encouraged both internal resistance and international intrigue against the queen. Two years later, as noted earlier, the piratical Sea Beggars, many of whom were Englishmen, occupied the port city of Brill in the Netherlands and aroused the surrounding countryside against the Spanish.

Following Don John's demonstration of Spain's awesome sea power at the famous naval battle of Lepanto in 1571, England signed a mutual defense pact with France. Also in the 1570s, Elizabeth's famous seamen John Hawkins (1532–1595) and Sir Francis Drake (1545?–1596) began to prey regularly on Spanish shipping in the Americas. Drake's circumnavigation of the globe between 1577 and 1580

Elizabeth I before Parliament. The artist shows the Queen small and in the background, and places Parliament prominently in the foreground, suggesting that England, despite the enormous power of the Queen, is a land where parliamentary government reigns supreme.
The Folger Shakespeare Library

was one in a series of dramatic demonstrations of English ascendancy on the high seas.

After the Saint Bartholomew's Day Massacre, Elizabeth was the only protector of Protestants in France and the Netherlands. In 1585 she signed the Treaty of Nonsuch, which provided English soldiers and cavalry to the Netherlands. Funds that had previously been funneled covertly to support Henry of Navarre's army in France now flowed openly.

MARY, QUEEN OF SCOTS   These events made a tinderbox of English–Spanish relations. The spark that finally touched it off was Elizabeth's execution of Mary, Queen of Scots (1542–1587).

Mary Stuart was the daughter of King James V of Scotland and Mary of Guise and had resided in France from the time she was six years old. This thoroughly French and Catholic queen had returned to Scotland after the death of her husband, the French king Francis II, in 1561. There she found a successful, fervent Protestant Reformation that had won legal sanction the year before in the Treaty of Edinburgh (1560). As hereditary heir to the throne of Scotland, Mary remained queen by divine and human right. She was not intimidated by the Protestants who controlled her realm. She established an international French court culture, the gaiety and sophistication of which impressed many Protestant nobles whose religion often made their lives exceedingly dour.

Mary was closely watched by the ever-vigilant Scottish reformer John Knox. He fumed publicly and always with effect against the queen's private mass and Catholic practices, which Scottish law made a capital offense for everyone else. Knox won support in his role of watchdog from Elizabeth and Cecil. Elizabeth personally despised Knox and never forgave him for writing the *First Blast of the Trumpet Against the Terrible Regiment of Women*, a work aimed at provoking a revolt against Mary Tudor, but published in the year of Elizabeth's ascent to the throne. Elizabeth and Cecil tolerated Knox because he served their foreign policy, never permitting Scotland to succumb to the young Mary and her French and Catholic ways.

In 1568, a public scandal forced Mary's abdication and flight to her cousin Elizabeth in England. Mary's reputed lover, the earl of Bothwell, was, with cause, suspected of having killed her legal husband, Lord Darnley. When a packed court acquitted Bothwell, he subsequently married Mary. The outraged reaction from Protestant nobles forced Mary to surrender the throne to her one-year-old son, who became James VI of Scotland (and, later, Elizabeth's successor as King James I of England). Because of Mary's clear claim to the English throne, she remained an international symbol of a possible Catholic England, and she was consumed by the desire to be queen of England. Her presence in England, where she resided under house arrest for nineteen years, was a constant discomfort to Elizabeth.

In 1583 Elizabeth's vigilant secretary, Sir Francis Walsingham, uncovered a plot against Elizabeth involving the Spanish ambassador Bernardino de Mendoza. After Mendoza's deportation in January 1584, popular antipathy toward Spain and support for

A portrayal of the execution of Mary, Queen of Scots and the apparent subsequent burning (left) of her body, so that no relics might survive for her followers to revere. Unknown Dutch artist. National Galleries of Scotland

An Unknown Contemporary Describes Queen Elizabeth

No sixteenth-century ruler governed more effectively than Elizabeth I of England (r. 1558–1603), who was both loved and feared by her subjects. An unknown contemporary has left the following description, revealing not only her intelligence and political cunning, but also something of her immense vanity.

❖ *How does this description compare with that of Mary I? How do the personal qualities and political skills of the two leaders differ?*

I will proceed with the description of the queen's disposition and natural gifts of mind and body, wherein she either matched or exceeded all the princes of her time, as being of a great spirit yet tempered with moderation, in adversity never dejected, in prosperity rather joyful than proud; affable to her subjects, but always with due regard to the greatness of her estate, by reason whereof she was both loved and feared.

In her later time, when she showed herself in public, she was always magnificent in apparel; supposing haply thereby that the eyes of her people (being dazzled by the glittering aspect of her outward ornaments) would not so easily discern the marks of age and decay of natural beauty; and she came abroad the more seldom, to make her presence the more grateful and applauded by the multitude, to whom things rarely seen are in manner as new.

She suffered not, at any time, any suitor to depart discontented from her, and though ofttimes he obtained not that he desired, yet he held himself satisfied with her manner of speech, which gave hope of success in the second attempt....

Latin, French, and Italian she could speak very elegantly, and she was able in all those languages to answer ambassadors on the sudden....Of the Greek tongue she was also not altogether ignorant. She took pleasure in reading of the best and wisest histories, and some part of Tacitus's *Annals* she herself turned into English for her private exercise. She also translated Boethius's *On the Consolation of Philosophy* and a treatise of Plutarch, *On Curiosity*, with divers others....

It is credibly reported that not long before her death, she had a great apprehension of her own age and declination by seeing her face (then lean and full of wrinkles) truly represented to her in a glass, which she a good while very earnestly beheld; perceiving thereby how often she had been abused by flatterers (whom she held in too great estimation) that had informed her the contrary.

From James Harvey Robinson, ed., *Readings in European History*, Vol. 2 (Boston: Athenaeum, 1906), pp. 191–193.

Protestant resistance in France and the Netherlands became massive throughout England.

In 1586 Walsingham uncovered still another plot against Elizabeth, the so-called Babington plot (after Anthony Babington, who was caught seeking Spanish support for an attempt on the queen's life). This time he had uncontestable proof of Mary's complicity. Elizabeth believed that the execution of a sovereign, even a dethroned sovereign, weakened royalty everywhere. She was also aware of the outcry that Mary's execution would create throughout the Catholic world, and Elizabeth sincerely wanted peace with English Catholics. But she really had no choice in the matter and consented to Mary's execution, which took place on February 18, 1587. This event dashed all Catholic hopes for a bloodless reconversion of Protestant England. After the execution of the Catholic queen of Scotland, Pope Sixtus V (r. 1585–1590), who feared Spanish domination almost as much as he abhorred English Protes-

tantism, could no longer withhold public support for a Spanish invasion of England. Philip II ordered his Armada to make ready.

THE ARMADA Spain's war preparations were interrupted in the spring of 1587 by Sir Francis Drake's successful shelling of the port city of Cádiz, an attack that inflicted heavy damage on Spanish ships and stores. After "singeing the beard of Spain's king," as he put it, Drake raided the coast of Portugal, further incapacitating the Spanish. The success of these strikes forced the Spanish to postpone their planned invasion of England until the spring of 1588.

On May 30 of that year, a mighty fleet of 130 ships bearing 25,000 sailors and soldiers under the command of the duke of Medina-Sidonia set sail for England. In the end, however, the English won a stunning victory. The invasion barges that were to transport Spanish soldiers from the galleons onto

English shores were prevented from leaving Calais and Dunkirk. The swifter English and Netherlandic ships, helped by what came to be known as an "English wind," dispersed the waiting Spanish fleet, over one-third of which never returned to Spain.

The news of the Armada's defeat gave heart to Protestant resistance everywhere. Although Spain continued to win impressive victories in the 1590s, it never fully recovered from that defeat. Spanish soldiers faced unified and inspired French, English, and Dutch armies. By the time of Philip's death on September 13, 1598, his forces had been successfully rebuffed on all fronts. His seventeenth-century successors were all inferior leaders who never knew responsibilities equal to his. Nor did Spain ever again know such imperial grandeur. The French soon dominated the Continent, while in the New World the Dutch and the English progressively whittled away Spain's once glorious overseas empire.

Elizabeth died on March 23, 1603, leaving behind her a strong nation poised to expand into a global empire. (See "An Unknown Contemporary Describes Queen Elizabeth.")

The Thirty Years' War (1618–1648)

The Thirty Years' War in the Holy Roman Empire was the last and most destructive of the wars of religion. Religious and political differences had long set Catholics against Protestants and Calvinists against Lutherans. What made the Thirty Years' War so devastating was the entrenched hatred of the various sides and their seeming determination to sacrifice all for their religious beliefs and extension of political power. As the conflicts multiplied, virtually every major European land became involved either directly or indirectly. When the hostilities ended in 1648, the peace terms shaped the map of northern Europe much as we know it today.

Preconditions for War

FRAGMENTED GERMANY In the second half of the sixteenth century, Germany was an almost ungovernable land of about 360 autonomous political entities. (See Map 12–2.) There were independent secular principalities (duchies, landgraviates, and marches); ecclesiastical principalities (archbishoprics, bishoprics, and abbeys); numerous free cities; and castle regions dominated by knights. The Peace of Augsburg (1555) had given each a significant degree of sovereignty within its own borders. Each levied its own tolls and tariffs and coined its own money, practices that made land travel and trade between the various regions dif-

ficult and sometimes impossible. In addition, many of these little lands were filled with great-power pretensions. Political decentralization and fragmentation characterized Germany as the seventeenth century opened; it was not a unified nation like Spain, England, or even strife-filled France.

Because of its central location, Germany had always been Europe's highway for merchants and traders going north, south, east and west. Europe's rulers pressed in on Germany both for reasons of trade and because some held lands or legal privileges within certain German principalities. German princes, in their turn, looked to import and export markets beyond German borders and opposed any efforts to consolidate the Holy Roman Empire, lest their territorial rights, confirmed by the Peace of Augsburg, be overturned. German princes were not loath to turn to Catholic France or to the kings of Denmark and Sweden for allies against the Habsburg emperor.

After the Council of Trent, Protestants in the empire suspected the existence of an imperial and papal conspiracy to re-create the Catholic Europe of pre-Reformation times. The imperial diet, which the German princes controlled, demanded strict observance of the constitutional rights of Germans, as set forth in agreements with the emperor since the mid-fourteenth century. In the late sixteenth century, the emperor ruled only to the degree to which he was prepared to use force of arms against his subjects.

RELIGIOUS DIVISION Religious conflict accentuated the international and internal political divisions. (See Map 12–3.) During this period, the population within the Holy Roman Empire was about equally divided between Catholics and Protestants, the latter having perhaps a slight numerical edge by 1600. The terms of the Peace of Augsburg had attempted to freeze the territorial holdings of the Lutherans and the Catholics (the so-called ecclesiastical reservation). In the intervening years, however, the Lutherans had gained and kept political control in some Catholic areas, as had the Catholics in a few previously Lutheran areas. Such territorial reversals, or the threat of them, only increased the suspicion and antipathy between the two sides.

The Lutherans had been far more successful in securing their rights to worship in Catholic lands than the Catholics had been in securing such rights in Lutheran lands. The Catholic rulers, who were in a weakened position after the Reformation, had made, but resented, concessions to Protestant communities within their territories. With the passage of time, they demanded that all ecclesiastical princes, electors, archbishops, bishops, and abbots who had deserted the Catholic for the Protestant side be immediately deprived of their religious offices and that their ecclesiastical holdings be promptly returned to Catholic

MAP 12–2 GERMANY IN 1547 *Mid-sixteenth-century Germany was an almost ungovernable land of about 360 autonomous political entities.* Originally "Map of Germany Showing It's Great Division/Fragmentation in the 16th Century" from Majo Holborn, *A History of Germany: The Reformation*, Copyright © 1982 by Princeton University Press. Reprinted by permission of Princeton University Press.

control in accordance with the ecclesiastical reservation. However, the Lutherans and, especially, the Calvinists in the Palatinate ignored this stipulation at every opportunity.

There was also religious strife in the empire between liberal and conservative Lutherans and between Lutherans and the growing numbers of Calvinists. The last half of the sixteenth century was a time of warring Protestant factions within German universities. And in addition to the heightened religious strife, a new scientific and material culture was becoming ascen-

dant in intellectual and political circles, increasing the anxiety of religious people of all persuasions.

CALVINISM AND THE PALATINATE As elsewhere in Europe, Calvinism was the political and religious leaven within the Holy Roman Empire on the eve of the Thirty Years' War. Unrecognized as a legal religion by the Peace of Augsburg, it gained a strong foothold within the empire when Frederick III (r. 1559–1576), a devout convert to Calvinism, became elector Palatine (ruler within the Palatinate; see Map 12–3) and made it the official religion of his domain. Heidelberg became a German Geneva in the 1560s: both a great intellectual center of Calvinism and a staging area for Calvinist penetration into the empire. By 1609, Palatine Calvinists headed a Protestant defensive alliance that received outside support from Spain's sixteenth-century enemies: England, France, and the Netherlands.

The Lutherans came to fear the Calvinists almost as much as they did the Catholics. Palatine Calvinists seemed to the Lutherans directly to threaten the Peace of Augsburg—and hence the legal foundation of the Lutheran states—by their bold missionary forays into the empire. Also, outspoken Calvinist criticism of the doctrine of Christ's real presence in the Eucharist shocked the more religiously conservative Lutherans. The elector Palatine once expressed his disbelief in transubstantiation by publicly shredding the host and mocking it as a "fine God." To Luther-

ans, such religious disrespect and aggressiveness disgraced the Reformation as well as the elector.

MAXIMILIAN OF BAVARIA AND THE CATHOLIC LEAGUE If the Calvinists were active within the Holy Roman Empire, so also were their Catholic counterparts, the Jesuits. Staunchly Catholic Bavaria, supported by Spain, became militarily and ideologically for the Counter-Reformation what the Palatinate was for Protestantism. From there, the Jesuits launched successful missions throughout the empire, winning such major cities as Strasbourg and Osnabrück back to the Catholic fold by 1600. In 1609 Maximilian, duke of Bavaria, organized a Catholic League to counter a new Protestant alliance that had been formed in the same year under the leadership of the Calvinist Elector Palatine, Frederick IV (r. 1583–1610). When the league fielded a great army under the command of Count Johann

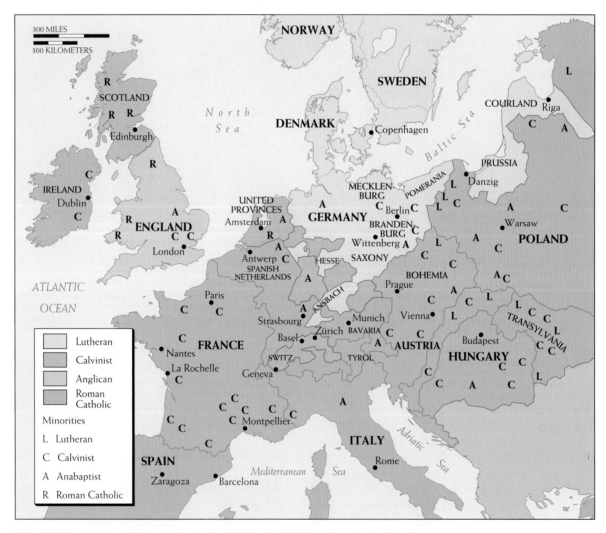

MAP 12–3 RELIGIOUS DIVISIONS ABOUT 1600 *By 1600, few could seriously expect Christians to return to a uniform religious allegiance. In Spain and southern Italy, Catholicism remained relatively unchallenged, but note the existence elsewhere of large religious minorities, both Catholic and Protestant.*

MAP 12–4 THE HOLY ROMAN EMPIRE ABOUT 1618 *On the eve of the Thirty Years' War, the Holy Roman Empire was politically and religiously fragmented, as revealed by this somewhat simplified map. Lutherans dominated the north and Catholics the south, while Calvinists controlled the United Provinces and the Palatinate and were important in Switzerland and Brandenburg.*

von Tilly, the stage was set, both internally and internationally, for the worst of the religious wars, the Thirty Years' War. (See Map 12–4.)

Four Periods of War

The war went through four distinguishable periods. During its course, it drew in every major western European nation—at least diplomatically and financially if not by direct military involvement. The four periods were the Bohemian (1618–1625); the Danish (1625–1629); the Swedish (1630–1635); and the Swedish–French (1635–1648).

THE BOHEMIAN PERIOD The war broke out in Bohemia after the ascent to the Bohemian throne in 1618 of the Habsburg Ferdinand, archduke of Styria, who was also in the line of succession to the imperial throne. Educated by the Jesuits and a fervent Catholic, Ferdinand was determined to restore the traditional faith to the eastern Habsburg lands (Austria, Bohemia, and Poland).

No sooner had Ferdinand become king of Bohemia than he revoked the religious freedoms of Bohemian Protestants. In force since 1575, these freedoms had even been recently broadened by Emperor Rudolf II (r. 1576–1612) in his Letter of Majesty in 1609. The Protestant nobility in Prague responded to Ferdi-

nand's act in May 1618 by literally throwing his regents out the window. The event has ever since been known as the "defenestration of Prague." (The three officials fell fifty feet into a dry moat that, fortunately, was padded with manure, which cushioned their fall and spared their lives.) In the following year Ferdinand became Holy Roman Emperor as Ferdinand II, by the unanimous vote of the seven electors. The Bohemians, however, defiantly deposed him in Prague and declared the Calvinist elector Palatine, Frederick V (r. 1616–1623), their overlord.

What had begun as a revolt of the Protestant nobility against an unpopular king of Bohemia thereafter escalated into an international war. Spain sent troops to Ferdinand, who found more immediate allies in Maximilian of Bavaria and the opportunistic Lutheran elector John George I of Saxony (r. 1611–1656), who saw a sure route to territorial gain by joining in an easy victory over the weaker elector Palatine. This was not the only time politics and greed would overshadow religion during the long conflict, although Lutheran–Calvinist religious animosity also overrode a common Protestantism.

Ferdinand's army under Tilly routed Frederick V's troops at the Battle of White Mountain in 1620. By 1622, Ferdinand had managed not only to subdue and re-Catholicize Bohemia, but to conquer the

The horror of the Thirty Years' War is captured in this painting by Jan Brueghel (1568–1625) and Sebastien Vranx (1573–1647). During the breaks in fighting, marauding armies ravaged the countryside, destroying villages and massacring the rural population.
Kunsthistorisches Museum, Vienna

Palatinate as well. Meanwhile, the duke of Bavaria pressed the conflict into northwestern Germany, laying claim to land as he went.

THE DANISH PERIOD   These events raised new fears that a reconquest and re-Catholicization of the empire now loomed, which was precisely Ferdinand II's design. The Lutheran King Christian IV (r. 1588–1648) of Denmark, who already held territory within the empire as the duke of Holstein, was eager to extend Danish influence over the coastal towns of the North Sea. Encouraged by the English, the French, and the Dutch, he picked up the Protestant banner of resistance, opening the Danish period of the conflict (1625–1629). Entering Germany with his army in 1626, he was, however, quickly humiliated by Maximilian and forced to retreat into Denmark.

As military success made Maximilian stronger and an untrustworthy ally, emperor Ferdinand sought a more pliant tool for his policies in Albrecht of Wallenstein (1583–1634), a powerful mercenary. Another opportunistic Protestant, Wallenstein had gained a great deal of territory by joining Ferdinand during the conquest of Bohemia. A brilliant and ruthless military strategist, Wallenstein carried Fer-

dinand's campaign into Denmark. By 1628 he commanded a crack army of more than 100,000 and also became a law unto himself, completely outside the emperor's control.

Wallenstein, however, had broken Protestant resistance so successfully that Ferdinand could issue the Edict of Restitution in 1629, a proclamation that dramatically reasserted the Catholic safeguards of the Peace of Augsburg (1555). It reaffirmed the illegality of Calvinism—a completely unrealistic move by 1629—and ordered the return of all church lands acquired by the Lutherans since 1552, an equally unrealistic mandate despite its legal basis. Compliance would have involved the return of no less than sixteen bishoprics and twenty-eight cities and towns to Catholic allegiance. The new edict struck panic in the hearts of Protestants and Habsburg opponents everywhere.

THE SWEDISH PERIOD   Gustavus Adolphus of Sweden (r. 1611–1632), a deeply pious king of a unified Lutheran nation, became the new leader of Protestant forces within the empire, opening the Swedish period of the war (1630–1635). He was bankrolled by two very interested bystanders: the French minister Cardinal Richelieu, whose foreign policy was to protect French interests by keeping Habsburg armies tied down in Germany, and the Dutch, who had not forgotten Spanish Habsburg domination in the sixteenth century. In alliance with the electors of Brandenburg and Saxony, the Swedish king won a smashing victory at Breitenfeld in 1630, one that so dramatically reversed the course of the war that it has been regarded as the most decisive engagement of the long conflict.

One of the reasons for the overwhelming Swedish victory at Breitenfeld was the military genius of Gustavus Adolphus. The Swedish king brought a new mobility to warfare by having both his infantry and his cavalry employ fire-and-charge tactics. At six deep, his infantry squares were smaller than the traditional ones, and he filled them with equal numbers of musketeers and pikemen. His cavalry also alternated pistol shots with charges with the sword. His artillery was lighter and more mobile in battle. Each unit of his army—infantry, cavalry, and artillery— had both defensive and offensive capability and could quickly change from one to the other.

Gustavus Adolphus died at the hands of Wallenstein's forces during the Battle of Lützen (November 1632)—a very costly engagement for both sides that created a brief standstill. Ferdinand had long been resentful of Wallenstein's independence, although he was the major factor in imperial success. In 1634, Ferdinand had Wallenstein assassinated. By that time, not only had Wallenstein served his purpose for the emperor, but, ever opportunistic, he was even trying openly to strike bargains with the Protestants for his services. The Wallenstein episode is a telling commentary on this war without honor. Despite the deep religious motivations, greed and political gain were the real forces at work in the Thirty Years' War. Even allies that owed one another their success were not above treating each other as mortal enemies.

In the Peace of Prague in 1635 the German Protestant states, led by Saxony, reached a compromise with Ferdinand. The Swedes, however, received continued support from France and the Netherlands. Desiring to maximize their investment in the war, they refused to join the agreement. Their resistance to settlement plunged the war into its fourth and most devastating phase.

THE SWEDISH–FRENCH PERIOD   The French openly entered the war in 1635, sending men and munitions as well as financial subsidies. After their entrance, the war dragged on for thirteen years, with French, Swedish, and Spanish soldiers looting the length and breadth of Germany—warring, it seemed, simply for the sake of warfare itself. The Germans, long weary of the devastation, were too disunited to repulse the foreign armies; they simply watched and suffered. By the time peace talks began in the Westphalian

cities of Münster and Osnabrück in 1644, an estimated one-third of the German population had died as a direct result of the war. It has been called the worst European catastrophe since the Black Death of the fourteenth century.

The Treaty of Westphalia

The Treaty of Westphalia in 1648 brought all hostilities within the Holy Roman Empire to an end. (See Map 12–5.) It rescinded Ferdinand's Edict of Restitution and firmly reasserted the major feature of the religious settlement of the Peace of Augsburg, with the ruler of each land again permitted to determine the religion there. The treaty also gave the Calvinists their long-sought legal recognition. The independence of the Swiss Confederacy and the United Provinces of Holland, long recognized in fact, was now proclaimed in law. And the treaty elevated Bavaria to the rank of an elector state. The provisions of the treaty made the German princes supreme over their principalities. Yet, as guarantors of the treaty, Sweden and France found many occasions to meddle in German affairs until the century's end, France to considerable territorial gain. Brandenburg–Prussia emerged as the most powerful northern German state. Because the treaty broadened the legal status of Protestantism, the pope opposed it altogether, but he had no power to prevent it.

France and Spain remained at war outside the empire until 1659, when French victories forced the humiliating Treaty of the Pyrenees on the Spanish. Thereafter France became Europe's dominant power, and the once vast Habsburg kingdom waned.

By confirming the territorial sovereignty of Germany's many political entities, the Treaty of Westphalia perpetuated German division and political weakness into the modern period. Only two German states attained any international significance during the seventeenth century: Austria and Brandenburg–Prussia. The petty regionalism within the empire also reflected on a small scale the drift of larger European politics. In the seventeenth century, distinctive nation–states, each with its own political, cultural, and religious identity, reached maturity and firmly established the competitive nationalism of the modern world.

In Perspective

Both religion and politics played major roles in each of the great conflicts of the Age of Religious Wars–the internal struggle in France, Spain's unsuccessful effort to subdue the Netherlands, England's successful

Swedish Dominions

Brandenburg Prussia

Spanish Monarchy

Austria Habsburg

Church Lands

Boundary of the Empire

MAP 12–5   *EUROPE IN 1648   At the end of the Thirty Years' War, Spain still had extensive possessions. Austria and Brandenburg–Prussia were prominent, the independence of the United Provinces and Switzerland was recognized, and Sweden held important river mouths in northern Germany.*

resistance of Spain, and the steady march of virtually every major European power through the hapless Holy Roman Empire during the first half of the seventeenth century. Parties and armies of different religious persuasions are visible in each conflict, and in each we also find a life-or-death political struggle.

The wars ended with the recognition of minority religious rights and a guarantee of the traditional boundaries of political sovereignty. In France, the Edict of Nantes (1598) brought peace by granting Huguenots basic religious and civil freedoms and by recognizing their towns and territories. With the departure of the Spanish, peace and sovereignty also came to the Netherlands, guaranteed initially by the Twelve Years' Truce (1609) and secured fully by the Peace of Westphalia (1648). The conflict between England and Spain ended with the removal of the Spanish threat to English sovereignty in politics and religion, which resulted from the execution of Mary, Queen of Scots (1587) and the English victory over the Armada (1588). In the Holy Roman Empire, peace came with the reaffirmation of the political principle of the Peace of Augsburg (1555), as the Peace of Westphalia brought the Thirty Years' War to an end by again recognizing the sovereignty of rulers within their lands and their right to determine the religious beliefs of their subjects. Europe at midcentury had real, if brief, peace.

REVIEW QUESTIONS

1. What part did politics play in the religious positions of the French leaders? How did the king (or his regent) decide which side to favor? What led to the infamous Saint Bartholomew's Day Massacre, and what did it achieve?
2. How did Spain achieve a position of dominance in the sixteenth century? What were its strengths and weaknesses as a nation? What were Philip II's goals? Which was he unable to achieve and why?
3. Henry of Navarre (Henry IV of France), Elizabeth I, and William of Orange were all *politiques*. Define the term and explain why it applies to these three rulers.
4. Discuss the background to the establishment of the Anglican church in England. What were the politics of Mary I? What was Elizabeth I's settlement, and how difficult was it to impose on all of England? Who were her detractors and what were their criticisms?
5. Why was the Thirty Years' War fought? To what extent did politics determine the outcome of the war? Discuss the Treaty of Westphalia in 1648. Could matters have been resolved without war?
6. It has been said that the Thirty Years' War is the outstanding example in European history of meaningless conflict. Evaluate this statement and provide specific reasons for or against it.

SUGGESTED READINGS

F. BRAUDEL, *The Mediterranean and the Mediterranean World in the Age of Philip the Second*, vols. 1 and 2 (1976). Widely acclaimed work of a French master historian.

N. Z. DAVIS, *Society and Culture in Early Modern France* (1975). Essays on popular culture.

R. DUNN, *The Age of Religious Wars, 1559–1689* (1979). Excellent brief survey of every major conflict.

J. H. ELLIOTT, *Europe Divided 1559–1598* (1968). Direct, lucid narrative account.

G. R. ELTON, *England under the Tudors* (1955). Masterly treatment.

J. H. FRANKLIN (ED. AND TRANS.), *Constitutionalism and Resistance in the Sixteenth Century: Three Treatises by Hotman, Beza, and Mornay* (1969). Three defenders of the right of people to resist tyranny.

P. GEYL, *The Revolt of the Netherlands, 1555–1609* (1958). The authoritative survey.

J. GUY, *Tudor England* (1990). The standard history and good synthesis of recent scholarship.

C. HAIGH, *Elizabeth I* (1988). Elizabeth portrayed as a magnificent politician and propagandist.

D. LOADES, *Mary Tudor* (1989). Authoritative and good storytelling.

J. LYNCH, *Spain under the Habsburgs I: 1516–1598* (1964). Political narrative.

G. MATTINGLY, *The Armada* (1959). A masterpiece and novellike in style.

J. E. NEALE, *The Age of Catherine de Médicis* (1962). Short, concise summary.

G. PARKER, *Europe in Crisis, 1598–1648* (1979). The big picture at a gallop.

J. G. RIDLEY, *John Knox* (1968). Large, detailed biography.

J. H. M. SALMON, *Society in Crisis: France in the Sixteenth Century* (1976). Standard narrative account.

A. SOMAN (ED.), *The Massacre of St. Bartholomew's Day: Reappraisals and Documents* (1974). Results of an international symposium on the anniversary of the massacre.

K. THOMAS, *Religion and the Decline of Magic* (1971). Provocative, much-acclaimed work focused on popular culture.

C. V. WEDGWOOD, *William the Silent* (1944). Excellent political biography of William of Orange.

J. WORMALD, *Mary, Queen of Scots: A Study in Failure* (1991). Mary portrayed as a queen who did not understand her country and was out of touch with the times.

Chapter 13

Charles I governed England from 1625 to 1649. His attempts to establish an absolutist government in matters of both church and state provoked clashes with the English Parliament and the outbreak of the Civil War in 1642. He was executed in 1649. Daniel Mytens/The Granger Collection

Paths to Constitutionalism and Absolutism:
England and France in the Seventeenth Century

Two Models of European Political Development

Constitutional Crisis and Settlement in Stuart England
James I
Charles I
Oliver Cromwell and the Puritan Republic
Charles II and the Restoration of the Monarchy
James II and Renewed Fears of a Catholic England
The "Glorious Revolution"

Rise of Absolute Monarchy in France
Henry IV and Sully
Louis XIII and Richelieu
Young Louis XIV and Mazarin

The Years of Louis's Personal Rule
King by Divine Right
Versailles
Suppression of the Jansenists
Government Geared for Warfare
Louis's Early Wars
Revocation of the Edict of Nantes
Louis's Later Wars
Louis XIV's Legacy

KEY TOPICS

- The factors behind the divergent political paths of England and France in the seventeenth century
- The conflict between Parliament and the king over taxation and religion in early Stuart England, the English Civil War, and the abolition of the monarchy
- The Restoration and the development of Parliament's supremacy over the monarchy after the "Glorious Revolution"
- The establishment of an absolutist monarchy in France under Louis XIV
- Religious policies of Louis XIV
- The wars of Louis XIV

During the seventeenth century, England and France moved in two very different political directions. By the close of the century, after decades of fierce civil war and religious conflict that pitted Parliament and monarch against each other, England had developed into a parliamentary monarchy with a policy of religious toleration. Parliament, composed of the House of Lords and the House of Commons, shared responsibility for government with the monarch. It met regularly, and the Commons, composed primarily of wealthy landed gentry, had to stand for election every three years. By contrast, France developed an absolutist, centralized form of government dominated by a monarchy that shared little power with any other national institutions. Its authority resided rather in a complex set of relationships with local nobility, guilds, and towns and in its ability to support the largest standing army in Europe. In the seventeenth century France also abandoned Henry IV's policy of religious toleration and proscribed all but the Roman Catholic church.

These English and French forms of government became models for other nations. The French model, termed absolutism in the nineteenth century, would be imitated by other monarchies across the continent during the eighteenth century. The English model would later inspire the political creed known in the nineteenth century as liberalism. Like all such political labels, these terms, although useful, can conceal considerable complexity. English "parliamentary monarchs" did not share all power with Parliament; they controlled the army, foreign policy, and much patronage. Likewise the "absolute monarchs" of France and their later imitators elsewhere in Europe were not truly absolute: laws, traditions, and many local institutions and customs limited their power.

Two Models of European Political Development

In the second half of the sixteenth century, changes in military organization, weapons, and tactics sharply increased the cost of warfare. Because traditional sources of revenue were inadequate to finance these growing costs—as well as the costs of government—monarchs sought new sources. Only monarchies that built a secure financial base which was not deeply dependent on the support of estates, diets, or assemblies of nobles achieved absolute rule. The French monarchy succeeded in this effort after midcentury, whereas the English monarchy failed. The paths to that success and failure led to the two models of government—absolutism in France and parliamentary monarchy in England—that shaped subsequent political development in Europe.

In their pursuit of adequate income, English monarchs of the seventeenth century threatened the local political interests and economic well-being of the country's nobility and others of great landed and commercial wealth. These politically active groups, invoking traditional English liberties in their defense, effectively resisted the monarchs' attempted intrusions throughout the century.

The experience of Louis XIV, the French king, was different. During the second half of the seventeenth century, he would make the French nobility dependent upon his goodwill and patronage. In turn, he would support their local influence and their place in a firm social hierarchy. But even the French king's dominance of the nobility was not complete. Louis accepted the authority of the noble-dominated *Parlement* of Paris to register royal decrees before they officially became law, and he permitted regional *parlements* to exercise considerable authority over local administration and taxation. Funds from taxes levied by the central monarchy found their way into many local pockets.

Religious factors also affected the political destinies of England and France. A strong Protestant religious movement known as Puritanism arose in England and actively opposed the Stuart monarchy. Puritanism represented a nonpolitical force that sought at first to limit and eventually to overturn the English monarchy. Louis XIV, in contrast, crushed the Protestant communities of France. He was generally supported in these efforts by Roman Catholics, who saw religious uniformity enforced by the monarchy working to their advantage.

There were also major institutional differences between the two countries. In Parliament, England possessed a political institution that had long bargained with the monarch over political issues. In the early seventeenth century, to be sure, Parliament did not meet regularly and was not the strong institution it would become by the close of the century. Nor was there anything certain or inevitable about the transformation it underwent over the course of the century. The institutional basis for it, however, was in place. Parliament was there and expected to be consulted from time to time. Its members—nobility and gentry—had experience organizing and speaking, writing legislation, and criticizing royal policies. Furthermore, the English had a legal and political tradition based on concepts of liberty to which members of Parliament and their supporters throughout the country could and did appeal in their conflict with the monarchy.

For all intents, France lacked a similarly strong tradition of broad liberties, representation, and bargaining between the monarchy and other national institutions. The Estates General had met from time to time to grant certain revenues to the monarch, but it played no role after the early seventeenth century. It met in 1614, but thereafter the monarchy was able to find other sources of income, and the Estates General was not called again until the eve of the French Revolution in 1789. Consequently, whatever political forces might have wished to oppose or limit the monarchy lacked both an institutional base from which to operate and a tradition of meetings during which the necessary political skills might have been developed.

Finally, personalities played an important role. During the first half of the century, France profited from the guidance of two of its most able statesmen: Cardinals Richelieu and Mazarin. Mazarin trained Louis XIV to be a hardworking, if not always wise, monarch. Louis drew strong and capable ministers about himself. The four Stuart monarchs of England, on the other hand, had trouble simply making people trust them. They did not always keep their word.

This elegant painting portays a very quiet London of the mid-1630s. During the next sixty years it would suffer wrenching political turmoil and the devastation of a great fire. Claude de Jongh (fl. 1615–1663), *The Thames at Westminster Stairs*, signed and dated 163(?1 or 7). Oil on panel, 18-1/4 × 31-1/2 in. (46.4 × 80 cm). B1973.1.31. Yale Center for British Art, Paul Mellon Collection

They acted on whim. They often displayed faulty judgment. In a political situation that demanded compromise, they rarely offered any. They offended significant groups of their subjects unnecessarily. In a nation that saw itself as strongly Protestant, they were suspected, sometimes accurately, of Catholic sympathies. Many of Charles's opponents in Parliament, of course, had flaws of their own, but the nature of the situation focused attention and criticism on the king.

In both England and France, the nobility and large landowners stood at the top of the social hierarchy and sought to protect their privileges and local interests. Important segments of the British nobility and landed classes came to distrust the Stuart monarchs, whom they believed sought to undermine their local political control and social standing. Parliamentary government was the result of the efforts of these English landed classes to protect their concerns and limit the power of the monarchy to interfere with life on the local level. The French nobility under Louis XIV, in contrast, eventually concluded that the best way to secure its own interests was to support his monarchy. He provided nobles with many forms of patronage, and he protected their tax exemptions, their wealth, and their local social standing.

The divergent developments of England and France in the seventeenth century would have surprised most people in 1600. It was not inevitable that the English monarchy would have to govern through Parliament or that the French monarchy would avoid dealing with

national political institutions that could significantly limit its authority. The Stuart kings of England certainly aspired to the autocracy Louis XIV achieved, and some English political philosophers eloquently defended the divine right of kings and absolute rule. At the beginning of the seventeenth century, the English monarchy was strong. Queen Elizabeth, after a reign of almost forty-five years, was much revered. Parliament met only when called to provide financial support to the monarch. France, on the other hand, was emerging from the turmoil of its religious wars. The strife of that conflict had torn the society asunder. The monarchy was relatively weak. Henry IV, who had become king in 1589, pursued a policy of religious toleration. The French nobles had significant military forces at their disposal and in the middle of the seventeenth century confronted the king with rebellion. These conditions would change dramatically in both nations by the late seventeenth century.

Constitutional Crisis and Settlement in Stuart England

James I

In 1603 without opposition or incident, James VI of Scotland (r. 1603–1625), the son of Mary Stuart, Queen of Scots, succeeded the childless Elizabeth as James I of England. His was a difficult situation. The elderly queen had been very popular and was totally identified with the nation. James was not well known, would never be popular, and, as a Scot, was an outsider. He inherited not only the crown, but also a large royal debt and a fiercely divided church—problems that his politically active subjects expected him to address. The new king strongly advocated the divine right of kings, a subject on which he had written a book—*A Trew Law of Free Monarchies*—in 1598. He expected to rule with a minimum of consultation beyond his own royal court.

James quickly managed to anger many of his new subjects, but he did not wholly alienate them. In this period, Parliament met only when the monarch summoned it, which James hoped to do rarely. Its chief business was to grant certain sources of income. The real value of these revenues, however, had been falling during the past half century, limiting their importance and thus the importance of Parliament to the king. To meet his needs, James developed other sources of income, largely by levying—solely on the authority of ill-defined privileges claimed to be attached to the office of king—new custom duties known as *impositions*. These were a version of the older customs duties known as *tonnage* and *poundage*. Members of Parliament resented these independent efforts to raise revenues as an affront to their authority over the royal purse, but they did not seek a serious confrontation. Rather, throughout James's reign, they wrangled and negotiated behind the scenes.

The religious problem also festered under James. Puritans within the Church of England had hoped that James's experience with the Scottish Presbyterian church and his own Protestant upbringing would incline him to favor their efforts to further the reformation of the English church. Since the days of Elizabeth, they had sought to eliminate elaborate religious ceremonies and replace the hierarchical episcopal system of church governance with a more representative Presbyterian form like that of the Calvinist churches on the Continent.

In January 1604, the Puritans had their first direct dealing with the new king. James responded in that month to a statement of Puritan grievances, the so-called Millenary Petition, at a special religious conference at Hampton Court. The political implications of the demands in this petition concerned him, and their tone offended him. To the dismay of the Puritans, he firmly declared his intention to maintain and even enhance the Anglican episcopacy. "A Scottish presbytery," he snorted, "agreeth as well with monarchy as God and the devil. No bishops, no king." James was not simply being arbitrary. Elizabeth also had not accommodated the Puritan demands. To have done so would have worsened the already existing strife within the Church of England.

Both sides left the conference with their suspicions of one another largely confirmed. The Hampton Court conference did, however, sow one fruitful seed: A commission was appointed to render a new translation of the Bible. That mission was fulfilled in 1611 with the publication of the eloquent authorized, or King James, version.

James also offended the Puritans with his opposition to their narrow view of human life and social activities. The Puritans believed that Sunday should be a day taken up largely with religious observances and little leisure or recreation. James believed that recreation and sports were innocent activities and good for his people. He also believed that Puritan narrowness discouraged Roman Catholics from converting to the Church of England. Consequently, in 1618 he issued the *Book of Sports*, which permitted games on Sunday for people who attended Church of England services. Many clergy refused to read his order from the pulpit, and he had to rescind it. (See "King James I Defends Popular Recreation Against the Puritans.")

It was during James's reign that some religious dissenters began to leave England. In 1620 Puritan separatists founded Plymouth Colony in Cape Cod Bay in North America, preferring flight from England to Anglican conformity. Later in the 1620s, a larger, better financed group of Puritans left England to found the Massachusetts Bay Colony. In each case, the colonists believed that reformation would or could not go far enough in England and that only in America could they worship freely and organize a truly reformed church.

Although James inherited a difficult situation, he also created special problems for himself. His court became a center of scandal and corruption. He governed by favorites, the most influential of whom was the duke of Buckingham, whom rumor made the king's homosexual lover. Buckingham controlled royal patronage and openly sold peerages and titles to the highest bidders—a practice that angered the nobility because it cheapened their rank. There had always been court favorites, but never before had a single person so controlled access to the monarch.

James's foreign policy also roused opposition. He regarded himself as a peacemaker. Peace reduced pressures on royal revenues and the need for larger debts. The less his demands for money, the less the king had to depend on the goodwill of Parliament. In 1604 he concluded a much-needed peace with Spain, England's chief adversary during the second half of the sixteenth century. His subjects viewed this peace as a sign of pro-Catholic sentiment. James further increased suspicions when he tried unsuccessfully to relax the penal laws against

King James I Defends Popular Recreation Against the Puritans

The English Puritans believed in strict observance of the Sabbath, disapproving any sports, games, or general social conviviality on Sunday. James I thought that these strictures prevented many Roman Catholics from joining the Church of England. In 1618, he ordered the clergy of the Church of England to read the Book of Sports *from their pulpits. In this declaration, he permitted people to engage in certain sports and games after church services. His hope was to allow innocent recreations on Sunday while encouraging people to attend the Church of England. Despite the king's good intentions, the order offended the Puritans. The clergy resisted his order and he had to withdraw it.*

❖ *What motives of state might have led James I to issue this declaration? How does he attempt to make it favorable to the Church of England? Why might so many clergy have refused to read this statement to their congregations?*

With our own ears we heard the general complaint of our people, that they were barred from all lawful recreation and exercise upon the Sunday's afternoon, after the ending of all divine service, which cannot but produce two evils: the one the hindering of the conversion of many [Roman Catholic subjects], whom their priests will take occasion hereby to vex, persuading them that no honest mirth or recreation is lawful or tolerable in our religion, which cannot but breed a great discontentment in our people's hearts, especially as such as are peradventure upon the point of turning [to the Church of England]: the other inconvenience is, that this prohibition barreth the common and meaner sort of people from using such exercises as may make their bodies more able for war, when we or our successors shall have occasion to use them; and in place thereof sets up filthy tipplings and drunkenness, and breeds a number of idle and discontented speeches in their ale-houses. For when shall the common people have leave to exercise, if not upon the Sundays and holy days, seeing they must apply their labor and win their living in all working days?...

[A]s for our good people's lawful recreation, our pleasure likewise is, that after the end of divine service our good people be not disturbed,...or discouraged from any lawful recreation, such as dancing, either men or women; archery for men, leaping, vaulting, or any other such harmless recreation, or from having of Hay-games, Whitsun-ales, and Morris-dances; and the setting up of May-poles and other sports therewith used;...but withal we do here account still as prohibited all unlawful games to be used upon Sundays only, as bear and bull-baitings...and at all times in the meaner sort of people by law prohibited, bowling.

And likewise we bar from this benefit and liberty all such known as recusants [Roman Catholics], either men or women, as will abstain from coming to church or divine service, being therefore unworthy of any lawful recreation after the said service, that will not first come to the church and serve God; prohibiting in like sort the said recreations to any that, though [they] conform in religion [i.e., members of the Church of England], are not present in the church at the service of God, before their going to the said recreations.

From Henry Bettenson, ed., *Documents of the Christian Church*, 2d ed. (London: Oxford University Press, 1963), pp. 400–403. By permission of Oxford University Press.

Catholics. The English had not forgotten the brutal reign of Mary Tudor and the acts of treason by Catholics during Elizabeth's reign. In 1618 James hesitated, not unwisely, to rush English troops to the aid of Protestants in Germany at the outbreak of the Thirty Years' War. This hesitation caused some to question his loyalty to the Anglican Church. These suspicions increased when he tried to arrange a marriage between his son Charles and the Spanish *Infanta* (the daughter of the king of Spain). In the king's last years, as his health failed and the reins of government passed increasingly to his son Charles and to Buckingham, parliamentary opposition and Protestant sentiment combined to undo his pro-Spanish foreign policy. In 1624, shortly before James's death, England entered a continental war against Spain largely in response to the pressures of members of Parliament.

Parliament Presents Charles I with the Petition of Right

After becoming monarch in 1625, Charles I (1625–1649) imposed unparliamentary taxes, coerced freemen, and quartered troops in transit in private homes. These actions deeply offended Parliament, which, in 1628, refused to grant him any funds until he rescinded those practices by recognizing the Petition of Right (June 1628). The Petition constituted a general catalog of the offenses associated with the exercise of arbitrary royal authority.

❖ *What limits does the Petition attempt to place on royal taxation? How did the Petition criticize arbitrary arrest? Why was the quartering of soldiers in private homes so offensive?*

[The Lords Spirit and Temporal, and commons in Parliament assembled] do humbly pray your Most Excellent Majesty, that no man hereafter be compelled to make or yield any gift, loan, benevolence, tax, or such like charge, without common consent by Act of parliament; and that none be called to make answer, to take such oath, or to give attendance, or be confined, or otherwise molested or disquieted concerning the same, or for refusal thereof; and that no freeman, in any such manner as in before-mentioned, be imprisoned or detained; and that your Majesty will be pleased to remove the said soldiers and mariners [who have been quartered in private homes], and that your people may not be so burdened in time to come; and that the foresaid commissions for proceeding by martial law, may be revoked and annulled; and that hereafter no commissions of like nature may issue forth to any person or persons whatsoever, to be executed as aforesaid, lest by colour of them any of your Majesty's subjects be destroyed or put to death, contrary to the laws and franchise of the land.

All which they most humble pray of your Most Excellent Majesty, as their rights and liberties according to the laws and statues of this realm.

The King's Reply: The King willeth that right be done according to the laws and customs of the realm; and that the statues be put in due execution, that his subjects may have no cause to complain of any wrong or oppressions, contrary to their just rights and liberties, to the preservation whereof he holds himself as well obliged as of his prerogative.

From *The Constitutional Documents of the Puritan Revolution*, ed. by Samuel R. Gardiner (Oxford: Clarendon Press, 1889), pp. 4–5.

Charles I

Parliament had favored the war with Spain, but would not adequately finance it because its members distrusted Buckingham. Unable to gain adequate funds from Parliament, Charles I (r. 1625– 1649), like his father, resorted to extraparliamentary measures. He levied new tariffs and duties and attempted to collect discontinued taxes. He even subjected the English people to a so-called forced loan (a tax theoretically to be repaid), imprisoning those who refused to pay. The government quartered troops in transit to war zones in private homes. All these actions intruded on life at the local level and challenged the power of the local nobles and landowners to control their districts.

When Parliament met in 1628, its members were furious. Taxes were being illegally collected for a war that was going badly for England and that now, through royal blundering, involved France as well as Spain. Parliament expressed its displeasure by making the king's request for new funds conditional on his recognition of the Petition of Right. (See "Parliament Presents Charles I with the Petition of Right.") This important declaration of constitutional freedom required that henceforth there should be no forced loans or taxation without the consent of Parliament, that no freeman should be imprisoned without due cause, and that troops should not be billeted in private homes. It was thus an expression of resentment and resistance to the intrusion of the monarchy on the local level. Though Charles agreed to the petition, there was little confidence that he would keep his word.

YEARS OF PERSONAL RULE   In August 1628, Charles's chief minister, Buckingham, with whom Parliament had been in open dispute since 1626, was assassinated. His death, while sweet to many, did not resolve the hostility between the king and Parliament. In January 1629, Parliament further underscored its resolve to limit royal prerogative. It declared that religious innovations leading to "popery"—the term used to condemn Charles's high-church policies—and the levying of taxes without parliamentary consent were acts of treason. Perceiving that things were getting out of hand, Charles promptly dissolved Parliament and did not call it again until 1640, when war with Scotland forced him to do so.

To conserve his limited resources, Charles made peace with France in 1629 and Spain in 1630. This policy again roused fears among some of his subjects that he was too friendly to Roman Catholic powers. The French and Roman Catholic background of Charles's wife furthered these suspicions. Part of her marriage contract permitted her to hear mass daily at the English court. Charles's attitude toward the Church of England also raised suspicions. He supported a group within the church, known as Arminians, who rejected many Puritan doctrines and favored elaborate, high-church practices. The Puritans were convinced these practices would bring a return to Roman Catholicism.

To allow Charles to rule without renegotiating financial arrangements with Parliament, his chief minister, Thomas Wentworth (after 1640, earl of Strafford), instituted a policy known as *thorough*. This policy imposed strict efficiency and administrative centralization in government. Its goal was absolute royal control of England. Its success depended on the king's ability to operate independently of Parliament, which no law required him to summon.

Charles's ministers exploited every legal fund-raising device. They enforced previously neglected laws and extended existing taxes into new areas. For example, starting in 1634, they gradually extended inland to the whole of England a tax called *ship money*, normally levied only on coastal areas to pay for naval protection. A great landowner named John Hampden mounted a legal challenge to the extension of this tax. Although the king prevailed in what was a close legal contest, his victory was costly. It deepened the animosity toward him among the powerful landowners, who would elect and sit in Parliament should he need to summon it.

During these years of personal rule, Charles surrounded himself with an elaborate court and patronized some of the greatest artists of the day. Like his father, he sold noble titles and knighthoods, lessening their value and the social exclusiveness conferred on those who already possessed them. Nobles and great landowners feared that the growth of the court, the king's relentless pursuit of revenue, and the inflation of titles and honors would reduce their local influence and social standing. They also feared that the monarch might actually succeed in governing without ever again calling Parliament into session.

Charles might very well have ruled indefinitely without Parliament had not his religious policies provoked war with Scotland. James I had allowed a wide variety of religious observances in England, Scotland, and Ireland. Charles, by contrast, hoped to impose religious conformity at least within England and Scotland. William Laud (1573–1645), who was first Charles's religious advisor and, after 1633, archbishop of Canterbury, held a high-church view of Anglicanism. He favored powerful bishops, elaborate liturgy, and personal religious observance and devotion rather than the preaching and listening favored by the Puritans. As a member of the Court of High Commission, Laud had already radicalized the English Puritans by denying them the right to publish and preach. In 1637 Charles and Laud, against the opposition of the English Puritans as well as the Scots, tried to impose on Scotland the English episcopal system and a prayerbook almost identical to the Anglican *Book of Common Prayer*.

The Scots rebelled, and Charles, with insufficient resources for a war, was forced to call Parliament. The members of Parliament opposed his policies almost as much as they wanted to crush the rebellion. Led by John Pym (1584–1643), they refused even to consider funds for war until the king agreed to redress a long list of political and religious grievances. The king, in response, immediately dissolved Parliament—hence its name, the Short Parliament (April–May 1640). When the Presbyterian Scots invaded England and defeated an English army at the Battle of Newburn in the summer of 1640, Charles reconvened Parliament, this time on its terms, for a long and most fateful duration.

THE LONG PARLIAMENT The landowners and the merchant classes represented by Parliament had resented the king's financial measures and paternalistic rule for some time. The Puritans in Parliament resented his religious policies and deeply distrusted the influence of the Roman Catholic queen. The Long Parliament (1640–1660) thus acted with widespread support and general unanimity when it convened in November 1640.

The House of Commons impeached both the earl of Strafford and Archbishop Laud. Disgraced and convicted by a parliamentary bill of attainder (a judgment of treason entailing loss of civil rights), Stafford was executed in 1641. Laud was imprisoned and also later executed (1645). Parliament abolished the Court of Star Chamber and the Court of High Commission, royal instruments of political and religious *thorough*, respectively. The levying of new taxes without the consent of Parliament and the inland extension of *ship money* now became illegal. Finally, Parliament resolved that no more than three years should elapse between its meetings and that it could not be dissolved without its own consent. Parliament was determined that neither Charles nor any future English king could again govern without consulting it.

Despite its cohesion on these initial actions, Parliament was divided over the precise direction to take on religious reform. Both moderate Puritans (the Presbyterians) and more extreme Puritans (the Independents) wanted the complete abolition of the episcopal system and the *Book of Common Prayer*. The majority Presbyterians sought to reshape England religiously along Calvinist lines, with local congregations subject to higher representative governing bodies (presbyteries). Independents wanted a much more fully decentralized church with every congregation as its own final authority. Finally, many conservatives in both houses of Parliament were determined to preserve the English church in its current form. Their numbers fell dramatically after 1642, however, when many of them left the House of Commons with the outbreak of civil war.

These divisions further intensified in October 1641, when a rebellion erupted in Ireland and Parliament was asked to raise funds for an army to suppress it. Pym and his followers, loudly reminding the House of Commons of the king's past behavior, argued that Charles could not be trusted with an army and that Parliament should become the commander-in-chief of English armed forces. Parliamentary conservatives, on the other hand, were appalled by such a bold departure from tradition.

ERUPTION OF CIVIL WAR Charles saw the division within Parliament as a chance to reassert his power. On December 1, 1641, Parliament presented him with the "Grand Remonstrance," a more-than-200-article summary of popular and parliamentary grievances against the crown. In January 1642, he invaded Parliament with his soldiers. He intended to arrest Pym and the other leaders, but they had been forewarned and managed to escape. The king then withdrew from London and began to raise an army. Shocked by his action, a majority of the House of Commons passed the Militia Ordinance, which gave Parliament authority to raise an army of its own. The die was now cast. For the next four years (1642–1646), civil war engulfed England.

Charles assembled his forces at Nottingham, and the war began in August. It was fought over two main issues:

- Would an absolute monarchy or a parliamentary government rule England?

- Would English religion be controlled by the king's bishops and conform to high Anglican practice or adopt a decentralized, Presbyterian system of church governance?

Charles's supporters, known as Cavaliers, were located in the northwestern half of England. The parliamentary opposition, known as Roundheads because of their close-cropped hair, had its stronghold in the southeastern half of the country. Supporters of both sides included nobility, gentry, and townspeople. The chief factor distinguishing them was religion; the Puritans tended to favor Parliament.

Oliver Cromwell and the Puritan Republic

Two factors led finally to Parliament's victory. The first was an alliance with Scotland consummated in 1643 when John Pym persuaded Parliament to accept the terms of the Solemn League and Covenant, an

Oliver Cromwell's New Model Army defeated the royalists in the English Civil War. After the execution of Charles I in 1649, Cromwell dominated the short-lived English republic, conquered Ireland and Scotland, and ruled as Lord Protector from 1653 until his death in 1658. Stock Montage, Inc./Historical Pictures Collection agreement that committed Parliament, with the Scots, to a Presbyterian system of church government. For the Scots, this policy meant that they would never again be confronted with an attempt to impose the English prayerbook on their religious services. The second factor was the reorganization of the parliamentary army under Oliver Cromwell (1599–1658), a middle-aged country squire of iron discipline and strong Independent religious sentiment. Cromwell and his "godly men" favored neither the episcopal system of the king nor the pure Presbyterian system of the Solemn League and Covenant. They were willing to tolerate an established majority church, but only if it also permitted Protestant dissenters to worship outside it. (See "John Milton Defends Freedom to Print Books.")

The allies won the Battle of Marston Moor in 1644, the largest engagement of the war. In June 1645, Cromwell's newly reorganized forces, known as the New Model Army, fighting with disciplined fanaticism, won a decisive victory over the king at Naseby. (See Map 13–1.)

Defeated militarily, Charles tried again to take advantage of divisions within Parliament, this time seeking to win the Presbyterians and the Scots over to the royalist side. But Cromwell and his army firmly foiled him. In December 1648, Colonel Thomas Pride physically barred the Presbyterians, who made up a majority of Parliament, from taking their seats. After "Pride's Purge," only a "rump" of fewer than fifty members remained. Though small in numbers, this Independent Rump Parliament did not hesitate to use its power. On January 30, 1649, after a trial by a special court, the Rump Parliament executed Charles as a public criminal and thereafter abolished the monarchy, the House of Lords, and the Anglican Church. What had begun as a civil war had at this point become a revolution.

From 1649 to 1660, England became officially a Puritan republic, although for much of that time it was dominated by Cromwell. During this period, Cromwell's army conquered Ireland and Scotland, creating the single political entity of Great Britain. Cromwell, however, was a military man and no politician. He was increasingly frustrated by what seemed to him to be pettiness and dawdling on the part of Parliament. When, in 1653, the House of Commons entertained a motion to disband his expensive army of 50,000, Cromwell responded by marching in and disbanding Parliament. He ruled thereafter as Lord Protector.

This military dictatorship, however, proved no more effective than Charles's rule had been and became just as harsh and hated. Cromwell's great army and foreign adventures inflated his budget to

MAP 13–1   THE ENGLISH CIVIL WAR. *This map shows the rapid deterioration of the royalist position in 1645.*

three times that of Charles's. Near chaos reigned in many places, and commerce suffered throughout England. Cromwell was as intolerant of Anglicans as Charles had been of Puritans. People deeply resented his Puritan prohibitions of drunkenness, theatergoing, and dancing. Political liberty vanished in the name of religious liberty.

Cromwell's challenge had been to devise a political structure to replace that of monarch and Parliament. He tried various arrangements, none of which worked. He quarreled with the various Parliaments that were elected while he was lord protector. By the time of his death in 1658, most of the English were ready to end the Puritan religious experiment and the republican political experiment and return to their traditional institutions of government. Negotiations between leaders of the

The bleeding head of Charles I is exhibited to the crowd after his execution on a cold day in January 1649. The contemporary Dutch artist also professed to see the immediate ascension of Charles's soul to heaven. In fact, many saw the king as a martyr.
An Eyewitness Representation of the Execution of King Charles I (1600–49) of England, 1649 (oil on canvas) by Weesop (fl. 1649–49). Private Collection/Bridgeman Art Library, London

army and the exiled Charles II (r. 1660–1685), son of Charles I, led to the restoration of the Stuart monarchy in 1660.

Charles II and the Restoration of the Monarchy

Charles II returned to England amid great rejoicing. A man of considerable charm and political skill, Charles set a refreshing new tone after eleven years of somber Puritanism. His restoration returned England to the status quo of 1642, with a hereditary monarch once again on the throne, no legal requirement that he summon Parliament regularly, and the Anglican Church, with its bishops and prayer book, supreme in religion.

The king, however, had secret Catholic sympathies and favored a policy of religious toleration. He wanted to allow all those outside the Church of England, Catholics as well as Puritans, to worship freely so long as they remained loyal to the throne. But in Parliament, even the ultraroyalist Anglicans did not believe that patriotism and religion could be separated. Between 1661 and 1665, through a series of laws known as the Clarendon Code, Parliament excluded Roman Catholics, Presbyterians, and Independents from the religious and political life of the nation. These laws imposed penalties for

attending non-Anglican worship services, required strict adherence to the *Book of Common Prayer* and the *Thirty-Nine Articles*, and demanded oaths of allegiance to the Church of England from all persons serving in local government.

At the time of the Restoration, England, again as under Cromwell in 1651, adopted navigation acts that required all imports to be carried either in English ships or in ships registered to the country from which the cargo originated. Dutch ships carried cargo from many nations, and such laws struck directly at Dutch dominance in the shipping industry. A series of naval wars between England and Holland ensued. Charles also attempted to tighten his grasp on the rich English colonies in North America and the Caribbean, many of which had been settled and developed by separatists who desired independence from English rule.

Although Parliament strongly supported the monarchy, Charles, following the pattern of his predecessors, required greater revenues than Parliament appropriated. These he obtained in part by increased customs duties. Because England and France were both at war with Holland, he also received aid from France. In 1670, England and France formally allied against the Dutch in the Treaty of Dover. In a secret portion of this treaty, Charles pledged to announce his conversion to Catholicism as soon as conditions in England permitted. In return for this announcement (which was never made), Louis XIV of France promised to pay a substantial subsidy to England.

In an attempt to unite the English people behind the war with Holland, and as a sign of good faith to Louis XIV, Charles issued the Declaration of Indulgence in 1672. This document suspended all laws against Roman Catholics and Protestant nonconformists. But again, the conservative Parliament proved less generous than the king and refused to grant money for the war until Charles rescinded the measure. After he did, Parliament passed the Test Act, which required all officials of the crown, civil and military, to swear an oath against the doctrine of transubstantiation—a requirement that no loyal Roman Catholic could honestly meet.

Parliament had aimed the Test Act largely at the king's brother, James, duke of York, heir to the throne and a recent devout convert to Catholicism. In 1678 a notorious liar named Titus Oates swore before a magistrate that Charles's Catholic wife, through her physician, was plotting with Jesuits and Irishmen to kill the king so that James could assume the throne. The matter was taken before Parliament, where Oates was believed. In the ensuing hysteria, known as the Popish Plot, several people were tried and executed. Riding the crest of anti-Catholic sentiment and led by the earl of Shaftesbury (1621–1683), opposition members of Parliament, called Whigs, made an impressive, but unsuccessful, effort to enact a bill excluding James from succession to the throne.

More suspicious than ever of Parliament, Charles II turned again to increased customs duties and the assistance of Louis XIV for extra income. By these means, he was able to rule from 1681 to 1685 without recalling Parliament. In those years, Charles suppressed much of his opposition. He drove the

---

John Milton Defends Freedom to Print Books

Certain Puritans were as concerned about resisting potential tyranny from Parliament as from the monarchy. During the English Civil War, the Parliament passed a very strict censorship measure. In "Areopagitica" (1644), John Milton, later the author of Paradise Lost *(1667), attacked this law and contributed one of the major defenses of the freedom of the press in the history of Western culture. In the passage that follows, he compares the life of a book with the life of a human being.*

❖ *Why does Milton think that it may be more dangerous and harmful to attack a book than to attack a person? Was life cheaper and intelligence rarer in his time? Does he have particular kinds of books in mind? What can a book do for society that people cannot?*

I deny not but that it is of greatest concern in the Church and Commonwealth to have a vigilant eye how books demean themselves as well as men; and thereafter to confine, imprison, and do sharpest justice on them as [if they were criminals]; for books are not absolutely dead things, but do contain a progeny of life in them to be as active as that soul was whose progeny they are; nay, they do preserve as in a vial the purest efficacy and extraction of that living intellect that bred them....He who kills a man kills a reasonable creature, God's Image; but he who destroys a good book, kills reason itself, kills the Image of God, as it were....Many a man lives [as] a burden to the Earth; but a good book is the precious lifeblood of a master spirit, embalmed and treasured up on purpose to a life beyond life. It is true, no age can restore a life, whereof, perhaps there is no great loss; and revolutions of ages do not oft recover the loss of a rejected truth, for the want of which whole nations fare the worse. We should be wary, therefore, what persecution we raise against the living labours of public men, how we spill that seasoned life of man preserved and stored up in books; since we see a kind of homicide may be thus committed, sometimes a martyrdom, and if it extends to the whole impression, a kind of massacre, whereof the execution ends not in the slaying of an elemental life, but strikes at that ethereal...essence, the breath of reason itself; slays an immortality rather than a life.

From J. A. St. John, ed., *The Prose Works of John Milton* (London: H. G. Bohn, 1843–1853), 2:8–9.

Charles II (r. 1660–1685) was a person of considerable charm and political skill. Here he is portrayed as the founder of the Royal Society. Robert Harding Picture Library

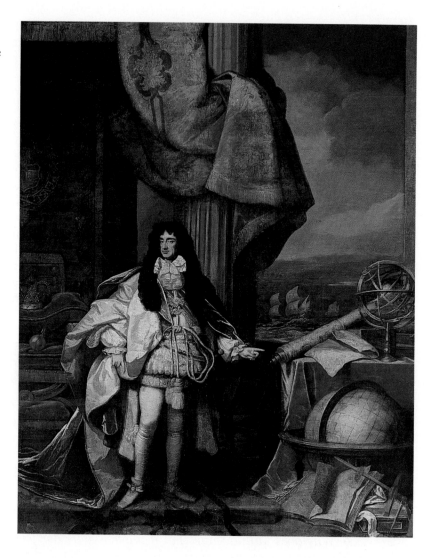

James II and Renewed Fears of a Catholic England

earl of Shaftesbury into exile, executed several Whig leaders for treason, and bullied local corporations into electing members of Parliament who were submissive to the royal will. When Charles died in 1685 (after a deathbed conversion to Catholicism), he left James the prospect of a Parliament filled with royal friends.

James II (r. 1685–1688) did not know how to make the most of a good thing. He alienated Parliament by insisting on the repeal of the Test Act. When Parliament balked, he dissolved it and proceeded openly to appoint known Catholics to high positions in both his court and the army. In 1687 he issued the Declaration of Indulgence, which suspended all religious tests and permitted free worship. Local candidates for Parliament who opposed the declaration were removed from their offices by the king's soldiers and were replaced by

Catholics. In June 1688, James went so far as to imprison seven Anglican bishops who had refused to publicize his suspension of laws against Catholics. Each of these actions represented a direct royal attack on the local power and authority of nobles, landowners, the church, and other corporate bodies whose members believed that they possessed particular legal privileges. James was attacking English liberty and challenging all manner of social privileges and influence.

Under the guise of a policy of enlightened toleration, James was actually seeking to subject all English institutions to the power of the monarchy. His goal was absolutism, and even conservative, loyalist Tories, as the royal supporters were called, could not abide this policy. The English feared, with reason, that James planned to imitate the religious intolerance of Louis XIV, who had, in 1685, revoked the Edict of Nantes (which had protected French Protestants for almost a century) and imposed Catholicism on the entire nation, using his dragoons against those who protested or resisted.

James soon faced united opposition. When his Catholic second wife gave birth to a son and Catholic male heir to the throne on June 20, 1688, opposition turned to action. The English had hoped that James would die without a male heir so that the throne would pass to Mary, his Protestant eldest daughter. Mary was the wife of William III of Orange, *stadtholder* of the Netherlands, great-grandson of William the Silent, and the leader of European opposition to Louis XIV's imperial designs. Within days of the birth of James's son, Whig and Tory members of Parliament formed a coalition and invited Orange to invade England to preserve "traditional liberties," that is, the Anglican Church and parliamentary government.

The "Glorious Revolution"

William of Orange arrived with his army in November 1688 and was received without opposition by the English people. In the face of sure defeat, James fled to France and the protection of Louis XIV. With James gone, Parliament declared the throne vacant and, on its own authority in 1689, proclaimed William and Mary the new monarchs, completing the successful bloodless "Glorious Revolution." William and Mary, in turn, recognized a Bill of Rights that limited the powers of the monarchy and guaranteed the civil liberties of the English privileged classes. Henceforth, England's monarchs would be subject to law and would rule by

England in the Seventeenth Century	
1603	James VI of Scotland becomes James I of England
1604	Hampton Court conference
1611	Publication of the authorized, or King James, version of the English Bible
1625	Charles I becomes English monarch
1628	Petition of Right
1629	Charles I dissolves Parliament and embarks on eleven years of personal rule
1640	April–May, Short Parliament November, Long Parliament convenes
1641	Grand Remonstrance
1642	Outbreak of the Civil War
1645	Charles I defeated at Naseby
1648	Pride's Purge
1649	Charles I executed
1649–1660	Various attempts at a Puritan Commonwealth
1660	Charles II restored to the English throne
1670	Secret Treaty of Dover between France and England
1672	Parliament passes the Test Act
1678	Popish Plot
1685	James II becomes king of England
1688	"Glorious Revolution"
1689	William and Mary proclaimed English monarchs
1701	Acts of Settlement provides for Hanoverian succession
1702–1715	Reign of Queen Anne, the last of the Stuarts

William and Mary became the monarchs of England in 1689. Their accession brought England's economic and military resources into the balance against the France of Louis XIV. Robert Harding Picture Library

the consent of Parliament, which was to be called into session every three years. The Bill of Rights also pointedly prohibited Roman Catholics from occupying the English throne. The Toleration Act of 1689 permitted worship by all Protestants but outlawed Roman Catholics and anti-Trinitarians (those who denied the Christian doctrine of the Trinity).

The measure closing this century of strife was the Act of Settlement in 1701. This bill provided for the English crown to go to the Protestant House of Hanover in Germany if none of the children of Queen Anne (r. 1702–1714), the second daughter of James II and the last of the Stuart monarchs, was alive at her death. She outlived all of her children, so in 1714, the elector of Hanover became King George I of England, the third foreign monarch to occupy the English throne in just over a century.

The Glorious Revolution of 1688 established a framework of government by and for the governed that seemed to bear out the arguments of John Locke's *Second Treatise of Government* (1690). In this work, Locke described the relationship of a king and his people as a bilateral contract. If the king broke that contract, the people, by whom Locke meant the privileged and powerful, had the right to depose him. Locke had written the essay before the revolution, but it came to be read as a justification for it. Although neither in fact nor in theory a "popular" revolution such as would occur in America and France a hundred years later, the Glorious Revolution did establish in England a permanent check on monarchical power by the classes represented in Parliament. At the same time, as will be seen in Chapter 15, in its wake the English government had achieved a secure financial base that would allow it to pursue a century of warfare.

Rise of Absolute Monarchy in France

Seventeenth-century France, in contrast to England, saw both discontent among the nobility and religious pluralism smothered by the absolute monarchy and the closed Catholic state of Louis XIV (r. 1643–1715). An aggressive ruler who sought glory (*la gloire*) in foreign wars, Louis XIV subjected his subjects at home to "one king, one law, one faith."

Historians once portrayed Louis XIV's reign as a time when the rising central monarchy exerted far-reaching, direct control of the nation at all levels. A somewhat different picture has now emerged. Louis's predecessors and their chief ministers, in the half century before his reign, had already tried to impose direct rule, arousing discontent and, at midcentury, a rebellion among the nobility. Louis's genius was to make the monarchy the most important and powerful political institution in France while also assuring the nobles and other wealthy groups of their social standing and political and social influence on the local level. Rather than destroying existing local social and political institutions, Louis largely worked through them. Once nobles understood that the king would support their local authority, they supported his central royal authority. In other words, the king and the nobles came to recognize that they needed each other. Nevertheless, Louis made it clear to all concerned that he was the senior partner in the relationship.

Louis's royal predecessors laid the institutional foundations for absolute monarchy and also taught him certain practices to avoid. Just as the emergence of a strong Parliament was not inevitable in England, neither was the emergence of an absolute monarchy in France.

Henry IV and Sully

Coming to the throne after the French wars of religion, Henry of Navarre who became Henry IV (r. 1589–1610; see Chapter 12) sought to curtail the privileges of the French nobility. His targets were the provincial governors and the regional *parlements*, especially the powerful *Parlement* of Paris, where a divisive spirit lived on. Here were to be found the old privileged groups, tax-exempt magnates who were largely preoccupied with protecting their self-interests. During the subsequent reign of Louis XIII (r. 1610–1643), royal civil servants known as *intendants* subjected these privileged groups to stricter supervision, implementing the king's will with some success in the provinces. An important function of the *intendants* was to prevent abuses from the sale of royal offices that conferred the right to collect revenues, sell licenses, or carry out other remunerative forms of administration. It was usually nobles who acquired these lucrative offices, which was one reason for their ongoing influence.

After decades of religious and civil war, an economy more amenable to governmental regulation emerged during Henry IV's reign. Henry and his finance minister, the duke of Sully (1560–1641), established government monopolies on gunpowder, mines, and salt, preparing the way for the mercantilist policies of Louis XIV and his minister, Colbert. They began a canal system to link the Atlantic and the Mediterranean by joining the Saône, the Loire, the Seine, and the Meuse rivers. They introduced the royal *corvée*, a labor tax that created a national force of drafted workers who were employed to improve roads and the conditions of internal travel. Sully even dreamed of organizing the whole of Europe politically and commercially into a kind of common market.

Louis XIII and Richelieu

Henry IV was assassinated in 1610, and the following year Sully retired. Because Henry's son and successor, Louis XIII, was only nine years old at his father's death, the task of governing fell to the queen mother, Marie de Médicis (d. 1642). Finding herself in a vulnerable position, she sought security abroad by signing a ten-year mutual defense pact with France's archrival Spain in the Treaty of Fontainebleau (1611). This alliance also arranged for the later marriage of Louis XIII to the Spanish *Infanta*, as well as for the marriage of the queen's daughter Elizabeth to the heir to the Spanish throne. The queen sought internal security against pressures from the French nobility by

Cardinal Richelieu laid the foundations for the political ascendancy of the French monarchy. Cardinal Richelieu by Philippe de Champaigne. The National Gallery, London

promoting the career of Cardinal Richelieu (1585–1642) as the king's chief adviser. Richelieu, loyal and shrewd, aspired to make France a supreme European power. He, more than any other person, was the secret of French success in the first half of the seventeenth century.

An apparently devout Catholic who also believed that the church best served both his own ambition and the welfare of France, Richelieu pursued a strongly anti-Habsburg policy. Although he supported the Spanish alliance of the queen and Catholic religious unity within France, he was determined to contain Spanish power and influence, even when that meant aiding and abetting Protestant Europe. It is an indication both of Richelieu's awkward political situation and of his diplomatic agility that he could, in 1631, pledge funds to the Protestant army of Gustavus Adolphus, the king of Sweden, while also insisting that Catholic Bavaria be spared from attack and that Catholics in conquered countries be permitted to practice their religion. One measure of the success of Richelieu's foreign policies can be seen in France's substantial gains in land and political influence when the Treaty of Westphalia (1648) ended hostilities in the Holy Roman Empire (see Chapter 12) and the Treaty of the Pyrenees (1659) sealed peace with Spain.

At home, Richelieu pursued centralizing policies utterly without qualm. Supported by the king, who let his chief minister make most decisions of state, Richelieu stepped up the campaign against separatist provincial governors and parlements. He made it clear that there was only one law, that of the king, and none could stand above it. When disobedient nobles defied his edicts, they were imprisoned and even executed. Such treatment of the nobility won Richelieu much enmity, even from the queen mother, who, unlike Richelieu, was not always willing to place the larger interests of the state above the pleasure of favorite nobles.

Richelieu started the campaign against the Huguenots that would end in 1685 with Louis XIV's revocation of the Edict of Nantes. Royal armies conquered major Huguenot cities in 1629. The subsequent Peace of Alais (1629) truncated the Edict of Nantes by denying Protestants the right to maintain garrisoned cities, separate political organizations, and independent law courts. Only Richelieu's foreign policy, which involved France in ties with Protestant powers, prevented the earlier implementation of the policy of extreme intolerance that marked the reign of Louis XIV. In the same year that Richelieu rescinded the independent political status of the Huguenots in the Peace of Alais, he also entered negotiations to make Gustavus Adolphus his counterweight to the expansion of Habsburg power within the Holy Roman Empire. By 1635, the Catholic soldiers of France were fighting openly with Swedish Lutherans against the emperor's army in the final phase of the Thirty Years' War. (See Chapter 12.)

Richelieu employed the arts and the printing press to defend his actions and to indoctrinate the French people in the meaning of *raison d'état* ("reason of state"). This also set a precedent for Louis XIV, who made elaborate use of royal propaganda and spectacle to assert and enhance his power.

Young Louis XIV and Mazarin

Although Richelieu helped lay the foundations for a much expanded royal authority, his immediate legacy was strong resentment of the monarchy among the French nobility and wealthy commercial groups. The crown's steady multiplication of royal offices, its replacement of local authorities by "state" agents, and its reduction of local sources of patronage undermined the traditional position of the privileged groups in French society. Among those affected were officers of the crown in the law courts and other royal institutions.

When Louis XIII died in 1643, Louis XIV was only five years old. During his minority, the queen mother, Anne of Austria (d. 1666), placed the reins of govern-

This medallion shows Anne of Austria, the wife of Louis XIII, with her son, Louis XIV. She wisely placed political authority in the hands of Cardinal Mazarin, who prepared Louis to govern France. Giraudon/Art Resource, N.Y.

ment in the hands of Cardinal Mazarin (1602–1661), who continued Richelieu's determined policy of centralization. During Mazarin's regency, long-building resentment produced a backlash: Between 1649 and 1652, in a series of widespread rebellions known as the *Fronde* (after the slingshot used by street boys), segments of the nobility and townspeople sought to reverse the drift toward absolute monarchy and to preserve local autonomy.

The *Parlement* of Paris initiated the revolt in 1649, and the nobility at large soon followed. Urging them on were the influential wives of princes whom Mazarin had imprisoned for treason. The many (the nobility) briefly triumphed over the one (the monarchy) when Mazarin released the imprisoned princes in February 1651. He and Louis XIV thereafter entered a short exile (Mazarin leaving France, Louis fleeing Paris). They returned in October 1652 after an interlude of inefficient and nearly anarchic rule by the nobility. The period of the *Fronde* convinced most French people that the rule of a strong king was preferable to the rule of many regional powers with competing and irreconcilable claims. At the same time, Louis XIV and his later advisors learned that heavy-handed policies like those of Richelieu and Mazarin could endanger the monarchy. Louis would ultimately concentrate unprecedented authority in the monarchy, but his means would be more clever than those of his predecessors.

The Years of Louis's Personal Rule

On the death of Mazarin, Louis XIV assumed personal control of the government. Unlike his royal predecessors, he appointed no single chief minister. One result was to make revolt more difficult. Rebellious nobles would now be challenging the king directly; they could not claim to be resisting only a bad minister.

Mazarin prepared Louis XIV well to rule France. The turbulent events of his youth also made an indelible impression on the king. Louis wrote in his memoirs that the *Fronde* caused him to loathe "kings of straw," and he followed two strategies to assure that he would never become one.

First, Louis and his advisors became masters of propaganda and the creation of a political image. Indoctrinated with a strong sense of the grandeur of his crown, Louis never missed an opportunity to impress it on the French people. When the *dauphin* (the heir to the French throne) was born in 1662, for example, Louis appeared for the celebration dressed as a Roman emperor.

Second, Louis made sure that the French nobles and other major social groups would benefit from the growth of his own authority. Although he maintained control over foreign affairs and limited the influence of noble institutions on the monarchy, he never tried to abolish those institutions or limit their authority at the local level. The crown, for example, usually conferred informally with regional *parlements* before making rulings that would affect them. Likewise, the crown would rarely enact economic regulations without consulting local opinion. Local *parlements* enjoyed considerable latitude in all regional matters. In an exception to this pattern, Louis did clash with the *Parlement* of Paris, with which he had to register laws, and eventually, in 1673, he curtailed much of its power. Many regional parlements and other regional authorities, however, had resented the power of that body.

Employing these strategies of propaganda and cooperation, Louis set out to anchor his rule in the principle of the divine right of kings, to domesticate the French nobility by binding them to the court rituals of Versailles, and to crush religious dissent. (See "Art & the West.")

King by Divine Right

Reverence for the king and the personification of government in his person had been nurtured in France since Capetian times. It was a maxim of French law and popular opinion that "the king of

Bishop Bossuet Defends the Divine Right of Kings

The revolutions of the seventeenth century caused many to fear anarchy far more than tyranny, among them the influential French bishop Jacques-Bénigne Bossuet (1627–1704), the leader of French Catholicism in the second half of the seventeenth century. Louis XIV made him court preacher and tutor to his son, for whom Bossuet wrote the celebrated Universal History. *In the following excerpt, Bossuet defends the divine right and absolute power of kings. He depicts kings as embracing in their person the whole body of the state and the will of the people they govern and, as such, as being immune from judgment by any mere mortal.*

❖ *Why might Bossuet have wished to make such extravagant claims for absolute royal power? How might these claims be transferred to any form of government? What are the religious bases of Bossuet's argument? How does this argument for absolute royal authority lead also to the need for a single uniform religion in France?*

The royal power is absolute....The prince need render account of his acts to no one. "I counsel thee to keep the king's commandment, and that in regard of the oath of God. Be not hasty to go out of his sight; stand not on an evil thing for he doeth whatsoever pleaseth him. Where the word of a king is, there is power; and who may say unto him, What doest thou? Whoso keepeth the commandment shall feel no evil thing" [Eccles. 8:2–5]. Without this absolute authority the king could neither do good nor repress evil. It is necessary that his power be such that no one can hope to escape him, and finally, the only protection of individuals against the public authority should be their innocence. This confirms the teaching of St. Paul: "Wilt thou then not be afraid of the power? Do that which is good" [Rom. 13:3].

God is infinite, God is all. The prince, as prince, is not regarded as a private person: he is a public personage, all the state is in him; the will of all the people is included in his. As all perfection and all strength are united in God, so all the power of individuals is united in the person of the prince. What grandeur that a single man should embody so much!...

Behold an immense people united in a single person; behold this holy power, paternal and absolute; behold the secret cause which governs the whole body of the state, contained in a single head: you see the image of God in the king, and you have the idea of royal majesty. God is holiness itself, goodness itself, and power itself. In these things lies the majesty of God. In the image of these things lies the majesty of the prince.

From *Politics Drawn from the Very Words of Holy Scripture*, as quoted in James Harvey Robinson, ed., *Readings in European History*, Vol. 2 (Boston: Athenaeum, 1906), pp. 275–276.

France is emperor in his realm" and the king's wish the law of the land. Building on this reverence, Louis XIV defended absolute royal authority on the grounds of divine right.

An important source for Louis's concept of royal authority was his devout tutor, the political theorist Bishop Jacques-Bénigne Bossuet (1627–1704). An ardent champion of the Gallican liberties—the traditional rights of the French king and church against the pope in matters of ecclesiastical appointments and taxation—Bossuet defended what he called the "divine right of kings." (See "Bishop Bossuet Defends the Divine Right of Kings.") In support of his claims, he cited examples of Old Testament rulers divinely appointed by, and answerable only to, God. As medieval popes had insisted that only God could judge a pope,

so Bossuet argued that none save God could judge the king. Kings may have remained duty-bound to reflect God's will in their rule—in this sense, Bossuet considered them always subject to a higher authority. Yet as God's regents on Earth, they could not be bound to the dictates of mere princes and parliaments. Such assumptions lay behind Louis XIV's alleged declaration, *"L'état, c'est moi"* ("I am the state").

Versailles

More than any other monarch of the day, Louis XIV used the physical setting of his royal court to exert political control. The palace court at Versailles on the outskirts of Paris became Louis's permanent residence after 1682. It was a true temple to royalty, architec-

Rigaud's Louis XIV:
The State Portrait

Even if Louis XIV may never actually have said, "I am the state," the famous remark attributed to him, most of his subjects and the other crowned heads of Europe certainly saw him as such. Hyacinthe Rigaud painted Louis as the embodiment of official political power and authority, establishing the model for what became known for the rest of the century as "the state portrait."

Previously, most portraits or statues of Louis—and there were many—set him in an allegorical setting where he embodied qualities of mythical heroes or in a historical setting in which he resembled a Roman emperor. Rigaud's portrait (1701) is largely, though not entirely, a painting of royal majesty and royal symbols. A mature Louis appears in his coronation robes, decorated with *fleurs-de-lis*, which he would not have worn for decades. The robes, along with the crown and the throne which rests beside and behind him in the background, suggest that each day he is again crowned by his accomplishments, his justice, and his divine right to rule. He holds the scepter of state as a staff that steadies him, as he presumably saw himself steadying the French nation after the decades of turmoil that had preceded his reign. The sword of state hangs by his side partially covered, though he had led the nation in war through most of his reign and would do so throughout the next decade as well. On the base of the column at the rear of the painting in the shadows resides the figure of justice.

The Italian sculptor Bernini, who sculpted a bust of Louis taken from a portrait, once wrote, "The secret of portraits is to exaggerate what is fine, add a touch of grandeur, and diminish what is ugly or petty or even suppress it when this is possible without flattery."[1] Rigaud followed this advice in his portrait of Louis, which

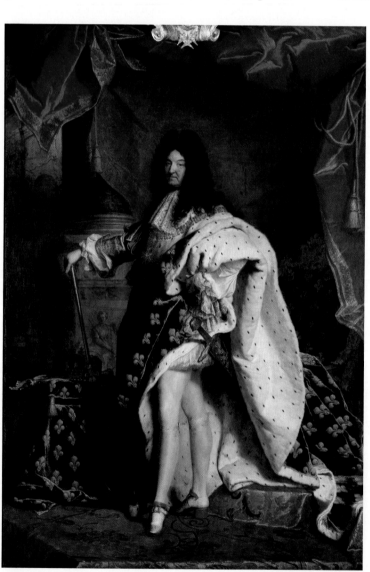

Hyacinthe Rigaud, *Louis XIV*, 1701. Giraudon/Art Resource, N.Y.

[1] Quoted in Peter Burke, *The Fabrication of Louis XIV* (New Haven, CT: Yale University Press, 1992), p. 23.

displays many ironies about which both Louis and the artist must have been aware. The full, long wig suggests a more youthful figure than the now aged king of sixty-three years. Furthermore, through disease early in his reign, Louis had lost much of his hair. By the time the portrait was painted, he was often ill with gout and other diseases. The portrait hid these facts, but Rigaud, presumably with Louis's encouragement, did give his sitter a face reflecting maturity and perhaps a kind of worldly wisdom. Louis may have been comfortable with such a portrayal, because, from the middle of the 1680s, he had led a very restricted personal life after marrying his strictly devout mistress, Madame de Maintenon. The dancing monarch of the early years of the reign, suggested by the remarkably handsome, athletic legs and red shoes, had given way to a more restrained person and one so rigorously devout, that in 1685 he had undertaken a policy of persecuting French Protestants.

This portrait is of a single person and carries the name of a single artist. The majesty of the lone Louis XIV concealed a multilayered network of royal ministers and bureaucrats working, negotiating, and compromising with hundreds of local officials, councils, and courts that really constituted the royal government, later termed absolutism. The attribution of the portrait to Rigaud alone concealed the fact that this painting, as was the custom with many other portraits and large paintings of the late seventeenth and eighteenth centuries, was completed in an artist's workshop. The master of the workshop, Rigaud, in this case would have personally painted the face and usually the hands. Different artists would have completed other elements of the picture, with, for example, some specializing in drapery and others in clothing. These workshops allowed the master artist to preside over a commercialized artistic business serving the expanding demand for the luxury good of a personal portrait on the part of aristocrats and members of the expanding commercial and professional classes. The business of art extended beyond these workshops into the world of engravers and printers, who could disperse commercially more inexpensive paper copies of important works of art for their own profit and, in the case of political portraits, for purposes of establishing a popular image of persons in public life.

Louis deeply admired this portrait. Originally, he had intended to send it to Philip V of Spain, the grandson he installed on the Spanish throne, thus provoking the greatest European war of his reign. But he decided to keep it for himself and had several copies made and distributed. When various councils or other ministerial bodies met at Versailles in his absence after 1701, the portrait was carried into the room to remind all those present of the monarch whom they served and whose policies they carried out.

Peter Burke, *The Fabrication of Louis XIV* (New Haven, CT: Yale University Press, 1992); Daniel Roche, *France in the Age of the Enlightenment* (Cambridge, MA: Harvard University Press, 1998), pp. 273–277; Germain Bazin, *Baroque and Rococo Art* (New York: Praeger, 1966); Marilyn Stockstad, *Art History* (New York: Harry N. Abrams, Inc., and Prentice Hall, Inc., Publishers, 1999),pp. 750–751.

Versailles, as painted in 1668 by Pierre Patel the Elder (1605–1676). The central building is the hunting lodge built for Louis XII earlier in the century. The wings that appear here were some of Louis XIV's first expansions. Pierre Patel, *Perspective View of Versailles*, Chateau, Versailles, France. Giraudon/Art Resource, NY

turally designed and artistically decorated to proclaim the glory of the Sun King, as Louis was known. A spectacular estate with magnificent fountains and acres of orange groves, it became home to thousands of the more important nobles, royal officials, and servants. Although its physical maintenance and new additions, which continued throughout Louis's lifetime, consumed over half his annual revenues, Versailles paid significant political dividends.

Because Louis ruled personally, he was the chief source of favors and patronage in France. To emphasize his prominence, he organized life at court around every aspect of his own daily routine. He encouraged nobles to approach him directly, but required them to do so through elaborate court etiquette. Polite and fawning nobles sought his attention, entering their names on waiting lists to be in attendance at especially favored moments. The king's rising and dressing in particular were times of rare intimacy, when nobles could whisper their special requests in his ear. Fortunate nobles held his night candle as they accompanied him to his bed.

Although only five feet four inches tall, the king had presence and was always engaging in conversation. He turned his own sexuality to political ends and encouraged the belief at court that it was an honor to lie with him. Married to the Spanish *Infanta* Marie Thérèse for political reasons in 1660, he kept many mistresses. After Marie's death in 1683, he settled down in a secret marriage to Madame de Maintenon and apparently became much less the philanderer.

Court life was a carefully planned and successfully executed effort to domesticate and trivialize the nobility. Barred by law from high government positions, the ritual and play kept them busy and dependent, so they had little time to plot revolt. Dress codes and high-stakes gambling contributed to their indebtedness and dependency on the king. Members of the court spent the afternoons hunting, riding, or strolling about the lush gardens of Versailles. Evenings were given over to planned entertainment in the large salons (plays, concerts, gambling, and the like), followed by supper at 10:00 P.M. Even the king's retirement was part of the day's spectacle.

Moments near the king were important to most court nobles because they were effectively excluded from the real business of government. Louis ruled through powerful councils that controlled foreign affairs, domestic relations, and economic regulations. Each day after morning mass, which Louis always observed, he spent hours with the chief ministers of these councils, whom he chose from families long in royal service or from among people just beginning to rise in the social structure. Unlike the nobles at court, they had no real or potential power bases in the provinces and depended solely on the king for their standing in both government and society.

Some nobles, of course, did not attend Versailles. Some tended to their local estates and cultivated their local influence. Many others were simply too poor to cut a figure at court. All the nobility understood, however, that Louis, unlike Richelieu and Mazarin, would not threaten their local social standing. Louis supported France's traditional social structure and the social privileges of the nobility.

Suppression of the Jansenists

Like Richelieu before him, Louis believed that political unity and stability required religious conformity. His first move in this direction, which came early in his personal reign, was against the Roman Catholic Jansenists.

The French crown and the French church had by long tradition—originating with the so-called Gallican liberties in the fourteenth century—jealously guarded their independence from Rome. A great influx of Catholic religious orders, the Jesuits prominent among them, followed Henry IV's conversion to Catholicism. Because of their leadership at the Council of Trent and their close connections to Spain, the Jesuits had been banned from France by Catherine de Médicis. Henry IV, however, lifted the ban in 1603, with certain conditions: He required members of the order to swear an oath of allegiance to the king, he limited the number of new colleges they could open, and he required them to have special licenses for public activities.

The Jesuits were not, however, easily harnessed. They rapidly monopolized the education of the upper classes, and their devout students promoted the religious reforms and doctrine of the Council of Trent throughout France. In a measure of their success, Jesuits served as confessors to Henry IV, Louis XIII, and Louis XIV.

Jansenism arose in the 1630s as part of an intra-Catholic opposition to the theology and the political influence of the Jesuits. Jansenists adhered to the Augustinian tradition that had also spawned many Protestant teachings. Serious and uncompromising, they particularly opposed Jesuit teachings about free will. They believed with Saint Augustine that original sin so corrupted humankind that individuals could do nothing good nor secure their own salvation without divine grace. The namesake of the movement, Cornelius Jansen (d. 1638), was a Flemish theologian and the bishop of Ypres. His posthumously published *Augustinus* (1640) assailed Jesuit teaching on grace and salvation.

A prominent Parisian family, the Arnaulds, became Jansenist allies, adding a political element to the Jansenists' theological objections to the Jesuits.

Versailles was a palace of unprecedented luxury for the French monarch and his court. Even Louis XIV's bedroom was a scene of court ritual and political intrigue with specially favored nobles being allowed to awake him or to escort him to the room in the evening. Navlet Victor (1819–1886), *Vue de la chambre a coucher de Louis XIV a Versailles en 1861.* 0.63 x 0.95. Chateaux de Versailles et de Trianon © Photo RMN

Like many other French people, the Arnaulds believed that the Jesuits had been behind the assassination of Henry IV in 1610.

The Arnaulds dominated Jansenist communities at Port-Royal and Paris during the 1640s. In 1643, Antoine Arnauld published a work entitled *On Frequent Communion* in which he criticized the Jesuits for confessional practices that permitted the easy redress of almost any sin. The Jesuits, in turn, condemned the Jansenists as "crypto-Calvinists."

On May 31, 1653, Pope Innocent X declared heretical five Jansenist theological propositions on grace and salvation. In 1656, the pope banned Jansen's *Augustinus* and the Sorbonne censured Antoine Arnauld. In the same year, Antoine's friend, Blaise Pascal (1623–1662), the most famous of Jansen's followers, published the first of his *Provincial Letters* in defense of Jansenism. A deeply religious man, Pascal tried to reconcile the "reasons of the heart" with growing seventeenth-century reverence for the clear and distinct ideas of the mind. (See Chapter 14.) He objected to Jesuit moral theology not only as being lax and shallow, but also because he felt that its rationalism failed to do full justice to the religious experience.

In 1660 Louis permitted the papal bull *Ad Sacram Sedem* (1656) to be enforced in France, thus banning Jansenism. He also closed down the Port-Royal community. Thereafter, Jansenists either retracted their views or went underground. Much later, in 1710, Louis lent his support to a still more thorough purge of Jansenist sentiment.

Jansenism had offered the prospect of a Catholicism broad enough to appeal to France's Protestant Huguenots. By suppressing it, Louis also eliminated the best hope for bringing peaceful religious unity to his country.

Government Geared for Warfare

Louis's France was in many ways like much of the rest of contemporary Europe. It had a largely subsistence economy, and its cities enjoyed only limited commercial prosperity. It did not, in other words, achieve the economic strength of a modern industrial economy. By the 1660s, however, France was superior to any other European nation in administrative bureaucracy, armed forces, and national unity. Louis had sufficient resources at his disposal to raise and maintain a large and powerful army. His enemies and some later historians claimed that Louis wished to dominate all Europe, but it would appear that his chief military and foreign policy goal was to achieve secure international boundaries for France. He was particularly concerned to secure the northern borders of France along the Spanish Netherlands, the Franche-Comté, Alsace, and Lorraine. The geography of these lands provided potential avenues of invasion into France. Louis also assumed that he must frustrate Habsburg ambitions that endangered France and, as part of that goal, sought to secure his southern borders toward Spain. Furthermore, external events, particularly problems

Throughout the age of splendor at the court of Louis XIV, millions of French peasants lived lives of poverty and hardship, as depicted in this 1640 painting, Peasant Family *by Louis LeNain.*
Erich Lessing/Art Resource, N.Y.

raised by succession issues in other states, provided the occasion of Louis's wars as often as his own personal ambition did. Nonethless, he saw himself as a warrior king and on more than one occasion personally accompanied his armies on their campaigns. Whether reacting to external events or pursuing his own ambitions, Louis's pursuit of French interests raised among neighboring states the most profound fears of extensive French aggression and fostered the formation of major coalitions against France.

Three remarkable French ministers established and supported Louis XIV's great war machine: Colbert, Louvois, and Vauban.

COLBERT AND THE FRENCH ECONOMY Jean-Baptiste Colbert (1619–1683), controller general of finances and Louis's most brilliant minister, created the economic base Louis needed to finance his wars. Colbert worked to centralize the French economy with the same rigor that Louis had worked to centralize the French government. Colbert tried, with modest success, to organize much economic activity under state supervision and, through tariffs, carefully regulated the flow of imports and exports. He sought to create new national industries and organized factories around a tight regimen of work and ideology. He simplified the administrative bureaucracy, abolished unnecessary positions, and reduced the number of tax-exempt nobles. He also increased the *taille*, a direct tax on the peasantry and a major source of royal income.

This kind of close government control of the economy came to be known as *mercantilism* (a term invented by later critics of the policy). Its aim was to maximize foreign exports and internal reserves of bullion, the gold and silver necessary for making war. Modern scholars argue that Colbert overcontrolled the French economy and cite his "paternalism" as a major reason for the failure of French colonies in the New World. Be that as it may, his policies unquestionably transformed France into a major commercial power, with foreign bases in Africa, in India, and in the Americas, from Canada to the Caribbean.

LOUVOIS, VAUBAN, AND THE FRENCH MILITARY Louis's army, about a quarter of a million strong, was the creation of Michel Tellier and his more famous son, the marquis of Louvois (1641–1691). Louis's war minister from 1677 to 1691, Louvois was a superior military tactician.

Before Louvois, the French army had been an amalgam of local recruits and mercenaries, uncoordinated groups whose loyalty could not always be counted on. Without regular pay or a way to supply their every-day needs, troops often lived by pillage. Louvois instituted good salaries and improved discipline, making soldiering a respectable profession. He limited military commissions and introduced a system of promotion by merit, bringing dedicated fighters into the ranks. Enlistment was for four years and was restricted to single men. *Intendants*, the king's ubiquitous civil servants, monitored conduct at all levels.

Because it was well disciplined, this new, large, and powerful standing army had considerable public support. Unlike its undisciplined predecessor, the new army no longer threatened the lives, homes, or well-being of the people it was supposed to protect. It thus provides an excellent example of the kinds of benefits many saw in the growing authority of the central monarchy.

What Louvois was to military organization, Sebastien Vauban (1633–1707) was to military engineering. He perfected the arts of fortifying and besieging towns. He also devised the system of trench warfare and developed the concept of defensive frontiers that remained basic to military tactics through World War I.

Louis's Early Wars

THE WAR OF DEVOLUTION Louis's first great foreign adventure was the War of Devolution (1667–1668). It was fought, as would be the later and more devastating War of the Spanish Succession, over Louis's claim to the Spanish Belgian provinces through his wife, Marie Thérèse (1638–1683). According to the terms of the Treaty of the Pyrenees (1659), Marie had renounced her claim to the Spanish succession on condition that a 500,000-crown dowry be paid to Louis within eighteen months of the marriage, a condition that was not met. When Philip IV of Spain died in September 1665, he left all his lands to his sickly four-year-old son by a second marriage, Charles II (r. 1665–1700) and explicitly denied any lands to his daughter. Louis had always harbored the hope of turning the marriage to territorial gain and even before Philip's death had argued that Marie was entitled to a portion of the inheritance.

Louis had a legal argument on his side, which gave the war its name. He maintained that in certain regions of Brabant and Flanders, which were part of the Spanish inheritance, property "devolved" to the children of a first marriage rather than to those of a second. Therefore, Marie had a higher claim than Charles II to these regions. Although such regional laws could hardly bind the king of Spain, Louis was not deterred from sending his armies, under the viscount of Turenne, into Flanders and the Franche-Comté in 1667. In response to this aggression,

MAP 13–2   THE WARS OF LOUIS XIV   *This map shows the territorial changes resulting from Louis XIV's first three major wars. The War of the Spanish Succession was yet to come.*

England, Sweden, and the United Provinces of Holland formed the Triple Alliance, a force sufficient to compel Louis to agree to peace under the terms in the Treaty of Aix-la-Chapelle (1668). The treaty gave him control of certain towns bordering the Spanish Netherlands. (See Map 13–2.)

INVASION OF THE NETHERLANDS   In 1670, with the signing of the Treaty of Dover, England and France became allies against the Dutch. Without the English,

the Triple Alliance crumbled. This left Louis in a stronger position to invade the Netherlands for a second time, which he did in 1672. This time he aimed directly at Holland, which had organized the Triple Alliance in 1667, foiling French designs in Flanders. Dutch gloating after the Treaty of Aix-la-Chapelle had offended Louis. Such cartoons as one depicting the sun (Louis was called the "Sun King") eclipsed by a great moon of Dutch cheese incensed him. Without neutralizing Holland, he knew he could never hope to acquire land in the Spanish Netherlands, much less fulfill his dreams of European hegemony.

Louis's invasion of the United Provinces in 1672 brought the downfall of the Dutch statesmen Jan and Cornelius De Witt. Replacing them was the twenty-seven-year-old Prince of Orange, destined after 1689 to become King William III of England. Orange was the great-grandson of William the Silent, who had repulsed Philip II and dashed Spanish hopes of dominating the Netherlands in the sixteenth century.

Orange, an unpretentious Calvinist who was in almost every way Louis's opposite, galvanized the seven provinces into a fierce fighting unit. In 1673 he united the Holy Roman Emperor, Spain, Lorraine, and Brandenburg in an alliance against Louis. His enemies now saw the French king as a "Christian Turk," a menace to the whole of western Europe, Catholic and Protestant alike. In the ensuing warfare, both sides experienced gains and losses. Louis lost his ablest generals, Turenne and Condé, in 1675, but a victory by Admiral Duquesne over the Dutch fleet in 1676 gave France control of the Mediterranean. The Peace of Nijmwegen, signed with different parties in successive years (1678 and 1679), ended the hostilities of this second war. There were various minor territorial adjustments, but no clear victor except the United Netherlands, which retained all of its territory.

Revocation of the Edict of Nantes

In the decade after his invasion of the Netherlands, Louis made his second major move to assure religious conformity. Following the proclamation of the Edict of Nantes in 1598, relations between the great Catholic majority (nine-tenths of the French population) and the Protestant minority remained hostile. There were about 1.75 million Huguenots in France in the 1660s, but their numbers were declining in the second half of the seventeenth century. The French Catholic Church had long denounced Calvinists as heretical and treasonous and had supported their persecution as both pious and patriotic.

Following the Peace of Nijmwegen in 1678–1679, which halted for the moment his aggression in Europe, Louis launched a methodical government campaign against the French Huguenots in a determined effort to unify France religiously. He hounded the Huguenots out of public life, banning them from government office and excluding them from such professions as printing and medicine. He used subsidies and selective taxation to encourage Huguenots to convert to Catholicism. And in 1681 he bullied them by quartering his troops in their towns. In the final stage of the persecution, Louis revoked the Edict of Nantes in October 1685. As a result, Protestant churches and schools were closed, Protestant ministers exiled, nonconverting laity forced to be galley slaves, and Protestant children ceremonially baptized by Catholic priests.

The revocation of the Edict of Nantes was a major blunder. Afterwards, Louis was viewed in Protestant countries as a new Philip II, intent on a Catholic reconquest of the whole of Europe, who must be resisted at all costs. The revocation prompted the voluntary emigration of more than a quarter million French people, who formed new communities and joined the resistance to France in England, Germany, Holland, and the New World. Thousands of French Huguenots served in the army of Louis's archfoe, William of Orange, later King William III of England. Many of those who remained in France became part of an uncompromising guerilla resistance to the king. Despite the many domestic and foreign liabilities it brought him, Louis, to his death, considered the revocation to be his most pious act, one that placed God in his debt.

Louis's Later Wars

THE LEAGUE OF AUGSBURG AND THE NINE YEARS' WAR After the Treaty of Nijmwegen, Louis maintained his army at full strength and restlessly probed beyond his perimeters. In 1681 his forces conquered the free city of Strasbourg, prompting new defensive coalitions to form against him. One of these, the League of Augsburg, created in 1686 to resist French expansion into Germany, had grown by 1689 to include England, Spain, Sweden, the United Provinces, and the electorates of Bavaria, Saxony, and the Palatinate. It also had the support of the Austrian emperor Leopold. In 1688 Louis's armies invaded the Palatinate, ostensibly to claim on very weak ground its succession for his sister-in-law Charlotte Elisabeth. A long, extraordinarily destructive war resulted. Between 1689 and 1697, the league and France battled each other in the Nine Years' War. During the same period, England and France struggled for control of North America in what came to be known as King William's War.

The Nine Years' War ended when stalemate and exhaustion forced both sides to accept an interim settlement. The Peace of Ryswick, signed in September 1697, was a triumph for William of Orange, now William III of England, and Emperor Leopold. It secured Holland's borders and thwarted Louis's expansion into Germany. (See "Louis IV's Sister-in-Law Grieves for Her Homeland.")

Louis XIV's Sister-in-Law Grieves for Her Homeland

Charlotte Elisabeth, Duchesse d' Orléans (1652–1722), who was married to the brother of Louis XIV of France, had been born the daughter of the Elector of the Palatinate. After her marriage in 1671, she moved to the French court and was never permitted to revisit her homeland. She did, however, carry out an extensive correspondence with friends and family in Germany throughout her life. In August, 1688, Louis XIV invaded the Palatinate under the guise of restoring it to his sister-in-law. He had no real purpose except the conquest of the German region. This invasion was important for two reasons. First, it opened a war that continued until 1697. Second, at the onset of the original invasion, the French forces committed enormous atrocities against the civilian population, killing many civilians and destroying their homes. In these letters to her aunt and foster mother, Charlotte Elisabeth recounts her sadness and anger over the plight of these civilians and the difficulty of her own situation in the French court.

❖ *How do these letters reflect the plight of a woman who had been required to enter a dynastic marriage when war broke out? How does she report Louis XIV's using her name to further his own political and financial ends in the Palatinate? What kind of destruction was Charlotte Elisabeth aware of in her homeland?*

March 20, 1689

I had barely began to recover somewhat from poor Carllutz's death [her brother] when the horrendous and piteous calamity was visited upon the poor Palatinate, and what pains me most is that my name is being used to cast these poor people into utter misery. And when I cry about it, I am treated to great annoyance and sulking [by those in the French royal court at Versailles]. But to save my life I cannot stop lamenting and bemoaning the thought that I am as it were, my fatherland's ruin, especially when I see all of the Elector's, my late father's, hard work and care suddenly reduced to rubble in poor Mannheim. I am so horrified by all the destruction that has been wrought that every night when I have finally dozed off, I imagine that I am in Mannheim and Heidelberg amidst all the destruction, and then I wake up with a dreadful start and cannot go back to sleep for two whole hours. Then I see in my mind how everything was in my day and in what state it is now, indeed in what state I am myself, and then I cannot hold back a flood of tears. It also grieves me deeply that the King [Louis XIV] waited to inflict the ultimate devastation precisely until I had begged him to spare Mannheim and Heidelberg.

June 5, 1689

Although I should be accustomed by now to the thought of my poor fatherland in flames, having heard nothing else for so long, I still cannot help being regretful and grieved every time I am told that yet another place has been put to the torch.... Recently Monsieur [her husband] told me something that annoys me to the depth of my soul and which I had not known before, namely that the King [Louis XIV] has all taxes in the Palatinate levied in my name; now these poor people must think that I am profiting from their misery and that I am the cause of it, and that makes me deeply sad.

October 30, 1689

Yesterday I was told something that touched my heart very deeply, and I could not hear it without tears; namely that the poor people of Mannheim have all returned and are living in their cellars as if they were houses and even hold a daily market as if the town were still in its previous state.

From *Louis XIV's Sister-in-Law Grieves for Her Homeland*, Elborg Forster, ed., in Von der Pfalz, *A Woman's Life in the Court of the Sun King*, pp. 61, 64, 68, © 1984 The Johns Hopkins University Press. Reprinted by permission.

The foreign policy of Louis XIV brought warfare to all of Europe. This eighteenth century painting by Benjamin West memorializes the British victory over France in the battle of La Hogue in 1692. National Gallery of Art

WAR OF THE SPANISH SUCCESSION: TREATIES OF UTRECHT AND RASTADT   After Ryswick, Louis, who seemed to thrive on partial success, made another attempt to secure and expand French interests against Habsburg influence. On November 1, 1700, Charles II of Spain, known as "the Sufferer" because of his genetic deformities and lingering illnesses, died.

Both Louis and the Austrian emperor Leopold had claims to the Spanish inheritance through their grandsons, Louis through his marriage to Marie Thérèse and Leopold through his marriage to her younger sister, Margaret Thérèse. Although Louis's grandson, Philip of Anjou, had the better claim (because Marie Thérèse was Margaret Thérèse's older sister), Marie Thérèse had renounced her right to the Spanish inheritance in the Treaty of the Pyrenees (1659), and the inheritance was expected to go to Leopold's grandson.

Louis nurtured fears that the Habsburgs would dominate Europe should they gain control of Spain as well as the Holy Roman Empire. Most of the nations of Europe, however, feared France more than the Habsburgs and determined to prevent a union of the French and Spanish crowns. As a result, before Charles II's death, negotiations began among the nations involved to partition his inheritance in a way that would preserve the existing balance of power.

Charles II upset these negotiations by leaving his entire inheritance to Philip of Anjou, Louis's grandson. At a stroke, Spain and its possessions had fallen to France. Although Louis had been party to the partition agreements that preceded Charles's death, he now saw God's hand in Charles's will; he chose to enforce its terms over those of the partition agreement. Philip of Anjou moved to Madrid and became Philip V of Spain. Louis, in what was interpreted as naked French aggression, sent his troops again into Flanders, this time to remove Dutch soldiers from Spanish territory in the name of the new French king of Spain. Louis also declared Spanish America open to French ships.

In September 1701, England, Holland, and the Holy Roman Empire formed the Grand Alliance to counter Louis. They sought to preserve the bal-

MAP 13–3 EUROPE IN 1714. *The War of the Spanish Succession ended in the year before the death of the aged Louis XIV. By then, France and Spain, although not united, were both ruled by members of the Bourbon family, and Spain had lost its non-Iberian possessions.*

ance of power by once and for all securing Flanders as a neutral barrier between Holland and France and by gaining for the emperor his fair share of the Spanish inheritance. After the formation of the Grand Alliance, Louis increased the stakes of battle by recognizing the claim of James Edward, the son of James II of England, to the English throne.

In 1701 the thirteen-year War of the Spanish Succession (1701–1714) began, and once again total war enveloped western Europe. France, for the first time, went to war with inadequate finances, a poorly equipped army, and mediocre military leadership. The English, in contrast, had advanced weaponry (flintlock rifles, paper cartridges, and ring bayonets) and superior tactics (thin, maneuverable troop columns rather than the traditional deep ones). John Churchill, the duke of Marlborough, who succeeded William of Orange as military leader of the alliance, bested Louis's soldiers in every major engagement. He routed French armies at Blenheim in August 1704 and on the plain of Ramillies in 1706—two decisive battles of the war. In 1708–1709 famine, revolts, and uncollectible taxes tore France apart internally. Despair pervaded the French court. Louis wondered aloud how God could forsake one who had done so much for him.

Though ready to make peace in 1709, Louis could not bring himself to accept the stiff terms of the alliance. These included a demand that he transfer all Spanish possessions to the emperor's grandson Charles and remove Philip V from Madrid. Hostilities continued, and a clash of forces at Malplaquet (September 1709) left carnage on the battlefield unsurpassed until modern times.

France finally signed an armistice with England at Utrecht in July 1713 and concluded hostilities with Holland and the emperor in the Treaty of Rastadt in March 1714. This agreement confirmed Philip V as king of Spain, but gave Gibraltar and the island of Minona to England, making it a Mediterranean power. (See Map 13–3.) It also won Louis's recognition of the right of the House of Hanover to accede to the English throne.

Spanish power declined in the wake of the war. Philip should have tried to consolidate his internal power and protect Spanish overseas trade. However, his second wife, Elizabeth Farnese, used Spanish power to secure thrones for her two sons in Italy. Such diversions of government resources allowed the nobility and the provinces to continue to assert their privileges against the monarchy. Not until the reign of Charles III (r. 1759–1788) did Spain have a

monarch concerned with efficient domestic and imperial administration and internal improvement. By the third quarter of the century, Spain was better governed, but it could no longer compete effectively in great-power politics.

Politically, the eighteenth century would belong to England as the sixteenth had belonged to Spain and the seventeenth to France. Although France remained intact and strong, the realization of Louis XIV's territorial ambitions had to await the rise of Napoleon Bonaparte. On his deathbed on September 1, 1715, Louis fittingly warned his heir, the *dauphin*, not to imitate his love of buildings and his liking for war.

Louis XIV's Legacy

Louis XIV left France a mixed legacy. His wars had brought widespread death and destruction and had sapped many of the nation's resources. Only a long period of peace could permit full economic recovery. Yet the years of war had established among both the army and much of the nobility a self-image of life in pursuit of military glory. Mid-eighteenth-century wars initiated in part from that outlook would undermine the recovering royal finances and cause an ongoing financial crisis that the monarchy never solved. Louis's policies of centralization would later make it difficult for France to develop effective institutions of representation and self-government The aristocracy, after its years of domestication at Versailles, would have difficulty providing the nation with effective leaders and ministers. Yet his reign had also laid the groundwork for a new French Empire by expanding trade into Asia and colonizing North America.

Despite his own ambitions for absolute rule and the association of the term "absolutism" with his mode of government, it is important to recognize that Louis's rule was not so absolute as to exert oppressive control over the daily lives of his subjects, as would be the case with police states of the nineteenth and twentieth centuries. His absolutism functioned primarily in the classic areas of European state action—the making of war and peace, the regulation of religion, and the oversight of economic activity. Even at the height of his power, local institutions, some controlled by townspeople and others by nobles, continued to exert administrative authority at the local level. The king and his ministers supported the high status and tax exemptions of these local elites. But in contrast to the Stuart kings of England, Louis firmly prevented them from capturing or significantly limiting his authority on the national level. Not until the French monarchy was so weakened by financial crisis at the end of the eighteenth century would it succumb to demands for a more representative form of government.

The Reign of Louis XIV (1643–1715)	
1643	Louis ascends the French throne at the age of five
1643–1661	Cardinal Mazarin directs the French government
1648	Peace of Westphalia
1649–1652	The *Fronde* revolt
1653	The pope declares Jansenism a heresy
1659	Treaty of Pyrenees between France and Spain
1660	Papal ban on Jansenists enforced in France
1661	Louis commences personal rule
1667–1668	War of Devolution
1670	Secret Treaty of Dover between France and Great Britain
1672–1679	French war against the Netherlands
1685	Louis revokes the Edict of Nantes
1689–1697	War of the League of Augsburg
1701	Outbreak of the War of the Spanish Succession
1713	Treaty of Utrecht between France and Great Britain
1714	Treaty of Rastatt between France and Spain
1715	Death of Louis XIV

In Perspective

In the seventeenth century, England and France developed divergent forms of government. England became the model for parliamentary monarchy, France for absolute monarchy.

The politically active English elite—the nobility, along with the wealthy landowning and commercial classes—struggled throughout the century to limit the authority of rulers—including Oliver Cromwell as well as the Stuart monarchs—over local interests. In the process, they articulated a political philosophy that stressed the need to prevent the central concentration of political power. The Bill of Rights of 1689 and the Toleration Act following the Glorious Revolution of William and Mary seemed to achieve the goals of this philosophy. These acts brought neither democracy nor full religious freedom in a modern sense; the Bill of Rights protected only the privileged, not all the English people, and the Toleration Act outlawed Catholics and Unitarians. Still, they firmly established representative government in England and extended legal recognition, at least in principle, to a variety of religious beliefs. The Bill of Rights required the monarch to call Parliament regularly.

In France, by contrast, the monarchy remained supreme. Although the king had to mollify privileged local elites by considering the interests of the nobility and the traditional rights of towns and regions, France had no national institution like Parliament through which he had to govern. Louis XIV was able, on his own authority, to fund the largest army in Europe. He could and did crush religious dissent. His own propaganda and the fear of his adversaries may have led to an exaggerated view of Louis's power, but his reign nonetheless provided a model of effective centralized power that later continental rulers tried to follow.

REVIEW QUESTIONS

1. By the end of the seventeenth century, England and France had different systems of government with different religious policies. What were the main differences? Similarities? Why did each nation develop as it did? How much did the particular personalities of the rulers of each nation determine the manner in which their political institutions emerged?

2. Why did the English king and Parliament come into conflict in the 1640s? What were the most important issues behind the war between them, and who bears more responsibility for it? What role did religion play in the conflict?

3. What was the Glorious Revolution and why did it take place? What were James II's mistakes, and what were the issues involved in the events of 1688? What kind of settlement emerged from the revolution? How did England in 1700 differ from England in 1600?

4. Discuss the development of absolutism in France. What policies of Henry IV and Louis XIII were essential in creating the absolute monarchy?

5. What were the chief ways Louis XIV consolidated his monarchy? What limits were there on his authority? What was Louis's religious policy?

6. Assess the success of Louis XIV's foreign policy. What were his aims? Were they realistic? To what extent did he attain them? To what extent did he forge events, and to what extent did he react to events outside France?

SUGGESTED READINGS

Robert Ashton, *Counter-Revolution: The Second Civil War and Its Origins, 1646–1648* (1995). A major examination of the resumption of civil conflict in England that ended with the abolition of the monarchy, House of Lords, and established church.

W. Beik, *Absolutism and Society in Seventeenth-Century France* (1985). An important study that questions the extent of royal power.

J. Bergin, *Cardinal Richelieu: Power and the Pursuit of Wealth* (1985). Considers the role of finance and private wealth in the rise of Richelieu.

R. Bonney, *Political Change in France under Richelieu and Mazarin, 1624–1661* (1978). A careful examination of how these two cardinals laid the foundation for Louis XIV's absolutism.

G. Burgess, *Absolute Monarchy and the Stuart Constitution* (1996). A new study that challenges many of the traditional interpretive categories.

P. Burke, *The Fabrication of Louis XIV* (1992). Examines the manner in which the public image of Louis XIV was forged in art.

P. Collinson, *The Religion of Protestants: The Church in English Society, 1559–1625* (1982). The best introduction to Puritanism.

J. H. Elliott and L. Brockliss, eds., *The Age of the Favourite* (1999). Explores, in the European setting, the political impact of those figures who received extraordinary royal favor and patronage.

T. Ertman, *Birth of the Leviathan: Building States and Regimes in Medieval and Early Modern Europe* (1997). An extensive survey by a sociologist.

R. Hutton, *Charles the Second, King of England, Scotland, and Ireland* (1989). Replaces all previous biographies.

M. KISHLANSKY, *A Monarchy Transformed: Britain, 1603–1714* (1996). The most recent overview.

J. R. MAJOR, *From Renaissance Monarchy to Absolute Monarchy: French Kings, Nobles and Estates* (1994). A major study by a leading scholar exploring the complexities of the relationship of the monarchy to other political and social groups.

R. METTAM, *Power and Faction in Louis XIV's France* (1988). Examines the political intricacies of the reign and suggests the limits to absolutism.

P. K. MONOD, *The Power of Kings: Monarchy and Religion in Europe, 1589–1715* (1999). An important and innovative examination of the roots of royal authority as early modern Europe became modern Europe.

G. PARKER, *The Military Revolution: Military Innovation and the Rise of the West, 1500–1800* (1988). Emphasizes the role of military organization and expenditures in the emergence of modern states.

H. PHILLIPS, *Church and Culture in Seventeenth-Century France* (1997). A clear examination of the major religious issues confronting France and their relationship to the larger culture.

O. RANUM, *The Fronde: A French Revolution, 1648–1652* (1993). The best recent work on the subject.

D. L. RUBIN (ED.), *The Sun King: The Ascendancy of French Culture During the Reign of Louis XIV* (1992). A collection of useful essays.

C. RUSSELL, *The Fall of the English Monarchies, 1637–1642* (1991). A major revisionist account.

K. SHARPE, *The Personal Rule of Charles I* (1992). An important narrative work.

J. SPUR, *The Restoration Church of England, 1646–1689* (1992). The standard work on this subject.

L. STONE, *The Causes of the English Revolution, 1529–1642* (1972). A classic survey stressing social history and ruminating over historians and historical method.

D. J. STURDY, *Louis XIV* (1998). A excellent brief overview with judicious comments on all major issues.

G. TREASURE, *Mazarin: The Crisis of Absolutism in France* (1996). An examination not only of Mazarin, but also of the larger national and international background.

R. D. TUMBLESON, *Catholicism in the English Protestant Imagination: Nationalism, Religion, and Literature, 1660–1745* (1998). Explores the impact of anti-Catholicism on English life during this critical period in the search for religious and political stability.

N. TYACKE, *Anti-Calvinists: The Rise of English Arminianism c. 1590–1640* (1987). The most important study of Archbishop Laud's policies and his predecessors.

D. UNDERDOWN, *Fire from Heaven: Life in an English Town in the Seventeenth Century* (1992). A lively account of a single English town.

J. B. WOLF, *Louis XIV* (1968). A very detailed political biography.

Chapter 14

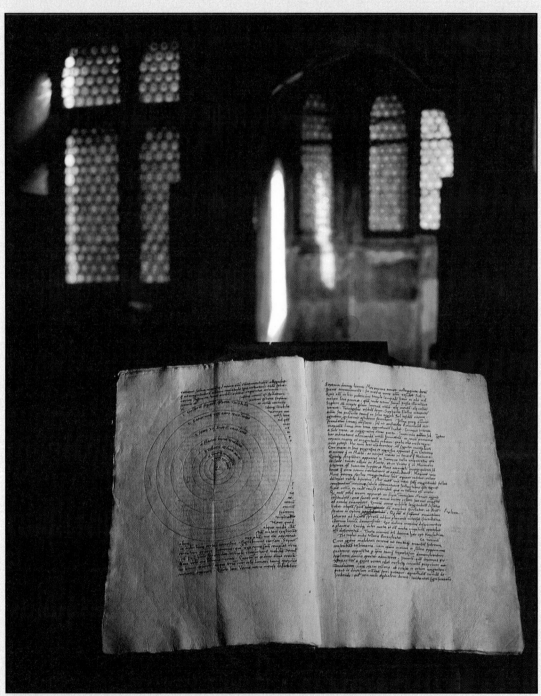

Nicolaus Copernicus's transforming view of the universe, with the sun in the center, is summarized in this diagram from his De Revolutionibus Orbium Coelestium (On the Revolutions of Heavenly Spheres), published in 1543.

Library of the Collegium Maius, Cracow, Poland. Erich Lessing/Art Resource.

New Directions in Thought and Culture in the Sixteenth and Seventeenth Centuries

KEY TOPICS

- The astronomical theories of Copernicus, Brahe, Kepler, Galileo, and Newton and the emergence of the scientific worldview
- Impact of the new science on philosophy
- Social setting of early modern science
- Women and the scientific revolution
- Approaches to science and religion
- Witchcraft and witch hunts

The sixteenth and seventeenth centuries witnessed a sweeping change in the scientific view of the universe. An Earth-centered picture gave way to one in which the Earth was only another planet orbiting about the sun. The sun itself became one of millions of stars. This transformation of humankind's perception of its place in the larger scheme of things led to a profound rethinking of moral and religious matters, as well as of scientific theory. Faith and reason needed new modes of reconciliation, as did faith and science. The new ideas and methods of science, usually termed natural philosophy at the time, challenged those modes of thought associated with late medieval times: Scholasticism, and Aristotelian philosophy.

The impact of the new science that explored the realm of the stars through the newly invented telescope and the world of microorganisms through the newly invented microscope must be viewed in the context of two other factors that simultaneously challenged traditional modes of European *thought and culture in the sixteenth and seventeenth centuries. The first of these was the Reformation, which permanently divided the religious unity of central and western Europe and fostered decades of warfare and theological dispute. Although by no means a complete break with medieval thought, the theology of the Reformation did question many ideas associated with medieval Christianity and society. The second factor was the cultural impact of the encounter of Europe with the New World of the Americas. The interaction with the Americas meant that Europeans directly or indirectly acquired knowledge of new peoples, plants, and animals wholly different from their own and about which people in neither ancient nor medieval times had any information. Consequently, new uncertainties and unfamiliar vistas confronted many Europeans as they considered their souls, geographical knowledge, and physical nature.*

Side by side with this new knowledge and science, however, came a new wave of superstition and persecution. The changing world of religion, politics, and knowledge also created profound fear and anxiety among both the simple and the learned, resulting in Europe's worst witch hunts.

The Scientific Revolution

The process which established the new view of the universe is normally termed the *Scientific Revolution*. The revolution-in-science metaphor must be used carefully, however. Not everything associated with the "new" science was necessarily new. Sixteenth- and seventeenth-century natural philosophers were often re-examining and rethinking theories and data from the ancient world and the late middle ages. Moreover, the word *revolution* normally denotes rapid, collective political change involving large numbers of people. The Scientific Revolution was *not* rapid. It was a complex movement with many false starts and brilliant people suggesting wrong as well as useful ideas. Nor did it involve more than a few hundred people who labored in widely separated studies and crude laboratories located in Poland, Italy, Bohemia, France, and Great Britain. Furthermore, the achievements of the new science were not simply the function of isolated brilliant scientific minds. The leading figures of the Scientific Revolution often drew upon the aid of artisans and craftspeople to help them construct new instruments for experimentation and to carry out those experiments. Thus, the Scientific Revolution involved a reappropriation of older knowledge as well as new discoveries. Additionally, because the practice of science involves social ac-

tivity as well as knowledge, the revolution also saw the establishment of new social institutions to support the emerging scientific enterprise.

Science as we know it today was only in the process of becoming during the era of the Scientific Revolution. In fact the word *scientist*, invented in the 1830s, did not yet exist in the seventeenth century nor did anything resembling the modern scientific career. Individuals devoted to natural philosophy might work in universities or in the court of a prince or possibly in their own homes and workshops. Only in the second half of the seventeenth century did formal societies and academies devoted to the pursuit of natural philosophy come into existence. Even then the entire process of the pursuit of natural knowledge was a largely informal one.

Yet by the close of the seventeenth century the new scientific concepts and the methods of their construction were so impressive that they set the standard for assessing the validity of knowledge in the Western world. From the early seventeenth century through the end of the twentieth century science achieved greater cultural authority in the Western world than any other form of intellectual activity, and the authority and application of scientific knowledge became one of the defining characteristics of modern Western civilization.

Although new knowledge emerged in many areas during the sixteenth and seventeenth centuries, including medicine, chemistry, and natural history, the scientific achievements that most captured the learned imagination and persuaded people of the cultural power of natural knowledge were those that occurred in astronomy.

Nicolaus Copernicus Rejects an Earth-centered Universe

Nicolaus Copernicus (1473–1543) was a Polish astronomer who enjoyed a high reputation during his life. He had been educated first in Cracow and later in Italy. He led a largely isolated intellectual career and had not been known for strikingly original or unorthodox thought. In 1543, the year of his death, Copernicus published *On the Revolutions of the Heavenly Spheres*. Copernicus's book was "a revolution-making rather than a revolutionary text."[1] What Copernicus did was to provide an intellectual springboard for a complete criticism of the then-dominant view of the position of the Earth in the universe.

[1] Thomas S. Kuhn, *The Copernican Revolution: Planetary Astronomy in the Development of Western Thought* (New York: Vintage, 1959), p. 135.

Copernicus Ascribes Movement to the Earth

Copernicus published De Revolutionibus Orbium Caelestium (On the Revolutions of the Heavenly Spheres) *in 1543. In his preface, addressed to Pope Paul III, he explained what had led him to think that the Earth moved around the sun and what he thought were some of the scientific consequences of the new theory.*

❖ *How does Copernicus justify his argument to the Pope? How important was historical precedent and tradition to the Pope? Might Copernicus have thought that the Pope would be especially susceptible to such argument, even though what Copernicus proposed (the movement of the Earth) contradicted the Bible?*

I may well presume, most Holy Father, that certain people, as soon as they hear that in this book about the Revolutions of the Spheres of the Universe I ascribe movement to the Earthly globe, will cry out that, holding such views, I should at once be hissed off the stage....

So I should like your Holiness to know that I was induced to think of a method of computing the motions of the spheres by nothing else than the knowledge that the Mathematicians [who had previously considered the problem] are inconsistent in these investigations.

For, first, the mathematicians are so unsure of the movements of the Sun and Moon that they cannot even explain or observe the constant length of the seasonal year. Secondly, in determining the motions of these and of the other five planets, they use neither the same principles and hypotheses nor the same demonstrations of the apparent motions and revolutions....Nor have they been able thereby to discern or deduce the principal thing—namely the shape of the Universe and the unchangeable symmetry of its parts....

I pondered long upon this uncertainty of mathematical tradition in establishing the motions of the system of the spheres. At last I began to chafe that philosophers could by no means agree on any one certain theory of the mechanism of the Universe, wrought for us by a supremely good and orderly Creator....I therefore took pains to read again the works of all the philosophers on whom I could lay hand to seek out whether any of them had ever supposed that the motions of the spheres were other than those demanded by the [Ptolemaic] mathematical schools. I found first in Cicero that Hicetas [of Syracuse, fifth century B.C.] had realized that the Earth moved. Afterwards I found in Plutarch that certain others had held the like opinion....

Thus assuming motions, which in my work I ascribe to the Earth, by long and frequent observations I have at last discovered that, if the motions of the rest of the planets be brought into relation with the circulation of the Earth and be reckoned in proportion to the circles of each planet, not only do their phenomena presently ensue, but the orders and magnitudes of all stars and spheres, nay the heavens themselves, become so bound together that nothing in any part thereof could be moved from its place without producing confusion of all the other parts of the Universe as a whole.

As quoted in Thomas S. Kuhn, *The Copernican Revolution: Planetary Astronomy in the Development of Western Thought* (New York: Vintage Books, 1959), pp. 137–139, 141–142.

THE PTOLEMAIC SYSTEM At the time of Copernicus, the standard explanation of the place of the Earth in the heavens combined the mathematical astronomy of Ptolemy, contained in his work entitled the *Almagest* (150 C.E.), with the physical cosmology of Aristotle. Over the centuries, commentators on Ptolemy's work had developed several alternative Ptolemaic systems, on the basis of which they made mathematical calculations relating to astronomy. Most of these writers assumed that the Earth was the center of the universe, an outlook known as *geocentricsm*. Drawing upon Aristotle, these commentators assumed that above the Earth lay a series of concentric spheres, probably fluid in character, one of which contained the moon, another the sun, and still others the planets and the stars. At the outer regions of these spheres lay the realm of God and the angels. The Earth had to be the center because of its heaviness. The stars and the other heavenly bodies had to be enclosed in the spheres so that they could move, since nothing could move unless something was actually moving it. The state of rest was presumed natural; motion required explanation. This was the astronomy found in such works as Dante's *Divine Comedy*.

Numerous problems were associated with the Ptolemaic model, and these had long been recognized. The most important was the observed motions of the planets. At certain times the planets actually appeared to be going backwards. The Ptolemaic model accounted for these motions primarily through *epicycles*. The planet moved uniformly about a small circle (an epicyle), while the center of the epicyle moved uniformly about a larger circle (called a deferent), with the Earth at or near its center. The combination of these two motions, as viewed from the Earth, was meant to replicate the changing planetary positions among the fixed stars—and did so to a high degree of accuracy. The circles employed in Ptolemaic systems were not meant to represent the actual paths of anything; that is, they were not orbits. Rather, they were the components of purely mathematical models meant to predict planetary positions. Other intellectual, but nonobservational, difficulties related to the immense speed at which the spheres had to move around the Earth. To say the least, the Ptolemaic systems were cluttered. They were effective, however, as long as one assumed Aristotelian physics.

COPERNICUS'S UNIVERSE Copernicus's *On the Revolutions of the Heavenly Spheres* challenged the Ptolemaic picture in the most conservative manner possible. (See "Copernicus Ascribes Movement to the Earth.") Copernicus adopted many elements of the Ptolemaic model, but transferred them to a *heliocentric* (sun-centered) model which assumed that the Earth moved about the sun in a circle. Copernicus's model, which retained epicycles, was actually no more accurate than Ptolemy's. However, Copernicus could claim certain advantages over the ancient model. In particular, the epicycles were smaller. The retrograde motion of the planets now stood explained as a result of an optical illusion arising from an observer viewing the planets from a moving Earth. The order of the planets from the sun became more clearly intelligible when it was understood as a result of their increasing periods of revolution based on the planets' increasing distance from the sun.

The repositioning of the Earth had not been Copernicus's goal. Rather, Copernicus appears to have set out to achieve new intelligibility and mathematical elegance to astronomy. The means of doing so was to reject Aristotle's cosmology and to remove the Earth from the center of the universe. His system was no more accurate than the existing ones for predicting the location of the planets. He had used no new evidence. The major impact of his work was to provide another

way of confronting some of the difficulties inherent in Ptolemaic astronomy. The Copernican system did not immediately replace the old astronomy, but it allowed other people who were also discontented with the Ptolemaic view to think in new directions. Indeed, for at least a century, the Copernican system was embraced by a distinct minority of natural philosophers and astronomers.

Tycho Brahe and Johannes Kepler Make New Scientific Observations

Tycho Brahe (1546–1601) took the next major step toward the conception of a sun-centered system. He did not embrace Copernicus's view of the universe and actually spent most of his life advocating an Earth-centered system. He suggested that the moon and the sun revolved around the Earth

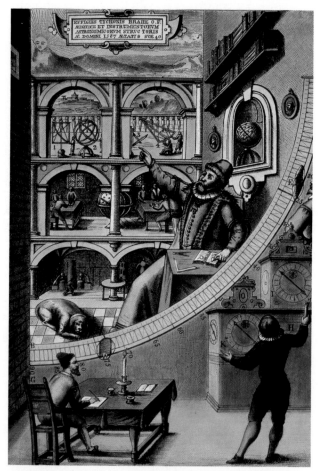

Tycho Brahe in the Uranienburg observatory on the Danish island of Hven (1587). Brahe made the most important observations of the stars since antiquity. Kepler used his data to solve the problem of planetary motion in a way that supported Copernicus's sun-centered view of the universe. Ironically, Brahe himself had opposed Copernicus's view. Bildarchiv Preussischer Kulturbesitz and that the other planets revolved around the sun. In pursuit of his own theory, Brahe constructed scientific instruments with which he made more extensive naked-eye observations of the planets than anyone previous to him. His labors produced a vastly expanded body of astronomical data from which his successors could work.

When Brahe died, these tables came into the possession of his assistant, Johannes Kepler (1571–1630), a German astronomer. Kepler was a convinced Copernican and a more consistently rigorous advocate of a heliocentric model than Copernicus himself. Deeply influenced by Renaissance Neoplatonism, which held the sun in special honor, Kepler was determined to find in Brahe's numbers mathematical harmonies that would support a sun-centered universe. After much work, Kepler discovered that to keep the sun at the center of things, he must abandon the circular components of Copernicus's model, particularly the epicycles. The mathematical relationships that emerged from his consideration of Brahe's observations suggested that the motions of the planets were elliptical. Then Kepler set forth the first astronomical model that actually portrayed motion—that is, the path of the planets—and those orbits were elliptical. Kepler published his findings in his 1609 book entitled *The New Astronomy*. He had solved the problem of planetary motion by using Copernicus's sun-centered universe and Brahe's empirical data.

Kepler had also defined a new problem. None of the available theories could explain why the planetary orbits were elliptical or, for that matter, why planetary motion was orbital at all rather than simply moving off along a tangent. That solution awaited the work of Sir Isaac Newton.

Galileo Galilei Argues for a Universe of Mathematical Laws

From Copernicus to Brahe to Kepler, there had been little new information about the heavens that might not have been known to Ptolemy. In 1609, however, the same year that Kepler published *The New Astronomy*, an Italian mathematician and natural philosopher named Galileo Galilei (1564–1642) first turned a telescope on the heavens. Using that recently-invented Dutch instrument, he saw stars where none had been known to exist, mountains on the moon, spots moving across the sun, and moons orbiting Jupiter. The heavens were far more complex than anyone had formerly suspected. These discoveries, with some work, could have been accommodated into the Ptolemaic model and even more

The telescope with which Galileo worked after 1609. He observed Earth's moon and the cyclical phases of the planet Venus and discovered the most prominent moons of Jupiter. These observations had revolutionary intellectual and theological implications in the seventeenth century. Muséo della Scienza, Florence, Italy. Scala/Art Resource, N.Y.

easily into Kepler's earth-centered model. Such accommodation would, however, have required a highly technical understanding of Ptolemaic astronomy. Galileo knew that few people who controlled patronage possessed such complex knowledge. Consequently, in the *Starry Messenger* (1610) and *Letters on Sunspots* (1613) he used his considerable rhetorical skills to argue that his newly observed physical evidence, most particularly the phases of Venus, required a Copernican interpretation of the heavens.

Galileo's career illustrates that the forging of the new science involved more than the presentation of arguments and evidence. In 1610 he had left the University of Padua for Florence, where he became the philosopher and mathematician to the Grand Duke of Tuscany, who was a Medici. Galileo was now pursuing natural philosophy in a princely court and had become dependent upon princely patronage. To win such support for both his continued work and the theories he propounded, he named the moons of Saturn after the Medicis. As a natural philosopher working with the new telescope, he had literally presented recently discovered heavenly bodies to his patron. By both his political skills and his excellent prose, he had transformed himself into a high-profile advocate of Copernicanism. Galileo's problems with the Roman Catholic Church, which are discussed later in the chapter, arose from both his ideas and his flair for self-advertisement.

Galileo not only popularized the Copernican system, but also articulated the concept of a universe subject to mathematical laws. More than any other writer of the century, he argued that nature displayed mathematical regularity in its most minute details:

Philosophy is written in that great book which ever lies before our eyes—I mean the universe—but we cannot understand it if we do not first learn the language and grasp the symbols in which it is written. This book is written in the mathematical language, and the symbols are triangles, circles, and other geometrical figures, without whose help it is impossible to comprehend a single word of it; without which one wanders through a dark labyrinth.[2]

The universe was rational; however, its rationality was not that of scholastic logic, but of mathematics. Copernicus had thought that the heavens conformed to mathematical regularity; Galileo saw this regularity throughout all physical nature.

A world of quantities was replacing one of qualities. All aspects of the world—including color, beauty, and taste—would increasingly be described in terms of the mathematical relationships among quantities. Mathematical models would eventually be applied even to social relations. The new natural philosophy portrayed nature as cold, rational, mathematical, and mechanistic. What was real and lasting was what was mathematically measurable. For many people, the power of the mathematical arguments that appeared irrefutable proved more persuasive than the new information from physical observation that produced so much controversy. Few intellectual shifts have wrought such momentous changes for Western civilization.

Isaac Newton Discovers the Laws of Gravitation

The question that continued to perplex seventeenth-century scientists who accepted the theories of Copernicus, Kepler, and Galileo was how the planets and other heavenly bodies moved in an orderly fashion. The Ptolemaic and Aristotelian answer had been the spheres and a universe arranged in the order of the heaviness of its parts. Many unsatisfactory theories had been set forth to deal with the question. It was this issue of planetary motion that the Englishman Isaac Newton (1642–1727) addressed and, in so doing, established a basis for physics that endured for more than two centuries.

In 1687 Newton published *The Mathematical Principles of Natural Philosophy*, better known by its Latin title of *Principia Mathematica*. Much of the research and thinking for this great work had taken place more than fifteen years earlier. Galileo's mathematical bias permeated Newton's thought, as did his view that inertia applied to bodies both at

Sir Isaac Newton discovered the mathematical and physical laws governing the force of gravity. Newton believed that religion and science were compatible and mutually supportive, and that the study of nature gave one a better understanding of the Creator. This portrait of Newton is by Sir Godfrey Kneller. Sir Godfrey Kneller, *Sir Isaac Newton.* Bildarchiv Preussicher Kulturbesitz

[2] Quoted in E. A. Burtt, *The Metaphysical Foundations of Modern Physical Science* (Garden City, NY: Anchor–Doubleday, 1954), p. 75.

rest and in motion. Newton reasoned that the planets and all other physical objects in the universe moved through mutual attraction, or gravity. Every object in the universe affected every other object through gravity. The attraction of gravity explained why the planets moved in an orderly, rather than a chaotic, manner. Newton had found that "the force of gravity towards the whole planet did arise from and was compounded of the forces of gravity towards all its parts, and towards every one part was in the inverse proportion of the squares of the distances from the part."[3] Newton proved this relationship mathematically; he made no attempt to explain the nature of gravity itself.

Newton was a great mathematical genius, but he also upheld the importance of empirical data and observation. Like Francis Bacon (see below), he believed that one must observe phenomena before attempting to explain them. The final test of any theory or hypothesis for him was whether it described what was actually observed. Newton was a great opponent of the rationalism of the French philosopher Descartes (see below), which he believed included insufficient guards against error. Consequently, as Newton's own theory of universal gravitation became increasingly accepted, so, too, was Baconian empiricism.

Philosophy Responds to Changing Science

The revolution in scientific thought contributed directly to a major reexamination of Western philosophy. Several of the most important figures in the Scientific Revolution, such as Bacon and Descartes, were also philosophers discontented with the scholastic heritage. Bacon stressed the importance of empirical research. Descartes attempted to find certainty through the exploration of his own thinking processes. Newton's interests likewise extended to philosophy; he wrote broadly on many topics, including scientific method and theology.

If a single idea informed all of these philosophers, though in different ways, it was the idea of *mechanism*. The proponents of the new science sought to explain the world in terms of mechanical metaphors, or the language of machinery. The image to which many of them turned was that of the clock. Johannes Kepler once wrote, "I am much occupied with the in-

vestigation of the physical causes. My aim in this is to show that the machine of the universe is not similar to a divine animated being, but similar to a clock."[4] Nature conceived as machinery removed much of the mystery of the world and the previous assumption of the presence of divine purpose in nature. The qualities that seemed to inhere in matter came to be understood as the result of mechanical arrangement. Some writers came to understand God as a kind of divine watchmaker or mechanic who had arranged the world as a machine that would thereafter function automatically. The drive to a mechanical understanding of nature also meant that the language of science and of natural philosophy would become largely that of mathematics. The emphasis that Galileo had placed on mathematics spread to other areas of thought.

This new mode of thinking transformed physical nature from a realm in which Europeans looked for symbolic or sacramental meaning related to the divine into a realm where they looked for utility or usefulness. Previously, philosophers had often believed that a correct understanding of the natural order would reveal divine mysteries or knowledge relating to sacred history. Henceforth, they would tend to see knowledge of nature as revealing nothing beyond itself—nothing about divine purposes for the life of humankind on earth. Natural knowledge became the path toward the physical improvement of human beings through their ability to command the processes of nature. Many people associated with the new science also believed that such knowledge would strengthen the power of their monarchs.

Francis Bacon: The Empirical Method

Bacon (1561–1626) was an Englishman of almost universal accomplishment. He was a lawyer, a high royal official, and the author of histories, moral essays, and philosophical discourses. Traditionally, he has been regarded as the father of empiricism and of experimentation in science. Much of this reputation was actually unearned. Bacon was not a natural philosopher, except in the most amateur fashion. His real accomplishment was setting an intellectual tone and helping to create a climate conducive to scientific work.

In books such as *The Advancement of Learning* (1605), the *Novum Organum* (1620), and the *New Atlantis* (1627), Bacon attacked the scholastic belief that most truth had already been discovered and only required explanation, as well as the scholastic reverence for authority in intellectual life. (See "Bacon Attacks the Idols That Harm Human Understanding.") He believed that scholastic thinkers paid too much attention to tradition and to the knowledge of the ancients. He urged contemporaries to strike out on their own

[3] Quoted in A. Rupert Hall, *From Galileo to Newton, 1630–1720* (London: Fontana, 1970), p. 300.

[4] Quoted in Steven Shapin, *The Scientific Revolution* (Chicago: University of Chicago Press, 1996), p. 33.

Sir Francis Bacon (1561–1626), champion of the inductive method of gaining knowledge. By courtesy of the National Portrait Gallery, London

syllogisms to examine the foundations of their thought and intellectual presuppositions. Bacon urged that philosophers and investigators of nature examine the evidence of their senses before constructing logical speculations. In a famous passage, he divided all philosophers into "men of experiment and men of dogmas" and then observed:

> The men of experiment are like the ant, they only collect and use; the reasoners resemble spiders, who make cobwebs out of their own substance. But the bee takes a middle course: it gathers its material from the flowers of the garden and of the field, but transforms and digests it by a power of its own. Not unlike this is the true business of philosophy.[6]

By directing natural philosophy toward an examination of empirical evidence, Bacon hoped that it would achieve new knowledge and thus new capabilities for humankind.

Bacon boldly compared himself with Columbus, plotting a new route to intellectual discovery. The comparison is significant, because it displays the consciousness of a changing world that appears so often in writers of the late sixteenth and early seventeenth centuries. They were rejecting the past not from simple contempt or overweening pride, but rather from a firm understanding that the world was much more complicated than their medieval forebears had thought. Neither Europe nor European thought could remain self-contained. Like the new worlds on the globe, new worlds of the mind were also emerging.

Most of the people in Bacon's day, including the intellectuals, thought that the best era of human history lay in antiquity. Bacon dissented vigorously from that view. He looked to a future of material improvement achieved through the empirical examination of nature. His own theory of induction from empirical evidence was unsystematic, but his insistence on appealing to experience influenced others whose methods were more productive. He and others of his outlook received almost daily support from the reports not only of European explorers, but also of ordinary seamen who now sailed all over the world and could describe wondrous cultures, as well as plants and animals, unknown to the European ancients.

Bacon believed that science had a practical purpose and its goal was human improvement. Some scientific investigation does have this character. Much pure research does not. Bacon, however, linked science and material progress in the public mind. This was a powerful idea and has continued to influence Western civilization to the present day. It has made science and those who can appeal to the authority of science major forces for change and

in search of a new understanding of nature. He wanted seventeenth-century Europeans to have confidence in themselves and their own abilities rather than in the people and methods of the past. Bacon was one of the first major European writers to champion the desirability of innovation and change.

Bacon believed that human knowledge should produce useful results—deeds rather than words. In particular, knowledge of nature should be brought to the aid of the human condition. These goals required the modification or abandonment of scholastic modes of learning and thinking. Bacon contended, "The [scholastic] logic now in use serves more to fix and give stability to the errors which have their foundation in commonly received notions than to help the search after truth."[5] Scholastic philosophers could not escape from their

[5] Quoted in Franklin Baumer, *Main Currents of Western Thought,* 4th ed. (New Haven, CT: Yale University Press, 1978), p. 281.

[6] Quoted in Baumer, p. 288.

Bacon Attacks the Idols That Harm Human Understanding

Francis Bacon wanted the men and women of his era to have the courage to change the way they thought about physical nature. In this famous passage from the Novum Organum *(1620), he attempted to explain why it is so difficult to ask new questions and seek new answers.*

❖ *Is Bacon's view of human nature pessimistic? Are people hopelessly trapped in overlapping worlds of self-interest and fantasy imposed by their nature and cultural traditions? How did Bacon expect people to overcome such formidable barriers?*

The idols and false notions which are now in possession of the human understanding and have taken deep root therein....so beset men's minds that truth can hardly find entrance....There are four classes of Idols which beset men's minds. To these for distinction's sake I have assigned names—calling the first class Idols of the Tribe; the second, Idols of the Cave; the third, Idols of the Marketplace; the fourth, Idols of the Theatre.

The Idols of the Tribe have their foundation in human nature itself; and in the tribe or race of men. For it is a false assertion that the sense of man is the measure of things. On the contrary, all perceptions as well as the sense as of the mind are according to the measure of the universe. And the human understanding is like a false mirror, which, receiving rays irregularly, distorts and discolours the nature of things by mingling its own nature with it.

The Idols of the Cave are the idols of the individual man. For every one (besides the errors common to human nature in general) has a cave

or den of his own, which refracts and discolours the light of nature; owing either to his own proper and peculiar nature; or to his education and conversation with others; or to the reading of books, and the authority of those whom he esteems and admires....

There are also Idols formed by the intercourse and association of men with each other, which I call Idols of the Marketplace, on account of the commerce and consort of men there. For it is by discourse that men associate; and words are imposed according to the apprehension of the vulgar. And therefore the ill and unfit choice of words wonderfully obstructs the understanding....

Lastly, there are Idols which have immigrated into men's minds from the various dogmas of philosophies, and also from wrong laws of demonstration. These I call Idols of the Theatre; because in my judgment all the received systems are but so many stage plays, representing worlds of their own creation after an unreal and scenic fashion.

From Francis Bacon, *Essays, Advancement of Learning, New Atlantis, and Other Pieces*, ed. by Richard Foster Jones (New York: Odyssey, 1937), pp. 278–280.

innovation. Thus, though not making any major scientific contribution himself, Bacon directed investigators of nature to a new method and a new purpose. As a person actively associated with politics, Bacon also believed that the pursuit of new knowledge would increase the power of governments and monarchies. Again, his thought in this area opened the way for the eventual strong linkage between governments and the scientific enterprise.

René Descartes: The Method of Rational Deduction

Descartes (1596–1650) was a gifted mathematician who invented analytic geometry. His most important contribution, however, was to develop a scientific method that relied more on deduction than empirical observation and induction.

In 1637 he published his *Discourse on Method*, in which he rejected scholastic philosophy and education and advocated thought founded on a mathematical model. (See "Descartes Explores the Promise of Science.") The work appeared in French rather than in Latin, because Descartes wanted it to have wide circulation and application. In the *Discourse*, he began by saying that he would doubt everything except those propositions about which he could have clear and distinct ideas. This approach rejected all forms of intellectual authority, except the conviction of his own reason. Descartes concluded that he could not doubt his own act of thinking and his own exis-

René Descartes (1596–1650) believed that because the material world operated according to mathematical laws, it could be accurately understood by the exercise of human reason. Sebastian Bourdon, *Portrait of philosopher René Descartes.* Louvre, Paris, France. Erich Lessing/Art Resource, N.Y.

speculation. Reason was to be applied only to the mechanical realm of matter or to the exploration of itself.

Descartes's emphasis on deduction, rational speculation, and internal reflection by the mind, all of which he explored more fully in his *Meditations* of 1641, exercised broad influence among philosophers. His deductive methodology, however, eventually lost favor to scientific induction, whereby the scientist draws generalizations derived from empirical observations.

Thomas Hobbes: Apologist for Absolutism

Nowhere did the impact of the methods of the new science so deeply affect political thought as in the thought of Thomas Hobbes (1588–1679), the most original political philosopher of the seventeenth century. In his low view of human nature and his concept of a commonwealth based on convenant between the community and an all-powerful sovereign, Hobbes's thought contained echoes of Calvinism. Yet Hobbes presented these arguments in a materialistic philosophical framework that led many of his contemporaries rightly or wrongly to regard him as an atheist.

An urbane and much-traveled man, Hobbes enthusiastically supported the new scientific movement. During the 1630s he visited Paris, where he came to know Descartes, and he spent time with Galileo in Italy as well. He took special interest in the works of William Harvey (1578–1657), who was famous for his discovery of the circulation of blood through the body. Hobbes was also a superb classicist. His earliest published work was the first English translation of Thucydides' *History of the Peloponnesian War* and is still being reprinted today. Part of the darkness of Hobbes's view of human nature would appear to derive from Thucydides' historical analysis.

Hobbes had written works of political philosophy before the English civil war, but the turmoil of that struggle led him in 1651 to publish his *Leviathan*, a work of contemporaneous controversy and lasting influence. He was deeply concerned with the problem of how a strong central political authority might receive rigorous philosophical justification. In the *Leviathan*, Hobbes portrayed human beings and society in a thoroughly materialistic and mechanical way. He traced all psychological processes to bare sensation and regarded all human motivations as egoistical, intended to increase pleasure and minimize pain. According to his analysis, human reasoning penetrated to no deeper reality or wisdom than those physical sen-

tence. From this base, he proceeded to deduce the existence of God. The presence of God was important to Descartes because God guaranteed the correctness of clear and distinct ideas. Since God was not a deceiver, the ideas of God-given reason could not be false.

On the basis of such an analysis, Descartes concluded that human reason could fully comprehend the world. He divided existing things into two basic categories: thinking things and things occupying space—mind and body, respectively. Thinking was the defining quality of the mind, and extension (the property in virtue of which things occupy space) was the defining quality of material bodies. Human reason could grasp and understand the world of extension, which became the realm of the natural philosopher. That world had no place for spirits, divinity, or anything nonmaterial. Descartes separated mind from body to banish such things from the realm of scientific

Descartes Explores the Promise of Science

In 1637, Descartes published his Discourse on Method. *He wrote against what he believed to be the useless speculations of scholastic philosophy. He championed the careful investigation of physical nature on the grounds that it would expand the scope of human knowledge beyond anything previously achieved and in doing so make human beings the masters of nature. This passage contains much of the broad intellectual and cultural argument that led to the ever-growing influence and authority of science from the seventeenth century onward.*

❖ *How does Descartes compare the usefulness of science with previous speculative philosophy? How does he portray science as an instrument whereby human beings may master nature? What, if any, limits does he place on the extension of scientific knowledge? Why does he place so much emphasis on the promise of science to improve human health?*

My speculations were indeed truly pleasing to me; but I recognize that other men have theirs, which perhaps please them even more. As soon, however, as I had acquired some general notions regarding physics, and on beginning to make trial of them in various special difficulties had observed how far they can carry us and how much they differ from the principles hitherto employed, I believed that I could not keep them hidden without grievously sinning against the law which lays us under obligation to promote, as far as in us lies, the general good of all mankind. For they led me to see that it is possible to obtain knowledge highly useful in life, and that in place of the speculative philosophy taught in the Schools we can have a practical philosophy, by means of which, knowing the force and the actions of fire, water, air, and of the stars, of the heavens, and of all the bodies that surround us—knowing them as distinctly as we know the various crafts of the artisans—we may in the same fashion employ them in all the uses for which they are suited, thus rendering ourselves the mas-

ters and possessors of nature. This is to be desired, not only with a view to the invention of an infinity of arts by which we would be enabled to enjoy without heavy labor the fruits of the earth and all its conveniences, but above all for the preservation of health, which is, without doubt, of all blessings in this life, the first of all goods and the foundation on which the others rest. For the mind is so dependent on the temper and disposition of the bodily organisms that if any means can ever be found to render men wiser and more capable than they have hitherto been, I believe that it is in the science of medicine that the means must be sought....With no wish to depreciate it, I am yet sure there is no one, even of those engaged in the profession, who does not admit that all we know is almost nothing in comparison with what remains to be discovered; and that we could be freed from innumerable maladies, both of body and of mind, and even perhaps from the infirmities of age, if we had sufficient knowledge of their causes and of the remedies provided by nature.

From René Descartes, *Discourse on Method*, in Norman Kemp Smith, ed., *Descartes's Philosophical Writings* (New York: The Modern Library, 1958), pp. 130–131. Reprinted by permission of Macmillan Press Ltd.

sations. Consequently, for Hobbes, unlike both previous Christian and ancient philosophers, human beings exist for no higher spiritual ends or larger moral purpose than those of meeting the needs of daily life. In his view, human beings could fulfill even those limited goals only within the confines of a sovereign commonwealth established by contract that prevented the exercise of the natural human pursuit of self-interest with all its attendant potential for conflict.

Much of the persuasive power of Hobbes's political philosophy lay in his brilliant myth or political fiction about the original state of humankind. According to his account, human beings in their natural state are inclined to a "perpetual and restless desire" for power. Because all people want and, in their natural state, possess a natural right to everything, their equality breeds enmity, competition, diffidence, and perpetual quarreling—"a war of every man against every man." As Hobbes put it in a famous summary,

A portrait of Thomas Hobbes (1588–1679), whose political treatise, Leviathan, *portrayed rulers as absolute lords over their lands, incorporating in their persons the individual wills of all their people.* Bildarchiv Preussischer Kulturbesitz

In such condition there is no place for industry, because the fruit thereof is uncertain; and consequently no culture of the Earth; no navigation nor use of the commodities that may be imported by sea; no commodious building; no instruments of moving and removing such things as require much force; no knowledge of the face of the Earth; no account of time; no arts; no letters; no society; and, which is worst of all, continual fear and danger of violent death; and the life of man solitary, poor, nasty, brutish, and short.[7]

As seen in this passage, Hobbes, contrary to Aristotle and Christian thinkers like Thomas Aquinas, did not believe that human beings were naturally sociable. Rather, they were self-centered creatures lacking a master. Whereas earlier and later philosophers saw the original human state as a paradise from which humankind had fallen, Hobbes saw it as a state of natural, inevitable conflict in which neither safety, security, nor any final authority existed. Human beings in this state of nature were constantly haunted by fear of destruction and death.

Human beings escaped this terrible state of nature, according to Hobbes, only by entering into a particular kind of political contract according to which they agreed to live in a commonwealth tightly ruled by a recognized sovereign. This contract obliged every person, for the sake of peace and self-defense, to agree to set aside personal rights to all things and to be content with as much liberty against others as he or she would allow others against himself or herself. All agreed to live according to a secularized version of the golden rule, "Do not that to another which you would not have done to yourself."[8]

Because, however, words and promises are insufficient to guarantee this state, the contract also established the coercive use of force to compel compliance. Believing the dangers of anarchy to be always greater than those of tyranny, Hobbes thought that rulers should be absolute and unlimited in their power, once established as authority. Hobbes's political philosophy has no room for protest in the name of individual conscience or for individual resistance to some other legitimate authority beyond the sovereign. In a reply to critics of his position on sovereign authority, Hobbes pointed out the alternative:

The greatest [unhappiness] that in any form of government can possibly happen to the people in general is scarce sensible in respect of the miseries and horrible calamities that accompany a civil war or that dissolute condition of masterless men, without subjection to laws and a coercive power to tie their hands from rapine and revenge.[9]

The specific structure of this absolute government was not of enormous concern to Hobbes. He believed that absolute authority might be lodged in either a monarch or a legislative body. But once that person or body had been granted authority, there existed no argument for appeal. For all practical purposes, obedience to the Hobbesian sovereign was absolute.

Hobbes's argument for an absolute political authority that could assure order aroused sharp opposition. Monarchists objected to his willingness to assign sovereign authority to a legislature. Republicans rejected his willingness to accept a monarchical authority. Some religious writers, including those who supported the divine right of kings, furiously criticized his materialist arguments for an absolute political authority. Other religious writers attacked his refusal to recognize the authority of either God or the Church as standing beside or above his secular sovereign. The influence of Hobbes's political analysis would grow over the next three centuries as political and religious authority in the West became increasingly separated.

[7] Thomas Hobbes, *Leviathan*, Parts I and II, ed. by H. W. Schneider (Indianapolis: Bobbs-Merrill, 1958), p. 86, 106–107.

[8] Hobbes, p. 130.

[9] Hobbes, p. 152.

The famous title page illustration for Hobbes's Leviathan. *The ruler is pictured as absolute lord of his lands, but note that the ruler incorporates the mass of individuals whose self-interests are best served by their willing consent to accept him and cooperate with him.*
Rare Books Division, The New York Public Library. Astor, Lenox and Tilden Foundations.

John Locke: Defender of Moderate Liberty and Toleration

Locke (1632–1704) proved to be the most influential philosophical and political thinker of the seventeenth century. Although he was less original than Hobbes, his political writings became a major source of criticism of absolutism and provided a foundation for later liberal political philosophy in both Europe and America. His philosophical works dealing with human knowledge became the most important work of psychology for the eighteenth century.

Locke's family had Puritan sympathies, and during the English civil war his father had fought for the parliamentary forces against the Stuart monarchy. Although a highly cerebral person who was well read in all the major seventeenth-century natural philosophers, Locke became deeply involved with the tumultuous politics of the English Restoration period. He was a close associate of Anthony Ashley Cooper, the earl of Shaftesbury, considered by his contemporaries to be a radical in both religion and politics. Shaftesbury organized an unsuccessful rebellion against Charles II in 1682, after which both he and Locke, who lived with him, were forced to flee to Holland.

During his years of association with Shaftesbury and the opposition to Charles II, Locke wrote two treatises on government, which were published in 1690. In the first of these, he rejected arguments for absolute government that based political authority on the patriarchal model of fathers ruling over a family. After the publication of this treatise, no major political philosopher again appealed to the patriarchal model. In that regard, though not widely read today, Locke's *First Treatise of Government* proved enormously important by clearing the philosophical decks, so to speak, of a long-standing traditional argument that could not stand up to rigorous analysis.

John Locke (1632–1704), defender of the rights of the people against rulers who think their power absolute.
By courtesy of the National Portrait Gallery, London

thority. In this respect, government exists to protect the best achievements and liberty of the state of nature, not to overcome them. Thus, by its very foundation, Locke's government is one of limited authority.

The warfare that Hobbes believed characterized the state of nature emerged for Locke only when rulers failed to preserve people's natural freedom and attempted to enslave them by absolute rule. The relationship between rulers and the governed is that of trust, and if the rulers betray that trust, the governed have the right to replace them. In this regard, Locke's position resembled that of St. Thomas Aquinas, who also permitted rebellion against government when it violated laws of nature.

In his *Letter Concerning Toleration* (1689), Locke used the premises of the as yet unpublished *Second Treatise* to defend extensive religious toleration, which he saw as an answer to the destructive religious conflict of the past two centuries. To make his case for toleration, Locke claimed that each individual stood charged with working out his or her own religious salvation and that these efforts might lead various people to join different religious groups. For its part, government existed by its very nature to preserve property, not to make religious decisions for its citizens. Governments that attempted to impose religious uniformity thus misunderstood their real purpose. Moreover, government-imposed religious uniformity could not achieve real religious ends, because assent to religious truth must be freely given by the individual's conscience rather than by force. Consequently, Locke urged a wide degree of religious toleration among differing voluntary Christian groups. He did not, however, extend toleration to Roman Catholics, whom he believed to have given allegiance to a foreign prince (i.e., the Pope), or

In his *Second Treatise of Government*, Locke presented an extended argument for a government that must necessarily be both responsible for and responsive to the concerns of the governed. Locke portrayed the natural human state as one of perfect freedom and equality in which everyone enjoyed, in an unregulated fashion, the natural rights of life, liberty, and property. Locke, contrary to Hobbes, regarded human beings in their natural state as creatures of reason and basic goodwill rather than of uncontrolled passion and selfishness. For Locke, human beings possess a strong capacity for dwelling more or less peacefully in society before they enter a political contract. What they experience in the state of nature is not a state of war, but a condition of competition and modest conflict that requires a political authority to sort out problems rather than to impose sovereign authority. They enter into the contract to form political society to secure and preserve the rights, liberty, and property that they already possess prior to the existence of political au-

Major Works of the Scientific Revolution

1543	*On the Revolutions of the Heavenly Spheres* (Copernicus)
1605	*The Advancement of Learning* (Bacon)
1609	*The New Astronomy* (Kepler)
1620	*Novum Organum* (Bacon)
1632	*Dialogues on the Two Chief World Systems* (Galileo)
1637	*Discourse on Method* (Descartes)
1651	*Leviathan* (Hobbes)
1687	*Principia Mathematica* (Newton)
1689	*Letter Concerning Toleration* (Locke)
1690	*An Essay Concerning Human Understanding* (Locke)
1690	*Treatises of Government* (Locke)

John Locke Explores the Sources of Human Knowledge

An Essay Concerning Human Understanding (1690) was probably the most influential philosophical work ever written in English. Locke's fundamental idea, which is explicated in the passage that follows, was that human knowledge is grounded in the experiences of the senses and in the reflection of the mind on those experiences. He rejected any belief in innate ideas. His emphasis on experience led to the wider belief that human beings are creatures of their environment. After Locke, numerous writers argued that human beings could be improved if the political and social environments in which they lived were reformed.

❖ *How does Locke explain how the human mind comes to be furnished? What does Locke mean by experience? How does reflection deal with external sensations? What role does the external environment play in Locke's psychology?*

Let us then suppose the mind to be, as we say, white paper void of all characters, without any ideas. Whence comes it to be furnished? Whence comes it by that vast store which the busy and boundless fancy of man has painted on it with an almost endless variety? Whence has it all the materials of reason and knowledge? To this I answer, from experience; in that all our knowledge is founded, and from that it ultimately derives itself. Our observation, employed either about external sensible objects, or about the internal operations of our minds perceived and reflected on by ourselves, is that which supplies our understanding with all the materials of thinking. These two are the fountains of knowledge, from whence all the ideas we have, or can naturally have, do spring.

First, our senses, conversant about particular sensible objects, do convey into the mind several distinct perceptions of things, according to those various ways wherein those objects do affect them. And thus we come by those ideas we have of yellow, white, heat, cold, soft, hard, bitter, sweet, and all those which we call sensible qualities....This great source of most of the ideas we have, depending wholly upon our senses, and derived by them to the understanding, I call SENSATION.

Secondly, the other fountain from which experience furnisheth the understanding with ideas is the perception of the operations of our own mind within us, as it is employed about the ideas it has got...and such are perception, thinking, doubting, believing, reasoning, knowing, willing, and all the different actings of our own minds....I call this REFLECTION, the ideas it affords being such only as the mind gets by reflecting on its own operations within itself.... These two, I say, viz., external material things as the objects of SENSATION, and the operations of our own minds within as the objects of REFLECTION, are to me the only originals from whence all our ideas take their beginnings...

The understanding seems to me not to have the least glimmering of any ideas which it doth not receive from one of these two.

From John Locke, *An Essay Concerning Human Understanding*, Vol. 1 (London, Everyman's Library, 1961), pp. 77–78.

to atheists, whom he believed could not be trusted to keep their word. Despite these limitations, Locke's *Letter Concerning Toleration* established a powerful foundation for the future extension of toleration, religious liberty, and the separation of church and state. His vision of such expansive toleration was partially realized in England after 1688 and most fully in the United States after the American Revolution.

Finally, just as Newton had set forth laws of astronomy and gravitation, Locke hoped to elucidate the basic structures of human thought. He did so in the most immediately influential of his books, his *Essay Concerning Human Understanding* (1690), which became the major work of European psychology during the eighteenth century. There, Locke portrayed a person's mind at birth as a blank tablet whose content would be determined by sense experience. (See "John Locke Explores the Sources of Human Knowledge.") His vision of the mind has been aptly compared to an early version of behaviorism. It was a reformer's psychology which believed that the human condition could be improved by changing the environment.

Locke's view of psychology rejected the Christian understanding of original sin, yet he believed that his psychology had preserved religious knowledge. He thought that such knowledge came through divine revelation in scripture and also from the conclusions that human reason could draw from observing nature. He hoped that this interpretation of religious knowledge would prevent human beings from falling into what he regarded as fanaticism arising from the claims of alleged private revelations and irrationality arising from superstition. For Locke, reason and revelation were compatible and together could sustain a moderate religious faith that would avoid religious conflict.

The New Institutions of Expanding Natural Knowledge

One of the most fundamental features of the expansion of science was the emerging idea that *genuinely new knowledge* about nature and humankind could be discovered. In the late Middle Ages, the recovery of Aristotle and the rise of humanistic learning looked back to the ancients to rediscover the kind of knowledge that later Europeans needed. Luther and other Reformers had seen themselves as recovering a better understanding of the original Christian message. By contrast, the proponents of the new natural knowledge and the new philosophy sought to pursue what Bacon called the advancement of learning. New knowledge would be continuously created. This outlook required new institutions.

There were powerful social implications to the expansion of natural knowledge. Both the new science and the philosophical outlook associated with it opposed Scholasticism and Aristotelianism. These were not simply disembodied philosophical outlooks, but ways of approaching the world of knowledge still espoused by most scholars in the universities of the day. Such scholars had a clear vested interest in preserving those traditional outlooks. As they saw it, they were defending the Ancients against the Moderns. Not surprisingly, the advanced thinkers of the seventeenth century often criticized the universities. For example, in his *Discourse on Method*, Descartes was highly critical of the education he had received. Hobbes filled the *Leviathan* with caustic remarks about the kind of learning then dominating schools and universities, and Locke advocated educational reform.

Some of the criticism of universities was exaggerated. Medical faculties, on the whole, welcomed the advancement of learning in their fields of study. Most of the natural philosophers had themselves received their education at universities. Moreover, however slowly new ideas might penetrate universities, the expanding world of natural knowledge would be taught to future generations. And with that diffusion of science into the universities came new supporters of scientific knowledge beyond the small group of natural philosophers themselves. Universities also provided much of the physical and financial support for the teaching and investigation of natural philosophy and employed many scientists, the most important of whom was Newton himself. University support of science did, however, vary according to country, with the Italian universities being far more supportive than the French.

Yet because of the reluctance of universities to rapidly assimilate the new science, its pioneers quickly understood that they required a framework for cooperation and sharing of information that went beyond existing intellectual institutions. Consequently, they and their supporters established what have been termed "institutions of sharing" that allowed information and ideas associated with the new science to be gathered, exchanged, and debated.[10] The most famous of these institutions was the Royal Society of London, founded in 1660, whose members consciously saw themselves as following the path Bacon had laid out almost a half century earlier. The Royal Society had been preceded by the Academy of Experiments in Florence in 1657 and was followed by the French Academy of Science in 1666. Germany only slowly overcame the destruction of the Thirty Years' War, with the Berlin Academy of Science being founded in 1700. In addition to these major academies, there were many local societies and academies at which the new science was discussed and experiments were carried out.

These societies provided organizations that met regularly to hear papers and observe experiments. One of the reasons many early experiments achieved credibility was that they had been observed by persons of social respectability who belonged to one or more of the societies and who, because of their social standing, were presumed to be truthful witnesses of what they had observed. These groups also published information relating to natural philosophy and often organized libraries for their members. Perhaps most important, they attempted to separate the discussion and exploration of natural philosophy from the religious and political conflicts of the day. They intended science to exemplify an arena for the polite exchange of ideas and for civil disagreement and debate. This particular function of science as fostering civility became one of its major attractions.

The activities of the societies also constituted a kind of crossroads between their own members always drawn from the literate classes, and people outside the

[10] Lewis Pyenson and Susan Sheets-Pyenson, *Servants of Nature: A History of Scientific Institutions, Enterprises and Sensibilities* (New York: W. W. Norton & Company, 1999), p. 75.

The sixteenth and seventeenth centuries saw Europeans expanding their knowledge into the ancient past, into the New World, and into the starry heavens. In this painting, The Sciences and the Arts, *the artist depicts recent paintings that connect contemporary culture with the ancient world and the Bible. In the same room, he sets globes depicting the New World and astronomical instruments used by natural philosophers exploring the heavens according to the the theories of Copernicus, Kepler, and Galileo. Yet throughout all of the expansion of mind and geographical knowledge, women were generally excluded as they are in this painting. For example, only on the rarest occasion were women permitted to visit the Royal Society of London.* Adriaen Stalbent, *The Sciences and the Arts.* Wood, 93 × 114 cm. Inv. 1405. Museo del Prado, Madrid, Spain. Erich Lessing/Art Resource, N.Y.

elite classes, whose skills and practical knowledge might be important for advancing the new science. The latter included craftspeople who could manufacture scientific instruments, sailors whose travels had taken them to foreign parts and who might report upon the plants and animals they had seen there, and workers who had practical knowledge of problems in the countryside. In this respect, the expansion of the European economy and the drive toward empire contributed to the growth of the scientific endeavor by bringing back to Europe specimens and experiences that required classification, analysis, and observation.

In good Baconian fashion, the members of the societies presented science as an enterprise that could aid the goals of government and the growth of the economy. For example, mathematicians portrayed themselves as being useful for solving surveying and

other engineering problems and for improving armaments. Furthermore, people who had ideas for improving production, navigation, or military artillery might seek the support of the associated societies. In the English context, these people became known as *projectors* and were satirized in Jonathan Swift's (1667–1745) *Gulliver's Travels.* (See "Jonathan Swift Satirizes Scientific Societies.")

The work, publications, and interaction of the scientific societies with both the government and private business established a distinct role and presence for scientific knowledge in European social life. By 1700 that presence was relatively modest, but it would grow steadily during the coming decades. The groups associated with the new science saw themselves as championing modern practical achievements of applied knowledge and urging religious toleration, mutual for-

Jonathan Swift Satirizes Scientific Societies

Swift was the greatest author of English satire in the eighteenth century. He was a deeply pessimistic person who thought that much of the promise held forth for the scientific enterprise would never be realized. In the "Third Voyage" of Gulliver's Travels, *published in 1726, Swift portrays Gulliver as visiting the land of Lagardo. In that country there exists a learned academy filled with scholars who pursue outlandish projects. Swift lists the efforts of a whole series of Projectors, each of whom is more impractical than the next. This passage in which Swift pillories the various people who hoped to receive patronage for projects from persons associated with the Royal Society of London remains one of the most famous satires of science in the English language. That Swift felt compelled to write it is a testimony to the cultural authority that science had achieved by the early eighteenth century.*

❖ *Why might Swift have so emphasized what he saw as the impracticality of science? How does this passage serve to refute the promise of science championed by Bacon and Descartes? How might Swift's presentation be seen as manifesting jealousy by a literary figure toward the growing influence of science?*

Gulliver reports a conversation he encountered while visiting Lagardo:

"The Sum of his Discourse was to this Effect. That about Forty Years ago, certain Persons went up to *Laputa*, either upon Business or Diversion; and after five Months Continuance, came back with a very little Smattering in Mathematics, but full of Volatile Spirits acquired in that Airy Region. That these Persons upon their Return, began to dislike the Management of every Thing below; and fell into Schemes of putting all Arts, Sciences, Languages, and Mechanics upon a new Foot. To this End they procured a Royal Patent for erecting an Academy of *Projectors* in *Lagado*; And the Humour prevailed so strongly among the People, that there is not a Town of any Consequence in the Kingdom without such an Academy. In these Colleges, the Professors contrive new Rules and Methods of Agriculture and Building, and new Instruments and Tools for all Trades and Manufactures, whereby, as they undertake, one Man shall do the Work of Ten; a Palace may be built in a Week, of Materials so durable as to last for ever without repairing. All the Fruits of the Earth shall come to Maturity at whatever Season we think fit to chuse; and increse an Hundred Fold more than they do at present; with innumerable other happy Proposals. The only Inconvenience is, that none of these Projects are yet brought to Perfection; and in the mean time, the whole Country lies miserably waste, the Houses in Ruins, and the People without Food or Cloaths. By all which, instead of

being discouraged they are Fifty Times more violently bent upon prosecuting their Schemes, driven equally on by Hope and Despair...."

Gulliver then reports what he found occurring in the rooms of an academy in Lagardo:

"The first Man I saw...had been Eight Years upon a Project for extracting Sun-Beams out of Cucumbers, which were to be put into Vials hermetically sealed, and let out to warm the Air in raw inclement Summers....

"I saw another at work to calcine ice into Gunpowder...

"There was another most ingenius Architect who had contrived a new Method for building Houses, by beginning at the Roof, and working downwards to the Foundation....

In another Apartment I was highly pleased with a Projector, who had found a Device of plowing the Ground with Hogs, to save the Charges of Plows, Cattle, and Labour. The Method is this: In an Acre of Ground you bury at six Inches Distance, and eight deep, a quantity of Acorns, Dates, Chesnuts, and other Masts or Vegatables whereof these Animals are fondest; then you drive six Hundred or more of them into the Field, where in a few Days they will root up the whole Ground in search of their Food, and make it fit for sowing, at the same time manuring it with their Dung. It is true, upon Experiment they found the Charge and Trouble very great, and they had little or no Crop. However, it is not doubted that this Invention may be capable of great Improvement."

From Jonathan Swift, *Gulliver's Travels*, Part III, chs. iv and v (New York: The Heritage Press, 1960), pp. 193–194, 197–199.)

bearance, and political liberty. Such people would form the social base for the eighteenth-century movement known as the Enlightenment.

Women in the World of the Scientific Revolution

The absence of women in the emergence of the new science of the seventeenth century has been a matter of much historical speculation. What characteristics of early modern European intellectual and cultural life worked against extensive contributions by women? Why have we heard so little of the activity by women that did actually occur in regard to the new science?

The same factors that had long excluded women from participating in most intellectual life continued to exclude them from working in the emerging natural philosophy. Traditionally, the institutions of European intellectual life had all but excluded women. Both monasteries and universities had been institutions associated with celibate male clerical culture. Except for a few exceptions in Italy, women had not been admitted to either medieval or early modern European universities; they would continue to be excluded from them until the end of the nineteenth century. Women could and did exercise much influence over princely courts where natural philosophers, such as Galileo, sought patronage, but they usually did not determine those patronage decisions or benefit from them. Queen Christina of Sweden was an exception by engaging René Descartes to provide the regulations for a new science academy. When various scientific societies were founded, women were not admitted to membership. In that regard, there were virtually no social spaces that might have permitted women easily to pursue science.

Yet a few isolated women from two different social settings did manage to engage in the new scientific activity—noblewomen and women from the artisan class. In both cases, they could do so only through their husbands or other men in their families.

The social standing of certain noblewomen allowed them to command the attention of ambitious natural philosophers who were part of their husband's social circle. Margaret Cavendish (1623–1673) actually made significant contributions to the scientific literature of the day. After she had been privately tutored and become widely read, her marriage to the duke of Newcastle introduced her into a circle of natural philosophers. She understood the new science, quarreled with the ideas of Descartes and Hobbes, and criticized the Royal Society for being more interested in novel scientific instruments than in solving practical problems. Her most important works were *Observations upon Experimental Philosophy* (1666) and

Grounds of Natural Philosophy (1668). She was the only woman in the seventeenth century to be allowed to visit a meeting of the Royal Society of London. (See "Margaret Cavendish Questions the Fascination with Scientific Instruments.")

Women associated with artisan crafts actually achieved greater freedom in pursuing the new sciences than did noblewomen. Traditionally, women had worked in artisan workshops, often with their husbands, and might take over the business when their spouse died. In Germany, much astronomy occurred in these settings, with women assisting their fathers or husbands. One such German female astronomer, Maria Cunitz, published a book on astronomy that many people thought her husband had written until he added a preface supporting her sole authorship. Elisabetha and Johannes Hevelius constituted a wife-and-husband astronomical team, as did Maria Winkelmann and her husband Gottfried Kirch. In each case, the wife served as the assistant to an artisan astronomer. Although Winkelmann discovered a comet in 1702, not until 1930 was the discovery ascribed to her rather than to her husband. Nonetheless, contemporary philosophers did recognize her abilities and understanding of astronomy. Winkelmann had worked jointly with her husband who was the official astronomer of the Berlin Academy of Sciences and was responsible for establishing an official calendar published by the Academy. When her husband died in 1710, Winkelmann applied for permission to continue the work, basing her application for the post on the guild's tradition of allowing women to continue their husband's work, in this case the completion of observations required for creating an accurate calendar. After much debate, the Academy formally rejected her application on the grounds of her gender, although its members knew of her ability and previous accomplishments. Years later, she returned to the Berlin Academy as an assistant to her son, who had been appointed astronomer. Again, the Academy insisted that she leave, forcing her to abandon astronomy. She died in 1720.

Such policies of exclusion, however, did not altogether prevent women from aquiring knowledge about the scientific endeavors of the age. Margaret Cavendish had composed a *Description of a New World, called the Blazing World* (1666) to introduce women to the new science. Other examples of scientific writings for a female audience were Bernard de Fontenelle's *Conversations on the Plurality of Worlds* and Francesco Algarotti's *Newtonianism for Ladies* (1737). During the 1730s, Emilie du Châtelet aided Voltaire in his composition of an important French popularization of Newton's science. Her knowledge of mathematics was more extensive than his and crucial to his completing his book.

Margaret Cavendish Questions the Fascination with Scientific Instruments

Margaret Cavendish, Duchess of Newcastle, was the most scientifically informed woman of seventeenth-century England. She read widely in natural philosophy and had many acquaintances who were involved in the new science. While she was enthusiastic about the promise of science, she also frequently criticized some of its leading proponents, including Descartes and Hobbes. She was skeptical of the activities of the newly established Royal Society of London, which she was once permitted to visit. She believed that some of its members had become overly enthusiastic about experimentation and new scientific instruments for their own sakes and had begun to ignore the practical questions that she thought science should address. In this respect, her criticism of the Royal Society and its experiments is a Baconian one. She thought the Society had replaced scholastic speculation with experimental speculation and that both kinds of speculation ignored important problems of immediate utility.

❖ *Why might Margaret Cavendish think that the experiments which were reported about new optical instruments dealt with superficial wonders? Why does she contrast experimental philosophy with the beneficial arts? Do you find a feminist perspective in her comparison of the men of the Royal Society with boys playing with bubbles?*

Art has intoxicated so many men's brains, and wholly imployed their thoughts and bodily actions about phaenomena, or the exterior figure of objects, as all better Arts and Studies are laid aside;...But though there be numerous Books written of the wonder of these [experimental optical] Glasses, yet I cannot perceive any such; at best, they are but superficial wonders, as I may call them. But could Experimental Philosophers find out more beneficial Arts then our Forefathers have done, either for the better increase of Vegetables and brute Animals to nourish our bodies, or better and commodious contrivances in the Art of Architecture to build us houses, or for the advancing of trade and traffick...it would not only be worth their labour, but of as much praise as could be given to them: But, as Boys that play with watry Bubbles...are worthy of reproof rather than praise, for wasting their time with useless sports; so those that addict themselves to unprofitable Arts, spend more time than they reap benefit thereby.

From Margaret Cavendish, *Observations Upon Experimental Philosophy; to which is added, the Description of a New Blazing World* (London, 1666), pp. 10–11 as quoted in Anna Battigelli, *Margaret Cavendish and the Exiles of the Mind* (Lexington, KY: University of Kentucky Press, 1998), p. 94.

Still, with only a few exceptions, women were barred from science and medicine until the late nineteenth century, and not until the twentieth century did they enter these fields in any significant numbers. Not only did the institutions of science exclude them, but also, the ideas associated with medical practice, philosophy, and biology suggested that women and their minds were essentially different from, and inferior to, men and theirs. By the early eighteenth century, despite isolated precedents of women pursuing natural knowledge, reading scientific literature, and engaging socially with natural philosophers, it had become a fundamental assumption of European intellectual life that the pursuit of natural knowledge was a male vocation.

The New Science and Religious Faith

In the minds of many contemporaries, the new science posed a potential challenge to religion. Three major issues were at stake. First, certain theories and discoveries did not agree with biblical statements about the heavens. Second, the question arose, Would church authorities or the natural philosophers decide conflicts between religion and science. Finally, for many religious thinkers, the new science offered only a materialistic universe, replacing one of spiritual meaning and significance. Yet most of the natural philosophers genuinely saw their work as contributing to a deeper knowledge of the divine, thus supporting religious belief. Their efforts and those of their supporters to reconcile faith and the new science constituted a fundamental factor in the spread of science and its widespread acceptance in educated European circles. The process was not an easy one. (See "Art & the West.")

The Case of Galileo

The condemnation of Galileo by Roman Catholic authorities in 1633 is the single most famous incident of conflict between modern science and religious institutions. For centuries it was interpreted as exemplifying the forces of religion smothering scientific knowledge. More recent research has modified that picture.

The condemnation of Copernicanism and of Galileo occurred at a particularly difficult moment in the history of the Roman Catholic Church. In response to Protestant emphasis on private interpretation of scripture, the Council of Trent (1545–1563) had stated that only the church itself possessed the authority to interpret the Bible. Furthermore, after the Council, the Roman Catholic Church had adopted a more literalist mode of reading the Bible in response to the Protestant emphasis on the authority of scripture. Galileo's championing of Copernicanism took place in this particular climate of opinion and practice when the Roman Catholic Church, on the one hand, could not surrender the interpretation of the Bible to a layman and, on the other, had difficulty moving beyond a literal reading of the Bible for fear of being accused by the Protestants of abandoning scripture.

In a *Letter to the Grand Duchess Christina* (1615), Galileo, as a layman, had published his own views about how scripture should be interpreted to accommodate the new science. (See "Galileo Discussed the Relationship of Science to the Bible.") To certain Roman Catholic authorities, his actions resembled that of a Protestant who looked to himself rather than the church to understand the Bible. In 1615 and 1616, he visited Rome and discussed his views openly and aggressively. In early 1616, however, the Roman Catholic Inquisition formally censured Copernicus's views, placing *On the Revolutions of the Heavenly Spheres* on the Index of Prohibited Books. The ground for the condemnation was the disagreement of Copernicus with the literal word of the Bible and the biblical interpretations of the Church Fathers. It should be recalled that at the

time there did not yet exist, even in Galileo's mind, fully satisfactory empirical evidence in support of Copernicus.

Galileo, who was not on trial in 1616, was formally informed of the condemnation of Copernicanism. It remains unclear exactly what agreement he and the Roman Catholic authorities reached as to what he would be permitted to write in regard to Copernicanism. It appears that he agreed not to advocate the physical truthfulness of Copernican astronomy, but to suggest only its theoretical possibility.

In 1623, however, a Florentine acquaintance of Galileo's was elected as Pope Urban VIII. He gave Galileo permission once again to discuss the Copernican system, which he did in *Dialogue on the Two Chief World Systems* (1632). The book clearly was designed to defend the physical truthfulness of Copernicanism. Moreover, the voices in the dialogue favoring the older system appeared slow-witted, and those voices presented the views of Pope Urban. Feeling both humiliated and personally betrayed, the Pope ordered an investigation of Galileo's book. The actual issue in Galileo's trial of 1633 was whether he had disobeyed the mandate of 1616, and it must have been clear to any observer that he had done so. Galileo was condemned, required to abjure his views, and placed under the equivalent of house arrest in his home near Florence for the last nine years of his life.

Although much more complicated than a simple case of a conflict between science and religion, the condemnation of Galileo cast a long and troubled shadow over the relationship of the emerging new science and the authority of the Roman Catholic Church. The controversy continued into the late twentieth century, when Pope John II formally ordered the reassessment of the Galileo case with the result that in 1992 the Roman Catholic Church admitted that errors had occurred, most particularly in the biblical interpretation of Pope Urban VIII's advisors.

Blaise Pascal: Reason and Faith

One of the most influential efforts to reconcile faith and the new science was presented by Pascal (1623–1662), a French mathematician and a physical scientist who surrendered his wealth to pursue an austere, self-disciplined life. He aspired to write a work that would refute both dogmatism (which he saw epitomized by the Jesuits) and skepticism. Pascal considered the Jesuits' casuistry (i.e., arguments designed to minimize and excuse sinful acts) a distortion of Christian teaching. He rejected the skeptics of his age be-

Vermeer's The Geographer and The Astronomer: Painting and The New Knowledge

During the sixteenth and seventeenth centuries, just as the theories and observations published by Copernicus, Kepler, and Galileo led to a new understanding of the heavens, the encounter with the Americas and the opening of new shipping lanes to Asia flooded Europe with new information about areas of the world previously unknown to Europeans. The Netherlands stood at a crucial juncture in both enterprises. Dutch opticians and metalworkers produced scientific instruments of the highest quality. Their boatyards constructed advanced ships that transported goods throughout the world as the Dutch established the first far-flung commercial empire. Religious toleration in the Netherlands permitted an active and open intellectual life, as did the Dutch policy of welcoming immigrants from everywhere. Dutch freedom of the press allowed the Netherlands to become a center for the publication of books that carried the new knowledge of astronomy, optics, geography and other sciences across Europe.

Two paintings of the late 1660s by the Dutch artist Jan Vermeer (1632–1675) reflect these developments: *The Astronomer* (1668) and *The Geographer* (1668–1669). Sales records suggest that Vermeer painted them as pendants; that is, they were meant to hang beside each other and to give meaning to each other. Astronomy and geography would have been closely related in the minds of a seventeenth-century Dutch artist and his contemporaries because the improved knowledge of the heavens was important for both navigation and calendars.

The geographer is shown consulting maps, which, over the course of the past two centuries, had seen the additions of new continents, islands, and rivers never recorded by the ancients. Used by Dutch fleets, those maps had opened the way for a worldwide trade that enriched the nation and led it into conflict with both France and England. Consequently, the geographer could look out through the window onto a wider world filled with more different kinds of goods and natural wonders than any Europeans had ever known. By placing on a map the regions where those goods originated and those wonders lay,

Vermeer van Delft, Jan, *The Geographer* (1668–69). Oil on canvas. Staedelsches Kunstinstitute, Frankfurt am Main. The Granger Collection

the geographer could make that expanding new world familiar to ordinary Europeans.

Vermeer's astronomer sits at his desk with his hand on a globe depicting the constellations of the night sky. On the side of the cabinet in the back of the room hangs a chart containing other astronomical information, and on the table is an instrument for making observations of the heavens. The scene portrays the kind of setting in which much theorizing about astronomy occurred. Clearly, science involved thinking and working through tables of observations as much as it did peering into the night sky. Through such mathematical theorizing, Newton would achieve the culmination of the Scientific Revolution about twenty years later with his publication of *Principia Mathematica* (1687). But the cultural fascination with astronomy predated that publication.

The Astronomer also depicts an important theme relating to science and religion. On the wall to the right, as a painting within the painting, hangs the *Finding of Moses*, an image artists often used to symbolize God's providential purposes. Because the *Finding of Moses* is at the side of the painting and the astronomer's back is to it, Vermeer might be suggesting that those practicing the new science must look to the light of nature alone, which streams in through the window. But as a Roman Catholic well aware of the fate of Galileo, Vermeer is probably suggesting that the new natural knowledge, like the life of Moses, did fulfill divine purposes. The presence of the astronomer with both the biblical painting and the astronomical globe thus appears to indicate that devout faith and the pursuit of rigorous science are compatible and mutually reinforcing.

Vermeer's method of painting as well as his content displays his fascination with optics, a subject that also interested many natural philosophers. In these and other paintings, Vermeer portrayed light illuminating interiors. He is believed to have used a *camera obscura*, a darkened box with a pinhole through which light projected the outside scene in precise detail and vibrant color. As one contemporary wrote, "I am certain that vision from these reflections in the dark can give no small light to the sight of the young artists; because besides gaining knowledge of nature, so one sees here what main or general [characteristics] should belong to a truly natural painting."[11] Vermeer's use of the *camera obscura* illustrates how the science and experiments of the new optics could influence the traditional craft of painting, expanding its capacity to portray the natural world.

Vermeer van Delft, Jan (1632–1675), *The Astronomer* (1668). Oil on canvas 31.5 × 45.5 cm. Louvre, Dep. des Peintures, Paris, France. Erich Lessing, Art Resource, NY

Mariet Westermann, *A Worldly Art: The Dutch Republic 1585–1718* (New York: Prentice Hall/Abrams, 1996); Arthur K. Wheelock, Jr., *Vermeer and the Art of Painting* (New Haven: Yale University Press, 1995); J. M. Montias, *Vermeer and His Milieu: A Web of Social History* (Princeton: Princeton University Press, 1989); Arthur K. Wheelock, Jr., *Perspective, Optics, and Delft Artists Around 1650* (New York: Garland Press, 1977)

[11] Arthur K. Wheelock, Jr., *Vermeer and the Art of Painting* (New Haven, CT: Yale University Press, 1995), p. 18.

Galileo Discusses the Relationship of Science to the Bible

The religious authorities were often critical of the discoveries and theories of six-teenth- and seventeenth-century science. For years before his condemnation by the Roman Catholic Church in 1633, Galileo had contended that scientific theory and religious piety were compatible. In his Letter to the Grand Duchess Christiana *(of Tus-cany), written in 1615, he argued that God had revealed truth in both the Bible and physical nature and that the truth of physical nature did not contradict the Bible if the latter were properly understood. Galileo encountered difficulties regarding this letter because it represented a layman telling church authorities how to read the Bible.*

❖ *Is Galileo's argument based on science or theology? Did the church believe that nature was as much a revelation of God as the Bible was? As Galileo describes them, which is the surer revelation of God, nature or the Bible? Why might the pope reject Galileo's argument?*

The reason produced for condemning the opin-ion that the Earth moves and the sun stands still is that in many places in the Bible one may read that the sun moves and the Earth stands still....

With regard to this argument, I think in the first place that it is very pious to say and prudent to affirm that the holy Bible can never speak untruth—whenever its true meaning is under-stood. But I believe nobody will deny that it is often very abstruse, and may say things which are quite different from what its bare words signify....

This being granted, I think that in discussions of physical problems we ought to begin not from the authority of scriptural passages, but from sense-ex-periences and necessary demonstrations; for the holy Bible and the phenomena of nature proceed alike from the divine Word, the former as the dictate of the Holy Ghost and the latter as the observant executrix of God's commands. It is necessary for the Bible, in order to be accommodated to the understanding of every man, to speak many things which appear to differ from the absolute truth so far as the bare mean-ing of the words is concerned. But Nature, on the other hand, is inexorable and immutable; she never transgresses the laws imposed upon her, or cares a whit whether her abstruse reasons and methods of operation are understandable to men. For that reason it appears that nothing physical which sense-expe-rience sets before our eyes, or which necessary demonstrations prove to us, ought to be called in question (much less condemned) upon the testimo-ny of biblical passages which may have some differ-ent meaning beneath their words. For the Bible is not chained in every expression to conditions as strict as those which govern all physical effects; nor is God any less excellently revealed in Nature's ac-tions than in the sacred statements of the Bible....

From this I do not mean to infer that we need not have an extraordinary esteem for the passages of holy Scripture. On the contrary, having arrived at any certainties in physics, we ought to utilize these as the most appropriate aids in the true exposition of the Bible and in the investigation of those mean-ings which are necessarily contained therein for these must be concordant with demonstrated truths. I should judge the authority of the Bible was designed to persuade men of those articles and propositions which, surpassing all human reason-ing, could not be made credible by science, or by any other means than through the very mouth of the Holy Spirit....

But I do not feel obliged to believe that the same God who has endowed us with senses, rea-son, and intellect has intended to forgo their use and by some other means to give us knowledge which we can attain by them.

From *Discoveries and Opinions of Galileo* by Galileo Galilei. Copyright © 1957 by Stillman Drake. Used by permission of Doubleday, a division of Bantam Doubleday Dell Publishing Group, Inc.

cause they either denied religion altogether (atheists) or accepted it only as it conformed to reason (deists). He never produced a definitive refutation of the two sides. Rather, he formulated his views on these mat-ters in piecemeal fashion in a provocative collection of reflections on humankind and religion published posthumously under the title *Pensées.*

Pascal allied himself with the Jansenists, seven-teenth-century Catholic opponents of the Jesuits. (See Chapter 13). His sister was a member of the Jansenist

Pascal invented this adding machine, the ancestor of mechanical calculators, around 1644. It has eight wheels with ten cogs each, corresponding to the numbers 0–9. The wheels move forward for addition, backward for subtraction. Bildarchiv Preussischer Kulturbesitz

convent of Port-Royal, near Paris. The Jansenists shared with the Calvinists Saint Augustine's belief in human beings' total sinfulness, their eternal predestination to heaven or hell by God, and their complete dependence on faith and grace for knowledge of God and salvation.

Pascal believed that in matters of religion, only the reasons of the heart and a "leap of faith" could prevail. For him, religion was not the domain of reason and science. He saw two essential truths in the Christian religion: that a loving God exists, and that human beings, because they are corrupt by nature, are utterly unworthy of God. He believed that the atheists and the deists of his age had overly estimated reason. To Pascal, reason itself was too weak to resolve the problems of human nature and destiny. Untimately, reason should drive those who truly heeded it to faith in God and reliance on divine grace.

Pascal made a famous wager with the skeptics. It is a better bet, he argued, to believe that God exists and to stake everything on his promised mercy than not to do so. This is because, if God does exist,

everything will be gained by the believer, whereas, should he prove not to exist, the loss incurred by having believed in him is by comparison slight.

Convinced that belief in God improved life psychologically and disciplined it morally (regardless of whether God proved in the end to exist), Pascal worked to strengthen traditional religious belief. He urged his contemporaries to seek self-understanding by "learned ignorance" and to discover humankind's greatness by recognizing its misery. He hoped thereby to counter what he believed to be the false optimism of the new rationalism and science.

The English Approach to Science and Religion

Francis Bacon established a key framework for reconciling science and religion that long influenced the English-speaking world. He had argued that there were two books of divine revelation: the Bible and nature. In studying nature, the natural philosopher could achieve a deeper knowledge of things divine, just as could the theologian studying the Bible. Because both books of revelation shared the same author, they must be compatible. Whatever discord might first appear between science and religion must eventually be reconciled. Natural theology based on a scientific understanding of the natural order would thus support theology derived from scripture.

Later in the seventeenth century, with the work of Newton, the natural universe became a realm of law and regularity. Many scientists were devout people who saw in the new picture of physical nature a new picture of God. The Creator of this rational, lawful nature must also be rational. To study nature was to come to a better understanding of that Creator. Science and religious faith were not only compatible, but mutually supportive. As Newton wrote, "The main Business of Natural Philosophy is to argue from Phaenomena without feigning Hypothesis, and to deduce Causes from Effects, till we come to the very first Cause, which certainly is not mechanical."[12]

The religious thought associated with such deducing of religious conclusions from nature became known as *physico-theology*. This reconciliation of faith and science allowed the new physics and astronomy to spread rapidly. At the very time when Europeans were finally tiring of the wars of religion, the new science provided the basis for a view of God that might lead away from irrational disputes and wars over religious doctrine. Faith in a rational God encouraged faith in the rationality of human beings and in their capacity to improve their lot once liberated from the traditions of the past. The Scientific Revolution provided the great model for the desirability of change and of criticism of inherited views.

Finally, the new science and the technological and economic innovations associated with its culture came again, especially among English thinkers, to be interpreted as part of a divine plan. By the late seventeenth century, natural philosophy and its practical achievements had become associated in the public mind with consumption and the market economy. Writers such as the Englishman John Ray in *The Wisdom of God Manifested in His Works of Creation* (1690) argued that it was evident that God had placed human beings in the world in order to understand it and then, having understood it, to turn it to productive practical use through rationality. Scientific advance and economic enterprise came to be interpreted in the public mind as the fulfillment of God's plan: Human beings were meant to improve

the world. This outlook provided a religious justification for the processes of economic improvement that would characterize much of eighteenth-century Western Europe.

Continuing Superstition

Despite the great optimism among certain European thinkers associated with the new ideas in science and philosophy, traditional beliefs and fears long retained their hold on the culture. During the sixteenth and seventeenth centuries, many Europeans remained preoccupied with sin, death, and the Devil. Religious people, including many among the learned and many who were sympathetic to the emerging scientific ideas, continued to believe in the power of magic and the occult. Until the end of the seventeenth century, almost all Europeans in one way or another believed in the power of demons.

Witch Hunts and Panic

Nowhere is the dark side of early modern thought and culture better seen than in the witch hunts and panics that erupted in almost every Western land. Between 1400 and 1700, courts sentenced an estimated 70,000–100,000 people to death for harmful magic (*maleficium*) and diabolical witchcraft. In addition to inflicting harm on their neighbors, these witches were said to attend mass meetings known as *sabbats*, to which they were believed to fly. They were also accused of indulging in sexual orgies with the Devil, who appeared at such gatherings in animal form, most often as a he-goat. Still other charges against them were cannibalism (they were alleged to be especially fond of small Christian children) and a variety of ritual acts and practices designed to insult every Christian belief and value.

Why did the great witch panics occur in the second half of the sixteenth and early seventeenth centuries? The misfortune created by religious division and warfare were major factors. Some argue that the Reformation was responsible for the witch panics. While the new theology portrayed demons and the Devil as still powerful, it weakened the traditional religious protections against them. Subsequently, the argument goes, people felt compelled to protect themselves by executing those perceived as witches. The new levels of violence exacerbated fears and hatreds and encouraged scapegoating, but political motives also played a role. As governments expanded control in their realms, they, like the church, wanted to eliminate all competition for the

---

[12] Quoted in Baumer, p. 323.

Three witches suspected of practicing harmful magic are burned alive on a pyre in Bade. On the left, two of them are shown feasting and cavorting with demons at a Sabbat. Bildarchiv Preussischer Kulturbesitz

loyalty of their subjects. Secular rulers, as well as the Pope, could pronounce their competitors "devilish." In fact, however, beliefs in witches and witch hunts had existed since the fifteenth century, well before the Reformation began.

Village Origins

The roots of the search for witches extended well beyond the world of the princes into both popular and elite cultures. In village societies, so-called cunning folk played a positive role in helping people cope with calamity. People turned to them for help when such natural disasters as plague and famine struck or when such physical disabilities as lameness or inability to conceive offspring be-

fell either humans or animals. The cunning folk provided consolation and gave people hope that such natural calamities might be averted or reversed through magic. In this way, they provided an important service and helped village life to keep functioning.

Possession of magical powers, for good or ill, made one an important person within village society. Not surprisingly, claims to such powers quite often were made by the people most in need of security and influence, namely, the old and the impoverished, especially single or widowed women. Belief in witches by village society may also have been a way of defying urban Christian society's attempts to impose its laws and institutions on the countryside. From this perspective, village Satanism became a fanciful substitute for an impossible social revolt, a way of spurning the values of one's new masters. It is also possible, although unlikely, that beliefs in witches among the rural population had a foundation in local fertility cults, whose semipagan practices, designed to ensure good harvests, may have acquired the features of diabolical witchcraft under church persecution.

Influence of the Clergy

Popular belief in magic was the essential foundation of the great witch hunts of the sixteenth and seventeenth centuries. Had ordinary people not believed that certain gifted individuals could aid or harm others by magical means, and had they not been willing to make accusations, the hunts could never have occurred. Yet the contribution of learned society was equally great. The Christian clergy also practiced magic, that of the holy sacraments, and the exorcism of demons had been one of its traditional functions within society. Fear of demons and the Devil, which the clergy actively encouraged, allowed clergymen to assert their moral authority over people and to enforce religious discipline and conformity.

In the late thirteenth century, the church declared that only its priests possessed legitimate magical power. Since such power was not human, theologians reasoned, it had to come either from God or from the Devil. If it came from God, then it was properly confined to, and exercised only on behalf of, the church. Those who practiced magic outside the church evidently derived their power from the Devil. From such reasoning grew accusations of "pacts" between non-Christian magicians and Satan. This made the witch hunts a life-and-death struggle against Christian society's worst heretics and foes: those who had directly sworn allegiance to the Devil himself.

The church based its intolerance of magic outside its walls on sincere belief in, and fear of, the Devil. But attacking witches was also a way for established Christian society to extend its power and influence into new areas. To accuse, try, and execute witches was a declaration of moral and political authority over a village or territory. As the cunning folk were local spiritual authorities, revered and feared by people, their removal became a major step in establishing a Christian beachhead in village society.

Why Women?

A good eighty percent of the victims of witch hunts were women, most between forty-five and sixty years of age and single. This suggests to some that misogyny fueled the witch hunts. Based on male hatred and sexual fear of women, and occurring at a time when women threatened to break out from under male control, witch hunts, it is argued, were simply woman hunts. Older single women may, however, have been vulnerable for a more basic social reason: They were a largely dependent social group in need of public assistance and hence became natural targets for the peculiar "social engineering" of the witch hunts. Some accused witches were women who sought to protect and empower themselves within their communities by claiming supernatural powers.

Gender, however, may have played a largely circumstantial role. Because of their economic straits, more women than men laid claim to the supernatural powers that made them influential in village society. For this reason, they found themselves on the front lines in disproportionate numbers when the church declared war against all who practiced magic without its blessing. Also, the involvement of many of these women in midwifery associated them with the deaths of beloved wives and infants and thus made them targets of local resentment and accusations. Both the church and midwives' neighbors were prepared to think and say the worst about these women. It was a deadly combination. (See "Why More Women than Men Are Witches.")

End of the Witch Hunts

Why did the witch hunts end in the seventeenth century? Many factors played a role. The emergence of a new, more scientific worldview made it difficult to believe in the powers of witches. When in the seventeenth century mind and matter came to be viewed as two independent realities, many people no longer believed that words and thoughts could affect the material world. A witch's curse was merely words. With advances in medicine and the beginning of insurance companies, people learned to rely on themselves when faced with natural calamity and physical affliction and no longer searched for supernatural causes and solutions. Witch hunts also tended to get out of hand. Accused witches sometimes alleged that important townspeople had also attended *sabbats*; even the judges could be so accused. At that point, the trials ceased to serve the purposes of those who were conducting them. They not only became dysfunctional, but threatened anarchy.

Although Protestants, like Catholics, hunted witches, the Reformation may also have contributed to an attitude of mind that put the Devil in a more manageable perspective. Protestants

Why More Women than Men Are Witches

A classic of misogyny, The Hammer of Witches *(1486), written by two Dominican monks, Heinrich Krämer and Jacob Sprenger, was sanctioned by Pope Innocent VIII as an official guide to the church's detection and punishment of witches. Here, Krämer and Sprenger explain why they believe that most witches are women rather than men.*

❖ *Why would two Dominican monks say such things about women? What are the biblical passages that they believe justify them? Do their descriptions have any basis in the actual behavior of women in that age? What is the rivalry between married and unmarried people that they refer to?*

Why are there more superstitious women than men? The first [reason] is that they are more credulous; and since the chief aim of the devil is to corrupt faith, therefore he rather attacks them....The second reason is that women are naturally more impressionable and ready to receive the influence of a disembodied spirit....The third reason is that they have slippery tongues and are unable to conceal from their fellow-women those things which by evil arts they know; and since they are weak, they find an easy and secret manner of vindicating themselves by witchcraft....[Therefore] since women are feebler both in mind and body, it is not surprising that they should come more under the spell of witchcraft. For as regards intellect, or the understanding of spiritual things, they seem to be of a different nature from men, a fact which is vouched for by the logic of the authorities, backed by various examples from the Scriptures....

But the natural reason [for woman's proclivity to witchcraft] is that she is more carnal than a man, as is clear from her many carnal abominations. And it should be noted that there was a defect in the formation of the first woman, since she was formed from a bent rib, that is, a rib of the breast, which is bent as it

were in a contrary direction to a man. And since through this defect she is an imperfect animal, she always deceives....

As to her other mental quality, her natural will, when she hates someone whom she formerly loved, then she seethes with anger and impatience in her whole soul, just as the tides of the sea are always heaving and boiling....

Truly the most powerful cause which contributes to the increase of witches is the woeful rivalry between married folk and unmarried women and men. This [jealousy or rivalry exists] even among holy women, so what must it be among the others...?

Just as through the first defect in their intelligence women are more prone [than men] to abjure the faith, so through their second defect of inordinate affections and passions they search for, brood over, and inflict various vengeances, either by witchcraft or by some other means. Wherefore it is no wonder that so great a number of witches exist in this sex....[Indeed, witchcraft] is better called the heresy of witches than of wizards, since the name is taken from the more powerful party [that is, the greater number, who are women]. Blessed be the Highest who has so far preserved the male sex from so great a crime.

From *Malleus Maleficarum*, trans. by Montague Summers (Bungay, Suffolk, U.K.: John Rodker, 1928), pp. 41–47. Reprinted by permission.

---

ridiculed the sacramental magic of the old church as superstition and directed their faith to a sovereign God absolutely supreme over time and eternity. Even the Devil was believed to serve God's purposes and acted only with his permission. Ultimately, God was the only significant spiritual force in the universe. This belief made the Devil a less fearsome creature. "One little word can slay him," Luther wrote of the Devil in

the great hymn of the Reformation, "A Mighty Fortress Is Our God."

Finally, the imaginative and philosophical literature of the sixteenth and seventeenth centuries, while continuing to display concern for religion and belief in the supernatural, also suggested that human beings have a significant degree of control over their own lives and need not be constantly fearing demons and resorting to supernatural aid.

In Perspective

The Scientific Revolution and the thought of writers whose work was contemporaneous with it mark a major turning point in the history of Western culture and eventually had a worldwide impact. The scientific and political ideas of the late sixteenth and seventeenth centuries gradually overturned many of the most fundamental premises of the medieval worldview. The sun replaced the Earth as the center of the solar system. The solar system itself came to be viewed as one of many possible systems in the universe. The new knowledge of the physical universe provided occasions for challenging the authority of the church and of scripture. Mathematics began to replace theology and metaphysics as the tool for understanding nature.

Parallel to these developments and sometimes related to them, political thought became much less concerned with religious issues. Hobbes generated a major theory of political obligation with virtually no reference to God. Locke theorized about politics with a recognition of God, but with little attention to scripture. He also championed greater freedom of religious and political expression. Locke produced a psychology that emphasized the influence of environment on human character and action. All of these new ideas gradually displaced or reshaped theological and religious modes of thought and placed humankind and life on Earth at the center of Western thinking. Intellectuals in the West consequently developed greater self-confidence in their own capacity to shape the world and their own lives.

None of this change came easily, however. The new science and enlightenment were accompanied by new anxieties that were reflected in a growing preoccupation with sin, death, and the Devil. The worst expression of this preoccupation was a succession of witch hunts and trials that took the lives of as many as 100,000 people between 1400 and 1700.

REVIEW QUESTIONS

1. Discuss the contributions of Copernicus, Brahe, Kepler, Galileo, and Newton to the Scientific Revolution. Which do you think made the most important contributions and why? What did Francis Bacon contribute to the foundation of scientific thought?

2. How would you define the term *Scientific Revolution*? In what ways was the event truly revolutionary? Which is more enduring, a political revolution or an intellectual one?

3. Compare and contrast the political philosophies of Thomas Hobbes and John Locke. How did each view human nature? Would you rather live under a government designed by Hobbes or by Locke? Why?

4. What factors prevented women from fully participating in the new science? How did family relationships help some women to become involved in the advance of natural philosophy?

5. What were the chief factors accounting for the condemnation of Galileo? How did Pascal seek to reconcile faith and reason? How did English natural theology support economic expansion?

6. How do you explain the phenomena of witchcraft and witch hunts in an age of scientific enlightenment? Why did the witch panics occur in the late sixteenth and early seventeenth centuries? How might the Reformation have contributed to them?

SUGGESTED READINGS

R. ASHCRAFT, *Revolutionary Politics and Locke's Two Treatises of Government* (1986). A major study emphasizing the radical side of Locke's thought.

J. BARRY, M. HESTER, AND G. ROBERTS, EDS. *Witchcraft in Early Modern Europe: Studies in Culture and Belief* (1998). A collection of recent essays.

M. BIAGIOLI, *Galileo Courtier: The Practice of Science in the Culture of Absolutism* (1993). A major revisionist work that emphasizes the role of the political setting on Galileo's career and thought.

H. BUTTERFIELD, *The Origins of Modern Science 1300–1800* (1949). A classic survey.

H. F. COHEN, *The Scientific Revolution: A Historiographical Inquiry* (1994). Supplants all previous discussions of the history of the concept of the Scientific Revolution.

J. DUNN, *The Political Thought of John Locke: An Historical Account of the "Two Treatises of Government"* (1969). Remains an excellent introduction.

M. A. FINOCCHIARO, *The Galileo Affair: A Documentary History* (1989). A collection of all the relevant documents and introductory commentary.

S. GAUKROGER, *Descartes: An Intellectual Biography* (1995). A major work that explores both the science and philosophy in Descartes's work.

A. GOLDGAR, *Impolite Learning: Conduct and Community in the Republic of Letters, 1680–1750* (1995). A lively survey of the structure of the European intellectual community.

I. HARRIS, *The Mind of John Locke: A Study of Political Theory in Its Intellectual Setting* (1994). The most comprehensive recent treatment.

P. HARRISON, *The Bible, Protestantism, and the Rise of Natural Science* (1998). Explores how the Protestant approach to the text of scripture contributed to the new scientific interpretation of nature.

E. HARTH, *Cartesian Women: Versions and Subversions of Rational Discourse in the Old Regime* (1992). A pioneering work on the relationship of educated French women to the new science.

A. JOHNS, *The Nature of the Book: Print and Knowledge in the Making* (1998). A brilliant study of the role of printing in the intellectual life of early modern Europe.

D. JOHNSTON, *The Rhetoric of* Leviathan: *Thomas Hobbes and the Politics of Cultural Transformation* (1986). An important study that links Hobbes's thought to the rhetoric of the Renaissance.

R. KIECKHEFER, *European Witch Trials: Their Foundations in Popular and Learned Culture 1300–1500* (1976). Excellent background for understanding the great witch panic.

A. KORS AND E. PETERS, EDS., *European Witchcraft, 1100–1700* (1972). Collection of major documents.

T. S. KUHN, *The Copernican Revolution* (1957). Remains the leading work on the subject.

C. LARNER, *Enemies of God: The Witchhunt in Scotland* (1981). Perhaps the most exemplary local study of the subject.

B. LEVACK, *The Witch Hunt in Early Modern Europe* (1986). Lucid survey.

D. LINDBERG AND R. L. NUMBERS, EDS., *God and Nature: Historical Essays on the Encounter Between Christianity and Science* (1986). An excellent collection of essays.

D. LINDBERG AND R. S. WESTMAN, EDS., *Reappraisals of the Scientific Revolution* (1990). Important essays pointing the way toward new understandings of the subject.

P. MACHAMER, ED., *The Cambridge Companion to Galileo* (1998). A wide-ranging collection of essays that aid the understanding of the entire spectrum of the new science.

O. MAYER, *Authority, Liberty, and Automatic Machinery in Early Modern Europe* (1986). A lively study that seeks to relate thought about machinery to thought about politics.

D. NOBLE, *A World Without Women: The Christian Clerical Culture of Western Science* (1992). A controversial account.

L. PYENSON AND S. SHEETS-PYENSON, *Servants of Nature: A History of Scientific Institutions, Enterprises, and Sensibilities* (1999). A history of the settings in which the creation and diffusion of scientific knowledge have occurred.

R. POPKIN, *The History of Scepticism from Erasmus to Spinoza* (1979). A classic study of the fear of loss of intellectual certainty.

R. PORTER AND M. TEICH, EDS., *The Scientific Revolution in National Context* (1992). Essays on the subject in each major European nation.

E. REEVES, *Painting the Heavens: Art and Science in the Age of Galileo* (1997). An exploration of the impact of Galileo's thought on the visual arts.

L. SCHIEBINGER, *The Mind Has No Sex? Women in the Origins of Modern Science* (1989). A major study of the subject.

S. SHAPIN, *The Scientific Revolution* (1996). The best brief introduction.

Q. SKINNER, *Reason and Rhetoric in the Philosophy of Hobbes* (1996). A major study by one of the leading scholars of Hobbes and early modern political thought.

L. STEWART, *The Rise of Public Science: Rhetoric, Technology, and Natural Philosophy in Newtonian Britain, 1660–1750* (1992). Examines how science became related to public life and economic development.

K. THOMAS, *Religion and the Decline of Magic* (1971). Provocative, much acclaimed work focused on popular culture.

R. TUCK, *Philosophy and Government 1572–1651* (1993). A continent-wide survey.

R. S. WESTFALL, *The Construction of Modern Science: Mechanisms and Mechanics* (1971). A classic work.

R. S. WESTFALL, *Never at Rest: A Biography of Isaac Newton* (1981). The major study.

N. WOLTERSTORFF, *John Locke and the Ethics of Belief* (1996). The best work on Locke's religious thought.

P. ZAGORIN, *Francis Bacon* (1998). A comprehensive treatment.

Chapter 15

Peter the Great (r. 1682–1725) seeking to make Russia a military power, reorganized the country's political and economic structures. His reign saw Russia enter fully into European power politics. The Apotheosis of Tsar Peter the Great 1672–1725 by unknown artist, 1710. Historical Museum, Moscow, Russia/E.T. Archive

Successful and Unsuccessful Paths to Power (1686–1740)

The Maritime Powers
The Netherlands: Golden Age
    to Decline
France after Louis XIV
Great Britain: The Age of Walpole

Central and Eastern Europe
Sweden: The Ambitions of Charles XII
The Ottoman Empire

Poland: Absence of Strong Central Authority
The Habsburg Empire and the Pragmatic
    Sanction
Prussia and the Hohenzollerns

**Russia Enters the European
Political Arena**
Birth of the Romanov Dynasty
Peter the Great

KEY TOPICS

- The Dutch Golden Age

- French aristocratic resistance to the monarchy

- Early eighteenth-century British political stability

- The efforts of the Habsburgs to secure their holdings

- The emergence of Prussia as a major power under the Hohenzollerns

- The efforts of Peter the Great to transform Russia into a powerful
  centralized nation along Western lines

The late seventeenth and early eighteenth centuries witnessed significant shifts of power and influence among the states of Europe. Nations that had been strong lost their status as significant military and economic units. Other countries that in some cases had figured only marginally in international relations came to the fore. Great Britain, France, Austria, Russia, and Prussia emerged during this period as the powers that would dominate Europe until at least World War I. Their political and economic dominance occurred at the expense of Spain, the United Netherlands, Poland, Sweden, and the Ottoman Empire. Equally essential to their rise was the weakness of the Holy Roman Empire after the Treaty of Westphalia (1648), which ended the Thirty Years' War.

The successful competitors for international power were those states that created strong central political authorities. Farsighted observers in the late seventeenth century already understood that in the future those domains that would become or remain great powers must imitate the political and military organization of Louis XIV's France. Strong monarchy alone could impose unity of purpose on the state. The turmoil of seventeenth-century civil wars and aristocratic revolts had impressed people with the value of a firm centralized monarch as the guarantor of minimum domestic tranquility.

Imitation of French absolutism involved more than belief in a firm centralized monarchy; it usually also required building a standing army, organizing an efficient tax structure to support the army, and establishing a bureaucracy to collect the taxes. Moreover, the political classes of the country—especially the nobles—had to be converted to a sense of duty and loyalty to the central government that was more intense than their loyalty to other competing political and social institutions.

The waning powers were those that failed to achieve such effective organization. They were unable to employ their political, economic, and human resources to resist external aggression or to overcome the forces of domestic dissolution. Internal and external failures were closely related. If a state did not maintain or establish a central political authority with sufficient power over the nobility, the cities, the guilds, and the church, it could not raise a strong army to defend its borders or its economic interests. More often than not, the key element leading to success or failure was the character, personality, and energy of the monarch.

The Maritime Powers

In western Europe, Britain and France emerged as the dominant powers. This development represented a shift of influence away from Spain and the United Netherlands. Both of the latter countries had been strong and important during the sixteenth and seventeenth centuries, but they became politically and militarily marginal during the eighteenth century. Neither, however, disappeared from the map, and both retained considerable economic vitality and influence. Spanish power declined after the War of the Spanish Succession (see Chapter 13). The case of The Netherlands was more complicated.

The Netherlands: Golden Age to Decline

The seven provinces that became the United Provinces of the Netherlands were the single genuinely new state to appear on the European scene during the early modern period. They emerged as a nation after revolting against Spain in 1572. Spain acknowledged their autonomy only in a truce of 1609, though other European powers had recognized Dutch independence in the 1580s. The Netherlands won formal independence from Spain in the Treaty of Westphalia (1648). These eighty years of on-again, off-again warfare forged much of the national identity of the Netherlands. During the middle of the seventeenth century, the Dutch engaged in a series of naval wars with England. Then, in 1672, the armies of Louis XIV invaded the Netherlands. William III, the *stadtholder* of Holland, the most important of the provinces, rallied the Dutch and eventually led the entire European

coalition against France. As a part of that strategy, he answered the invitation of Protestant English aristocrats in 1688 to assume, along with his wife Mary, the English throne. (See Chapter 13.)

During both the seventeenth and eighteenth centuries, the political and economic life of the Netherlands differed from that of the rest of Europe. The other major nations pursued paths toward strong central government, generally under monarchies, as with France, or in the case of England, under a strong parliamentary system. By contrast, the Netherlands was formally a republic. Each of the provinces retained considerable authority, and the central government, embodied in the States General that met in the Hague, exercised its authority through a kind of ongoing negotiation with the provinces. Prosperous and populous Holland dominated the States General. The Dutch deeply distrusted monarchy and the ambitions of the House of Orange. Nonetheless, when confronted with major military challenges, the Dutch would permit the House of Orange and, most notably, William III to assume dominant leadership. These political arrangements proved highly resilient and allowed the republic to establish itself permanently in the European state system during the seventeenth century. When William died in 1702 and the wars with France ended in 1714, the Dutch reverted to their republican structures.

Although the provinces making up the Netherlands were traditionally identified with the Protestant cause in Europe during their revolt against Spain and the wars against Louis XIV, extensive toleration marked Dutch religious life. The Calvinist Reformed Church was the official church of the nation, and most of the political elite belonged to it, but it was not an established church. There were always a significant number of Roman Catholics and Protestants living in the Netherlands who did not belong to the Reformed Church. The country also became a haven for Jews driven out of other lands, particularly those who had been expelled from Spain. Consequently, while other European states attempted to impose a single religion on their people or tore themselves apart in religious conflict, in the Netherlands peoples of differing religious faiths lived together peacefully.

URBAN PROSPERITY   Beyond the climate of religious toleration, what most amazed seventeenth-century contemporaries about the Dutch Republic was its economic prosperity. While the rest of Europe fought over religion, the Dutch enriched themselves and attained a high standard of living. Their remarkable economic achievement was built on the foundations of high urban consolida-

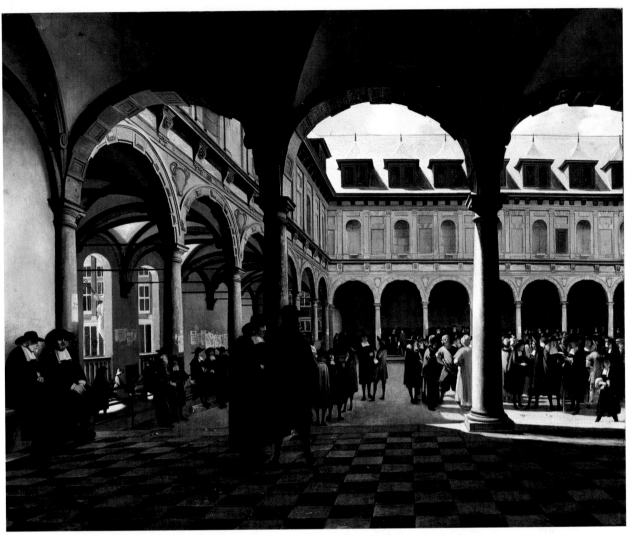

In the mid-eighteenth century, when this picture of the Amsterdam Exchange was paint-ed, Amsterdam had replaced the cities of Italy and south Germany as the leading bank-ing center of Europe. Amsterdam retained this position until the late eighteenth century.
Painting by Hiob A. Berckheyde, "The Amsterdam Exchange". Canvas 85 x 105 cm. Coll. Museum Boijmans Van
Beuningen, Rotterdam, The Netherlands

tion, transformed agriculture, extensive trade and finance, and an overseas commercial empire. (See "Art & the West.")

In the Netherlands, more people lived in cities than in any other area of Europe. By 1675, in Hol-land, the province where Amsterdam was located, at least sixty percent of the population were urban dwellers. Not until after the onset of industrial-ization in the late eighteenth century would such urban consolidation occur elsewhere, and then most notably in England. Trade, manufacture, shipbuilding, and finance were the engine of Dutch urban prosperity.

This urban concentration had been made possi-ble by key transformations in Dutch farming that served as the model for the rest of Europe. During the seventeenth century, the Dutch drained and reclaimed much land from the sea. The Dutch were able to use this reclaimed terrain for highly profitable farming because their shipping interests dominated the Baltic trade, which provided them with a steady supply of grain. The availability of this cheap grain meant that Dutch farmers could use their land to produce more profitable dairy products and beef. Dutch farmers also diversified into the cultivation of cash products such as tulip bulbs. So successful was tulip cultivation, that for a few years in the late 1630s, market speculation led to the sale of tulip bulbs at astounding prices.

The Baltic grain trade was just one example of the Dutch acting as the chief trading nation of Eu-rope. Their fishermen dominated the market for her-ring and supplied much of the continent's dried fish. The Dutch also supplied textiles to many parts of

Rachel Ruysch, Flower Still Life:
Flowers, Commerce, and Morality

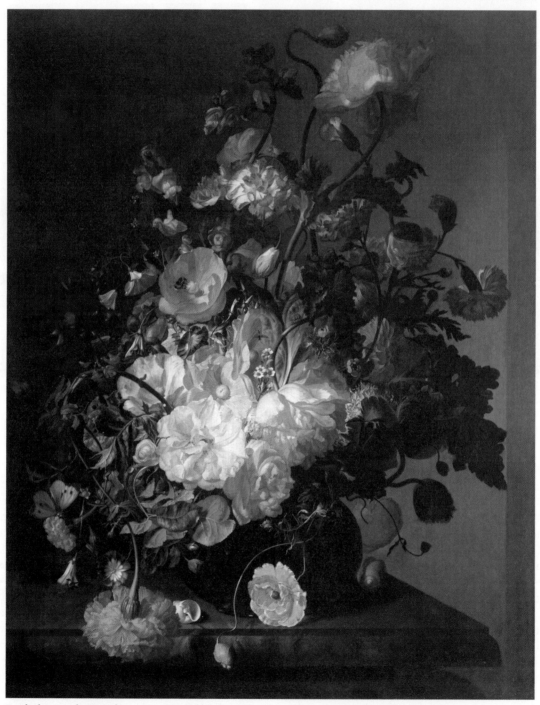

Rachel Ruysch, Dutch, 1664–1750, *Flower Still Life* (1956.57). The Toledo Museum of Art, Toledo, Ohio; Purchased with funds from the Libbey Endowment, Gift of Edward Drummond Libbey

$\mathcal{P}$aintings often are intended to convey more than first meets the eye. Such is more or less obvious in allegorical scenes in which themes appear in the guise of ancient gods or other mythological figures. But a painting of objects of everyday life arranged on tables, known as a *still life*, can also hold deep symbolic and cultural meaning. From the Middle Ages onward, particular flowers had religious meaning, but during the seventeenth century flowers took on more worldly associations.

Rachel Ruysch (1664–1750) was a Dutch woman artist living in Amsterdam who specialized in depicting elaborate arrangements of flowers. These paintings stand as very beautiful images, but they are also much more. The floral still life portrayed flowers usually raised from bulbs, a major Dutch commercial enterprise. Several decades before Ruysch completed this particular painting, *Flower Still Life* (after 1700), a financial mania had gripped Holland, with speculation in rare tulip bulbs reaching enormous extravagance before the bubble burst. Consequently, a painting such as this one from the early eighteenth century—and there were hundreds of such still-life floral works executed in seventeenth and eighteenth-century Holland—would have recalled that event.

The flowers in this and other Dutch floral paintings represent work and commerce, not the natural bounty of the Dutch countryside. Commercial growers and traders brought such flowers to the Netherlands from its overseas empire and trading partners, and the flowers came to symbolize Dutch interaction with the most far-flung regions of the globe.

The variety of flowers in the bowl suggests wealth and abundance; these are valuable species, not humble objects of ordinary life. And never, except on canvas, would these flowers have bloomed at one time. Only the painter can gather them together in a single place at a single moment, in effect overcoming the cycle of nature.

Paintings such as this one have been called "a dialogue between this newly affluent society and its material possessions" and "an expression of how the phenomenon of plenty is to be viewed and understood."[1] These rich still life paintings allowed the Calvinist Dutch to accommodate a morality that emphasized frugality and abstinence with life in the single wealthiest society in Europe. The melancholy surrounding the images conveys a lesson in the vanity and transience of earthly beauty and richness. All of these beautiful, valuable, rare natural objects, whether flowers or food, will soon decay. The flowers in this bowl, so stunning at the peak of their blossoming, will in a matter of days wilt and eventually rot. The insects buzzing about the flowers will also disappear. Even the empty snail shells on the table suggest that earthly life is only temporary. Similarly, the shadows in so many of the floral arrangements suggest the shadows that surround human life and the transience of both light and life. Yet, by owning a painting of an exquisite, diverse collection of flowers, one could possess an object of great beauty that would itself not decay.

The amazing attention to detail in Ruysch's work reflects the growth in botanical observation and knowledge during the previous century. Van Leeuwenhoek, the inventor of the microscope, hired artists to draw the organisms he could see through the instrument. That invention, as well as other Dutch optical achievements, such as the magnifying glass, led many artists to paint with enormous attention to detail.

Many of the most important illustrators of botanical manuals and other works of natural history were women. Among the leading figures was Anna Maria Sibylla Merian (1647–1717), a German woman who moved to the Netherlands and traveled to the Dutch colony of Surinam to study both plants and insects. Her work would have been enormously helpful to Ruysch, who would only rarely have worked from an actual bowl of real flowers.

Sources: Norman Bryson, *Looking at the Overlooked: Four Essays on Still Life Painting* (Cambridge, MA: Harvard University Press, 1990); Mariët Westermann, *A Worldly Art: The Dutch Republic, 1585–1718* (Upper Saddle River, NJ and New York: Prentice Hall Publishers, Inc., and Harry N. Abrahms, Inc., 1990); Marilyn Stokstad, *Art History*, rev. ed. (Upper Saddle River, NJ and New York: Prentice Hall Publishers, Inc., and Harry N. Abrahms, Inc., 1999) pp. 798–801.

[1]Norman Bryson, *Looking at the Overlooked: Four Essays on Still Life Painting* (Cambridge, MA: Harvard University Press, 1990), p. 104.

Europe. Dutch ships appeared in harbors all over the continent, with their captains purchasing goods that they then transported and resold at a profit to other nations. Or such goods might be returned to the Netherlands, stored, and then sold later at more advantageous prices. Many of the handsome merchant houses lining the canals of Amsterdam had storage facilities on their upper floors. The overseas trades also supported a vast domestic industry of shipbuilding and ship supplies.

All of this trade, commerce, and manufacturing was supported by the most advanced financial system of the day. Capital could be more easily raised in Amsterdam than anyplace else in the seventeenth century. Shares traded easily and often speculatively in the Amsterdam bourse. Dutch capital financed economic life outside its own borders.

The final foundation of Dutch prosperity was the Dutch seaborne empire. During the late sixteenth and early seventeenth centuries, Dutch traders established a major presence in East Asia, particularly in spice-producing areas of Java, the Moluccas, and Sri Lanka. The vehicle for this penetration was the Dutch East Indies Company (chartered in 1602), shares of which traded on the Amsterdam bourse. The Dutch East Indies Company eventually displaced Portuguese dominance in the spice trade of East Asia and for many years prevented English traders from establishing a major presence there. Initially, the Dutch had only wanted commercial dominance of the spice trade, but in time, that goal led them to move toward producing the spices themselves, which required them to control many of the islands that now constitute Indonesia. The Netherlands remained the colonial master of this region until after World War II.

ECONOMIC DECLINE The decline in political influence of the United Provinces of the Netherlands occurred within the eighteenth century. After the death of William III of Britain in 1702, the various local provinces prevented the emergence of another strong *stadtholder*. Unified political leadership therefore vanished. During the earlier long wars with Louis XIV and Britain, naval supremacy had slowly but steadily passed to the British. The fishing industry declined, and the Dutch lost their technological superiority in shipbuilding. Countries between which Dutch ships had once carried goods now traded directly with each other. For example, the British began to use their own vessels in the Baltic traffic with Russia.

Similar stagnation overtook the Dutch domestic industries, such as textile finishing, papermaking, and glassblowing. The disunity of the provinces and the absence of vigorous leadership hastened this economic decline and prevented action that might have slowed or halted it.

What saved the United Provinces from becoming completely insignificant in European affairs was their continued financial dominance. Well past the middle of the eighteenth century, their banks continued to finance European trade. Moreover, the Amsterdam bourse remained an important financial institution because, as will be seen later in this chapter, both France and England exprienced disastrously excessive and politically disruptive stock speculation in the early eighteenth century, which made them fearful of investment in shares.

France after Louis XIV

Despite its military reverses in the War of the Spanish Succession, France remained a great power. It was less strong in 1715 than in 1680, but it still possessed the largest European population, an advanced, if troubled, economy, and the administrative structure bequeathed it by Louis XIV. Moreover, even if France and its resources had been drained by the last of Louis's wars, the other major states of Europe were similarly debilitated. What France required was economic recovery and consolidation, wiser political leadership, and a less ambitious foreign policy. It did enjoy a period of recovery, but its leadership was at best indifferent. Louis XIV was succeeded by his five-year-old great-grandson Louis XV (r. 1715–1774). The young boy's uncle, the duke of Orléans, became regent and remained so until his death in 1720. The regency, marked by financial and moral scandals, further undermined the faltering prestige of the monarchy.

JOHN LAW AND THE MISSISSIPPI BUBBLE The duke of Orléans was a gambler, and for a time he turned over the financial management of the kingdom to John Law (1671–1729), a Scottish mathematician and fellow gambler. Law believed that an increase in the paper-money supply would stimulate France's economic recovery. With the permission of the regent, he established a bank in Paris that issued paper money. Law then organized a monopoly, called the Mississippi Company, on trading privileges with the French colony of Louisiana in North America.

The Mississippi Company also took over the management of the French national debt. The company issued shares of its own stock in exchange for government bonds, which had fallen sharply in value. To redeem large quantities of bonds, Law encouraged speculation in Mississippi Company stock. In 1719, the price of the stock rose handsomely. Smart

The impending collapse of John Law's bank triggered a financial panic throughout France. Desperate investors, such as those shown here in the city of Rennes, sought to exchange their paper currency for gold and silver before the banks supply of precious metals was exhausted. Collection Musée de Bretagne, Rennes

investors, however, took their profits by selling their stock in exchange for paper money from Laws bank, which they then sought to exchange for gold. The bank, however, lacked enough gold to redeem all the paper money brought to it.

In February 1720, all gold payments were halted in France. Soon thereafter, Law himself fled the country. The Mississippi Bubble, as the affair was called, had burst. The fiasco brought disgrace on the government that had sponsored Law. The Mississippi Company was later reorganized and functioned profitably, but fear of paper money and speculation marked French economic life for decades.

RENEWED AUTHORITY OF THE *PARLEMENTS* The duke of Orléans made a second decision that also lessened the power of the monarchy: He attempted to draw the French nobility once again into the decision-making processes of the government. Louis XIV had filled his ministries and bureaucracies with persons from nonnoble families. The regent, under pressure from the nobility, tried to restore a balance. He set up a system of councils on which nobles were to serve along with bureaucrats. The years of idle noble domestication at Versailles, however, had worked too well, and the nobility seemed to lack both the talent and the desire to govern. The experiment failed.

Despite this failure, the great French nobles did not surrender their ancient ambition to assert their rights, privileges, and local influence over those of the monarchy. The chief feature of eighteenth-century French political life was the attempt of the nobility to use its authority to limit the power of the monarchy. The most effective instrument in this process was the *parlements*, or courts dominated by the nobility.

The French *parlements* were different from the English Parliament. These French courts, the most important of which was the *Parlement* of Paris, could not legislate. Rather, they had the power to recognize or not to recognize the legality of an act or law promulgated by the monarch. By long tradition, their formal approval had been required to make a royal law valid. Louis XIV had often restricted stubborn, uncooperative *parlements*. In another major political blunder, however, the duke of Orléans had formally approved the full reinstitution of the *parlements'* power to allow or disallow laws. Thereafter, the growing financial and moral weakness of the monarchy allowed these aristocratic judicial institutions to reassert their authority. This situation meant that until the revolution in 1789 the *parlements* became natural centers for aristocratic resistance to royal authority.

ADMINISTRATION OF CARDINAL FLEURY In 1726, Cardinal Fleury (1653–1743) became the chief minister of the French court. He was the last of the great clerics who loyally and effectively served the French monarchy. Like his seventeenth-century predecessors, the cardinals Richelieu and Mazarin, Fleury was a realist. He understood the political ambition and incapacity of the nobility and worked quietly to block their undue influence. He was also aware of the precarious financial situation of the royal treasury. The cardinal, who was seventy-three years old when he came to office, was determined to give the country a period of peace. He surrounded himself with able assistants who tried to solve France's financial problems. Part of the national debt was repudiated. New industries enjoying special privileges were established and roads and bridges built. On the whole, the nation prospered, but Fleury could never draw sufficient tax revenues from the nobles or the church to put the state on a stable financial footing.

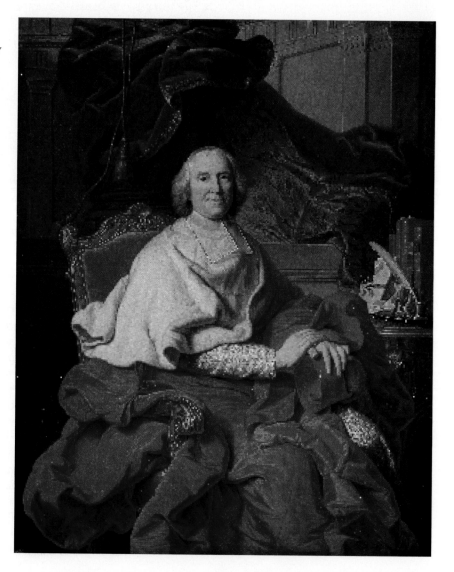

Cardinal Fleury (1653–1743) was the tutor and chief minister of Louis XV from 1726 to 1743. Fleury gave France a period of peace and prosperity, but was unable to solve the state's long-term financial problems. This portrait is by Hyacinthe Rigaud.
© Reunion des Musees Nationaux/ Art Resource, New York

Madame de Pompadour (1721–1764) was the mistress of Louis XV. She exercised considerable political influence at the court and was a notable patron of artists, craftspeople, and writers. This 1763 portrait is by Hubert Drouais (1727–1775). Liaison Agency, Inc.

Fleury died in 1743, having unsuccessfully attempted to prevent France from intervening in the war that was then raging between Austria and Prussia. The cost of this intervention was to undo all his financial pruning and planning.

Another failure must also be attributed to this elderly cleric. Despite his best efforts, he had not trained Louis XV to become an effective monarch. Louis XV possessed most of the vices and almost none of the virtues of his great-grandfather Louis XIV. He wanted to hold on to absolute power, but was unwilling to work the long hours required. He did not choose many wise advisers after Fleury. He was tossed about by the gossip and intrigues of the court. His personal life was scandalous. Louis XV was not an evil person, but a mediocre one. And in a monarch, mediocrity was unfortunately often a greater fault than vice. Consequently, it was not a lack of resources or military strength that plagued France, but the absence of political leadership to organize, direct, and inspire its people.

Great Britain: The Age of Walpole

In 1713 Britain had emerged as a victor over Louis XIV, but the nation required a period of recovery. As an institution, the British monarchy was not in the degraded state of the French monarchy, yet its stability was not certain.

THE HANOVERIAN DYNASTY In 1714 the Hanoverian dynasty, as designated by the Act of Settlement (1701), came to the throne. Almost immediately, George I (r. 1714–1727) faced a challenge to his new title. The Stuart pretender James Edward (1688–1766), the son of James II, landed in Scotland in December 1715. His forces marched southward, but met defeat less than two months later. Although militarily successful against the pretender, the new dynasty and its supporters saw the need for consolidation.

WHIGS AND TORIES During the seventeenth century, England had been one of the most politically restive countries in Europe. The closing years of Queen Anne's reign (1702–1714) had seen sharp clashes between the political factions of Whigs and Tories over whether to end the war with France. The Tories had urged a rapid peace settlement and after 1710 had opened negotiations with France. During the same period, the Whigs were seeking favor from the elector of Hanover, the future George I, who would soon be their monarch. His concern for his domains in Hanover made him unsympathetic to the Tory peace policy. In the final months of Anne's reign, some Tories, fearing that they would lose power under the waiting Hanoverian dynasty, opened channels of communication with the Stuart pretender; a few even rallied to his cause.

Under these circumstances, George I, on his arrival in Britain, clearly favored the Whigs. Previously, the differences between the Whigs and the Tories had been vaguely related to principle. The Tories emphasized a strong monarchy, low taxes for landowners, and firm support of the Anglican Church. The Whigs supported monarchy, but wanted Parliament to retain final sovereignty. They favored urban commercial interests as well as the prosperity of the landowners. They encouraged a policy of religious toleration toward the Protestant nonconformists in England. Socially, both groups supported the status quo.

Neither group was organized like a modern political party. Outside Parliament, each party consisted of political networks based on local connections and economic influence. Each group acknowledged a few national spokespeople, who articulated positions and principles. After the

Sir Robert Walpole (1676–1745), far left, is shown talking with the Speaker of the House of Commons. Walpole, who dominated British political life from 1721 to 1742, is considered the first prime minister of Britain. Time/Life Syndication.

Hanoverian accession and the eventual Whig success in achieving the firm confidence of George I, the chief difference between the Whigs and the Tories for almost forty years was that one group had access to public office and patronage and the other did not. This early Hanoverian proscription of Tories from public life was one of the most prominent features of the age.

THE LEADERSHIP OF ROBERT WALPOLE The political situation after 1715 remained in flux, until Robert Walpole (1676–1745) took over the helm of government. Though previously active in the House of Commons since the reign of Queen Anne and a cabinet minister, what gave Walpole special prominence under the new dynasty was a British financial scandal similar to the French Mississippi Bubble.

Management of the British national debt had been assigned to the South Sea Company, which exchanged government bonds for company stock. As in the French case, the price of the stock soared, only to crash in 1720 when prudent investors sold their holdings and took their speculative profits.

Parliament intervened and, under Walpole's leadership, adopted measures to honor the national debt. To most contemporaries, Walpole had saved the financial integrity of the country and had thus proved himself a person of immense administrative capacity and political ability.

George I gave Walpole his full confidence. For this reason, Walpole has often been regarded as the first prime minister of Great Britain and the originator of the cabinet system of government. Walpole generally demanded that all the ministers in the cabinet agree on policy, but he could not prevent frequent public differences among them. Unlike a modern English prime minister, he was not chosen by the majority of the House of Commons. The real sources of his power were the personal support of the king, first George I and later George II (r. 1727–1760), his ability to handle the House of Commons, and his ironfisted control of government patronage, which bought support for himself and his policies from people who wanted jobs, appointments, favors, and government contracts. Such corruption supplied the glue of political loyalty.

Walpole's favorite slogan was *"Quieta non movere"* (roughly, "Let sleeping dogs lie"). To that end, he pursued peace abroad and supported the status quo at home. In this regard he much resembled Cardinal Fleury.

THE STRUCTURE OF PARLIAMENT The structure of the eighteenth-century British House of Commons aided Walpole in his pacific policies. It was neither a democratic nor a representative body. Each of the counties into which Britain was divided elected two members. (See "Lady Mary Wortley Montagu Advises Her Husband on Election to Parliament.") But if the more powerful landed families in a county agreed on the candidates, there was no contest. Most members, however, were elected from a variety of units called *boroughs*. A few boroughs were large enough for

elections to be relatively democratic, but most had few electors. For example, a local municipal corporation or council of only a dozen members might have the right to elect a member of Parliament. In Old Sarum, one of the most famous corrupt, or "rotten," boroughs, the Pitt family simply bought up those pieces of property to which a vote was attached and thus in effect owned a seat in the House of Commons. Through proper electoral management, which involved favors to the electors, the House of Commons could be controlled.

The structure of Parliament and the manner in which the House of Commons was elected meant that the owners of property, especially wealthy nobles, dominated the government of England. They did not pretend to represent people and districts or to be responsive to what would later be called public opinion. They regarded themselves as representing various

Lady Mary Wortley Montagu (1689–1762) was a famous writer of letters and an extremely well-traveled woman of the eighteenth century. As the document on p. 494 suggests, she was also a shrewd and toughminded political advisor to her husband. National Portrait Gallery, London

This series of four Hogarth etchings satirizes the notoriously corrupt English electoral system. Hogarth shows the voters going to the polls after having been bribed and intoxicated with free gin. (Voting was then in public. The secret ballot was not introduced in England until 1872.) The fourth etching, "Chairing the Member," shows the triumphal procession of the victorious candidate, which is clearly turning into a brawl.

William Hogarth, *An Election Entertainment*, Print. The Metropolitan Museum of Art, Harris Brisbane Dick Fund, 1932. 32.35(212)

William Hogarth, *Canvassing for Votes*. Metropolitan Museum of Art, Harris Brisbane Dick Fund, 1932. 32.35 (213)

William Hogarth, *The Polling*, Print, H. 16 1/2 in. W, 20 5/8 in. (clipped impression). The Metropolitan Museum of Art, Gift of Sarah Lazarus, 1891. (91.1.75)

William Hogarth, *Chairing the Members*. Etching. Metropolitan Museum of Art, Harris Brisbane Dick Fund, 1932. 32.35 (214)

Lady Mary Wortley Montagu Advises Her Husband on Election to Parliament

In this letter of 1714, Lady Mary Wortley Montagu discussed with her husband the various paths that he might follow to gain election to the British House of Commons. Note her emphasis on knowing the right people and on having large amounts of money to spend on voters. Eventually, her husband was elected to Parliament in a borough that was controlled through government patronage.

❖ *What are the various ways in which candidates and their supporters used money to campaign? What role did friendships play in the campaigning? How important do the political ideas or positions of the candidates seem to be? Women could not vote in eighteenth-century parliamentary elections. Was there some other influence they exerted?*

You seem not to have received my letters, or not to have understood them: you had been chose undoubtedly at York, if you had declared in time; but there is not any gentleman or tradesman disengaged at this time; they are treating every night. Lord Carlisle and the Thompsons have given their interest to Mr. Jenkins. I agree with you of the necessity of your standing this Parliament, which, perhaps, may be more considerable than any that are to follow it; but, as you proceed, 'tis my opinion, you will spend your money and not be chose. I believe there is hardly a borough unengaged. I expect every letter should tell me you are sure of some place; and, as far as I can perceive you are sure of none. As it has been managed, perhaps it will be the best way to deposit a certain sum in some friend's hands, and buy some little Cornish borough: it would, undoubtedly, look better to be chose for a considerable town; but I take it to be now too late.

If you have any thoughts of Newark, it will be absolutely necessary for you to enquire after Lord Lexington's interest; and your best way to apply yourself to Lord Holdernesse, who is both a Whig and an honest man. He is now in town, and you may enquire of him if Brigadier Sutton stands there; and if not, try to engage him for you. Lord Lexington is so ill at the Bath, that it is a doubt if he will live 'till the elections; and if he dies, one of his heiresses, and the whole interest of his estate, will probably fall on Lord Holdernesse.

'Tis a surprize to me, that you cannot make sure of some borough, when a number of your friends bring in so many Parliament-men without trouble or expense. 'Tis too late to mention it now, but you might have applied to Lady Winchester, as Sir Joseph Jekyl did last year, and by her interest the Duke of Bolton brought him in for nothing; I am sure she would be more zealous to serve me, than Lady Jekyl.

From Lord Wharncliffe, ed., *Letters and Works of Lady Mary Wortley Montagu*, 3d ed., Vol. 1 (London: 1861), p. 211.

economic and social interests, such as the West Indian interest, the merchant interest, and the landed interest. These owners of property were suspicious of an administrative bureaucracy controlled by the crown or its ministers. To diminish royal influence, they or their agents served as local government administrators, judges, militia commanders, and tax collectors. In this sense, the British nobility and large landowners actually did govern the nation. And because they regarded the Parliament as the political sovereign, there was no absence of central political authority and direction. Consequently, the supremacy of Parliament gave Britain the unity that strong central monarchy provided elsewhere in Europe.

These parliamentary structures also helped to strengthen the financial position of the British government, which, under William III, had learned much about government finance from Dutch practices. The British monarch could not raise taxes the way his continental counterparts could, but the British government consisting of the monarch and Parliament could and did raise vast sums of tax revenue and loans to wage war throughout the eighteenth century. All Britons paid taxes; there were virtually no exemptions. The British credit market was secure through the regulation of the Bank of England, founded in 1693. This strong system of finance and tax collection was one of the cornerstones of eighteenth-century British power.

FREEDOM OF POLITICAL LIFE   British political life was genuinely more free than that on the Continent. There were real limits on the power of Robert Walpole. Parliament could not wholly ignore popular political pressure. Even with the extensive use of patronage, many members of Parliament maintained independent views. Newspapers and public debate flourished. There was freedom of speech and association. There was no large standing army. Those Tories barred from political office and the Whig enemies of Walpole could and did openly oppose his policies—which would have been far more difficult on the Continent.

For example, in 1733 Walpole presented a scheme to the House of Commons to expand the scope of the excise tax, a tax that resembled a modern sales tax. The outcry in the press, on the public platform, and in the streets was so great that he eventually withdrew the measure. What the British regarded as their traditional political rights raised a real and potent barrier to the power of the government. Again, in 1739, the public outcry over the alleged Spanish treatment of British merchants in the Caribbean pushed Britain into a war that Walpole opposed and deplored.

Walpole's ascendancy, which lasted until 1742, did little to raise the level of British political morality, but it brought a kind of stability that Britain had not enjoyed for a century. The nation's foreign trade grew steadily and spread from New England to India. Agriculture, in many cases following Dutch models, became more productive. All forms of economic enterprise seemed to prosper. The navy became stronger. As a result of this political stability and economic growth, Great Britain became a European power of the first order and stood at the beginning of its era as a world power. Its government and economy during the next generation became a model for all progressive Europeans.

Central and Eastern Europe

The major factors in the shift of political influence among the maritime nations were naval strength, economic progress, foreign trade, and sound domestic administration. The conflicts among them occurred less in Europe than on the high seas and in their overseas empires. These nations existed in well-defined geographical areas with established borders. Their populations generally accepted the authority of the central government.

Central and eastern Europe were different. The entire region was economically much less advanced than western Europe. Except for the Baltic ports, the economy was agrarian. There were fewer cities and many more large estates populated by serfs. The states in this region did not possess overseas empires; nor did they engage in extensive overseas trade of any kind, except for the supply of grain to western Europe, grain more often than not carried on west European ships.

Changes in the power structure normally involved changes in borders or in the prince who ruled a particular area. Military conflicts took place at home rather than overseas. The political structure of this region, which lay largely east of the Elbe River, was very "soft." The almost constant warfare of the seventeenth century had led to a habit of temporary and shifting political loyalties. The princes and aristocracies of small states and principalities were unwilling to subordinate themselves to a central monarchical authority. Consequently, the political life of the region and the kind of state that emerged there were different from those of western Europe.

During the last half of the seventeenth century, central and eastern Europe began to assume the political and social contours that would characterize it for the next two centuries. After the Peace of Westphalia, the Austrian Habsburgs recognized the basic weakness of the position of the Holy Roman Emperor and started to consolidate their power outside Germany. At the same time, Prussia emerged as a factor in North German politics and as a major challenger to Habsburg domination of Germany. Most important, Russia at the opening of the eighteenth century became a military and naval power of the first order. These three states (Austria, Prussia, and Russia) achieved their new status largely as a result of the political decay or military defeat of Sweden, Poland, and the Ottoman Empire.

France and Great Britain in the Early Eighteenth Century	
1713	Treaty of Utrecht ends the War of the Spanish Succession
1714	George I becomes king of Great Britain and establishes the Hanoverian dynasty
1715	Louis XV becomes king of France
1715–1720	Regency of the duke of Orléans in France
1720	Mississippi Bubble bursts in France and South Sea Bubble bursts in Great Britain
1720–1742	Robert Walpole dominates British politics
1726–1743	Cardinal Fleury serves as Louis XV's chief minister
1727	George II becomes king of Great Britain
1733	Excise-tax crisis in Britain

Sweden: The Ambitions of Charles XII

Under Gustavus Adolphus II (r. 1611–1632), Sweden had played an important role as a Protestant combatant in the Thirty Years' War. During the rest of the seventeenth century, Sweden had consolidated its control of the Baltic, thus preventing Russian possession of a Baltic port and permitting Polish and German access to the sea only on Swedish terms. The Swedes also possessed one of the better armies in Europe. Sweden's economy, however, based primarily on the export of iron, was not strong enough to ensure continued political success.

In 1697 Charles XII (r. 1697–1718) came to the throne. He was headstrong, to say the least, and perhaps insane. In 1700, Russia began a drive to the west against Swedish territory. The Russian goal was a foothold on the Baltic. In the resulting Great Northern War (1700–1721), Charles XII led a vigorous and often brilliant campaign, but one that eventually resulted in the defeat of Sweden. In 1700 he defeated the Russians at the Battle of Narva, but then he turned south to invade Poland. The conflict dragged on, and the Russians were able to strengthen their forces.

In 1708 the Swedish monarch began a major invasion of Russia, but became bogged down in the harsh Russian winter. The next year, his army was decisively defeated at the Battle of Poltava. Thereafter, the Swedes could maintain only a holding action against their enemies. Charles himself sought refuge in Turkey and did not return to Sweden until 1714. He was killed under uncertain circumstances four years later while fighting the Danes in Norway.

The Great Northern War came to a close in 1721. Sweden had exhausted its military and economic resources and had lost its monopoly on the Baltic coast. Russia had conquered a large section of the eastern Baltic, and Prussia had gained a part of Pomerania. Internally, after the death of Charles XII, the Swedish nobles were determined to reassert their power over the monarchy. They did so, but then quarreled among themselves. Sweden played a very minor role in European affairs thereafter.

The Ottoman Empire

At the southeastern extreme of Europe, the Ottoman Empire was a barrier to the territorial ambitions of the Austrian Habsburgs, Poland, and Russia. The empire in the late seventeenth century still controlled most of the Balkan Peninsula and the entire coastline of the Black Sea. In theory, the empire existed to enhance the spread of Islam. Its population, however, was exceedingly diverse both ethnically and religiously. The empire ruled these people not on a territorial, but on a religious, basis. That is, it created units, called *millets*, that included all persons of a particular religious faith. Various laws and regulations applied to the persons who belonged to a particular millet rather than to a particular administrative territory. Non-Islamic persons in the empire were known as *zimmis*. They could practice their religion, but they were second-class citizens who could not rise in the service of the empire or profit much from its successes. This mode of government maintained the self-identity of these various peoples but allowed for little religious integration or interaction.

From the fifteenth century onward, the Ottoman Empire had tried to push further westward in Europe. The empire made its deepest military invasion into Europe in 1683, when it unsuccessfully besieged Vienna. In addition, numerous Christians in the Balkans and on the Aegean islands had converted to Islam. Many of these people had previously been forced to convert to Roman Catholicism by the Venetians and welcomed the Turks and their Islamic faith as vehicles for political liberation. Much of the Islamic presence in the Balkans today dates to these conversions.

By the last third of the seventeenth century, however, the Ottomans had overextended themselves politically, economically, and militarily. From the mid-sixteenth century, the Ottoman rulers spent so much time at war that they could not attend to meetings of governmental bodies in Constantinople. As time passed, political groups in the capital resisted any substantial strengthening of the central government or of the role of the sultan. Rivalries for power among army leaders and nobles, as well as their flagrant efforts to enrich themselves, weakened the effectiveness of the government. In the outer provinces, such as Transylvania, Wallachia, and Moldavia (all parts of modern Romania), the empire depended on the goodwill of local rulers, who paid tribute, but never submitted themselves fully to the imperial power. The empire's economy was weak, and its exports were primarily raw materials. Moreover, the actual conduct of most of its trade had been turned over to representatives of other nations.

By the early eighteenth century, the weakness of the Ottoman Empire meant that a political vacuum that would expand during the next two centuries had come into existence on the southeastern perimeter of Europe. The various European powers that had created strong armies and bureaucracies would begin to probe and eventually dismember the Ottoman Empire. In 1699, the Turks concluded a treaty with their longtime Habsburg enemy and surrendered all pretensions of control over, and consequent receipt of, revenues from Hungary, Transylvania, Croatia, and Slavonia. From this time onward, Russia also attempted to extend its territory and influence at the expense of the empire. By the early nineteenth century, many of the peoples who lived in the Balkans and around the Black Sea would seek to create their own national states. The retreat and decay of the Ottoman Empire and the scramble of other states and regional peoples to assume control of south-eastern Europe would cause political and ethnic turmoil there from the eighteenth century to our own day.

Poland: Absence of Strong Central Authority

In no other part of Europe was the failure to maintain a competitive political position so complete as in Poland. In 1683, King John III Sobieski (r. 1674–1696) had led a Polish army to rescue Vienna from the Turkish siege. Following that spectacular effort, however, Poland became a byword for the dangers of aristocratic independence. In Poland as nowhere else on the Continent, the nobility became the single most powerful political factor in the country. Unlike the British nobility and landowners, the Polish nobility would not even submit to a central authority of their own making. There was no effective central authority in the form of either a king or a parliament.

The Polish monarchy was elective, but the deep distrust and divisions among the nobility prevented their electing a king from among themselves. Sobieski was a notable exception. Most of the Polish monarchs were foreigners and were the tools of foreign powers. The Polish nobles did have a central legislative body called the *Sejm*, or diet. It included only the nobles and specifically excluded representatives from corporate bodies, such as the towns. In the diet, however, there existed a practice known as the *liberum veto*, whereby the staunch opposition of any single member, who might have been bribed by a foreign power, could require the body to disband. Such opposition was termed "exploding the diet." This practice was most often the work of a group of dissatisfied nobles rather than of one person. Nonetheless, the requirement of unanimity was a major stumbling block to effective government. Localism reminiscent of the Middle Ages continued to hold sway as the nobles used all their energy to maintain their traditional "Polish liberties." There was no way to collect enough taxes to build up an army. The price of this noble liberty would eventually be the disappearance of Poland from the map of Europe during the latter half of the eighteenth century.

The Habsburg Empire and the Pragmatic Sanction

The close of the Thirty Years' War marked a fundamental turning point in the history of the Austrian Habsburgs. Previously, in alliance with the Spanish branch of the family, they had hoped to dominate all of Germany and to return it to the Catholic fold. They did not achieve either goal, and the decline of Spanish power meant that in future diplomatic relations the Austrian Habsburgs were on their own. The Treaty of Westphalia in 1648 permitted Protestantism within the Holy Roman Empire and also recognized the political autonomy of more than 300 corporate German political entities within the empire. These included large units (such as Saxony, Hanover, Bavaria, and Brandenburg) and scores of small cities, bishoprics, principalities, and petty territories of independent knights.

After 1648 the Habsburgs retained a firm hold on the title of Holy Roman Emperor, but the effectiveness of the title depended less on force of arms than on the cooperation that the emperor could elicit from the various political bodies in the empire. The diet of the empire sat at Regensburg from 1663 until the empire was dissolved in 1806. The diet and the emperor generally regulated the daily economic and political life of Germany. The post-Westphalian Holy Roman Empire resembled Poland in its lack of central authority. Unlike its Polish neighbor, however, the Holy Roman Empire was reorganized from within as the Habsburgs attempted to regain their authority. As will be seen shortly, Prussia set out on its course toward European power at the same time.

CONSOLIDATION OF AUSTRIAN POWER   While concentrating on their hereditary Austrian holdings among the German states, the Habsburgs also began to consolidate their power and influence within their other hereditary possessions. (See Map 15–1.) These included, first, the Crown of Saint Wenceslas, encompassing the kingdom of Bohemia (in the modern Czech Republic and Slovakia) and the duchies of Moravia and Silesia and, second, the Crown of Saint Stephen, which included Hungary, Croatia, and Transylvania. In the middle of the seventeenth century, much of Hungary remained occupied by the Turks and was liberated only at the end of the century.

In the early eighteenth century, the family extended its domains further, receiving the former Spanish (thereafter Austrian) Netherlands, Lombardy in northern Italy, and, briefly, the kingdom of Naples in southern Italy through the Treaty of Utrecht in 1713. During the eighteenth and nineteenth centuries, the

MAP 15–1   THE AUSTRIAN HABSBURG EMPIRE, 1521–1772   *The empire had three main units: Austria, Bohemia, and Hungary. Expansion was mainly eastward: East Hungary from the Ottomans (seventeenth century) and Galicia from Poland (1772). Meantime, Silesia was lost, but the Habsburgs retained German influences as Holy Roman emperors.*

Habsburgs' power and influence in Europe were based primarily on their territories outside Germany.

In the second half of the seventeenth century and later, the Habsburgs faced immense problems in these hereditary territories. In each, they ruled by virtue of a different title and had to gain the cooperation of the local nobility. The most difficult province was Hungary, where the Magyar nobility seemed ever ready to rebel. There was almost no common basis for political unity among peoples of such diverse languages, customs, and geography. Even the Habsburg zeal for Roman Catholicism no longer proved a bond for unity as they confronted the equally zealous Calvinism of many of the Magyar nobles. The Habsburgs established various central councils to chart common policies for their far-flung domains. Virtually all of these bodies dealt with only part of the Habsburgs' holdings. Repeatedly, the Habsburgs had to bargain with nobles in one part of of their empire to maintain their position in another.

Despite all these internal difficulties, Leopold I (r. 1657–1705) rallied his domains to resist the advances of the Turks and the aggression of Louis XIV. He achieved Ottoman recognition of his sovereignty over Hungary in 1699 and began the suppression of a long rebellion by his new Magyar subjects that lasted from 1703 to 1711. He also conquered much of

the Balkan Peninsula and western Romania. These southeastward extensions allowed the Habsburgs to hope to develop Mediterranean trade through the port of Trieste. The expansion at the cost of the Ottoman Empire helped them to compensate for their loss of domination over the Holy Roman Empire. The new strength in the East gave them somewhat greater political leverage in Germany. Leopold I was succeeded by Joseph I (r. 1705–1711), who continued Leopold's policies.

THE HABSBURG DYNASTIC PROBLEM   When Charles VI (r. 1711–1740) succeeded Joseph, he had no male heir, and there was only the weakest of precedents for a female ruler of the Habsburg domains. Charles feared that on his death the Austrian Habsburg lands might fall prey to the surrounding powers, as had those of the Spanish Habsburgs in 1700. He was determined to prevent that disaster and to provide his domains with the semblance of legal unity. To those ends, he devoted much of his energy throughout his reign to seeking the approval of his family, the estates of his realms, and the major foreign powers for a document called the Pragmatic Sanction.

This instrument provided the legal basis for a single line of inheritance within the Habsburg dynasty through Charles VI's daughter Maria Theresa (r. 1740–

1780). Other members of the Habsburg family recognized her as the rightful heir. The nobles of the various Habsburg domains did likewise after extracting various concessions from Charles. So, when Charles VI died in October 1740, he believed that he had secured legal unity for the Habsburg Empire and a safe succession for his daughter.

Charles VI had indeed established a permanent line of succession and the basis for future legal bonds within the Habsburg holdings. He had failed, however, to protect his daughter from foreign aggression, either through the Pragmatic Sanction or, more importantly, by leaving her a strong army and a full treasury. Less than two months after his death, the fragility of the foreign agreements became apparent. In December 1740, Frederick II of Prussia invaded the Habsburg province of Silesia. Maria Theresa had to fight to defend her inheritance.

Prussia and the Hohenzollerns

The Habsburg achievement had been to draw together into an uncertain legal unity a collection of domains possessed through separate feudal ti-

tles. The achievement of the Hohenzollerns of Brandenburg–Prussia was to acquire a similar collection of titular holdings and then to forge them into a centrally administered unit. Despite the geographical separation of their territories and the paucity of their natural economic resources, they transformed feudal ties and structures into bureaucratic ones. They subordinated every social class and most economic pursuits to the strengthening of the institution that united their far-flung realms: the army. They thus made the term "Prussian" synonymous with administrative rigor and military discipline.

A STATE OF DISCONNECTED TERRITORIES   The rise of Prussia occurred within the German power vacuum created after 1648 by the Peace of Westphalia. It is the story of the extraordinary Hohenzollern family, which had ruled the German territory of Brandenburg since 1417. (See Map 15–2.) Through inheritance, the family had acquired the duchy of Cleves and the counties of Mark and Ravensburg in 1609, the duchy of East Prussia in 1618, and the duchy of Pomerania in 1637. Except for Pomerania, none of these lands

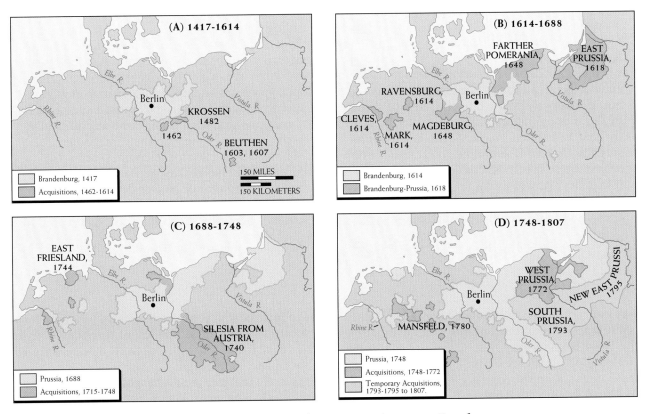

MAP 15–2   EXPANSION OF BRANDENBURG–PRUSSIA   *In the seventeenth century, Brandenburg–Prussia expanded mainly be acquiring dynastic titles in geographically separated lands. In the eighteenth century, it expanded through aggression to the east, seizing Silesia in 1740 and various parts of Poland in 1772, 1793, and 1795.*

The Great Elector Welcomes Protestant Refugees from France

*The Hohenzollern dynasty of Brandenburg–Prussia pursued a policy of religious tol-
eration. The family itself was Calvinist, whereas most of its subjects were Lutherans.
When Louis XIV of France revoked the Edict of Nantes in 1685, Frederick William,
the Great Elector, seized the opportunity to invite French Protestants into his realms.
As his proclamation indicates, he wanted to attract persons with productive skills who
could aid the economic development of his domains.*

❖ *In reading this document, do you believe that religious or economic concerns
more nearly led the elector of Brandenburg to welcome the French Protestants?
What specific privileges did the elector extend to them? To what extent were these
privileges a welcoming measure, and to what extent were they inducements to emigrate to Brandenburg? In what kind of economic activity does the elector expect the
French refugees to engage?*

We, Friedrich Wilhelm, by Grace of God Margrave
of Brandenburg...

Do hereby proclaim and make known to all
and sundry that since the cruel persecutions and
rigorous ill-treatment in which Our co-religionists of the Evangelical-Reformed faith have for
some time past been subjected in the Kingdom
of France, have caused many families to remove
themselves and to betake themselves out of the
said Kingdom into other lands, We now...have
been moved graciously to offer them through this
Edict...a secure and free refuge in all Our Lands
and Provinces....

Since Our Lands are not only well and amply
endowed with all things necessary to support life,
but also very well-suited to the reestablishment
of all kinds of manufactures and trade and traffic
by land and water, We permit, indeed, to those
settling therein free choice to establish themselves where it is most convenient for their profession and way of living....

The personal property which they bring with
them, including merchandise and other wares, is
to be totally exempt from any taxes, customs
dues, licenses, or other imposts of any description, and not detained in any way....

As soon as these Our French co-religionists of
the Evangelical-Reformed faith have settled in
any town or village, they shall be admitted to the
domiciliary rights and craft freedoms customary
there, gratis and without payments of any fee;
and shall be entitled to the benefits, rights, and
privileges enjoyed by Our other, native, subjects,
residing there....

Not only are those who wish to establish manufacture of cloth, stuffs, hats, or other objects in
which they are skilled to enjoy all necessary freedoms, privileges and facilities, but also provision
is to be made for them to be assisted and helped
as far as possible with money and anything else
which they need to realize their intention....

Those who settle in the country and wish to
maintain themselves by agriculture are to be
given a certain plot of land to bring under cultivation and provided with whatever they need to
establish themselves initially....

From C. A. Macartney, ed., *The Habsburg and Hohenzollern Dynasties in the Seventeenth and Eighteenth Centuries* (New
York: Walker, 1970), pp. 270–273.

was contiguous with Brandenburg. East Prussia
lay inside Poland and outside the authority of
the Holy Roman Emperor. All of the territories
lacked good natural resources, and many of them
were devastated during the Thirty Years' War.
At Westphalia the Hohenzollerns lost part of
Pomerania to Sweden, but were compensated by
receiving three more bishoprics and the promise
of the archbishopric of Magdeburg when it became vacant, as it did in 1680. By the late sev-

enteenth century, the scattered Hohenzollern
holdings represented a block of territory within
the Holy Roman Empire second in size only to
that of the Habsburgs.

Despite its size, the Hohenzollern conglomerate
was weak. The areas were geographically separate,
with no mutual sympathy or common concern among
them. In each, local noble estates limited the power
of the Hohenzollern prince. The various areas were
also exposed to foreign aggression.

FREDERICK WILLIAM, THE GREAT ELECTOR The person who began to forge these separated regions and diverse nobles into a modern state was Frederick William (r. 1640–1688), who became known as the Great Elector. (The ruler of Brandenburg was called an Elector because he was one of the princes who elected the Holy Roman Emperor.) He established himself and his successors as the central uniting power by breaking the local noble estates, organizing a royal bureaucracy, and establishing a strong army. (See "The Great Elector Welcomes Protestant Refugees from France.")

Between 1655 and 1660, Sweden and Poland engaged in a war that endangered the Great Elector's holdings in Pomerania and East Prussia. Frederick William had neither the military nor the financial resources to confront this threat. In 1655, the Brandenburg estates refused to grant him new taxes; however, he proceeded to collect the required taxes by military force. In 1659 a different grant of taxes, originally made in 1653, elapsed; Frederick William continued to collect them, as well as those he had imposed by his own authority. He used the money to build up an army that allowed him to continue to enforce his will without the approval of the nobility. Similar threats and coercion took place against the nobles in his other territories.

There did occur, however, a political and social trade-off between the elector and his various nobles: In exchange for their obedience to the Hohenzollerns, the *Junkers* received the right to demand obedience from their serfs. Frederick William also tended to choose as the local administrators of the tax structure men who would normally have been members of the noble estates. He thus co-opted potential opponents into his service. His taxes fell most heavily on the backs of the peasants and the urban classes.

As the years passed, sons of *Junkers* increasingly dominated the army officer corps, and this practice became even more pronounced during the eighteenth century. All officials and army officers took an oath of loyalty directly to the elector. The army and the elector thus came to embody the otherwise absent unity of the state. The existence of the army made Prussia a valuable potential ally and a state with which other powers needed to curry favor.

FREDERICK WILLIAM I, KING OF PRUSSIA Yet, even with the considerable accomplishments of the Great Elector, the house of Hohenzollern did not possess a crown. The achievement of a royal title was one of the few state-building accomplishments of Frederick I (r. 1688–1713). This son of the Great Elector was the least "Prussian" of his family during these crucial years. He built palaces, founded Halle University (1694), patronized the arts, and lived luxuriously. In 1701, however, at the outbreak of the War of the Spanish Succession, he put his army at the disposal of the Habsburg Holy Roman Emperor. In exchange for this loyal service, the emperor permitted Frederick to assume the title of "King in Prussia." Thereafter Frederick became Frederick I, and he passed the much-desired royal title to his son Frederick William I in 1713.

Frederick William I (r. 1713–1740) was both the most eccentric and one of the most effective Hohenzollerns. After giving his father a funeral that matched the luxury of his life, Frederick William I immediately imposed strict austerity. Some jobs were abolished and some salaries lowered. His political aims seem to have been the consolidation of an obedient, compliant bureaucracy and the establishment of a bigger army. He initiated a policy of *Kabinett* government, which meant that lower officials submitted all relevant documents to him in his office, or *Kabinett*. Then he alone examined the papers, made his decisions, and issued his orders. He thus skirted the influence of ministers and ruled alone.

Frederick William I organized the bureaucracy along military lines. He united all departments under the *General-Ober-Finanz-Kriegs-und-Domänen-Direktorium*, more happily known to us as the General Directory. He imposed taxes on the nobility and changed most remaining feudal dues into monetary payments. He sought to transform feudal

Austria and Prussia in the Late Seventeenth and Early Eighteenth Centuries

1640–1688	Reign of Frederick William, the Great Elector
1657–1705	Leopold I rules Austria and resists the Turkish invasions
1683	Turkish siege of Vienna
1688–1713	Reign of Frederick I of Prussia
1699	Peace treaty between Turks and Habsburgs
1711–1740	Charles VI rules Austria and secures agreement to the Pragmatic Sanction
1713–1740	Frederick William I builds up the military power of Prussia
1740	Maria Theresa succeeds to the Habsburg throne
1740	Frederick II violates the Pragmatic Sanction by invading Silesia

Though economically weak and with a small population, Prussia became an important state because it developed a large, well-trained army. Prussian troops were known for their discipline, the result of constant drill and harsh punishment. In this mideighteenth-century engraving one soldier is being whipped while another is about to run a gauntlet of other soldiers. Bildarchiv Preussischer Kulturbesitz

and administrative loyalties into a sense of duty to the monarch as a political institution rather than as a person. He once described the perfect royal servant as

an intelligent, assiduous, and alert person who after God values nothing higher than his king's pleasure and serves him out of love and for the sake of honor rather than money and who in his conduct solely seeks and constantly bears in mind his king's service and interests, who, moreover, abhors all intrigues and emotional deterrents.[2]

Service to the state and the monarch was to become impersonal, mechanical, and, in effect, unquestioning.

[2]Quoted in Hans Rosenberg, *Bureaucracy, Aristocracy, and Autocracy* (Boston: Beacon Press, 1958), p. 93.

THE PRUSSIAN ARMY   The discipline that Frederick William applied to the army was fanatical. During his reign, the size of the army grew from about 39,000 in 1713 to more than 80,000 in 1740. It was the third- or fourth-largest army in Europe, whereas Prussia ranked thirteenth in population. Rather than using recruiters, the king made each canton or local district responsible for supplying a quota of soldiers.

After 1725, Frederick William I always wore an officer's uniform. He formed one regiment from the tallest soldiers he could find in Europe. Separate laws applied to the army and to civilians. Laws, customs, and royal attention made the officer corps the highest social class of the state. Military service attracted the sons of *Junkers*. Thus, the army, the *Junker* nobility, and the monarchy were forged into a single political entity. Military priorities and values dominated Prussian government, society, and daily life as in no other state of Europe. It has often been said that whereas other nations possessed armies, the Prussian army possessed its nation.

Although Frederick William I built the best army in Europe, he avoided conflict. He wanted to drill his soldiers, but not to order them into battle. The army was for him a symbol of Prussian power and unity, not an instrument to be used for foreign adventures or aggression.

At his death in 1740, he passed to his son Frederick II, later known as "the Great" (r. 1740–1786), this superb military machine, but he could not also pass on the wisdom to refrain from using it. Almost immediately on coming to the throne, Frederick II upset the Pragmatic Sanction, invaded Silesia, and thus crystallized the Austrian–Prussian rivalry for control of Germany that would dominate central European affairs for over a century.

Russia Enters the European Political Arena

Though ripe with consequences for the future, the rise of Prussia and the new consolidation of the Austrian Habsburg domains seemed to many at the time only another shift in the long-troubled German scene. The emergence of Russia, however, as an active European power was a wholly new factor in European politics. Previously, Russia had been considered part of Europe only by courtesy, and before 1688 it did not even send minsters or ambassadors to western Europe. Geographically and politically, it lay on the periphery. Hemmed in by Sweden on the Baltic and by the Ottoman Empire on the Black Sea, Russia had no warm-water ports. Its chief outlet to the west was Archangel on the White Sea, which was ice free for only part of the year. There was little trade. What Russia did possess was a vast reserve of largely undeveloped natural and human resources.

Birth of the Romanov Dynasty

The reign of Ivan the Terrible, which had begun so well and closed so frighteningly, was followed by anarchy and civil war known as the "Time of Troubles." In 1613, hoping to restore stability, an assembly of nobles elected a seventeen-year-old boy named Michael Romanov (r. 1613–1654) as tsar. Thus began the dynasty that, despite palace revolutions, military conspiracies, assassinations, and family strife, ruled Russia until 1917.

Michael Romanov and his two successors, Alexis I (r. 1654–1676) and Theodore III (r. 1676–1682), brought stability and modest bureaucratic centralization to Russia. The country remained, however, weak and impoverished. After years of turmoil, the bureaucracy was still largely controlled by the *boyars*, the old nobility. This administrative apparatus could barely suppress a revolt of peasants and Cossacks (horsemen who lived on the steppe frontier) under Stepan Razin in 1670–1671. Furthermore, the government and the tsars faced the danger of mutiny from the *streltsy*, or guards of the Moscow garrison.

Peter the Great

In 1682, another boy—ten years old at the time—ascended the fragile Russian throne as co-ruler with his half brother. His name was Peter (r. 1682–1725), and Russia would never be the same after him. He and the sickly Ivan V had come to power on the shoulders of the *streltsy*, who expected to be rewarded for their support. Much vi-

Rise of Russian Power	
1533–1584	Reign of Ivan the Terrible
1584–1613	"Time of Troubles"
1613	Michael Romanov becomes tsar
1682	Peter the Great, age ten, becomes tsar
1689	Peter assumes personal rule
1696	Russia captures Azov on the Black Sea from the Turks
1697	European tour of Peter the Great
1698	Peter returns to Russia to put down the revolt of the *streltsy*
1700	The Great Northern War opens between Russia and Sweden; Russia defeated at Narva by Swedish Army of Charles XII
1703	Saint Petersburg founded
1709	Russia defeats Sweden at the Battle of Poltava
1718	Charles XII of Sweden dies
1718	Son of Peter the Great dies in prison under mysterious circumstances
1721	Peace of Nystad ends the Great Northern War
1721	Peter establishes a synod for the Russian church
1722	Peter issues the Table of Ranks
1725	Peter dies, leaving an uncertain succession

Peter the Great Issues a Table of Ranks

In 1722, after much consultation among his advisors and examination of how social and political ranks were established elsewhere in Europe, Peter the Great issued a Table of Ranks that became law in the vast Russian empire. This table indicated, with enormous precision, the hierarchy or official "pecking order" of the various offices among the military, the civilian bureaucracy, and the czarist court. In all cases, Peter declared that the military would take precedence over the other divisions. Note, significantly, that Peter omitted offices in the church from the ranks of state service.

The Table of Ranks was a cornerstone of Peter's effort to transform Russia into a modern European country. He was determined to establish a hierarchy of reward and social honor, as indicated in point 8 of the table, that would distinguish those people who served the state from those who possessed nobility merely by virtue of birth. Although he formally acknowledged that nobles by birth should receive all manner of formal courtesies, he reserved the highest honors to those serving the czar and the nation. Moreover, he made service to the state a formal path to ennoblement itself. Despite the precision of the listing of offices, there remained much confusion in the decades that followed about exactly which offices, degree of landholding, and the like permitted a person to receive a title of of nobility. Nonetheless, with later eighteenth- and nineteenth-century revisions, Peter's Table of Ranks essentially remained in force in Russia until the revolution in 1917.

These points listed from the Table of Ranks were intended to clarify the application and administration of the Table.

❖ *What steps did Peter take in these regulations to ensure that people did not attempt to go around the provisions of the Table of Ranks? How did he provide for the creation of new nobles through service to the state? How might the Table of Ranks and these provisions have fostered loyalty to the new social and political order that Peter sought to achieve?*

After announcing that all princes descended from himself and those married to such princes took precedence over all other ranks, these points of clarification followed:

3. Whoever shall demand honour higher than his rank or take a place higher than the rank given him, shall be fined two months pay for each offence...but this observance of each rank

---

olence and bloodshed had surrounded the disputed succession. Matters became even more confused when the boys' sister, Sophia, was named regent. Peter's followers overthrew her in 1689. From that date onward, Peter ruled personally, although in theory he shared the crown until Ivan died in 1696. The dangers and turmoil of his youth convinced Peter of two things: first, the power of the tsar must be made secure from the jealousy of the *boyars* and the greed of the *streltsy*; second, the military power of Russia must be increased. In both respects, he self-consciously resembled Louis XIV of France, who had experienced the turmoil of the *Fronde* during his youth and resolved to establish a strong monarchy safe from the noblity and defended by a powerful army.

Northwestern Europe, particularly the military resources of the maritime powers, fascinated Peter I, who eventually became known as Peter the Great. In 1697, he made a famous visit in transparent disguise to western Europe. There he dined and talked with the great and the powerful, who considered this almost seven-foot-tall ruler both crude and rude. His happiest moments on the trip were spent inspecting shipyards, docks, and the manufacture of military hardware in England and the Netherlands.

An imitator of the first order, Peter returned to Moscow determined to copy what he had seen abroad, for he knew that warfare would be necessary to make Russia a great power. He personally intervened in one project after anothis not demanded on such occasions as when good friends or neighbors get together, or in public assemblies, but only in churches during Divine Service, in Court ceremonies such as ambassadorial audiences, formal dinners, official meetings, weddings, christenings, and suchlike public festivity and business...

* * * * *

7. All married women occupy ranks according to the grades of their husbands, and when they act in a manner contrary to this they must pay a fine such as their husbands would have paid for the same offence.

8. Although We allow free entry before others of lower grade in public assembly where the Court is to be found to the sons of the Russians State's Princes, Counts, Barons, distinguished Nobility, and servants of the highest rank, because of their aristocratic birth, or because of the outstanding grades of their fathers, and although We keenly desire to see that they are distinguished from others according to their dignity in all cases; however We do not allow anybody rank, until they have rendered service to Us and the fatherland, and have received a character reference to this effect.

* * * * *

11. All Russian or foreign servants who are or actually were in the first eight ranks, their law-

ful children and descendants in perpetuity are considered equal to the best ancient Nobility in all honours and advantages, even though they are of low birth, and have never been promoted to Noble rank by Crowned Heads or granted coats of arms.

* * * * *

15. To military men of commoner origin who serve up to Commissioned rank, when one of them receives the aforementioned grade, he is a Noble and so are the children born while he holds the Commission....

* * * * *

19. Since...the prominence of and worthiness of the grade of any individual is often diminished, when the dress and behavior are not consonant with them, similarly on the other hand many are ruined when they have accoutrements higher than their grade and property: We therefore graciously point out that everybody should have the dress, equipage and livery as his position and character reference demand. All must act in this manner, and must beware of the ordained penalty and greatest punishment.

From Paul Dukes, trans. and ed., *Russia under Catherine the Great: Select Documents on Government and Society.* Oriental Research Partners, 1978, pp. 10–12. Reprinted by permission of Oriental Research Partners

er, displaying enormous energy and determination tied to equally enormous impulsiveness. The tsar's drive toward westernization, though unsystematic, had five interrelated general goals: taming the *boyars* and the *streltsy*, achieving secular control of the church, reorganizing the internal administration, developing the economy, and constructing a major army and navy. Peter pursued each of these goals ruthlessly. His effort was unprecedented in Russian history in both its intensity and scope.

TAMING THE *BOYARS* AND *STRELTSY* Peter made a sustained attack on the *boyars* and their attachment to traditional Russian culture. In 1698, immediately on his return from abroad, he personally

shaved the long beards of the court *boyars* and sheared off the customary long, hand-covering sleeves of their shirts and coats, which had made them the butt of jokes throughout Europe. More important, he demanded that the nobles serve his state. He faced considerable opposition, but eventually imposed his will.

A Table of Ranks, published in 1722, embodied Peter's policy of drawing the nobility into state service. (See "Peter the Great Issues a Table of Ranks.") That table equated a person's social position and privileges with his rank in the bureaucracy or the military, rather than with his lineage among the traditional landed nobility. Peter thus made the social standing of individual *boyars* a function of their willingness to serve the central

After Peter the Great of Russia returned from his journey to western Europe, he personally cut off the traditional and highly prized long sleeves and beards of the Russian nobles. His action symbolized his desire to see Russia become more powerful and more modern. The Granger Collection

state. Earlier tsars had created service nobles on the basis of merit, but none had envisioned drawing all nobles into state service. Unlike Prussian *Junkers*, however, the Russian nobility never became perfectly loyal to the state. They repeatedly sought to reassert their independence and their control of the Russian imperial court and to bargain with later tsars over local authority and the nobles' dominance of the serfs.

The *streltsy* fared less well than the *boyars*. In 1698, they had rebelled while Peter was on his European tour. On his return, he brutally suppressed the revolt. There were private tortures and public executions, in which Peter's own ministers took part. Almost 1,200 of the rebels were put to death, and their corpses remained on public display to discourage future disloyalty. The new military establishment that Peter built would serve the tsar and not itself.

ACHIEVING SECULAR CONTROL OF THE CHURCH
Peter quashed the potential independence of the Russian Orthodox Church with similar ruthlessness. Here again, he had to confront a problem that had arisen in the turbulent decades that had preceded his reign. The Russian church had long opposed the scientific, as well as the theological, thought of the West. In the mid-seventeenth century, a reformist movement led by Patriarch Nikon introduced changes into church texts and ritual. The Old Believers, a group of Russian Christians, strongly opposed these changes. Although condemned by the hierarchy, the Old Believers persisted in their opposition. Thousands of them committed suicide rather than submit to the new rituals. The Old Believers represented a rejection of change and innovation; their opposition discouraged the church hierarchy from making further substantial accommodations to modern thought.

In the future, Peter wanted to avoid two kinds of difficulties with the church: first, the clergy must not be able to oppose change and westernization; second, the hierarchy of the church must not be permitted to cause again the kind of controversy that had provoked the Old Believers. Consequently, in 1721, Peter simply abolished the position of patriarch. In its place he established a synod headed by a layman, called the procurator general, to rule the church in accordance with secular requirements. This action toward the church was the most radical transformation of a traditional institution in Peter's reign. It produced further futile opposition from the Old Believers, who saw the tsar as leading the church into new heresy.

REORGANIZING DOMESTIC ADMINISTRATION   In reorganizing his domestic administration, Peter looked to Swedish institutions called "colleges"—bureaus of several persons rather than departments headed by a single minister. These colleges, which he imposed on Russia, were to look after matters such as the collection of taxes, foreign relations, war, and economic affairs. This new organization was an attempt to breathe life into Russia's stagnant and inefficient administration.

In 1711, Peter created a central senate of nine members who were to direct the government when the tsar was away with the army. The purpose of these and other local administrative reforms was to establish a bureaucracy that could support an efficient army.

DEVELOPING THE ECONOMY AND WAGING WAR   The economic development advocated by Peter the Great was closely related to his military needs. He encouraged the establishment of an iron industry in the Ural Mountains, and by midcentury Russia had become the largest iron producer in Europe, although the industry later languished. He sent promising young Russians abroad to acquire technical and organizational skills. He tried to attract west European

Vüe des bords de la Neva en descendant la rivière entre le Palais d'hyver de Sa Majesté Impériale & les batimens de l'Académie des Sciences

Peter the Great built Saint Petersburg on the Gulf of Finland to provide Russia with better contact with western Europe. He moved Russia's capital there from Moscow in 1703. This is an eighteenth-century view of the city. The Granger Collection

Peter the Great Tells His Son to Acquire Military Skills

Enormous hostility existed between Peter the Great and his son Alexis. Peter believed that his son was not prepared to inherit the throne. In October 1715, he composed a long letter to Alexis in which he berated him for refusing to take military matters seriously. The letter indicates how an early eighteenth-century ruler saw the conduct of warfare as a fundamental part of the role of a monarch. Peter also points to Louis XIV of France as a role model. Peter and Alexis did not reach an agreement. Alexis died under mysterious circumstances in 1718, with Peter possibly responsible for his death.

❖ *How did Peter use the recent war with Sweden to argue for the necessity of his son acquiring military skills? What concept of leadership does Peter attempt to communicate to his son? Why did Peter see military prowess as the most important ability in a ruler?*

You cannot be ignorant of what is known to all the world, to what degree our people groaned under the oppression of the Swede before the beginning of the present war....

...You know what it has cost us in the beginning of this war...to make ourselves experienced in the art of war, and to put a stop to those advantages which our implacable enemies obtained over us....

But you even will not so much as hear warlike exercises mentioned: though it was by them that we broke through that obscurity in which we were involved, and that we make ourselves known to nations, whose esteem we share at present.

I do not exhort you to make war without lawful reasons: I only desire you to apply yourself to learn the art of it: for it is impossible well to govern without knowing the rules and discipline of it, was it for no other end than for the defense of the country.

...You mistake, if you think it is enough for a prince to have good generals to act under his order. Everyone looks upon the head; they study its inclinations and conform themselves to them: all the world own this....

You have no inclination to learn war. You do not apply yourself to it, and consequently you will never learn it: And how then can you command others, and judge of the reward which those deserve who do their duty, or punish others who fail of it? You will do nothing, nor judge of anything but by the assent and help of others, like a young bird that holds up his bill to be fed....

If you think there are some, whose affairs do not fail of success, though they do not go to war themselves; it is true: But if they do not go themselves, yet they have an inclination for it, and understand it.

For instance, the late King of France did not always take the field in person; but it is known to what degree he loved war, and what glorious exploits he performed in it, which make his campaigns to be called the theatre and school of the world. His inclinations were not confined solely to military affairs, he also loved mechanics, manufacture and other establishment, which rendered his kingdom more flourishing than any other whatsoever.

From Friedrich C. Weber, *The Present State of Russia* (London, 1722), 2:97-100; *The Global Experience*, 3/E, Vol. 2 by Riley, © 1999. Reprinted by permission of Prentice Hall, Inc., Upper Saddle River, NJ.

craftspeople to live and work in Russia. Except for the striking growth of the iron industry, these efforts had only marginal success.

But Peter did develop military support industries. What one historian has termed "Peter the Great's most revolutionary innovation" was his building of a Russian navy.[3] When Peter came to the throne, Rus-

sia had no real navy. In the mid-1690s, he oversaw the construction of ships to protect his interests in the Black Sea. Part of the reason for his subsequent trip to Western Europe was to learn how to build better warships. The construction of a Baltic fleet, largely built on the Finnish coast, was essential in the Great Northern War. By 1720, the Russian fleet was larger than that of either Sweden or Denmark. Only a decade earlier Russia had possessed no significant navy to launch against either Baltic power.

[3]Simon Dixon, *The Modernization of Russia, 1676–1825* (Cambridge: Cambridge University Press, 1999), p. 35.

The creation of a navy was one part of Peter's strategy to secure warm-water ports that would allow Russia to trade with the West and to influence European affairs. This ambition led him into wars with the Ottoman Empire and Sweden. His armies began fighting the Turks in 1695 and captured Azov on the Black Sea in 1696, though he was compelled to return the port in 1711.

Peter had more success against Sweden, where he profited from the inconsistency and irrationality of Charles XII. In 1700, Russia invaded the Swedish Baltic possessions. The Swedish king's failure to follow up his victory over the Russians at Narva in 1700 allowed Peter to regroup his forces and conserve his resources. In 1709, when Charles XII returned to fight Russia again, Peter was ready, and the Battle of Poltava sealed the fate of Sweden. In 1721 the Peace of Nystad, which ended the Great Northern War, confirmed the Russian conquest of Estonia, Livonia, and part of Finland. Henceforth, Russia possessed warm-water ports and a permanent influence on European affairs.

In the process of fighting these extensive wars, Peter reorganized the Russian army. He introduced effective and ruthless policies of conscription, drafting an unprecedented 130,000 soldiers during the first decade of the eighteenth century and almost 300,000 troops by the end of his reign. He had also adopted policies for the officer corps and general military discipline patterned on those of West European armies. In 1718–1719, he founded the College of War to administer the army. Such administration would be needed because, except for the 1720s, Russia was involved in war somewhere during every other decade of the eighteenth century.

At one point, the domestic and foreign policies of Peter the Great literally intersected. This was at the spot on the Gulf of Finland where he founded his new capital city of St. Petersburg in 1703. There he built government structures and compelled the *boyars* to construct town houses. He thus imitated those European monarchs who had copied Louis XIV by constructing smaller versions of Versailles. The founding of St. Petersburg went beyond establishing a central imperial court, however; it symbolized a new western orientation of Russia and Peter's determination to hold his position on the Baltic coast. He had begun the construction of the city and had moved the capital there even before his victory over Sweden was assured. Moreover, he and his successors employed architects from western Europe for many of the most prominent buildings in and around the city. Consequently, St. Petersburg looked different from other Russian cities. Both in Peter's day and later, many Russians saw St. Pe-

tersburg as a kind of illegitimate west European growth on Russian culture that symbolized Peter's autocracy and rejection of traditional Russian life and government.

Despite his notable successes, Peter's reign ended with a great question mark. He had long quarreled with his only son, Alexis. (See "Peter the Great Tells His Son to Acquire Military Skills.") Peter was jealous of the young man and feared that Alexis might undertake sedition. In 1718 Peter had his son imprisoned, and during this imprisonment Alexis died mysteriously. Thereafter Peter claimed the right to name a successor, but he could never bring himself to designate one. Consequently, when he died in 1725, there was no firm policy on the succession to the throne. For more than thirty years, soldiers and nobles again determined who ruled Russia. Peter had laid the foundations of a modern Russia, but he had failed to lay the foundations of a stable state.

In Perspective

By the second quarter of the eighteenth century, the major European powers were not nation–states in which the citizens felt themselves united by a shared sense of community, culture, language, and history. Rather, they were monarchies in which the personality of the ruler and the personal relationships of the great noble families exercised considerable influence over public affairs. The monarchs, except in Great Britain, had generally succeeded in making their power greater than the nobility's. The power of the aristocracy and its capacity to resist or obstruct the policies of the monarch were not destroyed, however. In Britain, of course, the nobility had tamed the monarchy, but even there tension between nobles and monarchs would continue throughout the rest of the century.

In foreign affairs, the new arrangement of military and diplomatic power established early in the century prepared the way for two long conflicts. The first was a commercial rivalry for trade and overseas empire between France and Great Britain. During the reign of Louis XIV, these two nations had collided over the French bid for dominance in Europe. During the eighteenth century, they dueled for control of commerce on other continents. The second arena of warfare was in central Europe, where Austria and Prussia fought for the leadership of the German states.

Behind these international conflicts and the domestic rivalry of monarchs and nobles, however, the society of eighteenth-century Europe began to change. The character and the structures of the societies over which the monarchs ruled were beginning to take on some features associated with the modern age. These economic and social developments would eventually transform the life of Europe to a degree beside which the state building of the early eighteenth-century monarchs paled.

REVIEW QUESTIONS

1. Explain why Britain and France remained leading powers in western Europe while the United Netherlands declined.
2. How did the structure of British government change under the political leadership of Robert Walpole? What were the chief sources of Walpole's political strength?
3. How was the Hohenzollern family able to forge a conglomerate of diverse landholdings into the state of Prussia? Who were the major personalities involved in this process, and what were their individual contributions? Why was the military so important in Prussia?
4. Compare and contrast the varying success with which the Hohenzollerns and Habsburgs each handled their problems. Which family was more successful and why? Why were Sweden, the Ottoman Empire, and Poland less successful?
5. How and why did Russia emerge as a great power? Discuss the character of Peter the Great. What were Russia's domestic problems before Peter came to power? What were his methods of reform? To what extent did he succeed? How were his reforms related to his military ambitions? Compare and contrast Peter the Great with Louis XIV of France.
6. Consider how between approximately 1685 and 1740 the problems and uncertainties of who would and could succeed to the thrones of the various states constutited one of the major political and diplomatic problems of European politics.

SUGGESTED READINGS

T. M. BARKER, *Army, Aristocracy, Monarchy: Essays in War, Society and Government in Austria, 1618–1780* (1982). Examines the intricate power relationships among these major institutions.

J. BLACK, *Eighteenth-Century Europe, 1700–1789* (1990). An excellent survey.

C. R. BOXER, *The Dutch Seaborne Empire* (1965). Remains the best treatment of the subject.

J. BREWER, *The Sinews of Power: War, Money and the English State, 1688–1783* (1989). An extremely important study of the financial basis of English power.

F. L. CARSTEN, *The Origins of Prussia* (1954). Discusses the groundwork laid by the Great Elector in the seventeenth century.

J. C. D. CLARK, *English Society: 1688–1832: Social Structure and Political Practice during the Ancien Régime* (1985). An important, controversial work that emphasizes the role of religion in English political life.

N. DAVIS, *God's Playground*, Vol. 1 (1991). Excellent on prepartition Poland.

W. DOYLE, *The Old European Order, 1660–1800* (1992). The most thoughtful treatment of the subject.

R. R. ERGANG, *The Potsdam Führer* (1941). The biography of Frederick William I.

R. J. W. EVANS, *The Making of the Habsburg Monarchy, 1550–1700: An Interpretation* (1979). Places much emphasis on intellectual factors and the role of religion.

F. FORD, *Robe and Sword: The Regrouping of the French Aristocracy after Louis XIV* (1953). An important book for political, social, and intellectual history.

L. HUGHES, *Russia in the Age of Peter the Great* (1998). Will likely stand for some time as the standard work.

C. J. INGRAO, *The Habsburg Monarchy, 1618–1815* (1994). The best recent survey.

J. I. ISRAEL, *The Dutch Republic, Its Rise, Greatness, and Fall, 1477–1806* (1995). The major survey of the subject.

R. A. KANN AND Z. V. DAVID, *The Peoples of the Eastern Habsburg Lands, 1526–1918* (1984). A helpful overview of the subject.

D. MCKAY AND H. M. SCOTT, *The Rise of the Great Powers, 1648–1815* (1983). Now the standard survey.

R. K. MASSIE, *Peter the Great: His Life and His World* (1980). A good popular biography.

G. PARKER, *The Military Revolution: Military Innovation and the Rise of the West (1500–1800)* (1988). A major work.

J. H. PLUMB, *The Growth of Political Stability in England, 1675–1725* (1969). Remains an important interpretive work.

J. L. PRICE, *The Dutch Republic in the Seventeenth Century* (1998). A sophisticated, concise introduction.

N. V. RIASANOVSKY, *The Image of Peter the Great in Russian History and Thought* (1985). Examines the legacy of Peter in Russian history.

S. SCHAMA, *An Embarrassment of Riches: An Interpretation of Dutch Culture in the Golden Age* (1987). Lively and controversial.

P. F. SUGAR, *Southeastern Europe under Ottoman Rule, 1354–1804* (1977). An extremely clear presentation.

Chapter 16

During the eighteenth century, with their employment opportunities tightly restricted, many unmarried women and widows served as governesses to children of the aristocracy and other wealthy groups in Europe. At the other end of the spectrum, many children born out of wedlock or to very poor parents might be left at foundling hospitals where many of them died quite young.

Chardin, Jean-Baptiste-Simeone: *The Governess* (#6432), National Gallery of Canada, Ottawa

Society and Economy Under the Old Regime in the Eighteenth Century

KEY TOPICS

- The varied privileges and powers of Europe's aristocracies in the Old Regime and their efforts to increase their wealth

- The plight of rural peasants

- Family structure and family economy

- The transformation of Europe's economy by the agricultural and industrial revolutions

- Urban growth and the social tensions that accompanied it

- The strains on the institutions of the Old Regime brought about by social change

During the French Revolution and the turmoil spawned by that upheaval, it became customary to refer to the patterns of social, political, and economic relationships that had existed in France before 1789 as the ancien régime, or the Old Regime. The term has come to be applied generally to the life and institutions of prerevolutionary Europe. Politically, it meant the rule of theoretically absolute monarchies with growing bureaucracies *and aristocratically led armies. Economically, a scarcity of food, the predominance of agriculture, slow transport, a low level of iron production, comparatively unsophisticated financial institutions, and, in some cases, competitive commercial overseas empires characterized the Old Regime. Socially, men and women living during the period saw themselves less as individuals than as members of distinct corporate bodies that possessed certain privileges or rights as a group.*

Tradition, hierarchy, a corporate feeling, and privilege were the chief social characteristics of the Old Regime. Yet it was by no means a static society. Change and innovation were fermenting in its midst. Farming became more commercialized, and both food production and the size of the population increased. The early stages of the Industrial Revolution made more consumer goods available, and domestic consumption expanded throughout the century. The colonies in the Americas provided strong demand for European goods and manufactures. Merchants in seaports and other cities were expanding their businesses. By preparing their states for war, European governments put new demands on the resources and the economic organizations of their nations. The spirit of rationality that had been so important to the Scientific Revolution of the seventeenth century continued to manifest itself in the economic life of the eighteenth century. The Old Regime itself fostered the changes that eventually transformed it into a different kind of society.

Major Features of Life in the Old Regime

Socially, prerevolutionary Europe was based on (1) aristocratic elites possessing a wide variety of inherited legal privileges; (2) established churches intimately related to the state and the aristocracy; (3) an urban labor force usually organized into guilds; and (4) a rural peasantry subject to high taxes and feudal dues. Of course, the men and women living during this period did not know it was the Old Regime. Most of them earned their livelihoods and passed their lives as their forebears had done for generations before them and as they expected their children to do after them.

Maintenance of Tradition

During the eighteenth century, the past weighed more heavily on people's minds than did the future. Few persons outside the government bureaucracies, the expanding merchant groups, and the movement for reform called the Enlightenment (see Chapter 18) considered change or innovation desirable. This was es-

pecially true of social relationships. Both nobles and peasants, for different reasons, repeatedly called for the restoration of traditional, or customary, rights. The nobles asserted what they considered their ancient rights against the intrusion of the expanding monarchical bureaucracies. The peasants, through petitions and revolts, called for the revival or the maintenance of the customary manorial rights that allowed them access to particular lands, courts, or grievance procedures.

Except for the early industrial development in Britain and the accompanying expansion of personal consumption, the eighteenth-century economy was also predominantly traditional. The quality and quantity of the grain harvest remained the most important fact of life for most of the population and the gravest concern for governments.

Hierarchy and Privilege

Closely related to this traditional social and economic outlook was the hierarchical structure of the society. The medieval sense of rank and degree not only persisted, but became more rigid during the century. In several continental cities, sumptuary laws regulating the dress of the different classes remained on the books. These laws forbade persons in one class or occupation from wearing clothes like those worn by their social superiors. The laws, which sought to make the social hierarchy easily visible, were largely ineffective by this time. What really enforced the hierarchy was the corporate nature of social relationships.

Each state or society was considered a community composed of numerous smaller communities. Eighteenth-century Europeans did not enjoy what Americans regard as "individual rights." Instead, a person enjoyed such rights and privileges as were guaranteed to the particular communities or groups of which she or he was a part. The "community" might include the village, the municipality, the nobility, the church, the guild, a university, or the parish. In turn, each of these bodies enjoyed certain privileges, some great and some small. The privileges might involve exemption from taxation or from some especially humiliating punishment, the right to practice a trade or craft, the right of one's children to pursue a particular occupation, or, for the church, the right to collect the tithe.

The Aristocracy

The eighteenth century was the great age of the aristocracy. The nobility constituted approximately 1 to 5 percent of the population of any given country. Yet in every country, the nobility was the single wealthiest sector of the population, had the widest degree of social, political, and economic power, and set the tone

The foundation of aristocratic life was the possession of land. English aristocrats and large landowners controlled local government as well as the English Parliament. This painting of Robert Andrews and his wife by Thomas Gainsborough (1728–1788) shows an aristocratic couple on their estate. The gun and the hunting dog in this portrait suggest the importance landowners assigned to the virtually exclusive hunting privileges they enjoyed on their land. © National Gallery, London

of polite society. In most countries, the nobility had their own separate house in the parliament, estates, or diet. Only nobles had any kind of representation in Hungary and Poland. Land continued to provide the aristocracy with its largest source of income, but aristocrats did not merely own estates: Their influence was felt throughout social and economic life. In much of Europe, however, it was felt that manual labor was regarded as beneath a noble. In Spain, it was assumed that even the poorer nobles would lead lives of idleness. In other nations, however, the nobility often fostered economic innovation and embraced the commercial spirit. Such willingness to change helped protect the nobility's wealth.

Varieties of Aristocratic Privilege

To be an aristocrat was a matter of birth and legal privilege. This much the aristocracy had in common across the Continent. In almost every other respect, they differed markedly from country to country.

BRITISH NOBILITY   The smallest, wealthiest, best-defined, and most socially responsible aristocracy resided in Great Britain. It consisted of about 400 families, and the eldest male members of each family sat

in the House of Lords. Through the corruptions of the electoral system, these families also controlled many seats in the House of Commons. The estates of the British nobility ranged from a few thousand to fifty thousand acres, from which they received rents. The nobles owned about one-fourth of all the arable land in the country. Increasingly, the British aristocracy invested its wealth in commerce, canals, urban real estate, mines, and even industrial ventures. Because only the eldest son inherited the title and the land, younger sons moved into commerce, the army, the professions, and the church. British landowners in both houses of Parliament levied taxes and also paid them. They had few significant legal privileges, but their direct or indirect control of local government gave them immense political power and social influence. The aristocracy dominated the society and politics of the English counties. Their country houses, many of which were built in the eighteenth century, were centers for local society.

FRENCH NOBILITY   The situation of the continental nobilities was less clear cut. In France, the approximately 400,000 nobles were divided between nobles "of the sword," or those whose nobility was derived from military service, and those "of the robe," or those who had acquired their titles either by serving in the bureaucracy or by having purchased them. The two groups had quarreled in the past, but often cooperated during the eighteenth century to defend their common privileges.

The French nobles were also divided between those who held office or favor with the royal court at Versailles and those who did not. The court nobility reaped the immense wealth that could be gained from holding high office. The nobles' hold on such offices intensified during the century. By the late 1780s, appointments to the church, the army, and the bureaucracy, as well as other profitable positions, tended to go to the nobles already established in court circles. Whereas these well-connected aristocrats were rich, the provincial nobility, called *hobereaux*, were often little better off than wealthy peasants.

Despite differences in rank, origin, and wealth, certain hereditary privileges set all French aristocrats apart from the rest of society. They were exempt from many taxes. For example, most French nobles did not pay the *taille*, or land tax, the basic tax of the Old Regime. The nobles were technically liable for payment of the *vingtième*, or the "twentieth," which resembled an income tax, but they rarely had to pay it in full. The nobles were not liable for the royal *corvées*, or forced labor on public works, which fell on the peasants. In addition to these exemptions, French nobles could collect feudal dues from their tenants and enjoyed exclusive hunting and fishing privileges.

EASTERN EUROPEAN NOBILITIES   East of the Elbe River, the character of the nobility became even more complicated and repressive. Throughout the area, the military traditions of the aristocracy remained important. In Poland, there were thousands of nobles, or *szlachta*, who were entirely exempt from taxes after 1741. Until 1768, these Polish aristocrats possessed the right of life and death over their serfs. Most of the Polish nobility were relatively poor. A few rich nobles who had immense estates exercised political power in the fragile Polish state.

In Austria and Hungary, the nobility continued to possess broad judicial powers over the peasantry through their manorial courts. They also enjoyed various degrees of exemption from taxation. The wealthiest of them, Prince Esterhazy of Hungary, owned ten million acres of land.

In Prussia, after the accession of Frederick the Great in 1740, the position of the Junker nobles became much stronger. Frederick's various wars required their full support. He drew his officers almost wholly from the Junker class. Nobles also

increasingly made up the bureaucracy. As in other parts of eastern Europe, the Prussian nobles had extensive judicial authority over the serfs.

In Russia, the eighteenth century saw what amounted to the creation of the nobility. Peter the Great's (r. 1682–1725) linking of state service and noble social status through the Table of Ranks (1722) established among Russian nobles a self-conscious class identity that had not previously existed. Thereafter, they were determined to resist compulsory state service. In 1736, Empress Anna (r. 1730–1740) reduced such service to twenty-five years. In 1762, Peter III (r. 1762) exempted the greatest nobles entirely from compulsory service. In 1785, in the Charter of the Nobility, Catherine the Great (r. 1762–1796) legally defined the rights and privileges of noble men and women in exchange for the assurance that the nobility would serve the state voluntarily. Noble privileges included the right of transmitting noble status to a nobleman's wife and children, the judicial protection of noble rights and property, considerable power over the serfs, and exemption from personal taxes.

Aristocratic Resurgence

The Russian Charter of the Nobility constituted one aspect of the broader European-wide development termed the "aristocratic resurgence." This was the nobility's reaction to the threat to their social position and privileges that they felt from the expanding power of the monarchies. This resurgence took several forms in the eighteenth century. First, all nobilities tried to preserve their exclusiveness by making it more difficult to become a noble. Second, they pushed to reserve appointments to the officer corps of the armies, the bureaucracies, the government ministries, and the church exclusively for nobles. By doing this, they hoped to resist the encroaching power of the monarchies.

Third, the nobles attempted to use the authority of existing aristocratically controlled institutions against the power of the monarchies. These institutions included the British Parliament, the French courts, or *parlements*, and the local aristocratic estates and provincial diets in Germany and the Habsburg Empire.

Fourth, the nobility sought to improve its financial position by gaining further exemptions from taxation or by collecting higher rents or long-forgotten feudal dues from the peasantry. The nobility tried to shore up its position by various appeals to traditional and often ancient privileges that had lapsed over time. This aristocratic challenge to the monarchies was a fundamental political fact of the day and potentially a very disruptive one.

The Land and Its Tillers

Land was the economic basis of eighteenth-century life and the foundation of the status and power of the nobility. Well over three-fourths of all Europeans lived in the country, and few of them ever traveled more than a few miles from their birthplace. Except for the nobility and the wealthier nonaristocratic landowners, most people who dwelled on the land were poor—in many regions, desparately poor. They lived in various states of economic and social dependency, exploitation, and vulnerability.

Peasants and Serfs

Rural social dependency related directly to the land. The nature of the dependency differed sharply for free peasants, such as English tenants and most French cultivators, and for the serfs of Germany, Austria, and Russia, who were legally bound to a particular plot of land and a particular lord. But everywhere, the class that owned most of the land also controlled the local government and the courts. For example, in Great Britain, all farmers and smaller tenants had the legal rights of English citizens. The justices of the peace, however, who presided over the county courts and who could call out the local militia, were always substantial landowners, as were the members of Parliament, who made the laws. In eastern Europe, the landowners presided over the manorial courts. On the Continent, the burden of taxation fell on the tillers of the soil.

OBLIGATIONS OF PEASANTS The power of the landlord increased as one moved across Europe from west to east. Most French peasants owned some land, but there were a few serfs in eastern France. Nearly all French peasants were subject to certain feudal dues, called *banalités*. These included the required use-for-payment of the lord's, or *seigneur's*, mill to grind grain and his oven to bake bread. The *seigneur* could also require a certain number of days each year of the peasant's labor. This practice of forced labor was termed the *corvée*. Because even landowning French peasants rarely possessed enough land to support their families, they had to rent more land from the *seigneur* and were also subject to feudal dues attached to those plots. In Prussia and Austria, despite attempts by the monar-

Eighteenth-century France had some of the best roads in the world, but they were often built with forced labor. French peasants were required to work part of each year on such projects. This system, called the corvée, *was not abolished until the French Revolution in 1789.* Claude Joseph Vernet, *Construction of a Road.* Louvre, Paris, France. Giraudon/Art Resource, NY

Russian Serfs Lament Their Condition

As with other illiterate groups in European history, it is difficult to recapture the voices of Russians serfs. The following verses from "The Slaves' Lament," a popular ballad from the era of the Pugachev Rebellion (1773–1775), indicate that the serfs were aware of how the legislation of that era which favored the landowning classes affected their lives. The verses embody the resentment that Pugachev's Rebellion ignited. Note how the verses suggest that the Tsar may be more favorable to serfs than their landowners are. Pugachev claimed to be Tsar Peter III, and many Russian serfs believed him and thus considered him a liberator from landlord tyranny. Throughout this ballad, serfs present themselves as slaves.

❖ *What specific complaints about landlords are expressed in these verses? What charges indicate that serfs may believe that their situation has worsened? What hope do they seem to place in the Tsar? What idealized picture of the world do the serfs believe they would themselves create?*

O woe to us slaves living for the masters!
We do not know how to serve their ferocity!
Service is like a sharp scythe;
And kindness is like the morning dew.

⋆ ⋆ ⋆ ⋆ ⋆

Brothers, how annoying it is to us
And how shameful and insulting
That another who is not worthy to be equal
   with us
Has so many of us in his power.

⋆ ⋆ ⋆ ⋆ ⋆

And if we steal from the lord one half
   kopeck,
The law commands us to be killed like a
   louse.
And if the master steals ten thousand,
Nobody will judge who should be hanged.
The injustice of the Russian sheriffs has
   increased:
Whoever brings a present is right beyond
   argument.
They have stopped putting their trust in the
   Creator for authority,
And have become accustomed to own us like
   cattle.
All nations rebuke us and wonder at our
   stupidity,
That such stupid people are born in Russia.
And indeed, stupidity was rooted in us long ago,
as each honour here has been given to vagrants.
The master can kill the servant like a gelding;
The denunciation by a slave cannot be believed.
Unjust judges have composed a decree

That we should be tyrannically whipped with a
   knout for that.

⋆ ⋆ ⋆ ⋆ ⋆

Better that we should agree to serve the tsar.
Better to live in dark woods
Than to be before the eyes of these tyrants;
They look on us cruelly with their eyes
And eat us as iron eats rye. No one wants to
   serve the tsar
But only to grind us down to the end.
And they try to collect unjust bribes,
And they are not frightened that people die cruelly.

⋆ ⋆ ⋆ ⋆ ⋆

Ah brothers, if we got our freedom,
We would not take the lands or the fields for
   ourselves.
We would go into service as soldiers, brothers,
And would be friendly among ourselves,
Would destroy all injustice
And remove the root of evil lords.

⋆ ⋆ ⋆ ⋆ ⋆

They [the landlords] sell all the good rye to
   the merchants,
And give us like pigs the bad.
The greedy lords eat meat at fast time,
And even when meat is allowed, the slaves
   must cook meatless cabbage soup.
O brothers, it is our misfortune
always to have rye kasha.
The lords drink and make merry,
And do not allow the slaves even to burst
   out laughing.

From Paul Dukes, trans. and ed., *Russia under Catherine the Great: Select Documents on Government and Society* (Oriental Research Partners, 1978), pp. 115–117. Reprinted by permission of Oriental Research Partners.

chies late in the century to improve the lot of the serfs, the landlords continued to exercise almost complete control over them. In many of the Habsburg lands, law and custom required the serfs to provide service, or *robot*, to the lords.

Serfs were worst off in Russia. There, nobles reckoned their wealth by the number of "souls," or male serfs, owned rather than by the acreage the landlord possessed. Russian landlords, in effect, regarded serfs merely as economic commodities. They could demand as many as six days a week of labor, known as *barshchina*, from the serfs. Like Prussian and Austrian landlords, they enjoyed the right to punish their serfs. On their own authority, Russian landlords could even exile a serf to Siberia. Serfs had no legal recourse against the orders and whims of their lords. There was little difference between Russian serfdom and slavery.

In southeastern Europe, where the Ottoman Empire held sway, peasants were free, though landlords tried to exert authority in every way. The domain of the landlords was termed a *çift*. The landlord was often an absentee who managed the estate through an overseer. During the seventeenth and eighteenth centuries, these landlords, like those elsewhere in Europe, often became more commercially oriented and turned to the production of crops, such as cotton, vegetables, potatoes, and maize, that could be sold in the market.

A scarcity of labor rather than the recognition of their legal rights supported the independence of the southeastern European peasants. A peasant might migrate from one landlord to another. Because the second landlord needed the peasant's labor, he had no reason to return him to the original landlord. During the seventeenth and eighteenth centuries, however, disorder originating in the capital of Constantinople (now Istanbul) spilled over into the Balkan Peninsula. In this climate, landlords increased their authority by offering their peasants protection from bandits or rebels who might destroy peasant villages. As in medieval times, the manor house or armed enclosure of a local landlord became the peasants' refuge. These landlords also owned all the housing and tools required by the peasants and furnished their seed grain. Consequently, despite legal independence, Balkan peasants under the Ottoman Empire became largely dependent upon the landlords, though never to the extent of serfs in eastern Europe or Russia.

PEASANT REBELLIONS The Russian monarchy itself contributed to the further degradation of the serfs. Peter the Great gave whole villages to favored nobles. Later in the century, Catherine the Great confirmed the authority of the nobles over their serfs in exchange for the landowners' political cooperation. Russia experienced vast peasant unrest, with well over fifty

Emelyan Pugachev (1726–1775) led the largest peasant revolt in Russian history. In this contemporary propaganda picture he is shown in chains. An inscription in Russian and German was printed below the picture decrying the evils of revolution and insurrection.
Bildarchiv Preussischer Kulturbesitz

peasant revolts occurring between 1762 and 1769. These culminated in Pugachev's Rebellion between 1773 and 1775, when Emelyan Pugachev (1726–1775) promised the serfs land of their own and freedom from their lords. (See "Russian Serfs Lament Their Condition.") All of southern Russia was in turmoil until the government brutally suppressed the rebellion. Thereafter, any thought of liberalizing or improving the condition of the serfs was set aside for a generation.

Pugachev's was the largest peasant uprising of the eighteenth century, but smaller peasant revolts or disturbances took place in Bohemia in 1775, in Transylvania in 1784, in Moravia in 1786, and in Austria in 1789. There were almost no revolts in western Europe, but England experienced many rural riots. Rural rebellions were violent, but the peasants and serfs normally directed their wrath against property rather than persons. The rebels usually sought to reassert traditional or customary rights against practices that they perceived as innovations. Their targets were carefully chosen and included unfair pricing, onerous new or increased feudal dues, changes in methods of payment or land use, unjust officials, or extraordinarily brutal overseers and landlords. Peasant revolts were thus conservative in nature.

Aristocratic Domination of the Countryside: The English Game Laws

One of the clearest examples of aristocratic domination of the countryside and of aristocratic manipulation of the law to its own advantage was English legislation on hunting.

Between 1671 and 1831, English landowners had the exclusive legal right to hunt game animals, including, in particular, hares, partridges, pheasants, and moor fowl. Similar legislation covered other animals such as deer, the killing of which by an unauthorized person became a capital offense in the eighteenth century. By law, only persons owning a particular amount of landed property could hunt these animals. Excluded from the right to hunt were all persons renting land, wealthy city merchants who did not own land, and poor people in cities, villages, and the countryside. The poor were excluded because the elite believed that allowing the poor to enjoy the sport of hunting would undermine their work habits. The city merchants were excluded because the landed gentry in Parliament wanted to demonstrate visibly and legally the superiority of landed wealth over commercial wealth. Thus, the various game laws upheld the superior status of the aristocracy and the landed gentry.

The game laws represent a prime example of legislation related directly to economic and social status. The gentry who benefitted from the laws and whose parliamentary representatives had passed them also served as the local justices of the peace who administered the laws and punished their violation. The justices of the peace could levy fines and even have poachers impressed into the army. Gentry could also take civil legal action against wealthier poachers, such as rich farmers who rented land, and thus saddle them with immense legal fees. The gentry also employed gamekeepers to protect game from poachers. The gamekeepers were known to kill the dogs belonging to people suspected of poaching. By the middle of the century, gamekeepers had devised guns to shoot poachers who tripped their hidden levers.

A small industry arose to circumvent the game laws, however. Many poor people living either on an estate or in a nearby village would kill game for food. They believed that the game actually belonged to the community, and this poaching increased during hard times. Poaching was thus one way for the poor to find food.

Even more important was the black market in game animals sustained by the demand of urban people for this kind of luxury meat. Here arose the possibility of poaching for profit, and indeed, poaching technically meant the stealing or killing of game for sale. Local people from both the countryside and the villages would steal the game and then sell it to intermediaries called *higglers*. Later, coachmen took over this function. The higglers and the coachmen would smuggle the game into the cities, where poulterers would sell it at a premium price. Everyone involved made a bit of money along the way. During the second half of the century, English aristocrats began to construct large game preserves. The rural poor, who had lost their rights to communal land as a result of its enclosure by the large landowners, deeply resented these preserves, which soon became hunting grounds to organized gangs of poachers.

Penalties against poaching increased in the 1790s after the outbreak of the French Revolution, but so did the amount of poaching as the economic hardships caused by Britain's participation in the wars of the era put a greater burden on poor people and as the demand for food in English cities grew along with their population. By the 1820s, both landowners and reformers called for a change in the law. In 1831 Parliament rewrote the game laws, retaining the landowners' possession of the game, but permitting them to allow other people to hunt it. Poaching continued, but the exclusive right of the landed classes to hunt game had ended.

Family Structures and the Family Economy

In preindustrial Europe, the household was the basic unit of production and consumption. Few productive establishments employed more than a handful of people not belonging to the family of the owner, and those rare exceptions were in cities. The overwhelming majority of Europeans, however, lived in rural areas. There, as well as in small towns and cities, the household mode of organization predominated on farms, in artisans' workshops, and in small merchants' shops. With that mode of economic organization, there developed what is known as the family economy. Its structure as described here had prevailed over most of Europe for centuries.

Households

What was a household in the preindustrial Europe of the Old Regime? There were two basic models, one characterizing northwestern Europe and the other eastern Europe.

NORTHWESTERN EUROPE   In northwestern Europe, the household almost invariably consisted of a married couple, their children through their early teenage years, and their servants. Except for the few wealthy people, households were small, usu-

During the eighteenth century, most goods were produced in small workshops such as this iron forge painted by Joseph Wright of Derby (1734–1797), or in the homes of artisans. Not until very late in the century, with the early stages of industrialization, did a few factories appear. In the small early workshops, it would not have been uncommon for the family of the owner to visit, as portrayed in this painting. The Iron Forge, 1772 (oil on canvas) by Joseph Wright of Derby (1734–97). Broadlands Trust, Hants/Bridgeman Art Library, London.

ally consisting of not more than five or six members. Furthermore, in these households, more than two generations of a family rarely lived under the same roof. High mortality and late marriage prevented formation of families of three generations. In other words, grandparents rarely lived in the same household as their grandchildren, and families consisted of parents and children. The family structure of northwestern Europe was thus nuclear rather than extended.

Prior to recent research into family structures, historians had assumed that before industrialization Europeans lived in extended familial settings, with several generations living together in a household. Demographic investigation has now sharply reversed this picture. Children lived with their parents only until their early teens. Then they normally left home, usually to enter the work force of young servants who lived and worked in another household. A child of a skilled artisan might remain with his or her parents to learn a valuable skill; but only rarely would more than one child do so, because children's labor was more remunerative outside the home.

Those young men and women who had left home would eventually marry and form an independent household of their own. This practice of moving away from home is known as *neolocalism*. These young people married relatively late. Men were usually over twenty-six, and women over twenty-three. The new couple usually had children as soon after marriage as possible. Frequently, the woman was already pregnant at marriage. Family and community pressure often compelled the man to marry her. In any case, premarital sexual relations were common, though illegitimate births were rare. The new couple would soon employ a servant, who, together with their growing children, would undertake whatever form of livelihood the household used to support itself.

The word *servant* in this context may be confusing. It does not refer to someone looking after the needs of wealthy people. Rather, in preindustrial Europe, a servant was a person—either male or female—who was hired, often under a clear contract, to work for the head of the household in exchange for room, board, and wages. The servant was usually young and by no means always socially inferior to his or her employer. Normally, the servant was an integral part of the household and ate with the family.

Young men and women became servants when their labor was no longer needed in their parents' household or when they could earn more money for their family outside the parental household. Being a servant for several years—often as many as eight or ten—allowed young people to acquire the productive skills and the monetary savings necessary to begin their own household. These years spent as servants largely account for the late age of marriage in northwestern Europe.

EASTERN EUROPE   As one moved eastward across the continent, the structure of the household and the pattern of marriage changed. In eastern Europe, both men and women usually married before the age of twenty. Consequently, children were born to much younger parents. Often—especially among Russian serfs—wives were older than their husbands. Eastern European households were generally larger than those in the West. Frequently a rural Russian household consisted of more than nine, and possibly more than twenty, members, with three or perhaps even four generations of the same family living together. Early marriage made this situation more likely. In Russia, marrying involved not starting a new household, but remaining in and expanding one already established.

The landholding structure in eastern Europe accounts, at least in part, for these patterns of marriage and the family. The lords of the manor who owned land wanted to ensure that it would be cultivated so they could receive their rents. Thus, in Poland, for example, landlords might forbid marriage between their own serfs and those from another estate. They might also require widows and widowers to remarry to assure adequate labor for a particular plot of land. Polish landlords also frowned on the hiring of free laborers—the equivalent of servants in the west—to help cultivate land. The landlords preferred to use other serfs. This practice inhibited the formation of independent households. In Russia, landlords ordered the families of young people in their villages to arrange marriages within a short, set time. These lords discouraged single-generation family households because the death or serious illness of one person in such a household might mean that the land assigned to it would go out of cultivation.

The Family Economy

Throughout Europe, most people worked within the family economy. That is to say, the household was the basic unit of production and consumption. Almost everyone lived within a household of some

kind because it was virtually impossible for ordinary people to support themselves independently. Indeed, except for members of religious orders, people living outside a household were viewed with great suspicion. They were considered potentially criminal, disruptive, or at least dependent on the charity of others. Everywhere beggars met deep hostility. (See "Rules for the Berlin Poor House.")

Depending on their ages and skills, everyone in the household worked. The need to survive poor harvests or economic slumps meant that no one could be idle. Within this family economy, all goods and income produced went to the benefit of the household rather than to the individual family member. On a farm, much of the effort went directly into raising food or producing other agricultural goods that could be exchanged for food. Few western Europeans, however, had enough land to support their household from farming alone. Thus, one or more family members might work elsewhere and send wages home. For example, the father and older children might work as harvesters or might fish or might engage in other labor, either in the neighborhood or farther from home. If the father was such a migrant worker, the burden of farmwork would fall on his wife and their younger children. This was not an uncommon pattern.

The family economy also dominated the life of skilled urban artisans. The father was usually the chief artisan. He normally employed one or more servants, but would expect his children to work in the enterprise also. His eldest child was usually trained in the trade. His wife often sold his wares or opened a small shop of her own. Wives of merchants also frequently ran their husbands' businesses, especially when the husband traveled to purchase new goods. In any case, everyone in the family was involved. If business was poor, family members would look for employment elsewhere—not to support themselves as individuals, but to ensure the survival of the family unit.

In western Europe, the death of a father often brought disaster to the economy of the household. The continuing economic life of the family usually depended on his land or skills. The widow might take on the farm or the business, or his children might do so. The widow usually sought to remarry quickly to restore the labor and skills of a male to the household and to prevent herself from becoming dependent on relatives or charity.

The high mortality rate of the time meant that many households were reconstituted second-family groups that included stepchildren. Because of the advanced age of the widow or economic hard times, however, some households might simply dissolve. The widow became dependent on charity or relatives. The children became similarly dependent or entered the work force of servants earlier than they

Rules for the Berlin Poor House

Poverty was an enormous problem in eighteenth-century Europe, often forcing family members to work away from home and creating thousands of migrant workers and beggars. Governments were hostile to beggars and sometimes migrant workers, whom they regarded as a potential source of crime and disorder. Many of these concerns are evident in the regulations for the Berlin Poor House.

❖ *What were the distinctions made between the poor who deserved sympathy and those who did not? How would such a distinction affect social policy? Why might beggars have been regarded as dangers to public order? What attitudes toward work are displayed in these regulations?*

Whereas His Majesty...has renewed the prohibition of begging in the streets and in houses and has made all giving of alms punishable; it is decided to inform the public of the present measures for the relief of the poor, and to acquaint it with the main outlines of the above order:

1. In the new workhouse,...the genuinely needy and the poor deserving sympathy shall be cared for better than hitherto, but the deliberate beggars shall more resolutely be made to work.

2. The past organization of this house has therefore been totally altered, so that all persons to be received in it shall be divided into two entirely separate main classes, differentiated both in the status of their work and its location, in their dormitory and in their board.

3. The first class is meant for the old and for other persons deserving help and sympathy, who cannot entirely live by their work and do not wish to beg. Those report to the Poor's Chest in the Town Hall of Berlin, with a certificate from the Minister of their Church, showing their hitherto unblemished character, and after their references have been checked, they shall be accepted. They spin in the house as much wool as their age and health permits, and if they spin more than the cost of their keep, the surplus shall be paid out to them....

5. The second main class is destined for those who do not wish to make use of this benefaction,

but would rather live by begging. These deliberate beggars will be arrested by the Poor Law Constables, if necessary with the assistance of the Police, irrespective of age or status, whether they be vagabonds, journeymen, citizens, discharged soldiers, their wives or children, and will be sent to the workhouse.

6. Those who are caught begging for the first time shall be put into this class for three months at least, for the second time, for a year, and for the third and later times for several years, according to circumstances, for life.

7. Similarly, this class is destined for those who after due process of law have been sent for punishment as runaway servants and apprentices, for a period of time determined by the Court.

8. All the persons under numbers 5, 6, and 7 shall be forced to spin and prepare wool, and shall be kept on a minimum standard, clearly differentiated from the first class, both in the status and quantity of their work in their board and their lodging.

9. The children shall be cared for separately,...and shall receive education for several hours a day....

10. Before a beggar is discharged, he must, in order that he shall not again become a public nuisance, prove an occupation in prospect or the existence of relations or of other persons, who will look after him and will put him up at once....

Kruegeger, *Geschichte der Manufacturen...*, as quoted and translated in S. Pollard and C. Holmes, eds., *Documents of European Economic History*, Vol. I (London: Edward Arnold, 1968), pp. 166–167. Reprinted by Permission of Edward Arnold Ltd.

---

would otherwise. In other cases, the situation could be so desperate that they would resort to crime or to begging. The personal, emotional, and economic vulnerability of the family cannot be overemphasized.

In eastern Europe, the family economy functioned in the context of serfdom and landlord domination. Peasants clearly thought in terms of their families

and expanding the land available for cultivation. The village structure may have mitigated the pressures of the family economy, as did the multigenerational family. Dependence on the available land was the chief fact of life. There were many fewer artisan and merchant households, and there was far less geographical mobility than in western Europe.

Women and the Family Economy

The family economy established many of the chief constraints on the lives and personal experiences of women in preindustrial society. Most of the historical research that has been undertaken on this subject relates to western Europe. There, a woman's life experience was largely the function of her capacity to establish and maintain a household. For women, marriage was an economic necessity, as well as an institution that fulfilled sexual and psychological needs. Outside a household, a woman's life was vulnerable and precarious. Some women succeeded in becoming economically independent. They were the exception. Normally, unless she were an aristocrat or a member of a religious order, a woman probably could not support herself solely by her own efforts. Consequently, a woman devoted much of her life first to maintaining her parents' household and then to devising some means of getting her own household to live in as an adult. Bearing and rearing children were usually subordinate to these goals.

By the age of seven, a girl would have begun to help with the household work. On a farm, this might mean looking after chickens, watering the animals, or carrying food to adults working the land. In an urban artisan's household, she would do light work, perhaps cleaning or carrying and later sewing or weaving. The girl would remain in her parents' home as long as she made a real contribution to the family enterprise or as long as her labor elsewhere was not more remunerative to the family.

An artisan's daughter might not leave home until marriage, because at home she could learn increasingly valuable skills associated with the trade. The situation was different for the much larger number of girls growing up on farms. Their parents and brothers could often do all the necessary farmwork, and a girl's labor at home quickly became of little value to her family. She would then leave home, usually between the ages of twelve and fourteen. She might take up residence on another farm, but more likely she would migrate to a nearby town or city. She would rarely travel more than thirty miles from her parents' household. She would then normally become a servant, once again living in a household, but this time in the household of an employer. (See "Art & the West.")

Having migrated from home, the young woman's chief goal was to accumulate enough capital for a dowry. Her savings would make her eligible for marriage, because they would allow her to make the necessary contribution to form a household with her husband. Marriage within the family economy was a joint economic undertaking, and the wife was expected to make an immediate contribution of capital for establishing the household. A young woman might well work for ten years or more to accumulate a dowry. This practice meant that marriage was usually postponed until her mid- to late twenties.

Within marriage, earning enough money or producing enough farm goods to ensure an adequate food supply dominated women's concerns. Domestic duties, childbearing, and child rearing were subordinate to economic pressures. Consequently, couples tried to limit the number of children they had, usually through the practice of *coitus interruptus*, the withdrawal of the male before ejaculation. Parents often placed young children with wet nurses so the mother could continue to make her economic contribution to the household. The wet nurse, in turn, contributed to the economic welfare of her own household. The child would be fully reintegrated into its own family when it was weaned and would then be expected to aid the family at an early age.

The work of married women differed markedly between city and country and was in many ways a function of their husbands' occupations. If the peasant household had enough land to support itself, the wife spent much of her time quite literally carrying things for her husband—water, food, seed, harvested grain, and the like. There were few such adequate landholdings, however. If the husband had to do work besides farming, such as fishing or migrant labor, the wife might actually be in charge of the farm and do the ploughing, planting, and harvesting. In the city, the wife of an artisan or a merchant might well be in charge of the household finances and actively participate in managing the trade or manufacturing enterprise. When her husband died, she might take over the business and perhaps hire an artisan. Finally, if economic disaster struck the family, it was usually the wife who organized what Olwen Hufton has called the "economy of expedients,"[1] within which family members might be sent off to find work elsewhere or even to beg in the streets.

Despite all this economic activity, women found many occupations and professions closed to them because they were women. They labored with less education than men, because in such a society women at all levels of life consistently found fewer opportunities for education than men. They often received lower wages than men for the same work. As will be discussed later in the chapter, all of these disabilities worsened as a result of the mechanization of agriculture and the textile industries.

---

[1] Olwen Hufton, "Women and the Family Economy in Eighteenth-Century France," *French Historical Studies*, 9 (1976): 19.

Children and the World of the Family Economy

For women of all social ranks, childbirth was a time of fear and personal vulnerability. Contagious diseases endangered both mother and child. Puerperal fever was frequent, as were other infections from unsterilized medical instruments. (See "An Edinburgh Physician Describe the Dangers of Childbirth.") Not all midwives were skillful practitioners. Furthermore, most mothers and children immediately encountered immense poverty and wretched housing. Assuming that both mother and child survived, the mother might nurse the infant, but often the child would be sent to a wet nurse. Convenience may have led to this practice among the wealthy, but economic necessity dictated it for the poor. The structures and customs of the family economy did not permit a woman to devote herself entirely to rearing a child. The wet-nursing industry was well organized, with urban children being frequently transported to wet nurses in the country, where they would remain for months or even years.

Throughout Europe, the birth of a child was not always welcome. The child might represent another economic burden on an already hard-pressed household. Or it might be illegitimate.

The number of illegitimate births seems to have increased during the eighteenth century, possibly because increased migration of the population led to fleeting romances.

Through at least the end of the seventeenth century, unwanted or illegitimate births could lead to infanticide, especially among the poor. The parents might smother the infant or expose it to the elements. These practices were one result of both the ignorance and the prejudice surrounding contraception.

The late seventeenth and the early eighteenth centuries saw a new interest in preserving the lives of abandoned children. Although foundling hospitals established to care for abandoned children had existed before, their size and number expanded during these years. Two of the most famous were the Paris Foundling Hospital (1670) and the London Foundling Hospital (1739). Such hospitals cared for thousands of European children, and the demand for their services increased during the eighteenth century. For example, early in the century, an average of 1,700 children a year were admitted to the Paris Foundling Hospital. In the peak year of 1772, however, that number rose to 7,676 children. Not all of those children came from Paris. Many had been brought to the city from the provinces, where local foundling homes and hospitals were overburdened. The London Foundling Hos-

An Edinburgh Physician Describes the Dangers of Childbirth

Death in childbirth was a common occurrence throughout Europe until the twentieth century. This brief letter from an Edinburgh physician illustrates how devastating infectious diseases could be to women at the time of childbirth.

❖ *How does the passage illustrate a health danger that only women confronted? How might the likelihood of the death of oneself or a spouse in childbirth have affected one's attitudes toward children? How does the passage illustrate limitations on knowledge about disease in the eighteenth century?*

We had puerperal fever in the infirmary last winter. It began about the end of February, when almost every woman, as soon as she was delivered, or perhaps about twenty-four hours after, was seized with it; and all of them died, though every method was tried to cure the disorder. What was singular, the women were in good health before they were brought to bed, though some of them had been long in the hospital before delivery. One woman had been dismissed from the ward before she was brought to bed; came into it some days after with her labor upon her; was easily delivered, and remained perfectly well for twenty-four hours, when she was seized with a shivering and the other symptoms of the fever. I caused her to be removed to another ward; yet notwithstanding all the care that was taken of her she died in the same manner as the others.

From a letter to Mr. White from a Dr. Young of Edinburgh, 21 November, 1774, cited in C. White, *Treatise on the Management of Pregnant and Lying-In Women* (London, 1777), pp. 45–46, as quoted in Bridget Hill, ed., *Eighteenth-Century Women: An Anthology* (London: George Allen & Unwin, 1984), p. 102.

Art & the West

The Breakfast *and* Return from Market: *Two Scenes of Domestic Life*

*W*hat are known as *genre* paintings depict scenes of everyday life. Largely pioneered by the Dutch, such paintings became widespread throughout Europe during the eighteenth century. Genre painting made no claim to convey a message of universal importance. Furthermore, because the subject matter was domestic, people could enjoy these paintings without an extensive knowledge of history, classical literature, or the Bible.

French genre painters focused mostly on what would become known as the "woman's sphere" in the home. But that female domestic sphere, as illustrated in these works of Boucher and Chardin, was a complex world with numerous compartments. The home might be the feminine empire, but it was an empire of many provinces, just as there were different kinds of homes among the various social classes.

Boucher's *The Breakfast* (1739) portrays the breakfast room of a wealthy, probably nonaristocratic, family, filled with the expensive consumer goods available in Paris shops drawn from around the world. (Note, for example, the Chinese porcelain figure sitting on the shelf.) This domestic interior lacks any suggestion of political awareness or engagement in economic productivity. It is a scene of domestic, feminine consumption and child rearing

such as Rousseau would advocate in *Emile* (1762). (See Chapter 18.)

Chardin's *The Return from the Market* (1738) presents another level of the domestic sphere: that of

F. Boucher. *The Breakfast*. 1739. Paris. Louvre. Scala/Art Resource, NY

526

the servant. The woman in the painting appears to work in the home of a person of moderate means, perhaps a merchant. In this and other of his paintings, Chardin avoids the world of domestic consumption that appears in Boucher's painting. His interiors are worlds of domestic order and tranquillity, set aside from the bustle of an eighteenth-century city street. Domestic servants in the eighteenth and nineteenth century were overwhelmingly women. Yet even among them, there existed a clear social hierarchy. This woman would have held a lower status than that of a governess who looked after the family's children. (See p. 512.)

Chardin was known for his remarkable ability to bring quiet dignity and warmth to the work of servants. He also suggests a certain dynamic element in the life of the family: The servant putting down the bread appears to be listening to the conversation in the other room. Later genre painters, such as the English artist Hogarth, would often suggest a strong moralizing tone, but Chardin is willing to portray his scenes without comment. He does not intrude upon the scene, which assumes a kind of timeless quality in the sense that households have needed to secure bread each day from time immemorial; this return from market is simply the most recent example. There is as much of a relaxed quality to Chardin's portrayal of this scene as there is a sense of energized arrangement in Boucher's. Chardin described his own painting as a kind of craft rather than a work of inspiration or academic rules. He seems to see his own painting as a kind of dignified everyday work, akin to the work performed by the woman returning from market.

Jean Baptiste Chardin, 1699–1799. *The Return from the Market* (*La Pourvoyeyse*). (1738). French. Musée Du Louvre, Paris/SuperStock

Albert Boime, *Art in an Age of Revolution, 1750–1800* (Chicago: University of Chicago Press, 1987); Norman Bryson, *Looking at the Overlooked: Four Essays on Still Life Painting* (Cambridge, MA.: Harvard University Press, 1990); Richard Rand, *Intimate Encounters: Love and Domesticity in Eighteenth-Century France* (Princeton, NJ: Princeton University Press, 1997).

Few children in the eighteenth century were as privileged as these in this landed English family. Most began working to help support their families as soon as they were physically able. It was during the eighteenth century, however, that Europeans apparently began to view childhood as a distinct period in human development. Even though Arthur Devis has painted these children to look something like little adults, he has included various toys associated with childhood. Arthur Devis (© 1711–1787), *Children in an Interior*, © 1742–1743, oil on canvas, 39 x 49 in. (99.0 x 125.5 cm), Yale Center for British Art, Paul Mellon Collection, B1978.43.5

pital lacked the income to deal with all the children brought to it. In the middle of the eighteenth century, the hospital found itself compelled to choose children for admission by a lottery system.

Sadness and tragedy surrounded abandoned children. Most of them were illegitimate infants from across the social spectrum. Many, however, were left with the foundling hospitals because their parents could not support them. There was a close relationship between rising food prices and increasing numbers of abandoned children in Paris. Parents would sometimes leave personal tokens or saints' medals on the abandoned baby in the vain hope that they might one day be able to reclaim the child. Few children were reclaimed. Leaving a child at a foundling hospital did not guarantee its survival. In Paris, only about 10 percent of all abandoned children lived to the age of ten.

Despite all of these perils of early childhood, children did grow up and come of age across Europe. The world of the child may not have received the kind of attention that it does today, but during the eighteenth century the seeds of that modern sensibility were sown. Particularly among the upper classes, new interest arose in the education of children. In most areas, education remained firmly in the hands of the churches. As economic skills became more demanding, literacy became more valuable, and literacy rates rose during the century. Yet most Europeans remained illiterate. Not until the late nineteenth century was the world of childhood inextricably linked to the process of education. Then children would be reared to become members of a national citizenry. In

the Old Regime, they were reared to make their contribution to the economy of their parents' family and then to set up their own households.

The Revolution in Agriculture

Thus far, this chapter has examined those groups that sought stability and that, except for certain members of the nobility, resisted change. Other groups, however, wished to pursue significant new directions in social and economic life. The remainder of the chapter will consider those forces and developments that would transform European life during the next century. These developments first appeared in agriculture.

The main goal of traditional peasant society was a stability that would ensure the local food supply. Despite differences in rural customs throughout Europe, the tillers resisted changes that might endanger the sure supply of food, which they generally believed that traditional cultivation would provide. The food supply was never certain, and the farther east one traveled, the more uncertain it became. Failure of the harvest meant not only hardship, but death from either outright starvation or protracted debility. Often, people living in the countryside had more difficulty finding food than did city dwellers, whose local government usually stored reserve supplies of grain.

Poor harvests also played havoc with prices. Smaller supplies or larger demand raised grain prices. Even small increases in the cost of food could exert heavy pressure on peasant or artisan families. If prices increased sharply, many of those families fell back on poor relief from their local municipality or county or the church.

Historians now believe that during the eighteenth century bread prices slowly but steadily rose, spurred largely by population growth. Since bread was their main food, this inflation put pressure on all of the poor. Prices rose faster than urban wages and brought no appreciable advantage to the small peasant producer. On the other hand, the rise in grain prices benefitted landowners and those wealthier peasants who had surplus grain to sell.

The rising grain prices gave landlords an opportunity to improve their incomes and lifestyle. To achieve those ends, landlords in western Europe began a series of innovations in farm production that became known as the Agricultural Revolution. Landlords commercialized agriculture and thereby challenged the traditional peasant ways of production. Peasant revolts and disturbances often resulted. The governments of Europe, hungry for new taxes and dependent on the goodwill of the nobility, used their armies and militias to smash peasants who defended the past.

NEW CROPS AND NEW METHODS The drive to improve agricultural production began during the sixteenth and seventeenth centuries in the Low Countries, where the pressures of the growing population and the shortage of land required changes in cultivation. Dutch landlords and farmers devised better ways to build dikes and drain land, so that they could farm more extensive areas. They also experimented with new crops, such as clover and turnips, that would increase the supply of animal fodder and restore the soil. These improvements became so famous that early in the seventeenth century English landlords hired Cornelius Vermuyden, a Dutch drainage engineer, to drain thousands of acres of land around Cambridge.

English landlords provided the most striking examples of eighteenth-century agricultural improvement. They originated almost no genuinely new farming methods, but they popularized ideas developed in the previous century either in the Low Countries or in England. Some of these landlords and agricultural innovators became famous. For example, Jethro Tull (1674–1741) was willing to conduct experiments himself and to finance the experiments of others. Many of his ideas, such as the rejection of manure as fertilizer, were wrong. Others, however, such as using iron plows to turn the earth more deeply and planting wheat by a drill rather than by casting, were excellent. His methods permitted land to be cultivated for longer periods without having to be left fallow.

Charles "Turnip" Townsend (1674–1738) encouraged other important innovations. He learned from the Dutch how to cultivate sandy soil with fertiliz-

ers. He also instituted crop rotation, using wheat, turnips, barley, and clover. This new system of rotation replaced the fallow field with one sown with a crop that both restored nutrients to the soil and supplied animal fodder. The additional fodder meant that more livestock could be raised. These fodders allowed animals to be fed during the winter and assured a year-round supply of meat. The larger number of animals increased the quantity of manure available as fertilizer for the grain crops. Consequently, in the long run, there was more food for both animals and human beings.

A third British agricultural improver was Robert Bakewell (1725–1795), who pioneered new methods of animal breeding that produced more and better animals and more milk and meat.

These and other innovations received widespread discussion in the works of Arthur Young (1741– 1820), who edited the *Annals of Agriculture*. In 1793 he became secretary of the British Board of Agriculture. Young traveled widely across Europe, and his books are among the most important documents of life during the second half of the eighteenth century.

ENCLOSURE REPLACES OPEN-FIELD METHOD Many of the agricultural innovations, which were adopted only slowly, were incompatible with the existing organization of land in England. Small cultivators who lived in village communities still farmed most of the soil. Each farmer tilled an assortment of unconnected strips. The two- or three-field systems of rotation left large portions of land fallow and unproductive each year. Animals grazed on the common land in the summer and on the stubble of the harvest in the winter. Until at least the middle of the eighteenth century, the decisions about what crops would be planted were made communally. The entire system discouraged improvement and favored the poorer farmers, who needed the common land and stubble fields for their animals. The village method precluded expanding pastureland to raise more animals that would, in turn, produce more manure, which could be used for fertilizer. Thus, the methods of traditional production aimed at a steady, but not a growing, supply of food.

In 1700, approximately half the arable land in England was farmed by this open-field method. By the second half of the century, the rising price of wheat encouraged landlords to consolidate or enclose their lands to increase production. The enclosures were intended to use land more rationally and to achieve greater commercial profits. The process involved the fencing of common lands, the reclamation of previously untilled waste, and the transfor-

Grain production lay at the heart of eighteenth-century farming. In this engraving, farm workers can be seen threshing wheat, winnowing the grain, and finally putting the grain in bags so it can be carried to a mill and ground into flour. In many cases, the mill would be owned by the local landlord, who would charge peasants for its use.
Bildarchiv Preussicher Kulturbesitz

mation of strips into block fields. These procedures brought turmoil to the economic and social life of the countryside. Riots often ensued.

Because many English farmers either owned their strips or rented them in a manner that amounted to ownership, the larger landlords usually resorted to parliamentary acts to legalize the enclosure of the land, which they owned but rented to the farmers. Because the large landowners controlled Parliament, such measures passed easily. Between 1761 and 1792, almost 500,000 acres were enclosed through acts of parliament, compared with 75,000 acres between 1727 and 1760. In 1801, a general enclosure act streamlined the process.

The enclosures were controversial at the time and have remained so among historians. They permitted the extension of both farming and innovation and thus increased food production on larger agricultural units. They also disrupted small traditional communities; they forced off the land independent farmers, who had needed the common pasturage, and poor cottage dwellers, who had lived on the reclaimed wasteland. The enclosures, however, did not depopulate the countryside. In some counties where the enclosures took place, the population increased. New soil had come into production, and services subsidiary to farming also expanded.

The enclosures did not create the labor force for the British Industrial Revolution. What the enclosures most conspicuously displayed was the introduction of the entrepreneurial or capitalistic attitude of the urban merchant into the countryside. This commercialization of agriculture, which spread from Britain slowly across the Continent during the next century, strained the paternal relationship between the governing and governed classes. Previously, landlords often had looked after the welfare of the lower orders through price controls or waivers of rent during depressed periods. As the landlords became increasingly concerned about profits, they began to leave the peasants to the mercy of the marketplace.

LIMITED IMPROVEMENTS IN EASTERN EUROPE   Improving agriculture tended to characterize farm production west of the Elbe. Dutch farming was quite efficient. In France, despite the efforts of the government to improve agriculture, enclosures were restricted. Yet there was much discussion in France about improving agricultural methods. These new procedures benefitted the ruling classes because better agriculture increased their incomes and assured a larger food supply, which discouraged social unrest.

In Prussia, Austria, Poland, and Russia, agricultural improvement was limited. Nothing in the relationship of the serfs to their lords encouraged innovation. In eastern Europe, the chief method of increasing production was to bring previously untilled lands under the plow. The landlords or their agents, and not the villages, normally directed farm management. By extending tillage, the great landlords sought to squeeze more labor from their serfs, rather than greater productivity from the soil. Eastern European landlords, like their western counterparts, sought to increase their profits, but they were much less ambitious and successful. The only significant nutritional gain achieved through their efforts was the introduction of maize and the potato. Livestock production did not increase significantly.

Expansion of the Population

The population explosion with which the entire world must contend today had its origins in the eighteenth century. Before that time, Europe's population had experienced dramatic increases, but plagues, wars, or famine had redressed the balance. Beginning in the second quarter of the eighteenth century, the population began to increase steadily. The need to feed this population caused food prices to rise, which spurred agricultural innovation. The need to provide everyday consumer goods for the expanding numbers of people fueled the demand side of the Industrial Revolution.

Our best estimates are that in 1700 Europe's population, excluding the European provinces of the Ottoman Empire, was between 100 million and 120 million people. By 1800 the figures had risen to almost 190 million and by 1850 to 260 million. The population of England and Wales rose from 6 million in 1750 to more than 10 million in 1800. France grew from 18 million in 1715 to about 26 million in 1789. Russia's population increased from 19 million in 1722 to 29 million in 1766. Such extraordinary sustained growth put new demands on all resources and considerable pressure on the existing social organization.

The population expansion occurred across the Continent in both the country and the cities. Only a limited consensus exists among scholars about the causes of this growth. There was a clear decline in the death rate. There were fewer wars and somewhat fewer epidemics in the eighteenth century. Hygiene and sanitation also improved. Better medical knowledge and techniques were once thought to have contributed to the decline in deaths. This factor is now discounted, because the more important medical advances came after the initial population explosion or would not have contributed directly to it.

Rather, changes in the food supply itself may have allowed population growth to be sustained. Improved and expanding grain production made one contribution. Another and even more important change was the cultivation of the potato. This tuber was a product of the New World and came into widespread European production during the eighteenth century. (See "The West & The World," p. 582.) On a single acre, enough potatoes could be raised to feed one peasant's family for an entire year. This more certain food supply enabled more children to survive to adulthood and rear children of their own.

The impact of the population explosion can hardly be overestimated. It created new demands for food, goods, jobs, and services. It provided a new pool of labor. Traditional modes of production and living had to be revised. More people lived in the countryside than could find employment there. Migration increased. There were also more people who might become socially and politically discontented. And because the population growth fed on itself, these pressures and demands continued to increase. The society and the social practices of the Old Regime literally outgrew their traditional bounds.

The Industrial Revolution of the Eighteenth Century

The second half of the eighteenth century witnessed the beginning of the industrialization of the European economy. That achievement of sustained economic growth is termed the *Industrial Revolution.* Previously, the economy of a province or a country might grow, but growth soon reached a plateau. Since the late eighteenth century, however, the economy of Europe has managed to expand at an almost uninterrupted pace. Depressions and recessions have been temporary, and even during such economic downturns, the Western economy has continued to grow.

At considerable social cost, industrialization made possible the production of more goods and more services than ever before in human history. Industrialization in Europe eventually overcame the economy of scarcity. The new means of production demanded new kinds of skills, new discipline in work, and a large labor force. The goods produced met immediate consumer demand and also created new demands. In the long run, industrialization clearly raised the standard of living and overcame the poverty that most Europeans, who lived during the eighteenth century and earlier, had taken for granted. It gave human beings greater control over the forces of nature than they had ever known before; yet by the middle of the nineteenth century, industrialism would also cause new and unanticipated problems with the environment.

During the eighteenth century, people did not call these economic developments a revolution. That term came to be applied to the British economic phenomena only after the French Revolution. Then continental writers observed that what had taken place in Britain was the economic equivalent of the political events in France, hence an *Industrial Revolution*. It was revolutionary less in its speed, which was on the whole rather slow, than in its implications for the future of European society.

A Revolution in Consumption

The most familiar side of the Industrial Revolution was the invention of new machinery, the establishment of factories, and the creation of a new kind of work force. Recent studies, however, have emphasized the demand side of the process and the vast increase in both the desire and the possibility of consuming goods and services that arose in the early eighteenth century.

The inventions of the Industrial Revolution increased the supply of consumer goods as never before in history. The supply of goods was only one side of the economic equation, however. The supply had been called forth by an unprecedented demand for humble goods of everyday life. Those goods included everyday consumer items such as clothing of all kinds, buttons, toys, china, furniture, rugs, kitchen utensils, candlesticks, brassware, silverware, pewterware, glassware, watches, jewelry, soap, beer, wines, and foodstuffs. It was the ever-increasing demand for these goods that sparked the ingenuity of designers and inventors. Furthermore, there seemed to be no limits to consumer demand.

Many social factors came into play to establish the markets for these consumer goods. During the seventeenth century, the Dutch had enjoyed enormous prosperity and had led the way in new forms of both everyday consumption and that of luxury goods. For reasons that are still not clear, during the eighteenth century, increasing numbers first of the English and then of people living on the Continent came to have more disposable income. This wealth may have resulted from the improvements in agriculture. Those incomes allowed people to buy consumer goods that previous generations had inherited or did not possess. What is key to this change in consumption is that it depended primarily upon expanding the various domestic markets in Europe.

This revolution, if that is not too strong a term, in consumption was not automatic. People became persuaded that they needed or wanted new consumer goods. Often, entrepreneurs caused it to happen by developing new methods of marketing. An enterprising manufacturer such as the porcelain manufacturer Josiah Wedgwood (1730–1795) first attempted to find customers among the royal family and the aristocracy. Once he had gained their business with luxury goods, he would then produce a somewhat less expensive version of the chinaware for middle-class customers. He also used advertising. He opened showrooms in London and had salespeople traveling all over England with samples and catalogs of his wares. On the Continent, he equipped salespeople with bilingual catalogs. There seemed to be no limit to the markets for different kinds of consumer goods that could be stimulated by social emulation on the one hand and advertising on the other.

Furthermore, the process of change in style itself became institutionalized. New fashions and inventions were always better than old ones. If new kinds of goods could be produced, there usually was a market for them. If one product did not find a market, its failure provided a lesson for the development of a different new product.

This expansion of consumption quietly, but steadily, challenged the social assumptions of the day. Fashion publications made all levels of society aware of new styles. Clothing fashions could be copied. Servants could begin to dress well if not luxuriously. There were changes in the consumption of food and drink that also called forth demand for new kinds of dishware for the home. Tea and coffee became staples. The brewing industry became fully commercialized. Those developments entailed the need for new kinds of cups and mugs and many more of them.

There would always be critics of this consumer economy. The vision of luxury and comfort it offered contrasted with the asceticism of ancient Sparta and contemporary Christian ethics. Yet ever-increasing consumption and production of the goods of everyday life became a hallmark of modern Western society from the eighteenth century to our own day. It would be difficult to overestimate the importance of the desire for consumer goods and the increasing material standard of living that they made possible in Western history after the eighteenth century. The presence and

Consumption of all forms of consumer goods increased greatly in the eighteenth century. This engraving illustrates a shop, probably in Paris. Here women, working apparently for a woman manager, are making dresses and hats to meet the demads of the fashion trade. As the document on page 540 demonstrates, some women writers urged more such employment opportunities for women. Bildarchiv Preussischer Kulturbesitz

accessibility of such goods became the hallmark of a nation's prosperity. It is perhaps relevant to note that it was the absence of such consumer goods, as well as of civil liberties, that during the 1980s led to such deep discontent with the communist regimes in Eastern Europe and the former Soviet Union.

Industrial Leadership of Great Britain

Great Britain was the home of the Industrial Revolution and, until the middle of the nineteenth century, maintained the industrial leadership of Europe. Several factors contributed to the early start in Britain.

Great Britain took the lead in the consumer revolution that expanded the demand for goods that could be efficiently supplied. London was by far the largest city in Europe. It was the center of a world of fashion and taste to which hundreds of thousands,

if not millions, of British citizens were exposed each year. In London, these people learned to want the consumer goods they saw on visits for business and pleasure. Newspapers thrived in Britain during the eighteenth century, allowing for advertising that increased consumer wants. The social structure of Britain allowed and even encouraged people to imitate the lifestyles of their social superiors. It seems to have been in Britain that a world of fashion first developed that led people to want to accumulate goods. In addition to the domestic consumer demand, the British economy benefitted from demand from the colonies in North America.

Britain was also the single largest free-trade area in Europe. The British had good roads and waterways without internal tolls or other trade barriers. The country was endowed with rich deposits of coal and iron ore. Its political structure was stable, and property was absolutely secure. The sound systems of banking and public credit established a stable climate for investment. Taxation in Britain was heavy, but it was efficiently and fairly collected, largely from indirect taxes. Furthermore, British taxes received legal approval through Parliament, with all social classes and all regions of the nation paying the same taxes. In contrast to the Continent, there was no pattern of privileged tax exemptions.

Finally, British society was mobile by the standards of the time. Persons who had money or could earn money could rise socially. The British aristocracy would receive into its midst people who had amassed large fortunes. Even persons of wealth not admitted to the aristocracy could enjoy their riches, receive social prominence, and exert political influence. No one of these factors preordained the British advance toward industrialism. Together, however, when added to the progressive state of British agriculture, they provided the nation with the marginal advantage to create a new mode of economic production.

New Methods of Textile Production

The industry that pioneered the Industrial Revolution and met growing consumer demand was the production of textiles for clothing. This industry provides the key example of industrialism emerging to supply the demands of an ever-growing market for everyday goods. Furthermore, it illustrates the surprising fact that much of the earliest industrial change took place not in cities, but in the countryside.

Although the eighteenth-century economy was primarily agricultural, manufacturing also permeated rural areas. The peasant family living in a one- or two-room cottage, rather than the factory, was the basic unit of production. The same peasants who tilled the land in spring and summer often spun thread or wove textiles in the winter.

Under what is termed the domestic, or putting-out, system, agents of urban textile merchants took wool or other unfinished fibers to the homes of peasants, who spun it into thread. The agent then transported the thread to other peasants, who wove it into the finished product. The merchant sold the wares. In thousands of peasant cottages from Ireland to Austria, there stood a spinning wheel or a handloom. Sometimes the spinners or weavers owned their own equipment, but more often than not by the middle of the century, the merchant capitalist owned the machinery as well as the raw material.

The domestic system of textile production was a basic feature of this family economy and would continue to be so in Britain and on the Continent well into the nineteenth century. By the mid-eighteenth century, however, a series of production bottlenecks had developed within the domestic system. The demand for cotton textiles was growing more rapidly than production, especially in Great Britain, which had a large domestic and North American market for cotton textiles. Inventors devised some of the most famous machines of the early Industrial Revolution in response to this consumer demand for cotton textiles.

THE SPINNING JENNY   Cotton textile weavers had the technical capacity to produce the quantity of fabric demanded. The spinners, however, did not have the equipment to produce as much thread as the weavers needed. James Kay's invention of the flying shuttle, which increased the productivity of the weavers, had created this imbalance during the 1730s. Thereafter, various groups of manufacturers and merchants offered prizes for the invention of a machine to eliminate this bottleneck.

About 1765, James Hargreaves (d. 1778) invented the spinning jenny. Initially, this machine allowed 16 spindles of thread to be spun, but by the close of the century its capacity had been increased to as many as 120 spindles.

THE WATER FRAME   The spinning jenny broke the bottleneck between the productive capacity of the spinners and the weavers, but it was still a piece of machinery used in the cottage. The invention that took cotton textile manufacture out of the home and put it into the factory was Richard Arkwright's (1732–1792) water frame, patented in 1769. This was a water-powered device designed to permit the production of a purely cotton fabric, rather than a cotton fabric containing linen fiber for durability. Eventually Arkwright lost his patent rights, and other manufacturers could use his invention freely. As a result, many factories sprang up in the countryside near streams that provided the necessary water power. From the 1780s onward, the cotton industry could meet an ever-expanding demand. Cotton output increased by 800 percent between 1780 and 1800. By 1815 cotton composed 40 percent of the value of British domestic exports and by 1830 just over 50 percent.

The Industrial Revolution had commenced in earnest by the 1780s, but the full economic and social ramifications of this unleashing of human productive capacity were not really felt until the early nineteenth century. The expansion of industry and the incorporation of new inventions often occurred rather slowly. For example, Edmund Cartwright (1743–1822) invented the power loom for machine weaving in the late 1780s. Yet not until the 1830s were there more power-loom weavers than handloom weavers in Britain. Nor did all the social ramifications of industrialism appear immediately. The first cotton mills used water power, were located in the country, and rarely employed more than two dozen workers. Not until the late-century application of the steam engine, perfected by James Watt (1736–1819) in 1769, to the running of textile machinery could factories easily be located in or near existing urban centers. The steam engine not only vastly increased and regularized the available energy, but also made possible the combination of urbanization and industrialization.

The Steam Engine

More than any other invention, the steam engine permitted industrialization to grow on itself and to expand into one area of production after another. This machine provided for the first time in human history a steady and essentially unlimited source of inanimate power. Unlike engines powered by water or the wind, the steam engine, driven by the burning of coal, provided a portable source of industrial power that did not fail or falter as the seasons of the year changed. Unlike human or animal power, the steam engine depended on mineral energy that did not tire during a day. Finally, the steam engine could be applied to many industrial and, eventually, transportation uses.

The first practical engine using steam power had been the invention of Thomas Newcomen (1663–1729) in the early eighteenth century. The piston of this device was moved when the steam that had been induced into the cylinder condensed, causing the piston to fall. The Newcomen machine was large, inefficient in its use of energy because both the condenser and the cylinder were heated, and practically untransportable. Despite these problems, English mine operators used the Newcomen machines to pump water out of coal and tin mines. By the third quarter of the eighteenth century, almost 100 Newcomen machines were operating in the mining districts of England.

During the 1760s, James Watt, a Scottish engineer and machine maker, began to experiment with a model of a Newcomen machine at the University of Glasgow. He gradually understood that separating the condenser from the piston and the cylinder would achieve much greater efficiency.

This painting shows the pithead of an eighteenth-century coal mine in England. The machinery on the left includes a steam engine that powered equipment to bring mined coal to the surface or to pump water from the mine. Britain's rich veins of coal were one of the factors contributing to its early industrialization. British School—A Pithead. Board of Trustees of the National Museums and Galleries on Merseyside, Walker Art Galley, Liverpool

In 1769 he patented his new invention, but transforming his idea into a practical application presented difficulties. His design required precise metalwork. Watt soon found a partner in Matthew Boulton (1728– 1809), a successful toy and button manufacturer in Birmingham, the city with the most skilled metalworkers in Britain. Watt and Boulton, in turn, consulted with John Wilkinson (1728–1808), a cannon manufacturer, to find ways to drill the precise metal cylinders required by Watt's design. In 1776, the Watt steam engine found its first commercial application pumping water from mines in Cornwall.

The use of the steam engine spread slowly because until 1800 Watt retained the exclusive patent rights. He was also reluctant to make further changes in his invention that would permit the engine to operate more rapidly. Boulton eventually persuaded him to make modifications and improvements that allowed the engines to be used not only for pumping, but also for running cotton mills. By the early nineteenth century, the steam engine had become the prime mover for all industry. With its application to ships and then to wagons on iron rails, the steam engine also revolutionized transportation.

Iron Production

The manufacture of high-quality iron has been basic to modern industrial development. Iron is the chief element of all heavy industry and land or sea transport. It has also been the material out of which most productive machinery itself has been manufactured. During the early eighteenth century, British ironmakers produced somewhat less than 25,000 tons annually. Three factors held back the production of the metal. First, charcoal rather than coke was used to smelt the ore. Charcoal, derived from wood, was becoming scarce and does not burn at as high a temperature as coke, derived from coal. Second, until the perfection of the steam engine, insufficient blasts could be achieved in the furnaces. Finally, the demand for iron was limited. The elimination of the first two problems also eliminated the third.

Eventually, British ironmakers began to use coke, and the steam engine provided new power for the blast furnaces. Coke was an abundant fuel because of Britain's large coal deposits. The existence of the steam engine both improved iron production and increased the demand for iron.

In 1784 Henry Cort (1740–1800) introduced a new puddling process, that is, a new method for melting and stirring the molten ore. Cort's process allowed

Major Inventions in the Textile-Manufacturing Revolution	
1733	James Kay's flying shuttle
1765	James Hargreaves's spinning jenny (patented 1770)
1769	James Watt's steam engine patent
1769	Richard Arkwright's water frame patent
1787	Edmund Cartwright's power loom

more slag (the impurities that bubbled to the top of the molten metal) to be removed and a purer iron to be produced. Cort also developed a rolling mill that continuously shaped the still-molten metal into bars, rails, or other forms. Previously, the metal had to be pounded into these forms.

All these innovations achieved a better, more versatile product at a lower cost. The demand for iron grew as its price became lower. By the early nineteenth century, the British produced over a million tons annually. The lower cost of iron, in turn, lowered the cost of steam engines and allowed them to be used more widely.

The Impact of the Agricultural and Industrial Revolutions on Working Women

The transformation of agriculture and industry, led to a series of seemingly modest changes that, taken collectively, diminished the importance and the role of those women already in the work force.

Women had been an important part of traditional European agriculture. They worked in the fields and often were permitted to glean the grain left over after the general harvest. Some women also managed industries like milking and cheese production. However, primarily in western Europe, increasing commercialization and mechanization eroded these traditional roles. Machinery operated by men displaced the work of women in the field and their industry skills in dairying and home industry, particularly in Britain. Even nonmechanized labor came to favor men. For example, during the late eighteenth century, heavy scythes wielded by men replaced the lighter sickles that women had used to harvest grain. Moreover, the drive to maximize profits led landlords to enclose lands and curtail customary rights like gleaning.

This transformation of farming constricted women's ability to earn their living from the land. Women in farming regions came to be viewed as opponents of agricultural improvement because of its negative impact on their economic life. As a result, proponents of the new agriculture often demeaned the role of women in farming and its related work. Indeed, the vast literature on agricultural improvement specifically advocated removing women from the agricultural work force.

A similar process took place in textile manufacturing, where mechanization deprived many women of one of their most traditional means of earning income. Before mechanization thousands of women worked at spinning wheels to produce thread that handloom weavers, who were often their husbands, then wove. The earlier, small spinning jennies did not immediately disrupt this situation because women could use them in the loft of a home, but the larger ones required a factory setting where men often ran the machinery. As a result, most women spinners were put out of work, and those women who did move into the factory labor force performed less skilled work than men. But in the long run, the mechanization of spinning left many other women without one of their most traditional means of earning income.

Many working women, displaced from spinning thread or from farming, slowly turned to cottage industries, such as knitting, button making, straw plaiting, bonnet making, or glove stitching, that invariably earned them less than their former occupations. In later generations, women who earlier would have been spinners or farm workers moved directly into cottage industries. The work and skills involved in these occupations were considered inferior; and because it paid so poorly, women who did this work might become prostitutes or engage in other criminal activity. Consequently, the reputations and social standing of many such working women suffered.

Among women who did not work in the cottage industries, thousands became domestic servants in the homes of landed or commercial families. During the nineteenth century, such domestic service became the largest area of female employment. It was far more respectable than the cottage industries, but was separate from the technologically advanced world of factory manufacture or transport.

By the end of the eighteenth century, the work and workplaces of men and women were becoming increasingly separate and distinct. In this respect, many people, such as the English writer Priscilla Wakefield, believed that the kinds of employment open to women had narrowed. Wakefield called for new occupations for women. (See "Priscilla Wakefield Demands More Occupations for Women.")

This shift in female employment, or what one historian has termed "this defamation of women workers,"[2] produced several long term results. First, women's work, whether in cottage industries or domestic service, became associated with the home rather than with places where men worked. Second, the laboring life of most women was removed from the new technologies present in the new farming, transportation, and manufacturing. Woman's work thus appeared traditional, and people assumed that women could do only such work. Third, during the nineteenth and early twentieth centuries, Europeans also assumed that most women worked only to supplement a spouse's income. Finally, because the work women did was considered marginal and only as supplementing a male income, men were paid much more than women. Most people associate the Industrial Revolution with factories, but for many working women, the result of these revolutions was a life located more in homes than ever before. Indeed, in the nineteenth century, one, though only one, motive behind efforts to restrict the hours and improve the conditions of women in factories was the belief that it was bad for them to be there in the first place. We will address the larger picture of the relationship of the new industrial workplace to family life in Chapter 21.

The Growth of Cities

Remarkable changes occurred in the pattern of city growth between 1500 and 1800. In 1500, within Europe (excluding Hungary and Russia) there were 156 cities with a population greater than 10,000. Only four of those cities—Paris, Milan, Venice, and Naples—had populations larger than 100,000. By 1800, 363 cities had 10,000 or more inhabitants, and 17 of them had populations larger than 100,000. The percentage of the European population living in urban areas had risen from just over 5 percent to just over 9 percent. There had also occurred a major shift in urban concentration from southern, Mediterranean Europe to the north.

Patterns of Preindustrial Urbanization

The eighteenth century witnessed a considerable growth of towns, closely related to the tumult of the day and the revolutions with which the cen-

---

[2]Deborah Valenze, *The First Industrial Woman* (New York: Oxford University Press, 1995), p. 183.

(a)

(b)

Francis Wheatley (1747–1801), an English artist, painted these and many other scenes of late eighteenth-century rural life. These four paintings portray a very idealized view of the farming family. Had Wheatley painted this family a half-century or more earlier, the women might have appeared with the father and husband in the fields, as workers or as gleaners picking up grain left by the harvesters.

After the mid-century changes in agricultural production, women worked in the home and men in the fields. Wheatley illustrates this division in the paintings shown here: Women work at home, or look after the needs of men and children. Men work in the fields and return home in the evening. During the early nineteenth century, much of the dairy work shown in the first painting would also have become mechanized, performed largely by male workers. Francis Wheatley (RA) (1747–1801) (a) *Morning,* (b) *Noon,* (c) *Evening,* (d) *Night,* signed and dated 1799, oil on canvas, each 17½ x 21½ in. (44.5 x 54.5 cm), Yale Center for British Art, Paul Mellon Collection B1977.14.120, B1977.14.119, B1977.14.118, B1977.14.121.

(c)

(d)

Priscilla Wakefield Demands More Occupations for Women

At the end of the eighteenth century, Priscilla Walkefield was one several English women writers who began to demand a wider life for women. She was concerned that women found themselves able to pursue only occupations that paid poorly. Often, they were excluded from work on the grounds of their alleged physical weakness. She also believed that women should receive equal wages for equal work. These issues reflected a narrowing of opportunities for women that had occurred in England during the second half of the eighteenth century. As a result of the mechanization of both agriculture and the textile industry, many women found traditional occupations closing to them. Wakefield is thus addressing a general question of opportunities available to women and more recent developments. Many of the issues she raised have yet to be adequately addressed on behalf of women.

❖ *From reading this passage, what do you understand to have been the arguments at the end of the eighteenth century to limit the kinds of employment that women might enter? Why did women receive lower wages for work similar to or the same as that done by men? What occupations traditionally filled by men does Wakefield believe women might also pursue?*

Another heavy discouragement to the industry of women, is the inequality of the reward of their labor, compared with that of men; an injustice which pervades every species of employment performed by both sexes.

In employments which depend on bodily strength, the distinction is just; for it cannot be pretended that the generality of women can earn as much as men, when the produce of their labor is the result of corporeal exertion; but it is a subject of great regret, that this inequality should prevail even where an equal share of skill and application is exerted. Male stay-makers, mantua-makers, and hair-dressers, are better paid than female artists of the same professions; but surely it will never be urged as an apology for this disproportion, that women are not as capable of making stays, gowns, dressing hair, and similar arts, as men; if they are not superior to them, it can only be accounted for upon this principle, that the prices they receive for their labor are not sufficient to repay them for the expense of qualifying themselves for their business; and that they sink under the mortification of being regarded as artisans of inferior estimation....

Besides these employments which are commonly performed by women, and those already shown to be suitable for such persons as are above the condition of hard labor, there are some professions and trades customarily in the hands of men, which might be conveniently exercised by either sex.—Watchmaking requiring more ingenuity than strength, seems peculiarly adapted to women; as do many parts of the business of stationer, particularly, ruling account books or making pens. The compounding of medicines in an apothecary's shop, requires no other talents than care and exactness; and if opening a vein occasionally be an indispensable requisite, a woman may acquire the capacity of doing it, for those of her own sex at least, without any reasonable objection.... Pastry and confectionery appear particularly consonant to the habits of women, though generally performed by men; perhaps the heat of the ovens, and the strength requisite to fill and empty them, may render male assistants necessary; but certain women are most eligible to mix up the ingredients, and prepare the various kinds of cakes for baking.—Light turnery and toy-making depend more upon dexterity and invention than force, and are therefore suitable work for women and children....

Farming, as far as respects the theory, is commensurate with the powers of the female mind: nor is the practice of inspecting agricultural processes incompatible with the delicacy of their frames if their constitution be good.

Priscilla Wakefield, *Reflections on the Present Condition of the Female Sex* (1798) (London, 1817), pp. 125–127, as quoted in Bridget Hill, ed., *Eighteenth-Century Women: An Anthology* (London: George Allen & Unwin, 1984), pp. 227–228.

tury closed. London grew from about 700,000 inhabitants in 1700 to almost 1 million in 1800. By the time of the French Revolution, Paris had more than 500,000 inhabitants. Berlin's population tripled during the century, reaching 170,000 in 1800. Warsaw had 30,000 inhabitants in 1730, but almost 120,000 in 1794. Saint Petersburg, founded in 1703, numbered more than 250,000 inhabitants a century later. In addition to the growth of these capitals, the number of smaller cities of 20,000–50,000 people increased considerably. This urban growth must, however, be kept in perspective. Even in France and Great Britain, probably somewhat less than 20 percent of the population lived in cities. And the town of 10,000 inhabitants was much more common than the giant urban center.

These raw figures conceal significant changes that took place in how cities grew and how the population distributed itself. The major urban development of the sixteenth century had been followed by a leveling off, and even a decline, in the seventeenth. New growth began in the early eighteenth century and accelerated during the late eighteenth and the early nineteenth centuries. Between 1500 and 1750, major urban expansion took place within already established and generally already large cities. After 1750, the pattern changed with the birth of new cities and the rapid growth of older smaller cities.

GROWTH OF CAPITALS AND PORTS In particular, between 1600 and 1750, the cities that grew most vigorously were capitals and ports. This situation reflects the success of monarchical state building during those years and the consequent burgeoning of bureaucracies, armies, courts, and other groups who lived in the capitals. The growth of port cities, in turn, reflects the expansion of European overseas trade—most especially, that of the Atlantic routes. Except for Manchester in England and Lyons in France, the new urban conglomerates were nonindustrial cities.

Furthermore, between 1600 and 1750, cities with populations of fewer than 40,000 inhabitants declined. These included older landlocked trading centers, medieval industrial cities, and ecclesiastical centers. They contributed less to the new political regimes, and the expansion of the putting-out system transferred to the countryside much production that had once occurred in medieval cities. Rural labor was cheaper than urban labor, and cities with concentrations of labor declined as production was moved from the urban workshop into the country.

EMERGENCE OF NEW CITIES AND GROWTH OF SMALL TOWNS In the middle of the eighteenth century, a new pattern emerged. The rate of growth of existing large cities declined, while new cities began to emerge and existing smaller cities began to grow. Several factors were at work in the process, which Jan De Vries has termed "an urban growth from below."[3] First, there was the general overall population increase. Second, the early stages of the Industrial Revolution, particularly in Britain, occurred in the countryside and fostered the growth of smaller towns and cities located near factories. Factory organization itself led to new concentrations of population.

Cities also grew as a result of the new prosperity of European agriculture, even where there was little industrialization. Improved agricultural production promoted the growth of nearby market towns and other urban centers that served agriculture or allowed more prosperous farmers to have access to the consumer goods and recreation they wanted. This new pattern of urban growth—new cities and the expansion of smaller existing ones—would continue into the nineteenth century.

Urban Classes

Social divisions were as marked in the cities of the eighteenth century as they were in the industrial centers of the nineteenth. Visible segregation often existed between the urban rich and the urban poor. The nobles and the upper-middle class lived in fashionable town houses, often constructed around newly laid-out green squares. The poorest town dwellers usually congregated along the rivers. Small merchants and artisans lived above their shops. Whole families might live in a single room. Modern sanitary facilities were still unknown. There was little pure water. Cattle, pigs, goats, and other animals walked the streets with the people. All reports on the cities of Europe during this period emphasize both the striking grace and beauty of the dwellings of the wealthy and the dirt, filth, and stench that filled the streets.

Poverty was not just an urban problem; it was usually worse in the countryside. In the city, however, poverty was more visible in the form of crime, prostitution, vagrancy, begging, and alcoholism. Many a young man or woman from the

[3]Jan De Vries, "Patterns of Urbanization in Pre-Industrial Europe, 1500–1800," in H. Schmal, ed., *Patterns of Urbanization Since 1500* (London: Croom Helm, 1981), p. 103.

countryside migrated to the nearest city to seek a better life, only to discover poor housing, little food, disease, degradation, and finally death. It did not require the Industrial Revolution and the urban factories to make the cities into hellholes for the poor and the dispossessed. The full darkness of London life during the midcentury "gin age," when consumption of that liquor blinded and killed many poor people, is evident in the engravings of William Hogarth (1697–1764).

Also contrasting with the serenity of the aristocratic and upper-commercial-class lifestyle were the public executions that took place all over Europe, the breaking of men and women on instruments of torture in Paris, and the public floggings in Russia. Brutality condoned and carried out by the ruling classes was simply a fact of everyday life.

THE UPPER CLASSES At the top of the urban social structure stood a generally small group of nobles, large merchants, bankers, financiers, clergy, and government officials. These upper-class men controlled the political and economic affairs of the town. Normally, they constituted a self-appointed and self-electing oligarchy that governed the city through its corporation or city council. These rights of self-government had usually been granted by some form of royal charter that gave the city corporation its authority and the power to select its own members. In a few cities on the Continent, artisan guilds controlled the corporations, but more generally, the councils were under the influence of the local nobility and the wealthiest commercial people.

THE MIDDLE CLASS Another group in the city was the prosperous, but not always immensely wealthy, merchants, tradespeople, bankers, and professional people. They were the most dynamic element of the urban population and constituted the persons traditionally regarded as the middle class, or bourgeoisie. The concept of the middle class was much less clear cut than that of the nobility. The middle class itself was and would remain diverse and divided, with persons employed in the professions often resentful of those who drew their incomes from commerce. Less wealthy members of the middle class of whatever occupation resented wealthier members who might be connected to the nobility through social or business relationships.

The middle class had less wealth than most nobles, but more than urban artisans. Middle-class people lived in the cities and towns, and their sources of income had little or nothing to do

with the land. In one way or another, they all benefitted from expanding trade and commerce, whether as merchants, as lawyers, or as small-factory owners. Theirs was a world in which the earning and saving of money allowed for rapid social mobility and change in lifestyle. They saw themselves as people willing to put their capital and energy to work, while they portrayed the nobility as idle. The members of the middle class tended to be economically aggressive and socially ambitious. People often made fun of them for these characteristics and were jealous of their success. The middle class normally supported reform, change, and economic growth. The bourgeoisie also wanted more rational regulations for trade and commerce, as did some of the more progressive aristocrats.

The middle class was made up of people whose lives fostered the revolution in consumption. On one hand, as owners of factories and of wholesale and retail businesses, they produced and sold goods for the expanding consumer market; on the other hand, members of the middle class were among the chief consumers. It was to their homes that the vast array of new consumer goods made their way. They were also the people whose social values clearly embraced the commercial spirit most fully. They might not enjoy the titles or privileges of the nobility, but they could enjoy considerable material comfort and prosperity. It was this style of life that less well-off people could still emulate as they sought to acquire consumer goods for themselves.

During the eighteenth century, the relationship between the middle class and the aristocracy was complicated. On one hand, the nobles, especially in England and France, increasingly embraced the commercial spirit associated with the middle class by improving their estates and investing in cities. On the other hand, wealthy members of the middle class often tried to imitate the lifestyle of the nobility by purchasing landed estates. The aspirations of the middle class for social mobility, however, conflicted with the determination of the nobles to maintain and reassert their own privileges and to protect their own wealth. The middle-class commercial figures—traders, bankers, manufacturers, and lawyers—often found their pursuit of both profit and prestige blocked by the privileges of the nobility and its social exclusiveness, by the inefficiency of monarchical bureaucracies dominated by the nobility, or by aristocrats who controlled patronage and government contracts.

The bourgeoisie was not rising to challenge the nobility; rather, both were seeking to add new dimensions to their existing political power and social prestige. The tensions that arose between the nobles and the middle class during the eighteenth century normally involved issues of power sharing or access to political influence, rather than clashes over values or goals associated with class.

The middle class in the cities also feared the lower-urban classes as much as they envied the nobility. The lower orders were a potentially violent element in society, a potential threat to property, and, in their poverty, a drain on national resources. The lower classes, however, were much more varied than either the city aristocracy or the middle class cared to admit.

ARTISANS   Shopkeepers, artisans, and wage earners were the single largest group in any city. They were grocers, butchers, fishmongers, carpenters, cabinet-makers, smiths, printers, handloom weavers, and tailors, to give a few examples. They had their own culture, values, and institutions. Like the peasants of the countryside, they were in many respects conservative. Their economic position was highly vulnerable. If a poor harvest raised the price of food, their own businesses suffered. These urban classes also contributed to the revolution in consumption, however. They could buy more goods than ever be-

fore, and, to the extent their incomes permitted, many of them sought to copy the domestic consumption of the middle class.

The lives of these artisans and shopkeepers centered on their work and their neighborhoods. They usually lived near or at their place of employment. Most of them worked in shops with fewer than a half dozen other artisans. Their primary institution had historically been the guild, but by the eighteenth century, the guilds rarely exercised the influence of their predecessors in medieval or early modern Europe.

Nevertheless, the guilds were not to be ignored. They played a conservative role. Rather than seeking economic growth or innovation, they tried to preserve the jobs and skills of their members. In many countries, the guilds were still able to determine who could pursue a particular craft. To lessen competition, they attempted to prevent too many people from learning a particular skill.

The guilds also provided a framework for social and economic advancement. At an early age, a boy might become an apprentice to learn a craft or trade. After several years, he would be made a journeyman. Still later, if successful and sufficiently competent, he might become a master. The artisan could also receive certain social benefits from the guilds, including aid for his family during sick-

This engraving illustrates a metalworking shop such as might have been found in almost any town of significance in Europe. Most of the people employed in the shop probably belonged to the same family. Note that two women are also working. The wife may very well have been the person in charge of keeping the accounts of the business. The two younger boys might be children of the owner or apprentices in the trade, or both.
Bildarchiv Preussischer Kulturbesitz

Manchester's Calico Printers Protest the New Machinery

The introduction of the new machines associated with the Industrial Revolution stirred much protest. With machines able to duplicate the skills of laborers, workers feared the loss of jobs and the resulting loss of status when their chief means of livelihood lay in their possession of those displaced and now mechanized skills. The following letter was sent anonymously to a Manchester manufacturer by English workers. It shows the outrage of those workers, the intimidation they were willing to use as threats, and their own economic fears.

❖ *How might new machines adversely affect the livelihood of workers? Did the workers have other complaints against Mr. Taylor in addition to the introduction of new machinery? How have these workers reached an agreement to protect the interests of James Hobson? How do the workers combine the threat of violent actions with claims that other actions they have taken are legal?*

Mr. Taylor, If you dont discharge James Hobson from the House of Correction we will burn your House about your Ears for we have sworn to stand by one another and you must immediately give over any more Mashen Work for we are determined there shall be no more of them made use of in the Trade and it will be madness for you to contend with the Trade as we are combined by Oath to fix Prices we can afford to pay him a Guinea Week and not hurt the fund if you was to keep him there till Dumsday therefore mind you comply with the above or by God we will keep our Words with you we will make some rare Bunfires in this Countey and at your Peril to call any more

Meetings mind that we will make the Mosney Pepel shake in their Shoes we are determined to destroy all Sorts of Masheens for Printing in the Kingdom for there is more hands then is work for so no more from the ingerd Gurnemen Rember we are a great number sworn nor you must not advertise the Men that you say run away from you when your il Usage was the Cause of their going we will punish you for that our Meetings are legal for we want nothing but what is honest and to work for selvs and familers and you want to starve us but it is better for you and a few more which we have marked to die then such a Number of Pore Men and their famerles to be starved.

From the *London Gazette*, 1786, p. 36, as reprinted in Douglas Hay, ed., *Albion's Fatal Tree* (New York: Pantheon Books, 1975), p. 318.

ness or the promise of admission for his son. The guilds were the chief protection for artisans against the operation of the commercial market. They were particularly strong in central Europe.

The Urban Riot

The artisan class, with its generally conservative outlook, maintained a rather fine sense of social and economic justice. These ideals were based largely on traditional practices. If the collective sense of what was economically "just" was offended, artisans frequently manifested their displeasure by rioting. (See "Manchester's Calico Printers Protest the New Machinery.") The most sensitive area was the price of bread, the staple food of the poor. If a baker or a grain merchant announced a price that was considered unjustly high, a bread riot might well ensue. Artisan leaders

would confiscate the bread or grain and sell it for what the urban crowd considered a "just price." They would then give the money paid for the grain or bread to the baker or merchant.

The potential for bread riots restrained the greed of merchants. Such disturbances represented a collective method of imposing the "just price" in place of the price set by the commercial marketplace. Thus, bread and food riots, which occurred throughout Europe, were not irrational acts of screaming, hungry people, but highly ritualized social phenomena of the Old Regime and its economy of scarcity.

Other kinds of riots also characterized eighteenth-century society and politics. The riot was a way in which people who were excluded in every other way from the political processes could make their will known. Sometimes urban rioters were incited by religious bigotry. For example, in 1753,

London Protestant mobs compelled the government ministry to withdraw an act to legalize Jewish naturalization. In 1780, the same rabidly Protestant spirit manifested itself in the Gordon riots. Lord George Gordon (1751–1793) had raised the specter of an imaginary Catholic plot after the government relieved military recruits from having to take specifically anti-Catholic oaths.

In these riots and in food riots, violence was normally directed against property rather than against people. The rioters themselves were not "riffraff," but usually small shopkeepers, freeholders, artisans, and wage earners. They usually wanted only to restore a traditional right or practice that seemed endangered. Nevertheless, considerable turmoil and destruction could result from their actions.

During the last half of the century, urban riots increasingly involved political ends. Though often simultaneous with economic disturbances, the political riot always had nonartisan leadership or instigators. In fact, the "crowd" of the eighteenth century was often the tool of the upper classes. In Paris, the aristocratic *Parlement* often urged crowd action in its disputes with the monarchy. In Geneva, middle-class citizens supported artisan riots against the local urban oligarchy. In Great Britain in 1792, the government incited mobs to attack English sympathizers of the French Revolution. Such outbursts of popular unrest indicate that the crowd or mob first entered the European political and social arena well before the revolution in France.

The Jewish Population: The Age of the Ghetto

Although the small Jewish communities of Amsterdam and other western European cities became famous for their intellectual life and financial institutions, the vast majority of European Jews lived in eastern Europe. In the eighteenth century and thereafter, the Jewish population of Europe was concentrated in Poland, Lithuania, and the Ukraine, where no fewer than three million Jews dwelled. There were perhaps as many as 150,000 Jews in the Habsburg lands, primarily Bohemia, around 1760. Fewer than 100,000 Jews lived in Germany. There were approximately 40,000 Jews in France. Much smaller Jewish populations resided in England and Holland, each of which had a Jewish population of fewer than 10,000. There were even smaller groups of Jews elsewhere.

In 1762, Catherine the Great of Russia specifically excluded Jews from a manifesto that welcomed foreigners to settle in Russia. She somewhat relaxed the exclusion a few years later, but Jews incorporated into the Russian Empire during her reign often felt that they needed to receive specific assurances of imperial protection for their livelihoods and religious practices against the ordinances of local officials. (See "Belorussian Jews Petition Catherine the Great.") After the first partition of Poland of 1772, to be discussed in Chapter 18, Russia included a large Jewish population. There were also larger Jewish communities in Prussia and under Austrian rule.

During the Old Regime, European Jews were separated from non-Jews, typically in districts known as ghettos. Relegated to the least desirable section of a city or to rural villages, most lived in poverty. This watercolor painting depicts a street in Kazimlesz, the Jewish quarter of Cracow, Poland. Judaica Collection, Max Berger, Vienna, Austria

Belorussian Jews Petition Catherine the Great

In the 1780s, through military expansion, Empress Catherine the Great of Russia (see Chapter 18) annexed Belorussia, bringing a new Jewish minority under her imperial government. In response to her decree, governing many aspects of the region's law and economy, Belorussian Jews petitioned the Empress to protect certain of their traditional rights regarding distillation and sale of spirits. They also petitioned for protection in court and for the right to retain their own traditional practices and courts for matters relating to their own community. The petition indicates how in Russia, as elsewhere in Europe, Jews were treated as a people apart. It also illustrates how Jews, like other minorities in Old Regime Europe, sought both to receive the protection of monarchies against arbitrary local officials and to maintain the integrity of long-standing social practices. The document also illustrates the Jews' dependence on the goodwill of the surrounding non-Jewish community.

❖ *In the first part of the petition, how do the petitioners attempt to appeal to long-standing custom to defend their interests? How do both parts of the petition suggest that Jewish law and practice distinct from the rest of the society governed Jewish social life? In the context of this petition, which non-Jewish authorities may actually or potentially influence Jewish life?*

...2. According to an ancient custom, when the squires built a new village, they summoned the Jews to reside there and gave them certain privileges for several years and then permanent liberty to distill spirits, brew beer and mead, and sell these drinks. On this basis, the Jews built houses and distillation plants at considerable expense....A new decree of Her Imperial Majesty...reserved [this right] to the squires....But a decree of the governor-general of Belorussia has now forbidden the squires to farm out distillation in their villages to Jews, even if the squires want to do this. As a result, the poor Jews who built houses in small villages and promoted both this trade and distillation have been deprived of these and left completely impoverished. But until all the Jewish people are totally ruined, the Jewish merchants suffer restraints equally with the poor rural Jews, since their law obliges them to assist all who share their religious faith. They therefore request an imperial decree authorizing the squire, if he wishes, to farm out distillation to Jews in rural areas.

3. Although, with Her Imperial Majesty's permission, Jews may be elected as officials..., Jews are allotted fewer votes than other people and hence no Jew can ever attain office. Consequently, Jews have no one to defend them in courts and find themselves in a desperate situation—given their fear and ignorance of Russian—in case of misfortune, even if innocent. To consummate all the good already bestowed, Jews dare to petition that an equal number of electors be required from Jews as from others (or, at least, that in matters involving Jews and non-Jews, a representative from the Jewish community hold equal rights with non-Jews, be present to accompany Jews in court, and attend the interrogation of Jews). But cases involving only Jews (except for promissory notes and debts) should be handled solely in Jewish courts, because Jews assume obligations among themselves, make agreements and conclude all kinds of deals in the Jewish language and in accordance with Jewish rites and laws (which are not known to others). Moreover, those who transgress their laws and order should be judged in Jewish courts. Similarly, preserve intact all their customs and holidays in the spirit of their faith, as is mercifully assured in the imperial manifesto.

From *From Supplication to Revolution: A Documentary Social History of Imperial Russia* by Gregory L. Freeze. Copyright © 1988 by Oxford University Press, Inc. Used by permission of Oxford University Press, Inc.

Jews dwelled in most nations without enjoying the rights and privileges of other subjects of the monarchs, unless such rights were specifically granted to them. They were regarded as a kind of resident alien whose residence might well be temporary or changed at the whim of local rulers or the monarchical government.

No matter where they dwelled, the Jews of Europe under the Old Regime lived apart in separate communities from non-Jewish Europeans. These communities might be distinct districts of cities known as ghettos or in primarily Jewish villages in the countryside. Jews were also treated as a distinct people religiously and legally. In Poland for much of the century, they were virtually self-governing. In other areas, they lived under the burden of discriminatory legislation. Except in England, Jews could not and did not mix in the mainstream of the societies in which they dwelled. This period, which really may be said to have begun with the expulsion of the Jews from Spain at the end of the fifteenth century, is known as the age of the ghetto, or separate community.

During the seventeenth century, a few Jews had helped finance the wars of major rulers. These financiers often became close to the rulers and were known as "court Jews." Perhaps the most famous was Samuel Oppenheimer (1630–1703), who helped the Habsburgs finance their struggle against the Turks and the defense of Vienna. Even these privileged Jews, including Oppenheimer, however, often failed to have their loans repaid. The court Jews and their financial abilities became famous. They tended to marry among themselves.

The overwhelming majority of the Jewish population of Europe, however, lived in poverty. They occupied the most undesirable sections of cities or poor rural villages. They pursued moneylending in some cases, but often worked at the lowest occupations. Their religious beliefs, rituals, and community set them apart. Virtually all laws and social institutions kept them apart from their Christian neighbors in situations of social inferiority.

Under the Old Regime, it is important to emphasize, all of this discrimination was based on religious separateness. Jews who converted to Christianity were welcomed, even if not always warmly, into the major political and social institutions of gentile European society. Until the last two decades of the eighteenth century, in every part of Europe, however, those Jews who remained loyal to their faith were subject to various religious, civil, and social disabilities. They could not pursue the professions freely, they often could not change residence freely, and they stood outside the political structures of the nations in which they lived. Jews could be expelled from the cities in which they resided, and their property could be confiscated. They were regarded as socially and religiously inferior. They could be required to listen to sermons that insulted them and their religion. Jews might find their children taken away from them and given Christian instruction. They knew that their non-Jewish neighbors might suddenly turn against them and kill them or their fellow religious believers.

As will be seen in subsequent chapters, the end of the Old Regime brought major changes in the lives of these Jews and in their relationship to the larger culture.

In Perspective

Near the close of the eighteenth century, European society was on the brink of a new era. That society had remained traditional and corporate largely because of an economy of scarcity. Beginning in the eighteenth century, the commercial spirit and the values of the marketplace, although not new, were permitted fuller play than ever before in European history. The newly unleashed commercial spirit led increasingly to a conception of human beings as individuals rather than as members of communities. In particular, that spirit manifested itself in agricultural and industrial revolutions, as well as in the drive toward greater consumption. Together, those two vast changes in production overcame most of the scarcity that had haunted Europe and the West generally. The accompanying changes in landholding and production would bring major changes to the European social structure.

The expansion of population provided a further stimulus for change. More people meant more labor, more energy, and more minds contributing to the creation and solution of social difficulties. Cities had to accommodate themselves to expanding populations. Corporate groups, such as the guilds, had to confront the existence of a larger labor force. New wealth meant that birth would eventually become less and less a determining factor in social relationships, except in regard to the social roles assigned to the two sexes. Class structure and social hierarchy remained, but the boundaries became somewhat blurred.

Finally, the conflicting ambitions of monarchs, the nobility, and the middle class generated innovation. In the pursuit of new revenues, the monarchs interfered with the privileges of the nobles. In the name of ancient rights, the nobles attempted to secure and expand their existing social privileges. The middle class, in all of its diversity, was growing wealthier from trade, commerce, and the practice of the professions. Its members wanted social prestige and influence equal to their wealth. They resented privileges, frowned on hierarchy, and rejected tradition.

All these factors meant that the society of the eighteenth century stood at the close of one era in European history and at the opening of another.

REVIEW QUESTIONS

1. Describe the life of an English aristocrat at the beginning of the eighteenth century and toward its close. How did the English aristocrat differ

from the French aristocrat in this regard? What kind of privileges separated European aristocrats from other social groups?

2. How would you define the term *family economy*? What were some of the particular characteristics of the northwestern European household as opposed to that in eastern Europe? In what ways were the lives of women constrained by the family economy in pre-industrial Europe?

3. What caused the Agricultural Revolution? How did technological innovations help change European agriculture? To what extent did the English aristocracy contribute to the Agricultural Revolution? What were some of the reasons for peasant revolts in Europe in the eighteenth century?

4. What factors explain the increase in Europe's population in the eighteenth century? What were the effects of the population explosion? How did population growth contribute to changes in consumption?

5. What caused the Industrial Revolution of the eighteenth century? What were some of the technological innovations and why were they important? Why did Great Britain take the lead in the Industrial Revolution? How did the consumer contribute to the Industrial Revolution?

6. Describe city life during the eighteenth century. Were all European cities of the same character? What changes had taken place in the distribution of population in cities and towns? Compare the lifestyle of the upper class with that of the middle and lower classes. What were some of the causes of urban riots?

SUGGESTED READINGS

I. T. BERND AND G. RANKI, *The European Periphery and Industrialization, 1780–1914* (1982). Examines the experience of eastern and Mediterranean Europe.

J. BLUM, *Lord and Peasant in Russia from the Ninth to the Nineteenth Century* (1961). A classic wide-ranging discussion.

J. BLUM, *The End of the Old Order in Rural Europe* (1978). Comprehensive treatment of rural Europe, especially in central and eastern Europe.

F. BRAUDEL, *The Structures of Everyday Life: The Limits of the Possible*, trans. by M. Kochan (1982). A magisterial survey.

J. BREWER AND R. PORTER, *Consumption and the World of Goods* (1993). A large, wide-ranging collection of essays.

J. CANON, *Aristocratic Century: The Peerage of Eighteenth-Century England* (1985). A useful treatment.

A. CLARKE, *The Struggle for the Breeches: Gender and the Making of the British Working Class* (1995). A major, deeply researched exploration of the subject.

P. DEANE, *The First Industrial Revolution*, 2d ed. (1979). A well-balanced and systematic treatment.

J. DE VRIES, *European Urbanization, 1500–1800* (1984). An important and far-ranging treatment.

W. DOYLE, *The Old European Order: 1660–1800* (1992). The best and most accessible one-volume study.

P. EARLE, *The Making of the English Middle Class: Business, Community, and Family Life in London, 1660–1730* (1989). The most careful study of the subject.

M. W. FLINN, *The European Demographic System, 1500–1820* (1981). A major summary.

P. GOUBERT, *The* Ancien Régime: *French Society, 1600–1750*, trans. by S. Cox (1974). A superb account of the peasant social order.

D. HAY (ED.), *Albion's Fatal Tree: Crime and Society in Eighteenth-Century England* (1975). Separate essays on a previously little explored subject.

O. H. HUFTON, *The Poor of Eighteenth-Century France, 1750–1789* (1975). A brilliant study of poverty and the family economy.

E. L. JONES, *Agriculture and Economic Growth in England, 1650–1815* (1968). A good introduction.

A. KAHAN, *The Plow, the Hammer, and the Knout: An Economic History of Eighteenth-Century Russia* (1985). An extensive and detailed treatment.

D. LANDES, *The Wealth and Poverty of Nations: Why Some Are So Rich and Some So Poor* (1998). A lively, opinionated overview of economic development.

F. E. MANUEL, *The Broken Staff: Judaism Through Christian Eyes* (1992). An important discussion of Christian interpretations of Judaism.

M. A. MEYER, *The Origins of the Modern Jew: Jewish Identity and European Culture in Germany, 1749–1824* (1967). Organized around individual case studies.

P. B. MUNSENE, *Gentlemen and Poachers: The English Game Laws, 1671–1831* (1981). An excellent analysis of these laws.

S. POLLARD, *Peaceful Conquest: The Industrialization of Europe, 1760–1970* (1981). A useful survey.

G. RUDÉ, *The Crowd in History, 1730–1848* (1964). A pioneering study.

H. SCHMAL, (ED.), *Patterns of European Urbanization Since 1500* (1981). Major revisionist essays.

L. STONE, *An Open Elite?* (1985). Raises important questions about the traditional view of open access to social mobility in England.

T. TACKETT, *Priest and Parish in Eighteenth-Century France: A Social and Political Study of the Curés in a Diocese of Dauphiné, 1750–1791* (1977). An important local study that displays the role of the church in the fabric of social life in the Old Regime.

D. VALENZE, *The First Industrial Woman* (1995). An elegant, penetrating volume

A. VICKERY, *The Gentleman's Daughter: Women's Lives in Georgian England* (1998). A richly documented study.

E. A. WRIGLEY, *Continuity, Chance and Change: The Character of the Industrial Revolution in England* (1988). A major conceptual reassessment.

Chapter 17

During the seventeenth and eighteenth centuries, European maritime nations established overseas empires, and set up trading monopolies within them, in an effort to magnify their economic strength. As this painting of the Old Custom House Quay in London suggests, trade from these empires and the tariffs imposed on it were expected to generate revenue for the home country. But behind many of the goods carried in the great sailing ships in the harbor and landed on these docks lay the labor of African slaves working on the plantations of North and South America. Samuel Scott *Old Custom House Quay* Collection. By Courtesy of the Trustees of the Victoria & Albert Museum

The Transatlantic Economy, Trade Wars, and Colonial Rebellion

Periods of European Overseas Empires

Mercantile Empires
Mercantilist Goals
French–British Rivalry

The Spanish Colonial System
Colonial Government
Trade Regulation
Colonial Reform under the Spanish
  Bourbon Monarchs

Black African Slavery, the Plantation System, and the Atlantic Economy
The African Presence in the Americas
Slavery and the Transatlantic Economy
The Experience of Slavery

Mid-Eighteenth-Century Wars
The War of Jenkins's Ear
The War of the Austrian Succession
  (1740–1748)
The "Diplomatic Revolution" of 1756
The Seven Years' War (1756–1763)

The American Revolution and Europe
Resistance to the Imperial Search
  for Revenue
The Crisis and Independence
American Political Ideas
Events in Great Britain
Broader Impact of the American
  Revolution

KEY TOPICS

- Europe's mercantilist empires
- Spain's vast colonial empire in the Americas
- Africa, slavery, and the transatlantic plantation economies
- The wars of the mid-eighteenth century in Europe and the colonies
- The struggle for independence in Britain's North American colonies

The middle of the eighteenth century witnessed a renewal of European warfare on a world-wide scale. The conflict involved two separate, but interrelated, rivalries. Austria and Prussia fought for dominance in central Europe, while Great Britain and France dueled for commercial and colonial supremacy. The wars were long, extensive, and costly in both effort and money. They resulted in a new balance of power on the Continent and on the high seas. Prussia emerged as a great power, and Great Britain gained a world empire.

The expense of these wars led every major European government after the Peace of Paris of 1763 to reconstruct its policies of taxation and finance. The revised fiscal programs produced internal conditions for the monarchies of Europe that had significant effects lasting the rest of the century, including the American Revolution, enlightened absolutism on the Continent, a continuing financial crisis for the French monarchy, and reform of the Spanish Empire in South America.

Periods of European Overseas Empires

Since the Renaissance, European contacts with the rest of the world have gone through four distinct stages. The first was that of the European discovery, exploration, initial conquest, and settlement of the New World. This phase also witnessed the penetration of southeast Asian markets by Portugal and the Netherlands, which established major imperial outposts and influence in the region. The period closed by the end of the seventeenth century.

The second era—that of the mercantile empires, which are largely the concern of this chapter—was one of colonial trade rivalry among Spain, France, and Great Britain. Although during the sixteenth and seventeenth centuries differing motives had led to the establishment of overseas European empires, by the eighteenth century they generally existed to foster trade and commerce. Those commerical goals, however, often led to intense rivalry and conflict in key imperial trouble spots. As a result, the various imperial ventures led to the creation of large navies and fostered a series of major naval wars at the mid-century—wars that in turn became linked to warfare on the European continent. The Anglo-French side of the contest has often been compared to a second Hundred Years' War, with theaters of conflict in Europe, the Americas, and India.

A fundamental element of these first two periods of European imperial ventures in the Americas was the presence of slavery. By the eighteenth century, the slave population of the New World consisted almost entirely of a black population either recently forcibly imported from Africa or born to slaves whose forebears had been forcibly imported from Africa. There existed no precedent in human history for so large a forced migration of peoples from one continent to another or for the mid-Atlantic plantation economies supported by such slave labor. The creation in the Americas of this slave-based plantation economy led directly to over three centuries of extensive involvement in the slave trade by Europeans and white Americans with Africa—most particularly, the societies of West Africa. In turn, the slave trade created on the American continent extensive communities of Africans from the Chesapeake region of Maryland and Virginia south to Brazil. The Africans brought to the American experience not only their labor, but their languages, customs, and ethnic associations. The Atlantic economy and the societies that arose in the Americas were consequently very much the creation of both Europeans and Africans, while, as a result of the Spanish conquest, native Americans were pressed toward the margins of those societies.

Finally, during the second period, both the British colonies of the North American seaboard and the Spanish colonies of Mexico and Central and South America emancipated themselves from European control. This era of independence, part of which is discussed in this chapter and part in Chapter 21, may be said to have closed during the 1820s.

The third stage of European contact with the non-European world occurred in the nineteenth century. During that period, European governments carved new formal empires involving the direct European administration of indigenous peoples in Africa and Asia. Those nineteenth-century empires also included new areas of European settlement, such as Australia, New Zealand, and South Africa. The bases of these empires were trade, national honor, Christian missionary enterprise, and military strategy.

The last period of European empire occurred during the mid- and late twentieth century, with the decolonization of peoples who had previously lived under European colonial rule.

During the four-and-one-half centuries before decolonization, Europeans exerted political dominance over much of the rest of the world that was far disproportional to the geographical size or population of Europe. Europeans frequently treated other peoples as social, intellectual, and economic inferiors. They ravaged existing cultures because of greed, religious zeal, or political ambition. These actions are major facts of both European and world history and remain significant factors in the contemporary relationship between Europe and its former colonies. What allowed the Europeans to exert such influence and domination for so long over so much of the world was not any innate cultural superiority, but a technological supremacy related to naval power and gunpowder. Ships and guns allowed the Europeans to exercise their will almost wherever they chose.

Mercantile Empires

Navies and merchant shipping were the keystones of the mercantile empires that were meant to bring profit to a nation rather than to provide areas for settlement. The Treaty of Utrecht (1713) established the boundaries of empire during the first half of the century.

Except for Brazil, which was governed by Portugal, Spain controlled all of mainland South America. In North America, it ruled Florida, Mexico, California, and the Southwest. The Spanish also governed Central America and the islands of Cuba, Puerto Rico, and half of Hispaniola.

The British Empire consisted of the colonies along the North Atlantic seaboard, Nova Scotia, Newfoundland, Jamaica, and Barbados. Britain also possessed a few trading stations on the Indian subcontinent.

The French domains covered the Saint Lawrence River valley and the Ohio and Mississippi River valleys. They included the West Indian islands of Saint Domingue (Hispaniola), Guadeloupe, and Martinique and also stations in India. To the French and British merchant communities, India appeared as a vast potential market for European goods, as well as the source of calicos and spices that were in much demand in Europe.

The Dutch controlled Surinam, or Dutch Guiana, in South America, and various trading stations in Ceylon and Bengal. Most important, they controlled the trade with Java in what is now Indonesia. The Dutch had opened these markets largely in the seventeenth century and had created a vast trading empire far larger in extent, wealth, and importance than the geographical size of the United Netherlands would have led one to expect. The Dutch had been daring sailors and made important technological innovations in sailing.

All of these powers also possessed numerous smaller islands in the Caribbean. So far as eighteenth-century developments were concerned, the major rivalries existed among the Spanish, the French, and the British.

Mercantilist Goals

Where any formal economic theory lay behind the conduct of eighteenth-century empires, it was mercantilism, that practical creed of hard-headed businesspeople. The terms *mercantilism* and *mercantile system* were invented by later opponents and critics of the system whereby governments heavily regulated trade and commerce in hope of increasing national wealth. Economic writers believed it necessary for a nation to gain a favorable trade balance of gold and silver bullion. They regarded bullion as the measure of a country's wealth, and a nation was truly wealthy only if it amassed more bullion than its rivals. (See "Jacques Savary Praises Trade.")

The mercantilist statesmen and traders regarded the world as an arena of scarce resources and economic limitation. The attitudes associated with mercantilist thinking assumed very modest levels of economic growth. Such thinking predated the expansion of agricultural and later industrial productivity discussed in the previous chapter. Prior to the beginning of such sustained economic growth, the wealth of one nation was assumed to grow or to be increased largely at the direct cost of another nation. That is to say, the wealth of one state might expand only if its armies or navies conquered the domestic or colonial territory of another state and thus gained the productive capacity of that area, or if a state expanded its trading monopoly over new territory, or if, by smuggling, it could intrude upon the trading monopoly of another state.

From beginning to end, the economic well-being of the home country was the primary concern of mercantilist writers. Colonies were to provide markets and natural resources for the industries of the home country. In turn, the home country was to furnish military security and political administration for the colonies. For decades,

The Dutch established a major trading base at Batavia in the East Indies. The city they called Batavia is now Djakarta, Indonesia.
Bildarchiv Preussicher Kulturbesitz

Jacques Savary Praises Trade

During the seventeenth century, certain writers believed it necessary to justify trade and commerce. At the time, many people associated wealth and social prestige with the aristocracy and with landed estates. Wealth in land appeared more certain and less likely to disappear through speculation than commercial wealth did. Jacques Savary was a Frenchman who in the 1670s wrote a treatise on merchants. He sought to explain why trade and commerce were part of the divine plan for humankind. He also explained how such trade could expand the wealth and power of monarchs. In writing for a French audience, Savary would appear to have in mind the commercial achievements of the Dutch, with whom France was then at war, as well as of the English.

❖ *How does Savary justify trade as part of God's plan for human society? How does he relate trade to the prosperity of kingdoms and to parts of the economy not directly engaging in overseas trade? How does he see commerce enriching monarchs?*

By the manner in which Divine Providence has dispersed things throughout the world, it is clear that God wished to create unity and love among all men, because He imposed upon them the state of always having need one of another. He did not choose to permit necessities of existence to be found in one place, but rather spread out his gifts, in order that men might have to trade together....it is this endless exchange of the commodities of life which gives birth to Trade, and it is also Trade which adds sweetness to life....

It was not enough that Trade be necessary; it was also essential that it be profitable, in order to compel some men to devote their energies to it; for there are a number of provinces, in which the plentiful supply of most of the goods needed for everyday life would have given rise to laziness, had not the desire for profit and social advancement been a goad which forced them to enter Trade.

One cannot question its usefulness; firstly, with reference to the individuals who practise commerce, because the largest part of the population makes an honest living by this occupation....

The usefulness of Trade extends also to kingdoms and to the princes who rule them; the more Trade there is within a country, the greater its wealth. There have been states which have gained immense wealth in a short time, but when war has disrupted Trade, their provinces have suffered, have sometimes been unable to pay their taxes, and in the end their fields have lain uncultivated.

The kings can also derive great benefit from Trade; because, apart from the dues which are paid to them on goods entering or leaving the kingdom, it is indeed true that all the ready money which is in he hands of the merchants and business men draw the immense sums of which the kings sometimes have need for financing great enterprises.

From Jacques Savary, *The Compleat Merchant* (first published 1675), as quoted in Roger Mettam, ed., *Government and Society in Louis XIV's France* (London: The Macmillan Press Ltd., 1977), pp. 172–173.

both sides assumed that the colonies were the inferior partner in the relationship. The home country and its colonies were to trade exclusively with each other. To that end, they tried to forge trade-tight systems of national commerce through navigation laws, tariffs, bounties to encourage production, and prohibitions against trading with the subjects of other monarchs. National monopoly was the ruling principle.

Mercantilist ideas had always been neater on paper than in practice. By the early eighteenth century, mercantilist assumptions were far removed

from the economic realities of the colonies. The colonial and home markets simply did not mesh. Spain could not produce enough goods for South America. Economic production in the British North American colonies challenged English manufacturing and led to British attempts to limit certain colonial industries, such as iron and hat making.

Colonists of different countries wished to trade with each other. English colonists could buy sugar more cheaply from the French West Indies than from English suppliers. The traders and merchants of one nation always hoped to break the monopoly of another. For all these reasons, the eighteenth century became what one historian many years ago termed the "golden age of smugglers."[1] The governments could not control the activities of all their subjects. Clashes among colonists could and did bring about conflict between governments.

French–British Rivalry

Major flash points existed between France and Britain in North America. Their colonists quarreled endlessly with each other. Both groups of settlers coveted the lower Saint Lawrence River valley, upper New England, and, later, the Ohio River valley. There were other rivalries over fishing rights, the fur trade, and alliances with Native American tribes.

The heart of the eighteenth-century colonial rivalry in the Americas, however, lay in the West Indies. These islands, close to the American continents, were the jewels of empire. The West Indies raised tobacco, cotton, indigo, coffee, and, above all, sugar, for which there existed strong markets in Europe. These commodities were becoming part of daily life, especially in western Europe. They represented one aspect of those major changes in consumption that marked eighteenth-century European culture. Sugar in particular had become a staple rather than a luxury. It was used in coffee, tea, and cocoa, for making candy and preserving fruits, and in the brewing industry. There seemed no limit to its uses, no limit to consumer demand for it, and, for a time, almost no limit to the riches that it might bring to plantation owners. Only slave labor allowed the profitable cultivation of these products during the seventeenth and eighteen centuries.

India was another area of French–British rivalry. On the Indian subcontinent, both France and Britain traded through privileged, chartered companies that enjoyed a legal monopoly. The East India Company was the English institution; the French equivalent was the *Compagnie des Indes*. The trade of India and Asia figured only marginally in the economics of empire. Nevertheless, enterprising Europeans always hoped to develop profitable commerce with India. Others regarded India as a springboard into the even larger potential market of China. The original European footholds in India were trading posts called *factories*. They existed through privileges granted by various Indian governments.

Two circumstances in the middle of the eighteenth century changed this situation in India. First, the indigenous administration and government of several Indian states had decayed. Second, Joseph Dupleix (1697–1763) for the French and Robert Clive (1725–1774) for the British saw the developing power vacuum as opportunities for expanding the control of their respective companies. To maintain their own security and to expand their privileges, each of the two companies began in effect to take over the government of some regions. Each group of Europeans hoped to checkmate the other.

The Dutch maintained their extensive commercial empire futher to the east in what today is Indonesia. By the eighteenth century, the other European powers more or less acknowledged Dutch predominance in that region.

The Spanish Colonial System

Spanish control of its American Empire involved a system of government and a system of monopolistic trade regulation. Both were more rigid in appearance than in practice. Actual government was often informal, and the trade monopoly was frequently breached. Until the middle of the eighteenth century, the primary purpose of the Spanish Emire was to supply Spain with the precious metals mined in the New World.

Colonial Government

Because Queen Isabella of Castile (r. 1474–1504) had commissioned Columbus, the technical legal link between the New World and Spain was the crown of Castile. Its powers both at home and in America were subject to few limitations. The Castilian monarch assigned the government of America to the Council of the Indies, which, with the monarch, nominated the viceroys of New Spain (Mexico) and Peru. These viceroys served as the chief executives in the New World and carried out the laws promulgated by the Council of the Indies.

Each of the viceroyalties was divided into several subordinate judicial councils, known as *audiencias*. There was also a variety of local officers, the most important of which were the *corregidores*, who presided over municipal councils. All of these offices provided the monarchy with a vast array of patronage, usually bestowed on persons born in Spain. Virtually all power flowed from the top of this political structure downward; in effect, local initiative or self-government scarcely existed.

Trade Regulation

The colonial political structures functioned largely to support Spanish commercial self-interest. The *Casa de Contratación* (House of Trade) in Seville reg-

[1]Walter Dorn, *Competition for Empire, 1740–1763* (New York: Harper, 1940), p. 266.

Visitors Describe the Portobello Fair

The Spanish tried to restrict all trade within their Latin American empire to a few designated ports. Each year, a fair was held in certain of these ports. The most famous such port was Portobello on the Isthmus of Panama. In the 1730s, two visitors saw the event and described it. This fair was the chief means of facilitating trade between the western coast of South America and Spain.

❖ *What products were sold at the fair? How does this passage illustrate the inefficiency of monopoly trade in the Spanish empire and the many chances for smuggling?*

The town of Portobello, so thinly inhabited, by reason of its noxious air, the scarcity of provisions, and the soil, becomes, at the time of the [Spanish] galleons one of the most populous places in all South America....

The ships are no sooner moored in the harbour, than the first work is, to erect, in the square, a tent made of the ship's sails, for receiving its cargo; at which the proprietors of the goods are present, in order to find their bales, by the marks which distinguish them. These bales are drawn on sledges, to their respective places by the crew of every ship, and the money given them is proportionally divided.

Whilst the seamen and European traders are thus employed, the land is covered with droves of mules from Panama, each drove consisting of above an hundred, loaded with chests of gold and silver, on account of the merchants of Peru. Some unload them at the exchange, others in the middle of the square; yet, amidst the hurry and confusion of such crowds, no theft, loss, or disturbance, is ever known. He who has seen this place during the *tiempo muerto*, or dead time, solitary, poor, and a perpetual silence reigning everywhere; the harbour quite empty, and every place wearing a melancholy aspect; must be filled with astonishment at the sudden change, to see

the bustling multitudes, every house crowded, the square and streets encumbered with bales and chests of gold and silver of all kinds; the harbour full of ships and vessels, some bringing by the way of Rio de Chape the goods of Peru, such as *cacao, quinquina,* or Jesuit's bark, Vicuña wool, and bezoar stones; others coming from Carthagena, loaded with provisions; and thus a spot, at all times detested for its deleterious qualities, becomes the staple of the riches of the old and new world, and the scene of one of the most considerable branches of commerce in the whole earth.

The ships being unloaded, and the merchants of Peru, together with the president of Panama, arrived, the fair comes under deliberation. And for this purpose the deputies of the several parties repair on board the commodore of the galleons, where, in the presence of the commodore, and the president of Panama, ...the prices of the several kinds of merchandizes are settled.... The purchases and sales, as likewise the exchanges of money, are transacted by brokers, both from Spain and Peru. After this, every one begins to dispose of his goods; the Spanish brokers embarking their chests of money, and those of Peru sending away the goods they have purchased, in vessels called *chatas* and *bongos*, up the river Chagres. And thus the fair of Portobello ends.

From George Juan and Antonio de Ulloa, *A Voyage to South America,* Vol. 1 (London, 1772), pp. 103–110, as quoted in Benjamin Keen, ed., *Readings in Latin-American Civilization, 1492 to the Present* (New York: Houghton Mifflin, 1955), pp. 107–108.

ulated all trade with the New World. Cádiz was the only port authorized for use in the American trade. The *Casa* was the most influential institution of the Spanish Empire. Its members worked closely with the *Consulado* (Merchant Guild) of Seville and other groups involved with American commerce in Cádiz.

A complicated system of trade and bullion fleets administered from Seville was the key to maintaining Spain's trade monopoly. Each year, a fleet of commercial vessels (the *flota*) controlled by Seville

merchants and escorted by warships carried merchandise from Spain to a few specified ports in America, including Portobello, Veracruz, and Cartagena on the Atlantic coast. (See "Visitors Describe the Portobello Fair.") There were no authorized ports on the Pacific Coast. Areas far to the south, such as Buenos Aires on the Rio de la Plata, received goods only after the shipments had been unloaded at one of the authorized ports. After selling their wares, the ships were loaded with silver and gold bullion, usually wintered in heavily fortified Caribbean ports, and then sailed back to Spain. The *flota* system always worked imperfectly, but trade outside it was illegal. Regulations prohibited the Spanish colonists within the American Empire from establishing direct trade with each other and from building their own shipping and commercial industry. Foreign merchants were also forbidden to breach the Spanish monopoly.

Colonial Reform under the Spanish Bourbon Monarchs

A crucial change occurred in the Spanish colonial system in the early eighteenth century. The War of the Spanish Succession (1701–1714) and the Treaty of Utrecht (1713) replaced the Spanish Habsburgs with the Bourbons of France on the Spanish throne. Philip V (r. 1700–1746) and his successors tried to use French administrative skills to reassert the imperial trade monopoly, which had decayed under the last Spanish Habsburgs and thus attempted to improve the domestic economy and revive Spanish power in European affairs.

Under Philip V, Spanish coastal patrol vessels tried to suppress smuggling in American waters. (See "Buccaneers Prowl the High Seas.") An incident arising from this policy (to be discussed later in the chapter) led to war with England in 1739, the year in which Philip established the viceroyalty of New Granada in the area that today includes Venezuela, Colombia, and Ecuador. The goal was to increase direct royal government in the area.

During the reign of Ferdinand VI (r. 1746–1759), the great midcentury wars exposed the vulnerability of the empire to naval attack and economic penetration. As an ally of France, Spain emerged as one of the defeated powers in 1763. Government circles became convinced that further changes in the colonial system had to be undertaken.

Charles III (r. 1759–1788), the most important of the royal imperial reformers, attempted to reassert Spain's control of the empire. Like his two Bourbon predecessors, Charles emphasized royal ministers rather than councils. Thus, the role of both the Council of the Indies and the *Casa de Contratación* diminished. After 1765, Charles abolished the monopolies of Seville and Cádiz and permitted other Spanish cities to trade with America. He also opened more South American and Caribbean ports to trade and authorized some commerce between Spanish ports in America. In 1776 he organized a fourth viceroyalty in the region of Rio de la Plata, which included much of present-day Argentina, Uruguay, Paraguay, and Bolivia. (See Map 17–1.)

While relaxing Spanish trade with and in America, Charles III attempted to increase the efficiency of tax collection and to end bureaucratic corruption. To achieve those ends, he introduced the institu-

tion of the *intendant* into the Spanish Empire. These loyal, royal bureaucrats were patterned on the French *intendants* made so famous and effective as agents of the absolutism of Louis XIV.

The late-eighteenth-century Bourbon reforms did stimulate the imperial economy. Trade expanded and became more varied. These reforms, however, also brought the empire more fully under direct Spanish control. Many *peninsulares* (persons born in Spain) entered the New World to fill new posts, which were often the most profitable jobs in the region. Expanding trade brought more Spanish merchants to Latin America. The economy remained export oriented, and economic life was still organized to benefit Spain. As a result of these policies, the *creoles* (persons of European descent born in the Spanish colonies) came to feel that they were second-class subjects. In time, their resentment would provide a major source of the discontent leading to the wars of independence in the early nineteenth century. The imperial reforms of Charles III were the Spanish equivalent of the new colonial measures undertaken by the British government after 1763, which led to the American Revolution.

Black African Slavery, the Plantation System, and the Atlantic Economy

Within various parts of Europe itself, slavery had existed since ancient times. Before the eighteenth century, little or no moral or religious stigma attached to slave owning or slave trading. It had a continuous existence in the Mediterranean world, where only the sources of slaves changed over the centuries. After the conquest of Constantinople in the mid-fifteenth century, the Ottoman Empire forbade the exportation of white slaves from regions under its control. The Portuguese then began to import African slaves into the Iberian Peninsula from the Canary Islands and West Africa. Black slaves from Africa were also not uncommon in other parts of the Mediterranean, and a few found their way into northern Europe. There they might be used as personal servants or displayed because of the novelty of their color in the courts of royalty or homes of the wealthy.

But from the sixteenth century onward, first within the West Indies and the Spanish and Portuguese settlements in South America and then in the British colonies on the South Atlantic seaboard of North America, slave labor became a fundamental social and economic factor. The development of those plantation economies based on slave labor led to an unprecedented interaction between the peoples of Europe and Africa and between the European settlers

Buccaneers Prowl the High Seas

By no means all of the trade in the Caribbean Sea occurred at the Portobello fair described in the previous document. Piracy was a major problem for transatlantic trade. There was often a fine line between freewheeling, buccaneering pirates operating for their own gain and privateers who in effect worked for various European governments that wanted to penetrate the commercial monopoly of the Spanish Empire. Alexander Exquemelin was a ship's surgeon who for a time plied his trade on board a pirate ship and then later settled in Holland. He wrote an account of those days in which he emphasizes the careful code of conduct among the pirates themselves and the harshness of their behavior toward both those on ships they captured and poor farmers and fishermen whom they robbed and virtually enslaved.

❖ *How did the restrictive commercial policy of the Spanish Empire encourage piracy and privateering? Was there a code of honor among the pirates? What kinds of people may have suffered most from piracy? To what extent did pirates have any respect for individual freedom? How romantic was the real world of pirates?*

When a buccaneer is going to sea he sends word to all who wish to sail with him. When all are ready, they go on board, each bringing what he needs in the way of weapons, powder and shot.

On the ship, they first discuss where to go and get food supplies....The meat is either [salted] pork or turtle...Sometimes they go and plunder the Spaniards' *corrales*, which are pens where they keep perhaps a thousand head of tame hogs. The rovers...find the house of the farmer...[whom] unless he gives them as many hogs as they demand, they hang...without mercy....

When a ship has been captured, the men decide whether the captain should keep it or not: if the prize is better than their own vessel, they take it and set fire to the other. When a ship is robbed, nobody must plunder and keep the loot to himself. Everything taken... must be shared..., without any man enjoying a penny more than his faire share. To prevent deceit, before the booty is distributed everyone has to swear an oath on the Bible that he has not kept for himself so much as the value of a sixpence... And should any man be found to have made a false

oath, he would be banished from the rovers, and never be allowed in their company....

When they have captured a ship, the buccaneers set the prisoners on shore as soon as possible, apart from two or three whom they keep to do the cooking and other work they themselves do not care for, releasing these men after two or three years.

The rovers frequently put in for fresh supplies at some island or other, often...lying off the south coast of Cuba.... Everyone goes ashore and sets up his tent, and they take turns to go on marauding expeditions in their canoes. They take prisoner...poor men who catch and set turtles for a living, to provide for their wives and children. Once captured, these men have to catch turtle for the rovers as long as they remain on the island. Should the rovers intend to cruise along a coast where turtle abound, they take the fishermen along with them. The poor fellows may be compelled to stay away from their wives and families four or five years, with no news whether they are alive or dead.

Alexander O. Exquemelin, *The Buccaneers of America*, Alexis Brown, tr. (Baltimore, Penguin Books, 1969) pp. 70–72.

in the Americas and Africa. It was from that point onward that Africa and Africans became drawn into the Western experience as never before in history.

The African Presence in the Americas

Once they had encountered and begun to settle the New World, the conquering Spanish and Portuguese faced a severe shortage of labor. They and

most of the French and English settlers who came later had no intention of undertaking manual work themselves. At first, they used Native Americans as laborers, but during the sixteenth century as well as afterwards, disease killed hundreds of thousands of the native population. As a result, labor soon became scarce. The Spanish and Portuguese then turned to the labor of imported African slaves. Settlers in the English colonies of

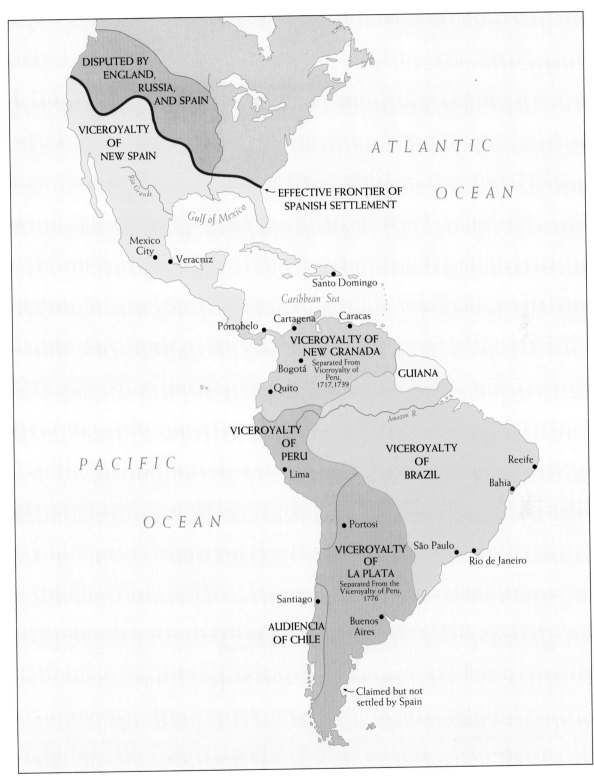

MAP 17–1   VICEROYALTIES IN LATIN AMERICA IN 1780   *The late-eighteenth-century viceroyalties in Latin America display the effort of the Spanish Bourbon monarchy to establish more direct conrol of the continent. They sought this control through the introductions of more royal officials and by establishing more governmental districts.*

This eighteenth-century print shows bound African captives being forced to a slaving port. It was largely African middlemen who captured slaves in the interior and marched them to the coast.
North Wind Picture Archives

North America during the seventeenth century turned more slowly to slavery, with the largest number coming to the Chesapeake Bay region of Virginia and Maryland and then later into the low country of the Carolinas. Which African peoples became sold into slavery during any given decade very largely depended upon internal African warfare and state-building. Such would continue to be the situation until the end of the transatlantic slave trade in the nineteenth century.

The major sources for slaves were slave markets in Central West Africa in Senegambia, Sierra Leone, the Gold Coast, the Bight of Benin, and the Bight of Biafra. Slavery and an extensive slave trade had existed in these as well as other regions of Africa for hundreds of years. Just as particular social and economic conditions in Europe had led to the voyages of exploration and settlement, political and military conditions in the African continent and warfare among various African nations similiarly created a supply of slaves that certain African societies were willing to sell to Europeans. In that respect, European slave traders did not confront a passive situation in West Africa over which they exercised their will by force and commerce. Rather, they encountered dynamic African societies working out their own internal historic power relationships and rivalries, one characteristic of which was Africans selling and acquiring other Africans from different regions and nations as slaves.

THE WEST INDIES, BRAZIL, AND SUGAR   To grasp the full impact of the forced immigration of Africans on the Americas, it is necessary to take into account both continents and the entire picture of the transatlantic economy. Far more slaves were imported into the West Indies and Brazil than into North America. Although citizens of the United States mark the beginning of slavery in 1619 with the arrival of African slaves on a Dutch ship in Jamestown, Virginia, over a century of slave trading in the West Indies and South America had preceded that event. Indeed, by the late sixteenth century, Africans had become a major social presence on the islands of the West Indies and in the major cities of both Spanish and Portuguese South America. That presence and influence in those regions would grow over the centuries. African labor and African immigrant slave communities were the most prominent social feature of those regions making the development of those economies and cultures what one historian has described as "a Euro-African phenomenon."[2] There, African slaves equaled or more generally surpassed the numbers of white European settlers in what soon constituted multiracial societies. Someone passing through the marketplace of those towns and cities would have heard a vast number of different African, as well as European, languages. Although Native American labor continued to be exploited on the South American continent, it was increasingly a marginal presence in the ever-expanding African slave-based plantation economy of the Atlantic seaboard, the Caribbean, and offshore islands.

Within much of Spanish South America, the numbers of slaves declined during the late seventeenth century, and slavery became somewhat

[2]John Thornton, *Africa and the Africans in the Making of the Atlantic World, 1400–1800*, 2d ed. (Cambridge, U.K.: Cambridge University Press, 1998), p. 140

In the American South, the islands of the Caribbean, and in Brazil, the slaves labored on sugar plantations under the authority of overseers. The Granger Collection

A vast increase in the number of Africans brought as slaves to the Americas occurred during the eighteenth century, with the majority arriving in the Caribbean or Brazil. Early in the century, as many as 20,000 new Africans a year arrived in the West Indies as slaves. By 1725, it has been estimated, almost 90 percent of the population of Jamaica was black slaves. After the middle of the century, for some time the numbers were even larger. The influx of new Africans in most areas—even in the British colonies—meant that the numbers of new forced immigrants outnumbered the slaves of African descent already present.

Newly imported African slaves were needed because the fertility rate of the earlier slave population was low and the death rate high from disease, overwork, and malnutrition. The West Indies proved a particularly difficult region in which to secure a stable, self-reproducing slave population. The conditions for slaves there simply led to very high rates of mortality with new slaves coming primarily from the ongoing slave trade. A similar situation prevailed in Brazil. Restocking through the slave trade meant that the slave population of those areas consisted of African-born persons rather than of persons of African descent. Consequently, one of the key factors in the social life of many of the areas of American slavery during the eighteenth century was the presence of persons newly arrived from Africa, carrying with them African languages, religion, culture, and local African ethnic identities that they would infuse into the already existing slave communities. Thus, the eighteenth century witnessed an enormous impact of a new African presence throughout the Americas.

Slavery and the Transatlantic Economy

Different nations dominated the slave trade in different periods. During the sixteenth century, the Portuguese and the Spanish were most involved. The Dutch supplanted them during most of the seventeenth century. Thereafter, during the late seventeenth and eighteenth century, the English constituted the chief slave traders. French traders also participated.

Slavery touched most of the economy of the transatlantic world. Colonial trade followed roughly a geographic triangle. European goods—quite often guns—were carried to Africa to be exchanged for slaves, who were then taken to the West Indies, where they were traded for sugar and other tropical products, which were then shipped

less fundamental there than elsewhere. Slavery continued to expand its influence, however, in Brazil and in the Caribbean through the spreading cultivation of sugar to meet the demand of the European market. By the close of the seventeenth century, the Caribbean islands were the world center for the production of sugar and the chief supplier for the ever-growing consumer demand for the product. The opening of new areas of cultivation and other economic enterprises required additional slaves during the eighteenth century, a period of major slave importation. The growing prosperity of sugar islands that had begun to be exploited in the late seventeenth century, as well as new sugar, coffee, and tobacco regions of Brazil, where gold mining also required additional slaves, accounts for this increase in slave commerce and allowed higher prices to be paid for slaves. In Brazil, the West Indies, and the southern British colonies, prosperity and slavery went hand in hand.

to Europe. Not all ships covered all three legs of the triangle. Another major trade pattern existed between New England and the West Indies with New England fish or ship stores being traded for sugar. At various moments, the prosperity of such cities as Amsterdam, Liverpool, England, and Nantes, France, rested very largely on the slave trade. Cities in the British North American colonies, such as Newport, Rhode Island, profited from slavery sometimes by trading in slaves, but more often by supplying other goods to the West Indian market. All the shippers who handled cotton, tobacco, and sugar depended on slavery, though they might not have had direct contact with the institution, as did all the manufacturers and merchants who produced the finished products for the consumer market. (See "Art & the West.")

As had been the case during previous centuries, eighteenth-century political turmoil in Africa, such as the Kongo civil wars, made possible the increasing supply of slaves during that period. These Kongo wars had originated in a dispute over succession in the late seventeenth century and con-

tinued into the eighteenth. In some cases, captives were simply sold to European slave traders calling at ports along the West African coast. In other cases, African leaders conducted slave raids so their captives could be sold to further finance the purchase of weapons for warfare. Similar political unrest and turmoil in the Gold Coast during the eighteenth century led to an increased supply of African captives to be sold into American slavery. Consequently, there existed a close relationship between warfare in West Africa, often far into the interior, and the economic development of the American Atlantic seaboard.

The Experience of Slavery

The Portuguese, Spanish, Dutch, French, and English slave traders forcibly transported several million (perhaps more than nine million, the exact numbers being in much dispute) Africans to the New World—the largest example of forced intercontinental migration in human history. During the first four centuries of settlement, far more black slaves came involuntarily to the New World

Loading plan for the main decks of the 320-ton slave ship Brookes. *The* Brookes *was only 25 feet wide and 100 feet long, but as many as 609 slaves were crammed on board for the nightmarish passage to the Americas. The average space allowed each person was only about 78 inches by 16 inches. The document from Thomas Phillips's journal describes the voyage across the Atlantic. (See "A Slave Trader Describes the Atlantic Passage.")* Photographs and Prints Division, Schomburg Center for Research in Black Culture, The New York Public Library, Astor, Lenox and Tilden Foundations

A Slave Trader Describes the Atlantic Passage

During 1693 and 1694, Captain Thomas Phillips carried slaves from Africa to Barbados on the ship Hannibal. *The financial backer of the voyage was the Royal African Company of London, which held an English crown monopoly on slave trading. Phillips sailed to the west coast of Africa, where he purchased the Africans who were sold into slavery by an African king. Then he set sail westward.*

❖ *Who are the various people described in this document who in one way or another were involved in or profited from the slave trade? What dangers did the Africans face on the voyage? What contemporary attitudes could have led this ship captain to treat and think of his human cargo simply as goods to be transported? What are the grounds of his self-pity for the difficulties he met?*

Having bought my complement of 700 slaves, 480 men and 220 women, and finish'd all my business at Whidaw [on the Gold Coast of Africa], I took my leave of the old king and his *cappasheirs* [attendants], and parted, with many affectionate expressions on both sides, being forced to promise him that I would return again the next year, with several things he desired me to bring from England.... I set sail the 27th of July in the morning, accompany'd with the East-India Merchant, who had bought 650 slaves, for the Island of St. Thomas...from which we took our departure on August 25th and set sail for Barbadoes.

We spent in our passage from St. Thomas to Barbadoes two months eleven days, from the 25th of August to the 4th of November following: in which time there happened such sickness and mortality among my poor men and Negroes. Of the first we buried 14, and of the last 320, which was a great detriment to our voyage, the Royal African Company losing ten pounds by every slave that died, and the owners of the ship ten pounds ten shillings, being the freight agreed on to be paid by the charter-party for every Negro delivered alive ashore to the African Company's agents at Barbadoes....The loss in all amounted to near 6500 pounds sterling.

The distemper which my men as well as the blacks mostly died of was the white flux, which was so violent and inveterate that no medicine would in the least check it, so that when any of our men were seized with it, we esteemed him a dead man, as he generally proved....

The Negroes are so incident to the small-pox that few ships that carry them escape without it, and sometimes it makes vast havock and destruction among them. But tho' we had 100 at a time sick of it, and that it went thro' the ship, yet we lost not above a dozen by it. All the assistance we gave the diseased was only as much water as they desir'd to drink, and some palm-oil to annoint their sores, and they would generally recover without any other helps but what kind nature gave them....

But what the small pox spar'd, the flux swept off, to our great regret, after all our pains and care to give them their messes in due order and season, keeping their lodgings as clean and sweet as possible, and enduring so much misery and stench so long among a parcel of creatures nastier than swine, and after all our expectations to be defeated by their mortality....

No gold-finders can endure so much noisome slavery as they do who carry Negroes; for those have some respite and satisfaction, but we endure twice the misery; and yet by their mortality our voyages are ruin'd, and we pine and fret ourselves to death, and take so much pains to so little purpose.

From Thomas Phillips, *"Journal," A Collection of Voyages and Travels*, Vol. VI, ed. by Awnsham and John Churchill (London, 1746), as quoted in Thomas Howard, ed., *Black Voyage: Eyewitness Accounts of the Atlantic Slave Trade* (Boston: Little, Brown and Company, 1971), pp. 85–87.

than did free European settlers or European indentured servants. The conditions of slaves' passage across the Atlantic were wretched. (See "A Slave Trader Describes the Atlantic Passage.") Quarters were unspeakably cramped, food was bad, disease was rampant. Many Africans died during the crossing. There were always more African men than women transported, so it was difficult to keep any form of traditional African extended family structures in place. During the passage and later, many Africans attempted to recreate such structures among themselves, even if

A Dramatic Moment in the Transatlantic World: Copley's Watson and the Shark

John Singleton Copley, American, 1738–1815. *Watson and the Shark*, 1778. Oil on canvas, 72 1/4 × 90 3/8 in. Gift of Mrs. George von Lengerke Meyer. Courtesy, Museum of Fine Arts, Boston. Reproduced with permission. © 1999 Museum of Fine Arts, Boston. All Rights Reserved.

*B*oth the career of the North American born painter John Singleton Copley (1738–1815) and his monumental painting, *Watson and the Shark* (1778) illustrate the economic and cultural interconnections of the eighteenth-century transatlantic world. Copley was born in Massachusetts and became an accomplished portrait painter of the Boston elite. When hostilities erupted between Britain and the colonies, Copley moved to London in 1774, where his reputation had preceded him. He never returned to America.

In Britain, he undertook commissions for *history painting*, then considered the most prestigious subject for artists. Traditionally, history painting drew its subject matter from mythology, biblical narratives, or ancient history, but Copley was interested in portraying contemporary events. His figures were modern people, dressed in modern clothing but striking poses taken from classical and Renaissance art.

History painting claimed to convey a moral message usually of heroism, patriotism, or self-sacrifice. In 1778 Copley completed *Watson and the Shark*, recounting the experience of Brook Watson's rescue, as a boy of 14 in 1749, from the jaws of a shark in the harbor of Havana, Cuba. Watson, who later became Lord Mayor of London, lost most of his leg in the attack, but regarded his rescue and subsequent success as a merchant as an inspiring example to others who had encountered adversity.

In portraying the terrifying moment just before Watson's rescue, Copley presents the event as a profound drama, which he invites the viewer to attend. By seeking to evoke a powerful emotional response from the viewer, Copley was working in the category of art known at the time as the *sublime*. Yet Copley also used his power as a portraitist to depict each man in the painting as a real person, not as some allegorical figure.

Watson and the Shark is also one of the first paintings to prominently depict an African American. The black man in the middle of the painting holds the rope that will soon be used to rescue Watson. His presence also places the action in the world of the plantation economy and transatlantic trade. It is not clear whether he is a slave or whether, like Olaudah Equiano in the following document, a former slave now working as a sailor in the commercial shipping trade.

In several respects, this painting illustrates the interconnectedness of the eighteenth-century transatlantic world. Copley is an American artist working in London. The action occurs in a Spanish colony during a commercial venture. The person being rescued is an English subject who will become a rich merchant. The boat holds a cross section of races and cultures from Africa, Europe, and the Americas that characterized the world of the plantation economies.

Watson and the Shark is also important in art history for another reason. Through the contrasts of light and dark, Copley set out to achieve a dramatic painting of human beings in combat with powerful natural forces—the sea, the wind, and the shark. This would become a major theme of the late eighteenth- and early nineteenth-century artistic and literary movement known as Romanticism. *Watson and the Shark* stands as a major forerunner of this new direction of painting and taste.

Sources: Jules Prown, *John Singleton Copley* (Cambridge, Mass.: Harvard University Press, 1966); John Wilmerding, *American Art* (New York: Penguin Books, 1976); Theodore Stebbins, Jr. et al., *A New World: Masterpieces of American Painting 1760–1910* (Boston: Museum of Fine Arts, 1983), pp. 210–211; Hugh Honour, *The Image of the Black in Western Art*, Vol 4, Part I., *From the American Revolution to World War I: Slave and Liberators* (Cambridge, Mass.: Harvard University Press, 1989).

they were not actually related by direct family ties. (See Olaudah Equiano Recalls His Experience at the Slave Market in Barbados.")

In the Americas, the slave population stood divided among new Africans recently arrived, old Africans who had lived there for some years, and creoles who were the descendants of earlier generations of African slaves. Plantation owners preferred the two latter groups, who were accustomed to the life of slavery. They sold for higher prices. The newly arrived Africans were subjected to a process known as *seasoning* whereby they were prepared for the laborious discipline of slavery and made to understand that they were no longer free. The process might involve receiving new names, acquiring new work skills, and learning, to an extent, the local European language. In some cases, newly arrived Africans would work in a kind of apprentice relationship to an older African slave of similar ethnic background. Other slaves were broken into slave labor through work on field gangs. Occasionally, plantation owners would prefer to buy younger Africans, whom they thought might be more easily acculturated to the labor conditions of the Americas. Generally, it was only such recently arrived Africans, seasoned in the West Indies, whom North American plantation owners were willing to purchase.

LANGUAGE AND CULTURE   The plantation to which the slaves eventually arrived always lay in a more or less isolated rural setting, but its inhabitants usually could visit their counterparts on other plantations or in nearby towns on market days. Within the sharply restricted confines of slavery, the recently arrived Africans were able at least for a time to sustain elements of their own culture and social structures. From the West Indies southward throughout the eighteenth century, there were more people whose first language was African rather than European. For example, Coromantee was the predominant language on Jamaica. In South Carolina and on St. Domingue, Kikongo was the language most commonly spoken among African slaves. It would take more than two generations for the colonial language to dominate, and even then what often resulted was a dialect combining an African and a European language.

Through these languages, Africans on plantation estates could organize themselves into *nations* with similar, though not necessarily identical, ethnic ties to regions of West Africa. The loyalty achieved through a shared African language in the American setting created a solidarity among African slaves that was wider than what in Africa had probably been a primary loyalty to a village. These nations

organized and sustained by the plantation experience might also become the basis for a wide variety of religious communities among African slaves that might have some kind of roots in their African experience. In this manner, some Africans maintained a loyalty to the Islamic faith of their homeland.

Many of the African nations on plantations, such as those of Brazil, organized lay brotherhoods that carried out various kinds of charitable work within the slave communities. In the Americas, the various African nations would elect their own kings and queens, who might preside over gatherings of the members of the nation drawn from various plantations.

The shared language of a particular African nation in an American setting provided a means for exclusive communication among slaves on the occasions of revolts such as that in South Carolina in 1739, in Jamaica in the early 1760s, and, most successfully, during the Haitian Revolution of the 1790s. In the South Carolina revolt, the slave owners believed that their slaves had communicated among themselves by playing African drums. In the aftermath of the revolt, the owners attempted to suppress the presence of such drum playing in the slave community.

DAILY LIFE   The life conditions of plantation slaves differed from colony to colony. Black slaves living in Portuguese areas had the fewest legal protections. In the Spanish colonies, the church attempted to provide some protection for black slaves, but devoted more effort toward protecting the Native Americans. Slave codes were developed in the British and the French colonies during the seventeenth century, but they provided only the most limited protection to slaves while assuring dominance to owners. Virtually all slave owners feared a revolt, and legislation and other regulations were intended to prevent one. All slave laws favored the master rather than the slave. Slave masters were permitted to whip slaves and inflict other exceedingly harsh corporal punishment. Furthermore, slaves were often forbidden to gather in large groups lest they plan a revolt. In most of these slave societies, the marriages of slaves were not recognized by law. Legally, the children of slaves continued to be slaves and were owned by the owner of their parents.

The daily life of most slaves during these centuries was one of hard agricultural labor, poor diet, and inadequate housing. Slave families could be separated by the owner during his life or sold separately after his death. Their welfare and their lives were sacrificed to the continuing expansion of the sugar, rice, and tobacco plantations that

Olaudah Equiano Recalls His Experience at the Slave Market in Barbados

Olaudah Equiano composed one of the most popular and influential slave narratives of the late eighteenth and early nineteenth centuries. He had led a remarkable life. Born in West Africa in what is today Nigeria, he spent his early life among the Ibo. He was captured and sold into slavery, making the dreaded Atlantic crossing described in the previous document. In the passage that follows, he recounts his arrival in Barbados and the experience of cultural disorientation, sale into slavery, and seeing Africans separated from their families. Equiano's life did not end in slavery, the most destructive aspects of which he also described in vivid detail. He achieved his freedom and then undertook an adventuresome life on various commercial and military ships plying the Caribbean, the Atlantic, and the Mediterranean. He also made a trip to the Arctic Ocean. Equiano's account consequently describes not only the life of a person taken from Africa and sold into American slavery, but also the life of a person who, once free, explored the entire transatlantic world. His autobiographical narrative, which first appeared in 1789 and displayed Equiano's wide reading, served two purposes for the antislavery campaign that commenced in the second half of the eighteenth century. (See "The West & the World," pp. 736–737.) First, it provided a firsthand report of the slave experience in crossing from Africa to America. Second, his powerful rhetoric and clear arguments demonstrated that, if free, Africans could achieve real personal independence. Many defenders of slavery had denied that Africans possessed the character and intelligence to be free persons.

❖ *What were the fears of the Africans on the slave ship as they approached the port? How were older slaves in Barbados used to calm their fears? How did the sale of slaves proceed? What happened to African families in the process of the sale?*

At last, we came in sight...of Barbados,...and we soon anchored...off Bridgetown. Many merchants and planters now came on board... They put us in separate parcels, and examined us attentively. They also made us jump, and pointed to the land, signifying we were to go there. We thought by this we should be eaten by these ugly men, as they appeared to us; and when, soon after we were all put down under the deck again, there was much dread and trembling among us, and nothing but bitter cries to be heard all the night from these apprehension, insomuch that at last the white people got some old slaves from the land to pacify us. They told us we were not to be eaten, but to work, and were soon to go on land, where were should see many of our country people. This report eased us much....We were conducted immediately to the merchant's yard, where we were all pent up together like so many sheep in a fold, without regard to sex or age. As every object was new to me, everything filled me with surprise...and indeed I thought these people were full of nothing but magical arts....We were not many days in the merchant's custody before we were sold after their usual manner which was this: On a signal given (as the beat of a drum), the buyers rush at once into the yard where the slaves are confined, and make choice of that parcel they like best. The noise and clamour with which this is attended, and the eagerness visible in the countenances of the buyers, serve not a little to increase the apprehension of the terrified Africans, who may well be supposed to consider them as the ministers of that destruction to which they think themselves devoted. In this manner, without scruple, relations and friends separate, most of them never to see each other again. I remember in the vessel in which I was brought over, in the men's apartment, there were several brothers who, in the sale, were sold in different lots; and it was very moving on this occasion to see and hear their cries at parting.... Surely this is a new refinement in cruelty, which, while it has no advantage to atone for it, thus aggravates distress, and adds fresh horrors even to the wretchedness of slavery.

From *The Interesting Narrative of the Life of Olaudah Equiano or Gustavus Vassa, The African, Written by Himself* (first published 1789), as quoted in Henry Louis Gates, Jr., and William L., Andrews, eds., *Pioneers of the Black Atlantic: Five Slave Narratives from the Enlightenment, 1772–1815* (Washington, DC: Counterpoint, 1998), pp. 221–223.

TO BE SOLD on board the Ship *Bance-Island*, on tuesday the 6th of *May* next, at *Ashley-Ferry*; a choice cargo of about 250 fine healthy **NEGROES**, just arrived from the Windward & Rice Coast. —The utmost care has already been taken, and shall be continued, to keep them free from the least danger of being infected with the SMALL-POX, no boat having been on board, and all other communication with people from *Charles-Town* prevented.

Austin, Laurens, & Appleby.

N. B. Full one Half of the above Negroes have had the SMALL-POX in their own Country.

Those Africans who survived the voyage across the Atlantic were immediately sold into slavery in the Americas. This slave-auction notice relates to a group of slaves whose ship had stopped at Charleston, South Carolina, and then landed elsewhere in the region to auction its human cargo. Notice the concern to assure potential buyers that the slaves were healthy. Corbis

made their owners wealthy and that produced goods for European consumers. Scholars have sometimes concluded that slaves in one area lived better than in another. Today, it is generally accepted that all the slaves in plantation societies led exposed and difficult lives with little variation among them.

CONVERSION TO CHRISTIANITY The African slaves who were transported to the Americas, were, like the Native Americans, eventually converted in most cases to Christianity. In the Spanish, French, and Portuguese domains, they became Roman Catholics, and in the English colonies they became Protestants of one denomination or another. Both forms of Christianity preached to slaves the acceptance of their situation and a natural social hierarchy with masters at the top.

While African religion of a systematic character eventually disappeared, especially in the British colonies, some African religious practices survived in muted forms, gradually separated from African religious belief. These included an African understanding of nature and the cosmos and the belief in witches and other people with special spiritual powers, such as conjurers, healers, and practitioners of voodoo. Although slaves did manage to mix Christianity with their previous African religions, their conversion to Christianity was nonetheless another example, like that of the Native Americans, of the crushing of a set of non-European cultural values in the context of the New World economies and social structures.

EUROPEAN RACIAL ATTITUDES The European settlers in the Americas and the slave traders also carried with them prejudices against black Africans. Many Europeans considered Africans to be savages or less than civilized. Still others looked down on them simply because they were slaves. Both Christians and Muslims had shared these attitudes in the Mediterranean world, where slavery had for so long existed. Furthermore, many European languages and cultures attached negative connotations to the idea and image of blackness. In virtually all these plantation societies, race was an important element in keeping black slaves in a position of marked subservience. Although racial thinking in regard to slavery became important primarily in the nineteenth century, the fact of slaves being differentiated from the rest of the population by race, as well as by their being chattel property, was fundamental to the system. All of these factors formed the racial prejudice that continues to plague society today in the former slave-owning regions.

The plantations that stretched from the middle Atlantic colonies of North America through the West Indies and into Brazil constituted a vast corridor of slave societies in which social and economic subordination was based on both involuntary servitude and race. These societies had not existed before the European discovery and exploitation of the resources of the Americas. In its extent and totality of dependence on slave labor and racial differences, this kind of society was novel in both European and world history. As already noted, its social and economic influence touched not only the plantation societies themselves, but West Africa, western Europe, and New England. It existed from the sixteenth century through the second half of the nineteenth century, when the emancipation of slaves had been completed through the slave revolt of Saint Domingue (1794), British outlawing of the slave trade (1807), the Latin American wars of independence, the Emancipation Proclamation of 1863 in the United States, and the Brazilian emancipation of 1888. To the present day, every society in which plantation slavery once existed still contends with the long-term effects of that institution.

Mid-Eighteenth-Century Wars

From the standpoint of international relations, the state system of the middle of the eighteenth century was quite unstable and tended to lead the major states of Europe into periods of prolonged warfare. The statesmen of the period generally assumed that warfare could be used to further national interests. There were essentially no forces or powers who saw it in their interest to prevent war or to maintain peace. Because eighteenth-century wars before the French Revolution were fought by professional armies and navies, civilian populations were rarely drawn deeply into the conflicts. Wars were not associated with domestic political or social upheaval, and peace was not associated with the achievement of international stability. Consequently, periods of peace at the conclusion of a war were often viewed simply as times when a nation might become strong enough to recommence warfare at a later period for the purpose of seizing another nation's territory or of invading another empire's area of trading monopoly.

There were two fundamental areas of great power rivalry: the overseas empires and central and eastern Europe. Alliances and general strategic concerns repeatedly interrelated these regions of conflict.

The War of Jenkins's Ear

In the middle of the eighteenth century, the West Indies had become a hotbed of trade rivalry. Spain attempted to tighten its monopoly, and English smugglers, shippers, and pirates attempted to pierce it. Matters came to a climax in the late 1730s.

The Treaty of Utrecht (1713) gave two special privileges to Great Britain in the Spanish Empire. The British received a thirty-year *asiento*, or contract, to furnish slaves to the Spanish. Britain also gained the right to send one ship each year to the trading fair at Portobello, a major Caribbean seaport on the Panamanian coast. These two privileges allowed British traders and smugglers potential inroads into the Spanish market. Little but friction arose from those rights. During the night, offshore, British ships often resupplied the annual legal Portobello ship with additional goods as it lay in port. Much to the chagrin of the British, the Spanish government took its own alleged trading monopoly seriously and maintained coastal patrols, which boarded and searched English vessels to look for contraband.

In 1731, during one such boarding operation, there was a fight, and the Spaniards cut off the ear of an English captain named Robert Jenkins. Thereafter he carried about his severed ear preserved in a jar of brandy. This incident was of little importance until 1738, when Jenkins appeared before the British Parliament, reportedly brandishing his ear as an example of Spanish atrocities to British merchants in the West Indies. The British merchant and West Indies interests put great pressure on Parliament to relieve Spanish intervention in their trade. Sir Robert Walpole (1676–1745), the British prime minister, could not resist these pressures. In late 1739, Great Britain went to war with Spain. This war might have been a relatively minor incident, but because of developments in continental European politics, it became the opening encounter to a series of European wars fought across the world until 1815.

The War of the Austrian Succession (1740–1748)

In December 1740, after being king of Prussia for less than seven months, Frederick II seized the Austrian province of Silesia in eastern Germany. The invasion shattered the provisions of the Pragmatic Sanction (see Chapter 15) and upset the continental balance of power as established by the Treaty of Utrecht. The young king of Prussia had treated the House of Habsburg simply as another German state rather than as the leading power in the region. Silesia itself rounded out Prussia's possessions, and Frederick was determined to keep his ill-gotten prize.

MARIA THERESA PRESERVES THE HABSBURG EMPIRE The Prussian seizure of Silesia could have marked the opening of a general hunting season on Habsburg holdings and the beginning of revolts by Habsburg subjects. Instead, it led to new political allegiances. Maria Theresa's great achievement was not the reconquest of Silesia, which eluded her, but the preservation of the Habsburg Empire as a major political power.

Maria Theresa was then only twenty-three and had succeeded to the Habsburg realms only two months before the invasion. She won loyalty and support from her various subjects not merely through her heroism, but, more specifically, by granting new privileges to the nobility. Most significant, the empress recognized Hungary as the most important of her crowns and promised the Magyars considerable local autonomy. She thus preserved the Habsburg state, but at considerable cost to the power of the central monarchy.

Hungary would continue to be, as it had been in the past, a particularly troublesome area in the Habsburg Empire. When the monarchy enjoyed periods of strength and security, guarantees made to Hun-

Maria Theresa of Austria provided the leadership that saved the Habsburg Empire from possible disintegration after the Prussian invasion of Silesia in 1740.
Kunsthistorisches Museum, Vienna

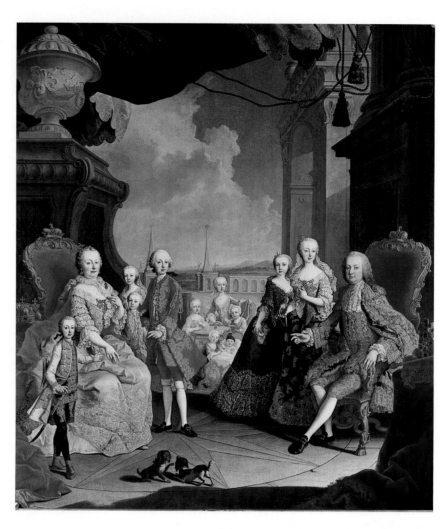

gary could be ignored. At times of weakness or when the Magyars could stir enough opposition, the monarchy promised new concessions.

FRANCE DRAWS GREAT BRITAIN INTO THE WAR   The war over the Austrian succession and the British–Spanish commercial conflict could have remained separate disputes. What quickly united them was the role of France. Just as British merchant interests had pushed Sir Robert Walpole into war, a group of aggressive court aristocrats compelled the elderly Cardinal Fleury (1653–1743), first minister of Louis XV, to abandon his planned naval attack on British trade and instead to support the Prussian aggression against Austria, the traditional enemy of France. This was among the more fateful decisions in French history.

In the first place, aid to Prussia consolidated a new and powerful state in Germany. That new power could, and indeed later did, endanger France. Second, the French move against Austria brought Great Britain into the Continental war, as Britain sought to make sure that the Low Countries remained in the friendly hands of Austria, not France. In 1744 the

British–French conflict expanded beyond the Continent, as France decided to support Spain against Britain in the New World. As a result, French military and economic resources were badly divided. France could not bring sufficient strength to the colonial struggle. Having chosen to continue the old struggle with Austria, France lost the struggle for the future against Great Britain. The war ended in stalemate in 1748 with the Treaty of Aix-la-Chapelle. Prussia retained Silesia, and Spain renewed the *asiento* agreement with Great Britain. Most observers rightly thought the treaty was a truce rather than a permanent peace.

The "Diplomatic Revolution" of 1756

Before the rivalries again erupted into war, a dramatic shift of alliances took place. In January 1756 Prussia and Great Britain signed the Convention of Westminster, a defensive alliance aimed at preventing the entry of foreign troops into the Germanies. Frederick II feared invasions by both Russia and France. The convention meant that Great

Britain, the ally of Austria since the wars of Louis XIV, had now joined forces with Austria's major eighteenth-century enemy.

Maria Theresa was despondent over this development. It delighted her foreign minister, Prince Wenzel Anton Kaunitz (1711–1794), however. He had long hoped for an alliance with France to help dismember Prussia. The Convention of Westminster made possible this alliance, which would have been unthinkable a few years earlier. France was agreeable because Frederick had not consulted with its ministers before coming to his understanding with Britain. So, later in May 1756, France and Austria signed a defensive alliance. Kaunitz had succeeded in completely reversing the direction that French foreign policy had followed since the sixteenth century. France would now fight to restore Austrian supremacy in central Europe.

The Seven Years' War (1756–1763)

Although the Treaty of Aix-la-Chapelle had brought peace in Europe, France and Great Britain continued to struggle unofficially on the colonial front. There were constant clashes between their settlers in the Ohio River valley and in upper New England. These were the prelude to what is known in American history as the French and Indian War. Once again, however, Frederick II precipitated a European war that extended into a colonial theater.

FREDERICK THE GREAT OPENS HOSTILITIES   In August 1756, Frederick II opened what would become the Seven Years' War by invading Saxony. Frederick considered this to be a preemptive strike against a conspiracy by Saxony, Austria, and France to destroy Prussian power. He regarded the invasion as a continuation of the defensive strategy of the Convention of Westminster. The invasion itself, however, created the very destructive alliance that Frederick feared. In the spring of 1757, France and Austria made a new alliance dedicated to the destruction of Prussia. They were eventually joined by Sweden, Russia, and many of the smaller German states.

Two factors in addition to Frederick's stubborn leadership (it was after this war that he came to be called Frederick the Great) saved Prussia. First, Britain furnished considerable financial aid. Second, in 1762 Empress Elizabeth of Russia died. Her successor was Tsar Peter III (he was murdered the same year), whose admiration for Frederick was boundless. He immediately made peace with Prussia, thus relieving Frederick of one enemy and allowing him to hold off Austria

and France. The Treaty of Hubertusburg of 1763 ended the continental conflict with no significant changes in prewar borders. Silesia remained Prussian, and Prussia clearly stood among the ranks of the great powers.

WILLIAM PITT'S STRATEGY FOR WINNING NORTH AMERICA   The survival of Prussia was less impressive to the rest of Europe than were the victories of Great Britain in every theater of conflict. The architect of these victories was William Pitt the Elder (1708–1778). Pitt was a person of colossal ego and administrative genius who had grown up in a commercial family. Although he had previously criticized British involvement with the Continent, once he became secretary of state in charge of the war in 1757, he reversed himself and pumped huge financial subsidies into the coffers of Frederick the Great. He regarded the German conflict as a way to divert French resources and attention from the colonial struggle. He later boasted of having won America on the plains of Germany.

North America was the center of Pitt's real concern. Put quite simply, he wanted all of North America east of the Mississippi for Great Britain, and that was exactly what he won. He sent more than 40,000 regular English and colonial troops

William Pitt the Elder guided Great Britain to a stunning victory in the Seven Years' War. National Portrait Gallery, London

against the French in Canada. Never had so many soldiers been devoted to a field of colonial warfare. He achieved unprecedented cooperation with the American colonies, whose leaders realized that they might finally defeat their French neighbors.

The French government was unwilling and unable to direct similar resources against the English in America. Their military administration was corrupt, the military and political commands in Canada were divided, and France could not adequately provision its North American forces. In September 1759, on the Plains of Abraham, overlooking the valley of the Saint Lawrence River at Quebec City, the British army under General James Wolfe defeated the French under Lieutenant General Louis Joseph de Montcalm. The French Empire in Canada was ending.

Pitt's colonial vision, however, extended beyond the Saint Lawrence Valley and the Great Lakes Basin. The major islands of the French West Indies fell to British fleets. Income from the sale of captured sugar helped finance the British war effort. British slave interests captured the bulk of the French slave trade. Between 1755 and 1760, the value of the French colonial trade fell by more than 80 percent. In India, the British forces under the command of Robert Clive defeated the French in 1757 at the Battle of Plassey. This victory opened the way for the eventual conquest of Bengal in northeast India and later of all India by the British East India Company. Never had Great Britain or any other European power experienced such a complete worldwide military victory.

THE TREATY OF PARIS OF 1763 The Treaty of Paris of 1763 reflected somewhat less of a victory than Britain had won on the battlefield. Pitt was no longer in office.

Conflicts of the Mid-Eighteenth Century

1713	Treaty of Utrecht
1739	Outbreak of War of Jenkins's Ear between England and Spain
1740	War of the Austrian Succession commences
1748	Treaty of Aix-la-Chapelle
1756	Convention of Westminster between England and Prussia
1756	Seven Years' War opens
1757	Battle of Plassey
1759	British forces capture Quebec
1763	Treaty of Hubertusburg
1763	Treaty of Paris

George III (r. 1760–1820) and Pitt had quarreled over policy, and the minister had departed. His replacement was the earl of Bute (1713–1792), a favorite of the new monarch. Bute was responsible for the peace settlement. Britain received all of Canada, the Ohio River valley, and the eastern half of the Mississippi River valley. Britain returned Pondicherry and Chandernagore in India and the West Indian sugar islands of Guadeloupe and Martinique to the French.

The Seven Years' War had been a vast conflict. Tens of thousands of soldiers and sailors had been killed or wounded. Major battles had been fought around the globe. At great internal sacrifice, Prussia had permanently wrested Silesia from Austria and had turned the Holy Roman Empire into an empty shell. Habsburg power now depended largely on the Hungarian domains. France, though still having sources of colonial income, was no longer a great colonial power. The Spanish Empire remained largely intact, but the British were still determined to penetrate its markets.

On the Indian subcontinent, the British East India Company was able to continue to impose its own authority on the decaying indigenous governments. The ramifications of that situation would extend until the middle of the twentieth century. In North America, the British government faced the task of organizing its new territories. From this time until World War II, Great Britain was a world power, not just a European one.

The quarter century of warfare also caused a long series of domestic crises among the European powers. The French defeat convinced many people in that nation of the necessity for political and administrative reform. The financial burdens of the wars had astounded all contemporaries. Every power had to begin to find ways to increase revenues to pay its war debt and to finance its preparation for the next combat. Nowhere did this search for revenue lead to more far-ranging consequences than in the British colonies in North America.

The American Revolution and Europe

The revolt of the British colonies in North America was an event in both transatlantic and European history. It erupted from problems of revenue collection common to all the major powers after the Seven Years' War. The War of the American Revolution also continued the conflict between France and Great Britain. The French support of the Americans deepened the existing financial and administrative difficulties of the French monarchy.

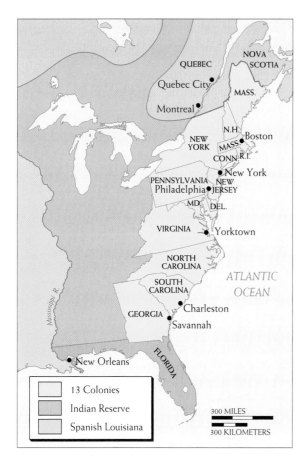

ed to produce more revenue from imports into the colonies by the rigorous collection of what was actually a lower tax. Smugglers who violated the law were to be tried in admiralty courts without juries. The next year, Parliament passed the Stamp Act, which put a tax on legal documents and certain other items such as newspapers. The British considered these taxes legal because the decision to collect them had been approved by Parliament. They regarded them as just because the money was to be spent in the colonies.

The Americans responded that they alone, through their assemblies, had the right to tax themselves and that they were not represented in Parliament. Furthermore, the expenditure in the colonies of the revenue levied by Parliament did not reassure the colonists. They feared that if colonial government were financed from outside, they would lose control over it. In October 1765, the Stamp Act Congress met in America and drew up a protest to the crown. (See "The Stamp Act Congress Addresses George III.") There was much disorder in the colonies, particularly in Massachusetts, roused by groups known as the Sons of Liberty. The colonists agreed to refuse to import British goods. In 1766 Parliament repealed the Stamp Act, but through the Declaratory Act said that it had the power to legislate for the colonies.

MAP 17–2   NORTH AMERICA IN 1763   *In the year of the victory over France, the English colonies lay along the Atlantic seaboard. The difficulties of organizing authority over the previous French territory in Canada and west of the Appalachian Mountains would contribute to the coming of the American Revolution.*

Resistance to the Imperial Search for Revenue

After the Treaty of Paris of 1763, the British government faced two imperial problems. The first was the sheer cost of empire, which the British felt they could no longer carry alone. The national debt had risen considerably, as had domestic taxation. Since the American colonies had been the chief beneficiaries of the conflict, the British felt that it was rational for the colonies henceforth to bear part of the cost of their protection and administration. The second problem was the vast expanse of new territory in North America that the British had to organize. This included all the land from the mouth of the Saint Lawrence River to the Mississippi River, with its French settlers and, more importantly, its Native American possessors. (See Map 17–2.)

The British drive for revenue began in 1764 with the passage of the Sugar Act under the ministry of George Grenville (1712–1770). The measure attempt-

This view of the "Boston Massacre" of March 5, 1770 by Paul Revere owes more to propaganda than fact. There was no order to fire and the innocent citizens portrayed here were really an angry, violent mob.
© Collection of The New-York Historical Society, New York City

The Stamp Act Congress Addresses George III

In 1765, the Stamp Act Congress met to protest the British imposition of taxes on the colonies. The resolutions of the Congress made it very clear that American leaders believed that Great Britain had no right to impose such taxation.

✢ *What are the rights of English citizens that the Americans claim? How has the Stamp Act violated them? Why do they believe that the British Parliament has no right to tax them? Do the colonists believe it possible for themselves to be represented in Parliament?*

The Members of this Congress, sincerely devoted, with the warmest sentiments of affection and duty to His Majesty's person and government...and with minds deeply impressed by a sense of the present and impending misfortunes of the British colonies on this continent; having considered as maturely as time will permit, the circumstances of the said colonies, esteem it our indispensable duty to make the following declarations of our humble opinion, respecting the most essential rights and liberties of the colonists, and of the grievances under which they labor, by reason of several late acts of Parliament.

I. That His Majesty's subjects in these colonies, own the same allegiance to the crown of Great Britain, that is owing from his subjects born within the realm, and all due subordination to that august body the Parliament of Great Britain.

II. That His Majesty's liege subjects in these colonies are entitled to all the inherent rights and liberties of his natural born subjects, within the kingdom of Great Britain.

III. That it is inseparably essential to the freedom of a people, and the undoubted right of Englishmen, that no taxes be imposed on them but with their own consent, given personally, or by their representatives.

IV. That the people of these colonies are not, and cannot, be represented in the House of Commons in Great Britain.

V. That the only representatives of the people of these colonies are persons chosen therein by themselves, and that no taxes ever have been, or can be constitutionally imposed on them, but by their respective legislatures.

VI. That all supplies to the crown being free gifts of the people, it is unreasonable and inconsistent with the principles and spirit of the British constitution, for the people of Great Britain to grant to His Majesty the property of the colonists.

VII. That trial by jury, is the inherent and invaluable right of every British subject in these colonies.

VIII. That the late act of Parliament entitled, An act for granting and supplying certain stamp duties, and other duties, in the British colonies and plantations, in America, etc. by imposing taxes on the inhabitants of these colonies, and the said act, and several other acts, by extending the jurisdiction of the courts of admiralty beyond its ancient limits, have a manifest tendency to subvert the rights and liberties of the colonists.

From the *Journal of the First Congress of the American Colonies...1765* (New York, 1845), pp. 27–29, as quoted in Oscar Handlin, ed., *Readings in American History* (New York: Alfred A. Knopf, 1957), pp. 116–117.

The Stamp Act crisis set the pattern for the next ten years. Parliament, under the leadership of a royal minister, would approve revenue or administrative legislation. The Americans would then resist by reasoned argument, economic pressure, and violence. Then the British would repeal the legislation, and the process would begin again. Each time, tempers on both sides became more frayed and positions more irreconcilable. With each clash, the Americans more fully developed their own thinking about political liberty.

The Crisis and Independence

In 1767 Charles Townshend (1725–1767), as Chancellor of the Exchequer, the British finance minister, led Parliament to pass a series of revenue acts relating to colonial imports. The colonists again resisted. The ministry sent over its own customs agents to administer the laws. To protect these new officers, the British sent troops to Boston in 1768. The obvious tensions resulted. In March 1770, the Boston Massacre, in which British troops killed

Thomas Paine was the author of Common Sense, *a political pamphlet published early in 1776 that helped galvanize American opinion in favor of independence.*
Bildarchiv Preussischer Kulturbesitz

five citizens, took place. That same year, Parliament repealed all of the Townshend duties except the one on tea.

In May 1773, Parliament passed a new law relating to the sale of tea by the East India Company. The measure permitted the direct importation of tea into the American colonies. It actually lowered the price of tea while retaining the tax imposed without the colonists' consent. In some cities, the colonists refused to permit the unloading of the tea; in Boston, a shipload of tea was thrown into the harbor.

The British ministry of Lord North (1732–1792) was determined to assert the authority of Parliament over the resistant colonies. During 1774, Parliament passed a series of laws known in American history as the Intolerable Acts. These measures closed the port of Boston, reorganized the government of Massachusetts, allowed troops to be quartered in private homes, and removed the trials of royal customs officials to England. The same year, Parliament approved the Quebec Act for the future administration of Canada. It extended the boundaries of Quebec to include the Ohio River valley. The Americans regarded the

Quebec Act as an attempt to prevent the extension of their mode of self-government westward beyond the Appalachian Mountains.

During these years, citizens critical of British policy had established committees of correspondence throughout the colonies. They made the various sections of the eastern seaboard aware of common problems and aided united action. In September 1774, these committees organized the gathering of the First Continental Congress in Philadelphia. This body hoped to persuade Parliament to restore self-government in the colonies and to abandon its attempt at direct supervision of colonial affairs. Conciliation, however, was not forthcoming. By April 1775, the Battles of Lexington and Concord had been fought. In June, the colonists suffered defeat at the Battle of Bunker Hill. Despite that defeat, the colonial assemblies soon began to meet under their own authority rather than under that of the king.

The Second Continental Congress gathered in May 1775. It still sought conciliation with Britain, but the pressure of events led it to begin to conduct the government of the colonies. By August 1775, George III had declared the colonies in rebellion. During the winter, Thomas Paine's (1737–1809) pamphlet *Common Sense* galvanized public opinion in favor of separation from Great Britain. A colonial army and navy were organized. In April 1776, the Continental Congress opened American ports to the trade of all nations. And on July 4, 1776, the Continental Congress adopted the Declaration of Independence. Thereafter, the War of the American Revolution continued until 1781, when the forces of George Washington defeated those of Lord Cornwallis at Yorktown. Early in 1778, however, the war had widened into a European conflict when Benjamin Franklin (1706–1790) persuaded the French government to support the rebellion. In 1779, the Spanish also came to the aid of the colonies. The 1783 Treaty of Paris concluded the conflict, and the thirteen American colonies had established their independence.

American Political Ideas

The political ideas of the American colonists had largely arisen out of the struggle of seventeenth-century English aristocrats and gentry against the absolutism of the Stuart monarchs. The American colonists looked to the English Revolution of 1688 as having established many of their own fundamental political liberties, as well as those of the English. The colonists claimed that, through the measures imposed from

The Horse America throwing his Master, an eighteenth-century cartoon (1779) mocking George III about the rebellion of the American colonies. Although he tried to reassert some of the monarchical influence on Britain's politics that had eroded under George I and George II, the first two Hanoverian kings, George III never sought to make himself a tyrant as his critics charged. The Granger Collection

1763 to 1776, George III and the British Parliament were attacking those liberties and dissolving the bonds of moral and political allegiance that had formerly united the two peoples. Consequently, the colonists employed a theory that had developed to justify an aristocratic rebellion to support their own popular revolution.

These Whig political ideas, largely derived from the writings of John Locke, were, however, only a part of the English ideological heritage that affected the Americans. Throughout the eighteenth century, they had become familiar with a series of British political writers called the Commonwealthmen, who held republican political ideas that had their intellectual roots in the most radical thought of the Puritan revolution. During the early eighteenth century, these writers, the most influential of whom were John Trenchard (1662–1723) and Thomas Gordon (d. 1750) in *Cato's Letters* (1720–1723), had relentlessly criticized the government patronage and parliamentary management of Sir Robert Walpole and his successors. They argued that such government was corrupt and that it undermined liberty. They regarded much parliamentary taxation as simply a means of financing political corruption. They also considered standing armies instruments of tyranny. In Great Britain, this republican political tradition had only a marginal impact. The writers were largely ignored because most British subjects regarded themselves as the freest people in the world. Three thousand miles away, however, colonists read the radical books and pamphlets and often accepted them at face value. The policy of Great Britain toward America following the Treaty of Paris of 1763 and certain political events in Britain had made many colonists believe that the worst fears of the Commonwealthmen were coming true. All of these events coincided with the accession of George III to the throne.

Events in Great Britain

George III (r. 1760–1820) believed that a few powerful Whig families and the ministries that they controlled had bullied and dominated his two immediate royal predecessors. George III also believed that he should have ministers of his own choice and that Parliament should function under royal rather than aristocratic management. When William Pitt resigned after a disagreement with George over war policy, the king appointed the earl of Bute as his first minister. In doing so, he ignored the great Whig families that had run the country since 1715. The king sought the aid of politicians whom the Whigs hated. Moreover, he tried to use the same kind of patronage techniques developed by Walpole to achieve royal control of the House of Commons.

Between 1761 and 1770, George tried one minister after another, but each in turn failed to gain enough support from the various factions in the House of Commons. Finally, in 1770 he turned to Lord North, who remained the king's first minister until 1782. The Whig families and other political spokespersons claimed that George III was attempting to impose a tyranny. What they meant was that the king was attempting to curb the power of a particular group of the aristocracy. George III certainly was seeking to restore more royal influence to the government of Great Britain, but he was not attempting to make himself a tyrant.

THE CHALLENGE OF JOHN WILKES   Then, in 1763 began the affair of John Wilkes (1725–1797). This London political radical and member of Parliament published a newspaper called *The North Briton*. In issue number 45 of this paper, Wilkes strongly criticized Lord Bute's handling of the peace negotiations with France. Wilkes was arrested under the authority of a general warrant issued by the secretary of state. He pleaded the privileges of a member of Parliament and was released. The courts also later ruled that the vague kind of general warrant by which he had been arrested was illegal. The House of Commons, however, ruled that issue number 45 of *The North Briton* constituted libel, and expelled Wilkes. He soon fled the country and was outlawed. Throughout these procedures there was widespread support for Wilkes, and many popular demonstrations were held in his cause.

In 1768, Wilkes returned to England and again stood for election to Parliament. He won the election, but the House of Commons, under the influence of George III's friends, refused to seat him. He was elected three more times. After the fourth election, the House of Commons simply ignored the results and seated the government-supported candidate. As had happened earlier in the decade, large, popular, unruly demonstrations of shopkeepers, artisans, and small-property owners supported Wilkes. He also received aid from some aristocratic politicians who wished to humiliate George III. Wilkes himself contended during all his troubles that his was the cause of English liberty. "Wilkes and Liberty" became the slogan of all political radicals and many noble opponents of the monarch. Wilkes was finally seated in 1774, after having become the lord mayor of London.

The American colonists followed these developments closely. Events in Britain confirmed their fears about a monarchical and parliamentary conspiracy against liberty. The king, as their Whig friends told them, was behaving like a tyrant. The Wilkes affair displayed the arbitrary power of the monarch, the corruption of the House of Commons, and the contempt of both for popular electors. That same monarch and Parliament were attempting to overturn the traditional relationship of Great Britain to its colonies by imposing parliamentary taxes. The

---

Events in Britain and America Relating to the American Revolution

1760	George III becomes king
1763	Treaty of Paris concludes the Seven Years' War
1763	John Wilkes publishes issue number 45 of *The North Briton*
1764	Sugar Act
1765	Stamp Act
1766	Sugar Act repealed and Declaratory Act passed
1767	Townshend Acts
1768	Parliament refuses to seat John Wilkes after his election
1770	Lord North becomes George III's chief minister
1770	Boston Massacre
1773	Boston Tea Party
1774	Intolerable Acts
1774	First Continental Congress
1775	Second Continental Congress
1776	Declaration of Independence
1778	France enters the war on the side of America
1778	Yorkshire Association Movement founded
1781	British forces surrender at Yorktown
1783	Treaty of Paris concludes War of the American Revolution

same government had then landed troops in Boston, changed the government of Massachusetts, and undermined the traditional right of jury trial. All of these events fulfilled too exactly the portrait of political tyranny that had developed over the years in the minds of articulate colonists.

MOVEMENT FOR PARLIAMENTARY REFORM The political influences between America and Britain operated both ways. The colonial demand for no taxation without representation and the criticism of the adequacy of the British system of representation struck at the core of the eighteenth-century British political structure. British subjects at home who were no more directly represented in the House of Commons than were the Americans could adopt the colonial arguments. The colonial questioning of the tax-levying authority of the House of Commons was related to the protest of John Wilkes. Both the Americans and Wilkes were challenging the power of the monarch and the authority of Parliament. Moreover, both the colonial leaders and Wilkes appealed over the head of legally constituted political authorities to popular opinion and popular demonstrations. Both were protesting the power of a largely self-selected aristocratic political body. The British ministry was fully aware of these broader political implications of the American troubles.

The American colonists also demonstrated to Europe how a politically restive people in the Old Regime could fight tyranny and protect political liberty. They established revolutionary, but orderly, political bodies that could function outside the existing political framework: the congress and the convention. These began with the Stamp Act Congress of 1765 and culminated in the Constitutional Convention of 1787. The legitimacy of those congresses and conventions lay not in existing law, but in the alleged consent of the governed. This approach represented a new way to found a government.

Toward the end of the War of the American Revolution, calls for parliamentary reform arose in Britain itself. The method proposed for changing the system was the extralegal Association Movement.

THE YORKSHIRE ASSOCIATION MOVEMENT By the close of the 1770s, many in Britain resented the mismanagement of the American war, the high taxes, and Lord North's ministry. In northern England in 1778, Christopher Wyvil (1740–1822), a landowner and retired clergyman, organized the Yorkshire Association Movement. Property owners, or freeholders, of Yorkshire met in a mass meeting to demand rather moderate changes in the corrupt system of parliamentary elections. They organized corresponding societies elsewhere. They intended that the association examine—and suggest reforms for—the entire government. The Association Movement was thus a popular attempt to establish an extralegal institution to reform the government.

The movement collapsed during the early 1780s because its supporters, unlike Wilkes and the American rebels, were not willing to appeal for broad popular support. Nonetheless, the agitation of the Association Movement provided many people with experience in political protest. Several of its younger figures lived to raise the issue of parliamentary reform after 1815.

Parliament was not insensitive to the demands of the Association Movement. In April 1780, the Commons passed a resolution that called for lessening the power of the crown. In 1782 Parliament adopted a measure for "economical" reform, which abolished some patronage at the disposal of the monarch. These actions, however, did not prevent George III from appointing a minister of his own choice. In 1783 shifts in Parliament obliged Lord North to form a ministry with Charles James Fox (1749–1806), a long-time critic of George III. The monarch was most unhappy with the arrangement.

In 1783 the king approached William Pitt the Younger (1759–1806), son of the victorious war minister, to manage the House of Commons. During the election of 1784, Pitt received immense patronage support from the crown and constructed a House of Commons favorable to the monarch. Thereafter, Pitt sought to formulate trade policies that would give his ministry broad popularity. In 1785, he attempted one measure of modest parliamentary reform. When it failed, the young prime minister, who had been only twenty-four at the time of his appointment, abandoned the cause of reform.

By the mid-1780s, George III had achieved a part of what he had sought since 1761. He had reasserted the influence of the monarchy in political affairs. It proved a temporary victory, because his own mental illness, which would eventually require a regency, weakened the royal power. The cost of his years of dominance had been high, however. On both sides of the Atlantic, the issue of popular sovereignty had been raised and widely discussed. The American colonies had been lost. Economically, this loss did not prove disastrous. British trade with America after independence actually increased.

Broader Impact of the American Revolution

The Americans—through their state constitutions, the Articles of Confederation, and the federal Constitution adopted in 1788—had demonstrated to

Europe the possibility of government without kings and hereditary nobilities. They had established the example of a nation in which written documents based on popular consent and popular sovereignty—rather than on divine law, natural law, tradition, or the will of kings—were the highest political and legal authority. The political novelty of these assertions should not be ignored.

As the crisis with Britain unfolded during the 1760s and 1770s, the American colonists had come to see themselves first as preserving traditional English liberties against the tyrannical crown and corrupt Parliament and then as developing a whole new sense of liberty. By the mid-1770s, the colonists had rejected monarchical government and embraced republican political ideals. They would govern themselves through elected assemblies without any presence of a monarchical authority. Once a constitution was adopted, they would insist on a Bill of Rights specifically protecting a whole series of civil liberties. The Americans would reject the aristocratic social hierarchy that had existed in the colonies. They would embrace democratic ideals—even if the franchise remained limited. They would assert the equality of white male citizens not only before the law, but in ordinary social relations. They would reject social status based on birth and inheritance and assert the necessity of the liberty for all citizens to improve their social standing and economic lot by engaging in free commercial activity. They did not free their slaves, nor did they address issues of the rights of women or of Native Americans. Yet in making their revolution, the American colonists of the eighteenth century produced a society more free than any the world had seen and one that would eventually expand the circle of political and social liberty. In all these respects, the American Revolution was a genuinely radical movement, whose influence would widen as Americans moved across the continent and as other peoples began to question traditional modes of European government.

In Perspective

During the sixteenth and seventeenth centuries the west European maritime powers established extensive commercial, mercantile empires in North and South America. The point of these empires was to extract wealth and to establish commercial advantage for the colonial power. The largest of these empires was that of Spain, but by the end of the seventeenth century Britain and France had also each established a major American presence. As a vast plantation economy emerged from the Chesapeake Bay through the southern North American Atlantic seaboard and the Caribbean south to Brazil, significant portions of these American empires became economically dependent upon slave labor, drawn from the forced immigration of Africans. Through this large slave labor force, African linguistic, social, and religious influences became major cultural factors in these regions.

During the eighteenth century, the great European powers engaged in warfare over their American empires and over their power in India. These colonial wars became entangled in dynastic wars in central and eastern Europe and resulted in worldwide mid century European conflict.

In the New World, Britain, France, and Spain battled for commercial dominance. France and Britain also clashed over their spheres of influence in India. By the third quarter of the century, Britain had succeeded in ousting France from most of its major holdings in North America and from any significant presence in India. Spain, though no longer a military power of the first order, had managed to maintain its vast colonial empire in Latin America and a large measure of its monopoly over the region's trade.

On the Continent, France, Austria, and Prussia collided over conflicting territorial and dynastic ambitions. Britain became involved to protect its continental interests and to use the continental wars to divert France from the colonial arena. With British aid, Prussia had emerged in 1763 as a major continental power. Austria had lost considerable territory to Prussia. France had accumulated a vast debt.

The midcentury conflicts in turn led to major changes in all the European states. Each of the monarchies needed more money and tried to govern itself more efficiently. This problem led Britain to attempt to tax the North American colonies, which led to a revolution and the colonies' independence. Already deeply in debt, the French monarchy aided the Americans, fell into a deeper financial crisis, and soon clashed sharply with the nobility as royal ministers tried to find new revenues. That clash eventually unleashed the French Revolution. Spain moved to administer its Latin American empire more efficiently, which increased revolutionary discontent in the early nineteenth century. In preparation for future wars, the rulers of Prussia, Austria, and Russia pursued a mode of activist government known as Enlightened Absolutism. This will be examined in the next chapter. In that regard, the mid-eighteenth-century wars set in motion most of the major political developments of the next half century.

REVIEW QUESTIONS

1. What were the fundamental ideas associated with mercantile theory? Did they work? Which European country was most successful in establishing a mercantile empire? Least successful? Why?
2. What were the main points of conflict between Britain and France in North America, the West Indies, and India? How did the triangles of trade function between the Americas, Europe, and Africa?
3. How was the Spanish colonial empire in the Americas organized and managed? What changes did the Bourbon monarchs institute in the Spanish Empire?
4. What was the nature of slavery in the Americas? How was it linked to the economies of the Americas, Europe, and Africa? In what respects was the plantation system unprecedented? What was the plantation system, and how did it contribute to the inhumane treatment of slaves?
5. The Seven Years' War was a major conflict, with battles fought around the globe. What were the results of this war? Which countries emerged in a stronger position and why?
6. Discuss the American Revolution in the context of European history. To what extent were the colonists influenced by European ideas and political developments? To what extent did their actions in turn influence Europe?

SUGGESTED READINGS

B. BAILYN, *The Ideological Origins of the American Revolution* (1967). Remains an important work illustrating the role of English radical thought in the perceptions of the American colonists.

B. BAILYN, *The Peopling of British North America: An Introduction* (1988). A study of the immigrants to the British colonies on the eve of the Revolution.

C. A. BAYLY, *Imperial Meridian: The British Empire and the World, 1780–1830* (1989). A major study of the empire after the loss of America.

I. BERLIN, *Many Thousands Gone: The First Two Centuries of Slavery in North America* (1998). The most extensive recent treatment emphasizing the differences in the slave economy during different decades.

L. BETHELL (ED.), *The Cambridge History of Latin America*, vols. 1 and 2 (1984). Excellent essays on the colonial era.

J. BLACK, *European Warfare, 1660–1815* (1994). A major, wide-ranging synthesis.

R. BLACKBURN, *The Making of New World Slavery from the Baroque to the Modern, 1492–1800* (1997). An extraordinary work.

D. BRADING, *The First America* (1991). A major study of colonial Latin America.

J. BREWER, *The Sinews of Power: War, Money, and the English State, 1688–1783* (1989). A study that emphasizes the financial power behind British military success.

J. BROOKE, *King George III* (1972). The best biography.

K. N. CHAUDHURI, *The Trading World of Asia and the English East India Company* (1978). Examines the impact of trade on both Asians and Europeans.

L. COLLEY, *Britons: Forging the Nation, 1707–1837* (1992). A major work with important discussions of the recovery from the loss of America.

P. CURTIN, *The Atlantic Slave Trade, a Census* (1969). Remains a major contribution.

D. B. DAVIS, *The Problem of Slavery in Western Culture* (1966). A brilliant and far-ranging discussion.

D. B. DAVIS, *The Problem of Slavery in the Age of Revolution, 1770–1823* (1975). A major work on both European and American history.

R. DAVIS, *The Rise of the Atlantic Economies* (1973). A major synthesis.

W. DORN, *Competition for Empire, 1740–1763* (1940). Still one of the best accounts of the mid-century struggle.

H. KLEIN, *The Middle Passage: Comparative Studies in the African Slave Trade* (1978). An overview of the movement of slaves from Africa to the Americas.

P. LANGFORD, *A Polite and Commercial People: England 1717–1783* (1989). An excellent survey covering social history, politics, the overseas wars, and the American Revolution.

J. LOCKHARDT AND S. B. SCHWARTZ, *Early Latin America: A History of Colonial Spanish America and Brazil* (1983). The standard work.

J. R. MCNEIL, *Atlantic Empires of France and Spain: Louisbourg and Havana, 1700–1763* (1985). An examination of imperial policies for two key overseas outposts.

P. MAIER, *American Scripture: Making the Declaration of Independence* (1997). Replaces previous works on the subject.

S. W. MINTZ, *Sweetness and Power: The Place of Sugar in Modern History* (1985). Traces the role of sugar in the world economy and how sugar has had an impact on world culture.

A. PAGDEN, *Lords of All the World: Ideologies of Empire in Spain, Britain, and France, 1492–1830* (1995). One of the few comparative studies of empire during this period.

J. H. PARRY, *Trade and Dominion: The European Overseas Empires in the Eighteenth Century* (1971). A comprehensive account with attention to the European impact on the rest of the world.

J. C. RILEY, *The Seven Years' War and the Old Regime in France: The Economic and Financial Toll* (1986). A useful analysis of pressures that would undermine the French monarchy.

G. RUDÉ, *Wilkes and Political Liberty* (1962). A close analysis of popular political behavior.

K. W. SCHWEIZER, *Frederick the Great, William Pitt, and Lord Bute: The Anglo–Prussian Alliance, 1756–1763* (1991). The most recent study of this complex diplomacy.

I. K. STEELE, *The English Atlantic, 1675–1740: An Exploration of Communication and Community* (1986). An exploration of culture and commerce in the transatlantic world.

R. L. STEIN, *The French Sugar Business in the Eighteenth Century* (1988). A study that covers all aspects of the French sugar trade.

J. THORNTON, *Africa and Africans in the Making of the Atlantic World, 1400–1800* (1998). A discussion of the role of Africans in the emergence of the transatlantic economy.

J. WEST, *Gunpower, Government, and War in the Mid-Eighteenth Century* (1991). A study of how warfare touched much of government.

G. S. WOOD, *The Creation of the American Republic, 1776–1787* (1969). A far-ranging work dealing with Anglo–American political thought.

G. S. WOOD, *The Radicalism of the American Revolution* (1991). A major interpretation.

The Columbian Exchange: Disease, Animals, and Agriculture

The European encounter with the Americas produced remarkable ecological transformations that have shaped the world to the present moment. The same ships that carried Europeans and Africans to the New World also transported animals, plants, and germs that had never before appeared in the Americas. There was a similar transport back to Europe and Africa. Alfred Crosby, the leading historian of the process, has named this cross-continental flow "the Columbian exchange."

Diseases Enter the Americas

With the exception of a few ships that had gone astray or, in the case of the Vikings, that had gone in search of new lands, the American continents had been biologically separated from Europe, Africa, and Asia for tens of thousands of years. In the Americas no native animals could serve as major beasts of burden except for the llama, which could not transport more than about 100 pounds. Nor did animals constitute a major source of protein for native Americans, whose diets consisted largely of maize, beans, peppers, yams, and potatoes. At the same time, the American continents included areas of vast grassland without grazing animals that would have transformed those plants into animal protein. Moreover, it also appears that native peoples had lived on the long-isolated American continents without experiencing major epidemics.

By the second voyage of Columbus (1493), that picture began to change in remarkable ways. On his return voyage to Hispaniola and other islands of the Caribbean, Columbus brought a number of animals and plants that were previously unknown to the New World. The men on all his voyages and those on subsequent European voyages also carried diseases novel to the Americas.

The diseases thus transported by Europeans ultimately accounted for the conquest of the people of the Americas as did much as the advanced European weaponry. Much controversy surrounds the question of the actual size of the populations of Native Americans in the Caribbean islands, Mexico, Peru and the North Atlantic coast. All accounts present those populations as quite significant, with those of Mexico in particular numbering many millions. Yet in the first two centuries after the encounter, wherever Europeans went either as settlers or as conquerors, extremely large numbers of Native Americans died from diseases they had never before encountered. The most deadly such disease was smallpox, which destroyed millions of people. Beyond the devastation wrought by that disease, bubonic plague, typhoid, typhus, influenza, measles, chicken pox, whooping cough, malaria, and diphtheria produced deadly results in more localized epidemics. For example, an unknown disease, but quite possibly typhus, caused major losses among the Native Americans of New England between approximately 1616 and 1619.

Native Americans appear to have been highly susceptible to these diseases because, with no earlier exposure, they lacked immunity. Wherever such outbreaks are recorded, Europeans either contracted or died from them at a much lower rate than the Native Americans. These diseases would continue to victimize Native Americans at a higher rate than Americans of European descent through the end of the nineteenth century when smallpox and measles still killed large numbers of the Plains Indian peoples of North America.

Although many historical and medical questions still surround the subject, it appears almost certain that syphilis, which became a rampant venereal dis-

Within one year of Columbus' encounter with the Americas, the event had been captured in a woodcut published in Giuliano Dati's Narrative of Columbus *(1493). Columbus' several voyages, and those of later Europeans as well, introduced not only European warfare but began a vast ecological exchange of plants, animals, and diseases between the Old and New Worlds.* The Granger Collection

ease in Europe at the close of the fifteenth century and eventually spread around the globe, originated in the New World. It seems to have been an entirely new disease, spawned through a mutation when the causal agent for yaws migrated from the Americas to new climatic settings in Europe. Until the discovery of penicillin in the 1940s, syphilis remained a major concern of public health throughout the world.

Animals and Agriculture

The introduction of European livestock to the Americas quite simply revolutionized the agriculture of two continents. The most important new animals were pigs, cattle, horses, goats, and sheep. Once transported to the New World, these animals multiplied at unprecedented rates. The

place where this first occurred was in the islands of the Caribbean, during the first forty years of Spanish settlement and exploitation. This situation established the foundation for the later Spanish conquest of both Mexico and Peru by providing the Spanish with strong breeds of animals, especially horses, acclimated to the Americas when they set out to conquer the mainland of South America.

The horse became first the animal of the conquest and then the animal of colonial Latin American culture. Native Americans had no experience with such large animals who would obey the will of a human rider. The mounted Spanish horseman struck fear into these people, and for good reason. After the conquest, however, the Americas from Mexico southward became the largest horse-breeding region of the

Nothing so destroyed the life of the Native Americans whom the Spanish encountered as the introduction of smallpox. With no immune defenses to this new disease, millions of Native Americans died of smallpox during the sixteenth and seventeenth centuries.
The Granger Collection.

world, with ranches raising thousands of animals. Horses became relatively cheap, and even Native Americans could acquire them. By the nineteenth century, the possession of horses would allow the Plains Indians of North America to resist the advance of their white conquerors.

The flourishing of pigs, cattle, and sheep allowed a vast economic exploitation of the Americas. These animals produced enormous quantities of hides and wool. Their presence in such large numbers also meant that the Americas from the sixteenth century through the present would support a diet more plentiful in animal protein than anywhere else in the world.

Europeans also brought their own plants to the New World, including peaches, oranges, grapes, melons, bananas, rice, onions, radishes, and various green vegetables. Socially, for three centuries the most significant of these was sugar cane, the cultivation of which created the major demand for slavery throughout the transatlantic plantation economy. Nutritionally, European wheat would, over the course of time, allow the Americas not only to feed themselves, but also to export large amount of grain throughout the world. This American production of wheat on the vast plains of the two continents contrasted sharply with the difficulty Europeans faced raising grain in the northern and northeastern parts of the continent, particularly in Russia.

No significant animals from the Americas, except the turkey, actually came to be raised in Europe. But the Americas did send to Europe a series of plants that eventually changed the European diet: maize, the potato, the sweet potato, the pepper, beans, manioc (tapioca), the peanut, squash, the pumpkin, pineapple, cocoa, and the tomato. All of these, to a greater or lesser degree, eventually entered the diet of Europeans and of European settlers and their descendants in the Americas. Maize and the potato, however, had the most transforming impact. Each of these two crops became a major staple in European farming, as well as the European diet. Both crops grow rapidly, supplying food quickly and steadily if not attacked by disease. Tobacco, we should note, originated in the Americas, too.

Maize was established as a crop in Spain within thirty years of the country's encounter with the New World. A century and a half later it was a commonplace in the Spanish diet, and its cultivation had spread to Italy and France. Maize produced more grain for the seed and farming effort than wheat did. Throughout Europe, maize was associated primarily with fodder for animals. But as early as the eighteenth-century travelers noted the presence of polenta in the peasant diet, and other forms of maize dishes, such as fried mush, spread.

The potato established its European presence more slowly than maize. The Spanish encountered the potato only when Pizarro conquered Peru, where it was a major part of the Native American food supply. It was adopted slowly by Europeans because it needed to be raised in climates more temperate than that of Spain and the Mediterranean. It appears to have become a major peasant food in Scotland, Ireland, and parts of Germany during the eighteenth century. It became more widely cultivated elsewhere in Europe only after new strains of the plant were imported from Chile in the late nineteenth century. In the middle of the seventeenth century, Irish peasants were urged to cultivate the potato as a major source of cheap nutrition that could grow in quantity on a small plot. The food shortages arising from the wars of Louis XIV and then during the eighteenth century led farmers in northern Europe to adopt the potato for similar reasons. It was nutrient insurance against failure of the grain harvest. There is good reason to believe that the cultivation of the potato was one of the major causes of the population increase in eighteenth- and nineteenth-century Europe. It was the quintessential food of the poor.

Many tragedies arose from the encounter between the people of the Americas and those of Europe, as well as the forging of new nations and civilizations in the Americas. But one of the last chapters of those tragedies to arise as a direct fallout of the Columbian exchange three centuries earlier was the Irish famine of the 1840s. Irish peasants had become almost wholly dependent upon the potato as a source of food. In the middle of the 1840s, an American parasite infected the Irish potato crop. The result of the failure of the crop was the death of hundreds of thousand of Irish peasants and the migration of still more hundreds of thousands to the Americas and elsewhere in the world.

❖ *Define the Columbian Exchange. What was the impact of European diseases on the Americas? Why was the impact so profound? Why could so many European crops grow well in the Americas? What was the cultural impact of animals taken from Europe to the Americas? How did food from the Americas change the diet of Europe and then later, as Europeans immigrated, the diet of the entire world?*

Part 4

1700–1850

	POLITICS AND GOVERNMENT	SOCIETY AND ECONOMY	RELIGION AND CULTURE
1700–1789	1713 **Peace of Utrecht** 1713–1740 **Frederick William I builds Prussian military** 1720–1740 **Walpole in England, Fleury in France** 1739 **War of Jenkins's Ear** 1740 **Maria Theresa succeeds to Habsburg throne** 1740–1748 **War of the Austrian Succession**	1715–1763 **Colonial rivalry in the Caribbean** 1733 **James Kay's flying shuttle**	1721 **Montesquieu, *Persian Letters*** 1733 **Voltaire, *Letters on the English*** 1738 **Voltaire, *Elements of the Philosophy of Newton*** Voltaire
	1756–1763 **Seven Years' War** 1767 **Legislative Commission in Russia** 1772 **First Partition of Poland** 1775–1783 **American Revolution** 1785 **Catherine the Great of Russia issues Charter of Nobility**	1750s **Agricultural Revolution in Britain** 1750–1840 **Growth of new cities** 1763 **British establish dominance in India** 1763–1789 **Enlightened absolutist rulers seek to spur economic growth** 1765 **James Hargreaves's spinning jenny** 1769 **Richard Arkwright's waterframe** 1771–1775 **Pugachev's Rebellion** 1780 **Gordon riots in London** 1787 **Edmund Cartwright's power loom**	1739 **Wesley begins field preaching** 1748 **Hume, *Inquiry into Human Nature*** 1748 **Montesquieu, *Spirit of the Laws*** 1750 **Rousseau, *Discourse on the Moral Effects of the Arts and Sciences*** 1751 **First volume of Diderot's *Encyclopedia*** 1762 **Rousseau, *Social Contract and Émile*** 1763 **Voltaire, *Treatise on Tolerance*** 1774 **Goethe, *Sorrows of Young Werther*** 1776 **Smith, *Wealth of Nations*** 1779 **Lessing, *Nathan the Wise***
1789–1815	1789 **Gathering of the Estates General at Versailles; fall of the Bastille; Declaration of the Rights of Man and Citizen** 1791 **French monarchy abolished** 1793 **Louis XVI executed; Second Partition of Poland** 1793–1794 **Reign of Terror** 1795 **Third Partition of Poland**	1789–1802 **Revolutionary legislation restructures French political and economic life**	1781 **Joseph II adopts toleration in Austria** 1781 **Kant, *Critique of Pure Reason*** 1789 **Blake, *Songs of Innocence*** 1790 **Civil Constitution of the Clergy; Burke, *Reflections on the Revolution in France*** 1792 **Wollstonecraft, *Vindication of the Rights of Woman*** 1793 **France proclaims Cult of Reason**

ENLIGHTENMENT AND REVOLUTION

1700–1850

POLITICS AND GOVERNMENT	SOCIETY AND ECONOMY	RELIGION AND CULTURE

1789–1815 (cont.)

POLITICS AND GOVERNMENT

1795 The Directory established in France

1799 Napoleon named First Consul in France

1803 War resumes between Britain and France

1804 Napoleonic Code; Napoleon crowned emperor

1805 Third Coalition formed against France; battles of Trafalgar and Austerlitz

1806 Napoleon establishes the Continental System

1807 Treaty of Tilsit between France and Russia

1808 Spanish resistance to Napoleon stiffens

1812 Napoleon invades Russia; meets defeat

1814 Napoleon abdicates; Congress of Vienna opens; Louis XVIII restored in France

1815–1850

1815 Napoleon defeated at Waterloo

1819 Carlsbad Decrees in Germanies; Peterloo Massacre and the Six Acts, Britain

1820 Spanish Revolution begins

1821 Greek Revolution begins

1823 France intervenes in Spanish Revolution

1825 Decembrist Revolt in Russia

1829 Catholic Emancipation Act in Great Britain

1830 Revolution in France, Belgium, and Poland; Serbia gains independence

1832 Great Reform Bill in Britain

1848 Revolutions sweep across Europe

SOCIETY AND ECONOMY

1794–1824 Wars of independence in Latin America break the colonial system

Napoleon Bonaparte

1810 Abolition of serfdom in Prussia

1800–1850 British industrial dominance

1825 Stockton and Darlington Railway opens

1828–1850 First European police departments

1830–1850 Railway building in western Europe

1833 English Factory Act to protect children

1834 German *Zollverein* established

1842 Chadwick, *Report on the Sanitary Condition of the Labouring Population*

1846 Corn Laws repealed in Britain

1847 Ten Hour Act passed in Britain

1848 Serfdom abolished in Austria and Hungary

RELIGION AND CULTURE

1794 France proclaims Cult of the Supreme Being

1798 Wordsworth and Coleridge, *Lyrical Ballads*; Malthus, *Essay on the Principle of Population*

1799 Schleiermacher, *Speeches on Religion to Its Cultured Despisers*

1802 Chateaubriand, *Genius of Christianity*

1802 Napoleon, Concordat with the Papacy

1806 Hegel, *Phenomenology of Mind*

1807 Fichte, *Addresses to the German Nation*

1808 Goethe, *Faust*, Part I

1812 Byron, *Childe Harold's Pilgrimage*

intellectual

1817 Ricardo, *Principles of Political Economy*

1819 Byron, *Don Juan*

1829 Catholic Emancipation Act in Great Britain

1830–1842 Comte, *The Positive Philosophy*

1830 Lyell, *Principles of Geology*

1833 Russia begins "Official Nationality" policy

1835 Strauss, *Life of Jesus*

1840 Villermé, *Catalogue of the Physical and Moral State of Workers*

1843 Kierkegaard, *Fear and Trembling*

1848 Marx and Engels, *Communist Manifesto*

Chapter 18

Philosopher, dramatist, poet, historian, and popularizer of scientific ideas, Voltaire (1694–1778) was the most famous and influential of the eighteenth-century philosophes. His sharp satire and criticism of religious institutions opened the way for a more general critique of the European political and social status quo.

Nicolas de Largilliere. Portrait of Voltaire at age 23, bust length, 1728. Private Collection, Musée de la Ville de Paris, Musée Carnavalet, Paris, France. Giraudon/Art Resource, NY.

The Age of Enlightenment:
Eighteenth-Century Thought

The *Philosophes*

**Formative Influences
on the Enlightenment**
Ideas of Newton and Locke
The Example of British Toleration
and Stability
Need for Reform in France
The Emergence of a Print Culture

The *Encyclopedia*

The Enlightenment and Religion
Deism
Toleration
Radical Enlightenment Criticism
of Religion
Jewish Thinkers in the Age
of Enlightenement

The Enlightenment and Society
Beccaria and Reform of Criminal Law
The Physiocrats and Economic Freedom
Adam Smith on Economic Growth
and Social Progress

Political Thought of the *Philosophes*
Montesquieu and *Spirit of the Laws*
Rousseau: A Radical Critique of Modern Society

**Women in the Thought and Practice
of the Enlightenment**

Enlightened Absolutism
Frederick the Great of Prussia
Joseph II of Austria
Catherine the Great of Russia
The Partition of Poland
The End of the Eighteenth Century
in Central and Eastern Europe

KEY TOPICS

- The intellectual and social background of the Enlightenment
- The *philosophes* of the Enlightenment and their agenda of intellectual and political reform
- Efforts of "enlightened" monarchs in central and eastern Europe to increase the economic and military strength of their domains
- The partition of Poland by Prussia, Russia, and Austria

D*uring the eighteenth century, the conviction began to spread throughout the literate sectors of European society that economic change and political reform were both possible and desirable. This attitude is now commonplace, but it came into its own only after 1700. It represents one of the primary intellectual inheritances from that age. The movement of people and ideas that fostered such thinking is called the* Enlightenment.

Its leading voices combined confidence in the human mind and human enterprise inspired by the Scientific Revolution and faith in the power of rational criticism to challenge the intellectual authority of tradition and the Christian past. These writers stood convinced that human beings could comprehend the operation of physical nature and mold it to the ends of material and moral improvement, economic growth, and political reform. They advocated agricultural improvement, commercial society, expanding consumption, and the application of innovative rational methods to traditional social and economic practices. The rationality of the physical universe became a standard against which the customs and traditions of society could be measured and criticized. Such criticism penetrated every corner of contemporary society, politics, and religious opinion. As a result, the spirit of innovation and improvement came to characterize modern Europe and Western society.

Some of the ideas and outlooks of the Enlightenment had a direct impact on several rulers in central and eastern Europe. These rulers, whose policies became known by the term "Enlightened Absolutism," sought to centralize their authority so as to reform their countries. They often attempted to restructure religious institutions and to sponsor economic growth. Although they frequently associated themselves with the Enlightenment, many of their military and foreign policies were in direct opposition to enlightened ideals. Nonetheless, both the Enlightenment writers and these monarchs were forces for modernization in European life.

The *Philosophes*

The writers and critics who forged the new attitudes favorable to change, who championed reform, and who flourished in the emerging print culture were the *philosophes*. Not usually philosophers in a formal sense, they sought rather to apply the rules of reason and common sense to nearly all the major institutions and social practices of the day. The most famous of their number included Voltaire, Montesquieu, Diderot, D'Alembert, Rousseau, Hume, Gibbon, Smith, Lessing, and Kant.

A few of these *philosophes* occupied professorships in universities. Most, however, were free agents who might be found in London coffeehouses, Edinburgh drinking spots, the salons of fashionable Parisian ladies, the country houses of reform-minded nobles, or the courts of the most powerful monarchs on the Continent. In eastern Europe, they were often to be found in the royal bureaucracies. They were not an organized group; they disagreed on many issues. Their relationship with each other and with lesser figures of the same turn of mind has quite appropriately been compared with that of a family, in which, despite quarrels and tensions, a basic unity remains.[1]

The chief bond among the *philosophes* was their common desire to reform thought, society, and government for the sake of human liberty. As Peter Gay

once suggested, this goal included "freedom from arbitrary power, freedom of speech, freedom of trade, freedom to realize one's talents, freedom of aesthetic response, freedom, in a word, of moral man to make his way in the world."[2] Though challenged over the last three centuries, no other single set of ideas has done so much to shape the modern world.

While expanding the realm of human action, much that the *philosophes* understood as freedom or improvement challenged traditional ideas, usually ideas associated with religion, a topic to be discussed shortly. Their call to rational improvement also embraced many of the economic changes of the day already considered in Chapter 16. In that regard, most of the advocates of agricultural improvement who sought to overturn so many of the customary practices also embodied the spirit of the Enlightenment. The same could be said of the inventors of the new textile machinery, the organizers of the early factory system, and the sponsors of the invention and spread of the steam engine and other improved means of transportation. The Enlightenment was a movement of intellectuals, but intellectuals deeply in touch with everyday life and intellectuals read by people who wished to transform everyday life.

The literary vehicles through which the *philosophes* delivered their message included books, pamphlets, plays, novels, philosophical treatises, encyclopedias, newspapers, and magazines. During the Reformation and the religious wars, writers had used the printed word to debate the proper mode of faith in God. The *philosophes* of the Enlightenment employed the printed word to proclaim a new faith in the capacity of humankind to improve itself without the aid of God.

The bulk of the readership of the *philosphes* was drawn from the prosperous commercial and professional people of the eighteenth-century towns and cities. These people discussed the reformers' writings and ideas in local philosophical societies, Freemason lodges, and clubs. They had enough income and leisure time to buy and read the *philosophes'* works. Although the writers of the Enlightenment did not consciously champion the goals or causes of the middle class, they did provide an intellectual ferment and a major source of ideas that could be used to undermine existing social practices and political structures. They taught their contemporaries how to pose pointed, critical questions. Moreover, the *philosophes* generally supported the growth, the expansion of trade, and the improvement of trans-

---

[1]Peter Gay, *The Enlightenment: An Interpretation*, vol. 1 (New York: Knopf, 1967), p. 4.

[2]Gay, p. 3.

port, which were transforming the society and the economy of the eighteenth century and enlarging the business and commerical classes.

The Enlightenment evolved over the course of the century and involved writers living at different times in various countries. Its early exponents popularized the rationalism and scientific ideas of the seventeenth century. (See Chapter 14.) They worked to expose contemporary social and political abuses and argued that reform was necessary and possible. Their progress in this cause was anything but steady. Among the obstacles they met were vested interests, political oppression, and religious condemnation. Yet, by midcentury, they had brought enlightened ideas to the European public in a variety of formats. They corresponded with each other, wrote for each other as well as for the public, and defended each other against the political and religious authorities.

By the second half of the century, they were sufficiently safe to quarrel among themselves on occasion. They had stopped talking in generalities, and their major advocates were addressing specific abuses. Their books and articles had become more specialized and more practical. They had become more concerned with politics than with religion. Having convinced Europeans that change was a good idea, they began to suggest exactly what changes were most desirable. They had become honored figures.

The *philosophes* believed that human society needed to and could be improved. But they were never certain that reform, if achieved, would be permanent. The optimism of the Enlightenment was a tempered hopefulness rather than a glib certainty. An undercurrent of pessimism characterized most of the works of the period. As D'Alembert wrote, "Barbarism lasts for centuries; it seems that it is our natural element; reason and good taste are only passing."[3]

What had been the forces in European life that gave rise to this group and their ideas?

Formative Influences on the Enlightenment

The Newtonian worldview, the stability and commerical prosperity of Great Britain after 1688, the need for administrative and economic reform in France after the wars of Louis XIV, and the consolidation of what is known as a print culture were the chief factors that fostered the ideas of the Enlightenment and the call for reform throughout Europe.

[3]Jean Le Rond d'Alembert, *Preliminary Discourse to the Encyclopedia of Diderot*, Richard N. Schwab, tr. (Indianapolis: ITT Bobbs-Merrill Educational Publishing Company Inc., 1985), p. 103.

Ideas of Newton and Locke

Isaac Newton (1642–1727) and John Locke (1632–1704) were the major intellectual forerunners of the Enlightenment. Newton's formulation of the law of universal gravitation exemplified the power of the human mind. By example and in his writing, he encouraged Europeans to approach the study of nature directly and to avoid metaphysics and supernaturalism. Newton had always insisted on empirical support for his general laws and constantly used empirical experience to check his rational speculations. This emphasis on concrete experience became a key feature of Enlightenment thought. (See Art & the West.)

Newton also seemed to have revealed a pattern of rationality in the physical world. During the eighteenth century, thinkers began to apply this insight to society. If nature was rational, they reasoned, society, too, should be organized rationally.

As explained in Chapter 14, Newton's success in physics inspired his countryman John Locke to explain human psychology in terms of experience. In *An Essay Concerning Human Understanding* (1690), Locke argued that all humans

This elaborate eighteenth-century engraving pays homage to Isaac Newton, who was a major intellectual influence on the Enlightenment. This engraving is in the collection of the British Museum. Corbis

Joseph Wright, An Experiment on a Bird in the Air-Pump: Science in the Drawing Room

Joseph Wright of Derby, *An Experiment on a Bird in the Air-Pump* (1768). National Gallery, London, Great Britain. The Bridgeman Art Library.

The air-pump, devised by the pioneering English natural philosopher Robert Boyle in the 1650s, stood for over a century as major symbol of the new experimental science championed by the Royal Society of London. The instrument permitted air to be pumped out of a spherical glass jar to create a vacuum for the purpose of demonstrating the qualities of air and air pressure. The early air-pumps often functioned quite poorly because air would seep in through leaky seals, invading the vacuum. By the middle of the eighteenth century, however, many provincial English scientific societies possessed effective models such as the one portrayed in Joseph Wright's *An Experiment on a Bird in the Air-Pump* (1768).

Wright, who lived near Derby in an early industrial region of England, was a close friend of manufacturers and other persons interested in science several of whom belonged to the Lunar Society. In this dramatically lit painting, Wright portrays the excited interest of fashionable upper-class audiences in experimental science. At the same time, though, he suggests genuine apprehension about the practice of science.

Wright presents the central figure, who is operating the pump, as a natural philosopher about to demonstrate his superior knowledge and scientific skill through an experiment meant to indicate the necessity of air for the life of an animal. The experimenter holds the life and death of the bird in his hands as he moves to turn the switch that will create the vacuum. One figure observes the experiment with a sense of amazement, while another looks on with an expression of stoic acceptance. The man speaking to the young women, one of whom appears fearful and the other cautiously curious, may be explaining the need to place rationality above feelings in the pursuit of knowledge. Sacrificing the bird would advance the progress of science.

In his depiction of women (including one more interested in her male companion than in the experiment), Wright seems to be suggesting the commonly-held view of the day that women may approach science and experiments as observers, but may lack the intellectual qualities required for active participation in the experimental method.

In art historical terms, Wright, an English artist, has taken a genre of painting known as the *conversation piece* and made a scientific experiment the center of attention. Wright has also made another important substitution of a scientific subject for a more traditional one. The painting dramatically contrasts light and dark, a technique originally devised to highlight elements in paintings of religious scenes. Here the drama of the light highlights a secular scientific experiment on a natural subject that, especially in England, many people believed might lead to a new understanding of the divine. Thus, Wright could see the reverence once reserved for religious subjects now being evoked by a scientific one.

His painting, though coming a century after the first air pump experiments, demonstrates the manner in which, by the mid-eighteenth century, experimental science had established its cultural presence within polite society and its ability to foster civil conversation in place of political and religious disputes. Rather than discussing the Bible or politics, this group is observing a scientific experiment that will provide them with the opportunity for polite and presumably noncontroversial conversation, or at least conversation that will not lead to destructive quarrels.

Although, as an artist, Wright explored the challenges of painting light, the setting of this experiment would also seem to suggest that even in the eighteenth century he and others saw science as an uncertain and possibly temporary light surrounded by darkness and potential superstition.

Sources: David H. Solkin, *Painting for Money: The Visual Arts and the Public Sphere in Eighteenth-Century England* (New Haven, CT: Yale University Press, 1993); Steven Shapin and Simon Schaffer, *Leviathan and the Air-Pump: Hobbes, Boyle, and the Experimental Life* (Princeton, NJ: Princeton University Press, 1985).

enter the world a *tabula rasa*, or blank page. (See p. 463.) Personality is the product of the sensations that impinge on an individual from the external world throughout his or her life. Thus, experience, and only experience, shapes character. The implication of this theory was that human nature is changeable and can be molded by modifying the surrounding physical and social environment. Locke's was a reformer's psychology. It suggested the possibility of improving the human condition. Locke's psychology also, in effect, rejected the Christian doctrine that human beings are permanently flawed by sin. Human beings need not wait for the grace of God or other divine aid to better their lives. They could take charge of their own destiny.

The Example of British Toleration and Stability

Newton's physics and Locke's psychology provided the theoretical basis for a reformist approach to society. The domestic stability of Great Britain after the Revolution of 1688 furnished a living example of a society in which, to many contemporaries, enlightened reforms appeared to function for the benefit of all. England permitted religious toleration to all except Unitarians and Roman Catholics, and even they were not actually persecuted. Relative freedom of the press and free speech prevailed. The authority of the monarchy was limited, and political sovereignty resided in Parliament. The courts protected citizens from arbitrary government action. The army was small. Furthermore, the domestic economic life of Great Britain displayed far less regulation than that of France or other continental nations. In the view of reformist observers on the Continent, these liberal policies had produced not disorder and instability, but prosperity, stability, and a loyal citizenry. This view may have been idealized, but England was nonetheless significantly freer than any other European nation at the time.

Need for Reform in France

If the example of Great Britain suggested that change and freedom need not be disastrous, France seemed to illustrate those aspects of European politics and society that most demanded reform. Its legacy from Louis XIV was absolute monarchy, a large standing army, heavy taxation, and religious persecution of Protestants and dissident Roman Catholic Jansenists. His successors continued to curb liberties. The regime restricted freedom of worship and censored the press and

literary expression. Authors often had their works printed in Switzerland to avoid these restraints. Critics of the regime were subject to arbitrary arrest, although some of them reached accommodations with the authorities. State regulations hampered economic growth. Many aristocrats, regarding themselves as part of a military class, upheld traditional militaristic values.

Yet France, because it confronted its political thinkers so sharply with the need for reform, became a major center for the Enlightenment. There one of the earliest and by far the most influential voice of Enlightenment was François Marie Arouet, known to posterity as Voltaire (1694–1778). His career embodied both the conviction of the need for change in France and the admiration of Britain.

During the 1720s, Voltaire had offended the French authorities by certain of his writings. He was arrested and put in prison for a brief time. Later Voltaire went to England, visiting its best literary circles, observing its tolerant intellectual and religious climate, relishing the freedom he felt in its moderate political atmosphere, and admiring its science and economic prosperity. In 1733 he published *Letters on the English*, which appeared in French the next year. The book praised the virtues of the English and indirectly criticized the abuses of French society. In 1738 he published *Elements of the Philosophy of Newton*, which popularized the thought of the great scientist. Both works were well received and gave Voltaire a reputation as an important writer.

Thereafter Voltaire lived part of the time in France and part near Geneva, just across the French border, where the royal authorities could not bother him. He wrote essays, history, plays, stories, and letters that made him the "literary dictator" of Europe. He used the bitter venom of his satire and sarcasm against one evil after another in French and European life. In his most famous satire, *Candide* (1759), he attacked war, religious persecution, and what he regarded as unwarranted optimism about the human condition.

The Emergence of a Print Culture

The Enlightenment was the first major intellectual movement of European history to flourish in a print culture, that is, a culture in which books, journals, newspapers, and pamphlets had achieved a status of their own. Although printed books and pamphlets played a significant role during the Reformation and Counter-Reformation, the powerful messages of those movements were spread mostly by preaching. During the eighteenth century, the volume of printed material—books, jour-

Printing shops were the productive centers for the book trade and newspaper publishing which spread the ideas of the Enlightenment.
The Granger Collection

nals, magazines, and daily newspapers—increased sharply throughout Europe, most notably in Britain. Prose came to be valued as highly as poetry, and the novel emerged as a distinct genre. The printed word had become the chief vehicle for the communication of ideas and would remain so until the electronic revolution of our own day.

A growing concern with everyday life and material concerns—with secular as opposed to religious issues—accompanied this expansion of printed forms. Toward the end of the seventeenth century, half the books published in Paris were religious; by the 1780s, only about 10 percent were.

Books were not inexpensive in this era, but they, and the ideas they conveyed, circulated in a variety of ways to reach a broad public. Private and public libraries grew in number, allowing single copies to reach many readers. Authors might also publish the same material in different formats. The English essayist, critic, and dictionary author Samuel Johnson (1709–1784), for example, published as books collections of essays that had first appeared in newspapers or journals.

Familiarity with books and secular ideas came increasingly to be expected within aristocratic and middle-class society. Popular publications, such as *The Spectator*, begun in 1711 by Joseph Addison (1672–1719) and Richard Steele (1672–1729), fostered the value of polite conversation and the reading of books. Coffeehouses became centers for the discussion of writing and ideas. The lodges of Freemasons, the meeting places for members of a movement that began in Britain and spread to the Continent, provided another site for the consideration of secular ideas in secular books.

The expanding market for printed matter allowed writers to earn a living from their work for the first time, making authorship an occupation. Parisian ladies sought out popular writers for their fashionable salons. Some writers, notably Alexander Pope (1688–1744) and Voltaire, grew wealthy, providing an example for their aspiring young colleagues. In a challenge to older aristocratic values, status for authors in this new print culture was based on merit and commercial competition, not heredity and patronage.

A division, however, soon emerged between high and low literary culture. Successful authors of the Enlightenment addressed themselves to monarchs, nobles, the upper middle classes, and professional groups and were read and accepted in these upper levels of society. Other authors found social and economic disappointment. They lived marginally, writing professionally for whatever newspaper or journal would pay for their pages. Many of these lesser writers grew resentful, blaming a corrupt society for their lack of success. From their anger, they often espoused radical ideas or carried Enlightenment ideas to radical extremes, transmitting them in this embittered form to their often lower class audience. The new print culture thus circulated the ideas of the Enlightenment to virtually all literate groups in society.

An expanding literate public and the growing influence of secular printed materials created a new and increasingly influential social force called public opinion. This force—the collective effect on political and social life of views circulated in print and discussed in the home, the workplace, and centers of leisure—seems not to have existed before the middle of the eighteenth century. Books and newspapers could have thousands of readers, who in effect supported the writers whose works they bought, discussing their ideas and circulating them widely. The writers, in turn, had to answer only to their readers. The result changed the cultural and political climate in Europe. In 1775 a new member of the French Academy declared that

A tribunal has arisen independent of all powers and that all powers respect, that appreciates all talents, that pronounces on all people of merit. And in an enlightened century, in a century in which each citizen can speak to the entire nation by way of print, those who have a talent for instructing men and a gift for moving them—in a word, men of letters—are, amid the public dispersed, what the orators of Rome and Athens were in the middle of the public assembled.[4]

Governments could no longer operate wholly in secret or with disregard to the larger public sphere. They, as well as their critics, had to explain and discuss their views and policies openly.

Continental European governments sensed the political power of the new print culture. They regulated the book trade, censored books and newspapers, confiscated offending titles, and imprisoned offending authors. The eventual expansion of freedom of the press represented also an expansion of the print culture—with its independent readers, authors, and publishers—and the challenge it posed to traditional intellectual, social, and political authorities.

The *Encyclopedia*

The midcentury witnessed the publication of the *Encyclopedia*, one the greatest monuments of the Enlightenment and its most monumental undertaking in the realm of print culture. Under the heroic leadership of Denis Diderot (1713–1784), and Jean le Rond d'Alembert (1717–1783), the first volume appeared in 1751. Eventually, numbering seventeen volumes of text and eleven of plates (illustrations), the project was completed in 1772.

The *Encyclopedia*, in part a collective plea for freedom of expression, reached fruition only after many attempts to censor it and to halt its publication. It was the product of the collective effort of more than 100 authors, and its editors had at one time or another solicited articles from all the major French *philosophes*. It included the most advanced critical ideas of the time on religion, government, and philosophy. To avoid official

censure, these ideas often had to be hidden in obscure articles or under the cover of irony. The *Encyclopedia* also included important articles and illustrations on manufacturing, canal building, ship construction, and improved agriculture, making it an important source of knowledge about eighteenth-century social and economic life. (See "The *Encyclopedia* Praises Mechanical Arts and Artisans.")

Between 14,000 and 16,000 copies of various editions of the *Encyclopedia* were sold before 1789. The project had been designed to secularize learning and to undermine intellectual assumptions that lingered from the Middle Ages and the Reformation. The articles on politics, ethics, and society ignored divine law and concentrated on humanity and its immediate well-being. The Encyclopedists looked to antiquity rather than to the Christian centuries for their intellectual and ethical models. For them, the future welfare of humankind lay not in pleasing God or following divine commandments, but rather in harnessing the power and resources of the Earth and in living at peace with one's fellow human beings. The good life lay here and now and was to be achieved through the application of reason to human relationships. With the publication of the *Encyclopedia*, Enlightenment thought became more fully diffused over the Continent, penetrating German and Russian intellectual and political circles.

The Enlightenment and Religion

For many, but not all, *philosophes* of the eighteenth century, ecclesiastical institutions were the chief impediment to human improvement and happiness. Voltaire's cry, "Crush the Infamous Thing," summed up the attitude of a number of *philosophes* toward the church and Christianity. Almost all varieties of Christianity, but especially Roman Catholicism, felt their criticism.

The critical *philosophes* complained that the churches hindered the pursuit of a rational life and the scientific study of humanity and nature. The clergy taught that humans were basically depraved, becoming worthy only through divine grace. According to the doctrine of original sin—either Protestant or Catholic—meaningful improvement in human nature on Earth was impossible. Religion thus turned attention away from this world to the world to come. For example, the *philosophes* argued that the Calvinist doctrine of predestination denied a relationship between virtuous actions in this life and the fate of the soul after death.

---

[4]Chrétien-Guillaume Malesherbes, as quoted in Roger Chartier, *The Cultural Origins of the French Revolution*, trans. by Lydia G. Cochran (Durham, NC: Duke University Press, 1991), pp. 30–31.

The *Encyclopedia* Praises Mechanical Arts and Artisans

The leading intellectuals and men of letters of the day wrote the articles of the En-cyclopedia. Yet the concrete reality of contemporaneous economic life in towns and the countryside fill its pages. Two of the most remarkable features of the Encyclopedia are the vast quantity of information it included in numerous articles about the mechanical arts and, in these articles, engravings that portrayed eighteenth-century French artisans in their workplace. The editors of the Encyclopedia believed that disseminating such information was necessary to aid the spirit of improvement and to promote economic growth. In the "Preliminary Discourse," which served as a general introduction to the Encyclopedia, D'Alembert explained the importance of the mechanical arts and the way the authors had explored these arts and the workshops where they were practiced.

❖ *How does D'Alembert defend the importance of the mechanical arts? Why does he think they have not always received proper attention and appreciation? How did the authors of the* Encyclopedia *familiarize themselves with such work? What kind of conversation might have occurred between one of those authors and a skilled artisan operating his machinery?*

The mechanical arts, which are dependent upon manual operation and are subjugated...to a sort of routine, have been left to those among men whom prejudices have placed in the lowest class. Poverty has forced these men to turn to such work more often than taste and genius have attracted them to it. Subsequently it became a reason for holding them in contempt... However, the advantage that the liberal arts have over the mechanical arts...is sufficiently counterbalanced by the quite superior usefulness which the latter for the most part have for us. It is this very usefulness which reduced them perforce to purely mechanical operations in order to make them accessible to a larger number of men. But while justly respecting great geniuses for their enlightenment, society ought not to degrade the hands by which it is saved....

Too much has been written on the sciences; not enough has been written well on the mechanical arts....Thus everything impelled us to go directly to the workers.

We approached the most capable of them....We took the trouble of going into their shops, of questioning them, of writing at their dictation, of developing their thoughts and of drawing therefrom the terms peculiar to their professions, of setting up tables of these terms and of working out definitions for them, of conversing with those from whom we obtained memoranda, and (an almost indispensable precaution) of correcting through long and frequent conversations with others what some of them imperfectly, obscurely, and sometimes unreliably had explained. There are some artisans who are also men of letters, and we would be able to cite them here; but their numbers are very small. Most of those who engage in the mechanical arts have embraced them only by necessity and work only by instinct....

But there are some trades so unusual and some operations so subtle that unless one does the work oneself, unless one operates a machine with one's own hands, and sees the work being created under one's own eyes, it is difficult to speak of it with precision. Thus several times we had to get possession of the machines, to construct them, and to put a hand to the work. It was necessary to become apprentices, so to speak, and to manufacture some poor object ourselves in order to learn how to teach others the way good specimens are made.

From Jean Le Rond d'Alembert, *Preliminary Discourse to the Encyclopedia of Diderot*, Richard N. Schwab, trans. (Indianapolis: ITT Bobbs-Merrill Educational Publishing Company, Inc., 1985), pp. 41–42, 122–123.

Mired in conflicts over obscure doctrinal differences, the churches promoted intolerance and bigotry, inciting torture, war, and other forms of human suffering.

With this attack, the *philosophes* were challenging not only a set of ideas, but also some of Europe's most powerful institutions. The churches were deeply enmeshed in the power structure of the old regime. They owned large amounts of land and collected tithes from peasants before any secular authority collected its taxes. Most clergy were legally exempt from taxes and made only annual voluntary grants to the government. The upper clergy in most countries were relatives of aristocrats. Clerics were actively involved in politics, serving in the British House of Lords and advising princes on the Continent. In Protestant countries, the leading local landowner usually appointed the clergyman of a particular parish. Across the Continent, membership in the predominant denomination of the kingdom gave certain subjects political advantages. Nonmembership often excluded other subjects from political participation. Clergy frequently provided intellectual justification for the social and political status quo, and they were active agents of religious and literary censorship.

Deism

The *philosophes*, although critical of many religious institutions and frequently anticlerical, were not opposed to all religion. In Scotland, for example, the enlightened historian William Robertson (1721–1793) was the head of the Scottish Kirk. In England, clergy of the established church did much to popularize the thought of Newton. What the *philosophes* sought, however, was religion without fanaticism and intolerance, a religious life that would largley substitute the authority of human reason for the authority of churches. The Newtonian worldview had convinced many writers that nature was rational. Therefore, the God who had created nature must also be rational, and the religion through which that God was worshiped should be rational. Most of them believed that the life of religion and of reason could be combined, giving rise to a movement known as *deism*.

The title of one of the earliest deist works, *Christianity Not Mysterious* (1696) by John Toland (1670–1722), indicates the general tenor of this religious outlook. Toland and later deist writers promoted religion as a natural and rational, rather than a supernatural and mystical, phenomenon. In this respect they differed from Newton and Locke, both of whom regarded themselves as distinctly Christian. Newton believed that God could interfere with the natural order, whereas the deists regarded God as a kind of divine watchmaker who had created the mechanism of nature, set it in motion, and then departed. Most of the deist writers were also strongly anticlerical and for that reason regarded as radical.

There were two major points in the deists' creed. The first was a belief in the existence of God, which they thought could be empirically justified by the contemplation of nature. Joseph Addison's poem on the spacious firmament (1712) illustrates this idea:

The spacious firmament on high,
With all the blue ethereal sky,
And spangled heav'n, a shining frame,
Their great Original proclaim:
Th' unwearied Sun, from day to day,
Does his Creator's power display,
And publishes to every land
The work of an Almighty hand.

Because nature provided evidence of a rational God, that deity must also favor rational morality. So the second point in the deists' creed was a belief in life after death, when rewards and punishments would be meted out according to the virtue of the lives people led on this Earth.

Deism was empirical, tolerant, reasonable, and capable of encouraging virtuous living. Voltaire wrote:

The great name of Deist, which is not sufficiently revered, is the only name one ought to take. The only gospel one ought to read is the great book of Nature, written by the hand of God and sealed with his seal. The only religion that ought to be professed is the religion of worshiping God and being a good man.[5]

Deists hoped that wide acceptance of their faith would end rivalry among the various Christian sects and with it religious fanaticism, conflict, and persecution. They also felt deism would remove the need for priests and ministers, who, in their view, were often responsible for fomenting religious differences and denominational hatred. Deistic thought led some contempraries to believe that God had revealed himself in various ways and that many religions might embody divine truth.

Toleration

According to the *philosophes*, religious toleration was a primary social condition for the virtuous life. Again Voltaire took the polemical lead in championing this cause. In 1762, the Roman Catholic political authorities in Toulouse ordered the execution of a Huguenot named Jean Calas. He stood accused of having murdered his son to prevent him from converting to Roman Catholicism. Calas was viciously tortured and publicly strangled without ever confessing his guilt. The confession would not have saved his life, but it would have given the Catholics good propaganda to use against Protestants.

Voltaire learned of the case only after Calas's death. He made the dead man's cause his own. In 1763, he published his *Treatise on Tolerance* and hounded the authorities for a new investigation. Finally, in 1765,

[5]Quoted in J. H. Randall, *The Making of the Modern Mind*, rev. ed. (New York: Houghton Mifflin, 1940), p. 292.

Voltaire Attacks Religious Fanaticism

The chief complaint of the philosophes *against Christianity was that it bred a fanaticism that led people to commit crimes in the name of religion. In this passage from Voltaire's* Philosophical Dictionary *(1764), he directly reminds his readers of the intolerance of the Reformation era and indirectly refers to examples of contemporary religious excesses. He argues that the philosophical spirit can overcome fanaticism and foster toleration and more humane religious behavior. Shocking many of his contemporaries, he praises the virtues of Confucianism over those of Christianity.*

❖ *What concrete examples of religious fanaticism might Voltaire have had in mind? Why does Voltaire contend that neither religion nor laws can contain religious fanaticism? Why does Voltaire admire the Chinese?*

Fanaticism is to superstition what delirium is to fever and rage to anger. The man visited by ecstasies and visions, who takes dreams for realities and his fancies for prophecies, is an enthusiast; the man who supports his madness with murder is a fanatic....

The most detestable example of fanaticism was that of the burghers of Paris who on St. Bartholomew's Night [1572] went about assassinating and butchering all their fellow citizens who did not go to mass, throwing them out of windows, cutting them in pieces.

Once fanaticism has corrupted a mind, the malady is almost incurable....

The only remedy for this epidemic malady is the philosophical spirit which, spread gradually, at last tames men's habits and prevents the disease from starting; for once the disease has made any progress, one must flee and wait for the air to clear itself. Laws and religion are not strong enough against the spiritual pest; religion, far from being healthy food for infected brains, turns to poison in them....

Even the law is impotent against these attacks of rage; it is like reading a court decree to a rav-

ing maniac. These fellows are certain that the holy spirit with which they are filled is above the law, that their enthusiasm is the only law they must obey.

What can we say to a man who tells you that he would rather obey God than men, and that therefore he is sure to go to heaven for butchering you?

Ordinarily fanatics are guided by rascals, who put the dagger into their hands; these latter resemble that Old Man of the Mountain who is supposed to have made imbeciles taste the joys of paradise and who promised them an eternity of the pleasures of which he had given them a foretaste, on condition that they assassinated all those he would name to them. There is only one religion in the world that has never been sullied by fanaticism, that of the Chinese men of letters. The schools of philosophy were not only free from this pest, they were its remedy; for the effect of philosophy is to make the soul tranquil, and fanaticism is incompatible with tranquility. If our holy religion has so often been corrupted by this infernal delirium, it is the madness of men which is at fault.

From Voltaire, *Philosophical Dictionary*, trans. by P. Gay (New York: Basic Books, 1962), pp. 267–269.

the judicial decision against the unfortunate man was reversed. For Voltaire, the case illustrated the fruits of religious fanaticism and the need for rational reform of judicial processes. (See "Voltaire Attacks Religious Fanaticism.") Somewhat later in the century, the German playwright and critic Gotthold Lessing (1729–1781) wrote *Nathan the Wise* (1779), a plea for toleration not only of different Christian sects, but also of religious faiths other than Christianity.

The premise behind all of these calls for toleration was, in effect, that life on Earth and human re-

lationships should not be subordinated to religion. Secular values and considerations were more important than religious ones.

Radical Enlightenment Criticism of Religion

Some *philosophes* went beyond the formulation of a rational religious alternative to Christianity and the advocacy of toleration to attack the churches and the clergy with great vehemence. Voltaire repeatedly questioned the truthfulness of priests and the morality of the Bible. In his *Philosophical Dictionary* (1764), he humorously pointed out inconsistencies in biblical narratives and immoral acts of the biblical heroes. The Scottish philosopher David Hume (1711–1776), in "Of Miracles," a chapter in his *Inquiry into Human Nature* (1748), argued that no empirical evidence supported the belief in divine miracles central to much of Christianity. For Hume, the greatest miracle was that people believed in miracles. In *The Decline and Fall of the Roman Empire* (1776), Edward Gibbon (1737–1794), the English historian, explained the rise of Christianity in terms of natural causes rather than the influence of miracles and piety.

A few *philosophes* went further. Baron d'Holbach (1723–1789) and Julien Offray de La Mettrie (1709–1751) embraced positions very near to atheism and materialism. Theirs was distinctly a minority position, however. Most of the *philosophes* sought not the abolition of religion, but its transformation into a humane force that would encourage virtuous living. In the words of the title of a work by the German philosopher Immanuel Kant, they sought to pursue *Religion within the Limits of Reason Alone* (1793).

Jewish Thinkers in the Age of Enlightenment

Despite their emphasis on toleration, the *philosophes'* criticisms of traditional religion often reflected an implicit contempt not only for Christianity but also, and sometimes more vehemently, for Judaism. Their attack on the veracity of biblical miracles and biblical history undermined the authority of the Hebrew scriptures as well as the Christian. They often aimed their satirical barbs at personalities from the Hebrew scriptures. Some *philosophes* characterized Judaism as a more primitive faith than Christianity and one from which philosophical rationalism provided a path of escape. The Enlightenment view of religion thus served in some ways to further stigmatize Jews and Judaism in the eyes of non-Jewish Europeans.

Enlightenment values also, however, allowed certain Jewish intellectuals to rethink the relationship of their communities to wider European culture from which they had largely lived apart. Two major Jewish writers—one a few decades before the opening of the Enlightenment and one toward the close—entered the larger debate over religion and the place of Jews in European life. These were Baruch Spinoza (1632–1677) who lived in the Netherlands and Moses Mendelsohn (1729–1786) who lived in Germany. Spinoza set the example for a secularized version of Judaism while Mendelsohn established the main outlines of an assimilationist position. While their approaches to the problem displayed certain similarities, there were also important differences.

Spinoza, the son of a Jewish merchant of Amsterdam, was deeply influenced by the new science of the mid-seventeenth century. Like his contemporaries, Hobbes and Descartes, he looked to the power of human reason to reconceptualize traditional thought. In that regard his thinking reflected the age of scientific revolution and looked toward the later Enlightenment.

In his *Ethics*, the most famous of his works, Spinoza so closely identified God and nature, or the spiritual and material worlds, that contemporaries condemned him. Many thought that he drew God and nature too intimately into a single divine substance, leaving little room for the possibility of a distinctly divine revelation to humankind in scripture. Both Christians and Jews also believed Spinoza's near pantheistic position meant that human beings might not be personally responsible for their actions and that there could be no personal, individual immortality of the human soul after death. During his lifetime the controversial character of his writings led both Jews and Protestants to criticize him as an athe-

The Dutch Jewish philosopher Baruch Spinoza was deeply influenced by the new science of the mid-seventeenth century. In his writings, Spinoza argued for rationality over traditional spiritual beliefs. Library of Congress ist. At the age of 24, he was excommunicated by his own synagogue and thereafter lived apart from the Amsterdam Jewish community.

In his *Theologico-Political Treatise* (1670), Spinoza directly anticipated much of the religious criticism of the Enlightenment and its attacks on the power of superstition in human life.Spinoza described the origins of religion in thoroughly naturalistic terms. He believed the Hebrew Bible provided Jews with divine legislation but not with specially revealed theological knowledge. In this respect, he was calling upon both Jews and Christians to use their own reason in religious matters and to read the Bible like other ancient books. Spinoza's extensive rational and historical criticism of the biblical narratives disturbed Christian and Jewish contemporaries who saw him as a writer seeking to lead people away from all religion. He actually argued, however, that the formally organized religious institutions of both Christianity and Judaism led people away from the original teaching of scripture and encouraged them to persecute those who disagreed with the leaders of their respective churches and synagogues.

Because of Spinoza's excommunication from his synagogue, the later *philosophes* viewed him as a martyr for rationality against superstition. He also symbolized a Jew who, through the use of his critical reason, had separated himself from traditional Jewish religion and practices and attempted to enter the mainstream society. In that regard, he left Judaism to pursue a secular existence with little or no regard for his original faith. Consequently, his life and his writings as one commentator has stated "made it possible for defenders of the Enlightenment to advocate toleration of Jews while simultaneously holding Judaism in contempt."[6] This stance of championing toleration while condemning Judaism itself would later characterize the outlook of many non-Jewish Europeans to the assimilation of Jews into European civic life. It was, however, an outlook that could not without much modification be welcomed by Jewish communities themselves.

Moses Mendelsohn, the leading Jewish philosopher of the eighteenth century and a person known as the "Jewish Socrates," writing almost a century later also advocated the entry of Jews into modern European life. In contrast to Spinoza, however, Mendelsohn argued for the possibility of loyalty to Judaism combined with adherence to rational, enlightenment values. Mendelsohn could hold this position in part because of the influence of Lessing's arguments for toleration. Indeed, Mendelsohn

had been the person on whose life Lessing had modeled the chief character of *Nathan the Wise*.

Mendelsohn's most influential work was *Jerusalem; or, On Ecclesiastical Power and Judaism* (1783) where he argued both for advancing extensive religious toleration and for maintaining the religious distinction of Jewish communities. Mendelsohn urged that religious diversity within a nation did not harm loyalty to the government; therefore, governments should be religiously neutral and Jews should enjoy the same civil rights as other subjects. Then in the spirit of the deists, he presented Judaism as one of many religious paths revealed by God. Jewish law and practice were intended for the moral benefit of Jewish communities; other religions similarly served other people. Consequently, various communities should be permitted to practice their religious faith alongside other religious groups.

Unlike Spinoza, Mendelsohn wished to advocate religious toleration while genuinely sustaining the traditional religious practices and faith of Judaism. Nevertheless, Mendelsohn believed that Jewish communities should *not* have the right to excommunicate their members over differences in theological opinions, but should tolerate within themselves a wide spectrum of outlooks. In this respect, Mendelsohn set forth a far more extensive vision of religious toleration than John Locke almost a century earlier, who had contended that numerous religious communities should be tolerated but that each should retain the right of excommunication (see Chapter 14.) Mendelsohn advocated broad toleration within the Jewish communities so that their members, if they wished, could embrace modern secular ideas without danger of excommunication. He thus sought both toleration *of* Jews within the broader non-Jewish European society and toleration *by* Jews of a wider spectrum of opinion within their own communities and congregations. His hope was that the rationalism of the Enlightenment would provide the foundation for both modes of toleration.

The Enlightenment and Society

Although the *philosophes* wrote much on religion, humanity was the center of their interest. As one writer in the *Encyclopedia* observed, "Man is the unique point to which we must refer everything, if we wish to interest and please amongst considerations the most arid and details the most dry."[7]

---

[6]Steven B. Smith, *Spinoza, Liberalism, and the Question of Jewish Identity* (New Haven, CT: Yale University Press, 1997), p. 166.

[7]Quoted in F. L. Baumer, *Main Currents of Western Thought*, 4th ed. (New Haven, CT.: Yale University Press, 1978), p. 374.

The *philosophes* believed that the application of human reason to society would reveal laws in human relationships similar to those found in physical nature. At the same time, the use of the word "man" in this passage was not simply an accident of language. Most *philosophes* were thinking primarily of men, not women, when they framed their reformist ideas. With a few exceptions, as will be seen later in the chapter, they had little interest in expanding women's intellectual and social opportunities.

Although the term did not appear until later, the idea of *social science* originated with the Enlightenment. *Philosophes* hoped to end human cruelty by discovering social laws and making people aware of them. These concerns are most evident in the *philosophes'* work on law and prisons.

Beccaria and Reform of Criminal Law

In 1764 Cesare Beccaria (1738–1794), an Italian *philosophe*, published *On Crimes and Punishments*, in which he applied critical analysis to the problem of making punishments both effective and just. He wanted the laws of monarchs and legislatures—that is, positive law—to conform with the rational laws of nature. He rigorously and eloquently attacked both torture and capital punishment. He thought that the criminal justice system should ensure a speedy trial and certain punishment and that the intent of punishment should be to deter further crime. The purpose of laws was not to impose the will of God or some other ideal of perfection; their purpose was to secure the greatest good or happiness for the greatest number of human beings. This utilitarian philosophy based on happiness in this life permeated most Enlightenment writing on practical reforms.

The Physiocrats and Economic Freedom

Economic policy was another area in which the *philosophes* saw existing legislation and administration preventing the operation of natural social laws. They believed that mercantilist legislation (designed to protect a country's trade from external competition) and the regulation of labor by governments and guilds actually hampered the expansion of trade, manufacture, and agriculture. In France, these economic reformers were called the *physiocrats*. Their leading spokespeople were François Quesnay (1694–1774) and Pierre Dupont de Nemours (1739–1817).

The physiocrats believed that the primary role of government was to protect property and to permit its owners to use it freely. They particularly felt that all economic production depended on sound agriculture. They favored the consolidation of small peasant holdings into larger, more efficient farms. Here as elsewhere, there was a close relationship between the rationalism of the Enlightenment and the spirit of improvement at work in eighteenth-century European economic life.

Adam Smith on Economic Growth and Social Progress

The most important economic work of the Enlightenment was Adam Smith's (1723–1790) *Inquiry into the Nature and Causes of the Wealth of Nations* (1776). Smith, who was for a time a professor at Glasgow, believed that economic liberty was the foundation of a natural economic system. As a result, he urged that the mercantile system of England—including the navigation acts, the bounties, most tariffs, special trading monopolies, and the domestic regulation of labor and manufacture—be abolished. These regulations were intended to preserve the wealth of the nation, to capture wealth from other nations, and to maximize the work available for the nation's laborers. Smith argued, however, that they hindered the expansion of wealth and production. The best way to encourage economic growth, he maintained, was to unleash individuals to pursue their own selfish economic interests. As self-interested individuals sought to enrich themselves by meeting the needs of others in the marketplace, the economy would expand. Consumers would find their wants met as manufacturers and merchants competed for their business.

It was a basic assumption of mercantilism that the earth's resources are limited and scarce, so that one nation can acquire wealth only at the expense of others. Smith's book challenged this assumption. He saw the resources of nature—water, air, soil, and minerals—as boundless. To him, they demanded exploitation for the enrichment and comfort of humankind. In effect, Smith was saying that the nations and peoples of Europe need not be poor.

Smith is usually regarded as the founder of *laissez-faire* economic thought and policy, which favors a limited role for the government in economic life. *The Wealth of Nations* was, however, a complex book. Smith was no simple dogmatist. For example, he did not oppose all government activity touching the economy. The state, he argued, should provide schools, armies, navies, and roads. It should also undertake certain commercial ventures, such as the opening of dangerous new trade routes that were economically desirable, but too expensive or risky for private enterprise.

Within *The Wealth of Nations*, Smith, like other Scottish thinkers of the day, embraced an important theory of human social and economic development, known as the *four-stage theory*. According to this theory, human societies can be classified as hunting and gathering, pastoral or herding, agricultural, and commercial. The hunters and gatherers have little or no settled life. Pastoral societies are groups of nomads who tend their herds and develop some private property. Agricultural or farming societies are settled and have clear-cut property arrangements. Finally, in the commercial state there exist advanced cities, the manufacture of numerous items for wide consumption, extensive trade between cities and the countryside, as well as elaborate forms of property and financial arrangements. Smith and other Scottish writers described the passage of human society through these stages as a movement from barbarism to civilization.

The four-stage theory implicitly evaluated the later stages of economic development and the people dwelling in them as higher, more progressive, and more civilized than the earlier ones. A social theorist using this theory could thus very quickly look at a society and, on the basis of the state of its economic development and organizations, rank it in terms of the stage it had achieved. In point of fact, the commercial stage, the highest rank in the theory, described society as it appeared in northwestern Europe. Thus, Smith's theory allowed Europeans to look about the world and always find themselves dwelling at the highest level of human achievement. This outlook served as one of the major justifications in the minds of Europeans for their economic and imperial domination of the world during the next century. They repeatedly portrayed themselves as bringing a higher level of civilization to people elsewhere who, according to the four-stage theory, lived in lower stages of human social and economic development. Europeans thus imbued with the spirit of the Enlightenment presented themselves as carrying out a civilizing mission to the rest of the world.

Political Thought of the *Philosophes*

Nowhere was the *philosophes'* reformist agenda, as well as tensions among themselves, so apparent as in their political thought. Most *philosophes* were discontented with certain political features of their countries, but they were especially discontented in France. There the corruptness of the royal court, the blundering of the administrative bureaucracy, the less-than-glorious midcentury wars, and the power of the church compounded all problems. Consequently, the most important political thought of the Enlightenment occurred in France. The French *philosophes*, however, stood quite divided as to the proper solution to their country's problems. Their attitudes spanned a wide political spectrum, from aristocratic reform to democracy to absolute monarchy.

Montesquieu and *Spirit of the Laws*

Charles Louis de Secondat, Baron de Montesquieu (1689–1755), was a lawyer, a noble of the robe, and a member of a provincial *parlement*. He also belonged to the Bordeaux Academy of Science, before which he presented papers on scientific topics.

Although living comfortably within the bosom of French society, he saw the need for reform. In 1721, he published *The Persian Letters* to satirize contemporary institutions. The book consisted of letters purportedly written by two Persians visiting Europe. They explained to friends at home how European behavior contrasted with Persian life and customs. Behind the humor lay the cutting edge of criticism and an exposition of the cruelty and irrationality of much contemporaneous European life.

Charles de Secondat, Baron de Montesquieu (1689–1755), was the author of Spirit of the Laws, *possibly the most influential work of political thought of the eighteenth century.* Corbis

Montesquieu Defends the Separation of Powers

Spirit of the Laws (1748) was probably the most influential political work of the Enlightenment. In this passage Montesquieu explains how the division of powers within a government would make that government more moderate and would protect the liberty of its subjects. This idea was adopted by the writers of the United States Constitution when they devised the checks and balances of the three branches of government.

❖ *What did Montesquieu mean by "moderate governments," and why did he associate political liberty with such governments? What might he have seen as such a government in his own day? How does Montesquieu define the liberty of a subject? Why does he regard a situation where the power of government is not divided as one where there can be no liberty?*

Democratic and aristocratic states are not in their own nature free. Political liberty is to be found only in moderate governments; and even in these it is not always found. It is there only when there is no abuse of power. But constant experience shows us that every man invested with power is apt to abuse it, and to carry his authority as far as it will go....

To prevent this abuse, it is necessary from the very nature of things that power should be a check to power....

In every government there are three sorts of power: the legislative; the executive in respect to things dependent on the law of nations; and the executive in regard to matters that depend on the civil law [the realm of the judiciary]....

The political liberty of the subject is a tranquillity of mind arising from the opinion each person has of his safety. In order to have this liberty, it is requisite that government be so constituted as one man need not be afraid of another.

When the legislative and executive powers are united in the same person, or in the same body of magistrates, there can be no liberty; because apprehensions may arise, lest the same monarchy or senate should enact tyrannical laws, to execute them in a tyrannical manner.

Again, there is no liberty, if the judiciary power be not separated from the legislative and executive. Were it joined with the legislative, the life and liberty of the subject would be exposed to arbitrary control; for the judge would be then the legislator. Were it joined to the executive power, the judge might behave with violence and oppression.

There would be an end of everything, were the same man or the same body, whether of the nobles or of the people, to exercise those three powers, that of enacting laws, that of executing the public resolutions, and of trying the causes of individuals.

Excerpted with permission of The Free Press, an imprint of Simon & Schuster, from *The Spirit of the Laws* by Baron de Montesquieu, trans. by Thomas Nugent. Copyright © 1949 by Hafner Publishing Company, pp. 150–152.

In his most enduring work, *Spirit of the Laws* (1748), Montesquieu held up the example of the British constitution as the wisest model for regulating the power of government. With his interest in science, his hope for reform, and his admiration for Britain, he embodied all the major elements of the Enlightenment mind. (See "Montesquieu Defends the Separation of Powers.")

Montesquieu's *Spirit of the Laws*, perhaps the single most influential book of the century, exhibits the internal tensions of the Enlightenment. In it, Montesquieu pursued an empirical method, taking illustrative examples from the political experience of both ancient and modern nations. From these, he concluded there could be no single set of political laws that applied to all peoples at all times and in all places. The good political life depended rather on the relationship among many political variables. Whether the best form of government for a country was a monarchy or a republic, for example, depended on that country's size, population, social and religious customs, economic structure, traditions, and climate. Only a careful examination and evaluation of these elements could reveal what mode of government would prove most beneficial to a particular people.

So far as France was concerned, Montesquieu had some definite ideas. He believed in a monarchical government tempered and limited by various sets of intermediary institutions, including the aristocracy, the towns, and the other corporate bodies that enjoyed liberties the monarch had to respect. These corporate bodies might be said to represent various segments of the general population and thus of public opinion. In France, he regarded the aristocratic courts, or *parlements*, as the major example of an intermediary association. Their role was to limit the power of the monarchy and thus to preserve the liberty of its subjects.

In championing these aristocratic bodies and the general role of the aristocracy, Montesquieu was a political conservative. He adopted this conservatism in the hope of achieving reform, however, for he believed that the oppressive and inefficient absolutism of the monarchy accounted for the degradation of French life.

One of Montesquieu's most influential ideas was that of the division of power in government. For his model of a government with authority wisely separated among different branches, he took contemporary Great Britain. There, he believed, executive power resided in the king, legislative power in the Parliament, and judicial power in the courts. He thought any two branches could check and balance the power of the other. His perception of the eighteenth-century British constitution was incorrect because he failed to see how patronage and electoral corruption allowed a handful of powerful aristocrats to dominate the government. Moreover, he was also unaware of the emerging cabinet system, which was slowly making the executive power a creature of the Parliament.

Nevertheless, Montesquieu's analysis illustrated his strong sense that monarchs should be subject to constitutional limits on their power and that a separate legislature, not the monarch, should formulate laws. For this reason, although he set out to defend the political privileges of the French aristocracy, Montesquieu's ideas had a profound and still-lasting effect on the constitutional form of liberal democracies for more than two centuries.

Rousseau: A Radical Critique of Modern Society

Jean-Jacques Rousseau (1712–1778) held a view of the exercise and reform of political power that was quite different from Montesquieu's. Rousseau was a strange, isolated genius who never felt particularly comfortable with the other *philosophes*. His own life was troubled. He could form few close friendships. He sired numerous children, whom he abandoned to foundling hospitals. Yet perhaps more than any other writer of the mid-eighteenth century, he transcended the political thought and values of his own time. Rousseau had a deep antipathy toward the world and the society in which he lived. It seemed to him impossible for human beings living according to the commercial values of his time to achieve moral, virtuous, or sincere lives. In 1750, in his *Discourse on the Moral Effects of the Arts and Sciences*, he contended that the process of civilization and enlightenment had corrupted human nature. In 1755, in his *Discourse on the Origin of Inequality*, Rousseau blamed much of the evil in the world on the uneven distribution of property.

In both works, Rousseau brilliantly and directly challenged the social fabric of the day. He drew into question the concepts of material and intellectual progress and the morality of a society in which commerce and industry were regarded as the most important human activities. The other *philosophes* generally believed that life would improve if people could enjoy more of the fruits of the Earth or could produce more goods. Rousseau raised the more fundamental question of what constitutes the good life. This question has haunted European social thought ever since the eighteenth century.

Jean-Jacques Rousseau (1712–1778) raised some of the most profound social and ethical questions of the Enlightenment. This portrait is by Maurice Quentin.
Maurice Quentin de la Tour, Jean Jacques Rousseau, ca. 1740. Original: Genf, Musée d'Art et d'Histoire. Bildarchiv Preussischer Kulturbesitz

Rousseau carried these same concerns into his political thought. His most extensive discussion of politics appeared in *The Social Contract* (1762). Although the book attracted rather little immediate attention, by the end of the century it was widely read in France. Compared with Montesquieu's *Spirit of the Laws*, *The Social Contract* is a very abstract book. It does not propose specific reforms, but outlines the kind of political structure that Rousseau believed would overcome the evils of contemporary politics and society.

In the tradition of John Locke, most eighteenth-century political thinkers regarded human beings as individuals and society as a collection of individuals pursuing personal, selfish goals. These writers wished to liberate individuals from the undue bonds of government. Rousseau picked up the stick from the other end. His book opens with the declaration, "All men are born free, but everywhere they are in chains."[8] The rest of the volume is a defense of the chains of a properly organized society over its members.

Rousseau suggested that society is more important than its individual members, because they are what they are only by virtue of their relationship to the larger community. Independent human beings living alone can achieve very little. Through their relationship to the larger community, they become moral creatures capable of significant action. The question then becomes, What kind of community allows people to behave morally? In his two previous discourses, Rousseau had explained that the contemporaneous European society was not such a community; it was merely an aggregate of competing individuals whose chief social goal was to preserve selfish independence in spite of all potential social bonds and obligations.

Rousseau envisioned a society in which each person could maintain personal freedom while behaving as a loyal member of the larger community. Drawing on the traditions of Plato and Calvin, he defined freedom as obedience to law. In his case, the law to be obeyed was that created by the general will. In a society with virtuous customs and morals in which citizens have adequate information on important issues, the concept of the general will is normally equivalent to the will of a majority of voting citizens. Democratic participation in decision-making would bind the individual citizen to the community. Rousseau believed that the general will, thus understood, must always be right and that to obey the general will is to be free. This argument led him to the notorious conclusion that under certain circumstances some people must be forced to

be free. Rousseau's politics thus constituted a justification for radical direct democracy and for collective action against individual citizens.

Rousseau had in effect launched an assault on the eighteenth-century cult of the individual and the fruits of selfishness. He stood at odds with the commercial spirit that was transforming the society in which he lived. Rousseau would have disapproved of the main thrust of Adam Smith's *Wealth of Nations*, which he may or may not have read, and would no doubt have preferred a study on the *virtue* of nations. Smith wanted people to be prosperous; Rousseau wanted them to be good even if being good meant that they might remain poor. He saw human beings not as independent individuals, but as creatures enmeshed in necessary social relationships. He believed that loyalty to the community should be encouraged. As one device to that end, he suggested that a properly governed society should decree a civic religion based on the creed of deism. Such a shared religion, the observance of which he thought should be enforced by repressive legislation, could, he argued, help unify a society.

Rousseau had only a marginal impact on his own time. The other *philosophes* questioned his critique of material improvement. Aristocrats and royal ministers could hardly be expected to welcome his proposal for radical democracy. Too many people were either making or hoping to make money to appreciate his criticism of commercial values. He proved, however, to be a figure to whom later generations returned. Many leaders in the French Revolution were familiar with his writing, and he influenced many writers in the nineteenth and twentieth centuries who were critical of the general tenor and direction of Western culture. Rousseau hated much about the emerging modern society in Europe, but he contributed much to modernity by exemplifying for later generations the critic who dared to call into question the very foundations of social thought and action.

Women in the Thought and Practice of the Enlightenment

Women, especially in France, helped significantly to promote the careers of the *philosophes*. In Paris, the salons of women such as Marie-Thérèse Geoffrin (1699–1777), Julie de Lespinasse (1733–1776), and Claudine de Tencin (1689–1749) gave the *philosophes* access to useful social and political contacts and a receptive environment in which to circulate their ideas. Association with a fashionable salon brought *philosophes* increased social status and added luster and respectability to their

[8]Jean-Jacques Rousseau, *The Social Contract and Discourses*, trans. by G. D. H. Cole (New York: Dutton, 1950), p. 3.

ideas. They clearly enjoyed the opportunity to be the center of attention that a salon provided, and their presence at them could boost the sales of their works. The women who organized the salons were well connected to major political figures who could help protect the *philosophes* and secure them pensions. The marquise de Pompadour, the mistress of Louis XV (1721–1764), played a key role in overcoming efforts to censor the *Encyclopedia*. She also helped block the circulation of works attacking the *philosophes*. Other salon hostesses purchased the writings of the *philosophes* and distributed them among their friends. Madame de Tencin was responsible for promoting Montesquieu's *Spirit of the Laws* in this way.

Despite this help and support from the learned women of Paris, the *philosophes* were on the whole not strong feminists. Many urged better and broader education for women. They criticized the education women did receive as overly religious, and they tended to reject ascetic views of sexual relations. But in general, they displayed rather traditional views toward women and advocated no radical changes in the social condition of women.

Montesquieu, for example, illustrates some of these tensions in the views of Enlightenment writers toward women. He maintained in general that the status of women in a society was the result of climate, the political regime, culture, and women's physiological nature. He believed that women were not naturally inferior to men and should have a wider role in society. He showed himself well aware of the kinds of personal, emotional, and sexual repression European women endured in his day. He sympathetically observed the value placed on women's appearance and the prejudice women met as they aged. In *The Persian Letters*, he included a long exchange about the repression of women in a Persian harem, condemning by implication the restrictions on women in European society. Yet there were limits to Montesquieu's willingness to consider social change in regard to the role of women in European life. Although in the *Spirit of the Laws* he indicated a belief in the equality of the sexes, he still retained a traditional view of marriage and family and expected men to dominate those institutions. Furthermore, although he supported the right of women to divorce and opposed laws directly oppressive of women, he upheld the ideal of female chastity.

The views about women expressed in the *Encyclopedia* were less generous than those of Montesquieu. It suggested some ways to improve women's lives, but in general, it did not include the condition of women as a focus of reform. The editors, Diderot and d'Alembert, recruited men almost exclusively as contributors, and there is no indication that they saw a need to include many articles by women. Most of the articles that dealt with women specifically or that discussed women in connection with other subjects often emphasized their physical weakness and inferiority, usually attributed to menstruation or childbearing. Contributors disagreed on the social equality of women. Some favored it, others opposed it, and still others were indifferent. The articles conveyed a general sense that women were reared to be frivolous and unconcerned with important issues. The Encyclopedists discussed women primarily in a family context— as daughters, wives, and mothers—and presented

The salon of Mme. Marie Thérèse Geoffrin (1699–1777) was one of the most important gathering spots for Enlightenment writers during the middle of the eighteenth century. Well-connected women such as Mme. Geoffrin were instrumental in helping the philosophes they patronized to bring their ideas to the attention of influential people in French society and politics.
Giraudon/Art Resource, N.Y.

Rousseau Argues for Separate Spheres for Men and Women

Rousseau published Émile, *a novel about education, in 1762. In it, he made one of the strongest and most influential arguments of the eighteenth century for distinct social roles for men and women. Furthermore, he portrayed women as fundamentally subordinate to men. In the next document, Mary Wollstonecraft, a contemporary, presents a rebuttal.*

❖ *How does Rousseau move from the physical differences between men and women to an argument for distinct social roles and social spheres? What would be the proper kinds of social activities for women in Rousseau's vision? What kind of education would he think appropriate for women?*

There is no parity between the two sexes in regard to the consequences of sex. The male is male only at certain moments. The female is female her whole life or at least during her whole youth. Everything constantly recalls her sex to her; and, to fulfill its functions well, she needs a constitution which corresponds to it. She needs care during her pregnancy; she needs rest at the time of childbirth; she needs a soft and sedentary life to suckle her children; she needs patience and gentleness, a zeal and an affection that nothing can rebuff in order to raise her children. She serves as the link between them and their father; she alone makes him love them and gives him the confidence to call them his own. How much tenderness and care is required to maintain the union of the whole family! And, finally, all this must come not from virtues but from tastes, or else the human species would soon be extinguished.

The strictness of the relative duties of the two sexes is not and cannot be the same. When woman complains on this score about unjust man-made inequality, she is wrong. This inequality is not a human institution—or, at least, it is the work not of prejudice but of reason. It is up to the sex that nature has charged with the bearing of children to be responsible for them to the other sex. Doubtless it is not permitted to any one to violate his faith, and every unfaithful husband who deprives

his wife of the only reward of the austere duties of her sex is an unjust and barbarous man. But the unfaithful woman does more; she dissolves the family and breaks all the bonds of nature....

Once it is demonstrated that man and woman are not and ought not be constituted in the same way in either character or temperament, it follows that they ought not to have the same education. In following nature's directions, man and woman ought to act in concert, but they ought not to do the same things. The goal of their labors is common, but their labors themselves are different, and consequently so are the tastes directing them....

The good constitution of children initially depends on that of their mothers. The first education of men depends on the care of women. Men's morals, their passions, their tastes, their pleasures, their very happiness also depend on women. Thus the whole education of women ought to relate to men. To please men, to be useful to them, to make herself loved and honored by them, to raise them when young, to care for them when grown, to counsel them, to console them, to make their lives agreeable and sweet—these are the duties of women at all times, and they ought to be taught from childhood. So long as one does not return to this principle, one will deviate from the goal, and all the precepts taught to women will be of no use for their happiness or for ours.

From Émile or On Education *by Jean-Jacques Rousseau by Allan Bloom, Translator. Copyright © 1979 by Basic Books, Inc. Reprinted by permission of BasicBooks, a member of Perseus Books, L.I.C.*

motherhood as their most important occupation. And on sexual behavior, the Encyclopedists upheld an unquestioned double standard.

In contrast to the articles, however, illustrations in the *Encyclopedia* showed women deeply involved in the economic activities of the day. The illustra-

tions also showed the activities of lower class and working-class women, about whom the articles had little to say.

One of the most surprising and influential analyses of the position of women came from Jean-Jacques Rousseau. This most radical of all Enlightenment political theorists urged a very traditional and conservative role for women. In his novel *Émile* (1762) (discussed again in Chapter 20), he set forth a radical version of the view that men and women occupy separate spheres. He declared that women should be educated for a position subordinate to men, emphasizing especially women's function in bearing and rearing children. In his vision, there was little else for women to do but make themselves pleasing to men. He portrayed them as weaker and inferior to men in virtually all respects, except perhaps for their capacity for feeling and giving love. He excluded them from political life. The world of citizenship, political action, and civic virtue was to be populated by men. Women were assigned the domestic sphere alone. (See "Rousseau Argues for Separate Spheres for Men and Women.") Many of these attitudes were not new—some have roots as ancient as Roman law—but Rousseau's powerful presentation and the influence of his other writings gave them new life in the late eighteenth century. Rousseau deeply influenced many leaders of the French Revolution, who, as will be seen in the next chapter, often incorporated his view on gender roles in the policies they implemented.

Paradoxically, in spite of these views and in spite of his own ill treatment of the woman who bore his many children, Rousseau achieved a vast following among women in the eighteenth century. He is credited with persuading thousands of upper-class women to breast-feed their own children rather than putting them out to wet nurses. One explanation for this influence is that his writings, although they did not advocate liberating women or expanding their social or economic roles, did stress the importance of their emotions and subjective feelings. He portrayed the domestic life and the role of wife and mother as a noble and fulfilling vocation, giving middle- and upper-class women a sense that their daily occupations had purpose. He assigned them a degree of influence in the domestic sphere that they could not have competing with men outside it.

In 1792, in *A Vindication of the Rights of Woman*, Mary Wollstonecraft (1759–1797) brought Rousseau before the judgment of the rational Enlightenment ideal of progressive knowledge. The immediate incentive for this essay was her opposition to certain policies of the French Revolution, unfavorable to women, which were inspired by Rousseau. Wollstonecraft (who, like so many women of her day, died of puerperal fever shortly after childbirth) accused Rousseau and others after him who upheld traditional roles for women of attempting to narrow women's vision and limit their experience. She argued that to confine women to the separate domestic sphere because of supposed limitations of their physiological nature was to make them the sensual slaves of men. Confined in this separate sphere, they were the victims of male tyranny, their obedience was blind, and they could never achieve their own moral or intellectual identity. Denying good education to women would impede the progress of all humanity. (See "Mary Wollstonecraft Criticizes Rousseau's View of Women.") With these arguments, Wollstonecraft was demanding for women the kind of liberty that male writers of the Enlightenment had been championing for men for more than a century. In doing so, she placed herself among the *philosophes* and broadened the agenda of the Enlightenment to include the rights of women as well as those of men.

Major Works of the Enlightenment and Their Publication Dates

1670	Spinoza's *Theologico-Political Treatise*
1677	Spinoza's *Ethics* (published pothumously)
1687	Newton's *Principia Mathematica*
1690	Locke's *Essay Concerning Human Understanding*
1696	Toland's *Christianity Not Mysterious*
1721	Montesquieu's *Persian Letters*
1733	Voltaire's *Letters on the English*
1738	Voltaire's *Elements of the Philosophy of Newton*
1748	Montesquieu's *Spirit of the Laws*
1748	Hume's *Inquiry into Human Nature*, with the chapter "Of Miracles"
1750	Rousseau's *Discourse on the Moral Effects of the Arts and Sciences*
1751	First volume of the *Encyclopedia*, edited by Diderot
1755	Rousseau's *Discourse on the Origin of Inequality*
1759	Voltaire's *Candide*
1762	Rousseau's *Social Contract* and *Émile*
1763	Voltaire's *Treatise on Tolerance*
1764	Voltaire's *Philosophical Dictionary*
1764	Beccaria's *On Crimes and Punishments*
1776	Gibbon's *Decline and Fall of the Roman Empire*
1776	Smith's *Wealth of Nations*
1779	Lessing's *Nathan the Wise*
1783	Mendelsohn's *Jerusalem; or, On Ecclesiastical Power and Judaism*
1792	Wollstonecraft's *Vindication of the Rights of Woman*
1793	Kant's *Religion within the Limits of Reason Alone*

Mary Wollstonecraft Criticizes Rousseau's View of Women

Mary Wollstonecraft published A Vindication of the Rights of Woman *in 1792, thirty years after Rousseau's* Émile *had appeared. In this pioneering feminist work, she criticizes and rejects Rousseau's argument for distinct and separate spheres for men and women. She portrays that argument as defending the continued bondage of women to men and as hindering the wider education of the entire human race.*

❖ *What specific criticisms does Wollstonecraft direct against Rousseau's views? Why does Wollstonecraft put so much emphasis on a new kind of education for women?*

The most perfect education...is such an exercise of the understanding as is best calculated to strengthen the body and form the heart. Or, in other words, to enable the individual to attain such habits of virtue as will render it independent. In fact, it is a farce to call any being virtuous whose virtues do not result from the exercise of its own reason. This was Rousseau's opinion respecting men: I extend it to women....

I may be accused of arrogance; still I must declare what I firmly believe, that all the writers who have written on the subject of female education and manners from Rousseau to Dr. Gregory [a Scottish physician], have contributed to render women more artificial, weak characters, than they would otherwise have been; and, consequently, more useless members of society....

...Strengthen the female mind by enlarging it, and there will be an end to blind obedience; but, as blind obedience is ever sought for by power, tyrants and sensualists are in the right when they endeavour to keep women in the dark, because the former only wants slaves, and the latter a play-thing. The sensualist, indeed, has been the most dangerous of tyrants, and women have been duped by their lovers, as princes by their ministers, whilst dreaming that they reigned over them.

...Rousseau declares that a woman should never, for a moment, feel herself independent, that she should be governed by fear to exercise her natural cunning, and made a coquettish slave in order to render her a more alluring object of desire, a sweeter companion to man, whenever he chooses to relax himself. He carries the arguments, which he pretends to draw from the indications of nature, still further, and insinuates that truth and fortitude, the corner stones of all human virtue, should be cultivated with certain restrictions, because, with re-spect to the female character, obedience is the grand lesson which ought to be impressed with unrelenting rigour.

What nonsense! when will a great man arise with sufficient strength of mind to put away the fumes which pride and sensuality have thus spread over the subject! If women are by nature inferior to men, their virtues must be the same in quality, if not in degree, or virtue is a relative idea; consequently, their conduct should be founded on the same principles, and have the same aim.

Connected with man as daughters, wives, and mothers, their moral character may be estimated by their manner of fulfilling those simple duties; but the end, the grand end of their exertions should be to unfold their own faculties and acquire the dignity of conscious virtue....

But avoiding...any direct comparison of the two sexes collectively, or frankly acknowledging the inferiority of women, according to the present appearance of things, I shall only insist that men have increased that inferiority till women are almost sunk below the standard of rational creatures. Let their faculties have room to unfold, and their virtues to gain strength, and then determine where the whole sex must stand in the intellectual scale....

...I...will venture to assert, that till women are more rationally educated, the progress of human virtue and improvement in knowledge must receive continual checks....

The mother, who wishes to give true dignity of character to her daughter, must, regardless of the sneers of ignorance, proceed on a plan diametrically opposite to that which Rousseau has recommended with all the deluding charms of eloquence and philosophical sophistry: for his eloquence renders absurdities plausible, and his dogmatic conclusions puzzle, without convincing, those who have not ability to refute them.

From Mary Wollstonecraft, *A Vindication of the Rights of Woman,* ed. by Carol H. Poston (New York: W. W. Norton & Co., Inc., 1975), pp. 21, 22, 24–26, 35, 40, 41.

Enlightened Absolutism

Most of the *philosophes* favored neither Montesquieu's reformed and revived aristocracy nor Rousseau's democracy as a solution to contemporary political problems. Like other thoughtful people of the day in other stations and occupations, they looked to the existing monarchies. Voltaire was a very strong monarchist. In 1759 he published a *History of the Russian Empire Under Peter the Great*, which declared, "Peter was born, and Russia was formed."[9] Voltaire and other *philosophes*, such as Diderot, who visited Catherine II of Russia, and the physiocrats, some of whom were ministers to the French kings, did not wish to limit the power of monarchs. Rather, they sought to redirect that power toward the rationalization of economic and political structures and the liberation of intellectual life. Most *philosophes* were not opposed to power if they could find a way of using it for their own purposes or if they could profit in one way or another from their personal relationships to strong monarchs.

During the last third of the century, it seemed to some observers that several European rulers had actually embraced many of the reforms set forth by the *philosophes*. "Enlightened Absolutism" is the term used to describe this phenomenon. It indicates monarchical government dedicated to the rational strengthening of the central absolutist administration at the cost of other lesser centers of political power. The monarchs most closely associated with it are Frederick II of Prussia, Joseph II of Austria, and Catherine II of Russia. Each had complicted relationships to the community of enlightened writers.

Frederick II corresponded with the *philosophes*, provided Voltaire with a place at his court for a time, and even wrote history and political tracts. Catherine II, adept at what would later be called public relations, consciously sought to create the image of being enlightened. She read and cited the works of the *philosophes*, provided financial subsidies to Diderot, and corresponded extensively with Voltaire, lavishing compliments on him, all in the hope that she would receive favorable comments from them, as she indeed did. Joseph II continued numerous initiatives begun by his mother, Maria Theresa. He imposed a series of religious, legal, and social reforms that contemporaries believed he had derived from suggestions of the *philosophes*.

The relationship between these rulers and the writers of the Enlightenment was, however, more complicated than these appearances suggest. The humanitarian and liberating zeal of the Enlightenment writers was only part of what motivated the policies of the rulers. Frederick II, Joseph II, and Catherine II were also determined that their nations would play major diplomatic and military roles in Europe. In no small measure, they adopted Enlightenment policies favoring the rational economic and social integration of their realms because these policies also increased their military strength. As explained in Chapter 17, all the states of Europe had emerged from the Seven Years' War knowing that they would need stronger armies for future wars and increased revenues to finance those armies. The search for new revenues and internal political support was one of the incentives prompting the "enlightened" reforms of the monarchs of Russia, Prussia, and Austria. Consequently, they and their advisers used rationality to pursue many goals admired by most *philosophes*, but also to further what some among the *philosophes* considered irrational militarism. The flattery of monarchs could bend the opinions of a *philososphe*. For example, Voltaire, who had written against war, could praise the military expansion of Catherine's Russia because it appeared in his mind to bring civilization to peoples he regarded as uncivilized and because he enjoyed being known as a literary confidant of the empress.

Frederick the Great of Prussia

Frederick II, the Great (r. 1740–1786), sought the recovery and consolidation of Prussia in the wake of its suffering and near defeat in the midcentury wars. He succeeded, at great military and financial cost, in retaining Silesia, which he had seized from Austria in 1740, and worked to promote it as a manufacturing district. Like his Hohenzollern forebears, he continued to import workers from outside Prussia. He directed new attention to Prussian agriculture. Under state supervision, swamps were drained, new crops introduced, and peasants encouraged and sometimes compelled to migrate where they were needed. For the first time in Prussia, potatoes and turnips came into general production. Frederick also established a land-mortgage credit association to help landowners raise money for agricultural improvements.

The impetus for these economic policies came from the state. The monarchy and its bureaucracy were the engine for change. Most Prussians, however, did not prosper under Frederick's reign. The burden of taxation continued to fall disproportionately on peasants and townspeople.

Frederick's noneconomic policies met with somewhat more success. Continuing the Hohenzollern policy of toleration, he allowed Catholics and Jews to settle in his predominantly Lutheran country, and he protected the Catholics living in Silesia. This policy

[9]Quoted in Larry Wolff, *Inventing Eastern Europe: The Map of Civilization on the Mind of the Enlightenment* (Palo Alto, CA: Stanford University Press, 1994), p. 200.

Frederick II, the Great (r. 1740–1786), sought to create prosperity for all parts of the Prussian economy and would make personal visits to factories and shops to inspect the goods being made and sold in his kingdom. Here, as portrayed in a late nineteenth-century painting, he visits a fashionable shop. Gemalde von Albert Baur, ca. 1901. *Frederick II, the Great, the house von der Leyen in Krefeld, on June 10, 1763.* Bildarchiv Preussischer Kulturbesitz

permitted the state to benefit from the economic contribution of foreign workers. Frederick, however, virtually always appointed Protestants to major positions in the government and army.

Frederick also ordered a new codification of Prussian law, completed after his death. His objective was to rationalize the existing legal system, making it more efficient, eliminating regional peculiarities, and reducing aristocratic influence. Frederick shared this concern for legal reform with the other enlightened monarchs, who saw it as a means of extending and strengthening royal power.

Reflecting an important change in the European view of the ruler, Frederick liked to describe himself as "the first servant of the State." The impersonal state was beginning to replace the personal monarchy. Kings might come and go, but the apparatus of government—the bureaucracy, the armies, the laws, the courts, and the combination of power, service, and protection that compelled citizens' loyalty—remained. The state as an entity separate from the personality of the ruler came into its own after the French Revolution, but it was born in the monarchies of the old regime.

Joseph II of Austria

No eighteenth-century ruler so embodied rational, impersonal force as the emperor Joseph II of Austria. He was the son of Maria Theresa and co-ruler with her from 1765 to 1780. During the next ten years he ruled alone. He was an austere and humorless person. During much of his life, he slept on straw and ate little but beef. He prided himself on a narrow,

passionless rationality, which he sought to impose by his own will on the various Habsburg domains. Despite his eccentricities and the coldness of his personality, Joseph II sincerely wished to improve the lot of his people. He was much less a political opportunist and cynic than either Frederick the Great of Prussia or Catherine the Great of Russia. The ultimate result of his well-intentioned efforts was a series of aristocratic and peasant rebellions extending from Hungary to the Austrian Netherlands.

CENTRALIZATION OF AUTHORITY   As explained in Chapter 15, of all the rising states of the eighteenth century, Austria was the most diverse in its people and problems. Robert Palmer likened it to "a vast holding company."[10] The Habsburgs never succeeded in creating either a unified administrative structure or a strong aristocratic loyalty. To preserve the monarchy during the War of the Austrian Succession (1740–1748), Maria Theresa had guaranteed the aristocracy considerable independence, especially in Hungary.

During and after the conflict, however, Maria Theresa took steps to strengthen the power of the crown outside of Hungary, building more of a bureaucracy than had previous Habsburg rulers. In Austria and Bohemia, through major administrative reorganization, she imposed a much more efficient system of tax collection that extracted funds even from the clergy and the nobles. She also established several central councils to deal with governmental problems. To assure her government a sufficient supply of educated offi-

[10]Robert R. Palmer, *The Age of Democratic Revolution*, vol. 1 (Princeton, NJ: Princeton University Press, 1959), p. 103.

cials, she sought to bring all educational institutions into the service of the crown. She also expanded primary education on the local level.

Maria Theresa was concerned about the welfare of the peasants and serfs. She brought them some assistance by extending the authority of the royal bureaucracy over local nobles and decreeing limits on the amount of labor, or *robot*, landowners could demand from peasants. Her concern was not particularly humanitarian; rather, it arose from her desire to assure a good pool from which to draw military recruits. In all these policies and in her general desire to stimulate prosperity and military strength by royal initiative, Maria Theresa anticipated the policies of her son.

Joseph II was more determined than his mother, and his projected reforms were more wide ranging. He aimed to extend the borders of his territories in the direction of Poland, Bavaria, and the Ottoman Empire. His greatest ambition, however, was to increase the authority of the Habsburg emperor over his various realms. He sought to overcome the pluralism of the Habsburg holdings by imposing central authority in areas of political and social life in which Maria Theresa had wisely chosen not to exert authority.

In particular, Joseph sought to reduce Hungarian autonomy. To avoid having to guarantee Hungary's existing privileges or extend new ones at the time of his coronation, he refused to have himself crowned king of Hungary and even had the Crown of Saint Stephen sent to the Imperial Treasury in Vienna. He reorganized local government in Hungary to increase the authority of his own officials. He also required the use of German in all governmental matters. The Magyar nobility resisted these measures, and in 1790 Joseph had to rescind most of them.

ECCLESIASTICAL POLICIES   Another target of Joseph's assertion of royal absolutism was the church. From the reign of Charles V in the sixteenth century to that of Maria Theresa, the Habsburgs had been the most important dynastic champion of Roman Catholicism. Maria Theresa was devout, but she had not allowed the church to limit her authority. Although she had attempted to discourage certain of the more extreme modes of Roman Catholic popular religious piety, such as public flagellation, she adamantly opposed toleration. (See "Maria Theresa and Joseph II of Austria Debate Toleration.")

Joseph II was also a practicing Catholic, but from the standpoint of both enlightenment and pragmatic politics, he favored a policy of toleration. In October 1781, Joseph issued a toleration patent or decree that extended freedom of worship to Lutherans, Calvinists, and the Greek Orthodox. They were permitted to have their own places of worship, to

sponsor schools, to enter skilled trades, and to hold academic appointments and positions in the public service. From 1781 through 1789, Joseph issued a series of patents and other enactments that relieved the Jews in his realms of certain taxes and signs of personal degradation. He also extended to them the right of private worship. Although these actions benefitted the Jews, they did not grant them full equality with other Habsburg subjects.

Joseph also sought to bring the various institutions of the Roman Catholic Church directly under royal control. He forbade direct communication between the bishops of his realms and the pope. Viewing religious orders as unproductive, he dissolved more than 600 monasteries and confiscated their lands. He excepted, however, certain orders that ran schools or hospitals. He dissolved the traditional Roman Catholic seminaries, which instilled in priests too great a loyalty to the papacy and too little concern for their future parishioners. In their place, he sponsored eight general

Joseph II of Austria (r. 1765–1790), shown here in the center, with his brother Leopold (later Leopold II) on his right, attempted to impose exceedingly rational policies on the Habsburg Empire. Joseph urged religious toleration and confiscated church lands. His attempts to tax the nobility stirred up a revolt that Leopold settled after Joseph's death by rescinding his policies. Pompeo Batoni (1708–1787). Kunsthistorisches Museum, Vienna

Maria Theresa and Joseph II of Austria Debate Toleration

In 1765 Joseph, the eldest son of the Empress Maria Theresa, had become co-regent with his mother. He began to believe that some measure of religious toleration should be introduced into the Habsburg realms. Maria Theresa, whose opinions on many political issues were quite advanced, adamantly refused to consider adopting a policy of toleration. This exchange of letters sets forth their sharply differing positions. The toleration of Protestants that is in dispute related only to Lutherans and Calvinists. Maria Theresa died in 1780; the next year Joseph issued an edict of toleration.

❖ *How does Joseph define toleration, and why does Maria Theresa believe that it is the same as religious indifference? Why does Maria Theresa fear that toleration will bring about political as well as religious turmoil? Why does Maria Theresa think that Joseph's belief in toleration has come from Joseph's acquaintance with wicked books?*

Joseph to Maria Theresa, July 20, 1777

It is only the word "toleration" which has caused the misunderstanding. You have taken it in quite a different meaning [from mine expressed in an earlier letter]. God preserve me from thinking it a matter of indifference whether the citizens turn Protestant or remain Catholic, still less, whether they cleave to, or at least observe, the cult which they have inherited from their fathers! I would give all I possess if all the Protestants of your states would go over to Catholicism.

The word "toleration," as I understand it, means only that I would employ any persons, without distinction of religion, in purely temporal matters, allow them to own property, practice trades, be citizens, if they were qualified and if this would be of advantage to the State and its industry. Those who, unfortunately, adhere to a false faith, are far further from being converted if they remain in their own country than if they migrate into another, in which they can hear and see the convincing truths of the Catholic faith. Similarly, the undisturbed practice of their religion makes them far better subjects and causes them to avoid irreligion, which is a far greater danger to our Catholics than if one lets them see others practice their religion unimpeded.

Maria Theresa to Joseph, Late July, 1777

Without a dominant religion? Toleration, indifference are precisely the true means of undermining everything, taking away every foundation; we others will then be the greatest losers.... He is no friend of humanity, as the popular phrase is, who allows everyone his own thoughts. I am speaking only in the political sense, not as a Christian; nothing is so necessary and salutary as religion. Will you allow everyone to fashion his own religion as he pleases? No fixed cult, no subordination to the Church—what will then become of us? The result will not be quiet and contentment; its outcome will be the rule of the stronger and more unhappy times like those which we have already seen. A manifesto by you to this effect can produce the utmost distress and make you responsible for many thousands of souls. And what are my own sufferings, when I see you entangled in opinions so erroneous? What is at stake is not only the welfare of the State but your own salvation....Turning your eyes and ears everywhere, mingling your spirit of contradiction with the simultaneous desire to create something, you are ruining yourself and dragging the Monarchy down with you into the abyss....I only wish to live so long as I can hope to descend to my ancestors with the consolation that my son will be as great, as religious as his forebears, that he will return from his erroneous views, from those wicked books whose authors parade their cleverness at the expense of all that is most holy and most worthy of respect in the world, who want to introduce an imaginary freedom which can never exist and which degenerates into license and into complete revolution.

As quoted in C. A. Macartney, ed., *The Habsburg and Hohenzollern Dynasties in the Seventeenth and Eighteenth Centuries* (New York: Walker, 1970), pp. 151–153. Reprinted by permission of Walker and Co.

seminaries whose training emphasized parish duties. He also issued decrees creating new parishes in areas with a shortage of priests, funding them with money from the confiscated monasteries. In effect, Joseph's policies made Roman Catholic priests the employees of the state, ending the influence of the Roman Catholic Church as an independent institution in Habsburg lands. In many respects, the ecclesiastical policies of Joseph II, known as *Josephinism*, prefigured those of the French Revolution.

ECONOMIC AND AGRARIAN REFORM   Like Frederick of Prussia, Joseph sought to improve the economic life of his domains. He abolished many internal tariffs and encouraged road building and the improvement of river transport. He went on personal inspection tours of farms and manufacturing districts. Joseph also reconstructed the judicial system to make laws more uniform and rational and to lessen the influence of local landlords. National courts with power over the landlord courts were established. All of these improvements were expected to bring new unity to the state and more taxes into the imperial coffers in Vienna.

Joseph's policies toward serfdom and the land were a far-reaching extension of those Maria Theresa had initiated. Over the course of his reign, he introduced a series of reforms that touched the very heart of the rural social structure. He did not seek to abolish the authority of landlords over their peasants, but he did seek to make that authority more moderate and subject to the oversight of royal officials. He abolished serfdom as a legally sanctioned state of servitude. He granted peasants a wide array of personal freedoms, including the right to marry, to engage in skilled work, and to have their children trained in skilled work without the landlord's permission.

Joseph reformed the procedures of the manorial courts and opened avenues of appeal to royal officials. He also encouraged landlords to change land leases so it would be easier for peasants to inherit them or to transfer them to other peasants. His goal in all of these efforts to reduce traditional burdens on peasants was to make them more productive and industrious farmers.

Near the end of his reign, Joseph proposed a new and daring system of land taxation. He decreed in 1789 that all proprietors of the land were to be taxed regardless of social status. No longer were the peasants alone to bear the burden of taxation. He abolished *robot* and commuted it into a monetary tax, only part of which was to go to the landlord, the rest reverting to the state. Resistant nobles blocked the implementation of this decree, and after Joseph died in 1790 it did not go into effect. This and other of Joseph's earlier measures, however, brought turmoil throughout the Habsburg realms. Peasants revolted over disagreements about the interpretation of their newly granted rights. The nobles of the various realms protested the taxation scheme. The Hungarian Magyars resisted Joseph's centralization measures and forced him to rescind them.

On Joseph's death, the crown went to his brother Leopold II (r. 1790–1792). Although sympathetic to Joseph's goals, Leopold found himself forced to repeal many of the most controversial decrees, such as that on taxation. In other areas, Leopold thought his brother's policies simply wrong. For example, he returned much political and administrative power to local nobles because he thought it expedient for them to have a voice in government. Still, he did not repudiate his brother's policies wholesale. He retained, in particular, Joseph's religious policies and maintained political centralization to the extent he thought possible.

Catherine the Great of Russia

Joseph II never grasped the practical necessity of forging political constituencies to support his policies. Catherine II (r. 1762–1796), who had been born

Catherine the Great ascended to the Russian throne after the murder of her husband. She tried initially to enact major reforms, but she never intended to abandon absolutism. She assured nobles of their rights and by the end of her reign had imposed press censorship.
The Granger Collection

Russia from Peter the Great Through Catherine the Great

1725	Death of Peter the Great
1725–1727	Catherine I
1727–1730	Peter II
1730–1741	Anna
1740–1741	Ivan VI
1741–1762	Elizabeth
1762	Peter III
1762	Catherine II (the Great) becomes empress
1767	Legislative Commission summoned
1769	War with Turkey begins
1771–1775	Pugachev's Rebellion
1772	First Partition of Poland
1774	Treaty of Kuchuk-Kainardji ends war with Turkey
1775	Reorganization of local government
1783	Russia annexes the Crimea
1785	Catherine issues the Charter of the Nobility
1793	Second Partition of Poland
1795	Third Partition of Poland
1796	Death of Catherine the Great

a German princess, but who became empress of Russia, understood only too well the fragility of the Romanov dynasty's base of power.

After the death of Peter the Great in 1725, the court nobles and the army repeatedly determined the Russian succession. As a result, the crown fell primarily into the hands of people with little talent. Peter's wife, Catherine I, ruled for two years (1725–1727) and was succeeded for three years by Peter's grandson, Peter II. In 1730, the crown devolved on Anna, a niece of Peter the Great. During 1740 and 1741, a child named Ivan VI, who was less than a year old, was the nominal ruler. Finally, in 1741, Peter the Great's daughter Elizabeth came to the throne. She held the title of empress until 1762, but her reign was not notable for new political departures or sound administration. Her court was a shambles of political and romantic intrigue. Much of the power possessed by the tsar at the opening of the century had vanished.

At her death in 1762, Elizabeth was succeeded by Peter III, one of her nephews. He was a weak ruler whom many contemporaries considered mad. He immediately exempted the nobles from compulsory military service and then rapidly made peace with Frederick the Great, for whom he held unbounded admiration. That decision probably saved Prussia from military defeat in the Seven

Years' War. The one positive feature of this unbalanced creature's life was his marriage in 1745 to a young German princess born in Anhalt Zerbst. This was the future Catherine the Great.

For almost twenty years, Catherine lived in misery and frequent danger at the court of Elizabeth. During that time, she befriended important nobles and read widely in the books of the *philosophes*. She was a shrewd person whose experience in a court crawling with rumors, intrigue, and conspiracy had taught her how to survive. She exhibited neither love nor fidelity toward her demented husband. A few months after his accession as tsar, Peter was deposed and murdered with Catherine's approval, if not her aid, and she was immediately proclaimed empress.

Catherine's familiarity with the Enlightenment and the general culture of western Europe convinced her that Russia was very backward and that it must make major reforms if it was to remain a great power. She understood that any major reform must have a wide base of political and social support, especially since she had assumed the throne through a palace coup. In 1767, she summoned a legislative commission to advise her on revisions in the law and government of Russia. There were more than 500 delegates, drawn from all sectors of Russian life. Before the commission convened, Catherine issued a set of instructions, partly written by herself. They contained many ideas drawn from the political writings of the *philosophes*. The commission considered the instructions as well as other ideas and complaints raised by its members. (See "Catherine the Great Issues an Instruction to the Legislative Commission.")

The revision of Russian law, however, did not occur for more than half a century. In 1768, Catherine dismissed the commission before several of its key committees had reported. Yet the meeting had not been useless, for a vast amount of information had been gathered about the conditions of local administration and economic life throughout the realm. The inconclusive debates and the absence of programs from the delegates themselves suggested that most Russians saw no alternative to an autocratic monarchy. For her part, Catherine had no intention of departing from absolutism.

LIMITED ADMINISTRATIVE REFORM   Catherine proceeded to carry out limited reforms on her own authority. She gave strong support to the rights and local power of the nobility. In 1777, she reorganized local government to solve problems brought to light by the legislative commission. She put most local offices in the hands of nobles rather than creating a royal bureaucracy. In 1785 Catherine issued the Charter of the Nobility, which guaranteed nobles many rights and privileges. In part, the empress had no choice but to favor the nobles. They had the capacity to topple her from the throne. There were too few educated subjects in her realm to establish an independent bureaucracy, and the treasury could not afford an army strictly loyal to the crown. So Catherine wisely made a virtue of necessity. She strengthened the stability of her crown by making convenient friends with her nobles.

ECONOMIC GROWTH Part of Catherine's program was to continue the economic development begun under Peter the Great. She attempted to suppress internal barriers to trade. Exports of grain, flax, furs, and naval stores grew dramatically. She also favored the expansion of the small Russian urban middle class that was so vital to trade. And through all of these departures Catherine tried to maintain ties of friendship and correspondence with the *philosophes*.

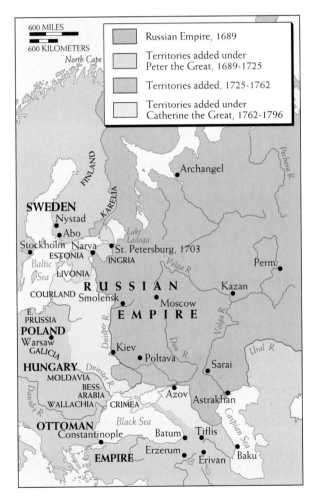

MAP 18–1 EXPANSION OF RUSSIA, 1689–1796 *The overriding territorial aim of Peter the Great in the first quarter, and of Catherine the Great in the latter half, of the eighteenth century was to secure year-round navigable outlets to the sea for the vast Russian Empire— hence Peter's push to the Baltic Sea and Catherine's to the Black Sea. Catherine also managed to acquire large areas of Poland through the partitions of that country.*

She knew that if she treated them kindly, they would be sufficiently flattered to give her a progressive reputation throughout Europe.

TERRITORIAL EXPANSION Catherine's limited administrative reforms and her policy of economic growth had a counterpart in the diplomatic sphere. The Russian drive for warm-water ports continued. (See Map 18–1.) This goal required warfare with the Turks. In 1769, as a result of a minor Russian incursion, the Ottoman Empire declared war on Russia. The Russians responded in a series of strikingly successful military moves.

During 1769 and 1770, the Russian fleet sailed all the way from the Baltic Sea into the eastern Mediterranean. The Russian army won several major victories that by 1771 gave Russia control of Ottoman provinces on the Danube River and the Crimean coast of the Black Sea. The conflict dragged on until 1774, when it was closed by the Treaty of Kuchuk-Kainardji. The treaty gave Russia a direct outlet on the Black Sea, free navigation rights in its waters, and free access through the Bosporus. Moreover, the province of the Crimea became an independent state, which Catherine painlessly annexed in 1783.

The Partition of Poland

The Russian military successes obviously brought Catherine much domestic political support, but they made the other states of eastern Europe uneasy. These anxieties were overcome by an extraordinary division of Polish territory known as the First Partition of Poland.

The Russian victories along the Danube River were most unwelcome to Austria, which also harbored ambitions of territorial expansion in that direction. At the same time, the Ottoman Empire was pressing Prussia for aid against Russia. Frederick the Great made a proposal to Russia and Austria that would give each something it wanted, prevent conflict among the powers, and save appearances. After long, complicated, secret negotiations, the three powers agreed that Russia would abandon the conquered Danubian provinces. In compensation, Russia received a large portion of Polish territory with almost two million inhabitants. As a reward for remaining neutral, Prussia annexed most of the territory between East Prussia and Prussia proper. This land allowed Frederick to unite two previously separate sections of his realm. Finally, Austria took Galicia, with its important salt mines, and other Polish territory with more than two and one-half million inhabitants. (See Map 18–2.)

In September 1772, the helpless Polish aristocracy, paying the price for maintaining internal liberties at the expense of developing a strong central government,

Catherine the Great Issues an Instruction to the Legislative Commission

Catherine the Great hoped to reform the laws of Russia along the lines of political theory associated with the Enlightenment. To that end, during the 1760s she and her advisors planned for a Legislative Commission, which eventually met in 1767. Catherine issued a set of broad instructions to the commission outlining the principles she expected it to follow in its deliberations. She personally wrote and edited significant portions of the Instruction. The commission did meet but, ultimately accomplished very little. Nonetheless, Catherine's Instruction went through a number of printings and translations during the second half of the eighteenth century. Occasionally, ministers and other administrators pointed to them as justifying certain of their decisions. Catherine took them very seriously throughout her reign. Even though the commission for which they were intended produced nothing lasting, Catherine's Instruction is the most important national document of broad political and legal principles written by a woman in the eighteenth century. Yet, the experience of most of Catherine's subjects in no manner reflected this Instruction, as during her reign Russian peasants were subjected to horrific punishment for rebelling and to complicated legal procedures governing most aspects of their life. The denunciation of Catherine by Alexander Radishchev toward the end of her reign (see next document) reflects the disillusionment created by the idealistic hopes she raised and the political reality of the government she pursued.

❖ *Why does Catherine insist that Russia must have an absolutist government? How do these instructions define liberty and attempt to reconcile it with strong monarchical authority? How does the concept of liberty included in the* Instruction *compare and contrast with those protests that the American colonists made to King George III during the Stamp Act Crisis? (See Chapter 17.) Why do Catherine's instructions emphasize the necessity of simplicity in the law.*

ratified this seizure of nearly one-third of Polish territory. The loss was not necessarily fatal to Poland's continued existence, and it inspired a revival of national feeling. Real attempts were made to adjust the Polish political structures to the realities of the time. These proved, however, to be too little and too late. The political and military strength of Poland could not match that of its stronger, more ambitious neighbors. The partition of Poland clearly demonstrated that any nation that had not established a strong monarchy, bureaucracy, and army could no longer compete within the European state system. It also demonstrated that the major powers in eastern Europe were prepared to settle their own rivalries at the expense of such a weak state. If such territory from a weaker state had not been available, the tendency of the international rivalries would have been to warfare.

Russia and Prussia partitioned Poland again in 1793, and Russia, Prussia, and Austria partitioned it a third time in 1795, removing it from the map

of Europe for more than a century. Each time, the great powers contended that they were saving themselves, and by implication the rest of Europe, from Polish anarchy. The fact of the matter was that Poland's political weakness left it vulnerable to plunderous aggression. The partitions of 1793 and 1795 took place in the shadow of the French Revolution, which left the absolute monarchies of eastern Europe concerned for their own stability. As a result, they reacted harshly even to minor attempts at reform by the Polish nobles, fearing that they might infect their own domains.

The End of the Eighteenth Century in Central and Eastern Europe

During the last two decades of the eighteenth century, all three regimes based on Enlightened Absolutism became more conservative and politically repressive. In Prussia and Austria, the

6. Russia is a European power....

9. The Sovereign is absolute, for no other than absolute Powers vested in one Person, can be suitable to the Extent of so vast an Empire.

10. An extensive Empire demands absolute Power in the person who rules it....

11. Any other than absolute Government, would not only be detrimental, but in the End destructive to Russia.

12. Another Reason is, that it is better to obey the Laws under the direction of one Master, than to be subject to the Wills of many.

13. What is the Object of absolute Government? Certainly not to deprive the People of their natural Liberty, but to direct their Conduct in such manner that the greatest good may be derived from all their Operations.

34. The Equality of Citizens consists in their being all subject to the same Laws.

35. This Equality requires a good Establishment which may prevent the Rich from oppressing the Poor, and from converting to their own private Advantage those Employments and Offices entrusted to them only for the benefit of the State.

36. Social or civil Liberty consists not in doing every one as he pleases.

37. In a State, that is in a Collection of People living in Society where Laws are established, Liberty can consist only in the Ability of doing what every one ought to desire, and in not being forced to do what should not be desired.

38.....Liberty is the right of doing whatever is permitted by the Laws....

39. Civil Liberty is a Tranquillity of Mind arising from the Opinion that every individual of the whole Society enjoys his personal Security, and that People may possess this Liberty, the Laws must be such as that no one Citizen need be in fear of another, but that all alike should fear the Laws only.

...448. Every Law must be wrote in words intelligible to all, and at the same time Concise....

...450. When in any Law Exceptions, Limitations and Modifications are unnecessary, it is much better not to use them....

...452. Laws must not be filled up with Subtleties arising from quickness of parts; they are made equally for People of moderate as well as of quick Understanding....

453. Sincerity must be observed throughout all the Laws, they are given to punish Vice and evil Doings, so that they themselves must include great Virtue and Innocence.

From Paul Dukes, trans. and ed., *Russia Under Catherine the Great, Volume II, Catherine the Great's Instruction* (Nakaz) *to the Legislative Commission, 1767* (Newtonville, MA: Oriental Research Partners, 1977), pp. 43–44, 46, 99.

innovations of the rulers stirred resistance among the nobility. In Russia, fear of peasant unrest was the chief factor.

Frederick the Great of Prussia grew remote during his old age, leaving the aristocracy to fill important military and administrative posts. A reaction to Enlightenment ideas also set in among Prussian Lutheran writers.

In Austria, Joseph II's plans to restructure society and administration in his realms provoked growing frustration and political unrest, with the nobility calling for an end to innovation. In response, Joseph turned increasingly to censorship and his secret police.

Russia faced a peasant uprising, the Pugachev Rebellion, between 1773 and 1775, and Catherine the Great never fully recovered from the fears of social and political upheaval that it raised. Once the French Revolution broke out in 1789, the Russian empress censored books based on Enlightenment thought and sent offensive authors into Siberian exile. (See "Alexander Radishchev Attacks Russian Censorship.")

By the close of the century, fear of, and hostility to, change permeated the ruling classes of central and eastern Europe. This reaction had begun before 1789, but the events in France bolstered and sustained it for almost half a century. Paradoxically, nowhere did the humanity and liberalism of the Enlightenment encounter greater rejection than in those states that had been governed by "enlightened" rulers.

The enlightened absolute monarchs had embraced the Enlightenment spirit of innovation that pressed in all directions against tradition. They wanted to change the political, social, and economic structures of their realms. From the close of the Seven Years' War (1763) until the opening of the French Revolution in 1789, the monarchies of both western and eastern Europe had been the major agents of insti-

Alexander Radishchev Attacks Russian Censorship

Alexander Radishchev (1749–1802) was an enlightened Russian landowner who published A Journey from Saint Petersburg to Moscow *in 1790. The book criticized many aspects of Russian political and social life, including the treatment of serfs. Shortly after its publication, Catherine the Great, fearing that the kind of unrest associated with the French Revolution might spread to Russia, had Radishchev arrested. He was tried and sentenced to death, but Catherine commuted the sentence to a period of Siberian exile. All but eighteen copies of his book were destroyed. It was not published in Russia again until 1905. These passages criticizing censorship illustrate how a writer filled with the ideas of the Enlightenment could question some of the fundamental ways in which an enlightened absolutist ruler, such as Catherine, governed.*

❖ *How does Radishchev satirize censorship and the censors? Why does he contend that public opinion rather than the government will act as an adequate censor? Would work censored by public opinion be truly free from censorship? Why might Catherine the Great or other enlightened absolutist rulers have feared opinions like these?*

Having recognized the usefulness of printing, the government has made it open to all; having further recognized that control of thought might invalidate its good intention in granting freedom to set up presses, it turned over the censorship or inspection of printed works to the Department of Public Morals. Its duty in this matter can only be the prohibition of the sale of objectionable works. But even this censorship is superfluous. A single stupid official in the Department of Public Morals may do the greatest harm to enlightenment and may for years hold back the progress of reason: he may prohibit a useful discovery, a new idea, and may rob everyone of something great. Here is an example on a small scale. A translation of a novel is brought to the Department of Public Morals for its imprimatur. The translator, following the author in speaking of love calls it "the tricky god." The censor in uniform and in the fullness of piety strikes out the expression saying, "It is improper to call a divinity tricky." He who does not understand should not interfere....

Let anyone print anything that enters his head. If anyone finds himself insulted in print, let him get his redress at law. I am not speaking in jest. Words are not always deeds, thoughts are not crimes. These are the rules in the *Instruction for a New Code of Laws*. But an offense in words or in print is always an offense. Under the law no one is allowed to libel another, and everyone has the right to bring suit. But if one tells the truth about another, that cannot, according to the law, be considered a libel. What harm can there be if books are printed without a police stamp? Not only will there be no harm; there will be an advantage, an advantage from the first to the last, from the least to the greatest, from the Tsar to the last citizen....

I will close with this: the censorship of what is printed belongs properly to society, which gives the author a laurel wreath or uses his sheets for wrapping paper. Just so, it is the public that gives its approval to a theatrical production, and not the director of the theater. Similarly the Censor can give neither glory nor dishonor to the publication of a work. The curtain rises, and every one eagerly watches the performance. If they like it, they applaud; if not, they stamp and hiss. Leave what is stupid to the judgment of public opinion, stupidity will find a thousand censors. The most vigilant policy cannot check worthless ideas as well as a disgusted public. They will be heard just once; they will die, never to rise again. But once we have recognized the uselessness of the censorship, or, rather, its harmfulness in the realm of knowledge, we must also recognize the vast and boundless usefulness of freedom of the press.

From Alexander Radishchev, *A Journey from Saint Petersburg to Moscow* (Cambridge, MA: Harvard University Press, 1958), pp. 9–19. Copyright © 1958 by the President and Fellows of Harvard College. Reprinted by permission of Harvard University Press. As quoted in Thomas Riha, ed., *Readings in Russian Civilization*, 2d ed., rev., Vol II (Chicago: University of Chicago Press, 1969), pp. 269–271.

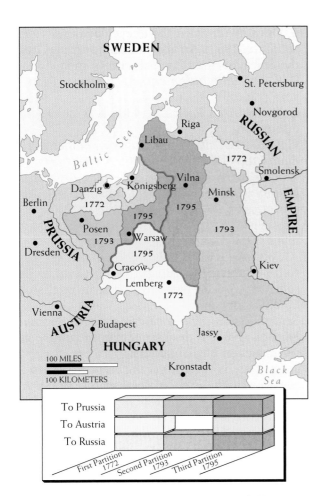

MAP 18–2 PARTITIONS OF POLAND, 1772, 1793 AND 1795 *The callous eradication of Poland from the map displayed eighteenth-century power politics at its most extreme. Poland, without strong central governmental institutions, fell victim to those states in central and eastern Europe that had developed such institutions.*

tutional change. In every case they provoked aristocratic, and sometimes popular, resistance and resentment. George III of Britain fought for years with Parliament and lost the colonies of North America in the process. Frederick II of Prussia succeeded with his program of reform only because he accepted new aristocratic influence over the bureaucracy and the army. Catherine II of Russia had to come to terms with Russia's nobility. Joseph II, who did not consult with the nobility of his domains, left those domains in turmoil.

These monarchs pushed for innovations from a desire for increased revenue. In France also, the royal drive for adequate fiscal resources led to aristocratic resistance. In France, however, neither the monarchy nor the aristocracy could control the social and political forces their quarrel unleashed.

In Perspective

The writers of the Enlightenment, known as philosophes, *charted a major new path in modern European and Western thought. They operated within a print culture that made public opinion into a distinct cultural force. Admiring Newton and the achievements of physical science, they tried to apply reason and the principles of science to the cause of social reform. They believed also that passions and feelings were essential parts of human nature. Throughout their writings they championed reasonable moderation in social life. More than any other previous group of Western thinkers, they strongly opposed the authority of the established churches and especially of Roman Catholicism. Most of them championed some form of religious toleration. They also sought to achieve a science of society that could discover how to maximize human productivity and material happiness. The great dissenter among them was Rousseau, who also wished to reform society, but in the name of virtue rather than material happiness.*

The political influence of these writers went in several directions. The founding fathers of the American republic looked to them for political guidance, as did moderate liberal reformers throughout Europe, especially within royal bureaucracies. The autocratic rulers of eastern Europe consulted the philosophes *in the hope that Enlightenment ideas might allow them to rule more efficiently. The revolutionaries in France would honor them. This diverse assortment of followers illustrates the diverse character of the* philosophes *themselves. It also shows that Enlightenment thought cannot be reduced to a single formula. Rather, it should be seen as an outlook that championed change and reform, giving central place to humans and their welfare on earth rather than to God and the hereafter.*

REVIEW QUESTIONS

1. How did the Enlightenment change basic Western attitudes toward reform, faith, and reason? What were the major formative influences on the *philosophes*? How important were Voltaire and the *Encyclopedia* in the success of the Enlightenment?
2. Why did the *philosophes* consider organized religion to be their greatest enemy? Discuss the basic tenets of deism. How did Jewish writers contribute to Enlightenment thinking about religion?

3. What were the attitudes of the *philosophes* toward women? What was Rousseau's view of women? What were the separate spheres he imagined men and women occupying? What were Mary Wollstonecraft's criticisms of Rousseau's view?

4. Compare the arguments of the mercantilists with those of Adam Smith in his book, *The Wealth of Nations*. How did both sides view the Earth's resources? Why might Smith be regarded as an advocate of the consumer? How did his theory of history work to the deteriment of less economically advanced non-European peoples.

5. Discuss the political views of Montesquieu and Rousseau. Was Montesquieu's view of England accurate? Was Rousseau a child of the Enlightenment or its enemy? Which did Rousseau value more, the individual or society?

6. Were the enlightened monarchs true believers in the ideal of the *philosophes*, or was their enlightenment a mere veneer? Were they really absolute in power? What motivated their reforms? What does the partition of Poland indicate about the spirit of enlightened absolutism?

SUGGESTED READINGS

G. J. BARKER-BENFIELD, *The Culture of Sensibility: Sex and Society in Eighteenth-Century Britain* (1992). A broad exploration of the role of women in society and literature in the age of Enlightenment.

R. P. BARTLETT, *Human Capital: The Settlement of Foreigners in Russia, 1762–1804* (1979). Examines Catherine's policy of attracting farmers and skilled workers to Russia.

D. BEALES, *Joseph II: In the Shadow of Maria Theresa, 1741–1780 (1987)*. The best treatment in English of the early political life of Joseph II.

C. B. A. BEHRENS, *Society, Government, and the Enlightenment: The Experiences of Eighteenth-Century France and Prussia* (1985). A wide-ranging comparative study.

D. D. BIEN, *The Calas Affair: Persecution, Toleration, and Heresy in Eighteenth-Century Toulouse* (1960). The standard treatment of the famous case.

R. CHARTIER, *The Cultural Origins of the French Revolution* (1991). A wide-ranging discussion of the emergence of the public sphere and the role of books and the book trade during the Enlightenment.

R. DARNTON, *The Literary Underground of the Old Regime* (1982). Essays on the world of printers, publishers, and booksellers.

R. DARNTON, *The Forbidden Best-Sellers of Pre-Revolutionary France* (1995). An exploration of what books the French read and the efforts of the government to control the book trade.

T. S. DOCK, *Women in the* Encyclopédie: *A Compendium* (1983). An analysis of the articles from the *Encyclopedia* that deal with women.

P. GAY, *The Enlightenment: An Interpretation*, 2 vols. (1966, 1969). A classic.

P. GAY, *Voltaire's Politics* (1988). A wide-ranging discussion.

C. C. GILLISPIE, *Science and Polity in France at the End of the Old Regime* (1980). A major survey.

D. GOODMAN, *The Republic of Letters: A Cultural History of the French Enlightenment* (1994). Concentrates on the role of salons.

N. HAMPSON, *A Cultural History of the Enlightenment* (1969). A useful introduction.

M. C. JACOB, *Living the Enlightenment: Freemasonry and Politics in Eighteenth-Century Europe* (1991). The best treatment in English of Freemasonry.

A. KERNAN, *Printing Technology, Letters, and Samuel Johnson* (1987). A discussion of print culture and its impact on English letters.

J. B. LANDES, *Women and the Public Sphere in the Age of the French Revolution* (1988). An extended essay on the role of women in public life during the eighteenth century.

J. P. LEDONNE, *The Russian Empire and the World, 1700–1917* (1996). An exploration of the major determinants in Russian expansion from the eighteenth to the early twentieth century.

C. A. MACARTNEY, *The Habsburg Empire, 1790–1918* (1971). Provides useful coverage of major mid-eighteenth century developments.

I. DE MADARIAGA, *Russia in the Age of Catherine the Great* (1981). The best discussion in English.

J. M. MCMANNERS, *Death and the Enlightenment: Changing Attitudes to Death among Christians and Unbelievers in Eighteenth-Century France* (1982). Explores a wide spectrum of religious beliefs.

M. A. MEYER, *The Origins of the Modern Jew: Jewish Identity and European Culture in Germany, 1749–1824* (1967). Remains a clear introduction.

S. NADLER, *Spinoza: A Life* (1999) The best recent biography.

C. ORWIN AND N. TARCOV, EDS., *The Legacy of Rousseau* (1997). Essays on the major themes of Rousseau's work.

D. ROCHE, *France in the Enlightenment* (1998). A brilliant work relating the society and government of eighteenth-century France to the Enlightenment agenda.

J. SCHWARTZ, *The Sexual Politics of Jean-Jacques Rousseau* (1984). A controversial reading of Rousseau's political thought organized around gender issues.

R. B. SHER, *Church and University in the Scottish Enlightenment: The Moderate Literati of Edinburgh* (1985). Examines the role of religious moderates in aiding the goals of the Enlightenment.

J. N. SHKLAR, *Men and Citizens, a Study of Rousseau's Social Theory* (1969). A thoughtful and provocative overview of Rousseau's political thought.

S. B. SMITH, *Spinoza, Liberalism, and the Question of Jewish Identity* (1997). A brilliant work.

D. SPADAFORA, *The Idea of Progress in Eighteenth Century Britain* (1990). A major study that covers many aspects of the Enlightenment in Britain.

S. I. SPENCER, *French Women and the Age of Enlightenment* (1984). An outstanding collection of essays that cover the political, economic, and cultural roles of women.

J. STAROBINSKI, *Jean-Jacques Rousseau: Transparency and Obstruction* (1971). A powerful analysis of Rousseau.

R. E. SULLIVAN, *John Toland and the Deist Controversy: A Study in Adaptation* (1982). An important and informative discussion.

A. M. WILSON, *Diderot* (1972). A splendid biography of the person behind the *Encyclopedia* and other major Enlightenment publications.

L. WOLFF, *Inventing Eastern Europe: The Map of Civilization on the Mind of the Enlightenment* (1994). A remarkable study of the manner in which Enlightenment writers recast the understanding of this part of the continent.

J. YOLTON, ED., *The Blackwell Companion to the Enlightenment* (1995). An excellent collection of essays.

Chapter 19

To symbolize the beginning of a new era in human history, French revolutionary legislators established a new calendar. The year 1793 became Year One in
this new calendar and all the months of the year were given new names. This
calendar for Year Two proclaims the indivisible unity of the revolution and the
goals of Liberty, Equality, and Fraternity. Bildarchiv Preussischer Kulturbesitz

The French Revolution

The Crisis of the French Monarchy
The Monarchy Seeks New Taxes
The Aristocracy and the Clergy
    Resist Taxation

The Revolution of 1789
The Estates General Becomes the National
    Assembly
Fall of the Bastille
The "Great Fear" and the Surrender of
    Feudal Privileges
The Declaration of the Rights of Man
    and Citizen
The Royal Family Forced to Return to Paris

The Reconstruction of France
Political Reorganization
Economic Policy
The Civil Constitution of the Clergy
Counterrevolutionary Activity

A Second Revolution
End of the Monarchy
The Convention and the Role of
    the *Sans-culottes*

Europe at War with the Revolution
Edmund Burke Attacks the Revolution
Suppression of Reform in Britain
The End of Enlightened Absolutism
    in Eastern Europe
War with Europe

The Reign of Terror
The Republic Defended
The "Republic of Virtue"
Progress of the Terror

The Thermidorian Reaction
The End of the Terror
Establishment of the Directory
Removal of the *Sans-culottes* from
    Political Life

KEY TOPICS

- The financial crisis that impelled the French monarchy to call the Estates General

- The transformation of the Estates General into the National Assembly, the Declaration of the Rights of Man and Citizen, and the reconstruction of the political and ecclesiastical institutions of France

- The second revolution, the end of the monarchy, and the turn to more radical reforms

- The war between France and the rest of Europe

- The Reign of Terror, the Thermidorian Reaction, and the establishment of the Directory

In the spring of 1789, the long-festering conflict between the French monarchy and the aristocracy erupted into a new political crisis. This dispute, unlike earlier ones, quickly outgrew the issues of its origins and produced the wider disruption known as the French Revolution. Before the turmoil settled, small-town provincial lawyers and Parisian street or-

ators exercised more influence over the fate of the Continent than did aristocrats, royal ministers, or monarchs. Armies commanded by people of low birth and filled by conscripted village youths emerged victorious over forces composed of professional soldiers led by officers of noble birth. The very existence of the Roman Catholic faith in France was challenged. Politically and socially, neither France nor Europe would ever be the same after these events.

The Crisis of the French Monarchy

Although the French Revolution was a turning point in modern European history, it grew out of the tensions and problems that characterized practically all late-eighteenth-century states. The French monarchy emerged from the Seven Years' War (1756–1763) both defeated and in debt and was unable afterward to put its finances on a sound basis. French support of the American revolt against Great Britain further deepened the financial difficulties of the government. On the eve of the revolution, the interest and payments on the royal debt amounted to just over one-half of the entire budget. Given the economic vitality of the nation, the debt was neither overly large nor disproportionate to the debts of other European powers. The problem lay with the inability of the royal government to tap the wealth of the French nation through taxes to service and repay the debt. Paradoxically, France was a rich nation with an impoverished government.

The Monarchy Seeks New Taxes

The debt was symptomatic of the failure of the late eighteenth-century French monarchy to come to terms with the resurgent social and political power of aristocratic institutions and, in particular, the *parlements*. For twenty-five years after the Seven Years' War, there was a standoff between them as one royal minister after another attempted to devise new tax schemes that would tap the wealth of the nobility, only to be confronted by the opposition of both the *Parlement* of Paris and provincial *parlements*. Both Louis XV (r. 1715–1774) and Louis XVI (r. 1774–1792) lacked the character and the resolution to carry the dispute to a successful conclusion. The moral and political corruption of their courts and the indecision of Louis XVI meant that the monarchy could not rally the French public to its side. In place of a consistent policy for dealing with the

growing debt and aristocratic resistance to change, the monarchy gave way to hesitancy, retreat, and even duplicity.

In 1770, Louis XV appointed René Maupeou (1714–1792) as chancellor. The new minister was determined to break the *parlements* and increase taxes on the nobility. He abolished the *parlements* and exiled their members to different parts of the country. He then began an ambitious program of reform and efficiency. What ultimately doomed Maupeou's policy was less the resistance of the nobility than the death of Louis XV in 1774. His successor, Louis XVI, in an attempt to regain what he conceived to be popular support, restored all the *parlements* and confirmed their old powers.

France's successful intervention on behalf of the American colonists against the British did nothing to relieve the government's financial difficulties. By 1781, as a result of the aid to America, its debt was larger and its sources of revenues were unchanged. The new director-general of finances, Jacques Necker (1732–1804), a Swiss banker, then produced a public report which suggested that the situation was not so bad as had been feared. He argued that if the expenditures for the American war were removed, the budget was in surplus. Necker's report also revealed that a large portion of royal expenditures went to pensions for aristocrats and other royal court favorites. This revelation angered court aristocratic circles, and Necker soon left office. His financial sleight of hand, nonetheless, made it more difficult for later government officials to claim a real need to raise new taxes.

The monarchy hobbled along until 1786. By this time, Charles Alexandre de Calonne (1734–1802) was the minister of finance. Calonne proposed to encourage internal trade, to lower some taxes, such as the *gabelle* on salt, and to transform peasants' services to money payments. More important, Calonne urged the introduction of a new land tax that would require payments from all landowners regardless of their social status. If this tax had been imposed, the monarchy could have abandoned other indirect taxes. The government would also have had less need to seek additional taxes that required approval from the aristocratically dominated *parlements*. Calonne also intended to establish new local assemblies to approve land taxes; in these assemblies the voting power would have depended on the amount of land owned rather than on the social status of the owner. All these proposals would have undermined both the political and the social power of the French aristocracy.

This late eighteenth-century cartoon satirizes the French social structure. It shows a poor man in chains, who represents the vast majority of the population, supporting an aristocrat, a bishop, and a noble of the robe. The aristocrat is claiming feudal rights, the bishop holds papers associating the church with religious persecution and clerical privileges, and the noble of the robe holds a document listing the rights of the noble-dominated parlements. Corbis

The Aristocracy and the Clergy Resist Taxation

Calonne's policies and the country's fiscal crisis made a new clash with the nobility unavoidable, and the monarchy had very little room to maneuver. The creditors were at the door; the treasury was nearly empty. In 1787, Calonne met with an Assembly of Notables drawn from the upper ranks of the aristocracy and the church to seek support and approval for his plan. The assembly adamantly refused any such action; rather, it demanded that the aristocracy be allowed a greater share in the direct government of the kingdom. The notables called for the reappointment of Necker, who they believed had left the country in sound fiscal condition. Finally, they claimed that they had no right to consent to new taxes and that such a right was vested only in the medieval institution of the Estates General of France, which had not met since 1614. The notables believed that calling the Estates General, which had been traditionally organized to allow aristocratic and church dominance, would produce a victory for the nobility over the monarchy.

Again, Louis XVI backed off. He dismissed Calonne and replaced him with Étienne Charles Loménie de Brienne (1727–1794), archbishop of Toulouse and the chief opponent of Calonne at the Assembly of Notables. Once in office, Brienne found, to his astonishment, that the situation was as bad as his predecessor had asserted. Brienne himself now sought to impose the land tax. The *Parlement* of Paris, however, took the new position that it lacked authority to authorize the tax and said that only the Estates General could do so. Shortly thereafter, Brienne appealed to the Assembly of the Clergy to approve a large subsidy to allow funding of that part of the debt then coming due for payment. The clergy, like the *Parlement* dominated by aristocrats, not only refused the subsidy, but also reduced its existing contribution, or *don gratuit*, to the government.

As these unfruitful negotiations were taking place at the center of political life, local aristocratic *parlements* and estates in the provinces were making their own demands. They wanted a restoration of the privileges they had enjoyed during the early seventeenth century, before Richelieu and

Louis XIV had crushed their independence. Consequently, in July 1788, the king, through Brienne, agreed to convoke the Estates General the next year. Brienne resigned and Necker replaced him. The institutions of the aristocracy—and to a lesser degree, of the church—had brought the French monarchy to its knees. In the country of its origin, royal absolutism had been defeated.

The Revolution of 1789

The year 1789 proved to be one of the most remarkable in the history of both France and Europe. The French aristocracy had forced Louis XVI to call the Estates General into session. Yet the aristocrats' triumph proved to be quite brief. From the moment the monarch summoned the Estates General, the political situation in France changed drastically. Social and political forces that neither the nobles nor the king could control were immediately unleashed.

From that calling of the Estates General to the present, historians have heatedly debated the meaning of the event and the turmoil that followed over the next decade. Many historians long believed that the calling and gathering of the Estates General unleashed a clash between the bourgeoisie and the aristocracy that had been building in the decades before 1789. More recently, other historians have countered that the two groups actually had much in common by 1789 and that many members of both the bourgeoisie and the aristocracy resented and opposed the clumsy absolutism of the late-eighteenth-century monarchy. This second group of historians contends that the fundamental issue of 1789 was the determination of various social groups to reorganize the French government to assure the future political influence of all forms of wealth.

As this complicated process was being worked out, the argument goes, distrust arose between the aristocracy and increasingly radical middle-class leaders. The latter then turned to the tradespeople of Paris, building alliances with them to achieve their goals. That alliance radicalized the revolution. When, in the mid-1790s, revolutionary policies and actions became too radical, aristocratic and middle-class leaders once again cooperated to reassert the security of all forms of private wealth

Well-meaning but weak and vacillating, Louis XVI (r. 1774–1792) stumbled from concession to concession until he finally lost all power to save his throne. Joseph Siffred Duplessis, *Louis XVI.* Versailles, France. Giraudon/Art Resource, NY

and property. According to this view, conflict did exist among different social groups during the years of the revolution, but its causes were immediate, not hidden in the depths of French economic and social development.

Other historians also look to the influence of immediate rather than long-term causes. They believe that the faltering of the monarchy and the confusion following the calling, election, and organization of the Estates General created a political vacuum. Various leaders and social groups, often using the political vocabulary of the Enlightenment, stepped into that vacuum, challenging each other for dominance. The precedent for such public debate had been set during the years of conflict between the monarchy and the *parlements* when the latter had begun to challenge the former as the true representative of the nation. These debates and conflicts over the language, and hence values, of political life and activity had been made possible by the emergence of the new print culture with its reading public and numerous channels for the circulation of books, pamphlets, and newspapers. Emerging from this culture were a large number of often-unemployed authors who were resentful of their situation and ready to use their skills to radicalize the discussion. The result was a political debate wider than any before in European history. The events of the era represented a continuing effort to dominate public opinion about the future course of the nation. The French Revolution, according to this view, thus illustrates the character of a new political culture created by changes in the technology and distribution of print communication.

Yet another group of historians maintains that the events of 1789 through 1795 are only one chapter in a longer-term political reorganization of France following the paralysis of monarchical government, a process that was not concluded until the establishment of the Third Republic in the 1870s. According to this interpretation, the core accomplishment of the revolution of the 1790s was to lay the foundations for a republic that could assure both individual liberty and the safety of property. It was not until the last quarter of the nineteenth century, however, that such a republic actually came into existence.

To some extent, how convincing one finds each of these interpretations depends on which years or even months of the revolution one examines. The various interpretations are not, in any case, always mutually exclusive. Certainly, the weakness and ultimate collapse of the monarchy influenced events more than was once acknowledged. All

sides did indeed make use of the new formats and institutions of the print culture. Individual leaders shifted their positions and alliances quite frequently, sometimes out of principle, more often for political expediency. Furthermore, the actual political situation differed from city to city and from region to region. The controversial and divisive religious policies of the revolutionary government itself were often determining factors in the attitudes that French citizens assumed toward the revolution. What does seem clear is that much of the earlier consensus—that the revolution arose almost entirely from conflict between the aristocracy and bourgeoisie—no longer stands, except with many qualifications. The interpretive situation is now much more complicated, and a new consensus has yet to emerge.

The Estates General Becomes the National Assembly

Almost immediately after the Estates General was called, the three groups, or Estates, represented within it clashed with each other. The First Estate was the clergy, the Second Estate the nobility, and the Third Estate theoretically everyone else in the kingdom, although its representatives were drawn primarily from wealthy members of the commercial and professional middle classes. All the representatives in the Estates General were men. During the widespread public discussions preceding the meeting of the Estates General, representatives of the Third Estate made it clear that they would not permit the monarchy and the aristocracy to decide the future of the nation.

A comment by the Abbé Siéyès (1748–1836) in a pamphlet published in 1789 captures the spirit of the Third Estate's representatives: "What is the Third Estate? Everything. What has it been in the political order up to the present? Nothing. What does it ask? To become something."[1] (See Abbé Siéyès Presents the Cause of the Third Estate.)

DEBATE OVER ORGANIZATION AND VOTING The initial split between the aristocracy and the Third Estate occurred before the Estates General gathered. The public debate over the proper organization of the body drew the lines of basic disagreement. The aristocracy made two moves to limit the influence of the Third Estate. First, they demanded an equal number of representatives for each estate. Second,

[1]Quoted in Leo Gershoy, *The French Revolution and Napoleon* (New York: Appleton-Century-Crofts, 1964), p. 102.

Abbé Siéyès Presents the Cause of the Third Estate

Among the many pamphlets that appeared after the calling of the Estates General, one of the most famous was What Is the Third Estate? *by Abbé Emmanuel Siéyès. In this pamphlet Siéyès contrasted the vital contributions of the Third Estate to the nation with its exclusion from political and social privilege. He presents an image of the Third Estate in direct conflict with the aristocracy rather than with the monarchy. On the basis of this pamphlet many later observers and historians argued that the revolution was a conflict between the middle class and the aristocracy. The social structure of France, however, and the interactions of those two groups was much more complicated than Siéyès suggests. Both groups were discontented with monarchical government.*

❖ *How does Siéyès define the Third Estate? What injustices does he claim it suffers? What are the complaints that he makes on behalf of the Third Estate against the aristocracy? Why does Siéyès make a distinction between the court and the monarchy?*

Who, then would dare to say that the third estate has not within itself all that is necessary to constitute a complete nation? It is the strong and robust man whose one arm remains enchained. If the privileged order were abolished, the nation would be not something less but something more. Thus, what is the third estate? Everything; but an everything shackled and oppressed....

The third estate must be understood to mean the mass of the citizens belonging to the common order. Legalized privilege in any form deviates from the common order, constitutes an exception to the common law, and, consequently, does not appertain to the third estate at all. We repeat, a common law and a common representation are what constitute ONE nation. It is only too true that one is NOTHING in France when one has only the protection of the common law; if one does not possess some privilege, one must resign oneself to enduring contempt, injury, and vexations of every sort....

But here we have to consider the order of the third estate less in its civil status than in its relation with the constitution. Let us examine its position in the Estates General.

Who have been its so-called representatives? The ennobled or those privileged for a period of years. These false deputies have not even been always freely elected by the people....

Add to this appalling truth that, in one manner or another, all branches of the executive power also have fallen to the case which furnishes the Church, the robe, and the Sword. A sort of spirit of brotherhood causes the nobles to prefer themselves...to the rest of the nation. Usurpation is complete; in truth they reign.

...it is a great error to believe that France is subject to a monarchical regime.

...it is the court, and not the monarch, that has reigned. It is the court that makes and unmakes, appoints and discharges ministers, creates and dispenses positions, etc. And what is the court if not the head of this immense aristocracy which overruns all parts of France; which though its members attains all and everywhere does whatever is essential in all parts of the commonwealth?

From *A Documentary Survey of the French Revolution*, by Stewart, John Hall, © 1951. Reprinted by permission of Prentice Hall, Inc., Upper Saddle River, NJ

in September 1788, the *Parlement* of Paris ruled that voting in the Estates General should be conducted by order rather than by head—that is, each estate, or order, rather than each member, should have one vote. This procedure would ensure that the aristocratic First and Second Estates could always outvote the Third. Both moves exposed the hollowness of the aristocracy's alleged concern for French liberty and revealed it as a group determined to maintain its privileges. Spokespeople for the Third Estate de-

nounced the arrogant claims of the aristocracy. Although the aristocracy and the Third Estate shared many economic interests and goals, and some intermarriage had occurred throughout the country between nobles and the elite of the Third Estate, a fundamental social distance separated the members of the two orders. There were far more examples of enormous wealth and military experience among the nobility than among the Third Estate; the latter also had experienced various forms of political and social

The Estates General opened at Versailles in 1789 with much pomp and splendor. This print shows the representatives of the three estates seated in the hall and Louis XVI on a throne at its far end. Convocation of the Estates General at Versailles. Bibliotheque Nationale, Paris, France. Giraudon/Art Resource, NY

discrimination from the nobility. The resistance of the nobility to voting by head simply confirmed the suspicions and resentments of the members of the Third Estate, who were overwhelmingly lawyers of substantial, but not enormous, economic means.

The royal council eventually decided that the cause of the monarchy and fiscal reform would best be served by a strengthening of the Third Estate. In December 1788, the council announced that the Third Estate would elect twice as many representatives as either the nobles or the clergy. This so-called doubling of the Third Estate meant that it could easily dominate the Estates General if voting were allowed by head rather than by order. It was correctly assumed that liberal nobles and clergy would support the Third Estate, confirming that, despite social differences, these groups shared important interests and reform goals. The method of voting was settled by the king only after the Estates General had gathered at Versailles in May 1789.

THE *CAHIERS DE DOLÉANCES* When the representatives came to the royal palace, they brought with them *cahiers de doléances*, or lists of grievances, registered by the local electors, to be presented to the king. Many of these lists have survived and provide considerable information about the state of the country on the eve of the revolution. The documents recorded criticisms of government waste, indirect taxes, church taxes and corruption, and the hunting rights of the aristocracy. They included calls for periodic meetings of the Estates General, more equitable taxes, more local control of administration, unified weights and measures to facilitate trade and commerce, and a free press. The overwhelming demand of the *cahiers* was for equality of rights among the king's subjects. (See "The Third Estate of a French City Petitions the King.")

These complaints and demands could not, however, be discussed until the questions of organization and voting had been decided. From the beginning, the Third Estate, whose members consisted largely of local officials, professionals, and other persons of property, refused to sit as a separate order as the king desired. For several weeks there was a standoff. Then, on June 1, the Third Estate invited the clergy and the nobles to join them in organizing a new legislative body. A few members of the lower clergy did so. On June 17, that body declared itself the National Assembly.

The Third Estate of a French City Petitions the King

The cahiers de doléances *were the lists of grievances brought to Versailles in 1789 by members of the Estates General. The particular* cahier *that follows originated in Dourdan, a city of central France, and reflects the complaints of the Third Estate. The first two articles refer to the organization of the Estates General. The other articles ask that the king grant various forms of equality before the law and in matters of taxation. These demands for equality appeared in practically all the* cahiers *of the Third Estate.*

❖ *Which of the following petitions relate to political rights and which to economic equality? The slogan most associated with the French Revolution was "liberty, equality, fraternity." Which of these petitions represents each of those values?*

The order of the third estate of the City...of Dourdan...supplicates [the king] to accept the grievances, complaints, and remonstrances which it is permitted to bring to the foot of the throne, and to see therein only the expression of its zeal and the homage of its obedience.

It wishes:

1. That his subjects of the third estate, equal by such status to all other citizens, present themselves before the common father without other distinction which might degrade them.

2. That all the orders, already united by duty and common desire contribute equally to the needs of the State, also deliberate in common concerning its needs.

3. That no citizen lose his liberty except according to law: that, consequently, no one be arrested by virtue of special orders, or, if imperative circumstances necessitate such orders, that the prisoner be handed over to regular courts of justice within forty-eight hours at the latest.

12. That every tax, direct or indirect, be granted only for a limited time, and that every collection beyond such term be regarded as peculation, and punished as such....

15. That every personal tax be abolished; that thus the *capitation* [a poll tax] and the *taille* [tax from which nobility and clergy were exempt] and its accessories be merged with the *vingtièmes* [an income tax] in a tax on land and real or nominal property.

16. That such tax be borne equally, without distinction, by all classes of citizens and by all kinds of property, even feudal...rights.

17. That the tax substituted for the *corvée* be borne by all classes of citizens equally and without distinction. That said tax, at present beyond the capacity of those who pay it and the needs to which it is destined, be reduced by at least one-half.

From *A Documentary Survey of the French Revolution*, by Stewart, John Hall, © 1951. Reprinted by permission of Prentice Hall, Inc., Upper Saddle River, NJ

THE TENNIS COURT OATH Three days later, finding themselves accidentally locked out of their usual meeting place, the National Assembly moved to a nearby tennis court. There its members took an oath to continue to sit until they had given France a constitution. This was the famous Tennis Court Oath. Louis XVI ordered the National Assembly to desist from its actions, but shortly afterward a majority of the clergy and a large group of nobles joined the assembly.

On June 27, the king capitulated and formally requested the First and Second Estates to meet with the National Assembly, where voting would occur by head rather than by order. Had nothing further occurred, the government of France would have been transformed. Government by privileged orders had ended. The National Assembly, which renamed itself the National Constituent Assembly, was composed of people from all three orders, who shared liberal goals for the administrative, constitutional, and economic reform of the country. The revolution in France against government by privileged hereditary orders had begun.

Fall of the Bastille

Two new forces soon intruded on the scene. The first was Louis XVI himself, who attempted to regain the political initiative by mustering royal troops near Versailles and Paris. It appeared that he might, following the advice of Queen Marie Antoinette (1755–1793), his brothers, and the most conservative nobles, be contemplating disruption of the National Constituent Assembly. On July 11, without consulting assembly leaders, Louis abrupt-

This painting of the Tennis Court Oath, June 20, is by Jacques-Louis David (1748–1825). In the center foreground are members of different Estates joining hands in cooperation as equals. The presiding officer is Jean-Sylvain Bailly, soon to become mayor of Paris. Jacques-Louis David, *Oath of the Tennis Court.* Chateau, Versailles, France. Giraudon/Art Resource, NY

ly dismissed his minister of finance, Necker. These actions marked the beginning of a steady, but consistently poorly executed, royal attempt to undermine the assembly and halt the revolution. Most of the National Constituent Assembly wished to establish some form of constitutional monarchy, but from the start Louis's refusal to cooperate thwarted that effort. The king fatally decided to throw his lot in with the conservative aristocracy against the emerging forces of reform drawn from across the social and political spectrum.

The second new factor to impose itself on the events at Versailles was the populace of Paris. The mustering of royal troops created anxiety in the city, where throughout the winter and spring of 1789 there had been several bread riots. The Parisians who had elected their representatives to the Third Estate had continued to meet after the elections. By June they were organizing a citizen militia and collecting arms. They regarded the dismissal of Necker as the opening of a royal offensive against the National Constituent Assembly and the city.

On July 14, somewhat more than 800 people, most of them small shopkeepers, tradespeople, artisans, and wage earners, marched to the Bastille in search of weapons for the militia. This great fortress, with ten-foot-thick walls, had once held political prisoners. Through miscalculations and ineptitude on the part of the governor of the fortress, the troops in the Bastille fired into the crowd, killing ninety-eight people and wounding many others. Thereafter, the crowd stormed the fortress and eventually gained entrance. They released the seven prisoners inside, none of whom was there for political reasons, and killed several troops and the governor. They found no weapons.

On July 15, the militia of Paris, by then called the National Guard, offered its command to the Marquis de Lafayette (1757–1834). This hero of the American Revolution gave the guard a new insignia: the red and blue stripes of Paris, separated by the white stripe of the king. The emblem became the revolutionary cockade (badge) and eventually the flag of revolutionary France.

On July 14, 1789, crowds stormed the Bastille, a prison in Paris. This event, whose only practical effect was to free a few prisoners, marked the first time the populace of Paris redirected the course of the revolution. France, 18th c., *Siege of the Bastille, 14 July, 1789.* Musée de la Ville de Paris, Musée Carnavalet, Paris, France. Giraudon/Art Resource, N.Y.

The attack on the Bastille marked the first of many crucial *journées*, days on which the populace of Paris redirected the course of the revolution. The fall of the fortress signaled that the National Constituent Assembly alone would not decide the political future of the nation. As the news of the taking of the Bastille spread, similar disturbances took place in provincial cities. A few days later, Louis XVI again bowed to the force of events and personally visited Paris, where he wore the revolutionary cockade and recognized the organized electors as the legitimate government of the city. The king also recognized the National Guard. The citizens of Paris were, for the time being, satisfied. They also had established themselves as an independent political force with which other political groups might ally for their own purposes.

The "Great Fear" and the Surrender of Feudal Privileges

Simultaneous with the popular urban disturbances, a movement known as the "Great Fear" swept across much of the French countryside. Rumors had spread that royal troops would be sent into the rural districts. The result was an intensification of the peasant disturbances that had begun during the spring. The Great Fear saw the burning of *châteaux*, the destruction of records and documents, and the refusal to pay feudal dues. The peasants were determined to take possession of food supplies and land that they considered rightfully theirs. They were reclaiming rights and property that they had lost through the aristocratic resurgence of the last quarter century, as well as venting their general anger against the injustices of rural life.

On the night of August 4, 1789, aristocrats in the National Constituent Assembly attempted to halt the spreading disorder in the countryside. By pre-arrangement, several liberal nobles and clerics rose in the assembly and renounced their feudal rights, dues, and tithes. In a scene of great emotion, hunting and fishing rights, judicial authority, and special exemptions were surrendered. These nobles gave up what they had already lost and what they could not have regained without civil war in the rural areas. Later they would also, in many cases, receive compensation for their losses. Nonetheless, after the night of August 4, all French citizens were subject to the same and equal laws. That dramatic session of the assembly paved the way for the legal and social reconstruction of the nation. Without those renunciations, the constructive work of the National Constituent Assembly would have been much more difficult. (See "The National Assembly Decrees Civic Equality in France.")

Both the attack on the Bastille and the Great Fear displayed characteristics of the rural and urban riots that had occurred often in eighteenth-century France.

Louis XVI first thought that the turmoil over the Bastille was simply another bread riot. Indeed, the popular disturbances were only partly related to the events at Versailles. A deep economic downturn had struck France in 1787 and continued into 1788. The harvests for both years had been poor, and food prices in 1789 were higher than at any time since 1703. Wages had not kept up with the rise in prices. Throughout the winter of 1788–1789, an unusually cold one, many people suffered from hunger. Several cities had experienced wage and food riots. These economic problems helped the revolution reach the vast proportions it did.

The political, social, and economic grievances of many sections of the country became combined. The National Constituent Assembly could look to the popular forces as a source of strength against the king and the conservative aristocrats. When the various elements of the assembly later fell into quarrels among themselves, the resulting factions appealed for support to the politically sophisticated and well-organized shopkeeping and artisan classes. They, in turn, would demand a price for their cooperation.

The National Assembly Decrees Civic Equality in France

These famous decrees of August 4, 1789, in effect created civic equality in France. The special privileges previously possessed or controlled by the nobility were removed.

❖ *What institutions and privileges are included in "the feudal regime"? How do these decrees recognize that the abolition of some privileges and former tax arrangements will require new kinds of taxes and government financing to support religious, educational, and other institutions?*

1. The National Assembly completely abolishes the feudal regime. It decrees that, among the rights and dues...all those originating in real or personal serfdom, personal servitude, and those which represent them, are abolished without indemnification; all others are declared redeemable, and that the price and mode of redemption shall be fixed by the National Assembly....

2. The exclusive right to maintain pigeon-houses and dove-cotes is abolished....

3. The exclusive right to hunt and to maintain unenclosed warrens is likewise abolished....

4. All manorial courts are suppressed without indemnification.

5. Tithes of every description and the dues which have been substituted for them...are abolished, on condition, however, that some other method be devised to provide for the expenses of divine worship, the support of the officiating clergy, the relief of the poor, repairs and rebuilding of churches and parsonages, and for all establishments, seminaries, schools, academies, asylums, communities, and other institutions, for the maintenance of which they are actually devoted....

7. The sale of judicial and municipal offices shall be suppressed forthwith....

8. Pecuniary privileges, personal or real, in the payment of taxes are abolished forever....

11. All citizens, without distinction of birth, are eligible to any office or dignity, whether ecclesiastical, civil or military....

From Frank Maloy Anderson, ed. and trans., *The Constitutions and Other Select Documents Illustrative of the History of France, 1789–1907*, 2d. ed., rev. and enl. (Minneapolis: H. W. Wilson, 1908), pp. 11–13.

The Declaration of the Rights of Man and Citizen

In late August 1789, the National Constituent Assembly decided that before writing a new constitution, it should set forth a statement of broad political principles. On August 27, the assembly issued the Declaration of the Rights of Man and Citizen. This declaration drew upon much of the political language of the Enlightenment and was also influenced by the Declaration of Rights adopted by Virginia in America in June 1776.

The French declaration proclaimed that all men were "born and remain free and equal in rights." The natural rights so proclaimed were "liberty, property, security, and resistance to oppression." Governments existed to protect those rights. All political sovereignty resided in the nation and its representatives. All citizens were to be equal before the law and were to be "equally admissible to all public dignities, offices, and employments, according to their capacity, and with no other distinction than that of their virtues and talents." There were to be due process of law and presumption of innocence until proof of guilt. Freedom of religion was affirmed. Taxation was to be apportioned equally according to capacity to pay. Property constituted "an inviolable and sacred right."[2]

[2]Quoted in Georges Lefebvre, *The Coming of the French Revolution*, trans. by R. R. Palmer (Princeton, NJ: Princeton University Press, 1967), pp. 221–223.

Civic equality was one of the hallmarks of the revolutionary era. This figure of Equality holds in her hand a copy of the Declaration of the Rights of Man and Citizen. Corbis

Although these statements were rather abstract, almost all of them were directed against specific abuses of the old aristocratic and absolutist regime. If any two principles of the future governed the declaration, they were civic equality and protection of property. The Declaration of the Rights of Man and Citizen has often been considered the death certificate of the Old Regime.

It was not accidental that the Declaration of the Rights of Man and Citizen specifically applied to men and not to women. As discussed in the previous chapter, much of the political language of the Enlightenment, and most especially that associated with Rousseau, separated men and women into distinct gender spheres. According to this view, which influenced the legislation of the revolutionary era, men were suited for citizenship, women for motherhood and the domestic life. Nonetheless, in the charged atmosphere of the summer of 1789, many politically active and informed Frenchwomen hoped that the guarantees of the declaration would be extended to them. Their issues of particular concern related to property, inheritance, family, and divorce. Some people saw in the declaration a framework within which women might eventually enjoy the rights and protection of citizenship.

The Royal Family Forced to Return to Paris

Louis XVI stalled before ratifying both the declaration and the aristocratic renunciation of feudalism. The longer he hesitated, the stronger grew suspicions that he might again try to resort to the use of troops. Moreover, bread continued to be scarce. On October 5, a crowd of as many as 7,000 Parisian women armed with pikes, guns, swords, and knives marched to Versailles demanding more bread. They milled about the palace, and many stayed the night. Intimidated by these Parisian women, the king agreed to sanction the decrees of the assembly. The next day he and his family appeared on a balcony before the crowd. The Parisians, however, were deeply suspicious of the monarch and believed that he must be kept under the watchful eye of the people. They demanded that Louis and his family return to Paris. The monarch had no real choice in

The women of Paris marched to Versailles on October 5, 1789. The following day the royal family was forced to return to Paris with them. Henceforth, the French government would function under the constant threat of mob violence. France, 18th c., *To Versailles, to Versailles.* The Women of Paris going to Versailles, 7 October, 1789. Musée de la Ville de Paris, Musée Carnavalet, Paris, France. Giraudon/Art Resource, NY the matter. On October 6, 1789, his carriage followed the crowd into the city, where he and his family settled in the palace of the Tuileries.

The march of the women of Paris was the first example of a popular insurrection employing the language of popular sovereignty directed against the monarch. The National Constituent Assembly also soon moved into Paris. Thereafter, both Paris and France remained relatively stable and peaceful until the summer of 1792. (See "Art & the West.")

The Reconstruction of France

Once established in Paris, the National Constituent Assembly set about reorganizing France. In government, it pursued a policy of constitutional monarchy; in administration, rationalism; in economics, unregulated freedom; and in religion, anticlericalism. Throughout its proceedings the assembly was determined to protect property in all its forms. In those policies, the aristocracy and the middle-class elite stood united. The assembly also sought to limit the impact on national life of the unpropertied elements of the nation and even of possessors of small amounts of property. Although championing civic equality before the law, the assembly spurned social equality and extensive democracy. In all these ways, the assembly charted a general course that, to a greater or lesser degree, nineteenth-century liberals across Europe would follow.

Political Reorganization

The Constitution of 1791, the product of the National Constituent Assembly's deliberations, established a constitutional monarchy. The major political authority of the nation would be a unicameral Legislative Assembly, in which all laws would originate. The monarch was allowed a suspensive veto that could delay, but not halt, legislation. Powers of war and peace were vested in the assembly.

ACTIVE AND PASSIVE CITIZENS   The constitution provided for an elaborate system of indirect elections intended to thwart direct popular pressure on the government. The citizens of France were divided into active and passive categories. Only active citizens—that is, men paying annual taxes equal to three days of local labor wages—could vote. They chose electors, who then in turn voted for the members of the legislature. At the level of electors or members, still further property qualifications were imposed. Only about fifty thousand citizens of a population of about twenty-five million could qualify as electors or members of the Legislative Assembly. Women could neither vote nor hold office.

These constitutional arrangements effectively transferred political power from aristocratic wealth to all forms of propertied wealth in the nation. Political authority would no longer be achieved through hereditary privilege or through purchase of titles, but through the accumulation of land and commercial property. These new political arrangements based on property rather than birth recognized the new complexities of French society that had developed over the past century and allowed more social and economic interests to have a voice in the governing of the nation.

The laws that excluded women from both voting and holding office did not pass unnoticed. In 1791 Olympe de Gouges (d. 1793), a butcher's daughter from Montauban who became a major revolutionary radical in Paris, composed a *Declaration of the Rights of Woman*, which she ironically addressed to Queen Marie Antoinette. Much of the document reprinted the Declaration of the Rights of Man and Citizen adding the word "woman" to the various original clauses. That strategy demanded that women be regarded as citizens and not merely as daughters, sisters, wives, and mothers of citizens. Olympe de Gouges further outlined rights that would permit women to own property and require men to recognize the paternity of their children. She called for equality of the sexes in marriage and improved education for women. She declared, "Women, wake up; the tocsin of reason is being heard throughout the whole universe; discover your rights."[3] Her declaration illustrated how the simple listing of rights in the Declaration of the Rights of Man and Citizen created a structure of universal civic expectations even for those it did not cover. The National Assembly had established a set of values against which it could itself be measured. It provided criteria for liberty, and those to whom it had not extended full liberties could demand to know why and could claim that the revolution was incomplete until they enjoyed those freedoms.

DEPARTMENTS REPLACE PROVINCES   In reconstructing the local and judicial administration, the National Constituent Assembly applied the rational spirit of the Enlightenment. It abolished the ancient French provinces, such as Burgundy and Brittany, and established in their place eighty-three departments, or *départements*, of generally equal size named after rivers, mountains, and other geographical features. (See Map 19–1.) The departments in turn were subdivided into districts, cantons, and communes. Most local elections

---

[3]Quoted in Sara E. Melzer and Leslie W. Rabine, eds., *Rebel Daughters: Women and the French Revolution* (New York: Oxford University Press, 1992), p. 88.

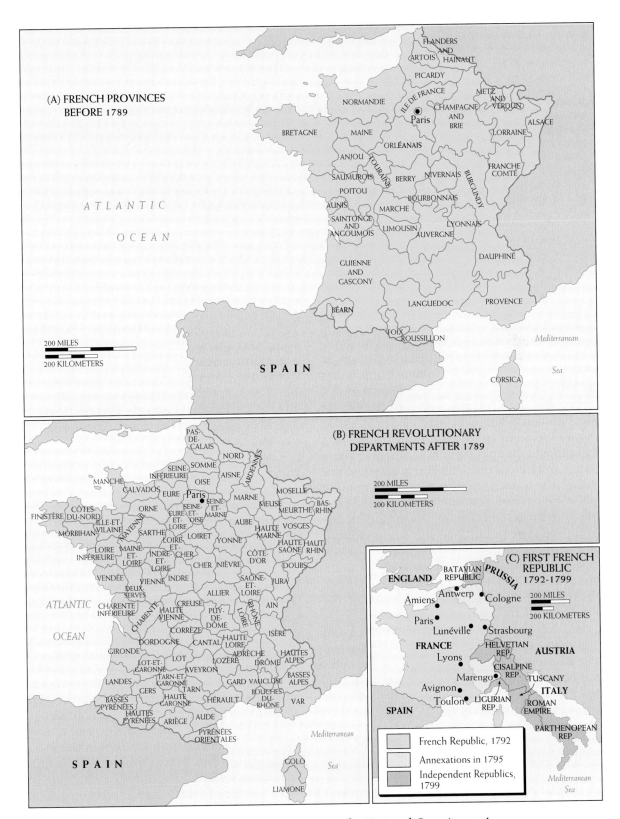

(A) FRENCH PROVINCES
BEFORE 1789

FLANDERS AND HAINAUT
ARTOIS
PICARDY
NORMANDIE
ILE DE FRANCE
Paris
CHAMPAGNE AND BRIE
METZ AND VERDUN
ALSACE
LORRAINE
BRETAGNE
MAINE
ORLÉANAIS
TOURAINE
FRANCHE COMTÉ
ANJOU
SAUMUROIS
BERRY
NIVERNAIS
BURGUNDY
POITOU
BOURBONNAIS
AUNIS
MARCHE
LYONNAIS
SAINTONGE AND ANGOUMOIS
LIMOUSIN
AUVERGNE
ATLANTIC OCEAN
DAUPHINÉ
GUIENNE AND GASCONY
BÉARN
LANGUEDOC
PROVENCE
FOIX ROUSSILLON
Mediterranean
Sea
SPAIN
CORSICA
200 MILES
200 KILOMETERS

(B) FRENCH REVOLUTIONARY
DEPARTMENTS AFTER 1789

PAS-DE-CALAIS
NORD
SEINE INFÉRIEURE
SOMME
AISNE
ARDENNES
MANCHE
OISE
CALVADOS
EURE
Paris
SEINE-ET-OISE
MARNE
MOSELLE
MEUSE
BAS-RHIN
CÔTES-DU-NORD
FINISTÈRE
ORNE
SEINE-ET-MARNE
MEURTHE
ILLE-ET-VILAINE
MAYENNE
SARTHE
EURE-ET-LOIRE
AUBE
HAUTE MARNE
VOSGES
HAUT-RHIN
MORBIHAN
LOIRE-ET-CHER
LOIRET
YONNE
CÔTE-D'OR
HAUTE SAÔNE
MAINE-ET-LOIRE
INDRE-ET-LOIRE
DOUBS
LOIRE INFÉRIEURE
CHER
NIÈVRE
VENDÉE
VIENNE
INDRE
SAÔNE-ET-LOIRE
JURA
DEUX-SÈVRES
ALLIER
AIN
CHARENTE INFÉRIEURE
CREUSE
RHÔNE
HAUTE VIENNE
PUY-DE-DÔME
LOIRE
ISÈRE
CORRÈZE
ATLANTIC OCEAN
CHARENTE
HAUTE LOIRE
GIRONDE
DORDOGNE
CANTAL
ARDÈCHE
DRÔME
HAUTES ALPES
LOT-ET-GARONNE
LOT
LOZÈRE
BASSES ALPES
LANDES
TARN-ET-GARONNE
AVEYRON
GARD
VAUCLUSE
GERS
TARN
HAUTE GARONNE
HÉRAULT
BOUCHES-DU-RHÔNE
VAR
BASSES PYRÉNÉES
HAUTES PYRÉNÉES
AUDE
ARIÈGE
PYRÉNÉES ORIENTALES
Mediterranean Sea
SPAIN
GOLO
LIAMONE
200 MILES
200 KILOMETERS

(C) FIRST FRENCH REPUBLIC 1792-1799

ENGLAND
BATAVIAN REPUBLIC
PRUSSIA
Amiens
Antwerp
Cologne
Paris
Lunéville
Strasbourg
FRANCE
HELVETIAN REP.
AUSTRIA
Lyons
CISALPINE REP.
Marengo
TUSCANY
Avignon
ITALY
Toulon
LIGURIAN REP.
ROMAN EMPIRE
SPAIN
PARTHENOPEAN REP.
Mediterranean Sea
200 MILES
200 KILOMETERS

French Republic, 1792
Annexations in 1795
Independent Republics, 1799

MAP 19–1   FRENCH PROVINCES AND THE REPUBLIC   *In 1789, the National Constituent Assembly redrew the map of France. The ancient provinces (A) were replaced with a larger number of new, smaller departments (B). This redrawing of the map was part of the assembly's effort to impose greater administrative rationality in France. The borders of the republic (C) changed as the French army conquered new territory.*

Jacques-Louis David Champions Republican Values: Lictors Bringing to Brutus the Bodies of His Sons

Jacques-Louis David (1748–1825) was the foremost French painter of the late eighteenth and early nineteenth centuries. Much of his art is associated with the movement called *neoclassicism*, which constituted a return to themes and topics drawn from antiquity and the copying in painting, sculpture, and architecture of major elements of classical models. Figures in such paintings rarely suggest movement and often seem to stand in a kind of tableau illustrating a moral theme. These paintings were didactic rather than emotional or playful. They usually pertained in some manner to public life or public morals, rather than to family life or daily routine. David was strongly critical of the old regime and used ancient republican themes in his paintings to point to the corruption of the current monarchical government.

David began the painting of *Lictors Bringing to Brutus the Bodies of His Sons* in 1789, before the revolutionary events of that year, but completed it only after the National Assembly had proclaimed itself. The work, which covers a very large canvas, though painted in literally the last days of old-regime France, conveys many of the political values and implies a social critique associated with the French Revolution itself.

The painting illustrates a famous incident in the history of republican Rome. Brutus, not to be confused with the later Brutus associated with the assassination of Julius Ceasar, had been instrumental in banishing the last king of Rome. He then became one of the two Consuls of the newly formed Roman Republic. Shortly thereafter, his two sons, Titus and Tiberius, became involved in an effort to restore the exiled king, who was a relative of their mother. Once the conspiracy was uncovered, Brutus, in his capacity as Consul, ordered and witnessed the execution of his sons who had betrayed the republic. This story, which formed the background for a famous play by Voltaire earlier in the century, embodied the concept of selfless republican patriotism as a virtue higher than ties to family. During the French revolution itself, Brutus assumed the status of a kind of cult figure who had opposed tyrannical kings.

David portrays the moment when the Lictors return the bodies of the two sons to Brutus's household. The painting has been described as "an interrogation of the idea of civic virtue" through its portrayal of the differing reactions of the parents.[4] David clearly illustrates the concept of separate spheres for men and women, which he may well have derived from Rousseau, a champion of the virtue of the ancient republics. The painting is sharply divided into an active male sphere on the left and a passive female sphere on the right. The male portion of the painting includes the world of politics, civic action, and republican virtue based on the rational values of law symbolized by the document in Brutus's hand.

The female portion of the painting depicts the mother and sisters of the executed sons, as well as a nurse, in various states of emotional distress, illustrating their presumed incapacity to place civic virtue above private family feelings. The basket, wool, and shears on the table, which form a still life within this large history painting, represent the domestic sphere of the daily routine of women. Moreover, their mother, according to Livy, had led the sons into the royal-

---

[4]Thomas Crow, *Emulation: Making Artists for Revolutionary France* (New Haven, CT: Yale University Press 1995), p. 108.

Jacques-Louis David (1748–1825), *Lictors bringing to Brutus the bodies of his sons.* 1789. Oil on canvas, 323 × 422 cm - Inv. 3693. Louvre, Paris, France. Erich Lessing/Art Resource, NY.

ist conspiracy. It has been suggested that a royalist *fleur-de-lis* appears in the cloth in the basket.

Brutus appears alone, separated from his family and from all other human emotions except dedication to the Roman Republic itself. The presence of the statue portraying the legend of Romulus and Remus suckled by the wolf symbolizes the manner in which the Roman Republic, at its origin, stood distinct from family life. Through this symbolism, David suggests that family loyalties and female influence stand in opposition to republican virtue. Indeed, loyalty to abstract political principles separated from human sympathies mark the years of the Terror, when revolutionary leaders often appealed directly to the experience of the ancient republics.

David himself was one of the great political survivors of the revolutionary era. He painted many of its events, became a strong Jacobin, was imprisoned for a time, and then emerged into public life to portray most of the major events of Napoleon's career. Under the restoration, he spent the end of his life in exile.

Robert Rosenblum and H. W. Janson, *Nineteenth-Century Art* (Englewood Cliffs, NJ and New York: Prentice Hall: Harry N. Abrams, Inc., 1984), pp. 24–50; Albert Boime, *Art in an Age of Revolution, 1750–1800* (Chicago: University of Chicago Press, 1987, pp. 417–421); Norman Bryson, *Looking at the Overlooked: Four Essays on Still Life Painting* (Cambridge, MA: Harvard University Press, 1900), pp. 156–158; and Thomas Crow, *Emulation: Making Artists for Revolutionary France* (New Haven, CT: Yale University Press, 1995).

were also indirect. The departmental reconstruction proved to be a permanent achievement of the assembly. The departments exist to the present day.

All the ancient judicial courts, including the seigneurial courts and the *parlements*, were also abolished. Uniform courts with elected judges and prosecutors were organized in their place. Procedures were simplified, and the most degrading punishments were removed from the books.

Economic Policy

In economic matters, the National Constituent Assembly continued the policies formerly advocated by Louis XVI's reformist ministers. It suppressed the guilds and liberated the grain trade. The assembly established the metric system to provide the nation with uniform weights and measures.

WORKERS' ORGANIZATIONS FORBIDDEN The new policies of economic freedom and uniformity disappointed both peasants and urban workers caught in the cycle of inflation. By decrees in 1789, the assembly placed the burden of proof on the peasants to rid themselves of the residual feudal dues for which compensation was to be paid. On June 14, 1791, the assembly crushed the attempts of urban workers to protect their wages by enacting the Chapelier Law, which forbade workers' associations. Peasants and workers were henceforth to be left to the freedom and mercy of the marketplace. (See "The Revolutionary Government Forbids Workers' Organizations.")

The Revolutionary Government Forbids Workers' Organizations

The Chapelier Law of June 14, 1791, was one of the most important pieces of revolutionary legislation. It abolished the kinds of labor organizations that had protected skilled workers under the Old Regime. The principles of this legislation prevented effective labor organization in France for well over half a century.

❖ *Why are workers' organizations declared to be contrary to the principles of liberty? Why were guilds seen as one of the undesirable elements of the Old Regime? What are the coercive powers that are to be brought to bear against workers' organizations? In light of this legislation, what courses of actions were left open to workers as they confronted the operation of the market economy?*

1. Since the abolition of all kinds of corporations of citizens of the same occupation and profession is one of the fundamental bases of the French Constitution, reestablishment thereof under any pretext or form whatsoever is forbidden.

2. Citizens of the same occupation or profession, entrepreneurs, those who maintain open shop, workers, and journeymen of any craft whatsoever may not, when they are together, name either president, secretaries, or trustees, keep accounts, pass decrees or resolutions, or draft regulations concerning their alleged common interests....

...4. If, contrary to the principles of liberty and the Constitution, some citizens associated in the same professions, arts, and crafts hold deliberations or make agreements among themselves tending to refuse by mutual consent or to grant only at a determined price the assistance of their industry or their labor, such deliberations and agreements, whether accompanied by oath or not, are declared unconstitutional, in contempt of liberty and the Declaration of the Rights of Man, and noneffective; administrative and municipal bodies shall be required so to declare them....

8. All assemblies composed of artisans, workers, journeymen, day laborers, or those incited by them against the free exercise of industry and labor appertaining to every kind of person and under all circumstances arranged by private contract, or against the action of police and the execution of judgments rendered in such connection, as well as against public bids and auctions of divers enterprises, shall be considered as seditious assemblies, and as such shall be dispersed by the depositories of the public force, upon legal requisitions made thereupon, and shall be punished according to all the rigor of the laws concerning authors, instigators, and leaders of the said assemblies, and all those who have committed assaults and acts of violence.

From *A Documentary Survey of the French Revolution*, by Stewart, John Hall, © 1951. Reprinted by permission of Prentice-Hall, Inc., Upper Saddle River, NJ.

CONFISCATION OF CHURCH LANDS   While these various reforms were being put into effect, the original financial crisis that had occasioned the calling of the Estates General persisted. The assembly did not repudiate the royal debt, because it was owed to the bankers, the merchants, and the commercial traders of the Third Estate. The National Constituent Assembly had suppressed many of the old, hated indirect taxes and had substituted new land taxes, but these proved insufficient. Moreover, there were not enough officials to collect them. The continuing financial problem led the assembly to take what may well have been, for the future of French life and society, its most decisive action. The assembly decided to finance the debt by confiscating and then selling the land and property of the Roman Catholic Church in France. The results were further inflation, religious schism, and civil war. In effect, the National Constituent Assembly had opened a new chapter in the relations of church and state in Europe.

THE *ASSIGNATS*   Having chosen to plunder the land of the church, the assembly authorized the issuance of *assignats*, or government bonds in December 1789. Their value was guaranteed by the revenue to be generated from the sale of church property. Initially, a limit was set on the quantity of *assignats* to be issued. The bonds, however, proved so acceptable to the public that they began to circulate as currency. The assembly decided to issue an ever-larger number of them to liquidate the national debt and to create a large body of new property owners with a direct stake in the revolution. Within a few months, however, the value of the *assignats* began to fall and inflation increased, putting new stress on the lives of the urban poor.

The Civil Constitution of the Clergy

The confiscation of church lands required an ecclesiastical reconstruction. In July 1790, the National Constituent Assembly issued the Civil Constitution of the Clergy, which transformed the Roman Catholic Church in France into a branch of the secular state. This legislation reduced the number of bishoprics from 135 to 83 and brought the borders of the dioceses into conformity with those of the new departments. It also provided for the election of priests and bishops, who henceforth became salaried employees of the state. The assembly consulted neither the Pope nor the French clergy about these broad changes. The king approved the measure only with the greatest reluctance.

The Civil Constitution of the Clergy was the major blunder of the National Constituent Assembly. It created embittered relations between the French church and state that have persisted to the present day. The measure immediately created immense opposition within the French church, even from bishops who had long championed Gallican liberties over papal domination. In the face of this resistance, the assembly unwisely ruled that all clergy must take an oath to support the Civil Constitution. Only seven bishops and about half the clergy did so. In reprisal, the assembly designated those clergy who had not taken the oath as "refractory" and removed them from their clerical functions.

Further reaction was swift. Refractory priests attempted to celebrate mass. In February 1791, the Pope condemned not only the Civil Constitution of the Clergy, but also the Declaration of the Rights of Man and Citizen. That condemnation marked the opening of a Roman Catholic offensive against liberalism and the revolution that continued throughout the nine-

The assignats were government bonds that were backed by confiscated church lands. They circulated as money. When the government printed too many of them, inflation resulted and their value fell.
Bildarchiv Preussischer Kulturbesitz

teenth century. Within France itself, the pope's action created a crisis of conscience and political loyalty for all sincere Catholics. Religious devotion and revolutionary loyalty became incompatible for many people. French citizens were divided between those who supported the constitutional priests and those who resorted to the refractory clergy. Louis XVI and his family favored the refractory clergy.

Counterrevolutionary Activity

The revolution had other enemies besides the Pope and the devout Catholics. As it became clear that the old political and social order was undergoing fundamental and probably permanent change, many aristocrats left France. Known as the *émigrés*, they settled in countries near the French border, where they sought to foment counterrevolution. Among the most important of their number was the king's younger brother, the count of Artois (1757–1836). In the summer of 1791, his agents and the queen persuaded Louis XVI to attempt to flee the country.

FLIGHT TO VARENNES   On the night of June 20, 1791, Louis and his immediate family, disguised as servants, left Paris. They traveled as far as Varennes on their way to Metz. At Varennes the king was recognized, and his flight was halted. On June 24, a company of soldiers escorted the royal family back to Paris. The leaders of the National Constituent Assembly, determined to save the constitutional monarchy, announced that the king had been abducted from the capital. Such a convenient public fiction could not cloak the realities that the chief counterrevolutionary in France now sat on the throne and that the constitutional monarchy might not last long.

DECLARATION OF PILLNITZ   Two months later, on August 27, 1791, under pressure from a group of *émigrés*, Emperor Leopold II of Austria, who was the brother of Marie Antoinette, and Frederick William II (r. 1786–1797), the king of Prussia, issued the Declaration of Pillnitz. The two monarchs promised to intervene in France to protect the royal family and to preserve the monarchy *if the other*

In June 1791, Louis XVI and his family attempted to flee France. They were recognized in the town of Varennes, where their flight was halted and they were returned to Paris. This ended any realistic hope for a constitutional monarchy. Corbis major European powers agreed. This provision rendered the declaration meaningless because, at the time, Great Britain would not have given its consent. The declaration was not, however, so read in France, where the revolutionaries saw the nation surrounded by aristocratic and monarchical foes.

The National Constituent Assembly drew to a close in September 1791. Its task of reconstructing the government and the administration of France had been completed. One of its last acts was the passage of a measure that forbade any of its own members to sit in the Legislative Assembly then being elected. The new body met on October 1 and had to confront the immense problems that had emerged during the earlier part of the year. Within the Legislative Assembly, major political divisions also soon developed over the future course of the nation and the revolution. Those groups whose members had been assigned to passive citizenship began to demand full political participation in the nation.

A Second Revolution

By the autumn of 1791, the government of France had been transformed into a constitutional monarchy. Virtually all the other administrative and religious structures of the nation had also been reformed. The situation both inside and outside France, however, remained unstable. Louis XVI had reluctantly accepted the constitution on July 14, 1790. French aristocrats resented their loss of position and plotted to overthrow the new order. In the west of France, peasants resisted the revolutionary changes, especially as they affected the church. In Paris, many groups of workers believed that the revolution had not gone far enough. Furthermore, during these same months, women's groups in Paris began to organize both to support the revolution and to demand a wider civic role and civic protection for women. Radical members of the new Legislative Assembly also believed that the revolution should go further. The major foreign powers saw the French Revolution as dangerous to their own domestic political order. By the spring of 1792, all these unstable elements had begun to overturn the first revolutionary settlement and led to a second series of revolutionary changes far more radical and democratically extensive than the first.

End of the Monarchy

The issues raised by the Civil Constitution of the Clergy and Louis XVI's uncertain trustworthiness undermined the unity of the newly organized nation. Factionalism plagued the Legislative Assembly throughout its short life (1791–1792). Ever since the

original gathering of the Estates General, deputies from the Third Estate had organized themselves into clubs composed of politically like-minded persons. The most famous and best organized of these clubs were the Jacobins, whose name derived from the fact that Dominican friars were called Jacobins and the group met in a Dominican monastery in Paris. The Jacobins had also established a network of local clubs throughout the provinces. They had been the most advanced political group in the National Constituent Assembly and had pressed for a republic rather than a constitutional monarchy. Their political language and rhetoric were drawn from the most radical thought of the Enlightenment. That thought and language became all the more effective because the events of 1789–1791 had destroyed the old political framework and the old monarchical political vocabulary was less and less relevant. The political language and rhetoric of a republic filled that vacuum and for a time supplied the political values of the day. The events of the summer of 1791 led to the reassertion of demands for establishing a republic.

In the Legislative Assembly, a group of Jacobins known as the Girondists (because many of them came from the department of the Gironde) assumed leadership.[5] They were determined to oppose the forces of counterrevolution. They passed one measure ordering the *émigrés* to return or suffer loss of property and another requiring the refractory clergy to support the Civil Constitution or lose their state pensions. The king vetoed both acts.

Furthermore, on April 20, 1792, the Girondists led the Legislative Assembly in declaring war on Austria, by this time governed by Francis II (r. 1792–1835) and allied to Prussia. The Girondists believed that the pursuit of the war would preserve the revolution from domestic enemies and bring the most advanced revolutionaries to power. Paradoxically, Louis XVI and other monarchists also favored the war. They thought that the conflict would strengthen the executive power (the monarchy). The king also entertained the hope that foreign armies might defeat French forces and restore the Old Regime. Both sides were playing dangerously foolish politics.

The war radicalized the revolution and led to what is usually called the second revolution, which overthrew the constitutional monarchy and established a republic. Both the country and the revolution seemed in danger. As early as March 1791, a group of women led by Pauline Léon had petitioned the Legislative Assembly for the right to bear arms and to fight for

---

[5]The Girondists are also frequently called the Brissotins after Jacques-Pierre Brissot (1754–1793), their chief spokesperson in early 1792.

French Women Petition to Bear Arms

The issue of women serving in the revolutionary French military appeared early in the revolution. In March 1791, Pauline Léon presented a petition to the National Assembly on behalf of more than 300 Parisian women asking the right to bear arms and train for military service for the revolution. Similar requests were made during the next two years. Some women did serve in the military, but in 1793 legislation specifically forbade women from participating in military service. The ground for that refusal was the argument that women belonged in the domestic sphere and military service would lead them to abandon family duties.

❖ Citoyenne *is the feminine form of the French word for citizen. How does this petition seek to challenge the concept of citizenship in the Declaration of the Rights of Man and Citizen? How do these petitioners relate their demand to bear arms to their role as women in French society? How do the petitioners relate their demands to the use of all national resources against the enemies of the revolution?*

Patriotic women come before you to claim the right which any individual has to defend his life and liberty.

...We are *citoyennes* [female citizens], and we cannot be indifferent to the fate of the fatherland.

...Yes, Gentlemen, we need arms, and we come to ask your permission to procure them. May our weakness be no obstacle; courage and intrepidity will supplant it, and the love of the fatherland and hatred of tyrants will allow us to brave all dangers with ease....

No, Gentlemen, We will [use arms] only to defend ourselves the same as you; you cannot refuse us, and society cannot deny the right nature gives us, unless you pretend the Declaration of Rights does not apply to women and that they should let their throats be cut like lambs, without the right to defend themselves. For can you believe the tyrants would spare us?...Why then not terrorize aristocracy and tyranny with all the resources of civic effort and the pure zeal, zeal which cold men can well call fanaticism and exaggeration, but which is only the natural result of a heart burning with love for the public weal?...

...If, for reasons we cannot guess, you refuse our just demands, these women you have raised to the ranks of *citoyennes* by granting that to their husbands, these women who have sampled the promises of liberty, who have conceived the hope of placing free men in the world, and who have sworn to live free or die—such women, I

say, will never consent to concede the day to slaves; they will die first. They will uphold their oath, and a dagger aimed at their breasts will deliver them from the misfortunes of slavery! They will die, regretting not life, but the uselessness of their death; regretting moreover, not having been able to drench their hands in the impure blood of the enemies of the fatherland and to avenge some of their own!

But, Gentlemen, let us cast our eyes away from these cruel extremes. Whatever the rages and plots of aristocrats, they will not succeed in vanquishing a whole people of united brothers armed to defend their rights. We also demand only the honor of sharing their exhaustion and glorious labors and of making tyrants see that women also have blood to shed for the service of the fatherland in danger.

Gentlemen, here is what we hope to obtain from your justice and equity:

1. Permission to procure pikes, pistols, and sabres (even muskets for those who are strong enough to use them), within police regulations.

2. Permission to assemble on festival days and Sundays on the Champ de la Fédération, or in other suitable places, to practice maneuvers with these arms.

3. Permission to name the former French Guards to command us, always in conformity with the rules which the mayor's wisdom prescribes for good order and public calm.

Excerpts from Leon, "Petition to the National Assembly on Woman's Rights to Bear Arms" in *Women in Revolutionary Paris 1789–1795*, edited and translated by Darline Gay Levy, Harriet Branson Applewhite, and Mary Durham Johnson. Copyright © 1979, by the Board of Trustees of the University of Illinois. Used with permission of the University of Illinois Press.

On August 10, 1792, the Swiss Guards of Louis XVI fought Parisians who attacked the Tuileries Palace. Several hundred troops and citizens were killed, and Louis XVI and his family were forced to take refuge with the Legislative Assembly. After this event, the monarch virtually ceased to influence events in France. Jean Duplessi–Bertaux, *The Siege of the Palais des Tuileries, August 10, 1792.* Chateau, Versailles, France. Giraudon/Art Resource, NY

the protection of the revolution. (See "French Women Petition to Bear Arms.") Even before that, Léon had led an effort to allow women to serve in the National Guard. These demands to serve, voiced in the universal language of citizenship, illustrated how the words and rhetoric of the revolution could be used to challenge traditional social roles and the concept of separate social spheres for men and women. Furthermore, the pressure of war raised the possibility that the military needs of the nation could not be met if the ideal of separate spheres were honored. Once the war began, some Frenchwomen did enlist in the army and served with distinction.

Initially, the war effort went quite poorly. In July 1792, the duke of Brunswick, commander of the Prussian forces, issued a manifesto promising the destruction of Paris if harm came to the French royal family. This statement stiffened support for the war and increased the already significant distrust of the king.

Late in July, under radical working-class pressure, the government of Paris passed from the elected council to a committee, or commune, of representatives from the sections (municipal

wards) of the city. On August 10, 1792, a very large Parisian crowd invaded the Tuileries palace and forced Louis XVI and Marie Antoinette to take refuge in the Legislative Assembly itself. The crowd fought with the royal Swiss guards. When Louis was finally able to call off the troops, several hundred of them and many Parisian citizens lay dead. The monarchy itself was also a casualty of that melee. Thereafter the royal family was imprisoned in comfortable quarters, but the king was allowed to perform none of his political functions. The recently established constitutional monarchy no longer had a monarch.

The Convention and the Role of the *Sans-culottes*

Early in September, the Parisian crowd again made its will felt. During the first week of the month, in what are known as the September Massacres, the Paris Commune summarily executed or murdered about 1,200 people who were in the city jails. Many of these people were aristocrats or priests, but the majority were

A Pamphleteer Describes a *Sans-culotte*

This document is a 1793 description of a **sans-culotte** *written either by one or by a sympathizer. It describes the* **sans-culotte** *as a hardworking, useful, patriotic citizen who bravely sacrifices himself to the war effort. It contrasts those virtues with the lazy and unproductive luxury of the noble and the personally self-interested plottings of the politician.*

❖ *What social resentments appear in this description? How could these resentments be used to create solidarity among the* **sans-culottes** *to defend the revolution? How does this document relate civic virtue to work? Do you see any relationship between the social views expressed in the document and the abolition of workers' organizations in a previous document? Where does this document suggest that the* **sans-culotte** *may need to confront enemies of the republic?*

A *sans-culotte* you rogues? He is someone who always goes on foot, who has no millions as you would all like to have, no chateaux, no valets to serve him, and who lives simply with his wife and children, if he has any, on a fourth or fifth story.

He is useful, because he knows how to work in the field, to forge iron, to use a saw, to use a file, to roof a house, to make shoes, and to shed his last drop of blood for the safety of the Republic.

And because he works, you are sure not to meet his person in the Café de Chartres, or in the gaming houses where others conspire and game; nor at the National theatre...nor in the literary clubs....

In the evening he goes to his section, not powdered or perfumed, or smartly booted in the hope of catching the eye of the citizenesses in the galleries, but ready to support good proposals with all his might, and to crush those which come from the abominable faction of politicians.

Finally, a *sans-culotte* always has his sabre sharp, to cut off the ears of all enemies of the Revolution; sometimes he even goes out with his pike; but at the first sound of the drum he is ready to leave for the Vendée, for the army of the Alps or for the army of the North....

From "Reply to an Impertinent Question: What is a Sans-culotte?" April 1793. Reprinted in Walter Markov and Albert Soboul, eds., *Die Sansculotten von Paris,* and republished trans. by Clive Emsley in Merryn Williams, ed., *Revolutions: 1775–1830* (Baltimore: Penguin Books, in association with the Open University, 1971), pp. 100–101.

simply common criminals. The crowd had assumed that the prisoners were all counterrevolutionaries.

The Paris Commune then compelled the Legislative Assembly to call for the election by universal male suffrage of a new assembly to write a democratic constitution. That body, called the Convention after its American counterpart of 1787, met on September 21, 1792. The previous day, the French army had halted the Prussian advance at the Battle of Valmy in eastern France. The victory of democratic forces at home had been confirmed by victory on the battlefield. As its first act, the Convention declared France a republic—that is, a nation governed by an elected assembly without a monarch.

GOALS OF THE *SANS-CULOTTES* The second revolution had been the work of Jacobins more radical than the Girondists and of the people of Paris known as the *sans-culottes*. The name of this group means "without breeches" and derived from the long trousers that, as

working people, they wore instead of aristocratic knee breeches. The *sans-culottes* were shopkeepers, artisans, wage earners, and, in a few cases, factory workers. The persistent food shortages and the revolutionary inflation had made their difficult lives even more burdensome. The politics of the Old Regime had ignored them, and the policies of the National Constituent Assembly had left them victims of unregulated economic liberty. The government, however, required their labor and their lives if the war was to succeed. From the summer of 1792 until the summer of 1794, their attitudes, desires, and ideals were the primary factors in the internal development of the revolution. (See "A Pamphleteer Describes a *Sans-culotte*.")

The *sans-culottes* generally knew what they wanted. The Parisian tradespeople and artisans sought immediate relief from food shortages and rising prices through price controls. They believed that all people had a right to subsistence and profoundly resented most forms of social inequality. This attitude made them intensely hostile to the aristocracy and the original leaders of the revolution of 1789, who they believed simply wanted to share political power, social prestige, and economic security with the aristocracy. The *sans-culottes'* hatred of inequality did not take them so far as to demand the abolition of property. Rather, they advocated a community of small property owners who would also participate in the political nation.

In politics they were antimonarchical, strongly republican, and suspicious even of representative government. They believed that the people should make the decisions of government to as great an extent as possible. In Paris, where their influence was most important, the *sans-culottes* had gained their political experience in meetings of the Paris sections. Those gatherings exemplified direct community democracy and were not unlike a New England town meeting. The economic hardship of their lives made them impatient to see their demands met.

THE POLICIES OF THE JACOBINS The goals of the *sans-culottes* were not wholly compatible with those of the Jacobins, republicans who sought representative government. Jacobin hatred of the aristocracy and hereditary privilege did not extend to a general suspicion of wealth. Basically, the Jacobins favored an unregulated economy. From the time of Louis XVI's flight to Varennes onward, however, the more extreme Jacobins began to cooperate with leaders of the Parisian *sans-culottes* and the Paris Commune for the overthrow of the monarchy. Once the Convention began its deliberations, these Jacobins, known as the Mountain because of their seats high in the assembly hall, worked with the *sans-culottes* to carry the revolution forward and to win the war. This willingness to cooperate with the forces of the popular revolution separated the Mountain from the Girondists, who were also members of the Jacobin Club.

EXECUTION OF LOUIS XVI By the spring of 1793, several issues had brought the Mountain and its *sans-culottes* allies to domination of the Convention and the revolution. In December 1792, Louis XVI was put on trial as mere "Citizen Capet," the family name of extremely distant forebears of the royal family. The Girondists looked for some way to spare his life, but the Mountain defeated the effort. Louis was convicted, by a very narrow majority, of conspiring against the liberty of the people and the security of the state. He was condemned to death and was beheaded on January 21, 1793.

Louis XVI was executed on January 21, 1793. Execution of Louis XVI. Aquatint. French, 18th century.
Musée de la Ville de Paris, Musée Carnavalet, Paris. France. Giraudon/Art Resource, NY

The next month, the Convention declared war on Great Britain, Holland, and Spain. Soon thereafter, the Prussians renewed their offensive and drove the French out of Belgium. To make matters worse, General Dumouriez (1739–1823), the Girondist victor of Valmy, deserted to the enemy. Finally, in March 1793, a royalist revolt led by aristocratic officers and priests erupted in the Vendée in western France and roused much popular support. Thus, the revolution found itself at war with most of Europe and much of the French nation. The Girondists had led the country into the war, but had proved themselves incapable either of winning it or of suppressing the enemies of the revolution at home. The Mountain stood ready to take up the task. Every major European power was now hostile to the revolution.

Europe at War with the Revolution

Initially, the rest of Europe had been ambivalent toward the revolutionary events in France. Those people who favored political reform regarded the revolution as wisely and rationally reorganizing a corrupt and inefficient government. The major foreign governments thought that the revolution meant that France would cease to be an important factor in European affairs for several years.

Edmund Burke Attacks the Revolution

In 1790, however, the Irish-born writer and British statesman Edmund Burke (1729–1799) argued a different position in *Reflections on the Revolution in France*. Burke regarded the reconstruction of French administration as the application of a blind rationalism that ignored the historical realities of political development and the complexities of social relations. He also forecast further turmoil as people without political experience tried to govern France. As the revolutionaries proceeded to attack the church, the monarchy, and finally the rest of Europe, Burke's ideas came to have many admirers. His *Reflections* and later works became the handbook of European conservatives for decades. (See "Burke Denounces the Extreme Measures of the French Revolution.")

By the outbreak of the war with Austria in April 1792, the other European monarchies recognized the danger of both the ideas and the aggression of

Edmund Burke (1729–1799) published Reflections on the Revolution in France *in 1790. It became the most famous of all conservative denunciations of the revolution.* National Portrait Gallery, London

Burke Denounces the Extreme Measures of the French Revolution

Edmund Burke was undoubtedly the most important and articulate foreign critic of the French Revolution. His first critique, Reflections on the Revolution in France, *appeared in 1790. He continued to attack the revolution in later years. In 1796 he composed* Letters on a Regicide Peace, *which opposed a peace treaty between Great Britain and revolutionary France. In that work, he summarized what he regarded as the most fundamental evils of the revolutionary government: the execution of the king, the confiscation of property of the church and nobles, and the policy of de-Christianization.*

❖ *To which of the major events in the French Revolution does Burke make reference? Why, by 1796, would Burke and others have attached so much importance to the religious policies of the revolution? Did Burke exaggerate the evils of the revolution? Who might have been persuaded by Burke's condemnation?*

A government of the nature of that set up at our very door has never been hitherto seen, or even imagined in Europe....France, since her revolution, is under the sway of a sect, whose leaders have deliberately, at one stroke, demolished the whole body of that jurisprudence which France had pretty nearly in common with other civilized countries....

Its foundation is laid in regicide, in Jacobinism, and in atheism, and it has joined to those principles a body of systematic manners, which secures their operation....

I call a commonwealth regicide, which lays it down as a fixed law of nature, and a fundamental right of man, that all government, not being a democracy, is an usurpation. That all kings, as such, are usurpers; and for being kings may and ought to be put to death, with their wives, families, and adherents. That commonwealth which acts uniformly upon those principles...—this I call regicide by establishment.

Jacobinism is the revolt of the enterprising talents of a country against its property. When private men form themselves into associations for the purpose of destroying the pre-existing laws and institutions of their country; when they secure to themselves an army, by dividing amongst the people of no property the estates of the ancient and lawful proprietors, when a state recognizes those acts; when it does not make confiscations for crimes, but makes crimes for confiscations; when it has its

principal strength, and all its resources, in such a violation of property...—I call this Jacobinism by establishment.

I call it atheism by establishment, when any state, as such, shall not acknowledge the existence of God as a moral governor of the world;...—when it shall abolish the Christian religion by a regular decree;—when it shall persecute with a cold, unrelenting, steady cruelty, by every mode of confiscation, imprisonment, exile, and death, all its ministers; —when it shall generally shut up or pull down churches; when the few buildings which remain of this kind shall be opened only for the purpose of making a profane apotheosis of monsters, whose vices and crimes have no parallel amongst men...When, in the place of that religion of social benevolence, and of individual self-denial, in mockery of all religion, they institute impious, blasphemous, indecent theatric rites, in honour of their vitiated, perverted reason, and erect altars to the personification of their own corrupted and bloody republic;...when wearied out with incessant martyrdom, and the cries of a people hungering and thirsting for religion, they permit it, only as a tolerated evil—I call this atheism by establishment.

When to these establishments of regicide, of Jacobinism, and of atheism, you add the correspondent system of manners, no doubt can be left on the mind of a thinking man concerning their determined hostility to the human race.

From *The Works of the Right Honourable Edmund Burke* (London: Henry G. Bohn, 1856), 5: 206–208.

revolutionary France. The ideals of the Rights of Man and Citizen were highly exportable and applicable to the rest of Europe. In response, one government after another turned to repressive domestic policies.

Suppression of Reform in Britain

In Great Britain, William Pitt the Younger (1759–1806), the prime minister, who had unsuccessfully supported moderate reform of Parliament during the 1780s, turned against both reform and popular movements. The government suppressed the London Corresponding Society, founded in 1792 as a working-class reform group. In Birmingham, the government sponsored mob action to drive Joseph Priestley (1733–1804), a famous chemist and a radical political thinker, out of the country. In early 1793, Pitt secured parliamentary approval for acts suspending *habeas corpus* and making it possible to commit treason in writing. With less success, Pitt attempted to curb freedom of the press. All political groups who dared oppose the government faced being associated with sedition.

The End of Enlightened Absolutism in Eastern Europe

In eastern Europe, the revolution brought an end to enlightened absolutism. The aristocratic resistance to the reforms of Joseph II in the Habsburg lands led his brother, Leopold II, to come to terms with the landowners. Leopold's successor, Francis II (r. 1792–1835), became a major leader of the counterrevolution. In Prussia, Frederick William II (r. 1786–1797), the nephew of Frederick the Great, looked to the leaders of the Lutheran church and the aristocracy to discourage any potential popular uprisings, such as those of the downtrodden Silesian weavers. In Russia, Catherine the Great burned the works of her one-time friend Voltaire. She also exiled Alexander Radishchev (1749–1802) to Siberia for publishing his *Journey from Saint Petersburg to Moscow*, a work critical of Russian social conditions. (See the document "Alexander Radishchev Attacks Russian Censorship" in Chapter 18.)

In 1793 and 1795, the eastern powers once again combined against Poland. In that unhappy land, aristocratic reformers had finally achieved the abolition of the *liberum veto* and had organized a new constitutional monarchy in 1791. Russia and Prussia, which already had designs on Polish territory, saw or pretended to see a threat of revolution in

the new Polish constitution. In 1793, they annexed large sections of the country. In 1795, Austria joined the two other powers in a final partition that removed Poland from the map of Europe until after World War I. The governments of eastern Europe had used the widely shared fear of further revolutionary disorder to justify old-fashioned eighteenth-century aggression.

War with Europe

In a paradoxical fashion, the very success of the revolution in France brought a rapid close to reform movements in the rest of Europe. The French invasion of the Austrian Netherlands and the revolutionary reorganization of that territory roused the rest of Europe to the point of active hostility. In November 1792, the Convention declared that it would aid all peoples who wished to cast off the burdens of aristocratic and monarchical oppression. The Convention had also proclaimed the Scheldt River in the Netherlands open to the commerce of all nations and thus had violated a treaty that Great Britain had made with Austria and Holland. The British were on the point of declaring war on France over this issue when the Convention issued its own declaration of hostilities in February 1793.

By April 1793, when the Mountain began to direct the French government, the nation was at war with Austria, Prussia, Great Britain, Spain, Sardinia, and Holland. The governments of those nations, allied in what is known as the First Coalition, were attempting to protect their social structures, political systems, and economic interests against the aggression of the revolution.

The Reign of Terror

The outbreak of war in the winter and spring of 1793 brought new, radical political actions within France. The government mobilized both itself and the nation for conflict. Throughout the nation, there was the sense that a new kind of war had erupted. In this war the major issue was not protection of national borders as such, but rather the defense of the bold new republican political and social order that had emerged during the past four years. The French people understood that the achievements of the revolution were in danger. To protect those achievements the government took extraordinary actions that touched almost every aspect of national life. (See "The Paris Jacobin Club Alerts the Nation to Internal Enemies of the Revolution.")

The Paris Jacobin Club Alerts the Nation to Internal Enemies of the Revolution

By early 1793, the revolutionary groups in Paris stood sharply divided amongst themselves. The Girondists (also known as Brissotins), who had led the nation into war, faced military reversals. General Dumouriez, a former revolutionary commander, had changed sides and was leading an army against France. At this point, on April 5, the radical Jacobin Club of Paris sent a circular to its provincial clubs, painting a dire picture of the fate of the revolution. While Dumouriez was marching against Paris, they accused members of the government and its administrators of conspiring to betray the revolution. The circular suggested that some people were cooperating with England in the war against France. The Jacobins also portrayed as counterrevolutionaries all those political figures who had opposed the execution of Louis XVI. The Paris Jacobins then called on their allies in the provinces to defend the revolution and to take vengeance against its internal enemies. The distortion of the motives of political enemies, the appeal to a possible reversal of the revolution, and the accusations of internal conspiracy served to justify the demand for justice against enemies of the revolution. The accusations embodied in this circular and the fears it sought to arouse represented the kind of thinking that informed the suspension of legal rights and due process associated with the Reign of Terror.

❖ *How did the Jacobins use the war to call for actions against their own domestic political enemies? What real and imagined forces did they see threatening the revolution? How did this circular constitute a smear campaign by one group of revolutionaries against other groups? What actions did the Jacobins seek?*

Friends, we are betrayed! To arms! To arms! The terrible hour is at hand when the defenders of the *Patrie* must vanquish or bury themselves under the bloody ruins of the Republic. Frenchmen, never was your liberty in such great peril! At last our enemies have put the finishing touch to their foul perfidy, and to complete it their accomplice Dumouriez is marching on Paris....

But Brothers, not all your dangers are to be found there!...You must be convinced of a grievous truth! Your greatest enemies are in your midst, they direct your operations. O Vengeance !!!....

Yes, brothers and friends, yes, it is in the Senate that parricidal hands tear at your vitals! Yes, the counter-revolution is in the Government..., in the National Convention! It is there, at the center of your security and your hope, that criminal delegates hold the threads of the web that they have woven with the horde of despots who come to butcher us!...It is there that a sacrilegious cabal is directed by the English court...and others....

Let us rise! Yes, let us rise! Let us arrest all the enemies of our revolution, and all suspected persons. Let us exterminate, without pity, all conspirators, unless we wish to be exterminated ourselves....

Let the departments, the districts, the municipalities, and all the popular societies unite and concur in protesting to the Convention, by dispatching thereto a veritable rain of petitions manifesting the formal wish for the immediate recall of all unfaithful members who have betrayed their duty by not wishing the death of the tyrant, and, above all, against those who have led astray so many of their colleagues. Such delegates are traitors, royalists, or fatuous men. The Republic condemns the friends of kings!...

Let us all unite equally to demand that the thunder of indictments be loosed against generals who are traitors to the Republic, against prevaricating ministers, against postal administrators, and against all unfaithful agents of the government. Therein lies our most salutary means of defence; but let us repel the traitors and tyrants.

The center of their conspiracy is here: it is in Paris that our perfidious enemies wish to consummate their crime. Paris, the cradle, the bulwark of liberty, is, without doubt, the place where they have sworn to annihilate the holy cause of humanity under the corpses of patriots.

From *A Documentary Survey of the French Revolution* by John Hall Stewart, © 1951. Reprinted by permission of Prentice-Hall, Inc., Upper Saddle River, NJ 07458.

The Republic Defended

To mobilize for war, the revolutionary government organized a collective executive in the form of powerful committees. These in turn sought to organize all French national life on a wartime footing. The result was an immense military effort dedicated to both the protection and the advancement of revolutionary ideals. Ironically, this war effort brought the suppression of many liberties within France itself and led ultimately to a destructive search for internal enemies of the revolution.

THE COMMITTEE OF PUBLIC SAFETY In April 1793, the Convention established a Committee of General Security and a Committee of Public Safety to carry out the executive duties of the government. The latter committee became more important and eventually enjoyed almost dictatorial power. The most prominent leaders of the Committee of Public Safety were Jaques Danton (1759–1794), who had provided heroic leadership in September 1792; Maximilien Robespierre (1758–1794), who became for a time the single most powerful member of the committee; and Lazare Carnot (1753–1823), who was in charge of the military. All of these men and the other figures on the committee were strong republicans who had opposed the weak policies of the Girondists. They conceived of their task as saving the revolution from mortal enemies at home and abroad. They enjoyed a working political relationship with the *sans-culottes* of Paris, but this was an alliance of expediency on the part of the committee.

THE *LEVÉE EN MASSE* The major problem for the Convention was to wage the war and at the same time to secure domestic support for the effort. In early June 1793, the Parisian *sans-culottes* invaded the Convention and successfully demanded the expulsion of the Girondist members. That action further radicalized the Convention and gave the Mountain complete control. On June 22, the Convention approved a fully democratic constitution, but delayed its implementation until the conclusion of the war. In point of fact, it was never implemented. On August 23, Carnot began a mobilization for victory by issuing a *levée en masse*, a military requisition on the entire population, conscripting males into the army and directing economic production to military purposes. On September 17, a ceiling on prices was established in accord with *sans-culotte* demands. During these same months, the armies of the revolution also successfully crushed many of the counterrevolutionary disturbances in the provinces.

Never before had Europe seen a nation organized in this way, nor one defended by a citizen army. Other events within France astounded Europeans

even more. The Reign of Terror had begun. Those months of quasi-judicial executions and murders stretching from the autumn of 1793 to the mid-summer of 1794 are probably the most famous or infamous period of the revolution. They can be understood only in the context of the war on one hand and the revolutionary expectations of the Convention and the *sans-culottes* on the other.

The "Republic of Virtue"

The presence of armies closing in on the nation made it easy to dispense with legal due process. The people who sat in the Convention and composed the Committee of Public Safety, however, did not see their actions simply in terms of expediency made necessary by war. They also believed they had created something new in world history, a "republic of virtue." In this republic, civic virtue would flourish in place of aristocratic and monarchical corruption. The republic of virtue manifested itself in many ways: in the renaming of streets from the egalitarian vocabulary of the revolution; in republican dress copied from that of the *sans-culottes* or the Roman Republic; in the absence of powdered wigs; in the suppression of plays that were insufficiently republican; and in a general attack against crimes, such as prostitution, that were supposedly characteristic of aristocratic society.

THE SOCIETY OF REVOLUTIONARY REPUBLICAN WOMEN Revolutionary women established their own distinct institutions during these months. In May 1793, Pauline Léon and Claire Lacombe founded the Society of Revolutionary Republican Women. Their purpose was to fight the internal enemies of the revolution. They saw themselves as militant citizens. Initially, the Jacobin leaders welcomed the organization. Its members and other women filled the galleries of the Convention to hear the debates and cheer their favorite speakers. The Society became increasingly radical, however. Its members sought stricter controls on the price of food and other commodities, worked to ferret out food hoarders, and brawled with working market women thought to be insufficiently revolutionary. The women of the Society also demanded the right to wear the revolutionary cockade usually worn only by male citizens. By October 1793, the Jacobins in the Convention had begun to fear the turmoil the Society was causing and banned all women's clubs and societies. The debates over these decrees show that the Jacobins believed that the Society opposed many of their economic policies, but the deputies used the Rousseauian language of separate spheres for men and women to justify their exclusion of women from active political life.

There were other examples of repression of women in 1793. Olympe de Gouges, author of the *Declaration of the Rights of Woman*, opposed the Terror and accused certain Jacobins of corruption. She was tried and guillotined in November 1793. The same year, women were formally excluded from serving in the French army. They were also excluded from the galleries of the Convention. In a very real sense, the exclusion of women from public political life was a part of the establishment of the Jacobin republic of virtue, because in such a republic men would be active citizens in the military and political sphere and women would be active in the domestic sphere.

DE-CHRISTIANIZATION The most dramatic departure of the republic of virtue, and one that illustrates the imposition of political values that would justify the Terror, was an attempt by the Convention to de-Christianize France. In November 1793, the Convention proclaimed a new calendar dating from the first day of the French Republic. There were twelve months of thirty days each, with names associated with the seasons and climate. Every tenth day, rather than every seventh, was a holiday. Many of the most important events of the next few years became known by their dates on the revolutionary calendar.[6] In November 1793, the Convention decreed the Cathedral of Notre Dame to be a "Temple of Reason." The legislature then sent trusted members, known as deputies on mission, into the provinces to enforce de-Christianization by closing churches, persecuting clergy and believers, and occasionally forcing priests to marry. This religious policy roused much opposition and deeply separated the French provinces from the revolutionary government in Paris.

ROBESPIERRE During the crucial months of late 1793 and early 1794, the person who emerged as the chief figure on the Committee of Public Safety

[6]From summer to spring, the months of the revolutionary calendar were *Messidor, Thermidor, Fructidor, Vendémiaire, Brumaire, Frimaire, Nivose, Pluviose, Ventose, Germinal, Floreal,* and *Prairial.*

Maximilien Robespierre (1785–1794) emerged as the most powerful revolutionary figure in 1793 and 1794, dominating the Committee of Public Safety. He considered the Terror essential for the success of the revolution. Giraudon/Art Resource, NY

was Robespierre. This complex Frenchman has remained controversial to the present day. He was utterly selfless and from the earliest days of the revolution had favored a republic. The Jacobin Club provided his primary forum and base of power. A shrewd and sensitive politician, Robespierre had opposed the war in 1792 because he feared it might aid the monarchy. He depended largely on the support of the *sans-culottes* of Paris, but he continued to dress as he had before the revolution and opposed de-Christianization as a political blunder. For him, the republic of virtue meant wholehearted support of republican government and the renunciation of selfish gains from political life. He once told the Convention:

If the mainspring of popular government in peacetime is virtue, amid revolution it is at the same time virtue and terror: virtue, without which terror is fatal; terror, without which virtue is impotent. Terror is nothing but prompt, severe, inflexible justice; it is therefore an emanation of virtue.[7]

[7]Quoted in Richard T. Bienvenu, *The Ninth of Thermidor: The Fall of Robespierre* (New York: Oxford University Press, 1968), p. 38.

Robespierre and those who supported his policies were among the first of a succession of secular ideologues of the left and the right who, in the name of humanity, would bring so much suffering to Europe in the following two centuries.

Progress of the Terror

The Reign of Terror manifested itself through a series of revolutionary tribunals established by the Convention during the summer of 1793. The mandate of these tribunals was to try the enemies of the republic, but the definition of "enemy" was uncertain and shifted as the months passed. It included those who might aid other European powers, those who endangered republican virtue, and, finally, good republicans who opposed the policies of the dominant faction of the government. In a very real sense, the Terror of the revolutionary tribunals systematized and channeled the popular resentment that had manifested itself in the September Massacres of 1792.

The first victims of the Terror were Marie Antoinette, other members of the royal family, and some aristocrats, who were executed in October 1793. They

On the way to her execution in 1793, Marie Antoinette was sketched from life by Jacques-Louis David as she passed his window. Jacques-Louis David, *Marie-Antoinette Taken to Her Execution.* Drawing. Bibliotheque Nationale, Paris, France. Giraudon/Art Resource, NY

were followed by certain Girondist politicians who had been prominent in the Legislative Assembly. These executions took place in the same weeks that the Convention had moved against the Society of Revolutionary Republican Women, whom it had also seen as endangering Jacobin control.

By the early months of 1794, the Terror had moved to the provinces, where the deputies on mission presided over the summary execution of thousands of people who had allegedly supported internal opposition to the revolution. One of the most infamous incidents occurred in Nantes, where several hundred people were simply tied to rafts and drowned in the river. The victims of the Terror were now coming from every social class, including the *sans-culottes*.

REVOLUTIONARIES TURN AGAINST THEMSELVES In Paris during the late winter of 1794, Robespierre began to orchestrate the Terror against republican political figures of the left and right. On March 24, he secured the execution of certain extreme *sans-culottes* leaders known as the *enragés*. They had wanted further measures regulating prices, securing social equality, and pressing de-Christianization. Robespierre then turned against more conservative republicans, including Danton. They were accused of being insufficiently militant on the war, profiting monetarily from the revolution, and rejecting any link between politics and moral virtue. Danton was executed during the first week in April. In this fashion, Robespierre exterminated the leadership from both groups that might have threatened his position.

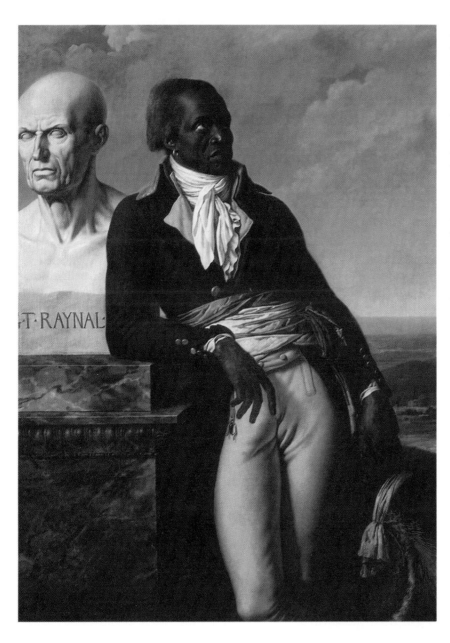

Jean-Baptiste Belley was a Senegalese African born in Gorée in 1747 and later taken to Saint-Domingue as a slave. In February, 1794, he was seated in the Convention along with two other people as representatives of citizens of Saint-Domingue. He had joined the French army there to resist counterrevolutionary forces, and once the representatives from Saint Domingue were seated, the Convention abolished slavery in the French colonies. Belley remained active in French revolutionary politics at least as late as 1797. He was one of several people of color from the Caribbean who served in either the Convention or the institutions of the Directory. Girodet de Roussy-Trioson Anne-Louis (1767–1824). *Portrait de Jean-Baptiste Belley, depute de Saint Dominique a la Convention (1747–1805). Chateaux de Versailles et de Tranon. © Photo RMN

*The Festival of the Supreme Being, which took place in June 1794, inaugurated Robe-
spierre's new civic religion. Its climax occurred when a statue of Atheism was burned
and another statue of Wisdom rose from the ashes.* Pierre-Antoine Demachy, *Festival of the
Supreme Being at the Champ de Mars on June 8, 1794.* Musée de la Ville de Paris, Musée Carnavalet, Paris,
France. Giraudon/Art Resource, NY

Finally, on June 10, he secured passage of the Law of
22 *Prairial*, which permitted the revolutionary tribunal to convict suspects without hearing substantial evidence. The number of executions was
growing steadily.

FALL OF ROBESPIERRE   In May 1794, at the height
of his power, Robespierre, considering the worship of "Reason" too abstract for most citizens,
abolished it and established the "Cult of the
Supreme Being." This deistic cult reflected
Rousseau's vision of a civic religion that would
induce morality among citizens. Robespierre,
however, did not long preside over his new religion. (See "The Convention Establishes the Worship of the Supreme Being.")

On July 26, Robespierre made an ill-tempered
speech in the Convention, declaring that other leaders of the government were conspiring against himself and the revolution. Usually, such accusations
against unnamed persons had preceded his earlier attacks. On July 27—the Ninth of *Thermidor*—members of the Convention, by prearrangement, shouted
him down when he rose to make another speech.
That night Robespierre was arrested, and the next

day he was executed. The revolutionary *sans-culottes* of Paris would not save him because he had
deprived them of their chief leaders. The other Jacobins turned against him because, after Danton's
death, they feared becoming the next victims. Robespierre had destroyed rivals for leadership without
creating supporters for himself. In that regard, he
was the selfless creator of his own destruction.

The fall of Robespierre might simply have been
one more shift in the turbulent politics of the revolution. Instincts of self-preservation rather than
major policy differences motivated those who
brought about his demise. They had generally supported the Terror and the executions. Yet within a
short time, the Reign of Terror, which ultimately
claimed more than 25,000 victims, came to a close.
The largest number of executions had involved
peasants and *sans-culottes* who had joined rebellions against the revolutionary government. By the
late summer of 1794, those provincial uprisings
had been crushed, and the war against foreign enemies was also going well. These factors, combined
with the feeling in Paris that the revolution had
consumed enough of its own children, brought the
Terror to an end.

The Convention Establishes the Worship of the Supreme Being

On May 7, 1794, the Convention passed an extraordinary piece of revolutionary legislation. It established the worship of the Supreme Being as a state cult. Although the law drew on the religious ideas of deism, the point of the legislation was to provide a religious basis for the new secular French state. The reader should pay particular attention to Article 7, which outlines the political and civic values that the Cult of the Supreme Being was supposed to nurture.

❖ *How does this declaration reflect the ideas of the Enlightenment? Why has it been seen as establishing a civil religion? What personal and social values was this religion supposed to nurture?*

1. The French people recognize the existence of the Supreme Being and the immortality of the soul.

2. They recognize that the worship worthy of the Supreme Being is the observance of the duties of man.

3. They place in the forefront of such duties detestation of bad faith and tyranny, punishment of tyrants and traitors, succoring of unfortunates, respect of weak persons, defence of the oppressed, doing to others all the good that one can, and being just towards everyone.

4. Festivals shall be instituted to remind man of the concept of the Divinity and of the dignity of his being.

5. They shall take their names from the glorious events of our Revolution, or from the virtues most dear and most useful to man, or from the greatest benefits of nature....

7. On the days of *décade* [the name given to a particular day in each month of the revolutionary calendar] it shall celebrate the following festivals:

To the Supreme Being and to nature; to the human race; to the French people; to the benefactors of humanity; to the martyrs of liberty; to liberty and equality; to the Republic; to the liberty of the world; to the love of the *Patrie* [Fatherland]; to the hatred of tyrants and traitors; to truth; to justice; to modesty; to glory and immortality; to friendship; to frugality; to courage; to good faith; to heroism; to disinterestedness; to stoicism; to love; to conjugal love; to paternal love; to maternal tenderness; to filial piety; to infancy; to youth; to manhood; to old age; to misfortune; to agriculture; to industry; to our forefathers; to posterity; to happiness.

From *A Documentary Survey of the French Revolution* by John Hall Stewart, © 1951. Reprinted by permission of Prentice-Hall, Inc., Upper Saddle River, NJ 07458.

The Thermidorian Reaction

This tempering of the revolution, called the Thermidorian Reaction, began in July 1794. It consisted of the destruction of the machinery of terror and the institution of a new constitutional regime. It was the result of a widespread feeling that the revolution had become too radical. In particular, it displayed a weariness of the Terror and a fear that the *sans-culottes* were exerting far too much political influence.

The End of the Terror

The influence of generally wealthy middle-class and professional people soon replaced that of the *sans-culottes*. Within days and weeks of Robespierre's execution, the Convention allowed the Girondists who had been in prison or hiding to return to their seats. There was a general amnesty for political prisoners. The Convention restructured the Committee of Public Safety, giving it much less power, and also repealed the notorious Law of 22 *Prairial*. Some, though by no means all, of the people responsible for the Terror were removed from public life. Leaders of the Paris Commune and certain deputies on mission were executed. The Paris Commune itself was outlawed. The Paris Jacobin Club was closed, and Jacobin clubs in the provinces were forbidden to correspond with each other.

The executions of former terrorists marked the beginning of "the white terror." Throughout the country, people who had been involved in the Reign

The closing of the Jacobin Club in November 1794 was a major event in the Thermidorean Reaction that began with the fall of Robespierre.   Roger-Viollet, © Collection Violett/Liaison Agency, Inc.

of Terror were attacked and often murdered. Jacobins were executed with little more due process than they had extended to their victims a few months earlier. The Convention itself approved some of these trials. In other cases, gangs of youths who had aristocratic connections or who had avoided serving in the army roamed the streets, beating known Jacobins. In Lyons, Toulon, and Marseilles, these "bands of Jesus" dragged suspected terrorists from prisons and murdered them much as alleged royalists had been murdered during the September Massacres of 1792.

The republic of virtue gave way, if not to one of vice, at least to one of frivolous pleasures. The dress of the *sans-culottes* and the Roman Republic disappeared among the middle class and the aristocracy. New plays appeared in the theaters, and prostitutes again roamed the streets of Paris. Families of victims of the Reign of Terror gave parties in which they appeared with shaved necks, like the victims of the guillotine, and with

red ribbons tied about them. Although the Convention continued to favor the Cult of the Supreme Being, it allowed Catholic services to be held. Many refractory priests returned to the country. One of the unanticipated results of the Thermidorian Reaction was a genuine revival of Catholic worship.

The Thermidorian Reaction also saw the repeal of legislation that had been passed in 1792 making divorce more equitable for women. As this suggests, the reaction did not result in any extension of women's rights or improvement in women's education. The Thermidorians and their successors had seen enough attempts at political and social change. They sought to return family life to its status before the outbreak of the revolution. Political authorities and the church articulated a firm determination to reestablish separate spheres for men and women and to reinforce traditional gender roles. As a result, Frenchwomen may have had somewhat less freedom after 1795 than before 1789.

Establishment of the Directory

The Thermidorian Reaction involved further political reconstruction. The fully democratic constitution of 1793, which had never gone into effect, was abandoned. In its place, the Convention issued the Constitution of the Year III, which reflected the Thermidorian determination to reject both constitutional monarchy and democracy. The new document provided for a legislature of two houses. Members of the upper body, or Council of Elders, were to be men over forty years of age who were either husbands or widowers. The lower Council of Five Hundred was to consist of men of at least thirty who were either married or single. The executive body was to be a five-person Directory chosen by the Elders from a list submitted by the Council of Five Hundred. Property qualifications limited the franchise, except for soldiers, who, though without property, were permitted to vote.

The term *Thermidor* has come to be associated with political reaction. If the French Revolution had originated in political conflicts characteristic of the eighteenth century, by 1795 it had become something very different. A political structure and a society based on rank and birth had given way to a political system based on civic equality and social status based on property ownership. People who had never been allowed direct, formal access to political power had, to different degrees, been granted it. Their entrance into political life had given rise to questions of property distribution and economic regulations that could not again be ignored. Representation had been established as a principle of politics. Henceforth, the question before France and eventually before all of Europe would be which new groups would be permitted representation. In the *levée en masse*, the French had demonstrated to Europe the power of the secular ideal of nationhood.

The post-Thermidorian course of the French Revolution did not void these stunning changes in the political and social contours of Europe. What triumphed in the Constitution of the Year III was the revolution of the holders of property. For this reason the French Revolution has often been considered a victory of the bourgeoisie, or middle class. The property that won the day, however, was not industrial wealth, but the wealth stemming from commerce, the professions, and land. The largest new propertied class to emerge from the revolutionary turmoil was the peasantry, who, as a result of the destruction of aristocratic privileges, now owned their land.

And unlike peasants liberated from traditional landholding in other parts of Europe during the next century, French peasants had to pay no monetary compensation.

Removal of the *Sans-culottes* from Political Life

The most decisively reactionary element in the Thermidorian Reaction and the new constitution was the removal of the *sans-culottes* from political life. With the war effort succeeding, the Convention severed its ties with the *sans-culottes*. True to their belief in an unregulated economy, the Thermidorians repealed the ceiling on prices. As a result, the winter of 1794–1795 brought the worst food shortages of the period. There were many food riots, which the Convention put down with force to prove that the era of the *sans-culottes journées* had come to a close. Royalist agents, who aimed to restore the monarchy, tried to take advantage of their discontent. On October 5, 1795–13 *Vendémiaire*—the sections of Paris led by the royalists rose up against the Convention. The government turned the artillery against the royalist rebels. A general named Napoleon Bonaparte (1769–1821) commanded the cannon, and with a "whiff of grapeshot" he dispersed the crowd.

By the Treaty of Basel in March 1795, the Convention concluded peace with Prussia and Spain. The legislators, however, feared a resurgence of both radical democrats and royalists in the upcoming elections for the Council of Five Hundred. Consequently, the Convention ruled that at least two-thirds of the new legislature must have been members of the older body. The Thermidorians did not even trust the property owners as voters.

The newly established Directory again faced social unrest. In Paris, Gracchus Babeuf (1760–1797) led the Conspiracy of Equals. He and his followers called for more radical democracy and for more equality of property. They declared at one point, "The aim of the French Revolution is to destroy inequality and to re-establish the general welfare.... The Revolution is not complete, because the rich monopolize all the property and govern exclusively, while the poor toil like slaves, languish in misery, and count for nothing in the *state*."[8] In a sense, they were correct. The Directory fully intended to resist any further social changes in France that

[8]Quoted in John Hall Stewart, *A Documentary Survey of the French Revolution* (New York: Macmillan, 1966), pp. 656–657.

The French Revolution

1789

May 5	The Estates General opens at Versailles
June 17	The Third Estate declares itself the National Assembly
June 20	The National Assembly takes the Tennis Court Oath
July 14	Fall of the Bastille in the city of Paris
Late July	The Great Fear spreads in the countryside
August 4	The nobles surrender their feudal rights at a meeting of the National Constituent Assembly
August 27	Declaration of the Rights of Man and Citizen
October 5–6	Parisian women march to Versailles and force Louis XVI and his family to return to Paris

1790

July 12	Civil Constitution of the Clergy adopted
July 14	A new political constitution is accepted by the king

1791

June 14	Chapelier Law
June 20–24	Louis XVI and his family attempt to flee France and are stopped at Varennes
August 27	The Declaration of Pillnitz
October 1	The Legislative Assembly meets

1792

April 20	France declares war on Austria
August 10	The Tuileries palace is stormed, and Louis XVI takes refuge with the Legislative Assembly
September 2–7	The September Massacres
September 20	France wins the Battle of Valmy

September 21	The Convention meets, and the monarchy is abolished

1793

January 21	King Louis XVI is executed
February 1	France declares war on Great Britain
March	Counterrevolution breaks out in the Vendée
April	The Committee of Public Safety is formed
June 22	The Constitution of 1793 is adopted, but not implemented
July	Robespierre enters the Committee of Public Safety
August 23	*Levée en masse* proclaimed
September 17	Maximum prices set on food and other commodities
October 16	Queen Marie Antoinette is executed
October 30	Women's societies and clubs banned
November 10	The Cult of Reason is proclaimed; the revolutionary calendar, beginning on September 22, 1792, is adopted

1794

March 24	Execution of the leaders of the *sans-culottes* known as the *enragés*
April 6	Execution of Danton
May 7	Cult of the Supreme Being proclaimed
June 8	Robespierre leads the celebration of the Festival of the Supreme Being
June 10	The Law of 22 *Prairial* is adopted
July 27	The Ninth of *Thermidor* and the fall of Robespierre
July 28	Robespierre is executed

1795

August 22	The Constitution of the Year III is adopted, establishing the Directory

might endanger property. Babeuf was arrested, tried, and executed. This minor plot became famous many decades later, when European socialists attempted to find their historical roots in the French Revolution.

The suppression of the *sans-culottes*, the narrow franchise of the constitution, the rule of the two-thirds, and the Catholic royalist revival pre-

sented the Directory with problems that it never succeeded in overcoming. It lacked any broad base of meaningful political support. It particularly required active loyalty because France remained at war with Austria and Great Britain. Consequently, the Directory came to depend on the power of the army, rather than on constitutional processes, for governing the country. All the soldiers could vote. Moreover, within the army, created and sustained by the revolution, were officers who were eager for power and ambitious for political conquest. The results of the instability of the Directory and the growing role of the army held profound consequences not only for France but for the entire Western world.

In Perspective

The French Revolution is the central political event of modern European history. It unleashed political and social forces that shaped events in Europe and much of the rest of the world for the next two centuries. The revolution began with a clash between the monarchy and the nobility. Once the Estates General gathered, however, discontent could not be contained within the traditional boundaries of eighteenth-century political life. The Third Estate, in all of its diversity, demanded real influence in government. Initially, that meant the participation of middle-class members of the Estates General, but quite soon the people of Paris and the peasants of the countryside made their demands known. Thereafter, popular nationalism exerted itself on French political life and the destiny of Europe.

Revolutionary legislation and popular uprisings in Paris, the countryside, and other cities transformed the social as well as the political life of the nation. Nobles surrendered traditional social privileges. The church saw its property confiscated and its operations brought under state control. For a time, there was an attempt to de-Christianize the nation. Vast amounts of landed property changed hands, and France became a nation of peasant landowners. Urban workers lost much of the protection they had enjoyed under the guilds and became much more subject to the forces of the marketplace.

Great violence accompanied many of the revolutionary changes. The Reign of Terror took the lives of thousands. France also found itself at war with virtually all of the rest of Europe. Resentment, fear, and a new desire for stability brought the Terror to an end. That desire for stability, combined with a determination to defeat the foreign enemies of the revolution and to carry it abroad, would in turn work to the advantage of the army. Eventually, Napoleon Bonaparte would claim leadership in the name of stability and national glory.

REVIEW QUESTIONS

1. It has been said that France was a rich nation with an impoverished government. Explain this statement. How did the financial weaknesses of the French monarchy lay the foundations of the revolution of 1789?
2. Discuss the role of Louis in the French Revolution. What were some of Louis XVI's most serious mistakes? Had Louis been a more able ruler, could the French Revolution have been avoided? Might a constitutional monarchy have succeeded? Or did the revolution ultimately have little to do with the competence of the monarch?
3. How was the Estates General transformed into the National Assembly? How does the Declaration of the Rights of Man and Citizen reflect the social and political values of the eighteenth-century Enlightenment? What were the chief ways in which France and its government were reorganized in the early years of the revolution? Why has the Civil Constitution of the Clergy been called the greatest blunder of the National Assembly?
4. Why were some political factions dissatisfied with the constitutional settlement of 1791? What was the revolution of 1792 and why did it occur? Who were the *sans-culottes* and how did they become a factor in the politics of the period? How influential were they during the Terror in particular? Why did the *sans-culottes* and the Jacobins cooperate at first? Why did that cooperation end?
5. Why did France go to war with Austria in 1792? What were the benefits and drawbacks for France of fighting an external war while in the midst of a domestic political revolution? What were the causes of the Terror? How did the rest of Europe react to the French Revolution and the Terror?
6. A motto of the French Revolution was "equality, liberty and fraternity." How did the revolution both support and violate this motto? Did French women benefit from the revolution? Did French peasants benefit from it?

SUGGESTED READINGS

K. M. BAKER AND C. LUCAS (EDS.), *The French Revolution and the Creation of Modern Political Culture,* 3 vols. (1987). A splendid collection of important original articles on all aspects of politics during the revolution.

K. M. BAKER, *Inventing the French Revolution: Essays on French Political Culture in the Eighteenth Century* (1990). Influential essays on political thought before and during the revolution.

T. C. W. Blanning (ed.), *The Rise and Fall of the French Revolution* (1996). A wide-ranging collection of essays illustrating the recent interpretive debates.

C. Blum, *Rousseau and the Republic of Virtue: The Language of Politics in the French Revolution* (1986). An exploration of the role of Rousseau's political ideals in the debates of the French Revolution.

R. Cobb, *The People's Armies* (1987). The best treatment in English of the revolutionary army.

K. Epstein, *The Genesis of German Conservatism* (1966). A major study of antiliberal forces in Germany before and during the revolution.

F. Fehér, *The French Revolution and the Birth of Modernity* (1990). A wide-ranging collection of essays on political and cultural facets of the revolution.

A. Forrest, *The French Revolution and the Poor* (1981). A study that expands consideration of the revolution beyond the standard social boundaries.

F. Furet, *Revolutionary France, 1770–1880* (1988). An important survey by a historian who argues the revolution must be seen in the perspective of an entire century.

J. Godechot, *The Taking of the Bastille, July 14, 1789* (1970). Places the fall of the Bastille in the context of crowd behavior in the eighteenth century.

J. Godechot, *The Counter-Revolution: Doctrine and Action, 1789–1803* (1971). An examination of opposition to the revolution.

C. Hesse, *Publishing and Cultural Politics in Revolutionary Paris* (1991). Probes the world of print culture during the French Revolution.

P. Higonnet, *Goodness beyond Virtue: Jacobins during the French Revolution* (1998). An outstanding work that clearly relates political values to political actions.

E. Kennedy, *A Cultural History of the French Revolution* (1989). An important examination of the role of the arts, schools, clubs, and intellectual institutions.

M. Kennedy, *The Jacobin Clubs in the French Revolution: The First Years* (1982). A careful scrutiny of the organizations chiefly responsible for the radicalizing of the revolution.

M. Kennedy, *The Jacobin Clubs in the French Revolution: The Middle Years* (1988). A continuation of the previously listed study.

G. Lefebvre, *The French Revolution*, 2 vols. (1962–1964). The leading study of the scholar noted for his subtle class interpretation of the revolution.

D. G. Levy, H. B. Applewhite, and M. D. Johnson (eds. and trans.), *Women in Revolutionary Paris, 1789–1795* (1979). A remarkable collection of documents on the subject.

G. Lewis and C. Lucas (eds.), *Beyond the Terror: Essays in French Regional and Social History, 1794–1815* (1983). Explorations of the counter-terror that followed in the wake of the Thermidorian Reaction.

H.-J. Lüsebrink and R. Reichardt, *The Bastille: A History of a Symbol of Despotism and Freedom*, N. Schürer, trans. (1997). A fascinating treatment of the Bastille as a political symbol in French and European political life.

T. W. Margadant, *Urban Rivalries in the French Revolution* (1992). Examines the political tensions between the central government in Paris and the cities and towns of the provinces.

S. E. Melzer and L. W. Rabine (eds.), *Rebel Daughters: Women and the French Revolution* (1992). A collection of essays exploring various aspects of the role and image of women in the French Revolution.

C. C. O'Brien, *The Great Melody: A Thematic Biography of Edmund Burke* (1992). The best recent biography.

M. Ozouf, *Festivals and the French Revolution* (1988). A pioneering study of the role of public festivals in the revolution.

R. R. Palmer, *Twelve Who Ruled: The Committee of Public Safety During the Terror* (1941). Classic analysis of the policies and problems of the committee.

R. R. Palmer, *The Age of Democratic Revolution: A Political History of Europe and America, 1760–1800*, 2 vols. (1959, 1964). An impressive survey of the political turmoil in the transatlantic world.

C. Proctor, *Women, Equality, and the French Revolution* (1990). An examination of how the ideas of the Enlightenment and the attitudes of revolutionaries affected the legal status of women.

W. J. Sewell, Jr., *A Rhetoric of Bourgeois Revolution: The Abbé Siéyès and What is the Third Estate* (1994). An important study of the political thought of Siéyès.

A. Soboul, *The Parisian* Sans-Culottes *and the French Revolution, 1793–94* (1964). Remains the best work on the subject.

B. S. Stone, *The French* Parlements *and the Crisis of the Old Regime* (1988). A study that considers the role of the aristocratic courts in bringing on the collapse of monarchical government.

D. G. Sutherland, *France, 1789–1815: Revolution and Counterrevolution* (1986). A major synthesis based on recent scholarship in social history.

T. Tackett, *Religion, Revolution, and Regional Culture in Eighteenth-Century France: The Ecclesiastical Oath of 1791* (1986). The most important study of this topic.

T. Tackett, *Becoming a Revolutionary: The Deputies of the French National Assembly and the Emergence of a Revolutionary Culture (1789–1790)* (1996). The best study of the early months of the revolution.

D. K. Van Kley, *The Religious Origins of the French Revolution: From Calvin to the Civil Constitution, 1560–1791* (1996). Examines the manner in which debates within French Catholicism influenced the coming of the revolution.

M. Walzer (Ed.), *Regicide and Revolution: Speeches at the Trial of Louis XVI* (1974). An important and exceedingly interesting collection of documents with a useful introduction.

Chapter 20

Napoleon Bonaparte used his military successes to consolidate his political leadership as First Consul and later as Emperor of France. In this heroic image, Jacques-Louis David portrays Napoleon as a force of nature conquering not only the armies of the enemies of France but also the Alps. On the rocks in the foreground his name follows those of Hannibal and Charlemagne, other great generals who had led armies over the Alps. Bildarchiv Preussischer Kulturbesitz

The Age of Napoleon and the Triumph of Romanticism

KEY TOPICS

- Napoleon's rise, his coronation as emperor, and his administrative reforms
- Napoleon's conquests, the creation of a French Empire, and Britain's enduring resistance
- The invasion of Russia and Napoleon's decline
- The reestablishment of a European order at the Congress of Vienna
- Romanticism and the reaction to the Enlightenment

By the late 1790s, there existed a general wish for stability in France, especially among property owners, who now included the peasants. The government of the Directory was not providing this stability. The one force that was able to take charge of the nation as a symbol of both order and popular national will was the army. The most politically astute of the army generals was Napoleon Bonaparte, who had been a radical during the early revo-

lution, a victorious general in Italy, and a supporter of the attempt to suppress revolutionary disturbances after Thermidor. Furthermore, as a general, he was a leader in the French army, the institution seen most clearly to embody the popular values of the nation and the revolution.

Once in power, Napoleon consolidated many of the achievements of the revolution. He also repudiated much of it by establishing an empire. Thereafter, his ambitions drew France into wars of conquest and liberation throughout the continent. For over a decade Europe was at war, with only brief periods of armed truce. In leading the French armies across the Continent, Napoleon spread many of the ideas and institutions of the revolution and overturned much of the old political and social order. He also provoked popular nationalism in opposition to his conquest. This new force and the great diplomatic alliances that arose against France eventually defeated Napoleon.

Throughout these Napoleonic years, new ideas and sensibilities, known by the term romanticism, grew across Europe. Many of the ideas had originated in the eighteenth century, but they flourished in the turmoil of the French Revolution and the Napoleonic Wars. The events and values of the revolution spurred the imagination of poets, painters, and philosophers. Some romantic ideas, such as romantic nationalism, supported the revolution; others, such as the emphasis on history and religion, opposed the values of the revolution.

The Rise of Napoleon Bonaparte

The chief danger to the Directory came from the royalists, who hoped to restore the Bourbon monarchy by legal means. Many of the *émigrés* had returned to France. Their plans for a restoration drew support from devout Catholics and from those citizens disgusted by the excesses of the revolution. Monarchy seemed to promise stability. The spring elections of 1797 replaced most incumbents with constitutional monarchists and their sympathizers, thus giving them a majority.

To preserve the republic and prevent a peaceful restoration of the Bourbons, the antimonarchist Directory staged a coup d'état on 18 *Fructidor* (September 4, 1797). They put their own supporters into the legislative seats won by their opponents. They then imposed censorship and exiled some of their enemies. At the request of the Directors,

Napoleon Bonaparte, the general in charge of the Italian campaign, had sent one of his subordinates to Paris to guarantee the success of the coup. In 1797, as in 1795, the army and Bonaparte had saved the day for the government installed in the wake of the Thermidorian Reaction.

Napoleon Bonaparte was born in 1769 to a poor family of lesser nobles at Ajaccio, Corsica. Because France had annexed Corsica in 1768, he went to French schools, pursued a military career, and in 1785 obtained a commission as a French artillery officer. He strongly favored the revolution and was a fiery Jacobin. In 1793, he played a leading role in recovering the port of Toulon from the British. As a reward for his service, he was appointed a brigadier general. His previous radical associations threatened his career during the Thermidorian Reaction, but his defense of the new regime on 13 *Vendémiaire* won him another promotion and a command in Italy.

Early Military Victories

By 1795, French arms and diplomacy had shattered the enemy coalition, but France's annexation of Belgium guaranteed continued fighting with Britain and Austria. The attack on Italy aimed at depriving Austria of the provinces of Lombardy and Venetia. In a series of lightning victories, Bonaparte crushed the Austrian and Sardinian armies. On his own initiative, and in many ways against the wishes of the government in Paris, he concluded the Treaty of Campo Formio in October 1797. The treaty took Austria out of the war and crowned Napoleon's campaign and independent policy with success. Before long, all of Italy and Switzerland had fallen under French domination.

In November 1797, the triumphant Bonaparte returned to Paris to be hailed as a hero and to confront France's only remaining enemy, Britain. He judged it impossible to cross the channel and invade England at that time. Instead, he chose to attack British interests through the eastern Mediterranean. He set out to capture Egypt from the Ottoman Empire. By this strategy, he hoped to drive the British fleet from the Mediterranean, cut off British communications with India, damage British trade, and threaten the British Empire.

Even though Napoleon overran Egypt, the invasion was a failure. Admiral Horatio Nelson (1758–1805) destroyed the French fleet at Abukir on August 1, 1798. Cut off from France, the French army could then neither accomplish anything of importance in the Near East nor get home. To make matters worse, the situation in Europe was deteriorating. The invasion of Egypt had alarmed Russia, which had its own ambitions in the Near East. The Russians, the Austrians, and the Ottomans soon joined Britain to form the Second Coalition. In 1799, the Russian and Austrian armies defeated the French in Italy and Switzerland and threatened to invade France.

The Constitution of the Year VIII

Economic troubles and the dangerous international situation eroded the already fragile support of the Directory. One of the Directors, the Abbé Siéyès, proposed a new constitution. The author of the pamphlet *What Is the Third Estate?* (1789) wanted to establish a vigorous executive body independent of the whims of electoral politics, a government based on the principle of "confidence from below, power from above." The change would require another coup d'état with military support. News of France's diplomatic misfortunes had reached Napoleon in Egypt. Without orders and leaving his doomed army behind, he returned to France in October 1799. Although some people thought that he deserved a court-martial for desertion, he received much popular acclaim. Soon he joined Siéyès. On 19 *Brumaire* (November 10, 1799), his troops drove out the legislators and ensured the success of the coup.

Siéyès appears to have thought that Napoleon could be used and then dismissed, but if so, he badly misjudged his man. The proposed constitution divided executive authority among three consuls. Bonaparte quickly pushed it aside, as he did Siéyès, and in December 1799, he issued the Constitution of the Year VIII. Behind a screen of universal male suffrage that suggested democratic principles, a complicated system of checks and balances that appealed to republican theory, and a Council of State that evoked memories of Louis XIV, the new constitution in fact established the rule of one man—the First Consul, Bonaparte. To find an appropriate historical analogy, one must go back to Caesar and Augustus and the earlier Greek tyrants. The career of Bonaparte, however, pointed forward to the dictators of the twentieth century. He was the first modern political figure to use the rhetoric of revolution and nationalism, to back it with military force, and to combine those elements into a mighty weapon of imperial expansion in the service of his own power and ambition.

The Consulate in France (1799–1804)

Establishing the Consulate in effect closed the revolution in France. The leading elements of the Third Estate—that is, officials, landowners, doctors, lawyers, and financiers—had achieved most of their goals by 1799. They had abolished hereditary privilege, and the careers thus opened to talent allowed them to achieve the wealth, status,

In this early nineteenth-century cartoon, England, personified by a caricature of Williams Pitt, and France, personified by a caricature of Napoleon, are carving out their areas of interest around the globe. Bildarchiv Preussischer Kulturbesitz

Napoleon Describes Conditions Leading to the Consulate

In late 1799 various political groups in France became convinced that the constitution that had established the Directory could not allow France to achieve military victory. They also feared domestic unrest and new outbreaks of the radicalism that had characterized the French Revolution during the mid-1790s. With the aid of such groups Napoleon Bonaparte seized power in Paris in November, 1799. Thereafter, under various political arrangements he governed France until 1814. He later gave his own version of the situation that brought him to power.

❖ *What are the factors that Napoleon outlines as having created a situation in which the government of France required change? In his narration how does he justify the use of military force? How does he portray himself as a savior of political order and liberty?*

On my return to Paris I found division among all authorities, and agreement upon only one point, namely, that the Constitution was half destroyed and was unable to save liberty.

All parties came to me, confided to me their designs, disclosed their secrets, and requested my support; I refused to be the man of a party.

The Council of Elders summoned me; I answered its appeal. A plan of general restoration had been devised by men whom the nation has been accustomed to regard as defenders of liberty, equality, and property; this plan required an examination, calm, free, exempt from all influence and all fear. Accordingly, the Council of Elders resolved upon the removal of the Legislative Body to Saint-Cloud; it gave me the responsibility of disposing the force necessary for its independence. I believed it my duty to my fellow citizens, to the soldiers perishing in our armies, to the national glory acquired at the cost of their blood, to accept the command....

I presented myself to the Council of Five Hundred, alone, unarmed, my head uncovered, just as the Elders had received and applauded me; I came to remind the majority of its wishes, and to assure it of its power.

The stilettos which menaced the deputies were instantly raised against their liberator; twenty assassins threw themselves upon me and aimed at my breast. The grenadiers of the Legislative Body whom I had left at the door of the hall ran forward, placed themselves between the assassins and myself. One of these brave grenadiers had his clothes pieced by a stiletto. They bore me out.

At the same moment cries of "Outlaw" were raised against the defender of the law. It was the fierce cry of assassins against the power destined to repress them.

They crowded around the president, uttering threats, arms in their hands; they commanded him to outlaw me. I was informed of this; I ordered him to be rescued from their fury, and six grenadiers of the Legislative Body secured him. Immediately afterwards some grenadiers of the Legislative Body charged into the hall and cleared it.

The factions, intimidated, dispersed and fled....

Frenchmen, you will doubtless recognize in this conduct the zeal of a soldier of liberty, a citizen devoted to the Republic. Conservative, tutelary, and liberal ideas have been restored to their rights through the dispersal of the rebels who oppressed the Councils....

From *A Documentary Survey of the French Revolution* by Stewart, John Hall, © 1951. Reprinted by permission of Prentice-Hall, Inc., Upper Saddle River, N.J.

and security for their property that they sought. The peasants were also satisfied. They had gained the land they had always wanted and had destroyed oppressive feudal privileges as well. The newly established dominant classes were profoundly conservative. They had little or no desire to share their new privileges with the lower social orders. Bonaparte seemed just the person to give them security. When he submitted his constitution to the voters in a plebiscite, they overwhelmingly approved it. (See "Napolean Describes Conditions Leading to the Consulate.")

Suppressing Foreign Enemies and Domestic Opposition

Bonaparte quickly justified the public's confidence by making peace with France's enemies. Russia had already quarreled with its allies and left the Second Coalition. A campaign in Italy brought another victory over Austria at Marengo in 1800. The Treaty of Luneville early in 1801 took Austria out of the war and confirmed the earlier settlement of Campo Formio. Britain was now alone and, in 1802, concluded the Treaty of Amiens, which brought peace to Europe.

Bonaparte also restored peace and order at home. He used generosity, flattery, and bribery to win over some of his enemies. He issued a general amnesty and employed in his own service persons from all political factions. He required only that they be loyal to him. Some of the highest offices were occupied by persons who had been extreme radicals during the Reign of Terror, others by persons who had fled the Terror and favored constitutional monarchy, and still others by former high officials of the old monarchical government.

On the other hand, Bonaparte was ruthless and efficient in suppressing opposition. He established a highly centralized administration in which prefects directly responsible to the central government in Paris managed all departments. He employed secret police. He stamped out once and for all the royalist rebellion in the west and made the rule of Paris effective in Brittany and the Vendée for the first time in many years.

Napoleon also used and invented opportunities to destroy his enemies. When a bomb plot on his life surfaced in 1804, the event provided an excuse to attack the Jacobins, though the bombing was the work of the royalists. Also in 1804, his forces violated the sovereignty of the German state of Baden to seize the Bourbon duke of Enghien (1772–1804). The duke was accused of participation in a royalist plot and put to death, though Bonaparte knew him to be innocent. The action was a flagrant violation of international law and of due process. Charles Maurice de Talleyrand-Périgord (1754–1838), Bonaparte's foreign minister, later termed the act "worse than a crime—a blunder," because it helped to provoke foreign opposition. On the other hand, it was popular with the former Jacobins, for it seemed to preclude the possibility of a Bourbon restoration. The executioner of a Bourbon was hardly likely to restore the royal family. The execution also seems to have put an end to royalist plots.

Concordat with the Roman Catholic Church

A major obstacle to internal peace was the steady hostility of French Catholics. Refractory clergy continued to advocate counterrevolution. The religious revival that dated from the Thermidorian Reaction increased discontent with the secular state created by the revolution. Bonaparte regarded religion as a political matter. He approved its role in preserving an orderly society, but was suspicious of any such power independent of the state.

In 1801, to the shock and dismay of his anticlerical supporters, Napoleon concluded a concordat with Pope Pius VII (r. 1800–1823). The settlement gave Napoleon what he most wanted. The agreement required both the refractory clergy and those who had accepted the revolution to resign. Their replacements received their spiritual investiture from the Pope, but the state named the bishops and paid their salaries and the salary of one priest in each parish. In return, the church gave up its claims on its confiscated property.

The concordat declared, "Catholicism is the religion of the great majority of French citizens." This was merely a statement of fact and fell far short of what the Pope had wanted: religious dominance for the Roman Catholic Church. The clergy had to swear an oath of loyalty to the state. The Organic Articles of 1802, which were actually distinct from the concordat, established the supremacy of state over church. Similar laws were applied to the Protestant and Jewish communities as well, reducing still further the privileged position of the Catholic Church. (See "Napoleon Makes Peace with the Papacy.")

The Napoleonic Code

In 1802 a plebiscite ratified Napoleon as consul for life, and he soon produced another constitution that granted him what amounted to full power. He thereafter set about reforming and codifying French law. The result was the Civil Code of 1804, usually known as the *Napoleonic Code*.

The Napoleonic Code safeguarded all forms of property and tried to make French society secure against internal challenges. All the privileges based on birth that had marked the Old Regime and that had been overthrown during the revolution remained abolished. Employment of salaried officials chosen on the basis of merit replaced the purchase of offices.

The conservative attitudes toward labor and women that had emerged during the revolutionary years also received full support. Workers' organizations remained forbidden, and workers had fewer rights than their employers. Within families, fathers were granted extensive control over their children and husbands over their wives. At the same time, laws of primogeniture remained abolished, and property was distributed among

Napoleon Makes Peace with the Papacy

In 1801, Napoleon concluded a concordat with Pope Pius VII. This document was the cornerstone of Napoleonic religious policy. The concordat, which was announced on April 8, 1802, allowed the Roman Catholic church to function freely in France only within the limits of Church support for the government as indicated in the oath included in Article 6.

❖ *Why was it to Napoleon's political advantage to make this agreement with the papacy? What privileges or advantages does the Church achieve in the document? Would the highest loyalty of a bishop who took the oath in Article 6 reside with the Church or the French state?*

The Government of the French Republic recognizes that the Roman, catholic and apostolic religion is the religion of the great majority of French citizens.

His Holiness likewise recognizes that this same religion has derived and in this moment again expects the greatest benefit and grandeur from the establishment of the catholic worship in France and from the personal profession of it which the consuls of the Republic make.

In consequence, after this mutual recognition, as well for the benefit of religion as for the maintenance of internal tranquility, they have agreed as follows:

1. The catholic, apostolic and Roman religion shall be freely exercised in France: its worship shall be public, and in conformity with the police regulations which the government shall deem necessary for the public tranquility....

4. The First Consul of the Republic shall make appointments, within the three months which shall follow the publication of the bull of His Holiness, to the archbishoprics and bishoprics of the new circumscription. His Holiness shall confer the canonical institution, following the forms established in relation to France before the change of government.

6. Before entering upon their functions, the bishops shall take directly, at the hands of the First Consul, the oath of fidelity which was in use before the change of government, expressed in the following terms:

"I swear and promise to God, upon the holy scriptures, to remain in obedience and fidelity to the government established by the constitution of the French Republic. I also promise not to have any intercourse, nor to assist by any counsel, nor to support any league, either within or without, which is inimical to the public tranquility; and if, within my diocese or elsewhere, I learn that anything to the prejudice of the state is being contrived, I will make it known to the government."

From Maloy Anderson, ed. and trans., *The Constitutions and Other Select Documents Illustrative of the History of France, 1789–1907*, 2d ed., rev. and enl. (Minneapolis: H. W. Wilson, 1908), pp. 296–297.

all children, males and females. Married women, however, could dispose of their own property only with the consent of their husbands. Divorce remained more difficult for women than for men. Before this code, French law had been a patchwork that differed from region to region. Within that confused set of laws, women had had opportunities to assert and protect their interests. The universality of the Napoleonic Code ended those possibilities.

Establishing a Dynasty

In 1804, Bonaparte seized on the bomb attack on his life to make himself emperor. He argued that establishing a dynasty would make the new regime secure and make further attempts on his life useless. Another new constitution was promulgated in which Napoleon Bonaparte was called Emperor of the French, instead of First Consul of the Republic. This constitution was also overwhelmingly ratified in a plebiscite.

To conclude the drama, Napoleon invited the Pope to Notre Dame to take part in the coronation. At the last minute, however, the Pope agreed that Napoleon should place the crown on his own head. The emperor had no intention of allowing anyone to think that his power and authority depended on the approval of the church. Henceforth, he was called Napoleon I.

The coronation of Napoleon, December 2, 1804, as painted by Jacques-Louis David. Having first crowned himself, the emperor is shown about to place the crown on the head of Josephine. Napoleon instructed David to paint Pope Pius VII with his hand raised in blessing. Giraudon/Art Resource, NY

Napoleon's Empire (1804–1814)

Between his coronation as emperor and his final defeat at Waterloo (1815), Napoleon conquered most of Europe in a series of military campaigns that astonished the world. France's victories changed the map of the continent. The wars put an end to the Old Regime and its feudal trappings throughout western Europe and forced the eastern European states to reorganize themselves to resist Napoleon's armies.

Everywhere, Napoleon's advance unleashed the powerful force of nationalism. His weapon was the militarily mobilized French nation, one of the achievements of the revolution. Napoleon could put as many as 700,000 men under arms at one time, risk as many as 100,000 troops in a single battle, endure heavy losses, and return to fight again. He could conscript citizen soldiers in unprecedented numbers, thanks to their loyalty to the nation and to their remarkable leader. No single enemy could match such resources. Even coali-

tions were unsuccessful, until Napoleon finally overreached himself and made mistakes that led to his own defeat.

Conquering an Empire

The Peace of Amiens (1802) between France and Great Britain was merely a truce. Napoleon's unlimited ambitions shattered any hope that it might last. He sent an army to restore the rebellious colony of Haiti to French rule. This move aroused British fears that he was planning the renewal of a French empire in America, because Spain had restored Louisiana to France in 1800. More serious were his interventions in the Dutch Republic, Italy, and Switzerland and his role in the reorganization of Germany. The Treaty of Campo Formio had required a redistribution of territories along the Rhine River, and the petty princes of the region engaged in a shameful scramble to enlarge their holdings. Among the results were the reduction of Austrian influence in Germany and the emergence of a smaller number of larger German states in the west, all dependent on Napoleon.

Admiral Viscount Horatio Nelson (1758–1805) was the greatest naval commander of his age. From the battle of Abukir in 1798 to his death at the battle of Trafalgar in 1805, he won a series of brilliant victories that gave Britain mastery of the seas. Corbis

BRITISH NAVAL SUPREMACY   The British found these developments alarming enough to justify an ultimatum. When Napoleon ignored it, Britain declared war in May 1803. William Pitt the Younger returned to office as prime minister in 1804 and began to construct the Third Coalition. By August 1805, he had persuaded Russia and Austria to move once more against French aggression. A great naval victory soon raised the fortunes of the allies. On October 21, 1805, the British admiral Horatio, Lord Nelson, destroyed the combined French and Spanish fleets at the Battle of Trafalgar just off the Spanish coast. Nelson died in the battle, but the British lost no ships. The victory of Trafalgar put an end to all French hope of invading Britain and guaranteed British control of the sea for the rest of the war.

NAPOLEONIC VICTORIES IN CENTRAL EUROPE   On land the story was different. Even before Trafalgar, Napoleon had marched to the Danube River to attack his continental enemies. In mid-October he forced a large Austrian army to surrender at Ulm

and soon occupied Vienna. On December 2, 1805, in perhaps his greatest victory, Napoleon defeated the combined Austrian and Russian forces at Austerlitz. The Treaty of Pressburg that followed won major concessions from Austria. The Austrians withdrew from Italy and left Napoleon in control of everything north of Rome. He was recognized as king of Italy.

Napoleon also made extensive political changes in Germany. In July 1806, he organized the Confederation of the Rhine, which included most of the western German princes. The withdrawal of these princes from the Holy Roman Empire led Francis II of Austria to dissolve that ancient political body and henceforth to call himself Emperor of Austria.

Prussia, which had carefully remained neutral up to this point, was now provoked into war against France. Napoleon's forces quickly crushed the famous Prussian army at the battles of Jena and Auerstädt on October 14, 1806. Two weeks later, Napoleon was in Berlin. There, on November 21, he issued the Berlin Decrees, forbidding his allies from importing British goods. On June 13, 1807, Napoleon defeated the Russians at Friedland and went on to occupy Königsberg, the capital of East Prussia. The French emperor was master of all Germany.

TREATY OF TILSIT   Unable to fight another battle and unwilling to retreat into Russia, Tsar Alexander I (r. 1801–1825) was ready to make peace. He and Napoleon met on a raft in the middle of the Niemen River while the two armies and the nervous king of Prussia watched from the bank. On July 7, 1807, they signed the Treaty of Tilsit, which confirmed France's gains. Moreover, the treaty reduced the Prussian state to half its previous size, and only the support of Alexander saved it from extinction. Prussia openly and Russia secretly became allies of Napoleon in his war against Britain.

Napoleon organized conquered Europe much like the domain of a Corsican family. The great French Empire was ruled directly by the head of the clan, Napoleon. On its borders lay several satellite states carved out as the portions of the several family members. His stepson ruled Italy for him, and three of his brothers and his brother-in-law were made kings of other conquered states. Napoleon denied a kingdom only to his brother Lucien, of whose wife he disapproved. The French emperor expected his relatives to take orders without question. When they failed to do so, he rebuked and even punished them. This establishment of the Napoleonic family as the col-

Napoleon's victory at the battle of Austerlitz is considered his most brilliant. A French army of 73,000 crushed an Austro-Russian army of 86,000 under the command of the tsar and the emperor of Austria.   Giraudon/Art Resource, NY

lective sovereigns of Europe was unpopular and provoked political opposition that needed only encouragement and assistance to flare up into serious resistance. (See "Napoleon Advises His Brother to Rule Constitutionally.")

The Continental System

After the Treaty of Tilsit, such assistance could come only from Britain, and Napoleon knew that he must defeat the British before he could feel safe. Unable to compete with the British navy, he continued the economic warfare begun by the Berlin Decrees. He planned to cut off all British trade with the European continent and thus to cripple British commercial and financial power. He hoped to cause domestic unrest and revolution, and thus to drive the British from the war. The Milan Decree of 1807 went further and attempted to stop neutral nations from trading with Britain.

Napoleon and the Continental System

1806	Napoleon establishes the Continental System prohibiting all trade with England
1807	The peace conference at Tilsit results in Russia joining the Continental System and becoming an ally of Napoleon
1809 and 1810	Napoleon at the peak of his power
1810	Russia withdraws from the Continental System and resumes relations with Britain; Napoleon plans to crush Russia militarily
1812	Napoleon invades Russia; the Russians adopt a scorched-earth policy and burn Moscow; the thwarted Napoleon deserts his dwindling army and rushes back to Paris

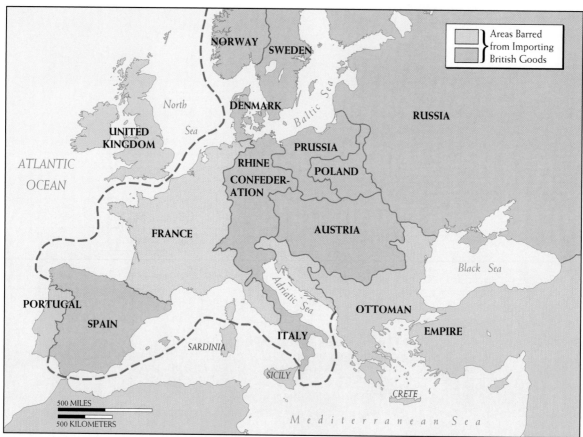

MAP 20–1   THE CONTINENTAL SYSTEM, 1806–1810   *Napoleon hoped to cut off all British trade with the European continent and thereby drive the British from the war.*

Despite initial drops in exports and domestic unrest, the British economy survived. British control of the seas assured access to the growing markets of North and South America and of the eastern Mediterranean. At the same time, the Continental System badly hurt the European economies. (See Map 20–1.) Napoleon rejected advice to turn his empire into a free-trade area. Such a policy would have been both popular and helpful. Instead, his tariff policies favored France, increased the resentment of foreign merchants, and made them less willing to enforce the system and more ready to engage in smuggling. It was in part to prevent smuggling that Napoleon invaded Spain in 1808. The resulting peninsular campaign in Spain and Portugal helped to bring on his ruin.

European Response to the Empire

Napoleon's conquests stimulated the two most powerful political forces in nineteenth-century Europe: liberalism and nationalism. The export of his version of the French Revolution directly and indirectly spread the ideas and values of the Enlightenment and the principles of 1789. Wherever Napoleon ruled, the Napoleonic Code was imposed, and hereditary social distinctions were abolished. Feudal privileges disappeared, and the peasants were freed from serfdom and manorial dues. In the towns, the guilds and the local oligarchies that had been dominant for centuries were dissolved or deprived of their power. New freedom thus came to serfs, artisans, workers, and entrepreneurs outside the privileged circles. The established churches lost their traditional independence and were made subordinate to the state. Church monopoly of religion was replaced by general toleration.

These reforms were not undone by the fall of Napoleon. Along with the demand for representative, constitutional government, they remained the basis of later liberal reforms. It also became clear, however, that Napoleon's policies were intended first for his own glory and that of France. The Continental System demonstrated that France, rather than Europe generally, was to be enriched by Napoleon's rule. Consequently, before long, the conquered states and peoples grew restive.

Napoleon Advises His Brother to Rule Constitutionally

As Napoleon swept through Europe, he set his relatives on the thrones of various conquered kingdoms and then imposed written constitutions on them. In this letter of November 1807, Napoleon sent his brother Jerome (1784–1860) a constitution for the Kingdom of Westphalia in Germany. The letter provides a good description of how Napoleon spread the political ideas and institutions of the French Revolution across Europe. Napoleon ignored, however, the possibility of nationalistic resentment that French conquest aroused, even when that conquest brought more liberal political institutions. Such nationalism would be one of the causes of his downfall.

❖ *What are the benefits that Napoleon believes his conquest and subsequent rule by his brother will bring to their new subjects? How does he believe that these, rather than military victory, will achieve new loyalty? How does Napoleon suggest playing off the resentment of the upper classes to consolidate power? What is the relationship between having a written constitution such as Napoleon is sending his brother and the power of public opinion that he mentions toward the close of the letter?*

I enclose the constitution for your Kingdom. You must faithfully observe it. I am concerned for the happiness of your subjects, not only as it affects your reputation, and my own, but also for its influence on the whole European situation.

Don't listen to those who say that your subjects are so accustomed to slavery that they will feel no gratitude for the benefits you give them. There is more intelligence in the Kingdom of Westphalia than they would have you believe; and your throne will never be firmly established except upon the trust and affection of the common people. What German opinion impatiently demands is that men of no rank, but of marked ability, shall have an equal claim upon your favour and your employment, and that every trace of serfdom, or of a feudal hierarchy between the sovereign and the lowest class of his subjects shall be done away with. The benefits of the Code Napoleon, public trial, and the introduction of juries, will be the leading features of your Government. And to tell you the truth, I count more upon their effects, for the extension and consolidation of your rule, than upon the most resounding victories. I want your subjects to enjoy a degree of liberty, equality, and prosperity hitherto unknown to the German people.... Such a method of government will be a stronger barrier between you and Prussia than the Elbe, the fortresses, and the protection of France. What people will want to return under the arbitrary Prussian rule, once it has tasted the benefits of a wise and liberal administration? In Germany, as in France, Italy, and Spain, people long for equality and liberalism. I have been managing the affairs of Europe long enough now to know that the burden of the privileged classes was resented everywhere. Rule constitutionally. Even if reason, and the enlightenment of the age, were not sufficient cause, it would be good policy for one in your position; and you will find that the backing of public opinion gives you a great natural advantage over the absolute kings who are your neighbors.

From J. M. Thompson, ed., *Napoleon's Letters* (London: Dent, 1954), pp. 190–191, as quoted in Maurice Hutt, ed., *Napoleon* (Englewood Cliffs, NJ: Prentice Hall, 1972), p. 34.

German Nationalism and Prussian Reform

The German response to Napoleon's success was particularly interesting and important. There had never been a unified German state. The great German writers of the Enlightenment, such as Immanuel Kant, Friedrich von Schiller, and Gotthold Lessing, were neither deeply politically engaged nor nationalistic.

At the beginning of the nineteenth century, the romantic movement had begun to take hold. One of its basic features in Germany was the emergence of nationalism, which went through two distinct stages there. Initially, nationalistic writers emphasized the unique and admirable qualities of

German culture, which, they argued, arose from the peculiar history of the German people. Such cultural nationalism prevailed until Napoleon's humiliation of Prussia at Jena in 1806.

At that point many German intellectuals began to urge resistance to Napoleon on the basis of German nationalism. The French conquest endangered the independence and achievements of all German-speaking people. Many nationalists were also critical of the German princes, who ruled selfishly and inefficiently and who seemed ever ready to lick the boots of Napoleon. Only a people united through its language and culture could resist the French onslaught. No less important in forging a German national sentiment was the example of France itself, which had attained greatness by enlisting the active support of the entire people in the patriotic cause. Henceforth, many Germans sought to solve their internal political problems by attempting to establish a unified German state, reformed to harness the energies of the entire people.

After Tilsit, only Prussia could arouse such patriotic feelings. Elsewhere German rulers were either under Napoleon's thumb or actively collaborating with him. Defeated, humiliated, and diminished, Prussia continued to resist, however feebly. To Prussia fled German nationalists from other states, calling for reforms and unification that were, in fact, feared and hated by Frederick William III (r. 1797–1840) and the Junker nobility. Reforms came about despite such opposition because the defeat at Jena had made clear the necessity of new departures for the Prussian state.

The Prussian administrative and social reforms were the work of Baron vom Stein (1757–1831) and Count von Hardenberg (1750–1822). Neither of these reformers intended to reduce the autocratic power of the Prussian monarch or to put an end to the dominance of the Junkers, who formed the bulwark of the state and of the army officer corps. Rather, they aimed at fighting French power with their own version of the French weapons. As Hardenberg declared,

Our objective, our guiding principle, must be a revolution in the better sense, a revolution leading directly to the great goal, the elevation of humanity through the wisdom of those in authority....Democratic rules of conduct in a monarchical administration, such is the formula...which will conform most comfortably with the spirit of the age.[1]

Although the reforms came from the top, they wrought important changes in Prussian society.

Stein's reforms broke the Junker monopoly of landholding. Serfdom was abolished. The power of the Prussian Junkers, however, did not permit the total end of the system in Prussia, as was occurring in the western principalities of Germany. In Prussia, peasants remaining on the land were forced to continue manorial labor, although they were free to leave the land if they chose. They could obtain the ownership of the land they worked only if they forfeited a third of it to the lord. The result was that Junker holdings grew larger. Some peasants went to the cities to find work, others became agricultural laborers, and some did actually become small freeholding farmers. In Prussia and elsewhere, serfdom had ended, but new social problems had been created as a landless labor force was enlarged by the population explosion.

Military reforms sought to increase the supply of soldiers and to improve their quality. Jena had shown that an army of free patriots commanded by officers chosen on merit rather than by birth could defeat an army of serfs and mercenaries commanded by incompetent nobles. To remedy the situation, the Prussian reformers abolished inhumane military punishments, sought to inspire patriotic feelings in the soldiers, opened the officer corps to commoners, gave promotions on the basis of merit, and organized war colleges that developed new theories of strategy and tactics.

These reforms soon enabled Prussia to regain its former power. Because Napoleon strictly limited the size of the Prussian army to 42,000 men, however, universal conscription could not be introduced until 1813. Before that date, the Prussians evaded the limit by training one group each year, putting them into the reserves, and then training a new group the same size. Prussia could thus boast an army of 270,000 by 1814.

The Wars of Liberation

SPAIN   In Spain more than elsewhere in Europe, national resistance to France had deep social roots. Spain had achieved political unity as early as the sixteenth century. The Spanish peasants were devoted to the ruling dynasty and especially to the Roman Catholic Church. France and Spain had been allies since 1796. In 1807, however, a French army came into the Iberian Peninsula to force Portugal to abandon its traditional alliance with Britain. The army stayed in Spain to protect lines of supply and communication. When a revolt broke out in Madrid in 1808, Napoleon used it as a pretext to depose the Spanish Bourbons and to place his brother Joseph (1768–1844) on the Spanish throne. Attacks on the privileges of the church increased public outrage. Many members of the upper classes were prepared to collaborate with Napoleon, but the peasants, urged on by the lower clergy and the monks, rose in a general rebellion. (See "Art & the West.")

[1]Quoted in Geoffrey Brunn, *Europe and the French Imperium* (New York: Harper & Row, 1938), p. 174.

A Commander Recalls an Incident in Spain

William Napier was a British officer during the Napoleonic Wars and later a distinguished leader in the British army. In the passage that follows, he describes his experiences in a battle that took place in 1811 during which he had difficulty leading his troops into battle and received a serious injury himself.

❖ *What were Napier's expectations of his men? of his officers? How does he explain the difficulties that his troops had in responding to his orders? How does he indicate his contempt for bad officers and yet a certain understanding that in war a person's character may display different faces?*

I arrived [with two companies] just in time to save Captain Dobbs, 52nd, and two men who were cut off from their regiment. The French were gathering fast about us, we could scarcely retreat, and Dobbs agreed with me that boldness would be our best chance; so we called upon the men to follow, and, jumping over a wall which had given us cover, charged the enemy with a shout which sent the nearest back....

Only the two men of the 52nd followed us, and we four arrived unsupported at a second wall, close to a considerable body of French, who rallied and began to close upon us. Their fire was very violent, but the wall gave cover. I was, however, stung by the backwardness of my men, and told Dobbs I would save him or lose my life by bringing up the two companies; he entreated me not, saying I could not make two paces from the wall and live. Yet I did go back to the first wall, escaped the fire, and, reproaching the men gave them the word again, and returned to Dobbs, who was now upon the point of being taken; but again I returned alone! The soldiers had indeed crossed the wall in their front, but kept edging away to the right to avoid the heavy fire. Being now maddened by this second failure, I made another attempt, but I had not made ten paces when a shot struck my spine, and the enemy very ungenerously continued to fire at me when I was down. I escaped death by dragging myself by my hands—for my lower extremities were paralyzed—towards a small heap of stones which was in the midst of

the field, and thus covering my head and shoulders....However, Captain Lloyd and my company, and some of the 52nd, came up at that moment, and the French were driven away.

The excuses for the soldiers were—1st That I had not made allowance for their exertions in climbing from the ravine up the hill-side with their heavy packs, and they were very much blown. 2nd Their own captains had not been with them for a long time, and they were commanded by two lieutenants, remarkable for their harsh, vulgar, tyrannical dispositions, and very dull bad officers withall; and one of them exhibited on this occasion such miserable cowardice as would be incredible if I had not witnessed it. I am sure he ordered the men not to advance, and I saw him leading them the second time to the right. This man was lying down with his face on the ground; I called to him, reproached him, bad him remember his uniform; nothing would stir him; until losing all patience I threw a large stone at his head. This made him get up, but when he got over the wall he was wild, his eyes staring and his hand spread out. He was a duellist, and had wounded one of the officers some time before. I would have broken him, but before I recovered my wound sufficiently to join, he had received a cannon-shot in the leg, and died at the old, desolate, melancholy mill below Sabugal. Everything combined to render death appalling, yet he showed no signs of weakness. Such is human nature, and so hard it is to form correct opinions of character!

Quoted in H. A. Bruce, *Life of Sir William Napier* (London: John Murray, 1864), 1:55–57.

In Spain, Napoleon faced a new kind of warfare. Guerrilla bands cut lines of communication, killed stragglers, destroyed isolated units, and then disappeared into the mountains. The British landed an army under Sir Arthur Wellesley (1769–1852), later the duke of Wellington, to support the Spanish insurgents. Thus began the long peninsular campaign that would drain French strength from elsewhere in Europe and play a critical role in Napoleon's eventual defeat. (See "A Commander Recalls an Incident in Spain.")

Francisco Goya Memorializes a Night of Executions: The Third of May, 1808

Goya y Lucientes, Francisco de Goya. *The Third of May, 1808.* 1814–1815. Oil painting on canvas. Museo del Prado, Madrid, Spain. Scala/Art Resource, NY

$\mathcal{N}$apoleon had begun to send troops into Spain in 1807 after the king of Spain had agreed to aid France against Portugal, which was assisting Britain. By early 1808 Spain had essentially become an occupied nation. On May 2 riots took place in Madrid between French troops, including many soldiers whom Napoleon had recruited in Egypt, and Spanish civilians. The Spaniards were attempting to prevent the departure of members of the Spanish royal family whom they considered to be French prisoners. In response to the riots, the French marshall Joachim Murat ordered numerous executions, especially of artisans and clergy, during the night of May 2 and 3. The events of these two days marked the opening of five years of the Spanish effort to free their country from French rule.

After the restoration of the Spanish monarchy, Francisco Goya (1745–1828) depicted the savagery of those executions in the most memorable war painting of the Napoleonic era, *The Third of May, 1808*. Because the executions had taken place at night, and the French chose their victims at random, Goya portrays a mechanical process of execution. One group has already been shot; another is being killed; and a third group, some of whom are covering their eyes, will be next. None of these people were necessarily heroes of the insurgency of the previous day. They were ordinary people being executed by troops of a nation that considered itself the champion of popular sovereignty. Goya's painting is one of the first works of art to illustrate victims of modern ideological wars.

In portraying these modern political executions, Goya recalled the traditional portrayal of Christian martyrdom–the pose of the central figure suggests a crucifixion. But more important, he drew on popular political prints of military firing squads, such as Paul Revere's famous print of the Boston Mas-

sacre. The painting thus presents the French as both infidels violating Christian Spaniards, and as a mechanical killing force picking out hapless civilians, as if in prophesy of the summary executions of civilians in modern warfare.

Goya's painting also illustrates two forces of modern warfare confronting each other: the professional solider and the guerilla (a term coined during this era). The guerilla is a civilian who must fight with what he finds. By contrast, the soldiers in this painting appear well disciplined and have modern rifles. They carry out the executions by the light of the large technologically advanced gas or oil lanterns with which Napoleon equipped his troops.

The Napoleonic conquest of Europe awakened the force of nationalism as ordinary people in the conquered nations resisted French domination. In *The Third of May*, Goya succeeds in making ordinary people, rather than elite officers, the symbolic heroes of the national war of liberation. But once the French were defeated and the royal family restored to the Spanish throne, the interpretation of the May 1808 events became more complicated.

In fact, Goya prepared this painting to please the royal family upon its return to Madrid in 1815. The conservative monarchy could not tolerate the insurgency as a popular uprising. It had to be seen as loyal humble citizens protecting the monarchy and the Church against Napoleon and an infidel France. The victims portrayed in his painting thus appeared in 1815 to be less martyrs for liberty than defenders of the evicted royal family.

Sources: Alfonso E. Perez Sanchez and Eleanor A. Sayre, *Goya and the Spirit of Enlightenment* (Boston: Museum of Fine Arts, 1989); Albert Boime, *Art in an Age of Bonapartism 1800–1815* (Chicago: University of Chicago Press, 1990), pp. 210–212, 297–300; Janis A. Tomlinson, *Goya in the Twilight of Enlightenment* (New Haven: Yale University Press, 1992), pp. 131–149; Robet Rosenblum and H. W. Janson, *19th-Century Art* (Englewood Cliffs, New Jersey: Prentice-Hall, Inc. and New York: Harry N. Abrams, Inc, Publishers: 1984), pp. 55–56.

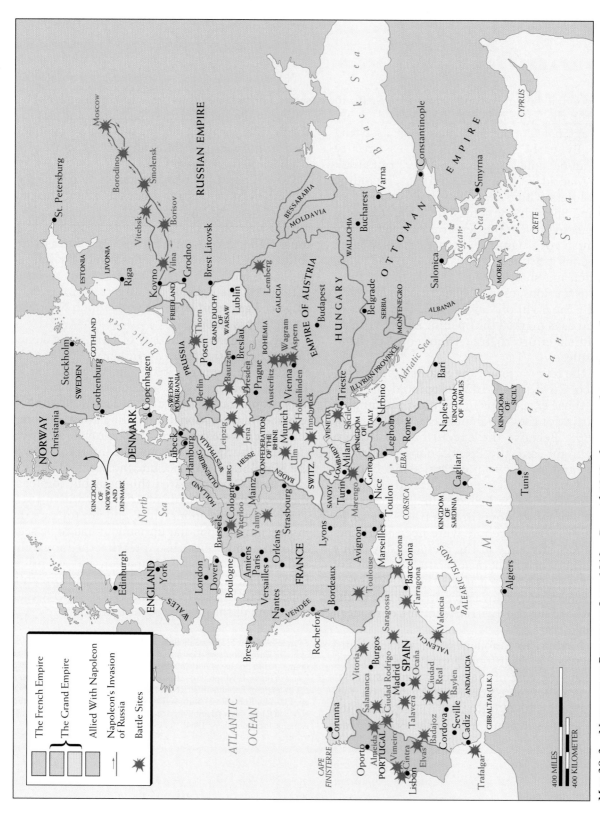

MAP 20–2   NAPOLEONIC EUROPE IN LATE 1812   *By mid-1812, the areas shown in peach were incorporated into France, and most of the rest of Europe was directly controlled by or allied with Napoleon. But Russia had withdrawn from the failing Continental System, and the decline of Napoleon was about to begin.*

AUSTRIA The French troubles in Spain encouraged the Austrians to renew the war in 1809. Since their defeat at Austerlitz, they had sought a war of revenge. The Austrians counted on Napoleon's distraction in Spain, French war weariness, and aid from other German princes. Napoleon was fully in command in France, however; and the German princes did not move. The French army marched swiftly into Austria and won the Battle of Wagram. The resulting Peace of Schönbrunn deprived Austria of much territory and 3½ million subjects.

Another spoil of victory was the Austrian archduchess Marie Louise (1791–1847), daughter of the emperor. Napoleon's wife, Josephine de Beauharnais (1763–1814), was forty-six and had borne him no children. His dynastic ambitions, as well as the desire for a marriage matching his new position as master of Europe, led him to divorce his wife and to marry the eighteen-year-old Austrian princess. Napoleon had also considered marrying the sister of Tsar Alexander, but had received a polite rebuff.

The Invasion of Russia

The failure of Napoleon's marriage negotiations with Russia emphasized the shakiness of the Franco–Russian alliance concluded at Tilsit. The alliance was unpopular with Russian nobles because of the liberal politics of France and because the Continental System prohibited timber sales to Britain. Only French aid in gaining Constantinople could justify the alliance in their eyes, but Napoleon gave them no help against the Ottoman Empire. The organization of the Grand Duchy of Warsaw as a Napoleonic satellite on the Russian doorstep and its enlargement in 1809 after the Battle of Wagram angered Alexander. Napoleon's annexation of Holland in violation of the Treaty of Tilsit, his recognition of the French Marshal Bernadotte (1763–1844) as the future King Charles XIV of Sweden, and his marriage to an Austrian princess further disturbed the tsar. At the end of 1810, Russia withdrew from the Continental System and began to prepare for war. (See Map 20–2.)

Napoleon was determined to end the Russian military threat. He amassed an army of more than 600,000 men, including a core of Frenchmen and more than 400,000 other soldiers drawn from the rest of his empire. He intended the usual short campaign crowned by a decisive battle, but the Russians disappointed him by retreating before his advance. His vast superiority in numbers—the Russians had only about 160,000 troops—made it foolish for them to risk a battle. Instead they followed a "scorched-

When their marriage failed to produce a male heir, Napoleon divorced his first wife, Josephine de Beauharnais (1763–1814). Many considered the action one aspect of Napoleon's betrayal of the Revolution, especially because he then married a daughter of the Habsburg emperor. This portrait is by F. P. Gerard.
Gerard Francois, *The Empress Josephine*. Chateau, Fontainebleau, France. 1808. Giraudon/Art Resource, NY

earth" policy, destroying all food and supplies as they retreated. The so-called Grand Army of Napoleon could not live off the country, and the expanse of Russia made supply lines too long to maintain. Terrible rains, fierce heat, shortages of food and water, and the courage of the Russian rear guard eroded the morale of Napoleon's army. Napoleon's advisers urged him to abandon the venture, but he feared that an unsuccessful campaign would undermine his position in the empire and in France. He pinned his faith on the Russians' unwillingness to abandon Moscow without a fight.

In September 1812, Russian public opinion forced the army to give Napoleon the battle he wanted despite the canny Russian General Kutuzov's (1745–1813) wish to avoid the fight and to let the Russian winter defeat the invader. At Borodino, not far west of Moscow, the bloodiest battle of the Napoleonic era

Napoleon's second wife, Marie Louise (1791–1847), bore him a son. It was clear that Napoleon hoped to establish a new imperial dynasty in France. This portrait is by J. B. Isabey. Marie Louise (1791–1847) and the King of Rome (1811–73) (oil on canvas) by Francois Pascal Simon Gerard, Baron (1770–1837). Chateau de Versailles, France/Bridgeman Art Library, London/Giraudon

cost the French 30,000 casualties and the Russians almost twice as many. Yet the Russian army was not destroyed. Napoleon won nothing substantial, and the battle was regarded as a defeat for him.

Fires set by the Russians soon engulfed Moscow and left Napoleon far from home with a badly diminished army lacking adequate supplies as winter came to a vast and unfriendly country. After capturing the burned city, Napoleon addressed several peace offers to Alexander, but the tsar ignored them. By October, what was left of the Grand Army was forced to retreat. By December, Napoleon realized that the Russian fiasco would encourage plots against him at home. He returned to Paris, leaving the remnants of his army to struggle westward. Perhaps only as many as 100,000 of the original army of more than 600,000 lived to tell the tale of their terrible ordeal.

European Coalition

Even as the news of the disaster reached the West, the final defeat of Napoleon was far from certain. He was able to put down his opponents in Paris and raise another 350,000 men. Neither the Prussians nor the Austrians were eager to risk another bout with Napoleon, and even the Russians hesitated. The Austrian foreign minister, Prince Klemens von Metternich (1773–1859), would have been glad to make a negotiated peace that would leave Napoleon on the throne of a shrunken and chastened France rather than see Europe dominated by Russia. Napoleon might have won a reasonable settlement by negotiation had he been willing to make concessions that would have split his jealous opponents. He would not consider that solution, however. As he explained to Metternich,

> Your sovereigns born on the throne can let themselves be beaten twenty times and return to their capitals. I cannot do this because I am an upstart soldier. My domination will not survive the day when I cease to be strong, and therefore feared.[2]

In 1813, patriotic pressure and national ambition brought together the last and most powerful coalition against Napoleon. The Russians drove westward, and Prussia and then Austria joined them. All were assisted by vast amounts of British money. From the west, Wellington marched his peninsular army into France. Napoleon's new army was inexperienced and poorly equipped. His generals had lost confidence and were tired. The emperor himself was worn out and sick. Still, he waged a skillful campaign in central Europe and defeated the allies at Dresden. In October, however, he was decisively defeated by the combined armies of the enemy at Leipzig in what the Germans called the Battle of the Nations. At the end of March 1814, the allied army marched into Paris. A few days later, Napoleon abdicated and went into exile on the island of Elba, off the coast of northern Italy.

The Congress of Vienna and the European Settlement

Fear of Napoleon and hostility to his ambitions had held the victorious coalition together. As soon as he was removed, the allies pursued their separate ambitions. The key person in achieving

[2]Quoted in Felix Markham, *Napoleon and the Awakening of Europe* (New York: Macmillan, 1965), pp. 115–116.

eventual agreement among them was Robert Stewart, Viscount Castlereagh (1769–1822), the British foreign secretary. Even before the victorious armies had entered Paris, he brought about the signing of the Treaty of Chaumont on March 9, 1814. It provided for the restoration of the Bourbons to the French throne and the contraction of France to its frontiers of 1792. Even more important was the agreement by Britain, Austria, Russia, and Prussia to form a Quadruple Alliance for twenty years to guarantee the peace terms and to act together to preserve whatever settlement they later agreed on. Remaining problems—and there were many—and final details were left for a conference to be held at Vienna.

Territorial Adjustments

The Congress of Vienna assembled in September 1814, but did not conclude its work until November 1815. Although a glittering array of heads of state attended the gathering, the four great powers conducted the important work of the conference. The only full session of the congress met to ratify the arrangements made by the big four. The easiest problem facing the great powers was France. All the victors agreed that no single state should be allowed to dominate Europe, and all were determined to see that France should be prevented from doing so again. The restoration of the French Bourbon monarchy, which was temporarily popular, and a nonvindictive boundary settlement were designed to keep France calm and satisfied.

The powers also built up a series of states to serve as barriers to any new French expansion. They established the kingdom of the Netherlands, including Belgium, in the north and added Genoa to Piedmont in the south. Prussia, whose power was increased by accessions in eastern Europe, was given important new territories along the Rhine River to deter French aggression in the west. Austria was given full control of northern Italy to prevent a repetition of Napoleon's conquests there. As for the rest of Germany, most of Napoleon's arrangements were left untouched. The venerable Holy Roman Empire, which had been dissolved in 1806, was not revived. (See Map 20–3.) In all these areas, the congress established the rule of legitimate monarchs and rejected any hint of the republican and democratic politics that had flowed from the French Revolution.

On these matters agreement was not difficult, but the settlement of eastern Europe sharply divided the victors. Alexander I of Russia wanted all Poland under his rule. Prussia was willing to give it to him in return for all of Saxony. Austria,

however, was unwilling to surrender its share of Poland or to see Prussian power grow or Russia penetrate deeper into central Europe. The Polish–Saxon question brought the congress to a standstill and almost caused a new war among the victors. But defeated France provided a way out. The wily Talleyrand, now representing France at Vienna, suggested that the weight of France added to that of Britain and Austria might bring Alexander to his senses. When news of a secret treaty among the three leaked out, the tsar agreed to become ruler of a smaller Poland, and Frederick William III of Prussia accepted only part of Saxony. Thereafter, France was included as a fifth great power in all deliberations.

The Hundred Days and the Quadruple Alliance

Unity among the victors was further restored by Napoleon's return from Elba on March 1, 1815. The French army was still loyal to the former emperor, and many of the French people thought that their fortunes might be safer under his rule than under that of the restored Bourbons. The coalition seemed to be dissolving in Vienna. Napoleon seized the opportunity, escaped to France, and was soon restored

MAP 20–3   THE GERMAN STATES AFTER 1815   *As noted, the German states were also recognized.*

Arthur Wellesley, the duke of Wellington, first led troops against Napoleon in Spain and later defeated him at the battle of Waterloo, June 18, 1815. Unlike his great naval contemporary, Nelson, he survived to become an elder statesman of Britian.   Bildarchiv Preussischer Kulturbesitz

to power. He promised a liberal constitution and a peaceful foreign policy. The allies were not convinced. They declared Napoleon an outlaw (a new device under international law) and sent their armies to crush him. Wellington, with the crucial help of the Prussians under Field Marshal von Blücher (1742– 1819), defeated Napoleon at Waterloo in Belgium on June 18, 1815. Napoleon again abdicated and was sent into exile on Saint Helena, a tiny Atlantic island off the coast of Africa, where he died in 1821.

The Hundred Days, as the period of Napoleon's return is called, frightened the great powers and made the peace settlement harsher for France. In addition to some minor territorial adjustments, the victors imposed a war indemnity and an army of occupation on France. Alexander proposed a Holy Alliance, whereby the monarchs promised to act together in accordance with Christian principles. Austria and Prussia signed; but Castlereagh thought it absurd and England abstained. The tsar, who was then embracing mysticism, believed his proposal a valuable tool for international relations. The Holy Alliance soon became a symbol of extreme political reaction.

Napoleonic Europe

Year	Event
1797	Napoleon concludes the Treaty of Campo Formio
1798	Nelson defeats the French navy in the harbor of Abukir in Egypt
1799	Consulate established in France
1801	Concordat between France and the papacy
1802	Treaty of Amiens
1803	War renewed between France and Britain
1804	Execution of Duke of Enghien
1804	Napoleonic Civil Code issued
1804	Napoleon crowned as emperor
1805 (October 21)	Nelson defeats French fleet at Trafalgar
1805 (December 2)	Austerlitz
1806	Jena
1806	Continental System established by Berlin Decrees
1807	Friedland
1807	Treaty of Tilsit
1808	Beginning of Spanish resistance to Napoleonic domination
1809	Wagram
1809	Napoleon marries Archduchess Marie Louise of Austria
1812	Invasion of Russia and French defeat at Borodino
1813	Leipzig (Battle of the Nations)
1814	Treaty of Chaumont (March) establishes Quadruple Alliance
1814 (September)	Congress of Vienna convenes
1815 (March 1)	Napoleon returns from Elba
1815 (June 18)	Waterloo
1815 (September 26)	Holy Alliance formed at Congress of Vienna
1815 (November 20)	Quadruple Alliance renewed at Congress of Vienna
1821	Napoleon dies on Saint Helena

The Quadruple Alliance among England, Austria, Prussia, and Russia was renewed on November 20, 1815. Henceforth, it was as much a coalition for the maintenance of peace as for the pursuit of victory over France. A coalition with such a purpose had not previously existed in European international relations. Its existence and later operation represented an important new departure in European affairs. Unlike the situation in the eighteenth century, certain powers were de-

LE CONGRÈS.

In this political cartoon of the Congress of Vienna, Tallyrand simply watches which way the wind is blowing, Castlereagh hesitates, while the monarchs of Russia, Prussia, and Austria form the dance of the Holy Alliance. The king of saxony holds onto his crown and the republic of Geneva pays homage to the Kingdom of Sardinia. Bildarchiv Preussischer Kulturbesitz

termined to prevent the outbreak of future war. The experiences of the statesmen at Vienna were very different from those of their eighteenth-century counterparts. They had seen the armies of the French Revolution change major frontiers of the European states. They had witnessed Napoleon overturning the political and social order of much of the continent. They had seen their nations experience unprecedented military organization and destruction. They knew that war affected not a relatively few people in professional armies and navies, but civilian populations and the entire social and political life of the continent. They were determined to prevent such upheaval and destruction from repeating itself.

Consequently, the chief aims of the Congress of Vienna were to prevent a recurrence of the Napoleonic nightmare and to arrange an acceptable settlement for Europe that might produce lasting peace. The leaders of Europe had learned that the previous peace treaties of the revolutionary era had failed and that the purpose of a treaty should be not to secure victory, but to secure future peace. The shared purpose of the diplomats was to establish a framework for future

stability, not to punish a defeated France. Through the Vienna Settlement, the great powers framed international relations in such a manner that the major powers would respect that settlement and not, as in the eighteenth century, use military force to change it.

The Congress of Vienna succeeded remarkably in achieving its goals. France accepted the new situation without undue resentment, in part because it was recognized not just as the defeated enemy of the revolutionary and Napoleonic eras, but also as a great power in the new international order. The victorious powers settled difficult problems among themselves and lesser states reasonably. They established a new legal framework whereby treaties were made between states rather than between monarchs. The treaties remained in place when a monarch died. Furthermore, during the quarter century of warfare, European leaders had come to calculate the nature of political and economic power in new ways that went beyond the simple vision of gaining a favorable balance of trade that had caused so many eighteenth-century wars. They took into account their natural resources, the technological structure of their

MAP 20–4   EUROPE 1815, AFTER THE CONGRESS OF VIENNA   *The Congress of Vienna achieved the post-Napoleonic territorial adjustments shown on the map. The most notable arrangements dealt with areas along France's borders (the Netherlands, Prussia, Switzerland, and Piedmont) and in Poland and northern Italy.*

economies, their systems of education, and the possibility of a general growth in agriculture, commerce, and industry whereby all states could prosper economically and not one at the expense of others.

The congress has been criticized for failing to recognize and provide for the great forces that would stir the nineteenth century—nationalism and democracy. Such criticism is inappropriate, however. At the time there were relatively few nationalist pressures; the general desire across the continent was for peace. The settlement, like all such agreements, was aimed at solving past ills, and in that it succeeded. The powers would have had to have been more than human to have anticipated future problems or to have yielded to forces of which they disapproved and which they believed threatened international peace and stability. It was unusual enough—indeed, virtually unprecedented—to produce an international settlement that remained essentially intact for almost half a century and that allowed Europe to suffer no general war for a hundred years. (See Map 20–4.)

The Romantic Movement

The years of the French Revolution and the conquests of Napoleon saw the emergence of a new and important intellectual movement throughout Europe. *Romanticism*, in its various manifestations, was a reaction against much of the thought of the Enlightenment. Romantic writers opposed what they considered the excessive scientific narrowness of the eighteenth-century *philosophes*. They accused the latter of subjecting everything to geometrical and mathematical models and thereby demeaning feelings and imagination. Romantic thinkers refused to conceive of human nature as primarily rational. They wanted to interpret both physical nature and human society in organic rather than mechanical terms and categories. The Enlightenment *philosophes* had often criticized religion and faith; the romantics, in contrast, saw religion as basic to human nature and faith as a means to knowledge.

Some historians, most notably Arthur O. Lovejoy, have warned against speaking of a single European-wide romantic movement. They have pointed out that a variety of such movements—occurring almost simultaneously in Germany, England, and France—arose independently and had their own particular courses of development. Such considerations have not, however, prevented the designation of a specific historical period, dated roughly from 1780 to 1830, as the *Age of Romanticism*, or the *romantic movement*.

Despite national differences, a shared reaction to the Enlightenment marked all of these writers and artists. They saw the imagination or some such intuitive intellectual faculty supplementing reason as a means of perceiving and understanding the world. Many of these writers urged a revival of Christianity, such as had permeated Europe during the Middle Ages. And unlike the *philosophes*, the romantics liked the art, literature, and architecture of medieval times. They were also deeply interested in folklore, folk songs, and fairy tales. The romantics were fascinated by dreams, hallucinations, sleepwalking, and other phenomena that suggested the existence of a world beyond that of empirical observation, sensory data, and discursive reasoning.

Romantic Questioning of the Supremacy of Reason

Several historical streams fed the romantic movement, including the individualism of the Renaissance and the Reformation, the pietism of the seventeenth century, and the eighteenth-century English Methodist movement. The influence of the last of these encouraged a heartfelt, practical religion in place of dogmatism, rationalism, and deism. The sentimental novels of the eighteenth century, such as Samuel Richardson's (1689–1761) *Clarissa* (1747), also paved the way for thinkers who would emphasize feeling and emotion. The so-called *Sturm und Drang*, "storm and stress," period of German literature and German idealist philosophy were important to the romantics. Two writers who were also closely related to the Enlightenment, however, provided the immediate intellectual foundations for romanticism: Jean-Jacques Rousseau and Immanuel Kant raised questions about the sufficiency of the rationalism so dear to the *philosophes*.

Rousseau and Education

It has already been pointed out in Chapter 18 that Jean-Jacques Rousseau, though sharing in the reformist spirit of the Enlightenment, opposed many of its other facets. What romantic writers especially drew from Rousseau was his conviction that society and material prosperity had corrupted human nature. In his works, Rousseau had portrayed humankind as happy and innocent by

In A Philosopher in a Moonlit Churchyard, *the British artist Philip James de Loutherbourg captured many of the themes of the Romantic movement. The painting suggests a sense of history, a love of Gothic architecture, a sense of the importance of religion, and a belief that the world is essentially mysterious.* Philip James de Loutherbourg (RA) (1740–1812), *A Philosopher in a Moonlit Churchyard*, signed and dated 1790. Oil on canvas, 34 × 27 in. (86.3 × 68.5 cm). B1974.3.4 Yale Center for British Art, Paul Mellon Collection.

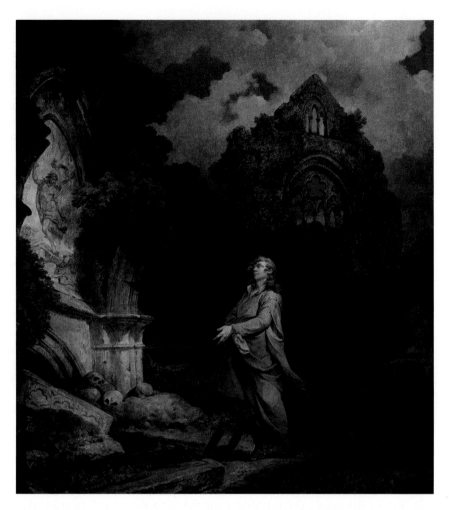

nature and originally living in a state of equilibrium, able to do what it desired and desiring only what it was able to do. To become happy again, humankind must remain true to its natural being while still attempting to realize the new moral possibilities of life in society. In his *Social Contract* (1762), Rousseau had provided his prescription for the reorganization of political life which might achieve that goal.

Rousseau set forth his view on the individual's development toward the good and happy life in his novel *Émile* (1762). (See Chapter 18.) Initially, this treatise on education was far more influential than the *Social Contract*. In *Émile*, Rousseau stressed the difference between children and adults. He distinguished the stages of human maturation and urged that children be raised with maximum individual freedom. Each child should be allowed to grow freely, like a plant, and to learn by trial and error what reality is and how best to deal with it. The parent or teacher would help most by providing the basic necessities of life and warding off what was manifestly harmful. Beyond that, the adult should

stay completely out of the way, like a gardener who waters and weeds a garden but otherwise lets nature take its course. As noted in Chapter 18, Rousseau thought that, because of their physical differences, men and women would naturally grow into social roles with different spheres of activity.

Rousseau also thought that the child's sentiments, as well as its reason, should be permitted to flourish. To romantic writers, this concept of human development vindicated the rights of nature over those of artificial society. They thought that such a form of open education would eventually lead to a natural society. In its fully developed form, this view of life led the romantics to value the uniqueness of each individual and to explore childhood in great detail. Like Rousseau, the romantics saw humankind, nature, and society as organically interrelated.

Kant and Reason

Immanuel Kant (1724–1804) wrote the two greatest philosophical works of the late eighteenth century: *The Critique of Pure Reason* (1781) and *The*

Critique of Practical Reason (1788). He sought to accept the rationalism of the Enlightenment and still to preserve a belief in human freedom, immortality, and the existence of God. Against Locke and other philosophers who saw knowledge rooted in sensory experience alone, Kant argued for the subjective character of human knowledge. For Kant, the human mind did not simply reflect the world around it like a passive mirror; rather, the mind actively imposed on the world of sensory experience "forms of sensibility" and "categories of understanding." The mind itself generated these categories. In other words, the human mind perceives the world as it does because of its own internal mental categories. This meant that human perceptions were as much the product of the mind's own activity as of sensory experience.

Kant found the sphere of reality that was accessible to pure reason to be quite limited. He believed, however, that beyond the phenomenal world of sensory experience, over which "pure reason" was master, there existed what he called the "noumenal" world. This world was a sphere of moral and aesthetic reality known by "practical reason" and conscience. Kant thought that all human beings possessed an innate sense of moral duty or an awareness of what he called a *categorical imperative*. This term referred to an inner command to act in every situation as one would have all other people always act in the same situation. Kant regarded the existence of this imperative of conscience as incontrovertible proof of humankind's natural freedom. On the basis of humankind's moral sense, Kant postulated the existence of God, eternal life, and future rewards and punishments. He believed that these transcendental truths could not be proved by discursive reasoning. Still, he was convinced that they were realities to which every reasonable person could attest.

To many romantic writers, Kantian philosophy constituted a decisive refutation of the narrow rationality of the Enlightenment. Whether they called it "practical reason," "fancy," "imagination," "intuition," or simply "feeling," the romantics believed in the presence of a special power in the human mind that could penetrate beyond the limits of largely passive human understanding as set forth by Hobbes, Locke, and Hume. Most of them also believed that poets and artists possessed these powers in abundance. Other romantic writers appealed to the limits of human reason to set forth new religious ideas or political thought that was often at odds with Enlightenment writers.

Romantic Literature

The term *romantic* appeared in English and French literature as early as the seventeenth century. Neoclassical writers then used the word to describe literature that they considered unreal, sentimental, or excessively fanciful. In the eighteenth century, the English writer Thomas Warton (1728–1790) associated romantic literature with medieval romances. In Germany, a major center of the romantic literary movement, Johann Gottfried Herder (1744–1803) used the terms *romantic* and *Gothic* interchangeably. In both England and Germany, the term came to be applied to all literature that did not observe classical forms and rules and that gave free play to the imagination.

As an alternative to such dependence on the classical forms, August Wilhelm von Schlegel (1767–1845) praised the "romantic" literature of Dante, Petrarch, Boccaccio, Shakespeare, the Arthurian legends, Cervantes, and Calderón. According to Schlegel, romantic literature was to classical literature what the organic and living were to the merely mechanical. He set forth his views in *Lectures on Dramatic Art and Literature* (1809–1811).

The romantic movement had peaked in Germany and England before it became a major force in France under the leadership of Madame de Staël (1766–1817) and Victor Hugo (1802–1885). (See "Madame de Staël Describes the New Romantic Literature of Germany.") So influential was the classical tradition in France that not until 1816 did a French writer openly declare himself a romantic. That was Henri Beyle (1783–1842), who wrote under the pseudonym Stendhal. He praised Shakespeare and Lord Byron and criticized his own countryman, the seventeenth-century classical dramatist Jean Racine (1639–1699).

The English Romantic Writers

The English romantics believed that poetry was enhanced by freely following the creative impulses of the mind. In this belief, they directly opposed Lockean psychology, which regarded the mind as a passive receptor and poetry as a mechanical exercise of "wit" following prescribed rules. For William Blake and Samuel Taylor Coleridge, the artist's imagination was God at work in the mind. As Coleridge expressed his views, the imagination was "a repetition in the finite mind of the eternal act of creation in the infinite I AM." So conceived of, poetry could not be con-

Madame de Staël Describes the New Romantic Literature of Germany

Anne Louise Germaine de Staël, known generally as Madame de Staël, was the daughter of the Jacques Necker, the finance minister of Louis XVI. In the years following the French Revolution, she was the friend of major French political liberals and was a firm critic of Napoleonic absolutism. More important for European literary life, Madame de Staël visited Germany, read widely in the emerging German romantic literature, and introduced it to both French and English-speaking Europe. Her book Concerning Germany *(1813) constituted a broad exploration of contemporary German culture. In the passage that follows, she gives a strong endorsement to the new literature then emerging in Germany. She points to the novelty of this Romantic poetry and then relates it to a new appreciation of Christianity and the Middle Ages. The Christian features which she associates with the poetry represent one strain among many of the religious revival that followed upon the de-Christianizing religious policies of the French Revolution.*

❖ *How does Madam de Staël characterize the new romantic school of poetry? Why does she contrast it with the literature that had its roots in ancient Greece and Rome? Why does she believe that the new literature will continue to grow? What is the relationship of the Middle Ages to the new poetry and other examples of the fine arts touched by romantic sensibilities?*

The word *romantic* has been lately introduced in Germany, to designate that kind of poetry which is derived from the songs of the Troubadours; that which owes its birth to the union of chivalry and Christianity. If we do not admit that the empire of literature has been divided between paganism and Christianity, the north and the south, antiquity and the middle ages, chivalry and the institutions of Greece and Rome, we shall never succeed in forming a philosophical judgment of ancient and of modern taste.

Some French critics have asserted that German literature is still in its infancy; this opinion is entirely false: men who are best skilled in the knowledge of languages, and the works of the ancients, are certainly not ignorant of the defects and advantages attached to the species of literature which they either adopt or reject; but their character, their habits, and their modes of reasoning, have led them to prefer that which is founded on the recollection of chivalry, on the wonders of the middle ages, to that which has for its basis the mythology of the Greeks. The literature of romance is alone capable of further improvement, because,

being rooted in our own soil, that alone can continue to grow and acquire fresh life: it expresses our religion; it recalls our history; its origin is ancient, although not of classical antiquity. Classic poetry, before it comes home to us, must pass through our recollections of paganism; that of the Germans is the Christian era of the fine arts; it employs our personal impressions to excite strong and vivid emotions; the genius by which it is inspired addresses itself immediately to our hearts; of all phantoms at once the most powerful and the most terrible....

The new school maintains the same system in the fine arts as in literature, and affirms that Christianity is the source of all modern genius; the writers of this school also characterize, in a new manner, all that in Gothic architecture agrees with the religious sentiments of Christians. It does not follow however from this, that the moderns can and ought to construct Gothic churches;...it is only of consequence to us, in the present silence of genius, to lay aside the contempt which has been thrown on all the conceptions of the middle ages.

From Madame De Staël, *Concerning Germany* (London, John Murray, 1814) as quoted in Howard E. Hugo, ed., *The Romantic Reader* (New York: Viking, 1957), pp. 64–66.

sidered idle play. Rather, it was the highest of human acts, humankind's self-fulfillment in a transcendental world.

BLAKE William Blake (1757–1827) considered the poet a seer and poetry to be translated vision. He thought it a great tragedy that so many people understood the world only rationally and could perceive no innocence or beauty in it. In the 1790s, he went through a deep personal depression that seems to have been related to his own inability to perceive the world as he believed it to be. The better one got to know the world, the more the life of the imagination and its spiritual values seemed to recede. Blake saw this problem as evidence of the materialism and injustice of English society. He was deeply impressed by the strong sense of contradiction between a true childlike vision of the world and conceptions of it based on experience.

COLERIDGE Samuel Taylor Coleridge (1772–1834) was the master of Gothic poems of the supernatural, such as "Christabel," and "The Rime of the Ancient Mariner." The latter relates the story of a sailor cursed for killing an albatross. The poem treats the subject as a crime against nature and God and raises the issues of guilt, punishment, and the redemptive possibilities of humility and penance. At the end of the poem, the mariner discovers the unity and beauty of all things. Having repented, he is delivered from his awful curse, which has been symbolized by the dead albatross hung around his neck:

O happy living things! no tongue
Their beauty might declare:
A spring of love gushed from my heart,
And I blessed them unaware...
The self-same moment I could pray;
And from my neck so free
The Albatross fell off, and sank
Like lead into the sea.

Coleridge also made major contributions to romantic literary criticism in his lectures on Shakespeare and in *Biographia Literaria* (1817), which presents his theories of poetry.

WORDSWORTH William Wordsworth (1770–1850) was Coleridge's closest friend. Together they published *Lyrical Ballads* in 1798 as a manifesto of a new poetry that rejected the rules of eighteenth-century criticism. Among Wordsworth's most important later poems is his "Ode on Intimations of Immortality" (1803), written in part to console Coleridge, who was suffering a deep personal cri-

sis. Its subject is the loss of poetic vision, something Wordsworth also keenly felt then in himself. Nature, which he had worshipped, no longer spoke freely to him, and he feared that it might never speak to him again:

There was a time when meadow, grove, and
  stream,
The earth, and every common sight,
To me did seem
Appareled in celestial light,
The glory and the freshness of a dream.
It is not now as it hath been of yore—
Turn whereso'er I may,
By night or day,
The things which I have seen I now can
see no more.

He had lost what he believed that all human beings lose in the necessary process of maturation: their childlike vision and closeness to spiritual reality. For both Wordsworth and Coleridge, childhood was the bright period of creative imagination. Wordsworth held a theory of the soul's preexistence in a celestial state before its creation. The child, being closer in time to its eternal origin and undistracted by worldly experience, recollects the supernatural world much more easily. Aging and urban living corrupt and deaden the imagination, making one's inner feelings and the beauty of nature less important. In his book-length

---

Publication Dates of Major Romantic Works

1762	Rousseau's *Émile*
1774	Goethe's *Sorrows of Young Werther*
1781	Kant's *Critique of Pure Reason*[*]
1788	Kant's *Critique of Practical Reason*[*]
1789	Blake's *Songs of Innocence*
1794	Blake's *Songs of Experience*
1798	Wordsworth and Coleridge's *Lyrical Ballads*
1799	Schlegel's *Lucinde*
1799	Schleiermacher's *Speeches on Religion to Its Cultured Despisers*
1802	Chateaubriand's *Genius of Christianity*
1806	Hegel's *Phenomenology of Mind*
1808	Goethe's *Faust*, Part I
1812	Byron's *Childe Harold's Pilgrimage*
1819	Byron's *Don Juan*

[*]Kant's books were not themselves part of the romantic movement, but they were fundamental to later romantic writers.

Lord Byron may well have been the most famous European poet of the first quarter of the nineteenth century. This portrait by the contemporary artist Géricault captures the poet in a brooding, introspective mood. Bildarchiv Preussischer Kulturbesitz

poem *The Prelude* (1850), Wordsworth presented a long autobiographical account of the growth of the poet's mind.

LORD BYRON   A true rebel among the romantic poets was Lord Byron (1788–1824). In Britain, even most of the other romantic writers distrusted and disliked him. He had little sympathy for their views of the imagination. Outside England, however, Byron was regarded as the embodiment of the new person of the French Revolution. He rejected the old traditions (he was divorced and famous for his paramours) and championed the cause of personal liberty. Byron was outrageously skeptical and mocking, even of his own beliefs. In *Childe Harold's Pilgrimage* (1812), he created a brooding, melancholy romantic hero. In *Don Juan* (1819), he wrote with ribald humor, acknowledged nature's cruelty as well as its beauty, and even expressed admiration for urban life.

The German Romantic Writers

Much romantic poetry was also written on the Continent, but almost all major German romantics wrote at least one novel. Romantic novels often were highly sentimental and borrowed material from medieval romances. The characters of romantic novels were treated as symbols of the larger truth of life. Purely realistic description was avoided. The first German romantic novel was Ludwig Tieck's (1773–1853) *William Lovell* (1793–1795). It contrasts the young Lovell, whose life is built on love and imagination, with those who live by cold reason alone and who thus become an easy prey to unbelief, misanthropy, and egoism. As the novel rambles to its conclusion, Lovell is ruined by a mixture of philosophy, materialism, and skepticism, administered to him by two women whom he naively loves.

Johann Wolfgang von Goethe (1749–1832), perhaps the greatest German writer of modern times, is portrayed here in the garb of a pilgrim against a Romantic background of classical ruins in the fields outside Rome. Tischbein, Johann Heinr. Wilh. 1751–1821. *Goethe in der romischen Campagna.* Stadelisches Kunstinstitut, Frankfurt/Artothek

SCHLEGEL   Friedrich Schlegel (1767–1845) wrote a progressive early romantic novel, *Lucinde* (1799), which attacked contemporaneous prejudices against women as capable of being little more than lovers and domestics. Schlegel's novel reveals the ability of the romantics to become involved in the social issues of their day. He depicted Lucinde as the perfect friend and companion, as well as the unsurpassed lover, of the hero. Like other early romantic novels, the work shocked contemporary morals by frankly discussing sexual activity and by describing *Lucinde* as equal in all ways to the male hero.

GOETHE   Towering above all of these German writers stood the figure of Johann Wolfgang von Goethe (1749–1832). Perhaps the greatest German writer of modern times, Goethe defies any easy classification. Part of his literary production fits into the romantic mold, and part of it was a condemnation of romantic excesses. The book that made his early reputation was *The Sorrows of Young Werther*, published in 1774. This novel, like many others in the eighteenth century, is composed of a series of letters. The hero falls in love with Lotte, who is married to another man. The letters explore their relationship and display the emotional sentimentalism that was characteristic of the age. Eventually Werther and Lotte part, but in his grief over his abandoned love, Werther takes his own life. This novel became popular through-

out Europe. Virtually all later romantic authors, and especially those in Germany, admired it because of its emphasis on feeling and on living outside the bounds of polite society.

Much of Goethe's early poetry was also erotic in nature. As he became older, however, Goethe became much more serious and self-consciously moral. He published many other works, including *Iphigenia at Tauris* (1787) and *Wilhelm Meister's Apprenticeship* (1792–1800), which explored how human beings come to live moral lives while still acknowledging the life of the senses.

Goethe's greatest masterpiece was *Faust*, a long dramatic work of poetry in two parts. Part I was published in 1808. It tells the story of Faust, who, weary of life, makes a pact with the Devil—he will exchange his soul for greater knowledge than other human beings possess. As the story progresses, Faust seduces a young woman named Gretchen. She dies, but is received into heaven as the grief-stricken Faust realizes that he must continue to live.

In Part II, completed in the year of Goethe's death (1832), Faust is taken through a series of strange adventures involving witches and various mythological characters. This portion of the work has never been admired so much as Part I. At the conclusion, however, Faust dedicates his life, or what remains of it, to the improvement of humankind. In his dedication, he feels that he has found a goal

Friedrich Schleiermacher (1768–1834) was the most important protestant theologian of the first half of the nineteenth century. He stressed the importance of feeling in religious experience. Bildarchiv Preussischer Kulturbesitz

that will allow him to overcome the restless striving that first induced him to make the pact with the Devil. That new knowledge breaks the pact. Faust then dies and is received by angels.

In this great work, Goethe obviously was criticizing much of his earlier thought and that of contemporary romantic writers. He was also attempting to portray the deep spiritual problems that Europeans would encounter as the traditional moral and religious values of Christianity were abandoned. Yet Goethe himself could not reaffirm those values. In that respect, both he and his characters symbolized the spiritual struggle of the nineteenth century.

Religion in the Romantic Period

During the Middle Ages, the foundation of religion had been the church. The Reformation leaders had appealed to the authority of the Bible. Then, later Enlightenment writers had attempted to derive religion from the rational nature revealed by Newtonian physics. Romantic religious thinkers, on the other hand, appealed to the inner emotions of humankind for the foundation of religion. Their forerunners were the mystics of Western Christianity. One of the first great examples of a religion characterized by romantic impulses—Methodism—arose in England.

Methodism

Methodism originated in the middle of the eighteenth century as a revolt against deism and rationalism in the Church of England. The Methodist revival formed an important part of the background of English romanticism. The leader of the Methodist movement was John Wesley (1703–1791). His education and religious development had been carefully supervised by his remarkable mother, Susannah Wesley, who bore eighteen children in addition to John.

While at Oxford, Wesley organized a religious group known as the "Holy Club." He soon left England for missionary work in Georgia in America, where he arrived in 1735. While he was crossing the Atlantic, a group of German Moravians on the ship had deeply impressed him. These German pietists exhibited unshakable faith and confidence during a violent storm at sea, while Wesley despaired of his life. Wesley concluded that they knew far better than he the meaning of justification by faith. When he returned to England in 1738 after an unhappy missionary career, Wesley began to worship with Moravians in London. There, in 1739, he underwent a conversion experience that he described in the words, "My heart felt strangely warmed." From that point on, he felt assured of his own salvation.

John Wesley (1703–1791) was the founder of Methodism. He emphasized the role of emotional experience in Christian conversion. Corbis

Chateaubriand Describes the Appeal of a Gothic Church

Throughout most of the eighteenth century, writers had harshly criticized virtually all aspects of the Middle Ages, then considered an unenlightened time. One of the key elements of romanticism was a new appreciation of all things medieval. In this passage from The Genius of Christianity, *Chateaubriand praises the beauty of the Middle Ages and the strong religious feelings produced by stepping into a Gothic church. The description exemplifies the typically romantic emphasis on feelings as the chief foundation of religion.*

❖ *Why does the capacity of a Gothic church to carry Chateaubriand back in time add to its power of inducing a religious feeling? How does Chateaubriand unite the church with nature to emphasize its religious character? Is this vision of religion dependent upon the authority of an organized church or of sacred writings, such as the Bible?*

You could not enter a Gothic church without feeling a kind of awe and a vague sentiment of the Divinity. You were all at once carried back to those times when a fraternity of cenobites [a particular order of monks], after having meditated in the woods of their monasteries, met to prostrate themselves before the altar and to chant the praises of the Lord, amid the tranquility and the silence of the night....

Everything in a Gothic church reminds you of the labyrinths of a wood; everything excites a feeling of religious awe, of mystery, and of the Divinity.

The two lofty towers erected at the entrance of the edifice overtop the elms and yew trees of the church yard, and produce the most picturesque effect on the azure of heaven. Sometimes their twin heads are illumined by the first rays of dawn; at others they appear crowned with a capital of clouds or magnified in a foggy atmosphere. The birds themselves seem to make a mistake in regard to them, and to take them for the trees of the forests; they hover over their summits, and perch upon their pinnacles. But, lo! confused noises suddenly issue from the tops of these towers and scare away the affrighted birds. The Christian architect, not content with building forests, has been desirous to retain their murmurs; and, by means of the organ and of bells, he has attached to the Gothic temple the very winds and thunders that roar in the recesses of the woods. Past ages, conjured up by these religious sounds, raise their venerable voices from the bosom of the stones, and are heard in every corner of the vast cathedral. The sanctuary reechoes like the cavern of the ancient Sibyl; loud-tongued bells swing over your head, while the vaults of death under your feet are profoundly silent.

Viscount François René de Chateaubriand, *The Genius of Christianity*, trans. by C. I. White (Baltimore: J. Murphy, 1862), as quoted in Howard E. Hugo, ed., The Romantic Reader (New York: Viking, 1957), pp. 341–342.

Wesley discovered that he could not preach his version of Christian conversion and practical piety in Anglican Church pulpits. Therefore, late in 1739, he began to preach in the open fields near the cities and towns of western England. Thousands of humble people responded to his message of repentance and good works. Soon he and his brother Charles (1707–1788), who became famous for his hymns, began to organize Methodist societies. By the late eighteenth century, the Methodists had become a separate church. They ordained their own clergy and sent missionaries to America, where they eventually achieved their greatest success and most widespread influence.

Methodism stressed inward, heartfelt religion and the possibility of Christian perfection in this life. John Wesley described Christianity as "an inward principle...the image of God impressed on a created spirit, a fountain of peace and love springing up into everlasting life."[3] True Christians were those who were "saved in this world from all sin, from all unrighteousness...and now in such a sense perfect as not to commit sin and...freed from evil thoughts and evil tempers."[4]

[3]Quoted in Albert C. Outler, ed., *John Wesley: A Representative Collection of His Writings* (New York: Oxford University Press, 1964), p. 220.

[4]*Ibid.*

Many people, weary of the dry rationalism that derived from deism, found Wesley's ideal relevant to their own lives. The Methodist preachers emphasized the role of enthusiastic emotional experience as part of Christian conversion. After Wesley, religious revivals became highly emotional in style and content.

New Directions in Continental Religion

Similar religious developments based on feeling appeared on the Continent. After the Thermidorian Reaction, a strong Roman Catholic revival took place in France. Its followers disapproved of both the religious policy of the revolution and the anticlericalism of the Enlightenment. The most impor-

tant book to express these sentiments was *The Genius of Christianity* (1802), by Viscount François René de Chateaubriand (1768–1848). In this work, which became known as the "Bible of romanticism," Chateaubriand argued that the essence of religion was "passion." The foundation of faith in the church was the emotion that its teachings and sacraments inspired in the heart of the Christian. (See "Chateaubriand Describes the Appeal of a Gothic Church.")

Against the Newtonian view of the world and of a rational God, the romantics found God immanent in nature. No one stated the romantic religious ideal more eloquently or with greater impact on the modern world than Friedrich Schleiermacher (1768–1834). In 1799, he published *Speeches on Religion to Its Cultured De-*

The philosopher J. G. Fichte (1762–1814), shown here in the uniform of a Berlin home guard. Fichte glorified the role of the great individual in history. Bildarchiv Preussischer Kulturbesitz *spisers*. It was a response to Lutheran orthodoxy, on the one hand, and to Enlightenment rationalism, on the other. The advocates of both were the "cultured despisers" of real, or heartfelt, religion. According to Schleiermacher, religion was neither dogma nor a system of ethics. It was an intuition or feeling of absolute dependence on an infinite reality. Religious institutions, doctrines, and moral activity expressed that primal religious feeling only in a secondary, or indirect, way.

Although Schleiermacher considered Christianity the "religion of religions," he also believed that every world religion was unique in its expression of the primal intuition of the infinite in the finite. He thus turned against the universal natural religion of the Enlightenment, which he termed "a name applied to loose, unconnected impulses," and defended the meaningfulness of the numerous world religions. Every such religion was seen to be a unique version of the emotional experience of dependence on an infinite being. In so arguing, Schleiermacher interpreted the religions of the world in the same way that other romantic writers interpreted the variety of unique peoples and cultures.

Romantic Views of Nationalism and History

A distinctive feature of romanticism, especially in Germany, was its glorification of both the individual person and individual cultures. Behind these

This colored lithograph of G. W. F. Hegel shows him attired in robes of a university professor. Hegel was the most important philosopher of history in the Romantic period.
Bildarchiv Preussischer Kulturbesitz

Hegel Explains the Role of Great Men in History

Hegel believed that behind the development of human history from one period to the next lay the mind and purpose of what he termed the "World-Spirit," a concept somewhat resembling the Christian God. Hegel thought particular heroes from the past (such as Caesar) and in the present (such as Napoleon) were the unconscious instruments of that Spirit. In this passage from his lectures on the philosophy of history, Hegel explained how these heroes could change history. All these concepts are characteristic of the romantic belief that human beings and human history are always intimately connected with larger, spiritual forces at work in the world. The passage also reflects the widespread belief of the time that the world of civic or political action pertained to men and that of the domestic sphere belonged to women.

❖ *How might the career of Napoleon have inspired this passage? What are the antidemocratic implications of this passage? In this passage, do great men make history or do historical developments make great men? Why do you think Hegel does not associate this power of shaping history with women as well as men? In that regard, note how he relates history with political developments rather than with those of the private social sphere.*

Such are all great historical men—whose own particular aims involve those large issues which are the will of the World-Spirit. They may be called Heroes, inasmuch as they have derived their purposes and their vocation, not from the calm, regular course of things, sanctioned by the existing order, but from a concealed fount—one which has not attained to phenomenal, present existence—from that inner Spirit, still hidden beneath the surface, which, impinging on the outer world as on a shell, bursts it in pieces, because it is another kernel than that which belonged to the shell in question. They are men, therefore, who appear to draw the impulse of their life from themselves; and whose deeds have produced a condition of things and a complex of historical relations which appear to be only their interest, and their work.

Such individuals had no consciousness of the general Idea they were unfolding, while prosecuting those aims of theirs; on the contrary, they were practical, political men. But at the same time they were thinking men, who had an insight into the requirements of the time—what was ripe for development. This was the very Truth for their age, for their world; the species next in order, so to speak, and which was already formed in the womb of time. It was theirs to know this nascent principle; the necessary, directly sequent step in progress, which their world was to take; to make this their aim, and to expend their energy in promoting it. World-historical men—the Heroes of an epoch—must, therefore, be recognized as its clear-sighted ones; their deeds, their words are the best of that time.

From G. W. F. Hegel, *The Philosophy of History*, trans. by J. Sibree (New York: Dover, 1956), pp. 30–31. Reprinted by permission.

views lay the philosophy of German idealism, which understood the world as the creation of subjective egos. J. G. Fichte (1762–1814), an important German philosopher and nationalist, identified the individual ego with the Absolute that underlies all existing things. According to him and similar philosophers, the world is truly the creation of humankind. The world is as it is because especially strong persons conceive of it in a particular way and impose their wills on the world and other people. Napoleon served as the contemporary example of such a great person. This philosophy has ever

since served to justify the glorification of great persons and their actions in overriding all opposition to their will and desires.

Herder and Culture

In addition to this philosophy, the influence of new historical studies lay behind the German glorification of individual cultures. German romantic writers went in search of their own past in reaction to the copying of French manners in eighteenth-century Germany, the impact of the French Revolution, and the imperialism of Napoleon. An early leader in this effort was Johann Gottfried Herder (1744–1803). Herder had early resented the French cultural preponderance in Germany. In 1778, he published an influential essay entitled "On the Knowing and Feelings of the Human Soul." In it, he vigorously rejected the mechanical explanation of nature so popular with Enlightenment writers. He saw human beings and societies as developing organically, like plants, over time. Human beings were different at different times and places.

Herder revived German folk culture by urging the collection and preservation of distinctive German songs and sayings. His most important followers in this work were the Grimm brothers, Jakob (1785–1863) and Wilhelm (1786–1859), famous for their collection of fairy tales. Believing that each language and culture were the unique expression of a people, Herder opposed both the concept and the use of a "common" language, such as French, and "universal" institutions, such as those imposed on Europe by Napoleon. These, he believed, were forms of tyranny over the individuality of a people. Herder's writings led to a broad revival of interest in history and philosophy. Although initially directed toward the identification of German origins, such work soon expanded to embrace other world cultures as well. Eventually the ability of the romantic imagination to be at home in any age or culture spurred the study of non-Western religion, comparative literature, and philology.

Hegel and History

The most important philosopher of history in the romantic period was the German, Georg Wilhelm Friedrich Hegel (1770–1831). He is one of the most complicated and significant philosophers in the history of Western civilization.

Hegel believed that ideas develop in an evolutionary fashion that involves conflict. At any given time, a predominant set of ideas, which he termed the *thesis*, holds sway. The thesis is challenged by other conflicting ideas, which Hegel termed the *antithesis*. As these patterns of thought clash, a *synthesis* emerges that eventually becomes the new thesis. Then the process begins all over again. Periods of world history receive their character from the patterns of thought predominating during them. (See "Hegel Explains the Role of Great Men in History.")

Several important philosophical conclusions followed from this analysis. One of the most significant was the belief that all periods of history have been of almost equal value because each was, by definition, necessary to the achievements of those that came later. Also, all cultures are valuable because each contributes to the necessary clash of values and ideas that allows humankind to develop. Hegel discussed these concepts in *The Phenomenology of Mind* (1806), *Lectures on the Philosophy of History* (1822–1831), and other works, many of which were published only after his death. During his lifetime, his ideas became widely known through his university lectures at Berlin.

In Perspective

The various romantic ideas made a major contribution to the emergence of nationalism, which proved to be one of the strongest motivating forces of the nineteenth and twentieth centuries. The writers of the Enlightenment had generally championed a cosmopolitan outlook on the world. By contrast, the romantic thinkers emphasized the individuality and worth of each separate people and culture. A people or a nation was defined by a common language, a common history, a homeland that possessed historical associations, and common customs. This cultural nationalism gradually became transformed into a political creed. It came to be widely believed that every people, ethnic group, or nation should constitute a separate political entity and that only when it so existed could the nation be secure in its own character.

The example of France under the revolutionary government and then Napoleon had demonstrated the power of nationhood. Other peoples came to desire similar strength and confidence. Napoleon's toppling of ancient political structures, such as the Holy Roman Empire, proved the need for new political organization in Europe. By 1815 these were the aspirations of only a few Europeans, but as time passed, such yearnings came to be shared by scores of peoples from Ireland to Ukraine. The Congress of Vienna could ignore such feelings, but for the rest of the nineteenth century, as will be seen in subsequent chapters, statesmen had to confront the growing reality of the power these feelings unleashed.

REVIEW QUESTIONS

1. How did Napoleon rise to power? What groups supported him? What were the stages by which he eventually made himself emperor? What were his major domestic achievements? Did his rule more nearly fulfill or betray the ideals of the French Revolution?

2. What regions made up Napoleon's realm and what status did each region have within it? How did Napoleon rule his empire? Did his administration show foresight, or did the empire ultimately become a burden he could not afford?

3. Why did Napoleon decide to invade Russia? Why did the operation fail? Can Napoleon be considered a "military genius"? Why or why not? To what extent was his brilliance dependent on the ineptitude of his enemies?

4. Who were the principal personalities, and what were the most significant problems, of the Congress of Vienna? What were the results of the Congress and why were they significant?

5. Compare the role of feelings for romantic writers with the role of reason for Enlightenment writers. What questions did Rousseau and Kant raise about reason?

6. Why did poetry become important to romantic writers? How did the romantic concept of religion differ from Reformation Protestantism and Enlightenment deism? How did romantic writers use the idea of history?

SUGGESTED READINGS

M. H. ABRAMS, *The Mirror and the Lamp: Romantic Theory and the Critical Tradition* (1958). A standard text on romantic literary theory that looks at English romanticism in the context of German romantic idealism.

M. H. ABRAMS, *Natural Supernaturalism: Tradition and Revolution in Romantic Literature* (1971). A brilliant survey of romanticism across western European literature.

J. S. ALLEN, *Popular French Romanticism: Authors, Readers, and Books in the Nineteenth Century* (1981). Relates romanticism to popular culture.

F. C. BEISER, *Enlightenment, Revolution, and Romanticism: The Genesis of Modern German Political Thought, 1790–1800* (1992). The best recent study of the subject.

L. BERGERON, *France under Napoleon* (1981). An in-depth examination of Napoleonic administration.

J. F. BERNARD, *Talleyrand: A Biography* (1973). A useful account.

E. CASSIRER, *Kant's Life and Thought* (1981). A brilliant work by one of the major philosophers of this century.

D. G. CHANDLER, *The Campaigns of Napoleon* (1966). A good military study.

D. G. CHARLTON, *New Images of the Natural in France* (1984). An examination of the changing attitude toward nature in France during the romantic era.

K. CLARK, *The Romantic Rebellion* (1973). A useful discussion that combines both art and literature.

O. CONNELLY, *Napoleon's Satellite Kingdoms* (1965). The rule of Napoleon and his family in Europe.

A. D. CULLER, *The Victorian Mirror of History* (1985). Studies in the writing of the nineteenth century with emphasis on romantic influences.

J. ENGELL, *The Creative Imagination: Enlightenment to Romanticism* (1981). An important book on the role of the imagination in romantic literary theory.

M. GLOVER, *The Peninsular War, 1807–1814: A Concise Military History* (1974). An interesting account of the military campaign that so drained Napoleon's resources in western Europe.

F. W. J. HEMMINGS, *Culture and Society in France: 1789–1848* (1987). Discusses French romantic literature, theater, and art.

H. HONOUR, *Romanticism* (1979). The best introduction to the subject in terms of the fine arts.

G. N. IZENBERG, *Impossible Individuality: Romanticism, Revolution, and the Origins of Modern Selfhood, 1787–1802* (1992). Explores the concepts of individualism in Germany, England, and France.

H. KISSINGER, *A World Restored: Metternich, Castlereagh and the Problems of Peace, 1812–1822* (1957). A provocative study by an author who became an American secretary of state.

S. KÖRNER, *Kant* (1955). A clear introduction to a brilliant thinker.

M. LEBRIS, *Romantics and Romanticism* (1981). A lavishly illustrated work that relates politics and romantic art.

G. LEFEBVRE, *Napoleon*, 2 vols., trans. by H. Stockhold (1969). The fullest and finest biography of the man.

F. MARKHAM, *Napoleon and the Awakening of Europe* (1954). Emphasizes the growth of nationalism.

R. MUIR, *Tactics and the Experience of Battle in the Age of Napoleon* (1998). A splendid account of the experience of troops in battle.

H. NICOLSON, *The Congress of Vienna* (1946). A good, readable account.

Z. A. PELCZYNSKI, *The State and Civil Society: Studies in Hegel's Political Philosophy* (1984). An important series of essays.

R. PLANT, *Hegel: An Introduction* (1983). Emphasis on his political thought.

R. PORTER AND M. TEICH (EDS.), *Romanticism in National Context* (1988). Essays on the phenomenon of romanticism in the major European nations.

B. M. G. REARDON, *Religion in the Age of Romanticism: Studies in Early Nineteenth-Century Thought* (1985). The best introduction to this important subject.

P. W. SCHROEDER, *The Transformation of European Politics, 1763–1848* (1994). A major synthesis of the diplomatic history of the period, emphasizing the new departures of the Congress of Vienna.

S. B. SMITH, *Hegel's Critique of Liberalism: Rights in Context* (1989). An excellent introduction to Hegelian political thought.

C. TAYLOR, *Hegel* (1975). The best one-volume introduction.

J. M. THOMPSON, *Napoleon Bonaparte: His Rise and Fall* (1952). A sound biography.

A. WALICKI, *Philosophy and Romantic Nationalism: The Case of Poland* (1982). Examines how philosophy influenced the character of Polish nationalism.

W. R. WARD, *The Protestant Evangelical Awakening* (1992). Examines the religious revivals of the eighteenth and nineteenth century from a transatlantic perspective.

B. YACK, *The Longing for Total Revolution: Philosophic Sources of Social Discontent from Rousseau to Marx and Nietzsche* (1986). A major exploration of the political philosophy associated with romanticism.

T. ZIOLKOWSKI, *German Romanticism and Its Institutions* (1990). An exploration of how institutions of intellectual life influenced creative literature.

Chapter 21

In 1830, Revolution again erupted in France as well as elsewhere on the continent. Eugène Delacroix's Liberty Leading the People was the most famous image recalling that event. Note how he portrays persons from different social classes and occupations joining the revolution led by the figure of Liberty. Eugène Delacroix, *Liberty Leading the People*, oil on canvas (1830), 260 × 325 cm – RF 129. Louvre – Department des Peintures, Paris, France. (c) Photograph by Erich Lessing. Art Resource, NY

The Conservative Order and the Challenges of Reform (1815–1832)

KEY TOPICS

- The challenges of nationalism and liberalism to the conservative order in the early nineteenth century

- The domestic and international politics of the conservative order from the Congress of Vienna through the 1820s

- The wars of Independence in Latin America

- The revolutions of 1830 on the Continent and the passage of the Great Reform Bill in Britain

The close of the Congress of Vienna was followed by a decade in which conservative political forces controlled virtually all of Europe. In the international arena, these forces sought to maintain peace and to prevent the outbreak of war that would unleash destruction and disorder. They did so through unprecedented forms of cooperation and mutual consultation. Domestically, they sought to maintain the authority of monarchies and aristocracies after the turmoil wrought by the French Revolution and Napoleon. Two sets of critics challenged this conservative order: Nationalists wished to see the map of Europe drawn according to the boundaries of nationalities or ethnic groups. Liberals sought moderate political reform and freer economic markets. The goals of nationalists and liberals threatened the dominance of landed aristocracies and the rule of monarchs who governed by virtue of dynastic inheritance rather than nationality. Still another challenge to the status quo came from the efforts of Europe's Latin American colonies to gain independence.

For the first fifteen years after the Congress of Vienna, the forces of conservatism were successful, except for their failure to retain control of Latin America. Late in the 1820s, however, the conservatives faced stronger challenges. Thereafter, certain major liberal goals were achieved when a revolution occurred in France in 1830 and a sweeping reform bill passed through the British Parliament in 1832. During the same period, however, Russia and other countries in eastern and central Europe continued to resist political and social change.

The Challenges of Nationalism and Liberalism

Observers have frequently regarded the nineteenth century as the great age of *isms*. Throughout the Western world, secular ideologies began to take hold of the learned and popular imaginations in opposition to the political and social status quo. These included nationalism, liberalism, republicanism, socialism, and communism. A noted historian has called all such words "trouble-breeding and usually thought-obscuring terms."[1] They are just that if one uses them as an excuse to avoid thinking or if one fails to see the variety of opinions concealed beneath each of them.

The Emergence of Nationalism

Nationalism proved to be the single most powerful European political ideology of the nineteenth and early twentieth centuries. It has reasserted itself in present-day Europe following the collapse of communist governments in Eastern Europe and in the former Soviet Union. As a political outlook, nationalism was and is based on the relatively modern concept that a nation is composed of people who are joined together by the bonds of a common language, as well as common customs, culture, and history, and who, because of those bonds, should be administered by the same government. That is to say, nationalists in the past and the present contend that political and ethnic boundaries should coincide. Political units had not been so defined or governed earlier in European history. The idea came into its own during the late eighteenth and the early nineteenth centuries.

OPPOSITION TO THE VIENNA SETTLEMENT   Early-nineteenth-century nationalism directly opposed the principle upheld at the Congress of Vienna that legitimate monarchies or dynasties, rather than ethnicity, provide the basis for political unity. Nationalists naturally protested multinational states such as the Austrian and Russian empires. They also objected to peoples of the same ethnic group, such as Germans and Italians, dwelling in political units smaller than that of the ethnic nation. Consequently, nationalists challenged both the domestic and the international order of the Vienna settlement.

Behind the concept of nationalism usually, though not always, lay the idea of popular sovereignty, since the qualities of peoples rather than their rulers determine a national character. But this aspect of nationalism frequently led to confusion or conflict because of the presence of minorities. Within many territories in which one national group has predominated, there have also existed significant minority ethnic enclaves that the majority has had every intention of governing with or without their consent. In some cases, a nationalistically conscious group would dominate in one section of a country, but people of the same ethnicity in another region would not have nationalistic aspirations. The former might then attempt to impose their aspirations on the latter.

CREATING NATIONS   In point of fact, it was nationalists who actually created nations in the nineteenth century. During the first half of the century, a particular, usually small, group of nationalistically minded writers or other intellectual elites, using the printed word spread a nationalistic concept of the nation. These groups were frequently historians who chronicled a people's past or writers and literary scholars who established a national literature by collecting and publishing earlier writings in the people's language. In effect, they gave a people a sense of their past and a literature of their own. As time passed, schoolteachers, by imparting a nation's official language and history, played an important role in spreading nationalistic ideas. These small groups of early nationalists established the cultural beliefs and political expectations upon which the later mass-supported nationalism of the second half of the century would grow.

The language to be used in the schools and in government offices was always a point of contention for nationalists. In France and Italy, official versions of the national language were imposed in the schools and replaced local dialects. In parts of Scandinavia and eastern Europe, nationalists attempted to resurrect from earlier times what they regarded as purer versions of the national language. Often, these resurrected languages were virtually invented by modern scholars or linguists. This process of establishing national languages led to far more linguistic uniformity in European nations than had existed prior to the nineteenth century. Yet even in 1850, perhaps less than half of the inhabitants of France spoke official French.

Language could become such an effective cornerstone in the foundation of nationalism thanks in large measure to the emergence of the print culture discussed in Chapter 18. The presence of large numbers of printed books, journals, magazines, and newspapers "fixed" language in a more permanent fashion than did the spoken word. This uniform language found in printed works could overcome regional spoken dialects and establish itself as dominant. In most countries, spoken and written proficiency in the official printed language became a path to social and political advancement. The growth of a uniform language helped to persuade people who had not thought of themselves as constituting a nation that they did so.

---

[1] Arthur O. Lovejoy, *The Great Chain of Being: A Study in the History of an Idea* (New York: Harper Torchbooks, 1963), p. 6.

MEANING OF NATIONHOOD Nationalists used a whole variety of arguments and metaphors to express what they meant by *nationhood*. Some argued that gathering, for example, Italians into a unified Italy or Germans into a unified Germany, thus eliminating the petty dynastic states that governed those regions, would promote economic and administrative efficiency. Adopting a tenet from political liberalism, certain nationalist writers suggested that nations determining their own destinies resembled individuals exploiting personal talents to determine their own careers. Some nationalists claimed that nations, like biological species in the natural world, were distinct creations of God. Other nationalists claimed a place for their nations in the divine order of things. (See "Mazzini Defines Nationality.") Throughout the nineteenth century, for example, Polish nationalists portrayed Poland as the suffer-

Mazzini Defines Nationality

No political force in the nineteenth and twentieth centuries was stronger than nationalism. It eventually replaced dynastic political loyalty with loyalty based on ethnic considerations. It received new standing after World War I when the concept of the self-determination of nations became one of the cornerstones of the Paris Peace Treaties. Still later, former European colonies embraced this powerful idea. In the passage that follows, written in 1835, the Italian nationalist and patriot Giuseppe Mazzini (1805–1872) explains his understanding of the concept. Note how he combines a generally democratic view of politics with a religious concept of the divine destiny of nations. As nationalism actually realized itself in various parts of Europe and the rest of the world, it was not always associated with democratic governments.

❖ *What are the specific qualities of a people that Mazzini associates with nationalism? How and why does Mazzini relate nationalism to divine purposes? How does this view of nationality relate to the goals of liberal freedoms? How might these ideals of nationalism lead to international or domestic conflict?*

The essential characteristics of a nationality are common ideas, common principles and a common purpose. A nation is an association of those who are brought together by language, by given geographical conditions or by the role assigned them by history, who acknowledge the same principles and who march together to the conquest of a single definite goal under the rule of a uniform body of law.

The life of a nation consists in harmonious activity (that is, the employment of all individual abilities and energies comprised within the association) towards this single goal....

But nationality means even more than this. Nationality also consists in the share of mankind's labors which God assigns to a people. This mission is the task which a people must perform to the end that the Divine Idea shall be realized in this world; it is the work which gives a people its rights as a member of Mankind; it is the baptismal rite which endows a people with its own character and its rank in the brotherhood of nations....

Nationality depends for its very existence upon its sacredness within and beyond its borders.

If nationality is to be inviolable for all, friends and foes alike, it must be regarded inside a country as holy, like a religion, and outside a country as a grave mission. It is necessary too that the ideas arising within a country grow steadily, as part of the general law of Humanity which is the source of all nationality. It is necessary that these ideas be shown to other lands in their beauty and purity, free from any alien mixture, from any slavish fears, from any skeptical hesitancy, strong and active, embracing in their evolution every aspect and manifestation of the life of the nation. These ideas, a necessary component in the order of universal destiny, must retain their originality even as they enter harmoniously into mankind's general progress.

The people must be the basis of nationality; its logically derived and vigorously applied principles its means; the strength of all its strength; the improvement of the life of all and the happiness of the greatest possible number its results; and the accomplishment of the task assigned to it by God its goal. This is what we mean by nationality.

From Herbert H. Rowen, ed., *From Absolutism to Revolution, 1648–1848*, 2d ed. © 1969. Reprinted by permission of Prentice-Hall, Inc., Upper Saddle River, NJ, pp. 277, 280.

ing Christ among nations, thus implicitly suggesting that Poland, like Christ, would experience resurrection and a new life.

A significant difficulty for nationalism was, and is, determining which ethnic groups could be considered nations, with claims to territory and political autonomy. In theory, any of them could, but in reality, nationhood came to be associated with groups that were large enough to support a viable economy, that had a history of significant cultural association, that possessed a cultural elite which could nourish and spread the national language, and that had the capacity to conquer other peoples or to establish and protect their own independence. Throughout the century many smaller ethnic groups claimed to fulfill these criteria, but could not effectively achieve either independence or recognition. They could and did, however, create domestic unrest within the political units they inhabited.

REGIONS OF NATIONALISTIC PRESSURE During the nineteenth century, nationalists challenged the political status quo in six major areas of Europe. England had brought Ireland under direct rule in 1800, allowing the Irish to elect members to the British Parliament in Westminster. Irish nationalists, however, wanted independence or at least larger measures of self-government. The "Irish problem," as it was called, would haunt British politics for the next two centuries. German nationalists sought political unity for all German-speaking peoples, challenging the multinational structure of the Austrian Empire and pitting Prussia and Austria against each other. Italian nationalists sought to unify Italian-speaking peoples on the Italian peninsula and to drive out the Austrians. Polish nationalists, targeting primarily their Russian rulers, struggled to restore Poland as an independent nation. In eastern Europe, a whole host of national groups, including Hungarians, Czechs, Slovenes, and others, sought either independence or formal recognition within the Austrian Empire. Finally, in southeastern Europe on the Balkan peninsula and eastward, national groups, including Serbs, Greeks, Albanians, Romanians, and Bulgarians, sought independence from Ottoman and Russian control. Although there were never disturbances in all six areas at one time, any one of them could erupt into turmoil. In each area, nationalist activity ebbed and flowed. The dominant governments often thought that they needed only to repress the activity or ride it out until stability returned. Over the course of the century, however, nationalists changed the political map and political culture of Europe.

Early Nineteenth-Century Political Liberalism

The word *liberal*, as applied to political activity, entered the European and American vocabulary during the nineteenth century. Its meaning has varied over time. Nineteenth-century European conservatives often regarded as *liberal* almost anyone or anything that challenged their own political, social, or religious values. For twentieth-century Americans, the word *liberal* carries with it meanings and connotations that have little or nothing to do with its significance to nineteenth-century Europeans. European conservatives of the last century saw liberals as more radical than they actually were; present-day Americans often think of nineteenth-century liberals as more conservative than they were.

POLITICAL GOALS Nineteenth-century liberals derived their political ideas from the writers of the Enlightenment, the example of English liberties, and the so-called principles of 1789 embodied in the French Declaration of the Rights of Man and Citizen. They sought to establish a political framework of legal equality, religious toleration, and freedom of the press. Their general goal was a political structure that would limit the arbitrary power of government against the persons and property of individual citizens. They generally believed that the legitimacy of government emanated from the freely given consent of the governed. The popular basis of such government was to be expressed through elected representative, or parliamentary, bodies. Most important, free government required that state or crown ministers be responsible to the representatives rather than to the monarch. Liberals sought to achieve these political arrangements through the device of written constitutions. Their desire was to see constitutionalism and constitutional governments installed across the Continent. (See "Benjamin Constant Discusses Modern Liberty.")

These goals may seem very limited, and they were. Responsible constitutional government, however, existed nowhere in Europe in 1815. Even in Great Britain, the cabinet ministers were at least as responsible to the monarch as to the House of Commons. Conservatives were suspicious of written constitutions, associating them with the French Revolution and Napoleonic regimes. They also were certain that not all necessary political wisdom could be reduced to writing.

Those who espoused liberal political structures often were educated, relatively wealthy people, usually associated with the professions or commercial life, who were excluded in one manner or another from the existing political processes. Because of their wealth and education, they felt that their exclusion was unjustified. Liberals were often academics, mem-

Benjamin Constant Discusses Modern Liberty

In 1819, the French liberal theorist Benjamin Constant (1767–1830) delivered lectures on the character of ancient and modern liberty. In the passage given here, he emphasizes the close relationship of modern liberty to economic freedom and a free private life. He then ties the desire for a free private life to the need for representative government.

❖ *According to Constant, what are the specific ways in which a modern citizen is free of government control and interference? What is Constant's defense of representative government? On the basis of this passage, why do you believe that Constant was opposed to democratic government? Compare Constant's views with those of Metternich in the next document.*

[Modern liberty] is, for each individual, the right not to be subjected to anything but the law, not to be arrested, or detained, or put to death, or mistreated in any manner, as a result of the arbitrary will of one or several individuals. It is each man's right to express his opinions, to choose and exercise his profession, to dispose of his property and even abuse it, to come and go without obtaining permission and without having to give an account of either his motives or his itinerary. It is the right to associate with other individuals, either to confer about mutual interests or profess the cult that he and his associates prefer or simply to fill his days and hours in the manner most conforming to his inclinations and fantasies. Finally, it is each man's right to exert influence on the administration of government, either through the election of some or all of its public functionaries, or through remonstrances, petitions, and demands which authorities are more or less obliged to take into account....

Just as the liberty we now require is distinct from that of the ancients, so this new liberty itself requires an organization different from that suitable for ancient liberty. For the latter, the more time and energy a man consecrated to the exercise of his political rights, the more free he believed himself to be. Given the type of liberty to which we are now susceptible, the more the exercise of our political rights leaves us time for our private interests, the more precious we find liberty to be. From this...stems the necessity of the representative system. The representative system is nothing else than an organization through which a nation unloads on several individuals what it cannot and will not do for itself. Poor men handle their own affairs; rich men hire managers. This is the story of ancient and modern nations. The representative system is the power of attorney given to certain men by the mass of the people who want their interests defended but who nevertheless do not always have the time to defend these interests themselves.

From Benjamin Constant, *Ancient and Modern Liberty*, as translated and quoted in Stephen Holmes, *Benjamin Constant and the Making of Modern Liberalism* (New Haven, CT: Yale University Press, 1984), pp. 66, 74.

bers of the learned professions, and people involved in the rapidly expanding commercial and manufacturing segments of the economy. They believed in, and were products of, a career open to talent. The monarchical and aristocratic regimes, as restored after the Congress of Vienna, often failed both to recognize their new status sufficiently and to provide for their economic and professional interests.

Although liberals wanted broader political participation, they did not advocate democracy. What they wanted was to extend representation to the propertied classes. Second only to their hostility to the privileged aristocracies was their general contempt for the lower, unpropertied classes. Liberals transformed the

eighteenth-century concept of aristocratic liberty into a new concept of privilege based on wealth and property rather than birth. As the French liberal theorist Benjamin Constant (1767–1830) wrote in 1814,

Those whom poverty keeps in eternal dependence are no more enlightened on public affairs than children, nor are they more interested than foreigners in national prosperity, of which they do not understand the basis and of which they enjoy the advantages only indirectly. Property alone, by giving sufficient leisure, renders a man capable of exercising his political rights.[2]

[2]Quoted in Frederick B. Artz, *Reaction and Revolution, 1814–1832* (New York: Harper, 1934), p. 94.

By the middle of the century, this widely shared attitude meant that throughout Europe liberals had separated themselves from both the rural and the urban working class, a division that was to have important consequences.

ECONOMIC GOALS The economic goals of nineteenth-century liberals also served to divide them from working people. The manufacturers of Great Britain, the landed and manufacturing middle class of France, and the commercial interests of Germany and Italy, following the Enlightenment ideas of Adam Smith, sought the removal of the economic restraints associated with mercantilism or the regulated economies of enlightened absolutists. They wanted to manufacture and sell goods freely. To that end, they favored the removal of international tariffs and internal barriers to trade. Economic liberals opposed the old paternalistic legislation that established wages and labor practices by government regulation or by guild privileges. They saw labor as simply one more commodity to be bought and sold freely.

Liberals wanted an economic structure in which people were at liberty to use whatever talents and property they possessed to enrich themselves. Such a structure, they contended, would produce more goods and services for everyone at lower prices and provide the basis for material progress.

Because the social and political circumstances of various countries differed, the specific programs of liberals also differed. In Great Britain, the monarchy was already limited and most individual liberties had been secured. With reform, Parliament could provide more nearly representative government. Links between land, commerce, and industry were in place. France likewise had many structures favored by liberals. The Napoleonic Code gave them a modern legal system. They could justify calls for greater rights by appealing to the widely accepted "principles of 1789." As in England, representatives of the different economic interests had worked together. The problem for liberals in both countries was to protect civil liberties, define the respective powers of the monarch and the elected representative body, and expand the electorate moderately while avoiding democracy.

The complex political situation in German-speaking Europe was different from that in France or Britain, and German liberalism differed accordingly from its French and British counterparts. Monarchs and aristocrats offered stiffer resistance to liberal ideas, leaving German liberals less access to direct political influence. A distinct social divide separated the aristocratic landowning classes, which filled the bureaucracies and officer corps, from the small middle-class commercial and industrial interests. There was little or no precedent for middle-class participation in the government or the military and no strong tradition of civil or individual liberty. From the time of Martin Luther through Kant and Hegel, freedom in Germany had meant conformity to a higher moral law rather than participation in politics.

Most German liberals favored a united Germany and looked either to Austria or to Prussia as the instrument of unification. As a result, they were more tolerant of strong state and monarchical power than other liberals were. They believed that a freer social and political order would emerge once unification had been achieved. Unfortunately, the monarchies in Austria and Prussia refused to cooperate with these dreams of unification, leaving German liberals frustrated and forcing them to be satisfied with more modest achievements such as the lowering of internal trade barriers.

RELATIONSHIP OF NATIONALISM TO LIBERALISM Nationalism was not necessarily or even logically linked to liberalism. Indeed, many aspects of nationalism were directly opposed to liberal political values. Some nationalists wished their own particular ethnic group to dominate minority national or ethnic groups within a particular region. This was true of the Hungarian Magyars, who sought political control over non-Magyar peoples living within the historical boundaries of Hungary. Nationalists also often defined their own national group in opposition to other national groups whom they might regard as cultural inferiors or as historical enemies. This darker side of nationalism would emerge starkly in the second half of the nineteenth century and would destructively poison European political life early and late in the twentieth century. Furthermore, conservative nationalists might seek political autonomy for their own ethnic group, but would have no intention of establishing liberal political institutions thereafter.

Nonetheless, although liberalism and nationalism were not identical, they were often compatible. By espousing the cause of representative government, civil liberties, and economic freedom, nationalist groups in one country could gain the support of liberals elsewhere in Europe who might not otherwise share their nationalist interests. Many nationalists in Germany, Italy, and much of the Austrian Empire adopted this tactic. Some nationalists took other symbolic steps to arouse sympathy. Nationalists in Greece, for example, made Athens their capital because they believed that it would associate their struggle for independence with ancient Athenian democracy, which English and French liberals revered.

Conservative Governments: The Domestic Political Order

Despite the challenges of liberalism and nationalism, the domestic political order established by the restored conservative institutions of Europe, particularly in Great Britain and eastern Europe, showed remarkable staying power. Not until World War I did their power and pervasive influence come to an end.

Conservative Outlooks

The major pillars of nineteenth-century conservatism were legitimate monarchies, landed aristocracies, and established churches. The institutions themselves were ancient, but the self-conscious alliance of throne, land, and altar was new. Throughout the eighteenth century, these groups had engaged in frequent conflict. Only the upheavals of the French Revolution and the Napoleonic era transformed them into natural, if sometimes reluctant, allies. In that regard, conservatism as an articulated outlook and set of cooperating institutions was as new a feature on the political landscape as nationalism and liberalism.

The more theoretical political and religious ideas of the conservative classes were associated with thinkers such as Edmund Burke (see Chapter 19) and Friedrich Hegel (see Chapter 20). Conservatives shared other, less formal attitudes forged by the revolutionary experience. The execution of Louis XVI at the hands of a radical democratic government convinced most monarchs that they could trust only aristocratic governments or governments of aristocrats in alliance with the wealthiest middle-class and professional people. The European aristocracies believed that their property and influence would rarely be safe under any form of genuinely representative government. All conservatives spurned the idea of a written constitution unless they were permitted to promulgate the document themselves. Even then, some could not be reconciled to the concept.

The churches were equally apprehensive of popular movements, except their own revivals. The ecclesiastical leaders throughout the Continent regarded themselves as entrusted with the educational task of supporting the social and political status quo. They also feared and hated most of the ideas associated with the Enlightenment, because those rational concepts and reformist writings enshrined the critical spirit and undermined revealed religion.

Conservative aristocrats retained their former arrogance, but not their former privileges or their old confidence. They saw themselves as surrounded by enemies and as standing permanently on the defensive against the forces of liberalism, nationalism, and popular sovereignty. They knew they could be toppled by political groups that hated them. They understood that revolution in one country could spill over into another.

All of the nations of Europe in the years immediately after 1815 confronted problems arising directly from their entering an era of peace after a quarter-century of armed conflict. The war effort, with its loss of life and property and its necessity of organizing people and resources, had distracted attention from other problems. The wartime footing had allowed all the belligerent governments to exercise firm control over their populations. War had fueled economies and had furnished vast areas of employment in armies, navies, military industries, and expanded agricultural activities. The onset of peace meant that citizens could raise new political demands and that there must be a major economic adjustment to peacetime economies. Soldiers and sailors came home and required nonmilitary employment. The vast demand of the military effort on other industries subsided and caused unemployment. The young were no longer growing up in a climate of war and could turn their minds to other issues. For all of these reasons, the conservative statesmen who led every major government in 1815 confronted new pressures that would cause various degrees of domestic unrest and that would lead them to use differing degrees of repressive action.

Liberalism and Nationalism Resisted in Austria and the Germanies

The early-nineteenth-century statesman who more than any other epitomized conservatism was the Austrian prince Metternich (1773–1859). This devoted servant of the Habsburg emperor had been, along with Britain's Viscount Castlereagh (1769–1822), the chief architect of the Vienna settlement. It was he who seemed to exercise chief control over the forces of the European reaction.

DYNASTIC INTEGRITY OF THE HABSBURG EMPIRE The Austrian government could make no serious compromises with the new political forces in Europe. To no other country were the programs of liberalism and nationalism potentially more dangerous. Germans and Hungarians, as well as Poles, Czechs, Slovaks, Slovenes, and other ethnic groups, peopled the Habsburg domains. Through puppet governments Austria also dominated the Italian peninsula.

Metternich Rejects Constitutionalism

Metternich was the chief minister of the Austrian Empire and the statesman who most opposed change in Europe after the Congress of Vienna. In 1820, following disturbances in German-speaking Europe, he wrote a political memoir for the monarchs and ministers who had assembled in the postwar congresses to halt the spread of revolution. In this portion of that memoir, Metternich points to the evil of human presumption, which he sees at the root of political liberalism and the demands for constitutions. Having rejected constitutionalism, he posed his own agenda for conservative monarchs.

❖ *Why might one say that Metternich's critique of presumption is actually a critique of Enlightenment political outlooks? Why does he associate these outlooks with the middle class? How is the changeable character he ascribes to calls for constitutions in different countries related to the political developments discussed in this chapter? How does he believe monarchs should prevent change and foster stability? Compare his views with those of Benjamin Constant in the previous document. How might Mazzini's ideal of nationalism also upset Metternich's agenda?*

Presumption makes every man the guide of his own belief, the arbiter of laws according to which he is pleased to govern himself, or to allow some one else to govern him and his neighbors; it makes him, in short, the sole judge of his own faith, his own actions, and the principles according to which he guides them....

It is principally the middle classes of society which this moral gangrene has affected....

There is...scarcely any epoch which does not offer a rallying cry to some particular factions. This cry, since 1815, has been *Constitution*. But do not let us deceive ourselves: this word, susceptible of great latitude of interpretation would be but imperfectly understood if we supposed that the factions attached quite the same meaning to it under different *régimes*. Such is certainly not the case. In pure monarchies it is qualified by the name of "national representation." In countries which have lately been brought under the representative *régime* [France under the Restoration monarchy] it is called "development," and promises charters and fundamental laws. In the only State which possesses an ancient national representation [Great Britain] it takes "reform" as its object. Everywhere it means change and trouble....

The Governments, having lost their balance, are frightened, intimidated, and thrown into confusion by the cries of the intermediary class of society, which, placed between the Kings and their subjects, breaks the scepter of the monarch, and usurps the cry of the people....The evil is plain....

We are convinced that society can no longer be saved without strong and vigorous resolutions on the part of the Governments still free in their opinions and actions....

The first principle to be followed by the monarchs...should be that of maintaining the stability of political institutions against the disorganized excitement which has taken possession of men's minds....

The first and greatest concern for the immense majority of every nation is the stability of the laws and their uninterrupted action—never their change. Therefore let the Governments govern, let them maintain the groundwork of their institutions....

Let them be just, but strong; beneficent, but strict.

Let them maintain religious principles in all their purity....

Let them suppress Secret Societies, that gangrene of society.

In short, let the great monarchs...prove to the world...that the principles which they profess are paternal and protective, menacing only the disturbers of public tranquillity.

From *Memoirs of Prince Metternich*, Prince Richard Metternich, ed., Mrs. Alexander Napier, trans. (New York: 1880–1882), 3: 458–475, as quoted in Raymond Phineas Stearns, *Pageant of Europe: Sources and Selections from the Renaissance to the Present Day* (New York: Harcourt, Brace and Company, 1848), pp. 470–471.

Prince Klemens von Metternich (1773–1859) epitomized nineteenth-century conservatism. Sir Thomas Lawrence (1769–1830), *Clemens Lothar Wenzel, Prince Metternich (1773–1859)* OM 905 WC 206. The Royal Collection © 2000 Her Majesty Queen Elizabeth II.

So far as Metternich and other Austrian officials were concerned, the recognition of the political rights and aspirations of any of the various national groups would mean the probable dissolution of the empire. If Austria permitted representative government, Metternich feared that the national groups would fight their battles internally at the probable cost of Austrian international influence.

Pursuit of dynastic integrity required Austrian domination of the newly formed German Confederation to prevent the formation of a German national state that might absorb the heart of the empire and exclude the other realms governed by the Habsburgs. The Congress of Vienna had created the German Confederation to replace the defunct Holy Roman Empire. It consisted of thirty-nine states under Austrian leadership. Each state remained more or less autonomous, but Austria was determined to prevent any movement toward constitutionalism in as many of them as possible. (See "Metternich Rejects Constitutionalism.")

DEFEAT OF PRUSSIAN REFORM   An important victory for this holding policy came in Prussia in the years immediately after the Congress of Vienna. In 1815 Frederick William III (r. 1797–1840), caught up in

the exhilaration that followed the War of Liberation, as Germans called the last part of their conflict with Napoleon, had promised some mode of constitutional government. After stalling on keeping his pledge, he formally reneged on it in 1817. Instead, he created a new Council of State, which, although it improved administrative efficiency, was not constitutionally based.

In 1819, the king moved further from reform. After a major disagreement over the organization of the army, his chief reform-minded ministers resigned, to be replaced with hardened conservatives. On their advice, in 1823 Frederick William III established eight provincial estates, or diets. These bodies were dominated by the Junkers and exercised only an advisory function. The old bonds linking monarchy, army, and landholders in Prussia had been reestablished. The members of this alliance would oppose the threats posed by the aspirations of German nationalists to the conservative social and political order.

STUDENT NATIONALISM AND THE CARLSBAD DECREES
Three southern German states—Baden, Bavaria, and Württemberg—had received constitutions after 1815 as their monarchs tried to secure wider political support. None of these constitutions, however, recognized popular sovereignty, and all defined political rights as the gift of the monarch. In the minds and hearts of many young Germans, however, nationalist and liberal expectations fostered by the defeat of the French armies remained alive.

The most important of these groups was composed of university students who had grown up during the days of the reforms of Stein and Hardenberg and the initial circulation of the writings of early German nationalists. Many of them or their friends had fought Napoleon. When they went to the universities, they continued to dream of a united Germany. They formed *Burschenschaften*, or student associations. Like student groups today, these clubs served numerous social functions, one of which was to sever old provincial loyalties and replace them with loyalty to the concept of a united German state. It should also be noted that these clubs were often anti-Semitic.

In 1817 in Jena, one such student club organized a large celebration for the fourth anniversary of the Battle of Leipzig and the tercentenary of Luther's Ninety-five Theses. There were bonfires, songs, and processions as more than 500 people gathered for the festivities. The event made German rulers uneasy, for it was known that some republicans were involved with the student clubs.

Two years later, in March 1819, a young man named Karl Sand (d. 1820), a *Burschenschaft* member, assassinated the conservative dramatist August

In May, 1820, Karl Sand, a German student and a member of a Burschenschaft, *was executed for his murder of the conservative playwright August von Kotzebue the previous year. In the eyes of many young German nationalists, Sand was a political martyr.*
Bildarchiv Preussischer Kulturbesitz

von Kotzebue (1761–1819). Sand, who was tried, condemned, and publicly executed, became a martyr in the eyes of some nationalists. Although the assassin had acted alone, Metternich decided to use the incident to suppress the student clubs and other potential institutions of liberalism.

In July 1819, Metternich persuaded representatives of the major German states to issue the Carlsbad Decrees, which dissolved the *Burschenschaften*. The decrees also provided for university inspectors and press censors. The next year the German Confederation promulgated the Final Act, which limited the subjects that might be discussed in the constitutional chambers of Bavaria, Württemberg, and Baden. The measure also asserted the right of the monarchs to resist demands of constitutionalists. For many years thereafter, the secret police of the various German states harassed potential dissidents. In the opinion of the princes, these included almost anyone who sought even moderate social or political change.

Postwar Repression in Great Britain

The years 1819 and 1820 marked a high tide for conservative influence and repression in western as well as eastern Europe. After 1815, Great Britain experienced two years of poor harvests. At the same time, discharged sailors and soldiers and out-of-work industrial workers swelled the ranks of the unemployed.

LORD LIVERPOOL'S MINISTRY AND POPULAR UNREST The Tory ministry of Lord Liverpool (1770–1828) was unprepared for these problems of postwar dislocation. Instead, it sought to protect the interests of the landed

and other wealthy classes. In 1815, Parliament passed a Corn Law to maintain high prices for domestically produced grain through import duties on foreign grain. The next year, Parliament abolished the income tax paid by the wealthy and replaced it with excise or sales taxes on consumer goods paid by both the wealthy and the poor. These laws continued a legislative trend that marked the abandonment by the British ruling class of its traditional role of paternalistic protector of the poor. In 1799 Parliament had passed the Combination Acts, outlawing workers' organizations or unions. During the war, wage protection had been removed. And many in the taxpaying classes called for the abolition of the Poor Law that provided public relief for the destitute and unemployed.

In light of these policies and the postwar economic downturn, it is hardly surprising that the lower social orders began to doubt the wisdom of their rulers and to call for a reform of the political system. Mass meetings calling for the reform of Parliament were held. Reform clubs were organized. Radical newspapers, such as William Cobbett's *Political Registrar*, demanded political change. In the hungry, restive agricultural and industrial workers, the government could see only images of continental *sans-culottes* crowds ready to hang aristocrats from the nearest lamppost. Government ministers regarded radical leaders, such as Cobbett (1763–1835), Major John Cartwright (1740–1824), and Henry "Orator" Hunt (1773–1835), as demagogues who were seducing the people away from allegiance to their natural leaders.

The government's answer to the discontent was repression. In December 1816, an unruly mass meeting took place at Spa Fields near London. This disturbance provided Parliament an excuse to pass the Coercion Act of March 1817. These measures temporarily suspended habeas corpus and extended existing laws against seditious gatherings.

"PETERLOO" AND THE SIX ACTS This initial repression, in combination with improved harvests, brought calm for a time to the political landscape. By 1819, however, the people were restive again. In the industrial north, many well-organized mass meetings were held to demand the reform of Parliament. The radical reform campaign culminated on August 16, 1819, with a meeting in Manchester at Saint Peter's Fields. Royal troops and the local militia were on hand to ensure order. As the speeches were about to begin, a local magistrate ordered the militia to move into the audience. The result was panic and death. At least eleven people in the crowd were killed; scores were injured. The event became known as the "Peterloo Massacre," a phrase that drew a contemptuous comparison with the victory at Waterloo.

Peterloo had been the act of the local Manchester officials, whom the Liverpool ministry felt it must support. The cabinet also decided to act once and for all to end these troubles. Most of the radical leaders were arrested and taken out of circulation. In December 1819, a few months after the German Carlsbad Decrees, Parliament passed a series of laws called the *Six Acts*, which (1) forbade large unau-thorized, public meetings, (2) raised the fines for seditious libel, (3) speeded up the trials of political agitators, (4) increased newspaper taxes, (5) prohibited the training of armed groups, and (6) allowed local officials to search homes in certain disturbed counties. In effect, the Six Acts attempted to remove the instruments of agitation from the hands of radical leaders and to provide the authorities with new powers.

Two months after the passage of the Six Acts, the Cato Street Conspiracy was unearthed. Under the guidance of a possibly demented figure named Thistlewood, a group of extreme radicals had plotted to blow up the entire British cabinet. The plot was foiled. The leaders were arrested and tried, and four of them were executed. Although little more than a half-baked plot, the conspiracy helped further to discredit the movement for parliamentary reform.

Bourbon Restoration in France

The abdication of Napoleon in 1814 opened the way for a restoration of Bourbon rule in the homeland of the great revolution. The new king was the former count of Provence and a brother of Louis XVI. The son of the executed monarch had died in prison. Royalists had regarded the dead boy as Louis XVII, and so his uncle became Louis XVIII (r. 1814–1824). This fat, awkward man had become a political realist during his more than twenty years of exile. He understood that he could not govern if he attempted to

In August, 1819, local troops dispersed a political rally in Manchester, killing a number of the participants. The event became known as the "Peterloo Massacre." Bildarchiv Preussischer Kulturbesitz

The French Bourbons were restored to the throne in 1815 but would rule only until 1830. This picture shows Louis XVIII, seated, second from left, and his brother, the Count of Artois, who would become Charles X, standing on the left. Notice the bust of Henry IV in the background, placed there to associate the restored rulers with their popular late-sixteenth–early-seventeenth-century forebear.
Bildarchiv Preussischer Kulturbesitz

turn back the clock. France had undergone too many irreversible changes. Consequently, Louis XVIII agreed to become a constitutional monarch, but under a constitution of his own making.

THE CHARTER   The constitution of the French restoration was the Charter. It provided for a hereditary monarchy and a bicameral legislature. The monarch appointed the upper house; the lower house, the Chamber of Deputies, was elected according to a very narrow franchise with a high property qualification. The Charter guaranteed most of the rights enumerated by the Declaration of the Rights of Man and Citizen. There was to be religious toleration, but Roman Catholicism was designated as the official religion of the nation. Most important for thousands of French people at all social levels who had profited from the revolution, the Charter promised not to challenge the property rights of the current owners of land that had been confiscated from aristocrats and the church. With this provision, Louis XVIII hoped to reconcile to his regime those who had benefitted from the revolution.

ULTRAROYALISM   This moderate spirit did not penetrate deeply into the ranks of royalist supporters whose families had suffered at the hands of the revolution. Rallying around the count of Artois (1757–1836), those people who were more royalist than the monarch now demanded their revenge. In the months after Napoleon's final defeat at Waterloo, royalists in the south and west carried out a White Terror against former revolutionaries and supporters of the deposed emperor. The king could do little or nothing to halt this bloodbath. Similar extreme royalist sentiment could be found in the Chamber of Deputies. The ultraroyalist majority

elected in 1816 proved so dangerously reactionary that the king soon dissolved the chamber. The majority returned by the second election was more moderate. Several years of political give-and-take followed with the king making mild accommodations to liberals.

In February 1820, however, the duke of Berri, son of Artois and heir to the throne after his father, was murdered by a lone assassin. The ultraroyalists persuaded Louis XVIII that the murder was the result of his ministers' cooperation with liberal politicians, and the king responded with repressive measures. Electoral laws were revised to give wealthy electors two votes. Press censorship was imposed, and people suspected of dangerous political activity were made subject to easy arrest. By 1821, the government placed secondary education under the control of the Roman Catholic bishops.

All these actions revealed the basic contradiction of the French restoration. By the early 1820s, the veneer of constitutionalism had worn away. Liberals were being driven out of politics and into a near-illegal status.

The Conservative International Order

At the Congress of Vienna, the major powers—Russia, Austria, Prussia, and Great Britain—had agreed to consult with each other from time to time on matters affecting Europe as a whole. Such consultation was one of the new departures in international relations achieved by the Congress. The vehicle for this consultation was a series of postwar congresses, or conferences. Later, as differences arose among the powers, the consultations became more informal. This new arrangement for resolving mutual foreign policy issues was known as the *Concert of Europe.* It prevented one nation from taking a major action in international affairs without the assent of the others. The initial goal of the Concert of Europe was to maintain the balance of power against new French aggression and against the military might of Russia. The Concert continued to function, however, on large and small issues until the third quarter of the century. Its goal—a novel one in European affairs—was to maintain the peace. In that respect, although the great powers sought to maintain conservative domestic governments, they were making genuinely new departures in regulating their international relations.

The Congress System

In the years immediately following the Congress of Vienna, the new congress system of mutual cooperation and consultation functioned well. The first congress took place in 1818 at Aix-la-Chapelle. As a result of this gathering, the four major powers re-

Tsar Alexander I (r. 1801–1825). A mild reformer when he succeeded to the throne, Alexander became increasingly reactionary after 1815. Corbis

moved their troops from France, which had paid its war reparations, and readmitted that nation to good standing among European nations. Despite unanimity on these decisions, the conference was not without friction. Tsar Alexander I (r. 1801–1825) suggested that the Quadruple Alliance (see Chapter 20) agree to uphold the borders and the existing governments of all European countries. Castlereagh, representing Britain, flatly rejected the proposal. He contended that the Quadruple Alliance was intended only to prevent future French aggression. These disagreements appeared somewhat academic until a series of revolutions began in southern Europe in 1820.

The Spanish Revolution of 1820

When the Bourbon Ferdinand VII of Spain (r. 1814–1833) was placed on his throne following Napoleon's downfall, he had promised to govern according to a written constitution. Once securely in power, however, he ignored his pledge, dissolved the *Cortés* (the parliament), and ruled alone. In 1820 a group of army officers who were about to be sent to suppress revolution in Spain's Latin American colonies rebelled. In March, Ferdinand once again announced that he would abide by the provisions of the constitution. For the time being, the revolution had succeeded.

Almost at the same time, in July 1820, revolution erupted in Naples, where the king of the Two Sicilies quickly accepted a constitution. There were other, lesser revolts in Italy, but none of them succeeded.

These events frightened the ever-nervous Metternich. Italian disturbances were especially troubling to him. Austria hoped to dominate the peninsula to provide a buffer against the spread of revolution on its own southern flank. The other powers were divided on the best course of action. Britain opposed joint intervention in either Italy or Spain. Metternich turned to Prussia and Russia, the other members of the Holy Alliance formed in 1815, for support. The three eastern powers, along with unofficial delegations from Britain and France, met at the Congress of Troppau in late October 1820. Led by Tsar Alexander, the members of the Holy Alliance issued the Protocol of Troppau. This declaration asserted that stable governments might intervene to restore order in countries experiencing revolution. Yet even Russia hesitated to authorize Austrian intervention in Italian affairs. That decision was finally reached in January 1821 at the Congress of Laibach. Shortly thereafter, Austrian troops marched into Naples and restored the king of the Two Sicilies to nonconstitutional government. Thenceforth, Metternich attempted to foster policies that would improve the efficient administration of the various Italian governments so as to give them more direct local support.

The final postwar congress took place in October 1822 at Verona. Its primary purpose was to resolve the situation in Spain. Once again, Britain balked at joint action. Shortly before the meeting, Castlereagh had committed suicide. George Canning (1770–1827), the new foreign minister, was much less sympathetic to Metternich's goals. At Verona, Britain, in effect, withdrew from continental affairs. Austria, Prussia, and Russia agreed to support French intervention in Spain. In April 1823, the French army crossed the Pyrenees, and within a few months it brutally suppressed the Spanish revolution and established its temporary occupation of the country, which ended in 1827.

What did not happen in Spain, however, was as important for the new international order as what did happen. The intervention had not been used as an excuse to aggrandize French power or territory. The same had been true of all the interventions under the congress system. Despite the conservative intention of the various interventions from the standpoint of domestic politics, they did not represent decisions taken by the great powers to achieve territorial conquest. Rather, they sought the maintenance of the international order established at Vienna. Such a situation stood in sharp contrast to the various alliances to invade or confiscate territory that had been forged among the European powers during the eighteenth century and the wars of the French Revolution and Napoleon. It was just this new mode of international restraint through formal and informal consultation that prevented war until the middle of the century and a general European conflict until 1914. As one historian has commented, "The statesmen of the Vienna generation...did not so much fear war because they thought it would bring revolution as because they had learned from bitter experience that war was revolution."[3]

There was a second diplomatic result of the Congress of Verona and the Spanish intervention. George Canning was much more interested in the fate of British commerce and trade than Castlereagh had been. Thus, Canning sought to prevent the politics of European reaction from being extended to Spain's colonies in Latin America, which were then in revolt (to be discussed later). He intended to exploit these South American revolutions to break the old Spanish trading monopoly with its colonies and gain access for Britain to Latin American trade. To that end, the British foreign minister supported the American Monroe Doctrine in 1823, prohibiting further colonization and intervention by European powers in the Americas. Britain soon recognized the Spanish colonies as independent states. Through the rest of the century, British commercial interests dominated Latin America. In this fashion, Canning may be said to have brought the War of Jenkins's Ear (1739) to a successful conclusion.

The Greek Revolution of 1821

While the powers were plotting conservative interventions in Italy and Spain, a third Mediterranean revolt erupted, in Greece. The Greek revolution became one of the most famous of the century, because it attracted the support and participation of many illustrious literary figures. Liberals throughout Europe, who were seeing their own hopes crushed at home, imagined that the ancient Greek democracy was being reborn. Lord Byron went to fight in Greece and died in 1824 in the cause of Greek liberty. Philhellenic societies were founded in nearly every major country.

The Greeks were rebelling against the Ottoman Empire. The weakness of that empire troubled Europe throughout the nineteenth century, raising what was known as "the Eastern question": What should the European powers do about Ottoman inability to assure political and administrative stability in its holdings in and around the eastern Mediterranean? Most of the major powers had a keen interest in those territories. Russia and Austria coveted land in the Balkans. France and Britain were concerned with the empire's commerce and with control of key naval positions in the eastern Mediterranean.

The Period of Political Reaction	
1814	French monarchy restored
1815	Russia, Austria, Prussia form Holy Alliance
1815	Russia, Austria, Prussia, and Britain renew Quadruple Alliance
1818	Congress of Aix-la-Chapelle
1819 (July)	Carlsbad Decrees
1819 (August 16)	Peterloo Massacre
1819 (December)	Great Britain passes Six Acts
1820 (January)	Spanish revolution
1820 (October)	Congress of Troppau
1821 (January)	Congress of Laibach
1821 (February)	Greek revolution
1822	Congress of Verona
1823	France helps crush Spanish revolution

[3]Paul W. Schroeder, *The Transformation of European Politics, 1763–1848* (Oxford: Clarendon Press, 1994), p. 802.

Also at issue was access for Christians to the shrines in the Holy Land. The goals of the great powers often conflicted with the desire for independence of the many national groups in the Ottoman Empire. But because the powers had little desire to strengthen the empire, they were often more sympathetic to nationalistic aspirations there than elsewhere in Europe.

These conflicting interests, as well as mutual distrust, prevented any direct intervention in Greek affairs for several years. Eventually, however, Britain, France, and Russia concluded that an independent Greece would benefit their strategic interests and would not threaten their domestic security. In 1827 they signed the Treaty of London, demanding Turkish recognition of Greek independence, and sent a joint fleet to support the Greek revolt. In 1828 Russia sent troops into the Ottoman holdings in what is today Romania, ultimately gaining control of that territory in 1829 with the Treaty of Adrianople. The treaty also stipulated that the Turks would allow Britain, France, and Russia to decide the future of Greece. In 1830, a second Treaty of London declared Greece an independent kingdom. Two years later, Otto I (r. 1832–1862), the son of the king of Bavaria, was chosen to be the first king of the new Greek royal dynasty.

Serbian Independence

The year 1830 also saw the establishment of a second independent state on the Balkan peninsula. Since the late eighteenth century, Serbia had sought independence from the Ottoman Empire. During the Napoleonic wars, its fate had been linked to Russian policy and Russian relations to the Ottoman Empire. Between 1804 and 1813, a remarkable leader, Karageorge (1762–1817), had led a guerilla war against the Ottoman authorities. This ultimately unsuccessful revolution helped build national self-identity and attracted the interest of the great powers.

In 1815 and 1816, a new leader, Milos (1780–1860), succeeded in negotiating greater administrative autonomy for some Serbian territory, but a majority of Serbs lived outside the borders of this new entity. In 1830 the Ottoman sultan formally granted independence to Serbia, and by the late 1830s the major powers had also extended it their recognition. The political structure of the new nation, however, remained in doubt for many years after 1830.

In 1833 Milos, now a hereditary prince, pressured the Ottoman authorities to extend the borders of Serbia, which they did. These new boundaries persisted until 1878. Serbian leaders continued to seek additional territory, however, creating tensions with Austria. The status of minorities, particularly Muslims, within Serbian territory, also created tensions.

Beginning in the mid-twenties, Russia became Serbia's formal protector, despite the Austrian territory that separated them. In 1856 Serbia came under the collective protection of the great powers, but the special relationship between Russia and Serbia would continue until the First World War and would play a decisive role in the outbreak of that conflict.

The Wars of Independence in Latin America

The wars of the French Revolution and, more particularly, those of Napoleon sparked movements for independence from European domination throughout Latin America. In less than two decades, between 1804 and 1824, France was driven from Haiti, Portugal lost control of Brazil, and Spain was forced to withdraw from all of its American empire except Cuba and Puerto Rico. Three centuries of Iberian colonial government over the South American continent came to an end. (See Map 21–1.)

Haiti achieved independence in 1804, following a slave revolt led by Toussaint L'Ouverture (1746–1803) and Jean-Jacques Dessalines (1758–1806) that began

Toussaint L'Ouverture (1743–1803) began the revolt that led to Haitian independence in 1804. Corbis

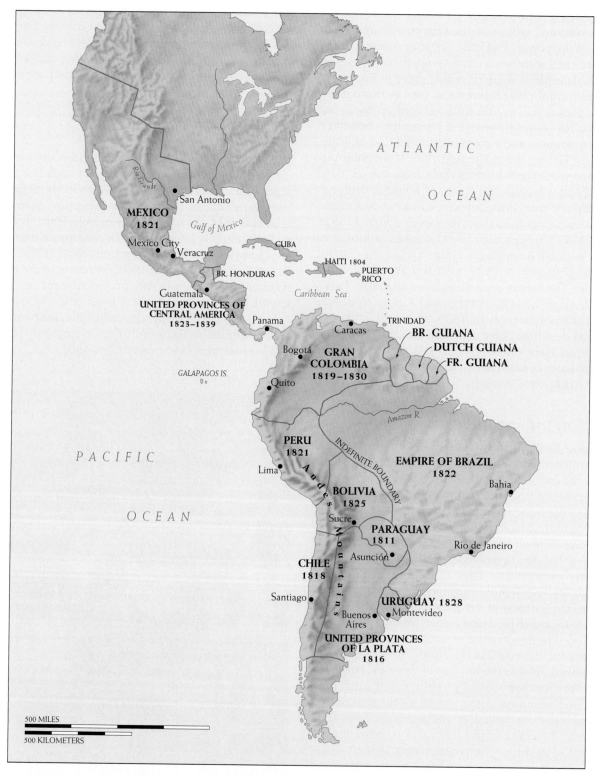

MAP 21–1 LATIN AMERICA IN 1830. *By 1830, Latin America had been liberated from European government. This map shows the initial borders of the states of the region, with the dates of their independence. The United Provinces of La Plata formed the nucleus of what later became Argentina.*

in 1794. Haiti's revolution, which involved the popular uprising of a repressed social group, proved to be the great exception in the Latin American drive for liberty from European masters. Generally speaking, on the South American continent it was the Creole elite—merchants, landowners, and professional people of Spanish descent—that led the movements against Spain and Portugal. Very few Native Americans, blacks, *mestizos*, mulattos, or slaves became involved in or benefitted from the end of Iberian rule. Indeed, the example of the Haitian slave revolt haunted the Creoles, as did the revolts of Indians in the Andes in 1780 and 1781. The Creoles were determined that any drive for political independence from Spain and Portugal should not cause social disruption or the loss of their existing social and economic privileges. In this respect, the Creole revolutionaries were not unlike American revolutionaries in the southern colonies who wanted to reject British rule but keep their slaves, or French revolutionaries who wanted to depose the king but not to extend liberty to the French working class.

CREOLE DISCONTENT   Creole discontent with Spanish colonial government had many sources. (The Brazilian situation will be discussed separately.) Latin American merchants wanted to trade more freely within the region and with North American and European markets. They wanted commercial regulations that would benefit them rather than Spain. They had also experienced increases in taxation by the Spanish crown.

Creoles were deeply resentful of Spanish policies favoring *peninsulares*—whites born in Spain—for political patronage, including appointments in the colonial government, church, and army. The Creoles believed that the *peninsulares* improperly secured all the best positions. Seen in this light, the royal patronage system represented another device with which Spain extracted wealth and income from America for its own people rather than its colonial subjects.

Creole leaders had read the Enlightenment *philosophes* and regarded their reforms as potentially beneficial to the region. They were also well aware of the events and the political philosophy of the American Revolution. Something more than reform programs and revolutionary example, however, was required to transform Creole discontent into revolt against the Spanish government. That transforming event occurred in Europe when Napoleon toppled the Portuguese monarchy in 1807 and the Spanish government in 1808 and then placed his own brother on the thrones of both countries. The Portuguese royal family fled to Brazil and established its government there. But the Bourbon monarchy of Spain stood, for the time being, wholly vanquished. That situation created an imperial political vacuum throughout Spanish Latin America and provided both the opportunity and the necessity for action by Creole leaders.

The Creole elite feared that a liberal Napoleonic monarchy in Spain would attempt to impose reforms in Latin America that would harm their economic and social interests. They also feared that a Spanish monarchy controlled by France would try to drain the region of the wealth and resources needed for Napoleon's wars. To protect their interests and to seize the opportunity to take over direction of their own political destiny, between 1808 and 1810 various Creole *juntas*, or political committees, claimed the right to govern different regions of Latin America. Many of them quite insincerely declared that they were ruling in the name of the deposed Spanish monarch Ferdinand VII. After the establishment of these local *juntas*, the Spanish would not again directly govern the continent; following ten years of politically and economically exhausting warfare, they were required to make Latin American independence permanent. The establishment of the *juntas* also ended the privileges of the *peninsulares*, whose welfare had always depended on the favors of the Spanish crown, and made positions in the government and army more easily available to Creoles.

SAN MARTÍN IN RIO DE LA PLATA   The vast size of Latin America, its geographical barriers, its distinct regional differences, and the absence of an even marginally integrated economy meant that there would be several different paths to independence. The first region to assert itself was the Rio de la Plata, or modern Argentina. The center of revolt was Buenos Aires, whose citizens, as early as 1806, had fought off a British invasion against the Spanish commercial monopoly and thus had learned that they could look to themselves rather than Spain for effective political and military action. In 1810 the *junta* in Buenos Aires not only thrust off Spanish authority, but also sent forces into both Paraguay and Uruguay in the cause of liberation from Spain and control by their own region. The armies were defeated, but Spanish control was nonetheless lost in the two areas. Paraguay asserted its own independence. Uruguay was eventually absorbed by Brazil.

The Buenos Aires government was not discouraged by these early defeats and remained determined to liberate Peru, the greatest stronghold of royalist power and loyalty on the continent. By 1814, José de San Martín (1778–1850) had become the leading general of the Río de la Plata forces. He organized a disciplined army and led his forces in a daring march over the Andes Mountains. By early 1817, he had occupied Santiago in Chile, where the Chilean independence leader Bernardo O'Higgins (1778–1842) was established as supreme dictator. From Santiago, San Martín oversaw the construction and organization of a naval force that, in 1820, he employed to carry his army by sea to an assault on Peru. The next year, San Martín drove royalist forces from Lima and took for himself the title of Protector of Peru.

SIMON BOLÍVAR'S LIBERATION OF VENEZUELA While the army of San Martín had been liberating the southern portion of the continent, Simón Bolívar (1783–1830) had been pursuing a similar task in the north. Bolívar had been involved in the organization of a liberating *junta* in Caracas, Venezuela, in 1810. He was a firm advocate of both independence and republican modes of government. Between 1811 and 1814, civil war broke out throughout Venezuela as both royalists, on one hand, and slaves and *llaneros* (Venezuelan cowboys), on the other, challenged the authority of the republican government. Bolívar had to go into exile first in Colombia and then in Jamaica. In 1816, with help from Haiti, he launched a new invasion against Venezuela. He first captured Bogotá, capital of New Granada (including modern Colombia, Bolivia, and Ecuador), to secure a base for attack on Venezuela. The tactic worked. By the summer of 1821, Bolívar's forces had captured Caracas and he had been named president.

Simón Bolívar was the liberator of much of Latin America. He inclined toward a policy of political liberalism. Hulton/Corbis

A year later, in July 1822, the armies of Bolívar and San Martín joined as they moved to liberate Quito. At a famous meeting of the two liberators in Guayaquil, a sharp disagreement occurred about the future political structure of Latin America. San Martín believed that monarchies were required; Bolívar maintained his republicanism. Not long after the meeting, San Martín quietly retired from public life and went into exile in Europe. Meanwhile, Bolívar purposefully allowed the political situation in Peru to fall into confusion, and in 1823 he sent in troops to establish his control. On December 9, 1824, at the Battle of Ayacucho, the Spanish royalist forces suffered a major defeat at the hands of the liberating army. This battle marked the conclusion of the Spanish effort to retain their American empire.

INDEPENDENCE IN NEW SPAIN The drive for independence in New Spain, which included present-day Mexico as well as Texas, California, and the rest of the southwest United States, illustrates better than that in any other region the socially conservative outcome of the Latin American colonial revolutions. As elsewhere, a local governing *junta* was organized. Before it had undertaken any significant measures, however, a Creole priest, Miguel Hidalgo y Costilla (1753–1811), issued a call for rebellion to the Indians in his parish. They and other repressed groups of black and *mestizo* urban and rural workers responded. Father Hidalgo set forth a program of social change, including hints of changes in land-holding. Soon he stood at the head of a loosely organized group of 80,000 followers, who captured several major cities and then marched on Mexico City. Hidalgo's forces and the royalist army that opposed them committed many atrocities. In July 1811, the revolutionary priest was captured and executed. Leadership of his movement then fell to José María Morelos y Pavón (1765–1815), a *mestizo* priest. Far more radical than Hidalgo, he called for an end to forced labor and for substantial land reforms. He was executed in 1815, ending five years of popular uprising.

The uprising and its demand for fundamental social reforms united all conservative political groups in Mexico, both Creole and Spanish. These groups were unwilling to undertake any kind of reform that might cause loss of their privileges. In 1820, however, they found their recently achieved security challenged from an unexpected source. As already explained, the revolution in Spain had forced Ferdinand VII to accept a liberal constitution. Conservative Mexicans feared that the new liberal monarchy would attempt to impose liberal reforms on Mexico. Therefore, for the most conservative of reasons,

Father Miguel Hidalgo y Costilla (d. 1811) led an unsuccessful peasant revolt in 1810–1811 that marked the beginning of Mexico's struggle for independence.
Reproduced with permission of the General Secretariat of the Organization of American States.

they rallied behind a former royalist general, Augustín de Iturbide (1783–1824), who declared Mexico independent of Spain in 1812. Shortly thereafter, Iturbide was declared emperor. His own regime did not last long, but an independent Mexico, governed by persons determined to resist any significant social reform, had been created.

BRAZILIAN INDEPENDENCE Brazilian independence, in contrast to that of Spanish Latin America, came relatively simply and peacefully. As already noted, the Portuguese royal family, along with several thousand government officials and members of the court, took refuge in Brazil in 1807. Their arrival immediately transformed Rio de Janeiro into a court city. The prince regent João addressed many of the local complaints, equivalent to those of the Spanish Creoles, by, for example, taking measures that expanded trade. In 1815 he made Brazil a kingdom, which meant that it was no longer to be regarded merely as a colony of Portugal. This change was in many respects long overdue, since Brazil

was far larger and more prosperous than Portugal itself. Then, in 1820, a revolution occurred in Portugal, and its leaders demanded João's return to Lisbon. They also demanded the return of Brazil to colonial status. João, who had become João VI in 1816 (r. 1816–1826), returned to Portugal, but left his son Dom Pedro as regent in Brazil and encouraged him to be sympathetic to the political aspirations of the Brazilians. In September 1822, Dom Pedro embraced the cause of Brazilian independence against the recolonizing efforts of Portugal. By the end of the year, he had become emperor of an independent Brazil, which maintained an imperial form of government until 1889. Thus, in contrast to virtually all other nations of Latin America, Brazil achieved independence in a way that left no real dispute as to where the center of political authority lay.

Two other factors aided the peaceful transition to independence in Brazil. First, the political leaders of Brazil were frightened by the destruction that had been unloosed in the Spanish American Empire by the wars of independence. They wanted to avoid that experience. Second, the political and social elite in Brazil had every intention of preserving slavery. The wars of independence elsewhere had generally led to the abolition of slavery or moved the independent states closer to abolition. Any attempt to gain independence from Portugal through warfare might have caused social as well as political turmoil that would open the slavery question.

CONSEQUENCES OF LATIN AMERICAN INDEPENDENCE The era of the wars of independence left Latin America liberated from direct colonial control but economically exhausted and politically unstable. Only Brazil prospered immediately. Independence there had come peacefully and resulted in the establishment of a clearly recognized political authority prepared to pursue policies desired by the economic elite. In contrast to Brazil, the new republics of the former Spanish Empire felt weak and vulnerable. Because the wars of independence had been largely civil wars, disaffected populations threatened all the new governments. Economic life contracted, and in 1830 overall production was lower than it had been in 1800. Mines had fallen into disrepair or had been flooded. Livestock had been confiscated or destroyed. There were few institutions to foster interregional trade or address the difficult terrain that impeded it. The disruption of old trade patterns reduced overseas trade. Funds for investment were scarce. Many wealthy *peninsulares* returned to Spain or went to Cuba. Consequently, Latin American governments and businesses looked to Britain for protection and for markets and capital investment.

The Conservative Order Shaken in Europe

During the first half of the 1820s, the institutions of the restored conservative order had in general successfully resisted the forces of liberalism. The two exceptions to this success, the Greek Revolution and the Latin American wars of independence, both occurred on the periphery of the European world. Beginning in the middle of the 1820s, however, the conservative governments of Russia, France, and Great Britain faced new stirrings of political discontent. (See Map 21–2.) In Russia the result was suppression, in France revolution, and in Britain, accommodation.

Russia: The Decembrist Revolt of 1825

Tsar Alexander I had come to the Russian throne in 1801 after a palace coup against his father, Tsar Paul (r. 1796–1801). After a brief flirtation with Enlightenment ideas, Alexander turned permanently away from reform. Both at home and abroad, he took the lead in suppressing liberalism and nationalism.

There would be no significant challenge to tsarist autocracy until his death.

UNREST IN THE ARMY As Russian forces drove Napoleon's army across Europe and then occupied defeated France, many Russian officers were exposed to the ideas of the French Revolution and the Enlightenment. Some of them, realizing how economically backward and politically stifled their own nation remained, developed reformist sympathies. Unable to express themselves openly because of Alexander's repressive policies, they formed secret societies. One of these, the Southern Society, was led by an officer named Pestel. It advocated representative government and the abolition of serfdom. Pestel himself even favored limited independence for Poland and democracy. Another secret society, the Northern Society, was more moderate. It favored constitutional monarchy and the abolition of serfdom, but wanted protection for the interests of the aristocracy. Both societies were very small and often in conflict with each other. They agreed only that Russia's government must change. Sometime during 1825, they apparently decided to carry out a coup d'état in 1826.

When the Moscow regiment refused to swear allegiance to Nicholas, he ordered the cavalry and artillery to attack them. Although a total failure, the Decembrist Revolt came to symbolize the yearnings of all Russian liberals in the nineteenth century for a constitutional government. The Insurrection of the Decembrists at Senate Square, St. Petersburg on 26th December, 1825 (w/c on paper) by Russian School (19th century). Private Collection/Bridgeman Art Library, London/Novosti

MAP 21–2 CENTERS OF REVOLUTION, 1820–1831 *The conservative order imposed by the great powers in post-Napoleonic Europe was challenged by various uprisings and revolutions, beginning in 1820–1821 in Spain, Naples, and Greece and spreading to Russia, Poland, France, and Belgium later in the decade.*

DYNASTIC CRISIS In late November 1825, Tsar Alexander I died unexpectedly. His death created two crises. The first was dynastic. Alexander had no direct heir. His brother Constantine, the next in line to the throne and at the time the commander of Russian forces in occupied Poland, had married a woman who was not of royal blood. He had thus excluded himself from the throne and was more than willing to renounce any claim to it. Through a series of secret instructions made public only after his death, Alexander had named his younger brother, Nicholas (r. 1825–1855), as the new tsar.

Once Alexander was dead, the legality of these instructions became uncertain. Constantine acknowledged Nicholas as tsar, and Nicholas acknowledged Constantine. This family muddle continued for about three weeks, during which, to the astonishment of all Europe, Russia actually had no ruler. Then, during the early days of December, the army command reported to Nicholas the existence of a conspiracy among certain officers. Able to wait no longer for the working out of legal niceties, Nicholas had himself declared tsar, much to the delight of the by-now-exasperated Constantine.

The second crisis then proceeded to unfold. Several junior officers had indeed plotted to rally the troops under their command to the cause of reform. On December 26, 1825, the army was to take the oath of allegiance to Nicholas, who was less popular than Constantine and who was regarded as more conservative. Nearly all regiments took the oath. But the Moscow regiment, whose chief officers, surprisingly, were not secret society members, marched into the Senate Square in Saint Petersburg and refused to swear allegiance. Instead, they called for a constitution and the installation of Constantine as tsar. Attempts to settle the situation peacefully failed. Late in the afternoon, Nicholas ordered the cavalry and the artillery to attack the insurgents. More than sixty people were killed. Early in 1826, Nicholas himself presided over the commission that investigated the Decembrist Revolt and the secret army societies. Five of the plotters were executed and more than 100 others were exiled to Siberia.

Although the Decembrist Revolt failed completely, it was the first rebellion in modern Russian history whose instigators had had specific political goals. They wanted constitutional government and the abolition of serfdom. As the century passed, the Decembrists, in their political martyrdom, came to symbolize the yearnings of all the never very numerous Russian liberals.

THE AUTOCRACY OF NICHOLAS I Although Nicholas was neither an ignorant nor a bigoted reactionary, he came to symbolize the most extreme form of nineteenth-century autocracy. He knew that economic growth and social improvement in Russia required reform, but he was quite simply afraid of change. In 1842 he told his State Council, "There is no doubt that serfdom, in its present form, is a flagrant evil which everyone realizes, yet to attempt to remedy it now would be, of course, an evil more disastrous."[4] To remove serfdom would necessarily, in his view, have undermined the nobles' support of the tsar. So Nicholas turned his back on this and practically all other reforms. Literary and political censorship and a widespread system of secret police flourished throughout his reign. There was little attempt to forge even an efficient and honest administration. The only significant reform of his rule was a codification of Russian law, published in 1833.

OFFICIAL NATIONALITY In place of reform, Nicholas and his closest advisers embraced a program called Official Nationality. Presiding over this program was Count S. S. Uvarov, minister of education from 1833 to 1849. Its slogan, published repeatedly in government documents, newspapers, journals, and schoolbooks, was "Orthodoxy, Autocracy, and Nationalism." The Russian Orthodox faith was to provide the basis for morality, education, and intellectual life. The church, which, since the days of Peter the Great, had been an arm of the secular government, controlled the schools and universities. Young Russians were taught to accept their place in life and to spurn social mobility.

[4]Quoted in Michael T. Florinsky, *Russia: A History and an Interpretation*, Vol. 2 (New York: Macmillan, 1953), p. 755.

The program of autocracy championed the unrestrained power of the tsar as the only authority that could hold the vast expanse of Russia and its peoples together. Political writers stressed that only under the autocracy of Peter the Great, Catherine the Great, and Alexander I had Russia prospered and exerted a major influence on world affairs.

Through the glorification of Russian nationality, Russians were urged to see their religion, language, and customs as a source of perennial wisdom that separated them from the moral corruption and political turmoil of the West. One result of this program was to leave serious Russian intellectuals profoundly alienated from the tsarist government.

REVOLT AND REPRESSION IN POLAND   Nicholas I was also extremely conservative in foreign affairs, as became apparent in Poland in the 1830s. That nation, which had been partitioned in the late eighteenth century and ceased to exist as an independent state, remained under Russian domination after the Congress of Vienna, but was granted a constitutional government. Under this arrangement, the tsar was Poland's ruler. Both Alexander and Nicholas delegated their brother, the Grand Duke Constantine (1779–1831), to run Poland's government. Although both tsars frequently infringed on the constitution and quarreled with the Polish diet, this arrangement held through the 1820s. Nevertheless, Polish nationalists continued to agitate for change.

In late November 1830, after news of the French and Belgian revolutions of that summer had reached Poland, a small insurrection of soldiers and students broke out in Warsaw. Disturbances soon spread throughout the rest of the country. On December 18, the Polish diet declared the revolution to be a nationalist movement. Early the next month, the diet voted to depose Nicholas as ruler of Poland. The tsar reacted by sending troops into the country and firmly suppressing the revolt. In February 1832, Nicholas issued the Organic Statute, declaring Poland to be an integral part of the Russian Empire. (See "Russia Reasserts Its Authority in Poland.") Although this statute guaranteed certain Polish liberties, the guarantees were systematically ignored. The Polish uprising had confirmed all the tsar's worst fears. Henceforth Russia and Nicholas became the *gendarme* of Europe, ever ready to provide troops to suppress liberal and nationalist movements.

Revolution in France (1830)

The Polish revolt was the most distant of several disturbances that flowed from the overthrow of the Bourbon dynasty in France during July 1830. When Louis XVIII had died in 1824, his brother, the count of Artois, the leader of the ultraroyalist faction at the time of the restoration, succeeded him as Charles X (r. 1824–1830). The new king was a firm believer in rule by divine right.

THE REACTIONARY POLICIES OF CHARLES X   Charles X's first action was to have the Chamber of Deputies in 1824 and 1825 indemnify aristocrats who had lost their lands in the revolution. He did this by lowering the interest rates on government bonds to create a fund to pay an annual sum to the survivors of the *émigrés* who had forfeited land. Middle-class bondholders, who lost income, naturally resented this measure. In another action, Charles restored the rule of primogeniture, whereby only the eldest son of an aristocrat inherited the family domains. And, in support of the Roman Catholic Church, he enacted a law that punished sacrilege with imprisonment or death. Liberals disapproved of all of these measures.

In the elections of 1827, the liberals gained enough seats in the Chamber of Deputies to compel conciliatory actions from the king. He appointed a less conservative ministry. Laws against the press and those allowing the government to dominate education were eased. The liberals, however, wanted a genuinely constitutional regime and remained unsatisfied. In 1829, the king decided that his policy of accommodation had failed. He replaced his moderate ministry with an ultraroyalist ministry headed by the Prince de Polignac (1780–1847). The opposition, in desperation, opened negotiations with the liberal Orléanist branch of the royal family.

THE JULY REVOLUTION   In 1830 Charles X called for new elections, in which the liberals scored a stunning victory. Instead of accommodating the new Chamber of Deputies, the king and his ministers decided to attempt a royalist seizure of power. In June and July 1830, Polignac had sent a naval expedition against Algeria. Reports of its victory and the founding of a French empire in North Africa reached Paris on July 9. Taking advantage of the euphoria created by this victory, Charles issued the Four Ordinances on July 25, 1830, staging what amounted to a royal coup d'état. These ordinances restricted freedom of the press, dissolved the recently elected Chamber of Deputies, restricted the franchise to the wealthiest people in the country, and called for new elections under the new royalist franchise.

The Four Ordinances provoked swift and decisive popular political reactions. Liberal newspapers called on the nation to reject the monarch's actions. The laboring populace of Paris, burdened since 1827 by an economic downturn, took to the streets and erected barricades. The king called out troops, and more than 1,800 people died during the ensuing battles in the city.

Russia Reasserts Its Authority in Poland

As a result of the three eighteenth-century partitions by Russia, Prussia, and Austria, an independent Poland had disappeared from the map of Europe. Russia governed the largest portion of the partitioned Polish lands. During 1830, Poland rebelled against Russian administration. The revolt failed after several months. Tsar Nicholas I then imposed even more direct and repressive control over Poland. This action constituted a direct rejection of the principle of nationalism, and Polish independence would become one of the major nationalist causes of the nineteenth century. An independent Poland emerged only as a result of the Paris Peace Settlement following World War I.

❖ *In what variety of specific ways does this proclamation attempt to offend and repress Polish nationalism? What rights are given to the Poles? What evidence is there of any institutions being established to protect those rights? Is there anything in the proclamation aimed at gaining the support of some parts of the Polish population? Compare this proclamation with the values espoused by Mazzini's vision of nationalism.*

Now that an end has been put by force of arms to the rebellion in Poland, and that the nation, led away by agitators, has returned to its duty, and is restored to tranquillity, we deem it right to carry into execution our plan with regard to the introduction of the new order of things, whereby the tranquillity and union of the two nations, which Providence has entrusted to our care, may be forever guarded against new attempts....The kingdom of Poland, again subject to our sceptre, will regain tranquillity, and again flourish in the bosom of peace, restored to it under the auspices of a vigilant government. Hence we consider it one of our most sacred duties to watch with paternal care over the welfare of our faithful subjects, and to use every means in our power to prevent the recurrence of similar catastrophes, by taking from the ill-disposed the power of disturbing public tranquillity....

Art. 1. The kingdom of Poland is forever to be reunited to the Russian empire and form an inseparable part of that empire....

Art. 2. The Crown of the kingdom of Poland is hereditary in our person and in our heirs and successors, agreeably to the order of succession to the throne prescribed by all the Russians.

Art. 3. The Coronation of the Emperors of all the Russians and Kings of Poland shall be one and the same ceremonial which shall take place at Moscow, in the presence of a deputation from the kingdom of Poland, which shall assist at that solemnity with the deputies from the other parts of the empire....

Art. 5. The freedom of worship is guaranteed....The Roman Catholic religion, being that of the majority of our Polish subjects, shall be the object of especial protection of the Government....

Art. 7. The protection of the laws is assured to all the inhabitants without distinction of rank or class....

Art. 13. Publication of sentiments by means of the press, shall be subjected to restrictions which will protect religion, the inviolability of superior authority, the interests of morals, and personal considerations....

Art. 14. The kingdom of Poland shall proportionably contribute to the general expenditure and to the wants of the empire....

Art. 20. Our army in the empire and in the kingdom shall compose one in common, without distinction of Russian or Polish troops....

Art. 21. Those of our subjects of the empire of Russia, who are established in the kingdom of Poland, who possess or shall possess, real property in that country, shall enjoy all the rights of natives. It shall be the same with those of our subjects in the kingdom of Poland, who shall establish themselves, and shall possess property, in the other provinces of the empire.

Published in Joseph Hordynaki, *History of the Late Polish Revolution and the Events of the Campaign* (Boston: Printed for Subscribers, 1833), pp. 424–428, as quoted in Alfred J. Bannan and Achilles Edelenyi, *Documentary History of Eastern Europe* (New York: Twayne Publishers, Inc., 1970), pp. 133–137.

On August 2, Charles X abdicated and left France for exile in England. The Chamber of Deputies named a new ministry composed of constitutional monarchists. In an act that finally ended the Bourbon dynasty, it also proclaimed Louis Philippe (r. 1830–1848), the duke of Orléans, the new king of France.

In the Revolution of 1830, the liberals of the Chamber of Deputies had filled a power vacuum created by the popular Paris uprising and the failure of effective royal action. Had Charles X provided himself with sufficient troops in Paris, the outcome could have been quite different. Moreover, had the liberals, who favored constitutional monarchy, not acted quickly, the workers and shopkeepers of Paris might have attempted to form a republic. By seizing the moment, the middle class, the bureaucrats, and the moderate aristocratic liberals overthrew the restoration monarchy and still avoided a republic. These liberals feared a new popular revolution such as had swept France in 1792. They had no desire for another *sansculottes* republic. A fundamental political and social tension thus underlay the new monarchy. The revolution had succeeded thanks to a temporary alliance between hard-pressed laborers and the prosperous middle class, but these two groups soon realized that their basic goals had been quite different.

MONARCHY UNDER LOUIS PHILIPPE   Politically, the July Monarchy, as it was called, was more liberal than the restoration government. Louis Philippe was called the "king of the French" rather than "king of France." The tricolor flag of the revolution replaced the white flag of the Bourbons. The new constitution was regarded as a right of the people rather than as a concession of the monarch. Catholicism became the religion of a majority of the people rather than "the official religion." The new government was strongly anticlerical. Censorship was abolished. The franchise became somewhat wider, but remained, on the whole, restricted. The king had to cooperate with the Chamber of Deputies; he could not dispense with laws on his own authority.

Socially, however, the Revolution of 1830 proved quite conservative. The hereditary peerage was abolished in 1831, but the everyday economic, political, and social influence of the landed oligarchy continued. Money was the path to power and influence in the government. There was much corruption.

Most important, the liberal monarchy displayed little or no sympathy for the lower and working classes. In 1830, the workers of Paris had called for the protection of jobs, better wages, and the preservation of the traditional crafts, rather than for the usual goals of political liberalism. The government of Louis Philippe ignored their demands and their plight. The laboring classes of Paris and the provincial cities seemed just one more possible source of disorder. In late 1831, troops suppressed a workers' revolt in Lyons. In July 1832, an uprising occurred in Paris during the funeral of a popular Napoleonic general. Again the govern-

Despite laws forbidding disrespect to the government, political cartoonists had a field day with Louis Philippe. Here, an artist emphasizes the king's resemblance to a pear and in the process, attacks restraints on freedom of the press. Corbis ment called out troops, and more than 800 people were killed or wounded. In 1834, a very large strike of silkworkers in Lyons was crushed. Such discontent might be smothered for a time, but without attention to the social and economic conditions creating it, new turmoil would eventually erupt.

Belgium Becomes Independent (1830)

The July Revolution in Paris sent sparks to other political tinder on the Continent. The revolutionary fires first lighted in neighboring Belgium. The former Austrian Netherlands, Belgium had been merged with the kingdom of Holland in 1815. The two countries differed in language, religion, and economy, however, and the Belgian upper classes never reconciled themselves to Dutch rule.

On August 25, 1830, disturbances broke out in Brussels following the performance of an opera about a rebellion in Naples against Spanish rule. To end the rioting, the municipal authorities and people from the propertied classes formed a provisional national government. When compromise between the Belgians and the Dutch failed, William of Holland (r. 1815–1840) sent troops and ships against Belgium. By November 10, 1830, the Dutch had been defeated. A national congress then wrote a liberal Belgian constitution, which was promulgated in 1831.

Although the major powers saw the revolution in Belgium as upsetting the boundaries established by the Congress of Vienna, they were not inclined to intervene to reverse it. Russia was preoccupied with the Polish revolt. Prussia and the other German states were suppressing small uprisings in their own domains. The Austrians were busy putting down disturbances in Italy. France under Louis Philippe favored an independent Belgium and hoped to dominate it. Britain felt that it could tolerate a liberal Belgium, as long as it was free of foreign domination.

In December 1830, Lord Palmerston (1784–1865), the British foreign minister, gathered representatives of the powers in London. Through skillful negotiations he persuaded them to recognize Belgium as an independent and neutral state. In July 1831, Leopold of Saxe-Coburg (r. 1831–1865) became king of the Belgians. Belgian neutrality was guaranteed by the Convention of 1839 and remained an article of faith in European international relations for almost a century.

Both Belgium and Serbia gained independence in 1830, and ironically, diplomatic circumstances involving both led to World War I. The assassination of an Austrian archduke by a Serbian nationalist in Sarajevo triggered the war, and German violation of Belgian neutrality brought Britain into it.

The Great Reform Bill in Britain (1832)

In Great Britain, the revolutionary year of 1830 saw the election of a House of Commons that debated the first major bill to reform parliament. The death of George IV (r. 1820–1830) and the accession of William IV (r. 1830–1837) required the calling of a parliamentary election, held in the summer of 1830. Historians once believed that the July revolution in France influenced voting in Britain, but close analysis of the time and character of individual county and borough elections has shown otherwise. The passage of the Great Reform Bill, which became law in 1832, was the result of a series of events very different from those that occurred on the Continent. In Britain, the forces of conservatism and reform made accommodations with each other.

POLITICAL AND ECONOMIC REFORM Several factors contributed to this spirit of accommodation. First, the commercial and industrial class was larger in Britain than in other countries. No matter what group might control the government, British prosperity required attention to their economic interests. Second, Britain's liberal Whig aristocrats, who regarded themselves as the protectors of constitutional liberty, represented a long tradition in favor of moderate reforms that would make revolutionary changes unnecessary. Early Whig sympathy for the French Revolution reduced their influence. After 1815, however, they reentered the political arena. Finally, British law, tradition, and public opinion all showed a strong respect for civil liberties.

In 1820, the year after the passage of the notorious Six Acts, Lord Liverpool shrewdly moved to change his cabinet. The new members continued to favor generally conservative policies, but they also believed that the government had to accommodate itself to the changing social and economic life of the nation. They favored policies of greater economic freedom and repealed the earlier Combination Acts that had prohibited labor organizations.

CATHOLIC EMANCIPATION ACT Economic considerations had generally led to the British moderate reforms. English determination to maintain the union with Ireland brought about another key reform. England's relationship to Ireland was similar to that of Russia to Poland or Austria to its several national groups. In 1800, fearful that Irish nationalists might again rebel as they had in 1798 and perhaps turn Ireland into a base for a French invasion, William Pitt the Younger had persuaded Parliament to pass the Act of Union between Ireland and England. Ireland now sent 100 members to the House of Commons. Only Protestant Irishmen,

At the first meeting of the House of Commons following the passage of the Great Reform Bill, most seats were still filled by the gentry and the wealthy. But the elimination of "rotten boroughs" and the election of members from the new urban centers began to transform the House into a representative national body. National Portrait Gallery, London

however, could be elected to represent their overwhelmingly Roman Catholic nation.

During the 1820s, under the leadership of Daniel O'Connell (1775–1847), Irish nationalists organized the Catholic Association to agitate for Catholic emancipation. In 1828 O'Connell secured his own election to Parliament, where he could not legally take his seat. The British ministry of the duke of Wellington realized that henceforth an entirely Catholic delegation might be elected from Ireland. If they were not seated, civil war might erupt across the Irish Sea. Consequently, in 1829, Wellington and Robert Peel steered the Catholic Emancipation Act through Parliament. Roman Catholics could now become members of Parliament. This measure, together with the repeal in 1828 of restrictions against Protestant nonconformists, ended the Anglican monopoly on British political life.

Catholic emancipation was a liberal measure passed for the conservative purpose of preserving order in Ireland. It included a provision raising the franchise in Ireland so that only the wealthier Irish could vote. Nonetheless, this measure alienated many of Wellington's Anglican Tory supporters in the House of Commons. The election of 1830 returned many supporters of parliamentary reform to Parliament. Even some Tories supported reform, because they thought that Catholic emancipation could have been passed only by a corrupt House of Commons. The Tories, consequently, were badly divided, and the Wellington ministry soon fell. King William IV then turned to the leader of the Whigs, Earl Grey (1764–1845), to form a government.

LEGISLATING CHANGE   The Whig ministry soon presented the House of Commons with a major reform bill that had two broad goals. The first was to abol-

ish "rotten boroughs," or boroughs that had very few voters, and to replace them with representatives for the previously unrepresented manufacturing districts and cities. Second, the number of voters in England and Wales was to be increased by about 50 percent through a series of new franchises. In 1831, the House of Commons narrowly defeated the bill. Grey called for a new election, in which a majority in favor of the bill was returned. The House of Commons

Events Associated with Liberal Reform and Revolution	
1824	Charles X becomes king of France
1825	Decembrist Revolt in Russia
1828	Repeal of restrictions against British Protestant noncomformists
1829	Catholic Emancipation Act passed in Great Britain
1830 (July 9)	News of French colonial conquest in Algeria reaches Paris
1830 (July 25)	Charles X issues the Four Ordinances
1830 (August 2)	Charles X abdicates; Louis Philippe proclaimed king
1830 (August 25)	Belgian revolution
1830 (November 29)	Polish revolution
1832	Organic Statute makes Poland an integral part of Russian Empire
1832	Great Reform Bill passed in Great Britain

passed the reform bill, but the House of Lords rejected it. Mass meetings were held throughout the country. Riots broke out in several cities. Finally, William IV agreed to create enough new peers to give a third reform bill a majority in the House of Lords. Under this pressure, the House of Lords yielded, and in 1832 the measure became law.

The Great Reform Bill expanded the size of the English electorate, but it was not a democratic measure. It increased the number of voters by more than 200,000, or almost 50 percent, but it kept a property qualification for the franchise. (Gender was also a qualification. No thought was given to enfranchising women.) Some members of the working class actually lost the right to vote because of the abolition of certain old franchise rights. New urban boroughs were created to allow the growing cities to have a voice in the House of Commons. Yet the passage of the reform act did not, as was once thought, consti-

tute the triumph of middle-class interests in England: For every new urban electoral district, a new rural district was also drawn, and the aristocracy was expected to dominate rural elections. What the bill permitted was a wider variety of property to be represented in the House of Commons. (See "Thomas Babington Macaulay Defends the Great Reform Bill.")

The success of the reform bill was to reconcile previously unrepresented property owners and economic interests to the political institutions of the country. The act laid the groundwork for further orderly reforms of the church, municipal government, and commercial policy. By admitting into the political forum people who sought change and giving them access to the legislative process, it made revolution in Britain unnecessary. In this manner, Great Britain maintained its traditional institutions of government while allowing an increasingly diverse group of people to influence them. (See "Art & the West.")

Thomas Babington Macaulay Defends the Great Reform Bill

Macaulay (1800–1859) was a member of the House of Commons, which passed the Great Reform Bill in 1831, only to have it rejected by the House of Lords before another measure was successfully enacted in 1832. His speeches in support of the bill reflect his views on the need for Parliament to give balanced representation to major elements in the population without embracing democracy. His arguments had wide appeal.

❖ *Who does Macaulay think should be represented in Parliament? Why does he oppose universal suffrage? Why does he regard the Reform Bill as "a measure of conservation"? Why would Metternich have seen little or nothing conservative about the measure?*

[The principle of the ministers] is plain, rational, and consistent. It is this,—to admit the middle class to a large and direct share in the Representation, without any violent shock to the institutions of our country.... I hold it to be clearly expedient, that in a country like this, the right of suffrage should depend on a pecuniary qualification. Every argument...which would induce me to oppose Universal Suffrage, induces me to support the measure which is now before us. I oppose Universal Suffrage, because I think that it would produce a destructive revolution. I support this measure, because I am sure that it is our best security against a revolution.... I...do entertain great apprehension for the fate of my country. I do in my conscience believe, that unless this measure, or some similar measure, be speedily adopted, great and terrible calamities will befall us.

Entertaining this opinion, I think myself bound to state it, not as a threat, but as a reason. I support this measure as a means of Reform: But I support it still more as a measure of conservation. That we may exclude those whom it is necessary to exclude, we must admit those whom it may be safe to admit.... All history is full of revolutions, produced by causes similar to those which are now operating in England. A portion of the community which had been of no account, expands and becomes strong. It demands a place in the system, suited, not to its former weakness, but to its present power. If this is granted, all is well. If this is refused, then comes the struggle between the young energy of one class, and the ancient privileges of another....Such...is the struggle which the middle classes in England are maintaining against an aristocracy of mere locality.

From *Hansard's Parliamentary Debates*, 3d series, Vol. 2, pp. 1191–1197.

John Constable's Harmonious Landscapes in Unstable Times

John Constable (1776–1837) was an English artist whose political views were as conservative as Jacque-Louis David's were radical (see "Art & the West," Chapter 19). The differences in their political outlooks and between the two eras in which they painted are evident in *Salisbury Cathedral, from the Meadows* (1831), one of Constable's many portrayals of the Gothic cathedral with the highest spire in England. His paintings are associated with romanticism because of his interest in nature, local history, and the Middle Ages and because of the very free application of paint. He paid enormous attention to clouds, of which he made many small studies, preparing for his larger paintings. The aim of painting, he wrote, was, "To give 'to one brief moment caught from fleeting time,' a lasting and sober existence, and to render permanent many of those splendid but evanescent Exhibitions, which are ever occurring in the changes of external Nature."[5]

In *Salisbury Cathedral, from the Meadows*, Constable created a landscape that suggests his politically conservative outlook. He was deeply concerned with portraying a landed order that was stable and unchallenged by either political turmoil or industrial development. Although the clouds and sky in the painting depict a severe storm, there is a powerful orderliness present in the works of both nature and humankind. The trees clearly have withstood the storm as they have done so for many years. The cathedral likewise has stood for centuries. Arching over the entire scene and giving it a sacramental nature is the rainbow, suggesting a divine presence.

Constable did not paint idealized classical landscapes, nor did he portray classical heroes dedicated to an abstract higher political good. His landscapes reproduced scenes of English rural and village life with great faithfulness to their appearance. People in Constable's paintings always are working, often at ordinary tasks. They seem to be an integral part of the natural order, suggesting no discontent with their lot. Constable and others of his era tended to look to rural life as the contemporary embodiment of what they regarded as the social stability of the Middle Ages. These artists and thinkers projected upon that era a sense of organic stability and religious reverence they saw absent from their own society.

In fact, though, social disruption and the potential for political upheaval marked the rural areas that Constable portrayed. The enclosures and early mechanization of farming had driven many people off the land, and many of the rural poor endured enormous suffering. During the Napoleonic Wars dairy farmers turned their land to grain raising, but after the war they could not reconvert the land efficiently enough to compete with Dutch dairy products. Wartime profits created wealthy farmers who separated themselves from the lives of their laborers. During the 1820s and 1830s rural riots broke out in East Anglia, the region of England that Constable knew best. In his paintings, he idealized a rural landscape and rustic society that had already largely disappeared. Moreover, Constable associated his vision of a staid, orderly landed society with various kinds of "natural" authority, such as family, community itself, and God. In the face of the radical politicalization of the countryside, his paintings depoliticized the landscape. People and nature stand in harmony, with their work part of the natural order.

Like many English conservatives of his day, Constable saw the church and the constitution as intimately related. Religious institutions served to withstand political radicalism. In private letters

[5]Quoted in Ann Bermingham, *Landscape and Ideology: The English Rustic Tradition, 1740–1860* (Berkeley, CA: University of California Press, 1986), p. 151

John Constable (1776–1837), *Salisbury Cathedral, from the Meadows*, 1831. Oil on canvas, 151.8 × 189.9. © The National Gallery, London.

Constable associated liberal reformers with the devil, leading some scholars to suggest that the lightning striking the back roof of the cathedral symbolizes those evil forces while the rainbow indicates the ongoing presence of the divine order of nature and society. Part of this argument is based on the fact that Constable would most certainly have known from his observations of weather that what he painted could never have occurred. Other commentators believe that the dark, boding qualities of this scene, with the rainbow suggesting hope, reflects Constable's inner sadness and turmoil over the death of his wife.

Sources: Ann Bermingham, *Landscape and Ideology: The English Rustic Tradition, 1740–1860* (Berkeley, CA: University of California Press, 1986); Michael Rosenthal, *Constable: The Painter and His Landscape* (New Haven, CT: Yale University Press, 1983); John Barrell, *The Darker Side of Landscape* (Cambridge, U.K.: Cambridge University Press, 1980).

In Perspective

Through the Congress System the major powers had responded to pressures on the Vienna Settlement without recourse to general warfare or territorial aggrandizement on the part of any state or collection of states. In the fifteen years between the conclusion of the Congress of Vienna and the Revolution of 1830 in France, with the exception only of the Greek revolution of 1821, no revolutionary disturbance had succeeded in Europe. In Russia, the Decembrist Revolt of 1825 failed almost before it had begun. The only truly successful revolutionary activity during these years occurred in Latin America, where wars of independence ended Spain's centuries-old colonial domination.

Nonetheless, during the 1820s, liberal political ideas and some liberal political figures began to make inroads into the otherwise conservative domestic order. In 1830, revolution and reform again began to move across Europe. The French rejected the restored Bourbon monarchy and established a more liberal monarchy. Belgium also achieved independence with a liberal government. Perhaps most important, Great Britain moved slowly toward a more liberal position. During the 1820s, Great Britain had become unenthusiastic about a political role that placed it in opposition to all change. For its own commercial reasons, it favored independence for Latin America. Popular pressures at home led the British aristocratic leadership to enact a moderate reform bill in 1832. Thereafter, Britain would be viewed as the leading liberal state in Europe and one that would support nationalistic causes.

REVIEW QUESTIONS

1. Define nationalism. What were the goals of nationalists? What were the difficulties they confronted in realizing those goals? Why was nationalism a special threat to the Austrian Empire? What areas saw significant nationalist movements between 1815 and 1830? Which were successful and which unsuccessful?

2. What were the tenets of liberalism? Who were the liberals and how did liberalism affect the political developments of the early nineteenth century? What relationship does liberalism have to nationalism?

3. What difficulties did the conservatives in Austria, Prussia, and Russia face in the years after the Napoleonic wars? How did they respond on both national and international levels? What were the aims of the Concert of Europe? How did international relations after the Congress of Vienna differ from the international relations of the eighteenth century?

4. What political changes took place in Latin America in the twenty years between 1804 and 1824? What were the main reasons for Creole discontent with Spanish rule, and to what extent were the Creole leaders influenced by Enlightenment political philosophy? Who were some of the primary leaders of Latin American independence, and why were they successful?

5. Describe the constitution of the restored monarchy in France. Was the government truly constitutional? What did Charles X hope to accomplish? How much support did he have? What were the causes of the revolution of 1830? What did this revolution achieve and at what cost?

6. Before 1820, Britain appeared to be moving down the same reactionary road as the other major powers. What factors led to a different outcome in Britain? What was the purpose of the Great Reform Bill? What did it achieve? Would you call it a "revolutionary" document?

SUGGESTED READINGS

P. ALTER, *Nationalism* (1985). A useful brief introduction.

B. ANDERSON, *Imagined Communities*, rev. ed. (1991). A discussion of the forces that have fostered national identity.

M. BERDAHL, *The Politics of the Prussian Nobility: The Development of a Conservative Ideology, 1770–1848* (1988). A major examination of German conservative outlooks.

G. DE BERTIER DE SAUVIGNY, *Metternich and His Times* (1962). Sympathetic, but not uncritical, study.

G. DE BERTIER DE SAUVIGNY, *The Bourbon Restoration* (trans., 1966). A clear survey of an era that has received relatively little attention.

R. J. BEZUCHA, *The Lyon Uprising of 1834: Social and Political Conflict in the Early July Monarchy* (1974). An excellent discussion of the tensions in France after the Revolution of 1830.

A. BRIGGS, *The Making of Modern England* (1959). Remains the best survey of English history during the first half of the nineteenth century.

M. BROCK, *The Great Reform Act* (1974). The standard work.

G. A. CRAIG, *The Politics of the Prussian Army, 1640–1945* (1955). A splendid study of the conservative political influence of the army on Prussian development.

D. DAKIN, *The Struggle for Greek Independence* (1973). An excellent explanation of the intricacies of the Greek independence question.

E. GELLNER, *Nations and Nationalism* (1983). A major theoretical work.

R. GILDEA, *Barricades and Borders: Europe 1800–1914* (1987). A useful survey.

L. GREENFELD, *Nationalism: Five Roads to Modernity* (1992). A major comparative study.

E. J. HOBSBAWM, *The Age of Revolution, 1789–1848* (1962). A comprehensive survey emphasizing the social ramifications of the liberal democratic and industrial revolutions.

E. J. HOBSBAWM, *Nations and Nationalism since 1780: Programme, Myth, Reality*, rev. ed. (1992). The best recent introduction to the subject.

S. HOLMES, *Benjamin Constant and the Making of Modern Liberalism* (1984). An outstanding study of a major liberal theorist.

A. JARDIN AND A. J. TUDESQ, *Restoration and Reaction, 1815–1848* (1984). Surveys this period in France.

B. JELAVICH, *Russia's Balkan Entanglements, 1899–1914* (1991). Now the standard discussion of this topic.

C. JELAVICH AND B. JELAVICH, *The Establishment of the Balkan National States, 1804–1920* (1977). A standard, clear introduction.

W. B. KAUFMANN, *British Policy and the Independence of Latin America, 1802–1828* (1951). A standard discussion of an important relationship.

W. B. LINCOLN, *Nicholas I: Emperor and Autocrat of All the Russians* (1978). A serious scholarly treatment.

J. LYNCH, *The Spanish American Revolutions, 1808–1826* (1973). An excellent one-volume treatment.

C. A. MACARTNEY, *The Habsburg Empire, 1790–1918* (1971). An outstanding survey.

P. MANENT, *An Intellectual History of Liberalism* (1994). A penetrating, succinct study.

A. PALMER, *Alexander I: Tsar of War and Peace* (1974). An interesting biography that captures much of the mysterious personality of this ruler.

P. PILBEAM, *The 1830 Revolution in France* (1991). An account that emphasizes the restoration's accommodation to various interest groups.

D. H. PINKNEY, *The French Revolution of 1830* (1972). The standard narrative account.

M. RAEFF, *The Decembrist Movement* (1966). An examination of the unsuccessful uprising, with documents.

N. V. RIASANOVSKY, *Nicholas I and Official Nationality in Russia, 1825–1855* (1959). A lucid discussion of the conservative ideology that made Russia the major opponent of liberalism.

C. A. RUUD, *Fighting Words: Imperial Censorship and the Russian Press, 1804–1906* (1982). Examines the government's attempt to shape and control public opinion.

J. SHEEHAN, *German History, 1770–1866* (1989). A very long work that is now the best available survey of the subject.

C. TILLY, *Popular Contention in Great Britain, 1758–1834* (1995). A major study by one of the chief scholars of popular uprisings.

A. B. ULAM, *Russia's Failed Revolutionaries* (1981). Contains a useful discussion of the Decembrists as a background for other nineteenth-century Russian revolutionary activity.

P. S. WANDYCZ, *The Lands of Partitioned Poland, 1795–1918* (1974). The best study of Poland during the nineteenth century.

I. WOLOCH, *The New Regime: Transformations of the French Civic Order, 1789–1820s* (1994). An important overview of just what had and had not changed in France after the quarter-century of revolution and war

The Abolition of Slavery in the Transatlantic Economy

One of the most important developments during the age of Enlightenment and Revolution was the opening of a crusade to abolish chattel slavery in the transatlantic economy. The antislavery movement constituted the greatest and most extensive achievement of liberal reformers during the eighteenth and nineteenth centuries. Indeed, it marked the first time in the history of the world that a society actually tried to abolish slavery. This achievement came as the result of the impact of Christian ethics, Enlightenment ideals, slave revolts, revolutionary wars in America and Europe, civil war in the United States, and economic dislocation in the slave economies themselves. In 1750, almost no one seriously questioned the existence of slavery, but by 1888 the institution no longer existed in the transatlantic economy.

Chattel slavery—the ownership of one human being by another—had existed in the West as well as elsewhere in the world since ancient times and had received intellectual and religious justification throughout the history of the West. Both Plato and Aristotle provided arguments for slavery based on the assertion that persons in bondage were intended by nature to be slaves. Christian writers similarly accommodated themselves to the institution. They contended that the most harmful form of slavery was the enslavement of the soul to sin rather than the enslavement of the physical body. They also argued that genuine freedom was realized through one's relationship to God and that problems relating to the injustices of inequality would be solved in the hereafter. Christian scholastic thinkers in the Middle Ages had portrayed slavery as part of the natural and necessary hierarchy of the universe.

Slavery Spreads to the Americas

Although a vast slave trade existed throughout the Mediterranean world through the end of the Middle Ages, slavery was no longer a dominant institution on the European continent or within the European economy. The European encounter with America at the end of the fifteenth century radically transformed that situation. The American continent and the West Indies presented opportunities for achieving great wealth, but a major labor shortage existed in these regions. Eventually slavery provided the means to resolve this labor shortage.

The establishment and maintenance of slavery in the transatlantic economy drew Europeans and Americans into various relationships with Africa. About the same time as the encounter with America, Europeans made contact with areas of West Africa where slavery already existed. This region became the chief source of slaves imported into the Americas. Four centuries later, during the antislavery movement, Europeans would seek to change the African economy by ending its dependence on the slave trade. Those efforts led to the penetration of Africa by European traders, missionaries, and finally colonial forces and administrators.

Although at one time or another slaves labored throughout the Americas, the system of slavery became primarily identified with the plantation economy stretching from Maryland south to Brazil, where tropical products, initially primarily sugar, were produced by slave labor. This plantation economy existed from approximately the late sixteenth through the late nineteenth century. The slaves upon whose labor this economy was based included Native Americans enslaved within both the Spanish Empire and North America, and Africans forcibly imported into the Americas. Consequently, the slaves were virtually always of a different race from their masters. Race itself soon became part of the justification for the social hierarchy of the plantation world.

In and of itself, the fact of slavery in the Americas was not unusual to the Western experience or to that of other societies in Africa or Asia. Slavery had existed at most times and places in human history. Far more unusual in the history of the West and for that matter in the experience of all other societies that had held and continued to hold slaves was the emergence after 1760 of an international movement to abolish chattel slavery in the transatlantic economy.

After 1807 the British Royal Navy patrolled the West African coast attempting to intercept slave-trading ships. In 1846 the British ship HMS Albatross captured a Spanish slave ship, the Albanoz and freed the slaves. A British officer depicted the appalling conditions in the slavehold in this watercolor. The Granger Collection, New York

The Crusade Against Slavery

The eighteenth-century crusade against slavery originated in a profound change in the religious and intellectual outlooks on slavery among small but influential groups in both America and Europe. The entire thrust of Enlightenment reasoning to the extent that it challenged or questioned the wisdom of existing institutions gnawed away at the older defenses of slavery, most particularly the concept of an unchanging social hierarchy. Although some writers associated with the Enlightenment, including John Locke, were reluctant to question slavery and even defended it, the general Enlightenment rhetoric of equality stood in sharp contrast to the radical inequality of slavery. Montesquieu sharply satirized slavery in *The Spirit of the Laws* (1748). Similarly, the emphasis of Adam Smith in *The Wealth of Nations* (1776) on free labor and efficiency of free markets undermined defenses of slavery.

Within much eighteenth-century literature, there emerged a tendency to idealize primitive peoples living in cultures very different from those of Europe. Previously such peoples had been regarded as backward and rebellious. Now numerous writers portrayed them as embodying a lost human virtue. This expanding body of literature transformed the way many people thought about slavery and allowed some Europeans to look upon African slaves in the Americas as having been betrayed and robbed of an original innocence. Additionally, much eighteenth-century European ethical thinking, as well as later romantic poetry, emphasized empathy and feeling. In such a climate, attitudes toward slavery were transformed. Once considered to be the natural and deserved result of some deficiency in slaves themselves, slavery now grew to be regarded as undeserved and unacceptable. The same kind of ethical thinking led reformers to believe that by working against slavery, for virtually the first time defined as an unmitigated evil, they would realize their own highest ethical character.

Religious movements became the single most important cultural force to foster the antislavery crusade. The evangelical religious revival associated with Methodism and with other forms of Protestant preaching emphasized the conversion experience and the change of heart as a sign of having received salvation. In 1774 John Wesley, the founder of Methodism, attacked slaveholding in *Thoughts on Slavery*. Turning against slaveholding and slave trading by plantation owners and slave traders served to illustrate one clear example of such a change of heart. Some slaveholders and slave traders feared they might be endangering their own salvation by their association with the institution. John Newton, a former slave trader who underwent an evangelical conversion, wrote the hymn "Amazing Grace."

The initial religious protest against slavery originated among English Quakers, a radical Protestant religious group founded by George Fox in the seventeenth century. By the early eighteenth century it had solidified itself into a small but relatively wealthy sect in England. Members of Quaker congregations at that time actually owned slaves in the West Indies and participated in the transatlantic slave trade. During the Seven Years' War (1756–1763), however, many Quakers experienced economic hardship. Furthermore, the war created other difficulties for the English population as a whole. Certain Quakers decided the presence of the evil of slavery in the world explained these troubles. They then sought to remove this evil from their own lives and that of their congregations and began to take action against the whole system of slavery that characterized the transatlantic economy.

Just as the slave system was a transatlantic affair, so was the crusade against it. Quakers in both Philadelphia and England soon moved against the institution. The most influential of the early antislavery writers was Anthony Benezet, a Philadelphia Quaker, whose most important publications were *Some Considerations on the Keeping of Negroes* (1754) and *A Short Account of That Part of Africa Inhabited by the Negroes* (1762). The latter work emphasized the manner in which the slave trade degraded African society itself. Benezet also drew heavily upon Montesquieu. This may not be surprising because Enlightenment writers often admired the English Quakers as exemplifying a religion of tolerance and reason.

By the earliest stages of the American Revolution a small group of reformers, normally spearheaded by Quakers, had established an antislavery network. They published pamphlets, sermons, and books on the subject. The Society for the Relief of Free Negroes Illegally Held in Bondage, the first antislavery society in the world, was founded in Philadelphia in 1775 and when reorganized in 1784 as the Pennsylvania Abolition Society, Benjamin Franklin became its president. In 1787, the Committee for the Abolition of the Slave Trade was organized in England. In France, the *Société des Amis des Noirs* was founded in 1778.

The turmoil of the American Revolution and the founding of the American republic gave these groups the occasion for some of their earliest successes. Emancipation gradually, but nonetheless steadily, spread among the northern states. In 1787, the Continental Congress forbade the presence of slavery in the newly organized Northwest Territory north of the Ohio River. What is important so far as the crusade against slavery is concerned is the disappearance of slavery in approximately half of the new nation and the commitment not to extend it to an important new territory.

Despite these American developments, Great Britain became and remained the center for the antislavery movement. In 1772, a decision by the chief justice affirmed that slaves brought into Great Britain could not forcibly be removed. The decision, though of less immediate importance than some thought at the time, gave further impetus to the small but growing group of antislavery reformers.

During the early 1780s, the antislavery reformers in Great Britain decided to work toward ending the slave trade rather than the institution of slavery. The horrors of the slave trade caught the public's attention in 1783 when the captain of the slave ship Zong threw more than 130 slaves overboard in order to collect insurance. For the reformers, attacking the trade rather than the institution appeared a less radical and a more achievable reform.

The Slave Revolt on the French Island of St. Dominique achieved the largest emancipation of slaves in the eighteenth century. In this print Toussant-L'Ouverture leads the revolt. Corbis

To many, the slave trade appeared a more obvious crime than the holding of slaves which seemed a more nearly passive act. Furthermore attacking slavery itself involved serious issues of property rights which might alienate potential supporters of the abolition of the slave trade. The antislavery groups also believed that if the trade were ended, planters would have to treat their remaining slaves more humanely.

By the end of the 1780s, the English Quakers were joined by evangelical Christians from the Church of England to form the Society for the Abolition of the Slave Trade. The most famous of the new leaders was William Wilberforce who, for the rest of his life, fought the slave trade. Year after year, he introduced a bill to abolish the slave trade. Finally, in 1807 he saw it passed.

Slave Revolts

While the British reformers worked for the abolition of the slave trade, slaves themselves in certain areas took matters into their own hands. The largest emancipation of slaves to occur in the eighteenth century came on the island of Saint Domingue (Haiti), France's wealthiest colony, as a result of the slave revolt of 1794 led by Toussaint L'Ouverture and Jean-Jacques Dessalines. The revolt in Haiti and Haiti's eventual independence in 1804 stood as a warning to slave owners throughout the West Indies. There would be other slave revolts such as those in Virginia led by Gabriel Prosser in 1800 and by Nat Turner in 1831, in South Carolina led by Denmark Vesey in 1822, in British-controlled Demarra in 1823 and 1824 and in Jamaica in 1831. Each of these was brutally suppressed.

Economic Pressures

Through the conclusion of the Seven Years' War, the West Indies interest group had been one of the most powerful in the British Parliament. During the second half of the eighteenth century and beyond, new and different economic interest groups began to displace the influence of that group. Within the West Indies themselves the planters were experiencing soil exhaustion and new competition from newly tilled islands controlled by France and other new islands opened for sugar cultivation. Some older plantations were being abandoned while others operated with low profitability. Now

with the new islands under cultivation there was a glut of sugar on the market, and as a consequence the price was falling.

Under these conditions some British West Indies planters, for reasons that had nothing to do with religion or humanitarianism, began to favor curtailing the slave trade. Without new slaves, French planters would lack the labor they needed to exploit their islands. During the Napoleonic Wars, the British captured a number of the valuable French islands. In order to protect the planters on the older British West Indies islands, in 1805 the British cabinet issued Orders in Council, which forbade the importation of slaves into the newly acquired French islands. By 1807 the abolition sentiment was strong enough for Parliament to pass Wilberforce's measure prohibiting slave trading from any British port.

The suppression of this trade through the navy became one of the fundamental pillars of nineteenth-century British foreign policy. Throughout the rest of the Napoleonic era the British attempted to draw allies into a policy of forbidding the slave trade. They also attempted unsuccessfully to incorporate the abolition of the slave trade into the settlement of the Congress of Vienna. In addition, the British navy maintained squadrons of ships around the coast of West Africa to halt slave traders. Although the French and Americans also patrolled the West African coast, neither was deeply committed to ending the slave trade. Nonetheless, in 1824 the American Congress had made slave trading a capital offense.

The French invasion of Spain in 1808, as discussed in Chapter 21, provided the spark for the Latin American wars of independence. The leaders of these movements had been influenced by the liberal ideas of the Enlightenment and were thus generally predisposed to disapprove of slavery. The political groups seeking independence from Spain also sought the support of slaves by promises of emancipation. Furthermore, the newly-independent nations needed good relations with Britain to support their economies and consequently most of them very quickly freed their slaves to gain such support. The actual freeing of slaves was gradual and often came some years after the emancipation legislation. Despite the gradual nature of this abolition, slavery would disappear by approximately the middle of the century from all of the newly-independent nations of Latin America. The great exception was Brazil.

Abolishing Slavery in the New World

British reformers gradually recognized that the abolition of the slave trade had not actually improved the lot of slaves. In 1823, they adopted as a new goal the gradual emancipation of slaves. The chief voices calling for this change were those of William Wilberforce and Thomas Clarkson, who were active in founding the Abolition Society. The savagery with which West Indian planters put down slave revolts in 1823 and 1824 and again in 1831 strengthened the resolve of the antislavery reformers. By 1830, the reformers had abandoned the goal of gradual abolition and demanded the complete abolition of slavery. In 1833, after the passage of the Reform Bill in Great Britain they achieved that goal when Parliament abolished the right of British subjects to hold slaves. In the British West Indies, 750,000 slaves were freed within a few years.

The other old colonial powers in the New World tended to be much slower in their own abolition of slavery. Portugal did little or nothing about slavery in Brazil, and when that nation became independent of Portugal, its new government continued slavery. Portugal ended slavery elsewhere in its American possessions in 1836; the Swedes, in 1847; the Danes, in 1848; but the Dutch not until 1863. France had witnessed a significant antislavery movement throughout the first half of the century, but slavery was not abolished in its West Indian possessions until the revolution of 1848.

During the first thirty years of the nineteenth century the institution of slavery revived and achieved strong new footholds in the transatlantic world. These areas were the lower south of the United States for the cultivation of cotton, Brazil for the cultivation of coffee, and Cuba for the cultivation of sugar. World demand for those products made the slave system economically viable in these regions. Consequently, despite the drive to emancipation, which had succeeded in the northern states of the United States, slavery persisted in much of the Caribbean and in most of Latin America.

An antislavery movement had existed in the United States since the end of the eighteenth century, but it took on a new life in the early 1830s. The British abolition of slavery in the West Indies served as an inspiration to a new generation of American antislavery leaders, the most famous of whom was William Lloyd Garrison. He and other American abolitionists raised the question of slavery throughout the 1830s and 1840s. It was, however, the disposition of lands the United States had acquired in the Mexican War of 1847 that placed slavery at the heart of American political debate. For over a decade the question of slavery sharply divided Americans. The election of Lincoln in 1860 brought those sectional tensions to a head, and the American Civil War erupted in the spring of 1861. In 1862 Lincoln issued the Emancipation Proclamation, which ended slavery in the combatant states. The passage of the Thirteenth Amendment to the American Constitution in 1865 abolished slavery in the United States.

The end of slavery in the United Sates left both Cuba, the most important remaining possession of the Spanish Empire in the Americas, and Brazil with slave economies. In 1868, an insurgency against Spanish colonial policy broke out in Cuba and lasted for ten years. This war disrupted much of the Cuban economy and saw some planters move toward using free labor. The Spanish forces attacked other planters by freeing their slaves. In 1870, the Spanish government passed a measure for gradual emancipation of slaves in both Cuba and Puerto Rico. In subsequent years, the sugar economy collapsed, making slavery unprofitable. Abolitionist agitation grew in Spain, and slavery was abolished in its new world colonies in 1886.

Brazil, under British pressure, had effectively ended the slave trade in 1850, but the question of the abolition of slavery was postponed for many years. In 1871, as a result of abolitionist agitation and because the Emperor Pedro II opposed slavery, a law providing for an extremely gradual abolition of slavery was passed. During the next two decades, abolitionist sentiment grew, and public figures from across the political spectrum voiced opposition to slavery. In 1888, Isabel Christiana, then regent while her father Pedro II was in Europe for medical treatment, signed a law abolishing slavery in Brazil without any form of compensation to the slave owners.

The abolition of slavery in Brazil ended a system of forced labor that had characterized the transatlantic economy for almost 400 years. Wherever slavery had existed, however, its presence left and would continue to leave long-term consequences for the realization of equality and social justice. The end of slavery consequently did not end the problems that slavery created in the transatlantic world.

Africa and the End of Slavery

The transatlantic slave trade itself had adversely affected the life of Africa both through the vast loss of population over the centuries as well as through the undermining of African society through the internal slave trade. Similarly, the crusade against transatlantic slavery had drawn Europeans much more deeply into the affairs of the African continent. The various efforts by antislavery groups began to impact Africa in the first half of the nineteenth century. Their goal was to transform the African economy by substituting new peaceful trade in tropical goods for the slave trade. The reformers hoped to spread both free trade and Christianity into Africa. "Christianity and civilization" and "Christianity and commerce" were popular slogans of the day. Missionaries and traders saw themselves as natural allies in the cause.

The first effort in this direction was the resettlement of black slaves or children of black slaves into Africa. In 1787 the British established a colony of poor free blacks from Britain in Sierra Leone. The effort went badly, but a few years later former slaves once owned by British loyalists in America were settled there. Then former slaves from the Caribbean were brought to Sierra Leone. The colony became relatively successful only after 1807, when the British navy landed slaves rescued from captured slave trading ships. Sierra Leone though quite small became a place on the coast of West Africa where Christianity and commerce rather than the slave trade flourished. The French established a smaller experiment at Libreville in Gabon. The most famous and lasting attempt to resettle former black slaves in Africa was the establishment of Liberia by the efforts of the American Colonization Society after 1817. Liberia became an independent republic in 1847. All of these efforts to move former slaves back to Africa had only modest success, but they did affect the life of West Africa.

Other antislavery reformers were less interested in establishing outposts for the settlement of former slaves than in transforming the African economy itself. In 1841, the African Civilization Society under the leadership of Thomas Fowell Buxton sent a group of paddle-steamer ships up the Niger River in the hope of creating the basis for new trade with Africa. The goal was to establish free trade between Britain and Africa in which the manufactured goods of the former, most particularly textiles, would be exchanged for tropical agricultural goods produced by Africans. The expedition failed because most of its members died of disease. Yet the impulse to penetrate Africa for purposes of spreading trade and Christianity would continue for the rest of the century.

The antislavery movement marked the first of the intrusions of the European powers well beyond the coast of West Africa into the heart of the continent. After the American Civil War finally halted any large-scale demand for slaves from Africa, the antislavery reformers began to focus on ending the slave trade in East Africa and the Indian Ocean. This drive against slavery and the slave trade in Africa itself became one of the rationales for European interference in Africa during the second half of the century and served as one of the foundations for the establishment of the late-century colonial empires.

The crusade against slavery in the transatlantic economy eventually touched most of the world. It radically transformed the economies and societies of both North and South America. It led to a transformation of the African economy and eventually to a significant European presence in the life of African societies. Efforts to eradicate slavery, particularly the efforts by British reformers, caused the spread of the reform movement into Asia. Slavery was not abolished throughout the world, and antislavery societies still exist though they receive little publicity. But the abolition of slavery in the transatlantic world stands as one of the most permanent achievements of the forces of eighteenth-century Enlightenment and Revolution.

❖ *What were the justifications of slavery prior to the eighteenth century? What religious and intellectual developments led some Europeans and some Americans to question and criticize the institution of slavery? Why did antislavery reformers first concentrate on the abolition of the slave trade? How did both slavery and antislavery lead Americans and Europeans to become involved with Africa? How did that involvement change between approximately 1600 and 1870?*

Chapter 22

The social and political tensions of the second quarter of the nineteenth century erupted in a series of revolutionary upheavals that swept across much of Europe in 1848. In The Uprising, the French artist Honoré Daumier recalled the drama of that year's revolution in Paris in a remarkable image of political and social protest Honoré Daumier, *The Uprising (L'Emeute)*, 1848 or later, Oil on canvas. 34 1/2 × 44 1/2 (87.6 × 113.0), Unsigned. Acquired 1925. The Phillips Collection, Washington, DC.

Economic Advance and Social Unrest (1830–1850)

Toward an Industrial Society
Britain's Industrial Leadership
Population and Migration
Railways

The Labor Force
Proletarianization of Factory Workers and
 Urban Artisans
Working-Class Political Action: The Example
 of British Chartism

Family Structures and the Industrial Revolution
The Family in the Early Factory System

Women in the Early Industrial Revolution
Opportunities and Exploitation in
 Employment
Changing Expectations in Working-Class
 Marriage

Problems of Crime and Order
New Police Forces
Prison Reform

Classical Economics
Malthus on Population
Ricardo on Wages
Government Policies Based on Classical
 Economics

Early Socialism
Utopian Socialism
Anarchism
Marxism

1848: Year of Revolutions
France: The Second Republic and Louis
 Napoleon
The Habsburg Empire: Nationalism Resisted
Italy: Republicanism Defeated
Germany: Liberalism Frustrated

KEY TOPICS

- The development of industrialism and its effects on the organization of labor and the family
- The changing role of women in industrial society
- The establishment of police forces and reform of prisons
- Early developments in European socialism
- The revolutions of 1848

B y 1830, Europe was headed toward an industrial society. Only Great Britain had already attained that status, but the pounding of new machinery and the grinding of railway engines soon began to echo across much of the Continent. Yet what characterized the second quarter of the century was not the triumph of industrialism but the final protests of those economic groups who opposed it. Intellectually, the period saw the formulation of the major creeds supporting and criticizing the newly emerging society.

These were years of uncertainty for almost everyone. Even the most confident entrepreneurs knew that the trade cycle might bankrupt them in a matter of weeks. For the industrial workers and the artisans, unemployment became a haunting and recurring problem. For *the peasants, the question was sufficiency of food. It was a period of self-conscious transition that culminated in 1848 with a continent-wide outbreak of revolution. People knew that one mode of life was passing, but no one knew what would replace it.*

Toward an Industrial Society

Britain's Industrial Leadership

The Industrial Revolution had begun in eighteenth-century Great Britain with the advances in textile production described in Chapter 16. Natural resources, adequate capital, native technological skills, a growing food supply, a social structure that allowed considerable mobility, and strong foreign and domestic demand for goods had given Britain an edge in achieving a vast new capacity for production in manufacturing. British factories and recently invented machines allowed producers to furnish customers with a greater number of products whose quality was higher and whose prices were lower than those of any competitors. Also, the French Revolution and the wars of Napoleon had finally destroyed the French Atlantic trade and had disrupted continental economic life for two decades. The Latin American wars of independence opened the markets of South America to British goods. In North America, both the United States and Canada demanded British products. Through its control of India, Britain commanded the markets of southern Asia.

The British textile industry was a vast worldwide economic network. For much of its raw cotton the industry depended on the labor of American slaves, although Britain itself had been trying to end the slave trade since 1807. In turn, the finished textiles were shipped all over the world along sea-lanes protected by the British navy. The wealth that Britain gained through textile production and its other industries of ironmaking, shipbuilding, china production, and the manufacture of other finished goods was invested all over the world, but especially in the United States and Latin America. This enormous activity provided the economic foundation for British dominance of the world scene in the nineteenth century.

Despite their economic lag, the continental nations were beginning to make material progress. By the 1830s, in Belgium, France, and Germany, the number of steam engines in use was growing steadily. Exploitation of the coalfields of the Ruhr and the Saar basins had begun. Coke was replacing charcoal in iron and steel production.

Industrial areas on the Continent were generally less concentrated than in Britain, and large manufacturing districts, such as the British Midlands, did not yet exist there. Major pockets of production, such as Lyons, Rouen, Liège, and Lille, did exist in western Europe, but most continental manufacturing still took place in the countryside. New machines were integrated into the existing domestic system. The extreme slowness of continental imitation of the British example meant that at midcentury peasants and urban artisans remained more important politically than industrial factory workers.

Population and Migration

While the process of industrialization spread, the population of Europe continued to grow on the base of the eighteenth-century population explosion. The number of people in France rose from 32.5 million in 1831 to 35.8 million in 1851. The population of Germany rose from 26.5 million to 33.5 million during approximately the same period. That of Britain grew from 16.3 million to 20.8 million. More and more of the people of Europe lived in cities. By midcentury, one-half of the population of England and Wales and one-quarter of the population of France and Germany had become town dwellers. Eastern Europe, by contrast, remained overwhelmingly rural, with little industrial manufacturing.

The sheer numbers of human beings put considerable pressure on the physical resources of the cities. Migration from the countryside meant that existing housing, water, sewers, food supplies, and lighting were completely inadequate. Slums with indescribable filth grew, and disease, especially cholera, ravaged the population. Crime increased and became a way of life for those who could make a living in no other manner. Human misery and degradation in many early-nineteenth-century cities seemed to have no bounds.

The situation in the countryside was scarcely better. During the first half of the century, the productive use of the land remained the basic fact of life for most Europeans. The enclosures of the late eighteenth century, the land redistribution of the French Revolution, and the emancipation of serfs in Prussia and later in Austria (1848) and Russia (1861) commercialized landholding. Liberal reformers had hoped that the legal revolution in ownership would transform peasants into progressive, industrious farmers. Instead, most peasants had become conservative landholders without enough land to make agricultural innovations or, often, even to support themselves.

It is important to note the differing dates of rural emancipation across Europe. In England, France, and the Low Countries, persons living in the countryside could move freely between country and town.

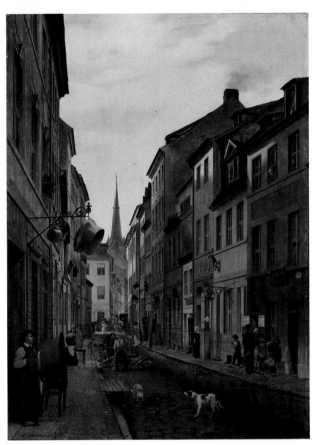

Cities all across the continent grew during the first half of the nineteenth century. Some developed with little planning into bewildering places. Others—as this Berlin street scene suggests—developed in ways more congenial to their residents, with neighborhoods that continued to combine workshops, stores, and residences. Bildarchiv Preussischer Kulturbesitz

In Germany, eastern Europe, and Russia, such migration was difficult until after emancipation of the serfs. Even when emancipation did occur, as throughout Germany early in the century, it did not make migration simple. So from Germany eastward, the pace of industrialization was much slower in part because of the absence of a fluid market for free labor moving to the cities.

The specter of poor harvests still haunted Europe. The worst such experience of the century was the Irish famine of 1845–1847. Perhaps as many as half a million Irish peasants with no land or small plots simply starved when disease blighted the potato crop. Hundreds of thousands emigrated. By midcentury, the revolution in landholding had led to greater agricultural production. It also resulted in a vast uprooting of people from the countryside into cities and from Europe into the rest of the world. The countryside thus provided many of the workers for the new factories, as well as people with few economic skills who slowly emigrated to cities in hope of finding work.

Railways

Industrial advance itself had also contributed to this migration. The 1830s and 1840s were the great age of railway building. The Stockton and Darlington Line opened in England in 1825. By 1830 another major line had been built between Manchester and Liverpool and had several hundred passengers a day. Belgium had undertaken railway construction by 1835. The first French line opened in 1832, but serious construction came only in the 1840s. Germany entered the railway age in 1835. At midcentury, Britain had 9,797 kilometers of railway, France 2,915, and Germany 5,856.

The railroads, plus canals and improved regular roads, meant that people could leave the place of their birth more easily than ever before. The improvement in transportation also allowed cheaper and more rapid passage of raw materials and finished products.

Railways epitomized the character of the industrial economy during the second quarter of the century. They represented investment in capital goods rather than in consumer goods. Consequently, there was a shortage of consumer goods at cheap prices. This favoring of capital over consumer production was one reason that the working class often found itself able to purchase so little for its wages. The railways in and of themselves also brought about still more industrialization. Embodying the most dramatic application of the steam engine, they created a sharply increased demand for iron and steel and then for a more skilled labor force. The new iron and steel capacity soon permitted the construction of ironclad ships and iron machinery rather than ships and machinery made of wood. These great capital industries led to the formation of vast industrial fortunes that would be invested in still newer enterprises. Industrialism had begun to grow on itself. (See "Art & the West.")

The Labor Force

The composition and experience of the early nineteenth-century labor force was varied. No single description could include all the factory workers, urban artisans, domestic craftspeople, household servants, miners, countryside peddlers, farmworkers, or railroad navvies. The work force was composed of some persons who were reasonably well off, enjoying steady employment and decent wages. It also numbered the "laboring poor," who held jobs, but who earned little more than subsistence wages. Then, there were others, such as the women and children who worked naked in the mines of Wales, whose conditions of life shocked all of Europe when a parliamentary report in the early

J. M. W. Turner, Rain, Steam, and Speed—The Great Western Railway

Joseph Mallord William Turner, *Rain, Steam, and Speed—The Great Western Railway*, 1844. Oil on canvas, 90.8 × 121.9.
© The National Gallery, London.

During the first half of the nineteenth century, Britain was the center of the new industrial economy. The railway, first in Britain, then across the world, was the most powerful transforming technology of the age. It embodied the industrial power and social shock of the early industrial revolution. Both the building of the railways and their daily operation tore across the physical and social structures of traditional rural life. The Great Western Railway shown here in Joseph Mallord William Turner's *Rain, Steam, and Speed—The Great Western Railway*, extended from London to the West Country of England and was the largest railway system yet constructed.

Turner's painting introduced the railway into the realm of high art. Turner (1775–1851) was an English artist who used the techniques of romantic painting to portray subjects as distinct as Hannibal crossing the Alps, warships, and, as in this work, the recently invented steam locomotive. Turner's ability to produce profound effects on his viewers from images filled with light and color rather than through precise linear portrayals, later influenced the French Impressionists, who themselves often painted scenes depicting railways. Turner was thus one of the pioneers in the movement that was revolutionizing Western art in the nineteenth century at the same time that technology was revolutionizing the economy and society.

Turner had begun as a painter of watercolors, and many of his paintings give a watercolor-like sense of transparency and of light emerging through the art itself. His paintings thus often appear as almost ethereal visions. One British newspaper could not decide wither *Rain, Steam, and Speed* represented "dazzling unrealities...or realities seized upon at a moment's glance."[1]

Despite the luminous quality of Turner's paintings, he sought to portray as much as possible from real life. In *Rain, Steam, and Speed*, the new technology is part of the natural world. The engine is made from iron. Its movement embodies speed itself as it passes through the rain and fog. Yet the bridges in the painting suggest a new human-constructed infrastructure.

Turner also was convinced that individual human beings loomed small before the forces of nature, history, and technology, For this reason, he is known as a painter of the sublime—that is, of subjects that aroused strong emotions like fear, dread, and awe, and that raise questions about our control over our lives. In *Rain, Steam, and Speed*, a farmer plows a field on the left while a much slower boat glides in the river on the right as the train seems to barrel ahead directly into the viewer. The farmer and the boat suggest the technologies of an earlier age that must yield to iron and steam. The steam locomotive, the chief symbol of the new technology of the day, thus surpasses animals, bypasses earlier technology, and moves boldly from the clouds of the past into a new era in human history.

[1]*The Times*, May 8, 1844, quoted in Martin Butlin & Evelyn Joll, *The Paintings of J. M. W. Turner*, rev. ed. (New Haven, CT: Yale University Press, 1984), p. 257.

Sources: Michael Freeman, *Railways and the Victorian Imagination* (New Haven, CT: Yale University Press, 1999); Gerard Finley, *Angel in the Sun: Turner's Vision of History* (Montreal, and Kingston, ON: McGill–Queen's University Press, 1999); Martin Butlin & Evelyn Joll, *The Paintings of J. M. W. Turner*, rev. ed. (New Haven, CT: Yale University Press, 1984).

A view of one of the first French railways, the line between Paris and the suburb of Saint Germain. The line was built by Baron James de Rothschild of the famous banking family. Liaison Agency, Inc.

1840s publicized them. Furthermore, the conditions of workers varied from decade to decade and from industry to industry within any particular decade.

Although historians have traditionally emphasized the role and experience of industrial factory workers, only the textile-manufacturing industry became thoroughly mechanized and moved into the factory setting during the first half of the century. Far more of the nonrural, nonagricultural work force consisted of skilled artisans living in cities or small towns. They were attempting to maintain the value of their skills and control over their trades in the face of changing features of production. All these working people faced possible unemployment, with little or no provision for their security. During their lives, they confronted the dissolution of many of the traditional social ties of custom and community.

Proletarianization of Factory Workers and Urban Artisans

During the nineteenth century, both artisans and factory workers underwent a process of proletarianization. This term is used to indicate the entry of workers into a wage economy and their gradual loss of significant ownership of the means of production, such as tools and equipment, and of control over the conduct of their own trades. The process occurred rapidly wherever the factory system arose. The factory owner provided the financial capital to construct the factory, to purchase the machinery, and to secure the raw materials. The factory workers contributed their labor for a wage. The process could also occur

outside the factory setting if a new invention, such as a mechanical printing press, could do the work of several artisans within a workshop setting.

Factory workers also submitted to various kinds of factory discipline that was virtually always unpopular and difficult to impose. This discipline meant that the demands for smooth operation of the machinery largely determined working conditions. Closing of factory gates to late workers, fines for such lateness, dismissal for drunkenness, and public scolding of faulty laborers were attempts to create human discipline that would match the regularity of the cables, wheels, and pistons. The factory worker had no direct say about the quality of the product or its price.

For all the difficulties of factory conditions, however, the economic situation was often better than for the textile workers who resisted the factory mode of production. In particular, English handloom weavers, who continued to work in their homes, experienced decades of declining trade and growing poverty in their unsuccessful competition with power looms.

Urban artisans in the nineteenth century experienced proletarianization more slowly than factory workers, and machinery had little to do with the process. The emergence of factories in and of itself did not harm urban artisans. Many even prospered from the development. For example, the construction and maintenance of the new machines generated major demand for metalworkers, who consequently prospered. The actual erection of factories and the expansion of cities benefitted all craftspeople in the building trades, such as carpenters, roofers, joiners, and masons. The lower prices for machine-made textiles aided artisans involved in the making of clothing, such as tailors and hatters, by reducing the costs of their raw materials. Where the urban artisans encountered difficulty and where they found their skills and livelihood threatened were in the organization of production.

In the eighteenth century, a European town or city workplace had usually consisted of a few artisans laboring for a master. They labored first as apprentices and then as journeymen, according to established guild regulations and practices. The master owned the workshop and the larger equipment, and the apprentices and journeymen owned their tools. The journeyman could expect to become a master. This guild system had allowed considerable worker control over labor recruitment and training, the pace of production, the quality of the product, and its price.

In the nineteenth century, it became increasingly difficult for artisans to continue to exercise corporate or guild direction and control over their trades. The legislation of the French Revolution had outlawed such organizations in France. Across Europe, political and economic liberals disapproved of labor and guild organizations and attempted to ban them.

Other destructive forces were also at work. The masters often found themselves under increased competitive pressure from larger, more heavily capitalized establishments or from the introduction of machine production into a previously craft-dominated industry. In many workshops masters began to follow a practice, known in France as *confection*, whereby goods, such as shoes, clothing, and furniture, were produced in standard sizes and styles rather than by special orders for individual customers.

This practice increased the division of labor in the workshop. Each artisan produced a smaller part of the more-or-less uniform final product. Thus, less skill was required of each artisan, and the particular skills possessed by a worker became less valuable. Masters also tried to increase production and reduce costs by lowering the wages paid for piecework. Those attempts often led to work stoppages or strikes. Migrants from the countryside or small towns into the cities created, in some cases, a surplus of relatively unskilled workers. They were willing to work for lower wages or under less favorable and protected conditions than traditional artisans. This situation made it much more difficult for urban journeymen ever to hope to become masters with their own workshops in which they would be in charge. Increasingly, these artisans became lifetime wage laborers whose skills were simply bought and sold in the marketplace.

Working-Class Political Action: The Example of British Chartism

By the middle of the century, such artisans, proud of their skills and frustrated in their social expectations, became the most radical political element in the European working class. From at least the 1830s onward, these artisans took the lead in one country after another in attempting to formulate new ways of protecting their social and economic interests.

By the late 1830s, significant numbers of people in the British working class linked the solution of their economic plight to a program of political reform known as *Chartism*. In 1836, William Lovett (1800–1877) and other London radical artisans

CAPITAL AND LABOUR.

A parliamentary report in the early 1840s revealed the deplorable conditions of women and children working underground in Welsh mines. The report had published illustrations of those conditions. This contemporary political cartoon draws upon those illustrations by portraying the wealthy and comfortable classes living a life based on the foundation of the misery of workers.
The Granger Collection, NY

formed the London Working Men's Association. In 1838 the group issued the Charter, demanding six specific reforms. The Six Points of the Charter included universal male suffrage, annual election of the House of Commons, the secret ballot, equal electoral districts, the abolition of property qualifications for members of the House of Commons, and payment of salaries to members of the House of Commons.

For more than ten years, the Chartists, who were never tightly organized, agitated for their reforms. On three occasions the Charter was presented to Parliament, which refused to pass it. Petitions with millions of signatures were presented to the House of Commons. Strikes were called. The Chartists published a newspaper, the *Northern Star*. Feargus O'Connor (1794–1855), the most important Chartist leader, made speeches across Britain. Despite this vast activity, Chartism as a national movement failed. Its ranks were split between those who favored violence and those who wanted to use peaceful tactics. On the local level, however, the Chartists scored several successes and controlled the city councils in Leeds and Sheffield.

As prosperity returned after the depression of the late 1830s and early 1840s, many working people abandoned the movement. Chartists' demonstrations in 1848 fizzled. Nevertheless, Chartism was the first large-scale European working-class political movement. It had specific goals and largely working-class leadership. Eventually, several of the Six Points were enacted into law. Continental working-class observers saw in Chartism the kind of mass movement that workers must eventually adopt if they were to improve their situation.

Family Structures and the Industrial Revolution

It is more difficult to generalize about the European working-class family structure in the age of early industrialism than under the Old Regime. Industrialism developed at such different rates across the Continent, and the impact of industrialism cannot be separated from that of migration and urbanization. Furthermore, industrialism did not touch all families directly; the structures and customs of many peasant families changed little for much of the nineteenth century.

Much more is known about the relationships of the new industry to the family in Great Britain than elsewhere. Many of the British developments foreshadowed those in other countries as the factory system spread.

The Family in the Early Factory System

Contrary to the opinion historians and other observers once held, the adoption of new machinery and factory production did not destroy the working-class family. Before the late-eighteenth-century revolution in textile production in England, the individual family involved in textiles was the chief unit of production. The earliest textile-related inventions, such as the spinning jenny, did not change that situation. As noted in Chapter 16, the new machine was initially simply brought into the home to spin the thread. It was the mechanization of weaving that led to the major change. The father who became a machine weaver was then employed in a factory. His work was thus separated from his home. Although one should not underestimate the changes and pressures in family life that occurred when the father left for the factory, the structure of early English factories allowed the father to preserve certain of his traditional family roles as they had existed before the factory system.

In the domestic system of the family economy, the father and mother had worked with their children in textile production as a family unit. They had trained and disciplined the children within the home setting. Their home life and their economic life were largely the same. Moreover, in the home setting, the wife who worked as a spinner might have earned as much or even more income than her husband. Early factory owners and supervisors permitted the father to employ his wife and children as his assistants. Thus, parental training and discipline could be transferred from the home into the early factory. In some cases, in both Britain and France, whole families would move near a new factory so that the family as a unit could work there. Those accommodations to family life nonetheless did not relieve any family members of having to face the new work discipline of the factory setting. Moroever, as will be discussed in a subsequent section, women assisting their husband in the factory often undertook less skilled work than they had pursued in their homes.

A major shift in this family and factory structure began in the mid-1820s in England and had been more or less completed by the mid-1830s. As spinning and weaving were put under one roof, the size of factories and of the machinery became larger. These newer machines required fewer skilled operators, but many relatively unskilled attendants. This relatively unskilled machine tending became the work of unmarried women and of children. Factory owners found that these workers would accept lower wages and were less likely than adult men to try to form worker or union organizations.

Factory wages for the more skilled adult males, however, became sufficiently high to allow some fathers to remove their children from the factory and to send them to school. The children who were left working in the factories as assistants were often the children of the economically depressed handloom weavers. The wives of the skilled operatives also usually no longer worked in the factories. So the original links of the family in the British textile factory that had existed for well over a quarter century largely disappeared. Men were supervising women and children who did not belong to their families.

CONCERN FOR CHILD LABOR It was at this point in the 1830s that workers became concerned about the plight of child-laborers, because parents were no longer exercising discipline over their own children in the factories. The English Factory Act of 1833 forbade the employment of children under age nine, limited the workday of children aged nine to thirteen to nine hours, and required that these children be given two hours of education a day, paid for by the factory owner. The effect was further to divide work and home life. The workday for adults and older teenagers remained twelve hours. Younger children often worked in relays of four or six hours. Consequently, the parental link was thoroughly broken. The education requirement began the process of removing nurturing and training from the home and family to a school, where a teacher rather than the parents was in charge of education.

After passage of the English Factory Act, many of the British working class demanded shorter workdays for adults. They desired to reunite, in some manner, the workday of adults with that of their children or at least to allow adults to spend more time with their children. In 1847, Parliament mandated a ten-hour workday. By present standards, this was long. At that time, however, it allowed parents and children more hours together as a domestic unit, since their relationship as a work or production unit had ceased wherever the factory system prevailed. By the middle of the 1840s, in the lives of industrial workers, the roles of men as breadwinners and as fathers and husbands had become distinct in the British textile industry. Furthermore, the concerns raised by reformers about the working conditions of women in factories and in mines arose in part from the relatively new view that the place of women was in the home rather than in either an industrial or even agrarian workplace.

CHANGING ECONOMIC ROLE FOR THE FAMILY What occurred in Britain presents a general pattern for what would happen elsewhere with the spread of industrial capitalism and public education. The European family was passing from being the chief unit of both production and consumption to becoming the chief unit of consumption alone. This development did not mean the end of the family as an economic unit. Parents and children, however, now came to depend on sharing wages often derived from several sources, rather than on sharing work in the home or factory.

Ultimately, the wage economy meant that families were less closely bound together than in the past. Because wages could be sent over long distances to parents, children might now move farther away from home. Once they moved far away, the economic link was, in time, often broken. On the other hand, when a family settled in an industrial city, the wage economy might, in that or the next generation, actually discourage children from leaving home as early as they had in the past. Children could find wage employment in the same city and then live at home until they had accumulated enough savings to marry and begin their own household. That situation meant that children often remained with their parents longer than in the past.

Women in the Early Industrial Revolution

As we noted in Chapter 16, the industrial economy ultimately produced an immense impact on the home and family life of women. First, it eventually took most productive work out of the home and allowed many families to live on the wages of the male spouse. That transformation prepared the way for a new concept of gender-determined roles in the home and in domestic life generally. Women came to be associated with domestic duties, such as housekeeping, food preparation, child rearing and nurturing, and household management, or with very poorly paid, largely unskilled cottage industries. Men came to be associated almost exclusively with supporting the family. Children were raised to conform to these expected gender patterns. Previously, this domestic division of labor into separate male and female spheres had prevailed only among the relatively small middle class and the gentry. During the nineteenth century, that division came to characterize the working class as well.

Opportunities and Exploitation in Employment

Because the early Industrial Revolution had begun in textile production, women and their labor were deeply involved from the start. While both spinning and weaving were still domestic industries, women usually worked in all stages of production. Hand spinning was virtually always a woman's task. At first, when spinning was moved into factories and involved large machines, women often were displaced by men. Furthermore, the higher wages commanded by male cotton-factory workers allowed many married women not to work or to work only to supplement their husbands' wages.

WOMEN IN FACTORIES With the next generation of machines in the 1820s, however, unmarried women rapidly became employed in the factories, where they often constituted the majority of workers. But their new jobs often demanded fewer skills than those they had previously exercised in the home production of textiles. Women's factory work also required fewer skills than most work done by men. Tending a machine required less skill than actually spinning or weaving or acting as forewoman. There was thus a certain paradox in the impact of the factory on women: Many new jobs were opened to them, but the level of skills was lowered. The supervisors of women were almost invariably men.

Moreover, almost always, the women in the factories were young, single women or widows. Upon marriage or perhaps after the birth of the first child,

As textile production became increasingly automated in the nineteenth century, textile factories required fewer skilled workers and more unskilled attendants. To fill these unskilled positions, factory owners turned increasingly to unmarried women and widows, who worked for lower wages than men and were less likely to form labor organizations. Bildarchiv Preussischer Kulturbesitz

young women usually found that their husbands earned enough money for them to leave the factory. Or they found themselves unwanted by the factory owners, who disliked employing married women because of the likelihood of pregnancy, the influence of their husbands, and the duties of child rearing. Widows might return to factory work, because they lacked their husbands' former income.

WORK ON THE LAND AND IN THE HOME In Britain and elsewhere by midcentury, industrial factory work still accounted for less than half of all employment for women. The largest group of employed women in France continued to work on the land. In England, they were domestic servants. Through western Europe, domestic cottage industries, such as lace making, glove making, garment making, and other kinds of needlework, employed a vast number of women. In almost all such cases, their conditions of labor were harsh, whether they worked in their homes or in sweatshops. It cannot be overemphasized that *all* work by women commanded low wages and involved low skills. They had virtually no effective modes of protecting themselves from exploitation. The charwoman, a common sight across the Continent, symbolized the plight of working women.

The low wages of female workers in all areas of employment sometimes led to their becoming prostitutes to supplement their wage income. This situation prevailed across Europe throughout the century. In 1844 Louise Aston (1814–1871), a German political radical, portrayed this situation in a poem looking at the experience of a Silesian weaver as she confronts a factory owner upon whom her family depends to purchase the cloth they have woven:

The factory owner has come,
And he says to me: "My darling child,
I know your people
Are living in misery and sorrow;
So if you want to lie with me
For three or four nights,
See this shiny gold coin!
It's yours immediately."[2]

Such sexual exploitation of women was hardly new to European society, but the particular pressures of the transformation of the economy from one of skilled artisans to that of unskilled factory workers made many women especially vulnerable. (See "Women Industrial Workers Explain Their Economic Situation.")

[2]As quoted in Lia Secci, "German Women Writers and the Revolution of 1848," in John C. Fout, ed., *German Women in the Nineteenth Century: A Social History* (New York: Holmes & Meier, 1984), p. 162.

Women Industrial Workers Explain Their Economic Situation

In 1832, there was much discussion in the British press about factory legislation. Most of that discussion was concerned with the employment of children, but the Examiner *newspaper made the suggestion that any factory laws should not only address the problem of child labor, but also, in time, eliminate women from employment in factories. That article provoked the following remarkable letter to the editor, composed by or on behalf of women factory workers, which eloquently stated the real necessity of such employment for women and the unattractive alternatives.*

❖ *What are the reasons these women enumerate to prove the necessity of their holding manufacturing jobs? What changes in production methods have led women from the home to the factory? How does the situation of these women relate to the possibility of their marrying? Compare the plight of these English working-class women with that of the French middle-class woman in the next document.*

Sir,

Living as we do, in the densely populated manufacturing districts of Lancashire, and most of us belonging to that class of females who earn their bread either directly or indirectly by manufactories, we have looked with no little anxiety for your opinion on the Factory Bill....You are for doing away with our services in manufactories altogether. So much the better, if you had pointed out any other more eligible and practical employment for the surplus female labour, that will want other channels for a subsistence. If our competition were withdrawn, and short hours substituted, we have no doubt but the effects would be as you have stated, "not to lower wages, as the male branch of the family would be enabled to earn as much as the whole had done," but for the thousands of females who are employed in manufactories, who have no legitimate claim on any male relative for employment or support, and who have, through a variety of circumstance, been early thrown on their own resources for a livelihood, what is to become of them?

In this neighbourhood, hand-loom has been almost totally superseded by power-loom weaving, and no inconsiderable number of females, who must depend on their own exertions, or their parishes for support, have been forced, of necessity, into the manufactories, from their total inability to earn a livelihood at home.

It is a lamentable fact, that, in these parts of the country, there is scarcely any other mode of employment for female industry, if we except servitude and dressmaking. Of the former of these, there is no chance of employment for one-twentieth of the candidates that would rush into the field, to say nothing of lowering the wages of our sisters of the same craft; and of the latter, galling as some of the hardships of manufactories are (of which the indelicacy of mixing with the men is not the least), yet there are few women who have been so employed, that would change conditions with the ill-used genteel little slaves, who have to lose sleep and health, in catering to the whims and frivolities of the butter-flies of fashion.

We see no way of escape from starvation, but to accept the very tempting offers of the newspapers, held out as baits to us, fairly to ship ourselves off to Van Dieman's Land [Tasmania] on the very delicate errand of husband hunting, and having safely arrived at the "Land of Goshen," jump ashore, with a "Who wants me?"...

The Female Operatives of Todmorden

From *The Examiner*, February 26, 1832, as quoted in Ivy Pinchbeck, *Women Workers and the Industrial Revolution, 1750–1850* (New York: Augustus M. Kelley, 1969), pp. 199–200.

Changing Expectations in Working-Class Marriage

Moving to cities and entering the wage economy gave women wider opportunities for marriage. Cohabitation before marriage was not uncommon. Parents had less to do with arranging marriages than in the past. (See "A Young Middle-Class Frenchwoman Writes to Her Father about Marriage.") Marriage now usually meant that a woman would leave the work force to live on her husband's earnings. If all went well, that arrangement might improve her situation.

A Young Middle-Class Frenchwoman Writes to Her Father about Marriage

Stéphanie Jullien was a young middle-class woman whose father wished her to marry a man who was courting her. She had already rejected one suitor, and her father was greatly concerned about her future. In this letter, she explains to her father the matters that disturb her and make her wish to delay her decision. Ultimately, she did marry the man in question, and the marriage appears to have been happy.

❖ *How does Stéphanie Jullien distinguish between the vocational and social opportunities available to a woman and those to a man? What are her expectations of a relationship with a husband? What does the letter also tell you about her sense of her relationship to her father? Compare this letter with the preceding letter by English working-class women. What problems do the women share? How are their lives different? What does a comparison of the two letters tell you about the difference in class experience in the early nineteenth century?*

You men have a thousand occupations to distract you: society, business, politics, and work absorb you, exhaust you, upset you.... As for us women who, as you have said to me from time to time, have only the roses in life, we feel more profoundly in our solitude and in our idleness the sufferings that you can slough off. I don't want to make a comparison here between the destiny of man and the destiny of woman: each sex has its own lot, its own troubles, its own pleasures. I only want to explain to you that excess of moroseness of which you complain and of which I am the first to suffer.... I am not able to do anything for myself and for those around me. I am depriving my brothers in order to have a dowry. I am not even able to live alone, being obliged to take from others, not only in order to live but also in order to be protected, since social convention does not allow me to have independence. And yet the world finds me guilty of being the only person that I am at liberty to be; not having useful or productive work to do, not having any calling except marriage, and not being able to look by myself for someone who will suit me, I am full of cares and anxieties....

I am asking for more time [before responding to a marriage proposal]. It is not too much to want to see and know a man for ten months, even a year when it is a matter of passing one's life with him. There is no objection to make, you say. But the most serious and the most important presents itself: I do not love him. Don't think I am talking about a romantic and impossible passion or an ideal love, neither of which I ever hope to know. I am talking of a feeling that makes one want to see someone, that makes his absence painful and his return desirable, that makes one interested in what another is doing, that makes one want another's happiness almost in spite of oneself, that makes, finally, the duties of a woman toward her husband pleasures and not efforts. It is a feeling without which marriage would be hell, a feeling that cannot be born out of esteem, and which to me, however, seems to be the very basis of conjugal happiness. I can't feel these emotions immediately.... Let me have some time. I want to love, not out of any sense of duty, but for myself and for the happiness of the one to whom I attach my life, who will suffer if he only encounters coldness in me, when he brings me love and devotion.

From the Jullien Family Papers, 39 AP 4, Archives Nationales, Paris, trans. by Barbara Corrado Pope, as quoted in Erna Olafson Hellerstein, Leslie Parker Hume, and Karen M. Offen, eds., *Victorian Women: A Documentary Account of Women's Lives in Nineteenth-Century England, France, and the United States* (Stanford, CA: Stanford University Press, 1981), pp. 247–248.

If the husband became ill or died, however, or if he deserted his wife, she would have to reenter the market for unskilled labor at an advanced age.

Despite these changes, many of the traditional practices associated with the family economy survived into the industrial era. As a young woman came of age, both family needs and her desire to marry still directed what she would do with her life. The most likely early occupation for a young woman was domestic service. A girl born in the country normally migrated to a nearby town or city for such employment, often living initially with a relative. As in the past, she would try to earn enough in wages to give her a dowry, so that she might marry and set up her own household. If she became a factory worker, she would probably live in a supervised dormitory. These dormitories helped attract young women into their employ by convincing parents that their daughters would be safe.

The life of young women in the cities was more precarious than earlier. There were fewer family and community ties. There were also perhaps more available young men. These men, who worked for wages rather than in the older apprenticeship structures, were more mobile, so that relationships between men and women often were more fleeting. In any case, illegitimate births increased; fewer women who became pregnant before marriage found the father willing to marry them.

Marriage in the wage industrial economy was also different in certain respects from marriage in earlier times. It still involved the starting of a separate household, but the structure of gender relationships within the household was different. Marriage was less an economic partnership. The husband's wages might well be able to support the entire family. The wage economy and the industrialization separating workplace from home made it difficult for women to combine domestic duties with work. When married women worked, it was usually in the nonindustrial sector of the economy. More often than not, it was the children rather than the wife who were sent to work. This may help explain the increase in the number of births within marriages, as children in the wage economy usually were an economic asset. Married women worked outside the home only when family needs, illness, or the death of a spouse forced them to do so.

In the home, working-class women were by no means idle. Their domestic duties were an essential factor in the family wage economy. If work took place elsewhere, someone had to be directly in charge of maintaining the home front. Homemaking came to the fore when a life at home had to be organized separately from the place of work. Wives were concerned primarily with food and cooking, but they often also were in charge of the family's finances. The role of the mother expanded when the children still living at home became wage earners. She was now providing home support for her entire wage-earning family. She created the environment to which the family members returned after work. The longer period of home life of working children may also have increased and strengthened familial bonds of affection between those children and their hardworking, homebound mothers. In all these respects, the culture of the working-class marriage and family tended to imitate the family patterns of the middle and upper classes, whose members had often accepted the view of separate gender spheres set forth by Rousseau and popularized in hundreds of novels, journals, and newspapers.

Problems of Crime and Order

Throughout the nineteenth century, the political and economic elite in Europe were profoundly concerned about social order. The revolutions of the late eighteenth and early nineteenth centuries made them fearful of future disorder and threats to life and property. The processes of industrialization and urbanization also contributed to this problem of order. Thousands of Europeans migrated from the countryside to the towns and cities. There, they often encountered poverty or unemployment and general social frustration and disappointment. Cities became places associated with criminal activity, especially crimes against property, such as theft and arson. Throughout the first sixty years of the nineteenth century, crime appears to have increased slowly but steadily before more or less reaching a plateau.

Historians and social scientists are divided about the reasons for this rise in the crime rate. So little is known about crime in rural settings, that comparisons with the cities are difficult. There are also many problems with crime statistics in the nineteenth century. No two nations kept them in the same manner. Different legal codes and systems of judicial administration were in effect in different areas of the Continent, thus giving somewhat different legal definitions of criminal activity. The result has been confusion, difficult research, and tentative conclusions.

New Police Forces

From the propertied elite classes, two major views about containing crime and criminals emerged during the nineteenth century: prison reform and better systems of police. The result of these efforts was the triumph in Europe of the idea of a policed society. This concept means the presence of a paid, professionally trained group of law-enforcement officers charged with keeping order, protecting property and lives, investigating crime, and apprehending offenders. These officers are distinct from the army and are charged specifically with domestic security. It is to them that the civilian population normally turns for law enforcement. One of the key features of the theory of a policed society is that crime may be prevented by the visible presence of law-enforcement officers. These police forces, at least in theory, did not perform a political role, although in many countries that distinction was often ignored. Police forces also became one of the major areas of municipal government employment.

London policeman. Professional police forces did not exist before the early nineteenth century. The London police force was created in 1828. Peter Newark's Pictures

Such professional police forces did not really exist until the early nineteenth century. They differed from one country to another in both authority and organization, but their creation proved to be one of the main keys to the emergence of an orderly European society. The prefect of Paris set forth the chief principles that lay behind the founding of all of these new police units when he announced in 1828 that

Safety by day and night, free traffic movement, clean streets, the supervision of and precaution against accidents, the maintenance of order in public places, the seeking out of offences and their perpetrators....The municipal police is a parental police.[3]

Professional police forces appeared in Paris in 1828. The same year, the British Parliament passed legislation sponsored by Sir Robert Peel (1788–1850) that placed police on London streets. They were soon known as *bobbies*, after the sponsor of the legislation. Similar police departments were deployed in

[3]Quoted in Clive Emsley, *Policing and Its Context, 1750–1870* (London: Macmillan, 1983), p. 58.

Berlin after the Revolution of 1848. All of these forces were distinguished by an easily recognizable uniform. Police on the Continent were armed; those in Britain were not.

Although citizens sometimes viewed police with a certain suspicion, by the end of the century, most Europeans held friendly views toward police and regarded them as their protectors. Persons from the upper and middle classes felt their property to be more secure. Persons from the working class also frequently turned to the police to protect their lives and property and to aid them in other ways in emergencies. Of course, such was not the attitude toward political or secret police, who were hated and dreaded wherever governments created them.

Prison Reform

Before the nineteenth century, European prisons were local jails or state prisons, such as the Bastille. Governments also sent criminals to prison ships, called *hulks*. Some Mediterranean nations sentenced prisoners to naval galleys, where, chained to their benches, they rowed until they died or were eventually released. In prisons, inmates lived under wretched conditions. Men, women, and children were housed together. Persons guilty of minor offenses were left in the same room with those guilty of the most serious offenses.

Beginning in the late eighteenth century, the British government used the penalty of transportation for persons convicted of the most serious offenses. Transportation to the colony of New South Wales in Australia was regarded as an alternative to capital punishment and was used by the British until the middle of the nineteenth century, when the colonies began to object. Thereafter, the British government established public works prisons in Britain to house long-term prisoners.

By the close of the eighteenth century and in the early decades of the nineteenth century, reformers, such as John Howard (1726–1790) and Elizabeth Fry (1780–1845) in England and Charles Lucas (1803–1889) in France exposed the horrendous conditions in prisons and demanded change. Reform came slowly because of the expense of constructing new prisons and a general lack of sympathy for criminals.

In the 1840s, however, both the French and the English undertook several bold efforts at prison reform. These efforts would appear to indicate a shift in opinion whereby crime was seen not as an assault on order or on authority but as a mark of a character fault in the criminal. Thereafter, part of the goal of imprisonment was to rehabilitate or transform the prisoner during the period of incarceration. The result of this change was the creation

In many prisons, treadmills like these were the only source of exercise available to English prisoners. Bildarchiv Preussischer Kulturbesitz

of exceedingly repressive prison systems designed according to the most advanced scientific modes of understanding criminals and criminal reform.

Europeans used various prison models originally established in the United States. All these experiments depended on separating prisoners from each other. One was known as the Auburn system after Auburn Prison in New York State. According to it, prisoners were separated during the night but could associate while working during the day. The other was the Philadelphia system, in which prisoners were kept rigorously separated at all times.

The chief characteristics of these systems were an individual cell for each prisoner and long periods of separation and silence among prisoners. The most famous example of this kind of prison in Europe was Pentonville Prison near London. There, each prisoner occupied a separate cell and was never allowed to speak to or see another prisoner. Each prisoner wore a mask when in the prison yard; in the chapel, each had a separate stall. The point of the system was to turn the prisoner's mind in on itself to a mode of contemplation that would reform criminal tendencies. As time passed, the system became more relaxed because the intense isolation often led to mental collapse.

In France, imprisonment became more repressive as the century passed. The French constructed prisons similar to Pentonville in the 1840s. In 1875, the French also adopted a firm general policy of isolation of inmates in prison. Sixty prisons based on this principle were constructed by 1908. Prisoners were

supposed to be trained in some kind of trade or skill while in prison so that they could reemerge as reformed citizens.

The vast increase in repeat offenses led the French government in 1885 to declare transportation the penalty for repeated serious crimes. It did this long after the British had abandoned the practice. The French sent serious repeat offenders to places such as the infamous Devil's Island off the coast of South America, literally to purge the nation of its worst criminals and to ensure that they would never return.

All of these attempts to create a police force and to reform prisons illustrate the new post-French Revolution concern about order and stability on the part of European political and social elites. On the whole, by the end of the century, an orderly society had been established, and the new police and prisons had no small role in that development.

Classical Economics

Economists whose thought derived largely from Adam Smith's *Wealth of Nations* (1776) dominated private and public discussions of industrial and commercial policy. Their ideas are often associated with the phrase *laissez-faire*. Although they thought that the government should perform many important functions, the classical economists favored economic growth through competitive free enterprise. They conceived of society as consisting of atomistic individuals whose competitive efforts met the demands of consumers in the marketplace. They believed that most economic decisions should be made through the mechanism of the marketplace. They distrusted government action, believing it to be mischievous and corrupt. The government should maintain a sound currency, enforce contracts, protect property, impose low tariffs and taxes, and leave the remainder of economic life to private initiative. The economists naturally assumed that the state would maintain enough armed forces and naval power to protect the nation's economic structure and foreign trade. The emphasis on thrift, competition, and personal industriousness voiced by the political economists appealed to the middle classes.

Malthus on Population

The classical economists suggested complicated and pessimistic ideas about the working class. Thomas Malthus (1766–1834) and David Ricardo (1772–1823), probably the most influential of all these writers, suggested, in effect, that the condition of the working class could not be improved. In 1798, Malthus published the first edition of his *Essay on the Principle of Population*. His ideas have haunted the world ever since. He contended that population must eventually outstrip the food supply. Although the human population grows geometrically, the food supply can expand only arithmetically. There was little hope of averting the disaster, in Malthus's opinion, except through late marriage, chastity, and contraception, the last of which he considered a vice. It took three-quarters of a century for contraception to become a socially acceptable method of containing the population explosion.

Malthus contended that the immediate plight of the working class could only become worse. If wages were raised, the workers would simply produce more children, who would, in turn, consume both the extra wages and more food. Later in his life, Malthus suggested, in a more optimistic vein, that if the working class could be persuaded to adopt a higher standard of living, their increased wages might be spent on consumer goods rather than on begetting more children.

Ricardo on Wages

In his *Principles of Political Economy* (1817), David Ricardo transformed the concepts of Malthus into the "iron law of wages." If wages were raised, more children would be produced. They, in turn, would enter the labor market, thus expanding the number of workers and lowering wages. As wages fell, working people would produce fewer children. Wages would then rise, and

Harriet Martineau (1802–1876) popularized the ideas of the British classical economists, using moral tales to illustrate their principles. Corbis

the process would start all over again. Consequently, in the long run, wages would always tend toward a minimum level. (See "Ricardo Enunciates the Iron Law of Wages.") These arguments simply supported employers in their natural reluctance to raise wages and also provided strong theoretical support for opposition to labor unions. The ideas of the economists were spread to the public during the 1830s through journals, newspapers, and even short stories, such as Harriet Martineau's (1802–1876) series entitled *Illustrations of Political Economy*.

Government Policies Based on Classical Economics

The working classes of France and Great Britain, needless to say, resented the attitudes of the economists, but the governments embraced them. Louis Philippe (1773–1850) and his minister François Guizot (1787–1874) told the French to go forth and enrich themselves. People who simply displayed sufficient energy need not be poor. A number of the French middle class did just that. The July Monarchy

Ricardo Enunciates the Iron Law of Wages

Political economy emerged as a science of society and economic life in the late eighteenth and early nineteenth centuries. The English economist David Ricardo was one of its most distinguished and influential practioners and a person to whom the government looked for advice. Ricardo held a very pessimistic view of the nature of wages for working people. He believed that in the long run wages would move toward a minimum level. The reason for this assumption was his conviction that, as workers achieved more prosperity, they would necessarily have more children. That rise in population would increase the size of the work force and thus drive wages to a minimum. For that reason, he argued that those who wished to see the work force prosper should encourage workers to enjoy a high standard of consumption so that they would spend money on consumer goods rather than upon larger families. He also believed that government interference would only make the situation worse.

❖ *What is the difference between the natural and market price of labor? What assumptions does Ricardo make about human nature and family life? Why does he think a high expectation of consumer comforts will prevent an increase in population leading to a lower market price for labor?*

The natural price of labour is that price which is necessary to enable the labourers, one with another, to subsist and to perpetuate their race, without either increase or diminution.

...The natural price of labour, therefore, depends on the price of the food, necessaries, and conveniences required for the support of the labourer and his family.

The market price of labour is the price which is really paid for it...; labour is dear when it is scarce, and cheap when its is plentiful....

It is when the market price of labour exceeds its natural price that the condition of the labourer is flourishing and happy, that he has it in his power to command a greater proportion of the necessaries and enjoyments of life, and therefore to rear a healthy and a numerous family. When, however, by the encouragement which high wages give to the increase of population, the number of labourers is increased, wages again fall to their natural price, and indeed from a reaction sometimes below it.

When the market price of labour is below its natural price, the condition of the labourers is most wretched.... It is only after their privations have reduced their number, or the demand of

labour has increased, that the market price will rise to its natural price, and that the labourer will have the moderate comforts which the natural rate of wages will afford....

The friends of humanity cannot but wish that in all countries the labouring classes should have a taste for comforts and enjoyments, and that they should be stimulated by all legal means in their exertion to procure them. There cannot be a better security against a superabundant population. In those countries, where the labouring classes have the fewest wants, and are contented with the cheapest food, the people are exposed to the greatest vicissitudes and miseries. They have no place of refuge from calamity; they cannot seek safety in a lower station; they are already so low, that they can fall no lower. On any deficiency of the chief article of their subsistence, there are few substitutes of which they can avail themselves, and dearth to them is attended with almost all the evils of famine....

...Like all other contracts, wages should be left to the fair and free competition of the market, and should never be controlled by the interference of the legislature.

From David Ricardo, *On the Principles of Political Economy and Taxation,* in P. Sraffa and M. H. Dobb, ed., *The Works and Correspondence of David Ricardo* (Cambridge, UK: Cambridge University Press for the Royal Economic Society, 1951), 1: 93, 94, 100–101, 105. Reprinted with the permission of Cambridge University Press.

(1830–1848) saw the construction of major capital-intensive projects, such as roads, canals, and railways. Little, however, was done about the poverty in the cities and the countryside.

In Germany, the middle classes made less headway. After the Napoleonic wars, however, the Prussian reformers had seen the desirability of abolishing internal tariffs that impeded economic growth. In

1834 all the major German states, except Austria, formed the *Zollverein*, or free trading union. Classical economics had less influence in Germany because of the tradition dating from the enlightened absolutism of state direction of economic development. The German economist Friedrich List (1789–1846) argued for this approach to economic growth during the second quarter of the century.

Britain was the home of the major classical economists, and their policies were widely accepted. The utilitarian thought of Jeremy Bentham (1748–1832) increased their influence. Although utilitarianism did not originate with him, Bentham sought to create codes of scientific law that were founded on the principle of utility, that is, the greatest happiness for the greatest number. In his *Fragment on Government* (1776) and *The Principles of Morals and Legislation* (1789), Bentham explained that the application of the principle of utility would overcome the special interests of privileged groups who prevented rational government. He regarded the existing legal and judicial systems as burdened by traditional practices that harmed the very people whom the law should serve. The application of reason and utility would remove the legal clutter that prevented justice from being realized. He believed that the principle of utility could be applied to other areas of government administration.

Bentham gathered round him political disciples who combined his ideas with those of classical economics. In 1834, the reformed House of Commons passed a new Poor Law that had been prepared by followers of Bentham. This measure established a Poor Law Commission that set out to make poverty the most undesirable of all social situations. Government poor relief was to be disbursed only in workhouses. Life in the workhouse was consciously designed to be more unpleasant than life outside. Husbands and wives were separated, the food was bad, and the enforced work was distasteful. The social stigma of the workhouse was even worse. The law and its administration presupposed that people would not work because they were lazy. The laboring class, not unjustly, regarded the workhouses as new "bastilles."

The second British monument to applied classical economics was the repeal of the Corn Laws in 1846. The Anti-Corn Law League, organized by manufacturers, had sought this goal for more than six years. The league wanted to abolish the tariffs protecting the domestic price of grain. That change would lead to lower food prices, which would then allow lower wages at no real cost to the workers. In turn, the prices on British manufactured goods could also be lowered to strengthen their competitive position in the world market.

The actual reason for Sir Robert Peel's repeal of the Corn Laws in 1846 was the Irish famine. Peel had to open British ports to foreign grain in order to feed the starving Irish. He realized that the Corn Laws could not be reimposed. Peel accompanied the abolition measure with a program for government aid to modernize British agriculture and to make it more efficient. The repeal of the Corn Laws was the culmination of the lowering of British tariffs that had begun during the 1820s. The repeal marked the opening of an era of free trade that continued until late in the century.

Early Socialism

During the twentieth century, the socialist movement, in the form of either Communist or social democratic political parties, constituted one of the major political forces in Europe. Less than 150 years ago, the advocates of socialism lacked any meaningful political following, and their doctrines appeared blurred and confused to most of their contemporaries. It is important to understand their early ideas and then to see, as we shall in later chapters, how those ideas, which for many years appeared on the margins of European political life, came to assume great importance in the late nineteenth century.

The early socialists generally applauded the new productive capacity of industrialism. They denied, however, that the free market could adequately produce and distribute goods the way the classical economists claimed. In the capitalist order, the socialists saw primarily mismanagement, low wages, maldistribution of goods, and suffering arising from the unregulated industrial system. Moreover, the socialists thought that human society should be organized as a community, rather than merely as a conglomerate of atomistic, selfish individuals.

Utopian Socialism

Among the earliest people to define the social question were a group of writers called the *utopian socialists* by their later critics. They were considered utopian because their ideas were often visionary and because they frequently advocated the creation of ideal communities. They were called socialists because they questioned the structures and values of the existing capitalistic framework. In some cases, they actually deserved neither description. A significant factor in the experience of almost all these groups was the discussion, and sometimes the practice, of radical ideas in regard to sexuality and the family. People who might have been sympathetic to their economic concerns were profoundly unsympathetic to their views on free love and open family relationships.

SAINT-SIMONIANISM Count Claude Henri de Saint-Simon (1760–1825) was the earliest of the socialist pioneers. As a young liberal French aristocrat, he had fought in the American Revolution. Later he welcomed the French Revolution, during which he made and lost a fortune. By the time of Napoleon's ascendancy, he had turned to a career of writing and social criticism.

Above all else, Saint-Simon believed that modern society would require rational management. Private wealth, property, and enterprise should be subject to an administration other than that of its owners. His ideal government would have consisted of a large board of directors organizing and coordinating the activity of individuals and groups to achieve social harmony. In a sense, he was the ideological father of technocracy. Not the *redistribution* of wealth, but its *management* by experts, would alleviate the poverty and social dislocation of the age.

When Saint-Simon died in 1825, he had persuaded only a handful of people that his ideas were correct. Nonetheless, Saint-Simonian societies were always centers for lively discussion of advanced social ideals. Some of the earliest debates in France over feminism took place within those societies. During the late 1820s and 1830s, the Saint-Simonians became well known for advocating sexuality outside marriage. Interestingly enough, several of Saint-Simon's disciples became leaders in the French railway industry during the 1850s.

OWENISM The major British contributor to the early socialist tradition was Robert Owen (1771–1858), a self-made cotton manufacturer. In his early twenties, Owen became a partner in one of the largest cotton factories in Britain at New Lanark, Scotland. Owen was a firm believer in the environmentalist psychology of the Enlightenment. If human beings were placed in the correct surroundings, they and their character could be improved. Moreover, Owen saw no incompatibility between creating a humane industrial environment and making a good profit.

At New Lanark, he put his ideas into practice. Workers were provided with good quarters. Recreational possibilities abounded, and the children received an education. There were several churches, although Owen himself was a notorious freethinker on matters of religion and sex. In the factory itself, various rewards were given for good work. His plant made a fine profit. Visitors flocked from all over Europe to see what Owen had accomplished through enlightened management.

In numerous articles and pamphlets, as well as in letters to influential people, Owen pleaded for a reorganization of industry based on his own successful model. He envisioned a series of communities shaped like parallelograms in which factory workers and farmworkers might live together and produce their goods in cooperation. During the 1820s, Owen sold his New Lanark factory and then went to the United States, where he established the community of New Harmony, Indiana. When quarrels among the members led to the community's failure, he refused to give up his reformist causes. He returned to Britain, where he became the moving force behind the organization of the Grand National Union, an attempt to draw all British trade unions into a single body. It collapsed with other labor organizations during the early 1830s.

FOURIERISM Charles Fourier (1772–1837) was the French intellectual counterpart of Owen. He was a commercial salesperson who never succeeded in attracting the same kind of public attention as Owen. He wrote his books and articles and waited at home each day at noon, hoping to meet a patron who would undertake his program. No one ever arrived to meet him. Fourier believed that the industrial order ignored the passionate side of human nature. Social discipline ignored all the pleasures that human beings naturally seek.

Fourier advocated the construction of communities, called *phalanxes*, in which liberated living would replace the boredom and dullness of industrial existence. Agrarian rather than industrial production would predominate in these communities. Sexual activity would be relatively free, and marriage was to be reserved only for later life. Fourier also urged that no person be required to perform the same kind of work for the entire day. People would be both happier and more productive if they moved from one task to another. Through his emphasis on the problem of boredom, Fourier isolated one of the key difficulties of modern economic life.

Saint-Simon, Owen, and Fourier expected some existing government to carry out their ideas. They failed to confront the political difficulties of their envisioned social transformations. Other figures paid more attention to the politics of the situation. In 1839, Louis Blanc (1811–1882) published *The Organization of Labor*. Like other socialist writers, this Frenchman demanded an end to competition, but he did not seek a wholly new society. He called for political reform that would give the vote to the working class. Once so empowered, workers could use the vote to turn the political processes to their own economic advantage. A state controlled by a working-class electorate would finance workshops to employ the poor. In time, such workshops might replace private enterprise, and industry would be organized to ensure jobs. Blanc recognized the power of the state to improve life and the conditions of labor. The state itself could become the great employer of labor.

Anarchism

Other writers and activists of the 1840s, however, rejected both industry and the dominance of government. These were the anarchists. They are usually included in the socialist tradition, although they do not exactly fit in there. Some favored programs of violence and terrorism; others were peaceful. Auguste Blanqui (1805–1881) was a major spokesperson for terror. He spent most of his adult life in jail. Seeking the abolition of both capitalism and the state, Blanqui urged the development of a professional revolutionary vanguard to attack capitalist society. His ideas for the new society were vague, but in his call for professional revolutionaries, he foreshadowed Lenin.

Pierre Joseph Proudhon (1809–1865) represented the other strain of anarchism. In his most famous work, *What Is Property?* (1840), Proudhon attacked the banking system, which rarely extended credit to small-property owners or the poor. He wanted credit expanded to allow such people to engage in economic enterprise. Society should be organized on the basis of mutualism, which amounted to a system of small businesses. There would be peaceful cooperation and exchange of goods among these groups. With such a social system, the state as it then existed would be unnecessary. His ideas later influenced the French labor movement, which was generally less directly political in its activities than the movements in Britain and Germany.

Marxism

Too often, the history of European socialism is regarded as a linear development leading naturally or necessarily to the late-century triumph of Marxism within the major socialist political parties. Nothing could be further from the truth. Marxist socialist ideas did eventually triumph over much, though not all, of Europe, but only through competition with other socialist formulas and largely as a result of the political situation in Germany during the last quarter of the century. At midcentury, the ideas of Karl Marx were simply one more contribution to a heady mixture of concepts and programs criticizing the emerging industrial capitalist society. Marxism differed from its competitors in its claims to scientific accuracy, its rejection of reform, and its call for revolution, though the character of that revolution was not well defined. Furthermore, Marx set the emergence of the industrial work force into the context of a world historical development from which he drew sweeping political conclusions. With the collapse of the Soviet Union and of the communist governments in Eastern Europe in the last quarter of the twentieth century, it is difficult for many people to recapture the power that Marx's political and social vision exerted over Europe and then many other parts of the world for more than a hundred years.

Karl Marx's socialist philosophy eventually triumphed over most alternative versions of socialism in Europe, but his monumental work became subject to varying interpretations, criticisms, and revisions that continue to this day. Bildarchiv Preussischer Kulturbesitz

Karl Marx (1818–1883) was born in the Rhineland. His family was Jewish, but his father had converted to Lutheranism, and Judaism played no role in his education. Marx's middle-class parents sent him to the University of Berlin, where he became deeply involved in Hegelian philosophy and radical politics. During 1842 and 1843, he edited the radical *Rhineland Gazette* (*Rheinische Zeitung*). Soon the German authorities drove him from his native land. He lived as an exile in Paris, then in Brussels, and finally, after 1849, in London.

PARTNERSHIP WITH ENGELS In 1844 Marx met Friedrich Engels (1820–1895), another young middle-class German, whose father owned a textile factory in Manchester, England. The next year Engels published *The Condition of the Working Class in England*, which presented a devastating picture of industrial life. The two men became fast friends. Late in 1847, they were asked to write a pamphlet for a newly organized and ultimately short-lived secret Communist League. *The Communist Manifesto*, published in German, appeared early in 1848. Marx, Engels, and the league had adopted the name *communist* because the term was much more self-consciously radical than *socialist*. Communism implied the outright abolition of private property, rather than some less extensive rearrangement of society. A work of fewer than fifty pages, the *Manifesto* would become the most influential political document of modern European and possibly world history, but that development lay in the future. At the time, it was simply one more political tract. Moreover, neither Marx nor his thought had any effect on the revolutionary events of 1848.

SOURCES OF MARX'S IDEAS The major ideas of the *Manifesto* and of Marx's later work, including *Capital* (vol. I, 1867), were derived from German Hegelianism, French socialism, and British classical economics. Marx applied to concrete, historical social and economic developments Hegel's abstract philosophical concept that thought develops from the clash of thesis and antithesis into a new intellectual synthesis. For Marx, the conflict between dominant and subordinate social groups generated conditions that led to the emergence of a new dominant social group. These new social relationships, in turn, generated new discontent, conflict, and development.

The French socialists provided Marx with a portrayal of the problems of capitalist society and had raised the issue of property redistribution. Both Hegel and Saint-Simon led Marx to see society and economic conditions as developing through historical stages. The classical economists had produced the analytical tools for an empirical, scientific examination of industrial capitalist society.

Using the intellectual tools provided by Hegel, the French socialists, and the British classical economists, Marx fashioned a philosophy that gave a very special role or function to the new industrial work force as the single most important driving force of contemporary history. Marx later explained to a friend:

What I did that was new was to prove: (1) that the existence of classes is bound up with particular historical phases in the development of production; (2) that the class struggle necessarily leads to the dictatorship of the proletariat; (3) that this dictatorship itself only constitutes the transition to the abolition of all classes and to a classless society.[4]

In the *Communist Manifesto* and his numerous other writings, Marx equated the fate of the proletariat— that is, the new industrial labor force—with the fate of humanity itself. According to Marx, as the proletariat came to liberate itself from its bondage to the capitalist mode of industrial production, such liberation would eventually amount to the liberation of all humanity. It was this utopian vision of human emancipation, no matter how the actual later development of the European and world economy failed to conform to Marx's predictions, that drew many people from Europe and elsewhere to embrace much of his thought and to base their political actions upon their understanding of his philosophy. But besides this wider vision, the details of Marx's argument were important as well for later nineteenth-century and twentieth-century European political life.

REVOLUTION THROUGH CLASS CONFLICT In the *Communist Manifesto*, Marx and Engels contended that human history must be understood rationally and as a whole. History is the record of humankind's coming to grips with physical nature to produce the goods necessary for survival. That basic productive process determines the structures, values, and ideas of a society. Historically, the organization of the means of production has always involved conflict between the classes that owned and controlled the means of production and the classes that worked for them. That necessary conflict has provided the engine for historical development; it is not an accidental byproduct of mismanagement or bad intentions. Thus, piecemeal reforms cannot eliminate the social and economic evils that are inherent in the very structures of production. A radical social transformation is required. The development of capitalism will make such a revolution inevitable.

In Marx's and Engels's eyes, the class conflict that had characterized previous Western history had become simplified during the early nineteenth century into a struggle between the bourgeoisie and the proletariat, or between the middle class associated with industry and commerce on the one hand and the workers on the other. The character of capitalism itself ensured the sharpening of the struggle. Capitalist production and competition would steadily increase the size of the unpropertied proletariat. Large-scale mechanical production crushed both traditional and smaller industrial producers into the ranks of the proletariat. As the business structures grew larger and larger, the competitive pressures would squeeze out smaller middle-class units. Competition among the few remaining giant concerns would lead to more intense suffering for the proletariat. The process also meant that the proletariat itself would continue to expand to include more and more people. As this ever-expanding body of workers suffered increasingly from the competition among the ever-enlarging firms, Marx contended, they would eventually begin to foment revolution. Finally, they would overthrow the few remaining owners of the means of production. For a

---

[4]Albert Fried and Ronald Sanders, eds., *Socialist Thought: A Documentary History* (Garden City, NY: Anchor Doubleday, 1964), p. 295.

Major Works of Economic and Political Commentary
1776 Adam Smith, *The Wealth of Nations*
1798 Thomas Malthus, *Essay on the Principle of Population*
1817 David Ricardo, *Principles of Political Economy*
1830s Harriet Martineau, *Illustrations of Political Economy*
1839 Louis Blanc, *The Organization of Labor*
1845 Friedrich Engels, *The Condition of the Working Class in England*
1848 Karl Marx and Friedrich Engels, *The Communist Manifesto*

time, the workers would organize the means of production through a dictatorship of the proletariat. This would eventually give way to a propertyless and classless communist society.

This proletarian revolution was inevitable, according to Marx and Engels. The structure of capitalism required competition and consolidation of enterprise. Although the class conflict involved in the contemporary process resembled that of the past, it differed in one major respect: The struggle between the capitalistic bourgeoisie and the industrial proletariat would culminate in a wholly new society that would be free of class conflict. The victorious proletariat, by its very nature, could not be a new oppressor class: "The proletarian movement is the self-conscious, independent movement of the immense majority, in the interest of the immense majority."[5] The result of the proletarian victory would be "an association, in which the free development of each is the condition for the free development of all."[6] The victory of the proletariat over the bourgeoisie would represent the culmination of human history. For the first time in human history, one group of people would not be oppressing another.

The economic environment of the 1840s had conditioned Marx's analysis. The decade had seen much unemployment and deprivation. During the later part of the century, however, capitalism did not collapse as he had predicted, nor did the middle class become proletarianized. Rather, more and more people came to benefit from the industrial system. Nonetheless, within a generation Marxism had captured the imagination of many socialists, especially in Germany, and

large segments of the working class. Marxist doctrines appeared to be based on the empirical evidence of hard economic fact. This scientific claim of Marxism helped spread the ideology as science became more influential during the second half of the century. But at its core, the attraction of the ideology was its utopian vision of ultimate human liberation, no matter how illiberal or authoritarian the governments were that embraced that vision in the twentieth century.

1848: Year of Revolutions

In 1848, a series of liberal and nationalistic revolutions erupted across the Continent. No single factor caused this general revolutionary groundswell; rather, similar conditions existed in several countries. Severe food shortages had prevailed since 1846. Grain and potato harvests had been poor. The famine in Ireland was simply the worst example of a more widespread situation. The commercial and industrial economy was also depressed. Unemployment was widespread. All systems of poor relief were overburdened. These difficulties, added to the wretched living conditions in the cities, heightened the sense of frustration and discontent of the urban artisan and laboring classes.

The dynamic force for change in 1848 originated, however, not with the working classes, but with the political liberals, who were generally drawn from the middle classes. Throughout the Continent, liberals were pushing for their program of more representative government, civil liberty, and unregulated economic life. The repeal of the English Corn Laws and the example of peaceful agitation by the Anti-Corn Law League encouraged them. The liberals on the Continent wanted to pursue similar peaceful tactics. To put additional pressure on their governments, however, they began to appeal for the support of the urban working classes. The goals of the latter were improved working and economic conditions, rather than a liberal framework of government. Moreover, the tactics of the working classes were frequently violent rather than peaceful. The temporary alliance of liberals and workers in several states overthrew or severely shook the old order; then the allies began to fight each other.

Finally, outside France, nationalism was an important common factor in the uprisings. Germans, Hungarians, Italians, Czechs, and smaller national groups in eastern Europe sought to create national states that would reorganize or replace existing political entities. The Austrian Empire, as usual, was the state most profoundly endangered by nationalism. At the same time, however, various national groups clashed with each other during these revolutions.

The immediate results of the 1848 revolutions were stunning. Never in a single year had Europe

[5]Robert C. Tucker, ed., *The Marx–Engels Reader* (New York: W.W. Norton, 1972), p. 353.

[6]*Ibid.*

known so many major uprisings. The French monarchy fell, and many other thrones were badly shaken. Yet the revolutions proved a false spring for progressive Europeans. Without exception, the revolutions failed to establish genuinely liberal or national states. The conservative order proved stronger and more resilient than anyone had expected. Moreover, the liberal middle-class political activists in each country discovered that they could no longer push for political reform without also raising the social question. The liberals refused to follow political revolution with social reform and thus isolated themselves from the working classes. Once separated from potential mass support, the liberal revolutions became an easy prey to the armies of the reactionary classes.

France: The Second Republic and Louis Napoleon

As had happened twice before, the revolutionary tinder first blazed in Paris. The liberal political opponents of the corrupt regime of Louis Philippe and his minister Guizot had organized a series of political banquets. These occasions were used to criticize the government and to demand further middle-class admission to the political process. The poor harvests of 1846 and 1847 and the resulting high food prices and unemployment brought working-class support to the liberal campaign. On February 21, 1848, the government forbade further banquets. A large one had been scheduled for the next day. On February 22, disgruntled Parisian workers paraded through the streets demanding reform and Guizot's ouster. The next morning the crowds grew, and by afternoon Guizot had resigned. The crowds had erected barricades, and numerous clashes had occurred between the citizenry and the municipal guard. On February 24, 1848, Louis Philippe abdicated and fled to England.

THE NATIONAL ASSEMBLY AND PARIS WORKERS   The liberal opposition, led by the poet Alphonse de Lamartine (1790–1869), organized a provisional government. The liberals intended to call an election

During the February days of the French Revolution of 1848, crowds in Paris burned the throne of Louis Philippe. Bildarchiv Preussischer Kulturbesitz

for an assembly that would write a republican constitution. The various working-class groups in Paris, however, had other ideas: They wanted a social as well as a political revolution. Led by Louis Blanc, they demanded representation in the cabinet. Blanc and two other radical leaders were made ministers. Under their pressure, the provisional government organized national workshops to provide work and relief for thousands of unemployed workers.

On Sunday, April 23, an election based on universal male suffrage chose the new National Assembly. The result was a legislature dominated by moderates and conservatives. In the French provinces, there had been much resentment against the Paris radicals. The church and the local notables still exercised considerable influence. Small landowning peasants feared possible confiscation of their holdings by Parisian socialists. The new conservative National Assembly had little sympathy for the expensive national workshops, which they incorrectly perceived to be socialistic. (See "Paris Workers Complain about the Actions of the Second Republic.")

Throughout May, government troops and the Parisian crowd of unemployed workers and artisans clashed. As a result, the assembly closed the workshops to new entrants and planned the removal of many enrolled workers. By late June, barricades again appeared in Paris. On June 24, under orders from the government, General Cavaignac (1802–1857), with troops drawn largely from the conservative countryside, moved to destroy the barricades and to quell potential disturbances. During the next two days, more than

During June 1848, troops moved against the insurrection in Paris. This edition of a French journal is reporting those events and illustrates a moment before a clash between troops and revolutionaries.
Bildarchiv Preussischer Kulturbesitz

Paris Workers Complain about the Actions of the Second Republic

In the late spring of 1848, the government of the recently formed Second French Republic abolished the national workshops that it had created a few weeks earlier to provide aid for the unemployed. The first selection presented illustrates the anger felt by the workers. The second selection describes the experience of a cabinet worker who, for a time, had enrolled in one of the workshops.

❖ *Each of these statements reflects political disillusionment, but how does each reflect a different kind of disillusionment? How does the first statement reflect a sense of an expected economic reward for political action? How does the second statement reflect a belief in a political philosophy of cooperation among different classes or social groups?*

To the Finance Minister of the Republic

Are you really the man who was the first finance minister of the Republic, of the Republic won at the cost of blood thanks to the workers' courage, of this Republic whose first vow was to provide bread every day for all its children by proclaiming the universal right to work. Work, who will give it to us if not the state at a time when industry has everywhere closed its workshops, shops and factories? Yesterday martyrs for the Republic out on the barricades, today its defenders in the ranks of the national guard, the workers might consider it owed them something....

Why do the national workshops so rouse your reprobation...? You are not asking for their reform, but for their total abolition. But what is to be done with this mass of 100,000 workers who are waiting each day for their modest pay, for the means of existence for themselves and their families? Are they to be left a prey to the evil influences of hunger and of the excesses that follow in the wake of despair?

A Letter to a Newspaper Editor

I live in the *fauborg* [a working-class neighborhood]; by trade I am a cabinet-maker and I am enrolled in the national workshops, waiting for trade to pick up again.

I went into the workshops when I could no longer find bread elsewhere. Since then people have said we were given charity there. But when I went in I did not think that I was becoming a beggar. I believed that my brothers who were rich were giving me a little of what they had to spare simply because I was their brother.

I admit that I have not worked very hard in the national workshops, but then I have done what I could. I am too old now to change my trade easily—that is one explanation. But there is another: the fact is that, in the national workshops, there is absolutely nothing to do.

From Roger Price, ed. and trans, *1848 in France* (Ithaca, NY: Cornell University Press, 1975), pp. 103–104.

---

400 people were killed. Thereafter, troops hunted down another 3,000 persons in street fighting. The drive for social revolution had ended.

EMERGENCE OF LOUIS NAPOLEON The so-called June Days confirmed the political predominance of conservative property holders in French life. They wanted a state that was safe for small property. This search for social order received further confirmation late in 1848. The victor in the presidential election was Louis Napoleon Bonaparte (1808–1873), a nephew of the great emperor. For most of his life,

he had been an adventurer living outside France. Twice he had attempted to lead a coup against the July Monarchy. The disorder of 1848 gave him a new opportunity to enter French political life. After the corruption of Louis Philippe and the turmoil of the early months of the Second Republic, the voters turned to the name of Bonaparte as a source of stability and greatness.

The election of the "Little Napoleon" doomed the Second Republic. Louis Napoleon was dedicated to his own fame rather than to republican institutions. He was the first of the modern dictators who, by playing on unstable politics and social insecurity, greatly changed European life. He constantly quarreled with the National Assembly and claimed that he, rather than they, represented the will of the nation. In 1851, the assembly refused to amend the constitution to allow the president to run for reelection. Consequently, on December 2, 1851, the anniversary of the great Napoleon's victory at Austerlitz, Louis Napoleon personally seized power. Troops dispersed the assembly, and the president called for new elections. More than 200 people died resisting the coup, and more than 26,000 persons were arrested throughout the country. Almost 10,000 persons who opposed the coup were transported to Algeria.

Yet, in the plebiscite of December 21, 1851, more than 7.5 million voters supported the actions of Louis Napoleon and approved a new constitution that consolidated his power. Only about 600,000 citizens dared to vote against him. A year later, in December 1852, an empire was proclaimed, and Louis Napoleon became Emperor Napoleon III. Again a plebiscite approved the action. For the second time in just over fifty years, France had turned from republicanism to Caesarism. (See "Karl Marx Ponders the Revolutionary History of France and Louis Napoleon's Coup.")

FRENCHWOMEN IN 1848   The years between the February Revolution of 1848 and the Napoleonic coup of 1852 saw major feminist activity on the part of Frenchwomen. Especially in Paris, women seized the opportunity of the collapse of the July Monarchy to voice demands for reform of their social conditions. They joined the wide variety of political clubs that emerged in the wake of the revolution. Some of these clubs particularly emphasized women's rights. Some women even tried unsuccessfully to vote in the various elections of 1848. Both middle-class and working-class women were involved in these activities. The most radical group of women called themselves the Vesuvians, after the volcano in Italy. They claimed it was time for the demands of women to come forth like pent-up lava. They demanded full domestic household equality between men and women, the right of women to serve in the military, and similarity in dress for both sexes. They also conducted street demonstrations. The radical character of their demands and actions lost them the support of more moderate women.

Certain Parisian women quickly attempted to use for their own cause the liberal freedoms that suddenly had become available. They organized the *Voix des femmes* (*The Women's Voice*), a daily newspaper that addressed issues of concern to women. The newspaper insisted that improving the lot of men would not necessarily improve the condition of women. They soon organized a society with the same name

as the newspaper. Many of the women involved in the newspaper and society had earlier been involved in Saint-Simonian or Fourierist groups. Members of the *Voix des femmes* group were relatively conservative feminists. They cooperated with male political groups, and they urged the integrity of the family and fidelity in marriage. They furthermore warmly embraced the maternal role for women, but tried to use that social function to raise the importance of women in society. Because motherhood and child rearing are so important to a society, they argued, women must receive better education, the right to work, economic security, equal civil rights, property rights, and the right to vote. The provisional government made no move to enact these rights, although some members of the assembly supported the women's groups. The emphasis on family and motherhood represented in part a defensive strategy to prevent conservative women and men from accusing the advocates of women's rights of seeking to destroy the family and traditional marriage.

The fate of French feminists in 1848 was similar to that of the radical workers. They were thoroughly defeated and their efforts wholly frustrated. Once the elections were held that spring, the new government expressed no sympathy for their causes. The closing of the national workshops adversely affected women workers as well as men and blocked one outlet that women had used to make their needs known. The conservative crackdown on political clubs closed another arena in which women had participated. Women were soon specifically forbidden to participate in political clubs either by themselves or with men. These repressive actions repeated what had happened to politically active Frenchwomen and their organizations in 1793.

At this point, women associated with the *Voix des femmes* attempted to organize workers' groups to improve the economic situation for working-class women. Two leaders of this effort, Jeanne Deroin (d. 1894) and Pauline Roland (1805–1852), were arrested, tried, and imprisoned for these activities. The former eventually went into exile from France; the latter was sent off to Algeria during the repression after the coup of Louis Napoleon. By 1852, the entire feminist movement that had sprung up in 1848 had been thoroughly eradicated.

The Habsburg Empire: Nationalism Resisted

The events of February 1848 in Paris immediately reverberated throughout the Habsburg domains. The empire was susceptible to revolutionary challenge on every score. Its government rejected liberal

Karl Marx Ponders the Revolutionary History of France and Louis Napoleon's Coup

Besides being a major political philosopher, Karl Marx was a gifted newspaper journalist noted for his biting sarcasm and wit. In late 1851 and early 1852, he contributed to a German-language journal published in New York City a series of articles on the recent coup of Louis Napoleon. Marx used the articles in part to outline his understanding of the constraints within which human beings could function as historical actors. He saw them as repeatedly attempting to interpret their present historical actions in terms of those of the past. He emphasized how the events in France from 1848 through 1851 had appeared to some people to repeat those of the French Revolution of the late eighteenth century. The attraction of Louis Napoleon caricatured the attraction of his much greater uncle. Marx, however, went beyond commenting on events in France to suggest that the future social revolution of the nineteenth century that he hoped to foster must be different than previous revolutions in France and must seek different goals and look to different actors.

❖ *What constraints does Marx say limit human beings as historical actors? Why do people attempt to depict their actions as repetitions of earlier eras? Why does Marx write so contemptuously of Louis Napoleon? Why does he believe that the social revolution of the nineteenth century must be different from revolutions of the past?*

Hegel remarks somewhere that all facts and personages of great importance in world history occur, as it were twice. He forgot to add: the first time as tragedy, the second as farce....

Men make their own history, but they do not make it just as they please; they do not make it under circumstances chosen by themselves, but under circumstances directly encountered, given and transmitted from the past. The tradition of all the dead generations weighs like a nightmare on the brain of the living. And just when they seem engaged in revolutionizing themselves and things, in creating something that has never yet existed, precisely in such periods of revolutionary crisis they anxiously conjure up the spirits of the past to their service and borrow from them names, battle-cries and costumes in order to present the new scene of world history in this time-honored disguise and this borrowed language. Thus Luther donned the mask of the apostle Paul, the revolution of 1789 to 1814 draped itself alternately as the Roman Republic and the Roman Empire, and the revolution of 1848 knew nothing better to do than to parody, now 1789, now the revolutionary tradition of 1793 to 1795.

In like manner a beginner who has learnt a new language always translates it back into his mother tongue, but he has assimilated the spirit of the new language and can freely express himself in it only when he finds his way into it without recalling the old and forgets his native tongue in the use of the new....

...The French, so long as they were engaged in revolution, could not get rid of the memory of Napoleon....They hankered to return from the perils of revolution to the fleshpots of Egypt, and December 2, 1851 was the answer. They have not only a caricature of the old Napoleon, they have the old Napoleon himself, caricatured as he must appear in the middle of the nineteenth century.

The social revolution of the nineteenth century cannot draw its poetry from the past, but only from the future. It cannot begin with itself before it has stripped off all superstition about the past. Earlier revolutions required recollections of past world history in order to dull themselves to their own content. In order to arrive at its own content, the revolution of the nineteenth century must let the dead bury their dead.

From Karl Marx, *The Eighteenth Brumaire of Louis Napoleon*, in Karl Marx, *Selected Writings*, Lawrence H. Simon, ed. © 1994 International Publishers Co., pp. 188–189, 190. Reprinted by permission of International Publishers Co.

When revolution broke out in Vienna, Metternich resigned his leadership of the government.
Bildarchiv Preussischer Kulturbesitz

institutions. Its borders cut across national lines. Its society perpetuated serfdom. During the 1840s, even Metternich had urged reform, but none was forthcoming. In 1848, the regime confronted major rebellions in Vienna, Prague, Hungary, and Italy. It was also intimately concerned about the disturbances that broke out in Germany.

THE VIENNA UPRISING The Habsburg troubles began on March 3, 1848, when Louis Kossuth (1802–1894), a Magyar nationalist and member of the Hungarian diet, attacked Austrian domination of Hungary, called for the independence of Hungary, and demanded a responsible ministry under the Habsburg dynasty. Ten days later, inspired by Kossuth's speeches, students led a series of major disturbances in Vienna. The army failed to restore order. Metternich resigned and fled the country. The feebleminded Emperor Ferdinand (r. 1835–1848) promised a moderately liberal constitution. Unsatisfied, the radical students then formed democratic clubs to press the revolution further. On May 17, the emperor and the imperial court fled to Innsbruck. The government of Vienna at this point lay in the hands of a committee of more than 200 persons concerned primarily with alleviating the economic plight of Viennese workers.

What the Habsburg government actually most feared was not the urban rebellions but a potential uprising of the serfs in the countryside. Already there had been isolated instances of serfs invading manor houses and burning records. Consequently, almost immediately after the Vienna uprising, the imperial government had emancipated the serfs in

much of Austria. The Hungarian diet also abolished serfdom in March 1848. These actions smothered the most serious potential threat to order in the empire. The emancipated serfs now had little reason to support the revolutionary movement in the cities. These emancipations were one of the most important permanent results of the Revolutions of 1848.

THE MAGYAR REVOLT The Vienna revolt had further encouraged the Hungarians. The Magyar leaders of the Hungarian March Revolution were primarily liberals supported by nobles who wanted their aristocratic liberties guaranteed against the central government in Vienna. The Hungarian diet passed the March Laws, a series of laws that ensured equality of religion, jury trials, the election of a lower chamber, a relatively free press, and payment of taxes by the nobility. Emperor Ferdinand approved these measures because in the spring of 1848 he could do little else.

The Magyars also hoped to establish a separate Hungarian state within the Habsburg domains. They would retain considerable local autonomy while Ferdinand remained their emperor. As part of this scheme for a partially independent state, the Hungarians attempted to annex Transylvania, Croatia, and other eastern territories of the Habsburg Empire. That policy of annexation would have brought Romanians, Croatians, and Serbs under Magyar government. These national groups resisted the drive toward Magyarization, the most important element of which was the imposition upon them of the Hungarian language. The national groups now being repressed by the Hungarians believed that they had a better chance of maintaining their national or ethnic identity, their languages, and their economic self-interest under Habsburg control. In late March, the Vienna government sent Count Joseph Jellachich (1801–1859) to aid the national groups who were rebelling against the rebellious Hungarians. By early September 1848, he was leading an invasion force against Hungary with the strong support of the national groups who were resisting Magyarization. These events in Hungary represented a prime example of the clash between liberalism and nationalism. The state that the Hungarian March Laws would have governed was liberal in political structure, but it would not have allowed autonomy to the non-Magyar peoples within its borders.

CZECH NATIONALISM   In the middle of March 1848, with Vienna and Budapest in revolt, Czech nationalists demanded that Bohemia and Moravia be permitted to constitute an autonomous Slavic state within the empire similar to that just constituted in Hungary. Conflict immediately developed, however, between the Czechs and the Germans living in these regions. The Czechs summoned a congress of Slavs, including Poles, Ruthenians, Czechs, Slovaks, Croats, Slovenes, and Serbs, which met in Prague during early June. Under the leadership of Francis Palacky (1798–1876), this first Pan-Slavic Congress issued a manifesto calling for the national equality of Slavs within the Habsburg Empire. The manifesto also protested the repression of all Slavic peoples under Habsburg, Hungarian, German, and Ottoman domination. The document raised the vision of a

vast East European Slavic nation or federation of Slavic states that would extend from Poland south and eastward through Ukraine and within which Russian interests would surely dominate. (See "The Pan-Slavic Congress Calls for the Liberation of Slavic Nationalities.") Although such a state never came into being, the prospect of a unified Slavic people freed from Ottoman and Habsburg control was an important political factor in later European history. Pan-slavism would become a tool that Russia would use in attempts to gain the support of nationalist minorities in eastern Europe and the Balkans and to bring pressure against both the Habsburg Empire and Germany.

On June 12, the day the Pan-Slavic Congress closed, a radical insurrection broke out in Prague. General Prince Alfred Windischgraetz (1787–1862), whose wife had been killed by a stray bullet, moved his troops against the uprising. The local middle class was happy to see the radicals suppressed, as they were by June 17. The Germans in the area approved the smothering of Czech nationalism. The policy of "divide and conquer" had succeeded.

REBELLION IN NORTHERN ITALY   While repelling the Hungarian and Czech bids for autonomy, the Habsburg government also faced war in northern Italy. A revolution against Habsburg domination began in Milan on March 18. Five days later, the Austrian commander General Count Joseph Wenzel Radetzky (1766–1858) retreated from the city. King Charles Albert of Piedmont (r. 1831–1849), who wanted to expand the influence of his kingdom in

Louis Kossuth, a Magyar nationalist, seeking to raise troops to fight for Hungarian independence during the revolutionary disturbances of 1848.
Bildarchiv Preussischer Kulturbesitz

The Pan-Slavic Congress Calls for the Liberation of Slavic Nationalities

The first Pan-Slavic Congress met in Prague in June 1848. It called for the reorganization of the Austrian Empire and the political reorganization of most of the rest of eastern Europe. Its calls for changes in the national standing of the various Slavic peoples would have touched the Russian, Austrian, and Ottoman empires, as well as some of the then disunited states of Germany. The national aspirations voiced in the manifesto of the Congress would affect Europe from that time to the present. Note that the authors recognize that the principle of nationality, as adapted to the political life of Slavic peoples, is relatively new in 1848.

❖ *How did the authors of the manifesto apply the individual freedoms associated with the French Revolution to the fate of individual nations? What are the specific areas of Europe that these demands would have changed? What potential national or ethnic differences among the Slavic peoples does the manifesto ignore or gloss over?*

The Slavic Congress in Prague is something un-heard-of, in Europe as well as among the Slavs themselves. For the first time since our appearance in history, we, the scattered members of a great race, have gathered in great numbers from distant lands in order to become reacquainted as brothers and to deliberate our affairs peacefully. We have understood one another not only through our beautiful language, spoken by eighty millions, but also through the consonance of our hearts and the similarity of our spiritual qualities....

It is not only in behalf of the individual within the state that we raise our voices and make known our demands. The nation, with all its intellectual merit, is as sacred to us as are the rights of an individual under natural law....

In the belief that the powerful spiritual stream of today demands new political forms and that the state must be re-established upon altered principles, if not within new boundaries, we have suggested to the Austrian Emperor, under whose constitutional government we, the majority [of Slavic peoples] live, that he transform his imperial state into a union of equal nations....

...We raise our voices vigorously in behalf of our unfortunate brothers, the Poles, who were robbed of their national identity by insidious force. We call upon the governments to rectify this curse and these old onerous and hereditary sins in their administrative policy, and we trust in the compassion of all Europe....We demand that the Hungarian Ministry abolish without delay the use of inhuman and coercive means toward the Salvic races in Hungary, namely the Serbs, Croats, Slovaks, and Ruthenians, and that they promptly be completely assured of their national rights. Finally, we hope that the inconsiderate policies of the Porte will no longer hinder our Slavic brothers in Turkey from strongly claiming their nationality and developing it in a natural way. If, therefore, we formally express our opposition to such despicable deeds, we do so in the confidence that we are working for the good of freedom. Freedom makes the peoples who hitherto have ruled more just and makes them understand that injustice and arrogance bring disgrace not to those who must endure it but to those who act in such a manner.

From the "Manifesto of the First Pan-Slavic Congress," trans. by Max Riedlsperger from I. I. Udalzow, *Aufzeichnungen über die Geschichte des nationalen und politischen Kampfes in Böhme im Jahre 1848* (Berlin: Rutten & Loening, 1953), pp. 223–226, as quoted in Stephen Fischer-Galati, ed., *Man, State, and Society in East European History* (New York: Praeger Publishers, 1970), pp. 156–159. Copyright © 1970 by Praeger Publishers. Reproduced by permission of Greenwood Publishing Group, Inc., Wesport, CT.

Lombardy (the province of which Milan is the capital), aided the rebels. The Austrian forces fared badly until July, when Radetzky, reinforced by new troops, defeated Piedmont and suppressed the revolution. For the time being, Austria had held its position in northern Italy.

Vienna and Hungary remained to be recaptured. In midsummer, the emperor returned to the capital. A newly elected assembly was trying to write a constitution, while within the city the radicals continued to press for further concessions. The imperial government decided to reassert its control. When a new insurrection occurred in October, the imperial army bombarded Vienna and crushed the revolt. On December 2, Emperor Ferdinand, now clearly too feeble to govern, abdicated in favor of his young nephew Francis Joseph (r. 1848–1916). Real power now lay with Prince Felix Schwarzenberg (1800–1852), who intended to use the army with full force.

On January 5, 1849, troops occupied Budapest. By March the triumphant Austrian forces had imposed military rule over Hungary, and the new emperor repudiated the recent constitution. The Magyar nobles attempted one last revolt. In August, Austrian troops, reinforced by 200,000 soldiers happily furnished by Tsar Nicholas I of Russia (r. 1825–1855), finally crushed the Hungarian revolt. Croatians and other nationalities that had resisted Magyarization welcomed the collapse of the revolt. The imperial Habsburg government had survived its gravest internal challenge because of the divisions among its enemies and its own willingness to use military force with a vengeance.

Italy: Republicanism Defeated

The brief Piedmont–Austrian war of 1848 marked only the first stage of the Italian revolution. Many Italians hoped that King Charles Albert of Piedmont would drive Austria from the peninsula and thus prepare the way for Italian unification. The defeat of Piedmont was a sharp disappointment to them. Liberal and nationalist hopes then shifted to the Pope. Pius IX (r. 1846–1878) had a liberal reputation. He had reformed the administration of the Papal States. Nationalists believed that some form of a united Italian state might emerge under the leadership of this pontiff.

In Rome, however, as in other cities, political radicalism was on the rise. On November 15, 1848, a democratic radical assassinated Count Pelligrino Rossi (r. 1787–1848), the liberal minister of the Papal States. The next day, popular demonstrations forced the Pope to appoint a radical ministry. Shortly thereafter, Pius IX fled to Naples for refuge. In February 1849, the radicals proclaimed the Roman Republic. Republican nationalists from all over Italy, including Giuseppe Mazzini (1805–1872) and Giuseppe Garibaldi (1807–1882), two of the most prominent, flocked to Rome. They hoped to use the new republic as a base of operations to unite the rest of Italy under a republican government.

In March 1849, radicals in Piedmont forced Charles Albert to renew the patriotic war against Austria. After the almost immediate defeat of Piedmont at the Battle of Novara, the king abdicated in favor of his son, Victor Emmanuel II (r. 1849–1878). The defeat meant that the Roman Republic must defend itself alone. The troops that attacked Rome and restored the Pope came from France. The French wanted to prevent the rise of a strong, unified state on their southern border. Moreover, protection of the Pope was good domestic politics for the French Republic and its president, Louis Napoleon. In early June 1849, 10,000 French soldiers laid siege to Rome. By the end of the month, the Roman Republic had dissolved. Garibaldi attempted to lead an army north against Austria, but was defeated. On July 3, Rome fell to the French forces, which stayed there to protect the Pope until 1870.

Pius IX returned, having renounced his previous liberalism. He became one of the archconservatives of the next quarter century. Leadership toward Italian unification would have to come from another direction.

Germany: Liberalism Frustrated

The revolutionary contagion had also spread rapidly through numerous states of Germany. Württemberg, Saxony, Hanover, and Bavaria all experienced insurrections calling for liberal government and greater German unity. The major revolution, however, occurred in Prussia.

REVOLUTION IN PRUSSIA By March 15, 1848, large popular disturbances had erupted in Berlin. Frederick William IV (r. 1840–1861), believing that the trouble stemmed from foreign conspirators, refused to turn his troops on the Berliners. He even announced certain limited reforms. Nevertheless, on March 18, several citizens were killed when troops cleared a square near the palace.

The monarch was still hesitant to use his troops forcefully, and there was much confusion in the government. The king also called for a Prussian constituent assembly to write a constitution. The next day, as angry Berliners crowded around the palace, Frederick William IV appeared on the balcony to salute the corpses of his slain subjects. He made further concessions and implied that henceforth Prussia would aid the movement toward German unification. For all practical purposes, the Prussian monarchy had capitulated.

Frederick William IV appointed a cabinet headed by David Hansemann (1790–1864), a widely respected moderate liberal. The Prussian constituent assembly, however, proved to be radical and democratic. As time passed, the king and his conservative supporters decided that they would ignore the assembly. The liberal ministry resigned and was replaced by a conservative one. In April

The Revolutionary Crisis of 1848–1851

1848

February 22–24	Revolution in Paris forces the abdication of Louis Philippe
February 26	National workshops established in Paris
March 3	Kossuth attacks the Habsburg domination of Hungary
March 13	Revolution in Vienna
March 15	The Habsburg emperor accepts the Hungarian March Revolution Laws in Berlin
March 18	Frederick William IV of Prussia promises a constitution; Revolution in Milan
March 19	Frederick William IV is forced to salute the corpses of slain revolutionaries in Berlin
March 22	Piedmont declares war on Austria
April 23	Election of the French National Assembly
May 15	Worker protests in Paris lead the National Assembly to close the national workshops
May 17	Habsburg emperor Ferdinand flees from Vienna to Innsbruck
May 18	The Frankfurt Assembly gathers to prepare a German constitution
June 2	Pan-Slavic Congress gathers in Prague
June 17	A Czech revolution in Prague is suppressed
June 23–26	A workers' insurrection in Paris is suppressed by the troops of the National Assembly
July 24	Austria defeats Piedmont
September 17	General Jellachich invades Hungary
October 31	Vienna falls to the bombardment of General Windischgraetz
November 15	Papal minister Rossi is assassinated in Rome
November 16	Revolution in Rome
November 25	Pope Pius IX flees Rome
December 2	Habsburg Emperor Ferdinand abdicates and Francis Joseph becomes emperor
December 10	Louis Napoleon is elected president of the Second French Republic

1849

January 5	General Windischgraetz occupies Budapest
February 2	The Roman Republic is proclaimed
March 12	War is resumed between Piedmont and Austria
March 23	Piedmont is defeated, and Charles Albert abdicates the crown of Piedmont in favor of Victor Emmanuel II
March 27	The Frankfurt Parliament completes a constitution for Germany
March 28	The Frankfurt Parliament elects Frederick William IV of Prussia to be emperor of Germany
April 21	Frederick William IV of Prussia rejects the crown offered by the Frankfurt Parliament
June 18	The remaining members of the Frankfurt Parliament are dispersed by troops
July 3	Collapse of the Roman Republic after invasion by French troops
August 9–13	The Hungarian forces are defeated by Austria, aided by Russian troops

1851

December 2	Coup d'état of Louis Napoleon

1849, the assembly was dissolved, and the monarch proclaimed his own constitution. One of its key elements was a system of three-class voting. All adult males were allowed to vote. They voted, however, according to three classes arranged by ability to pay taxes. Thus, the largest taxpayers, who constituted only about 5 percent of the population, elected one-third of the Prussian Parliament. This system prevailed in Prussia until 1918. In the finally revised Prussian constitution

of 1850, the ministry was responsible to the king alone. Moreover, the Prussian army and officer corps swore loyalty directly to the monarch.

THE FRANKFURT PARLIAMENT While Prussia was moving from revolution to reaction, other events were unfolding in Germany as a whole. On May 18, 1848, representatives from all the German states gathered in Saint Paul's Church in Frankfurt to revise the organization of the German Confederation. The

Frankfurt Parliament intended to write a moderately liberal constitution for a united Germany. The liberal character of the Frankfurt Parliament alienated both German conservatives and the German working class. The offense to the conservatives was simply the challenge to the existing political order. The Frankfurt Parliament lost the support of the industrial workers and artisans by refusing to restore the protection once afforded by the guilds. The liberals were too attached to the concept of a free labor market to offer meaningful legislation to workers. This failure marked the beginning of a profound split between German liberals and the German working class. For the rest of the century, German conservatives would be able to play on that division.

As if to demonstrate its disaffection from workers, in September 1848 the Frankfurt Parliament called in troops of the German Confederation to suppress a radical insurrection in the city. The liberals in the parliament wanted nothing to do with workers who erected barricades and threatened the safety of property.

The Frankfurt Parliament also floundered on the issue of unification. Members differed over whether to include Austria in the projected united Germany. The "large German [*grossdeutsch*] solution" favored inclusion, whereas the "small German [*kleindeutsch*] solution" advocated exclusion. The latter formula prevailed because Austria rejected the whole notion of German unification, which raised too many other nationality problems within the Habsburg domains. Consequently, the Frankfurt Parliament looked to Prussian rather than Austrian leadership.

On March 27, 1849, the parliament produced its constitution. Shortly thereafter, its delegates offered the crown of a united Germany to Frederick William IV of Prussia. He rejected the offer, asserting that kings ruled by the grace of God rather than by the permission of man-made constitutions. On his refusal, the Frankfurt Parliament began to dissolve. Not long afterward, troops drove off the remaining members.

German liberals never fully recovered from this defeat. The Frankfurt Parliament had alienated the artisans and the working class without gaining any compensating support from the conservatives. The liberals had proved themselves to be awkward, hesitant, unrealistic, and ultimately dependent on the armies of the monarchies. They had failed to unite Germany or to confront effectively the realities of political power in the German states. The various revolutions did achieve an extension of the franchise in some of the German states and the establishment of conservative constitutions. The gains were not negligible, but they were a far cry from the hopes of March 1848.

In Perspective

The first half of the nineteenth century witnessed enormous, unprecedented social change in Europe. The foundations of the industrial economy were laid. Virtually no existing institution was untouched by that emerging economy. Railways crossed the Continent. New consumer goods were available. Family patterns changed, as did the social and economic expectations of women. The crowding of cities presented new social and political problems. Issues of social order came to the fore with the new concern about crime and the establishment of police forces. An urban working class became one of the chief facts of both political and social life. The ebb and flow of the business cycle caused increased economic anxiety for workers and property owners alike.

While all these fundamental social changes took place, Europe was also experiencing continuing political strife. The turmoil of 1848 through 1850 ended the era of liberal revolution that had begun in 1789. Liberals and nationalists had discovered that rational argument and small insurrections would not achieve their goals. The political initiative passed for a time to the conservative political groups. Henceforth, nationalists were less romantic and more hardheaded. Railways, commerce, guns, soldiers, and devious diplomacy, rather than language and cultural heritage, became the future weapons of national unification. The working class also adopted new tactics and a new organization. The era of the riot and urban insurrection was ending; in the future, workers would turn to trade unions and political parties to achieve their political and social goals.

Perhaps most important after 1848, the European middle class ceased to be revolutionary. It became increasingly concerned about protecting its property against radical political and social movements associated with socialism and, increasingly, as the century passed, with Marxism. The middle class remained politically liberal only so long as liberalism seemed to promise economic stability and social security for its own style of life.

REVIEW QUESTIONS

1. What inventions were particularly important in the development of industrialism? What changes did industrialism make in society? Why were the years covered in this chapter so difficult for artisans? What is meant by "the proletarianization of workers"?

2. In what ways did the industrial economy change the working-class family? What roles and duties did various family members assume? Most specifically, how did the role of women change in the new industrial era?

3. What were the goals of the working class in the new industrial society, and how did they differ from middle-class goals? How do you explain the separation of working-class and middle-class goals?

4. How did police change in the nineteenth century, and why were new systems of enforcement instituted? In what ways were prisons improved, and how do you account for the reform movement that led to the improvements?

5. How would you define socialism? What were the chief ideas of the early socialists? How did the ideas of Karl Marx differ from those of earlier writers?

6. What factors, old and new, led to the widespread outbreak of revolutions in 1848? Were the causes in the various countries essentially the same, or did each have its own particular set of circumstances? Why did these revolutions fail throughout Europe? What roles did liberals and nationalists play in the revolutions? Why did they sometimes clash?

SUGGESTED READINGS

B. S. ANDERSON AND J. P. ZINSSER, *A History of Their Own: Women in Europe from Prehistory to the Present*, vol. II (1988). A wide-ranging survey.

I. BERLIN, *Karl Marx: His Life and Environment*, 4th ed., (1996). A classic introduction.

P. BROCK, *The Slovak National Awakening* (1976). A standard work.

E. D. BROSE, *The Politics of Technological Change in Prussia: Out of the Shadow of Antiquity, 1809–1848* (1993). Examines the roles of the various social groups in the economic growth and industrialization of Prussia.

R. B. CARLISLE, *The Proffered Crown: Saint-Simonianism and the Doctrine of Hope* (1987). The best treatment of the broad social doctrines of Saint-Simonianism.

A. CLARK, *The Struggle for the Breeches: Gender and the Making of the British Working Class* (1995). An examination of the manner in which industrialization made various relationships between men and women problematical.

J. COFFIN, *The Politics of Women's Work* (1996). Examines the situation in France.

W. COLEMAN, *Death Is a Social Disease: Public Health and Political Economy in Early Industrial France* (1982). One of the first works in English to study this problem.

I. DEAK, *The Lawful Revolution: Louis Kossuth and the Hungarians, 1848–1849* (1979). The most significant study of the topic in English.

J. ELSTER, *An Introduction to Karl Marx* (1985). Provides the best discussion of Marx's fundamental concepts.

T. HAMEROW, *Restoration, Revolution, and Reaction: Economics and Politics in Germany, 1815–1871* (1958). Traces the forces that worked toward the failure of revolution in Germany.

R. F. HAMILTON, *The Bourgeois Epoch: Marx and Engels on Britain, France, and Germany* (1991). Examines Marx's and Engels's observations against what is known to have been the situation in each nation.

J. F. C. HARRISON, *Quest for the New Moral World: Robert Owen and the Owenites in Britain and America* (1969). The standard work.

G. HIMMELFARB, *The Idea of Poverty: England in the Early Industrial Age* (1984). A major work covering the subject from the time of Adam Smith through 1850.

M. IGNATIEFF, *A Just Measure of Pain: The Penitentiary in the Industrial Revolution, 1750–1850* (1978). An important treatment of early English penal thought and practice.

K. KOLAKOWSKI, *Main Currents of Marxism: Its Rise, Growth, and Dissolution*, 3 vols. (1978). An important and comprehensive survey.

D. LANDES, *The Unbound Prometheus: Technological Change and Industrial Development in Western Europe from 1750 to the Present* (1969). The best one-volume treatment of technological development in a broad social and economic context.

R. MAGRAW, *A History of the French Working Class*, 2 vols. (1992). A major overview based on the most recent literature.

F. MANUEL, *The Prophets of Paris* (1962). Remains a stimulating treatment of French utopian socialism and social reform.

T. W. MARGADANT, *French Peasants in Revolt: The Insurrection of 1851* (1979). A study of the rural resistance to Louis Napoleon.

J. M. MERRIMAN, *The Agony of the Republic: The Repression of the Left in Revolutionary France, 1848–1851* (1978). A major study of how the Second French Republic and popular support for it were suppressed.

C. G. MOSES, *French Feminism in the Nineteenth Century* (1984). Includes important chapters on French feminism in 1848.

H. PERKIN, *The Origins of Modern English Society, 1780–1880* (1969). A provocative attempt to look at the society as a whole.

I. PINCHBECK, *Women Workers and the Industrial Revolution, 1750–1850* (1930, rep. 1969). A pioneering study that remains of great value.

D. H. PINKNEY, *Decisive Years in France, 1840–47* (1986). A detailed and careful examination of the years leading up to the Revolution of 1848.

P. ROBERTSON, *An Experience of Women: Pattern and Change in Nineteenth-Century Europe* (1982). A useful survey.

W. H. SEWELL, JR., *Work and Revolution in France: The Language of Labor from the Old Regime to 1848* (1980). A fine analysis of French artisans.

D. SORKIN, *The Transformation of German Jewry, 1780–1840* (1987). An examination of the decades of Jewish emancipation in Germany.

J. SPERBER, *The European Revolution, 1841–1851* (1993). An excellent synthesis.

L. S. STRUMINGHER, *Women and the Making of the Working Class: Lyon, 1830–1870* (1979). A local study from which broader generalizations can be made.

D. THOMPSON, *The Chartists: Popular Politics in the Industrial Revolution* (1984). An important study.

E. P. THOMPSON, *The Making of the English Working Class* (1964). A classic work.

L. A. TILLY AND J. W. SCOTT, *Women, Work, and Family* (1978). A useful and sensitive survey.

D. WINCH, *Riches and Poverty: An Intellectual History of Political Economy in Britain, 1750–1834* (1996). A superb survey from Adam Smith through Thomas Malthus.

A. S. WOHL, *Endangered Lives: Public Health in Victorian Britain* (1983). A wide-ranging examination of the health problems created by urbanization and industrialization.

H. ZEHR, *Crime and the Development of Modern Society: Patterns of Criminality in Nineteenth-Century Germany and France* (1976). An examination of crimes against property in urban society.

Part 5

1850–1939

	POLITICS AND GOVERNMENT	SOCIETY AND ECONOMY	RELIGION AND CULTURE
1850–1890	1851 Louis Napoleon seizes power in France	1850–1910 Height of European outward migration	1850–1880 Jewish emancipation in much of Europe
	1854–1856 Crimean War	1853–1870 Haussmann redesigns Paris	1853–1854 Gobineau, *Essay on the Inequality of the Human Races*
	1861 Proclamation of the kingdom of Italy	1857 Bessemer steelmaking process	1857 Flaubert, *Madame Bovary*
	1862 Bismarck becomes prime minister of Prussia	1861 Serfdom abolished in Russia	1859 Darwin, *The Origin of Species*
	1864 First International founded		
	1867 Austro–Hungarian Dual Monarchy founded		
	1868 Gladstone becomes British prime minister		
	1869 Suez Canal completed		

Charles Darwin

	POLITICS AND GOVERNMENT	SOCIETY AND ECONOMY	RELIGION AND CULTURE
	1870 Franco–Prussian War; French Republic proclaimed	1870 Education Act and first Irish Land Act, Britain	1864 Pius IX, *Syllabus of Errors*
	1871 German Empire proclaimed; Paris Commune		1867 Mill, *The Subjection of Women*
	1874 Disraeli becomes British prime minister		1869 Disestablishment of the Irish Church
	1875 Britain gains control of Suez	1875 Public Health and Artisan Dwelling Acts, Britain	1871 Darwin, *The Descent of Man*; Religious tests abolished at Oxford and Cambridge
	1880s Britain establishes Protectorate in Egypt		1872 Nietzsche, *The Birth of Tragedy*
	1881 People's Will assassinates Alexander II; Three Emperors' League is renewed	1881 Second Irish Land Act	1873–1876 Bismarck's *Kulturkampf*
	1882 Italy, Germany, Austria form Triple alliance		1879 Ibsen, *A Doll's House*
	1884–1885 Germany forms African protectorates		1880s Growing anti-Semitism in Europe
			1880 Zola, *Nana*
	1888 William II becomes German emperor	1886 Daimler invents internal combustion engine	1883 Mach, *The Science of Mechanics*
1890–1918	1894 Dreyfus convicted in France; Nicholas II becomes tsar of Russia	1890s Oil begins to have impact on world economy	1883 Nietzsche, *Thus Spake Zarathustra*
	1898 Germany begins to build a battleship navy	1894 Union of German Women's Organizations founded	1892 Ibsen, *The Master Builder*
	1902 British Labour Party formed	1895 Diesel engine invented	1893 Shaw, *Mrs. Warren's Profession*
	1903 Bolshevik–Menshevik split	1897 German and Czech language equality in Austrian Empire; Russia mandates eleven-and-a-half hour workday	1896 Herzl, *The Jewish State*
	1904 Britain and France in Entente Cordiale		1899 Bernstein, *Evolutionary Socialism*
		1901 National Council of French Women founded	1900 Freud, *The Interpretation of Dreams*; Key, *The Century of the Child*
			1902 Lenin, *What Is to Be Done?*

Toward the Modern World

1850–1939

POLITICS AND GOVERNMENT	SOCIETY AND ECONOMY	RELIGION AND CULTURE

1890–1918 (cont.)

POLITICS AND GOVERNMENT

1905 Revolution in Saint Petersburg suppressed; first Moroccan Crisis

1906 Dreyfus conviction set aside

1908–1909 Bosnian crisis

1911 Second Moroccan crisis

1912 Third Irish Home Rule Bill passed

1912–1913 First and Second Balkan wars

1914–1918 World War I

1917 Russian Revolution; Bolsheviks seize power

SOCIETY AND ECONOMY

1903 Third Irish Land Act; British Women's Social and Political Union founded; Wright brothers fly the first airplane

1906 Land redemption payments canceled for Russian peasants

1907 Women vote on national issues in Norway

1918 Vote granted to some British women

RELIGION AND CULTURE

1903 Shaw, *Man and Superman*

1905 Weber, *The Protestant Ethic and the Spirit of Capitalism*; Termination of the Napoleonic Concordat in France

1907 Bergson, *Creative Evolution*

1908 Sorel, *Reflections of Violence*

1910 Pope Pius X requires anti-Modernist oath

1914 Joyce, *Portrait of the Artist as a Young Man*

1918–1939

POLITICS AND GOVERNMENT

1919 Paris Peace Conference; Weimar constitution proclaimed in Germany

1922 Mussolini takes power in Italy

1923 France invades the Ruhr; Hitler's Beer Hall *Putsch*; first Labour government in Britain

1924 Death of Lenin

1925 Locarno Agreements

1931 National Government formed in Great Britain

1933 Hitler appointed chancellor of Germany

1935 Nuremburg Laws; Italy invades Ethiopia

1936 Popular Front in France; purge trials in the Soviet Union; Spanish Civil War begins

1938 Munich Conference; *Kristallnacht* in Germany

1939 Germany invades Poland, starts World War II

SOCIETY AND ECONOMY

1920s Worldwide commodity crisis

1921 Soviet Union begins New Economic Policy

1922 French Senate rejects vote for women

1923 Rampant inflation in Germany

1926 General strike in Great Britain

1928 Britain extends full franchise to women

1928–1933 First Five-Year Plan and agricultural collectivization in the Soviet Union

1929 Wall Street crash

1932 Lausanne Conference ends German reparations

mid-1930s Nazis stimulate German economy through public works and defense spending

RELIGION AND CULTURE

1919 Barth, *Commentary on the Epistle to the Romans*

1920 Keynes, *Economic Consequences of the Peace*

1922 Joyce, *Ulysses*

1924 Hitler, *Mein Kampf*

1925 Woolf, *Mrs. Dalloway*

1927 Heidegger, *Being and Time*; Mann, *Buddenbrooks*

1927 Woolf, *To the Lighthouse*; Mann, *Magic Mountain*

1929 Woolf, *A Room of One's Own*

1936 Keynes, *General Theory of Employment, Interest, and Money*

1937 Orwell, *Road to Wigan Pier*

1938 Sartre, *Nausea*

Chapter 23

Prince Otto von Bismarck (1815–1898) was the most important statesmen of the second half of the nineteenth century. He used warfare and shrewd diplomacy to lead Prussia to unify Germany. Having achieved this goal, he worked for the rest of his career to keep the peace. Franz von Lenbach (1836–1904) *Prince Otto von Bismark in uniform with Prussian helmet.* Canvas. Kunsthistorisches Museum, Gemaeldegalerie, Vienna, Austria. (c) Photograph by Erich Lessing. Art Resource, NY

The Age of Nation–States

The Crimean War (1853–1856)

Italian Unification
Romantic Republicans
Cavour's Policy
The New Italian State

German Unification
Bismarck
The Franco–Prussian War and the German
    Empire (1870–1871)

**France: From Liberal Empire
to the Third Republic**
The Paris Commune
The Third Republic
The Dreyfus Affair

The Habsburg Empire
Formation of the Dual Monarchy
Unrest of Nationalities

**Russia: Emancipation
and Revolutionary Stirrings**
Reforms of Alexander II
Revolutionaries

**Great Britain:
Toward Democracy**
The Second Reform Act (1867)
Gladstone's Great Ministry
    (1868–1874)
Disraeli in Office (1874–1880)
The Irish Question

KEY TOPICS

- The unification of Italy and Germany
- The shift from empire to republic in France
- The emergence of a dual monarchy in Austria–Hungary
- Reforms in Russia, including the emancipation of the serfs
- The emergence of Great Britain as the exemplary liberal state and its confrontation with Irish nationalists

The revolutions of 1848 had collapsed in defeat for both liberalism and nationalism. Throughout the early 1850s, conservative regimes entrenched themselves across the Continent. Yet only a quarter century later, many of the major goals of early nineteenth-century liberals and nationalists had been accomplished. Italy and Germany were each finally united under constitutional monarchies. The Habsburg emperor accepted constitutional government and recognized the liberties of the Magyars of Hungary. In Russia, the tsar emancipated the serfs. France was again a republic. Liberalism and even democracy flourished in Great Britain.

Paradoxically, most of these developments occurred under conservative leadership. Events within European international affairs compelled some governments to pursue new policies at home as well as abroad. They had to find novel methods of maintaining the loyalty of their subjects. Some conservative leaders preferred to carry out a popular policy on their own terms, so that they, rather than the liberals, would receive credit. Other leaders acted as they did because they had no choice.

The Crimean War (1853–1856)

As has so often been true in modern European history, the impetus for change originated in war. The Crimean War (1853–1856) was rooted in the long rivalry between Russia and the Ottoman Empire. Two disputes led to the conflict. First, the Ottoman Empire had recently granted Catholic France rather than Orthodox Russia oversight of the Christian shrines in the Holy Land. Second, Russia wanted to extend its control over the Ottoman provinces of Moldavia and Walachia (now in Romania). The tsar's duty to protect Orthodox Christians in the Ottoman Empire furnished the pretext for the Russian aggression. Russia occupied the two provinces in the summer of 1853. The Ottoman Empire declared war on Russia in the autumn of that year.

The other great powers soon became involved, and a war among major European states resulted. Both France and Great Britain opposed Russian expansion in the eastern Mediterranean, where they had extensive naval and commercial interests. Napoleon III also thought that an activist foreign policy would shore up domestic support for his regime. On March 28, 1854, France and Britain declared war on Russia. Much to the disappointment of Tsar Nicholas I, Austria and Prussia remained neutral. The Austrians had their own ambitions in the Balkans, and, for the moment, Prussia followed Austrian leadership.

Both sides conducted the conflict ineptly. The ill-equipped and poorly commanded armies became bogged down along the Crimean coast of the Black Sea. In September 1855, after a long siege, the Russian fortress of Sevastopol finally fell to the French and British. In March 1856, a conference in Paris concluded the Treaty of Paris, which required Russia to surrender territory near the mouth of the Danube River, to recognize the neutrality of the Black Sea, and to renounce claims of protection over Christians in the Ottoman Empire. Even before the conference, Austria had forced Russia to withdraw from Moldavia and Walachia. The image of an invincible Russia that had prevailed across Europe since the close of the Napoleonic wars was shattered.

Also shattered was the Concert of Europe (see Chapter 21) as a means of dealing with international relations on the Continent. Following the successful repression of the 1848 uprisings, the great powers feared revolution less than they had earlier in the century, and consequently they displayed much less reverence for the Vienna settlement. As historian Gordon Craig once commented, "After 1856 there were more powers willing to fight to overthrow the existing order than there were to take up

During the Crimean War, Florence Nightingale of Great Britain organized nursing care for the wounded. Corbis

arms to defend it."[1] Napoleon III had little respect for the Congress of Vienna and favored redrawing the map along lines of nationality. Hoping to compensate for their failure to act during the Crimean War, the Austrians tried to assert more influence within the German Confederation. Prussia became increasingly discontented with a role in Germany subordinate to Austria's. Russia, which had been among the chief defenders of the Vienna settlement, now sought to overcome the disgrace of the 1856 Treaty of Paris. The mediocre display of British military prowess led that nation to hesitate about future continental involvement.

Consequently, for about twenty-five years after the Crimean War, European affairs were unstable, producing a period of largely unchecked adventurism in foreign policy. Without the restraining influence of the Concert of Europe, each nation believed that only the limits of its military power and its diplomatic influence should constrain its international ambitions. Moreover, foreign policy increasingly became an instrument of domestic policy. The two most significant achievements to result from this new international situation were the unifications of Italy and Germany. Those events, in turn, put further pressures on their neighbors.

Giuseppe Mazzini was a fervent republican nationalist. He aroused emotional support for Italian unity, but also frightened moderate Italians. Bildarchiv Preussischer Kulturbesitz

Italian Unification

Nationalists had long wanted to unite the small, absolutist principalities of the Italian peninsula into a single state. During the first half of the century, however, opinion differed about the manner and goals of Italian unification.

Romantic Republicans

One approach to the issue was *romantic republicanism*. After the Congress of Vienna, secret republican societies were founded throughout Italy, the most famous of which was the *Carbonari* ("charcoal burners"). They were singularly ineffective.

Following the failure of nationalist uprisings in 1831, the leadership of romantic republican nationalism passed to Giuseppe Mazzini (1805–1872). He became the most important nationalist leader in all Europe and brought new emotional fervor to the cause. He once declared, "Nationality is the role assigned by God to a people in the work of humanity. It is its mission, its task on earth, to the end that God's thought may be

realized in the world."[2] In 1831, he founded the Young Italy Society to drive Austria from the peninsula and establish an Italian republic.

During the 1830s and 1840s, Mazzini and his fellow republican Giuseppe Garibaldi (1807–1882) led insurrections. Both were deeply involved in the ill-fated Roman Republic of 1849. Throughout the 1850s, they continued to conduct what amounted to guerilla warfare. Because both men spent much time in exile, they became well known across the Continent and in the United States.

Republican nationalism frightened moderate Italians, who wanted to rid themselves of Austrian domination, but not at the cost of establishing a republic. For a time, these people had looked to the papacy as a possible vehicle for unification. That solution became impossible after the experience of Pius IX with the Roman Republic in 1849. Consequently, at midcentury, "Italy" remained a geographical expression rather than a political entity.

Yet between 1852 and 1860, the Italian peninsula was transformed into a nation–state governed

[1]*The New Cambridge Modern History*, Vol. 10 (Cambridge, U.K.: Cambridge University Press, 1967), p. 273.

[2]Quoted in William L. Langer, *Political and Social Upheaval, 1832–1852* (New York: Harper Torchbooks, 1969), p. 115.

by a constitutional monarchy. The process was carried out not by romantic republican nationalists, but by Count Camillo Cavour (1810–1861), the moderately liberal prime minister of Piedmont. The method of unification was force of arms tied to secret diplomacy. The spirit of Machiavelli must have smiled over the enterprise.

Cavour's Policy

Piedmont (officially styled the Kingdom of Sardinia), in northwestern Italy, was the most independent state on the peninsula. The Congress of Vienna had restored the kingdom as a buffer between French and Austrian ambitions. As we have seen, during 1848 and 1849, King Charles Albert of Piedmont, after having promulgated a conservative constitution, twice unsuccessfully fought Austria. Following the second defeat, he abdicated in favor of his son, Victor Emmanuel II (r. 1849–1878). In 1852, the new monarch chose Count Camillo Cavour as his prime minister.

A cunning statesman, Cavour had begun political life as a strong conservative, but had gradually moved toward a moderately liberal position. He had made a fortune by investing in railroads, reforming agriculture on his own estates, and editing a newspaper. He was deeply imbued with the ideas of the Enlightenment, classical economics, and utilitarianism. Cavour was a nationalist of a new breed who had no respect for Mazzini's ideals. A strong monarchist, Cavour rejected republicanism. It was economic and material progress rather than romantic ideals that required a large, unified state on the Italian peninsula.

Cavour believed that if Italians proved themselves to be efficient and economically progressive, the great powers might decide that Italy could govern itself. He joined the Piedmontese Cabinet in 1850 and became premier two years later. He worked for free trade, railway construction, expansion of credit, and agricultural improvement. He felt that such material and economic bonds, rather than fuzzy Romantic yearnings, must unite the Italians. Cavour also recognized the need to capture the loyalties of those Italians who believed in other varieties of nationalism. He thus fostered the Nationalist Society, which established chapters in other Italian states to press for unification under the leadership of Piedmont. Finally, the prime minister believed that Italy could be unified only with the aid of France. The recent accession of Napoleon III in France seemed to open the way for such aid.

FRENCH SYMPATHIES   Cavour used the Crimean War to bring Italy into European politics. In 1855, Piedmont joined the conflict on the side of France and Britain and sent 10,000 troops to the front. This small but significant participation in the war allowed Cavour to raise the Italian question at the Paris conference. (See "Cavour Explains Why Piedmont Should Enter the Crimean War.") He left Paris with no diplomatic reward, but his intelligence and political capacity had impressed everyone. Cavour also gained the sympathy of Napoleon III. During the rest of the decade, he achieved further international respectability for Piedmont by opposing various plots of Mazzini, who was still attempting to lead nationalist uprisings. By 1858, Cavour represented a moderate liberal alternative to both republicanism and reactionary absolutism in Italy.

Cavour continued to bide his time. Then, in January 1858, an Italian named Orsini attempted to assassinate Napoleon III. The incident made the French emperor, who had once belonged to a nationalist group, newly concerned about the Italian issue. He saw himself continuing his more famous uncle's liberation of the peninsula. He also saw Piedmont as a potential ally against Austria. In July 1858, Cavour and Napoleon III met at Plombières in southern France. Riding alone in a carriage, with the emperor at the reins, the two men plotted to provoke a war in Italy that would permit them to defeat Austria. A formal treaty in December 1858 confirmed the agreement. France was to receive French-speaking Nice and Savoy from Piedmont for its aid.

WAR WITH AUSTRIA   In early 1859, tension grew between Austria and Piedmont as Piedmont mobilized its army. On April 22, Austria demanded that Piedmont demobilize. That demand allowed Piedmont to claim that Austria was provoking a war. France intervened to aid its ally. On June 4, the Austrians were defeated at Magenta, and on June 24 at Solferino. Meanwhile, revolutions had broken out in Tuscany, Modena, Parma, and the Romagna provinces of the Papal States.

With the Austrians in retreat and the new revolutionary regimes calling for union with Piedmont, Napoleon III feared too extensive a Piedmontese victory. On July 11, he independently concluded a peace with Austria at Villafranca. Piedmont received Lombardy, but Venetia remained under Austrian control. Cavour felt betrayed by France, but the war had driven Austria from most of northern Italy. Later that summer, Parma, Modena, Tuscany, and the Romagna provinces voted to unite with Piedmont. (See Map 23–1.)

GARIBALDI'S CAMPAIGN   At this point, the forces of romantic republican nationalism compelled Cavour to pursue the complete unification of northern and southern Italy. In May 1860, Garibaldi landed in Sicily with more than 1,000 troops, who had been outfitted in the north. He captured Palermo and

MAP 23–1   THE UNIFICATION OF ITALY   *Beginning with the association of Sardinia and Piedmont by the Congress of Vienna in 1815, unification was achieved through the expansion of Piedmont between 1859 and 1870. Both Cavour's statesmanship and the campaigns of ardent nationalists played large roles.*

Giuseppe Garibaldi represented the forces of romantic Italian nationalism. The landing of his Redshirts on Sicily and their subsequent invasion of southern Italy in 1860 forced Cavour to unite the entire peninsula sooner than he had intended. Bildarchiv Preussischer Kulturbesitz

prepared to attack the mainland. By September he controlled the city and kingdom of Naples, probably the most corrupt example of Italian absolutism. For more than two decades Garibaldi had hoped to form a republican Italy, but Cavour forestalled him. He rushed Piedmontese troops south to confront Garibaldi. On the way, they conquered the rest of the Papal States except the area around Rome, which was protected for the Pope by French troops. Garibaldi's nationalism won out over his republicanism, and he unhappily accepted the Piedmontese domination. In late 1860, Naples and Sicily voted to join the northern union forged by Piedmont.

The New Italian State

In March 1861, Victor Emmanuel II was proclaimed king of Italy. Three months later Cavour died. The new state more than ever needed his skills, because Italy had, in effect, been more nearly conquered than united by Piedmont. The republicans resented the treatment of Garibaldi. The clericals resented the conquest of the Papal States. In the south, armed resistance against the imposition of Piedmontese-style administration continued until 1866. The economies of north and south Italy were incompatible. The south was rural, poor, and backward. The north was industrializing, and its economy was increasingly linked to that of the rest of Europe. The social structures of the two regions reflected those differences, with large landholders and peasants dominant in the south and an urban working class emerging in the north.

The political framework of the united Italy could not overcome these problems. The constitution, which was that promulgated for Piedmont in 1848, provided for a conservative constitutional monarchy. Parliament consisted of two houses: a senate appointed by the king and a chamber of deputies elected on a narrow franchise. Ministers were responsible to the monarch, not to Parliament. These arrangements did not foster vigorous parliamentary life. Political leaders often simply avoided major problems. In place of efficient, progressive government, such as Cavour had brought to Piedmont, a system called *transformismo* developed. Political opponents were "transformed" into government supporters through bribery, favors, or a seat in the cabinet. Italian politics became a byword for corruption.

Nor was unification complete. Many Italians believed that other territories should be added to their nation. The most important of these were Venetia and Rome. The former was gained in 1866 in return for Italy's alliance with Prussia in the Austro–Prussian War. Rome and the papacy continued to be guarded by French troops, first sent there in 1849, until the Franco–Prussian War of 1870 forced their withdrawal. The Italian state then annexed Rome and made it the capital. The papacy confined itself to the Vatican, and it remained hostile to the Italian state until the two sides concluded a treaty, the Lateran Accord of 1929.

By 1870, only the small province of Trent and the city of Trieste, both ruled by Austria, remained outside Italy. In and of themselves, these areas were not

Cavour Explains Why Piedmont Should Enter the Crimean War

As prime minister of Piedmont, Cavour tried to prove that the Italians were capable of progressive government. In 1855, addressing the Parliament of Piedmont, he urged entry into the Crimean War, so that the other Europeans would consider Piedmont a military power. Earlier, politics in Italy had been characterized by petty absolute princes and romantic nationalist conspiracies, both of which Cavour scorned. He understood that in the nineteenth century a nation must possess good government, economic prosperity, and a strong army.

❖ *Why does Cavour feel it necessary to condemn conspiracies as a political device? What does Cavour believe Italy must do to raise its reputation? Why is war the test of strength and character for Italy?*

The experience of recent years and previous centuries has proved (at least in my opinion) how little Italy has benefited by conspiracies, revolutions and disorderly uprisings. Far from helping her, they have been a tremendous calamity for this beautiful part of Europe. And not only, gentlemen, because individual people so often suffered from them, not only because revolutions became the cause or pretext for repression, but above all because continual conspiracies, repeated revolutions and disorderly uprisings damaged the esteem and, up to a certain point, the sympathy that other European peoples cherished for Italy.

Now, gentlemen, I believe that the principal condition for the improvement of Italy's fate, the condition that stands out above all others, is to lift up her reputation once more, so to act that all the peoples of the world, those governing and those governed, may do justice to her qualities. And for this two things are necessary: first, to prove to Europe that Italy has sufficient civic sense to govern herself freely and according to law, and that she is in a condition to adopt the very best forms of government; second, to prove that her military valor is as great as that of her ancestors.

You have done Italy one service by your conduct over the last seven years. You have shown Europe in the most luminous way that Italians are capable of governing themselves with wisdom, prudence, and trustworthiness. But it still remains for you to do Italy an equal, if not a greater, service; it is our country's task to prove that Italy's sons can fight valiantly on battlefields where glory is to be won. And I am sure, gentlemen, that the laurels that our soldiers will win in Eastern Europe will help the future state of Italy more than all that has been done by those people who hoped to regenerate her by rhetorical speeches and writings.

As quoted in Denis Mack Smith, ed. and trans., *The Making of Italy, 1796–1870* (New York: Walker and Company, 1968), pp. 199–200.

important, but they fueled the continued hostility of Italian nationalists toward Austria. The desire to liberate *Italia irredenta*, or "unredeemed Italy," was one reason for the Italian support of the Allies against Austria and Germany during World War I.

German Unification

The construction of a united Germany was the single most important political development in Europe between 1848 and 1914. (See Map 23–2.) It transformed the balance of economic, military, and international power. Moreover, the method of its creation largely determined the character of the new German state. Germany was united by the conservative army, the monarchy, and the prime minister of Prussia, among whose chief motives was the outflanking of Prussian liberals. A unified Germany, sought for two generations by German liberals, was actually achieved for the most illiberal of reasons.

During the 1850s, German unification still seemed remote. The major states continued to trade with each other through the *Zollverein* (tariff union), and railways linked their economies. Frederick William IV of Prussia had given up thoughts of unification under Prussian leadership. Austria continued to oppose any closer union that might lessen its influence. Liberal nationalists had not recovered from the humiliating experiences of 1848 and 1849. What quickly modified

MAP 23–2   THE UNIFICATION OF GERMANY   *Under Bismarck's leadership, and with the strong support of its royal house, Prussia used diplomatic and military means, on both the German and international stages, to forcibly unify the German states into a strong national entity.*

this situation was a series of domestic political changes and problems within Prussia.

In 1858 Frederick William IV was adjudged insane, and his brother William assumed the regency. William I (r. 1861–1888), who became king in his own right in 1861, was less idealistic than his brother and more of a Prussian patriot. In the usual Hohenzollern tradition, his first concern was to strengthen the Prussian army. In 1860 his war minister and chief of staff proposed to enlarge the army, to increase the number of officers, and to extend the period of conscription from two to three years. The Prussian Parliament, created by the Constitution of 1850, refused to approve the necessary taxes. The liberals, who dominated the body, sought to avoid placing additional power in the hands of the monarchy. For two years, monarch and Parliament were deadlocked.

Bismarck

In September 1862, William I turned for help to the person who, more than any other single individual, shaped the next thirty years of European history:

Otto von Bismarck (1815–1898). Bismarck came from Junker (noble landlord) stock. He attended a university, joined a *Burschenschaft* (a student society), and displayed an interest in German unification. Then he retired to his father's estate. During the 1840s he was elected to the provincial diet, where his stand was so reactionary as to disturb even the king. Yet he had made his mark. From 1851 to 1859, Bismarck served as the Prussian minister to the Frankfurt diet of the German Confederation. Later he became Prussian ambassador to Russia, and he had just been named ambassador to France when William I appointed him prime minister of Prussia.

Although Bismarck entered public life as a reactionary, he had mellowed into a conservative. He opposed parliamentary government, but not a constitutionalism that provided for a strong monarch. He understood that Prussia—and later, Germany—must have a strong industrial base. His years in Frankfurt arguing with his Austrian counterpart had hardened his Prussian patriotism. In politics, he was a pragmatist who put more trust in power and action than in ideas. As he declared in his first speech as prime minister, "Germany is not looking to Prussia's liberalism but to her power....The great questions of the day will not be decided by speeches and majority decisions—that was the mistake of 1848–1849—but by iron and blood."[3] Yet this same minister, after having led Prussia into three wars, spent the next nineteen years seeking to preserve peace.

Upon becoming prime minister in 1862, Bismarck immediately moved against the liberal Parliament. He contended that even without new financial levies, the Prussian constitution permitted the government to carry out its functions on the basis of previously granted taxes. Therefore, taxes could be collected and spent despite the parliamentary refusal to vote them. The army and most of the bureaucracy supported this interpretation of the constitution. In 1863, however, new elections sustained the liberal majority in the Parliament. Bismarck had to find some way to attract popular support away from the liberals and toward the monarchy and the army. He therefore set about uniting Germany through the conservative institutions of Prussia.

THE DANISH WAR (1864)

Bismarck pursued a *kleindeutsch*, or small German, solution to unification. Austria was to be excluded from a united German state. This goal required complex diplomacy. The Schleswig–Holstein problem gave Bismarck the handle for his policy. These two northern duchies had long been ruled by the kings of Denmark without being part of Denmark itself. Their populations were a mixture of Germans and Danes. Holstein, where Germans predominated, belonged to the German Confederation. In 1863, the Danish Parliament moved to incorporate both duchies into Denmark. The smaller states of the German Confederation proposed an all-German war to halt this move. Bismarck wanted Prussia to act alone or only in cooperation with Austria. Together, the two large states easily defeated Denmark in 1864.

The Danish defeat increased Bismarck's personal prestige, and over the next two years he maneuvered Austria into war with Prussia. In August 1865, the two powers negotiated the Convention of Gastein, which put Austria in charge of Holstein and Prussia in charge of Schleswig. Bismarck then moved to mend other diplomatic fences. He had gained Russian sympathy by supporting the 1863 suppression of a Polish revolt, and he persuaded Napoleon III to promise neutrality in an Austro–Prussian conflict. In April 1866, Bismarck concluded a treaty with Italy promising that Italy would get Venetia if it attacked Austria in support of Prussia when war broke out. Now Bismarck had to provoke his war.

THE AUSTRO–PRUSSIAN WAR (1866)

Constant Austro–Prussian tension had arisen over the administration of Schleswig and Holstein. Bismarck ordered the Prussian forces to be as obnoxious as possible to the Austrians. On June 1, 1866, Austria appealed to the German Confederation to intervene in the dispute. Bismarck claimed that the request violated the terms of the 1864 alliance and the Convention of Gastein. The Seven Weeks' War, which resulted in the summer of 1866, led to the decisive defeat of Austria at the Battle of Königgrätz in Bohemia.

The Treaty of Prague, which ended the conflict on August 23, was lenient toward Austria, which only lost Venetia, ceded to Napoleon III, who in turn ceded it to Italy. Austria refused to give Venetia directly to Italy because the Austrians had crushed the Italians during the war. The treaty and the military defeat permanently excluded the Habsburgs from German affairs. Prussia had thus established itself as the only major power among the German states.

THE NORTH GERMAN CONFEDERATION

In 1867, the states of Hanover, Hesse, and Nassau and the city of Frankfurt, which had all supported Austria during the war, were annexed by Prussia, and their rulers were deposed. Under Prussian Leadership, all Germany north of the Main River now formed a federation known as the North German Confederation. Each state retained its own local government, but all military forces were under federal control. The president of the federation was the king of Prussia, represented by his chancellor, Bismarck. A legislature consisted of two houses: a federal council, or *Bundesrat*, composed of members appointed by the governments of the states, and a lower house, or *Reichstag*, chosen by universal male suffrage.

Bismarck had little fear of this broad franchise, because he sensed that the peasants would vote for conservatives. Moreover, the Reichstag had little real power, because the ministers were responsible only to the monarch. The Reichstag could not even originate legislation. All laws had to be proposed by the chancellor. The legislature did have the right to approve military budgets, but these were usually submitted to cover several years at a time. The constitution of the confederation, which after 1871 became the constitution of the German Empire, possessed some of the appearances, but none of the substance, of liberalism. Germany was in effect a military monarchy.

The spectacular success of Bismarck's policy overwhelmed the liberal opposition in the Prussian

---

[3]Quoted in Otto Pflanze, *Bismarck and the Development of Germany: The Period of Unification: 1815–1871* (Princeton, NJ: Princeton University Press, 1963), p. 177.

Heinrich von Treitschke Demands the Annexation of Alsace and Lorraine

The Franco–Prussian War witnessed outbursts of extreme nationalistic rhetoric on both sides. One such voice was that of the German historian Heinrich von Treitschke (1834–1896). In a newspaper article, he demanded the annexation of Alsace and Lorraine from France. He did so even though that the population of Alsace wished to remain part of France and German was not the dominant language in the region. He appealed to an earlier time when the region had been German in language and culture, and he asserted a policy that "might makes right" to assure German domination. This passage should be read in conjunction with Lord Acton's condemnation of nationalism. (See "Lord Acton Condemns Nationalism," p. 802.)

❖ *On what grounds does Treitschke base the German claim to Alsace and Lorraine? Why does he contend that it is proper to ignore the wishes of the people involved? What, if any, political morality informs his views?*

The sense of justice to Germany demands the lessening of France....

What is demanded by justice is, at the same time, absolutely necessary for our security....

Every State must seek the guarantees of its own security in itself alone....

In view of our obligation to secure the peace of the world, who will venture to object that the people of Alsace and Lorraine do not want to belong to us? The doctrine of the right of all the branches of the German race to decide on their own destinies, the plausible solution of demagogues without a fatherland, shiver to pieces in presence of the sacred necessity of these great days. These territories are ours by the right of the sword, and we shall dispose of them in virtue of a higher right—the right of the German nation, which will not permit its lost children to remain strangers to the German Empire. We Germans, who know Germany and France, know better than these unfortunates themselves what is good for the people of Alsace.... Against their will we shall restore them to their true selves. We have seen with joyful wonder the undying power of

Parliament. The liberals were split between those who prized liberalism and those who supported unification. In the end, nationalism proved more attractive. In 1866, the Prussian Parliament retroactively approved the military budget that had been disputed earlier. Bismarck had crushed the Prussian liberals by making the monarchy and the army the most popular institutions in the country. The drive toward unification had achieved his domestic political goal.

The Franco–Prussian War and the German Empire (1870–1871)

Bismarck now awaited an opportunity to complete unification by bringing the states of southern Germany into the confederation. Events in Spain gave him the excuse. In 1868 a military coup deposed the corrupt Bourbon queen of Spain, Isabella II (r. 1833–1868). In searching for a new monarch, the Spaniards chose Prince Leopold of Hohenzollern–Sigmaringen, a Catholic cousin of William I of Prussia. On June 19, 1870, Leopold accepted the Spanish crown with Prussian blessings. Bismarck knew that France would react strongly against the idea of a Hohenzollern Spain.

On July 2, the Spanish government announced Leopold's acceptance, and the French reacted as expected. France sent its ambassador Count Vincent Benedetti (1817–1900) to consult with William I, who was vacationing at Bad Ems. They discussed the matter at several meetings. On July 12, Leopold's father renounced his son's candidacy for the Spanish throne, fearing that the issue would cause war between Prussia and France. William was relieved that conflict had been avoided and that he had not had to order Leopold to renounce the Spanish throne.

There the matter might have rested had it not been for the impetuosity of the French and the guile of Bismarck. On July 13, the French government instructed Benedetti to ask William for assurances that he would tolerate no future Spanish candidacy for Leopold. The king refused, but said that he might take the question under further considerathe moral forces of history, manifested far too frequently in the immense changes of these days, to place much confidence in the value of a mere popular disinclination. The spirit of a nation lays hold, not only of the generation which live beside it, but of those who are before and behind it. We appeal from the mistaken wishes of the men who are there to-day to the wishes of those who were there before them. We appeal to all those strong German men who one stamped the seal of our German nature on the language and manners, the art and the social life of the Upper Rhine. Before the nineteenth century closes the world will recognize that...we were only obeying the dictates of national honor when we made little account of the preferences of the people who live in Alsace to-day....

At all times the subjection of a German race to France has been an unhealthy thing; to-day it is an offence against the reason of History—a vassalship of free men to half-educated barbarians....

...There is no perfect identity between the political and national frontier of any European country.

Not one of the great Powers, and Germany no more than the rest of them, can ever subscribe to the principle that "language alone decides the formation of States." It would be impossible to carry that principle into effect....

The German territory which we demand is ours by nature and by history....In the tempests of the great Revolution the people of Alsace, like all the citizens of France, learned to forget their past....

Most assuredly, the task of reuniting there the broken links between the ages is one of the heaviest that has ever been imposed upon the political forces of our nation....

The people of Alsace are already beginning to doubt the invincibility of their nation, and at all events to divine the mighty growth of the German Empire. Perverse obstinancy, and a thousand French intrigues creeping in the dark, will make every step on the newly conquered soil difficult for us: but our ultimate success is certain, for on our side fights what is stronger than the lying artifices of the stranger—nature herself and the voice of common blood.

From Heinrich von Treitschke,"What We Demand from France" (1870) in Heinrich von Treitschke, *Germany, France, Russia and Islam* (New York: G. P. Putnam's Sons, 1915), pp. 100, 102, 106, 109, 120, 122, 134–135, 153, 158.

tion. Later that day he sent Bismarck, who was in Berlin, a telegram reporting the substance of the meeting. The chancellor, who desperately wanted a war with France to complete unification, had been disappointed by the peaceful resolution of the controversy. The king's telegram gave him a new opportunity to incite a war. Bismarck released an edited version of the dispatch. The revised Ems telegram made it appear that William had insulted the French ambassador. The idea was to goad France into declaring war.

The French government fell for Bismarck's bait and declared war on July 19. Napoleon III was sick and not eager for war, but his government believed that victory over the North German Confederation would give the empire renewed popular support. Once the conflict erupted, the southern German states, honoring treaties of 1866, enthusiastically joined Prussia against France, whose defeat was not long in coming. On September 1, at the Battle of Sedan, the Germans not only beat the French army, but also captured

Napoleon III. By late September, Paris was besieged; it finally capitulated on January 28, 1871.

Ten days earlier, in the Hall of Mirrors at the Palace of Versailles, the German Empire had been proclaimed. During the war the states of southern Germany had joined the North German Confederation, and their rulers requested William to accept the imperial title of German emperor. The princes remained heads of their respective states within the new federation. From the peace settlement with France, Germany received the additional territory of Alsace and part of Lorraine. (See "Heinrich von Treitschke Demands the Annexation of Alsace and Lorraine.")

Both the fact and the manner of German unification produced long-range effects in Europe. A powerful new state had been created in north central Europe. It was rich in natural resources and talented citizens. Militarily and economically, the German Empire would be far stronger than Prussia had been alone. The unification of Germany was

German and Italian Unification

1854	Crimean War opens
1855	Cavour leads Piedmont into the war on the side of France and England
1856	Treaty of Paris concludes the Crimean War
1858	(January 14) Attempt to assassinate Napoleon III
1858	(July 20) Secret conference between Napoleon III and Cavour at Plombières
1859	War of Piedmont and France against Austria
1860	Garibaldi lands his forces in Sicily and invades southern Italy
1861	(March 17) Proclamation of the Kingdom of Italy
1861	(June 6) Death of Cavour
1862	Bismarck becomes prime minister of Prussia
1864	Danish–Prussian War
1865	Convention of Gastein
1866	Austro–Prussian War
1866	Venetia ceded to Italy
1867	North German Confederation formed
1870	(June 19–July 12) Crisis over Hohenzollern candidacy for the Spanish throne
1870	(July 13) Bismarck publishes the edited Ems dispatch
1870	(July 19) France declares war on Prussia
1870	(September 1) France defeated at Sedan and Napoleon III captured
1870	(September 4) French Republic proclaimed
1870	(October 2) Italian state annexes Rome
1871	(January 18) Proclamation of the German Empire at Versailles
1871	(March 28–May 28) Paris Commune
1871	(May 23) Treaty of Frankfurt ratified between France and Germany

also a blow to European liberalism, because the new state was a conservative creation. Conservative politics was now backed not by a weak Austria or an economically retrograde Russia, but by the strongest state on the Continent.

The two nations most immediately affected by German and Italian unification were France and Austria. The emergence of the two new united states revealed the weakness of both France and the Habsburg Empire. Change had to come in each. France returned to republican government, and the Habsburgs came to terms with their Magyar subjects.

France: From Liberal Empire to the Third Republic

Historians have traditionally divided the reign of Emperor Napoleon III (r. 1851–1870) into the years of the authoritarian empire and those of the liberal empire. The point of division is the year 1860. Initially, after the coup in December 1851, Napoleon III had controlled the legislature, strictly censored the press, and harassed political dissidents. His support came from the army, property owners, the French Catholic Church, and businesspeople. They approved the security he ensured for property, his protection of the Pope, and his aid to commerce and railroad construction. The French victory in the Crimean War had further confirmed the emperor's popularity.

From the late 1850s onward, Napoleon III began to modify his policy. In 1860, he concluded a free-trade treaty with Britain and permitted freer debate in the legislature. By the late 1860s, he had relaxed the press laws and had permitted labor unions. In 1870 he allowed the leaders of the moderates in the legislature to form a ministry, and he also agreed to a liberal constitution that made the ministers responsible to the legislature.

Napoleon III's liberal concessions sought to shore up domestic support to compensate for his failures in foreign policy. By 1860, he had lost control of the diplomacy of Italian unification. Between 1861 and 1867, he had supported a disastrous military expedition against Mexico led by Archduke Maximilian of Austria that ended in defeat and Maximilian's execution. In 1866, France had watched passively while Bismarck and Prussia reorganized German affairs. The war of 1870 against Germany had been the French government's last and most disastrous attempt to shore up its foreign policy and secure domestic popularity.

The Second Empire, but not the war, came to an inglorious end with the Battle of Sedan in September 1870. The emperor was captured, imprisoned, and then allowed to go to England, where he died in 1873. Shortly after news of the Sedan disaster reached Paris, a republic was proclaimed, and a government of national defense was established. Paris itself was soon under Prussian siege, and the government was transferred to Bordeaux. Paris finally surrendered in January 1871, but the rest of France had been ready to sue for peace long before.

The Paris Commune

The division between the provinces and Paris became sharper after the fighting with Germany stopped. Monarchists dominated the new National Assembly elected in February. For the time being, the assembly

The siege of Paris during the Franco-Prussian War led to extreme food shortages. Aminals in the zoo were slaughtered and domestic dogs and cats were butchered to feed the hungry citizens. Sketches such as this one, made early in 1871, were published in London newspapers after being sent from Paris by balloon post. The Granger Collection

gave executive power to Adolphe Thiers (1797–1877), who had been active in French politics since 1830. He negotiated a settlement with Prussia (the Treaty of Frankfurt) whereby France was charged a large indemnity and remained occupied by Prussian troops until the indemnity had been paid. France also lost Alsace and part of Lorraine. The treaty was officially ratified on May 23.

Many Parisians, having suffered during the siege, resented what they regarded as a betrayal by the monarchist National Assembly sitting at Versailles. The Parisians elected a new municipal government, called the Paris Commune, which was formally proclaimed on March 28, 1871. The Commune intended to administer Paris separately from the rest of France. (See "The Paris Commune Is Proclaimed.") At one time or another, political radicals and socialists of all stripes participated in the Paris Commune. The National Assembly moved rapidly in early April to surround Paris with an army. On May 8, this army bombarded the city. On May 21, the assembly's forces broke through the city's defenses. During the next seven days, the troops restored order to Paris and killed about 20,000 inhabitants. The communards claimed their own victims as well.

The short-lived Paris Commune quickly became a legend throughout Europe. Marxists regarded it as a genuine proletarian government that the French

bourgeoisie had suppressed. This interpretation is mistaken. The Commune, though of shifting composition, was dominated by petty bourgeois members. The socialism of the Commune had its roots in Blanqui's and Proudhon's anarchism rather than in Marx's concept of class conflict. The goal of the Commune was not a worker's republic, but a nation composed of relatively independent, radically democratic enclaves. Its suppression thus represented not only the protection of property, but also the triumph of the centralized nation–state over an alternative political organization. Just as the armies of Piedmont and Prussia had united the small states of Italy and Germany, the army of the French National Assembly destroyed the particularistic political tendencies of Paris and, by implication, those of any other French community.

The Third Republic

The National Assembly backed into a republican form of government indirectly and much against its will. The monarchists, who constituted its majority, were divided in loyalty between the House of Bourbon and the House of Orléans. They could have surmounted this problem, because the Bourbon claimant, the count of Chambord, had no children and agreed to accept the Orléanist heir as his successor. Chambord refused to become king, how-

The Paris Commune Is Proclaimed

In September 1870, the French Republic was proclaimed, and shortly thereafter a National Assembly was elected. Paris, which had held out against Prussia longer than any other part of France, was hostile to the National Assembly. On March 18, 1871, a revolt against the assembly occurred in Paris. The National Guard of Paris sought to organize the city as a separate part of France. What follows is an excerpt of the proclamation of March 28 of Paris as an autonomous commune separate from the rest of France. The rebellious Parisians wanted all of France to be organized into a federation of politically autonomous communes. This communal concept was directly opposed to that of the large national state. Two months after the proclamation, the troops of the assembly crushed the commune.

❖ *How does this document interpret the French defeat at the hands of Prussia as a punishment? How does the declaration portray the proclamation of the commune as a continuation of the French Revolution? What are the specific political goals and values of the commune, according to this declaration?*

By its revolution of the 18th March, and the spontaneous and courageous efforts of the National Guard, Paris has regained its autonomy....On the eve of the sanguinary and disastrous defeat suffered by France as the punishment it has to undergo for the seventy years of the Empire, and the monarchical, clerical, parliamentary, legal and conciliatory reaction, our country again rises, revives, begins a new life, and retakes the tradition of the Communes of old and of the French Revolution. This tradition, which gave victory to France, and earned the respect and sympathy of past generations, will bring independence, wealth, peaceful glory and brotherly love among nations in the future.

Never was there so solemn an hour. The Revolution which our fathers commenced and we are finishing...is going on without bloodshed, by the might of the popular will....To secure the triumph of the Communal idea...it is necessary to determine its general principles, and to draw up...the programme to be realized....

The Commune is the foundation of all political states, exactly as the family is the embryo of human society. It must have autonomy; that is to say, self-administration and self-government, agreeing with its particular genius, traditions, and wants; preserving, in its political, moral, national, and special groups its entire liberty, its own character, and its complete sovereignty, like a citizen of a free town.

To secure the greatest economic development, the national and territorial independence, and security, association is indispensable; that is to say, a federation of all communes, constituting a united nation.

The autonomy of the Commune guarantees liberty to its citizens; and the federation of all the communes increases, by the reciprocity, power, wealth, markets, and resources of each member, the profit of all. It was the Communal idea...which triumphed on the 18th of March, 1871. It implies, as a political form, the Republic, which is alone compatible with liberty and popular sovereignty.

From G. A. Kertesz, ed., *Documents in the Political History of the European Continent, 1815–1939* (Oxford, U.K.: Clarendon Press, 1968), pp. 312–313.

ever, if France retained the revolutionary tricolor flag. Even the conservative monarchists would not return to the white flag of the Bourbons, which symbolized extreme political reaction.

While the monarchists quarreled among themselves, time passed, and events marched on. By September 1873, the indemnity had been paid, and the Prussian occupation troops had withdrawn. Thiers was ousted from office because he had displayed clear republican sentiments. The monarchists wanted a more sympathetic executive. They elected as president a conservative army officer, Marshal MacMahon (1808–1893), who was expected to prepare for a monarchist restoration. In 1875 the National Assembly, still monarchist in sentiment, but unable to find a king, decided to regularize the political system.

It adopted a law that provided for a Chamber of Deputies elected by universal male suffrage, a Senate chosen indirectly, and a president elected by the two legislative houses. This rather simple republican system had resulted from the bickering and frustration of the monarchists.

After numerous quarrels with the Chamber of Deputies, MacMahon resigned in 1879. His departure meant that dedicated republicans generally controlled the national government despite lingering opposition from the church, wealthy families, and a part of the army.

The political structure of the Third Republic proved much stronger than many citizens suspected at the time. It survived challenges to its leadership from persons such as General Georges Boulanger (1837–1891), who would have imposed stronger executive authority. It also survived several scandals, such as those involving sales of awards of the Legion of Honor and widespread corruption of politicians by a company that tried to construct a canal in Panama, which made its politics appear increasingly sleazy to conservatives. The institutions of the republic, however, allowed new ministers to replace those whose corruption was exposed. (See "Art & the West.")

The Dreyfus Affair

The greatest trauma of the Third Republic occurred over what became known as the "Dreyfus affair." On December 22, 1894, a French military court found Captain Alfred Dreyfus (1859–1935) guilty of passing secret information to the German army. The evidence against him was flimsy and was later revealed to have been forged. Someone in the officer corps had been passing documents to the Germans, and it suited the army investigators to accuse Dreyfus, who was Jewish. After Dreyfus had been sent to Devil's Island, a notorious prison in French Guiana, however, secrets continued to flow to the German army. In 1896, a new head of French counterintelligence reexamined the Dreyfus file and found evidence of forgery. A different officer was implicated, but a military court acquitted him of all charges.

By then the affair had provoked widespread and sometimes near-hysterical public debate. The army, the French Catholic Church, political conservatives, and vehemently antisemitic newspapers repeatedly contended that Dreyfus was guilty. Such anti-Dreyfus opinion was dominant at the beginning of the affair. In 1898, however, the novelist Émile Zola published

The prosecution of Captain Alfred Dreyfus, who is shown here standing on the right at his military trail, provoked the most serious crisis of the Third Republic. Corbis

Édouard Manet,
A Bar at the Folies-Bergère:
Painting Modern Life

The decade of the 1870s witnessed enormous political turmoil in France. It also witnessed the flowering of new painting dedicated to depicting contemporary society. In the mid-nineteenth century, primarily in Paris, European painting began to change in ways that would dominate art for the next century and a half. Two major characteristics marked this new art. First, instead of portraying religious, mythological, and overtly political themes, painters began to depict modern life itself, focusing on the social life and leisured activities of the urban middle and lower middle class. Second, many of these artists were fascinated with light, color, and the representation of momentary, largely yet unfocused, visual experience. Contemporaries called these paintings *impressionistic* and considered them curious and artistically shocking when they were first displayed in Paris.

Édouard Manet (1832–1883), was probably the most influential painter of the second half of the nineteenth century. He did not consider himself an Impressionist, but by the time of his early death in 1883, Manet had begun to adopt many of the techniques of the Impressionists, particularly their use of bright colors. *A Bar at the Folies-Bergère* was Manet's last major work. From the time it was first displayed in 1882, its technique and its meaning have been controversial.

The new paintings of modern life by Manet and the Impressionists, including Claude Monet, Camille Pissaro, Pierre-August Renoir, and Edgar Degas, recorded the middle- and lower-middle classes of Paris attending cafes, dance halls, concerts, picnics, horse races, boating excursions, and beach parties. The backdrop for these works was Paris as it had been reconstructed under Napoleon III into a city of wide boulevards and many places for middle-class leisure. The sites often included these paintings allowed people from different classes to mix socially, while pursuing a leisure activity. One such meeting place was the *Folies-Bergère*, a café–concert hall where patrons could enjoy a wide variety of popular entertainment, including singers, musicians, dancers, gymnasts, and animal shows. Paris had many such establishments, but the *Folies-Bergère* was one of the largest and most expensive.

In *A Bar at the Folies-Bergère*, Manet has painted a young barmaid standing behind a table holding liquor and wine bottles and in front of a very large mirror that reflects the activity occurring in front of her. (Manet actually painted this picture in his studio with a woman who worked as a barmaid posing as his model.) The table, together with its bottles, fruit, vase, and flowers, constitutes a formal still-life composition, but unlike traditional still-lifes, this one shows objects of commercial consumption in a setting where leisure itself is commercially consumed. The mirror reflects the table and its contents, the music hall itself with the legs of a trapeze artist appearing in the top left corner, the audience for the performance, the back of the barmaid, and a man whom she is serving. Manet took great pains to paint the interior light of the hall, which appears to be coming from the newly invented electric lightbulbs.

The mirror in *A Bar at the Folies-Bergère* has provoked enormous comment. Nothing reflected in the mirror exactly relates to the objects in the foreground. The reflected barmaid is leaning; the woman before the mirror is not. The painting seems to demand that we visualize the male figure whom we see only by reflection. Indeed, a contemporary cartoonist published a drawing of the painting with the male patron standing in front of the table with his back to the viewer. Many art historians believe that Manet intended this painting as a comment on late-nineteenth-century urban life—a time of uncertain

Édouard Manet (1832–1883), *A Bar at the Folies–Bergère*, 1882. Oil on canvas, 96 × 130 cm. Signed, dated. Courtauld gift 1932. Courtauld Institute of Gallaries, London.

class relations and growing fears that prosperity would be destroyed by an economic downturn or war. The problem of the reflections in the mirror and their uncertain relationship to the real world may indicate that absence of security in social life.

One of the great questions of the painting is the meaning and expression of the barmaid. The hub-bub and restlessness of the reflected audience and the noise and excitement of the performance music do not register on her face. One art historian has called her a "disconcerting figure because her mat-ter-of-fact, cool glance seems to lack expression."[4] The barmaid's expression may suggest the anonymi-

ty of so many social encounters in modern urban life. Because it was commonly assumed in Paris that many barmaids and shop girls needed to supplement their meager wages through prostitution, some scholars have also suggested that the woman in this painting, like the liquor and the fruit, is simply an-other object of commerce. Does the slightly fore-boding reflected male image suggest that possibility? Or is the barmaid simply an attractive young woman, hired to encourage the sale of alcohol?

Sources: T. J. Clark, *The Painting of Modern Life: Paris in the Art of Manet and His Followers* (Princeton, NJ: Princeton University Press, 1984); Anne Coffin Hanson, *Manet and the Modern Tradition* (New Haven, CT: Yale University Press, 1977); Robert L. Herbert, *Impression-ism: Art, Leisure, and Parisian Society* (New Haven, CT: Yale Universi-ty Press, 1988); Bradford R. Collins, ed., *Twelve Views of Manet's Bar* (Princeton, NJ: Princeton University Press, 1996).

[4]Robert L. Herbert, *Impressionism: Art, Leisure, and Parisian Society* (New Haven, CT: Yale University Press, 1988) , p. 80.

Major Dates in the History of the Third French Republic	
1870	Defeat by Prussia and proclamation of republic
1871	Paris Commune
1873	Prussian occupation troops depart
1873	Marshal MacMahon elected president
1875	Major political institutions of Third Republic organized
1894	Captain Dreyfus convicted
1906	Dreyfus's conviction set aside

a newspaper article entitled *"J'accuse"* ("I accuse") in which he contended that the army had consciously denied due process to Dreyfus and had plotted to suppress or forge evidence. Zola was convicted of libel and received a one-year prison sentence, which he avoided by fleeing to England.

Political discourse in the Third French Republic was harsh. The cover of this anticlerical journal presents the French Roman Catholic Church as the enemy of the nation. A menacing figure symbolizing the church holds the recently built Basilica of the Sacred Heart. Corbis

Zola was only one of numerous liberals, radicals, and socialists who had begun to demand a new trial for Dreyfus. Although these forces of the political left had come to Dreyfus's support rather slowly, they soon realized that his cause could aid their own public image. They portrayed the conservative institutions of the nation as having denied Dreyfus the rights belonging to any citizen of the republic. They also claimed, and properly so, that Dreyfus had been singled out, so that the guilty persons, who were still in the army, could be protected. In August 1898, further evidence of forged material came to light. The officer responsible for those forgeries committed suicide in jail, but a new military trial again convicted Dreyfus. The president of France immediately pardoned him, however, and eventually, in 1906, a civilian court set aside the results of both military trials.

The Dreyfus case divided France as no issue had done since the Paris Commune. By its conclusion, the conservatives were on the defensive. They had allowed themselves to persecute an innocent person and to manufacture false evidence against him to protect themselves from disclosure. They had also embraced violent anti-Semitism. On the political left, radicals, republicans, and socialists developed an informal alliance, which outlived the fight over the Dreyfus case itself. These groups realized that republican institutions must be supported if the political left were to achieve its goals. Nonetheless, the political, religious, and racial divisions and suspicions growing out of the Dreyfus affair continued to divide the Third Republic until France's defeat by Germany in 1940.

The Habsburg Empire

After 1848, the Habsburg Empire was a problem both to itself and for the rest of Europe. An ungenerous critic remarked that a standing army of soldiers, a kneeling army of priests, and a crawling army of informers supported the empire. In the age of national states, liberal institutions, and industrialism, the Habsburg domains remained primarily dynastic, absolutist, and agrarian. The Habsburg response to the revolts of 1848–1849 had been the reassertion of absolutism. Francis Joseph, who became emperor in 1848 and ruled until 1916, was honest and hardworking, but unimaginative. He reacted to events, but rarely commanded them.

During the 1850s, Francis Joseph's ministers attempted to impose a centralized administration on the empire. The system amounted to a military and bureaucratic government dominated by German-speaking Austrians. The Vienna government abolished all internal tariffs in the empire. It divided Hungary, which had been so revolutionary in 1848, into military districts. The Roman Catholic Church acquired control of education. National groups, such as the Croats and Slovaks, who had supported the empire against the Hungarians, received no rewards for their loyalty. Although this domestic system of neo-absolutism provoked resentment and opposition, it eventually floundered because of setbacks in Habsburg foreign affairs.

Austrian refusal to support Russia during the Crimean War meant that the new tsar would no longer help preserve Habsburg rule in Hungary, as Nicholas I had done in 1849. An important external prop of Habsburg power for the past half-century thus disappeared. The Austrian defeat in 1859 at the hands of France and Piedmont and the subsequent loss of territory in Italy confirmed the necessity for a new domestic policy. For seven years the emperor, the civil servants, the aristocrats, and the politicians tried to construct a viable system of government.

Formation of the Dual Monarchy

In 1860 Francis Joseph issued the October Diploma, which created a federation among the states and provinces of the empire. There were to be local diets dominated by the landed classes and a single imperial parliament. The Magyar nobility of Hungary, however, rejected the plan.

Consequently, in 1861, the emperor issued the February Patent, which set up an entirely different form of government. It established a bicameral imperial parliament, or *Reichsrat*, with an upper chamber appointed by the emperor and an indirectly elected lower chamber. Again the Magyars refused to cooperate in a system designed to give political dominance in the empire to German-speaking Austrians. The Magyars sent no delegates to the legislature. Nevertheless, for six years, the February Patent governed the empire, and it prevailed in Austria proper until World War I. Ministers were responsible to the emperor, not the *Reichsrat*, and civil liberties were not guaranteed. Armies could be levied and taxes raised without parliamentary consent. When the *Reichsrat* was not in session, the emperor could simply rule by decree.

Meanwhile, negotiations continued secretly between the emperor and the Magyars. They produced no concrete result until the Prussian defeat of Austria in the summer of 1866 and the consequent exclusion of Austria from German affairs. The military disaster compelled Francis Joseph to come to terms with the Magyars. The subsequent *Ausgleich*, or Compromise, of 1867 transformed the Habsburg Empire into a dual monarchy, thereafter generally known as Austria–Hungary. (See "The Austrian Prime Minister Explains the Dual Monarchy.")

Francis Joseph was crowned king of Hungary in Budapest in 1867. Except for the common monarch, Austria and Hungary became almost wholly separate states. They shared ministers of foreign affairs, defense, and finance, but the other ministers were different for each state. There were also separate parliaments. Each year, sixty parliamentary delegates from each state met to discuss mutual interests. Every ten years, Austria and Hungary renegotiated their trade relationship. By this cumbersome machinery, unique in European history, the Magyars were reconciled to Habsburg rule. They had achieved the free hand they had long wanted in Hungary.

Unrest of Nationalities

The Compromise of 1867 had introduced two different principles of political legitimacy into the two sections of the Habsburg Empire. In Hungary, political loyalty was based on nationality because Hungary had been recognized as a distinct part of the monarchy on the basis of nationalism. In effect, Hungary was a Magyar nation under the Habsburg emperor. In the rest of the Habsburg domains, the principle of legitimacy meant dynastic loyalty to the emperor. Many of the other nationalities wished to achieve the same type of settlement that the Hungarians had won, or to govern themselves, or to unite with fellow nationals who lived outside the empire. (See Map 23–3.)

Many of those other national groups—including the Czechs, the Ruthenians, the Romanians, and the Croatians—opposed the Compromise of 1867 that, in effect, had permitted the German-speaking Austrians and the Hungarian Magyars to dominate all other nationalities within the empire. The most vocal critics were the Czechs of Bohemia. They favored a policy of "trialism," or triple monarchy, in which the Czechs would be given a position similar to that given the Hungarians. In 1871, Francis Joseph was willing to accept this concept. The Magyars, however, vetoed it lest they be forced to make similar concessions to their own subject nationalities. Furthermore, the Germans of Bohemia were afraid that the Czech language would be imposed on them and their children.

For more than twenty years, the Czechs were placated by generous patronage and posts in the bureaucracy. By the 1890s, however, Czech nationalism

MAP 23–3   NATIONALITIES WITHIN THE HABSBURG EMPIRE   *The patchwork appearance reflects the unusual problem of the numerous ethnic groups that the Habsburgs could not, of course, meld into a modern national state. Only the Magyars were recognized in 1867, leaving nationalist Czechs, Slovaks, and the others chronically dissatisfied.*

Major Dates in the Late Nineteenth-Century Habsburg Empire

1848	Francis Joseph becomes emperor
1860	October Diploma
1861	February Patent
1866	Defeat by Prussia
1867	Compromise between emperor and Hungary, establishing the Dual Monarchy
1897	Ordinances giving equality of language between Germans and Czechs in Austria
1907	Universal male suffrage introduced for Austria

again became more strident. In 1897, Francis Joseph gave the Czechs and the Germans equality of language in various localities. Thereafter, the Germans in the Austrian *Reichsrat* opposed these measures by disrupting Parliament. The Czechs replied in kind. By the turn of the century, this obstructionism, which included the playing of musical instruments in the *Reichsrat*, had paralyzed parliamentary life. The emperor ruled by imperial decree through the bureaucracy. In 1907, Francis Joseph introduced universal male suffrage in Austria (but not in Hungary), but this action did not eliminate the chaos in the *Reichsrat*. In effect, by 1914 constitutionalism was a dead letter in Austria. It flourished in Hungary, but only because the Magyars relentlessly exercised political supremacy over all other competing national groups except Croatia, which was permitted considerable autonomy.

There is reason to believe that nationalism became stronger during the last quarter of the nineteenth century. It was then that language became the single most important factor in defining a nation. The expansion of education made this possible. In all countries where nationalistic groups

The Austrian Prime Minister Explains the Dual Monarchy

The multinational character of the Austrian Empire had long been a source of internal weakness and political discontent. After the defeat of Austria by Prussia in 1866, the Austrian government attempted to regain the loyalty of the Hungarians by making Hungary a separate kingdom within a dual monarchy, known thereafter as Austria–Hungary.

❖ *How does the Austrian prime minister define the problems of nationality within the empire? Why does he distinguish Hungary from the other national groups that seek independence or association with another nation? What are the principles he claims lie behind the establishment of the dual monarchy?*

The dangers which Austria has to face are of a twofold nature. The first is presented by the tendency of her liberal-minded German population to gravitate toward that larger portion of the German-speaking people....the second is the diversity of language and race in the empire. Of Austria's large Slav population, the Poles have a natural craving for independence after having enjoyed and heroically fought for it for centuries; while the other nationalities are likely at a moment of dangerous crisis to develop pro-Russian tendencies.

Now my object is to carry out a bloodless revolution—to show the various elements of this great empire that it is to the benefit of each of them to act in harmony with its neighbor.... But to this I have made one exception. Hungary is an ancient monarchy, more ancient as such than Austria proper.... I have endeavoured to give Hungary not a new position with regard to the Austrian empire, but to secure her in the one which she has occupied. The Emperor of Austria is King of Hungary; my idea was that he should revive in his person the Constitution of which he and his ancestors have been the heads. The leading principles of my plan are...the resuscitation of an old monarchy and an old Constitution; not the separation of one part of the empire from the other, but the drawing together of the two component parts by the recognition of their joint positions, the maintenance of their mutual obligations, their community in questions affecting the entire empire, and their proportional pecuniary responsibility for the liabilities of the whole State. It is no plan of separation that I have carried out: on the contrary, it is one of close union, not by the creation of a new power, but by the recognition of an old one....

From *Memoirs of Friedrich Ferdinand Count von Beust*, Vol. I, ed. by Baron Henry de Worms (London: Remington, 1887), pp. xx–xxvi.

prospered, their membership was dominated by intellectuals, students, and educated members of the middle class, all of whom were literate in the literary version of particular national languages. Furthermore, it was during these same years, as will be seen in Chapter 25, that racial thinking became important in Europe. Racial thought maintained that there was a genetic basis for ethnic and cultural groups which had hitherto been generally defined by a common history and culture. Once language and race became the ways to define an ethnic or national group, the lines between such groups became much more sharply drawn. (See "Lord Acton Condemns Nationalism.")

The unrest of the various nationalities within the Habsburg Empire not only caused internal political difficulties; it also became a major source of political instability for all of central and eastern Europe. Each of the nationality problems normally had ramifications for both foreign and domestic policy. Both the Croats and the Poles wanted an independent state in union with their fellow nationals who lived outside the empire—and in the case of the Poles, with fellow nationals in the Russian Empire. Other national groups, such as Ukrainians, Romanians, Italians, and Bosnians, saw themselves as potentially linked to Russia, Romania, Serbia, Italy, or a yet-to-be established south Slavic, or Yugoslav, state. Many of these nationalities looked to Russia to protect their interests or influence the government in Vienna. The Romanians were also concerned about the Romanian minority in Hungary. Serbia sought to expand its

Lord Acton Condemns Nationalism

Lord Acton (1834–1902) was a major nineteenth-century English historian and commentator on contemporary religious and political events. In all his writings, he was deeply concerned with the character and preservation of liberty. His was one of the earliest voices to warn against the political dangers of nationalism.

❖ *Why does Acton see the principle of nationality as dangerous to liberty? Why does he see nationalism as a threat to minority groups? Why does he see nationalism as a threat to democracy?*

The greatest adversary of the rights of nationality is the modern theory of nationality. By making the State and the nation commensurate with each other in theory, it reduces practically to a subject condition all other nationalities that may be within the boundary. It cannot admit them to an equality with the ruling nation which constitutes the State, because the State would then cease to be national, which would be a contradiction of the principle of its existence. According, therefore, to the degree of humanity and civilization in that dominant body which claims all the rights of the community, the inferior races are exterminated, or reduced to servitude, or outlawed, or put in a condition of dependence.

If we take the establishment of liberty for the realization of moral duties to be the end of civil society, we must conclude that those states are substantially the most perfect which, like the British and Austrian Empires, include various distinct nationalities without oppressing them. Those in which no mixture of races has occurred are imperfect; and those in which its effects have disappeared are decrepit. A State which is incompetent to satisfy different races condemns itself; a State which labors to neutralize, to absorb, or to expel them, destroys its own vitality; a State which does not include them is destitute of the chief basis of self-government. The theory of nationality, therefore, is a retrograde step in history....

...[N]ationality does not aim either at liberty or prosperity, both of which it sacrifices to the imperative necessity of making the nation the mold and measure of the State. Its course will be marked with material as well as moral ruin, in order that a new invention may prevail over the works of God and the interests of mankind. There is no principle of change, no phrase of political speculation conceivable, more comprehensive, more subversive, or more arbitrary than this. It is a confutation of democracy, because it sets limits to the exercise of the popular will, and substitutes for it a higher principle.

From John Emerich Edward Dalbert-Acton, First Baron Acton, *Essays in the History of Liberty*, ed. by J. Rufus Fears (Indianapolis: Liberty Classics, 1985), pp. 431–433.

borders to include Serbs who lived within Habsburg or Ottoman territory. Out of these Balkan tensions emerged much of the turmoil that would spark the First World War. Many of the same ethnic tensions account for warfare in the former Yugoslavia.

The dominant German population of Austria proper was generally loyal to the emperor. A part of it, however, yearned to join the united German state being established by Bismarck. These nationalistic Austro–Germans often hated the non-German national groups of the empire, and many of them were anti-Semites. Such attitudes would influence the youth and the young adulthood of Adolph Hitler.

For the next century of European and even world history, the significance of this nationalist unrest within the late-nineteenth-century Austrian Empire and its neighbors can hardly be overestimated. Nationality problems touched all three of the great central and eastern European empires—the German, the Russian, and the Austrian. All had large Polish populations, and Russia had many minority groups. Each nationality regarded its own aspirations and discontents as more important than the larger good or even survival of the empires that they inhabited. The weakness of the Ottoman Empire allowed both Austria and Russia to compete in the Balkans for greater influence and thus further inflame nationalistic resentments. Such nationalistic stirrings affected the fate of all three empires from the 1860s through the outbreak of World War I. The government of each of those empires would be overturned during the war, and the Austrian Empire would disappear. Those same unresolved problems of central and eastern European nationalism would then lead directly to World War II. They continue to fester today.

Russia: Emancipation and Revolutionary Stirrings

Russia changed remarkably during the last half of the nineteenth century. The government finally both addressed the long-standing problem of serfdom and undertook a broad range of administrative reforms. During the same period, however, radical revolutionary groups began to organize. These groups tried to draw the peasants into revolutionary activity and assassinated major government officials, including the tsar. The government's response was a new era of repression following the years of reform.

Reforms of Alexander II

Russia's defeat in the Crimean War and its humiliation of the Treaty of Paris compelled the government to reconsider its domestic policies. Nicholas I had died in 1855 during the conflict. Because of extensive travel in Russia and an early introduction to government, his son Alexander II (r. 1855–1881) was familiar with the chief difficulties facing the nation. The debacle of the war had made reform both necessary and possible. Alexander II took advantage of this turn of events to institute the most extensive restructuring of Russian society and administration since Peter the Great. Like Peter, Alexander imposed his reforms from the top.

ABOLITION OF SERFDOM In every area of economic and public life, a profound cultural gap separated Russia from the rest of Europe. Nowhere was this more apparent than in the survival of serfdom. In

Life in Russian villages during the 1870s was very difficult. Tsar Alexander II abolished serfdom in 1861, but peasants were required to pay compensation to the government for 49 years and living standards remained dismal. This painting shows peasants waiting patiently outside a government office while officials inside take their time over lunch.
Bildarchiv Preussischer Kulturbesitz

Russia, the institution had changed very little since the eighteenth century, although every other nation on the Continent had abandoned it. Russian landowners still had a free hand with their serfs, and the serfs had little recourse against the landlords. In March 1856, at the conclusion of the Crimean War, Alexander II announced his intention to abolish serfdom. He had decided that only its abolition would permit Russia to organize its human and natural resources to maintain its status as a great power.

Serfdom had become economically inefficient. There was always the threat of revolt, and the serfs forced into the army had performed poorly in the Crimean conflict. Moreover, nineteenth-century moral opinion condemned serfdom. Only Russia, Brazil, and certain portions of the United States among the Western nations still retained such forms of involuntary servitude. For five years, government commissions wrestled over how to implement the tsar's desire. Finally, in February 1861, against much opposition from the nobility and the landlords, Alexander II promulgated the long statute ending serfdom in Russia.

The actual emancipation statute proved to be a disappointment, however, because freedom was not accompanied by land. Serfs immediately received the personal right to marry without their landlord's permission, as well as the rights to purchase and sell property freely, to engage in court actions, and to pursue trades. What they did not receive was free title to their land. They had to pay the landlords over a period of forty-nine years for allotments of land that were frequently too small to support them. They were also charged interest during this period. The serfs made the payments to the government, which had already reimbursed the landlords for their losses. The serfs would not receive title to the land until the debt was paid.

The procedures were so complicated and the results so limited that many serfs believed that real emancipation was still to come. The redemption payments led to almost unending difficulty. Poor harvests made it impossible for many peasants to keep up with the payments, and they fell increasingly behind in their debt. The situation was not remedied until 1906, when, during the widespread revolutionary unrest following the Japanese defeat of Russia in 1905, the government grudgingly completed the process of emancipation by canceling the remaining debts.

REFORM OF LOCAL GOVERNMENT AND THE JUDICIAL SYSTEM   The abolition of serfdom required the reorganization of local government and the judi-

cial system. The authority of village communes replaced that of the landlord over the peasant. The village elders settled family quarrels, imposed fines, issued internal passports, and collected taxes. Often, also, it was the village commune rather than individual peasants who owned the land. The nobility were permitted a larger role in local administration through a system of provincial and county *zemstvos*, or councils, organized in 1864. These councils were to oversee local matters, such as bridge and road repair, education, and agricultural improvement. Because the councils received inadequate funds, however, local governments were never vitalized.

The flagrant inequities and abuses of the pre-emancipation judicial system could not continue. In 1864, Alexander II promulgated a new statute on the judiciary. For the first time, western European legal principles were introduced into Russia. These included equality before the law, impartial hearings, uniform procedures, judicial independence, and trial by jury. The new system was far from perfect. The judges were not genuinely independent, and the tsar could increase, as well as reduce sentences. Certain offenses, such as those involving the press, were not tried before a jury. Nonetheless, the new courts were both more efficient and less corrupt than the old system.

MILITARY REFORM   The government also reformed the army. Russia possessed the largest military force on the Continent, but it had floundered badly in the Crimean War. The usual period of service for a soldier was twenty-five years. Villages had to provide quotas of serfs to serve in the army. Often, the recruiters simply appeared in the villages and seized serfs from their families. Once in the army, the recruits rarely saw their homes again. Life in the army was harsh, even by the brutal standards of most midcentury armies. In the 1860s, the army lowered the period of service to fifteen years and relaxed discipline slightly. In 1874, the enlistment period was lowered to six years of active duty, followed by nine years in the reserves. All males were subject to military service after the age of twenty.

REPRESSION IN POLAND   Alexander's reforms became more measured shortly after the Polish Rebellion of 1863. As in 1830, Polish nationalists attempted to overthrow Russian dominance. Once again the Russian army suppressed the rebellion. Alexander II then moved to Russify Poland. In 1864, he emancipated the Polish serfs to punish the politically restive Polish nobility. Russian law, language, and administration were imposed on all areas of Polish life. Henceforth,

until the close of World War I, Poland was treated as merely another Russian province.

As the Polish suppression demonstrated, Alexander II was a reformer only within the limits of his own autocracy. His changes in Russian life failed to create new loyalty to, or gratitude for, the government among his subjects. The serfs felt that their emancipation had been inadequate. The nobles and the wealthier educated segments of Russian society resented the tsar's persistent refusal to allow them a meaningful role in government and policy making. Consequently, although Alexander II became known as the Tsar Liberator, he was never popular. He could be indecisive and closed minded. These characteristics became more pronounced after 1866, when an attempt was made on his life. Thereafter, Russia increasingly became a police state. This new repression fueled the activity of radical groups within Russia. Their actions, in turn, made the autocracy more reactionary.

Revolutionaries

The tsarist regime had long had its critics. One of the most prominent was Alexander Herzen (1812–1870), who lived in exile. From London, he published a newspaper called *The Bell*, in which he set forth reformist positions. The initial reforms of Alexander II had raised great hopes among Russian students and intellectuals, but they soon became discontented with the limited character of the reforms. Drawing on the ideas of Herzen and other radicals, these students formed a revolutionary movement known as Populism. They sought a social revolution based on the communal life of the Russian peasants. The chief radical society was called *Land and Freedom*.

In the early 1870s, hundreds of young Russians, including both men and women, took their revolutionary message into the countryside. They intended to live with the peasants, to gain their trust, and to teach them about the peasant's role in the coming revolution. The bewildered and

Tsar Alexander II (r. 1855–1881) was assassinated on March 1, 1881. The assassins first threw a bomb that wounded several Imperial guards. When the tsar stopped his carriage to see the wounded, the assassins threw a second bomb, killing him. Bildarchiv Preussischer Kulturbesitz

The People's Will Issues a Revolutionary Manifesto

In the late 1870s, an extreme revolutionary movement appeared in Russia calling itself The People's Will. It advocated the overthrow of the tsarist government and the election of an Organizing Assembly to form a government based on popular representation. It directly embraced terrorism as a path toward its goal of the Russian people governing themselves. Members of this group assassinated Alexander II in 1881.

❖ *Which of the group's seven demands might be associated with liberalism, and which go beyond liberalism in their radical intent? Why does the group believe that it must engage in terrorism as well as propaganda? Would there have been any reforms or steps toward reform that the Russian government might have taken which might have satisfied this group or dissuaded them from terrorist action?*

Although we are ready to submit wholly to the popular will, we regard it as none the less our duty, as a party, to appear before the people with our program....It is as follows:

1. Perpetual popular representation...having full power to act in all national questions.

2. General local self-government, secured by the election of all officers, and the economic independence of the people.

3. The self-controlled village commune as the economic and administrative unit.

4. Ownership of the land by the people.

5. A system of measures having for their object the turning over to the laborers of all mining works and factories.

6. Complete freedom of conscience, speech, association, public meeting, and electioneering activity.

7. The substitution of a territorial militia for the army....

In view of the stated aim of the party its operations may be classified as follows:

1. Propaganda and agitation. Our propaganda has for its object the popularization, in all social classes, of the idea of a political and popular revolution as a means of social reform, as well as popularization of the party's own program. Its essential features are criticism of the existing order of things, and a statement and explanation of revolutionary methods. The aim of agitation should be to incite the people to protest as generally as possible against the present state of affairs, to demand such reforms as are in harmony with the party's purposes, and, especially, to demand the summoning of an Organizing Assembly....

2. Destructive and terroristic activity. Terroristic activity consists in the destruction of the most harmful persons in the Government, the protection of the party from spies, and the punishment of official lawlessness and violence in all the more prominent and important cases in which such lawlessness and violence are manifested. The aim of such activity is to break down the prestige of Governmental power, to furnish continuous proof of the possibility of carrying on a contest with the Government, to raise in that way the revolutionary spirit of the people and inspire belief in the practicability of revolution, and, finally, to form a body suited and accustomed to warfare.

Quoted in George Kennan, *Siberia and the Exile System*, Vol. 2 (New York: The Century Co., 1891), pp. 495–499.

distrustful peasants turned most of the youths over to the police. In the winter of 1877–1878, almost 200 students were tried. Most were acquitted or given light sentences, because they had been held for months in preventive detention and because the court believed that a display of mercy might lessen public sympathy for the young revolutionaries. The court even suggested that the tsar might wish to pardon those students given heavier sentences. The tsar refused and let it become known that he favored heavy penalties for all persons involved in revolutionary activity.

Thereafter, the revolutionaries decided that the tsarist regime must be attacked directly. They adopted a policy of terrorism. In January 1878, Vera Zasulich (1849–1919) attempted to assassinate the

Major Dates in Late Nineteenth-Century Russia	
1855	Alexander II becomes tsar
1856	Defeat in Crimean War
1861	Serfdom abolished
1863	Suppression of Polish rebellion
1864	Reorganization of local government
1864	Reform of judicial system
1874	Military enlistment period reduced
1878	Attempted assassination of military governor of Saint Petersburg
1879	Land and Freedom splits
1881	The People's Will assassinates Alexander II
1881	Alexander III becomes tsar
1894	Nicholas II becomes tsar

military governor of Saint Petersburg. A jury acquitted her because the governor she had shot had a reputation for brutality. Some people also believed that Zasulich had a personal rather than a political grievance against her victim. Nonetheless, the verdict further encouraged the terrorists.

In 1879, Land and Freedom split into two groups. One advocated educating the peasants, and it soon dissolved. The other, known as *The People's Will*, was dedicated to the overthrow of the autocracy. Its members decided to assassinate the tsar himself. (See "The People's Will Issues a Revolutionary Manifesto.") Several attempts failed, but on March 1, 1881, a bomb hurled by a member of The People's Will killed Alexander II. Four men and two women were sentenced to death for the deed. All of them had been willing to die for their cause. The emergence of such dedicated revolutionary opposition was as much a part of the reign of Alexander II as were his reforms. The limited character of those reforms convinced many Russians that the autocracy could never truly redirect Russian society.

The reign of Alexander III (r. 1881–1894) strengthened that pessimism. He possessed all the autocratic and repressive characteristics of his grandfather, Nicholas I, and none of the better qualities of his father, Alexander II. Some slight improvements were made to conditions in Russian factories, but Alexander III sought primarily to roll back his father's reforms. He favored the centralized bureaucracy over the *zemstvos*. He strengthened the secret police and increased censorship of the press. In effect, he confirmed all the evils that the revolutionaries saw as inherent in autocratic

government. His son, Nicholas II (r. 1894–1917), would discover that autocracy could not survive the pressures of the twentieth century.

Great Britain: Toward Democracy

While the continental nations became unified and struggled toward internal political restructuring, Great Britain continued to symbolize the confident liberal state. Britain was not without its difficulties and domestic conflicts, but it seemed able to deal with these through existing political institutions. The general prosperity of the third quarter of the century mitigated the social hostility of the 1840s. All classes shared a belief in competition and individualism. Even the leaders of trade unions during these years asked mainly to receive more of the fruits of prosperity and to have their social respectability acknowledged. Parliament itself remained an institution through which new groups and interests were absorbed into the existing political processes. In short, the British did not have to create new liberal institutions and then learn how to live within them.

The Second Reform Act (1867)

By the early 1860s, most observers realized that the franchise would again have to be expanded. The prosperity and social respectability of the working class convinced many politicians that the workers deserved the vote. Organizations such as the Reform League, led by John Bright (1811–1889), were agitating for parliamentary action. In 1866, Lord Russell's Liberal ministry introduced a reform bill that was defeated by a coalition of traditional Conservatives and antidemocratic Liberals. Russell resigned, and the Conservative Lord Derby (1799–1869) replaced him. What then occurred surprised everyone.

The Conservative ministry, led in the House of Commons by Benjamin Disraeli (1804–1881), introduced its own reform bill in 1867. As the debate proceeded, Disraeli accepted one amendment after another and expanded the electorate well beyond the limits proposed earlier by the Liberals. When the final measure was passed, the number of voters had been increased from approximately 1,430,000 to 2,470,000. Britain had taken a major step toward democracy. Large numbers of male working-class voters had been admitted to the electorate.

Disraeli hoped that by sponsoring the measure, the Conservatives would receive the gratitude of the new voters. Because reform was inevitable, it was best for the Conservatives to enjoy the credit for it. Disraeli thought that eventually significant portions of the working class would support Conservative candidates who were responsive to social issues. He also thought that the growing suburban middle class would become more conservative. In the long run, his intuition proved correct. The Conservative Party dominated British politics in the twentieth century.

The immediate election of 1868, however, dashed Disraeli's hopes. William Gladstone (1809–1898) became the new prime minister. Gladstone had begun political life in 1833 as a strong Tory, but over the next thirty-five years he became steadily more liberal. He had supported Robert Peel, free trade, repeal of the Corn Laws, and efficient administration. As chancellor of the exchequer (finance minister) during the 1850s and early 1860s, he had lowered taxes and government expenditures. He had also championed Italian nationalism. Yet he had continued to oppose a new reform bill until the early 1860s. In 1866, he had been Russell's spokesperson in the House of Commons for the unsuccessful Liberal reform bill.

Gladstone's Great Ministry (1868–1874)

Gladstone's ministry of 1868–1874 witnessed the culmination of classical British liberalism. Those institutions that remained the preserve of the aristocracy and the Anglican Church were opened to people from other classes and religious denominations. In 1870, competitive examinations for the civil service replaced patronage. In 1871, the purchase of officers' commissions in the army was abolished. The same year, Anglican religious requirements for the faculties of Oxford and Cambridge universities were removed. The Ballot Act of 1872 introduced voting by secret ballot.

The most momentous measure of Gladstone's first ministry was the Education Act of 1870. For the first time in British history, the government assumed the responsibility for establishing and running elementary schools. Previously, British education had been a task relegated to the religious denominations, which received small amounts of state support for the purpose. Henceforth, the government would establish schools where the efforts of religious denominations to establish them had proved inadequate.

All of these reforms were typically liberal. They sought to remove long-standing abuses

William Ewart Gladstone served in the British Parliament from the 1830s through the 1890s. Four times the Liberal Party prime minister, he was responsible for guiding major reforms through Parliament. Bildarchiv Preussischer Kulturbesitz

without destroying existing institutions and to permit all able citizens to compete on the grounds of ability and merit. They tried to avoid the potential danger to a democratic state of an illiterate citizenry. These reforms also constituted a mode of state building, because they created new bonds of loyalty to the nation by abolishing many sources of discontent.

Disraeli in Office (1874–1880)

The liberal policy of creating popular support for the nation by extending political liberties and reforming abuses had its conservative counterpart in concern for social reform. Disraeli succeeded Gladstone as prime minister in 1874, when the election produced sharp divisions among Liberal Party voters over religion, education, and the sale of alcohol.

The two men had stood on different sides of most issues for over a quarter century. Whereas Gladstone looked to individualism, free trade, and competition to solve social problems, Disraeli believed in paternalistic legislation. Disraeli also

Benajmin Disraeli served as British prime minister from 1874 to 1880. He is regarded as the founder of modern British conservatism because of his efforts to convince the Conservative Party to accept a democratic electorate, which he believed would vote conservative more often than not. Bildarchiv Preussischer Kulturbesitz

believed in state action to protect the weak. In his view, such paternalistic legislation would alleviate class antagonisms.

Disraeli talked a better line than he produced. He had few specific programs or ideas. The significant social legislation of his ministry stemmed primarily from the efforts of his home secretary, Richard Cross (1823–1914). The Public Health Act of 1875 consolidated previous legislation on sanitation and reaffirmed the duty of the state to interfere with private property on matters of health and physical well-being. Through the Artisans Dwelling Act of 1875, the government became actively involved in providing housing for the working class. That same year, in an important symbolic gesture, the Conservative majority in Parliament gave new protection to British trade unions and allowed them to raise picket lines. The Gladstone ministry, although recognizing the legality of unions, had refused such protection.

The Irish Question

In 1880, a second Gladstone ministry took office after an agricultural depression and an unpopular foreign policy undermined the Conservative government. In 1884, with Conservative cooperation, a third reform act gave the vote to most male farmworkers. The major issue of the decade, however, was Ireland. From the late 1860s onward, Irish nationalists had sought to achieve home rule for Ireland, by which they meant Irish control of local government.

During his first ministry, Gladstone had addressed the Irish question through two major pieces of legislation. In 1869 he had disestablished the Church of Ireland, the Irish branch of the Anglican church. Henceforth, Irish Roman Catholics would not pay taxes to support the hated Protestant Church, to which few of the Irish belonged. Second, in 1870, the Liberal ministry sponsored a land act that provided compensation to those Irish tenants who were evicted and loans for those who wished to purchase their land. Throughout the 1870s, the Irish question continued to fester. Land remained the center of the agitation. Today, Irish economic development seems more complicated, and who owned the land seems less important than the methods of management and cultivation. Nevertheless, the organization of the Irish Land League in the late 1870s led to intense agitation and intimidation of landlords, who were often English. The leader of the Irish movement for a just land settlement and for home rule was Charles Stewart Parnell (1846–1891). In 1881, the second Gladstone ministry passed another Irish land act that strengthened tenant rights. It was accompanied, however, by a Coercion Act to restore law and order to Ireland.

By 1885, Parnell had organized eighty-five Irish members of the House of Commons into a tightly disciplined party that often voted as a bloc. They frequently disrupted Parliament to gain attention for the cause of home rule. They bargained with the two English political parties. In the election of 1885, the Irish Party emerged holding the balance of power between the English Liberals and Conservatives. (See "Parnell Calls for Home Rule for Ireland.") Irish support could decide which party took office. In December 1885, Gladstone announced his support of home rule for Ireland. Parnell gave his votes to the formation of a Liberal ministry. The home rule issue then split the Liberal Party. In 1886, a group known as the Liberal Unionists joined with the Conservatives to defeat Gladstone's Home Rule Bill. Gladstone called for a new election, in which the Liberals were defeated.

Parnell Calls for Home Rule for Ireland

Since 1800, Ireland had been governed as part of Great Britain, sending representatives to the British Parliament in Westminster. Throughout the century, there had been tension and violent conflict between the Irish and their English governors. Agitation for home rule whereby the Irish would directly control many of their own affairs reached a peak in the 1880s. Charles Stewart Parnell was the chief leader for the cause of Irish nationalism during that decade. His program at the time was home rule for Ireland, by which he meant Irish administration of Irish domestic affairs in the context of a continuing ill-defined union with England. In 1885, he made a speech in which he outlined the resentments the Irish had felt toward the English since the Act of Union of 1800. He also drew direct parallels between the relationship of Ireland to England and that of Hungary to Austria. His remarks should be compared with those of the Austrian Prime Minister explaining the dual monarchy in the document, "The Austrian Prime Minister Explains the Dual Monarchy," p. 801. The efforts toward achieving home rule failed during the nineteenth century.

❖ *How does Parnell say the Act of Union affected Irish sentiment toward England? What parallel does he draw with Hungary and Austria? Why might Parnell be regarded as a moderate nationalist?*

It is not possible for human intelligence to forecast the future in the matter; but we can point to this—we can point to the fact that under 85 years of parliamentary connection with England, Ireland has become intensely disloyal and intensely disaffected; that notwithstanding the Whig policy of so-called conciliation, alternative conciliation and coercion...that disaffection has broadened, deepened and intensified from day to day. Am I not, then, entitled to assume that one of the roots of this disaffection and feeling of disloyalty is the assumption by England of the management of our affairs. It is admitted that the present system can't go on, and what are you going to put in its place? My advice to English statesmen considering this question would be this—trust the Irish people altogether or trust them not at all....Whatever chance the English rulers may have of drawing to themselves the affection of the Irish people lies in destroying the abominable system of legislative union between the two countries by conceding fully and freely to Ireland their right to manage her own affairs. It is impossible for us to give guarantees, but we can point to the past; we can show that the record of English rule is a constant series of steps from bad to worse, that the condition of English power is more insecure and more unstable at the present moment than it has ever been. We can point to the example of other countries; of Austria and of Hungary—to the fact that Hungary having been conceded self-government became one of the strongest factors in the Austrian empire. We can show the powers that have been freely conceded in the colonies [such as Canada and Australia have led to loyalty]...I am confident that the English statesman who is great enough... to carry out these teachings...to give Ireland full legislative liberty, full power to manage her own domestic concerns will be regarded in the future by his countrymen as one who has removed the greatest peril to the English empire—a peril, I firmly believe, which if not removed will find some day...an opportunity of revenging itself to the destruction of the British empire for the misfortunes, the oppressions, and the misgovernment of our country.

From Charles Stewart Parnell, "Speech at Wicklow," October 5, 1885, as quoted in Raymond Phineas Stearns, *Pageant of Europe: Sources and Selections from the Renaissance to the Present Day* (New York: Harcourt, Brace and Company, 1948), pp. 634–635.

Major Dates in Late Nineteenth-Century Britain	

Year	Event
1867	Second Reform Act
1868	Gladstone becomes prime minister
1869	Disestablishment of Church of Ireland
1870	Education Act and first Irish Land Act
1871	Purchase of army officers' commissions abolished
1871	Religious tests abolished at Oxford and Cambridge
1872	Ballot Act
1874	Disraeli becomes prime minister
1875	Public Health Act and Artisan Dwelling Act
1880	Beginning of Gladstone's second ministry
1881	Second Irish Land Act and Irish Coercion Act
1884	Third Reform Act
1885	Gladstone announces support of Irish home rule
1886	Home Rule Bill defeated and Lord Salisbury becomes the Conservative prime minister
1892	Gladstone begins his third ministry; second Irish Home Rule Bill defeated
1903	Third Irish Land Act
1912	Third Irish Home Rule Bill passed
1914	Provisions of Irish Home Rule Bill suspended because of the outbreak of World War I

They remained permanently divided, and Ireland remained firmly under English administration.

The new Conservative ministry of Lord Salisbury (1830–1903) attempted to reconcile the Irish to English government through public works and administrative reform. The policy, which was tied to further coercion, had only marginal success. In 1892, Gladstone returned to power. A second Home Rule Bill passed the House of Commons, but was defeated in the House of Lords. There the Irish question stood until after the turn of the century. The Conservatives sponsored a land act in 1903 that carried out the final transfer of land to tenant ownership. Ireland became a country of small farms. In 1912, a Liberal ministry passed the third Home Rule Bill. Under the provisions of the House of Lords Act of 1911, which curbed the power of that body, the bill had to pass the Commons three times over the Lords' veto to become law. The third passage occurred in the summer of 1914, but the implementation of the home rule provisions of the bill was suspended for the duration of World War I.

The Irish question affected British politics in a manner not unlike that of the Austrian nationalities problem. Normal British domestic issues could not be resolved because of the political divisions created by Ireland. The split of the Liberal Party proved especially harmful to the cause of further social and political reform. People who could agree about reform could not agree about Ireland, and the Irish problem seemed more important. Since the two traditional parties failed to deal with the social questions by the turn of the century, a newly organized Labour Party began to fill the vacuum.

In Perspective

Between 1850 and 1875, the major contours of the political systems that would dominate Europe until World War I had been drawn. Those systems and political arrangements solved, so far as such matters can be solved, many of the political questions and problems that had troubled Europeans during the first half of the nineteenth century. On the whole, the concept of the nation–state had triumphed. Support for governments no longer stemmed from loyalty to dynasties, but from various degrees of citizen participation. Moreover, the unity of nations was no longer based on dynastic links, but on ethnic, cultural, linguistic, and historical bonds. The parliamentary governments of western Europe were different from the autocracies of eastern Europe, but both political systems had been compelled to recognize the force of nationalism and the larger role of citizens in political affairs. Only Russia failed to make such concessions, but the emancipation of serfs had been one concession to popular opinion.

The major sources of future discontent would arise from the demands of labor to enter the political processes and the still unsatisfied aspirations of subject nationalities. Those two areas of unrest would trouble Europe for the next forty years and would eventually undermine the political structures created during the third quarter of the nineteenth century.

REVIEW QUESTIONS

1. Why was it so difficult to unify Italy? What groups were urging unification? Who was Camillo Cavour, and how did he achieve what others failed to do? What were Garibaldi's contributions to Italian unification?

2. Who was Otto von Bismarck and why did he try to unify Germany? What attempts had preceded Bismarck's efforts and why did they fail? What was Bismarck's policy of unification and why did he succeed? What effect did the unification of Germany have on the rest of Europe?

3. Discuss the transformation in France from the Second Empire of Napoleon III to the establishment of the Third Republic. Why did the Second Empire fall and what problems faced the new republic? Why did the Paris Commune become a legend throughout Europe? What effect did the Dreyfus affair have on the politics of the Third Republic?

4. Describe the governmental changes in Austria after 1848. What unique problems did Austria have? Were they solved? Why was nationalism a more pressing problem for Austria than for any other nation?

5. What reforms were instituted by Tsar Alexander II in Russia? Were they effective in solving some of Russia's domestic problems? Can Alexander II be regarded as a "visionary" reformer? Why or why not?

6. How would you contrast the British Liberal and Conservative parties between 1860 and 1890? Who were the leaders of each? What problems did they face in those years and what different solutions did they favor? Specifically, how did British politicians handle the Irish question? What are the parallels between England's relationship with Ireland and the nationality problem of the Austrian Empire?

SUGGESTED READINGS

M. BENTLEY, *Politics Without Democracy, 1815–1914* (1984). A well-informed survey of British development.

D. BLACKBOURN, *The Long Nineteenth Century: A History of Germany, 1780–1918* (1998). An outstanding survey based on up-to-date scholarship.

R. BLAKE, *Disraeli* (1967). Remains the best biography of the man.

J. BLUM, *Lord and Peasant in Russia from the Ninth to the Nineteenth Century* (1961). A clear discussion of emancipation in the later chapters.

G. CHAPMAN, *The Dreyfus Affair: A Reassessment* (1955). A detached treatment of a subject that still provokes strong feelings.

G. CRAIG, *Germany, 1866–1945* (1978). An excellent survey.

S. EDWARDS, *The Paris Commune of 1871* (1971). A useful examination of a complex subject.

S. ELWITT, *The Making of the Third Republic: Class and Politics in France, 1868–1884* (1975). An excellent introduction.

S. ELWITT, *The Third Republic Defended: Bourgeois Reform in France, 1880–1914* (1986). A study that continues the survey of the previously listed volume.

E. HOBSBAWM, *The Age of Empire, 1875–1914* (1987). A stimulating survey that covers cultural as well as political developments.

I. V. HULL, *The Entourage of Kaiser Wilhelm II, 1888–1918* (1982). An important discussion of the scandals of the German court.

R. A. KANN, *The Multinational Empire*, 2 vols. (1950). The basic treatment of the nationality problem of Austria–Hungary.

R. R. LOCKE, *French Legitimists and the Politics of Moral Order in the Early Third Republic* (1974). An excellent study of the social and intellectual roots of monarchist support.

A. J. MAY, *The Habsburg Monarchy, 1867–1914* (1951). Narrates in considerable detail and with much sympathy the fate of the dual monarchy.

J. F. MCMILLAN, *Napoleon III* (1991). The best recent study.

N. M. NAIMARK, *Terrorists and Social Democrats: The Russian Revolutionary Movement under Alexander III* (1983). Useful discussion of a complicated subject.

C. C. O'BRIEN, *Parnell and His Party* (1957). An excellent treatment of the Irish question.

J. P. PARRY, *The Rise and Fall of Liberal Government in Victorian Britain* (1994). An outstanding study.

O. PFLANZE, *Bismarck and the Development of Germany*, 3 vols. (1990). A major biography and history of Germany for the period.

A. PLESSIS, *The Rise and Fall of the Second Empire, 1852–1871* (1985). A useful survey of France under Napoleon III.

R. SHANNON, *Gladstone: 1809–1865* (1982). Best coverage of his early career.

D. M. SMITH, *The Making of Italy, 1796–1870* (1968). A narrative that incorporates the major documents.

D. M. SMITH, *Cavour* (1984). An excellent biography.

A. J. P. TAYLOR, *The Habsburg Monarchy, 1809–1918* (1941). An opinionated but highly readable work.

R. TOMBS, *The War Against Paris, 1871* (1981). Examines the role of the army in suppressing the Commune.

A. B. ULAM, *Russia's Failed Revolutionaries* (1981). A study of revolutionary societies and activities prior to the Revolution of 1917.

F. VENTURI, *The Roots of Revolution* (trans., 1960). A major treatment of late-nineteenth-century revolutionary movements.

H. S. WATSON, *The Russian Empire, 1801–1917* (1967). A far-ranging narrative.

H. U. WEHLER, *The German Empire, 1871–1918* (1985). An important, controversial work.

J. WERTHEIMER, *Unwelcome Strangers: East European Jews in Imperial Germany* (1987). Examines the difficult position of Jews in Wilhelm's Germany.

C. B. WOODHAM-SMITH, *The Reason Why* (1953). A lively account of the Crimean War and the charge of the Light Brigade.

T. ZELDIN, *France: 1848–1945*, 2 vols. (1973, 1977). Emphasizes the social developments.

R. E. ZELNICK, *Labor and Society in Tsarist Russia: The Factory Workers of Saint Petersburg, 1855–1870* (1971). An important volume that considers the early stages of the Russian industrial labor force in the era of emancipation of the serfs.

Chapter 24

Railways were an important part of late nineteenth-century middle-class life.
They helped promote the development of suburbs, allowing breadwinners to
commute into the city to work, leaving their families at home. They also pro-
moted travel to the vacation spots that were being developed across Europe
during this era. Zeichnung von A. Beltrame, 1899, "Im Londoner Hauptbahnhof." Bildarchiv
Preussischer Kulturbesitz. Photo: Alfredo Dagli Orti, 1991

The Building of European Supremacy:
Society and Politics to World War I

KEY TOPICS

- The transformation of European life by the Second Industrial Revolution
- Urban sanitation, housing reform, and the redesign of cities
- The condition of women in late-nineteenth-century Europe and the rise of political feminism
- The development of labor politics and socialism in Europe to the outbreak of World War I
- Industrialization and political unrest in Russia

The growth of industrialism between 1860 and 1914 increased Europe's productive capacity to unprecedented and unparalleled levels. Newly erected steel mills, railways, shipyards, and chemical plants reflected an expanding supply of capital goods in the second half of the nineteenth century. By the first decade of the new century, the age of the automobile, the airplane, the bicycle, the refrigerated ship, the telephone, the radio, the typewriter, and the electric lightbulb had dawned. The world's economies, based on the gold standard, became increasingly interdependent. European manufactured goods and financial capital flowed into markets all over *the globe. In turn, Europeans imported foreign raw materials and foodstuffs. Within Europe itself, the countries toward the eastern part of the continent tended to import finished goods from the west and to export agricultural products.*

During this half century, European political, economic, and social life assumed many of its current characteristics. Nation–states with large electorates, political parties, and centralized bureaucracies emerged. Business adopted large-scale corporate structures, and the labor force organized itself into trade unions. Increasing numbers of white-collar workers appeared. Urban life came to predominate throughout western Europe. Socialism became a major ingredient in the political life of all nations. The foundations of the welfare state and of vast military establishments were laid. Taxation increased accordingly.

Europe had also quietly become dependent on the resources and markets of the rest of the world. Changes in the weather conditions in Kansas, Argentina, or New Zealand might now affect the European economy. Before World War I, however, that dependence was concealed by Europe's industrial, military, and financial supremacy. Many Europeans assumed their supremacy to be natural and enduring, but the twentieth century would reveal it to have been temporary.

Population Trends and Migration

The proportion of Europeans in the world's total population was apparently greater around 1900—estimated at about 20 percent—than ever before or since. The number of Europeans had risen from approximately 266 million in 1850 to 401 million in 1900 and 447 million in 1910. Thereafter, birth and death rates declined or stabilized in Europe and other developed regions, and population growth began to slow in those areas but not elsewhere. The result has been the demographic differential between the developed and undeveloped world—stable or slowly growing populations in developed countries and large, rapidly growing populations in undeveloped regions—that contributes to the world's present food and resource crisis.

Europe's peoples were on the move in the latter half of the century as never before. The midcentury emancipation of peasants lessened the authority of landlords and made legal movement and migration easier. Railways, steamships, and better roads increased mobility. Cheap land and better wages accompanied economic development in Europe, North America, Latin America, and Australia, enticing people to move.

European emigrants from eastern Europe wait to board a ship that will carry them to the United States. Between 1846 and 1932, more than 50 million Europeans immigrated to the United States, Canada, South America, Australia, and South Africa. Bildarchiv Preussischer Kulturbesitz

Europeans migrated away from their continent in record numbers. Between 1846 and 1932, more than 50 million Europeans left their homelands. The major areas to benefit from this movement were the United States, Canada, Australia, South Africa, Brazil, and Argentina. At midcentury, most of the emigrants were from Great Britain (especially Ireland), Germany, and Scandinavia. After 1885, migration from southern and eastern Europe rose. This exodus helped to relieve the social and population pressures on the Continent. The outward movement of peoples, in conjunction with Europe's economic and technological superiority, contributed heavily to the Europeanization of the world. Not since the sixteenth century had European civilization produced such an impact on other cultures.

The Second Industrial Revolution

During the third quarter of the nineteenth century, the gap that had long existed between British and continental economic development closed. The basic heavy industries of Belgium, France, and Germany underwent major expansion. In particular, the growth of all areas of German industry was stunning. German steel production surpassed that of Britain in 1893 and was nearly twice that of Britain by the outbreak of World War I. This emergence of an industrial Germany was the major fact of European economic and political life at the turn of the century.

New Industries

Initially, the economic expansion of the third quarter of the century involved the spread of industries similar to those pioneered earlier in Great Britain. In particular, the expansion of railway systems on the Continent spurred economic growth. Thereafter, however, wholly new industries emerged. It is this latter development that is usually termed the Second Industrial Revolution. The first Industrial Revolution was associated with textiles, steam, and iron; by contrast, the second was associated with steel, chemicals, electricity, and oil.

In the 1850s, Henry Bessemer (1830–1898), an English engineer, discovered a new process, named after him, for manufacturing steel cheaply in large quantities. In 1860 Great Britain, Belgium, France, and Germany had produced 125,000 tons of steel. By 1913, the figure had risen to 32,020,000 tons.

The chemical industry also came of age during this period. The Solway process of alkali production replaced the older Leblanc process, allowing the recovery of more chemical by-products. The new process permitted increased production of sulfuric acid and laundry soap. New dyestuffs and plastics were also developed. Formal scientific research played an important role in this growth of the chemical industry, marking the beginning of a direct link between science and industrial development. As in so many other aspects of the Second Industrial Revolution, Germany was a leader in forging this link, fostering scientific research and education.

The most significant change for industry and, eventually, for everyday life involved the application of electrical energy to production. Electricity was the most versatile and transportable source of power ever discovered. It could be delivered almost anywhere to run either large or small machinery, making the locations of factories more flexible and factory construction more efficient. The first major public power plant was constructed in 1881 in Great Britain. Soon electric poles, lines, and generating stations dotted the European landscape. Homes began to use electric lights. Streetcar and subway systems were electrified.

The internal combustion engine was invented in 1886. When the German engineer Gottlieb Daimler (1834–1900) put it on four wheels and obtained a French patent in 1887, the automobile was born. France initially took the lead in auto manufacturing, but for many years the car remained a novelty item that only the wealthy could afford. It was the American, Henry Ford (1863–1947), who later made the automobile accessible to large numbers of people.

The automobile and new industrial and chemical uses for petroleum had, by the turn of the century, created the first significant demand for oil. Then as now, Europe depended on imported supplies. The major oil companies were Standard Oil of the United States, British Shell Oil, and Royal Dutch Petroleum.

Economic Difficulties

Despite the multiplication of new industries, the second half of the nineteenth century was not a period of uninterrupted or smooth economic growth. Both industry and agriculture generally prospered from 1850 to 1873, but in the last quarter of the century economic advance was slower. Bad weather and foreign competition put grave pressures on European agriculture. Although these problems for agriculture lowered consumer food prices, they also put a drag on the economy. Many of the emigrants who left Europe during these years came from the countryside or from the least industrialized parts of Europe.

Major Dates of the Second Industrial Revolution

1856–1870	Passage of laws permitting joint stock companies: 1856, Britain; 1863, France; 1870, Prussia
1857	Bessemer process for making steel
1873	Beginning of major economic downturn
1876	Alexander Graham Bell invents the telephone
1879	Edison perfects the electric lightbulb
1881	First electric power plant in Britain
1886	Daimler invents the internal combustion engine
1887	Daimler's first automobile
1895	Diesel engine invented
1895	Wireless telegraphy invented
1890s	Decade of first major impact of petroleum
1903	Wright brothers make first successful airplane flight
1909	Ford manufactures the Model T

Several large banks failed in 1873, and the rate of capital investment slowed. Some industries then entered a two-decade-long period of stagnation that many contemporaries regarded as a depression. Overall, however, the general standard of living in the industrialized nations improved in the second half of the nineteenth century. Both prices and wages, as well as profits, fell, so real wages generally held firm and even rose in some countries. Yet many workers still lived and labored in abysmal conditions. There were pockets of *unemployment* (a word that was coined during this period), and strikes and other forms of labor unrest were common. The economic difficulties fed the growth of trade unions and socialist political parties.

The new industries produced consumer goods, and expansion in consumer demand brought the economy out of stagnation by the end of the century. Lower food prices eventually allowed all classes to spend a marginally larger amount of their income on consumer goods. Urbanization naturally created larger markets. People living in cities simply saw more things they wanted to buy than they would have seen in the countryside. New forms of retailing and marketing appeared—department stores, chain stores, packaging techniques, mail-order catalogs, and advertising—simultaneously stimulating and feeding consumer demand. (See "Paris Department Stores Expand Their Business.") Overseas imperialism also opened new markets for European consumer goods.

The Middle Classes in Ascendancy

The sixty years before World War I were the age of the middle classes. The London Great Exhibition of 1851 held in the Crystal Palace had displayed the products and the new material life they had forged. Thereafter, the middle classes became the arbiter of consumer taste. After the revolutions of 1848, the middle classes ceased to be a revolutionary group. Once the question of social equality and equality of property had been raised, large and small property owners across the Continent moved to protect what they possessed against demands from socialists and other working-class groups.

Social Distinctions Within the Middle Classes

The middle classes, never perfectly homogeneous, grew increasingly diverse. Their most prosperous members—the owners and managers of great businesses and banks—lived in splendor that rivaled, and sometimes exceeded, that of the aristocracy. Some, such as W. H. Smith (1825–1891), the owner of railway newsstands in England, were made members of the House of Lords. The Krupp family of Germany were pillars of the state and received visits from the German emperor and his court.

Only a few hundred families gained such wealth. Beneath them were the comfortable small entrepreneurs and professional people, whose incomes permitted private homes, large quantities of furniture, pianos, pictures, books, journals, education for their children, and vacations. Also in this group were the shopkeepers, schoolteachers, librarians, and others who had either a bit of property or a skill derived from education that provided respectable, nonmanual employment.

Finally, there was a wholly new element— "white-collar workers"—who formed the lower middle class, or *petit bourgeoisie.* They included secretaries, retail clerks, and lower-level bureaucrats in business and government. They often had working-class origins and might even belong to unions, but they had middle-class aspirations and consciously sought to distance themselves from a lower-class lifestyle. They actively pursued educational opportunities and chances for even the slightest career advancement for themselves and, more especially, for their children. Many of them spent a considerable portion of their disposable income on consumer goods, such as stylish clothing

Paris Department Stores Expand Their Business

The department store in Europe and the United States became a major institution of retailing in the last half of the nineteenth century. It was one of the reasons for the expansion in late-century consumer demand. The description that follows, written by the Frenchman E. Levasseur in 1907, follows the growth of such stores in Paris and explains why they exerted such economic power. The reader will notice how many of their techniques of retailing are still used today.

❖ *Why should the various French governments have favored the growth of department stores? Where did these stores stand in the process of economic production and sales? Why was the volume of sales so important? What kinds of people might have benefitted from the jobs available in these stores?*

It was in the reign of Louis Philippe [1830–1848] that department stores for fashion goods and dresses...began to be distinguished. The type was already one of other notable developments of the Second Empire; it became one of the most important ones of the Third Republic. These stores have increased in number and several of them have become extremely large. Combining in their different departments all articles of clothing, toilet articles, furniture and many other ranges of goods, it is their special object so to combine all commodities as to attract and satisfy customers who will find conveniently together an assortment of a mass of articles corresponding to all their various needs. They attract customers by permanent display, by free entry into the shops, by periodic exhibitions, by special sales, by fixed prices, and by their ability to deliver the goods purchased to customers' homes, in Paris and to the provinces. Turning themselves into direct intermediaries between the producer and the consumer, even producing sometimes some of their articles in their own workshops, buying at lowest prices because of their large orders

and because they are in a position to profit from bargains, working with large sums, and selling to most of their customers for cash only, they can transmit these benefits in lowered selling prices. They can even decide to sell at a loss, as an advertisement or to get rid of out-of-date fashions.

The success of these department stores is only possible thanks to the volume of their business, and this volume needs considerable capital and a very large turnover. Now capital, having become abundant, is freely combined nowadays in large enterprises....[The] large urban agglomerations, the ease with which goods can be transported by the railways, the diffusion of some comforts to strata below the middle classes, have all favoured these developments....

According to the tax records of 1891, these stores in Paris, numbering 12, employed 1,708 persons and rated their site values at 2,159,000 francs; the largest had then 542 employees. These same stores had, in 1901, 9,784 employees; one of them over 2,000 and another over 1,600; their site value was doubled.

Krueger, *Gesischte der Manufacturen...*, as quoted and translated in Sidney Pollard and Colin Holmes, eds., *Documents of European Economic History*, Vol. 1 (London: Edward Arnold, 1968), pp. 166–167. Reprinted by permission of Edward Arnold Ltd.

and furniture, that were distinctively middle class in appearance.

Significant tensions and social anxieties marked relations among the various middle-class groups. Small shopkeepers resented the power of the great capitalists, with their department stores and mail-order catalogs. There is some evidence that the professions were becoming overcrowded. People who had only recently attained a middle-class lifestyle feared losing it in bad economic times. Nonetheless, the decades immediately before the World War I saw the middle classes setting the values and goals for most of the society.

Late Nineteenth-Century Urban Life

Europe became more urbanized than ever in the latter half of the nineteenth century as migration to the cities continued. Between 1850 and 1911, urban dwellers rose from 25 to 44 percent of the population in France and from 30 to 60 percent of the population in Germany. Other western European countries experienced similar increases.

The rural migrants to the cities were largely uprooted from traditional social ties. They often faced poor housing, social anonymity, and, because they rarely possessed the right kinds of skills, unemployment. People from different ethnic backgrounds found themselves in proximity to one another and had difficulty mixing socially. Competition for jobs generated new varieties of political and social discontent, such as the anti-Semitism directed at the thousands of Russian Jews who had migrated to western Europe. Indeed, much of the political anti-Semitism of the latter part of the century had its roots in the problems generated by urban migration.

The Redesign of Cities

The inward urban migration placed new social and economic demands on already strained city resources and gradually produced significant transformations in the patterns of urban living. National and municipal governments redesigned the central portions of many major European cities during the second half of the century. Previously, the central urban areas had been places where many people from all social classes both lived and worked. From the middle of the century onward, planners transformed these districts into areas where businesses, government offices, large retail stores, and theaters were located, but where fewer people resided. Commerce, trade, government, and leisure activities now dominated central cities.

THE NEW PARIS   The most famous and extensive transformation of a major city occurred in Paris. Like so many other European cities, Paris had expanded from the Middle Ages onward with little or no design or planning. Great public buildings and

squalid hovels stood near each other. The Seine River was little more than an open sewer. The streets were narrow, crooked, and crowded. It was impossible to cross easily from one part of the city to another either on foot or by carriage. In 1850 a fully accurate map of the city did not even exist. Of more concern to the government of Napoleon III, the city's streets had for sixty years provided battlegrounds for urban insurrections that had toppled French governments on numerous occasions, most recently in 1848.

Napoleon III personally determined that Paris must be redesigned. He appointed Georges Haussmann (1809–1891), who, as prefect of the Seine from 1853 to 1870, oversaw a vast urban reconstruction program. Whole districts were destroyed to open the way for the broad boulevards and streets that became the hallmark of modern Paris. Much, though by no means all, of the purpose of this street planning was political. The wide vistas not only were beautiful, but also allowed for the quick deployment of troops to put down riots. The eradication of the many small streets and alleys removed areas where barricades could be, and had been, erected.

The project was also political in another sense. In addition to the new boulevards, parks such as the Bois de Boulogne and major public buildings such as the Paris Opera were also constructed or completed. These projects, along with the demolition and street building, created thousands of public jobs. Many other laborers found employment in the private construction that accompanied the public works.

Further rebuilding and redesign occurred under the Third Republic after the destruction that accompanied the suppression of the Commune. Many department

The Eiffel Tower, shown under construction in this painting, was to become a symbol of the newly redesigned Paris and its steel structure a symbol of French industrial strength. Liaison Agency, Inc.

stores, office complexes, and largely middle-class apartment buildings were constructed. By the late 1870s, mechanical trams were operating in Paris. After much debate, construction of a subway system (the *métro*) began in 1895, long after that of London (1863). New railway stations were also erected near the close of the century. This transport linked the refurbished central city to the suburbs.

In 1889 the Eiffel Tower was built, originally as a temporary structure for the international trade exposition of that year. Not all the new structures of Paris bespoke the impact of middle-class commerce and the reign of iron and steel, however. Between 1873 and 1914, the French Roman Catholic Church oversaw the construction of the Basilica of the Sacred Heart high atop Montmartre as an act of national penance for the sins that had led to French defeat in the Franco–Prussian War. Those two landmarks—the Eiffel Tower and the Basilica of the Sacred Heart—visibly symbolized the social and political divisions between liberals and conservatives in the Third Republic.

DEVELOPMENT OF SUBURBS Commercial development, railway construction, and the clearing of slums displaced many city dwellers and raised urban land values and rents. Consequently, both the middle classes and the working class began to seek housing elsewhere. The middle classes looked for neighborhoods removed from urban congestion. The working class looked for affordable housing. The result, in virtually all countries, was the development of suburbs surrounding the city proper. These suburbs housed families whose breadwinners worked in the central city or in a factory located within the city limits. European suburbs, unlike those that developed in the United States, often consisted of apartment buildings or private houses built closely together with small lawns and gardens.

The expansion of railways with cheap workday fares and the introduction of mechanical and, later, electric tramways, as well as subways, allowed tens of thousands of workers from all classes to move daily between the city and the outlying suburbs. For hundreds of thousands of Europeans, home and work became more physically separated than ever before.

Urban Sanitation

The efforts of governments and of the increasingly conservative middle classes to maintain public order after 1848 led to a growing concern with the problems of public health and housing for the poor. A widespread feeling arose that only when the health and housing of the working class were improved would middle-class health also be secure and the political order stable.

Growth of Major European Cities (FIGURES IN THOUSANDS)			
	1850	1880	1910
Berlin	419	1,122	2,071
Birmingham	233	437	840
Frankfurt	65	137	415
London	2,685	4,470	7,256
Madrid	281	398	600
Moscow	365	748	1,533
Paris	1,053	2,269	2,888
Rome	175	300	542
St. Petersburg	485	877	1,962
Vienna	444	1,104	2,031
Warsaw	160	339	872

IMPACT OF CHOLERA Concerns with health and housing first manifested themselves as a result of the great cholera epidemics of the 1830s and 1840s. Unlike many other common deadly diseases of the day that touched only the poor, cholera struck all classes, impelling the middle class to demand a solution. Before the development of the bacterial theory of disease late in the century, physicians and sanitary reformers believed that cholera and other diseases were spread through infection from miasmas in the air. These miasmas, the presence of which was marked by their foul odors, were believed to arise from filth. The way to get rid of the dangerous, foul-smelling air was to clean up the cities.

During the 1840s, many physicians and some government officials began to publicize the dangers posed by the unsanitary conditions associated with overcrowding in cities and with businesses such as basement slaughterhouses. In 1840, Louis René Villermé published his *Tableau de l'état physique et moral des ouvriers* (*Catalog of the Physical and Moral State of Workers*). In 1842, Edwin Chadwick's (1800–1890) *Report on the Sanitary Condition of the Labouring Population* shocked the English public. In Germany, Rudolf Virchow (1821–1902) published similar findings. These and various other private and public-commission reports closely linked the issues of wretched living conditions and public health. They also demonstrated that sanitary reform would remove the dangers. The reports, incidentally, now provide some of the best information available about working-class living conditions in the middle of the nineteenth century. (See "A French Physician Describes a Working-Class Slum in Lille Before the Public Health Movement.")

NEW WATER AND SEWER SYSTEMS The proposed solution to the health hazard was cleanliness, to be achieved through new water and sewer systems.

*Urban slums such as this one in Glasgow, Scotland,
aroused the concern of sanitary and housing reformers.*
Service Photographique des Musées Nationaux, Paris/Photo R.M.N.

These facilities were constructed slowly, beginning usually in capital cities and then much later in provincial cities. Some major urban areas did not have good water systems until after the turn of the century. Nonetheless, the building of such systems was one of the major health and engineering achievements of the second half of the nineteenth century. The sewer system of Paris was a famous part of Haussmann's rebuilding program. In London, the construction of the Albert Embankment along the Thames involved not only large sewers discharging into the river, but gas mains and water pipes as well; all were encased in thick walls of concrete, one of the new building materials of the day, and granite. Wherever these sanitary facilities were installed, the mortality rate dropped considerably.

EXPANDED GOVERNMENT INVOLVEMENT IN PUBLIC HEALTH   The concern with public health led to an expansion of governmental power on various levels. In Britain the Public Health Act of 1848, in France the Melun Act of 1851, and various laws in the still-disunited German states, as well as later legislation, introduced new restraints on private life and enterprise. This legislation allowed medical officers and building inspectors to enter homes and other structures in the name of public health. Pri-

vate property could be condemned for posing health hazards. Private land could be excavated for the construction of the sewers and water mains required to protect the public. New building regulations put restraints on the activities of private contractors.

Full acceptance at the close of the century of the bacterial theory of disease associated with the discoveries of Louis Pasteur (1822–1895) in France, Robert Koch (1843–1910) in Germany, and Joseph Lister (1827–1912) in Britain made cleanliness an even more prominent public concern. Throughout Europe, issues related to the maintenance of public health and the physical well-being of national populations repeatedly opened the way for new modes of government intervention in the lives of citizens.

Housing Reform and Middle-Class Values

The information about working-class living conditions brought to light by the sanitary reformers also led to heated debates over the housing problem. The wretched dwellings of the poor were themselves a cause of poor sanitation and thus became a newly perceived health hazard. Furthermore, middle-class reformers and bureaucrats found themselves shocked by the domestic arrangements of the poor, whose large families might live in a single room lacking all forms of personal privacy. A single toilet facility might serve a whole block of tenements. After the revolutions of 1848, the overcrowding in housing and the social discontent that it generated were also seen to pose a political danger.

Middle-class reformers thus turned to housing reform to solve the medical, moral, and political dangers posed by slums. Proper, decent housing would foster a good home life, in turn leading to a healthy, moral, and politically stable population. As A. V. Huber, one of the early German housing reformers, declared,

Certainly it would not be too much to say that the home is the communal embodiment of family life. Thus the purity of the dwelling is almost as important for the family as is the cleanliness of the body for the individual. Good or bad housing is a question of life and death if ever there was one.[1]

Later advocates of housing reform, such as Jules Simon in France, saw good housing as leading to good family life and, ultimately, to strong patriotic feeling. It was widely believed that providing the poor and the working class with adequate, respectable, cheap housing would alleviate social and

[1]Quoted in Nicholas Bullock and James Read, *The Movement for Housing Reform in Germany and France, 1840–1914* (Cambridge, U.K.: Cambridge University Press, 1985), p. 42.

A French Physician Describes a Working-Class Slum in Lille before the Public Health Movement

It is difficult to conceive of the world before the sanitation movement. The work of medical doctors frequently carried them into working-class areas of industrial cities rarely visited by other members of the middle class. Louis Villermé was such a French physician. He wrote extensive descriptions of the slums and the general living conditions of industrial workers. The passage here, published in 1840, describes a particularly notorious section of Lille, a major cotton-manufacturing town in northern France.

❖ *What does this physician find most disturbing about the scene he describes? How is his description possibly designed to call forth sympathy and concern from a middle-class reader? How might the conditions described have led the poor of France toward socialism or radical politics? How would addressing the problems described have led to a larger role for government?*

The poorest live in the cellars and attics. These cellars...open onto the streets or courtyards, and one enters them by a stairway which is very often at once the door and the window....Commonly the height of the ceiling is six or six and a half feet at the highest point, and they are only ten to fourteen or fifteen feet wide.

It is in these somber and sad dwellings that a large number of workers eat, sleep, and even work. The light of day comes an hour later for them than for others, and the night an hour earlier.

Their furnishings normally consist, along with the tools of their profession, of a sort of cupboard or a plank on which to deposit food, a stove...a few pots, a little table, two or three poor chairs, and a dirty pallet of which the only pieces are a straw mattress and scraps of a blanket....

In their obscure cellars, in their rooms, which one would take for cellars, the air is never renewed, it is infected; the walls are plastered with garbage....If a bed exists, it is a few dirty, greasy planks; it is damp and putrescent straw; it is a coarse cloth whose color and fabric are hidden by a layer of grime; it is a blanket that resembles a sieve....The furniture is dislocated, worm-eaten, covered with filth. Utensils are thrown in disorder all over the dwelling. The windows, always closed, are covered by paper and glass, but so black, so smoke-encrusted, that the light is unable to penetrate...everywhere are piles of garbage, of ashes, of debris from vegetables picked up from the streets, of rotten straw; of animal nests of all sorts; thus, the air is unbreathable. One is exhausted, in these hovels, by a stale, nauseating, somewhat piquante odor, odor of filth, odor of garbage....

And the poor themselves, what are they like in the middle of such a slum? Their clothing is in shreds, without substance, consumed, covered, no less than their hair, which knows no comb, with dust from the workshops. And their skin?...It is painted, it is hidden, if you wish, by indistinguishable deposits of diverse exudations.

From Louis René Villermé, *Tableau de l'état physique et moral des ouvriers employés dans les manufactures de coton, de laine et de soie* (Paris, 1840), as quoted and trans. in William H. Sewell, Jr., *Work and Revolution in France: The Language of Labor from the Old Regime to 1848* (Cambridge, U.K.: Cambridge University Press, 1980), p. 224.

political discontent. It was also believed that the personal saving and investment required for owning a home would lead the working class to adopt the thrifty habits of the middle classes.

Private philanthropy made the first attack on the housing problem. Companies operating on low profit margins or making low-interest loans encouraged housing for the poor. Firms such as the German Krupp armaments concern, seeking to ensure a contented, healthy, and stable work force, constructed model housing projects and industrial communities.

By the mid-1880s, the migration into cities had made housing a political issue. Legislation in England in 1885 lowered the interest rates for the construction of cheap housing, and soon thereafter government authorities began public housing projects. In Germany, action on housing came later in the century through the initiative of local municipalities. In 1894, France made inexpensive credit available for constructing housing for the poor. None of these governments, however, adopted wide-scale housing experiments.

Major Dates Relating to Sanitation Reform

1830s and 1840s	Cholera epidemics
1840	Villermé's *Catalog of the Physical and Moral State of Workers*
1842	Chadwick's *Report on the Sanitary Condition of the Labouring Population*
1848	British Public Health Act
1851	French Melun Act

Nonetheless, by 1914, the housing problem had been fully recognized if not adequately addressed. The goal of housing reform across western Europe came to be to provide homes for the members of the working class that would allow them to enjoy a family life more or less like that of the middle class. Such a home would be in the form of a detached house or some kind of affordable city apartment with several rooms, a private entrance, and separate toilet facilities.

Varieties of Late Nineteenth-Century Women's Experiences

Late-nineteenth-century women and men led lives that reflected their social rank. Yet, within each rank, the experience of women was distinct from that of men. Women remained, generally speaking, in positions of economic dependence and legal inferiority, whatever their social class.

Social Disabilities Confronted by All Women

At the middle of the nineteenth century, virtually all European women faced social and legal disabilities in three areas: property rights, family law, and education. By the close of the century, there had been some improvement in each area.

WOMEN AND PROPERTY   Until the last quarter of the century in most European countries, married women could not own property in their own names, no matter what their social class. For all practical purposes, upon marriage, women lost to their husbands' control any property they owned or that they might inherit or earn by their own labor. Their legal identities were subsumed in their husbands', and they had no independent standing before the law. The courts saw the theft of a woman's purse as a theft of her husband's property. Because European society was based

on private property and wage earning, these disabilities put married women at a great disadvantage, limiting their freedom to work, to save, and to move from one location to another.

Reform of women's property rights came very slowly. By 1882, Great Britain had passed the Married Woman's Property Act, which allowed married women to own property in their own right. In France, however, a married woman could not even open a savings account in her own name until 1895, and not until 1907 were married women granted possession of the wages they earned. In 1900, Germany allowed women to take jobs without their husbands' permission, but except for her wages, a German husband retained control of most of his wife's property. Similar laws prevailed elsewhere in Europe.

FAMILY LAW   Virtually all European family law also worked to the disadvantage of women. Legal codes actually required wives to "give obedience" to their husbands. The Napoleonic Code and the remnants of Roman law still in effect made women legal minors throughout Europe. Divorce was difficult everywhere for most of the century. In England before 1857, divorce required an act of Parliament. Thereafter, divorce could be procured, with difficulty, through the Court of Matrimonial Causes. Most nations did not permit divorce by mutual consent. French law forbade divorce between 1816 and 1884. Thereafter, the chief recognized legal cause for divorce was cruelty and injury, which had to be proven in court. In Great Britain, adultery was the usual cause for divorce, but to obtain a divorce, a woman had to prove her husband's adultery plus other offenses, whereas a man only had to prove his wife's adultery. In Germany, only adultery or serious maltreatment were recognized as reasons for divorce. Across Europe, some version of the double standard prevailed whereby extramarital sexual relations of husbands were tolerated to a greater degree than those of wives. Everywhere, divorce required legal hearings and the presentation of legal proof, making the process expensive and all the more difficult for women who did not control their own property.

The authority of husbands also extended to children. A husband could take children away from their mother and give them to someone else for rearing. Only the husband, in most countries, could permit his daughter to marry. In some countries, he could virtually force his daughter to marry the man of his choice. In cases of divorce and separation, the husband normally assumed authority over children, no matter how he had treated them previously.

The issues surrounding the sexual and reproductive rights of women that have been so widely debated recently could hardly be discussed in the nineteenth century. Until well into the twentieth century, both contraception and abortion were illegal. The law surrounding rape normally worked to the disadvantage of women. Wherever they turned with their problems—whether to physicians or lawyers— women confronted an official or legal world almost wholly populated and controlled by men.

EDUCATIONAL BARRIERS Throughout the nineteenth century, women had less access to education than men had and what was available to them was inferior to that available to men. Not surprisingly, the percentage of illiterate women exceeded that of men. Most women were educated only enough for the domestic careers they were expected to follow.

University and professional education remained reserved for men until at least the third quarter of the century. The University of Zurich first opened its doors to women in the 1860s. The University of London admitted women for degrees in 1878. Women's colleges were founded at Cambridge during the last quarter of the century. Women could take Oxford and Cambridge university examinations, but were not awarded degrees at Oxford until 1920 and at Cambridge until 1921. Women could not attend Sorbonne lectures until 1880. Just before the turn of the century, universities and medical schools in the Austrian Empire allowed women to matriculate, but Prussian universities did not admit women until after 1900. Russian women did not attend universities before 1914, but other institutions that awarded degrees were open to them. Italian universities proved themselves more open to both women students and women instructors than similar institutions elsewhere in Europe. In many countries, there were frequently more foreign than native women attending university classes. This was especially the case in Zurich, where many Russian women studied for medical degrees. Many of the American women who founded or taught in the first women's colleges in the United States studied at European universities.

The absence of a system of private or public secondary education for women prevented most of them from gaining the qualifications they needed to enter a university whether or not the university prohibited them. Considerable evidence suggests that educated, professional men feared that their professions would be overcrowded if they admitted women. Women who attended universities and medical schools, like the young Russian women who studied medicine at Zurich, were sometimes labeled political radicals.

Women only gradually gained access to secondary and university education during the second half of the nineteenth century and the early twentieth century. Young women on their way to school, the subject of this 1880 English painting, would thus have been a new sight when it was painted. Sir George Clausen (RA) (1852–1944) *Schoolgirls, Haverstock Hill*, signed and dated 1880, oil on canvas, 20-1/2 × 30-3/8 in. (52 × 77.2 cm), Yale Center for British Art/ Paul Mellon Collection B1985.10.1

By the turn of the century, some men in the educated elites feared the challenge educated women posed to traditional gender roles in the home and workplace. Restricting women's access to secondary and university education helped bar them from social and economic advancement. Women would benefit only marginally from the expansion of professional employment that occurred during the late nineteenth and early twentieth centuries. Some women did enter the professions, most particularly medicine, but their number remained few. Most nations refused to allow women to become lawyers until after World War I.

Schoolteaching at the elementary level, which had come to be seen as a "female job" because of its association with the nurturing of children, became a professional haven for women. Trained at institutions that were equivalent to normal schools, women schoolteachers at the elementary level were regarded as educated, but not as university educated. Secondary education remained largely the province of men.

The few women who pioneered in the professions and on government commissions and school boards or who dispersed birth control information faced grave social obstacles, personal humiliation, and often outright bigotry. These women and their male supporters were challenging that clear separation into male and female spheres that had emerged in middle-class European social life during the nineteenth century. Women themselves were often hesitant to support feminist causes or expanded opportunities for females because they had been so thoroughly acculturated into the recently stereotyped roles. Many women, as well as men, saw a real conflict between family responsibilities and feminism.

New Employment Patterns for Women

During the decades of the Second Industrial Revolution, two major developments affected the economic lives of women. The first was a significant expansion in the variety of jobs available outside the better-paying learned professions. The second was a significant withdrawal of married women from the work force. These two seemingly contradictory developments require some explanation.

AVAILABILITY OF NEW JOBS   The expansion of governmental bureaucracies, the emergence of corporations and other large-scale businesses, and the vast growth of retail stores opened many new employment opportunities for women. The need for elementary school teachers, usually women, grew as governments adopted compulsory education laws. Technological inventions and innovations, such as the typewriter and, eventually, the telephone exchange, also fostered female employment. Women by the thousands became secretaries and clerks for governments and for private businesses. Still more thousands became shop assistants.

Although these jobs did open new and often somewhat better employment opportunities for women, they nonetheless required low-level skills and involved minimal training. They were occupied primarily by unmarried women or widows. Women were rarely to be found in more prominent positions.

Employers continued to pay women low wages, because they assumed, quite often knowing better, that a woman did not need to support herself independently, but could expect additional finan-

Women working in the London Central Telephone Exchange. The invention of the telephone opened new employment opportunities for women.   Mary Evans Picture Library

Although new opportunities opened to them in the late nineteenth century, many working-class women, like these women ironing in a laundry, remained in traditional occupations. As the wine bottle suggests, alcoholism was a problem for women as well as for men engaged in tedious and boring work. The painting is by Edgar Degas (1834–1917). Service Photographique des Musée Nationaux, Paris/Photo R.M.N.

cial support from her father or from her husband. Consequently, a woman who did need to support herself independently was almost always unable to find a job paying an adequate income—or a position that paid as well as one held by a man who was supporting himself independently.

WITHDRAWAL FROM THE LABOR FORCE Most of the women filling the new service positions were young and unmarried. Upon marriage, or certainly after the birth of her first child, a woman normally withdrew from the labor force. Either she did not work or she worked at some occupation that could be pursued in the home. This pattern was not new, but it had become significantly more common by the end of the nineteenth century. The kinds of industrial occupations that women had filled in the middle of the nineteenth century, especially textile and garment making, were shrinking. There were thus fewer opportunities for employment in those industries for either married or unmarried women. Employers in offices and retail stores preferred young, unmarried women whose family responsibilities would not interfere with their work. The decline in the number of children being born also meant that fewer married women were needed to look after other women's children.

The real wages paid to male workers increased during this period, so families had a somewhat reduced need for a second income. Also, thanks to improving health conditions, men lived longer than before, so wives were less likely to be thrust into the work force by the death of their husbands. The smaller size of families also lowered the need for supplementary wages. Working children stayed at home longer and continued to contribute to the family's wage pool.

Finally, the cultural dominance of the middle class established a pattern of social expectations, especially for wives. The more prosperous a working-class family became, the less involved in employment its women were supposed to be. Indeed, the less income-producing work a wife did, the more prosperous and stable the family was considered.

Yet behind these generalities stands the enormous variety of social and economic experiences late-nineteenth-century women actually encountered. As might be expected, the chief determinant of these individual experiences was social class.

Working-Class Women

Although the textile industry and garment making were much less dominant than earlier in the century, they continued to employ large numbers of women. The German clothing-making trade illustrates the kind of vulnerable economic situation that women could encounter as a result of their limited skills and the organization of the trade. The system of manufacturing mass-made clothes of uniform sizes in Germany was complex. It was designed to require minimal capital investment on the part of the manufacturers and to protect them from significant risk. A major manufacturer would arrange for the production of clothing through what was called a *putting-out system*. The manufacturer would purchase the material and then put it out for tailoring. The clothing was produced not in a factory, but usually in numerous, independently owned, small sweatshops or by workers in their homes.

In Berlin in 1896, there were more than 80,000 garment workers, mostly women, who were so employed. When business was good and demand strong, employment for these women was high. As the seasons shifted or business became poor, however, less and less work was put out, idling many of them. In effect, the workers who actually sewed the clothing carried much of the risk of the enterprise. Some women did work in factories, but they, too, were subject to layoffs. Furthermore, women in the clothing trade were nearly always in positions less skilled than those of the male tailors or the middlemen who owned the workshops.

The expectation of separate social and economic spheres for men and women and the definition of women's chief work as pertaining to the home contributed mightily to the exploitation of women workers outside the home. Because their wages were regarded merely as supplementing their husbands', they became particularly vulnerable to the kind of economic exploitation that characterized the German putting-out system for clothing production and similar systems elsewhere. Women were nearly always treated as casual workers everywhere in Europe.

Poverty and Prostitution

A major, but little recognized, social fact of most nineteenth-century cities was the presence of a surplus of working women who did not fit the stereotype of wife or daughter supplementing a family's income. There were almost always many more women seeking employment than there were jobs. The economic vulnerability of women and the consequent poverty many of them faced were among the chief causes of prostitution. In any major late-nineteenth-century European city, there were thousands of prostitutes.

Prostitution was, of course, not new. It had always been one way for very poor women to find some income. In the late nineteenth century, however, it was closely related to the difficulty encountered by indigent women who were trying to make their way in an overcrowded female labor force. On the Continent,

prostitution was generally legalized and was subject to governmental and municipal regulations passed by male legislatures and councils and enforced by male police and physicians. In Great Britain, prostitution received only minimal regulation.

Many myths and misunderstandings have surrounded the subject of prostitution. The most recent studies of the subject in England emphasize that most prostitutes were active on the streets for a very few years, generally from their late teens to about age twenty-five. They often were very poor women who had recently migrated from nearby rural areas. Others were born in the towns where they became prostitutes. Certain cities—those with large army garrisons or naval ports or those, like London, with large transient populations—attracted many prostitutes. There were far fewer prostitutes in manufacturing towns, where there were more opportunities for steady employment and where community life was more stable.

Women who became prostitutes usually came from families of unskilled workers and had minimal skills and education themselves. Many had been servants. They also often were from broken homes or were orphaned. Contrary to many sensational late-century newspaper accounts, there were few child prostitutes. Furthermore, rarely were women seduced into prostitution by middle-class employers or middle-class clients, although working-class women were always potentially subject to such pressure. The customers of poor working-class prostitutes were primarily working-class men.

Women of the Middle Class

A vast social gap separated poor working-class women from their middle-class counterparts. As their fathers' and husbands' incomes permitted, middle-class women participated in the vast expansion of consumerism and domestic comfort that marked the end of the nineteenth century and the early twentieth century. They filled their homes with manufactured items, including clothing, china, furniture, carpets, drapery, wallpaper, and prints. They enjoyed all the improvements of sanitation and electricity. They could command the services of numerous domestic servants. They moved into the fashionable new houses being constructed in the rapidly expanding suburbs.

THE CULT OF DOMESTICITY   For the middle classes, the distinction between work and family, defined by gender, had become complete and constituted the model for all other social groups. Middle-class women, if at all possible, did not work. More than any other women, they became limited to the roles of wife and mother. As a result, they might enjoy

Family was central to the middle-class conception of a stable and respectable social life. This portrait of the Bellelli family is by Edgar Degas. Notice that the husband and father sits at his desk, suggesting his association with business and the world outside their home, whereas the wife and mother stands with their children, suggesting her domestic role. Giraudon/Art Resource, NY

great domestic luxury and comfort, but their lives, talents, ambitions, and opportunities for applying their intelligence were markedly circumscribed.

Middle-class women became, in large measure, the product of a particular understanding of social life. Home life was to be very different from the life of business and the marketplace. The home was to be a private place of refuge, a view set forth in scores of women's journals across Europe.

As studies of the lives of middle-class women in northern France have suggested, this image of the middle-class home and of the role of women in the home is quite different from the one that had existed earlier in the nineteenth century. During the first half of the century, the spouse of a middle-class husband might very well contribute directly to the business, handling accounts or correspondence. These women also frequently had little to do with rearing their children, leaving that task first to nurses and later to governesses. The reasons for the change over the course

of the century are not certain, but it appears that men began to insist on doing business with other men. Magazines and books directed toward women began to praise motherhood, domesticity, religion, and charity as the proper work of women in accordance with the concept of separate spheres. (See "The Virtues of a French Middle-Class Lady Praised.")

For middle-class Frenchwomen, as well as for middle-class women elsewhere, the home came to be seen as the center of virtue, children, and the proper life. Marriages were usually arranged for some kind of family economic benefit. Romantic marriage was viewed as a danger to social stability. Most middle-class women in northern France married by the age of twenty-one. Children were expected to follow very soon after marriage, and the first child was often born within the first year. The rearing and nurturing of her children was a woman's chief task. She would receive no experience or training for any role other than that of dutiful daughter, wife, and mother.

The Virtues of a French Middle-Class Lady Praised

One of the chief social roles assigned to middle-class Frenchwomen was that of charitable activity. This obituary of Mme. Émile Delesalle from a Roman Catholic Church paper of the late nineteenth century describes the work of that woman among the poor. It is a very revealing document because it clearly shows the class divisions that existed in the giving of charity. Also through the kinds of virtues it praises, it gave instruction to its women readers. Note the emphasis on home life, spirituality, and the instruction of children in charitable acts.

❖ *What assumptions about the character of women allowed writers to see charity as a particularly good occupation for women? What middle-class attitudes toward the poor are displayed in this passage? How did the assignment of charity work to women lead to their being excluded from other kinds of work and the learned professions?*

The poor were the object of her affectionate interest, especially the shameful poor, the fallen people. She sought them out and helped them with perfect discretion which doubled the value of her benevolent interest. To those whom she could approach without fear of bruising their dignity, she brought, along with alms to assure their existence, consolation of the most serious sort—she raised their courage and their hopes. To others, each Sunday, she opened all the doors of her home, above all when her children were still young. In making them distribute these alms with her, she hoped to initiate them early into practices of charity.

In the last years of her life, the St. Gabriel Orphanage gained her interest. Not only did she accomplish a great deal with her generosity, but she also took on the task of maintaining the clothes of her dear orphans in good order and in good repair. When she appeared in the courtyard of the establishment at recreation time, all her protégés surrounded her and lavished her with manifestations of their profound respect and affectionate gratitude.

Quoted in Bonnie G. Smith, *Ladies of the Leisure Class: The Bourgeoises of Northern France in the Nineteenth Century* (Princeton, NJ: Princeton University Press, 1981) pp. 147–148. Copyright © 1981 by Princeton University Press. Reprinted by permission of Princeton University Press.

Within the home, a middle-class woman performed major roles. She was largely in charge of the household. She oversaw virtually all domestic management and child care. She was in charge of the home as a unit of consumption, which is why so much advertising was directed toward women. All this domestic activity, however, occurred within the limits of the approved middle-class lifestyle that set strict limits on a woman's initiative. In her conspicuous position within the home and family, a woman symbolized first her father's and then her husband's worldly success.

RELIGIOUS AND CHARITABLE ACTIVITIES The cult of domesticity in France and elsewhere assigned firm religious duties to women, which the Roman Catholic Church strongly supported. Women were expected to attend mass frequently and assure the religious instruction of their children. They were charged with observing meatless Fridays and with participating in religious observances. Prayer was a major part of their lives and daily rituals. They internalized those portions of the Christian religion that stressed meekness and passivity. In other countries as well, religion and religious activities became part of the expected work of women. For this reason, women were regarded by political liberals as especially susceptible to the influence of priests. This close association between religion and a strict domestic life for women was one of the reasons for later tension between feminism and religious authorities.

Another important role for middle-class women was the administration of charity. Women were judged especially qualified for this work because of their presumed innate spirituality and their capacity to instill domestic and personal discipline. Middle-class women were often in charge of clubs for poor youth, societies to protect poor young women, schools for infants, and societies for visiting the poor. Women were supposed to be particularly interested in the problems of poor women, their families, and their children. Quite often, charity from middle-class women required the poor recipient to demonstrate good character. By the end of the century, middle-class women seeking to expand their spheres of activity became social workers for the church, for private charities, or for the government. These vocations were a natural extension of the roles socially assigned to them.

SEXUALITY AND FAMILY SIZE   The world of the middle-class wife and her family is now understood to have been much more complicated than was once thought. Neither they nor their families all conformed to the stereotypes. Recent studies have suggested that the middle classes of the nineteenth century enjoyed sexual relations within marriage far more than was once thought. Diaries, letters, and even early medical and sociological sex surveys indicate that sexual enjoyment rather than sexual repression was fundamental to middle-class marriages. Much of the inhibition about sexuality stemmed from the dangers of childbirth rather than from any dislike or disapproval of sex itself.

One of the major changes in this regard during the second half of the century was the acceptance of a small family size among the middle classes. The birthrate in France dropped throughout the nineteenth century. It began to fall in England steadily from the 1870s onward. During the last decades of the century, various new contraceptive devices became available, which middle-class couples used. One of the chief reasons for the apparently conscious decision of couples to limit their family size was to maintain a relatively high level of material consumption. Children had become much more expensive to rear, and at the same time, more material comforts had become available. Fewer children probably meant more attention for each of them, possibly bringing mothers and their children emotionally closer.

The Rise of Political Feminism

Plainly, liberal society and its values had neither automatically nor inevitably improved the lot of women. In particular, it did not give women the vote or access to political activity. Male liberals feared that granting the vote to women would benefit political conservatives, because women were thought to be unduly controlled by Roman Catholic priests. A similar apprehension existed about the alleged influence of the Anglican clergy over women in England. Consequently, anticlerical liberals often had difficulty working with feminists.

OBSTACLES TO ACHIEVING EQUALITY   But women also were often reluctant to support feminist causes. Political issues relating to gender were only one of several priorities for many women. Some were very sensitive to their class and economic interests. Others subordinated feminist political issues to national unity and patriotism. Still others would not support particular feminist organizations because of differences over tactics. The various social and tactical differences among women led quite often to sharp divisions within the feminists' own ranks. Except in England, it was often difficult for working-class and middle-class women to cooperate. Roman Catholic feminists were uncomfortable with radical secularist feminists. And there were other disagreements about which goals for improvement in women's legal and social conditions were most important.

Although liberal society and law presented women with many obstacles, they also provided feminists with many of their intellectual and political tools. As early as 1792 in Britain, Mary Wollstonecraft (1759–1797), in *The Vindication of the Rights of Woman*, had applied the revolutionary doctrines of the rights of man to the predicament of the members of her own sex. (See Chapter 18.) John Stuart Mill (1806–1873), together with his wife, Harriet Taylor (1804–1858), had applied the logic of liberal freedom to the position of women in *The Subjection*

Major Dates in Late Nineteenth-Century and Early Twentieth-Century Women's History

1857	Revised English divorce law
1865	University of Zurich admits women for degrees
1869	John Stuart Mill's *The Subjection of Women*
1878	University of London admits women as candidates for degrees
1882	English Married Woman's Property Act
1894	Union of German Women's Organizations founded
1901	National Council of French Women founded
1903	British Women's Social and Political Union founded
1907	Norway permits women to vote on national issues
1910	British suffragettes adopt radical tactics
1918	Vote extended to some British women
1918	Weimar constitution allows German women to vote
1920–1921	Oxford and Cambridge Universities award degrees to women
1922	French Senate defeats bill extending vote to women
1928	Britain extends vote to women on same basis as men

of Women (1869). The arguments for utility and efficiency so dear to middle-class liberals could be used to expose the human and social waste implicit in the inferior role assigned to women.

Furthermore, the socialist criticism of capitalist society often, though by no means always, included a harsh indictment of the social and economic position to which women had been relegated. The earliest statements of feminism arose from critics of the existing order and were often associated with people who had unorthodox opinions about sexuality, family life, and property. This hardened resistance to the feminist message, especially on the Continent.

These difficulties prevented continental feminists from raising the kind of massive public support or mounting the large demonstrations that feminists in Great Britain and the United States could. Everywhere in Europe, however, including Britain, the feminist cause was badly divided over both goals and tactics. (See "An English Feminist Defends the Cause of the Female Franchise.")

VOTES FOR WOMEN IN BRITAIN Europe's most advanced women's movement was in Great Britain. There, Millicent Fawcett (1847–1929) led the moderate National Union of Women's Suffrage Societies. She believed that Parliament would grant women the vote only if it were convinced that they would be respectable and responsible in their political activity. In 1908, the National Union could rally almost half a million women in London. Fawcett's husband was a former Liberal Party cabinet minister and economist. Her tactics were those of English liberals.

Emmeline Pankhurst (1858–1928) led a different and much more radical branch of British feminists. Pankhurst's husband, who died near the close of the century, had been active in both labor and Irish nationalist politics. Irish nationalists had developed numerous disruptive political tactics. Early labor politicians had also sometimes had confrontations with police over the right to hold meetings. In 1903 Pankhurst and her daughters, Christabel and Sylvia, founded the Women's Social and Political Union. For several years they and their followers, known derisively as *suffragettes*, lobbied publicly and privately for the extension of the vote to women. By 1910, having failed to move the government, they turned to the violent tactics of arson, breaking windows, and sabotage of postal boxes. They marched en masse on Parliament. The Liberal government of Herbert Asquith imprisoned many of the demonstrators and force-fed those who went on hunger strikes in jail. The government refused to extend the franchise. Only in 1918, and then as a result of their contribution to the war effort, did some British women receive the vote.

POLITICAL FEMINISM ON THE CONTINENT The contrast between the women's movement in Britain and those in France and Germany shows how advanced the British women's movement was. In France, when Hubertine Auclert (1848–1914) began campaigning for the vote in the 1880s, she stood virtually alone. During the 1890s, several women's organizations emerged. In 1901 the National Council of French Women (CNFF) was organized among upper-middle-class women, but it did not support the vote for women for several years. French Roman Catholic feminists such as Marie Mauguet (1844–1928) supported the franchise. Almost all French feminists, however, rejected any form of violence. They also

The creator of this poster cleverly reveals the hypocrisy and absurdity of denying the vote to women. The Bridgeman Art Library International

An English Feminist Defends the Cause of the Female Franchise

Frances Power Cobbe (1822–1904) wrote widely on many religious and social issues of the second half of the century. She had been a feminist since early adulthood. In this letter to a British feminist magazine in 1884, she explains why women should seek the vote.

❖ *What motives does Cobbe assign to the pursuit of the right to vote? Why does she emphasize the issue of "womanliness" as one that must not be allowed to undermine the cause of women? What is Cobbe's attitude toward violence? Why would later British advocates of votes for women turn to violent tactics?*

If I may presume to offer an old woman's counsel to the younger workers in our cause, it would be that they should adopt the point of view—that it is before all things our duty to obtain the franchise. If we undertake the work in this spirit, and with the object of using the power it confers, whenever we gain it, for the promotion of justice and mercy and the kingdom of God upon earth, we shall carry on all our agitation in a corresponding manner, firmly and bravely, and also calmly and with generous good temper. And when our opponents come to understand that this is the motive underlying our efforts, they, on their part, will cease to feel bitterly and scornfully toward us, even when they think we are altogether mistaken....

The idea that the possession of political rights will destroy "womanliness," absurd as it may seem to us, is very deeply rooted in the minds of men; and when they oppose our demands, it is only just to give them credit for doing so on grounds which we should recognize as valid, if their premises were true. It is not so much that our opponents (at least the better part of them) despise women, as that they really prize what women now are in the home and in society so highly that they cannot bear to risk losing it by any serious change in their condition. These fears are futile and faithless, but there is nothing in them to affront us. To remove them, we must not use violent words, for every such violent word confirms their fears; but, on the contrary, show the world that while the revolutions wrought by men have been full of bitterness and rancor and stormy passions, if not of bloodshed, we women will at least strive to accomplish our great emancipation calmly and by persuasion and reason.

From letter to the *Woman's Tribune*, May 1, 1884, quoted in Frances Power Cobbe, *Life of Frances Power Cobbe by Herself*, Vol. 2 (Boston: Houghton Mifflin, 1894), pp. 532–533.

---

were never able to organize mass rallies. The leaders of French feminism believed that the vote could be achieved through careful legalism. In 1919, the French Chamber of Deputies passed a bill granting the vote to women, but in 1922 the French Senate defeated the bill. It was not until after World War II that Frenchwomen received the right to vote.

In Germany, feminist awareness and action were even more underdeveloped. German law actually forbade German women from political activity. Because no group in the German Empire enjoyed extensive political rights, women were not certain that they would benefit from demanding them. Any such demand would be regarded as subversive not only of the state, but also of society.

In 1894, the Union of German Women's Organizations (BDFK) was founded. By 1902, it was supporting a call for the right to vote. But it was largely concerned with improving women's social conditions, their access to education, and their right to other protections. The group also worked to see women admitted to political or civic activity on the municipal level. Their work usually included education, child welfare, charity, and public health. The German Social Democratic Party supported women's suffrage, but that socialist party was so disdained by the German authorities and German Roman Catholics, that its support served only to make suffrage more suspect in their eyes. Women received the vote in Germany only in 1918, when the constitution of the Weimar Republic was promulgated after German defeat in war and revolution at home.

Throughout Europe in the years before World War I, women demanded rights widely and vocally. The tactics they used and the success they achieved, however, varied from country to country depending on political and class structures. Before World War I, only in Norway (1907) could women vote on national issues.

Jewish Emancipation

The emancipation of European Jews from the narrow life of the ghetto into a world of equal or nearly equal citizenship and social status was a major accomplishment of political liberalism and had an enduring impact on European life. The process of emancipation, slow and never fully completed, began in the late eighteenth century and continued throughout the nineteenth. It moved at different paces in different countries.

Differing Degrees of Citizenship

In 1782 Joseph II, the Habsburg emperor, issued a decree that placed the Jews of his empire under more or less the same laws as Christians. In France, the National Assembly recognized Jews as French citizens in 1789. During the turmoil of the Napoleonic wars, Jewish communities in Italy and Germany were allowed to mix on a generally equal footing with the Christian population. These various steps toward political emancipation were always somewhat uncertain and were frequently limited or partially repealed with changes in rulers or governments. Certain freedoms were granted, only to be partially withdrawn later. Even in countries that had advanced Jews some political rights, they could not own land and could be subject to special discriminatory taxes. Nonetheless, during the first half of the century, European Jews in western Europe, and to a much lesser extent in central and eastern Europe, began to gain significant rights that brought them equal or more nearly equal citizenship.

In Russia, and in Poland under Russian rule, the traditional modes of prejudice and discrimination continued unabated until World War I. Jews were treated as aliens under Russian rule. The government undermined Jewish community life, limited the publication of Jewish books, restricted areas where Jews might live, required internal passports from Jews, banned Jews from many forms of state service, and excluded Jews from many institutions of higher education. The police and others were allowed to conduct *pogroms*—organized riots—against Jewish neighborhoods and villages.

Broadened Opportunities

After the revolutions of 1848, European Jews saw a general improvement in their situation that lasted for several decades. In Germany, Italy, the Low Countries, and Scandinavia, Jews attained full rights of citizenship. After 1858, Jews in Great Britain could sit in Parliament. Austria–Hungary extended full legal rights to Jews in 1867. Indeed, from about 1850 to 1880, there was relatively little organized or overt prejudice against Jews. They entered the professions and other occupations once closed to them. They participated fully in the literary and cultural life of their nations. They were active in the arts and music. They became leaders in science and education. Jews intermarried freely with non-Jews as legal secular prohibitions against such marriages were repealed during the last quarter of the century.

Outside of Russia, Jewish political figures entered cabinets and served in the highest offices of the state. Politically, they often were aligned with

The era of Jewish emancipation allowed more freedom to European Jews and a wider recognition of their faith and culture. This painting by G. E Opitz portrays the dedication of a new synagogue in Alsace in 1820.
Jewish Museum, N.Y./Art Resource, NY

liberal parties because these groups had championed equal rights. Later in the century, especially in eastern Europe, many Jews became associated with socialist parties.

The prejudice that had been associated with Christian religious attitudes toward Jews seemed for a time to have dissipated, although it still appeared in Russia and other parts of eastern Europe. Hundreds of thousands of European Jews migrated from these regions to western Europe and the United States. Almost anywhere in Europe, Jews might encounter prejudice on a personal level. But in western Europe, including England, France, Italy, Germany, and the Low Countries, Jews felt fairly secure from the legalized persecution and discrimination that had so haunted them in the past.

That newfound security began to erode during the last two decades of the nineteenth century. Anti-Semitic voices began to be heard in the 1870s, attributing the economic stagnation of the decade to Jewish bankers and financial interests. In the 1880s, organized anti-Semitism erupted in Germany, as it did in France at the time of the Dreyfus Affair. As will be seen in the next chapter, these developments gave rise to the birth of Zionism, initially a minority movement within the Jewish community. Most Jewish leaders believed the attacks on Jewish life were merely temporary recurrences of older modes of prejudice; they felt their communities would remain safe under the liberal legal protections that had been extended over the course of the century. That analysis would be proved disastrously wrong during the second quarter of the twentieth century.

Labor, Socialism, and Politics to World War I

The late-century industrial expansion wrought further changes in the life of the labor force. In all industrializing continental countries, the numbers of the urban proletariat rose. The proportion of artisans and highly skilled workers declined, and for the first time factory wage earners predominated. The number of people engaged in unskilled work associated with shipping, transportation, and building also grew considerably.

Workers still had to look to themselves to improve their lot. After 1848, however, European workers stopped rioting in the streets to voice their grievances. They also stopped trying to revive the paternal guilds and similar institutions of the past. After midcentury, workers turned to new institutions and ideologies. Chief among these were trade unions, democratic political parties, and socialism.

Trade Unionism

Trade unionism came of age as governments extended legal protections to unions during the second half of the century. Unions became fully legal in Great Britain in 1871 and were allowed to picket in 1875. In France, Napoleon III at first used troops against strikes, but as his political power waned, he allowed weak labor associations in 1868. The Third French Republic fully legalized unions in 1884. In Germany, unions were permitted to function with little disturbance after 1890. Union participation in the political process was at first marginal. As long as the representatives of the traditional governing classes looked after labor interests, members of the working class rarely sought office themselves.

Unions directed their midcentury organizational efforts toward skilled workers and the immediate improvement of wages and working conditions. By the close of the century, industrial unions for unskilled workers were being organized. With thousands of workers, these large unions met intense opposition from employers. They frequently had to engage in long strikes to convince employers to accept their demands. Europe suffered a rash of strikes in the prewar decade as unions sought to keep wages in line with inflation. Despite union advances, however, and the growth of union membership (in 1910 to approximately 3 million in Britain, 2 million in Germany, and 977,000 in France), most of Europe's labor force was never unionized in this period. What the unions did represent for workers was a new collective form of association for confronting economic difficulties and improving security.

Democracy and Political Parties

Except for Russia, all the major European states adopted broad-based, if not perfectly democratic, electoral systems in the late nineteenth century. Great Britain passed its second voting reform act in 1867 and its third in 1884. Bismarck brought universal male suffrage to the German Empire in 1871. The French Chamber of Deputies was democratically elected. Universal male suffrage was adopted in Switzerland in 1879, in Spain in 1890, in Belgium in 1893, in the Netherlands in 1896, and in Norway in 1898. Italy finally fell into line in 1912. The broadened franchise meant that politicians could no longer ignore workers and discontented groups could now voice their grievances and advocate their programs within the institutions of government rather than from the outside.

The advent of democracy brought organized mass political parties like those already in existence in the United States to Europe for the first time. In the

Trade Unions continued to grow in late-century Great Britain. The effort to curb the unions eventually led to the formation of the Labour Party. The British unions often had quite elaborate membership certificates, such as this one for the National Union of Gas Workers and General Labourers of Great Britain and Ireland. The Granger Collection

liberal European states with narrow electoral bases, most voters had been people of property who knew what they had at stake in politics. Organization had been minimal. The expansion of the electorate brought into the political process many people whose level of political consciousness, awareness, and interest was quite low. This electorate had to be organized and taught the nature of power and influence in the liberal democratic state.

The organized political party—with its workers, newspapers, offices, social life, and discipline—was the vehicle that mobilized the new voters. The largest single group in these mass electorates was the working class. The democratization of politics presented the socialists with opportunities and required the traditional ruling classes to vie with the socialists for the support of the new voters.

During these years, socialism as a political ideology and plan of action opposed nationalism. The problems of class were supposed to be transnational, and socialism was supposed to unite the working classes across national borders. European socialists,

however, badly underestimated the emotional drawing power of nationalism. Many workers had both socialist and nationalist sympathies, which were rarely in conflict with each other. When the outbreak of war in 1914 did bring them into conflict, however, nationalist feelings prevailed.

The major question for late-century socialist parties throughout Europe was whether the improvement of the lot of the working class would come about through revolution or democratic reform. This question sharply divided all socialist parties and most especially those whose leadership adhered to the intellectual legacy of Karl Marx. (See "Art & the West.")

Karl Marx and the First International

Karl Marx himself made considerable accommodation to the new practical realities that developed during the third quarter of the century. Although he continued to predict the disintegration of capitalism, his practical, public political activity reflected a somewhat different approach.

In 1864, a group of British and French trade unionists founded the International Working Men's Association. Known as the *First International*, its membership encompassed a vast array of radical political types, including socialists, anarchists, and Polish nationalists. In the inaugural address for the International, Marx supported and approved efforts by workers and trade unions to reform the conditions of labor within the existing political and economic processes. In his private writings he often criticized such reformist activity, but these writings were not made public until near the end of the century, years after his death.

The violence involved in the rise and suppression of the Paris Commune (see Chapter 23), which Marx had declared a genuine proletarian uprising, cast a pall over socialism throughout Europe. British trade unionists, who received legal protections in 1871, wanted no connection with the events in Paris. The French authorities used the uprising to suppress socialist activity. Under these pressures, the First International held its last European congress in 1873. It soon transferred its offices to the United States, where it was dissolved in 1876.

The short-lived First International had a disproportionately great impact on the future of European socialism. Throughout the late 1860s, the organization had gathered statistics, kept labor groups informed of mutual problems, provided a forum for the debate of socialist doctrine, and extravagantly proclaimed its own influence over contemporary events. From these debates and activities, Marxism emerged as the single most important strand of socialism. Marx and his supporters defeated or drove out anarchists and advocates of other forms of socialism. The apparently scientific character of Marxism made it attractive, science being more influential than at any previous time in European history. German socialists, who were to establish the most powerful socialist party in Europe, were deeply impressed by Marx's thought and were the chief vehicle for preserving and developing it. The full development of German socialism also, however, involved the influence of non-Marxist socialists in Great Britain.

Great Britain: Fabianism and Early Welfare Programs

Neither Marxism nor any other form of socialism made significant progress in Great Britain, the most advanced industrial society of the day. There trade unions grew steadily, and their members normally supported Liberal Party candidates. The "new unionism" of the late 1880s and the 1890s organized the dockworkers, the gas workers, and similar unskilled groups. In 1892, Keir Hardie became the first independent working man to be elected to Parliament, but the small socialist Independent Labour Party founded a year later remained ineffective. Until 1901, general political activity on the part of labor remained quite limited. In that year, however, the House of Lords, through the Taff Vale decision, removed the legal protection previously accorded union funds. The Trades Union Congress responded by launching the Labour Party. In the election of 1906, the fledgling party sent twenty-nine members to Parliament. Their goals as trade unionists, however, did not yet include socialism. In this same period, the British labor movement became more militant. In scores of strikes before the war, workers fought for wages to meet the rising cost of living. The government took a larger role than ever before in mediating these strikes, which in 1911 and 1912 involved the railways, the docks, and the mines.

British socialism itself remained primarily the preserve of non-Marxist intellectuals. The Fabian Society, founded in 1884, was Britain's most influential socialist group. The society took its name from Q. Fabius Maximus, the Roman general whose tactics against Hannibal involved avoiding direct conflict that might lead to defeat. The name reflected the society's gradualist approach to major social reform. Its

Beatrice and Sidney Webb, in a photograph from the late 1920s. These most influential British Fabian socialists wrote many books on governmental and economic matters, served on special parliamentary commissions, and agitated for the enactment of socialist policies. UPI/Corbis

Georges Seurat and Giuseppe Pellizza da Volpedo: European Society in Conflict

Georges Seurat, (French, 1859–1891), *A Sunday on La Grande-Jatte—1884.* Oil on canvas, 1884–86, 207.6 × 308 cm. Helen Birch Barlett Memorial Collection, 1926.224. Photograph © 1999, The Art Institute of Chicago. All rights reserved.

*M*any contemporaries saw late nineteenth-century European society divided into hostile political and social camps. In one nation after another labor unions and socialists politically galvanized recently enfranchised workers, while liberal parties appealed to the propertied middle classes. European artists whose political allegiances extended across the political spectrum portrayed this social division.

Georges Seurat (1859–1891) was a young French painter who read extensively in contemporary scientific works about light, color, and vision. These studies led him to a technique of painting known as *pointillism* whereby the artist applied very small dots or points of paint to the canvas. Through this laborious process he hoped to decompose colors into their basic units leaving it to the eye of the viewer to mix

Giuseppe Pellizza da Volpedo, *I1 Quarto Stato (The Fourth Estate)*, 1901. Oil on canvas, 283 cm × 550 cm. Civica Galleria d'Arte Moderna–Milano. Photo by Marcello Saporetti

those dots into the desired color or shade of color. Seurat is counted among the first *Post-Impressionists* because he saw himself bringing the new painting of modern life back into touch with earlier artistic traditions. In that regard, he once described *A Sunday on La Grande-Jatte—1844* as "a new version of Phidias's Panathenaic procession on the Parthenon frieze, with 'the moderns moving about...friezelike, stripped down to their essentials.'"[2]

Seurat also introduced implicit social commentary into the previous Impressionist portrayal of leisured activity. The Grande-Jatte was an island in the Seine beyond Paris where Parisians would gather on Sundays. In Seurat's painting, shadows in the foreground suggest that all is not entirely sunny for the largely middle class afternoon crowd. The boatman smoking the pipe indicates a brooding working-class presence in the foreground of their lives. All of the figures resemble the manikins that appeared in the fashionable new Paris department stores. Except for the one child who is running, the figures appear almost mechanical, like the manufacturing processes which produced their clothing and their other domestic consumer goods. These figures, compared by one contemporary critic to lead soldiers, stand bored and perhaps puzzled by their situation of comfort, leisure, and ease.

Giuseppe Pellizza da Volpedo (1868–1907) was a powerfully committed Italian socialist artist who throughout *The Fourth Estate* (1898–1901) used Seurat's pointillist technique. He took his title from the French socialist Jean Jaurès who believed that workers would soon displace the traditional three estates of the clergy, aristocracy, and commoners. Pellizza and other artists embracing *social realism* moved painting away from nostalgic, sentimental, depictions of peasants to images of industrial or farm laborers experiencing hunger, poverty, and awakening political consciousness. Pellizza originally intended to display this vast seventeen foot wide painting at the Paris World Fair of 1900, where it would have challenged the Fair's glorification of industrialism, imperialism, and middle-class consumerism, but he failed to complete the painting in time.

Pellizza described *The Fourth Estate* as a "Social painting...a crowd of people, workers of the soil, who are intelligent, strong, robust, united, who advance like a torrent, overthrowing every obstacle in their path, who thirst for justice."[3] The woman and child with a male figure in the foreground recall earlier Christian paintings of Jesus, Mary, and Joseph, but are here transformed into secular figures demanding social justice on earth. It is significant that Pellizza portrayed agricultural laborers marching in protest because in contrast to the rest of Europe, farm workers in Italy were among the most extensively organized worker groups and introduced women in leadership roles.

Pelliza's was one of many paintings of the last quarter of the century to portray groups of people previously largely excluded from politics and social engagement walking toward the viewer and demanding a place in the viewer's world, that is the world of middle-class prosperity and political activity. (See also Sir George Clausen's *Schoolgirls, Haverstock Hill*, 1880, p. 825).

[3] Robert Rosenblum and H. W. Janson, *19th-Century Art* (Englewood Cliffs, N.J.: Prentice Hall and New York: Harry N. Abrahms, 1984), p. 463.

Sources: T. J. Clark, *The Painting of Modern Life: Paris in the Art of Manet and His Followers* (Princeton: Princeton University Press, 1984); Robert Rosenblum and H. W. Janson, *19th-Century Art* (Englewood Cliffs, N.J.: Prentice Hall and New York: Harry N. Abrahms, 1984).

[2] T. J. Clark, *The Painting of Modern Life: Paris in the Art of Manet and His Followers* (Princeton: Princeton University Press, 1984), p. 266.

leading members were Sidney Webb (1859–1947) and Beatrice Webb (1858–1943), H. G. Wells (1866–1946), Graham Wallas (1858–1932), and George Bernard Shaw (1856–1950). Many Fabians were civil servants who believed that the problems of industry, the expansion of ownership, and state direction of production could be achieved gradually, peacefully, and democratically. They sought to educate the country about the rational wisdom of socialism. They were particularly interested in modes of collective ownership on the municipal level, the so-called gas-and-water socialism.

The British government and the major political parties responded slowly to these various pressures. In 1903, Joseph Chamberlain (1836–1914) launched his unsuccessful campaign to match foreign tariffs and to finance social reform through higher import duties. The campaign badly split the Conservative Party. After 1906, the Liberal Party, led by Sir Henry Campbell-Bannerman (1836–1908) and, after 1908, by Herbert Asquith (1852–1928), pursued a two-pronged policy. Fearful of losing seats in Parliament to the new Labour Party, they restored the former protection of the unions. Then, after 1909, with Chancellor of the Exchequer David Lloyd George (1863–1945) as its guiding light, the Liberal ministry undertook a broad program of social legislation that included the establishment of labor exchanges, the regulation of certain trades, such as tailoring and lace making, and the passage of the National Insurance Act of 1911, which provided unemployment benefits and health care.

The financing of these programs brought the House of Commons into conflict with the Conservative-dominated House of Lords. The result was the Parliament Act of 1911, which allowed the Commons to override the legislative veto of the upper chamber. The new taxes and social programs meant that in Britain, the home of nineteenth-century liberalism, the state was taking on an expanded role in the life of its citizens. The early welfare legislation was only marginally satisfactory to labor, many of whose members still thought they could gain more from the direct action of strikes.

France: "Opportunism" Rejected

At the turn of the century, Jean Jaurès (1859–1914) and Jules Guesde (1845–1922) led the two major factions of French socialists. Jaurès believed that socialists should cooperate with middle-class Radical ministries to ensure the enactment of needed social legislation. Guesde opposed this policy, arguing that socialists could not, with integrity, support a bourgeois cabinet that they were theoretically dedicated to overthrow. The government's response to the Dreyfus affair brought the quarrel to a head. In 1899, seeking to unite

all supporters of Dreyfus, Prime Minister René Waldeck-Rousseau (1846–1904) appointed the socialist Alexander Millerand (1859–1943) to the cabinet.

The Second International had been founded in 1889 in a new effort to unify the various national socialist parties and trade unions. By 1904 the Amsterdam Congress of the Second International debated the issue of "opportunism," as such cabinet participation by socialists was termed. The Congress condemned "opportunism" in France and ordered French socialists to form a single party. Jaurès accepted the decision. Thereafter French socialists began to work together, and by 1914 the recently united Socialist Party had become the second largest group in the Chamber of Deputies. But Socialist Party members would not again serve in a French cabinet until the Popular Front Government of 1936.

The French labor movement, with deep roots in anarchism, was uninterested in either politics or socialism. French workers usually voted socialist, but the unions themselves, unlike those in Great Britain, avoided active political participation. The Confédération Générale du Travail, founded in 1895, regarded itself as a rival to the socialist parties. Its leaders sought to improve the workers' conditions through direct action. They embraced the doctrines of syndicalism, which had been most persuasively expounded by Georges Sorel (1847–1922) in *Reflections on Violence* (1908). This book enshrined the general strike as a device for generating worker unity and power. The strike tactic often conflicted with the socialist belief in aiding labor through state action. Strikes were common between 1905 and 1914, and the middle-class Radical ministry used troops to suppress them on more than one occasion.

Germany: Social Democrats and Revisionism

The negative judgment rendered by the Second International against French socialist participation in bourgeois ministries reflected a policy of permanent hostility to nonsocialist governments previously adopted by the German Social Democratic Party, or SPD. The organizational success of this party, more than any other single factor, kept Marxist socialism alive during the late nineteenth and early twentieth centuries.

The SDP had been founded in 1875. Its origins lay in the labor agitation of Ferdinand Lasalle (1825–1864), who sought worker participation in German politics. Wilhelm Liebknecht (1826–1900) and August Bebel (1840–1913), who were Marxists and opposed reformist politics, soon joined the party. Thus, from its founding, the SPD was divided between those who advocated reform and those who advocated revolution.

BISMARCK'S REPRESSION OF THE SPD   Twelve years of persecution under Bismarck forged the character of the SPD. The so-called Iron Chancellor believed that socialism would undermine German politics and society. He used an assassination attempt on William I in 1878, in which the socialists were not involved, to steer several antisocialist laws through the Reichstag. The measures suppressed the organization, meetings, newspapers, and other public activities of the SPD. Thereafter, to remain a socialist meant to remove oneself from the mainstream of respectable German life and possibly to lose one's job. The antisocialist legislation proved politically counterproductive. From the early 1880s onward, the SPD steadily polled more and more votes in elections to the *Reichstag*.

As simple repression failed to isolate German workers from socialist loyalties, Bismarck undertook a program of social welfare legislation. In 1883, the German Empire adopted a health insurance measure. The next year saw the enactment of accident insurance legislation. Finally, in 1889, Bismarck sponsored a plan for old age and disability pensions. These programs, to which both workers and employers contributed, represented a paternalistic, conservative alternative to socialism. The state itself would organize a system of social security that did not require any change in the system of property holding or politics. Germany became the first major industrial nation to enjoy this kind of welfare program.

THE ERFURT PROGRAM   After forcing Bismarck's resignation, Emperor William II (r. 1888–1918) allowed the antisocialist legislation to expire, hoping to build new political support among the working class. Even under the repressive laws, members of the SPD could sit in the *Reichstag*. With the repressive measures lifted, the party needed to decide what attitude to assume toward the German Empire.

The answer came in the Erfurt Program of 1891, formulated under the political guidance of Bebel and the ideological tutelage of Karl Kautsky (1854–1938). In good Marxist fashion, the program declared the imminent doom of capitalism and the necessity of socialist ownership of the means of production. The party intended to pursue these goals through legal political participation rather than by revolutionary activity. Kautsky argued that because capitalism by its very nature must collapse, the immediate task for socialists was to work for the improvement of workers' lives rather than for the revolution, which was inevitable. So, although in theory the SPD was vehemently hostile to the German Empire, in practice the party functioned within its institutions. The SPD members of the *Reichstag* maintained clear political consciences by refusing to enter the cabinet (to which they were not invited anyway) and by refraining for many years from voting in favor of the military budget.

THE DEBATE OVER REVISIONISM   The dilemma of the SPD, however, generated the most important challenge within the socialist movement to the orthodox Marxist analysis of capitalism and the socialist revolution. The author of this socialist heresy, Eduard Bernstein (1850–1932), had spent over a decade of his life in Great Britain and was familiar with the Fabians. Bernstein questioned whether Marx and his later orthodox followers, such as Kautsky, had been correct in their pessimistic appraisal of capitalism and the necessity of revolution. In *Evolutionary Socialism* (1899), Bernstein pointed to conditions that did not meet orthodox Marxists' expectations. The standard of living was on the rise in Europe. Ownership of capitalist industry was becoming more widespread through stockholding. The middle class was not falling into the ranks of the proletariat and was not identifying its problems with those of the workers. The inner contradictions of capitalism as expounded by Marx had simply not developed. Moreover, the extension of the franchise to the working class meant that parliamentary methods might achieve revolutionary social change. For Bernstein, social reform through democratic institutions replaced revolution as the path to a humane socialist society. (See "Eduard Bernstein Criticizes Orthodox Marxism.")

Bernstein's doctrines, known as *Revisionism*, generated heated debate among German socialists, who finally condemned them. His critics argued that evolution toward social democracy might be possible in liberal, parliamentary Britain, but not in authoritarian, militaristic Germany, with its basically powerless *Reichstag*. Nonetheless, while still calling for revolution, the SPD pursued a course of action similar to that advocated by Bernstein. Its trade union members, prospering within the German economy, did not want revolution. Its grassroots members wanted to consider themselves patriotic Germans as well as good socialists. Its leaders feared any actions that might renew the persecution that they had experienced under Bismarck.

Consequently, the SPD worked for electoral gains, expansion of its membership, and short-term political and social reform. It prospered and became one of the most important institutions of imperial Germany. Even some middle-class Germans voted for it as a way to oppose the illiberal institutions of the empire. And in August 1914, after long debate among themselves, the SPD members of the *Reichstag* abandoned their former practice and unanimously voted for the war credits that would finance Germany's participation in World War I.

Eduard Bernstein Criticizes Orthodox Marxism

Eduard Bernstein was responsible for the emergence of "Revisionism" within the German Social Democratic Party. He was a dedicated socialist who recognized that the Communist Manifesto *(1848) had not predicted the actual future of the European working classes. He believed that there would be no sudden collapse or catastrophe in the capitalist system and that socialists should change their tactics to work to achieve political rights and pursue reform instead of revolution.*

❖ *According to Bernstein, what specific predictions in the* Communist Manifesto *failed to materialize? Why is the advance of democracy important to his argument? Why does he see the extension of political rights to German workers as so important?*

I set myself against the notion that we have to expect shortly a collapse of the bourgeois economy, and that social democracy should be induced by the prospect of such an imminent, great, social catastrophe to adapt its tactics to that assumption....

The adherents of this theory of a catastrophe, base it especially on the conclusion of the *Communist Manifesto.* This is a mistake in every respect....

Social conditions have not developed to such an acute opposition of things and classes as is depicted in the *Manifesto....* The number of members of the possessing classes is to-day not smaller but larger. The enormous increase of social wealth is not accompanied by a decreasing number of large capitalists but by an increasing number of capitalists of all degrees....

In all advanced countries we see the privileges of the capitalist bourgeoisie yielding step by step to democratic organizations.... Factory legislation, the democratizing of local government, and the extension of its area of work, the freeing of trade unions and systems of co-operative trading from legal restrictions, the consideration of standard conditions of labour in the work undertaken by public authorities—all these characterize this phase of the evolution....

The conquest of political power by the working classes, the expropriation of capitalists, are not ends in themselves but only means for the accomplishment of certain aims and endeavours. As such they are demands in the program of social democracy....Nothing can be said beforehand as to the circumstances of their accomplishment; we can only fight for their realization. But the conquest of political power necessitates the possession of political *rights;* and the most important problem of tactics which German social democracy has at the present time to solve, appears to me to be to devise the best ways for the extension of the political and economic rights of the German working classes.

From Eduard Bernstein, *Evolutionary Socialism: A Criticism and Affirmation, 1899* (New York: Schocken Books, 1961), pp. xxiv–xxvi, xxix–xxx.

Russia: Industrial Development and the Birth of Bolshevism

During the last decade of the nineteenth century, Russia entered the industrial age and confronted many of the problems that the more advanced nations of the Continent had experienced fifty or seventy-five years earlier. Unlike those other countries, Russia had to deal with major political discontent and economic development simultaneously. Russian socialism reflected that peculiar situation.

WITTE'S PROGRAM FOR INDUSTRIAL GROWTH Alexander III (r. 1881–1894) and, after him, Nicholas II (r. 1894–1917) were determined that Russia should become an industrial power. Only by doing so, they believed, could the country maintain its European military position and diplomatic role. It was Sergei Witte (1849–1915) who led Russia into the industrial age. After a career in railways and other private business, he was appointed finance minister in 1892. Witte, who pursued a policy of planned economic development, protective tariffs, high taxes, the gold standard, and efficiency, epitomized the nineteenth-century modernizer. He established strong financial relationships with the French money market, which later led to diplomatic cooperation between Russia and France.

Witte favored heavy industries. Between 1890 and 1904, the Russian railway system grew from 30,596 to 59,616 kilometers. The 5,000-mile Trans-Siberian Railroad was almost completed. Coal output more than tripled during the same period. There was a vast increase in pig-iron production, from 928,000 tons in 1890 to 4,641,000 tons in 1913. During the same period, steel production rose from 378,000 to 4,918,000 tons. Textile manufacturing continued to expand and was still the single largest industry. The factory system began to be used more extensively throughout the country.

Industrialism brought considerable social discontent to Russia, as it had elsewhere. Landowners felt that foreign capitalists were earning too much of the profit. The peasants saw their grain exports and tax payments finance development that did not measurably improve their lives. A small, but significant, industrial proletariat emerged. At the turn of the century, there were approximately three million factory workers in Russia. Their working and living conditions were poor by any standard. They enjoyed little state protection, and trade unions were illegal. In 1897, Witte did enact a measure providing

A Russian Social Investigator Describes the Condition of Children in the Moscow Tailoring Trade

E. A. Oliunina was a young Russian woman who had been active among union organizers during the Revolution of 1905. Later, as a student at the Higher Women's Courses in Moscow, a school for women's postsecondary education, she began to investigate and to write about child garment workers. The clothes produced by these children might have ended up in Russian department stores that copied those in Paris, described in an earlier document in this chapter.

❖ *Why might the parents of these children have allowed them to work in sweatshops? Why was alcoholism such a prevalent problem? Why does Oliunina regard schools as the solution to this problem?*

Children begin their apprenticeship between the ages of twelve and thirteen, although one can find some ten- and eleven-year-olds working in the shops....

Apprenticeship is generally very hard on children. At the beginning, they suffer enormously, particularly from the physical strain of having to do work well beyond the capacity of their years. They have to live in an environment where the level of morality is very low. Scenes of drunkenness and debauchery induce the boys to smoke and drink at an early age.

For example, in one subcontracting shop that made men's clothes, a fourteen-year-old boy worked together with twelve adults. When I visited there at four o'clock one Tuesday afternoon, the workers were half-drunk. Some were lying under the benches, others in the hallway. The boy was as drunk as the rest of them and lay there with a daredevil look on his face, dressed only in a pair of longjohns and a dirty, tattered shirt. He had been taught to drink at the age of twelve and could now keep up with the adults.

"Blue Monday" is a custom in most subcontracting shops that manufacture men's clothes. The whole workshop gets drunk, and work comes to a standstill. The apprentices do nothing but hang around. Many of the workers live in the workshop, so the boys are constantly exposed to all sorts of conversations and scenes. In one shop employing five workers and three boys, "Blue Monday" was a regular ritual. Even the owner himself is prone to alcoholic binges. In these kinds of situations, young girls are in danger of being abused by the owner or his sons....

In Russia, there have been no measures taken to improve the working conditions of apprentices. As I have tried to show, the situation in workshops in no way provides apprentices with adequate training in their trade. The young workers are there only to be exploited. Merely limiting the number of apprentices would not better their position, nor would it eradicate the influx of cheap labor. An incomparably more effective solution would be to replace apprenticeship with a professional educational system and well-established safeguards for child workers. However, the only real solution to the exploitation of unpaid child labor is to introduce a minimum wage for minors.

Quoted in Victoria E. Bonnell, *The Russian Worker: Life and Labor Under the Tsarist Regime* (Berkeley, CA: University of California Press, 1983), pp. 177, 180–181, 182–183. Reprinted by permission of the University of California Press.

for an 11-1/2 hour workday. But needless to say, discontent and strikes continued. (See "A Russian Social Investigator Describes the Condition of Children in the Moscow Tailoring Trade.")

Similar social and economic problems arose in the countryside. Russian agriculture had not revived after the emancipation of the serfs in 1861. The peasants remained burdened with redemption payments, local taxes, excessive national taxes, and falling grain prices. Free peasants owned their land communally through the *mir*, or village. They farmed the land inefficiently through strip farming or the tilling of small plots. Many free peasants with too little land to support their families had to work on larger noble estates or for more prosperous peasant farmers, known as *kulaks*. Between 1860 and 1914, the population of European Russia rose from approximately 50 million to approximately 103 million people. Land hunger and intense discontent spread among the peasants. Uprisings in the countryside were a frequent problem.

New political departures accompanied economic development. The membership and intellectual roots of the Social Revolutionary Party, founded in 1901, reached back to the Populists of the 1870s. The new party opposed industrialism and looked to the communal life of rural Russia as a model for the future. In 1903 the Constitutional Democratic Party, or Cadets, was formed. This liberal party drew its members from people who participated in local councils called *zemstvos*. Modeling themselves on the liberal parties of western Europe, the Cadets wanted a parliamentary regime with responsible ministries, civil liberties, and economic progress.

LENIN'S EARLY THOUGHT AND CAREER   The situation of Russian socialists differed radically from that of socialists in other major European countries. Russia had no representative institutions and only a small working class. The compromises and accommodations achieved elsewhere were meaningless in Russia, where socialists believed that in both theory and practice they must be revolutionary. The repressive policies of the tsarist regime required the Russian Social Democratic Party, founded in 1898, to function in exile. The party members greatly admired the German Social Democratic Party and adopted its Marxist ideology.

The leading late-nineteenth-century Russian Marxist was Gregory Plekhanov (1857–1918), who wrote from exile in Switzerland. At the turn of the century, his chief disciple was Vladimir Ilyich Ulyanov (1870–1924), who later took the name of Lenin. The future leader of the communist revolution was the son of a high bureaucrat. His older brother, while a student in Saint Petersburg, had become involved in radical politics; arrested for participating in a plot against Alexander III, he was executed in 1887. In 1893 Lenin moved to Saint Petersburg, where he studied law. Soon he, too, was drawn to the revolutionary groups among the factory workers. He was arrested in 1895 and exiled to Siberia. In 1900, after his release, Lenin left Russia for the West. He spent most of the next seventeen years in Switzerland.

Once in Switzerland, Lenin became deeply involved in the organizational and policy disputes of the exiled Russian Social Democrats. They all considered themselves Marxists, but they differed on the meaning of a Marxist revolution for primarily

In this photograph taken in 1895, Lenin sits at the table among a group of other young Russian radicals from Saint Petersburg. Corbis

Lenin Argues for the Necessity of a Secret and Elite Party of Professional Revolutionaries

Social democratic parties in western Europe had mass memberships and generally democratic structures of organization. In this passage from What Is to Be Done? *(1902), Lenin explains why the autocratic political conditions of Russia demanded a different kind of organization for the Russian Social Democratic Party. Lenin's ideas became the guiding principles of Bolshevik organization.*

❖ *What does Lenin mean by "professional revolutionaries"? Why are such revolutionaries especially needed in Russia? How does Lenin reconcile his antidemocratic views to the goal of aiding the working class?*

I assert that it is far more difficult [for government police] to unearth a dozen wise men than a hundred fools. This position I will defend, no matter how much you instigate the masses against me for my "anti-democratic" views, etc. As I have stated repeatedly, by "wise men," in connection with organization, I mean professional revolutionaries, irrespective of whether they have developed from among students or working men. I assert: (1) that no revolutionary movement can endure without a stable organization of leaders maintaining continuity; (2) that the broader the popular mass drawn spontaneously into the struggle, which forms the basis of the movement and participates in it, the more urgent the need for such an organization, and the more solid this organization must be...; (3) that such an organization must consist chiefly of people professionally engaged in revolutionary activity; (4) that in an autocratic state [such as Russia], the more we confine the membership of such an organization to people who are professionally engaged in revolutionary activity and who have been professionally trained in the art of combating the political police, the more difficult will it be to unearth the organization; and (5) the greater will be the number of people from the working class and from other social classes who will be able to join the movement and perform active work in it....

The only serious organization principle for the active workers of our movement should be the strictest secrecy, the strictest selection of members, and the training of professional revolutionaries.

From Albert Fried and Ronald Sanders, eds., *Socialist Thought: A Documentary History* (Garden City, NY: Anchor Doubleday, 1964), pp. 460, 468.

rural Russia and on how to structure their own party. Unlike the backward-looking Social Revolutionaries, the Social Democrats were modernizers who favored further industrial development. The majority believed that Russia must develop a large proletariat before the revolution could come. This same majority hoped to build a mass political party like the German SPD.

Lenin dissented from both positions. In *What Is to Be Done?* (1902), he condemned any accommodations, such as those practiced by the German SPD. He also criticized trade unionism that settled for short-term gains rather than true revolutionary change for the working class. Lenin further rejected the concept of a mass democratic party composed of workers. He declared that revolutionary consciousness would not arise spontaneously from the working class. Rather, "people who make revolutionary activity their profession" must carry that consciousness to the workers.[4] Only a small, tightly organized, elite party could possess the proper dedication to revolution and prove able to resist penetration by police spies. The guiding principle of that party should be "the strictest secrecy, the strictest selection of members, and the training of professional revolutionaries."[5] Within the context of turn-of-the-century European socialist debates, Lenin thus rejected both Kautsky's view that revolution was inevitable and Bernstein's view that it would arrive democratically. Lenin substituted the small, professional, nondemocratic revolutionary party for Marx's proletariat as the instrument of revolutionary change. (See "Lenin Argues for the Necessity of a Secret and Elite Party of Professional Revolutionaries.")

[4]Quoted in Albert Fried and Ronald Sanders, eds., *Socialist Thought: A Documentary History* (Garden City, NY: Anchor Doubleday, 1964), p. 459.

[5]Fried and Sanders, p. 468.

Major Dates in the Development of Socialism

1864	International Working Men's Association (the First International) founded
1875	German Social Democratic Party founded
1876	First International dissolved
1878	German antisocialist laws passed
1884	British Fabian Society founded
1889	Second International founded
1891	German antisocialist laws permitted to expire
1891	German Social Democratic Party's Erfurt Program
1895	French *Confédération Générale du Travail* founded
1899	Eduard Bernstein's *Evolutionary Socialism*
1902	Formation of the British Labour party
1902	Lenin's *What Is to Be Done?*
1903	Bolshevik–Menshevik split
1904	"Opportunism" debated at the Amsterdam Congress of the Second International

In 1903, at the London Congress of the Russian Social Democratic Party, Lenin forced a split in the party ranks. During much of the congress, he and his followers lost many votes on various questions put before the body, but near the close they mustered a very slim majority. Thereafter Lenin's faction assumed the name *Bolsheviks*, meaning "majority," and the other, more moderate, democratic revolutionary faction came to be known as the *Mensheviks*, or "minority." There was, of course, a considerable public relations advantage to the name *Bolshevik*. (In 1912, the *Bolsheviks* organized separately.)

In 1905, Lenin complemented his organizational theory with a program for revolution in Russia. In *Two Tactics of Social Democracy in the Bourgeois–Democratic Revolution,* he urged the socialist revolution to unite the proletariat and the peasantry. Lenin grasped better than any other revolutionary the profound discontent in the Russian countryside. He believed that the tsarist government probably could not suppress an alliance of workers and peasants in rebellion.

Lenin's two principles—an elite party and a dual social revolution—guided later *Bolshevik* activity. The *Bolsheviks* ultimately seized power in November 1917, transforming the political landscape of the modern world. But they did so only after the turmoil of World War I had undermined support for the tsar and only after other political forces had toppled the tsarist government earlier in 1917. Prior to World War I, the *Bolsheviks* constituted the odd man out in European socialist politics; they exerted no significant prewar influence on other socialist groups, who, in general, ignored them. For their part, the *Bolsheviks* responded by holding in contempt the west European socialist parties who worked within their nations' political systems. Between the turn of the century and World War I, the government of Nicholas II managed to confront political upheaval more or less successfully.

On Bloody Sunday, January 22, 1905, troops of Tsar Nicholas II fired on a peaceful procession of workers who sought to present a petition at the Winter Palace in Saint Petersburg. After this event, there was little chance of reconciliation between the Tsarist government and the Russian working class. Bildarchiv Preussischer Kulturbesitz

THE REVOLUTION OF 1905 AND ITS AFTERMATH The quarrels among the exiled Russian socialists and Lenin's doctrines had no immediate influence on events in Russia. Industrialization proceeded and continued to stir resentment in many sectors. In 1903, Nicholas II dismissed Witte, hoping to quell the criticism. The next year Russia went to war against Japan, partly in hopes that the conflict would rally public opinion to the tsar. Instead, the Russians lost the war and the government faced an internal political crisis. The Japanese captured Port Arthur early in 1905. A few days later, on January 22, a priest named Father Gapon led several hundred workers to present a petition to the tsar for the improvement of industrial conditions. As the petitioners approached the Winter Palace in Saint Petersburg, the tsar's troops opened fire. About 100 people were shot down in cold blood, and many more were wounded on what became known as Bloody Sunday.

During the next ten months, revolutionary disturbances spread throughout Russia. Sailors mutinied, peasant revolts erupted, and property was attacked. The uncle of Nicholas II was assassinated. Liberal leaders of the Constitutional Democratic Party from the *zemstvos* demanded political reform. Student strikes occurred in the universities. Social Revolutionaries and Social Democrats agitated among urban working groups. In early October 1905, strikes broke out in Saint Petersburg, and for all practical purposes, worker groups, called *soviets*, controlled the city. Nicholas II recalled Witte and issued the *October Manifesto*, which promised Russia constitutional government.

Early in 1906, Nicholas II announced the election of a representative body, the *Duma*, with two chambers. He reserved to himself, however, ministerial appointments, financial policy, military matters, and foreign affairs. The April elections returned a highly radical group of representatives. (See "Two Examples of Russian Social and Political Protest: 1906.") The tsar then dismissed Witte and replaced him with P.A. Stolypin (1862–1911), who had little sympathy for parliamentary government. Stolypin persuaded Nicholas to dissolve the *Duma*. A second assembly was elected in February 1907. Again, cooperation proved impossible, and the tsar dissolved that *Duma* in June. A third *Duma*, elected in late 1907 on the basis of a more conservative franchise, proved sufficiently pliable for the tsar and his minister. Thus, within two years of the 1905 Revolution, Nicholas II had recaptured much of the ground he had conceded.

Stolypin set about repressing rebellion, removing some causes of the revolt, and rallying property owners behind the tsarist regime. Early in

	Major Dates in Turn-of-the-Century Russian History
1892	Witte appointed finance minister
1895	Lenin arrested and sent to Siberia
1897	Eleven-and-a-half-hour workday established
1898	Russian Social Democratic Party founded
1900	Lenin leaves Russia for western Europe
1901	Social Revolutionary Party founded
1903	Constitutional Democratic Party (Cadets) founded
1903	Bolshevik–Menshevik split
1903	Witte dismissed
1904	Russo–Japanese War begins
1905 (January)	Japan defeats Russia
1905 (January 22)	Revolution breaks out in Saint Petersburg after Bloody Sunday massacre
1905 (October 20)	General strike
1905 (October 26)	*October Manifesto* establishes constitutional government
1906 (May 10)	Meeting of first *Duma*
1906 (June)	Stolypin appointed prime minister
1906 (July 21)	Dissolution of first *Duma*
1906 (November)	Land redemption payments canceled for peasants
1907 (March 5–June 16)	Second *Duma* seated and dismissed
1907	Franchise changed and a third *Duma* elected, which sits until 1912
1911	Stolypin assassinated by a Social Revolutionary
1912	Fourth *Duma* elected
1914	World War I breaks out

1907, special field courts-martial tried rebellious peasants, condemning almost 700 to death. Before undertaking this repression, the minister, in November 1906, had canceled any redemptive payments that the peasants still owed the government from the emancipation of the serfs in 1861. He took this step in order to encourage peasants to assume individual proprietorship of their landholdings and to abandon the communal system associated with the *mirs*. Stolypin believed that farmers would be more productive working for themselves. Combined with a program to in-

Two Examples of Russian Social and Political Protest: 1906

The Revolution of 1905 in Russia and the calling of a Duma unleashed more open, public political activity than ever before in Russian history. It was a time of enormous expectations for both social and political reform. Following are two political manifestos of the day. The first is a call for the union organization of Plumbers' Apprentices. The second is the introduction to a much longer document outlining the goals of the Women's Progressive Party. In both selections, observe the strident rhetoric of protest that then gives way to statements of goals which combine the political ideas of the French Revolution and the language of reform rather than outright revolution. Such was characteristic of many of the Russian political groups of 1905 and 1906, who believed that such programs of advanced reform could solve the nation's problems. In the Russian context, these were radical proposals, but they were, of course, moderate compared to the Bolshevik revolution that erupted in 1917.

✤ *To what conditions of employment do the advocates of the Plumbers' union appeal to gain members? How much do their complaints relate to working conditions and how much to their economic situation? About what specific legal and social disabilities does the Women's Progressive Party protest? What political values and outlooks do the union and the party share? How do they differ?*

A. Proclamation of the Union of Plumbers' Apprentices, January 1906

Comrade Plumbers!

Your condition is unbearably onerous. Your wages, compared to the inflation of prices, are so insignificant that every worker is doomed to slow death by starvation....You work in stifling, disgustingly filthy shops, in stinking manholes, underground and in water, out in the frost (where your feet even freeze in your boots)—wherever there are dirty, harmful places, where your weak strength is quickly drained and you are overcome by every kind of disease, which quickly carries you to a premature death...the slightest caprice of the proprietor or foreman—and you workers are mercilessly thrown into the street, into famine, into the cold in penury..... But there is a way out of this terrible condition. Though powerless as individuals, you can make yourself into a great power by joining together in a union of plumber–workers. This union sets as its goal the organization and defense of the proletariat in order to form a unified family of workers, aimed at one and the same goal: the pursuit, for each Russian worker, of the right of man and citizen, and a striving for final victory of living human labor over a soulless capitalism.

B. Program of the Women's Progressive Party, 30 January 1906

Women are the most rightless, dispossessed part of the population. They find themselves in subordination to men and in complete dependence upon their will. They are deprived of their human personality and enslaved by the exiting laws and their economic dependence on the ruling sex. Because of their subordination, economic dependence and lack of rights, women cannot develop all their spiritual abilities and render active assistance to the perfection of mankind (in spiritual and physical respects) and improvement of the social order. Because lack of political rights is one of the main causes of the enslavement of women, the Women's Progressive Party makes its immediate goal the attainment of complete political equality of women with men.

The Women's Progressive Party regards it as necessary to struggle with all the shortcomings of contemporary life and to realize general human ideals: truth, equality, fraternity, freedom, justice and humanitarianism. It holds that realization of these ideals is only possible through a peaceful, evolutionary path.

Gregory L. Freeze, *From Supplication to Revolution: A Documentary Social History of Imperial Russia* (New York: Oxford University Press, 1988), pp. 264–265, 303. Copyright © 1988 by Oxford University Press, Inc. Used by permission of Oxford University Press, Inc.

struct peasants in better farming methods, this policy did improve agricultural production. The very small-proprietor peasants who sold their land increased the size of the industrial labor force.

The moderate liberals who sat in the *Duma* approved of the new land measures. They liked the idea of competition and individual property ownership. The Constitutional Democrats wanted a more genuinely parliamentary mode of government, but they compromised out of fear of new revolutionary disturbances. Hatred of Stolypin was still widespread, however, among the country's older conservative groups, and industrial workers remained antagonistic to the tsar. In 1911, Stolypin was assassinated by a Social Revolutionary, who may have been a police agent in the pay of conservatives. Nicholas II found no worthy successor. His government simply continued to muddle along.

Meanwhile, at court, the monk Grigory Efimovich Rasputin (1871?–1916) came into ascendancy because of his alleged power to heal the tsar's hemophilic son, the heir to the throne. The undue influence of this strange, uncouth man, as well as continued social discontent and conservative resistance to any further liberal reforms, rendered the position and the policy of the tsar uncertain after 1911. Once again, as in 1904, he and his ministers thought that some bold move on the diplomatic front might bring the regime the broad popular support that it so desperately needed.

In Perspective

The years from 1860 through 1914 saw the emergence of two apparently contradictory developments in European social life. On one hand, the lifestyle of the urban middle classes came to dominate, becoming the model to which much of society aspired. The characteristics of this lifestyle included a relatively small family living in its own house or large apartment, servants, and a wife who did not earn an income. The middle classes in general benefitted from the many material comforts generated by the Second Industrial Revolution.

During the same period, the forces of socialism and labor unions assumed a new and major role in European political life. Their leaders demanded greater social justice and a fairer distribution of the vast quantities of consumer goods being produced in Europe. Some socialists sought in one way or another to work within existing political systems.

Others—most particularly, those in Russia—advocated revolution. The growth in wealth and the availability of new goods and services magnified the injustices suffered by the poor and the contrast between them and the middle classes, contributing to the stridency of the demands of labor and the socialists. In Russia, the strains of the early stages of industrialization intensified social unrest. These strains, compounded by a humiliating defeat in a war against Japan, triggered the unsuccessful revolution of 1905.

The working class, however, was not alone in seeking change. Women, for the first time in European history, began in significant ways to demand a political role and to protest the gender inequalities embedded in law and family life. They were beginning to enter the professions in small numbers and were taking a significant role in the service economy, such as the new telephone companies. These changes, as much as the demands of socialists, would in time raise questions about the adequacy of the much admired late nineteenth-century middle-class lifestyle.

REVIEW QUESTIONS

1. How was European society transformed by the Second Industrial Revolution? What new industries developed, and which do you think had the greatest impact in the twentieth century? How do you account for European economic difficulties in the second half of the nineteenth century?

2. How would you describe living conditions in European cities during the late nineteenth century? Why were European cities redesigned during this period? In what ways were they redesigned? Why were housing and health key issues for urban reform? Be specific in your examples.

3. What was the status of European women in the second half of the nineteenth century? Why did they grow discontented with their lot? What factors led to change? To what extent had they improved their position by 1914? What tactics did they use in effecting change? Was the emancipation of women inevitable? How did women approach their situation differently from country to country?

4. What were the major characteristics of Jewish emancipation in the nineteenth century?

5. What was the status of the proletariat in 1860? Had it improved by 1914? What caused the growth in trade unions and organized mass political parties? Why were the debates over "opportunism" and "revisionism" important to the Western European socialist parties?

6. Assess the value of industrialism for Russia. Were the tsars wise in attempting to modernize their country, or would they have been better off leaving it as it was? How did Lenin's view of socialism differ from that of the socialists in western Europe?

SUGGESTED READINGS

J. Albisetti, *Schooling German Girls and Women: Secondary and Higher Education in the Nineteenth Century* (1988). Contains much information on the subject beyond Germany.

H. Anderson, *Utopian Feminism: Women's Movements in Fin-de-Siècle Vienna* (1992). Examines movements to improve the status of women in the Austrian Empire.

I. M. Aronson, *Troubled Waters: The Origins of the 1881 Anti-Jewish Pogroms in Russia* (1990). The best discussion of this subject.

J. Auerbach, *The Great Exhibition of 1851: A Nation on Display* (1999). Explores the most influential exhibition of manufactured goods of the nineteenth century in its larger cultural and national setting.

L. R. Berlanstein, *The Working People of Paris, 1871–1914* (1985). Interesting and comprehensive.

N. Bullock and J. Read, *The Movement for Housing Reform in Germany and France, 1840–1914* (1985). An important and wide-ranging study of the housing problem.

C. M. Cipolla, *The Economic History of World Population* (1962). A basic introduction.

T. W. Clyman and J. Vowles, *Russia through Women's Eyes: Autobiographies from Tsarist Russia* (1996). A splended collection of relatively brief memoirs.

L. Frader and S. Rose (eds.), *Gender and Class in Modern Europe* (1996). A wide-ranging collection of essays.

S. P. Frank, *Crime, Cultural Conflict, and Justice in Rural Russia, 1856–1914* (1999). An extensively documented study of the interaction of Russian peasants and the Czarist state during the decades of the abolition of serfdom.

J. Frankel and S. Zipperstein, *Assimilation and Community: The Jews in Nineteenth-Century Europe* (1992). A major collection of essays that ranges widely over the continent.

P. Gay, *The Dilemma of Democratic Socialism: Eduard Bernstein's Challenge to Marx* (1952). A clear presentation of the problems raised by Bernstein's revisionism.

A. Geifman, *Thou Shalt Kill: Revolutionary Terrorism in Russia, 1894–1917* (1993). An examination of political violence in late imperial Russia.

J. Harsin, *Policing Prostitution in Nineteenth-Century Paris* (1985). A major study of this very significant subject in French social history.

S. C. Hause, *Women's Suffrage and Social Politics in the French Third Republic* (1984). A wide-ranging examination of the question.

P. Hilden, *Working Women and Socialist Politics in France, 1880–1914* (1986). A study that traces both cooperation and tension between socialism and feminism in the French working class.

G. Himmelfarb, *Poverty and Compassion: The Moral Imagination of the Late Victorians* (1991). The best examination of late Victorian social thought.

E. J. Hobsbawm, *The Age of Capital* (1975). Explores the consolidation of middle-class life after 1850.

L. Holcombe, *Wives and Property: Reform of the Married Women's Property Law in Nineteenth-Century England* (1983). The standard work on the subject.

S. S. Holton, *Feminism and Democracy: Women's Suffrage and Reform Politics in Britain, 1900–1918* (1986). An excellent treatment of the subject.

T. Hoppen, *The Mid-Victorian Generation, 1846–1886* (1998). The most extensive treatment of the subject.

P. Joyce, *Visions of the People: Industrial England and the Question of Class, 1848–1914* (1991). Based on important explorations of what actually occurred in the workplace.

S. Kern, *The Culture of Love: Victorians to Moderns* (1992). A major discussion of how Europeans have thought and behaved in regard to love, family, and sexuality.

K. Kolakowski, *Main Currents of Marxism: Its Rise, Growth, and Dissolution*, 3 vols. (1978). The sections on the last years of the nineteenth century and the early years of the twentieth are especially good.

D. Landes, *The Unbound Prometheus: Technological Change and Industrial Development in Western Europe from 1750 to the Present* (1969). Includes excellent discussions of late-nineteenth-century development.

W. O. McCagg, Jr., *A History of Habsburg Jews, 1670–1918* (1989). An excellent examination of the political and economic life of the Jews under Habsburg rule.

G. L. Mosse, *German Jews Beyond Judaism* (1985). Sensitive essays exploring the relationship of Jews to German culture in the nineteenth and early twentieth centuries.

P. G. Nord, *The Republican Moment: Struggles for Democracy in Nineteenth-Century France* (1996). A major new examination of nineteenth-century French political culture.

H. PELLING, *The Origins of the Labour Party, 1880–1900* (1965). Examines the sources of the party in the activities of British socialists and trade unionists.

M. PERROT, *Workers on Strike: France, 1871–1890* (1987). A major exploration of the social and cultural dimensions of strikes.

D. H. PINKNEY, *Napoleon III and the Rebuilding of Paris* (1958). A classic study.

T. RICHARDS, *The Commodity Culture of Victorian England: Advertising and Spectacle, 1851–1914* (1990). A study of how consumers were persuaded of their need for new commodities.

H. ROGGER, *Jewish Policies and Right-Wing Politics in Imperial Russia* (1986). A very learned examination of Russian anti-Semitism.

M. L. ROZENBLIT, *The Jews of Vienna, 1867–1914: Assimilation and Identity* (1983). Covers the cultural, economic, and political life of Viennese Jews.

C. E. SCHORSKE, *German Social Democracy, 1905–1917* (1955). The classic study of the difficulties of the Social Democrats under the empire.

B. G. SMITH, *Ladies of the Leisure Class: The Bourgeoises of Northern France in the Nineteenth Century* (1981). Emphasizes the importance of the reproductive role of women.

N. STONE, *Europe Transformed* (1984). A sweeping survey that emphasizes the difficulties of late-nineteenth-century liberalism.

R. STUART, *Marxism at Work: Ideology, Class, and French Socialism during the Third Republic* (1992). The most extensive examination of French Marxism during this period.

F. M. L. THOMPSON, *The Rise of Respectable Society: A Social History of Victorian Britain, 1830–1900* (1988). A major survey.

J. TOSH, *A Man's Place: Masculinity and the Middle-Class Home in Victorian England* (1999). A pioneering work.

A. B. ULAM, *The Bolsheviks: The Intellectual and Political History of the Triumph of Communism in Russia* (1965). Early chapters discuss prewar developments and the formation of Lenin's doctrines.

A. M. VERNER, *The Crisis of Russian Autocracy: Nicholas II and the 1905 Revolution* (1990). A major study of this crucial event.

J. R. WALKOWITZ, *Prostitution and Victorian Society: Women, Class, and the State* (1980). A work of great insight and sensitivity.

E. WEBER, *Peasants into Frenchmen: The Modernization of Rural France, 1870–1914* (1976). An important and fascinating work on the transformation of French peasants into self-conscious citizens of the nation–state.

M. J. WIENER, *English Culture and the Decline of the Industrial Spirit, 1850–1980* (1981). The best study of the problem.

T. ZELDIN, *France, 1848–1945*, 2 vols. (1973, 1977). Covers many areas of French social life.

Chapter 25

The German physicist Albert Einstein's theory of relativity, published in 1905, set the fundamental theory of physics in a new direction. His work was part of a multi-faceted series of intellectual developments that changed and challenged much Western thought not only in science but also in literature, politics, and philosophy, redirecting Western thinking in ways that were often quite different from those of the Enlightenment. Corbis

The Birth of Modern European Thought

The New Reading Public
Advances in Primary Education
Reading Material for the Mass Audience

Science at Midcentury
Comte, Positivism, and the Prestige of Science
Darwin's Theory of Natural Selection
Science and Ethics

Christianity and the Church under Siege
Intellectual Skepticism
Conflict between Church and State
Areas of Religious Revival
The Roman Catholic Church
  and the Modern World

Toward a Twentieth-Century Frame of Mind
Science: The Revolution in Physics
Literature: Realism and Naturalism
Modernism
Friedrich Nietzsche and the Revolt
  against Reason
The Birth of Psychoanalysis
Retreat from Rationalism in Politics
Racism
Anti-Semitism and the Birth of Zionism
Science, Racial Thought,
  and the Non-Western World

Women and Modern Thought
Antifeminism in Late-Century Thought
New Directions in Feminism

KEY TOPICS

- The dominance of science in the thought of the second half of the nineteenth century
- The conflict between church and state over education
- The effect of modernism, psychoanalysis, and the revolution in physics on intellectual life
- Racism and the resurgence of anti-Semitism
- Late-nineteenth- and early-twentieth-century developments in feminism

During *the same period that the modern nation–state developed and the Second Industrial Revolution laid the foundations for the modern material lifestyle, the ideas and concepts that have marked European thought for much of the last century took shape. Like previous intellectual changes, these arose from earlier patterns of thought. The Enlightenment provided late-nineteenth-century Europeans with a heritage of rationalism, toleration, cosmopolitanism, and appreciation of science. Romanticism led them to value feelings, imagination, national identity, and the autonomy of the artistic experience.*

By 1900, these strands of thought had become woven into a new fabric. Many of the traditional intellectual signposts were disappearing. The death of God had been proclaimed. Christianity had experienced the most severe intellectual attack in its history. The picture of the physical world prevailing since Newton had undergone major modification. The work of Darwin and Freud had challenged the special place that Western thinkers had assigned to humankind. Writers began to question the value long ascribed to rationality. The political and humanitarian ideals of liberalism and socialism gave way to new, aggressive nationalism. At the turn of the century, European intellectuals were more daring than ever before, but they were also probably less certain and less optimistic.

Many of the new ideas shaking Europe were not particularly sympathetic to the women's movement, but women could use the challenge to tradition for their own ends. In new ways, small groups of European feminists began to challenge the idea of separate gender spheres.

The New Reading Public

The social context of intellectual life changed in the latter half of the nineteenth century. For the first time in Europe, a mass reading public came into existence as more people than ever before became drawn into the world of print culture. In 1850, about half the population of western Europe and a much higher proportion of Russians were illiterate. Even those people who could technically read and write often did so poorly. That situation changed during the next half century.

Advances in Primary Education

Literacy on the Continent improved steadily from the 1860s onward, as one government after another undertook state-financed education. Hungary provided elementary education in 1868, Britain in 1870, Switzerland in 1874, Italy in 1877, and France between 1878 and 1881. The already advanced education system of Prussia was extended in various ways throughout the German Empire after 1871. The attack on illiteracy proved most successful in Britain, France, Belgium, the Netherlands, Germany, and Scandinavia, where approximately 85 percent or more of the people could read by 1900. Italy, Spain, Russia, Austria–Hungary, and the Balkans lagged well behind, with illiteracy rates of between 30 and 60 percent.

The new primary education in the basic skills of reading, writing, and elementary arithmetic reflected and generated social change. Both liberals and conservatives regarded such minimal training as necessary for orderly political behavior by the newly enfranchised voters. They also hoped that literacy might help the poor to help themselves and might create a better, more productive labor force. This side of the educational crusade

Public education became widespread in Europe during the second half of the nineteenth century and women came to dominate the profession of schoolteaching, especially at the elementary level. This 1905 photograph shows English schoolchildren going through morning drills. Corbis embodied the Enlightenment rationalist faith that right knowledge would lead to right action.

Literacy and its extension, however, soon became forces in their own right. The schoolteaching profession grew rapidly in numbers and prestige and, as noted in the previous chapter, became a major area for the employment of women. Those people who learned to read the little they were taught could continue to read much more on their own. They soon discovered that much of the education that led to better jobs and political influence was still open only to those who could afford it. Having created systems of primary education, the major nations had to give further attention to secondary education by the time of World War I. In yet another generation, the question would become one of democratic university instruction.

Reading Material for the Mass Audience

The expanding literate population created a vast market for new reading material. There was a veritable explosion of printed matter of every variety. Advances in printing and paper technology lowered production costs. The number of newspapers, books, magazines, mail-order catalogs, and libraries grew rapidly. Cheap mass-circulation newspapers, such as *Le Petit Journal* of Paris and the *Daily Mail* and *Daily Express* of London, enjoyed their first heyday. Such newspapers carried advertising that alerted readers to the new consumer products made available through the Second Industrial Revolution. Other publishers produced newspapers with specialized political or religious viewpoints. The number of monthly and quarterly journals for families, women, and freethinking intellectuals increased. Probably more people with different ideas could get into print in the late nineteenth century than ever before in European history. And more people could read their ideas than ever before.

Because many of the new readers were only marginally literate and still ignorant about many subjects, the books and journals catering to them often were mediocre. The cheap newspapers prospered on stories of sensational crimes and political scandal and on pages of advertising. Religious journals depended on denominational rivalry. A brisk market existed for pornography. Newspapers with editorials on the front page became major factors in the emerging mass politics. The news could be managed, but in central Europe more often by the government censor than by the publisher.

Social and artistic critics were correct in pointing to the low level of public taste. Nevertheless, the new education, the new readers, and the hundreds of new books and journals permitted a monumental popularization of knowledge that has become a hallmark of the contemporary world. The new literacy was the intellectual parallel of the railroad and the steamship. People could leave their original intellectual surroundings, since literacy is not an end in itself, but leads to other skills and the acquisition of other knowledge.

Science at Midcentury

In about 1850, Voltaire would still have felt at home in a general discussion of scientific concepts. The basic Newtonian picture of physical nature that he had popularized still prevailed. Scientists continued to believe that nature operated as a vast machine according to mechanical principles. At midcentury, learned persons regarded the physical world as rational, mechanical, and dependable. Its laws could be ascertained objectively through experiment and observation. Scientific theory purportedly described physical nature as it really existed. Moreover, by 1850 science had come to have a strong institutional life in French and German universities and in new professional societies. The word *scientist* had been invented in the early 1830s by William Whewell of Cambridge University and had entered common usage by the end of the century.

Comte, Positivism, and the Prestige of Science

During the early nineteenth century, science had continued to establish itself as the model for all human knowledge. The French philosopher Auguste Comte (1798–1857), a late child of the Enlightenment and a one-time follower of Saint-Simon, developed a philosophy of human intellectual development that culminated in science. In *The Positive Philosophy* (1830–1842), Comte argued that human thought had developed in three stages. In the first, or theological, stage, physical nature was explained in terms of the action of divinities or spirits. In the second, or metaphysical, stage, abstract principles were regarded as the operative agencies of nature. In the final, or positive, stage, explanations of nature became matters of exact description of phenomena, without recourse to an unobservable operative principle.

Physical science had, in Comte's view, entered the positive stage, and similar thinking should penetrate other areas of analysis, he thought. In particular, Comte believed that positive laws of social behavior could be discovered in the same fashion as laws of physical nature. He is thus generally regarded as the father of sociology. Works like Comte's helped to convince learned Europeans that genuine knowledge in any area must resemble scientific knowledge.

From the middle of the nineteenth century onward, the links of science to the technology of the Second Industrial Revolution made the general European public aware of science and technology as never before. The British Fabian socialist Beatrice Webb (1858–1943) recalled this situation from her youth:

> Who will deny that the men of science were the leading British intellectuals of that period; that it was they who stood out as men of genius with international reputations; that it was they who were the self-confident militants of the period; that it was they who were routing the theologians, confounding the mystics, imposing their theories on philosophers, their inventions on capitalists, and their discoveries on medical men; whilst they were at the same time snubbing the artists, ignoring the poets, and even casting doubts on the capacity of the politicians?[1]

Her remarks would have applied in virtually every industrialized nation in Europe. During the third quarter of the century, writers spoke of a religion of science that would explain all nature without resorting to supernaturalism. Popularizers, such as Thomas Henry Huxley (1825–1895) in Britain and Ernst Haeckel (1834–1919) in Germany, wrote and lectured widely on scientific topics. They argued that science held the answer to the major questions of life. They worked for government support of scientific research and for the inclusion of science in the schools and universities.

In two works of seminal importance, The Origin of Species *(1859) and* The Descent of Man *(1871), Charles Darwin articulated the theory of evolution by natural selection and applied that theory to human beings. The result was a storm of controversy that affected not only biology but also religion, philosophy, sociology, and even politics.* Bildarchiv Preussischer Kulturbesitz

Darwin's Theory of Natural Selection

In 1859 Charles Darwin (1809–1882) published *The Origin of Species*, which carried the mechanical interpretation of physical nature into the world of living things. The book proved to be one of the seminal works of Western thought and earned Darwin the honor of being regarded as the "Newton of biology." Both Darwin and his book have been much misunderstood. He did not originate the concept of evolution, which had been discussed widely before he wrote. What he and Alfred Russel Wallace (1823–1913) did, working independently, was to formulate the principle of natural selection, which explained how species had changed or evolved over time. Earlier writers had believed *that* evolution might occur; Darwin and Wallace explained *how* it could occur.

Drawing on Malthus, the two scientists contended that more seeds and living organisms come into existence than can survive in their environment. Those organisms having some marginal advantage in the struggle for existence live long enough to propagate their kind. This principle of

survival of the fittest Darwin called *natural selection*. The principle was naturalistic and mechanistic. Its operation required no guiding mind behind the development and change in organic nature. What neither Darwin nor anyone else in his day could explain was the origin of those chance variations that provided some living things with the marginal chance for survival. Only after 1900, when the work on heredity of the Austrian monk, Gregor Mendel (1822–1884), received public attention, did the mystery of those variations begin to be unraveled.

Darwin's and Wallace's theory represented the triumph of naturalistic explanation, which removed the idea of purpose from organic nature. Eyes were not made for seeing according to the rational wisdom and purpose of God, but had developed mechanistically over time. Thus, the theory of evolution through natural selection not only contradicted the biblical narrative of the Creation, but also undermined the deistic argument for the existence of God from the design of the universe. Moreover, Darwin's work undermined the whole concept of fixity in nature or the universe at large. The world was a realm of flux and change. The idea that physical and organic nature might be constantly changing allowed people in the late nineteenth

[1] Beatrice Webb, *My Apprenticeship* (London: Longmans, Green, 1926), pp. 130–131.

century to believe that society, values, customs, and beliefs should also change.

In 1871 Darwin carried his work a step further. In *The Descent of Man*, he applied the principle of evolution by natural selection to human beings. Darwin was hardly the first person to treat human beings as animals, but his arguments brought greater plausibility to that point of view. He contended that humankind's moral nature and religious sentiments, as well as its physical frame, had developed naturalistically largely in response to the requirements of survival. Neither the origin nor the character of humankind on Earth, in Darwin's view, required the existence of a God for their explanation. Not since Copernicus had removed the Earth from the center of the universe had the pride of Western human beings received so sharp a blow.

Darwin's theory of evolution by natural selection was controversial from the moment of the publication of *The Origin of Species*. It encountered criticism from both the religious and the scientific communities. By the end of the century, scientists widely accepted the concept of evolution, but not yet Darwin's mechanism of natural selection. The acceptance of the latter within the scientific community really dates from the 1920s and 1930s, when Darwin's theory was combined with the insights of modern genetics.

Science and Ethics

One area in which science came to have a new significance was social thought and ethics. Certain philosophers modeled theories of ethics on science. They applied the concept of the struggle for survival to human social relationships. The phrase "survival of the fittest" pre-dated Darwin and reflected the competitive outlook of classical economics. Darwin's use of the phrase gave it the prestige associated with advanced science.

The most famous advocate of evolutionary ethics was Herbert Spencer (1820–1903), a British philosopher. Spencer, a strong individualist, believed that human society progressed through competition. If the weak received too much protection, the rest of humankind was the loser. In Spencer's work, struggle against one's fellow human beings became a kind of ethical imperative. The concept could be applied to justify the avoidance of aiding the poor and the working class or to justify the domination of colonial peoples or to advocate aggressive competition among nations. Evolutionary ethics and similar concepts, all of which are usually termed *social Darwinism*, often came close to saying that might makes right.

One of the chief opponents of such thinking was Thomas Henry Huxley, the great defender of Darwin.

In 1893, Huxley declared that the physical cosmic process of evolution was at odds with the process of human ethical development. The struggle in nature held no ethical implications except to demonstrate how human beings should *not* behave. (See "T. H. Huxley Criticizes Evolutionary Ethics.")

Scientists and their admirers enjoyed a supreme confidence during the last half of the century. They genuinely believed that they had, for all intents and purposes, discovered all that might be discovered. The issues for science in the future would be the extension of acknowledged principles and the refinement of measurement. The turn of the century, however, held a much more brilliant and rapidly expanding horizon for science as a much more complicated picture of nature developed. Before examining those new departures, we must see how the cult of science affected religious thought and practice.

Christianity and the Church under Siege

The nineteenth century was one of the most difficult periods in the history of the organized Christian churches. Many European intellectuals left the faith. The secular, liberal nation–states attacked the political and social influence of the church. The expansion of population and the growth of cities challenged its organizational capacity to meet the modern age. Yet during all of this turmoil, the Protestant and Catholic churches still made considerable headway at the popular level.

Intellectual Skepticism

The intellectual attack on Christianity arose on the grounds of its historical credibility, its scientific accuracy, and its pronounced morality. The *philosophes* of the Enlightenment had delighted in pointing out contradictions in the Bible. The historical scholarship of the nineteenth century brought new issues to the fore.

HISTORY   In 1835, David Friedrich Strauss (1808–1874) published *The Life of Jesus*, in which he questioned whether the Bible provided any genuine historical evidence about Jesus. Strauss contended that the story of Jesus was a myth that had arisen from the particular social and intellectual conditions of first-century Palestine. Jesus' character and life represented the aspirations of the people of that time and place, rather than events that had actually occurred. Other authors also published skeptical examinations of the life of Jesus.

During the second half of the century, scholars such as Julius Wellhausen (1844–1918) in Germany, Ernst

T. H. Huxley Criticizes Evolutionary Ethics

T. H. Huxley (1825–1895) was a British scientist who had been among Darwin's strongest defenders. He was also an outspoken advocate for the advancement of science in the late nineteenth century. Huxley, however, became a major critic of social Darwinism, which attempted to deduce ethical principles from evolutionary processes involving struggle in nature. Drawing a strong distinction between the cosmic process of evolution and the social process of ethical development, he argued in Evolution and Ethics *(1893) that human ethical progress occurred through combating the cosmic process.*

❖ *What does Huxley mean by the "cosmic process"? Why does he equate "social progress" with the "ethical process"? In this passage, does Huxley present human society as part of nature or as something that may be separate from nature?*

Men in society are undoubtedly subject to the cosmic process. As among other animals, multiplication goes on without cessation, and involves severe competition for the means of support. The struggle for existence tends to eliminate those less fitted to adapt themselves to the circumstances of their existence. The strongest, the most self-assertive, tend to tread down the weaker. But the influence of the cosmic process on the evolution of society is the greater the more rudimentary its civilization. Social progress means a checking of the cosmic process at every step and the substitution for it of another, which may be called the ethical process; the end of which is not the survival of those who may happen to be the fittest, in respect of the whole of the conditions which obtain, but of those who are ethically the best.

As I have already urged, the practice of that which is ethically best—what we call goodness or virtue—involves a course of conduct which, in all respects, is opposed to that which leads to success in the cosmic struggle for existence. In place of ruthless self-assertion it demands self-restraint; in place of thrusting aside, or treading down, all competitors, it requires that the individual shall not merely respect, but shall help his fellows; its influence is directed, not so much to the survival of the fittest, as to the fitting of as many as possible to survive. It repudiates the gladiatorial theory of existence.

It is from neglect of these plain considerations that the fanatical individualism of our time attempts to apply the analogy of cosmic nature to society....

Let us understand, once for all, that the ethical progress of society depends, not on imitating the cosmic process, still less in running away from it, but in combating it.

From T. H. Huxley, *Evolution and Ethics* (London: Macmillan & Co., 1894), as quoted in Franklin L. Baumer, *Main Currents of Western Thought: Readings in Western European Intellectual History from the Middle Ages to the Present*, 3d ed., rev. (New York: Alfred A. Knopf, 1970), pp. 561–562.

Renan (1823–1892) in France, and William Robertson Smith (1847–1894) in Great Britain contended that human authors had written and revised the books of the Bible with the problems of Jewish society and politics in mind. The Bible was not an inspired book, but had, like the Homeric epics, been written by normal human beings in a primitive society. This questioning of the historical validity of the Bible caused more literate men and women to lose faith in Christianity than any other single cause.

SCIENCE The march of science also undermined Christianity. This blow was particularly cruel because many eighteenth-century writers had led Christians to believe that the scientific examination of nature provided a strong buttress for their faith. William Paley's (1743–1805) *Natural Theology* (1802) and books by numerous scientists had enshrined that belief. The geology of Charles Lyell (1797–1875) suggested that the Earth was much older than the biblical records contended. By looking to natural causes to explain floods, mountains, and valleys, Lyell removed the miraculous hand of God from the physical development of the Earth. Darwin's theory cast doubt on the doctrine of the Creation. His ideas and those of other writers suggested that the moral nature of humankind could be explained without appeal to God. Finally, anthropologists, psychologists, and sociologists proposed that religion itself and religious sentiments were just one more set of natural phenomena. (See "A German Scientist Announces the End of the Idea of Design in Nature.")

A German Scientist Announces the End of the Idea of Design in Nature

Ernst Haeckel (1834–1919) was a German biologist and philosopher who wrote widely on scientific topics and vigorously attacked traditional religious faith. In 1899 he published The Riddle of the Universe, *one of the era's most wide-ranging proclamations of the power of science. He made sweeping claims to establish the supremacy of science as a mode of thought and scientists as important citizens. In the passage that follows, he contends that the concept of a divine design has been banished from all scientific thinking, including biological thought. Two points should be noted. First, Haeckel used a more aggressive language than Darwin did. Second, at the very time that he declared that Darwin had "proved" certain things, Darwin's ideas remained hotly contested within the scientific community itself, often for reasons that had nothing to do with religion.*

❖ *What role, if any, does Haeckel see for the concept of design in contemporary science? How does he present Darwin as having banished the idea of design from the biological sciences? What is the significance of his stating that so long as questions surrounding human nature are set aside, design does not play a role in the biological sciences?*

At the close of the nineteenth century...no scientist ever asks seriously of the "purpose" of any single phenomenon...Is any astronomer likely to inquire seriously to-day into the purpose of planetary motion, or a mineralogist to seek design in the structure of a crystal? Does the physicist investigate the purpose of electric force, or the chemist that of atomic weight? We may confidently answer in the negative—certainly not, in the sense that God, or a purposive natural force, had at some time created these fundamental laws of the mechanism of the universe with a definite design, and causes them to work daily in accordance with his rational will. The anthropomorphic notion of a deliberate architect and ruler of the world has gone forever from this field; the "eternal, iron laws of nature" have taken his place.

But the idea of design has a very great significance and application in the *organic* world. We do undeniably perceive a purpose in the structure and in the life of an organism. The plant and the animal seem to be controlled by definite design in the combination of their several parts, just as clearly as we see in the machines which man invents, and constructs....

Darwin was the first to point out that the "struggle for life" is the unconscious regulator which controls the reciprocal action of heredity and adaptation in the gradual transformation of species; it is the great "selective divinity" which, by a purely "natural choice," without preconceived design, creates new forms, just as selective man creates new types by an "artificial choice" with a definite design....

Throughout the whole of astronomy, geology, physics, and chemistry there is no question to-day of a "moral order," or a personal God, whose "hand hath disposed all things in wisdom and understanding." And the same must be said of the entire field of biology, the whole constitution and history of organic nature, if we set aside the question of man for the moment. Darwin has not only proved by his theory of selection that the orderly processes in the life and structure of animals and plants have arisen by mechanical laws without any preconceived design, but he has shown us in the "struggle for life" the powerful natural force which has exerted supreme control over the entire course of organic evolution for millions of years.

From Ernest Haeckel, *The Riddle of the Universe*, Joseph McCambe, tr. (New York: Harper and Brothers, 1901), as quoted in Franklin L.Baumer, *Main Currents of Western Thought: Readings in Western European Intellectual History from the Middle Ages to the Present*, 3d ed., rev. (New York: Alfred A. Knopf, 1970), pp. 565–567.

MORALITY Other intellectuals questioned the morality of Christianity. The old issue of immoral biblical stories was again raised. Much more important, the moral character of the Old Testament God came under fire. His cruelty and unpredictability did not fit well with the progressive, tolerant, rational values of liberals. They also wondered about the morality of the New Testament God, who would sacrifice for his own satisfaction the only perfect being ever to walk the Earth. Many of the clergy began to ask themselves if they could honestly preach doctrines they felt to be immoral.

During the last quarter of the century, this moral attack on Christianity came from another direction. Writers like Friedrich Nietzsche (1844–1900) in Germany portrayed Christianity as a religion of sheep that glorified weakness rather than the strength life required. Christianity demanded a useless and debilitating sacrifice of the flesh and spirit, rather than full-blooded heroic living and daring. Nietzsche once observed, "War and courage have accomplished more great things than love of neighbor."[2]

These widespread skeptical intellectual currents directly influenced only the upper levels of educated society. Yet they created a climate in which Christianity lost much of its intellectual respectability. Fewer educated people joined the clergy. More and more people found that they could lead their lives with little or no reference to Christianity. The secularism of everyday life proved as harmful to the faith as the direct attacks. This situation was especially prevalent in the cities, which were growing faster than the capacity of the churches to meet the

---

[2]Walter Kaufmann, ed. and trans., *The Portable Nietzsche* (New York: Viking, 1967), p. 159.

challenge. There was not even enough room in urban churches for potential worshipers to sit. Whole generations of the urban poor grew up with little or no experience of the church as an institution or of Christianity as a religious faith.

Conflict between Church and State

The secular state of the nineteenth century clashed with both the Protestant and the Roman Catholic churches. Liberals generally disliked the dogma and the political privileges of the established churches. National states were often suspicious of the supranational character of the Roman Catholic Church. The primary area of conflict between the state and the churches, however, was the expanding systems of education. Previously, most education in Europe had taken place in schools run by religious orders or denominations. The churches feared that future generations would emerge from the new state-financed schools without the rudiments of religious teaching. From 1870 through the turn of the century, religious education was heatedly debated in every major country.

GREAT BRITAIN In Great Britain, the Education Act of 1870 provided for the construction of state-supported schools run by elected school boards, whereas earlier the government had given small grants to religious schools. The new schools were to be built in areas where the religious denominations did not provide satisfactory education. There was rivalry not only between the Anglican Church and the state, but also between the Anglican Church and the Nonconformist denominations—that is, those Protestant denominations that were not part

The conflict between church and state disrupted German politics during the 1870s. In this contemporary cartoon, Bismarck and Pope Pius IX seek to checkmate each other in a game of chess. Bildarchiv Preussischer Kulturbesitz

Zwischen Berlin und Rom.

of the Church of England. There was intense local hostility among all these groups. The churches of all denominations had to oppose improvements in education because these increased the costs of their own schools. In the Education Act of 1902, the government decided to provide state support for both religious and nonreligious schools, but imposed the same educational standards on each.

FRANCE The British conflict was calm compared with that in France, which had a dual system of Catholic and public schools. Under the Falloux Law of 1850, the local priest provided religious education in the public schools. The conservative French Catholic Church and the Third French Republic were hostile to each other. Between 1878 and 1886, the government passed a series of educational laws sponsored by Jules Ferry (1832–1893). The Ferry Laws replaced religious instruction in the public schools with civic training. Members of religious orders could no longer teach in the public schools, the number of which was to be expanded. After the Dreyfus affair, the French Catholic Church again paid a price for its reactionary politics. The Radical government of Pierre Waldeck-Rousseau (1846–1904), drawn from pro-Dreyfus groups, suppressed the religious orders. In 1905 the Napoleonic Concordat was terminated, and church and state were totally separated.

GERMANY AND THE *KULTURKAMPF* The most extreme example of church–state conflict occurred in Germany during the 1870s. At unification, the German Catholic hierarchy had wanted freedom for the churches guaranteed in the constitution. Bismarck left the matter to the discretion of each federal state, but he soon felt that the activity of the Roman Catholic Church and the Catholic Center Party threatened the political unity of the new German Empire. Through administrative orders in 1870 and 1871, Bismarck removed both Catholic and Protestant clergy from overseeing local education in Prussia and set education under state direction. This secularization of education represented the beginning of a concerted attack on the independence of the Catholic Church in Germany.

The "May Laws" of 1873, which applied to Prussia, but not to the entire German Empire, required priests to be educated in German schools and universities and to pass state-administered examinations. The state could veto the appointments of priests. The legislation abolished the disciplinary power of the Pope and the church over the clergy and transferred it to the state. When the bishops and many of the clergy refused to obey these laws, Bismarck used the police against them. In 1876, he had either arrested or driven out all the Catholic bishops from Prussia.

In the end, Bismarck's *Kulturkampf* ("cultural struggle") against the Catholic Church failed. Not for the first time, Christian martyrs aided resistance to persecution. By the end of the 1870s, the chancellor had abandoned his attack. He had gained state control of education and civil laws governing marriage only at the price of provoking long-term Catholic resentment against the German state. The *Kulturkampf* was probably the greatest blunder of Bismarck's career.

Areas of Religious Revival

The successful German Catholic resistance to the intrusions of the secular state illustrates the continuing vitality of Christianity during this period of intellectual and political hardship facing the church. In Great Britain, both the Anglican Church and the Nonconformist denominations experienced considerable growth in their membership and raised vast sums of money for new churches and schools. In Ireland, the 1870s saw a widespread Catholic devotional revival. In France, after the defeat by Prussia, priests organized special pilgrimages by train to shrines for thousands of penitents who believed that France had been defeated because of their sins. The cult of the miracle of Lourdes grew during these years. There were efforts by churches of all denominations to give more attention to the urban poor.

In effect, the last half of the nineteenth century witnessed the final great effort to Christianize Europe. It was well organized, well led, and well financed. It failed not from want of effort, but because the population of Europe had simply outstripped the resources of the churches. This persistent liveliness of the churches accounts in part for the intense hostility of its enemies.

The Roman Catholic Church and the Modern World

The most striking feature of Christian religious revival amidst turmoil and persecution was the resilience of the papacy. The brief hope for a liberal pontificate from Pope Pius IX (r. 1846–1878) vanished on the night he fled the turmoil in Rome in November 1848. In the 1860s, embittered by the process of Italian unification, he launched a counteroffensive against liberalism in thought and deed. In 1864 he issued the *Syllabus of Errors*, which condemned all the major tenets of political liberalism and modern thought. He set the Roman Catholic Church squarely against contemporary science, philosophy, and politics.

In 1869, the Pope summoned the First Vatican Council. The next year, through the political manipulations of the pontiff and against much opposition from many bishops, the council promulgated the dogma of the infallibility of the Pope when speaking officially on matters of faith and morals. No earlier Pope had gone so far in asserting centralized authority within the Church. The First Vatican Council ended in 1870, when Italian troops invaded Rome at the outbreak of the Franco–Prussian War. Thereafter the territory of the papacy was limited to the Vatican City, and the papacy made no formal accommodation to the Italian state until well into the twentieth century. The key to understanding the papacy of Pius IX is the recognition that he and many other Roman Catholics among both clergy and laity believed that the only way the Roman Catholic Church could sustain itself in the modern world of nation–states with large electorates was to center the authority of the Church in the papacy itself. In this regard, the spiritual authority of the papacy came to be a substitute for its previous political and temporal authority.

Pius IX died in 1878 and was succeeded by Leo XIII (r. 1878–1903). The new Pope, who was sixty-eight years old at the time of his election, sought to make accommodations to the modern age and to address the great social questions. He looked to the philosophical tradition of Thomas Aquinas (1225– 1274) to reconcile the claims of faith and reason. Leo's encyclicals of 1885 and 1890 permitted Catholics to participate in the politics of liberal states.

Leo's most important prouncement on public issues was the encylical *Rerum Novarum* (1891). In that document, he defended private property, religious education, and religious control of the marriage laws and he condemned socialism and Marxism. He also declared, however, that employers should treat their employees justly, pay them proper wages, and permit them to organize labor unions. He supported laws and regulations to protect the conditions of labor. The Pope urged that modern society be organized according to corporate groups, including people from various classes, who might cooperate according to Christian principles. The corporate society, based on medieval social organization, was to be an alternative to both socialism and competitive capitalism. On the basis of Leo XIII's pronouncements, democratic Catholic political parties and Catholic trade unions were founded throughout Europe. (See "Leo XIII Considers the Social Question in European Politics.")

Pius X, who reigned from 1903 to 1914 and who has been proclaimed a saint, hoped to resist the intrusions of modern thought and to restore traditional devotional life. Between 1903 and 1907, he condemned Catholic modernism, a movement of modern biblical criticism within the church, and in 1910 he required all priests to take an anti-Modernist oath. Pius X thus set the church once more squarely against the intellectual currents of the day, and the struggle between Catholicism and modern thought continued. Although Pius X did not strongly support the social policy of Leo XIII, the Catholic Church continued to permit its members to participate actively in social and political movements.

Toward a Twentieth-Century Frame of Mind

The last quarter of the nineteenth century and the first decade of the twentieth century constituted the crucible of modern Western and European thought. During this period, the kind of fundamental reassessment that Darwin's work had previously made necessary in biology and in understanding the place of human beings in nature became writ large in other areas of thinking. Philosophers, scientists, psychologists, and artists began to portray physical reality, human nature, and human society in ways different from those of the past. Their new concepts challenged the major presuppositions of mid-nineteenth-century science, rationalism, liberalism, and bourgeois morality.

Science: The Revolution in Physics

The changes in the scientific worldview originated within the scientific community itself. By the late 1870s, considerable discontent existed over the excessive realism of midcentury science. It was thought that many scientists believed that their mechanistic models, solid atoms, and absolute time and space actually described the real universe.

In 1883 Ernst Mach (1838–1916) published *The Science of Mechanics*, in which he urged that scientists consider their concepts descriptive not of the physical world, but of the sensations experienced by the scientific observer. Scientists could describe only the sensations, not the physical world that underlay those sensations. In line with Mach, the French scientist and mathematician Henri Poincaré (1854–1912) urged that the concepts and theories of scientists be regarded as hypothetical constructs of the human mind rather than as descriptions of the true state of nature. In 1911, Hans Vaihinger (1852–1933) suggested that the concepts of science be considered "as if" descriptions of the physical world. By World War I, few scientists believed any longer that they could portray the "truth" about physical reality. Rather, they saw themselves as recording the observations of instruments and as setting forth useful hypothetical or symbolic models of nature.

Leo XIII Considers the Social Question in European Politics

In his 1891 encyclical Rerum Novarum, *Pope Leo XIII addressed the social question in European politics, providing the Catholic Church's answer to secular calls for social reforms. The Pope denied the socialist claim that class conflict was the natural state of affairs. He urged employers to seek just and peaceful relations with workers.*

❖ *How does Leo XIII reject the concept of class conflict? What responsibilities does he assign to the rich and to the poor? Are the two classes' responsibilities equal? What kinds of social reform might emerge from these ideas?*

The great mistake that is made in the matter now under consideration is to possess oneself of the idea that class is naturally hostile to class; that rich and poor are intended by Nature to live at war with one another. So irrational and so false is this view that the exact contrary is the truth....Each requires the other; capital cannot do without labour, nor labour without capital. Mutual agreement results in pleasantness and good order; perpetual conflict necessarily produces confusion and outrage. Now, in preventing such strife as this, and in making it impossible, the efficacy of Christianity is marvelous and manifold....Religion teaches the labouring man and the workman to carry out honestly and well all equitable agreements freely made; never to injure capital, or to outrage the person of an employer; never to employ violence in representing his own cause, or to engage in riot or disorder; and to have nothing to do with men of evil principles, who work upon the people with artful promises and raise hopes which usually end in disaster and in repentance when too late. Religion teaches the rich man and the employer that their work people are not their slaves; that they must respect in every man his dignity as a man and as a Christian; that labour is nothing to be ashamed of, if we listen to right reason and to Christian philosophy, but is an honourable employment, enabling a man to sustain his life in an upright and creditable way; and that it is shameful and inhuman to treat men like chattels to make money by, or to look upon them merely as so much muscle or physical power. Thus, again, Religion teaches that, as among the workman's concerns are Religion herself and things spiritual and mental, the employer is bound to see that he has time for the duties of piety; that he be not exposed to corrupting influences and dangerous occasions; and that he be not led away to neglect his home and family or to squander his wages. Then, again, the employer must never tax his work people beyond their strength, nor employ them in work unsuited to their sex or age. His great and principal obligation is to give every one that which is just.

As quoted in F. S. Nitti, *Catholic Socialism*, trans. by Mary Mackintosh (London: S. Sonnenschein, 1895), p. 409.

X-RAYS AND RADIATION   Discoveries in the laboratory paralleled the philosophical challenge to nineteenth-century science. With those discoveries, the comfortable world of supposedly "complete" nineteenth-century physics vanished forever. In December 1895, Wilhelm Roentgen (1845–1923) published a paper on his discovery of X-rays, a form of energy that penetrated various opaque materials. Major steps in the exploration of radioactivity followed within months of the publication of his paper.

In 1896 Henri Becquerel (1852–1908), through a series of experiments that built upon Roentgen's work, discovered that uranium emitted a similar form of energy. The next year, J. J. Thomson (1856–1940), working in the Cavendish Laboratory of Cambridge University, formulated the theory of the electron. The interior world of the atom had become a new area for human exploration, which continues to this day. In 1902 Ernest Rutherford (1871–1937), who had been Thomson's assistant, explained the cause of radiation through the disintegration of the atoms of radioactive materials. Shortly thereafter, he speculated on the immense store of energy present in the atom.

THEORIES OF QUANTUM ENERGY, RELATIVITY, AND UNCERTAINTY   The discovery of radioactivity and discontent with the existing mechanical models led to revolutionary theories in physics. In 1900, Max Planck (1858–1947) pioneered the articulation of the quantum theory of energy, according to which energy is a series of discrete quantities, or packets, rather than a continuous stream. In 1905, Albert Einstein (1879–1955) published his first epoch-making papers on relativity

Marie Curie (1869–1934) and Pierre Curie (1859–1906) were two of the most important figures in the advance of physics and chemistry. Marie was born in Poland but worked in France for most of her life. She is credited with the discovery of radium, for which she was awarded the Nobel Prize in Chemistry in 1911. Bildarchiv Preussischer Kulturbesitz

in which he contended that time and space exist not separately, but rather as a combined continuum. Moreover, the measurement of time and space depends on the observer as well as on the entities being measured.

In 1927 Werner Heisenberg (1901–1976) set forth his famous uncertainty principle, according to which the behavior of subatomic particles is a matter of statistical probability rather than of exactly determinable cause and effect. Much that only fifty years earlier had seemed certain and unquestionable about the physical universe had now become ambiguous.

The mathematical complexity of twentieth-century physics meant that, despite valiant efforts on the part of scientific writers, science would rarely again be successfully popularized. At the same time, through applied technology and further research in chemistry, physics, and medicine, science affected daily living more than ever before in human history.

Scientists from the late nineteenth century onward became the most successful group of Western intellectuals in gaining the financial support of governments and private institutions for the pursuit of their research. They did so by relating the success of science to the economic progress, military security, and the health of their various nations. In all those regards, science, through pure research, medical knowledge, and technological change, has affected modern life more significantly than any other intellectual activity.

Literature: Realism and Naturalism

Between 1850 and 1914, the moral certainties of learned and middle-class Europeans underwent changes no less radical than their concepts of the physical universe. The realist movement in literature portrayed the hypocrisy, the physical and psychic brutality, and the dullness that underlay bourgeois life and society. The realist and naturalist writers brought scientific objectivity and observation to their work. By using the midcentury cult of science so vital to the middle class, they confronted readers with the harsh realities of life around them. Realism rejected the romantic idealization of nature, the poor, love, and polite society. Realist novelists portrayed the dark, degraded, and dirty side of life, almost, some people thought, for its own sake.

An earlier generation of writers, including Charles Dickens (1812–1870) and Honoré de Balzac (1799–1850), had portrayed the cruelty of industrial life and of a society based wholly on money. Other authors, such as George Eliot (born Mary Ann Evans, 1819–1880), had paid close attention to the details of the scenes and the characters she portrayed. There had, however, always been room in their works for imagination, fancy, and artistry. They had felt a better moral world possible through Christian values or humane efforts or, for Eliot, through an appreciation of humanity arising from Auguste Comte's thought.

The major figures of late-century realism examined the dreary and unseemly side of life without being certain whether a better life was possible. In good Darwinian fashion, they regarded and portrayed human beings as subject to the passions, the materialistic determinism, and the pressures of the environment like any other animals. Most of them, however, also saw society itself as perpetuating evil.

FLAUBERT AND ZOLA Critics have often considered Gustave Flaubert's (1821–1880) *Madame Bovary* (1857), with its story of colorless provincial life and a woman's hapless search for love in and outside of marriage, as the first genuinely realistic novel. The work portrayed life without heroism, purpose, or even simple civility.

But the author who turned realism into a movement was Émile Zola (1840–1902). He found artistic inspiration in Claude Bernard's (1813–1878) *Introduction to the Study of Experimental Medicine* (1865). Zola argued that he could write an experimental novel in which he would observe and report the characters and their actions as the scientist might relate events within a laboratory experiment. He once declared, "I have simply done on living bodies the work of analysis which surgeons perform on corpses."[3] He believed that absolute physical and psychological determinism ruled human events in the same manner as determinism prevailed in the physical world. (See "Émile Zola Defines the Naturalistic Novel.")

Between 1871 and 1893, Zola published twenty volumes of novels exploring subjects normally untouched by writers. In *L'Assommoir* (1877) he discussed the problem of alcoholism, and in *Nana* (1880) he examined the life of a prostitute. In other works, he considered the defeat of the French army in 1870 and the social strife arising from attempts to

[3]Quoted in George J. Becker, *Documents of Modern Literary Realism* (Princeton, NJ: Princeton University Press, 1963), p. 159.

Émile Zola of France was the master of the realistic novel. Émile Zola, 1840–1902. Franzosischer Schriftsteller. Gemalde von Edouard Manet, 1868. Original: Paris, Louvre. Photograph: Lauros–Giraudon. (c) Bildarchiv Preussischer Kulturbesitz, Berlin.

Henrick Ibsen's plays challenged middle-class values in one area of life after another. He particularly questioned the values surrounding marriage and the family, Bildarchiv Preussischer Kulturbesitz

organize labor. Zola refused to turn his pen or his readers' thoughts away from the most ugly aspects of life. Nothing in his purview received the light of hope or the aura of romance. Although polite critics faulted his taste and middle-class moralists condemned his subject matter, Zola enjoyed a wide following in France and elsewhere. As noted in Chapter 23, he took a leading role in the public defense of Captain Dreyfus.

IBSEN AND SHAW The Norwegian playwright Henrik Ibsen (1828–1906) carried realism into the dramatic presentation of domestic life. He sought to achieve new modes of social awareness and to strip away the illusory mask of middle-class morality. His most famous play is *A Doll's House* (1879). Its chief character, Nora, has a narrow-minded middle-class husband who cannot tolerate any independence of character or thought on her part. She finally confronts this situation, and the play ends as she leaves him, slamming the door behind her. In *Ghosts* (1881), a respectable middle-class woman must deal with a son suffering from syphilis inherited from her husband. In *The Master Builder* (1892), an aging architect kills himself while trying to impress a young woman who perhaps loves him. Ibsen's works were extremely controversial. He had dared to attack

Émile Zola Defines the Naturalistic Novel

No single European novelist became so identified with naturalism in literature as the French writer Émile Zola. In an essay first published in a Russian newspaper and then in a collection of essays in 1880, Zola directly linked the methods and goals of the experimental novel to those of contemporary science. He suggested that through precise exploration of the lives of his characters, the novelist might contribute to the social sciences and to future legislation. He criticized as idealistic writers who looked to fiction and metaphysics rather than to the precise insights of science.

❖ *How does Zola attempt to allow the novel to benefit from the contemporary prestige of science? Why does he see his effort as a moral one? Why might he think that it was necessary for readers to believe that the novel possessed social utility? How might one argue that Zola surrenders any independent moral or social value of literature by making it subservient to science and social improvement?*

We shall enter upon a century in which man...will make use of nature and will utilize its law to produce upon the earth the greatest possible amount of justice and freedom.... Here is our role as intelligent beings to penetrate to the wherefore of things, to become superior to these things, and to reduce them to a condition of subservient machinery.

Well, this dream of the physiologist and the experimental doctor is also that of the novelist, who employs the experimental method in his study of man as a simple individual and as a social animal. Their object is ours; we also desire to master certain phenomena of an intellectual and personal order, to be able to direct them. We are... experimental moralists, showing by experiment in what way a passion acts in a certain social condition. The day which we gain control of the mechanism of this passion we can treat it and reduce it, or at least make it inoffensive as possible. And in this consists the practical utility and high morality of our naturalistic works which experiment on man, and which dissect piece by piece this human machinery in order to set it going through the influence of the envi-

ronment.... In this way we shall construct a practical sociology, and our work will be a help to political and economic sciences. I do not know...of a more noble work, nor of a grander application. To be the master of good and evil, to regulate life, to regulate society...to give justice a solid foundation by solving through experiment the questions of criminality—is not this being the most useful and the most moral workers in the human workshop?

...In our role as experimental moralists we show mechanism of the useful and the useless, we disengage the determinism of the human and social phenomena so that, in their turn, the legislators can one day dominate and control these phenomena. In a word we are working with the whole country toward that great object, the conquest of nature and the increase of man's power a hundredfold. Compare with ours the work of the idealistic writers, who rely upon the irrational and the supernatural, and whose every flight upward is followed by a deeper fall into metaphysical chaos. We are the ones who possess strength and morality.

From Émile Zola, "Naturalism on the Stage," (1880), from Émile Zola, *The Experimental Novel and Other Essays*, Belle M. Sherman, tr., copyright © Haskell House, New York.

sentimentality, the ideal of the female "angel of the house," and the cloak of respectability that hung so insecurely over the middle-class family.

One of Ibsen's greatest champions was the Irish writer George Bernard Shaw (1856–1950), who spent most of his life in England. During the late 1880s, Shaw vigorously defended Ibsen's work. He

went on to make his own realistic onslaught against romanticism and false respectability. In *Mrs. Warren's Profession* (1893), a play long censored in England, he explored prostitution. In *Arms and the Man* (1894) and *Man and Superman* (1903) he heaped scorn on the romantic ideals of love and war, and in *Androcles and the Lion*

(1913) he pilloried Christianity. Shaw added to the impact of his plays by writing long critical prefaces in which he emphasized his social criticism.

These and many other realist writers believed it the duty of the artist to portray reality and the commonplace. In dissecting what they considered the "real" world, they helped to change the moral perception of the good life. They refused to let existing public opinion dictate what they wrote about or how they treated their subjects. By presenting their audiences with unmentionable subjects, they sought to remove the veneer of hypocrisy that had previously forbidden such discussion. They hoped to destroy social and moral illusions and to compel the public to face reality. That change in itself seemed good. Few of the realist writers who raised these problems posed solutions to them. They often left their readers unable to sustain old values and uncertain about where to find new ones.

Modernism

From the 1870s onward throughout Europe, a new multifaceted movement usually called modernism touched virtually all the arts. Like realism, modernism was critical of middle-class society and accepted morality. Modernism, however, whether in music, art, or literature, was not deeply concerned with social issues. What drove the modernists in every field was a concern for the aesthetic or the beautiful. The English essayist Walter Pater (1839–1903) set the tone of the movement when he declared in 1877 that art "constantly aspires to the condition of music."

Across the spectrum of the arts, modernists tried to break the received forms and to create new forms. To many contemporaries, the new forms seemed formless. Practitioners of the modern believed that each of the arts should and could influence the others. Painters gave their works musical titles, as did James Abbott McNeill Whistler (1834–1903) in *Nocturnes*. Musicians combined material from many sources. In his at first notorious and then famous ballet, *The Rite of Spring* (1913), Igor Stravinsky (1882–1971) combined jazz rhythms, dissonance, and anthropological theory. Pablo Picasso (1881–1973) and other artists associated with cubism constructed paintings that involved viewing objects from a variety of angles at the same time and drew inspiration from primitive masks they saw in Paris anthropological museums. In England, practitioners of what was called the *New Sculpture* mixed various materials in richly sensuous statues. Other sculptors rejected traditional forms entirely. For all of these artists, the immediate aesthetic experience of a work of art, whatever its medium, dominated other concerns. (See "Art & the West.")

Virginia Woolf charted the changing sentiments of a world with most of the nineteenth-century social and moral certainties removed. In A Room of One's Own, *quoted in the document selection on p. 883, she also challenged some of the accepted notions of feminist thought, asking whether women writers should bring to their work any separate qualities they possessed as women, and concluding that men and women writers should strive to share each other's sensibilities.*
Hulton Getty/Archive Photos

Among the chief proponents of modernism in England were the members of the Bloomsbury Group, including authors Virginia Woolf (1882–1941) and Leonard Woolf (1880–1969), artists Vanessa Bell (1879–1961) and Duncan Grant (1885–1978), the historian and literary critic Lytton Strachey (1880–1932), and the economist John Maynard Keynes (1883–1946). These authors challenged what they regarded as the inherited values of their Victorian forebears. In *Eminent Victorians* (1918), Strachey used a series of biographical sketches less to write history than to heap contempt on his subjects. Grant and Bell looked to the modern artists on the Continent for their models. Keynes eventually challenged much of the structure of nineteenth-century economic theory. In both personal practice and theory, all in the Bloomsbury

Cubism Changes the Shape of Painting

Cubism was the single most important new departure in the twentieth-century art of the West. A contemporary critic first coined the term to describe the paintings of Pablo Picasso (1881–1973) and Georges Braque (1882–1963). Cubism emerged in the heady turn-of-the century cultural climate that also fostered the new physics, philosophies that questioned the adequacy of rationality, psychoanalysis, atonality in music, and growing sensitivities to non-Western cultures. Each of these developments in a very real sense led to a refocusing of Western thought just as Cubism led to a refocusing of perspective in painting.

For over five hundred years painting in the West had sought to reproduce the appearance of reality. From the time of the Renaissance, paintings functioned as a kind of window on an artistic depiction of the real world. Even the most advanced art of the nineteenth century, including the Impressionists and post-Impressionists, essentially stood in this tradition as seen in Manet's *A Bar at the Folies-Bergère* and Seurat's *A Sunday on La Grande-Jatte— 1884.* (See pp. 796–797 and 838–839).

During the late nineteenth century artists generally, though not always, working in Paris undertook a number of experiments in both the content and style of painting. In reaction to the Impressionists' fascination with light, Paul Cezanne, working largely in isolation, attempted to bring form and solidity back into painting. A new sensitivity also arose in regard to non-Western peoples and their art. Paul Gaugin, for example, produced works portraying peoples living in the South Pacific. Other artists collected African masks or studied such objects in the anthropological museum in Paris. Whereas Cezanne had given artists a new way of looking at and then shaping reality, the art of Africa and of the Pacific gave artists examples of remarkably beautiful works that had no relationship to the longstanding Western artistic tradition.

Beginning in 1907 Picasso and Braque rejected the idea of a painting as constituting a window looking onto the depiction of the real world.

Rather, they saw painting as an autonomous realm of art itself with no purpose beyond itself. Braque once commented, "The painter thinks in forms and colors. The aim is not to *reconstitute* an anecdotal fact but to *constitute* a pictorial fact . . .One does not imitate the appearance; the appearance is the result."[4] Echoing the art of Egypt, medieval primitives, and Africa, Picasso and Braque represented only two dimensions in their painting. They made little or no effort to go beyond the flatness of the surface itself. They attempted to include at one time on a single surface as many different perspectives, angles, or views of the object painted as possible. "Reality" was the construction of their experience of multiple perceptions. The space in the paintings was literally the space of two dimensions filled with geometric shapes as well as geometric voids. The shapes stand dismantled, set in new and usually unexpected positions, communicating a sense of dislocation.

Braque's still life *Violin and Palette* (1909 and 1910) represents the Cubist determination to present "a new, completely non-illusionistic and non-imitative method of depicting the visual world."[5]Various shapes seem to flow into other shapes. Portions of the violin and of the palette are recognizable, but as shapes, not as objects in and of themselves. The violin appears at one moment from a host of perspectives, but the violin has interest only in its relationship to the other shapes of color in the painting. As one moves to the right of the painting there are no elements that reproduce a recognizable object. The painting exists as its own world and as the construction of the artist. Throughout the painting Braque is quite literally taking apart the violin and other objects so that he and the viewer can analyze

[4] Quoted in Max Kozloff, *Cubism/Futurism* (New York: Charterhouse, 1973), p. 11.

[5] Edward F. Fry, *Cubism* (New York: McGraw-Hill Book Company, 1966), p. 38.

them. As one commentator explained in 1919 in regard to Cubism, "...the true picture will constitute an individual object, which will possess an existence of its own apart from the subject that has inspired it."[6] The elements of the palette, the violin, and the notes of a musical score floating on folded paper tents hold interest and meaning in this painting only because they are in the painting, not because they are imitations of a violin, a palette, or a musical score.

At the same time the appearance of elements of these objects in a single painting may indicate Braque's desire to unify the arts. It is known that he was interested in achieving in painting the kind of abstract purity that informed the radically innovative musical compositions of Igor Stravinsky and Arnold Schoenberg. It was also a commonplace modernist outlook that all art aspired to the condition of music. Braque's painting may indicate his aesthetic ambition to carry painting toward the condition of music.

Georges Braque, *Violin and Palette (Violon et Palette)*, 1909–1910. Oil on canvas. 91.7 x 42.8 cm (36 1/8 x 16 7/8 inches). Solomon R. Guggenheim Museum, New York, 154.1412. Photography by Lee B. Ewing, © The Solomon R. Guggenheim Foundation, New York. © 2001 Artists Rights Society (ARS), New York/ADAGP, Paris

[6] Maurice Raynal, "Some Intentions of Cubism," 1919, as quoted in Fry, *Cubism*, p. 153.

Sources: Max Kozloff, *Cubism/Futurism* (New York: Charterhouse, 1973); Edward F. Fry, *Cubism* (New York: McGraw-Hill Book Company, 1966); Douglas Cooper, *The Cubist Epoch* (New York: Paidon, 1970); Christopher Green, *Cubism and Its Enemies* (New Haven: Yale University Press, 1987); Christine Poggi, *In Defiance of Painting: Cubism, Futurism, and the Invention of Collage* (New Haven: Yale University Press, 1992); Marilyn Stokstad, *Art History* (Englewood Ciffs, N.J.: Prentice Hall and New York: Harry N. Abrahms, 1999).

Group rejected what they regarded as the repressive sexual morality of their parents' generation.

No one charted these changing sensibilities with more care and eloquence than Virginia Woolf. Her novels, such as *Mrs. Dalloway* (1925) and *To the Lighthouse* (1927), portrayed individuals seeking to make their way in a world with most of the nineteenth-century social and moral certainties removed.

On the Continent, one of the major practitioners of modernism in literature was Marcel Proust (1871–1922). In his seven-volume novel *In Search of Time Past* (*À la Recherche du temps perdu*), published between 1913 and 1927, he adopted a stream-of-consciousness format that allowed him to explore his memories. He would concentrate on a single experience or object and then allow his mind to wander through all the thoughts and memories it evoked. In Germany, Thomas Mann (1875–1955), through a long series of novels, the most famous of which were *Buddenbrooks* (1901) and *The Magic Mountain* (1924), explored both the social experience of middle-class Germans and how they dealt with the immediate intellectual heritage of the nineteenth century. In *Ulysses* (1922), James Joyce (1882–1941), who was born in Ireland, but spent much of his life on the Continent, wholly transformed not only the novel, but also the structure of the paragraph. Joyce encountered enormous diffi-

Dates of Major Works of Fiction	
1857	Flaubert, *Madame Bovary*
1877	Zola, *L'Assommoir*
1879	Ibsen, *A Doll's House*
1880	Zola, *Nana*
1881	Ibsen, *Ghosts*
1892	Ibsen, *The Master Builder*
1893	Shaw, *Mrs. Warren's Profession*
1894	Shaw, *Arms and the Man*
1901	Mann, *Buddenbrooks*
1903	Shaw, *Man and Superman*
1913	Shaw, *Androcles and the Lion*
1913	Proust, first volume of *In Search of Time Past*
1922	Joyce, *Ulysses*
1924	Mann, *The Magic Mountain*
1925	Woolf, *Mrs. Dalloway*
1927	Woolf, *To the Lighthouse*

culty getting this novel published because of its challenging form and its frank sexuality.

Modernism in literature arose before World War I and flourished after the war, nourished by the turmoil and social dislocation it created. The war removed many of the old political structures and

James Joyce transformed the novel and drew his readers into new modes of realism. In 1922 Sylvia Beach published his highly controversial novel, Ulysses. *Here, Joyce and Beach sit in her Paris bookstore, Shakespeare and Company, with a poster for* Ulysses *in the background.* Corbis

Friedrich Nietzsche (1844–1900) became the most influential German philosopher of the late nineteenth century. His books, which challenged existing morality and values, have exerted a powerful influence on twentieth-century literature and philosophy. Detail from a portrait by Kurt Stoeving, 1904. Bildnis Friedrich Nietzsche von kurt Stoeving, 1904; Original: Staatliche Museen zu Berlin–Preussischer Kulturbesitz Nationalgalerie. Photograph: Klaus Goken, 1992. Bildarchiv Preussischer Kulturbesitz

social expectations. After its appalling violence, readers found themselves much less shocked by upheavals in literary forms and the moral content of novels and poetry.

Friedrich Nietzsche and the Revolt against Reason

During the second half of the century, philosophers began to question the adequacy of rational thinking to address the human situation. No late-nineteenth-century writer better exemplified this new attitude than the German philosopher Friedrich Nietzsche (1844–1900), who had been educated as a classical philologist rather than as an academic philosopher. His books remained unpopular until late in his life, when his brilliance had deteriorated into an almost totally silent insanity. He was wholly at odds with the predominant values of the age. At one time or another, he attacked Christianity, democracy, nationalism, rationality, science, and progress. He sought less to change values than to probe the sources of values in the human mind and character. He wanted not only to tear away the masks of

respectable life, but also to explore how human beings made such masks.

His first important work was *The Birth of Tragedy* (1872) in which he urged that the nonrational aspects of human nature were as important and noble as the rational characteristics. Here and elsewhere, he insisted on the positive function of instinct and ecstasy in human life. To limit human activity to strictly rational behavior was to impoverish human life and experience. In this work, Nietzsche regarded Socrates as one of the major contributors to Western decadence because of the Greek philosopher's appeal for rationality in human affairs. In Nietzsche's view, the strength for the heroic life and the highest artistic achievement arose from sources beyond rationality.

In later works, such as the prose poem *Thus Spake Zarathustra* (1883), Nietzsche criticized democracy and Christianity. Both would lead only to the mediocrity of sheepish masses. He announced the death of God and proclaimed the coming of the Overman (*Übermensch*), who would embody heroism and greatness. The term was frequently interpreted as some mode of superman or superrace, but such was not Nietzsche's intention. He was highly critical of contemporary racism and anti-Semitism. He sought a return to the heroism that he associated with Greek life in the Homeric age. He thought that the values of Christianity and of bourgeois morality prevented humankind from achieving life on a heroic level. Those moralities forbade too much of human nature from fulfilling and expressing itself.

Two of Nietzsche's most profound works are *Beyond Good and Evil* (1886) and *The Genealogy of Morals* (1887). Both are difficult books. Much of the former is written in brief, ambiguous aphorisms. Nietzsche sought to discover not what is good and what is evil, but the social and psychological sources of the judgment of good and evil. He declared, "There are no moral phenomena at all, but only a moral interpretation of phenomena."[7] He dared to raise the question of whether morality itself was valuable: "We need a critique of moral values; the value of these values themselves must first be called in question."[8] In Nietzsche's view, morality was a human convention that had no independent existence apart from humankind. For Nietzsche, this discovery did not condemn morality, but liberated human beings to create life-affirming instead of life-denying values. Christianity, utilitarianism, and middle-class respectability could, in good conscience, be abandoned. Human beings could, if they so willed, create a new moral order for themselves that would glorify pride, assertiveness, and strength rather than meekness, humility, and weakness.

In his appeal to feelings and emotions and in his questioning of the adequacy of rationalism, Nietzsche drew on the Romantic tradition. The kind of creative impulse that earlier Romantics had considered the gift of artists Nietzsche saw as the burden of all human beings. The character of the human situation that this philosophy urged on its contemporaries was that of an ever-changing flux in which little or nothing but change itself was permanent. Human beings had to forge from their own inner will and determination the truth and values that were to exist in the world.

The Birth of Psychoanalysis

A determination to probe beneath surface or public appearance united the major figures of late-nineteenth-century science, art, and philosophy. They sought to discern the various undercurrents, tensions, and complexities that lay beneath the smooth, calm surfaces of hard atoms, respectable families, rationality, and social relationships. As a result of their theories and discoveries, articulate, educated Europeans could never again view

Sigmund Freud forced a reconsideration of the role of rationality in human motivation. After Freud it was no longer possible to see reason as the sole determinant of behavior. Bildarchiv Preussischer Kulturbesitz

the surface of life with smugness or complacency or even much confidence. No single intellectual development more clearly and stunningly exemplified this trend than the emergence of psychoanalysis through the work of Sigmund Freud (1856–1939).

DEVELOPMENT OF FREUD'S EARLY THEORIES   Freud was born into an Austrian Jewish family that settled in Vienna. He originally planned to become a lawyer, but soon moved to the study of physiology and then to medicine. In 1886 he opened his medical practice in Vienna, where he lived until driven out by the Nazis in 1938. Freud conducted all his research and writing from the base of his medical practice. His earliest medical interests had been psychic disorders, to which he sought to apply the critical method of science. In late 1885 he had studied for a few months in Paris with Jean-Martin Charcot (1825–1893), who used hypnosis to treat cases of hysteria. In Vienna, he collaborated with another physician, Josef Breuer (1842–1925), and in 1895 they published *Studies in Hysteria*.

[7]*The Basic Writings of Nietzsche*, ed. and trans. by Walter Kaufman (New York: The Modern Library, 1968), p. 275.

[8]Kaufman, p. 456.

In the mid-1890s, Freud changed the technique of his investigations. He abandoned hypnosis and allowed his patients to talk freely and spontaneously about themselves. Repeatedly, he found that they associated their particular neurotic symptoms with experiences related to earlier experiences, going back to childhood. He also noted that sexual matters were significant in his patients' problems. For a time, he thought that perhaps sexual incidents during childhood accounted for their illnesses.

By 1897, however, Freud had privately rejected this view. In its place he formulated a theory of infantile sexuality, according to which sexual drives and energy already exist in infants and do not simply emerge at puberty. For Freud, human beings were sexual creatures from birth through adulthood. He thus questioned in the most radical manner the concept of childhood innocence. He also portrayed the little-discussed or little-acknowledged matter of sexuality as one of the bases of mental order and disorder.

FREUD'S CONCERN WITH DREAMS During the same decade, Freud also examined the psychic phenomena of dreams. Romantic writers had taken dreams seriously, but few psychologists had examined them scientifically. As a rationalist, Freud believed that the seemingly irrational content of dreams must have a reasonable, scientific explanation. His research led him to reconsider the general nature of the human mind. He concluded that dreams allow unconscious wishes, desires, and drives that had been excluded from everyday conscious life and experience to enjoy freer play in the mind. "The dream," he wrote, "is the [disguised] fulfillment of a [suppressed, repressed] wish."[9] During the waking hours, the mind represses or censors certain wishes, which are as important to the individual's psychological makeup as conscious thought is. In fact, Freud argued, unconscious drives and desires contribute to conscious behavior. Freud developed these concepts and related them to his idea of infantile sexuality in his most important book, *The Interpretation of Dreams*, published in 1900.

FREUD'S LATER THOUGHT In later books and essays, Freud continued to maintain the significance of the human unconscious. He developed a new model of the internal organization of the mind. According to this model, the mind is an arena of struggle and conflict among three entities: the id, the ego, and the superego. The id consists of amoral, irrational, driving instincts for sexual gratification, aggression, and general physical and sensual pleasure. The superego embodies the external moral imperatives

and expectations imposed on the personality by society and culture. The ego mediates between the impulses of the id and the asceticism of the superego. The ego allows the personality to cope with the inner and outer demands of its existence. Consequently, everyday behavior displays the activity of the personality as its inner drives are partially repressed through the ego's coping with external moral expectations, as interpreted by the superego.

In his acknowledgment of the roles of instinct, will, dreams, and sexuality, Freud reflected the Romantic tradition of the nineteenth century. In other respects, however, he was a son of the Enlightenment. Like the *philosophes*, he was a realist who wanted human beings to live free of fear and illusions by rationally understanding themselves and their world. He saw the personalities of human beings as being determined by finite physical and mental forces in a finite world. He was hostile to religion and spoke of it as an illusion. Freud, like the writers of the eighteenth century, wished to see civilization and humane behavior prevail. More fully than those predecessors, however, he understood the immense sacrifice of instinctual drives required for rational civilized behavior. It has been a grave misreading of Freud to see him as urging humankind to thrust off all repression. He did indeed believe that excessive repression could lead to mental disorder, but he also believed that civilization and the survival of humankind required some repression of sexuality and aggression. Freud thought that the sacrifice and struggle were worthwhile, but he was pessimistic about the future of civilization in the West.

DIVISIONS IN THE PSYCHOANALYTIC MOVEMENT By 1910 Freud had gathered around him a small, but able, group of disciples. Several of his early followers soon moved toward theories of which the master disapproved. The most important of these dissenters was Carl Jung (1875–1961), a Swiss whom for many years Freud regarded as his most distinguished and promising student. Before World War I, the two men had, however, come to a parting of the ways. Jung had begun to question the primacy of sexual drives in forming human personality and in contributing to mental disorder. He also put much less faith in the guiding light of reason.

Jung believed that the human subconscious contained inherited memories from previous generations. These collective memories, as well as the personal experience of an individual, constituted his or her soul. Jung regarded human beings in the twentieth century as alienated from these useful collective memories. In *Modern Man in Search of a Soul* (1933) and other works, Jung tended toward mysticism and saw positive values in religion. Freud was highly critical of most of Jung's work. If Freud's

[9]*The Basic Writings of Sigmund Freud*, trans. by A. A. Brill (New York: The Modern Library, 1938), p. 235.

thought derived primarily from the Enlightenment, Jung's was more dependent on romanticism.

By the 1920s, the psychoanalytic movement had become even more fragmented. Nonetheless, in its several varieties, it influenced not only psychology, but also sociology, anthropology, religious studies, and literary theory. In recent years, psychoanalysis has confronted considerable criticism. Whether or not it survives as a model for understanding human behavior, however, there can be no question that it profoundly influenced the intellectual life of the twentieth century.

Retreat from Rationalism in Politics

Nineteenth-century liberals and socialists agreed that rational principles could guide society and politics. Rational analysis could discern the problems of society and prepare solutions. These thinkers generally felt that, once given the vote, individuals would behave according to their rational political self-interest. The improvement of society and the human condition would be possible through education. By the close of the century, these views had come under attack in both theory and practice. Political scientists and sociologists painted politics as frequently irrational. Racial theorists questioned whether rationality and education could affect human society at all.

WEBER   During this period, however, one major social theorist was profoundly impressed by the role of reason in human society. The German sociologist Max Weber (1864–1920) regarded the emergence of rationalism throughout society as the major development of human history. Such rationalization displayed itself in both the development of scientific knowledge and the rise of bureaucratic organization.

Weber saw bureaucratization as the basic feature of modern social life. He used this view to oppose Marx's concept of the development of capitalism as the driving force in modern society. Bureaucratization involved the extreme division of labor as each individual began to fit himself or herself into a particular small role in much larger organizations. Furthermore, Weber believed that in modern society people derived their own self-images and sense of personal worth from their positions in these organizations.

Weber also contended—again, in contrast to Marx—that noneconomic factors might account for major developments in human history. For example, in his best-known essay, *The Protestant Ethic and the Spirit of Capitalism* (1905), Weber traced much of the rational character of capitalist enterprise to the ascetic religious doctrines of Puritanism. The Puritans, in his opinion, had accumulated

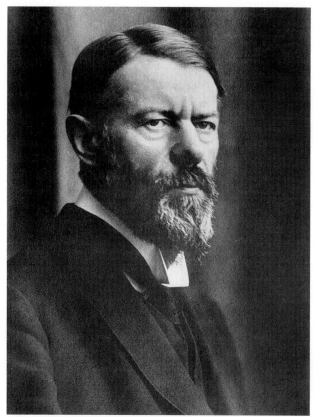

Max Weber considered bureaucratization as the basic feature of modern social life. In contrast to Marx and Freud, Weber stressed the role of the individual and of rationality in human affairs. Bildarchiv Preussischer Kulturbesitz

wealth and worked for worldly success less for its own sake than to assure themselves that they stood among the elect of God. The theory has generated both much historical research and critical debate from its publication to the present.

THEORISTS OF COLLECTIVE BEHAVIOR   In his emphasis on the individual and on the dominant role of rationality, Weber differed from many contemporary social scientists, such as Gustave LeBon (1841–1931), Émile Durkheim (1858–1917), and Georges Sorel (1847–1922) in France, Vilfredo Pareto (1848–1923) in Italy, and Graham Wallas (1858–1932) in England. LeBon was a psychologist who explored the activity of crowds and mobs. He believed that in crowd situations rational behavior was abandoned. In *Reflections on Violence* (1908), Sorel argued that people did not pursue rationally perceived goals but were led to action by collectively shared ideals. Durkheim and Wallas became deeply interested in the necessity of shared values and activities in a society. These elements, rather than a logical analysis of the social situation, bound human beings together. Instinct, habit, and affections, instead of reason, directed human social behavior. Besides playing down the function of reason in society, all of these theorists emphasized the role of collective groups in politics, rather than that of the individual formerly championed by liberals.

Racism

The same tendencies to question or even to deny the constructive activity of reason in human affairs and to sacrifice the individual to the group manifested themselves in theories of race. Racial thinking had long existed in Europe. Renaissance explorers had displayed considerable prejudice against nonwhite peoples. Since at least the eighteenth century, biologists and anthropologists had classified human beings according to the color of their skin, their language, and their stage of civilization. After late-eighteenth-century linguistic scholars observed similarities between many of the European languages and Sanskrit, they postulated the existence of an ancient race called the Aryans, who had spoken the original language from which the rest derived. During the romantic period, writers had called the different cultures of Europe races.

The debates over slavery in the European colonies and the United States had given further opportunity for the development of racial theory. In the late nineteenth century, however, race emerged as a single dominant explanation of the history and the character of large groups of people. What transformed racial thinking at the end of the century was its association with the biological sciences. The prestige associated with biology and science in general became transferred to racial thinking, whose advocates now claimed to possess a materialistic, scientific basis for their thought. They came to claim that racial science could support a hierarchy of superior and inferior races within Europe and among the various peoples outside Europe.

GOBINEAU   Count Arthur de Gobineau (1816–1882), a reactionary French diplomat, enunciated the first important theory of race as the major determinant of human history. In his four-volume *Essay on the Inequality of the Human Races* (1853–1854), Gobineau portrayed the troubles of Western civilization as being the result of the long degeneration of the original white Aryan race. He claimed that it had unwisely intermarried with the inferior yellow and black races, thus diluting the qualities of greatness and ability that originally existed in its blood. Gobineau was deeply pessimistic, because he saw no way to reverse the degeneration that had taken place. (See "Alexis de Tocqueville Forecasts the Danger of Gobineau's Racial Thought.")

Gobineau's essay remained little known for many years. In the meantime, a growing literature by anthropologists and explorers helped to spread racial thinking. In the wake of Darwin's theory, thinkers applied the concept of survival of the fittest to races and nations. The recognition of the animal nature of humankind made the racial idea all the more persuasive.

CHAMBERLAIN   At the close of the century, Houston Stewart Chamberlain (1855–1927), an Englishman who settled in Germany, drew together these strands of racial thought into the two volumes of his *Foundations of the Nineteenth Century* (1899). He championed the concept of biological determinism through race, but he was somewhat more optimistic than Gobineau. Chamberlain believed that through genetics the human race could be improved and even that a superior race could be developed. (See, "H. S. Chamberlain Exalts the Role of Race.")

Chamberlain brought anti-Semitism to prominence in racial theory. He pointed to the Jews as the major enemy of European racial regeneration. Chamberlain's book and the works on which it drew aided the spread of anti-Semitism in European political life. Also in Germany, the writings of Paul de Lagarde (1827–1891) and Julius Langbehn (1851–1907) emphasized the supposed racial and cultural dangers posed by the Jews to traditional German national life.

LATE-CENTURY NATIONALISM   Racial thinking was one part of a wider late-century movement toward more aggressive nationalism. Previously, nationalism had in general been a movement among European literary figures and liberals. The former had sought to develop what they regarded as the historically distinct qualities of particular national or ethnic literatures. The liberal nationalists had hoped to redraw the map of Europe to reflect ethnic boundaries. The drive for the unification of Italy and Germany had been major causes, as had been the liberation of Poland from foreign domination. The various national groups of the Habsburg Empire had also sought emancipation from Austrian domination.

From the 1870s onward, however, nationalism became a movement with mass support, well-financed organizations, and political parties. Nationalists often redefined nationality in terms of race and blood. The new nationalism opposed the internationalism of both liberalism and socialism. The ideal of nationality was used to overcome the pluralism of class, religion, and geography. The nation and its duties replaced religion in the lives of many secularized people. It sometimes became a secular religion in the hands of state schoolteachers, who were replacing the clergy as the instructors of youth. Nationalism of this aggressive racist variety would

Alexis De Tocqueville Forecasts the Danger of Gobineau's Racial Thought

Alexis De Tocqueville is best known for having written Democracy in America *(2 vols., 1835, 1840). He was also a major historian of the French Revolution, an active politician, and an important commentator on the events and ideas of his time. He knew Arthur De Gobineau and read the first volume of the latter's* Essay on the Inequality of the Human Races *shortly after it was published in 1853. Tocqueville then wrote Gobineau a letter in which he sharply criticized the idea of the racial determination of human actions. Tocqueville also pointed to how dangerous it would be if the idea ever influenced the political life of nations with mass electorates.*

❖ *Why does Tocqueville see Gobineau's idea as a kind of materialistic determinism? Why does he think Gobineau's views to be wrong? Why does he see political danger in racial thinking?*

Your doctrine is rather a sort of fatalism, of predestination, if you wish, but at any rate, very different from that of St. Augustine, from the Jansenists, and from the Calvinists...You continually speak about races regenerating or degenerating, losing, or acquiring through an infusion of new blood social capacities which they have not previously had.... I must frankly say that, to me, this sort of predestation is a close relative of the purest materialism. And be assured that should the masses, whose reasoning always follows the most beaten tracks, accept your doctrines, it would lead them straight from races to individuals and from social capacities to all sorts of potentialities. Whether the element of fatality should be introduced into the material order of things, or whether God willed to make different kinds of men so that He imposed special burdens of race on some, witholding from them a capacity

for certain feelings, for certain thoughts, for certain habits, for certain qualities—all this has nothing to do with my own concern with the practical consequences of these philosophical doctrines. The consequence of both theories is that of a vast limitation, if not a complete aboliton, of human liberty. Thus I confess that after having read your book I remain, as before, opposed in the extreme to your doctrines. I believe that they are probably quite false; I know that they are certainly very pernicious. Surely among the different families which compose the human race there exist certain tendencies, certain proper aptitudes resulting from thousands of different causes. But that these tendencies, that these capacities should be insuperable has not only never been proved but no one will ever be able to prove it since to do so one would need to know not only the past but also the future.

From Alexis De Tocqueville to Arthur De Gobineau, 17 November, 1853, in Alexis de Tocqueville, *The European Revolution and Correspondence with Gobineau*, J. Lukacs, ed. (Gloucester, MA: Peter Smith, 1968), pp. 227–228.

prove to be the most powerful ideology of the early twentieth century and would reemerge after the collapse of communism late in the century.

Anti-Semitism and the Birth of Zionism

Political and racial anti-Semitism, which cast such dark shadows across the twentieth century, developed in part from the prevailing atmosphere of racial thought and the retreat from rationality in politics. Religious anti-Semitism dated from at least the Middle Ages. Since the French Revolution, West

European Jews had gradually gained entry into the civil life of Britain, France, and Germany. Popular anti-Semitism, however, continued to exist, with the Jewish community being identified with money and banking interests. During the last third of the century, as finance capitalism changed the economic structure of Europe, many non-Jewish Europeans pressured by the changes became hostile toward the Jewish community.

ANTI-SEMITIC POLITICS In Vienna, Mayor Karl Lueger (1844–1910) used anti-Semitism as a major attraction for his successful Christian Socialist

Party. In Germany, the ultraconservative Lutheran chaplain Adolf Stoecker (1835–1909) revived anti-Semitism. The Dreyfus affair in France allowed a new flowering of hatred toward the Jews.

To this already ugly atmosphere, racial thought contributed the belief that no matter to what extent Jews assimilated themselves and their families into the culture of their country, their Jewishness—and thus their alleged danger to the society—would remain. According to racial thinkers, the problem of race was not in the character, but in the blood of the Jew. An important Jewish response to this new, rabid outbreak of anti-Semitism was the launching in 1896 of the Zionist movement to found a separate Jewish state. Its founder was the Austro–Hungarian Theodor Herzl (1860–1904).

HERZL'S RESPONSE   The conviction in 1894 of Captain Dreyfus in France and the election of Karl Lueger in 1895 as mayor of Vienna, as well as personal experience of discrimination, deeply influenced Herzl. He became convinced that liberal politics and the institutions of the liberal state could not protect the Jews in Europe or ensure that they would be treated justly. In 1896 Herzl published *The Jewish State*, in which he called for the organization of a separate state in which all Jews might be assured of those rights and liberties that they should be enjoying in the liberal states of Europe. Furthermore, Herzl followed the tactics of late-century mass democratic politics by directing his appeal particularly to the economically poor Jews who lived in the ghettos of eastern Europe and the slums of western Europe. The original call to Zionism thus combined a rejection of the anti-Semitism of Europe

H. S. Chamberlain Exalts the Role of Race

Houston Stewart Chamberlain's Foundations of the Nineteenth Century *(1899) was one of the most influential late-century works of racial thought. Chamberlain believed that most people in the world were racially mixed and that this mixture weakened those human characteristics most needed for physical and moral strength. He also believed that people who were assured of their racial purity could act with the most extreme self-confidence and arrogance. Chamberlain's views had a major influence on the Nazi Party in Germany and on others who wished to establish their alleged racial superiority for political purposes.*

❖ *What does Chamberlain mean by "Race" in this passage? How, in his view, does race, as opposed to character or environment, determine human nature? How might a nationalist use these ideas?*

Nothing is so convincing as the consciousness of the possession of Race. The man who belongs to a distinct, pure race, never loses the sense of it. The guardian angel of his lineage is ever at his side, supporting him where he loses his foothold, warning him like the Socratic Daemon where he is in danger of going astray, compelling obedience, and forcing him to undertakings which, deeming them impossible, he would never have dared to attempt. Weak and erring like all that is human, a man of this stamp recognises himself, as others recognise him, by the sureness of his character, and by the fact that his actions are marked by a certain simple and peculiar greatness, which finds its explanation in his distinctly typical and super-personal qualities. Race lifts a man above himself; it endows him with extraordinary—I might almost say supernatural—powers, so entirely does it distinguish him from the individual who springs from the chaotic jumble of peoples drawn from all parts of the world: and should this man of pure origin be perchance gifted above his fellows, then the fact of Race strengthens and elevates him on every hand, and he becomes a genius towering over the rest of mankind, not because he has been thrown upon the earth like a flaming meteor by a freak of nature, but because he soars heavenward like some strong and stately tree, nourished by thousands and thousands of roots—no solitary individual, but the living sum of untold souls striving for the same goal.

From Houston Stewart Chamberlain, *Foundations of the Nineteenth Century*, Vol. 1, trans. by John Lees (London: John Lane, 1912), p. 269.

Theodor Herzl's visions of a Jewish state would eventually lead to the creation of Israel in 1948. BBC Hulton/Corbis

and a desire to realize some of the ideals of both liberalism and socialism in a state outside Europe. (See "Herzel Calls for a Jewish State.")

Science, Racial Thought, and the Non-Western World

The European embrace of science during the nineteenth century became intertwined with the relationship of Europeans to the non-Western world. This relationship had three elements.

First, scientists were actively involved with the world outside Europe. European geologists explored sites on all the continents as they sought to develop and confirm their theories of the earth's past. Naturalists, such as Darwin and Wallace, traveled widely in South America, the Pacific, and Asia. Anthropologists observed native peoples to understand how their socities functioned. Astronomers took their equipment to Africa and India to record solar eclipses. Engineers pursued vast railway and mining construction projects all over the world. Major European botanical gardens, such as Kew Garden near London, fostered an active exchange of plants for agricultural experimentation. Physicians and public health officials helped administer the new

colonial empires (see Chapter 26). In all these respects, nineteenth-century science was deeply intertwined with colonialism.

Second, Europeans used the power of their science and technology to justify their governing less economically and technologically advanced regions. They portrayed themselves as carrying civilization to "backward" peoples or races. Europeans assumed the role of cultural and economic improvers of non-European peoples. In turn, some non-Europeans, especially the Japanese, recognized that the basis of European power lay in the possession of technology that they could master and imitate. To that end, during the second half of the nineteenth century, the Japanese government pursued a concerted, successful westernizing policy to copy European methods of manufacture, armament, and government administration.

The third manner in which European science touched the non-European world was through racial theory. Here the story is more complex. Some Europeans celebrated technological superiority, but did *not* believe in European racial superiority. Others, however, used racial theory to support harsh, condescending treatment of colonial peoples in the late nineteenth and early twentieth centures. They were convinced that white Europeans were racially superior to the peoples of color whom they governed and that these peoples would always be socially and politically inferior to Europeans and people of European descent. Racial theory also informed attitudes toward peoples of color in the West as was the case with the racial inferiority ascribed to African Americans and Native Americans in the United States.

Women and Modern Thought

The ideas that so shook Europe from the publication of *The Origin of Species* through the opening of World War I raised questions about much of the European intellectual legacy. Religion, science, art, and society came under new forms of criticism. Yet these new ideas and intellectual movements produced, at best, mixed results for women. Within the often radically new ways of thinking about the world, views of women and their roles in society often remained remarkably unchanged.

Antifeminism in Late-Century Thought

The influence of biology on the thinking of intellectuals during the late nineteenth century and their own interest in the nonrational side of human behavior led many of them to sustain what had become stereotyped views of women. The emphasis

Herzl Calls for a Jewish State

In 1896, Theodor Herzl published his pamphlet The Jewish State. *Herzl had lived in France during the turmoil and anti-Semitism associated with the Dreyfus affair. He became convinced that only the establishment of a separate state for Jews would halt the outbreaks of anti-Semitism that characterized late-nineteenth-century European political and cultural life. Following the publication of this pamphlet, Herzl began to organize the Zionist movement among Jews in both eastern and western Europe.*

❖ *Why does Herzl define what he calls the Jewish Question as a national question? What objections does he anticipate to the founding of a Jewish state? Why does he believe the founding of a Jewish state will be an effective move against anti-Semitism?*

The idea which I develop in this pamphlet is an age-old one: the establishment of a Jewish State.

The world resounds with outcries against the Jews, and this is what awakens the dormant idea.

...I believe I understand anti-Semitism, a highly complex movement. I view it from the standpoint of a Jew, but without hatred or fear. I think I can discern in it the elements of vulgar sport, of common economic rivalry, of inherited prejudice, of religious intolerance—but also of a supposed need for self-defense. To my mind, the Jewish Question is neither a social nor a religious one, even though it may assume these and other guises. It is a national question, and to solve it we must first of all establish it as an international political problem which will have to be settled by the civilized nations of the world in council.

We are a people, one people.

Everywhere we have sincerely endeavored to merge with the national communities surrounding us and to preserve only the faith of our fathers. We are not permitted to do so....

And will some people say that the venture is hopeless, because even if we obtain the land and the sovereignty only the poor people will go along? They are the very ones we need first! Only desperate men make good conquerors.

Will anybody say, Oh yes, if it were possible it would have been done by now?

It was not possible before. It is possible now. As recently as a hundred, even fifty years ago it would have been a dream. Today it is all real. The rich, who have an epicurean acquaintance with all technical advance, know very well what can be done with money. And this is how it will be: Precisely the poor and plain people, who have no idea of the power that man already exercises over the forces of Nature, will have the greatest faith in the new message. For they have never lost their hope of the Promised Land....

Now, all this may seem to be a long-drawn-out affair. Even in the most favorable circumstances it might be many years before the founding of the State is under way. In the meantime, Jews will be ridiculed, offended, abused, whipped, plundered, and slain in a thousand different localities. But no; just as soon as we begin to implement the plan, anti-Semitism will immediately grind to a halt everywhere.

From Theodor Herzl, *The Jewish State* (New York: The Herzl Press, 1970), pp. 27, 33, 109, as quoted in William W. Hallo, David B. Ruderman, and Michael Stanislawski, eds., *Heritage: Civilization and the Jews Source Reader* (New York: Praeger, 1984), pp. 234–235.

on biology, evolution, and reproduction led intellectuals to concentrate on women's mothering role. Their interest in the nonrational led them to reassert the traditional view that feeling and the nurturing instinct were basic to women's nature. Many late-century thinkers and writers of fiction also often displayed real fear and hostility toward women, portraying them as creatures susceptible to overwhelming and often destructive feelings and instincts. A genuinely misogynist strain emerged in late-century fiction and painting.

Much of the biological thought that challenged religious ideas and the accepted wisdom in science actually reinforced the traditional view of women as creatures weaker and less able than men. Darwin himself held such views of women, and he expressed them directly in his scientific writings. Medical thought of the late century similarly sustained these views. Whatever social changes were to be wrought through science, significant changes in the organization of the home and the relationship between men and women were not among them.

This conservative and hostile perception of women manifested itself in several ways within the scientific community. In London in 1860, the Ethnological Society excluded women from its discussions on the grounds that the subject matter of the customs of primitive peoples was unfit for women and that women were amateurs whose presence would lower the level of the discussion. T. H. Huxley, the great defender of Darwin, took the lead in this exclusion, as he had in a previous exclusion of women from meetings of the Geological Society. Male scientists also believed women should not discuss reproduction or other sexual matters. Huxley, in public lectures, claimed to have found scientific evidence of the inferiority of women to men. Karl Vogt (1817–1895), a leading German anthropologist, held similar views about the character of women. Darwin would repeat the ideas of both Huxley and Vogt in his *Descent of Man*. Late-Victorian anthropologists tended likewise to assign women, as well as nonwhite races, an inferior place in the human family. Still, despite their otherwise conservative views on gender, both Darwin and Huxley supported the expansion of education for women.

The position of women in Freud's thought has always been controversial. Many of his earliest patients, upon whose histories he developed his theories, were women. Critics have claimed, nonetheless, that Freud portrayed women as incomplete human beings who might be inevitably destined to unhappy mental lives. He saw the natural destiny of women as motherhood and the rearing of sons as their greatest fulfillment. The first psychoanalysts were trained as medical doctors, and their views of women reflected contemporary medical education, which, like much of the rest of the scientific establishment, tended to portray women as inferior. Distinguished women psychoanalysts, such as Karen Horney (1885–1952) and Melanie Klein (1882–1960), would later sharply challenge Freud's views on women, and other writers would try to establish a psychoanalytic basis for feminism. Nonetheless, the psychoanalytic profession would remain dominated by men, as would nonpsychoanalytic academic psychology. Since psychology would increasingly influence child-rearing practices and domestic relations law in the twentieth century, it would, ironically, give men a large impact in the one area of social activity that had been dominated by women.

The social sciences of the late nineteenth and early twentieth centuries similarly reinforced traditional gender roles. Virtually all major theorists believed that women's role in reproduction and child rearing demanded a social position inferior to men. Auguste Comte, whose thought in this area owed much to Rousseau, portrayed women as biologically and intellectually inferior to men. Herbert Spencer, although an advocate for improving women's lot, thought they could never achieve genuine equality with men. Émile Durkheim portrayed women as essentially creatures of feeling and family rather than of intellect. Max Weber favored improvements in the social condition of women, but did not really support significant changes in their social roles or in their relationship to men. Virtually all of the early sociologists took a conservative view of marriage, the family, child rearing, and divorce.

New Directions in Feminism

The close of the century witnessed a revival of feminist thought in Europe that would grow as the twentieth century passed. The role of feminist writers during these years was difficult. Many women's organizations, as seen in the previous chapter, concentrated on achieving the vote for women, but feminist writers and activists raised other questions as well. Women became more clearly conscious of their problems as women in a variety of ways, confronting them not only by seeking the vote. Some organizations forged new ways of thinking about women, redefining their relationships to men and the larger society. Few of these groups were large, and their victories were rare. Nonetheless, late in the last century and early in this one, they defined the issues that would become more fully and successfully explored after World War II.

SEXUAL MORALITY AND THE FAMILY In various nations, middle-class women began to challenge the double standard of sexual morality and the traditional male-dominated family. Often, this challenge took the form of action relating to prostitution.

Between 1864 and 1886, English prostitutes were subject to the Contagious Diseases Acts. The police in certain cities with naval or military bases could require any woman identified as, or suspected of being, a prostitute to undergo an immediate internal medical examination for venereal disease. Those found to have a disease could be confined for months to lock hospitals (women's hospitals for the treatment of venereal diseases) without legal recourse. The law took no action against their male customers. Indeed, the purpose of the laws was to protect men, presumably sailors and soldiers, and not the women themselves, from infection.

These laws angered English middle-class women who believed that the working conditions and the poverty imposed on so many working-class women were the true causes of prostitution. They framed the issue in the context of their own efforts to prove that women were as human and rational as men and thus properly subject to equal treatment. They saw poor women being made victims of the same kind

The Swedish feminist Ellen Key maintained that motherhood was so crucial to society that the support of mothers and children should be a government responsibility.
Hulton Getty/Archive Photos

of discrimination that prevented themselves from entering the universities and professions. The Contagious Diseases Acts assumed that women were inferior to men and treated them as less than human and less than rational creatures. The laws literally took women's bodies from their own control and put them under the control of male customers, male physicians, and male law enforcement personnel. They denied to poor women the freedoms that all men enjoyed in English society.

By 1869 the Ladies' National Association for the Repeal of the Contagious Diseases Acts, a distinctly middle-class organization led by Josephine Butler (1828–1906), began actively to oppose those laws. The group achieved the suspension of the acts in 1883 and their repeal in 1886. The issue of government and police regulation of prostitution roused similar movements in other nations, which adopted the English movement as a model. In Vienna during the 1890s, the General Austrian Women's Association, led by Auguste Ficke (1833–1916), combated the introduction of legally regulated prostitution,

which would have put women under the control of police authorities. In Germany, women's groups divided between those who would have penalized prostitutes and those who saw them as victims of male society. By the turn of the century, the latter had come to dominate, although tensions between the groups would remain for some time.

The feminist groups that demanded the abolition of laws that punished prostitutes without questioning the behavior of their customers were challenging the double standard and, by extension, the traditional relationship of men and women in marriage. In their view, marriage should be a free union of equals with men and women sharing responsibility for their children. In Germany, the Mothers' Protection League (*Bund für Mutterschutz*) contended that both married and unmarried mothers required the help of the state, including leaves for pregnancy and child care. This radical group emphasized the need to rethink all sexual morality. In Sweden, Ellen Key (1849–1926), in *The Century of the Child* (1900) and *The Renaissance of Motherhood* (1914), both widely read in Europe, maintained that motherhood was one of women's chief roles and was so crucial to society that the government, rather than husbands, should support mothers and their children.

Virtually all turn-of-the-century feminists in one way or another supported wider sexual freedom for women, often claiming that it would benefit society as well as improve women's lives. Many of the early advocates of contraception had also been influenced by social Darwinism. They hoped that limiting the number of children would allow a larger proportion of both healthy and intelligent children to survive. Such was the outlook of Marie Stopes (1880–1958), an Englishwoman with a doctorate in geology, who pioneered contraception clinics in the poor districts of London.

WOMEN DEFINING THEIR OWN LIVES For Josephine Butler and Auguste Ficke, as well as other continental feminists, achieving legal and social equality for women would be one step toward transforming Europe from a male-dominated society to one in which both men and women could control their own destinies. Ficke wrote, "Our final goal is therefore not the acknowledgment of rights, but the elevation of our intellectual and moral level, the development of our personality."[10] Increasingly, feminists would concentrate on freeing and developing women's personalities through better education and government financial support for women engaged in traditional social roles, whether or not they had gained the vote.

[10]Quoted in Harriet Anderson, *Utopian Feminism: Women's Movements in Fin-de-Siècle Vienna* (New Haven, CT.: Yale University Press, 1992), p. 13.

Publication Dates of Major Nonfiction Works	
1830	Lyell, *Principles of Geology*
1830–1842	Comte, *The Positive Philosophy*
1835	Strauss, *The Life of Jesus*
1853–1854	Gobineau, *Essay on the Inequality of the Human Races*
1859	Darwin, *The Origin of Species*
1864	Pius IX, *Syllabus of Errors*
1865	Bernard, *An Introduction to the Study of Experimental Medicine*
1871	Darwin, *The Descent of Man*
1872	Nietzsche, *The Birth of Tragedy*
1883	Mach, *The Science of Mechanics*
1883	Nietzsche, *Thus Spake Zarathustra*
1891	Leo XIII, *Rerum Novarum*
1893	Huxley, *Evolution and Ethics*
1896	Herzl, *The Jewish State*
1899	Chamberlain, *The Foundations of the Nineteenth Century*
1900	Freud, *The Interpretation of Dreams*
1900	Key, *The Century of the Child*
1905	Weber, *The Protestant Ethic and the Spirit of Capitalism*
1908	Sorel, *Reflections of Violence*
1929	Woolf, *A Room of One's Own*
1933	Jung, *Modern Man in Search of a Soul*

Some women also became active within socialist circles. There they argued that the socialist transformation of society should include major reforms for women. Socialist parties usually had all-male leadership. By the close of the century, most male socialist leaders, including Lenin and later Stalin, were intolerant of demands for changes in the family or greater sexual freedom for either men or women. Nonetheless, socialist writings began to include calls for improvements in the economic situation of women that were compatible with more advanced feminist ideals.

It was within literary circles, however, that feminist writers often most clearly articulated the problems that they now understood themselves to face. Distinguished women authors were actually doing, on a more or less equal footing, something that men had always done, leading some to wonder whether simple equality was the main issue. Virginia Woolf's *A Room of One's Own* (1929) became one of the fundamental texts of twentieth-century feminist literature. In it, she meditated first on the difficulties that women of both brilliance and social standing encountered in being taken seriously as writers and intellectuals. She concluded that a woman who wished

to write required both a room of her own, meaning a space not dominated by male institutions, and an adequate independent income. But Woolf was concerned with more than asserting the right of women to participate in intellectual life. Establishing a new stance for feminist writers, she asked whether women, as writers, must imitate men or whether they should bring to their endeavors separate intellectual and psychological qualities that they possessed as women. As she had challenged some of the literary conventions of the traditional novel in her fiction, she challenged some of the accepted notions of feminist thought in *A Room of One's Own* and concluded that male and female writers must actually be able to think as both men and women and share the sensibilities of each. In this sense, she sought to open the whole question of gender definition. (See, "Virginia Woolf Urges Women to Write.")

By World War I, feminism in Europe, fairly or not, had become associated in the popular imagination with challenges to traditional gender roles and sexual morality and with either socialism or political radicalism. So when extremely conservative political movements arose between the world wars, their leaders often emphasized traditional roles for women and traditional ideas about sexual morality. Lenin and Stalin would follow a similar path in the Soviet political experiment.

In Perspective

By the opening of the twentieth century, European thought had achieved contours that seem familiar to us today. The study of science had led to virtually revolutionary changes in thinking about both biological and physical nature. Physicists had transformed the traditional views of matter and energy as they probed the mysteries of the atom. Research in evolutionary biology had revealed human beings as part of the natural order, not something distinct from it. In the minds of some writers, science was expected to provide human beings with a basis for new ethical knowledge and moral values. Christianity had experienced the strongest challenge in modern times. In part, this was a result of the strong new role for science, but also because of other intellectual changes arising from the study of history and philosophy and the goals of the politicians in secular national states.

Simultaneous with this struggle between religion and science, there arose a tendency among certain major nonreligious thinkers and writers to question the primacy of reason. Nietzsche and Freud, in their

Virginia Woolf Urges Women to Write

In 1928 Virginia Woolf, the English novelist, delivered two papers at women's colleges at Cambridge University that became the basis for A Room of One's Own, *published a year later. There, discussing the difficulty a woman writer confronted in finding women role models, she outlined obstacles that women faced in achieving the education, the time, and the income that would allow them to write. In the passage that follows, which closes her essay, she urges women to begin to write so that future women authors will have models. She then presents an image of Shakespeare's sister, who, lacking such models, had not written anything, but who, through the collective efforts of women, might in the future emerge as a great writer because she would have the literary models of the women Woolf addressed to follow and to imitate.*

❖ *How does Woolf's fiction of Shakespeare's sister establish a benchmark for women writers? What does Woolf mean by the common life through which women will need to work to become independent writers? Why does she emphasize the need for women to have both income and space if they are to become independent writers?*

A thousand pens are ready to suggest what you should do and what effect you will have. My own suggestion is a little fantastic, I admit; I prefer, therefore, to put it in the form of fiction.

I told you in the course of this paper that Shakespeare had a sister; but do not look for her in Sir Sidney Lee's life of the poet. She died young—alas, she never wrote a word. She lies buried where the omnibuses now stop, opposite the Elephant and Castle [a London intersection]. Now my belief is that this poet who never wrote a word and was buried at the cross-roads still lives. She lives in you and in me, and in many other women who are not here to-night, for they are washing up the dishes and putting the children to bed. But she lives; for great poets do not die; they are continuing presences; they need only the opportunity to walk among us in the flesh. This opportunity, as I think, it is now coming within your power to give her. For my belief is that if we live another century or so—I am talking of the common life which is the real life and not of the little separate lives which we live as individuals—and have five hundred [pounds income] a year each of us and rooms of our own; if we have the habit of freedom and the courage to write exactly what we think; if we escape a little from the common sitting-room and see human beings not always in their relation to each other but in relation to reality; and the sky, too, and the trees or whatever it may be in themselves;...if we face the fact, for it is a fact, that there is no arm to cling to, but that we go alone and that our relation is to the world of reality and not only to the world of men and women, then the opportunity will come and the dead poet who was Shakespeare's sister will put on the body which she has so often laid down. Drawing her life from the lives of the unknown who were her forerunners, as her brother did before her, she will be born. As for her coming without that preparation, without that effort on our part, without that determination that when she is born again she shall find it possible to live and write her poetry, that we cannot expect, for that would be impossible. But I maintain that she would come if we worked for her, and that so to work, even in poverty and obscurity, is worth while.

From Virginia Woolf, *A Room of One's Own* (London: The Hogarth Press, 1974), pp. 170–172.

different ways, questioned whether human beings were primarily creatures of reason. Weber and other social and political theorists doubted that politics could be entirely rational. All these developments challenged the rational values associated with the Enlightenment. The racial theorists questioned whether mind and character were as important as alleged racial characteristics carried in the blood.

Racial thinking also allowed Europeans to believe that they were somehow inherently superior to other peoples and cultures of the world. Such racial thinking fostered anti-Semitism in Europe and discrimination against other ethnic minority groups. Similar racial attitudes also informed the thinking of virtually all the colonial administrators of the European imperial powers.

The feminists of the turn of the century, more than any of their predecessors, demanded a rethinking of gender roles. They urged equal treatment for women under the law, but no less important, they contended that the relationship between men and women within marriage and the family required rethinking. They set forth much of the feminist agenda for the twentieth century.

REVIEW QUESTIONS

1. How would you account for the dominance of science in the thought of the second half of the nineteenth century? What were some of the major changes in the scientific outlook between 1850 and 1914? Comment especially on advances in physics. How would you define *positivism*? Describe Darwin's and Wallace's theory of natural selection. What effect did it have on theories of ethics, on Christianity, and on European views of human nature?

2. How and why did Christianity come under attack in the late nineteenth century? Discuss the politics of Pius IX, Leo XIII, and Pius X. Why was Leo regarded as a liberal Pope? How do you account for the resilience of the papacy during this period of attack on the church?

3. How had the social conditions of literature changed in the late nineteenth century? What was the significance of the explosion of literary matter? What was literary realism? How was it influenced by science? How did the realists undermine middle-class morality? How did literary modernism differ from realism?

4. How did Nietzsche and Freud challenge traditional middle-class and religious morality? Would you describe Freud more as a product of the Enlightenment or of the Age of Romanticism?

5. How do you account for the fear and hostility many late-nineteenth-century intellectuals displayed toward women? How did Freud view the position of women? What were some of the social and political issues affecting women in the late nineteenth and early twentieth centuries, and how did reformers confront them? What new directions did feminism take?

6. What was the character of late-nineteenth-century racism? How did it become associated with anti-Semitism? What personal and contemporary political experiences led Herzl to develop the idea of Zionism?

SUGGESTED READINGS

M. ADAS, *Machines as the Measure of Men: Science, Technology, and Ideologies of Western Dominance* (1989). The best single volume on racial thinking and technological advance as forming ideologies of European colonial dominance.

C. ALLEN, *The Human Christ: The Search for the Historical Jesus* (1998). A broad survey of the issue for the past two centuries.

R. ARON, *Main Currents in Sociological Thought*, 2 vols. (1965, 1967). An introduction to the founders of the science.

S. ASCHHEIM, *The Nietzsche Legacy in Germany 1890–1990* (1992). Examines the influence of Nietzsche.

S. AVINERI, *The Making of Modern Zionism: The Intellectual Origins of the Jewish State* (1981). An excellent introduction to the development of Zionist thought.

M. D. BIDDIS, *Father of Racist Ideology: The Social and Political Thought of Count Gobineau* (1970). Sets the subject in the more general context of nineteenth-century thought.

P. BOWLER, *Evolution: The History of an Idea* (1989). An outstanding survey of the subject.

O. CHADWICK, *The Secularization of the European Mind in the Nineteenth Century* (1975). The standard treatment.

C. M. CIPOLLA, *Literacy and Development in the West* (1969). Traces the explosion of literacy in the past two centuries.

F. J. COPPA, *The Modern Papacy since 1789* (1999). A straightfoward survey.

A. DANTO, *Nietzsche as Philosopher* (1965). A helpful and well-organized introduction.

A. DESMOND AND J. MOORE, *Darwin* (1992). A brilliant biography.

J. EFRON, *Defenders of the Race: Jewish Doctors and Race Science in Fin-de-Siècle Europe* (1994). How Jewish physicians responded to anti-Semitic racial thought.

P. GAY, *Freud: A Life for Our Time* (1988). The new standard biography.

P. GAY, *Pleasure Wars* (1998). An expansive analysis of changing tastes among the upper middle class.

A. HARRINGTON, *Reenchanted Science: Holism in German Culture from Wilhelm II to Hitler* (1996). A superb analysis of the conflation of science and cultural ideologies.

R. HARRIS, *Lourdes: Body and Soul in a Secular Age* (1999). The best available discussion of Lourdes in its religious and cultural contexts.

R. HELMSTADTER, ED., *Freedom and Religion in the Nineteenth Century* (1997). Major essays on the relationship of church and state.

H. S. HUGHES, *Consciousness and Society: The Reorientation of European Social Thought, 1890–1930* (1958). A wide-ranging discussion of the revolt against positivism.

C. JUNGNICKEL AND R. MCCORMMACH, *Intellectual Mastery of Nature: Theoretical Physics from Ohm to Einstein*, 2 vols. (1986). A demanding, but powerful, exploration of the creation of modern physics.

J. KATZ, *From Prejudice to Destruction: Anti-Semitism, 1700–1933* (1980). An excellent and far-reaching analysis.

T. A. KSELMAN, *Miracles and Prophesies in Nineteenth-Century France* (1983). A study of popular religion.

W. LACQUEUR, *A History of Zionism* (1989). The most extensive one-volume treatment.

E. MAYR, *The Growth of Biological Thought: Diversity, Evolution, and Inheritance* (1982). A major survey by a scientist of note.

G. L. MOSSE, *Toward the Final Solution: A History of European Racism* (1978). A sound introduction.

R. NOLL, *The Jung Cult: Origins of a Charismatic Movement* (1994). A highly critical account of the origins of Jung's thought in nineteenth-century occult science.

M. R. O'CONNELL, *Critics on Trial: An Introduction to the Catholic Modernist Crisis* (1994). An extensive, accessible account.

L. POLIAKOV, *The Aryan Myth: A History of Racist and Nationalist Ideas in Europe* (1971). The best introduction to the problem.

P. G. J. PULZER, *The Rise of Political Anti-Semitism in Germany and Austria* (rev. 1989). A sound discussion of anti-Semitism in the world of central European politics.

A. RABINBACH, *The Human Motor: Energy, Fatigue, and the Origins of Modernity* (1990). A broad study of the impact of metaphors of energy as related to the study of human nature.

L. RAINEY, *Institutions of Modernism* (1999). A superb exploration of how modernist writers got their books published.

C. E. SCHORSKE, *Fin de Siècle Vienna: Politics and Culture* (1980). Classic essays on the explosively creative intellectual climate of Vienna.

R. SMITH, *Civic Ideals: Conflicting Visions of Citizenship in U. S. History* (1997). How ideas discussed in this chapter shaped American understandings of citizenship.

W. SMITH, *Politics and the Sciences of Culture in Germany, 1840–1920* (1991). A major survey of the interaction between science and the various social sciences.

F. STERN, *Einstein's German World* (1999). An exploration of German science from the turn of the century to the rise of Hitler.

F. STERN, *The Politics of Cultural Despair: A Study in the Rise of the German Ideology* (1965). An important examination of antimodern and anti-Semitic thought in imperial Germany.

F. M. TURNER, *Contesting Cultural Authority: Essays in Victorian Intellectual Life* (1993). Essays on the relationship between science and religion.

D. VITAL, *A People Apart: The Jews in Europe 1789–1939* (1999) A remarkably broad and deeply researched volume.

J. P. VON ARX, *Progress and Pessimism: Religion, Politics, and History in Late Nineteenth Century Britain* (1985). A major study that casts much new light on the nineteenth-century view of progress.

A. N. WILSON, *God's Funeral* (1999). Explores the thinkers who contributed to religious doubt during the nineteenth and twentieth centuries.

Chapter 26

India was "the jewel in the crown" of the British Empire, its most profitable and valued possession. This engraving from 1875 pictures the Prince of Wales entering the Indian town of Baroda on an elephant. The Granger Collection

Imperialism, Alliances, and War

KEY TOPICS

- The economic, cultural, and strategic factors behind Europe's New Imperialism in the late nineteenth and early twentieth centuries
- The formation of alliances and the search for strategic advantage among Europe's major powers
- The origins and progress of World War I
- The Russian Revolution
- The peace treaties ending World War I

During the second half of the nineteenth century, and especially after 1870, Europe exercised unprecedented influence and control over the rest of the world. North and South America, as well as Australia and New Zealand, almost became part of the European world as great streams of European immigrants populated them. Until the nineteenth century, Asia (with the significant exception of India) and most of Africa had gone their own ways, having little contact with Europe. But in the latter part of that century, almost all of Africa was divided among a number of European nations. Europe also imposed its economic and political power across Asia. By the next century, European dominance had brought every part of the globe into a single world economy. Events in any corner of the world had significant effects thousands of miles away.

These developments might have been expected to lead to greater prosperity and good fortune. Instead, they helped to foster competition and hostility among the great powers of Europe and to bring on a terrible war that undermined Europe's strength and its influence in the world. The peace settlement, proclaimed as "a peace without victors," disillusioned idealists in the West. It treated Germany almost as harshly as Germany would have treated its foes if it had been victorious. Also, the new system failed to provide realistic and effective safeguards against a return to power of a vengeful Germany. The withdrawal of the United States into a disdainful isolation from world affairs destroyed the basis for keeping the peace on which the hopes of Britain and France relied. The frenzy for imperial expansion that seized Europeans in the late nineteenth century had done much to destroy Europe's peace and prosperity and its dominant place in the world.

Expansion of European Power and the New Imperialism

The explosive developments in nineteenth-century science, technology, industry, agriculture, transportation, communication, and military weapons provided the chief sources of European power. They made it possible for a few Europeans (or Americans) to impose their will, by force or the threat of force, on other peoples many times

their number. Institutional as well as material advantages allowed westerners to have their way. The growth of national states that commanded the loyalty, service, and resources of their inhabitants to a degree previously unknown was a Western phenomenon. It permitted the European nations to deploy their resources more effectively than ever before.

The Europeans also possessed another, less tangible, weapon: They considered their civilization and way of life to be superior to all others. This gave them a self-confidence that was often unpleasantly arrogant and fostered their expansionist mood.

The expansion of European influence was not anything new. Spain, Portugal, France, Holland, and Britain had controlled territories overseas for centuries, but by the mid-nineteenth century, only Great Britain still had extensive holdings. The first half of the century was generally hostile to colonial expansion. Even the British had been sobered by their loss of the American colonies. The French acquired Algeria and part of Indochina, and the British added territory to their holdings in Canada, India, Australia, and New Zealand. The dominant doctrine of free trade, however, opposed political interference in other lands as economically unprofitable.

Britain ruled the waves and had great commercial advantages as a result of being the first country to experience the Industrial Revolution. Therefore, the British were usually content to trade and invest overseas without annexations. Yet they were prepared to interfere forcefully if a

Queen Victoria (r. 1837–1901) works on state papers in 1893. Note the Indian attendant. The Queen was also Empress of India, which was by far the most important possession in the British Empire. Hill & Sanders/National Portrait Gallery, London less industrialized country placed barriers in the way of their trade. Still, at midcentury, in Britain as elsewhere, most people opposed further political or military involvement overseas.

In the last third of the century, however, the European states swiftly spread their control over perhaps 10 million square miles and 150 million people—about one-fifth of the world's land area and one-tenth of its population. During this period, European expansion went forward with great speed, and participation in it came to be regarded as necessary for a great power. The movement has been called the *New Imperialism.*

The New Imperialism

The word *imperialism* is now so loosely used that it has almost lost real meaning. It may be useful to offer a definition that might be widely accepted: "the policy of extending a nation's authority by territorial acquisition or by establishing economic and political hegemony over other nations."[1] That definition seems to apply equally well to ancient Egypt and Mesopotamia and to the European performance in the late nineteenth century. But there were new elements in the latter case. Previous imperialisms had taken the form either of seizing land and settling it with the conqueror's people or of establishing trading centers to exploit the resources of the dominated area. The New Imperialism did not completely abandon these devices, but it also introduced new ones.

The usual pattern of the New Imperialism was for a European nation to invest capital in a "less industrialized" country, to develop its mines and agriculture, to build railroads, bridges, harbors, and telegraph systems, and to employ great numbers of natives in the process. The local economy and culture were thereby transformed. To safeguard its investments, the dominant European state would make favorable arrangements with the local government, either by loaning the rulers money or by intimidating them.

If these arrangements proved inadequate, the dominant power would establish more direct political control. Sometimes this meant full annexation and direct rule as a colony, or it could be a protectorate status, whereby the local ruler became a figurehead controlled by the dominant European state and maintained by its military power. In other instances, the European state established "spheres of influence" in which it received special commercial and legal privileges without direct political involvement.

THE DEVILFISH IN EGYPTIAN WATERS.

An American cartoonist in 1888 depicted John Bull (England) as the octopus of imperialism, grabbing land on every continent. The Granger Collection

Motives for the New Imperialism: The Economic Interpretation

The predominant interpretation of the motives for the New Imperialism has been economic, in the form given by the English radical economist J. A. Hobson (1858–1928) and later adapted by Lenin. As Lenin put it, "Imperialism is the monopoly stage of capitalism,"[2] the last stage of a dying system. Competition inevitably eliminates inefficient capitalists and therefore leads to monopoly. Powerful industrial and financial capitalists soon run out of profitable areas of investment in their own countries and persuade their governments to gain colonies in "less developed" countries. Here they can find higher profits from their investments, new markets for their products, and safe sources of raw materials.

Facts do not support this viewpoint, however. The European powers did invest considerable capital abroad, but not in a way that fit the model of Hobson and Lenin. Britain, for example, made heavier investments abroad before 1875 than during the next two decades. Only a small percentage of British and European investments overseas, moreover, went to their new colonies. Most

[1]*American Heritage Dictionary of the English Language,* 3d ed. (New York: Houghton Mifflin, 1993), p. 681.

[2]V. I. Lenin, *Imperialism, the Highest Stage of Capitalism* (New York: International Publishers, 1939), p. 88.

Social Darwinism and Imperialism

One of the intellectual foundations of the New Imperialism was the doctrine of "social Darwinism," a pseudoscientific application of Darwin's ideas about biology to nations and races. The impact of social Darwinism was substantial. In the selection that follows, an Englishman, Karl Pearson (1857–1936), attempts to connect concepts from evolutionary theory—the struggle for survival and the survival of the fittest—to the development of human societies.

❖ *How does the author connect Darwin's ideas to the concept of human progress? Is it reasonable to equate biological species with human societies, races, or nations? How do the author's ideas justify imperial expansion? What arguments can you make against the author's assertions?*

History shows me one way, and one way only, in which a state of civilisation has been produced, namely, the struggle of race with race, and the survival of the physically and mentally fitter race.

This dependence of progress on the survival of the fitter race, terribly black as it may seem to some of you, gives the struggle for existence its redeeming features; it is the fiery crucible out of which comes the finer metal. You may hope for a time when the sword shall be turned into the ploughshare, when American and German and English traders shall no longer compete in the markets of the world for raw materials, for their food supply, when the white man and the dark shall share the soil between them, and each till it as he lists. But, believe me, when that day comes mankind will no longer progress; there will be nothing to check the fertility of inferior stock; the relentless law of heredity will not be controlled and guided by natural selection. Man will stagnate....

The path of progress is strewn with the wreck of nations; traces are everywhere to be seen of the hecatombs of inferior races, and of victims who found not the narrow way to the greater perfection. Yet these dead peoples are, in very truth, the stepping stones on which mankind has arisen to the higher intellectual and deeper emotional life of today.

From Karl Pearson, *National Life from the Standpoint of Science*, 2d ed. (Cambridge, U.K.: Cambridge University Press, 1907), pp. 21, 26–27, 64.

capital went into other European countries or to older, well-established areas like the United States, Canada, Australia, and New Zealand. Even when investments were made in new areas, they were not necessarily put into colonies held by the investing country.

The facts are equally discouraging for those who emphasize the need for markets and raw materials. Colonies were not usually important markets for the great imperial nations, and all these states were forced to rely on areas that they did not control as sources of vital raw materials. It is not even clear that control of the new colonies was particularly profitable, though Britain, to be sure, benefited greatly from its rule of India. It is also true that some European businesspeople and politicians hoped that colonial expansion would cure the great depression of 1873–1896.

Nevertheless, as one of the leading students of the subject has said, "No one can determine whether the accounts of empire ultimately closed with a favorable cash balance."[3] That is true of the European imperial nations collectively, but it is certain that for some of them, like Italy and Germany, empire was a losing proposition. Some individuals and companies, of course, made great profits from particular colonial ventures, but such people were able to influence national policy only occasionally. Economic motives certainly played a part, but a full understanding of the New Imperialism requires a search for other motives.

Cultural, Religious, and Social Interpretations

Advocates of imperialism gave various justifications for it. Some argued that the advanced European nations had a duty to bring the benefits of their higher

[3]D. K. Fieldhouse, *The Colonial Empires* (New York: Delacorte, 1966), p. 393.

culture and superior civilization to more "backward" peoples. (See "Social Darwinism and Imperialism.") Religious groups demanded that Western governments furnish political and even military support for Christian missionaries. Some politicians and diplomats supported imperialism as a tool of social policy. In Germany, for instance, some people suggested that imperial expansion would deflect public interest away from domestic politics and social reform. Yet Germany acquired few colonies, and such considerations played little, if any, role in its colonial policy.

In Britain, Joseph Chamberlain (1836–1914), the colonial secretary from 1895 to 1903, argued for the empire as a source of profit and economic security that would finance a great program of domestic reform and welfare. These arguments were not important as motives for British imperial expansion, because they were made well after Britain had acquired most of its empire.

Another common and apparently plausible justification for imperialism was that colonies would attract a European country's surplus population. In fact, most European emigrants went to areas *not* controlled by their countries, chiefly North and South America and Australia.

Strategic and Political Interpretations: The Scramble for Africa

Strategic and political considerations were more important in bringing on the New Imperialism. The scramble for Africa in the 1880s is one example. (See Maps 26–1 and 26–2.)

GREAT BRITAIN   Britain was the only great power with extensive overseas holdings on the eve of the scramble. The completion of the Suez Canal in 1869 made Egypt vitally important to the British because it sat astride the shortest route to India. Under Disraeli, Britain purchased a major, but not a controlling, interest in the canal in 1875. When internal troubles threatened Egypt's stability in the 1880s, the British established control. Then, to protect Egypt, they advanced into the Sudan.

FRANCE AND SMALLER NATIONS   France became involved in North Africa in 1830 by sending an expedition to attack pirates in Algiers. The French gradually extended their control, and thousands of Europeans settled in the country. By the 1880s, France was in full control of Algeria. In 1882, to prevent Tunisia from falling into Italy's hands, France took over that country also. In addition, the French annexed much of West Africa, the Congo, and the island of Madagascar.

France's imperialism always reflected its sense of its unique cultural superiority, and the French liked to think of themselves as benevolently sharing it with the colonial people they ruled. This magazine cover from 1911 shows the symbol of France bringing civilization, peace, and prosperity to Morocco. The Granger Collection

Soon smaller states like Belgium, Portugal, Spain, and Italy were acquiring new African colonies or expanding old ones. By the 1890s, their intervention had compelled Britain to expand northward from the Cape of Good Hope into what is now Zimbabwe and Zambia. Britain may have had significant strategic reasons for protecting the Suez and Cape routes to India, but France and the other European nations did not. Their motives were political as well as economic, for they equated political status (Britain was the chief model) with the possession of colonies. They therefore sought colonies to buttress their own importance.

GERMANY   Bismarck appears to have pursued an imperial policy, however briefly, from cold political motives. In 1884 and 1885, Germany declared protectorates over Southwest Africa (Namibia), Togoland, the Cameroons, and East Africa (Tanzania).

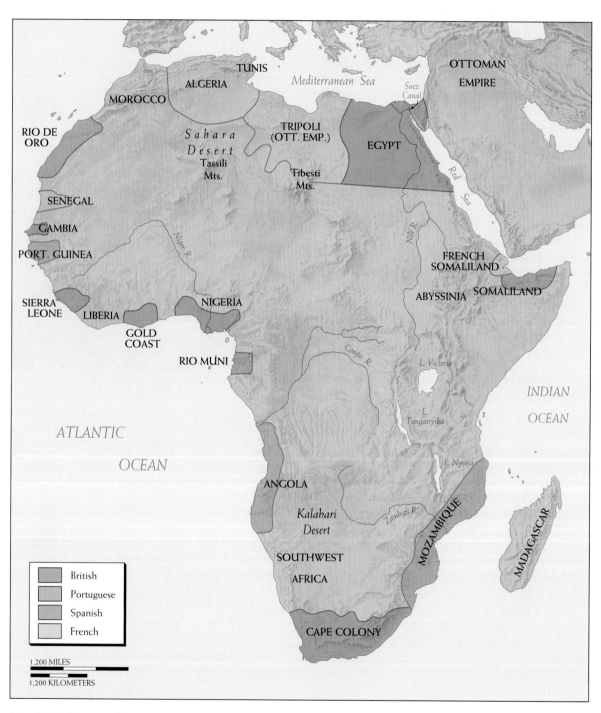

MAP 26–1   IMPERIAL EXPANSION IN AFRICA TO 1880   *Until the 1880s, few European countries held colonies in Africa, mostly on its fringes.*

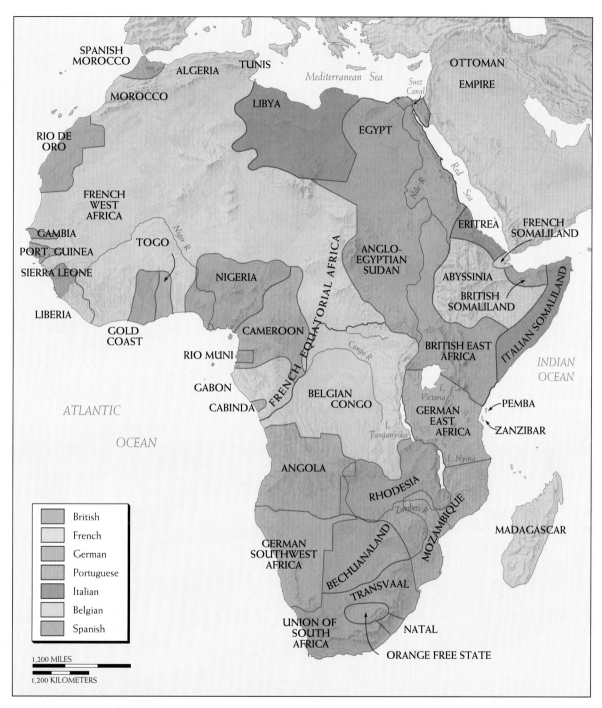

MAP 26–2   PARTITION OF AFRICA, 1880–1914   *Before 1880, the European presence in Africa was largely the remains of early exploration by old imperialists and did not penetrate the heart of the continent. By 1914, the occupying powers included most large European states; only Liberia and Abyssinia remained independent.*

MAP 26–3   ASIA, 1880–1914   *As in Africa, the decades before World War I saw imperialism spread widely and rapidly in Asia. Two new powers, Japan and the United States, joined the British, French, and Dutch in extending control both to islands and to the mainland and in exploiting an enfeebled China.*

In the Spanish–American War of 1898, Spain was driven from the Western Hemisphere and Cuba came under U.S. influence. This lithograph shows the Ninth and Tenth Cavalry Regiments, composed of black Americans, engaged in the Battle of Quasimas, near Santiago, Cuba, on June 24, 1898.
The Granger Collection

(See "Carl Peters Demands Colonies for Germany.") None of these places was particularly valuable or of intrinsic strategic importance. Bismarck himself had no interest in overseas colonies and once compared them to fine furs worn by impoverished Polish nobles who had no shirts underneath. His concern lay in Germany's exposed position in Europe. On one occasion he said, "My map of Africa lies in Europe. Here is Russia, and there is France, and here in the middle are we. That is my map of Africa."[4] He acquired colonies chiefly to improve Germany's diplomatic position in Europe. He hoped that colonial expansion would divert French hostility against Germany. Also, German colonies in Africa could be used as a subtle weapon with which to persuade the British to be reasonable.

The Irrational Element

Germany's annexations started a wild scramble by the other European powers to acquire what was left of Africa. By 1890, almost all the continent had been parceled out. Great powers and small had expanded into areas neither profitable nor strategic for reasons less calculating and rational than Bismarck's. "Empire in the modern period," D. K. Fieldhouse observed, "was the product of European power: its reward was power or the sense of power."[5]

Such motives were not new. They had been well understood by the Athenian spokesman at Melos in 416 B.C.E., whose words were reported by Thucydides: "Of the gods we believe and of men we know clearly that by a necessity of their nature where they have the power they rule."[6]

In Asia, the emergence of Japan as a great power frightened the other powers that were interested in China. (See Map 26–3.) The Russians were building a railroad across Siberia to Vladivostok and were afraid of any threat to Manchuria. Together with France and Germany, they applied diplomatic pressure that forced Japan out of the Liaotung Peninsula in northern China and its harbor, Port Arthur. All pressed feverishly for concessions in China. Fearing that China, its markets, and its investment opportunities would soon be closed to U.S. citizens, the United States proposed the Open Door Policy in 1899. This policy opposed foreign annexations in China and allowed entrepreneurs of all nations to trade there on equal terms. The support of Britain helped win acceptance of the policy by all the powers except Russia.

The United States had only recently emerged as a force in international affairs. After freeing itself of British rule and consolidating its independence during the Napoleonic wars, the Americans had busied themselves with westward expansion on the North American continent until the end of the nineteenth century. The Monroe Doctrine of 1823 had, in effect, made the entire Western Hemisphere an American

---

[4]Quoted in J. Remak, *The Origins of World War I, 1871–1914* (New York: Holt, Rinehart & Winston, 1967), p. 5.

[5]Fieldhouse, p. 393.

[6]Thucydides, *The Peloponnesian War*, 5, 105:2.

Carl Peters Demands Colonies for Germany

Germany was a late arrival in the competition for colonies. The territories still available were neither profitable nor attractive for settlement by Europeans. Carl Peters (1856–1918) was one of the growing number of Germans, who, nevertheless, were eager to acquire a colonial empire. He was the founder of German East Africa, now Tanzania. His arguments based on economic advantage and the prospects of German emigration proved to be absurd and provided a mask for less rational motives.

❖ *What reasons does Peters give for Germany to seek colonies? What assumptions does he make about their advantages? Are those assumptions correct? What do you think were the most important motives for colonization to Peters and those who supported his policy?*

Manifesto of the Society for German Colonization, April 1884

In the partition of the earth, as it has proceeded from the beginning of the fifteenth century up to our times, the German nation received nothing. All the remaining European culture-bearing peoples possess areas outside our continent where their languages and customs can take firm root and flourish. The moment that the German emigrant leaves the borders of the Reich behind him, he is a stranger sojourning on foreign soil. The German Reich, great in size and strength through its bloodily achieved unity, stands in the leading position among the continental European powers: her sons abroad must adapt themselves to nations which look upon us with either indifference or even hostility. For centuries the great stream of German emigration has been plunging down into foreign races where it is lost sight of. Germandom outside Europe has been undergoing a perpetual national decline.

This fact, so painful to national pride, also represents a great economic disadvantage for our *Volk*. Every year our Fatherland loses the capacity of approximately 200,000 Germans. The greatest amount of this capacity flows directly into the camp of our economic competitors and increases the strength of our rivals. Germany's imports of products from tropical zones originate in foreign settlements whereby many millions of German capital are lost every year to alien nations. German exports are dependent upon the discretion of foreign tariff policies. Our industry lacks an absolutely safe market for its goods because our *Volk* lacks colonies of its own.

The alleviation of this national grievance requires taking practical steps and strong action.

In recognition of this point of view, a society has been organized in Berlin with the goal of mobilizing itself for such steps and such action. The Society for German Colonization aims to undertake on its own, in a resolute and sweeping manner, carefully chosen colonization projects and thereby supplement the ranks of organizations with similar tendencies.

Its particular tasks will be:

1. to provide necessary sums of capital for colonization;
2. to seek out and lay claim to suitable districts for colonization;
3. to direct German emigrants to these regions.

Imbued as we are with the conviction that it is no longer permissible to hesitate in energetically mobilizing ourselves for this great national task, we venture to come before the German *Volk* with a plea for active support of the endeavors of our Society! The German nation has proven time and again its willingness to make sacrifices for general patriotic undertakings: may she also bring her full energies to play in the solution of this great historical task.

Every German whose heart beats for the greatness and the honor of our nation is entreated to come to the side of our Society. What is at stake is compensation for centuries of deprivation: to prove to the world that, along with the splendor of the Reich, the German *Volk* has inherited the old German national spirit of its forefathers!

Carl Peters, *Die Grundung von Deutsch-Ostafrika* [*The Foundation of German East Africa*] (Berlin, 1906), pp. 43–45, as trans. in Ralph A. Austen, *Modern Imperialism* (Lexington, MA: D. C. Heath, 1969), pp. 62–63. ©1969 by D. C. Heath and Company. Reprinted by permission of Houghton Mifflin Company protectorate. Cuba's attempt to gain independence from Spain was the spark for the new U.S. involvement in international affairs. Sympathy for the Cuban cause, U.S. investments on the island, the desire for Cuban sugar, and concern over the island's strategic importance in the Caribbean all helped persuade the United States to fight Spain.

Victory in the Spanish-American War of 1898 brought the United States an informal protectorate over Cuba and the annexation of Puerto Rico and drove Spain completely out of the Western Hemisphere. The United States forced Spain to sell the Philippine Islands and Guam, and Germany bought the other Spanish islands in the Pacific. The United States and Germany also divided Samoa between them. The remaining Pacific Islands were taken by France and Britain. Hawaii had been under American influence for some time and was annexed in 1898. This burst of activity after the Spanish War made the United States an imperial and Pacific power.

Thus, by the turn of the century, most of the world had come under the control of the industrialized West. The one remaining area of great vulnerability was the Ottoman Empire. Its fate, however, was closely tied up with European developments and must be treated in that context.

Emergence of the German Empire and the Alliance Systems (1873–1890)

Prussia's victories over Austria and France and its creation of a large, powerful German Empire in 1871 revolutionized European diplomacy. A vast new political unit had united the majority of Germans to form a nation of great and growing population, wealth, industrial capacity, and military power. Its sudden appearance created new problems and upset the balance of power that had been forged at the Congress of Vienna. Britain and Russia retained their positions, although the latter had been weakened by the Crimean War.

Austria, however, had been severely weakened, and the forces of nationalism threatened it with disintegration. French power and prestige were badly damaged by the Franco–Prussian War and the German annexation of Alsace–Lorraine. The French were both afraid of their powerful new neighbor and resentful of their defeat, their loss of territory, and the loss of France's traditional position as the dominant western European power.

Bismarck's Leadership (1873–1890)

Until 1890, Bismarck continued to guide German policy. After 1871 he insisted that Germany was a satisfied power and wanted no further territorial gains, and he meant it. He wanted to avoid a new war that might undo his achievement. He tried to assuage French resentment by pursuing friendly relations and by supporting French colonial aspirations. He also prepared for the worst. If France could not be conciliated, it must be isolated. Bismarck sought to prevent an alliance between France and any other European power—especially Austria or Russia—that would threaten Germany with a war on two fronts.

WAR IN THE BALKANS Bismarck's first move was to establish the Three Emperors' League in 1873. The League brought together the three great conservative empires of Germany, Austria, and Russia. The league soon collapsed as a result of Austro–Russian rivalry in the Balkans that arose from the Russo–Turkish War that broke out in 1875. The tottering Ottoman Empire was held together chiefly because the European powers could not agree about how to partition it. Ottoman weakness encouraged Serbia and Montenegro to come to the aid of their fellow Slavs in Bosnia and Herzegovina when they revolted against Turkish rule. Soon the rebellion spread to Bulgaria.

Then Russia entered the fray and turned it into a major international crisis. The Russians hoped to pursue their traditional policy of expansion at Ottoman expense and especially to achieve their most cherished goal: control of Constantinople and the Dardanelles. Russian intervention also reflected the influence of the Pan-Slavic movement, which sought to unite all the Slavic peoples, even those under Austrian or Ottoman rule, under the protection of Holy Mother Russia.

The Ottoman Empire was weak and soon was forced to sue for peace. The Treaty of San Stefano of March 1878 was a Russian triumph. The Slavic states in the Balkans were freed of Ottoman rule, and Russia itself obtained territory and a large monetary indemnity. The terms of the settlement, however, alarmed the other great powers. Austria feared that the Slavic victory and the powerful increase in Russian influence in the Balkans would threaten its own Balkan provinces. The British were alarmed both by the effect of the Russian victory on the European balance of power and by the possibility of Russian control of the Dardanelles, which would make Russia a Mediterranean power and threaten Britain's control of the Suez Canal. Disraeli was determined to resist, and British public opinion supported him. A music-hall song that became popular gave the language a new word for superpatriotism: *jingoism.*

We don't want to fight,
But by jingo if we do,
We've got the men,
We've got the ships,
We've got the money too!
The Russians will not have Constantinople!

THE CONGRESS OF BERLIN Even before the Treaty of San Stefano, Disraeli sent a fleet to Constantinople. After the magnitude of Russia's appetite was known, Britain and Austria forced Russia to agree to an international conference at which the other great powers would review the provisions of San Stefano. The resulting Congress of Berlin met in June and July of 1878 under the presidency of Bismarck. The choice of site and presiding officer was a clear recognition of Germany's new importance and of Bismarck's claim that Germany wanted no new territory and sought to preserve the peace.

Bismarck referred to himself as an "honest broker," and the title was justified. He agreed to the congress simply because he wanted to avoid a war between Russia and Austria into which he feared Germany would be drawn with nothing to gain and much to lose. From the collapsing Ottoman Empire, he wanted nothing. "The Eastern Question," he said, "is not worth the healthy bones of a single Pomeranian musketeer."[7]

The decisions of the congress were a blow to Russian ambitions. Bulgaria, a Russian client, was reduced in size by two-thirds and was deprived of access to the Aegean Sea. Austria–Hungary was given Bosnia and Herzegovina to "occupy and administer," although those provinces remained formally under Ottoman rule. Britain received Cyprus, and France was encouraged to occupy Tunisia. These territories were compensation for the gains that Russia was permitted to keep. Germany asked for nothing, but still earned Russian resentment. The Russians believed that they had saved Prussia in 1807 from complete dismemberment by Napoleon and had expected a show of German gratitude. They were bitterly disappointed, and the Three Emperors' League was dead.

All of the Balkan states were also annoyed by the Berlin settlement. Romania wanted Bessarabia, which Russia kept; Bulgaria wanted a return to the borders of the Treaty of San Stefano; and Greece wanted a part of the Ottoman spoils. The major trouble spot, however, was in the south Slavic states of Serbia and Montenegro. They deeply resented the Austrian occupation of Bosnia and Herzegovina, as did many of the natives of those provinces. The south Slavic question, no less than the estrangement between Russia and Germany, was a threat to the peace of Europe.

GERMAN ALLIANCES WITH RUSSIA AND AUSTRIA For the moment, Bismarck could ignore the Balkans, but he could not ignore the breach in his eastern alliance system. With Russia alienated, he concluded a secret treaty with Austria in 1879. The resulting Dual Alliance provided that Germany and Austria would come to each other's aid if either were attacked by Russia. If either were attacked by another country, each promised at least to maintain neutrality.

The treaty was for five years and was renewed regularly until 1918. As the anchor of German policy, it was criticized at the time, and in retrospect, some have considered it an error. It appeared to tie German fortunes to those of the troubled Austro–Hungarian Empire and thus to borrow trouble for Germany. And, by isolating the Russians, it pushed them to seek alliances in the West.

Bismarck was fully aware of these dangers, but discounted them with good reason. He never allowed the alliance to drag Germany into Austria's Balkan quarrels. As he put it, in any alliance there is a horse and a rider, and he meant Germany to be the rider. He made it clear to the Austrians that the alliance was purely defensive and that Germany would never be a party to an attack on Russia. "For us," he said, "Balkan questions can never be a motive for war."[8]

Bismarck believed that monarchical, reactionary Russia would not seek an alliance either with republican, revolutionary France or with increasingly democratic Britain. In fact, he expected the news of the Austro–German negotiations to frighten Russia

[7]Quoted in Hajo Holborn, *A History of Modern Germany, 1840–1945* (New York: Knopf, 1969), p. 239.

[8]Quoted in Remak, p. 14.

into seeking closer relations with Germany, and he was right. Russian diplomats soon approached him, and by 1881 he had concluded a renewal of the Three Emperors' League on a firmer basis. The three powers promised to maintain friendly neutrality in case any of them was attacked by a fourth power. Other clauses included the right of Austria to annex Bosnia–Herzegovina whenever it wished and the support of all three powers for closing the Dardanelles to all nations in case of war.

The agreement allayed German fears of a Russian–French alliance and Russian fears of a combination of Austria and Britain against it, of Britain's fleet sailing into the Black Sea, and of a hostile combination of Germany and Austria. Most importantly, the agreement aimed to resolve the conflicts in the Balkans between Austria and Russia. Though it did not end such conflicts, it was a significant step toward peace.

THE TRIPLE ALLIANCE In 1882 Italy, ambitious for colonial expansion and bothered by the French occupation of Tunisia, asked to join the Dual Alliance.

Bismarck and the young Kaiser William II meet in 1888. The two disagreed over many issues, and in 1890 William dismissed the aged chancellor. German Information Center

The provisions of its entry were defensive and were directed against France. At this point, Bismarck's policy was a complete success. He was allied with three of the great powers and friendly with the other, Great Britain, which held aloof from all alliances. France was isolated and no threat. Bismarck's diplomacy was a great achievement, but an even greater challenge was to maintain this complicated system of secret alliances in the face of the continuing rivalries among Germany's allies. Despite another Balkan war that broke out in 1885 and that again estranged Austria and Russia, he succeeded.

Although the Three Emperors' League lapsed, the Triple Alliance (Germany, Austria, and Italy) was renewed for another five years. To restore German relations with Russia, Bismarck negotiated the Reinsurance Treaty of 1887, in which both powers promised to remain neutral if either was attacked. All seemed smooth, but a change in the German monarchy soon upset Bismarck's arrangements.

In 1888, William II (r. 1888–1918) came to the German throne. He was twenty-nine years old, ambitious, and impetuous. He was imperious by temperament and believed that he ruled by divine right. He had suffered an injury at birth that left him with a withered left arm. He compensated for this disability with vigorous exercise, a military bearing and outlook, and an often embarrassingly bombastic rhetoric.

Like many Germans of his generation, William II was filled with a sense of Germany's destiny as the leading power of Europe. He wanted to achieve recognition of at least equality with Britain, the land of his mother and of his grandmother, Queen Victoria. To achieve a "place in the sun," he and his contemporaries wanted a navy and colonies like Britain's. These aims, of course, ran counter to Bismarck's limited continental policy. When William argued for a navy as a defense against a British landing in North Germany, Bismarck replied, "If the British should land on our soil, I should have them arrested." This was only one example of the great distance between the young emperor, or Kaiser, and his chancellor. In 1890, William used a disagreement over domestic policy to dismiss Bismarck.

As long as Bismarck held power, Germany was secure, and there was peace among the great European powers. Although he made mistakes and was not always successful, there was much to admire in his understanding and management of international relations in the hard world of reality. He had a clear and limited idea of his nation's goals. He resisted pressures for further expansion with few and insignificant exceptions. He understood and used the full range of diplomatic weapons: appeasement and deterrence, threats and promises, secrecy and openness. He understood the needs and hopes of other countries and, where possible, tried to help them satisfy their needs or used those countries to his own advantage. His system of alliances created a stalemate in the Balkans and ensured German security.

During Bismarck's time, Germany was a force for European peace and was increasingly understood to be so. This position would not, of course, have been possible without its great military power. It also required, however, the leadership of a statesman who was willing and able to exercise restraint and who understood what his country needed and what was possible.

Forging of the Triple Entente (1890–1907)

FRANCO–RUSSIAN ALLIANCE   Almost immediately after Bismarck's retirement, his system of alliances collapsed. His successor was General Leo von Caprivi (1831–1899), who had once asked, "What kind of jackass will dare to be Bismarck's successor?" Caprivi refused the Russian request to renew the Reinsurance Treaty, in part because he felt incompetent to continue Bismarck's complicated policy and in part because he wished to draw Germany closer to Britain. The results were unfortunate, as Britain remained aloof and Russia was alienated.

Even Bismarck had assumed that ideological differences would prevent a Franco–Russian alliance. Political isolation and the need for foreign capital, however, unexpectedly drove the Russians toward France. The French, who were even more isolated, were glad to encourage their investors to pour capital into Russia if it would help produce an alliance and security against Germany. In 1894, a defensive Franco–Russian alliance against Germany was signed.

BRITAIN AND GERMANY   Britain now became the key to the international situation. Colonial rivalries pitted the British against the Russians in central Asia and against the French in Africa. Traditionally, Britain had also opposed Russian control of Constantinople and the Dardanelles and French control of the Low Countries. There was no reason to think that Britain would soon become friendly to its traditional rivals or abandon its accustomed friendliness toward the Germans.

Yet within a decade of William II's accession, Germany had become the enemy in British minds. Before the turn of the century, popular British thrillers about imaginary wars portrayed the French as the invader; after the turn of the century, the enemy was always Germany. This remarkable transformation has often been attributed to economic rivalry between Germany and Britain, in which Germany made vast strides to challenge and even overtake British production in various materials and markets. Certainly, Germany made such gains and many Britons resented them. Yet the problem was not a serious cause of hostility, and it waned during the first decade of the century. The real problem lay in the foreign and naval policies of the German emperor and his ministers.

William II admired Britain's colonial empire and mighty fleet. At first, Germany tried to win the British over to the Triple Alliance, but when Britain clung to its "splendid isolation," German policy changed. The idea was to demonstrate Germany's worth as an ally by withdrawing support and even making trouble for Britain. This odd manner of gaining an ally reflected the Kaiser's confused feelings toward Britain, which mixed dislike and jealousy with admiration. These feelings were shared by many Germans, especially in the intellectual community. Like William, they were eager for Germany to pursue a "world policy" rather than Bismarck's limited one that confined German interests to Europe. They, too, saw England as the barrier to German ambitions. Their influence in the schools, the universities, and the press guaranteed popular approval of actions and statements hostile to Britain.

The Germans began to exert pressure against Britain in Africa by barring British attempts to build a railroad from Capetown to Cairo. They also openly sympathized with the Boers of South Africa in their resistance to British expansion. In 1896 William insulted the British by sending a congratulatory telegram to Paul Kruger (1825–1904), president of the Transvaal, for repulsing a British raid "without having to appeal to friendly powers [i.e., Germany] for assistance."

In 1898, William began to realize his dream of a German navy with the passage of a naval law providing for nineteen battleships. In 1900, a second law doubled that figure. The architect of the new navy was Admiral Alfred von Tirpitz (1849–1930), who openly proclaimed that Germany's naval policy was aimed at Britain. His "risk" theory argued that Germany could build a fleet strong enough, not to defeat the British, but to do enough damage to make the British navy inferior to that of other powers like France or the United States. The theory was, in fact, absurd, because as Germany's fleet became menacing, the British would certainly build enough ships to maintain their advantage, and Britain had greater financial resources than Germany.

The naval policy, therefore, was doomed to failure. Its main achievements were to waste German resources and to begin a great naval race with Britain. Eventually, the threat posed by the German navy so antagonized and alarmed British opinion that the British abandoned their traditional attitudes and policies.

At first, however, Britain was not unduly concerned. The British were embarrassed by the general hostility of world opinion during the Boer War (1899–1902), in which their great empire crushed a rebellion by South African farmers, and their isolation no longer seemed so splendid. The Germans had acted with restraint during the war. Between 1898 and 1901, Joseph Chamberlain, the colonial secretary, made several attempts to conclude an alliance with Germany. The Germans, confident that a British alliance with France or Russia was impossible, refused and expected the British to make greater concessions in the future.

THE ENTENTE CORDIALE The first breach in Britain's isolation came in 1902, when it concluded an alliance with Japan to defend British interests in the Far East against Russia. Next, Britain abandoned its traditional antagonism toward France and in 1904 concluded a series of agreements with the French, collectively called the *Entente Cordiale*. It was not a formal treaty and had no military provisions, but it settled all outstanding colonial differences between the two nations. In particular, Britain gave France a free hand in Morocco in return for French recognition of British control over Egypt. The Entente Cordiale was a long step toward aligning the British with Germany's great potential enemy.

Britain's new relationship with France was surprising, but in 1904 hardly anyone believed that the British whale and the Russian bear would ever come together. The Russo–Japanese War of 1904–1905 made such a development seem even less likely, because Britain was allied with Russia's enemy. But Britain had behaved with restraint, and the Russians were chastened by their unexpected and humiliating defeat, which also led to the Russian Revolution of 1905. Although the revolution was put down, it weakened Russia and reduced British apprehensions about Russian power. The British were also concerned that Russia might again drift into the German orbit.

THE FIRST MOROCCAN CRISIS At this point, Germany decided to test the new understanding between Britain and France and to press for colonial gains. In March 1905, Emperor William II landed at Tangier, made a speech in favor of Moroccan independence, and by implication asserted Germany's right to participate in Morocco's destiny. This was a challenge to France. Germany's chancellor, Prince Bernhard von Bülow (1849–1929), intended to show France how weak it was and how little support it could expect from Britain. He also hoped to gain significant colonial concessions.

The Germans demanded an international conference to show their power more dramatically. The conference met in 1906 at Algeciras in Spain. Austria sided with its German ally, but Spain, which also had claims in Morocco, Italy, and the United States, voted with Britain and France. The Germans had overplayed their hand, receiving trivial concessions, and the French position in Morocco was confirmed. German bullying had, moreover, driven Britain and France closer together. In the face of the threat of a German attack on France, Sir Edward Grey (1862–1933), the British foreign secretary, without making a firm commitment, authorized conversations between the British and French general staffs. Their agreements became morally binding as the years passed. By 1914 French and British military and naval plans were so mutually dependent that the two countries were effectively, if not formally, allies.

BRITISH AGREEMENT WITH RUSSIA Britain's fear of Germany's growing naval power, its concern over German ambitions in the Near East (as represented by the German-sponsored plan to build a railroad from Berlin to Baghdad), and its closer relations with France made it desirable for Britain to become more friendly with France's ally, Russia. With French support, in 1907 the British concluded an agreement with Russia much like the Entente Cordiale with France. It settled Russo–British quarrels in central Asia and opened the door for wider cooperation. The Triple Entente, an informal, but powerful, association of Britain, France, and Russia, was now ranged against the Triple Alliance. Italy was an unreliable ally, however, which meant that Germany and Austria–Hungary were encircled by two great land powers and Great Britain.

William II and his ministers had turned Bismarck's nightmare of the prospect of a two-front war with France and Russia into a reality. They had made it more horrible by adding Britain to their foes. The equilibrium that Bismarck had worked so hard to achieve was destroyed. Britain would no longer support Austria in restraining Russian ambitions in the Balkans. Germany, increasingly alarmed by a sense of being encircled, was less willing to restrain the Austrians for fear of alienating them, too. In the Dual Alliance of Germany and Austria, it had become less clear who was the horse and who the rider.

Bismarck's alliance system had been intended to maintain peace, but the new alliance increased the risk of war and made the Balkans a likely spot for it to break out. Bismarck's diplomacy had left France isolated and impotent; the new arrangement associated France with the two greatest powers in Europe besides Germany. The Germans could rely only on Austria, and Austria's troubles made it less likely to provide aid than to need it.

World War I

The Road to War (1908–1914)

The weak Ottoman Empire still controlled the central strip of the Balkan Peninsula running west from Constantinople to the Adriatic. North and south of it were the independent states of Romania, Serbia, and Greece, as well as Bulgaria, technically still part of the empire, but legally autonomous and practically independent. The Austro–Hungarian Empire included Croatia and Slovenia and, since 1878, had "occupied and administered" Bosnia and Herzegovina.

Except for the Greeks and the Romanians, most of the inhabitants of the Balkans spoke variants of the same Slavic language and felt a cultural and historical kinship with one another. For centuries they had been ruled by Austrians, Hungarians, or Turks, and the growing nationalism that characterized late-nineteenth-century Europe made many of them eager for independence. The more radical among them longed for a union of the south Slavic, or Yugoslav, peoples in a single nation. They looked to independent Serbia as the center of the new nation and hoped to detach all the Slavic provinces (especially Bosnia, which bordered on Serbia) from Austria. Serbia believed that its destiny was to unite the Slavs at the expense of Austria, as Piedmont had united the Italians and Prussia the Germans.

In 1908, a group of modernizing reformers called the *Young Turks* brought about a revolution in the Ottoman Empire. Their actions threatened to revive the life of the empire and to interfere with the plans of the European jackals preparing to pounce on the Ottoman corpse. These events brought on the first of a series of Balkan crises that would eventually lead to war.

THE BOSNIAN CRISIS   In 1908, the Austrian and Russian governments decided to act quickly before Turkey became strong enough to resist. They struck a bargain in which Russia agreed to support the Austrian annexation of Bosnia and Herzegovina in return for Austrian backing for opening the Dardanelles to Russian warships.

Austria, however, declared the annexation before the Russians could act. The British and French, eager for the favor of the Young Turks, refused to agree to the Russian demand for the opening of the Dardenelles. The Russians were humiliated and furious, but too weak to do anything but protest. Their "little brothers," the Serbs, were frustrated and angered by the Austrian annexation of Bosnia, which they had hoped one day to annex themselves.

Germany had not been warned in advance of Austria's plans and was unhappy because the action threatened their relations with Russia. Germany felt so dependent on the Dual Alliance, however, that it nevertheless assured Austria of its support. Austria had been given a free hand, and to some extent, German policy was being made in Vienna. It was a dangerous precedent. Also, the failure of Britain and France to support Russia strained the Triple Entente. This made it harder for them to oppose Russian interests in the future if they were to keep Russian friendship.

THE SECOND MOROCCAN CRISIS   The second Moroccan crisis, in 1911, emphasized the French and British need for mutual support. When France sent an army to Morocco to put down a rebellion, Germany took the opportunity to "protect German interests" there as a means of extorting colonial concessions in the French Congo. To add force to their demands, the Germans sent the gunboat *Panther* to the Moroccan port of Agadir, purportedly to protect German citizens there. Once again, as in 1905, the Germans went too far. The *Panther*'s visit to Agadir provoked a strong reaction in Britain. For some time Anglo–German relations had been growing worse, chiefly because of the intensification of the naval race. In 1907 Germany had built its first new dreadnought, a new type of battleship that Britain had launched in 1906. In 1908, Germany had passed still another naval law that accelerated the challenge to British naval supremacy.

These actions frightened and angered the British because they threatened the security of the island kingdom and its empire. The German actions also forced Britain to increase taxes to pay for new armaments just when the Liberal government in Britain was launching its expensive program of social legislation. Negotiations failed to persuade William II and Tirpitz to slow down naval construction.

In this atmosphere, the British heard of the *Panther*'s arrival in Morocco. They wrongly believed that the Germans meant to turn Agadir into a naval base on the Atlantic. The crisis passed when France yielded some insignificant bits of the Congo and Germany recognized the French protectorate over Morocco. The main result was to increase British fear and hostility and to draw Britain closer to France. Specific military plans were formulated for a British expeditionary force to defend France in case of German attack, and the British and French navies agreed to cooperate. Without any formal treaty, the German naval construction and the Agadir crisis had turned the *Entente Cordiale* into a de facto alliance. If Germany attacked France, Britain must defend the French, for its own security was inextricably tied up with that of France.

WAR IN THE BALKANS   The second Moroccan crisis also provoked another crisis in the Balkans. Italy sought to gain colonies and to take its place among the great powers. It wanted Libya, which, though worth little before the discovery of oil in the 1950s, was at least available. Italy feared that the recognition of the French protectorate in Morocco would encourage France also to move into Libya. So, in 1911, Italy attacked the Ottoman Empire to preempt the French, defeated the faltering Turks, and forced Turkey to cede Libya and the Dodecanese Islands in the Aegean. The Italian victory demonstrated Turkish weakness and encouraged the Balkan states to try their luck. In 1912 Bulgaria, Greece, Montenegro, and Serbia jointly attacked the Ottoman Empire and won easily. (See Map 26–4.) After this First Balkan War, the victors fell out among themselves over the division of Macedonia, and in 1913 a Second Balkan War erupted. This time, Turkey and Romania joined the other states against Bulgaria and stripped away much of what the Bulgarians had gained in 1878 and 1912.

After the First Balkan War, the alarmed Austrians were determined to limit Serbian gains and especially to prevent the Serbs from gaining a port on the Adriatic. This policy meant keeping Serbia out of Albania, but the Russians backed the Serbs, and tensions mounted. An international conference sponsored by Britain in early 1913 resolved the matter in Austria's favor and called for an independent kingdom of Albania. Austria, however, felt humiliated by the public airing of Serbian demands, and the Serbs defied the powers and continued to occupy parts of Albania. Under Austrian pressure they eventually withdrew, but they returned to Albania in September 1913, after the Second Balkan War. Finally, in mid-October, Austria unilaterally issued an ultimatum, and Serbia again withdrew its forces from Albania.

During this crisis, many people in Austria had wanted an all-out attack on Serbia to remove its threat to the empire once and for all. Those demands had been resisted by Emperor Francis Joseph and the heir to the throne, Archduke Francis Ferdinand. At the same time, Pan-Slavic sentiment in Russia pressed Tsar Nicholas II to take a firm stand, but Russia once again let Austria have its way in its confrontation with Serbia. Throughout the crisis, Britain, France, Italy, and Germany restrained their allies, although each worried about seeming too reluctant to help its friends.

The lessons learned from this crisis of 1913 profoundly influenced behavior in the final crisis in 1914. As in 1908, the Russians had been embarrassed by their passivity; and their allies were more reluctant to restrain them again. The Austrians were embarrassed by the results of accepting an international conference and were determined not to do it again. They had gotten better results from a threat of direct force; they and their German allies did not miss the lesson.

	Central Powers
	Allies of the Central Powers
	Berlin–Baghdad Railway

(A) THE BALKANS, 1912   (B) THE BALKANS, 1913   (C) CENTRAL EUROPE, 1914

MAP 26–4   THE BALKANS, 1912–1913   *Two maps show the Balkans (a) before and (b) after the two Balkan wars; note the Ottoman retreat. In (c), we see the geographical relationship of the Central Powers and their Bulgarian and Turkish allies.*

Sarajevo and the Outbreak of War (June–August 1914)

THE ASSASSINATION   On June 28, 1914, a young Bosnian nationalist shot and killed Archduke Francis Ferdinand, heir to the Austrian throne, and his wife as they drove in an open car through the Bosnian capital of Sarajevo. The assassin was a member of a conspiracy hatched by a political terrorist society called *Union or Death*, better known as the *Black Hand*. The chief of intelligence of the Serbian army's general staff had helped plan and prepare the crime. Though his role was not actually known at the time, it was generally believed throughout Europe that Serbian officials were involved. The glee of the Serbian press after the assassination lent support to that belief.

Above: The Austrian Archduke Francis Ferdinand and his wife in Sarajevo on June 28, 1914. Later in the day the royal couple were assassinated by young revolutionaries trained and supplied in Serbia, igniting the crisis that led to World War I. Below: Moments after the assassination the Austrian police captured one of the assassins.   Brown Brothers

The archduke was not popular in Austria, and his funeral evoked few signs of grief. He had been known to favor a form of federal government for Austria that would have raised the status of the Slavs in the empire. This position alienated the conservatives among the Habsburg officials and the Hungarians. It also alarmed radical Yugoslav nationalists, who feared that Habsburg reform might end their dream of an independent south Slav state.

GERMANY AND AUSTRIA'S RESPONSE   News of the assassination produced outrage and condemnation everywhere in Europe except in Serbia. To those Austrians who had long favored an attack on Serbia as a solution to the empire's Slavic problem, the opportunity seemed irresistible. But it was never easy for the Dual Monarchy to make a decision. Conrad von Hotzendorf (1852–1925), chief of the Austrian general staff, urged an attack, as he had often done before. Count Stefan Tisza (1861–1918), speaking for Hungary, resisted. Count Leopold von Berchtold (1863–1942), the Austro–Hungarian foreign minister, felt the need for strong action, but he knew that German support would be required in the likely event that Russia should decide to intervene to protect Serbia. He also knew that nothing could be done without Tisza's approval and that only German support could persuade the Hungarians to accept the policy of war. The question of peace or war against Serbia, therefore, had to be answered in Berlin.

William II and Chancellor Theobald von Bethmann-Hollweg (1856–1921) readily promised German support for an attack on Serbia. It has often been said that they gave the Austrians a "blank check," but their message was more specific than that. They urged the Austrians to move swiftly while the other powers were still angry at Serbia. They also made the Austrians feel that they would view a failure to act as evidence of Austria–Hungary's weakness and uselessness as an ally. (See "The Austrian Ambassador Gets a 'Blank Check' from the Kaiser.") Therefore, the Austrians never wavered in their determination to make war on Serbia. They hoped, with the protection of Germany, to fight Serbia alone, but they were prepared to risk a general European conflict. The Germans also knew that they risked a general war, but they too hoped to "localize" the fight between Austria and Serbia.

Some scholars believe that Germany had long been plotting war, and some even think that a specific plan for war in 1914 was set in motion as early as 1912. The vast body of evidence on the crisis of 1914, however, gives little support to such notions. The German leaders plainly reacted to a crisis that they had not foreseen and just as plainly made decisions in response to events. The fundamental

The Austrian Ambassador Gets a "Blank Check" from the Kaiser

It was at a meeting at Potsdam on July 5, 1914, that the Austrian ambassador received assurance from the Kaiser that Germany would support Austria in the Balkans, even at the risk of war.

✣ *Why did the Austrians need to consult the Germans? How did the Kaiser's response compare with German policy in recent crises? Was the check "written" by the Kaiser really blank? How important for the coming of the war was this meeting?*

After lunch, when I again called attention to the seriousness of the situation, the Kaiser authorised me to inform our gracious Majesty that we might in this case, as in all other, rely upon Germany's full support. He must, as he said before, first hear what the Imperial Chancellor has to say, but he did not doubt in the least that Herr von Bethmann Hollweg would agree with him. Especially as far as our action against Serbia was concerned. But it was his [William II's] opinion that this action must not be delayed. Russia's attitude will no doubt be hostile, but to this he had been for years prepared, and should a war between Austria–Hungary and Russia be unavoidable, we might be convinced that Germany, our old faithful ally, would stand at our side. Russia at the present time was in no way prepared for war, and would think twice before it appealed to arms. But it will certainly set other powers on to the Triple Alliance and add fuel to the fire in the Balkans. He understands perfectly well that His Apostolic Majesty in his well-known love of peace would be reluctant to march into Serbia; but if we had really recognised the necessity of warlike action against Serbia, he [William II] would regret if we did not make use of the present moment, which is all in our favour.

From *Outbreak of the World War: German Documents Collected by Karl Kautsky, Max Montgelas and Walther Schücking* (eds.) (New York: Carnegie Endowment for International Peace, 1924), p. 76.

decision to support Austria, however, made war difficult, if not impossible, to avoid. That decision was made by the emperor and chancellor without significant consultation with either their military or diplomatic advisers.

William II appears to have reacted violently to the assassination. He was moved by his friendship for the archduke and by outrage at an attack on royalty. A different provocation would probably not have moved him so much. Bethmann-Hollweg was less emotional, but under severe pressure. To resist the decision would have meant flatly opposing the emperor. The powerful military circles favored by William suspected the chancellor of being "soft." It would have been difficult for him to take a conciliatory position.

Moreover, Bethmann-Hollweg, like many other Germans, feared for the future. Russia was recovering its strength and would reach a military peak in 1917. The Triple Entente was growing closer and more powerful, and Germany's only reliable ally was Austria. The chancellor recognized the danger of supporting Austria, but he believed it to be even more dangerous to withhold that support. If Austria did not crush Serbia, it would soon collapse before the onslaught of Slavic nationalism defended by Russia. If Germany did not defend its ally, the Austrians might look elsewhere for help. His policy was one of "calculated risk."

Unfortunately, the calculations proved to be incorrect. Bethmann-Hollweg hoped that the Austrians would strike swiftly and present the powers with a fait accompli while the outrage of the assassination was still fresh. And he felt that German support would deter Russian involvement. Failing that, he was prepared for a continental war against France and Russia. This policy, though, depended on British neutrality, and the German chancellor convinced himself that the British could be persuaded to stand aloof.

The Austrians, however, were slow to act. They did not even deliver their deliberately unacceptable ultimatum to Serbia until July 24, when the general hostility toward Serbia had begun to subside. Serbia further embarrassed the Austrians by returning so soft and conciliatory an answer that even the mercurial German emperor thought it removed all reason for war. But the Austrians were determined not to turn back. On July 28, they declared war on Serbia, even though the army would not be ready to attack until mid-August.

The Coming of World War I

1871	The end of the Franco–Prussian War; creation of the German Empire; German annexation of Alsace–Lorraine
1873	The Three Emperors' League (Germany, Russia, and Austria–Hungary)
1875	The Russo–Turkish War
1878	The Congress of Berlin
1879	The Dual Alliance between Germany and Austria
1881	The Three Emperors' League is renewed
1882	Italy joins Germany and Austria in the Triple Alliance
1888	William II becomes the German emperor
1890	Bismarck is dismissed
1894	The Franco–Russian alliance
1898	Germany begins to build a battleship navy
1899–1902	Boer War
1902	The British alliance with Japan
1904	The Entente Cordiale between Britain and France
1904–1905	The Russo–Japanese War
1905	The first Moroccan crisis
1907	The British agreement with Russia
1908–1909	The Bosnian crisis
1911	The second Moroccan crisis
1911	Italy attacks Turkey
1912–1913	The First and Second Balkan wars
1914	Outbreak of World War I

THE TRIPLE ENTENTE'S RESPONSE   The Russians, previously so often forced to back off, responded angrily to the Austrian demands on Serbia. The most conservative elements of the Russian government opposed war, fearing that it would lead to revolution, as it had in 1905. But nationalists, Pan-Slavs, and most of the politically conscious classes in general demanded action. The government responded by ordering partial mobilization, against Austria only. This policy was militarily impossible, but its intention was to put diplomatic pressure on Austria to refrain from attacking Serbia.

Mobilization of any kind, however, was a dangerous weapon because it was generally understood to be equivalent to an act of war. It was especially alarming to the German general staff. The possibility that the Russians might start mobilization before the Germans could move would upset the delicate timing of Germany's only battle plan, the Schlieffen Plan, which required an attack on France before the Russians were ready to act, and would put Germany

in great danger. From this point on, the general staff pressed for German mobilization and war. The pressure of military necessity soon became irresistible.

France and Britain were not eager for war. France's president and prime minister were on their way back from a visit to Russia when the crisis flared on July 24. The Austrians had, in fact, timed their ultimatum precisely so that these two men would be at sea when it was delivered to the Serbs. Had they been in Paris, they might have tried to restrain the Russians. The French ambassador to Russia gave the Russians the same assurances, however, that Germany had given its ally. The British worked hard to resolve the crisis by traditional means: a conference of the powers. Austria, still smarting from its humiliation after the London Conference of 1913, would not hear of it. The Germans privately supported the Austrians, but publicly took on a conciliatory tone in the hope of keeping the British neutral.

Soon, however, Bethmann-Hollweg came to realize what he should have known from the first: If Germany attacked France, Britain must fight. Until July 30, his public appeals to Austria for restraint were a sham. Thereafter, he sincerely tried to persuade the Austrians to negotiate and avoid a general war, but it was too late. The Austrians could not turn back without losing their own self-respect and the respect of the Germans.

On July 30, Austria ordered mobilization against Russia. Bethmann-Hollweg resisted the enormous pressure to mobilize, not because he hoped to avoid war, but because he wanted Russia to mobilize against Germany first and appear to be the aggressor. Only in that way could he win the support of the German nation for war, especially the support of pacifist Social Democrats. His luck was good for a change. The news of Russian general mobilization came only minutes before Germany would have mobilized in any case. The Schlieffen Plan went into effect. The Germans occupied Luxembourg on August 1 and invaded Belgium, which resisted, on August 3. The invasion of Belgium violated the treaty of 1839 in which the British had joined the other powers in guaranteeing Belgian neutrality. This factor undermined sentiment in Britain for neutrality and united the nation against Germany, which then invaded France. On August 4, Britain declared war on Germany.

The Great War had begun. As Sir Edward Grey, the British foreign secretary, put it, the lights were going out all over Europe. They would come on again, but Europe would never be the same.

Although debate on the causes of the war continues, the most common opinion today is that German ambitions for a higher place in the international order under the new Kaiser William II led to a new challenge to the status quo. Germany adopted a bullying policy resulting in a series of crises that led to the final crisis in July 1914, when Germany supported—indeed, pushed—its only reliable ally Austria into a war against Serbia that touched off the World War. The deeper causes of that war are seen to be Germany's new ambitions to become a world power like Great Britain and to become the dominant power on the European continent. Germany's decision to build a battleship navy aimed at Great Britain and strong enough at least to make the British stand aside and permit this vast change in the balance of power threatened Britain's interests and security. The British became so alarmed at the prospect, that they launched an expensive and unwelcome naval race to maintain their superiority at sea and abandoned their cherished "splendid isolation" and long-standing competitions with their colonial rivals France and Russia. In an unprecedented reversal of policy, they made an alliance with Japan and agreements with France and Russia to form the "Triple Entente," which grew from a set of colonial accords to an informal, but visible, check on German ambitions. This new international configuration alarmed Germany, which complained that it was being "encircled" by jealous and hostile forces. The Germans feared the growing power of the country's enemies, and consequently, Germany did not seek any serious attempt at negotiations to ease the tension. Instead, a new arms race ensued, and Germany assumed a rigid stance in the final crisis that ended in war.

Strategies and Stalemate: 1914–1917

Throughout Europe, jubilation greeted the outbreak of war. No general war had been fought since Napoleon, and few understood the horrors of modern warfare. The dominant memory was of Bismarck's swift and decisive campaigns, in which the costs and casualties were light and the rewards great. After the repeated crises of recent years and the fears and resentments they had created, war came as a release of tension. The popular press had increased public awareness of, and interest in, foreign affairs and had fanned the flames of patriotism. The prospect of war moved even a rational man of science like Sigmund Freud to say, "My whole libido goes out to Austria–Hungary."[9]

[9]Quoted in Remak, p. 134.

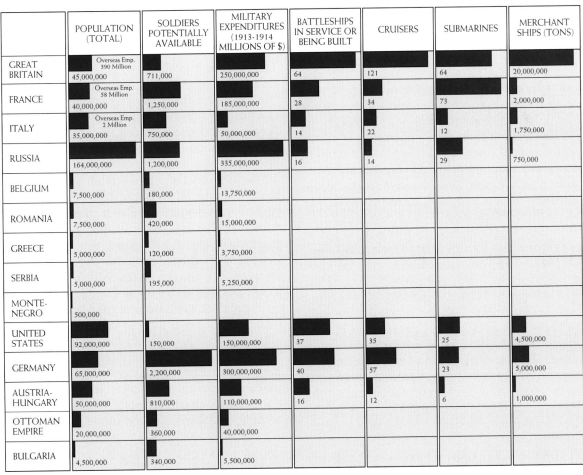

	POPULATION (TOTAL)	SOLDIERS POTENTIALLY AVAILABLE	MILITARY EXPENDITURES (1913-1914 MILLIONS OF $)	BATTLESHIPS IN SERVICE OR BEING BUILT	CRUISERS	SUBMARINES	MERCHANT SHIPS (TONS)
GREAT BRITAIN	Overseas Emp. 390 Million / 45,000,000	711,000	250,000,000	64	121	64	20,000,000
FRANCE	Overseas Emp. 58 Million / 40,000,000	1,250,000	185,000,000	28	34	73	2,000,000
ITALY	Overseas Emp. 2 Million / 35,000,000	750,000	50,000,000	14	22	12	1,750,000
RUSSIA	164,000,000	1,200,000	335,000,000	16	14	29	750,000
BELGIUM	7,500,000	180,000	13,750,000				
ROMANIA	7,500,000	420,000	15,000,000				
GREECE	5,000,000	120,000	3,750,000				
SERBIA	5,000,000	195,000	5,250,000				
MONTE-NEGRO	500,000						
UNITED STATES	92,000,000	150,000	150,000,000	37	35	25	4,500,000
GERMANY	65,000,000	2,200,000	300,000,000	40	57	23	5,000,000
AUSTRIA-HUNGARY	50,000,000	810,000	110,000,000	16	12	6	1,000,000
OTTOMAN EMPIRE	20,000,000	360,000	40,000,000				
BULGARIA	4,500,000	340,000	5,500,000				

FIGURE 26–1 *Relative strengths of the combatants in World War I.*

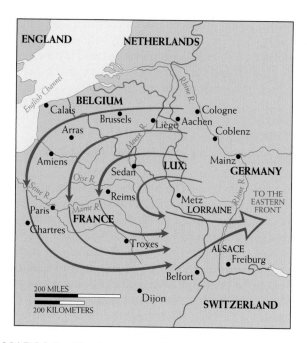

MAP 26–5   THE SCHLIEFFEN PLAN OF 1905 *Germany's grand strategy for quickly winning the war against France in 1914 is shown by the wheeling arrows on the map. In the original plan, the crushing blows at France were to be followed by the release of troops for use against Russia on Germany's eastern front. The plan, however, was not adequately implemented, and the war on the Western Front became a long contest in place.*

Both sides expected to take the offensive, force a battle on favorable ground, and win a quick victory. The Triple Entente powers—or the Allies, as they called themselves—held superiority in numbers and financial resources, as well as command of the sea. (See Figure on p. 907.) Germany and Austria, the Central Powers, had the advantages of possessing internal lines of communication and having launched their attack first.

After 1905 Germany's only war plan was the one developed by Count Alfred von Schlieffen (1833–1913), chief of the German general staff from 1891 to 1906. (See Map 26–5.) It aimed at going around the French defenses by sweeping through Belgium to the Channel and then wheeling to the south and east to envelop the French and crush them against the German fortresses in Lorraine. The secret of success lay in making the right wing of the advancing German army immensely strong and deliberately weakening the left opposite the French frontier. The weakness of the left was meant to draw the French into attacking the wrong place while the war was decided on the German right. As one keen military analyst has explained,

It would be like a revolving door—if a man pressed heavily on one side, the other side would spring round and strike him in the back. Here lay the real subtlety of the plan, not in the mere geographical detour.[10]

In the east, the Germans planned to stand on the defensive against Russia until France had been crushed, a task they thought would take only six weeks.

The apparent risk, besides the violation of Belgian neutrality and the consequent alienation of Britain, lay in weakening the German defenses against a direct attack across the frontier. The strength of German fortresses and the superior firepower of German howitzers made that risk more theoretical than real. The true danger was that the German striking force on the right through Belgium would not be powerful enough to make the swift progress vital to success. Schlieffen is said to have died uttering the words, "It must come to a fight. Only make the right wing strong."

The execution of his plan, however, was left to Helmuth von Moltke (1848–1916), the nephew of Bismarck's most effective general. Despite Schlieffen's warning, Moltke (chief of staff 1906–1914) added divisions to the left wing and even weakened the Russian front for the same purpose. As a result of this hesitant strategy and of theoretical mistakes by German commanders in the field, the Schlieffen Plan failed by a narrow margin.

THE WAR IN THE WEST   The French had also put their faith in the offensive, but with less reason than the Germans. They badly underestimated the numbers and effectiveness of the German reserves and overestimated the importance of the courage and spirit of their own troops. Courage and spirit could not win against machine guns and heavy artillery. The French offensive on Germany's western frontier failed totally. This defeat probably was preferable to a partial success, because it released troops for use against the main German army. As a result, the French and the British were able to stop the German advance on Paris at the Battle of the Marne in September 1914. (See Maps 26–6 and 26–7.)

Thereafter, the nature of the war in the west became one of position instead of movement. Both sides dug in behind a wall of trenches protected by barbed wire that stretched from the North Sea to Switzerland. Strategically placed machine-gun nests made assaults difficult and dangerous. Both sides, nonetheless, attempted massive attacks preceded by artillery bombardments of unprecedented and hor-

---

[10]B. H. Liddell Hart, *The Real War, 1914–1918* (Boston: Little, Brown, 1964; first published in 1930), p. 47.

MAP 26–6   WORLD WAR I IN EUROPE   *Despite the importance of military action in the Far East, in the Arab world, and at sea, the main theaters of activity in World War I were in the European areas.*

MAP 26–7   THE WESTERN FRONT, 1914–1918   *This map shows the crucial western front in detail.*

rible force and duration. Still, the defense was always able to recover and to bring up reserves fast enough to prevent a breakthrough.

Sometimes assaults that cost hundreds of thousands of lives produced advances of only hundreds of yards. The introduction of poison gas to resolve the problem proved ineffective. In 1916 the British introduced the tank, which eventually proved to be the answer to the machine gun, but the Allied command was slow to understand this, and until the end of the war, defense was supreme. For three years after its establishment, the western front moved only a few miles in either direction. (See "Art & the West.")

THE WAR IN THE EAST   In the east, the war began auspiciously for the Allies. The Russians advanced into Austrian territory and inflicted heavy casualties, but Russian incompetence and German energy soon reversed the situation. A junior German officer, Erich Ludendorff (1865–1937), under the command of the elderly General Paul von Hindenburg (1847–1934), destroyed or captured an entire Russian army at the Battle of Tannenberg and defeated another one at the Masurian Lakes. In 1915 the Central Powers pressed

their advantage in the east and drove into the Baltic states and Russian Poland, inflicting more than two million casualties in a single year.

As the battle lines hardened, both sides sought new allies. Turkey (because of its hostility to Russia) and Bulgaria (the enemy of Serbia) joined the Central Powers.

Both sides bid for Italian support with promises of the spoils of victory. Because what the Italians wanted most was held by Austria, the Allies could promise more. In a secret treaty of 1915, they agreed to deliver to Italy after victory most of *Italia Irredenta* (i.e., the South Tyrol, Trieste, and some of the Dalmatian Islands), plus new colonies in Africa and a share of the Turkish Empire. By the spring of 1915, Italy was engaging Austrian armies. The Italian campaign weakened Austria and divided some German troops, but the Italian alliance was generally a disappointment to the Allies and never produced significant results. Romania joined the Allies in 1916, but was quickly defeated and driven from the war.

In the Far East, Japan honored its alliance with Britain and entered the war. The Japanese quickly overran the German colonies in China and the Pacific and used the opportunity to improve their own position against China.

Both sides also appealed to nationalistic sentiment in areas held by the enemy. The Germans supported nationalist movements among the Irish, the Flemings in Belgium, and the Poles and the Ukrainians under Russian rule. They even tried to persuade the Turks to lead a Muslim uprising against the British in Egypt and India and the French in North Africa.

The Allies made the same appeals with greater success. They sponsored movements of national

The 33rd division in a front line trench near Forges, France fires through a fence of barbed wire and sticks.
National Archives

British tanks moving toward the battle of Cambrai in Flanders late in 1917. Tanks were impervious to machine-gun fire. Had they been used in great numbers they might have broken the stalemate in the west. Bildarchiv Preussischer Kulturbesitz

autonomy for the Czechs, the Slovaks, the south Slavs, and the Poles that were under Austrian rule. They also favored a movement of Arab independence from Turkey. Guided by Colonel T. E. Lawrence (1888–1935), this last scheme proved especially successful later in the war.

In 1915, the Allies undertook action to break the deadlock on the western front by going around it. The idea came chiefly from Winston Churchill (1874–1965), first lord of the British admiralty. He proposed to attack the Dardanelles and capture Constantinople. This policy would knock Turkey from the war, bring help to the Balkan front, and ease communications with Russia. The plan was daring, but promising, and in its original form, presented little risk. British naval superiority and the element of surprise would allow the forcing of the straits and the capture of Constantinople by purely naval action. Even if the scheme failed, the fleet could escape with little loss.

The success of Churchill's plan depended on timing, speed, and daring leadership, but all of these were lacking. Worse, the execution of the attack was inept and overly cautious. Troops were landed, and as Turkish resistance continued, the Allied commitment in-

creased. Before the campaign was abandoned, the Allies lost almost 150,000 men and diverted three times that number from more useful occupations.

RETURN TO THE WEST Both sides turned back to the west in 1916. General Erich von Falkenhayn (1861–1922), who had succeeded Moltke in September 1914, sought success by an attack on the French stronghold of Verdun. His plan was not to take the fortress or to break through the French line, but to inflict enormously heavy casualties on the French, who would have to defend Verdun against superior firepower from several directions. He, too, underestimated the superiority of the defense. The French were able to hold Verdun with comparatively few men and to inflict almost as many casualties as they suffered. The commander of Verdun, Henri Pétain (1856–1951), became a national hero, and "They shall not pass" became a slogan of national defiance.

The Allies tried to end the impasse by launching a major offensive along the River Somme in July. Aided by a Russian attack in the East that drew off some German strength and by an enormous artillery bombardment, they hoped at last to break through. Once again, the defense was superior. Enormous ca-

John Singer Sargent, Gassed: The Horrors of Modern War

John Singer Sargent, *Gassed*, 1918–1919. Imperial War Museum, London

Many new weapons were used extensively for the first time in the Great War of 1914–1918, including machine guns, barbed wire, tanks, airplanes, and several kinds of poison gas. The Germans were the first to employ gas as a weapon, firing a nonlethal kind of tear gas at the Russians on the eastern front in January 1915. By April, they had learned how to use the poison gas chlorine against the Allies on the western front. Releasing it from pressurized cylinders, they counted on favorable winds to blow it at the enemy, to kill or disable soldiers, and permit a breakthrough that was otherwise not possible. In time, they brought other horrible gases into play on both fronts, but the device—which killed, blinded, and permanently disabled many—was not militarily effective. Wind proved an unreliable means of propulsion, and better gas masks further reduced the value of such attacks. The use of poison gas as a weapon and the dreadful character of its effects especially caught the public's imagination as a symbol of the horrors of modern war.

The American painter John Singer Sargent (1856–1925) chose one of these attacks as the subject of a vast painting, twenty feet long by seven-and-one-half feet wide, that now hangs in the Imperial War Museum in London. Sargent might be thought an unlikely artist to carry out such an assignment. Born in Florence of American parents, he was trained in Paris in the 1870s. He is best known as the favorite portrait painter of the American and British upper classes. Later in his career, he specialized in watercolor pictures of European landscapes done in the style of the Impressionist painters, and even when the war broke out, he continued with the same subjects.

Propaganda was an important part of the war effort on both sides, and artists, too, were called on to do their part. In 1918, the British War Memorials Committee and Britain's Prime Minister Lloyd George asked Sargent to come to England and paint a very large picture that would show British soldiers and their new American allies cooperating in the fighting. The painter agreed, but changed the subject to a picture of soldiers after a gas attack. He went to France and made sketches on which he based the painting. A friend who traveled with him wrote an account of what they saw:

Gassed cases kept coming in, led along in parties of six just as Sargent depicted them, by an orderly. They sat or lay down on the grass, there may have been several hundred, evidently suffering a great deal, chiefly, I fancy from their eyes which were covered by a piece of lint.

The gas was mustard which causes temporary blindness from swelling the conjunctiva and lids. Sargent was very struck by the scene and immediately made a lot of notes. It was a very fine evening and the sun toward setting.[11]

Gassed has been compared with ancient Greek friezes depicting mythical battles, and there is a clear resemblance, in part because of the shape and size of the canvas and because of the common subject of men at war. There is, however, an important difference in treatment: Where the Greek sculptures always portrayed an element of heroism along with death and suffering, Sargent's painting reveals only the horror of battle.

[11]Quotation from Website of the Imperial War Museum in London, viewed September 1, 1999.

Sources: John Keegan, *The First World War* (New York: Alfred A. Knopf, 1999); Martin Gilbert, *The First World War* (New York: Henry Holt and Co., 1994); Radcliff Carter, *John Singer Sargent* (Abbeville Press, 1982); Website, Imperial War Museum, London.

The Allies promoted Arab efforts to secure independence from Turkey in an effort to remove Turkey from the war. Delegates to the peace conference of 1919 in Paris included British Colonel T. E. Lawrence, who helped lead the rebellion, and representatives from the Middle Eastern region. Prince Feisal, the third son of King Hussein, stands in the foreground of this picture; Colonel T. E. Lawrence is in the middle row, second from the right; and Brigadier General Nuri Pasha Said of Baghdad is second from the left. Corbis

sualties on both sides brought no result. On all fronts, the losses were great and the results meager. The war on land dragged on with no end in sight.

THE WAR AT SEA As the war continued, control of the sea became more important. The British ignored the distinction between war supplies (which were contraband according to international law) and food or other peaceful cargo (which was not subject to seizure). They imposed a strict blockade meant to starve out the enemy, regardless of international law. The Germans responded with submarine warfare meant to destroy British shipping and starve the British. They declared the waters around the British Isles a war zone, where even neutral ships would not be safe. Both policies were unwelcome to neutrals, and especially to the United States, which conducted extensive trade in the Atlantic. Yet the sinking of neutral ships by German submarines was both more dramatic and more offensive than the British blockade.

In May 1915, a German submarine torpedoed the British liner *Lusitania*. Among the 1,200 who drowned were 118 Americans. President Woodrow Wilson (1856–1924) warned Germany that a repetition would have grave consequences; the Germans desisted for the time being, rather than further anger the United States. This development gave the Allies a considerable advantage: Thereafter, the German fleet that had cost so much money and had caused so much trouble played no significant part in the war. The only battle it fought was at Jutland in the spring of 1916. The battle resulted in a standoff and confirmed British domination of the surface of the sea.

AMERICA ENTERS THE WAR In December 1916, President Woodrow Wilson of the United States intervened to try to bring about a negotiated peace. Neither side, however, was willing to renounce war

Major Campaigns and Events of World War I

August 1914	Germans attack in West
August–September 1914	First Battle of the Marne; Battles of Tannenberg and the Masurian Lakes
April 1915	British land at Gallipoli, start of Dardanelles campaign
May 1915	Germans sink British ship *Lusitania*
February 1916	Germans attack Verdun
May–June 1916	Battle of Jutland
February 1917	Germans declare unrestricted submarine warfare
March 1917	Russian Revolution
April 1917	United States enters war
November 1917	Bolsheviks seize power
March 1918	Treaty of Brest–Litovsk
March 1918	German offensive in the West
November 1918	Armistice

aims that its opponent found unacceptable. The war seemed likely to continue until one or both sides reached exhaustion.

Two events early in 1917 changed the situation radically. On February 1, the Germans announced the resumption of unrestricted submarine warfare, which led the United States to break off diplomatic relations. On April 6, the United States declared war on the Central Powers. One of the deterrents to an earlier American intervention had been the presence of autocratic tsarist Russia among the Allies. Wilson could conceive of the war only as an idealistic crusade "to make the world safe for democracy." That problem was resolved in March of 1917 by a revolution in Russia that overthrew the tsarist government.

The Russian Revolution

The March Revolution in Russia was neither planned nor led by any political faction. It was the result of the collapse of the monarchy's ability to govern. Although public opinion in Russia had strongly supported the country's entry into the war, the conflict put far too great demands on Russia's resources and the efficiency of the tsarist government.

Nicholas II was weak and incompetent and was suspected of being under the domination of his German wife and the insidious peasant faith healer Rasputin, who was assassinated by a group of Russian noblemen in 1916. Military and domestic failures produced massive casualties, widespread hunger, strikes by workers, and disorganization in the army. The peasant discontent that had plagued the countryside before 1914 did not subside during the conflict. In 1916 the tsar adjourned the *Duma*, Russian's parliament, and proceeded to rule alone. All political factions were discontented.

The Provisional Government

In early March 1917, strikes and worker demonstrations erupted in Petrograd, as Saint Petersburg had been renamed. The ill-disciplined troops in the

Petrograd Munitions workers demonstrating in 1917. Ria-Novosti/Eastfoto

The Outbreak of the Russian Revolution

The great Russian Revolution of 1917 started with a series of ill-organized demonstrations in Petrograd early in March. The nature of these actions and the ineffectuality of the government's response are described in the memoirs of Maurice Paléologue (1859–1944), the French ambassador.

❖ *What elements contributing to the success of the March Revolution emerge from this selection? Why might the army have been unreliable? Why did the two ambassadors think a new ministry should be appointed? What were the grievances of the revolutionaries? Why is there no discussion of the leaders of the revolution? What role did the emperor (tsar) play in these events?*

Monday, March 12, 1917

At half-past eight this morning, just as I finished dressing, I heard a strange and prolonged din which seemed to come from the Alexander Bridge. I looked out: there was no one on the bridge, which usually presents such a busy scene. But, almost immediately, a disorderly mob carrying red flags appeared at the end which is on the right bank of the Neva, and a regiment came towards it from the opposite side. It looked as if there would be a violent collision, but on the contrary the two bodies coalesced. The army was fraternizing with revolt.

Shortly afterwards, someone came to tell me that the Volhynian regiment of the Guard had mutinied during the night, killed its officers and

was parading the city, calling on the people to take part in the revolution and trying to win over the troops who still remain loyal.

At ten o'clock there was a sharp burst of firing and flames could be seen rising somewhere on the Litenny Prospekt which is quite close to the embassy. Then silence.

Accompanied by my military attaché, Lieutenant-Colonel Lavergne, I went out to see what was happening. Frightened inhabitants were scattering through the streets. There was indescribable confusion at the corner of the Liteïny. Soldiers were helping civilians to erect a barricade. Flames mounted from the Law Courts. The gates of the arsenal burst open with a crash. Suddenly the crack of machine-gun fire split the air: it was the regulars who had just taken up

city refused to fire on the demonstrators. (See "The Outbreak of the Russian Revolution.") The tsar abdicated on March 15. The government of Russia fell into the hands of members of the reconvened *Duma*, who soon formed a provisional government composed chiefly of Constitutional Democrats (Cadets) with Western sympathies.

At the same time, the various socialists, including both Social Revolutionaries and Social Democrats of the Menshevik wing, began to organize the workers into *soviets*, councils of workers and soldiers. Initially, they allowed the provisional government to function without actually supporting it. As relatively orthodox Marxists, the Mensheviks believed that a bourgeois stage of development must come to Russia before the revolution of the proletariat could be achieved. They were willing to work temporarily with the Constitutional Democrats in a liberal regime, but they became estranged when the Cadets failed to control the army or to purge "reactionaries" from the government.

In this climate, the provisional government decided to remain loyal to the existing Russian alliances and to continue the war against Germany. The provisional government thus accepted tsarist foreign policy and associated itself with the source of much domestic suffering and discontent. Its fate was sealed by the collapse of the last Russian offensive in the summer of 1917. Disillusionment with the war, shortages of food and other necessities at home, and the growing demand by the peasants for land reform undermined the government. This occurred even after its leadership had been taken over by the moderate socialist Alexander Kerensky (1881–1970). Moreover, discipline in the army had disintegrated.

Lenin and the Bolsheviks

Ever since April, the Bolshevik wing of the Social Democratic Party had been working against the provisional government. The Germans, in their most position near the Nevsky Prospekt. The revolutionaries replied. I had seen enough to have no doubt as to what was coming. Under a hail of bullets I returned to the embassy with Lavergne who had walked calmly and slowly to the hottest corner out of sheer bravado.

About half-past eleven I went to the Ministry for Foreign Affairs, picking up Buchanan [the British ambassador to Russia] on the way.

I told Pokrovski [the Russian foreign minister] everything I had just witnessed.

"So it's even more serious than I thought," he said.

But he preserved unruffled composure, flavoured with a touch of scepticism, when he told me of the steps on which the ministers had decided during the night:

"The sitting of the Duma has been prorogued to April and we have sent a telegram to the Emperor, begging him to return at once. With the exception of M. Protopopov [the Minister of the Interior, in charge of the police], my colleagues and I all thought that a dictatorship should be established without delay; it would be conferred upon some general whose prestige with the army is pretty high, General Russky for example."

I argued that, judging by what I saw this morning, the loyalty of the army was already too heavily shaken for our hopes of salvation to be based on the use of the "strong hand," and that the immediate appointment of a ministry inspiring confidence in the *Duma* seemed to me more essential than ever, as there is not a moment to lose. I reminded Pokrovski that in 1789, 1830, and 1848, three French dynasties were overthrown because they were too late in realizing the significance and strength of the movement against them. I added that in such a grave crisis the representative of allied France had a right to give the Imperial Government advice on a matter of internal politics.

Buchanan endorsed my opinion.

Pokrovski replied that he personally shared our views, but that the presence of Protopopov in the Council of Ministers paralyzed action of any kind.

I asked him:

"Is there no one who can open the Emperor's eyes to the real situation?"

He heaved a despairing sigh.

"The Emperor is blind!"

Deep grief was writ large on the face of the honest man and good citizen whose uprightness, patriotism and disinterestedness I can never sufficiently extol.

From *Maurice Paléologue, An Ambassador's Memoirs* (London: Doubleday & Company, Inc., and Hutchinson Publishing Group, Ltd., 1924), pp. 221–225.

---

successful attempt at subversion, had rushed the brilliant Bolshevik leader V. I. Lenin in a sealed train from his exile in Switzerland across Germany to Petrograd. They hoped that he would cause trouble for the revolutionary government.

Lenin saw the opportunity to achieve the political alliance of workers and peasants that he had discussed before the war. In speech after speech, he hammered away on the theme of peace, bread, and land. The Bolsheviks demanded that all political power go to the *soviets*, which they controlled. The failure of the summer offensive encouraged them to attempt a coup, but the effort was a failure. Lenin fled to Finland, and his chief collaborator, Leon Trotsky (1879–1940), was imprisoned.

The failure of a right-wing countercoup gave the Bolsheviks another chance. Trotsky, released from prison, led the powerful Petrograd *soviet*. Lenin returned in October, insisted to his doubting colleagues that the time was ripe to take power, and by the extraordinary force of his personality persuaded them to act. Trotsky organized the coup that took place on November 6 and that concluded with an armed assault on the provisional government. The Bolsheviks, almost as much to their own astonishment as to that of the rest of the world, had come to rule Russia.

The Communist Dictatorship

The victors moved to fulfill their promises and to assure their own security. The provisional government had decreed an election for late November to select a Constituent Assembly. The Social Revolutionaries won a large majority over the Bolsheviks. When the assembly gathered in January, it met for only a day before the Red Army, controlled by the Bolsheviks, dispersed it. (See "Lenin Establishes His Dictatorship.") All other political parties also ceased to function in any meaningful fashion. In November and January, the Bolshevik government issued decrees that nationalized the land and turned it over to its peasant proprietors. Factory workers were put

Lenin Establishes His Dictatorship

After the Bolshevik coup in October, elections for the Constituent Assembly were held in November. The results gave a majority to the Social Revolutionary Party and embarrassed the Bolsheviks. Using his control of the Red Army, Lenin closed the Constituent Assembly in January 1918, after it had met for only one day, and established the rule of a revolutionary elite and his own dictatorship. Here is the crucial Bolshevik decree.

❖ *What reasons does Lenin give for closing the legitimately elected Constituent Assembly? What other reasons might he have had? What were the* soviets? *Did they have a legitimate claim to the monopoly of political power? Was the dissolution of the assembly a temporary or permanent measure? What defense can be made for the Bolsheviks' action? Is it enough to justify that action?*

The Constituent Assembly, elected on the basis of lists drawn up prior to the October Revolution, was an expression of the old relation of political forces which existed when power was held by the compromisers and the Cadets. When the people at the time voted for the candidates for the Socialist-Revolutionary Party, they were not in a position to choose between the Right Socialist-Revolutionaries, the supporters of the bourgeoisie, and the Left Socialist-Revolutionaries, the supporters of Socialism. Thus the Constituent Assembly, which was to have been the crown of the bourgeois parliamentary republic, could not but become an obstacle in the path of the October Revolution and the Soviet power.

The October Revolution, by giving the power to the Soviets, and through the Soviets to the toiling and exploited classes, aroused the desperate resistance of the exploiters, and in the crushing of this resistance it fully revealed itself as the beginning of the socialist revolution....the majority in the Constituent Assembly which met on January 5 was secured by the party of the Right Socialist-Revolutionaries, the party of Kerensky, Avksentyev and Chernov. Naturally, this party refused to discuss the absolutely clear, precise, and unambiguous proposal of the supreme organ of Soviet power, the Central Executive Committee of the Soviets, to recognize the program of the Soviet power, to recognize the "Declaration of Rights of the Toiling and Exploited People," to recognize the October Revolution and the Soviet power....

The Right Socialist-Revolutionary and Menshevik parties are in fact waging outside the walls of the Constituent Assembly a most desperate struggle against the Soviet power....

Accordingly, the Central Executive Committee resolves: The Constituent Assembly is hereby dissolved.

Reprinted from *A Documentary History of Communism: Communism in Russia*, Vol. 1, Robert V. Daniels, ed., by permission of University Press of New England; pp. 91–92, "The Dissolution of the Constituent Assembly," Copyright 1984 by the Trustees of the University of Vermont.

in charge of their plants. Banks were taken from their owners and seized for the state, and the debt of the tsarist government was repudiated. Property of the church reverted to the state.

The Bolshevik government also took Russia out of the war, which they believed benefited only capitalism. They signed an armistice with Germany in December 1917. On March 3, 1918, they accepted the Treaty of Brest–Litovsk, by which Russia yielded Poland, the Baltic states, and the Ukraine. Some territory in the Transcaucasus region went to Turkey. The Bolsheviks also agreed to pay a heavy war indemnity.

These terms were a terribly high price to pay for peace, but Lenin had no choice. Russia was incapable of renewing the war effort, and the Bolsheviks needed time to impose their rule on a devastated and chaotic Russia. Moreover, Lenin believed that communist revolutions would soon occur across Europe as a result of the war and the Russian example.

Until 1921 the new Bolshevik government met major domestic resistance. A civil war erupted between the "Red" Russians, who supported the revolution, and the "White" Russians, who opposed it. In the summer of 1918, the Bolsheviks murdered the tsar and his family. Loyal army officers continued to fight the revolution and eventually received aid from the Allied armies. Under the leadership of Trotsky, however, the Red Army eventually overcame the domestic opposition. By 1921, Lenin and his supporters were in firm control.

The End of World War I

The collapse of Russia and the Treaty of Brest–Litovsk were the zenith of German success. The Germans controlled eastern Europe and its resources, especially food, and by 1918 they were free to concentrate their forces on the western front.

These developments would probably have been decisive had they not been balanced by American intervention. Still, American troops would not arrive in significant numbers for about a year, and both sides tried to win the war in 1917.

An Allied attempt to break through in the west failed disastrously. Losses were heavy and the French army mutinied. The Austrians, supported by the Germans, defeated the Italians at Caporetto and threatened to overrun Italy, until they were checked with the aid of Allied troops. The deadlock continued, but time was running out for the Central Powers.

Germany's Last Offensive

In March 1918, the Germans decided to gamble everything on one last offensive. (In this decision they were persuaded chiefly by Ludendorff, by then quartermaster-general, second in command

Women munitions workers in England. World War I demanded more from the civilian populations than had previous wars, resulting in important social changes. The demands of the munitions industries and a shortage of men (so many of whom were in uniform) brought many women out of traditional roles at home and into factories and other war-related work.

Hulton Getty/Archive Photos

to Hindenburg, but the real leader of the army.) The German army pushed forward and even reached the Marne again, but got no farther. They had no more reserves, and the entire nation was exhausted. The Allies, on the other hand, were bolstered by the arrival of American troops in ever-increasing numbers. They were able to launch a counteroffensive that proved to be irresistible. As the Austrian fronts in the Balkans and Italy collapsed, the German high command knew that the end was imminent.

Ludendorff was determined that peace should be made before the German army could be thoroughly defeated in the field and that the responsibility for ending the war should fall on civilians. For some time, he had been the effective ruler of Germany under the aegis of the emperor. He now allowed a new government to be established on democratic principles and to seek peace immediately. The new government, under Prince Max of Baden, asked for peace on the basis of the Fourteen Points that President Wilson had declared as the American war aims. These were idealistic principles, including self-determination for nationalities, open diplomacy, freedom of the seas, disarmament, and the establishment of a league of nations to keep the peace. Wilson insisted that he would deal only with a democratic German government because he wanted to be sure that he was dealing with the German people and not merely their rulers.

German Republican Government Accepts Defeat

The disintegration of the German army forced William II to abdicate on November 9, 1918. The majority branch of the Social Democratic Party proclaimed a republic to prevent the establishment of a soviet government under the control of their radical, Leninist wing, which had earlier broken away as the Independent Socialist Party. Two days later, this republican, socialist-led government signed the armistice that ended the war by accepting German defeat. The German people were, in general, unaware that their army had been defeated in the field and was crumbling. No foreign soldier stood on German soil. Many Germans expected a negotiated and mild settlement. The real peace was quite different and embittered the Germans. Many of them came to believe that Germany had not been defeated, but had been tricked by the enemy and betrayed—even stabbed in the back—by republicans and socialists at home.

The victors rejoiced, but they also had much to mourn. The casualties on all sides came to about ten million dead and twice as many wounded. The economic and financial resources of the European states were badly strained. The victorious Allies, formerly creditors to the world, became debtors to the new American colossus, itself barely touched by the calamities of war.

The Great War, as contemporaries called it, the First World War to those who lived through its horrible offspring, lasted more than four years, doing terrible damage. Battle casualties alone counted 4 million dead and 8.3 million wounded among the Central Powers and 5.4 million dead and 7 million wounded from their opponents, while millions of civilians died from the war and causes arising from it. Among the casualties also were the German, Austro–Hungarian, Russian, and Turkish empires. The American intervention in 1917 thrust the United States into European affairs with a vengeance, and the collapse of the Russian autocracy brought the Bolshevik revolution and the reality of a great communist state. Disappointment, resentment, and economic dislocations caused by the war brought various forms of fascism to Italy, Germany, and other countries. The comfortable nineteenth-century assumptions of inevitable progress based on reason, science and technology, individual freedom, democracy, and free enterprise gave way in many places to cynicism, nihilism, dictatorship, statism, official racism, and class warfare. It is widely agreed that the First World War was the mother of the Second and to most of the horrors of the rest of the century.

These kinds of changes affected the colonial peoples ruled by the European powers, and overseas empires would never again be as secure as they had seemed before the war. Europe was no longer the center of the world, free to interfere when it wished or to ignore the rest of the world if it chose. The memory of that war lived on to shake the nerve of the victorious Western powers as they faced the new conditions of the postwar world.

The Settlement at Paris

The representatives of the victorious states gathered at Versailles and other Parisian suburbs in the first half of 1919. Wilson speaking for the United States, David Lloyd George (1863–1945) for Britain, Georges Clemenceau (1841–1929) for France, and Vittorio Emanuele Orlando (1860–1952) for Italy made up the Big Four. Japan also had an important part in the discussions. The diplomats who met in Paris had a far more difficult task than those who had sat at Vienna a century earlier. Both groups attempted to restore order to the world after long and costly wars. At the earlier conference, however,

The German delegation signs the peace treaty ending World War I in the Hall of Mirrors of the Palace of Versailles on June 28, 1919. This painting by Sir William Orpen, completed in 1921, now hangs in the Imperial War Museum in London. Imperial War Museum, London/Bildarchiv Preussicher Kulturbesitz

Metternich and his associates could confine their thoughts to Europe. France had acknowledged defeat and was willing to take part in and uphold the Vienna settlement. The diplomats at Vienna were not much affected by public opinion; and they could draw the new map of Europe along practical lines determined by the realities of power and softened by compromise.

Obstacles Faced by the Peacemakers

The negotiators at Paris in 1919 were less fortunate. They represented constitutional, generally democratic governments, and public opinion had become a mighty force. Though there were secret sessions, the conference often worked in the full glare of publicity. Nationalism had become almost a secular religion, and Europe's many ethnic groups could not be relied on to remain quiet while they were distributed on the map at the whim of the great powers. World War I, moreover, had been transformed by pro-

paganda and especially by the intervention of Woodrow Wilson into a moral crusade to achieve a peace that would be just as well as secure. The Fourteen Points set forth the right of nationalities to self-determination as an absolute value; but in fact, the map of Europe could not be drawn to match ethnic groups perfectly with their homelands. All these elements made compromise difficult.

Wilson's idealism, moreover, came into conflict with the more practical war aims of the victorious powers and with many of the secret treaties that had been made before and during the war. The British and French people had been told that Germany would be made to pay for the war. Russia had been promised control of Constantinople in return for recognition of the French claim to Alsace–Lorraine and British control of Egypt. Romania had been promised Transylvania at the expense of Hungary.

Some of the agreements contradicted others. Italy and Serbia had competing claims to the islands and shore of the Adriatic. During the war, the British had encouraged Arab hopes of an independent Arab state carved out of the Ottoman Empire. Those plans, however, contradicted the Balfour Declaration (1917), in which the British seemed to accept Zionist ideology and to promise the Jews a national home in Palestine. Both of these plans conflicted with an Anglo–French agreement to divide the Near East between themselves.

The continuing national goals of the victors presented further obstacles to an idealistic "peace without victors." France was painfully conscious of its numerical inferiority to Germany and of the low birthrate that would keep it inferior. So France was naturally eager to weaken Germany permanently and preserve French superiority. Italy continued to seek the acquisition of *Italia Irredenta*, Britain continued to look to its imperial interests, and Japan pursued its own advantage in Asia. The United States insisted on freedom of the seas, which favored American commerce, and on its right to maintain the Monroe Doctrine.

Finally, the peacemakers of 1919 faced a world still in turmoil. The greatest immediate threat appeared to be the spread of Bolshevism. While Lenin and his colleagues were distracted by civil war, the Allies landed small armies at several places in Russia to help overthrow the Bolshevik regime. The revolution seemed likely to spread as communist governments were established in Bavaria and Hungary. Berlin also experienced a dangerous communist uprising led by the "Spartacus group." The Allies were sufficiently worried by these developments to support their suppression by right-wing military forces. They even allowed an army of German volunteers to operate against the Bolsheviks in the Baltic states.

Fear of the spread of communism affected the diplomats at Versailles, but it was far from dominant. The Germans played on such fears to get better terms, but the Allies, especially the French, would not hear of it. Fear of Germany remained the chief concern for France. More traditional and more immediate interests governed the policies of the other Allies.

The Peace

The Paris settlement consisted of five separate treaties between the victors and the defeated powers. Formal sessions began on January 18, 1919, and the last treaty was signed on August 10, 1920. (See Map 26–8.) Wilson arrived in Europe to unprecedented popular acclaim. Liberals and idealists expected a new kind of international order achieved in a new and better way, but they were soon disillusioned. "Open covenants openly arrived at" soon gave way to closed sessions in which Wilson, Clemenceau, and Lloyd George made arrangements that seemed cynical to outsiders.

The notion of "a peace without victors" became a mockery when the Soviet Union (as Russia was now called) and Germany were excluded from the peace conference. The Germans were simply presented with a treaty and compelled to accept it, fully justified in their complaint that the treaty had been dictated, not negotiated. The principle of national self-determination was violated many times, as was unavoidable. Still, the diplomats of the small nations were angered by their exclusion from decisions. The undeserved adulation accorded Wilson on his arrival gradually turned into equally undeserved scorn. He had not abandoned his ideals lightly, but had merely given way to the irresistible force of reality.

THE LEAGUE OF NATIONS   Wilson could make unpalatable concessions without abandoning his ideals because he put great faith in a new instrument for peace and justice: the League of Nations. Its covenant was an essential part of the peace treaty. The league was to be not an international government, but a body of sovereign states that agreed to pursue common policies and to consult in the common interest, especially when war threatened. The members promised to submit differences among themselves to arbitration, an international court, or the League Council. Refusal to abide by the results would justify league actions in the form of economic sanctions and even military intervention. The league was unlikely to be effective, however, because it had no armed forces at its disposal. Furthermore, any action required the unanimous consent of its council, consisting permanently of Britain, France, Italy, the United States, and Japan, as well as four other states that had temporary seats. The Covenant of the League bound its members to "respect and preserve" the territorial integrity of all its members; this was generally seen as a device to ensure the security of the victorious powers. The exclusion of Germany and the Soviet Union from the League Assembly further undermined its claim to evenhandedness.

COLONIES   Another provision of the covenant dealt with colonial areas. These were called mandates and were placed under the "tutelage" of one of the great powers under league supervision and encouraged to advance toward independence. This provision had no teeth, and little advance was made. Provisions for disarmament were equally ineffective. Members of the league remained fully sovereign and continued to pursue their own na-

MAP 26–8 WORLD WAR I PEACE SETTLEMENT IN EUROPE AND THE MIDDLE EAST   *The map of central and eastern Europe, as well as that of the Middle East, underwent drastic revision after World War I. The enormous territorial losses suffered by Germany, Austria–Hungary, the Ottoman Empire, Bulgaria, and Russia were the other side of the coin represented by gains for France, Italy, Greece, and Romania and by the appearance or reappearance of at least eight new independent states from Finland in the north to Yugoslavia in the south. The mandate system for former Ottoman territories outside Turkey proper laid foundations for several new, mostly Arab, states in the Middle East. In Africa, the mandate system placed the former German colonies under British, French, and South African rule. (See Map 26–2.)*

tional interests. Only Wilson put much faith in the league's future ability to produce peace and justice. To get the other states to agree to the league, he approved territorial settlements that violated his own principles.

GERMANY   In the West, the main territorial issue was the fate of Germany. Although a united Germany was less than fifty years old, no one seems to have thought of undoing Bismarck's work and dividing the country into its component parts. The French would have liked to set the Rhineland up as a separate buffer state, but Lloyd George and Wilson would not permit it. Still, they could not ignore France's need for protection against a resurgent Germany. France received Alsace–Lorraine and the right to work the coal mines of the Saar for fifteen years. Germany west of the Rhine and fifty kilometers east of it was to be a demilitarized zone; Allied troops could stay on the west bank for fifteen years.

In addition to this physical barrier to a new German attack, the treaty provided that Britain and the United States would guarantee aid to France if it were attacked by Germany. Such an attack was made more unlikely by the permanent disarmament of that country. Germany's army was limited to 100,000 men on long-term service, its fleet was reduced to a coastal defense force, and it was forbidden to have warplanes, submarines, tanks, heavy artillery, or poison gas. As long as these provisions were observed, France would be safe.

THE EAST   The settlement in the East reflected the collapse of the great defeated empires that had ruled it for centuries. Germany lost part of Silesia, and East Prussia was cut off from the rest of Germany by a corridor carved out to give the revived state of Poland access to the sea. The Austro–Hungarian Empire disappeared entirely, giving way to five small successor states. Most of its German-speaking people were gathered in the Republic of Austria, cut off from the Germans of Bohemia and forbidden to unite with Germany.

The Magyars were left with the much-reduced kingdom of Hungary. The Czechs of Bohemia and Moravia joined with the Slovaks and Ruthenians to the east to form Czechoslovakia, and this new state included several million unhappy Germans plus Poles and Magyars. The southern Slavs were united in the Kingdom of Serbs, Croats, and Slovenes, or Yugoslavia. Italy gained Trentino and Trieste. Romania was enlarged by receiving Transylvania from Hungary and Bessarabia from Russia. Bulgaria lost territory to Greece, Romania, and Yugoslavia. Russia lost vast territories in the west.

Finland, Estonia, Latvia, and Lithuania became independent states, and most of Poland was carved out of formerly Russian soil.

REPARATIONS   Perhaps the most debated part of the peace settlement dealt with reparations for the damage done by Germany during the war. Before the armistice, the Germans promised to pay compensation "for all damages done to the civilian population of the Allies and their property." The Americans judged that the amount would be between $15 billion and $25 billion and that Germany would be able to pay that amount. France and Britain, however, worried about repaying their war debts to the United States, were eager to have Germany pay the full cost of the war, including pensions to survivors and dependents.

There was general agreement that Germany could not afford to pay such a huge sum, whatever it might be, and no sum was fixed at the conference. In the meantime, Germany was to pay $5 billion annually until 1921. At that time, a final figure would be set, which Germany would have to pay in thirty years. The French did not regret the outcome. Either Germany would pay and be bled into impotence, or Germany would refuse to pay and French intervention would be warranted.

To justify these huge reparation payments, the Allies inserted the notorious Clause 231 into the treaty:

> The Allied and Associated Governments affirm, and Germany accepts, the responsibility of Germany and her allies for causing all the loss and damage to which the Allied and Associated Governments and their nationals have been subjected as a consequence of the war imposed upon them by aggression of Germany and her allies.

The Germans, of course, did not believe that they were solely responsible for the war and bitterly resented the charge. They had lost territories containing badly needed natural resources. Yet they were presented with an astronomical and apparently unlimited reparations bill. To add insult to injury, they were required to admit to a war guilt that they did not feel.

Finally, to heap insult upon insult, they were required to accept the entire treaty as it was written by the victors, without any opportunity for negotiation. Germany's Prime Minister Philipp Scheidmann (1865–1939) spoke of the treaty as the imprisonment of the German people and asked, "What hand would not wither that binds itself and us in these fetters?" But there was no choice. The Social Democrats and the Catholic Center Party formed a new government, and their representatives signed the treaty. These parties formed the backbone of the Weimar government that ruled Germany until 1933. They never overcame the stigma of having accepted the Treaty of Versailles.

Evaluation of the Peace

Few peace settlements have undergone more severe attacks than the one negotiated in Paris in 1919. It was natural that the defeated powers should object to it, but the peace soon came under bitter criticism in the victorious countries as well. Many of the French objected that the treaty tied French security to promises of aid from the unreliable Anglo–Saxon countries. In England and the United States, a wave of bitter criticism arose in liberal quarters because the treaty seemed to violate the idealistic and liberal aims that the Western leaders had professed.

It was not a peace without victors. It did not put an end to imperialism, but attempted to promote the national interests of the winning nations. It violated the principles of national self-determination by leaving significant pockets of minorities outside the borders of their national homelands.

THE ECONOMIC CONSEQUENCES OF THE PEACE   The most influential economic critic of the treaty was John Maynard Keynes (1883–1946), a brilliant British economist who took part in the peace conference. He resigned in disgust when he saw the direction it was taking. His book, *The Economic Consequences of the Peace* (1920), was a scathing attack, especially on reparations and the other economic aspects of the peace. It was also a skillful assault on the negotiators and particularly on Wilson, who was depicted as a fool and a hypocrite. Keynes argued that the Treaty of Versailles was both immoral and unworkable. He called it a Carthaginian peace, referring to the utter destruction of Carthage by Rome after the Third Punic War. He argued that such a peace would bring economic ruin and war to Europe unless it were repudiated.

Keynes's argument had a great effect on the British, who were already suspicious of France and glad of an excuse to withdraw from continental affairs. The decent and respectable position came to be one that supported revision of the treaty in favor of Germany. Even more important was the book's influence in the United States. It fed the traditional American tendency toward isolationism and gave powerful weapons to Wilson's enemies. Wilson's own political mistakes helped prevent American ratification of the treaty. Thus, America was out of the League of Nations and not bound to defend France. Britain, therefore, was also free from its obligation to France. France was left to protect itself without adequate means to do so for long.

Many of the attacks on the Treaty of Versailles are unjustified. It was not a Carthaginian peace. Germany was neither dismembered nor ruined.

Reparations could be and were scaled down. Until the great world depression of the 1930s, the Germans recovered a high level of prosperity. Complaints against the peace should also be measured against the peace that the victorious Germans had imposed on Russia at Brest-Litovsk and their plans for a European settlement in case of victory. Both were far more severe than anything enacted at Versailles. The attempt at achieving self-determination for nationalities was less than perfect, but it was the best effort Europe had ever made to do so.

DIVISIVE NEW BOUNDARIES AND TARIFF WALLS   The peace, nevertheless, was unsatisfactory in important ways. The elimination of the Austro–Hungarian Empire, however inevitable, created several serious problems. Economically, it was disastrous, for it separated raw materials from manufacturing areas and producers from their markets by new boundaries and tariff walls. In hard times, this separation created friction and hostility that aggravated other quarrels also created by the peace treaties. Poland contained unhappy German and Ukrainian minorities, and Czechoslovakia was a collection of nationalities that did not find it easy to live together as a nation. Disputes over territories in eastern Europe promoted further tension.

The peace was inadequate on another level as well. It rested on a victory that Germany did not admit. The Germans believed that they had been cheated rather than defeated. And the high moral principles proclaimed by the Allies undercut the validity of the peace, for it plainly fell far short of those principles.

FAILURE TO ACCEPT REALITY   Finally, the great weakness of the peace was its failure to accept reality. Germany and Russia must inevitably play an important part in European affairs, yet they were excluded from the settlement and from the League of Nations. Given the many discontented parties, the peace was not self-enforcing; yet no satisfactory machinery for enforcing it was established. The League of Nations was never a serious force for this purpose. It was left to France, with no guarantee of support from Britain and no hope of help from the United States, to defend the new arrangements. Finland, the Baltic states, Poland, Romania, Czechoslovakia, and Yugoslavia were expected to be a barrier to the westward expansion of Russian communism and to help deter a revival of German power. Most of these states, however, would have to rely on France in case of danger, and France was simply not strong enough to protect them if Germany were to rearm.

The tragedy of the Treaty of Versailles was that it was neither conciliatory enough to remove the desire for change, even at the cost of war, nor harsh enough to make another war impossible. The only hope for a lasting peace was that Germany would remain disarmed while the more obnoxious clauses of the peace treaty were revised. Such a policy required continued attention to the problem, unity among the victors, and farsighted leadership; but none of these was consistently present during the next two decades.

In Perspective

The outburst of European imperialism in the last part of the nineteenth century brought the Western countries into contact with almost all the inhabited areas of the world. They intensified their activity in places where they had already been interested. The growth of industry, increased ease of transportation and communication, and the burgeoning of a world economic system all brought previously remote and isolated places into the orbit of the West.

By the time of the outbreak of the war, European nations had divided Africa among themselves for exploitation in one way or another. The vast subcontinent of India had long been a British colony. The desirable parts of China were under European commercial control. Indochina was under French rule, and the islands of the Pacific had been divided among the powers. Much of the Near East was under the nominal control of the Ottoman Empire, in its death throes and under European influence. The Monroe Doctrine made Latin America a protectorate of the United States. Japan, pushed out of its isolation, had itself become an imperial power at the expense of China and Korea.

But the world created by the New Imperialism did not last long. What began as yet another Balkan war involving the European powers became a general war that profoundly affected much of the rest of the world. As the terrible war of 1914–1918 dragged on, the real motives that had driven the European powers to fight gave way to public affirmations of the principles of nationalism and self-determination. The peoples under colonial rule took the public statements—and promises sometimes made to them in private—seriously and sought to win their independence and nationhood.

Mostly, they were disappointed by the peace settlement. The establishment of the League of Nations and the system of mandates in place of the previous system of open colonial rule changed lit-

tle. The British Empire grew even larger as it inherited vast territories from the defeated German and the defunct Ottoman empires. The French retained and expanded their holdings in Africa, the Pacific, and the Near East. The Americans added to the islands they controlled in the Pacific. Japanese imperial ambitions were rewarded at the expense of China.

A glance at the new map of the world could give the impression that the old imperial nations, especially Britain and France, were more powerful than ever, but that impression would be superficial and misleading. The great western European powers had paid an enormous price in lives, money, and will for their victory in the war. Colonial peoples pressed for the rights that were proclaimed as universal by the West, but denied to their colonies; and some influential minorities in the countries that ruled those colonies sympathized with colonial aspirations for independence. Tension between colonies and their ruling nations was a cause of serious instability in the world created by the Paris treaties of 1919.

REVIEW QUESTIONS

1. To what areas of the world did Europe extend its power after 1870? How and why did European attitudes toward imperialism change after 1870? What features differentiate the New Imperialism from previous imperialistic movements? What features did they have in common?

2. What role in the world did Bismarck envisage for the new Germany after 1871? How successful was he in carrying out his vision? What was Bismarck's attitude toward colonies? Was he wise to tie Germany to Austria–Hungary?

3. Why and in what stages did Britain abandon its policy of "splendid isolation" at the turn of the century? Were the policies it pursued instead wise ones, or should Britain have followed a different course altogether?

4. How did developments in the Balkans lead to the outbreak of World War I? What was the role of Serbia? Of Austria? Of Russia? What was the aim of German policy in July 1914? Did Germany want a general war?

5. Why did Germany lose World War I? Could Germany have won, or was victory never a possibility? Assess the settlement of Versailles. What were its benefits to Europe, and what were its drawbacks? Was the settlement too harsh or too conciliatory? Could it have secured lasting peace in Europe? How might it have been improved?

6. Why was Lenin successful in establishing Bol-

shevik rule in Russia? What role did Trotsky play? Was it wise policy for Lenin to take Russia out of the war?

SUGGESTED READINGS

L. ALBERTINI, *The Origins of the War of 1914, 3 VOLS. (1952, 1957)*. Discursive, but invaluable.

M. BALFOUR, *The Kaiser and His Times* (1972). A fine biography of William II.

V. R. BERGHAHN, *Germany and the Approach of War in 1914* (1973). A work similar in spirit to Fischer's 1967 book (see later), but stressing the importance of Germany's naval program.

R. BOSWORTH, *Italy and the Approach of the First World War* (1983). A fine analysis of Italian policy.

L. CECIL, *Wilhelm II, Prince and Emperor, 1859–1900* (1989). The first part of a projected two-volume history of the kaiser.

S. B. FAY, *The Origins of the World War*, 2 vols. (1928). The best and most influential of the revisionist accounts.

N. FERGUSON, *The Pity of War* (1999). An analytic study of important aspects of the First World War with controversial interpretations, especially of why it began and why it ended.

D. K. FIELDHOUSE, *The Colonial Experience: A Comparative Study from the Eighteenth Century* (1966). An excellent recent study.

F. FISCHER, *Germany's Aims in the First World War* (1967). An influential interpretation that stirred an enormous controversy by emphasizing Germany's role in bringing on the war.

F. FISCHER, *War of Illusions* (1975). A long and diffuse book that tries to connect German responsibility for the war with internal social, economic, and political developments.

I. GEISS, *July 1914* (1967). A valuable collection of documents by a student of Fritz Fischer. The emphasis is on German documents and responsibility.

O. J. HALE, *The Great Illusion, 1900–1914* (1971). A fine survey of the period, especially good on public opinion.

M. B. HAYNE, *The French Foreign Office and the Origins of the First World War* (1993). An examination of the work of the influence on French policy of the professionals in the foreign service.

H. HERWIG, *The First World War: Germany and Austria, 1914–18* (1997). A fine study of the war from the losers' perspective.

J. N. HORNE, *Labour at War: France and Britain, 1914–1918* (1991). An examination of a major issue on the home fronts.

J. JOLL, *The Origins of the First World War* (1984). A brief, but thoughtful, analysis.

J. KEEGAN, *The First World War* (1999). A vivid and readable narrative account.

P. KENNEDY, *The Rise of the Anglo–German Antagonism, 1860–1914* (1980). An unusual and thorough analysis of the political, economic, and cultural roots of important diplomatic developments.

W. L. LANGER, *The Diplomacy of Imperialism* (1935). An excellent study of the diplomatic history of the years 1890–1902.

W. L. LANGER, *European Alliances and Alignments*, 2d ed. (1966). An admirable diplomatic history of the years 1871–1890.

D. C. B. LIEVEN, *Russia and the Origins of the First World War* (1983). A good account of the forces that shaped Russian policy.

W. J. MOMMSEN, *Theories of Imperialism* (1980). A study of the debate on the meaning of imperialism.

G. SCHÖLLGEN, *Escape Into War? The Foreign Policy of Imperial Germany* (1990). A valuable collection of interpretive essays.

J. STEINBERG, *Yesterday's Deterrent* (1965). An excellent study of Germany's naval policy and its consequences.

Z. STEINER, *Britain and the Origins of the First World War* (1977). A perceptive and informed account of the way British foreign policy was made before the war.

A. J. P. TAYLOR, *The Struggle for Mastery in Europe, 1848–1918* (1954). Clever, but controversial.

L. C. F. TURNER, *Origins of the First World War* (1970). Especially good on the significance of Russia and its military plans.

S. R. WILLIAMSON, JR., *Austria–Hungary and the Origins of the First World War* (1991). A valuable new study of a complex subject.

Imperialism: Ancient and Modern

The concept of "empire" does not win favor today, and the word *imperialism*, derived from it, has carried an increasingly pejorative meaning since it was coined in the nineteenth century. Both words imply forcible domination by a nation or a state that exploits an alien people for its own benefit. Although, in our time, the charge of "imperialism" arises whenever a large and powerful nation influences weaker ones, exertion of influence alone is not imperialism. To be true to historical experience, one nation's actions toward another are imperialistic only if the dominant nation exerts both political and military control over the weaker one. In that sense, the last great empire in the modern world was the conglomeration of republics and ostensibly independent satellite states dominated by Russia prior to the USSR's collapse. But the Russians and the other imperial powers after World War II took no public pride in their domination. In our day, ruling an "empire" or engaging in "imperialism" is generally considered among the worst acts a nation can commit.

Such views are rare, perhaps unique, in the history of civilization. A major source for this opinion is the Christian religious tradition, especially parts of the New Testament that deprecate power and worldly glory and praise humility. But in fact, Christianity was not hostile to power and empire, for it took control of the Roman Empire in the fourth century C.E. and has lived comfortably with "empire" until our own century. The rise of democracy and nationalism in the last two centuries may have been more influential in changing attitudes toward imperialism because these movements exalt the freedom and autonomy of a people. But perhaps the modern disdain for empire-building has its principal origins in the extraordinary horror of modern warfare and the historical knowledge that competition for empire has often led to war.

If, however, we are to understand the widespread experience of empire throughout history, we must be alert to the great gap that separates the views of most people throughout history from our current opinions. The earliest empires go back more than four thousand years to the valleys of the Nile and the Tigris-Euphrates, and empires arose later in China, Japan, India, Iran, and Central and South America, among other areas. Typically, they were led by rulers who were believed to be gods or the representatives of gods, or at least were godlike in their ability to rule over many people. To their own people they brought wealth and prosperity, power, and reflected glory, all considered highly desirable. No one appears to have questioned the propriety of conquering another people and taking their lands, property, and persons to benefit the conquerors. Empire seemed to be part of the order of things—good for the rulers, usually bad for the ruled.

The Greeks: Ambiguities of Power

In most respects, the Greeks resembled other ancient peoples in their attitudes toward power, conquest, empire, and the benefits that came with them. Their Olympian gods held sway over Earth, heaven, and the underworld because of victorious wars over other deities, and they gloried in their rule. The heroes in the epic poems that formed the Greek system of values won glory and honor through battle, conquest, and rule over other people. They viewed the world as a place of intense competition in which victory and domination, which brought fame and glory, were the highest goals, while defeat and subordination brought ignominy and shame.

When the legendary world of aristocratic heroes gave way to the world of city-states (*poleis*), competition was elevated from contests among individuals, households, and clans to contests and wars among *poleis*. In 416 B.C.E., more than a decade after the death of Pericles (c. 490–429 B.C.E.), Athenian spokesmen explained to some Melian officials their view of international relations: "Of the gods we believe, and of men we know, that by a necessity of their nature they always rule wherever they have the power." (Thucydides 5.105) Although their language was shockingly blunt, it reflected the views of most Greeks.

Yet this was also a dramatic presentation of the morally problematic status of the Athenian Empire. The Athenians' harsh statement would have struck a sympathetic chord among the Greeks. They appreciated power and the security and glory it can bring, but their own historical experience was dif-

Exile of the Israelites. In 1722 B.C.E. the northern part of Jewish Palestine, the kingdom of Israel, was conquered by the Assyrians. Its people were driven from their homeland and exiled all over the vast Assyrian empire. This wall carving in low relief comes from the palace of the Assyrian king Sennacherib at Nineveh. It shows the Jews with their cattle and baggage going into exile. Erich Lessing/Art Resource, N.Y.

ferent from that of other ancient nations. Their culture had been shaped by small, autonomous, independent city-states, and they considered freedom natural for people raised in such an environment. Citizens, they believed, should be free in their persons, free to maintain their own constitutions, laws, and customs, and their city-states should be free to conduct their own foreign relations and to compete for power and glory. The free, autonomous *polis*, they thought, was greater than the mightiest powers in the world, and the sixth-century B.C.E. poet Phocylides was prepared to compare it to the great Assyrian Empire: "A little *polis* living orderly in a high place is greater than block-headed Nineveh." (Fragment 5)

When *poleis* fought one another, the victor typically took control of a piece of border land that was usually the source of the dispute. They did not normally enslave the defeated enemy or annex and occupy its land. In these matters, as in many others, the Greeks distinguished themselves from alien peoples who did not speak Greek and were not shaped by the Greek cultural tradition. These people were called barbarians, *barbaroi*, because their speech sounded to the Greeks like "bar bar." Since they had not been raised as people in free communities, but lived as subjects to a ruler, they were, it seemed, slaves by nature. To the Greeks, then, dominating and enslaving such people was perfectly acceptable. Greeks, on the other hand, viewed themselves as naturally free, as they demonstrated by creating and living in the free institutions of the *polis*. To rule over such people, to deny them their freedom and autonomy, would be wrong. So the Greeks thought, but they did not always act accordingly. The early Spartans, for instance, had changed the status of the conquered Greeks of Laconia and Messenia to *Helots*, or slaves of the state.

The Greeks shared still another belief that interfered with the comfortable acceptance of great power and empire: They thought that any good thing amassed by humans to excess, beyond moderation, eventually led to *hybris*, a condition of wanton violence arising from arrogant pride in one's greatness. Those overcome by *hybris* were thought to have overstepped the limits established for human beings, to have shown contempt for the gods and, thereby, to have incurred *nemesis*, or divine anger and retribution. The great example to the Greeks of the fifth century of the workings of *hybris* and *nemesis* was the fate of Xerxes (r. 486–465 B.C.E.), Great King of the Persian Empire. His power became so great that it filled him with a blind arrogance that led him to try to extend his rule over the Greek mainland and thus brought disaster to himself and his people. When, therefore, the Athenians undertook the leadership of a Greek alliance after the Persian War, and that leadership brought them wealth and power and, in fact, turned into what was frankly acknowledged to be an empire, their response was ambiguous and contradictory. These developments were a source of pride and gratification, but also of embarrassment and, to some Athenians, shame.

The Macedonian conquest of the Greek city-states in 338 B.C.E. marked a return to an older attitude toward empire. Alexander the Great (r. 340–323 B.C.E.) conquered the vast Persian Empire, itself the successor of empires that had stretched from the Nile to the Indus valley. The death of Alexander led to its division and eventual absorption by the emergent Roman Empire by the second century B.C.E.

The Romans: A Theory of Empire

The Romans had fewer hesitations about the desirability of imperial power than the Greeks. Their culture, which arose from a world of farmers accustomed to hard work, deprivation, and subordination to authority, venerated the military virtues. Roman society valued power, glory, and the responsibilities of leadership, even domination, without embarrassment. In time, the Romans formulated a theory of empire that claimed that Roman rule brought great advantages to its subjects: prosperity, justice, the rule of law, and, most valuable of all, peace. In the words of their great epic poet Vergil (70–19 B.C.E.), it was the Roman practice "To humble the arrogant and be sparing to their

The philosopher–emperor Marcus Aurelius was compelled to spend much of his time fighting against tribal invaders on Rome's northern frontiers. This relief from the triumphal arch dedicated to him in Rome (176–180) shows him mounted, on campaign. Nimatallah/Art Resource

subjects." These claims had considerable foundation, and the Romans could not have ruled so vast an empire with a relatively small army for more than half a millennium if their subjects had not enjoyed these benefits. Some of the conquered had a different viewpoint, however. As one British chieftain put it in the first century C.E.: "They make a wilderness and call it peace."

Muslims, Mongols, and Ottomans

The rise of Islam in the seventh century C.E. produced a new kind of empire that derived its energy from religious zeal. Bursting out of Arabia, the Muslim armies swiftly gained control of most of the territory held by the old Persian Empire, North Africa, and Spain.

In the twelfth and thirteenth centuries, the great Mongol Empire, at its height, dominated Eurasia from the Pacific to central Europe, ruling Russia for more than two centuries. As in most ancient empires, the Mongols demanded taxes and military service from the conquered. They also imposed their rule over the mighty and long-standing Chinese Empire, parts of India, and much of the Islamic world before their power declined.

Still another great empire that spanned Europe and Asia was that of the Ottomans, a Turkish people, originally from central Asia. In the fourteenth century, they established a kingdom in Anatolia (Asia Minor) and soon conquered the ancient Byzantine Empire, seizing Constantinople in 1453. In the next century, the Ottoman Empire dominated southeastern Europe, the Black Sea, North Africa from Morocco to Egypt, Palestine, Syria and Arabia, Mesopotamia and Iraq, and Kurdistan and Georgia in the Caucasus. As late as 1683, Ottoman armies threatened to take Vienna and push into western Europe. Over the next two centuries, however, Ottoman power declined as the European national states grew stronger. Russia, in particular, inflicted defeats that left Turkey in the late nineteenth century, "the sick man of Europe."

European Expansion

Europe, divided first by feudalism, then by the emergence of multiple nascent national states, had been the victim of Islamic imperial expansion during the Middle Ages, first at the hands of the Arabs, then the Turks. The crusades had produced small and transitory conquests. It was only in the late 1400s that Europeans began the economic and political expansion that culminated in their command of much of the planet by 1900. The first phase of European expansion involved the "discovery," exploration, conquest, exploitation, and settlement of the Americas. It was made possible by important developments in naval and military technology, the dynamism inherent in early commercial and financial capitalism, and the freedom to compete for wealth and power unleashed by the division into separate states.

Spain and Portugal took the lead, founding empires in central and South America, sometimes conquering existing empires ruled by native peoples. In Central America the Aztecs exacted labor and taxes from their subject peoples, using some of them as human sacrifices. In the Andes the Incas ruled a great empire that also required military service and forced labor from its subjects. Both Native American empires were overthrown by Spain, which then established a vast American empire whose resources, especially gold and silver, formed the basis of the great Spanish Empire in Europe. Portugal exploited the agricultural and mineral riches of Brazil using slaves imported from Africa.

The seventeenth century saw the establishment of European trading posts and then colonies on the Indian subcontinent and in the East Indies, chiefly by the Dutch, British, and French. In North America Spain held Mexico, Florida, and California. Of more lasting significance were French and British settlements in Canada and what was to become the United States. The British colonies, especially, represented a special kind of European overseas settlement in which concern for commerce was less important than the acquisition of land for farming.

The wars of the eighteenth century ultimately cleared North America and India of French competition, leaving both as British monopolies and important bases of what would become a world-wide British Empire. The largest and most populous empire in the history of the world, it included colonies of one sort or another on all the inhabited continents; the sun, as the saying went, never set on the British Empire. Whether European colonialism was profitable for the imperial powers is still controversial, but Great Britain certainly benefited more than the others. Unlike most colonial powers, the British

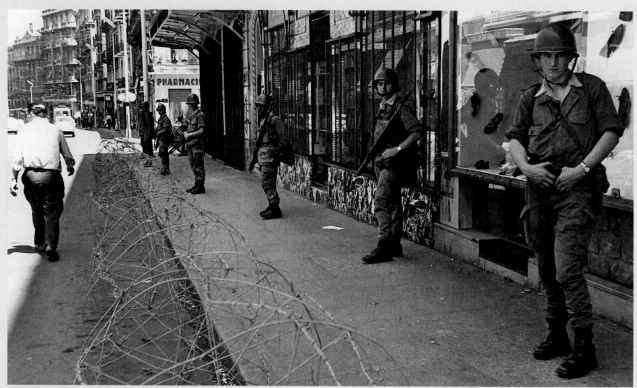

The period in which the European imperial powers were compelled to abandon their colonies was sometimes difficult and painful for both sides. The French departure from Algeria, under French control for more than a century, was especially agonizing. This picture shows the Rue Michelet, one of Algiers' chief shopping streets, patrolled by armed troops in 1962. [AFP/Archive Photos]

imported great quantities of natural resources from their colonies and carried on a high percentage of their trade with them. Even more singular, the British Empire included such self-governing areas as Canada, Australia, New Zealand, and South Africa, ruled by emigrants from Britain who remained loyal to the mother country and were willing to assist it in wartime. The jewel in Britain's imperial crown, as another saying went, was India. With a population of some 300,000,000, it contained perhaps 80 percent of the empire's subjects and provided much of the imperial profit.

At the height of its power in the mid-nineteenth century, it is remarkable how little money and effort Britain needed to spend to maintain these desired conditions. The cost of its armed services, including its great navy, during these years was only about 2 to 3 percent of its gross national product—a low figure compared with other nations, and incredibly low

considering Britain's status as the world's greatest empire. The British army was the smallest among the European powers: By 1880 it numbered fewer than a quarter of a million men, less than half the size of France's and barely a quarter of Russia's.

France returned to its imperial pursuits after its defeat in the Napoleonic Wars, especially in North Africa and Southeast Asia, and in the last quarter of the century, Germany and Italy joined the competition for colonies. The latter part of the century brought the European partition of Africa and the establishment of European economic and political power throughout Asia. Modernized Japan, too, became a colonial power, modeling itself on the imperialist policies of the European powers. (See Chapter 26.)

By the next century, European dominance had created a single global economy and had made events in any corner of the world significant thousands of miles away. The possession of colonies became part of the definition of a great power, and competition for colonies helped bring on World War I.

Toward Decolonization

The weakening of the European colonial powers in the World War II began the process of decolonization. The economic value of most colonies had proved to be much smaller than anticipated, and the colonial powers lacked both the capacity and the incentive to restore their former rule. Nationalist movements in the old colonies, moreover, would make such attempts costly and unpleasant. These movements flourished under the banner of national self-determination, self-government, and independence, ideas that came from and were cherished by the European colonial powers themselves. The example of Nazi Germany, moreover, had discredited theories of racial superiority that had justified much of European imperial rule. For European imperialism the handwriting was on the wall, although some colonial powers held on more fiercely than others. The French, for instance, fought at great cost—but in vain—to retain Algeria and Indo–China. By the 1970s a post-colonial world had emerged, and the concept of empire had become unclean. (See Chapter 31.)

❖ *What were the major ancient attitudes toward imperialism? What are the major modern attitudes? How do you account for the differences? What justifications and explanations have modern people used in connection with imperialism? Which do you think are the most important? Do you think ancient and modern reasons for imperialism are fundamentally different?*

Chapter 27

Anxiety over the spread of the Bolshevik Revolution was a fundamental factor of European politics during the 1920s and 1930s. Images like this Soviet portrait of Lenin as a heroic revolutionary conjured fears among people in the rest of Europe of a political force determined to overturn their social, political, and economic institutions. Gemälde von A. M. Gerassimow, *Lenin as Agitator* /Bildarchiv Preussischer Kulturbesitz

Political Experiments of the 1920s

KEY TOPICS

- Economic and political disorder in the aftermath of World War I
- The Soviet Union's far-reaching political and social experiment
- Mussolini and the Fascist seizure of power in Italy
- French determination to enforce the Versailles treaty
- First Labour government and general strike in Britain
- The development of authoritarian governments in all the successor states to the Austrian Empire except Czechoslovakia
- Reparations, inflation, political turmoil, and the rise of Nazism in the German Weimar Republic

Experimentation in politics and the pursuit of normality in economic life marked the decade following the conclusion of the Paris peace settlement, also known throughout the period as the Versailles settlement. These treaties, as examined in the last chapter, established a bold new experiment in European diplomatic relations. The Paris settlement instituted the League of Nations and imposed economic and military arrangements that fostered friction among all the powers and deep resentment in Germany. Through war and revolution the Habsburg Empire *collapsed, and its peoples formed several small successor states, only one of which became a successful democracy. In Russia, the Bolsheviks, after seizing control of the government in 1917 and then winning the civil war, proceeded to reorganize every aspect of life, transforming the state into the Soviet Union. In Italy, the political turmoil and social strains of the postwar era resulted in the emergence of the authoritarian movement known as fascism. In Great Britain, the Labour Party came to power for the first time, and most of Ireland became an independent nation. Germany, after suffering a humiliating military defeat, jettisoned the imperial monarchy and set out on the experiment of the Weimar Republic, which encountered numerous determined and violent opponents. All of those transformations involved considerable domestic violence for at least five years after the close of the war itself.*

Many of these political experiments failed, and the economic and social normality so many Europeans sought proved elusive. By the close of the 1920s, the political path had been paved for the nightmares of brutally authoritarian governments and international aggression that were to mark the 1930s and 1940s. Yet many of the people who had survived the Great War had hoped and worked for a better outcome. Authoritarianism and aggression were not the inescapable destiny of Europe. They emerged from the failure to secure alternative modes of democratic political life and stable international relations and from the inability to achieve long-term economic prosperity.

Political and Economic Factors after the Paris Settlement

New Governments

In 1919, experimental political regimes studded the map of Europe. From Ireland to Russia, new governments were seeking to gain the active support of their citizens and to solve the grievous economic problems caused by the war. In the Soviet Union, the Bolsheviks regarded themselves as forging a new kind of civilization, one built on achieving communism. To that end, they constructed a vast authoritarian state apparatus.

The situation was different elsewhere on the Continent. In many, though not all, countries, the turn to liberal democracy resulted in the right to vote being given to women and previously disenfranchised males. For the first time in European history, the governments handling diplomatic and economic matters were responsible to mass electorates. Even where the authoritarian, military empires of Germany and Austria–Hungary had previously held sway, democratically elected parliamentary governments took form. Their goals were substantially more modest and less utopian than those of the Bolsheviks. Yet to pursue parliamentary politics where it had never been meaningfully practiced proved no simple task. The Wilsonian vision of democratic, self-determined nations foundered on the harsh realities of economics, aggressive nationalism, and revived political conservatism. Too often, nations that had been given democratic, parliamentary government lacked both the will and the political skill to make the new system work. Many of the constitutional arrangements were themselves deeply flawed, containing the seeds of their own destruction. Moreover, in many of the new democracies, important sectors of the citizenry believed that parliamentary politics was inherently corrupt or unequal to great nationalistic enterprises. Economics and politics had become more intimately connected than ever before. The economic and social anxieties of the electorate, as well as nationalistic ambitions, could, and eventually did, overcome political scruples.

Demands for Revision of the Paris Settlement

The Paris peace treaties themselves became domestic political issues. Usually, the objections arose from nationalistic concerns and resentments. Germany had been humiliated. The arrangements for reparations led to endless haggling over payments. Various national groups in the successor states of eastern Europe also felt that they had been treated unjustly or been denied self-determination. There were important demands for further border adjustments because significant national minorities, particularly German, still resided outside national boundaries, as drawn in Paris. On the other side, the victorious powers, and especially France, often believed that the provisions of the treaty were not being adequately enforced. So, throughout the 1920s, calls either to revise or to enforce the Paris treaties contributed to domestic political turmoil across the Continent. Many political figures were willing to fish in these troubled international waters for a large catch of domestic votes.

Postwar Economic Problems

Along with the move toward political experimentation and the demands for revision of the new international order, there existed a widespread desire to return to the economic prosperity of the prewar years. After 1918, however, it was impossible to restore in the economic realm what American President Warren Harding (1865–1923) would shortly term "normalcy." During the Great War, Europeans had turned the vast military and industrial power that they had created during the previous century against themselves and their civilization. What had been "normal" in economic and social life during the previous half century could not be reestablished.

More than 750,000 British soldiers had perished. The combat deaths for France and Germany were 1,385,000 and 1,808,000, respectively. Russia had lost no fewer than 1,700,000 troops. Hundreds of thousands more from other nations had also been killed. Still more millions had been wounded. These casualties represented not only a waste of human life and talent, but also the loss of producers and consumers.

Another casualty of the conflict was the financial dominance and independence of Europe. At the opening of hostilities, Europe had been the financial and credit center of the world. At the close of the fighting, European states were deep in debt to each other and to the United States. The Bolsheviks had repudiated the debt of the tsarist government, much of which was owed to French creditors. Other nations could not pursue this revolutionary course. The Paris settlement had imposed heavy financial obligations on Germany and its allies. The United States refused to ask reparations from Germany, but demanded repayment of war debts from its own allies.

On one hand, the reparation and debt structure meant that no nation was fully in control of its own economic life. On the other hand, the absence of international economic cooperation meant that, more than ever, individual nations felt compelled to pursue or to try to pursue selfish, nationalistic economic aims. It was perhaps the worst of all possible international economic worlds.

The market and trade conditions that had prevailed before 1914 had also changed radically. In addition to the unprecedented loss of human life, much of Europe's transport facilities, mines, and industry had been damaged or destroyed. Russia all but withdrew from the European economic order. The political reconstruction of eastern and central Europe into a multitude of small states broke up the trade region formerly encompassed by Germany and Austria–Hungary. Most of those new states had weak economies hardly capable of competing in modern economic life. The new political boundaries separated raw materials from the factories that used them. Railway systems on which finished and unfinished products traveled might now lie under the control of two or more nations. Political and economic nationalism went together. Nations raised new customs barriers where before there had been none.

International trade also followed novel patterns. The United States became less dependent on European production and was now a major competitor. During the war, the belligerents had been forced to sell many of their investments on other continents to finance the conflict. As a consequence, European dominance over the world economy weakened. Slow postwar economic growth or even the decline of economic activity within colonies or former colonies lowered the international demand for European goods. The United States and Japan began to penetrate markets in Latin America and Asia that European producers and traders had previously dominated.

New Roles for Government and Labor

Throughout Europe, the war had given labor new prominence. In every country, the unions had actively supported the war effort. They had ensured labor peace for wartime production. In turn, their members had received better wages, and their leaders had been admitted to high political councils. This wartime cooperation of unions and labor leaders with the various national governments destroyed the internationalism of the prewar labor movement. It also, however, meant that henceforth government could not ignore the demands of labor. After the war, many wages were lowered, but rarely to prewar levels. European workers intended to receive their just share of the fruits of their labor. Collective bargaining and union recognition brought on by the war were also there to stay. This improvement in both the status and the effective influence of labor was one of the most significant social and political changes to flow from World War I.

Throughout the 1920s, people from the various segments of the middle class remained suspicious of the new role of labor and of socialist political parties. This suspicion and fear of potential loss of property by the middle classes led them to seek to perpetuate the status quo and to fend off further social and economic advances by the working classes. Thus, the European middle classes, once the vanguard of the liberal revolution, became a generally conservative political force in the 1920s. Their conservatism deepened as fear of Bolshevism spread across the Continent.

The Soviet Experiment Begins

The consolidation of the Bolshevik Revolution in Russia established the most extensive and durable of all the twentieth-century authoritarian governments that came to power in the political turmoil of World War I and its aftermath. The Communist Party of the Soviet Union retained power from 1917 until the end of 1991, and its presence influenced the political history of Europe during this century as did no other single factor. The Communist Party was neither a mass party nor a nationalistic one. Its early membership rarely exceeded one percent of the Russian population. For several years after 1917, the party faced widespread domestic opposition, and the Communist leaders long felt that their hold on the country was insecure. Yet the Communists also regarded their government and their revolution not as local events in a national history, but as epoch-making events in the history of the world and the development of humanity. Communism was an exportable commodity that could disrupt the political life of other nations, and throughout the history of the Soviet Union, its leaders sought to export its ideology and doctrines. Fear of communism and a determination to stop its spread became one of the leading political forces in western Europe and the United States for most of the rest of the century.

War Communism

Within the Soviet Union, the Red Army, under the organizational direction of Leon Trotsky (1879–1940), eventually suppressed internal and foreign military opposition to the new government. The White Russian armies, which fought the Red Army for several years, could not adequately organize themselves, and Allied help was inadequate to defeat the Bolsheviks. The existence of a military threat allowed the Bolsheviks rapidly to pursue authoritarian policies. Within months of the revolution, a new secret police, known as the *Cheka*, appeared. Throughout the civil war, Lenin had declared that the Bolshevik Party, as the vanguard of the revolution, was imposing the dictatorship of the proletariat. Political and economic administration became highly centralized. All major decisions flowed from the top in a nondemocratic manner. Under the economic policy of *war communism*, the revolutionary government confiscated and then operated the banks, the transport system, and heavy industry. The state also seized grain from the peasants to feed the army and the workers in the cities. The fact of the civil war permitted the Bolsheviks to suppress resistance to this economic policy. Throughout the period of the civil war, the government headed by Lenin carried out extensive repression of all actual or potential sources of opposition. (See "Trotsky Urges the Use of Terror.")

War communism aided the victory of the Red Army. The revolution had survived and triumphed. The policy, however, generated domestic opposition to the Bolsheviks, who in 1920 numbered only about 600,000 members. The alliance of workers and peasants forged by the slogan of "Peace, Bread, and Land" had begun to come apart at the seams. Many Russians were no longer willing to make the sacrifices demanded by the central party bureaucrats. In 1920 and 1921, large strikes occurred in many factories. Discontented peasants resisted the requisition of grain as they had since 1918. In March 1921, the Baltic fleet mutinied at Kronstadt. The Red Army crushed the rebellion with grave loss of life.

Each of these incidents suggested that the proletariat itself was opposing the dictatorship of the proletariat as embodied in the Communist Party. Also, by late 1920 it had become clear that revolution was not going to erupt across the rest of

During the civil war in the Soviet Union hunger and starvation haunted the countryside. Here a group of malnourished children posed for a photograph. Bildarchiv Preussischer Kulturbesitz

Trotsky Urges the Use of Terror

Leon Trotsky led the Red Army to victory in the brutal and extensive civil war that followed the Bolshevik Revolution in 1918. He became a major opponent, and later a victim, of Stalin. In this 1920 discussion, he explains how terror and intimidation must be used to achieve communist revolution. He contends that capitalist society itself came to power through the use of force and that only force will allow the working class to establish its dominance. He argues that there is no real moral argument against the use of terror and violence. In particular, he directs his remarks toward liberals, who thought that social change could be achieved by parliamentary means, and against the German Marxist socialists, the Kautskians, who had argued that historical forces would bring about the revolution of the working class without the use of violence. These words of Trotsky help explain the fear of Bolshevism that swept across much of Europe immediately after World War I, a fear right-wing politicians manipulated during the 1920s and 1930s.

❖ *How does Trotsky's justification of terror compare with that associated with the Reign of Terror during the French Revolution? How might the circumstances of the Russian civil war have led Trotsky to these views? Do you agree that the communist terror advocated by Trotsky differed from the repressive police policies of the tsars?*

The problem of revolution, as of war, consists in breaking the will of the foe, forcing him to capitulate and to accept the conditions of the conqueror. The will, of course, is a fact of the physical world, but in contradistinction to a meeting, a dispute, or a congress, the revolution carries out its object by means of the employment of material resources—though to a lesser degree than war. The bourgeoisie itself conquered power by means of revolts, and consolidated it by the civil war. In the peace period, it retains power by means of a system of repression. As long as class society, founded on the most deep-rooted antagonisms, continues to exist, repression remains a necessary means of breaking the will of the opposing side.

Even if, in one country or another, the dictatorship of the proletariat grew up within the external framework of democracy, this would by no means avert the civil war. The question as to who is to rule the country, i.e., of the life or death of the bourgeoisie, will be decided on either side, not by references to the paragraphs of the constitution, but by the employment of all forms of violence....

The question of the form of repression, or of its degree, of course, is not one of "principle." It is a question of expediency....

...Terror can be very efficient against a reactionary class which does not want to leave the scene of operations. Intimidation is a powerful weapon of policy, both internationally and internally. A victorious war, generally speaking, destroys only an insignificant part of the conquered army, intimidating the remainder and breaking their will. The revolution works in the same way: it kills individuals, and intimidates thousands. In this sense, the Red Terror is not distinguishable from the armed insurrection, the direct continuation of which it represents. The State terror of a revolutionary class can be condemned "morally" only by a man who, as a principle, rejects (in words) every form of violence whatsoever—consequently, every war and every uprising. For this one has to be merely and simply a hypocritical Quaker.

"But, in that case, in what do your tactics differ from the tactics of Tsarism?" we are asked by the high priests of Liberalism and Kautskianism.

You do not understand this, holy men? We shall explain to you. The terror of Tsarism was directed against the proletariat. The gendarmerie of Tsarism throttled the workers who were fighting for the Socialist order. Our Extraordinary Commissions shoot landlords, capitalists, and generals who are striving to restore the capitalist order. Do you grasp this—distinction? Yes? For us Communists it is quite sufficient.

From Leon Trotsky, *Terrorism and Communism*, 1920; English trans., *Dictatorship vs. Democracy: A Reply to Karl Kautsky* (New York: Workers' Party of America, 1922), pp. 54, 57–59, as quoted in Robert V. Daniels, *A Documentary History of Communism*, rev. ed., Vol. 1 (Hanover, NH and London: University Press of New England, 1984), pp. 121–122.

Europe. For the time being, the Soviet Union would be a vast island of revolutionary socialism in the worldwide sea of capitalism.

The New Economic Policy

Under these difficult conditions, Lenin made a crucial strategic retreat. In March 1921, following the Kronstadt mutiny and in the face of continuing peasant resistance to the requisition of grain needed to feed the urban population, he outlined the New Economic Policy, normally called NEP. Apart from what he termed "the commanding heights" of banking, heavy industry, transportation, and international commerce, the government would tolerate private economic enterprise. In particular, peasants could farm for profit. They would pay taxes like other citizens, but they could sell their surplus grain on the open market. The New Economic Policy was in line with Lenin's earlier conviction that the Russian peasantry held the key to the success of the revolution.

After 1921 the countryside did become more stable, and a more secure food supply seemed assured for the cities. Similar free enterprise flourished within light industry and domestic retail trade. The implementation of the New Economic Policy, however, was not fully successful, because there were virtually no con-

After the Bolshevik Revolution there were many shortages in the cities of the new Soviet Union. This painting shows citizens buying and selling goods in a Moscow street market in the early 1920s. Alfredo Dagli Orti/Bildarchiv Preussischer Kulturbesitz

sumer goods for the peasants to purchase with the money they received for their grain. Yet by 1927, industrial production had reached its 1913 level. The revolution seemed to have transformed Russia into a land of small, if frequently discontented, family farmers and owners of small private shops and businesses.

Stalin Versus Trotsky

The New Economic Policy had caused sharp disputes within the Politburo, the highest governing committee of the Communist Party. Some members considered the partial return to capitalism a betrayal of Marxist principles. These frictions increased when Lenin's firm hand disappeared. In 1922, he suffered a stroke and never again dominated party affairs. In 1924, Lenin died.

The resulting power vacuum led to an intense struggle for the leadership of the party. Two factions emerged. One was led by Leon Trotsky, the other by Joseph Stalin (1879–1953), who had become general secretary of the party in 1922. Shortly before his death, Lenin had criticized both men, but was especially harsh toward Stalin. Stalin's power base, however, lay with the party membership and in the day-to-day management of party affairs. Consequently, he was able to withstand the posthumous strictures of Lenin.

The issue between the two factions was power within the party, but the struggle was fought out over the question of Russia's path toward industrialization and the future of the communist revolutionary movement. Trotsky, speaking for what became known as the *left wing*, urged rapid industrialization financed through the expropriation of farm production. Agriculture should be collectivized, and the peasants should be made to pay for industrialization. Trotsky further argued that the revolution in Russia could succeed only if new revolutions took place elsewhere. Russia needed the skills and wealth of other nations to build its own economy. As Trotsky's influence within the party waned, he also demanded that party members be permitted to criticize the policies of the government and the party. Trotsky was, however, a latecomer to the advocacy of open discussion. When he had controlled the Red Army, he had been an unflinching disciplinarian.

A faction known as the *right wing* opposed Trotsky. Its chief ideological voice was that of Nikolai Bukharin (1888–1938), the editor of *Pravda* (*Truth*), the official party newspaper. Stalin was the major political manipulator of this group. In the mid-1920s, in the face of uncertain economic recovery, the right wing pressed for the continuation of Lenin's NEP and for relatively slow industrialization. At the time, this position

Lenin and Trotsky (saluting) in Red Square in Moscow in 1919, from a documentary film made by Herman Axelbank. Trotsky's organizational skill was largely responsible for the Red Army's victory in the Russian civil war of 1918–1920. By 1921, as a result of war, revolution, and civil war, the Russian economy had all but collapsed. Roger-Violett/Liaison Agency, Inc.

represented an economic policy based largely on decentralized economic planning and the toleration of modest free enterprise and small landholdings. Stalin emerged as the victor in these intraparty rivalries.

Stalin had been born in 1879 into a poor family. Unlike the other early Bolshevik leaders, he had not spent a long period of exile in western Europe and was much less intellectual and internationalist in his outlook. He was also much more brutal. During his tenure as Commissar of Nationalities, Stalin's handling of various recalcitrant national groups within Russia after the revolution had shocked even Lenin, though not enough for Lenin to dismiss him. As the Party General Secretary, a post that party intellectuals disdained as merely clerical, Stalin amassed power through his command of bureaucratic and administrative methods. He was neither a brilliant writer nor an effective public speaker. He did, however, master the crucial, if dull, details of party structure, including admission to the party and promotion within it. That mastery meant that he had the support of the lower levels of the party apparatus when he clashed with other leaders.

In the mid-1920s, Stalin expediently supported Bukharin's position on economic development. In 1924 he also enunciated, in opposition to Trotsky, the doctrine of "socialism in one country." Stalin urged that socialism could be achieved in Russia alone. Russian success did not depend on the fate of revolutions elsewhere. Stalin thus nationalized the previously international scope of the Marxist revolution. He cunningly used his control over the Central Committee of the Communist Party to edge out Trotsky and his supporters.

By 1927 Trotsky had been removed from all his offices, expelled from the party, and exiled to Siberia. In 1929 he was forced out of Russia, and eventually he moved to Mexico, where he was murdered in 1940, presumably by one of Stalin's agents. With Trotsky de-feated, Stalin was firmly in control of the Soviet state. It remained to be seen where he would take it and what "socialism in one country" would mean in practice.

The Third International

The Bolshevik Revolution in Russia stunned the world of west European socialism. In the West, prior to the war, as seen in Chapter 24, the various social democratic parties had debated among themselves the degree to which they might participate in the existing parliamentary structures. While Marxist in ideology, they had generally come to expect that the lot of the proletariat would be improved by evolutionary rather than revolutionary means. They had regarded the Russian Bolsheviks as political and Marxist extremists. The Bolshevik victory required west European social democrats to rethink their position within the world of international socialism. For their part, the Bolsheviks regarded such social democrats with their reformist agendas as a major enemy. The Bolsheviks intended to establish themselves as the international leaders of Marxism.

To that end, in 1919 the Soviet Communists founded the Third International of the European socialist movement, better known as the *Comintern*. The Comintern worked to make the Bolshevik model of socialism, as developed by Lenin, the rule for all socialist parties outside the Soviet Union. In 1920, a year after its inception, the Comintern imposed its Twenty-one Conditions on any other socialist party that wished to join it. These conditions included acknowledging Moscow's leadership, rejecting reformist or revisionist socialism, repudiating previous socialist leaders, and adopting the Communist Party name. In effect, the Comintern sought to destroy all democratic socialism, which it accused of having betrayed the working class through reform policies and parliamentary accommodation.

In 1919, the new Soviet government established the Comintern to sponsor and organize communist parties outside the Soviet Union. In this Bolshevik propaganda poster the banner declares, "You have nothing to lose but your chains, but the world will soon be yours." The figures in the foreground represent peoples from around the globe as an indication of the Soviet ambition to spread Communism far beyond the borders of the Soviet Union. Museum of the Revolution, Moscow/Bridgeman Art Library, London

The decision whether to accept these conditions split every major European socialist party. As a result, separate communist and social democratic parties emerged in many countries. The communist parties modeled themselves after the Soviet party, and Moscow dictated their policies. The social democratic parties attempted to pursue both social reform and liberal parliamentary politics. Throughout the 1920s and early 1930s, the communists and social democrats fought each other more intensely than they fought either capitalism or conservative political parties. Their fierce conflict was one of the fundamental features of the interwar European political landscape.

These policies of the Comintern directly affected the rise of the Fascists and the Nazis in western Europe. It is difficult to exaggerate the fears that Soviet political rhetoric and Communist Party activity aroused throughout Europe during the 1920s and 1930s. These fears, often exaggerated, were manipulated by conservative and right-wing political groups. The presence of separate communist parties in western Europe meant that right-wing

politicians always had a convenient target that they could justly accuse of seeking to overthrow the existing government and to impose Soviet-style political and economic experiments in their respective nations. Furthermore, right-wing politicians continued to accuse the democratic socialist parties of supporting policies that might facilitate a communist takeover. The division of the European political left also meant that right-wing political movements rarely had to confront a united left-wing opposition.

The Fascist Experiment in Italy

Italy witnessed the first authoritarian political experiment in western Europe that arose in part from fears of the spread of Bolshevism. From the Italian fascist movement of Benito Mussolini (1883–1945) came the general term *fascist*, frequently used to describe a number of right-wing dictatorships that arose across Europe between the wars.

Both historians and political scientists disagree about the exact meaning of *fascism* as a political term. Most scholars agree, however, that the government regimes regarded as fascist were antidemocratic, anti-Marxist, antiparliamentary, and frequently anti-Semitic. These governments claimed to hold back the spread of Bolshevism, which, because of Soviet rhetoric and the activity of domestic communist parties, seemed at the time a real threat. They sought to make the world safe for the middle class, small businesses, owners of moderate amounts of property, and small farmers. The fascist regimes rejected the political inheritance of the French Revolution and of nineteenth-century liberalism. Fascist movements were invariably nationalistic in response to the feared international expansion of communism.

Fascists believed that normal parliamentary politics and parties sacrificed national honor and greatness to petty disputes. They wanted to overcome the class conflict of Marxism and the party conflict of liberalism by consolidating the various groups and classes within the nation for great national purposes. As Mussolini declared in 1931, "The fascist conception of the state is all-embracing, and outside of the state no human or spiritual values can exist, let alone be desirable."[1] The fascist governments were usually single-party dictatorships characterized by terrorism and police surveillance. In contrast to the Communist Party of the Soviet Union, they were rooted in the base of mass political parties.

[1]Quoted in Denis Mack Smith, *Italy: A Modern History* (Ann Arbor, MI: University of Michigan Press, 1959), p. 412.

The Rise of Mussolini

The Italian *Fasci di Combattimento*, or "Bands of Combat," was founded in 1919 in Milan. Its members came largely from Italian war veterans who felt that the Paris conference had cheated Italy of the hard-won fruits of victory. They especially resented Italy's failure to gain Fiume (now Rijeka) on the northeast coast of the Adriatic Sea. They also feared the spread of socialism and the effects of inflation.

Their leader, Benito Mussolini, had been born the son of a blacksmith. He had worked as a schoolteacher and a day laborer before becoming active in Italian socialist politics. By 1912, he had become editor of the socialist newspaper *Avanti* (meaning "forward"). In 1914, Mussolini broke with the socialists and supported Italian entry into the war on the side of the Allies. His interventionist position lost him the editorship of *Avanti*. He had in effect moved from championing the proletariat to championing the nation. Nationalism replaced socialism as his ideology for a national revolution that would transform what he and many other regarded as a weak liberal state. He soon established his own paper, *Il Popolo d'Italia* (*The People of Italy*). Later he served in the army and was wounded. In 1919, although of some prewar political stature, Mussolini was simply one of many Italian politicians, and his *Fasci* organization was just one more small political group in a country full of them. As a politician, Mussolini was an opportunist par excellence. He could change his ideas and principles to suit every new occasion. Action for him was always more important than thought or rational justification. His one real goal was political survival. (See "Mussolini Heaps Contempt on Political Liberalism.")

POSTWAR ITALIAN POLITICAL TURMOIL Postwar Italian politics was a muddle. During the conflict, the Italian Parliament had virtually ceased to function, and it allowed ministers to rule by decree. Many Italians, however, were already dissatisfied with the parliamentary system. Italian nationalists—not just Mussolini's followers—felt that Italy had not been treated as a great power at the peace conference and had not received the territories it deserved.

The main spokesperson for this discontent was the extreme nationalist writer Gabriele D'Annunzio (1863–1938). In 1919, he seized Fiume with a force of patriotic Italians. He was eventually driven out, but D'Annunzio had shown how a nongovernmental military force could be put to political use. Moreover, the use of force against D'Annunzio embarrassed the Italian government and made it appear less patriotic than the ultranationalists.

Between 1919 and 1921, Italy also experienced considerable internal social turmoil. Many industrial strikes occurred, and workers occupied factories. Peasants seized uncultivated land from large estates. Parliamentary and constitutional government seemed incapable of dealing with this unrest. The Socialist Party had captured a plurality of seats in the Chamber of Deputies in the 1919 election. The sharp division between socialists and communists had not yet emerged, and the Socialist Party included many people who were soon to become communists. A new Catholic Popular Party had also done well in the election. Both appealed to the working and agrarian classes. Neither party, however, would cooperate with the other; parliamentary deadlock resulted. Under these conditions, many Italians honestly, and still others conveniently, believed that the social upheaval and political paralysis would lead to a communist revolution.

EARLY FASCIST ORGANIZATION Initially, Mussolini was uncertain of the direction of the political winds. He first supported the factory occupations and land seizures. Never one to be concerned with consistency, however, he soon reversed himself. He had discovered that many upper-class and middle-class Italians, pressured by inflation and fearing the loss of their property, had no sympathy for the workers or the peasants. They wanted order, rather than some vague social justice that might harm their own interests. Moreover, Mussolini was coming to see any social group pursuing its own goals as undermining great national purposes and national unity. The Socialists became easy and obvious targets because they had always espoused internationalism as well as working-class interests.

Consequently, Mussolini and his Fascists took direct action in the face of government inaction. They formed local squads of terrorists who disrupted Socialist Party meetings, beat up Socialist leaders, and intimidated Socialist supporters. They attacked strikers and farmworkers and protected strikebreakers. Conservative land and factory owners were grateful. The officers and institutions of the law simply ignored the crimes of the Fascist squads. By early 1922 the Fascists had turned to intimidation through arson, beatings, and murder against local officials in cities such as Ferrara, Ravenna, and Milan. They controlled the local government in much of northern Italy.

MARCH ON ROME In the election of 1921, Italian voters sent Mussolini and thirty-four of his followers to the Chamber of Deputies. Their importance grew as the local Fascists gained more direct power. The movement now had hundreds of thousands of supporters. In October 1922, the Fascists, dressed in their characteristic black shirts, began a rather haphazard march on Rome, which became known as the *Black Shirt March*. King Victor

Mussolini Heaps Contempt on Political Liberalism

The political tactics of the Italian Fascists wholly disregarded the liberal belief in the rule of law and the consent of the governed. In 1923, Mussolini explained why the Fascists so hated and repudiated these liberal principles. Note his emphasis on the idea of the twentieth century as a new historical epoch requiring a new kind of politics and his undisguised praise of force in politics.

❖ *Who would be some nineteenth-century liberal political leaders included in Mussolini's attack? Why might Mussolini's audience have been receptive to these views? What events or developments within liberal states allowed Mussolini to portray liberalism as so corrupt and powerless?*

Liberalism is not the last word, nor does it represent the definitive formula on the subject of the art of government.... Liberalism is the product and the technique of the 19th century.... It does not follow that the Liberal scheme of government, good for the 19th century, for a century, that is, dominated by two such phenomena as the growth of capitalism and the strengthening of the sentiment of nationalism, should be adapted to the 20th century, which announces itself already with characteristics sufficiently different from those that marked the preceding century....

I challenge Liberal gentlemen to tell if ever in history there has been a government that was based solely on popular consent and that renounced all use of force whatsoever. A government so constructed there has never been and never will be. Consent is an ever-changing thing like the shifting sand on the sea coast. It can never be permanent: It can never be complete.... If it be accepted as an axiom that any system of government whatever creates malcontents, how are you going to prevent this discontent from overflowing and constituting a menace to the stability of the State? You will prevent it by force. By the assembling of the greatest force possible. By the inexorable use of this force whenever it is necessary. Take away from any government whatsoever force— and by force is meant physical, armed force—and leave it only its immortal principles, and that government will be at the mercy of the first organized group that decides to overthrow it. Fascism now throws these lifeless theories out to rot....The truth evident now to all who are not warped by [liberal] dogmatism is that men have tired of liberty. They have made an orgy of it. Liberty is today no longer the chaste and austere virgin for whom the generations of the first half of the last century fought and died. For the gallant, restless and bitter youth who face the dawn of a new history there are other words that exercise a far greater fascination, and those words are: order, hierarchy, discipline....

Know then, once and for all, that Fascism knows no idols and worships no fetishes. It has already stepped over, and if it be necessary it will turn tranquilly and step again over, the more or less putrescent corpse of the Goddess of Liberty.

Benito Mussolini, "Force and Consent" (1923), as trans. in Jonathan F. Scott and Alexander Baltzly, eds., *Readings in European History Since 1814* (New York: F. S. Crofts, 1931), pp. 680–682.

Emmanuel III (r. 1900–1946), because of both personal and political concerns, refused to sign a decree that would have authorized the army to stop the marchers. Probably no other single decision so ensured a Fascist seizure of power. The cabinet resigned in protest. On October 29, the monarch telegraphed Mussolini in Milan and asked him to become prime minister. The next day, Mussolini arrived in Rome by sleeping car and greeted his followers as head of the government when they entered the city. Although the March on Rome became a famous moment in Fascist history, Mussolini would not have achieved authority if he had not made allies within the political system during the months preceding the march.

Technically, Mussolini had come into office by legal means. The monarch had the constitutional authority to appoint the prime minister. Mussolini, however, had no majority or even near majority in the Chamber of Deputies. Behind the legal facade of his coming to power lay months of terrorist disruption and intimidation and the threat of the Fascist march itself. The non-Fascist politicians, whose ineptitude had prepared the way for Mussolini, believed that his ministry, like others since 1919, would be brief. They did not comprehend that he was not a traditional Italian politician.

The Fascists in Power

Mussolini had not really expected to be appointed prime minister. He moved cautiously to shore up his support and to consolidate his power. His success was the result of the impotence of his rivals, his own effective use of his office, his power over the masses, and his sheer ruthlessness. On November 23, 1922, the king and Parliament granted Mussolini dictatorial authority for one year to bring order to local and regional government. Wherever possible, Mussolini appointed Fascists to office.

REPRESSION OF OPPOSITION Late in 1924, under Mussolini's guidance, Parliament changed the election law. Previously, parties had been represented in the Chamber of Deputies in proportion to the popular vote cast for them. According to the new election law, the party that gained the largest popular vote (if they won at least 25 percent) received two-thirds of the seats in the chamber. Coalition government, with all its compromises and hesitant policies, would no longer be necessary. In the election of 1924, the Fascists won a great victory and complete control of the Chamber of Deputies. They used that majority to end legitimate parliamentary life. A series of laws passed in 1925 and 1926 permitted Mussolini, in effect, to rule by decree. In 1926, all other political parties were dissolved. By the close of that year, Mussolini had transformed Italy into a single-party dictatorial state.

Their growing dominance over the government had not, however, diverted the Fascists from their course of violence and terror. Fascists were put in charge of the police force, and the terrorist squads became a government militia. In late 1924, their thugs murdered Giacomo Matteotti (1885–1924), a leading noncommunist socialist leader and member of Parliament. He had persistently criticized Mussolini and had exposed the criminality of the fascist movement. In protest against the murder, most opposition deputies withdrew from the Chamber of Deputies. That tactic gave Mussolini an even freer hand. The deputies were refused readmission.

In October, 1922, Mussolini's Fascist followers staged a highly publicized march on Rome. Although Mussolini had been asked to form a government shortly before the arrival of his followers, Fascists created a myth that their march was what had put him into office. This picture, taken from the Victor Emmanuel monument in Rome, shows the gathering of the Fascists at the base of the monument. Once in power Mussolini would often make speeches from a balcony in this square.
Hulton Getty/Archive Photos

PARALLEL STRUCTURE OF PARTY AND GOVERNMENT
The parallel organizations of the party and the government sustained support for the regime. For every government institution, there was a corresponding party organization. The Fascist Party thus dominated Italy's political structure at every level. When all other political parties were outlawed, the citizens had to look to the Fascists in their community for political favors. They also knew the high price of opposition. By the late 1920s, the Grand Council of the party, which Mussolini controlled, had become an organ of the state. It decided who would stand for election to the Chamber of Deputies and on which policies the chamber would vote.

The party used propaganda to great effect. A cult of personality surrounded Mussolini. His skills in oratory and his general intelligence allowed him to hold his own with both large crowds and prominent individuals, foreign as well as Italian. Many respectable Italians tolerated and even admired Mussolini because they believed that he had saved them from Bolshevism. Those who did have the courage to oppose him were usually driven into exile, and some, like Matteotti, were murdered.

ACCORD WITH THE VATICAN Mussolini made one important domestic departure that brought him significant political dividends. Through the Lateran Accord of February 1929, the Roman Catholic Church and the Italian state made peace with each other. Ever since the armies of Italian unification had seized papal lands in the 1860s, the church had been hostile to the state. The Popes had remained secluded in the Vatican after 1870. The agreement of 1929 recognized the Pope as the temporal ruler of Vatican City. The Italian government agreed to pay an indemnity to the papacy for the territory it had confiscated. The state also recognized Catholicism as the religion of the nation, exempted church property from taxes, and allowed church law to govern marriage. The Lateran Accord brought further respectability to Mussolini's authoritarian regime.

Joyless Victors

France and Great Britain, with the aid of the United States, had won the war. France became the strongest military power on the Continent. Britain had escaped with almost no physical damage. Both nations, however, had lost vast numbers of young men in the conflict. Their economies were weakened, their overseas investments and power much diminished. Compared with events in Russia and Italy, the interwar political development of the two major democracies seems rather tame. Neither experienced a revolution or a shift to authoritarian government. Yet this surface calm was largely illusory. Both France and Britain were troubled democracies. To neither did victory in war bring the good life in peace.

France: The Search for Security

At the close of World War I, as after Waterloo, the revolution of 1848, and the defeat of 1871, the French voters elected a doggedly conservative Chamber of Deputies. The preponderance of military officers in blue uniforms among its members led to the nickname of the "Blue Horizon Chamber." The overwhelmingly conservative character of the chamber was registered in 1920 when it defeated Georges Clemenceau's bid for the presidency. The crucial factor had been, of all things, the alleged leniency of the Paris treaties and Clemenceau's failure to establish a separate Rhineland state. The deputies wanted to achieve future security against Germany and Russian communism. They intended to make as few concessions to domestic social reform as possible. The 1920s were marked by frequent changes of ministries and drift in domestic policy. The political turnstile remained ever active. Between the end of the war and January 1933, France was governed by no fewer than twenty-seven different cabinets.

NEW ALLIANCES During the first five years after the conclusion of the Paris settlement, France accepted its role as the leading European power. The French plan was to enforce strictly the clauses of the treaty that were meant to keep Germany weak and also to build a system of eastern alliances to replace the prewar alliance with Russia. In 1920 and 1921, three eastern states that had much to lose from revision of the Versailles treaty—Czechoslovakia, Romania, and Yugoslavia—formed the Little Entente. Before long, France made military alliances with these states and with Poland. A border dispute with Czechoslovakia prevented the Poles from joining the Little Entente, but Poland's independence depended on the maintenance of the Paris settlement.

This new system of eastern pacts was the best France could do, but it was far weaker than the old Franco–Russian alliance. Even combined, the new states were no match for the former power of tsarist Russia, and they were neither united nor reliable. Poland and Romania were more concerned about Russia than about Germany, and the main target of the Little Entente was Hungary. If one of these states was threatened by a resurgent Germany, it could not rely on the others to come to its aid.

The formation of this new alliance system heightened the sense of danger and isolation felt by the two excluded powers, Germany and the Soviet Union. In 1922, while the European states were holding an economic conference at Genoa, the Russians and the Germans met at nearby Rapallo and signed a treaty

The French invasion of the German Ruhr began a crisis that brought strikes and rampant inflation in Germany. Here French troops have commandeered a German locomotive during one of the strikes. UPI/Corbis

of their own. It established diplomatic and economic relations that proved useful to each of them. Although the treaty contained no secret political or military clauses, other governments suspected that such arrangements did exist. And it is now known that the Germans did help train the Russian army, and their own army got valuable experience in the use of tanks and planes in the Soviet Union. Rapallo confirmed the French in their belief that Germany would not live up to the terms of the Versailles treaty and helped move them to strong action.

QUEST FOR REPARATIONS   In early 1923, the Allies, and France in particular, declared Germany to be in technical default on payment of its reparations. Raymond Poincaré (1860–1934), France's powerfully nationalistic prime minister, decided to teach the Germans a lesson and force them to comply. On January 11, 1923, to ensure receipt of the hard-won reparations, the French government ordered its troops to occupy Germany's borderland Ruhr mining and manufacturing district. In response, the German government ordered passive resistance. The policy amounted to calling a general strike in the largest industrial region of Germany. Confronted with this tactic, Poincaré sent French civilians to run the German mines and railroads. France prevailed.

The Germans paid, but France's victory was costly. The English were alienated by the French heavy-handedness and took no part in the occupation. They became more suspicious of France and more sympathetic to Germany. The cost of the Ruhr occupation, moreover, vastly increased French as well as German inflation and hurt the French economy. The Ruhr invasion demonstrated how the uncertainties surrounding the Versailles treaty could harm even the nations whom it was intended to benefit.

In 1924, Poincaré's conservative ministry gave way to a coalition of leftist parties, the so-called *Cartel des Gauches*, led by Edouard Herriot (1872–1957). The new cabinet recognized the Soviet Union and adopted a more conciliatory policy toward Germany. This policy was the work of Aristide Briand (1862–1932), who was foreign minister for the remainder of the decade. He championed the League of Nations and tried to persuade France that its military power did not give it unlimited influence in the foreign affairs of Europe.

Under the leftist coalition, a mild inflation also occurred. It had begun under the conservatives, but picked up intensity in 1925. When the value of the franc fell sharply on the international money market in 1926, Poincaré returned to office as head of a national government of several parties. The value of the franc recovered somewhat, and inflation cooled. For the rest of the 1920s, the conservatives remained in power, and France enjoyed a general prosperity that lasted until 1931, longer than any other nation did.

Great Britain: Economic Confusion

World War I profoundly changed British politics if not the political system. In 1918, Parliament expanded the electorate to include all men aged twenty-one and women aged thirty. (In 1928, the age for women voters was also lowered to twenty-one.) The prewar structure of parties and leadership shifted. A coalition cabinet of Liberal, Conservative, and Labour ministers had directed the war effort. The wartime ministerial participation of the Labour Party helped dispel its radical image. For the Liberal Party, however, the conflict brought further division.

Until 1916, Liberal Prime Minister Herbert Asquith (1852–1928) had presided over the cabinet.

As disagreements over war management developed, he was ousted by fellow Liberal David Lloyd George (1863–1945). The party split sharply between followers of the two men. In 1918, against the wishes of both the Labour Party and the Asquith Liberals, Lloyd George decided to maintain the coalition through the tasks of the peace conference and the domestic reconstruction. In December 1918, the wartime coalition, now minus its Labour members, won a stunning victory at the polls. Lloyd George, however, could thereafter remain prime minister only as long as his dominant Conservative partners wished to keep him.

During the election campaign, there had been much talk about creating "a land fit for heroes to live in." It did not happen. Except for the three years immediately after the war, the British economy was depressed throughout the 1920s. There was no genuine postwar recovery. Unemployment never dipped below 10 percent and often hovered near 11 percent. There were never fewer than a million workers unemployed. Government insurance programs to cover unemployed workers, widows, and orphans were expanded. There was no similar meaningful expansion in the number of jobs available. From 1922 onward, accepting the "dole" with little expectation of future employment became a wretched and degrading way of life for scores of thousands of poor British families.

THE FIRST LABOUR GOVERNMENT   In October 1922, the Conservatives replaced Lloyd George with Andrew Bonar Law (1858–1923), one of their own. A Liberal would never again be prime minister. Stanley Baldwin (1867–1947) soon replaced Law, who had fallen victim to throat cancer. Baldwin decided to attempt to cure Britain's economic plight by abandoning free trade and imposing protective tariffs. The voters rejected that policy in 1923. In the election, the Conservative Party lost its majority in the House of Commons, but only votes from both Liberal and Labour party members could provide an alternative majority.

Labour had elected the second largest group of members to the Commons. Consequently, in December 1923, King George V (r. 1910–1936) asked Ramsay MacDonald (1866–1937) to form the first Labour ministry in British history. The Liberal Party did not serve in the cabinet, but provided the necessary votes to give Labour a working majority in the House of Commons.

The Labour Party was socialistic in its platform, but democratic and distinctly nonrevolutionary. The party had expanded beyond its early trade-union base. MacDonald himself had opposed World War I and for a time had also broken with the party. His own version of socialism owed little, if anything, to Marx. His program consisted of plans for extensive social reform rather, than for the nationalization or public seizure

of industry. A sensitive politician, if not a great leader, MacDonald understood that the most important task facing his government was proving to the nation that the Labour Party was both respectable and responsible. His nine months in office achieved that goal, if little else of major importance. The establishment of Labour as a viable governing party signaled the permanent demise of the Liberal Party. It has continued to exist, but the bulk of its voters have drifted into either the Conservative or the Labour ranks.

THE GENERAL STRIKE OF 1926   The Labour government fell in the autumn of 1924 over charges of inadequate prosecution of a communist writer. Stanley Baldwin returned to office, where he remained until 1929. The stagnant economy remained uppermost in the public mind. Business and political leaders continued to believe that all would be well if they could restore the prewar conditions of trade. A major element in these conditions had been the gold standard as the basis for international trade. In 1925 the Conservative government returned to the gold standard, abandoned during the war, in hopes of re-creating the former monetary stability. The government, however, set the conversion rate for the pound too high against other currencies and thus, in effect, raised the price of British goods to foreign customers.

To make their products competitive on the world market, British management attempted to lower prices by cutting wages. The coal industry was the sector most directly affected by the wage cuts. It was inefficient and poorly managed and had been in trouble since the end of the war.

Labor relations in the coal industry long had been unruly. In 1926, after cuts in wages and a breakdown in negotiations, the coal miners went on strike. Soon thereafter, in May 1926, sympathetic workers in other industries engaged in a general strike lasting nine days. There was much tension but little violence. In the end, the miners and the other unions capitulated. With such high levels of unemployment, organized labor was in a weak position. After the general strike, the Baldwin government attempted to reconcile labor primarily through new housing and reforms in the poor laws. Despite the economic difficulties of these years, the actual standard of living of most British workers, including those receiving government insurance payments, actually improved. (See "Stanley Baldwin Reflects on the British General Strike.")

EMPIRE   World War I also modified Britain's imperial position. The aid given by the dominions, such as Canada and Australia, demonstrated a new independence on their part. Empire was a two-way proposition. The idea of self-determination as applied to Europe filtered

Stanley Baldwin Reflects on the British General Strike

After halting much economic activity for more than a week in 1926, the British general strike came to a peaceful conclusion. Stanley Baldwin, who was the Conservative Prime Minister at the time, thought that the outcome spoke well for British character and British freedom. In examining the impact of the strike, he was particularly concerned to present British institutions in a favorable light, as contrasted with the new social order then emerging in the Soviet Union. He hoped that communist doctrines would not come to influence the British labor movement.

❖ *In discussing the general strike, how did Baldwin seek to downplay the strife and class conflict present in the event? How did Baldwin appeal to patriotism to overcome political and social divisions in the wake of the strike? How do the language and rhetoric of this prime minister of a liberal democracy compare with the language and rhetoric of contemporary leaders of authoritarian political movements also presented in this chapter?*

It may have been a magnificent demonstration of the solidarity of labour, but it was at the same time a most pathetic evidence of the failure of all of us to live and work together for the good of all....But if that strike showed solidarity, sympathy with the miners—whatever you like—it showed something else far greater. It proved the stability of the whole fabric of our own country, and to the amazement of the world not a shot was fired. We were saved by common sense and the good temper of our own people. We have been called a stupid people; but the moment the public grasped that what was at stake was not the solidarity of labour nor the fate of the miners, but the life of the State, then there was a response to the country's need deep and irresistible. And mark this: in my view there was that feeling in the country because the leaders of the strike and the men who were on strike felt it in their innermost hearts, too. They felt a conflict of loyalties. They knew that same conflict was raging in the breasts of thousands of men who had fought for their country ten years ago. Many of the strikers were uneasy in their minds and their consciences, because the British workman, as I known him, does not like breaking contracts, as so many of them did. I do not think many of them like stopping food supplies and shutting down the Press. I sometimes amuse myself with wondering what their language would have been like if these things had been done by the Government. And, after all, when all has been said about England, about the mistakes we make, and about our stupidity, and about how much better they do things in Russia, yet how many of those men or any of us, would prefer to have been born and brought up in any country in the world but this, or to send our children to be brought up there. In these postwar years, in spite of the depression, in spite of all our troubles, never before has the wealth of this country, through the taxes and the rates, been so distributed to those less fortunate and for the provision of those thrown out of work....

I want to see out British Labour movement free from alien and foreign heresy. I want to see it pursued and developed on English lines, led by English men. The temptations that beset the growth of these vast organizations [the labour unions], in many respects as they are today outside the law, controlling multitudes of men and large sums of money—the temptation to set such a machine in motion and make people follow it is great indeed.

From Stanley Baldwin, *Our Inheritance* (London: Hodder and Stroughton, 1928), pp. 222–224.

into imperial relationships. In India, the Congress Party, led by Mohandas Gandhi (1869–1948), was beginning to attract widespread support. The British started to talk more about eventual self-government for India. Moreover, during the 1920s, the government of India achieved the right to impose tariffs to protect its own industry rather than for the advantage of British manufacturers. British textile producers no longer had totally free access to the vast Indian market.

IRELAND   A new chapter was written in the unhappy relations between Britain and Ireland during and after the war. In 1914 the Irish Home Rule Bill had passed Parliament, but its implementation was postponed

Eamon De Valera inspects troops of the Irish Republican Army during the Irish Civil War. Archive Photos

until after the war. As the war dragged on, Irish nationalists determined to wait no longer. On Easter Monday in April 1916, a nationalist uprising occurred in Dublin. It was the only rebellion of a national group to occur against any government engaged in the war. The British suppressed it in less than a week, but then made a grave tactical blunder: They executed the Irish nationalist leaders who had been responsible for the uprising. Overnight those rebels became national martyrs. Leadership of the nationalist cause quickly shifted from the Irish Party in Parliament to the extremist *Sinn Fein*, or "Ourselves Alone," movement.

In the election of 1918, the Sinn Fein Party won all but four of the Irish parliamentary seats outside Ulster. They refused to go to the Parliament at Westminster. Instead, they constituted themselves into a *Dail Eireann*, or Irish Parliament. On January 21, 1919, they declared Irish independence. The military wing of Sinn Fein became the Irish Republican Army (IRA). The first president was Eamon De Valera (1882–1975), who had been born in the United States. What amounted to a guerrilla war broke out between the IRA and the British army, with the latter supported by auxiliaries known as the Black and Tans. There was intense bitterness and hatred on both sides.

In late 1921, the two governments began secret negotiations. In the treaty concluded in December 1921, the Irish Free State took its place beside the earlier dominions in the British Commonwealth: Canada, Australia, New Zealand, and South Africa. The six counties of Ulster, or Northern Ireland, were permitted to remain part of what was now called the United Kingdom of Great Britain and Northern Ireland, with provisions for home rule. No sooner had the treaty been signed than a new civil war broke out between Irish moderates and diehards. The moderates supported the treaty; the diehards wanted to abolish the oath to the British monarch and establish

a totally independent republic. The second civil war continued until 1923. De Valera, who supported the diehards, resigned the presidency and organized resistance to the treaty. In 1932, he was again elected president. The next year, the *Dail Eireann* abolished the oath of allegiance to the monarch.

During World War II, the Irish Free State remained neutral. In 1949, it declared itself the wholly independent republic of Eire.

Trials of the Successor States in Eastern Europe

Only the barest outline can be given of the dreary political story of the *successor states* of eastern Europe. They were termed the successor states because they succeeded all or portions of the overturned German, Austro–Hungarian, and Russian empires. Their story is significant because, except for Austria after 1956, the interwar era provided those lands with their only modern experience of political independence before the revolutions of 1989 toppled their communist regimes.

It had been an article of faith among nineteenth-century liberals sympathetic to nationalism that only good could flow from the demise of Austria–Hungary, the restoration of Poland, and the establishment of nation–states throughout eastern Europe. These new states were to embody the principle of national self-determination and to provide a buffer against the westward spread of Bolshevism. They were, however, in trouble from the beginning.

Both France and Great Britain had long experience in liberal democratic government. Their primary challenges during the 1920s lay in responding to economic pressures and allowing new groups, such as the Labour Party, to share political power. In Germany, Poland, Austria, Czechoslovakia, and the other successor states, the challenge for the 1920s was to make new parliamentary governments function in a satisfactory and stable manner. Before the war, the elected parliaments of both Germany and Austria–Hungary had not exercised genuine political power. The question after the war became whether those groups that had previously sat powerless in parliaments could assume both power and responsibility. Another question was how long conservative political groups and institutions, such as the armies, would tolerate or cooperate with the liberal experiments.

Economic and Ethnic Pressures

All the new states faced immense postwar economic difficulties. None of them possessed the kind of strong economy that nation–states such as France and Germany had developed in the nineteenth century. Indeed, political independence disrupted the previous economic relationships that each of them had developed as part of one of the prewar empires. None of the new states was financially independent; except for Czechoslovakia, all of them depended on foreign loans to finance economic development. Nationalistic antagonisms often prevented these states from trading with each other, and as a consequence, most became highly dependent upon trade with Germany. The successor states of eastern Europe were poor and overwhelmingly rural nations in an industrialized world. The depression hit them especially hard, because they had to import finished goods for which they paid with agricultural exports whose value was falling sharply.

Finally, throughout eastern Europe, the collapse of the old German, Russian, and Austrian empires allowed various ethnic groups—large and small—to pursue nationalistic goals unchecked by any great power or central political authority. The major social and political groups in these countries were generally unwilling to make compromises lest they undermine their nationalist identity and independence. Each state included minority groups that wanted to be independent or to become part of a different nation in the region. Again, except for Czechoslovakia, all of these states succumbed to some form of domestic authoritarian government.

It is important to recognize these interwar economic difficulties and nationalistic pressures, because many of them reemerged in the region in the 1990s. Indeed, to a considerable extent, the breakup of Yugoslavia and Czechoslovakia, the present turmoil in the former Soviet Union, and the efforts at political reorganization in the rest of the areas, dominated by the Soviet Union constitute one more attempt by the peoples of eastern Europe to achieve political and economic stability in the wake of the upheaval in that region caused by the events surrounding World War I.

Poland: Democracy to Military Rule

The nation whose postwar fortunes probably most disappointed liberal Europeans was Poland. For more than 100 years, the country had, as a result of the late eighteenth-century partitions, been erased from the map. Restoration of an independent Poland had been one of Woodrow Wilson's Fourteen Points. When the country was finally reconstructed in 1919, nationalism proved an insufficient bond to overcome political disagreements stemming from class differences, diverse economic interests, and regionalism. The new Poland had been constructed from portions governed by Germany, Russia, and Austria for over a century. Each of those regions of partitioned Poland had different administrative systems and laws, different economies, and different degrees of experience with electoral institutions. A vast number of small political parties bedeviled the new Polish Parliament. The constitution assigned too little power to the executive. In 1926 Marshal Josef Pilsudski (1857–1935) carried out a military coup. Thereafter, he ruled, in effect, personally until his death, when the government passed into the hands of a group of his military followers.

Czechoslovakia: Successful Democratic Experiment

Only one central European successor state escaped the fate of self-imposed authoritarian government. Czechoslovakia possessed a strong industrial base, a substantial middle class, and a tradition of liberal values. During the war, Czechs and Slovaks had cooperated to aid the Allies. They had learned to work together and to trust each other. After the war, the new government had broken up large estates in favor of small peasant holdings. In the person of Thomas Masaryk (1850–1937), the nation possessed a gifted leader of immense integrity and fairness. The country had a real chance of becoming a viable modern nation–state.

Czechoslovakia encountered discontent among its smaller national groups, including the German population of the Sudetenland, which the Paris settlement had placed within Czech borders. The parliamentary regime might have been able to deal with this problem, but extreme German nationalists in the Sudetenland looked to Hitler for aid. For his part, the German dictator wished to expand into eastern Europe. In 1938, at Munich, the great powers first divided liberal Czechoslovakia to appease Hitler's aggressive instincts and then watched passively as he occupied the country.

Thomas Masaryk was the first president of the Czechoslovak Republic, which was the only successful democratic state in eastern Europe during the interwar period. Bildarchiv Preussischer Kulturbesitz

Hungary: Turmoil and Authoritarianism

Hungary was one of the defeated powers of World War I. In that defeat, it achieved its long-desired separation from Austria, but at a high political and economic price. In Hungary during 1919, Bela Kun (1885–1937), a communist, established a short-lived Hungarian Soviet Republic, which received support from the socialists as well. The Allies authorized an invasion by Romanian troops to remove the communist danger. The Hungarian landowners then established Admiral Miklós Horthy (1858–1957) as regent, a position he held until 1944. After the collapse of the Kun government, thousands of Hungarians were either executed or imprisoned. It was in part in reaction to Kun's cooperation with socialists that Lenin ordered the Comintern to reject such cooperation in the future. Kun himself was later murdered by Stalin in purges of the late 1930s.

There was also deep resentment in Hungary over the territory it had lost in the Paris settlement. The largely agrarian Hungarian economy suffered from a general stagnation. During the 1920s, the effective ruler of Hungary was Count Stephen Bethlen (1874–1947). He presided over a government that was parliamentary in form, but aristocratic in character. In 1932 he was succeeded by General Julius Gömbös (1886–1936), who pursued anti-Semitic policies and rigged elections. No

matter how the popular vote turned out, the Gömbös party controlled Parliament. After his death in 1936, anti-Semitism lingered in Hungarian politics.

Austria: Political Turmoil and Nazi Conquest

The situation in Austria was little better than that in the other successor states. A quarter of the eight million Austrians lived in Vienna. Viable economic life was almost impossible, and the Paris settlement forbade union with Germany. Throughout the 1920s, the leftist Social Democrats and the conservative Christian Socialists contended for power. Both groups employed small armies to terrorize their opponents and to impress their followers.

In 1933, the Christian Socialist Engelbert Dollfuss (1892–1934) became chancellor. He tried to steer a course between the Austrian Social Democrats and the German Nazis, who had surfaced in Austria. In 1934 he outlawed all political parties except the Christian Socialists, the agrarians, and the paramilitary groups, which composed his own Fatherland Front. He used troops against the Social Democrats, but was shot later that year during an unsuccessful Nazi coup. His successor, Kurt von Schuschnigg (1897–1977) presided over Austria until Hitler annexed it in 1938.

Southeastern Europe: Royal Dictatorships

In southeastern Europe, revision of the arrangements in the Paris settlement was less of an issue. Parliamentary government floundered there nevertheless. Yugoslavia had been founded by the Corfu Agreement of 1917 and was known as the Kingdom of the Serbs, Croats, and Slovenes until 1929. Throughout the interwar period, the Serbs dominated the government and were opposed by the Croats. The two groups clashed violently, but the Serbs had the advantage of having had an independent state with an army prior to World War I, whereas the Croats and Slovenes had been part of the Austro–Hungarian Empire. The Croats generally were Roman Catholic, better educated, and accustomed to reasonably incorrupt government administration. The Serbs were Orthodox, somewhat less well educated, and considered to be corrupt administrators by the Croats. Furthermore, although each group predominated in certain areas of the country, each had isolated enclaves in other parts of the nation. Bosnia–Herzegovina, in addition to Serbs and Croats, had a significant Muslim population. The Slovenes, Muslims, and other small national groups often played the Serbs and the Croats against each other. All of the political parties except the small Communist Party represented a particular ethnic group rather than the nation of Yugoslavia. The violent clash of nationalities eventually led to a royal dictatorship in 1929 under King Alexander I (r. 1921–1934), himself a Serb. He outlawed political parties and jailed popular politicians. Alexander was assassinated in 1934, but the authoritarian government continued under a regency for his son.

Other royal dictatorships were imposed elsewhere in the Balkans: in Romania by King Carol II (r. 1930–1940) and in Bulgaria by King Boris III (r. 1918–1943). They regarded their own illiberal regimes as preventing the seizure of power by more extreme antiparliamentary movements and as quieting the discontent of the varied nationalities within their borders. In Greece, the parliamentary monarchy floundered amidst military coups and calls for a republic. In 1936, General John Metaxas (1871–1941) instituted a dictatorship that, for the time being, ended parliamentary life in Greece.

The fate of the eastern European successor states disappointed those who had hoped that political liberty would result from the dissolution of the Habsburg Empire and from the restoration of an independent Poland. By the early 1930s, in most of those states, the authoritarianism of the Habsburgs had been replaced by that of other rulers. Meanwhile, Germany conducted the most momentous democratic experiment between the wars. There, after a century of frustration and disappointment, Germans had constructed a liberal state. It was in Germany that parliamentary democracy and its future in Western civilization faced its major trial.

The Weimar Republic in Germany

The German Weimar Republic was born amidst the defeat of the imperial army, the revolution of 1918 against the Hohenzollerns, and the hopes of German Liberals and Social Democrats. Its name derived from the city of Weimar, in which its constitution was written and promulgated in August 1919. While the constitution was being debated, the republic, headed by the Social Democrats, accepted the humiliating terms of the Versailles treaty, the part of the Paris settlement that applied to Germany. Although it had signed only under the threat of an Allied invasion, the republic was nevertheless permanently associated with the national disgrace and the economic burdens of the treaty.

Throughout the 1920s, the government of the republic was required to fulfill the economic and military provisions imposed by the Paris settlement. It became all too easy for German nationalists and military figures, whose policies had brought on the tragedy and defeat in the war, to blame the young republic and the socialists for the military defeat and its grievous social and political results. In Germany, more than in other countries, all political groups shared the desire to revise the treaty, though they differed about the means. Some wished to oppose its provisions whenever good tactical opportunities arose; others simply assumed a position of total opposition to the treaty. Because of those revisionist desires, there were different degrees of loyalty among Germans to the political arrangements of the Weimar constitution, which many of them associated with the Paris settlement.

Constitutional Flaws

The Weimar constitution was in many respects a highly enlightened document. It guaranteed civil liberties and provided for direct election, by universal suffrage, of the Reichstag and the president. It also contained, however, certain crucial structural flaws that eventually allowed its liberal institutions to be overthrown. It provided for proportional representation for all elections. This system made it relatively easy for small parties to gain seats in the Reichstag. Ministers were technically responsible to the Reichstag, but the president appointed and removed the chancellor. Perhaps most important, Article 48 allowed the president to rule by decree in an emergency. The constitution thus permitted a temporary presidential dictatorship.

Lack of Broad Popular Support

Beyond the burden of the Paris settlement and these potential constitutional pitfalls, the Weimar Republic did not command the sympathy or loyalty of many Germans. No social revolution had accompanied the new political structure. Many important political figures favored a constitutional monarchy. The schoolteachers, civil servants, and judges of the republic were generally the same people who had served the kaiser and the empire. Before the war, they had distrusted or even hated the Social Democratic Party, which figured so prominently in the establishment and the politics of the republic.

The officer corps was also deeply suspicious of the government and profoundly resentful of the military provisions of the peace settlement. Its leaders and other nationalistic Germans perpetuated the myth that the German army had surrendered on foreign soil only because it had been stabbed in the back by civilians at home. Thus, many Germans in significant social and political positions wanted both to revise the peace treaty and to modify the system of government. The early years of the republic only reinforced those sentiments.

Major and minor humiliations, as well as considerable economic instability, impinged on the new government. In March 1920, the right-wing *Kapp Putsch*, or "armed insurrection," erupted in Berlin. Led by a conservative civil servant and supported by army officers, the attempted coup failed. But the *putsch* collapsed only after the government had fled the city and German workers had carried out a general strike. In the same month, strikes took place in the Ruhr. The government sent in troops. Such extremism from both the left and the right would haunt the republic for all its days.

In May 1921, the Allies presented a reparations bill for 132 billion gold marks. The German republican government accepted this preposterous demand only after new Allied threats of occupation. Throughout the early 1920s, there were numerous assassinations or attempted assassinations of important republican leaders. Violence marked the first five years of the republic.

Invasion of the Ruhr and Inflation

Inflation brought on the major crisis of the period. Borrowing to finance the war and the continued postwar deficit spending generated an immense rise in prices. Consequently, the value of German currency fell. By early 1921, the German mark traded against the American dollar at a ratio of 64 to 1, compared with a ratio of 4.2 to 1 in 1914. German bankers contended that the mark could not be stabilized until the reparations issue had been solved. In the meantime, the printing presses kept pouring forth paper money, used to redeem government bonds as they fell due.

The French invasion of the Ruhr in January 1923 and the German response of economic passive resistance produced cataclysmic inflation. The Weimar government subsidized the Ruhr labor force, which had laid down its tools. Unemployment soon spread from the Ruhr to other parts of the country, creating a new drain on the treasury and also reducing tax revenues. By this point, the printing presses had difficulty providing enough paper currency to keep up with the daily rise in prices. In November 1923, an American dollar was worth more than 800 million German marks. Money was literally not worth the paper it was printed on. Stores were unwilling to exchange goods for the worthless currency, and farmers withheld produce from the market.

The social and economic consequences of the great inflation of 1923 were disastrous for many Germans. Middle-class savings, pensions, and insurance policies were wiped out, as were investments in government bonds. Simultaneously, debts and mortgages could easily be paid off. Speculators in land, real estate, and industry made great fortunes. Union contracts generally allowed workers to keep up with rising prices. Farmers who supplied food to the cities did well, as did food stores whose proprietors benefitted from the barter that took place. The inflation thus was not a disaster to everyone. To the middle class and the lower middle class, however, the infla-

In 1923, Germany suffered from cataclysmic inflation. Paper money became worthless and children used packets of it as building blocks. Bettmann/Hulton Deutsch/Corbis

tion was another trauma coming hard on the heels of the military defeat and the peace treaty. Only when the social and economic upheaval of these months is grasped can the later German desire for order and security at almost any cost be comprehended.

Hitler's Early Career

Late in 1923, Adolf Hitler (1889–1945) made his first major appearance on the German political scene. He was born in 1889, the son of a minor Austrian customs official. By 1907 he had gone to Vienna, where his hopes of becoming an artist were soon dashed. He lived for a time off money sent by relatives and later off his Austrian orphan's allowance. He also painted and sold postcards and worked as a day laborer. In Vienna, he became acquainted with Mayor Karl Lueger's (1844–1910) Christian Social Party, which prospered on an anti-Semitic ideology.

Hitler also absorbed much of the rabid German nationalism, racism, and extreme anti-Semitism that flourished in Vienna. He came to hate Marxism, which he associated with Jews. During World War I, Hitler fought in the German army and was wounded; he was promoted to the rank of corporal and awarded the Iron Cross for bravery. The war gave him his first sense of purpose.

After the conflict, Hitler settled in Munich and lived there during a postwar year of violent tumult when social democrats briefly governed the city. There he became associated with a small nationalistic, anti-Semitic political party, which in 1920 adopted the name of National Socialist German Workers' Party, better known simply as the *Nazis*. The same year, the group began to parade under a red-and-white banner with a black swastika. It issued a platform, or program, known as the *Twenty-five Points*, which called for the repudiation of the Versailles treaty, the unification of Austria and Germany, the exclusion of Jews from German citizenship, agrarian reform, the prohibition of land speculation, the confiscation of war profits, state administration of the giant cartels, and the replacement of department stores with small retail shops. (See "Hitler Denounces the Versailles Treaty.") In the two years after the war, Hitler seems to have firmly adopted and frequently voiced anti-Semitism as a fundamental part of his political outlook.

Originally, the Nazis had called for a broad program of nationalization of industry in an attempt to compete directly with the Marxist political parties for the vote of the workers. When the tactic failed, the Nazis redefined the meaning of the word *socialist* in their name to suggest a nationalistic outlook. In 1922 Hitler said,

Whoever is prepared to make the national cause his own to such an extent that he knows no higher ideal than the welfare of his nation; whoever has understood our great national anthem, *Deutschland, Deutschland, Über Alles* ["Germany, Germany, Over All"], to mean that nothing in the wide world surpasses in his eyes this Germany, people and land, land and people—that man is a Socialist.[2]

This definition, of course, had nothing to do with traditional German socialism. The "socialism" that Hitler and the Nazis had in mind was not state ownership of the means of production, but the subordination of all economic enterprise to the welfare of the nation. It often implied protection for small economic enterprises. Increasingly, the Nazis discovered that their party appealed to virtually any economic group that was experiencing pressure and instability. They often tailored their messages to the particular local problems these groups confronted in different parts of Germany. The Nazis found considerable support among war veterans, who faced economic and social displacement in Weimar society.

Soon after the promulgation of the Twenty-five Points, the storm troopers, or SA (*Sturmabteilung*), were organized under the leadership of Captain Ernst Roehm (1887–1934). (See "Ernst Roehm Demands a Return to German Military Values.") The SA was a paramilitary organization that initially provided its members with food and uniforms and eventually also paid them. In the mid-1920s, the SA adopted its infamous brown-shirted uniform. The storm troopers were the chief Nazi instrument for terror and intimidation before the party controlled the government. They were a law unto themselves. They attacked socialists and communists. The organization was a means of preserving military discipline and values outside the small army permitted by the Paris settlement. The existence of such a private party army was a sign of the potential for violence in the Weimar Republic. It also represented widespread contempt for the law and the institutions of the republic. In response to Nazi force, both the Social Democrat and the Communist Parties organized paramilitary organizations, but in neither size nor discipline could they rival the Nazis. These paramilitary forces greatly weakened the Weimar Republic. (See "Art & the West.")

The social and economic turmoil following the French occupation of the Ruhr and the German inflation provided the fledgling Nazi Party with an opportunity for direct action against the Weimar Republic, which seemed incapable of giving Germany military or economic security. Because of his immense oratorical skills and organizational abilities, Hitler personally dominated the Nazi Party.

During a Nazi Party rally in Nuremberg in 1927, Adolf Hitler stops his motorcade to receive the applause of the surrounding crowd. In the late 1920s, the Nazi movement was only one of many bringing strife to the Weimar Republic. Heinrich Hoffman/Bildarchiv Preussischer Kulturbesitz

[2]Quoted in Alan Bullock, *Hitler: A Study in Tyranny*, rev. ed. (New York: Harper & Row, 1962), p. 76.

Hitler Denounces the Versailles Treaty

One of the chief complaints of the National Socialist movement was the unfairness of the Versailles treaty of 1919. Virtually all German public figures, including leaders of the Weimar Republic, hoped to revise that settlement. Hitler and his followers made denunciation of the treaty their most uncompromising declaration. In this speech of April 17, 1923, Hitler explained how the treaty had undermined the German nation.

❖ *How might the French invasion of the Ruhr and the resulting inflation have made this speech particularly effective? To what extent was Hitler's condemnation of the controls imposed on Germany by the Versailles treaty correct? How does Hitler contrast his young Nazi movement with the young Weimar Republic? Why does the one appear a strong and the other a weak supporter of German national goals?*

With the armistice begins the humiliation of Germany. If the Republic on the day of its foundation had appealed to the country: "Germans, stand together! Up and resist the foe! The Fatherland, the Republic expects of you that you fight to your last breath," then millions who are now the enemies of the Republic would be fanatical Republicans. To-day they are the foes of the Republic not because it is a Republic but because this Republic was founded at the moment when Germany was humiliated, because it so discredited the new flag that men's eyes must turn regretfully towards the old flag.

It was no Treaty of Peace which was signed, but a betrayal of Peace.

The Treaty was signed which demanded from Germany that she should perform what was for ever impossible of performance. But that was not the worst; after all that was only a question of material values. This was not the end: Commissions of Control were formed! For the first time in the history of the modern world there were planted on a State agents of foreign Powers to act as Hangmen, and German soldiers were set to serve the foreigner. And if one of these Commissions was "insulted," a company of the German army had to defile before the French flag. We no

longer feel the humiliation of such an act; but the outside world says, "What a people of curs!"

So long as this Treaty stands there can be no resurrection of the German people: no social reform of any kind is possible! The Treaty was made in order to bring 20 million Germans to their deaths and to ruin the German nation. But those who made the Treaty cannot set it aside. At its foundation our Movement formulated three demands:

1. Setting aside of the Peace Treaty.
2. Unification of all Germans.
3. Land and soil to feed our nation.

Our Movement could formulate these demands, since it was not our Movement which caused the War, it has not made the Republic, it did not sign the Peace Treaty.

There is thus one thing which is the first task of this Movement: it desires to make the German once more National, that his Fatherland shall stand for him above everything else. It desires to teach our people to understand afresh the truth of the old saying: He who will not be a hammer must be an anvil. An anvil are we today, and that anvil will be beaten until out of the anvil we fashion once more a hammer, a German sword!

From Norman H. Baynes, ed., *The Speeches of Adolph Hitler, April 1922–1939* (Oxford University Press for the Royal Institute of International Affairs, London, 1942), Volume 1, pp. 56-57. Reprinted by permission of the Royal Institute of International Affairs).

On November 9, 1923, Hitler and a band of followers, accompanied by General Ludendorff, attempted a *putsch* from a beer hall in Munich that was unsuccessful. When the local authorities crushed the uprising, sixteen Nazis were killed. Hitler and Ludendorff were arrested and tried for treason. The general was acquitted. Hitler used the trial to make himself into a national figure. In his defense, he condemned the republic, the Versailles treaty, the Jews, and the weak-

ened condition of his adopted country. He was convicted and sentenced to five years in prison, but was paroled after serving only a few months.

During his time in prison, Hitler dictated *Mein Kampf*, or *My Struggle*, from which he eventually made a great deal of money. In this book, not taken seriously enough at the time, he outlined key political views from which he never swerved, including a fierce racial anti-Semitism, a powerful opposition to Bolshevism, which he associated with Jews, and a conviction that Germany must expand eastward beyond the borders established at Versailles to achieve greater "living space." Such expansion assumed the recovery of German military might vanquished by the war and the peace. In effect, Hitler transferred the foreign policy goals and racial outlooks previously associated with German overseas imperialism to the politics of central and eastern Europe. The natural targets of implementating these ideas would be Jews, the succes-

sor states of eastern Europe, the Soviet Union, and any groups within Germany that opposed Hitler's vision of national unity and purpose. In the midtwenties, most observers discounted the likelihood of any German political party's carrying out such policies.

During the same months of imprisonment, Hitler reached two other decisions. First, it appears that this was the moment when he came to see himself as the leader who could transform Germany from a position of weakness to strength. Second, he decided that he

Ernst Roehm Demands a Return to German Military Values

Ernst Roehm (1887–1934) was the early Nazi leader who headed the SA (Sturmabteilung, or storm troopers). He had fought in the First World War and saw himself primarily as a soldier. In this passage from his autobiography, he emphasizes a soldier's understanding of German nationalism and how National Socialism could contribute to German renewal. Roehm himself was executed in 1934 along with other SA officers when Hitler consolidated his personal power at their expense.

❖ *Why would this speech have appealed to the tens of thousands of German World War I veterans? Why does Roehm favor nationalistic and military values over those of peace and prosperity? Why are "politicians" such a convenient target for his attack?*

I am a believer in plain talk and have not hid my heart like a skeleton in the closet.

I must write without fear, with defiance—just as it comes from my soul....

Soldierly comradeship, cemented with blood, can perhaps temporarily relax, but it can never be torn out of the heart, it cannot be exterminated.

Still, all of Germany has not been awakened yet—despite National Socialism. My words shall be a trumpet call to those who are still asleep.

I am not appealing to the hustling and sneaky trader who has made accursed gold his God, but to the warrior who is struggling in the battle of life, who wants to win freedom and with it the kingdom of heaven.

I approve of whatever serves the purpose of German Freedom. I oppose whatever runs counter to it. Europe, aye, the whole world, may go down in flames—what concern is it of ours? Germany must live and be free.

One may call me a bigoted fool—I can't help that. I am opposed to sport in its present form and to its effects. Moreover, I consider it a definite national danger. We cannot rebuild the Fatherland with champions and artificially nurtured "big guns of sport." Only the most careful develop-

ment which provides physical strength and capability, with spiritual elasticity and ethical backbone, can be of use to the Volk community....

The Germans have forgotten how to hate.

Virile hate has been replaced by feminine lamentation. But he who is unable to hate cannot live either. Fanatical love and hate—their fires kindle flames of freedom.

Passionlessness, matter-of-factness, objectivity, are impersonality, are sophistry.

Only passion gives knowledge, creates wisdom.

"Peace and order" is the battle cry of people living on pensions. In the last analysis you cannot govern a state on the basis of the needs of pensioners....

"Irresponsible dreamers" for years and years have called upon the people to rise up against enslavement and oppression. The "responsible politicians" of the new Germany in these same years have sold Germany lock, stock, and barrel....

From time immemorial Germany was not suited to "diplomacy" and "politics." The sword has always determined the greatness of its history....

Only the soldier could lead his people and Fatherland out of wretchedness and shame to freedom and honor.

From Ernst Roehm, *Die Geschichte eines Hochverraters* (Munich: Verlang Frz. Eher Nachf., 1928), pp. 365–367 (7th ed., 1934), as quoted in George L. Mosse, *Nazi Culture: Intellectual, Cultural, and Social Life in the Third Reich* (New York: Grosset & Dunlap, 1966), pp. 101–103.

George Grosz Satirizes Germany's Social and Political Elite

George Grosz, *Pillars of Society*, 1926. Bildarchiv Preussischer Kulturbesitz.

The 1920s saw enormous turmoil and social unrest in the Weimar Republic. Anger over the loss of World War I and bitterness about the Versailles Treaty and its punishing attitude toward Germany poisoned the life of the young republic. The forces of political reaction blamed the problems on the socialists and communists, who in turn blamed the conservative classes.

More than any artist of the day, George Grosz (1893–1959) captured the strife and despair that marked Weimar politics and social life. He had criticized the German government's role in the outbreak of the First World War, but enlisted anyway, knowing that he would soon be drafted. Grosz believed that ordinary Germans had blindly followed the ruling elite into the war. He hated what he regarded as the hypocrisy of the conservative middle class and representatives of the old German imperial order. Their economic greed and irrational patriotism, Grosz believed, had led Germany into the war. A socialist himself, Grosz joined the Communist party in 1919.

Pillars of Society (1926) is one of Grosz's most bitter attacks on the German social elite (1926). Although he had become disgusted with what he saw as the hypocrisy of the Communist Party, he still considered the conservative classes the greatest danger to the Weimar Republic. They would lead Germany into new disasters, he believed, just as they had headed the country into the First World War.

Pillars of Society is a savage attack on the German social and political elite. Toward the top of the painting, an elderly officer stands with sword and pistol drawn. Just below him to the left a clergyman preaches patriotism. Grosz was consistently anticlerical, attacking what he saw as the German churches' support for a resurgent Germany and their unwillingness to oppose militarism. The bloated figure on the left with his flag and the pamphlet in his pocket declaring "Socialism at Work" represents German nationalism. The top of his head is sliced and excrement spews out. Even the pacifist with the palm leaf has a nasty aggressive face. The nationalistic papers that he is carrying and the chamber pot he wears suggest that he is a hypocrite. The most menacing figure in the painting is the Nazi at the bottom with the swastika on his tie. The beer mug in his hand reminds the viewer of Hitler's abortive Beer Hall Putsch in Munich in 1923. Like the officer at the top of the painting, the Nazi carries a sword. This parallel and the mounted soldier rising from the Nazi's head suggests a future alliance between traditional German militarism and the aggressiveness of Nazi ideology and foreign policy that would lead to war and the destruction of the republic. Grosz grasped the danger of the then small and discredited Nazi party as early as 1926.

By late 1932, the Nazis were on the verge of taking power, and Grosz fled to the United States. His art represented all that the Nazis and Hitler personally despised. In 1937 they organized an infamous exhibition of "degenerate art." Grosz's work was included.

Sources: Richard Cork, *A Bitter Truth: Avant-Garde Art and the Great War* (New Haven: Yale University Press, 1994); Bärbel Schrader and Jürgen Scheber, *The "Golden" Twenties: Art and Literature in the Weimar Republic* (New Haven: Yale University Press, 1988).

and the party must pursue power by legal means. But as Hitler emerged from his imprisonment, he was still a regional politician (albeit one in the process of transforming himself into a national figure).

The Stresemann Years

Elsewhere, the officials of the republic were trying to repair the damage from the inflation. Gustav Stresemann (1878–1929) was primarily responsible for the reconstruction of the republic and for giving it a sense of self-confidence. As chancellor from August to November 1923, Stresemann abandoned the policy of passive resistance in the Ruhr. The country simply could not afford it. Then, with the aid of the banker Hjalmar Schacht (1877–1970), he introduced a new German currency. The rate of exchange was one trillion of the old German marks for one new *Rentenmark*.

Stresemann also moved against challenges from the left and the right. He supported the crushing of both Hitler's abortive *putsch* and smaller Communist disturbances. In late November 1923, he resigned as chancellor and became foreign minister, a post that he held until his death in 1929. He continued to exercise considerable influence over the affairs of the republic.

In 1924, the Weimar Republic and the Allies agreed to a new system of reparation payments. The Dawes Plan, submitted by the American banker Charles Dawes, lowered the annual payments and allowed them to vary according to the fortunes of the German economy. The last French troops left the Ruhr in 1925. (See Map 27–1.)

The same year, Friedrich Ebert (1871–1925), the Social Democratic president of the republic, died. Field Marshal Paul von Hindenburg (1847–1934), a military hero and a conservative monarchist, was elected as his successor. He governed in strict accordance with the constitution, but his election suggested that German politics had become more conservative. It looked as if conservative Germans had become reconciled to the republic. This conservatism was in line with the prosperity of the later 1920s. The new political and economic stability meant that foreign capital flowed into Germany, and employment rose smartly. In the steel and chemical industries, large combines spread. The prosperity helped to broaden the acceptance of, and appreciation for, the republic.

In foreign affairs, Stresemann was conciliatory. He fulfilled the provisions of the Paris settlement, even as he attempted to revise it by diplomacy. He was willing to accept the settlement in the west, but was a determined, if sometimes secret, revisionist in the east. He aimed to recover German-speaking territories lost to Poland and Czechoslovakia and possibly to unite with Austria, chiefly by diplomatic means. The first

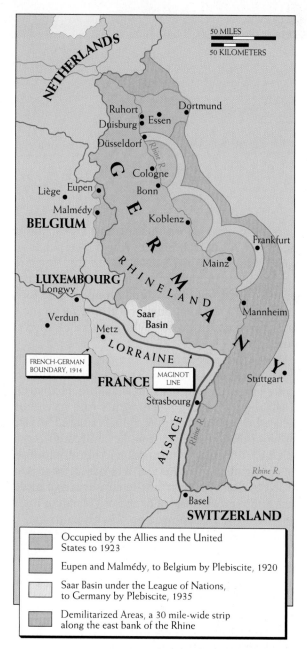

Map 27–1 GERMANY'S WESTERN FRONTIER *The French–Belgian–German border area between the two world wars was sensitive. Despite efforts to restrain tensions, there were persistent difficulties related to the Ruhr, Rhineland, Saar, and Eupen–Malmédy regions that required strong defenses.*

step, however, was to achieve respectability and economic recovery. That goal required a policy of accommodation and "fulfillment," for the moment at least.

Locarno

These developments gave rise to the Locarno Agreements of October 1925. The spirit of conciliation led foreign secretary Austen Chamberlain (1863–1937) for

Britain and Aristide Briand for France to accept Stresemann's proposal for a fresh start. France and Germany both accepted the western frontier established at Paris as legitimate. Britain and Italy agreed to intervene against whichever side violated the frontier or if Germany sent troops into the demilitarized Rhineland. Significantly, no such agreement was reached about Germany's eastern frontier. The Germans signed treaties of arbitration with Poland and Czechoslovakia, however, and France strengthened its ties with the Little Entente. France supported German membership in the League of Nations and agreed to withdraw its occupation troops from the Rhineland in 1930, five years earlier than specified at Paris.

Locarno pleased everyone. Germany was satisfied to have achieved respectability and a guarantee against another Ruhr occupation, as well as to have been afforded the possibility of revision in the east. Britain was pleased to be allowed to play a more evenhanded role. Italy was glad to be recognized as a great power. The French were happy, too, because the Germans voluntarily accepted the permanence of their western frontier, also guaranteed by Britain and Italy, while France maintained its allies in the east.

The Locarno Agreements brought a new spirit of hope to Europe. Germany's entry into the League of Nations was greeted with enthusiasm. Chamberlain and Dawes received the Nobel Peace Prize in 1925, and Briand and Stresemann were awarded it in 1926. The spirit of Locarno was carried even further when the leading European states, Japan, and the United States signed the Kellogg–Briand Pact in 1928, renouncing "war as an instrument of national policy."

The joy and optimism were not justified. France had merely recognized its inability to coerce Germany without help. Britain had shown its unwillingness to uphold the Paris settlement in the east. Austen Chamberlain declared that no British government would ever "risk the bones of a British grenadier" for the Polish corridor. Germany remained unreconciled to the eastern settlement. It continued its clandestine military connections with the Soviet Union, which had begun with the Treaty of Rapallo, and planned to continue to press for revision of the Paris settlement.

In both France and Germany, moreover, the conciliatory politicians represented only a part of the nation. In Germany, especially, most people continued to reject Versailles and regarded Locarno as only an extension of it. When the Dawes Plan ran out in 1929, it was replaced by the Young Plan. Named after the American businessman Owen D. Young (1874–1962), who devised it on behalf of the Allies, this plan lowered German reparation payments, put a limit on how long they had to be made, and removed Germany entirely from outside supervision and control. The intensity of the outcry in Germany against the

Major Political Events of the 1920s	
1919 (August)	Constitution of the Weimar Republic promulgated
1920	*Kapp Putsch* in Berlin
1921 (March)	Kronstadt mutiny leads Lenin to initiate his New Economic Policy
1921 (December)	Treaty between Great Britain and the Irish Free State
1922 (April)	Treaty of Rapallo between Germany and the Soviet Union
1922 (October)	Fascist march on Rome leads to Mussolini's assumption of power
1923 (January)	France invades the Ruhr
1923 (November)	Hitler's Beer Hall *Putsch*
1923 (December)	First Labour government in Britain
1924	Death of Lenin
1925	Locarno Agreements
1926	General strike in Britain
1928	Kellogg–Briand Pact
1929 (January)	Trotsky expelled from the Soviet Union
1929 (February)	Lateran Accord between the Vatican and the Italian state

continuation of *any* reparations showed how far the Germans were from accepting their situation.

Despite these problems, major war was by no means inevitable. Europe, aided by American loans, was returning to prosperity. German leaders like Stresemann would unquestionably have continued to press for change, but they would certainly not have resorted to force, much less to a general war. Continued prosperity and diplomatic success might have won the loyalty of the German people to the Weimar Republic and moderate revisionism. But the Great Depression of the 1930s brought new forces into play.

In Perspective

At the close of the 1920s, Europe appeared finally to have emerged from the difficulties of the World War I era. The Soviet Union, regarded in the West as a communist menace, was isolated by the other powers and had withdrawn into its own internal power struggles. Elsewhere, the initial resentments over the Versailles peace settlement seemed to have abated. The major powers were cooperating. Democracy was still functioning in Germany. The Labour Party was about to form its second ministry in Britain. France had settled into a less assertive international role. Mussolini's Fascism seemed to have little relevance to the rest of the Continent. The successor states had not fulfilled the democratic hopes of the Paris conference, but their troubles were their own.

The European economy seemed finally to be on an even keel. The frightening inflation of the early years of the decade was over, and unemployment had eased. American capital was flowing into the Continent. The reparation payments had been systematized by the Young Plan. Yet this economic and political stability proved illusory and temporary. What brought it to an end was the deepest economic depression in the modern history of the West. As governments and electorates responded to the economic collapse, the search for liberty yielded in more than one instance to a search for security. The political experiments of the 1920s gave way to the political tragedies of the 1930s.

REVIEW QUESTIONS

1. How did the Bolshevik Revolution pose a challenge to the rest of Europe? Why did Lenin institute the New Economic Policy? Was it successful? Could the Russian Revolution have succeeded without Lenin? How did Lenin's policies lead to divisions among western socialist parties?
2. Discuss the rise of Joseph Stalin. How did he overcome the opposition of Trotsky and establish himself as head of the Soviet state?
3. Define *fascism*. How and why did the fascists succeed in obtaining power in Italy? What tactics did they use? To whom did they appeal? To what extent did Mussolini deserve the credit for his success? Was there a difference between the right-wing fascist dictatorship of Mussolini and the left-wing communist dictatorship of Stalin?
4. Why were Britain and France "joyless victors" after World War I? What weakness did each have? How did World War I change British politics? Discuss the decline and fall of the Liberal Party. How successful was the general strike of 1926? By what stages did Ireland win its independence?
5. Discuss France's foreign policy problems after the Versailles treaty. By what means could the country best obtain security? Was the invasion of the Ruhr wise? Should France have signed the Locarno pact?
6. Why did all but one of the successor states in eastern and central Europe fail to establish viable democracies?
7. Could the Weimar Republic have taken root in Germany, or was its failure inevitable? Between 1919 and 1929, what were the republic's greatest strengths and weaknesses? To what extent did its fate depend on personalities rather than on underlying trends? Why did the Versailles Treaty loom so large in domestic German politics?

SUGGESTED READINGS

I. BANAC, *The National Question in Yugoslavia: Origins, History, Politics* (1984). An outstanding treatment of the reorganization of eastern European political life.

I. T. BEREND, *Decades of Crisis: Central and Eastern Europe before World War II* (1998). The best recent discussion of a remarkably troubled region of the early twentieth century.

R. BESSEL, *Political Violence and the Rise of Nazism: The Storm Troopers in Eastern Germany, 1925–1934* (1984). A study of the uses of violence by the Nazis.

K. D. BRACHER, *The German Dictatorship* (1970). A comprehensive treatment of both the origins and the functioning of the Nazi movement and government.

A. BULLOCK, *Hitler: A Study in Tyranny*, rev. ed. (1964). Classic biography of Hitler.

E. H. CARR, *A History of Soviet Russia*, 14 vols. (1950–1978). A study by a historian sympathetic to Soviet policies.

S. F. COHEN, *Bukharin and the Bolshevik Revolution: A Political Biography, 1888–1938* (1973). An interesting examination of Stalin's chief opponent on the Communist right.

I. DEUTSCHER, *The Prophet Armed* (1954), *The Prophet Unarmed* (1959), and *The Prophet Outcast* (1963). A major biography of Trotsky.

G. FELDMAN, *The Great Disorder: Politics, Economics, and Society in the Germany Inflation, 1914–1924* (1993). The best work on the subject.

O. FIGES, *Peasant Russia, Civil War: The Volga Countryside in Revolution (1917–1921)* (1989). An important study of the Russian Civil War in a single district.

L. FISCHER, *The Life of Lenin* (1964). A sound biography by an American journalist.

S. FITZPATRICK, *The Russian Revolution, 1917–1932* (1994). An excellent brief introduction.

F. FURET, *The Passing of an Illusion: The Idea of Communism in the Twentieth Century* (1995). A brilliant account of the manner in which Communism shaped politics and thought outside the Soviet Union.

P. FUSSELL, *The Great War and Modern Memory* (1975). A brilliant account of the literature arising from World War I during the 1920s.

P. GAY, *Weimar Culture: The Outsider as Insider* (1968). A sensitive analysis of the intellectual life of Weimar Germany.

H. J. GORDON, *Hitler and the Beer Hall Putsch* (1972). An excellent account of the event and the political situation in the early Weimar Republic.

N. GREENE, *From Versailles to Vichy: The Third Republic, 1919–1940* (1970). A useful introduction to a difficult subject.

H. GRUBER, *International Communism in the Era of Lenin: A Documentary History* (1967). An excellent collection of difficult-to-find documents.

H. GRUBER, *Red Vienna: Experiment in Working-Class Culture, 1919–1934* (1991). A discussion of social democratic policies in Vienna after the fall of the Habsburgs.

B. HAMANN, *Hitler's Vienna: A Dictator's Apprenticeship* (1999). Probing study of the politics and society of Vienna as experienced by the young Hitler.

J. HELD (ED.), *The Columbia History of Eastern Europe in the Twentieth Century* (1992). Individual essays on each of the nations.

B. JELAVICH, *History of the Balkans*, vol. 2 (1983). The standard work.

L. JONES, *German Liberalism and the Dissolution of the Weimar Party System, 1918–1933* (1988). A major study of the parties that failed during the experiment of the Weimar Republic.

I. KERSHAW, *Hitler, 1889–1936: Hubris* (1998). The best treatment of Hitler's early life and rise to power.

P. KENEZ, *The Birth of the Propaganda State: Soviet Methods of Mass Mobilization, 1917–1929* (1985). An examination of how the Communist government inculcated popular support.

B. KENT, *The Spoils of War: The Politics, Economics, and Diplomacy of Reparations, 1918–1932* (1993). A comprehensive account of the intricacies of the reparations problem of the 1920s.

B. LINCOLN, *Red Victory: A History of the Russian Civil War* (1989). An excellent narrative account.

A. LYTTLETON, *Seizure of Power* (1973). A good narrative of the Italian fascist rise to power.

C. S. MAIER, *Recasting Bourgeois Europe: Stabilization in France, Germany, and Italy in the Decade After World War I* (1975). An important interpretation written from a comparative standpoint.

A. MARWICK, *The Deluge: British Society and the First World War* (1965). Full of insights into both major and more subtle minor social changes.

M. MCAULEY, *Bread and Justice: State and Society in Petrograd, 1917–1922* (1991). A study that examines the impact of the Russian Revolution and Leninist policies on a major Russian city.

R. PIPES, *The Formation of the Soviet Union*, 2d ed. (1964). A study of internal policy with emphasis on Soviet minorities.

R. PIPES, *The Unknown Lenin: From the Secret Archive* (1996). A collection of previously unpublished documents that indicate the repressive character of Lenin's government.

J. F. POLLARD, *The Vatican and Italian Fascism 1929–32: A Study in Conflict* (1985). Provides the background to the Lateran pacts.

J. ROTHSCHILD, *East Central Europe Between the Two World Wars* (1974). A detailed and authoritative survey.

H. SETON-WATSON, *Eastern Europe Between the Wars, 1918–1941* (1946). Somewhat dated, but still a useful work.

D. P. SILVERMAN, *Reconstructing Europe After the Great War* (1982). Examines the difficulties faced by the major powers.

D. M. SMITH, *Italy: A Modern History*, rev. ed. (1969). Good chapters on the fascists and Mussolini.

D. M. SMITH, *Italy and Its Monarchy* (1989). A major treatment of an important neglected subject.

R. J. SONTAG, *A Broken World, 1919–1939* (1971). An exceptionally thoughtful and well-organized survey.

M. STEINBERG, *Sabers and Brownshirts: The German Students' Path to National Socialism, 1918–1935* (1977). An interesting study of the recruitment of young Germans.

Z. STERNHELL, *The Birth of Fascist Ideology: From Cultural Rebellion to Political Revolution* (1994). A controversial examination of the roots of Mussolini's ideology.

A. J. P. TAYLOR, *English History, 1914–1945* (1965). Lively and opinionated.

M. TRACTENBERG, *Reparations in World Politics: France and European Economic Diplomacy, 1916–1923* (1980). Points to the special role of reparations in French calculations.

R. TUCKER, *Stalin as Revolutionary, 1879–1929: A Study in History and Personality* (1973). A useful and readable account of Stalin's rise to power.

N. TUMARKIN, *Lenin Lives: The Lenin Cult in Soviet Russia* (1983). An interesting work on the uses of Lenin's reputation after his death.

E. G. WALTERS, *The Other Europe: Eastern Europe to 1945* (1988). An excellent introduction to the problems in the region.

T. WILSON, *The Downfall of the Liberal Party, 1914–1935* (1966). A close examination of the surprising demise of a political party in Britain.

J. WINTER, *Sites of Memory, Sites of Mourning: The Great War in European Cultural History* (1995). A distinguished analysis of the impact of the war on European art, literature, and society.

R. WOHL, *The Generation of 1914* (1979). An important work that explores the effect of the war on political and social thought.

Chapter 28

Thousands of German troops listen to a speech by Hitler at a Nuremberg rally in 1936. Corbis

Europe and the Great Depression of the 1930s

KEY TOPICS

- Financial collapse and depression in Europe
- The emergence of the National Government in Great Britain and the Popular Front in France in response to the political pressures caused by the depression
- The Nazi seizure of power, the establishment of a police state, and the imposition of racial laws in Germany
- Planned industrialism, agricultural collectivization, and purges in the Soviet Communist Party and Soviet army under Stalin

I n Europe, unlike the situation in the United States, the 1920s had not been "roaring." Economically, it had been a decade of insecurity, of a search for elusive stability, of a short-lived upswing, followed by collapse in finance and production. The Great Depression that began in 1929 was the most severe downturn ever experienced by the capitalist economies. High unemployment, low production levels, financial instability, and shrinking trade arrived and would not depart. Capitalist business and political leaders despaired over the failure of the market mechanism to save them. Marxists and, indeed, many other observers thought that the final downfall of capitalism was at hand.

European voters looked for new ways out of the doldrums, and politicians sought escapes from the pressures that the depression had brought on them. One result of the fight for economic security was the establishment of the Nazi dictatorship in Germany. Another was the piecemeal construction of what has since become known as the mixed economy; that is, governments became directly involved in economic decisions alongside business and labor. In both cases, most of the political and economic guidelines of nineteenth-century liberalism were abandoned for good. Two other casualties of these years were decency and civility in political life.

Toward the Great Depression

Three factors combined to bring about the intense severity and the extended length of the Great Depression. First, there was a financial crisis that stemmed directly from the war and the peace settlement. Second, a crisis arose in the production and distribution of goods in the world market. These two problems became intertwined in 1929 and, so far as Europe was concerned, reached the breaking point in 1931. Finally, both difficulties became worse because neither the major western European nations nor the United States offered strong economic leadership or acted responsibly. Without cooperation or leadership in the Atlantic economic community, the economic collapse in finance and production simply lingered and deepened.

The Financial Tailspin

Most European nations emerged from World War I with inflated currencies. Immediately after the armistice, the unleashed demand for consumer and industrial goods drove up prices. The price and wage increases generally subsided after 1921. Yet the problem of maintaining the value of their national currencies still haunted political leaders—and was intensified after the German financial disaster of 1923. The frightening German example of uncontrolled inflation helped explain the later refusal of most governments to run budget deficits when the depression struck. They feared inflation as a source of social instability and political turmoil the way that European governments since World War II have feared unemployment.

REPARATIONS AND WAR DEBTS   Reparation payments and international war-debt settlement further complicated the picture. Here France and the United States were the stumbling blocks. France had twice paid reparations as a defeated nation, once after 1815 and again after 1871. As a victor, it now intended both to receive reparations and to finance its postwar recovery through them. The 1923 invasion of the Ruhr demonstrated French determination on this question.

The United States was no less determined to be repaid for the wartime loans it had made to its allies. Moreover, the European Allies owed various debts to each other. It soon became apparent that German reparations were to provide the means by which other European nations intended to repay all these debts. Most of the money that the Allies collected from each other eventually went to the United States.

In 1922, Great Britain announced that it would insist on payment for its own loans only to the extent that the United States required payments from Britain. The American government, however, would not

Major Dates of the Economic Crisis

1923	German inflation following French invasion of Ruhr
1924	Dawes Plan on reparations
1929 (June)	Young Plan on reparations
1929 (October)	Wall Street crash
1931 (May)	Collapse of *Kreditanstalt* in Vienna
1931 (June)	Hoover announces moratorium on reparations
1932	Lausanne Conference ends reparations

relent. The reparations and the war debts made normal business, capital investment, and international trade difficult and expensive for the European nations. Governments exercised various controls over credit, trade, and currency. Currency speculation drew funds away from capital investment in productive enterprise. The monetary problems reinforced the general tendency toward high tariff policies. If a nation imported too many goods from abroad, it might have difficulty meeting those costs and the expenses of debt or reparation payments. The financial and money muddle thus discouraged trade and production and, in consequence, hurt employment.

AMERICAN INVESTMENTS   In 1924 the Dawes Plan reorganized the administration and transfer of reparations, which procedures in turn smoothed the debt repayments to the United States. Thereafter, private American capital flowed into Europe—especially Germany. Much of the money, which provided the basis for Europe's brief prosperity after 1925, was in the form of short-term loans.

In 1928, this lending began to contract as American money was withdrawn from European investments into the booming New York stock market. In the Wall Street crash of October 1929—the result of virtually unregulated financial speculation—huge amounts of money were lost. United States banks had made large loans to customers, who then invested the money in the stock market. When stock prices collapsed, the customers could not repay the banks. Consequently, within the United States, all kinds of credit that had been available shrank severely or disappeared, and many banks failed. Thereafter, little American capital was available for investment in Europe. Furthermore, loans already made to Europeans were not renewed, as American banks strove to cover domestic shortages.

THE END OF REPARATIONS   When the credit to Europe began to run out, a major financial crisis struck the continent. In May 1931, the *Kreditanstalt*, a major

Crowds gathered on Wall Street in New York on October 29, 1929, the day the stock market crashed. The Great Depression in the United States dried up American capital previously available for investment in Europe. Brown Brothers

bank in Vienna, collapsed. It was a primary lending institution for much of central and eastern Europe. The German banking system came under severe pressure and was saved only through government guarantees. It became clear, however, that in this crisis Germany would be unable to make its next reparation payment as stipulated in the 1929 Young Plan. In June 1931, as the German difficulties mounted, American President Herbert Hoover (1874–1964) announced a one-year moratorium on all payments of international debts.

The Hoover moratorium was a prelude to the end of reparations. Hoover's action was a sharp blow to the French economy, for which the flow of reparations had continued to be important. The French agreed to the moratorium only reluctantly, as they really had little alternative because the German economy had all but collapsed. The Lausanne Conference in the summer of 1932 in effect ended the era of reparations. The next year, the debts owed to the United States were settled either through small token payments or simply through default. Nevertheless, the financial politics of the 1920s had done its damage.

Problems in Agricultural Commodities

In addition to the dramatic financial turmoil and collapse, a less dramatic, but equally fundamental, downturn occurred in production and trade. The 1920s saw the market demand for European goods shrink relative to the Continent's capacity to produce goods. This meant idle factories and fewer jobs. Part of the problem originated within Europe, part outside.

In both instances, the difficulty arose from agriculture. Better methods of farming, improved strains of wheat, expanded tillage, and more extensive transport facilities all over the globe vastly increased the world supply of grain. World wheat prices fell to record lows. This development was, of course, initially good for consumers. The collapse in grain prices, however, meant lower incomes for European farmers, especially those of central and eastern Europe.

Also, higher industrial wages raised the cost of the industrial goods used by farmers or peasants. The farmers could not purchase those products. Moreover, farmers began to have difficulty paying off their mortgages and normal annual operational debts. Normally, they borrowed money to plant their fields, expecting to pay the debt when the crops were sold, but the fall in commodity prices made it difficult for the farmers to repay those debts.

Farm problems became especially pressing in eastern Europe. Immediately after the war, the new governments there had undertaken land-reform programs. The democratic franchise in the successor states had opened the way for considerable redistribution of tillable soil. In Romania and Czechoslovakia, large amounts of land changed hands. In Hungary and Poland, it occurred to a lesser extent.

The new small farms, however, proved to be inefficient, and the farmers who worked them were unable to earn sufficient incomes. Protective tariffs often prevented the export of grain among European countries. The credit and cost squeeze on eastern European farmers and on their counterparts in Germany played a major role in their disillusionment with liberal politics. For example, farmers in Germany were a major source of political support for the Nazis.

Outside Europe, similar problems affected other producers of agricultural commodities. The prices that they received for their products plummeted. Government-held reserves of agricultural commodities accumulated to record levels. The glut involved the supplies of wheat, sugar, coffee, rubber, wool, and lard. The people who produced these goods in underdeveloped nations in Asia, Africa, and Latin America could no longer make enough money to buy finished goods from industrial Europe. As world credit collapsed, the economic position of these commodity producers worsened. Commodity production had simply outstripped world demand.

The collapse in agricultural prices and the financial turmoil resulted in stagnation and depression for European industry. European coal, iron, and textiles had depended largely on international markets. Unemployment spread from these industries to those producing finished consumer goods. The persistent unemployment in Great Britain and to a lesser extent in Germany during the 1920s had already meant "soft" domestic markets in those countries. The policies of reduced government spending with which the governments confronted the depression further weakened domestic demand. By the early 1930s, the Great Depression was growing on itself.

Depression and Government Policy

The Great Depression did not mean absolute economic decline. Nor did it mean that everyone was out of a job. People with work always well outnumbered those without work. New economic sectors, such as the production of automobiles, radios, and synthetics, and the service industries around them did develop. But the economic downturn made people extremely anxious. People in nearly all walks of life feared that their own economic security and lifestyle would suffer next. The depression also frustrated social and economic expectations. People with jobs improved their standard of living or were promoted much more slowly than might have been the case under sound economic conditions. They were working, but in their own eyes they seemed to be going nowhere. Their anxieties created a major source of social discontent.

The governments of the late 1920s and the early 1930s were not well fitted in either structure or ideology to confront these problems. The Keynesian theory of governments' spending the economy out of depression was not yet available. John Maynard Keynes's (1883–1946) *General Theory of Employment, Interest, and Money* was not published until 1936. Before Keynes, orthodox economic policy

called for cuts in government spending to prevent inflation. Eventually, the market mechanism was supposed to bring the economy back to prosperity.

Nonetheless, the length and severity of the depression, plus direct political pressure from the new mass electorates, led governments across Europe to interfere with the economy as never before. Government participation in economic life was not new; one need only recall the mercantilistic policies of the seventeenth and eighteenth centuries and the government encouragement of railway building in the nineteenth century. From the early 1930s onward, however, government involvement increased rapidly. Private economic enterprise became subject to new trade, labor, and currency regulations. The political goals of restoring employment and providing for defense established new state-related economic priorities. As in the past, state intervention generally increased as one moved from west to east across the Continent. These new economic policies usually also involved further political experimentation.

Confronting the Great Depression in the Democracies

The Great Depression ended the business-as-usual attitude that had marked the political life of Great Britain and France during the late 1920s. In Britain, the emergency led to a new coalition government and the abandonment of economic policies considered sacred for a century. The economic stagnation in France proved to be the occasion for a bold political and economic program sponsored by the parties of the left. The relative success of the British venture gave the nation new confidence in the democratic processes; the new departures in France created social and political hostilities that undermined faith in republican institutions.

Great Britain: The National Government

In 1929 a second minority Labour government, headed by Ramsay MacDonald, took office. As the number of British unemployed rose to more than 2.5 million workers in 1931, the ministry became divided over what to do. MacDonald believed that the budget should be slashed, government salaries reduced, and unemployment benefits cut. This was a bleak program for a Labour government. MacDonald's strong desire to make the Labour Party respectable led him to reject more radical programs. Many of the cabinet ministries resisted

MacDonald's proposals. They refused to take income away from the poor and the unemployed. The prime minister requested the resignations of his entire cabinet and arranged for a meeting with King George V.

Everyone assumed that the entire Labour ministry was about to leave office. However, to the surprise of his party and the nation, MacDonald did not resign. At the urging of the king and probably of his own ambition, MacDonald formed a coalition ministry, called the *National Government*, composed of Labour, Conservative, and Liberal ministers. The bulk of the Labour Party believed that their leader had sold them out. In the election of 1931, the National Government received a comfortable majority. After the election, however, MacDonald, who remained prime minister until 1935, was little more than a tool of the Conservatives. They held a majority in their own right in the House of Commons, but the appearance of a coalition was useful for imposing unpleasant programs.

The National Government took three decisive steps to attack the depression. First, to balance the budget, it raised taxes, cut insurance benefits to the unemployed and the elderly, and lowered government salaries. Its leaders argued that the fall in prices that had taken place meant that those reductions did not appreciably cut real income. Second, in September 1931, Britain went off the gold standard. The value of the British pound on the international money market fell by about 30 percent. This move stimulated exports somewhat. Third, in 1932 Parliament passed the Import Duties Bill, which placed a 10 percent *ad valorem* tariff (a tax levied in proportion to the value of each imported good) on all imports except those from the empire. In the context of previous British policy, these steps were extraordinary. Gold and free trade, the hallmarks of almost a century of British commercial policy, were abandoned.

The policies of the National Government produced significant results. Great Britain avoided the banking crisis that hit other countries. By 1934, industrial production had expanded beyond the level for 1929. Britain was the first nation to restore that level of production. Of course, the mediocre British industrial performance of the 1920s made the British task easier. The government also encouraged lower interest rates, which, in turn, led to the largest private housing boom in British history. Industries related to housing and the furnishing of homes prospered.

Those people who were employed generally improved their standard of living. Nonetheless, the hard core of unemployment remained. In 1937 the number of jobless had fallen to just below 1.5 million. That same year, when George Orwell (1903–1950) described the laboring districts of Britain in *The Road*

to Wigan Pier, the poverty and the idle days without work of the people he met dominated his picture. (See "George Orwell Observes a Woman in the Slums.")

Britain had entered the depression with a stagnant economy and left the era with a stagnant economy. Yet the British political system was not fundamentally challenged. There were demonstrations by the unemployed, but social insurance, though hardly generous, did support them. To the employed citizens of the country, the National Government seemed to pursue a policy that avoided the extreme wings of both the Labour and the Conservative parties. When MacDonald retired in 1935, Stanley Baldwin again took office. He was succeeded in 1937 by Neville Chamberlain (1869–1940). The new prime minister is today known for the disastrous Munich agreement, but when he took office, he was considered one of the more progressive thinkers on social issues in the Conservative Party.

One movement in Britain did flirt with the extreme right-wing politics of the Continent. In 1932, Sir Oswald Mosley (1896–1980) founded the British Union of Fascists. He had held a minor position in the second Labour government and was disappointed by its feeble attack on unemployment. Mosley urged a program of direct action through a new corporate

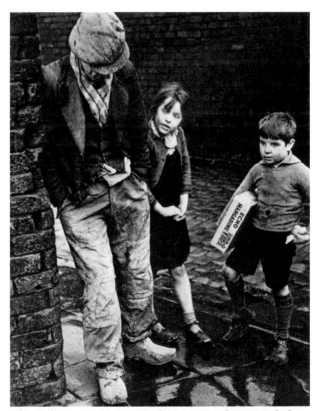

Throughout Europe, unemployment in the 1930s led to profound social and political discontent as the lives and families of unemployed workers, such as this British miner, collapsed. The Granger Collection

George Orwell Observes a Woman in the Slums

Although Great Britain was beginning to emerge from the Great Depression by the late 1930s, much poverty and human degradation remained. This scene, described in 1937 by the social critic and novelist George Orwell (1903–1950), captures a glimpse of the sadness and hopelessness that many British citizens experienced every day of their lives.

❖ *How does Orwell's descriptive language evoke sympathy for the woman he portrays? What economic conditions led to such poverty? What class attitudes does Orwell begin to explore in this passage?*

The train bore me away, through the monstrous scenery of slag-heaps, chimneys, piled scrap-iron, foul canals, paths of cindery mud crisscrossed by the prints of clogs....As we moved slowly through the outskirts of the town we passed row after row of little grey slum houses running at right angles to the embankment. At the back of one of the houses a young woman was kneeling on the stones, poking a stick up the leaden waste-pipe which ran from the sink inside, and which I suppose was blocked. I had time to see everything about her—her sacking apron, her clumsy clogs, her arms reddened by the cold....She had a round pale face, the usual exhausted face of the slum girl who is twenty-five and looks forty, thanks to miscarriages and drudgery; and it wore, for the second in which I saw it, the most desolate, hopeless expression I have ever seen. It struck me then that we are mistaken when we say that "It isn't the same for them as it would be for us," and that people bred in the slums can imagine nothing but the slums. For what I saw in her face was not the ignorant suffering of an animal. She knew well enough what was happening to her—understood as well as I did how dreadful a destiny it was to be kneeling there in the bitter cold, on the slimy stones of a slum backyard, poking a stick up a foul drain-pipe.

Excerpt from *The Road to Wigan Pier* by George Orwell. U.S.: copyright 1958 and renewed 1986 by the Estate of Sonia B. Orwell, reprinted by permission of Harcourt Brace & Company. Canada: copyright © George Orwell, 1937. Reprinted with permission of Bill Hamilton as the Literary Executor of the Estate of the Late Sonia Brownell Orwell, Martin Seeker & Warburg, Ltd.

structure for the economy. His group wore black shirts and attempted to hold mass meetings. Even at the height of his popularity, he gained only a few thousand adherents. Thereafter his anti-Semitism began to alienate supporters, and by the close of the decade, he was little more than a political oddity.

France: The Popular Front

The timing of the Great Depression in France was the reverse of that in Britain. It came later and lasted longer. Only in 1931 did the economic slide begin to affect the French economy. Even then, unemployment did not become a major problem. Rarely were more than half a million French workers without jobs. In one industry after another, however, wages were lowered. The government raised tariffs to protect French goods and especially French agriculture. (Ever since that time, French farmers have enjoyed unusual protection by the government.) These measures helped maintain the home market, but did little to overcome industrial stagnation. Relations between labor and management were tense. (See "Art & the West.")

The first political fallout of the depression was the election of another Radical coalition government in 1932. Fearful of contributing to inflation as they had after 1924, the Radicals pursued a generally deflationary policy. In the same year that the new ministry took office, reparation payments upon which the French economy depended stopped. As the economic crisis tightened, normal parliamentary and political life became difficult and confused.

RIGHT-WING VIOLENCE   Outside the Chamber of Deputies, politics grew ugly. Various right-wing groups with authoritarian tendencies became active. These leagues included the *Action Française,* founded before World War I in the wake of the Dreyfus affair, and the *Croix de Feu* or "Cross of Fire," composed of army veterans. These and similar groups had a total of more than two million members. Some of them wanted a monarchy; others favored what would have amounted to military rule. They were hostile to parliamentary government, socialism, and communism. They wanted what they regarded as the greater good and glory of France to be

René Magritte, The Human Condition: *Exploring Illusion and Reality*

At first glance, René Magritte's (1898–1967) *The Human Condition* (1933) seems to be just a picture of an oil painting, on an easel, before a window that looks out onto a slightly overgrown lawn. But look again. Why does Magritte's painting-within-a-painting perfectly match the landscape we can see through the window? Is that landscape also painted, or is the picture on the easel itself a kind of window? And what does all this say about being human?

Such open-ended questions and enigmatic images are a trademark of Magritte's work. Although like many European painters who followed Picasso, Magritte began as an abstract artist, from the mid-1920s until his death he worked in the eerily realist style exemplified by this painting. Magritte's work is "surreal"; it turns straightforward and "realistic" scenes into paradoxes of unresolved meaning. In this, he was influenced by a variety of non-artistic sources, from advertising to Sigmund Freud's *The Interpretation of Dreams*. In that work, Freud had argued that dreams are a mechanism through which the human unconscious "speaks" desires and fears that were repressed in everyday conscious life. Like other Surrealist artists, Magritte was fascinated by dreams. For him they embody the "surreality" of everyday life.

This painting, as well as other surrealism of the period, indicates that even in the midst of the depression and the rise of authoritarian movements across the continent some artists retreated from the engagement with public life seen in the George Grosz painting of the previous chapter and explored their own inner lives and fantasies. Such an approach to art was easier in Western Europe, where unlike Weimar, the democracies were stable even if troubled.

The Human Condition could be a dream-image. It could also illustrate the nature of dreaming itself: Just as in Magritte's painting, dreams confuse distinctions between image and reality, revealing truths about seemingly straightforward "real" life in the most fantastic forms. Magritte himself opposed any such direct interpretations of his work, however. Instead, he claimed to create "encounters" among diverse images and ideas. In this, he confronted one of the stumbling blocks of Surrealist theory: For if dreams are a product of the unconscious, how can an artist make an adequate conscious representation of them?

Perhaps the best way to understand *The Human Condition* is as a reflection of the challenges to accepted scientific truths, from Freud's psychoanalysis to Einstein's General Theory of Relativity, that shook the intellectual life of the West in the early 1900s. In an era in which previously held absolutes seemed to be falling one after the other, Magritte saw uncertainty itself—what is real and what is illusion?—as the very condition of being human.

Today, his speculations seem more relevant than ever. In the twenty-first century, "virtual reality" is no longer just the concern of avant-garde artists.

René Magritte (Belgian, 1898–1967), *The Human Condition*, (*La Condition Humaine*), 1933. Oil on canvas, 1.000 × .810 × .016. National Gallery of Art, Washington. Gift of Collectors Committee.

set above the petty machinations of political parties. They thus resembled the Fascists and the Nazis.

The activities and propaganda of the right-wing leagues weakened loyalty to republican government and made French political life more bitter and vindictive. They also led to an incident of extraordinary havoc that produced important long-range political consequences.

This incident grew out of the Stavisky affair, the last of those curious scandals that punctuated the political fortunes of the Third Republic. Serge Stavisky (d. 1934) was a small-time gangster who appears to have had good connections within the government. In 1933 he became involved in a fraudulent bond scheme. When finally tracked down by the police, he committed suicide in January 1934. The official handling of the matter suggested a political cover-up. It was alleged that people in high places wished to halt the investigation. To the right wing in France, the Stavisky incident symbolized all the seaminess, immorality, and corruption of republican politics.

On February 6, 1934, a large demonstration of the right-wing leagues took place in Paris. The exact purpose and circumstances of the rally remain uncertain, but the crowd did attempt to march on the Chamber of Deputies. Violence erupted between right and left political groups and between them and the police. Fourteen demonstrators were killed; scores of others were injured. It was the largest disturbance in Paris since the Commune of 1871.

In the wake of the night of February 6, the Radical ministry of Édouard Daladier (1884–1970) resigned and was replaced by a national coalition government composed of all living former premiers. The Chamber of Deputies permitted the ministry to deal with economic matters by decree. The major result of the right-wing demonstrations, however, was a political self-reassessment by the parties of the left. Radicals, Socialists, and Communists began to realize that a right-wing coup might be possible in France.

EMERGENCE OF SOCIALIST–COMMUNIST COOPERATION
Between 1934 and 1936, the French left began to make peace within its own ranks. This was not easy. French Socialists, led by Léon Blum (1872–1950), had been the major target of the French communists since the split over joining the Comintern in 1920. Only Stalin's fear of Hitler as a danger to the Soviet Union made this new cooperation possible. Despite deep suspicions on all sides, the Popular Front of all left-wing parties had been established by July 1935. Its purpose was to preserve the republic and press for social reform.

The election of 1936 gave the Popular Front a majority in the Chamber of Deputies. The Socialists were the largest single party for the first time in French history. They organized the cabinet as they had long promised they would do when they constituted the majority party of a coalition. Léon Blum assumed the premiership on June 5, 1936. From the early 1920s, this Jewish intellectual and humanitarian had opposed the communist version of socialism. Cast as the successor to Jean Jaurès (1859–1914), who had been assassinated in 1914, Blum pursued socialism in the context of democratic, parliamentary government.

BLUM'S GOVERNMENT   During May 1936, before the Popular Front came to power, strikes had begun to spread throughout French industry. Immediately after assuming office on June 6, the Blum government faced further spontaneous work stoppages involving over half a million workers who had occupied factories in sit-down strikes. These were the most extensive labor disturbances in the history of the Third Republic. They aroused new fears in the conservative business community, already frightened by the election of the Popular Front.

Blum acted swiftly to bring together representatives of labor and management. On June 8, he announced the conclusion of an accord that reorganized labor–management relations in France. Wages were immediately raised between 7 and 15 percent, depending on the job involved. Employers were required to recognize unions and to bargain collectively with them. Workers were given annual paid two-week vacations. The forty-hour week was established throughout French industry. Blum hoped to overcome labor hostility to French society, to establish a foundation for justice in labor–management relations, and to increase the domestic consumer demand of the nation.

Blum followed his labor policy with other bold departures. He raised the salaries of civil servants and instituted a program of public works. Government loans were extended to small industry. Spending on armaments was increased, and some armament industries were nationalized. A National Wheat Board was set up to manage the production and sale of grain. Initially, Blum had promised to resist devaluation of the franc. By the autumn of 1936, however, international monetary pressure forced him to devalue. He did so again in the spring of 1937. The devaluations came too late to help French exports.

These moves enraged the conservative banking and general business communities. In March 1937, they brought enough influence to bear on the ministry to cause Blum to halt the program of reform. It was not taken up again. Blum's Popular Front colleagues considered the pause in reform an unnecessary compromise. In June 1937, Blum resigned. The Popular Front ministry itself held on until April 1938, when it was

Depression Years in Great Britain and France

1929	Second Labour government comes to power in Britain with Ramsay MacDonald as prime minister
1931	Formation of National Government in Britain
1931	British government goes off the gold standard
1932	Oswald Mosley founds British Union of Fascists
1933–1934	Stavisky affair in France
1934 (February 6)	Right-wing riots in Paris
1935	Stanley Baldwin becomes British prime minister
1936 (June 5)	Popular Front government in France under Blum
1936 (June 8)	Labor accord in France
1937	Neville Chamberlain becomes British prime minister
1938	Popular Front replaced by Radical ministry in France

replaced by a Radical ministry under Daladier. Not until 1939 did French industrial production reach the level of 1929.

By the close of the 1930s, citizens from all walks of life had begun to wonder whether the republic was worth preserving. The left remained divided. Business people found the republic inefficient and too subject to socialist pressures. The right wing hated the republic in principle. When the time came in 1940 to defend the republic, too many French citizens were not sure that it was worth defending.

Germany: The Nazi Seizure of Power

The most remarkable political event caused by the uncertainty and turmoil of the Great Depression was the coming to power of the National Socialists (Nazis) in Germany. By the late 1920s, the Nazis were a major presence in the Weimar Republic, but were not yet real contenders for political dominance. The financial crisis, economic stress, and social anxiety associated with the onset of the depression rapidly changed that situation. All the fragility of the Weimar constitution stood exposed, and the path opened for the most momentous and far-reaching event of the decade: the Nazi seizure of power.

Depression and Political Deadlock

The outflow of foreign—especially American—capital from Germany beginning in 1928 undermined the brief economic prosperity of the Weimar Republic. The resulting economic crisis brought parliamentary government to an end. In 1928, a coalition of center parties and the Social Democrats governed. All went reasonably well until the depression struck. Then the coalition partners disagreed sharply on economic policy. The Social Democrats refused to reduce social and unemployment insurance. The more conservative parties, remembering the inflation of 1923, insisted on a balanced budget. The coalition dissolved in March 1930.

To resolve the parliamentary deadlock in the Reichstag, President von Hindenburg appointed Heinrich Brüning (1885–1970) as chancellor. Lacking a majority in the Reichstag, Brüning governed through emergency presidential decrees, as authorized by Article 48 of the constitution. The party divisions in the Reichstag prevented the parliament from overriding the decrees. The Weimar Republic was thus transformed into an authoritarian regime.

German unemployment rose from 2,258,000 in March 1930 to more than 6,000,000 in March 1932. There had been persistent unemployment during the 1920s, but nothing of such magnitude or duration. The economic downturn and the parliamentary deadlock worked to the advantage of the more extreme political parties. In the election of 1928, the Nazis had won only 12 seats in the Reichstag, and the Communists had won 54 seats. After the election of 1930, the Nazis held 107 seats and the Communists 77.

For the Nazis, politics meant the capture of power by terror and intimidation as well as by legal elections. All decency and civility in political life vanished. Thousands of unemployed joined the storm troopers (SA), which had 100,000 members in 1930 and almost 1 million in 1933. The SA freely and viciously attacked communists and Social Democrats, who also went on fighting each other. The Nazis held mass rallies that resembled religious revivals. They gained powerful supporters and sympathizers in business, military, and newspaper circles. Some intellectuals were also sympathetic. The Nazis transformed this new enthusiasm born of economic despair and nationalistic frustration into impressive electoral results.

Hitler Comes to Power

For two years Brüning governed with the confidence of his president, Hindenburg. The economy did not improve, however, and the political situation deteriorated. In 1932, the eighty-three-year-old president

Hitler's mastery of the techniques of mass politics and propaganda—including huge staged rallies like this one in 1938—was an important factor in his rise to power. Bildarchiv Preussischer Kulturbesitz

stood for reelection. Hitler ran against him and forced a runoff. The Nazi leader got 30.1 percent of the first vote and 36.8 percent in the runoff. Although Hindenburg remained in office, the results of the poll convinced him that Brüning no longer commanded sufficient confidence from conservative German voters.

On May 30, 1932, Hindenburg dismissed Brüning. The next day, Hindenburg appointed Franz von Papen (1878–1969) as chancellor. The new chancellor was one of a small group of extremely conservative advisers on whom the aged Hindenburg had become increasingly dependent. Others included the president's son and several military figures. With the continued paralysis in the Reichstag, their influence over the president virtually amounted to control of the government. Thus, only a handful of people made the crucial decisions of the next several months.

Papen and the circle around the president wanted to find some way to draw the Nazis into cooperation with them without giving any effective power to Hitler. The government needed the mass popular support that only the Nazis seemed able to generate. The Hindenburg circle decided to convince

Hitler that the Nazis could not come to power on their own. Papen removed the ban on Nazi meetings that Brüning had imposed. Furthermore, he called a Reichstag election for July 1932. The Nazis won 230 seats and polled 37.2 percent of the vote. As the price for his entry into the cabinet, Hitler demanded that he be appointed chancellor. Hindenburg refused. The government called another election in November, partly to wear down the Nazis' financial resources, which it did. The Nazis lost 34 seats, and their popular vote dipped to 33.1 percent. The advisers around Hindenburg still refused to appoint Hitler to office.

In November 1932, Papen resigned, and the next month General Kurt von Schleicher (1882–1934) became chancellor. Fear of civil war between the left and the right mounted. Schleicher tried to build a broad-based coalition of conservative groups and trade unionists. The prospect of such a coalition, including groups from the political left, frightened the Hindenburg circle even more than the prospect of Hitler. They did not trust Schleicher's motives, which were never clear. Consequently, they persuaded Hindenburg to appoint Hitler as chancellor. To control Hitler and to see that he did little

Josef Goebbels Explains How to Use Radio for Political Propaganda

Radio revolutionized communications during the interwar years. It also created an entirely new industry while many other areas of the economy stagnated. Radio, as popular at that time as television is today, also became an important political instrument. Most of the early radio stations were government owned and controlled. Political leaders could address their nations as they never could before. Communication became instant and could enter every home with a radio. Unlike newspapers, radio did not depend upon the literacy of its audience. Shortly after coming into power, Josef Goebbels (1897–1945), who was in charge of Nazi propaganda, discussed the role of radio in the new Nazi order. Note how he urges his listeners, who were broadcasters, never to be boring. All radio broadcasting had to be interesting to audiences so that they would be receptive to its political messages.

❖ *Why does Goebbels emphasize the Nazi monopoly on broadcasting? What new attitudes did Goebbels want radio to bring to its audience? What advantages did radio have over newspapers as a propaganda device?*

We make no bones about the fact that the radio belongs to us and to no one else. And we will place the radio in the service of our ideology [*Idee*] and...no other ideology will find expression here....The radio must subordinate itself to the goals which the Government of the national revolution has set itself. The Government will give the necessary instructions....

I consider radio to be the most modern and the most crucial instrument that exists for influencing the masses. I also believe—one should not say that out loud—that radio will in the end replace the press....

First, principle: At all costs avoid being boring. I put that before *everything*....So do not think that you have the task of creating the correct attitudes, of indulging in patriotism, of blasting out military music and declaiming patriotic verse—no, that is not what this new orientation is all about. Rather you must help to bring forth a nationalist art and culture which is truly appropriate to the

pace of modern life and to the mood of the times. The correct attitudes must be conveyed but that does not mean they must be boring. And simply because you have the task of taking part in this national enterprise you do not have carte blanche to be boring. You must use your imagination, an imagination which is based on sure foundations and which employs all means and methods to bring to the ears of the masses the new attitude in a way which is modern, up to date, interesting, and appealing; interesting, instructive but not schoolmasterish. Radio must never go down with the proverbial disease—the intention is clear and it puts you off.

I am placing a major responsibility in your hands for you have in your hands the most modern instrument in existence for influencing the masses. By means of this instrument you are the creators of public opinion. If you carry this out well we shall win over the people and if you do it badly in the end the people will once more desert us....

J. Noakes and G. Pridham, eds., *Nazism 1919–1945: Vol. 2, State, Economy and Society, 1933–39, A Documentary Reader,* Exeter Studies in History, No. 8 (Exeter, U.K.: University of Exeter Press, © 1984), p. 386. Reprinted by permission.

---

mischief, the Hindenburg circle appointed Papen as vice-chancellor and named other traditional conservatives to the cabinet. On January 30, 1933, Adolf Hitler became the chancellor of Germany.

Hitler had come into office by legal means. All the proper legal forms and procedures had been observed. This was important, for it permitted the civil service, the courts, and the other agencies of

the government to support him in good conscience. He had forged a rigidly disciplined party structure and had mastered the techniques of mass politics and propaganda. (See "Josef Goebbels Explains How to Use Radio for Political Propaganda.") He understood how to touch the raw social and political nerves of the electorate. His support appears to have come from across the social spectrum and not simply from the lower middle class, as was once thought to be the case. Pockets of resistance appeared among Roman Catholic voters in the country and small towns. Otherwise, support for Hitler was particularly strong among groups such as farmers, war veterans, and the young, who had especially suffered from the insecurity of the 1920s and the depression of the early 1930s. Hitler promised them security against communists and socialists, effective government in place of the petty politics of the other parties, and an uncompromising nationalist vision of a strong, restored Germany.

German big business once received much of the credit for the rise of Hitler. There is little evidence, however, that business contributions made any crucial difference to the Nazis' success or failure. Hitler's supporters were frequently suspicious of business and giant capitalism. They wanted a simpler world, one in which small property would be safe from both socialism and large-scale capitalist consolidation. These people looked to Hitler and the Nazis rather than to the Social Democrats because the latter, though concerned with social issues, never appeared sufficiently nationalistic. The Nazis won out over other conservative nationalistic parties because, unlike those conservatives, the Nazis did address the problem of social insecurities.

Hitler's Consolidation of Power

Once in office, Hitler moved with almost lightning speed to consolidate his control. This process had three facets: the capture of full legal authority, the crushing of alternative political groups, and the purging of rivals within the Nazi Party itself.

On February 27, 1933, a mentally ill Dutch communist set fire to the *Reichstag* building in Berlin. The Nazis quickly claimed that the fire proved the existence of an immediate communist threat against the government. To the public,

The Reichstag *fire in 1933 provided Hitler with an excuse to consolidate his power.* Bildarchiv Preussischer Kulturbesitz

it was plausible that the communists might attempt some action against the state now that the Nazis were in power. Under Article 48, Hitler issued an emergency decree suspending civil liberties and proceeded to arrest communists or alleged communists. This decree was not revoked for as long as Hitler ruled Germany.

In early March, another Reichstag election took place. The Nazis still received only 43.9 percent of the vote and won 288 seats. The arrest and removal of all communist deputies, however, and the political fear aroused by the fire enabled Hitler to control the Reichstag. On March 23, 1933, the Reichstag passed an Enabling Act that permitted Hitler to rule by decree. Thereafter, there were no legal limits on his exercise of power. The Weimar constitution was never formally repealed or amended; it had simply been supplanted by the February Emergency Decree and the March Enabling Act.

Perhaps better than anyone else, Hitler understood that he and his party had not inevitably come to power, so in a series of complex moves, Hitler outlawed or undermined any German institution that might have served as a rallying point for opposition. In early May 1933, the Nazi Party, rather than any government agency, seized the offices, banks, and newspapers of the free trade unions and arrested their leaders. In late June and early July, all other German political parties were outlawed. By July 14, 1933, the National Socialists were the only legal party in Germany. During the same months, the Nazis moved against the governments of the individual federal states in Germany. By the close of 1933, all major institutions of potential opposition had been eliminated.

The final element in Hitler's consolidation of power involved the Nazi Party itself. By late 1933 the SA, or storm troopers, consisted of approximately 1 million active members and a larger number of reserves. The commander of this party army was Ernst Roehm (1887–1934), a possible rival to Hitler himself. The German army officer corps, on whom Hitler depended to rebuild the national army, were jealous of the SA leadership. So, to protect his own position and to shore up support with the regular army, on June 30, 1934, Hitler personally ordered the murder of key SA officers, including Roehm. Between June 30 and July 2, more than 100 persons were killed, including former chancellor General Kurt von Schleicher and his wife. The German army, the only institution that might have prevented the murders, did nothing.

A month later, on August 2, 1934, President Hindenburg died. Thereafter, Hitler combined the offices of chancellor and president and became head of state as well as the head of the government. He was now the sole ruler of Germany and the Nazi Party.

Major Dates in the Nazi Seizure of Power	
1928	National Socialists win 12 seats in the *Reichstag*
1930	National Socialists win 107 seats in the *Reichstag*
1930	Brüning appointed chancellor
1932 (April 10)	Hindenburg defeats Hitler for presidency
1932 (May 31)	Von Papen replaces Brüning
1932 (July 31)	National Socialists win 230 seats in the *Reichstag*
1932 (November 6)	Indecisive *Reichstag* election; National Socialists lose 34 seats
1932 (November 17)	Von Papen resigns
1932 (December 2)	Von Schleicher appointed chancellor
1933 (January 28)	Von Schleicher resigns
1933 (January 30)	Hitler appointed chancellor
1933 (February 27)	*Reichstag* fire
1933 (March 5)	National Socialists win 288 seats in the *Reichstag*
1933 (March 23)	Enabling Act passed
1933 (July 14)	National Socialists declared the only legal party
1934 (June 30)	Murder of SA leadership
1934 (August 2)	Death of Hindenburg
1935	Passage of Nuremberg Laws
1938 (November 9 and 10)	*Kristallnacht* (nights of attacks on Jewish businesses and synagogues)

The Police State and Anti-Semitism

Terror and intimidation had been major factors in the Nazi march to office. As Hitler consolidated his power, he oversaw the organization of a police state. The chief vehicle of police surveillance was the SS (*Schutzstaffel*, or "protective force"), or security units, commanded by Heinrich Himmler (1900–1945). This group had originated in the mid-1920s as a bodyguard for Hitler and had become a more elite paramilitary organization than the much larger SA. In 1933 there were approximately 52,000 members of the SS, which was the instrument that carried out the blood purges of the party in 1934. By 1936, Himmler had become head of all police matters in Germany and stood second only to Hitler in power and influence.

The police character of the Nazi regime was all pervasive, but the people who most consistently experienced the terror of the police state were the German Jews. A key plank of the Nazi program was an anti-Semitism based on biological racial

Soon after seizing power, the Nazi government began harassing German Jewish businesses. Non-Jewish German citizens were urged not to buy merchandise from shops owned by Jews. Paulmann/Bildarchiv Preussischer Kulturbesitz

theories stemming from late-nineteenth-century thought rather than from religious discrimination. Before World War II, the Nazi attack on the Jews went through three stages of increasing intensity. First, in 1933, shortly after assuming power, the Nazis excluded Jews from the civil service. They also tried to enforce boycotts of Jewish shops and businesses, but these won little public support.

Second, in 1935, a series of measures known as the Nuremberg Laws robbed German Jews of their citizenship. The professions and the major occupations were closed to those defined as Jews. Marriage and sexual intercourse between Jews and non-Jews were prohibited. Legal exclusion and humiliation of the Jews became the order of the day. The definition of a Jew was confusing in this law, because the Nazis found that they could not produce regulations based on a racial concept alone. The Nazi legal definitions of who was a Jew took into account the number of Jewish parents or grandparents, as well as, whether certain persons being defined as Jewish practiced the Jewish faith. All persons with at least three Jewish grandparents were defined as Jews, but persons with two Jewish grandparents were accounted Jewish only if practicing the Jewish faith, or if married to a Jew, or if born to a marriage with one Jewish parent, or if born out of wedlock with one Jewish parent.

Third, the persecution of the Jews increased again in 1938. Business careers were forbidden to them. On November 9 and 10, 1938, under Nazi Pary orders, thousands of Jewish stores and synagogues were burned or otherwise destroyed on what became known as *Kristallnacht*. (See "An American Diplomat Witnesses *Kristallnacht* in Leipzig.") The Jewish community itself was required to pay for the destruction because the government confiscated the insurance money that was paid to cover the damages. In many other ways, large and petty, German Jews were harassed. This persecution allowed the Nazis to inculcate the rest of the population with the concept of a master race of pure German "Aryans" and also to display their own contempt for civil liberties.

Finally, after the war broke out, Hitler decided in 1941 and 1942 to destroy the Jews in Europe. More than six million Jews, mostly from eastern Europe, died as a result of that staggering decision, unprecedented in its scope and implementation. (See Chapters 29 and 30.)

Nazi Economic Policy

Besides consolidating power and pursuing anti-Semitic policies, Hitler still had to confront the Great Depression. German unemployment had

In early November, 1938, the Nazi authorities in Germany increased their persecution of Jews. On what has come to be called Kristallnacht, *Nazis destroyed Jewish businesses and burned synagogues.* Bildarchiv Preussischer Kulturbesitz

helped propel him to power. The Nazis attacked this problem with a success that astonished and frightened Europe. By 1936, while the rest of the European economy remained stagnant, the specter of unemployment and other difficulties associated with the Great Depression no longer haunted Germany.

As far as the economic crisis was concerned, Hitler had become the most effective political leader in Europe. This success was a most important source of the internal strength and support for his tyrannical regime. The Nazi success against the Great Depression gave the regime considerable credibility. Behind the direction of both business and labor stood the Nazi terror and police. The Nazi economic

experiment proved that, by sacrificing all political and civil liberty, destroying a free trade-union movement, preventing the private exercise of capital, and ignoring consumer satisfaction, full employment to prepare for war and aggression could be achieved.

Nazi economic policies maintained private property and private capitalism, but subordinated all significant economic enterprise and decisions about prices and investment to the goals of the state. Hitler reversed the deflationary policy of the cabinets that had preceded him. He instituted a massive program of public works and spending. Many of these projects related directly or indirectly to rearmament. The government sponsored canal

Young women among an enthusiastic crowd extend the Nazi salute at a party rally in 1938. Nazi ideology encouraged women to favor traditional domestic roles over employment in the workplace and to bear many children. The onset of the war, however, forced the government to recruit women workers. (See Chapter 30 for discussion of women in Nazi Germany.) Bildarchiv Preussischer Kulturbesitz

An American Diplomat Witnesses *Kristallnacht* in Leipzig

A key event in the Nazi attack on Jews in Germany occurred on November 9 and 10, 1938, during nights of destructive terror known as Kristallnacht *because of the vast quantity of shattered plate glass from the broken windows of Jewish-owned businesses. David Buffum, the American consul in Leipzig, wrote an extensive report of what happened in that city. In addition to providing the information in the passage that follows, he observed that most German citizens seemed stunned by what had occurred and deeply disapproved of it. But as his observations of the events in the Leipzig Zoo indicate, Germans were intimidated by the Nazi tactics. Buffum also reported that many German Jews came to the American consulate to find aid for emigration or help in locating husbands and sons taken to concentration camps. Both the United States and the nations of western Europe admitted only limited numbers of Jewish refugees from Germany and, later, from Nazi-occupied Europe. The events recorded in this document should be compared with the predictions that Alexis De Tocqueville made to Count Arthur De Gobineau about what might happen when racial thinking affected mass politics. (See p. 876.)*

❖ *Why did the Nazis claim that the destruction of life and property in Leipzig and other German cities arose from spontaneous actions? What steps did the Nazi perpetrators of* Kristallnacht *take to intimidate Jewish citizens? What aid that was available to other German citizens was denied to Jews during these destructive events? How might one account for the failure of other German citizens to oppose the Nazi actions against the Jews?*

At 3 A.M. on 10 November 1938 was unleashed a barrage of Nazi ferocity that has had no equal hitherto in Germany....

Jewish shop windows by the hundreds were systematically and wantonly smashed throughout the entire city at a loss estimated at several millions of marks.... According to reliable testimony, the debacle was executed by SS men and Stormtroopers not in uniform, each group having been provided with hammers, axes, crowbars and incendiary bombs.

Three synagogues in Leipzig were fired simultaneously by incendiary bombs and all sacred objects and records desecrated or destroyed, in most cases hurled through the windows and burned in the streets.... All the synagogues were irreparably gutted by flames....One of the largest clothing stores in the heart of the city was destroyed by flames from incendiary bombs, only the charred walls and gutted roof having been left standing. As was the case with the synagogues, no attempts on the part of the fire brigade were made to extinguish the fire... It is extremely difficult to believe, but the owners of the clothing store were actually charged with setting the fire and on that basis were dragged from their beds at 6 A.M. and clapped into prison.

Tactics which closely approached the ghoulish took place at the Jewish cemetery where the temple was fired together with a building occupied by caretakers, tombstones uprooted and graves violated....

Ferocious as was the violation of property, the most hideous phase of the so-called 'spontaneous' action has been the wholesale arrest and transportation to concentration camps of male German Jews between the ages of sixteen and sixty, as well as Jewish men without citizenship.... Having demolished dwellings and hurled most of the movable effects onto the streets, the insatiably sadistic perpetrators threw many of the trembling inmates into a small stream that flows through the Zoological Park, commanding horrified spectators to spit at them, defile them with mud and jeer at their plight. The latter incident has been repeatedly corroborated by German witnesses who were nauseated in telling the tale. The slightest manifestation of sympathy evoked a positive fury on the part of the perpetrators, and the crowd was powerless to do anything but turn horror-stricken eyes from the scene of abuse, or leave the vicinity. These tactics were carried out...without police intervention and they were applied to men, women, and children.

J. Noakes and G. Pridham, eds., *Nazism, 1919–1945: Vol. 2, State, Economy and Society, 1933–39: A Documentary Reader*, Exeter Studies in History No. 8 (Exeter, U.K.: University of Exeter Press, © 1984), pp. 555–556. Reprinted by permission.

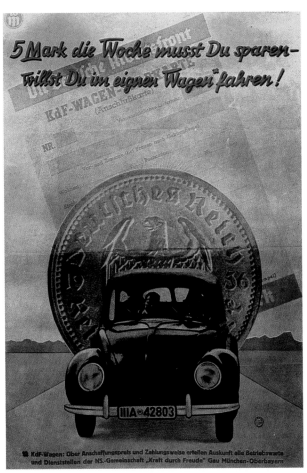

The Volkswagen, which first appeared in 1938, was intended to provide inexpensive transportation for German workers. This advertisement declares that saving five marks a week is all it takes to buy one.
Bildarchiv Preussischer Kulturbesitz

building, land reclamation, and the construction of a large highway system with clear military uses. The government returned some unemployed workers to farms if they had originally come from there. Other laborers were not permitted to change jobs.

In 1935, the renunciation of the military provisions of the Versailles treaty led to open rearmament and expansion of the army with little opposition, as will be explained in Chapter 29. These measures essentially restored full employment. In 1936 Hitler instructed Hermann Göring (1893–1946), who had headed the air force since 1933, to undertake a four-year plan to prepare the army and the economy for war. The government determined that Germany must be economically self-sufficient. Armaments received top priority. This economic program satisfied both the yearning for social and economic security and the desire for national fulfillment.

With the crushing of the trade unions in 1933, strikes became illegal. There was no genuine collective bargaining. The government handled labor disputes through compulsory arbitration. It also required workers and employers to participate in the Labor Front, an organization intended to demonstrate that class conflict had ended. The Labor Front sponsored a "Strength Through Joy" program that provided vacations and other forms of recreation for the labor force.

Italy: Fascist Economics

The fascists had promised to stabilize Italian social and economic life. Discipline was a substitute for economic policy and creativity. During the 1920s, Mussolini undertook vast public works, such as draining the Pontine Marshes near Rome for settlement. The government subsidized the shipping industry and introduced protective tariffs. Mussolini desperately sought to make Italy self-sufficient. He embarked on the "battle of wheat" to prevent foreign grain from appearing in products on Italian tables. Wheat farming in Italy expanded enormously. These policies, however, did not keep the Great Depression from affecting Italy. Production, exports, and wages fell. Even the increased wheat production backfired. So much poor marginal land that was expensive to cultivate came into production, that the domestic price of wheat, and thus of much other food, actually rose.

Syndicates

Both before and during the depression, the fascists sought to steer an economic course between socialism and a liberal *laissez-faire* system. Their policy was known as *corporatism*. It was a planned economy linked to the private ownership of capital and to government arbitration of labor disputes. Major industries were first organized into syndicates representing labor and management. The two groups negotiated labor settlements within this framework and submitted differences to compulsory government arbitration. The fascists contended that class conflict would be avoided if both labor and management looked to the greater goal of productivity for the nation.

Whether this arrangement favored workers or managers is still in dispute. From the mid-1920s, however, Italian labor unions lost the right to strike and to pursue independent economic goals. In that respect, management clearly profited.

Corporations

After 1930, the industrial syndicates were further organized into entities called *corporations*. These bodies included all industries relating to a major area of production, such as agriculture or metallurgy, from raw materials through finished products and distribution. Twenty-two such corporations were established to encompass the whole economy. In 1938, Mussolini abolished the Italian Chamber of Deputies and replaced it with a Chamber of Corporations.

This vast organizational framework did not increase production; instead, bureaucracy and corruption proliferated. The corporate state allowed the government to direct much of the nation's economic life without a formal change in ownership. Consumers and owners could no longer determine what was to be produced. The Fascist government gained further direct economic power through the Institute for Industrial Reconstruction, which extended loans to businesses that were in financial difficulty. The loans, in effect, established partial state ownership of those businesses.

How corporatism might have affected the Italian economy in the long run is unknown. In 1935 Italy invaded Ethiopia, and economic life was put on a formal wartime footing. The League of Nations imposed economic sanctions, urging member nations to refrain from purchasing Italian goods. The sanctions had little effect. Thereafter, taxes rose. During 1935, the government imposed a forced loan on the citizenry by requiring property owners to purchase bonds. Wages continued to be depressed. As international tensions increased during the late 1930s, the Italian state assumed more and more direction over the economy. The order that fascism brought to Italy had not proved to be the order of prosperity; rather, it had brought economic dislocation and a falling standard of living.

The Soviet Union: Central Economic Planning and Party Purges

While the capitalist economies of western Europe floundered in the doldrums of the Great Depression, the Soviet Union undertook a tremendous industrial advance. As in similar past eras of Russian economic progress, the direction and impetus came from the top. Stalin far exceeded his tsarist predecessors in the intensity of state coercion and terror he brought to the task. Russia achieved its stunning economic growth during the 1930s only at the cost of literally millions of human lives and the degradation of still other millions. Stalin's economic policy clearly proved that his earlier rivalry with Trotsky had been a political power struggle rather than one over substantial ideological differences.

The Decision for Rapid Industrialization

Through 1927, Lenin's New Economic Policy (NEP), as championed by Bukharin with Stalin's support, had charted the course of Soviet economic development. The government permitted private ownership and enterprise to flourish in the countryside to ensure an adequate food supply for the workers in the cities. Although the industrial production level of 1913 had been achieved by 1927, industrial growth had slowed. During 1927, the Party Congress decided to push for rapid industrialization. As implemented through what has been termed "industrialization by political mobilization," this policy, which began in 1928, marked a sharp departure from the NEP.[1]

The drive to rapid industrialization represented a major pillar in Stalin's undertaking of "Socialism in One Country." It was to be the path whereby the communist Soviet Union would overtake the productive capacity of capitalist nations and thus protect itself against capitalist enemies. Such a policy required the rapid construction of heavy industries, such as iron, steel, electricity-generating stations, the machine tool industry, and tractor manufacturing. Stalin's organizational vehicle for industrialization was a series of five-year plans, starting in 1928. The State Planning Commission, or *Gosplan*, oversaw the program, setting goals for production and attempting to organize the economy to meet them. The task of coordinating all facets of production was immensely difficult and complicated. Deliveries of materials from mines or factories had to be assured before the next unit could carry out its part of the plan. Enormous disruption occurred throughout the economy as the *Gosplan* carried out its goals of building power plants and steel mills and increasing the production of mines. Capital projects were consistently favored over consumer production. The entire process of planning also saw growth over the years in the number of centralized agencies or ministries involved in the effort. They often functioned in competition, rather than coordination, with each other.

The rapid expansion of the industrial base actually created the first genuinely large factory labor force in what had been Russia. Workers were recruited from the countryside and from the unemployed in the towns and cities. New cities and new work districts in existing cities arose during these years. More often than not, the workers themselves lived in deplorable conditions around the new factories, electric works, or rising industrial cities such

---

[1]Validmir Andrle, *A Social History of Twentieth-Century Russia* (London: Arnold, 1994), p. 161.

An enormous propaganda effort accompanied the Soviet five-year plans. This poster proclaims, "For the betterment of the Soviet people we are building an electricity plant." Bildarchiv Preussischer Kulturbesitz

as Magnitogorsk, a new center of metallurgy in the Urals. The situation of laborers' work and personal lives was worse than anything Marx and Engels had decried in the middle of the nineteenth century.

The government and the Communist Party undertook a vast program of propaganda to sell the five-year plans to the Russian people and to elicit their cooperation. The government boasted of the sheer size of the plants being constructed and the new town being organized. Such efforts were necessary because industrial workers had to be recruited from displaced peasants from the countryside who had no previous factory experience and who often resisted industrial discipline. The party appealed to the idealism of the young in proclaiming its goals of rapidly modernizing the nation. Workers, such as a legendary coal miner named Stakhanov, who exceeded their assigned goals received rewards and publicity.

But there was a sharp contrast between, on the one hand, the boasts of government propaganda, and on the other hand, the often disorganized state of factories and work sites and the poor equipment with which the laborers were supposed to undertake new production. And despite all the publicity, the industrial labor force soon found itself subject to the same regimentation that, as will be seen in the next section, was being imposed on the peasants. By the late 1930s, laborers had to carry a "workbook" that indicated any infractions of work discipline of which they had been guilty. In effect, the drive to rapid industrialization allowed the government to reimpose the kind of discipline that had existed during the years of the civil war immedi-

ately following the revolution in 1918. Those people who in some way questioned the process or wished to revise it—and they were very few—or whose work fell short of the assigned quotas could be, and were, accused of political opposition.

Throughout these years, the Communist Party and the government claimed that Bolsheviks could storm all fortresses. During the depression years, the industrialization of the Soviet Union did achieve what amounted to a fully employed labor force, but a labor force with an astoundingly low standard of living and with no political liberties or ability to organize independent labor unions. Moreover, with Stalin's explicit approval, there existed considerable wage differentials within the industrial labor force, as well as between industrial workers and more skilled professionals such as engineers. Workers who observed discipline, or who sought the more skilled job, or who pursued technical education could improve their situation. The Soviet system thus combined a generally harsh system of work discipline with the possibility of significant rewards to those who worked within the system.

By the close of the 1930s, the results of the three five-year plans were truly impressive. The Russian economy grew more rapidly than that of any other nation in the Western world during any similar period. By even the conservative estimates of Western observers, Soviet industrial production rose approximately 400 percent between 1928 and 1940. Industries that had never before existed in Russia now challenged and, in some cases, such as tractor production, surpassed their counterparts in the rest of the world. Large, new industrial cities had been built and populated by hundreds of thousands of people. The social and human cost of this effort had, however, been astounding.

The Collectivization of Agriculture

The decision to industrialize rapidly brought enormous consequences for Soviet agriculture. Under the NEP, a few farmers, the *kulaks*, had become prosperous. Probably numbering less than five percent of the rural population, they, together with other farmers, were discontented with their situation, because there were few consumer goods to purchase with the cash they received for their crops. They had frequently withheld grain from the market in the 1920s and did so again during 1928 and 1929. Food shortages then occurred in the cities, and the government worried about potential unrest.

During these troubled months, Stalin came to a momentous decision. Agriculture must be collectivized to produce enough grain for food and export, to achieve control over the farm sector of the economy, and to free peasant labor for the factories in the expanding industrial sector. The implementation of this program of collectivization, which basically embraced Trotsky's earlier economic position, unleashed a second Russian revolution and unprecedented violence in the countryside.

In 1929, Stalin ordered party agents into the countryside to confiscate any hoarded wheat and to carry out a program of collectivization of agriculture. The *kulaks* were blamed for the grain shortages. As part of the general plan to erase the private ownership of land and to collectivize farming, the government decided to eliminate the *kulaks* as a class. (See "Stalin Calls for the Liquidation of the *Kulaks* as a Class.") The definition of a *kulak*, however, soon embraced any peasants and farmers, of

Collective farmers bringing grain to a shipment center. Note that horse-drawn wagons are the only form of transport in this picture; there are no trucks or tractors. Bildarchiv Preussischer Kulturbesitz

Stalin Calls for the Liquidation of the *Kulaks* as a Class

The core of Stalin's agricultural policy undertaken in the late 1920s and early 1930s was the eradication of private farms and their replacement with large collective farms. The greatest obstacle to this policy was the kulaks, *peasants who owned substantial farms. In this remarkable speech of 1929, Stalin first explains why small peasant farming must be replaced with collective farms to achieve an adequate food supply for the cities and the industrial sector of the population. He then calls for the liquidation of the* kulaks *as a class. As might be expected, the* kulaks *resisted collectivization by destroying crops and farm animals. In turn, Communist Party agents killed millions of peasants to achieve collectivization.*

❖ *What were the goals of the collectivization of farms in the Soviet Union? How did the* kulaks *stand in the way of collectivization? How does Stalin dehumanize the* kulaks *as people by discussing them entirely as a class and as part of the capitalistic system?*

Can we advance our socialized industry at an accelerated rate as long as we have an agricultural base, such as is provided by small-peasant farming, which is incapable of expanded reproduction, and which, in addition, is the predominant force in our national economy? No, we cannot....

What, then, is the solution? The solution lies in enlarging the agricultural units, in making agriculture capable of accumulation, of expanded reproduction, and in thus transforming the agricultural bases of our national economy.

...[T]he *socialist* way [to enlarge farming units], which is to introduce collective farms and state farms in agriculture, the way which leads to the amalgamation of the small-peasant farms into large collective farms, employing machinery and scientific methods of farming, and capable of developing further, for such agricultural enterprises can achieve expanded reproduction....

The characteristic feature in the work of our Party during the past year is that we, as a Party, as the Soviet power,

(a) have developed an offensive along the whole front against the capitalist elements in the countryside;

(b) that this offensive, as you know, has brought about and is bringing about very palpable, *positive* results.

What does this mean? It means that we have passed from the policy of *restricting* the exploiting proclivities of the *kulaks* to the policy of *eliminating* the *kulaks* as a class....

Until recently the Party adhered to the policy of *restricting* the exploiting proclivities of the *kulaks*....

...Could we have undertaken such an offensive against the *kulaks* five years or three years ago? Could we then have counted on success in such an offensive? No, we could not. That would have been the most dangerous adventurism. It would have been playing a very dangerous game at offensive. We would certainly have failed, and our failure would have strengthened the position of the *kulaks*. Why? Because we still lacked a wide network of state and collective farms in the rural districts which could be used as strongholds in a determined offensive against the *kulaks*. Because at that time we were not yet able to *substitute* for the capitalist production of the *kulaks* the socialist production of the collective farms and state farms....

...Now we are able to carry on a determined offensive against the *kulaks*, to break their resistance, to eliminate them as a class and substitute for their output the output of the collective farms and state farms. Now, the *kulaks* are being expropriated by the masses of poor and middle peasants themselves, by the masses who are putting solid collectivization into practice. Now, the expropriation of the *kulaks* in the regions of solid collectivization is no longer just an administrative measure. Now, the expropriation of the *kulaks* is an integral part of the formation and development of the collective farms. Consequently it is now ridiculous and foolish to discourse on the expropriation of the *kulaks*. You do not lament the loss of the hair of one who has been beheaded.

From Stalin, "Problems of Agrarian Policy in the USSR," speech at a conference of Marxist students of the agrarian question, December 27, 1929, in *Problems of Leninism*, pp. 391–393, 408–409, 411–412, as quoted in Robert V. Daniels, *A Documentary History of Communism*, rev. ed. (Hanover, NH, and London: University Press of New England, 1984), pp. 224–227.

all levels of wealth, who resisted collectivization. Determined to keep their land, stubborn peasants sabotaged collectivization by slaughtering millions of horses and cattle between 1929 and 1933. The situation in the countryside amounted to open warfare, with the communist military force directed against peasant resistance. In March 1930, Stalin called a brief halt to the process, justifying the slowdown on the grounds of "dizziness from success."

After the harvest of that year had been secured, the drive to collectivize the farms was renewed with vehemence, and the costs remained very high. Even with the recent opening of the Soviet archives, it is difficult to know how many peasants were killed as a result of collectivization. The number would appear to have been in the millions, with many millions more removed from the land. Initially, because of the turmoil on the land, agricultural production fell. Then, in 1932 and 1933, an extensive famine resulted in even more deaths in the countryside. This famine was one of the major human disasters to occur in twentieth-century Europe outside the context of war. As the collectivization process continued, uprooted peasants were moved to thousand-acre collective farms, where the state provided the machinery for these units through machine-tractor stations. The state monopoly in heavy farm machines, as well as in seed, was a powerful weapon of control over the recalcitrant countryside.

As will be discussed more fully in Chapter 31, collectivization changed Russian farming dramatically. In 1928, approximately 98 percent of Russian farmland consisted of small peasant holdings. Ten years later, despite all opposition, more than 90 percent of the land had been collectivized, and the quantity of farm produce directly handled by the government had risen by 40 percent. Those shifts in control meant that the government now controlled the food supply, although by the middle of the decade the government had compromised, allowing peasants to cultivate small personal plots of land that actually became a significant factor in the Soviet food supply. Yet, the farmers and peasants could no longer cause instability or unrest in the Soviet cities by withholding grain. Stalin and the Communist Party had won the battle of the wheat fields, but they had not solved the problem of producing enough grain. That difficulty would plague the Soviet Union until its collapse in 1991, and indeed, it remains a problem today for the new Commonwealth of Independent States.

Foreign Reactions and Repercussions

Many foreign contemporaries looked at the Soviet economic experiment naïvely. While the capitalist world lay in the throes of the Great Depression, the Soviet economy had grown at a pace never realized in the West. After a trip to Russia, the American writer Lincoln Steffens (1866–1936) reported, "I have seen the future and it works." Beatrice and Sidney Webb, the British Fabian Socialists, spoke of "a new civilization" in the Soviet Union. These and similar observers ignored the shortages in consumer goods and the poor housing. More important, they had little idea of the social cost of the Soviet achievement. Millions of human beings had been killed and millions more uprooted. The total picture of suffering and human loss during those years will probably never be known; however, the deprivation and sacrifice of Soviet citizens far exceeded anything described by Marx and Engels in relation to nineteenth-century industrialization in western Europe.

The internal difficulties caused by collectivization and industrialization led Stalin to make an important shift in foreign policy. In 1934, he began to fear that the nation might be left isolated against future aggression by Nazi Germany. The Soviet Union was not yet strong enough to withstand such an attack. So that year he ordered the Comintern to permit communist parties in other countries to cooperate with noncommunist parties against Nazism and Fascism. This reversed the Comintern policy established by Lenin as part of the Twenty-one Conditions in 1919. The new Stalinist policy allowed the formation of the Popular Front Government in France.

The Purges

Stalin's decisions to industrialize rapidly, to move against the peasants, and to reverse the Comintern policy aroused internal political opposition. Each policy was a departure from the policies of Lenin. In 1929 Stalin forced Bukharin, the fervent supporter of the NEP and his own former ally, off the Politburo. Little detailed information is known about further opposition, but it seems to have existed among lower-level party followers of Bukharin and other opponents of rapid industrialization. At its most extensive, however, such opposition was quite modest.

In 1933, with turmoil in the countryside and economic dislocation in the industrializing sectors, Stalin and others in the central Soviet bureaucracy began to fear that they were losing control of the country and the party apparatus, and that effective rivals might emerge. These apprehensions, which were exaggerated, were part of Stalin's own penchant for paranoia and resulted in the Great Purges, which remain one of the most mysterious and horrendous political events of the twentieth century. The purges were not understood at the time and have not been fully comprehended since, either inside or outside the former Soviet Union, even with the recent opening of Soviet archives.

By the mid 1930s Stalin's purges had eliminated many leaders and other members from the Soviet Communist Part. This photograph of a meeting of a party congress in 1936 shows a number of the surviving leaders with Stalin, who sits fourth from the right in the front row. To his left is Vyacheslav Molotov, long-time foreign minister. The first person on the left in the front row is Nikita Khruschev, who headed the Soviet Union in the late 1950s and early 1960s. Itar–Tass/Sovfoto/Eastfoto

On December 1, 1934, Sergei Kirov (1888–1934), the popular party chief of Leningrad (formerly and now again Saint Petersburg) and a member of the Politburo, was assassinated. In the wake of the shooting, thousands of people were arrested, and still more were expelled from the party and sent to labor camps. At the time, it was believed that opponents of the regime had murdered Kirov. Direct or indirect complicity in the crime became the normal accusation against those whom Stalin attacked. It has long been thought that Stalin himself authorized Kirov's assassination because he was afraid of him. The available documentary evidence does not allow us to know for sure whether Stalin was involved, but he quickly used Kirov's death for his own internal party purposes. Under Stalin, the Soviet Communist Party had already shown that it could punish

dissent within its ranks. The debates of the 1920s within the party had established a clear precedent for exercising firm discipline, and in the confusion surrounding the implementation of the five-year plans, persons accused of sabotage and disloyalty had been executed. The purges, however, went beyond any of these precedents.

The purges that took place immediately after Kirov's death were just the beginning of a larger and longer process. Between 1936 and 1938, a series of spectacular show trials were held in Moscow. Former high Soviet leaders, including some who had belonged to the Politburo, such as Bukharin, publicly confessed to political crimes and were convicted and executed. It is still not certain why they made their palpably false confessions, although this seems to have been the kind of ritual confession of faults and shortcomings that had characterized previous internal Com-

Major Dates in Soviet History During the Five-Year Plans and Purges
1927 Decision to move toward rapid industrialization
1928 First five-year plan begins
1929 Beginning of collectivization of agriculture
1929 Expulsion of Bukharin from Politburo affirms Stalin's central position
1930 Stalin's call for moderation in his policy of agricultural collectivization because of "dizziness from success"
1934 Assassination of Kirov
1936–1938 Major purge trials

munist Party life. They had also been interrogated under the most difficult conditions, including torture, and feared for their families' lives. Other lower-level party members were tried in private and shot. Hundreds of thousands of people received no trial at all and were either executed or deported to slave labor camps. The purges touched persons in all areas of party life, as well as their families. Within the party itself, hundreds of thousands of members were expelled, and applicants for membership were removed from the rolls. After the civilian party members had been purged, followed by the purging of major party leaders, the prosecutors turned against the Soviet army, convicting and executing important officers, including heroes of the civil war. The exact number of executions, imprisonments, interrogations, and expulsions is unknown, but ran into the millions.

The rational explanations of the purges probably lie in two directions. First, over the several years of the purges, different portions of the party leadership moved against others. Initially, the central Moscow leadership used the purges to discipline and gain more centralized control over lower levels of the party in the far-flung regions of the Soviet Union. In addition to supporting Stalin's authority, these central bureaucratic groups wanted to eliminate any opposition to their positions in the party or their policies. By 1937, however, Stalin seems to have become distrustful of the central party elite, and he began to find enemies within its ranks. Moreover, by that date, local communist groups were allowed to designate their own victims with little direction from Moscow. Thereafter, a self-destructive flurry of accusations, imprisonments, and executions occurred throughout the party and within its highest levels. The Communist Party leadership at all levels appeared to be consuming itself. This

situation has been termed "centrally authorized chaos."[2] (See "A Prosecutor and Victim of the Purges States His Case to the Court.")

Second, no matter how much attention is paid to the tensions and relationships among the different levels and regions of the Communist Party, Stalin's fears for his own power cannot be ignored. He and other leaders who survived the purges selected certain victims and determined the fate of their families. In effect, the purges created a new party structure absolutely subservient and loyal to Stalin. The "old Bolsheviks" of the October Revolution were among his earliest targets. They and others active in the first years of the revolution knew how far Stalin had moved from Lenin's policies. New, younger members replaced the party members who were executed or expelled. The newcomers knew little about old Russia or the ideals of the original Bolsheviks. They had not been loyal to Lenin, Trotsky, or any other Soviet leader except Stalin himself.

In Perspective

By the middle of the 1930s, dictators of the right and the left had established themselves across much of Europe. Political tyranny was hardly new to Europe, but several factors combined to give these rulers unique characteristics. They drew their immediate support from well-organized political parties. Except for the Bolsheviks, these were mass parties. The roots of support for the dictators lay in nationalism, the social and economic frustration of the Great Depression, and political ideologies that promised to transform the social and political order. As long as the new rulers seemed successful, they did not lack support. Many citizens believed that these leaders had ended the pettiness of everyday politics.

After coming to power, the dictators possessed a practical monopoly over mass communications. Through armies, police forces, and party discipline, they also monopolized terror and coercive power. They could propagandize large populations and compel people to obey them and their followers. Finally, as a result of the Second Industrial Revolution, they commanded a vast amount of technology and a capacity for immense destruction. Earlier rulers in Europe may have shared the ruthless ambitions of Hitler, Mussolini, and Stalin, but they had lacked the ready implements of physical force to impose their wills.

[2]J. Arch Getty and Oleg V. Naumov, *The Road to Terror: Stalin and the Self-Destruction of the Bolsheviks, 1932–1939,* Benjamin Sher, trans. (New Haven, CT: Yale University Press, 1999), p. 583.

A Prosecutor and Victim of the Purges
States His Case to the Court

N. I. Yezhov had joined the Communist Party well before the revolution of 1917. He served in the Soviet bureaucracy and had consistently supported Stalin. From 1936 to 1938, he had been the People's Commissar of the USSR for Internal Affairs and had overseen the purging of many people, including Bukharin. Yezhov was arrested in 1939 for reasons he did not understand and was tried early in 1940. The formal charge against him was spying for Poland. He believed that he was being brought down by his enemies within the Commissariat for Internal Affairs. He also clearly believed that it had been necessary to purge a vast number of enemies of Stalin and the Communist Party. In his statement to the military court, only recently made public from the Soviet archives, he both confessed faults and attempted to defend himself, though he knew he would be convicted. Indeed, Yezhov was found guilty and shot shortly after making this statement. The confessions by victims of the purges made to the courts tended to be long and rambling. The portion quoted gives only a brief sense of such statements.

❖ *How does Yezhov indicate his loyalty to the Communist Party and to Stalin? What actions does he boast about? How had he been treated? How can a man who had committed so many injustices against his fellow communists present himself as innocent? What do the personal favors he requests indicate about the purges? What, if any, regrets for his actions does he show?*

At the preliminary investigation I said that I was not a spy, that I was not a terrorist, but they didn't believe me and beat me up horribly. During the 25 years of my party work I have fought honorably against enemies and have exterminated them....

I did not organize any conspiracy against the party and the government. On the contrary, I used everything at my disposal to expose conspiracies....

....I purged 14,000 *chekists* [enemies], but my great guilt lies in the fact that I purged so few of them. My practice was as follows: I would hand over the task of interrogating the person under arrest to one or another department head while thinking to myself: "Go on, interrogate him today—tomorrow I will arrest you." All around me were enemies of the people, my enemies. I purged *chekists* everywhere. It was only in Moscow, Leningrad, and the Northern Caucasus that I did not purge them. I thought they were honest, but it turned out, in fact, that I had been harboring under my wings saboteurs, wreckers, spies, and enemies of the people of other stripes....

....I understand and honestly declare that the only cause for sparing my life would be for me to admit that I am guilty of the charges brought against me, to repent before the party and to implore it to spare my life....

I'll now finish my final address. I ask the military collegium to grant me the following requests: 1. My fate is obvious. My life, naturally, will not be spared...I ask only one thing: shoot me quietly, without putting me through any agony. 2. ...If my mother is alive, I ask that she be provided for in her old age, and that my daughter be taken care of. 3. I ask that my relatives—nephews—not be subjected to punitive measures because they are not guilty of anything.... 5. I request that Stalin be informed that I have never in my political life deceived the party, a fact known to thousands of persons who know my honesty and modesty. I request that Stalin be informed that I am a victim of circumstances and nothing more, yet here enemies I have overlooked may have also had a hand in this. Tell Stalin that I shall die with his name on my lips.

N. I. Yezhov's statement before a secret judicial meeting of the Military Collegium of the Supreme Court of the USSR, February 3, 1940, as quoted in J. Arch Getty and Oleg V. Naumov, *The Road to Terror: Stalin and the Self-Destruction of the Bolsheviks, 1932–1939*, Benjamin Sher, trans. (New Haven, CT: Yale University Press, 1999), pp. 561–562.

Mass political support, the monopoly of police and military power, and technological capacity meant that the dictators of the 1930s held more extensive sway over their nations than any other group of rulers who had ever governed on the Continent. Soon the issue would become whether they would be able to maintain peace among themselves and with their democratic neighbors.

REVIEW QUESTIONS

1. Explain the causes of the Great Depression of the 1930s. Why was it more severe and longer lasting than previous depressions? Could it have been avoided?

2. Compare the relative success of Britain's National Government and France's Popular Front in dealing with their respective economic problems. How would you account for the differences? Why did France's Third Republic have so few supporters?

3. How did the Great Depression affect Germany? Discuss Hitler's rise to power between 1929 and 1934. Was his dictatorship inevitable? Was his seizure of power due more to personalities than to impersonal forces?

4. Discuss Hitler's economic policies. Why were they successful? Compare and contrast his economic policies with those used in Britain, Italy, and France. Why were some nations more successful than others in addressing the Great Depression?

5. What were the characteristics of a "police state"? How necessary is terror and intimidation in the consolidation of an authoritarian regime? How did Hitler, Mussolini, and Stalin use terror to achieve their goals? What were the particular characteristics of Nazi racial policy?

6. Why did Stalin decide that Russia had to industrialize rapidly? Why did this require the collectivization of agriculture? What obstacles stood in the way of collectivization, and how did Stalin overcome them? What were the causes of the purges in the Soviet Union? What groups became the special targets of the purges?

SUGGESTED READINGS

W. S. Allen, *The Nazi Seizure of Power: The Experience of a Single German Town, 1930–1935*, rev. ed. (1984). A classic treatment of Nazism in a microcosmic setting.

K. E. Bailes, *Technology and Society Under Lenin and Stalin: Origins of the Soviet Technical Intelligentsia, 1917–1941* (1978). An important study of the people who actually put the programs of modernization into place.

N. Branson and M. Heinemann, *Britain in the Nineteen Thirties* (1971). Primarily considers the social and economic problems of the day.

M. Burleigh and W. Wipperman, *The Racial State: Germany 1933–1945* (1991). Emphasizes the manner in which racial theory influenced numerous areas of policy.

D. Carroll, *French Literary Fascism: Nationalism, Anti-Semitism, and the Ideology of Culture* (1995). A study of right-wing political theories in France.

J. Colton, *Léon Blum: Humanist in Politics* (1966). One of the best biographies of any twentieth-century political figure.

R. Conquest, *The Great Terror: Stalin's Purges of the Thirties* (1990). Remains the most useful treatment of the subject to date.

R. Conquest, *The Harvest of Sorrow: Soviet Collectivization and the Terror–Famine* (1986). A study of how Stalin used starvation against his own people.

G. Craig, *Germany, 1866–1945* (1978). An important survey.

R. W. Davies, *The Socialist Offensive: The Collectivization of Soviet Agriculture, 1929–1930* (1980). Examines the crucial years when Stalin moved against the *kulaks*.

I. Deutscher, *Stalin: A Political Biography*, 2d ed. (1967). A major biography.

B. Eichengreen, *Golden Fetters: The Gold Standard and the Great Depression, 1919–1939* (1992). A remarkable study of the role of the gold standard in the economic policies of the interwar years.

S. Fitzpatrick, *Stalin's Peasants: Resistance and Survival in the Russian Village after Collectivization* (1994). A pioneering study.

R. Gellately, *The Gestapo and German Society: Enforcing Racial Policy, 1933–1945* (1990). A discussion of how the police state supported Nazi racial policies.

J. A. Getty and O. V. Naumov, *The Road to Terror: Stalin and the Self-Destruction of the Bolsheviks, 1933–1939* (1999). A major collection of newly available documents revealing much new information about the purges.

R. F. Hamilton, *Who Voted for Hitler?* (1982). An important examination of voting patterns.

E. C. Helmreich, *The German Churches Under Hitler: Background, Struggle, and Epilogue* (1979). A useful study.

J. JACKSON, *The Politics of Depression in France, 1932–1936* (1985). A detailed examination of the political struggles prior to the Popular Front.

J. JACKSON, *The Popular Front in France: Defending Democracy, 1934–1938* (1988). An extensive treatment.

H. JAMES, *The German Slump: Politics and Economics, 1914–1936* (1986). A difficult, but informative, examination of the German experience of the Great Depression.

I. KERSHAW, *Hitler 1889–1936: Hubris* (1998). The best biography now available.

C. KINDLEBERGER, *The World in Depression, 1929–1939* (1973). An account by a leading economist whose analysis is comprehensible to the layperson.

M. LEWIN, *The Making of the Soviet System: Essays in the Social History of Interwar Russia* (1985). A pioneering treatment written before the opening of the archives.

E. MENDELSOHN, *The Jews of East Central Europe Between the World Wars* (1983). An excellent survey of the subject.

I. MUELLER, *Hitler's Justice: The Courts of the Third Reich* (1991). An account of how German courts cooperated with the Nazis.

D. J. K. PEUKERT, *Inside Nazi Germany: Conformity, Opposition, and Racism in Everyday Life* (1987). An excellent discussion of life under Nazi rule.

P. PULZER, *Jews and the German State: The Political History of a Minority, 1848–1933* (1992). A detailed study by a major historian of European minorities.

R. PROCTOR, *Racial Hygiene: Medicine Under the Nazis* (1988). An exploration of how medical science contributed to racism.

L. J. RUPP, *Mobilizing Women for War: German and American Propaganda, 1939–1945* (1978). Although concentrating on a later period, includes an excellent discussion of general Nazi attitudes toward women.

D. SCHOENBAUM, *Hitler's Social Revolution: Class and Status in Nazi Germany* (1966). A fascinating analysis of Hitler's appeal to various social classes.

D. M. SMITH, *Mussolini's Roman Empire* (1976). A general description of the fascist regime in Italy.

W. D. SMITH, *The Ideological Origins of Nazi Imperialism* (1986). A study that links Nazi expansionist thought to earlier German foreign policy.

A. SOLZHENITSYN, *The Gulag Archipelago*, 3 vols. (1974–1979). A major examination of the labor camps under Stalin by one of the most important contemporary writers.

R. SOUCY, *French Fascism: The Second Wave, 1933–1939* (1995). A study of the right-wing leagues.

J. STEPHENSON, *The Nazi Organization of Women* (1981). Examines the attitude and policies of the Nazis toward women.

H. A. TURNER, JR., *German Big Business and the Rise of Hitler* (1985). An important major study of the subject.

H. A. TURNER, JR., *Hitler's Thirty Days to Power* (1996). A narrative of the events leading directly to the Nazi seizure of power.

E. WEBER, *The Hollow Years: France in the 1930s* (1995). Examines France between the wars.

L. YAHIL, *The Holocaust: The Fate of the European Jewry, 1932–1945* (1990). A major recent study of this fundamental subject in twentieth-century history.

Reference should also be made to the works cited in Chapters 27, 29 and 31.

Part 6

1939–2000

POLITICS AND GOVERNMENT	SOCIETY AND ECONOMY	RELIGION AND CULTURE

1939–1960

POLITICS AND GOVERNMENT

1939 World War II begins

Jewish children at Auschwitz, Poland

1941 Japan attacks Pearl Harbor, US enters war

1942 Battle of Stalingrad

1944 Normandy invasion

1945 Yalta Conference; Germany surrenders; atomic bombs dropped on Japan; Japan surrenders; United Nations founded

1946 Churchill gives Iron Curtain speech

1947 Truman Doctrine

1948 Communist takeover in Czechoslovakia and Hungary; State of Israel proclaimed

1948–1949 Berlin blockade

1949 NATO founded; East and West Germany emerge as separate states

1950–1953 Korean War

1953 Death of Stalin

1954 French defeat at Dien Bien Phu

1955 Warsaw Pact founded

1956 Khrushchev denounces Stalin; Polish Communist Party crisis; Suez crisis; Soviet invasion of Hungary

SOCIETY AND ECONOMY

1945–1951 Attlee ministry establishes the Welfare State in Great Britain

Churchill, Roosevelt, Stalin at Yalta

1947 Marshall Plan to rebuild Europe instituted

1949 Europe divided into Eastern and Western blocs

1950s and 1960s Increase in agricultural production

1957 European Economic Community founded

RELIGION AND CULTURE

1940 Koestler, *Darkness at Noon*

1942 Lewis, *The Screwtape Letters*

1943 Sartre, *Being and Nothingness*

1947 Camus, *The Plague*; Gramsci, *Letters from Prison*

1949 de Beauvoir, *The Second Sex*; Crossman, *The God That Failed*

1958 Pasternak forbidden to accept Nobel Prize for *Dr. Zhivago*; John XXIII becomes pope

GLOBAL CONFLICT, COLD WAR, AND NEW DIRECTIONS

1939–2000

	POLITICS AND GOVERNMENT	SOCIETY AND ECONOMY	RELIGION AND CULTURE
1960–1980	1960 Khruschev aborts Geneva summit	1960s Rapid growth of student population in universities; migration of workers from eastern and southern to northern and western Europe; migration of non-European workers to northern and western Europe	1960s The Beatles take world by storm
	1961 Berlin Wall erected		
	1962 Cuban Missile Crisis		
	1963 Test Ban Treaty		
	1963–1973 Major US involvement in Vietnam		
	1964–1982 Brezhnev era in Soviet Union		
	1967 Six Days' War between Israel and Arab states		
	1968 Soviet invasion of Czechoslovakia		

The Beatles

			1962–1965 Second Vatican Council
			1963 Solzhenitsyn, *One Day in the Life of Ivan Denisovich*; Robinson, *Honest to God*
		1972 Club of Rome founded	1968 Student rebellion in Paris
	1973 Yom Kippur War between Israel and Egypt	1973–1974 Arab oil embargo	
	1975 Helsinki Accords		1974 Solzhenitsyn expelled from Soviet Union
	1978 Camp David Accords; Solidarity founded in Poland		1978 John Paul II becomes pope
	1979–1988 Soviet troops in Afghanistan	1980s and 1990s Internal migration from Eastern to Western Europe; racial and ethnic tensions in Western Europe	
1980–2000	1981–1983 Martial law in Poland		1980s Growth of the environmental movement
	1985 Gorbachev comes to power in the Soviet Union		1990s Expanding influence of Roman Catholic Church in independent eastern Europe
	1989 Revolutions sweep across Eastern Europe		
	1990 German reunification; Yugoslavia breaks up		1990s Feminists continue the critical tradition of Western culture
	1991 Persian Gulf War; civil war in former Yugoslavia; August coup in Moscow; Gorbachev resigns; Soviet Union dissolved		1990s Era of the Internet opens

Berlin Wall Opens, November, 1989

	1992–1999 Ascendancy of Yeltsin in Russia		
	1995 Bosnia recognized as independent		
	1997 Hong Kong returns to China		
	1999 NATO military campaign against Serbia	1990s Changes in Eastern Europe and Soviet Union open way for economic growth and new trade relations across Europe	
	2000 Putin elected President of Russia		

Internet use explodes in China

Chapter 29

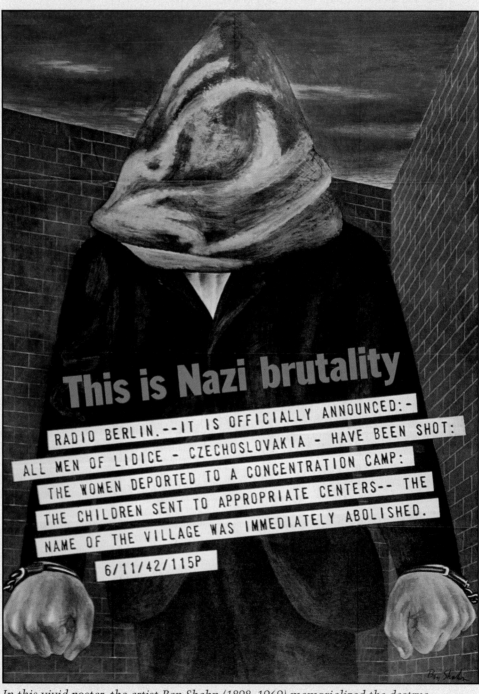

In this vivid poster, the artist Ben Shahn (1898–1969) memorialized the destruction of Lidice. The Czechoslovakian town was obliterated by the Nazis on June 11, 1942, in vengeance for the resistance by Czechs against their Nazi rulers.
The Granger Collection

World War II

KEY TOPICS

- The origins of World War II
- The course of the war
- Racism and the Holocaust
- The impact of the war on the people of Europe
- Relationships among the victorious allies and the preparations for peace

The more idealistic survivors of World War I, especially in the United States and Great Britain, thought of it as "the war to end all wars" and a war "to make the world safe for democracy." Only thus could they justify the horrible slaughter, expense, and upheaval of that terrible conflict. How appalled they would have been had they known that only twenty years after the peace treaties a second great war would break out that would be more terribly global than the first. In this war, the democracies would be fighting for their lives against militaristic, nationalistic, authoritarian, and totalitarian states in Europe and Asia, and they would be allied with the communist Soviet Union in the struggle. The defeat of the militarists and dictators would not bring the peace they longed for, but a Cold War in which the European states would become powers of the second class, subordinate to two new superpowers, partially or fully non-European: the Soviet Union and the United States.

Again the Road to War (1933–1939)

World War I and the Versailles treaty had only a marginal relationship to the world depression of the 1930s. In Germany, however, where the reparations settlement had contributed to the vast inflation of 1923, economic and social discontent focused on the Versailles settlement as the cause of all ills. Throughout the late 1920s, Adolf Hitler and the Nazi Party had denounced Versailles as the source of all of Germany's troubles. The economic woes of the early 1930s seemed to bear them out. Nationalism and attention to the social question, along with party discipline, had been the sources of Nazi success. They continued to influence Hitler's foreign policy after he became chancellor in January 1933. Moreover, the Nazi destruction of the Weimar constitution and of political opposition meant that Hitler himself totally dominated German foreign policy. Consequently, it is important to know what his goals were and how he planned to achieve them.

Hitler's Goals

From the first expression of his goals in a book written in jail, *Mein Kampf* (*My Struggle*), to his last days in the underground bunker in Berlin where he killed himself, Hitler's racial theories and goals were at the center of his thought. He meant to go far beyond Germany's 1914 boundaries, which were the limit of the vision of his predecessors. He meant to bring the entire German people—the *Volk*—understood as a racial group, together into a single nation.

The new Germany would include all the Germanic parts of the old Habsburg Empire, including Austria. This virile and growing nation would need more space to live, or *Lebensraum*, which would be taken from the Slavs, who, according to Nazi theory, were a lesser race, fit only for servitude. The new Germany would be purified by the removal of the Jews, another inferior race according to Nazi theory. The plans required the conquest of Poland and Ukraine as the primary areas for the settlement of Germans and for the provision of badly needed food. Neither *Mein Kampf* nor later statements of policy were blueprints for action. Rather, Hitler was a brilliant improviser who exploited opportunities as they arose. He never lost sight of his goal, however, which would almost certainly require a major war. (See "Hitler Describes His Goals in Foreign Policy.")

GERMANY REARMS When Hitler came to power, Germany was far too weak to permit a direct approach toward reaching his aims. The first problem he set out to resolve was to shake off the fetters of Versailles and to make Germany a formidable military power. In October 1933, Germany withdrew from an international disarmament conference and also from the League of Nations. Hitler argued that because the other powers had not disarmed as they had promised, it was wrong to keep Germany helpless. These acts alarmed the French, but were merely symbolic. In January 1934, Germany signed a nonaggression pact with Poland that was of greater concern to France, for it undermined France's chief means of containing the Germans. At last, in March 1935, Hitler formally renounced the disarmament provisions of the Versailles treaty with the formation of a German air force, and soon he reinstated conscription, which aimed at an army of half a million men.

THE LEAGUE OF NATIONS FAILS Hitler's path was made easier by growing evidence that the League of Nations could not keep the peace and that collective security was a myth. In September 1931, Japan occupied Manchuria, provoking an appeal to the League of Nations by China. The league responded by sending out a commission under a British diplomat, the earl of Lytton (1876–1951). The *Lytton Report* condemned the Japanese for resorting to force, but the powers were unwilling to impose sanctions. Japan withdrew from the league and kept control of Manchuria.

When Hitler announced his decision to rearm Germany, the league formally condemned that action, but it took no steps to prevent Germany's rearming. France and Britain opposed German rearmament, but they felt unable to object forcefully because they had not carried out their own promises to disarm. Instead, they met with Mussolini in June 1935 to form the so-called Stresa Front, promising to use force to maintain the status quo in Europe. This show of unity by the three powers was short lived, however. Britain, desperate to maintain superiority at sea, violated the spirit of the Stresa accords and sacrificed French security needs to make a separate naval agreement with Hitler. The pact allowed him to rebuild the German fleet to 35 percent of the British navy. Italy's expansionist ambitions in Africa soon brought it into conflict with the Western powers. Hitler had taken a major step toward his goal without provoking serious opposition.

Italy Attacks Ethiopia

In October 1935, Mussolini, using a border incident as an excuse, attacked Ethiopia. This attack made the impotence of the League of Nations and the timidity of the Allies clear. Mussolini's purpose was to avenge a humiliating defeat that the Italians had

Hitler Describes His Goals in Foreign Policy

From his early career, Hitler had certain long-term general views and goals. They were set forth in his Mein Kampf (My Struggle), *which appeared in 1925 and called for consolidation of the German* Volk *(people), more land for the Germans, and contempt for such "races" as Slavs and Jews. Here are some of Hitler's views about land.*

❖ *What is the basic principle on which Hitler's policy is founded? How does he justify his plans for expansion? What reasons does he give for hostility to France and Russia? What is the basis for Hitler's claim of a right of every man to own farmland? Was that a practical goal for Germany in the 1930s? Was there any way for Hitler to achieve his goals without a major war?*

The National Socialist movement must strive to eliminate the disproportion between our population and our area—viewing this latter as a source of food as well as a basis for power politics—between our historical past and the hopelessness of our present impotence....

The demand for restoration of the frontiers of 1914 is a political absurdity of such proportions and consequences as to make it seem a crime. Quite aside from the fact that the Reich's frontiers in 1914 were anything but logical. For in reality they were neither complete in the sense of embracing the people of German nationality, nor sensible with regard to geomilitary expediency....

As opposed to this, we National Socialists must hold unflinchingly to our aim in foreign policy, namely, to secure for the German people the land and soil to which they are entitled on this earth....

...The soil on which some day German generations of peasants can beget powerful sons will sanction the investment of the sons of today, and will some day acquit the responsible statesmen of blood-guilt and sacrifice of the people, even if they are persecuted by their contemporaries....

Much as all of us today recognize the necessity of a reckoning with France, it would remain ineffectual in the long run if it represented the whole of our aim in foreign policy. It can and will achieve meaning only if it offers the rear cover for an enlargement of our people's living space in Europe....

If we speak of soil in Europe today, we can primarily have in mind only Russia and her vassal border states....

...See to it that the strength of our nation is founded, not on colonies, but on the soil of our European homeland. Never regard the Reich as secure unless for centuries to come it can give every scion of our people his own parcel of soil. Never forget that the most sacred right on this earth is a man's right to have earth to till with his own hands, and the most sacred sacrifice the blood that a man sheds for this earth.

Excerpts from *Mein Kampf* by Adolf Hitler, trans. by Ralph Manheim. Copyright © 1943, renewed 1971 by Houghton Mifflin Company, pp. 646, 649, 652, 653, 656. Reprinted by permission of Houghton Mifflin Co. All rights reserved.

suffered in 1896, to begin the restoration of Roman imperial glory, and, perhaps, to distract Italian public opinion from domestic problems.

France and Britain were eager to appease Mussolini in order to offset the growing power of Germany. They were prepared to allow him the substance of conquest if he would only maintain Ethiopia's formal independence. For Mussolini, however, the form was more important than the substance. His attack outraged opinion in the West, and the French and British governments were forced to at least appear to resist.

The League of Nations condemned Italian aggression and, for the first time, voted economic sanctions. It imposed an arms embargo that limited loans and credits to, and imports from, Italy. Britain and France were afraid of alienating Mussolini, however, so they refused to embargo oil, the one economic sanction that could have prevented Italian victory. Even more important, the British fleet allowed Italian troops and munitions to use the Suez Canal. The results of this wavering policy were disastrous. The League of Nations and collective security were totally discredited, and Mussolini was alienated as well. He now turned to Germany, and by November 1, 1936, he could speak publicly of a Rome–Berlin "Axis."

Remilitarization of the Rhineland

No less important a result of the Ethiopian affair was its effect on Hitler's evaluation of the strength and determination of the Western powers. On

March 7, 1936, he took his greatest risk yet, sending a small armed force into the demilitarized Rhineland. This was a breach not only of the Versailles treaty, but of the Locarno Agreements of 1925 as well—agreements Germany had made voluntarily. It also removed a crucial element of French security. France and Britain had every right to resist, and the French especially had a claim to retain the only element of security left to them after the failure of the Allies to guarantee France's defense. Yet neither power did anything but register a feeble protest with the League of Nations. British opinion would not permit support for France, and the French would not act alone. They were paralyzed by internal division and by a military doctrine that concentrated on defense and shunned the offensive. Both countries were further weakened by a growing pacifism.

In retrospect, the Allies lost a great opportunity in the Rhineland to stop Hitler before he became a serious menace. The failure of his gamble, taken against the advice of his generals, might have led to his overthrow; at the least, it would have made German expansion to the east dangerous if not impossible. Nor is there much reason to doubt that the French army could easily have routed the tiny German force in the Rhineland. As the German general Alfred Jodl (1890–1946) said some years later, "The French covering army would have blown us to bits."[1]

A Germany that was rapidly rearming and that had a defensible western frontier presented a completely new problem to the Western powers. Their response was the policy of "appeasement," based on the assumption that Germany had real grievances and that Hitler's goals were limited and ultimately acceptable. They believed that the correct policy was to negotiate and make concessions before a crisis could lead to war.

Behind this approach was the universal dread of another war. Memories of the horrors of the last war were still vivid, and the prospect of aerial bombardment made the thought of a new war even more terrifying. A firmer policy, moreover, would have required rapid rearmament. British leaders especially were reluctant to pursue this path because of the expense and the widespread belief that the arms race had been a major cause of the last war. As Germany armed, the French huddled behind their newly constructed defensive wall, the Maginot Line, and the British hoped for the best.

The Spanish Civil War

The new European alignment that found the Western democracies on one side and the fascist states on the other was made clearer by the Spanish Civil War, which broke out in July 1936. (See Map 29–1.) In 1931 the monarchy had collapsed, and Spain became a democratic republic. The new government followed a program of moderate reform that antagonized landowners, the Catholic Church, nationalists, and conservatives without satisfying the demands of peasants, workers, Catalán separatists, or radicals. Elections in February 1936 brought to power a Spanish Popular Front government ranging from republicans of the left to communists and anarchists. The losers, especially the Falangists, the Spanish fascists, would not accept defeat at the polls. In July, General Francisco Franco (1892–1975) led an army from Spanish Morocco against the republic.

Thus began the Spanish Civil War, which lasted almost three years, cost hundreds of thousands of lives, and provided a training ground for World War II. Germany and Italy supported Franco with troops, airplanes, and supplies. The Soviet Union sent equipment and advisers to the republicans. Liberals and leftists from Europe and America volunteered to fight in the republican ranks against fascism.

The civil war, fought on blatantly ideological lines, profoundly affected world politics. It brought Germany and Italy closer together, leading to the Rome–Berlin Axis Pact in 1936. Japan joined the Axis powers that year in the Anti-Comintern Pact, ostensibly directed against international communism, but really a new and powerful diplomatic alliance. Western Europe, especially France, had a great interest in preventing Spain from falling into the hands of a fascist regime closely allied with Germany and Italy. Appeasement reigned, however. Although international law permitted the sale of weapons and munitions to the legitimate republican government, France and Britain forbade the export of war materials to either side, and the United States passed new neutrality legislation to the same end. When Barcelona fell to Franco early in 1939, the fascists had won effective control of Spain. (See "Art & the West.")

Austria and Czechoslovakia

Hitler made good use of his new friendship with Mussolini. He had always planned to annex his native Austria. In 1934, the Nazi Party in Austria assassinated the prime minister and tried to seize

---

[1]Quoted in W. L. Shirer, *The Collapse of the Third Republic* (New York: Simon & Schuster, 1969), p. 281.

Picasso's Guernica

Pablo Picasso, *Guernica*, 1937. Oil on Canvas. 11′5 × 25′5 3/4. Museo Nacional Centro de Arte Reina Sofia/© 1998 Estate of Pablo Picasso/Artists Rights Society (ARS), New York.

*I*n July 1936, right-wing rebels based in Spanish Morocco and led by General Francisco Franco landed in Spain and launched an attack on the legitimate government, the Popular Front, a leftist coalition that ranged from moderate republicans to communists and anarchists. The Spanish Civil War that followed divided Europe, with fascist Italy and Nazi Germany assisting Franco, and Soviet Russia aiding the Republic. The war served as a sort of preview of the horrors that would follow in World War II. Before its end in 1939, the war in Spain took some 500,000 lives.

Pablo Picasso, probably the most famous painter of the twentieth century, was asked by the government of the Republic to paint a mural in the Spanish pavilion for the Paris World's Fair. Soon after he accepted the commission, on April 26, 1937, planes from the German Condor Legion bombed the Basque town of Guernica, killing some 1,000 men, women, and children and destroying about seventy percent of the buildings. It was the most effective aerial bombardment of a city up to that time, and its purpose was simply to create terror.

Picasso seized upon Guernica as the subject of his mural. The painting was an enormous success, serving the enemies of Franco, Mussolini, and Hitler as a powerful symbol of their evil. When it was taken to the Metropolitan Museum in New York soon after, it had an enormous impact. "*Guernica* helped to push a whole segment of Western opinion, including the magazines *Time* and *Newsweek*, over to the Republican side."[2]

The style of *Guernica* is greatly influenced by the surrealists, especially the Spaniard Joan Miró. The painting does not show the attack, but depicts its terrible effects on its victims. It has been called "a stark and surrealistic nightmare" by a scholar who offers the following interpretation: "Expressively distorted women, one with her dead child, wail at the carnage. Above a fallen, broken warrior is a screaming horse, symbolizing the suffering republic. To our left is a bull, thought to symbolize either Franco or Spain. An electric light and a woman holding a lantern suggest Picasso's desire to reveal the event in all its horror."[3]

Sources: H. W. Janson and Anthony F. Janson, *History of Art*, rev. 5th ed. (Upper Saddle River, NJ: Prentice Hall, 1997), p. 82; R. O. Paxson, *Europe in the Twentieth Century* (New York: Harcourt, Brace, 1975), pp. 289–398; Paul Johnson, *Modern Times* (New York: Harper and Row, 1983), pp. 321–337; Marilyn Stokstad, *Art History* (New York: Harry N. Abrams, 1999), p. 109.

[2]Paul Johnson, *Modern Times*. (New York: Harper and Row, 1983), p. 336.

[3]Stokstad, *Art History*. (New York: Harry N. Abrams, 1999), p. 1090.

MAP 29–1   THE SPANISH CIVIL WAR, 1936–1939   *The purple area on the map shows the large portion of Spain quickly overrun by Franco's insurgent armies during the first year of the war. In the next two years, progress came more slowly for the fascists as the war became a kind of international rehearsal for the coming World War II. Madrid's fall to Franco in the spring of 1939 had been preceded by that of Barcelona a few weeks earlier.*

power. Mussolini had not yet allied with Hitler and was suspicious of German intentions. He quickly moved an army to the Austrian border, thus preventing German intervention and causing the coup to fail.

In 1938, the new diplomatic situation encouraged Hitler to try again. He perhaps hoped to achieve his goal by propaganda, bullying, and threats, but Austrian Chancellor Kurt Schuschnigg (1897–1977) refused to be intimidated. Schuschnigg announced a plebiscite for March 13, in which the Austrian people themselves could decide whether to unite with Germany. To forestall the plebiscite, Hitler sent his army into Austria on March 12. To his great relief, Mussolini did not object, and Hitler rode to Vienna amid the cheers of his Austrian sympathizers.

The *Anschluss*, or union of Germany and Austria, was another clear violation of Versailles. The treaty, however, was now a dead letter, and the West remained passive. The *Anschluss* had great strategic significance, however, because Germany now surrounded Czechoslovakia, one of the bulwarks of French security, on three sides.

In fact, the very existence of Czechoslovakia was an affront to Hitler. It was democratic and pro-Western; it had been created partly as a check on Germany and was allied both to France and to the Soviet Union. It also contained about 3.5 million Germans who lived in the Sudetenland, near the German border. These Germans had belonged to the dominant nationality group in the old Austro–Hungarian Empire and resented their new minority position. Supported by Hitler and led by Konrad Henlein (1898–1945), the chief Nazi in Czechoslovakia, they made ever-increasing demands for privileges and autonomy within the Czech state. The Czechs made many concessions, but Hitler did not really want to improve the lot of the Sudeten Germans. He wanted to destroy Czechoslovakia. He told Henlein, "We must always demand so much that we can never be satisfied."[4]

As pressure mounted, the Czechs grew nervous. In May 1938, they received false rumors of an imminent attack by Germany and mobilized their army. The French, British, and Russians all warned that they would support the Czechs. Hitler, who had not planned an attack at that time, was forced to publicly deny any designs on Czechoslovakia. The public humiliation infuriated him, and he planned a military attack on the Czechs. The affair stiffened Czech resistance, but it frightened the French and British. The French,

[4]Quoted in Alan Bullock, *Hitler, a Study in Tyranny* (New York: Harper & Row, 1962), p. 443.

as had become the rule, deferred to British leadership. The British prime minister was Neville Chamberlain (1869–1940), a man thoroughly committed to the policy of appeasement. He was determined not to allow Britain to go to war again. He pressed the Czechs to make further concessions to Germany, but no concession was enough.

On September 12, 1938, Hitler made a provocative speech at the Nuremberg Nazi Party rally. His rhetoric led to rioting in the Sudetenland, and the Czechs declared martial law. German intervention seemed imminent. Chamberlain, aged sixty-nine, who had never flown before, made three flights to Germany between September 15 and September 29 in an attempt to appease Hitler at Czech expense and thus to avoid war. At Hitler's mountain retreat, Berchtesgaden, on September 15, Chamberlain accepted the separation of the Sudetenland from Czechoslovakia. And he and the French premier, Édouard Daladier (1884–1970), forced the Czechs to agree by threatening to abandon them if they did not. A week later, Chamberlain flew yet again to Germany, only to find that Hitler had raised his demands. He wanted cession of the Sudetenland in three days and immediate occupation by the German army.

Munich

Chamberlain returned to England, and France and Britain prepared for war. At Chamberlain's request and at the last moment, Mussolini proposed a conference of Germany, Italy, France, and Britain. It

On September 29–30, 1938, Hitler met with the leaders of Britain and France at Munich to decide the fate of Czechoslovakia. The Allied leaders abandoned the small democratic nation in a vain attempt to appease Hitler and avoid war. Hitler sits in the center of the picture. To his right is Prime Minister Neville Chamberlain of Britain. Ullstein Bilderdienst

MAP 29–2   PARTITIONS OF CZECHOSLOVAKIA AND POLAND, 1938–1939   *The immediate background of World War II is found in the complex international drama unfolding on Germany's eastern frontier in 1938 and 1939. Germany's expansion inevitably meant the victimization of Austria, Czechoslovakia, and Poland. With the failure of the Western powers' appeasement policy and the signing of a German–Soviet pact, the stage for the war was set.*

met on September 29 at Munich. Hitler received almost everything he had demanded. (See Map 29–2.) The Sudetenland, the key to Czech security, became part of Germany, thus depriving the Czechs of any chance of self-defense. In return, Hitler agreed to spare the rest of Czechoslovakia. He promised, "I have no more territorial demands to make in Europe." Chamberlain returned to England with the Munich agreement and told a cheering crowd that he had brought "peace with honour. I believe it is peace for our time."

Even in the short run, the appeasement of Hitler at Munich was a failure. Czechoslovakia did not survive. Soon Poland and Hungary tore more territory from it, and the Slovaks demanded a state of their own. Finally, on March 15, 1939, Hitler broke his promise and occupied Prague, putting an end to the Czech state and to illusions that his only goal was to restore Germans to the Reich. Defenders of the appeasers have argued that their policy was justified because it bought valuable time in which the West

could prepare for war. But that argument was not made by the appeasers themselves, who thought that they were achieving peace, nor does the evidence support it.

If the French and the British had been willing to attack Germany from the west while the Czechs fought in their own defense, their efforts might have been successful. High officers in the German army were opposed to Hitler's risky policies and might have overthrown him. Even failing such developments, a war begun in October 1938 would have forced Hitler to fight without the friendly neutrality and material assistance of the Soviet Union—and without the resources of eastern Europe that became available to him as a result of appeasement and Soviet cooperation. If, moreover, the West ever had a chance of concluding an alliance with the Soviet Union against Hitler, the exclusion of the Russians from Munich and the appeasement policy helped destroy it. Munich remains an example of shortsighted policy that helped bring on war in disadvantageous circumstances because of the very fear of war and the failure to prepare for it. (See "Churchill's Response to Munich.")

Hitler's occupation of Prague discredited appeasement in the eyes of the British people. In the summer of 1939, a Gallup Poll showed that three-quarters of the British public believed it worth a war to stop Hitler. Though Chamberlain himself had not lost all faith in his policy, he felt he had to respond to public opinion, and he responded to excess.

Poland was the next target of German expansion. In the spring of 1939, the Germans put pressure on Poland to restore the formerly German city of Danzig and to allow a railroad and a highway through the Polish Corridor to connect East Prussia with the rest of Germany. When the Poles would not yield, the usual

---

Churchill's Response to Munich

In the parliamentary debate that followed the Munich conference at the end of September 1938, Winston Churchill was one of the few critics of what had been accomplished. In the following selections from his speech, he expresses his concerns.

❖ *What was decided at Munich? Why were the representatives of Czechoslovakia not at the meeting? Why did Chamberlain think the meeting was successful? Munich was the high point of the policy called appeasement. How would its advocates defend this policy? Churchill was a leading opponent of appeasement. What are his objections to it?*

I will begin by saying what everybody would like to ignore or forget but which must nevertheless be stated, namely, that we have sustained a total and unmitigated defeat, and that France has suffered even more than we have...

We really must not waste time after all this long debate upon the difference between the positions reached at Berchtesgaden, at Godesberg and at Munich. They can be very simply epitomized if the House will permit me to vary the metaphor. One pound was demanded at the pistol's point. When it was given, £2 were demanded at the pistol's point. Finally, the dictator consented to take £1 17s. 6d. and the rest in promises of good will for the future...

All is over. Silent, mournful, abandoned, broken, Czechoslovakia recedes into the darkness. She has suffered in every respect by her association with the Western democracies and with the League of Nations, of which she has always been an obedient servant...

We have been reduced in those five years from a position of security so overwhelming and so unchallengeable that we never cared to think about it. We have been reduced from a position where the very word "war" was considered one which could be used only by persons qualifying for a lunatic asylum. We have been reduced from a position of safety and power—power to do good, power to be generous to a beaten foe, power to make terms with Germany, power to give her proper redress for her grievances, power to stop her arming if we chose, power to take any step in strength or mercy or justice which we thought right—reduced in five years from a position safe and unchallenged to where we stand now...

The responsibility must rest with those who have had the undisputed control of our political affairs. They neither prevented Germany from rearming, nor did they rearm ourselves in time. They quarreled with Italy without saving Ethiopia. They exploited and discredited the vast institution of the League of Nations and they neglected to make alliances and combinations which might have repaired previous errors, and thus they left us in the hour of trial without adequate national defense or effective international security...

We are in the presence of a disaster of the first magnitude which has befallen Great Britain and France. Do not let us blind ourselves to that. It must now be accepted that all the countries of Central and Eastern Europe will make the best terms they can with the triumphant Nazi power. The system of alliances in Central Europe upon which France has relied for her safety has been swept away, and I can see no means by which it can be reconstituted. The road down the Danube Valley to the Black Sea, the road which leads as far as Turkey, has been opened...

From Winston S. Churchill, *Blood, Sweat, and Tears* (New York: G. P. Putnam's Sons, 1941), pp. 55–56, 58, 60–61. Reproduced with permission of Curtis Brown Ltd., on behalf of the Estate of Sir Winston S. Churchill. Copyright Winston S. Churchill propaganda campaign began, and the pressure mounted. On March 31, Chamberlain announced a Franco–British guarantee of Polish independence. Hitler appears to have expected to fight a war with Poland, but not with the Western allies, for he did not take their guarantee seriously. He had come to hold their leaders in contempt. He knew that both countries were unprepared for war and that large segments of their populations were opposed to fighting for Poland.

Moreover, France and Britain had no means of getting effective help to the Poles. The French, still dominated by the defensive mentality of the Maginot Line, had no intention of attacking Germany. The only way to defend Poland was to bring Russia into the alliance against Hitler, but a Russian alliance posed many problems. Each side was profoundly suspicious of the other. The French and the British were hostile to communism, and since Stalin's purge of the Red Army, they were skeptical of the military value of a Russian alliance. Besides, the Russians could not help Poland without being given the right to enter Poland and Romania. Both nations, suspicious of Russian intentions—and with good reason—refused to grant these rights. As a result, Western negotiations for an alliance with Russia made little progress.

The Nazi–Soviet Pact

The Russians had at least equally good reason to hesitate. They resented being left out of the Munich agreement. They were annoyed by the low priority that the West gave to negotiations with Russia, compared with the urgency with which they dealt with Hitler. They feared, quite rightly, that the Western powers meant them to bear the burden of the war against Germany. As a result, they opened negotiations with Hitler, and on August 23, 1939, the world was shocked to learn of a Nazi–Soviet nonaggression pact.

The secret provisions of the pact, which were easily guessed and soon carried out, divided Poland between the two powers and allowed Russia to occupy the Baltic states and to take Bessarabia from Romania. The most bitter ideological enemies had become allies. Communist parties in the West changed their line overnight from the ardent advocacy of resistance to Hitler to a policy of peace and quiet. Ideology gave way to political and military reality. The West offered the Russians immediate danger without much prospect of gain. Hitler offered Stalin short-term gain without immediate danger. There could be little doubt about Stalin's decision.

The Nazi–Soviet pact sealed the fate of Poland, and the Franco–British commitment guaranteed a general war. On September 1, 1939, the Germans invaded Poland. Two days later, Britain and France declared war on Germany. World War II had begun.

The Coming of World War II	
1919 (June)	The Versailles treaty
1923 (January)	France occupies the Ruhr
1925 (October)	The Locarno Agreements
1931 (Spring)	Onset of the Great Depression in Europe
1931 (September)	Japan occupies Manchuria
1933 (January)	Hitler comes to power
1933 (October)	Germany withdraws from the League of Nations
1935 (March)	Hitler renounces disarmament, starts an air force, and begins conscription
1935 (October)	Mussolini attacks Ethiopia
1936 (March)	Germany reoccupies and remilitarizes the Rhineland
1936 (July)	Outbreak of the Spanish Civil War
1936 (October)	Formation of the Rome–Berlin Axis
1938 (March)	*Anschluss* with Austria
1938 (September)	The Munich conference and the partition of Czechoslovakia
1939 (March)	Hitler occupies Prague; France and Great Britain guarantee Polish independence
1939 (August)	The Nazi–Soviet pact
1939 (September 1)	Germany invades Poland
1939 (September 3)	Britain and France declare war on Germany

World War II (1939–1945)

World War II has a better claim to its name than its predecessor, for it was truly global. Fighting took place in Europe and Asia, on the Atlantic and the Pacific oceans, and in the Northern and Southern Hemispheres. The demand for the fullest exploitation of material and human resources for increased production, the use of blockades, and the intensive bombing of civilian targets made the war of 1939 even more "total"—that is, comprehensive and intense—than that of 1914.

The German Conquest of Europe

The German attack on Poland produced swift success. The new style of "lightning warfare," or *Blitzkrieg*, employed fast-moving, massed armored columns supported by airpower. The Poles had no tanks and few planes, and their defense soon collapsed. The speed of

German troops march down the Champs-Elysées in Paris in September, 1940, after the rapid collapse of French defenses. Roger-Viollet/Liaison Agency, Inc.

the German victory astonished the Russians, who hastened to collect their share of the booty before Hitler could deprive them of it.

On September 17, Russia invaded Poland from the east, dividing the country with the Germans. Stalin then forced the encircled Baltic countries to allow the Red Army to occupy them. By 1940, Estonia, Latvia, and Lithuania had become puppet republics within the Union of Soviet Socialist Republics (USSR), or the Soviet Union. In June 1940, the Russians forced Romania to cede Bessarabia. In November 1940, the Russians invaded Finland, but the Finns resisted fiercely for six months. Although they were finally worn down and compelled to yield territory and bases to Russia, the Finns remained independent. Russian expansionism and the poor performance of the Red Army in Finland may well have encouraged Hitler to invade the Soviet Union in June 1941, just twenty-two months after the 1939 treaty.

Until the spring of 1940, the western front was quiet. The French remained behind the Maginot Line, while Hitler and Stalin swallowed Poland and the Baltic states. Britain rearmed hastily, and the British navy blockaded Germany. Cynics in the West called it the *phony war*, or *Sitzkrieg*, but Hitler shattered the stillness in the spring of 1940. In April, without warning and with swift success, the Germans invaded Denmark and Norway. Hitler's northern front was

secure, and he now had both air and naval bases closer to Britain. A month later, a combined land and air attack struck Belgium, the Netherlands, and Luxembourg. German airpower and armored divisions were irresistible. The Dutch surrendered in a few days; the Belgians, though aided by the French and the British, gave up less than two weeks later.

The British and French armies in Belgium were forced to flee to the English Channel to seek escape on the beaches of Dunkirk. The heroic efforts of hundreds of Britons manning small boats saved more than 200,000 British and 100,000 French soldiers. Casualties, however, were high, and valuable equipment was abandoned.

The Maginot Line ran from Switzerland to the Belgian frontier. Until 1936, the French had expected the Belgians to continue the fortifications along their German border. After Hitler remilitarized the Rhineland without opposition, the Belgians lost faith in their French alliance and proclaimed their neutrality, leaving the Maginot Line exposed on its left flank. Hitler's swift advance through Belgium therefore circumvented France's main line of defense.

The French army, poorly and hesitantly led by aged generals who did not understand how to use tanks and planes, collapsed. Mussolini, eager to claim the spoils of victory when it was clearly safe to do so, invaded southern France on June 10. Less than a week later, the new French government, under the ancient hero of Verdun, Marshal Henri Philippe Pétain (1856–1951), asked for an armistice. In two months Hitler had accomplished what Germany had failed to achieve in four years of bitter fighting in the previous war.

The Battle of Britain

The fall of France left Britain isolated, and Hitler expected the British to come to terms. He was prepared to allow Britain to retain its empire in return for a free hand for Germany on the Continent. The British had never been willing to accept such an arrangement and had fought the long and difficult war against Napoleon to prevent the domination of the Continent by a single power. If there was any chance that the British would consider such terms, it disappeared when Winston Churchill (1874–1965) replaced Chamberlain as prime minister in May of 1940.

Churchill had been an early and forceful critic of Hitler, the Nazis, and the policy of appeasement. He was a descendant and biographer of the duke of Marlborough (1650–1722), who had fought to prevent the domination of Europe by Louis XIV in the eighteenth century. Churchill's sense of history, his feeling for British greatness, and his hatred of tyranny and love of freedom made him reject any thought of compromise with Hitler. His skill as a speaker and a writer enabled him to inspire the British people with his own courage and determination and to undertake what seemed a hopeless fight. Hitler and

The close cooperation between Prime Minister Winston Churchill of Britain and President Franklin Roosevelt of the United States greatly helped to assure the effective cooperation of their two countries in World War II.
UPI/Corbis

his allies, including the Soviet Union, controlled all of Europe. Japan was having its way in Asia. The United States was neutral, dominated by isolationist sentiment, and determined to avoid involvement outside the Western Hemisphere.

One of Churchill's greatest achievements was establishing a close relationship with the American President Franklin D. Roosevelt (1882–1945). Roosevelt found ways to help the British despite strong political opposition. In 1940 and 1941, before the United States was at war, America sent military supplies, traded badly needed warships for leases on British naval bases, and even convoyed ships across the Atlantic to help the British survive.

As weeks passed and Britain remained defiant, Hitler was forced to contemplate an invasion, and that required control of the air. The first strikes by the German air force (*Luftwaffe*), directed against the airfields and fighter planes in southeastern England, began in August 1940. If these attacks had continued, Germany might soon have gained control of the air and, with it, the chance of a successful invasion.

In early September, however, seeking revenge for some British bombing raids on German cities, the *Luftwaffe* switched its main attacks to London. For two months, London was bombed every night. Much of the city was destroyed and about 15,000 people were killed. The theories of victory through airpower alone, however, proved false. Casualties were much less than expected, and morale was not shattered. In fact, the bombings united the British people and made them more resolute.

The Royal Air Force (RAF) inflicted heavy losses on the *Luftwaffe*. Aided by the newly developed radar and an excellent system of communications, the British Spitfire and Hurricane fighter planes destroyed more than twice as many enemy planes as were lost by the RAF. Hitler had lost the Battle of Britain in the air and was forced to abandon his plans for invasion.

The German Attack on Russia

The defeat of Russia and the conquest of the Ukraine to provide *Lebensraum*, or "living space," for the German people had always been a major goal for Hitler. Even before the assault on Britain, he had informed his staff of his intention to attack Russia as soon as conditions were favorable. In December 1940, even while the bombing of England continued, he ordered his generals to prepare for an invasion of Russia by May 15, 1941. (See Map 29–3.) He apparently thought that a *Blitzkrieg* victory in the east would also destroy any further British hope of resistance.

MAP 29–3 AXIS EUROPE, 1941 *On the eve of the German invasion of the Soviet Union, the Germany–Italy Axis bestrode most of western Europe by annexation, occupation, or alliance—from Norway and Finland in the north to Greece in the south and from Poland to France. Britain, the Soviets, a number of insurgent groups, and, finally, America, had before them the long struggle of conquering this Axis "fortress Europe."*

Operation Barbarossa, the code name for the invasion of Russia, was aimed at destroying Russia before winter could set in. Success depended in part on an early start, but here Hitler's Italian alliance proved costly. Mussolini was jealous of Hitler's success and annoyed by the treatment he had received from the German dictator. His invasion of France was a fiasco, even though the main French forces were being simultaneously crushed by the Germans. Hitler did not allow Mussolini to annex French territory in Europe or North Africa. Mussolini instead launched

an attack against the British in Egypt and drove them back some sixty miles. Encouraged by this success, he also invaded Greece from his base in Albania (which he had seized in 1939). His purpose was revealed by his remark to his son-in-law, Count Ciano: "Hitler always faces me with a *fait accompli*. This time I am going to pay him back in his own coin. He will find out in the newspapers that I have occupied Greece."[5]

[5]Quoted in Gordon Wright, *The Ordeal of Total War, 1939–1945* (New York: Harper & Row, 1968), pp. 35–36.

Mussolini inspecting Italian troops at the Florence train station in October 1940 as he awaits a visit from Hitler. Mussolini's military reverses in North Africa and the Balkans would divert German resources in 1941 and delay the beginning of Hitler's planned invasion of Russia. Popperfoto/Archive Photos

In North Africa, however, the British counterattacked and drove the Italians back into Libya. The Greeks themselves pushed into Albania. In March 1941, the British sent help to the Greeks, and Hitler was forced to divert his attention to the Balkans and Africa. General Erwin Rommel (1891–1944), later to earn the title of "Desert Fox," went to Africa and soon drove the British out of Libya and back into Egypt. In the Balkans, the German army swiftly occupied Yugoslavia and crushed Greek resistance. The price, however, was a delay of six weeks. The diversion caused by Mussolini's vanity proved to be costly the following winter in the Russian campaign.

Operation Barbarossa was launched against Russia on June 22, 1941, and it almost succeeded. Despite their deep suspicion of Germany (and the excuse later offered by apologists for the Soviet Union that the Nazi–Soviet pact was meant to give Russia time to prepare), the Russians were taken quite by surprise. Stalin appears to have panicked. He had not fortified his frontier, nor did he order his troops to withdraw when attacked. In the first two days, 2,000 Russian planes were destroyed on the ground. By November, Hitler had gone further into Russia than Napoleon. The German army stood at the gates of Leningrad, on the outskirts of Moscow, and on the Don River. Of the 4.5 million troops with which the Russians had begun the fighting, they had lost 2.5 million; of their 15,000 tanks, only 700 were left. Moscow was in panic, and a German victory seemed imminent.

Yet the Germans could not deliver the final blow. In August, they delayed their advance while Hitler decided strategy. The German general staff wanted to drive directly for Moscow and take it before winter. This plan probably would have brought victory. Unlike its status in Napoleon's time, Moscow was the hub of the Russian system of transportation. Hitler, however, diverted a significant part of his forces to the south. By the time he was ready to return to the offensive near Moscow, it was too late. Winter devastated the German army, which was neither dressed nor equipped to face it.

Given precious time, Stalin restored order and built defenses for the city. Even more important, troops arrived from Siberia, where they had been placed to check a possible Japanese attack. In November and December, the Russians counterattacked. The *Blitzkrieg* had turned into a war of attrition, and the Germans began to have nightmares of duplicating Napoleon's retreat.

Hitler's Plans for Europe

Hitler often spoke of the "new order" that he meant to impose after he had established his Third Reich (Empire) throughout Europe. The first two German empires were those of Charlemagne in the ninth century and Bismarck in the nineteenth. Hitler predicted that his own would last for a thousand years. If his organization of Germany before the war is a proper guide, he had no single plan of government, but relied frequently on intuition and pragmatism. His organization of conquered Europe had the same patchwork characteristics. Some conquered territory was annexed to Germany, some was not annexed, but administered directly by German officials, and other lands were nominally autonomous, but ruled by puppet governments.

Hitler's regime was probably unmatched in history for carefully planned terror and inhumanity. His plan of giving *Lebensraum* to the Germans was to be accomplished at the expense of people he deemed inferior. Hitler established colonies of Germans in parts of Poland, driving the local people from their land and employing them as cheap labor. He had similar plans on an even greater scale for Russia. The Russians would be driven eastward to central Asia and Siberia; they would be kept in check by frontier colonies of German war veterans. European Russia would be settled by Germans.

Hitler's long-range plans included germanization as well as colonization. In lands inhabited by people racially akin to the Germans, like the Scandinavian countries, the Netherlands, and Switzerland, the natives would be absorbed into the German nation. Such peoples would be reeducated and purged of dissenting elements, but there would be little or no colonization. Hitler even had plans, only slightly realized, of adopting selected people from the lesser races into the master race. One of these plans involved bringing half a million Ukrainian girls into Germany as servants and finding German husbands for them; about 15,000 were actually sent to Germany.

Hitler regarded the conquered lands as a source of plunder. From eastern Europe, he removed everything useful, including entire industries. In Russia and Poland, the Germans simply confiscated the land itself. In the West, the conquered countries were forced to support the occupying army at a rate several times above the real cost. The Germans used the profits to buy up everything desirable, stripping the conquered peoples of most necessities. The Nazis were frank about their policies. One of Hitler's high officials said, "Whether nations live in prosperity or starve to death interests me only insofar as we need them as slaves for our culture."[6]

Racism and the Holocaust

The most horrible aspect of the Nazi rule in Europe arose not from military or economic necessity but from the inhumanity and brutality inherent in Hitler's racial doctrines. He considered the Slavs *Untermenschen*, subhuman creatures like beasts who need not be thought of or treated as people. In parts of Poland, the upper and professional classes

[6]Quoted in Wright, p. 117.

In the spring of 1943, when only a fraction of the many Jews whom the Germans imprisoned in the Warsaw Ghetto were still alive, about a thousand of them took up hidden arms to offer what they knew would be a doomed resistance. Before the fighting was over the Germans suffered many casualties and had to call for reinforcements. Archive Photos were entirely removed—either jailed, deported, or killed. Schools and churches were closed. The Nazis limited marriage to keep down the Polish birth rate and imposed harsh living conditions.

In Russia, things were even worse. Hitler spoke of his Russian campaign as a war of extermination. Heinrich Himmler (1900–1945), head of Hitler's elite SS formations, planned to eliminate 30 million Slavs to make room for the Germans; he formed extermination squads for this purpose. Six million Russian prisoners of war and deported civilians may have died under Nazi rule.

Hitler had special plans for the Jews. He meant to make all Europe *Judenrein*, or "free of Jews." For a time, he thought of sending them to the island of Madagascar. Later, he arrived at the "final solution of the Jewish problem"— extermination. The Nazis built extermination camps in Germany and Poland and used the latest technology to achieve the most efficient means of killing millions of men, women, and children simply because they were Jews. Before the war was over, perhaps 6 million Jews had died in what has come to be called the Holocaust. Only about a million European Jews remained alive, most of them in pitiable condition. (See Chapter 30.)

As interest in the Holocaust has grown since the 1960s, so has debate about its character and meaning. Was it a unique event of such a special kind of evil that it is unprecedented and unparalleled, or was it one specific instance of a more general human wickedness to be found throughout human history? Are its roots to be found in flaws in human nature as a whole, or are they unique to the experience of the West or, perhaps,

to the German people? Some scholars point to the horrible mass murders committed in the twentieth century by communist regimes under Stalin in the Soviet Union and Mao in China, each of which killed many more people than did Hitler, as evidence of the more general character of the phenomenon. Others argue that the Holocaust was unique because its goal was the annihilation of a whole people, from infants to the aged, just because of who they were. Some focus on the wickedness personified by Hitler, who was driven by his fixation on the myth of Jewish power and evil.

Perhaps we should think of the problem from the standpoint of two questions: Why were the Jews the main target of Hitler's policy of extermination? How was it possible to carry out such a vast mass murder? Surely, an essential part of an answer to the first is the persistence of anti-Semitism in Christianity and Western culture, from the church fathers to Luther and to the teachings of churches in modern times. Some would combine this religious and historical anti-Semitism with the coming of the Enlightenment and the social sciences, which gave rise to pseudo-scientific racial theories that lent a new twist to the old hatred of the Jews. Pseudoscientific racism appears to have been the most powerful influence on Hitler, but it could not have found widespread support without deeply rooted religious and social anti-Semitism.

As to how it was possible to murder six million people, part of the answer must lie in the parochial nationalism that arose during and after the French Revolution. For many pepole, nationalism divided the world into one's fellow nationals and all others. It encouraged, excused, and even justified all sorts of

These are some of the dead at the Nordhausen concentration camp, which was liberated by the American army in April 1945. The Nazis set up their first concentration camps in Germany in 1933 to hold opponents of their regime. After the conquest of Poland, new camps were established there as part of the "final solution," the extermination of the Jews. About six million Jews were murdered in these camps. Even in those camps not dedicated to extermination—in which political prisoners and "undesirables" such as Gypsies, homosexuals, and Jehovah's Witnesses were held—conditions were brutal in the extreme, and tens of thousands died. The crimes of the Nazi regime have no precedent in human history. National Archives

An Observer Describes the Mass Murder of Jews in Ukraine

After World War II, the victorious powers put some German officers and officials on trial at Nuremberg for crimes they were charged with having committed during the war. The selections that follow, from the testimony of a German construction engineer who witnessed the mass murder of Jews at Dubno in the Ukraine on October 5, 1942, reveal the brutality with which Hitler's attempt at a "final solution of the Jewish problem" was carried out.

❖ *Why did the German government commit these atrocities? Why were they directed chiefly at Jews? Was there a cost to Germany in pursuing such a policy? Why did ordinary Germans participate?*

On October 5, 1942, when I visited the building office at Dubno, my foreman told me that in the vicinity of the site, Jews from Dubno had been shot in three large pits, each about 30 metres long and 3 metres deep. About 1,500 persons had been killed daily. All the 5,000 Jews who had still been living in Dubno before the pogrom were to be liquidated. As the shooting had taken place in his presence, he was still much upset.

Thereupon, I drove to the site accompanied by my foreman and saw near it great mounds of earth, about 30 metres long and 2 metres high. Several trucks stood in front of the mounds. Armed Ukrainian militia drove the people off the trucks under the supervision of an S.S. man. The militiamen acted as guards on the trucks and drove them to and from the pit. All these people had the regulation yellow patches on the front and back of their clothes, and thus could be recognized as Jews.

My foreman and I went directly to the pits. Nobody bothered us. Now I heard rifle shots in quick succession from behind one of the earth mounds. The people who had got off the trucks—men, women and children of all ages—had to undress upon the orders of an S.S. man, who carried a riding or dog whip. They had to put down their clothes in fixed places, sorted according to shoes, top clothing and underclothing. I saw a heap of shoes of about 800 to 1,000 pairs, great piles of underlinen and clothing.

Without screaming or weeping, these people undressed, stood around in family groups, kissed each other, said farewells, and waited for a sign

from another S.S. man, who stood near the pit, also with a whip in his hand. During the fifteen minutes that I stood near I heard no complaint or plea for mercy. I watched a family of about eight persons, a man and a woman both about fifty with their children of about one, eight and ten, and two grown-up daughters of about twenty to twenty-nine. An old woman with snow-white hair was holding the one-year-old child in her arms and singing to it and tickling it. The child was cooing with delight. The couple were looking on with tears in their eyes. The father was holding the hand of a boy about ten years old and speaking to him softly; the boy was fighting his tears. The father pointed to the sky, stroked his head, and seemed to explain something to him.

At that moment the S.S. man at the pit shouted something to his comrade. The latter counted off about twenty persons and instructed them to go behind the earth mound. Among them was the family which I have mentioned. I well remember a girl, slim and with black hair, who, as she passed close to me pointed to herself and said "23." I walked around the mound and found myself confronted by a tremendous grave. People were closely wedged together and lying on top of each other so that only their heads were visible. Nearly all had blood running over their shoulders from their heads. Some of the people shot were still moving. Some were lifting their arms and turning their heads to show that they were still alive. The pit was already two-thirds full. I estimated that it already contained about 1,000 people.

From the Nuremberg Proceedings, as quoted in Louis L. Snyder, *Documents of German History* (New Brunswick, NJ: Rutgers University Press, 1958), pp. 462–464.

terrible and violent acts performed on behalf of one's fatherland. Another part of the answer may derive from the utopian visions also unleashed by the Enlightenment, which promised to achieve perfect

societies through social engineering, regardless of the human cost. To this were added the scientific and technological advances that gave the modern state new power to command its people, to persuade them to obey by controlling the media of propaganda, and to enforce its will with efficient brutality. All of these permitted the creation of a totalitarian state that, for the first time in history, could conduct mass murder on the scale of the Holocaust. (See "An Observer Describes the Mass Murder of Jews in Ukraine.")

These questions and their possible answers are but suggestions meant to encourage further and deeper thought in what will surely be a continuing debate among scholars and the general public.

World War II was unmatched in cruelty in modern times. When Stalin's armies conquered Poland and entered Germany, they raped, pillaged, and deported millions to the east. The British and American bombing of Germany killed thousands of civilians, and the dropping of atomic bombs on Japan killed and maimed tens of thousands more. The bombings, however, were thought of as acts of war that would help defeat the enemy. Stalin's atrocities were not widely known in the West at the time or even today.

The victorious Western allies were shocked by what they saw when they came upon the Nazi extermination camps and their pitiful survivors. Little wonder it was that they were convinced that the effort of resistance to the Nazis and all the pain it had cost were well worth it. (For more on the Holocaust, see Chapter 30.)

Japan and the United States Enter the War

The American government was very pro-British. The various forms of assistance that Roosevelt gave Britain would have justified a German declaration of war. Hitler, however, held back. The U.S.

The successful Japanese attack on the American base at Pearl Harbor in Hawaii on December 7, 1941, together with simultaneous attacks on other Pacific bases, brought the United States into war against the Axis powers. This picture shows the battleships USS West Virginia and USS Tennessee in flames as a small boat rescues a man from the water. US Army Photograph government might not have overcome isolationist sentiment and entered the war in the Atlantic if war had not been thrust on America in the Pacific.

Since the Japanese conquest of Manchuria in 1931, American policy toward Japan had been suspicious and unfriendly. The outbreak of the war in Europe emboldened the Japanese to accelerate their drive to dominate Asia. They allied themselves with Germany and Italy, made a treaty of neutrality with the Soviet Union, and penetrated Indochina at the expense of defeated France. They also continued their war in China and planned to gain control of Malaya and the East Indies at the expense of beleaguered Britain and the conquered Netherlands. The only barrier to Japanese expansion was the United States.

The Americans had temporized, unwilling to cut off vital supplies of oil and other materials for fear of provoking a Japanese attack on Southeast Asia and Indonesia. The Japanese occupation of Indochina in July 1941 changed that policy, which had already begun to stiffen. The United States froze Japanese assets and cut off oil supplies; the British and Dutch did the same. Japanese plans for expansion could not continue without the conquest of the Indonesian oil fields and Malayan rubber and tin.

In October, a war faction led by General Hideki Tojo (1885–1948) took power in Japan and decided to risk a war rather than yield. On Sunday morning, December 7, 1941, while Japanese representatives were discussing a settlement in Washington, Japan launched an air attack on Pearl Harbor, Hawaii, the chief American naval base in the Pacific. The technique was similar to the one Japan had used against the Russian fleet at Port Arthur in 1904, and it caught the Americans equally by surprise. Much of the American fleet and many airplanes were destroyed; the American capacity to wage war in the Pacific was negated for the time being. The next day, the United States and Britain declared war on Japan. Three days later, Germany and Italy declared war on the United States.

The Tide Turns

The potential power of the United States was enormous, but America was ill prepared for war. Though conscription had been introduced in 1940, the army was tiny, inexperienced, and poorly supplied. American industry was not ready for war. The Japanese swiftly captured Guam, Wake Island, and the Philippine Islands. Also, they attacked Hong Kong, Malaya, Burma, and the Dutch East Indies. By the spring of 1942, they controlled these places and the Southwest Pacific as far as New Guinea. They were poised for an attack on Australia, and it seemed that nothing could stop them.

In 1942, the Germans also advanced deeper into Russia and almost reached the Caspian Sea in their drive for Russia's oil fields. In Africa, too, Axis fortunes were high. Rommel drove the British back into Egypt toward the Suez Canal until he was stopped at El Alamein, only seventy miles from Alexandria. Relations between the democracies and their Soviet ally were not close. German submarine warfare was threatening British supplies. The Allies were being thrown back on every front, and the future looked bleak.

The first good news for the Allied cause in the Pacific came in the spring of 1942. A naval battle in the Coral Sea sank many Japanese ships and gave security to Australia. A month later, the United States defeated the Japanese in a fierce air and naval battle off Midway Island; they thus blunted the chance of another assault on Hawaii and did enough damage to halt the Japanese advance. Soon American marines landed on Guadalcanal in the Solomon Islands and began to reverse the momentum of the war. The war in the Pacific was far from over, but the check to Japan allowed the Allies to concentrate their efforts on Europe.

More than twenty nations located all over the world were opposed to the Axis powers. The main combatants, however, were Great Britain, the Soviet Union, and the United States. The two Western democracies cooperated to an unprecedented degree, but suspicion between them and the Soviet Union continued. The Russians accepted all the aid they could get. Nevertheless, they did not trust their allies, complained of inadequate help, and demanded that the democracies open a "second front" on the mainland of Europe.

In 1942, American preparation and production were inadequate for an invasion of Europe. German submarines made the Atlantic unsafe for crossing by the vast numbers of troops needed for such an invasion. Not until 1944 were conditions right for the invasion, but in the meantime other developments forecast the doom of the Axis.

ALLIED LANDINGS IN AFRICA, SICILY, AND ITALY In November 1942, an Allied force landed in French North Africa. (See Map 29–4.) Even before that landing, after stopping Rommel at El Alamein, British Field Marshal Bernard Montgomery (1887–1976) had begun a drive to the west. Now, the American General Dwight D. Eisenhower (1890–1969) pushed eastward through Morocco and Algeria. The two armies caught the German army between them in Tunisia and crushed it. The Allies now controlled the Mediterranean and could attack southern Europe.

In July and August 1943, the Allies took Sicily. Mussolini was driven from power, but the Germans occupied Italy. The Allies landed in Italy,

MAP 29–4   NORTH AFRICAN CAMPAIGNS, 1942–1945   *Control of North Africa would give the Allies access to Europe from the south. The map illustrates this theater of the war from Morocco to Egypt and the Suez Canal.*

and Marshal Pietro Badoglio (1871–1956), the leader of the new Italian government, went over to their side, declaring war on Germany. Churchill had spoken of Italy as the "soft underbelly" of the Axis, but the Germans there resisted fiercely. Still, the need to defend Italy diverted the Germans' energy and resources and left them vulnerable on other fronts.

BATTLE OF STALINGRAD   The Russian campaign became especially demanding. In the summer of 1942, the Germans resumed the offensive on all fronts, but were unable to get far except in the south. (See Map 29–5.) Their goal was the oil fields near the Caspian Sea. Stalingrad, on the Volga, was a key point on the flank of the German army in the south. Hitler was determined to take the city and Stalin was equally determined to hold it. The Battle of Stalingrad raged for months with unexampled ferocity. The Russians lost more men in this one battle than the Americans lost in combat during the entire war, but their heroic defense prevailed. Because Hitler again overruled his generals and would not allow a retreat, an entire German army was lost at Stalingrad.

Stalingrad marked the turning point of the Russian campaign. Thereafter, the Americans provided material help. Even more important, increased production from their own industry, which had been moved to or built up in the safety of the central and eastern regions of the USSR, allowed the Russians to gain and keep the offensive. As the Germans' resources dwindled, the Russians inexorably advanced westward.

STRATEGIC BOMBING   In 1943, the Allies also gained ground in production and logistics. The industrial might of the United States began to come into full force, and new technology and tactics greatly reduced the submarine menace.

In the same year, the American and British air forces began a series of massive bombardments of Germany by night and day. The Americans were more committed to the theory of "precision bombing" of military and industrial targets vital to the enemy war effort, so they flew the day missions. The British considered precision bombing impossible and therefore useless. They preferred indiscriminate "area bombing," aimed at destroying the morale of the German people; this kind of bombing could be done at night. Neither kind of bombing had much

MAP 29–5   DEFEAT OF THE AXIS IN EUROPE, 1942–1945   *Here we see some major steps in the progress toward Allied victory against Axis Europe. From the south through Italy, the west through France, and the east through Russia, the Allies gradually conquered the Continent to bring the war in Europe to a close.*

effect on the war until 1944, when the Americans introduced long-range fighters that could protect the bombers and allow accurate missions by day.

By 1945, the Allies had virtually cleared the skies of German planes and could bomb at will. Concentrated attacks on industrial targets, especially communication centers and oil refineries, did extensive damage and helped to shorten the war. Terror bombing continued, too, with no useful result. The bombardment of Dresden in February 1945 was especially savage and destructive. It was much debated within the British government and has raised moral questions since. Whatever else it accomplished, the aerial war over Germany did take a heavy toll of the German air force and diverted vital German resources away from other military purposes.

The Defeat of Nazi Germany

On June 6, 1944 ("D-Day"), American, British, and Canadian troops landed in force on the coast of Normandy. The "second front" was opened. General

Dwight D. Eisenhower, the commander of the Allied armies, faced a difficult problem. The European coast was heavily fortified. Amphibious assaults, moreover, are especially vulnerable to changes of wind and weather. Success depended on meticulous planning, advance preparation by heavy bombing, and feints to mask the point of attack. The German defense was strong, but the Allies were able to establish a beachhead and then break out of it. In mid-August, the Allies landed in southern France to put more pressure on the enemy. By the beginning of September, France had been liberated.

THE BATTLE OF THE BULGE   All went smoothly until December, when the Germans launched a counterattack in Belgium through the Ardennes Forest. Because the Germans were able to push forward into the Allied line, this was called the Battle of the Bulge. Although the Allies suffered heavy losses, the Bulge was the last gasp for the Germans in the West. The Allies soon recovered their momentum and pushed eastward. They crossed the Rhine in

Allied troops landed in Normandy on D-Day, June 6, 1944. This photograph, taken two days later, shows long lines of men and equipment moving inland from the beach to reinforce the troops leading the invasion. Archive Photos

March of 1945, and German resistance rapidly crumbled. This time there could be no doubt that the Germans had lost the war on the battlefield.

THE CAPTURE OF BERLIN   In the East, the Russians swept forward no less swiftly, despite fierce German resistance. By March 1945, they were near Berlin. Because the Allies insisted on unconditional surrender, the Germans fought on until May. Hitler and his intimates committed suicide in an underground bunker in Berlin on May 1, 1945. The Russians occupied Berlin by agreement with their Western allies. The Third Reich had lasted a dozen years instead of the thousand predicted by Hitler.

Fall of the Japanese Empire

The war in Europe ended on May 8, 1945, and by then, victory over Japan was also in sight. The original Japanese attack on the United States had been

a calculated risk against the odds. Japan was inherently weaker than the United States. The longer the war lasted, the more American superiority in industrial production and population counted.

AMERICANS RECAPTURE THE PACIFIC ISLANDS   In 1943 the American forces, still small in number, began a campaign of "island hopping." They did not try to recapture every Pacific island held by the Japanese, but selected major bases and strategic sites along the enemy supply line. (See Map 29–6.) Starting from the Solomon Islands, they moved northeast toward Japan itself. By June 1944, they had reached the Mariana Islands, usable as bases for bombing the Japanese in the Philippines, China, and Japan itself.

In October of the same year, the Americans recaptured most of the Philippines and drove the Japanese fleet back into its home waters. In 1945 Iwo Jima and Okinawa fell, despite a determined Japanese

MAP 29–6   WORLD WAR II IN THE PACIFIC   *As in Europe, the Pacific war involved Allied recapture of areas that had been quickly taken earlier by the enemy. The enormous area represented by the map shows the initial expansion of Japanese holdings to cover half the Pacific and its islands, as well as huge sections of eastern Asia, and the long struggle to push the Japanese back to their homeland and defeat them by the summer of 1945.*

The ruins of Hiroshima after the explosion of the atom bomb.
Hulton Getty/Archive Photos

resistance that included kamikaze attacks, suicide missions in which specially trained pilots deliberately flew their explosive-filled planes into American warships. From these new bases, closer to Japan, the American bombers launched a terrible wave of bombings that destroyed Japanese industry and disabled the Japanese navy. Still the Japanese government, dominated by a military clique, refused to surrender.

Confronted with Japan's determination, the Americans made plans for a frontal assault on the Japanese homeland. They calculated that it might cost a million American casualties and even greater losses for the Japanese. At this point, science and technology presented the Americans with another choice.

THE ATOMIC BOMB   Since early in the war, a secret program had been in progress. Its staff, made up in significant part of exiles from Hitler's Europe, was working to use atomic energy for military purposes. On August 6, 1945, an American plane dropped an atomic bomb on the Japanese city of Hiroshima. The city was destroyed, and more than 70,000 of its 200,000 residents were killed. Two days later, the Soviet Union declared war on Japan and invaded Manchuria. The next day, a second atomic bomb fell, this time on Nagasaki. Even then, the Japanese cabinet was prepared to resist further, to face an invasion rather than give up.

The unprecedented intervention of Emperor Hirohito (r. 1926–1989) finally forced the government to surrender on August 14. Even then, the Japanese set forth the condition that Japan must keep its emperor. Although the Allies had continued to insist on unconditional surrender, President Harry S Truman (1884–1972), who had come to office on April 12,

1945, on the death of Franklin D. Roosevelt, accepted the condition. Peace was formally signed aboard the USS *Missouri* in Tokyo Bay on September 2, 1945.

Revulsion and horror at the use of atomic bombs, as well as hindsight arising from the Cold War, have made the decision to use the bomb against Japanese cities controversial. Some have suggested that the bombings were unnecessary to win the war and that their main purpose was to frighten the Russians into a more cooperative attitude after the war. Others have emphasized the bureaucratic, almost automatic nature of the decision, once it had been decided to develop the bomb. To the decision makers and their contemporaries, however, matters were simpler. The bomb was a way to end the war swiftly and save American lives. The decision to use it was conscious, not automatic, and required no ulterior motive.

The Cost of War

World War II was the most terrible war in history. Military deaths are estimated at some 15 million, and at least as many civilians were killed. If deaths linked indirectly to the war, from disease, hunger, and other causes, are included, the number of victims might reach as high as 40 million. Most of Europe and significant parts of Asia were devastated. Yet the end of so terrible a war brought little opportunity for relaxation. The dawn of the atomic age and the dramatic end it brought to the war made people conscious that another major war might extinguish humanity. Everything depended on concluding a stable peace, but even as the fighting ended, conflicts among the victors made the prospects of a lasting peace doubtful.

Major Campaigns and Events of World War II

September 1939	Germany and the Soviet Union invade Poland
November 1939	The Soviet Union invades Finland
April 1940	Germany invades Denmark and Norway
May 1940	Germany invades Belgium, the Netherlands, Luxembourg, and France
June 1940	Fall of France
August 1940	Battle of Britain begins
June 1941	Germany invades the Soviet Union
July 1941	Japan takes Indochina
December 1941	Japan attacks Pearl Harbor; United States enters war against Axis Powers
June 1942	Battle of Midway Island
November 1942	Battle of Stalingrad begins
July–August 1943	Allies take Sicily, land in Italy
June 1944	Allies land in Normandy
May 1945	Germany surrenders
August 1945	Atomic bombs dropped on Hiroshima and Nagasaki
September 1945	Japan formally surrenders

The Domestic Fronts

World War II represented an effort at total war by all the belligerents. Never in European or world history had so many men and women and so many resources been devoted to military effort. One result was the carnage that occurred on the battlefields, at sea, and in the air. Another was an unprecedented organization of civilians on the various home fronts. Each domestic effort and experience was different, but few escaped the impact of the conflict. Everywhere there were shortages, propaganda campaigns, and new political developments.

Germany: From Apparent Victory to Defeat

Hitler had expected to defeat all his enemies by a series of rapid strokes, or *Blitzkriegs*. Such campaigns would have required little change in Germany's society and economy. During the first two years of the war, in fact, Hitler demanded few important sacrifices from the German people. Spending on domestic projects continued, and food was plentiful; the economy as a whole was not on a full wartime footing. Germany's failure to quickly overwhelm the Soviet Union changed everything. Food could no longer be imported from the east in needed quantities, Germany had to mobilize for total war, and the government demanded major sacrifices from the people.

A great expansion of the army and of military production began in 1942. As minister for armaments and munitions, Albert Speer (1905–1981) directed the economy, and Germany met its military needs instead of making consumer goods. The government sought the cooperation of major German business enterprises to aid the growth of wartime production. Between 1942 and late 1944, the output of military products tripled; as the war went on, more men were drafted from industry into the army, and military production suffered.

As the manufacture of armaments replaced the production of consumer goods, shortages of everyday products became serious. Prices and wages were controlled, but the standard of living of German workers fell. Burdensome food rationing began in April 1942, and shortages were severe until the Nazi government seized more food from the occupied regions of Europe. To preserve their own home front, the Nazis passed on the suffering to their defeated neighbors.

By 1943, there were also serious labor shortages. The Nazis required German teenagers and retired men to work in the factories, and increasing numbers of women joined them. To achieve total mobilization, the Germans closed retail businesses, raised the age of eligibility of women for compulsory service, shifted non-German domestic workers to wartime industry, moved artists and entertainers into military service, closed theaters, and reduced such basic public services as mail and railways. Finally, the Nazis compelled thousands of people from conquered lands to do forced labor in Germany.

Hitler assigned women a special place in the war effort. The celebration of motherhood continued, with an emphasis on women who were the mothers of important military figures. Films portrayed ordinary women who became especially brave and patriotic during the war and remained faithful to their husbands who were at the front. Women were thereby shown as mothers and wives who sent their sons and husbands off to war. The government pictured other wartime activities of women as the natural fulfillment of their maternal roles. As air-raid wardens, they protected their families; as factory workers in munitions plants, they aided their sons on the front lines. Women working on farms were providing for their soldier sons and husbands; as housewives, they were helping to win the war by conserving food and managing their households frugally. Finally, by their

The Allied campaign of aerial bombardment did terrible damage to German cities. This photograph shows the devastation it delivered to the city of Cologne on the Rhine. UPI/Corbis

faithful chastity, German women were protecting racial purity. They were not to marry or to engage in sexual relations with men who were not German.

The war years also saw an intensification of political propaganda on the domestic front beyond what occurred in other countries. Hitler and other Germans genuinely believed that weak domestic support had led to Germany's defeat in World War I; they were determined that this situation would not happen again. Nazi propaganda blamed the outbreak of the war on the British and the Jews and its prolongation on the policies of Germany's opponents. It also stressed the power of Germany and the inferiority of its foes.

Propaganda Minister Josef Goebbels (1897–1945) used both radio and films to boost the Nazi cause. Movies of the collapse of Poland, Belgium, Holland, and France were shown in Germany to demonstrate German military might. Throughout the conquered territories, the Nazis used the same mass media to frighten inhabitants about the possible consequences of an Allied victory. Later in the war, the ministry broadcast exaggerated claims of Nazi victories. As the German armies were checked on the battlefield, especially in Russia, propaganda became

a substitute for victory. To stiffen German resolve, propaganda now aimed to frighten Germans about the consequences of defeat.

After May 1943, when the Allies began their major bombing offensive over Germany, the German people had much to fear. One German city after another was devastated, but German morale was not undermined. The bombing may even have increased German resistance by seeming to confirm the regime's propaganda about the ruthlessness of Germany's opponents.

World War II increased the power of the Nazi Party in Germany. Every area of the economy and society came under the direct influence or control of the party. The Nazis were determined that they, rather than the traditionally honored German officer corps, would profit from the new authority that the war effort was giving to the central government. Throughout the war years, there was virtually no serious opposition to Hitler or his ministers. In 1944, a small group of army officers attempted to assassinate Hitler; the effort failed, and there were few indications of significant popular support for this act.

The war brought great changes to Germany, but what transformed the country most was the experience of vast physical destruction, invasion, and occupation. Hitler and the Nazis had brought Germany to such a complete and disastrous defeat, that only a new kind of state with new political structures could emerge.

France: Defeat, Collaboration, and Resistance

The terms of the 1940 armistice between France, under Pétain, and Germany, signed June 22, allowed the Germans to occupy more than half of France, including the Atlantic and English Channel coasts. To prevent the French from continuing the fight from North Africa, and even more to prevent them from turning their fleet over to Britain, Hitler left southern France unoccupied until November 1942. Marshal Pétain set up a dictatorial regime at the resort city of Vichy and followed a policy of close collaboration with the Germans in hopes of preserving as much autonomy as possible.

Some of the collaborators believed that the Germans were sure to win the war and wanted to be on the victorious side. A few sympathized with the ideas and plans of the Nazis. Many conservatives regarded the French defeat as a judgment on what they saw as the corrupt, secularized, liberal ways of the Third Republic. Most of the French were not active collaborators, but were helpless and demoralized by defeat and the evidence of German power.

Many conservatives and extreme rightists saw in the Vichy government a way to reshape the French national character and to halt the decadence they associated with political and religious liberalism. The Roman Catholic clergy, which had lost power and influence under the Third Republic, gained status under Vichy. The church supported Pétain, and his government restored religious instruction in the state schools and increased financial support for Catholic schools. Vichy adopted the church's views on the importance of family and spiritual values. The government forbade divorce during the first three years of marriage and made subsequent divorce difficult; large families were encouraged and subsidized.

The Vichy regime also encouraged an intense, chauvinistic nationalism. It exploited the long-standing prejudice against foreigners working in France and fostered resentment even against French men and women who were not regarded as genuinely "French." The chief victims were French Jews. Anti-Semitism was not new in France, as the Dreyfus affair had demonstrated. Even before Germany undertook Hitler's "final solution" in 1942, the French had begun to remove Jews from positions of influence in government, education, and publishing. In 1941, the Germans began to intern Jews living in occupied France; soon they carried out assassinations and imposed large fines collectively on the Jews of the occupied zone. In the spring of 1942, they began to deport Jews from France—ultimately more than 60,000—to the extermination camps of eastern Europe. The Vichy government had no part in these decisions, but it made no protest, and its own anti-Semitic policies made the whole process easier to carry out.

A few French, most notably General Charles de Gaulle (1890–1969), fled to Britain after the defeat of France. There they organized the French National Committee of Liberation, or "Free French." Until the end of 1942, the Vichy government controlled French North Africa and the navy, but the Free French began operating in central Africa. From London, they broadcast hope and defiance to their compatriots in France.

Serious internal resistance to the German occupiers and the Vichy government, however, began to develop only late in 1942. The Germans tried to force young people in occupied France to work in German factories; some of them joined the Resistance, but the number of all the resisters was small. Many were deterred by fear of harsh punishment by the Germans. Some disliked the violence inevitably connected with resistance to a powerful ruthless nation. So long as it appeared that the Germans would win the war, moreover, resistance seemed imprudent and futile. For these reasons, the organized Resistance never attracted vast numbers of followers; well under five percent of the adult French population appears to have been involved.

By early 1944, the tide of battle had shifted. The Allies seemed sure to win, and the Vichy government would clearly not survive; only then did a large-scale active movement of resistance assert itself. General de Gaulle spoke confidently for Free France from his base in London and urged the French people to resist their conquerors and the German lackeys in the Vichy government. Within France, Resistance groups joined forces to plan for a better day. From Algiers on August 9, 1944, the Committee of National Liberation declared the authority of Vichy illegitimate. Soon French soldiers joined in the liberation of Paris and established a government for Free France. On October 21, 1945, France voted to end the Third Republic and adopted a new constitution as the basis of the Fourth Republic. The French people had experienced defeat, disgrace, deprivation, and suffering in the war. Hostility and bitter quarrels over who had done what during the occupation and under Vichy divided them for decades.

Great Britain: Organization for Victory

On May 22, 1940, the British Parliament gave the government emergency powers. Together with others already in effect, this measure allowed the government to institute compulsory military service, food rationing, and various controls over the economy.

To deal with the crisis facing them, all British political parties joined in a national government under Winston Churchill. Churchill and the British war cabinet moved as quickly as possible to mobilize the nation. Perhaps the most pressing immediate need was the production of airplanes to fight the Germans in the Battle of Britain. This effort was led by Lord Beaverbrook (1879–1964), one of Britain's most important newspaper publishers. The demand for more planes and other armaments inspired a massive campaign to reclaim scrap metal. Wrought-iron fences, kitchen pots and pans, and every conceivable kind of scrap metal were collected for the war effort. This was only one successful example of the many ways the civilian population was enthusiastically engaged in the struggle.

By the end of 1941, British production had already surpassed Germany's. To meet the heavy demands on the labor force, factory hours were extended, and many women were brought into the work force. Unemployment disappeared, and the working classes had more money to spend than they had enjoyed for many years. To avoid inflation caused by increased demand for an inadequate supply of consumer goods, savings were encouraged, and taxes were raised to absorb the excess purchasing power.

The "blitz" air attacks of the winter and spring of 1940–1941 were the most immediate and dramatic experience of the war for the British people themselves. The German air raids killed thousands of people and left many others homeless. Once the bombing began, many families removed their children to the countryside. Ironically, the rescue effort improved the standard of living of many of the chil-

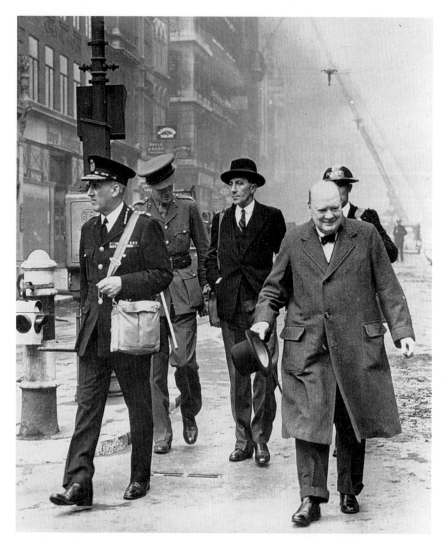

Winston Churchill walks through the rubble-strewn streets of London after the city had experienced a night of German bombing. Despite many casualties and widespread devastation, the German bombing of London did not break British morale or prevent the city from functioning. UPI/Corbis

The aerial bombardment of British cities, begun in earnest in the summer of 1940, continued throughout the war, causing destruction and loss of life, but failing to fulfill expectations that it would prove decisive in the war. This photograph, taken in May 1941, shows a postman on his rounds in the devastation of historic Watling Street.
HultonGetty/Archive Photos

dren, for the government paid for their food and medication. Gas masks were issued to thousands of city dwellers, who were frequently compelled to take shelter from the bombs in the London subways.

After the spring of 1941, Hitler needed most of his air force on the Russian front, but the bombing of Britain continued, killing more than 30,000 people by the end of the war. Terrible as it was, this toll was much smaller than the number of Germans killed by Allied bombing in the war. In England, as in Germany, however, the bombing, far from breaking the people's spirit, may well have made them more determined.

The British made many sacrifices. Transportation facilities were strained simply from carrying enough coal for domestic heating and for running factories. Food and clothing for civilians were scarce, and the government adopted strict rationing to achieve a fair distribution. Every scrap of land was farmed, increasing the productive portion by almost four million acres. Gasoline was scarce, and private vehicles almost vanished.

The British established their own propaganda machine to influence the Continent. The British Broadcasting Company (BBC) sent programs to every country in Europe in the local language, to encourage resistance against the Nazis. At home, the government used the radio to unify the nation. Soldiers at the front heard the same programs as their families at home. The most famous program, second only to Churchill's speeches, was *It's That Man Again*, a humorous broadcast filled with imaginary figures that the entire nation came to treasure.

Strangely, for the broad mass of the population, the standard of living improved during the war. The general health of the nation also improved, for reasons that are still not clear. These improvements should not be exaggerated, but they did occur, and many connected them with the active involvement of the government in the economy and in the lives of the citizens. This wartime experience may have contributed to the Labour Party's victory in 1945; many feared that a return to Conservative Party rule would also mean a return to the economic problems and unemployment of the 1930s.

The Soviet Union: "The Great Patriotic War"

The war against Germany came as a great surprise to Stalin and the Soviet Union. The German attack violated the 1939 pact with Hitler and put the government of the Soviet Union on the defensive militarily and politically. It showed the failure of Stalin's foreign policy and the ineptness of his preparation for war. He claimed that the pact had given the nation an extra year and a half to prepare for war, but this was clearly a lame and implausible excuse in light of the ease of Germany's early victories. Within days, German troops occupied much of the western Soviet Union. The communist government feared that Soviet citizens who had been conquered by the Germans—many of whom were not ethnic Russians—might welcome the conquerors as liberators; these Soviet citizens had been harshly oppressed by the Stalinist regime.

No nation suffered greater loss of life or more extensive physical destruction during World War II than the Soviet Union. Perhaps as many as 16 million people were killed, and vast numbers of Soviet troops were taken prisoner. Hundreds of cities and towns and well over half of the industrial and transportation facilities of the country were devastated. From 1942, thousands of Soviet prisoners worked in German factories as forced labor. The Germans also served their own war effort with grain, mineral resources, and oil confiscated from the Soviet Union.

Stalin conducted the war as virtual chief of the armed forces, and the State Committee for Defense provided strong central coordination. In the decade before the war, Stalin had already made the Soviet Union a highly centralized state; he had tried to manage the entire economy from Moscow through the five-year plans, the collectivization of agriculture, and the purges. The country was thus already on what amounted to a wartime footing long before the conflict erupted. When the war began, millions of citizens entered the army, but the army itself did not grow in influence at the expense of the state and the Communist Party— that is, of Stalin. He was suspicious of the generals, though he had presumably eliminated officers of doubtful loyalty in the purges of the late 1930s. As the war continued, however, the army gained some degree of independence, and eventually the generals were no longer subservient to party commissars. The army thus gained some freedom of action. It was, however, still sharply limited by the power of Stalin and by the nature of Soviet government and society.

Soviet propaganda was different from that of other nations. Because the Soviet government distrusted the loyalty of its citizens, it confiscated radios to prevent the people from listening to German or British propaganda. In cities, the government broadcast to the people over loudspeakers in place of radios. During the war, Soviet propaganda emphasized Russian patriotism rather than traditional Marxist themes that stressed class conflict. The struggle against the Germans was called "The Great Patriotic War."

Great Russian novels of the past were republished; more than half a million copies of Tolstoy's *War and Peace* were printed during the siege of Leningrad (Saint Petersburg). Other authors wrote straightforward propaganda fostering hatred of the Germans. Serge Eisenstein (1898–1948), the great filmmaker, produced a vast epic entitled *Ivan the Terrible*, which glorified this brutal tsar of the Russian past. Composers, such as Dimitri Shostakovich (1906–1975), produced scores that sought to contribute to the struggle and evoke heroic emotions. The most important of these was Shostakovich's *Seventh Symphony*, also known as the *Leningrad Symphony*.

The pressure of war led Stalin to make peace with the Russian Orthodox Church, allowing church leaders to enter the Kremlin. Stalin hoped that this new policy would give him more support at home and permit the Soviet Union to be viewed more favorably in eastern Europe, where the Orthodox Church predominated.

Within occupied portions of the western Soviet Union, an active resistance movement arose against the Germans. The swiftness of the German invasion had stranded thousands of Soviet troops behind German lines. Many were shipped to Germany as prisoners of war, but others escaped and carried on guerrilla resistance warfare behind enemy lines. Stalin supported partisan forces in lands held by the enemy for two reasons: He wanted to cause as much difficulty as possible for the Germans, and Soviet-sponsored resistance reminded the peasants in the conquered regions that the Soviet government, with its policies of collectivization, had not disappeared. Stalin feared that the peasants' hatred of the communist government might lead them to collaborate with the invaders. When the Soviet army moved westward toward the end of the war, it incorporated the partisans into the regular army.

As its armies reclaimed the occupied areas and then moved across eastern and central Europe, the Soviet Union established itself as a world power second only to the United States. Stalin had entered the war a reluctant belligerent, but he emerged a major victor. In that respect, the war and the extraordinary patriotic effort and sacrifice it generated consolidated the power of Stalin and the party more effectively than the political and social policies of the previous decade.

Preparations for Peace

The split between the Soviet Union and its wartime allies should cause no surprise. As the self-proclaimed center of world communism, the Soviet Union was openly dedicated to the overthrow of the capitalist nations. This message, however, was muted when the occasion demanded. On the other side, the Western allies were no less open about their hostility to communism and its chief purveyor, the Soviet Union. Although they had been friendly to the early stages of the 1917 Russian Revolution, they had intervened to try to overthrow the Bolshevik regime during the civil war resulting from the Revolution. The United States did not grant formal recognition to the USSR until 1933. The Western powers' exclusion of the Soviets from the Munich conference and Stalin's pact with Hitler did nothing to improve relations between them during the war.

Nonetheless, the need to cooperate against a common enemy and strenuous propaganda efforts helped improve Western feeling toward the Soviet ally. Still, Stalin remained suspicious and critical of the Western war effort, and Churchill was determined to contain the Soviet advance into Europe. Roosevelt perhaps had been more hopeful that the Allies could continue to work together after the war, but even he was losing faith by 1945. Differences in historical development and ideology, as well as traditional conflicts over political power and influence, soon dashed hopes of a mutually satisfactory peace settlement and continued cooperation to uphold it.

The Atlantic Charter

In August 1941, even before the Americans were at war, Roosevelt and Churchill had met on a ship off Newfoundland and agreed to the Atlantic Charter. This broad set of principles in the spirit of Wilson's Fourteen Points provided a theoretical basis for the peace they sought. When Russia and the United States joined Britain in the war, the three powers entered a purely military alliance in January 1942, leaving all political questions aside. The first political conference was the meeting of foreign ministers in Moscow in October 1943. The ministers reaffirmed earlier agreements to fight on until the enemy surrendered unconditionally and to continue cooperating after the war in a united-nations organization.

Tehran: Agreement on a Second Front

The first meeting of the leaders of the "Big Three" (as the USSR, Britain, and the United States were known) took place at Tehran, the capital of Iran, in 1943. Western promises to open a second front in France the next summer (1944) and Stalin's agreement to join in the war against Japan when Germany was defeated created an atmosphere of goodwill in which to discuss a postwar settlement. Stalin wanted to retain what he had gained in his pact with Hitler and to dismember Germany. Roosevelt and Churchill were conciliatory, but they made no firm commitments.

The most important decision was the one that chose Europe's west coast as the main point of attack instead of the Mediterranean. That meant, in retrospect, that Soviet forces would occupy eastern Europe and control its destiny. At Tehran in 1943, the Western allies did not foresee this clearly, for the Russians were still fighting deep within their own frontiers, and military considerations were still paramount.

CHURCHILL AND STALIN By 1944, the situation was different. In August, Soviet armies were before Warsaw, which had revolted against the Germans in expectation of liberation. But the Russians halted, allowing the Polish rebels to be annihilated while they [the Russians] turned south into the Balkans. They gained control of Romania and Hungary, advances that centuries of expansionist tsars had only dreamed of achieving. Alarmed by these developments, Churchill went to Moscow and met with Stalin in October. They agreed to share power in the Balkans on the basis of Soviet predominance in Romania and Bulgaria, Western predominance in Greece, and equality of influence in Yugoslavia and Hungary. These agreements were not enforceable without American approval, and the Americans were known to be hostile to such un-Wilsonian devices as "spheres of influence."

GERMANY The three powers easily agreed on Germany—its disarmament, denazification, and division into four zones of occupation by France and the Big Three. Churchill, however, began to balk at Stalin's demand for $20 billion in reparations as well as forced labor from all the zones, with Russia to get half of everything. These matters were left to fester and cause dissension in the future.

EASTERN EUROPE The settlement of eastern Europe was an equally thorny problem. Everyone agreed that the Soviet Union deserved to have friendly neighboring governments, but the West insisted that they also be autonomous and democratic. The Western leaders, particularly Churchill, were not eager to see eastern Europe fall under Russian domination. They were also, especially Roosevelt, committed to democracy and self-determination.

Stalin, however, knew that independent, freely elected governments in Poland and Romania could not be counted on to be friendly to Russia. He had already established a puppet government in Poland in competition with the Polish government-in-exile in London. Under pressure from the Western leaders, however, he agreed to reorganize this government and include some Poles friendly to the West in it. He also signed a Declaration on Liberated Europe, promising self-determination and free democratic elections.

Stalin may have been eager to avoid conflict before the war with Germany was over. He was always afraid that the Allies would make a separate peace with Germany and betray him. And he probably thought it worth endorsing some hollow principles as the price of continued harmony. In any case, he wasted little time violating these agreements.

Yalta

The next meeting of the Big Three was at Yalta in the Crimea in February 1945. The Western armies had not yet crossed the Rhine, but the Soviet army was within a hundred miles of Berlin. (See Map 29–7.) The war with Japan continued, and no atomic explosion had yet taken place. Roosevelt, faced with a prospective invasion of Japan and heavy losses, was eager to

Negotiations Among the Allies	
August 1941	Churchill and Roosevelt meet off Newfoundland to sign Atlantic Charter
October 1943	American, British, and Soviet foreign ministers meet in Moscow
November 1943	Churchill, Roosevelt, and Stalin meet at Tehran
October 1944	Churchill meets with Stalin in Moscow
February 1945	Churchill, Roosevelt, and Stalin meet at Yalta
July 1945	Attlee, Stalin, and Truman meet at Potsdam

bring the Russians into the Pacific war as soon as possible. As a true Wilsonian, he also suspected Churchill's determination to maintain the British Empire and Britain's colonial advantages. The Americans thought that Churchill's plan to set up British spheres of influence in Europe would encourage the Russians to do the same and would lead to friction and war. To encourage Russian participation in the war against Japan, Roosevelt and Churchill made extensive concessions to Russia, ceding the Soviets Sakhalin and the Kurile Islands, and accommodating some of their desires in Korea and in Manchuria.

Again in the tradition of Wilson, Roosevelt laid great stress on a united-nations organization: "Through the United Nations, he hoped to achieve a self-enforcing peace settlement that would not require American troops, as well as an open world without spheres of influence in which American enterprise could work freely."[7] Soviet agreement on these points seemed well worth concessions elsewhere.

Potsdam

The Big Three met for the last time in the Berlin suburb of Potsdam in July 1945. Much had changed since the previous conference. Germany had been defeated, and news of the successful experimental explosion of an atomic weapon reached the American president during the meetings. The cast of characters was also different: President Truman replaced the deceased Roosevelt, and Clement Attlee (1883–1967), leader of the Labour Party that had defeated Churchill's Conservatives in a general election, replaced Churchill as

MAP 29–7   YALTA TO THE SURRENDER   *"The Big Three"—Roosevelt, Churchill, Stalin—met at Yalta in the Crimea in February of 1945. At the meeting, concessions were made to Stalin concerning the settlement of Eastern Europe because Roosevelt was eager to bring the Russians into the Pacific war as soon as possible. This map shows the positions held by the victors when Germany surrendered.*

[7]Robert O. Paxton, *Europe in the Twentieth Century* (New York: Harcourt Brace Jovanovich, 1975), p. 487.

This photograph shows the leaders of the Big Three at Potsdam. By the summer of 1945, only Stalin (right) remained of the original leaders of the major Allies. Roosevelt and Churchill had been replaced by Harry Truman (center) and Clement Atlee. Corbis

Britain's spokesperson during the conference. Previous agreements were reaffirmed, but progress on undecided questions was slow.

Russia's western frontier was moved far into what had been Poland and included most of German East Prussia. In compensation, Poland was allowed "temporary administration" over the rest of East Prussia and Germany east of the Oder–Neisse river, a condition that became permanent. In effect, Poland was moved about a hundred miles west, at the expense of Germany, to accommodate the Soviet Union. The Allies agreed that Germany would be divided into occupation zones until the final peace treaty was signed. Germany remained divided until 1990.

A Council of Foreign Ministers was established to draft peace treaties for Germany's allies. Growing disagreements made the job difficult, and Italy, Romania, Hungary, Bulgaria, and Finland did not sign treaties until February 1947. The Russians were dissatisfied with the treaty that the United States made with Japan in 1951 and signed their own agreements with the Japanese in 1956. These disagreements were foreshadowed at Potsdam.

In Perspective

The second great war of the twentieth century (1939–1945) grew out of the unsatisfactory resolution of the first. In retrospect, the two wars appear to some people to be one continuous conflict, a kind of twentieth-century "Thirty Years' War," with the two main periods of fighting separated by an uneasy truce. To others, that point of view oversimplifies and distorts the situation by implying that the second war was the inevitable result of the first and its inadequate peace treaties. The latter opinion seems more sound, for, whatever the flaws of the treaties of Paris, the world suffered an even more terrible war than the first because of failures of judgment and will on the part of the victorious democratic powers.

Between the two wars, the United States, which had become the wealthiest and potentially the strongest nation in the world, disarmed almost entirely and withdrew into a shortsighted and foolish isolation. Therefore, it could play no important part in restraining the angry and ambitious dictators who brought on the war. Britain and France refused to face the threat posed by the Axis powers until the most deadly war in history was required to put it down. If the victorious democracies had remained strong, responsible, and realistic, they could easily have remedied whatever injustices or mistakes arose from the treaties without endangering the peace.

The second war itself was so plainly a world war that little need be said to indicate its global character. There is good reason to think that if the Japanese occupation of Manchuria in 1931 was not technically a part of that war, it was a significant precursor. Moreover, there were Italy's attack on the African nation of Ethiopia in 1935, the Italian, German, and Soviet interventions in the Spanish Civil War (1936–1939), and Japan's attack on China in 1937. These acts revealed that aggressive forces were on the march around the globe and that the defenders of the world order lacked the will to stop them. The formation of the Axis incorporating Germany, Italy, and Japan guaranteed that when the war came, it would be fought around the world.

There was fighting and suffering in Asia, Africa, the Pacific islands, and Europe; and men and women from all the inhabited continents took part in it. The use of atomic weapons brought the frightful struggle to a close. Still, what are called conventional weapons did almost all the damage; their level of destructiveness threatened the survival of civilization, even without the use of atomic or nuclear devices.

The Second World War ended not with unsatisfactory peace treaties, but with no treaty at all in the European arena, where the war had begun. The world quickly split into two unfriendly camps: the western, led by the United States, and the eastern, led by the Soviet Union. This division, among other things, hastened the liberation of former colonial territories. The bargaining power of the new nations that emerged from them was temporarily increased as the two rival superpowers tried to gain their friendship or allegiance. It has become customary to refer to these nations as "the Third World," with the former Soviet Union and the United States and their respective allies being the first two. The passage of time has shown that the differences among Third World nations are so great as to make the term all but meaningless.

The surprising treatment received by the defeated powers of the second war was also largely the result of the emergence of the Cold War. Instead of holding them back, the Western powers installed democratic governments in Italy, West Germany, and Japan, took them into the Western alliances designed to contain communism, and helped them recover economically. Japan and Germany are now among the richest nations in the world, and Italy is more prosperous than it has ever been.

By the last decade of the twentieth century, Japan had become one of the greatest industrial, commercial, and financial powers in the world and a major investor in the American economy. Its manufacturers have offered stiff competition to their counterparts in the United States and Western Europe, provoking concern and calls for protective tariffs.

Germany, divided between East and West by the war, never ceased to hope for eventual unification. The startling events of 1989, in which the Soviet Union gave up its hold over Eastern Europe, made unification suddenly possible, and it occurred in 1990. One result of this unification has been to open again a question that lay behind the two great wars of the twentieth century: the place of a unified Germany in Europe.

REVIEW QUESTIONS

1. What were Hitler's foreign policy aims? Was he bent on conquest in the east and dominance in the west, or did he simply want to return Germany to its 1914 boundaries?

2. Why did Britain and France adopt a policy of appeasement in the 1930s? What were its main features? Did the appeasers buy the West valuable time to prepare for war by their actions at Munich in 1938?

3. How was Hitler able to defeat France so easily in 1940? Why was the air war against Britain a failure? Why did Hitler invade Russia? Why did the invasion ultimately fail? Could it have succeeded?

4. Why did Japan attack the United States at Pearl Harbor? What was the significance of American intervention in the war? Why did the United States drop atomic bombs on Japan? Did President Truman make the right decision when he ordered the bombs used?

5. What impact did World War II have on the civilian population of Europe? How did experiences on the domestic front in Great Britain differ from those in Germany and France? What impact did "the Great Patriotic War" have on the people of the Soviet Union? Did the Soviet Union's participation in World War II solidify Stalin's hold on power?

6. What was Hitler's "final solution" to the Jewish problem? Why did Hitler want to eliminate Slavs as well? Some historians have looked at the twentieth century and have seen a period of great destruction as well as of great progress. Was the twentieth century truly a "century of Holocaust"? Discuss the ramifications of these questions.

SUGGESTED READINGS

A. ADAMTHWAITE, *France and the Coming of the Second World War, 1936–1939* (1977). A careful account making good use of the French archives.

J. ADLER, *The Jews of Paris and the Final Solution: Communal Response and Internal Conflicts, 1940–1944* (1987). Written by a former member of the French Resistance.

E. R. BECK, *Under the Bombs: The German Home Front, 1942–1945* (1986). An interesting examination of a generally unstudied subject.

A. BULLOCK, *Hitler: A Study in Tyranny*, rev. ed. (1964). A brilliant biography.

W. S. CHURCHILL, *The Second World War*, 6 vols. (1948–1954). The memoirs of the great British leader.

J. L. GADDIS, *We Now Know: Rethinking Cold War History* (1998). A fine account of the early years of the Cold War, making use of new evidence emerging since the collapse of the Soviet Union.

J. L. GADDIS, P. H. GORDON, AND E. MAY, eds., *Cold War Statesmen Confront the Bomb: Nuclear Diplomacy Since 1945* (1999). A collection of essays discussing the effect of atomic and nuclear weapons on diplomacy since World War II.

H. W. GATZKE, *Stresemann and the Rearmament of Germany* (1954). An important monograph.

M. GILBERT AND R. GOTT, *The Appeasers*, rev. ed. (1963). A revealing study of British policy in the 1930s.

M. GILBERT, *The Holocaust: A History of the Jews of Europe During the Second World War* (1985). The best and most comprehensive treatment.

M. HARRISON, *Soviet Planning in Peace and War, 1938–1945* (1985). An examination of the Soviet wartime economy.

A. IRIYE, *Pearl Harbor and the Coming of the Pacific War* (1999). Essays on how the Pacific war came about, including a selection of documents.

J. KEEGAN, *The Second World War* (1990). A lively and penetrating account by a master military historian.

M. KNOX, *Mussolini Unleashed* (1982). An outstanding study of Fascist Italy's policy and strategy in World War II.

W. L. LANGER AND S. E. GLEASON, *The Challenge of Isolation* (1952). American foreign policy in the 1930s.

S. MARKS, *The Illusion of Peace* (1976). A good discussion of European international relations in the 1920s and early 1930s.

V. MASTNY, *Russia's Road to the Cold War* (1979). Written by an expert on the Soviet Union and Eastern Europe.

W. MURRAY, *The Change in the European Balance of Power, 1938–1939* (1984). A brilliant study of the relationships among strategy, foreign policy, economics, and domestic politics in the years before the war.

R. OVERY, *Why the Allies Won* (1997). An analysis of the reasons for the victory of the Allies with special emphasis on technology.

N. RICH, *Hitler's War Aims*, 2 vols. (1973–1974). The best study of the subject in English.

M. SHERWIN, *A World Destroyed: The Atomic Bomb and the Grand Alliance* (1975). An analysis of the role of the atomic bomb in the years surrounding the end of World War II.

R. J. SONTAG, *A Broken World, 1919–1939* (1971). An excellent survey.

A. J. P. TAYLOR, *The Origins of the Second World War* (1966). A lively, controversial, and even perverse study.

H. THOMAS, *The Spanish Civil War*, 3d ed. (1986). The best account in English.

P. WANDYCZ, *The Twilight of French Eastern Alliances, 1926–1936* (1988). A well-documented account of the diplomacy of central and eastern Europe in a crucial period.

G. L. WEINBERG, *A World at Arms: A Global History of World War II* (1994). A thorough and excellent narrative account.

G. WRIGHT, *The Ordeal of Total War, 1939–1945* (1968). An excellent survey.

Chapter 30

The forced migration of peoples as a result of war and other state violence was one of the chief social experiences of Europeans in the first half of the twentieth century. The Soviet collectivization of farms, the Nazi attempt to exterminate European Jews, and the change in borders after World War II caused the dislocation of millions of Europeans. Similar dislocation would occur in the former Yugoslavia at the end of the century. Here Jewish survivors of the Nazi-organized Lodz ghetto, located in Poland, make their way back into Germany in the months after World War II. © Hulton Getty/Liaison Agency

Faces of the Twentieth Century:
European Social Experiences

State Violence in Twentieth-Century Europe

Women in Early Twentieth-Century Authoritarian Regimes
Women and the Family in the Early Soviet Union
Motherhood for the Nation in Fascist Italy
Racial Ideology and the Lives of Women in Nazi Germany

The Social Experience of Stalinism
The Social Experience of Collectivization
The Attack on Religion
Life on the Collective Farm
Flight to the Soviet Cities
Urban Consumer Shortages

The Destruction of the Polish Jewish Community
Polish Jews at the End of World War I
Polish Jewry between the Wars
Polish Anti-Semitism
Political Alternatives for Polish Jews
The Nazi Assault on the Jews of Poland

The Twentieth-Century Movement of Peoples
Displacement through War
External Migration
Economic Growth and Internal Migration

The Welfare State

New Patterns in the Work and Expectations of Women
Feminism
Modern European Household Structure
More Married Women in the Work Force
New Work Patterns
Women in the New Eastern Europe

Transformations in Knowledge and Culture
Communism and Western Europe
Existentialism
Expansion of the University Population and Student Rebellion
The Americanization of Europe
Rock Music and Political Protest
A Consumer Society
Environmentalism

The Christian Heritage
Neo-Orthodoxy
Liberal Theology
Roman Catholic Reform

Late Twentieth-Century Technology: The Arrival of the Computer
The Demand for Calculating Machines
Early Computer Technology
The Development of Desktop Computers
The Social Impact of the Computer

KEY TOPICS

- Social impact of state violence on women, Russian peasants, and Polish Jews
- Migration in twentieth-century Europe
- Changing status and role of women in Europe
- New cultural forces and continuing influence of Christianity
- The impact of computer technology

*T*he Second World War was an event that politically divided the twentieth century, closing the era of European world domination and opening the era of the Cold War conflict between the United States and the Soviet Union which ended with the collapse of Communism. The war, however, did not constitute a major divide in European social history. Rather it was an event of enormous destruction during a century that witnessed the unleashing of destructive military and political forces that shaped and reshaped much of the social experience of Europe. In this chapter, we will examine the social experience of twentieth-century Europe, before and after World War II.

Historians have tended to regard social history as primarily the study of private life lived largely outside the concerns of politics and the state. Indeed, social historians many years ago, though less so today, often defined their work as standing more or less in opposition to political, diplomatic, and military history. When, however, one turns to the social history of Europe in the twentieth century that distinction is difficult, if not impossible, to maintain. To separate the private lives of the mass of twentieth-century Europeans from the political and military events of the era would falsify any account of their personal lives as they lived them. Consequently, in this chapter, the intermeshing of social and political history will feature more prominently than it has in our previous considerations of social experience.

State Violence in Twentieth-Century Europe

Governments certainly touched the private lives of Europeans well before the twentieth century, but they did so in relatively modest and often quite inefficient ways. Two major factors changed that situation in the twentieth century. First, the militarization of Europe that began before the First World War and persisted through the Cold War turned Europe into an armed camp for the entire century. This bellicose climate increased the power of governments and the resources they could claim through taxation and borrowing for military preparedness. The mobilization of whole nations for war—a mobilization more complete and extensive because of the technologies that were available—disrupted and changed the social role of large groups of Europeans, especially women. The wars of the twentieth century killed tens of millions of Europeans prematurely. Those deaths in turn affected many more millions of survivors and their social expectations. The fear from early in the century until the collapse of the Soviet Union that

world war might break out at any time meant that defense spending in both large and small nations diverted enormous resources from nondefense purposes. This diversion of resources imposed limits on what Europeans could hope to achieve in their private lives.

Second, the various and sharply differing political ideologies of communist, fascist, national socialist, democratic socialist, and democratic welfare states assumed that, to some extent, the central state should pursue social and economic policies that directly shaped the lives and social expectations of individual citizens and their families. The political outlooks associated with democratic socialism and welfare legislation were essentially reformist in their appeal to state intervention. They generally saw the state as providing the kinds of remedial aid that would supplement the free functioning of the marketplace, employers, charitable agencies, and the family. Many of the proponents of such remedial policies favored them to prevent more radically expansive social agendas from being implemented.

But far more important for European social history during the twentieth century were the visions associated with communism, fascism, and national socialism, which called for total social transformations. Fulfilling the goals of these "isms" involved moving whole groups of people or attempting to eradicate those whom the state defined as racially different or genetically deficient.

Behind war and ideology stood the ever-expanding technological revolutions of the twentieth century. On the one hand, these placed greater mechanical and industrial power in the hands of political leaders, who now possessed the technological capacity for massive transformations and destruction. On the other hand, the new technologies, with their capacity for improving health, expanding industrial production, providing better food, and generating more rapid transportation and communication, made the vision of a radically transformed society seem genuinely possible for the first time, often within a single generation.

During the first half of the twentieth century the groups whose personal and social lives were most dramatically reshaped as a result of the radical transformations imposed by authoritarian governments were women, Soviet peasants, and central and Eastern European Jews. Each of their stories might stand as an independent section of the history of the dictatorships or of the events of World War II, but that approach would separate them from their place in the larger fabric of European social experience determined by the forces of state violence.

Women in Early Twentieth-Century Authoritarian Regimes

In the first two decades of the twentieth century, the lives of European women expanded considerably. As noted in Chapter 24, in many parts of Europe, universities and the professions had opened to women of the upper classes. Elsewhere in the social structure, the growth of office work and public school systems created new economic opportunities for women. World War I marked a major moment of significant, if not always permanent, transformation, as thousands of women entered the workforce to replace the men who were fighting the war. Many women could now imagine social roles for themselves in addition to those of wives and mothers. The war also saw greater sexual freedom and experimentation. After the war, women also entered more fully into the political life of Europe. Yet in the face of these advances, despite enormous differences in their ideologies, the policies of the authoritarian governments of the Soviet Union, Italy, and Germany placed new constraints on women's lives even while giving them some paternalistic protections. In each nation, various political rhetorics described new roles for women, but each of those rhetorics collided with the realities of the economy, politics, and everyday life.

Women and the Family in the Early Soviet Union

Nowhere did the rhetoric and reality surrounding women's issues involve so many contradictions as in the Soviet Union, where the Communist Party declared itself to be building a new civilization and actually to be creating new kinds of human beings—the "Soviet Man" and the "Soviet Woman."

EARLY SOVIET UTOPIANISM REGARDING WOMEN AND THE FAMILY Communist views toward women and the family assumed that the traditional family embodied middle-class capitalist values that were at odds with what was socially good and with the liberty of the proletariat. In the early years of the Russian Revolution, this outlook led to utopian projections of what the life of women and the family would resemble under socialism. The most famous such utopian writer was Alexandra Kollontai (1872–1952). In *Communism and the Family* (1918) and other works, she envisioned a new kind of family that she thought would liberate both women and men. (See "Alexandra Kollontai Demands a New Family Life.") Her views included both the expansion of sexual freedom and the radical shar-

ing of tasks about the home between wives and husbands. She wanted to replace what she regarded as egoistic, exploitative family relationships with families based on love and comradeship. Few people in the Soviet Union, even among the communists, agreed with Kollontai, but her views became well known and were often assumed to reflect those of a wide spectrum of the Soviet leadership and citizenry. At a time when the Soviet Union was isolated from the rest of the world, people on the outside could imagine that Kollontai's visions were the reality of the bold new life being forged there. Both fascists and Nazis contrasted their own traditionalist views of women with these radical views.

FAMILY LEGISLATION FROM REFORM TO REPRESSION Soon after achieving power in late 1917, the Bolsheviks began to issue laws pertaining to women. Divorce became far easier, marriage was no longer a religious ceremony, and both legitimate and illegitimate children came to have the same rights. Various protections were extended to women in the workplace and within marriage. Abortion was legalized in late 1920. All of these measures were enacted to create a socialist society. Women obtained high positions in the Communist Party, and voting among women rose steadily, but in fact, women did not have any significant impact on Soviet government.

The dislocations flowing from the civil war, the confiscation of property, shifting economic policies, and the general reordering of Soviet society during the 1920s seriously disrupted Soviet family life. Domestic violence appears to have been common. The birthrate fell, while the number of both abortions and abandoned children rose. The new divorce law made it easy for husbands to abandon their wives, while a housing shortage made it difficult for divorced couples to live separately.

During the 1930s the general political repression associated with both the collectivization of farming and the purges within the Communist Party led to a general tightening of policies regarding women, the family, and sexuality. Women in *kulak* families were condemned as class enemies, their property was seized, and they were deported along with their husbands. In 1937, except for medical reasons, abortion became illegal, and divorce procedures became more difficult about the same time. Once the purges began, women could be condemned, exiled, or impoverished simply for being married or related to an "enemy of the people." During World War II, legislation ended the validity of common-law marriage and made divorce virtually impossible. Only in the later 1950s, after the death of Stalin in 1953, was this legislation relaxed.

Alexandra Kollontai Demands a New Family Life

While Lenin sought to consolidate the Bolshevik revolution against internal and external enemies, there existed within the young Soviet Union a vast utopian impulse to change and reform virtually every social institution that had existed before the revolution or that was associated in the communists' minds with capitalist society. Alexandra Kollontai (1872–1952) was a spokesperson of the extreme political left within the early Soviet Union. In communist circles, there had been much speculation on how the end of bourgeois society might change the structure of the family and the position of women. In the passage that follows, written in 1920, Kollontai states one of the most radically idealistic visions of this change. During the years immediately after the revolution, rumors circulated in both Europe and America about sexual and family experimentation in the Soviet Union. Statements such as this one fostered such rumors. Kollontai herself later became a supporter of Stalin and a Soviet diplomat.

❖ *Why did Kollontai see the restructuring of the family as essential to the establishment of a new kind of communist society? Would these changes make people loyal to that society? What changes in society does the kind of economic independence she seeks for women presuppose? What might childhood be like if the state, rather than their parents, assumed responsibility for their children?*

There is no escaping the fact: the old type of family has seen its day. It is not the fault of the Communist State, it is the result of the changed conditions of life. The family is ceasing to be a necessity of the State, as it was in the past; on the contrary, it is worse than useless, since it needlessly holds back the female workers from more productive and far more serious work....But on the ruins of the former family we shall soon see a new form rising which will involve altogether different relations between men and women, and which will be a union of affection and comradeship, a union of two equal members of the Communist society, both of them free, both of them independent, both of them workers. No more domestic "servitude" of women. No more inequality within the family. No more fear on the part of the woman lest she remain without support or aid with little ones in her arms if her husband should desert her. The woman in the Communist city no longer depends on her husband but on her work. It is not her husband but her robust arms which will support her. There will be no more anxiety as to the fate of her children. The State of the Workers will assume responsibly for these. Marriage will be purified of all its material elements, of all money calculations, which constitute a hideous blemish on family life in our days....

The woman who is called upon to struggle in the great cause of the liberation of the workers—such a woman should know that in the new State there will be no more room for such petty divisions as were formerly understood: "These are my own children, to them I owe all my maternal solicitude, all my affection; those are your children, my neighbour's children; I am not concerned with them. I have enough to do with my own." Henceforth the worker–mother, who is conscious of her social function, will rise to a point where she no longer differentiates between yours and mine; she must remember that there are henceforth only our children, those of the Communist State, the common possession of all the workers.

The Worker's State has need of a new form of relation between the sexes. The narrow and exclusive affection of the mother for her own children must expand until it embraces all the children of the great proletarian family. In place of the indissoluble marriage based on the servitude of woman, we shall see rise the free union, fortified by the love and mutual respect of the two members of the Workers' State, equal in their rights and in their obligations. In place of the individual and egotistic family there will arise a great universal family of workers, in which all the workers, men and women, will be, above all, workers, comrades.

From Alexandra Kollontai, *Communism and the Family*, as reprinted in Rudolf Schlesinger, ed. and trans., *The Family in the USSR* (London: Routledge and Kegan Paul, 1949), pp. 67–69. Reprinted by permission of Taylor & Francis Books, Ltd.

In the 1920s and 1930s and after, women could advance through the party structures into leadership positions. They could also achieve leadership in the newly collectivized farms. Educational opportunities for women were readily available, yet women who worked, even in professional careers, were still expected to do the housework, and there was no significant structure of child care. Typically, women were paid less than men.

Sociological studies of the Soviet Union during the third quarter of the century indicated the presence of enormous stress in family life arising from women who found themselves laboring in jobs and then working the equivalent of another job as wives and mothers. Throughout the history of the Soviet Union, the culture of economic shortage of consumer goods affected women more than any other group. It was they who most often had to stand in the long lines, cope with an absence of goods, and somehow make their own lives and those of their families hang together.

During the upheavals of the collectivization of farming, starvation in the Soviet countryside was not uncommon. The Soviet government used famine against political enemies, and collective farms that failed to meet their quotas might see their own food rations reduced. Here, a woman and her son search for food.
Hulton Deutsch Collections/Corbis

Motherhood for the Nation in Fascist Italy

Fascist policy toward women has been called "a complex mix of paternalistic protectionism and benign neglect, positive incentives and mean constraints."[1] Its paternalism represented a rejection of late nineteenth and early twentieth-century liberalism that had left the situation of women, as that of other groups in the population, to be shaped largely by the force of the marketplace. The new policies combined Roman Catholic social traditionalism with goals of national expansion. The fascist rhetoric portraying man as the wage earner and woman as mother and homemaker reflected Catholic social policy, but dominating all fascist policy toward women was a desire to expand the size of the Italian population for national self-aggrandizement.

THE CULT OF MOTHERHOOD   Mussolini wanted Italian women to have more children and to remain in the home to rear them for the good of the Italian state. To that end, the government instituted policies such as maternity leaves, insurance, subsidies to large families, and the dissemination of information about sound child-rearing practices. Other legislation outlawing contraception and abortion and discouraging the publication of information about sexuality and reproduction made it more difficult for women to limit the size of their families.

Mussolini portrayed mothers as having the duty to rear their children for the good of the state. They were expected to see that their children attended fascist school programs. Government agencies provided modest benefits to mothers and their children, which tended to make them dependent on the government because Italian wages were low. In this respect, under fascism, the home became a kind of extension of state policy.

WOMEN IN THE ITALIAN WORK FORCE   Despite the government's emphasis on the home and child rearing and the image of the father as earning a wage to support his family, 25 percent of the Italian work force was women, a percentage of women workers second only to Sweden. The fascist government, however, discouraged female participation in the work force or sought to keep women in lower skilled jobs. For example, although the fascists opened civil service jobs to

[1]Victorian de Grazia, "How Mussolini Ruled Italian Women," in Françoise Thébaud, ed., *A History of Women in the West, Volume V: Toward a Cultural Identity in the Twentieth Century* (Cambridge, MA: The Belknap Press of Harvard University Pres, 1994), p. 145.

women, over the years they made it more difficult for women to compete with male workers. Laws favored the employment of skilled workers when, in Italy as elsewhere in Europe, most women worked in less skilled jobs. Laws that protected women from exploitation also limited their access to the labor market. In 1938, the government forbade both government and private offices from having more than 10% women employees. While most of these exclusions were modified when Italy entered the Second World War, the policies had succeeded in degrading women's work. By 1940, women's particpation in the Italian labor force was more part time and low skilled than it had been before the fascists took power. For example, while the number of domestic servants declined elsewhere in Western Europe during the 1920s and 1930s, it increased in Italy.

Racial Ideology and the Lives of Women in Nazi Germany

Certain aspects of Nazi social policy toward women and the family resembled those of Italy, but there were also important distinctions. Nazi writers portrayed women as wives and mothers first and foremost. In a period of high unemployment, this Nazi attitude also appealed to many men, because it discouraged women from competing with men in the workplace. Hitler and other Nazis thought that there were natural, separate social spheres for men and women—the world of action for men and the home for women—and that the two spheres should not mix. Women who sought liberation and who adopted roles traditionally followed by men in public life were considered symptoms of cultural decline and weakness.

Although Nazi ideology emphasized motherhood, in 1930 the party vowed to protect the jobs of working women, and the actual number of women working in Germany rose steadily under the Nazi regime. The Nazis recognized that in the midst of the depression many women needed to work, but the party urged them to pursue employment that was "natural" to their character as women. Such employment included agricultural labor, teaching, nursing, social service, and domestic service. The Nazis also intended women to be educators of the young. In that role, whether as mothers or as members of the serving professions, women became special protectors of German cultural values. Through cooking, dress, music, and stories, mothers were to instill a love for the nation in their children. As consumers for the home, women were to support German-owned shops, buy German-made goods, and boycott Jewish merchants.

A few Nazi feminists hoped that women could achieve new standing in the Nazi order. They appealed to ancient German history to prove that German men and women had once been equal. They also contended that only by allowing women to play a broader role could Nazi society actually reach its goals. They argued that if sons were not reared to respect their mothers, then those mothers could not carry out their role as educators of children for the nation. Most of these Nazi feminists seem to have been professional women who hoped both to support the party and to maintain their position in German society. They had only minimal influence on the policies of the party and none on the major Nazi leaders.

The Nazis were less interested in expanding the population as a whole, which was Mussolini's policy, than in producing a population of racially pure Germans. In their role as mothers, German women had the special task of preserving racial purity and giving birth to more pure Germans who were healthy in mind and body. Hitler championed this view of women. They were to breed strong sons and daughters for the German nation. Nazi journalists often compared the role of women in childbirth to that of men in battle. Each served the state in particular social and gender roles. In both cases, the good of the nation was more important than that of the individual. (See "Hitler Rejects the Emancipation of Women.")

Nazi racial ideology, however, focused on women as the carriers and bearers of both the desired and undesired races. Government policy as rigorously attempted to eradicate the latter as it did to foster the former. Nazi policy favored motherhood only for those its adherents regarded as fit for motherhood. As early as late 1933, the government raised the issue of what kind of persons were fit to bear children for the nation. This policy disapproved of fostering motherhood among those people condemned by Nazi racism—most particularly the Jews, but also Slavs and Gypsies. During the mass executions of Jews in the Holocaust, Jewish women were specifically targeted for death, in part to prevent them from bearing a new generation.

Nazi theorists also discriminated among the healthy and unhealthy, the desirable and undesirable, in the German population itself. The government sought to sterilize such undesirables, a policy that led to both the sterilization and death of many women, often on the alleged grounds of some form of mental degeneracy. In some cases, pregnant women slated for sterilization were forced to have abortions. The Nazis' population policy was, in effect, one of selective breeding or anti-natalism that profoundly affected the lives of women.

Hitler Rejects the Emancipation of Women

According to Nazi ideology, women's place was in the home, producing and rearing children and supporting their husbands. In this speech, Hitler urges this view of the role of women. He uses anti-Semitism to discredit those writers who urged the emancipation of women from their traditional roles and occupations. Hitler returns here to the "separate spheres" concept of the relationship of men and women. His traditional view of women was directed against contrary views that were associated with the Soviet experiment during the interwar years. Contrast the Nazi outlook on women and the family with the view expressed by the young Bolshevik Alexandra Kollontai in the preceding document. Ironically, once World War II began, the Nazi leadership demanded that women leave the home and work in factories to support the war effort.

❖ *What are the social tasks Hitler assigns to women? Why does he associate the emancipation of women with Jews and intellectuals? How does he attempt to subordinate the lives of women to the supremacy of the state?*

The slogan "Emancipation of Women" was invented by Jewish intellectuals and its content was formed by the same spirit. In the really good times of German life the German woman had no need to emancipate herself. She possessed exactly what nature had necessarily given her to administer and preserve; just as the man in his good times had no need to fear that he would be ousted from his position in relation to the woman....

If the man's world is said to be the State, his struggle, his readiness to devote his powers to the service of the community, then it may perhaps be said that the woman's is a smaller world. For her world is her husband, her family, her children, and her home. But what would become of the greater world if there were no one to tend and care for the smaller one? How could the greater world survive if there were no one to make the cares of the smaller world the content of their lives? No, the greater world is built on the foundation of this smaller world. This great world cannot survive if the smaller world is not stable. Providence has entrusted to the woman the cares of that world which is her very own, and only on the basis of this smaller world can the man's world be formed and built up. The two worlds are not antagonistic. They complement each other, they belong together just as man and woman belong together.

We do not consider it correct for the woman to interfere in the world of the man, in his main sphere. We consider it natural if these two worlds remain distinct. To the one belongs the strength of feeling, the strength of the soul. To the other belongs the strength of vision, of toughness, of decision, and of the willingness to act. In the one case this strength demands the willingness of the woman to risk her life to preserve this important cell and to multiply it, and in the other case it demands from the man the readiness to safeguard life.

The sacrifices which the man makes in the struggle of his nation, the woman makes in the preservation of that nation in individual cases. What the man gives in courage on the battle field, the woman gives in eternal self-sacrifice, in eternal pain and suffering. Every child that a woman brings into the world is a battle, a battle waged for the existence of her people....

So our women's movement is for us not something which inscribes on its banner as its programme the fight against men, but something which has as its programme the common fight together with men. For the new National Socialist national community acquires a firm basis precisely because we have gained the trust of millions of women as fanatical fellow-combatants, women who have fought for the common life in the service of the common task of preserving life....

Whereas previously the programmes of the liberal, intellectualist women's movements contained many points, the programme of our National Socialist Women's movement has in reality but one single point, and that point is the child, that tiny creature which must be born and grow strong and which alone gives meaning to the whole life-struggle.

From J. Noakes and G. Pridham, eds., *Nazism, 1919–1945, Vol. 2: State, Economy and Society, 1933–39: A Documentary Reader,* Exeter Studies in History No. 8 (Exeter, U.K.: University of Exeter Press, © 1984), pp. 449–450. Reprinted by permission.

To support motherhood among those whom they believed should have children, the Nazis provided loans to encourage early marriage, tax breaks for families with children, and child allowances. In this respect, Nazi legislation resembled that passed elsewhere in Europe during the decade. The Nazi subsidies and other family payments were sent to husbands rather than wives, in an effort to make married fatherhood seem preferable to bachelorhood. Furthermore, all of these policies were administered on the premise that only racially and physically desirable children received support.

The Social Experience of Stalinism

The emphasis on building for the future and the creation of the new "Soviet Man" and "Soviet Woman" were a fundamental feature of twentieth-century Soviet society and culture. The Communist Party portrayed itself as an engine of change leading Soviet society from backwardness to a bright socialist future. This effort to transform the Soviet Union affected the smallest details of the social life of its citizens.

The collectivization of farming, the rapid industrialization, and the purges that occurred in the Soviet Union during the 1930s touched every part of Soviet society. Since the collapse of the Soviet Union, survivors from the era have told interviewers that the vastly disruptive political processes through which they lived affected some of the most intimate moments of their personal lives. Rarely has politics so profoundly shaped individuals' social experience.

The Social Experience of Collectivization

During the 1920s throughout much of the Soviet Union, the New Economic Policy, begun by Lenin and continued until late in the decade, had led to a considerable amount of small commerce. Furthermore, ambitious, entrepreneurial farmers had been encouraged to work hard to expand the urban food supply, which was always troubled. The shopkeepers and energetic farmers thought they were doing just what the Soviet state wished them to do.

This situation became transformed almost literally overnight when Stalin decided to collectivize Soviet agriculture in 1929. (See Ch. 28.) The successful farmers of the 1920s became transformed into the despised *kulaks*, whom Stalin declared must be destroyed as a class. Collectivization and the destruction of the *kulaks* were carried out by urban members of the Communist Party, who went into the countryside with only the vaguest set of orders as to what exactly collectivization meant. More than 400,000 *kulak* households, which amounted to over 2 million people, were forcibly removed from their homes and their land. They were transported to distant areas of the Soviet Union or to prison camps. The closest experience that most of the readers of this volume have seen to these expulsions was the actions taken against ethnic Albanians in Kosovo during 1998 and 1999.

However, unlike the Kosovars, the *kulaks* saw no one come to their aid. Because of the controlled press in the Soviet Union, many people had no detailed knowledge of what was happening. The social experience of what was termed *dekulakization* did not end with the expulsions, forced marches, and transport to unknown distant destinations in overcrowded cattle cars. Even if they survived that ordeal, the *kulaks* then had to patch together some kind of life in Siberia or another inhospitable province, where many of them became industrial workers. Throughout the 1930s, the children of *kulaks* faced ongoing discrimination and were regarded as politically subversive.

The Attack on Religion

Kulaks were not the only village people to be persecuted during collectivization: The party also targeted priests of the Russian Orthodox Church. The Soviet Communist Party, formally atheistic in its ideology, had always opposed religion and the church, but only with collectivization were many priests attacked and churches closed or transformed into structures to store grain, manufacture alcohol, or house local administrators. Jewish rabbis, Catholic priests, and Islamic mullahs often received the same harsh treatment.

Life on the Collective Farm

The peasants, frequently with women in the lead, forcibly resisted collectivization in many regions. As noted in Chapter 28, they slaughtered enormous numbers of livestock. Their resistance contributed to a widespread famine in 1932 and 1933. Those peasants who refused to cooperate with collectivization were themselves then attacked as *kulaks*. In some regions, the Soviet government manipulated the distribution of scarce food to turn the famines to its own political ends.

The peasants who remained in the village—and the collectivized farm was actually a village—found themselves subject to the administration of party members who expected them to produce the quantities of grain demanded by the central government. By 1937, approximately 90 percent of peasant households were located on collectivized farms that had not existed a decade earlier. Collective farms that failed to meet their requisitions might experience collective punishment, including lower food allotments for their own members.

Peasants on the collective farms throughout the Soviet period could not keep horses, though by the end of the 1930s they were permitted a cow and a small private plot of land. Within the world of the collective farms, there was little personal security against both serious and petty crime. Villages became sharply divided between peasants who hoped to gain favor by producing crops beyond what was demanded and those who dragged their feet to resist the entire process.

The living conditions on the collectives were poor in terms of food, electricity, water, and sanitation. In contrast to this dreary reality, government propaganda in newspapers, posters, paintings, and movies depicted happy peasants working to further socialism. (See "Art & the West.") The standard of living on the collective farms did not improve appreciably until late in the Khrushchev era, and not substantially until the 1970s, when prices paid to farmers were raised and the retirement age lowered. The general standard of living in the countryside remained below that of the cities. Pensions and other benefits on the collectives were usually lower than those for industrial workers.

Until the standard of living improved in the third quarter of the century (and the improvement was often marginal), many peasants in the Soviet Union saw collectivization as a second serfdom, even though education in the countryside increased and rural literacy rose substantially with collectivization.

Flight to the Soviet Cities

An immediate social fallout of Soviet collectivization was an enormous peasant flight from the land to the cities. In the 1930s, the number of peasant households dropped by approximately 20 percent. Between 1928 and 1932, approximately 12 million peasants left the countryside, an unprecedented migration in European history. In the years immediately after the drive toward collectivization, the populations of major cities grew rapidly. Moscow's population almost doubled. Between 1939 and 1980, the proportion of the Soviet population living on the land fell from two-thirds to one-third.

The greatest number of people to depart the countryside were young males, leaving a disproportionate number of women and elderly people in the villages, where they lived in enormous poverty. Although the trend throughout Europe in the twentieth century has been toward greater urbanization,

in the Soviet Union urbanization arose directly from the government-sponsored turmoil and disruption in the countryside.

Urban Consumer Shortages

Much of the housing shortage that plagued the Soviet Union for the rest of its history originated in the 1930s. In the newly founded industrial cities, the most famous of which was Magnitogorsk, workers lived in barracks. In the older cities, individuals and families had difficulty finding apartments of their own. Those apartments they did find were extremely small and several families often had to share toilets and baths. People who were not related and who had no common background often had to share the most private aspects of their lives. Life in such cramped quarters led people to value even more what few possessions they had, including pots and pans and small pieces of furniture. Enormous resentments arose, which led to political denunciations during the purges as the 1930s proceeded.

For urban dwellers, in addition to the shortage of housing, the most fundamental fact of everyday life under Stalin and subsequent Soviet leaders was an ongoing shortage of the most basic consumer goods, including food, clothing, and particularly shoes. From the end of the New Economic Policy through the collapse of the Soviet Union in 1991, city shops had few goods. Throughout the 1930s, Russians consumed less food each year than they had before the revolution, and the famines affected everyone's life. What goods did appear were often sold in separate stores reserved for party members. A sharp inequality constantly distinguished the small minority of party members and leaders from the general Soviet population. One of the most common experiences of Soviet citizens was standing in line for bread. Ordinary materials for home repair and home improvement were also in short supply.

Except for certain showplaces in Moscow and St. Petersburg (Leningrad until the fall of the Soviet Union), Soviet cities generally lacked the kind of urban infrastructure that Western European cities had long enjoyed. The transport systems were too small for the rapidly expanding populations. Even cities as large and important as Stalingrad (today, Volgograd) lacked sewer systems in the mid-1930s. In the new industrial cities even running water was rare, and there were few paved streets and poor electric lighting. All of these cities had extensive crime and disease.

How did this Soviet society sustain itself? There was much black marketeering, and food was raised on private plots. Informal systems of exchange arose alongside those sponsored by the state. This whole informal mode of coping became known as the *blat*.

Cultural Divisions
and the Cold War

While they may seem like products from different centuries, the Soviet painter Tatjiana Yablonskaya's (b. 1917) sun-strewn *Bread* (1949) and the American Jackson Pollock's (1912–1956) dizzyingly abstract *One (Number 31, 1950)* were painted only one year apart. The stark differences between these two works mirror the cultural divisions of the early Cold War.

Bread, measuring over six feet high and twelve feet wide, is a monumental example of Socialist Realism. Established as the official doctrine of Soviet art and literature in 1934, Socialist Realism sought to create optimistic and easily intelligible scenes of a bold socialist future, in which prosperity and solidarity would reign. Manual laborers and prominent historical and political figures were painted in a traditional and often rigid figurative manner. With the spread of Soviet control after World War II, Socialist Realism became the dominant artistic model throughout Eastern Europe, only waning when Nikita Khrushchev liberalized Soviet cultural policy toward the end of the 1950s.

Although *Bread*'s bountiful harvest, streaming sunlight, and happy workers are typical Soviet Realist idealizations—in contrast to the harsh reality of life and food shortages under Stalin—Yablonskaya's painting can also be seen as a tribute to the role of women in Soviet economic life. Between 1928 and 1950, the number of working women in the USSR grew dramatically. By the late 1940's, about half of the USSR's female labor force worked in agriculture occupations.

The looping skeins of paint in *One (Number 31, 1950)* may seem completely different from the kind of "realistic" propaganda visible in *Bread*, but Pol-

Tatjiana Yablonskaya, *Bread*, 1949. Ria Novosti/Sovfoto/Eastfoto

Jackson Pollock, *One (Number 31, 1950)*. Oil and enamel on unprimed canvas, 8 ft. 10 in. x 17 ft. 5 5/8 in. (269.5 x 530.8 cm). The Museum of Modern Art, New York. Sidney and Harriet Janis Collection Fund (by exchange). Photograph © 2000 The Museum of Modern Art, New York. 00007.68 © 2000 Pollock–Krasner Foundation/Artists Rights Society (ARS), NY.

lock's painting is in fact a central document of postwar American cultural life. Flinging paint from sticks and brushes onto his floorbound canvas, Pollock freed his lines from representing any figure or outline. The result, in *One (Number 31, 1950)*, which is over eight feet high and 17 feet wide, is a writhing tangle of pure visual energy. In the politically charged atmosphere of the early Cold War, Pollock's exuberant "drip" paintings were seen as the embodiment of American cultural freedom, just as the Wyoming-born Pollock was celebrated as a kind of artist cowboy.

Lurking behind such interpretations was the awareness that the Soviets had forcibly imposed Socialist Realism on Eastern Europe, and that the Nazis had persecuted avant-garde artists. As skeptical as many viewers might have been about the merits of abstract art (*Time* magazine, for instance, dismissively called Pollock "Jack the dripper" in 1947), it came to be seen in the West as the antithesis of Socialist Realist totalinarianism.

Indeed, New York City—not Paris—emerged as the international center of modern art after World War II, a position it still holds today. As the home of growing collections of twentieth-century art and dozens of European avant-garde figures who had fled from the Nazis, New York became a fertile training ground for young artists such as Pollock. And just as American political and economic structures became models for the postwar redevelopment of Western Europe, so did American cultural developments. By the time Pollock's first posthumous retrospective toured Europe in 1958, much European painting resembled an elegant imitation of his frenetic lines.

Yablonskaya and Pollock together illustrate the two central poles of twentieth-century art: realism and abstraction. While artistic style is no longer as closely associated with political programs as it once was, these two poles still frame the work of countless artists today.

Bown, Matthew Cullerne. *Art under Stalin*. Oxford: Phaidon, 1991. Bowlt, John E. (ed.) *Russian Art of the Avant-Garde: Theory and Criticism 1902–1934*. New York: Viking Press, 1976. McAuley, Alastair. *Women's Work and Wages in the Soviet Union*. London: Allen & Unwin, 1981. O'Conner, Francis V. *Jackson Pollock*. New York: Museum of Modern Art, 1967. Varnedoe, Kirk and Pepe Karmel. *Jackson Pollock*. New York: Museum of Modern Art, 1998.

But for much of the century, the Soviet people sustained themselves in the face of these difficulties mainly through the conviction that they were enduring their present troubles to build a greater socialist future in which the world would be set right and all the goods people needed would be available. During World War II, this emphasis changed to protecting the fatherland. After the war, the emphasis again fell on a better future, but that future never came.

The Destruction of the Polish Jewish Community

Before the Second World War, the Jewish community of Poland was the largest in Europe. It consisted of over 3 million people, or about 10 percent of Poland's population. Approximately 90 percent of that Jewish community would perish during the war and the Holocaust. Those events destroyed an entire way of life among Polish Jews and other Jewish communities in central and eastern Europe.

Polish Jews at the End of World War I

A large Jewish community had dwelled within Polish lands for centuries, often in a climate of religious and cultural anti-Semitism. As a result of that anti-Semitism, Polish Jews had long lived in their own villages and then later in their own urban neighborhoods. After the late-eighteenth-century partitions of Poland and the Congress of Vienna, most of Poland came under Russian rule. Through the policy of Official Nationalism, the nineteenth-century tsars defined their nation ideologically within the confines of Russian Orthodox Christianity. Polish Jews thus constituted a non-Christian minority that became subject to a wide variety of discriminatory legislation. Consequently, during the nineteenth century, Polish Jews did not experience any of the forms of Jewish emancipation that had occurred in western Europe. (See Ch. 24.)

The Paris Peace Settlement of 1919 established an independent Polish state. Shortly after the end of World War I and the organization of the new Polish republic, anti-Jewish violence swept Poland. The new Poland defined itself in terms of Polish nationalism, which, no less than Russian Orthodoxy, had defined Jews as outside the national fold. Polish nationalists resented the guarantees of the Minorities Treaty of 1919 as conditions outside powers had imposed on Poland. Although Ukrainians constituted the largest single ethnic minority within Poland, the Jews became the most problematical, because, unlike the Ukrainians, they were a minority people without a nearby ethnic homeland.

Polish Jewry between the Wars

The Polish Jewish community was the single most distinctive of the various European Jewish communities and was perceived as such. Polish Jews were more religiously observant than other Jewish communities, a social situation that sharply separated them from the Roman Catholicism that characterized Polish culture and nationalism. Hebrew was the Polish Jews' chief written, and Yiddish their primary spoken, language. Many Jews, particularly older ones, continued to wear distinctive dress. Their food differed from that of most Poles. Finally, although the Jewish population was not concentrated in any particular geographical section of Poland, individual neighborhoods in cities and some small towns might be overwhelmingly Jewish. Jews also constituted a higher proportion of urban populations than other minority groups and were regarded as an overwhelmingly urban people in a rural nation. Thus, religion, language, dress, and place of residence distinguished Jews from the rest of the Polish population.

Jews were also among the poorest people in Poland. It has been estimated that during the early 1920s only one-third of Polish Jews were gainfully employed, a far lower percentage than the non-Jewish population. Jews tended to be self-employed merchants, peddlers, or craftspeople. A high proportion of Jewish workers in all industries were women, but the proportion was even higher in particular industries identified as Jewish, such as textiles, clothing, and paper. By the nature of their employment, few belonged to trade unions.

These conditions made Polish Jews economically vulnerable during the economic turmoil of the 1920s and especially of the 1930s. Hundreds of thousands of Polish Jews lived in desperate poverty. Many relied on communal charity from other Jewish families. What made such relief so distinctive in Poland was that it often went to people who were actually holding jobs, but earning too little to support themselves.

Polish Anti-Semitism

During the interwar years, the Polish government pursued policies that were directly anti-Semitic. Because Jews filled a disproportionate number of jobs in commerce, shopkeeping, peddling, and crafts, any legislation affecting such occupations disproportionately touched their lives. The Polish government nationalized the matches, salt, tobacco, and alcohol industries and then enacted legislation that discriminated against hiring Jews in those government monopolies. Other legislation made it

Before World War II, Jews pursued their lives openly in relative freedom in western Europe, but in a much more uncertain atmosphere in eastern Europe. At left, Dutch Jews, Hilde and Gerrit Verdoner pose on their wedding day with their bridesmaids. Below, the Kornhausers, a family of Hungarian Jews, enjoy a day at a beach near Budapest, and four Jewish schoolgirls walk together on a street in Sosnowiec, Poland in 1938. All of this normal, everyday social life would end with the Nazi advance throughout Europe. Indeed, Hilde Verdoner would be deported to Westerbork, and from there to Auschwitz, where she perished. Her husband and their three children survived the war in hiding.
United States Holocaust Memorial Museum

difficult for Jews to observe the Sabbath while keeping their jobs. Regulations requiring businesses to be closed on Sunday meant that Jewish shops had to close two days of the week. By the late 1930s, the government required businesses to display their owners' names prominently, which made it easy for people to avoid doing business in Jewish shops. Since Jews were excluded from the civil service, they moved into law and medicine, where their presence led to further resentment. Spokesmen for the Polish Roman Catholic Church, which was

closely associated with Polish nationalism, supported such discriminatory policies.

The path of assimilation into the larger culture that many European Jewish leaders had advocated during the nineteenth century hit a dead end in Poland because Poles generally refused to regard even secular, assimilated Jews as members of the Polish nation. Yet many Jews attempted to embrace the social practices, dress, and language of the Polish majority without actually expecting to be considered Polish. In this respect, they saw themselves as moving from a traditional style of life to a more modern, more Polish one. Jewish newspapers and other publications began to be published in Polish.

Political Alternatives for Polish Jews

Although Polish independence had neither improved the Jews' economic condition nor given them a fundamentally more friendly government than they had endured under the tsars, the new Polish constitution did allow them to participate in political life. Because of the large size of the Polish Jewish community, it became the arena between the wars in which different Jewish cultural and political groups contested their various strategies to remedy the Jewish plight. The Zionists urged active participation in Polish life and politics until the envisioned Jewish state in Palestine had been established and Jews could emigrate to it. Approximately 140,000 Polish Jews did emigrate to Palestine between the wars, the largest single group from Europe. Yet the difficulties associated with emigration and British barriers to Jewish immigration into Palestine made mass emigration impractical.

The second Jewish political faction in prewar Poland was the Polish *Bund*, a group of generally young secular, socialist Jews that was organized around 1900. Their outlook combined Marxism and Jewish nationalism. The *Bund* welcomed women members. Bundists believed that Polish Jews should identify their plight with that of the working class in general and seek a socialist solution. They could not, however, cooperate with the Soviet communists because, prior to the Russian Revolution, they had been one of the socialist groups that had quarreled with Lenin's Bolsheviks. Their goal was to maintain the safety of Polish Jews and to regard Poland as their homeland. They worked to create an alliance with the Polish working class and largely ignored the anti-Semitism that was rife in Polish working-class culture. The *Bundists* generally rejected Zionism as a middle-class outlook and championed Yiddish as the language of Polish Jews, while the Zionists strongly favored Hebrew.

Finally, Jewish leaders of a traditionalist outlook essentially urged their fellow Jews to retreat into their distinct communities, observe their religion, and preserve their faith. They thought it unwise to quarrel with the new Polish government, as they had also thought it unwise to challenge the tsars. They refused to cooperate with other minorities in Poland. They were often both skeptical of Zionism and hostile to the secular Jews of the *Bund*.

The debate among the Jews had assumed that an independent Poland would continue to exist and that any improvement in the Jews' situation had to take place within that nation. The conquest of Poland in 1939 by Germany, a nation governed by a party embracing an ideology of racial nationalism and anti-Semitism, rendered this debate irrelevant. The events of the war and the Holocaust destroyed the community within which the debate had taken place.

The Nazi Assault on the Jews of Poland

The joint German–Soviet invasion of Poland brought millions of Jews under either German or Soviet authority. The total Jewish population of Germany was small—indeed, not much more than the Jewish population of Warsaw. By conquering Poland, the Nazi government could carry out the destruction of Jewish communities to an extent far beyond anything possible in Germany itself. From the Nazi standpoint, the destruction of the Polish Jewish community held special importance. Polish Jewry was large and had produced many religious, cultural, and political leaders. Moreover, because it was so large, it had constituted the single most important source for Jewish emigration beyond eastern Europe. The racial thinking of the Nazis thus saw Poland literally as the chief breeding ground of Europe for Jews populating the rest of the world.

By late autumn of 1939, the Germans had begun to move against Polish Jews. The Nazi government first thought that it might herd virtually all the Jews of occupied Europe into the Lublin region of Poland. By early 1940, the Nazis decided to move as many Jews as possible into ghettos, where they would be separated from the rest of the Polish population. The most famous of these ghettos were Lodz and Warsaw, each of which had populations of several hundred thousand. Jews from all over Poland and, eventually, other occupied regions were moved by rail into these ghettos, which were then sealed with police guards and walls. The ghettos were administered by Jewish councils, which were torn between responsibility to their communities and the necessity of responding to German orders. The personal property and businesses of the Jews who were herded into the ghettos were confiscated and sold. Jewish laborers were sent out of the ghettos to work as contract labor while their families remained in the ghettos.

By 1941, the Polish Jews had lost all their civic standing and property. They had been located in segregated communities within Poland where typhus, tuberculosis, and influenza were rampant and where the food supply was meager. Approximately 20 percent of the population of both the Lodz and Warsaw ghettos died of disease and malnourishment. (See "Oskar Rosenfeld Describes the Food Supply in the Lodz Ghetto.")

Once the Nazis moved into eastern Europe, Jews living in the region became one of their chief targets. Above, Jews from Sandomierz, Poland, wearing armbands, pass Nazi guards as they board a ferry that will transport them across the Vistula River for resettlement in the Krakow ghetto, 1940. In the bottom picture, a group of Jews, all but one of whom are women, dig ditches in a fenced-in lot in Krakow as German troops look on. United States Holocaust Memorial Museum

A member of the German SS supervises the boarding of Jews from the Krakow ghetto onto box cars that will carry them to one of the several concentration camps in eastern Europe where millions perished. In the photo [right], Jewish children stand behind a barbed wire fence at Auschwitz, Poland. [Left] United States Holocaust Memorial Museum. [Right] Hulton Getty/Archive Photos

The outbreak of war between Germany and the Soviet Union in June 1941 further transformed the situation of Jews in Poland. (See Ch. 29.) The advancing German forces killed tens of thousands of Jews in the Soviet Union during 1941 and hundreds of thousands more the next year. Bolsheviks and Jews became conflated in German thinking and propaganda. During the second half of 1941, the Nazi government decided to exterminate the Jews of Europe. From late 1941 through 1944, the German authorities in Poland transported Jews from the ghettos by rail to a series of death camps located in Poland, including Kulmhof, Belzen, Sobibor, Treblinka, Birkenau, and Auschwitz. One or more of the camps were in operation from 1941 to 1944, with Auschwitz being the last closed. In those camps, Jews were systematically killed in gas chambers. Through execution in the camps, death by disease and starvation in the ghettos, and loss of life in the turmoil of war, approximately 90 percent of the pre-1939 Jewish population of Poland was destroyed. The largest Jewish community in Europe had ceased to exist.

The Nazi authorities regarded this process as a major part of their "final solution" to the Jewish question. Immediately after the war, the tiny minority of Polish Jews who had survived faced bitter anti-Semitism under the Soviet-dominated government. Many eventually immigrated to Israel, leaving only a few thousand Jews within the borders of a nation where they had numbered in the millions and where they had created a rich religious, cultural, and political community.

The Twentieth-Century Movement of Peoples

The forced removal of Russian peasants by Soviet communists and the deportations and executions of European Jews by the Nazis were only the most dramatic movements of people in twentieth-century Europe. Both the Second World War and the economic transformation of the continent after the war brought about extensive migration. The most pervasive trend in this migration was the continuing move from the countryside to cities. Today, except for Albania, at least one-third of the population of every European nation lives in large cities. In Western Europe, city dwellers are approximately 75 percent of the population.

Displacement through War

World War II created a vast refugee problem. An estimated 46 million people were displaced in central and Eastern Europe and the Soviet Union alone between 1938 and 1948. Many cities in Germany and in central and Eastern Europe had been bombed or overrun by invading armies. Hundreds of thousands of foreign workers had been moved into Germany to contribute to the war effort. Hundreds of thousands more were prisoners of war. Some of these people were returned to their homeland willingly; others, particularly Soviet prisoners fearful of being executed in the Soviet Union, left unwillingly. Hundreds of thousands of Baltic, Polish, and Yugoslav prisoners found asylum in Western Europe.

Oskar Rosenfeld Describes the Food Supply in the Lodz Ghetto

Tens of thousands of Jews were relocated to ghettos in Poland. These were cities sealed off from the rest of the world. Entrances and exits were closely guarded by the German Nazi occupiers. Maintaining the food supply was an enormous challenge for these communities of imprisonment. Oskar Rosenfeld, a professional journalist and one of the inhabitants of Lodz who, along with others, maintained a chronicle of the life of the ghetto, discussed the food supply in the early summer of 1943. Rosenfeld died in 1944, as did most of the people who had lived in the Lodz ghetto.

❖ *Why would the cares of everyday life have seemed, as Rosenfeld asserts, more of a burden than the psychological burden of life in the ghetto? What steps had the inhabitants of the ghetto been required to take to look after their own food supply? Why were potatoes more important for nutrition than vegetables? How does this passage suggest what Rosenfeld terms "the nightmare of the ghetto"?*

In general, one can say that people have grown accustomed to living surrounded by barbed wire and tolerate that state as almost natural, as a thing ordained by fate. For, in comparison with the cares of everyday life, the constant psychic constraints seem less burdensome.

....Since the offices of food supply are unable to provide the 85,000 inhabitants of the ghetto with the fresh vegetables they need, the gardeners are required to surrender a portion of their produce to the population....In the early morning hours one can see groups of people, with agricultural tools in their hands and on their shoulders, marching through the streets to till the soil—heading out to the vegetable gardens....No such figures were to be seen previously, just as there were no vegetable and potato beds on the grounds of the ghetto. The ghetto has been reconstructed; and as a result, we are supplied with vegetables not only by the [German] Ghetto Administration, but also by our own soil....

During this first week, the month of June was a good friend to the ghetto dwellers. It brought them the most precious food that can be wished

for the in the ghetto: potatoes. When the carts appeared in the streets—whether horse drawn or in handcarts—passersby halted and stared hopefully at the round of fruits of the earth. What do the hungry care whether the potatoes are first or second quality as long as there are potatoes?...Suddenly, the potato shipments stopped. Potatoes were replaced by vegetables—spinach, lettuce, red beets, carrots, radishes—too little to fill empty stomachs. And since no more potatoes came in during the second half of June the allocated supplies had already been consumed, hunger and despair loomed in the horizon once again. The end of this month of June is reminiscent of last year's "starvation" June....

The first truckloads of green vegetables are now rolling through the streets, causing renewed hope. Just hold out for a few more weeks, and then there will be potatoes again—the fresh young potatoes, not the sort of which half has to be thrown into the trash as unfit for consumption. This thought can be read on the face in the ghetto....Ultimately, no one escapes the nightmare of the ghetto.

From Luchan Dobroszycki, *The Chronicle of the Lodz Ghetto*, copyright © 1984 Yale University Press, pp. 355–357. Reprinted by permission of Yale University Press.

Changes in borders after the war also caused many people to move or be moved. For example, Poland, Czechoslovakia, and Hungary forcibly and brutally expelled millions of ethnic Germans from their territories and sent them to Germany. This transfer of over 12 million Germans in effect "solved" the problem of German minorities living outside Germany's national boundaries that had been one of Hitler's excuses for aggression against neighboring countries. In another case of forced migration, hundreds of thousands of

Poles were transferred to within Poland's new borders from territory annexed by the Soviet Union. Other minorities, such as Ukrainians in Poland and Italians along the Yugoslav coast, were driven into their ethnic homelands. As one historian has commented, "War, violence and massive social dislocation turned Versailles's dream of national homogeneity into realities."[2]

[2]Mark Mazower, *Dark Continent: Europe's Twentieth Century* (New York: Alfred Knopf, 1999), p. 218.

External Migration

Between 1945 and 1960, approximately half a million Europeans left Europe ech year. This was the largest outward migration since the 1920s, when the rate had been approximately 700,000 persons annually. In the second half of the nineteenth century, the immigrants had mostly been from rural areas. After World War II, they often included educated city dwellers. Immediately after the war, some governments encouraged migration because they were afraid that, as in the 1930s, their economies would not be able to provide adequate employment for all their citizens.

Decolonization in the postwar period led many European colonials to return to Europe from overseas. The most dramatic example of this phenomenon was the more than 1 million French colonials who moved to France after the end of the Algerian War in 1962. British citizens returned from various parts of the British Empire, Dutch came back to the Netherlands from Indonesia in the late 1940s, and Portuguese returned from Mozambique and Angola in the 1970s.

Decolonization also led non-European inhabitants of the former colonies to migrate to Europe. Great Britain, for example, received thousands of immigrants from the Caribbean, India and Pakistan, and some of its former African colonies. France received many immigrants from its former colonies in Africa, Indochina, and the Arab world. This influx proved to be a long-term source of social tension and conflict. In Britain, racial tension was high during the 1980s. France faced similar difficulties, which contributed to the emergence of the National Front, an extreme right-wing group led by Jean-Marie LePen (b. 1928). This group has drawn strength from the racial and ethnic tensions that have developed as a tight job market provokes resentment among some working-class voters toward North African immigrants. Similar pressures have arisen in Germany and Austria. Such tension did not arise only from immigrants from Africa and Asia; internal European migration also changed the social and economic face of the continent.

Economic Growth and Internal Migration

Although the Soviet Union made it difficult for citizens of its subject nations in eastern Europe to migrate, many did leave, especially if young and able to go on their own without having to relocate families. The motivations for such east-to-west migration were the desire to live and live better in a free society. For example, before the construction of the Berlin Wall in 1961, an estimated 3 million East Germans migrated to West Germany via Berlin.

But economic growth in western Europe, rather than political factors, primarily accounted for internal migration from the late 1950s onward. The increasingly prosperous nations of northern and western Europe enjoyed expanding job markets that paid good wages and provided excellent benefits, often subsidized by the state. Germany made agreements with southern European countries to facilitate labor migration into Germany. Thus, workers from the poorer countries of Turkey, Greece, Yugoslavia, Italy, Spain, and Portugal flowed into the wealthier countries of France, West Germany, Switzerland, and the Scandinavian and Benelux nations. The establishment of the European Economic Community in 1957 made this movement of labor much easier.

The migration of workers into northern Europe swelled after 1960. Several hundred thousand workers would enter France and Germany each year. Virtually all these migrants settled in cities. The host countries usually welcomed them during years of prosperity. When, however, European economies began to slow in the early 1980s and 1990, these guest workers, as they were sometimes called, met increasing resentment. In Germany during the early 1990s, guest workers whom the German government had originally invited into the country began to be attacked.

In the late 1980s, politics again became a major factor in European migration. The pressure of thousands of refugees seeking to escape from Eastern Europe to the West contributed to the collapse of the communist governments of Eastern Europe in 1988 and 1989. Since 1989, people from throughout Eastern Europe have migrated to Western European nations. The civil war in the former Yugoslavia has also created many refugees, and the entire world watched in horror at the forced removal of peoples from regions of that country.

The Welfare State

The Great Depression, the rise of authoritarian states in the wake of economic dislocation and unemployment, and World War II, which involved more people in a war effort than ever before, led to a marked change in how numerous Europeans thought about social welfare. The result was the emergence of the modern European welfare state, which took different forms, but which bore certain general characteristics.

Before World War II, except in Scandinavia, the two basic models for social legislation were the German and the British. Bismarck had introduced some forms of social insurance in Germany during the 1880s. His purpose was to undermine the German Social Democratic Party. In effect, he had the imperial German government provide workers with social insurance and thus some sense of social security while denying them significant political participation. In early twentieth-century Great Britain, where all classes had access to the political system, social insurance was targeted toward the very poor. According to both approaches, workers should be insured against the risks arising from disease, injury on the job, and old age. Although various legislative efforts had been made to address unemployment, it was assumed to be only a short-term problem and often one that workers brought on themselves. People higher up in the social structure would look out for themselves and not need help.

After World War II, the concept emerged that social insurance against predictable risks was a social right and should be universally available to all citizens. This concept had been most famously set forth in Great Britain by William B. Beveridge (1879–1963) in 1942. Paradoxically, making coverage universal, as Beveridge recommended, was attractive to conservatives as well as socialists. If medical care, old age pensions, and other benefits were available to all, they would not be seen as a device for redistributing income from one portion of the population to another.

The first European nation to begin to create a welfare state was Great Britain, during the 1945–1951 Labour Party ministry of Clement Attlee (1883–1967). The most important element of this early legislation was the creation of the National Health Service. France and Germany did not adopt similar health care legislation until the 1970s, because their governments initially refused to consider making coverage universal.

The spread of welfare legislation (including various forms of unemployment insurance) within Western Europe was closely related to the both Cold War and domestic political and economic policy. The communist states were promising their people enormous social security as well as full employment. The capitalist states came to believe that they had to produce similar security for their people. But in fact, the social security of the communist states was often more rhetoric than reality.

Western European attitudes toward the welfare state have reflected what are generally regarded as the three periods that have marked economic life since the end of the war. The first period was one of reconstruction from 1945 through the early 1950s. It was followed by the second period—almost twenty-five years of generally steady and expanding economic growth. The third period brought first an era of inflation in the late 1970s and then one of relatively low growth and high unemployment that persisted throughout the 1990s. During each of the first two periods, a general conviction existed, based on Keynesian

economics, that the foundation of economic policy was government involvment in a mixed economy. From the late 1970s, more people came to believe that the market should be allowed to regulate itself and that government should be less involved—though not completely withdrawn from—the economy.

The systems of government-furnished services now found across Europe in varying forms are beginning to encounter resistance. The payment systems on which they are based assume a growing population and low unemployment. As the proportion of the population consuming the services of the welfare state—the sick, the injured, and the elderly—increases relative to the able-bodied employed population that pays for them, the costs of those services rise. The significant leveling off of population growth in Europe thus imperils the now expected benefits of the welfare state. Furthermore, during the past two decades, significant levels of unemployment in major Western European nations have placed increased demands on various welfare payments. The low fertility rates across the continent mean that there will be fewer people in the next working generation to support the retired elderly population. Middle-class taxpayers have also become reluctant to support existing systems. The general growth of confidence in the ability of market forces rather than government intervention to sustain social cohesion has also spread in the past twenty years and has raised questions about the existing welfare structures. Governments across the continent, including those normally associated with left-of-center politics, such as the British Labour Party and the German Social Democratic Party, have limited further growth of the welfare state and reduced current benefits. In that respect, Europeans in the next few decades may look at the second half of the twentieth century as the Golden Age of welfare states and may find their own societies dealing with the issues of social welfare differently.

New Patterns in the Work and Expectations of Women

The decades since World War II have witnessed striking changes in the work patterns and social expectations of European women. In all social ranks, women have begun to assume larger economic and political roles. More women have entered the "learned professions," and more are filling major managerial positions than ever before in European history. At the same time, certain more or less traditional patterns continue to describe the position of women in both family and economic life. Despite enormous gains during the second half of the twentieth century, and despite the collapse of those authoritarian governments whose social policies inhibited the advancement of women into the mainstream of society, gender inequality remained a major characteristic of the social life of Europe at the opening of the twenty-first century.

Feminism

Since World War II, European feminism, although less highly organized than American feminism, has set forth a new agenda. The most widely read postwar work on women's issues was undoubtedly Simone de Beauvoir's (1908–1986) *The Second Sex*, published in 1949. In that work, de Beauvoir explored the difference it had made in her life to be a woman rather than a man. She was part of the French intellectual establishment and thus wrote from a privileged position. Over the years, however, she and other European feminists argued that at all levels, European women experienced distinct social and economic disadvantages. (See "Simone de Beauvoir Urges Economic Freedom for Women.") In the courts, for example, divorce and family laws favored men. European feminists also called attention to the social problems that were particular to women, including spousal abuse.

In contrast to earlier feminism, recent feminism has been less a political movement pressing for specific rights than a social movement offering a broader critique of European culture. More radical European feminists have asserted that their society, as presently organized, inherently represses women. They have been equally critical of all political parties—from conservative to socialist—that avoid a full airing of women's issues.

Several new feminist publications appeared during the 1970s, many of which are still published: *Courage, Emma—Magazine by Women for Women*, and *Spare Rib*. A statement in *Spare Rib*, an English magazine, captures the spirit of these publications:

Spare Rib aims to reflect women's lives in all their diverse situations so that they can recognize themselves in its pages. This is done by making the magazine a vehicle for their writing and their images. Most of all, *Spare Rib* aims to bring women together and support them in taking control of their lives.[3]

This emphasis on women controlling their own lives may be the most important element of recent European feminism. Whereas in the past feminists sought

and, in significant measure, gained legal and civil equality with men, they are now pursuing personal independence and issues that are particular to women.

The women's movement and the environmental movement have come to play a significant new role in European politics and culture. The collapse of communism in Eastern Europe has raised questions about socialism and challenged the credibility of the cultural criticism it generated. Feminist and environmental groups now provide the continuing critique of society that had been the role of socialist parties. In this sense, feminism is an important manifestation of the critical tradition in Western culture.

Modern European Household Structure

Despite the media attention devoted to unconventional lifestyles, the number of married people in Europe increased in the half century after World War II. Before then, a significant number of women remained single all their lives, but many fewer do so now. Women are also marrying at a younger age than before, particularly in Eastern and southern Europe. Overall, more people in the last half century have married, and have married at an earlier age, than in all of previous European history.

At the same time, many of the traditional ideas and expectations about marriage have changed. Family size fell and divorce rates rose during the twentieth century. Divorce laws have eased throughout Europe, although not until after 1980 in Ireland and the nations of southern Europe, where the Roman Catholic Church remains influential.

In the Scandinavian countries, more children are born out of wedlock. Their parents often live together, but are not married. Government-sponsored programs directed toward the care of children have made such arrangements, as well as single motherhood, economcally possible. Despite the attention these arrangements have received, they have not become the norm anywhere in Europe.

More Married Women in the Work Force

One of the patterns firmly established in 1900 has reversed itself. The number of married women in the work force has risen sharply. Both middle-class and working-class married women have sought jobs outside the home. Because of the low birthrate in the 1930s, few young single women were employed in the years just after World War II. Married women entered the job market to replace them. Some factories changed their work shifts to accommodate the needs of married women. Consumer conveniences and improvements in health care also made it easier for

---

[3]Quoted in Bonnie S. Anderson and Judith P. Zinsser, *A History of Their Own: Women in Europe from Prehistory to the Present*, Vol. 2 (New York: Harper Perennial, 1988), p. 412.

Simone de Beauvoir Urges Economic Freedom for Women

Simone de Beauvoir was the single most important feminist voice of mid-twentieth-century Europe. In The Second Sex, *published in France in 1949, she explored the experience of women coming of age in a world of ideas, institutions, and social expectations shaped historically by men. Much of the book discusses the psychological strategies that modern European women had developed to deal with their status as "the second sex." Toward the end of her book, Beauvoir argues strongly that economic freedom and advancement for women are fundamental to their personal fulfillment.*

❖ *Why does de Beauvoir argue that the achievement of civic rights must be accompanied by economic freedom for women? Why does the example of the small number of professional women illustrate issues for European women in general? How does she indicate that even professional women must overcome a culture in which the experience of women is fundamentally different from that of men? Do de Beauvoir's comments seem relevant for women at the opening of the twenty-first century? What similarities do you see to the views of Priscilla Wakefield (Chapter 16), Mary Wollstonecraft (Chapter 18), and Virginia Woolf (Chapter 25)?*

According to French law, obedience is no longer included among the duties of a wife, and each woman citizen has the right to vote; but these civil liberties remain theoretical as long as they are unaccompanied by economic freedom....It is through gainful employment that woman has traversed most of the distance that separated her from the male; and nothing else can guarantee her liberty in practice. Once she ceases to be a parasite, the system based on her dependence crumbles; between her and the universe there is no longer any need for a masculine mediator.

...When she is productive, active, she regains her transcendence; in her projects she concretely affirms her status as subject; in connection with the aims she pursues, with the money and the rights she takes possession of, she makes trial of and senses her responsibility.....

There are...a fairly large number of privileged women who find in their professions a means of economic and social autonomy. These come to mind when one considers woman's possibilities and her future...[E]ven though they constitute as

yet only a minority; they continue to be the subject of debate between feminists and antifeminists. The latter assert that the emancipated women of today succeed in doing nothing of importance in the world and that furthermore they have difficulty in achieving their own inner equilibrium. The former exaggerate the results obtained by professional women and are blind to their inner confusion. There is no good reason...to say they are on the wrong road; and still it is certain that they are not tranquilly installed in their new realm: as yet they are only halfway there. The woman who is economically emancipated from man is not for all that in a moral, social, and psychological situation identical with that of man. The way she carried on her profession and her devotion to it depends on the context supplied by the total pattern of her life. For when she begins her adult life she does not have behind her the same past as does a boy; she is not viewed by society in the same way; the universe presents itself to her in a different perspective. The fact of being a woman today poses peculiar problems for an independent human individual.

By Simone de Beauvoir, from *The Second Sex*, trans. by H. M. Parshley. Copyright 1952 and renewed 1980 by Alfred A. Knopf, Inc. Reprinted by permission of Alfred A. Knopf, a division of Random House Inc.

married women to enter the work force by reducing the demands child care made on their time. At the same time, all surveys indicate that the necessity of providing care for their children is the most important difficulty women find in the workplace. This situation is a main reason that women remain overwhelmingly in forms of part-time employment.

In the twentieth century, children were no longer expected to contribute substantially to family in-

come. They now spend years in compulsory education. When families need more income than one worker can provide, both parents will work, bringing many married women with children into the work force. Such financial necessity led many married women back to work. Evidence also suggests that married women began to work to escape the boredom of housework and to find company among other adult workers.

In Europe, as in the United States, women have gained access to new roles and opportunities. Geraldine Bridgewater was the first woman to hold a seat on the London Stock Exchange. Liaison Agency, Inc.

New Work Patterns

The work pattern of European women has been far more consistent in the twentieth century than it had been in the nineteenth. Single women enter the work force after their schooling and continue to work after marriage. They may stop working to care for their young children, but return to work when the children begin school. Several factors created this new pattern, but women's increasing life expectancy is one of the most important.

When women died relatively young, child rearing filled a large proportion of their lives. As a longer life span has shortened that proportion, women throughout the West are seeking ways to lead satisfying lives after their children have grown. Decisions regarding when to have children and how many children to have have also shaped the late-twentieth-century work pattern for women. Many women have begun to choose to limit the number of children they bear or to forgo childbearing and child rearing altogether. The age at which women have decided to bear children has risen, to the early twenties in Eastern Europe and to the late twenties in Western Europe. In urban areas, childbearing is later and the birthrate lower than elsewhere. These various personal decisions leave many years free for developing careers and for staying in the work force.

Controversy over abortion has fueled recent public debate and legislation in Europe. Two factors have triggered the debate: the emergence of the European Union and the collapse of communism. From before the formation of the European Union until the Treaty of Masstricht, each nation of Western Europe had its own legislation on the subject. By the 1990s, abortion with various degrees of difficulty of access was legal throughout Western Europe (except Ireland), including the traditionally Roman Catholic Mediterranean countries. The process of working through the details of the European Union provoked debate over abortion as countries with either liberal or conservative policies had to work their way to a common policy. In Eastern Europe before the collapse of communism, abortion was legalized. In the Soviet Union, the 1936 Stalinist prohibition was lifted after his death. With the opening of political life since 1989, abortion has become a matter of new public debate. It also complicated the unification of East and West Germany, because the former had a more liberal policy toward abortion than the latter.

Women in the New Eastern Europe

Many paradoxes surround the situation of women in Eastern Europe now that communists no longer govern the region. Under communism, women generally enjoyed social equality, as well as a broad spectrum of government-financed benefits. A significant proportion (normally well over 50 percent) of women worked in these societies, both because they could and because they were expected to. There were, however, no significant women's movements, since they, like all independent associations, were regarded with suspicion.

The new governments of the region are free, but have so far shown little concern with women's issues. Indeed, the economic difficulties the new governments face may endanger their funding various health and welfare programs that benefit women and children. For example, a free-market economy may limit the extensive maternity benefits to which Eastern European women were previously entitled. Moreover, the high proportion of women in the work force could leave them more vulnerable than men to the region's economic troubles. Women may well find themselves being laid off before men and hired later than men for lower pay.

Transformations in Knowledge and Culture

Knowledge and culture in Europe have rapidly transformed themselves in the twentieth century. Institutions of higher education have reached out to an increasingly large and diverse student body, making knowledge more widely available than ever before. Also, intellectual movements, such as existentialism, challenged many traditional intellectual attitudes. Concerns about the environment have also brought new issues to the fore. Throughout this ferment, representatives of the Christian faith have tried to keep their religion relevant.

Communism and Western Europe

Until the final decade of the twentieth century, Western Europe had organized communist parties, as well as groups of intellectuals sympathetic to communism. After the Bolshevik victory in the Russian Revolution and the subsequent civil war, the Western European socialist movement divided into independent democratic socialist parties and Soviet-dominated communist parties that followed the directions of the Third International. Throughout the 1920s and 1930s, those two groups fought each other with only rare moments of cooperation, such as that achieved during the French Popular Front in 1936.

THE INTELLECTUALS During the 1930s, as liberal democracies floundered in the face of the Great Depression and as right-wing regimes spread across the Continent, many people saw communism as a vehicle for protecting humane and even liberal values. Throughout Europe, students in the universities were often affiliated with the Communist Party. They and older intellectuals visited the Soviet Union and praised Stalin's achievements. Some of these intellectuals may not have known of Stalin's terror. Others simply closed their eyes to it, believing that humane ends might come from inhumane methods. Still others actually defended Stalinist terror. During the late

1920s and the 1930s, communism became a substitute religion for some Europeans. One group of former communists, writing after World War II, described their attraction toward, and later disillusionment with, communism in a book entitled *The God That Failed* (1949).

Four events proved crucial to the disillusionment of the intellectuals: the great public purge trials of the late 1930s, the Spanish Civil War (1936–1939), the Nazi–Soviet pact of 1939, and the Soviet invasion of Hungary in 1956. Arthur Koestler's (1905–1983) novel *Darkness at Noon* (1940) recorded a former communist's view of the purges. George Orwell (1903–1950), who had never been a communist, but who had sympathized with the party, expressed his disappointment with Stalin's policy in Spain in *Homage to Catalonia* (1938). The Nazi–Soviet pact destroyed the image of Stalin as an opponent of fascism. Other intellectuals, such as the French philoso-

George Orwell (1903–1950), shown here with his son, was an English writer of socialist sympathies who wrote major works opposing Stalin and communist authoritarianism. Felix H. Man/Bildarchiv Preussischer Kulturbesitz

pher Jean-Paul Sartre (1905–1980), continued to believe in the Soviet Union during and after the war, but the Hungarian Revolution cooled their ardor. The later invasion of Czechoslovakia simply confirmed a general disillusionment with Soviet policies by even left-wing Western European intellectuals.

Yet disillusionment with the Soviet Union or with Stalin did not always mean disillusionment with Marxism or with radical socialist criticisms of European society. Some writers and social critics looked to the establishment of alternative communist governments based on non-Soviet models. During the decade after World War II, Yugoslavia provided such an example. Beginning in the late 1950s, radical students and a few intellectuals found inspiration in the Chinese Revolution. Other groups hoped that a European Marxist system would develop. Among the more important contributors to this non-Soviet tradition was the Italian communist Antonio Gramsci (1891–1937), especially in his work *Letters from Prison* (published posthumously in 1947). The thinking of such non-Soviet communists became important to Western European communist parties, such as the Italian Communist party, that hoped to gain office democratically.

Another way to accommodate Marxism within mid-twentieth-century European thought was to redefine the basic message of Marx himself. During the 1930s, many of Marx's previously unprinted essays were published. These books and articles, written before the *Communist Manifesto* of 1848, are abstract and philosophical. They make the "young Marx" appear to belong more nearly to the humanist than to the revolutionary tradition of European thought. Since World War II, works such as *Philosophic Manuscripts of 1844* and *German Ideology* have been widely read. Today, many people are more familiar with them than with the *Manifesto* or *Capital*. They allowed some people to consider themselves sympathetic to Marxism without also seeing themselves as revolutionaries or supporters of the Soviet Union. With the collapse of the communist governments of Eastern Europe and the Soviet Union, what influence Marxism will continue to have on European intellectual life in the future is unclear.

Existentialism

The intellectual movement that perhaps best captured the predicament and mood of mid-twentieth-century European culture was existentialism. Like the modern Western mind in general, existentialism, which has been termed the "philosophy of Europe in the twentieth century," was badly divided; most of the

philosophers associated with it disagreed with each other on major issues. The movement represented in part a continuation of the revolt against reason that began in the nineteenth century.

Roots in Nietzsche and Kierkegaard Friedrich Nietzsche, discussed in Chapter 25, was a major forerunner of existentialism. Another was the Danish writer Søren Kierkegaard (1813–1855), who received little attention until after World War I. Kierkegaard was a rebel against both Hegelian philosophy and the Lutheran Christianity of Denmark. In works such as *Fear and Trembling* (1843), *Either/Or* (1843), and *Concluding Unscientific Postscript* (1846), he maintained that the truth of Christianity could not be contained in creeds, doctrines, and church organizations. It could be grasped only in the living experience of those who faced extreme human situations.

Kierkegaard also criticized Hegelian philosophy and, by implication, all modes of academic rational philosophy. Its failure, he felt, was the attempt to contain all of life and human experience within abstract categories. Kierkegaard spurned this faith in the power of mere reason. "The conclusions of passion," he once declared, "are the only reliable ones."[4]

The intellectual and ethical crisis of World War I brought Kierkegaard's thought to the fore and also created new interest in Nietzsche's critique of reason. The war led many people to doubt whether human beings were actually in control of their own destiny. Its destructiveness challenged faith in human rationality and improvement. Indeed, the war's most terrible weapons were the products of rational technology. The pride in rational human achievement that had characterized much nineteenth-century European civilization lay in ruins. The sunny faith in rational human development and advancement had not withstood the extreme experiences of war.

Questioning of Rationalism Existentialist thought thrived in this climate and received further support from the trauma of World War II. The major existential writers included the Germans Martin Heidegger (1889–1976) and Karl Jaspers (1883–1969) and the French Jean-Paul Sartre (1905–1980) and Albert Camus (1913–1960). Their books are often difficult and in some cases obscure. Although they frequently disagreed with each other, they all, in one way or another, questioned the primacy of reason and scientific understanding as ways of coming to grips with the human situation. Heidegger, a philosopher deeply

---

[4]Quoted in Walter Kaufman, ed., *Existentialism from Dostoevsky to Sartre* (Cleveland: The World Publishing Company, 1962), p. 18.

Jean-Paul Sartre (1905–1980) and Simone de Beauvoir (1908–1986) were two leading mid-century French intellectuals. His was a major voice in the existentialist movement, and she wrote extensively on the social position, experience, and psychology of women.
Bildarchiv Preussischer Kulturbesitz

compromised by his association with the Nazis, argued "Thinking only begins at the point where we have come to know that Reason, glorified for centuries, is the most obstinate adversary of thinking."[5]

The romantic writers of the early nineteenth century had also questioned the primacy of reason, but they did so in a much less radical manner than the existentialists. The romantics emphasized the imagination and intuition, but the existentialists dwelled primarily on the extremes of human experience. Death, dread, fear, and anxiety provided their themes. The titles of their works illustrate their sense of foreboding and alienation: *Being and Time* (1927), by Heidegger; *Nausea* (1938) and *Being and Nothingness* (1943), by Sartre; *The Stranger* (1942) and *The Plague* (1947), by Camus. The touchstone of philosophic truth became the experience of the individual under extreme conditions. (See "Sartre Discusses the Character of His Existentialism.")

According to the existentialists, human beings are compelled to formulate their own ethical values and cannot depend on traditional religion, rational philosophy, intuition, or social customs for ethical guidance. The opportunity and need to define values endow humans with a dreadful freedom.

The existentialists were largely protesting against a world in which reason, technology, and politics produced only war and genocide. Their thought reflected

the uncertainty of social institutions and ethical values in the era of the two world wars. Since the 1950s, however, their works and ideas have found their way into university curriculums around the world, making them objects of study, if not the source of intellectual ferment they had been. They will probably continue to be subjects of philosophy and literature classes, but their former popularity is probably past.

European intellectuals were attracted to communism and existentialism before and just after World War II, but in the 1960s, the turmoil over Vietnam and the youth rebellion brought other intellectual and social issues to the fore. Even before the collapse of communism, these had begun to redirect European intellectual interests.

Expansion of the University Population and Student Rebellion

As rapid changes in communications technology vastly expanded access to information, increasing numbers of Europeans received some form of university education. At the turn of the century, only a few thousand people were enrolled in universities in any major European country. By the 1980s that figure had risen to hundreds of thousands, although university education is still less common in Europe than in the United States. Higher education is now available to people from a variety of social and economic backgrounds and, for the first time, is readily available to women.

[5]Quoted in William Barrett, *Irrational Man* (Garden City, NY: Doubleday, 1962), p. 20.

Sartre Discusses the Character of His Existentialism

Jean-Paul Sartre, dramatist, novelist, and philosopher, was the most important French existentialist. In the first paragraph of this 1946 statement, Sartre asserted that all human beings must experience a sense of anguish or the most extreme anxiety when undertaking a major commitment. That anguish arises because, consciously or unconsciously, they are deciding whether all human beings should make the same decision. In the second paragraph, Sartre argued that the existence or nonexistence of God would make no difference in human affairs. What humankind must do is to discover the character of its own situation by itself.

❖ *How might the experiences of fascism in Europe and the fall of France to the Nazis have led Sartre to emphasize the need of human beings to choose? Why does Sartre believe that existentialism must be related to atheism? Why did Sartre regard existentialism as optimistic?*

The existentialist frankly states that man is in anguish. His meaning is as follows—When a man commits himself to anything, fully realizing that he is not only choosing what he will be, but is thereby at the same time a legislator deciding for the whole of mankind—in such a moment a man cannot escape from the sense of complete and profound responsibility. There are many, indeed, who show no such anxiety. But we affirm that they are merely disguising their anguish or are in flight from it. Certainly, many people think that in what they are doing they commit no one but themselves to anything: and if you ask them, "What would happen if everyone did so?"they shrug their shoulders and reply, "Everyone does not do so."But in truth, one ought always to ask oneself what would happen if everyone did as one is doing; nor can one escape from that disturbing thought except by a kind of self-deception. The man who lies in self-excuse, by saying, "Everyone will not do it" must be ill at ease in his conscience, for the act of lying implies the universal value which it denies. By its very disguise his anguish reveals itself.

Existentialism is nothing else but an attempt to draw the full conclusions from a consistently atheistic position. Its intention is not in the least that of plunging men into despair. And if by despair one means—as the Christians do—any attitude of unbelief, the despair of the existentialist is something different. Existentialism is not atheist in the sense that it would exhaust itself in demonstration of the nonexistence of God. It declares, rather, that even if God existed that would make no difference from its point of view. Not that we believe God does exist, but we think that the real problem is not that of His existence; what man needs is to find himself again and to understand that nothing can save him from himself, not even a valid proof of the existence of God. In this sense existentialism is optimistic. It is a doctrine of action, and it is only by self-deception, by confusing their own despair with ours that Christians can describe us as without hope.

From Jean-Paul Sartre, *Existentialism and Humanism*, trans. by Philip Mairet (London: Methuen), in Walter Kaufman, ed., *Existentialism from Dostoevsky to Sartre* (New York: Meridian Books, 1956), pp. 292, 310–311.

This expanding population of university-educated people is closely related to a surge of intense self-criticism among Europeans. Millions of citizens have acquired the critical intellectual skills and familiarity with critical writers that in previous centuries were usually the preserve of small literate elites. Television has given critical voices an even wider audience. Indeed, in Great Britain, the Open University uses television to provide university training to thousands of people.

Previously known only to a privileged few, the "student experience"—leaving home and settling for several years in a community composed primarily of late adolescents—has come to be widely shared. Since World War II, it has become a major feature of European society.

The expanding student population in Europe and elsewhere required an increase also in the number of university teachers. As a result, there have been more scientists, historians, economists, literary critics, and other professional intellectuals during the last seventy-five years than in all previous human history. Not since the early years of the Reformation have university intellectuals exerted such widespread influence. The major intellectual developments of the seventeenth, eighteenth, and nineteenth centuries took place primarily outside the university. In the twentieth century, the university has become the most likely home for the intellectual. And the symbol of success for writers in almost any field has been the inclusion of their work in the university curriculum.

One of the most striking and unexpected results of this rising population of students and intellectuals was the student rebellion of the 1960s. This development is still not well understood. Student uprisings began in the early 1960s in the United States and assumed major proportions as opposition grew to the war in Vietnam. The student rebellion then spread into Europe and other parts of the world. It was almost always associated with a radical political critique of the United States, although in Eastern Europe resentment was also directed toward the Soviet Union. The movement was generally antimilitarist. In addition to their political concerns, students questioned middle-class values and traditional sexual mores and family life.

The student movement reached its peak in 1968, when students in the United States demonstrated forcibly against U.S. involvement in Vietnam. In the same year, students at the Sorbonne in Paris seriously challenged the government of Charles de Gaulle, and in Czechoslovakia, students were in the forefront of the liberal socialist experiment. These protests failed to have an immediate effect on the policies of the governments at which they were directed. The United States stayed in Vietnam until 1973, De Gaulle remained president of France, and the Soviets suppressed the Czech experiment.

By the early 1970s, the era of student rebellion seemed to have passed. Students remained active in European movements against nuclear weapons and particularly against the placement of American nuclear weapons in Germany and elsewhere in Europe. From the mid-1970s, however, although often maintaining a radical political stance, they generally abandoned the kind of disruptive protests that marked the 1960s.

Nothing has so characterized both student and youth culture in the second half of the twentieth century as rock music, which first emerged in the 1950s. Now part of the fabric of contemporary European life, rock music abounds on radio and television. The lyrics of the Beatles, the British rock group that became wildly popular on both sides of the Atlantic in the 1960s, may be by now the most widely dispersed poetry in the history of the world. Yet rock music had originated in the United States, and its impact on Europe represented part of the wider postwar influence of American popular culture in Europe. As will be seen, such music affected European politics.

The Americanization of Europe

During the past half century, through the Marshall Plan, leadership of NATO, the stationing of hundreds of thousands of military personnel in

Popular entertainment has been one of the most prominent areas to reflect the Americanization of European culture. In late 1999, hundreds of Parisians waited outside an American-style multiplex theatre to see an American-made movie. The year before, only six French films were among the most popular in France.
Bruno Schacht/SIPA Press

Europe, student exchanges, and tourism, the United States has exerted enormous influence on Europe, especially Western Europe. The word *Americanization*, often appearing as a term of criticism in European publications, refers in part to this economic and military influence, but also to concerns about cultural loss. Many Europeans feel that American popular entertainment and economic enterprises threaten to extinguish some of the unique qualities of their nations and regions. American banks, other financial institutions, and law firms often have European branches. Large American corporations, such as the McDonald's fast-food chain, have established a presence in European cities from Dublin to Moscow. American liquor companies and distilleries now sell their goods in Europe. Styles of clothing, such as blue jeans, first popular in America, are now equally popular in Europe. Shopping centers and supermarkets, first pioneered in America, are displacing neighborhood shopping areas. American television programs and movies are readily available. Furthermore, as Europe moves toward greater economic cooperation, English seems to be emerging as the most common language of business, technology, and even some academic fields. And American influence, not British, lies behind this trend.

Rock Music and Political Protest

One of the most pervasive examples of the Americanization of European culture is the manner in which American rock music has come to dominate much of the continent. Moreover, just as when, during the Vietnam War, American popular music served as a major source of the popular criticism of that conflict, rock music in Europe has become part of a continuing critique of contemporary society.

Many lyrics emphasized the need for love, the anguish of isolation, a desire for sexual liberation, and hopes for community and peace. During the 1960s, rock music in the West was an integral feature of the antiwar movement and a vehicle for expressing discontent with the older generation. In the 1970s and 1980s, it emerged as a major vehicle for cultural and political criticism in Eastern Europe and the Soviet Union. Rock stars came to symbolize daring and even heroism. Their music emphasized subjectivity and individualism. Lyrics directly criticized communist governments, as in this example from "Get Out of Control," sung at a rock concert in Leningrad in 1986:

We were watched from the days of kindergarten.
Some nice men and kind women
Beat us up. They chose the most painful places
And treated us like animals on the farm.
So we grew up like a disciplined herd.
We sing what they want and live how they want
And we look at them downside up, as if we're
    trapped.
We just watch how they hit us
Get out of control!
Get out of control!
And sing what you want
And not just what is allowed
We have a right to yell![6]

This song later became popular throughout Eastern Europe. Sentiments like these were common in popular songs and undoubtedly contributed to the dramatic changes that swept through the region at the close of the 1980s. (See Ch. 31.)

A Consumer Society

Although European economies came under pressure during the 1990s and experienced high levels of unemployment, the consumer sector has expanded to an extraordinary degree during most of the last half century.

The consumer orientation of the Western European economy emerged as one of the most important characteristics differentiating it from Eastern Europe. Those differences produced important political results. Throughout the Soviet Union and the nations it dominated in Eastern Europe, economic planning overwhelmingly favored capital investment and military production. Those nations produced inadequate food for their people and few consumer goods. Long lines for food and nonfood staples, such as shoes and clothing, were common; automobiles were a luxury, and housing was inadequate. The quality of all consumer goods was shoddy.

By contrast, in the last fifty years, consumer goods have steadily become more available elsewhere in Europe. By the early 1950s, Western Europeans enjoyed an excellent food supply that has continued to improve. The variety of fresh and frozen foods and vegetables available to Western consumers has steadily increased. And in a sign of

---

[6]Quoted in Artemy Troitsky, *Back in the USSR: The True Story of Rock in Russia* (Boston: Faber & Faber, 1987), p. 127, as cited in Sabrina P. Ramet, *Social Currents in Eastern Europe: The Sources and Meaning of the Great Transformation* (Durham, N.C.: Duke University Press, 1991), p. 239.

the strength of Western Europe's consumer economy, if not the healthfulness of its diet, fast-food outlets have multiplied in number.

Western Europe has enjoyed a similarly great expansion of virtually all other kinds of consumer goods and services. Automobiles have become widely accessible. The number of people owning refrigerators, washing machines, electric ranges, televisions, and now microwaves, videocassette recorders, computers, compact disc players, and other small electronic consumer items has grown rapidly. A wide variety of everyday clothing has become available, from woolen goods to blue jeans and sneakers. Like their American counterparts, Western Europeans now have a whole gamut of products, such as disposable diapers and prepared baby foods, to help them raise their children. They take foreign vacations year round, prompting the expansion of ski resorts in the Alpine countries and beach resorts on the Mediterranean.

This vast expansion of consumerism, which, as noted in Chapter 16, began in the eighteenth century, became a defining characteristic of Western Europe in the late twentieth century. It stood in marked contrast to the consumer shortages in Eastern Europe. Yet through even the limited number of radios, televisions, movies, and videos available to them, people in the East grew increasingly aware of the discrepancy between their lifestyle and that of the West. They saw Western consumerism clearly linked to democratic governments, free societies, and economic policies that favored the free market and only limited government planning. Thus, the expansion of consumerism in the West, deplored by many commentators and Christian moralists, helped generate the discontent that brought down the communist governments of Eastern Europe and the Soviet Union.

Environmentalism

After World War II, shortages of consumer goods created a demand that fueled postwar economic reconstruction and growth into the 1950s and 1960s. In those expansive times, there was little room for public debate about the ethics of economic expansion and efficiency and their effects on the environment. Concerns about pollution began to emerge in the 1970s, and by the 1980s, environmentalists had developed real political clout. Among the most important environmental groups were the Club of Rome, founded in 1972, and the German Greens. The Greens formed a political party in 1979 that immediately became an electoral force. During these same years, concern for envi-

Pollution of waterways poses danger to human health in many parts of Europe and has been one of the conditions giving rise to the European environmental movement. Here, a German factory pours its refuse and chemicals into a river. Such pollution has been a particular problem in the former Soviet block nations.
Frischmuth/Argos/SABA Press Photos, Inc.

ronmental issues, such as global warming and the pollution of water and the atmosphere with substances endangering human health, commanded the attention of governments outside Europe and the agencies of the United Nations.

Several developments lay behind this new concern about dangers to the environment. The Arab oil embargo of 1973–1974 pressed home two key messages to Europeans and other nations in the Northern Hemisphere: First, natural resources are limited, and second, supplies of several critical resources only could come from foreign countries. By the 1970s, too, the environmental consequences of three decades of economic expansion were becoming increasingly apparent. Fish were dying in the Thames River in England. Industrial pollution was destroying the rivers of Germany and France. Acid rain had begun to kill trees from Sweden to Germany. Finally, long-standing apprehensions about nuclear weapons merged with concerns about their environmental effects, strengthening antinuclear groups and generating opposition to the placement of nuclear weapons in Europe.

The German Green movement originated among the radical student groups of the late 1960s. Like them, it was anticapitalist, holding business responsible for pollution. The Greens and other European environmental groups were also strongly antinuclear. Unlike the students of the 1960s, the Greens avoided violence and mass demonstrations, seeking instead to enter the electoral process directly. They elected a few representatives to the West German Parliament and to local offices.

The 1986 disaster at the Chernobyl nuclear reactor in the Soviet Union heightened concern about environmental issues and raised questions that no European government could ignore. The Soviet government had to confront casualties at the site and relocate tens of thousands of people. Clouds of radioactive fallout spread westward across Europe. Environmentalists had always contended that their issues transcended national borders. The Chernobyl fire proved them right.

After Chernobyl, virtually all European governments, East and West, began to respond to environmental concerns. Some observers believe that the environment may become a major political issue across the Continent. In Western Europe, environmental groups command a significant share of votes. Economic and political integration opens the possibility of transnational cooperation on environmental matters. As the European Economic Community solidifies, it and its member nations will likely impose environmental regulations on business and industry. The nations of Eastern Europe face the daunting task of cleaning up vast areas polluted by industrial development during the communist era and devising policies that combine environmental protection with economic growth.

The Christian Heritage

In most ways, Christianity in Europe has continued to be as hard pressed during the twentieth century as it had been in the late nineteenth. Material prosperity, political ideologies, environmentalism, gender politics, and simple indifference have replaced religious faith in many people's lives. Still, despite the loss of much of their popular support and former legal privileges, the European Christian churches continue to exercise considerable social and political influence. In Germany, the churches were one of the few major institutions that the Nazis did not wholly subdue. Lutheran clergy, such as Martin Niemöller (1892–1984) and Dietrich Bonhoeffer (1906–1945), were leaders of the opposition to Hitler. After the war, in Poland and elsewhere in Eastern Europe, the Roman Catholic Church opposed the influence of communism.

In Western Europe, religious affiliation provided much of the initial basis for the Christian democratic parties. Across Europe, the churches have raised critical questions about colonialism, nuclear weapons, human rights, and other moral issues. Consequently, even in this most secular of all ages, Christian churches have influenced state and society.

Neo-Orthodoxy

Liberal theologians of the nineteenth century often softened the concept of sin and portrayed human nature as close to the divine. The horror of World War I destroyed that optimistic faith, leaving many Europeans feeling that evil had stalked the continent.

The most important Christian response to this experience appeared in the theology of Karl Barth (1886–1968). In 1919, this Swiss pastor published *A Commentary on the Epistle to the Romans*, which reemphasized the transcendence of God and the dependence of humankind on the divine. Barth portrayed God as wholly other than, and different from, humankind. In a sense, Barth was returning to the Reformation theology of Luther, but the work of Kierkegaard had profoundly influenced his reading of the reformer. Like the Danish writer, Barth regarded the lived experience of men and women as the best testimony to the truth of Luther's theology. Those extreme moments of life described by Kierkegaard provided the basis for a real knowledge of humankind's need for God.

This view challenged outright much nineteenth-century writing about human nature. Barth's theology, which came to be known as *neo-Orthodoxy*, proved influential throughout the West in the wake of new disasters and suffering.

Liberal Theology

Neo-Orthodoxy did not, however, sweep away liberal theology, which had a strong advocate in Paul Tillich (1886–1965). This German–American theologian tended to regard religion as a human, rather than a divine, phenomenon. Whereas Barth saw God as dwelling outside humankind, Tillich believed that evidence of the divine had to be sought in human nature and human culture.

Other liberal theologians, such as Rudolf Bultmann (1884–1976), continued to work on the problems of naturalism and supernaturalism that had troubled earlier writers. Bultmann's major writing took place before World War II, but was popularized thereafter in Anglican Bishop John Robinson's *Honest to God* (1963). Another liberal Christian writer from Britain, C. S. Lewis (1878–1963), attracted millions of readers during and after World War II. This layman and scholar of medieval literature often expressed his thoughts on theology in the form of letters and short stories. His most famous work is *The Screwtape Letters* (1942). In recent years, however, European religious thought has produced few major Protestant voices.

Pope John Paul II, elected in 1978, is the first non-Italian pope since 1522. He has reasserted many traditional Roman Catholic practices and values while also extending the presence of the Roman Catholic Church in Africa and Asia and working to foster improved relations and understanding between Jews and Christians.
Deville–Gallarde/Liaison Agency, Inc.

Roman Catholic Reform

Among Christian denominations, the most significant postwar changes have been in the Roman Catholic Church. Pope John XXIII (r. 1958–1963) initiated these changes, the most extensive in Catholicism for more than a century and, some would say, since the Council of Trent in the sixteenth century. In 1959, Pope John summoned the Twenty-first Ecumenical Council (the first had been called by Emperor Constantine in the fourth century), which came to be called Vatican II. The council finished its work in 1965 under John's successor, Pope Paul VI (r. 1963–1978). Among many changes in Catholic liturgy, the council required that mass be celebrated in the vernacular languages rather than Latin. It also permitted freer relations with other Christian denominations, fostered a new spirit toward Judaism, and gave more power to bish-

ops. In recognition of the growing importance to the church of the world outside Europe and North America, Pope Paul appointed several cardinals from the former colonial nations, transforming the church into a truly world body.

In contrast to these liberal changes, however, Pope Paul and his successors have firmly upheld the celibacy of priests, maintained the church's prohibition on contraception, and opposed moves to open the priesthood to women. The church's unyielding stand on clerical celibacy has caused many men to leave the priesthood and many men and women to leave religious orders. The prohibition on contraception has caused resentment and rebellion among the laity.

John Paul II, the former Karol Wojtyla, archbishop of Cracow in Poland, was elected in 1978 after the death of John Paul I, whose reign lasted only 34 days. The youngest Pope since Pius IX (r. 1846–1878), John Paul II has pursued a three-pronged policy. First, he has maintained a traditional policy in doctrinal matters, stressing the authority of the papacy and attempting to limit doctrinal and liturgical experimentation. Second, he has encouraged the expansion of the church in the non-Western world, stressing the need for social justice, but limiting the political activity of priests. (See "John Paul II Discusses International Social Justice.")

Finally, taking a firm stand against communism, he directly contributed to the spirit of freedom in Eastern Europe that brought down the communist regimes. As a cardinal in Poland, he had clashed with the communist government. After his election, he visited Poland, lending support to the activities of the Solidarity movement. His Polish origins undoubtedly helped make him an important factor in the popular resistance to Eastern Europe's communist governments that developed during the 1980s. In this respect, his actions, both public and private, opened a new chapter in the relationship between church and state in modern Europe.

Late Twentieth-Century Technology: The Arrival of the Computer

Technology played an unprecedented role in Western life during the twentieth century, crossing international borders the way popular culture did. As with other areas of European life and society, technology originating in America had an unprece-

Pope John Paul II Discusses International Social Justice

Pope John Paul II issued his encyclical, The Social Concerns of the Church, *in 1988. In the passages given here, he attempted to set concerns for justice among developed and developing nations into the larger context of Christian moral theology.*

❖ *How does the Pope relate the fate of the poorest nations to the international system of trade and finance? What evidence is there that the Pope did not favor radical social action on the part of Roman Catholic clergy? How does this encyclical illustrate the Pope's concerns for non-European parts of the world?*

The Church's social doctrine is not a "third way" between liberal capitalism and Marxist collectivism, nor even a possible alternative to other solutions less radically opposed to one another: rather, it constitutes a category of its own. Nor is it an ideology, but rather the accurate formulation of the results of a careful reflection on the complex realities of human existence, in society and in the international order, in the light of faith and of the Church's tradition. Its main aim is to interpret these realities, determining their conformity with or divergence from the lines of the Gospel teaching on man and his vocation, a vocation which is at once earthly and transcendent; its aim is thus to guide Christian behavior. It therefore belongs to the field, not of ideology, but of theology and particularly moral theology....

The international trade system today frequently discriminates against the products of the young industries of the developing countries and discourages the producers of raw materials. There exists, too, a kind of international division of labor, whereby the low-cost products of certain countries which lack effective labor laws or which are too weak to apply them are sold in other parts of the world at considerable profit for the companies engaged in this form of production, which knows not frontiers....

...[H]umanity today is in a new and more difficult phase of its genuine development. It needs a greater degree of international ordering, at the service of the societies, economies and cultures of the whole world....

It is desirable, for example, that nations of the same geographical area should establish forms of cooperation which will make them less dependent on more powerful producers; they should open their frontiers to the products of the area; they should examine how their products might complement one another; they should combine in order to set up those services which each one separately is incapable of providing; they should extend cooperation to the monetary and financial sector....

The Church well knows that no temporal achievement is to be identified with the Kingdom of God, but that all such achievements simply reflect and in a sense anticipate the glory of the Kingdom, the Kingdom which we await at the end of history, when the Lord will come again. But that expectation can never be an excuse for lack of concern for people in their concrete personal situations and in their social, national, and international life, since the former is conditioned by the latter, especially today.

The *New York Times*, February 20, 1988, p. 4. Copyright © 1988 by The *New York Times* Co. Reprinted by permission.

---

dented impact on the continent, whether in the guise of the first airplanes or Henry Ford's method of producing affordable automobiles. But it seems certain that no single American technological achievement of the twentieth century will so influence Western life on both sides of the Atlantic, as well as throughout the rest of the world, as the computer. Though always linked to forecasts about the future, the arrival of the computer on the world scene had its origins in the Scientific Revolution of

the seventeenth century, the nation building of the nineteenth century, and the economic growth and wars of the twentieth century.

The Demand for Calculating Machines

All of the greatest figures of the Scientific Revolution—Kepler, Galileo, Descartes, and Newton—believed that mathematics held the key to the understanding and eventual command of nature.

Beginning in the seventeenth century, thinkers associated with the new science—most famously, the French mathematician and philosopher Blaise Pascal—attempted to construct machines that would carry out mathematical calculations. Their goal and that of their successors for the next two centuries was to construct machinery that could carry out complex mathematical calculations that human beings would find essentially impossible because of the tedium and the large amount of time involved in them.

Starting in the late nineteenth century, the governments of the consolidating nation–states of Europe and of the United States confronted new administrative tasks that involved collecting and organizing vast amounts of data about national censuses, tax collection, economic statistics, and the administration of pension plans and welfare legislation. During the same years, private businesses sought calculating machinery to handle and organize growing amounts of economic and business data. Such machines became technologically possible through the development of complex circuitry for electricity, the most versatile mode of energy in human history. Moreover, inventions that were dependent on electricity, including the telephone, the telegraph, underwater cables, and the wireless, created a new communications industry that in and of itself also required the organization of large databases of customer information to deliver their services. By the late 1920s, companies like National Cash Register, Remington Rand, and International Business Machines Corporation had begun to manufacture such business machinery.

Early Computer Technology

As has happened so often in history, warfare was the chief catalyst of change. After World War I and during World War II, the major powers developed new weapons that required exact mathematical ballistic calculations to effectively strike targets with bombs delivered by aircraft or long-range guns. The war effort and the Cold War diverted large investments to research in computing that might have been spent on other projects in a peace-time economy. Moreover, the efforts to break various German codes during the Second World War had further advanced computer science theory.

The first machine genuinely recognizable as a modern digital computer was the Electronic Numerical Integrator and Computer (ENIAC), built and designed at Moore Laboratories of the University of Pennsylvania and put into use by the U.S. Army in 1946 for ballistics calculation. The ENIAC was an enormous piece of equipment with 40 panels, 1,500 electric relays, and 18,000 vacuum tubes. It also used thousands of punch cards, and a separate tabulator had to print the data from them. Further computer engineering occurred at the Institute for Advanced Research in Princeton, New Jersey, in laboratories at the Massachusetts Institute of Technology, and in other laboratories run by the U.S. government and by private businesses, especially IBM. The other primary site for computer development was British university and government laboratories.

During their first decade of operation, computers were not objects of everyday life. The general public rarely saw these machines, except in magazine pictures or when television news broadcasters used them to predict election outcomes before all the votes were tabulated. Most people assumed that computing machinery, which occupied large amounts of space, would be used only by the military, government agencies, or the largest corporations. Few understood that, beyond their capacity for calculation, these machines could store, sort, transmit, manage, and transform a variety of information, as long as it could be reduced to a numerical base.

During the 1950s the invention of the transistor revolutionized electronics, permitting a miniaturization of circuitry that made vacuum tubes obsolete. Transistors allowed computers to become somewhat smaller and much more dependable, because unlike the vacuum tube, the transistor did not burn out. Nonetheless, computers remained large, unconnected mainframes accessible only to government and large corporate users. Furthermore, throughout the 1950s and 1960s, computers had to be programmed with difficult computer languages by persons expertly trained to use them.

The Development of Desktop Computers

During the late 1960s, two remarkable innovations tranformed the technology of computing and opened the way for the social impact of computing that characterizes life around the globe at the turn of the millennium. First, direction for the control of the computer became transferred to a bitmap covering the screen of a computer monitor. The mouse, invented in 1964, eased the movement of the cursor around the computer screen. Second, engineers associated with the Intel Corporation—then a California start-up company—invented the microchip, which became the heart of all future computers.

The bitmap on the screen, operated through the mouse, in effect embedded complicated computer language in the machine, hidden from the user, who simply manipulated images on the screen with the mouse. People who were by no means computer experts could thus learn to operate computers. At the same time, the tiny microchip, itself a miniature computer or microprocessor, permitted computer technology to abandon the mainframe and move to still smaller computers. In the world of computing, small proved beautiful in every way. The smaller the computer could be made, the more potential applications became available. Such downsizing was essential to all the computer applications that have made computers not only transportable but also capable of being installed in other machinery.

In the late 1970s, the technology associated with user accessibility and miniaturization coalesced into a different social vision of computing. The path was rapid, but not entirely smooth. First, at Xerox Corporation, engineers devised a small computer using a mouse, but the machine never achieved commercial success. By 1982, IBM had produced a small personal computer, but temporarily lost the race for commercialization to a then small company called Apple Computer Corporation. The design features originally developed at Xerox informed the ideas of the Apple engineers, who, in early 1984, produced a small, highly accessible, commercially successful computer, known as the Macintosh, that would fit on a desktop in the home or office. IBM soon adopted the Apple concept with different engineering and marketing approaches and manufactured a product called the Personal Computer, or PC. By the mid-1980s, for a relatively modest cost (and one that has continued to drop), individuals had available for their own personal use in their offices or homes computers with far more power than the old mainframes. The Apple Macintosh and the IBM PC transformed computers into objects of everyday life and, in doing so, initiated a transformation of everyday life itself. During the 1990s, that transformation became even more revolutionary with the development of the World Wide Web, which, in less than a decade, made possible the most rapid communication and access to information in human history. The most surprising and unanticipated result of the Internet use of computers has been the rapid development of e-commerce.

The Social Impact of the Computer

The skills involved in devising, applying, and using computers resemble the skill of reading. Both skills lead to the acquisition of new and unanticipated skills, with all the rewards and dangers such a situation implies. Computers are themselves open-ended devices that can be used

in myriad ways. In that respect, they resemble electricity, which has many uses instead of being an end in itself. Furthermore, the personal computer, integrated with the World Wide Web of the 1990s, has increased democratization by opening unparalleled access to information, just as the first relatively inexpensive automobile increased democratization earlier in the century by providing unparalleled access to geographical mobility.

Computer technology opens the possibility of transforming the idea and the reality of the workplace. The industrial revolution in the textile industry eventually drew workers out of their homes and into factories. The computer revolution is allowing many workers in service industries to spend much more time in their home offices. The computer may enable both fathers and mothers to do their work while staying at home with their children at least for part of the week. Students are already taking university courses on the computer without having physically to go to class. This new setting for learning is radically changing the idea that higher education has to take place in a particular collegiate location.

Nonetheless, the chief contemporary uses of computers still derive from the institutions that first created demand for them. Computers serve the core demands of the military and have transformed the modern battlefield, as both the Persian Gulf War of 1991 and the NATO bombing of Yugoslavia in 1999 demonstrated. The computer is now essential to governmental administration at virtually all levels. The most extensive civilian uses for computer technology have been in the telephone industry, followed by banking and finance, automobile operation, and airline reservation systems.

The computer has also begun to transform private life. People in their own homes can communicate not only with friends, but with faceless strangers, trade stocks and transfer money, access information from around the globe, read foreign newspapers even before they appear on the streets of the cities where they are published, launch their own ideas and opinions into cyberspace, establish their own on-line businesses, order goods and services worldwide, wander through the corridors of famous museums, and inspect the bedrooms of small inns before making reservations.

Despite the potential democratizing character of computer technology, the computer revolution has also introduced new concepts of "haves" and "have nots" to societies around the world. Computers, whatever their possible shortcomings, give their users the ability to do things that nonusers cannot do. Whether in poor school districts in the

United States or in poor countries of the former Soviet block, students who graduate without significant computer skills will have difficulty making their way in the world's rapidly computerizing economy. Some commentators also fear that boys in schools are more likely than girls to receive important technological training in computers. Nations whose governments and businesses become networked into the world of computers will prosper more fully than those whose access to computer technology is deficient. In that regard, the possession of computers and the ability to use them will probably determine future economic competition, just as they have determined recent military competition.

In China, web use—and dotcom advertising—have exploded. From 1996 to 2000, the number of Chinese online rose from fewer than 1 million to ten million.
Reuters/Natalie Behring/Archive Photos.

In Perspective

The twentieth century was the most destructive in human history. The wars of the first half of the century destroyed the lives of millions of Europeans and disrupted the fabric of European society across the continent. The authoritarian governments of the Bolsheviks, Fascists, and National Socialists sought to remake whole societies according to utopian visions that resulted in political repression, death, and social relocation of numerous minority groups. All of these ideologically driven governments sharply circumscribed the lives of women. Never before in European history had such a vast scheme as the collectivization of Soviet agriculture been undertaken in so short a time or with such disregard for law and human rights. The racial ideology of National Socialism led to the attempt to destroy the Jews of Europe and eradicated virtually all the Jewish community in Poland as well as those in other regions under Nazi control. The Holocaust stands as much a part of the social experience of this century as a part of its political history.

With the defeat of National Socialism and Fascism, society in Western Europe developed along more peaceful lines with powerful economic and cultural influence coming from the American presence. Migration reshaped the societies of many western nations as did the economic growth of the second half of the century. Welfare systems provided a network of security. The role and opportunities for women in the society expanded. More and more Europeans in both the west and the east attended universities. The Soviet-dominated portions of the continent lagged badly in terms of both political, intellectual and religious freedom

and never achieved a satisfactory level of consumer goods.

By the close of the century Europe like much of the rest of the world had entered a new age of technological revolution through the computer and improved health through advances in medical care. Economic growth slowed in the last decade of the century, but most of Europe outside the former communist-dominated regions continued to enjoy a high standard of living under liberal democratic governments. In the regions of the former Soviet Union and its empire the challenge became how to realize economic growth in some form of market economy without the former centralized state planning.

REVIEW QUESTIONS

1. What are major examples of state violence in twentieth-century Europe? How did this violence affect social life?
2. Compare and contrast the ideas and policies affecting women under communism, fascism, and National Socialism.
3. Describe the impact on peasant life of Stalin's policy of collectivization. How did these policies also affect city dwellers? How did the shortages in consumer goods affect everyday life in the Soviet Union?
4. What were the major features of the Jewish society in Poland between the two world wars? What were the major factors leading to the destruction of that community?
5. How has migration affected twentieth-century European social life?

6. In what specific ways was Europe American-ized in the second half of the twentieth century? How do you account for the trend toward a consumer society?

7. How have women's social and economic roles changed in the second half of the twentieth century? What tensions and difficulties have new work patterns created for women? What changes and problems have women faced amidst the political instability in Eastern Europe?

8. Discuss the changes in the pursuit and diffusion of knowledge in the twentieth century. What has been the effect of the communications revolutions? Of the boom in universities? Has Western intellectual life become more unified or less so? Why?

9. Discuss the contributions of Nietzsche and Kierkegaard to existentialism. What does Sartre mean when he says that existentialism is a philosophy of anguish and despair? How was existentialism a response to the various crises of the twentieth century?

10. Trace the major technological steps in the emergence of the computer. What are the major areas of computer application? What are the most likely changes that computers will bring in the next decade?

SUGGESTED READINGS

G. Ambrosius and W. H. Hubbard, *A Social and Economic History of Twentieth-Century Europe* (1989). The best one-volume treatment of the subject.

A. Applebaum, *Between East and West: Across the Borderlands of Europe* (1995). A travelogue recounting the state of numerous regions of Europe in the aftermath of the collapse of communism.

B. S. Anderson and J. P. Zinsser, *A History of Their Own: Women in Europe from Prehistory to the Present*, vol. 2 (1988). A broad-ranging survey.

G. Bock and P. Thane, eds., *Maternity and Gender Politics: Women and the Rise of the European Welfare States, 1880s–1950s* (1991). Explores politics relating to population, families, and mothers in the emergence of welfare legislation.

E. Bramwell, *Ecology in the 20th Century: A History* (1989). Traces the environmental movement to its late-nineteenth-century origins.

C. Browning, *Ordinary Men* (1993). Examines a single Nazi death squad.

M. Burleigh and W. Wippermann, *The Racial State: Germany, 1933–1945* (1991). A powerful examination of how racial policy affected every aspect of Nazi government.

S. Collinson, *Beyond Borders: West European Migration Policy and the 21st Century* (1993). An exploration of a major contemporary European social issue.

R. Crossman (ed.), *The God That Failed* (1949). Essays by former communist intellectuals.

L. Dobroszycki, ed., *The Chronicle of the Lodz Ghetto, 1941–1944* (1984). A collection of the official documents of daily life and administration.

B. A. Engel and A. Posadskaya-Vanderbeck, *A Revolution of Their Own: Voices of Women in Soviet History* (1998). Long interviews and autobiographical recollections by women who lived through the Soviet era.

C. Fink, P. Gasert, and D. Junker, *1968: The World Transformed* (1998). The single best collection of essays on a momentous year.

S. Fitzpatrick, *Everyday Stalinism, Ordinary Life in Extraordinary Times: Soviet Russia in the 1930s* (1999). A major study based on newly available materials.

S. Fitzpatrick, *Stalin's Peasants: Resistance and Survival in the Russian Village after Collectivization* (1994). An extensive social history.

T. Forester, ed., *The Microelectronics Revolution* (1980). Discusses the basic inventions in electronics that have created the structures for the new computers.

H. H. Goldstine, *The Computer from Pascal to von Neuman* (1972). A clear history of the technological development of the computer.

B. Graham, *Modern Europe: Place, Culture, Identity* (1998). Thoughtful essays on the future of Europe by a group of geographers.

C. S. Heller, *On the Edge of Destruction: Jews of Poland between the Two World Wars* (1994). A probing examination of the subject.

J. Herf, *Divided Memory: The Nazi Past in the Two Germanies* (1997). An exploration of the manner in which writers in East and West Germany interpreted the Nazi years.

R. Hilberg, *The Destruction of the European Jews*, 3 vols. (1985). Now the classic account of the political and administrative processes that supported the Holocaust.

H. S. Hughes, *Sophisticated Rebels: The Political Culture of European Dissent, 1968–1987* (1988). A series of thoughtful essays on recent cultural critics.

T. Judt, *Past Imperfect: French Intellectuals, 1944–1956* (1992). An important study of French intellectuals and communism.

Thomas K. Landauer, *The Trouble with Computers: Usefulness, Usability, and Productivity* (1997). An informed skeptical commentary on the impact of computers.

R. Maltby (ed.), *Passing Parade: A History of Popular Culture in the Twentieth Century* (1989). A collection of essays on a topic just beginning to receive scholarly attention.

R. Marrus, *The Unwanted: European Refugees in the 20th Century* (1985). An important work on a disturbing subject.

E. Mendelsohn, *The Jews of East Central Europe between the World Wars* (1983). An excellent introduction.

D. Meyer, *Sex and Power: The Rise of Women in America, Russia, Sweden, and Italy* (1987). A lively, useful survey.

G. Montefiore, *Philosophy in France Today* (1983). A good introduction to one of the major centers of contemporary thought.

D. Ofer and L. J. Weitzman, eds., *Women in the Holocaust* (1998). A major collection of essays.

M. Poster, *Existential Marxism in Postwar France* (1975). An excellent and clear work.

S. Strasser, C. McGovern, and M. Judt, *Getting and Spending: Eurpean and American Consumer Societies in the Twentieth Century* (1998). An extensive collection of comparative essays.

F. Thébaud, ed., *A History of Women in the West, Vol. V: Toward a Cultural Identity in the Twentieth Century* (1994). A collection of wide-ranging essays of the very highest quality.

D. Vital, *A People Apart: The Jews in Europe, 1789–1939* (1999). A major survey with excellent discussions of the interwar years.

Chapter 31

***The opening of the Berlin Wall in November 1989, more than any other
event, symbolized the collapse of the Communist governments in Eastern
Europe.*** R. Bossu/Corbis Sygma Photo News

The Cold War Era and the Emergence of the New Europe

The Emergence of the Cold War
"Containment" in American Foreign Policy
Soviet Assertion of Domination of Eastern Europe
The Postwar Division of Germany
NATO and the Warsaw Pact
The Creation of the State of Israel
The Korean War

The Khrushchev Era in the Soviet Union
The Last Years of Stalin
Khrushchev's Domestic Policies

The Three Crises of 1956
The Suez Intervention
Poland's Efforts toward Independent Action
Uprising in Hungary

Later Cold War Confrontations
Collapse of the 1960 Paris Summit Conference
The Berlin Wall
The Cuban Missile Crisis
Brezhnev and the Invasion of Czechoslovakia

The European Retreat from Empire
The Effects of World War II
Major Areas of Colonial Withdrawal

France, the United States, and Vietnam
Resistance to French Colonial Rule

The Geneva Settlement and Its Aftermath
The U.S. Involvement

Western European Political Developments during the Cold War
Christian Democratic Parties
Economic Concerns within Western Europe

Toward Western European Unification
Postwar Cooperation
The European Economic Community
The European Union

The Brezhnev Era in the Soviet Union and Eastern Europe
The United States and Détente
Invasion of Afghanistan
Communism and *Solidarity* in Poland
Relations with the Reagan Administration

The Collapse of European Communism
Gorbachev Redirects the Soviet Union
1989: Year of Revolution in Eastern Europe
The Collapse of the Soviet Union
The Yeltsin Decade
The Collapse of Yugoslavia and Civil War
Problems in the Wake of the Collapse
    of Communism

Europe at the Opening of the Global Century

KEY TOPICS

- The origins of the Cold War and the division of Europe into Eastern and Western blocs following World War II
- Decolonization and the conflicts in Korea and Vietnam
- Political and economic developments in Western Europe during the Cold War
- Polish protests against Soviet domination of Eastern Europe
- *Perestroika* and *glasnost* in the Soviet Union
- The collapse of communism in Eastern Europe and the Soviet Union
- The civil war in Yugoslavia
- Europe in the twenty-first century

During the second half of the twentieth century, the social development of Europe occurred in the climate of the rivalry and potential nuclear conflict of two superpowers whose military, economic, and political influence dominated much of the continent. From the end of World War II in 1945 until the collapse of the Soviet Union and its subject regimes in Eastern Europe between 1989 and 1991, the Soviet Union and the United States—two nuclear-armed superpowers—confronted each other in a simmering conflict known as the Cold War. While it lasted, this conflict dominated global politics and threatened the peace of Europe, which stood divided between the U.S.-dominated North Atlantic Treaty Organization (NATO) and the Soviet-dominated Warsaw Pact.

Undertaking an active role in Europe and the rest of the world constituted a major shift in foreign policy for the United States, reflecting its leaders' awareness of the dangers to which the country had been exposed when it retreated from the world scene after World War I. Moving to oppose what it regarded as the expansion of Soviet power and communist influence across the globe, the United States assumed a position of military, political, and economic leadership. This policy of active international leadership prompted the Marshall Plan, the formation of NATO, and military interventions in Korea and Vietnam.

The Cold War rapidly became globalized as regional conflicts outside Europe were drawn into the orbit of the U.S.–Soviet rivalry. As the nations of Europe retreated from empire, the rivalry between the two superpowers expanded into a contest for dominance in the postcolonial world. Superpower intervention aggravated local conflicts on every continent. Southeast Asia in particular developed into a battleground. In its efforts to limit communism, the United States became embroiled in bitter wars in Korea and Vietnam. The struggle between Israel and the Arab nations likewise became an arena of superpower conflict.

The communist government of the Soviet Union, established in 1917 and consolidated under Stalin's dictatorship, underwent many changes and attempts at redirection after World War II. The turmoil of World War I and Bolshevik victory in the civil war that followed had allowed the Soviet Union to come into existence; the turmoil of World War II permitted it to establish hegemony over eastern Europe. From the late 1940s through the 1980s, the Soviet Union tried to retain dominance in Eastern Europe and to challenge the United States around the globe.

The Soviet Union pursued two not always compatible foreign policy goals. One was to lead the international communist movement, ideologically dedicated to the overthrow of capitalism throughout the world. Recently opened archives indicate that Marxist–Leninist ideology genuinely shaped Soviet decisions and was not just a language that hid more traditional geopolitical motives. The other goal was to secure its own national interests, which sometimes put it at odds with communist movements elsewhere. Eventually, harsh rivalries emerged between the Soviet Union and other communist nations, notably the People's Republic of China. The leaders of the Soviet Union, meanwhile, failed to build lasting support for their goals, either internally or in their eastern European dependencies. Nonetheless, the Soviet Union maintained its position as a superpower and its Cold War antagonism to the United States through the early 1980s.

The Emergence of the Cold War

The tense relationship between the United States and the Soviet Union began in the closing months of World War II. Some scholars attribute the hardening of the atmosphere between the two countries to Harry Truman's assumption of the presidency in April 1945, after the death of the more sympathetic Franklin Roosevelt, and to the American possession of an effective atomic bomb. Evidence suggests, however, that Truman was trying to carry Roosevelt's policies forward and that Roosevelt himself had become distressed by Soviet actions in Eastern Europe. Some have also argued that Truman did not use the atomic bomb to try to keep Russia out of the Pacific. On the contrary, he worked hard to ensure Russian intervention against Japan at the end of the war. In part, the new coldness between the Allies arose from the mutual feeling that each had violated previous agreements. The Russians were plainly asserting permanent control of Poland and Romania under puppet communist governments. The United States, on the other hand, was taking a harder line about the extent of German reparation payments to the Soviet Union.

In retrospect, however, and as more information emerges from the previously closed Soviet archives, it appears unlikely that friendlier styles on either side could have avoided a split that arose from basic differences of ideology and interest. The Soviet Union's attempt to extend its control westward into central Europe and the Balkans and southward into the Middle East continued the general thrust of the foreign policy of tsarist Russia.

Britain had traditionally tried to restrain Russian expansion into these areas, and it was not surprising that the United States should inherit that task as Britain's power waned.

The Americans made no attempt to roll back Soviet power where it existed at the close of World War II. (See Map 31–1.) At the time, Amer-

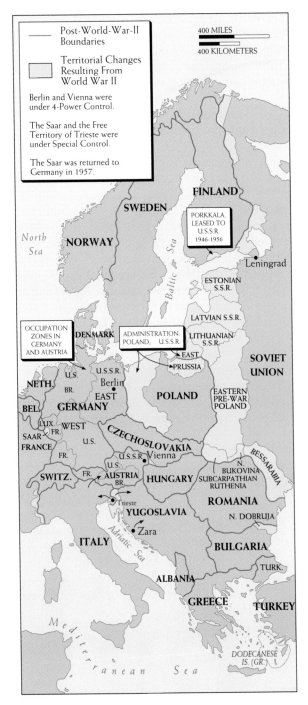

MAP 31–1 TERRITORIAL CHANGES AFTER WORLD WAR II *The map shows the shifts in territory following the defeat of the Axis. No treaty of peace formally ended the war with Germany.*

ican military forces were the greatest in U.S. history, American industrial power was unmatched in the world, and atomic weapons were an American monopoly. In less than a year from the war's end, the Americans had reduced their forces in Europe from 3.5 million to half a million. The speed of the withdrawal reflected domestic pressure to "get the boys home," but was also fully in accord with America's peacetime plans and goals, which included support for self-determination, autonomy, and democracy in the political sphere, and free trade, freedom of the seas, no barriers to investment, and an Open Door policy in the economic sphere. Those goals reflected American principles and served American interests well. As the strongest, richest nation in the world—the one with the greatest industrial base and the strongest currency—the United States would benefit handsomely from an international order based on such goals.

Although postwar American hostility to colonial empires created tensions with France and Britain, the main conflict lay with the Soviet Union. The growth in France and Italy of large, popular communist parties taking orders from Moscow led the Americans to believe that Stalin was engaged in a worldwide plot to subvert capitalism and democracy. From the Soviet perspective, extending the borders of the USSR and dominating the formerly independent successor states of Eastern Europe would provide needed security and compensate for the fearful losses the Soviet people had endured in the war. The Soviets could thus see American resistance to their expansion as a threat to their security and their legitimate aims. They considered American objections to Soviet actions in Poland and other states as an effort to undermine regimes friendly to Russia and to encircle the Soviet Union with hostile neighbors. The Soviets could also use this point of view to justify their own attempts to overthrow regimes friendly to the United States in Western Europe and elsewhere.

Evidence of the new mood of postwar hostility between the former allies was soon apparent. In February 1946, both Stalin and his foreign minister, Vyacheslav Molotov (1890–1986), publically spoke of the Western democracies as enemies. A month later, Churchill gave a speech in Fulton, Missouri, in which he declared that an "Iron Curtain" had descended on Europe, dividing a free and democratic West from an East under totalitarian rule. He warned against communist subversion and urged Western unity and strength against the new menace. In this atmosphere, difficulties grew.

"Containment" in American Foreign Policy

The resistance of Americans and Western Europeans to what they increasingly perceived as Soviet intransigence and communist plans for subversion and expansion took clearer form in 1947. The American policy became known as one of "Containment," the purpose of which was to resist the extension of Soviet expansion and influence in the expectation that eventually the Soviet Union would collapse from internal pressures and the burdens of its foreign oppression. This strategy, devised by American policymakers in the late 1940s, would direct the broad outlines of American foreign policy for the next four decades, until the Soviet Union did collapse from exactly such pressures. "Containment" marked a major departure in American foreign policy and transformed the international situation during the second half of the twentieth century. The execution of the policy led the United States to enter overseas alliances, to make formal and informal commitments of support, to undertake enormous military expenditures, and to send large amounts of money abroad. In all these respects, the United States assumed the kind of long-term foreign policy responsibilities that it had not done before in its history. The United States thus became a permanent player in European international relations and in areas of the world where only European nations had been involved earlier in the century.

THE TRUMAN DOCTRINE   Since 1944, civil war had been raging in Greece between the royalist government restored by Britain and insurgents supported by the communist countries, chiefly Yugoslavia. In 1947, Britain informed the United States that it could no longer financially support the Greeks. On March 12, President Truman asked Congress to provide funds to support Greece and Turkey, then under Soviet pressure to yield control of the Dardanelles, and Congress complied. In a speech to Congress that gave these actions much broader significance, the president set forth what came to be called the Truman Doctrine. He advocated a policy of support for "free people who are resisting attempted subjugation by armed minorities or by outside pressures," by implication, anywhere in the world. (See "The Truman Doctrine Declared.")

THE MARSHALL PLAN   American aid to Greece and Turkey took the form of military equipment and advisers. For Western Europe, where postwar poverty and hunger fueled the menacing growth of communist parties, the Americans devised the European Recovery Program. Named the Marshall Plan after George C. Marshall (1880–1959), the secretary of state who introduced it, this program provided broad economic aid to European states on the sole condition that they work together for their mutual benefit. The Soviet Union and its satellites were invited to participate. Finland and Czechoslovakia were willing to do so, and Poland and Hungary showed interest. The Soviets, however, fearing that American economic aid would attract their satellites out of the Soviet orbit, forbade them to take part.

The Marshall Plan restored prosperity to Western Europe and set the stage for Europe's unprecedented postwar economic growth. In addition to the vast

President Harry Truman greets Secretary of State George Marshall returning from Europe. Truman and Marshall were the architects of American foreign policy during the early years of the Cold War. Archive Photos

The Truman Doctrine Declared

In 1947, the British informed the United States that they could no longer support the Greeks in their fight against a communist insurrection supported from the outside. On March 12 of that year, President Truman asked Congress for legislation in support of both Greece and Turkey, which was also in danger. The principle behind that request, which became known as the Truman Doctrine, appears in the selections that follow from Truman's speech to the Congress.

❖ *How does Truman relate the goals of the Second World War to the emerging Cold War with the Soviet Union? What are the qualities that Truman associates with free governments, and how were those qualities absent in the Soviet Union and the nations of eastern Europe under its domination? How does this speech establish guidelines that might be applied to U.S. policy in parts of the world beyond Greece?*

One of the primary objectives of the foreign policy of the United States is the creation of conditions in which we and other nations will be able to work out a way of life free from coercion. This was a fundamental issue in the war with Germany and Japan. Our victory was won over countries which sought to impose their will, and their way of life, upon other nations.

To insure the peaceful development of nations, free from coercion, the United States has taken a leading part in establishing the United Nations. The United Nations is designed to make possible lasting freedom and independence for all its members. We shall not realize our objectives, however, unless we are willing to help free peoples to maintain their free institutions and their national integrity against aggressive movements that seek to impose upon them totalitarian regimes....

At the present moment in world history nearly every nation must choose between alternative ways of life. The choice is too often not a free one.

One way of life is based upon the will of the majority, and is distinguished by free institutions, representative government, free elections, guaranties of individual liberty, freedom of speech and religion, and freedom from political oppression.

The second way of life is based upon the will of a minority forcibly imposed upon the majority. It relies upon terror and oppression, a controlled press and radio, fixed elections, and the suppression of personal freedoms.

I believe that it must be the policy of the United States to support free peoples who are resisting attempted subjugation by armed minorities or by outside pressures.

I believe that we must assist free peoples to work out their own destinies in their own way.

I believe that our help should be primarily through economic and financial aid, which is essential to economic stability and orderly political processes.

From Senate Committee on Foreign Relations, *A Decade of American Foreign Policy: Basic Documents, 1941–1949* (1950), pp. 1235–1237.

program of American economic aid, the strong Christian Democratic movement that dominated the politics of Italy, France, and West Germany worked to keep communist influence at bay outside the Soviet sphere in Eastern Europe.

Soviet Assertion of Domination of Eastern Europe

For the Soviets, the determination to control Eastern Europe had both historical and ideological roots. Western European powers had invaded the lands of the Soviet Union twice in the nineteenth century (under Napoleon and during the Crimean War) and already twice more in the twentieth century. For its part, tsarist Russia had governed most of Poland for over a century and had intervened at the request of the Austrian Empire to put down the Hungarian revolution in 1849. Russia's interests in Turkey and the lands around the Black Sea were similarly long standing. Given this history and the Soviet Union's extraordinary losses in World War II, it is not surprising that Soviet leaders sought to use their Eastern European satellites as a buffer against future invasions.

The Cominform Issues a Manfesto

The Soviet Union sponsored the formation of the Cominform, an organization of European communist parties, in the autumn of 1947, only a few months after the ennunciation of the Truman Doctrine and the announcement of the Marshall Plan. The Cominform, which resembled the earlier Comintern, was a direct response to those initiatives. Its purpose was to model all socialist parties on the Soviet Communist Party and bring them under its direction. The proclamation of the Cominform, issued on October 5, 1947, set forth the Soviet vision of events and goals among the various former Allies of World War II. Compare this document with the statement of the Truman Doctrine, which had clarified the American understanding of those developments.

❖ *How does this proclamation reinterpret the war aims of the World War II Allies? How and why did the Cominform present itself as a supporter of anti-imperialism and democracy? Which nations would appear to be the audience for the proclamation? Why does the proclamation attack noncommunist socialist parties in Western Europe? How does the proclamation appear to be a reply to the Truman Doctrine?*

In the international situation brought about by the Second World War and in the period that followed fundamental changes took place. The characteristic aspect of these changes is a new balance of political forces interplaying in the world arena, a shift in the relationship between states which were the victors in the Second World War, and their reevaluation.

As long as the war lasted the Allied states fighting against Germany and Japan marched in step and were one. Nevertheless, in the Allies' camp already during the war there existed differences regarding the aims of the war as well as the objectives of the post-war and world organization. The Soviet Union and the democratic countries believed that the main objective of the war was the rebuilding and strengthening of democracy in Europe, the liquidation of fascism and the prevention of a possible aggression on behalf of Germany, and that its further aim was an achievement of an all-around and lasting cooperation between the nations of Europe.

The United States of America and with them England placed as their war aim a different goal—the elimination of competition on the world market (Germany and Japan) and the consolidation of their dominant position. This difference in the definition of war aims and post-war objective has begun to deepen in the post-war period.

Two opposite political lines have crystallized. On one extreme the USSR and the democratic countries aim at whittling down imperialism and the strengthening of democracy. On the other hand the United States of America and England aim at the strengthening of imperialism and choking democracy....

In this way there arose two camps—the camp of imperialism and anti-democratic forces, whose chief aim is an establishment of a world-wide American imperialists' hegemony and the crushing of democracy; and an anti-imperialist democratic camp whose chief aim is the elimination of imperialism, the strengthening of democracy, and the liquidation of the remnants of fascism....

In these conditions the anti-imperialist democratic camp has to close its ranks and draw up and agree on a common platform to work out its tactics against the chief forces of the imperialist camp, against American imperialism, against its English and French allies, against the Right-Wing Socialists above all in England and France. To frustrate those imperialistic plans of aggression we need the efforts of all democratic and anti-imperialist forces in Europe...

As quoted in Edward H. Judge and John W. Langdon, eds., *The Cold War: A History through Documents,* © 1999, p. 38. Reprinted by permission of Prentice Hall, Inc., Upper Saddle River, NJ.

Stalin may have seen containment as a renewed attempt by the West to isolate and encircle the USSR. In Eastern Europe, the Soviet Union found numerous supporters among those segments of the population who had opposed the various right-wing movements in those countries before the war and who had fought German Nazism during the war. In the autumn of 1947, Stalin called a meeting in Warsaw of all communist parties around the globe. There they organized the Communist

Information Bureau (Cominform), a revival of the old Comintern, dedicated to spreading revolutionary communism throughout the world. (See "The Cominform Issues a Manifesto.") In Western Europe the establishment of the Cominform officially ended the era of the popular front during which communists had cooperated with noncommunist parties. Communist leaders in the West who favored friendship, collaboration, and reform were replaced by hard-liners who attempted to sabotage the new structures.

In February 1948, in Prague, Stalin gave a dramatic and brutal display of his new policy of bringing the government of eastern Europe under direct Soviet control. The communists expelled the democratic members of what had been a coalition government and murdered Jan Masaryk (1886–1948), the foreign minister and son of the founder of Czechoslovakia, Thomas Masaryk. President Eduard Beneš (1884–1948) was forced to resign, and Czechoslovakia was brought fully under Soviet rule. There and elsewhere in eastern Europe, it was clear that there would be no multiparty political system.

During the late 1940s, the Soviet Union moved to dominate the other subject governments in Eastern Europe. It required them to impose Stalinist policies, including one-party political systems, close military cooperation with the Soviet Union, the collectivization of agriculture, Communist Party domination of universities and other institutions of education, and attacks on the churches. Long-time Communist Party officials were purged and subjected to show trials like those that had taken place in Moscow during the late 1930s. The catalyst for this harsh tightening probably was the success of Marshal Josip "Broz" Tito (1892–1980), the leader of communist Yugoslavia, in freeing his country from Soviet domination. Stalin feared that other Eastern European states might follow the Yugoslav example and moved to prevent them from doing so.

The Postwar Division of Germany

Soviet actions, especially those in Czechoslovakia, increased the determination of the United States to go ahead with its own arrangements in Germany.

Disagreements over Germany During the war, the Allies had never decided how to treat Germany after its defeat. At first they all agreed it should be dismembered, but they differed on how. By the time of Yalta, Churchill had come to fear Russian control of Eastern and Central Europe and began to oppose dismemberment.

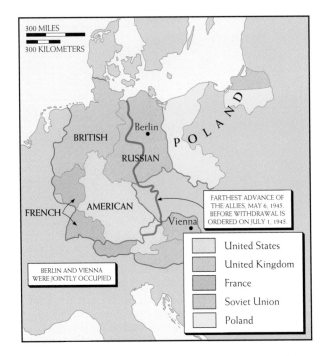

MAP 31–2 OCCUPIED GERMANY AND AUSTRIA *At the war's end, defeated Germany, including Austria, was occupied by the victorious Allies in the several zones shown here. Austria, by prompt agreement, was reestablished as an independent, neutral state, no longer occupied. The German zones hardened into an "East" Germany (the former Soviet zone) and a "West" Germany (the former British, French, and American zones). Berlin, within the Soviet zone, was similarly divided.*

The Allies also differed on economic policy. The Russians swiftly dismantled German industry in the eastern zone, but the Americans acted differently in the western zone. (See Map 31–2.) They concluded that if they followed the Soviet policy, the United States would have to support Germany economically for the foreseeable future. It would also cause political chaos and open the way for communism. They preferred, therefore, to try to make Germany self-sufficient, and this meant restoring, rather than destroying, its industrial capacity. To the Soviets, the restoration of a powerful industrial Germany, even in the western zone only, was frightening and unacceptable. The same difference of approach hampered agreement on reparations. The Soviets claimed the right to the industrial equipment in all the zones, and the Americans resisted their demands.

Berlin Blockade When the Western powers agreed to go forward with a separate constitution for the western sectors of Germany in February 1948, the Soviets walked out of the joint Allied Control Commission. In the summer of that year, the Western powers issued a new currency in

Located deep within communist East Germany, West Berlin was suddenly cut off from the West when Josef Stalin blockaded all surface traffic in an attempt to take over the war-torn city. Between June 1948 and May 1949, British and U.S. pilots made 272,000 flights, dropping food and fuel to civilians. the Berlin Airlift successfully foiled the blockade, and the Soviet Union reopened access on May 12. Brown Brothers

their zone. Berlin, though well within the Soviet zone, was governed by all four powers. The Soviets feared the new currency, which was circulating in Berlin at better rates than their own currency. They chose to seal the city off by closing all railroads and highways that led from Berlin to West Germany. Their purpose was to drive the Western powers out of Berlin.

The Western allies responded to the Berlin blockade by airlifting supplies to the city for almost a year. In May 1949, the Russians were forced to back down and to reopen access to Berlin. The incident, however, was decisive. It increased tensions and suspicions between the opponents and hastened the separation of Germany into two states. West Germany formally became the German Federal Republic in September 1949, and the eastern region became the German Democratic Republic a month later. Ironically, Germany had been dismembered in a way no one had planned or expected. The two Germanies and the divided city of Berlin, isolated within East Germany, would remain central fixtures in the geopolitics of the Cold War until it ended in 1989.

NATO and the Warsaw Pact

Meanwhile, the nations of Western Europe had been coming closer together. The Marshall Plan encouraged international cooperation. In March 1948, Belgium, the Netherlands, Luxembourg, France,

and Britain signed the Treaty of Brussels, providing for cooperation in economic and military matters. In April 1949, these nations joined with Italy, Denmark, Norway, Portugal, and Iceland to sign a treaty with Canada and the United States that formed the North Atlantic Treaty Organization (NATO), which committed its members to mutual assistance in case any of them was attacked. The NATO treaty transformed the West into a bloc. A few years later, West Germany, Greece, and Turkey joined the alliance. For the first time in history, the United States was committed to defend allies outside the Western Hemisphere.

A series of bilateral treaties providing for close ties and mutual assistance in case of attack governed Soviet relations with the states of Eastern Europe. In 1949, these states formed the Council of Mutual Assistance (COMECON) to integrate their economies. Unlike the NATO states, the Eastern alliance system was under direct Soviet domination through local communist parties controlled from Moscow and overawed by the presence of the Red Army. The Warsaw Pact of May 1955, which included Albania, Bulgaria, Czechoslovakia, East Germany, Hungary, Poland, Romania, and the Soviet Union, merely gave formal recognition to the system that already existed. Europe was divided into two unfriendly blocs. The Cold War had taken firm shape in Europe. (See Map 31–3.)

The strategic interests and ambitions of the United States and the Soviet Union would not, however, permit the Cold War to be limited to the European continent. Major flash points would erupt around the world during the decades that followed, most particularly in the Middle East and in Asia. The establish-

Major Dates of Early Cold War Years	
1945	Yalta Conference
1945	Founding of the United Nations
1946	Churchill's Iron Curtain speech
1947	(March) Truman Doctrine regarding Greece and Turkey
1947	(June) Announcement of Marshall Plan
1948	Communist takeover in Czechoslovakia
1948	Communist takeover in Hungary
1948–1949	Berlin blockade
1949	NATO founded
1949	East and West Germany emerge as separate states
1950–1953	Korean conflict
1955	Warsaw Pact founded

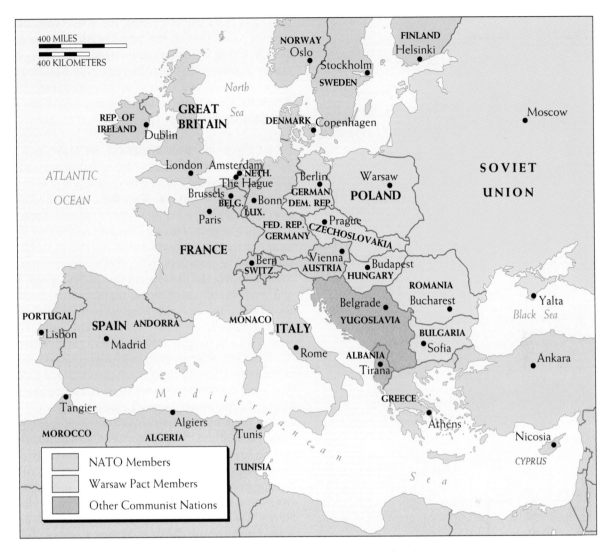

MAP 31–3   MAJOR COLD WAR EUROPEAN ALLIANCE SYSTEMS   *The North Atlantic Treaty Organization, which includes both Canada and the United States, stretched during the Cold War era as far east as Turkey. By contrast, the Warsaw Pact nations were the contiguous communist states of Eastern Europe, with the Soviet Union, of course, as the dominant member.*

ment of a communist government in Cuba after 1959 would bring the conflict to the American hemisphere as well. In each case, the Cold War rivalry drew what might otherwise have been regional conflicts into the realm of superpower strategic concerns.

The Creation of the State of Israel

One of the areas of ongoing regional conflict that became a major point of Cold War rivalry was the Middle East. Following World War I, Great Britain had exercised the chief political influence in the region under various postwar mandates. After World War II, both the Zionist movement seeking to establish an independent Jewish state and Arab nationalists seeking to achieve self-determination challenged British authority and influence.

BRITISH BALFOUR DECLARATION   The modern state of Israel was the achievement of the world Zionist movement, founded in 1897 by Theodor Herzl and later led by Chaim Weizmann (1874–1952). The British Balfour Declaration of 1917 had favored establishing a national home for the Jewish people in Palestine. Between the wars, thousands of Jews, mainly from Europe, immigrated to the area, then governed by Great Britain under a mandate of the League of Nations. During the interwar period, the *Yishuv*, or Jewish community in Palestine, developed its own political parties, press, labor unions, and educational system. There were many conflicts with the Arabs already living in Palestine, who considered the Jewish settlers intruders. The British tried, but failed, to mediate those clashes.

This situation might have prevailed longer in Palestine, except for the outbreak of World War II

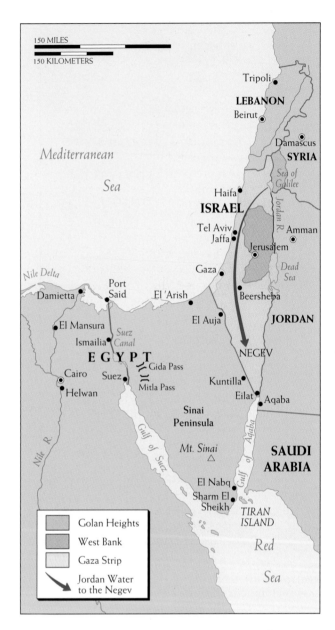

MAP 31–4   ISRAEL AND ITS NEIGHBORS IN 1949   *The terri-tories gained by Israel in 1949 did not secure peace in the region. In fact, the disposition of those lands and the Arab refugees who live there has constituted the core of the region's unresolved problems to the present day.*

passed a resolution calling for a division of the territory into two states, one Jewish and one Arab. The Arabs in Palestine and the surrounding Arab states resisted this resolution. Not unnaturally, they resented the influx of new settlers. Many Palestinian Arabs were displaced and became refugees themselves.

ISRAEL DECLARES INDEPENDENCE   In May 1948, the British officially withdrew from Palestine and the *Yishuv* declared the independence of a new Jewish state called Israel on May 14. Two days later, the United States, through the personal intervention of President Truman, recognized the new nation, whose first prime minister was David Ben-Gurion (1886–1973). Almost immediately, Lebanon, Syria, Jordan, Egypt, and Iraq invaded Israel. The fighting continued throughout 1948 and 1949. By the end of its war of independence against the Arabs, Israel had expanded its borders beyond the limits originally set forth by the United Nations. (See Map 31–4.) Jerusalem was divided. Jordan controlled the Old City of Jerusalem, but Israel retained control of the New City. By 1949, Israel had secured its exis-tence, but not the acceptance of its Arab neighbors. So long as Egypt, Jordan, Syria, Lebanon, Iraq, and Saudi Arabia, to name those nations closest, withheld diplo-matic recognition, the peace was only an armed truce.

The Arab–Israeli conflict would inevitably draw in the superpowers. The dispute directly involved Europe because many of the citizens of Israel had emigrated from there, and Europe, like the United States, was highly dependent on oil from Arab coun-tries. Furthermore, both the United States and the Soviet Union believed that they had major strate-gic and economic interests in the region.

By 1949, the United States had established itself as a firm ally of Israel. Gradually, the Soviet Union began to furnish aid to the Arab nations. The bipo-lar tensions that had settled over Europe were thus transferred to the Middle East.

The Korean War

While early stages of the Cold War took place in Europe and the Arab–Israeli conflict developed in the Middle East, the United States confronted armed aggression in Asia. As part of a UN police action, it intervened militarily in Korea, following the same principle of containment that directed its actions in Europe.

Between 1910 and 1945, Japan, as an Asian colo-nial power, had occupied and exploited Korea, but at the close of World War II, the Japanese were repelled. The United States and the Soviet Union divided Korea into two parts along the thirty-eighth parallel of lati-tude. Korea was supposed to be reunited. By 1948, however, two separate states had been organized: the

and Hitler's attempt to exterminate the Jews of Europe. The Nazi persecution united Jews through-out the world behind the Zionist ideal of a Jewish state in Palestine, and touched the conscience of the United States and other Western powers. It seemed morally right to do something for Jewish refugees from Nazi concentration camps.

THE UNITED NATIONS RESOLUTION   In 1947, the British turned over to the United Nations the problem of the relationship of Arabs and Jews in Palestine. That same year, the United Nations

Democratic People's Republic of Korea in the North, supported by the Soviet Union, and the Republic of Korea in the South, supported by the United States.

In late June 1950, after border clashes, North Korea invaded South Korea across the thirty-eighth parallel. (See Map 31–5.) The United States intervened and was soon supported by a United Nations mandate. Great Britain, Turkey, Australia, and other countries sent token forces. The Korean police action was technically a UN venture to halt aggression. (It had been made possible when the Soviet ambassador boycotted the United Nations when the key vote was taken.) For the United States, the point of the Korean conflict was to contain the spread and halt the aggression of communism.

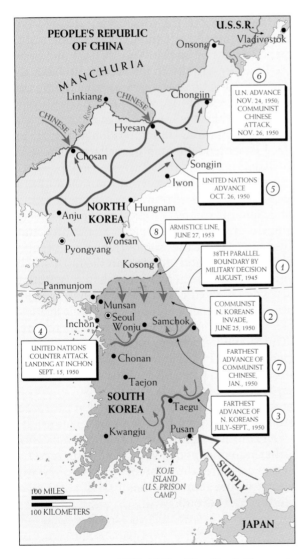

MAP 31–5   KOREA, 1950–1953   *The North Korean invasion of South Korea in 1950 and the bitter three-year war to repulse the invasion and stabilize a firm boundary near the thirty-eighth parallel are outlined here. The war was a dramatic application of the American policy of "containment" of communism.*

Late in 1950 the Chinese, responding to the approach of UN forces near their border, sent troops to support North Korea. The American forces had to retreat. The U.S. policymakers believed that the Chinese, who, since 1949, had been under the communist government of Mao Tse-tung (1893–1976), were simply the puppets of the Soviet Union. Accordingly, the Americans viewed the movement of Chinese troops into South Korea as another example of communist pressure against a noncommunist state, similar to what had previously happened in Europe. Today it is clear that tension existed between Moscow and the People's Republic of China, but that was little known or appreciated at the time.

On June 16, 1953, the Eisenhower administration concluded an armistice ending the Korean War and restoring the border near the thirty-eighth parallel. American troops would, however, remain stationed in Korea for the rest of the century. The lessons of the Cold War learned in Europe appeared to have been successfully applied to Asia. The American government's faith in Containment was confirmed. The Korean conflict transformed the Cold War into a global encounter and rivalry that ranged well beyond the borders of Europe.

The formation of NATO and the Korean conflict capped the first round of the Cold War. In 1953, Stalin's death and the armistice in Korea fostered hopes that international tensions might ease. In early 1955, Soviet occupation forces left Austria after that nation accepted neutral status. Later that year the leaders of France, Great Britain, the Soviet Union, and the United States held a summit conference in Geneva. Nuclear weapons and the future of divided Germany were the chief items on the agenda. Despite public displays of friendliness, the meeting produced few substantial agreements on major problems, and the rivalry and polemics of the Cold War soon resumed.

The Khrushchev Era in the Soviet Union

The Last Years of Stalin

No other nation had suffered greater losses or more deprivation during World War II than the Soviet Union. Many Russians had hoped that the end of the war would signal a reduction in the scope of the police state and a redirection of the economy away from heavy industry to consumer products. They were disappointed. Stalin did little or nothing to modify the character of the regime he had created. If anything, his determination to centralize his authority and a desire to undertake a new wave of internal purges continued until his death on March 6, 1953.

For a time, no single leader replaced Stalin. Rather, the presidium (the renamed politburo) pursued a policy of collective leadership. Gradually, however, power and influence began to devolve on Nikita Khrushchev (1894–1971), who had been named party secretary in 1953. Three years later, he became premier. Khrushchev's rise ended collective leadership, but he never commanded the extraordinary powers of Stalin.

Khrushchev's Domestic Policies

The Khrushchev era, which lasted until the autumn of 1964, witnessed a marked retreat from Stalinism, though not from authoritarianism. Khrushchev sought to reform the Soviet system, but to maintain the firm dominance of the Communist Party. Intellectuals were somewhat freer to express their opinions. Although Boris Pasternak (1890–1960), the author of *Dr. Zhivago* (1957), was not permitted to receive the Nobel prize for literature in 1958, a dissident author such as Aleksandr Solzhenitsyn (b. 1918) could publish *One Day in the Life of Ivan Denisovich* (1963). Khrushchev's economic policy also differed somewhat from Stalin's, with modest efforts to meet the demand for more consumer goods and decentralize economic planning and execution. In agriculture, Khrushchev removed many of the more restrictive regulations on private cultivation and sought to expand the area available for wheat cultivation. At first this program led to record grain production, but inappropriate farming techniques soon caused soil erosion on the newly farmed lands, reducing yields. The agricultural problem grew, forcing the Soviet Union to import vast quantities of grain from the United States and other countries.

THE SECRET SPEECH OF 1956 In February 1956, Khrushchev made an extraordinary departure from expected practice by directly attacking the policies of the Stalin years. At the Twentieth Congress of the Communist Party, Khrushchev gave a secret speech (later published outside the Soviet Union) in which he denounced Stalin and his crimes against socialist justice during the purges of the 1930s. The speech caused shock and consternation in party circles, but it also opened the way for genuine, if limited, internal criticism of the Soviet government and for many of the changes in intellectual and economic life cited earlier. Gradually, Khrushchev removed the strongest supporters of Stalinist policies from the presidium. By 1958, all Stalin's former supporters were gone, and none had been executed. (See "Khrushchev Denounces the Crimes of Stalin: The Secret Speech.")

Khrushchev's speech had repercussions well beyond the borders of the Soviet Union. Communist leaders in Eastern Europe took it as a signal that they could govern with greater leeway than before and retreat from Stalinist policies. Indeed, Khrushchev's speech was simply the first of a number of important and extraordinary events in 1956.

The Three Crises of 1956

The Suez Intervention

In July 1956, Egypt's President Gamal Abdel Nasser (1918–1970), who had seized power in that country in 1952, nationalized the Suez Canal, until then controlled by British and French interests. Egyptian control of the canal threatened the access of Great Britain and France to Persian Gulf oil supplies, essential to their industrial economies. In October 1956 war broke out between Egypt, then receiving arms from the Soviet Union, and the new state of Israel, closely tied to the West. Britain and France seized the opportunity to intervene. Although they justified their actions as a way to separate the combatants, their real motive was to regain control of the canal and reassert their influence in the region. Israel joined with France and Britain. Although this alliance helped Israel fend off Arab guerrilla attacks, it also associated Israel with the former imperial powers.

Although the Suez intervention was a military success, with Israel seizing the Sinai and Britain and France landing troops in the canal zone, it ended in a humiliating diplomatic defeat. The United States refused to support the Anglo–French intervention, and the Soviet Union protested in the most strident terms. The Anglo–French forces had to withdraw, and Egypt retained control of the canal. A United Nations peacekeeping force separated the armies of Israel and Egypt, and Israel withdrew from the Sinai.

The Suez intervention proved that without the support of the United States the nations of Western Europe could no longer use military force to impose their will on the rest of the world. Also, the United States and the Soviet Union showed that they would restrain their allies from actions that might result in a wider conflict. At the same time, the Arab–Israeli conflict remained unresolved. The Arab states refused to recognize the existence of Israel. The Middle East would remain a major flash point of the Cold War and beyond.

Poland's Efforts toward Independent Action

The autumn of 1956 saw important developments in Eastern Europe, based in large measure on miscalculations about the real meaning of Khruschev's secret speech attacking Stalin.

Khrushchev Denounces the Crimes of Stalin: The Secret Speech

In 1956, Khrushchev denounced Stalin in a secret speech to the Party Congress. The New York Times *published a text of that speech, smuggled from Russia.*

❖ *What are the specific actions on the part of Stalin that Khrushchev denounced? Why does Khrushchev pay so much attention to Stalin's creation of the concept of an "enemy of the people"? Why does Khrushchev draw a distinction between the actions of Stalin and those of Lenin?*

Stalin acted not through persuasion, explanation, and patient cooperation with people, but by imposing his concepts and demanding absolute submission to his opinion. Whoever opposed this concept or tried to prove his viewpoint and the correctness of his position was doomed to removal from the leading collective [group] and to subsequent moral and physical annihilation....

Stalin originated the concept of "enemy of the people." This term automatically rendered it unnecessary that the ideological errors of a man or men engaged in a controversy be proved; this term made possible the usage of the most cruel repression violating all norms of revolutionary legality, against anyone who in any way disagreed with Stalin, against those who were only suspected of hostile intent, against those who had bad reputations.

This concept "enemy of the people" actually eliminated the possibility of any kind of ideological fight or the making of one's views known on this or that issue, even those of a practical character. In the main, and in actuality, the only proof of guilt used, against all norms of current legal science, was the "confession" of the accused himself; and, as a subsequent probing proved, "con-

fessions" were acquired through physical pressures against the accused....

Lenin used severe methods only in the most necessary cases, when the exploiting classes were still in existence and were vigorously opposing the revolution, when the struggle for survival was decidedly assuming the sharpest forms, even including civil war.

Stalin, on the other hand, used extreme methods and mass repressions at a time when the revolution was already victorious, when the Soviet State was strengthened, when the exploiting classes were already liquidated and Socialist relations were rooted solidly in all phases of national economy, when our party was politically consolidated and had strengthened itself both numerically and ideologically. It is clear that here Stalin showed in a whole series of cases his intolerance, his brutality and his abuse of power. Instead of proving his political correctness and mobilizing the masses, he often chose the path of repression and physical annihilation, not only against actual enemies, but also against individuals who had not committed any crimes against the party and the Soviet Government....

From The *New York Times*, June 5, 1956, pp. 13–16. Copyright © 1956 The *New York Times*. Reprinted by permission.

The Polish Communist Party had been subjected to Stalinist discipline during the late 1940s. One of the Communist leaders who had been imprisoned was Wladyslaw Gomulka (1905–1982). Toward the end of 1954 the authorities released him, and he stood ready to reenter a leadership position. The opportunity presented itself in June 1956, when a workers' uprising took place in Poznan, indicating discontent with the highly disciplined communist regime. By October, the hard-line Stalinist leadership of Poland was resigning. Gomulka began to exercise considerable influence and was attending government meetings. The Russians were sufficiently concerned to order troop movements and send a delegation, in-

cluding Khrushchev, to Warsaw. In the end, Gomulka emerged as the new communist leader of Poland. The choice of the Polish communists, he also proved acceptable to the Soviets because he was genuinely a communist, promised to continue economic and military cooperation, and, most important to the Soviets, continued Polish membership in the Warsaw Pact. Within those limits, he moved to halt the collectivization of Polish agriculture and to improve the relationship between the communist government and the Polish Roman Catholic Church. This resolution more or less allowed the Polish Communist Party to manage its own affairs, leading another Eastern European country to seek similar autonomy.

Uprising in Hungary

In late October, as the Polish problem was nearing resolution, Hungarians in Budapest demonstrated in sympathy for the Poles. Hungary's communist government moved to stop the demonstrations, and street fighting erupted. The Hungarian Communist Party then installed a new government headed by former premier Imre Nagy (1896–1958).

Although a communist, Nagy sought greater independence for Hungary. He demanded more than Gomulka had in Poland and appealed to noncommunist groups in Hungary for support. He wanted the Soviets to withdraw their troops and Hungary to become a neutral state. Nagy even called for Hungarian withdrawal from the Warsaw Pact. These demands were wholly unacceptable to the Soviet Union. In early November, Soviet troops invaded Hungary, deposed Nagy (who was executed in 1958), and installed Janos Kadar (1912–1989) as premier.

The Polish and Hungarian disturbances showed the limits of the Soviet Union's tolerance for independence within its bloc, notwithstanding Khrushchev's criticisms of Stalinism. They also demonstrated that the countries of Eastern Europe would not be permitted to imitate Austrian neutrality. It should also be noted that the Suez intervention had distracted international attention and permitted the Soviet Union

Major Dates of the Early Khrushchev Era	
1953	Death of Stalin
1955	Austria established as a neutral state
1955	Geneva summit
1956	(February) Khrushchev's secret speech denouncing Stalin
	(Autumn) Polish crisis
	(October) Suez crisis
	(October) Hungarian uprising
1957	Sputnik launched

freer action within its sphere of influence. Finally, the failure of the United States to support the Hungarian uprising demonstrated the hollowness of American political rhetoric about liberating the captive nations of Eastern Europe.

The events of 1956 in the Middle East and Eastern Europe solidified the position of the United States and the Soviet Union as superpowers. In different ways and to differing degrees, the two superpowers had demonstrated this new political reality to their allies. The nations of Western Europe would be able to make independent policy among themselves within Europe,

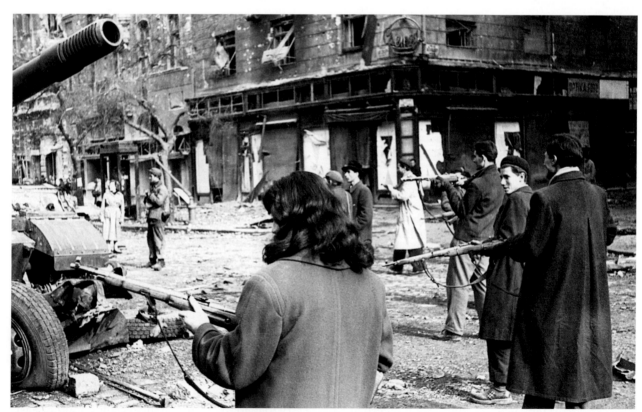

In Budapest in October 1956, street battles raged for several days until Soviet tanks put down the Hungarian revolt.
Darolle/Corbis Sygma Photo News

but were generally curtailed from independent action on the broader international scene. For approximately twenty-five years, the nations of Eastern Europe would be permitted virtually no autonomous actions in either the domestic or the international sphere.

Later Cold War Confrontations

Collapse of the 1960 Paris Summit Conference

After 1956, the Soviet Union began to talk about "peaceful coexistence" with the United States. With the 1957 launch of *Sputnik*, the Soviet Union appeared to have achieved enormous technological superiority over the West. In 1958, the two countries began negotiations toward limiting the testing of nuclear weapons. The same year, however, the Soviet Union demanded the West grant formal diplomatic recognition to East Germany and then announced that the status of West Berlin must be changed and the Allied occupation forces withdrawn. These demands were refused, but they had made Germany, and particularly Berlin, the center of East–West tension. In 1959, matters relaxed sufficiently for several Western leaders to visit Moscow and for Khrushchev to tour the United States. A summit meeting was scheduled for May 1960, and President Eisenhower was to go to Moscow.

Just before the Paris Summit Conference, the Soviet Union shot down an American U-2 aircraft that was flying reconnaissance over Soviet territory. Khrushchev demanded an apology from Eisenhower for this air surveillance. Eisenhower accepted full responsibility for the surveillance policy, but refused to apologize publicly. Khrushchev then refused to take part in the summit conference, just as the participants arrived in the French capital. The conference, as well as Eisenhower's proposed trip to the Soviet Union, was thus aborted.

The Soviets did not scuttle the summit meeting on the eve of its opening simply because of the American spy flights. They had long been aware of these flights and had other reasons for protesting them when they did. By 1960, the communist world itself had split between the Soviets and the Chinese. The latter were portraying the Russians as lacking sufficient revolutionary zeal. Destroying the summit was, in part, a way to demonstrate the Soviet Union's hardline attitude toward the capitalist world.

The Berlin Wall

The aborted Paris conference opened the most difficult period of the Cold War. In 1961 the new U.S. president, John F. Kennedy (1917–1963), and Premier Khrushchev met in Vienna. The conference was inconclusive, but the American president left wondering whether the two nations could avoid war.

Throughout 1961, thousands of refugees from East Germany crossed the border into West Berlin. The western sector of the city was the single point in Eastern Europe where persons living under Soviet dominance might escape to a free political climate. This outflow of people embarrassed East Germany and hurt its economy. It also demonstrated the Soviet Union's inability to control events in Eastern Europe.

In August 1961, the East Germans, with the support of the Soviet Union, erected a concrete wall along the border between East and West Berlin, shutting the two parts of the city off from each other. In June 1963, President Kennedy himself appeared in Berlin, making a famous speech in which he declared, *"Ich bin ein Berliner"* ("I am a Berliner"). Despite speeches and symbolic support from the West, the wall halted the flow of refugees and brought the United States' commitment to West Germany into doubt.

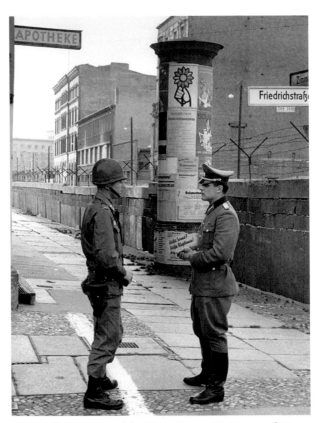

The wall constructed in 1961 separating East and West Berlin became the single most important symbol of the Cold War. Along the wall there was a series of check points where troops were stationed to control the very limited flow of people between the sections of the divided city. Here a U.S. Army officer (left) and an Eastern German officer face each other at the Friedrichstrasse checkpoint. UPI/Corbis

The Cuban Missile Crisis

The most dangerous days of the Cold War occurred during the Cuban missile crisis of 1962, which represented another facet of the globalization of the Cold War, on this occasion into the Americas. Cuba lies less than 100 miles from the United States. In 1957 Fidel Castro (b. 1926) launched a communist insurgency in Cuba, which toppled the dictatorship of Flugencio Batista (1901–1973) on New Year's Day of 1959. Thereafter Castro established a communist government, and Cuba became an ally of the Soviet Union. These events caused enormous concern within the United States.

In 1962, the Soviet Union secretly began to place nuclear missiles in Cuba. Now concern turned to confrontation. The American government, under President Kennedy, blockaded Cuba, halted the shipment of new missiles, and demanded the removal of existing installations. After a tense week, during which communications between Washington and Moscow were permeated with admonitions and threats, the Soviets backed down, and the crisis ended. This adventurism in foreign policy undermined Khrushchev's credibility in the ruling circles of the Soviet Union and caused other non-European communist regimes to question the Soviet Union's commitment to their security and survival. It also increased the influence of the People's Republic of China in communist circles and convinced Soviet military leaders of the need to strengthen their forces, so that they would be as strong as, or stronger than, those of the United States in any future confrontation.

If the Cuban missile crisis had led to war, the United States could have launched missiles over Europe or from European bases into the Soviet Union. The crisis

Major Dates of Later Cold War Years	
1959	Khrushchev visit to the United States
1960	Failed Paris Summit
1961	Soviet Union erects Berlin Wall
1962	Cuban missile crisis
1963	Test Ban Treaty between Soviet Union and the United States
1964	Khrushchev falls from power
1968	Soviet invasion of Czechoslovakia
1972	Strategic Arms Limitation Treaty

thus threatened Europe directly, but it was the last major Cold War confrontation to do so. In 1963, the United States and the Soviet Union concluded a nuclear test ban treaty. This agreement marked the beginning of a lessening in the overt tensions between the two powers. By 1964, many in the Soviet Communist Party had concluded that Khrushchev had tried to do too much too soon and had done it poorly. On October 16, 1964, Khrushchev was forced to resign. He was replaced by Alexei Kosygin (1904–1980) as premier and Leonid Brezhnev (1906–1982) as party secretary. Brezhnev eventually emerged as the dominant figure.

Brezhnev and the Invasion of Czechoslovakia

In 1968, during what became known as the *Prague Spring*, the government of Czechoslovakia, under Alexander Dubcek (1921–1992), began

President John F. Kennedy announcing on television the strategic blockade of Cuba, and his warning to the Soviet Union about missile sanctions during the Cuban missile crisis. Hutton Getty/Archive Photos

to experiment with a more liberal communism. Dubcek expanded freedom of discussion and other intellectual rights at a time when they were being suppressed in the Soviet Union. In the summer of 1968, the Soviet government and its allies in the Warsaw Pact sent troops into Czechoslovakia and installed communist leaders more to its own liking.

At the time of the invasion, Soviet Party Chairman Brezhnev, in what came to be termed the *Brezhnev Doctrine*, declared the right of the Soviet Union to interfere in the domestic politics of other communist countries. Whereas the Truman Doctrine of 1947 had supported democratic governments and offered help to resist further communist penetration in Europe, the Brezhnev Doctrine of 1968 sought to sustain the communist governments of Eastern Europe and prevent any liberalization in the region. No further direct Soviet interventions occurred in Eastern Europe after 1968, yet the invasion of Czechoslovakia showed that any political experimentation involving greater liberalization could trigger Soviet military repression. (See "The Warsaw Pact Justifies the Invasion of Czechoslovakia.")

The European Retreat from Empire

At the opening of the twentieth century, European powers had dominated or directly ruled most of Africa and large parts of Asia, while the United States ruled the Philippines. After World War I, many of the colonial peoples had argued unsuccessfully for their independence at the Paris Peace Conference in 1919. Before World War II, nationalist political movements arose in a number of these colonial empires. After the war, these movements burgeoned throughout most of the colonial world and drove out the Europeans.

Consequently, the first two decades of Cold War conflict and tension within Europe took place against the backdrop of the breakup of the great European empires in Africa, the Middle East, and Asia. Virtually all of those colonial holdings would be abandoned by the end of the third quarter of the twentieth century. The one exception to this movement, known at the time as *decolonization*, was the vast empire of the Soviet Union itself that had been established by the tsars.

The nations that emerged from the former colonial status were generally termed the Third World, because, in the Cold War context, most of them having

In the summer of 1968, Soviet tanks rolled into Czechoslovakia, ending that country's experiment in liberalized communism. This picture shows defiant, flag-waving Czechs on a truck rolling past a Soviet tank in the immediate aftermath of the invasion. Archive Photos

The Warsaw Pact Justifies the Invasion of Czechoslovakia

In 1968, the Soviet Union and its Warsaw Pact allies invaded Czechoslovakia to halt the political liberalization being carried out by that portion of the Czech Communist Party led by Alexander Dubcek. Their intention was to place other, less liberal, communists into power. This invasion provided the occasion for the declaration of the Brezhnev Doctrine, *according to which Warsaw Pact members had the right to interfere in the internal affairs of their communist neighbors.*

❖ *On what grounds does the Soviet Union justify its invasion of Czechoslovakia? Why does this justification invoke the possibility of the Czechs' involvement with foreign enemies? What limits does the justification place on political experimentation in Eastern European nations dominated by the Soviet Union? How could the principles of this justification be applied to other nations under Soviet control?*

Tass [the Soviet Government news agency] is authorized to state that [Communist] party and Government leaders of the Czechoslovak Socialist Republic have asked the Soviet Union and other allied states to render the fraternal Czechoslovak people urgent assistance, including assistance with armed forces. This request was brought about by the threat that has arisen to the socialist system existing in Czechoslovakia and to the statehood established by the Constitution—the threat emanating from the counterrevolutionary forces that have entered into a collusion with foreign forces hostile to socialism.

The events in Czechoslovakia and around her were repeatedly the subject of exchanges of views between leaders of fraternal socialist countries, including the leaders of Czechoslovakia. These countries are unanimous in that the support, consolidation and defense of the people's socialist gains is a common internationalist duty of all the socialist states....

The Soviet Government and the Governments of the allied countries—the People's Republic of Bulgaria, the Hungarian People's Republic, the German Democratic Republic, the Polish People's Republic—proceeding from the principles of inseparable friendship and cooperation and in ac-

cordance with the existing contractual commitments, have decided to meet the above-mentioned request for rendering necessary help to the fraternal Czechoslovak people.

The decision is fully in accord with the right of states to individual and collective self-defense envisaged in treaties of alliance concluded between the fraternal socialist countries. This decision is also in line with vital interests of our countries in safeguarding European peace against forces of militarism, aggression and revenge, which have more than once plunged the peoples of Europe into wars.

Soviet armed units, together with armed units of the above-mentioned allied countries, entered the territory of Czechoslovakia on Aug. 21 [1968]. They will be immediately withdrawn from the Czechoslovak Socialist Republic as soon as the obtaining threat to the gains of socialism in Czechoslovakia, the threat to the security of the socialist countries, is eliminated and lawful authorities find that further presence of these armed units there is no longer necessary.

The actions which are being taken are not directed against any state and in no measure infringe state interests of anybody. They serve the purpose of peace and have been prompted by concern for its consolidation.

From The *New York Times*, December 5, 1989, p. A15. Copyright © 1989 The *New York Times*. Reprinted by permission.

just emerged from colonial dominance wished to remain unaligned with the two superpowers. Nonetheless, both the United States and the Soviet Union were apprehensive about the potential alignment of the new nations and moved to create spheres of influence and, in some cases, alliances. Certain nations, such as India, fiercely pursued policies of neutrality in hopes of receiving aid and support from both sides.

The Effects of World War II

Decolonization after1945 was a direct result of both the war itself and the rise of indigenous nationalist movements within Africa, Asia, and the Middle East. World War II drew the military forces of the colonial powers back to Europe. The Japanese conquests in east Asia helped force the European pow-

The Pan-African Congress Issues a Declaration to the Colonial Powers

For more than two centuries before World War II, European powers had dominated or directly ruled large parts of Africa, the Middle East, and Asia. The costs of fighting World War II meant that the European powers had less wealth with which to govern their colonies. The principles of the victorious Allies in Europe were also inconsistent with colonialism, as was the foreign policy of the United States, now the dominant Western power. In 1945, representatives to the Fifth Pan-African Congress met in Manchester, England, where they set forth their demand for freedom from colonialism in terms that echoed the political values of the Western Allies.

❖ *How did the Pan-African Congress use the values of the Western Allies in the Second World War to support their own demands for liberty? What did the Congress expect to achieve through independence for African nations? How might the Proclamation of the Cominterm that appeared in a previous document be considered a response to the demands of the Pan African Congress and other groups that sought to resist European colonialism?*

The delegates believe in peace. How could it be otherwise, when for centuries the African peoples have been the victims of violence and slavery? Yet if the Western world is still determined to rule mankind by force, then Africans, as a last resort, may have to appeal to force in the effort to achieve freedom, even if force destroys them and the world.

We are determined to be free. We want education. We want the right to earn a decent living; the right to express our thoughts and emotions, to adopt and create forms of beauty. We demand for Black Africa autonomy and independence so far and no further than it is possible in this One World for groups and peoples to rule themselves subject to inevitable world unity and federation.

We are not ashamed to have been an age-long patient people. We continue willingly to sacrifice and strive. But we are unwilling to starve any longer while doing the world's drudgery, in order to support by our poverty and ignorance a false aristocracy and a discarded imperialism.

We condemn the monopoly of capital and the rule of private wealth and industry for private profit alone. We welcome economic democracy as the only real democracy.

Therefore, we shall complain, appeal and arraign. We will make the world listen to the fact of our condition. We will fight in every way we can for freedom, democracy, and social betterment.

From Molefi Kete Asante and Abus S. Abarry, *African Intellectual Heritage: A Book of Sources.* Copyright © 1996 Temple University Press, pp. 520–521. Reprinted by permission of Temple University Press.

ers from that area and demonstrated that their presence might not be permanent. After the military and political dislocations of the war came the immediate postwar European economic collapse, which left the European colonial powers less able to afford to maintain their positions abroad.

The war aims of the Allies had also undermined colonialism. It was difficult to fight against tyranny in Europe while maintaining colonial dominance abroad. The general embrace of the doctrine of the self-determination of nations that had driven European politics since 1919 proved powerful within their empires. Within the colonies, nationalist movements of varying strength had arisen before World War II and became stronger after that conflict. Gifted political

leaders who had been educated in Europe often led these movements. Among the most important of these leaders were Mohandas Gandhi (1869–1948) in India, Ho Chi Minh (1892–1969) in Vietnam, Kwame Nkrumah (1909–1972) in Ghana, and Jomo Kenyatta (1889–1978) in Kenya. The names of colonial leaders became household words in the European press and political discussion. The leaders used the values and political ideologies they had learned in Europe, liberal in some cases and socialist or communist in others, to attack the colonial situation. Such leadership, as well as the frequently blatant injustice imposed on colonial peoples, helped make the nationalist movements effective. (See "The Pan-African Congress Issues a Declaration to the Colonial Powers.")

MAP 31–6   DECOLONIZATION IN AFRICA AND ASIA AFTER WORLD WAR II   *The map shows when the European possessions in Africa and Asia achieved independence from the late 1940s to the 1970s.*

The postwar policy of the United States, which opposed the continuation of European empires, and the emergence of the civil rights movement also encouraged Europe's retreat from empire. Under the leadership of Reverend Martin Luther King, Jr., the U.S. civil rights movement echoed many of the values and ideologies that would turn the European powers away from empire.

This mid-twentieth-century process of decolonization marked the conclusion of almost five centuries of European dominance of much of the world outside Europe. From the voyages of discovery in the late fifteenth century, Europeans in possession of advanced technologies and driven by a confusing mixture of motives, including greed, missionary goals, and humanitarian impulses, had come to dominate, govern, and administer vast areas of the globe. The first retreat from empire—the general European abandonment of the Americas—occurred between approximately 1776 and 1830 with the American and Haitian Revolutions and the wars of independence in Latin America. Many of the ideas inspiring the people of both North and South America had come from the European enlightenment. The twentieth-century retreat from empire in Africa, the Caribbean, the Middle East, and Asia repeated that experience, with the nationalist movements also often drawing their ideas

from European political ideologies. Furthermore, the leadership of resistance to empire in the Americas and then a century and a half later in Africa, the Middle East, and Asia tended to come from the local elites who were weary of economic exploitation and discrimination and who were capable of galvanizing popular support. During both eras of imperial retreat, the governments of Europe generally did not go willingly or without resistance.

Major Areas of Colonial Withdrawal

Decolonization was anything but a systematic process. The British under the postwar Labor government were the nation most prepared to accept what many had come to regard as the inevitable retreat from empire. India was the largest single imperial holding of any nation. In 1947 Britain left India, which, as a result of religious disputes, broke into two states, India and Pakistan. In 1948, Burma and Sri Lanka (formerly Ceylon) became independent. As already observed, Britain was also forced from the Middle East by the formation of the state of Israel and Arab nationalist movements. During the 1950s, the British tried to prepare colonies for self-government. Ghana (formerly the Gold Coast) and Nigeria—which became self-governing in 1957 and

1960, respectively—were the major examples of planned decolonization. In other areas, such as Malta and Cyprus, the British withdrew under the pressure of militant nationalist movements.

The smaller colonial powers had much less choice. The Dutch were forced from the East Indies possessions, which they had governed since the seventeenth century, in 1949 as the independent nation of Indonesia emerged. In the late 1950s, Belgium believed that it had to leave Africa quickly in order to avoid a long colonial conflict. In 1960, the Belgian Congo, became independent in the midst of great turmoil. For some time, France tried to maintain its position in Southeast Asia, but was defeated in 1954. It was similarly driven from Algeria in 1962 in a conflict that disrupted internal French political life. President Charles de Gaulle carried out a policy of referendums on independence within the French colonial possessions in sub-Saharan Africa. By the late 1960s, only Portugal remained a traditional colonial power. Following a revolution in Portugal in 1974, its African colonies of Mozambique and Angola were finally liberated in 1974 and 1975, respectively. (See Map 31–6.)

The development of these former colonies in the second half of the twentieth century has followed two distinct paths. The more recent history of the independent states in Africa has, in general, been marked by political instability and poverty. By contrast, Asia has been an area of general political stability and remarkable economic growth, challenging the economies of both the United States and Western Europe.

Ho Chi Minh (1892–1969), center, and advisers meet during the war against the French in 1954. Black Star

France, the United States, and Vietnam

French decolonization in particular became an integral part of the Cold War and led directly to the long military involvement of the United States in the southeast Asian country of Vietnam.

Resistance to French Colonial Rule

During the years of the Korean conflict, another war was being fought in Asia, between France and the Viet Minh nationalist movement in Indochina. In its push for empire, France had occupied this territory (which contained Laos, Cambodia, and Vietnam) between 1857 and 1893.

Ho Chi Minh's Leadership
By 1930, Ho Chi Minh (1892–1969) had turned a movement against French colonial rule into the Indochinese Communist Party. After organizing

this party, he traveled in Asia and spent time in the Soviet Union. Throughout the 1930s, however, the French suppressed most activities by the Communist Party in their colony. World War II provided new opportunities for Ho Chi Minh and other nationalists as they fought both the Japanese who occupied Indochina in 1941 and the pro-Vichy French colonial administration that collaborated with the Japanese. Thus, action against the Japanese thereafter meshed neatly with action against the French. The war established Ho Chi Minh as a major nationalist leader. He was a communist to be sure, but he had achieved his position in Vietnam during the war without the support of the Chinese communists.

In September 1945, Ho Chi Minh declared the independence of Vietnam under the Viet Minh, a coalition of nationalists that the communists soon dominated. In 1946 France and the Viet Minh reached a short-lived armistice, which was followed the next year by the outbreak of full-fledged war. In 1948 the French established a friendly Vietnamese government that was independent, but retained a loose union with France, an arrangement unacceptable to both the Viet Minh and most other nationalists.

Until 1949, the United States had displayed minimal concern about the Indochina War. The establishment of the Communist People's Republic of China that year dramatically changed the U.S. outlook. The United States now saw the French colonial war against Ho Chi Minh as an integral part of the Cold War conflict. Even though the United States supported the French effort in Vietnam financially, it was not prepared, despite divisions among policymakers, to intervene militarily.

The Geneva Settlement and Its Aftermath

In the spring of 1954, during a conference in Geneva on the future of Vietnam, the French stronghold of Dien Bien Phu fell to Viet Minh forces. By late June, a complicated and generally unsatisfactory peace accord had been secured.

NORTH AND SOUTH VIETNAM The Geneva conference divided Vietnam at the seventeenth parallel of latitude. North of the parallel, centered in Hanoi, the Viet Minh were in charge; below it, centered in Saigon, the French were in charge. This was to be a temporary border. By 1956, elections were to be held to reunify the country. The prospect of elections meant that, theoretically, both groups could function politically in the territory of the other. In effect,

MAP 31–7 VIETNAM AND ITS NEIGHBORS *This map identifies important locations in the long and complex struggle centered in Vietnam.*

the conference attempted to transform a military conflict into a political one.

The United States was less than happy about the results of the Geneva discussions. Its first major response came in September 1954, with the formation of the Southeast Asia Treaty Organization (SEATO). In some respects, this collective security agreement paralleled the European NATO alliance. It did not, however, involve the integration of military forces the way NATO did, nor did it include all the major states of the region. Its membership consisted of the United States, Great Britain, France, Australia, New Zealand, Thailand, Pakistan, and the Philippines.

By 1955, American policymakers had begun to think about the Indochina region, and particularly Vietnam, largely in terms of the Korean example. The U.S. government assumed that, like the government of North Korea, the government in North Vietnam was basically a communist puppet. The same year, French troops began to withdraw from South Vietnam. As they left, the various Vietnamese political groups began to fight for power.

THE UNITED STATES AND THE DIEM GOVERNMENT The United States stepped into the turmoil in Vietnam with military and economic aid. Among the Vietnamese politicians, it chose to support Ngo Dinh Diem (1901–1963), a strong noncommunist nationalist who had not collaborated with the French. Because the United States had been publicly and deeply committed to the French, however, Vietnamese nationalists would view any government it supported with suspicion. In October 1955, Diem established a Republic of Vietnam in the territory for which the Geneva conference had made France responsible. Diem announced that he and his newly established government were not bound by the Geneva agreements and that elections would not be held in 1956. The American government, which had not signed the Geneva documents, supported his position. Diem undertook an anticommunist campaign which began a program of political repression that soon created internal resistance in South Vietnam. In 1960 the National Liberation Front was founded, with the goals of overthrowing Diem, unifying the country, reforming the economy, and ousting the Americans. It was anticolonial, nationalist, and communist. Its military arm was called the Viet Cong and was aided by the government of North Vietnam. (See Map 31–7.) Diem, a Roman Catholic, also faced mounting criticism from Buddhists and the army. His response to these pressures was further repression and dependence on an ever-smaller group of advisers.

United States armed forces patrol in Vietnam. At the war's peak, more than 500,000 American troops were stationed in South Vietnam. The United States struggled in Vietnam for more than a decade, seriously threatening its commitment to Western Europe.
C. Simonpietri/Corbis Sygma Photo News

Major Dates in the Vietnam Conflict	
1945	Ho Chi Minh proclaims Vietnamese independence from French rule
1947–1954	War between France and Vietnam
1950	U.S. financial aid to France
1954	Geneva conference on Southeast Asia opens
1954	French defeat at Dien Bien Phu
1954	Southeast Asia Treaty Organization founded
1955	Diem establishes Republic of Vietnam in the south
1960	Founding of National Liberation Front to overthrow the Diem government
1961	Six hundred American troops and advisers in Vietnam
1963	Diem overthrown and assassinated
1964	Gulf of Tonkin Resolution
1965	Major U.S. troop commitment
1969	Nixon announces policy of "Vietnamization"
1973	Ceasefire announced
1975	Saigon falls to North Vietnamese troops

The U.S. Involvement

The Eisenhower and Kennedy administrations continued to support Diem while demanding reforms in his government. The American military presence grew from about 600 people in early 1961 to more than 16,000 troops in late 1963. The political situation in Vietnam became increasingly unstable. On November 1, 1963, Diem was overthrown and murdered in an army coup in which the United States was deeply involved. The United States hoped that a new government in South Vietnam would generate popular support. Thereafter, the United States sought to find a leader who could fulfill that hope. It finally settled on Nguyen Van Thieu (b. 1923), who governed South Vietnam from 1966 to 1975.

President Kennedy was assassinated on November 22, 1963. His successor, Lyndon Johnson, vastly expanded the commitment to South Vietnam. In August 1964, after an attack on an American ship in the Gulf of Tonkin, Johnson authorized the first

bombing of North Vietnam. In February 1965, major bombing attacks began. They continued, with only brief pauses, until early in 1973. The land war grew until more than 500,000 Americans were stationed in South Vietnam.

In 1969 President Richard Nixon began a policy known as "Vietnamization," which involved the gradual withdrawal of American troops from Vietnam while the South Vietnamese army took over the full military effort. Peace negotiations had begun in Paris in the spring of 1968, but a ceasefire was not finally arranged until January 1973. American troops left South Vietnam, and North Vietnam interred its American prisoners of war. In early 1975, an evacuation of South Vietnamese troops from the northern part of their country turned into a complete rout as they were attacked by the North Vietnamese. On April 30, 1975, Saigon fell to the Viet Cong and the North Vietnamese army.

The United States intervention in Vietnam, which grew out of a power vacuum left by decolonization, affected the entire Western world. For a decade after the Cuban missile crisis, Vietnam largely diverted the attention of the United States from Europe. American prestige suffered, and the U.S. policy in Southeast Asia made many Europeans question the basic wisdom of the American government and its commitment to Western Europe. Many young Europeans—and not a few Americans—born after World War II came to regard the United States not as a protector of liberty, but as an ambitious, aggressive, and cruel power trying to keep colonialism alive after the end of the colonial era.

Western European Political Developments during the Cold War

During the decades spanning the Cold War, the U.S. involvement in Vietnam, and the continuing Soviet domination of Eastern Europe, the nations of Western Europe achieved unprecedented economic prosperity and maintained or inaugurated independent liberal democratic governments. Most of them confronted the problems associated both with decolonization and with maintaining economic growth.

The end of the Second World War saw vast constitutional changes in much of Western Europe, except for Portugal and Spain, which remained dictatorships until the mid-1970s. Either before or during the war, Germany, Italy, and France had experienced authoritarian governments. The construction of stable liberal democratic political frameworks became a major goal of their postwar political leaders, as well as of the United States. All concerned recognized that the earlier political stuctures in those nations had not been able to resist the rise of right-wing, antidemocratic movements. It became widely recognized in light of the Great Depression that democracy required a social and economic base, as well as a political structure. Most Europeans came to feel that government ought to ensure economic prosperity and social security. Success at doing so, they believed, would stave off the kind of turmoil that had brought on tyranny and war and that could lead to communism.

Christian Democratic Parties

Except for the British Labour Party, the vehicles of the new postwar politics were not, as might have been expected, the democratic socialist parties. On the whole, those parties did not prosper after the onset of the Cold War. They were opposed by both communists and conservatives. Rather, various Christian democratic parties, usually leading coalition governments, introduced the new policies.

These parties were a major new feature of postwar politics. They were largely Roman Catholic in leadership and membership. Catholic parties had existed in Europe since the late nineteenth century. Until the 1930s, however, they had been conservative and had protected the social, political, and educational interests of the church. They had traditionally opposed communism, but proposed few positive programs of their own. The postwar Christian democratic parties of Germany, France, and Italy, however, were progressive and welcomed non-Catholic members. Democracy, social reform, economic growth, and anti-communism were their hallmarks.

The events of the war years largely determined the political leadership of the postwar decade. On the Continent, those groups and parties, including communist parties, that had been active in the resistance against Nazism and fascism held an initial advantage. After 1947, however, in a policy naturally favored by the United States, communists were systematically excluded from all Western European governments.

The most immediate postwar domestic problems included not only those created by the physical damage of the conflict but often also those that had existed in 1939. The war, however, opened new opportunities for solving those prewar difficulties.

Economic Concerns within Western Europe

Except for France, the economy dominated all other political issues from the end of World War II onward. The most remarkable success story of those years was what became known as the "economic miracle" of West Germany. That nation, under both Christian Democratic and Social Democratic ministries, achieved unprecedented prosperity. In Great Britain, the Labour ministry of Clement Attlee, which governed from 1945 to 1951, introduced the welfare state and nationalized major industries like coal mining and steel. From the 1960s through the 1970s, clashes between unions and business became commonplace. When Margaret Thatcher (b. 1925), the first woman prime minister of Great Britain, took office in 1979, she moved strongly against the unions and pressed for a more nearly free market economy. In 1997, after eighteen years of Conservative government, the Labour Party returned to power, but on a platform of much more limited state intervention. Elsewhere in Europe parties of the traditional political left also were elected to office, but without exception, at the close of the century they favored retreat from government involvement and government-sponsored welfare programs.

Toward Western European Unification

The unprecedented steps toward economic cooperation and unity that Western European nations have taken during the past five decades are the single most important success story of the second half of the century. The process arose originally from American encouragement in response to the Soviet domination of Eastern Europe and from the Western European states' own sense that they lacked effective political power.

Postwar Cooperation

The movement toward unity could have occurred in at least three ways: politically, militarily, or economically. Economic cooperation, unlike military and political cooperation, involved little or no immediate loss of sovereignty. Furthermore, it brought material benefits to all the states involved, increasing popular support for their governments. Moreover, the administration of the Marshall Plan and the organization of NATO gave the countries involved new experience in working with each other and demonstrated the productivity and efficiency that resulted from mutual cooperation.

The first effort toward economic cooperation was the formation of the European Coal and Steel Community in 1951 by France, West Germany, Italy, and the "Benelux" countries (Belgium, the Netherlands, and Luxembourg). The community

Margaret Thatcher, Britain's first woman prime minister, took office in 1979. She moved against trade unions and promoted a more nearly free-market economy.
Peter Marlow/Corbis Sygma Photo News

both benefitted from and contributed to the immense growth of material production in Western Europe during this period. Its success reduced the suspicions of government and business groups about coordination and economic integration.

The European Economic Community

It took more than the prosperity of the European Coal and Steel Community to draw European leaders toward further unity, however. The unsuccessful Suez intervention and the resulting diplomatic isolation of France and Britain persuaded many Europeans that they could only significantly influence the two superpowers or control their own destinies by acting together. So, in 1957, through the Treaty of Rome, the six members of the Coal and Steel Community agreed to form a new organization: the European Economic Community (EEC). The members of the *Common Market*, as the EEC was soon known, envisioned more than a free-trade union: They sought to achieve the eventual elimination of tariffs, a free flow of capital and labor, and similar wage and social benefits in all their countries.

The Common Market achieved stunning success during its early years. By 1968, well ahead of schedule, all tariffs among the six members had been abolished. Trade and labor migration among the members grew steadily. Moreover, nonmember states began to copy the EEC and, later, to seek membership. In 1959, Britain, Denmark, Norway, Sweden, Switzerland, Austria, and Portugal formed the European Free Trade Area. By 1961, however, Great Britain had decided to seek Common Market membership. Twice, in 1963 and 1967, President de Gaulle of France vetoed British membership. He felt that Britain was too closely tied to the United States to support the EEC wholeheartedly. Finally, in 1973, Great Britain, Ireland, and Denmark became members. Throughout the late 1970s, however, and into the 1980s, momentum slowed. Norway and Sweden, with relatively strong economies, declined to join. Although in 1982 Spain, Portugal, and Greece applied for membership and were eventually admitted, sharp disagreements and a sense of stagnation within the EEC continued.

The European Union

In 1988, the leaders of the EEC reached an important decision. By 1992 the EEC was to be a virtual free-trade zone with no trade barriers or other restrictive trade policies. In 1991, the Treaty of Maastricht made a series of specific proposals leading to a unified EEC currency (the Euro) and a strong central bank. The treaty was submitted to referendums in several European states. Initially, it failed to be adopted in Denmark,

The move to achieve economic unity within Europe by eliminating all internal trade barriers and restrictive trade policies has encountered organized resistance. These French farmers are demonstrating against EEC policies.   Liaison Agency, Inc.

and it passed only narrowly in France and Great Britain, making clear that it could not be enforced without wider popular support. When the treaty took effect in November 1993, the EEC was renamed the European Union. Throughout the 1990s, the Union grew in influence. Its most notable achievement was the launching in early 1999 of the Euro, which has become the common denominator of most West European currencies and which will become the single circulating currency in most of Western Europe early in the twenty-first century.

Several major political concerns at present confront the European Union. First, it must decide how to relate to the host of newly independent states in Eastern Europe whose economies and governments are less strong than those of the present members of the Union. Second, the profound influence of Germany, now the most populous country of Europe, and of the German economy, Europe's largest, makes many Europeans uneasy. Europeans do not want the further development of the European Union to lead to German economic and political domination. Third,

whereas in the past it was primarily the bureaucracy of the European Commission headquartered in Brussels that shaped the policies of the European Union, the political leaders of the member states and the European Parliament, which sits in Strasbourg, will have more influence. Finally, no one knows what the full impact of a common currency and interest rate policies set by a new central bank will be.

The European Union encountered a new, unexpected challenge just after the turn of the century in Austria. In order to form a government, the Austrian chancellor turned to a coalition with the Freedom Party led by Jörg Haider, who made compromising statements about the Nazi era in Austrian history. The party itself has been associated with anti-immigration policies regarded as racially motivated by many observers. The European Union took various steps, including downgrading its diplomatic relations with Austria, to isolate the new Austrian government on the grounds that it had broken the implicit politically liberal character of the Union.

The Brezhnev Era in the Soviet Union and Eastern Europe

While Western Europe moved toward unity and experienced democracy and considerable prosperity during the seventies and early eighties, the Soviet Union resisted change both internally and within Eastern Europe. Under Brezhnev, who governed from 1964 to 1982, the Soviet government became markedly more repressive at home, suggesting a return to Stalinist policies.

Brezhnev made virtually no effort to draw younger persons into the administration of the government or the party. The entire governing structure literally aged without finding sources of renewal. However, the membership of the Soviet Communist Party itself, never a large percentage of the population, did expand. That meant finding jobs for new party members, who also sought to enjoy various perks and privileges from their party membership. A general climate of corruption set in. In the various republics, party members from the local ethnic groups were allowed to take over the party leadership to a greater extent than ever before in Soviet history. These leaders came to have a loyalty both to the party and to local constituencies. This potentially divided loyalty would prove to be important in the late 1980s.

The Brezhnev years were also a time of general repression. The terrors of Stalinism were not revived, but police surveillance was pervasive. In 1974 the government expelled Aleksandr Solzhenitsyn. It also began to harass Jewish citizens, creating bureaucratic obstacles for those who wanted to emigrate to Israel.

This internal repression gave rise to a dissident movement. Certain Soviet citizens dared to criticize the regime in public and to demonstrate against it. They accused the government of violating the human rights provision of the 1975 Helsinki Accords, discussed in the next section. The dissidents included prominent citizens, such as the Nobel prize-winning physicist Andrei Sakharov (1921–1989). The government responded with further repression, placing some opponents in psychiatric hospitals and others under what amounted to house arrest.

The United States and Détente

Foreign policy under Brezhnev combined attempts to reach an accommodation with the United States with continued efforts to expand Soviet influence and maintain Soviet leadership of the communist movement.

Although the Soviet Union sided with North Vietnam in its war with the United States, Soviet support was restrained. Under President Richard Nixon (1969–1974), the United States began a policy of détente with the Soviet Union, and the two countries concluded agreements on trade and on reducing strategic arms. Despite these agreements, Soviet spending on defense, and particularly on its navy, grew, damaging the consumer sectors of the economy.

During Gerald Ford's presidency (1974–1977), both the United States and the Soviet Union along with other European nations signed the Helsinki Accords. The Accords recognized the Soviet sphere of influence in Eastern Europe, but they also recognized the human rights of the signers' citizens, which every government, including the Soviet Union, agreed to protect. President Jimmy Carter (1977–1981), a strong advocate of human rights, sought to induce the Soviet Union to comply with this commitment, a policy that cooled relations between the two countries.

Throughout this period of detente, in addition to its military presence in Eastern Europe, the Soviet Union pursued an activist foreign policy. During the 1970s, it financed Cuban military intervention in Angola, Mozambique, and Ethiopia. Soviet funds also flowed to the Sandinista forces in Nicaragua and to Vietnam, which permitted the Soviets to use naval bases after North Vietnam conquered the south in 1975. The Soviet Union provided funds and weapons to various Arab governments for use against Israel. Each of these actions represented either Soviet support for what it viewed as its own strategic interests or pressures against those of the United States. Even more important, following its backdown in the Cuban missile crisis, the Soviet government determined to build up its military forces. By the early 1980s, the Soviet Union possessed the largest armed force in the world and had achieved virtual nuclear parity with the United States.

Invasion of Afghanistan

It was at this moment of great military strength in 1979 that the Brezhnev government decided to invade Afghanistan, a strategic decision of enormous long-range consequences for the future of the Soviet Union. Although the Soviet Union already had a presence in Afghanistan, the Brezhnev government, for reasons that remain unclear, determined to send in troops to ensure its influence in central Asia and to support a client Afghan government.

The invasion brought a sharp response from the United States. The U.S. Senate refused to ratify a second Strategic Arms Limitation agreement that President Carter had signed earlier that year. The United States also embargoed grain shipments to the Soviet Union, boycotted the 1980 Olympic Games in Moscow, and sent aid to the Afghan rebels through various third parties, as did several Islamic nations. The U.S. Central Intelligence Agency also became directly involved. China thoroughly disapproved of the invasion as well and helped the rebels.

Eventually, the Soviet forces bogged down in Afghanistan and could not defeat their guerrilla enemies. The Afghans killed approximately 2000 Soviet troops a year and inflicted many other casualties. The morale and prestige of the Soviet army plummeted. At first, few Soviets knew about the problems in Afghanistan, but during the 1980s, the military failure became common knowledge in the Soviet Union. Although the Afghan War did not make daily headline news in the Western press, it sapped Soviet strength for ten years and had a demoralizing effect on the Soviet Union not unlike that which the Vietnam conflict had caused in the United States.

Communism and *Solidarity* in Poland

Events in Poland commencing in 1980—a time when the Soviet government was becoming increasingly rigidified and involved in Afghanistan—challenged both the authority of the Polish Communist Party and the influence of the Soviet Union.

After the events of late 1956 when the Polish Communist Party had accommodated itself to Soviet domination, Poland was plagued by chronic economic mismanagement and persistent shortages of food and consumer goods for twenty-five years. In 1978, the election of Karol Wojtyla, cardinal archbishop of Cracow, as Pope proved important for Polish resistance to Communist control and Soviet domination. An outspoken Polish opponent of Communism now occupied a position of authority and enormous public visibility well beyond the reach of Soviet Communist control. The new Pope visited his homeland in 1979 and received a tumultuous welcome.

In August 1980, Polish workers struck the shipyard at Gdansk, demanding the right to be represented by their own independent union, Solidarity. *Here, strikers display the* Solidarity *banner.*   Liaison Agency, Inc.

In July 1980, the Polish government raised meat prices, leading to hundreds of protest strikes across the country. On August 14, workers occupied the Lenin shipyard at Gdansk. The strike soon spread to other shipyards, transport facilities, and factories connected with the shipbuilding industry. The strikers, led by Lech Walesa (b. 1944), refused to negotiate through any of the traditionally government-controlled unions. The Gdansk strike ended on August 31 after the government promised the workers the right to organize an independent union called *Solidarity*. In September, the head of the Polish Communist Party was replaced, the Polish courts recognized *Solidarity* as an independent union, and the state-controlled radio broadcast a Roman Catholic mass for the first time in thirty years.

The summer of 1981 saw events that were no less remarkable occur within the Polish Communist Party itself. For the first time in any European communist state, secret elections for the party congress were permitted with real choices among the candidates. Poland remained a nation governed by a single party,

Major Dates of the Brezhnev Era

1974	Solzhenitsyn expelled
1975	Helsinki Accords
1979	Soviet invasion of Afghanistan
1980	U.S. Olympic Games boycott
1981	Martial law declared in Poland in response to Solidarity
1982	Death of Brezhnev

but for the time being, the party congress permitted real debate within its ranks.

This extraordinary Polish experiment, however, ended abruptly. In 1981, General Wojciech Jaruzelski (b. 1923) became head of the Polish Communist Party and the army imposed martial law in December. (See "Poland Declares Martial Law.") Several of the leaders of *Solidarity* were arrested. The Polish military acted to preserve its own position and perhaps to prevent a Soviet invasion similar to the one in Czechoslovakia in 1968. Martial law continued in effect until late in 1983, but the Polish Communist Party continued to fail to solve Poland's major economic problems.

Although, by the time of Brezhnev's death in 1982, the Soviet system appeared to observers inside and outside the country to have become rigid and corrupt, virtually no one expected rapid change in the Soviet Union or its satellites. The nations of Eastern Europe were expected to continue with one-party governments, their aspirations for self-determination smothered, and with only limited possibilities for independent political action. Almost everyone assumed that the political situation that had lasted forty years would endure far into the future. Almost no one anticipated the vast changes that were imminent throughout both the Soviet Union and Eastern Europe.

Relations with the Reagan Administration

Early in the administration of President Ronald Reagan (1981–1989), the United States relaxed its grain embargo and placed less emphasis on human rights. At the same time, however, Reagan intensified Cold War rhetoric, famously describing the Soviet Union as an "evil empire." More important, the Reagan administration increased U.S. military spending, slowed arms limitation negotiations, deployed a major new missile system in Europe, and proposed the Strategic Defense Initiative (dubbed "Star Wars"

Poland Declares Martial Law

On December 13, 1981, General Wojciech Jaruzelski, the premier of Poland and the head of the Polish Communist Party, announced the imposition of martial law. The action was taken after months of liberal reform in Poland, led by the independent trade union Solidarity. The government turned to military rule out of fear that the political activity of Solidarity would endanger the rule of the Communist Party in Poland. The reason that was announced for the imposition of martial law was to prevent disorder.

❖ *What events in Poland had led to the imposition of martial law? How did Jaruzelski use fear of disorder to justify his action? Why did both the Polish Communist government and the Soviet Union so fear the activities of Solidarity? Are there any indications in this statement that Jaruzelski may have feared a Soviet invasion of Poland if the Polish Communist government did not itself take action?*

Our country is on the edge of the abyss. Achievements of many generations, raised from the ashes, are collapsing into ruin. State structures no longer function. New blows are struck each day at our flickering economy. Living conditions are burdening people more and more.

Through each place of work, in many Polish people's homes, there is a line of painful division. The atmosphere of unending conflict, misunderstanding and hatred sows mental devastation and damages the traditions of tolerance.

Strikes, strike alerts, protest actions have become standard. Even students are dragged into it....

With our aims, it cannot be said that we [the Communist Party government] did not show good will, moderation, patience, and sometimes there was probably too much of it. It cannot be said the Government did not honor the social agreements [made with Solidarity in 1980 at Gdansk]. We even went further. The initiative of the great national understanding was backed by the millions of Poles. It created a chance, an op-portunity to deepen the system of democracy of people ruling the country, widening reforms. Those hopes failed.

Around the negotiating table there was no leadership from Solidarity. Words said...in Gdansk [strike calls and political demands from Solidarity] showed the real aims of its leadership. These aims are confirmed by everyday practice, growing aggressiveness of the extremists, clearly aiming to take apart the Polish state system.

How long can one wait for a sobering up? How long can a hand reached for accord meet a fist? I say this with a broken heart, with bitterness. It could have been different in our country. It should have been different. But if the current state had lasted longer, it would have led to a catastrophe, to absolute chaos, to poverty and starvation....

I declare that today the army Council of National Salvation has been constituted, and the Council of State obeying the Polish Constitution declared a state of emergency at midnight on the territory of Poland....

From The *New York Times*, December 14, 1981, p. 16.

by the press), involving a high-technology space-based defense against nuclear attack. The Star Wars proposal, although controversial in the United States, was a major issue in later arms control negotiations with the Soviet Union. Star Wars and the Reagan defense spending forced the Soviet Union to increase its own defense spending when it could ill afford to do so and contributed to the economic problems that helped bring about its collapse. Yet even during Reagan's first term (1980–1984), no major transformation of the Soviet Union seemed to be in the offing.

The Collapse of European Communism

The withdrawal of Soviet influence from Eastern Europe and the internal collapse of the Soviet Union are the most important events of the second half of the twentieth century. These events had virtually no parallel in modern European history. All of the other major governments that had disappeared in Europe earlier in the century had fallen either as the result of domestic revolution brought on by military defeat, as happened in tsarist Russia, Germany, and Austria after World War I and Italy during World War II, or military defeat followed by military occupation, as was the case with Germany after 1945 and the Third Republic in France in 1940. By contrast, the Soviet Union essentially imploded from within and then divided into separate successor states. There was no foreign invasion, no military defeat, and no internal revolution. Many of the factors leading to the Soviet collapse remain to be investigated, but a relatively clear narrative of what occurred can be set forth.

Gorbachev Redirects the Soviet Union

Although economic stagnation, party corruption, and the lingering Afghan War had long been undermining Soviet authority, what brought those forces to a head and began the dramatic collapse of the Soviet Empire was the accession to power of Mikhail S. Gorbachev (b. 1931) in 1985 after both of Brezhnev's two immediate successors, Yuri Andropov (1914–1984) and Constantin Chernenko (1911–1985) died within thirteen months of each other. In what proved to be the last great attempt to reform the Soviet system, Gorbachev immediately began the most remarkable changes that the Soviet Union had witnessed since the 1920s. These reforms loosed forces that, within seven years, would force him to retire and would end both communist rule and the Soviet Union as it had existed since the Bolshevik Revolution of 1917.

In his earlier administrative career, Gorbachev had become impatient with the inefficiencies of the Soviet system and disappointed that the Communist Party had failed to fulfill its socialist promises. He believed that only drastic change could restore the Soviet Union's political and economic health and allow it to achieve its socialist agenda. As a reformer, Gorbachev never repudiated socialism or the intellectual framework of Soviet communism. He hoped to rejuvenate the original Bolshevik vision, which he believed that corruption and political terror had prevented from being realized. However, his reforms unleashed political and social forces that he could not control, and he was ultimately overwhelmed by them.

ECONOMIC *PERESTROIKA* Gorbachev's primary goal was to revive the Russian eonomy in order to raise the country's standard of living. Initially, he and his supporters, most of whom he had appointed himself, challenged traditional party and bureaucratic management of the Soviet government and economy. Under the policy of *perestroika*, or "restructuring," they proposed major economic and political reforms of the various centralized economic ministries, which were reduced in size and importance. During these same years, Gorbachev also confronted labor discontent. A major strike by coal miners occurred

in July 1989 in Siberia. Gorbachev had to settle their grievances quickly, because the economy desperately needed their output. He promised them better wages and wider political liberties. By early 1990, in a clear abandonment of traditional Marxist ideology, Gorbachev had begun to advocate private ownership of property and liberalization of the economy toward free market mechanisms. He may have been following Lenin's model of the New Economic Policy of the early 1920s, which had allowed some free markets within the Soviet economy.

In the Soviet context, Gorbachev's approach was genuinely radical. It challenged centralized planning and Communist Party control, as well as the corruption and inefficiencies in the economy and the party bureaucracy. His policies, however, did not achieve what they had hoped for them. Despite many organizational changes, the Soviet economy remained stagnated and even declined. Shortages of food, consumer goods, and housing became chronic. The failure of Gorbachev's economic policies affected his political policies. To some extent, he pursued bold political reform because he failed to achieve economic progress.

GLASNOST Gorbachev allowed an extraordinary public discussion and criticism of Soviet history and Soviet Communist Party policy. This development was termed *glasnost*, or openness. The contributions to Soviet history of such figures from the 1920s as Bukharin, whom Stalin had purged, received official public recognition. Workers were permitted to criticize party officials and the economic plans of the party and the government. Censorship was relaxed and free expression encouraged. Dissidents were released from prison. In the summer of 1988, Gorbachev presided over a party congress that witnessed full debates.

The policy of open discussion allowed national minorities within the Soviet Union to demand political autonomy. Throughout its history, the Soviet Union had remained a vast empire of subject peoples. The tsars had conquered some of those groups, Stalin had incorporated others, such as the Baltic states, into the Soviet Union. *Glasnost* quickly brought to the fore the discontent of all such peoples, no matter how or when they had been subjugated. Gorbachev proved inept in addressing these ethnic complaints. He badly underestimated the unrest internal national discontent could generate.

Gorbachev soon moved from *glasnost* to *perestroika* in the political arena. In 1988, a new constitution permitted openly contested elections. After real political campaigning—a new experience for the Soviet Union—the Congress of People's Deputies was elected in 1989. One of the new members of the congress was Andrei Sakharov, the dissident physicist who had been persecuted under Brezhnev. After lively debate, the Supreme Soviet, another elected body, although one dominated by the Communist Party, formally elected Gorbachev president in 1989.

PERESTROIKA **AND THE ARMY** The role of the armed forces in the Soviet Union is too large and complicated for more than brief comment, but it was a significant element in the story of the Soviet collapse.

The army was perhaps the single most important national institution of the Soviet Union. It had been the institution through which a people with many different national and ethnic loyalties had been given a national identity. As a result of the victory in Word War II, the Soviet Army enjoyed enormous prestige. Throughout the Soviet period, the armed forces had also enjoyed enormous expenditures of public funds to support them.

By the late 1980s, Gorbachev had concluded that only a significant redeployment of expenditures from military purposes to nonmilitary domestic concerns could stimulate the economic growth that he sought and improve the Soviet standard of living. The political and military structures of the Soviet Union allowed a relatively small group of people to decide to cut the defense budget with little public debate. Gorbachev began to retreat from the Afghan War and reduce expenditures on weaponry. These measures seem to have confused the military leadership and, along with the Afghan war, hurt morale. Furthermore, military spending and manufacture were so large a part of Soviet economic life that any effort to convert more resources to domestic spending caused massive dislocations in what was still a centrally planned economy.

The Soviet military soon faced a new problem. Between 1986 and 1991 the Soviet army was ordered to put down several instances of domestic unrest involving either ethnic groups fighting among themselves (Georgia in 1989 and Azerbaijan, 1990) or national minoritites challenging the central government (in Lithuania, 1990). The greater openness in the press and on television meant that the media covered these clashes between the Soviet army and Soviet citizens. Furthermore, in certain cases, the central government let the army take the blame for the incidents even when the army was following the government's orders. Again, morale and military prestige suffered.

Finally, Gorbachev undermined the military just by cutting its size. He carried out this policy, as he had the cuts in defense spending, to convince the West that the Soviet Union was serious about arms reduction in the hope that the West would also reduce such spending. Gorbachev forced through reductions in the size of the army at home and, as will be discussed in the next section, massive military withdrawals from eastern Europe. Furthermore, some of the Soviet republics began to organize their own national military forces. This development represented movement to-

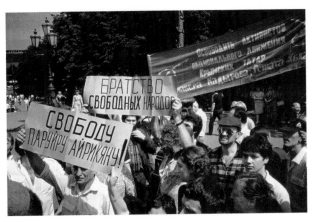

One of the chief factors to undermine Gorbachev's reform efforts was the unrest of nationalities in the former Soviet Union. The most important unrest took place in the Baltic Republics. Here in the summer of 1988 Lithuanians demonstrate against the Soviet government in Vilnius, the capital of Lithuania.
Corbis Sygma Photo News

ward national autonomy and showed disrespect for the Soviet army itself. Finally, there appears to have been resistance against conscription into the army, with various republics failing to fulfill their draft quotas. Again, resistance to conscription indicated the discontent of national groups and their determination to resist central Soviet government policy.

Gorbachev's efforts to reduce the size and predominance of military spending thus contributed to the disintegration of the Soviet armed forces without his having intended to do so. As other events unfolded, officers lacked the means to support any particular political or national group. Nor could the army function any longer as a national force to fill the political vacuum that would begin to emerge in the early 1990s.

1989: Year of Revolution in Eastern Europe

SOLIDARITY **REEMERGES IN POLAND** In the early 1980s, Poland's government relaxed martial law, and it eventually released all the *Solidarity* prisoners, although Jaruzelski remained in control as president. In 1988, new strikes occurred that surprised even the leaders of *Solidarity*. This time, the communist government could not reimpose control. After consultations between the government and *Solidarity*, the union was legalized. Lech Walesa again took center stage, as a kind of mediator between the government and the more independent elements of the trade union movement he had founded.

Jaruzelski began some political reforms with the tacit consent of the Soviet Union. He promised free elections to a parliament with increased powers. When elections were held in 1989, the communists lost overwhelmingly to *Solidarity* candidates. Late in the summer, Jaruzelski, unable to find a communist who could forge a majority coalition in Parliament, turned to *Solidarity* and appointed the first noncommuist prime minister of Poland since 1945. Gorbachev expressly approved the appointment.

Throughout 1989, as these events unfolded within Poland, one Soviet-dominated state after another in Eastern Europe moved toward independence. Early in the year, the Hungarian government opened its border with Austria, permitting free travel between the two countries. This breech in the Iron Curtain immediately led thousands of East Germans to move into Austria through Hungary. From Austria, they went to West Germany. In May, Janos Kadar, who had been installed after the Soviet intervention in 1956, was stripped of his position as president of the Hungarian Communist Party. Thousands of Hungarians gave an honorary burial to the body of Imre Nagy, whom Kadar had executed in 1958. The Hungarian Communist Party changed its name to the Socialist Party, permitted other opposition political parties to engage, and promised free elections by October.

In the autumn of 1989, popular demonstrations erupted in East German cities. Adding to the pressure, Gorbachev told the leaders of the East German Communist Party that the Soviet Union would not use force to support them. With startling swiftness, the East German government resigned, making way for a younger generation of Communist leaders who remained in office only for a few weeks. In November 1989, in one of the most emotional moments in European history since 1945, the government of East Germany ordered the opening of the Berlin Wall. That week, tens of thousands of East Berliners crossed into West Berlin to celebrate, to visit their families, and to shop with money provided by the West German government. Shortly thereafter, free travel began between East and West Germany. (See Map 31–8.)

Within days of these dramatic events, West Germany and the other Western nations faced the issue of German reunification. Helmut Kohl (b. 1930), the Chancellor of West Germany, became the leading force in moving toward full unification. Late in 1989, the European Economic Community accepted, in principle, the unification of Germany. By February 1990, some form of reunification had become a forgone conclusion, accepted by the United States, the Soviet Union, Great Britain, and France.

Revolution in Czechoslovakia rapidly followed the breach of the Berlin Wall. The popular new Czech leader who led the forces against the party was Vaclav Havel (b. 1936), a playwright of international standing whom the communist government had frequently imprisoned. In December 1989, the tottering communist government, togetehr with the Soviet Union and other Warsaw pact states, acknowledged that the invasion of 1968 had been a mistake. Shortly thereafter, Havel's group, known as Civic Forum, forced Gustav Husak (b. 1913), who had been president of Czechoslovakia since 1968, to resign. On December 28, 1989, Alexander Dubcek became chairman of the Parliament, and the next day, Havel was elected president.

East Berliners return home through the Invalidenstrasse crossing point, after a shopping trip in West Berlin. Shortages of consumer goods in the former Soviet Union, and in those Eastern European nations dominated by it, were a major source of discontent with communism.
Reuters/Juergen Schwartz/Archive Photos

MAP 31–8   THE BORDERS OF GERMANY IN
THE TWENTIETH CENTURY   *Map A shows
the borders of Imperial Germany at the
outbreak of World War I. Map B shows the
borders of Germany after the Versailles
peace settlement. Map C shows the borders of Germany after Hitler's invasion of
the Rhineland, the Anschluss with Austria, the Munich Pact, the invasion of
Czechoslovakia, and the invasion of
Poland. Map D illustrates the division of
Germany into the German Federal Republic (West Germany) and the German Democratic Republic (East Germany) in the
aftermath of World War II. Map E illustrates the borders of Germany after reunification in 1990.*

Major Events in the Revolutions of 1989

January 11	Independent parties permitted in Hungary
April 5	Solidarity legalized in Poland and free elections accepted by government
May 2	Hungary dismantles barriers along its borders
May 8	Janos Kadar removed from office in Hungary
May 17	Polish government recognizes Roman Catholic Church
June 4	Solidarity victory in Polish parliamentary elections
July 25	Solidarity asked to join coalition government
August 24	Solidarity member appointed premier in Poland
October 18	Erich Honecker removed from office in East Germany
October 23	Hungary proclaims itself a republic
October 25	Gorbachev renounces Brezhnev Doctrine
November 9	Berlin Wall opened
November 17	Large antigovernment demonstration in Czechoslovakia crushed by police
November 19	Czechoslovak opposition groups organize into Civic Forum and demand resignation of communist leaders responsible for 1968 invasion
November 24	Czechoslovak communist leadership resigns
December 1	New Czechoslovak communist leaders denounce 1968 invasion; Soviet Union and Warsaw Pact express regret over 1968 invasion
December 3	Czechoslovak government announces ministry with noncommunist members
December 16–17	Massacre of civilians in Timisoara, Romania
December 22	Ceausescu government overthrown in Romania with many casualties
December 25	Announcement of Ceausescu's execution
December 28	Alexander Dubcek elected chairman of Czechoslovak Parliament
December 29	Vaclav Havel elected president of Czechoslovakia

The only revolution of 1989 that involved significant violence occurred in Romania. There, in mid-December, the forces of President Nicolae Ceausescu (1918–1989), who had governed without opposition since 1965, fired on crowds protesting conditions in the country. By December 22, Bucharest was in full revolt. Ceausescu and his wife attempted to flee, but were captured, secretly tried, and shot on December 25.

THE SOVIET STANCE ON REVOLUTIONARY DEVELOPMENTS
None of the revolutions of 1989 could have taken place unless the Soviet Union had refused to intervene militarily, in contrast to 1956 and 1968. As events unfolded, it became clear that Gorbachev would not rescue the old-line communist governments and party leaderships in Eastern Europe. In October 1989, he formally renounced the Brezhnev Doctrine. For the first time since the end of World War II, Eastern Europeans could shape their own political destiny without the fear of Soviet military intervention. Once they realized that the Soviets would not act, thousands of ordinary citizens took to the streets to denounce Communist Party domination and assert their desire for democracy. The major question facing the Soviet Union became the peaceful withdrawal of its troops from Eastern Europe back home. The haphazard nature of that withdrawal and the general poverty to which those troops returned were another factor undermining the Soviet armed forces.

The peaceful character of most of these revolutions was not inevitable. It may, in part, have resulted from the shock with which much of the world responded to the violent repression of prodemocracy protesters in Beijing's Tiananmen Square by the People's Republic of China in May 1989. The Communist Party officials of Eastern Europe and the Soviet Union clearly decided in 1989 that they could not offend world opinion with a similar attack on democratic demonstrators.

The Collapse of the Soviet Union

Gorbachev clearly believed, as his behavior toward Eastern Europe in 1989 showed, that the Soviet Union could no longer afford to support communist governments in that region or intervene to uphold their authority while seeking to restructure its own economy. He also had concluded that the Communist Party in the Soviet Union must restructure itself and its relationship to the Soviet state and society.

RENUNCIATION OF COMMUNIST POLITICAL MONOPOLY
In early 1990, Gorbachev formally proposed to the Central Committee of the Soviet Communist Party

Gorbachev Proposes that the Soviet Communist Party Abandon Its Monopoly of Power

On February 5, 1990, President Mikhail Gorbachev proposed to the Central Committee of the Soviet Communist Party that it abandon its position as the single legal party as provided in Article 6 of the Soviet constitution. His proposal followed similar actions by several of the Communist Parties of Eastern Europe. From the time of Lenin through Brezhnev, the Soviet Communist Party portrayed itself as the sole vanguard of the revolution. Gorbachev argued that it should abandon that special role and compete for political power with other political parties. Within two years, the party was no longer in power, Gorbachev had resigned, and the Soviet Union no longer existed.

❖ *Why did Gorbachev argue that the Soviet Communist Party must reform itself? To what extent did his speech call for the abandonment of traditional Communist Party goals? How did he think the Soviet Communist Party could function in a pluralistic political system?*

The main thing that now worries Communists and all citizens of the country is the fate of *perestroika*, the fate of the country and the role of the Soviet Communist Party at the current, probably most crucial, stage of revolutionary transformation.

[It is important to understand]...that the party will only be able to fulfill the mission of political vanguard if it drastically restructures itself, masters the art of political work in the present conditions and succeeds in cooperating with forces committed to *perestroika*.

The crux of the party's renewal is the need to get rid of everything that tied it to the authoritarian–bureaucratic system, a system that left its mark not only on methods of work and inter-relationships within the party, but also on ideology, ways of thinking and notions of socialism.

The [newly proposed] platform says: our ideal is a humane, democratic socialism, expressing the interests of the working class and all working people; and relying on the great legacy of Marx, Engels and Lenin, the Soviet Communist Party is creatively developing socialist ideals to match present-day realities and with due account for the entire experience of the 20th century.

The platform states clearly what we should abandon. We should abandon the ideological dogmatism that became ingrained during past decades, outdated stereotypes in domestic policy and outmoded views on the world revolutionary process and world development as a whole.

We should abandon everything that led to the isolation of socialist countries from the mainstream of world civilization. We should abandon the understanding of progress as a permanent confrontation with a socially different world....

The party's renewal presupposes a fundamental change in its relations with state and economic bodies and the abandonment of the practice of commanding them and substituting for their functions.

The party in a renewing of society can exist and play its role as vanguard only as a democratically recognized force. This means that its status should not be imposed through constitutional endorsement.

The Soviet Communist Party, it goes without saying, intends to struggle for the status of the ruling party. But it will do so strictly within the framework of the democratic process by giving up any legal and political advantages, offering its program and defending it in discussions, cooperating with other social and political forces, always working amidst the masses, living by their interests and their needs.

From The *New York Times*, February 6, 1990, p. A16.

that the party abandon its monopoly of power. (See "Gorbachev Proposes that the Soviet Communist Party Abandon Its Monopoly of Power.") After intense debate, the Committee adopted his proposal, abandoning the Leninist position that only a single elite party could act as the vanguard of the revolution and forge a new Soviet society. Gorbachev seems not to have wanted wholly to abandon communism and certainly not socialism, but he did want to open the political process to genuine com-

The collapse of Communist Party governments in Eastern Europe and the Soviet Union is the most important political event of the closing years of the twentieth century. It was accompanied by the destruction of the public symbols of those governments. Throughout the region gigantic statues of Communist Party leaders were torn down. Here, Hungarians explore a toppled statue of Lenin. Corbis Sygma Photo News

petition. He was determined, however, that the Soviet Union should remain a strong state with a powerful central government.

NEW POLITICAL FORCES   Gorbachev confronted challenges from three major political forces by 1990. One consisted of those groups—considered conservative in the Soviet context—whose members wanted to preserve the influence of the Communist Party and the Soviet army. The country's economic stagnation and political and social turmoil deeply disturbed them. They still appeared to control significant groups in the economy and society. During late 1990 and early 1991, Gorbachev, who himself seems to have been disturbed by the nation's turmoil, began to appoint members of these factions to key positions in the government. In other words, he seemed to be making a strategic retreat.

Gorbachev initiated these moves because he was now facing opposition from a second group—those who wanted much more extensive and rapid change. Their leading spokesman was Boris Yeltsin (b. 1931). He and his supporters wanted to move quickly to a market economy and a more democratic government. Like Gorbachev, Yeltsin had risen through the ranks of the Communist Party and had then become disillusioned with its policies. Throughout the late 1980s, he had been critical of Gorbachev. In 1990, he was elected president of the Russian Republic, the largest and most important of the Soviet Union's constituent republics. In the new political climate, that position gave him a firm political base from which to challenge Gorbachev's authority and increase his own.

The third force that came into play from 1989 onward was growing regional unrest in some of the republics of the Soviet Union. These republics had experienced considerable discontent in the past, but it

had been repressed by military or Communist Party action. Initially, the greatest unrest came from the three Baltic republics of Estonia, Latvia, and Lithuania, which had been independent states until the eve of World War II. In accord with secret arrangements in the Soviet–German nonaggression pact of 1939, the Soviet Union had occupied them in 1940. That prewar pact with Nazi Germany provided the only seemingly legal basis for the Soviet Union's continued control. In these republics, many local communist leaders began to see themselves as leaders of their national groups rather than of the party.

During 1989 and 1990, the parliaments of the Baltic republics tried to increase their independence from the Soviet Union, and Lithuania actually declared independence. Gorbachev used military force to resist these moves. Discontent also arose in the Soviet Islamic republics in central Asia. Riots broke out in Azerbaijan and Tajikistan, where the army was used as a police force against Soviet citizens. Throughout 1990 and 1991, Gorbachev sought to negotiate new constitutional arrangements between the republics and the central government. His failure to effect such arrangements may have been the single most important reason for the rapid collapse of the Soviet Union.

THE AUGUST 1991 COUP   The turning point in all of these events came in August 1991, when the conservative forces that Gorbachev had brought into the government attempted a coup. Armed forces occupied Moscow, and Gorbachev himself was placed under house arrest while on vacation in the Crimea. The forces of political and economic reaction—led by people who, at the time, were associated with Gorbachev—had at last tried to seize control. The day of the coup, Boris Yeltsin climbed on a tank in front of the Russian Parliament building to denounce the coup and ask the world for help maintain the Soviet Union's movement toward democracy.

Within two days, the coup collapsed. Gorbachev returned to Moscow, but in humiliation, having been victimized by the groups to whom he had turned for support. One of the largest public demonstrations in Russian history—perhaps even the largest—celebrated the failure of the coup in Moscow. From that point on, Yeltsin steadily became the dominant political figure in the nation. In the months immediately afterward, the Communist Party, compromised by its participation in the coup, collapsed as a political force. The constitutional arrangements between the central government and the individual republics were revised. On December 25, 1991, the Soviet Union ceased to exist, Gorbachev left office, and the Commonwealth of Independent States came into being. (See Map 31–9.)

The Yeltsin Decade

Boris Yeltsin emerged as the strongest leader within the new commonwealth. As president of Russia, he was head of the largest and most powerful of the new states. His popularity was high both in Russia and in the commonwealth in 1992, but within a year he faced serious economic and political problems. The Russian Parliament, most of whom were former communists, opposed Yeltsin personally and his policies of economic and political reform. Relations between the president and Parliament reached an impasse, crippling the government. In September 1993, Yeltsin suspended Parliament, which responded by deposing him. Parliament leaders tried to incite popular uprisings against Yeltsin in Moscow. The military, however, backed Yeltsin, and he surrounded the parliament building with troops and tanks. On

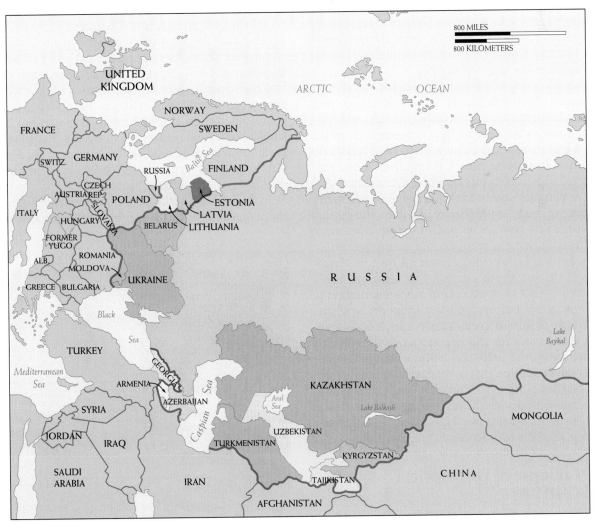

MAP 31–9   THE COMMONWEALTH OF INDEPENDENT STATES   *In December 1991, the Soviet Union broke up into its fifteen constituent republics. Eleven of these are now loosely joined in the Commonwealth of Independent States (CIS). Those not in the new union are Estonia, Latvia, Lithuania, and Georgia.*

October 4, 1993, after pro-Parliament rioters rampaged through Moscow, Yeltsin ordered the tanks to attack the Parliament building, crushing the opposition.

These actions consolidated Yeltsin's authority. The major Western powers, deeply concerned by the turmoil in Russia, supported him. In December 1993, Russians voted for a new Parliament and approved a new constitution. In 1994 the central government found itself at war in the Islamic province of Chechnya in the Caucasus, a conflict that the central government lost. The defeat further diminished the small remaining prestige and morale of the army. This conflict and lesser pressures from other Islamic republics demonstrated the government's limited capacity to deal with significant resistance.

In the parliamentary elections of late 1995, the Communist Party reasserted its political presence, winning over one-third of the seats in the Russian Parliament. The Party leadership claimed that it did not intend to return to its former authoritarian ways. Those elections represented a major defeat for the Yeltsin government, which had become increasingly unpopular. Yet by deft political maneuvers, Yeltsin defeated the Communist Party candidate for the presidency in the summer of 1996.

Thereafter the situation in Russia remained highly confused. President Yeltsin, who suffered from poor health, thereafter faced remarkably steady opposition in the Russian Parliament. The economic life of the nation remained stagnated at best. In 1998 Russia defaulted on its debt payments. Political assassinations occurred. The economic downturn contributed to furthur political unrest. In the face of these problems, Yeltsin resigned the presidency in a dramatic gesture just as the new century opened. His resignation made Vladimir Putin, his premier, the acting president. Putin achieved the presidency on his own in March, 2000. Putin carried out a renewed war against Chechnyan rebels that resulted in enormous destruction in the province but strong political support elsewhere. The future of Russia remains uncertain. It is also possible that Russia for the next decade will resemble Mexico during the 1920s and 1930s, when in the wake of its own revolution that country experienced almost two decades of uncertain political stability while financing itself through the sale of natural resources to the rest of the world. (See "Aleksandr Solzhenitsyn Ponders the Future of Russian Democracy.")

The Collapse of Yugoslavia and Civil War

The communist government of Yugoslavia had long been distinct from those of the other Eastern bloc nations that the Soviet Union dominated. Yugoslavia's leader, Marshal Tito, had defied Stalin in the late

1940s. Thereafter, Yugoslavia pursued a foreign policy that was independent of the Soviet Union. After Tito's death in 1980, Yugoslavia became increasingly unstable until it broke apart in a series of civil wars.

Yugoslavia was created after World War I. Its borders included seven major national groups—Serbs, Croats, Slovenes, Montenegrins, Macedonians, Bosnians, and Albanians—among whom there have been ethnic disputes for centuries. (See Map 31–10.) The Croats and Slovenes are Roman Catholic and use the Latin alphabet. The Serbs, Montenegrins, and Macedonians are Eastern Orthodox and use the Cyrillic alphabet. The Bosnians and many of the Albanians are Islamic. Most members of each group reside in a region with which they are associated historically—Serbia, Croatia, Slovenia, Montenegro, Macedonia, and Bosnia–Herzegovina—and these regions constituted individual republics within Yugoslavia. The Albanians live in Kossovo, historically a part of Serbia that came to have an Albanian majority under the Ottoman Empire. Many Serbs, however, live outside Serbia proper.

Tito muted these ethnic differences by encouraging a cult of personality around himself and by a complex arrangement of political power sharing. In addition to the central government, each state had its own government, and Kosovo enjoyed a degree of autonomy within Serbia. After Tito's death, economic difficulties undermined the authority of the Yugoslavian central government. Because the presidency rotated among the leaders of the six republics, however, no strong leader could emerge to deal with the country's problems.

In the late 1980s, the old ethnic differences came to the fore again in Yugoslav politics. Nationalist lead-

An elderly parishioner walks through the ruins of St. Mary's Roman Catholic Church in Sarajevo. The church was destroyed by Serb shelling in May 1992.
Reuters/Corbis

Aleksandr Solzhenitsyn Ponders the Future of Russian Democracy

Aleksandr Solzhenitsyn, the foremost Russian novelist of his generation, was one of the most outspoken critics of the communist government of the Soviet Union. He was expelled from the country in 1974 and lived for many years in the United States. After the collapse of the Soviet Union and of the Soviet communist government, he returned to live in Russia. In recent years, he has been highly critical of the new Russian government. In January 1997, he outlined his criticism in The New York Times.

❖ *What are Solzhenitsyn's chief criticisms of the structure of the new Russian government? Why does he not consider it democratic? Why does he emphasize the necessity of establishing structures of local self-government? Why does he believe corruption could undermine democracy in Russia? Have events in Russia since 1997 alleviated those concerns?*

What is known today as "Russian democracy" masks a Government of a completely different sort. *Glasnost*—freedom of the press—is only an instrument of democracy, not democracy itself. And to a great extent freedom of the press is illusory, since the owners of newspapers erect strict taboos against discussion of issues of vital importance, while in the outlying parts of the country newspapers get direct pressure from the province authorities.

Democracy in the unarguable sense of the word means the rule of the people—that is a system in which the people are truly in charge of their daily lives and can influence the course of their own historical fate. There is nothing of the sort in Russia today.

In August 1991, the "councils of people's deputies," though only window dressing under the rule of the Communist Party, were abolished throughout the country. Since then, the united resistance of the President's machine, the Government, State *Duma* [Parliament], leaders of the political parties and majority of governors has prevented the creation of any agencies of local self-government.

Legislative assemblies do exist at the regional level but are entirely subordinate to the governors, if only because they are paid by the province's executive branches. (The election of governors is only a recent development and far from widespread; most governors were appointed by the President.)

There exists no legal framework or financial means for the creation of local self-government; people will have no choice but to achieve it through social struggle. All that really exists is the government hierarchy, from the President and national Government on down.

...The Constitution of 1993, which was passed hastily and not in a manner to inspire confidence, groans under the weight of the President's power. The rights it allocates to the State *Duma* are exceedingly constrained.

...This system of centralized power cannot be called a democracy.

It could be said that throughout the last 10 years of frenetic reorganization our Government has not taken a single step unmarked by ineptitude. Worse, our ruling circles have not shown themselves in the least morally superior to the Communists who preceded them. Russia has been exhausted by crime, by the transfer into private hands of billions of dollars' worth of the nation's wealth. Not a single serious crime has been exposed, nor has there been a single public trial. The investigatory and judicial systems are severely limited in both their actions and their resources.

The destructive course of events over the last decade has come about because the Government, while ineptly imitating foreign models, has completely disregarded the country's creativity and particular character as well as Russia's centuries-old spiritual and social traditions. Only if those paths are freed up can Russia be delivered from its near fatal condition.

From The *New York Times*, January 4, 1997, p. 23. Copyright © 1997 by The *New York Times* Co. Reprinted by permission.

ers—notably Slobodan Milosevic (b. 1941) in Serbia and Franjo Tudjman (1922-2000) in Croatia—gained increasing authority. The Serbs contended that Serbia did not exercise sufficient influence in Yugoslavia and that Serbs living in other parts of Yugoslavia were discriminated against, especially by Croats and Albanians. The Croats and Slovenes believed that they could prosper economically by pursuing a market economy more rapidly. Ethnic tension and violence soon resulted. During the summer of 1990, in the wake of the changes in the former Soviet bloc nations, Slovenia and Croatia declared independence from the central Yugoslav government. Within a year, several European nations, including, most importantly, Germany, recognized their independence. Recognition from the full European community soon followed.

From this point on, violence escalated steadily. Serbia—concerned about Serbs living in Croatia and about the loss of lands and resources there—was determined to maintain a unitary Yugoslav state that it would dominate. Croatia was equally determined to secure independence. Croatian Serbs demanded safeguards against discrimination and violence, providing the Serbian army with a pretext to move against Croatia. By June 1991, full-fledged war had erupted between the two republics. Serbia accused Croatia of reviving fascism, while Croatia accused

Serbia of maintaining a Stalinist regime. At its core, however, the conflict is ethnic and, as such, highlights the potential for violent ethnic conflict also within the former Soviet Union.

The conflict took a new turn in 1992 when Croatian and Serbian forces determined to divide Bosnia–Herzegovina. The Muslims in Bosnia—who had lived alongside Serbs and Croats in the region for generations—were soon crushed between the opposing forces. The Serbs in particular, pursuing a policy called "ethnic cleansing," a euphemism redolent of some of the worst horrors of World War II, killed or forcibly evicted many Bosnian Muslims.

The unremitting bombardment of Sarajevo, the capital of Bosnia–Herzegovina, brought the violence of the Yugoslav civil war to the attention of the world. In long negotiations, the United Nations failed to mediate the conflict and instead imposed sanctions, which had little impact. Early in 1994, however, a shell exploded in the marketplace in Sarajevo, killing dozens of people. Thereafter, NATO threatened to bomb Serbian military positions if the Serbs did not withdraw their artillery from around Sarajevo. NATO's ultimatum and the military actions taken to enforce it—the first such actions in NATO history—were successful. Serb forces withdrew from the city.

MAP 31–10   THE ETHNIC COMPOSITION OF BOSNIA–HERZEGOVINA, CROATIA, AND SERBIA IN THE FORMER YUGOSLAVIA   *The rapid changes in Eastern Europe during the close of the 1980s brought to the fore various long-standing ethnic tensions in the former Yugoslavia. This map shows national and ethnic borders and major ethnic enclaves within areas generally dominated by a single ethnic group. [Source: CIA]*

The civil war came to a head in 1995, when NATO forces carried out strategic air strikes. Later that year, under the aegis of the United States, the leaders of the warring forces completed a peace agreement in Dayton, Ohio. The agreement recognized an independent Bosnia. NATO troops, including those from the United States, were to enforce the terms of the pact.

Toward the end of the 1990s, Serbian aggression against ethnic Albanians in Kosovo again drew NATO into Yugoslav affairs. For months, through television and other media, the world watched the Serbian military force ethnic Albanians out of Kosovo. The tactics closely resembled those the Serbs had previously used in Bosnia. There were many casualities, atrocities, and deaths. Early in 1999, NATO carried out an air campaign that was the largest military action in Europe since the close of World War II. The result was the withdrawal of Serbian forces and the introduction of NATO forces into Kosovo to restore the ethnic Albanians. An uncertain peace has descended on the former Yugoslavia, although there is considerable political discontent in each of its successor states, and the future remains troubled.

Problems in the Wake of the Collapse of Communism

The collapse of communism in Eastern Europe and the Soviet Union has presented Europe with new problems and opportunities. The opportunities include the possibility of establishing democratic governments and market economies throughout the region and the restoration of civil liberties in countries where they have not been known for over half a century. If the countries of the former Soviet bloc reorganize their economies successfully, their citizens may come to enjoy the kinds of consumer goods—and the standard of living these goods make possible—that have long been available in Western Europe. As the past decade has demonstrated, however, realizing these opportunities will be a slow process and will require much patience. (See "Art & the West.")

The problems in the new political and economic situation are enormous. Unemployment is widespread throughout the former Soviet Union and Eastern Europe. The plants and factories that the communist governments built are obsolete. Many also are so polluting that they have left the former communist nations with some of the worst environmental problems in the world. These nations now recognize that, by the standards of Western Europe, they are poor. As a result, hundreds of thousands of East Europeans have migrated to Western Europe looking for work. In Western countries such as Ger-

The Breakup of Yugoslavia	
June 1991	Slovenia declares independence; Croatia declares independence
April 1992	War erupts in Bosnia and Herzegovina after Muslims and Croats vote for independence
November 1995	Peace agreement reached in Dayton, Ohio
January 1992	Macedonia declares independence
April 1992	Serbia and Montenegro proclaim a new Federal Republic of Yugoslavia
March 1998	War breaks out in Kosovo, a province of Serbia
March 1999	NATO bombing of Serbia begins

many, however, these immigrants, like those from the Third World, have encountered resentment, opposition, and violence. In response to ethnic tensions, Western countries have restricted immigration.

Western Europeans are also grappling with another issue. How should the former communist economies relate to the European Union, which has moved rapidly during the past ten years to secure its economic dominance of the continent? Many Eastern Europeans want speedy economic integration, but Western European leaders fear that Eastern Europe's economic difficulties could threaten prosperity in the West.

The political challenges that the collapse of communism has created are no less great than the economic ones. Civil war has raged in Yugoslavia. Ethnic violence has already erupted in the former Soviet Union, where nuclear weapons are still available. The Czechs and the Slovaks, unable to establish a stable, unified state, divided Czechoslovakia into two separate nations in 1993. The liberty made possible by the end of the communist governments has thus far tended to be used in pursuit of ethnic goals, leading almost inevitably to domestic political turmoil. Except for Romania, Bulgaria, and Greece, all of the nations between Germany and the Commonwealth of Independent States have existed as distinct political units within more or less their present borders only since World War I, although many of the national groups in them enjoyed some form of political autonomy decades or centuries earlier. Moreover, between World War I and 1989, all of them found themselves under either a fascist or a communist government at one time or another. After World War II, West Germany and Austria developed strong democratic institutions, but elsewhere this did not happen. The key ques-

Architecture and Internationalism: Guggenheim Museum Bilbao, Spain

Frank O. Gehry. *Guggenheim Museum Bilbao, Spain*, 1997. Javier Bauluz Stringer/AP/Wide World Photos.

*H*ailed as a masterpiece in 1997, Frank Gehry's (b. 1929) Guggenheim Museum Bilbao, Spain has become a beacon of artistic innovation and cultural cooperation at the turn of the millennium. While the museum's wave-like titanium canopies recall Bilbao's shipbuilding past, they also point to the city's—and Europe's—future.

The Solomon R. Guggenheim Foundation was founded in New York City in 1937, dedicated solely to modern art. As one of five Guggenheim "branches" across the globe, the Bilbao museum joins Frank Lloyd Wright's 1959 New York City Guggenheim as a milestone of twentieth-century architecture. The Bilbao building could only be finished with the help of an advanced computer program that simulated the final construction of its twisting sculptural forms. With one gallery measuring over four hundred feet long and eighty-five feet high, the museum, which appears on the horizon as a huge metallic flower, is both an engineering and aesthetic marvel.

Bilbao is an unlikely site for such a cultural landmark. Spain's fourth-largest city, Bilbao is better known for shipyards and ironworks than for artistic attractions. Located in the Basque Country, an autonomous region in northeastern Spain with its own flag, parliament, and president, Bilbao has also long been plagued by separatist violence. Indeed, a Bilbao policeman was killed just days before the museum's opening, when he caught separist terrorists attempting to plant explosives outside the building.

Spain itself was ruled by the dictator Francisco Franco from 1939 until his death in 1975, although the country then rapidly became a democracy integrated with the rest of Europe. This quick democratic transition has been due largely to the kind of innovative and far-sighted planning that led to the development of the Guggenheim Bilbao. Faced with economic recession in the mid-1980s, Basque officials developed an urban renewal plan for the city that included a new subway, a renovated airport, and high-tech offices. The plan also envisaged a new

museum for contemporary art. However, the city had no art collection with which to fill it. Hence, Bilbao entered a partnership with the New York-based Guggenheim Foundation in 1991, leading to the construction of the Bilbao museum on an abandoned riverfront site between 1993 and 1997.

Frank Gehry, the Bilbao Guggenheim's Canadian-American architect, first gained wide attention for the 1978 renovation of his own California home, which integrated industrial materials like corrugated metal and chain-link fence into the redesign of a traditional clapboard structure. Since then, Gehry has designed a series of major projects that combine unconventional materials and ever-more-whimsical forms, creating buildings that continually test architectural limits. This ambitious spirit has attracted millions of visitors to Bilbao. The museum has spearheaded an economic and cultural renaissance in Bilbao's once-depressed industrial center.

As Europe enters a new millennium in which international partnerships are replacing Cold War divisions, the Guggenheim Museum Bilbao provides a model for new forms of political and cultural thought. Just as the museum's billowing forms composed of titanium, limestone, and glass expand conceptions of what a building is—combining a puzzle of individual parts (it even snakes under an adjacent highway bridge) into an elegantly unified whole—so must twenty-first-century Europe aspire to combine diversity and unity under the banner of pluralistic democracy. This is not an easy task, as recent conflicts in war-torn Yugoslavia and Chechnya demonstrate. Gehry's Bilbao masterpiece, nevertheless, remains a testament to the power of artistic and governmental innovation.

Bruggen, Coosje van. *Frank O. Gehry: Guggenheim Musem Bilbao*. New York: Guggenheim Museum Publications, 1997. Forster, Kurt Walter. *Frank O. Gehry: Guggenheim Bilbao Museum*. Stuttgart and London: Edition Axel Menges, 1998. Muschamp, Herbert. *The Miracle in Bilbao. New York Times* (September 7, 1997), section 6, page 54. Reid, T. R. *The Art of Rejuvenation. Washington Post* (March 31, 1999), page A16.

Vaclav Havel Reflects on the Future of Europe

In October 1993, Vaclav Havel, the president of the Czech Republic, gave a speech in which he outlined many of the problems confronting Europe after the collapse of communism. Havel was addressing the General Assembly of the Council of Europe, so his general theme was European unity. He discussed the danger of resurgent ethnic nationalism and noted nationalism had caused two major wars in Europe in the twentieth century. He was seeking to convince European leaders and nationalist groups to think differently about their interests in the future and to create a European, rather than a particular national, ethos.

❖ *What are the values around which Havel believes European nations might integrate and unify themselves? How does he portray special interests as undermining cooperation? What specific dangers does he associate with the appearance of new forms of nationalism?*

All of us—whether from the west, the east, the south, or the north of Europe—can agree that the common basis of any effort to integrate Europe is the wealth of values and ideas we share. Among them are respect for the uniqueness and the freedom for each human being, the principles of a democratic and pluralistic political system, a market economy, and a civic society with the rule of law. All of us respect the principle of unity in diversity and share a determination to foster creative cooperation between the different nations and ethnic, religious, and cultural groups—and the different spheres of civilization—that exist in Europe....

Despite general agreement on the values upon which European integration should stand, this process today,...has encountered a number of obstacles....

There are many reasons for this state of affairs, but I feel strongly that they all have one thing in common: the erroneous belief that the great European task before us is a purely technical, a purely administrative, or a purely systematic matter....

To put it more succinctly: Europe today lacks an ethos; it lacks imagination, it lacks generosity, it lacks the ability to see beyond the horizon of its own particular interests, be they partisan or otherwise....Europe does not appear to have achieved a genuine and profound sense of responsibility for itself as a whole, and thus for the future of all those who live in it....

The former Yugoslavia is the first great testing ground for Europe in the era that was initiated by the end of the cold war....

Another one consists in how we deal with the temptation to open the back gate to the demons of nationalist collectivism with an apparently innocent emphasis on minority rights and on the right of minorities to self-determination. At first sight, this emphasis would seem harmless and beyond reproach. But one real consequence could be new unrest and tension, because demands for self-determination inevitably lead to questioning the integrity of the individual states and the inviolability of their present borders, and even the validity of all postwar treaties. Attempts of this kind are dangerous chiefly because they look not to the future, but to the past, for they call in question the very principle of civil society and the indivisible rights of the individual, as well as the certainty that only democracy, individual rights and freedoms, and the civil principle can guarantee the genuinely full development of even that aspect of one's identity represented by membership in a nationality....

If various Western states cannot rid themselves of their desire for a dominant position in their own sphere of interests, if they don't stop trying to outwit history by reducing the idea of Europe to a noble backdrop against which they continue to defend their own petty concerns, and if the post-Communist states do not make radical efforts to exorcise the ghosts their newly won freedom has let loose, then Europe will only with great difficulty be able to respond to the challenge of the present and fulfill the opportunities that lie before it.

From Vaclav Havel, Address to the General Assembly of the Council of Europe, October 9, 1993, *New York Review of Books,* November 18, 1993, p. 3.

tion is whether the democratic governments can survive in the midst of the resulting confusion, economic stagnation, and competing ethnic claims or whether they will succumb to some authoritarian alternative. (See "Varlov Havel Reflects on the Future of Europe.")

The collapse of European communism has broader implications as well. It has closed the era in which Marxism domianted European socialism that began in the 1870s with the German socialists' adoption of Marxist thought. The Bolshevik victory in the Russian Revolution seemed to validate Marxism, and the policies of Lenin and Stalin sought to extend it around the world. Now the Soviet Union and the communist governments of Eastern Europe—heirs to the Bolshevik Revolution—have vanished, and the economies they built have collapsed. As a result, Marxist socialism has been discredited, and socialism in general may find itself on the defensive in the future. Other groups—feminists and environmentalists, for example—may now provide the kind of social criticism that had previously flowed from socialism. To play a role in the new era taking shape in Europe, socialists must come to grips with the benefits of markets, economic decentralization, and political democracy.

The collapse of European communism has also profoundly altered international relations within Europe. The demise of the Warsaw Pact has brought the future of NATO to the fore. NATO's primary function had been to deter a Soviet attack on Western Europe. As that danger has disappeared, the purpose of the alliance has become unclear. Many argue that NATO should be kept as an instrument to preserve international order. Its hesitancy to play an effective role in ending the Yugoslav civil war, however, has raised doubts that it could counter the kinds of problems Europe may face in the future. At the same time, NATO's air campaign during the Kosovo crisis, which relied primarily on United States aircraft, has led some European leaders to urge the buildup of European armed forces to diminish Europe's dependence on the American military. Much debate also now centers on the possible admission of some Eastern European nations, once members of the Warsaw Pact, into NATO. Poland, the Czech Republic, and Hungary have already joined NATO to protect themselves from any future Russian aggression and to integrate themselves more fully into the Western European economy. Russia has indicated its disapproval of the expansion of NATO. At present, it appears that while NATO will continue to expand, it will try to allay Russian concerns.

Europe at the Opening of the Global Century

In 1900, the major European nations dominated the entire world. Their wealth in terms of manufacturing, investment banking, and consumer demand profoundly influenced the lives of millions of people on every continent. Their military power, particularly their navies, and their colonial administrators, controlled enormous regions of Africa and Asia. Many Europeans were emigrating abroad especially into the Americas. Wherever Europeans traveled or governed they could expect that people on the other continents would look to Europe as a model for industrial development, accumulation of wealth, and high culture in the arts and sciences. It was the apex of the European era that began at the close of the fifteenth century. In 1900, almost no one could have predicted the enormous human tragedies that would occur in Europe during the next half century or the retreat from world dominance that would mark the European experience during the rest of the twentieth century. Since 1991, and the collapse of the Soviet Union, for the first time in five hundred years no European power can even imagine itself dominating the world. What that new situation will mean for Europeans is not yet clear and probably will not become so for many years.

Consequently, it would be foolish to predict the contours of the new century let alone the new millenium. Yet some elements of at least the opening years of that century seem more or less clear. Europeans will see themselves more than at any previous time in their history as part of a global economy and global culture in which they will play a major role, but not the dominant role they imagined a hundred years ago. Electronic technology will play a leading role in Europe's integration into the global order. But globalization goes beyond the economy and technology; it also relates to religious life. Whereas early in the twentieth century, Christianity was largely a European religion, it is now much more nearly a world religion, stagnating in Europe but growing overseas. At the same time, a very significant Islamic immigration characterizes many European cities where mosques mark skylines and Islamic worshippers outnumber those of many Christian denominations.

That imperative to placing themselves in the global setting will no doubt continue to spur European economic integration and in all likelihood greater political integration. Language barriers, ethnic prejudices, and the desire of individual nation–state bureaucracies to preserve themselves will make such integration difficult, but it will occur. As the integration moves forward, the questions of constitutionalism and rule of law will be central to the new vision of the continent. What many Europeans experienced under Fascism, National Socialism, and Communism was the absence of the rule of law, due process, and respect for the institutions of civil society. It is just those values and institutions that appear to stand in the forefront of European civic thinking and political development today. Their achievement will be as difficult in the new century as in past centuries.

The collapse of communism, as well as the emergence of the European Community, has opened the way for new ways of thinking about Europe as a single community. Europeans, however, have not yet decided if they wish such a community or what price they are willing to pay to achieve it. Beyond that question is the issue of whether the enormous prosperity that forms a geographical line beginning in London, then going through the Benelux countries, France, Germany and finally into northern Italy, can be expanded into areas of Europe which have been traditionally poorer. Will the East-West tension of the Cold War years be replaced by tensions between prosperous and poor regions? In that respect, the perennial question of the place of Russia in European civilization—a question that has concerned Europeans since the age of Peter the Great—again presents itself.

It does seem safe to conclude that however Europeans forge their lives and civilization in the next century, the major themes we have explored in this volume will persist. The traditional features of European life—concern for constitutionalism, tension between church and state, pursuit of science and rationalism, and a penchant for self-criticism—have not ensured that its civilization, as well as the results flowing from it, will be morally good. Rather they have meant that Western civilization has possessed in itself the possibility of correcting and redirecting itself and of raising questions about what are the good life and the good society. The possibility of asking those questions is necessary before the desired improvement and reform can be attained. Perhaps the chief carriers of Western culture in the new century will be those who, within its midst, most criticize it and demand that it justify itself.

REVIEW QUESTIONS

1. How did the United States and the Soviet Union come to dominate Europe after 1945? Trace the stages of the Cold War. Why were 1956 and 1962 particularly crucial years?
2. How would you define the policy of "containment"? Give some specific examples of how the United States instituted that policy throughout the world from 1945 to 1982.
3. How did Khrushchev's policies and reforms change the Soviet state after the repression of Stalin? Why did many people inside and outside the Soviet Union regard Khrushchev reckless?
4. After World War II, Europe "achieved unprecedented economic prosperity and maintained liberal democratic governments." How did Western Europe move toward political unity? What were the chief steps in this process?
5. Trace the process of European decolonization. Why did the nations of Europe give up their empires? Was the retreat orderly? How did the United States become involved in Vietnam? How did the Vietnam War affect Europe?
6. What internal political pressures did the Soviet Union experience in the 1970s and early 1980s? What steps did the Soviet government take to repress those protests? What role did Gorbachev's attempted reforms play in the collapse of the Soviet Union?
7. What were the major events in eastern Europe—particularly Poland—that contributed to the collapse of communism?
8. What are the major economic and political challenges facing Europe as it enters a new century?

SUGGESTED READINGS

F. ANSPRENGER, *The Dissolution of Colonial Empires* (1989). A broad survey.

T. G. ASH, *The Uses of Adversity* (1989). Important essays on central European culture and politics prior to the events of 1989.

T. G. ASH, *The Magic Lantern: The Revolution of '89 Witnessed in Warsaw, Budapest, Berlin and Prague* (1990). Essays by a long-time observer of central Europe.

I. BANAC (ED.), *Eastern Europe in Revolution* (1992). Excellent articles on the events of 1989 and afterward.

J. H. BILLINGTON, *Russia Transformed: Breakthrough to Hope, Moscow, August, 1991* (1992). A thoughtful essay on the attempted coup.

C. D. BLACK AND G. DUFFY (EDS.), *International Arms Control Issues and Agreements* (1985). A discussion of arms issues as they stood near the close of the Cold War.

E. BOTTOME, *The Balance of Terror: Nuclear Weapons and the Illusion of Security, 1945–1985* (1986). An examination of the role of nuclear weapons in the Cold War climate.

A. BROWN, *The Gorbachev Factor* (1996). Reflections by a thoughtful observer.

T. BUCHANAN AND M. CONWAY, *Political Catholicism in Europe, 1918–1965 (1996)*. Examines the background of Christian democracy.

M. E. CHAMBERLAIN, *Decolonization: The Fall of the European Empires* (1985). A useful treatment.

M. ELLMAN AND V. KONTOROVICH, *The Disintegration of the Soviet Economic System* (1992). An overview of the economic strains that the Soviet Union experienced during the 1980s.

R. EMERSON, *From Empire to Nation: The Rise to Self-assertion of Asian and African Peoples* (1960). An important early discussion of the origins of decolonization.

B. B. FALL, *The Two Vietnams: A Political and Military Analysis*, rev. ed. (1967). A discussion by a journalist who spent many years on the scene.

H. FEIS, *From Trust to Terror: The Onset of the Cold War, 1945–1950* (1970). The best general account.

J. L. GADDIS, *The United States and the Origins of the Cold War, 1941–1947* (1992). The most important recent discussion.

B. GWERTZMAN AND M. T. KAUFMAN (EDS.), *The Collapse of Communism* (1991). A collection of contemporary news accounts.

B. GWERTZMAN AND M. T. KAUFMAN (EDS.), *The Decline and Fall of the Soviet Empire* (1992). Another collection of contemporary news accounts.

W. F. HANRIEDER, *Germany, America, and Europe: Forty Years of German Foreign Policy* (1989). A major survey.

M. J. HOGAN (ED.), *The End of the Cold War: Its Meaning and Implications* (1992). A collection of essays by contributors from a wide political spectrum.

K. H. JARAUSCH, *The Rush to German Unity* (1994). Examines the events and background of the reunification of Germany.

P. JENKINS, *Mrs. Thatcher's Revolution: The Ending of the Socialist Era* (1988). The best work on the subject.

L. JOHNSON, *Central Europe: Enemies and Neighbors and Friends* (1996). Examines the various nations of central Europe with an eye to the recent changes in the region.

J. KEEP, *Last of the Empires: A History of the Soviet Union, 1945–1991* (1995). An outstanding one-volume survey.

F. LEWIS, *Europe: Road to Unity* (1992). A discussion of contemporary Europe by a thoughtful journalist.

L. MARTIN (ED.), *Strategic Thought in the Nuclear Age* (1979). A collection of useful essays on an issue that lay at the core of the American relationship to Western Europe.

D. MCKAY, *Rush to Union: Understanding the European Federal Bargain* (1996). Examines the background of the Maastricht treaty.

L. P. MORRIS, *Eastern Europe Since 1945* (1984). Concentrates on the political and economic organization of the then Soviet-dominated states.

J. MORRISON, *Boris Yeltsin* (1992). A useful biography.

D. E. MURPHY, S. A. KONDRASHEV, AND G. BAILEY, *Battleground Berlin: CIA vs. KGB in the Cold War* (1997). One of the best of a growing literature on Cold War espionage.

B. NAHAYLO AND V. SWOBODA, *Soviet Disunion: A History of the Nationalities Problem in the USSR* (1990). A discussion of one of the major areas of political difficulty today.

D. OBERDORFER, *The Turn: How the Cold War Came to an End: The United States and the Soviet Union, 1983–1990* (1992). A major narrative by a Washington journalist.

W. E. ODOM, *The Collapse of the Soviety Military* (1999). A study more wide-ranging than the title suggests.

S. P. RAMET (ED.), *The Religious Policy in the Soviet Union* (1993). Essays on an important subject that has often received little attention.

D. REMNICK, *Lenin's Tomb: The Last Days of the Soviet Empire* (1993). An excellent account by an American journalist working in the Soviet Union.

J. ROTHSCHILD, *Return to Diversity: A Political History of East Central Europe Since World War II* (1989). A clear, well-organized introduction.

L. SCHAPIRO, *The Communist Party of the Soviet Union* (1960). A classic analysis of the most important institution of Soviet Russia.

H. SIMONIAN, *The Privileged Partnership: Franco–German Relations in the European Community (1969–1984)* (1985). An important examination of the dominant roles of France and Germany.

H. A. TURNER, *Germany from Partition to Reunification* (1992). The best brief introduction.

A. ULAM, *Expansion and Coexistence: The History of Soviet Foreign Policy, 1917–1967* (1968). A classic treatment.

A. ULAM, *The Communists: The Story of Power and Lost Illusions: 1948–1991* (1992). The best account to date of the days of communist strength and collapse.

M. WALKER, *The Cold War and the Making of the Modern World* (1994). A major new survey.

H. WALLACE (ED.), *Policy-Making in the European Union* (1996) A useful introduction to the institutions of European integration.

Energy and the Modern World

No single technological factor so determines the social relationships and standard of living of human beings as energy. The more energy a society can command for each of its members the stronger and more influential it will be. Throughout recorded human history, those societies that have found ways to improve their access to sources of energy, and have then efficiently applied the energy, have dominated both their immediate environments and much of the world beyond. Indeed, the possession of, or the lack of, efficient, inexpensive sources of energy in large measure determines which nations will be wealthy and which will be poor.

Animals, Wind, and Water

For civilization to advance technologically, energy had to be applied to tasks. The earliest source of such energy was animal power, which was used all over the world except among the peoples on the American continent prior to the arrival of the Europeans. Oxen, water buffalo, and horses were the major draft animals. Of these, horses were the most efficient.

Throughout the world until the eighteenth century, however, wind and water furnished most of the energy for machinery. Sailing ships had been used since ancient times for travel, fishing, and the transport of goods. The wind also worked mills that pumped water and ground grain. Waterwheels proved to be highly flexible machines and by the eighteenth century constituted the major sources of mechanical power in Europe and much of the rest of the world. But wind and water were uncertain sources of energy. The wind could cease; drought could dry up streams. Waterpowered machinery had to be located near the stream furnishing the water. Consequently, most of the mills employing such machinery were located in the countryside.

Although animals, wind, and water provided energy for relatively complicated machines capable of manufacturing and transporting high-quality goods, the economic and political transformations that have driven the history of the world for the past two and a half centuries could only have occurred through a qualitative as well as quantitative leap in the manner in which human beings commanded energy. The twin sources of this world-transforming energy have been fossil fuels and electricity.

Until the second half of the eighteenth century fossil fuels—coal, petroleum, and to a lesser extent natural gas—contributed only a small portion of

Until the eighteenth century sailing ships were powered by wind alone. In this fourteenth-century manuscript illustration, sailors navigate with the help of an astrolabe. Bridgeman Art Library International

human energy requirements. Their use as meaningful sources of energy required a series of inventions that allowed the energy of heat to be changed into mechanical energy.

Steam Power and the Age of Coal

Although peoples living near coal deposits had used it as a household fuel for a very long time, only the invention of the steam engine, patented by James Watt in 1769, established a major industrial demand for coal. The steam engine first permitted the pumping of water from coal mines to increase production. But as the industrial uses for the steam engine grew, the invention itself drove the demand for greater quantities of coal as fuel.

Coal-fueled steam power changed the face of human society during the nineteenth century and continues to provide the energy for the most powerful turbogenerators at the dawn of the twenty-first century. Steampowered machines could be made larger and more flexible than those powered by wind or water, and so long as coal was available, they could run steadily day and night. Steam engines, in contrast to waterwheels, were transportable. Factories could be moved away from streams in the countryside to urban areas where a ready workforce existed. And goods produced in factories powered by steam engines could be carried around the world by steampowered locomotives and ships. Those expanding markets in turn called forth more steampowered factories and even greater use of coal. Furthermore, steampowered factories could also produce military weapons that could be placed on steampowered naval vessels constructed of iron and steel in vast coal-fueled blast furnaces. When Theodore Roosevelt sent the United States fleet around the world, it was a testimony to the power of coal and steam as well as to the power of the American navy.

The age of steam was the age of coal. The nations possessing large coal deposits dominated much nineteenth-century economic life as the nations that possess oil reserves dominate much contemporary economic life. For many decades, Great Britain dominated the world's production and delivery of coal, which was transported over the entire world. Its domination was challenged only in the late nineteenth century as the United States and later Russia and China began to produce vast quantities of the fuel. Coal remained the chief fuel for the United States until after World War I and for Western Europe until after World War II. It remains the chief fuel for China.

66   *The Ladies* HOME JOURNAL   February, 1925

Cancel distance & conquer weather

The woman who drives her own Ford Closed Car is completely independent of road and weather conditions in any season.

It enables her to carry on all those activities of the winter months that necessitate travel to and fro—in or out of town. Her time and energy are conserved; her health is protected, no matter how bitterly cold the day, or how wet and slushy it is underfoot.

A Ford Sedan is always comfortable—warm and snug in winter, and in summer with ventilator and windows open wide, as cool and airy as an open car.

This seasonal comfort is combined with fine looks and Ford dependability; no wonder there is for this car so wide and ever-growing a demand.

FORD MOTOR COMPANY, DETROIT, MICHIGAN

TUDOR SEDAN, $580 .·.   FORDOR SEDAN, $660
COUPE, $530 .·.   ALL PRICES F. O. B. DETROIT

Ford

CLOSED CARS

Until 1924, Henry Ford had disdained national advertising for his cars. But as General Motors gained a competitive edge by making yearly changes in style and technology, Ford was forced to pay more attention to advertising. This ad was directed at "Mrs. Consumer," combining appeals to both female independence and motherly duties. Ford Motor Company

Coal generated a rising standard of living in Europe and the expansion of European and later American power, but coal also generated a number of social problems. The most shocking conditions of exploited labor occurred in coal mines, where parliamentary reports of the 1840s described and illustrated half-clad women and children drawing coal carts from the depths of the mines to the surface. Throughout the nineteenth and twentieth centuries thousands of miners died in mining disasters. Work in the mines injured the health of miners, as did the pollution sent into the atmosphere by coal fires from both factories and homes. By the early twentieth century, observers had begun to note the damage to the environment caused by strip mining of coal and the later abandonment of the regions.

The Internal Combustion Engine: The Age of Oil

As with coal, the impact of petroleum, the second major fossil fuel, also depended upon the invention of machinery to use it. Originally, the use for oil was limited to kerosene, the fuel used for lighting around much of the world by 1900. It was upon the world demand for lamp oil that John D. Rockefeller founded the Standard Oil Company. The invention of the internal combustion engine in 1882 by Rudolf Daimler and the diesel engine in 1892 by Rudolf Diesel transformed the demand for oil. Toward the close of the nineteenth century extensive oil production had begun in the United States, with Russia, Romania, Sumatra, Mexico, Iran, and Venezuela starting to tap their own oil resources before World War I.

Just as the steam engine had spurred the expansion of the coal industry, the internal combustion engine drove the oil industry. Fuel oil would begin to replace coal, not so much because it was cheaper but rather because it was more efficient, easier to store and transport, and cleaner to burn. Initially fuel oil tended to be used in those countries where it could be produced relatively near the point of use. Until the end of World War II, the United States was the primary world producer and user of oil. As fuel for the internal combustion engine, oil became the driving force of automobiles, locomotives, airplanes, ships, factory machinery, and electric generators. It revolutionized agricultural machinery and world food production, but as a fuel for transportation, it fostered a social transformation over much of the world.

Starting in the United States and then spreading elsewhere, owning an automobile introduced a new mobility factor into social relationships. People could move easily across long distances to join a new community or to start a new job. Inexpensive gasoline for cars and public transport buses permitted the development of suburbs ever farther removed from traditional urban centers. In turn, retailing moved away from city centers to shopping malls. At the same time wherever the mechanization of farming through improved farm machinery took place, there usually followed a movement of people from farming communities to urban areas.

Electricity Increases the Demand for Oil

The manufacture of automobiles and other forms of transport using the internal combustion or diesel engine was central to all modern industrial life. As those industries expanded, so did the construction of extensive road systems. These in turn created new demands for fuel oil.

But the greatest demand for fuel oil arose from the application of electricity to the needs of everyday life. Electricity proved to be the most flexible and versatile source of energy for the twentieth century, and its generation provided the single greatest source of demand for both coal and oil. Electricity generation would also employ new modes of water power in the forms of hydroelectric generators.

The scientific basis for the production of electric energy was Michael Faraday's study of electromagnetic induction. In 1831, he demonstrated that mechanical energy under the proper conditions could be converted into electric energy. Even more important, the reverse was also true. Electricity could be generated in one location and applied far away wherever electrical lines could be extended. The applications of electrical power have appeared to be limited only by the limitations of the inventive imagination.

During the second half of the nineteenth century a whole host of inventors, such as Thomas Alva Edison, worked through the production and application of electrical power to service large regions. Electricity found applications across the spectrum of human society, actions, and enterprises. Access to electricity in the course of the twentieth century became the key factor for an improved standard of living. A fundamental moment in the decision by Japan to modernize during the late nineteenth century was the construction of the Tokyo Electric Light Company in 1888. The extension of electrical lines into the American countryside was one of the major accomplishments of Franklin Roosevelt's New Deal. Electrical power transformed the workplace, but even more strikingly it transformed homes. Without access to electrical power, domestic households could not make use of any of the growing array of labor-saving appliances such as electric washing machines, electric irons, electric stoves, and electric vacuum cleaners. Electric lights brightened whole cities. Electricity replaced both coal and oil as the source of power for many locomotives; it powered public tram systems and opened the way for the telegraph, the telephone, the wireless, the motion picture camera, and television. It planted the seeds for the computer revolution in communication and information. Electricity allowed manufacturing plants and office complexes to be built wherever electric lines could be

In 1989, when a supertanker spilled 35,000 tons of crude oil into Alaska's Prince William Sound, rescue workers struggled to save the lives of sea birds and animals. Nevertheless, thousands died. Ron Levy/Liaison Agency, Inc.

carried. Indeed, the spread of access to electrical power has been the single best indication of economic advance for any nation or region.

Yet within this era of ever-expanding electrification, coal and oil—the fundamental fossil fuels—would still provide the underpinnings of the world's energy. In fact, more oil and coal are used to generate electricity than for any other single purpose. Throughout the twentieth century the demand for these fuels led to the refinement of their production techniques to permit the extraction of coal from ever-deeper seams and the strip-mining of it from regions where previously it would have been economically unproductive to do so. The effort to discover, extract, and transport oil would have major consequences for the world's physical and geopolitical environment far into the twentieth century.

Oil and Global Politics in the Twentieth Century

As the century began, the United States was by far the largest producer and exporter of petroleum. Yet by the 1920s, the American government began to worry about running out of oil. So, too, did the British, who depended on imported oil for all of their military and industrial needs. During the 1920s and 1930s, both governments encouraged oil companies to forge agreements for the drilling and export of oil from the Middle East. These arrangements fit into the pattern of formal and informal colonialism that still characterized the interwar period.

After World War II, Western Europe, the Soviet Union, and the nations of the Warsaw Pact began to turn from coal to oil as the basis for economic growth. (Japan followed this course during the 1960s.) By 1947, the United States had begun to import more oil than it produced. These two developments—a new dependence on oil by the industrialized nations and the expanded search for oil by the West—formed the basis for the new role that the nations of the Middle East would play in the world economy as the chief oil exporters. Simultaneously, as the world's industrialized economies were growing dependent on Middle East oil production, nationalistic leaders in that region were denouncing former colonial domination and rejecting relationships with the West and with Israel, a country which received strong political support from the United States and Western Europe. The stage was thus set for oil to play a new role in the geopolitical conflicts of the Cold War era.

Playing a major role in those conflicts was the Organization of Petroleum Exporting Nations (OPEC), founded in 1960. Regardless of their differences, OPEC members were united in two things: First, they deeply resented former colonial control of their oil supplies, and second, they were determined that their own governments, not foreign oil companies, would control those vital resources. (Mexico had brought its own petroleum industry under state control before World War II.) In 1973, during the Yom Kippur War, OPEC acted, sharply raising oil prices to nations whose governments supported Israel. The action caused severe economic consequences in the West and spurred new efforts to develop local oil reserves in politically safe locations such as in the North Sea.

OPEC would attempt similar actions on other occasions, most successfully in 1979. In that year, a revolution in Iran overthrew the government which had long been supported by the United States. OPEC cut off oil shipments to the West, causing severe dislocations. Concerns about securing oil supplies in the West were again sparked by the Persian Gulf War and other political tensions in the region.

In addition to the political problems associated with Middle East oil production, the industrial world's reliance on oil has had severe environmental consequences. Generally, when the United States dominated oil production, the oil refineries were located near the source of oil production. As the exploitation of oil reserves moved to the Middle East and then later in the century to Alaska and to the North Sea, oil refineries became separated from the drilling locations. Crude oil was shipped to refineries on enormous tankers. More than once, these supertankers have hit shoals or gone aground, causing large oil spills, calamitous to both animals and humans.

The Promise and Danger of Nuclear Energy

Following World War II, nuclear power became a new source for the generation of electrical energy. The power of the atom, first released in the 1940s for military purposes, held the promise of virtually infinite quantities of energy. The world would no longer be dependent upon finite supplies of fossil fuel located in politically tense regions of the world. The generation of such energy, however, required the most complex sets of machinery ever devised to produce electrical energy. France and Great Britain began to build nuclear reactors in the 1950s with the United States, the Soviet Union, and various other European nations following in the 1960s. Nations outside the West, such as India and Pakistan, looked to the construction of nuclear power stations as a means of moving more rapidly toward the achievements of industrialization and a rising standard of living through extensive electrification. Nations with limited supplies of fossil fuel, such as Japan, hoped nuclear energy would solve their energy supply problem. The oil shock of the mid-1970s brought new enthusiasm to the adoption of nuclear energy, but the economic downturn of the late 1970s and early 1980s slowed the construction of nuclear generating stations. The construction of breeder reactors, which would produce their own fuel in the process of generating electrical energy, seemed to promise a world liberated from dependence upon a finite supply of fossil fuels. Furthermore, unlike coal and oil, which have many uses besides that of fuel, uranium had no other economic use. The workers in the field of atomic energy were scientists and engineers rather than the kind of industrial labor force that produced coal and oil.

Yet, the technology of nuclear energy production proved to be exceedingly dangerous. The atomic reactors produced spent radioactive waste that would remain hazardous for hundreds of years. After many years of warnings of such danger, the Chernobyl nuclear generating plant in the former Soviet Union caused enormous, lasting damage in the spring of 1986. In 1979 the possibility of a similar disaster had occurred at the Three Mile Island plant in Pennsylvania. Both the promise and danger of nuclear power continue to inform the political life of all nations using such power. It is wholly unclear, for example, what will be done with the radioactive spent fuel. Furthermore, the construction of nuclear generating plants has allowed nations who lack atomic weapons to train scientists and other experts who might be able to use that knowledge to develop atomic weapons. Whereas in the United States and Europe the military uses of atomic power came first and were followed by peaceful energy uses, the reverse has been the case in nations such as India and Pakistan. Despite its initial promise, nuclear power has contributed far less to energy production than we originally imagined.

The problem of energy remains with us in the new century. Environmental pollution, and all the issues surrounding the nuclear generation of energy will demand increasing attention and expenditure of public funds. Similarly, the political pressures and tensions surrounding the oil supplies of the Middle East will not disappear, as advanced nations seek to secure and protect energy reserves while the nations that possess those reserves seek to secure a rising standard of living for themselves.

❖ *Trace the transformation of energy used in the West from wind and water to petroleum. How did coal transform both the industry and the military power of the West? How did inventions, such as the internal combustion engine, change the demands on sources of energy? Why did the rise of electrical power increase the need for petroleum? What opportunities and dangers has nuclear energy posed?*

Glossary

absolutism   Term applied to strong centralized continental monarchies that attempted to make royal power dominant over aristocracies and other regional authorities.

Acropolis (ACK-row-po-lis)   The religious and civic center of Athens. It is the site of the Parthenon.

Act of Supremacy   The declaration by Parliament in 1534 that Henry VIII, not the Pope, was the head of the Church in England.

agape (AG-a-pay)   Meaning "love feast." A common meal that was part of the central ritual of early Christian worship.

agora (AG-o-rah)   The Greek marketplace and civic center. It was the heart of the social life of the polis.

Agricultural Revolution   The innovations in farm production that began in the eighteenth century and led to a scientific and mechanized agriculture.

Albigensians (Al-bi-GEN-see-uns)   Thirteenth-century advocates of a dualist religion. They took their name from the city of Albi in southern France. Also called Cathars.

Anabaptists   Protestants who insisted that only adult baptism conformed to Scripture.

anarchism   The theory that government and social institutions are oppressive and unnecessary and that society should be based on voluntary cooperation among individuals.

Anschluss (AHN-shluz)   Meaning "union." The annexation of Austria by Germany in March 1938.

anti-Semitism   Prejudice, hostility, or legal discrimination against Jews.

apostolic primacy   The doctrine that the Popes are the direct successors to the Apostle Peter and as such heads of the Church.

Apostolic Succession   The Christian doctrine that the powers given by Jesus to his original disciples have been handed down from bishop to bishop through ordination.

appeasement   The Anglo–French policy of making concessions to Germany in the 1930s to avoid a crisis that would lead to war. It assumed that Germany had real grievances and that Hitler's aims were limited and ultimately acceptable.

Areopagus   The governing council of Athens, originally open only to the nobility. It was named after the hill on which it met.

Arete (AH-ray-tay)   Manliness, courage, and the excellence appropriate to a hero. It was considered the highest virtue of Homeric society.

Arianism (AIR-ee-an-ism)   The belief formulated by Arius of Alexandria (ca. 280–336 C.E.) that Jesus was a created being, neither fully man nor fully God, but something in between. It did away with the doctrine of the Trinity.

aristocratic resurgence   Term applied to the eighteenth-century aristocratic efforts to resist the expanding power of European monarchies.

Arminians (are-MIN-ee-ans)   A group within the Church of England who rejected Puritanism and the Calvinist doctrine of predestination in favor of free will and an elaborate liturgy.

Asia Minor   Modern Turkey. Also called Anatolia.

asiento (ah-SEE-ehn-tow)   The contract to furnish slaves to the Spanish colonies.

assignants (as-seen-YAHNTS)   Government bonds based on the value of confiscated Church lands issued during the early French Revolution.

Atomists   School of ancient Greek philosophy founded in the fifth century B.C.E. by Leucippus of Miletus and Democritus of Abdera. It held that the world consists of innumerable, tiny, solid, indivisible, and unchangeable particles called atoms.

Attica (AT-tick-a)   The region of Greece where Athens is located.

Augsburg (AWGS-berg) **Confession**   The definitive statement of Lutheran belief made in 1530.

Augustus (AW-gust-us)   The title given to Octavian in 27 B.C.E. and borne thereafter by all Roman emperors. It was a semireligious title that implied veneration, majesty, and holiness.

Ausgleich (AWS-glike)   Meaning "compromise." The agreement between the Habsburg Emperor and the Hungarians to give Hungary considerable administrative autonomy in 1867. It created the Dual Monarchy or Austria–Hungary.

autocracy (AW-to-kra-see)   Government in which the ruler has absolute power.

Axis   The alliance between Nazi Germany and Fascist Italy. Also called the Pact of Steel.

banalities   Exactions that the lord of a manor could make on his tenants.

baroque (bah-ROWK)   A style of art marked by heavy and dramatic ornamentation and curved rather than straight lines that flourished between 1550 and 1750. It was especially associated with the Catholic Counter-Reformation.

beguines (bi-GEENS)   Lay sisterhoods not bound by the rules of a religious order.

benefice Church offices granted by the ruler of a state or the Pope to an individual. It also meant "fief" in the Middle Ages.

bishop Originally a person elected by early Christian congregations to lead them in worship and supervise their funds. In time bishops became the religious and even political authorities for Christian communities within large geographical areas.

Black Death The bubonic plague that killed millions of Europeans in the fourteenth century.

blitzkrieg (BLITZ-kreeg) Meaning "lightning war." The German tactic early in World War II of employing fast-moving, massed armored columns supported by airpower to overwhelm the enemy.

Bolsheviks Meaning the "majority." Term Lenin applied to his faction of the Russian Social Democratic Party. It became the Communist Party of the Soviet Union after the Russian Revolution.

boyars The Russian nobility.

Bronze Age The name given to the earliest civilized era, c. 4000 to 1000 B.C.E. The term reflects the importance of the metal bronze, a mixture of tin and copper, for the peoples of this age for use as weapons and tools.

Bund A secular Jewish socialist organization of Polish Jews.

Caesaro-papism (SEE-zer-o-PAY-pi-zim) The direct involvement of the ruler in religious doctrine and practice as if he were the head of the Church as well as the state.

cahiers de doleances (KAH-hee-ay de dough-LAY-ahnce) Meaning "lists of grievances." Petitions for reforms submitted to the French Crown when the Estates General met in 1789.

caliphate (KAH-li-fate) The true line of succession to Muhammad.

capital goods Machines and tools used to produce other goods.

carbonari (car-buh-NAH-ree) Meaning "charcoal burners." The most famous of the secret republican societies seeking to unify Italy in the 1820s.

categorical imperative According to Emmanuel Kant (1724–1804), the internal sense of moral duty or awareness possessed by all human beings.

Catholic Emancipation The grant of full political rights to Roman Catholics in Britain in 1829.

catholic Meaning "universal." The body of belief held by most Christians enshrined within the Church.

censor Official of the Roman republic charged with conducting the census and compiling the lists of citizens and members of the Senate. They could expel senators for financial or moral reasons. Two censors were elected every five years.

Chartism The first large-scale European working-class political movement. It sought political reforms that would favor the interests of skilled British workers in the 1830s and 1840s.

chiaroscuro (kyar-eh-SKEW-row) The use of shading to enhance naturalness in painting and drawing.

civic humanism Education designed to promote humanist leadership of political and cultural life.

civilization A form of human culture marked by urbanism, metallurgy, and writing.

classical economics The theory that economies grow through the free enterprise of individuals competing in a largely self-regulating marketplace with government intervention held to a minimum.

clientage (KLI-ent-age) The custom in ancient Rome whereby men became supporters of more powerful men in return for legal and physical protection and economic benefits.

Cold War The ideological and geographical struggle between the U.S. and its allies and the U.S.S.R. and its allies that began after World War II and lasted until the dissolution of the U.S.S.R. in 1989.

Collectivization The bedrock of Stalinist agriculture, which forced Russian peasants to give up their private farms and work as members of collectives, large agricultural units controlled by the state.

coloni (CO-loan-ee) Farmers or sharecroppers on the estates of wealthy Romans.

Commonwealthmen British political writers whose radical republican ideas influenced the American revolutionaries.

Concert of Europe Term applied to the European great powers acting together (in "concert") to resolve international disputes between 1815 and the 1850s.

Conciliar Theory The argument that General Councils were superior in authority to the Pope and represented the whole body of the faithful.

condottieri (con-da-TEE-AIR-ee) Military brokers who furnished mercenary forces to the Italian states during the Renaissance.

Congress System A series of international meetings among the European great powers to promote mutual cooperation between 1818 and 1822.

conquistadores (kahn-KWIS-teh-door-hez) Meaning "conquerors." The Spanish conquerors of the New World.

conservatism Support for the established order in Church and state. In the nineteenth century it implied support for legitimate monarchies, landed aristocracies, and established Churches. Conservatives favored only gradual, or "organic," change.

Consulate French government dominated by Napoleon from 1799 to 1804.

consuls (CON-suls) The two chief magistrates of the Roman state.

Consumer Revolution The vast increase in both the desire and the possibility of consuming goods and services that began in the early eighteenth century and created the demand for sustaining the Industrial Revolution.

Containment The U.S. policy during the Cold War of resisting Soviet expansion and influence in the expectation that the U.S.S.R. would eventually collapse.

Convention French radical legislative body from 1792 to 1794.

Corn Laws British tariffs on imported grain that protected the price of grain grown within the British Isles.

corporatism The planned economy of Fascist Italy that combined private ownership of capital with government direction of Italy's economic life and arbitration of labor disputes. All major areas of production were organized into state-controlled bodies called corporations, which were represented in the Chamber of Corporations that replaced the Chamber of Deputies. The state, not consumers and owners, determined what the economy produced.

corvee (cor-VAY) A French labor tax requiring peasants to work on roads, bridges, and canals.

Council of Nicaea (NIGH-see-a) The council of Christian bishops at Nicaea in 325 C.E. that formulated the Nicene Creed, a statement of Christian belief that rejected Arianism in favor of the doctrine that Christ is both fully human and fully divine.

Counter-Reformation The sixteenth-century reform movement in the Roman Catholic Church in reaction to the Protestant Reformation.

coup d'état (COO DAY-ta) The sudden violent overthrow of a government by its own army.

creed A brief statement of faith to which true Christians should adhere.

creoles (KRAY-ol-ez) Persons of Spanish descent born in the Spanish colonies.

Crusades Religious wars directed by the Church against infidels and heretics.

culture The ways of living built up by a group and passed on from one generation to another.

cuneiform (Q-nee-i-form) A writing system invented by the Sumerians that used a wedge-shaped stylus, or pointed tool, to write on wet clay tablets that were then baked or dried ("cuneus" means wedge in Latin). The writing was also cut into stone.

Curia (CURE-ee-a) The papal government.

Cynic (SIN-ick) **School, The** A fourth-century philosophical movement that ridiculed all religious observances and turned away from involvement in the affairs of the polis. Its most famous exemplar was Diogenes of Sinope (ca. 400-325 B.C.E.).

deacon Meaning "those who serve." In early Christian congregations, deacons assisted the presbyters, or elders.

deism A belief in a rational God who had created the universe, but then allowed it to function without his interference according to the mechanisms of nature and a belief in rewards and punishments after death for human action.

Delian (DEE-li-an) An alliance of Greek states under the leadership of Athens that was formed in 478–477 B.C.E. to resist the Persians. In time the league was transformed into the Athenian Empire.

deme (DEEM) A small town in Attica or a ward in Athens that became the basic unit of Athenian civic life under the democratic reforms of Clisthenes in 508 B.C.E.

demesne (di-MAIN) The part of a manor that was cultivated directly for the lord of the manor.

divine right of kings The theory that monarchs are appointed by and answerable only to God.

Domesday (DOOMS-day) **Book** A detailed survey of the wealth of England undertaken by William the Conqueror between 1080 and 1086.

domestic system of textile production Method of producing textiles in which agents furnished raw materials to households whose members spun them into thread and then wove cloth, which the agents then sold as finished products.

Donatism The heresy that taught that the efficacy of the sacraments depended on the moral character of the clergy who administered them.

Duce (DO-chay) Meaning "leader." Mussolini's title as head of the Fascist Party.

Duma (DOO-ma) The Russian parliament, after the Revolution of 1905.

Electors Nine German princes who had the right to elect the Holy Roman Emperor.

emigrés (em-ee-GRAYS) French aristocrats who fled France during the Revolution.

empiricism (em-PEER-ih-cism) The use of experiment and observation derived from sensory evidence to construct scientific theory or philosophy of knowledge.

enclosure The consolidation or fencing in of common lands by British landlords to increase production and achieve greater commercial profits. It also involved the reclamation of waste land and the consolidation of strips into block fields.

encomienda (en-co-mee-EN-da) The grant by the Spanish Crown to a colonist of the labor of a specific number of Indians for a set period of time.

ENIAC The Electronic Numerical Integrator and Computer. The first genuine modern digital computer, developed in the 1940s.

Enlightenment The eighteenth-century movement led by the philosophies that held that change and reform were both desirable through the application of reason and science.

Epicureans (EP-i-cure-ee-ans) School of philosophy founded by Epicurus of Athens (342–371 B.C.E.). It sought to liberate people from fear of death and the supernatural by teaching that the gods took no interest in human affairs and that true happiness consisted in pleasure, which was defined as the absence of pain. This could be achieved by attaining ataraxia, freedom from trouble, pain, and responsibility by withdrawing from business and public life.

equestrians (EE-quest-ree-ans) Literally "cavalrymen" or "knights." In the earliest years of the Roman Republic those who could afford to serve as mounted warriors. The equestrians evolved into a social rank of well-to-do businessmen and middle-ranking officials. Many of them supported the Gracchi.

Estates General The medieval French parliament. It consisted of three separate groups, or "estates:" clergy, nobility, and commoners. It last met in 1789 at the outbreak of the French Revolution.

Etruscans (EE-trus-cans) A people of central Italy who exerted the most powerful external influence on the early Romans. Etruscan kings ruled Rome until 509 B.C.E.

Eucharist (YOU-ka-rist) Meaning "thanksgiving." The celebration of the Lord's Supper. Considered the central ritual of worship by most Christians. Also called Holy Communion.

Euro The common currency created by the EEC in the late 1990s.

European Economic Community (EEC) The economic association formed by France, Germany, Italy, Belgium, the Netherlands, and Luxembourg in 1957. Also known as the Common Market.

European Union The new name given to the EEC in 1993. It included most of the states of Western Europe.

excommunication Denial by the Church of the right to receive the sacraments.

Existentialism The post-World War II Western philosophy that holds that human beings are totally responsible for their acts and that this responsibility causes them dread and anguish.

Führer (FYOOR-er) Meaning "leader." The title taken by Hitler when he became dictator of Germany.

Fabians British socialists in the late 19th and early 20th century who sought to achieve socialism through gradual, peaceful, and democratic means.

family economy The basic structure of production and consumption in preindustrial Europe.

fascism Political movements that tend to be antidemocratic, anti-Marxist, antiparliamentary, and often anti-Semitic. Fascists were invariably nationalists and exhalted the nation over the individual. They supported the interests of the middle class and rejected the ideas of the French Revolution and nineteenth-century liberalism. The first fascist regime was founded by Benito Mussolini (1883–1945) in Italy in the 1920s.

fealty An oath of loyalty by a vassal to a lord, promising to perform specified services.

feudal (FEW-dull) **society** The social, political, military, and economic system that prevailed in the Middle Ages and beyond in some parts of Europe.

fief Land granted to a vassal in exchange for services, usually military.

foederati (FAY-der-ah-tee) Barbarian tribes enlisted as special allies of the Roman Empire.

folk culture The distinctive songs, sayings, legends, and crafts of a people.

Fourteen Points President Woodrow Wilson's (1856–1924) idealistic war aims.

Fronde (FROHND) A series of rebellions against royal authority in France between 1649 and 1652.

gabelle (gah-BELL) The royal tax on salt in France.

Gaul (GAWL) Modern France.

German Confederation Association of German states established at the Congress of Vienna that replaced the Holy Roman Empire from 1815 to 1866.

ghetto Separate communities in which Jews were required by law to live.

Glasnost (GLAZ-nohst) Meaning "openness." The policy initiated by Mikhail Gorbachev (MEEK-hail GORE-buh-choff) in the 1980s of permitting open criticism of the policies of the Soviet Communist Party.

Glorious Revolution The largely peaceful replacement of James II by William and Mary as English monarchs in 1688. It marked the beginning of constitutional monarchy in Britain.

gold standard A monetary system in which the value of a unit of a nation's currency is related to a fixed amount of gold.

Golden Bull The agreement in 1356 to establish a seven-member electoral college of German princes to choose the Holy Roman Emperor.

Great Depression A prolonged worldwide economic downturn that began in 1929 with the collapse of the New York Stock Exchange.

Great Purges The imprisonment and execution of millions of Soviet citizens by Stalin between 1934 and 1939.

Great Reform Bill (1832) A limited reform of the British House of Commons and an expansion of the electorate to include a wider variety of the propertied classes. It laid the groundwork for further orderly reforms within the British constitutional system.

Great Schism The appearance of two and at times three rival popes between 1378 and 1415.

Green Movement A political environmentalist movement that began in West Germany in the 1970s and spread to a number of other Western nations.

grossdeutsch (gross-DOYCH) Meaning "great German." The argument that the German-speaking portions of the Habsburg Empire should be included in a united Germany.

guild An association of merchants or craftsmen that offered protection to its members and set rules for their work and products.

hacienda (ha-SEE-hen-da) A large landed estate in Spanish America.

Hegira (HEJ-ear-a) The flight of Muhammad and his followers from Mecca to Medina in 622 C.E. It marks the beginning of the Islamic calendar.

heliocentric (HE-li-o-cen-trick) **theory** The theory, now universally accepted, that the Earth and the other planets revolve around the Sun. First proposed by Aristarchos of Samos (310–230 B.C.E.). Its opposite, the geocentric theory, which was dominant until the sixteenth century C.E., held that the Sun and the planets revolved around the Earth.

helots (HELL-ots) Hereditary Spartan serfs.

heretic (HAIR-i-tick) A person whose beliefs were contrary to those of the Catholic Church.

Hieroglyphics (HI-er-o-gli-phicks) The complicated writing script of ancient Egypt. It combined picture writing with pictographs and sound signs. Hieroglyph means "sacred carvings" in Greek.

Holocaust The Nazi extermination of millions of European Jews between 1940 and 1945. Also called the "final solution to the Jewish problem."

Holy Roman Empire The revival of the old Roman Empire, based mainly in Germany and northern Italy, that endured from 870 to 1806.

Home Rule The advocacy of a large measure of administrative autonomy for Ireland within the British Empire between the 1880s and 1914.

Homo sapiens (HO-mo say-pee-ans) The scientific name for human beings, from the Latin words meaning "Wise man." Homo sapiens emerged some 200,000 years ago.

honestiores (HON-est-ee-or-ez) The Roman term formalized from the beginning of the third century C.E. to denote the privileged classes: senators, equestrians, the municipal aristocracy, and soldiers.

hoplite phalanx (FAY-lanks) The basic unit of Greek warfare in which infantrymen fought in close order, shield to shield, usually eight ranks deep. The phalanx perfectly suited the farmer-soldier-citizen who was the backbone of the polis.

hubris (WHO-bris) Arrogance brought on by excessive wealth or good fortune. The Greeks believed that it led to moral blindness and divine vengeance.

Huguenots (HYOU-gu-nots) French Calvinists.

humanism The study of the Latin and Greek classics and of the Church Fathers both for their own sake and to promote a rebirth of ancient norms and values.

humanitas (HEW-man-i-tas) The Roman name for a liberal arts education.

humiliores (HEW-mi-lee-orez) The Roman term formalized at the beginning of the third century C.E. for the lower classes.

Hussites (HUS-Its) Followers of John Huss (d. 1415) who questioned Catholic teachings about the Eucharist.

iconoclasm (i-KON-o-kla-zoom) A heresy in Eastern Christianity that sought to ban the veneration of sacred images, or icons.

id, ego, superego The three entities in Sigmund Freud's model of the internal organization of the human mind. The id consists of the amoral, irrational instincts for self-gratification. The superego embodies the external morality imposed on the personality by society. The ego mediates between the two and allows the personality to cope with the internal and external demands of its existence.

Iliad (ILL-ee-ad) **and the Odyssey** (O-dis-see), **The** Epic poems by Homer about the "Dark Age" heroes of Greece who fought at Troy. The poems were written down in the eighth century B.C.E. after centuries of being sung by bards.

imperator (IM-per-a-tor) Under the Roman Republic it was the title given to a victorious general. Under Augustus and his successors it became the title of the ruler of Rome meaning "Emperor."

imperialism The extension of a nation's authority over other nations or areas through conquest or political or economic hegemony.

imperium (IM-pear-ee-um) In ancient Rome the right to issue commands and to enforce them by fines, arrests, and even corporal and capital punishment.

indulgences Remission of the temporal penalty of punishment in purgatory that remained after sins had been forgiven.

Industrial Revolution Mechanization of the European economy that began in Britain in the second half of the eighteenth century.

insulae (IN-sul-lay) Meaning "islands." The multistoried apartment buildings of Rome in which most of the inhabitants of the city lived.

intendents (in-TEN-duhnts) Royal officials under the French monarchy who supervised the provincial governments in the name of the king.

Intolerable Acts Measures passed by the British Parliament in 1774 to punish the colony of Massachusetts and strengthen Britain's authority in the colonies. The laws provoked colonial opposition, which led immediately to the American Revolution.

Investiture Struggle The medieval conflict between the Church and lay rulers over who would control bishops and abbots, symbolized by the ceremony of "investing" them with the symbols of their authority.

Ionia (I-o-knee-a) The part of western Asia Minor heavily colonized by the Greeks.

Islam (IZ-lahm) Meaning "submission." The religion founded by the prophet Muhammad.

Italia Irredenta (ee-TAHL-ee-a ir-REH-dent-a) Meaning "unredeemed Italy." Italian-speaking areas that had been left under Austrian rule at the time of the unification of Italy.

Jacobins (JACK-uh-bins) The radical republican party during the French Revolution that displaced the Girondins.

jacquerie (jah-KREE) Revolt of the French peasantry.

Jansenism A seventeenth-century movement within the Catholic Church that taught that human beings were so corrupted by original sin that they could do nothing good nor secure their own salvation without divine grace. (It was opposed to the Jesuits).

Judah (JEW-da) The southern Israelite kingdom established after the death of Solomon in the tenth century B.C.E.

Julian Calendar The reform of the calendar by Julius Caesar in 46 B.C.E. It remained in use throughout Europe until the sixteenth century and in Russia until the Russian Revolution in 1917.

July Monarchy The French regime set up after the overthrow of the Bourbons in July 1830.

junkers (YOONG-kerz) The noble landlords of Prussia.

jus gentium (YUZ GEN-tee-um) Meaning "law of peoples." The body of Roman law that dealt with foreigners.

jus naturale (YUZ NAH-tu-rah-lay) Meaning "natural law." The Stoic concept of a world ruled by divine reason.

Ka'ba (KAH-bah) A black meteorite in the city of Mecca that became Islam's holiest shrine.

Keynesian Economics The theory of John Maynard Keynes (CANES) (1883–1946) that governments could spend their economies out of a depression by running deficits to encourage employment and stimulate the production and consumption of goods.

kleindeutsch (kline-DOYCH) Meaning "small German." The argument that the German-speaking portions of the Habsburg Empire should be excluded from a united Germany.

Kristallnacht (KRIS-tahl-NAHKT) Meaning "crystal night" because of the broken glass that littered German streets after the looting and destruction of Jewish homes, businesses, and synagogues across Germany on the orders of the Nazi Party in November, 1938.

kulaks (koo-LAKS) Prosperous Russian peasant farmers.

Kulturkampf (cool-TOOR-cahmff) Meaning the "battle for culture." The conflict between the Roman Catholic Church and the government of the German Empire in the 1870s.

laissez-faire (lay-ZAY-faire) French phrase meaning "allow to do." In economics the doctrine of minimal government interference in the working of the economy.

latifundia (LAT-ee-fun-dee-a) Large plantations for growing cash crops owned by wealthy Romans.

Latium (LAT-ee-um) The region of Italy in which Rome is located. Its inhabitants were called Latins.

League of Nations The association of sovereign states set up after World War I to pursue common policies and avert international aggression.

Lebensraum (LAY-benz-rauhm) Meaning "living space." The Nazi plan to colonize and exploit the Slavic areas of Eastern Europe for the benefit of Germany.

levée en masse (le-VAY en MASS) The French Revolutionary conscription (1792) of all males into the army and the harnessing of the economy for war production.

liberal arts The medieval university program that consisted of the trivium (TRI-vee-um): grammar, rhetoric, and logic, and the quadrivium (qua-DRI-vee-um): arithmetic, geometry, astronomy, and music.

liberalism In the nineteenth century, support for representative government dominated by the propertied classes and minimal government interference in the economy.

Logos (LOW-goz) Divine reason, or fire, which according to the Stoics was the guiding principle in nature. Every human had a spark of this divinity, which returned to the eternal divine spirit after death.

Lollards (LALL-erds) Followers of John Wycliffe (d. 1384) who questioned the supremacy and privileges of the Pope and the Church hierarchy.

Lower Egypt The Nile delta.

Luftwaffe (LUFT-vaff-uh) The German airforce in World War II.

Magna Carta (MAG-nuh CAR-tuh) The "Great Charter" limiting royal power that the English nobility forced King John to sign in 1215.

Magna Graecia (MAG-nah GRAY-see-a) Meaning "Great Greece" in Latin, it was the name given by the Romans to southern Italy and Sicily because there were so many Greek colonies in the region.

Magyars (MAH-jars) The majority ethnic group in Hungary.

Mandates The assigning of the former German colonies and Turkish territories in the Middle East to Britain, France, Japan, Belgium, Australia, and South Africa as de facto colonies under the vague supervision of the League of Nations with the hope that the territories would someday advance to independence.

mannerism A style of art in the mid-to late-sixteenth century that permitted the artist to express his or her own "manner" or feelings in contrast to the symmetry and simplicity of the art of the High Renaissance.

manor Village farms owned by a lord.

Marshall Plan The U.S. program named after Secretary of State George C. Marshall of providing economic aid to Europe after World War II.

Marxism The theory of Karl Marx (1818–1883) and Friedrich Engels (FREE-drick Eng-ulz) (1820–1895) that history is the result of class conflict, which will end in the inevitable triumph of the industrial proletariat over the bourgeoisie and the abolition of private property and social class.

Mein Kampf (MINE KAHMFF) Meaning "my struggle." Hitler's statement of his political program published in 1924.

Mensheviks Meaning the "minority." Term Lenin applied to the majority moderate faction of the Russian Social Democratic Party opposed to him and the Bolsheviks.

mercantilism Term used to describe close government control of the economy that sought to maximize exports and accumulate as much precious metals as possible to enable the state to defend its economic and political interests.

Mesopotamia (MEZ-o-po-tay-me-a) Modern Iraq. The land between the Tigris and Euphrates Rivers where the first civilization appeared around 3000 B.C.E.

Messiah (MESS-eye-a) The redeemer whose coming Jews believed would establish the kingdom of God on earth. Christians considered Jesus to be the Messiah (Christ means Messiah in Greek).

Methodism An English religious movement begun by John Wesley (1703–1791) that stressed inward, heartfelt religion and the possibility of attaining Christian perfection in this life.

millets Administrative units of the Ottoman Empire that were not geographic but consisted of ethnic or religious minorities to whom particular laws and regulations applied.

Minoans (MIN-o-ans) The Bronze Age civilization that arose in Crete in the third and second millenia B.C.E.

missi dominici (MISS-ee dough-MIN-ee-chee) Meaning "the envoys of the ruler." Royal overseers of the king's law in the Carolingian Empire.

mobilization The placing of a country's military forces on a war footing.

modernism The movement in the arts and literature in the late nineteenth and early twentieth centuries to create new aesthetic forms and to elevate the aesthetic experience of a work of art above the attempt to portray reality as accurately as possible.

moldboard plow A heavy plow introduced in the Middle Ages that cut deep into the soil.

monophysitism (ma-NO-fiz-it-ism) A Christian heresy that taught that Jesus had only one nature.

monotheism The worship of one, universal God.

Mycenaean (MY-cen-a-an) The Bronze Age civilization of mainland Greece that was centered at Mycenae.

"mystery" religions The cults of Isis, Mithra, and Osiris, which promised salvation to those initiated into the secret or "mystery" of their rites. These cults competed with Christianity in the Roman Empire.

nationalism The belief that one is part of a nation, defined as a community with its own language, traditions, customs, and history that distinguish it from other nations and make it the primary focus of a person's loyalty and sense of identity.

natural selection The theory originating with Darwin that organisms evolve through a struggle for existence in which those that have a marginal advantage live long enough to propagate their kind.

naturalism The attempt to portray nature and human life without sentimentality.

Nazis The German Nationalist Socialist Party.

Neolithic (NEE-o-lith-ick) **Revolution, The** The shift beginning 10,000 years ago from hunter-gatherer societies to settled communities of farmers and artisans. Also called the Age of Agriculture, it witnessed the invention of farming, the domestication of plants and animals, and the development of technologies such as pottery and weaving. The earliest Neolithic societies appeared in the Near East about 8,000 B.C.E. "Neolithic" comes from the Greek words for "new stone."

Neoplatonism (KNEE-o-play-ton-ism) A religious philosophy that tried to combine mysticism with classical and rationalist speculation. Its chief formulator was Plotinus (205–270 C.E.).

New Economic Policy (NEP) A limited revival of capitalism, especially in light industry and agriculture, introduced by Lenin in 1921 to repair the damage inflicted on the Russian economy by the Civil War and War Communism.

New Imperialism The extension in the late nineteenth and early twentieth centuries of Western political and economic dominance to Asia, the Middle East, and Africa.

nomes regions or provinces of ancient Egypt governed by officials called nomarchs.

oikos (OI-cos) The Greek household, always headed by a male.

Old Believers Those members of the Russian Orthodox Church who refused to accept the reforms of the seventeenth century regarding Church texts and ritual.

Old Regime Term applied to the pattern of social, political, and economic relationships and institutions that existed in Europe before the French Revolution.

optimates (OP-tee-ma-tes) Meaning "the best men." Roman politicians who supported the traditional role of the Senate.

orthodox Meaning "holding the right opinions." Applied to the doctrines of the Catholic Church.

Ottoman Empire The imperial Turkish state centered in Constantinople that ruled large parts of the Balkans, North Africa, and the Middle East until 1918.

Paleolithic (PAY-lee-o-lith-ick) **Age, The** The earliest period when stone tools were used, from about 1,000,000 to 10,000 B.C.E. From the Greek meaning "old stone."

Panhellenic (PAN-hell-en-ick) ("all-Greek")   The sense of cultural identity that all Greeks felt in common with each other.

Panslavism   The movement to create a nation or federation that would embrace all the Slavic peoples of eastern Europe.

papal infallibility   The doctrine that the Pope is infallible when pronouncing officially in his capacity as head of the Church on matters of faith and morals, enumerated by the First Vatican Council in 1870.

Papal States   Territory in central Italy ruled by the Pope until 1870.

parlements (par-luh-MAHNS)   French regional courts dominated by hereditary nobility. The most important was the Parlement of Paris, which claimed the right to register royal decrees before they could become law.

patricians (PA-tri-she-ans)   The hereditary upper class of early Republican Rome.

Peloponnesian (PELL-o-po-knees-ee-an) **Wars**   The protracted struggle between Athens and Sparta to dominate Greece between 465 and Athens final defeat in 404 B.C.E.

Peloponnesus (PELL-o-po-knee-sus)   The southern peninsula of Greece where Sparta was located.

peninsulares (pen-in-SUE-la-rez)   Persons born in Spain who settled in the Spanish colonies.

Perestroika (pare-ess-TROY-ka)   Meaning "restructuring." The attempt in the 1980s to reform the Soviet government and economy.

petit bourgeoisie (peh-TEE BOOSH-schwa-zee)   The lower middle class.

Pharisees (FAIR-i-sees)   The group that was most strict in its adherence to Jewish law.

pharoah (FAY-row)   The god-kings of ancient Egypt. The term originally meant "great house" or palace.

philosophes (fee-lou-SOPHS)   The eighteenth-century writers and critics who forged the new attitudes favorable to change. They sought to apply reason and common sense to the institutions and societies of their day.

Phoenicians (FA-nee-shi-ans)   The ancient inhabitants of modern Lebanon. A trading people, they established colonies throughout the Mediterranean.

physiocrats   Eighteenth-century French thinkers who attacked the mercantilist regulation of the economy, advocated a limited economic role for government, and believed that all economic production depended on sound agriculture.

Plantation Economy, The   The economic system stretching between Chesapeake Bay and Brazil that produced crops, especially sugar, cotton, and tobacco, using slave labor on large estates.

plebeians (PLEB-bee-ans)   The hereditary lower class of early Republican Rome.

plenitude of power   The teaching that the Popes have power over all other bishops of the Church.

pogroms (PO-grohms)   Organized riots against Jews in the Russian Empire.

polis (PO-lis) (plural, poleis)   The basic Greek political unit. Usually, but incompletely, translated as "city state," the Greeks thought of the polis as a community of citizens theoretically descended from a common ancestor.

polygyny (po-LIJ-eh-nee)   The practice of having two or more wives or concubines at the same time.

polytheism (PAH-lee-thee-ism)   The worship of many gods

pontifex maximus (PON-ti-feks MAK-suh-muss)   Meaning "supreme priest." The chief priest of ancient Rome. The title was later assumed by the Popes.

Popular Front   A government of all left-wing parties that took power in France in 1936 to enact social and economic reforms.

populares (PO-pew-lar-es)   Roman politicians who sought to pursue a political career based on the support of the people rather than just the aristocracy.

Positivism   The philosophy of Auguste Comte that science is the final, or positive, stage of human intellectual development because it involves exact descriptions of phenomena, without recourse to unobservable operative principles, such as gods or spirits.

Pragmatic Sanction   The legal basis negotiated by the Emperor Charles VI (r. 1711–1740) for the Habsburg succession through his daughter Maria Theresa (r. 1740–1780).

predestination   The doctrine that God had foreordained all souls to salvation (the "elect") or damnation. It was especially associated with Calvinism.

Presbyterians   Scottish Calvinists and English Protestants who advocated a national church composed of semi-autonomous congregations governed by "presbyteries."

presbyter (PRESS-bi-ter)   Meaning "elder." A person who directed the affairs of early Christian congregations.

proconsulship (PRO-con-sul-ship)   In Republican Rome the extension of a consul's imperium beyond the end of his term of office to allow him to continue to command an army in the field.

Protestant Ethic   The theory propounded by Max Weber in 1904 that the religious confidence and self-disciplined activism that were supposedly associated with Protestantism produced an ethic that stimulated the spirit of emergent capitalism.

Ptolemaic (tow-LEM-a-ick) **System**   The pre-Copernican explanation of the universe, with the Earth at the center of the universe, originated in the ancient world.

Punic (PEW-nick) **Wars**   Three wars between Rome and Carthage for dominance of the western Mediterranean that were fought from 264 B.C.E. to 146 B.C.E.

Puritans   English Protestants who sought to "purify" the Church of England of any vestiges of Catholicism.

Qur'an (kuh-RAN)   Meaning "a reciting." The Islamic bible, which Muslims believe God revealed to the prophet Muhammad.

racism   The pseudo-scientific theory that biological features of race determine human character and worth.

raison d'etat (RAY-suhn day-TAH)   Meaning "reason of state." Concept that the interests of the state justify a course of action.

realism   The style of art and literature that seeks to depict the physical world and human life with scientific objectivity and detached observation.

Reformation   The sixteenth-century religious movement that sought to reform the Roman Catholic Church and led to the establishment of Protestantism.

regular clergy   Monks and nuns who belong to religious orders.

Reichstag (RIKES-stahg)   The German parliament, which existed in various forms, until 1945.

Reign of Terror   The period between the summer of 1793 and the end of July 1794 when the French Revolutionary state used extensive executions and violence to defend the Revolution and suppress its alleged internal enemies.

relativity   The scientific theory associated with Einstein that time and space exist not separately but as a combined continuum whose measurement depends as much on the observer as on the entities that are being measured.

Renaissance   The revival of ancient learning and the supplanting of traditional religious beliefs by new secular and scientific values that began in Italy in the fourteenth and fifteenth centuries.

reparations   The requirement incorporated into the Versailles Treaty that Germany should pay for the cost of World War I.

revisionism   The advocacy among nineteenth-century German socialists of achieving a humane socialist society through the evolution of democratic institutions, not revolution.

robot (ROW-boht)   The amount of labor landowners demanded from peasants in the Habsburg Monarchy before 1848.

Romanitas (row-MAN-ee-tas)   Meaning "Romanness." The spread of the Roman way of life and the sense of identifying with Rome across the Roman Empire.

Romanticism   A reaction in early nineteenth century literature, philosophy, and religion against what many considered the excessive rationality and scientific narrowness of the Enlightenment.

SA   The Nazi parliamentary forces, or storm troopers.

sans-culottes (SAHN coo-LOTS)   Meaning "without kneebreeches." The lower-middle classes and artisans of Paris during the French Revolution.

Schlieffen (SHLEE-fun) **Plan**   Germany's plan for achieving a quick victory in the West at the outbreak of World War I by invading France through Belgium and Luxembourg.

scholasticism   The method of study based on logic and dialectic that dominated the medieval schools. It assumed that truth already existed; students had only to organize, elucidate, and defend knowledge learned from authoritative texts, especially those of Aristotle and the Church Fathers.

scientific induction   Scientific method in which generalizations are derived from data gained from empirical observations.

Scientific Revolution   The sweeping change in the scientific view of the universe that occurred in the sixteenth and seventeenth centuries. The new scientific concepts and the method of their construction became the standard for assessing the validity of knowledge in the West.

scutage   Monetary payments by a vassal to a lord in place of the required military service.

Second Industrial Revolution   The emergence of new industries and the spread of industrialization from Britain to other countries, especially Germany and the United States, in the second half of the nineteenth century.

secular clergy   Parish clergy who did not belong to a religious order.

seigneur (sane-YOUR)   A noble French landlord.

Sejm (SHEM)   The legislative assembly of the Polish nobility.

serfs   Peasants tied to the land they tilled.

Shi-a (SHE-ah)   The minority of Muslims who trace their beliefs from the caliph Ali who was assassinated in 661 C.E.

Sinn Fein (SHIN FAHN)   Meaning "ourselves alone." An Irish political movement founded in 1905 that advocated complete political separation from Britain.

Social Darwinism   The application of Darwin's concept of "the survival of the fittest" to explain evolution in nature to human social relationships.

Sophists (SO-fists)   Professional teachers who emerged in Greece in the mid-fifth century B.C.E. who were paid to teach techniques of rhetoric, dialectic, and argumentation.

soviets   Workers and soldiers councils formed in Russia during the Revolution.

spinning jenny   A machine invented in England by James Hargreaves around 1765 to mass-produce thread.

SS   The chief security units of the Nazi state.

Stoics (STOW-icks) A philosophical school founded by Zeno of Citium (335–263 B.C.E.) that taught that humans could only be happy with natural law. Human misery was caused by passion, which was a disease of the soul. The wise sought apatheia, freedom from passion.

studia humanitatis (STEW-dee-a hew-MAHN-ee tah-tis) During the Renaissance a liberal arts program of study that embraced grammar, rhetoric, poetry, history, philosophy, and politics.

Sturm und Drang (SHTURM und DRAHNG) Meaning "storm and stress." A movement in German romantic literature and philosophy that emphasized feeling and emotion.

suffragettes British women who lobbied and agitated for the right to vote in the early 20th century.

summa (SUE-ma) An authoritative summary in the Middle Ages of all that was allegedly known about a subject.

Sunna (SOON-ah) Meaning "tradition." The dominant Islamic group.

symposium (SIM-po-see-um) The carefully organized drinking party that was the center of Greek aristocratic social life. It featured games, songs, poetry, and even philosophical disputation.

syncretism (SIN-cret-ism) The intermingling of different religions to form an amalgam that contained elements from each.

syndicalism French labor movement that sought to improve workers' conditions through direct action, especially general strikes.

Table of Ranks An official hierarchy established by Peter the Great in Imperial Russia that equated a person's social position and privileges with his rank in the state bureaucracy or army.

tabula rasa (tah-BOO-lah RAH-sah) Meaning a "blank page." The philosophical belief associated with John Locke that human beings enter the world with totally unformed characters that are completely shaped by experience.

taille (TIE) The direct tax on the French peasantry.

"Ten lost tribes" The Israelites who were scattered and lost to history when the northern kingdom of Israel fell to the Assyrians in 722 B.C.E.

tertiaries (TER-she-air-ees) Laypeople affiliated with the monastic life who took vows of poverty, chastity, and obedience but remained in the world.

tetrarchy (TET-rar-key) Diocletian's (r. 306–337 C.E.) system for ruling the Roman Empire by four men with power divided territorially.

Thermidorean Reaction The reaction against the radicalism of the French Revolution that began in July 1794. Associated with the end of terror and establishment of the Directory.

thesis, antithesis, and synthesis G.W.F. Hegel's (HAY-gle) (1770–1831) concept of how ideas develop. The thesis is a dominant set of ideas. It is challenged by a set of conflicting ideas, the antithesis. From the clash of these ideas, a new pattern of thought, the synthesis, emerges and eventually becomes the new thesis.

Third Estate The branch of the French Estates General representing all of the kingdom outside the nobility and the clergy.

Third Reich (RIKE) Hitler's regime in Germany, which lasted from 1933 to 1945.

Thirty-Nine Articles (1563) The official statement of the beliefs of the Church of England. They established a moderate form of Protestantism.

three-field system A medieval innovation that increased the amount of land under cultivation by leaving only one-third fallow in a given year.

transportation The British policy from the late eighteenth to the mid-nineteenth centuries of shipping persons convicted of the most serious offenses to Australia as an alternative to capital punishment.

transubstantiation The doctrine that the entire substances of the bread and wine are changed in the Eucharist into the body and blood of Christ.

tribunes (TRIB-unes) Roman officials who had to be plebeians and were elected by the plebeian assembly to protect plebeians from the arbitrary power of the magistrates.

ulema (oo-LEE-mah) Meaning "persons with correct knowledge." The Islamic scholarly elite who served a social function similar to the Christian clergy.

Upper Egypt The part of Egypt that runs from the delta to the Sudanese border.

utilitarianism The theory associated with Jeremy Bentham (1748–1832) that the principle of utility, defined as the greatest good for the greatest number of people, should be applied to government, the economy, and the judicial system.

utopian socialism Early nineteenth century theories that sought to replace the existing capitalist structure and values with visionary solutions or ideal communities.

vassal A person granted an estate or cash payments in return for accepting the obligation to render services to a lord.

vernacular The everyday language spoken by the people as opposed to Latin.

vingtieme (VEN-tee-em) Meaning "one twentieth." A tax on income in France before the Revolution.

Vulgate The Latin translation of the Bible by Jerome (348–420 C.E.) that became the standard bible used by the Catholic Church.

Waldensians (wahl-DEN-see-ens)   Medieval heretics who advocated Biblical simplicity in reaction to the worldliness of the Church.

War Communism   The economic policy adopted by the Bolsheviks during the Russian Civil War to seize the banks, heavy industry, railroads, and grain.

War Guilt Clause   Clause 231 of the Versailles Treaty, which assigned responsibility for World War I solely to Germany.

water frame   A water-powered device invented by Richard Arkwright to produce a more durable cotton fabric. It led to the shift in the production of cotton textiles from households to factories.

Weimar (Why-mar) **Republic**   The German democratic regime that existed between the end of World War I and Hitler's coming to power in 1933.

White Russians   Those Russians who opposed the Bolsheviks (the "Reds") in the Russian Civil War of 1918–1921.

zemstvos (ZEMPST-vohs)   Local governments set up in the Russian Empire in 1864.

Zionism   The movement to create a Jewish state in Palestine (the Biblical Zion).

Zollverein (TZOL-fuh-rine)   A free trade union established among the major German states in 1834.

Index

John Paul II, pope (Karol Wojtyla), 1061, *1061,*
    1062, 1095
Johnson, Lyndon, 1091
Johnson, Samuel, 595
Joinville, treaty of (1584), 403
Joseph I, of Austria, 498
Joseph II, of Austria, 612–615, *613,* 834
Josephine de Beauharnais, 682, *682*
Journey from Saint Petersburg to Moscow
    (Radishchev), 652
Joyce, James, 870, *870*
Judaism, 30, 31, 600–601
Judith of Bavaria, 221
Jugurthine War, 133–135, 151
Julia, daughter of Augustus, 150, 160
Julia, daughter of Caesar, 139
Julian the Apostate, 174–175, 179
Julius Excluded from Heaven (Erasmus), 334
Julius II, pope, 328, 330, 331, 333–334, 358
Jung, Carl, 873–874
Junkers, 501, 502–503, 678
Jus gentium (law of peoples), 151
Jus naturale (natural law), 151, 152
Justinian, emperor, 93, 152, 200–204, *200,* 272
Juvenal, 163, 164

K

Ka'ba, 205, 206
Kadar, Janos, 1082, 1100
Kant, Immanuel, 677, 690–691
Kappel, battles of (1529 and 1531), 364
Karageorge, 719
Kassites, 13, 27
Kaunitz, Wenzel Anton, 571
Kautsky, Karl, 841
Kay, James, 534
Kellogg-Briand Pact (1928), 961
Kempis, Thomas à, 355
Kennedy, John F., 1083, 1084, 1091
Kenyatta, Jomo, 1087
Kepler, Johannes, 453, 455
Kerensky, Alexander, 916
Key, Ellen, 881, *881*
Keynes, John Maynard, 867, 925, 968
Kharijites, 206
Khrushchev, Nikita, *987,* 1080–1084
Kierkegaard, Søren, 1054
Kiev, 313–314
King, Martin Luther, Jr., 1088
Kingdom of the Serbs, Croats, and
    Slovenes, 952
King Lear (Shakespeare), 385
King William's War, 441
Kirov, Sergei, 987
Klein, Melanie, 880
Knighthood, 258–259
Knights Templars, 235–236, 271, 308
Knox, John, 395, 404, 406
Koch, Robert, 822
Koestler, Arthur, 1053
Kohl, Helmut, 1100
Kollontai, Alexandra, 1033, 1034
Korean War (1950–1953), 1078–1079
Kosovars, 1038
Kossovo, 1106, 1109
Kossuth, Louis, 770, *771*

Kosygin, Alexei, 1084
Kotzebue, August von, 713–714, *714*
Krämer, Heinrich, 477
Kreditanstalt, 966–967
Kristallnacht, 978, *979,* 980
Kristeller, Paul O., 322
Kruger, Paul, 900
Kuchuk-Kainardii, treaty of (1774), 617
Kulaks, 844, 984–986, 1038
Kulturkampf, 861
Kun, Bela, 952
Kyd, Thomas, 385

L

Labor
    See also Employment
    child, 751
    factory workers in 19th century, 748–750, 752
    in the 1920s, 937
    servitude in the Americas, 348
    unions, 835, *836*
    of women, 751–753
Lacombe, Claire, 654
Ladies' National Association for the Repeal of the
    Contagious Diseases Acts, 881
Lafayette, Marquis de, 633
Lagarde, Paul de, 875
Lagash, 10, 11
Laibach, congress of (1821), 717
Laissez-faire economics, 602, 757–758, 981
Lamartine, Alphonse de, 765
Lancaster, House of, 337–338
Land and Freedom, 805, 807
Langbehn, Julius, 875
Laocoon, 105, *106*
Lasalle, Ferdinand, 840
Las Casas, Bartolomé de, 376, 377
L'Assommoir (Zola), 865
Lateran Accord (1929), 786, 946
Latifundia, 128, 130
Latimer, Hugh, 404
Latin America
    See also under name of country
    early exploration of, 344
    viceroyalties in, *559*
    wars of independence, 719–723
Latin League, 119
Latium, 113
Latvia, 924, 1005
Laud, William, 423
Lausanne Conference, 967
Law
    Byzantine Empire, 200–201
    Code of Hammurabi, 11, 13, 17, *17*
    Enlightenment and, 602
    Napoleonic Code, 671–672
    19th century and family, 824–825
    revival of Roman, in Middle Ages, 272–273
    Roman Empire, 151, 152
Law, Andrew Bonar, 948
Law, John, 486–487, *487*
Lawrence, T. E., 911, *914*
League of Cognac (1526), 360
League of Nations, 922, 925, 996, 997
League of Venice (1495), 333, 334
LeBon, Gustave, 874

160° 140° 120° 100° 80° 60° 40° 20°

80°

GREENLAND
(DENMARK)

60°

U.S.

CANADA

IC

UNITED KING

ALEUTIAN ISLANDS

ATLANTIC

IRELAN

40°

OCEAN

ANDO

PACIFIC

UNITED   STATES

PORTUGA

OCEAN

MOR

MEXICO

BAHAMAS

WESTERN
SAHARA
(MOROCCO)

Tropic of Cancer

CUBA

PUERTO RICO (U.S.)

20°

U.S.

HAITI

MAURITANIA

JAMAICA

ST. KITTS AND NEVIS
ANTIGUA AND BARBUDA
DOMINICA
ST. VINCENT AND
THE GRENADINES
BARBADOS

CAPE VERDE   SENEGAL

BELIZE

DOMINICAN
REPUBLIC

GAMBIA

HONDURAS

GUINEA-BISSAU

GUATEMALA

GRENADA

GUINEA

NICARAGUA

TRINIDAD AND TOBAGO

SIERRA LEONE

EL SALVADOR

VENEZUELA

GUYANA

LIBERIA

COSTA RICA

SURINAME

IVORY COAS

PANAMA

FRENCH
GUIANA
(FR)

GHA

COLOMBIA

CENTRAL AFRICAN

Equator

GALAPAGOS
ISLANDS
(ECUADOR)

ECUADOR

SÃO TOMÉ AN

EQUATOR

PERU

B R A Z I L

WESTERN
SAMOA

BOLIVIA

20°

TONGA

PARAGUAY

Tropic of Capricorn

CHILE

A R G E N T I N A

URUGUAY

ATLANTIC

40°

PACIFIC

OCEAN

OCEAN

60°

Antarctic Circle

80°